APPLEGATE
AUG 2017

T0040613

THE ROUGH GUIDE TO
AUSTRALIA

This twelfth edition updated by
**Melanie Ball, Mark Chipperfield, Shafik Meghji,
Lee Mylne, Helen Ochyra, Amy Palfreyman,
Philip Tang and Greg Ward**

**ROUGH
GUIDES**

Contents

Introduction to
Australia

More than most other countries, Australia seizes the imagination. For many visitors its name is synonymous with endless summers where the living is easy. This is where the adventures are as vast as the horizons and the jokes flow as freely as the beer – a country of can-do spirit and laidback friendliness. No wonder Australians call theirs the Lucky Country.

Every aspect of Australian life and culture, whether its matey attitudes or its truly great outdoors, is a product of the country's scale and population – or lack of it. Australia rivals the USA in size, but is home to only 24 million people, giving it one of the lowest population densities on earth. The energy of its contemporary culture is in contrast to a landscape that is ancient and often looks it: much of central and western Australia – the bulk of the country – is overwhelmingly arid and flat. In contrast, its cities, most founded as recently as the mid-nineteenth century, burst with a vibrant, youthful energy.

The most iconic scenery is the **Outback**, the vast fabled desert that spreads west of the Great Dividing Range into the country's epic interior. Here, vivid blue skies, cinnamon-red earth, deserted gorges and geological features as bizarre as the wildlife comprise a unique ecology, one that has played host to the oldest surviving human culture for up to 70,000 years (just 10,000 years after *Homo sapiens* is thought to have emerged from Africa).

This harsh interior has forced modern Australia to become a **coastal country**. Most of the population lives within 20km of the ocean, the majority of these occupying a suburban, southeastern arc that extends from southern Queensland to Adelaide. Urban Australians celebrate the typical New World values of material self-improvement through hard work and hard play, with an easy-going vitality that visitors, especially Europeans, often find refreshingly hedonistic. A sunny climate also contributes to this exuberance, with an outdoor life in which a thriving beach culture and the congenial backyard "barbie" are central.

Although visitors might eventually find this low-key, suburban lifestyle rather prosaic, there are opportunities – particularly in the Northern Territory – to experience

ABOVE CAMEL TOUR, CABLE BEACH, KIMBERLEY **RIGHT** WHITEHAVEN BEACH, WHITSUNDAY ISLAND

Australia's indigenous peoples and their culture through visiting ancient art sites, taking tours and, less easily, making personal contact. Many Aboriginal people – especially in central Australia – have managed to maintain a traditional lifestyle (albeit with modern amenities), speaking their own languages and living by their own laws. Conversely, most Aboriginal people in cities and country towns are trapped in a destructive cycle of racism, poverty and lack of meaningful employment opportunities, often resulting in health problems and substance abuse. To give just one example, life expectancy rates for Aboriginal Australians are ten years lower than those of the rest of the population. There's still a long way to go before black and white people in Australia can exist on genuinely equal terms.

Where to go

For visitors, deciding where to go can mean juggling distance, money and time. You could spend months driving around the Outback, exploring the national parks, or hanging out at beaches; or you could take an all-in, two-week "Sydney, Reef and Rock" package, encompassing Australia's outstanding trinity of must-sees.

FACT FILE

- With an **area** of just over 7.5 million square kilometres, Australia is the **sixth-largest country** in the world.

- Australia's **population** is estimated at just over 24 million, of whom some 85 percent live in urban areas. About 92 percent are of European ancestry, two percent Aboriginal, and around six percent of Asian origin.

- Much of Australia is arid and flat. One-third is **desert** and another third steppe or semi-desert. Only six percent of the country rises above 600m in elevation, and its **tallest peak**, Mount Kosciuszko, is just 2228m high.

- Australia's main **exports** are minerals, metals, fossil fuels, cotton, wool, wine and beef, and its most important **trading partners** are Japan, China and the USA.

- At 5614km the **dingo fence** is the longest of its kind in the world, stretching from Jimbour to the cliffs of the Nullarbor Plain. It's around twice the length of the Great Wall of China.

- Australia ranks proudly second in the **Human Development Index**, which measures a country's progress by its life expectancy, education and income. Norway comes first.

- Around 22 percent of Australians are descended from **convicts**.

INDONESIA

*TIMOR
SEA*

Darwin

Katherine

*INDIAN
OCEAN*

Kununurra

**NORTHERN
TERRITORY**

Halls
Creek

*TANAMI
DESERT*

Broome

Tennant Creek

Port Hedland

*GREAT SANDY
DESERT*

Newman

Tropic of Capricorn

Alice Springs

GIBSON DESERT

Uluru
(Ayers Rock)

Carnarvon

**WESTERN
AUSTRALIA**

Meekatharra

Wiluna

Coober Pedy

Leonora

*GREAT VICTORIA
DESERT*

Geraldton

Kalgoorlie-
Boulder

Perth

*Great Australian
Bight*

Bunbury

Esperance

Albany

SOUTHERN OCEAN

0   800

kilometres

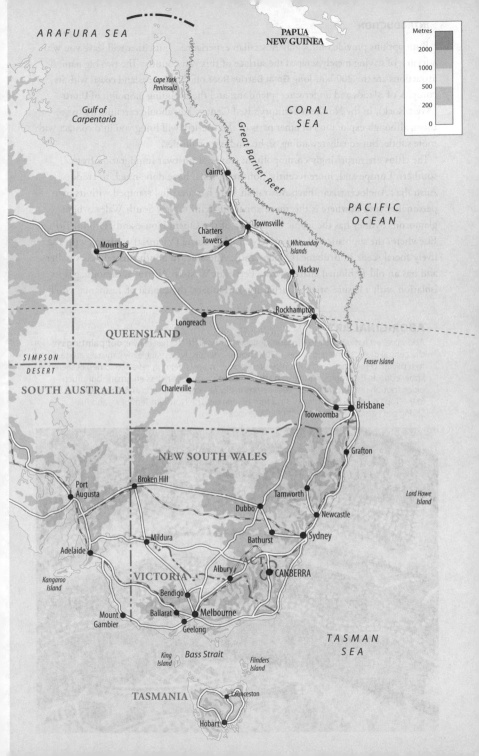

Both options provide thoroughly Australian experiences, but either will leave you with a feeling of having merely scraped the surface of this vast country. The two big natural attractions are the 2000km-long **Great Barrier Reef** off the Queensland coast, with its complex of islands and underwater splendour, and the brooding monolith of **Uluru** (Ayers Rock), in the Northern Territory's Red Centre. You should certainly try to see them, although exploration of other parts of the country will bring you into contact with more subtle, but equally rewarding, sights and opportunities.

The **cities** are surprisingly cosmopolitan: waves of postwar immigration from southern Europe and, more recently, Southeast Asia, have done much to erode Australia's Anglocentrism. Each Australian state has a capital stamped with its own personality, and nowhere is this more apparent than in New South Wales, where glamorous Sydney has the iconic landmarks of the Opera House and Harbour Bridge. Elsewhere, the sophisticated café society of Melbourne (Victoria) contrasts with the lively social scene in Brisbane (Queensland). Adelaide, in South Australia, is smaller and has an old-fashioned charm, while Perth, in Western Australia, camouflages its isolation with a leisure-oriented urbanity. In Hobart, the capital of Tasmania, you'll

ABORIGINAL ART

Aboriginal art has grown into a million-dollar industry since the first canvas **dot paintings** of the central deserts emerged in the 1970s. Though seemingly abstract, early canvases are said to replicate ceremonial sand paintings – temporary "maps" fleetingly revealed to depict sacred knowledge. In the tropics, figurative **bark** and **cave** paintings are less enigmatic but much older, though until recently they were ceremonially repainted. The unusual **X-ray style** found in the Top End details the internal structure of animals. The Northern Territory – and Alice Springs, in particular – are the best places to look.

encounter a relaxed small city with a distinct maritime feel. The purpose-built administrative centre of Canberra, in the Australian Capital Territory, often fails to grip visitors, but Darwin's continuing regeneration enlivens an exploration of the distinctive "Territory".

Away from the suburbs, with their vast shopping malls and quarter-acre residential blocks, is the transitional "bush", and beyond that the wilderness of the **Outback** – the quintessential Australian environment. Protected from the arid interior, the **east coast** has the pick of the country's greenery and scenery, from the north's tropical rainforests and the Great Barrier Reef to the surf-lined beaches further south. The east coast is backed by the Great Dividing Range, which steadily decreases in elevation as it extends from Mount Kosciuszko (2228m) in New South Wales north into tropical Queensland. Though often overlooked, **Tasmania** is worth the trip across the Bass Strait: you'll be rewarded with vast tracts of temperate wilderness and a wealth of scenery, from jagged alpine mountains to almost English bucolic villages.

When to go

Australia's **climate** has become less predictable in recent times, with phenomena such as the cyclic El Niño effect probably part of a long-term pattern. In mid-2016, Tasmania suffered its worst floods in decades, with Queensland and New South Wales

LEFT BOOMERANGS DECORATED WITH ABORIGINAL ART, QUEEN VICTORIA MARKET, MELBOURNE **ABOVE** OPERA BAR, SYDNEY

ECCENTRIC AUSTRALIA

It could be part of the Australian psyche that celebrates renegades. Perhaps it is just the standard set by such utterly odd wildlife as the platypus. Whatever the cause, Australia enjoys **eccentricity** like few other first-world nations, even down to the playful rough-and-tumble of its slang, Strine. The further you go from the big cities, the quirkier Australia gets. You could base an entire visit around a tour of **kitsch sights** like the Big Banana at Coffs Harbour, the Big Pineapple at Nambour or the Big Prawn at Ballina; for more inspiration see ⓦwilmap.com.au/bigstuff. Country and especially Outback **pubs** are often reliable outposts of the weird and wonderful. Yet for true glorious weirdness head to small **festivals** like the World Cockroach Races staged in Brisbane every Australia Day, or Darwin's riotous Beer Can Regatta in July, with boat races in craft made entirely from beer cans.

also devastated by the same storm. This followed on from severe flooding across much of the country in 2008–09 and 2010–11. There have also been record-breaking heatwaves and numerous huge bushfires in recent years. With freak weather increasingly becoming a misnomer, some climate scientists suggest that storm clouds are gathering over the Lucky Country.

Visitors from the northern hemisphere should remember that, as early colonials observed, in Australia "nature is horribly reversed": when it's winter or summer in the northern hemisphere, the opposite season prevails down under, a principle that becomes harder to apply to the transitional seasons of spring and autumn. To confuse things further, the four seasons only really exist in the southern half of the country, **outside of the tropics**. Here, you'll find reliably warm summers at the coast with regular, but brief, heatwaves in excess of 40°C. Head inland, and the temperatures rise further. Winters, on the other hand, can be miserable, particularly in Victoria, where the short days add to the gloom. Tasmania is cooler year-round: while weather in the highlands is unpredictable at all times, summer is a reliable time to explore the island's outdoor attractions.

In the **coastal tropics**, weather basically falls into two seasons. The best time to visit is during the hot and cloudless Dry (from April to November), with moderate coastal humidity maintaining a pleasant temperature day and night and cooler nights inland. In contrast, the Wet – particularly the "Build Up" in November or December before the rains commence – can be very uncomfortable, with stifling, near-total humidity. As storm clouds gather, rising temperatures, humidity and tension can provoke irrational behaviour in the psychologically unacclimatized – something known as "going troppo". Nevertheless, the mid-Wet's daily downpours and enervating mugginess can be quite intoxicating, compelling a hyper-relaxed inactivity for which these regions are known; furthermore, the countryside – if you can reach it – looks its best at this time.

Australia's **interior** is an arid semi-desert with very little rain, high summer temperatures and occasionally freezing winter nights. Unless you're properly equipped to cope with these extremes, you'd be better off coming here during the transitional seasons between April and June or October and November.

In general, the best time to visit the south is during the Australian summer, from December to March, though long summer holidays from Christmas through January

AVERAGE TEMPERATURES AND RAINFALL

	Jan	Feb	March	April	May	June	July	Aug	Sept	Oct	Nov	Dec
ADELAIDE												
Temp. (°C)	28	27	25	22	18	16	14	15	17	21	22	25
Rainfall (mm)	20	20	25	45	65	70	65	60	55	40	25	20
ALICE SPRINGS												
Temp. (°C)	36	35	32	27	22	21	19	21	25	30	32	35
Rainfall (mm)	35	40	25	20	25	25	20	20	10	25	30	35
BRISBANE												
Temp. (°C)	27	27	26	25	23	21	23	22	24	25	26	27
Rainfall (mm)	160	160	150	80	70	60	55	50	50	75	100	140
CAIRNS												
Temp. (°C)	31	31	30	29	28	25	25	27	27	28	30	31
Rainfall (mm)	400	440	450	180	100	50	30	25	35	35	90	160
CANBERRA												
Temp. (°C)	27	25	23	20	15	13	12	13	15	18	22	25
Rainfall (mm)	55	50	50	45	50	30	30	50	50	70	65	65
DARWIN												
Temp. (°C)	31	30	31	32	31	30	30	31	32	32	33	32
Rainfall (mm)	400	430	435	75	50	10	5	10	15	70	110	310
HOBART												
Temp. (°C)	21	21	20	17	14	12	11	12	15	18	19	20
Rainfall (mm)	50	45	50	55	50	45	50	50	55	55	50	50
MELBOURNE												
Temp. (°C)	26	26	24	21	16	15	14	15	17	19	21	20
Rainfall (mm)	45	50	55	60	55	50	50	50	55	65	55	55
PERTH												
Temp. (°C)	30	30	28	25	22	20	19	19	20	22	25	28
Rainfall (mm)	10	15	25	50	125	185	175	145	80	75	25	20
SYDNEY												
Temp. (°C)	25	25	24	23	20	17	16	17	19	22	23	24
Rainfall (mm)	100	105	125	130	125	130	110	75	60	75	70	75

All temperatures are in Celsius: to convert to Fahrenheit multiply by 9, divide by 5 and add 32.

mean that prices are higher and beaches more crowded at this time. In the tropical north, the best months are from May to October, while in the centre they are from October to November and from March to May. If you want to tour extensively, keep to the southern coasts in summer and head north for the winter.

Author picks

Our authors have crossed the length and breadth of Australia in search of the most impressive landscapes, sumptuous food and memorable sights. Here's a list of their personal highlights.

Enjoying Art Deco Katoomba This tiny Blue Mountains town is lined with Art Deco buildings, modest in scale yet glamorous in their effect. The pinnacle is the *Paragon Café*, which features classical friezes and a back room inspired by an ocean liner. See p.161

Heading to the Outback playground The wild Western MacDonnell Ranges unfurl from Alice Springs, reaching a scenic high point at Ormiston Gorge. Trekking the Larapinta Trail allows you to take in the whole glorious chain. See p.539

Catching sight of a cassowary These rare and idiosyncratic birds can be spotted at the Sanctuary on Mission beach. See p.393

Exploring Port Arthur A vivid sense of the hardship and horror of convict life is conjured at this World Heritage Site. See p.914

Listening to live music Melbourne is renowned for its vibrant live music scene, whether folk, indie or alternative. See p.775

Sampling Adelaide's Italian culinary heritage Head to the city's 140-year-old Central Market, where you'll find everything from handmade *gelati* to Neapolitan pizza. See p.660

Soaking up Mad Max scenery Dust storms, subterranean homes, high plateaus: isolated Coober Pedy has it all. See p.715

Donning a hard hat Get a sense of what mining life was like with a tour of Day Dream Mine near Broken Hill, where a seam of silver is still visible running through the rock. See p.294

Swimming with whale sharks Put on a snorkel and go for a dip with the world's largest fish, which appears for a few months each year off the coast of Exmouth. See p.619

> Our author recommendations don't end here. We've flagged up our favourite places – a perfectly sited hotel, an atmospheric café, a special restaurant – throughout the Guide, highlighted with the ★ symbol.

26
things not to miss

It's not possible to see everything that Australia has to offer in one trip – and we don't suggest you try. What follows, in no particular order, is a selective taste of the country's highlights: beautiful beaches, outstanding national parks, spectacular wildlife and lively festivals. All highlights have a page reference to take you straight into the Guide, where you can find out more.

1 KAKADU NATIONAL PARK (NT)
Page 502

Abundant wildlife and fascinating Aboriginal rock art in Australia's largest national park, a World Heritage-listed wilderness that featured in *Crocodile Dundee*.

2 SPORT AT THE MCG (VIC)
Page 743

Taking in a game of cricket or, better still, Aussie Rules football at the venerable Melbourne Cricket Ground (MCG) is a must for any sports fan.

3 SYDNEY HARBOUR (NSW)
Pages 66, 70 & 72

Scale the bridge, take a harbour ferry to Manly or just marvel at the Opera House sails at the most iconic location in Sydney, a shorthand for Australia itself.

4 ATHERTON TABLELANDS (QLD)
Page 407

With its rainforest, crater lakes and
abundant wildlife, you could spend days
exploring the Atherton Tablelands.

5 FRASER ISLAND (QLD)
Page 350

The giant dunes and freshwater lakes of
the world's largest sand island form the
backdrop to popular 4WD safaris.

6 ULURU (NT)
Page 547

Visit at dawn or dusk and you'll understand
why Uluru, aka Ayers Rock, is a sacred site
for Aboriginal people.

7 SURFING
Page 50

Whether point, reef or beach breaks, there
are world-famous waves on most coasts
and warm water to boot.

8 WILPENA POUND (SA)
Page 722

There are some fantastic hikes in the
Flinders Ranges National Park but few top
the spectacular scenery at the elevated
basin of Wilpena Pound.

4

5

12

9 SAILING IN THE WHITSUNDAYS (QLD)
There's fantastic sailing and diving – and whale watching in season – in the white-sand Whitsunday Islands.

10 GREAT OCEAN ROAD (VIC)
On two wheels or four, the 280km route along the surf-battered cliffs bordering the Great Ocean Road is perfect road-trip material.

11 THE FRANKLIN RIVER (TAS)
The Franklin River not only provides one of the wildest whitewater roller-coasters on earth, it is the only means of access to an astounding rainforest wilderness.

12 EATING OUT IN MELBOURNE (VIC)
Nowhere in Australia does food culture better: edgy urban cafés, stylish bohemian bistros and glamorous fine-food restaurants.

13 RIDING THE RAILS
For the ultimate in romantic travel, take a ride on one of Australia's famous long-distance trains, the *Ghan* or the *Indian Pacific*.

13

14 **INDIGENOUS TOURS (NT)**
Page 489
Seek a small-group Aboriginal-run tour in the Territories to get a taste of 70,000 years of Australian culture.

15 **BLUE MOUNTAINS (NSW)**
Page 156
World Heritage-listed, the Blue Mountains are a wonderland of ancient forests, deep valleys and lookouts from sheer cliffs, all just an hour or so from Sydney.

16 **THE KIMBERLEY (WA)**
Page 630
Regarded as Australia's last frontier, the Kimberley is a sparsely populated, untamed wilderness that contains some stunning landscapes.

17 **PERTH'S SMALL BAR SCENE (WA)**
Page 568
Follow the cool kids to rooftop and laneway bars serving Asian-inspired cocktails, rare whiskies and WA craft beers.

18 **BUSHTUCKER**
Page 43
Never mind wattle seeds and witchetty grubs, in Australia you can slap rooburgers on the barbie and eat emu steaks in a restaurant.

19 **CROCODILES (NT)**
Page 510
Head up north to see the Territory's population of fearsome crocs.

16

17

18

1º

25

26

20 KANGAROO ISLAND (SA)
Page 688
Fantastic coastal scenery and a huge variety of wildlife on a pristine island.

21 MARDI GRAS (NSW)
Page 136
Sydney's irreverent Oxford Street parade, from "dykes on bikes" to the "Melbourne marching boys", ends the summer season.

22 COOBER PEDY (SA)
Page 715
This bone-dry, baking-hot opal-mining town is the embodiment of the Outback spirit.

23 SOUTH AUSTRALIA'S WINERIES (SA)
Pages 679, 675, 685, 705, 697
The Barossa Valley, Adelaide Hills, McLaren Vale, Clare Valley and Coonawarra vineyards are all wonderful places to unwind.

24 TALL TIMBER COUNTRY (WA)
Page 589
These primeval karri forests are one of WA's greatest natural sights. Get a bird's-eye view from the Tree Top Walk.

25 BONDI BEACH (NSW)
Page 102
Sand, surf and café culture: Sydney's famous beach has something for everyone.

26 THE OVERLAND TRACK (TAS)
Page 954
The 80km route from Cradle Mountain to Lake St Clair is Australia's greatest extended bushwalk: five or more days of exhilarating exhaustion and stupendous scenery.

Itineraries

Given Australia's vast scale, it makes more sense to focus on one, two or perhaps three regions, depending on your time frame. The following itineraries showcase both classic attractions and less well-known gems, from the elegant attractions of the coastal cities to the mesmerizing desert interior.

TOP TO BOTTOM

An adventurous itinerary for which you need a minimum of two weeks. From Darwin, make a foray into the Kakadu National Park. Then take the Outback *Ghan* train via Alice Springs to visit Uluru, winding up in Adelaide.

❶ Darwin An ocean city with a revitalized waterfront area. Fast-growing and multicultural, it's a great place for food: the sunset markets provide Malay *laksa*, peanut satays and even bushtucker. **See p.487**

❷ Kakadu National Park This Aboriginal-managed region features weird and wonderful wildlife, including freshwater crocodiles, jabiru birds and dingoes. The indigenous rock art, including images in the X-ray style, is outstanding. **See p.502**

❸ The Ghan Cutting into the Red Centre, the legendary *Ghan* train takes its name from the nineteenth-century camel drivers who explored the Australian interior. Red earth and inky blue skies provide a fantastic panorama. **See p.534**

❹ Alice Springs The modern desert town of Alice Springs makes an attractive stop-off, where you can browse art galleries and find some welcome good-quality cafés and restaurants. It's a great place to shop for Aboriginal art. **See p.528**

❺ Uluru Perhaps Australia's defining sight, this mighty monolith is also a keystone in the country's cultural history. Once seen by visitors as simply a challenging lump of rock to climb, it is now recognized for its deep significance to the local Aboriginal population. **See p.547**

❻ Adelaide Elegant Adelaide is the end of this particular line, with attractions including bountiful botanic gardens, bluestone mansions and a host of museums and cultural centres. **See p.655**

WESTERN AUSTRALIA

This two-week trip takes you along the Indian Ocean coast, from tropical Broome in the north to cosmopolitan Perth in the south. Treats en route include sparkling beaches, river gorges and opportunities to dolphin-spot.

❶ Broome Broome is a bustling little place, first made wealthy by an 1880s pearl rush; remnants of the industry still pervade the town, and you can visit one of the world's oldest cinemas. **See p.630**

❷ Dampier If you fancy a bit of bushcamping, make a stop at the northern beaches here. You'll find some lovely white-sand stretches and isolated creeks. **See p.627**

❸ Ningaloo Reef Take to the waters to snorkel and dive among the corals, and five hundred species of fish. **See p.622**

ABOVE THE CITY SKYLINE FROM KINGS PARK, PERTH

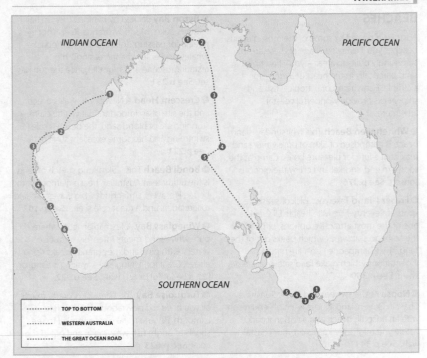

INDIAN OCEAN

PACIFIC OCEAN

SOUTHERN OCEAN

TOP TO BOTTOM

WESTERN AUSTRALIA

THE GREAT OCEAN ROAD

❹ Monkey Mia You're pretty much guaranteed to see dolphins here, which is the main draw, but there's also a lovely beach, and plenty of resorts and attractions to explore in the enclosing Shark Bay. **See p.616**

❺ Kalbarri The river and coastal gorges at Kalbarri comprise a spectacular national park which features wonderful hiking trails. **See p.611**

❻ Nambung National Park As you wend your way south, don't miss the extraordinary limestone pinnacles of this park: the Pinnacles Desert Discovery Centre fills you in on the geological detail. **See p.606**

❼ Perth Sunny Perth is an ideal stopover after the great outdoors. Check out the fine collection of galleries, see rare flora at the Botanic Garden, and catch up on some nightlife. **See p.560**

THE GREAT OCEAN ROAD

This is a classic drive, taking in dramatic rock formations, submerged shipwrecks and some lively and attractive beach resorts. Allow a week to explore the road at leisure, including a couple of days immersed in the café culture and arts scene of Melbourne.

❶ Melbourne Australia's "European" city, with large Greek and Italian communities, stand-out restaurants, arts festivals and ornate Victorian architecture. There's a varied selection of live music venues and some excellent galleries. **See p.732**

❷ Lorne Picturesque seaside Lorne is an ideal holiday resort, combining a laidback surfie vibe with some fine restaurants, delis and boutiques. Plunge into the chilly waters, then warm up on a hiking trail among the ferns and eucalypts. **See p.815**

❸ Great Otway National Park A triangle of national park designated an Important Bird Area for its populations of bristlebirds, fieldwrens and pink robins. The lush hills and gullies are hugely scenic, and don't miss the historic Cape Otway Lighthouse. **See p.819**

❹ Twelve Apostles These ocean-set limestone pillars are an icon of the Great Ocean Road, rising up to 65m. Watch out for the fairy penguins crowding onto the shore at dusk. **See p.820**

❺ Port Fairy A lovely place to end your trip, this early whaling settlement has some of the oldest houses you'll see in Australia, as well as enticing beaches. The sight of umpteen muttonbirds roosting here is unforgettable. **See p.823**

BEACHES

Australia is ringed by some of the most glorious beaches you'll ever see. Many of these are in surprisingly built-up areas – you'll find pristine sand practically in the heart of Sydney, for example. Elsewhere, coral, tropical fish and shipwrecks provide wonderful coastal adventures.

❶ **Whitehaven Beach** This Whitsunday Island beach is comprised of 5km of pure white sand, making it a lure for pleasure boats. Camp at the southern end, snorkel and enjoy the glorious sunsets. **See p.376**

❷ **Fraser Island** Take your pick of seashore spots at Seventy-Five Mile Beach. Eli Creek is one of the most attractive options, or head for the Maheno shipwreck which peeks out of the sand. The Champagne Pools are natural indentations which make for a safe and serene swim. **See p.350**

❸ **Noosa** At the swisher end of the Sunshine Coast in Queensland, Noosa is a high-end resort with an unspoilt beach and a national park, where you might see koalas on your coastal walk. **See p.343**

❹ **Byron Bay** Backed by rainforest, Byron Bay features 30km of sandy strands. Keep your eyes peeled for passing dolphins and humpback whales, and enjoy the increasingly hip restaurant scene and nightlife once the sun has set. **See p.231**

❺ **Crescent Head** A New South Wales beach, and the site of an important native title claim. A stunning arc of blond sand, the beach is safe for swimming and has some excellent surf spots. **See p.221**

❻ **Bondi Beach** This 1.5km-long stretch of sand is the ultimate in Australian beach glamour, with buffed lifesavers, surfer dudes, big waves, passing rollerbladers and a great café scene. **See p.102**

❼ **Wineglass Bay** A Tasmanian icon, where pure white sand meets intensely turquoise waters, with pink and grey granite peaks rising above. Great for fishing, sea-kayaking, sailing, or just a beautiful beach walk. **See p.922**

❽ **Turquoise Bay** The name says pretty much all you need to know about this beach near Exmouth. Be sure to take your snorkel to see shoals of bright fish weaving in and out of the coral. **See p.623**

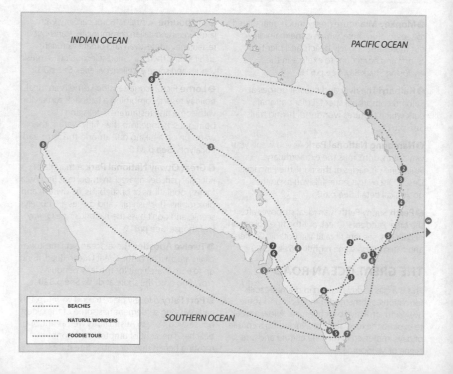

INDIAN OCEAN

PACIFIC OCEAN

SOUTHERN OCEAN

········· BEACHES
········· NATURAL WONDERS
········· FOODIE TOUR

NATURAL WONDERS

The country is blessed with spectacular and varied landscapes, from eucalyptus-cloaked hills to epic desert and the great monolith of Uluru. Hiking is the best way to explore the flora, fauna and rock art.

❶ **Undara Lava Tubes** Vast subterranean pipes formed by an ancient volcano, which shelter microbats and brown tree snakes, known as "night tigers", which hang from the trees. **See p.476**

❷ **The Kimberley** Western Australian frontier land, with a crocodile coast, wide rivers and deep isolated gorges. A unique sight here is the bulbous boab tree, whose nuts are carved by Aboriginal artists. **See p.630**

❸ **Uluru** Epic and elemental, this massive rock is one of the country's great natural sights. Aboriginal and ranger-led tours introduce you to some fascinating wildlife, including more than seventy reptile species. **See p.547**

❹ **Mungo National Park** Take a camping trip in a desert wilderness where Australia's megafauna once roamed: you'll see crowds of emus and kangaroos. The dome of stars in the night sky in this remote region is a sight in itself. **See p.297**

❺ **Kangaroo Island** Just off South Australia, the country's third-largest island is remarkably unspoilt. As well as having a spectacular coastline, sand dunes and cave networks to explore, the island simply teems with wildlife. **See p.688**

❻ **Cradle Mountain** Tasmanian wilderness cut through by iconic hiking trails. Look out for wombats, echidnas and platypus. In the same region is Lake St Clair, Australia's deepest lake. **See p.953**

❼ **Blue Mountains** Endlessly receding mountain ranges, tinged blue by gum oil in the atmosphere. The region is home to the Wollemi pine, or dinosaur tree, which dates back sixty million years and until recently was thought only to exist in fossil form. **See p.156**

❽ **Lord Howe Island** A tiny island ringed by coral, with unique flora, rare flightless birds, umpteen sea birds and dazzling tropical fish. Snorkellers might catch sight of imposing but unthreatening Galapagos sharks. **See p.241**

FOODIE TOUR

Immigrants to Australia from Mediterranean Europe and the Far East have brought some wonderful food traditions to the country, and the sunny climate means bountiful produce. The food-obsessed coastal cities in particular offer a top-notch range of eating opportunities.

❶ **Sydney** You'll find no end of top-notch restaurants in Sydney, the most famous being Japanese/French *Tetsuya's*, which offers a ten-course degustation. **See p.123**

❷ **Orange** At F.O.O.D. Week in April you can learn about local food, browse markets, meet producers, listen to talks, and take part in the justly popular FORAGE walk, a gentle stroll with chances to gather and devour local produce. **See p.253**

❸ **High Country Gourmet Regions** Some of Victoria's finest food, wine and beer can be found in the "High Country" of the Victorian Alps and along the Murray River. The vineyards, fields, orchards and olive groves result in some wonderful produce, including handmade butter and artisan cheeses. **See p.875**

❹ **Melbourne** From funky up-cycled coffee shops to high-end rooftop restaurants and bountiful farmers' markets, Melbourne is a city that takes food seriously. Just listen to your waiter effuse about the specials and you'll see what we mean. **See p.767**

❺ **Tasmania** The temperate Tasmanian climate results in excellent fruit and veg, cool-climate wine and high-quality beef, cheeses, beers and honey. The island's oysters are also renowned. **See p.884**

❻ **Adelaide** With strong Greek and Italian influences, Adelaide has a lively eating and drinking scene, focused on the Central Market, home to scores of great stalls, cafés and restaurants. **See p.655**

❼ **Barossa Valley** You'll find terrific wine across the country, but the Barossa region near Adelaide is the largest and best-established region. Visit between March and May for the harvest; the Barossa Vintage Festival is celebrated from Easter Monday in odd-numbered years. **See p.679**

❽ **The Kimberley** Catch your own mangrove jack or barramundi on a wilderness cruise and have it cooked up on board. You might also get a bite from a golden snapper, blue bone groper or red emperor. **See p.630**

ROAD SIGN ON THE NULLARBOR PLAIN

Basics

Getting there

There are daily flights to various Australian cities from across Europe, North America and Southeast Asia. Fares depend on the season, the highest being the two weeks either side of Christmas. Fares drop during the "shoulder" seasons – which run from late February to May and from mid-August to November – and you'll get the best prices during the low season, June to mid-August. Because of the distance from most popular departure points, flying on weekends does not alter the price.

In addition to flight comparison sites like Skyscanner (Ⓦ skyscanner.net), **specialist flight agents** can also help find cheap deals, and may offer special student and youth fares as well as organize travel insurance, rail passes, car rental and tours. If Australia is a stop on a longer journey, consider a round-the-world (RTW) ticket (see below); Australia is a fixture in RTW tickets offered by most travel agents. With the exception of New Zealanders, all tourists – including those on one-year working visas – are required to arrive with a return ticket.

Flights from the UK and Ireland

The journey to Sydney and other eastern cities **from London** takes a minimum of 21 hours including stops to refuel. Sydney and Melbourne are served by the greatest number of airlines, the former usually being slightly cheaper, though carriers like Qantas (Ⓦ qantas.com) charge similar prices to fly to any eastern city between Cairns and Adelaide; flights to Darwin and Perth are generally a little bit cheaper.

Notwithstanding the stop to refuel, often in Dubai, Singapore or Kuala Lumpur, direct flights depart from London's Heathrow and Gatwick airports, although you can check luggage through if you fly with the same operator from regional UK airports to connect with international flights.

The cheapest return ticket costs around £600 during the low season (June to mid-August). The **most expensive time** to fly is around Christmas, when there are few tickets under £1000 return: you need to book at least six months in advance to secure a cheap flight. Prices also blip upwards from mid-July to mid-August, coinciding with the European holiday period. The shoulder seasons of mid-August to November and mid-January to March can provide better deals if you're flexible.

An alternative to the long direct flight is a **multi-stopover ticket**, typically in Asia though often in the US or Middle East, which can cost the same or just a little more than the price of an ordinary return (and also breaks up the journey).

There are currently no direct flights to Australia **from Ireland**, so most journeys involve a change in a European air hub – London, Paris or Frankfurt – in order to transfer to a long-haul airline. Return fares in the low season are usually around the €850–1000 mark, €1500 plus in high season.

RTW tickets

Round-the-world (RTW) tickets often incorporate Australia within a package of global flights. The permutations are tantalizing: typically stopovers allow overland travel in Asia, the Pacific and North America, but you can pretty much devise your own fantasy itinerary (for example, including destinations in South America and the Pacific). A good travel agency such as STA Travel (see p.31) or Round The World Flights (see p.31) will be able to piece together sector fares from various airlines; to give you an idea of prices, a simple London–Bangkok–Sydney–Dubai–London deal can cost as little as £650; more complicated routings will be more like £1200–1700.

Flights from the US and Canada

It is possible to **fly nonstop** from Los Angeles to Sydney in around fourteen hours. Qantas, United (Ⓦ united.com) and Air Canada (Ⓦ aircanada.com) all operate direct to the east coast of Australia. National Asian airlines usually stop in their capital city

---

A BETTER KIND OF TRAVEL

At Rough Guides we are passionately committed to travel. We believe it helps us understand the world we live in and the people we share it with – and of course tourism is vital to many developing economies. But the scale of modern tourism has also damaged some places irreparably, and climate change is accelerated by most forms of transport, especially flying. All Rough Guides' flights are carbon-offset, and every year we donate money to a variety of environmental charities.

(Singapore, Tokyo, Hong Kong, etc); their fares on the Pacific route from the west coast of North America to the east coast of Australia are generally a bit higher than their American and Australian competitors.

Many of the major airlines offer stopover deals in **Pacific Rim destinations** such as Tokyo, Honolulu or Kuala Lumpur, or at South Pacific locations such as Fiji. Either there will be a flat surcharge on your ticket or they may offer you a higher-priced ticket allowing you to make as many stops as you like, within certain parameters, over a fixed period of time.

As an idea of prices, standard scheduled **return fares** for the low/high seasons cost around US$1500/2200. The price of an **open-jaw ticket** (ie flying into one city and returning from another) will be the average of the return fares to the two cities. If you plan to fly around Australia, a Qantas AirPass can pay dividends, though due to price slashing by budget domestic flights this is not necessarily the case – do the sums first.

RTW or Circle Pacific tickets

If you don't mind setting an itinerary in advance, the best deal will most likely be a round-the-world (RTW) ticket from North America that has stop-offs in Australia and New Zealand, typically via Southeast Asia or Europe but also South America. As you would expect, prices vary hugely, depending on the travel agent. However, a sample **RTW itinerary** of Los Angeles–London–Dubai–Bangkok–Sydney–Auckland–Los Angeles costs around US$1500. Circle Pacific tickets are similar but restricted to the Pacific region, which includes North America and Asia. Check out the websites of agents such as STA Travel and Round The World Flights (see opposite) for deals.

Flights from New Zealand and South Africa

New Zealand–Australia routes are busy and competition is fierce, resulting in an ever-changing range of economical deals; your best bet is to check the latest prices with flight websites that pool all airlines' prices or consult a specialist travel agent (see below). Budget **airlines** have cut fares, with the likes of Virgin Australia (ⓦvirginaustralia .com) offering daily deals. Ultimately, the price you pay will depend on how much flexibility you want; many of the cheapest deals are hedged with restrictions (typically, a maximum stay of thirty days and a fourteen-day advance-purchase requirement). Air New Zealand (ⓦairnewzealand .co.nz) and Virgin Australia fly from Auckland,

Christchurch, Queenstown and Wellington. Flight times between Auckland and Sydney are about three and a half hours.

Flying **from South Africa**, the journey time is around fourteen hours, travelling from Johannesburg to Sydney or around ten to Perth. The main carriers for this route are Qantas and South African Airways (ⓦflysaa.com); expect to pay around ZAR20,000 for a return to Sydney in peak season.

Getting there from Southeast Asia

For many European backpackers, the journey to Australia via Southeast Asia is a rite of passage, thanks to the boundless opportunities for adventures at (generally) wallet-friendly prices. Travelling **overland through Southeast Asia** should not make too much of a difference to the price of your plane ticket, since many Asian airlines stop in their regional hub en route to Australia: Thai Airways in Bangkok (ⓦthaiairways.com), Singapore Airlines in Singapore (ⓦsingaporeair.com), Malaysia Airways in Kuala Lumpur (ⓦmalaysiaairlines.com), and Air China in Beijing (ⓦairchina.com). If you want to continue overland between, for example, Bangkok and Bali, from where it is a short flight over to Darwin in Australia's Northern Territory, consider buying a round-the-world ticket (see p.29) with an overland component. Be aware, too, that if you buy a one-way ticket from Bali, you will still need a return ticket out of Australia to get through immigration.

Agents and tour operators

If time is short and you're reasonably sure of your plans, it is worth prebooking your accommodation and tours; see below for a list of operators and Australian tour specialists.

AGENTS AND OPERATORS

AAT Kings UK ☎ 020 8225 4220, Australia ☎ 1300 228 546, NZ ☎ 0800 500 146; ⓦ aatkings.com. A long-established Australian agency that operates right across the country and is particularly popular with older travellers.

Abercrombie and Kent UK ☎ 01242 547 760, US ☎ 1800 554 7016, ⓦ abercrombiekent.com. This high-end agent excels in tailored, small-group tours and interesting experiences themed by family fun, adventure, highlights or icons. It also has several fixed-itinerary tours.

North South Travel UK ☎ 01245 608 291, ⓦ northsouthtravel .co.uk. Small, competitive agency with discounted airfares. Profits support projects in the developing world, especially the promotion of sustainable tourism.

Round The World Flights UK ☎ 02 0 7704 5700, ⓦ roundtheworldflights.com. As the name suggests, this knowledgeable agency has an extensive range of RTW flights, including customizable itineraries.

STA Travel UK ☎ 0871 230 0040, US ☎ 1800 781 4040, Australia ☎ 134 782, NZ ☎ 0800 474 400, South Africa ☎ 0861 781 781; ⓦ statravel.co.uk. Worldwide specialists in independent travel, STA has good discounts for students and under-26s, plus student IDs, travel insurance, car rental, rail passes and more.

Swain Destinations US ☎ 1-866 429 9722, ⓦ swaindestinations .com. A wide range of customizable tours covering all of Australia, as well as food-, wine- and wildlife-themed itineraries.

Tasmanian Odyssey UK ☎ 01534 735 449, ⓦ tasmanianodyssey .com. Well-chosen accommodation and tour experiences curated by the only specialist Tassie agency in the UK.

Trailfinders UK ☎ 0845 054 6060, Ireland ☎ 01677 7888, Australia ☎ 1300 780 212; ⓦ trailfinders.com. One of the best-informed, helpful and most efficient agents for independent travellers to Australia (and beyond).

Travel CUTS Canada ☎ 1800 667 2887, US ☎ 1800 592 2887; ⓦ travelcuts.com. Canadian youth and student travel firm, good for trip bookings, ISIC cards and student discounts, and working holidays.

USIT Ireland ☎ 01602 1906, Northern Ireland ☎ 028 9032 7111; ⓦ usit.ie. Ireland's main student and youth travel specialists can also help to arrange working holidays in Australia.

World Expeditions UK ☎ 020 8545 9030, US & Canada ☎ 1800 567 2216, Australia ☎ 1300 720 000, NZ ☎ 09 368 4161; ⓦ worldexpeditions.co.uk. This Australian-owned adventure company runs small-group active wilderness holidays; as well as cycling, canoeing, rafting, 4WD excursions, walking and camping trips.

Visas and red tape

All visitors to Australia, except for New Zealanders, require a visa – either electronic or paper – to enter the country. Almost all applications are now made and paid for online.

The easiest way to find out which visa suits you is to visit the Department of Immigration and Border Protection's website (ⓦ border.gov.au), which has links to visa application pages based on a few multiple-choice questions. For nationals of European countries (including the UK and Ireland), the US, Canada, Malaysia, Singapore, Japan, Hong Kong, South Korea and some Middle Eastern countries who intend to stay for less than three months, this will be a free eVisitor visa (for European nationals) or ETA (for US, Canadian and some Asian and Middle Eastern nationals). These computerized visas replace a stamp in your passport and are valid for multiple entries into Australia over periods of three months, six months or one year. Apply prior to travelling, or through travel agents and airlines for a small administration fee when you book your flight. While processing is usually fast – from five minutes to a day or two – officially visas can take up to two weeks to process. Get an application in early unless you particularly enjoy a spot of pre-trip panic.

Citizens of other countries, including South Africa, should apply for a **tourist visa**, valid for three, six or twelve months, which costs $135–340, and can be lodged online (ⓦ immi.gov.au), in person or by post to the relevant embassy or consulate. There is no longer a guarantee of multiple entries for visa holders, so check on receipt.

Twelve-month **working holiday visas** are available to citizens aged 18–30 of many European countries (including the UK and Ireland), Canada, Hong Kong, Japan, Taiwan and Korea. The stress is on casual employment – no single job is meant to last more than six months – and visas must be sought several months in advance of arrival. Working visas cost $440, plus $80 administration if not applied for online; some travel agents such as STA Travel (see above) can arrange them for you. A Work and Holiday Visa (subclass 462) offers the same deal for nationals of the US, Turkey, Thailand, Malaysia, Chile and Bangladesh (among others).

Note that Australia has strict **quarantine laws** on importing fruit, vegetables, fresh and packaged food, seed, vegetative and some animal products into the country, and when travelling interstate. For the same reasons it is suspicious of walking boots and camping equipment used in many parts of the developing world. Counterfeit or pirated goods may be seized and there are also strict laws prohibiting drugs, steroids, firearms, protected wildlife, and heritage-listed products. Sniffer dogs and X-ray scanners for luggage are commonplace – if you are in doubt about an item declare it as you enter rather than risk a fine. You are allowed $900 worth of goods, including gifts and souvenirs, while visitors aged 18 or over are given a **duty-free allowance** of 2.25 litres of alcohol and 50 cigarettes or 50g of tobacco. To find out more about specific prohibited goods before you travel, visit the Australian Immigration and Border Protection website (ⓦ border.gov.au).

Getting around

Given the country's vast size, internal travel is a major factor of any visit to Australia. In general, public transport plies only the major highways to capital

cities, the bigger towns between them, and to popular tourist destinations; to get off the beaten track you'll have to consider renting – or even buying – a vehicle.

If you're planning to cross states overland, it is important to factor in ample travel time. It's easy to underestimate **distances and conditions** – you may well be letting yourself in for a three-day bus journey, or planning to drive 500km on bad roads. Bear in mind, too, what the **weather** will be doing; you don't necessarily want to head into central Australia in a battered car during summer, or into the northern tropics in the wet season.

By plane

Flying is the most common means of interstate travel in Australia, and **budget operators** like Jetstar (Ⓦ jetstar.com.au), Tiger (Ⓦ tiger.com.au) and Virgin Australia (Ⓦ virginaustralia.com) compete with the national operator, Qantas (Ⓦ qantas .com.au). As a rough idea of prices, a typical one-way flight from Sydney to Melbourne costs from around $75 and from Perth to Darwin $275. These three airlines cover the majority of interstate flights. **Regional routes** are served by smaller airlines such as Regional Express, also called Rex (Ⓦ rex.com.au), which focuses on New South Wales, Victoria, South Australia and Tasmania, and state-based companies such as Air North (Ⓦ airnorth .com.au) in the Northern Territory.

If flying with Qantas, you could save money with a **Walkabout Air Pass**, which covers up to multiple discounted domestic (and selected New Zealand) flights; you'll need to purchase it when you book as part of a package with your international flight. As ever, prices fluctuate by the season, and, in the US and Canada, according to your departure point. If you know your travel plans and can face the extra effort, it is worth double-checking that the pass will actually save money; some travellers discover that budget airline bargains can work out cheaper than the discounted flights included in a pass.

Sightseeing flights are available throughout Australia – the best and most spectacular are included in the relevant sections of the Guide and local tourist boards can also advise. They cover everything from biplane spins above cities to excursions to the Great Barrier Reef and flights over well-known landscapes. A flight from Alice Springs to Uluru in a small plane, for example, enables you to visit the Rock in a day, but also observe the impressive central Australian landforms from the air. In addition, helicopter and hot-air balloon rides are also offered.

By train

The southeast has a reasonably comprehensive rail service: interstate railways link the entire east coast from Cairns to Sydney, and on to Melbourne and Adelaide. Each state operates its own rail network. For rail buffs, Australia has two great (or perhaps just long) journeys: the **Indian Pacific** from Perth to Sydney, travelling for three nights and 4352km across the Nullarbor Plain ("gold" sleeper single/twin from $2269/2529 per person; "platinum" sleeper from $3919); and the **Ghan**, which takes three days to go from Adelaide to Darwin via Alice Springs ("gold" sleeper single/twin from $1819/2029 per person; "platinum" sleeper from $3409). Both services are operated by Great Southern Railway (☎ 13 21 47, Ⓦ greatsouthernrail.com.au), and are geared towards the travel experience more than the act of getting from A to B. Great Southern Railway also runs the *Overland* 828km interstate service between Melbourne and Adelaide (11hr; from $79).

There's also the option of transportation for vehicles up to 7m long, with prices dependent upon the distance and direction travelled, plus the length of the vehicle: for example, while it costs from $649 from Adelaide to Darwin, the reverse journey costs from $379. Other than these lines, there are a couple of inland tracks in Queensland – to Mount Isa, Longreach and Charleville, plus the rustic Cairns–Forsayth run and isolated Croydon–Normanton stretch – and suburban networks around some of the major cities. Only around Sydney does this amount to much, with decent services to most of New South Wales. There are no passenger trains in Tasmania.

Trains are usually more comfortable than buses and can be a little faster – Brisbane to Cairns takes 25 hours by train, and 29 hours by coach – for only a little extra expense. Some also get seriously booked up – Queensland trains, for example, require a month's advance booking during holiday season. Generally, it's cheaper – and faster – to fly, though far less atmospheric.

By bus

Thanks to the spread of budget flights, bus travel is no longer necessarily the cheapest way to get around, and is certainly the most tiresome. It also often means arriving or departing in the middle of the night. Nor are services daily, as you might think, especially in Western Australia and the Northern Territory. Where buses are useful is access: the network reaches much further than the train network and visits small towns between cities; occasional bargain fares crop up on popular routes like Sydney–Byron Bay.

The buses are about as comfortable as they can be, with reclining seats, air conditioning, toilets and DVDs. Try to plan for a stopover every twenty hours – if you endure a sixty-hour marathon trip, you'll need a day or more to get over it. **Discounts** (ten percent, or fifteen percent if you buy your ticket before entering Australia) are available on many fares if you have a YHA, ISIC or recognized backpacker card such as VIP (see box, p.39), or if you are a pensioner.

The major **interstate bus company** on the mainland is Greyhound Australia (☎1300 473 946, ⍟greyhound.com.au), which covers the entire country. Along the east coast, Premier Motor Service (☎13 34 10, ⍟premierms.com.au) calls in every-where along the highway between Melbourne and Cairns, while in Western Australia, Integrity Coach Lines (☎1800 226 339, ⍟integritycoachlines.com.au) goes from Perth to Broome, looping inland, too. Firefly Express (☎1300 730 740, ⍟fireflyexpress.com.au) runs from Sydney to Adelaide via Canberra and Melbourne and usually has the cheapest fares for these routes. Tasmania is covered by Tassielink (☎1300 300 520, ⍟tassielink.com.au) and Tasmanian Redline Coaches (☎1300 360 000, ⍟www.tasredline.com.au).

A **one-way fare** from Sydney costs about $130 to Adelaide (23hr), $110 to Brisbane (16hr), and $120 to Melbourne (12hr). Longer trips to, say, Darwin or Alice Springs will be several hundred, so are not worth considering unless you are passionately anti-flying. Return fares are only marginally cheaper than two singles.

Where bus travel scores over air (aside from its environmental impact) is its plethora of **passes**, though bear in mind that you won't save money over shorter routes and that passes are non-refundable. Greyhound offers a range of passes lasting between three days and twelve months on which you can break your journey as often as you like and travel in any direction. Year-long **Kilometre Passes** are the most flexible, giving you unlimited travel up to 25,000km in any direction until you have used up the distance paid for – these work out around 10–11¢ per kilometre; 1000km ($189) will get you from Sydney to Melbourne, 25,000km will get you all around Australia ($2675). Greyhound also has dedicated holiday packages that combine travel and activities.

By car

If you stick to the east coast, public transport will cover most of your needs. But to explore Australia fully, you'll really **need your own vehicle**. Only then will the national parks, remote beaches and isolated Outback towns that make the country so unique be within reach. If your trip is of four months or more then **buying a vehicle** may be the cheapest way to go. For shorter trips **renting** is the best bet – if not for the whole time then at least for short periods between bus rides, thereby allowing you to explore an area in depth.

Most foreign licences are valid for a year in Australia. An International Driving Permit (which is available from national motoring organizations) may be useful if you come from a non-English-speaking country. In mid-2016, **fuel** prices averaged $1.19 per litre for unleaded petrol: prices increase a bit in Darwin, and significantly along the Outback highways and in remote stations. The **rules of the road** are similar to those in the UK and US: drive on the left (as in the UK), and wear seat belts at all times. The speed limit in all built-up areas is 50kph or less. Outside built-up areas, maximums are either 90kph or 110kph on longer stretches, except in the Northern Territory, where common sense is your only limit between towns. Whatever else you do in a vehicle, respect the distances in Australia. Never drive tired and be tempted to push on through; similarly, get out of the car every few hours. Drinking alcohol is also forbidden: random breath tests are common even in rural areas, especially during the Christmas season and on Friday and Saturday nights. One rule that might catch you out in towns is that **roadside parking** must be in the same direction as the traffic; in other words, don't cross oncoming traffic to park on the right.

DRIVING INTERSTATE
When driving across state borders bear in mind that your car may be subject to a **customs search** by officers on the lookout for fruit and fresh produce, which often cannot be carried from one state to another, to minimize the spread of plant pests and viruses. You'll see large bins at the side of the road as you approach a state border line for this purpose: dump any perishables here before crossing; otherwise, you risk receiving a large fine if pulled over and caught with them.

SHORTEST DRIVING DISTANCES IN KILOMETRES

	Adelaide	Alice Springs	Brisbane	Broken Hill	Broome	Cairns
Adelaide	x	1533	1959	508	3274	2854
Alice Springs	1533	x	2700	1638	1745	2163
Brisbane	1959	2700	x	1458	4250	1700
Broken Hill	508	1638	1458	x	3383	2344
Broome	3274	1745	4250	3383	x	3411
Cairns	2854	2163	1700	2344	3411	x
Canberra	1164	2561	1212	929	4305	2545
Darwin	3025	1489	3426	3135	1868	2596
Melbourne	731	2255	1690	835	3999	2812
Perth	2690	2475	4260	2802	2176	4638
Sydney	1371	2768	929	1160	4741	2414
Townsville	2532	1773	1361	2022	3319	348
Uluru	1582	440	3149	1690	2185	2603

The main **hazards** are boredom and fatigue, and animal collisions – a serious problem everywhere (and not just in the Outback), particularly at dawn, dusk and night-time. Driving in the Outback is by far the most dangerous tourist pursuit in Australia and every year several people get killed in single-vehicle rollovers or head-on collisions, particularly Europeans on short see-it-all holidays in cumbersome 4WDs or motorhomes. Beware of 50m-long **road trains**: these colossal trucks can't stop quickly or pull off the road safely, so if there's the slightest doubt, get out of their way; only overtake a road train if you can see well ahead and are certain your vehicle can manage it. On dirt roads be doubly cautious, or just pull over and let the road train pass.

Roads, Outback driving and breakdowns

Around the cities the only problem you're likely to face is inept signposting, but the quality of some interstate roads isn't always great and some minor routes are pretty shabby. **Conditions**, especially on unsealed roads, are unpredictable, and some roads will be impassable after a storm, so always seek reliable advice (from local police or a roadhouse) before starting out into the big nothingness. Make

---

FOUR-WHEEL DRIVING TIPS

The Outback is not the place to learn how to handle a 4WD and yet this is exactly where many tourists try to do so. Take essential spares – spark plugs, fuses, fuel filters, radiator hoses and a fan belt – plus a shovel, hi-lift jack and gloves, and one of the "how to" manuals easily found in bookshops. The following basic hints should help.

- Know how to operate everything – including free-wheeling hubs (where present) and how to change a wheel – before you need it.
- Always cross deep water and very muddy sections on foot first.
- Don't persevere if you're stuck – wheel spin will only dig you further in – and reverse out. Momentum is key on slippery surfaces such as mud or sand – as long as you're moving forward, however slowly, resist the temptation to change gear, and so lose traction.
- Reducing tyre pressures down to 1 bar (15lb psi) dramatically increases traction in mud and sand, but causes tyre overheating, so keep speeds down. Carry a compressor or reinflate as soon as possible.
- If stuck, clear all the wheels, create a shallow ramp (for all wheels), engage four-wheel drive, lower pressures if necessary, and drive or reverse out in low-range second.
- Keep to tracks – avoid unnecessary damage to the environment.
- On beaches observe other vehicles' tracks and be aware of tidal patterns.
- Consider a rented satellite phone for remote travel (see p.58).

Canberra	Darwin	Melbourne	Perth	Sydney	Townsville	Uluru
1164	3025	731	2690	1371	2532	1582
2561	1489	2255	2475	2768	1773	440
1212	3426	1690	4260	929	1361	3149
929	3135	835	2802	1160	2022	1690
4305	1868	3999	2176	4741	3319	2185
2545	2596	2812	4638	2414	348	2603
x	3947	666	3724	286	2161	2612
3947	x	3752	3983	3926	2509	1937
666	3752	x	3419	875	2480	2310
3724	3983	3419	x	3932	4823	2035
286	3926	875	3932	x	2070	2820
2161	2509	2480	4823	2070	x	2219
2612	1937	2310	2035	2820	2219	x

it clear what sort of vehicle you're driving and remember that their idea of a "good" or "bad" road may be radically different from yours. Some so-called "4WD only" tracks are navigable in ordinary cars as long as you take it easy – high ground clearance, rather than four-driven wheels, is often the crucial factor.

Rain and flooding – particularly in the tropics and central Australia – can close roads to all vehicles within minutes, so driving through remote regions or even along the coastal highway in the wet season can be prone to delays. The spectacular stretches of highway between Broome and Kununurra and Cairns to Townsville are notorious for flooding during summer cyclone season. Several remote and unsealed roads through central Australia (the Sandover and Plenty highways, the Oodnadatta, Birdsville and Tanami tracks, and others) are theoretically open to all vehicles in dry winter weather, but unless you're well-equipped with a tough car, don't attempt a crossing during summer, when extreme temperatures strain both driver and vehicle.

On **poor roads and dirt tracks**, the guidelines are to keep your speed down to 80kph, stick to the best section and never assume that the road is free from potholes and rocks. Long corrugated stretches can literally shake a vehicle apart – check radiators, fuel tanks and battery connections after rough stretches; reducing tyre pressures slightly softens the ride but can cause the tyres to overheat, making them more prone to punctures. Windscreens are often shattered by flying stones from passing traffic, so slow down and pull over to the left when passing other cars.

At all times carry plenty of **drinking water** and **fuel**, and if you're heading to the Outback let someone know your timetable, route and destination so that a rescue can be organized if you don't report in. Carry a detailed map, and don't count on finding regular signposts. It's advisable to carry a high-frequency (HF) radio transceiver to pick up the Royal Flying Doctor Service bases. Better still, hire a satellite phone (see p.58) and Global Positioning System (GPS) finder – an extra cost worth bearing when it is literally a lifesaver.

In the event of a breakdown in the Outback, **always stay with your vehicle**: it's more visible to potential rescuers and you can use it for shade. If you're off a main track, as a last resort, burn a tyre or anything plastic – the black smoke will be distinctive from the average bushfire.

Car, 4WD and campervan rental

To **rent** a car you will need a full, clean driver's licence and to be at least 21 years old, rising to 25 for 4WDs and motorcycles. As ever, make sure you double-check the small print before signing: mileage limits, extras, and the extent of the accident cover are all things to pay particular attention to. The multinational operators Hertz, Budget, Avis and Thrifty all have offices in major cities and at airports, but a lack of competition makes standard **rates** expensive at $70–80 a day for a small car. Local firms – of which there are many in the cities – are generally better value, though we have heard tales of unscrupulous operators who sting travellers with unwarranted fees; expect to pay around $60 a day with unlimited kilometres. One-way rental might appear handy, but is usually very expensive due to drop-off fees.

Four-wheel-drive vehicles are best reserved for specific areas rather than long term because rental at around $100–150 a day is steep even without fuel. **Campervans**, typically a Toyota Hiace, cost from $80 a day for a two-berth campervan in low season (prices can double in high season) with unlimited kilometres – good value when you factor in the saving on accommodation costs – plus one-way rental is often possible. Like cars, most campervans are limited to sealed roads, but they give you the chance to create your own tour across Australia. Remember, though, that the sleeping capacity stated is an absolute maximum, which you wouldn't want to endure too long. Furthermore, in the tropics the interior never really cools overnight unless you leave the doors open – which brings the bugs in. Consider sleeping outside under a mosquito dome or inner tent.

Larger operators – nationwide firms like Britz, Apollo and Kea, for example, plus larger local outfits – rent **4WD campervans** fitted with 180-litre fuel tanks that are only limited off-road by your 4WD experience or roof heights. Average prices for 4WD campers average $180–220 per day year-round. The downside of all campervans is that they are thirsty and require drivers to appreciate the altered driving dynamics of an already high vehicle fitted with a heavy body. Novice renters regularly drift off the road, overcompensate and roll a heavy camper. Finally, note that a few companies such as Spaceships rent out modern hybrid campervans. These are basically converted "people-movers", so more car than van, that make up in driving comfort and fuel economy what they lack in accommodation; they are a good option if you have a tent, too.

CAR RENTAL AGENCIES

Avis Ⓦ avis.com.au.
Budget Ⓦ budget.com.au.
Europcar Ⓦ europcar.com.
Hertz Ⓦ hertz.com.au.
Holiday Autos Ⓦ holidayautos.com.au.
National Ⓦ nationalcar.com.au.
Rent-A-Bomb Ⓦ rentabomb.com.au.
Thrifty Ⓦ thrifty.com.

CAMPERVAN AND MOTORHOME RENTAL AGENCIES

Apollo Motorhome Holidays Ⓦ apollocamper.com.au.
Backpacker Campervans Ⓦ backpackercampervans.com.
Britz Australia Ⓦ britz.com.au.
Kea Campers Ⓦ www.keacampers.com.
Maui Ⓦ maui-rentals.com.
Spaceships Ⓦ spaceshiprentals.com.au.
Travellers Autobarn Ⓦ travellers-autobarn.com.au.
Wicked Campervans Ⓦ wickedcampers.com.au.

Buying a car

Buying a used vehicle need not be an expensive business, and a well-kept car should resell at about two-thirds to half the purchase price at the end of your trip. A good place to check vehicle prices and availability online is at Ⓦ tradingpost .com.au.

If you don't know your axle from your elbow but are not too gullible, you'll find **car yards** can provide advice – some in Sydney even cater specifically to travellers – but don't forget that you're dealing with used-car salesmen. Buying privately saves money. **Backpackers' notice-boards** in cities and major tourist destinations are the best places to look. A huge advantage of buying from backpackers is that you usually get all sorts of useful stuff thrown in – such as camping gear, eskies and spares. The disadvantages are high mileage and low mainten ance. Unless you know what you're doing, call in the experts: state automobile associations offer rigorous pre-purchase inspections for about $200, which isn't much if it saves you from buying a wreck. The Australian Automobile Association (Ⓦ aaa.asn.au) holds a huge backlist of vehicle tests online, which might help make a decision.

You'll also need a roadworthiness certificate to have the vehicle transferred from its previous owner to you. This means having a garage check it over; legally, the previous owner should do this, and theoretically it guarantees the car is mechanically sound – but don't rely on it. You take the document to the local Department of Transport with the certifi-cate, a receipt of purchase, your driver's licence and passport; it is then registered in your name for a percentage of the price. For Western Australia-regis-tered cars, the process is the same, except that a roadworthiness certificate is not required.

If the annual **vehicle registration** is due or you bought a vehicle interstate, you'll have to pay extra for registration (aka "rego"), which is around $300/600 for six/twelve months depending on the state and engine size. Note that cars with interstate registration can be difficult to sell.

Registration includes the legal minimum third-party personal **insurance**. We advise increasing this cover to protect against third-party damage and theft, or better still, comprehensive insurance. Joining one of the **automobile clubs** for another $150 or so buys you the peace of mind of free roadside assistance (within certain limits), and discounts on road maps and other products. Each state has its own club, but membership is reciprocal with overseas equivalents.

By motorcycle

Motorcycles, especially large-capacity trail bikes, are ideal for the Australian climate, although long distances place a premium on their comfort and fuel range. If you aim to return to your starting point, look out for dealers with a buy-back option as bikes can be more difficult to sell privately than cars. Whether you're planning to ride off or on the bitumen, plenty of water-carrying capacity is essential in the Outback. **Outback night-riding** is risky due to the possibility of collisions with wildlife; make sure your lights and brakes are up to it and keep your speed down to under 100kph. Motorcycle **rental** is widely in the main southern cities. In Sydney, Bikescape (W bikescape.com.au) has a good selection. *The Adventure Motorcycling Handbook* (W adventure-motorcycling.com) is a definitive manual for preparation and riding off the beaten track and includes Outback tracks.

Hitching

The official advice for hitching in Australia is don't. A much better option is to line up lifts through backpackers' notice boards and websites such as W catchalift.com and W coseats.com and share the fuel costs. This gives you the chance to meet the driver in advance, and most likely stop to see sights en route. In out-of-the-way locations, roadhouses are a good place to try as the owners often know of people who'll be heading in your direction. We strongly advise against a thumb on the open road. If this is the only option, **never hitch alone** and ensure you are dropped at a settlement. Remember that you don't have to get into a vehicle just because it stops: choose whom to get in with and don't be afraid to ask questions before you do. Ask the driver where he or she is going rather than say where you want to go. Try to keep your pack with you; having it locked in the boot makes a quick escape difficult.

Accommodation

Finding somewhere to stay is rarely a problem in Australia, even in the smallest of towns. However, on the east coast it is a good idea to book ahead for Christmas, January and the Easter holidays, as well as for long weekends, especially when big sporting events are held.

The term "**hotel**" in Australia means a pub or bar. They were once legally required to provide

TOP 5 HOTELS
ADGE Apartment Hotel Sydney.
See p.121
Cicada Lodge Nitmiluk National Park.
See p.520
Como The Treasury Perth. See p.565
Henry Jones Art Hotel Hobart. See p.897
Kingfisher Bay Resort Fraser Island.
See p.355

somewhere for customers to sleep off a skinful and most still provide accommodation. They're usually cheap and sometimes even cheerful, though because these are still primarily places to drink, a hotel stay can be loud – a case of if you can't sleep through 'em, join 'em, perhaps.

The flip side of this is that many places that would call themselves hotels in any other country instead call themselves motels, resorts, "private hotels" (in the cities), or boutique hotels. There are also a growing number of B&Bs and farmstays.

Australia caters extremely well for budget travellers, with a huge array of excellent hostels for backpackers (both old and young) and caravan parks that offer accommodation as permanent on-site vans and cabins or chalets, as well as campervan facilities and tent spaces. In general, city accommodation is more expensive than rural, and prices in Perth and Western Australia mining towns are noticeably steeper, powered northwards by the state's resources boom.

Hotels and motels

Rooms in Australian **hotels** (what in the UK would be pubs) tend to be basic – no TV, and shared bathrooms and plain furnishings – and aren't the best choice for peace and quiet. In rural areas hotels are often the social centre of town, especially at weekends. But with double rooms at around $80–130 and singles from around $60, they can be better value – and more private – than hostel accommodation. **Motels** are a comfortable if rather bland choice, often found en masse at the edge of town on arterial routes and priced on average upwards of $120 for a double room with TV and bath, not including breakfast. They rarely have single rooms, but they may have larger units for families, often with basic cooking facilities.

Cities have hotels in the conventional sense. Those at the cheaper end may describe themselves as "**private hotels**" to distinguish themselves from pubs. Some of these, especially in inner cities, can be

ACCOMMODATION PRICES

The room prices given throughout this book are the official "rack-rates" for the cheapest double in high season. In practice, you may find cheaper walk-up and online rates, and prices will certainly reduce out of season. Camping prices (unless otherwise specified) are for a pitch for a standard-sized tent for two people. Wi-fi access is included in the rates, unless stated otherwise in the review.

rather shabby at best, sleazy at worst, but others are pleasant guesthouses, often family run. As a guide, double rooms generally average from $140; more expensive hotels in the cities are standard inter national chain fare stuff, while in resorts and tourist areas they're more like upmarket motels. Prices can vary from around $150 to well over $400 in five-star establishments: a typical city three-star will probably cost you above $160–180. Similar places in a resort or country area charge $100 or more.

Numerous nationwide hotel and **motel chains** – among them familiar names such as Best Western, Ibis and Travelodge, as well as Australian ones such as Budget, Golden Chain and Flag – are dependable if not particularly exciting.

Resorts and self-catering apartments

Many establishments call themselves **resorts** but the term is fairly hazy. At the bottom end of the scale, price, appearance and facilities may be of motel standard, while top-flight places can be exclusive (and expensive) hideaways. Originally, the name implied that the price was all-inclusive of accommodation, drinks, meals, activities and so on, but this isn't always the case. These places tend to be set in picturesque locations – the Barrier Reef islands swarm with them – and are often brilliant value if you can wangle a standby or off-season price.

Self-catering apartments or country cabins can be a great deal for families and larger groups. Whether larger units at a motel or purpose-built apartment hotels, they are usually excellent value.

ACCOMMODATION ALTERNATIVES

The following websites all provide alternatives to standard hotel and hostel accommodation:
CouchSurfing ⓦcouchsurfing.org.
Vacation Rentals by Owner ⓦvrbo.com.
Airbnb ⓦairbnb.com.au.
Homestay.com ⓦhomestay.com.

Cooking facilities are variable, but there'll always be a TV and fridge; bed linen is not always included but can be rented for a small charge.

Farmstays and B&Bs

Another option in rural areas is **farmstays** on working farms, and **B&Bs** or **guesthouses**; the last two, predominantly found in the south and east and Tasmania, can be anything from someone's home to your own colonial cottage. Farmstays are even more variable; some are very comfortable, at others you'll bunk down in vacant shearers' quarters. Their attraction is that they are always in out-of-the-way locations, and may provide a chance to participate in the working of the farm, or take advantage of guided tours around the property on horseback or by 4WD.

Hostels

There is an extensive range of budget accommoda-tion in Australia, and although more shambolic operations don't survive for long, standards are variable. There are numerous – generally high quality – **YHA youth hostels** (ⓦyha.com.au), with stiff competition provided by a range of smaller private operators. So, a private network like the **VIP Backpacker Card** (see box opposite) is generally as useful as the **International Youth Hostels Association/Hostelling International** (ⓦyha.com.au) membership. Another well-known name is **Nomads** (ⓦnomadsworld.com), which also issues a membership card entitling holders to plenty of discounts.

At their best, hostels and backpackers' accommo-dation are excellent value and good places to meet other travellers. There's often a choice of dormitories, double or family rooms, plus bike rental, a kitchen, laundry facilities, a games room, TV, wi-fi and help with finding work or planning trips. Most have excellent notice boards, and offer organized activities and tours. At their worst, however, their double rooms are poorer value than local hotel accommodation, and some are simply grubby, rapid-turnover dives. Affiliation to an

TOP 5 HOSTELS

Flashpackers Noosa. See p.345
Fremantle Prison YHA Fremantle.
See p.573
The Nunnery Melbourne. See p.764
Port Elliot Beach House YHA Port Elliot.
See p.687
Sydney Harbour YHA Sydney. See p.118

organization also does not necessarily ensure quality. Hostels generally charge around $25–40 or more for a dormitory bed, with doubles and twins – if available – from around $70.

Some establishments ban the use of personal sleeping bags (for hygiene reasons) and instead provide all bedding, generally free or at a small charge. It might be a good idea to carry at least a sheet sleeping bag for the few hostels that don't provide bed linen.

Camping, caravan parks and roadhouses

Perhaps because Australian hostels are so widespread and (generally speaking) inexpensive, few foreign travellers bother to **camp**. It's their loss, however, as national parks and nature reserves offer great camping grounds, most with mod cons like an amenities block with toilets, hot and cold showers, drinking water, plus a barbecue and picnic tables. Others provide nothing except perhaps a pit toilet – basic, certainly, but going wild is part of the appeal for many travellers. Still, come prepared in national parks, where **bush camping** is the norm. That great Aussie invention, the swag, a sort of roll-up easy-pitch tent for one or two, is a good buy if you're touring in national parks. Vital equipment includes ground mats and a range of pegs – wide

for sand, and narrow for soil. Fuel stoves are recommended, but if you do build a fire keep it under strict control and always observe fire bans. Prices depend on state policy and site facilities, and you'll usually need a permit from the local NPWS (National Parks & Wildlife Service) office, details of which are given throughout the Guide. Payment will be either by self-registration (fill in a form, pay the fee and post both into a box on the campground), or a park ranger will collect money.

Camping rough by the road is not a good idea, even if you take the usual precautions of setting up away from the roadside and avoiding dry river beds. If you have to do it, try to ensure you're not visible: having a group of drunks pitch into your camp at midnight is not an enjoyable experience. Animals are only likely to pose a threat to your food – keep it in your car, not your tent, or in a sealed container, unless you enjoy possums and currawongs raiding your supplies.

Australian **caravan parks** (sometimes called holiday parks) are usually superbly equipped: in addition to an amenities block and a coin-operated laundry, you'll often get a camp kitchen, a coin-operated (or free) barbecue, a kiosk of minor supplies, possibly a pool, maybe even a children's playground and a tennis court. If you are travelling without a tent, renting an on-site van (ie a caravan or trailer with cooking facilities but shared amenities) is a cheap, if basic, option. Cabins usually come with cooking facilities and a bathroom. In some upmarket caravan parks, cabins can be slightly more expensive than a motel room, but are larger and better equipped, so are a good choice for families or groups.

Expect to pay $10–30 per tent for an unpowered site, about $5–15 more for a powered site, or $60–180 for a van or cabin, depending on its location, age, size and equipment. Highway

HOSTEL PASSES

The following **hostel passes** provide discounts – generally five to ten percent off – on accommodation at member establishments, as well as on everything from bus tickets and tours to vehicle hire and food.

VIP Backpacker Card ⓦ vipbackpackers.com. Probably of most use in Australia, this card also includes an Australian SIM card with discounted international minutes. At present, there are around 125 member hostels around the country, and your card is also valid at one hundred more in New Zealand. $47/year.
Nomads ⓦ nomadsworld.com. The Nomad MAD card doubles as a rechargeable internet and phone card. Its network comprises about twenty hostels in Australia, many of them in old

pubs, a few of them "working hostels" in country areas. The network's span is global, with affiliated hostels on most continents. $19/year.
IYHA ⓦ yha.com.au. The International YHA card is available online, and through YHA hostels in Australia and your home country. HA Membership and Travel Centres can be found in state capitals and at many YHA hostels. Australian YHA hostels number around ninety, with over four thousand more worldwide. $25/year.

roadhouses are similar, combining a range of accommodation with fuel and restaurants for long-distance travellers.

Health

Australia has high standards of hygiene, and there are few exceptional health hazards – at least in terms of disease. No vaccination certificates are required unless you've come from a yellow-fever zone within the past week. Standards in Australia's hospitals are also very high, and medical costs are reasonable in comparison to Europe and the US.

The national healthcare scheme, **Medicare**, offers a reciprocal arrangement – free essential health care – for New Zealanders, British and Irish citizens, and some Europeans. If you are a resident of a country without a reciprocal healthcare agreement, such as South Africa, the US or Canada, among others, make sure that you have adequate health insurance coverage in place before you travel. Similarly, you will need extended cover if you plan to take part in adventure activities such as diving and climbing. Most policies cover bushwalking and surfing, though it pays to check before you travel.

Nationals of the UK, Ireland, New Zealand, Italy, Belgium, Malta, Finland, the Netherlands, Norway, Slovenia and Sweden have, under their country's reciprocal health agreement, access to medically necessary treatment in hospitals and at GPs. Each country's specific arrangement varies; check ⓦ humanservices.gov.au for full details. In general this arrangement allows for medically necessary treatment in public hospitals and casualty departments (though the ambulance ride to get you there isn't covered). For most under the scheme, but not New Zealand or Ireland, visits to the GP are also included. You pay upfront (about $50 minimum), with two-thirds of your fee reimbursed by Medicare, or fill in a bulk bill form and the doctor bills Medicare directly (so you don't pay anything).

Reimbursements are collected from a Medicare Centre by presenting your doctor's bill together with a **Medicare Card**, which is available from any Medicare Centre. It's advisable to obtain one if you are eligible and staying in Australia for a while, particularly if on extended working holidays. You'll need an Australian bank account. Bring your passport and home country National Health documents.

Dental treatment, however, is not included in the reciprocal health agreements. If you find yourself in need of dental treatment in one of the larger cities, try the dental hospital, where dental students may be able to treat you at a reasonable price.

The sun

Australia's biggest health issue is also one of its prime attractions: **sunshine**. You might think that by now every visitor would be aware that a sunny day in London, Toronto or even Miami is not the same as one in Cairns, and that Australian ultraviolet rays are so damaging. Apparently not – most visitors still get burned at some point, so special care is essential.

Two out of three Australians are likely to develop **skin cancer** in their lifetime, the world's highest incidence rate. Around 95–99 percent of this is caused by exposure to the sun and about five percent of these cancers will develop into fatal melanomas; over two thousand Australians die from skin cancer each year. Looking at the ravaged complexions of some older Australians (who had prolonged exposure before there was an awareness of skin cancer) should be enough to make you use lashings of the highest-factor **sunblock** (SPF 35+).

Sunscreen should not be used on babies less than six months old: instead, keep them out of direct sunlight. The war paint on the noses of surfers and small children is actually zinc cream; the thick, sticky, waterproof cream provides a total blockout and is particularly useful when applied to protruding parts of the body, such as noses and shoulders.

Australians are now fully aware of the sun's dangers, and you're constantly reminded to "Slip, Slop, Slap", an old government catchphrase to remind Aussies to slip on a T-shirt, slop on some sunblock and slap on a hat – still sound advice. Pay attention to any moles on your body: if you notice any changes, either during or after your trip, see a doctor; cancerous melanomas are generally easily removed if caught early. To prevent headaches – and, in the long term, cataracts – wear sunglasses; look for "UV block" ratings when you buy a pair.

The sun can also cause **heat exhaustion** and **sunstroke**, so as well as covering up, stay in the shade if you can. Drink plenty of liquids: on hot days when walking, experts advise drinking a litre of water an hour. Alcohol and sun don't mix well; remember that more than one cold beer will dehydrate you.

Other health hazards

In the hot and humid north, **tropical ear**, a painful fungal infection of the ear canal, is an issue. Treatment is with ear drops, and if you think you might be susceptible, use them after getting wet regardless.

Water purity is a potential issue when bushwalking – gone are the days when you could guarantee that every creek and borehole in the bush was safe. E. coli and giardia are the main concerns – dehydration from gastroenteritis is a real danger in the bush – so boil, filter or treat water supplies to guarantee their purity. Better still, seek local knowledge before you walk.

Wildlife dangers

The danger from **wildlife** is much over-rated, but should not be discounted. Snake and spider bites are central to the perilous Outback myth, and crocodile and shark attacks are widely publicized, but all are extremely rare. The widest-spread threat is disease passed on by mosquitoes (see below). Jellyfish can be venomous and the stings are extremely painful. Reefs have their own minor hazards to keep in mind (see p.359).

Mosquitoes

Mosquitoes are spread across the country, and, while malaria has been eradicated, in the tropical north there are outbreaks of **Ross River fever** and **dengue fever**, both chronically debilitating viruses transmitted by mosquito bite that are potentially fatal to children and the elderly. Outbreaks of Ross River fever are most common in coastal marshy areas of the Northern Territory, Queensland and north Western Australia but can occur as far south as South Australia – reason enough not to be too blasé about mosquito bites.

Crocodiles

To minimize the danger from **saltwater crocodiles** (which actually range far inland), keep your distance. If you're camping in the bush within 100km of the northern coast between Broome (WA) and Rockhampton (QLD), make sure your tent is at least 50m from waterholes or creeks, don't collect water at the same spot every day or leave any rubbish out, and always seek local advice before pitching camp. Four-wheel drivers should take extra care when walking creeks prior to driving across.

Snakes

Snakes almost always try to avoid people, and you'll probably never even see one. They're more likely to be active in hot weather, when you should be more careful, and keep an eye out in open patches of woodland or scrub in the morning, when they often sunbathe. Treat snakes with respect and you're unlikely to be bitten: most bites occur when people try to catch or kill them. Wear boots and long trousers when hiking through undergrowth, collect firewood carefully, and, in the event of a confrontation, back off. **Sea snakes** sometimes find divers intriguing, and may even wrap themselves around limbs, but they're seldom aggressive. If you are **bitten** by a snake, use a crepe bandage to bind the entire limb firmly and splint it as if for a sprain; this slows the distribution of venom into the lymphatic system. Don't clean the bite area (venom around the bite can identify the species, making treatment easier), and don't slash the bite or apply a tourniquet. Treat all bites as serious and always seek immediate medical attention, but remember: not all snakes are venomous, not all venomous snakes inject a lethal dose of venom every time they bite, and death from snakebite is rare.

Spiders

Two **spiders** whose bites could be fatal are the funnel-web, a black, stocky creature found in the Sydney area, and the small redback usually found in dark, dry locations all over Australia (ie outdoor toilets, among shrubs, and under rocks and timber logs), although they are less common in colder regions like Tasmania. Both are prolific in January and February, when there is the greatest danger of bites – that said, there hasn't been a fatality from either species since antivenoms were developed in 1981 and 1956 respectively. Treat funnel-web bites as for snakebites, and apply ice to redback wounds to relieve pain; if bitten by either, get to a hospital immediately. Other spiders, centipedes, scorpions and ants can deliver painful wounds but only cause health problems if you have allergies.

Ticks, mites and leeches

The bane of bushwalkers, ticks, mites and leeches can be kept off of legs and out of socks with gaiters or repellent sprayed over shoes and leggings. **Ticks** are venomous – they produce the most toxins during feeding in spring – and can transmit disease. They attach themselves to long grass and bushes, latching on to passing animals that brush past. The most common complaint is discomfort and allergic reactions. However, the paralysis tick, a native of Australia, can be found from Cairns to Lakes Entrance, east Victoria, and is life-threatening. This tick causes more problems to humans because the

---

BUSHFIRES

The sheer devastation caused by bushfires over the last fifteen years has led Australia to take its fire-hazard more seriously than ever. Although you're highly unlikely to find yourself in the path of a raging **bushfire** – government warnings are now excellent – it certainly does not hurt to know survival basics. The government advice is to take shelter if you cannot escape a fire front: stay in the house when the fire front is passing – usually five to fifteen minutes – and take shelter furthest from the front, albeit while maintaining an easy escape route from the building. A room with two exits and a water supply such as a laundry or a kitchen are advised; people have died sheltering in bathrooms and single-entry rooms. If you must **evacuate** do so into an area that has already been burnt and go as far from the approaching fire as possible – toxic smoke and fumes from houses are a danger. And wear long sleeves, long trousers and strong leather boots against radiant heat.

---

tick can feed undiscovered over several days, thereby passing on toxins.

Check yourself over after a hike: look for local stinging and swelling (usually just inside the hairline) and you'll find either a tiny black dot or a pea-sized animal attached, depending on which species has bitten you. Use fine-pointed tweezers and grasp it as close to the skin as possible, and gently pull the tick out, trying to avoid squeezing the animal's body, which will inject more venom. Seek medical attention if you are not successful – a medic will need to cut out the tick's mouthparts with a scalpel. Incidentally, old bushwalker tales about dabbing kerosene, alcohol or insect repellent on the ticks before pulling them out are ill-advised – medical advice suggests this causes the ticks to inject more toxins into the host.

Mites cause an infuriating rash known as "scrub itch" wherever your clothes are tightest, such as around the hips and ankles. Unfortunately, there's not much you can do except take antihistamines and wait a day or two for the itching to stop. **Leeches** are gruesome but harmless: slide your fingernail under the sucker to get one off your skin, or twirl it gently with a fingertip until it lets go, then flick it off. Bites may bleed heavily for some time.

Jellyfish

The threat from various **jellyfish** (commonly known as "stingers") in coastal tropical waters in summer needs to be taken seriously. Unfortunately, both the tiny irukandji and saucer-sized box jellyfish are virtually invisible in water. **Irukandji** have initially painless stings, but their venom causes "irukandji syndrome", which can be fatal. Its symptoms are somewhat similar to those of decompression illness: elevated heart rate and increased blood pressure and, in addition, excruciating pain, anxiety and an overwhelming sense of dread. **Box jellyfish** stings leave permanent red

weals, and the venom can cause rapid unconsciousness and even kill by paralysing the heart muscles. Treat stinger victims by dousing the sting area (front and back) with liberal amounts of vinegar – which you may find in small stands on affected beaches, such as North Queensland. Never rub with sand or towels, or attempt to remove tentacles from the skin – both could trigger the release of more venom; apply mouth-to-mouth resuscitation if needed, and get the victim to hospital for treatment. Whatever the locals are doing, don't risk swimming anywhere on tropical beaches during stinger season (roughly Oct–May) – tiny irukandji can pass through the nets designed to stop box jellyfish.

Better known as a Portuguese Man o'War, bluebottle jellyfish (or "bluies") are widespread. They deliver a searing sting and a rash for an hour or so, but are only dangerous if you are allergic to the venom. Quickly wash off any tentacles stuck to the skin.

Food and drink

When it comes to food, Australia is almost two separate nations. In the cities – most notably Melbourne and Sydney – and the more populated regions there is an extensive range of cosmopolitan restaurants, cafés and bars featuring cuisines from across the globe. There's an exceptionally high ratio of places to eat, which survive because people dine out so much – three times a week is not unusual. Remote country areas, however, are the antithesis of this: often the only options other than meat pies and fast food is the straightforward food served at the local hotel, local restaurant or, perhaps, Chinese joint.

Traditionally, Australian food has its roots in the British meat-and-two-veg vein. But **immigration** and the range of superb, locally produced fresh ingredients have had a profound effect on mainstream Australian food. Fifteen years or so ago, it led to the emergence of "modern Australian" cuisine (or **mod Oz**), a fusion of flavours from around the world – particularly Asia and the Mediterranean. It still dominates Aussie menus, so even the average pub restaurant is likely to serve decent curries, dolmades, pasta and fish and seafood dishes, alongside standards like steaks and fish and chips, even if more high-end places follow global culinary trends. At its best, the result has a lot in common with Californian cooking styles where the watchwords are healthy, eclectic and, above all, fresh.

Food

Meat is plentiful, cheap and generally excellent in Australia: steak forms the mainstay of the pub-counter meal and of the ubiquitous **barbie**, as Australian an institution as you could hope to find: free or coin-operated barbecues are in car parks, campsites and beauty spots all over the country. As well as the usual beef, chicken, lamb and pork, wallaby, emu and buffalo may be served, but the most common "unusual" meats are kangaroo (or wallaby) – a rich, tender and virtually fat-free meat – and occasionally crocodile, which tastes, inevitably enough, like a mix of chicken and pork, and is at its best when grilled. On the coast, there's tremendous **seafood** – prawns and oysters, squid, mud crabs, lobster and yabbies (crayfish) – and a wide variety of fresh- and seawater fish. Flathead is a mainstay, flake is gummy shark, trumpeter and blue-eye is good and barramundi has a reputation as one of the finest, but is easily beaten by sweetlips or coral trout.

Fruit is good, too, from Tasmanian cherries and pears to tropical bananas, pawpaw (papaya), mangoes, avocados, citrus fruits, custard apples, lychees, pineapples, passion fruit, star fruit and coconuts – few of them native, but delicious nonetheless. **Vegetables** are similarly good, with everything from pumpkin, cauliflowers and potatoes to bok choy and Indian bitter gourds available. Note that in Australia aubergine is known as eggplant, courgettes as zucchini and peppers as capsicums.

Vegetarians are better served than you might expect of meat-centred Australia, at least in the cities, where veggie cafés have cultivated a wholesome image that suits Australians' health-conscious nature. Similarly, you'll find that organic products and gluten-free breads are almost standard. In the country, things are trickier, but most restaurants will have one vegetarian option at least.

A quick word on **eskies**: these insulated food containers vary from handy "six-pack" sizes to sixty-litre trunks able to swallow a weekend's worth of food or beer. No barbie or camping trip is complete without one.

International food

As you would expect, Australia's multicultural make-up is reflected in its dining options. An array of Asian cuisines – especially Chinese, Vietnamese, Malaysian, Thai, Japanese and Indian – can be found throughout the country. European cuisines have also made their mark, with Italian food an enormous influence, and Greek, Turkish and Lebanese also very popular.

BUSHTUCKER

Before the first European colonists settled on the continent, **Aborigines** followed a nomadic lifestyle within extensive tribal boundaries, following seasonal game and plants and promoting both by annually burning off grassland.

Along the coast, indigenous people speared turtles and dugong from outrigger canoes, and even cooperated with dolphins to herd fish into shallows. On land, animals caught were possums, snakes, goannas, emus and kangaroos, while more meagre pickings were provided by honey and green ants, water-holding frogs, moths and various grubs – the witchetty (or *witjuti*) being the best known. Plants were used extensively and formed the bulk of the diet. This food became known as **bushtucker**.

Until 1993, it was illegal to sell or serve kangaroo or emu anywhere outside of South Australia, but following legislation that allowed their consumption in other states, emu, kangaroo and even crocodile are now readily available on **restaurant** menus.

There are also several bushtucker tours and safaris available (particularly in the Northern Territory), which give an introduction to living off the land.

Eating out

Restaurants in Australia are no longer such good value compared with the UK, the US and Canada. Inflated by a (relatively) solid economy and the strong dollar, prices for visitors are on the steep side: a main course in a pub is likely to cost between $20 and $30, while $25 to $45 is the norm in a mid-range restaurant.

Cafés are one of the great joys of modern Australian life. Imported by southern European immigrants in the fifties, café culture in cities and resort towns is excellent, with most places acting as places to hang out with the morning papers and a coffee as much as venues for healthy food throughout the day.

The **hotel** (ie pub) counter meal is another Aussie mainstay, and in places may be all that's available: if it is, make sure you get there in time – meals in pubs are generally served from noon to 2.30pm and from 6pm to 8pm, and sometimes not at all on Sunday evening. The food is often simple but substantial; typically steaks/fish and chips, perhaps a daily pie or curry, and a pasta dish. In smarter areas and in cities you'll find more gastro-pub fare.

In cities and bigger resorts, **food courts**, where dozens of small stalls compete to offer Thai, Chinese, Japanese or Italian food as well as burgers, steaks and sandwiches, often in the basements of office buildings or in shopping malls, are a good bet for a meal on the go. On the road, you may be limited to what's available at the roadhouse, usually the lowest common denominator of reheated meat pies and microwaved ready-meals.

Drink

Australians have a reputation for enjoying a drink, and the local **hotel**, pub, tavern, inn or bar has as central a place in Aussie culture as it does in British. Traditionally, public bars were male enclaves, the place where mates met after work on their way home, with the emphasis more on the beer and banter than the surroundings. Nowadays, many city hotels are comfortable, relaxed bars for all, but a lot of Outback pubs remain pretty basic and daunting for strangers of either sex, though you'll find the barriers come down if you're prepared to join in the conversation.

Friday and Saturday are the party nights, when there's likely to be a band and – in the case of some Outback establishments – everybody for 100km around jammed into the building. **Opening hours** vary from state to state; they're usually 11am to 11pm, but are often much later, with early closing on Sunday. Some places are also "early openers", with hours from 6am to 6pm.

Off-licences or liquor stores are known as **bottle shops**. These are usually in a separate section attached to a pub or supermarket – in many states, you can't buy alcohol from supermarkets or grocery stores. There are also **drive-in** bottle shops, sometimes attached to pubs, where you can load bulk purchases directly into your car. If you plan to visit **Aboriginal communities** in the Outback, bear in mind that some are "dry". Respect their regulations and don't take any alcohol with you, even if members of the communities ask you for "grog".

Beer

As any Aussie will tell you, the only way to drink **beer** in a hot country is cold and fast. Tubular foam or polystyrene coolers are often supplied for **tinnies** (cans) or **stubbies** (short-necked bottles) to make sure that they stay icy. Glasses are always on the small side and, rather confusingly, have different names state by state. The standard ten-ounce (half-pint) serving is known as a **pot** in Victoria and Queensland, and a **middie** in New South Wales and Western Australia, where the situation is further complicated by the presence of fifteen-ounce **schooners**. A **carton** or **slab** is a box of 24–30 tinnies or stubbies, bought in bulk from a bottle shop. A "Darwin stubby", with typically

---

TOP 5 RESTAURANTS

Bluebonnet Barbecue Melbourne. See p.770
Hanuman Darwin. See p.498
Lamont's Margaret River. See p.588
Peacock & Jones Hobart. See p.899
Watergate Port Douglas. See p.418

BYO

In a restaurant, **BYO**, or **Bring Your Own**, means that diners may bring their own wine to enjoy with their meal. Some establishments add "wine only" after BYO, but the understanding is generally that you may not bring spirits or beer. A small corkage fee is usually charged, either per bottle or per head. Some licensed restaurants also allow BYO wine, but throw in a steep corkage fee to the price of your bottle – you might as well stick to their wine list.

INFAMOUS AUSTRALIAN FOODS

Some foods are all Aussie. Here's a selection sure to make any expat antipodean long for home.

Chiko Roll Imagine a wrapper of stodgy breadcrumbed dough filled with a mess of beef, veg, thickeners and flavourings, then deep-fried. Inspired by the spring roll, they say, but you could only get away with it in Australia.

Damper Sounding positively wholesome by comparison is this swagman's staple – soda bread baked in a pot buried in the ashes of a fire. It's not hard to make after a few attempts. The secret is in the heat of the coals – and a splash of beer.

Lamington A chocolate-coated sponge cube rolled in shredded coconut.

Pavlova (or "pav"). A dessert concoction of meringue with layers of cream and fruit; named after the eminent Russian ballerina. Made properly with fresh fruit and minimum quantities of cream and sugar, it's not bad at all.

Pie floater The apotheosis of the meat pie; a "pie floater" is an inverted meat pie swamped in mashed green peas and tomato sauce. Floaters can be surprisingly good, or horrible enough to put you off both pies and peas for life.

Vegemite Regarded by the British as an inferior form of Marmite and by almost every other nationality with total disgust, Vegemite is an Australian institution – a strong, dark, yeast spread.

Witchetty grubs (witjuti). The king of Aussie bushtucker, these delicacies about the size of your little finger are dug from the roots of mulga trees. Eating them plump, fawn-coloured caterpillars live (as is traditional) takes some nerve, so give them a brief roast in embers. Either way, they're oddly reminiscent of peanut butter.

Territorian eccentricity, is two litres of beer in an oversized bottle.

Traditionally Australian beers are lager- or pilsner-style, and even the big mass-produced ones are pretty good – at least once you've worked up a thirst. They're considerably stronger than their US equivalents, equivalent to the average British lager at just under five percent alcohol. Each state has its own **label** and there are fierce local loyalties, even though most are sold nationwide.

However, in recent years, Australians have discovered there's more to slake a thirst than icy lager. A number of smaller breweries now produce hoppy ales with less fizz and arguably more taste. As in Britain and the US, Australia has caught onto the appeal of pale ales, porters and more hoppy lagers. A rapidly growing number of microbreweries and specialist beer makers are manufacturing craft beers. Similarly, a number of pubs stock imported beers, but outside cities (where Irish pubs often serve decent Guinness) it's rare that you'll find anything foreign on tap.

Incidentally, Fosters is treated as a joke in Australia, fit only for export.

Wines and spirits

As the sixth-largest exporter of wine in the world – in 2015 exports were worth over $2.1bn, up fourteen percent on the previous year – the Aussie wine industry has a global reputation. The likes of Jacob's Creek and Oxford Landing, Yalumba, Lindemans, Wolf Blass, Penfolds and Hardys are fixtures in most European supermarkets. And even if Australia is still stereotyped as a nation of beer-drinkers, Australian viticulture has a long pedigree – vine cuttings from the Cape of Good Hope were shipped with the First Fleet.

Shiraz, Cabernet Sauvignon, Merlot, Chardonnay, Sauvignon blanc, Sémillon and Riesling are the principal grape varieties, and winemakers in recent years have moved away from a weakness for big, powerful wines which packed a punch in terms of fruit and jams as much as alcohol levels. Aussie **wines** today tend to be more subtle affairs: spicy or silky, mouth-filling or aromatic reds; fresh crisp whites packed with citrus or tropical fruits that are tailor-made for quaffing with the barbie; and vibrant summery rosés. Nor are they particularly pricey: even an inexpensive bottle will be better than just drinkable, while pricier varieties can produce something really special.

Most states in the southern half of the country have wine-growing regions and, as in America, most vineyards welcome guests. You can easily lose a few happy days pottering around vineyards, sampling wines and chatting to makers. The most celebrated wine-producing **regions** are the Hunter Valley in New South Wales and the Barossa Valley in South Australia, but you will also find superb vineyards in the Yarra Valley, Victoria, and the Clare Valley, South Australia. More recently, Margaret River in southwest Western Australia has emerged

WINE-TASTING TIPS

The smaller wineries tend to have more charm and intrinsic interest than the larger commercial operators and it's here you'll often get to talk personally to the winemaker or snare some wines not generally available in wine shops. Groups are welcomed by most wineries but are encouraged to book, although some places are too small to accommodate them. You're under no obligation to buy wine, but coming away with a few of your favourites of the day and some fruity adjectives to describe them is part of the fun.

For a novice, **wine tasting** can be an intimidating experience. On entering the tasting area (or cellar door) you'll be shown a list of wines that may be tasted, divided into whites through to reds, all printed in the order that the winemaker considers best on the palate. This is fine, but if you are visiting several wineries and are only interested in reds, by all means concentrate on the reds. Always look at the colour and clarity of the wine first, then give it a swirl and a sniff. Then take a deeper sniff with your nose inside the rim of the glass to try to appreciate the aroma or bouquets you can pick up. Take a sip, rolling it around on your tongue before swallowing; there's always a spittoon if you don't want to swallow. A great way to learn more is to think about what you can pick up on your palate and then check it against the winemaker's notes. Don't be shy about discussing the wines with the person serving – that's what they're there for, and even wine snobs are down-to-earth Australians at heart.

as a gourmet hotspot of world-class wineries and restaurants. If you buy at the wineries themselves, you'll be able to sample in advance (see box above). That said, most bottle shops have a good range of reasonably priced options from around the country, and at some specialist bottle shops staff can advise on varieties to suit your palette.

The Australian wine industry also makes port and brandy as a sideline and there are two (in)famous dark **rums** from Queensland's sugar belt that are well worth tasting: the sweet, smoky Bundaberg and the more conventionally flavoured Beenleigh. They're of average strength, normally 33 percent alcohol, but beware of "overproof" variations, which will floor you if you try to drink them like ordinary spirits.

Finally, a word about whisky. Scots will dispute the malts as second rate, but the Australian whisky industry is winning plaudits from connoisseurs. Tasmania, the most Scottish of Aussie states, with similar peaty streams and pure environment, is the centre of production, with fine single malts produced by distilleries such as Lark, Hellyer, Nant and Sullivans Cove.

Coffee

Australia has a thriving coffee culture, thanks largely to the waves of European (and most notably Italian) immigration in the 1950s. You can get a good cup right across the country, with standards particularly high in Melbourne. Australia is also the birthplace of the flat white: an espresso topped with milk that has been heated to produce "micro foam" but is not frothy. Meanwhile, a "short black" is the local term for an espresso, and a "long black" is an Americano (without milk).

Festivals and sporting events

The nationwide festivals listed below all include, necessitate and are, in some cases, the imaginative product of prolonged beer-swilling. Why else would you drive to the edge of the Simpson Desert to watch a horse race? More seriously, each mainland capital tries to elevate its sophistication quotient with a regular celebration and showcase of art and culture, of which the biennial Adelaide Festival of Arts is the best known.

Besides the major events listed below, there's a host of smaller, local events, many of which are detailed throughout the Guide. All cities and towns also have their own agricultural "shows", which are high points of the local calendar. The Christmas and Easter holiday periods, especially, are marked by celebrations at every turn, all over the country.

JANUARY

Sydney Festival Sydney, NSW; starts the first week
Ⓦ sydneyfestival.org.au. See p.142. Three weeks of festivities all over the city – in parks, theatres and cinemas – with something for everyone, from new film and outdoor jazz to contemporary art and current-events lectures.

MoFo TAS; mid-Jan Ⓦ mofo.net.au. See p.900. This is a hip Hobart festival of alternative rock and arts curated by the cutting-edge Mona gallery. The Flaming Lips, Kate Tempest and Gilbert & George all featured at the 2016 event.

Australian Open Tennis Championship Melbourne, VIC; mid- to end Jan Ⓦ australianopen.com. The year's first Grand Slam attracts hordes of tennis fans to see the best players in the world compete for two weeks at Melbourne Park.

Tamworth Country Music Festival NSW; mid-Jan Ⓦ tcmf .com.au. Ten days of country music, with around 700 musicians and bands, 2800 events, attracting over 50,000 people and culminating in the Australian Country Music Awards.

FEBRUARY

Sydney Gay and Lesbian Mardi Gras NSW; early Feb to early March Ⓦ mardigras.org.au. See p.136. Sydney's proud gay community's festival runs throughout Feb and culminates at the beginning of March with an extravagant parade and an all-night dance party.

Perth International Arts Festival Perth, WA; mid-Feb to early March Ⓦ perthfestival.com.au. Australia's oldest and largest arts festival, attracting renowned international artists, performers and attendees to indoor and outdoor events all over the city for three weeks.

Adelaide Festival of Arts SA; March Ⓦ adelaidefestival.com.au. See p.672. The country's best-known and most innovative annual arts festival, featuring opera, theatre, music and dance, and including the largest literary festivals in the world. Not to be missed.

MARCH

Australian Grand Prix Melbourne, VIC Ⓦ grandprix.com.au. Formula 1 mania takes over Melbourne for four days, with action centred on the purpose-built Albert Park race track. As well as the high-adrenaline 58-lap race, which takes place on Sun, off-track entertainment includes air displays, rides, go-karting and glamour in the form of the pit girls.

Womadelaide Adelaide, SA; first or second weekend Ⓦ womadelaide.com.au. See p.672. Part of the Womad festival circuit; three-day festival featuring world music, folk, blues and jazz.

Moomba Festival Melbourne, VIC; second weekend. A long weekend of partying in Melbourne, beginning and ending with fireworks, with lots of water-based fun on the Yarra River in between. Don't miss the "Birdman Rally" in which various flying contraptions assemble at Princes Bridge and attempt to defy gravity.

APRIL

Melbourne International Comedy Festival Melbourne, VIC; Ⓦ comedyfestival.com.au. Leading comedy fest that attracts more than a thousand home-grown and international stand-ups and acts. Based around the Melbourne Town Hall, but with programmes in over fifty other city venues, spanning stand-up comedy, plays, film, TV and street theatre.

JUNE

Sydney International Film Festival Sydney, NSW; early June Ⓦ sff.org.au. Influential film festival, running for over two weeks and based at four CBD venues including the glorious State Theatre.

Barunga Cultural and Sports Festival Katherine, NT; Queen's Birthday weekend (second weekend) Ⓦ barungafestival.com.au. This three-day festival, held on Aboriginal land near Katherine, offers a rare and enjoyable opportunity to encounter Aboriginal culture in the NT. No alcohol.

Laura Dance and Cultural Festival Cape York, QLD; third weekend (held in odd-numbered years) Ⓦ lauradancefestival.com. Three-day celebration of authentic Aboriginal culture, attracting over five thousand people and five hundred performers.

JULY

Imparja Camel Cup Alice Springs, NT; second Sat Ⓦ camelcup .com.au. This event originated with camels charging down the dry Todd River; the camel-racing now takes place at Blatherskite Park, with free buses to the site.

Darwin Beer Can Regatta NT; early Sun Ⓦ beercanregatta .org.au. Mindil Beach is the venue for the recycling of copious empties into a variety of "constructed" seacraft. Also a thong-throwing contest; Territorian eccentricity personified.

Melbourne International Film Festival VIC; end July to mid-Aug Ⓦ miff.com.au. The country's largest and most prestigious film festival, lasting for nineteen days, with a focus on Australian, cult and arty films, plus a multimedia component.

AUGUST

Isa Rodeo Mount Isa, QLD; second or third weekend Ⓦ isarodeo .com.au. Australia's largest rodeo – a gritty, down-to-earth encounter with bulls, horses and their riders.

Henley-on-Todd Regatta Alice Springs, NT; third Sat Ⓦ henleyontodd.com.au. Wacky races in bottomless boats running down the dry Todd River; the event is heavily insured against the river actually flowing.

SEPTEMBER

Birdsville Races QLD; first weekend Ⓦ birdsvilleraces.com. Once a year, the remote Outback town of Birdsville (population approx. 120) comes alive for a weekend (Fri & Sat) of drinking and horseracing – a well-known and definitive Australian oddity.

Brisbane Festival Brisbane, QLD; mid-Sept Ⓦ brisbanefestival .com.au. Huge seventeen-day festival featuring performing arts, food and drink, music, writing, kids' stuff and fireworks.

Royal Melbourne Show VIC; mid-Sept Ⓦ royalshow.com.au. Eleven-day agricultural bonanza, featuring sheepshearing, dog and horse shows and performing pigs. Rides, candyfloss and contests for everything from Jersey-Holstein cows to wood-choppers.

Shinju Matsuri Festival Broome, WA; third weekend Ⓦ shinjumatsuri.com.au. Probably the most remote of the big festivals, but the town packs out for WA's ten-day Asian-themed pearl festival.

AFL Grand Final Melbourne, VIC; last Sat Ⓦ afl.com.au. Huge, testosterone-charged sporting event. The Australian Football League final is held at Melbourne's MCG and is accompanied by lots of beer drinking and celebrating, depending on which team wins.

OCTOBER

Australian Motorcycle Grand Prix Phillip Island, VIC Ⓦ motogp
.com.au. Held over one weekend, this is one of the last races of the World
Championship and a popular pilgrimage for all motorbike enthusiasts.
Melbourne Festival VIC; mid-Oct Ⓦ festival.melbourne. One of
Australia's pre-eminent annual arts events, this seventeen-day festival
has a cast of thousands drawn from the fields of music, multimedia,
opera, dance and theatre. Ticketed and free performances are held both
indoors at various venues and on Melbourne's streets.

NOVEMBER

Melbourne Cup Flemington Racecourse, VIC; first Tues
Ⓦ flemington.com.au/melbourne-cup-carnival. Australia's Ascot,
dating back to 1861, this horse race brings the entire country to a
standstill around the radio or TV.
Targa Tasmania Statewide, TAS; first or second weekend Ⓦ targa
.com.au. One of Australia's top motor events, with three hundred cars,
many vintage, on a six-day, 2000km rally. A petrolhead's paradise.

DECEMBER

Christmas Day Sydney, NSW. Australia's largest festive day event is
held on Sydney's Bondi Beach – usually with bands and DJs and a fair
slug of alcohol. The days of free partying are long gone and the festivities
are now by ticket only (Ⓦ sunburntchristmas.com.au), although a
section of the beach remains accessible to the public.
New Year's Eve Sydney, NSW. The fireworks display from Sydney
Harbour Bridge is a grand show, and a fine example to the rest of the
world of how to welcome in the New Year. For the best views along the
water's edge, get there while it's still light.
Sydney–Hobart Yacht Race Sydney, NSW Ⓦ rolexsydneyhobart
.com. Crowds flock to the harbour to witness the start of this classic
regatta, which departs Sydney at 1pm on Boxing Day and arrives in
Hobart three days later.

Sports and outdoor activities

**Australians famously love their sports,
especially cricket, Aussie Rules football,
rugby (both League or Union), tennis and
racing, be it horse, camel or cockroach. No
matter what it is, it'll draw a crowd – with
thousands more watching on TV – and a
crowd means a party. Even unpromising-
sounding activities such as surf lifesaving
and yacht racing (the start of the Sydney-
to-Hobart race just after Christmas is a
massive social event) are hugely popular.**

Football

The football (**footy**) season in Australia lasts from
March to September, and comes in two varieties.
Football as most of the world knows it is "soccer" to
differentiate it from Australian Rules footy, which in
the 1950s was considered the game "real Australians"
played. Soccer's A-League competition (Ⓦ a-league
.com.au), with ten teams from Australia and New
Zealand, is about commitment rather than the slick
skills of top European and South American leagues,
though standards are slowly improving. The best
players invariably play overseas but unite for Australia's national team, the **Socceroos**, whose never-say-
die performances in recent World Cups have
boosted interest in the sport.

Australian Rules ("**Aussie Rules**") football
dominates Victoria, Tasmania, South Australia and
Western Australia. It's an anarchic, no-holds-barred,
eighteen-a-side brawl, most closely related to
Gaelic football. The ball can be propelled by any
means necessary, and the fact that players aren't
sent off for misconduct ensures a lively, skilful and,
above all, gladiatorial confrontation. The aim is to
get a ball similar to that used in rugby or American
football through central uprights for a goal (six
points). There are four twenty-minute quarters,
though the clock is stopped each time the ball is
out of play, so quarters can go on for longer.
Despite the violence on the pitch (or perhaps
because of it), Aussie Rules fans tend to be well
behaved, with a high proportion of women and
children in crowds. It's also worth noting that fans
aren't segregated at matches. Victoria has traditionally been the home of the game and has ten out of
the sixteen AFL clubs, and an all-Victorian Grand
Final held in September usually warrants a sell-out
crowd at the MCG (see p.743).

Rugby

In New South Wales and Queensland, **Rugby
League** attracts the fanatics, especially for the hard-
fought State of Origin matches. The thirteen-a-side
game is one at which Australians excel – national
team the **Kangaroos** have won the World Cup in
ten of the fourteen tournaments to date – despite
having a relatively small professional league. Rugby
League is huge in Sydney and the majority of the
sixteen NRL teams are based there. One consequence of mass-media promotion of the sport has
been the loss of some traditional inner-city clubs
through mergers. Many people also resent the way
in which this one-time bastion of working-class
culture has been co-opted by pay TV.

Rugby Union is very much a minority interest
domestically. However, the introduction of a

GAMBLING

Australians are obsessive about gambling, though legalities vary from state to state. Even small towns have their own racetracks, and there are government TAB betting agencies everywhere; you can often bet in pubs, too. Many states have huge casinos and clubs, open to anyone, with wall-to-wall one-armed bandits (poker machines or "pokies"), often packed into pubs too.

Super 12 – which, since 2016, has become a Super 18 – competition, involving teams from Australia, New Zealand, South Africa, Argentina and Japan, has generated greater interest in what was an elitist sport, and the national team, the **Wallabies**, are hugely popular. Both the League and Union rugby season runs from April to September.

Cricket

Cricket is played from October to March, and is a great spectator sport – for the crowd, the sunshine and the beer, as much as the play. Every state is involved, and the three- or four-day Sheffield Shield matches of the interstate series are interspersed with one-day games and internationals, as well as full five-day international test matches. In recent years the Big Bash Twenty20 league has rapidly gained in popularity, drawing players from across the cricketing world.

The international competition that still arouses greatest interest is the biennial series (the next competition is in 2017–18) between Australia and England – **The Ashes**. Having been around for 135 years, this is perhaps the oldest sporting rivalry between nations. The "trophy" dates from 1882, when an Australian touring side defeated England at the Oval in South London by seven runs, and the *Sporting Times* was moved to run a mock obituary for the death of English cricket. A set of bails was cremated, and then preserved in a funerary urn. This never actually leaves Lord's cricket ground in London – what's up for grabs is a crystal glass replica and prestige. In 2006, Australia took the Ashes back down under after demolishing England in the first series whitewash since 1920. The Poms got their revenge in 2011 by walloping Australia on their home turf, their first win on Australian soil since the mid-1980s and the only one in which a team has won three Tests by innings margins. They won again in 2013, then the Aussies gained their revenge in 2014, and then

NATIONAL PARKS

Each state and territory has its own protected area management authority; departmental names vary from state to state, but Australians tend to generically dub them the **National Parks and Wildlife Service (NPWS)**. The thousand-odd **national parks** range from suburban commons to the Great Barrier Reef, and from popular hiking areas within striking distance of the cities to wilderness regions that require days in a 4WD simply to reach. They protect everything within their boundaries: flora, fauna and landforms as well as Aboriginal art and sacred sites, although not always to the exclusion of mineral exploitation in Western Australia or the Northern Territory.

Entry and camping **fees** are variable. Some parks or states have no fees at all, some charge entry fees but often don't police the system, some charge for use of camping facilities, while others require permits – free or for a small fee – obtained in advance. Each state offers a pass (generally lasting anything from one month to a year) – which makes it cheaper if you want to visit many national parks and for longer periods – but no national pass is available. If you're camping you can usually pay on site, but booking ahead can be a good idea during the Christmas, Easter and school holidays.

Some parks have cabin accommodation, either self-catering or bunk-style with a camp kitchen, but nearby resorts or alternative accommodation are always independently run. For details on the names and vagaries of each state or territory's system, consult the websites listed below.

Australian Dept of the Environment Ⓦ environment.gov.au
New South Wales & ACT Ⓦ nationalparks.nsw.gov.au
Northern Territory Ⓦ nt.gov.au/leisure/parks-reserves
Queensland Ⓦ npsr.qld.gov.au

South Australia Ⓦ environment.sa.gov.au/parks
Tasmania Ⓦ parks.tas.gov.au
Victoria Ⓦ parkweb.vic.gov.au
Western Australia Ⓦ dpaw.wa.gov.au

England claimed another victory on home territory. The rivalry is far from dead.

Outdoor pursuits

The cities are fun, but if Australia is about anything, it is its great outdoors: the vast and remote wilderness of the bush, the Outback, and thousands of kilometres of unspoilt coastline. With one of the world's best adventure playgrounds in the backyard it's no wonder that Aussies participate in a huge range of **outdoor pursuits** – hiking, surfing, diving, fishing, even skiing – especially in the national parks that cover the country. The best sources of information tend to be the local tourist visitor centres, which publicize what is available in their area: from detailed maps of national parks with walking trails, swimming holes and activities to specialist tour operators. You'll find tour operators providing just about any activity you can think of, usually with all gear supplied. If you want to go it alone, plenty of places will rent or sell you equipment. Either way, check your insurance cover beforehand (see p.56).

Be aware, too, that the Australian interior does not suffer fools – every year tourists die here by underestimating the harshness of the environment – and the coast conceals **dangers**, too: sunstroke and dehydration are risks everywhere, and riptides, strong currents and large waves can be fatal on exposed coasts. In remote regions, isolation and lack of surface water compromise energetic outdoor activities such as bushwalking or mountain biking, which for novices are better practised in the cooler and more populated south.

Watersports

Beach culture is hardwired into the Aussie mentality and with around ninety percent of the population living within two hours of the beach, Australians have found countless ways of getting in, on or under the water.

In the century since Hawaiian legend Duke Kahanamoku paddled out at North Sydney's Freshwater Beach to demonstrate the wave-riding of his homeland, Australians have made **surfing** their own, thanks to world-class waves on all coastlines except the north. Forget any impressions of surfing as the counterculture activity of beach bums, however – in Australia it is a mainstream sport where the standard is high and the mentality is territorial; cliquey at best, aggressive at worst. Learners, therefore, should familiarize themselves with a lesson or two at resorts such as Byron Bay first, and keep clear of the pack. Similarly, beginners should seek advice if they hire gear and always select breaks patrolled by lifeguards.

Sailing is also hugely popular. Prime destinations are Queensland's Whitsunday Islands, a concentrated dose of azure sea and white powder beaches, and also Sydney Harbour and Western Australia's Fremantle and Coral Bay. Tourist sailing trips are a fixture in Sydney; in Western Australia, check at local visitor information centres or ask at local yacht clubs.

For many, what lies underwater is reason alone to visit Australia. A huge draw for **divers**, the Great Barrier Reef is the world's largest living organism, a kaleidoscope of coral and tropical fish – the dilemma is which bit of its 2000km to visit, and whether to go with a liveaboard dive school or day-trip. Far less commercial is the superb Ningaloo

---

TOP DIVE SITES

Cod Hole Far North Reef, Great Barrier Reef, QLD. Where giant potato cod and divers meet. Trips from Cairns. See p.403

Geographe Bay WA. The HMS *Swan* was scuppered off Cape Naturaliste. Trips from Dunsborough. See p.584

Lord Howe Island NSW. The world's southernmost reef surrounds one of its most beautiful islands. See p.241

Ningaloo Reef WA. Whale sharks from April to June. Tours from Exmouth or Coral Bay. Snorkelling from the beaches of Cape Range National Park. See p.622

Port Lincoln SA. These waters are a last bastion for the unfairly maligned great white shark. Shark-cage diving trips from Port Lincoln. See p.709

SS Yongala QLD. Huge fish and the wreck of an early twentieth-century passenger liner sunk by a cyclone. Trips from Townsville (p.383) and Cairns (p.400).

Tasman Peninsula TAS. Caves and kelp forests in the world's most accessible underwater wilderness. Trips from Eaglehawk Neck. See box, p.914

Marine Park (see p.622) in Western Australia The proximity of the continental shelf provides for sublime **snorkelling** straight off the beach – if you want to swim with whale sharks, the gentle giants of the deep, this is your place.

Bushwalking

Bushwalking in Australia means self-sufficient hikes, lasting anything from a day to a week or more. You will find trails marked in almost every national park, as well as local bushwalking clubs and dedicated bushwalk tour operators.

Given the harshness of the environment in Australia, it is impossible to stress enough that you must be **properly equipped** for all conditions you might encounter. Make sure that you carry a proper walking map, know the trail markers, and stay on the route. Ideally, let someone know where you're going and confirm your safe return – many park rangers insist on this for overnight walks, which may well require registration.

The essentials, even for a short walk, are adequate clothing, including a wide-brimmed hat, enough food (with extra in case of problems) and, above all, plenty of water. Other useful items include a torch, matches or lighter, penknife, sunblock, insect repellent, a fuel stove, toilet paper (often with a trowel to bury it), a first-aid kit and a whistle or mirror to attract attention.

Most of the long-distance tracks are in the south, with Tasmania's wilderness being the biggest draw for many travellers; particularly fabulous are the 80km Overland Track (see p.954) and the South Coast Track (see p.966). In 2015 the Three Capes Track (W threecapestrack.com.au) around the Tasman Peninsula also opened. On the mainland, the Blue Mountains, a two-hour train ride from Sydney, the Snowy Mountains further south, and Victoria's spectacular Grampians are all popular regions for longer, marked walks.

BUSH ESSENTIALS

There are four things to remember above all when you are in the bush:

FIRE

The driest continent on earth, Australia is always at risk from **bushfires** (see box, p.42). In February 2009 wildfires in Victoria destroyed over a million acres of bushland and killed 173 people in the country's worst bushfire disaster. New South Wales experienced sweeping fires in in 2013, though thankfully only two people died as an indirect result. Western Australia was badly affected by bushfires in 2016.

Even in wet years, there's a constant red alert during summer months. Ideally, use a fuel-stove – a requisite for cooking in national park areas. Elsewhere, always use an established fireplace where available, or dig a shallow pit and ring it with stones. Keep fires small and make absolutely sure embers are smothered before going to sleep or moving on. Similarly, never leave a burning fire unattended nor discard burning cigarette butts from cars. Periodic total fire bans – announced in the local media – prohibit any fire in the open, including wood, gas or electric barbecues, with heavy fines for offenders.

Check on the local fire danger before you go bushwalking – some walking trails are closed in risky periods (summer – Dec, Jan & Feb – in the south; the end of the dry season – Sept/Oct – in the north). If driving, carry blankets and a full water container, listen to the radio and watch out for roadside fire-danger indicators.

WATER

Carry plenty of **water** and do not contaminate local water resources: soaps and detergents can render water undrinkable and kill livestock and wild animals. Avoid washing in standing water, especially tanks and small lakes or reservoirs.

WASTE

As the saying goes, take only photographs, leave only footprints. This means carrying out all **rubbish** – never burn or bury it – and urinating and burying excrement at least 50m from the nearest campsite or water source.

HYPOTHERMIA

Prepare for four seasons in a day when you are in the **highlands of Tasmania**, where the weather is notoriously changeable, even in summer; the conditions can go from sunburn to snow between breakfast and lunch.

South Australia's **Flinders Ranges**, 300km north of Adelaide, are accessible along the Heysen Trail (see p.684) from the Fleurieu Peninsula, the walk into the 1000m-high natural basin of Wilpena Pound being the highlight (see p.722). In temperate southwestern WA, the 960km **Bibbulmun Track** (see p.589) is an old Aboriginal trail through the region's giant eucalypt forests, from Albany to Kalamunda near Perth, while the 220km Larapinta Trail (see p.539) runs along the McDonnell Ranges west of Alice Springs. Queensland's rainforested coastal strip offers plenty more opportunities for walks, including the Lamington area in the south, and around northern Atherton Tablelands and Hinchinbrook Island.

Off-road driving

Australia's wilderness is an ideal venue for extended **off-road driving** and **motorbiking**, although permission may be needed to cross station- and Aboriginal-owned lands, and the fragile desert ecology should be respected at all times. Northern Queensland's Cape York and WA's Kimberley are the most adventurous destinations, 4WD-accessible in the dry season only. The great **Outback tracks** pushed out by explorers or drovers, such as the Warburton Road and Sandover Highway and the Tanami, Birdsville and Oodnadatta tracks, are actually two-wheel driveable in dry conditions, but can be hard on poorly prepared vehicles. Getting right to the tip of Queensland's 800km-long Cape York Peninsula will definitely require a 4WD or trail bike, while the Kimberley's notoriously corrugated Gibb River Road in Western Australia is also popular in the Dry.

Other pursuits

Alice Springs' wide-open spaces make it the country's **hot-air-ballooning** capital, as well as the main base for **camel treks** into the surrounding desert.

More traditional **riding**, on horseback, is offered all over the country – anything from a gentle hour at walking pace to a serious cattle roundup. **Cycling** and mountain biking are tremendously popular, too, and a good way of getting around resorts; many hostels rent bikes, and we've listed other outlets throughout this book.

Finally, you may not associate Australia with **skiing**, but there's plenty of it in the 1500m-high Australian Alps on the border of Victoria and New South Wales (see p.878), based around the winter resorts of Thredbo, Perisher, Falls Creek and Mount Hotham; the season usually runs from late June until the end of September.

Travelling with children

With beautiful beaches, parks and playgrounds, and all sorts of wildlife to discover, travelling Australia with kids can be great fun. Australians have an easy-going attitude to children and in most places they are welcome – small luxury hotels may stipulate no under-12s and tots are discouraged in some smarter restaurants.

In the cities and larger towns, general facilities are good – changing tables are found in most restaurants and public toilets, and staff in cafés may warm a bottle if they have time. Breastfeeding in public has been a legal right in Australia since 1984 – something to remember if you receive comments in small country towns – and individual states have implemented laws to protect you from harassment.

Getting around

The catch with travelling around Australia with children is the country's size – fail to appreciate the distances involved in road travel and the jolly family holiday can be a disaster of fourteen-hour drives. **Domestic airlines** may be the best bet for interstate travel. Some airlines offer discounts for children between 2 and 11 years. However, you may find that a discounted adult ticket is even cheaper. Infants usually travel free.

Long-distance bus travel with kids verges on the masochistic; most interstate buses offer discounts for under-14s. **Long-distance train** travel, though limited, has the advantage of sleepers and a bit more freedom of movement. Discounts are generally available up to 11 or 12 years old and children under 4 generally go free. Most train companies offer family fares, too, allowing discounted or free travel for children who travel with at least one adult. Otherwise, there's always the option of self-drive. **Car rental** is reasonably priced, and motorhomes and campervans are also available for rental (see p.35).

Within cities, metropolitan buses and trains give discounts of around fifty percent for children and many allow children under 4 or 5 to travel free.

Accommodation

While resorts and motels often provide child discounts and may offer a babysitting service or organized activities, most families on extended trips find that **self-catering** provides the most flexibility. Similarly, **hostels** are not exclusively for backpackers and most have affordable family rooms – some en-suite. A few modern hostels are positively luxurious, and most are in good locations. All have communal kitchens, lounge areas and television, and there are usually plenty of books and games.

Aside from camping, the most economical way to see the country is the thousands of **caravan parks**. Most have on-site vans or self-contained cabins at reasonable family rates. Check with visitor centres for details.

Eating out

Since they take a relaxed attitude to dining, Aussies welcome children in most cafés, restaurants and pubs, with some providing a decent **children's menu**. Smart restaurants are (generally speaking) the exception.

The ubiquity of British and Italian favourites such as fish and chips and pasta, plus the fast, casual service typical of Chinese and Thai restaurants make for kid-friendly dining. Children are allowed in the dining section of most **pubs** (they are banned from the gaming and bar sections, however), and typical counter-meal menus and eating hours of 5 to 8pm will suit. Modern pubs in large towns are generally child-friendly too. Elsewhere, it's a judgement call – Aussie pubs can be fairly rowdy even though you'll be in a separate dining room, and some maintain an over-18s-only policy. Most country towns also have an **RSL club** (Returned Servicemen's League), a bastion of older, usually male, diners but an inexpensive way to feed the family on pub grub.

Kids' gear

Airlines will allow you to carry a pram, pushchair or travel cot for free. For **car seats**, Australian law requires that all children below six months are in a rear-facing safety seat; from six months to four years are in a rear- or forward-facing child seat; and those from four to seven are in a forward-facing seat or on a booster seat. Exemptions are in taxis. Car and van rental companies provide child safety seats at a cost. Keep in mind that your own seat may not fit standard attachments in Australian cars.

Sun care

The Australian **sun** is ferocious, so sensible skincare is essential for outdoor activities; (see p.40). A "no hat, no play" policy operates in school playgrounds and most kids wear legionnaire-style caps, or broad-brimmed sun hats. Most kids wear UV-resistant Lycra swim tops or wetsuit-style all-in-ones to the beach.

Working in Australia

It has become something of a right of passage for younger longer-term visitors to come to Australia with a Working Holiday Visa (see p.31). If you are between 18 and 30 and are prepared to try anything (officially for no more than six months at a time), you are allowed to work to fund your travels – or simply work to experience Aussie life at ground level.

In practice, the only jobs open will be temporary and generally unskilled. Old faithfuls are harvesting or farm labouring – the **Harvest Trail** (☏ 1800 062 332, ⓦ jobsearch.gov.au/job/search/harvest) has information about such jobs, but remember that crop-picking means hard work for low wages (usually paid on a commission basis). It is also worth noting that harvest work is often on farms or plantations some distance from a town. Many employers will provide transport to and from a workers' hostel in a nearby town – sometimes, but not always, free of charge. In other cases, you will be given basic accommodation on the farm or be required to pitch your own tent.

For casual work – for example bar or restaurant, construction and factory work – Sydney-based agency **Travellers' Contact Point** (☏ 02/9221 7900, ⓦ travellers.com.au) has a branch in most of the major cities. Other dedicated traveller job agencies include **Travellers At Work** (ⓦ taw.com.au) and **Work & Travel Company** (ⓦ worktravelcompany .com); both are based in Sydney. All of these help with every aspect of working, from organizing tax file numbers to actually finding jobs, but either take a commission for finding work or charge a membership fee. Specialized **temping agencies** in cities (basic office computer work, accountancy, nursing, catering and so on) have better, higher-paid jobs on their books, though they often require full-time or longer commitments. Finally, travellers, hostel staff and **notice boards** may be the best sources of all, especially in remote areas. In fact, some hostels occasionally offer free nights in lieu of cleaning work – and some even pay you.

TAX

Due to the threat of fines on employers for cash-in-hand labour, it's difficult to avoid paying income **tax**. In 2015–16, this was not levied at earnings under $18,200, then levied at nineteen percent for every dollar from $18,201–$37,000, deducted at source. To become part of the system you'll need a **tax file number** (apply online via Ⓦato.gov.au, call ☎13 2861 or visit an Australian Tax Office centre; locations are provided on the ATO website), for which you'll need a passport with a relevant work visa. Your employer will give you thirty days' grace to get a number, after which you'll be taxed at 46.5 percent. Nowadays, it's hard to claim a tax rebate, no matter how little you earn; however, it's worth a try, and possibly a trip to a tax advisor. Alternatively, go to Ⓦtaxback.com, which offers a hassle-free service to reclaim tax and superannuation refunds.

One word of warning: Australia is tough on people who work on tourist visas or expired working visas. If you're caught, your visa will be cancelled, you will be asked to leave the country immediately, or taken into detention in the interim. Furthermore, you are extremely unlikely to be granted another visa even after the set three-year period.

STUDY AND WORK PROGRAMMES

AFS Intercultural Programs Ⓦ afs.org. Intercultural exchange organization with programmes in over sixty countries, including Australia.
American Institute for Foreign Study Ⓦ aifs.com. Cultural immersion and study programmes.
BUNAC Ⓦ bunac.org. Travel and work agency that helps members find work **and volunteering opportunities** through resource centres nationwide.
Conservation Volunteers Ⓦ conservationvolunteers.com.au. Volunteer work on conservation projects in reserves and parks across Australia from one day to four weeks. About $40–50/day charged for food and accommodation on some projects.
Council on International Educational Exchange (CIEE) Ⓦ ciee.org. Leading NGO offering study programmes in Australia.
Earthwatch Institute Ⓦ earthwatch.org. Scientific expedition project that spans over fifty countries with environmental and archeological ventures.
Volunteering Australia Ⓦ volunteering australia.org. Offers an extensive range of volunteering opportunities across the country.
Visitoz Ⓦ australiaworkingadventures.com. Work on Outback farms and stations organized before you arrive in Australia. Previous experience not required – participants stay on a training farm for five

days, during which suitable work is found – but a driving licence is required for many jobs.
WWOOF (Willing Workers on Organic Farms) Ⓦ wwoof.com.au. A popular way to experience rural Australia in which you work for board and lodging not cash, so no work visa is required. Four to six hours daily, minimum stay two nights; everything else is negotiable. A one-year membership costs $70, and buys you a book or an app with over 2600 host farms to contact (plus email updates and an online forum) and basic work insurance.

LGBT travellers

Australia is a fixture on the queer map thanks to its great climate and laidback lifestyle. Sydney is Australia's gay-friendly capital, especially in March when hundreds of thousands of people pour in for the Sydney Gay & Lesbian Mardi Gras (see p.136). Despite its reputation as a macho culture, the country revels in a large and active scene: you'll find an air of confidence and a sense of community that is often missing in other parts of the world.

Australia is testimony to the power of the **pink dollar**: there's an abundance of gay venues, services, businesses, travel clubs, country retreats and the like. The scene obviously makes full use of sun and sport, and while it's far from limited to the toned muscle crowd, it's worth packing your swimming and especially clubbing gear to make the most of a thriving community that, in cities at least, is fully integrated. Australian dykes are refreshingly open – a relief after the cliquey European scene. The flip side of such fearlessness is the predominance of S&M on the scene.

Dyke and gay scenes are nothing if not mercurial, and Australia is no exception. We've done our best to list bars, clubs and meeting places, but be warned that venues open, change name, shut, get relaunched and finally go out of business at frightening speed.

The **age of consent** varies: in ACT, NSW, the Northern Territory, Victoria and Western Australia (16) and SA and Tasmania (both 17), it is the same as the heterosexual age. In Queensland, the age of consent for homosexuals depends on the sexual act practised, with anal sex outlawed until 18, but otherwise 16.

Where to go

Sydney is the jewel in Australia's navel. Famous as one of the world's great gay cities, it attracts lesbian and gay visitors from around the world. Melbourne closely follows, but there are scenes in Brisbane and the Gold Coast, and to a lesser extent in Perth, Adelaide, Hobart and Darwin.

Away from the cities, things get more discreet, but a lot of **country areas** do have friendly local scenes – impossible to pinpoint, but easy to stumble across. However, **Outback** mainstays of mining and cattle ranching are not famed for their tolerance of homosexuality, so tread carefully in remote destinations.

LGBT CONTACTS

Gay News Network Ⓦ gaynewsnetwork.com.au. LGBT news, features and lifestyle from across the country.

DNA Ⓦ dnamagazine.com.au. The nation's best-selling LGBT title, an upmarket lifestyle magazine for gay men.

LOTL (Lesbians on the Loose) Ⓦ lotl.com. Joint website of two leading lesbian lifestyle magazines: *LOTL Magazine* and *Curve*.

Pinkboard Ⓦ pinkboard.com.au. Popular, long-running website with useful "Graffiti Walls" full of LGBT parties, personal ads and classifieds sections with everything from house-shares, party tickets for sale, employment, and a help and advice section. Posting ads is free.

The Pink Directory Ⓦ thepinkdirectory.com.au. Online directory of LGBT business and community information.

Star Observer Ⓦ ssonet.com.au. Website of Sydney's free LGBT newspaper, now an online magazine that covers news nationwide.

TOURIST SERVICES AND TRAVEL AGENTS

GALTA (Gay and Lesbian Tourism Australia) Ⓦ galta.com.au. An online resource and nonprofit organization that promotes the gay and lesbian tourism industry with good links.

Gay Travel Ⓦ gaytravel.com. Online travel agent, concentrating mostly on accommodation across the globe, including Australia.

International Gay and Lesbian Travel Association Ⓦ iglta.org. Trade group with lists of gay-owned or gay-friendly travel businesses.

Travel essentials

Costs

Prices in Australia always came as a shock if you had arrived from Southeast Asia, but are now often higher than in Europe or North America, especially for food and drink. This is most noticeable in Sydney, Melbourne, Perth and the mining towns of Western Australia – the cost of living continues to creep up and any prolonged length of time spent in these places will quickly drain savings.

If you're prepared to camp and cook all meals, the absolute minimum **daily budget** is around $60 (circa £34/US$45/€41), but count on spending around $90 (£52/US$68/€62) a day for food, board and transport

if you stay in hostels, travel on buses and eat and drink fairly frugally. Stay in motels and B&Bs (assuming you're sharing costs) and eat out well, regularly, and you'll need to budget at least $160 (£92/US$121/€110). Extras such as scuba diving, clubbing, car rental, petrol and tours will all add to your costs.

Under the Tourist Refund Scheme (TRS), visitors can claim **Goods and Services Tax** (GST) refunds for goods purchased in Australia as they clear customs (goods need to be worn or taken within hand luggage), providing individual receipts exceed $300, and the claim is made within sixty days of purchase.

Crime, personal safety and the law

Australia is a relatively safe country. This is not to say that there's no petty crime, but you're more likely to fall victim to another traveller or an opportunist: theft does happen in hostels and many provide lockers. That said, if you leave valuables lying around or unguarded, you can expect them to vanish.

You're most likely to see violence in or outside pubs – nearly always alcohol-fuelled and usually on a Friday or Saturday night in untouristed small towns or in major cities. Strangers are rarely involved without provocation, though keep your wits about you in city nightlife hotspots such as Kings Cross in Sydney, also a focus of drug-related crime.

Marijuana use may be widespread, but you'd be foolish to carry it when you travel and crazy to carry any other illegal narcotics. Each state has its own penalties, and while a small amount of grass may mean no more than confiscation and an on-the-spot fine, they're generally pretty tough – especially in Queensland. **Drink driving** is taken extremely seriously, so don't risk it – random breath tests are common around all cities and larger towns.

There are all sorts of controls on where and when you can drink, and taking alcohol onto Aboriginal lands can be a serious offence. Keep in mind that nude or topless sunbathing may be quite acceptable in many places, but absolutely not in others; follow the locals' lead. **Smoking** is banned in all public places, including bars, pubs, restaurants and train stations; in 2010 Hobart even banned it around bus stops in the city centre.

Electricity

Australia's electrical current is 240v, 50Hz AC. British appliances require a plug adaptor, while American and Canadian 110v appliances will also need a transformer.

Insurance

Even if you're entitled to free emergency health care from Medicare (see p.40), some form of travel insurance is essential to help plug the gaps and to cover you in the event of losing your baggage, missing a plane and the like. A typical policy covers the loss of baggage, tickets and – up to a certain limit – cash and cheques, as well as cancellation or curtailment of your journey. Be aware that "high-risk" activities such as scuba diving, skiing or even just hiking require an extra premium; check the small print before you take out a policy. For medical coverage, ascertain whether benefits will be paid as treatment proceeds or only after your return home, and whether there is a 24-hour medical emergency number. When securing baggage cover, make sure that the per-article limit will cover your most valuable possession. If you need to make a claim, you should keep receipts for medicines and medical treatment, and in the event you have anything stolen, you must obtain an official written statement from the police.

Internet

Internet access – whether wi-fi or in cyber cafés – is widespread, easy and (generally) inexpensive. In the cities, wi-fi is widely available in cafés, most hostels and many hotels, generally for free nowadays or for a small daily rate. Otherwise, most hostels and hotels provide terminals for their guests, typically costing $3–6 an hour. Access is also available in libraries, though, again, you'll need to pay for it.

Laundry

These are known as laundromats in Australia and are rare outside urban centres. Hostels have at least one coin-operated washing machine and a dryer, as do most caravan parks, holiday units and many motels.

Maps

In Australia, most book and travel shops stock national, regional and city maps of varying sizes and quality by the likes of UBD and Gregory's (both ⓦ hardiegrant.com.au), HEMA (ⓦ hemamaps.com), Westprint (ⓦ westprint.com.au) and state-produced AusMap. HEMA produce regional and themed maps: cities, states, national parks, fishing, hiking, 4WD and wine are some of the many themes covered. State motoring organizations have regularly updated touring guides, with regional maps and listings.

Money

The national **currency** is the Australian dollar, or "buck", written as $ or Aus$ and divided into 100 cents. The waterproof notes come in $100, $50, $20, $10 and $5 denominations, along with $2, $1, 50¢, 20¢, 10¢ and 5¢ coins. Irregular bills such as $1.98 are rounded up or down to the closest five cents. To check the latest exchange rate, visit ⓦ xe.com. At the time of writing, $1 was worth £0.50/ US$.73/€0.65/ZAR11.

While small towns may not have a local **bank**, there will be a local agency that handles bank business – usually at the general store, post office or roadhouse – though not necessarily a 24-hour **ATM**. Credit and debit cards are universally accepted, but have some cash on you for small purchases before leaving bigger towns, especially at weekends. The major four banks are Westpac (ⓦ westpac.com.au), ANZ (ⓦ anz.com), the Commonwealth (ⓦ commbank.com.au) and the National Australia Bank (ⓦ national.com.au). Banks are generally open Monday to Thursday 9.30am to 4pm, Friday 9.30am to 5pm. Saturday-morning openings are limited to cities. In rural areas, banks may close at lunch or on certain days of the week. Banks are closed on national holidays.

All **post offices** act as Commonwealth or National Australia Bank agents, which means there's a fair chance of withdrawing money even in the smallest Outback settlement. However, be aware that quantities are limited by a lack of ready cash.

If you're spending some time in Australia, and plan to work or move around, **open a bank account**. To do this you'll need to take along every piece of ID documentation you own – a passport may not be enough – but it's otherwise a fairly straightforward process. Of the big four, Commonwealth Bank and Westpac are probably the most widespread options, and their cards give you access to anywhere that offers **EFTPOS** facilities (Electronic Funds Transfer at Point of Sale). Though not as prevalent as it was, this is still available in many Outback service stations and supermarkets and acts like a debit card to pay for goods as well as to withdraw cash. As ever, shop around before you open an account to check charges on accounts or cards.

Discount cards soon pay for themselves in savings. If you're a full-time student, it's worth applying for an **International Student ID Card** (ISIC; Ⓦ isic.org), which entitles the bearer to prove they're a student, so receive discounts on transport, museums, theatres and other attractions. The card cost varies per location: UK £12; US$25; Can$20; NZ$30; and $30 in Australia itself. Non-students aged 26 or younger qualify for the similarly priced **International Youth Travel Card**; there are also cards available for teachers. For all cards, visit the ISIC website to source points of sale such as branches of STA, or order online.

Opening hours

Shops and services are generally open Monday to Saturday 9am to 4pm, though places in small towns can close at lunchtime on Saturday. In cities and larger towns, shops may stay open late on Thursday or Friday evening – usually until 9pm – and shopping malls and department stores in major cities are often open on Sunday. Banks have generally shorter hours, but may be open on Saturday mornings.

In remote country areas, **roadhouses** provide all the essential services for the traveller and, on the major highways, are generally open 24 hours a day. **Visitor centres** – even ones well off the beaten track – are often open every day from 9am to 5pm or at least through the week plus weekend mornings; urban visitor centres are more likely to conform to normal shopping hours.

Tourist attractions such as museums or art galleries are usually open every day, though in rural communities hours become erratic. Almost without exception, all of them are closed on Good Friday and Christmas Day, but most are open during school and other public holidays. Specific opening hours are given throughout this book.

Phones

Public telephones take coins or phone cards, which are sold in most newsagents, as well as other stores. Some bars and restaurants still have orange or blue payphones, which are more expensive than a regular call box. No payphone accepts incoming calls. Local calls are **untimed**, and on a public phone are good value. Many businesses and services have freephone numbers, prefixed ☎1800, while others have six-digit numbers beginning ☎13 or ☎1300 charged at a local-call rate – all can only be dialled from within Australia. Numbers starting ☎1900 are premium-rate private information services.

Phone cards offer a cheap way to call cross-country or abroad. A head-spinning variety of

---

HOLIDAYS

National holidays are New Year's Day, Australia Day (Jan 26), Good Friday, Easter Monday, Anzac Day (April 25), Queen's Birthday (second Mon in June; Sept/Oct in Western Australia), Christmas Day and Boxing Day (except South Australia). Note that when a public holiday falls on a weekend, Australians take the following Monday off. State holidays are listed in the capital-city accounts of each state or territory. **School holidays** can transform a visit: beaches become bucket-and-spade war zones, national park campsites fill to overflowing. Dates vary by year and state, but generally things get busy from mid-December to the end of January or beginning of February (Jan is the worst, as many people stay home until after Christmas), for two weeks around Easter, for a fortnight in late June to early July, and over two weeks in late September to early October. January and Easter are the **busiest periods**, and accommodation is booked up accordingly.

CALLING AUSTRALIA FROM HOME

Dial the relevant international access code + 61 + area code, omitting the initial zero.

The **international access code** for the UK, the Republic of Ireland, New Zealand and South Africa is ✆00; for the US and Canada ✆011.

---

brands is available, and most post offices and some newsagents sell them. Rates can be as low as 5¢ a minute.

Most travellers bring their **mobile phones**. You can buy an Australian SIM card for your handset (assuming it is unlocked) for a couple of dollars. Telstra has the widest coverage; Optus, Virgin and Vodafone are also major networks. Each has a coverage map/checker on its website – worth a look since reception drops off in remote areas. One solution for guaranteed reception (albeit at higher call charges) is a **satellite phone**. Little bigger than a conventional mobile, these can be rented from ⓦrentasatphone.com.au from around $18 a day for up to a fortnight's rental, or $8 a day for up to three months, and can run both standard and satellite SIM cards.

Post

Every town has a **post office** or an Australia Post agency, usually at the general store. Post offices and agencies are officially open Monday to Friday 9am to 5pm; big-city GPOs sometimes open earlier and later, generally on Saturday morning, too. Out in the country, it's rare to see post boxes.

Same-state postage takes up to two business days, as does interstate post between metropolitan areas. Interstate between country areas is around four working days. International mail is efficient, taking up to around five working days to the UK, six to the US and seven to Canada. **Stamps** are sold at post offices and agencies; most newsagents sell them for standard local letters only. Large **parcels** are reasonably cheap to send home by sea mail – but it will take up to three months. Air mail is a good compromise for packages that you want to see soon (up to 20kg) – expect up to five working days to Europe. For more information on postage rates, and delivery times, visit ⓦaustpost.com.au.

Shopping

You'll find plenty of shops and markets to tempt you to part with your cash, from surf and skate stores to designer boutiques, flea markets to craft fairs. Australians also do vintage very well; around Chapel Street in Melbourne and Paddington in Sydney are particularly good hunting grounds.

Excellent weekly **markets** in cities and resort towns sell everything from secondhand clothes and New Age remedies to delicious fresh food; popular ones are Mindil Beach in Darwin (see p.499), Queen Victoria Market in Melbourne (see p.792) and Hobart's Salamanca Market (see p.892). In Sydney, Paddington Market is a great place to pick up one-off new designer clothes, while Glebe's Saturday market is more alternative.

There's also no shortage of souvenir shops selling Australiana: mass-produced tat such as stuffed koalas, painted boomerangs and the like. The best place to shop for Aboriginal art, however, is Alice Springs, where many galleries sell on behalf of the artist and the money goes back to the Aboriginal communities. **Gemstones** such as the Australian opal are a popular purchase, though the quality and price varies, so shop around. Broome in Western Australia has long been the "pearl capital" of Australia, and sells all manner of mother-of-pearl trinkets. Note that if you buy goods worth more than $300 in a single transaction, you can claim the tax back under the **Tourist Refund Scheme** (see p.55).

Time

Australia has three different time zones: Eastern Standard Time (QLD, NSW, VIC, TAS, VIC), Central Standard Time (NT, SA) and Western Standard Time (WA). Eastern Standard Time is ten hours ahead of Greenwich Mean Time (GMT) and fifteen hours ahead of US Eastern Time. (Don't forget that daylight saving in home countries will affect this by an hour either way.) Central Standard Time is thirty minutes behind Eastern Standard, and Western Standard two hours behind Eastern. Daylight saving

---

SEASONS

The seasons are reversed in the southern hemisphere: **summer** lasts from December to February, **winter** from June to September. Of course, it's not that simple: in the tropical north, the important seasonal distinction is between the **Wet**, effectively summer, and the **Dry**, over the winter months.

(Oct–March) Is adopted everywhere except QLD, NT and WA; clocks are put forward one hour.

Tipping

Tipping is not as widespread in Australia as it is in Europe and the US. In cafés and restaurants you might leave the change or round up the bill, while taxi drivers will usually expect you to round up to the nearest dollar. Only in posher restaurants is a service charge of ten percent the norm. Note that on public holidays cafés and restaurants in cities may add a surcharge of ten percent.

Tourist information

The Australian Tourist Commission's website (ⓦaustralia.com) has plenty of useful information, links and features. Local information is available by the sackful once you're in the country. Each state or territory has a **tourist authority** that maintains visitor information offices throughout its area and in major cities. One tier below this is a host of regional and community-run visitor centres and information kiosks. Even the smallest Outback town has one – or at the very least an information board at a roadside rest spot. **Hostels** are also excellent sources of information for backpackers, and often have good noticeboards.

Travellers with disabilities

Much of Australia's tourist **accommodation** is suitable for people with disabilities as buildings tend to be built out rather than up; all new buildings in the country must comply with a legal minimum accessibility standard.

Some of Australia's major tourist attractions, even those way out in the wilderness, have taken accessibility into account. For example, you'll find you can access rock art sites at Kakadu National Park, tour around the base of Uluru, snorkel on the Great Barrier Reef, cruise around Sydney Harbour, and see penguins at Phillip Island.

Easy Access Australia by wheelchair-user Bruce Cameron (ⓦeasyaccessaustralia.com.au; individual chapters are available by PDF download) is a comprehensive guide aimed at anyone with mobility difficulties, and has information on all the states, with maps, and a section featuring hotel-room floor plans.

USEFUL WEBSITES

Broadsheet ⓦbroadsheet.com.au/melbourne (or "/sydney")
Guardian Australia ⓦtheguardian.com/au
The Hungry Australian blog ⓦhungryaustralian.com
Sydney Morning Herald ⓦsmh.com.au
Time Out Sydney ⓦtimeout.com/sydney (or "/melbourne", "/adelaide", "/perth", etc.)
UK Foreign & Commonwealth Office (Australia travel advice section) ⓦgov.uk/foreign-travel-advice/australia
Visit Australia ⓦaustralia.com

USEFUL CONTACTS

NDS (National Disability Service) ☎02/6283 3200, ⓦnds.org.au. Regional offices provide lists of state-based help organizations, accommodation, travel agencies and tour operators.
NICAN (National Information Communication Awareness Network) ☎02/6241 1220 or ☎1800 806 769, ⓦnican.com.au. Free information service on recreation, sport, tourism, the arts and more, nationwide. Has a database of over 4500 organizations – such as wheelchair-accessible accommodation, sports organizations and vehicle rental.
Paraplegic and Quadriplegic Association of NSW ☎02/8741 5600 or ☎1300 886 601, ⓦparaquad.org.au. A body serving the needs of spinally injured people in NSW, with independent offices in each state capital.
Vision Australia ☎1300 847 466, ⓦvisionaustralia.org. Support and advice for people with blindness and low vision.

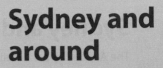

Sydney and around

SYDNEY HARBOUR

1

Sydney and around

The Aussie city par excellence, Sydney stands head and shoulders above any other in Australia. Taken together with its surrounds, it's in many ways a microcosm of the country as a whole – if only in its ability to defy your expectations and prejudices as often as it confirms them. A thrusting, high-rise business centre, a clutch of fascinating museums, vibrant art galleries, a high-profile gay community and inner-city deprivation of unexpected harshness are as much part of the scene as the beaches, the bodies and the sparkling harbour. Its sophistication, cosmopolitan population and exuberant nightlife are a long way from the Outback, and yet Sydney has the highest Aboriginal population of any Australian city, and bushfires are an annual threat.

It might seem surprising that Sydney is not Australia's **capital**: the creation of Canberra in 1927 – intended to stem the intense rivalry between Sydney and Melbourne – has not affected the view of many Sydneysiders that their city remains the country's true capital, and certainly in many ways it feels like it. The city has a tangible sense of **history**: the old stone walls and well-worn steps in the backstreets around **The Rocks** are an evocative reminder that Sydney has more than two hundred years of white history behind it.

You'll need at least five days in this unique city to ensure you see not only its glorious **harbourside** but also its wider treasures. Delving into the **inner-city areas** of Paddington, Surry Hills and Glebe reveal more of the Sydney psyche. And no trip to the city would be complete without at least one visit to the **eastern-suburb beaches** – for a true taste of Sydney, take a long afternoon stroll along the coastal path that stretches from Bondi to Coogee.

The surrounding areas – all the places covered in this chapter are within day-trip distance – offer a taste of virtually everything you'll find in the rest of the country, with the exception of desert. There are magnificent **national parks** – Ku-ring-gai Chase and

HUNTER VALLEY VINEYARDS

Highlights

1 Sydney Opera House Catch a show or relax with a drink at the *Opera Bar*. **See p.70**

2 Sydney Harbour Bridge Drive, walk, cycle or even climb the famous "coathanger" for a giddy vision of the city. **See p.72**

3 Newtown Arty, quirky and with restaurants representing every flavour of multicultural Sydney. **See p.94**

4 Sydney Harbour National Park Multiple pockets of astounding natural beauty with great views of the harbour. **See p.96**

5 Bondi Beach Bold, brash Bondi is synonymous with Australian beach culture. **See p.102**

6 Cruise the harbour Sydney is at its best from the harbour; take it in cheaply on the popular Manly Ferry. **See p.106**

7 Manly Beach A hub of watersports, with a holiday-village feel. **See p.106**

8 Mardi Gras The world's biggest celebration of LGBT culture. **See p.136**

9 Hunter Valley wineries A famous wine-growing region with a plethora of culinary and cultural activities to choose from. **See p.153**

10 Blue Mountains Take a weekend break in the World Heritage-listed Blue Mountains. **See p.156**

HIGHLIGHTS ARE MARKED ON THE MAPS ON P. 64, PP.68–69, P.72 & P.94

1

Royal being the best known – and native wildlife within an hour's drive from the centre of town; while further north stretch endless **ocean beaches**, great for surfers, and more enclosed waters for safer swimming and sailing. Inland, the gorgeous **Blue Mountains** – UNESCO World Heritage-listed – offer isolated bushwalking and scenic viewpoints. On the way are historic colonial towns that were among the earliest foundations in the country – Sydney itself was the very first. The commercial and industrial heart of the state of New South Wales, especially the central coastal region, is bordered by **Wollongong** in the south and much more enticing **Newcastle** in the north. Both were synonymous with coal and steel, but the smokestack industries that supported them for decades are now in severe decline. This is far from an industrial wasteland, though: the heart of the coal-mining country is the **Hunter Valley**, northwest of Newcastle, but to visit it you'd never guess, because this is also Australia's oldest, and

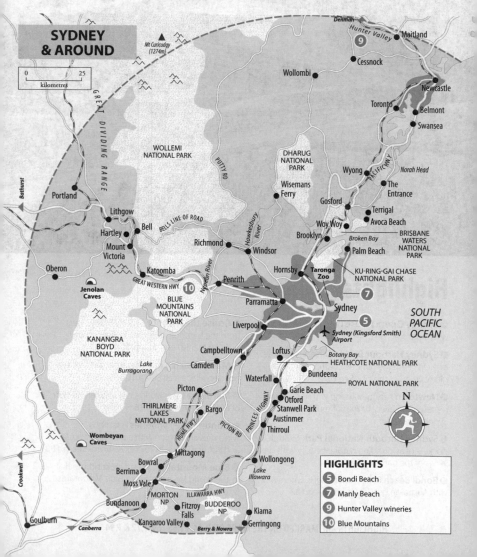

SYDNEY & AROUND

HIGHLIGHTS

5 Bondi Beach
7 Manly Beach
9 Hunter Valley wineries
10 Blue Mountains

arguably its best-known, wine-growing region, where you can not only sample the fine wines but enjoy some of the best food in the state.

Brief history

The city of Sydney was founded as a penal colony, amid brutality, deprivation and despair. In January 1788, the **First Fleet**, carrying over a thousand people, 736 of them convicts, arrived at **Botany Bay** expecting the "fine meadows" that Captain James Cook had described eight years earlier. In fact, what greeted them was mostly swamp, scrub and sand dunes. An unsuccessful scouting expedition prompted Commander Arthur Phillip to move the fleet a few kilometres north, to the well-wooded Port Jackson, where a stream of fresh water was found. This settlement was named **Sydney Cove** after Viscount Sydney, then Secretary of State in Great Britain.

Hunger and conflict

In the first three years of settlement, the new colony nearly starved to death several times; the land around Sydney Cove proved to be barren. When supply ships did arrive, they inevitably came with hundreds more convicts to further burden the colony. It was not until 1790, when land was successfully farmed further west at **Parramatta**, that the hunger began to abate. Measure this suffering, however, with that of the original occupants, the **Eora Aborigines**: their land had been invaded, their people virtually wiped out by smallpox, and now they were stricken by hunger as the settlers shot at their game. Under the leadership of **Pemulwuy**, a skilled Aboriginal warrior, the Eora commenced a guerrilla war against the colony for much of the 1790s. However, the numbers and firepower of the settlers proved too great, and in 1802 Pemulwuy was captured and killed, his severed head sent back to England. The Eora's resistance soon ended.

The colony grows

By the early 1800s, Sydney had become a stable colony and busy trading post. Army officers, exploiting their access to free land and cheap labour, became rich farm-owners

---

FREE SYDNEY

In the last few years, Sydney has become one of the **world's most expensive cities** to live in and visit. While even paying for a coffee may have you groaning at the expense, the good news is there's lots to do in this beautiful city that will cost you little or nothing. Here are some ideas:

Art Gallery of New South Wales Take a free tour on different aspects of the collection (see p.83).
Bondi Beach Check out the waves – and the lifeguards (see p.102).
Botanic Gardens Enjoy a guided tour of the gardens (daily 10.30am; see p.84).
Bronte Baths Take a dip in an ocean-fringed pool (see p.164).
Cliff walk Catch the breeze on the 6km walk between Coogee and Bondi (see box, p.105).
I'm Free walking tour Tours leave the Town Hall daily at 10.30am, 2.30pm & 6pm (see p.117).
Possum spotting Spot marsupials among the fig trees in Hyde Park (see p.81).
State Library Take in an exhibition at the glamorous public library (where there's free wi-fi, too; see p.79).
Sydney Festival In January, don't miss the free street party that kicks off this major festival (see box, pp.142–143).
Sydney fish market Marvel at the second-largest fish market in the world (and grab a cheap snack; see p.87).
Sydney Mint Visit this historic building in the Sydney Hospital (see p.79).
Walking Harbour Bridge Save a small fortune and walk across the bridge (see p.72) instead of climbing it: the views are almost as impressive.
Whale-spotting Look out for whales off the North Head shore in the June–July and August–October migration periods (see p.102).
Writers' Walk Explore literary Australia as you walk round Circular Quay; informative plaques are embedded in the ground (see p.67).

1

SYDNEY ORIENTATION

Port Jackson carves Sydney in two halves, linked by the Harbour Bridge and Harbour Tunnel. The **South Shore** is the hub of activity, and it's here that you'll find the **city centre** and most of the things to see and do. Many of the classic images of Sydney are within sight of **Circular Quay**, making this busy waterfront area on Sydney Cove a logical – and pleasurable – point to start discovering the city, with the **Sydney Opera House** and the expanse of the Royal Botanic Gardens to the east of Sydney Cove and the historic area of **The Rocks** to the west. By contrast, gleaming, slightly tawdry **Darling Harbour**, at the centre's western edge, is a shiny redeveloped tourist and entertainment area.

and virtually established a currency based on rum. The **military**, known as the New South Wales Corps (or more familiarly as "the rum corps"), became the supreme political force in 1809, even overthrowing the governor (mutiny-plagued Captain Bligh himself). This was the last straw for the government back home, and the rebellious officers were finally brought to heel when the reformist governor **Lachlan Macquarie** arrived from England with forces of his own. He liberalized conditions, supported the prisoners' right to become citizens after they had served their time, and appointed several to public offices.

By the 1840s, the transportation of convicts to New South Wales had ended, the explorers Lawson and Blaxland had found a way through the Blue Mountains to the Western Plains, and **gold** had been struck in Bathurst. The population soared as free settlers arrived in ever-increasing numbers. In the Victorian era, Sydney's population became even more starkly divided into the **haves** and the **have-nots**: while the poor lived in slums where disease, crime, prostitution and alcoholism were rife, the genteel classes – self-consciously replicating life in the mother country – took tea on their verandas and erected grandiloquent monuments such as the Town Hall, the Strand Arcade and the Queen Victoria Building in homage to English architecture of the time. An outbreak of the plague in The Rocks at the beginning of the twentieth century made wholesale slum clearances inevitable, and with the demolitions came a change in attitudes. Strict new vice laws meant the end of the bad old days of backstreet knifings, drunk-filled taverns and makeshift brothels.

Suburban Sydney

Over the next few decades, Sydney settled into comfortable **suburban living**. The metropolis sprawled westwards, creating a flat, unremarkable city with no real centre, an appropriate symbol for the era of shorts and knee socks and the stereotypical, BBQ-loving Bruce and Sheila – an international image that still plagues Australians. Sydney has come a long way since the parochialism of the 1950s, however, and today, Sydney's citizens don't look inwards – and they certainly don't look towards England. Thousands of immigrants from around the globe have given Sydney a truly cosmopolitan air, and it's a city as thrilling and alive as any.

Circular Quay

At the southern end of Sydney Cove, **Circular Quay** is the launchpad for harbour and river ferries and sightseeing boats, and is the terminal for buses from the eastern and southern suburbs. It's also home to a major suburban train station – some of the best views of the harbour can be seen from the above-ground station platforms. Circular Quay itself is always bustling with commuters during the week, and at the weekend it fills up with people out to enjoy themselves. Restaurants, cafés and fast-food outlets line the Quay, buskers entertain the crowds, and vendors of newspapers and trinkets add to the general hubbub. The sun reflecting on the water, and its heave and splash as the ferries come and go, make for a dreamy setting – best appreciated over an expensive beer at a waterfront bar.

The inscribed bronze pavement-plaques of **Writers' Walk** beneath your feet as you stroll around the Circular Quay waterfront provide an introduction to the Australian literary canon. There are short biographies of writers ranging from Miles Franklin, author of *My Brilliant Career*, through Peter Carey and Patrick White, to Germaine Greer, and quotable citations on what it means to be Australian.

You could then embark on a sightseeing **cruise** or enjoy a ferry ride on the harbour (see box below). Staying on dry land, you're only a short walk from most of the city-centre sights, along part of a continuous foreshore walkway beginning under the Harbour Bridge and passing through the historic area of Sydney's first settlement, The Rocks, then extending beyond the Opera House to the Royal Botanic Gardens.

Overseas Passenger Terminal

Besides ferries, Circular Quay still acts as a passenger terminal for ocean liners; head north past the Museum of Contemporary Art to Circular Quay West. It's a long time since the crowds regularly waved their hankies from the **Overseas Passenger Terminal**, looking for all the world like the deck of a ship itself, but you may still see an ocean liner docked here; even if there's no ship, take the escalator and the flight of stairs up

---

HARBOUR CRUISES

Sydney offers a wide choice of **harbour cruises**, almost all of them leaving from Wharf 6, Circular Quay, and the rest from Darling Harbour. While many offer a good insight into the harbour and an intimate experience of its bays and coves, the altogether much cheaper ordinary ferry rides, enjoyable cruises in themselves, are worth experiencing first. The best of these is the gorgeous thirty-minute ride to Manly, but there's a ferry going somewhere worth checking out at almost any time of the day.

The Australian Travel Specialists (ATS) at Jetty 6, Circular Quay and the Harbourside Shopping Centre at Darling Harbour (☎02 9211 3192, ⓦ atstravel.com.au) book all cruises.

CRUISE OPERATORS

Captain Cook and Matilda Captain Cook: ☎1800 804 843, ⓦ captaincook.com.au; Matilda: ☎02 8270 5188, ⓦ matilda.com.au. The majority of cruises are offered by the combined forces of these two operators (while they retain separate names). The Captain Cook Breakfast (Sat & Sun Nov–March 9.30am; 1.5hr; $49) and High Tea (Wed & Sat 2.30pm; 1.5hr; $55) cruises are probably the most popular and affordable of the private cruises, allowing you to venture into quaint little bays and coves, with commentary on local history and ecology.

Harbour Jet ☎1300 887 373, ⓦ harbourjet.com. Harbour Jet runs the "Jet Blast" (35min; $65), and the "Sydney Harbour Adventure" (50min; $80) on a boat that roars along at 75kph, executing spins, power breaks and fishtails.

Ocean Extreme ☎1300 604 080, ⓦ oceanextreme .com.au. Some alternative cruise companies go for maximum thrills (but also more noise pollution for the locals): Ocean Extreme offers "Offshore Blast" (35min; $75), a trip out to the heads and back, reaching almost 100kph.

Sydney Ferries ☎02 9246 8363, ⓦ transport.nsw .gov.au/customers/ferries/sydney-ferries. The public ferry network makes for varied makeshift tours of the harbour. Any ferry from Circular Quay will cruise by the Opera House, but get onboard quick to snag an outdoor seat, especially on busy Sundays to Manly when unlimited public transport costs $2.50 all day.

Sydney Harbour Tall Ships ☎1300 664 410, ⓦ sydneytallships.com.au. Sydney Harbour Tall Ships operates the *Svanen*, a beautiful, three-masted Danish ship, built in 1922, which moors at Campbell's Cove. "Lunch" and "Twilight" cruises (both: 2hr; $79 Mon–Thurs, $99 Fri–Sun) sail past iconic harbour sights while guests devour gourmet seafood BBQ offerings. One of a number of more romantic sailing options.

Sydney Heritage Fleet ☎02 9298 3888, ⓦ shf .org.au. Sydney's oldest sailing ship, the *James Craig*, an 1874 three-masted iron barque, is part of the Sydney Heritage Fleet based at Wharf 7, 58 Pirrama Rd, Pyrmont, near Star City Casino, and does full-day cruises on Sat and Sun (9.30am–4pm; $170; over-12s only; refreshments and lunch provided).

1

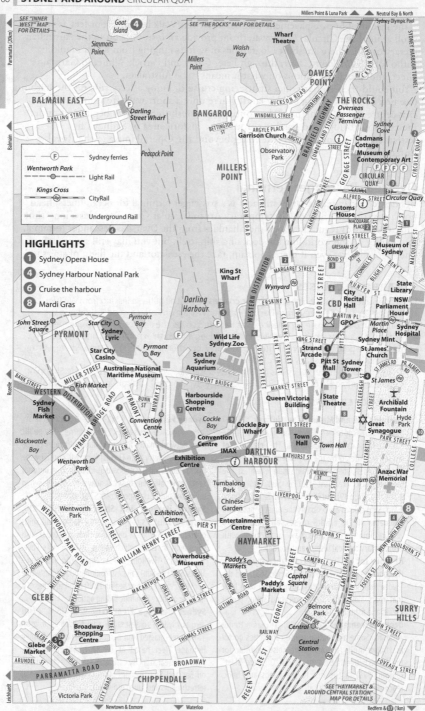

SEE "INNER WEST" MAP FOR DETAILS

Millers Point & Luna Park ▲ ▲ Neutral Bay & North
Sydney Olympic Pool

SEE "THE ROCKS" MAP FOR DETAILS

Goat Island **4**

Simmons Point

Walsh Bay

Wharf Theatre

DAWES POINT

Parramatta (20km)

Millers Point

HICKSON ROAD

SYDNEY HARBOUR TUNNEL

BALMAIN EAST

DARLING STREET

F Darling Street Wharf

Peacock Point

BANGAROO

HICKSON ROAD

WINDMILL STREET

ARGYLE PLACE

Garrison Church

BETTINGTON ST

ARGYLE

Observatory Park

MILLERS POINT

KENT STREET

HICKSON ROAD

THE ROCKS

Overseas Passenger Terminal

Sydney Cove

CIRCULAR QUAY

Cadmans Cottage
Museum of Contemporary Art

F F F F

CIRCULAR QUAY

3

Balmain ◀

F Sydney ferries

Wentworth Park ━━━ Light Rail

Kings Cross ━━━ CityRail

━━━ Underground Rail

4

HIGHLIGHTS

1 Sydney Opera House

4 Sydney Harbour National Park

6 Cruise the harbour

8 Mardi Gras

CUMBERLAND HIGHWAY

BRADFIELD HIGHWAY

CAHILL

ALFRED STREET *Circular Quay*

Customs House **i**

MACQUARIE PLACE

BRIDGE STREET

GRESHAM ST   SPRING

BOND ST

Museum of Sydney

GEORGE STREET

LOFTUS ST

YOUNG ST

PHILLIP ST

MACQUARIE ST

1

King St Wharf

MARGARET STREET

2

Wynyard

ERSKINE ST

CLARENCE STREET

KENT STREET

SUSSEX STREET

Darling Harbour

Pyrmont Bay

Star City ◯

F

John Street Square

PYRMONT

Sydney Lyric

Pyrmont Bay

Star City Casino

Miller Street

Australian National Maritime Museum

Fish Market

WESTERN DISTRIBUTOR

Sydney Fish Market **6**

BANK STREET

Blackwattle Bay

PYRMONT BRIDGE ROAD

BUNN ST

MURRAY ST

Convention Centre **7**

HARRIS STREET

ALLEN STREET

Wentworth Park

Wild Life Sydney Zoo

Sea Life Sydney Aquarium

PYRMONT BRIDGE

Harbourside Shopping Centre **7**

Cockle Bay

Convention Centre

IMAX

Exhibition Centre

DARLING HARBOUR **i**

Cockle Bay Wharf **3**

Town Hall

Town Hall

BATHURST ST

O'CONNELL ST

BLIGH ST

PHILLIP ST

HUNTER ST

BENT ST

GEORGE STREET

City Recital Hall

CBD

Martin PL **M** GPO

KING STREET

MARKET STREET

DRUITT STREET

ELIZABETH STREET

CASTLEREAGH STREET

State Library

NSW Parliament House

Sydney Hospital

Martin Place

Sydney Mint

St James' Church

St James

Sydney Tower

Queen Victoria Building

State Theatre **8**

Great Synagogue

Archibald Fountain

Hyde Park

Strand Arcade **1**

Pitt St Mall **3**

PR. ALBERT RD

ST JAMES RD

PARK STREET **10**

WILMOT ST

Museum

Anzac War Memorial

LIVERPOOL ST

GOULBURN ST

HAYMARKET

PITT STREET

DIXON ST

HARBOUR STREET

Tumbalong Park

Chinese Garden

Entertainment Centre

Exhibition Centre

PIER ST

ULTIMO

WILLIAM HENRY STREET

DARLING DRIVE

BULWARRA RD

QUARRY ST

JONES ST

HARRIS STREET

WATTLE STREET

WENTWORTH PARK ROAD

Wentworth Park

Powerhouse Museum

Paddy's Markets

Paddy's Markets

Capitol Square

Belmore Park

ULTIMO ROAD

THOMAS STREET

QUAY'S ST

DARLING ST

GEORGE

PITT STREET

HAY ST

CAMPBELL ST

8

WENTWORTH AVENUE

GOULBURN ST

FOSTER STREET

HUNT ST

11

SURRY HILLS

ALBION STREET

Central

EDDY AVE

RAILWAY SQ

Central Station

LEE ST

REGENT STREET

ELIZABETH STREET

CASTLEREAGH STREET

FOVEAUX STREET

GLEBE

ST JOHNS ROAD

MITCHELL ST

COWPER STREET

BAY STREET

GLEBE POINT ROAD

Broadway Shopping Centre **14**

MACARTHUR ST

BULWARRA RD

JONES ST

MARY ANN STREET

THOMAS STREET

7

Glebe Market **15**

ARUNDEL ST

PARRAMATTA ROAD

CHIPPENDALE

BROADWAY

CITY ROAD

Victoria Park

Leichhardt ◀

Newtown & Enmore ▼   Waterloo ▼

SEE "HAYMARKET & AROUND CENTRAL STATION" MAP FOR DETAILS

Redfern & **17** (1km) ▼

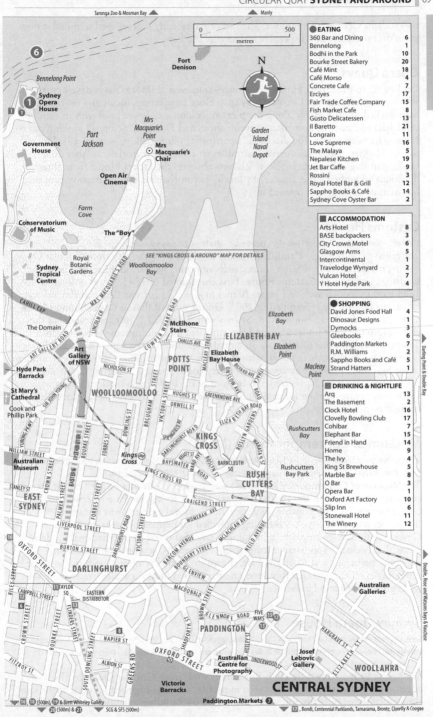

Taronga Zoo & Mosman Bay   Manly

0   500
metres

N

EATING

360 Bar and Dining	6
Bennelong	1
Bodhi in the Park	10
Bourke Street Bakery	20
Café Mint	18
Café Morso	4
Concrete Cafe	7
Erciyes	17
Fair Trade Coffee Company	15
Fish Market Cafe	8
Gusto Delicatessen	13
Il Baretto	21
Longrain	11
Love Supreme	16
The Malaya	5
Nepalese Kitchen	19
Jet Bar Caffe	9
Rossini	3
Royal Hotel Bar & Grill	12
Sappho Books & Café	14
Sydney Cove Oyster Bar	2

ACCOMMODATION

Arts Hotel	8
BASE backpackers	3
City Crown Motel	6
Glasgow Arms	5
Intercontinental	1
Travelodge Wynyard	2
Vulcan Hotel	7
Y Hotel Hyde Park	4

SHOPPING

David Jones Food Hall	4
Dinosaur Designs	1
Dymocks	3
Gleebooks	6
Paddington Markets	2
R.M. Williams	7
Sappho Books and Café	5
Strand Hatters	1

DRINKING & NIGHTLIFE

Arq	13
The Basement	2
Clock Hotel	16
Clovelly Bowling Club	17
Cohibar	7
Elephant Bar	15
Friend in Hand	14
Home	9
The Ivy	4
King St Brewhouse	5
Marble Bar	8
O Bar	3
Opera Bar	1
Oxford Art Factory	10
Slip Inn	6
Stonewall Hotel	11
The Winery	12

Fort
Denison

Bennelong Point

Sydney
Opera
House

Government
House

Port
Jackson

Mrs
Macquarie's
Point

Mrs
Macquarie's
Chair

Garden
Island
Naval
Depot

Open Air
Cinema

Farm
Cove

Conservatorium
of Music

The "Boy"

SEE "KINGS CROSS & AROUND" MAP FOR DETAILS

Sydney
Tropical
Centre

Royal
Botanic
Gardens

Woolloomooloo
Bay

Elizabeth
Bay

CAHILL EXP

The Domain

Art
Gallery
of NSW

ELIZABETH BAY

Elizabeth
Point

ART GALLERY ROAD

MRS MACQUARIE'S ROAD

LINCOLN CR

COWPER WHARF ROAD

McElhone
Stairs

CHALLIS AVE

Elizabeth
Bay House

MACLEAY STREET

BILLYARD AVE

Macleay
Point

Hyde Park
Barracks

NICHOLSON ST

POTTS
POINT

St Mary's
Cathedral

SIR JOHN YOUNG CR

WOOLLOOMOOLOO

HUGHES ST

GREENKNOWE AVE

Rushcutters
Bay

Cook and
Phillip Park

BROUGHAM ST

VICTORIA STREET

DOWLING ST

ORWELL ST

ELIZA BE ER BAY ROAD

ROSLYN GARDENS

WILLIAM STREET

SPRINGFIELD AV

DARLINGHURST RD

KINGS
CROSS

ROSLYN ST

WARATAH ST

Rushcutters
Bay Park

Australian
Museum

Kings
Cross

BAYSWATER RD

WARD AVE

BARNCLEUTH
SQ

RUSH-
CUTTERS
BAY

CROWN STREET

FORBES ST

KINGS CROSS RD

TILLEY ST

ROSLYN ST

STANLEY ST

EAST
SYDNEY

PALMER STREET

FORBES STREET

BOURKE STREET

EASTERN
DISTRIBUTOR

CRAIGEND STREET

WOMERAH AVE

MCLACHLAN AVE

NEILD AVENUE

Liverpool Street

BURTON STREET

DARLINGHURST RD

VICTORIA STREET

BARCOM AVENUE

BOUNDARY STREET

GLENVIEW

RILEY ST

OXFORD STREET

DARLINGHURST

CAMPBELL STREET

TAYLOR
SQ

MACDONALD

BROWN STREET

Australian
Galleries

CROWN STREET

BOURKE STREET

FLINDERS STREET

GLENMORE ROAD

FIVE
WAYS

PADDINGTON

NAPIER ST

HARGRAVE ST

Josef
Lebovic
Gallery

WOOLLAHRA

FITZROY ST

SOUTH DOWLING STREET

ALBION ST

GREENS RD

OXFORD STREET

SHADFORTH STREET

HEELEY ST

UNDERWOOD ST

Australian
Centre for
Photography

ELIZABETH ST

Victoria
Barracks

CENTRAL SYDNEY

Darling Point & Double Bay

Double Point, Rose and Watsons Bays & Vaucluse

1

for excellent views of the harbour. The rest of the recently redeveloped terminal is now given over to trendy and expensive restaurants and bars.

Opera Quays

Leading up to the Opera House is the once-controversial **Opera Quays** development, which runs the length of **Circular Quay East**. Since its opening, locals and tourists alike have flocked to promenade along the pleasant colonnaded lower level with its outdoor cafés, bars and bistros, upmarket souvenir shops and Dendy Cinema, all looking out to sublime harbour views. The distasteful apartment building above was described by Robert Hughes, the famous expat Australian art critic and historian, as "that dull, brash, intrusive apartment block which now obscures the Opera House from three directions". Dubbed "The Toaster" by locals, its construction caused massive protests, but went up anyway and opened in 1999.

Customs House

31 Alfred St • Mon–Fri 10am–7pm, Sat 11am–4pm, closed public hols • Free • ⓦ sydneycustomshouse.com.au

The railway and the ugly Cahill Expressway block views to the city from Circular Quay, cutting it off from Alfred Street immediately opposite, with its architectural gem, the sandstone and granite **Customs House**. First constructed in 1845, it was redesigned in 1885 by the colonial architect James Barnet to give it its current Classical Revival-style facade; its interior was revamped in 2005. On the ground floor a **City Exhibition Space** keeps pace with the development of Sydney with a detailed 1:500 scale model of the city set into the floor under glass and accompanied by a multimedia presentation. Temporary exhibitions often focus on **global cities**, and Sydney's premier public library is housed on the first three floors, with free wi-fi. On the top floor is the only reminder of the building's previous incarnation, a pricey contemporary brasserie, *Cafe Sydney* (see p.123), with postcard harbour views. In front of the building, a modern forecourt space incorporates seating for cafés and bars that, on weekday evenings, buzz with a twilight post-work euphoria.

Museum of Contemporary Art (MCA)

On the western side of Circular Quay with another entrance at 140 George St • Daily 10am–5pm, Thurs till 9pm; free tours Mon–Fri 11am & 1pm, Thurs also 7pm, Sat & Sun also 3pm • Permanent collection free • ☎ 02 9252 2400, ⓦ mca.com.au

The **Museum of Contemporary Art** (**MCA**) was developed out of a bequest by the art collector John Power in the 1940s to Sydney University to purchase international contemporary art. The growing collection finally found a permanent home in 1991 in the former Maritime Services Building, provided for peppercorn rent by the State Government. The striking 1950s building is now dedicated to international modern art, with an eclectic approach encompassing lithographs, sculpture, film, video, drawings, paintings and Aboriginal art, shown in themed temporary exhibitions. The museum's excellent and superbly sited café has shaded outdoor tables overlooking the waterfront and Opera House.

Sydney Opera House

Bennelong Point **Guided tours** Daily 9am–5pm; 1hr • $35 **Backstage tours** Daily 7am; 2hr • $150 • **Opera Australia** Season runs Feb–March & June–Nov • Prices vary • **Australian Ballet** Season runs mid-March to May & Nov–Dec • Prices vary ☎ 02 9250 7250, ⓦ sydneyoperahouse.com

The iconic **Sydney Opera House** is just a short stroll from Circular Quay, by the water's edge on **Bennelong Point**. It's best seen in profile, when its high white roofs, at the same time evocative of full sails and white shells, give the building an almost ethereal quality.

BUILDING THE OPERA HOUSE

Some say that the inspiration for the distinctive design of the Opera House came from the simple peeling of an orange into segments, though perhaps Danish architect **Jørn Utzon**'s childhood as the son of a yacht designer had something to do with the sail-like shapes – he certainly envisaged a building that would appear to "float" on water. Despite its familiarity, or perhaps precisely because you already feel you know it so well, it's quite breathtaking at first sight. Close up, you can see that the shimmering effect is created by thousands of white tiles.

The feat of structural engineering required to bring to life Utzon's "sculpture", which he compared to a Gothic church and a Mayan temple, made the final price tag $102 million, ten times the original estimate. Now almost universally loved and admired, it's hard to believe quite how controversial a project this was during its long haul from plan – as a result of an international competition in the late 1950s – to completion in 1973. For sixteen years, construction was plagued by quarrels and scandal, so much so that Utzon, who won the competition in 1957, was forced to resign in 1966. Seven years and three Australian architects later, the interior, which at completion never matched Utzon's vision, was finished: the focal Concert Hall, for instance, was designed by **Peter Hall** and his team.

Utzon did have a final say, however: in 1999, he was appointed as a design consultant to prepare a Statement of Design Principles for the building, which has become a permanent reference for its conservation and development. The Reception Hall has been refurbished to Utzon's specifications and was renamed the **Utzon Room** in 2004. He also remodelled the western side of the structure, with a colonnade and nine new glass openings, giving previously cement-walled theatre foyers a view of the harbour. Utzon died in November 2008.

"Opera House" is actually a misnomer: it's really a performing-arts centre, one of the busiest in the world, with five performance venues inside its shells, plus restaurants, cafés and bars, and a stash of upmarket souvenir shops on the lower concourse. The building's initial impetus, in fact, was as a home for the Sydney Symphony Orchestra, and it was designed with the huge **Concert Hall**, seating 2690, as the focal point; the smaller **Opera Theatre** (1547 seats) is used as the Sydney performance base for **Opera Australia** and the **Australian Ballet**. There are three theatrical venues: the **Drama Theatre**, used primarily by the **Sydney Theatre Company**; **The Playhouse**, used by travelling performers; and the more intimate **The Studio**.

If you're not content with gazing at the outside, guided and backstage **tours** are available. But of course the best way to appreciate the Opera House is to attend an evening **performance**, which might include modern musicians such as Beach House, Blur and Tame Impala. You could also **eat** at one of Sydney's best restaurants, *Bennelong* (see p.123), overlooking the city skyline, or take a **drink** at the spectacularly sited *Opera Bar* on the lower concourse (see p.131). Good-value **packages**, which include tours, meals, dinner cruises, drinks and performances, can be purchased at the Opera House or via the website.

The Rocks

Rocks Walking Tours, Shop 4a Clocktower Square, cnr Argyle St and Harrington St • Daily 10.30am & 1.30pm; 1hr 30min • $25 • ☎ 02 9247 6678, ⓦ rockswalkingtours.com.au

The Rocks, immediately beneath the Harbour Bridge, is the heart of historic Sydney. On this rocky outcrop between Sydney Cove and Walsh Bay, Captain Arthur Phillip proclaimed the establishment of Sydney Town in 1788, the first permanent European settlement in Australia. Within decades, the area degenerated into little more than a slum of dingy dwellings, narrow alleys and dubious taverns and brothels. In the 1830s and 1840s, merchants began building fine stone warehouses here, but as the focus for Sydney's shipping industry moved from Circular Quay, the area fell into decline. By the 1870s and 1880s, the notorious Rocks "pushes", gangs of "larrikins" (louts), mugged

1

passers-by and brawled with each other: the narrow street named **Suez Canal** was a favourite place to hide in wait. Some say the name is a shortening of Sewers' Canal, and indeed the area was so filthy that whole streetfronts had to be torn down in 1900 to contain an outbreak of the bubonic plague. It remained a run-down, depressed quarter until the 1970s, when there were plans to raze the historic cottages, terraces and warehouses to make way for office towers. However, due to the foresight of a radical building-workers' union that opposed the demolition, the restored and renovated **historic quarter** is now one of Sydney's major tourist attractions and, despite a passing resemblance to a historic theme park, it's worth exploring. It's also the best place for souvenir shopping, especially at weekends when **The Rocks Market** (see p.141) takes over the northern end of George and Playfair streets; also on Playfair Street, **Rocks Walking Tours** provide excellent guided tours of the area.

Sydney Harbour Bridge

Toll to drive across $4, payable only when heading south; walking or cycling across is free

The charismatic **Sydney Harbour Bridge**, connecting the The Rocks and the rest of South Sydney to Milsons Point in North Sydney, has straddled the channel since 1932. The largest arch bridge in the world when it was built, its construction costs weren't paid off until 1988. Pedestrians should head up the steps to the bridge from Cumberland Street, opposite the *Glenmore Hotel* in The Rocks, and walk along the eastern side for fabulous views of the harbour and Opera House (cyclists keep to the western side).

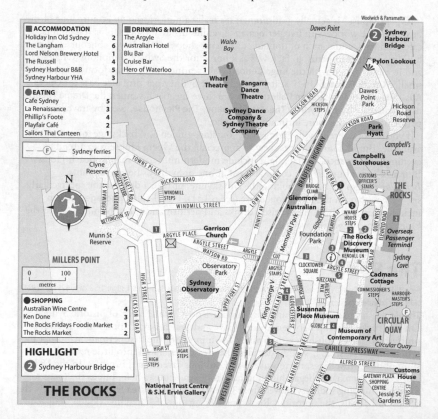

Bridge Climb

5 Cumberland St • Full trip 3hr 30min, Bridge Climb Sampler (halfway up) 1hr 30min • Feb–Nov: day climb Mon–Fri $268, Sat & Sun $283, night climb $228, twilight & dawn climb $333–353; Dec & Jan: day climb $283, night climb $243, twilight & dawn climb $353; no under-10s • Booking advised on ☎ 02 8274 7777, ⓦ bridgeclimb.com

The bridge demands full-time maintenance, and is protected from rust by continuous painting in trademark steel-grey. Comedian Paul Hogan, of *Crocodile Dundee* fame, worked as a rigger on the "coathanger" before being rescued by a *New Faces* talent quest in the 1970s. To check out Hogan's vista, you can follow a rigger's route and climb the bridge with **Bridge Climb**, who take specially equipped groups (maximum 12) to the top of the bridge from sunrise until after dark. The ascents climb over the arch of the bridge to its summit, for impressive views of the harbour and Opera House. As you gradually ascend, the guide points out landmarks and offers interesting background snippets.

The grey *Star Trek*-style suits, designed to blend in with the bridge, make you feel as if you're preparing to go into outer space. It's not as scary as it looks – harnessed into a cable system, there's no way you can fall off. So that nothing can be dropped onto cars or people below, cameras cannot be taken on the walk, limiting scope for one of the world's greatest photo opportunities.

Pylon Lookout

Daily 10am–5pm • $13 • ⓦ pylonlookout.com.au • 5min walk north from Cumberland St to the entrance, then walk up 200 steps in the pylon

If you can't stomach (or afford) the Bridge Climb, there's a viewpoint, **Pylon Lookout**, actually inside the bridge's southeastern pylon. As well as gazing out across the harbour, you can study a photo exhibition on the bridge's history, and find information on the daring exploits of the men who built the structure.

The Rocks Discovery Museum

Kendall Lane • Daily 10am–5pm • Free • ☎ 02 9240 8680

Tucked away down Kendall Lane and housed in a restored 1850s sandstone warehouse, **The Rocks Discovery Museum** offers excellent background information and displays on The Rocks' rich history, from the lives of the original Cadigal inhabitants to the dramatic story of the 1970s protests that helped preserve the area from major redevelopment.

Susannah Place Museum

58–64 Gloucester St • Daily 2–5pm; visit by guided tour only • $8; book ahead at busy times • ☎ 02 9241 1893, ⓦ hht.net.au

The **Susannah Place Museum** is a row of four brick terraces built in 1844 and occupied until 1990. It's now a fascinating "house museum" (including a recreated 1915 corner store), which conserves the domestic history of Sydney's working class. The lively tours use oral history anecdotes to bring the former inhabitants of the threadbare interiors to vivid life.

Argyle Street and around

Exploring the narrow alleys and streets hewn out of the original rocky spur, which involves climbing and descending several stairs and cuts to different levels, is the area's chief delight. From Argyle Street, wander north up (and in between) Playfair Street, Kendall Lane and George Street, then nip down cobbled pedestrian back-alleys to the south towards Suez Canal and Nurses Walk, or take coffee or lunch in the charming old-world courtyard of *La Renaissance* (see p.123). Leafy Argyle Street hosts **The Rocks Fridays Foodie Market** (see p.141), where you can taste and buy delectable local produce.

1

Cadmans Cottage

110 George St

Next to the Museum of Contemporary Art, in a small tree-filled reserve, is **Cadmans Cottage**, the oldest private house still standing in Sydney, built in 1816 for John Cadman, ex-convict and government coxswain. Unfortunately, the cottage is closed to the public; however, it is also the departure point for a captivating the Rocks Dreaming Aboriginal Heritage Tour of the harbour (see p.117).

Campbell's Cove

North along the waterfront walkway, past the Overseas Passenger Terminal, is **Campbell's Cove**, where the beautifully restored 1830s **Campbell's Storehouses**, once part of the private wharf of the merchant Robert Campbell, now house a shopping and eating complex. A replica of Captain Bligh's ship, the *Bounty*, is moored here between cruises, while a luxury hotel, the *Park Hyatt*, overlooks the whole area.

Dawes Point Park

The waterfront walkway runs adjacent to Hickson Road to **Dawes Point Park**, which sits beneath the Harbour Bridge offering brilliant views, particularly at sunset. Looking out past the Opera House, you can see **Fort Denison** on a small island in the harbour: "Pinchgut", as the island is still known, was originally used as a special prison for the tough nuts the penal colony couldn't crack. During the Crimean Wars in the mid-nineteenth century, however, old fears of a Russian invasion were rekindled and the fort was built as part of a defence ring around the harbour.

Wharf Theatre

Pier 4/5 • Tours Tues 10.30am; 1hr • $10; booking essential • ☎ 02 9250 1777, ⓦ sydneytheatre.com.au

On the west side of Dawes Point Park, Hickson Road passes several luxurious old wharves, now renovated as luxury housing, and the **Wharf Theatre**, home to the Sydney Theatre Company and the Sydney Dance Company. From the restaurant and its bar, you can revel in the sublime view across Walsh Bay to Balmain, Goat Island and the North Shore. Guided **tours** include the costume department and a peek at set construction. The area around the theatre, Walsh Bay, is also emerging, with new restaurants and artistic companies filling the old storage wharves with culture and character.

Barangaroo

West along Hickson Road, a once derelict-looking shipping area has seen massive development over the last few years as a new precinct for Sydney, called **Barangaroo**. The area includes a new public park on the harbour, exhibition spaces, residences and commercial outlets. There are future plans for a ferry hub, a pedestrian bridge from Wynyard station and, controversially, a second casino for the city, justified on the dubious grounds that it'll be geared up for Chinese high-rollers, rather than domestic punters.

Sydney Observatory

Watson Rd, Observatory Hill • Daily 10am–5pm • Free • Night tours 8.15pm; 2hr tours include a lecture, film, exhibition, guided view of the telescopes and a look at the sky, weather permitting; $20–22; booking essential, usually up to a week in advance • ☎ 02 9217 0111, ⓦ sydneyobservatory.com.au

Observatory Park on Observatory Hill, with its shady Moreton Bay figs, benches and lawns, features a marvellous view over the whole harbour. It's also easy to reach the park from the **Bridge Stairs** off Cumberland Street by the Argyle Cut.

Set among some very pretty gardens in the park, the **Sydney Observatory** is a museum of astronomy. Every evening, you can view the sky through telescopes and learn about the Southern Cross and other southern constellations. The small planetarium is used during night visits when the sky is not clear enough for observation.

Argyle Cut

Located under the Bradfield Highway, the **Argyle Cut** slices through solid stone connecting Millers Point and Circular Quay. The cut took sixteen years to complete, carved first with chisel and hammer by convict chain gangs who began the work in 1843; when transportation ended ten years later the tunnel was still unfinished, and it took explosives and hired hands to complete it in 1859.

Once you've passed through the cut, look out for the **Argyle Steps**, which lead back up to Cumberland Street. The Harbour Bridge is accessible by foot from here via the pylon staircase, or you can sit back and enjoy the splendid views from a couple of fine old boozers, the *Glenmore* and the *Australian*.

Millers Point

Surrounding the wharves, on the western side of the Bradfield Highway (Sydney Harbour Bridge), **Millers Point** is a reminder of how The Rocks used to be; it has a genuine community feel that's surprising, so close to the tourist hype of The Rocks. Much of the housing is government- or housing association-owned, though with threats of a sell-off, local residents are having to campaign to keep things that way. The area has its upmarket pockets, but for the moment the traditional street-corner pubs and shabby terraced houses on the hill are reminiscent of the raffish atmosphere once typical of the whole area, and the mostly peaceful residential streets are a delight to wander through.

You can reach the area through the Argyle Cut or from the end of George Street, heading onto Lower Fort Street, where you could stop for a drink at the **Hero of Waterloo** at no. 81 (see p.132), built from sandstone excavated from the Argyle Cut in 1844. Afterwards, peek in at the **Garrison Church** (daily 9am–5pm) on the corner of Argyle Street, the place of worship for the military stationed at Dawes Point fort (the fort was demolished in the 1920s to make way for the Harbour Bridge) from the 1840s. Beside the church, **Argyle Place** has some of the area's prettiest old terraced houses.

Central Business District (CBD)

From Circular Quay south as far as King Street is Sydney's **Central Business District (CBD)**, with **Martin Place** as its commercial nerve centre, a pedestrian mall stretching from George Street to **Macquarie Street**, lined with imposing banks and investment companies.

Along Martin Place, plans have been made for four hundred illuminated flower symbols to be inlaid in the ground as a permanent **memorial** to the two people killed in the overnight siege of the *Lindt Café* in December 2014. The enduring memorial will reflect the vast number of bouquets placed here in the days that followed the attack – a random act of terrorism by a solo madman in an otherwise extremely safe Sydney. Martin Place bears little other trace of the tragedy; all year round, fruit and flower stalls line the street, and in summer, street performances are still held at the little amphitheatre.

General Post Office

1 Martin Place • Mon–Thurs 8am–10pm, Fri 8am–11pm, Sat 9am–11pm, Sun 10am–10pm

The vast **General Post Office (GPO)**, built between 1865 and 1887, with its landmark clock tower added in 1900, broods over the George Street end in all its Victorian-era

1

pomp. The upper floors have been incorporated into part of a five-star luxury hotel, the *Westin Sydney*; the rest of the hotel resides in the 31-storey tower behind. The old building and the new tower meet in the grand Atrium Courtyard, on the lower ground floor, with its restaurants, bars and classy designer stores.

Museum of Sydney

37 Phillip St, at Bridge St • Daily 10am–5pm • $10 • ⓦ hht.net.au

North of Martin Place stands the **Museum of Sydney**. The site itself is the reason for the museum's existence: a ten-year archeological dig starting here in 1983 unearthed the foundations of the first Government House built by Governor Phillip in 1788, which was home to eight subsequent governors of New South Wales before being demolished in 1846. The museum, built next to the site, is totally original in its approach, presenting history in an interactive manner, through exhibitions, film, photography and multimedia. Around half the exhibition space is taken up with special exhibitions.

First Government Place, a public square in front of the museum, preserves the site of the original Government House: its foundations are marked out in different-coloured sandstone on the pavement. It's easy to miss, as your eye is naturally drawn to the forest of vertical poles at the western end. This is **Edge of the Trees**, an emotive sculptural installation that was a collaboration between a European and an Aboriginal artist, and attempts to convey the complexity of a shared history that began in 1788. Each pole represents one of the original 29 clans that lived in the greater Sydney area.

Entering the museum, you hear a dramatized dialogue between the Eora woman Patyegarang and the First Fleeter Lieutenant Dawes, giving a strong impression of the meeting and misunderstanding between the two cultures. Straight ahead is a video screen that projects images of the bush, sea and Sydney sandstone across all three levels, stylistically linking together what is in fact quite a small museum. Head up to the Level 2 auditorium for short movies of mid-twentieth-century Sydney life and the construction of the Harbour Bridge, then work your way down past wonderful **panoramas** of Sydney Harbour, the **Bond Store Tales** section, in which holographic "ghosts" relate tales of old Sydney as an ocean port, and the **Trade Wall**, full of anecdotes and facts about goods Sydney imported in its early days – rice from Batavia, cheroots from India, ginger wine from the West Indies and tar from Sweden.

Victorian arcades

South of Martin Place, the streets get a little more interesting. The rectangle between Elizabeth, King, George and Park streets is Sydney's prime shopping area, with the only surviving restored **Victorian arcade** – beautiful Strand Arcade – and Queen Victoria Building both worth a look. The space also houses Sydney's two **department stores**, the very upmarket David Jones on the corner of Market and Elizabeth streets (see p.140), established in 1838, and Myers on Pitt Street Mall, a pedestrianized zone.

Sydney Tower

100 Market St, at Castlereagh St • **Tower** Daily 9am–10.30pm • $26; free with Unlimited Attractions pass (p.117) **Skywalk** Daily 10am–8pm, every 30min–1hr; 45min • $70, online $50; free with Ultimate Sydney Pass • **4D Cinema Experience** 4min • Included in Skywalk ticket • ⓦ sydneytower.com.au

The landmark **Sydney Tower** (still referred to by many locals as Centrepoint, its pre-2001 name) is the tallest poppy in the Sydney skyline – a giant golden gearstick thrusting up 305m. The 360-degree view from the top is especially fine at sunset, and on clear days you can even see the Blue Mountains, 100km away. Once up at the observation level you can opt for the **Skywalk**, a harnessed-up walking tour of the exterior of the tower complete with vertiginous, glass-floored viewing platforms, one of which extends out over the abyss. It obviously imitates the popular Harbour Bridge climb, the original and still the best thrill for your money (see p.73). No cameras are permitted, but your guide can take photos for purchase afterwards. The ticket also includes **4D Cinema Experience** at the base of the tower, a tacky 3D "virtual ride" introduction to a clichéd Australia, with added wind effects.

To enjoy the Sydney Tower view without the crowds, save your ticket money and put it towards a meal at one of the **revolving restaurants** at the top of the tower instead (see p.123). The revolution takes about one hour and ten minutes, and nearly all the tables are by the windows.

State Theatre

49 Market St • **Tours** Mon–Wed 10am & 1pm; 2hr • $22.50 **Retro Café** Mon–Wed & Fri 7.30am–8pm, Thurs till 7.30am–10.30pm, Sat 8am–8pm • ☏ 136 100; ⓦ statetheatre.com.au

If heaven has a hallway, it surely must resemble that of the restored **State Theatre**, just across from the Pitt Street Mall. Step inside and take a look at the glorious interior of this picture palace, opened in 1929, whose lavishly painted, gilded and sculpted corridor leads to the lush, red and wood-panelled foyer. To see more of the interior, you'll need to attend the Sydney Film Festival (see p.138) or other events held here, such as concerts and plays, or you can take a guided tour. Otherwise, pop into the beautiful little *Retro Café* next door for a coffee.

Queen Victoria Building

455 George St, at Druid St • Mon–Fri 9am–6pm, Sat 10am–4pm, Sun 11am–4pm • ⓦ qvb.com.au

The stately **Queen Victoria Building** (or **QVB**), takes up the block bounded by Market, Druitt, George and York streets. Stern and matronly, a huge statue of Queen Victoria herself sits outside the impressive building. Built as a market hall in 1898, two years before Victoria's death, the long-neglected building was beautifully restored and reborn in 1986 as an upmarket shopping mall with a focus on fashion: from the basement up, the four levels become progressively exclusive. The interior is magnificent, with its beautiful woodwork, gallery levels and antique lifts; Charles I is beheaded on the hour, every hour, by figurines on the mechanical **Royal Automata Clock** on Level 2. From Town Hall station, you can walk right through the basement level (mainly bustling food stalls) and continue via Sydney Central Plaza to Myers department store, emerging on Pitt Street and Sydney Tower without having to go outside.

Town Hall

483 George St • Mon–Fri 8am–6pm • ⓦ sydneytownhall.com.au

In the realm of architectural excess, the sandstone **Town Hall** – across from the QVB on the corner of George and Druitt streets – is king. It was built during the boom years of the 1870s and 1880s as a homage to Victorian England. Inside is a vast organ with nearly nine thousand pipes – the world's largest at the time – which was restored in 2015 and is used for recitals.

Macquarie Street

Macquarie Street neatly divides business from pleasure, separating the office towers and cramped streets of the CBD from the open spaces of The Domain. The southern end of Governor Macquarie's namesake street (see box, p.78) is lined with the grand edifices that were the result of his dreams for a stately city: **Hyde Park Barracks**, **Parliament House**, the **State Library** and the **hospital** he and his wife designed. The new Sydney – wealthy and

1

LACHLAN MACQUARIE IN SYDNEY

Lachlan Macquarie, reformist governor of New South Wales between 1809 and 1821, gave the early settlement its first imposing public buildings, clustered on the southern half of his namesake **Macquarie Street**. He established Sydney's street plan, and had a vision of an elegant, prosperous city, although the Imperial Office in London didn't share his enthusiasm for expensive civic projects. Refused both money and expertise by the British government, Macquarie was forced to be resourceful: many of the city's finest buildings were designed by the ex-convict architect **Francis Greenway** and paid for with rum money, the proceeds of a monopoly on liquor sales.

Macquarie's influence on the physical city is still evident: he may have actually designed what is now the Parliament House of New South Wales, the wide verandas inspired by **colonial architecture** he saw in India. And the grand stables Macquarie commissioned for Government House, known as a "palace for horses", now form part of the Sydney Conservatorium of Music.

international – shows itself on the corner of Bent and Macquarie streets in the curved glass sails of ABN AMRO's 41-storey **Aurora Place** tower, completed in 2000 to a design by Italian architect Renzo Piano, co-creator of the Georges Pompidou Centre in Paris.

St James' Church

173 King St • Mon–Fri 10am–4pm, Sat 9am–1pm, Sun 7am–4pm • ⓦ sjks.org.au

Immediately north of Hyde Park, the Anglican **St James' Church** is Sydney's oldest existing place of worship, completed in 1824. It was one of Macquarie's schemes built to ex-convict Greenway's design, and the architect originally planned it as a courthouse – you can see how the simple design was converted into a graceful church. It's worth popping into the crypt (separate entrance on Phillip St) to see the richly coloured **Children's Chapel** mural painted in the 1930s.

Hyde Park Barracks

Queens Square/10 Macquarie St • Daily 10am–5pm • $10 • ⓦ hht.net.au

The **Hyde Park Barracks**, bordering the park, were designed by convict-architect Francis Greenway to house six hundred male convicts. Built in 1819, without permission from London, it is the oldest institutional building in Australia and one of the most complete convict barracks in the former British Empire. Now a **museum** of the social and architectural history of Sydney, it's a great place to visit for a taste of prison life during the early years of the colony. Start on the **top floor**, where you can swing in recreations of the prisoners' rough hammocks suspended from exposed beams. You can do a digital search for information on a selection of convicts' histories and backgrounds – several of those logged were American sailors nabbed for misdeeds while in Dublin or English ports (look up poor William Pink). Later, the Barracks took in single immigrant women, many of them Irish, escaping the potato famine; an exhibition on the middle level looks specifically at the lives of Irish orphan girls, over four thousand of whom passed through the barracks between 1848 and 1850. Next door, you can see how buildings here were adapted to cope with the changing needs in a series of detailed scale models.

Ground-floor exhibits explore why the Australian colonies were set up in the first place: the reconstruction of one of the prison hulks that used to line the Thames in London gives a clear indication of how bad the situation had become once Britain could no longer transport its criminals to America after independence. Look out, too, for the excellent **temporary historical exhibitions**, as well as the room stripped back to reveal the building's original construction.

Sydney Hospital

8 Macquarie St

Next door to Hyde Park Barracks, sandstone **Sydney Hospital**, the so-called "Rum Hospital", funded by liquor-trade profits, was Macquarie's first enterprise, commissioned in 1814 and therefore one of the oldest buildings in Australia. Outside the hospital, you can't miss *Il Porcellino*, a bronze copy of the lolling Florentine boar, donated to the city in 1968.

Sydney Mint

10 Macquarie St • Mon–Fri 9am–5pm • Free • ⓦ hht.net.au

One of the original wings of the hospital was long ago converted into **Sydney Mint**, originally a branch of the Royal Mint, opened in response to the first Australian gold rush. It closed in 1927 and after several incarnations received an award-winning $14 million redevelopment, which combined historic restoration with contemporary architecture. It now houses the head office of the Historic Houses Trust, which maintains a small display on how the building was restored. On site is also the *Mint Café*, which extends onto the veranda looking over Macquarie Street.

New South Wales Parliament House

6 Macquarie St • Mon–Fri 9am–5pm • ⓦ parliament.nsw.gov.au

The northernmost hospital wing is now the **New South Wales Parliament House** where, as early as 1829, local councils called by the governor started to meet, making it by some way the oldest parliament building in Australia. However, it wasn't until the May 2003 state elections that an Aboriginal Australian was elected to the New South Wales Parliament – Linda Burney, former head of the New South Wales Department of Aboriginal Affairs and now Labour member for multicultural Canterbury as well as minister for State Plan and Community Services. You can listen in on the politicians during **question time**, when Parliament is sitting. Look out for the varied exhibitions in the foyer, which change every fortnight or so; all represent community or public-sector interests and range from painting, craft and sculpture to excellent, often overtly political, photographic displays.

State Library

Macquarie St • Mon–Thurs 9am–8pm, Fri 9am–5pm, Sat & Sun 10am–5pm; Mitchell Library Special Collections closed Sun; film screenings Thurs noon • Free • ⓦ sl.nsw.gov.au

The row of public architecture along Macquarie Street ends with the **State Library of New South Wales**. The complex of old and new buildings includes the 1906 sandstone **Mitchell Library**, its imposing Neoclassical facade gazing across to the Botanic Gardens. Inside the foyer, the **Tasman Map** floor mosaic replicates an original drawn by the Dutch explorer Abel Tasman in the 1640s and now held in the library's collection. It depicts the Australian continent, still without an east coast, and its northern extremity joined to Papua New Guinea.

A walkway links the Mitchell Library with the modern building housing the **General Reference Library**. Free exhibitions relating to Australian history, art, photography and literature are a regular feature of the Reference Library vestibules, while lectures, films and video shows often take place in the **Metcalfe Auditorium**. The library's **bookshop** on the ground floor has one of the best collections of Australia-related books in Sydney, and every Thursday the Metcalfe Auditorium hosts **free movies** from the extensive film and documentary archive.

Haymarket

The section of the city centre south from Liverpool Street down to Central Station is known as **Haymarket**, a lively area that's effectively a downmarket southern extension of the CBD. Between Town Hall and Central Station, **George Street** shifts gear as businesspeople and shoppers give way to backpackers, who jam the area's

1

abundant hostels, and students from the University of Technology. It's also a markedly East Asian area with its own distinct **Chinatown**, a growing **Koreatown** and **Thaitown**, as well as plenty of street-food-style food courts.

The short stretch between the Town Hall and Liverpool Street is for the most part teenage territory, a frenetic zone of **multiscreen cinemas**, arcade game halls and fast-food joints, though the **Metro Theatre** is one of Sydney's best live-music venues (see p.134). The stretch is trouble-prone on Friday and Saturday nights, when there are more pleasant places to catch a film (see p.138). Things change pace at Liverpool Street, where Sydney's **Spanish Corner** is gradually being taken over by Korean restaurants.

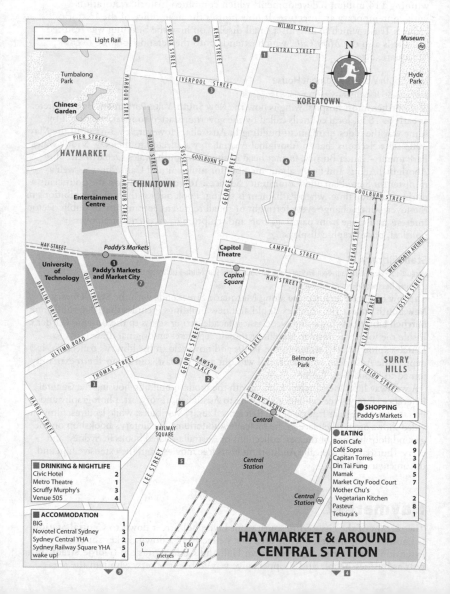

■ DRINKING & NIGHTLIFE

Civic Hotel	2
Metro Theatre	1
Scruffy Murphy's	3
Venue 505	4

■ ACCOMMODATION

BIG	1
Novotel Central Sydney	3
Sydney Central YHA	2
Sydney Railway Square YHA	5
wake up!	4

● SHOPPING

Paddy's Markets	1

■ EATING

Boon Cafe	6
Café Sopra	9
Capitan Torres	3
Din Tai Fung	4
Mamak	5
Market City Food Court	7
Mother Chu's Vegetarian Kitchen	2
Pasteur	8
Tetsuya's	1

HAYMARKET & AROUND CENTRAL STATION

Chinatown

Chinatown is a more full-blooded affair than Spanish Corner and probably the most active of the city's ethnic enclaves. Through the ornate Chinese gates, pedestrianized **Dixon Street** is the main official thoroughfare (though arguably Chinatown stretches north up to the Town Hall), buzzing day and night as people crowd into numerous restaurants, pubs, cafés, cinemas, food courts and Asian grocery stores. Towards the end of January or in the first weeks of February, Chinese New Year is celebrated here with gusto: traditional dragon and lion dances, food festivals and musical entertainment compete with the noise and smoke from strings of Chinese crackers. For a calmer retreat, on the edge of Chinatown, at the southern fringes of Darling Harbour, is the serene **Chinese Garden** (see p.85).

The area immediately south of Chinatown is enlivened by Sydney's oldest market, bustling **Paddy's Market** (Wed–Sun 9am–5pm), in its undercover home in between Thomas and Quay streets: a good place to buy cheap vegetables, seafood, clothes, souvenirs and bric-a-brac. Above Paddy's, the multilevel **Market City Shopping Centre** (ⓦmarketcity.com.au) has a modern Asian feel as well as some excellent discounted-fashion outlets. There's also a first-rate Asian food court (see p.124) on the top floor next to the multiscreen cinema.

Hyde Park

Hyde Park was fenced off by Governor Macquarie in 1810 to mark the outskirts of his township (see box, p.78), and with its war memorials and church, and peripheral museum and Catholic cathedral, is still very much a formal city park. Park Street divides the park into two sections linked by a main north–south axis, shaded by enormous fig trees. In the northern half, the 1932 **Archibald Fountain** commemorates the alliance of Australia and France during World War I and is dripping in Greek and Roman iconography – all gods and minotaurs in a large hexagonal pool.

Anzac Memorial

Daily 9am–5pm • Free

The southern focus of the park is the **Anzac Memorial**, Sydney's most potent monument to those fallen in wartime. Fronted by the tree-lined Pool of Remembrance (currently undergoing remodelling into a cascading water feature), the 30m-high cenotaph, unveiled in 1934, is classic Art Deco right down to the stylized soldier figures that solemnly decorate the exterior. Inside, the domed ceiling is covered in 120,000 tiny golden stars representing each serviceman and woman from New South Wales who fought overseas during World War I. Downstairs, a mainly photographic exhibition looks at Australian wartime experiences.

Great Synagogue

187 Elizabeth St • Tours Thurs and first & third Tues at noon • $10 • ⓦ greatsynagogue.org.au

On the west side of Hyde Park, the 1878 **Great Synagogue** was inspired by English synagogues of the time in London and Liverpool and is the most beautiful in Australia, with domed towers flanking the wrought-iron gates and a big rose window facing Hyde Park.

Australian Museum

6 College St • Daily 9.30am–5pm • $12, 5–15 yrs $8 or free on weekends, under-5s free; special exhibitions usually extra • ⓦ australianmuseum.net.au

Facing Hyde Park across College Street, the **Australian Museum** is primarily a museum of natural history, with an interest in human evolution and Aboriginal culture and

1

history. The collection was founded in 1827, but the actual building, a grand sandstone affair with a facade of Corinthian pillars, wasn't fully finished until the 1860s and has been extended several times since. As well as the permanent exhibitions below, there are also **special exhibitions** throughout the year.

The core of the old museum is the three levels of the **Long Gallery**, Australia's first exhibition gallery, opened in 1855 to a Victorian public keen to gawk at the colony's curiosities. Many of the classic displays of the following hundred years remain here, Heritage-listed, contrasting with a very modern approach in the rest of the museum.

Ground floor

On the **ground floor**, the compelling **First Australians** exhibition looks at the history of Australia's Aboriginal people from the Dreamtime to the more contemporary issues of the Stolen Generation and freedom rides. The ground-floor level of the Long Gallery houses the **Skeletons** exhibit, where you can see a skeletal human going through the motions of riding a bicycle, for example, and the elegantly complex bone structure of a python.

Levels 1 & 2

Level 1 is devoted to **minerals**, but far more exciting are the disparate collections on **Level 2** – especially the Long Gallery's **More Than Insects** exhibition, which includes chilling contextual displays of dangerous spiders such as redbacks and funnelwebs. On the same floor, adaptation is the key to **Surviving Australia**, which explores how monotremes, marsupials and humans have coped with the extremes of the Australian climate, or ultimately failed to in the case of the ancient marsupial lion or the Tasmanian tiger. Ancient beasts also form the bulk of the **Dinosaurs** exhibit, where the fun design-o-saurus programme allows you to create your own dinosaur on-screen amid displays of dinosaur eggs and explanations of how this primeval world came to an end 65 million years ago.

Children, of course, will love the dinosaurs, and can pass an hour in **Kids' Space**, a fun play-space for under-5s, while adults and older children will appreciate **Search and Discover Centre**, a flora and fauna identification centre with internet access and reference books.

Cook and Phillip Park

Recreation centre Mon–Fri 6am–10pm, Sat & Sun 7am–8pm • Pool $7.20 • ⓦ cookandphillip.org.au

The northern stretch of College Street flanks the large **Cook and Phillip Park** with its impressive submerged **recreation centre**, which includes a 50m swimming pool and gym. All sorts of classes are available including yoga and swimming, and you can refuel at the lovely *Bodhi in the Park* (see p.123).

St Mary's Cathedral

St Mary's Rd • Mon–Fri & Sun 6.30am–6.30pm, Sat 8am–6.30pm • ⓦ stmaryscathedral.org.au

Overlooking Cook and Phillip Park, Catholic **St Mary's Cathedral** is a huge Gothic-style church opened in 1882, though the foundation stone was laid in 1821. In 1999, the cathedral at last gained the twin stone spires originally planned for the two southern towers by architect William Wardell in 1865.

The Domain

Cook and Phillip Park fills in the green gap between Hyde Park and **The Domain**, a much larger, plainer open space that stretches from behind the historic precinct on

Macquarie Street to the waterfront, divided from the **Royal Botanic Gardens** by the ugly Cahill Expressway and Mrs Macquarie's Road. In the early days of the settlement, The Domain was the governor's private park; now it's a popular place for a stroll or a picnic, with the **Art Gallery of New South Wales**, an **outdoor swimming pool** and **Mrs Macquarie's Chair** to provide distraction. On Sundays, assorted cranks and revolutionaries assemble here for Speakers' Corner, and every January thousands of people gather on the lawns to enjoy the free open-air concerts of the **Sydney Festival** (see p.138).

Art Gallery of New South Wales

Art Gallery Rd • Daily 10am–5pm, Wed till 10pm; Art After Hours Wed 5–10pm • Free except for special exhibitions; guided tours free; excellent audio tour $5 or free download from website • ⓦ artgallery.nsw.gov.au

Beyond St Mary's Cathedral, Art Gallery Road runs through The Domain to the **Art Gallery of New South Wales**. The collection was begun in 1874, moved into this building in 1897 and has been expanding ever since, most recently in 2003, when a gigantic cube of white glass, dubbed the "**lightbox**", was grafted onto the eastern Woolloomooloo facade to contain the gallery's Asian collection. As well as a wonderful permanent collection spanning European, colonial, Aboriginal and contemporary art, there's a strong programme of **temporary exhibits**.

You enter the gallery at Ground Level from where stairs lead down to three lower levels. Ground Level principally contains a large collection of **European art** dating from the eleventh to the twenty-first centuries and includes a vast, gilt-framed canvas by Edward John Poynter depicting *The Queen of Sheba before Solomon* in luminous detail. You should also be able to spot Cézanne's *Bords de la Marne*: the painting was bought for over $16 million in 2008, making it the most expensive work ever purchased by an Australian public gallery.

Classic **Australian paintings** to look out for are Frederick McCubbin's *On the Wallaby Track* from 1855, Tom Roberts' romanticized shearing-shed scene *The Golden Fleece* (1894) and an altogether less idyllic look at rural Australia in Russell Drysdale's *Sofala* (1947), a depressing vision of a drought-stricken town. Other luminaries such as Sidney Nolan and Brett Whitely are usually well represented, though works on show rotate from the greater collection. The **photographic collection** includes Max Dupain's iconic *Sunbaker* (1937), an early study of Australian hedonism that looks as if it could have been taken yesterday.

On Lower Level 3, the **Yiribana** gallery is devoted to the art and cultural artefacts of Aboriginal and Torres Strait Islanders – painting, sculpture, photography and multimedia installations. Try to visit during "**Art After Hours**" on Wednesday evenings for the free programme of events including exhibition talks, celebrity talks, films and live music in the *Artbar*. There's also an excellent bookshop, a café (Lower Level 1) and a well-regarded restaurant (Ground Level).

Mrs Macquarie's Chair

Mrs Macquarie's Rd

The northern part of Art Gallery Road turns into the beginning of one of Sydney's most popular jogging routes – Mrs Macquarie's Road, built in 1816 at the urging of the governor's wife, Elizabeth. The road curves down from Art Gallery Road to Mrs Macquarie's Point, which separates idyllic Farm Cove from the grittier Woolloomooloo Bay. At the end is the celebrated lookout point known as **Mrs Macquarie's Chair**, a bench seat fashioned out of the rock. From here, Elizabeth could admire her favourite view of the harbour on her daily walk in what was then the governor's private park. Continue walking along the water to get to the Opera House.

1

The "Boy"

1C Mrs Macquarie's Rd • Sept–April daily 6am–7pm • $6.20 • ⓦ abcpool.org

On the route down to Mrs Macquarie's Point, the Andrew "Boy" Charlton Pool – "**The Boy**", as the locals fondly call it – is an open-air, chlorinated saltwater swimming pool safely isolated from the harbour waters on the Woolloomooloo side of the promontory, with views across to the engrossingly functional Garden Island Naval Depot. The pool was named after the gold-medal-winning Manly swimmer, who turned 17 during the 1924 Paris Olympics. It's a popular hangout for trendy Darlinghurst types and gay sun-worshippers.

Royal Botanic Garden

Mrs Macquarie's Rd **Gardens** Daily 7am–sunset, visitor centre daily 9.30am–4.30pm; tours daily at 10.30am (1hr 30min), March–Nov also Mon–Fri at 1pm (1hr) • Free **Choo Choo Express** Daily 10am–4.30pm, every 30min • Hop-on-hop-off $10 • ⓦ rbgsyd.nsw.gov.au

The **Royal Botanic Garden**, established in 1816, occupies the area between this strip of The Domain and the Sydney Opera House, around the headland on Farm Cove where the first white settlers struggled to grow vegetables for the hungry colony. While duck ponds, a romantic rose garden and fragrant herb garden strike a very English air, look out for native birds and, at dusk, the fruit bats flying overhead (hundreds of the giant bats hang by day in the Palm Grove area near the restaurant) as the nocturnal possums begin to stir. There are examples of trees and plants from all over the world, although it's the huge, gnarled, native Moreton Bay figs that stand out. The gardens provide some of the most stunning **views** of Sydney Harbour and are always crowded with workers at lunchtime, picnickers on fine weekends, and lovers entwined beneath the trees.

Free **tours** of the gardens commence from the **visitor centre** at Palm Grove in the centre of the Gardens. The **Choo Choo Express** trackless train, which runs through the gardens, stops here; the main pick-up point is the entrance near the Opera House, and there are more stops along the way.

Darling Harbour and around

Immediately east of the city centre lies **Darling Harbour**, once a grimy industrial docks area which lay moribund until the 1980s when the State Government chose to pump millions of dollars into the regeneration of this prime city real estate as part of the 1988 Bicentenary Project. The huge redevelopment scheme around **Cockle Bay**, which opened in 1988, included the building of the above-ground monorail – now dismantled – as well as a massive new shopping and entertainment precinct. In many ways, it's a thoroughly stylish redevelopment of the old wharves, and Darling Harbour has plenty of attractions: an aquarium, entertainment areas, a shopping mall, an IMAX cinema, a children's playground, gardens, and a convention and exhibition centre. However, it's only recently that Sydneysiders themselves have embraced it. Sneered at for years by locals as tacky and touristy, it took the Cockle Bay and King Street Wharf developments on the eastern side of the waterfront – with upmarket cafés, good bars and restaurants – to finally lure them.

The eastern side of Darling Harbour blends straight into the CBD, with office and apartment blocks overlooking the yacht-filled water. Across the old **Pyrmont Bridge**, the western side is a different matter. Push beyond the wharfside developments and you're onto the Pyrmont–Ultimo Peninsula, an altogether older industrial quarter comprising the suburbs of **Pyrmont** and **Ultimo**, both of which have only started to smarten up since the turn of the millennium. It still has a good way to go, and there's pleasure in just wandering around marking the changes in between visits to the **Star City Casino**, the **Sydney Fish Market** and the superb **Powerhouse Museum**.

By ferry Getting to the wharf outside the Sydney Aquarium by ferry from Circular Quay gives you a chance to see a bit of the harbour – STA ferries stop at McMahons Point, on the North Shore, and Balmain en route. The *Matilda Ferry* runs from the Harbourmaster's Steps, outside the MCA, and goes via Luna Park (every 45min; 20min).

By bus The #443 goes from Circular Quay via the QVB, Pyrmont and the casino, and the #449 runs between the casino, the Powerhouse Museum, Broadway Shopping Centre and Glebe.

By light rail The L1 Dulwich Hill Line of the light rail loops around the perimeter of Darling Harbour, stopping at several stations along the way, before heading east towards Central Station or west towards Lilyfield and Dulwich Hill.

By People Mover The harbour can be navigated on the dinky People Mover train (daily 10am–5pm, full circuit 20min; $5).

On foot It's only a 10min walk from the Town Hall to get to Darling Harbour; from the QVB, down Market St and along the overhead walkway. Further south, there's a pedestrian bridge from Bathurst St, or cut through on Liverpool St to Tumbalong Park.

Visitor Centre There are always festivals and events here, particularly during school holidays; to find out what's on, visit the Darling Harbour Visitor Centre (daily 9.30am–5.30pm; ☎02 9240 8788, ⓦ darlingharbour .com.au), next door to the IMAX Theatre.

Tumbalong Park and Cockle Bay

The southern half of Darling Harbour, around **Cockle Bay**, is focused on **Tumbalong Park**, reached from the city via Liverpool Street. Backed by the Exhibition Centre, this is the "village green" of Darling Harbour – complete with water features and some interesting sculptures and public artworks – and serves as a venue for open-air concerts and free public entertainment. The area surrounding it can be Darling Harbour's most frenetic – at least on weekends and during school holidays – as most of the attractions, including a free playground and a stage for holiday concerts, are aimed at children. For some peace and quiet, head for the adjacent **Chinese Garden** (daily 9.30am–5pm; $6), completed for the Bicentenary in 1988, as a gift from Sydney's sister city Guangdong; the "Garden of Friendship" is designed in the traditional southern-Chinese style.

Sea Life Sydney Aquarium

1–5 Wheat Rd • Daily 9am–7pm, last entry 6pm • $40, under-16s $28; free with Unlimited Attractions pass (see p.117); check the website for discounts ⓦ sydneyaquarium.com.au

At the eastern end of **Pyrmont Bridge** is the impressive **Sea Life Sydney Aquarium**, which, if you're not going to get the chance to explore the Great Barrier Reef, makes a good substitute. The highlights are the three vast ocean tanks. The first two cover the **Southern Oceans**, with underwater walkways allowing you to wander along as sharks, seals and gigantic stingrays swim overhead. There's a similarly grand approach to the **Northern Oceans** exhibit, where exotic species from the **Great Barrier Reef** drift past behind huge sheets of glass. Try to come at a quiet time (early or late in the day) when it can be breathtaking: black-and-yellow-spotted butterfly fish drift by, undulating moon jellyfish loom into view, iridescent blue starfish glow and a spotted leopard shark seems disinterested in it all. The Great Barrier Reef Oceanarium finishes with a huge **floor-to-ceiling tank** where you can sit and watch the underwater world while classical music plays. Another section displays dangerous creatures like the moray eel and venomous sea urchins, and Little penguins try to keep cool.

Wild Life Sydney Zoo

1–5 Wheat Rd • Daily 9am–8pm • $40, under-16s $25; free with Unlimited Attractions pass (see p.117); check the website for discounts • ⓦ myfun.com.au/wild-life-sydney-zoo

Impressive **Wild Life Sydney Zoo** is a mesh-domed centre with free-flying birds and a compact collection of over 130 species of animals found throughout Australia. The elegant glass displays are carefully thought out, giving a good impression of the

1

animals' natural environment. Koalas and kangaroos are the inevitable highlights, but snakes, spiders and other creepy-crawlies make interesting viewing, and you might even get the chance to handle some non-venomous species.

Powerhouse Museum

500 Harris St • Daily 10am–5pm • $15, under-16s free; special exhibitions extra • ⓦ powerhousemuseum.com • Exhibition Centre light rail

From Tumbalong Park, a signposted walkway leads to the **Powerhouse Museum**, located, as the name suggests, in a former power station – though plans are underway to move the museum all the way to Parramatta, in western Sydney. Arguably the best museum in Sydney, it's a huge, fresh and exciting place dedicated to **science and design**. Set aside at least a couple of hours to investigate the four-level museum properly, more if you visit one of the temporary exhibitions.

You enter on Level 3, which is dominated by the huge **Boulton and Watt Steam Engine**, the oldest rotative steam engine in the world, first put to use in 1785 in a British brewery and used for over a hundred years. Still operational, the engine is often loudly demonstrated.

Downstairs, the old destination board from Sydney's Central Station is set to look as it would have on a Sunday in 1937, although the board was in use until 1982. It overlooks the **transport section**, including the venerable red-and-cream Rose Bay tram and one of the solar racers that competed in transcontinental races – effectively a streamlined solar panel on wheels.

Elsewhere, you'll find ¡Inspired!, an excellent **design exhibit** usually featuring pieces of furniture by top Australian industrial designer Marc Newsom, including his classic Lockheed Lounge Chair (1986), with aluminium panels riveted into a deliciously organic form.

The **Kings Cinema** on Level 2, with its original Art Deco fittings, aptly shows the sorts of newsreels and films a Sydneysider would have watched in the 1930s. Judging by the tears at closing time, the **special children's areas** go down a treat.

Pyrmont

Long an integral part of Sydney's industrial waterfront, with shipbuilding yards, a sugar refinery and wool stores, **Pyrmont**, which juts out into the water between Darling Harbour and Blackwattle Bay, was also Sydney's answer to Ellis Island. In the 1950s, thousands of immigrants disembarked here at the city's main overseas passenger terminal, Pier 13. Today, the former industrial suburb, which had a population of only nine hundred in 1988, has been transformed into a residential suburb of some twenty thousand, with $2 billion worth of investment, and slick modern blocks and warehouse renovations to show for it. The area has certainly become glitzier, with the gleaming **Australian National Maritime Museum**, Sydney's **casino** and the Channel Ten TV company based here. Harris Street has filled up with shops and cafés, and the area's old pubs have been given a new lease of life, attracting the young and upwardly mobile.

Australian National Maritime Museum

2 Murray St • Daily 9.30am–5pm; Jan till 6pm • Free; special exhibitions vary • ⓦ anmm.gov.au • Pyrmont Bay light rail

The imposing **Australian National Maritime Museum** celebrates Australia's intimate relationship with the sea, from the earliest days of exploration to immigration and sport. Permanent collections feature **Aboriginal objects** adorned with marine motifs, including shell work from Tasmania, **Art Deco-styled galleries** exploring ocean liner travel and historic **explorer icons** such as a piece from Captain Cook's ship HMS *Resolution* and the 1602 Blaeu celestial globe, the first to show constellations of the southern hemisphere. There are often hands-on exhibitions for children, such as **Horrible Histories Pirates**.

1

The Star Casino
80 Pyrmont St • 24hr • Ⓦ star.com.au • Star City light rail

The Star Casino on Pyrmont Bay is Sydney's spectacularly tasteless 24-hour gambling spot. As well as the two hundred gaming tables (from blackjack to pai gow – there are lots of Asian games, and gamblers), a big betting lounge and sports bar, and 1500 noisy poker machines, the building houses over a dozen restaurants, cafés (good for late-night eats) and theme bars, two theatres and a nightclub. Dress code is smart casual; you can just wander in and have a look around or a drink, without betting.

Sydney Fish Market
Cnr Pyrmont Bridge Rd & Bank St • Daily 7am–4pm • **Auctions** Mon–Fri, though the biggest is on Fri; buyers begin viewing fish at 4.30am, auctions begin at 5.30am, public viewing platform opens at 7am • **Tours** Weekdays except Tues 6.40am, 1hr 30min • $35, including coffee and $5 voucher; enclosed shoes required; booking essential **Sydney Seafood School** Cookery lessons $90/2hr, $130/3hr, $165/4hr; Seafood BBQ course Sat & Sun $165/4hr – book at least three months in advance on ☎ 02 9004 1111 • ☎ 02 9004 1108, Ⓦ sydneyfishmarket.com.au • Fish Market light rail

A ten-minute walk via Pyrmont Bridge Road from Darling Harbour is the **Sydney Fish Market**, the second-largest seafood market in the world after the Tsukiji market in Tokyo. You need to visit early in the morning to see the weekday **auctions**. Buyers log into computer terminals to register their bids in a Dutch-style auction: the price drops steadily until a bid is made, and the first bid gets the fish. You don't get much of a view from the public platform, so to get a taste of the action on the auction floor and stand among buyers bidding for sashimi-grade yellowfin tuna, join one of the informative fish market **tours**. The tours also visit the rooms used by the **Sydney Seafood School**, which offers cookery lessons, from Thai-style to Provençale, under the expert tuition of resident home economists as well as guest chefs from the city's top restaurants. The most popular course is the "Seafood BBQ".

EATING	SYDNEY FISH MARKET

You can **take away** oysters, prawns and cooked seafood and (if you don't mind being pestered by seagulls) eat picnic-style on waterfront tables watching the boats come in. Everything is set up for throwing together an impromptu meal – there's a **bakery**, the **Blackwattle Deli** (with an extensive cheese selection), a **bottle shop** and a **grocer**.

Doyles on the Wharf ☎ 02 9337 6214, Ⓦ doyles.com.au. The casual and slightly more affordable version of the famous fish restaurant of the same name at Watsons Bay (see p.128), *Doyles* serves decent lunchtime options such as creamy half-lobster mornay ($31). For a classic Australian dish, go for barramundi and chips and salad ($20). Daily 11am–5pm.
Fish Market Café ☎ 02 9660 4280, Ⓦ sydneyfishmarket .com.au. Come here for dirt-cheap fish and chips (from $9) or a crack-of-dawn espresso. Mon–Fri 4am–4pm, Sat & Sun 5am–5pm.

Sushi bar ☎ 02 9552 2269, Ⓦ sydneyfishmarket .com.au. This excellent sushi joint offers fresh sashimi either at quiet interior tables or taking in the full sights, sounds and smells on stools at the bar. Everything is prepared by a highly skilled chef from Osaka, Japan, who knows his stuff. A mixed plate ($10.90–13.50) is a good deal, or go for the ten pieces of buttery salmon sashimi ($14.90). Mon–Fri 10am–4.30pm, Sat & Sun 9.30am–4.30pm.

The inner east

To the **east** of the city centre, the adjacent districts of **Kings Cross** and Potts Point comprise one of the city's major entertainment districts and a popular spot for tourists (particularly backpackers). To the north you can descend a series of steps to **Woolloomooloo** with its busy naval dockyards and stylish Finger Wharf. South of Kings Cross, **Darlinghurst** and **Paddington** were once rather scruffy working-class suburbs, but were gradually taken over and revamped by the young, arty and upwardly mobile.

Oxford Street runs from the city southeast through **Taylor Square**, the heart of gay Sydney, and on through the designer shopping and art gallery areas of Darlinghurst

1

> ### HOW WOOLLOOMOOLOO GOT ITS NAME
>
> There are several explanations of how this area came by its sonorous **Aboriginal name**, perhaps the least plausible being the local story that the area's first settler, John Palmer, found a **sheep** in his bathroom and exclaimed, "There's wool on my loo." Other possible meanings include: **burial place**; **place of plenty**; **young black kangaroo**; **young male kangaroo**; and **field of blood**, due to the tribal fights said to have been held in the area. The name has also been rumoured to be a mispronunciation of **windmill**, from one that sat on Darlinghurst ridge until the 1850s. It's pronounced *wooller* (rhyming with fuller)-*ma-loo*.

and Paddington to old-money **Woollahra** and the open grasslands of **Centennial Parklands**.

Oxford Street marks the northern boundary of rapidly gentrifying **Surry Hills**. While cutting-edge galleries and bars are still filling the area's backstreets, others are looking south to go-ahead **Waterloo** and even edgier **Redfern**.

Kings Cross

Take a train (Eastern Suburbs line) or bus (#311, #324 or #325 from Circular Quay; many others from the city to Darlinghurst Rd), or walk straight up William St from Hyde Park; for a quieter route than William St, head up from The Domain via Cowper Wharf Rd in Woolloomooloo, and then up the McElhone Stairs to Victoria St

The preserve of Sydney's bohemians in the 1950s, **Kings Cross** became an R&R spot for American soldiers during the Vietnam War and has long been considered Sydney's seedy red-light district. In recent years, however, the brothels have moved out to the suburbs and a facility for drug users has taken substance abuse off the streets. What remains of the sex industry is a 700m-long stretch of Darlinghurst Road, where a handful of strip shows cling on – though their days here are probably numbered, as no new places are allowed to open up.

"The Cross" remains lively, with places to eat, drink and dance that stay open late, but following the **lockout laws** (last entry at 1.30am and last drinks at 3am for bars and clubs) the streets are subdued late at night, and some businesses have been forced to close down, so do check ahead before heading out. Friday and Saturday nights can be rumbustious, but the constant flow of people (and police officers) makes it relatively safe. Generally, the area is much quieter during the day, with a slightly hungover feel to it; local residents emerge, and it's a good time to hang out in the cafés.

Eastbound from the city centre, **William Street** heads straight for the giant neon Coca-Cola sign that heralds Kings Cross. The street is an uneasy blend of cheap car and van rental places and dealerships for Ferrari, Lamborghini and Maserati.

Fitzroy Gardens

The **Fitzroy Gardens** feature the distinctive **El Alamein fountain**: the centre of the action. At weekends, people from the suburbs arrive in droves, emerging from the underground Kings Cross Station, near the beginning of the Darlinghurst Road "sin" strip, to wander the streets licking ice creams, as touts try to haul them into the strip joints and sleazy clubs. This same stretch is increasingly being populated with hostels and budget travel agencies catering to the travellers staying in the area.

Woolloomooloo

Best reached on foot from Kings Cross by taking the McElhone Stairs or the Butlers Stairs from Victoria St, or from the Royal Botanic Gardens by walking south around the foreshore from Mrs Macquarie's Chair; alternatively, take bus #311 from Kings Cross, Circular Quay or Central Station

North of William Street, just below Kings Cross, **Woolloomooloo** occupies the old harbourside quarter between The Domain and the grey-painted fleet of the **Garden**

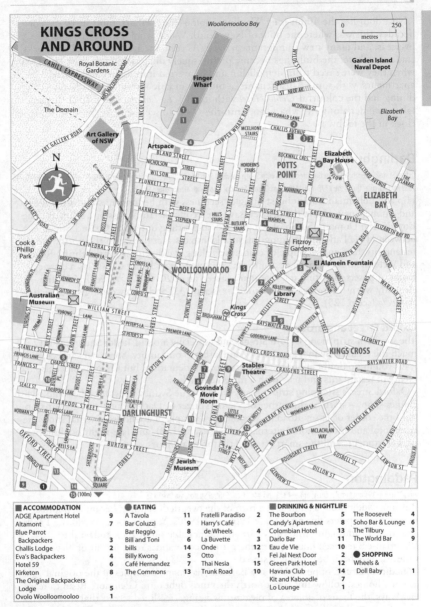

KINGS CROSS AND AROUND

ACCOMMODATION		EATING				DRINKING & NIGHTLIFE			
ADGE Apartment Hotel	9	A Tavola	11	Fratelli Paradiso	2	The Bourbon	5	The Roosevelt	4
Altamont	7	Bar Coluzzi	9	Harry's Café		Candy's Apartment	8	Soho Bar & Lounge	6
Blue Parrot		Bar Reggio	8	de Wheels	4	Colombian Hotel	13	The Tilbury	3
Backpackers	3	Bill and Toni	6	La Buvette	3	Darlo Bar	11	The World Bar	9
Challis Lodge	2	bills	14	Onde	12	Eau de Vie	10		
Eva's Backpackers	4	Billy Kwong	5	Otto	1	Fei Jai Next Door	2	SHOPPING	
Hotel 59	6	Café Hernandez	7	Thai Nesia	15	Green Park Hotel	12	Wheels &	
Kirketon	8	The Commons	13	Trunk Road	10	Havana Club	14	Doll Baby	1
The Original Backpackers						Kit and Kaboodle	7		
Lodge	5					Lo Lounge	1		
Ovolo Woolloomooloo	1								

Island Naval Depot. Once a narrow-streeted slum, Woolloomooloo is quickly being transformed, though its upmarket apartment developments sit uneasily side by side, and sometimes in conflict with, community housing, and you should still be careful in the backstreets at night. There are some lively pubs and some quieter, more old-fashioned drinking holes, as well as the legendary **Harry's Café de Wheels** on Cowper Wharf Road, a late-closing pie-cart operating since 1945 and popular nowadays with Sydney cabbies and hungry clubbers (see p.125).

1

Next door lies the 400m-long Woolloomooloo **Finger Wharf**, built in 1915. For decades, this was where the bulk of New South Wales' wool left for markets overseas, and many new immigrants arrived. As containerization shifted the docks' trade elsewhere, the buildings became picturesquely dilapidated until the late 1980s, when they were saved from demolition and converted into luxury residential apartments, with some A-list tenants, a number of chic restaurants with alfresco dining and the colourful *Ovolo Hotel* with its slick *Lo Lounge* (see p.132). If you take a wander along the wharf, pop into the *Ovolo* to see the 86kg Swedish-designed clock in the lobby.

Darlinghurst

Oxford St strikes southeast from the intersection with South Dowling St in Darlinghurst – buses heading in this direction include #380 and #389 from Circular Quay; the #378 and #440, from Central Station, also heads along Oxford St

Hip and bohemian **Darlinghurst** mingles seediness with hedonism: some art students and clubbers never leave the district, save for a coffee at The Cross or a swim at "The Boy" in The Domain. South of Kings Cross and strung out along Oxford Street between Hyde Park and Paddington, it falls into distinct halves. In the north, the restaurants, bars and a couple of chic hotels along the diverging Darlinghurst Road and **Victoria Street** seem like a southern continuation of Kings Cross. It's a classic haunt of posers, boasting the legendary, street-smart *Bar Coluzzi* (see p.125), the elegantly worn-in, lounge-style *Darlo Bar* (see p.132) and funky dining spots such as *A Tavola* (see p.125).

Oxford Street and around

The southern strip along **Oxford Street**, and especially around **Taylor Square**, is very much the focus of Sydney's active **gay and lesbian** community. Some bars and clubs leave you in no doubt about the punters' sexual orientation, but Oxford Street also has plenty of restaurants and bars with a mixed clientele.

Oxford Street's **shopping strip** – many would argue Sydney's best for labels and stylish clothes shops – starts at the corner of Victoria Street in Darlinghurst and doesn't stop until the corner of Jersey Road in Woollahra. A couple of art-house cinemas show the latest local and international alternative flicks (see p.138), and late-night bookshops pack in students and the smart set alike till the small hours.

Paddington

Bus #380 or #389 from Circular Quay, or the #378 and #440 from Central Station, via Oxford St

Bustling **Paddington**, a slum at the turn of the twentieth century, became a popular hangout for hipsters during the late 1960s and 1970s. Yuppies took over in the 1980s and turned Paddington into the smart and fashionable suburb it is today: the Victorian-era terraced houses, with their iron-lace verandas reminiscent of New Orleans, have been beautifully restored.

Shadforth Street, opposite Victoria Barracks, has many examples of the original artisans' homes. Follow this street north then turn right onto Glenmore Road to reach **Five Ways**, the focus of an area of pleasant, winding, tree-lined streets that make a great place for a stroll, and offer a chance to wander into speciality stores, cafés and numerous small art galleries.

The area's swankiest clothes **shopping** is around the junction of Glenmore Road and Oxford Street, and there are more classy shops further east on Elizabeth Street, which runs off Oxford Street almost 1km further southeast. Photo fans shouldn't miss the **Australian Centre for Photography** (see p.139) with exhibitions of photo-based art from established and new international and Australian artists.

Victoria Barracks

Oxford St • Museum Thurs 10am–1pm; barracks tours 10am • $2 donation; bring photo ID • ☎ 02 8335 5330, ⓦ armymuseumnsw.com.au

Many of Paddington's terraces were originally built in the 1840s to house the artisans who worked on the graceful, sandstone **Victoria Barracks** on the southern side of Oxford Street, its walls stretching seven blocks, from Greens Road to just before the Paddington Town Hall on Oatley Road. The barracks are still used by the army, though you can visit a small **museum** of uniforms, medals and firearms. Free weekly barracks **tours** include an army band recital.

Paddington Markets

Uniting Church grounds, 395 Oxford St • Sat 10am–4pm • ⓦ paddingtonmarkets.com.au

On Saturday, when everyone descends on **Paddington Markets**, the area is heaving. The markets just keep getting bigger, selling everything from handmade jewellery to local artwork, cheap but fresh flowers and vintage clothes; you can even get a massage or a tarot reading between a cup of coffee and an organic sandwich. Australian label Sass & Bide started from a humble stall here.

Centennial Parklands

Daily sunrise to sunset • ⓦ centennialparklands.com.au • To get to the Paddington entrance of Centennial Parklands, take a bus along Oxford St: either the #378 or #440 from Railway Square and Central Station or the #380 from Circular Quay; alternatively, head straight into the heart of the park from Central Station (#372, #393 or #395)

South of Paddington and Woollahra, lies the great green expanse of **Centennial Parklands**, opened to the citizens of Sydney at the Centennial Festival in 1888. With its vast lawns, rose gardens and extensive network of ponds complete with ducks, it resembles an English country park, but is reclaimed at dawn and dusk by distinctly Antipodean residents, including possums and flying foxes. The park is crisscrossed by walking paths and tracks for cycling, rollerblading, jogging and horseriding: you can rent a bike or rollerblades nearby (see p.117) or hire a horse from the adjacent equestrian centre and then recover from your exertions in the café with its pleasant outdoor tables or, in the finer months, stay on until dark and catch an outdoor film at the Moonlight Cinema (see p.138).

The Sydney Cricket Ground (SCG)

Cnr of Moore Park & Driver Ave • **Matches** Tickets for all matches can be bought at the gates on the day, subject to availability, or purchased in advance from ⓦ ticketek.com • **Tours** Mon–Sat 10am (non-match days only), 1hr 30min • $30 • General enquiries ☎ 02 9360 6601, tour booking ☎ 1300 724 737, ⓦ scgt.nsw.gov.au • Bus #1 from Chalmers St outside Central Station runs to Moore Park Bus Station when events are on

The venerated institution of the **Sydney Cricket Ground** earned its place in cricketing history for Don Bradman's score of 452 not out in 1929, and for the controversy over England's bodyline bowling techniques in 1932. Ideally, proceedings are observed from the lovely 1886 Members Stand, while sipping an ice-cold gin and tonic – but unless you're invited by a member, you'll end up elsewhere, probably drinking beer from a plastic cup. Cricket spectators aren't a sedate lot in Sydney, and the noisiest barrackers will probably come from the Victor Trumper Stand. The Brewongle Stand provides consistently good viewing, although beware the blinding afternoon sun. Best of all is the Bradman Stand, with a view directly behind the bowler's arm, and adjacent to the exclusive stand occupied by members, commentators and ex-players. The Test to see here is, of course, **The Ashes**; the Sydney leg of the five tests, each for five days, begins on New Year's Day.

Die-hard cricket fans can go on a **tour** of the SCG on non-match days, which also covers the **Sydney Football Stadium** next door, where the focus is on international and national rugby league and rugby union, and Aussie Rules football matches, when Sydneysiders come out to support their local team, The Swans.

1

Surry Hills

A short walk uphill from Central Station (Devonshire St or Elizabeth St exit): take Foveaux or Devonshire sts and you'll soon hit Crown St, or it's a quicker stroll from Oxford St, Darlinghurst, heading south along Crown or Bourke sts; several buses run from Circular Quay, including the #301 and #303, both to Crown St; bus #352 runs from Newtown along Cleveland St to Crown St and on to Bondi Junction

South of Darlinghurst's Oxford Street and due east of Central Station, **Surry Hills** was traditionally the centre of the rag trade. Rows of tiny terraces once housed its poor, working-class population, many of them of Irish origin. Considered a slum by the rest of Sydney, the dire and overcrowded conditions were given fictional life in Ruth Park's *The Harp in the South* trilogy (see p.998), set in the Surry Hills of the 1940s. The area became something of a cultural melting pot as a result of European postwar immigration, and doubled as a grungy, student heartland in the 1980s.

By the mid-1990s, the slickly fashionable scenes of neighbouring Darlinghurst and Paddington had finally taken over Surry Hills' twin focal points of **Crown Street**, filled with cafés, swanky restaurants, funky clothes shops and designer galleries, and parallel **Bourke Street**, where a couple of Sydney's best cafés lurk among the trees. As rents have gone up, only **Cleveland Street**, running west to Redfern and east towards Moore Park and the Sydney Cricket Ground (see p.91), traffic-snarled and lined with cheap Indian, Lebanese and Turkish restaurants, retains its ethnically varied population.

Surry Hills is always a good area for a coffee, a meal, a few drinks or just a general mooch around the shops, particularly along Crown Street.

Brett Whiteley Gallery

2 Raper St, off Davies St • Fri–Sun 10am–4pm • Free • ⓦ artgallery.nsw.gov.au/brett-whiteley-studio

If you have an interest in the city's art scene, don't miss the **Brett Whiteley Gallery**. Whiteley, who died of a heroin overdose in 1992 at the age of 53, was one of Australia's best-known contemporary painters. His work includes wild self-portraits and expressive female nudes, but it is his sensual paintings of Sydney Harbour for which he is best known. In 1986, Whiteley converted this former T-shirt factory into a studio and living space, and since his death it has become a museum and gallery showing his paintings and memorabilia, left chaotically scattered with works in progress.

Waterloo

As Surry Hills becomes ever more gentrified, galleries in search of cheaper rent and restaurants out to create a buzz have gone in search of a new playground. They've found it on **Danks Street**, around its junction with Young Street on the northern fringes of **Waterloo**, about half a kilometre south of Cleveland Street. Although surrounded by uninspiring residential housing, Danks Street is a world apart, and it's worth making the effort to visit **2 Danks Street Galleries** (ⓦ 2danksstreet.com.au), which contain eight contemporary art galleries, a jewellery studio and café, or to pop into one of the gourmet cafés or ethical food stores dotted along the street.

Redfern

Redfern train station

There's a resurgent feel to **Redfern**, northwest of Waterloo and less than 2km south of Central Station. The days as Sydney's underbelly are long gone, and you'll now find ever-new cafés and budget Asian restaurants opening amid the more mundane shops and what remains of the pubs. **Carriageworks**, at 245 Wilson St (ⓦ carriageworks.com.au), is a hub for contemporary artistic endeavour in Sydney, hosting both international and local artists, from dance and photographic exhibitions to music and avant-garde theatre. Redfern is perhaps best known, at least among Sydneysiders, for **Eveleigh Street**, where Australia's biggest urban **Aboriginal community** lives in "the Block", a squalid streetscape of derelict terraced houses and rubbish-strewn streets not far from Redfern train station;

this is the closest Sydney has to a no-go zone. The Aboriginal Housing Company, set up as a cooperative in 1973, has been unable to pay for repairs and renovation work, and Eveleigh Street appears in shocking contrast to Paddington's twee restored terraces. Derelict houses have been knocked down in recent years and residents relocated, upsetting many who want to keep the community together.

The inner west

West of the centre, immediately beyond Darling Harbour, the inner-city areas of **Glebe** and **Newtown** surround Sydney University, their vibrant artistic communities and cultural mix enlivened by large student populations. On a peninsula north of Glebe and west of The Rocks, **Balmain** is a gentrified former working-class dock area popular for its village atmosphere, while west of Glebe, **Leichhardt** is a focus for Sydney's Italian community.

Glebe

Buses #431, #433 and #434 run to Glebe from Millers Point, George St and Central Station, while #431 and #434 run right down the length of Glebe Point Rd to Jubilee Park, with the #434 continuing on to Balmain and the #433 running halfway, turning at Wigram Rd and heading on to Balmain; from Coogee beach, the #370 runs to Glebe via the University of New South Wales and Newtown, or it's a 15min walk from Central Station up Broadway to the beginning of Glebe Point Rd; Glebe light rail station is near the busy restaurant area at the Bridge Rd and Glebe Point Rd intersection; the quieter, northern end of Glebe Point Rd is served by Jubilee Park light rail, a 5min walk away

Right by Australia's oldest university, **Glebe** is very much the centre of established alternative culture in Sydney. Its main thoroughfare, Glebe Point Road, lined with a mix of cafés with leafy courtyards, restaurants, organic food stores, healing centres, yoga schools, bookshops and secondhand shops, runs uphill from **Broadway**, becoming quietly residential as it slopes down towards the water of Rozelle Bay. The side streets here are fringed with renovated two-storey terraced houses with white-iron lacework verandas; not surprisingly, Glebe is popular with backpackers and offers several hostels (see p.121). The large **Broadway Shopping Centre** on Broadway, linked to Glebe by an overhead walkway, is useful if you're staying in the area.

Glebe is at its best on Saturday, when **Glebe Market** (10am–4pm), which takes place on the shady primary-school playground on Glebe Point Road, is in full swing. On sale are mainly secondhand clothes and accessories, CDs, the inevitable crystals and a bit of bric-a-brac. Across the road at no. 49 is the brilliant **Gleebooks** (see p.141). Just before the beginning of Glebe Point Road, on Broadway, **Victoria Park** has a pleasant, heated outdoor swimming pool (Mon–Fri 6am–8pm, Sat & Sun 7am–8pm; $6.20; ⊚vppool .com.au) with attached gym and a sophisticated café.

Sydney University

Buses heading west from the city along Parramatta Rd or towards Newtown stop at the university; Redfern station is a 20min walk away

From Victoria Park, a path and steps lead up into **Sydney University**, inaugurated in 1850; your gaze is led from the walkway up to the Main Quadrangle and its very Oxford-reminiscent clock tower and Great Hall. You can wander freely around the university grounds, and there are several free museums and galleries to visit.

Jubilee Park

Jubilee Park light rail; buses #431, #433 and #434

Glebe Point Road trails off into a more residential area as it runs northwest of Victoria Park, petering out at **Jubilee Park**. The pleasantly landscaped waterfront park, complete with huge, shady Moreton Bay fig trees, children's playground and picturesque Harbour Foreshore Walk around Blackwattle Bay, offers an unusual view of far-off Sydney Harbour Bridge framed within the cabled Anzac Bridge.

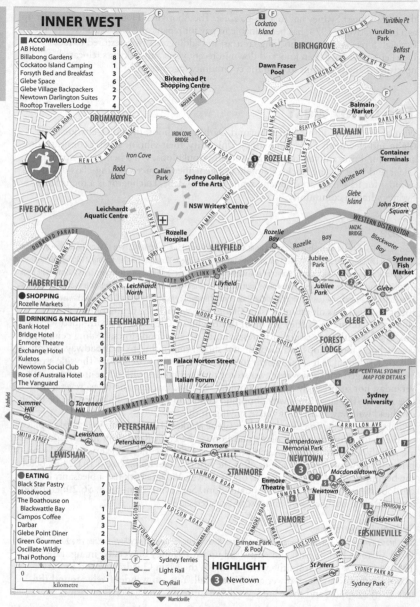

INNER WEST

ACCOMMODATION

AB Hotel	5
Billabong Gardens	8
Cockatoo Island Camping	1
Forsyth Bed and Breakfast	3
Glebe Space	6
Glebe Village Backpackers	2
Newtown Darlington Suites	7
Rooftop Travellers Lodge	4

SHOPPING

Rozelle Markets	1

DRINKING & NIGHTLIFE

Bank Hotel	5
Bridge Hotel	2
Enmore Theatre	6
Exchange Hotel	3
Kuletos	1
Newtown Social Club	9
Rose of Australia Hotel	8
The Vanguard	4

EATING

Black Star Pastry	7
Bloodwood	9
The Boathouse on Blackwattle Bay	1
Campos Coffee	5
Darbar	3
Glebe Point Diner	2
Green Gourmet	4
Oscillate Wildly	6
Thai Pothong	8

Sydney ferries
Light Rail
CityRail

HIGHLIGHT
3 Newtown

Newtown

Buses #M30, #422, #423, #426 and #428 run to Newtown from Circular Quay via Castlereagh St, Railway Square and City Rd, going down King St as far as Newtown station, where the #422 continues to St Peters while the others turn off to Enmore and Marrickville; from Bondi Junction take bus #352; from Coogee beach, take the #370 bus to Glebe, which goes via Newtown, or catch a train to Newtown, St Peters or Erskineville stations

Newtown, separated from Glebe by Sydney University and easily reached by train, is a hip inner-city neighbourhood. What was once a working-class district – a hotchpotch of derelict factories, junkyards and cheap accommodation – has transformed into a trendy, offbeat area where body piercing, shaved heads and quirky fashions can be seen among the gentrified residents. The area is characterized by a large population of artists, devotees of numerous alternative cultures, a strong gay and lesbian community, a rich ethnic mix, and a healthy dose of students and lecturers from the nearby university. It also has an enviable number of cafés and diverse restaurants, especially Thai, making it an agreeable location for an evening meal, late-night drink or fortifying brunch. The highlight of the year is the huge **Newtown Festival** on the second Sunday of November each year, which takes over nearby Camperdown Memorial Park with an eclectic mix of over two hundred stalls and live music on three stages.

King Street becomes less crowded south of Newtown station as it heads for 1km towards St Peters train station, but it's well worth strolling down to look at the more unusual speciality shops (such as those devoted to buttons or upcycled designer spectacles), as well as some small art galleries and yet more retro clothes shops.

Enmore Road
Newtown station; buses #423, #426 and #428

Enmore Road, stretching west from King Street, opposite Newtown station, offers a similar mix of shops and evidence of a migrant population – such as the African International Market at no. 2 and Amera's Palace Bellydancing Boutique at no. 83 (ⓦ ameraspalace.com.au). It's generally much quieter than King Street, except when a big-name band or comedian is playing at the Art Deco **Enmore Theatre** at no. 130. Beyond here, the multicultural, lively but down-at-heel **Marrickville** stretches south, and has dozens of Vietnamese and Greek restaurants as well as a growing reputation as a new hipster haven, bursting with gastro pubs and cafés to pose in.

Leichhardt
Bus #440 from The Rocks (30min); also buses #436, #437 and #438 from George St in the city centre

Leichhardt is Sydney's "Little Italy", where the famous **Norton Street** strip of cafés and restaurants runs off unattractive, traffic-jammed **Parramatta Road**. Close to Parramatta Road, at 23 Norton Street, is the **Italian Forum**, an upmarket shopping and dining centre and showcase for all things Italian, while a ten-minute walk further down at no. 171 is the lively, much-loved *Bar Italia* – a Leichhardt institution. In between, the upmarket cinema complex, the **Palace Norton Street**, hosts a two-week Italian film festival in late October.

Rozelle
The #445 bus from Leichhardt runs along Rozelle High St and down the hill to Balmain's waterfront; bus #440 runs all the way from Bondi Beach through the CBD to Leichhardt and then Rozelle High St

Rozelle, once very much the down-at-heel, poorer sister to Balmain, has emerged as a sophisticated and stylish area, with the **Sydney College of the Arts** and the **NSW Writers' Centre** now based here, in the grounds of the 150-acre waterfront **Callan Park** on Balmain Road. Darling Street has a string of cafés, bookshops, speciality shops, gourmet grocers, restaurants, refurbished pubs, and designer homeware stores. The street is at its liveliest at the weekend, when **Rozelle Markets**, a huge flea market, takes place (see p.141).

Balmain
Balmain, directly north of Glebe, is less than 2km from the Opera House, but stuck out on a spur in the harbour and kept apart from the city centre by Darling Harbour and Johnston's Bay, it has a degree of separation that has helped it retain its village-like atmosphere and made it the favoured abode of many writers and film-makers. Like

1

better-known Paddington, Balmain was once a working-class quarter of terraced houses that has gradually been gentrified. Although the docks at White Bay no longer operate, the pubs that used to fuel the dockworkers still abound, and **Darling Street** and the surrounding backstreets are blessed with enough watering holes to warrant a pub crawl – two classics are the *London Hotel* (see p.133) and the *Exchange Hotel* (see p.133). Darling Street, which stretches down through Rozelle, also rewards a leisurely stroll, with a bit of browsing in its quirky shops (focused on clothes and gifts), and grazing in its restaurants and cafés. The best time to come is on Saturday, when the lively **Balmain Market** (Sat 7.30am–4pm) occupies the grounds of St Andrews Church, on the corner opposite the *London Hotel*.

ARRIVAL AND INFORMATION
BALMAIN

By ferry The most appealing way to get to Balmain is to catch a ferry from Circular Quay to Darling St Wharf in Balmain East, where the #442 bus waits to take you up Darling St to Balmain proper (or it's about a 10min walk).
By bus Buses #432 and #433 run out to Balmain via George St, Railway Square and Glebe Point Rd and down Darling St. A quicker option is the #442 from the QVB, which crosses Anzac Bridge and heads to Balmain Wharf.

Tours For a self-guided tour of Balmain and Birchgrove, buy a *Balmain Walks* leaflet ($2.20) from Balmain Library, 370 Darling St (Mon–Fri 9.30am–8pm, Sat & Sun 10am–4pm; ☏02 9367 9211, ⓦleichhardt .nsw.gov.au/library), or from the well-stocked Bray's Books, at no. 268 (Mon & Sat 9am–6pm, Tues–Fri 9am–7pm, Sun 9.30am–6pm; ☏02 9810 5613, ⓦbraysbooks.com).

The Harbour

Loftily flanking the mouth of **Sydney Harbour** are the rugged sandstone cliffs of North Head and South Head, providing spectacular viewing points across the calm water to the city 11km away, where the Harbour Bridge spans the sunken valley at its deepest point. The many coves, bays, points and headlands of Sydney Harbour, and their parks, bushland and swimmable beaches are rewarding to explore. However, harbour beaches are not always as clean as ocean ones, and swimming is often banned during and after storms. Finding your way by ferry is the most pleasurable method: services run to much of the **North Shore** and to harbourfront areas of the **eastern suburbs**. The eastern shores are characterized by a certain glitziness and are, fundamentally, the haunt of the nouveaux riches, while the leafy North Shore is largely the domain of Sydney's old money. Both sides of the harbour have pockets of bushland that have been incorporated into **Sydney Harbour National Park**, along with several harbour islands: Cockatoo Island, the largest and easily reached via Sydney Ferries (see box, p.57); Shark Island, a popular picnic destination; former penal site Fort Denison; and Goat Island, site of a well-preserved gunpowder-magazine complex, all visitable with the Matilda or Captain Cook cruise companies (see box, p.67); and Clark Island and Rodd Island, reachable by private vessel only.

Rushcutters Bay Park is wonderfully set against a backdrop of the yacht- and cruiser-packed marina in the bay; the marina was revamped for the 2000 Olympics sailing competition. You can take it all in from the tables outside the very popular *Rushcutters Bay Kiosk*.

WALKING FROM ELIZABETH BAY TO SOUTH HEAD

Woollahra Council (ⓦwoollahra.nsw.gov.au) has brochures detailing three **waterside walks**: the 5.5km (3hr) **Rushcutters Bay to Rose Bay** harbour walk, which can then be continued with the 8km (4hr 30min) walk to **Watsons Bay**, and the fascinating 5km cliffside walk from Christison Park in **Vaucluse** (off Old South Head Rd) to Watsons Bay and **South Head**, with shipwreck sites, old lighthouses and military fortifications along the way.

1

Elizabeth Bay House

7 Onslow Ave • Fri–Sun 10am–4pm • $8 • ⓦ hht.net.au/museums/ebh • Bus #311 from either Railway Square or Circular Quay; 10min walk from Kings Cross station

Barely five minutes' walk northeast of Kings Cross, **Elizabeth Bay** is a well-heeled residential area, centred on **Elizabeth Bay House**, a grand Regency residence with harbour views, built in 1835 and once known as the "finest house in the colony". Constructing the gracious mansion nearly bankrupted colonial secretary Alexander Macleay, and it was never finished, though the wonderful domed saloon and Greek Revival detailing remain intact.

Darling Point, Double Bay and Rose Bay

Ferries from Circular Quay stop at Darling Point, Double Bay and Rose Bay; otherwise, catch bus #327 for Darling Point and Double Bay or #323, #324, or #325 for all three destinations

At **Darling Point**, McKell Park provides a magnificent view across to **Clarke Island** and **Bradleys Head**, both part of Sydney Harbour National Park; follow Darling Point Road.

Double Bay is dubbed "Double Pay" for obvious reasons. The noise and traffic of New South Head Road are redeemed by several excellent antiquarian and secondhand bookshops, while in the quieter "village", some of the most exclusive shops in Sydney are full of imported designer labels and expensive jewellery. Eastern-suburbs socialites meet on **Cross Street**, **Knox Street** and the small pedestrian lanes feeding them, where the swanky pavement cafés are filled with well-groomed women in Armani outfits.

Double Bay's hidden gem is **Redleaf Pool** (Sept–May daily dawn–dusk; free), a peaceful, shady harbour beach enclosed by a wooden pier you can dive off or just laze on; there's also an excellent café here.

A ferry to **Rose Bay** from Circular Quay gives you a chance to check out the waterfront mansions of **Point Piper** as you skim past. Rose Bay itself is a haven of exclusivity, with the verdant expanse of the members-only Royal Sydney Golf Course.

Nielson Park

Café Tues–Fri 8.30am–4pm Sat & Sun 8am–4pm • ⓦ nielsenpark.com.au • **Greycliffe House** Mon–Fri 10am–4pm • ⓦ npws.nsw .gov.au • Buses #324 and #325 from Circular Quay go to Nielson Park, a short walk from Greycliffe House

Sydney Harbour National Park emerges onto the waterfront at Bay View Hill, where the delightful 1.5km **Hermitage walking track** to Nielson Park begins; the starting point, Bay View Hill Road, is off South Head Road between the Kambala School and Rose Bay. The walk takes about an hour, with great views of the Opera House and Harbour Bridge, some lovely little coves to swim in, and a picnic ground and sandy beach at yacht-filled **Hermit Point**. Extensive, tree-filled **Nielson Park**, on Shark Bay, is one of Sydney's delights, a great place for a swim, a picnic, or refreshment at the popular café. The decorative Victorian-era mansion, **Greycliffe House**, built for William Wentworth's daughter in 1852, is now the headquarters of Sydney Harbour National Park and provides excellent information and maps on all waterfront walks. With views across the harbour to the city skyline, the park is a prime spot to watch both the New Year's Eve fireworks and the Sydney-to-Hobart yachts racing out through the heads on Boxing Day.

Vaucluse House

Wentworth Rd • **Gardens** 24hr • Free • **House** Wed–Sun 10am–4pm • $8 • ⓦ hht.net.au • Walk from Nielson Park along Coolong Rd or take bus #325

Beyond Shark Bay, Vaucluse Bay shelters the magnificent Gothic-style 1803 **Vaucluse House** and its large estate, which has tearooms in the grounds for refreshment. The house's original owner, explorer and reformer William Wentworth, was a member of the first party to cross the Blue Mountains. Beyond Vaucluse Bay, narrow **Parsley Bay**'s shady park is a popular picnic and swimming spot, and is crossed by a picturesque pedestrian suspension bridge.

Watsons Bay

Buses terminate just opposite The Gap – the #324, #325, and faster #L24 from Circular Quay, and the #380 from Circular Quay via Bondi Beach; ferries run regularly from Circular Quay (20min) and Manly (15–20min)

On the finger of land culminating in South Head, with an expansive sheltered harbour bay on its west side, and the treacherous cliffs of The Gap on its ocean side, **Watsons Bay** was one of the earliest settlements outside of Sydney Cove. In 1790, Robert Watson was one of the first signalmen to man the clifftop flagstaffs nearby, and by 1792 the bay was the focus of a successful fishing village; the quaint old wooden fishermen's cottages are still found on the narrow streets around Camp Cove. It's an appropriate location for one of Sydney's longest-running fish restaurants, *Doyles* (see p.128), by the old Fishermans Wharf, now the ferry terminal. In fact, *Doyles* has taken over the waterfront here, with two restaurants, a takeaway, and a seafood bistro in the bay-front beer-garden of *Doyles Palace Hotel*.

Spectacular ocean views are just a two-minute walk away through grassy Robertson Park, across Gap Road to **The Gap**, whose high cliffs are notorious as a place to commit suicide. You can follow a walking **track** north from here to South Head through another chunk of Sydney Harbour National Park, past the HMAS *Watson* Military Reserve. The track heads back to the bay side, and onto Cliff Street, which leads to pretty **Camp Cove**, a tiny, palm-fronted, unnetted harbour beach.

South Head

South Head sits at the lower jaw of the harbour mouth affording sweeping views of Port Jackson and the city, via Sydney's best-known **nudist beach**, "Lady Jane" (officially Lady Bay), a favourite gay haunt. It's not very private, however: a lookout point on the track provides full views, and ogling tour boats cruise past all weekend. From Lady Bay, it's a further fifteen minutes' walk along a boardwalked path to South Head itself, past nineteenth-century fortifications, lighthouse cottages, and the picturesquely red-and-white-striped Hornby Lighthouse.

Luna Park

Opening times vary • Access free, unlimited-ride day-pass $52 • ⓦ lunaparksydney.com • The ferry to Milsons Point Wharf from Circular Quay or Darling Harbour pulls up right outside, or take the train to Milsons Point station

Beside the Harbour Bridge, on Lavender Bay at **Milsons Point**, you can't miss the enormous and iconic laughing clown's face that belongs to **Luna Park**. Generations of Sydneysiders have walked through the grinning mouth, and the park's old rides and conserved 1930s fun hall, complete with period wall murals, slot machines, silly mirrors and giant slippery dips, have great nostalgia value for locals. Entry is free – it's worth a look, even if you don't want to ride.

North Sydney Olympic Pool

Alfred South St • Mon–Fri 5.30am–9pm, Sat & Sun 7am–7pm • $7.50 • Ferry to Milsons Point Wharf from Circular Quay or Darling Harbour, or train to Milsons Point station

Right next door to Luna Park is Sydney's most picturesquely sited public swimming pool, with terrific vistas of the Harbour Bridge – the heated **North Sydney Olympic Pool**. There's an indoor 25m pool as well as a 50m outdoor pool, a gym, sauna, spa, café, and an expensive restaurant, *Aqua*.

1

Kirribilli

Ferry from Circular Quay to Neutral Bay (15min); Milson's Point train station

Just east of the Harbour Bridge and immediately opposite the Opera House, **Kirribilli** and adjacent Neutral Bay are mainly residential areas, although Kirribilli hosts a great general **market** on the fourth Saturday of the month (7am–3pm) in Bradfield Park, the best and biggest of several rotating markets on the North Shore (see p.141). On Kirribilli Point, **Kirribilli House** is the Prime Minister's official Sydney residence, while next door, Admiralty House is the Sydney home of the Governor General, where the British royal family stay when they're in town.

Nutcote

5 Wallaringa Ave, Neutral Bay • Wed–Sun 11am–3pm • $10 • Ⓦ maygibbs.com.au • Ferry from Circular Quay to Neutral Bay (15min)

Upmarket **Neutral Bay** features spacious period homes dotted around a leafy hillscape. A five-minute walk from Neutral Bay ferry wharf via Hayes Street and Lower Wycombe Road is **Nutcote**, the former home for 45 years of May Gibbs, the author and illustrator of the famous Australian children's book, *Snugglepot and Cuddlepie*, about two little gumnuts who come to life; published in 1918, it's an enduring classic.

Cremorne Point

Mosman Bay ferry from Circular Quay to Cremorne Point Wharf (20min)

Bush-covered **Cremorne Point**, which juts out from Neutral Bay into the harbour, is worth a jaunt. The ferry from Circular Quay arrives a short stroll from a quaint open-access sea pool; from here, you can walk right around the point to **Mosman Bay** (just under 2km), and in the other direction, past the pool, there's a very pretty walk into **Shell Cove** (1km).

Taronga Zoo

Bradleys Head Rd, Mosman • **Zoo** Daily 9.30am–5pm • $46, 4–15 yrs $26, under-4s free • **Koala photos** Daily 11am–2.45pm • $25 for a group up to four; book at the zoo's Animal Encounters Shop • Ⓦ taronga.org.au • Ferries run from Circular Quay to Taronga Zoo Wharf every 30min; alternatively, take bus #247 from Wynyard or the QVB

Taronga Zoo has a superb hilltop position overlooking the city. The wonderful views and the natural bush surrounds are as much an attraction as the chance to get up close to the animals. The zoo houses bounding Australian marsupials, native birds, reptiles, and sea lions and seals from the sub-Antarctic region. You'll also find exotic beasts from around the world, including giraffes, gorillas and chimpanzees. The **Wild Asia** exhibit includes five Asian elephants.

You can get close to kangaroos and wallabies in the **Australian Walkabout** area, and the **koala house** gives you eye-level views; to get closer, arrange to have your photo taken next to a koala. Keeper talks and feeding sessions – including a free-flight bird show and a seal show – run through the day; details are on the map handed out on arrival.

Although there's a lower entrance near the wharf on Athol Road, it's best to start your visit from the upper entrance and spend several leisurely hours winding downhill to exit for the ferry. State Transit buses meet the ferries for the trip uphill, but a better option is to take the **Sky Safari** cable car included in the entry price.

Bradleys Head

About a 15min walk from Taronga Zoo Wharf (ferries from Circular Quay every 30min); bus #247 from Wynyard or the QVB

At the termination of Bradleys Head Road, beyond the zoo, **Bradleys Head** is marked by an enormous mast that once belonged to HMAS *Sydney* (1912), a victorious World War I Royal Australian Navy battleship (not to be confused with the recently recovered ship of the same name, built in 1934). The rocky point is a peaceful spot with a dinky lighthouse and, of course, a fabulous view back over the south shore. A colony of ringtail possums nests here, and boisterous flocks of rainbow lorikeets visit. The headland comprises another large chunk of Sydney Harbour National Park: you can walk to Bradleys Head via the 6km **Ashton Park walking track**, which starts near Taronga Zoo Wharf, and continues beyond the headland to picturesque Taylors Bay and Chowder Head, finishing at **Clifton Gardens**, where there's a jetty and sea baths on **Chowder Bay**. It is worth wandering the streets of Clifton Gardens: the lofty hillside mansions here are arguably the most beautiful and superbly sited on the harbour. The now defunct **military reserve** that separates Chowder Bay from another chunk of Sydney Harbour National Park on Middle Head is open to the public, reached by a boardwalk from the northern end of Clifton Gardens.

Middle Harbour

Bus #144 runs to Spit Rd from Manly Wharf, taking a scenic route uphill overlooking the Spit marina; to get to Castlecrag, take bus #203 from Wynyard

Middle Harbour is the largest inlet of Port Jackson, its two sides joined across the narrowest point at **The Spit**. The Spit Bridge opens regularly to let tall-masted yachts through – much the best way to explore its pretty, quiet coves and bays. Crossing the Spit Bridge, you can walk all the way to Manly Beach along the 10km Manly Scenic Walkway (see box, p.106). The area also hides some architectural gems: the mock-Gothic 1889 bridge leading to **Northbridge**, and the idyllic enclave of **Castlecrag**, which was designed in 1924 by **Walter Burley Griffin**, fresh from planning Canberra and intent on building an environmentally friendly suburb that would be "for ever part of the bush".

Middle Head

Military reserve Free • Daily sunrise–sunset **Tours** Oct–May on the fourth Sun of the month, 10.15am at car entrance; 2hr • $20 • ☎ 1300 072 757, ⊛ nationalparks.nsw.gov.au • Entrance accessible from the northern end of Clifton Gardens, or walkable from Balmoral Beach

Between Clifton Gardens and Balmoral Beach, for over a century a military reserve and naval depot at **Chowder Bay** blocked coastal access by foot to both **Georges Head** and the more spectacular **Middle Head**. Since the military's 1997 withdrawal from the site, walkers can trek all the way between Bradleys Head and Middle Head. Used in the 1890s as a military settlement, Middle Head is now open to visitors as a reserve, and the NPWS offers monthly **tours** exploring the underground fortifications. On the Hunters Bay (Balmoral) side of Middle Head, tiny **Cobblers Beach** is officially **nudist**, and is a much more peaceful, secluded option than the more famous Lady Bay at South Head.

Balmoral Beach

Catch a ferry from Circular Quay to Taronga Zoo Wharf and then bus #238 via Bradleys Head Rd, or, after 7pm Mon–Sat, the ferry to South Mosman (Musgrave St) Wharf, at nearby Mosman, then bus #233

The bush of Middle Head provides a gorgeous backdrop to the shady, tree-lined **Balmoral Beach** on Hunters Bay, which is very popular with families. Fronting the beach, there's something very Edwardian and genteel about palm-filled, grassy Hunters Park and its bandstand, which is still used for Sunday jazz concerts and Shakespeare performances in summer. The antiquated air is enhanced by the pretty, white-painted **Bathers Pavilion** at the northern end, now converted into a restaurant and café (see p.128). There are two sections of beach at Balmoral, separated by **Rocky Point**, a picturesque promontory and noted picnicking spot. South of Rocky Point, the "**baths**" – actually a netted bit of beach with a boardwalk and lanes for swimming laps – have been here in one form or another since 1899; you can rent sailboards, catamarans, kayaks and canoes, while lessons are available from Balmoral Sailing Club (see p.140).

1

Ocean beaches

Sydney's **beaches** are among its great natural joys. The water and sand seem remarkably clean – people actually eat fish caught in the harbour – and at Long Reef, just north of Manly, you can find rock pools teeming with starfish, anemones, sea snails and crabs, and even a few shy moray eels. In recent years, whale populations have recovered to such an extent that humpback and southern right **whales** have been regularly sighted from the Sydney headlands in June and July on their migratory path from the Antarctic to the tropical waters of Queensland, and southern right whales even occasionally make an appearance in Sydney Harbour itself.

Topless bathing for women, while legal, is accepted on many beaches but frowned on at others, so if in doubt, do as the locals do. There are two official **nudist** beaches around the harbour (see p.99 & p.101).

Bondi Beach

Bondi Beach is synonymous with Australian beach culture, and indeed the 1.5km-long curve of golden sand must be one of the best-known beaches in the world. It's also the closest ocean beach to the city centre, 7km from town. Big, brash and action-packed, it's probably not the best place for a quiet sunbathe and swim, but the sprawling sandy crescent really is spectacular. Red-tiled houses and apartment buildings crowd in to catch the view, many of them erected in the 1920s when Bondi was a working-class suburb. Although still residential, it's long since become a popular gathering place for backpackers from around the world.

The beachfront **Campbell Parade** is both cosmopolitan and highly commercialized, lined with cafés and shops. For a gentler experience, explore some of the side streets, such as **Hall Street**, where an assortment of kosher bakeries and delis serve the area's Jewish community, and some of Bondi's best cafés are hidden. On Sunday, the **Bondi Beach Markets**, in the grounds of the primary school at Campbell Parade and Warners Avenue facing the northern end of the beach (10am–4pm), are good for fashion and jewellery, and there are also the **Bondi Beach Farmers' Markets** (9am–1pm). Between Campbell Parade and the beach, **Bondi Park** slopes down to the promenade, and is always full of sprawling bodies.

BEACH SAFETY

Don't be lulled into a false sense of security: the beaches do have **perils** as well as pleasures. Some are protected by special shark nets, but they don't keep out stingers such as bluebottles, which can suddenly swamp an entire beach; listen for loudspeaker announcements that will summon you from the water in the event of shark sightings or other dangers. Pacific **currents** can be very strong indeed – inexperienced swimmers and those with small children would do better sticking to the sheltered **harbour beaches** or **sea pools** at the ocean beaches. Ocean beaches are generally patrolled by **surf lifesavers** during the day between October and April (all year at Bondi): red and yellow flags (generally up from 6am till 6 or 7pm) indicate the safe areas to swim, avoiding dangerous rips and undertows. It's hard not to be impressed as **surfers** paddle out on a seething ocean, but don't follow them unless you're confident you know what you're doing. If you're a beginner surfer, get some lessons with one of Sydney's many surf schools (see p.139) in order to build your confidence. You can check daily surf reports on ⓦrealsurf.com.

The final hazard, despite the apparent cleanliness, is **pollution**. Monitoring shows that it is nearly always safe to swim at all of Sydney's beaches – except after storms, when storm water, currents and onshore breezes wash up sewage and other rubbish onto harbour beaches, making them (as signs will indicate) unsuitable for swimming and surfing. To check pollution levels, consult the Beachwatch Bulletin (ⓣ1800 036 677, ⓦenvironment.nsw.gov.au).

CHRISTMAS DAY ON BONDI

For years, backpackers and Bondi Beach on **Christmas Day** were synonymous. The beach was transformed into a drunken party scene, as those from colder climes lived out their fantasy of spending Christmas on the beach under a scorching sun. The behaviour and litter began getting out of control, and after riots in 1995, and a rubbish-strewn beach, the local council began strictly controlling the whole performance, with the idea of trying to keep a spirit of goodwill towards the travellers while also tempting local families back to the beach. Nowadays, alcohol is banned from the beach and surrounding area on Christmas Day, and police enforce the rule with on-the-spot confiscations. However, the **Sunburnt Christmas party** is organized in the Pavilion, with a bar, DJs, food and entertainment running from noon to 10pm. Up to three thousand revellers cram into the Pavilion, while thousands of others – including a greater proportion of the desired family groups – enjoy the alcohol-free beach outside. Buy **tickets** for the Pavilion bash at Moshtix (☎1300 438 849, ⓦmoshtix.com.au) or Ticketek (☎13 28 49, ⓦticketek.com.au).

Bondi Pavilion
Art Gallery: Mon–Fri 9am–5pm, Sat & Sun 10am–5pm • Free

The focus of Campbell Promenade is the arcaded, Spanish-style **Bondi Pavilion**, built in 1928 as a deluxe changing-room complex and converted into a **community centre** hosting an array of workshops, classes and events, from drama and comedy in the theatre and the Seagull Room (the former ballroom) to the outdoor Bondi Short Film Festival (ⓦbondishortfilmfestival.com) in the courtyard, held in late November. A community-access **art gallery** on the ground floor features changing exhibitions by local artists. In September, the day-long Festival of the Winds, Australia's largest **kite festival**, takes over the beach.

The beach
Surfing is part of the Bondi legend, the big waves ensuring that there are always groups of young people hanging around, bristling with surfboards. However, the beach is carefully delineated, with surfers using the southern end. There are two sets of flags for swimmers and boogie-boarders, with families congregating at the northern end near the sheltered saltwater pool (free), and everybody else using the middle flags. The beach is netted and there hasn't been a shark attack since 1929.

Topless bathing is condoned at Bondi – a far cry from conditions up to the late 1960s when stern beach inspectors were constantly on the lookout for indecent exposure.

Bondi Icebergs Club
Notts Ave • Pool Mon–Wed & Fri 6am–6.30pm, Sat & Sun 6.30am–6.30pm • $6.50 • ⓦicebergs.com.au

If the sea is too rough, or if you want to swim laps, head for the seawater swimming pool at the southern end of the beach under the **Bondi Icebergs Club**, where there's a 50m lap pool, kids' pool, gym, sauna, massage service and poolside café. The Icebergs Club has been part of the Bondi legend since 1929 – members must swim throughout the winter, and media coverage of their plunge, made truly wintry with the addition of huge chunks of ice, heralds the first day of winter. The very dilapidated club building was knocked down and rebuilt in 2002; the top floor houses the posh *Icebergs Dining Room and Bar*, while the floor below has the club's less salubrious *Icebergs Bistro* (see p.130), which shares the fabulous view over pool and beach.

ARRIVAL AND INFORMATION   BONDI BEACH

By bus Bus #333, #380 or #389 from Circular Quay, or #440 from Central Station, via Oxford St and Bondi Junction.
By train Take any Eastern Suburbs line to Bondi Junction station (under 15min from Central or Town Hall station),

then transfer to the buses listed above, or to the #361, #381 and #382 (10min).
By car From the city centre (20min), travel via the Cross City Tunnel, up Ocean St, then left into Syd Einfeld Drive and

1

BONDI'S SURF LIFESAVERS

Surf lifesavers are what made Bondi famous, so naturally a bronze sculpture of one is given pride of place outside the Bondi Pavilion. The surf lifesaving movement began in 1906 with the founding of the Bondi Surf Life Bathers' Lifesaving Club in response to the **drownings** that accompanied the increasing popularity of **swimming**. From the beginning of the colony, swimming was harshly discouraged as an unsuitable bare-fleshed activity. However, by the 1890s, swimming in the ocean had become the latest fad, and a Pacific Islander introduced the concept of catching waves – or bodysurfing – that was to become an enduring national craze. Although "wowsers" (teetotal puritanical types) attempted to put a stop to it, by 1903 all-day swimming was every Sydneysider's right.

The bronzed and muscled surf lifesavers in their distinctive red-and-yellow caps are a highly photographed, world-famous Australian image. Surf lifesavers (members of what are now called Surf Life Saving Clubs, abbreviated to SLSC) are volunteers who work the beach at weekends, so come then to watch their exploits – or look out for a **surf carnival**. Lifeguards, on the other hand, are employed by the council and work all week during swimming season (year-round at Bondi).

left again into Bondi Rd. Car parking is limited, so public transport is an easier option.
Beach hire Located below the lifeguard lookout tower, Beached at Bondi (☎ 02 9389 5836) rents out everything from surf gear to swimsuits and beach umbrellas, plus has lockers for valuables.

Tamarama Bay

Bus #360 or #361 from Bondi Junction, or a 30min walk from the station

Tamarama Bay ("Glamarama" to the locals) is a deep, narrow beach favoured by the smart set and a gay crowd, as well as surfers. Tamarama is generally thought to be the most dangerous of the patrolled beaches, due to its ocean swell. Take special heed of the designated swimming areas.

Bronte Beach

Mini-train ride Sat & Sun 11am–4pm • Bus #378 or #440 from Central Station via Oxford St and Bondi Junction; 5min walk from Tamarama Bay

The next beach along from Tamarama Bay is **Bronte Beach**, on Nelson Bay. Something of a family affair, with a large green park, a popular café strip and sea baths, the **northern end** as you arrive from Tamarama has inviting flat-rock platforms, popular as fishing and relaxation spots, and the beach here is cliff-backed, providing some shade. The **park** beyond is extensive, with Norfolk Island pines for shade; a **mini-train ride** for small children has been operating here since 1947, while further back there's a children's playground. At the **southern end** of the beach, palm trees lend a holiday feel as you relax at one of the outside tables of Bronte Road's cafés – there are several to choose from, plus a fish-and-chip shop. Back on the water at this end, a natural rock enclosure, the "Bogey Hole", makes a calm area for snorkelling and kids' swimming, and there are rock ledges to lie on around the enclosed sea swimming pool known as **Bronte Baths**, often a better option than the surf here, which can be very rough.

Waverley Cemetery

Waverley Cemetery, just south of Bronte Beach, is a fantastic spot to spend eternity. Established in 1877, it contains the graves of many famous Australians, with the bush poet contingent well represented. **Henry Lawson**, described on his headstone as poet, journalist and patriot, languishes in section 3G 516, while **Dorothea Mackellar**, who penned the famous poem *I love a sunburnt country*, is in section 6 832–833.

Clovelly Bay

Bus #339 from Millers Point via Central Station and Albion St in Surry Hills, the #360 from Bondi Junction or the weekday peak-hour #X39 from Wynyard

A ten-minute walk from Bronte Beach is the channel-like **Clovelly Bay**, with concrete platforms on either side and several sets of steps leading into the very deep water. Rocks at the far end keep out the waves, and the sheltered bay is popular with lap-swimmers and snorkellers; you're almost certain to see one of the bay's famous blue groupers. There's also a free swimming pool. A grassy park with several terraces extends back from the beach and is a great place for a picnic. The divinely sited café is packed at weekends, and the beachside *Clovelly Bowling Club* is popular for its cheap drinks and fantastic views (see p.128).

Coogee

Bus #373 or #374 from Circular Quay via Randwick, or #372 from Eddy Ave, outside Central Station (about 25min), or bus #313 or #314 from Bondi Junction via Randwick, or bus #376 from Newtown; from Gordon Bay, a walkway leads around the waterfront to Major St and then onto Dunningham Reserve overlooking the northern end of Coogee Beach – the walk to Coogee proper takes about 15min in all

Laidback **Coogee** is a long-popular seaside resort, almost on a par with Manly and Bondi, and teeming with young travellers who flock to the backpackers' hostels here. With its hilly streets of Californian-style apartment blocks looking onto a compact, pretty beach enclosed by two craggy, green-covered headlands, Coogee has a snugness that Bondi just can't match. Everything is close to hand: beachside **Arden Street** is dominated by the extensive *Coogee Bay Hotel* (see box, p.130), one of Sydney's best-known music venues; while the main shopping street, **Coogee Bay Road**, runs uphill from the beach and has a choice selection of coffee spots and restaurants, plus a big supermarket.

The imaginatively modernized promenade is a great place to stroll and hang out; between it and the **beach**, a grassy park has free electric BBQs, picnic tables and shelters. The beach is popular with families (there's an excellent children's playground above the southern end), while at the northern end you'll find the popular backpacker drinking spot *Coogee Pavillion* (see p.134), a 1980s restoration of the 1887 Coogee Palace Aquarium.

Coogee Baths

Coogee Women's Pool Daily noon–5pm • 20¢ **Wylies Baths** Daily 7am–7pm, April–Oct till 5pm • $5 • ⓦ wylies.com.au

The **Coogee baths**, beyond the southern end of the beach, are one of the resort's chief pleasures. The first, the secluded, volunteer-run McIvers Baths, traditionally for women only (and boys up to age 3), is known by locals as **Coogee Women's Pool**. Just south of the women's pool is the 1917 **Wylies Baths**, a unisex saltwater pool on the edge of the sea, with big decks to lie on and solar-heated showers; its kiosk serves excellent coffee.

Manly

Manly, just above the North Head of Sydney Harbour, is doubly blessed, with both ocean and harbour **beaches**. It is this combination, and its easy accessibility from

---

WALKING THE EASTERN BEACHES COASTAL WALKWAY

Sydney's eastern beaches stretch from Bondi down to Maroubra. Heading south from Bondi, you can walk right along the coast to its smaller, less brazen but very lively cousin **Coogee** in a leisurely three hours, passing through gay-favourite **Tamarama**, family-focused, café-cultured **Bronte**, narrow **Clovelly** and **Gordons Bay**, the last of these with an underwater nature trail. Randwick Council has designed the "**Coastal Walkway**" from Clovelly to Coogee and beyond to more downmarket **Maroubra**, with stretches of boardwalk and interpretive boards detailing environmental features. A free guide can be picked up at visitor centres, or for a preview and online guide of each step, visit ⓦ bonditocoogeewalk.com.au. It's also possible to walk north all the way from Bondi to South Head along the cliffs.

1

MANLY ADVENTURE SPORTS

Manly wharf is now a hub for **adventure activities**: three watersports companies based here offer parasailing (from $99/hr), kayaking (double kayak from $75/2hr) or rigid-inflatable-boat tours through crashing surf to North Head; ask at the visitor centre (see opposite) for details. Manly Kayak Centre (daily 9.30am–4pm; Ⓦ manlykayakcentre.com.au) also offers stand-up paddleboarding lessons for $70 for a private lesson.

central Sydney, that gives it the feeling of a holiday village still within the city limits. When Captain Arthur Phillip, the commander of the First Fleet, was exploring Sydney Harbour in 1788, he saw a group of well-built Aboriginal men onshore, proclaimed them to be "manly" and named the cove in the process. During the Edwardian era it became fashionable as a recreational retreat from the city, with the promotional slogan "Manly – seven miles from Sydney, but a thousand miles from care". An excellent time to visit is over the Labour Day long weekend in early October, for the **Jazz Festival** (see box, p.142).

The ferry trip out to Manly has always been half the fun: the legendary **Manly Ferry** (see p.113) has run from Circular Quay since 1854. Ferries terminate at **Manly Wharf** (Ⓦ manlywharf.com.au) where there are cafés, shops and a **visitor centre** (see opposite).

What's known as **Manly Beach** is actually made up of Queenscliff, North Steyne, and South Steyne. Northeast of Manly Wharf, **The Corso** cuts directly across the isthmus, 500m to South Steyne beach. The Corso is lined with surf shops, cafés, bakeries, restaurants and pubs, while **South Steyne** beach is characterized by the stands of Norfolk pine that line the shore. A 6km-long shared pedestrian and **cycle path** begins at South Steyne and runs north to Seaforth, past North Steyne Beach and Queenscliff.

Around **Cabbage Tree Bay**, on Manly's eastern shore, there are two very pretty – and protected – green-backed beaches at either end: **Fairy Bower** to the west and **Shelley Beach** to the east.

Belgrave Street, running north from Manly Wharf, is Manly's alternative strip, with good cafés, interesting shops, yoga schools and the Manly Environment Centre at no. 41, whose aim is to educate the community about the local biodiversity and the issues affecting it.

Manly Sea Life Sanctuary

West Esplanade • Daily 9.30am–5pm; shark feeding Mon, Wed & Fri 9.30am • $25, under-16s $15, under-4s free; Shark Dive Extreme: qualified diver $299 • ☎ 1800 078 446, Ⓦ manlysealifesanctuary.com.au

From Manly Wharf, you can walk north along West Esplanade to **Manly Sea Life Sanctuary**, where clear acrylic walls hold back the water so you can saunter along the harbour floor, gazing at sharks and stingrays. It's not a patch on the Sydney Aquarium at Darling Harbour, but is considerably cheaper, and kids love it. Divers hand-feed sharks three times a week, and you can also organize dives among the big grey nurse sharks with **Shark Dive Extreme**.

THE MANLY SCENIC WALKWAY

One of the finest harbourside walks anywhere in Sydney is the **Manly Scenic Walkway** (10km one-way; 3–4hr; mostly flat), which follows the harbour shore inland from Manly Cove all the way west to Spit Bridge on Middle Harbour, where you can catch a bus (#180 and many others) back to Wynyard station in the city centre (20min). This wonderful walk takes you through some of the area's more expensive neighbourhoods before heading into a section of Sydney Harbour National Park (free entry), past a number of small beaches and coves (perfect for stopping off for a dip), Aboriginal middens and some subtropical rainforest. The walk can be easily broken up into six sections with obvious exit/entry points; pick up a map from the Manly visitor centre (see opposite) or NPWS offices.

Manly Art Gallery and Museum

Cnr West Esplanade & Commonwealth Parade • Tues–Sun 10am–5pm, closed public hols • Free • ☎ 02 9976 1420, ⓦ www.manly.nsw.gov.au

The **Manly Art Gallery and Museum** has a collection, started in the 1920s, of Australian paintings, drawings, prints and etchings, and a stash of fun retro beach memorabilia including huge old wooden surfboards and old-fashioned swimming costumes. A smaller gallery features work by artists from the Northern Beaches region, and holds solo shows, retrospectives and group exhibitions.

ARRIVAL AND DEPARTURE   MANLY

By ferry From Circular Quay (Mon–Fri 6am–11.45pm, Sat 8am–11.45pm, Sun 8am–11pm; every 30–40min; $7 one-way).

By bus Bus #152 from the centre to Belgrave St (every 30min; 40min); night bus #151 from Wynyard station (hourly; 40min).

INFORMATION, TOURS AND ACTIVITIES

Tourist information The visitor centre (Mon–Fri 9am–4pm, Sat & Sun 10am–4pm; ☎ 02 9976 1430, ⓦ hellomanly.com.au) is at Manly Wharf.

Manly Beach Hire Manly Beach Hire (winter daily 9am–5pm, summer varying extended hours; ⓦ manlybeachhire.com.au) rents out just about anything

to make the beach more fun, from surfboards to snorkel sets, and also has lockers for your valuables.

Manly Bike Tours Join a 2hr guided bike tour around interesting corners of Manly (54 West Esplanade; daily 10.30am; $99; ☎ 02 8005 7368, ⓦ manlybiketours.com. au), or rent a bike for $31/day.

North Head

Bus #135 from Manly Wharf

The Sydney Harbour National Park can be explored at **North Head**, the harbour mouth's upper jaw, where you can follow the short, circuitous Fairfax Walking Track to three lookout points, including the **Fairfax Lookout**, for splendid views. Keep an eye out for whales during the June–July and August–October migration periods.

Q Station

North Head Scenic Drive • Tours (2hr) $35–44, 5–16 yrs $22 • ☎ 02 9977 5145, ⓦ quarantinestation.com.au • Fast ferry from Circular Quay via Manly $8.60 one-way; bus #135 from Manly

There's a modern twist to historic Sydney at **Q Station**, a reworking of the old Quarantine Station, on the harbour side of North Head. From 1832 until 1984, arriving passengers and crew who had a contagious disease were set down here to serve forty days of isolation. Sydney residents, too, were forced here, most memorably during the plague that broke out in The Rocks in 1900, when 1828 people were quarantined (104 plague victims are buried in the grounds). The old quarantine accommodation has now been given an interesting conversion into a historic luxury resort.

Although you can't just wander around the site, you can join a tour, attend a performance or dine at the *Boilerhouse Restaurant* – no bad thing in itself. To get a general feel for the old Quarantine Station, join one of the **tours**, which mostly take place at weekends: the "**Quaratine Wander**" is a fairly straightforward 45min walking visit, while "**Quarantine Station Story**" takes a more interactive approach, with clues guiding you around the quarantine station as you get a sense of what it was like here during the 1918 flu epidemic. **Ghost tours** come in various guises: the child-friendly "Ghost Trackers"; the more nerve-wracking "Ghostly Encounters" and "Extreme Ghost Tour"; the "Paranormal Investigation Nights", during which a medium takes you ghost-hunting; and the nerves-of-steel "Ghostly Sleepover".

Freshwater to Palm Beach

Freshwater, just beyond Manly, sits snugly between two rocky headlands on Queenscliff Bay, and is one of the most picturesque of the northern beaches. There's

1

plenty of surf culture around the headland at Curl Curl, and a walking track at its northern end, commencing from Huston Parade, will take you above the rocky coastline to the curve of **Dee Why Beach**.

Collaroy to Bangin Bay

The long, beautiful sweep of **Collaroy Beach** with its YHA (see p.122) shades into **Narrabeen Beach**, an idyllic spot backed by the extensive, swimmable and fishable **Narrabeen Lakes**, popular with anglers, kayakers and families. Beyond Narrabeen, **Mona Vale** is a long, straight stretch of beach with a large park behind and a sea pool dividing it from sheltered **Bongin Bay**.

Pittwater to Avalon

After Bongin Bay, the Barrenjoey Peninsula begins, with calm **Pittwater** on its western side and ocean beaches running up its eastern side. **Newport** is best known for the gargantuan beer-garden deck of *The Newport*, overlooking Heron Cove at Pittwater (see box, p.130). Unassuming **Bilgola Beach**, next door to Newport and nestled at the base of a steep cliff, is one of the prettiest of the northern beaches, with its distinctive orange sand. From Bilgola Beach, a trio of Sydney's best beaches, for both surf and scenery, runs up the eastern fringe of the hammerhead peninsula. One of the most convenient is **Avalon Beach**, popular surfer territory backed by a set of shops.

Palm Beach

At the northern point of the Barrenjoey Peninsula is **Palm Beach**, a hangout for the rich and famous, and a popular city escape. It's also the location of "Summer Bay" in the long-running Aussie soap *Home and Away*, with the picturesque bush-covered Barrenjoey Head – part of **Ku-ring-gai Chase National Park** – regularly in shot.

Barrenjoey Lighthouse

Entry by tour only: Sun 11am–3pm; 30min tours every 30min • $5 • ☏ 02 9472 9300 • The lighthouse is 1km from the car park, up a 110m ascent; it's about a 40min–1hr round-trip walk

Barrenjoey Peninsula is topped by the 1881 **Barrenjoey Lighthouse**, which can be reached by a steep walking path from the car park at the base; your reward is a stunning panorama of Palm Beach, Pittwater and the Hawkesbury River. You might recognize the lighthouse from the Aussie TV soap opera *Home and Away*.

ARRIVAL AND INFORMATION   **FRESHWATER TO PALM BEACH**

By bus The northern beaches can be reached by regular bus from various city bus terminals, or from Manly Wharf. Take bus #136 or #156 from Manly Wharf, or bus #151, #169 or #178 from outside the QVB. Buses #190 and #L90 run up the peninsula from Railway Square at Central via Wynyard to Avalon, continuing to Palm Beach via the Pittwater side; change at Avalon for bus #193 to Whale Beach. Bus #L88 goes from Central and Wynyard to Avalon, and the #187 from Milsons Point in The Rocks to Newport.

Information Pick up the excellent, free *Sydney's Northern Beaches Map* from the Manly visitor centre (see p.107).

Botany Bay

The southern suburbs of Sydney, arranged around huge **Botany Bay**, are seen as the heartland of red-tiled-roof suburbia, a terracotta sea spied from above as the planes land at **Mascot**. Clive James, the area's most famous son, hails from Kogarah – described as a 1950s suburban wasteland in his tongue-in-cheek *Unreliable Memoirs*. The popular perception of Botany Bay is coloured by its proximity to an airport, a high-security prison (Long Bay), an oil refinery, a container terminal and a sewerage outlet. Yet the surprisingly clean-looking water is fringed by quiet, sandy beaches and the marshlands shelter a profusion of birdlife. Whole areas of the waterfront, at

La Perouse, with its associations with eighteenth-century French exploration, and on the **Kurnell Peninsula** where Captain Cook first set anchor, are designated as part of **Botany Bay National Park**, and large stretches on either side of the Georges River form a State Recreation Area. **Brighton-Le-Sands**, the busy suburban strip on the west of the bay, is a hive of bars and restaurants and is something of a focus for Sydney's Greek community. Its long beach is also a popular spot for windsurfers and kitesurfers.

La Perouse

NPWS visitor centre ☎ 02 9311 3379, Sun 10am–4pm • **Boatshed Cafe** Daily 11.30am–4pm, Sat also 5.30pm–late, Sun also 8.30–10.30am • Bus #394 or #399 from Circular Quay via Darlinghurst and Moore Park, #393 from Railway Square via Surry Hills and Moore Park, or the #L94 express from Circular Quay

La Perouse, tucked into the northern shore of Botany Bay where it meets the Pacific Ocean, contains Sydney's oldest Aboriginal settlement, the legacy of a mission. The suburb took its name from the eighteenth-century French explorer, **Laperouse**, who set up camp here for six weeks, briefly and cordially meeting Captain Arthur Phillip, who was making his historic decision to forgo swampy Botany Bay and move on to Port Jackson. After leaving Botany Bay, the La Perouse expedition was never seen again.

The headlands and foreshore surrounding La Perouse have been incorporated into the northern half of **Botany Bay National Park** (the other half is across Botany Bay on the Kurnell Peninsula). An **NPWS visitor centre** in the La Perouse Museum building provides details of walks, including a fine one past Congwong Bay Beach to Henry Head and its lighthouse (5km round trip), though it's only open on Sundays. The idyllic veranda of **The Boatshed café**, on the small headland between Congwong and Frenchmans bays, sits right over the water, with a white-sand beach arcing from below and cranes puncturing the distant shoreline. La Perouse is at its most lively on Sunday afternoons (and on public holidays) when, following a tradition established at the start of the twentieth century, **Aboriginal people** come down to sell boomerangs and other crafts, and demonstrate snake-handling skills and boomerang throwing.

La Perouse Museum

Anzac Parade • Sun 10am–4pm • $5.50 • ⓦ laperousemuseum.org

A monument erected in 1825 and the excellent NPWS-run **La Perouse Museum**, which sits on a grassy headland between the pretty beaches of Congwong Bay and Frenchmans Bay, tell the whole fascinating story of the mysterious disappearance of the eighteenth-century La Perouse expedition. There is also an exhibition that looks at the Aboriginal history and culture of the area.

Bare Island

Tours Sun 1.30pm, 2.30pm & 3.30pm; 45min • $10 • No booking required; wait at the gate to the island 15min prior to tour time

There are tours of the nineteenth-century fortifications on **Bare Island**, which is joined to La Perouse by a thin walkway; the island was originally built amid fears of a Russian invasion, and featured in *Mission Impossible II*. The island can only be visited one day a week on a guided tour.

Captain Cook's Landing Place

NPWS Discovery Centre Mon–Fri 11am–3pm, Sat & Sun 10am–4.30pm • Car $8 • ☎ 02 9668 2000 • Train to Cronulla and then Kurnell Bus Services route #987

From La Perouse, you can see across Botany Bay to Kurnell and the red buoy marking the spot where Captain James Cook and the crew of the *Endeavour* anchored on April 29, 1770, for an eight-day exploration. Back in England, many refused to believe that the uniquely Australian plants and animals they had recorded actually existed – the kangaroo and platypus in particular were thought to be a hoax. **Captain Cook's Landing Place** is now the south head of **Kamay Botany Bay National Park**, where the informative

1

NPWS Discovery Centre looks at the wetlands ecology of the park and tells the story of Cook's visit and its implications for Aboriginal people. Set aside as a public recreation area in 1899, the heath and woodland of the park is unspoilt and there are some secluded beaches for swimming; you may even spot parrots and honeyeaters.

Cronulla

Train from Central Station on the Sutherland line (40 min); surfboards carried free

On the ocean side of the **Kurnell Peninsula** sits Sydney's southernmost beach suburb and its longest stretch of beach – just under 5km; the sandy stretch of Bate Bay begins at **Cronulla** and continues as deserted, dune-backed **Wanda Beach**. This is prime **surfing** territory – and the only Sydney beach accessible by train. Steeped in surf culture, everything about Cronulla centres on watersports and a laidback beach lifestyle, from the multitude of surf shops on Cronulla Street (which becomes a pedestrianized mall between Kingsway and Purley Place), to the outdoor cafés on the beachfront and the surfrider clubs and boating facilities on the bay. Even the *Cronulla Beach YHA* (see p.122) is aimed primarily at surfers, with excursions to Garie and free use of boogie-boards.

ARRIVAL AND DEPARTURE   SYDNEY

The dream way to **arrive** in Sydney is, of course, by ship, cruising in below the great "coathanger" of the Harbour Bridge to tie up at the Overseas Passenger Terminal alongside Circular Quay. The reality of the functional airport, bus and train stations is a good deal less romantic.

BY PLANE
Kingsford Smith Airport Sydney's airport (☎ 13 12 23, ⓦ sydneyairport.com.au), referred to as "Mascot" after the suburb where it's located, is 8km south of the city, near Botany Bay. Bureau de change offices at terminals are open daily from 5am till last arrival, with rates comparable to major banks. On the ground floor (arrivals) of the international terminal, the Sydney Visitor Centre (daily 5am till last arrival; ☎ 02 9667 9386) can arrange car rental and city-bound shuttle-bus tickets, plus they can book hotels anywhere in Sydney and New South Wales. Most hostels advertise on an adjacent notice board; there's a freephone line for reservations, and many of them will refund your bus fare; a few also offer free airport pick-ups.
Airlines (domestic) Jetstar ☎ 13 15 38, ⓦ jetstar.com; Regional Express (REX) ☎ 13 17 13, ⓦ rex.com.au; Virgin Australia ☎ 13 67 89, ⓦ virginaustralia.com.
Transferring between terminals If travelling with Qantas or Virgin Australia, you may be eligible for a free transfer between the domestic and international terminals; otherwise, pay $6 (varies on Opal Card) for the Airport Link shuttle (5am–midnight).
Domestic destinations Adelaide (16 daily; 2hr 10min); Albury (8 daily; 1hr 20min); Alice Springs (1 daily; 3hr 15min); Armidale (4 daily; 1hr 10min); Ballina (4–7 daily; 1hr 40min); Bathurst (3 daily Mon–Fri; 40min); Bourke (1 daily except Sat; 3hr 10min); Brisbane (42 daily; 1hr 30min); Broken Hill (1 daily; 1hr 50min); Cairns (8 daily; 3hr 10min); Canberra (20–25 daily; 45min); Cobar (2 daily except Sat; 2hr 25min); Coffs Harbour (7 daily; 1hr 15min); Cooma (1–2 daily; 1hr); Darwin (1 daily; 4hr 25min);

Dubbo (5–7 daily Mon–Fri; 1hr); Fraser Coast (1–2 daily; 1hr 40min); Gold Coast (17 daily; 1hr 20min); Grafton (1 daily; 2hr); Griffith (3–4 daily; 1hr 25min); Hamilton Island (2 daily; 2hr 25min); Hobart (8 daily; 1hr 50min); Inverell (1–2 daily; 1hr 55min); Launceston (2 daily; 1hr 40min); Lismore (3–4 daily; 1hr 35min); Lord Howe Island (1 daily; 1hr 50min); Melbourne (58 daily; 1hr 20min); Merimbula (3 daily; 1hr 35min); Mildura (1 daily; 2hr 40min); Moruya (2 daily; 50min); Mudgee (2 daily Mon–Fri, 1 daily Sat & Sun; 1hr); Narrandera (2 daily; 1hr 30min); Newcastle (1 daily except Sun; 40min); Norfolk Island (4 weekly; 2hr 20min); Orange (3–4 daily; 45min); Parkes (2–3 daily; 1hr); Perth (8 daily; 4hr 50min); Port Macquarie (6 daily; 1hr); Port Stephens (Mon–Fri 1 daily; 1hr); Prosperine (1 daily; 2hr 30min); Rockhampton (1 daily; 2hr); Sunshine Coast (4 daily; 1hr 30min); Tamworth (4 daily; 1hr); Taree (2–3 daily; 50min); Townsville (1 daily; 2hr 40min); Uluru (2 daily; 3hr 30min); Wagga Wagga (3–6 daily; 1hr 10min).

GETTING INTO TOWN
By train There are rail stations at all terminals – follow the clear signage once you leave the arrivals lounge – with Airport Link trains ($13.40 from the domestic or international terminals on an Opal Card; ⓦ airportlink.com.au) to whisk you into the city centre in under 20min. Services from each terminal ply a slightly different route, so check in advance which one gets you closest to your accommodation.
By bus STA's daily east–west commuter route #400 stops frequently at the international and domestic terminals bound for Bondi Junction ($4.50) via Maroubra and Randwick in one direction, and to Burwood in the other. To get into the city you

can get a T-Bus (every 30min; $5.50). KST Sydney Transporter ($15 one-way, $28 return; ⓣ 02 9666 9988, ⓦ kst.com.au) is a private bus service dropping off at hotels or hostels in the area bounded by Kings Cross and Darling Harbour. Service leaves when the bus is full. Premier Motor Service (ⓣ 13 34 10, outside Australia ⓣ 02 4423 5233, ⓦ premierms.com.au) departs daily at 9.30am and 3.35pm from the domestic terminals, 10min later from the international terminal, to south-coast towns as far as Eden ($80), though the 3.35pm service continues to Melbourne ($95). Booking essential.

By taxi Taxis leave from the rank outside the concourse and charge $50–60 to take you to the centre.

BY TRAIN

All local and interstate trains arrive at Central Station on Eddy Ave, just south of the city centre. There are no lockers, but you can store luggage here at Baggage Storage, Grand Concourse (daily 6am–10pm; $16/day per bag, $101/week). From outside Central Station and neighbouring Railway Square, you can hop onto nearly every major bus route, and from within Central Station you can take a CityRail train to any city or suburban station. All out-of-town trains depart from the country trains terminal of Central Station (information and booking at the travel centre 6.30am–10pm; ⓣ 13 22 32, ⓦ nswtrainlink.info). The *Indian Pacific*, the *Ghan* and the *Overland* are managed by Great Southern Railway (ⓣ 13 21 47, ⓦ gsr.com.au). Interstate trains should be booked as early as possible, especially the *Indian Pacific* and Brisbane–Cairns trains.

Destinations Adelaide (*Indian Pacific*; Sat & Wed 2.55pm; 24hr 10min); Albury (2 daily; 7hr 30min); Armidale (1 daily; 8hr 15min), via Tamworth (6hr 15min); Bowral (2–3 daily; 1hr 50min); Brisbane (2 daily; 14hr 10min); Broken Hill (1 daily; 15hr); Bundanoon (2 daily; 2hr); Canberra (2 daily; 4hr 15min); Cootamundra (2–3 daily; 5hr 15min); Dubbo (2 daily; 6hr 30min); Gosford (every 30min; 1hr 30min); Goulburn (4 daily; 2hr 45min); Griffith (Sat only; 8hr 50min); Hawkesbury River (every 30min; 1hr); Katoomba (29 daily; 2hr 10min); Kiama (1 daily; 1hr); Maitland (6 daily; 2hr 45min); Melbourne (2 daily; 11hr; plus daily bus/train Speedlink via Albury; 12–13hr); Menindee (Mon only; 12hr); Mittagong (2 daily; 1hr 40min); Moree (1 daily; 8hr 40min) via Gunnedah (6hr 20min) and Narrabri (7hr 20min); Murwillumbah (3 daily; 13hr 45min); Newcastle (28 daily; 2hr 45min); Orange (1–2 daily; 5hr 45min); Parkes (daily coach connection at Lithgow; 6hr 30min); Perth (*Indian Pacific*; Sat & Wed 2.55pm; 67hr 45min); Richmond (14 daily; 2hr); Scone (daily; 4hr); Wagga Wagga (2 daily; 6hr 15min); Waterfall (every 20–40min; 1hr); Windsor (14 daily; 1hr 45min); Wollongong (32 daily; 1hr 30min).

BY BUS

All buses to Sydney arrive and depart from Eddy Ave and Pitt St, bordering Central Station. The area is well set up, with decent cafés, a 24-hour police station and a huge YHA hostel (see p.119), as well as the Sydney Coach Terminal (Mon–Fri 6am–6pm, Sat & Sun 8am–6pm; ⓣ 02 9281 9366), which has a left-luggage room ($5–10/day per bag) and an internet kiosk, and can book accommodation, tours and coach tickets and passes. Most bus services from Sydney depart from Eddy Ave, alongside Central Station; buy tickets from the Sydney Coach Terminal or direct from bus companies.

Interstate services There are four interstate services: Greyhound Australia has Australia-wide services (ⓣ 1300 473 946, ⓦ greyhound.com.au); Firefly Express (ⓣ 1300 730 740, ⓦ fireflyexpress.com.au), twice daily to Melbourne and connecting to Adelaide; Murray's (ⓣ 13 22 51, ⓦ murrays.com.au; also from Strathfield station), to Canberra many times daily, with onward services to the southeast coast (Batemans Bay, Moruya and Narooma) or the Snowy Mountains; while Premier Motor Service departs just around the corner at 490 Pitt St (ⓣ 13 34 10, ⓦ premierms.com.au), heading to Cairns via the north coast, and to Melbourne via the south coast.

New South Wales services Most bus services to destinations within New South Wales also depart from Eddy Ave: Rover Coaches (ⓣ 02 4990 1699, ⓦ rovercoaches.com.au; also from *Four Seasons Hotel*, The Rocks), daily to Cessnock and Hunter Valley resorts; Port Stephens Coaches (ⓣ 02 4982 2940 or ⓣ 1800 045 949, ⓦ pscoaches.com.au), daily to Port Stephens via Newcastle outskirts; Selwoods (ⓣ 02 6362 7963, ⓦ selwoods.com.au), daily to Orange via the Blue Mountains, Lithgow and Bathurst; Prior's Scenic Express departs from Parramatta, Liverpool and Campbelltown train stations (ⓣ 02 4472 4040 or ⓣ 1800 816 234), daily except Sat to the Southern Highlands and Kangaroo Valley, and from there to Moruya or Narooma via the south coast including Batemans Bay and Ulladulla.

Destinations Adelaide (3 daily; 22hr); Albury (4 daily; 8hr 30min); Armidale (2 daily; 8hr 30min); Batemans Bay (2 daily; 5hr 20min); Bathurst (1 daily; 3hr 15min); Bega (2 daily; 8hr); Brisbane (9 daily; 15–17hr, with connections to Cairns and Darwin); Broken Hill (1 daily; 15hr 40min); Byron Bay (7 daily; 13hr 15min); Canberra (11–14 daily; 4hr); Cessnock (1 daily; 2hr 30min); Coffs Harbour (7 daily; 9hr); Eden (2 daily; 8hr 30min–9hr 30min); Forster (1 daily; 6hr); Glen Innes (2 daily; 10hr); Gosford (1 daily; 1hr 30min); Goulburn (1 daily; 3hr 30min); Grafton (3 daily; 10hr); Kiama (1 daily; 2hr); Melbourne (6 daily; 12–18hr); Mildura (3 daily; 16hr); Mittagong (4 daily; 2hr 20min); Moss Vale (1 daily; 2hr 45min); Muswellbrook (1 daily; 3hr 30min); Narooma (2 daily; 8hr); Newcastle (8 daily; 3hr); Nowra (2 daily; 3hr–4hr 20min); Orange (1 daily; 4hr 15min); Perth (2–3 daily; 52–56hr); Port Macquarie (6 daily; 7hr); Port Stephens (1 daily; 3hr); Scone (1 daily; 6hr); Tamworth (1 daily; 7hr); Taree (2 daily; 6hr 30min); Tenterfield (1 daily; 12hr); Wollongong (2–3 daily; 2hr).

1

BY CAR

The Big 4 car-rental companies offer expensive new-model cars and charge from $50/day for a small manual, with much cheaper rates for five-to-seven-day and longer rentals.

Car rental Avis, airport (☎ 02 8374 2847, ⊚ avis.com.au) and 200 William St, Kings Cross (☎ 02 9357 2000); Budget, airport (☎ 02 9207 9165, ⊚ budget.com.au) and 93 William St, Kings Cross (☎ 02 8255 9600); Hertz (bookings ☎ 13 30 39, international ☎ 613 9698 2555, ⊚ hertz .com.au), airport (☎ 02 8337 7500) and corner of William and Riley sts, Kings Cross (☎ 02 9360 6621); Thrifty, airport (☎ 1300 367 227 or ☎ 612 8337 2700, ⊚ thrifty.com.au) and 75 William St, Kings Cross (☎ 02 8374 6177). There are cheaper deals with the popular Bayswater, 180 William St, Kings Cross (☎ 02 9360 3622, ⊚ bayswatercarrental .com.au), which has low rates often linked, however, with limited kilometres; Travellers Auto Barn, 177 William St, Kings Cross (☎ 02 9360 1500 or ☎ 1800 674 374, ⊚ travellers-autobarn.com.au), does cheap one-way rentals to Melbourne, Brisbane or Cairns, but with a minimum ten-day hire.

BY MOTORBIKE

Bikescape, at 183 Parramatta Rd, Annandale (☎ 02 9569 4111, ⊚ bikescape.com.au), offer scooters from $90/day and motorbikes from $130 (cheaper weekend and longer-term rates available).

BY CAMPERVAN AND 4WD

All Seasons Campervans, 20 Hattersley St, Arncliffe (☎ 1800 226 737, ⊚ camper.com.au), is south of the centre and offers a wide range of campervans and motorhomes with linen, sleeping bags and free delivery within the CBD. Britz Campervan Rentals, 653 Gardeners Rd, Mascot (domestic ☎ 1800 331 454, international ☎ 00 800 200 80 801, ⊚ britz.com), has campervans, 4WD campers and camping gear, available one-way to Adelaide, Alice Springs, Brisbane, Cairns, Darwin, Melbourne and Perth.

CARS: BUYING AND SELLING

Sydney is the most popular place to buy a **car** or **campervan** for travelling around Australia. The information below is specific to buying a car in New South Wales. Before you start looking, it's a good idea to join the **NRMA** motoring association, 74 King St, City (☎ 13 21 32, international ☎ 612 9848 5201, ⊚ mynrma.com.au; $55 joining fee plus $110 annual charge per vehicle, or $199 for extra benefits); overseas motoring association members may have reciprocal membership. Membership entitles you to roadside assistance, though the NRMA often refuses to cover overseas travellers for third-party insurance. The NRMA's website has an excellent "Motoring" section and *The Red Book* (⊚ redbook.com.au) provides detailed, up-to-date information on the value of all makes of new and used cars. The Office of Fair Trading's useful *The Car Buyers Handbook: Buying and Maintaining a Car in NSW* can be viewed online (☎ 13 32 20, ⊚ fairtrading.nsw.gov.au).

NEWSPAPER LISTINGS

The *Weekly Trading Post* (⊚ tradingpost.com.au) has a big **secondhand car** section, while the *Sydney Morning Herald*'s Friday "Drive" supplement (⊚ drive.com.au) has ads for **secondhand dealers** (most on Parramatta Rd from Annandale onwards) and private used cars for sale at the pricier end of the market. Both have good websites; try your luck with Gumtree (⊚ gumtree.com.au) for more direct sales. Demand to see a **"pink slip"** (certificate of roadworthiness) that is less than 42 days old. You can contact REVS (☎ 13 32 20, ⊚ revs.com.au) to check if there are any payments owing, and call the Roads and Traffic Authority (RTA; ☎ 13 22 13, ⊚ rta.nsw.gov.au) to check that registration is still current.

DEALERSHIPS

Sydney is well equipped with **dealerships** who will arrange to **buy back** the vehicle they've sold you at the end of your trip – expect to get 30–50 percent back. The longest running is Travellers Auto Barn, 177 William St, Kings Cross (☎ 1800 674 374, ⊚ travellers-autobarn.com. au), with offices in Melbourne, Brisbane, Cairns, Perth and Darwin, or The Sydney Travellers Car Market, Level 2, Ward Avenue Car Park, King's Cross (Mon–Sat 10am–5pm; ☎ 02 9331 4361, ⊚ sydneytravellerscarmarket.com.au), specifically aimed at travellers, with paperwork assistance and contract exchange provided. It's also one of the few places where you will be able to sell a car registered in another state. Dealers are barred, and fees for sellers are $60/wk with a pink slip. Many of the vehicles come equipped with **camping gear** and other extras. Third-party property **insurance** is no longer arranged but staff can offer advice. It's worth checking the Car Market's website, where sellers can advertise for $50.

Travel Car Centre, 26 Orchard Rd, Brookvale (℡ 02 9905 6928, ⊕ travelcar.com.au), has been established for over twenty years and has hatchbacks, station wagons, campervans and 4WDs available for long- or short-term rental. Travellers Auto Barn (see opposite) also offers budget campervan and 4WD bush-camper rentals.

GETTING AROUND

Sydney's **public transport network** is wide-reaching and relatively comprehensive, but not always punctual, and since the system relies heavily on buses, traffic jams can be a problem. **State Transit Authority (STA)** operates buses, trains and ferries, and there's also the privately run light-rail system which whizzes about the city centre 24/7. **Taxis** and Ubers (app needed, ⊕ uber.com) are plentiful. For all public transport information, routes and timetables, call ℡ 13 15 00 (24hr) or check ⊕ transportnsw.info.

BY BUS

Within the central area, buses – hailed from yellow-signed bus stops – are the most convenient, widespread mode of transport, and cover more of the city than the trains. Bus information, including route maps, timetables and passes, is available from booths at Carrington St, Wynyard; at Circular Quay on the corner of Loftus and Alfred streets; and at the Queen Victoria Building on York St. You can also view timetables and route maps on Sydney Buses' website (⊕ sydneybuses.info). With few exceptions, buses radiate from the centre, with major interchanges at Railway Square near Central Station (especially southwest routes), at Circular Quay (range of routes), from York and Carrington streets outside Wynyard station (North Shore), and at Bondi Junction station (eastern suburbs and beaches). The corner of Argyle and Kent streets, Millers Point, is a terminus for several useful bus routes; buses #431–434 go along Castlereagh St to Railway Square and from there to various locations including Glebe and Balmain, while #339 goes to the eastern beaches suburb of Clovelly via Elizabeth St in the city and Surry Hills.

Fares An Opal Card is required for all fares (see box, p.115), and you cannot top-up or buy tickets onboard. You must tap on and off the bus or you will be automatically charged the maximum fare of $4.50. When you tap off, you will be charged either $2.10 (0–3km), $3.50 (3–8km) or $4.50 (over 8km), depending on the distance travelled.

Night buses Buses stop around midnight, though several services towards the eastern and northern beaches, such as the #380 to Bondi Beach, the #372 and #373 to Coogee and the #151 to Manly, run through the night. Otherwise, a pretty good network of NightRide buses – which use the Opal Card – shadows the train routes to the suburbs from midnight to 4.30am, with extra services on weekends. The buses depart from Town Hall station (in front of the Energy Australia Building on George St) and stop at train stations, where taxis wait at designated ranks.

Sydney & Bondi Explorer The red Sydney Explorer (from Circular Quay daily 8.30am–7.30pm, every 20min; 24hr ticket $40, 48hr ticket $60; ⊕ theaustralianexplorer.com. au) takes in all the important sights in the city and inner suburbs, via 26 hop-on-hop-off stops (1hr 30min circuit). Included on the same ticket is the Bondi Explorer (daily from Central 8.30am–6.30pm; approx every 30min), which covers the waterside eastern suburbs. Neither bus uses the Opal Card.

BY TRAIN

Trains, operated by CityRail (see p.111), will get you where you're going faster than buses, especially at rush hour and when heading out to the suburbs, but you need to transfer to a bus or ferry to get to most harbourside or beach destinations. There are seven train lines, mostly over ground, each of which stops at Central and Town Hall stations. Trains run from around 5am to midnight. All platforms are painted with designated "nightsafe" waiting areas and all but two or three train carriages are closed after about 8pm, enforcing a cattle-like safety in numbers. Security guards also patrol trains at night; at other times, if the train is deserted, sit in the carriage nearest the guard – marked by a blue light.

Fares An Opal Card (see box, p.115) is required to travel on the train network, and top-ups can be made at station machines. Fare prices depend on distance – you will automatically be charged the best fare when you tap off. Most journeys you're likely to make will be under 10km and cost the minimum fare of $3.38, or $2.36 off-peak (eg Central to Bondi Junction, Mascot or Circular Quay). The next band up (10–20km) costs $4.20, or $2.94 off-peak (eg Central to Bankstown or Chatswood). The maximum fare (over 65km) is $8.30, or $5.81 off-peak (eg Central to Katoomba or Newcastle). Peak hours are Mon–Fri 7–9am and 4–6.30pm. On-the-spot fines for fare evasion start from $200, and transit officers patrol frequently.

BY FERRY

Sydney's distinctive green-and-yellow ferries are the fastest means of transport from Circular Quay to the North Shore, and to most places around the harbour. Even if you don't want to go anywhere, a ferry ride is a must – it's a chance to get out on the water and see the city from the harbour.

Routes Ferries chug off in various directions from the wharves at Circular Quay (see p.66); cruises depart from Wharf 6. The Manly Ferry (30min) operates until 12.20am. Other ferry routes, such as those to Parramatta and

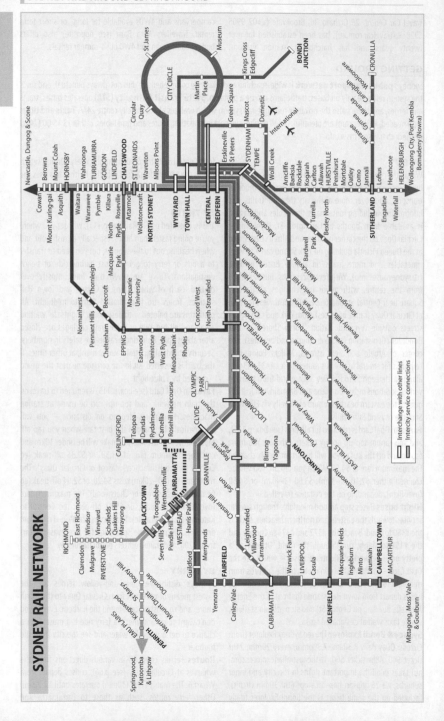

SYDNEY RAIL NETWORK

OPAL CARD

All public transport in Sydney works with a rechargeable **Opal Card** (ⓦopal.com.au). You must tap your Opal Card on and off at the machines at all train station gates, and bus and light rail entrances and exits. If you don't tap off, you will be charged the maximum fare – except on ferries, where you only need to tap on. The benefit of Opal Cards is that they are able to calculate the best fare for you – so there's no need to work out if you would have been better off with a weekly ticket – and they provide other discounts, outlined below. Opal Cards are available at most newsagents, convenience stores and train stations (including airport stations). The cards are free but must be purchased with an initial minimum-journey top-up fee.

Daily and Sunday $2.50 cap Once you hit $15 on trips on any given day, all other trips that day are free, on any mode of transport. The daily cap on Sun is only $2.50, meaning you could travel all day on ferries and even from Central Station to Katoomba in the Blue Mountains and back for only $2.50. Plus, no matter where you go, you will never pay more than $60 for a week of travel. Excludes Sydney airports.

Weekly cap There is no separate weekly travel card with Opal Card. Instead, once you've paid for eight journeys in a week period from Mon to Sun (not including transfers between bus, train, ferry or light rail), all trips for the rest of the week are half-price (until late 2016, they were free), and you'll never pay more than $60 for a week's travel, Mon–Sun. Excludes Sydney airports.

Opal 60 minute transfer You can change bus/train/light rail within 60min and get a $2 discount on each transfer you make. If you use the same mode of transport, eg get off the bus, have a coffee, and then continue on a bus in the same direction within 60min, you will not be charged a second fare. This is useful for stopping at the supermarket on the way home, for example, as you get charged for one trip, not two. All exclude Sydney airports.

Off-peak trains Travelling by train outside of peak times (Mon–Fri 7–9am and 4–6.30pm) is thirty percent cheaper than during rush hour.

Airports When you tap on or off at Sydney Domestic Airport or International Airport stations, you are charged a fee of $13.40, in addition to your regular train fare. Even if you've reached a daily cap, you still pay this fee, and it doesn't count towards any caps. The Opal 60 minute transfer is also void. There is a separate weekly cap of $25 for the Airport.

Pyrmont Bay, run only till 10.30pm, while ferries to closer locations, including Neutral Bay and Balmain, continue till around 11.40pm. Except for the Manly Ferry, Sunday services are greatly reduced and often finish earlier. Timetables for each route are available at Circular Quay and on the Sydney Ferries website ⓦ sydneyferries.info.

Fares Trips are only by Opal Card and one-way fares are either $5.74 (eg Circular Quay to Taronga Zoo, Darling Harbour or Eastern Suburbs) or $7.18 (Circular Quay to Manly, Sydney Olympic Park or Parramatta). Daily, weekly and especially Sunday caps can offer substantial savings (see box above).

BY LIGHT RAIL

Light rail The city's leisurely light rail (ⓣ 13 15 00, ⓦ transportnsw.info) runs from Central Station to Dulwich Hill in the inner west. There are 23 stops on the route, which links Central Station with Chinatown and Paddy's Markets, Darling Harbour, the fish markets at Pyrmont, Star City Casino, Wentworth Park's greyhound racecourse, Glebe (with stops near Pyrmont Bridge Rd, Jubilee Park, and Rozelle Bay by Bicentennial Park), Lilyfield (not far from Darling St), Rozelle, and now Leichhardt and Dulwich Hill, next to the train station. The service operates 24/7, every 8–30min. There are 2 zones: Zone 1 is from Central to Convention Centre in Darling Harbour ($1.05), and Zone 2

runs from Pyrmont Bay to Dulwich Hill ($1.75 from Central). An Opal Card is used for all fares and must be tapped on and off at machines at the stops, not onboard. Another route (CBD and South East Light Rail) is in the works and will run from Circular Quay to the southeast suburb of Kingsford by 2019 or 2020. Useful stations on the way will include Town Hall, Chinatown, Central Station, Surry Hills, and the University of New South Wales.

BY TAXI

Taxis are vacant if the rooftop light is on, though they are notoriously difficult to find at 3pm, when the shifts change over. The four major city taxi ranks are outside the *Four Seasons Hotel* at the start of George St, The Rocks; on Park St outside Woolworths, opposite the Town Hall; outside David Jones department store on Market St; and at the Pitt St ("CountryLink") entrance to Central Station. Drivers don't expect a tip but often need directions – try to have some idea of where you're going. Check that the correct tariff rate is displayed: tariff 2 (10pm–6am) is twenty percent more than tariff 1 (6am–10pm). Taxi-like service Uber can be cheaper and as reliable as taxis; you'll need the app to order one (ⓦ uber.com).

Taxi companies Legion (ⓣ 13 14 51, ⓦlegioncabs.com.au); Premier (ⓣ13 10 17, ⓦpremiercabs.com.au); St George

1

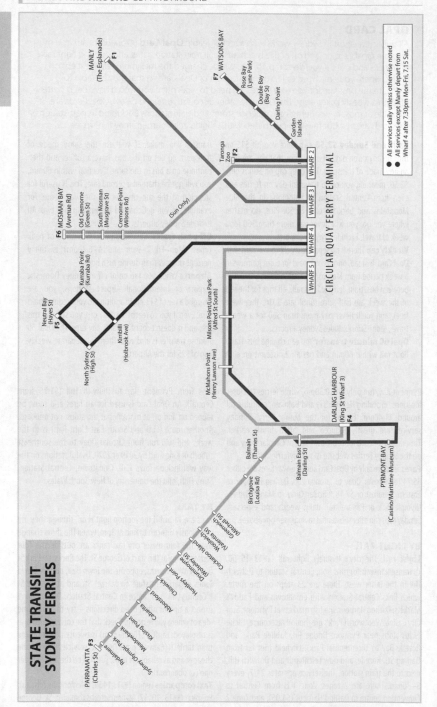

STATE TRANSIT SYDNEY FERRIES

CIRCULAR QUAY FERRY TERMINAL

- All services daily unless otherwise noted
- ● All services except Manly depart from Wharf 4 after 7.30pm Mon–Fri, 7.15 Sat.

WHARF 2
WHARF 3
WHARF 4
WHARF 5

F1 MANLY (The Esplanade)

F7 WATSONS BAY
Rose Bay (Lyne Park)
Double Bay (Bay St)
Darling Point
Garden Islands

F2 Taronga Zoo

(Sun Only)

F6 MOSMAN BAY (Avenue Rd)
Old Cremorne (Green St)
South Mosman (Musgrave St)
Cremorne Point (Milsons Rd)

Kurraba Point (Kurraba Rd)

F5 Neutral Bay (Hayes St)
Kirribilli (Holbrook Ave)
North Sydney (High St)

Milsons Point/Luna Park (Alfred St South)

McMahons Point (Henry Lawson Ave)

DARLING HARBOUR (King St Wharf 3)

F4 Balmain (Thames St)
Balmain East (Darling St)

PYRMONT BAY (Casino/Maritime Museum)

Birchgrove (Louisa Rd)
Woolwich (Valentia St)
Greenwich (Mitchell St)
Cockatoo Island
Dunmymo Point (Wolseley St)
Huntleys Point
Chiswick
Abbotsford
Cabarita
Kissing Point
Sydney Olympic Park
Rydalmere
Meadowbank

F3 PARRAMATTA (Charles St)

(☎13 21 66, ⓦstgeorgecabs.com.au); Taxis Combined (☎13 33 00, ⓦtaxiscombined.com.au). For harbour water taxis, call Water Taxis Combined (☎02 9555 8888, ⓦwatertaxis.com.au).

BY BIKE

Bicycles can be carried for free on Sydney trains and ferries at all times. The Roads and Traffic Authority (RTA; ☎1800 060 607, ⓦrta.nsw.gov.au) produces a fold-out map, *Sydney Cycleways*, showing off-road paths and bicycle routes, which you can order by post or download on the useful website ⓦsydneycycleways.net. Another good source of information is the organization Bicycle NSW, Level 5, 822 George St (Mon–Fri 9am–5.30pm; ☎02 9218 5400, ⓦbicyclensw.org.au). A useful downloadable publication

is *Bike It Sydney* (PDF $8.95; ⓦbike-it.com.au), which shows backstreet inner-city bike routes. Centennial Parklands and the bike path that runs from Manly are popular cycling spots.

Bike rental Recommended central bike shops include Clarence Street Cyclery, 104 Clarence St (☎02 9299 4962, ⓦcyclery.com.au); Woolys Wheels, 82 Oxford St, Paddington (☎02 9331 2671, ⓦwoolyswheels.com); and Inner City Cycles, 151 Glebe Point Rd, Glebe (☎02 9660 6605, ⓦinnercitycycles.com.au). Clarence Street Cyclery also rents hybrid bikes ($29/half-day), as does Inner City Cycles ($33/24hr, $55/weekend). For a leisurely ride in the park, Centennial Park Cycles, 50 Clovelly Rd, Randwick (☎02 9398 5027, ⓦcyclehire.com.au), rents various types of bikes (from $15/hr), as well as pedal cars ($30–50/hr).

INFORMATION

Tourist information There are two Sydney Visitor Centres offering comprehensive information, accommodation and tour-booking facilities; they also sell transport tickets and sightseeing passes and offer free maps and brochures. Both are centrally located, one on the corner of Argyle and Playfair streets in The Rocks, the other at Darling Harbour, beside the IMAX cinema (both daily 9.30am–5.30pm; ☎02 9240 8788 or ☎1800 067 676, ⓦshfa.nsw.gov.au). Tourism New South Wales (☎13 20 77, ⓦvisitnsw.com) runs the City Host information kiosks (daily 9am–5pm) at Circular Quay (cnr of Pitt & Alfred sts), Martin Place and Town Hall, providing brochures, maps and information.

Passes The Sydney Visitor Centres sell the iVenture Card (☎1300 661 711, ⓦseesydneypass.iventurecard.com). The Unlimited Attractions pass comes in three- and seven-day versions (to be used over consecutive days),

and includes unlimited admission to over thirty attractions in Sydney and the Blue Mountains, one day on the Sydney Explorer, plus a range of discounts. Attractions include Sea Life Sydney Aquarium, Manly Sea Life Sanctuary, Taronga Zoo, Sydney Opera House tour, Sydney Tower Eye and Captain Cook Cruises (three-day $245, seven-day $295). If an action-packed, fast-paced itinerary is your thing, the card can be good value, and it's certainly a convenient way to bypass the queues. The Flexi Attractions Pass is less expensive (three attractions $105; five $155) and covers your choice of one-time entry into the same attractions.

Listings Several free magazines are worth picking up at tourist offices: the quarterly *This Week in Sydney* is best for general information, while *TNT Magazine* is aimed at backpackers. The *Time Out* website (ⓦau.timeout.com) is also a good place to find out about what's happening.

TOURS

I'm Free tour Volunteers give free tours of different Sydney sites, open to anybody who shows up (☎0405 515 654, ⓦimfree.com.au). The Sydney Sights free tour meets at the Town Hall (483 George St) at 10.30am and 2.30pm daily and covers the history and lesser-known bars of the CBD (3hr). The Rocks tour meets daily at 6pm at Cadman's Cottage (110 George St), taking you through little laneways and covering convict history (1hr 30min). Look for guides in green T-shirts, who wait in all weather and are friendly and knowledgeable; they appreciate (and deserve) a tip at the end. The tours are an excellent way to orient yourself.

The Rocks Dreaming Aboriginal Heritage Tour Starting at Cadmans Cottage, at 110 George St in The Rocks, this tour (daily 10.30am; 1hr 30min; $42; ☎02 9240 8788; ⓦdreamtimesouthernx.com.au) evokes the culture of the Cadigal people, from the medicinal properties of plants to Dreamtime stories and the uses of ochre. Above all, the experience provides you with an alternative geography of the city centre: the area now occupied by the Botanical Gardens, for example, was where men went through their initiation rites, and it's hard to imagine that gaudy Darling Harbour was a sacrosanct area where Cadigal women gave birth.

ACCOMMODATION

There are a tremendous number of places to stay in Sydney, and fierce competition helps keep prices down. Finding somewhere is usually only a problem around Christmas, throughout Jan, in late Feb/early March during the Gay Mardi Gras, and at Easter: at these times, **book ahead**. All types of accommodation offer a (sometimes substantial) discount for **weekly bookings**, and may also cut prices considerably during the **low season** (from May–Sept, school hols excepted).

WHERE TO STAY

For short visits, you'll want to stay in the city centre or the immediate vicinity: The Rocks, the CBD and Darling Harbour have the greatest concentration of **expensive hotels**, while Haymarket is well endowed with **backpackers' hostels**, a couple of fine YHAs and a few mid-range hotels. Kings Cross makes an excellent base, as it's only a ten-minute walk from the city, has its own train station and is always lively. In recent years, it has shaken the worst of its red-light and drug-abuse sleaze and is once again popular with backpackers who frequent the dense cluster of hostels and **cheap hotels** in The Cross and along leafy Victoria Street. Fashionable new restaurants and bars are opening up all the time in adjacent Potts Point, Woolloomooloo and Darlinghurst, and the buzz has attracted a cluster of chic **boutique hotels** and **refined B&Bs** to the area.

There's far less choice in southern Darlinghurst, Paddington and Surry Hills, though the vibrant gay scene along Oxford Street ensures there are **gay-friendly places** to stay. Few are exclusively gay, but there are several welcoming places that we've included in our general listings: try *BIG* (see opposite), the *Kirketon* (see p.120) and *Arts Hotel* (see p.121).

To the west, verdant and peaceful Glebe is another slice of prime travellers' territory, featuring several backpackers' and a number of small, **luxurious guesthouses**. For longer stays, consider somewhere further out, on the North Shore, where you'll get more of a feel for Sydney as a city. Kirribilli, Neutral Bay or Cremorne Point, only a short ferry ride from Circular Quay, offer serenity and affordable water views. Large old private hotels out this way are increasingly being converted into hostels, particularly on Carabella Street in Kirribilli.

This being Sydney, the **beaches** are a huge draw, and thanks to the good ferry and train system, it's quite possible to stay at the beach and still sightsee quite comfortably. The closest ocean beach to the city is Bondi, which has a couple of great hostels and a boutique hotel, while there's a more casual feel to Coogee, a couple of headlands to the south. A frequent and fast ferry service makes Manly, the first of the northern beaches, a good base. This seaside suburb with ocean and harbour beaches, just thirty minutes from Circular Quay, has a concentration of hostels and a limited supply of more upmarket accommodation. Lastly, the beaches to the north of Manly offer a couple of hostels and B&Bs that are inconvenient for visiting the city but make good spots for a **short break**.

THE ROCKS

HOTELS AND B&BS

Holiday Inn Old Sydney 55 George St ☎ 02 9252 0524, ⓦ holidayinn.com; map p.72. Right in the heart of The Rocks, this hotel is impressively designed around a central atrium with a remarkable feeling of space. The best rooms have harbour views, but the rooftop pool (plus spa and sauna) also offers sensational vistas. $\underline{\$525}$

The Langham 89–113 Kent St ☎ 02 9256 2222, ⓦ sydney.langhamhotels.com.au; map p.72. A glamorous option in a quiet location, with famous afternoon teas and a spacious underground pool. Some rooms look over to Observatory Hill and Walsh Bay. $\underline{\$450}$

★ **Lord Nelson Brewery Hotel** 19 Kent St, at Argyle St ☎ 02 9251 4044, ⓦ lordnelson.com.au; map p.72.

Colonial-style B&B in a historic pub with ten cosy, variably priced rooms: best is the corner room with views of Argyle St. Serves beer brewed on the premises, plus bar food daily and upmarket meals from its first-floor brasserie (lunch Wed–Fri, dinner Tues–Sat). Continental breakfast included. $\underline{\$180}$

The Russell 143A George St ☎ 02 9241 3543, ⓦ therussell.com.au; map p.72. A small hotel with popular shared-bathroom rooms, plus en-suite options; the priciest have views of Circular Quay. There's a rooftop garden with a small restaurant serving the included Continental breakfast. $\underline{\$180}$

Sydney Harbour B&B 140–142 Cumberland St ☎ 02 9247 1130, ⓦ bbsydneyharbour.com.au; map p.72. This elegant B&B is located in two historic boarding houses in the heart of The Rocks. Enjoy your substantial breakfast (included) inside or in the courtyard garden. $\underline{\$165}$

HOSTEL

★ **Sydney Harbour YHA** 106–128 Cumberland St ☎ 02 9261 1111, ⓦ yha.com.au; map p.72. Built in 2009, and with gorgeous harbour views, this is the pick of Sydney's youth hostels — and the only budget accommodation in

---

TOP 5 ROOMS WITH A VIEW

Ovolo Woolloomooloo See p.120
Cremorne Point Manor See p.122
DIVE See p.122
Intercontinental See opposite
Sydney Harbour YHA See below

FLAT-SHARES

If you're staying longer than a month, consider a **flat-share** as an alternative to hotels or hostels – you'll feel more at home, and it will probably cost less. Sites like ⓦairbnb.com.au (user-rated, though remember to factor in the booking fee) and ⓦgumtree.com.au offer longer-term apartments and shares. Furnished Property Group (☎02 8669 3678, ⓦfurnishedproperty.com.au) offers shared and independent short-term accommodation in apartments and houses in all the best areas. The average shared-house room price is around $220 a week excluding bills (usually two weeks in advance, plus a bond/deposit of four weeks' rent); you'll usually need your own bed linen and towels, and furnished rooms are rarer than unfurnished. Check Wednesday and Saturday's real-estate section of the *Sydney Morning Herald* and café notice boards, especially on King Street in Newtown, Glebe Point Road in Glebe, or Hall Street in Bondi Beach. If you feel unsure about renting in a foreign city, contact the New South Wales Tenants Union (☎02 9251 6590, ⓦtenants.org.au) for information on lease agreements and tenants' rights.

The Rocks. It also doubles as an innovative Archaeology Education Centre (the "Big Dig") – with the YHA's structure suspended over early nineteenth-century remains uncovered in the 1990s. Very popular, so book well in advance. Dorms $48; doubles $162

CENTRAL BUSINESS DISTRICT (CBD)

HOTELS

★**Intercontinental** 117 Macquarie St ☎02 9253 9000, ⓦihg.com; map pp.68–69. The sandstone facade of the 1851 former Treasury building forms the lower floors of this 31-storey, five-star hotel, with stunning views of the Botanic Gardens, Opera House and harbour. Pool and gym on the top floor. Summer rates from around $395, more for city and harbour views. $355

Travelodge Wynyard 7–9 York St ☎02 9274 1222, ⓦtfehotels.com; map pp.68–69. This 22-storey hotel close to The Rocks has the usual motel-style rooms but excels with its spacious studios, which come with a kitchen area. There's also a small gym and a pleasant café-brasserie. Cheaper weekend packages. $275

Y Hotel Hyde Park 5–11 Wentworth Ave ☎1800 994 994, ⓦyhotels.com.au; map pp.68–69. Surprisingly stylish and very comfortable YWCA (both sexes welcome) near Hyde Park, catering to solo travellers and groups. Standard and deluxe rooms are available, and facilities include a café, laundry and safe. Prices include a light breakfast, but there's no kitchen. $115

HOSTELS

BASE Backpackers 477 Kent St ☎1800 24 BASE, ⓦstayatbase.com; map pp.68–69. This huge, modern, 360-bed hostel is well set up with two TV rooms, laundry and kitchen. Well-furnished rooms and dorms (four-, six-, eight- and ten-bed) all have a/c with shared bathrooms. The women-only "Sanctuary" features hairdryers in the bathrooms, Aveda haircare products and feather pillows. Dorms $29; doubles $130

HAYMARKET AND AROUND CENTRAL STATION

HOTEL

Novotel Central Sydney 169–179 Thomas St, Haymarket ☎1800 252 588, ⓦnovotelsydneycentral .com.au; map p.80. This modern eighteen-storey tower with plain decor in a quiet street near Central Station and Chinatown is fronted by the charming nineteenth-century facade of the site's former hospital. A heated outdoor pool and spa, as well as a terrace garden with BBQ area, are further pluses. $135

HOSTELS

BIG 212 Elizabeth St, Haymarket ☎1800 212 244, ⓦbighostel.com; map p.80. Central, boutique-style hostel with well-equipped, sunny rooms – eight-bed dorms, an en-suite double and a family room – decorated in a contemporary style. The ground-floor lobby doubles as the common area with designer lounges and a high-tech guest kitchen to the side where the free buffet breakfast is served. There's also a great roof-terrace BBQ area, guest laundry and free bikes. Dorms $32, double $110

Sydney Central YHA 11–23 Rawson Place at Pitt St, opposite Central Station ☎02 9281 9111, ⓦyha .com.au; map p.80. A listed building transformed into a snazzy hostel with over 550 beds, which are almost always full, with spacious four- and six-bed dorms and private rooms (some en-suite). There are hotel-like facilities, but it still feels very sociable: a travel agency, rooftop pool, sauna and BBQ area are all on site, and movies are organized nightly. Dorms $40, doubles $118

★**Sydney Railway Square YHA** 8–10 Lee St (cnr Upper Carriage Lane & Lee St or entry via the Henry Deane Plaza) ☎02 9281 9666, ⓦyha.com.au; map p.80. This cute and unusual hostel is located in a historic packing shed right by Central Station, but feels surprisingly tucked away. Offers dorms, hotel-quality doubles, and there are even beds in burgundy-painted

1

CAMPSITES AROUND SYDNEY

Big cities usually offer few options for camping, but Sydney is an exception, with walk-in camping right in the middle of Sydney Harbour at Cockatoo Island, and several more distant drive-in sites. The four **campsites** and **caravan parks** listed below are the closest sites to the centre. Camping rates rise in the listed peak season; expect to pay $10 less in low season.

Cockatoo Island Camping Cockatoo Island, Sydney Harbour ☎02 8898 9774, ⓦwww.cockatooisland .gov.au; map pp.68–69. Arguably one of the world's most uniquely sited campsites, with magnificent views of the city across the water. Includes a campsite kitchen, BBQs, fridge, hot showers and access to the island's café. Glamping packages ($150) are available and include a tent, mattresses, chairs and a lantern. Prices rise by ten to twenty percent Fri–Sun. Access is via ferry on the Parramatta River service or Woolwich service (cars must be parked near one of the wharfs). Unpowered sites $45

Lane Cove River Tourist Park Plassey Rd, North Ryde, 14km northwest of the city ☎02 9888 9133, ⓦnationalparks.nsw.gov.au. Wonderful bush location beside Lane Cove National Park, right on the river, in Sydney's northern suburbs. Great facilities include a bush kitchen (with fridge), TV room, wi-fi and

pool. Train to Chatswood, then bus #545. Un/powered sites $37/39; en-suite cabins $155

Sheralee Tourist Caravan Park 88 Bryant St, Rockdale, 13km south of the city ☎02 9567 7161, ⓦsheraleetouristcaravanpark.com.au. Small, basic park, six blocks from Botany Bay, with good, clean facilities and friendly staff. Train to Rockdale station, then a 10min walk. Un/powered sites $35/40

Sydney Lakeside Holiday Park Lake Park Rd, Narrabeen, 26km north of the city ☎1800 008 845, ⓦsydneylakeside.com.au. Spacious campsite in a great spot by Narrabeen Lakes on Sydney's northern beaches, with camp kitchens and coin-operated gas BBQs, and only a 10min walk to the supermarket. Prices increase by twenty percent on peak holiday weekends. Bus #L90 from Railway Square by Central Station. Powered sites $58; en-suite sites $71

train carriages. Excellent communal areas make for a lively atmosphere, though it's not too party oriented. Dorms $32, doubles $96

wake up! 509 Pitt St, opposite Railway Square ☎02 9288 7888, ⓦwakeup.com.au; map p.80. Trendy mega-backpackers' complex with over five hundred beds. Highly styled, right down to the black-clad staff in the huge foyer, where you'll find internet terminals and a travel/jobs desk. Rooms are light and well furnished; only nine doubles are en suite. Dorms have lockers, there's a laundry on every floor and security is very good. Facilities include a café, bar and a huge modern kitchen. Pay wi-fi. Dorms $35, doubles $107

DARLING HARBOUR AND AROUND

Glasgow Arms 527 Harris St, Ultimo ☎02 9211 2354, ⓦglasgowarms.com.au; map pp.68–69. This pleasant pub has good-value accommodation upstairs. Polished-floor, a/c rooms with double-glazed windows keep out the bar noise. Light in-room breakfast included. $100

Vulcan Hotel 500 Wattle St, Ultimo ☎02 9211 3283, ⓦvulcanhotel.com.au; map pp.68–69. Classy reworking of a Heritage-listed 1894 former pub in a quiet part of Ultimo, but close to Darling Harbour. Smallish rooms in the old wing (some with bathtubs) and larger modern rooms are all decorated in muted tones and come with a/c and fridge, and some have kitchenettes. Breakfast (included if booked on their website) is served in the *Hummingbird* restaurant downstairs. $135

KINGS CROSS AND AROUND
HOTELS AND B&BS

Challis Lodge 21–23 Challis Ave, Potts Point ☎02 9358 5422, ⓦbudgethotelssydney.com; map p.89. An old renovated mansion with polished timber floors set on a quiet, tree-filled street a short walk from Woolloomooloo and Kings Cross. All rooms have TV, fridge and sink; there's a laundry but no kitchen. It looks rather more enticing online than in real life, but the rates are a bargain. $125

Hotel 59 59 Bayswater Rd, Kings Cross ☎02 9360 5900, ⓦhotel59.com.au; map p.89. Small hotel (just nine rooms), reminiscent of a pleasant European pension, with a friendly owner and small and very clean, if slightly dated, a/c rooms. A cooked breakfast (included) is served in the downstairs café. The good-value ($140) four-person family room has a small kitchenette and bathtub. Very popular – book in advance. $135

Kirketon 229 Darlinghurst Rd, Darlinghurst ☎1800 332 920, ⓦkirketon.com.au; map p.89. Fashionable place in an excellent location, with lovely staff, slick service and great restaurants (including several Asian ones) and cafés on the doorstep. $149

Ovolo Woolloomooloo 6 Cowper Wharf Rd, Woolloomooloo ☎02 9331 9000, ⓦovolohotels.com; map p.89. This luxury establishment has bags of colourful contemporary style and is located on the water's edge in a redeveloped wharf lined with fashionable cafés and restaurants. Eclectic rooms retain much of the building's original features; loft rooms boast city views. There's also a day-spa, indoor heated pool and gym. **$475**

HOSTELS

★**Blue Parrot Backpackers** 87 Macleay St, Potts Point ☎02 9356 4888, ⓦblueparrot.com.au; map p.89. A family-run 18–35s hostel in a great position in the trendy (and quieter) part of Potts Point, this converted mansion is sunny, airy and brightly painted. Rooms consist of mostly six- and eight-bed dorms. There's a common room with cable TV and gas fire, and the huge courtyard garden has wooden furniture and shady trees. Dorms **$39**

Eva's Backpackers 6–8 Orwell St, Potts Point ☎1800 802 517, ⓦevasbackpackers.com.au; map p.89. It's worth the extra couple of dollars to stay at this excellent, family-run hostel away from Darlinghurst Rd's clamour. Rooms and common areas are colourful and clean, and there's a peaceful rooftop garden with table umbrellas, greenery, BBQ area and fantastic views over The Domain. The guest kitchen/dining room, positioned at street level, feels like a café and has a sociable feel, though this isn't a "party" hostel. Dorms **$35**, doubles **$92**

The Original Backpackers Lodge 160–162 Victoria St, Kings Cross ☎1800 807 130, ⓦoriginalbackpackers .com.au; map p.89. In a spacious Victorian mansion with ornate ceilings, this upscale hostel tends to have a quieter clientele. All rooms have a TV and fridge and there are security lockers and a laundry available at the 24hr reception. A newer wing has small but stylish en-suite doubles. Dorms **$29**; doubles **$99**

PADDINGTON AND SURRY HILLS

★**ADGE Apartment Hotel** 222 Riley St, Surry Hills ☎02 8093 9888, ⓦadgehotel.com.au; map p.89. Technicolour, modern designer decor, friendly staff and nice details such as a free welcome drink and cosy slippers. Somewhere between a serviced apartment and a hotel, and highly recommended. **$379**

Arts Hotel 21 Oxford St, Paddington ☎02 9361 0211, ⓦartshotel.com.au; map pp.68–69. Medium-sized hotel in a trendy location, run by staff tuned into the local scene (free guided walking tour of Paddington included). Comfortable, modern en-suite rooms with TV. There's free (but limited) parking, as well as a garden courtyard and swimming pool, in-house movies, free guest bicycles, fitness room and laundry. The on-site café is open for a huge and delicious buffet breakfast for $20 per person. **$144**

City Crown Motel 289 Crown St, Surry Hills ☎1800 358 666 ⓦcitycrownmotel.com.au; map pp.68–69. Standard motel in a great location. The smart a/c units come with free in-house movies and the added

bonus of a large balcony looking onto Crown St. Limited parking. **$129**

GLEBE AND NEWTOWN

B&BS

★**Forsyth Bed and Breakfast** 3 Forsyth St, Glebe ☎02 9552 2110, ⓦforsythbnb.com; map p.94. A sweet Victorian brick-built villa with a cleverly modernized interior. The level of customer care is outstanding, and superb breakfasts (included) are served in the Japanese courtyard. There is a $15 loading for weekend stays, and $30 for single-night stays. **$195**

Newtown Darlington Suites 30 Golden Grove St, at Abercrombie St ☎02 8003 7333, ⓦbedbreakfastsydney .com.au; map p.96. Choose between two stylish apartments: the upstairs one has lofty ceilings and a roof garden, while the downstairs option features a grassed backyard with a wood-fired oven and BBQ. Free breakfast. Airport pick-up available at an additional cost. Apartments **$167**

HOSTELS

Billabong Gardens 5–22 Egan St, off King St, Newtown ☎02 9550 3236, ⓦbillabonggardens .com.au; map p.94. In a quiet street but close to the action, this long-running hostel is arranged around a peaceful inner courtyard with swimming pool, and has excellent communal facilities. Clean dorms (four- to six-bed, mostly en suite), as well as private rooms and motel-style en suites. Car park and wi-fi available for a fee. Dorms **$29**; doubles **$85**

Glebe Space 8 Missenden Rd, Camperdown ☎02 9697 3923, ⓦhotelspace.com.au/glebe; map p.94. On the fringe of the University of Sydney campus, this student accommodation, opened up for visitors, is handily positioned for Newtown and Glebe, and makes for a quirky budget option. There's a rooftop terrace, and rooms have kitchenettes. Most availability is during university holidays. **$115**

Glebe Village Backpackers 256 Glebe Point Rd, Glebe ☎02 9660 8133 or ☎1800 801 983, ⓦglebevillage. com; map p.94. Three large old houses with a mellow, friendly atmosphere – the laidback guests socialize in the streetside fairy-lit garden, and young local staff know what's going on around town. Dorms **$25**, doubles **$99**

Rooftop Travellers Lodge 146 Glebe Point Rd, Glebe ☎02 9660 7711, ⓦrooftoptravellerslodge .com.au; map p.94. This excellent-value budget retreat for short and long stays is right in the heart of Glebe. There's a large kitchen, while most rooms have a double and a single bed, a/c, and a PC with free unlimited broadband. Fabulous city views from the rooftop; parking included. Dorms **$25**

1

NORTH SHORE

★Cremorne Point Manor 6 Cremorne Rd, Cremorne Point ☎02 9953 7899, ⓦcremornepointmanor.com.au. Huge, restored Federation-style villa. Some rooms are en suite, while others have their own toilet and sink, and all have TV and fridge; some pricier rooms have harbour views. There's a communal kitchen and laundry facilities, plus a light breakfast is included. Ferry to Cremorne Point Wharf. $109

Glenferrie Lodge 12A Carabella St, Kirribilli ☎02 9955 1685, ⓦglenferrielodge.com. Another made-over Kirribilli mansion: clean, light and secure with 24hr reception. Single, double or family rooms (all shared bath). Some pricier rooms have their own balcony and harbour glimpses, but guests can also hang out in the garden and on the verandas. Ferry to Kirribilli Wharf or train to Milsons Point. Prices include breakfast. $95

BONDI BEACH

Bondi Beachouse YHA 63 Fletcher St ☎02 9365 2088, ⓦbondibeachouse.com.au. Actually nearer to peaceful Tamarama Beach than lively Bondi, but still close enough to the action, this well-run and fully equipped hostel has a sunny internal courtyard with BBQ, and a rooftop deck with fabulous ocean views. Spacious, high-ceilinged dorms (with lockers) and private rooms – some en suite, with fridges and kettles – all have ceiling fans. Free surfboards and body-boards. Book well ahead to get a beach-view room. Dorms $29, doubles $81

Noah's Bondi Beach 2 Campbell Parade ☎1800 226 662, ⓦwww.noahsbondibeach.com. Huge hostel right opposite the beach with spectacular ocean views from the rooftop deck and BBQ area. Clean and well run with beach-view private rooms and decent dorms, but cramped bathrooms. On-site bar with bargain meals, TV room and pool table. Excellent security. Dorms $27, doubles $70

Ravesi's 118 Campbell Parade, at Hall St ☎02 9365 4422, ⓦravesis.com.au. The first-floor restaurant and most of the twelve rooms at this boutique hotel have glorious ocean views. Minimalist interiors are very modern, and some rooms have French windows opening onto small balconies. $210

COOGEE

★DIVE 234 Arden St ☎02 9665 5538, ⓦthedivehotel.com. Wonderful sixteen-room hotel opposite the beach, with interiors that combine clean, modern lines with original Art Nouveau tiling and high, decorative plaster ceilings. Two larger rooms at the front have splendid sea views; one at the back has its own balcony and all have designer blue-tiled little bathrooms, cable TV, queen-size beds and a handy kitchenette. Breakfast included. $210

MANLY AND THE NORTHERN BEACHES

Ivanhoe House B&B 10 Birkley Rd, Manly ☎02 9977 6474, ⓦmanlybandb.com.au. Nestled in the green spaces of Manly, Ivanhoe makes for a peaceful place to rest yet is still a leisurely stroll from the action of Manly. $150

Novotel Manly Pacific Sydney 55 North Steyne, Manly ☎02 9977 7666, ⓦnovotelmanlypacific.com.au. Beachfront, multistorey, four-star hotel with 24hr reception and additional add-ons such as room service, spa, sauna, gym and heated rooftop pool. The ocean-view rooms are spectacular and worth forking out extra for. $259

Sydney Beachouse YHA 4 Collaroy St, Collaroy Beach ☎02 9981 1177, ⓦsydneybeachouse.com.au. Relaxed, purpose-built YHA across the road from the beach, with heated outdoor pool, sun deck, BBQs, open fireplaces, video lounge and games and pool rooms. Too far out for your entire Sydney stay (a 45min bus ride from the city), it's a good base for kicking back on the sand or exploring the northern beaches; bikes are free for guests, and kayaking and sailing can be organized. Bus #L90 from Railway Square by Central Station. Dorms $27, doubles $144

CRONULLA BEACH

Cronulla Beach YHA 40 Kingsway, Cronulla ☎02 9527 7772, ⓦcronullabeachyha.com. No-fuss working hostel in this unpretentious, surf-oriented suburb, 2min from the sand and even less to the shops and restaurants of Cronulla Mall. Also well situated for day-trips to the Royal National Park. Staff can help guests who have working holiday visas find employment. Dorms $32, doubles $105

EATING

If the fact that its chefs are regularly poached by restaurants overseas is any indication, Sydney has blossomed into one of the world's great culinary capitals, offering a wonderful range of cosmopolitan **restaurants**, covering every imaginable cuisine. For a personal touch, check out ⓦgrabyourfork.blogspot.com, a good foodie blog with lots of restaurant reviews. The many fascinating **ethnic** enclaves, representing the city's diverse communities, serve up authentic cuisines, including Jewish on Hall St, Bondi Beach; Chinese in Haymarket and Ashfield; Korean in Strathfield and on Pitt St in the CBD; Turkish and Indian on Cleveland St, Surry Hills; Italian in East Sydney, Leichhardt and Haberfield; Portuguese on New Canterbury Rd, Petersham; Greek in Brighton-Le-Sands; and Indonesian on Anzac Parade, in Kingsford and Kensington. Much further out, reached by train, Cabramatta is very much a Little Vietnam, as is Marrickville in the inner west.

THE CBD AND CIRCULAR QUAY

The cafés and food stalls in the business and shopping districts of the CBD cater mainly for lunchtime crowds, and

there are lots of food courts serving fast food and snacks. Check out the selection in the basements of the QVB, the Westfield Sydney, Quayside Shopping Centre on Alfred St,

1

TOP 5 VEGGIE/VEGGIE-FRIENDLY RESTAURANTS

Bodhi in the Park See below
Fair Trade Coffee Company See p.127
Green Gourmet See p.128
Mother Chu's Vegetarian Kitchen See p.124
Nepalese Kitchen See p.127

Circular Quay, Regent's Place between the George St cinema and Town Hall, Myers department store in Pitt Street Mall and the MLC Centre near Martin Place, but the classiest is the foodie's paradise in the basement of the David Jones department store on Market St. There are lots of great Italian espresso bars throughout the CBD, and many museums and tourist attractions also have surprisingly good cafés – notably the MCA, the Australian Museum, Hyde Park Barracks and the Art Gallery of New South Wales.

360 Bar and Dining Sydney Westfield Centre, Level 4/100 Market St, CBD ☏ 02 8223 3883, ⓦ trippaswhite group.com.au; map pp.68–69. A la carte restaurant with a spectacular revolving view from the Sydney Tower (two-course dinner $75–85, three-course $95). Excellent fresh produce and stylish modern Aussie cooking, with dishes such as pan-fried barramundi and roasted lamb rump. Daily noon–2pm & 5.30–9pm.

★**Bodhi in the Park** Cook & Phillip Park, 2–4 College St ☏ 02 9360 2523, ⓦ bodhi.id.au; map pp.68–69. Top-notch Chinese vegetarian and vegan *yum cha* ($6.50–8.50) using predominantly organic and biodynamic produce; faux Peking "duck" is a signature dish (mains $18–23). A good option near the Australian Museum, particularly on a sunny day when the outside seating is a treat; at night it's enchantingly candlelit. *Yum cha* daily 11am–4pm; dinner Tues–Sun 5–10pm.

★**Bennelong** Sydney Opera House, Bennelong Point ☏ 02 9241 1999, ⓦ bennelong.com.au; map pp.68–69. Australian chef Peter Gilmore took control of the Opera House's top-notch restaurant, located in one of the iconic building's renovated shells, in 2015; the huge windows provide stunning harbour views. If you're going to have one splash-out, romantic meal in Sydney, come here. The dishes (two-course lunch $100, three-course dinner $135) are equally Aussie, showcasing indigenous ingredients with a hint of multicultural Sydney, such as Fraser Island crabs with palm hearts over polenta. You can always just opt for a cocktail at the bar ($19–23). Daily 6.30–10pm, Fri–Sun also noon–2pm.

Jet Bar Caffe QVB, 455 George St, at Druitt St, CBD ☏ 02 9283 5004, ⓦ jetbarcaffe.com; map pp.68–69. Very lively Italian café-bar, on the corner of the QVB looking across to Town Hall, with big glass windows and outdoor seating providing people-watching opportunities. Coffee is predictably excellent, and the menu is big on breakfast ($12–21). The rest of the day, choose from pasta, risotto, soups, salads and sandwiches. Daily 7.30am–11pm.

Rossini Wharf 5, Circular Quay ☏ 02 9247 8026, ⓦ rossini.com.au; map pp.68–69. Quality alfresco Italian fast food while you're waiting for a ferry or just watching the quay. *Panzerotti* – big, cinnamon-flavoured and ricotta-filled doughnuts ($8.50) – are a speciality. Pricey but excellent coffee. Takes bookings. Daily 7am–9.30pm.

Sydney Cove Oyster Bar Circular Quay East ☏ 02 9247 2937, ⓦ sydneycoveoysterbar.com; map pp.68–69. This place is en route to the Opera House, and the quaint little building housing the bar and kitchen was once a public toilet, but don't let that put you off. The outdoor tables right on the water's edge provide a magical location to sample Sydney Rock Pacific oysters (around $25 a half-dozen), or just come for coffee, cake and the view. Mon–Fri 9am–late, Sat & Sun 8am–late.

Tetsuya's 529 Kent St, CBD ☏ 02 9267 2900, ⓦ tetsuyas.com; map p.80. Stylish premises – a Japanese timber interior and beautiful garden outside – and exquisite Japanese/French-style food created by the internationally renowned chef Tetsuya Wakuda. As Sydneysiders will attest, an evening here is a once-in-a-lifetime experience, and the month-long waiting list is worth it to sample the ten-course tasting menu ($230); wine teamed with each course starts from $75 (though it's also BYO). Tues–Fri 6–11pm, Sat noon–3pm & 6.30–11pm.

THE ROCKS

There are several good pubs in The Rocks (see p.131), many of which serve food, and some reasonably priced cafés with calm courtyards or street seating, as well as a choice of expensive restaurants, popular for business lunches.

Cafe Sydney Level 5 Customs House, 31 Alfred St, Circular Quay ☏ 02 9251 8683, ⓦ cafesydney.com; map p.72. The views of the Harbour Bridge and Opera House from the balcony are jaw-dropping, and the contemporary Australian cuisine with a seafood focus comes highly rated. Service is great and the atmosphere is fun (the Sun lunch jazz, acoustic and percussion session is popular). Mains such as tandoori-roasted Tasmanian ocean trout from $35. Mon–Fri noon–late, Sat 5pm–late, Sun noon–3pm.

★**La Renaissance** 47 Argyle St ☏ 02 9241 4878, ⓦ larenaissance.com.au; map p.72. Quite simply the best cake shop in Sydney. Try the Mousse Picasso or the shop's very own, tear-shaped creation Larme de Gaugin (both $10.50). The Parisian-style café is located in a historic sandstone building and has a large, cool courtyard. The service can be a little abrupt at times, but it is efficient and fast. Daily 8am–5.30pm.

Phillip's Foote 101 George St ☏ 02 9241 1485, ⓦ phillipsfoote.com.au; map p.72. Cook yourself a steak to your own taste in a Heritage-listed building, just up from

1

TOP 5 BREAKFAST OPTIONS

The Bathers Pavilion See p.128
bills See p.126
Café Mint See p.126
Fair Trade Coffee Company See p.127
Icebergs Bistro See p.130

Circular Quay. Meals are well priced: $30 for steak, all-you-can-eat salads, potatoes and bread. Mon–Sat noon–midnight, Sun noon–10pm.

Playfair Café Shop 21, The Rocks Centre, Playfair St; ☎ 02 9251 3317. map p.72. In a quaint old-meets-new pedestrian street, this small, stylish hole-in-the-wall with mod plastic outdoor seating beneath a perspex awning serves the best coffee in The Rocks. Also deals in tasty frittatas, sandwiches, wraps and burgers from $8. Daily 8am–5pm.

Sailors Thai Canteen 106 George St, The Rocks ☎ 02 9251 2466, ⊛ sailorsthai.com.au; map p.72. Cheaper version of the much-praised, pricey downstairs restaurant housed in the restored Sailors' Home. The ground-level canteen with a long stainless-steel communal table looks onto an open kitchen, where the chefs chop away to produce simple, delectable meals. Mains such as Isaan-style barbecued chicken marinated in ginger cost $24–38. Daily 5.30–10.30pm, Mon–Fri also noon–3pm.

HAYMARKET, CHINATOWN AND AROUND CENTRAL STATION

The southern end of George St and its backstreets have plenty of cheap restaurants of variable quality. Chinatown around the corner is a better bet: many places here specialize in *yum cha*, and there are several late-night eating options. Inexpensive Asian food courts are also common and serve authentic street-food style dishes, and a couple of blocks northeast of Chinatown there's an array of Spanish places on Liverpool St, almost all of them boisterous, though mostly geared towards tourists. Further along Liverpool St, up to Pitt St, the casual restaurants in Little Korea are booming.

Boon Cafe 425 Pitt St, Haymarket ☎ 02 9281 2114, ⊛ booncafe.com; map p.80. A modern Italian bistro serving Thai food, *Boon* whips up noodles and inventive sandwiches by day such as chicken, chilli squid and holy basil on sourdough ($14). Evenings delight with excellent Isaan flavours: punchy sourness and chilli explodes in thirteen types of *som dtum* (green papaya salads), including tasty dried shrimps ($13) or tastebud-daring snails with pork crackling and bamboo shoots ($15). There are plenty of (non-creamy) curries too ($14–20). Daily 8am–midnight.

Din Tai Fung World Square, 644 George St, Haymarket ☎ 02 9264 6010, ⊛ dintaifung.com.au; map p.80. If you have just one Sydney dumpling experience, make it here – you won't soon forget it. The delicious pork *xiao long bao*

(dumpling soup), delivered in a tasty broth, bursts in your mouth. Set in a shopping centre, the restaurant looks like a modern dining hall, so forget dragons and red velvet – but do expect a queue to get in. Mon–Wed & Sun 11.30am–9pm, Thurs–Sat 11.30am–10pm.

★**Mamak** 15 Goulburn St, Haymarket ☎ 02 9211 1668, ⊛ mamak.com.au; map p.80. There's often a queue at this budget Malaysian place, but you're kept entertained while you wait, as you watch the chefs whip up super-flaky *roti canai*. Share dishes such as tangy fish curry, stir-fried beans in shrimp paste or *nasi goreng* ($15–20), and leave space for the impressively conical sweet *roti* with ice cream ($8–10). BYO ($2 a bottle). Daily 11.30am–2.30pm & 5.30–10pm, Fri & Sat till 2am.

Market City Food Court Level 3, Market City Shopping Centre, above Paddy's Markets; map p.80. Almost entirely Asian cuisine at this bustling food court – Japanese, Chinese, Malaysian, Indian, Cambodian, Thai and Singaporean. Try the Korean "Seoul *bibimbap*" from Asago ($12). Daily 10am–7pm.

Mother Chu's Vegetarian Kitchen 367 Pitt St, Chinatown ⊛ motherchusvegetarian.com.au; map p.80. Inexpensive, Taiwanese-Buddhist cuisine, with heavy use of tempeh and mock meats, set in suitably plain surrounds, and – true to its name – family-run. Despite the absence of onion and garlic, the dishes ($9–17) are far from bland. No alcohol. Mon–Sat noon–3pm & 5–10pm.

Pasteur 709 George St, Haymarket; ☎ 02 9212 5622; map p.80. Popular Vietnamese cheapie specializing in *pho*, a rice-noodle soup, served with fresh herbs, lemon and bean sprouts. Most noodles (mainly pork, chicken and beef) are $12, and there's nothing over $15. Refreshing pot of jasmine tea included. BYO. Daily 10am–9.30pm.

DARLING HARBOUR AND AROUND

The Cockle Bay Wharf restaurant precinct is home to some excellent-quality food. Beyond Darling Harbour, you can eat well at the Sydney Fish Market.

Café Morso 108 Lower Deck, West Side Jones Bay Wharf, 26–32 Pirrama Rd, Pyrmont ☎ 02 9692 0111; map pp.68–69. Right on the harbourfront, offering fusion Italian lunch platters such as delicious salt-and-pepper squid in tamarind ($22) or beetroot cured salmon ($20). Mon–Fri 7am–3.30pm, Sat 9am–2.30pm, Sun 8am–3.30pm.

Fish Market Cafe Sydney Fish Market, Pyrmont ☎ 02 9660 4280; map pp.68–69. Located on the left-hand side after the entrance of the undercover market, this is the pick of the hawkers for its excellent-value seafood platter with Kilpatrick oysters, scallops, calamari and more (£35 for 2). Mon–Fri 4am–4pm, Sat & Sun 5am–5pm.

The Malaya 39 Lime St, King St Wharf, Darling Harbour ☎ 02 9279 1170, ⊛ themalaya.com.au; map pp.68–69.

Popular, veteran Chinese–Malaysian place in swish surrounds, serving some of the best and spiciest *laksa* ($29) in town. Mon–Fri noon–3pm & 6–11pm, Sat noon–3pm & 5.30–11pm, Sun 5.30–11pm only.

KINGS CROSS, POTTS POINT AND WOOLLOOMOOLOO

Many of the coffee shops and restaurants in "The Cross" cater for the tastes (and wallets) of the area's backpackers, though there are also increasing numbers of stylish restaurants, particularly in Potts Point. Several of the places in the Darlinghurst listings (see opposite) are only a few steps away.

Billy Kwong 1/28 Macleay St, Potts Point ☎02 9332 3300, ⓦbillykwong.com.au; map pp.89. Traditional Chinese cooking gets a stylish slant at this restaurant owned by celebrity chef Kylie Kwong. The space itself – all dark polished wood and Chinese antiques but brightly lit and with contemporary fittings – complements the often adventurous combination of dishes and flavours. Mains $23–46. Licensed and BYO ($10/bottle). Mon–Thurs 5.30–10pm, Fri & Sat 5.30–11pm, Sun noon–9pm.

Café Hernandez 60 Kings Cross Rd, Kings Cross ☎02 9331 2343, ⓦcafehernandez.com.au; map p.89. Veteran Argentinian-run all-hours coffee shop. Relaxed and friendly – you can linger for ages and no one will make you feel unwelcome. Spanish food is served – *churros*, tortilla ($8.50) and good pastries (from $7) – but the coffee is the focus. 24hr.

Fratelli Paradiso 12–16 Challis Ave, Potts Point ☎02 9357 1744, ⓦfratelliparadiso.com; map p.89. This place has everything, from gorgeous wallpaper and a dark furniture fit-out to flirty waiting staff and a diverse wine list. The moderately priced food is incredible – calamari, veal, pizzas and pastries (from $22) – with a blackboard menu that changes daily. Mon–Sat 7am–11pm, Sun 7am–10pm.

★Harry's Café de Wheels Cowper Wharf Rd, Woolloomooloo, ⓦharryscafedewheels.com.au; map p.89. Sometimes, there's nothing like a good old-fashioned pie, and this little cart has been serving them up since 1945. Some gourmet and vegetarian options have made it onto the menu, but the standard meat pie with mashed peas and gravy ($6.20) is still the favourite. Daily 9am–2am or later.

La Buvette 35 Challis Ave, Potts Point; ⓦfacebook .com/labuvette.pottspoint; map p.89. Hole-in-the-wall coffee shop with streetside seating usually packed with mid-morning caffeine-seekers. The blackboard menu features some yummy delicacies such as baked egg with spinach, sun-dried tomatoes, goat's cheese and caramelized onion or vanilla French toast brioche. Steak frites and wine or beer $25. Mon, Sat & Sun 7am–5pm, Tues–Fri 7am–10pm.

Otto The Wharf, 6 Cowper Wharf Rd, Woolloomooloo ☎02 9368 7488, ⓦottoristorante.com.au; map p.89. Trendy and glamorous, with a location not just by the water but *on* it. Exquisite Italian cuisine – very fresh seafood – coupled with friendly service and a lively atmosphere. Mains ($26–49) include vegan options such as battered courgette flowers. Daily noon–10.30pm.

DARLINGHURST AND EAST SYDNEY

South of Kings Cross, Darlinghurst's Victoria St has a thriving café and restaurant scene that spills west down the hill to East Sydney, focused on the intersection of Stanley St and Crown St. Once an Italian stronghold, it has now branched out. Further south you hit Oxford St, which is lined with restaurants, cafés and fast food from one end to the other. Taylor Square and its surroundings (the heart of the city's gay community) is a particularly busy area, with lots of ethnic restaurants and several pubs.

A Tavola 348 Victoria St, Darlinghurst ☎02 9331 7871, ⓦatavola.com.au; map p.89. Stylish Italian restaurant with a modern approach to traditional dishes selected from the daily blackboard menu. Mains (from $24) such as rabbit and home-made ravioli are supplemented by superb salads and desserts. Mon–Sat noon–3pm & 6–10.30pm.

Bar Coluzzi 322 Victoria St, Darlinghurst ☎0412 253 782; map p.89. Veteran Italian café that's almost a Sydney legend: tiny and always packed with a diverse crew of regulars spilling out onto wooden stools on the pavement and partaking in the standard menu of focaccias, muffins, bagels (all from $7) and, of course, coffee (reputedly Sydney's best). Daily 5am–7pm.

Bar Reggio 135 Crown St, East Sydney ☎02 9332 1129, ⓦbarreggio.com.au; map p.89. Hugely popular neighbourhood Italian joint serving good food (mains $15-30), like pasta with chilli mussels, in sizeable portions to an eager clientele. Not the place for a romantic dinner. BYO ($1 a head). Mon–Sat noon–11pm.

Bill and Toni 74 Stanley St, East Sydney ☎02 9360 4702, ⓦbillandtonis.com.au; map p.89. Cheap-and-cheerful Italian, where it's worth the queue up the stairs for the huge servings of simple home-made pasta and sauces (around $15). The café downstairs serves tasty Italian sandwiches (daily 6am–midnight). BYO. Daily noon–2.30pm & 6–10.30pm.

TOP 5 PIZZA JOINTS

Da Orazia Pizza and Porchetta See p.130
Delucas See p.149
Exchange Hotel See p.133
Love Supreme See p.126
The Oaks Hotel See box, p.130

1

★ **bills** 433 Liverpool St, Darlinghurst ☎ 02 9360 9631, ⓦ bills.com.au; map p.89. Owned by celebrity chef Bill Granger, this sunny corner café-restaurant in the quieter Darlinghurst backstreets is one of Sydney's favourite breakfast spots. Linger over ricotta hotcakes with honeycomb butter and banana ($22), muffins and newspapers. It's definitely worth a visit for breakfast (though expect to queue at weekends); the modern Australian lunches start at about $22. Mon–Sat 7.30am–3pm, Sun 8am–3pm.

The Commons 32 Burton St, Darlinghurst ☎ 02 9358 1487, ⓦ thecommons.com.au; map p.89. Cute wine bar and restaurant conveniently located just off Oxford St. The food is simple and tasty – the chicken parmigiana with leg ham, confit of cherry tomatoes and fresh mozzarella ($24) is delicious. It's popular, so you may need to wait downstairs at the cocktail bar – in itself a great place to visit. Tues & Wed 6pm–midnight, Thurs & Fri noon–3pm & 6pm– midnight, Sat & Sun 8.30am–3pm & 6pm–midnight.

Onde 346 Liverpool St, Darlinghurst ☎ 02 9331 8749, ⓦ onderestaurant.com; map p.89. People keep returning to this French-owned restaurant, on the corner of a Darlinghurst side street, which serves outstanding and very authentic bistro-style food, with mains (mostly $25–31) such as steak frites or confit of duck, plus a fish dish. Portions are generous, service excellent and desserts decadent. Daily 5.30pm–late.

Thai Nesia 243 Oxford St, Darlinghurst ☎ 02 9361 4817, ⓦ thainesia.com.au; map p.89. Ever-popular, low-key place serving delectable Thai dishes. Get the juices flowing with the betel leaf with prawn ($4) then choose from the likes of pumpkin chicken curry ($19) and roast duck salad ($23). It's great value and attracts a strong gay following. BYO ($2 a head). Daily 5.30–10.30pm.

Trunk Road 163 Crown St, Darlinghurst ☎ 0476 172 471, ⓦ trunkroad.com.au; map p.89. The main event here is naan bread with excellent Indian toppings such as butter chicken ($10) or lamb with spiced yoghurt ($12). These delicious snack-sized creations are made to go, thus the name, "roadies". If you want to eat in, take it slow with the curry of the day (5–9pm only) with pilau rice or *roti* ($18) and a sweet, rum lassi cocktail ($12). Tues–Thurs 5–10pm, Fri–Sun noon–3pm & 5–10pm.

PADDINGTON

Oxford St becomes gradually more upmarket as it heads east from the city through Paddington; the majority of restaurants here are attached to gracious old pubs, and most have had a complete culinary overhaul, now offering far more than the steak-and-two-veg option of times past.

Gusto Delicatessen 2A Heeley St, Five Ways, ☎ 02 9361 5640, ⓦ facebook.com/gustopaddo; map pp.68– 69. Sit at the breakfast bar at this relaxed local café to tuck into mushrooms on sourdough, a croissant and coffee or

one of the salads, quiches and cold meats from the counter; mains are around $14. Daily 6.30am–7pm.

Love Supreme 180 Oxford St ☎ 02 9331 1779, ⓦ lovesupreme.com.au; map pp.68–69. Delicious, thin-based pizzas (three sizes: $14, $19 & $25) served up in a sometimes frenetic atmosphere. Try Ya Basta! (ham, pumpkin, chilli and pecorino) with a rocket salad, followed by one of their delicious desserts. Always popular, this place can get pretty stifling on a hot day, when you may prefer to take away. Mon–Fri 5–11pm, Sat & Sun noon– 3pm & 5pm–midnight.

Royal Hotel Bar & Grill Royal Hotel, 237 Glenmore Rd, Five Ways ☎ 02 9331 2604, ⓦ royalhotel.com.au; map pp.68–69. Grand old triple-storey pub-restaurant serving some of the most mouthwatering steaks ($26–38) in Sydney. Eating on the veranda is a real treat, with views over the art gallery and Five Ways action below. Tables fill fast, and there are no bookings. There's also *Elephant Bar* upstairs (see p.133). Daily noon–3pm & 5.30–9.30pm.

SURRY HILLS AND REDFERN

Surry Hills' Crown St, and the streets running off either side, are home to numerous boho-chic cafés and some upmarket restaurants. At its southern end, Cleveland St, running west towards Central Station, is lined with Turkish, Lebanese and Indian restaurants, which are among the cheapest and most atmospheric in Sydney. And half a kilometre further south, cool Danks St is the focus of Waterloo's resurgence.

★ **Bourke Street Bakery** 633 Bourke St, Surry Hills ☎ 02 9699 1011, ⓦ bourkestreetbakery.com.au; map pp.68–69. Superb bakery-café with just three mini-tables inside, and some seats outside that catch the afternoon sun. Great for tucking into a chicken and lime-pickle pie ($5.50) or a pear and rhubarb muffin ($4.50). Mon–Fri 7am–6pm, Sat & Sun 7am–5pm.

Café Mint 579 Crown St, Surry Hills ☎ 02 9319 0848, ⓦ cafemint.com.au; map pp.68–69. Wonderful smart-casual café that gives a Mediterranean–Middle Eastern twist to the usual urban breakfasting scene. Try the beautifully presented Turkish breakfast of roast tomato, spinach, boiled egg, olives, grilled halloumi and *za'atar* toast ($16.90). At dinner you might tuck into spice-crusted lamb with charred cauliflower, pearl couscous and a pomegrante reduction ($26.50). No bookings; cash only. Daily 11am–3pm, Tues–Thurs & Sun also 5.30–10pm, Fri & Sat also 5.30–11pm.

Café Sopra Above Fratelli Fresh, 52 Mitchell Rd, Alexandria ☎ 02 9699 3174, ⓦ fratellifresh.com.au; map p.80. Amiable modern Italian café (part of *Fratelli Fresh* restaurant) serving dishes such as butternut, pumpkin, roast garlic and mozzarella risotto, and braised squid with peas and potatoes. Popular, and they don't take bookings, so aim for an off-peak time. Most mains $18–24. Daily noon–10pm.

Erciyes 409 Cleveland St, Surry Hills ☎ 02 9319 1309, ⓦ erciyesrestaurant.com.au; map pp.68–69. Among the offerings of this busy, family-run Turkish restaurant is delicious $15 *pide* – a bit like pizza – available with thirty different toppings, many vegetarian; there's a takeaway section, too. Reservations are essential on Fri & Sat nights, when there's belly-dancing. BYO. Daily 10.30am–11.30pm.

Il Baretto 496 Bourke St, Surry Hills ☎ 02 9361 6163, ⓦ ilbarettosydney.com; map pp.68–69. A small space with big, hearty Italian meals – the pappardelle with duck ragu ($27) is a must. Well-priced items and a BYO ($3 per person) policy make for an affordable experience. No bookings, cash only. The lovely *Fico Bar*, only a few doors down, is a great place to wait for your table. Tues–Sat noon–3pm & 6–10pm.

Longrain 85 Commonwealth St, Surry Hills ☎ 02 9280 2888, ⓦ longrain.com; map pp.68–69. Hip restaurant and bar in a converted warehouse on a quiet edge of Surry Hills. The contemporary Thai flavours are much raved-about – try the grilled octopus, black bean and persimmon – and dining is on three-long community-style wooden tables. Mains around $35. Mon–Fri 6–10pm, Sat & Sun 5.30–10pm.

Nepalese Kitchen 481 Crown St, Surry Hills ☎ 02 9319 4264; ⓦ nepalesekitchen.com.au; map pp.68–69. Peaceful establishment with cosy wooden furniture, religious wall hangings and traditional music. The speciality is goat curry, served with freshly cooked relishes that traditionally accompany the mild Nepalese dishes, and simple but delicious *momos* (stuffed handmade dumplings). There are vegetarian options and a lovely courtyard for warmer nights. Mains $12.50–19. BYO. Daily 5.30–10pm.

GLEBE

Glebe has a bit of everything: both cheap and upmarket restaurants, ethnic takeaways and delis. Glebe Point Rd is dominated by cafés – with a cluster of particularly good places at the Broadway end.

The Boathouse on Blackwattle Bay Coastal end of Ferry Rd ☎ 02 9518 9011, ⓦ boathouse.net.au; map p.94. Atmospheric restaurant above Sydney Women's Rowing Club, with wonderful views across the bay. Unsurprisingly, seafood is the thing here (and this is one of the best places to sample some), from the six different kinds of oysters to the raved-about snapper pie. Expensive, at $42–48 for mains, but worth it. Daily 6–11pm, Thurs–Sun also noon–3pm.

Darbar 134 Glebe Point Rd ☎ 02 9660 5666, ⓦ darbar .com.au; map p.94. A cavernous old sandstone building with stone pillars and arched doors and windows provides a gorgeous setting for a surprisingly inexpensive – but superb – Indian meal. Mains $18–24. Both licensed and

BYO. Daily 5.30–10pm, Wed–Sun also noon–2.30pm.

Fair Trade Coffee Company 33 Glebe Point Rd, ☎ 02 9660 0621, ⓦ fairtradecoffeecompany.com.au; map pp.68–69. Warm, earthy tones and a delightful ambience, with great music and vegetarian dishes from around the world – Colombia, Morocco, Indonesia and the Middle East are all featured, with nothing over $17. The all-day cooked breakfast is fantastic. Breakfast, lunch & dinner daily. Mon–Fri 6.30am–9.30pm, Sat & Sun 8.30am–10pm.

★**Glebe Point Diner** 407 Glebe Point Rd ☎ 02 9660 2646, ⓦ glebepointdiner.com.au; map p.94. Contemporary, upmarket dishes ($29–36) – try the duck "to share" for starters and save room for the amazing desserts. Reservations essential, with two sittings a night (6–6.30pm & 8–8.30pm). End the evening with a walk to the end of Glebe Point and see the city lights sparkle. Mon & Tues 6–9.30pm, Wed–Sun noon–2.30pm & 6–9.30pm, Sun noon–2.30pm.

Sappho Books & Café 51 Glebe Point Rd ⓦ sapphobooks.com.au; map pp.68–69. Colourful graffiti and murals (remnants of a grittier past) combine beautifully with rainforest plants, timber lattice side walls, parasols and a sail shelter in this quintessential Glebe courtyard café, joined to a secondhand bookstore. Great coffee is the focus here, but the panini ($9–13) and salads ($16–17) satisfy, and there is a long vegan menu – plus who could resist hot toasted banana bread with ricotta ($12)? Mon & Tues 8.30am–6.30pm, Wed–Sat 8.30am–11.30pm, Sun 9am–6.30pm.

NEWTOWN

On the other side of Sydney University from Glebe, King St and Enmore Rd in Newtown are lined with cafés, takeaways and restaurants of every ethnic persuasion, particularly Thai.

Black Star Pastry 277 Australia St, Newtown ☎ 02 9557 8656, ⓦ blackstarpastry.com.au; map p.94. Three words: strawberry watermelon cake. People travel (and queue) from afar for the delightful layers of fresh fruit, pistachios and dried rose petals in this exceptional dessert ($7.50). Other favourites include vegan chocolate cake topped with caramel popcorn and raspberries ($7) and savoury pies ($5.50). Savoury dishes $4–10. Daily 7am–5pm.

Bloodwood 416 King St ☎ 02 9557 7699, ⓦ bloodwoodnewtown.com; map p.94. Great food, decor and value at this mod-Oz restaurant. It's good for groups, with many dishes designed as "share plates" – polenta chips ($9) are a must, particularly with the gorgonzola dipping sauce. The trifle ($12) is a clear winner among the desserts. No bookings, so arrive early to avoid disappointment or a long wait. Mon–Fri 5pm–midnight, Sat noon–midnight, Sun noon–10pm.

1

Campos Coffee 193 Missenden Rd, just off King St ☎02 9516 3361, ⓦcamposcoffee.com; map p.94. Superb coffee (among the best in Sydney; around $5) is what this pocket-sized timber café does best – roasted, blended and ground in-house and served up to perfection by trained baristas. The only nibbles on offer are a few delicious biscuits and pastries. Mon–Fri 7am–4pm, Sat & Sun 8am–5pm.

Green Gourmet 115 King St ☎02 9519 5330, ⓦgreengourmet.com.au; map p.94. Loud and busy Chinese vegan place, which always has plenty of Asian customers, including the odd Buddhist monk. The devout Buddhist owner's creativity is reflected in the divine tofu variations on offer. Order off the menu (mains around $15), try the *yum cha* at weekend lunch, or get a taste of everything at the nightly buffet. The owners also run the excellent Vegan's Choice Grocery next door. Daily noon–3pm & 6–10pm, Fri & Sat noon–3pm & 6–11pm.

Oscillate Wildly 275 Australia St, Newtown ☎02 9517 4700, ⓦoscillatewildly.com.au; map p.94. Newtown has plenty of fine places to eat, but to treat yourself with some tasty contemporary cuisine, try the eight-course tasting menu here ($100; vegetarian available), which is exceptional, with unusual flavour combinations such as whiting with radish and squid ink. Tues–Sat 6.30–11pm.

Thai Pothong 294 King St, Newtown ☎02 9550 6277, ⓦthaipothong.com.au; map p.94. King St was home to over thirty Thai restaurants at its peak, but now a mere dozen or so remain. This kingdom-sized restaurant rules the competition, with its delicate decor fit for royalty and reliably good classic cuisine. Dishes tend towards sweet, but standouts like barramundi green mango salad ($25) and flash-fried tamarind prawns ($23) kick back with mouthwatering sourness. Mains $14–31. Daily noon–3pm, Mon–Thurs also 6–10.30pm, Fri & Sat also 6–11pm, Sun also 5.30–10pm.

THE HARBOUR

Military Rd, running from Neutral Bay to Mosman, has a string of good restaurants, mainly on the expensive side, but there are a number of tempting pastry shops and well-stocked delis. The intersection of Willoughby Rd and the Pacific Hwy in Crows Nest, north of North Sydney, also has a great range of options. At South Head, Watsons Bay is known for its famous seafood restaurant, *Doyles*.

The Bathers Pavilion 4 The Esplanade, Balmoral Beach ☎02 9969 5050, ⓦbatherspavilion.com.au. Indulgent beach-house-style dining in the former (1930s) changing rooms on Balmoral Beach. The very pricey restaurant and café double act is presided over by one of Sydney's top chefs, Serge Dansereau. Fixed-price menu (vegetarian available) in the restaurant is $115 for five courses. Weekend breakfast in the café is a North Shore

ritual – expect to queue to get in – while the wood-fired pizzas are popular later in the day. Daily noon–5pm & 6.30pm–midnight.

The Colonial 1/19 Grosvenor St, Neutral Bay ☎02 8068 6462, ⓦthecolonialrestaurant.com.au. The Indian dishes here have to pass the taste test of the local British community, and excel with nicely balanced lamb vindaloo ($20) and spicy okra ($16). Mon 5–10pm, Tues–Sun noon–10pm.

Doyles on the Beach and **Doyles Wharf Restaurant** 11 Marine Parade, Watsons Bay ☎02 9337 2007 (beach) ☎02 9337 1572 (wharf). The beach branch is the original of this long-running Sydney fish-restaurant institution, but both serve great (if overpriced at around $42 for mains) seafood and have wonderful views of the city across the water. The adjacent boozer offers pub versions in its beer garden, with slightly more affordable takeaway options. A ferry or water taxi can transport you from Circular Quay to Watsons Bay. Daily 5.30–9pm, Mon–Fri also noon–3pm, Sat & Sun also noon–4pm.

★**Radio Cairo** 83 Spofforth St, Cremorne ☎02 9908 2649. Oozing African exotica – with African art, crafts, artefacts and ornate brass-framed flat-screen monitors showing *Tarzan*, *Tin Tin* and *Casablanca* – this funky café, directly opposite the fabulous Orpheum cinema, features a creative and varied menu with a strong emphasis on African flavours – complemented by a superb selection of wines and cocktails (try the "Cosmic Cairo"). Mains $19–27. Licensed & BYO. Daily 6–11pm.

OCEAN BEACHES

Bondi is a cosmopolitan centre with the area's many Eastern European and Jewish residents giving its cafés a continental flair; there are also some excellent kosher restaurants, delis and cake shops. The Bondi Beach area is full of cheap takeaways, fish-and-chip shops and beer gardens, as well as some seriously trendy cafés and restaurants. South of Bondi, Bronte's beachfront café strip is wonderfully laidback, and Coogee has a thriving café scene, too. At the northern mouth of the harbour, Manly offers something for every taste and budget.

Barzura 62 Carr St, Coogee ☎02 9665 5546, ⓦbarzura .com.au. Fantastic spot, up close to the shore. Both a café and a fully fledged restaurant, with wholesome breakfast until 1pm, snacks until 7pm, and restaurant meals – such as seafood spaghetti or grilled kangaroo rump – served at lunch and dinner. Unpretentious, though stylish service encourages a large local crowd. Mains $24–35. Licensed & BYO. Daily 7.30am–11pm.

Clovelly Bowling Club 1 Ocean St, Clovelly Bay ☎02 9665 1507, ⓦclovellybowlingclub.com.au. Many a weary coastal walker has been relieved to see this unexpected rectangle of green lawn perched above the ocean. It must

1

have the best views of any lawn bowls club in the world, and drinks are sold at rock-bottom-prices. Barefoot bowls is $15 per person per game. Mon, Wed & Fri 10am–7.30pm, Tues & Thurs 9.30am–7.30pm, Sat & Sun 9am–7.30pm.

Da Orazio Pizza and Porchetta 3/75–79 Hall St, Bondi ☎02 8090 6969, ⓦdaorazio.com. Wood-fired, Neapolitan-style pizzas that give individual ingredients their time to shine are what draws happy customers here after a day at nearby Bondi beach. The *foccacia con porchetta* is a bonus – roasted pork and succulent eggplant stuffed into an indulgent marriage of pizza and sandwich. Mains $18–28. Mon–Fri 5pm–late, Sat & Sun noon–late.

Garfish 1/39 East Esplanade, Manly ☎02 9977 0707, ⓦgarfish.com.au. Blessed with a combination of stunning views across Manly beach and excellent seafood, Garfish is worth the extra bucks for fine fish and chips ($26) or jerk-spiced, grilled chicken ($30) and steaks. Mains $26–48. Mon–Sat noon–3pm & 5.30–10pm, Sun noon–3pm & 5.30–9pm.

Gertrude & Alice Cafe Bookstore 46 Hall St, Bondi Beach ☎02 9130 5155, ⓦgertrudeandalice.com.au. It's hard to decide if *Gertrude & Alice* is a café or a secondhand bookshop. With small tables crammed into every available space, a big communal table and a comfy couch to lounge on, it can be tough going for browsers to get to the books at busy café times. A homely hangout with

generous, affordable servings of Greek and Mediterranean food ($12–15), great cakes, even greater coffee and soy chai, and lots of conversation. Daily 7.30am–9.30pm.

★**Icebergs Bistro** 1 Notts Ave, Bondi Beach ☎02 9130 3120, ⓦicebergs.com.au. Effectively the clubrooms of the Icebergs swimming club, this straightforward bistro shares the fabulous view of the far flashier *Icebergs Dining Room* on the floor above. Just show a photo ID, sign in and settle down for a beer and everything from a fry-up breakfast to half a dozen oysters ($17) or roast duck with mango ($29). There are often cover bands playing at weekends. Mon–Sat 11am–9pm, Sat & Sun from 9am–9pm.

North Bondi Fish 120 Ramsgate Ave, North Bondi ☎02 9130 2155, ⓦnorthbondifish.com.au. This sprawling seafood restaurant offers the ideal combination of gorgeous beach views and wonderful food with a smart-casual vibe. The standard fish and chips ($29) show up, but the stars are in the twists, like whiting tacos or Moreton Bay bug linguine ($36). Buzzes on weekends. Daily noon–late.

Sabbaba 82 Hall St, Bondi ☎02 9365 7500, ⓦsabbaba .com.au. Excellent-value non-kosher Israeli-run café (*sabbaba* is Hebrew for "great" or "cool") in the heart of Bondi's small Jewish quarter. Great falafel (around $11), grilled chicken, salads, tabbouleh and a selection of gooey baklava made from all sorts of different nuts. Daily 11am–10pm.

DRINKING AND NIGHTLIFE

The differences between a **restaurant**, **bar**, **pub** and **nightclub** are often blurred in Sydney, and one establishment may be a combination of all these under one roof. Sydney's low-key, pub-dominated wilderness has disappeared in the inner city and you'll find a fashionable bar on almost every corner, offering everything from poetry readings and art classes to

---

LEGENDARY BEER GARDENS

Many Sydney pubs have an outdoor drinking area, perfect for enjoying the sunny weather – the five listed below, however, are outright legends.

Coogee Bay Hotel Arden St, Coogee ☎02 9315 6063, ⓦcoogeebayhotel.com.au. Loud, rowdy and crammed with backpackers, this enormous beer garden across from the beach is renowned in the eastern suburbs. The hotel has six bars in all, including a big-screen sports bar for all international sporting events. Revellers can buy jugs of beer and cook their own meat. Daily 9.30am till late.

Courthouse Hotel Australia St, Newtown ☎02 9519 8273, ⓦbit.ly/courthousesydney. A typical Australian pub at the front, and out the back a relaxed and inviting beer garden. It's a favourite local hangout, with modern pub cuisine. Mon–Sat 10am–midnight, Sun 10am–10pm.

The Newport Beaconsfield St, Newport ☎02 9997 4900, ⓦnewportarms.com.au. Famous beer-garden pub established in 1880, with a huge deck looking out

over Heron Cove at Pittwater. Good for families, with a children's play area. The bistro's range of pasta, pizza, grills and salads complements a large wine list. Mon–Wed & Sun 10am–11pm, Thurs–Sat 10am–midnight.

The Oaks Hotel 118 Military Rd, Neutral Bay ☎02 9953 5515, ⓦoakshotel.com.au. The North Shore's most popular pub takes its name from the huge oak tree that shades the entire beer garden. Cook your own (expensive) steak, or order a gourmet pizza from the restaurant inside. Mon–Sat 10am–midnight, Sun noon–midnight.

Watsons Bay Hotel 11 Marine Parade, Watsons Bay ☎02 9337 5444, ⓦwatsonsbayhotel.com.au. The beer garden here gives uninterrupted views across the harbour, which you can enjoy with fresh fish and chips from the renowned *Doyles* kitchen (see p.128) or a steak from the outdoor BBQ. Daily 7am–10pm.

LOCKOUT LAWS

Sydney's infamous **lockout laws** prevent punters from entering a bar or club after 1.30am, or buying drinks inside after 3am. The laws were supposedly implemented to curb drunken violence, but many see it as nanny-state action to protect the interests of The Star Casino, which is exempt from the laws. The zone covers the "Sydney CBD Entertainment Precinct", which stretches from parts of Surry Hills and Darlinghurst to the city and the Rocks, and from King's Cross to Cockle Bay. You cannot buy alcohol to take away after 10pm across the whole state. Full details at ⓦ nsw.gov.au/newlaws.

Sunday-afternoon jazz or DJ sessions. Surry Hills and Darlinghurst are the places to go for "pop-up" bars, as well as a variety of drinking holes for all tastes. Circular Quay and King Street Wharf are more touristy, yet have harbour views that even locals still savour now and again. Not to be outdone, the traditional hotels are getting in renowned chefs and putting on food far beyond the old pub grub. Sydney has many Art Deco pubs, a style notably seen in the tilework; we've included some of the best below. **Opening hours** vary considerably, and have been cut back due to the city's **lockout laws** (see box above): traditional pubs and beer gardens will be open 11am–11pm or later, while some cocktail bars may not open until the evening, closing at 2am (perhaps 4am or later at weekends).

BARS AND PUBS

THE CBD, CIRCULAR QUAY AND DARLING HARBOUR

Civic Hotel 388 Pitt St, cnr of Goulburn St, Haymarket ☎02 8267 3186, ⓦ civichotel.com.au; map p.80. Beautiful 1940s Art Deco-style pub, its original features in great condition. Upstairs, there's a glamorous dining room and cocktail bar. Handy meeting point for Chinatown and George St cinema trips. Daily 11am–3pm & 5–10pm.

Cohibar Harbourside Shopping Centre, Darling Harbour ☎02 9281 4440, ⓦ cohibar.com.au; map p.80. Classy cocktail bar across the water from the main Darling Harbour strip. The "cigar loft" is perfect for a leisurely Cohiba along with great city views. Limited bar food; DJs at weekends. Mon–Thurs noon–late, Fri–Sun 10am–late.

King St Brewhouse 22 The Promenade, King St Wharf ☎02 8270 7901, ⓦ kingstbrewhouse.com.au; map pp.68–69. Beer drinkers will enjoy a visit to this harbourfront bar as it serves the entire range of James Squires beer on tap and has a microbrewery on site, offering speciality brews. The food is also of a high standard and caters well for vegetarians. Daily 11am–late.

Marble Bar 259 Pitt St, CBD ☎02 9266 2000, ⓦ marblebarsydney.com.au; map pp.68–69. A sightseeing stop as well as a great place for a drink: this was the original 1893 basement bar of the *Tattersalls Hotel*, and the stunningly ornate *fin de siècle* interior is now encased within the 1973 *Hilton Hotel*. Drinks are modestly priced and there's free comedy or music most nights. Also check out the glamorous *Zeta Bar* on Level 4 of the same building. Mon–Thurs & Sun 4pm–12.30am, Fri & Sat 3pm–2am.

0 Bar Level 47, Australia Square, 264 George St, CBD ☎02 9247 7777, ⓦ obardining.com.au; map pp.68–69. The views from this stylish revolving bar are best when darkness falls and the city is dramatically lit up, with glimpses of the Harbour Bridge and Opera House, all seen from the 47th floor of Australia's first Manhattan-style skyscraper. The drinks list is very James Bond (try the delicious mandarin and orange blossom mojito, $22), and there's bar food. Open all night when custom justifies it. Daily 5pm–late, Fri from noon.

★**Opera Bar** Lower Concourse Level, Sydney Opera House ⓦ operabar.com.au; map pp.68–69. Stunningly located – a tiered deck beneath the Opera House sails – with alfresco bar, tables and stylish parasols overlooking the Quay, the Bridge and the harbour, and a sleek glass-walled interior – the *Opera Bar* is almost perfect (though drinks aren't cheap). Some of Sydney's best DJs and live music nightly from 8.30pm (2pm at weekends). The crowd is a pleasant mix of locals and visitors. Mon–Thurs 8am–midnight, Fri 8am–1am, Sat 9am–1am, Sun–9am–midnight.

Scruffy Murphy's 43 Goulburn St, CBD ☎02 9211 2002, ⓦ scruffymurphys.com.au; map p.80. Rowdy Irish pub with Guinness on tap, of course; phenomenally popular with travellers and expats, who come for some hearty home cooking, including $9 meal deals. 24hr.

Slip Inn 111 Sussex St ☎02 8295 9999, ⓦ merivale .com.au/slipinnevents; map pp.68–69. Now famous as the place where Mary Donaldson met her Prince Frederick of Denmark, this huge three-level place has several bars, a Mexican-inspired bistro and *The Chinese Laundry* nightclub, overlooking Darling Harbour. The front bars have a pool room, while downstairs a boisterous beer garden fills up on balmy nights, with the quieter, more sophisticated *Sand Bar* beside it. Excellent wine list, with lots available by the glass; bar food includes Thai. Mon–Fri noon–midnight, Sat noon–4am, Sun noon–10pm.

THE ROCKS

The Argyle 18 Argyle St ☎02 9247 5500, ⓦ theargylerocks.com; map p.72. A slick blend of the best of the past and the future in a vast, multi-zoned glass, stone and timber playground. Early nineteenth-century wool stores have been transformed with chic cubic furniture, sleek bars, impressive use of recycled timber and a suspended glass DJ booth. Numerous Bavarian beers and diverse food and cocktail menus. Mon–Wed & Sun 11am–midnight, Thurs 11am–1am, Fri & Sat 11am–3am.

Australian Hotel 100 Cumberland St ☎02 9241 3262, Ⓦaustralianheritagehotel.com; map p.72. This corner hotel is seemingly always full of visitors from around the world. Inside, original fittings give a lovely old-pub feel while convivial outside tables let you take in the neighbourhood's historic charm. Known and loved for its Bavarian-style draught beer brewed in Picton, plus delicious gourmet pizzas with extravagant toppings that extend to native animals – emu, kangaroo and crocodile ($21). Daily 10.30am–midnight.

Blu Bar Shangri-La Hotel, 176 Cumberland St ☎02 9250 6000, Ⓦshangri-la.com; map p.72. The top-floor bar of the five-star *Shangri-La Hotel* has a stunning 270-degree view – the Opera House, Darling Harbour, Middle Harbour and Homebush Bay to the Blue Mountains. The mega-expensive lounge is worth it for the view alone. Dress smart; cocktails are a must. Mon–Thurs 5pm–midnight, Fri & Sat 5pm–1am, Sun 5–11pm.

Cruise Bar Levels 1–3 Overseas Passenger Terminal, Circular Quay West ☎02 9251 1188, Ⓦcruisebar.com.au; map p.72. Glass walls and a cute patio make for stunning views of the Harbour Bridge and Opera House. A busy vibe on level 1 (especially on Fri & Sat); retreat to the next level for an excellent restaurant and cocktail lounge. Mon–Wed 11am–midnight, Thurs–Sun 11am–3am.

★**Hero of Waterloo** 81 Lower Fort St, Millers Point, The Rocks ☎02 9252 4553, Ⓦheroofwaterloo.com.au; map p.72. One of Sydney's oldest pubs, built in 1843 from sandstone dug out from the Argyle Cut, this place is redolent with history, the atmosphere enhanced by a complete absence of TV monitors and with blazing fireplaces in winter. There's live music almost nightly, from folk through to dirty blues, traditional Irish and jazz – check out the classic jazz quartet on weekend afternoons. Good, simple, hearty food is served in the pub, or upstairs in the elegant dining room: the Hero Burger is $17, fish'n'chips $22.50. Mon–Wed 10am–11.30pm, Thurs–Sat 10am–midnight, Sun 10am–10pm.

KINGS CROSS AND WOOLLOOMOOLOO

The Bourbon 24 Darlinghurst Rd, Kings Cross ☎02 9035 8888, Ⓦthebourbon.com.au; map p.89. Established in 1968 when it was frequented by US soldiers on R&R, this infamous late-opening Kings Cross restaurant and drinking hole has been given a swish look, which hasn't done much to deter some of its more colourful regulars. There's a terrace upstairs, a lounge bar out back, a happy hour (daily 6–9pm), live music every night and

all-day $10 steaks. Cover bands and DJs at weekends. This is one of only two bars in the area exempt from the Sydney lockout laws – you can enter after 1.30am, though no alcohol is served after that. Mon–Thurs & Sun 9am–4am, Fri & Sat 8am–6am.

Fei Jai Next Door 31 Challis Ave, Potts Point ☎02 8668 4424, Ⓦfeijai.com; map p.89. Where the beautiful people (and aspiring) sip and nibble. Not just a cocktail bar, but also an intimate, chic spot for fancy dumplings – prawn and scallop are nicely indulgent ($15). Try the "chinegroni" ($18): apricot gin and chai-infused vermouth with campari. Drinks $8–20. Mon–Fri 6–10pm, Sat & Sun noon–10pm.

Lo Lounge Ovolo Hotel, 6 Cowper Wharf Rd, Woolloomooloo Ⓦovolohotels.com; map p.89. Colourful and semi-industrial (but definitely classy) with retro touches like video-game machines, the large spaces of this bar are busiest 5.30–6.30pm, when hotel guests drink for free. Non-guests are welcome to come for cocktails ($19) or lager on tap ($7) and use the space as a fancy office on its superspeed wi-fi. Share some cumin eggplant with shaved macadamia and manchego ($22) or rosemary salt fries ($9). 24hr.

The Roosevelt 32 Orwell St, Potts Point ☎02 8096 1787, Ⓦtheroosevelt.com.au; map p.89. An oh-so-fancy nod to the Fifties and Sixties, this is the place to splash out on the pure theatre of a liquid nitrogen martini. If those cool flavours aren't smooth enough, there are oysters on hand too. Tues–Fri 5pm–midnight, Sat noon–midnight, Sun 3–10pm.

The Tilbury 12–18 Nicholson St, Woolloomooloo ☎02 9368 1955, Ⓦtilburyhotel.com.au; map p.89. Gentrified to the max, *The Tilbury* was once the stomping ground of sailors and the like. Now a light, airy hangout with mood lighting and tonnes of outdoor space, it attracts a relaxed yet stylish crowd for after-work drinks and regular BBQ evenings. Mon–Thurs & Sun 11am–10pm, Fri & Sat 11am–midnight.

DARLINGHURST, PADDINGTON AND SURRY HILLS

Clock Hotel 470 Crown St, Surry Hills ☎02 9331 5333, Ⓦclockhotel.com.au; map pp.68–69. Classy former pub with fashionable clientele draped around the chocolate-coloured lounge bar and filling the booths and tables downstairs. It's popular for after-work drinks, and the restaurant really excels, with prime position seating on the veranda and a satisfying menu of burgers, pasta and risotto dishes (mains $19–28) with plenty of creative touches; tapas are available too. Daily noon–midnight.

Darlo Bar 306 Liverpool St, Darlinghurst ☎02 9331 3672, Ⓦdarlobar.com.au; map p.89. Popular meeting place with a lounge-room atmosphere. Comfy colourful chairs and sofas have a 1950s feel, but there aren't enough to accommodate the mixed and unpretentious crowd who are there to play pool or just curl up under the lamps and chat. Bottles of wine start at $30, and cocktails cost $18; beers from $5 in happy hour (4–7pm). At night, you can order from the menus of local restaurants (Thai, pizza, etc), and they'll fetch the food for you. Daily 10am–midnight.

Eau de Vie 229 Darlinghurst Rd, Darlinghurst ☎ 02 9331 2604, ⓦ eaudevie.com.au; map pp.89. Part theatre, part secret club, this leather-and-dark-wood bar is a cocktail extravaganza, conjuring magic from over five hundred spirits. Arty creations include the Kentucky Kickstarter, a bacon-infused bourbon with ice cream, and bitters in a glass milk carton. Cocktails $19–24. Mon–Sat 6pm–1am, Sun 6pm–midnight.

Elephant Bar Royal Hotel, 237 Glenmore Rd, Paddington ☎ 02 9331 2604, ⓦ royalhotel.com.au; map pp.68–69. The top-floor bar of this beautifully renovated, Victorian-era hotel has knockout views of the city, best appreciated at sunset (and happy hour is 5.30–6.30pm). The small interior is great, too, with its fireplaces, paintings and elephant prints. As it gets crowded later on, people pack onto the stairwell, creating a party atmosphere. Mon–Sat 10am–midnight, Sun 11am–10pm.

Green Park Hotel 360 Victoria St, Darlinghurst ☎ 02 9380 5311, ⓦ greenparkhotel.com.au; map p.89. A Darlinghurst stalwart, partly because of the pool tables in the back room, but mainly thanks to the unpretentious vibe. The bar couldn't be more unassuming; there's nothing decorating the walls, and humble bar tables with stools and a few lounges out back accommodate the regular arty crowd. Very popular with gay men on Sun evening. Mon–Wed 11am–midnight, Thurs–Sat 11am–2am, Sun noon–midnight.

★**The Winery** 285A Crown St, Surry Hills ☎ 02 9331 0833, ⓦ thewinerysurryhills.com.au; map pp.69–69. A whimsical and wine-focused venue offering the likes of Peacock Spritz (gin, Prosecco and muscat, $15). Great in the afternoon with its kitsch courtyard and city skyline views. Excellent nosh, too, with seafood, meaty and vegan options (mains $25–44). The hardest part is finding a table. Daily noon–midnight.

INNER WEST: GLEBE, NEWTOWN AND BALMAIN

AB Hotel 225 Glebe Point Rd, Glebe ☎ 02 9660 1417, ⓦ abhotel.com.au; map p.94. This lively pub, popular with the area's travellers, is a stylish boozer, with a sleek upstairs "Pacific Penthouse" area sporting the world's largest fish-tank bar, professional poker tournaments (Thurs, Fri & Sat), DJs on weekend nights, live jazz, soul and blues on Thurs night and world music on Sun afternoon. The food is Asian and mod-Oz (check out the $7.50–12 "value meals") and goes down well in the Spanish-style courtyard. Mon–Sat 10am–midnight, Sun 10am–10pm.

Bank Hotel 324 King St, next to Newtown station ☎ 02 8568 1900, ⓦ bankhotel.com.au; map p.94. Smart-looking pub open late and always packed with local arty residents and visiting musos. Upstairs, the stylish Velvet Room, with a side deck for smokers, is usually good for a dance and has lesbian nights on Wed, while downstairs, the cocktail bar leads out to timber decking, lovely in summer. Modern pub food, such as roasted-prawn flatbread pizzas ($23) and spinach empanadas ($17), is served in the leafy beer garden below. Mon–Wed 11am–1am, Thurs 11am–2am, Fri & Sat 11am–4am, Sun 11am–midnight.

Exchange Hotel 94 Beattie St, at Mullens St, Balmain ☎ 02 8755 2555, ⓦ exchangehotel.com.au; map p.94. This classic Balmain backstreet corner pub, built in 1885 and popular with the locals, has a stylish and comfortably furnished wrought-iron balcony upstairs. Relax with a beer or combine a hearty breakfast with a Bloody Mary on the balcony at the "Bloody Mary Breakfast Club" on Sat and Sun (10am–3pm). The gourmet pizzas are also popular. Mon–Sat 8am–11pm, Sun 8am–10pm.

Friend in Hand 58 Cowper St, Glebe ☎ 02 9660 2326, ⓦ friendinhand.com.au; map pp.68–69. A fun, popular backpacker haunt in the leafy backstreets of Glebe, with all manner of curious objects dangling from the walls and ceilings. Diverse entertainment takes place in the upstairs bar (where you can also play pool), from poetry to stand-up comedy and crab-racing nights – call to check what's on. There's also a good bistro with daily specials; try the fish of the day on Thurs ($12). Mon–Fri 8am–midnight, Sat 10am–midnight, Sun 10am–10pm.

Kuletos 157 King St, Newtown ☎ 02 9519 6369, ⓦ kuletos.com.au; map p.94. From 6 to 7.30pm on a weeknight, *Kuletos* is the best place to be on King St, packed with locals and university students for its Cocktail Happy Hour (Mon–Sat 5.30–7.30pm). The bar on level 1 is more relaxed, and the place is a gaming-free zone. Daily 4pm–late.

London Hotel 234 Darling St, Balmain ☎ 02 9555 1377, ⓦ londonhotel.com.au. A long-time favourite with locals, this cosy pub offers a distant view of the Sydney Harbour Bridge from the balcony. Inside, at the back, biodynamic steaks ($34–44) are served in the classy dining area. Mon–Sat 11am–midnight, Sun 11.30am–10pm.

OCEAN BEACHES

4 Pines Brewing Company 43 The Esplanade, Manly ☎ 02 9976 2300, ⓦ 4pinesbeer.com.au. Slick yet casual bar with polished concrete floors, recycled timber tables and a harbour-view deck. Its own microbrewery produces toothsome handcrafted beers, typically including a pale ale, a bitter, a Hefeweizen and a Kölsch (light ale from Cologne), plus seasonal brews. Good, modern bar meals for around $20. Daily 11am–midnight.

1

Coogee Pavillion 169 Dolphin St, Coogee ☎02 9240 3000, Ⓦmerivale.com.au/coogeepavilion. In its heyday, this hotel had a gigantic dance floor that could accommodate three thousand pleasure-seekers; today it's is a popular drinking spot for a young and drunken crowd, made up of locals, beach babes and backpackers, who crowd out its oceanfront balcony. Five bars, two restaurants and a great view of the beach from the balcony under the distinctive dome. Daily 11am–late.

Bondi Icebergs Club 1 Notts Ave, Bondi Beach Ⓦicebergs.com.au. Famous for its winter swimming club, *Icebergs* is a delightful place to sip a beer on the balcony and soak up the views and atmosphere of Bondi Beach. The bistro within the club serves mussels ($21), Porterhouse steak, salad and chips ($29), burgers and more. Cover bands often play at weekends. Daily 11am–late.

Manly Wharf Hotel Manly Wharf, Manly ☎02 9977 1266, Ⓦmanlywharfhotel.com.au. Modern, light and airy pub that makes a great spot to catch the afternoon sun and sunset over the city. With four bars, there's something to suit everyone, including the *Harbour Bar* restaurant serving great seafood, grills ($20–32) and pizza ($22–24). Mon–Fri 11.30am–midnight, Sat 11am–1am, Sun 11am–midnight.

LIVE MUSIC

The live-music scene in Sydney has passed its boom time, and pub venues keep closing down to make way for the dreaded poker machines. However, there are still enough venues to just barely nourish a steady stream of local, interstate and overseas acts passing through, peaking in summer with a well-established open-air festival circuit. Bands in pubs and clubs are often free, especially if you arrive early; door charge is usually from $5, with $30 the top price for smaller international acts or the latest interstate

sensation. Sunday afternoon and early evening is a mellow time to catch some music, particularly jazz, around town.

The Basement 29 Reiby Place, Circular Quay ☎02 9251 2797, Ⓦthebasement.com.au; map pp.68–69. This dark and moody venue attracts the great and rising names in jazz, funk, acoustic and world music, as well as a roster of the world's most renowned blues performers. To take in a show, book a table and dine in front of the low stage; otherwise, you'll have to stand all night at the bar at the back.

Bridge Hotel 119 Victoria Rd, Rozelle ☎02 9810 1260, Ⓦfacebook.com/thebridgehotel; map p.94. Legendary inner-west venue specializing in blues, jazz and pub rock, with the occasional big international act (B.B. King and Jon Cleary have played here), but mostly hosting local performers. Laidback, no-frills atmosphere.

Enmore Theatre 130 Enmore Rd, Newtown Ⓦenmoretheatre.com.au; map p.94. Atmospheric venue that's one of Australia's oldest. All seating has a decent view of the stage, and performers include well-known Australian/ international rock bands, hip-hop acts and comedians.

Metro Theatre 624 George St, CBD Ⓦmetrotheatre .com.au; map p.80. One of Sydney's best live-music venues, situated in the heart of George St's bustling entertainment district and hosting many international and Australian acts. Arrive early to get a seat in the gallery, as floor space is limited.

Oxford Art Factory 38–46 Oxford St, Darlinghurst ☎02 9332 3711, Ⓦoxfordartfactory.com; map pp.68–69. Andy Warhol-inspired cultural hub and arts space with an industrial feel. As well as running a bar and cutting-edge art gallery, it puts on a vast range of shows – from album launches and avant-garde plays to gigs and DJ nights.

Rose of Australia Hotel 1 Swanson St, Erskineville ☎02 9565 1441, Ⓦroseofaustralia.com; map p.94. Trendy inner-city types mix with goths, locals and gays to sample

---

ENTERTAINMENT AND NIGHTLIFE LISTINGS

To find out **what's on** in Sydney, get Friday's *Sydney Morning Herald*, which offers a weekly entertainment supplement, also online Ⓦsmh.com.au/entertainment. In addition to this and the rather bland tourist monthlies, there is a plethora of **free listings magazines** for more alternative goings-on – clubbing, bands, fashion, padding and the like – which can be found in the cafés, record shops and boutiques of Bondi, Paddington, Darlinghurst, Glebe, Newtown and Kings Cross: these include *The Brag* (Ⓦthebrag.com) and *The Music* (Ⓦthemusic.com.au), with their weekly band listings and reviews. *City Hub*, a politically aware, free weekly newspaper, also has excellent events listings, and the monthly *Time Out Sydney* (Ⓦau.timeout. com/sydney) has listings and plenty of ideas on how to spend your time. The official Sydney website (Ⓦsydney.com) has details of film, theatre and music events.

BOOKING AGENCIES

The main **booking agencies** are Ticketek (outlets at Hum, 55 Oxford St; Ticketek@Park, 50 Park St, and the Theatre Royal; ☎13 28 49, Ⓦticketek.com.au), Ticketmaster (outlets include the State Theatre, Market St, and CBD; ☎13 61 00, Ⓦticketmaster.com.au) and Moshtix (outlets at Utopia Records, 233 Broadway; and The Music Shop, Shop 5050, Level 5, Westfield, 500 Oxford St, Bondi Junction; ☎1300 438 849, Ⓦmoshtix.com.au).

OUTDOOR MUSIC FESTIVALS

Sydney loves to party, nowhere more so than at these **outdoor music festivals** . We list other festivals separately (see box, pp.142–143).

Field Day This long-running, one-day indie and dance music festival ($147; ⓦfieldday.sydney), taking place on New Year's Day, has seen recent acts such as Broods, MØ, and Australian Alison Wonderland in the Domain.

Good Vibrations (mid-Feb; around $100; ⓦfacebook.com/goodvibrationstx). A one-day dance/hip-hop festival held at Centennial Park.

Laneway Festival Held across four stages in Callan Park in Rozelle for one day (around $165; ⓦsydney.lanewayfestival.com). Lots of smaller acts and left-field (if non-political), unconvential musicians have played here, like Beach House, Grimes, Shamir and Vince Staples.

Newtown Festival With three stages, two hundred stalls and varied live music, this event is held at the Camperdown Memorial Park on the second Sunday of November (ⓦnewtownfestival.org)

some favourites of the pub circuit. Line-up changes regularly, and there are no set days for performances (check the free magazine *The Music*). Catch anything from an original rock act through to a country-and-western cover band; music is from 9pm and usually free.

Newtown Social Club 387 King St, Newtown ☎02 9557 1254, map p.94. The former "Sando" Sandringham Hotel continues a long tradition of promoting local and interstate indie bands, who play on the stage upstairs ($15–25; big shows $25) or the "Ground Floor" stage downstairs, next to a cosy cocktail lounge. There is also a fancy meatballs menu. Mon–Thurs 4pm–late, Fri & Sat noon–2am, Sun noon–10pm.

The Vanguard 42 King St, Newtown ☎02 9557 7992, ⓦthevanguard.com.au; map p.94. Billed as bringing jazz, blues and roots to Newtown, this 1920s-style venue – resplendent in racy crimson – with restaurant and cocktail bar, attracts some important international acts, plus some excellent raw local talent. Most acts play from 7pm till 11.45pm.

Venue 505 280 Cleveland St, Surry Hills ⓦvenue505 .com; map p.80. Jazz, roots, reggae, funk, gypsy, Latin, instrumental and vocal entertainment, with a focus on supporting local artists.

CLUBS

From dark den to opulent fantasy, Sydney's thriving club scene, attracting international DJ celebrities and impressive local talent, is likely to satisfy. A long strip of clubs stretches from Kings Cross to Oxford St and down towards Hyde Park. The scene can be pretty snobby, with door gorillas frequently vetting your style, so don your finest threads and spruce up. Along with the places listed below, most of the clubs in our LGBT listings (see box, pp.136–137) have a fairly mixed clientele. Admission ranges from $10 to $30; many clubs stay open until 5am or 6am on Sat and Sun mornings. Be aware, however, that this area is covered by the lockout laws and last entry is 1.30am, so plan your bar-hopping early. There are also good clubs attached to several of the drinking spots

listed in the bars and pubs section (see p.130). Here we list the bigger venues or places with something unusual to offer.

★**Candy's Apartment** 22 Bayswater Rd, Kings Cross ☎02 9380 5600, ⓦcandys.com.au; map p.89. One of the loudest places in town, this music portal transforms itself every night with the coolest DJs playing gigs early and then churning out fresh dance mixes as the night progresses. $10–20. Wed–Sun 10pm–4am.

Home 101/1–5 Wheat Rd, Darling Harbour ⓦhomesydney.com; map pp.68–69. The first really big club venture in Sydney, lavish *Home* can cram two thousand punters into its cool, cavernous interior. There's also a mezzanine, a chill-out room, and outdoor balconies. Decks are often manned by big-name DJs, drinks are expensive, and staff beautiful. Packed with a younger crowd on Fri for its flagship night "Sublime", with four musical genres across four levels. On Sat, "Homemade" plays progressive and funky house. $25–35. Fri & Sat 11pm till late.

The Ivy 330 George St, CBD ⓦmerivale.com.au/ivy; map pp.68–69. With several distinct areas spread over different levels, and draped around a central courtyard, *The Ivy* is unashamedly extravagant – men must wear blazers at weekends – and comprises a grill restaurant, a Japanese eatery, a lounge space and the dramatic, turquoise-walled Den where DJs play. Check the website for the specific opening times of various areas. Mon–Fri noon–late, Sat 6.30pm–late.

The World Bar 24 Bayswater Rd, Kings Cross ⓦtheworldbar.com; map, p.89. With a relatively relaxed door policy, *The World Bar* is popular with a fun, party-loving crowd of travellers, who move to different sounds each night – funk, jazz, Latin, dub, cabaret, live bands – in a pleasant Victorian-era building with a big front balcony. Daily 2pm–7am.

LGBT BARS AND CLUBS

The last few years have seen a quiet diminishing of specifically gay and lesbian bars, and due to Sydney's restrictive licensing laws, the smaller venues vanish and

1

the large ones just get bigger. The city's LGBT scene (see box below) is concentrated in two areas, so it's easy to bar-hop (as long as it's before the 1.30am lockout laws in the inner east): in the inner east around Oxford St, Darlinghurst, including Surry Hills and Kings Cross, and in the inner west in adjoining Newtown and Erskineville. Those wanting a comfortable place to drink with a mixed clientele should also check out pubs such as the *Green Park Hotel* (see p.133). Entry is free unless otherwise indicated.

Arq 16 Flinders St, at Taylor Square, Darlinghurst ⓦarqsydney.com.au; map pp.68–69. Huge, state-of-the-art mainstream club with everything from DJs and drag shows to pool competitions. The "Arena", on the top floor, is mostly gay, while the ground-floor "Vortex" is a quieter, less crowded mix of gay and straight, with pool tables. Chill-out booths, laser lighting, viewing decks and fish tanks add to the fun, friendly atmosphere. Sat and Sun are the big nights. Check website for events. Fri $10, Sat $15 before 11pm ($25 after), Sun $5. Thurs–Sun from 9pm.

Colombian Hotel 117 Oxford St, at Crown St, Darlinghurst ⓦcolombian.com.au; map p.89. Mixed-clientele bar where people come to get revved up in the evenings and renew their energy the day after. The downstairs bar offers an airy, comfortable space to drink, dance and chat, with open windows onto the street. Upstairs, there's a more intimate cocktail bar featuring a giant red tribal mask. Different DJs and musical styles (Wed–Sun), from R&B to funky house and drag-cum-variety nights Wed & Thurs. Thurs is glamour night in the cocktail lounge. Retro cool but not pretentious. Thurs–Sun 9pm till late.

Stonewall Hotel 175 Oxford St, at Taylor Square, Darlinghurst ☎02 9360 1963, ⓦstonewallhotel.com; map pp.68–69. With three action-packed levels, this pub is a big hit with young gay and lesbian punters and their straight friends – it gets packed out on weekends. Every night is a different event, such as Tues Karaoke, Fri drag shows and Sat Madonna tribute shows. The music is generally the usual commercial dance and house. Mon–Fri noon–6am, Sat & Sun 9am–6am.

LGBT SYDNEY

Sydney is indisputably one of the world's great gay cities. There's something for everyone – whether you want to lie on a beach during the warmer months or party hard year-round. You'll see same-sex couples walking hand in hand on the streets, particularly in the inner-city and eastern areas. In fact, in recent years there has been a decline in gay-specific bars and clubs, as bars have evolved to become generally more mixed and gay-friendly.

Even if you can't be here for Mardi Gras (see below), you'll still find the city has much to offer. **Oxford Street** (mostly around Taylor Square) is Sydney's official "pink strip" of gay-frequented restaurants, coffee shops, bookshops and bars. However, the gay–straight divide in Sydney has less relevance for the younger generation, perhaps as a result of Mardi Gras' mainstream success. Several of the long-running gay venues on and around Oxford Street have closed down and many of those remaining attract older customers, as younger gays and lesbians embrace inclusiveness and party with their straight friends and peers or choose to meet new friends in apps instead of in bars. **King Street**, Newtown and nearby **Erskineville** are quieter centres of gay culture, while lesbian communities have carved out territory of their own in **Leichhardt** (known affectionately as "Dykehart") and **Marrickville**.

Little of the **accommodation** in Sydney is gay-exclusive, but anywhere within a stone's throw of Taylor Square will be very gay-friendly. Best bets in our accommodation listings are *City Crown Motel* (see p.121), *Kirketon* (see p.120), *Arts Hotel* (see p.121) and the *BIG* hostel (see p.119). Most of the cafés and **restaurants** in the same area have a strong gay following. Weekly event listings are included in the free magazines.

If you've come for the sun, popular **gay beaches** are Tamarama (see p.104), Bondi (see p.119) and "clothing-optional" Lady Jane, while swimming pools of choice are Redleaf harbour pool at Double Bay (see p.98) and the appropriately named Andrew "Boy" Charlton pool in The Domain (see p.84). The Coogee Women's Pool, at the southern end of Coogee Beach (see p.105), are popular with lesbians.

MARDI GRAS

The year's highlight is the **Sydney Gay & Lesbian Mardi Gras** (☎02 9568 8600, ⓦmardigras .org.au): three weeks of exhibitions, performances and other events, including the **Mardi Gras Film Festival** (ⓦqueerscreen.com.au), showcasing the latest in queer cinema. Mardi Gras starts the second week of **February**, kicking off with a free Fair Day in Victoria Park, Camperdown, and culminating with a massive parade and party, usually on the first weekend of March. The first parade was held in 1978 as a gay-rights protest, and today it's the biggest

CLASSICAL MUSIC, THEATRE, DANCE AND COMEDY

Sydney's **arts scene** is vibrant and varied. The Sydney Symphony Orchestra plays at the Opera House, and sometimes at the City Recital Hall, while the Australian Ballet performs at the Opera House and the Capitol Theatre. The Sydney Theatre and Dance companies are located centrally in The Rocks, and with the many new restaurants and bars in the area, create a good night out. The free outdoor performances in The Domain, under the auspices of the Sydney Festival, are one of the year's highlights, with crowds gathering to enjoy the music with a picnic. Sydney's Comedy Festival held in April showcases a number of local and international acts. Try also the *Friend In Hand* pub (see p.133), which has Thursday comedy nights.

Bangarra Dance Theatre Pier 4, Hickson Rd, Millers Point, The Rocks ☎02 9251 533, ⓦbangarra.com.au. Formed in 1989, Bangarra's innovative style fuses contemporary movement with the traditional dances and culture of the Yirrkala Community in the Northern Territory's Arnhem Land. Although based here, the company performs at other venues in Sydney and tours nationally and internationally.

Belvoir St Theatre 25 Belvoir St, Surry Hills ☎02 9699 3444, ⓦbelvoir.com.au. Highly regarded two-stage venue for a wide range of contemporary Australian and international theatre, as well as the reworking of many classics. Great ambience and strong theatrical work. If you are going to see one piece of theatre while in Sydney, see it here.

Capitol Theatre 13 Campbell St, Haymarket ☎02 8512 9020, ⓦcapitoltheatre.com.au. One of the oldest theatres in Sydney with an atmospheric interior, staging mainly musical theatre.

City Recital Hall Angel Place, between George & Pitt sts, CBD ☎02 8256 2222, ⓦcityrecitalhall.com. Opened in 1999, this classical music venue right next to Martin Place was specifically designed for chamber music. It seats twelve hundred, but on three levels, giving it an intimate atmosphere.

celebration of gay and lesbian culture in the world. The main event is the exuberant night-time **parade** down Oxford Street, when up to half a million gays and straights jostle for the best viewing positions, before the Dykes on Bikes – traditional leaders of the parade since 1988 – roar into view. Participants devote months to the preparation of outlandish floats and outrageous costumes at Mardi Gras workshops, and even more time is devoted to the preparation of beautiful bodies in Sydney's packed gyms. The **parade** begins at 7.45pm (finishing around 10.30pm), but people line the barricades along Oxford Street from mid-morning, brandishing stolen milk crates to stand on for a better view. If you can't get to Oxford Street until late afternoon, your best chance of finding a spot is along Flinders Street near Moore Park Road, where the parade ends. Otherwise, AIDS charity The Bobby Goldsmith Foundation (ⓦbgf.org.au) has around seven thousand grandstand ("Glamstand") seats on Flinders Street, from $155 each.

The all-night **dance party** that follows the parade attracts up to 25,000 people and is held in several differently themed dance spaces at The Entertainment Quarter in Moore Park. You may have to plan ahead if you want to get a **ticket**: party tickets, from Ticketek (see box, p.134) sometimes sell out by the end of January. The *Sydney Gay & Lesbian Mardi Gras Guide*, available from mid-December, can be picked up from bookshops, cafés and restaurants around Oxford Street or viewed online on the Mardi Gras website.

GROUPS AND INFORMATION

First stop for **information** on gay Sydney is The Bookshop, 207 Oxford St, Darlinghurst (☎02 9331 1103, ⓦthebookshop.com.au), a friendly place with a complete stock of gay- and lesbian-related books, cards and magazines. You can pick up the free gay and lesbian weeklies *Sydney Star Observer* (ⓦstarobserver.com.au), *SX* (ⓦgaynewsnetwork.com.au) and the lesbian-specific monthly *LOTL* (*Lesbians on the Loose*; ⓦlotl.com) here and in other gay-friendly businesses in the eastern suburbs and inner west. The websites are good for trip planning, and the mags will tell you where and when the weekly dance parties are being held, and where you can buy tickets.

Support networks include: the Gay & Lesbian Counselling Service (daily 5.30–10.30pm; ☎02 8594 9596, ⓦtwenty10.org.au); the AIDS Council of New South Wales (ACON), 9 Commonwealth St, Surry Hills (☎1800 063 060, ⓦacon.org.au); Albion Street Centre, 150–154 Albion St, Surry Hills (☎02 9332 1090, ⓦthealbioncentre.org.au), which offers counselling, a free HIV rapid testing clinic, information and a library; and the Anti-Discrimination Board (☎02 9268 5544, ⓦwww.antidiscrimination.justice.nsw.gov.au).

1

BIG VENUES

The venues for **major events**, with bookings direct or through Ticketek, Ticketmaster or Moshtix (see box, p.134), are the **Hordern Pavilion** at Driver Avenue, Entertainment Quarter, Moore Park (☎02 9921 5333); the **Capitol Theatre**, 13 Campbell St, Haymarket (☎02 9320 5000); the **Enmore Theatre**, 130 Enmore Rd, just up from Newtown (☎02 9550 3666); the centrally located **Metro Theatre**, 624 George St (also ☎02 9550 3666); and the **State Theatre**, on Market Street in the city (☎13 61 00).

Conservatorium of Music Royal Botanic Gardens, off Macquarie St, CBD ☎02 9351 1438, ⓦmusic .sydney.edu.au. Students of the "Con" give lunchtime recitals every Wed at 1.10pm during term-time in Verbrugghen Hall (donation expected). Other concerts, both free and ticketed ($10–35), are given by students and staff both here and at venues around town; check website for details.

Ensemble Theatre 78 McDougall St, Kiribilli ☎02 9929 0644, ⓦensemble.com.au. The country's longest running professional theatre, the Ensemble hosts Australian contemporary and classic plays.

NIDA 215 Anzac Parade, Kensington ☎02 9697 7613, ⓦnida.edu.au. Australia's premier dramatic training ground, the National Institute of Dramatic Art – where the likes of Mel Gibson, Judy Davis and Colin Friels started out – offers student productions for talent-spotting.

Stables Theatre 10 Nimrod St, Darlinghurst ☎02 9361 3817, ⓦgriffintheatre.com.au. Home to the Griffin Theatre Company, whose mission is to develop and foster new Australian playwrights.

Sydney Comedy Store Entertainment Quarter, Driver Ave, Moore Park ☎02 9357 1419, ⓦcomedystore .com.au. International (often American) and Australian stand-up comics Tues–Sat; doors open 8.15pm; shows start 8.30pm. Meals aren't available, but nearby restaurants offer meal discounts for *Comedy Store* ticket-holders. Prices vary depending on shows and comedy festival events, but range from $10–30 plus booking fees. Bookings

recommended. Thurs–Sun.

Sydney Dance Company Pier 4, Hickson Rd, Millers Point, The Rocks ☎02 9221 4811, ⓦsydneydancecompany .com. Raises the bar with ambitious sets and beautifully designed costumes. The company is based here but tours nationally and internationally.

Sydney Lyric Star City Casino, Pirrama Rd, Pyrmont ☎1300 795 267, ⓦsydneylyric.com.au. *The* place to see big musical extravaganzas imported from the West End and Broadway. The casino's smaller theatre, the Star City Showroom, puts on more offbeat musicals – such as the *Rocky Horror Picture Show* – and comedy.

Sydney Opera House Bennelong Point ☎02 9250 7777, ⓦsydneyoperahouse.com. The Opera House is, of course, the place for the most prestigious performances in Sydney, hosting not just opera and classical music but also theatre and ballet in its many auditoriums. Forget quibbles about ticket prices (classical concerts from $50, ballet from $70, opera from $100) – the quintessential Sydney icon is worth it.

Sydney Theatre Company Pier 4, Hickson Rd, Millers Point, The Rocks ☎02 9250 1777, ⓦsydneytheatre .com.au. Cate Blanchett and her husband, Andrew Upton, are artistic directors of this reputable and long-running company. They produce Shakespeare and modern pieces in a waterfront location, with three performance spaces, including the recently built Sydney Theatre nearby on Hickson Rd itself. Also has a good restaurant, *The Theatre Bar at the End of the Wharf*.

FILM

FILM FESTIVALS

Sydney Film Festival ⓦsff.org.au. An exciting two-week programme of features, shorts, documentaries and retrospective screenings from Australia and around the world. June.

Tropfest The Domain ⓦtropfest.com/au. The world's largest short-film festival is held in all Australian state capitals; the Sydney event takes place in The Domain, with huge crowds turning up to picnic and watch the screening. End Feb.

OPEN-AIR CINEMAS

Moonlight Cinema Centennial Park Amphitheatre, Oxford St, Woollahra entrance ⓦmoonlight.com.au. Shows classic, art-house and cult films. Tickets ($19) are

available when gates open from 7pm. Dec–March Tues–Sun, films start at sundown (about 8–8.30pm).

Open Air Cinema Mrs Macquarie's Point, the Royal Botanic Gardens ☎1300 366 649, ⓦstgeorgeopenair. com.au. Picturesque harbour screening, backed by the Opera House and Harbour Bridge; mainly mainstream recent releases and some classics ($38). Jan and Feb; tickets from 6.30pm.

CINEMAS

Cinema Paris Entertainment Quarter, 122 Lang Rd ☎02 9332 1633, ⓦhoyts.com.au. Hoyts' four-screen art-house option also has mini-film festivals and events throughout the year.

1

Cremorne Orpheum 380 Military Rd, Cremorne ☎02 9908 4344, ⓦorpheum.com.au. Charming, Heritage-listed, six-screen cinema built in 1935, with a splendid Art Deco interior and old-fashioned, friendly service. The main cinema has never dispensed with its Wurlitzer organ recitals before Sat-night and Sun-afternoon films. Shows both mainstream and foreign new releases ($21). Discount Tues ($13.50).

Govinda's Movie Room 112 Darlinghurst Rd, Darlinghurst ☎02 9380 5155, ⓦgovindas.com.au. Run by the Hare Krishnas, Govinda's shows two films every night, from a range of classics and recent releases, in a pleasantly unorthodox screening room with cushions. The movie-and-dinner deal (all-you-can-eat vegetarian buffet) is popular – $22.80 for the meal with an extra $12 to see a movie. Buy your film ticket when you order your meal, or you may miss out on busy nights. Film-only is $17.90, but diners are given preference.

Palace Cinemas ⓦpalacecinemas.com.au. Chain of inner-city cinemas showing foreign-language, art-house and new releases: Academy Twin, 3A Oxford St, at South Dowling St, Paddington (☎02 9361 4453); Verona, 17 Oxford St, at Verona St, Paddington (☎02 9360 6099), which has a bar; Norton, 99 Norton St, Leichhardt (☎02 9550 0122), the newest, with a bookshop and café. Discount Mon.

ART GALLERIES AND EXHIBITIONS

The official Sydney website (ⓦsydney.com) has comprehensive listings of **art galleries** and current **exhibitions**, while Friday's entertainment section of the *Sydney Morning Herald* offers reviews of recently opened shows. Galleries tend to be concentrated in Paddington and Surry Hills, with a few smaller ones on King St, Newtown.

Artspace The Gunnery Arts Centre, 43–51 Cowper Wharf Rd, Woolloomooloo ☎02 9356 0555, ⓦartspace .org.au. In a wonderful location, this place shows provocative young artists, with a focus on installations and new media. Mon–Fri 11am–5pm, Sat & Sun 11am–6pm.

Australian Centre for Photography 66 Oxford St, Paddington ☎02 9332 1455, ⓦacp.org.au. Free exhibitions of photo-based art from established and new international and Australian artists, shown in four galleries. Emerging photographers are showcased, and there is an extensive specialist library, photography courses, and a darkroom, studio and digital-media suite hire. At the time of writing, the gallery was in the process of moving to 66 Oxford St. Check the website for details. Tues–Fri noon–7pm, Sat & Sun 10am–6pm.

Australian Galleries 15 Roylston St, Paddington ☎02 9360 5177, ⓦaustraliangalleries.com.au. A serene gallery selling and exhibiting contemporary Australian art, including works by Gary Shead, Jeffrey Smart and John Coburn. Daily 10am–6pm.

Josef Lebovic Gallery 34 Paddington St, Paddington ☎02 9332 1840, ⓦjoseflebovicgallery.com. Renowned print and graphic gallery specializing in Australian and international prints from the nineteenth, twentieth and twenty-first centuries, as well as vintage photography. Advance appointments are recommended, though you can sometimes just walk in, if you're lucky. Wed–Fri 1–6pm, Sat 11am–5pm.

Ray Hughes Gallery 270 Devonshire St, Surry Hills ☎02 9698 3200, ⓦrayhughesgallery.com. Influential dealer with a stable of high-profile, contemporary Australian, New Zealand and Chinese artists. Openings monthly, with two artists per show. Tues–Sat 9am–6pm.

SPORTS AND OUTDOOR ACTIVITIES

Diving Pro Dive Coogee (27 Alfreda St, Coogee ☎02 9665 6333, ⓦprodivesydney.com) offers boat and shore dives anywhere between Camp Cove (Watsons Bay) and La Perouse, plus dives all over Sydney. Dive Centre Manly (10 Belgrave St, Manly ☎02 9977 4355, ⓦdivesydney.com.au) offers shore dives to Shelley Beach, Fairlight and Little Manly, plus Harbord if conditions are good, and boat dives off North and South heads and Long Reef (boat dives, double $195; shore dives twice daily; single shore dive $125, double $145; "Discover Scuba" $195; rates include equipment).

Scenic flights Sydney Harbour Seaplanes, Rose Bay (☎02 9388 1978, ⓦseaplanes.com.au), can take you on a 15min scenic flight over Sydney Harbour and Bondi Beach ($200pp, min two people, max eight), or the harbour and the Northern beaches ($265), or the Blue Mountains ($440), or Hunter Valley flight and golf ($3000 return).

Spectator sports Sydney Cricket Ground, at the corner of Moore Park and Driver Ave (☎02 9360 6601, ⓦsydneycricketground.com.au; see p.91); Allianz Stadium (rugby), Moore Park Rd, Paddington (☎02 9360 6601).

Surfing Lets Go Surfing, 128 Ramsgate Ave, North Bondi (daily 9am–6pm; ☎02 9365 1800, ⓦletsgosurfing .com.au), sells surfing gear, rents boards ($25/2hr, $40/day, plus $15–30 for a wetsuit) and offers lessons: a group lesson (2hr; $99) includes board and wetsuit, or go for a private lesson (1hr; $140). Manly Surf School (Balmoral, Collaroy, Long Reef, Manly, Narrabeen and Palm beaches; ☎02 9977 6977, ⓦmanlysurfschool.com) run $70 group lessons and offer private lessons for $100/hr per person.

Swimming pools Most pools are outdoors and unheated, and open from the long weekend in Oct until Easter. Those

1

HORSERACING IN SYDNEY

There are horseracing meetings on Wednesday, Saturday and most public holidays throughout the year, but the best times to hit the track are during the **spring and autumn carnivals** (Aug–Sept & March–April), when prize money rockets, and the quality of racing rivals the best in the world. The venues are well maintained, and peopled with colourful characters, and often massive crowds. Principal racecourses are: Royal Randwick (Alison Rd, Randwick), which featured in *Mission: Impossible II*; Rosehill Gardens (James Ruse Drive, Rosehill); and Canterbury Park (King St, Canterbury), which has midweek racing, plus floodlit Thursday-night racing from September to March. Entry is around $15, or $20–25 on carnival days. Contact the Australian Turf Club (☎02 9663 8400, ⓦaustralianturfclub.com.au) for details of many other picturesque country venues. Every Friday, the *Sydney Morning Herald* publishes its racing guide, "The Form". Bets are placed at TAB shops; these are scattered throughout the city, and most pubs also have TAB access.

detailed in this chapter, with times and prices given, are: Cook and Phillip Park Aquatic and Leisure Centre, near Hyde Park (see p.82); Andrew "Boy" Charlton in The Domain (see p.84); North Sydney Olympic Pool, North Sydney (see p.99); Victoria Park, City Rd, next to Sydney University (see p.93); and the pool of champions, the Sydney International Aquatic Centre at Homebush Bay (see p.155).

Tennis Rushcutters Bay Tennis Centre, 7 Waratah St, Rushcutters Bay (daily 7am–11pm; courts $24/hr, $29 after 5pm and on Sat & Sun; racket rental $3; ☎02 9357 1675). If you don't have anyone to play, the managers will try to provide a partner for you.

Watersports Balmoral Windsurfing, Sailing and Kayaking School, at the Balmoral Sailing Club, southern end of the Esplanade (Oct–April; ☎02 9960 5344, ⓦsailingschool. com.au), rents out kayaks (single/double $25/50/hr) and

windsurf kits (from $66/hr), and offers sailing courses (4hr; $297), plus courses for kids (from $167). Northside Sailing School, Spit Bridge, Mosman (☎02 9969 3972), specializes in weekend dinghy sailing courses on Middle Harbour (Sept–April; 2hr; $120). Sydney by Sail, Darling Harbour (☎02 9280 1110, ⓦsydneybysail.com.au), has "Learn To Sail" yachting programmes year-round. Try also the NSW Yachting Association (☎02 8073 4900, ⓦnsw.yachting .org.au). Natural Wanders Sea Kayak Adventures (☎02 9899 1001, ⓦkayaksydney.com) arrange sea-kayaking in the harbour, including the Balmain Island Paddle (3hr 30min; $120). Manly Surf School (☎02 9932 7000, ⓦmanlysurfschool.com) offers daily private ($70) stand-up paddle surfing (SUP) lessons. Kite Sessions (ⓦkitesessions. com.au) offer private one-on-one kitesurfing lessons ($250/2hr) or two-person ($550/3hr) lessons.

SHOPPING

Sydney's main shopping focus is the stretch between Martin Place and the QVB in the CBD, and its charming old nineteenth-century arcades and two **department stores**, David Jones and Myers. If you've run out of time to buy presents and souvenirs, don't worry: the revamped **Sydney Airport** is attached to one of the biggest shopping malls in Sydney, with outlets for everything from surfwear to R.M. Williams bush outfitters, at the same prices as the downtown stores. The Rocks is the best place for souvenir and duty- and GST-free (VAT-free) shopping.

FASHION AND CLOTHING

Oxford St in Paddington is the place to go for interesting fashion, with outlets of most Australian designers along the strip. You'll find more expensive designer gear in the city, at the Strand Arcade, 412 George St, and David Jones department store. For striking street fashion, check out Crown St in Surry Hills and head to King St in Newtown running up to St Peters, where you'll also find cheaper styles, retro clothes and interesting accessories. If it's interesting surfwear you're after, head for an array of surf shops at Manly and Bondi Beach.

Dinosaur Designs 77 Strand Arcade, CBD ☎02 9223 2953, ⓦdinosaurdesigns.com.au; map pp.68–69. Funky Australian jewellery with lots of use of resin, as well as silver, brass and glass elements. Mon–Wed & Fri

9.30am–5.30pm, Thurs 9.30am–8pm, Sat 10am–5pm, Sun 11am–4pm.

R.M. Williams 389 George St, CBD ⓦrmwilliams .com.au; map pp.68–69. This quality Australian bush outfitters is great for moleskin trousers, Drizabone coats and Akubra hats. Mon–Wed & Fri 9am–6pm, Thurs 9am–9pm, Sat 9am–5pm, Sun 10am–5pm.

Strand Hatters 8/412 George St, CBD ⓦstrandhatters .com.au; map pp.68–69. A wide range of Australian Akubra hats, as well as top hats, fedoras, sombreros and panamas. Mon–Wed & Fri 9am–5.30pm, Thurs 9am–8pm, Sat 9.30am–4.30pm, Sun 11am–4pm.

Wheels & Doll Baby 259 Crown St, Darlinghurst ☎02 9361 3286, ⓦwheelsanddollbaby.com; map p.89. Cult designer with a fresh aesthetic and celebrity clients including Sadie Frost, Kelly Osborne, Katy Perry and Pink. The clothes are Australian-made and handcrafted with vintage inspired and sourced fabrics. Mon–Wed, Fri & Sat 10am–6pm, Thurs 10am–8pm, Sun 11am–5pm.

FOOD AND DRINK

Australian Wine Centre 3/1 Alfred St, at George St, Circular Quay ☎ 02 9247 2755, ⓦ australianwinecentre .co.uk; map p.72. Sells more than a thousand wines from around Australia and even has an in-house wine bar. Mon & Sun 10am–7pm, Tues–Thurs & Sat 9.30am–8pm, Fri 9.30am–9pm.

David Jones Food Hall 65–77 Market St, CBD ☎ 02 9266 5544, ⓦ davidjones.com.au; map pp.68–69. In this Australian-owned department store, the food hall is piled with delicious fresh and packaged produce, and features an oyster bar, grills, sushi and noodles, as well as an espresso joint. Mon–Wed 9.30am–7pm, Thurs & Fri 9.30am–9pm, Sat & Sun 10am–7pm.

MARKETS

Kirribilli Markets Kirribilli Bowling Green ⓦ kirribillimarkets.com. Scenically sited Kirribilli is the best known of markets on the North Shore. Some two hundred stalls feature new and secondhand fashion (especially on Sun), local designers, arts and crafts, fresh produce and gourmet grub. Fourth Sat & second Sun of month 8.30am–3pm.

Paddington Markets 395 Oxford St, Paddington ⓦ paddingtonmarkets.com.au; map pp.68–69. Paddington supports a hundred and fifty stalls with an eclectic offering: Australian fashion, crafts and jewellery, homeware and food. Sat 10am–4pm.

Paddy's Markets Thomas St, Haymarket ⓦ paddysmarkets.com.au; map p.80. Located near Chinatown, this is Sydney's oldest market, selling fresh produce and deli items, plus large quantities of bargain-basement clothes and toys. Wed–Sun 10am–6pm.

The Rocks Fridays Foodie Market George St, The Rocks ⓦ therocks.com; map p.72. Delectable farmers market with local produce sold in the heart of The Rocks, from hot dogs to Japanese pancakes. Fri 9am–3pm.

The Rocks Market Northern end of George & Playfair sts, The Rocks ⓦ therocks.com; map p.72. Long-established and very local market featuring the work of new young designers and artisans. As well as fashion and homeware, you'll find beauty products, original photographic prints and jewellery. Sat & Sun 10am–5pm.

Rozelle Markets Rozelle School, 663 Darling St, Rozelle ⓦ rozellemarkets.com.au; map p.94. Flea market piled high with furniture, bric-a-brac, vinyl and books, with a strong presence of vintage clothing and jewellery. Plus food stalls, massages and even tarot readings. The long-running market is changing management from Jan 2017 and may move location; check website for details. Sat & Sun 9am–4pm.

BOOKS

Dymocks 424 George St, CBD ☎ 02 9235 0155, ⓦ dymocks.com.au; map, pp.68–69. One of the biggest bookshops in the city is the long running, Australian-owned Dymocks, on several floors with an impressive Australian selection and a café. Mon–Wed & Fri 9am–7pm, Thurs 9am–9pm, Sat 9.30am–6pm, Sun 10am–6pm.

Gleebooks 49 Glebe Point Rd, Glebe ☎ 02 9660 2333, ⓦ gleebooks.com.au; map pp.68–69. One of Australia's best bookshops, specializing in academic and alternative books, contemporary Australian and international literature. Book launches and other literary events are regularly held. Mon–Wed & Sun 9am–7pm, Thurs–Sat till 9pm.

Sappho Books and Café 51 Glebe Point Rd, Glebe ☎ 02 9552 4498, ⓦ sapphobooks.com.au; map pp.68–69. Characterful bookshop piled with secondhand volumes. At night, the wine and tapas bar draws a diverse intellectual crowd. Mon & Tues 8.30am–6.30pm, Wed–Sat 8.30am–11.30pm, Sun 9am–6.30pm.

DIRECTORY

Banks and exchange Head offices of banks are mostly in the CBD, around Martin Place. There's a travelex bureaux de change at the airport (daily 5am–11pm), and at 570 George St (Mon–Fri 9.30am–4pm) and 28 Bridge St (Mon–Thurs 9.30am–4pm, Fri 9.30am–5pm); for more locations, visit ⓦ travelex.com.au/StoreLocator.

Consulates Embassies are all in Canberra, and it's usually easier to call them when in difficulty than to go to the consulates in Sydney: Canadian, Level 5, 111 Harrington St, The Rocks (☎ 02 9364 3000); New Zealand, Level 10, 55 Hunter St, CBD (☎ 02 8256 2000); UK, Level 16, Gateway Building, 1 Macquarie Place, CBD (☎ 02 9247 7521); US, Level 59, MLC Centre, 19–29 Martin Place, CBD (☎ 02 9373 9200).

Hospitals with emergency departments St Vincent's, 390 Victoria St, at Burton St, Darlinghurst (☎ 02 8382 1111); Royal Prince Alfred, Missenden Rd, Camperdown (☎ 02 9515 6111); Prince of Wales, Barker St, Randwick (☎ 02 9382 2222). Medical centres listed below.

Immigration Department of Immigration, 26 Lee St, near Central Station, CBD (☎ 13 18 81).

Internet There's free internet access at the State Library, Macquarie St.

Left luggage There are lockers at the airport, and left luggage services at Baggage Storage, Grand Concourse and Central Station (daily 6am–10pm; $16/day, or $101/week).

1

FESTIVALS AND EVENTS

The Sydney year is interspersed with **festivals and events** of various sorts that reach their peak in the summer – check the City of Sydney Council's online "What's On" website (**ⓦ**whatson .cityofsydney.nsw.gov.au). We list outdoor music festivals earlier on in this chapter (see box, p.135).

JANUARY–FEBRUARY

New Year New Year begins with a spectacular midnight fireworks display from the Harbour Bridge and Darling Harbour.

Sydney Festival Exhaustive and exhausting arts event (**ⓣ**02 8248 6500, **ⓦ**sydneyfestival .org.au) that lasts for most of January and ranges from concerts, plays and outdoor art installations to circus performances. Numerous free events are based around urban public spaces, focusing on Circular Quay, The Domain, Darling Harbour and Sydney Olympic Park; the remainder – mostly international performances – can cost a packet.

Australia Day A huge celebration in Sydney that takes place on January 26, with activities focused on the water (**ⓦ**australiaday.com.au). Sydney's passenger ferries race from Fort Denison to the Harbour Bridge, via Shark Island, and there's a Tall Ships Race from Bradleys Head to the Harbour Bridge, as well as an aerial display of military planes. The Australia Day Regatta takes place in the afternoon, with hundreds of yachts racing all over the harbour, from Botany Bay to the Parramatta River. There are also free events at The Rocks, Hyde Park, and at Darling Harbour, where the day culminates with the Australia Day Spectacular at around 9pm with a "multimedia symphony of light, sound and music" concluding with a massive fireworks display. In addition, many museums let visitors in for free or half-price. Many locals simply head to the beach for a barbecue. Yabun, which celebrates Aboriginal culture and acts as an antidote to the mainstream, white Australia Day festivities, is held at Victoria Park, Broadway (free; contact Koori Radio on **ⓣ**02 9384 4000 or check **ⓦ**gadigal .org.au).

Surf carnivals Impressive summer events staged regularly by local surf lifesaving clubs (**ⓣ**02 9984 7188, **ⓦ**surflifesaving.com.au).

Sydney Gay and Lesbian Mardi Gras The city's explosive and outrageous gay festival, with parades and partying at the end of Feb (**ⓦ**mardigras.org.au; see box, pp.136–137).

Libraries The State Library, Macquarie St, CBD (see p.79).

Maps Map World, 280 Pitt St, CBD (**ⓣ**02 9261 3601, **ⓦ**mapworld.net.au), has Sydney's biggest selection of maps and travel guides. We list more maps in the "Parks and wildlife" section below.

Medical centres Broadway General Practice, Level 1, Broadway Shopping Centre, 1 Bay St, near Glebe (Mon–Wed & Fri 8.30am–7pm, Thurs 8.30am–9pm, Sat 9am–6pm, Sun 10am–6pm; no appointment necessary; **ⓣ**02 8245 1500, **ⓦ**broadwaygeneralpractice.com.au); Sydney Sexual Health Centre, Sydney Hospital, Macquarie St, CBD (**ⓣ**02 9382 7440 or **ⓣ**1800 451 624, **ⓦ**sshc.org. au); The Travel Doctor, 7th Floor, 428 George St, CBD (**ⓣ**02 9221 7133, **ⓦ**traveldoctor.com.au).

Parks and wildlife information The NPWS, Cadmans Cottage, 110 George St, The Rocks (**ⓣ**02 9247 5033, **ⓦ**nationalparks.nsw.gov.au), is the information centre for Sydney Harbour National Park and books tours to its islands. The Sydney Map Shop, part of the Surveyor-General's Department, at 22 Bridge St, CBD (**ⓣ**02 9228 6111), sells detailed National Park, State Forest and bushwalking maps of New South Wales.

Pharmacy (late-night) Crest Hotel Pharmacy, 91–93 Darlinghurst Rd, Kings Cross (daily 8am–midnight; **ⓣ**02 9358 1822).

Police 151–241 Goulburn St, Surry Hills (**ⓣ**02 9265 4144); emergency **ⓣ**000.

Post office The General Post Office (GPO) is at 1 Martin Place, CBD (Mon–Fri 8.15am–5.30pm, Sat 10am–2pm).

Public holidays In addition to the Australia-wide public holidays (see box, p.57), the following are celebrated only in New South Wales: Bank Holiday (first Mon in Aug); Labour Day (first Mon in Oct); Queen's Birthday (first Mon in June).

Travel agents Backpackers World Travel, 234 Sussex St, CBD (**ⓣ**02 8268 6001, **ⓦ**backpackersworld.com.au), arranges everything from international flights to bus passes; offices also at 91 York St, CBD (**ⓣ**02 8268 5000); 488 Pitt St, near Central Station (**ⓣ**02 9282 9711); 212 Victoria St, Kings Cross (**ⓣ**02 9380 2700); and 2B Grosvenor St, Bondi Junction (**ⓣ**02 9369 2011). Flight Centre, 52 Martin Place, CBD (**ⓣ**13 18 66), also at several other locations, offers cheap domestic and international air tickets. STA Travel has many branches, including Town Hall Square, 464 Kent St, CBD (**ⓣ**02 9262 9763), or try Student Flights (**ⓣ**1300 762 410), with several offices including 140 King St, Newtown; 50 Spring St, Bondi

MARCH–APRIL

Sydney Royal Easter Show An agricultural and garden show based at the Showground at Sydney Olympic Park (W easter show.com.au). For twelve consecutive days, the country comes to the city for a frantic array of amusement-park rides, fireworks, parades of prize animals, a rodeo and wood-chopping displays. The second weekend is always the Easter weekend.

MAY

Sydney Writers Festival A week-long programme of mostly free events which takes place in the very scenically located Wharf Theatre complex (W swf.org.au).

JUNE–AUGUST

Sydney Film Festival With two weeks of screenings, this is the highlight of the country's cinematic calendar (W sff.org.au; see p.138).

Biennale of Sydney Every even-numbered year, the Biennale of Sydney takes place over six weeks between March and June, staging provocative contemporary art exhibitions at various venues and public spaces around town (W biennaleofsydney.com.au).

City to Surf Race A 14km fun-run from the city to Bondi, held in August (W city2surf.com.au).

OCTOBER–NOVEMBER

Manly International Jazz Festival Labour Day weekend in early October is marked by the Manly Jazz Festival, with several free waterfront events and a few indoor concerts charging entry (W manlyaustralia.com.au).

Sculpture By The Sea The coast between Bondi and Tamarama is transformed for two weeks in late October / early November by this magical exhibition (W sculpturebythesea.com).

DECEMBER

Sydney to Hobart Yacht Race The year is brought to a close on December 26 by the yacht race, when it seems that half of the city turns up at the harbour to cheer on the start of this classic regatta and watch the colourful spectacle of two hundred or so yachts setting sail for a 630-nautical-mile slog (W rolexsydneyhobart.com).

Junction; and 87 Glebe Point Rd, Glebe. There's a travel agent at *Sydney Central YHA* (T 02 9218 9000, W yha.com.au), offering an excellent range of Sydney tours.

Travellers with disabilities Sydney For All (W www .sydneyforall.com) has useful access maps and ratings for top Sydney attractions. Most national parks have wheelchair-accessible walks; check W nationalparks.nsw .gov.au. Many train stations are wheelchair accessible; check W cityrail.nsw.gov.au. All taxi companies take wheelchair bookings.

Work If you have a working holiday visa, you shouldn't have too much trouble finding some sort of employment, particularly in hospitality or retail. Offices of the government-run Centrelink (T 13 28 50) have a database of jobs. Centrelink also refers jobseekers to several private "Job Network" agencies, searchable at W jobsearch.gov.au. The private agency Troys, at Level 11, 89 York St, CBD (T 02 9290 2955, W troys.com.au), specializes in the hospitality industry. If you have some office or professional skills, there are plenty of temp agencies keen to take on travellers: search for "Employment Services" in the *Yellow Pages* (W yellowpages .com.au). For a range of work, from unskilled to professional, the multinational Manpower is a good bet (W manpower .com.au), as is Seek (W seek.com.au). Otherwise, scour hostel notice boards and the *Sydney Morning Herald*'s employment pages – Sat's bumper edition is best. Working hostels, like *Cronulla Beach YHA* (see p.122), actively help guests look for work and maintain a database of opportunities.

Around Sydney

If life in the fast lane is taking its toll, Sydney's residents can easily get away from it all. Right on their doorstep, golden beaches and magnificent national parks beckon, interwoven with intricate waterways. Everything in this part of the chapter can be done as a day-trip from the city, although some require an overnight stay to explore more fully, and there is a huge variety of tours on offer (see box, p.144).

1

North of Sydney, the Hawkesbury River flows into the jagged jaws of the aptly named **Broken Bay**. The entire area is surrounded by bush, with the huge spaces of the **Ku-ring-gai Chase National Park** in the south and the **Brisbane Waters National Park** in the north. Beyond Broken Bay, the **Central Coast** between Gosford and Newcastle is an ideal spot for a bit of fishing, sailing and lazing around. **Newcastle** is escaping its industrial-city tag: an up-and-coming, attractive beach metropolis, with a surfing, student, café and music culture all part of the mix. Immediately beyond are the wineries of the **Hunter Valley**.

To the **west**, you escape suburbia to emerge at the foot of the beautiful World Heritage-listed **Blue Mountains**, while the scenic Hawkesbury–Nepean river valley is home to historic rural towns such as **Windsor**.

As you head **south**, the **Royal National Park** is an hour's drive away, while on the coast beyond is a string of small, laidback towns – Waterfall, Stanwell Park, Wombarra – with beautiful, unspoilt **beaches**. The industrial city of **Wollongong** and neighbouring Port Kembla are impressively located between the Illawarra Escarpment and the sea, but of paltry interest to visitors, although more interesting spots cluster around. Inland, the **Southern Highlands** are covered with yet more national parks, punctuated by pleasing towns such as **Berrima** and **Bundanoon**.

TOURS FROM SYDNEY

Day-tours from Sydney range from a sedentary bus trip to a wildlife park to a day of canyoning in the Blue Mountains, and there are many **overnight trips**, too. You'll almost certainly have a better time with one of the outfits specializing in **small-group tours**, quite often with an emphasis on physical activities such as bushwalking, horseriding, whitewater rafting or abseiling, as opposed to travelling with one of the commercial bus-tour operators. **One-way tours** can be the next best thing to going by car: small groups in minibuses travel from Sydney to Melbourne (for example), taking detours to attractions along the way that you'd never be able to reach on public transport. As well as booking direct, you can book most of the tours below through YHA Travel (☎02 9261 1111, ⓦyha.com.au).

DAY- AND OVERNIGHT TRIPS AROUND SYDNEY

Oz Trek ☎02 9666 4262 or ☎1300 66 1234, ⓦoztrek .com.au. Recommended active full-day tours to the Blue Mountains ($69, with lunch), with a choice of bushwalks. Small groups (max twenty). The trip can be extended to overnight packages with either abseiling ($255) or a Jenolan Caves visit ($210–230). CBD, Glebe, Kings Cross, Bondi and Coogee pick-ups.

Waves Surf School ☎02 9369 3010 or ☎1800 851 101, ⓦwavessurfschool.com.au. "Learn To Surf" trips to the Royal National Park, Seal Rocks or up the north coast to Byron Bay, learning surfing technique and etiquette and beach safety, with a chance to spot

wildlife. Prices start from $99 (one day, with lunch) and go up to $595 for five days, meals included. CBD, Bondi and Coogee pick-ups.

Wildframe Ecotours ☎02 9440 9915, ⓦwildframe .com. Two full-day tours to the Blue Mountains ($95) and overnight tours starting at $136. The "Grand Canyon Ecotour" is for fit walkers as it includes a small-group bushwalk (max 21) through the Grand Canyon (5km; 3hr), with BYO lunch in Katoomba. The "Blue Mountains Bush Tour" is more relaxed, with several short bushwalks and BYO lunch in Blackheath. Kangaroo spotting promised on both trips.

EXTENDED AND ONE-WAY TOURS

Ando's Outback Tours ☎0416 220 452 or ☎1800 228 828, ⓦoutbacktours.com.au. Popular five-day tour from Sydney to Byron Bay but getting well off the beaten track inland via the Blue Mountains, the Warrumbungles, Coonabarabran and Lightning Ridge ($935 all-inclusive; departs Sydney every Sun); includes a stay on the rural property of the true-blue family who run the tours. Finding farm work is a common bonus.
Autopia Tours ☎03 9419 8878 or ☎1800 000 507,

ⓦautopiatours.com.au. This excellent, long-established Melbourne-based tour company has a one-day Hunter Valley "Wine & Dine" tour of the wineries ($139; includes pizza lunch).

Oz Experience ☎02 9213 1766 or ☎1300 300 028, ⓦozexperience.com. A cross between transport and tours that go a little off the beaten track, with a hop-on-hop-off component lasting six months; accommodation and meals not included (eg Sydney–Cairns from $639).

Ku-ring-gai Chase National Park

24km north of the centre of Sydney • Daily sunrise–sunset; Bobbin Head Information Centre daily 10am–4pm • $12 per vehicle per day • ☎ 02 9472 8949, ⓦ nationalparks.nsw.gov.au

Ku-ring-gai Chase National Park is the best known of New South Wales' national parks and, with the Pacific Highway running all the way up one side, is also the easiest to get to. The bushland scenery is crisscrossed by walking tracks, which you can explore to seek out Aboriginal rock carvings, or just to get away from it all and see the forest and its wildlife.

The park's most popular picnic spot is at **Bobbin Head**, 6km east of the Sydney–Newcastle Freeway, essentially just a colourful marina with a café, picnic area and NPWS **Bobbin Head Information Centre**, located inside the Art Deco sunlit café *Bobbin Inn* (ⓦ bobbininncafe.com.au). From here, the **Mangrove Boardwalk** (10min return) pleasantly traces the water's edge past thousands of bright red crabs and continues as the **Gibberagong Track** (additional 20min return) through a small sandstone canyon to some Aboriginal rock art featuring figures and axe-grinding grooves.

To the northeast, West Head Road leads to West Head, which juts into Broken Bay, marking the entrance to **Pittwater**, a deep, 10km-long sheltered waterway. There are superb views from here across to Barrenjoey Head and Barrenjoey Lighthouse at Palm Beach on the eastern shore of Pittwater. From West Head, the **Garigal Aboriginal Heritage Walk** (3.5km loop; 2–3hr) leads past the Aboriginal rock-engraving site, the most accessible Aboriginal art in the park.

ARRIVAL AND DEPARTURE · KU-RING-GAI CHASE NATIONAL PARK

By bus Two direct buses run to Church Point: #E86 from Central Station or #156 from Manly Wharf (Mon–Sat, hourly; 1hr).

By ferry Without your own transport, it's most rewarding to explore the Pittwater and eastern Ku-ring-gai by ferry, which provides access to a couple of great places to stay. Take the ferry from Church Point Wharf (hourly, last departure Mon–Fri 7pm, Sat & Sun 6.30pm; 40min round trip; $15 return; ☎ 02 9999 3492, ⓦ churchpointferryservice.com).

ACCOMMODATION

The Basin Western foreshores of Pittwater, Ku-ring-gai Chase National Park ☎ 02 9974 1011, ⓦ nationalparks.nsw.gov.au. The only place to camp on Pittwater, reached via the Palm Beach Ferry Service. Facilities at the site are minimal, so bring everything with you. Unpowered sites $32.80

Pittwater YHA Halls Wharf ☎ 02 9999 5748, ⓦ yha .com.au. If you want to stay in the park in rather more

---

CLOSE WILDLIFE ENCOUNTERS AROUND SYDNEY

Australian Reptile Park Off the Pacific Hwy, just south of Gosford turn-off; ⓦ reptilepark.com.au. Around 65km north of Sydney, this park offers photographic opportunities with koalas and has roaming kangaroos, though its real stars are the reptiles, with native Australian species well represented and visible all year round thanks to heat lamps in the enclosures. The highlights are Elvis, New South Wales' largest saltwater crocodile, and the sizeable Central Australian perentie lizard. There are reptile shows and talks throughout the day, including giant Galapagos tortoise feeding (daily 10.45am), alligator feeding (Sat & Sun noon) and a crocodile show (Sat & Sun 1.30pm), featuring five-metre Elvis. Daily 9am–5pm; $34, under-16s $18.

Featherdale Wildlife Park 217 Kildare Rd, Doonside; ⓦ featherdale.com.au. Located 30km west of Sydney off the M4 motorway between Parramatta and Penrith, this wildlife park hosts feeding sessions and talks throughout the day focused on koalas, flying foxes, dingoes and other animals. Train to Blacktown station, then bus #725. Daily 9am–5pm; $31, under-16s $17.

Koala Park Sanctuary Castle Hill Rd, West Pennant Hills, near Pacific Hwy; ⓦ koalapark.com.au. Established as a safe haven for koalas in 1935, this sanctuary, around 25km north of Sydney, has since opened its gates to wombats, possums, kangaroos and native birds of all kinds. Koala-feeding sessions (daily 10.20am, 11.45am, 2pm & 3pm) are the photo-opportunity times, with wombat feeding 15min before the koalas. Train to Pennant Hills then bus #651 or #655 towards Glenorie (Mon–Sat). Daily 9am–5pm; $27, under-15s $15.

comfort than under canvas, there's the very popular *Pittwater YHA*. One of New South Wales' most scenically sited hostels, it's set in a rambling old house overlooking the water (kayaks available) and surrounded by spectacular bushwalks. Accessed by regular ferry from Church Point

Wharf (15min; see p.145) or water taxi (freephone at the wharf), alighting at Halls Wharf and walking 15min up the hill. Bring supplies with you – the last food (and bottle) shop is at Church Point. Booking essential; reserve well in advance for weekends. Dorms $\overline{27}$; doubles $\overline{67.50}$

Newcastle

NEWCASTLE was founded in 1804 for convicts too hard even for Sydney to cope with, but the river is the real reason for the city's existence: coal, which lies in great abundance beneath the Hunter Valley, was and still is ferried from the countryside to be exported around the country and the world. The proximity of the mines encouraged the establishment of other **heavy industries**, though the production of steel here ceased in late 2000 and most of the slag heaps have been worked over, but the docks are still functional, particularly with the through traffic of coal from the Hunter Valley.

New South Wales' second city, with a population of over a quarter of a million, Newcastle has long suffered from comparison with nearby Sydney. However, for a former major industrial city, it's surprisingly attractive in parts, a fact now being more widely recognized, and old icons have been redeveloped, such as the *Great*

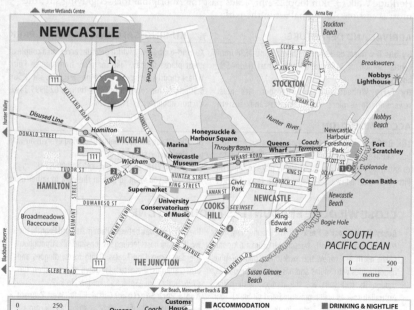

■ ACCOMMODATION	
Backpackers Newcastle	2
Clarendon Hotel	3
The Grand Hotel	5
Newcastle Beach YHA	4
Quality Hotel	
Noah's on the Beach	1

● EATING	
Apothecary Kitchen	3
Delucas	4
Estabar	2
Goldbergs Coffee House	7
Harry's Café de Wheels	5
Rolador	1
Scratchleys On The Wharf	6

■ DRINKING & NIGHTLIFE	
The Beach Hotel	5
Cambridge Hotel	3
Cazador	7
Great Northern Hotel	6
The Kent	1
Lass O'Gowrie	2
The Terrace Bar	4

Northern Hotel (see p.150). The large and lively student community keeps the atmosphere vibrant, and there's a serious **surf culture** too – many surfwear- and surfboard-makers operate here, several champion surfers hail from the city, and there's a big contest, Surfest, in March. You might not choose to spend too much time here, but it can be a good base for excursions, particularly to the wineries of the nearby Hunter Valley.

Newcastle Harbour Foreshore Park

Newcastle has whole streetscapes of beautiful **Victorian terraces** to rival Sydney's – pick up a free *Newcastle Visitor Guide* from the tourist office, to steer you around some of the old buildings. A couple of buildings in **Newcastle Harbour Foreshore Park** show the trend for the city's wealth of disused public architecture: on one corner of the park stands the beautiful, Italianate, brick **Customs House**, now a popular pub. Nearby is the wooden two-storey **Paymasters House**, where you can sit with a coffee in its fine veranda café and contemplate the water.

Fort Scratchley

Nobbys Rd • Mon & Wed–Sun 10am–4pm • Free, tours $16 • ⓦ fortscratchley.com.au

The mound occupied by **Fort Scratchley** was recognized as being of strategic significance back in 1804; in 1828, an earthwork battery called Fort Battlesticks was constructed and equipped with guns. By the 1870s, with the fear of Russian attack escalating, the current fort was built, with gun emplacements carved into the hillside. The guns were fired in anger in 1942, when a Japanese submarine emerged and began shelling Newcastle: the Japanese shells caused little damage, and Fort Scratchley's guns missed their mark. To see the whole site and to hear about the fort's unique history, take a guided tour.

Queens Wharf and Honeysuckle

The restored **Queens Wharf**, a landmark with its distinctive observation tower, is located on the south bank of the Hunter River. It's linked to the city centre by an elevated walkway from Hunter Street Mall. Further along the foreshore is the **Honeysuckle** development, an assortment of renovated rail sheds, wharves, pristine walkways and smart apartments centring on **Harbour Square**. You'll find a string of stylish cafés, restaurants and bars here, definitely worthy of a twilight drink or mid-morning slap-up breakfast.

Newcastle Museum

Workshop Way, Honeysuckle • Tues–Sun 10am–5pm • Free • ⓣ 4974 1421 • ⓦ newcastlemuseum.com.au

The new **Newcastle Museum** is dramatically located in Newcastle's expansive nineteenth-century railway workshops. The emphasis is on social history, with photography projects by Novocastrians and a particularly effective large-scale display on the city's steelworking past. The Supernova section is a light-and-sound-filled attempt to interest children in maths, science and engineering. Call ahead to ask when a free museum tour is on.

Newcastle Region Art Gallery

1 Laman St • Tues–Sun 10am–5pm • Free • ⓦ nag.org.au

The **Newcastle Region Art Gallery** is considered one of the best in Australia, holding an impressive collection of works by esteemed Australian artists such as Brett Whitely, Arthur Boyd and Russell Drysdale, as well as regularly hosting touring exhibitions of significant local, national and international artists. Sadly, Newcastle's local administration recently vetoed a much-needed expansion, and few of the more than five hundred artworks can be displayed at any one time. Nevertheless, it's a beautiful modernist building, and inspired curation makes the gallery well worth a visit.

1

Newcastle Beach and Nobbys Beach

The city centre, positioned on a narrow length of land between the Hunter River to the west and the Pacific Ocean to the east, has several popular and pleasantly low-key beaches close by. **Newcastle Beach**, only a few hundred metres from the city on Shortland Esplanade, has patrolled swimming between flags, a sandy saltwater pool perfect for children, shaded picnic tables and good surfing at its southern end. At the northern end, the beautifully painted, Art Deco-style, free **Ocean Baths** houses the changing pavilions for the huge saltwater pool, which has its own diving board. North of Newcastle Beach, beyond Fort Scratchley, is the long, uncrowded stretch of **Nobbys Beach**, with a lovely old beach pavilion. A walkway leads to Nobbys Head and its nineteenth-century lighthouse.

Beaches south of town

If you follow Shortland Esplanade south from Newcastle Beach, you'll come to the huge, undulating expanse of **King Edward Park**, with good walking paths and cliff views over this rocky stretch of waterfront. One section of the rock ledge holds Australia's first man-made ocean pool, the **Bogie Hole**, chiselled out of the rock by convicts in the early nineteenth century for the Military Commandant's personal bathing pleasure. The cliffs are momentarily interrupted by **Susan Gilmore Beach**, arguably Newcastle's most beautiful beach, and definitely its most visually unadulterated – cliff-rimmed and secluded enough to indulge in some nude bathing, this is a great place for a swim. Further around the rocks is **Bar Beach**, a popular surfing spot with a good beachfront café and ugly surrounding development. The longer **Merewether Beach** next door has a fabulous ocean bath at its southern end and a separate children's pool; overlooking the beach is *The Beach Hotel*, a good place for a drink (see p.150).

Stockton Beach

Just two minutes by ferry from Queens Wharf across the Hunter River, the beachside suburb of **Stockton** is the starting point for the vast, extraordinary **Stockton Beach**, which extends 32km north to **Anna Bay**. Two kilometres wide at some points and covered in moving sand dunes up to 30m high, Stockton Bight, as it's officially known, looks strikingly like a mini desert.

Blackbutt Reserve

New Lambton Heights • Daily 9am–5pm • Free • ⓦ newcastle.nsw.gov.au • Bus #222 or #224 to the main Carnley Ave entrance (for the best enclosures, including koalas), or for the entrances on Lookout Rd, take bus #363; the tourist office produces a free map

Inland, **Blackbutt Reserve** is a large slab of beautiful bushland in the middle of Newcastle suburbia, about 10km southwest of the city with a number of multi-award-winning wildlife exhibits. Consisting of four valleys, it includes a remnant of rainforest, creeks, lakes and ponds, and 20km of walking tracks to explore them. En route, you'll see kangaroos, koalas, wombats, emus and other native animals in the reserve's wildlife enclosures.

Hunter Wetlands Centre

Sandgate Rd, Shortland • Daily 9am–4pm; feeding talks daily 11am • $5 • ☎ 02 4951 6466, ⓦ wetlands.org.au • Train from Newcastle to Sandgate, from where it's a 10min walk

Some 13km northwest of the city, the **Hunter Wetlands Centre** is situated on Hexham Swamp by Ironbark Creek, and is home to a plethora of birdlife. There are walking and cycling trails here, and you can rent canoes ($10/2hr per person) or participate in canoe tours, ecotours or bird- and reptile-feeding talks.

ARRIVAL AND INFORMATION	NEWCASTLE

By train The closure of the main city train station has made train travel from Sydney inconvenient. To get here by train, alight at Broadmeadow or Hamilton stations, from where shuttle buses take you to the city centre. This arrangement is constantly changing, so visit ⓦ visitnewcastle.com.au for the latest.

By bus The coach terminal is situated on the corner of Scott and Watt streets in the city centre.

Tourist information The very helpful visitor centre (Mon–Fri 9am–5pm, Sat & Sun 10am–3pm; ☎02 4974 2999 or ☎1800 654 558, ⓦvisitnewcastle.com.au) at 361 Hunter St, opposite Civic station, provides free maps and local information on self-guided walks, cycling trails and arts and entertainment – all downloadable from the website.

GETTING AROUND

By bus It's easy to get around using Newcastle's public transport system, which now runs on the Opal Card system (☎13 15 00, ⓦopal.com.au). Bus fares must be pre-purchased with an Opal Card. There's also a free shuttle bus loop (every 20min) around town starting at the coach terminal (daily 9am–2.40pm, Sat & Sun till 5.40pm).

By tram You can familiarize yourself with the city sights on Newcastle's Famous Tram (Mon–Fri & school hols 11am & 1pm; 1hr; $15; ☎02 4977 2270), the usual twee coach-done-out-as-a-tram deal, departing from Newcastle station.

Car rental A.R.A, 86 Belford St, Broadmeadow (☎02 4962 2488 or ☎1800 243 122, ⓦararental.com.au); Thrifty, 272 Pacific Hwy, Charlestown (☎02 4942 2266, ⓦthrifty.com.au).

Taxis Newcastle Taxis ☎13 33 00.

ACCOMMODATION

Backpackers Newcastle 42 & 44 Denison St, Hamilton ☎02 4969 3436, ⓦbackpackersnewcastle.com.au. A home-style hostel and guesthouse run by a friendly family, with dorms and doubles set in two adjacent wooden bungalows with a pool out back. Located 3km from the city centre and beach but only a few mins' walk from lively Beaumont St; take a bus (#100, #104, #111, #118) to Tudor St, or call for a free pick-up. The owner runs people down to the beach most days and offers free surfing lessons (boogie-boards free, surfboards $20/day). Backyard camping per person $18; dorm $30; doubles $80

Clarendon Hotel 347 Hunter St ☎02 4907 6700, ⓦclarendonhotel.com.au. This central Art Deco pub has been beautifully renovated, with original features In the bar downstairs. The stylish, vibrantly coloured rooms are contemporary and offer great value. A bright café-bistro with a huge courtyard serves good-value meals from breakfast onwards. $170

The Grand Hotel 32 Church St ☎02 4929 3489, ⓦthegrandhotel.net.au. The small monochrome rooms and neat bathrooms at this CBD hotel might sound a bit business-like, but are actually modern and chic. The balconies and downstairs bistro make for extra relaxation after a day at nearby Newcastle Beach. Doubles $130

Newcastle Beach YHA 30 Pacific St, at King St ☎02 4925 3544, ⓦyha.com.au. Relaxed hostel in an impressively restored, spacious old building complete with wood-panelled ballroom (once a gentlemen's club), huge timber staircases, a lounge with a fireplace and leather armchairs, a pool table and courtyard with BBQ, plus the usual YHA facilities. Dorms, doubles, twins and family rooms ($84) all available. Just 50m from the surf and right in the centre of town; free boogie-boards, plus surfboards ($5/hr) and bikes ($5/3hr) to rent. Dorms $28; doubles $82

Quality Hotel Noah's on the Beach Shortland Esplanade ☎02 4929 5181, ⓦnoahsonthebeach.com.au. Upmarket, modern multistorey motel opposite Newcastle Beach. There's room service, and most rooms have ocean views. $189

EATING

The two streets to head for are **Darby St** and **Beaumont St**. Perpetually buzzy Darby St, close to the city centre, has a multicultural mix of restaurants and some very hip cafés, as well as some secondhand bookshops and retro clothes stores to browse in between coffees. Beaumont St, in Hamilton, 3km northwest of the city centre (train to Hamilton station or bus #235 from Scott St or Hunter St, west of Hunter Mall), also has great cafés and a concentration of Italian places, as well as Turkish, Lebanese, Indonesian, Thai and Indian; it's jam-packed Friday and Saturday nights.

Apothecary Kitchen Shop, 103 Tudor St, Hamilton ☎02 4961 2020, ⓦapothecarykitchen.com.au. A bistro-style café serving excellent single-origin coffee and tasty breakfasts, lunches and pastries with a focus on healthy food without being dull; plenty of different salads and vegan options. The fig tarts ($11) are incredible, and forget what you know about coleslaws – their "wonderslaw" will leave you feeling empowered. Mon–Sat 8am–3pm.

Delucas 159 Darby St ☎02 4929 3555, ⓦbit.ly/delucaspizza. This dimly lit, groovy little place, populated by hip locals, dishes out delicious Italian cuisine. There are fabulous pizzas and pastas, the risottos are lovely ($20–25) and the tiramisu is out of this world ($11). Tues–Sun 5pm till late.

Estabar Shop 1, 61 Shortland Esplanade. A brilliant (all-day) breakfast option, with muesli, salmon and egg combos, and croissants. Light meals and salads (from $12) served from 11am. Picture windows look across the road to the surf. Mon–Thus 6.30am–4pm, Fri–Sun 6.30am–6pm.

1

★**Goldbergs Coffee House** 137 Darby St ☎02 4929 3122. This perennially popular Darby St institution has a cosy, boho feel, with green walls and wooden floors. The emphasis is on the excellent coffee, plus very reasonably priced, eclectic modern meals – try the Afghani cornbread with bacon for $15 for breakfast. Has a great outside courtyard. Licensed. Daily 7am–midnight.

★**Rolador** 1 Beaumont St, Hamilton ☎02 4969 1786, ⓦfacebook.com/rolador. Fabulous music and coffee, and divine, cheap meals in this artfully assembled hip establishment; owner Fiona Smart is a bona fide queen on the Melbourne café scene. The menu is diverse and interesting – try the pumpkin, spinach and polenta loaf served with avocado and fresh tomato ($13.50). Mon–Fri 6am–4pm, Sat & Sun 7am–3pm.

Scratchleys On The Wharf 200 Wharf Rd ☎02 4929 1111, ⓦscratchleys.com.au. Opposite *Harry's Café de Wheels* on the waterfront, this is a great seafood restaurant. Dine in the beautiful, airy glass-walled interior (mains $29– 45) or get takeaway and devour it happily on the grass overlooking the water. Daily 11.30am–3pm & 5.30–9pm, takeaway daily 10.30am–9pm.

DRINKING AND NIGHTLIFE

During term-time, the students of Newcastle University bring a buzz to the city, but there's a thriving **live-music scene** year-round. On Friday and Saturday nights, the city pubs on Hunter St and parallel King St are lively and there are a few **clubs**, too. For **nightlife listings**, check out ⓦnewcastlelive.com.au.

The Beach Hotel 99 Frederick St, at Ridge St, opposite Merewether Beach ☎02 4963 1574, ⓦthebeachhotel. com.au. With a huge, beachfront beer garden, this is popular all weekend and has free live bands. Daily 11am– midnight, live music Thurs–Sun from 8pm.

Cambridge Hotel 789 Hunter St, West Newcastle ☎02 4962 2459, ⓦyourcambridge.com. A medium-sized venue with good acoustics, which attracts touring interstate and international bands. Gigs Fri–Sun from 8pm.

Cazador 148 Hunter St, West Newcastle ☎02 4929 4880, ⓦcazador.com.au. With dim lighting and lots of leather and wood, this styling bar is a rare find so close to the beach. A good place to share a jug of white-wine sangria ($30) with some tapas or paella. Cocktails $17. Tues–Sun 8.30am–3pm, Wed & Thurs also 5–10pm, Fri & Sat also 5pm–midnight.

Great Northern Hotel 89 Scott St ☎02 4927 5729, ⓦthegreatnorthern.com.au. Built in 1938, this venerable old gig-hosting hotel benefited from a $3 million face-lift; however, at the time of writing it was closed while undergoing further renovations. Check the website for updates and new hours.

The Kent 59 Beaumont St, at Cleary St, Hamilton ☎02 4961 3303, ⓦthekenthotel.com.au. This beautifully renovated old pub and music venue is busy most nights with pool competitions, quizzes, karaoke, and bands Fri–Sun. You can take refuge from the noise in the plant-filled beer garden, big upstairs balcony or the decent bistro. Daily 9am–3pm, Sun 10am–midnight.

Lass O'Gowrie 14 Railway St, Wickham ☎02 4962 1248, ⓦlassogowriehotel.com.au. This down-to-earth Aussie pub near Wickham station attracts a hip, alternative crowd. Its beer garden has a backyard feel, and local bands bash out original tunes Wed–Sun (from 9pm). Good, cheap pub grub, too. The *Moulin Rouge*-esque ladies' toilets are a sight to behold. Take bus #100, #104, #111 or #118 (free). Tues–Sun noon–late.

The Terrace Bar 529 Hunter St, West Newcastle ☎02 4962 2459, ⓦtheterracebar.wordpress.com. Recently renovated and under new management, *The Terrace Bar* hosts interstate and international bands and serves craft beer. Soul, deep house and disco nights. Thurs–Sat 5pm–midnight, Sun 5–10pm.

ENTERTAINMENT

The area known as "**the cultural precinct**", near Civic Park on King, Hunter and Auckland streets, is the location for the city's major **arts venues**: the Civic Theatre, City Hall and the Playhouse. Wheeler Place, flanking Civic Theatre and the mushroom-like Newcastle City Council building, is a palm-tree-fringed, attractive space hosting occasional outdoor community events.

Civic Theatre 375 Hunter St ☎02 4929 1977, ⓦcivictheatrenewcastle.com.au. The grand, Art Deco Civic Theatre, with its opulent 1920s interior, has a diverse programme featuring dance, theatre, comedy, film and shows for children.

Event Cinema 183 King St ☎02 4926 2233, ⓦevent cinemas.com.au. Mainstream cinema and the odd art-house release are on offer at the three-screen Greater Union.

Playhouse 375 Hunter St ☎02 4929 1977, ⓦcivictheatrenewcastle.com.au. Newly refurbished venue for the performing arts (at the same location as Civic Theatre), with a thirty-year history.

University Conservatorium of Music Auckland St ☎02 4921 6836, ⓦnewcastle.edu.au. There are free lunchtime concerts (1pm) on Thurs, as well as Fri-evening performances (7.30pm; $20).

NEWCASTLE FESTIVALS

Try to time your visit to Newcastle with the **This Is Not Art** festival (☎02 4927 0470, ⓦthisisnotart.org), a dynamic, multidisciplinary experimental arts festival with free performances, exhibitions and talks all over the city over the October long weekend; the **Mattara Festival** (Festival of Newcastle; ⓦmattarafestival.org.au) is held at the same time. It's also worth investigating the **Street Performers Festival** and **Surfest** in March (ⓦsurfest .com) and the **Newcastle Jazz Festival** in August (ⓦnewcastlejazz.com.au).

DIRECTORY

Left luggage At the train station (daily 8am–5pm; $2 per article for one day; $5.50 each day after).
Post office Newcastle GPO, 1 Market St (Mon–Fri 8.45am–5pm).
Supermarket Coles, cnr of King & National Park sts; open 24hr.

The Hunter Valley

New South Wales' best-known wine region and Australia's oldest, the **Hunter Valley** is an area long synonymous with fine **wine** – in particular, its golden, citrusy **Sémillon** and soft and earthy **Shiraz**. In recent years, the region has become equally prized for its restaurant

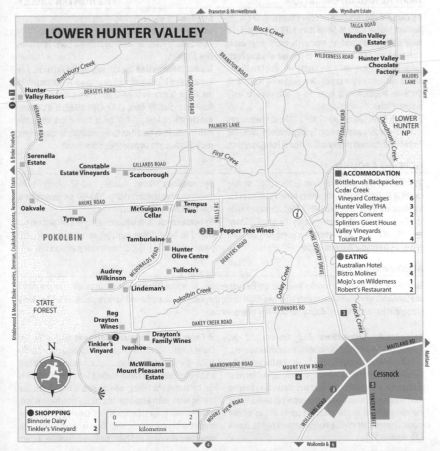

1

and cultural scene: visitors are treated to some of the best the country has to offer in the way of fine dining, gourmet delis, arts and crafts, and outdoor events and festivals.

Wine, however, is still the main attraction. The first vines were planted in 1828, and some still-existing winemaker families, such as the Draytons, date back to the 1850s. In what seems a bizarre juxtaposition, this is also a very important **coal-mining region**, in the **Upper Hunter Valley** especially. By far the best-known wine area is the **Lower Hunter Valley**, nestled under the picturesque **Brokenback Range**, fanning north from the main town of **Cessnock** to the main wine-tasting area of **Pokolbin**. Cessnock, unfortunately, is a depressingly unattractive introduction to the salubrious wine culture surrounding it, though its big old country pubs offer cheaper accommodation options. **Broke Fordwich** is an easy fifteen-minute drive from the hectic centre of Pokolbin and also has many wonderful wineries, many of them boutique.

The area can seem a little like an exhausting winery theme park; to experience the real appeal of the Hunter Valley wine country, explore the region's periphery. Take the scenic, winding Wollombi Road to the charming historic town of **Wollombi**, 28km southwest of Cessnock; or try the Lovedale/Wilderness Road area, to the northeast, and the still unspoilt **Upper Hunter**, west of Muswellbrook, with its marvellous ridges and rocky outcrops.

ARRIVAL AND INFORMATION
THE HUNTER VALLEY

By car and motorbike The Lower Hunter Valley is 2hr north of Sydney along National Hwy 1 (F3 Freeway). For a more scenic route, and an eminently more pleasurable start to your stay, turn off the F3 to join the winding Peats Ridge Rd and continue to the pretty village of Wollombi on the outskirts of the region. A meandering route from the Blue Mountains via Putty Rd is also popular with motorcyclists.

By coach Rover Coaches (📞 02 4990 1699, 🌐 rovercoaches .com.au) run daily services from Sydney Central Station, The Rocks and Chatswood to Cessnock, and on to Pokolbin resorts.

By plane If you're feeling flush, you might consider arriving in style on a scenic amphibious seaplane flight from Sydney Harbour with Sydney Harbour Seaplanes (see p.139).

Tourist information You can pick up the excellent, free *Hunter Valley Wine Country* guide with a pull-out map from the Visitor Centre on Wine Country Drive, Pokolbin (daily 9am–5pm, Sun till 4pm; 📞 02 4990 0900). If it's closed, you can still pick up the free guide from a rack under the shelter outside, or read it on 🌐 winecountry.com.au, where you'll also find info on numerous other events.

GETTING AROUND

By bike You can rent bikes from Grapemobile, on the corner of McDonalds Rd and Palmers Lane, Pokolbin ($35/ day; booking required on 📞 02 4998 7660, 🌐 grapemobile .com.au); alternatively, Hunter Valley Cycling ($35/day; 📞 0418 281 480, 🌐 huntervalleycycling.com.au) will deliver a bike to your accommodation.

By minibus Rover Coaches (📞 02 4990 1699, 🌐 rovercoaches.com.au) charge $40–50 per person for a full-day driver and minibus.

By horse coach Those who are feeling extravagant can get around in horse-drawn carriages on a group tour ($88/ person, 📞 0408 161 133, 🌐 huntervalleycarriages.com.au).

ACCOMMODATION

Since the Hunter Valley is a popular weekend trip for Sydneysiders, accommodation **prices** can as much as double on Fri and Sat nights when most places only offer two-night deals; the prices below are for midweek rooms. Advance **booking** is essential for weekends and during the Oct–Nov events season.

Bottlebrush Backpackers 26B Cumberland St, Cessnock 📞 02 4991 3278, 🌐 bottlebrushbackpackers. com. A convenient budget choice for visiting the vineyards. The weatherboard house is in an excellent central location in Cessnock, with public transport and places to eat within short walking distance. Rooms are simple but with a/c, and you can book out dorms (sleeping up to six) as private rooms. Discounts for staying more than three nights. Dorms __$30__; doubles __$75__

★**Cedar Creek Vineyard Cottages** Wollombi Rd, Cedar Creek, 10km northwest of Wollombi 📞 02 4998 1576, 🌐 cedarcreekcottages.com.au. An idyllic choice on a 550-acre deer- and cattle-stocked farm. The vineyard is run by Stonehurst Wines, who operate a tiny chapel-like tasting room, with wine from insecticide-free, handpicked, estate-grown grapes. Delightful self-catering cottages, for couples or big groups, are made from recycled timber with views over vineyards and bush-clad mountainsides. Expect

WINE TASTING IN THE HUNTER VALLEY

Nearly a hundred and fifty wineries cluster around the Lower Hunter Valley, and fewer than twenty in the Upper Hunter; almost all offer **free wine tastings**. Virtually all are open daily, at least between 10am and 4pm, and many offer **guided tours**. Try to tour the wineries during the week; at weekends, both the number of visitors and accommodation prices go up, and the area can get booked out completely when there's a concert on in the valley. Below are a handful of our favourites, but you'll inevitably discover your own gems.

VINEYARD TOURS

A huge range of vineyard tours are on offer, and many of the wineries themselves offer guided tours.

Hunter Valley Day Tours ☎02 4951 4574, ⓦhuntervalleydaytours.com.au. The excellent, long-established Hunter Valley Day Tours offers a wine-and-cheese tasting tour, taking you through various wineries in the region ($95 for Hunter Valley pick-ups; restaurant lunch included), with very informative commentary.

Hunter Valley Resort 917 Hermitage Rd, Pokolbin ☎02 4998 7777, ⓦhunterresort.com.au. Runs a recommended wine course (daily 9–11am; $60; bookings essential), including a tour and followed by a tasting instruction tutorial.

Hunter Vineyard Tours ☎02 4991 1659, ⓦhuntervineyardtours.com.au. The family-run Hunter Vineyard Tours visits five wineries (Hunter Valley pick-up $70; Newcastle, Maitland or Wollombi $80; restaurant lunch $29 extra).

McWilliams Mount Pleasant Estate 401 Marrowbone Rd, Pokolbin ☎02 4998 7505, ⓦmountpleasantwines.com.au. A winery with a pedigree of award-winning wines such as Old Hill Shiraz. Wine tastings are run by very knowledgeable guides (daily 11am; $3.30, no booking required).

WINERIES

Constable Estate Vineyards 205 Gillards Rd, Pokolbin ⓦconstablevineyards.com.au. Established in 1981 by two best friends from England, this small establishment offers unhurried wine tastings. The thirty-acre vineyard under the Brokenback Ranges has five formal gardens – Sculpture, Camellia, Rose, Herb and Secret; the gardener leads a tour Mon & Wed–Fri at 10.30am. Mon & Wed–Sun 10am–5pm.

Drayton's Family Wines 555 Oakey Creek Rd, Pokolbin ⓦdraytonswines.com.au. Friendly, down-to-earth winery, established in 1853. All processes are still carried out on site, and the excellent free tours (Mon–Fri 11am; 40min) guide you through. A pretty picnic area with wood-fired BBQ overlooks a small dam and vineyards. Mon–Fri 8am–5pm, Sat & Sun 10am–5pm.

Krinklewood 712 Wollombi Rd, Broke ⓦkrinklewood .com. Stunning cellar door with European-styled courtyard and gardens – the most beautiful winery in the region. Biodynamic *Krinklewood* does all the classic Hunter varieties of Sémillon, Chardonnay, Verdelho and Shiraz, with younger plantings including French varieties Viognier and Mourvèdre and the popular Spanish Tempranillo. Fri, Sat & Sun 10am–5pm or by appointment.

Mount Broke Wines 30 Adams Peak Rd, Broke Fordwich ☎02 65791314, ⓦmtbrokewines.com.au. This boutique winery has recently won awards for its stunning Chardonnay (buy a couple or even a case if you're here in Dec/Jan when it's bottled). The pretty courtyard makes a pleasant tasting spot, and lunch can be organized if you phone ahead. Fri & Sat 10am–5pm.

Scarborough 179 Gillards Rd, Pokolbin ⓦscarboroughwine.com.au. Small, friendly winery specializing in Chardonnay and Pinot Noir, and with a reputation for outstanding wines. Pleasantly relaxed sit-down tastings are held in a small cottage on Hungerford Hill with wonderful valley views. Daily 9am–5pm.

Tamburlaine 358 Mcdonalds Rd, Pokolbin ⓦtamburlaine.com.au. The jasmine-scented garden outside provides a hint of the flowery, elegant wines within. Tastings are well orchestrated and delivered with a heap of experience. Daily 9am–5pm.

Tempus Two Broke Rd, at McDonalds Rd, Pokolbin ⓦtempustwo.com.au. This huge, contemporary winery – all steel, glass and stone – has a high-tech, urban-chic exterior. The place is owned by Lisa McGuigan, of the well-known winemaking family, whose unique-tasting wines are the result of using lesser-known varieties such as Pinot Gris, Viognier and Marsanne. The attached Japanese-Thai *Oishi* (daily 11.30am–9.30pm; ☎02 4998 7051, ⓦoishii.com.au) has surprisingly moderate prices (mains $23–28), and there's a lounge area where you can relax over an espresso. Daily 10am–5pm.

Tyrrell's Broke Rd, Pokolbin ⓦtyrrells.com.au. The oldest independent family vineyards, producing consistently fine wines. The tiny ironbark slab hut, where Edward Tyrrell lived when he began the winery in 1858, is still in the grounds, and the old winery with its cool earth floor is much as it was. It's in a beautiful setting against the Brokenback Range. Tours run daily at 10.30am ($5). Mon–Sat 9am–5pm, Sun 10am–4pm.

1

HUNTER VALLEY FESTIVALS AND EVENTS

A Day on the Green On multiple dates from November to February, Bimbadgen Estate holds A Day on the Green, featuring local and international performers. Tickets $108–204, bookable through ⓦticketek.com.au or ⓦadayonthegreen.com.au.

Jazz in the Vines A day of fine food, wine and music in later October at Jazz in the Vines, based at Tyrrell's vineyard (see box, p.153; $69–89; ⓦjazzinthevines.com.au).

Lovedale Long Lunch Every year over a mid-May weekend, around eight wineries along and around the scenic Lovedale and Wilderness roads team up with local restaurants to host the Lovedale Long Lunch (weekend package, including 2 meals $90; ☎02 4990 4526, ⓦlovedalelonglunch.com.au).

Opera in the Vineyards In late October, Wyndham Estate in Dalwood hosts the night-time Opera in the Vineyards ($85; ⓦoperainthevineyards.com.au).

Sculpture in the Vineyards From early October to mid-January, the Wollombi region hosts Sculpture in the Vineyards, in which surreal and innovative site-specific sculptures dazzle among the vineyards, valleys, dirt roads and bushy ridges of picturesque Wollombi's wineries (ⓦsculptureinthevineyards.com.au).

---

queen-sized beds, wood combustion stoves, ceiling fans and a/c, stylish decor, breakfast hampers (for a fee) and a BBQ. There's a $20 surcharge for a single night and $30 extra per night on weekends. **$169**

Hunter Valley YHA 100 Wine Country Drive, Nulkaba ☎02 4991 3278, ⓦyha.com.au. A single-storey long timber building with wraparound balcony offering everything you'd expect: a communal kitchen, fridge, laundry and TV lounge, plus a sauna and swimming pool. Bicycles to rent, cheap tours to local vineyards and, for nightlife, *Potters Hotel and Brewery* is only 400m away. Dorms **$33.50**; doubles **$76.50**

Peppers Convent Halls Rd, Pokolbin ☎02 4993 8999, ⓦpeppers.com.au. The swankiest place to stay in the Hunter Valley, with a price to match (weekends from $359). The guesthouse, converted from an old nunnery, is decidedly regal, with fireplaces, low beams and luxurious

rooms, and is part of the Pepper Tree Winery, with fine dining at *Robert's Restaurant* (see opposite) just a stroll away. **$209**

Splinters Guest House 617 Hermitage Rd, Pokolbin ☎02 6574 7118, ⓦsplinters.com.au. Traditional home and cottages with wraparound balconies and pitched roofs set in ten acres of land, with sweeping views of the Brokenback Ranges. Decor is stylish and the welcome exceptionally warm: the owner will advise on where to eat and imbibe in the area. Double **$230**; cottage **$300**

Valley Vineyards Tourist Park Mount View Rd, 2km northwest of Cessnock ☎02 4990 2573, ⓦvalleyvineyard.com.au. High-standard campsite with kitchen, BBQ area, pool and on-site Thai restaurant. Cabins (sleep two to four; BYO linen) have external bathrooms; villas (sleeps four to six; linen included) have en-suite facilities. Cabin **$100**; villa **$200**

EATING AND DRINKING

Many of the Hunter's excellent (and pricey) **restaurants** are attached to wineries or are among vineyards rather than in the towns (see box, p.153), while the large old **pubs** dish out less fancy but more affordable grub.

Australian Hotel 136 Wollombi Rd, Cessnock ☎1800 104 010, ⓦaustraliahotel.com.au. The excellent bistro here is popular with the locals, and the pub showcases the Hunter's coal-mining roots with mining paraphernalia and related art. Though steaks hit the $28 mark, mains average $15–26 and there are excellent $10 lunch deals; the menu encompasses stir-fries, gourmet salads and vegetarian dishes. Daily noon–3pm & 6–11pm.

Bistro Molines Tallavera Grove, 749 Mount View Rd, Mount View ☎02 4990 9553, ⓦbistromolines.com.au. Valley and vineyard views, great wines and excellent food make for a lovely, if isolated, restaurant. As the name suggests, the chef is French; try the excellent baked figs wrapped in gorgonzola and prosciutto ($27), followed by

local Hunter duckling with orange glaze ($40). Splash out and stay in the cottage, if you can't make it home ($270). Mon & Thurs–Sun noon–3pm, also Fri & Sat 7–9pm.

★**Mojo's on Wilderness** Wilderness Rd, Lovedale ☎02 4930 7244, ⓦmojos.com.au. A British Michelin-rated chef and his Australian chef wife create the divine modern British-Australian food at this bush-set restaurant with a warm, arty interior, flowery courtyard with hillside views, cheerful staff and a laidback vibe. The set-dinner menu (2 courses $62, 3 courses $75) has suggested wines for each course, available by the glass. The attached deli (Mon–Fri 10am–5pm; Sat & Sun 9am–4pm) serves scrumptious gourmet pizzas ($10), panini ($10) and desserts ($3–12), as well as coffee; consume it all on

brightly coloured beanbags on a lush green lawn beneath stylish parasols – or take away. Daily 6.30–11pm.
Robert's Restaurant Pepper Tree Winery, Halls Rd, Pokolbin ☎ 02 4998 7330. This restaurant in a fairy-tale wooden farmhouse (built 1876) is as romantic a dining experience as one could possibly wish for. Oodles of dark

polished timber contrast with cream walls and gleaming white tablecloths, while gothic antiques, candles and flowers do the rest. The modern European cuisine is outstanding – but pricey. Mains $40–56; tasting menu (highly recommended) $150. Booking essential. Daily 6–11pm, Sat & Sun also noon–3pm.

SHOPPING

Just about every winery and accommodation place in the valley has a BBQ or cooking facilities – **picnic** or **self-catering** supplies are a budgeter's necessity in this area. Other places where you can taste the local wares include:

Binnorie Dairy 1 Mistletoe Lane, Pokolbin ☎ 02 4998 6660, ⍟ binnorie.com.au. Just across from the Hunter Resort, the Binnorie Dairy stock their own award-winning soft fresh cheeses. Mon–Sat 10am–5pm, Sun 10am–4pm.
Tinkler's Vineyard Pokolbin Mountain Rd ☎ 02 4998

7435, ⍟ tinklers.com.au. The single-vineyard wines here are fruity and come from small batches. Seasonal produce is also on sale here, including grapes, peaches, nectarines, avocados, figs and citrus fruits, plus jams, marmalades, pickles and relishes. Daily 10am–5pm.

Sydney Olympic Park

Homebush Bay **Aquatic Centre** Mon–Fri 5am–9pm, Sat & Sun 6am–7pm • $7.50 • **ANZ Stadium tours** Daily 11am, 1pm & 3pm • $28.50 • Turn up at Gate C, but check it's a non-event day first by contacting ☎ 02 8765 2300 or checking ⍟ anzstadium.com.au • ⍟ sydneyolympicpark.com.au • Ferry up the Parramatta River: the RiverCat from Circular Quay (40min; $7.18 one-way) or direct train from Central, four times daily on weekdays (at weekends, change at Lidcombe station, from where trains depart every 10min)

The main focus of the 2000 Olympic events was **Sydney Olympic Park** at Homebush Bay, since transformed into a family-oriented entertainment and sporting complex, with events such as free outdoor movies, multicultural festivals and children's holiday activities. The **Aquatic Centre** here has a pool for laps and a splash-and-play area complete with wave pool and slide. The **ANZ Stadium** (originally Telstra Stadium), the venue for the opening and closing Olympic ceremonies, track and field events, and marathon and soccer finals, is Sydney's largest stadium, used for Australian Rules football, cricket, rugby league, rugby union, soccer and concerts. Tours of the stadium with commentary are available daily.

Bicentennial Park and Newington Armory

Park: Daily sunrise–sunset • Free • **Armory**: Daily 24hr • Free • **Bike hire**: Next to *Lilies on the Park* café in Bicentennial Park • From $15/hr, $30/half-day • ⍟ bikehiresydneyolympicpark.com.au • Bikes can be taken on trains and ferries, though charges apply during peak hours

Opposite the Olympic site is the huge **Bicentennial Park**; more than half of the expanse is conservation wetlands – a delightful, zigzagging boardwalk explores thick subtropical mangroves, and there's a bird hide from which to observe a profusion of native birds. **Newington Armory** (formerly the Royal Australian Naval Armament Depot, or RANAD), is also close by and features over one hundred heritage buildings, set amid a vast riverside landscape of hills and woodlands. The best way to explore both of these areas is by **bike**; there's a rental outlet in Bicentennial Park.

Parramatta

Situated on the Parramatta River, a little over 20km upstream from the harbour mouth, **PARRAMATTA** was the first of Sydney's rural satellites – the first farm settlement in Australia, in fact. It's hard to believe today, but the fertile soil of "Rosehill", as it was originally called, saved the fledgling colony from starvation with its first wheat crop of 1789. Dotted here and there among the malls and busy roads are a few remnants from that time – eighteenth-century public buildings and original settlers' dwellings that warrant a visit if you're interested in Australian history.

1

Parramatta today is a modern multicultural suburban town with a wealth of international restaurants around Church and Phillip streets, and bargain shops and factory outlets on its outskirts.

Old Government House

Parramatta Park • Tues–Sun 10am–4pm • $10 • ☎ 02 9635 8149, ⓦ nationaltrust.org.au

Parramatta's most important historic feature is the National Trust-owned **Old Government House** in **Parramatta Park** by the river. Entered through the 1885 gatehouse on O'Connell Street, the park – filled with native trees – rises up to the gracious old Georgian-style building, the oldest remaining public edifice in Australia. It was built between 1799 and 1816 and used as the Viceregal residence until 1855; one wing has been converted into a pleasant teahouse.

ARRIVAL AND INFORMATION   PARRAMATTA

By train It's a 30min train ride from Central Station to Parramatta.

By ferry The most enjoyable way to get to Parramatta is on the River Express from Circular Quay up the Parramatta River (50min; $8 one-way). The wharf is on Phillip St.

Tourist information The visitor centre (daily 9am–5pm; ☎ 02 8839 3311, ⓦ discoverparramatta.com) is at 346A Church St, by the convict-built Lennox Bridge. The Parramatta Heritage Centre is in the same building. The centre hands out free walking-route maps detailing its many historical attractions.

Penrith

1hr train ride from Central Station

The Western Highway and the rail lines head on from Parramatta to **PENRITH**, the westernmost of Sydney's satellite towns, in a curve of the Nepean River at the foot of the Blue Mountains (on the way out here you pass **Featherdale Wildlife Park**; see box, p.145). Penrith has an old-fashioned Aussie feel to it – a tight community that is immensely proud of the Panthers, its boisterous rugby league team. The area is also the home of the extensive International Regatta Centre on Penrith Lakes, spreading between Castlereagh and Cranebrook roads north of the town centre, and used in the Olympics; at **Penrith Whitewater Stadium** you can go whitewater rafting (1hr 30min; $94; ☎ 02 4730 4333, ⓦ penrithwhitewater.com.au).

Blue Mountains region

The section of the Great Dividing Range nearest Sydney gets its name from the blue mist that rises from millions of eucalyptus trees and hangs in the mountain air, tinting the sky and the range alike. In the colony's early days, the **Blue Mountains** were believed to be an insurmountable barrier to the west. The first expeditions followed the streams in the valleys until they were defeated by cliff faces rising vertically above them. Only in 1813, when the explorers Wentworth, Blaxland and Lawson followed the ridges instead of the valleys, were the "mountains" (actually a series of canyons) finally conquered, allowing the western plains to be opened up for settlement. The range is surmounted by a plateau at an altitude of more than 1000m where, over millions of years, rivers have carved deep valleys into the sandstone, and winds and driving rain have helped to deepen the ravines, creating a spectacular scenery of sheer precipices and walled canyons.

Before white settlement, the Daruk Aborigines lived here, dressed in animal-skin cloaks to ward off the cold. An early coal-mining industry, based in **Katoomba**, was followed by tourism, which snowballed after the arrival of the railway in 1868; by 1900, the first three mountain stations of Wentworth Falls, Katoomba and Mount Victoria had been established as fashionable resorts, extolling the health-giving benefits of eucalyptus-infused mountain air. In 2000, the Blue Mountains became a **UNESCO**

FROM TOP MARDI GRAS (P.136); TARONGA ZOO (P.100) >

1

SAFETY IN THE BLUE MOUNTAINS

Walkers go missing in the Blue Mountains with distressing regularity. The mountains are extremely wild, and you can lose your bearings quickly. Never leave the **marked paths**, and use a **guide** for long-distance walks. Bear in mind that due to the high elevation, night-time temperatures dip pretty low in winter, when you should take an extra layer and waterproofs.

World Heritage Site, joining the Great Barrier Reef; the listing came after abseiling was finally banned on the mountains' most famous scenic wonder, the **Three Sisters**, after forty years of clambering had caused significant erosion. The Blue Mountains stand out from other Australian forests in particular for the **Wollemi pine**, discovered in 1994 (see box, p.161), a "living fossil" that dates back to the dinosaur era.

All the villages and towns of the romantically dubbed "**City of the Blue Mountains**" lie on a ridge, connected by the Great Western Highway. Around them is the **Blue Mountains National Park**, the state's fourth-largest national park and to many minds the best. The region makes a great weekend break from the city, with stunning views and clean air complemented by a wide range of accommodation, cafés and restaurants. But be warned: at weekends, and during the summer holidays, Katoomba is thronged with escapees from the city, and prices escalate accordingly. Even at their most crowded, though, the Blue Mountains offer somewhere where you can find peace and quiet, and even solitude – the deep gorges and high rocks make much of the terrain inaccessible except to bushwalkers and mountaineers. Climbing schools (see p.164) offer courses in rock climbing, abseiling and canyoning for both beginners and experienced climbers, while Glenbrook is a popular mountain-biking spot.

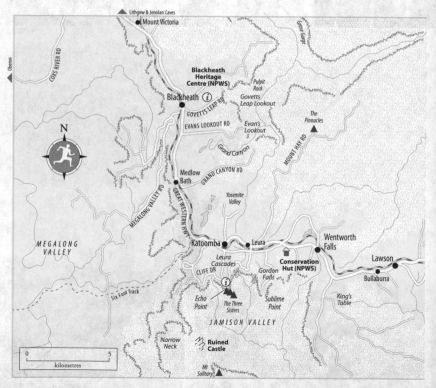

Glenbrook

The first stop off the busy Highway 32 heading west from Sydney is **GLENBROOK**, a pleasant village with an adventure shop and a strip of cafés. The section of the Blue Mountains National Park here ($8/vehicle per day) is popular for **mountain biking** along the Oaks Fire Trail and for the Aboriginal rock art in the Red Hands Cave. The part-time NPWS office is at the outside end of Bruce Road (hours variable; ☎02 4739 2950).

Red Hands Cave

Blue Mountains National Park, Glenbrook • Daily 9am–4.30pm • Cave free, $8 per vehicle park entry • ☎02 4787 8877, ⓦ nationalparks .nsw.gov.au • Vehicle required for access

The hand stencils at the **Red Hands Cave** are a fascinating example of Aboriginal art. The handprints alternate between white and ochre red, positive and negative, many blurry but some with startling clarity despite the age – they range from 500 to 1600 years old. The prints were made by blowing a mix of water and ochre (a natural earth pigment) over hands, and can be rather moving to see close up.

Wentworth Falls

The small town of **WENTWORTH FALLS** was named after William Wentworth, one of the famous trio who conquered the mountains in 1813. A signposted road leads from the highway to the **Wentworth Falls Reserve**, with superb views of the waterfall tumbling down into the Jamison Valley; walkers should take the scenic 2.5km Charles Darwin Walk, avoiding the road. Once at the car park by the Falls, see the information boards for details of **walks**, from short strolls to the four- to five-hour Wentworth Pass route, which has an additional two- to three-hour detour to Vera Falls.

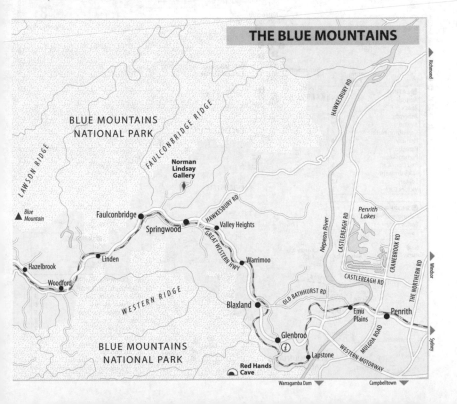

THE BLUE MOUNTAINS

1

Leura

Just 2km west of Wentworth Falls, well-heeled **LEURA**, packed with cafés and antiques stores, is a scenic spot with views across the Jamison Valley to the imposing plateau that is **Mount Solitary**. The main shopping strip, **Leura Mall**, has a wide grassy area lined with cherry trees and makes a popular picnicking spot.

Gardens

Leura Gardens Festival At around a dozen gardens in the region; check website for current list • Early to mid-Oct • $5 per garden, $25 all gardens • Ⓦ leuragardensfestival.com.au • **Everglades Gardens** 37 Everglades Ave, 2km southeast of Leura Mall • Daily 10am–5pm • $13 • Ⓦ everglades.org.au

Leura is renowned for its beautiful **gardens**, and nine are open to the public during the **Leura Gardens Festival**. Open all year round, though, is the beautiful National Trust-listed **Everglades Gardens**, which has wonderful Jamison Valley views from its formal terraces, a colourful display of azaleas and rhododendrons, an arboretum, and a simple tearoom.

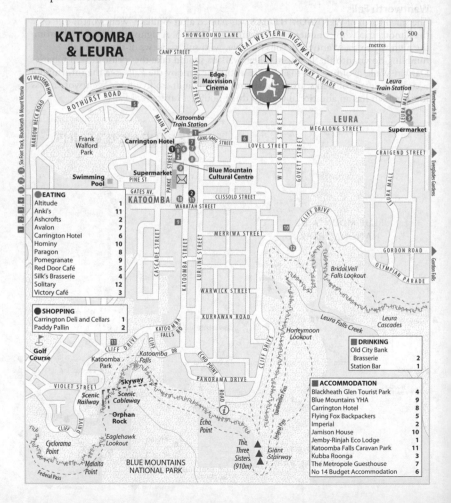

KATOOMBA & LEURA

● EATING	
Altitude	1
Anki's	11
Ashcrofts	2
Avalon	7
Carrington Hotel	6
Hominy	10
Paragon	8
Pomegranate	9
Red Door Café	5
Silk's Brasserie	4
Solitary	12
Victory Café	3

● SHOPPING	
Carrington Deli and Cellars	1
Paddy Pallin	2

■ DRINKING	
Old City Bank	
Brasserie	2
Station Bar	1

■ ACCOMMODATION	
Blackheath Glen Tourist Park	4
Blue Mountains YHA	9
Carrington Hotel	8
Flying Fox Backpackers	5
Imperial	2
Jamison House	10
Jemby-Rinjah Eco Lodge	1
Katoomba Falls Caravan Park	11
Kubba Roonga	3
The Metropole Guesthouse	7
No 14 Budget Accommodation	6

Gordon Falls and the Leura Cascades

Just over 1km south of Leura Mall is the **Gordon Falls** picnic area on Lone Pine Avenue, where Leura's mansions and gardens give way to the bush of the **Blue Mountains National Park**; it's an easy ten-minute return walk to the lookout over the falls, and there's a canyon walk (1.5hr return; medium difficulty) via Lyre Bird Dell and the Pool of Siloam, which takes in some of the Blue Mountains' distinctive hanging swamps, an Aboriginal rock shelter and cooling rainforest; the walk leaves from the far end of the picnic area. From Gordon Falls, a 45-minute bushwalk partway along the Prince Henry Cliff Walk (see p.162) heads to **Leura Cascades** picnic area off **Cliff Drive** (the scenic route around the cliffs that extends from Leura to beyond Katoomba) where there are several bushwalks, including a two- to three-hour circuit walk to the base of the cascading **Bridal Veil Falls** (not to be confused with Bridal Veil Falls on the north side of Leura at Grose Valley). To the east of Gordon Falls, Sublime Point Road leads to the aptly named **Sublime Point** lookout, from where there are panoramic views of the Jamison Valley.

Katoomba and around

KATOOMBA, 103km west of Sydney, is the biggest town in the Blue Mountains and the area's commercial heart; it's also the best located for the major sights of Echo Point and the Three Sisters. There's a lively café scene on **Katoomba Street**, which runs downhill from the train station; the street is also full of vintage clothes shops, secondhand bookstores, outdoor supplies, antiques dealers and gift shops. Katoomba's Art Deco buildings, with their pastel colours, stained glass and glamorous original fittings, make for an enticing wander. If you're dependent on public transport, Katoomba makes the best base in the region; facilities and services are concentrated here.

Blue Mountains Cultural Centre

30 Parke St • Mon–Fri 10am–5pm, Sat & Sun 10am–4pm • $5 • ☎ 02 4780 5410, ⓦ bluemountainsculturalcentre.com.au

A very stylish addition to the town, the **Blue Mountains Cultural Centre** is located in a new ecofriendly building and features wonderful mountain views. There's a strong programme of temporary exhibitions, a gallery featuring Aboriginal art and an excellent high-tech immersive display on the history, geology and fauna of the Blue Mountain region. They also have a café and shop selling art books, jewellery and homewares.

Carrington Hotel

15–47 Katoomba St • Tours by reservation 1hr–1hr 30min • $25 • ☎ 02 4754 5726, ⓦ thecarrington.com.au

When Katoomba was first discovered by fashionable city-dwellers in the late nineteenth century, the grandiose **Carrington Hotel** (see p.165), prominently located at the top of Katoomba Street, was the height of elegance. It's been restored to its former glory, with elegant sloping lawns running down to the street, half of which has been taken over by a new **town square**. Learn the secrets of the hotel in a tour given by a historian.

> ## WOLLEMI PINE
>
> A famous feature of the Katoomba region is the "dinosaur trees", a stand of 30m-high **Wollemi pine**, previously known only from fossil material over sixty million years old. The trees – miraculously still existing – survive deep within a sheltered rainforest gully in the **Wollemi National Park**, north of Katoomba, and they made headlines when they were first discovered in 1994 by a group of canyoners. The first cultivated Wollemi pine was planted in 1998 at Sydney's Royal Botanic Gardens, and you can see one in the YHA hostel in Katoomba (see p.165).

1

Echo Point and the Three Sisters

A 25min walk south from the train station down Katoomba St and along Lurline St and Echo Point Rd, or by tour, or by regular Opal Card bus #686 from outside the Carrington Hotel

From the projecting lookout platform at **Echo Point**, between the visitor centre (see opposite) and the souvenir shops and eating places, breathtaking vistas take in the Kedumba and Jamison valleys, Mount Solitary, the Ruined Castle, Kings Tableland and the Blue Mountains' most famous landmark, the **Three Sisters** (910m). These three gnarled, rocky points take their name from an Aboriginal Dreamtime story that relates how the Kedumba people were losing a battle against the rival Nepean people: the Kedumba leader, fearing that his three beautiful daughters would be carried off by the enemy, turned them to stone, but was killed before he could reverse his spell.

Giant Stairway

1hr 45min walk, one-way

The Three Sisters are accessed via the **Giant Stairway**, the beginning of the very steep eight hundred steps into the 300m-deep **Jamison Valley** below, passing **Katoomba Falls** en route. There's a popular walking route, taking about two hours and graded medium, down the stairway and partway along the **Federal Pass** to the **Landslide**, and then on to the Scenic Railway or Cableway (see below), either of which you can take back up to the ridge. Otherwise, if you have the energy, follow the signs along the path to take the steep Federal Steps.

Scenic World

At the end of Violet St, off Cliff Drive • Scenic Skyway, Scenic Railway & Scenic Cableway daily 9am–4.50pm; every 10min • $39; cableway only $19 • ⓦ scenicworld.com.au • Regular Opal Card bus #686 from outside the Carrington Hotel

To spare yourself the trek down into the Jamison Valley or the walk back up, head for the very touristy **Scenic World**. Apart from housing a small cinema showing a documentary of the area (free with any ticket), you can take a short and pricey glass-bottomed cable-car ride over the valley in the **Scenic Skyway** or choose between two modes of transport to get to the valley floor: the original **Scenic Railway** or the modern **Scenic Cableway**. The Railway and Cableway offer steep descents to the valley floor with fantastic views of the Three Sisters, and end up about 100m away from each other, making it easy to go down by one and up by the other. Once at the bottom, a 2km, wheelchair-accessible boardwalk meanders through the rainforest, with boards detailing natural features and history. For the more energetic, there's a tranquil but moderately difficult 12km return bushwalk to the **Ruined Castle**, or link up with paths to the Three Sisters (see above).

Cliff Drive

A short walk from the Scenic World complex along **Cliff Drive** is the **Katoomba Falls picnic area** in Katoomba Park, where there's a kiosk and several bushwalking options. The **Prince Henry Cliff Walk** (9km one-way; 3hr; easy) is a long, pleasant stroll along the plateau clifftop via Echo Point all the way to **Gordon Falls** (see p.161) with glorious lookouts. A scenic drive following Cliff Drive southwest of Katoomba Falls leads to several other spectacular lookouts: Eaglehawk, the Landslide and Narrow Neck – a great sunset spot, with views into both the Jamison and Megalong valleys.

Blackheath

Two train stops beyond Katoomba, and 11km further northwest along the Great Western Highway, there are more lookout points at **BLACKHEATH** – just as impressive as Echo Point and much less busy. One of the best is **Govetts Leap**, at the end of Govetts Leap Road (just over 2km east of the highway through the village centre), near the **Blue Mountains Heritage Centre** at Blackheath, which acts as the Blue Mountains National Park headquarters (see p.164). The 2km **Fairfax Heritage Track** from the NPWS centre is wheelchair- and pram-accessible and takes in the Govetts Leap Lookout with its marvellous panorama of the Grose Valley and the much-photographed Bridal Veil Falls. Many walks start from the centre, but one of the most popular, **The Grand Canyon** (5km; 3hr 30min; medium difficulty), begins from Evans Lookout Road at the south end of town, west of the Great Western Highway.

Govetts Leap Road and its shady cross-street, Wentworth Street, have lots of antiques and craft shops, an antiquarian bookshop, and great cafés and restaurants. Some 10km southwest of Blackheath, across the railway line, the beautiful, unspoilt **Megalong Valley** is reached via winding Megalong Road; it's popular for **horseriding** (see p.164), and there are creeks with swimmable waterholes.

Mount Victoria

At the top of the Blue Mountains, secluded and leafy **MOUNT VICTORIA**, 6km northwest of Blackheath along the Great Western Highway and the last mountain-settlement proper, is the only one with an authentic village feel. The great old pub, the *Imperial* (see p.165) is good for a drink or meal. Several antiques shops and secondhand bookstores are worth a browse. Some short walks start from the Fairy Bower picnic area, a ten-minute walk from the Great Western Highway via Mount Piddington Road.

Norman Lindsay Gallery

14 Norman Lindsay Crescent, Faulconbridge • Daily 10am–4pm; tours 10.30am and 11.30am • Museum $15 • ☎ 02 4751 1067, ⓦ normanlindsay.au.au • From Springwood station (on the Katoomba or Lithgow lines, 1hr 30min from central Sydney), a shuttle bus departs at 10.50am Mon–Fri and returns at 2.40pm

The main highlight of the Falcounbridge region is the **Norman Lindsay Gallery**. Half of the allure of this museum is down to the infamous nude studies of this pioneering Australian artist; and the other is the stately cottage and garden that the gallery is housed in. Don't miss the knowledgeable guided tours, as they are the only way to access the painting and etching studios. The on-site café makes a good rest stop.

ARRIVAL AND DEPARTURE　　　　　　　　　　　　BLUE MOUNTAINS

By car Public transport to the mountains is pretty decent, but your own vehicle will give you much greater flexibility, allowing you to take detours to old mansions, cottage gardens and the lookout points scattered along the ridge. The drive takes an hour or so from the Sydney CBD.

By train Trains leave from Central Station for Mount Victoria and/or Lithgow and follow the highway, stopping at all the major towns en route; there are frequent departures until the last train at about midnight. The trains take around 2hr to get to the Blue Mountains, and you need an Opal Card to travel. From Central Station to Katoomba or other Blue Mountain destinations costs $8.30 ($5.81 off-peak) one-way, and the Opal Card daily cap is $15 (Sun cap $2.50; see box, p.115).

GETTING AROUND

By bus Blue Mountains Bus Company (☎ 02 4751 1077, ⓦ bmbc.com.au) run Trolley Tours (ⓦ trolleytours .com.au) services every 30min to Blackheath, Mount Victoria (Mon–Fri only), Echo Point and the Scenic World complex, Leura, Wentworth Falls and North Katoomba for $25. A cheaper option is to use the regular Opal Card (see box, p.115) local buses that leave from Katoomba St outside the *Carrington Hotel* (see p.165) and opposite the *Savoy*, and that run the loop to Echo Point and Scenic World. You can also get around the region on the Blue Mountains Explorer Bus (see p.164), but the routes are the same as those of public buses.

By taxi Taxis wait outside the main train stations to meet arrivals. If you need to call a cab, for the upper mountains try Katoomba Radio Cabs (☎ 02 4782 1311, ⓦ katoombataxis.com.au), and for the middle mountains try Blue Mountains Taxi Cabs (☎ 02 4759 3000).

Car rental Hertz, 78–82 Megalong St, 15min walk west of Leura station (☎ 02 4784 1043, ⓦ hertz.com.au).

By bike For mountain-bike rental, try Rocksports Adventure Glenbrook, 1A Ross St, Glenbrook ($40/day including helmet and repair kit; ☎ 02 4739 3152).

INFORMATION

Tourist information The Blue Mountains Information Centre (daily 9am–4.30pm; ☎ 1300 653 408, ⓦ bluemts .com.au) is on the Great Western Hwy at Glenbrook (see p.159), the gateway to the Blue Mountains. The other

1

BLUE MOUNTAINS FESTIVALS

The Blue Mountains Music Festival is a three-day, mid-March festival of folk, roots and blues, held in Katoomba and featuring Australian and international musicians on several indoor and outdoor stages ($165 weekend, $95 day and night, $65–70 night only; ⓦ bmff.org.au).

The Winter Magic Festival (ⓦ wintermagic.com.au), celebrating the winter solstice in late June, consists of a number of events over several weeks culminating on the final Saturday, when Katoomba Street is closed off to traffic and taken over by performers and a parade of locals in colourful pagan garments.

official tourist information centre is at Echo Point, near Katoomba (daily 9am–5pm; ⓣ 1300 653 408); both offices offer a free accommodation booking service. Check the online publications the *Blue Mountains Gazette* (ⓦ bluemountainsgazette.com.au), which has local news and an events guide. The only point where you must pay vehicle entry into the park is at Glenbrook ($7).

Ranger station The Blue Mountains National Park has its main ranger station at Blackheath (Govetts Leap Rd; daily 9am–4.30pm; ⓣ 02 4787 8877), where you can get comprehensive walking and camping information – there are car-accessible NPWS camping and picnic sites near Glenbrook, Woodford, Wentworth Falls, Blackheath and Oberon, and bush camping is allowed in most areas.

TOURS

Most tours of the Blue Mountains start from Sydney (see box, p.144). The two Katoomba-based, hop-on-hop-off **tour buses** have offices by the train station exit on Main St; passes include discounts to some of the attractions en route.

Blue Mountains Explorer Bus ⓣ 02 4782 1866 or ⓣ 1300 300 915, ⓦ explorerbus.com.au. The Blue Mountains Explorer Bus links Katoomba and Leura in a hop-on, hop-off red double-decker bus (departs Katoomba roughly hourly 9.45am–4.05pm, last return 5.15pm; 29 stops; $44 seven-day pass). There's no commentary with the Explorer Bus, but you do get a guide with maps detailing bushwalk and sightseeing options.

Blue Mountains Walkabout ⓣ 0408 443 822, ⓦ bluemountainswalkabout.com. The excellent Blue Mountains Walkabout offers all-day ($95) off-the-beaten-track bush roams (around 10km) between Faulconbridge and Springwood, led by an Aboriginal guide.

Fantastic Aussie Tours 283 Main St, Katoomba

ⓣ 02 4782 1866, ⓦ fantastic-aussie-tours.com.au. Large-group coach tours to the Jenolan Caves: a day-tour (daily; $70–78 with one cave entry), or adventure caving ($105).

Tread Lightly Eco Tours ⓣ 02 4788 1229, ⓦ treadlightly.com.au. Small-group, expert-guided, half-day and full-day bushwalk, 4WD and kangaroo-spotting tours from Katoomba. From $135 with picnic lunch.

Trolley Tours ⓣ 1800 801 577, ⓦ trolleytours.com.au. A minibus decked out like a tram, which does a scenic circuit with commentary from Katoomba to Leura around Cliff Drive to the Three Sisters and back, taking in 29 attractions (departs Katoomba hourly 9.45am–4.45pm; $25 all-day pass also valid on all ordinary bus routes).

ACTIVITIES

CLIMBING AND ABSEILING

Australian School of Mountaineering Paddy Pallin, 166 Katoomba St, Katoomba (ⓣ 02 4782 2014, ⓦ asmguides.com). Offers daily day-long abseiling courses ($180), plus canyoning to Grand, Empress or Fortress canyons (Oct–May daily 9am; $180; also less frequent trips to other canyons), rock climbing and bush-survival courses.

High 'n' Wild Mountain Adventures 3–5 Katoomba St, Katoomba (ⓣ 02 4782 6224, ⓦ high-n-wild.com.au). Another long-established operator, High 'n' Wild Mountain Adventures has great beginners' courses in abseiling ($135/

half-day, $175/day), canyoning (from $190), rock climbing ($169/half-day, $190/day), plus guided bushwalking and bushcraft courses. Both include lunch on full-day courses.

HORSERIDING

Megalong Horseriding Adventures Pick-ups from Blackheath (ⓣ 02 4787 8188, ⓦ megalong.cc). A range of escorted trail rides in the Megalong Valley and along the Coxs River, from the beginners' 1hr "Wilderness Ride" ($60) to the experienced riders' Cox's River Ride, a 4hr adventure along the river (from $195).

ACCOMMODATION

Accommodation rates rise on Fri and Sat nights; weekdays are quieter and cheaper. The tourist offices at Glenbrook and Echo Point have a booking service. Katoomba is the obvious choice for those on a budget, since it has several **hostels** to choose from. There are unusual and interesting **guesthouses** in Katoomba, Leura and Blackheath.

HOTELS, MOTELS AND GUESTHOUSES
KATOOMBA AND LEURA
★**Carrington Hotel** 15–47 Katoomba St ☎02 4782 1111, ⊚thecarrington.com.au; map p.160. When it opened in 1882, this was the region's finest hotel. Now fully restored, original features include stained-glass windows, open fireplaces, a splendid dining room and ballroom, cocktail bar, snooker and games room, library and guest lounges. The spacious en-suite rooms are beautifully decorated in rich heritage colours. **$149**

Jamison House 48 Merriwa St, at Cliff Drive, Leura ☎02 4782 1206, ⊚jamisonhouse.com; map p.160. Built as a guesthouse in 1903, this enchanting place has amazing, unimpeded views across the Jamison Valley. The feel is of a small European hotel, enhanced by the French restaurant, *The Rooster*, with its gorgeous dining room full of original fixtures. Upstairs, a breakfast room gives splendid views and there's a sitting room with a fireplace. Breakfast included. **$160**

The Metropole Guesthouse Cnr Gang Gang St & Lurline St ☎02 4782 5544, ⊚metropolekatoomba .com.au; map p.160. Just after stepping off the train you can be transported into another era with old-world charm. Think oil heaters, ceiling fans, polished brass and the clunk of cedar. Rooms are small but comfortable. Good-value singles available ($75). **$149**

MOUNT VICTORIA
Imperial 1 Station St ☎02 4787 1233, ⊚hotelimperial .com.au; map p.160. Gorgeously restored nineteenth-century resort that once hosted croquet-playing ministers and royalty. Its old-world charms are still in evidence: there are beautifully appointed en-suite rooms ($120) and spacious, pleasantly decorated guesthouse-style shared-bathroom options, as well as more basic pub-style dorm rooms that sleep four. Breakfast included. Dorms **$40**, doubles **$80**

BLACKHEATH
Jemby-Rinjah Eco Lodge 336 Evans Lookout Rd, 4km from Blackheath ☎02 4787 7622, ⊚jemby.com.au; map p.160. Accommodation in idyllic one- and two-bedroom timber cabins sleeping two to six, each with a wood fire, and located amid tranquil bushland near the Grose Valley. Wine is served in the common area, where the focal point is the huge circular "fire pit". The restaurant operates on demand, so book in advance. Bushwalks can be organized for guests. Cabins **$250**

★**Kubba Roonga** 9 Brentwood Ave ☎02 4787 5224, ⊚kubbaroongaguesthouse.com; map p.160. In a peaceful part of Blackheath, this charming boutique guesthouse dates from 1915 and offers warm service, a large guest lounge and seven sympathetically restored en-suite bedrooms. Enjoy complimentary port by the roaring fireplace in winter, or in warmer months relax under the large oak tree

in the garden. You can tuck into a full, complimentary gourmet breakfast, and then burn it off on the stunning Braeside walk, which starts only moments away. **$170**

HOSTELS
KATOOMBA
★**Blue Mountains YHA** 207 Katoomba St ☎02 4782 1416, ⊚yha.com.au; map p.160. Huge two-hundred-bed YHA right in the town centre, with private, four- and eight- bed rooms (some en-suite). The former 1930s guesthouse has been modernized but retains its charming lead-lighted windows, Art Deco decor, huge ballroom and an old-fashioned mountain-retreat ambience, with an open fire in the reading room and games room (with pool table). There's also wi-fi and a pleasant courtyard. Friendly reception staff. Dorms **$27.50**, doubles **$74**

Flying Fox Backpackers 190 Bathurst Rd ☎02 4782 4226, ⊚theflyingfox.com.au; map p.160. Colourful, homely and comfortable bungalow near the station, with spacious seven-bed dorms and artistically furnished doubles (all shared bath). Cosy lounge area, plus a courtyard and a popular chill-out hut with a fire, and a bush-outlook campsite ($19pp). There's free tea and coffee, a kitchen, and fridge space. Simple breakfast included. Camping gear is rented out at reasonable rates and the knowledgeable managers offer information on bushwalks and camping, and free transport to walks. Dorms **$29**, doubles **$75**

★**No. 14 Budget Accommodation** 14 Lovel St ☎02 4782 7104, ⊚no14.com.au; map p.160. This relaxed hostel in a restored former guesthouse – polished floors, cosy fireplace and original features – is like a home from home, run by an informative, friendly young couple. Mostly twin and double rooms (some en-suite) plus four-person dorms with comfy beds instead of bunks; all centrally heated. Free cereal available for breakfast. The peaceful veranda is surrounded by pretty plants and valley views. Dorms **$34**, doubles **$85**

CAMPING AND CARAVAN PARKS
As well as the campsites below, you can also camp in the grounds of *Flying Fox Backpackers*, and in the bush at several NPWS sites.

Blackheath Glen Tourist Park Prince Edward St ☎02 4787 8101, ⊚bmtp.com.au; map p.160. Lovely grassy campsite with good amenities, a communal "camp kitchen" and one-, two- and three-bedroom cabins. Cabins **$118**, un/powered sites **$37/45**, en-suite sites **$56**

Katoomba Falls Caravan Park Katoomba Falls Rd ☎02 4782 1835, ⊚bmtp.com.au; map p.160. An idyllic location, with bushwalks possible from the site, and two-bedroom cabins for those not wanting to camp. Discounts for longer stays. Cabins **$125**, un/powered sites **$37/45**, en-suite sites **$56**

1

EATING

Cuisine in the Blue Mountains has gone way beyond the ubiquitous "Devonshire teas", with many well-regarded **restaurants**, and a real **café culture** in Katoomba and Leura.

BLACKHEATH

Altitude 20 Govetts Leap Rd ☎02 4787 6199; map p.160. Great coffee and sandwiches made to order. Try the well-priced, delicious egg and bacon rolls (from $6). Daily 9am–5pm.

Ashcrofts 18 Govetts Leap Rd ☎02 4787 8297, ⓦ ashcrofts.com; map p.160. Award-winning restaurant serving innovative yet substantial food with Middle Eastern and Japanese influences (mains $22–30), accompanied by an excellent wine list. They serve highly recommended breakfasts, such as the indulgent scrambled eggs on sourdough toast with truffles ($25), and the knowledgeable staff are welcoming. Don't forget to check out the gallery upstairs. Thurs 6–10.30pm, Fri–Sun 8am–2pm & 6–10.30pm.

Victory Café 17 Govetts Leap Rd ☎02 4787 6777, ⓦ victorytheatre.com.au; map p.160. A very pleasant space in the front of an old Art Deco theatre now converted into an antiques centre. The menu offers gourmet sandwiches and café favourites with an interesting spin, with daily specials such as grilled barramundi with Thai curry sauce and jasmine rice. Generous breakfasts are served till 2pm, and there's plenty for vegetarians. Mains from $15. Daily 8am–4pm.

KATOOMBA

Anki's 54 Waratah St, Katoomba St ☎02 4782 5536, ⓦ bit.ly/AnkiKatoomba; map p.160. A lovely Indian dinner at cosy *Anki's* is a warming reward after a chilly hike. The garlic naan is perfectly flaky, and the mango chicken ($11) and other mains are large and filling. There are plenty of vegetarian and vegan options, all with home-cooked flavours. Daily 5–9pm.

Avalon 18 Katoomba St ☎02 4782 5532, ⓦ avalonkatoomba.com; map p.160. Stylish place with the ambience of a quirky café, in the dress circle of the old Savoy Theatre, with many Art Deco features. Beautiful views down the valley, too – turn up for lunch or early dinner to see them. Moderately expensive menu (mains $24.50–33.50), but generous servings and to-die-for desserts. BYO & licensed. Wed–Fri 6–11pm, Sat & Sun noon–3pm & 6–11pm.

Carrington Hotel 15–47 Katoomba St ☎02 4782 1111, ⓦ thecarrington.com.au; map p.160. The hotel (see p.165) has a host of bars in and around its grand old building: *Champagne Charlie's Cocktail Bar* has a decorative glass ceiling dome and chandeliers, and serves tasty polysyllabic cocktails. There are cheaper drinks and a livelier atmosphere at the bottom of the *Carrington's* driveway at stately *Old City Bank Brasserie* (live music most

Fri & Sat evenings) with its award-winning upstairs brasserie serving great pizzas ($15–19) and other mains such as mushroom penne ($22) and lemongrass and ginger duck ($28). The *Carrington Public Bar*, with a separate entrance around the corner on Bathurst St, is more down-to-earth, and upstairs is the *Baroque Bar & Nightclub*, a dimly illuminated Art Deco retreat hosting a mix of DJs and live music (Fri & Sat 10pm till late). Daily 8am–midnight.

Hominy 185 Katoomba St ☎02 4782 9816; map p.160. Great for picnic takeaways: sourdough, sandwiches, good croissants and cakes. No eating area of its own, but the street's public picnic tables are just outside. Daily 6am–5.30pm.

Paragon 65 Katoomba St ☎02 4782 2928, ⓦ facebook.com/TheParagonCafe; map p.160. A wonderfully historic Viennese-style tearoom founded by a Greek family, and Australia's most famous café in the 1920s. The Art Deco styling is superb, from the Grecian friezes in the front room to the pre-Columbian-inspired Banquet Hall and the Blue Room with its ocean liner feel. They serve classic afternoon teas and light meals, and also operate a film club. Mon–Fri 9am–5pm, Sat 10am–10.30pm, Sun 10am–4pm.

Pomegranate 49 Katoomba St ☎02 0452 199 708; map p.160. Excellent food is assured at this café, which is popular for all-day breakfasts, with organic sourdough ($19) and their baked frittata ($11) plus excellent coffee. The banana bread is also a worthy favourite. Tues–Sun 7.30am–3pm.

WENTWORTH FALLS

Il Postino 13 Station St, opposite the train station, Wentworth Falls ☎02 4757 1615. Relaxed café in the old post office; there are some tables outside on a street-facing courtyard. The menu is Italian, with plenty for vegetarians (nothing over $8). Excellent breakfast options. Daily 8.30am–5pm.

LEURA

★ **Red Door Café** 134 The Mall, Leura ☎02 4784 1328; map, p.160. This wood-panelled café is both chic and homely, serving excellent coffee, snacks and fabulous specials such as barramundi fillet with saffron relish ($18.50). Daily 7am–4pm, Sat & Sun from 8am.

Silk's Brasserie 128 The Mall, Leura ☎02 4784 2534, ⓦ silksleura.com; map p.160. Parisian-style bar with excellent service and great food. For dinner, there are sophisticated European-style dishes, from confit of duck to Tasmanian salmon (two-courses $59–65). They offer both fine dining and cheaper, more relaxed food ($26–42) at lunch. Daily noon–3pm & 6–10pm.

★**Solitary** 90 Cliff Drive, Leura Falls ☎02 4782 1164, ⓦsolitary.com.au; map p.160. Perched on a hairpin bend on the mountains' scenic cliff-hugging road, the views of the Jamison Valley and Mount Solitary from this mod-Oz restaurant are sublime. Expect beautifully laid tables, eager service, a reasonably priced wine list and superb food, such as pan-seared ocean trout ($33). There's a fireplace in the back room and rattan tables and chairs beneath parasols on the lawn outside overlooking the valley. You can enjoy it all more cheaply when it morphs into the laidback *Solitary Kiosk* (most mains under $17). Kiosk: Wed–Sun 11am–4.30pm; restaurant: Sat 6.30–10pm.

DRINKING

KATOOMBA

Old City Bank Brasserie Carrington Hotel, 15–47 Katoomba St, Katoomba ☎02 4782 1111; map p.160. Yes, it still looks like an old bank with clunky wood furniture, and brass and glass lamps. The service is old-world too, with friendly staff serving up wine, beer and good food created by the owners of the respected Carrington Hotel. A lively place on weekends, despite appearances. Daily noon–9pm.

Station Bar 287 Bathurst Rd, Katoomba ☎02 4782 4782, ⓦstationbar.com.au; map p.160. A classic friendly, noisy Aussie pub, with craft beers, good ciders and a cocktail menu. There are passable thin-crust pizzas too. Daily noon–midnight.

SHOPPING

Carrington Deli and Cellars 15–47 Katoomba St, Katoomba ☎02 4782 09999, ⓦthecarrington.com.au; map p.160. A friendly upscale deli behind the *Carrington Hotel*, selling regional and European produce including chutneys, pasta, pulses and teas, as well as local cheeses and salami. There's an impressive wine collection, including Bathurst and Mudgee wines. They have plans to construct an adjoining microbrewery, and an upstairs café.

Mon–Thurs 9am–7pm, Fri 9am–9pm, Sat 9am–8pm, Sun 10am–6.30pm.

Paddy Pallin 166 Katoomba St, Katoomba ☎02 4782 4466, ⓦpaddypallin.com.au; map p.160. Sells camping gear and a good range of topographic maps and bushwalking guides and supplies. For cheap gear, go to K-Mart (next to Coles supermarket, Katoomba St). Daily 8.30am–5.30pm.

DIRECTORY

Hospital Blue Mountains District Anzac Memorial, Katoomba (☎02 4784 6500).

Library 30 Parke St, Katoomba. Has free wi-fi, as well as epic mountain views (Mon–Fri 10am–5pm, Sat 10am–4pm, Sun noon–4pm).

Pharmacies Blooms Springwood Pharmacy, 161 Macquarie Rd, Springwood (Mon–Fri 8.30am–9pm, Sat & Sun 9am–7pm; ☎02 4751 2963); Greenwell & Thomas,

145 Katoomba St, Katoomba (Mon–Fri 8.30am–7pm, Sat & Sun 9am–6pm; ☎02 4782 1066).

Post office Katoomba Post Office, Pioneer Place, off Katoomba St, Katoomba (Mon–Fri 9am–5pm).

Swimming pool Katoomba Aquatic Centre, Gates Ave, Katoomba (Mon–Fri 6am–8pm, Sat & Sun 8am–6pm; $6.20; ☎02 4782 5156), has outdoor and indoor complexes with a toddlers' pool, sauna, spa and gym.

The Jenolan Caves

Daily 9.30am–5.30pm • Tours: "Central River Adventure Cave" $220 (7hr); Lucas Cave $35 (1hr 30min); "Plughole" $100 (2hr); Temple of Baal $41 (1hr 30min); River Cave $48.50 (2hr); adult-oriented ghost tours (Sat 8pm; 2hr; $48.50) • ☎02 6359 3911, ⓦjenolancaves.org.au

The **Jenolan Caves** lie 30km southwest across the mountains from Katoomba on the far edge of the Kanangra Boyd National Park – over 80km by road – and contain New South Wales' most spectacular limestone formations. There are ten "show" caves, with daily guided tours at various times throughout the day. If you're coming for just a day, plan to see one or two caves: the best general one is the **Lucas Cave**, though more spectacular is the **Temple of Baal**, while the extensive **River Cave**, with its tranquil Pool of Reflection, is the longest and priciest. The system of caves is surrounded by the **Jenolan Karst Conservation Reserve**, a fauna and flora sanctuary with picnic facilities and walking trails to small waterfalls and lookout points. It and the caves are administered by the Jenolan Caves Trust, which also offers **adventure caving** in various other caves. The Jenolan Caves Trust also looks after several places to stay in the vicinity.

1

ARRIVAL AND DEPARTURE   **THE JENOLAN CAVES**

By car The caves are a 3hr drive from Sydney centre and under 1hr 30min from Katoomba.

On a tour There's transport to Jenolan Caves with Fantastic Aussie Tours (see p.164; 1hr 30min; $35; departs Katoomba 11.15am; departs Jenolan Caves 3.45pm), designed as an

overnight rather than a day-return service; otherwise, the same company offers day-tours from Katoomba, as do several other operators, and there are also several tours from Sydney (see box, p.144).

ACCOMMODATION

Jenolan Caves Cottages 4655–4669 Jenolan Caves Rd ☏ 02 6359 3900, ⓦ jenolancaves.org.au. About 10min by car from the caves, in a secluded woodland setting at Binda Flats; reception is at *Jenolan Caves House*. Cabins sleep six; BYO linen. Cabins $170

Jenolan Caves House 4655–4669 Jenolan Caves Rd

☏ 02 6359 3900, ⓦ jenolancaves.org.au. The most convenient place to stay for the caves, and a charming old hotel that was a popular honeymoon destination in the 1920s. In the old section, there's a good restaurant, a bar and a more casual bistro. $138

The Southern Highlands and the road to Canberra

Heading southwest out of Sydney through Campbelltown along the speedy South Western Motorway (M5), you'll eventually find yourself on the Hume Highway bound for Goulburn and Canberra. It's a straightforward drive, but best broken by detours into the picturesque **Southern Highlands**, a favourite weekend retreat for Sydneysiders since the 1920s. The pretty Highlands towns are full of cafés, restaurants, antiques shops and secondhand bookstores, and there's an emerging wine industry, too. The cooler-climate wines produced here are building a good reputation, and visiting the wineries – an excellent alternative to the better-known Hunter Valley – is a great way to enjoy the beautiful countryside of the area.

Southwest of Campbelltown, **Mount Annan Botanical Garden**, where you'll find a great restaurant (see p.171), and **Wirrimbirra Sanctuary** (daily 9am–4pm; ⓦ wirrimbirra.com.au) make appealing short stops. To get into the Highlands proper, you'll need to continue to Mittagong, a base for accessing the limestone underworld of **Wombeyan Caves**. All true-blue Australians know that the world's best ever batsman, Donald Bradman, grew up in **Bowral**, a short drive from historic **Berrima** with its ancient inn. **Bundanoon** sits on the edge of the wild Morton National Park, where **Fitzroy Falls** are a justified highlight. Further south, fabulous views are the main reward for visiting the Illawarra Fly **treetops walkway**, while the boardwalk at **Minnamurra** highlights the charms down at floor level. The last stop before the coast is **Kangaroo Valley**, another quaint and ancient little village, with some lovely kayaking through Shoalhaven Gorge.

Camden and around

About 40km south of Parramatta, the Camden Valley Way heads west from the motorway to **CAMDEN** on the Nepean River, where John Macarthur pioneered the breeding of merino sheep in 1805. The town still has a rural feel and several well-preserved nineteenth-century buildings, the oldest of which dates from 1816. En route, you'll pass **Mount Annan Botanical Garden** (daily 10am–5pm; free; ⓦ rbgsyd.nsw.gov.au). The native-plant section of the Royal Botanic Gardens in Sydney, this outstanding collection of flora is the largest of its kind in Australia.

Wombeyan Caves

Daily 9am–4.30pm • Figtree Cave $18 (self-guided); tours $21 per cave (1hr–1hr 30min); Explorer Pass $40 (includes two tours and Figtree Cave) • Two daily trains (1hr 40min) and one daily bus (2hr 30min) from Sydney to the caves

Just over 100km south of Sydney, the small agricultural and tourist town of **Mittagong** is mostly visited on the way to the limestone, NPWS-run **Wombeyan Caves**, 65km west on a tortuously winding road. Take as long as you like in the self-guided Figtree

Cave, with its wild formations inventively lit; other caves are visited on tours. There's a well-run **campsite** near the caves (see p.171).

Bowral

Two to three daily trains from Sydney (1hr 50min); one or two buses daily from Batemans Bay (3hr 30min), and one from Wollongong (1hr 30min)

BOWRAL, 6km southwest of Mittagong, is a busy, well-to-do town; its main strip, Bong Bong Street, is full of upmarket clothes and homeware shops and it has a good bookstore and a cinema. It was also the birthplace of cricket legend Don Bradman, celebrated in the local museum.

Bradman Museum

St Jude St • Daily 10am–5pm • $20 • ☎ 02 4862 1247, ⓦ bradman.com.au

Cricket fans should check out the **Bradman Museum** (also known as the International Cricket Hall of Fame) on Jude Street, in an idyllic spot between a park and the well-used cricket oval and club. Inside, a history of the game's development in Australia is accompanied by great 1930s and 1940s films of "The Don", and a chance to try your hand at Bradman's childhood game, using a golf ball and a stump as a bat, playing knock-back against the brick base of a water tank – he claimed this as the foundation of his skills.

Berrima

Buses run here from Moss Vale (Mon–Sat 2–5 daily; 30min)

The picturesque village of **BERRIMA**, 7km west of Bowral, boasts a complement of well-preserved and restored old buildings, including the *Surveyor General Inn*, which has been serving beer since 1835. The **visitor centre** (daily 10am–4pm; ☎ 02 4877 1505) is inside the 1838 sandstone **Courthouse Museum** (daily 10am–4pm; $7; ⓦ berrimacourthouse.org.au) on the corner of Argyle and Wiltshire streets, while across the road is the still-operational **Berrima Gaol**, which once held the infamous bushranger Thunderbolt, and acted as an internment camp for POWs and immigrants in wartime; it also has the dubious distinction of being the first place in Australia to execute a woman, in 1841.

Bundanoon

Trains run to Bundanoon station from Sydney (2 daily; 2hr)

Some 30km south of Bowral is **BUNDANOON**, famous for the April celebration of its Scottish heritage with the annual Highland Games – Aussie-style. The town is in an attractive spot, set in hilly countryside scarred by deep gullies and with splendid views over the gorges and mountains of the huge **Morton National Park** (car fee $8), which extends east from Bundanoon to near Kangaroo Valley.

Glow Worm Glen

25min walk from Bundanoon via the end of William St, or an easy 40min signposted trek from Riverview Road in the national park

A pleasant way to start your Bundanoon explorations is by setting off at sunset armed with a torch on an evening stroll to **Glow Worm Glen**; after dark, the small sandstone grotto is transformed by the naturally flickering lights of these insects, and you may be lucky enough to see wombats along the way.

Budderoo National Park

Daily 9am–5pm • $4.40

As you leave the Southern Highlands via Moss Vale, one route to the coast heads southwest past Fitzroy Falls to Kangaroo Valley and Berry, while a second initially follows the **Illawarra Highway** due east then cuts southeast at **Robertson**, 25km east of Moss Vale. This runs through **Budderoo National Park** past the impressive, 50m-high

1

Carrington Falls, 8km southeast of Robertson off Jamberoo Mountain Road, which can be accessed by a short bushwalk leading to lookout points over the waterfalls.

Minnamurra Rainforest Centre

Daily 9am–5pm • $12/car • ☎ 02 4236 0469

A turn-off on the Jamberoo Mountain Road leads to the **Minnamurra Rainforest Centre**, which hugs the base of the escarpment. From the centre, you can wander along a wheel-chair-accessible elevated **boardwalk** (1.6km return; 30min–1hr; last entry 4pm) that winds through cabbage tree palms, staghorn ferns and impressive Illawarra fig trees, with the distinctive call of whipbirds and the undergrowth rustle of lyrebirds for company. Midway along the boardwalk, a **path** (2.6km return; last entry 3pm) spurs off steeply uphill – quickly gaining 100m – to a platform with views to the delicate 25m-tall **Upper Minnamurra Fall**. A second platform allows you to peer down the 50m lower fall as it cascades into a dark slot canyon. From Minnamurra, it's a further 17km south to coastal Kiama.

Illawarra Fly

182 Knights Hill Rd • Daily 9am–5pm • Treetop walk $25, zipline tour $60 (2.5hr) • ⓦ illawarrafly.com.au

Just outside Budderoo National Park is **Illawarra Fly**, where you can walk out on a massive 500m-long **treetop walkway** cantilevered out over the edge of the Illawarra Escarpment. On a fine day, the views can seem never-ending, north and south along the coast, and down into the gum trees below. There's also a fun **zipline tour** across a series of elevated cable spans.

Fitzroy Falls

Daily 9am–5.30pm, May–Sept till 5pm • Parking $4 • NPWS visitor centre ☎ 02 4887 7270

Nowra Road heads directly southeast from Moss Vale and after 15km reaches **Fitzroy Falls**, on the fringes of Morton National Park. A short boardwalk from the car park takes you to the falls, which plunge 80m into the valley below, with glorious views of the Yarrunga Valley beyond. The NPWS visitor centre at the falls has a buffet-style café with a very pleasant outside deck, and can provide detailed information about the many walking tracks and scenic drives in the park.

Kangaroo Valley

Kangaroo Valley Road winds steeply down 20km from Fitzroy Falls to **KANGAROO VALLEY**. Hidden between the lush dairy country of Nowra and the Highlands, the town is a popular base for walkers and canoeists, and is brimming with cafés, craft and gift shops, plus an imposing old distinctive pub, *The Friendly Inn*.

Just over 1km west of the township, the road from Fitzroy Falls crosses the Kangaroo River on the picturesque 1898 **Hampden Suspension Bridge**, with its castellated turrets made from local sandstone. Lying to one side of the bridge, the **Pioneer Museum Park** (Feb–Nov: Mon, Wed & Fri–Sun 10am–4pm; Dec & Jan daily 10am–4pm; $10; ⓦ kangaroovalleymuseum.com) provides an insight into the origins of the area, in and around an 1850 homestead.

ARRIVAL AND ACTIVITIES

THE SOUTHERN HIGHLANDS

By train Transport down south is good; the Southern Highlands are well served by a frequent train service between Sydney and Canberra, stopping at Picton, Mittagong, Bowral, Moss Vale, Bundanoon and Goulburn.

By bus Priors (☎ 1800 816 234) run a once-daily (except Sat) bus service through the region from Campbelltown train station with stops at Mittagong, Bowral, Fitzroy Falls

and Kangaroo Valley before continuing to the coast. Berrima Buslines provides a local bus service (☎ 02 4871 3211, ⓦ berrimabuslines.com.au). Bus access to Kangaroo Valley is with Priors, whose buses stop at 5.25pm southbound and 10.45am northbound.

Kayaking Kangaroo Valley Safaris (☎ 02 4465 1502, ⓦ kangaroovalleycanoes.com.au) offer leisurely self-guided kayak trips along the placid Kangaroo River and between the escarpments of the Shoalhaven Gorge. Rates include basic instruction, maps, waterproof containers and a return bus trip so you only need to paddle downstream.

ACCOMMODATION

Kangaroo Valley Tourist Park Moss Vale Rd ☏ 1300 559 977, ⓦ kangaroovalleytourist.asn.au. You can venture out in kayaks and canoes rented from this very pleasant campsite, which offers camping lots, a bunkhouse and en-suite timber a/c cabins sleeping between two and seven. Un/powered sites per person $\underline{$11/13}$, bunkhouse $\underline{$20}$ per person, cabins $\underline{$90}$

Tall Trees B&B 8 Nugents Creek Rd ☏ 02 4465 1208, ⓦ talltreesbandb.com.au. A kilometre east of

Opt for a day-trip ($40–70pp) or an overnight trip ($120–140pp), camping beside the river. They also rent tents ($65) and cooking stoves ($35).

Kangaroo Village, *Tall Trees B&B* is a home from home, with great views and hearty breakfasts (included; room-only options available). Self-contained accommodation in a studio or tree house is also available (both $180). $\underline{$160}$

Wombeyan Caves Camping ☏ 02 4843 5976, ⓦ nationalparks.nsw.gov. Large and leafy campground with a communal kitchen, as well as areas where you can light fires. Unpowered sites per person $\underline{$14}$

EATING

General Café 151 Moss Vale Rd, Kangaroo Valley ☏ 02 4465 1660, ⓦ facebook.com/thegeneralcafekv. Of the many cafés in Kangaroo Valley, *Café Bella* stands out from the crowd with its relaxed, friendly feel, good-value breakfasts and delicious lunches. It also opens on Fri and Sat evenings with a small but well-chosen menu (mains $15–30). BYO. Fri & Sat 8am–2pm & 6–9pm, Sun 8am–2pm.

Melaleuca House Mount Annan Botanical Garden, Camden ☏ 02 4647 1363, ⓦ melaleucahouse.com.au. Within the garden grounds, you can eat well at this

idyllically sited restaurant and café, with outside tables surrounded by trees. Try the Moroccan lamb skewers with a feta salad ($23). Mon–Fri 8.30am–4pm, Sat & Sun 8am–4pm.

Jing Jo Café 2038 Moss Vale Rd, Kangaroo Valley ☏ 02 4465 1314, ⓦ jingjo.com.au. You can sit beneath a shady veranda and enjoy a cup of tea at *Jing Jo Café* restaurant by the Hampden Suspension Bridge, where there's a modern-Australian daytime menu and a Thai menu in the evening (mains $19.50–22.50). Wed 6–11pm, Thurs–Sun 9am–2.30pm & 6–11pm.

Royal National Park

Daily 7am–8.30pm • $12 per car (drive through without stopping free) • The NPWS Visitor Centre (daily 8.30am–4.30pm; ☏ 02 9542 0648, ⓦ nationalparks.nsw.gov.au) is at the Triangle car park in Audley, in the northwest corner of the park • Train to Loftus station, from where there's a tram to the Park (Sun only); 40min drive to north side from Sydney

The **Royal National Park** is a huge nature reserve right on Sydney's doorstep, only 36km south of the city. Established in 1879, it was the second national park in the world (after Yellowstone in the US). The railway between Sydney and Wollongong marks its western border, and from the train the scenery is sensational. If you want to explore more closely, get off at one of the stations along the way – Loftus, Engadine, Heathcote, Waterfall or Otford – all starting points for walking trails into the park. On the eastern side, from Jibbon Head to Garie Beach, the park falls away abruptly to the ocean, creating a spectacular coastline of steep cliffs broken here and there by creeks cascading into the sea and little coves with fine sandy beaches; the remains of **Aboriginal rock carvings** are the only traces of the original Dharawal people.

You can also drive in at various points: so long as you don't stop, cars are allowed right through the park without paying, exiting at **Waterfall** on the Princes Highway or **Stanwell Park** at the start of Grand Pacific Drive.

Approaching the park from the north, stop 3km south of Loftus at the easy, concrete Bungoona Lookout **nature trail** (1km return; 20min; flat) with its panoramic views, or continue 1km to the NPWS Visitor Centre at tiny **Audley**. Here, beside the Hacking River, you can rent a bike or canoe or just laze around with a picnic.

Deeper into the park, on the ocean shore, **Wattamolla** and **Garie beaches** have good surfing waves; the two beaches are connected by a walking track. There are kiosks at Audley, Wattamolla and Garie Beach.

1

Bush camp Southern precinct of park ☎ 02 9542 0648, ⓦ nationalparks.nsw.gov.au. The bush camp at North Era requires a permit from the visitor centre; you'll often need to book weeks in advance at weekends, and the permit can be posted out to you (which can take up to five days), or you can buy it before leaving Sydney at the NPWS centre at 110 George St (see p.142). $12 per person

Heathcote National Park

The best train station for the park is Waterfall (every 30min from Central Station; 1hr); you can't drive in the park, but you can reach the picnic area at Woronora Dam on its western edge by car: turn east off the Princes Hwy onto Woronora Rd (free entry; parking available) – the *Royal National Park Tourist Map* ($6.50 from NPWS) is invaluable for route finding

Heathcote National Park, across the Princes Highway from the Royal National Park, is much smaller and quieter. This is a serious bushwalkers' park with no roads and a ban on trail bikes. You can follow the fairly hilly **Bullawarring Track** (12km one-way; 5hr; moderate difficulty) north from Waterfall station and join a later train from Heathcote. The track weaves through a variety of vegetation, including scribbly gums with their intriguing bark patterns, and spectacular gymea lilies, which have bright red flowers atop tall flowering spears in the spring. Along the path are several swimmable pools fed by Heathcote Creek – the carved sandstone of the **Kingfisher Pool** is the largest and most picturesque.

Kingfisher Pool ☎ 1300 072 757, ⓦ nationalparks .nsw.gov.au. There's a small, very basic six-pitch campsite here perched above the Kingfisher Pool, which can only be accessed on foot (bring drinking water; no fires permitted). $12 per person

Mirang Pool ☎ 1300 072 757, ⓦ nationalparks .nsw.gov.au. The remote no-facilities campsite at Mirang Pool is accessed by foot only, with space for just four tents (bring drinking water, no fires permitted). $12 per person

South down the coast

For a **scenic drive from Sydney**, follow the Princes Highway south, exiting into the Royal National Park after Loftus onto Farnell Drive; the entry fee at the gate is waived if you are just driving through without stopping. The road through the national park emerges above the cliffs at **Otford**, beyond which runs **Lawrence Hargrave Drive** (Route 68), part of the newly dubbed **Grand Pacific Drive**, which ends south of Wollongong.

Bald Hill

A couple of kilometres south of Otford is **Bald Hill**, a great viewpoint looking down the coast past the 665m-long Sea Cliff Bridge, which curls around the sea cliffs. It's above **Stanwell Park** where you're likely to see the breathtaking sight of **hang-gliders** taking off (see opposite)

Austinmer

By the time you get to **AUSTINMER**, a northern suburb of Wollongong some 10km south of Bald Hill, you're at a break in the stunning cliffs and into some heavy surf territory. The down-to-earth town has a popular, very clean, patrolled **surf beach** that gets packed out on summer weekends.

Thirroul

THIRROUL, 2km south of Austinmer, is the spot where English novelist D.H. Lawrence wrote *Kangaroo* during his short Australian interlude in 1922 (the bungalow he stayed in is at 3 Craig St, but not open to visitors). The town and surrounding area are described in some depth in the novel, though he renamed the then-sleepy village

Mullumbimby. Today, Thirroul is gradually being swallowed up by the suburban sprawl of Wollongong but makes a lively spot to stop for a coffee. At the southern end of Thirroul's beach, **Sandford Point** (labelled Bulli Point on maps) is a famous surfing break. A 60km cycle track runs from Thirroul south along the coast through Wollongong to Lake Illawarra.

Illawarra Escarpment

After Thirroul, Lawrence Hargrave Drive joins up with the Princes Highway going south into Wollongong (Route 60) or heading northwest, uphill to a section of the forested **Illawarra Escarpment** and the **Bulli Pass**. There are fantastic views from the Bulli Lookout, which has its own café, and further towards Sydney at the appropriately named **Sublime Point Lookout**. You can explore the escarpment using the **walking tracks** that start from the lookouts, and there's an extensive part of the **Illawarra Escarpment State Recreation Area**, about 10km west of Wollongong's city centre on Mount Kembla and Mount Keira.

ACTIVITY	SOUTH DOWN THE COAST
Hang-gliding The Sydney Hang Gliding Centre at Stanwell Park (☎ 02 4294 4294, ⓦ hanggliding.com.au)	offers tandem flights with an instructor ($245 midweek, $295 weekends) and runs courses (from $580/2 days).

EATING	
Samuels 382 Lawrence Hargrave Drive, Thirroul ☎ 02 4268 2244, ⓦ samuelsrestaurantthirroul.com.au. Come here for a sophisticated but moderately priced dinner. Interesting mains such as Chinese chicken crêpes with cucumber, spring onion and hoisin average $30. Tues–Fri 6–10pm, Sat noon–3pm & 6–10pm.	**Tin Shed** 364 Lawrence Hargrave Drive, Thirroul ☎ 02 4268 0009. Breakfast is the main event at this cute café (from $12), as well as omelettes, bagels, *brushetta*, pastas and salads, and bakery items such as friands ($4). Eat in the bamboo-fringed garden. Daily 8am–2.30pm.

Wollongong

Although it's New South Wales' third-largest city, **WOLLONGONG** has more of a country-town feel; the students of Wollongong University give it extra life in term-time, and it enjoys a big dose of surf culture too – the city centre is set right on the ocean. Some 80km south of Sydney, Wollongong is essentially a working-class industrial centre – Australia's largest steelworks at nearby Port Kembla looms unattractively over Wollongong City Beach – but the Illawarra Escarpment (see above), rising dramatically beyond the city, provides a lush backdrop.

There's not much to see in the **city centre** itself (concentrated between Wollongong train station and the beach), which has been swallowed up by a giant shopping mall on **Crown Street**. If you continue east down Crown Street and cross Marine Drive, you'll hit **Wollongong City Beach**, a surf beach that stretches over 2km to the south.

Science Centre

Squires Way • Daily 10am–4pm, closed Wed during term-time; planetarium shows daily noon, 1pm & 3pm (30min) • $14, children $10 • ⓦ sciencecentre.uow.edu.au

Just over 2km north of the city centre, off Grand Pacific Drive, is the $6-million **Science Centre**, remodelled in 2016, where attractions include the state's best **planetarium** and over one hundred themed kid-friendly, hands-on exhibits. There is also a short film, which is popular with older kids (and adults).

Wollongong Art Gallery

Burelli St, at Kembla St • Tues–Fri 10am–5pm, Sat & Sun noon–4pm • Free • ⓦ wollongongartgallery.com

The regional art centre, the **Wollongong Art Gallery** shows changing exhibitions and has a permanent collection with an emphasis on colonial Illawarra and contemporary

1

Aboriginal artists; the core of the collection is a bequest from a local labourer, who came to Australia from Lithuania in the 1950s and spent his weekends and spare earnings acquiring artworks in Sydney.

City Walk

One of the most pleasant activities in Wollongong is simply wandering along the coastal **City Walk**, which starts at the eastern end of Crown Street and runs 2km north to **North Wollongong Beach** where you'll find the excellent *Diggies* café (see below). The walk passes Flagstaff Point, a grassy headland overlooking the lovely **Wollongong Harbour,** with its fishing fleet, fish market, seafood restaurants, and a picturesque nineteenth-century lighthouse on the breakwater.

Nan Tien Buddhist Temple

Berkeley Rd, Berkeley • Tues–Sun & public hols 9am–4pm; *Dew Drop Inn Tea House* Tues–Fri 10.30am–4.30pm, Sat & Sun 9.30am–4.30pm • Free, though there are small charges for tours; check online for retreat details and prices • ⓦ nantien.org.au • Well signposted off the Princes Hwy; a 20min walk from the Unanderra CityRail train station, 2 stops south of Wollongong

Some 8km south of Wollongong centre, the vast **Nan Tien Buddhist Temple** is the largest in Australia. The Fo Guang Shan Buddhists welcome visitors to the temple, and offer a variety of speciality teas and a vegetarian lunch menu at the *Dew Drop Inn Tea House,* as well as weekend meditation and Buddhist activity **retreats** in peaceful and surprisingly upmarket guesthouse accommodation, the *Pilgrim Lodge.*

ARRIVAL AND DEPARTURE   WOLLONGONG

By train The best and cheapest way to get to Wollongong from Sydney by public transport is the frequent South Coast Line train service from Central Station (hourly; 1hr 30min), which hugs the coast and stops at most of the small towns en route. Wollongong station is right in the centre, just off Crown St.

ACCOMMODATION AND EATING

Boat Harbour Motel 7–9 Wilson St, at Campbell St ☎ 02 4228 9166, ⓦ boatharbour-motel.com.au. Large, central motel with comfortable and spacious rooms with balconies, some with sea views. Restaurant on site. Prices increase by around a third at weekends. <u>$75</u>

★ **Caveau** 122 Keira St ☎ 02 4226 4855, ⓦ caveau .com.au. The food at Wollongong's finest, award-winning restaurant is French, immaculately presented and eased down with superb old-world wines. The menu is seasonal and changes regularly; sample dishes might include confit duck croquettes and cured duck breast with beets, parsnip, roasted spelt, bitter chocolate and ice plant. Lunch $45, dinner $65, seven-course tasting menu $105 ($150 with five wines). Reservations essential. Tues–Sat 6–11pm.

Corrimal Beach Tourist Park Lake Parade, Corrimal, 6km north of the centre ☎ 02 4285 5688, ⓦ wollongongtouristparks.com.au/corrimal. This is just

back from the beach at the mouth of Towradgi Lagoon, and has good facilities. The one-, two- and three-bedroom cabins are clean, comfortable and modern. The park is generally quiet, with plenty of permanent caravan residents. Un/powered sites <u>$27/34</u>, cabins <u>$147</u>

★ **Diggies** 1 Cliff Rd, North Wollongong ☎ 02 4226 2688, ⓦ diggies.com.au. A beachside location, top coffee and excellent café dishes make this a very popular place, especially for weekend brunch. Mains include lobster roll ($21) and crispy barramundi with quinoa ($26). You might want to move to their takeaway kiosk next door, where the food is cooked in the same kitchen, views from the outdoor tables are similar, and prices much lower. Daily 6.30am–11pm (winter opening hours vary).

Novotel Northbeach 2–14 Cliff Rd, North Wollongong ☎ 02 4224 3111, ⓦ novotelnorthbeach.com.au. Wollongong's finest hotel, with sea views, a pool, gym, restaurant and bars. <u>$169</u>

Kiama

Of the coastal resorts south of Sydney, **KIAMA**, 35km south of Wollongong, is probably the most attractive. A large resort and fishing town, Kiama is famous for its star attraction, the Blowhole. A few kilometres north, **Cathedral Rocks**' rocky outcrops drop abruptly to the ocean.

Blowhole

A 5min walk from the train station on Blowhole Point

Stemming from a natural fault in the cliffs, the **Blowhole** explodes into a waterspout when a wave hits with sufficient force. It's impressive, but also potentially dangerous: freak waves can be thrown over 60m into the air and have swept several over-curious bystanders into the raging sea – so stand well back.

ARRIVAL AND INFORMATION   KIAMA

By train South Coast Line train service from Central Station (hourly; 1hr 30min).

Tourist information The visitor centre on Blowhole Point Rd (daily 9am–5pm; ☎ 02 4232 3322, ⓦ kiama .com.au), books accommodation and supplies details of other local attractions.

ACCOMMODATION AND EATING

Hanoi on Manning 10 Manning St ☎ 02 4232 3315, ⓦ hanoionmanning.com.au. Very popular and welcoming Vietnamese restaurant: go for the mostly-seafood-based chef's specials, such as *chà cá Lã Vong* (grilled fish with Hanoi-style marinade) for $25. Daily except Tues 11.30am–2.30pm & 5–9.30pm.

Kiama Harbour Cabins Blowhole Point Rd ☎ 1800 823 824, ⓦ kiamacoast.com.au. Swanky cabins (one-two-or three-bedroom) with great views of the harbour and coast; there's a two-night minimum at weekends. **$220**

Surf Beach Holiday Park Bourrool St ☎ 02 4232 1791, ⓦ kiamacoast.com.au. Convenient camping right in town. Most of the cabins have excellent views of Kiama beach; the beds and TVs are adequate, but far from modern or luxurious. Powered sites **$34**, en-suite sites **$49**, cabins **$155**

New South Wales and the ACT

SURFERS, BYRON BAY

New South Wales and the ACT

New South Wales is Australia's premier state in more ways than one. The oldest of the six states, and also the most densely populated, its 7.3 million residents make up a third of the country's population. The vast majority occupy the urban and suburban sprawl that straggles along the state's thousand-plus kilometres of Pacific coastline, and the consistently mild climate and many beaches draw a fairly constant stream of visitors, especially during the summer holiday season, when thousands of Australians descend on the coast to enjoy the extensive surf beaches and other oceanside attractions.

South of Sydney, the coast offers a string of low-key family resorts and fishing ports, good for watersports and idle pottering. To the **north,** the climate gradually becomes warmer and the coastline more popular, but there are still plenty of tiny national parks and inland towns where you can escape it all. One of the most enjoyable beach resorts in Australia is **Byron Bay**, chic these days but still retaining something of its slightly offbeat, alternative appeal, radiating from the thriving hippy communes of the lush, hilly **north coast hinterland**. For those with a true desire to escape the crowds, there are the Pacific islands far off the north coast of New South Wales: subtropical **Lord Howe Island**, 700km northeast of Sydney, and **Norfolk Island**, 900km further northeast, inhabited by the descendants of the *Bounty* mutineers.

Just over 280km southwest of Sydney is the **Australian Capital Territory** (**ACT**), which was carved out of New South Wales at the beginning of the twentieth century as an independent base for the new national capital. While **Canberra** struggles to shed its dull image, it is the principal gateway to the **Snowy Mountains**, which offer skiing in winter and glorious hiking in summer.

Inland New South Wales may not be a stand-alone holiday destination but it gives a real insight into the Australian way of life and covers a strikingly wide range of landscapes, from the rugged slopes of the **Great Dividing Range** to the red-earth desert of the Outback. Inland towns such as **Bathurst** and **Dubbo** date back to the early days of Australian exploration. Free (non-convict) settlers appropriated vast areas of rich pastureland here and made immense fortunes off the back of sheep farming, establishing the agricultural prosperity that continues to this day. When gold was discovered near Bathurst in 1851, and the first **gold rush** began, New South Wales' fortunes were assured.

As you move west, the land becomes increasingly desolate and arid as you head into the harsh **Outback** regions, where the mercury can climb well above the 40°C mark in summer, and even places that look large on the map turn out to be tiny, isolated communities. The small town of **Bourke** is traditionally regarded as the beginning of the real Outback; other destinations in the area include the eccentric opal-mining town of **Lightning Ridge** and, in the far west of the state almost at the South Australian border, the surprisingly arty mining settlement of **Broken Hill**.

MUNGO NATIONAL PARK

Highlights

❶ Australian War Memorial, Canberra
This moving museum commemorates
Australia's war dead from Gallipoli to
Afghanistan. **See p.189**

❷ Snowy Mountains Cosy lodges and good
skiing in winter, fine bushwalking in summer,
and spectacular drives year round. **See p.209**

❸ Byron Bay Come and enjoy the laidback
lifestyle of the locals, the 30km of sandy beaches
and the vibrant nightlife. **See p.231**

❹ Lord Howe Island A dreamy Pacific Island
paradise with pristine beaches, jungles,
mountains and some of the world's best dive
sites. **See p.241**

❺ Tamworth Boot-scoot with country music
fans from all over the world during Tamworth's
famous annual festival. **See p.270**

❻ Waterfall Way Drive through verdant
rainforests and pass spectacular waterfalls on
this lesser-known scenic drive. **See p.275**

❼ Lightning Ridge Discover underground
sandstone sculptures, unique black opal and
Outback art in this offbeat mining outpost.
See p.283

❽ Mungo National Park Enjoy sunset on the
Walls of China dunes, camp under the stars or
take a morning drive past kangaroos and emus.
See p.297

HIGHLIGHTS ARE MARKED ON THE MAP ON PP.180–181

QUEENSLAND

CURRAWINYA
NATIONAL PARK

STURT
NATIONAL PARK

Tibooburra

Wanaaring

MITCHELL HWY

Brewarrina

Bourke

Louth

White
Cliffs

Darling River

Tilpa

Macquarie R.

MUTAWINTJI
NATIONAL PARK

Wilcannia

BARRIER HWY

Cobar

Nyngan

BARRIER HWY

Silverton

Broken Hill

NEW SOUTH WALES

KINCHEGA
NATIONAL PARK

Ivanhoe

ROUND HILL
NATURE
RESERVE

NOMBINNIE
NATURE
RESERVE

Lachlan R.

MUNGO
NATIONAL
PARK

WILLANDRA
NATIONAL PARK

8

MID WESTERN HWY

COCOPARRA
NATIONAL
PARK

Wentworth

Mildura

Murrumbidgee R.

Griffith

Leeton

Balranald

Hay

Narrandera

SOUTH AUSTRALIA

MURRAY SUNSET
NATIONAL PARK

HATTAH-KULKYNE
NATIONAL PARK

STURT HWY

Ouyen

WYPERFELD
NATIONAL PARK

Deniliquin

Corowa

Albury

Wodonga

HIGHLIGHTS

1 Australian War Memorial, Canberra

2 Snowy Mountains

3 Byron Bay

4 Lord Howe Island

5 Tamworth

6 Waterfall Way

7 Lightning Ridge

8 Mungo National Park

Echuca

Shepparton

N

Benalla

GREAT ALPINE RD

Bright

HUME HWY

Seymour

2

NATIONAL PARKS IN NEW SOUTH WALES

The **National Parks and Wildlife Service (NPWS)** charges **entrance fees** at many of its most popular parks – usually $8 a day per vehicle (bring plenty of coins for the ticket machines). If you intend to "go bush" a lot in New South Wales you can buy an **annual pass** for $190, which includes all parks. Remember that the pass is vehicle specific and can't be transferred.

Because of its popularity as a skiing destination, entrance to Kosciuszko is a steep $29 per car per day in winter and $17 per car per day at other times – if you plan on spending a fair length of time here, it's worth considering the annual pass. Passes can be bought at NPWS offices and some park entry stations, over the phone using a credit card or online (☎ 1300 072 757, ⓦ nationalparksnsw.gov.au; allow five to ten working days for delivery).

You can **camp** in most national parks. Camping in the bush is generally free, but where there is a ranger station and a designated campsite with facilities, fees of $5–14 per person per night apply, according to a grading system that reflects the type of amenities on offer. Campsites often have hot showers and electric or gas barbecues, but you'll need a fuel stove for hard-core camping. Open **fires** are banned in most parks and forbidden everywhere on days when there is high danger of fire – it's worth checking with the NPWS for details of any current bushfires and park closures before you visit.

GETTING AROUND

BY PLANE

The main airlines operating in NSW are: Qantas (☎ 13 13 13, ⓦ qantas.com.au); Jetstar (☎ 13 15 38, ⓦ jetstar.com); Virgin Australia (☎ 13 67 89, ⓦ virginaustralia.com); Regional Express (Rex; ⓦ rex.com.au) and Tiger Air (☎ 1300 174 266, ⓦ tigerair.com.au)

BY TRAIN

Inland New South Wales still has a fairly extensive rail network, although the operator NSW TrainLink has replaced many train services with buses. The train journey from Sydney to Broken Hill ($97–139; 13hr) is a direct service on Mondays) is a great way to see the vast desert in air-conditioned comfort – if you're lucky the train will pass through one of the huge sandstorms that ravage the region from time to time.

BY BUS

The most extensive bus networks along the coast of New South Wales are run by NSW TrainLink, who offer many services integrated with their train network; and Greyhound, supplemented by several regional companies

with limited range. Greyhound also operates a number of inland New South Wales services.

NSW TrainLink ☎ 13 22 32, ⓦ nswtrainlink.info. Frequent services along the east coast from Melbourne via Sydney to Brisbane, stopping at many places en route. A one-month Discovery Pass ($275) with NSW TrainLink will get you just about anywhere in the state.

Greyhound ☎ 1300 473 946, ⓦ greyhound.com.au. Greyhound buses run through Scone, Tamworth, Armidale and Glen Innes en route between Sydney and Brisbane via the New England Hwy, and along the coast north of Sydney stopping at Port Macquarie, Coffs Harbour and Byron Bay. There are also buses from Sydney out to Canberra, Orange, Wagga Wagga and Griffith.

New England Coaches ☎ 02 6732 1051, ⓦ newenglandcoaches.com.au. Services between Tamworth and the north coast as far as Port Macquarie.

Premier Motor Service ☎ 13 34 10, ⓦ premierms .com.au. Services along the coast between Sydney and Brisbane and Sydney and Eden, stopping at a number of destinations en route.

Canberra

The first European squatters settled in the valleys and plains north of the Snowy Mountains in the 1820s, though until 1900 this remained a remote rural area. When the Australian colonies united in the **Commonwealth of Australia** in 1901, a capital city had to be chosen, with Melbourne and Sydney the two obvious and eager rivals. After much wrangling, and partly in order to avoid having to decide on one of the two, it was agreed to establish a brand-new capital instead. In 1909, Limestone Plains, south of Yass, was chosen out of several possible sites as the future seat of the Australian government. An area of 2368 square kilometres was excised from the state of New South Wales and named the **Australian Capital Territory**, or **ACT**. The name for the

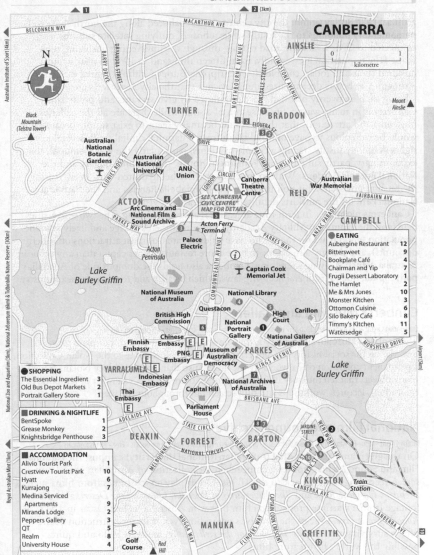

CANBERRA

● EATING
Aubergine Restaurant	12
Bittersweet	9
Bookplate Café	4
Chairman and Yip	7
Frugii Dessert Laboratory	1
The Hamlet	2
Me & Mrs Jones	10
Monster Kitchen	3
Ottoman Cuisine	6
Silo Bakery Café	8
Timmy's Kitchen	11
Watersedge	5

● SHOPPING
The Essential Ingredient	3
Old Bus Depot Markets	2
Portrait Gallery Store	1

■ DRINKING & NIGHTLIFE
BentSpoke	1
Grease Monkey	2
Knightsbridge Penthouse	3

■ ACCOMMODATION
Alivio Tourist Park	1
Crestview Tourist Park	10
Hyatt	6
Kurrajong	7
Medina Serviced Apartments	9
Miranda Lodge	2
Peppers Gallery	3
QT	5
Realm	8
University House	4

future capital was supposedly taken from the language of local Aborigines: **Canberra** – the meeting place.

In 1912 **Walter Burley Griffin**, an American landscape architect from Chicago, won the international competition for the design of the future Australian capital. His plan envisaged a garden city for about 25,000 people based in five main centres, each with separate city functions, located on three axes: land, water and municipal. Roads were to be in concentric circles, with arcs linking the radiating design.

Construction started in 1913, but political squabbling and the effects of World War I, the Depression and World War II prevented any real progress being made until 1958, when growth began in earnest. In 1963 the Molonglo River was dammed to form long, artificial **Lake Burley Griffin**; the city centre, **Civic**, coalesced along the north shore to face **parliamentary buildings** to the south; while a host of outlying **satellite suburbs**, each connected to Civic by a main road cutting through the intervening bushland, took shape. The population grew rapidly, from fifteen thousand in 1947 to nearly four hundred thousand today, completely outstripping Burley Griffin's original estimates – though Canberra's decentralized design means that the city never feels crowded.

Being such an overtly planned place populated by civil servants and politicians, Canberra is in many ways a city in search of a soul: while there are all the galleries, museums and attractions that there should be, many seem to exist simply because it would be ridiculous to have omitted them from a national capital. Still, several key sights definitely justify staying a couple of nights, particularly the **War Memorial**, the extraordinary, partly subterranean **Parliament House**, the **National Gallery** and the **National Botanic Gardens**. With so much of the city being dotted with trees, visiting the bush might seem a bit pointless, but the **Brindabella Ranges** and the **Namadgi National Park** on the outskirts definitely warrant a short visit.

Canberra's **nightlife** – in term-time at least – is alive and kicking. The two universities here (and the Duntroon Military Academy) mean that there's a large and lively **student population** (good news for those who have student cards, as most attractions offer hefty discounts), and the city also claims to have more **restaurants** per capita than any other in Australia, which is saying something. Canberra also holds the dubious title of Australia's **porn capital**, due to its liberal licensing laws, which legalize and regulate the sex industry.

Canberra Museum and Gallery

Cnr London Circuit and City Square • Mon–Fri 10am–5pm, Sat & Sun noon–4pm • Free • ⊛ cmag.com.au

The **Canberra Museum and Gallery** is the one real sight in Civic and it displays good material on the social history of Canberra and the ACT. It is home to the Nolan Collection, a permanent collection of 24 works by the great Australian painter Sidney Nolan, as well as many objects that tell the story of Canberra itself. There are also a number of temporary exhibitions, lectures, workshops and film screenings throughout the year.

National Film and Sound Archive

McCoy Circuit • Mon–Fri 9am–5pm; Fri eve, Sat & Sun for advertised events, see website for details • Free • ⊛ nfsa.gov.au

On the green and spacious **ANU (Australian National University)** campus, the **National Film and Sound Archive** houses a comprehensive collection of Australian sound and screen recordings dating back to the 1890s. On display are costumes from films such as *Picnic at Hanging Rock* and *The Adventures of Priscilla, Queen of the Desert*, and there is footage from a wartime propaganda film that won Australia its first Oscar in 1942, *Kokoda Front Line*. One of the Archive's gems, however, is its reconstruction of the fifteen surviving minutes of *The Story of the Kelly Gang*, made in 1906 and quite possibly the world's first feature film.

National Museum of Australia

Lawson Crescent, Little Acton Peninsula • Daily 9am–5pm • Free • Highlights Tour 10am & 1pm, $10 • ⊛ nma.gov.au

The **National Museum of Australia** is an unmistakeable, piecemeal building on the shores of Lake Burley Griffin, topped by a giant black and orange loop. This is one sight that people either love or hate, as traditional gallery and museum displays are largely shunned in favour of experience spaces. Style doesn't completely overshadow the content, however, which might cover anything from the country's early Greek cafés to the sad decline of Tasmania's **thylacine**, or marsupial wolf, which became extinct in the 1930s. Look out for a working windmill, a Holden Prototype No. 1 and Phar Lap's abnormally large heart, then head down to Kspace to help design the future and see

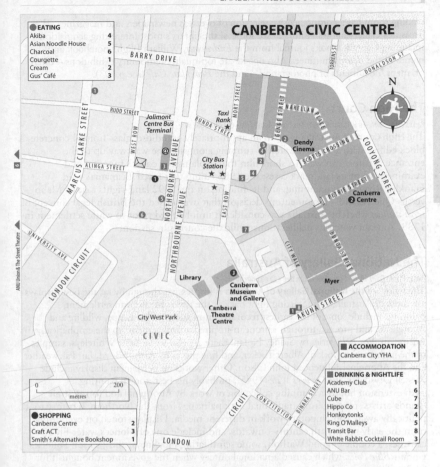

CANBERRA CIVIC CENTRE

EATING

Akiba	4
Asian Noodle House	5
Charcoal	6
Courgette	1
Cream	2
Gus' Café	3

ACCOMMODATION

Canberra City YHA	1

DRINKING & NIGHTLIFE

Academy Club	1
ANU Bar	6
Cube	7
Hippo Co	2
Honkeytonks	4
King O'Malleys	5
Transit Bar	8
White Rabbit Cocktail Room	3

SHOPPING

Canberra Centre	2
Craft ACT	3
Smith's Alternative Bookshop	1

your house or car design in 3D on the theatre screen. Outside, the **Garden of Australian Dreams** is a challenging and initially baffling map-like installation that attempts to marry colonial and Aboriginal geopolitical perspectives.

Questacon

King Edward Terrace • Daily 9am–5pm • $23 • W canberra.questacon.edu.au

The hands-on National Science and Technology Centre (Questacon) is great fun, especially for children, with heaps of interactive exhibits explaining geology, sound, light and other bits of physics; favourites include a simulated earthquake and lightning storm, a roller-coaster simulator, and the Mini Q section for under-6s. You'll easily kill a couple of hours here, though it does get very busy during school holidays.

National Library

Parkes Place • Main reading room Mon–Thurs 10am–8pm, Fri & Sat 10am–5pm; gallery exhibitions Mon–Sat 10am–5pm • Free • Guided tour daily 11.30am; behind the scenes tour Thurs 2pm; free • W nla.gov.au

Looming behind Questacon's oddly shaped, truncated tower is the **National Library**, whose reading room has a comprehensive selection of overseas newspapers and magazines. The Treasures Gallery allows visitors to see some of the library's most interesting acquisitions, including Captain Cook's journal from the *Endeavour*, William Bligh's notebook and the names of the *Bounty* mutineer. Also on site are top-quality temporary exhibitions – often on maps, documents or photography – and the *Bookplate Café* (see p.193).

The High Court

Parkes Place • Mon–Fri 9.45am–4.30pm, Sun noon–4pm • Free • W hcourt.gov.au

The **High Court of Australia** is set in an appropriately grandiose, glass-fronted concrete-block edifice with a stylized waterfall running alongside the walkway up to the entrance. Visitors can watch a short film that explains the court's function and examines two of its landmark cases: the 1983 ruling that saved Tasmania's wild Franklin River from damming, and its finding on the 1992 land-rights case of Mabo versus Queensland – a momentous decision that overturned the British legal concept of *terra nullius* whereby Australia was considered uninhabited prior to white settlement in 1788. You can watch its deliberations while the court is in session.

The National Gallery of Australia

Parkes Place • Daily 10am–5pm • Tours daily; free • W nga.gov.au

The whole of the **National Gallery of Australia** is impressive, though by far the best displays are those of Australian art. Starting right back at the time of European settlement, paintings include some of the earliest recorded impressions of landscape, wildlife and Aborigines, and proceed through European-inspired art movements to the emphatically Australian *Ned Kelly* series by Sidney Nolan; there are also some Brett Whiteleys, samples of the nightmarish work of Albert Tucker, and fine pieces by Arthur Boyd, Ian Fairweather and the Aboriginal-influenced John Olson. Other works on permanent display include Russell Drysdale's *The Drover's Wife* (1945), probably his best-known painting.

An extension houses a stunning collection of work by **Aboriginal and Torres Strait Islands artists**, ranging from traditional bark paintings from the Northern Territory to politically aware contemporary work in different media. Displays touch on everything from the early nineteenth century onwards, and include one of Monet's water-lily canvases, a couple of good Warhols, some scintillating Hockneys, and Jackson Pollock's vibrant *Blue Poles*, which caused a national outcry when the government bought it for $1.3 million in 1973.

There's a fine display of **Indian and Southeast Asian antiquities**, including some wonderful textiles, a lovely gilt Buddha and a twelfth-century Shiva, all strikingly displayed amid the concrete brutalism of the gallery. **East Asian art** can be found on the lower ground floor, where there are some interesting contemporary pieces including a Jewish Kiddush cup made in Japan in 2004, and Zhang Xiaogang's *Bloodline (Two Comrades with Red Baby)*.

Outside, the **Sculpture Garden** overlooking Lake Burley Griffin includes a dispersed version of Rodin's freestanding bronze statues, *The Burghers of Calais*. Visible and audible across the water from here is the **National Carillon**, stranded on Aspen Island, whose three elegant bell towers and 55 bronze bells – ranging from tiny to huge – were a gift from the British government to mark Canberra's fiftieth birthday.

National Portrait Gallery

King Edward Terrace • Daily 10am–5pm • Free except for special exhibitions • W portrait.gov.au

Containing oils, photos, drawings and sculptures of more than four hundred prominent Australians, the **National Portrait Gallery of Australia** is home to images dating from the eighteenth century to the present day. Look out for Howard Arkley's colourful Nick Cave, the paperweight depicting Australia's seventh PM Billy Hughes and a number of stars of the silver screen. Often the most interesting sections are the temporary shows, which change every few weeks.

Museum of Australian Democracy

King George Terrace • Daily 9am–5pm • $2 • ⓦ moadoph.gov.au

At the foot of Capital Hill is the **Museum of Australian Democracy** at **Old Parliament House**, a grand, white Neoclassical wedding cake of a building, in use between 1927 and 1988. Tours show just how crowded and inconvenient the building actually was, all imposingly gloomy, Victorian-style wood panelling and moulded plaster, though the leather seats in the old senate are pretty comfortable.

Outside, you can wander in the adjacent **Senate Rose Garden**, or take a look at the so-called **Aboriginal Tent Embassy** on the lawn in front, which has been here, on and off, since 1972 and serves as a focus for the million-odd representatives of Australia's oldest culture – you'll be welcomed for a cup of tea and a (political) chat.

National Archives of Australia

Queen Victoria Terrace, Parkes • Daily 9am–5pm • Free • ⓦ naa.gov.au

Built in 1927, this was once Canberra's first post office, and for a time housed the Australian security services, but has been occupied by the National Archives since 1998. You can use the reading rooms here for research and there are temporary exhibitions as well as the permanent **Memory of a Nation**. Documents on display include passenger cards and medical forms, album covers of once-banned music and photographs of Australians from the 1950s and 1960s. Those who want to see Australia's "birth certificate", the Royal Commission of Assent from 1900, and other key documents will need to book in advance to visit the Federation Gallery.

Parliament House

Capital Hill • Daily 9am–5pm; 30–40min guided tours daily 9.30am, 11am, 1pm, 2pm and 3pm; Question Time in the public galleries 2pm when Parliament is in session: to guarantee a seat at busy times (like budget day), book in advance • Free • ☎ 02 6277 7111 • ⓦ aph.gov.au

Behind Old Parliament House, (New) **Parliament House** is an extraordinary construction that appears to be built into Capital Hill. All you see from a distance are grassy slopes leading up to the landmark, four-legged **flagpole**, though closer inspection reveals a modern, white, colonnaded entry. Designed by the American-Italian architect (and now Canberra resident) Romaldo Giurgola, it opened in May 1988 to much derision but, twenty years on, it is ageing well and most now concede that, while not an iconic building, it is still a good one – impressive in scale and concept, with over 4500 rooms tucked away from prying eyes.

Outside the ground-floor entrance level is a **mosaic** by the Aboriginal artist Michael Nelson Jagamara – a piece that conveys the idea of a sacred meeting place. It is all explained next to the original painting on which it is based, which can be found inside the cool and serene **foyer**. The foyer is dominated by marble staircases and over forty columns clad in grey-green and rose-pink marble, representing a eucalypt forest. Around the walls, wood panels feature delightful marquetry designs of native flora.

Simply wandering around the remaining public areas isn't very instructive, so catch one of the **guided tours**, which visit both chambers of parliament when they're not sitting. When Parliament is in session – usually from sixty to eighty days a year – you can sit in the **public galleries** and watch the proceedings in the House of Representatives (the lower chamber of Parliament) or the Senate (the upper chamber of the legislature), though the former makes for better viewing.

Beyond the foyer, the **Great Hall** sports a 20m-high **tapestry** based on a painting of blackened trees by Arthur Boyd: guides will point out the cockatoo and Halley's

Comet, which was in the sky when the weavers were at work. In the adjacent **Members' Hall**, you can admire Queen Victoria's writing desk and one of only four extant original copies of the **Magna Carta**, this one bought for the National Archive in 1952.

The diplomatic quarters

No political sightseeing tour is complete without a trip among the upmarket suburban homes in Canberra's diplomatic quarters – **Yarralumla** and **Forrest**. The consulates and high commissions were asked to construct buildings that exemplified the typical architecture of the countries they represent – look out for the eye-catching embassies of Thailand, Indonesia, China, Papua New Guinea and Finland.

Royal Australian Mint

Denison St, Deakin • Mon–Fri 8.30am–5pm, Sat & Sun 10am–4pm • Free • ⓦ ramint.gov.au

Australia's coins are produced at the **Royal Australian Mint**, where you can see robots in action, admire historic Australian currency including gold bars and "holey" dollars, and stamp out your own dollar coin from a polished blank.

Lake Burley Griffin

Canberra is oriented around **Lake Burley Griffin**, which stretches for 11km from west to east and is ringed by a **cycle track**. Commonwealth Avenue Bridge, spanning the lake between Civic and Parliament, overlooks the **Captain Cook Memorial Jet** (daily 2–4pm), which spurts a column of water 140m into the air. It was built in 1970 to mark the bicentenary of Captain Cook's "discovery" of Australia. **Commonwealth Park**, immediately behind it, is the venue for all sorts of outdoor shows, from the springtime **Floriade** (Sept–Oct) flower festival to New Year's Eve firework displays.

Black Mountain Telstra Tower

Black Mountain Drive • Daily 9am–10pm • $7.50 • ⓦ blackmountaintower.com.au

Black Mountain rises just north of Lake Burley Griffin's midpoint, with the **Telstra Tower** poking upwards from the summit like a 195m-high homing beacon for the city, visible from many kilometres away. There are magnificent panoramic views of Canberra from the 66m-high viewing platform or the revolving restaurant just below.

Australian National Botanic Gardens

Clunies Ross St • Daily 8.30am–5pm • Visitor centre daily 9.30am–4.30pm • Tours daily 11am & 2pm • Free • ⓦ anbg.gov.au

The **Australian National Botanic Gardens** has done an amazing job recreating a wide swathe of native habitats in what was a dairy farm until the 1950s. Strolling through the lush rainforest section, it is astonishing to consider that this was a dry valley until 1968. You can spend a couple of tranquil hours here walking through the undergrowth and spotting reptiles and birds, including rare **gang-gang cockatoos**. The visitor centre has a leaflet on the Aboriginal walk, highlighting significant plants and how they were used. The outdoor **café** (daily 8.30am–4.30pm) is beautifully set among shaded fern gardens and lawns.

National Zoo and Aquarium

999 Lady Denman Drive • Daily 10am–5pm • $40 • Zooventure tour daily 3.30pm; Mon–Fri $120, Sat & Sun $145; zoo entry included; advance booking required • ⓦ nationalzoo.com.au

The **National Zoo and Aquarium** sits on Lake Burley Griffin's far western shore, 6km west of Civic. All the usual native suspects are here, but the zoo's best feature is its collection of

big cats, including tigers, lions, cheetahs and snow leopards. The two-hour **Zooventure tour** lets you hand-feed most of these, along with some of the native animals.

Australian War Memorial

Treloar Crescent • Daily 10am–5pm; tours 10am–4.15pm • Free • ⓦ awm.gov.au

The **Australian War Memorial** does an admirable job of positively commemorating Australia's war dead while avoiding any glorification of war itself – a notable achievement for a country that sees participation in world wars as key to its identity.

The centrepiece is the Byzantine-style, domed **Hall of Memory**, approached past an eternal flame rising from a rectangular pond. Look up to see mosaics depicting veterans of World War II (the walls and ceiling are covered with more than six million tiles), while the lovely blue stained-glass windows commemorate those who fought in World War I. In the centre is the tomb of the Unknown Australian Soldier, while over 102,000 names of the fallen are etched onto the walls outside. This, the commemorative area, is where you should be just before closing time when the story of one of the soldiers named on the roll of honour is read out, and a bugler plays the **Last Post** in moving testament to the dead.

The centrepiece of the museum is the shiny new $34 million Australia In The Great War gallery, which has replaced the rather stiff battle dioramas of old with well-designed modern displays, some highly artistic. The collection includes many newly acquired objects such as the Bullecourt Tank, General Sir John Monash's uniform and relics from the Pheasant Wood mass grave, excavated in 2010.

Don't miss the vast ANZAC Hall with its giant Lancaster bomber, Messerschmitt fighters and a Japanese mini submarine which attacked Sydney in 1942. Kids will love

---

THE ANZACS

Travelling around Australia you'll notice that almost every town, large or small, has a war memorial dedicated to the memory of the Anzacs, the **Australia and New Zealand Army Corps**. When war erupted in Europe in 1914, Australia was overwhelmed by a wave of pro-British sentiment. On August 5, 1914, one day after Great Britain had declared war against Germany, the Australian prime minister summed up the feelings of his compatriots: "When the Empire is at war so Australia is at war." On November 1, 1914, a contingent of twenty thousand enthusiastic volunteers – the **Anzacs** – left from the port of Albany in Western Australia to assist the mother country in her struggle.

In Europe, Turkey had entered the war on the German side in October 1914. At the beginning of 1915, military planners in London (Winston Churchill prominent among them) came up with a plan to capture the strategically important Turkish peninsula of the Dardanelles with a surprise attack near **Gallipoli**, thus opening the way to the Black Sea. On April 25, 1915, sixteen thousand Australian soldiers landed at dawn in a small bay flanked by steep cliffs: by nightfall, two thousand men had died in a hail of Turkish bullets from above. The plan, whose one chance of success was surprise, had been signalled by troop and ship movements long in advance; by the time it was carried out, it was already doomed to failure. Nonetheless, Allied soldiers continued to lose their lives for another eight months without ever gaining more than a foothold. In December, London finally issued the order to withdraw. Eleven thousand Australians and New Zealanders had been killed, along with as many French and Indians and three times as many British troops. The Turks lost 86,000 men.

Official Australian historiography continues to mythologize the battle for Gallipoli, elevating it to the level of a national legend on which Australian identity is founded. From this point of view, in the war's baptism of fire, the Anzac soldiers proved themselves heroes who did the new nation proud, their loyalty and bravery evidence of how far Australia had developed. It was "the birth of a nation", and at the same time a loss of innocence, a national rite of passage – never again would Australians so unquestioningly involve themselves in foreign ventures. Today the legend is as fiercely defended as ever, the focal point of Australian national pride, commemorated each year on April 25, **Anzac Day**.

the Biggles-style multi-screen film, *Over The Front*, which recreates a dog fight between Australian and German pilots in World War 1. Other new attractions include Mephisto, a sinister German tank from the same era – the only one of its type still in existence.

The Australian Institute of Sport

Leverrier St, Bruce • Tours daily 10am, 11.30am, 1pm & 2.30pm; 1hr 30min • $19 • Swimming pools Mon–Fri 6.15am–2pm; $6.40; ⓦ experienceais.com • Bus #7

Some 7km northwest of Civic is the ultramodern **Australian Institute of Sport (AIS)**. Founded to improve the national sports profile after Australia's dismal showing in the 1976 Olympics (when they won just three medals), AIS has since churned out world-beating athletes with such regularity that other countries now copy their training techniques. **Tours** are guided by athletes and introduce you to their intensive training schedules, while the **Sportex** interactive zone gives you the chance to test your prowess at virtual football, cycling, rowing, wheelchair basketball and rock climbing. Visitors can also use the centre's two immaculate swimming pools.

National Arboretum

Forest Drive, Weston Creek • Daily 9am–4pm • Free, parking $2/hr • ⓦ nationalarboretum.act.gov.au

The **National Arboretum** opened in 2013 on land that had been badly damaged by bushfires. The plan is for the six-hundred-acre site to be home to one hundred forests of rare, symbolic and endangered trees from Australia and around the world. As you might expect, the site is still finding its feet and many of the trees are in their infancy, so the main reason to visit is to enjoy the views over Canberra and admire the miniature trees of the National Bonsai and Penjing Collection. There are free guided tours, a children's play area and picnic spots, and the Village Centre is home to a shop and café.

ARRIVAL AND INFORMATION
CANBERRA

By plane Canberra Airport (ⓦ canberraairport.com.au), 7km east of the city, is served by both domestic and international flights. The Airport Express shuttle bus ($12 one-way, $20 return; ☎ 1300 368 897, ⓦ royalecoach.com.au) runs between the airport and West Row, the National Convention Centre and the YHA every 50min or so (Mon–Fri 8am–6.50pm, less frequently Sat & Sun 9.15am–6pm).

Destinations Adelaide (1–5 daily; 1hr 50min); Brisbane (9–11 daily; 1hr 45min); Melbourne (10–15 daily; 1hr 10min); Newcastle (1–3 daily; 1hr 10min); Sydney (20–30 daily; 55min).

By train The train station is 2km southeast of central Canberra, on Wentworth Avenue in Kingston, within walking distance of Kingston's accommodation options and around fifteen minutes by bus from Civic. The one-way fare from Sydney is around $48.

Destination Sydney (2–3 daily; 4hr 20min).

By bus The long-distance bus terminal is in Civic at the Jolimont Centre, 65–67 Northbourne Ave. The centre has a tourist information point with a free telephone line to the main visitor centre. Tickets are available here for direct services with Greyhound to Sydney and Melbourne; and Murrays Coaches to Sydney, Bateman's Bay, Wollongong and, during winter, a Snow Express to Thredbo. The Transborder Express runs services to Yass, and in season to Thredbo via Cooma and Jindabyne.

Destinations Batemans Bay (daily; 2hr 25min); Cooma (2 daily; 1hr 20min); Goulburn (daily; 1hr 10min); Melbourne (2 daily; 8–9hr); Moss Vale (daily; 2hr); Narooma (daily; 4hr 30min); Sydney (15–19 daily; 3hr 30min); Thredbo (winter 2 daily; 3hr); Wollongong (daily; 3hr 30min); Yass (5 daily; 1hr).

Tourist information The Visitor Information Centre (Mon–Fri 9am–5pm, Sat & Sun 9am–4pm; ☎ 1300 554 114, ⓦ visitcanberra.com.au) is at Regatta Point, Barrine Drive, Parkes. Regatta Park is served by direct buses from the City Bus Station.

GETTING AROUND

By bus City buses run by ACTION (☎ 13 17 10, ⓦ action .act.gov.au) operate daily from around 6.30am to 11.30pm or later, though weekend services are greatly reduced. Almost all services pass through the City Bus Station in Civic, a set of open-air bays around the eastern end of Alinga St. Tickets are available from drivers, and cost $4.70 for a single journey (including transfers), $9 for a day-pass. If you're planning to use a lot of buses, a MyWay smartcard works out cheaper – you can get these from a newsagent or MyWay kiosk; the cards come pre-loaded with credit (minimum $20), which can be topped up at any time, and can be used on any ACTION buses. An inexpensive way to tour the main attractions on the north side of the lake is to take ACTION bus route #981 (Sat & Sun only); places of interest on the south side are served by routes #2 and #3 (Mon–Fri), or #934 (Sat & Sun). Another option is the free City Loop service (every 15min Mon–Fri 7am–7pm) to the Canberra Centre, Baddon precinct, Northbourne Avenue, the ANU and NewAction precinct.

By car Canberra is an expensive place to rent a car, but relatively good deals are available with Redspot Car Rentals at Canberra Airport (☎ 02 6248 9966, ⊛ redspot.com.au). All of the big hire companies have outlets at the airport, including: Avis (☎ 02 6219 3033), Budget (☎ 02 6219 3040), Hertz (☎ 02 6249 6211) and Thrifty (☎ 02 6248 9081). If you're driving, make sure you carry a GPS – Canberra's baffling concentric street plan can turn

navigating the city's roads into a Kafka-esque nightmare. You typically pay $3 an hour for parking in the city centre. Note that many of the main museums and galleries also have parking available.

By taxi There's a taxi rank on Bunda St, Civic, outside the cinema. One recommended company is Canberra Elite (☎ 13 22 27, ⊛ canberraelite.com.au). Uber is also available (download app first).

By bike With Canberra's sights so spread out, you'd have to be very enthusiastic to consider walking everywhere. A good option is to rent a bike and take advantage of the city's excellent network of cycle paths; many city buses have racks for two bikes on the front. Damn Fine Bike Hire (☎ 02 6257 1122), next to the ferry dock on the north side of the lake, rents out bikes ($20/hr or $40/day) and four-wheel pedal cars ($40/hr). Bring photo ID and a credit card.

TOURS

Red Bus ☎ 0418 455 099, ⊛ canberradaytours.com.au. The Red Bus circuits the city's major sights around five times a day (Mon–Fri 9.30am–3.30pm, Sat with advance booking only). Go for a stay-on-the-bus sightseeing tour (1hr) or a hop-on-hop-off day-pass; both cost $30, with accommodation pick-ups available on request.

Lake cruises ☎ 0419 418 846, ⊛ lakecruises.com.au. A cruise on the lake is one of the most pleasant ways to see the city; cruises (Mon–Sat 10.30am, noon, 1.30pm &

3pm, Sun 1.30pm & 4pm; $18) depart from the Acton Ferry Terminal less than 1km southwest of Civic. There are also 2hr tea cruises on Sun at 10am ($18, bookings essential).

Dawn Drifters ☎ 02 6248 8200, ⊛ dawndrifters .com.au. The ever-popular sunrise hot-air ballooning trips with Dawn Drifters are a great way to see Canberra. An hour-long flight costs $290 (Sat & Sun $340) and you can add in a champagne breakfast for $40.

ACCOMMODATION

Most of Canberra's **accommodation** is located either in Civic or south of the lake at Kingston, both on bus routes and within striking distance of sights and places to eat. **Rates** fall at weekends, when the city empties, but hotel rooms can become scarce during big **conferences**, or when the House is sitting. If you have a vehicle it's better to stay outside Civic where **parking** is easier and cheaper.

HOTELS, MOTELS AND GUESTHOUSES

Hyatt 120 Commonwealth Ave, Yarralumla ☎ 02 6270 1234, ⊛ canberra.park.hyatt.com; map p.183. One of the most stylish hotels in Canberra, in glamorous 1930s buildings surrounded by lawns and gardens. Facilities include a fitness centre, swimming pool and off-street parking. Don't miss afternoon tea in the famous *Tea Lounge*. **$239**

★**Kurrajong** 8 National Circuit, Barton ☎ 02 6234 4444, ⊛ tfehotels.com; map p.183. Fresh from an extensive renovation, this beautiful heritage building can now be rated as Canberra's most elegant pied-a-terre, with 1920s style decor, tastefully decorated rooms, including 26 in the heritage wing, and an upscale restaurant: *Chifley's Bar & Grill*. **$129**

Medina Serviced Apartments 11 Giles St, Kingston ☎ 02 6239 8100, ⊛ adinahotels.com.au; map p.183. Good-value apartment hotel in a great location near shops and restaurants. Apartments are equipped with kitchenettes, laundries and balconies or courtyards. There

is a small indoor pool, a spa, and undercover parking. **$178**

Miranda Lodge 534 Northbourne Ave, Downer, 4km north of Civic ☎ 02 6249 8038, ⊛ mirandalodge .com.au; map p.183. Good, motel-style B&B with limited off-street parking and a bus stop nearby. There's a relaxed, old-fashioned feel and the owner is friendly and helpful. Consider asking for a room at the back to escape any traffic noise. Breakfast included. **$115**

Peppers Gallery 15 Edinburgh Ave, Civic ☎ 02 6175 2222, ⊛ peppers.com.au; map p.185. One of Canberra's most reliable mid-size hotels, offering eighty rooms, suites and apartments, plus a fitness centre, bar and restaurant. The rooms are simply furnished, with a few decorative flourishes and luxurious bathrooms. **$359**

QT 1 London Circuit ☎ 02 6247 6244, ⊛ qthotelsand resorts.com; map p.185. The Australia-wide QT chain is known for its camp interiors, photogenic staff and Pop Art excess, and the Canberra branch is no exception. There are amazing views from the upper floors, a buzzy (and quite noisy) restaurant and an old-school barber shop. Rooms are

2

2

contemporary, with thoughtful touches such as cocktail-making kits, work desks and designer chairs. Breakfast included. **$252**

Realm 18 National Circuit, Canberra ☏ 02 6163 1888, ⓦ hotelrealm.com.au; map p.183. This sophisticated, discreet and beautifully designed hotel is one of Canberra's best secrets. Guest rooms are spacious, with king-size beds, Nespresso machines and luxurious bathrooms – and there's a health club, with a 25m heated pool, and a spa. **$209**

University House 1 Balmain Crescent, Acton ☏ 1800 814 864, ⓦ anu.edu.au/unihouse; map p.183. Clubhouse-style hotel run by the Australian National University on the edge of its huge, semi-rural campus. There are affordable single rooms, suites, family rooms and two-bed apartments, all of which stay true to their 1950s origins. There's also a restaurant, library and bar on site. **$159**

HOSTELS AND CARAVAN PARKS

There are caravan parks near the centre of Canberra but many are in desperate need of renovation, particularly the facilities made available to campers. Ask to see your cabin or caravan site before committing.

EATING

NORTH OF THE LAKE: CIVIC, BRADDON AND DICKSON

Akiba 40 Bunda St ☏ 02 6162 0602, ⓦ akiba.com.au; map p.185. Asian street food is still a novelty in Canberra – and this cavernous space is ahead of the pack. The well-priced menu stretches across southeast Asia and China and includes a good selection of sushi dishes, savoury buns and noodles. Particularly recommended are the pork-belly bun ($8), ocean trout ceviche ($13) or salt and Sichuan pepper squid. Good drinks list, including cocktails. Mon–Fri 7.30am–10.30pm, Sat & Sun 11.30am–10.30pm.

Asian Noodle House 49 Northbourne Ave ☏ 02 6247 5145, ⓦ noodlehouse.net.au; map p.185. Predominantly Thai and Lao cheapie serving good *laksa* ($14.50–17), chow mein noodles ($13.50) and tangy noodle dishes like pad thai ($13.50). It's a Canberra institution, with other branches in Tuggeranong, Woden and Belconnen. Daily 11.30am–10pm.

Chairman and Yip 1 Burbury Cl, Barton ☏ 02 6162 1220, ⓦ chairmangroup.com.au/chairmanyip; map p.185. This stylish and eccentric restaurant offers eastern Chinese classics such as meltingly tender, aromatic *shantung* lamb ($32) alongside imaginative fusion dishes like pan-seared prawns with green papaya salad ($17.50). Tues–Fri noon–2.30pm & 6–11pm, Sat 6–11pm.

Charcoal 61 London Circuit ☏ 02 6248 8015; map p.185. Charcoal-grilled steak, in shamelessly large servings, is the mainstay here and all cuts are served with a baked potato and vegetables ($47–63). Not one for vegetarians but they do offer grilled fish, and chicken and

★ **Alivio Tourist Park** 20 Kunzea St, O'Connor ☏ 02 6247 5466, ⓦ aliviogroup.com.au; map p.183. Just four kilometres from Civic, this family-friendly holiday camp is a cut above the others, with modern cabins, functional caravan sites and facilities that include a swimming pool, tennis courts, shop, guest laundry and a slick cafeteria. Powered sites **$49**, cabins **$140**

Canberra City YHA 7 Akuna St, Civic ☏ 02 6248 9155, ⓦ yha.com.au; map p.185. This large, modern and well-organized hostel is located right in the heart of Civic, a short hop from the bus terminals, and comes with basement pool, sauna, roof terrace, 24hr check-in and decent-sized rooms. Note that there's no parking. Dorms **$33**, doubles **$103**

Crestview Tourist Park 81 Donald Rd, Queanbeyan, 13km southeast of Parliament ☏ 02 6297 2443, ⓦ crestviewtouristpark.com.au; map p.183. Technically in NSW, this park is about 20min from the city centre. There are a number of cabin options, as well as powered and en-suite sites. Facilities are clean, and there's a BBQ, small pool and play area. Not the prettiest place but it's quiet. Powered sites **$39**, cabins **$90**

veal dishes – and a couple of salad options. Mon–Fri noon–2.30pm & 6–10pm, Sat 6–10pm.

Courgette 54 Marcus Clarke St ☏ 02 6247 4042, ⓦ courgette.com.au; map p.185. Some of Canberra's finest cooking is served up at this smart yet intimate restaurant, a mainstay of the city's dining scene for the past decade. Modern European leanings inform a menu that might include flaked ocean trout, maple-glazed duck or seared cauliflower steak. Four-course dinner menu $66. Mon–Sat noon–3pm, 6.30–9.30pm.

Cream Cnr Bunda and Grange Sts ☏ 02 6162 1448, ⓦ creamcafebar.com.au; map p.185. Decent, moderately priced food is served with panache at this modern, always-buzzing spot. The menu is fairly broad with dishes ranging from burgers (from $18) to pad thai ($26) and veal saltimbocca ($32). On a warm evening, head for the marble cocktail bar or shun the echoey interior for the streetside seating. Mon–Tues 7am–6pm, Wed–Fri 7am–late, Sat 7am–late, Sun 7.30am–4pm.

Frugii Dessert Laboratory 30 Lonsdale St, Braddon ☏ 0438 366 368, ⓦ frugii.com; map p.183. More like a shrine to sorbet and ice cream than a laboratory, this all-white space serves up icy desserts ($5/scoop) laced with interesting flavours, such as lavender, blood orange, gin and tonic, salted caramel and rosewater. They also serve thick shakes and exquisite cake, alongside other options. Wed–Sun noon–11pm.

Gus' Café Garema Arcade, Bunda St ☏ 02 6248 8118; map p.185. This long-standing café serves inexpensive food throughout the day; the lunch menu includes toasted sandwiches, burgers and pasta ($17–21.90), with lots of choice for vegetarians. Popular with students and an arty crowd, and has outside tables under vines. Daily 7.30am–11pm.

The Hamlet 16 Lonsdale St, Braddon ☏ 0407 283 218; ⊚ bit.ly/thehamlet; map p.183. What is the collective noun for a group of food vans? Well, in Canberra it's *The Hamlet*. This former car yard is now occupied by a collection of vans and temporary stalls selling Indian, Peruvian, Italian and vegetarian cuisine, among others – try the pulled-pork sandwich ($13) or strip steam empanadas ($7) from *Mr Papa*. Wed–Sat noon–9pm, Sun noon–3pm.

★ **Monster Kitchen & Bar** 25 Edinburgh Avenue ☏ 02 6287 6286, ⊚ monsterkitchen.com.au; map p.183. Part of the stunning *Hotel Hotel* art and accommodation complex, this place looks ridiculously pretentious but is in fact quite the reverse, with friendly service, fresh regional food and a laid-back vibe. Guests can choose from the formal restaurant or more relaxed bistro. The bistro menu includes such delights as Wagyu beef bresaola ($28) and yabby – a freshwater crayfish – jaffle ($20). Daily 6.30am–1am.

SOUTH OF THE LAKE: PARKES, KINGSTON, GRIFFITHS AND MANUKA

Aubergine Restaurant 18 Barker St, Griffiths ☏ 02 6260 8666, ⊚ aubergine.com.au; map p.183. Dedicated foodies should make a bee-line to this elegant restaurant in the 'burbs. The emphasis here is firmly on food and wine matching; the four-course menu ($135 with wine) is terrific value, boasting the likes of strawberry gazpacho, spiced duck and beef rib-eye. Mon–Sat 6–9.30pm.

Bittersweet Green Square, Kingston ☏ 02 6260 7263; map p.183. With hessian coffee bags decorating the walls and a house blend for sale, the coffee here is as good as you'd expect. The big breakfast ($19.90) is a popular choice; lunch is soups, salads, wraps and burgers. Service can slow when the place gets busy. Mon–Fri 7.30am–4.30pm, Sat & Sun 7am–4pm.

Bookplate Café National Library, Parkes Place ☏ 02 6262 1154; map p.183. The best café in the Parliamentary district. Sit inside surrounded by modern stained glass, or out

on the sunny terrace overlooking the lake. The lunch menu includes a meze platter ($13.50) and a Moroccan veggie salad ($17.80), plus wines by the glass. Mon–Thurs 7.30am–5.30pm, Fri 7.30am–4pm, Sat & Sun 9am–4pm.

Me & Mrs Jones Cnr Giles & Kennedy sts, Kingston ☏ 02 6162 3355, ⊚ mmjones.com.au; map p.183. A busy and stylish restaurant with exposed brick walls, wines on display and seating inside and out. The menu ranges from snacks such as pulled brioche sliders ($6.50) to wild mushroom cannelloni ($26). Mon–Fri 7am–9pm, Sat 8am–9pm, Sun 8am–4pm.

Ottoman Cuisine Cnr Broughton & Blackall sts, Barton ☏ 02 6273 6111, ⊚ ottomancuisine.com.au; map p.183. There's an *Arabian Nights* feel to the entrance, but inside it's all crisp white linen – a swanky setting for top-end Turkish dishes such *hiramassa* kingfish skewers ($33) or thyme and sea salt seasoned Cowra lamb cutlets ($33). Tues–Fri noon–2.30pm & 6–10pm, Sat 6–10pm.

Silo Bakery Café 36 Giles St, Kingston ☏ 02 6260 6060, ⊚ silobakery.com.au; map p.183. Narrow and cramped yet always packed with Canberra's smart set, *Silo* is a specialist cheese shop, bakery and café. Excellent coffee, bread, pastries and imaginative breakfasts, such as vegan salad ($18) have made it justly popular, so be prepared to wait. Tues–Sat 7am–4pm.

Timmy's Kitchen Cnr Furneaux & Bougainville sts, Manuka ☏ 02 6295 6537; map p.183. This friendly and very popular Chinese and Malay restaurant is particularly good for seafood. Dishes include *laksa* ($14.50–18.50) and Mongolian beef ($15), as well as Szechuan-style seafood. BYO. Tues–Thurs 11.30am–2.30pm & 5–10pm, Fri 11.30am–2.30pm & 5–11pm, Sat 11.30am–2.30pm & 5–10.30pm, Sun 11.30am–2.30pm & 5.30–10pm.

Watersedge 40 Parkes Place, Parkes ☏ 02 6273 5066, ⊚ watersedgecanberra.com.au; map p.183. One of Canberra's longest-running upmarket restaurants is handy for the National Gallery – and enjoys pleasant views over Lake Burley Griffin. The dishes here are solidly French, so expect the likes of goat's cheese millefeuille ($22), confit of duck leg ($36) and other elaborate creations. Ideal for a long lunch. Wed–Sun noon–3pm, 6–9pm.

NIGHTLIFE AND ENTERTAINMENT

Canberra has a lively entertainment scene, though it's nothing you'd make a special journey for. Most of the **drinking** action is in Civic, but Braddon (immediately north) and Dickson (4km north) also have small scenes. South of the lake there are a couple of worthwhile bars among the restaurants of Kingston. Canberra's **clubs** are mostly in Civic. The best **live music** is usually at the university's *ANU Bar*; *Transit Bar* hosts local bands and some overseas acts. For information about upcoming **events**, the daily *Canberra Times* is your best bet; the most extensive listings are published every Thurs in the "Good Times" supplement. For details of gigs and club nights, check out the entertainment magazine *BMA* (⊚ bmamag .com), available from record shops, hostels and bars, and accessible online.

PUBS AND BARS

BentSpoke 38 Mort St, Braddon ☏ 02 6257 5220, ⊚ bentspokebrewing.com.au; map p.183. One for the

craft beer aficionados, this brand new microbrewery and tap house in the heart of Braddon serves eighteen ales and ciders, plus some seasonal specials. Two-litre refillable

2

containers are also available to take away. They also serve food, a cut above the usual pub offerings. Daily 11am–late.

Grease Monkey 19 Lonsdale St, Braddon 02 6174 1401, greasys.com.au; map p.183. Boisterous industrial space that lives up to its name, serving less than healthy delights like burgers, fried chicken and jam doughnuts. Try the Nimbin (vegetarian) burger ($17). Expect a lively crowd and plenty of craft beers on tap, plus a good choice of boutique wines, ciders and cocktails. On warmer evenings, grab a table in the beer garden. Daily 11am–late.

Honkytonks 5 Garema Place, Civic; map p.185. Sit on one of the high stools and watch the world go by or take in the colourful decor, the hard-to-miss mural and the exhibition of local art. You can soak up the booze with a taco or a honkydog. Mon–Thurs 4pm–2am, Fri 3pm–2am, Sat & Sun noon–2am.

King O'Malleys 131 City Walk, Civic; map p.185. This vibrant Irish-style pub in the heart of town hosts regular live music nights and gets busy at weekends. At quieter times it's a good spot for bar meals such as beef-and-Guinness pie. Mon–Wed & Sun 11am–midnight, Thurs 11am–1am, Fri 11am–3am, Sat 11am–midnight.

Knightsbridge Penthouse 1/34 Mort St, Braddon; map p.185. Sleek cocktail bar a short walk north of Civic that has a good party vibe at weekends, with DJs on duty. It's like being in someone's (large) lounge but with a cocktail menu that changes with the season. Tues & Wed 5pm–midnight, Thurs–Sat 5pm–2am.

White Rabbit Cocktail Room 65 Northbourne Ave, Civic; map p.185. An Alice in Wonderland-inspired cocktail lounge serving sharing plates ($14–28) and an amusingly named range of lush cocktails ($18–23), such as The Walrus and Pocket Watch. Tues–Sat 5pm–late.

CLUBS AND LIVE MUSIC

Academy Club 50 Bunda St academyclub.com.au; map p.185. One of Canberra's top nightclubs for more than a decade, with a capacity to hold six hundred people and a state-of-the-art sound and lighting system. Thursday is Uni Night, with great deals on drinks and all the hits on high rotation. A mix of visiting and resident DJs play here. Thurs–Sat 9pm–5am.

ANU Bar University Ave, Civic anuunion.com.au; map p.185. Also known as the *Uni Bar* and not to be

FESTIVALS

Floriade floriadeaustralia.com. This month-long spring festival is the city's biggest event of the year, taking place in Commonwealth Park and marked by floral displays, music and entertainers. Mid-Sept to mid-Oct.

The Canberra International Film Festival ciff. com.au From late Oct to early Nov around sixty feature

confused with the *Uni Pub*, this venue hosts mostly small to mid-range touring bands and DJs. Stays open later on nights when a band's playing. Mon–Wed noon–6.30pm, Thurs & Fri noon–7.30pm.

Cube 33 Petrie Plaza, Civic cubenightclub.com.au; map p.185. This is Canberra's main gay and lesbian venue. There are regular drag shows, theme nights and guest DJs and the party carries on well into the early hours. Thurs–Sun 10pm–5am.

Hippo Co 17 Garema Place, Civic hippoco.com.au; map p.185. Stylish, hard-to-spot lounge bar in Civic offering live music, whisky tastings and even cocktail masterclasses. Expect ground-breaking new cocktails and more than two hundred different varieties of whisky, displayed on the vintage-style black and gold whisky board. Live jazz every Wed. Mon–Thurs & Sat 5pm–late, 2am, Fri 4pm–late.

Transit Bar 7 Akuna St, Civic transitbar.com.au; map p.185. Tucked away near the YHA, this is a popular live music venue but there are also karaoke and trivia nights. Stocks a good range of bottled beers, and pizza for the peckish. Mon–Sat noon–10pm, Sun 2–8pm.

THEATRE AND CINEMA

Arc Cinema National Film and Sound Archive, McCoy Circuit 02 6248 2000, nfsa.gov.au/arc. Excellent art-house movies from around the world, many of them historic, though with occasional new releases. Mostly Thurs & Sat.

Canberra Theatre Centre London Circuit 02 6275 2700, canberratheatrecentre.com.au. Canberra's main performing arts space, with several theatres hosting plays, concerts, dance performances and travelling shows.

Dendy Cinema Canberra Centre, 149 Bunda St, Canberra 02 6221 8900, dendy.com.au. Independent multiplex showing mainstream films and a smattering of international and art-house films.

Palace Electric 2 Phillip Law St, Acton 02 6222 4900, palacecinemas.com.au. Eight screens showing art-house films and new releases. Also home to film festivals and a bar.

The Street Theatre Cnr Childers St & University Ave 02 6247 1223, thestreet.org.au. An alternative venue offering offbeat music, theatre and opera performances. Close to ANU.

films and documentaries from around the world are screened over a period of twelve days.

The Royal Canberra Show canberrashow.org.au. An agricultural fair lasting three days over the last weekend in Feb.

CANBERRA DISTRICT WINERIES

The cool-climate wines of the ACT are enjoying increasing recognition for their quality. Although many varieties can be found here, visitors should ensure they try a Shiraz or Riesling.

There are more than one hundred wineries in the Canberra region and more than thirty within half an hour of the city. Pick up a map from the visitor centre (see p.190) or visit the website Ⓦ canberrawines.com.au for details of wineries with tours and restaurants. If you're at a loss for where to start, visit **Clonakilla** (Ⓦ clonakilla.com.au; daily 10am–5pm) and try its famous Shiraz Viognier, or sip the impressive Sauvignon Blanc and Riesling wines at **Brindabella Hills** winery (Ⓦ brindabellahills.com.au; tastings Sat & Sun 10am–5pm). Don't miss the **Wiley Trout** vineyard (Ⓦ poacherspantry.com.au; daily 9.30am–5pm) as it shares space with the *Poachers Pantry*, which dishes up gourmet meals using fresh and local produce, as well as meats smoked on site.

2

SHOPPING

Canberra Centre Bunda St. This is Canberra's main shopping complex, home to the Myer and David Jones department stores as well as other well-known high-street brands. There are a number of eating options on site and the Dendy cinema (see opposite). Mon–Thurs 9am–5.30pm, Fri 9am–9pm, Sat 9am–5pm, Sun 10am 4pm.

Craft ACT: Craft and Design Centre 1st Floor, North Building, 180 London Circuit, Civic. The shop next to the Contemporary Design Exhibition Space offers original and high-quality handmade jewellery and homewares which make excellent gifts or souvenirs. Tues–Fri 10am–5pm, Sat noon–4pm.

The Essential Ingredient 25 Jardine St, Kingston. A large space dedicated to all things foodie, from cookbooks to dinosaur-shaped cookie cutters. There is also a speciality cheese counter and condiments galore on sale. Mon–Fri 9.30am–5.30pm, Sat 9am–4pm, Sun 10am–3pm.

Old Bus Depot Markets 21 Wentworth Ave, Kingston.

An opportunity to see what creative Canberra has been up to. This busy indoor market offers the chance to admire and buy handcrafted goods, tuck into some local food and listen to live music. Sun 10am–4pm, also Sat in the run-up to Christmas.

Portrait Gallery Store National Portrait Gallery. A great range of titles is for sale here, including biographies and novels and of course books covering art and architecture. There are also ceramics, jewellery and craft by Australian designers and some interesting children's toys and gifts. Daily 10am–5pm.

Smiths Alternative Bookshop 76 Alinga St, opposite the post office, Ⓦ smithsalternative.com. A small shop selling books and vintage clothes and accessories; the counter also serves as a café/bar. Hosts a number of interesting events, from spoken word to gigs to debates. Mon–Thurs 7am–midnight, Fri 7am–3pm, Sat 9am–3pm, Sun noon–midnight.

DIRECTORY

Banks ANZ, Commonwealth, HSBC Australia, National Australia Bank and Westpac all have branches in Civic.

Embassies and high commissions There are more than seventy in Canberra (all the following are in Yarralumla, unless otherwise stated): Britain, Commonwealth Ave (☎02 6270 6666); Canada, Commonwealth Ave (☎02 6270 4000); China, 15 Coronation Drive (☎02 6273 4780); Ireland, 20 Arkana St (☎02 6214 0000); Malaysia, 7 Perth Ave (☎02 6120

0300); New Zealand, Commonwealth Ave (☎02 6270 4211); Singapore, 17 Forster Crescent (☎02 6271 2000); Thailand, 111 Empire Circuit (☎02 6206 0100); USA, 21 Moonah Place (☎02 6214 5600).

Hospitals Calvary Hospital (cnr Haydon & Belconnen Way, ☎02 6201 6111); The Canberra Hospital, Yamba Drive, Garran (☎02 6244 2222).

Post office Alinga St, Canberra, ACT 2600 (Mon–Fri 8.30am–5.30pm, Sat 9.30am–1pm; ☎13 13 18).

Namadgi National Park

The **Namadgi National Park**, a subalpine region occupying almost half of the ACT, is well worth visiting. Its mountain ranges and high plains rise to 1900m, have a far more severe climate than low-lying Canberra, and give rise to the Cotter River and many smaller streams. Landscapes here range from the highest peak of Mount Bimberi, above snowline, to grassy frost hollow valleys, alpine meadows and snow gum woodlands. The park is home to 35 species of mammals including swamp wallabies, eastern grey kangaroos, echidnas, wombats, emus and pygmy possums, alongside numerous reptiles.

2

Canberra Deep Space Communication Centre

421 Discovery Drive, Tidbinbilla · Daily 9am–5pm · Free · Ⓦ cdscc.nasa.gov

Amid the foothills of the Tidbinbilla Range, 30km southwest of Canberra, you'll glimpse the big white satellite dishes of the **Canberra Deep Space Communication Centre**. They're the largest in Australia and are operated in conjunction with NASA for communicating with spacecraft exploring the solar system; there are only two others in the world – one near Madrid, the other in Goldstone, California. In their shadow, a small visitor centre gives fairly pedestrian but interesting coverage of their activities. It is all slotted into displays on understanding the universe, space exploration and general rocketry, including a 1970s vintage minicomputer (all big brown switches and hubcap-sized hard disk) once used for mission control. There's enough interactive stuff to keep kids happy for a while.

Tidbinbilla Nature Reserve

Paddy's River Rd, Tharwa · Daily: June–Aug 7.30am–6pm; Dec–Feb 7.30am–8pm · Day-pass $11.50 (per vehicle) · ☎ 02 6205 1233, Ⓦ tidbinbilla.com.au

The small **Tidbinbilla Nature Reserve** is an enjoyable place of rocks and gum trees with relatively easy walks, picnic grounds, a good chance of seeing emus, and even the possibility of spotting platypus. Consequently, it's popular on long weekends and during the school holidays, especially with families.

The area around the park entrance and **visitor centre** is home to kangaroos and wallabies in spacious bush enclosures, and you can also see koalas, birds and **corroboree frogs**, an extremely rare alpine amphibian. From here, a 16km sealed loop road runs through the reserve with short trails off to panoramic viewpoints and historic sites – a once heavily used Aboriginal shelter rock and the spire-like Church Rock, where services were held in pioneering times. The reserve's highlight is the **Sanctuary**, a few acres fenced off from predators where a 2km wheelchair-accessible boardwalk winds though some wetlands. Landscaping allows you to get a duck's-eye view of one lake, and the signage is entertaining and informative.

Lanyon Homestead

Tharwa Drive, Tharwa · Tues–Sun 10am–4pm · $7, admission to grounds free · Ⓦ historicplaces.com.au

Some 4km north of the little hamlet of Tharwa, and some 30km south of Canberra, the convict-built **Lanyon Homestead** dates back to the earliest European settlement of the region. The house itself has been thoroughly restored to its original mid-Victorian style and is a prime example of how life in colonial Australia was lived, at least for wealthy landowners. It also houses a small display outlining the history of the area before Canberra existed.

GETTING AROUND AND INFORMATION

By car You really need a vehicle to explore the park. The best route is the 80km loop from Canberra, which takes in all the sights mentioned above.

Tourist information The Namadgi Visitor Centre at Naas

NAMADGI NATIONAL PARK

Rd, 7km south of Lanyon Homestead (Mon–Fri 9am–4pm, Sat & Sun 9am–4.30pm; ☎ 02 6207 2900, Ⓦ tams.act .gov.au), provides tours on request and has displays and films about the park, plus advice on camping.

ACCOMMODATION

The Namadgi National Park campsites need to be booked in advance through the visitor centre or via Ⓦ tams.act.gov.au. Bring your own drinking water and wood, and be sure to take your rubbish with you when you leave.

Honeysuckle Apollo Rd, 23km from Namadgi Visitor Centre. A simple drive-in campsite with composting toilets, accessed via a sealed road. It's near the Honeysuckle Creek Tracking Station, which was in use until 1981.

Unpowered sites per person $8

Mt Clear Boboyan Rd. The most remote of the Namadgi campsites and close to the NSW border, this site is accessed by unsealed road and has pit toilets. You can walk up the Nass Valley to Horse Gully Hut (18km return) from here; ask at the visitor centre for a map. Unpowered sites per person $10

Orroral Orroral Rd, 22km from Namadgi Visitor Centre.

Shady tent sites under gum trees beside a river, access is via a sealed road, and there are flush toilets. The 6km Orroral Heritage Walking Track starts from here. Unpowered sites per person $8

The south coast

The **south coast** of New South Wales is all rather low-key and family-oriented, with lush dairy farms and small fishing villages. There are a few wildlife and amusement parks to keep the children happy, and plenty of opportunities to cast a rod or relax on a sunny beach. Exposed parts on this stretch of the coast are perfect for **surfing**, while the numerous coastal lakes, bays and inlets are suited for **swimming**, windsurfing, sailing or canoeing. Away from the ocean there's some superb rugged scenery, with some great **bushwalking** and **horseriding** in the forest-clad, mountainous hinterland.

Give yourself four or more days to drive the scenic **Princes Highway** and appreciate the beautiful coastline. The area between **Jervis Bay** and **Batemans Bay** in particular can get busy during the summer months, especially from Christmas to the end of January, and prices rise accordingly. Winter (June to August) is a great time to visit if you want to avoid the crowds and still enjoy the great outdoors, but you'll find many businesses, especially adventure tour operators and restaurants, closed during the off season.

Berry

On the Princes Highway some 65km south of Wollongong, **BERRY** is a pretty, historic town with many listed buildings, surrounded by dairy country and green hills. The main reason to stop is to eat well, do a little craft and homewares shopping, then eat some more. The main drag, **Queen Street**, is packed with upmarket shops, cafés and restaurants. Understandably enough, Berry is a favourite with weekending Sydneysiders, and the place can get unbearably crowded. The town's popularity is further enhanced by the proximity of **Kangaroo Valley** (16km west), the beach at **Gerringong** (18km east) and a monthly market (March–Jan first Sun of the month). Wineries are another draw: Coolangatta Estate (daily 10am–5pm; ☎02 4448 7131, ⓦcoolangattaestate.com.au), just 5km southeast of Berry on Bolong Road, and Silos Estate (daily 11am–5pm; ☎02 4448 6082, ⓦthesilos.com), 8km southwest at Jasper's Brush, are among the best.

ARRIVAL AND INFORMATION   BERRY

By train Berry is easily reached by train on CityRail's South Coast Line from Sydney, change at Kiama (5 daily; 2hr 40min).

Tourist information The Shoalhaven region visitor information centre (daily 9am–5pm; ☎1300 662 808,

ⓦshoalhavenholidays.com.au) is located 18km south of Berry on the Princes Hwy at Nowra, just after the Shoalhaven River road bridge. Check their website for details of rural B&Bs in the hills around town.

ACCOMMODATION

The Berry Inn 122 Queen St ☎02 4464 2064, ⓦberryinn.com.au. Four-room B&B in a heritage building, with a lovely leafy garden and small swimming pool. Every room is different; the modern stables accommodation includes one wheelchair-accessible unit and one with a kitchen. $140

Berry Showground Camping 35 Alexander St ☎0427 605 200, ⓔberryshowgroundcamping@gmail.com. Nestled on the edge of the town's playing fields, this

pleasant campsite offers 48 powered and unpowered sites, plus hot showers, a communal kitchen and horse stables. No wi-fi. Un/powered sites $18/$24

Silos Estate Jaspers Bush, 8km south ☎02 4448 6082, ⓦthesilos.com. Boutique accommodation on a vineyard with cosy suites and a two-bedroom cottage, with plenty of breakfast supplies provided. There's also a good restaurant on site. Minimum two-night stay on weekends. $195

2

EATING

Berry Sourdough Bakery & Café 23 Prince Alfred St ☎02 4464 1617, ⓦberrysourdoughcafe.com.au. Virtually everything is made on the premises at this wonderful bakery/café just off the main street. Lunch might included delights like courgette flower and buffalo feta omelette ($17.50) or rigatoni with Spanish pork sausage ($20). They also have an outlet on the main street, Milkwood Bakery, which sells breads and pastries to take away. Wed–Sun 8am–3pm.

Emporium Food Co 127B Queen St ☎02 4464 1570. An inviting deli and café selling pasta, condiments, smoked meats and imported and local farmhouse cheeses. Lunch options also include soup of the day ($11.50) and gourmet sandwiches and wraps ($8–12). Mon–Sat 9am–5pm, Sun 10am–4.30pm.

The Hungry Duck 85 Queen St ☎02 4464 2323, ⓦhungryduck.com.au. A contemporary Asian restaurant with an emphasis on sharing: dishes include sashimi ($18) and home-made steamed Wagyu beef tongue buns ($16). There's also a five- or nine-course banquet option. Book in advance. Wed–Mon 6–10pm.

Il Locale Gelati 114 Queen St ☎02 4464 3355. This cute little Italian-style café-cum-art gallery serves delicious *gelato* made from locally sourced milk (two scoops, $6), plus excellent coffee ($3.50), light snacks (lunch $10) and home-made biscuits in various flavours. Daily 8am–6pm.

Jervis Bay

Around 40km south of Berry, the sheltered waters of **Jervis Bay** (often mispronounced Jarvis Bay), now a marine reserve, are surrounded by small towns. On the southern hook of the bay is the town of the same name, which, by a political quirk, is technically part of the ACT, in order to provide Canberra with theoretical access to the sea.

Huskisson

Of the several villages dotted around the bay and its vicinity, the main focus is **HUSKISSON**, at the midpoint of the bay, which isn't much more than a few streets centred on the small marina backed by a handful of cafés, takeaways and watersports operators. There is, however, the **Jervis Bay Maritime Museum** (daily 10am–4pm; ☎02 4441 5675, ⓦjervisbaymaritimemuseum.asn.au), which is home to a large collection of maritime artefacts, historic vessels and nautical equipment, plus photographs, paintings and other objects telling the story of the Jervis Bay area. A market is held here on the playing field (next to the bowling club) on the second Sunday (8am–1pm) of the month.

Booderee National Park

The visitor information centre (Mon–Thurs 9.30am–3pm, Fri–Sun 9am–4pm; ☎02 4443 0977, ⓦ parksaustralia.gov.au) is at the entrance to the park on Village Rd; walking maps are available, and you also pay the entry fee here • $11 per vehicle for 48hr; NSW Parks passes are not valid

The beautiful coast of **Booderee National Park** ("bay of plenty", or "plenty of fish"), at the southern end of the bay, is very popular: rugged cliffs face the pounding ocean along its eastern boundary, while the park's northern side, within the confines of the bay, is marked by tranquil beaches of dazzling white sand and clear water. Inland, heaths, wetlands and forests offer strolls and bushwalks; there's also great snorkelling from the park and around nearby Bowen Island, with a chance of spotting a range of marine life including dolphins, stingrays and – around the island – a penguin colony.

Booderee Botanic Gardens

Cave Beach Rd • May–Sept daily 9am–4pm; Oct–April Mon–Fri 9am–5pm, Sat & Sun 8am–6pm • Included in park entrance fee

Booderee Botanic Gardens focuses on regional coastal flora, and has a combination of cultivated areas and natural bushland. Covering almost two hundred acres of parkland, there are a number of pleasant walks along well-marked tracks here and interpretive boards allow visitors to learn more about the Koorie people's use of local plants.

GETTING AROUND AND INFORMATION
JERVIS BAY

By bus Nowra Coaches (☎02 4423 5244, ⓦwww .nowracoaches.com.au) runs a local service from Nowra to Jervis Bay (Mon–Fri 4 daily; 2hr; single $10.40).

By bike Bikes can be hired from Dive Jervis Bay ($15/hr; see opposite).

Tourist information The visitor information centre in

Nowra (see p.197) has the most comprehensive information on the area, though there's a small information centre at the Jervis Bay Maritime Museum (daily 10am–4pm; ☎02 4441 5999) in Huskisson at 11 Dent St.

ACTIVITIES

Sealife-watching Tours are available with eco-certified Dolphin Watch Cruises, 50 Owen St (1hr 30min to half-day; $35–1800; ☎02 4441 6311, ⬤dolphinwatch.com.au), which run year-round; from Sept to Nov you may see whales. **Diving and snorkelling** Dive Jervis Bay, 64 Owen St (☎02 4441 5255, ⬤divejervisbay.com), offer diving in pristine waters – surprisingly enough, it's the second most popular dive spot in Australia after the Great Barrier Reef,

with an extremely diverse range of marine life. Four-hour, two-dive trips go for $130 ($190 including all gear) or choose a half-day snorkelling trip for $95.
Kayaking Jervis Bay Kayak & Paddlesports Co, 13 Hawke St (☎02 4441 7157, ⬤jervisbaykayaks.com), run a wide range of trips including a half-day Discover Jervis Bay tour ($109). They also rent out kayaks, stand-up paddleboards and scooters.

ACCOMMODATION

Booderee National Park campsites ☎02 4443 0977, ⬤booderee.gov.au. The Booderee National Park visitor information centre handles all bookings for the three insanely popular unpowered campsites in the park – a ballot is held in Aug for spots over the Christmas holiday period. The *Cave Beach* site is the most sought after, despite its cold showers and 300m walk-in, but *Bristol Point* and *Green Patch* (where the sites vary in size) also get plenty of guests; the latter is the only one of the three suitable for campervans. Unpowered sites: *Cave Beach* $49, *Bristol Point* and *Green Patch* $12–49
Huskisson B&B 12 Tomerong St, Huskisson ☎02 4441 7551, ⬤huskissonbnb.com.au. Lovely B&B in a 1913 weatherboard cottage with bright, beach-house-chic rooms and a multitude of home comforts. Massages and other pampering services can be arranged. Rates include breakfast. $195
★ **Hyams Beach Seaside Cottages** 53–55 Cyrus St, Hyams Beach ☎0412 029 096, ⬤hyamsbeachseaside cottages.com.au. These pastel-coloured wooden beach cottages, 10km south of Huskisson, are reminiscent of what

an Australian seaside holiday once was – uncomplicated, laidback and fairly modest. The cottages are compact but superbly equipped, with queen-size beds, small kitchens, spa baths and BBQs; Hyams Beach, a family-friendly stretch of sand, is just across the road. No wi-fi. $320
Jervis Bay Caravan Park 785 Woollamia Rd, 2km northwest of Huskisson ☎02 4441 5046, ⬤jervisbaycaravanpark.com.au. A campsite that's right on the water, with some popular cabins, a solar-heated swimming pool, kids splash zone, renovated ablutions block and undercover BBQs. Un/powered sites $25/35, cabins $80
Paperbark Camp 571 Woollamia Rd, 4km northwest of Huskisson ☎02 4441 6066, ⬤paperbarkcamp .com.au. Unusual luxury eco-resort set in the middle of the bush, with accommodation in twelve romantic en-suite safari tents on stilts (some with baths), solar-powered lighting and a superb restaurant (see below). Rates include the use of bikes and canoes; there is no wi-fi in the tents. Massages and beauty treatments are available for a fee. Closed July and Aug. $395

EATING

The Gunyah Paperbark Camp, 571 Woollamia Rd, 4km northwest of Huskisson ☎02 4441 7299. Fabulously sited in the treetops, this airy restaurant allows you to view the resident possums and sugar gliders through the windows. The three-course set menu ($70; no a la carte option) changes daily and includes dishes such as fresh papperdelle with rabbit, local fish and pepperberry kangaroo. A vegetarian version is also available. Sept– June daily 6.30–10pm.
Supply Café 54 Owen St, Huskisson ☎02 4441 5815, ⬤supplyjervisbay.com.au. This combined café, juice bar and shop covers a lot of culinary territory – from hearty

breakfasts and wholesome lunches to fresh fruit and vegetables, gourmet produce and kitchenware. Try the Maxi Breakfast (eggs, tomato, mushrooms, bacon and Turkish toast) for $18; coffee $3.50. Mon–Sat 7.30am–5pm, Sun 7.30am–3pm.
5 Little Pigs 64–66 Owen St, Huskisson ☎02 4441 7056, ⬤5littlepigs.com.au. This modern café serves classic Aussie food but with a cosmopolitan twist. Try the lime, chilli and salt squid ($17.50) or *huevos rancheros* ($16.50), or just drop in for a classic milkshake, organic tea or a cup of locally roasted Swell coffee. Mon–Thurs & Sun 7am–4pm, Fri & Sat 7am–5pm.

Ulladulla and around

ULLADULLA, 60km south of Jervis Bay, is a pleasant but uninspiring fishing port arranged along the Princes Highway, whose saving grace is its small, pretty harbour. There are attractive river mouths, beaches and lakes along the coast in both directions.

Pretty **Lake Conjola** (10km north), **Lake Burrill** (5km south) and **Lake Tabourie** (13km south) are popular with anglers, canoeists and campers. The best local beach is **Mollymook**, 2km north, which has a few shops, motels and cafés.

Milton

It's worth taking a detour 7km north along the Princes Highway to the village of **Milton**, a vaguely alternative place that's home to several craft shops, cafés and the **Milton Theatre** (w miltontheatre.com.au), which attracts predominantly acoustic acts – anything from classical to world music.

Morton National Park

Ulladulla and Milton are set within a beautiful area, dominated by the sandstone plateau of the **Morton National Park** to the west, one of the biggest and wildest national parks in New South Wales. Towards the south of the park in the Budawang Ranges there's a good bushwalk to the top of the 720m **Pigeon House Mountain** (5.3km return; 3–4hr; 500m ascent), a fairly steep affair with some ladders for the final ascent. To get there, turn west off the Princes Highway 8km south of town along Wheelbarrow Road then follow signs 26km inland.

ARRIVAL AND INFORMATION

ULLADULLA AND AROUND

By bus Premier Motor Service (t 13 34 10, w premierms .com.au) operates a regular coach service from Central Station in Sydney to Ulladulla and other south-coast towns – and onward to Melbourne.

Tourist information Shoalhaven Visitor Information Centre Princes Hwy (Mon–Fri 9am–5pm, Sat & Sun 9am–2pm; t 02 4455 1269, w shoalhavenholidays.com. au) provides a range of brochures and maps, plus a booking service tours and accommodation.

ACTIVITIES

Swimming There's swimming at Ulladulla's free seawater pool by the wharf (Nov–April Wed–Mon 7am–6pm).

Scuba diving Ulladulla Dive & Adventure, 211 Princes Hwy (t 02 4455 3029, w ulladulladive.com.au), offer a range of dive courses and daily dives; sites are only a short distance from shore.

Walking The local Budamurra Aboriginal community has constructed an interesting cultural trail, "One track for all", at Ulladulla Head; turn off the highway at North St and keep going.

ACCOMMODATION

Bannisters By The Sea 191 Mitchell Parade, Mollymook, 5km north of Ulladulla t 02 4455 3044, w bannisters.com.au. Just southeast of Milton, this former motel owes its popularity to the Rick Stein restaurant on the site – a magnet for Sydney's foodie brigade. However, the 32 rooms and suites, recycled from an earlier motel, do not live up to its star billing, though there is an element of glamour, if not luxury, about the place. Facilities include a modest swimming pool, funky bar and spa. Breakfast included. **$370**

Seaspray Motel 70 Ocean St, Mollymook t 02 4455 5311, w mollymookseaspray.com.au. Pleasant, mainstream motel just across from Mollymook beach. The rooms at the front have the best views and facilities, others are a little dated. Breakfast provisions provided. **$100**

Ulladulla Headland Tourist Park 14 Did-Dell St, Ulladulla t 1300 733 021, w holidayhaven.com.au. This well-maintained campsite offers a clifftop location overlooking the harbour, plus excellent amenities, including a swimming pool, tennis court and playground. Also has access to the beach. Un/powered sites **$26/35**, cabins **$105**

Ulladulla Lodge 63 Princes Hwy, 500m north of Ulladulla t 02 4454 0500, w ulladullalodge.com.au. Small backpackers' with clean, bright rooms, a cosy lounge and well-equipped kitchen. There are doubles and four- to six-bed dorms, all with shared bathrooms, or you can rent the whole lodge ($590). Surfboard and wetsuit rental available, and a wealth of outdoor activities can be arranged. Dorms **$35**, doubles **$80**

EATING

Cupitt's Kitchen Restaurant 58 Washburton Road, Ulladulla t 02 4455 7888, w cupitt.com.au. A few minutes' drive inland, you'll find this delightful hilltop winery which also happens to house one of the region's very best restaurants. The food is rustic, warming and inventive, with dishes such as seared scallops, black angus bresaola and pan-fried kingfish (three-course degustation $70). The property also offers delightful cottage accommodation;

$475 for a midweek stay (two-night minimum booking). Wed–Sun noon–2pm, Fri & Sat 6–8.30pm.

Pilgrims Vegetarian Café 9 Princes Hwy, Milton ☎ 02 4455 3421, ⊛ pilgrimsmenu.com. Excellent family-friendly vegetarian wholefood place. Their buttermilk pancakes with banana, yoghurt and maple syrup ($16) make a great breakfast, and the millennium burger ($11), made with curried lentils, goes nicely with a mango lassi. Evening meals focus on Mexican food such as burritos and enchiladas. Bookings recommended. Mon–Wed & Sun 9am–3pm, Thurs–Sat 9am–3pm & 6–9pm.

Rick Stein at Bannisters 191 Mitchell Parade, Mollymook, 5km north of Ulladulla ☎ 02 4455 3044, ⊛ bannisters.com.au. When he first arrived here seven years ago, British chef Rick Stein was treated with some scepticism but his passion for local seafood has won over the critics who now flock here. The menu brims with classic seafood dishes from around the globe; try the Madras Fish Curry ($46) or the signature Bannisters Fish Pie ($44). Wed & Sun 12.30–2pm & 6–8.30pm, Thurs 6–8.30pm, Fri 6–9.15pm, Sat 12.30–2pm & 6–9.15pm.

Treehouse Café 4 Boree St, Ulladulla ☎ 02 4455 3991. A friendly veggie/vegan café with quirky decor, such as old trunks for tables, and an on-site massage therapist. Breakfast includes banana bread ($6.50) and killer hot chocolate; for lunch try the slow-cooked beef burger ($14). Mon–Fri 8am–4pm, Sat 8am–3pm.

Ulladulla Oyster Bar 107 Princes Hwy, Ulladulla ☎ 0419 219 275, ⊛ ulladullaoysterbar.com .au. Originally launched as a fishmonger's selling locally caught seafood, this modest shop is now a must-do destination for all oyster fans. Diners can enjoy local rock oysters *au naturel* or with a variety of hot and cold toppings (dozen oysters $28). The tapas-style menu also includes pizza, Italian meatballs and tortilla. Tues & Wed 10am–8pm, Thurs–Sat 10am–10pm.

Batemans Bay

At the mouth of the Clyde River and the end of the highway from Canberra, **BATEMANS BAY** is a favourite escape for the landlocked residents of the capital, just 152km away. It's not the most exciting place on the coast, but it's a fair-sized beach destination with plenty to do. The town itself is focused around Clyde and Orient streets, which run into one another. Beach Road runs alongside the river to the pleasant marina, then southeast past a string of good beaches – the further you go, the nicer they get.

There are a number of small zoos and theme parks dotted around town, including **Birdland Animal Park** (55 Beach Rd; daily 9.30am–4.30pm; $24; ⊛ birdlandanimalpark .com.au), where you can feed the wallabies, watch koalas being fed, cuddle wombats and get draped in snakes. **Murramarang National Park** ($8 per vehicle for 24hr) can be found to the north of town and offers good camping. It's popular with kangaroos: they come here at dawn and dusk to frolic on the beach – especially Pebbly Beach.

ARRIVAL AND INFORMATION   BATEMANS BAY

By bus Premier Motor Service buses (☎ 13 34 10, ⊛ premierms.com.au) call at Batemans Bay from Sydney, stopping where Orient St becomes Clyde St.
Destinations Eden (2 daily; 3hr 30min); Merimbula (2 daily; 2hr 45min); Narooma (2 daily; 1hr); Nowra (2 daily; 1hr 50min); Sydney (2 daily; 5–6hr); Ulladulla (2 daily; 50min); Wollongong (2 daily; 4hr).

Tourist information The visitor information centre (daily: Sept–June 9am–5pm; July–Sept 9am–4pm; ☎ 1800 802 528, ⊛ eurobodalla.com.au) is on the corner of Princes Hwy and Beach Rd.

ACTIVITIES

Cruises You can take a cruise on the Clyde River with Merinda Cruises (3hr; $30; ☎ 02 4472 4052), whose trips include a 30min stopover at the pretty village of Nelligen, 6km upstream (which is also accessible off the road to Canberra). Cash only.

Cycling Bikes can be rented from Batemans Bay Cycles ($20/hr; ☎ 02 4472 1777) at 23b Vesper St, but ring ahead to check availability.

Kayaking Explore the inland and coastal waters by kayak with Bay and Beyond Sea Kayak Tours (☎ 02 4478 7777, ⊛ bayandbeyond.com.au), who offer tours and kayak rental.

ACCOMMODATION

Araluen Motor Lodge 226 Beach Rd, Batehaven ☎ 02 4472 6266, ⊛ araluenmotorlodge.com.au. Well-appointed motel with its own heated pool, laundry, restaurant and a good range of rooms and apartments. Located across the road from Corrigans Beach. $135

2

Batemans Bay Beach Resort 51 Beach Rd ☏ 02 4472 4541 or ☏ 1800 217 533, ⓦ beachresort.com.au. Smart, spacious resort with very plush beachfront cabins, some prime camping spots overlooking the water and all the facilities you'd expect of a Big4 resort. Facilities include tennis courts, a swimming pool and minigolf. Un/powered sites $68/84, cabins $375

Batemans Bay YHA Cnr Old Princes Hwy & South St, ☏ 02 4472 4972, ⓦ yha.com.au. This hostel, 800m south of the town centre, is showing its age and is a little cramped. There are two six-bed dorms and a twin, and in summer guests who want private rooms are accommodated in caravans. Facilities include bicycles, swimming pool and a food store. Dorms $25, doubles $51

Pebbly Beach Campground Mount Agony Rd, ☏ 02 4478 6582, ⓦ nationalparks.nsw.gov.au. Drive-in campsite 21km north of Bateman's Bay with cold showers, drinking water (boil before drinking), wood BBQs, and lots of kangaroos. Book early in summer as this is a popular spot. Suitable for tents and small campervans only. There's an additional daily fee of $8 to enter the Yuraygir National Park. Unpowered sites $23

EATING AND DRINKING

Barkala Kitchen & Bar 3 Orient St ☏ 02 4472 1888, ⓦ barkala.wix.com. Chic tapas bar with sea views, designer decor, a great list of wines, sherries and cocktails, and delicious nibbles and classic Spanish favourites to share. Try the *patatas bravas* ($8) or grilled swordfish *bocadillo* ($14.50). Mid-July to April Tues–Sat 7pm–10pm.

Innes' Boatshed Clyde St ☏ 02 4472 4052. Long-standing waterfront chippy that's excellent for fresh local seafood. It has a few seats inside and a deck at the back with seating overlooking the water. Opt for the eat-in special and tuck into fish, chips, salad and tea or coffee for $14. Cash only. Mon–Thurs & Sun 8.30am–7pm, Fri & Sat 8.30am–8pm.

On the Pier 2 Old Punt Rd, just over the bridge to the north ☏ 02 4472 6405, ⓦ onthepier.com.au. The nicest restaurant in town by a stretch, this is a bright, breezy place with good lounging possibilities, a great Aussie wine list and imaginative seafood mains like tempura king prawns with plum dipping sauce and lemon ($26). Tues–Sat noon–2.30pm & 6–8.30pm; Sun 10am–late.

Oyster Shed 5 Wray St ☏ 02 4472 6771, ⓦ oystershed .com.au. Fresh is always best when it comes to seafood and it doesn't get any fresher than this classic old shed, a farm gate for a family-owned oyster lease on the Clyde River. These are the best-value oysters you'll find; a dozen unopened oysters cost $9.50. You can sit at outdoor tables or take away. Daily 9am–5pm.

Narooma and around

Surrounded on three sides by beautiful beaches, inlets and coastal lakes, **NAROOMA**, 70km south of Batemans Bay, is perfect for aquatic pursuits, and lies at the heart of an area famous for its succulent **freshwater oysters**. The town is spread out along the Princes Highway – first Wagonga then Campbell Street as it runs through the centre – with a marina down to the west and beaches to the east. First impressions are best from the pretty, 350m-long **Mill Bay Boardwalk**, which skirts the northern shore of Wagonga Inlet. Southern right and humpback whales migrate past the bay from September to early November; there's also a decent chance of seeing seals from the lookout at the end of Bar Rocks Road, particularly in spring.

Montague Island

You can sail to the town's star attraction, **Montague Island**, a sanctuary for sea birds, seals and Little penguins 9km offshore. To actually disembark on the island, you'll need to book a tour with one of the NSW National Parks & Wildlife-approved vessels such as Narooma Charters (see opposite), since it's a protected wildlife reserve. Morning tours include a nature walk on the island with an NPWS guide, while evening tours have time set aside to see the penguins come ashore.

Tilba Valley Wines

947 Old Hwy • May–July & Sept Wed–Sun 11am–5pm; Oct–April daily 10am–5pm • ⓦ tilba.com.au

Some 12km south of Narooma, stop for a little wine tasting at **Tilba Valley Wines**. Situated beside Corunna Lake, the winery provides an idyllic spot for a home-made lunch on the terrace or a game of croquet with the English owner. There's live music every first and third Sunday of the month.

ARRIVAL AND INFORMATION

By bus Murray's Coaches run buses to Narooma from Canberra and Batemans Bay, while Premier Motor Service buses operate from Sydney.

Destinations Batemans Bay (daily; 1hr 50min); Canberra (daily; 4hr 30min); Sydney (2 daily; 7hr 30min).

Tourist information The visitor information centre

NAROOMA AND AROUND

(daily 9am–5pm; ☎02 4476 2881, ⊛narooma.org.au) is on the Princes Hwy.

Festival If you're in town over the long weekend at the start of Oct, don't miss the annual Great Southern Blues Festival (⊛narooma.org.au), which is now combined with the Narooma Oyster Festival.

ACTIVITIES

Cruises Scenic inlet cruises through the mangroves are available aboard the *Wagonga Princess* (daily during peak season, otherwise Wed, Fri & Sun; 3hr; $35; ☎02 4476 2665, ⊛wagongainletcruises.com), a charming little pine ferry very different from the usual glass-bottomed tourist hulks. Tours include a rainforest walk and an oyster-shucking demonstration.

Cycling Narooma Bike Hire, 8 Noorooma Crescent (☎04 0315 7290), rents out bikes from $14/hr.

Kayaking Narooma Marina on Riverside Drive (☎02 4476

2126, ⊛naroomamarine.com.au) rent out two-seater canoes and pedal boats for $30/hr; you can canoe on the Wagonga Inlet.

Sailing and scuba diving Narooma Charters (☎0407 909 111, ⊛naroomacharters.com.au) offer diving and snorkelling, often combining time underwater with a trip to Montague Island for a small additional cost. There are also whale-watching trips in season. They charge $80 for a single dive, $110 for a tour of Montague Island plus seal snorkel (3–4hr).

ACCOMMODATION

Ecotel Narooma 44 Princes Hwy, on the northern side of the inlet ☎02 4476 2217, ⊛ecotel.com.au. Good-value motel in a peaceful spot, with decent-sized rooms, though bathrooms are a little dated. Environmentally friendly features include wind and solar power, and responsible water management. $68

Lyrebird Lodge 99 Armitage Rd, 13km southwest of Narooma ☎02 4476 3370, ⊛tilba.com.au/lyrebirdlodge.htm. Ecofriendly three-bedroom cottage among the gum trees, roughly equidistant from Narooma and Central Tilba; worth the drive for its simple but lovely interior and tranquil setting. A cheese platter and bottle of wine are provided on arrival. No wi-fi. $185

Pub Hill Farm B&B 566 Wagonga Scenic Drive ☎02 4476 3177, ⊛pubhillfarm.com. Great country-style B&B with four well-decorated en-suite rooms (all with private entrances). The location is very scenic, right on Punkallah Creek and overlooking Wagonga Inlet and Mount Dromedary. The rate includes a hearty breakfast of bacon, mushrooms, hash browns and chipolatas. $135

Surfbeach Holiday Park Ballingalla St ☎02 4476 2275, ⊛naroomaholidayaccommodation.com.au. Adjoining the much-celebrated Narooma Golf Club, the beach and a creek, this holiday park is spacious, well situated and far nicer than the caravan parks in town. Un/powered sites $25/30, cabins $145

EATING

Casey's Café Cnr Canty & Wagonga sts ☎02 4476 1241. A bright, cheery establishment, serving healthy, hearty food with many veggie options, giant smoothies and the best coffee in town. Try *Casey's* crunchie nut salad ($12.50). Daily 8am–4.30pm.

Lynch's Restaurant 135 Wagonga St ☎02 4476 3022. Posh pub serving a good range of salads ($21–25), some Nepali curries ($18–29), and even local oysters ($22–28). The $10 lunch specials are very popular during the week. Tues–Fri 11.30am–2.30pm & 5.30–9pm, Sat 5.30–9.30pm.

Montague Coffee 40 Princes Hwy ☎02 4405 9523, ⊛montaguecoffee.com.au. This small roastery and café is the place to come for good coffee, handmade chocolates or a cake. If you want something a little more substantial there are also simple ham and

cheese toasties ($5.50), and they sell bags of freshly roasted beans. Mon–Fri 6.30am–4pm, Sat 7.30am–noon.

Quarterdeck 13 Riverside Drive, by the marina ☎02 4476 2723. An eclectic and colourful café with a great deck that is famous for its live music during the summer months. The menu ranges from natural oysters to tapas, pasta, salads and fish and chips ($20.50). Thurs–Mon 8am–3.30pm.

The Whale Restaurant 102 Wagonga St ☎02 4476 2411. White tablecloths and river views set the tone for this slow-food restaurant run by an award-winning chef who blends Italian, Middle Eastern and Asian influences, making superb use of home-grown produce in dishes such as Wagyu rib-eye fillet with kumera puree, beets, turnips and crispy kale ($37). Mon–Sat 6–9pm.

2

Central Tilba and Tilba Tilba

There are a couple of tiny, picturesque villages signposted off the highway south of Narooma, **CENTRAL TILBA** and **Tilba Tilba**. **Central Tilba** is by far the quaintest village on the south coast, beautifully set against the forested slopes of Mount Dromedary and invariably packed at weekends; there's a growers market on Saturday mornings. Almost everything happens on Bate Street, where there are many shops selling art, fudge, jewellery and gourmet foodstuffs, and where Central Tilba's 1891 **ABC Cheese Factory** (daily 9am–5pm) can be found. It is open for visits and free tastings, and there's cheese for sale here as well. Locals may also suggest you walk up Paradise Hill to the lookout, which is just where the water tank stands, but the views are impressive. To appreciate the village properly, you should probably stay overnight.

Some 2km south along the loop road, pretty **Tilba Tilba** is a tiny community with a pleasant walking trail up to the 797m-high summit of **Mount Dromedary** (14km return; 5–6hr; 600m ascent), which starts from Pam's Store.

ACCOMMODATION AND EATING   CENTRAL TILBA AND TILBA TILBA

CENTRAL TILBA

The Bryn 1km down Bate St on the Tilba–Punkalla Rd ☎ 02 4473 7385, ⓦ thebrynattilba.com.au. A great B&B boasting bucolic views and a sunny veranda, with four immaculate, light-filled bedrooms and a self-contained cottage ($215). Rates – other than for the cottage – include a generous home-cooked breakfast. <u>$225</u>

Tilba Teapot 17 Bate St ☎ 02 4473 7811. This country-style cottage dates back to 1895 and serves all-day breakfast, including buttermilk pancakes ($12) and lunchtime meals such as hot roast roll ($8) and a variety of burgers or salads. Take a seat on the balcony at the back and enjoy the view. Daily 9am–4pm.

The Two Story Guesthouse 2 Bate St ☎ 02 4473 7290, ⓦ tilbatwostory.com. A delightful, if chintzy, B&B with one room downstairs and two up, plus a common area for guests; rates include a delicious breakfast. <u>$170</u>

Bermagui and around

South of Narooma the Princes Highway cuts inland for the next 85km down to Merimbula and it's better to stick to the slower coast road, which heads for the cute fishing village of **Tathra**, 60km south – as pleasant a drive as you'll find in this area. **BERMAGUI** is the one place you will likely stop on this route; it's a busy port town with a few places to stay and eat, and the snazzy Fishermen's Wharf that looks slightly out of place. To the south of Bermagui, unsealed tracks branch off the coast road to **Mimosa Rocks National Park**, where there are opportunities for bushwalking, camping and swimming.

INFORMATION   BERMAGUI AND AROUND

Tourist information Bunga St, Bermagui (daily 9am–4pm; ☎ 02 6493 3054).

BURNUM BURNUM: ABORIGINAL ACTIVIST

Wallaga Lake is the birthplace of one of Australia's most celebrated Aboriginal figures, the elder named **Burnum Burnum**, an ancestral name meaning "great warrior". He was best known for his flamboyant political stunts, which included planting the Aboriginal flag at Dover to claim England as Aboriginal territory in Australia's bicentennial year, in order to highlight the dispossession of his native country. He was born under a sacred tree by Wallaga Lake in January 1936. His mother died soon afterwards and he was taken by the Aborigines Protection Board and placed in a mission at Bomaderry, constituting one of the "stolen generation" of indigenous children removed from their families in this period. After graduating in law and playing professional rugby union for New South Wales, he became a prominent political activist in the 1970s. He was involved in various environmental and indigenous protests, including erecting the "tent embassy" outside the Federal Parliament in Canberra, and standing twice, unsuccessfully, for the senate. Burnum Burnum died in August 1997 and his ashes were scattered near the tree where he was born.

ACCOMMODATION AND EATING

Bellbird Cottage B&B 88 Nutleys Creek Rd, Bermagui ☎02 6493 5274, ⓦbellbirdcottage-bnb.com. A homely B&B offering a room with private access and a terrace overlooking the forest, where you can tuck into your gourmet breakfast. There are even good views from the bath. Breakfast included. $215

Cream Patisserie 28 Wallaga St, Bermagui ☎02 6493 5445. Eating options tend to narrow the further you drive south, so this contemporary European café comes as a delightful surprise, serving excellent coffee, freshly made cakes, doughnuts, chocolate éclairs and gourmet sandwiches ($10), among other treats. Mon–Sat 9am–5pm.

Il Passaggio Fishermen's Wharf, Bermagui ☎02 6493 5753, ⓦilpassaggio.com.au. This Italian restaurant, right on the wharf, delivers a straightforward menu (pizza $20, pasta $30) using fresh regional ingredients, including locally sourced seafood. Wed & Thurs 6–9.30pm, Fri–Sun noon–2.30pm & 6–9.30pm.

Ocean Lake Caravan Park 891 Wallaga Lake Rd, 6km from Bermagui ☎02 6493 4055, ⓦoceanlakecaravan park.com.au. This peaceful spot, on the shore of Lake Wallaga, offers a good range of grassy camping sites and some pleasant, self-contained villas. Canoe rental is available, and there's a shop and a tennis court in addition to the usual facilities. No wi-fi. Un/powered site $60/60, deluxe villa $225

Saltwater Restaurant 59 Lamont St, Bermagui ☎02 6493 4328. This stylish waterfront restaurant specializes in – as you'd expect – fresh, local seafood. Choose from natural oysters (dozen $24), Thai fish cakes ($13.50) or fish and chips ($21) – grilled, crumbed or battered. There are steaks, pasta and quiche to satisfy non-fish-eaters. Daily 7.30am–8pm.

Merimbula

The holiday town of **MERIMBULA** is surrounded by lagoons, lakes, rivers and ocean, making it ideal for watersports or an evening stroll along the shore. By day, you can explore **Merimbula Lake** (actually the wide mouth of the Merimbula River) and **Pambula Lake**, and there are also some good **dive** sites around town. You've a chance in a million of seeing a whale while you're underwater, but it has happened.

To see sharks and tropical fish that are firmly under control, check out the **Merimbula Aquarium** (Lake St; daily 10am–5pm; $22; ⓦmerimbulawharf.com.au) where the fish feeding on Monday, Wednesday and Friday at 11.30am is always popular. If you'd rather get up close and personal with wombats and koalas, and learn something about Australia's diverse environment, visit **Potoroo Palace** (2372 Princes Hwy; daily 10am–4pm; $20; ⓦpotoroopalace.com). This not-for-profit wildlife sanctuary is 9km north of town and is also home to kangaroos and echidnas.

ARRIVAL AND INFORMATION

By plane Daily flights run between Merimbula and Sydney (1hr 45min) or Melbourne (2–3 daily; 1hr 30min). Merimbula Airport is a 5min drive south of the town centre, across the causeway.

By bus Merimbula is well served with buses: Premier Motor Service down the coast from Sydney; NSW TrainLink from Canberra, Cooma and Eden; and V/Line from Melbourne and Batemans Bay (☎1800 800 007, ⓦvline .com.au).

Destinations Batemans Bay (3 daily; 2hr 45min); Canberra (daily; 4hr 20min); Cooma (daily; 1hr 55min); Eden (daily; 30min); Melbourne (2 daily; 9hr); Sydney (2 daily; 8hr 30min).

Tourist information The visitor information centre is at 2 Beach St (Mon–Fri 9am–5pm, Sat 9am–4pm, Sun 10am–4pm; ☎02 6495 1129, ⓦmerimbulatourism .com.au). For national park information visit the NPWS office (Mon–Fri 8.30am–4.30pm; ☎02 6495 5000) on the corner of Sapphire Coast Drive and Merimbula Drive.

ACTIVITIES

Boat tours Merimbula Marina (☎02 6495 1686, ⓦmerimbulamarina.com) runs dolphin tours, boat rental, fishing charters and whale-watching tours (May–Dec; $69).

Diving *Merimbula Divers Lodge* at 15 Park St (☎02 6495 3611, ⓦmerimbuladiverslodge.com.au) offer single and double boat dives ($77/120) .

Cycling and surfing Cycle 'N' Surf, 1B Marine Parade (☎02 6495 2171, ⓦcyclensurf.com.au), rent bikes, surf boards and bodyboards.

ACCOMMODATION

★ **Coast Resort Merimbula** 68/1 Elizabeth St ☎02 6495 4930, ⓦcoastresort.com.au. This contemporary holiday development offers swish modern apartments, two swimming pools and a tennis court – all two minutes' from the beach and a good alternative to the local (and fairly drab) motels. $198

Merimbula Beach Cabins 47–65 Short Point Rd ☎ 02 6495 1216, ⊛ beachcabins.com.au. A choice between quirky pentagon and more modern cabins, all surrounded by natural bushland overlooking the ocean. Facilities include laundry, playground, heated pool and BBQs; no wi-fi in the cabins. $125

NRMA Merimbula Beach Holiday Park 2 Short Point Rd ☎ 02 6499 8999, ⊛ merimbulabeachholidaypark .com.au. The nicest of several caravan parks in town,

scenically located in a breezy spot above lovely Short Point Beach, with a great swimming pool. The park has a wide range of camping sites – some of the powered sites have their own private bathroom facilities – plus an impressive choice of villas, beach houses and condos, including a honeymoon retreat. Un/powered sites $33/38, cabins $120

Wandarrah Lodge YHA 8 Marine Parade ☎ 02 6495 3503, ⊛ yha.com.au. This hostel is close to both the beach and lake. Rooms are a little dated, and have shared bathrooms, but are bright and clean with lockers. There are good communal areas. Dorms $32, doubles $77

2

EATING

Bar Beach Café Bar Beach Rd ☎ 0422 286 708, ⊛ barbeachkiosk.com. Fun café serving coffee, snacks and freshly made cakes – just a hop and a skip from the surf. Lunch options include a salad of grilled vegetables, halloumi, brown rice and almonds ($11) and Middle Eastern meatballs, tabbouleh and flatbread ($15). Daily 7.30am–4pm.

★ **Dulcie's Cottage** 60 Main St ⊛ dulcies.com.au. A rickety old wooden cottage serving craft beer, well-mixed cocktails and gourmet standard burgers (served on organic milk buns). The excellent fish burger ($17) features grilled ling fillets, lettuce, vine-ripened tomato, pickled daikon and seaweed mayonnaise. Look out for the fairy lights and food truck in the garden. Daily noon–late.

Wheelers Seafood Restaurant 162 Arthur Kaine Dr, Pambula ☎ 02 6495 6330, ⊛ wheelersoysters.com.au.

It's worth making the ten-minute drive to this convivial seafood restaurant near the airport. Open for lunch and dinner, the menu includes freshly shucked oysters (dozen for $28), yellowtail kingfish ceviche ($18) and a classic Aussie Surf and Turf ($42). Tours of the nearby oyster farm are also available. Mon–Sat noon–2.30pm & 6.30–9.30pm, Sun noon–2.30pm.

Zanzibar Café Cnr Market & Main sts ☎ 02 6495 3636, ⊛ zanzibarmerimbula.com.au. Upmarket restaurant serving inventive modern Australian cuisine and showcasing the finest south coast ingredients, such as free-range pork, rock oysters, mussels, farmhouse cheese and figs. Choose from the Locavore Sample Menu ($90) or five-course degustation ($140, with matching wines). Wed–Sun 6–10pm.

Eden

EDEN, on pretty Twofold Bay, is just about the last seaside stop before the Princes Highway heads south towards Victoria, and is perhaps the nicest coastal village in the south. In 1818 the first **whaling station** on the Australian mainland was established here, and **whaling** remained a major industry until the 1920s. Today Eden is touristy in a quiet sort of way, with good fishing and plenty of reminders of the old days. The busy main **wharf** in Snug Cove, at the bottom of Imlay Street, is the best area for eating and a good place for a stroll, as are the two pretty **beaches**, Aslings and Cocora. In November, the town hosts the **Whale Festival** weekend, a series of whale-related events to celebrate their southern migration.

Eden Killer Whale Museum

184 Imlay St • Mon–Sat 9.15am–3.45pm, Sun 11.15am–3.45pm • $10 • ⊛ killerwhalemuseum.com.au

The **Killer Whale Museum** is looking a little dated these days but still has some excellent displays. The star attraction is the huge skeleton of "Old Tom", an orca that used to herd baleen whales into the bay then lead whaling boats towards the pods, in order to get his chops around the discarded bits of carcass. There are also plenty of old whale bones, boats, some interesting Aboriginal history, and a (literally) incredible account of a man being swallowed by a sperm whale and coming out alive fifteen hours later.

Sapphire Coast Marine Discovery Centre

253 Imlay St • Mon–Fri 10am–3.30pm • $10 • ⊛ sapphirecoastdiscovery.com.au

The **Marine Discovery Centre** promotes interactive learning, and kids with an interest in the ocean are bound to enjoy themselves. Enthusiastic and knowledgeable staff are on hand to explain more about the displays, there's a shell collection children can

2

handle, a touch tank with an elephant snail, and a decorator crab. The centre also offers educational activity programmes.

ARRIVAL AND INFORMATION

By bus Premier buses from Sydney (2 daily; 9hr) stop here, while NSW TrainLink buses link the town with Canberra (daily; 5hr), Cooma (daily; 3hr) and Merimbula (daily; 30min), and V/Line from Victoria continue up the coast to

EDEN

Batemans Bay (2 weekly; 10hr 30min).
Tourist information The visitor information centre (daily 9am–5pm; ☏ 02 6495 7031, ⓦ visiteden.com.au) is at the corner of Mitchell St and Princes Hwy.

ACTIVITIES

Cruises Cat Balou Cruises (☏ 0427 962 027, ⓦ catbalou.com.au), based at the main wharf, offer a Twofold Bay Highlights Cruise ($40), two-hour Twofold Bay discovery cruises ($35), and half-day whale-watching cruises (mid-Sept to Nov; $85).
Fishing Freedom Charters (☏ 02 6496 1209,

ⓦ freedomcharters.com.au) are the town's fishing specialists; they also offer whale-watching trips in season ($75).
Sea-kayaking Coastlife Adventures (☏ 1300 762 993, ⓦ coastlife.com.au) offers a range of stand-up paddleboarding lessons and kayak tours along the south coast ($60–65).

ACCOMMODATION AND EATING

★ **Cocora Cottage** 2 Cocora St ☏ 02 6496 1241, ⓦ cocoracottage.com. A pretty, heritage-listed B&B with fine rooms, a cute garden and a stunning sun deck where you can breakfast. In winter there's a fire in the lounge, and nice touches such as home-made cake. Breakfast included. **$160**
Eden Smokehouse 20 Weecoon St ☏ 02 6496 2331, ⓦ edensmokehouse.com.au. Traditional smokehouses like this are making a welcome return to Australia; come here for smoked delights like salmon, hoki, Mexican chilli mussels and eel, plus delicacies such as gravlax and smoked garlic. Mon–Fri 7.30am–4pm.
Garden of Eden Caravan Park Cnr Princes Hwy and Barclay St ☏ 02 64956 1172, ⓦ edengarden.biz. A

peaceful, shady park on the banks of Lake Curalo: the beach can be reached via a boardwalk. Facilities are clean and modern, and the park has a pool and tennis courts. Un/powered sites **$28/37**, cabins **$130**
Heritage House 178 Imlay St ☏ 02 6496 1657, ⓦ heritagehouseunits.com. Pleasant, spacious and clean motel rooms and well-equipped apartments right in the centre of Eden with shops, supermarket and the museum within walking distance. **$140**
Wharfside 253 Imlay St ☏ 02 6496 1855, ⓦ wharfsidecafe.com.au. A friendly café with great views over the wharf. Seafood is fresh from the boats: enjoy the home-made fish cakes ($16) or just settle for a panini. The coffee is good, too. Daily 8am–3.30pm.

Ben Boyd National Park

$8 per vehicle for 24hr

Heading south from Eden, you become increasingly surrounded by the vast temperate rainforests that characterize southeastern Australia. Roads lead off the highway to the east into the magnificent **Ben Boyd National Park**, which hugs the coast to the north and south of Eden. As well as lovely beaches you can seek out the nineteenth-century folly of Boyds Tower and the Green Cape light station. The tower and light station can be linked by walking the **Light to Light Walk** (31km one-way; two days), which is predominantly coastal but also traverses heathland areas. There's no public transport, so the easiest way to tackle it is to base yourself midway at *Saltwater Creek* campsite and explore north and south on successive days.

ACCOMMODATION

Green Cape Lightstation Green Cape Rd ☏ 02 6495 5000, ⓦ nationalparks.nsw.gov.au. These three atmospheric lighthouse-keeper's cottages offer fully equipped kitchens, wood-burning fireplaces and nautical decor. Each cottage sleeps six, and free lighthouse tours can be arranged for guests. Bring your own food and drink, and a pair of binoculars for dolphin and whale watching. Linen and towels can be rented on site. No wi-fi. **$280**

BEN BOYD NATIONAL PARK

Saltwater Creek Camping Ground Saltwater Rd ☏ 02 6495 5000, ⓦ nationalparks.nsw.gov.au. Popular campsite reached via an unsealed road. BBQs and toilet facilities available but bring your own drinking water. Book in advance by phone or online, particularly at Christmas and Easter school holidays. A vehicle entry fee of $8 applies. No wi-fi. Unpowered sites **$23**

The Snowy Mountains

Australia's and the Great Dividing Range's highest terrain is in the **Snowy Mountains**, which peak at the 2228m **Mount Kosciuszko**, named in 1840 by the Polish-born explorer Paul Strzelecki, after the Polish freedom fighter General Tadeusz Kosciuszko. The Snowies are just one section of the Australian Alps that sprawl from northeast Victoria into New South Wales via the Crackenback Range, and they have Australia's best skiing and, in summer, some fine bushwalking.

2

Kosciuszko National Park

Much of the New South Wales section of the Snowies falls within **Kosciuszko National Park**. This is the state's largest national park, extending 200km north to south and encompassing ten peaks above 2100m, forested valleys, and a beautiful plateau with glacial lakes and rivers. Compared to the high mountain ranges of other continents, the "roof of Australia" is relatively low and the rounded and granite-strewn mountaintops lie below the line of permanent snow. Nonetheless, in **winter** (June–July), skiers and snowboarders flock to Australia's most concentrated cluster of **ski resorts** (see box, p.210).

The downhilling isn't world-class and the snow is rarely dry, but it's better than you might think, and if you're into back-country skiing, the Snowy Mountains offer a paradise of huge, empty valleys, snow-gum forests and wildlife. In summer, some of the resorts close completely but the towns are less crowded and work as bases for excellent hiking, mountain biking, horse trekking, fishing and whitewater rafting in crystal-clear mountain rivers. The main resort town is **Thredbo**, which operates ski lifts throughout the year up to a high plateau, from where you can bushwalk across the wild-flower-covered high country and reach Australia's highest summit. The other main ski town is lakeside **Jindabyne**, 35km further west along the scenic Alpine Way and just outside the eastern boundary of the park. It doesn't have its own ski-field but provides access along Kosciuszko Road to a string of resorts that virtually close down in summer.

Eastern access to the region is through the small town of **Cooma**, from where you can head for the northern reaches of the park and **Yarrangobilly Caves**.

ESSENTIALS | KOSCIUSZKO NATIONAL PARK

Entry fees Visitors to Cooma and Jindabyne (both outside the park) and those driving through without stopping do not have to pay, but visitors to Thredbo, all the ski resorts and Yarrangobilly Caves must pay the vehicle entry fee (June to early Oct $29, early Oct to May $17), which is charged per 24hr period. Pay at the entrance station between Jindabyne and Thredbo, the Snowy Region Visitor Centre in Jindabyne or the newsagent in Thredbo and attach the sticker to your windscreen. Arriving by bus, you'll still have to make a one-off payment of $11.45 ($6.60 in summer) but many companies now include this in the ticket price. The New South Wales annual park pass ($190) is a wise investment if you're planning to spend more than seven days here.
Information See ⊛ nationalparks.nsw.gov.au/kosciuszko

and look out for the free *Snowy Times*, which has resort information, maps, and listings of skiing prices and packages.
Accommodation In summer you're better off staying in Jindabyne or Thredbo: rates are considerably lower off-peak and you should have little difficulty finding somewhere. Hikers can also camp for free in most of the national park, except day areas and within 200m of any road. In winter, prices in Cooma are lower and availability is a little easier, while accommodation in Jindabyne and Thredbo is expensive and hard to get during the ski season, especially during school holidays and at weekends. Rooms in Thredbo are almost impossible to come by without a reservation; minimum stays are enforced and prices are high and often rise at weekends.

ARRIVAL AND DEPARTURE

By plane In season, Regional Express flies from Sydney to the Snowy Mountains Airport southwest of Cooma (1–3 daily; 1hr 10min). The Alpine Resort Shuttle (⊛ alpineresortshuttle .com.au) meets all flights and shuttles visitors to Jindabyne ($32), the Skitube ($35; see p.210) and Thredbo ($45).

By car In summer there is no useful public transport into or around the park so a car is pretty much essential. The Snowy Mountains Hwy leads straight through the mountain ranges across the northern section of the Kosciuszko National Park. If you want to see more of the alpine scenery, head along the spectacular Alpine Way, turning off the highway at Kiandra in the heart of the park and heading south via Khancoban to Thredbo. In winter, check road conditions before driving anywhere; snow chains must be carried by two-wheel drives between June and early October, and are recommended for 4WD: some roads might be closed altogether.

By bus Numerous winter bus services operate around the area. The most useful is Transborder Alpinexpress (☏1800 780 935, ⓦtransborder.com.au), which links Canberra, Cooma, Jindabyne and Thredbo daily. Cooma is also accessible from Canberra and Melbourne with V/Line. A number of small bus companies link Jindabyne and all the ski-fields in the winter – contact the visitor centre in Jindabyne (see opposite) for details.

By rack railway Winter road access to the resorts of Perisher Valley and Mount Blue Cow is quite hairy and usually requires chains, but there's an intriguing alternative in the form of the Skitube (late June to Sept daily every 20–30min; open return $86; ⓦperisher.com.au). This rack railway ascends 8.5km (6.3km in tunnels) under the mountains from Bullocks Flat, roughly midway between Jindabyne and Thredbo, up to the resorts.

Cooma and around

The small town of **COOMA** is outside the national park and at least an hour from the nearest resort, but it successfully functions as a service centre for skiers. It's a fairly interesting place in its own right, with a number of fine old buildings on Lambie and Vale streets in particular; the visitor centre has a map of the 5km "Lambie Town Walk".

Snowy Hydro Discovery Centre

Monaro Hwy, 2km north of Cooma • Mon–Fri 8am–5pm, Sat & Sun 8am–2pm • ⓦsnowyhydro.com.au

If you're interested in the history and technical details of the Snowy hydroelectric project, which utilizes the water of the area's rivers to provide electricity to the ACT, New South Wales and Victoria and took 25 years to build, check out the **Snowy Hydro Discovery Centre**. It's surprisingly popular and there's a café on site.

INFORMATION AND ACTIVITIES

COOMA AND AROUND

Tourist information The visitor centre (daily 9am–3pm; ☏1800 636 525, ⓦvisitcooma.com.au) is on the main road, Sharp St; they have details of local farmstays.

Horseriding The long-established Yarramba Trail Rides (1hr; $65; ☏02 6453 7204, ⓦyarramba.com.au) is located 25km northwest of town on Dry Plains Rd, on the way to Adaminaby.

ACCOMMODATION AND EATING

Alpine Hotel 170 Sharp St ☏02 6452 1466, ⓦalpinehotel.com.au. There are a few en suites in this refurbished Art Deco pub, but most rooms are basic with shared baths. The restaurant serves decent food and the noise from the bar is minimal. **$100**

Bunkhouse Motel 28–30 Soho St ☏02 6452 2983, ⓦbunkhousemotel.com.au. Long-established homely motel set around a pleasant courtyard, in a very central

---

SKIING AND SNOWBOARDING IN THE SNOWY MOUNTAINS

The easiest option for **skiing in the Snowy Mountains** is to arrange a **ski package** departing from Sydney or Canberra – always check exactly what's included in the price. Be aware that snow conditions can let you down and that the resorts' interpretation of "good" conditions may not match yours, so check an independent source like the excellent ⓦski .com.au (which also has links for accommodation) before you go.

The longest **downhill runs** are at Thredbo (ⓦthredbo.com.au), while the Perisher Valley/Mount Blue Cow/Smiggin Holes/Guthega complex (known as Perisher; all one lift pass; ⓦperisher.com.au) is the largest and most varied; other resorts include family-oriented Selwyn Snowfields (ⓦselwynsnow.com.au), in the far north of the park, and Charlotte Pass (ⓦcharlottepass.com.au), which has more advanced runs. If you have your own equipment and vehicle, and don't need a package, check out the resort websites for details of lift pass prices and lift-and-lesson deals. Resorts are generally **child-friendly**, particularly Thredbo's Friday Flats area and Perisher's Smiggin Holes.

The Mountain Adventure Centre (☏1800 623 459, ⓦmountainadventurecentre.com.au) in Jindabyne runs all manner of cross-country ski trips, plus mountain biking in summer. Sydney-based Ski Kaos (☏02 9908 8111, ⓦskikaos.com.au) offer two-day deals from $229 – you'll have to add food, lift pass and equipment to this.

spot. Some rooms are timber-clad for a cosy chalet feel. Also offers singles ($65) and triples ($110). $95

Cooma Snowy Mountains Tourist Park 286 Sharp St ☎ 02 6452 1828, ⓦ coomatouristpark.com.au. While pretty basic, this is the only option in town for campers. Non-campers can stay in cabins or shearers' huts –the latter is a decent budget option – where linen is provided, and there's a basic camp kitchen, tennis court and children's playground. Un/powered sites $28/33, shearer's huts $60, cabins $125

The Lott Foodstore 177–9 Sharp St ☎ 02 6452 1414, ⓦ lott.com.au. A smart café turning out good breakfasts and lunches, enjoyed by the warmth of the log fire. Lunch options include ham and cheese panini ($13.50), smoked trout risotto ($16.50) and pulled-pork salad ($16.50).

The attached food shop sells kitchen utensils and various condiments. Mon–Thurs 7.30am–3.30pm, Fri 7.30am–4pm, Sat & Sun 8am–4pm.

Pha Thai's Kitchen 121 Sharp St ☎ 02 6452 5489, ⓦ phaskitchen.com.au. Popular with locals and visitors, this place serves plenty of spicy Thai favourites such as *tom yum* soup ($15.90), *pad thai* ($17.90) and *massaman* curry ($19.90). Lunch dishes all $10. As you'd expect, vegetarians are well catered for. Tues–Fri 11am–2.30pm & 5–9.30pm, Sat & Sun 11am–9.30pm.

White Manor Motel 252 Sharp St ☎ 02 6452 1152, ⓦ whitemanor.com. Far more pleasant than the majority of motels, with large, bright and warm rooms and a friendly welcome. There's an abundance of potted plants and an acceptable helping of chintz. $138

Yarrangobilly Caves

6.5km off the Snowy Mountains Highway near Kiandra, 110km northwest of Cooma and 70km southwest of Canberra • Visitor centre daily 9am–5pm; most caves daily 9am–4pm, South Glory cave 9.30am–4pm; tours: Oct to early June 10.30am, 11.45am, 1.45pm & 3pm, mid-June to Sept 11am, 1pm & 3pm • Self-guided tour $18, two-day cave pass $30, guided tour $22 • ☎ 02 6454 9597

In the northern reaches of Kosciuszko National Park, the **Yarrangobilly Caves**, a vast system of about sixty limestone caves at the edge of a rocky plateau surrounded by unspoilt bushland, are one of the few specific sights in the park. There's a **visitor centre** where you can fix up guided tours to the **Jersey**, **Jillabenan** and **North Glory** caves. A fourth cave, the **South Glory Cave**, can be explored on a self-guided tour. From walking trails along the edge of the rock plateau there are panoramic views of the Yarrangobilly Gorge, and a steep trail leads from the Glory Hole car park to a **thermal pool** at the bottom of the gorge near the Yarrangobilly River. The spring-fed pool, which you can swim in, has a year-round temperature of 27°C.

Jindabyne

A scenic settlement beside the man-made lake of the same name, **JINDABYNE**, 63km west of Cooma, is the jumping-off point for most of the national park's ski resorts. From here, Kosciuszko Road heads north then west, passing Smiggin Holes on the way and finishing up at Charlotte Pass.

The town itself sits just outside the national park and was created in the 1960s after the Snowy Mountains Scheme dammed the Snowy River and drowned the original settlement. There's good fishing on the lake and in summer you can also swim and sail – equipment is available to rent in town.

INFORMATION   JINDABYNE

Tourist information The Snowy Region Visitor Centre (daily 8.30am–5pm; ☎ 02 6450 5600) in Jindabyne is the park's main visitor centre, and has details of walking trails, ranger-guided tours and campsites. There are also small

NPWS visitor centres at Perisher Valley (☎ 1300 655 811), Khancoban (☎ 02 6076 9373), Yarrangobilly (☎ 02 6454 9597) and Tumut (☎ 02 6947 7025).

ACCOMMODATION

Bimblegumbie 942 Alpine Way, Crackenback, 10km west of Jindabyne ☎ 02 6456 2185, ⓦ bimblegumbie .com.au. The most interesting place to stay in the mountains by a long way: a tranquil cluster of arty, eclectically decorated self-contained cottages set in

sculpture-filled bushland, and four rooms in the main house with breakfast included. Two-night minimum. $590

Discovery Holiday Park Junction of Alpine Way and Kosciuszko Rd, 3km west of Jindabyne ☎ 1800 248 148,

2

ⓦdiscoveryholidayparks.com.au. Right on the lakeshore, this excellent campsite has a range of accommodation from budget cabins to more luxurious villas (5–6 people). There's also a spa/sauna, tennis court, and motorboat and canoe rental. Un/powered sites $36/42, cabins $87, villas $174

Snowy Mountains Backpackers 2/3 Gippsland St,

Jindabyne ⓣ1800 333 468, ⓦsnowybackpackers .com.au. Pleasant hostel with clean dorms, some with balcony access, as well as one double, family rooms, and a wheelchair-accessible room. There's a comfy kitchen and common area and a laundry, plus ski rental next door. Dorms $40, doubles $100

EATING

Cafe Darya Snowy Mountains Plaza ⓣ02 6457 1867 ⓦcafedarya.com.au. This popular Persian restaurant serves dishes such as *khoresht-e-boz*, slow-cooked goat in a cardamom and carrot sauce ($32). There are some vegetarian options available. Mon & Tues 11am–10pm, Wed–Sun 11.30am–11pm.

CBD Coffee Beats Drinks Nuggets Crossing Shopping Centre ⓣ02 6456 1692, ⓦfacebook.com/ coffeebeatsdrinks. A small café serving bagels, soup, and a range of hot chocolates as well as good coffee. With chalkboard-covered walls, staff with attitude and milk-crate seating, this place is so trendy it's painful, but remains popular. Bagels from $8. Opens early in peak season. Daily 7am–3pm.

Snow Vineyard Estate 255 Werralong Rd, Dalgety ⓣ1300 766 608, ⓦsnowywine.com. For something a

little different, drop into this combined winery and microbrewery on the banks of the Snowy River. The brewery produces a small range of ales, including pale ale, red ale and strong ale, as well as a range of cold climate wines; tastings, tours and lunches are all available. They offer brunch and lunch, with tasting plates and lovely mains such as whole rainbow trout sauteed in lemon butter with parsley sauce ($28). Wed–Sun 10am–5pm.

Wild Brumby Wollondibby Rd, Crackenback, 11km west of Jindabyne ⓣ02 6457 1447, ⓦwildbrumby.com. A modern schnapps distillery making all manner of vodkas, gins and fruit liqueurs, from pear to peppermint, plus a handful of estate grown wines. The attached café serves great late breakfasts and lunches such as Monaro lamb ragout slow-cooked with vegetables ($24). Daily 10am–5pm.

Thredbo

From Jindabyne, the Alpine Way continues 35km west into the national park to **THREDBO**, an attractive, bustling little village at 1380m, entirely devoted to the needs of hikers, bikers and winter-sports enthusiasts. The array of pitched-roof houses and condos huddles against the mountainside in a narrow valley between the road and the infant Thredbo River. Once the snows have melted, some of the valley trails are open for **mountain biking**.

Unlike the other resorts, Thredbo is reasonably lively in summer, with activity focused on the Village Square where the bulk of the restaurants, bars and shops stay open year-round.

HIKING AROUND THREDBO

Once the snows have melted, hikers take over the hills, with the main **hiking season** running from December through to April or May. Some of Australia's most interesting and beautiful bushwalking tracks pass through the area. Initially you might find yourself between beautiful snow gums with multicoloured bark in greens and yellows, before climbing up to the barren tops. Thredbo's Kosciuszko Express **chairlift** (daily 9am–4pm; one-way $29, day-pass $35) carries you 560m up to the *Eagles Nest* restaurant (and back down), giving easy access to hiking in the high country. You can book guided **walks** through ⓦthredbo.com.au.

MT Kosciuszko Summit This relatively gentle hike (13km return; 4–6hr; 300m ascent) starts at the top of the chairlift on the edge of a high plateau. The altitude here will have you struggling to catch your breath, and it can be -5°C even in summer, so check conditions at the bottom. Views are particularly panoramic from Kosciuszko Lookout (after 2km), from where Australia's highest peak seems barely higher than the surrounding country. A guided sunset walk can be arranged ($99; ⓦthredbo.com.au).

Main Range Walk Perhaps the best hike in the park (32km loop; 8–10hr; 600m ascent), this starts from the top of the chairlift and follows the Kosciuszko Summit track, then skirts a beautiful glacial lake before dropping down to Charlotte Pass ski resort and looping back via the stone Seaman's Hut. If undertaking this walk, a topographical map and a compass are required.

Merritts Nature Track A picturesque alternative to riding the Kosciuszko Express chairlift. Best done downhill, unless you relish the slog (4km one-way; 2–3hr; 560m ascent).

INFORMATION AND ACTIVITIES   THREDBO

Tourist information The visitor centre (daily 10am–4pm or later; ☎02 6459 4198, ⓦ thredbo.com.au) on Friday Drive, has details of annual events such as the Thredbo Blues Festival (ⓦ thredboblues.com.au) in mid-January and the Thredbo Jazz Festival (ⓦ thredbojazz.net.au) in early May.

Bobsled Thredbo Bobsled offers luge-style rides (1 ride $7, 10 rides $50) throughout the summer – take it easy on your first run, as you'll probably go faster than you expect.

Cycling Bikes can be rented from Thredbo MTB ($140;

☎02 6459 4100, ⓦ thredbo.com.au). To get onto the fantastically steep runs down the ski slopes, go for the full-day package ($216), which includes fully sprung bike, lift ticket, full-face helmet with body armour and a compulsory first run down with an instructor.

Swimming When the weather turns foul, head for the Thredbo Leisure Centre (ⓦ thredbo.com.au), which has a 50m heated pool with waterslide, plus gym and squash courts. You can rent a towel if needs be.

ACCOMMODATION

The Denman 21 Diggings Terrace ☎02 9657 6222, ⓦ thedenman.com.au. Smart boutique hotel in the heart of the village with upmarket, minimalist rooms, a day-spa and a swanky cocktail bar and restaurant (see below). Rooms vary in price and size, some have mountain views, some balconies. **$560**

Kasees Apartments & Mountain Lodge 4 Banjo Drive ☎02 6457 6370, ⓦ kasees.com.au. An excellent guesthouse centred around an alpine-style lounge with a

piano for après-ski singalongs. The rooms are large, with fantastic mountain views, and there's a sauna on site. Two-night minimum stay. **$412**

Thredbo YHA 2 Buckwong Pl ☎02 6457 6376, ⓦ yha .com.au. Central and spacious hostel with cosy fires and communal areas, and great views across the mountains – the only downside is the hefty price tag on winter weekends. There are lockers available for those who arrive when reception is closed. No parking. Dorms **$122**, doubles **$314**

EATING AND DRINKING

Apres Bar and The Terrace The Denman, 21 Diggings Terrace ☎02 6457 6039, ⓦ thedenman.com.au. With its glowing yellow bar, admirable cocktail list and prices no more expensive than the rest of town, *The Denman* hotel's *Apres Bar* has long been a Thredbo favourite and is a great place to work up an appetite for dinner at upstairs *The Terrace*, which has won awards for its elegant seasonal cuisine (such as Parisian gnocchi with roast pumpkin, sage and pine nuts, $34). Ring to check opening times in summer. June–Sept daily: Apres Bar 4pm–late, The Terrace 6pm–late.

Bernti's Mountain Inn 4 Mowomba Place ☎02 6457 6332, ⓦ berntis.com.au. Cheerful restaurant serving

hearty mountain cuisine such as Berkshire pork cutlet ($34), slow-cooked osso bucco ($32) and confit of duck with saffron potato ($34), but this place is best known for its high-quality grain-fed steaks ($30–46). June–Sept daily 5pm–late, Tues–Sun 5pm–late during the rest of the year.

T-Bar Restaurant Village Square ☎02 6457 6355, ⓦ tbar-restaurant.com.au. Snug, rustic place with a lot of wood and a relaxed vibe. Serves gourmet pizzas that range from the traditional margherita ($27) to a mango prawn offering ($37), as well as filling dishes such as braised lamb shanks ($40). Daily noon–2.30pm & 6–9pm, Oct–May evenings only.

The north coast

The coast from Sydney **north to Queensland** is more densely populated and much more touristy than its southern counterpart, with popular holiday destinations such as **Port Stephens**, **Port Macquarie** and **Coffs Harbour** strung along the coast north of Newcastle. Since the 1970s, the area around **Byron Bay** has been a favoured destination for people seeking an alternative lifestyle; this movement has left in its wake not only disillusioned hippy farmers (as well as a few who've survived with their illusions intact), but also a firmly established artistic and alternative scene.

As in the south, the **coastline** consists of myriad inlets, bays and coastal lakes, interspersed with white, sandy beaches and rocky promontories. Parallel to the coast are the rocky plateaus of the **Great Dividing Range**, whose national parks provide bushwalkers with remote, rugged terrain to explore. Numerous streams tumble down from the escarpment in mighty waterfalls, creating fertile river valleys where the predominant agricultural activity is cattle breeding; in the north, subtropical and tropical agriculture takes over, especially the cultivation of bananas. In essence, the further you go, the better this coast gets.

2

Port Stephens

Just north of Newcastle, the wide bay of **Port Stephens**, which extends inland for some 25km, offers calm waters and numerous coves ideal for swimming, watersports and fishing, while the ocean side has good surf and wide, sandy beaches. In January, thousands of families arrive to take their annual holiday in the area dubbed "Blue Water Paradise". The main township of **NELSON BAY** is perched near the tip of the bay's southern arm, together with the smaller settlements of Shoal Bay, Soldiers Point, Fingal Bay and Anna Bay. Stockton Beach in the Worimi Conservation Lands, to the south, has some of the largest sand dunes in the eastern Australian mainland.

From May to November you might see **whales** as they migrate first north then south, while **dolphin cruises** are available all year round, most leaving from d'Albora Marinas in Nelson Bay.

ARRIVAL AND INFORMATION
PORT STEPHENS

By bus Getting around the bay is easiest if you have your own vehicle, though Greyhound and Premier Motor Service buses from Sydney and Newcastle stop at Karuah, midway around the bay. Port Stephens Coaches (ⓦ pscoaches.com.au) links all the smaller beach settlements with Nelson Bay throughout the day, and runs an express service from Sydney and a service from Newcastle.

Destinations Canberra (daily; 5hr); Coffs Harbour (4

daily; 5hr 30min); Newcastle (4 daily; 45min); Sydney (5 daily; 3hr 30min).

Tourist information The visitor information centre (Mon–Sat 9am–5pm, Sun 9am–4pm; ☎ 1800 808 900, ⓦ portstephens.org.au) is at Victoria Parade in Nelson Bay, and offers an accommodation, tour and cruise booking service. Enquire here, or check their website, for details of surfing, horseriding, parasailing, sea-kayaking and jet-skiing opportunities.

ACTIVITIES

4WD tours Port Stephens 4WD Tours (☎ 02 4984 4760, ⓦ portstephens4wd.com.au), 35 Stockton St, Nelson Bay, run trips to the impressive sand dunes – try sandboarding or driving down the slopes in a 4WD; the black, metallic pyramids rising out of the sand (World War II anti-tank defences) give the experience a sci-fi twist.

Dolphin cruises Dolphin cruises are available all year round, most leaving from d'Albora Marinas in Nelson Bay. Imagine Cruises run satisfyingly ecofriendly trips aboard a 15m sailing catamaran (dolphin-watching cruise around 1hr 30min, $29; whale-and-dolphin cruise from May–Nov,

3hr–3hr 30min, $63; ☎ 02 4984 9000, ⓦ imaginecruises .com.au). Alternatives include Moonshadow Cruises (1hr 30min; $25; ☎ 02 4984 9388, ⓦ moonshadow.com.au) or the Port Stephens Ferry Service (☎ 04 1268 2117, ⓦ portstephensferryservice.com.au), which runs lunch cruises (3hr; $30) and ferries between Nelson Bay and Tea Gardens ($20 return); you can usually see dolphins.

Scuba diving To get underwater among the marine life contact Feet First (☎ 02 4984 2092, ⓦ feetfirstdive .com.au). They organize boat dives from $65 ($115 with rental) and run PADI Open Water courses.

ACCOMMODATION

Melaleuca Surfside Backpackers 2 Koala Place, Boat Harbour ☎ 02 4981 9422, ⓦ melaleucabackpackers .com.au. Red cedar timber cabins, a shared bunkhouse and camping set in tranquil bushland roamed by koalas, possums and a pet kangaroo, minutes from an excellent surf beach. Two-night minimum stay at weekends. Unpowered sites $20, dorms $32, cabins $100

Samurai Beach Bungalows YHA Cnr Frost Rd & Robert Connell Close, Anna Bay ☎ 02 4982 1921, ⓦ samuraiportstephens.com.au. A wonderfully mellow, southeast Asian-influenced place set in lush

gardens, with shared or private timber cabins arranged around a covered bush kitchen and a delightful saltwater pool; Port Stephens Coaches stop nearby. Dorms $35.50, cabins $129

Wanderers Retreat 7 Koala Place, One Mile Beach ☎ 02 4982 1702, ⓦ wanderersretreat.com. A gorgeous, ecofriendly hideaway set in mature woodland, with "treehouses" (cabins on stilts) and cottages, all with composting loos and an abundance of luxurious touches. Facilities include a swimming pool, guest laundry and BBQ. Wi-fi only reaches some rooms. $245

EATING

★ **Little Nel Café** 1 Government Rd, Nelson Bay ☎ 02 4916 4600, ⓦ littlenel.com.au. The funkiest café along

this part of the coast, with barista-made coffee and a good selection of breakfast and brunch food. Try the salad of watermelon, strawberries and pomegranate ($12). Expect a crowd. Mon–Fri 7–11.30am, Sat & Sun 7.30–11.30am.

The Point Restaurant 1 Soldiers Point Marina, Sunset Boulevarde, Soldiers Point ☎ 02 4984 7111, ✆ thepointrestaurant.com.au. The poshest eating option around, with great views from the balcony and dining room. There's lots of fresh seafood on offer, ranging from mixed grilled seafood ($27) to squid and sticky pork belly ($28). The place to come for a treat or special occasion. Mon–Fri 11am–11pm, Sat & Sun 8am–11pm.

Myall Lakes National Park

From Port Stephens the Pacific Highway continues north past the beautiful **Myall Lakes National Park**, which well rewards a day or so of exploration. About 20km before the small town of **Bulahdelah**, turn right onto Tea Gardens Road for a heavenly drive to **Mungo Brush**, along the shores of Myall Lake. There are plenty of gentle walking tracks around here, while a more challenging 21km hike leads back to **Hawks Nest**, on Port Stephens Bay. Just after Mungo Brush, the charming Bombah Point Ferry (daily 8am–6pm; every 30min; $6; ☎ 02 6591 0300) takes you and your car over Myall Lake and back to Bulahdelah and the highway via the unsealed Bombah Point Road; the service is occasionally suspended when water is low or due to mechanical problems, so always call ahead.

The Lakes Way

Heading north again towards Forster–Tuncurry, you can turn east just after Bulahdelah onto the extremely scenic **Lakes Way** (Tourist Drive 6). At Bungwahl, a turn-off leads down mostly unsealed roads to **Seal Rocks**, a remote, unspoilt fishing village and the only settlement in the Myall Lakes National Park. The first beach you come to, the inspirationally named Number One Beach, is truly beautiful, with crystal-clear waters marooned between two headlands. Two minutes to the south, there are great waves for surfing. **Sugar Loaf Point Lighthouse** is around ten minutes' walk up a steep path; the grounds offer fantastic 360-degree views, and the lookout below leads down to a deserted, rocky beach. Seal Rocks' seasonal agglomerations of nurse sharks make it one of the best **dive sites** in New South Wales.

Back on the Lakes Way, an exhilarating drive through the tiny **Booti Booti National Park** takes you through endless forests, and over a narrow spit of land between Wallis Lake and Elizabeth Bay where it's hard to keep your eyes on the road, especially at sunset. Further north, a bridge connects the twin holiday towns of **Forster–Tuncurry**, the former set on the strip of land separating **Wallis Lake** from the ocean. The lake is very pretty, but Forster itself decidedly isn't, being somewhat blighted by high-rise development. It's a good base for all manner of cruises and watersports though, and famous for its **oysters** and playful resident **dolphins**. Tobwabba Art Gallery (Mon–Fri 9am–5pm; free; ✆ tobwabba.com.au), a couple of streets inland at 10 Breckenridge Street, has some wonderful indigenous art by the Worimi people.

ARRIVAL AND INFORMATION   MYALL LAKES NATIONAL PARK

By bus Busways service between Sydney, Newcastle and Taree runs along the Lakes Way, and Greyhound and Premier Motor Service buses both serve Forster, with Greyhound also stopping at Bulahdelah.

Destinations Bulahdelah (daily; 1hr); Newcastle (2 daily; 2hr 55min); Port Macquarie (daily; 1hr 50min); Sydney (6 weekly; 5hr 30min); Taree (daily; 45min).

By car To explore the Myall Lakes National Park in your own time you really need a vehicle, and this is the only way to experience the Lakes Way.

Tourist information The well-organized visitor information centre (Mon–Fri 9am–5pm, Sat & Sun 9am–4pm; ☎ 1800 802 692, ✆ greatlakes.org.au), on Little St in Forster, is responsible for the Myall Lakes area and offers an accommodation booking service. There is also a visitor centre in Bulahdelah (Mon–Sat 9am–4pm; ☎ 02 4997 4981, ✆ greatlakes.org.au) on Crawford St.

ACTIVITIES

Dolphin watching Amaroo Cruises (10am most days; 2hr; $45; ☎ 0419 333 445, ⓦ amaroocruise.com.au), on Memorial Drive, Forster, run dolphin-watching trips.

Diving Dive Forster (☎ 02 6554 7478, ⓦ diveforster.com.

au), on the corner of Memorial Drive and Little St, Forster, offers diving at Seal Rocks (double boat dive $120) and swimming with dolphins ($80).

ACCOMMODATION

If you want to stay in the area overnight, camping is an appealing option; check the national parks website (ⓦ environment .nsw.gov.au) for listings. There are scores of holiday apartments and motels in Forster.

Mobys Beachside Retreat Boomerang Beach, Pacific Palms ☎ 1800 655 322, ⓦ mobysretreat.com.au. These stylish self-contained beach houses come with all mod cons and are minutes from the beach. There's a chic restaurant serving up creative cuisine and a bar on site. **$150**

Myall Shores NRMA Holiday Park Bomba Point Rd, Bombah Point ☎ 1300 795 913, ⓦ myallshores.com.au. Beautifully located, tranquil holiday park, boasting rather stylish waterfront villas (among other options) and a smart café-restaurant, plus loads of activities including canoe,

boat and bike rental. Popular with families. Un/powered sites **$27/$31**, villas **$176**

North Coast Holiday Parks Seal Rocks Kinka Rd, Seal Rocks ☎ 02 4997 6164 or ☎ 1800 112 234, ⓦ northcoastholidayparks.com.au. Glorious, unspoilt site right on beautiful Number One Beach that's a big hit with families. Although there's a small general store in the settlement, you should bring supplies in with you. Facilities include camp kitchen and laundry. Un/powered sites **$32/$36**, cabins **$192**

EATING

Bella Bellissimo Italian Restaurant Memorial Drive, Forster ☎ 02 6555 6411. This has long been a local favourite, offering pizza, pasta and risotto, along with a number of gluten-free options. Great waterfront location and very child-friendly. Book in advance at weekends. Tues–Sun noon–3pm & 5.30–9.30pm.

Little Lucifers Wharf St ☎ 02 6557 2702, ⓦ littlelucifers .com.au. Cosy little place serving delicious breakfast, artisan

coffees, tapas and cocktails. The breakfast menu includes corn tortillas stacked with bacon, corn and salsa ($14) and green eggs on toast ($14.50). Wine and craft beer available. Tues–Fri 11am–10pm, Sat & Sun 7am–10pm.

Reef Bar Grill Wharf St, Forster ☎ 02 6555 7092, ⓦ reefbargrill.com.au. Boasting one of the best waterfront locations, serving deliciously fresh seafood, including local Wallis Lake oysters ($36. dozen). Daily 11am–10pm.

Barrington Tops and around

Heading from Forster–Tuncurry via Nabiac and Gloucester, you arrive at the World Heritage-listed **Barrington Tops National Park**. It's gentle, hilly farming country up to the country town of **Gloucester**; about 40km beyond here, unsealed roads lead through the park.

The Barrington Tops themselves are two high, cliff-ringed plateaus, **Barrington** and **Gloucester**, which rise steeply from the surrounding valleys. The changes in altitude within the park are so great – the highest point is 1586m – that within a few minutes you can pass from areas of subtropical rainforest to high, windswept plateaus covered with snow gums, meadows and subalpine bog. Up on the plateau, snow is common from the end of April to early October.

Travelling on to Port Macquarie via Wingham you can call at the 200m-high **Ellenborough Falls**, one of the most spectacular waterfalls on the whole coast; the falls are located near Elands on Bulga Forest Drive – unsealed for much of the way.

ARRIVAL AND ACTIVITIES

By public transport The closest you'll get to the park with public transport is on the train from Sydney or Newcastle (change at Broadmeadow) to Gloucester (daily; 2hr–4hr 20min) or Dungog (daily; 1hr 10min–3hr 30min).

Adventure tours Barrington Outdoor Adventure Centre

ACTIVITIES BARRINGTON TOPS AND AROUND

(☎ 02 6558 2093, ⓦ boac.com.au), at 126 Thunderbolts Way, Gloucester, offers mountain biking and kayaking tours in the Barrington Tops region, as well as abseiling. They also rent out canoes, kayaks and mountain bikes.

National park tours The Dungog Visitor Information

Centre, corner Dowling & Brown streets (Mon–Fri 9am–5pm, Sat & Sun 10am–3pm; ☎02 4992 2212, ⓦ visitdungog.com.au), and the Gloucester Visitor Centre, 27 Denison St (Mon–Fri 9am–4.30pm, Sat & Sun 10am–3pm; ☎02 6538 5252, ⓦ visitgloucester.com.au), can help with tours into the national park. There are plenty of picnic grounds, walking trails and scenic lookouts in the park.

ACCOMMODATION

Other than camping, accommodation in the area is relatively pricey but there are lots of options. You'll find a range of cheaper alternatives, from snug cottages to larger lodges, listed on ⓦ visitbarringtontops.com.au.

Camping A 4WD is often required to access the many campsites in the forest: check out the New South Wales National Parks and Wildlife website (ⓦ environment .nsw.com.au) or contact the NPWS in Gloucester (☎02 6538 5300) or Scone (☎02 6540 2300) for locations and advice. Free, with facilities $5 per person

Salisbury Lodges 2930 Salisbury Rd, Salisbury, 40km northwest of Dungog ☎02 4995 3285, ⓦ salisburylodges.com.au. Timber chalets and motel-style rooms in a gorgeous rainforest setting that are perfect for a cosy country weekend. There's a good restaurant on site, too. One of the closest places to the park. $299

Port Macquarie

The fast-growing town of **PORT MACQUARIE**, at the mouth of the Hastings River, has a beautiful natural setting. Long, sandy **beaches** extend far along the coast, while the hinterland is dotted with forests, mountains and pretty towns. The town was established in 1821 as a place of secondary punishment for convicts who continued their criminal ways after arrival in New South Wales, though by the late 1820s the **penal settlement** was closed and the area opened up to free settlers. An increasing number of independent travellers call into "Port", but it remains primarily a family-focused resort. The **activities** on offer are really the thing here, with wildlife and nature parks, cruises on the Hastings River, horseriding and, above all, watersports, all vying for your attention. Horton Street is the main downtown street, running north to the Hastings River.

The river foreshore

With its anglers and pelican colony, the river foreshore is a pleasant place for a peaceful sunset stroll or to grab some fish and chips. Floating offices, where you can book anything from dolphin tours to seaplane flights, are located along its western end, towards the town wharf.

Beaches

A string of fine beaches runs down the ocean-facing side of town (Town, Flynn's and Lighthouse are patrolled); perhaps the best way to spend a day in Port Macquarie is to rent a bike and explore the clifftop paths and roads that link them all.

Historical Society Museum

22 Clarence St • Mon–Sat 9.30am–4.30pm • $7

Port Macquarie has a tendency to destroy reminders of its past, though a few early buildings survive, including the convict-built St Thomas' Anglican Church; pick up a historic walk leaflet at the visitor centre (see p.219). The 1835 **Historical Society Museum**, opposite the 1869 **Courthouse**, illuminates early life in the penal settlement, and houses a rather gruesome convict-whipping stool complete with fake blood that should frighten the kids into good behaviour.

Mid-North Maritime Museum

6 William St • Daily 10am–4pm • $5

The quaint **Mid-North Maritime Museum** in the Pilot Station Cottages near Town Beach

2

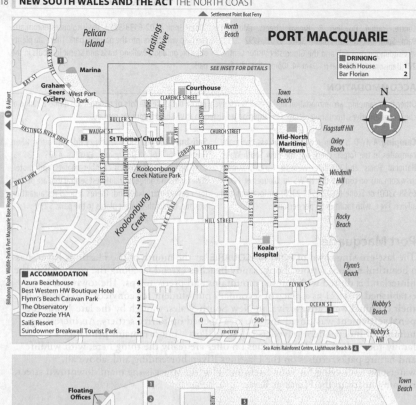

DRINKING
Beach House 1
Bar Florian 2

ACCOMMODATION
Azura Beachhouse 4
Best Western HW Boutique Hotel 6
Flynn's Beach Caravan Park 3
The Observatory 7
Ozzie Pozzie YHA 2
Sails Resort 1
Sundowner Breakwall Tourist Park 5

EATING
Carlos & Co 3
Cassegrain Wines 1
The Corner Restaurant 4
Fusion 7 6
The Latin Loafer 5
Off The Hook 2

contains the usual mix of nautical artefacts, photographs and model boats. Some objects date back to the arrival of the first convicts to Port Macquarie in 1821.

The Glasshouse

Cnr Clarence & Hay sts • Mon–Fri 9am–5pm, Sat & Sun 9am–4pm • Free • Ⓦ glasshouse.com.org.au

The **Glasshouse** is a regional visual and performing arts venue incorporating an art and photography gallery, a theatre with capacity for almost six hundred people and it is also home to the Visitor Information Centre (see opposite).

Kooloonbung Creek Nature Park

Always open • Free

A large bushland reserve remarkably close to the Central Business District (CBD), **Kooloonbung Creek Nature Park** is the best attraction in town. From the entrance at the corner of Horton and Gordon streets, you walk trails among casuarinas, eucalypts and swampy mangroves, visit a cemetery containing the graves of eminent early settlers, or sweat through a small patch of rainforest – were it not for the boardwalks and faint hum of traffic, it'd be amazingly easy to believe that you were lost in the bush.

Koala Hospital

Lord St • Daily 8am–4pm; feeding 8am, guided tour 3pm • Free • ⓦ koalahospital.org.au

In the grounds of Roto House is the **Koala Hospital**, Australia's oldest. Here you can see the koalas being fed, learn more about the work of the koala hospital, take an afternoon guided tour, and adopt one of the "patients" if you get particularly attached.

Sea Acres Rainforest Centre

4km south of town on Pacific Drive at Shelly Beach • Daily 9am–4.30pm • Free • Guided walks at regular intervals, including bushtucker walks with indigenous guides

The impressive **Sea Acres Rainforest Centre** features a 1.3km boardwalk through the rare subtropical rainforest of Sea Acres National Park. Begin your visit by dropping into the Sea Acres Rainforest centre, which has valuable information about the bushtucker and discovery tours. Enjoy the birds and other wildlife at close quarters, and pay a visit to the ecology centre to learn more about the local Aboriginal culture and the surrounding rainforest.

Billabong Koala & Wildlife Park

61 Billabong Drive, off the Oxley Highway west of the town centre • Daily 9am–5pm; pat a koala 10.30am, 1.30pm & 3.30pm • $26.50 • ⓦ billabongkoala.com.au

The **Billabong Koala & Wildlife Park** is home to koalas as well as wombats, emu chicks, kangaroos, monkeys and reptiles. There are opportunities to pat a koala and have your photograph taken, watch the monkeys being fed and see a reptile show.

ARRIVAL AND INFORMATION

PORT MACQUARIE

By plane You can fly to Port Macquarie from Sydney with QantasLink or Virgin Australia; Virgin Australia also flies from Brisbane. Busways operates services to town (6km; 25min) from near the terminal throughout the day.

Destinations Brisbane (daily; 6hr 20min); Lord Howe Island (summer only; weekly; 1hr 30min); Sydney (3–8 daily; 1hr).

By train NSW TrainLink trains from Sydney (daily; 6hr 30min) stop in Wauchope, 22km to the west, from where there's a connecting bus service.

By bus Greyhound and Premier Motor Service stop at Port Macquarie on their runs between Sydney and Brisbane, while New England Coaches run to Tamworth, Nambucca Heads, Coffs Harbour, Bellingen and Dorrigo. Long-distance buses arrive and depart from the Coach Terminal at 109 Gordon St. Busways buses (ⓦ busways.com.au) operate from their depot at 6–8 Denham St and offer connections to many places on the central and mid-north coast.

Destinations Ballina (4 daily; 6hr); Bellingen (3 weekly; 2hr 45min); Byron Bay (4 daily; 7hr); Coffs Harbour (6 daily; 2hr 30min); Dorrigo (3 weekly; 3hr 15min); Grafton (4 daily; 3hr 15min); Nambucca Heads (6 daily; 2hr).

Tourist information The helpful visitor information centre (Mon–Fri 9am–5.30pm, Sat & Sun 9am–4pm; ☎ 02 6581 8000 or ☎ 1300 303 155, ⓦ portmacquarieinfo .com.au) is at the Glasshouse on Clarence St (see opposite).

Services The post office can be found at Shop 2, Palm Court Centre, 14–16 Short St. Port Macquarie Hospital (☎ 02 6581 2000) is on Wright's Rd. (☎ 02 6581 2000) is on Wright's Rd. For Police call ☎ 02 6583 0199.

GETTING AROUND

The town's attractions are far-flung and local transport isn't great: the best option is cycling.

By bike Graham Seers Cyclery, Shop 1, Port Marina, Park St (☎ 02 6583 2333, ⓦ grahamseercyclery.com.au) rent bikes for $30/half-day or $50/day.

By bus You can get around much of town with Busways buses (ⓦ busways.com.au) local services. No. 322 will take you along Pacific Drive past the beaches.

2

By car Car rental companies include Hertz, 7 Jindalee St (☎ 1300 767 339), and Thrifty, 101 Hastings River Drive (☎ 02 6584 2122).

By taxi Port Macquarie Taxicabs ☎ 02 6581 0081 or ☎ 131 008.

ACTIVITIES

Boat rental The Settlement Point Boatshed (☎ 02 6583 6300), 2km north of the CBD next to the Settlement Point Ferry (follow Park St north over the road bridges), rents out canoes and boats at low hourly rates.

Camel safari Port Macquarie Camel Safaris (☎ 04 3767 2080, ⓦ portmacquariecamels.com.au) offer half-hour rides ($35) from Lighthouse Beach (daily except Sat, 9.30am–2pm, weather permitting).

Cruises Boats leave from the Town Wharf: Port Macquarie Cruise Adventures (☎ 0414 897 444, ⓦ cruiseadventures .com.au) offer dolphin-spotting cruises (2hr; $15) and Everglades trips (6hr; $79); Port Venture Cruises (☎ 02 6583 3058, ⓦ portventure.com.au) offer BBQ lunch cruises (4hr 30min; $40) and twilight tours (1hr 30min; $17). Both also run whale-watching trips May–Nov. You can embark on a fish-and-chip lunch tour on a Chinese junk (2hr; $30) with

Junk Cruises (ⓦ 04 0974 4270, ⓦ junkcruises.com.au).

Diving Rick's Dive School (☎ 02 6584 7759 or ☎ 0422 063 528, ⓦ ricksdiveschool.com.au) offer dive courses and snorkelling.

Horseriding Rides with Bellrowan Valley Horse Riding (☎ 02 6587 5227, ⓦ bellrowanvalley.com.au), a 30min drive from Port Macquarie in beautiful bushland, range from a one-hour trip ($65) to a two-day tour with overnight pub stay ($395).

Paddleboarding Stand Up Paddle (☎ 04 5764 9429, ⓦ standuppaddlepmq.com.au) offer both equipment rental and lessons.

Surfing Port Macquarie Surf School (☎ 02 6584 7733, ⓦ portmacquariesurfschool.com.au) offer 2hr group lessons, as well as one-on-one sessions, and rent out boards.

ACCOMMODATION

Azura Beachhouse B&B 109 Pacific Drive ☎ 02 6582 2700, ⓦ azura.com.au. A rather smart B&B close to Shelly Beach with modern, comfortable rooms. The considerate hosts provide picnics on request and rustle up very nice breakfasts on the wooden veranda, overlooking lush gardens. $140

Best Western HW Boutique Hotel 1 Stewart St ☎ 02 6583 1200, ⓦ hwboutique.com.au. Comfortable, modern, executive-friendly motel with tastefully decorated rooms. It's in a fine location overlooking Town Beach, and there's a great view from the breakfast room. Also has a small pool. $139

Flynn's Beach Caravan Park 22 Ocean St, 2.5km from the centre ☎ 02 6583 5754, ⓦ flynnsbeachcaravanpark .com.au. A great little leafy park just 200m from Flynn's Beach with a range of cabins set amid ferns and gum trees, a pool, BBQ areas and a camp kitchen. Un/powered sites $28/32, cabins $86

The Observatory 40 William St, Town Beach ☎ 02 6586 8000, ⓦ observatory.net.au. These stylish contemporary rooms and apartments are sleek and spacious with all mod cons and balconies with stunning sea

views. There's a pool on site, as well as a popular café. $199

Ozzie Pozzie YHA 36 Waugh St ☎ 02 6583 8133 or ☎ 1800 620 020, ⓦ ozziepozzie.com. Friendly, vibrantly painted place set around a small central courtyard, with good kitchen facilities, a games room and a garage converted into a TV room complete with DVDs and comfy armchairs. Dorms range from four- to ten-bed, and there are very smart doubles (some en-suite) and even private single rooms. There's also a small pool and bike rental. Dorms $25, doubles $63

Sails Resort 20 Park St ☎ 1800 025 271, ⓦ rydges .com. This waterfront property may look pretty swanky but the 86 guest rooms and suites are very affordable – especially if you hunt for an online deal. Rooms are stylish, well equipped and comfortable. $189

Sundowner Breakwall Tourist Park 1 Munster St ☎ 02 6583 2755, ⓦ breakwall.sundownerholidays.com. Right in the heart of town next to the river, this family-orientated park is superbly located but amenities are a little dated and sites are tightly packed. Also offers some backpacker dorm accommodation and attractive cottages. Un/powered sites $28/38, dorms $80, cabins $148

EATING

Carlos & Co 73 Clarence St ☎ 02 6583 9009, ⓦ carlosandcocafe.com.au. A Mexican restaurant serving Vietnamese rolls and Canadian waffles, this family-friendly place takes genre-hopping to new heights. The lunch menu includes a lamb taco ($15.90) and BBQ pork roll ($12.50); try the huevos rancheros ($14.90) for breakfast. Mon–Sat 7.30am–2.30pm, Sun 9am–2.30pm.

Cassegrain Wines 764 Fernbank Creek Rd, off the Pacific Hwy west of town ☎ 02 6582 8377, ⓦ cassegrain-restaurant.com.au. Cassegrain wines appear on many a wine list in these parts; here, you can enjoy them at the source, along with French brasserie-style food such as *lapin a la cocotte* ($34) and *pot au feu* ($44), their signature winter dish, prepared from local ingredients. Daily 10am–4pm.

Cedro 70 Clarence St ☎02 6583 5529. Breakfast and lunch are so good at this casual café that locals wish it was open for dinner. The menu includes delights such as goat's cheese and shallot scramble, served on sourdough toast with a rasher of bacon ($17.50) and various Mediterranean-meets-Middle East lunchtime specials, such as halloumi salad ($18.50). Mon–Sun 7.30am–2pm.

The Corner Restaurant 11 Clarence St ☎02 6583 3300, ⓦcornerrestaurant.com.au. This modern, light-filled restaurant is the ideal place for an early breakfast, relaxed lunch or tasty evening meal. Breakfast items include thick-cut raisin toast ($8), coconut and almond toasted muesli ($15) and house-made pancakes ($15). The Campos coffee blend is excellent. Mon–Sat 7am–3pm & 6–11pm, Sun 7am–3pm.

Fusion 7 6/124 Horton St ☎02 6584 1171, ⓦfusion7 .com.au. Aussie chef Lindsey Schwab perfected the art of Pacific Rim fusion cuisine while working in London under Paul Gordon; back home, he now artfully applies his talents to dishes such as seared Hokkaido sea scallops ($24.50) and pan-roasted duck breast with sweet potato skordalia, green papaya and *umeboshi* salad ($36). Tues–Sat 6pm–9pm.

The Latin Loafer 74 Clarence St ☎02 6583 9481, ⓦlatinlaofer.com.au. This bohemian bar serves surprisingly excellent Spanish tapas and well-priced drinks. Try the kingfish ceviche ($18) or the chorizo in red wine ($16). Live music most nights. Tues–Thurs noon–3pm & 5–10pm, Fri–Sun noon–11pm.

Off The Hook 5/2 Horton St. Ever-popular fish and chip takeaway (serving fresh oysters, barramundi, basa, flake and local flathead) with just a few tables but handily located thirty seconds from the river. The fisherman's basket ($30.50, including fish fillets, prawn cutlets, calamari, scallops and chips) is a great choice for sharing. Daily 11am–10pm.

DRINKING

Beach House 1 Horton St ☎02 6584 6011. Waterside bar in an 1887 building with a wraparound veranda: a great spot for a morning coffee or sunset drinks. There's a decent choice of wines, beers, ciders and cocktails and plenty of bar food to choose from. Live music at weekends. Daily 7.30am–midnight.

Bar Florian 6–14 Clarence St ☎02 6584 7649, ⓦbarflorian.com.au. This stylish Italian bar is a welcome addition to the local gastronomic scene, offering a good range of small plates, pizza and desserts, plus an extensive list of wines and spirits. Pop by for a Vespa dry martini ($16) or Aperol Spritz ($14). Wed–Sat 4–11pm, Sun 2–8pm.

The coast north to Nambucca Heads

The coastline between Port Macquarie and Nambucca Heads, 115km to the north, has some beautiful locations, including **CRESCENT HEAD**, a small seaside town with safe swimming beaches, some wonderful waterfront campsites and popular surf spots for long boarders. If surfing, come during term-time and you may have the waves to yourself.

Slightly further up the coast is **Hat Head National Park** and the small town of **SOUTH WEST ROCKS**, perched on a picturesque headland. Further north, back on the Pacific Highway, you'll pick up signs for **TAYLORS ARM** and its famous pub, **The Pub with No Beer**, one of two hostelries that market themselves as the inspiration for the popular Australian folk song of the same name, penned by Slim Dusty and Gordon Parsons.

ACCOMMODATION

THE COAST NORTH TO NAMBUCCA HEADS

Waves Campground 954 Point Plomer Rd ☎02 6566 0144. Set in secluded bushland but offering modern amenities, this campsite a 10min drive from Crescent Head has BBQs, a bush kitchen, hot-water showers, a small kiosk and a complimentary guest laundry. No internet. Un/powered sites $20/55

Hat Head Holiday Park Straight St, Hat Head ☎02 6567 7501, ⓦmvcholidayparks.com.au. With beach and river access and surrounded by the national park, this is a lovely spot. There's a small kiosk on site, as well as a covered camp kitchen and access to some great surf. No internet. Un/powered site $29/36, cabin $95

Nambucca Heads

Further north again is the laidback holiday town of **NAMBUCCA HEADS**. There's some excellent **surf** on Main, Beilby's and Shelly beaches, and great **swimming** in the crystal-clear water at the extremely scenic river mouth. Whales can be sighted from Scotts Head, a popular surfing spot to the south, during their southern migration (July–Oct).

2

By train The town is on the main Sydney–Brisbane NSW TrainLink train routes. Nambucca Heads Station is located on Railway Rd, 5min walk from the centre of town.

Destinations Brisbane (3 daily; 8hr 44min); Coffs Harbour (3 daily; 40min); Grafton (3 daily; 1hr 50min); Sydney (3 daily; 9hr 13min).

By bus Greyhound, Premier Motor Service and Busways operate a daily service to Urunga and Coffs Harbour. The Greyhound service continues on to Byron Bay and the Busways to Bellingen.

Destinations Bellingen (4 daily; 1hr 40min); Byron Bay (2 daily; 4hr); Coffs Harbour (5–9 daily; 35min); Port Macquarie (3 daily; 2hr); Urunga (5–9 daily; 15min).

ACCOMMODATION AND EATING

Marcel Towers Holiday Apartments 12–14 Wellington Drive ☎ 02 6568 7041, ⓦ marceltowers .com.au. These comfy one- and two-bed apartments have wonderful river and ocean views, and come with well-equipped kitchens. Use of kayaks and rowing boats is also included in the rate. $170

Matilda's Restaurant 6 Wellington Drive ☎ 02 6568 6024. A long-standing favourite with locals, chef Kel and his wife Cissy serve up delicious seafood and steak (mains $25–35) in a cute little building. Check the board for specials. BYO. Mon–Sat 6–10pm.

V-Wall Tavern Wellington Drive ☎ 02 6568 6344. Good pub grub such as a seafood basket ($40) or schnitzel with a creamy sauce ($30) served on a veranda overlooking the lagoon. Sun lunch specials. Mon–Sat 11.30am–2pm & 5.30–11pm, Sun 5.30–11pm.

White Albatross Caravan & Holiday Park 12–14 Wellington Drive ☎ 02 6568 6468, ⓦ whitealbatross .com.au. In splashing distance of the sea and lagoon, this park is in a great location, with camping facilities (some en-suite spaces) and a selection of one- or two-bedroom cabins. There's a kiosk on site and a pub nearby (see above) – a bonus if you don't feel like cooking. Limited wi-fi available. Powered sites $43, cabins $130

The Bellinger Region

The **Bellinger Region** is a beautiful area just south of Coffs Harbour, which truly has something for everyone. It comprises the country village of **Dorrigo** and its spectacular plateau, the charming town of **Bellingen** and the Bellinger Valley, and the pristine seaboard around **Urunga** and **Mylestom**. The Bellinger River was the setting for Peter Carey's 1988 novel *Oscar and Lucinda*, later turned into a film starring Ralph Fiennes and Cate Blanchett.

Urunga

URUNGA, 20km north of Nambucca Heads, is a small and peaceful beachside town where the Bellinger and Kalang rivers meet the sea. It's a popular holiday spot for families, and offers pretty beaches, safe swimming and an interesting boardwalk through mangroves.

Mylestom

MYLESTOM, 7km further down the highway from Urunga, is an undeveloped backwater occupying a stunningly beautiful spot on the wide Bellinger River. You can take advantage of its riverside setting at the **Alma Doepel Reserve**'s sheltered, sandy river beach. Two minutes' walk to the east is a gorgeous sweep of surf beach – often gloriously deserted. There's a place to **stay** overnight, along with a couple of basic restaurants, but you're better off having a quick swim, then heading inland up into the valley.

Bellingen

Just after Urunga, a turn-off heads 12km west to the bewitching town of **BELLINGEN**, one of the prettiest and most beguiling spots in New South Wales. This laidback town is awash with cafés, restaurants, organic produce, and artistic and creative types. Most people come to "Bello" for a day-trip and end up staying a week.

On your way into town, don't miss the 100-year-old **Old Butter Factory** (1 Doepel St; daily 9am–5pm), a former dairy that is now a complex of art galleries, craft shops and home to a pleasant café. If you need a break from crafts and culture, however, walk for five minutes down Waterfall Way before hopping over a white gate and heading down to the river; the **rope swings** here are popular, and you can **swim** back into town.

ARRIVAL AND ACTIVITIES   BELLINGEN

By bus Busways operates bus services from Coffs Harbour (2–6 daily; 1hr) and Urunga (2–6 daily; 30min) – the bus stop is at the corner of Hyde and Church streets – but if you're arriving by long-distance bus it's more convenient to arrange a pick-up from Urunga.

Tourist information The Waterfall Way visitor centre (daily 9am–5pm; ☎02 6655 1522, ⓦ bellingermagic.com) is at 29–31 Hyde St.

Festivals Bellingen's lively annual programme of community festivals and cultural events includes a jazz festival in Aug.

Canoeing Out of town in Fernmount is the much-loved Bellingen Canoe Adventures (☎02 6655 9955, ⓦ canoeadventures.com.au), whose daily meanders down the tranquil Bellinger River bring sightings of koalas, eagles and the odd dolphin. Half-day tours cost $48, while sunset and full-moon trips with champagne are also available (1hr; $25).

ACCOMMODATION

There are a number of cottages and B&Bs in the surrounding countryside, and campers can set up at the showground where there are powered and unpowered sites available.

Bellingen YHA 2 Short St ☎02 6655 1116, ⓦ bellingenyha.com.au. Located in a beautiful two-storey timber house with wide verandas, this hostel boasts a lovely garden of jacaranda trees that come alive with flying foxes at dusk. They arrange excursions to Dorrigo National Park and have bikes for rent, pick-ups from Urunga, free morning yoga and a legendary wall of nudey pics. Dorms $27, doubles $72

Koompartoo Retreat Cnr Rawson & Dudley sts ☎02 6655 2326, ⓦ koompartoo.com.au. Set amid acres of rainforest rich in birdlife 5min walk from town. The four hardwood chalets have stained-glass windows, cosy rooms inside and big verandas out. No breakfast; limited free wi-fi near the owner's office. $155

Lilp Pily Country House 54 Sunny Corner Rd ☎02 6655 0522, ⓦ lilypily.com.au. This peaceful place can be found out of town, overlooking the river. The three rooms are contemporary and comfortable, and breakfast (included) is delicious. Champagne is served on arrival. $280

EATING AND DRINKING

★ **Bellingen Gelato Bar** 101 Hyde St ☎04 0330 6995, ⓦ bellingengelato.com.au. Stylish *gelateria* with 1950s-style decor, a cool old jukebox, delicious cakes and mouthwatering ice cream (two scoops $6), handmade on the premises. Daily 10am–6pm.

Federal Hotel 77 Hyde St ☎02 6655 1003, ⓦ federalhotel.com.au. With a breezy, lacework veranda and battered brown-leather sofas, this renovated heritage-listed pub is Bello's social hub. *Relish*, an above-average brasserie, serving dishes such as Thai-style BBQ pork ($25), and live music draw large crowds most nights of the week. Mon–Sat 10am–11.30pm, Sun 11.30am–10pm; food stops around 8.30pm.

5 Church Street 5 Church St ☎02 6655 0155, ⓦ 5churchstreet.com. This bistro is dedicated to the ethical and responsible use of resources, so the menu features plenty of local organic and bio-dynamic produce, such as vegan pizza ($16). A great place to sample craft beer from the local Bellingen brewery. Daily 8am–8pm.

Oak Street Food & Wine 2 Oak St ☎02 6655 9000, ⓦ oakstreetfoodandwine.com.au. This multiple-award-winning restaurant rustles up some truly stunning contemporary Australian food in a cute, candlelit heritage cottage. Try the twelve-hour herb and Parmesan crusted lamb shoulder ($36). Book ahead. Wed–Sat 6.30–10pm.

The Vintage Nest 62 Hyde St ☎02 6655 0015. A popular little café that sells coffees, cakes and savoury snacks (from $4), as well as vintage furniture and clothes. Sink into the comfy sofas and admire the decor or browse the secondhand treasures. Mon–Fri 7am–4.30pm, Sat & Sun 8am–2pm.

SHOPPING

Bellingen Community Markets The enjoyable Bellingen Community Markets (third Sat of the month; 9am–2.30pm), in Bellingen Park, is one of Australia's largest local markets, with plenty of buskers and over 250 stalls selling arts, crafts, clothes and organic food.

Didgeridoos 2/25 Hyde St. At Heartland Didgeridoos, opposite the Shell garage, you can buy a didj from the craftsmen themselves. Mon–Fri 10am–5pm, Sat 10am–4pm.

Growers' Market The predominantly foodie Growers' Market is held on the second and fourth Saturday (8am–1pm) at Bellingen Showground.

Dorrigo

The Waterfall Way winds steeply from Bellingen up to **DORRIGO**, past some spectacular lookouts. Dorrigo is a quiet country town with sleepy, wide streets lined with plenty of little shops, art galleries and cafés, which, in combination with the natural attractions nearby, make it well worth a day or so of exploration. Aside from visiting the magnificent Dangar Falls, 2km north along Hickory Street, there isn't much to do in town, but Dorrigo is the gateway to the **Dorrigo National Park**. This protected area contains a beautiful remnant of World Heritage-listed rainforest in a region that was once intensively logged for its valuable stocks of Australian cedar.

The Rainforest Centre

2km east of town on Dome Rd • Daily 9am–4.30pm • $2 donation • ☎ 02 6657 2309

The **Rainforest Centre** is a wonderful facility with interpretive displays on flora and fauna, a café and walking-trail maps. Right behind the centre is the 200m boarded **Skywalk**, which offers spectacular views from canopy level. Several **trails** start nearby, ranging from the 600m Satinbird Stroll up to the Wonga Walk (6.6km return), which winds through the rainforest and underneath the Crystal Shower and Tristania Falls. It's cool, misty and slightly eerie down on the forest floor, and easy to believe you're kilometres from anywhere as huge trees and vines soar overhead. All the walks starting behind the centre are open from 5am to 10pm daily, so visitors can observe the forest's nocturnal creatures.

ARRIVAL AND INFORMATION
DORRIGO

By car To reach Dorrigo you really need your own transport, as buses from Coffs Harbour generally only run once a week. **Tourist information** The visitor centre (daily 10am–4pm; ☎ 02 6657 2486) at 36 Hickory St can advise

you on the many farmstays in the area.
Festivals The Dorrigo Folk and Bluegrass Festival (ⓦ dorrigofolkbluegrass.com.au) is held in late Oct each year.

ACCOMMODATION AND EATING

Canopy Café Dome Rd ☎ 02 6657 1541, ⓦ canopycafedorrigo. An ecofriendly café with forest views. Pop in for a delicious breakfast, lunch or snack; expect dishes like king prawn coconut *laksa* on rice vermicelli ($19) or grilled barramundi fillet ($21). Daily 9am–4.30pm.

Mossgrove B&B 589 Old Coast Rd ☎ 02 6657 5388, ⓦ mossgrove.com.au. An elegant Federation-style guesthouse set on two acres of manicured gardens and offering two spacious rooms. Guests have the use of a pleasant sitting room. Breakfast included. **$225**

Coffs Harbour

COFFS HARBOUR – or "Coffs" – is beautifully set at a point where the mountains of the Great Dividing Range fall into the South Pacific Ocean, and boasts glorious expanses of white sand to the north. The town itself is far less pretty but a lot of fun, with tons of outdoor activities, such as the charming creek walk and cycle trail that begins on Coffs Street and winds its way down the creek's southern bank to the sea. Coffs' major shops and services can be found in the CBD and mall, clustered around the western end of Harbour Drive and Grafton Street, while a little further on is The Promenade, a breezy boutique shopping centre on Harbour Drive. It is the boat-filled marina, however, with its adjacent Jetty Beach and historic pier, that is the nicest part of Coffs, and the perfect place for a pre-dinner sunset stroll.

Offshore, the **Solitary Islands** are notable for diving, fringed with coral reefs and home to a plethora of fish, while migrating whales pass by between late May and late November.

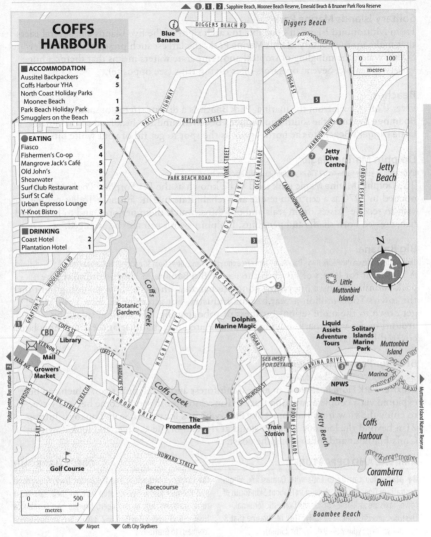

2

Botanic Gardens

Hardacre St • Daily 9am–5pm • Donation • W ncrbg.com.au

Delightfully tranquil, the subtropical **Botanic Gardens** feature a range of native and exotic flora. There's a mangrove boardwalk to explore, as well as a sensory garden with roses, camellia hedge and information about the culinary and medicinal properties of the herbs on display.

Muttonbird Island Nature Reserve

Sunrise–sunset • Free

A fifteen-minute walk from the marina, **Muttonbird Island Nature Reserve** offers fantastic views back over Coffs Harbour, its beaches and the Great Dividing Ranges beyond. Thousands of wedge-tailed shearwaters, or muttonbirds, travel to the island from Southeast Asia each year to breed (Aug–April).

2

Solitary Islands Marine Park

From Muttonbird Island, it's possible to catch sight of the five islands and several islets that make up the **Solitary Islands Marine Park**, the largest such preserved area in New South Wales; the mingling of tropical and temperate waters means that there's a huge variety of sea life. Several operators offer diving trips (see opposite).

Beaches

Over Coffs Creek from the marina, **Park Beach** is a decent stretch of sand, as is **Boambee Beach** to the south and **Digger's Beach** around the headland to the north. **Little Digger's Beach**, to the north again, is the spot to get rid of your white bits.

Dolphin Marine Magic

65 Orlando St • Daily 9am–4pm • $36 • ⓦ dolphinmarinemagic.com.au

The **Dolphin Marine Magic** park used to be known as the Pet Porpoise Pool, and was opened in 1970 as a centre to rescue and rehabilitate marine animals. Today, people visit to receive "kisses" from seals and dolphins, watch them perform, and to hand-feed fish, crested horn sharks and penguins. Dolphin swims can also be arranged.

Big Banana

3km north of Coffs on the Pacific Hwy • Daily 9am–5pm • Free entry; rides and shows from $6 each • ⓦ bigbanana.com

A highlight for lovers of kitsch is the iconic **Big Banana**, a "horticultural theme park" dominated by a big yellow concrete banana. There's a show shedding light on the town's $600-million-a-year banana industry, but after you've seen it you can get down to the more serious business of tobogganing, ice-skating, splashing around in the water park, buying banana-related merchandise and eating chocolate-covered bananas.

Bruxner Park Flora Reserve

5km northwest of Coffs • Daily 8am–dusk • Free

Bruxner Park Flora Reserve is an area of rainforest and eucalyptus trees, which can be explored via a couple of walking tracks. The reason most people come here, however, is to enjoy the view from the **Forest Sky Pier**, which is located at Sealy Lookout. Jutting 21m beyond the lookout, you can stand at the end of the sky pier and look down on Coffs Harbour and south along the coast.

ARRIVAL AND DEPARTURE

COFFS HARBOUR

By plane You can fly to Coffs with QantasLink, Virgin Australia or Tiger Airways; the airport is about 5km south of town. Taxis are available outside the Domestic Terminal.
Destinations Brisbane (1–2 daily; 1hr); Melbourne (Sat & Sun daily; 2hr); Sydney (4–9 daily; 1hr 25min).
By train The train station is by the harbour. NSW TrainLink runs services daily from Sydney and Brisbane to Coffs.
Destinations Brisbane (daily; 5hr); Sydney (3 daily; 8hr 50min).
By bus All long-distance buses stop at the bus station on

the corner of McLean St and the Pacific Hwy; Greyhound and Premier Motor Service stop here on their east-coast runs; Busways run to Bellingen, Urunga and Nambucca Heads; and Ryan's (☎ 02 6652 3201, ⓦ ryansbusservice .com.au) to Grafton.
Destinations Bellingen (Mon–Fri 4–5 daily, Sun daily; 1hr); Byron Bay (8 daily; 3hr 50min); Dorrigo (3 weekly; 1hr 10min); Grafton (8–12 daily; 1hr 10min); Nambucca Heads (6–1 daily; 1hr); Port Macquarie (6–7 daily; 2hr 40min); Urunga (6–1 daily; 40min).

GETTING AROUND

By bus Coffs is rather spread out, and if you haven't rented a car you'll have to use either taxis or the Busways bus that runs between the town centre, Coffs Jetty and Park Beach. The three distinct areas of interest in town are the CBD and mall; the jetty, around 2km to the east; and Sapphire, Moonee and Emerald beaches 10–20km to

the north – Ryan's (see above) run buses to all three (Mon–Fri 8 daily, Sat 2 daily).
By car For car rental try Europcar ☎ 02 6658 9009, Hertz ☎ 02 6651 1899 or Thrifty ☎ 02 6652 8622.
By taxi Call Coffs Harbour Taxis ☎ 13 10 08.

INFORMATION

Tourist information The visitor information centre (daily 9am–5pm; ☎02 6648 4990 or ☎1300 369 070, ⓦcoffscoast.com.au) is located at the Big Banana on the Pacific Hwy (see opposite).

Market There's a growers' market on Thursdays (8am–3.30pm) at City Square. It's a good place to stock up on fresh produce and buy a tasty lunch from one of the stands.

Services The hospital is at 345 Pacific Hwy (☎02 6656 7000) and police at 2 Beryl St (☎02 6691 0799). There are three post office branches in Coffs: Park Beach Shopping Centre, The Palms Centre and at 354 Harbour Drive.

ACTIVITIES

Canoeing *Mangrove Jack's Café*, 321 Harbour Drive (☎02 6652 5517, ⓦmangrovejackscafe.com.au; see below), rents out canoes ($30/hr), kayaks (single $15/hr) and paddleboards ($20/hr).

Cruises Pacific Explorer (☎0422 210 338, ⓦpacificexplorer.com.au) offers whale-watching trips, 3hr cruises in search of dolphins, and snorkelling excursions.

Diving Jetty Dive Centre, 398 Harbour Drive(☎02 6651 1611, ⓦjettydive.com.au), offers a range of PADI courses and trips (including to the Solitary Islands). Snorkelling and whale-watching also available.

Horseriding Valery Trails, 758 Valery Rd, 20km southwest of Coffs off the Pacific Hwy at Bonville (☎02 6653 4301, ⓦvalerytrails.com.au), run twice-daily, 2hr excursions

($65). Other options include a breakfast ride, BBQ ride or a two-day trip overnighting at the pub in Bellingen.

Skydiving Coffs City Skydivers, 64 Aviation Drive (☎02 6651 1167, ⓦcoffsskydivers.com.au), offer tandem skydives for $269.

Surfing There are about six surf schools operating in the area, including East Coast Surf School, Digger's Beach (☎0412 257 233, ⓦeastcoastsurfschool.com.au), which runs introductory lessons (2hr 30min; $55) and five-lesson courses ($200).

Watersports Liquid Assets Adventure Tours, 38 Marina Drive (☎02 6658 0850, ⓦsurfrafting.com), offer sea- and river-kayaking, surf rafting (all $50/half-day) and trips inland to go whitewater rafting on the Goolang ($80/half-day) or Nymboida ($185/day) rivers.

ACCOMMODATION

Aussitel Backpackers 312 Harbour Drive ☎02 6651 1871 or ☎1800 330 335, ⓦaussitel.com. Hugely friendly and popular hostel with good facilities and helpful management; there's also a heated pool, lots of free activities, bikes to rent and sports gear to borrow. Dorms __$27__, doubles __$65__

Coffs Harbour YHA 51 Collingwood St ☎02 6652 6462, ⓦyha.com.au. This large hostel has good facilities and very helpful staff who can sign you up for an avalanche of activities. Bikes are available to rent ($5), and there's a pleasant pool area. Doubles are motel style, with en suite and TV. Dorms __$25__, doubles __$72__

North Coast Holiday Parks Moonee Beach Moonee Beach Rd, Moonee Beach, 12km north, off the Pacific Hwy ☎02 6653 6552 or ☎1800 184 120, ⓦnorthcoastholidayparks.com.au. A magical camping

spot in bush surroundings, with coastal wilderness to explore. Guests have the use of a camp kitchen, a good BBQ spot, tennis courts and laundry. Un/powered sites __$28/36__, cabins __$95__

Park Beach Holiday Park 1 Ocean Parade, Coffs Harbour ☎02 6648 4888, ⓦcoffscoastholidayparks.com.au. Large well-ordered caravan and camping ground in a good spot across the road from the beach, with BBQ, pool, tennis court, playground and a camp kitchen. Un/powered sites __$35/41__, cabins __$89__

Smugglers on the Beach 36 Sandy Beach Rd ☎02 6653 6166, ⓦsmugglers.com.au. These comfortable, fully self-contained apartments are set in a pleasant garden, right on the beach. Some have ocean views. There's also a heated pool, tennis racquets and bodyboards to borrow. __$225__

EATING

CAFÉS AND RESTAURANTS

★**Fiasco** 22 Orlando St ☎02 6651 2006, ⓦfiascorestaurant.com.au. Hip, noisy *ristorante* delivering delicious traditional Italian food, including wonderful pizza from the wood-fired oven ($18–27) and pasta dishes such as squid ink spaghetti with mussels, garlic and chilli ($32). Tues–Sat 5–11pm.

Fishermen's Co-op The Marina. First-class takeaway attached to a superb fishmonger, where you can stock up on fish and seafood fresh from the boat. Eat your hoki and chips or salt and pepper squid and chips ($10) here, or take

your meal over to the tables overlooking the fishing fleet. Daily 9am–6pm.

Mangrove Jack's Café The Promenade, 321 Harbour Dr ☎02 6652 5517, ⓦmangrovejackscafe.com.au. Tuck into filling food such as black mussels in a chilli tomato sauce ($18) or fish of the day ($32), served up in simple surrounds with fine creek views. Mon–Thurs & Sun 7.30am–3pm, Fri & Sat 7.30am–3pm & 5–9.15pm.

Old John's 360 Harbour Drive ☎02 6699 2909. This cool, friendly café has mismatched furniture, a wooden spaceship in the window and good coffee. There are nice touches like fresh flowers on the tables, and the food doesn't disappoint. Try the ginger-spiced chicken wings ($6) or Mexican sliders. Has a good range of craft beers and cocktails. Mon & Tues–Sun 7am–4pm, Wed–Sat also 5pm–11am.

Shearwater Restaurant & Café The Promende, 321 Harbour Drive ☎02 6651 6053, ⓦshearwater restaurant.com.au. Grab a sheltered veranda table overlooking Coffs Creek and try the ricotta hot cakes with spiced dates, lemon curd and mascarpone ($13.50) for breakfast or the Thai Chicken salad ($19.90) for lunch. Dinner features heavier meat and seafood dishes ($30–34 mains). Mon–Sat 8am–3pm & 6–9pm, Sun 8am–10pm.

Surf Club Restaurant & Bar 23 Surf Club Rd ☎02 6652 9870, ⓦsurfclubparkbeach.com. A cavernous canteen-style dining room, attached to the local surf club, which serves well-priced unpretentious fare, and amazingly cheap drinks. The menu includes salt and pepper calamari ($24) and excellent fish and chips ($19), and there are also plenty of non-seafood options available.

Daily 7am–2.30pm.

Surf St Cafe 104 Fiddaman Rd, Emerald Beach, 20km north of Coffs Harbour ☎02 6656 1888, ⓦsurfstreet .com.au. This sophisticated all-day place is one of the north coast's few truly beachside restaurants. The seasonal lunch menu may include Szechuan-spiced squid ($15) and Cuban pork *bocadillo* ($18). Wed & Sun 8am–4pm, Thurs–Sat 8am–10pm.

Urban Espresso Lounge 384A Harbour Drive ☎02 6651 1989, ⓦurbanespressolounge.com.au. Popular coffee lounge, serving healthy yet still filling breakfasts and lunches – a magnet for local workers. The lunch menu includes burgers ($15.50), salads ($16.50) and gourmet sandwiches ($14.50). Daily 7am–3.30pm.

YKnot Bistro Coffs Harbour Yacht Club, 30 Marina Drive ☎02 6651 1741, ⓦyknotbistro.com.au. With unbeatable sea views and friendly, professional service, Coffs Harbour Yacht Club is a welcoming spot for drinks and tasty bistro meals such as beer-battered fish and chips ($21.90) and 250g eye fillet ($36.90). Daily 7am–9pm.

DRINKING

Coast Hotel 2 Moonee St ☎02 6652 3007, ⓦcoasthotel .com.au. A lively pub with a good atmosphere and an attractive outdoor seating area that's best appreciated on a Sun afternoon. Live music at weekends and events most nights; they also do $10 lunch specials. Mon–Sat 10am–midnight, Sun 11am–midnight.

Plantation Hotel 88 Grafton St ☎02 6652 3855,

ⓦplantationhotel.com.au. Serves large portions of decent food at reasonable prices, such as pasta bolognaise ($15.90) and seafood basket ($18.90). This pub attracts a young crowd at weekends with its club nights. The backpacker accommodation is popular with seasonal workers (dorms $30, doubles $70). Discounted cocktails served on Fri and Sat evenings. Daily 10am–late.

Grafton

GRAFTON, north of Coffs Harbour, is a pleasant country town on a bend of the wide **Clarence River**, which almost encircles the city. It's a genteel, old-fashioned place with wide, tree-lined avenues; Victoria and Fitzroy streets are lined with pretty, Federation-style houses, while the main commercial strip is Prince Street. The week-long **Jacaranda Festival** (see opposite) celebrates the town's jacaranda and flame trees, which come ablaze with mauve, maroon and white blossoms in the spring. Out of festival time this is a tranquil place, where the main attraction is visiting some of the historic buildings preserved by the National Trust. **Schaeffer House**, at 190 Fitzroy Street (Tues–Thurs & Sun 1–4pm; $5), dating to 1900, has a collection of beautiful china, glassware and period furniture. On the same street at no. 158 is the **Grafton Regional Gallery** (Tues–Sun 10am–4pm; free; ⓦgraftongallery.nsw.gov.au), which has some fine temporary exhibitions and local artwork.

ARRIVAL AND DEPARTURE GRAFTON

By train NSW TrainLink train services along the north coast stop at Grafton station, close to the river crossing in South Grafton. It's a half-hour walk into the town proper, across a fine, split-level road-and-rail bridge, or Busways operate regular buses between the town and South Grafton. Destinations Coffs Harbour (3 daily; 1hr 10min); Sydney (3 daily; 10hr 10min).

By bus Long-distance buses stop near the visitor centre, and Grafton is on the main Sydney–Brisbane Greyhound and Premier Motor Service routes. Ryan's also run to Coffs Harbour.
Destinations Byron Bay (4 daily; 3hr); Coffs Harbour (4–8 daily; 1hr 15min); Port Macquarie (daily; 3hr 15min); Sydney (4 daily; 9hr 10min).

INFORMATION

Tourist information The Clarence River Visitor Information Centre (daily 9am–5pm; ☎02 6643 0800, ⓦclarencetourism.com) can be found on the Pacific Hwy at the corner of Spring St in South Grafton. The staff here can give you information on scenic drives, national parks and other activities, and there's a great deal of information on the surrounding area.

Festival The Jacaranda Festival (late Oct to early Nov; ⓦjacarandafestival.org.au) dates back to 1934 and is a community affair with a Jacaranda Ball and a Jacaranda Queen, as well as a number of events such as the open garden competition.

ACCOMMODATION AND EATING

Crown Hotel Motel 1 Prince St ☎02 6642 4000, ⓦcrownhotelmotel.com. Overlooking the river, choose from pub rooms (some with en suites) or motel-style units in a separate building. Of the motel rooms, those with a river view are best. **$85**

Gateway Lifestyle Grafton 598 Summerland Way ☎02 6642 4225, ⓦthegatewayvillage.com.au. A large, well-ordered caravan park, and the best one in town by a long way. Options include camping sites, villas and motel units,

and facilities include BBQs, a tennis court and a kitchen area. Un/powered sites **$20/$25**, cabins **$95**, doubles **$110**

Roches Family Hotel 85 Victoria St ☎02 6642 2866, ⓦroches.com.au. One of Grafton's oldest pubs, *Roches* serves pub staples and daily specials that can be enjoyed in the public bar, restaurant or courtyard. Don't miss T-Bone Tuesday when you can grab a steak, chips and a salad for $13. There are also very good-value pub rooms. Mon–Sat 11.30am–2pm & 6–8.30pm, Sun 11.30am–2pm. **$55**

Yamba and Iluka

The twin settlements of **YAMBA** and **ILUKA** are two pretty holiday villages facing each other across the mouth of the Clarence River. Iluka is famous for its fishing, and Iluka Bluff Beach is recommended for swimming, while Yamba is a holiday resort popular with families and retirees, and boasts postcard-perfect scenery, superlative surfing and a laidback vibe.

A few kilometres south of Yamba is **Yuraygir National Park**, which has plenty of basic but attractive camping and a spectacular strip of sand at Angourie Point, which became New South Wales's first **surfing reserve** in 2007.

ARRIVAL AND INFORMATION

YAMBA AND ILUKA

By bus Busways run daily services to both settlements from Grafton.

By ferry Clarence River Ferries shuttle between the two communities (foot passengers only; 1–2 daily; $8; ☎02

6646 6423) and also cruise along the river.

Tourist information Clarence Valley Information Centre on the Pacific Hwy at Maclean (☎02 6643 0800) offers advice, maps, brochures, wi-fi and a booking service.

ACCOMMODATION

Anchorage Holiday Park Marandowrie Drive, Iluka ☎02 6646 62010, ⓦanchorageholidaypark.com.au. Just a short distance from town, this caravan park is family friendly and has a heated pool. Note that river-view sites don't actually have views of the river. Powered sites **$45**, cabins **$120**

Calypso Holiday Park Harbour St, Yamba ☎02 6646 8847, ⓦcalypsoyamba.com.au. A thin, pretty, riverfront campsite in the centre of Yamba with a nice pool, BBQ areas and good amenities. Good value. Wi-fi available for a fee. Un/powered sites **$30/$36**, cabins **$92**

Pacific Hotel 18 Pilot St, Yamba ☎02 6646 2466, ⓦpacifichotelyamba.com.au. Staying here is really all about the ocean views. Rooms themselves are clean but fairly basic, and range from those with balconies and en suites, to standard motel rooms and backpacker bunks with shared bathrooms. Some are subject to noise from

the bar. Wi-fi available for a fee. Dorms **$30**, doubles **$90**

Yamba YHA 26 Coldstream St, Yamba ☎02 6646 3397, ⓦyha.com.au. So central you might miss it, this hostel shares the ground floor with a busy café, and offers four- and eight-bed dorms, modern bathrooms, a pool and a lovely rooftop decking area. Can organize surf lessons and a place on Shane's famous "Ten Buck Tour" of Yamba. Dorms **$25**, doubles **$86**

Yuraygir National Park campgrounds ☎02 6441 1500, ⓦenvironment.nsw.gov.au. Plenty of options here for basic camping in beautiful surroundings, including some spots by the beach. Sites are available on a first come, first served basis. Facilities include picnic tables, BBQs and non-flush toilets. Note that a vehicle entrance fee ($8) to the national park still applies. No wi-fi. Unpowered sites per person **$11.50**

EATING

Caperberry Café Cnr Coldstream St and Yamba St ☎ 02 6646 2322. A popular spot for breakfast or lunch, come here for toasties ($9.50), gourmet burgers, summer salads or one of the house specialities, such as a grilled vegetarian halloumi stack ($12.90). Mon–Fri 6am–5pm, Sat 6am–4pm, Sun 6am–3pm.

Pacific Hotel 18 Pilot St, Yamba ☎ 02 6646 2466, ⓦ pacifichotelyamba.com.au. Commanding views over Main Beach and good live music (Thurs–Sun) make this hotel's unpretentious bistro a local favourite. Enjoy panoramic ocean views and dishes such as pork cutlet ($25) and ocean trout with creamy mash, green beans and lemon-caper butter. Mon–Thurs 10am–midnight, Sat 10am–1.30am, Sun 10am–10pm.

Ballina

The old port of **BALLINA**, at the mouth of the Richmond River, is a tranquil holiday town – a **Big Prawn** marks the entrance to town on the highway from Grafton.

On Regatta Avenue, near the visitor centre, the **Maritime Museum**'s (daily 9am–4pm; $5; ⓦ ballinamaritimemuseum.org.au) star exhibit is a raft from the 1973 Las Balsas expedition, in which three vessels set sail from Ecuador with the aim of proving that ancient South American civilizations could have traversed the Pacific. A mere 179 days and 14,400km later the twelve-strong crew arrived in Ballina, sporting some choice facial hair.

The **Northern Rivers Community Gallery** (44 Cherry St; Wed–Fri 10am–4pm, Sat & Sun 9.30am–2.30pm; free) showcases work by local artists in a wide variety of media, and there is also a small shop selling jewellery and other crafts. The biggest draw, however, is the **Gallery Café** (see opposite).

ARRIVAL AND INFORMATION

By plane Virgin Australia, Regional Express and Jetstar all operate domestic flights into Ballina Byron Gateway Airport. The airport is only 5km from Ballina, and a 25min drive from Byron Bay (see opposite).
Destinations Melbourne (2–6 weekly; 2hr 10min); Newcastle (6 weekly; 1hr 20min); Sydney (5 daily; 1hr 25min).

By bus Greyhound and Premier Motor Service connect Ballina to all stops between Sydney and Brisbane; Northern River Buslines (☎ 02 6626 1499, ⓦ nrbuslines.com.au) run to Lismore, while Blanch's (☎ 02 6686 2144, ⓦ blanchs .com.au) operate services to Lennox Head, Bangalow,

Mullumbimby and Byron Bay. Buses arrive and depart from the bus zone on Tamar St.
Destinations Brisbane (4 daily; 3hr 55min–5hr); Byron Bay (3–8 daily; 55min); Lennox Head (3–8 daily; 25min); Lismore (3–9 daily; 1hr); Sydney (4 daily; 12hr 45min).

Tourist information The visitor centre (daily 9am–5pm; ☎ 02 6686 3484, ⓦ discoverballina.com) is in Las Balsas Plaza.

Market Ballina Market takes place on the first and third Sun of the month (7am–1pm) at the East Ballina Lions Club on Canal Rd.

ACTIVITIES

Boat rental Visit Ballina Boat Hire (☎ 04 028 767), at 268 River St, to rent out a tinnie (runabout).
Cruises Richmond River Cruises (2hr; $36; ☎ 0427 699317)

run morning and/or afternoon tea cruises downriver where you can tuck into scones with jam and cream and enjoy the views. The dock is just down from the visitor centre.

ACCOMMODATION

Ballina Manor 25 Norton St ☎ 02 6681 5888, ⓦ ballinamanor.com.au. Ballina's most atmospheric option, this heritage house was once a girls' school and now offers rooms with big brass beds, ceiling fans and lace curtains. Sizes of rooms vary, as do prices. Tours of the house are available for non-residents. Breakfast included. **$294**
Ballina Travellers Lodge Motel 36 Tamar St ☎ 02 6686 6737, ⓦ ballinatravellerslodge.com.au. This former hostel is now a budget motel and it's quiet, neat and the rooms are good value. It also has a small swimming pool and a communal kitchen. There are super-saver rooms available with shared bathrooms. **$145**

Discovery Parks Ballina 25 Fenwick Drive ☎ 02 6686 3953, ⓦ ballinalakeside.com.au. Right next to the lagoon, this is a popular choice with families, offering plenty of facilities including a pool, minigolf and a camp kitchen. For non-campers there is a good choice of spacious modern villas and more basic cabins. Powered sites **$42**, villas **$154**
Flat Rock Tent Park 38 Flat Rock Rd (off Coast Rd, 5km northeast of town) ☎ 02 6686 4848, ⓦ flatrockcamping .com.au. A friendly, tent-only campsite in a great location, right on Angels Beach. Sites are large and well maintained, and there's a kiosk for essentials, plus BBQs, and well-kept amenities. No wi-fi. Unpowered sites **$33**

2

EATING

Ballina Manor 25 Norton St ☎02 6681 5888, ⓦballinamanor.com.au. Very civilized fine dining in an elegant wood-panelled room. Food is old-school regional cooking using the finest local produce, including seafood, grass-fed beef and garden vegetables. The dinner menu includes classic dishes such as slow-roasted pork belly ($36), grilled ocean trout ($35) and pan-seared lamb rack ($34). Daily 7am–9pm.

Gallery Café 44 Cherry St ☎02 6681 3888, ⓦballinagallery.com.au. This welcoming café is part of the community art gallery complex (see opposite), housed in a building that was once the council chambers. Enjoy breakfasts such as blueberry buttermilk pancakes ($16.90) or a lunch of beer-battered barramundi ($23.90) or spanner crab fettuccine ($25.90) among the paintings, or out on the veranda or lawn. Wed–Sun 7.30am–3pm.

2

Lennox Head

LENNOX HEAD, 11km north of Ballina, is a small, relaxed town with a surfie feel and is worth a stop before the madness of Byron Bay. At the southern end of the fabulous Seven-Mile Beach, The Point rates among the best **surfing** spots in the world, and professionals congregate here for the big waves in May, June and July. Adding to Lennox Head's appeal is the calm, fresh water of **Lake Ainsworth**; stained dark by the tea trees around its banks, it's a popular swimming spot for families seeking refuge from the crashing surf in the soft medicinal water (it's effectively diluted tea-tree oil).

ARRIVAL AND DEPARTURE   LENNOX HEAD

By bus Since Lennox Head is off the Pacific Hwy, no long-distance bus services call here; jump on a local service to/from Ballina or Lismore with Northern Rivers Buslines or Blanch's, or catch the Greyhound and Premier Motor

Service buses at Ballina.
Destinations Ballina (3–8 daily; 25min); Byron Bay (3–8 daily; 40min); Lismore (5 weekly; 1hr).

ACCOMMODATION AND EATING

Lennox Beach Resort 7 Park Lane ☎02 6618 0000, ⓦlennoxbeachresort.com.au. A family-friendly beachside getaway offering a range of smart one-, two- and three-bedroom apartments, close to centre of town. Facilities include a heated pool, steam room, BBQ area, jacuzzi, half-court tennis, restaurant and bar. **$179**
Mi Thai 76 Ballina St ☎02 6687 5820, ⓦmithai .com.au. Terrific Thai food with a dynamic and interesting menu. Expect the classics such as pad thai ($19.50) and choo chee curry with king prawns ($25). Look out for the weekly blackboard specials, which might include Indian-style butter chicken ($24.50). Takeaway available. Wed–Sun 5.30–9pm.
North Coast Holiday Parks Lennox Head Cnr Ross St

& Pacific Parade ☎02 6687 7249 or ☎1800 833 792, ⓦnorthcoastholidayparks.com.au. A large but fairly standard holiday park superbly located right by the water and popular with young families, within walking distance from town. The camp kitchen is large and well equipped and amenities blocks are new. Un/powered sites **$33/38**, villas **$175**
Quattro 90–92 Ballina St ☎02 6687 6950, ⓦquattro-restaurant.com. Lively Italian joint serving breakfast, lunch and dinner. Famous for its wood-fired pizzas ($18–26) and breads, Quattro also serves a delicious range of mains, including fresh seafood and dishes such as handmade pumpkin ravioli ($26.40). Takeaway available. Daily 9am–10pm.

Byron Bay and around

Situated at the end of a long, sweeping bay, the vibrant township of **BYRON BAY** boasts 30km of almost unbroken sandy beaches and is high on most travellers' lists. Once a favourite with barefoot hippies, Byron's small-community feel and bohemian atmosphere have been disappearing over the past few years, and it now has stylish hotels, restaurants, lively pubs, chic boutiques and a fascinating mix of subcultures as surfie meets soap starlet meets free spirit.

As you would expect, Byron Bay offers a huge variety of alternative therapies, New Age bookshops, crystals, palmists and tarot readers – all with a good dose of capitalism, as prices are hiked during the lucrative summer months. Expect to see plenty of street performers, artists, surfers and freelance exhibitionists from around the globe.

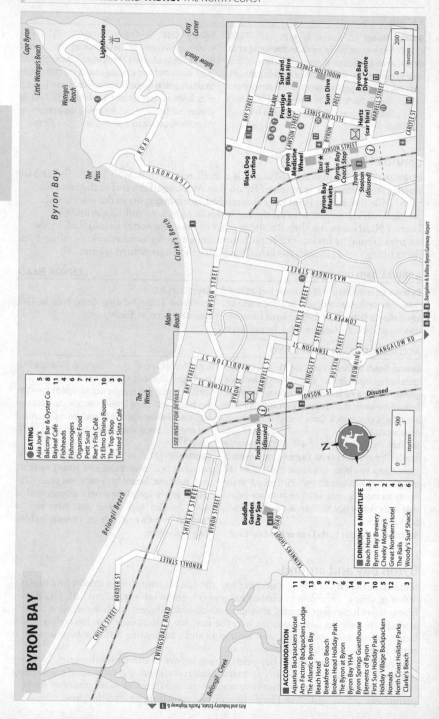

BYRON BAY

Lighthouse

Cape Byron

Little Wategos Beach

Wategos Beach

Byron Bay

The Pass

Clarke's Beach

Cosy Corner

Tallow Beach

LIGHTHOUSE ROAD

The Wreck

Main Beach

Belongil Beach

The Wreck

Belongil Creek

SHIRLEY STREET

BYRON STREET

CHILDE STREET

BORDER ST

EWINGSDALE ROAD

KENDALL STREET

SKINNERS SHOOT

ROAD

LAWSON STREET

MASSINGER STREET

CARLYLE STREET

KINGSLEY STREET

RUSKIN STREET

BROWNING ST

TENNYSON ST

COWPER ST

BAY STREET

MIDDLETON ST

FLETCHER ST

MARVELL ST

BYRON ST

JONSON ST

BANGALOW RD

Buddha Garden Day Spa

Train Station (disused)

Disused

SEE INSET FOR DETAILS

Arts and Industry Estate, Pacific Highway & 1

Bangalow & Ballina Byron Gateway Airport

● **EATING**
Asia Joe's	5
Balcony Bar & Oyster Co	8
Bayleaf Café	11
Fishheads	4
Fishmongers	6
Orgasmic Food	7
Petit Snail	2
Rae's Fish Café	1
St Elmo Dining Room	10
The Top Shop	3
Twisted Sista Café	9

■ **ACCOMMODATION**
Aquarius Backpackers Motel	11
Arts Factory Backpackers Lodge	4
The Atlantic Byron Bay	13
Beach Hotel	9
Breakfree Eco Beach	7
Broken Head Holiday Park	2
The Byron at Byron	6
Byron Bay YHA	14
Byron Springs Guesthouse	8
Elements of Byron	1
First Sun Holiday Park	10
Holiday Village Backpackers	5
Nomads	12
North Coast Holiday Parks	
Clarke's Beach	3

■ **DRINKING & NIGHTLIFE**
Beach Hotel	3
Byron Bay Brewery	1
Cheeky Monkeys	2
Great Northern Hotel	4
The Rails	5
Woody's Surf Shack	6

N

0 — 500 metres

Inset (town centre)

BAY STREET

BAY LANE

LAWSON STREET

MIDDLETON STREET

FLETCHER STREET

BYRON STREET

MARVELL STREET

CARLYLE ST

JONSON STREET

Black Dog Surfing

Byron Medicine Wheel

Surf and Bike Hire

Prestige (car hire)

Sun Dive

Byron Bay Dive Centre

Hertz (car hire)

Taxi rank

Byron Bay Coach Stop

Train Station (disused)

Byron Bay Markets

0 — 200 metres

Cape Byron and the lighthouse
Lighthouse Rd • Daily 9.30am–dusk • $8 for car

If you want to explore, one of the first places to visit is the **lighthouse** on the rocky promontory of **Cape Byron**. The cape is the easternmost point of the Australian mainland and is a popular spot to greet the dawn; with a bit of luck you'll see **dolphins**, which like to sport in the surf off the headland, or **humpback whales**, which pass this way heading north in June or July and again on their return south in September or October.

Most people walk up to the lighthouse (2hr return) and there's a café there if you need a pick-me-up; you can also drive, although parking is limited and you have to pay to enter the main precinct. The lighthouse itself is open, there's a museum on the ground floor and free guided tours of the tower. There are wonderful views from the top.

Beaches
Main Beach in town is as good as any to swim from, and usually has relatively gentle surf. One reason why Byron Bay is so popular with surfers is because its beaches face in all directions, so there's almost always one with a good swell; conversely, you can usually find somewhere for a calmer swim. West of Main Beach, you can always find a spot to yourself on **Belongil Beach**, from where there's sand virtually all the way to **Brunswick Heads**.

To the east, Main Beach curves round towards Cape Byron to become **Clarke's Beach**; The Pass, a famous surfing spot, is at its eastern end and there's a good café there as well. This and neighbouring **Watego's Beach** – beautifully framed between two rocky spurs – face north, and usually have the best surfing. On the far side of the cape, **Tallow Beach** extends towards the **Broken Head Nature Reserve**, 6km south of the town centre at Suffolk Park; there's good surf at Tallow just around the cape at Cosy Corner, and also at Broken Head.

Dive spots
The diversity of marine life in the waters of Byron Bay makes it a prime place to **dive** (see p.234), though these are rock – rather than coral – reefs. Tropical marine life and creatures from warm temperate seas mingle at the granite outcrop of **Julian Rocks Aquatic Reserve**, 3km offshore; by far the most popular spot here is **Cod Hole**, an extensive underwater cave inhabited by large moray eels and other fish. Between April and June is the best time to dive, before the plankton bloom.

Bangalow
Just 14km from Byron Bay is the much quieter town of **Bangalow**, which has an attractive main street crammed with cafés, restaurants, boutiques and antique shops. Come here to escape the bustle of Byron Bay and walk by the river, or pick up a copy of the self-guided heritage walk from the newsagent-cum-visitor-centre and take in the historic buildings, including the **Heritage House Museum** (Wed–Sat 10am–3pm).

ARRIVAL AND DEPARTURE **BYRON BAY AND AROUND**

By plane The closest airport is Ballina Byron Gateway Airport, 39km south (25min drive), served by Jetstar, Virgin Australia and Regional Express. Blanch's (☎ 02 6686 2144, ⓦ blanchs.com.au) run a connecting bus service (3–7 daily; $9.60), and there's a regular shuttle service, the Byron Easy Bus (☎ 02 6685 7447; ⓦ byronbayshuttle.com.au) between the airport and Byron Bay ($40 return). A number of shuttle companies also connect Byron Bay with Brisbane airport and the Gold Coast airport (Coolangatta), such as Airport Express (☎ 02 6685 7447, ⓦ byronbayshuttle.com.au), Brisbane 2 Byron (☎ 1800 626 222, ⓦ brisbane2byron.com) and Xcede (☎ 02 6620 9200, ⓦ byronbay.xcede.com.au).

Destinations Melbourne (2–6 weekly; 2hr 10min); Newcastle (6 weekly; 1hr 20min); Sydney (5 daily; 1hr 25min). **By bus** Byron Bay's campaign to get its railway line reopened has yet to succeed; instead, a NSW TrainLink bus service runs here from a large number of east-coast destinations. Greyhound and Premier Motor Service also stop in town on east-coast runs, and drop you at the bus stop on Jonson St. Local bus services include Northern River Buslines, which run to Bangalow, Lismore, Brunswick Heads, Lennox Head and Ballina; and Blanch's, which call at Ballina, Lennox Head and Mullumbimby.

2

Destinations Ballina (13–22 daily; 40min); Brisbane (9 daily; 2hr 30min); Brunswick Heads (10–13 daily; 15min); Buladelah (6 daily; 9hr 20min); Coffs Harbour (8 daily; 4hr); Forster (daily; 8hr 45min); Grafton (8 daily; 3hr); Karuah (7 daily; 9hr 45min); Lennox Head (8–12 daily; 25min); Lismore (6–10 daily; 2hr 5min); Maclean (5 daily; 2hr 15min); Murwillumbah (5 daily; 55min); Nambucca Heads (6 daily; 3hr 30min); Port Macquarie (5 daily; 8hr); Surfers Paradise (9 daily; 1hr 20min); Sydney (4 daily; 14hr 15min); Tweed Heads (4–5 daily; 1hr 20min); Urunga (6 daily; 3hr 20min).

GETTING AROUND

By car Car rental companies include Hertz, 5 Marvel St (☏ 02 6680 7925), and Prestige Car Hire 3/13 Lawson St (☏ 0431 288 973, ⊕ byronprestigecarhire.com.au).

By taxi Byron Bay Taxis ☏ 02 6685 5008. There's a taxi rank on Jonson St at weekends, opposite the *Great Northern Hotel*.

INFORMATION

Tourist information The visitor information centre (daily 9am–5pm; ☏ 02 6680 8558, ⊕ visitbyronbay.com) is in the old Stationmaster's Cottage at 80 Jonson St, near the bus stop. There is a plethora of other "information centres" along Jonson St that are really private travel agencies selling adventure tours.

Festivals Many of Byron Bay's festivals and events are held in venues in the hinterland. There's plenty of activity in summer: New Year's Eve is such a big event that the council has taken to closing the town off, so come early. Byron's music festivals also always draw huge crowds and the main ones are Bluesfest (⊕ bluesfest.com.au) at Tyagarah Tea Tree Farm, outside town, over Easter, and Splendour in the Grass (⊕ splendourinthegrass.com), usually held in June/July. The Byron Bay Writers' Festival (⊕ byronbaywritersfestival .com.au) is held annually around the beginning of August; check the website for exact dates and details of readings, workshops and film screenings.

ACTIVITIES

Alternative therapies Notice boards around town advertise hundreds of conventional and slightly wackier therapies. Found in the Byron Bay Brewery complex, Buddha Gardens Day Spa (1 Skinners Shoot Rd; ☏ 02 6680 7844, ⊕ buddhagardendayspa.com.au) offers some good old-fashioned pampering, with massages, body wraps and facials, as well as a host of other packages. At the other end of the spectrum, Byron Medicine Wheel (84 Jonson St; ☏ 02 6685 8366, ⊕ byronmedicinewheel.com.au) is very New Age, and offers a wide range of treatments from massage and reflexology to tarot readings, crystal healing and empathic communication.

Ballooning Watch the sun rise over the hinterland on a Byron Bay Ballooning trip (☏ 1300 889 660, ⊕ byronbayballooning.com.au; $350 for an hour, includes champagne breakfast).

Circus School Circus Arts (☏ 02 6685 6566, ⊕ circusarts .com.au) will have you swinging from the chandeliers and generally clowning about in no time. Trapeze workshops (1hr 30min) cost $66.

Cycling Most hostels have bikes that can either be used free or rented by guests; otherwise try Surf & Bike Hire Byron Bay (☏ 02 6680 7066, ⊕ byronbaysurfandbikehire .com.au) on Lawson St. Mountain Bike Tours (☏ 0429 122 504, ⊕ mountainbiketours.com.au) offer tours through the rainforest that will satisfy both the casual cyclist and the rabid downhiller, full-day tours in the Nightcap National Parks ($99), or shorter coastal runs.

Diving Sundive, next door to *Cape Byron YHA* on Byron St (☏ 02 6685 7755, ⊕ sundive.com.au), and Byron Bay Dive Centre at 9 Marvell St (☏ 02 6685 8333, ⊕ byronbaydivecentre .com.au) both offer Open Water courses ($560) and run dives at Julian Rocks for qualified divers.

Hang-gliding Byron Airwaves Hang Gliding School (☏ 02 6629 0354, ⊕ byronair.com) offers 30min tandem flights for $145.

Kayaking Paddle into the bay with Cape Byron Kayaks (☏ 02 6680 9555, ⊕ capebyronkayaks.com) to watch wild dolphins and turtles with expert guides, then recharge your batteries with drinks and snacks on the beach (3hr; $69).

Skydiving Skydive Byron Bay (☏ 1300 663 634, ⊕ skydive.com.au) offer Australia's highest tandem jump (14,000ft) at several locations on the east coast, including Byron Bay ($334).

Surfing Black Dog Surfing, 11 Byron St (☏ 02 6680 9828, ⊕ blackdogsurfing.com), are the best of many outlets offering gear rental and lessons; they aim to get you to stand up on your first lesson, a bold claim worth testing out. Intro lessons start at $60. If you really want to learn to surf, Surfari (☏ 02 6566 0009, ⊕ surfaris.com) offer a great way of doing it. For $650 you'll spend five days living with gnarly wave-riders who'll chuck you in the water every day until you get it.

Wildlife tours Vision Walks (☏ 0405 275 743, ⊕ visionwalks.com) lead a number of small group tours into the scenic hinterland around Byron Bay, introducing visitors to a pristine environment sacred to the Bundjalung people. Choose from its Wildlife Tour, Rainforest Walk, Yowie Tour or Night Vision Walk during which night-vision goggles are strapped to your head – a unique way to observe nocturnal wildlife ($125).

ACCOMMODATION

During school holidays, in December and January especially, demand for accommodation far exceeds supply, and it's essential to book well in advance – think months or weeks for hostels, months ahead for hotels and apartments, and a year ahead for caravan parks. The **backpackers'** in Byron Bay are among Australia's liveliest, but prices and stress levels rise dramatically in summer due to overcrowding. **Holiday apartments** (booked through the visitor centre, estate agents in town and Airbnb) are a great-value option, especially for groups. The list below is just a small selection; for more options contact the dedicated accommodation desk at the visitor centre (daily 9am–5pm; ☎02 6680 8558, ⓦbyronbayaccom .net), and if everything's full, try **Brunswick Heads**, about 18km further up the coast, **Lennox Head** about 12km south (see p.231), or **Bangalow**.

MOTELS, HOTELS, GUESTHOUSES AND APARTMENTS

The Atlantic Byron Bay 13 Marvell St ☎02 6685 5118, ⓦatlanticbyronbay.com.au. A slice of the 70s Aussie seaside comes to rest on a quiet suburban street. This tropical oasis is a retreat for grown-up hipsters, complete with fire pit, lap pool and communal kitchen. Rooms are comfy, white and uncluttered. __$350__

Beach Hotel Bay St ☎02 6685 6402, ⓦbeachotel .com.au. Byron's famous waterfront pub, directly opposite the beach, has spacious rooms and suites set around a lush garden and pool. Things are beginning to look a little dated though, but this place is really all about location. __$480__

Breakfree Eco Beach 35–37 Shirley St ☎132 007, ⓦbreakfree.com.au. Clean, stylish contemporary motel free of the dreadful interior design tendencies that usually bedevil this type of place. There's a tiny but pristine pool, a garden and BBQ area. Book a room at the back away from the road. No wi-fi. __$168__

The Byron at Byron 77–97 Brokenhead Rd ☎02 6639 2000, ⓦthebyronatbyron.com.au. Stunningly set amid 45 acres of rainforest and landscaped garden, this stylish resort is Byron's most exclusive, with yoga each day, spa treatments on offer, and a restaurant and bar. __$440__

Byron Springs Guesthouse 2 Oodgeroo Gardens, cnr of Mahogany Drive ☎02 6680 8101, ⓦbyronspringsguesthouse.com. This lovely, light and airy guesthouse, set amid tropical gardens, offers very tasteful rooms; the shared bathroom options are ideal for budget travellers who are over the backpacker scene. Shared kitchen and living area. Generous breakfast included. __$175__

Elements of Byron 144 Bayshore Dr ☎2 6639 1500, ⓦelementsofbyron.com.au. Glam beach resort, a 10min drive north of Byron, set on 50 acres of land fronting a pristine, and usually empty, beach. The property offers eco-friendly studios and villas, a luxurious spa, lagoon pool, restaurant and sexy bar. Rates includes Continental breakfast and a yoga class. __$355__

HOSTELS

Aquarius Backpackers Motel 16 Lawson St ☎1800 029 909, ⓦaquarius-backpackers.com.au. Excellent hostel boasting split-level en-suite dorms (eight- to ten-bed, and a female-only option) with fridge, motel-style doubles and some cute apartments for couples. There's also a pool, a bar with a daily happy hour and a café serving good-value meals. Dorms __$28__, doubles __$60__, apartments __$180__

Arts Factory Backpackers Lodge 1 Skinners Shoot Rd ☎02 6685 7709, ⓦbyron-bay.com/artsfactory. In a bushland setting with a hippy atmosphere, this is a love-it-or-hate-it kind of place, and the sheer number of backpackers wanting to stay here means it can be a bit of a scrum. There's a huge array of "funky abodes", including tents, tepees and "love shacks" as well as standard dorms, plus plenty of activities like didgeridoo-making and a reasonably priced café. Dorms __$28__, doubles __$80__

Byron Bay YHA 7 Carlyle St ☎02 6685 8853, ⓦyha .com.au. Central but peaceful option with friendly, professional staff, above-average communal areas and a decent pool. An excellent choice if you're not that into Byron's party-hostel scene. Bikes for rent, too. Dorms __$27__, doubles __$90__

Holiday Village Backpackers 116 Jonson St ☎02 6685 8888, ⓦbyronbackpackers.com.au. Opposite *Cheeky Monkeys* (see p.237) so a popular backpacker choice, this is a friendly, social hostel. There are standard dorms as well as some doubles in apartments, plus a small pool area, free use of bikes and surfboards, and free wi-fi in the lounge. Dorms __$23__, doubles __$60__

Nomads Lawson Lane ☎02 6680 7966 or ☎1800 666 237, ⓦnomadsworld.com. Very central hostel with bags of offbeat style and an up-for-it attitude, which attracts a young crowd. There's a travel desk, communal kitchen, cinema and a jacuzzi; be warned, however, that they put their prices up for the Christmas season earlier than the other hostels. Wi-fi available for a fee. Dorms __$39__, doubles __$165__

CAMPSITES

Broken Head Holiday Park 184 Beach Rd, Broken Head, 6km south ☎02 6685 3245, ⓦbrokenheadholidaypark .com.au. The best of the bay's holiday parks but a distance from Byron Bay, this site has good facilities and gentle, wooded inclines that afford great sea views over Tallow Beach. Un/powered sites __$31/$38__, cabins __$96__

First Sun Holiday Park Lawson St ☎02 6685 6544, ⓦfirstsunholidaypark.com.au. Excellent central location on Main Beach with superb facilities, including two camp kitchens you'd be happy to have at home, BBQs, kiosk and modern shower blocks. Bikes and board rental can be

arranged. Un/powered sites $60/80, cabins $200
North Coast Holiday Parks Clarke's Beach 1 Lighthouse Rd ☎ 02 6685 6496, ⓦ northcoastholidayparks.com.au/ park/info/clarkes-beach. Pleasant wooded site with

standard, though modern, amenities but in a fantastic setting right on Clarke's Beach – and only a short walk to town. Un/powered sites $48/56, cabins $240

EATING

CAFÉS AND TAKEAWAYS

Asia Joe's 4 Bay Lane ☎ 02 6680 8787, ⓦ asiajoes.com. Popular joint with tiny tables, cooking up tasty, pan-Asian stir-fries and noodle dishes at fair prices, such as *nasi goreng* ($10.30), green chicken curry ($11.30) and Malaysian satay stir-fry ($10.30). There's a $5 beer or glass of wine with every meal. Takeaway available. Daily noon–3pm & 5.30–10pm.

Bayleaf Café 2 Marvell St ☎ 02 6685 8900. Busy little spot with casual perches at which to enjoy warm organic porridge ($10.50) and stewed spiced rhubarb ($9.50) for breakfast or leafy sandwiches and salads for lunch, plus there's great coffee. Catches the morning sun. Daily 6.30am–5pm.

Fishheads 1 Jonson St ☎ 02 6680 7632, ⓦ restaurantbyronbay.com.au. Right by Main Beach, sit on the deck and tuck into a mixed seafood grill ($38), prawn and calamari linguine ($30) or good old fish and chips, complemented by a compact list of wine and beers. Takeaway available. Daily 7.30am–11.30pm.

Fishmongers 1/9 Bay Lane ☎ 0412 059 771. Locals and visitors alike love this stylish little fish-and-chip place for its freshly shucked Sydney Rock oysters, marinated and chargrilled octopus, and tempura battered fish with hand-cut chips ($15.50). If you're feeling healthy you can order grilled fish with rice or salad. Daily noon–10.30pm.

Orgasmic Food 11 Bay Lane ☎ 02 6680 7778. A popular Middle Eastern café with wooden chairs and tables, best known for its falafel in pitta ($7.50) but you can also share a Mediterranean platter of dips, salad, pitta and falafel ($41, for 2–3 people). Daily 11am–9pm.

The Top Shop 65 Carlyle St ☎ 02 6685 6495. A friendly, bright spot with upbeat music and a steady stream of regulars. There are pastries, cakes and sandwiches in a glass cabinet, and small breakfast (breakfast burger $13) and lunch (steak sandwich $14) menus on the blackboard. Also sells freshly baked sourdough on Tues, Thurs and Sat. Daily 6.30am–4pm.

Twisted Sista Café 4 Lawson St ☎ 02 6685 6810. A funky pavement café serving fairly wholesome breakfast

and lunch options, such as an open chicken wrap ($14.95), plus some wickedly indulgent cakes, milkshakes and desserts. Look for the salted caramel popcorn ($12.95). Daily 7am–5pm.

RESTAURANTS

★**Balcony Bar & Oyster Co** Lawson St ☎ 02 6680 9666, ⓦ balcony.com.au. An early-evening cocktail on the balcony of this Byron Bay institution is a relaxing way to kick off your night. Delicious food is served at breakfast (weekends only), lunch and dinner, when the style is New York Grill meets Spain under the direction of UK-born chef Sean Connolly. The small menu includes a range of tapas dishes and posh mains such as beef and lamb ragout ($28) and crispy-skinned ocean trout ($32). There's a limited menu available 3–6pm. Mon–Fri 11.30am–9.30pm, Sat & Sun 9am–9.30pm.

Petit Snail 5 Carlyle St ☎ 02 6685 8526, ⓦ thepetitsnail.com.au. A small, friendly French restaurant where you'll be served dishes such as snails in garlic butter ($18) and Charolais tenderloin steak in red-wine sauce ($45) by French staff. Finish with the macarons or crêpes suzette, or a selection of French cheeses. Also offers cooking classes. Booking are essential. Wed–Sat 6.30–10pm.

Rae's Fish Café Watego's Beach ☎ 02 6685 5366, ⓦ raes.com.au. The romantic atmosphere is reason enough to book a table at this superb restaurant, but head chef Guy Skinner-Hutchison's artful cuisine is another (such as spanner crab linguine, $38, and Moreton Bay bug ravioli, $45). Opening hours are shorter during low season; ring to check. Daily noon–11.30pm.

St Elmo Dining Room & Bar Cnr Fletcher St and Lawson Lane ☎ 02 6680 7426, ⓦ stelmodining.com. A dark and moody space serving modern, surprisingly good, Spanish tapas (*jamón serrano* $13.50), or more substantial dishes such as saffron and garlic fish stew ($33) and slow-cooked brisket ($29.50). Also has a good wine and sherry list. Mon–Sat 4pm–midnight, Sun 4–10pm.

DRINKING AND NIGHTLIFE

Byron's **nightlife** caters to all tastes, from quiet cocktails in the early evening to some of the best **live music** around and partying backpacker-style into the early hours. Check out Tuesday's *Byron Shire Echo* for gig guides. Some places may have shorter opening hours in the low season.

Beach Hotel Cnr Jonson & Bay sts ☎ 02 6685 6402. The large sunny terrace here attracts a mix of locals and visitors, and there's live music from Thurs–Sun year-round, and

every night in high season, including jazz and soul sessions on Sun afternoon. Mon–Sat 10am–1am, Sun 10am–midnight.

Byron Bay Brewery 1 Skinners Shoot Rd ☎ 02 6685 5833. Brewery-bar and restaurant next door to the *Arts Factory* (see p.235), and popular with backpackers. There's frequent live music and pub meals are served inside and out, in the shade of a giant fig tree. Home to Byron Bay Premium Ale, you can watch your beer being brewed as you eat and drink. Tours are available on request. The Pig House Flicks cinema (see below) is also on site. If there's more than six of you, ring for a free pick-up. Mon–Fri 4pm–midnight, Sat noon–midnight, Sun noon–10pm.

Cheeky Monkeys 115 Jonson St ☎ 02 6685 5886. Renowned backpacker party zone, with loud music, lots of frolicking, prizes to be won, and junk food from 7pm to see you through to closing time. Some hostels even lay on a shuttle to get you here. Mon–Sat 7pm–2am, Sat 6pm–midnight.

Great Northern Hotel Cnr Jonson & Byron sts ☎ 02 6685 6454, ⓦ greatnorthernhotel.com.au. Huge, very central and occasionally raucous Aussie pub with nightly live music (national, international and local bands) in high season. During the day the pavement seating is a popular place to spend time, and tuck into the pub grub and enjoy a beer. Mon–Sat 10am–3am, Sun noon–midnight.

The Rails 86 Johnson St ☎ 02 6685 7662. Good local bands rock the mic at this busy place, also known as the *Railway Friendly Bar*, a few times a week, and with its covered outdoor area it's a better bet than the pub. It also serves tasty food, including some interesting salads and burgers. Daily 10am–midnight.

Woody's Surf Shack The Plaza, near Woolworths ☎ 02 6680 7677. A backpacker bar with, in case you couldn't guess, a surf theme. There's dancing, drinking, a surfboard giveaway on Wed and live music on Thurs. Mon–Sat 8pm–3am.

2

SHOPPING

In town, Jonson St is lined with shops selling clothes and locally made **crafts**, particularly **jewellery**, and in winter you can usually find some good deals on **swimwear**, wetsuits etc. The Arts and Industry Estate, 3km west of town off Ewingsdale Rd (the road to the Pacific Hwy), is a browser's dream: several of the light industrial units here house gallery shops selling artisan-made furniture, jewellery, art and glassware.

Markets Local arts and crafts are on sale at the Byron Bay market, held on the first Sun of each month on Butler St, behind the train station from 8am–4pm. There is also a farmers' market there every Thurs (8–11am). There are other markets in Mullumbimby, Uki (north of Nimbin), Lismore, Alstonville and Bangalow, 13km southwest of Byron.

DIRECTORY

Cinema Located in the Byron Bay Brewery complex (ⓦ pighouseflicks.com.au), Pig House Flicks shows art-house and international blockbusters. The interior has been renovated but the front row of seats where you can lie down has been retained. Palace Cinemas Byron Bay (ⓦ palacecinemas.com.au) in the centre of Byron is part of the Palace chain and shows more obscure foreign art-house films, as well as general new releases.

Hospital Byron District Hospital, Wordsworth St, off Shirley St ☎ 02 6685 6200.

Police 2 Shirley St ☎ 02 6685 9499.

Post office 61 Jonson St.

Far north coast hinterland

The beautiful **far north coast hinterland** lies between the major service town of **Lismore**, in the fertile Richmond River valley to the south, and **Murwillumbah**, in the even lusher valley of the Tweed River near the Queensland border. Much of the area dances to a different tune, with hippies, communes and Kombi vans very much the norm in this "Rainbow Region". The hinterland's three rainforest national parks and several reserves are World Heritage-listed: **Mount Warning National Park** rises in the middle of a massive caldera, on whose northwest and southern rims lie the **Border Ranges** and **Nightcap national parks**, the latter near countercultural **Nimbin** and **The Channon**, home to the largest and most colourful craft market in the area.

You need your own **vehicle** to get the best out of the area, particularly to complete one of the most **scenic drives** in New South Wales, the short round trip over the mountainous, winding country roads north and northeast of Lismore to Nimbin, The Channon and Clunes, and then via Eltham and Bexhill, from where there are superb views from the ridges and hilltops.

2

Nimbin

Some 50km inland from Byron via Lismore is **NIMBIN**, site of the famed Aquarius Festival that launched Australian hippy culture in 1973. The surrounding rainforest is dotted with as many as fifty communes, while the town itself is a friendly little place, famous for live music, crafts and New Age therapies, but mainly **marijuana**. Visitors are invariably offered dope as soon as they set foot in town and you'll see it smoked openly on the streets; however, that doesn't mean to say you can wave joints around and expect not to get arrested should the police make one of their infrequent visits. The tiny centre of Nimbin is aglow with buildings painted in bright, psychedelic designs, while small stores sell health food and incense sticks; everything of interest is on the main strip, Cullen Street.

Try to time your visit to coincide with the annual **Mardi Grass and Cannabis Law Reform Rally** (Ⓦ nimbinmardigrass.com), held on the first weekend in May, when the town becomes a tent city and a high proportion of the temporary population have dreadlocks – bong throwing, joint rolling and campaigning rallies are among the activities on offer. Alternatively, aim to make it here on the fourth or fifth Sunday of the month for **market** day.

Nimbin Environmental Centre

54 Cullen St • Daily 10am–5pm

If you have Green leanings, the **Nimbin Environmental Centre** might be of interest – they campaign on environmental issues and offer information to take away, as well as selling relevant books and a variety of bumper stickers and local foodstuffs. They can arrange visits to the **Djanbung Gardens Permaculture Centre** (74 Cecil St; Ⓦ permaculture.com.au), a showcase for a system of sustainable agriculture that has gained ground worldwide.

The Hemp Embassy and the Hemp Bar

51 Cullen St • Daily 10am–5pm • Ⓦ hempembassy.net

At the **Hemp Embassy** you can learn why the Hemp Party believe the herb should be legalized, and shop for hemp-related products ranging from hemp seed to T-shirts. Next door is the **Hemp Bar** (daily 10am–5pm), serving hempburgers and other hempseed foods (as well as just plain eggs on toast).

Nimbin Artists Gallery

49 Cullen St • Daily 10am–5pm • Ⓦ nimbinartistsgallery.org

The **Nimbin Artists Gallery** exhibits and sells work by a number of artists living in and around Nimbin. As well as paintings, there are ceramics, clothes and jewellery on offer, and some great cards. The gallery also curates the **Nimbin Autumn Arts Extravaganza**, which takes place over three weeks during Easter and also includes dance and performance art.

ARRIVAL AND INFORMATION   NIMBIN

By bus There's very little regular public transport to the town and most visitors arrive on a day-trip from Byron Bay. Day-trips are run by Grasshoppers ($55; ☎ 0438 269 076, Ⓦ grasshoppers.com.au), which includes lunch and wild swimming in a rainforest creek. It is possible, however, to catch a Waller's bus between Lismore and Nimbin (5 daily Mon–Fri; 3min) and Gosel's buses (daily Mon–Fri; 1hr) between Nimbin and Murwillumbah. The visitor centre has more information on getting around by bus.

Tourist information There is a visitor information centre at 3/46 Cullen St (daily 10am–4pm; ☎ 02 6689 1388, Ⓦ visitnimbin.com.au) where you can pick up a map of the village with the main sights highlighted. There are also free copies of *The Nimbin Good Times* newspaper, if you want to learn more about what's happening locally.

Market day The Nimbin market is held on the fourth and fifth Sun of the month at 81 Cullen St by the Community Centre. Catch some music, buy some crafts and eat great organic Indian food. There is also a farmers' market every Wed from 3–6pm, where you can stock up on local produce.

ACCOMMODATION

Grey Gum Lodge 2 High St ☎02 6689 1713, Ⓦgreygumlodge.com. Just a few minutes' walk from town, this comfortable, laidback guesthouse in an old Queenslander (a house on stilts with verandas) is about as smart as they get here. Relax on the balcony and enjoy the view. No wi-fi. $85

Nimbin Backpackers & Granny's Farm 112 Cullen St ☎02 6689 1333, Ⓦnimbinbackpackers.com. A tidy place on the edge of town with dorms, singles and some double rooms with great views. There is a grassy, creekside area for camping, an entertainment room and a welcoming log-burning stove in the kitchen area. Unpowered sites $30, dorms $25, doubles $60

Nimbin Rox YHA 74 Thorburn St ☎02 6689 0022, Ⓦyha.com.au. The pick of the hostels, this friendly, well-managed place has colourful rooms, canvas lodges (one with a fantastic view), a tepee and a very pretty pool. It's set in a superb rural location just outside town and you may well see wallabies. Dorms $25, doubles $61

Rainbow Retreat 75 Thorburn St ☎02 6689 1262, Ⓦrainbowretreat.net. The hippiest place in town, accommodation is in an assortment of shacks, dorms and tents in a leafy setting. The property shares a stretch of Goolmanger Creek with the resident platypus. Some tours from Byron will drop you here. Unpowered sites $30, dorms $25, doubles $60

EATING, DRINKING & NIGHTLIFE

Contented Tummy 2/45 Cullen St ☎02 6689 0590. Located in the centre of town, and with shaded outdoor seating, this café has a new-look menu featuring fish or chicken and salad, hamburgers, wraps, smoothies and milkshakes. The coffee here is made from beans grown on the Byron hinterland. Daily 7am–3pm.

Nimbin Hotel 53 Cullen St ☎02 6689 1246, Ⓦnimbinhotel.com.au. This place sees plenty of live music and some interesting local characters, and there's a bistro on site and some backpacker accommodation (doubles $80). Mon–Fri 10am–10pm, Sat & Sun 11am–11pm.

Nimbin Trattoria & Pizzeria 70 Cullen St ☎02 6689 1427. A long-established favourite offering gargantuan pizzas ($16) topped with local produce, as well as pasta dishes and salads. Also sells pizza slices to take away ($3).

Check out the dessert window. Book in advance. Daily 5–9pm.

Phoenix Rising Café 2 Blue Knob Rd ☎02 6699 111, Ⓦphoenixrisingcafe.net. This hippy café is housed in the old butter factory, just 5min walk from the centre of Nimbin, and serves healthy meals, snacks and drinks, plus offers lovely views of Mulgum Creek. The lunch menu includes salads ($12.50), wraps ($9) and burgers ($15), and specials are written up on a blackboard. Daily 9am–5pm.

Pot of Gold Café 1/45 Cullen St ☎02 6689 1199. A successor to the legendary *Rainbow Café* which is sadly no more, this retro-style café serves a good selection of no-nonsense dishes including burgers and wraps ($11) and salads ($8), plus daily specials such as moussaka. Daily 7.30am–8.30pm.

The Channon

A 26km drive south of Nimbin, **THE CHANNON** is a pretty village on the banks of **Terania Creek**. It's home to the **Channon Craft Market** (second Sun of the month), the best – and the first – of its type in the Rainbow Region. Begun in 1976 to provide the rapidly starving hippies with some cash, the rule that you have to "make it or bake it" still holds fast – it's a colourful spectacle and well worth a trip.

Nightcap National Park

A 14km drive into the **Nightcap National Park**, along the unsealed Terania Creek Road, brings you to **Protestors Falls** and a rainforest valley filled with ancient brush box trees, saved by the 1979 protest, which was the first successful anti-logging campaign in Australia. You can walk down to the bottom of the falls, named after the dispute, to the Terania Creek Picnic Area. Also within the park are the 100m cascades of **Minyon Falls**, often more of a trickle in summer; a steep walk (2hr return) leads down to the base.

Murwillumbah and around

MURWILLUMBAH is a quiet, inland town on a bend of the Tweed River, a little over 30km northwest of Byron Bay. It's a good base for exploring the beautiful Tweed Valley and the mountains that extend to the Queensland border, and is home to some beautiful Art Deco buildings.

2

Tweed River Regional Art Gallery

2 Mistral Rd, 2km from centre · Wed–Sun 10am–5pm; tours 11.30am Wed–Sun · Free · ⓦ artgallery.tweed.nsw.gov.au

It's well worth dropping by the superb **Tweed River Regional Art Gallery**, which displays the work of Australian artists and features travelling exhibitions. The gallery now features the impressive Margaret Olley Art Centre, dedicated to the life and work of this celebrated Australian artist and including a recreation of her chaotic studio in Sydney.

Tropical Fruit World

Duranbah Rd · Daily 10am–4pm · $44, children $25 · ⓦ tropicalfruitworld.com.au

At the Murwillumbah exit on the Pacific Highway, the **Big Avocado** lures the visitor towards **Tropical Fruit World**. An avocado, macadamia and fruit plantation that has been turned into a miniature theme park complete with small zoo featuring native animals, it also offers fruit tastings, boat rides and rainforest walking trails.

Tweed Valley

The **Tweed Valley** and the surrounding land close to the Queensland border are among the most beautiful areas of New South Wales, ringed by mountain ranges that are the remains of an extinct volcano. Some twenty million years ago a huge shield **volcano** spewed lava through a central vent onto the surrounding plain. Erosion carved out a vast bowl around the centre of the resultant mass of lava, while the more resistant rocks around the edges stood firm. Right at the bowl's heart is **Mount Warning** (1157m), or Wollumbin ("cloud catcher") to the local **Bundjalung** Aborigines, the original vent of the volcano, whose unmistakeable, twisted profile rises like a sentinel from the Tweed Valley. The mountain is a place of great cultural significance to the Bundjalung, who believe that only expressly chosen people may attempt the steep three-hour path to the summit; however, as at Uluru, many visitors can't resist the dazzling views on offer.

North of Murwillumbah is Tourist Drive 40, a 57km **scenic drive** through the **Tweed Valley**, which takes in some of its best features en route from Murwillumbah up to Tweed Heads and the state border.

ARRIVAL AND INFORMATION   MURWILLUMBAH AND AROUND

By bus Greyhound and Premier Motor Service long-distance buses from both Sydney and Brisbane stop in town.

Tourist information The visitor centre (Mon–Sat 9am–4.30pm, Sun 9.30am–4pm; ☏ 02 6672 1340, ⓦ tweedtourism.com.au) is located in the World Heritage Rainforest Centre at the corner of Tweed Valley Way and Alma St. There are permanent displays on local ecology, a small art gallery and a painted panorama of the view from Wollumbin Mount Warning.

ACCOMMODATION AND EATING

Milk & Honey 5/59a Station St, Mullumbimby ☏ 02 6684 1422; ⓦ milkandhoneymullumbimby.com.au. A laidback restaurant offering delicious, artisan wood-fired pizzas ($21–25) and a frequently changing menu showcasing seasonal, locally sourced produce. There's an interesting selection of local and imported wines and craft beers, several brewed in this region. Tues–Sat 5–9pm.

Gallery Café 2 Mistral Rd ☏ 02 6670 2790. This café attached to the Tweed River Art Gallery has breathtaking views from the balcony and you may want to spend all afternoon here. The food is fairly straightforward, ranging from frittata ($15.50) to sandwiches and salads (warm roasted pumpkin salad $19.50), and there's a good selection of fresh cakes and a good wine list. Wed–Sun 9am–5pm.

Mount Warning Forest Hideaway 460 Byrill Creek Rd, near the village of Uki ☏ 02 6679 7277, ⓦ foresthideaway.com.au. Make the most of the countryside by staying in this rural accommodation southwest of town. Occupying a hundred acres of lush forest, the *Hideaway* offers motel-style units with cooking facilities, plus a saltwater swimming pool. $97

★**Mount Warning Riverside YHA** 1 Tumbulgum Rd ☏ 02 6672 3763, ⓦ yha.com.au. A truly wonderful find, this cosy hostel is in an atmospheric old sea captain's house overlooking the picturesque Tweed River, and is near cafés and shops. Free use of bikes if you stay two nights or more. Dorms $30, doubles $60

Lord Howe Island

World Heritage-listed **LORD HOWE ISLAND** is a kind of Australian Galapagos, and a favourite destination for ecotourists attracted by its rugged beauty. Situated 700km northeast of Sydney, on the same latitude as Port Macquarie, it is technically a part of New South Wales, despite its distance from the mainland. Its nearest neighbour is **Norfolk Island**, 900km further northeast (see p.246). Just 11km long and 2.8km across at its widest point, two-thirds of the crescent-shaped island is designated as Permanent Park Reserve. As you fly in, you'll get a stunning view of the whole of the volcanic island: the towering summits of rainforest-clad **Mount Gower** (875m) and **Mount Lidgbird** (777m) at the southern end; the narrow centre with its idyllic lagoon and a **coral reef** extending about 6km along the west coast; and a group of tiny islets off the lower northern end of the island providing sanctuary for the prolific **birdlife**. Much of the surrounding waters and islands fall within Lord Howe's protective **marine park**.

The emphasis here is on tranquillity and most of the four hundred visitors allowed at any one time are couples and families. Though it's expensive to get to the island, once here you'll find that cruises, activities and bike rental are all relatively affordable. The island's **climate** is subtropical, with temperatures rising from a mild 19°C in winter to 26°C in the summer, and an annual rainfall of 1650mm. It's cheaper to visit in the winter, though some restaurants and tour operators close during colder months.

Brief history

Lord Howe Island was discovered in 1788 by Lieutenant Henry Lidgbird Ball (who named the island after the British admiral Richard Howe), commander of the First Fleet ship *Supply*, during a journey from Sydney to found a penal colony on Norfolk Island. The island wasn't inhabited for another 55 years, however; the first **settlers** came in 1833, and others followed in the 1840s. In 1853 two white men arrived with three women from the Gilbert Islands in the central Pacific, and it is from this small group

LORD HOWE ECOLOGY

Seven million years ago, a volcanic eruption on the sea floor created Lord Howe Island and its 27 surrounding islets and outcrops – the island's boomerang shape is a mere remnant (around two percent) of its original form, mostly eroded by the sea. While much of the **flora** on the island is similar to that of Australia, New Zealand, New Caledonia and Norfolk Island, the island's relative isolation has led to the evolution of many **new species** – of the 241 native plants found here, 113 are endemic, including the important indigenous **kentia palm**.

Similarly, until the arrival of settlers, fifteen species of flightless **land birds** (nine of which are now extinct) lived on the island. However, in the nineteenth century Lord Howe became a port of call for ships en route to Norfolk Island, whose hungry crews eradicated the island's stocks of **white gallinule** and **white-throated pigeon**. The small, plump and flightless **woodhen** managed to survive, protected on Mount Gower, and an intensive captive breeding programme in the early 1980s (aided by eradication of feral goats, pigs and cats) saved the species. There are now about 250 woodhens on the island, and you'll often spot them pecking around your lodging.

About one million **sea birds** – fourteen species – nest on Lord Howe annually: it is one of the few known breeding grounds of the providence petrel; has the world's largest colony of red-tailed tropic birds; and is the most southerly breeding location of the sooty tern, the noddy tern and the masked booby.

The cold waters of the **Tasman Sea**, which surround Lord Howe, host the world's southernmost **coral reef**, a tropical oddity that is sustained by the warm summer current sweeping in from the Great Barrier Reef. There are about sixty varieties of brilliantly coloured and fantastically shaped coral, and the meeting of warm and cold currents means that a huge variety of both **tropical and temperate fish** can be spotted in the crystal-clear waters. Beyond the lagoon, the water becomes very deep, with particularly good diving in the seas around the **Admiralty Islets**, which have sheer underwater precipices and chasms.

2

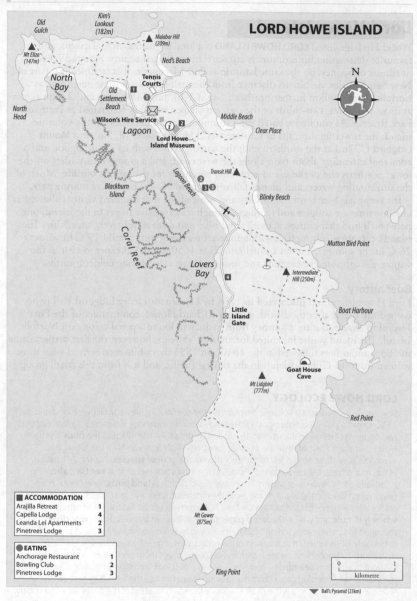

LORD HOWE ISLAND

Old Gulch
Kim's Lookout (182m)
Mt Eliza (147m)
Malabar Hill (209m)
Ned's Beach
North Bay
North Head
Tennis Courts
Old Settlement Beach
Lagoon
Wilson's Hire Service
Middle Beach
Clear Place
Lord Howe Island Museum
Blackburn Island
Transit Hill
Blinky Beach
Lagoon Beach
Coral Reef
Lovers Bay
Mutton Bird Point
Intermediate Hill (250m)
Boat Harbour
Little Island Gate
Goat House Cave
Mt Lidgbird (777m)
Red Point
Mt Gower (875m)
King Point
Ball's Pyramid (23km)

0   1
kilometre

■ ACCOMMODATION	
Arajilla Retreat	1
Capella Lodge	4
Leanda Lei Apartments	2
Pinetrees Lodge	3

● EATING	
Anchorage Restaurant	1
Bowling Club	2
Pinetrees Lodge	3

that many of Lord Howe's present population are descended. In the 1840s and 1850s the island served as a stopover for **whaling ships** from the US and Britain, with as many as fifty ships a year passing through.

With the decline of whaling, economic salvation came in the form of the **kentia palm**, which was in demand as a Victorian house plant, making its seeds a lucrative export. **Tourism** later became the mainstay – Lord Howe was a popular cruise-ship stopover before World War II, and after the war it began to be visited by holiday-makers from Sydney, who came by seaplane.

Lord Howe Island Museum

Lagoon Rd • Sept–May daily 9am–3pm, June–Aug shorter hours – check with the visitor information centre • Free • Slide show Sept–May Mon, Thurs, Fri & Sun 5.30pm; $6 • ⓦ lhimuseum.com

A good way to kick off your island idyll is with a trip to the **Lord Howe Island Museum**, which shares space with the visitor information centre (see p.244). There are artefacts charting the history of the island, as well as photographs, stamps and an environmental gallery showcasing the island's biodiversity. From September to May, the museum hosts slide shows on island history and ecology a few evenings a week narrated by Ian Hutton, the island naturalist, and local expert Chris Murray.

North Bay

At the island's **northern end**, Lagoon Road ends at Old Settlement Beach, a good starting point for lovely, easy to moderate **hikes** around the top of the island. Memorial Track is a steep 2km hike over a hill to **North Bay**, also accessible by boat with Islander Cruises (see p.244), where there's a picnic area, toilets and barbecue. It's a good place to hang out for the day, perhaps swimming, snorkelling or taking in a couple more short hikes. There's a twenty-minute trek to the summit of **Mount Eliza** (147m; closed Sept–March to allow sooty terns to nest). Also from **North Bay**, a five-minute walk through forest leads to **Old Gulch**, a beach of boulders, where at low tide you can rock-hop to the **Herring Pools** at the base of the cliff front and examine the colourful marine life before returning to the picnic area.

Ned's Beach

Some 500m northwest of the centre, **Ned's Beach** is a popular place to feed trevally, whiting and kingfish; the best way to experience the frenzy is to **snorkel**. Harmless but menacing-looking, metre-long Galapagos sharks are usually around, and coral lies only 10m from the shore. Consider returning at dusk for the clumsy arrival of the **muttonbirds** (sooty shearwaters; here Sept–May) at their burrows among the palms at the back of the beach.

Mount Gower

The lofty summit of Mount Gower (875m), in the far south, gives vistas over the whole island and out to sea towards the world's tallest sea stack, Balls Pyramid (548m), a spike of volcanic rock that breaks dramatically up out of the ocean 23km southeast of Lord Howe. This walk should be undertaken with a licensed guide (see p.244) and is extremely strenuous – one section runs precariously along a narrow cliff face above the sea, and in parts the track is so steep that you have to pull yourself up the guide ropes. You can see rare endemic plants here, including the island apple and the blue plum, as well as birds such as the providence petrel.

The lagoon

The lagoon has some lovely beaches and sensational swimming, snorkelling and diving sites, including **Sylphs Hole**, off Old Settlement Beach. The combination of temperate and tropical waters makes double-headed wrasse, lobsters and angelfish a common sight.

ARRIVAL AND DEPARTURE | LORD HOWE ISLAND

Package deals Rooms are considerably pricier than on the mainland, and have to be arranged before you book your flight, as the number of tourists staying each night is limited. It's therefore often much easier – and better value – to buy an accommodation and flights package deal. Prices for seven nights on the island start from around $1400 in winter and from $2100 in summer: try Oxley Travel (☎ 1800 671 546, ⌨ oxleytravel.com.au) or Pinetrees Travel (☎ 02 9262 6585; ⌨ pinetrees.com.au). **By plane** You can fly to Lord Howe Island with Qantas from Sydney (6 weekly; 1hr 50min) and Brisbane (Sat & Sun daily; 1hr 45min) from around $1300 return in summer and $970 in winter. There are weekly flights from Port Macquarie (1hr 30min) from Feb to June and Sept to Dec. Overseas visitors can fly to Lord Howe as an add-on fare on an air pass. The airport is located in the narrow central part of the island, south of the small settled area people jokingly refer to as the CBD. There are no taxis on the island; your hotel or resort will arrange airport transfers. No flights operate between Lord Howe and Norfolk islands.

GETTING AROUND

The island has few **roads**, a small number of cars and no taxis; the speed limit is just 25km/h. The majority of places you want to go are within 3km of each other so many people get around on foot or rent a **bicycle**; there are also some good minibus **tours**. There are sporadic streetlights down Lagoon Road, but if you are walking or cycling after dark you'll need a torch.

INFORMATION

Tourist information The visitor information centre (Mon–Thurs, Sat & Sun 10am–1pm, ☎ 02 6563 2114, ⌨ lordhoweisland.info) is on Lagoon Rd, set back from Lagoon Beach.

Services Thompson's General Store (daily 9am–5pm; ☎ 02 6563 2155) is where you can buy most things, from bait to fresh bread and roast chickens (pre-order), and rent fishing or snorkelling gear. There is a Westpac (Neds Beach Rd) and Commonwealth Bank (Bouker Ave) on the island and another ATM can be found at the Bowling Club. Credit and debit cards are fairly widely accepted. The post office (Mon–Fri 10am–4pm) is located in the CBD.

ACTIVITIES

Cruises Islander Cruises (☎ 02 6563 2298, ✉ islandercruises @gmail.com) run glass-bottom boat tours and specialist snorkel tours (both $50), while Marine Adventures (Lagoon Rd ☎ 02 6563 2448, ⌨ marineadventures.com.au) are water activities specialists with loads of options, from snorkelling to turtle spotting and fishing charters; two-hour cruises around the island cost $75.

Diving Pro Dive (Lagoon Rd; ☎ 02 6563 2253, ⌨ prodivelordhoweisland.com.au), open Sept–May, offers introductory dives for $26, Ball's Pyramid dives for $280 and an Advanced Open Water Course for $450.

Nature tours Lord Howe Nature Tours (☎ 02 6563 2447, ✉ ianhutton@clearmail.com.au) runs specialist tours with the island's fabulously knowledgeable naturalist, Ian Hutton. Private half-day tours are $400.

Walks Sea to Summit Expeditions (☎ 02 6563 2218, ⌨ lordhoweislandtours.net) run excellent and informative guided hikes up Mount Gower (Mon & Thurs; 8hr; $70) with fifth-generation islander, Jack Shick, whose grandfather started treks up the peak.

Watersports A good place for rental of all types of gear is Wilson's Hire Service (☎ 02 6563 2045) on Lagoon Rd, which rents out cars, bikes, kayaks, snorkelling gear and surfboards. You can also rent snorkelling gear from the hut at Ned's Beach. Stand Up paddleboards and glass-bottom kayaks can be hired from Pro Dive (see above).

ACCOMMODATION

Arajilla Retreat Lagoon Rd ☎ 1800 063 928, ⌨ arajilla .com.au. The twelve refurbished suites at this luxury lodge nestle among the kentia palms and banyan trees, linked by sinuous boardwalks. There's all the pampering and seclusion you could want, and the beach is just a few steps away. Full board only. **$900**

Capella Lodge Lagoon Rd ☎ 02 9918 4355, ⌨ lordhowe.com. Nestling under Mount Gower and Mount Lidgbird, this is the most luxurious place to stay on the island. Facilities include a spa, infinity pool, cocktail bar and a stylish restaurant that serves contemporary Australian cuisine. The suites are immaculate, with sweeping ocean and mountain views and the latest entertainment systems. Rates are half board. **$750**

Leanda Lei Apartments Middle Beach Rd ☎ 02 6563 2195, ⌨ leandalei.com.au. This lush tropical property offers nineteen self-contained studios and apartments in lush manicured grounds close to Lagoon Beach. Car and bike rental is available, plus specialist aquatic tours with Lord Howe Marine Adventures. **$300**

★ **Pinetrees Lodge** 1 Lagoon Rd ☎ 02 9262 6585, ⌨ pinetrees.com.au. Family-friendly motel-style units and cottages (all of which have been recently updated) arranged around the island's original guesthouse, in extensive, forested grounds with a tennis court. There's also a games room and a massage deck. Choose between B&B rates or an all-inclusive rate; excellent winter discounts available. No wi-fi. Doubles **$225**

2

EATING AND DRINKING

Anchorage Restaurant Ned's Beach Rd ☎02 6563 2287. This all-day café, located in the heart of the main settlement, includes an on-site bakery and licensed bar. Choose from indoor or garden seating options. Start your day with quality coffee and smoked salmon on toast ($16) and return in the evening for something more substantial such as pan-fried ricotta gnocchi ($30) or slow-braised lamb shank ($36). Daily 8am–8pm.

Bowling Club ("The Bowlo") ☎02 6563 2171. The bar here opens at 4.30pm, about an hour before the kitchen starts serving. Fresh local fish is a favourite and

is on the menu most nights, and there are also the daily specials. It's good value; meals start from around $15. Mon–Thurs, Sat & Sun 5.30–8pm.

Pinetrees Lodge Lagoon Rd ☎02 6563 2177, ⓦpinetrees.com.au. The fish fry ($65) here on Mon evenings is a quintessential Lord Howe experience, including vast plates of sushi, fried kingfish, chips, salads and desserts. The à la carte menu includes the likes of roast pumpkin and coconut soup, grain-fed fillet steak and passionfruit and coconut sorbet. Four-course set menu $60. Daily noon–2.30pm & 6–8pm.

Norfolk Island

Just 8km long and 5km wide, tiny, isolated **NORFOLK ISLAND** is an External Territory of Australia, located 1450km east of Brisbane and geographically closer to New Zealand. The island has had an eventful history, being linked with early convict settlements and later with the descendants of Fletcher Christian and other rebels associated with the mutiny on HMS *Bounty* (1789). It's a unique place, forested with grand indigenous pine trees, and with a mild subtropical **climate** ranging between 12°C and 19°C in the winter and from 19°C to 28°C in the summer; Norfolk is also said to have some of the world's **cleanest air** after Antarctica.

Today, it attracts honeymooners and retirees, and is also an ornithologist's paradise, with nine endemic **land-bird** species, including the endangered **Norfolk Island green parrot**, with its distinctive chuckling call. Once a refuge for millionaires seeking to escape Australia's relentless tax system – its tax-free status was revoked in 2016 – tourism in Norfolk Island is pitched at wealthier travellers. The cost of airfares and accommodation tends to deter the average backpacker.

Brief history

Norfolk is one of a handful of islands created by a violent **volcanic eruption** three million years ago. **Captain Cook** "discovered" the then-uninhabited islands in 1774, noting that the tall **Norfolk pines** would make fine ships' masts, but it's now known that migrating Polynesian people lived here as far back as the tenth century – their main settlement at Emily Bay has been excavated and stone tools found. The first European settlement was founded in 1788, only six weeks after Sydney, but was short-lived – the island lacked a navigable harbour and the pine timber turned out to be too weak for purpose. The site was abandoned in 1814, its buildings destroyed to discourage settlement by other powers.

Around ten years later, Norfolk began a thirty-year stint as a **prison** and up to two thousand convicts were held here, overseen by sadistic commandants. The island was again abandoned in 1855, but this time the buildings remained and were taken over a year later by the 194-strong population of **Pitcairn Island** who left their overcrowded conditions over 6000km east across the Pacific to establish a new life here. The new settlers had only eight family surnames among them – five of which (Christian, Quintal, Adams, McCoy and Young) were the names of the original mutineers of the *Bounty*. These names – especially Christian – are still common on the island, and today about one in three can claim descent from the mutineers. **Bounty Day**, the day the Pitcairners arrived, is celebrated in Kingston on June 8.

From 1979 to 2015, Norfolk Island was a self-governing Australian territory, with its own parliament, government services and welfare system. But the island economy faltered after the 2008–09 financial crisis and, in 2010, the local Legislative Assembly voted to surrender its **tax-free status** in return for a bail-out from the Federal Government. Five years later – despite 68 percent of residents voting against the move in a referendum – the island assembly was dissolved and power transferred to New South Wales.

Burnt Pine

The island's main settlement, **BURNT PINE**, is a relatively modern affair crammed with shops selling everything from cosmetics to electrical goods, all at almost duty-free prices; some shops are closed on Wednesday and Saturday afternoons and all day Sunday. The island's ecotourism attraction, **A Walk in the Wild**, is located on Grassy Road (daily 2–5pm; free), and educates visitors about the fragile, disappearing rainforest and its birdlife.

Kingston and around

KINGSTON is the place to come for a taste of Norfolk Island history. This is the site of the second settlement penal colony and is now Norfolk's administrative centre. There's an excellent view from the **Queen Elizabeth Lookout** over the **Kingston and Arthur's Vale Historic Area** and the poignant seafront **cemetery**, which contains a number of graves from the brutal second settlement in 1825, when the island formally became a British colony. A string of houses known as **Quality Row** bears some of the world's most impressive examples of Georgian **military architecture**.

Norfolk Island Museum

Pier St • Mon–Sat 11am–3pm • $25 for a museum pass, $10 for a single visit • ⓦ norfolkislandmuseum.com.au

The fascinating **Norfolk Island Museum** is spread over four locations, all within walking distance of one another: the Commissariat Store, No. 10 Quality Row, HMS *Sirius* and Pier Store. The collection of buildings also includes the Museum Theatre and the *Reo Café*. No. 10 Quality Row, a beautifully restored 1844 residence, houses convict-era furniture, ceramics and other objects recovered from archeological digs on the island, while the basement of the 1835 Commissariat Store contains pre-colonial artefacts alongside whips, leg irons, glass beads and other objects from the two European settlements. The Pier Store tells the story of the *Bounty* mutineers, with recordings of the Norfolk language (also known as Norfuk, a blend of eighteenth-century English and Tahitian) and objects recovered from HMS *Bounty*, including canons, kettles, carvings and bibles. HMS *Sirius*, on Bounty Street, is dedicated to the ship of the same name which was wrecked on the island in 1790.

Slaughter Bay

The Kingston area is also the site of the island's main swimming **beaches**, which are protected by a small reef. Immediately in front of the walls of the ruined barracks is **Slaughter Bay**, which has a sandy beach dotted with interestingly gnarled and eroded basalt rock formations; the small hard-coral reef is excellent for **snorkelling**. At low tide you can take a **glass-bottomed boat cruise** ($45) from nearby Emily Bay, which is also a beautiful, safe swimming area backed by a large pine forest.

St Barnabas Chapel

West of Burnt Pine, along Douglas Drive, you'll find the exquisite **St Barnabas Chapel**, once the property of the Melanesian Mission (Anglican), which relocated gradually here from New Zealand between 1866 and 1921. The chapel's rose window was designed by William Morris and some of the others are by Sir Edward Burne-Jones; the altar was carved by Solomon Islanders – ancestral masters of the craft.

Botanic Gardens

Just south of the national park, on Pitt Road, the tranquil rainforest of the **Botanic Gardens** (unrestricted access) is worth a stroll. Here you can observe the forty endemic plant species, including the pretty native hibiscus, the native palm, and the island's best-known symbol, the **Norfolk pine**, which can grow as tall as 57m with a circumference of up to 11m.

ARRIVAL AND DEPARTURE

By plane Air New Zealand fly once a week from Auckland for around $1150 return, and twice a week from Sydney and Brisbane for around $700 and $1400 respectively (but keep a look out for specials). There are no scheduled flights between Lord Howe and Norfolk islands. The airport is on the west side of the island, just outside Burnt Pine; most

NORFOLK ISLAND

hotels will provide transfers. Package deals, including flights and accommodation, are very popular – prices for seven nights start at around $1200 in winter and $1600 in summer: try Oxley Travel (☎ 1800 671 546, ☒ oxleytravel .com.au) or Burnt Pine Travel (☎ 006 723 22195; ☒ burntpinetravel.com).

GETTING AROUND

By car No public transport operates on Norfolk Island and it's rather hilly, so getting around by car is the best option. Many accommodation places offer a car as part of the package or give you a big discount on car rental. It's very cheap anyway, with rates around $45/day. The speed limit is 50km/h (40km/h in town). Aloha Rent A Car (☎ 006 7232 2510, ☒ aloha.nlk.nf) is based opposite the airport.

By bike Bikes are available for rent from Land and Sea on Taylors Rd, Burnt Pine (Mon, Tues and Fri 9am–5pm, Wed & Sat 9am–12.30pm, Thurs 9.15am–5pm; ☎ 006 7232 3418). Several hotels also hire out bikes.
By taxi The island only has one taxi; booked in advance on ☎ 006 7235 0371.

INFORMATION AND ACTIVTIES

Tourist information The visitor information centre (Mon, Tues, Thurs & Fri 8.30am–5pm, Wed 8.30am–4pm, Sat & Sun 8.30am–3pm; ☎ 006 7232 2147, ☒ norfolkisland .com.au) is in the Bicentennial Complex on Taylors Rd in Burnt Pine.
Services There are branches of Westpac and the Commonwealth Bank on Taylors Rd; the latter has an ATM – the only one on the island. Credit and debit cards are fairly widely accepted. The post office is at P & R Groceries on Taylors Rd, south of Burnt Pine, in Kingston (Mon–Fri 9am–5pm, Sat 9am–noon).

Cultural tours Pinetree Tours (☎ 006 7232 2424, ☒ pinetreetours.com), on the main street next to the Commonwealth Bank, is the agent for an array of sightseeing and cultural tours, including a half-day bus trip around the island ($44), a convict settlement tour ($49), and a three-course dinner in islanders' homes ($84).
Kayaking Crystal Kayak Tours (☎ 006 7232 2147; ☒ norfolkisland.com.au) offers half-day tours along the pristine coastline with a local guide – no previous paddling experience is required ($190).

ACCOMMODATION

The **price** of accommodation on Norfolk is higher than on the mainland, though lower than on Lord Howe. With no camping and no hostel, the only **budget options** are the several comfortable 1970s-style motels that dot the island. All places below include a small car in the rates.

Christian's of Bucks Point 22 Martin's Rd, Bucks Point ☎ 006 7232 3833, ☒ christiansofbuckspoint.com. This charming timber house dates from 1914 and offers three luxurious bedrooms, a country-style kitchen (self-catering), lounge, gas BBQ and shady veranda. Couples or groups welcome; the rate includes breakfast provisions for the first day. $490
Forrester Court Clifftop Cottages Mill Rd ☎ 006 7232 2838, ☒ forrestercourt.com. Three upmarket one- or two-bedroom cottages with open-plan living rooms and inspiring views over Cascade Bay; breakfast included. In-house massage, babysitting and the services of a private

chef can also be arranged. $350
Heritage Hill Taylor's Rd ☎ 006 7232 2255, ☒ heritagehill.nf. Welcoming hotel with a pool, restaurant and a choice of motel-style rooms, cottages or apartments. The best rooms have views over Kingston towards Phillip Island. Rates include an introductory tour and breakfast. $162
Tintoela of Norfolk Harper's Rd ☎ 006 7232 2946, ☒ norfolkislandaccommodation.com. Very comfortable, homely cottages in a garden setting, plus a large wooden house, sleeping up to ten, with panoramic views of Cockpit Valley and Cascade Bay. $375

EATING AND DRINKING

The only place to buy wine, spirits and beer on the island is at the Liquor Mart on Taylors Rd (Mon–Thurs 10am–6pm, Fri & Sat 10am–6.30pm).

Dino's at Bumboras 89 Bumboras Rd, south of the airport ✆ 006 7232 4225. A quality licensed place serving Italian-influenced contemporary dishes made with local produce, such as local beef with a red wine and thyme jus ($35.50) or prosciutto and spicy sausage pizza ($20). Dining is inside surrounded by art-covered walls or on the veranda of the late 1800s house. Book ahead. Thurs, Fri & Sat 5.30pm–late; Sun 11.30am–3pm.

Golden Orb Bookshop Café Taylor's Rd, Burnt Pine ✆ 006 7232 4295. Peaceful subtropical sanctuary just off the main street that serves wholesome café meals such as pie of the day with salad ($15.50) and ploughman's plate ($17), as well as a variety of snacks, good coffee, juices and cakes. There's also a decent range of books, many of local interest. Daily 8am–2pm.

Norfolk Blue 100 Acre Farm, west of the airport ✆ 006 7232 2068, ⓦ norfolkblue.com. Dine on the veranda shaded by a huge Morton Bay fig, tucking into the likes of handmade pasta *rotolo* ($35) or slow-cooked beef shin ($36). The restaurant specializes in its own locally reared Norfolk Blue beef dishes. It's a great spot if you're exploring the west coast, and they also offer a shuttle service on request. Daily noon–2.30pm & 6–10.30pm.

Norfolk Island Leagues Club 17 Ferny Lane, Kingston ✆ 006 7232 2440, ⓦ facebook.com/NorfolkIslandLeagues SquashClub. This friendly club is the closest thing to a pub on the island, offering a good range of alcoholic drinks, a pool table, wide-screen TVs, sporting memorabilia and a bistro serving well-priced Asian and Australian fare. Mon–Wed, Sat & Sun 2pm–late, Thurs & Fri 11am–late.

The central west

The **central west** of New South Wales is rich farmland, and the undulating green hills provide both seasonal work and easy hiking tracks. Although **Dubbo** is the region's major hub, and home to a famous zoo, **Bathurst** is the most sophisticated town, celebrated for its fine Victorian architecture and numerous museums. **Cowra**'s fame derives from the breakout of Japanese prisoners here during World War II, while **Young** was the site of the Lambing Flat Riots against Chinese miners in 1861, significant events in Australian history. Both towns lack major draws though, and could easily be overlooked. **Parkes**' main attractions are its nearby observatory and its annual Elvis Festival. While not tremendously cosmopolitan, the central west is picking up its culinary act and **Orange** is now widely known for its F.O.O.D Week in March/April, which showcases the region's cool-climate wines and fresh produce. There are also large numbers of wineries, both large and small, around **Mudgee** and **Young** – lunch at one of these is *de rigueur* for Sydneysiders escaping the city at weekends and makes for a lovely break from the road.

Bathurst and around

The pleasant city of **BATHURST**, elegantly situated on the western slopes of the Great Dividing Range, 207km west of Sydney, is Australia's oldest inland settlement. Its cool climate – proximity to the mountains means it can be cold at night – as well as its beautifully preserved nineteenth-century architecture, quirky shops, lively arts scene and good cafés, make it an enjoyable overnight stop, and it has a very different feel to anywhere on the baking plains further west. The settlement was founded by Governor Macquarie in 1815, but Bathurst remained nothing more than a small convict and military settlement for years, only slowly developing into the main supply centre for the rich surrounding pastoral area. It was the discovery of **gold** nearby at Lewis Ponds Creek at Ophir in 1851, and on the Turon River later the same year, which changed the life of the town and the colony forever. Soon rich fields of alluvial gold were discovered in every direction and, being the first town over the mountains for those on the way to the goldfields, Bathurst prospered and grew.

Although there's still the odd speck of gold and a few gemstones (especially sapphires) to be found in the surrounding area, modern Bathurst has reverted to its role as capital of one of the richest fruit- and grain-growing districts in Australia. The presence of the **Charles Sturt University**, one of Australia's leading institutes, gives the city an academic feel and adds to its liveliness. Car enthusiasts, however, probably associate it with racing and during the second weekend in October, rev-heads turn up for the big annual motor-racing meetings – centred on the famous **Bathurst 1000** endurance race – at the Mount Panorama Racing Circuit.

Courthouse Museum

Russell St • Tues–Sat 10am–4pm, Sat & Sun 11am–2pm • $5

The 1880 Courthouse contains a little **museum** displaying relics and archives of regional pioneer history along with some interesting Aboriginal artefacts.

Bathurst Regional Art Gallery

70–78 Keppel St • Tues–Sat 10am–5pm, Sun 11am–2pm • Free • Ⓦ bathurstart.com.au

The **Regional Art Gallery** houses a fine collection strong on ceramics and paintings by Lloyd Rees (though not always on display), as well as regular special and travelling exhibitions. The gallery also manages the Hill End artist-in-residence programme and often exhibits works associated with it.

Australian Fossil and Mineral Museum

224 Howick St • Mon–Sat 10am–4pm, Sun 10am–2pm • $14 • Ⓦ somervillecollection.com.au

The **Australian Fossil and Mineral Museum** does a fantastic job of displaying a fairly small but broad-ranging collection, compiled entirely by local geologist Warren Somerville, a lecturer at Charles Sturt University. It includes Australia's only complete *Tyrannosaurus rex* skeleton, and there's a world-class array of trilobites along with superb amber (including one piece with an entire preserved gecko) and a perfectly preserved crab captured in the defence position.

Chifley Home

10 Busby St • Guided tours Mon, Sat & Sun 10am & noon • $13 • ☎ 02 6333 6111, Ⓦ chifleyhome.org.au

The well-preserved **Chifley Home**, southwest of the city centre, was once the residence of Ben Chifley, Bathurst's most famous son. Chifley was born to a blacksmith in 1885, became an engine driver on the railways by age 24, and after becoming involved in Labor politics served as prime minister of Australia between 1945 and 1949.

Mount Panorama

Panorama Ave • **National Motor Racing Museum** Daily 9am–4.30pm • $15 • Ⓦ nmrm.com.au

West of the centre is **Mount Panorama** and its famous 6km-long racing circuit, providing panoramic city views. The circuit is a public road that's accessible by car when it's not a race day, so you can realize any childhood dreams of racing on an official track (albeit at 60kph).

The **National Motor Racing Museum**, at Murray's Corner at the beginning of the circuit, features around 110 famous racing cars and bikes, plus photographs and memorabilia from races since the 1930s. One wing is dedicated to Australian supercar legend Peter Brock, who won "The Great Race" nine times before his untimely death in 2006.

ARRIVAL AND INFORMATION

BATHURST

By plane You can fly to Bathurst with Regional Express (☎ 13 17 13, Ⓦ rex.com.au) from Sydney (3 daily; 50min).

By train NSW TrainLink has daily train services from Sydney (1–2 daily; 3hr 30min), which carry on to Orange and Dubbo. There is a service from Broken Hill on Tues (10hr 15min). Bathurst Railway Station (Keppel St) is in the town centre.

By bus Australia Wide Coaches (☎ 02 9516 1300, Ⓦ austwidecoaches.com.au) run services from Sydney to Orange stopping at Bathurst, and Orange Buslines (☎ 02 6362 3197, Ⓦ orangebuslines.com.au) runs between Orange and Bathurst via Millthorpe. NSW TrainLink also runs services to Lithgow and beyond.

Destinations Cowra (daily; 1hr); Lithgow (daily; 1hr); Sydney (daily; 3hr 30min); Orange (daily; 40min).
Tourist office The visitor information centre (daily

9am–5pm; ☎02 6332 1444, ⓦvisitbathurst.com.au) is on the eastern edge of town at 1 Kendall Avenue.

ACCOMMODATION

Bathurst Heritage Apartments 108 William St ☎02 6332 4920, ⓦbathurstheritage.com.au. A collection of swish apartments spread around town, including Royal Hotel, a jewel-in-the-crown heritage building where two antique-filled mews apartments take up the top floor, complete with access to the wide veranda with views over the King's Parade Park. **$209**
Big4 Bathurst Panorama Holiday Park 250 Sydney Rd (Great Western Hwy), 4km east of town ☎1800 669 911, ⓦbig4.com.au. A spacious, well-kept park, with a large swimming pool, laundry, family-friendly movies at weekends, good (outdoor) camp kitchen and a BBQ area. The tent spots are right by the road, so it can be noisy. Un/

powered sites $30/$35, cabins $130
Jack Duggans Irish Pub 135 George St ☎02 6331 2712, ⓦjackduggans.com.au. Standard, neat rooms above a pub with TVs, shared bathrooms and a small communal kitchen space. Very little noise from downstairs and a good restaurant on site (see below). $65
Rydges Mount Panorama 1 Conrad Straight, Mount Panorama ☎02 6338 1888, ⓦrydges.com. Modern, self-contained rooms with views of the Mount Panorama Racetrack and the surrounding countryside. Facilities include a pool, spa, gym, and a contemporary restaurant and bar. Breakfast included. $190

EATING AND DRINKING

Church Bar + Woodfired Pizza 1 Ribbon Gang Lane (enter from William St) ☎02 6334 2300, ⓦchurchbar .com.au. Drinks and tasty wood fired pizzas both traditional and quirky (crocodile with wild lime and ginger $25) in the impressive surrounds of the neo-Gothic Old School House; you can eat inside, or out in the leafy courtyard. Mon–Sat noon–midnight, Sun noon–10pm.
Cobblestone Lane 173–179 George St ☎02 6331 2202, ⓦthecobblestonelane.com.au. Bathurst's best restaurant, a casual affair located in the historic Webb building serving mod-Oz cuisine such as rabbit and thyme terrine, toasted brioche with anchovy, apple, rhubarb and celeriac salad ($18) and Cowra lamb fillet served with pumpkin, chickpea, pomegranate and curd salad ($45). Two-course lunches available for $40. Daily noon–2pm & 6–9pm.
The Hub 52 Keppel St ☎02 6332 1565. A popular café with a wide range of breakfast options, from sweet-potato rosti with poached eggs, chorizo and mushroom ($18.90) to burritos with scrambled egg, avocado, fried onion, halloumi and spinach ($17.90) and some excellent lunch dishes, including lemon and garlic chicken salad ($18.90). Afternoon tea from 3pm, and they also host live music. Daily 7am–5pm.

Maalouf's 52 George St ☎02 6331 1477. Basic eat-in and takeaway Lebanese place serving authentic versions of Middle Eastern favourites such as falafel roll ($7), fattoush salad ($10.50), shawarma plate ($24.90) and kebabs. BYO. Mon–Fri 11am–2pm & 5–10pm, Sat 5–10pm.
Ma Duggan's Kitchen Jack Duggans Irish Pub, 135 George St ☎02 6331 2712, ⓦjackduggans.com.au. Hearty Irish fare such as Auld Ma's Irish Lamb Stew ($18) and Arthur's Steak and Guinness Pot Pie ($22), as well as pub grub like nachos, burgers and schnitzels. Curry night on Tues. The attached pub stays open until late and hosts live music at weekends. Daily 11.30am–3pm & 5.30–9pm.
The Oxford Hotel Cnr William & Piper sts ☎02 6331 5500, ⓦtheoxfordbathurst.com.au. Popular among students, with regular club nights on Fri and Sat. This huge alfresco bar has plasma screens blasting out music videos and good-value meals from its *Piper Bistro* upstairs, such as pulled-pork pizza ($17), braised lamb *ragu* with pappardelle ($22) and baked salmon fillet ($29). Mon–Wed 11.30am–10pm, Thurs 11.30am–2am, Fri 11.30am–3am, Sat 11.30am–4am, Sun noon–10pm.

Abercrombie Karst Conservation Reserve

Abercrombie Caves Rd, 72km south of Bathurst • Mon & Thurs–Sun 9am–4.30pm; daily in school holidays • Self-guided cave tour $18, guided tour $22 ☎02 6368 8603, ⓦnationalparks.nsw.gov.au

An enjoyable excursion from Bathurst is to the spectacular **Abercrombie Caves**, in the middle of a large conservation reserve. The principal and most impressive cavern, the **Abercrombie Archway** is 221m long and in some places over 30m high – it's said to be the largest natural limestone arch in the southern hemisphere. More than eighty other caves are dotted around the reserve; the best-known sights are Archway, Bushranger's Cave and King Solomon's Temple, where miners constructed a dance floor 130 years ago, and where concerts and church services still take place.

2

Hill End

The gold-rush town of **HILL END** is located on a plateau above the Turon Valley. In 1870, Hill End was the largest inland centre in New South Wales, a booming gold-mining town with a population of about twenty thousand, with 53 hotels and all the accoutrements of a wealthy settlement. Within ten years, however, gold production had faltered and Hill End became a virtual ghost town. Efforts to r estore the town have since been made, but it is a strange place with less than a hundred residents living in the remaining buildings, all widely scattered across the grassy reserve. Hill End has an **open day** in April and October, during which time visitors can see inside some of the historic buildings and the artists-in-residence open their studios.

ARRIVAL AND INFORMATION   HILL END

By car From Sofala, a 12km unsealed road leads to Hill End but those who want to avoid this can travel from Mudgee or Bathurst via Turondale. The Bridle Track that follows the Turon River is no longer a through road.

Tourist information You can pick up a leaflet at the NPWS visitor centre in the old hospital (daily 9.30am–12.30pm & 1.30–4.30pm; ☎02 6337 8206), where there's also a small museum ($2.20); ask about the ghost tours ($35) which explore the town's darker history.

Mudgee

About 120km north of Bathurst on good roads, the large, old country town of **MUDGEE** (meaning "the nest in the hills" in the Wiradjuri language) is the centre of an important wine region that's the original home of Aussie Chardonnay. The town is set along the lush banks of the Cudgegong River, and the countryside appears to have more grazing cows and sheep than vineyards. Dotted with original boutiques and local produce shops, it's popular with the Sydney crowd.

MUDGEE WINERIES: FIVE OF THE BEST

The majority of the forty-odd cellar doors are immediately north of Mudgee and offer free **tastings**. Consider cycling around the vineyards on a bike rented from Countryfit (36–42 Short St; ☎02 6372 3955).

Botobolar Vineyard 89 Botobolar Rd, 16km northeast of town ☎02 6373 3840, ⓦbotobolar .com. Australia's first organic winery is known for its Marsanne, with tastings on a shady terrace. There's also a picnic area and BBQs. Daily except Wed 11am–4pm.

Di Lusso Estate 162 Eurunderee Lane, 5km north of town ☎02 6373 3125, ⓦdilusso.com.au. A winery specializing entirely in Italian varieties and blends, founded by a doctor eighty years ago and now run by the charming Robert Lane. Enjoy fourteen different Italian wines paired with wood-fired pizzas. Also stages an Italian film festival every three to four months. Mon–Sat 10am–5pm, Sun 10am–4pm.

Huntington Estate Wines 641 Ulan Rd, 6km northeast of town ☎02 6373 3825, ⓦhuntingtonestate.com.au. Delicious wines, notably the young Semillons and the intense, heady Cabernet Sauvignons. Hosts an excellent annual chamber-music festival in Nov. Mon–Sat 10am–5pm,

Sun 10am–4pm.

Pieter Van Gent Winery & Vineyard 141 Black Springs Rd, 6km northwest of town ☎02 6373 3030, ⓦpvgwinery.com.au. Daily tastings in a delightful setting: beautiful nineteenth-century choir stalls on cool earth floors, overshadowed by huge old barrels salvaged from Penfolds Winery. Try the Pipeclay Port, a tawny specimen aged in wood. The winemaker is Dutch, and the herbs he uses in his traditional vermouth are specially imported from the Netherlands. Mon–Sat 10am–5pm, Sun 10am–4pm.

Robert Oatley Vineyards 815 Craigmoor Rd, 2km north of town ☎02 6372 4320, ⓦrobertoatley .com.au. The oldest winery in Mudgee (established in 1858) and still one of the best. Known for its Montrose label and the fact that Australian Chardonnay began life here. There's an interesting museum featuring old winemaking equipment, too. The café is temporarily closed. Daily 10am–4pm.

ARRIVAL AND INFORMATION

MUDGEE

By train and bus NSW TrainLink trains run from Sydney to Lithgow (1–3 daily; 2hr 20min), just east of Bathurst, where you connect with a bus on to Mudgee.

Tourist information The useful visitor information centre (daily 9am–5pm; ☎02 6372 1020, ⓦvisitmudgeeregion.com.au) at 84 Market Street has detailed winery information and maps.

ACCOMMODATION

Cobb & Co Court 97 Market St ☎02 6372 7245, ⓦcobbandcocourt.com.au. Luxurious option with sixteen rooms around the dining courtyard, featuring crisp white bedding, plush furnishings, Art Deco tiled bathrooms (some with jacuzzis) and a chic restaurant (see below). The one- and two-bed apartments are particularly spacious. **$175**

Mudgee Riverside Caravan & Tourist Park 22 Short St ☎02 6372 2531, ⓦmudgeeriverside.com.au. The most central of the caravan parks, this site's leafy foliage provides shade and there's a good BBQ area/camp kitchen and kids' playground. It's an easy walk to restaurants and shops. No wi-fi. Un/powered sites **$24/31**, cabin **$90**

The Tannery 48 Lawson St ☎0411 020 574, ⓦthetannerymudgee.com.au. Central, stylish renovation of an 1850s cottage into a two-bedroom suite with all the luxuries you need and a small garden with a terrace. Breakfast provisions included. **$200**

Winning Post Motor Inn 101 Church St ☎02 6372 3333, ⓦwinnlngpostmotorinn.com.au. Quiet and friendly motel-style accommodation a 5min walk from the centre with a pool and an on-site restaurant. Breakfast included. **$210**

EATING AND DRINKING

Blue Wren Winery 433 Ulan Rd, 3km northeast ☎02 6372 6205, ⓦbluewrenwines.com.au. For a treat, visit this winery restaurant which uses mainly local produce. The menu includes dishes such as seared scallops with pancetta, corn purée and crustacean oil ($19) and slow-roasted beef sirloin ($26). Mon–Thurs, Sat & Sun noon–2.30pm, Fri noon–2.30pm & 6–9pm.

Butcher Shop Café 49 Church St. The place to go for great in-house roasted coffee, all-day breakfasts ($5–17) and tasty lunches, ranging from a butcher's burger ($14) to chilli, garlic and prawn pasta ($17). There's not much for veggies though. Mon–Fri 8am–5pm, Sat 8am–3pm, Sun 8am–2pm.

My Thai 69 Market St ☎02 6372 9898. This tiny place serves a good range of meat, seafood and vegetarian dishes, including *tom kha* soup ($9), *panang* curry ($13.90) and prawn salad ($17.50). Mon & Sun 5–8pm, Tues–Sat 5–9pm,.

The Quick Brown Fox 79 Market St ☎02 6372 9949. A quirky, friendly café with old signs on the walls and books on display. Come for a home-made muffin ($4.50), pumpkin quiche ($6.95) or the chicken pasta salad ($9.50). Mon–Fri 7.30am–4.30pm, Sat 7.30am–2.30pm.

Wineglass Bar & Grill 97 Market St ☎02 6372 7245, ⓦcobbandcocourt.com.au. Regional, seasonal produce that you can enjoy in the courtyard sunshine or inside the classic dining room. Try the antipasto ($24.95, including a glass of beer or wine) or the slow-roasted chilli jam lamb rump ($39.45). Leave room for a pudding, such as the petit pavlova or Toblerone mousse. Daily 6am–11pm.

Orange

ORANGE, 55km west of Bathurst on the Mitchell Hwy en route to Dubbo, is a pretty town of around 40,000 set amid rolling countryside. There's not an orange tree to be seen – the Surveyor General apparently named it after William, Prince of Orange, under whom he fought Napoleon – but the hills hereabouts are draped in **fruit**, principally apples, cherries and grapes. You can find apple-picking **work** here from late February into April, while cherry picking takes place from late November to early January – contact Harvest Trail (see p.53). Many growers have rough accommodation on their properties but demand often outstrips supply, so bring a tent. If you want to sample the local produce rather than pick it, turn up for **F.O.O.D Week** (ⓦorangefoodweek.com.au) in March/April or **Wine Week** (ⓦwinesoforange.com.au) in October. There's also a great little **farmers' market** on the second Saturday of every month.

Orange Regional Art Gallery

Byng St • Tues–Sat 10am–4pm, Sun noon–4pm • Free

The **Regional Art Gallery** can be found behind the visitor information centre. It is home to three galleries that display the permanent collection (including work by Sidney Nolan), as well as temporary exhibits with an emphasis on local artists.

2

Botanic Gardens

Kearney's Drive • Daily 7.30am–dusk • Free

The **Botanic Gardens** on the northern outskirts of town feature an impressive native and exotic plant collection, typical of those found in a cool climate, and makes a pleasant afternoon diversion.

Mount Canobolas

Just out of town, a drive 15km southwest will take you to the 1395m summit of **Mount Canobolas**, with great views all around and lots of rosellas. The route is dotted with **vineyards** and cellar doors, should you fancy stocking up. Also out this way is **Lake Canobolas**, a great spot for picnicking, fishing and canoeing.

ARRIVAL AND INFORMATION   ORANGE

By plane You can fly here from Sydney (4 daily; 50min) with Regional Express (☎ 13 17 13, ⓦ rex.com.au).

By train NSW TrainLink has daily train services from Sydney (1–2 daily; 4hr 45min) and Dubbo (daily; 1hr 40min).

By bus Australia Wide Coaches (☎ 02 9516 1300, ⓦ austwidecoaches.com.au) run services from Sydney to Orange stopping at Bathurst. There are NSW TrainLink buses from Orange to Dubbo, and to Parkes stopping at Canowindra and Forbes.

Destinations Bathurst (1–6 daily; 40min–1hr); Cootamundra (3 weekly; 3hr); Dubbo (daily; 2hr); Parkes (1–6 daily; 1hr 45min–2hr)

Tourist information The visitor information centre (daily 9am–5pm; ☎ 1800 069 466, ⓦ visitorange.com.au) on Byng Street in Civic Square has information on local attractions including fossicking for gold in the Ophir Reserve. They can also give you a food and wine map and information on wine tours in the area.

ACCOMMODATION

Arancia B&B 69 Wrights Lane, 5km southwest of town ☎ 02 6365 3305, ⓦ arancia.com.au. Luxurious B&B with stunning views of Mount Canobolas and the valley below. Rooms are opulent, stylish and well appointed, and each has its own entrance. Rates include a full cooked breakfast. Two-night minimum on weekends. **$250**

Cotahele 177 Anson St, two blocks south of the centre ☎ 02 6361 2520, ⓦ cotehele.com.au. Occupies an 1878 magistrate's home with high ceilings; the six en-suite rooms are all distinctively decorated. Breakfast included. **$210**

Sundowner Oriana Motel 178 Woodward St, 1km west of the centre ☎ 02 6362 3066, ⓦ sundownerhotels .com.au. Part of the Sundowner chain, offering clean and comfortable motel-style accommodation with a/c and a fridge in the rooms, and a pool and restaurant on site. **$165**

EATING AND DRINKING

Mr Sushi King 297 Summer St ☎ 02 5310 6480. A busy, friendly Japanese restaurant with menus made from manga comics. Choose from bento boxes ($28–33), chicken *karage udon* ($16.50), *donburi* ($20) and a range of sushi and sashimi. At lunchtime there's a sushi train and a daily special. Mon 5–9.30pm, Tues–Sun noon–2.30pm & 5–9.30pm.

Sweet Sour Salt 116 Summer St ☎ 02 6362 5191, ⓦ sweetsoursalt.com.au. A cool Asian restaurant serving contemporary dishes such as deep-fried soft-shell crab ($34), pork wanton ($18), and slow-roasted pork shoulder ($30). Tues–Thurs & Sat 6–9pm, Fri noon–2pm & 6–9pm.

Union Bank Wine Bar & Dining 84 Byng St ☎ 02 6361 4441, ⓦ unionbank.com.au. A classy and long-established but not too expensive wine cellar and bar that serves great tapas-style dishes ($5–18) and bistro meals such as grass-fed sirloin steak ($20). There's also a compact courtyard. Mon–Sat noon–midnight, Sun noon–10pm.

Millthorpe

The historic village of **Millthorpe**, 22km south of Orange, has in recent years become a fashionable weekend jaunt and been granted living-museum status thanks to its buildings, which are made of Australian blue stone. It is an attractive little place offering a number of great dining options, and makes an interesting side trip from Orange or Bathurst.

ARRIVAL AND DEPARTURE   MILLTHORPE

By bus Orange Buslines (ⓦ buslinesgroup.com.au/ orange) operates a service to Millthorpe from both Orange (2 daily Mon–Fri; 30min) and Bathurst (2 daily Mon–Fri; 35min).

EATING

★**Tonic** 30 Victoria St ☎02 6366 3811, ⓦtonicmillthorpe.com.au. One of the most awarded restaurants in regional NSW, *Tonic* is a must-do culinary experience serving dishes such as slow-roasted pork shoulder and baked quail with cassoulet and white-bean puree. Enjoy a two-course lunch for $65 or three courses for $75. Book in advance. Thurs & Fri 6.30–9pm, Sat noon–3pm & 6.30–9pm, Sun noon–3pm.

Forbes

FORBES, 110km west of Orange on the Lachlan River, is a graceful old place famous as the stomping ground of the nineteenth-century bushranger **Ben Hall**, who is buried in the town's cemetery. The area boomed after gold was discovered in 1861 but gradually agriculture took over and it became the country town you see today. On Good Friday, Forbes hosts **camel races** that attract people from all over.

ARRIVAL AND DEPARTURE   FORBES

By train Forbes is serviced from Sydney (5 weekly; 5hr 40min) by NSW TrainLink, with a changeover to a bus at Lithgow.

By bus NSW TrainLink buses link Forbes with the small town of Parkes (6 weekly; 30min).

ACCOMMODATION

Big4 Forbes Holiday Park 141 Flint St ☎1800 641 207, ⓦbig4forbesholidaypark.com.au. A well-kept park, with a pool, play area, and BBQ and camp kitchen. There are a range of accommodation options, from lodges with shared bathrooms to villas sleeping seven, as well as slabs and grass sites. No wi-fi. Un/powered sites $30/38, cabins $115

Country Mile Motor Inn 14 Cross St ☎02 6852 4099, ⓦgoldenchain.com.au. *Country Mile* offers standard motel rooms but they're clean and the welcome is friendly. There's also a pool and a laundry room. $128

Parkes

PARKES considers itself the "Elvis Capital of Australia" and puts on an **Elvis Festival** (ⓦparkeselvisfestival.com.au) dedicated to The King each January. The five-day event features look-alike contests and impersonator performances; during the festival the population almost doubles. Parkes is also well known, however, for its observatory and "dish".

Henry Parkes Centre

Pioneer Park, Newell Hwy • Mon–Fri 9am–5pm, Sat & Sun 10am–4pm • $12 for entry to all four museums • ⓦhenryparkescentre.com.au

The Henry Parkes Centre is home to the visitor information centre, as well as three museums and a collection of antique machinery. Former Wiggles star Greg Page has used his fortune to garner an impressive collection of Elvis memorabilia and this is on display at **The King's Castle**. It includes a gold lamé suit, the shirt Elvis wore in the film *Jailhouse Rock* and handwritten letters to his parents and girlfriends. Included in the entry fee is access to the **Motor Museum**, which features some impressive automobiles from as far back as 1920, and the last Cadillac Elvis ever owned. The quirky **Henry Parkes Museum** features artefacts and local memorabilia from the last century.

Parkes Observatory

Newell Hwy, 20km north of Parkes • Daily 8.30am–4.15pm • Free • ⓦparkes.atnf.csiro.au

The **Parkes Observatory** radio telescope was used for tracking the Apollo 11 mission to the moon, and featured in the 2000 film *The Dish*. The observatory's visitor centre has displays on space and the observatory's work, and continuously screens the 22-minute *Invisible Universe* and a changing roster of short 3D films. Unfortunately, the observatory's long-term future is currently in limbo following government funding cutbacks to the national scientific agency, CSIRO, in 2016.

2

By plane You can fly here from Sydney (1–6 daily; 1hr–1hr 40min) with Regional Express. The airport is 5km from town; there are hire-car outlets and taxis (☎ 02 6862 2222) available at the terminal.

By train There's a weekly direct service from Sydney to Parkes (Mon; 6hr 35min), or a daily (except Sat) service with a change to a bus at Lithgow. During the festival,

TrainLink runs the special *Elvis Express* between Sydney and Parkes, but it's very popular, so book well ahead (W parkeselvisfestival.com.au).

By bus TrainLink buses to Forbes (6 weekly; 30min).

Tourist information The town's visitor information centre (daily 9am–5pm; ☎ 02 6862 6000, W visitparkes .com.au) is located in the Henry Parkes Centre.

ACCOMMODATION

Coachman Hotel Motel 48–54 Welcome St ☎ 02 6862 2622, W coachman.com.au. Centrally located and comfortable enough for a night but it's showing its age, and the TVs are ancient. Rooms are en suite, and there's a nice pool and a bar. **$99**

Station Motel 82 Peak Hill Rd ☎ 02 6862 8444, W stationmotel.com.au. Large, clean motel rooms that are tastefully furnished and come with toaster and microwave. There's also an on-site restaurant. Good online deals. **$140**

Dubbo

Named after an Aboriginal word meaning "red earth", **DUBBO** lies on the banks of the Macquarie River 420km northwest of Sydney and about 200km from Bathurst. The regional capital for the west of the state (with around 40,000 people), it supports many agricultural industries and is located at a vital crossroads where the Melbourne–Brisbane Newell Highway meets the Mitchell Highway and routes west to Bourke or Broken Hill. As such, it's well used to people passing through, but not staying long. The only real attraction is the Taronga Western Plains Zoo, which can easily fill a day.

Taronga Western Plains Zoo

Obley Rd, 5km south of Dubbo off the Newell Hwy • Daily 9am–4pm • $47 ticket valid for two consecutive days • Bike rental $15/day; electric cart $69/3hr • Billabong Camp $169 • ☎ 02 6881 1400, W taronga.org.au

The open-range **Taronga Western Plains Zoo** is easily the biggest attraction in the area. This vast zoo-cum-safari-park is mostly populated with Australian and African animals used to a hot, dry climate similar to Dubbo's. Beasts – white rhinos, giraffes, Sumatran tigers and so on – roam in expansive landscaped habitats separated by moats, giving a good approximation of being on safari. Close encounters include face-to-face photo ops with giraffes (10.10am, $7), and the chance to hand-feed lions and tigers from behind a strong mesh fence ($59, book in advance). You can even get inside the meerkat enclosure and feed them live invertebrates.

The zoo is threaded by a 6km road you can drive round, or you can walk or cycle along the many paths, or rent an electric cart. Start early – temperatures can become unbearable by noon and the animals sometimes slink off out of sight into the shade.

Early birds can opt for the Morning Walk (every Sat & Sun, plus Wed & Fri during school holidays, 6.45am; $15), which is a good opportunity to get close to the animals without the crowds. Even better is waking up with the sound of roaring lions, possible in a couple of ways: the family-oriented Billabong Camp package is available at weekends and includes a night under canvas, dinner and breakfast, guided animal encounters and general zoo access or there's the African-style *Zoofari Lodge* (see opposite).

Dundullimal Homestead

23L Obley Rd, 2min drive from the zoo • Tues–Sat 11am–3pm • $8 • W nationaltrust.org.au

The National Trust-owned **Dundullimal Homestead** deserves a quick look and is best combined with a trip to the zoo, as it is just a few kilometres further up Obley Road. This 1840s timber slab house is one of the oldest in the district, and there are traditional sandstone stables on the property that house a blacksmith's forge. Devonshire teas are served in a 1920s shed.

Old Dubbo Gaol

90 Macquarie St • Daily 9am–4pm • $16.50 • W olddubbogaol.com.au

In the centre of town, **Old Dubbo Gaol** is worth an hour or so. Back in the 1880s, this fortress-style building housed some of the west's most notorious criminals, and today it glories in the details of nineteenth-century prison life, giving loving attention to the macabre – the gallows, the hangman's kit and the criminal careers of some of those who were executed here.

Western Plains Cultural Centre

76 Wingewarra St • Wed–Mon 10am–4pm • Free • W westernplainsculturalcentre.org

The lovely **Western Plains Cultural Centre** houses both the **Art Gallery**, which has regularly changing exhibitions and where the collection is built around the theme of animal representations in the visual arts, and the **Dubbo Regional Museum**, showing pastoral scenes of early settlers. There's also a café on site.

ARRIVAL AND INFORMATION

DUBBO

By plane Dubbo's airport, 5km northwest of town, receives daily Regional Express and Qantas link flights from Sydney (4–11 daily; 1hr 10min), and Regional Express flights from Broken Hill (1–2 daily except Sat; 2hr). Dubbo Radio Cabs (☏ 13 10 08) charge around $15 for the trip into Dubbo. Country Care Hire (W countrycarhire.com.au) rents cars from $55 a day and can arrange for you to pick up a vehicle from the airport.

By train The railway station is on Talbragar St and NSW TrainLink services from Bathurst (daily; 3hr), Orange (daily; 1hr 50min) and Sydney (daily; 6hr 30min) stop here.

By bus NSW TrainLink buses arrive just outside the railway station from Broken Hill, Bourke and Lightning Ridge. Sid Fogg's Coachlines (☏ 02 4928 1088) runs services between Dubbo and Newcastle.

Destinations Bathurst (daily; 2hr 25min); Bourke (4 weekly; 4hr 30min); Broken Hill (daily; 9hr 40min); Cobar (daily; 3hr 30min); Lightning Ridge (daily; 4hr 30min); Newcastle (daily; 5hr 40min); Orange (daily; 2hr); Parkes (daily; 1hr 20min).

Tourist information The visitor information centre (daily 9am–5pm; ☏ 02 6801 4450, W dubbo.com.au) is set in a riverside park at the corner of Erskine and Macquarie streets, just off the Newell Hwy.

ACCOMMODATION

Dubbo Parklands 154 Whylandra St, 2km south of Dubbo off the Newell Hwy near the Western Plains Zoo ☏ 02 6884 8633, W discoveryholidayparks.com.au. Typically anodyne but well-appointed caravan park, in a green spot right on the river, though the luxurious cabins (some even have spas) are expensive. There's also the safari-style tent glamping option of a Serengeti suite ($99). Un/powered sites $30/35, cabins $129

No. 95 95 Cobra St ☏ 02 6882 7888, W no95.com.au. The trendiest option in town, with stylish motel-style rooms, king-size beds, a pool, wi-fi throughout (1hr free) and a restaurant (closed Sun) serving mod-Oz cuisine. Rates include breakfast. $145

Tallarook Motor Inn 17 Stonehaven Ave ☏ 02 6882 7066, W tallarookmotorinn.com. Comfortable, spacious rooms with basic kitchen facilities; those upstairs have balconies. The motel is just across from the park, and there's

a pool on site. $120

Terramungamine Reserve Barraway Rd, follow signs from Brocklehurst on the Newell Hwy. Free camping in a pretty spot next to the Macquarie River on a historic Aboriginal site – note the ancient grinding grooves in rocks where Aborigines would shape their spears. Toilets, but no showers. Look out for the galahs and cockatoos. No wi-fi. **Free**

Zoofari Lodge Taronga Western Plains Zoo, Obley Rd ☏ 02 6881 1488, W zoofari.com.au. A good option for families; choose between a deluxe Savannah (sleeps four) and Serengeti (sleeps six) lodge, both with private en suites. All linens are provided, there's underfloor heating in winter, and you can watch giraffe, eland and oryx grazing from the viewing area. Rates include two days' general zoo admission, bike rental, a behind-the-scenes tour, dinner and breakfast. Wi-fi (free) in public areas. $359

EATING AND DRINKING

Grapevine Café 144 Brisbane St. A low-key, relaxed daytime café with a lovely shady courtyard. Serves delicious meals in generous portions ($14–20); for something lighter try the soup ($10.95) or a pie. Mon–Fri 7.30am–4pm, Sat & Sun 8.30am–4pm.

Rose Garden 33–34 Whylandra St ☏ 02 6884 3884. Superb Thai restaurant and takeaway that's a cut above the average (but no more expensive). Choose from freshly prepared curries, stir-fries and noodle dishes. The $16.50 lunch special (starter, main and soft drink or tea) is great value. Daily noon–2.30pm & 5.30–10pm.

Sticks and Stones 215A Macquarie St 📞 02 6885 4852, 🌐 sticksandstonespizza.com.au. Located in a former doctor's house, four long blocks south of the visitor centre, this places serves wood-fired pizzas from $18 (with the option of gluten free), as well as salads and pasta dishes. Some breakfast options are available until 3pm. Daily 7.30am–8.30pm.

Two Doors Tapas And Wine Bar 215B Macquarie St 📞 02 6885 2333, 🌐 twodoors.com.au. Occupying a lovely stone cellar below *Sticks and Stones*, and with a leafy courtyard, this place is perfect for a few glasses of wine and something from the Spanish-influenced menu, also sold as half-portion tapas. Expect the likes of pan-fried smoky chicken skewers ($16) and chilli-salted squid and chorizo ($25). Tues–Fri 4–11.30pm, Sat 10am–11.30pm.

Cowra

Nestled on the banks of the Lachlan River 107km southwest of Bathurst along the Mid-Western Hwy, **COWRA** is a green little town, though it doesn't invite you to stay longer than necessary. Its only claim to fame is the **Cowra Breakout** of World War II. August 5, 1944, saw the escape of 1104 Japanese prisoners of war armed with baseball bats, staves, home-made clubs and sharpened kitchen knives – those who were sick and remained behind hanged or disembowelled themselves, unable to endure the disgrace of capture. It took nine days to recapture all the prisoners, during which time four Australian soldiers and 231 Japanese died. The breakout was little known until the publication of Harry Gordon's excellent 1970s account *Die Like the Carp* (republished as *Voyage of Shame*). There's a great holographic explanation of the breakout at the visitor centre (see below), and an anti-war symbol in the shape of the **World Peace Bell** on Civic Square, a replica of the one in New York City.

POW Camp and Japanese War Cemetery

You can see the site of the **POW camp**, now just ruins and fields, on Sakura Avenue on the northeast edge of town. The graves of the escapees, who were buried in Cowra, were well cared for by members of the local Returned Servicemen's League, a humanitarian gesture that touched Japanese embassy officials who then broached the idea of an official **Japanese War Cemetery**. Designed by Shigeru Yura, the tranquil burial ground lies north of the camp, on Doncaster Drive.

Japanese Garden

Daily 8.30am–5pm • $15, audioguide $2

The theme of Japanese–Australian friendship and reconciliation continued in Cowra with the establishment of the **Japanese Garden** in 1979, with funding from Japanese and Australian governments and companies. The large, tranquil garden, designed to represent the landscape of Japan, is set on a hill overlooking the town, on a scenic drive running north off Kendal Street, the main thoroughfare. Rent the audioguide for a more thorough and highly enjoyable insight into Japanese garden design and symbolism.

ARRIVAL AND INFORMATION   COWRA

By bus The only public transport here is NSW TrainLink buses from Bathurst (6 weekly; 1hr 35min).

Tourist information The visitor information centre (daily 9am–5pm; 🌐 cowratourism.com.au) can be found at the junction of the Olympic Hwy, Lachlan Valley Way and

Mid-Western. Staff can provide information about the ten or so wineries dotting the area.

Seasonal work If you're interested in some grape-picking work, contact Harvest Trail (see p.53).

Young

The hilly town of **YOUNG**, 70km southwest of Cowra along the Olympic Hwy, is a good spot to pick up some **cherry-picking** work during the season (around six weeks from the first week of November); being monotonous rather than strenuous, the work is very popular with backpackers following the Harvest Trail. You can also pick your own from mid-November until Christmas. The long weekend in October generally coincides with the **cherry blossoms** being in full bloom – a glorious sight – and there's an annual three-day **Cherry Festival** in December which celebrates the cherry harvest with games and competitions. There are also several **vineyards** on the slopes of the undulating area, which is known as the **Hilltops wine** region and is gaining recognition around the country.

A former gold-mining centre previously known as Lambing Flat, the town was the scene of racist violence – the notorious **Lambing Flat Riots** – against Chinese miners in June 1861. As the gold ran out, European miners resented what they saw as the greater success of the more industrious Chinese, and troops had to be called in when the Chinese were chased violently from the diggings and their property destroyed. Carried at the head of the mob was a flag made from a tent flysheet, with the Southern Cross in the centre and the slogan "Roll Up, Roll Up, No Chinese" painted on. Following the riots, the Chinese Immigration Restriction Act was passed, one of the first steps on the slippery slope towards the White Australia Policy of 1901 (see p.974). You can see the original flag and other exhibits relating to the Lambing Flat Riots at the **Lambing Flat Folk Museum** in the Community Art Centre on Campbell Street (daily 10am–4pm; $5; ☎02 6382 2248). The museum is a lot bigger than you might expect and houses local artefacts that range from nineteenth-century wedding dresses to mining lamps and a wine press.

ARRIVAL AND INFORMATION

By bus There are NSW TrainLink buses from Dubbo (3 weekly; 3hr 25min), Bathurst (4 weekly; 3hr 10min) and Cootamundra (daily; 3hr 50min).

By train There is a daily NSW TrainLink train from Melbourne to Cootamundra (2 daily; 6hr), from where you can catch a bus to Young.

Tourist information The visitor information centre (Mon–Fri 9am–5pm, Sat & Sun 9am–4pm; ☎02 6382 3394, ⓦvisityoung.com.au) is in the old railway station on Lovell St.

Seasonal work Contact MADEC Australia on ☎1800 062 332. accommodation and eating

The Country Providore 143 Boorowa St

YOUNG

☎02 6382 7255. A licensed café serving some local wines, this is a good place to stop for breakfast or lunch. Options include aubergine and courgette bruschetta ($13.50) and beetroot risotto with goat's cheese ($17) and seared scallop with avocado, pine nuts and prosciutto chips. Mon–Thurs 8am–3pm, Fri & Sat 8am–10pm.

Young Caravan Park 17 Edwards St ☎02 6283 2190. A shady campsite not far from the visitor centre, with a BBQ area and a camp kitchen. Guests can choose from cabins, powered and unpowered sites; some of the powered sites have their own bathroom facilities. No wi-fi. Un/powered sites $25/30, cabins $83

WINERIES

There are a number of cellar doors in the area and the visitor centre has a map you can take away. Note that a couple only offer tasting by appointment, particularly during the winter months.

Chalkers Crossing 285 Henry Lawson Way ☎02 6382 24200, ⓦchalkerscrossing.com.au. Wine varieties you can taste here include Riesling, Semillon and Cabernet Sauvignon. Mon–Fri 9.30am–4.30pm.

Lindsays Woodonga Hill Winery 10km north of

Young on Olympic Hwy ☎02 6382 2972, ⓦlindsayswine.com.au. A small, family-run winery, which offers tours as well as tastings of its Chardonnay, Shiraz, Riesling, Tempranillo and Merlot. Daily 9am–5pm.

The Hume Highway and the Riverina

The rolling plains of southwestern New South Wales, spreading west from the Great Dividing Range, are bounded by two great rivers: the **Murrumbidgee** to the north and the **Murray** to the south, the latter forming the border with the state of Victoria. This area is now known as the **Riverina**. The land the explorer John Oxley described as "uninhabitable and useless to civilized man" began its transformation to fertile fruit bowl when the ambitious **Murrumbidgee Irrigation Scheme** was launched in 1907. The area around **Griffith** normally produces ninety percent of Australia's rice, most of its citrus fruits and twenty percent of its wine grapes, so if you're looking for **work** on the land, you've a reasonable chance of finding it here.

The eastern limit of the region is defined by the **Hume Highway**, the rather tedious route between Sydney and Melbourne. It is often choked with trucks, particularly at night, and still occasionally narrows to one lane either way, so you'll want to keep your wits about you. Better still, stop off at towns along the way, many of them truly and typically Australian – rich in food, wine, flora and fauna, and friendly locals. Tick off the big sheep at **Goulburn**, but don't miss the town's historic brewery. **Yass** has associations with Hamilton Hume – after whom the highway is named – while **Gundagai** is more famous for a fictional dog's behaviour. You'll have to detour 50km off route to visit likeable **Wagga Wagga**, the capital of the central Riverina and the largest inland town in New South Wales, while the last stop in the state is **Albury**, twinned with Wodonga on the Victorian shore of the Murray River.

Head west for **Narrandera**, which really only justifies a meal stop, while **Griffith** is good for wine tasting and fruit picking. There are several festivals in the region, including Taste Riverina food festival (w tasteriverina.com.au) every October, and Griffith's La Festa (w lafesta.org.au), an orgy of Aussie wine, food and culture held over the Easter weekend.

Goulburn

GOULBURN, just off the Hume Highway, is a large regional centre and home to a quality **wool industry**, established in the 1820s. The town, with its wide streets, has a conservative country feel, but boasts some large and impressive public buildings. The **Cathedral of Saint Saviour** on Church Street (daily 10am–4pm), completed in 1884, is one of the most attractive old churches in Australia, with some beautiful stained glass and a fine organ.

Big Merino

Cnr Hume & Sowerby sts, near the Hume Hwy southern exit • Daily 8.30am–5pm • Free

Goulburn's wool traditions have been immortalized by the **Big Merino**, a 15m-high, 97-tonne concrete sheep standing proudly at the town entrance – pop inside for a display on the industry and to shop for knitwear and sheepskin products. You can also climb up to the lookout.

Goulburn War Memorial and Museum

Memorial Drive • Lookout daily; Museum Sat & Sun 7am–5pm • Donation

The **war memorial** was built in 1925 and presides over the town from Rocky Hill. Climb to the top to enjoy fantastic views of the surrounding countryside from the viewing platform. Also on site is a **museum** displaying artefacts of war such as weapons and uniforms, and some personal memorabilia including medals.

Riversdale

2 Twynam Dr • Mon, Tues, Thurs & Sun 10am–2pm • $6

There are several historic places to visit in Goulburn, including the National Trust property **Riversdale**, an 1840 coaching inn on Maud Street that later became the home of the district surveyor Edward Twynam and his family. His descendants occupied the house for almost a hundred years before it was acquired by the National Trust. The property includes its original paddocks and outbuildings, plus an impressive collection of colonial furniture and artefacts.

ARRIVAL AND INFORMATION
GOULBURN

By bus Greyhound buses from Sydney (daily; 3hr) to Melbourne stop here, as do services from Canberra (daily; 1hr 10min) to Sydney.

By train There are regular trains from Sydney that stop in

Goulburn (4–5 daily; 3hr 15min) en route to Canberra.

Tourist information The visitor centre (Mon–Fri 9am–5pm, Sat & Sun 10am–4pm; ☎ 1800 353 646, w igoulburn.com) is opposite the shady, flower-filled

Belmore Park at 201 Sloane St. It stocks brochures detailing self-guided walks around town.

Tours Enjoy a glimpse into Australian country life at Pelican Sheep Station (T 02 4821 4668, W pelicansheepstation.com.au); the 1hr 15min tour includes a shearing demonstration and the chance to see sheepdogs being put through their paces – kids can cuddle newborn lambs in April. Book at least 48hr in advance.

ACCOMMODATION AND EATING

Grit Café 3–5 Sowerby St T 02 4822 1191. Just off the Highway near the Big Merino, this popular little café serves soups, cakes, bagels and a decent cup of espresso, with an emphasis on raw food and home baking. Food allergies are well catered for. Mon–Fri 6am–4pm, Sat & Sun 7am–4pm.

Governors Hill Carapark 77 Sydney Rd, 3km northeast of town T 1800 227 373, W governors-hill-carapark .nsw.big4.com.au. This smart little caravan park, run by the national Big4 chain, offers a store, kitchen, BBQs and a TV room. There's even a miniature garden railway. Free wi-fi. Powered sites $36, cabins $128

Mandelson's 160 Sloane St T 02 4821 0707, W mandelsons.com.au. A cross between a B&B and a hotel, *Mandelson's* offers luxurious rooms with modern bathrooms in a heritage building, furnished with antiques. Breakfast included. $160

Paragon Café 174 Auburn St T 02 4821 3566. This café, which dates back to the 1940s, is the essential Goulburn eating experience but come for the decor rather than the food. It serves up inexpensive breakfasts, steaks and Italian dishes, and a daily lunchtime two-course meal ($15). You may have to reserve in advance if you're after a booth seat. Daily 7.30am–9.30pm.

The Bungonia National Park

Check for scheduled park closures on T 02 4827 4700 • $8 per vehicle for 24hr • W nationalparks.nsw.gov.au

The **Bungonia National Park**, 35km east of Goulburn, covers a rugged strip of the Southern Tablelands containing some of the deepest **caves** in Australia, the spectacular limestone Bungonia Gorge and the Shoalhaven River. There are also plenty of bushwalking tracks with good river and canyon views.

Wombeyan Caves

Daily 9am–4pm • Self-guided tour of Fig Tree Cave $18, guided tours of one additional cave $30, two additional caves $40 • W nationalparks.nsw.gov.au

Some 70km north of Goulburn are the huge and accessible **Wombeyan Caves**, some of which have been open to the public since 1875. The **Fig Tree Cave** can be visited on a self-guided tour – look out for the cave coral; Wollondilly, Junction, Kooringa and Mulwaree caves can be discovered on a variety of guided tours. It's possible to swim in nearby Wombeyan Gorge, or just explore the surrounding area via the many walking trails.

Yass

YASS, 87km west of Goulburn just off the Hume Hwy, is an appealing little place with a rural feel, kept green by the Yass River. Before European settlement, the town had a large

HAMILTON HUME

The explorer Hamilton Hume was different from many of his contemporaries in that he was born in Australia – to free settlers in Parramatta in 1797. When the family moved to Appin, Hume began to explore the bush and his later explorations would rely on the first-hand knowledge he acquired during this time as well as the Aboriginal skills and languages he had learned.

Hume's best-known exploration was in 1828 when he paired with **Hovell**, an English sea captain, to head for Port Phillip Bay; you can follow in their footsteps on the **Hume and Hovell Walking Track** (W takeawalk.com.au; full map kits are available from the visitor centre in Yass), which starts at Yass and runs over 440km southwest to Albury. Hume also assisted Sturt in tracing the Murray and Darling rivers, before retiring to Yass with his wife in 1839 and moving into Cooma Cottage (see p.262).

Aboriginal population, who gave the town its name, "yharr", meaning running water. The famous explorer **Hamilton Hume** chose to retire here, and is the town's main claim to fame.

The **Yass and District Museum** on Comur Street (mid-Sept to early June Sat & Sun 10am–4pm; $5) contains displays on what the town looked like back in the 1890s. The National Trust-owned **Cooma Cottage** (Thurs–Sun 10am–4pm; $5; ⓦnationaltrust .org.au), a well-preserved nineteenth-century homestead 4km south of Yass on the Canberra road (and down a dirt track), was Hamilton Hume's former home and is now a museum, set in 100 acres of rolling countryside and containing excellent material on Hume and his expeditions.

ARRIVAL AND INFORMATION   YASS

By bus Both NSW TrainLink and Greyhound pass through the town, as do Transborder (ⓣ02 6299 3722, ⓦtransborder.com.au) services. There are regular services to Sydney (4 daily; 3hr 55min).
Tourist information The visitor centre (Mon–Fri

9am–4.30pm; ⓣ1300 886 014, ⓦyassvalley.com.au) at 259 Comur St has maps outlining an informative, 2km walk through town and will point you to good wineries in this up-and-coming cool-climate wine region.

ACCOMMODATION AND EATING

Kaffeine 2582 175 Comur St ⓣ02 6226 1263. Café and boutique selling pretty things; if you like the chair you're sitting on you may well be able to buy it. Settle onto a banquette covered in colourful cushions and try smoked salmon quiche with cream cheese and capers ($14). Cash only. Mon–Fri 7am–4pm, Sat & Sun 8am–3pm.
Kerrowgair 24 Grampian St ⓣ02 6226 4932,

ⓦkerrogair.com.au. There are some lovely B&Bs in Yass and this is one of the best. The three rooms in this elegant historical residence are all en suite, and rates include breakfast provisions. **$150**
Thunderbird Motel 264 Comur St ⓣ02 6226 1158, ⓦthunderbirdmotelyass.com.au. Opposite the visitor centre, this motel has comfortable units, a pool and a restaurant, plus BBQ facilities and a DVD library. **$140**

Wee Jasper and around

For some downtime away from the Hume Highway, head south from Yass along Tourist Route 7, which rejoins the Hume south of Gundagai. After around 50km you reach the picturesque, tiny village of **WEE JASPER**.

Carey's Caves, 6km northwest, are home to some of Australia's most spectacular limestone rock formations. The caves can only be explored by guided tour (Mon & Fri noon & 1.30pm, Sat & Sun noon, 1.30pm & 3pm; 1hr 15min; $16.50; ⓦweejaspercaves.com), which take visitors into some of the seven chambers that make up the cave system. Carey's Caves also hosts concerts and theatre productions, and if you want to, you can bring your instrument with you on a tour to take advantage of the acoustics.

Gundagai

GUNDAGAI sits on the banks of the Murrumbidgee, some 100km west of Yass at the foot of the rounded bump of Mount Parnassus, and lacks much character. The town was once situated on the alluvial flats north of the river, despite warnings from local Aborigines that the area was prone to major flooding. Proving them correct, old Gundagai was the scene of Australia's worst flood disaster in 1852, when 89 people drowned. Gold was eventually discovered here in 1858, and by 1864 Gundagai had become a boom town, preyed upon by the romantically dubbed bushranger Captain Moonlight. The relocated town, on the main route between Sydney and Melbourne until bypassed by the Hume Highway, became a favoured overnight stopping point among pioneers heading into the interior by bullock cart. A large punt was the only means of crossing the Murrumbidgee until the pretty wooden **Prince Alfred Bridge** was erected in 1867.

Gundagai found immortality through a **Jack Moses** poem, in which "the dog sat on the tuckerbox, nine miles from Gundagai" and stubbornly refused to help its master pull the bogged bullock team from the creek. Somehow the image became elevated from that of a disobedient dog and a cursing teamster to a symbol of the pioneer with his faithful hound at his side. As a consequence, a statue of the dog was erected 8km north of town at **Five Mile Creek**, where pioneers used to camp overnight – it's still a very pleasant spot to take a break.

ARRIVAL AND INFORMATION GUNDAGAI **2**

By train There are NSW TrainLink services from Sydney (6 weekly; 5hr); catch the train as far as Wagga Wagga or Cootamundra and then change to a bus. The bus journey takes around 55min.
By bus Greyhound buses between Sydney and Canberra service the town on a regular basis.

Destinations Albury (daily; 3hr 15min); Canberra (daily; 2hr 5min); Goulburn (daily; 3hr 25min); Sydney (daily; 7hr); Wagga Wagga (daily; 1hr).
Tourist information The visitor centre (daily 9am–4.30pm; ☎ 02 6944 0250, ⓦ visitgundagai.com.au) is at 249 Sheridan St.

Wagga Wagga

WAGGA WAGGA, known simply as "Wagga" (and pronounced "Wogga"), is capital of the Riverina region and by far its largest town with around 63,000 inhabitants. Its curious name is thought to come from the Wiradjuri, the most numerous of the New South Wales Aboriginal peoples: "wagga" means crow, and its repetition signifies the plural (though some claim it means "dancing men").

Despite its size, Wagga remains a green and pleasant place, and visitors will find the town's main attractions on the outskirts. Baylis Street is the main strip (and Fitzmaurice Street, its continuation), and it extends from the bridge spanning the Murrumbidgee River south through town.

Botanic Gardens

Willians Hill, Macleay St · Zoo and aviary daily 10am–4pm · Free

It's a thirty-minute walk south of the town centre to reach the huge and impressive **Botanic Gardens**, which have a rose garden, a cactus and succulent garden, and a rainforest and fern area that is misted throughout the day to create the right conditions. The gardens are also home to a walk-through bird aviary, a mini zoo, bush trails and picnic areas.

Museum of the Riverina

Lord Baden Powell Drive and the Civic Centre · Tues–Sat 10am–4pm, Sun 10am–2pm · Free · ⓦ wagga.nsw.gov.au/museum

The **Museum of the Riverina** has two sites: one near the Botanic Gardens on Lord Baden Powell Drive, which concentrates on the people and events of Wagga Wagga and is home to the Sporting Hall of Fame; and the other back in town at the **Civic Centre**, which often hosts travelling exhibitions.

Wagga Wagga Art Gallery

Civic Centre · Tues–Sat 10am–4pm, Sun 10am–2pm · Free · ⓦ waggaartgallery.org

The **Wagga Wagga Art Gallery** is home to a collection of more than twelve hundred original Australian prints (some usually on display) and the **National Art Glass Collection**, comprising around four hundred pieces, mostly non-representational studio glass made since the 1970s.

ARRIVAL AND DEPARTURE WAGGA WAGGA

By plane There are daily Qantas and Regional Express flights between Wagga and both Sydney (6–9 daily; 1hr 10min) and Melbourne (3–7 daily; 1hr 10min). The airport is about 6km from town. There are car-rental outlets in the terminal and a taxi rank just outside.
By train A twice-daily train connects Wagga with Sydney

2

(7hr 10min) and Melbourne (5hr 20min).

By bus The train station is also the stop for interstate Greyhound buses travelling to Sydney, Melbourne and Canberra.

Destinations Canberra (1–2 daily; 3hr); Hay (daily; 4hr 50min); Goulburn (daily; 5hr 5min)

INFORMATION AND ACTIVITIES

Tourist information The visitor centre (Mon–Fri 9am–5pm, Sat 9am–4pm, Sun 9.30am–2pm; ☏ 1300 100 122, ⓦ waggawaggaaustralia.com.au) at 183 Tarcutta St, can provide timetables for the local bus routes.

Market Myer car park, O'Reilly St. On the third Sun on the month, stalls sell secondhand clothes and books, crafts, local produce and knick knacks. There are also miniature-pony rides for kids. Entry is free but a small ("gold coin") donation is welcome. Sun 7.30am–noon.

Wine tasting The city's Charles Sturt University boasts a well-regarded wine course and has its own on-campus winery (McKeown Drive, off Coolamon Rd; Mon–Fri 11am–5pm, Sat & Sun 11am–4pm; ☏ 02 6933 2435, ⓦ csu.edu.au/winery) open for tastings and sales. The cellar door also has handmade cheese – try the unusual lemon myrtle – and olive oil.

ACCOMMODATION

Mercure Wagga Wagga 1 Morgan St ☏ 02 6921 6444, ⓦ accorhotels.com.au. This four-star property is part of the global Mercure hotel chain and provides dependable if unexciting accommodation, with a good choice of rooms, a fitness centre and swimming pool. **$154**

Townhouse Hotel 70 Morgan St ☏ 02 6921 4337, ⓦ townhousewagga.com. A very central and stylish hotel with tastefully furnished rooms and suites, some with private balcony and a useful desk and chair. Free swim/gym pass for the local sports centre, and a good on-site restaurant (see below). **$129**

Wagga Beach Caravan Park 2 Johnston St ☏ 02 6931 0603, ⓦ wwbcp.com.au. The town's best-situated caravan park, this shady and tranquil place accesses the town beach and is a 5min walk north of the main shops. Facilities include kiosk, BBQ area and children's playground. Powered sites **$30**, cabins **$80**

EATING AND DRINKING

Indian Tavern Tandoori Restaurant 81 Peter St ☏ 02 6921 3121, ⓦ indiantavern.com.au. A popular spot with authentic dishes, such as fish tikka ($22.90) and tandoori chicken ($20.90) and a good range of vegetarian options. Can be a bit liberal with the chilli sauce but there are some mild offerings marked on the menu. Daily 5.30–9pm.

The Oakroom Kitchen & Bar 70 Morgan St ☏ 02 6921 4337, ⓦ townhousewagga.com. Attached to the *Townhouse Hotel*, this is one of the classiest eateries in Wagga. Food is mod-Oz and includes dishes such as Riverina lamb with roasted pepper pesto ($37) and grain-fed Wagyu rump ($44). The menu also offers a selection of small plates like prawn dumplings and slow-roasted pork belly. Mon–Sat 7–9am & 6–9pm.

Thirsty Crow Brewery 31 Kincaid St ☏ 02 6921 7470, ⓦ thirstycrow.com.au. A microbrewery with a great atmosphere and pizzas that range from the likes of blue cheese, brie and basil ($21) to Sunday roast complete with gravy and peas ($23). Brewery snacks include fried calamari ($15) and beef-cheek nachos ($16). You can also book brewery tours ($15). Daily 7am–11pm.

Uneke Lounge 140 Fitzmaurice St ☏ 02 6925 8143, ⓦ unekelounge.com.au. This place is usually packed, particularly for Sunday brunch (big breakfast $18.50), but find a spot on a comfy sofa and you can try a rump burger, wrap or BLT ($15.50). Mon–Wed 8.30am–4pm, Thurs–Sat 8.30am–5.30pm, Sun 8.30am–3pm.

Victoria Hotel 55 Baylis St ☏ 02 6921 5233, ⓦ vichotelwagga.com.au. One of the city's most happening pubs, the *Victoria* offers a traditional front bar alongside a modern bistro and upstairs nightclub. The menu includes the likes of Thai beef salad ($16) to chimichanga ($13). Live music and DJs on Wed, Fri and Sat nights in the front bar. Daily noon–2pm & 6–9pm.

Junee

JUNEE, 37km north of Wagga Wagga, can be visited on a day-trip. It is a small, attractive town with a surprising number of grand buildings, and a history marked by the railways. One of the main things to do in Junee is tour the Green Grove Organics **Junee Liquorice and Chocolate Factory**, situated in a restored flour mill at 45 Lord Street (daily 9.30am–4.30pm; free; tours every hour from 10am–3pm, $5; ⓦ greengroveorganics.com.au). There is also the restored 1884 **Monte Cristo Homestead** (1 Homestead Lane; Fri–Mon 10am–4pm; $12), said to be haunted by its former owner, Christopher Crawley (among others).

Albury and around

The small city of **ALBURY** and its smaller twin **Wodonga**, across the Murray River in Victoria, are traditionally regarded as a stopping point between Sydney and Melbourne. The Hume Highway now cuts through the twin cities, but if you stop here you'll likely spend most of your time in Albury. There are a few key sights in the area northeast of the junction of Dean and Kiewa streets.

Library Museum

Cnr Kiewa & Swift sts • Mon, Wed & Thurs 10am–7pm, Tues & Fri 10am–5pm, Sat 10am–4pm, Sun noon–4pm • Free • ⓦ alburycity
.nsw.gov.au/librarymuseum

The excellent, modern **Library Museum** has a small but well-presented display on the city's history and culture including material on Bonegilla (see p.266) and a great poster showing *Spirit of Progress*, one of the sleek trains that once called at the train station here. Always on display are three oils by Australian artist Russell Drysdale (1912–81), who lived in the area in the 1920s and married into a local family.

Murray Art Museum Albury (MAMA)

546 Dean St • Mon, Tues, Wed & Fri 10am–5pm, Thurs 10am–7pm, Sat & Sun 10am–4pm• Free • ⓦ mamalbury.com.au

The **Murray Art Museum Albury (MAMA)** is an exciting new regional art gallery which offers seven exhibition spaces, a restaurant and shop. The permanent collection includes 2400 works by the likes of Rupert Bunny, Donald Friend, Lloyd Rees and many other Australian greats.

Albury Botanical Gardens

Dean St • Dawn–dusk • Free

The historic **Albury Botanical Gardens** house some impressive old trees, including a huge Queensland kauri pine and an English elm dating from 1887, as well as over a thousand native and exotic plant species. The gardens are very family friendly, with a special children's garden to explore.

Noreuil Park

Off Wodonga Place • Always open • Free

At their southern end, Albury Botanical Gardens abut **Noreuil Park**, a peaceful place looking across to a bush-covered riverbank in Victoria. People swim in the river and picnic under the large gum trees here – one of which was marked by the explorer Hovell at the point where he and Hume crossed the Murray.

ARRIVAL AND DEPARTURE   ALBURY AND AROUND

By plane There are regular Regional Express and Virgin Australia flights between Albury and Sydney (5–6 daily; 1hr 25min) and Regional Express flights to Melbourne (1–3 daily; 1hr).

By train Trains from Sydney (2 daily; 7hr 30min), Melbourne (2 daily; 3hr 20min) and Wagga Wagga (2 daily; 1hr 25min) all stop at the magnificent train station, 100m

east of the shops and cafés of Dean St and 10min walk from the Cultural Precinct and Botanic Gardens.

By bus NSW TrainLink and V/Line long-distance buses to/from Victoria stop at the train station, connecting Albury with Corowa (3 weekly; 50min) and Melbourne (4 daily; 3hr 50min).

INFORMATION AND ACTIVITIES

Tourist information There's a visitor centre (daily 9am–5pm; ☎ 1300 252 879, ⓦ visitalburywodonga.com) on Railway Place in Albury.

Canoeing To get out on the water, rent a canoe from Murray River Canoe Hire (Noreuil Park, Wodonga Place;

$30/half-day, $45/day, two-day camping trip $85; ☎ 0417 691 339, ⓦ murrayrivercanoehire.com.au). They generally drop you upstream and let you paddle back into town, where you'll be picked up.

2

ACCOMMODATION

Albury Tourist Park 372 Wagga Rd, 4.5km north ☎ 02 6040 2999, ⓦ alburymotorvillage.com.au. A Big4 holiday park with pool, camp kitchen and BBQ area, and a range of cabins (linen provided with the deluxe options) but no tent or unpowered sites. Powered sites $35, cabin $115

Clifton Motel 424 Smollett St ☎ 02 6021 7126, ⓦ cliftonmotel.com. In a good, central spot near the railway and bus station, this motel offers good-value, clean and tastefully decorated rooms. Breakfast included. $82

Fraunfelder Cottage 791 David St, 1km north ☎ 02 6023 5948, ⓦ frauenfeldercottagealbury.com.au. This charming stone cottage dating from 1857 sleeps four people in comfort; rate includes breakfast provisions but wi-fi is not available. The cottage is surrounded by beautiful lawns, established trees and flower beds. $130

EATING

Bended Elbow 480 Dean St ☎ 02 6023 6266, ⓦ thebendedelbow.com.au. A lively English-style pub with good meal deals – such as beef and Guinness pie for $22. Also hosts karaoke, trivia nights, club nights at weekends and has a great rooftop beer garden. Mon–Thurs 11am–11pm, Fri–Sun 11am–late.

Electra Café 441 Dean St at Macauley St. Popular with locals for great breakfasts in a retro setting, and you can also sit out on the pavement. Try the pancakes for breakfast or the roasted lamb and pumpkin salad ($18) for lunch. Excellent coffee. Mon–Wed 7.30am–3pm, Thurs–Sun 7.30am–4.30pm.

Mr Benedict 664 Dean St ☎ 02 6041 1840, ⓦ mrbenedict.com.au. Sit in the courtyard and enjoy breakfast eggs on toast ($9) washed down with one of many hangover cures, including a Bloody Mary ($12.50), or a lunch of pan-fried gnocchi with brussel sprouts, pea pesto and smoky bacon ($16.50). Wed–Sun 7.30am–3pm.

Bonegilla Migrant Experience

82 Bonegilla Rd, 15km east of Wodonga • Daily 10am–4pm • Free • ⓦ bonegilla.org.au

Thousands of older Australians have strong memories (fond or otherwise) of the **Bonegilla**, the Migrant Reception and Training Centre. It was set up after World War II to cope with immigrants from more than thirty countries wanting a new life in "the lucky country". Between 1947 and 1971 more than three hundred thousand people were processed here, most staying just a couple of months before being shipped off to where labour was in short supply, many to the Snowy Mountains hydroelectric scheme nearby. It was the largest and longest-operating centre of its kind in Australia. When it closed, most of the 26 self-contained living areas were flattened, but Block 19 has been restored and contains an interpretive centre, the starting point for a self-guided tour around the rest of the site.

Corowa

It's 56km northwest from Albury to the pleasant town of **COROWA**, across the Murray from Victoria's Rutherglen wine region (see p.873). Corowa is the birthplace of the Australian Commonwealth (see p.974), since the Federation Conference of 1893 was held at Corowa's courthouse on Queen Street. Today, the courthouse is the site of the **Corowa Federation Museum** (Sat & Sun 1–4pm; $4) on Queen Street, which contains documents and photos of the Federation Conference along with displays on local artists including Aboriginal artist Tommy McRae, who painted around here.

ARRIVAL AND INFORMATION COROWA

By bus The NSW TrainLink bus runs from Albury to Corowa (daily; 50min), stopping at the IGA supermarket on Riesling St.

Tourist information The visitor centre (Mon–Fri 10am–5pm, Sat 10am–3pm, Sun 10am–1pm; ☎ 02 6033 3221, ⓦ corowa.nsw.gov.au/visitors) is at 100 Edward St.

Narrandera

Almost 100km northwest of Wagga Wagga, at the junction of the Sturt and Newell highways, leafy **NARRANDERA** is a popular and laidback overnight stop. It's a pleasant place, set on the **Murrumbidgee River** – fishing fans can try for some Murray cod, yellowbelly and redfin – with streets lined with tall native trees; its white cedars, which blossom in November, are particularly beautiful. In mid-March the town hosts the **John O'Brien Festival** (🖥 johnobrien.com.au), a commemoration of the famous poet-priest who lived here in the early 1900s.

A good place to cool down is **Lake Talbot**, a willow-fringed expanse of water flowing from the Murrumbidgee River. Right next to the lake are the **Lake Talbot Pools** (Nov–March daily 10am–dusk; $3.50), a family-friendly complex with picnic areas, barbecues, water slides and an Olympic-sized swimming pool. Nearby, the riverside **Koala Regeneration Reserve** (dawn to dusk; free) has been set aside for a disease-free colony of koalas; to get there, follow the Bundidgerry Walking Track (map from visitor centre) around Lake Talbot and the Murrumbidgee River.

ARRIVAL AND INFORMATION NARRANDERA

By plane Regional Express flies daily to Narrandera from Griffith (2–3 daily; 25min) and Sydney (1–3 daily; 1hr 20min).

By bus NSW TrainLink buses between Griffith and Wagga Wagga stop outside the train station. Greyhound stops at

Narrandera South en route to Adelaide, Brisbane, Melbourne or Sydney.

Tourist information The friendly visitor centre (Mon–Sat 9am–5pm, Sun 10am–2pm; ☎ 02 6959 5545, 🖥 narrandera .com.au) is in Narrandera Park on the Newell Highway.

ACCOMMODATION AND EATING

Café Shazaray 124 East St ☎ 02 6959 1411. A good daytime option with tasty sandwiches, wraps, and light meals such as soup and sweet potato tart and salad. The coffee's good, too. Mon–Fri 8.30am–5pm, Sat 8.30am–4pm, Sun 8am–2pm.

Lake Talbot Caravan Park Gordon St, southeastern edge of town ☎ 1800 106 601, 🖥 laketalbot.com.au. Quiet and shady camping, with some nice grassy sites, and well positioned above the lake and pool. There are also brick cabins, a camp kitchen and BBQs. Un/powered sites **$25/35**, cabins **$75**

Murrumbidgee Hotel 159 East St ☎ 02 6959 2011. A classic country hotel, complete with iron lace balconies. The rooms are simple, clean and good value (with shared bathrooms) but expect some noise from the pub below. No wi-fi. **$40**

New Criterion 100 East St ☎ 02 6959 1122, 🖥 newcriterion.com.au. A fine country hotel that offers eighteen tastefully decorated rooms (en-suite or with shared bathrooms). There's also a comfortable communal lounge, and Continental breakfast is included in the rate. **$120**

Griffith

Citrus orchards line the way into **GRIFFITH**, 96km northwest of Narrandera, with a range of low hills in the background. The major centre of the Murrumbidgee Irrigation Area (MIA), it's known for its large **Italian population**, the descendants of immigrants who came in the 1920s, having already tried mining in Broken Hill, and again after World War II. Needless to say, excellent Italian cafés and restaurants line the tree-filled main street of Banna Avenue, and many **wineries** are run by Italian families. The city was laid out by **Walter Burley Griffin**, the landscape architect from Chicago who was also responsible for Canberra's confusing layout; although Griffith suffers from a similar charm deficit, it does have a rather spacious feel.

Probably the main reason you'll visit the off-the-beaten-track area around Griffith is to find **work**. There's abundant fruit picking available roughly between August and March – check with the Harvest Trail service (see p.53).

The best way to get an overview of the area is to head for **Scenic Hill**, the escarpment that forms the northern boundary of the city, where **Sir Dudley de Chair's Lookout** gives a panoramic view of the horticultural enterprises below. Immediately beneath this rocky outcrop is the **Hermit's Cave**, where Italian immigrant Valerio Recetti (1898–1932) lived alone and undetected for 23 years, working only at night and early in the morning with Stone Age tools to create a home in the caves.

In an extensive bushland setting 2km north from the city centre on Remembrance Drive, **Pioneer Park** (daily 9.30am–4pm; $10) has more than forty buildings recreating the era of the early MIA. This open-air complex also houses the **Italian Museum**, which gives an overview of early immigrants and their traditions.

ARRIVAL AND INFORMATION

GRIFFITH

By plane Regional Express (📞13 17 13, 🌐rex.com.au) flies daily between Griffith and Sydney (3–5 daily; 1hr 20min). The airport is 4km from town. Rental cars and taxis are available from the terminal.

By train There's just one direct train a week from Sydney (Sat; 9hr).

By bus NSW Trainlink offers bus services from Wagga Wagga. NSW TrainLink buses pull up at the railway station; Greyhound buses and local services stop outside the combined Griffith Travel and Transit Centre (📞02 6962

7199) and visitor centre, on the corner of Jondaryan and Banna avenues.

Destinations Narrandera (daily; 1hr 15min); Sydney (daily; 11hr 30min); Wagga Wagga (daily; 2hr 40min).

Tourist information The visitor centre (daily 9am–5pm; 📞1800 681 141, 🌐visitgriffith.com.au) can provide information on nearby wineries, while the NPWS office (Mon–Fri 8.30am–4.30pm; 📞02 6966 8100) at 200 Yambil St has details of camping and bushwalking in the nearby national parks.

ACCOMMODATION

Globe Backpackers 26 Wayeela St 📞02 6962 3619, 🌐theglobebackpackersgriffith.com.au. Very central and reasonably well-equipped hostel, offering four-bed dorms and eight-bed apartments. Good work connections. Rates go down if you stay for more than three nights. $30

Griffith Tourist Caravan Park 919 Willandra Ave, 2km south of the centre 📞02 6964 2144, 🌐griffithtouristcaravanpark.com.au. Popular with fruit-pickers and other labourers, with a range of accommodation

from bunkhouses (sleeping six) with shared kitchens to cabins and self-contained motel units. Facilities include a swimming pool, tennis court, BBQ area and TV room. Un/powered sites $28/33, bunkhouses $70, motel units $90

Victoria Hotel 384 Banna Ave 📞02 6962 1299, 🌐hotelvictoria.com.au. The best option in the centre of town, with basic en-suite rooms, a covered courtyard, and quality bistro meals downstairs (with an $11 meal Tues–Thurs). Cooked breakfast included. $110

EATING

Bertoldo's Bakery 324 Banna Ave. Italian-style bakery serving fresh breads, cakes, biscuits and hot drinks. There's an extensive lunch menu, including inexpensive pasta dishes, gourmet pies and hot rolls, plus a range of delicious *gelato*. Mon–Fri 8am–5.30pm, Sat & Sun 8am–midday.

Il Corso Café 140 Banna Ave 📞02 6964 4500. Popular mainstream Italian restaurant serving authentic pizza and well-priced pasta dishes (both from $16.50), plus a good

selection of mains, including saltimbocca, *fritto misto* and *pollo rustica*. Licensed. Takeaway available. Daily 8am–10pm.

Vita's Restaurant 252–254 Banna Ave 📞02 6962 7999. One of the more upmarket Italian places, serving fresh seafood, risotto, pasta and substantial mains like veal scallopini with mushrooms ($28) and grain-fed eye fillet ($34). The covered terrace is a good place for people watching. Mon 6–11pm, Tues–Sat 10am–2pm & 6–11pm.

WINERIES

Griffith is said to be the largest wine-producing region in Australia, and there are seventeen wineries around the town, nine of them open to the public (some by appointment only). There's virtually no public transport, but Bella Vita offers half-day winery tours ($125; 📞0437 927 651), visiting several wineries and cellar doors, plus the chance to sample other artisan produce along the way.

De Bortoli Wines De Bortoli Rd, Bilbul 📞02 6966 0111, 🌐debortoli.com.au. One of the more celebrated vineyards, and the birthplace of the sensational Noble One Botrytis Semillon dessert wine, which has raked in more than three hundred gold medals across the world. Mon–Sat 9am–5pm & Sun 9am–4pm.

McWilliam's Hanwood Estate Jack McWilliam Rd 📞02 6963 3404, 🌐mcwilliams.com.au. The region's oldest winery, McWilliam's Hanwood Estate was established in 1913 and holds tastings in a building resembling a wine barrel. Tues–Sun 10am–4pm.

Cocoparra National Park

Northeast of Griffith via Yenda • Always open • Free • Take extra supplies in case you get rained in

Cocoparra National Park, 35km northeast of Griffith, is draped across the wooded Cocoparra Range, the blue-green cypresses contrasting with the classic red Aussie rocks.

The park has several walking tracks, most taking less than an hour, though **Mount Brogden** (4km; 3hr) is moderately difficult and turns back at a trig point with long views to Murrumbidgee River. NPWS in Griffith (see opposite) has information on walks and drive-in camping.

Willandra National Park

Reached via Hillston (110km from Griffith) on the unsealed Hillston–Mossgiel road • Always open • $8 per vehicle for 24hr • Wet weather makes all the roads to Willandra impassable, so check at the NPWS office in Griffith (see opposite) before setting out and take extra supplies in case you get rained in

On the flat plains 185km northwest of Griffith is **Willandra National Park**. The park was created in 1971 from a section of the vast Big Willandra pastoral station, a famous stud-merino property founded in the 1860s. As well as allowing you to experience the semi-arid riverine plains country at close quarters, a visit to the 1918 **homestead** gives an insight into station life and the wool industry.

Hay and Shear Outback: The Australian Shearers' Hall of Fame

120km west of Griffith, at the junction of Sturt and Cobb highways • Daily 9am–5pm • $20 • ⓦ shearoutback.com.au • Shearing demonstrations daily 10.30am, 1pm & 3.30pm

The Riverina town of Hay is principally known for **The Australian Shearer's Hall Of Fame**. The centre provides an insight into Australia's farming heritage. With its clear and vibrant descriptions of Outback station life and the history of Australian pastoralism, this striking, interpretive centre-cum-museum perfectly complements a visit to the great former sheep stations at Willandra or Kinchega national parks. Along with exhibits on sheep-shearing technology, there's wool art, a woolshed relocated from Murray Downs (120km to the southwest), and, of course, shearing demonstrations.

The New England Plateau

The **New England Plateau** rises parallel to the coast, extending from the northern end of the Hunter Valley, some 200km north of Sydney, all the way to the Queensland border. At the top it's between 1000m and 1400m above sea level, and on the eastern edge an escarpment falls away steeply towards the coast. This eastern rim consists of precipitous cliff faces, deep gorges, thickly forested valleys, streams and mighty waterfalls, and because of its inaccessibility remains a largely undisturbed wilderness. On the plateau itself the scene is far more pastoral, as sheep and cattle graze on the undulating highland. Because of the altitude, the **climate** up here is fundamentally different from the subtropical coast, a mere 150km or so away: winters are cold and frosty, with occasional snowfalls, while in summer the fresh, dry air can offer welcome relief after the coastal heat and humidity. Even during a heat wave the nights will be pleasantly cool.

GETTING AROUND AND ACCOMMODATION — THE NEW ENGLAND PLATEAU

By car The New England Hwy, one of the main links between Brisbane and Sydney, passes all the major towns – Tamworth, Armidale, Glen Innes and Tenterfield – from where scenic side roads branch off towards the coast.

By train Sydney's Cityrail trains go as far north as Scone, while NSW TrainLink has services to Tamworth where the line forks, continuing to Moree to the west, and, to the east, Tenterfield and points north.

By bus The area is well served by bus: Greyhound Australia has daily services between Sydney or Canberra and Brisbane, and between Brisbane and Melbourne, both via New England. New England Coaches (ⓦ newenglandcoaches.com.au) runs a service from Coffs Harbour to Tamworth via Bellingen, Dorrigo, Armidale and Uralla three times a week.

Accommodation Farms and stations all over the highlands provide farmstay accommodation, offering horseriding and other activities.

Scone and around

The upper end of the **Hunter Valley** is Australia's main horse-breeding area, with at least thirty stud farms; sires are flown in from all over the world to breed with the local mares. The pretty township of **SCONE** is at the centre of the horse trade here and you can get further details of the business from the visitor information centre. The best time to visit is during the Scone Horse Festival (ten days in May) which features local prize specimens in horse shows, rodeos and races including the Scone Cup; book your accommodation well in advance. Any time of the year, ask at the visitor information centre about regular races held in the area, and visits to the studs (particularly during breeding season, September to Christmas).

There are cattle- and sheep-breeding stations up here too, while the fertile soils of the Upper Hunter also yield a harvest of cereals and fruits including, of course, grapes. In recent years, coal seam gas exploration has become a hotly contested political issue in the region, and you'll see many protest signs outside houses and on country fences.

Burning Mountain

About 20km north of Scone, **Burning Mountain** can be found near the village of Wingen. The smoking vents don't indicate volcanic activity but rather a seam of coal burning 30m under the surface – one of only three such in the world: the fire was ignited naturally, perhaps by a lightning strike or spontaneous combustion, more than a thousand years ago. The area, protected as a nature reserve, can be reached via a signposted **walking trail** that starts at the picnic grounds at the foot of the hill, just off the New England Highway; pick up the informative NPWS guide to the area's walking tracks from Scone's NPWS office (see below). You might also see aquatic fossils on your walk – this area was once under the ocean.

ARRIVAL AND INFORMATION

SCONE AND AROUND

By train NSW TrainLink trains run daily from Sydney to Scone, while Cityrail has three services per day (change in Hamilton for Sydney); the trip is around four hours.

By bus Greyhound buses stop daily at Murrurundi and Scone en route between Sydney and Brisbane. New England Coaches operates a service three times a week between Coffs Harbour and Tamworth.

Tourist information The visitor information centre (daily 9am–5pm; ☏ 02 6540 1300, ⓦ upperhuntertourism .com.au) is on the corner of Susan and Kelly streets and also has a wine centre attached. The National Parks & Wildlife Service office (Mon–Fri 8.30am–4.30pm; ☏ 02 6540 2300) is at 137 Kelly St.

ACCOMMODATION AND EATING

Asser House Café 202 Kelly St ☏ 02 6545 3571. A small, popular café with shady outdoor seating. There's the usual breakfast offerings, and sandwiches for lunch ($7–10) include ham and cheese toasties or roast beef and tomato chutney. Open for dinner on Thursday and Friday during festival time. Mon–Fri 6.30am–4pm, Sat & Sun 8am–4pm.

INN Scone 112 St Aubins St ☏ 02 6545 3848, ⓦ innscone.com.au. In the centre of Scone, just off the main road, are these modern, stylish and self-contained studio and one-bed apartments in what used to be a tannery. Two apartments open out onto a private courtyard. $189

Kerv Espresso Bar 108 Liverpool St ☏ 02 6545 3111. This café serves hearty breakfast and a good range of lunch options ($10–20) such as pork dumplings with Asian broth, as well as delicious scones for afternoon tea. Dinner is also served three nights a week. Mon–Wed & Sun 8am–7pm, Thurs–Sat 8am–9pm.

Segenhoe View B&B 429 Glenbawn Rd, Segenhoe ☏ 02 6545 2081, ⓦ segenhoeview.com.au. This spacious modern farmhouse, a five-minute drive from Scone, offers two charming bedrooms, with access to a guest lounge and breakfast room. A cooked breakfast is included, and evening meals are available. $200

Tamworth

TAMWORTH – on the New England Highway – is also known as the "City of Lights" because it was the first in Australia to be fitted with electric street lighting, in 1888. To most Australians, however, Tamworth means **country music** – it's a sort of antipodean

Nashville and recently became the Texas town's sister city. If country music isn't your thing, there are **art galleries** and craft studios around, and the city is gradually building its reputation as a food and wine destination. In late April it hosts the **Taste Tamworth** festival, which is ten days of food-related activities. In the second half of January each year, fans from all over Australia and beyond descend on the city for the ten-day **Tamworth Country Music Festival**. Every pub, club and hall in the city hosts gigs, record launches and bush poetry, culminating in the presentation of "Golden Guitars", the Australian Country Music Awards – for information and bookings, contact the visitor centre (see below).

Outside of festival time Tamworth is a lot less atmospheric but there is still enough to keep you busy. For panoramic views of the city and the Peel River Valley, head to the **Oxley Lookout and Nature Reserve** at the end of White Street.

Big Golden Guitar

Cnr The Ringers Rd & New England Hwy • Daily 9am–5pm • Museum $10; Bradman Collection $5 • ⓦ biggoldenguitar.com.au

The 12m-high golden guitar in front of the **Golden Guitar Complex**, on the southern edge of town, sums up the town's role as the country music capital of Australasia. Inside you'll find a waxwork museum displaying Australian country stars such as Chad Morgan, Buddy Williams, Smoky Dawson and his horse Flash, Slim Dusty, Reg Lindsay and Tex Morton. A separate **Bradman Collection** brings together the biggest cache memorabilia associated with the great Australian cricketer Sir Don Bradman.

Walk a Country Mile

561 Peel St • ⓣ 02 6766 9696 • Mon–Fri 10am–4pm, Sat 10am–2pm • $7

Now part of the larger Australian Country Music Hall of Fame, this special feature offers interactive displays, film and music clips, and old albums which allow visitors to explore the music and artists that have been pivotal in shaping Australian Country Music.

Hands of Fame and the Smoky Dawson statue

There's yet more musical memorabilia at the corner of Brisbane Street and Kable Avenue, where the **Hands of Fame** cornerstone bears the palm prints of various country greats. Outside the council offices on Peel Street is a **statue of Smoky Dawson** sitting on a bench, and you can pop yourself down next to him and ask someone to take a photo.

Tamworth Regional Gallery

466 Peel St • Tues–Fri 10am–5pm, Sat 10am–4pm • Free • ⓦ tamworthregionalgallery.com.au

The **Tamworth Regional Gallery**, above the library, has frequently changing exhibitions, with good contemporary and Aboriginal art. It is also the home of the Tamworth Textile Triennial and every three years the best of textile art from around the country is displayed here.

ARRIVAL AND DEPARTURE — TAMWORTH

By train NSW TrainLink train services run daily between Sydney (6hr 10min) and Armidale (1hr 50min) via Tamworth.

By bus Both Greyhound and New England Coaches buses pass through on a regular basis, the former en route between Sydney and Brisbane. New England coaches make the trip to Coffs Harbour, stopping at Uralla and Bellingen. Destinations Armidale (daily; 1hr 40min); Dorrigo (daily; 3hr 45min); Port Macquarie (2 weekly; 7hr 15min); Scone (weekly; 1hr 45min); Tenterfield (daily; 4hr).

INFORMATION AND ACTIVITIES

Tourist information The visitor information centre (daily 9am–5pm; ⓣ 02 6767 5300, ⓦ visittamworth.com) is located at the Big Golden Guitar on The Ringers Rd (see above).

Market The Tamworth Farmers Market (ⓦ tamworthfarmersmarket.com) is held on the second Sunday of the month in Bicentennial Park on Kable Avenue (9am–1pm) and sells fresh produce, dairy products and goodies to eat as you browse.

Jackeroo and Jilleroo school Leconfield in Kootingal, 50km east of Tamworth (ⓣ 02 6769 4328, ⓦ leconfield .com) offers a five-day residential school (\$625) where you learn to ride and groom horses, shear and throw fleeces, lasso, whip crack and muster. Pick-up from *Tamworth YHA*.

ACCOMMODATION

Big4 Paradise Tourist Park 575 Peel St ☎ 02 6766 3120 or ☎ 1800 330 133, ⓦ big4.com.au. The closest place to town for campers and caravanners, this Big4 site is on the river about a 5min walk from the centre and has a camp kitchen and pool. Two-night minimum for cabins. Un/powered sites $34/39, cabins $174

Quality Hotel Powerhouse Cnr East St & Armidale Rd ☎ 02 6766 7000, ⓦ qualityhotelpowerhouse.com.au. This smart motel has a corporate feel, large, clean rooms, and five-star facilities, including room service, a gym and a swimming pool. Breakfast extra. There's also a restaurant on site. $192

Tamworth YHA 169 Marius St ☎ 02 6761 2600, ⓦ yha.com.au. Bang opposite the train station, this hostel is very friendly and makes a comfortable base. Dorms and rooms are showing their age, but there's a sunny courtyard, TV room, laundry and a courtesy bus. Dorms $30.50, doubles $61

EATING

Hog's Breath Café 265–267 Peel Sy ☎ 02 6766 9522, ⓦ hogsbreath.com.au. In the land of beef, a steak house, even one that is part of global chain, is the natural choice – and a better option than most of the pubs in town. The menu includes Aussie prime ribs ($36.95) and Byron Bay chilli prime rib ($33.95). All steaks include a choice of steamed vegetables or salad, and fried, baked or mashed potato. Daily 11.30am–9.30pm.

Hopscotch Kiosk Cnr Kable Ave & Hill St ☎ 02 6766 8422; ⓦ hopscotchrestaurant.com.au/kiosk. This child-friendly little place offers a range of takeaway snacks and cakes, plus excellent coffee. Have a brioche brekky burger ($12) in the morning, or a satisfying lunch main later on, such as crab-meat mac and cheese ($17). Ingredients are sourced locally where possible. Mon, Tues & Sun 7am–3pm, Wed–Sat 7am–10pm.

Le Pruneau 83 Bridge St ☎ 02 6765 3666, ⓦ lepruneau .com.au. An easy-to-miss French restaurant on a residential street that prides itself on using organic and local produce; the menu changes regularly. Breakfast offerings include dukkah-spiced eggs, tabbouleh, baba ganoush, labna and toast ($17) while the lunch menu offers soup, warm wraps, pasta and blinis ($18). They also make their own bread. Daily 7.30am–6pm.

The Old Bell Tower 152 Marius St ☎ 02 6761 2785, ⓦ theoldbelltower.net.au. A repurposed old church that's part café and part shop selling furniture, gifts and antiques. Sip tea and eat lemonade scones under the stained-glass windows or lounge outside in the flower-filled garden with a burger ($17.50). Mon–Fri 8.30am–5pm, Sat & Sun 7.30am–4pm.

Uralla and around

URALLA is an old gold town on the New England Highway with a small but thriving population of around two and a half thousand. Many people choose to drive straight through without stopping, but Uralla has small-town charm and the **Historic Building Walk** takes you past the highlights (pick up a leaflet from the visitor centre). Look out for **McCrossin's Mill Museum** (daily 10am–5pm; $7), a historic redbrick, three-storey flour mill on Salisbury Street. The **New England Brewing Company** operates out of an old wool store in town and you can drop by for tastings (Thurs–Sat 11am–6pm; ☎ 04 3387 5209), or take a brewery tour, held on Saturdays at 1pm.

Walcha

The town of **WALCHA** (pronounced "Wol-ka"), 41km south of Uralla on Thunderbolt's Way, is surrounded by national parks, making it a great base for nature enthusiasts and trout anglers. There are some scenic drives in the surrounding area, as well as good fossicking opportunities. While in Walcha itself, pick up a map from the visitor centre to discover the **sculptures** by Australian and international artists that are displayed around town.

Oxley Wild Rivers National Park

Easily reached from Uralla, Walcha and Armidale (see p.274), **Oxley Wild Rivers National Park**, 20km east of Walcha, is home to dramatic gorges and waterfalls as well as some tracts of rare dry rainforest. Admire **Dangars Falls** from the lookout and explore the network of walking tracks around **Dangars Gorge** and **Apsley Gorge**. Serious and well-prepared walkers may want to take on the four-day **Green Gully Track** into the Apsley and Macleay gorges.

INFORMATION AND ACTIVITIES

Tourist information The Uralla visitor information centre (Mon–Fri 9.30am–4.30pm, Sat & Sun 10am–3pm; 📞 02 6778 4496, ⓦ uralla.com) is on Bridge St, and the NPWS office is at 188 North St (Mon–Fri 9am–4pm; 📞 02 6777 4700).

Fossicking Fossicking is possible at the Wooldridge Recreation and Fossicking Reserve, 6km west of Uralla. The visitor centre rents equipment for $10/day (with a $50 deposit) and has a sheet of gold-panning instructions for novices.

2

Armidale

Australia's highest city, at 980m, **ARMIDALE** is home to the **University of New England**, which, together with a couple of famous boarding schools, gives an unexpectedly academic feel to a place so far upcountry. Significantly cooler than the surrounding plains, Armidale is also a place of considerable natural beauty, especially in autumn, when its many parks are transformed into a sea of red and gold. The central pedestrian mall, **Beardy Street**, is flanked by quaint Australian country pubs with wide, iron-lace verandas and on the last Sunday of the month the street comes alive with an extensive morning **market** complete with buskers.

New England Regional Art Museum

106 Kentucky Street • Tues–Sun 10am–4pm • Free • ⓦ neram.com.au

The excellent **New England Regional Art Museum** includes a fantastic collection of pieces by English-born Howard Hinton (1867–1948) and displays by Arthur Streeton and Tom Roberts, plus big-name temporary exhibits from Sydney.

Aboriginal Centre and Keeping Place

128 Kentucky Street • Mon–Fri 9am–4pm, Sat 10am–2pm • Free

The arresting modern building with the distinctive ochre-coloured tin roof is the indigenous-run **Aboriginal Centre and Keeping Place**, an educational, visual and performing arts centre.

Mount Yarrowyck Nature Reserve

West of Armidale, 27km along the Bundarra Road, is the **Mount Yarrowyck Nature Reserve**, where an Aboriginal cave-painting site can be accessed via a 3km circuit walk.

ARRIVAL AND INFORMATION

By plane QantasLink and Regional Express (Rex) both fly between Armidale and Sydney (3–5 daily; 1hr 15min). The airport is 8km from town; there's a taxi service (📞 02 6771 1455) available from the terminal.

By train There's a NSW TrainLink train to/from Sydney (daily; 8hr 10min), which also calls at Tamworth (daily; 1hr). The train station is on Brown St, in the town centre.

By bus The bus terminal adjoins the visitor centre. NSW TrainLink, New England Coaches and Greyhound services arrive and depart from here for Brisbane (1–2 daily; 7hr 30min); Port Macquarie (3 weekly; 5hr 50min); Sydney (daily; 8hr); Tamworth (daily; 1hr 25min); Tenterfield (2–3 daily; 2hr 25min).

Tourist information Armidale has a helpful visitor information centre (daily 9am–5pm; 📞 02 6772 3888, ⓦ armidaletourism.com.au) at 82 Marsh St.

GETTING AROUND

By car Plenty of places offer car rental, among them Budget, at Armidale airport (📞 02 6772 5872), and Realistic Car Rentals, at Armidale Exhaust Centre on the corner of Rusden and Dangar streets (📞 02 6772 8078). You can pick up a self-drive tour leaflet from the visitor information centre.

By bus A free bus tour of the city with Heritage Tours departs from the visitor information centre daily at 10am (2hr 30min; bookings essential, 📞 02 6770 3888).

By bike One of the best ways to get around town is by bike: there's a signposted city tour, as well as a bike path to the university campus. Bikes can be rented from Armidale Bicycle Centre, 244 Beardy St (📞 02 6772 3718).

By taxis Call Armidale Radio Taxis 📞 13 10 08.

2

ACCOMMODATION

Armidale Tourist Park 39 Waterfall Way, 2km east of town ⊕ 02 6772 6470, ⓦ armidaletouristpark.com.au. This tourist park, 2km from the town centre, has good facilities including a pool, tennis court, minigolf and a camp kitchen. There's even a herb and vegetable garden. Accommodation ranges from campsites to two- and three-bedroom cabins. Wi-fi hotspot available for a fee. Un/powered sites $26/38, dorms $41, cabins $90

Glenhope B&B 59 Red Gum Lane ⊕ 02 6772 1940, ⓦ glenhopebnb.com.au. For a real country feel and the chance to get close to a herd of cute alpacas, head 4km northwest of the city to this working alpaca farm. The cosy, self-contained doubles with kitchenette have exposed brick walls and alpaca duvets and boast a scenic location overlooking the farm. Breakfast include. $145

EconoLodge Hideaway 70 Glen Innes Rd, 2km west of town ⊕ 02 6772 5177, ⓦ econolodgearmidale.com.au. A very clean and friendly motel with good-sized rooms that are tastefully decorated and have microwaves. Bathrooms are a little dated, but it's good value and there is a small pool. $125

Poppy's Cottage Dangarsleigh Rd ⊕ 02 6775 1277, ⓦ poppyscottage.com.au. A B&B set in a farm cottage a 5min drive from town and close to a local vineyard. Guests have their own garden cottage filled with reading material and with home-made Anzac biscuits to nibble on. A cooked breakfast is included and a three-course evening meal can be arranged. $165

EATING

Archie's On The Park 63 Moore Park Lane ⊕ 02 6772 2358, ⓦ mooreparkinn.com.au. Set in a delightful old homestead, Archie's is one of the town's most elegant restaurants. The seasonal dinner menu offers a good choice of meat, seafood and pasta dishes, such as Mediterranean terrine ($12), cajun-spiced snapper fish ($37) and rack of lamb ($39). Mon–Sat 6–10pm.

Bistro On Cinders 14 Cinders Lane, behind the post office ⊕ 02 6772 42 73. A stylish restaurant serving contemporary dishes. The seasonal menu changes regularly and is chalked up on the board: try the ricotta gnocchi ($21.50), Thai calamari salad ($21.50) or slow-cooked pork belly ($23.50). Mon–Sat 8.30am–3pm.

Ten Koo 175 Beardy St ⊕ 02 6771 2102. A small Japanese restaurant offering daily lunch specials such as teriyaki chicken on rice ($9) and bento boxes ($10). There are also sushi lunch packs and sushi rolls, including vegan, veggie and brown rice options. Only four tables but takeaway is available. Mon–Fri 9.30am–3pm.

NIGHTLIFE

The New Armidale Hotel 196 Beardy St. Locally known as The Newie, this classic Australian country pub attracts a good crowd on Fri and weekends. The property has a brasserie, a cocktail bar and a veranda upstairs as well as the usual public bar, plus there's a dance floor. Daily 10am–midnight.

White Bull 117 Marsh St. A smart pub with comfy sofas, a good range of beers on tap and sports on TV. There is a decent bar menu with salads, burgers, chicken schnitzel and generous steaks ($20–26). Daily 10am–10pm.

Wicklow Hotel Cnr Dumaresq & Marsh sts. The region's oldest licensed establishment,with a good food menu, an impressive wine list and sixteen beers on tap, including their very own Wicklow Gold craft brew. The pub has two log fires for winter nights, and a sunny courtyard for warm summer days. Daily 10am–midnight.

The Waterfall Way

ⓦ visitwaterfallway.com.au

Armidale makes a good staging-post north through the **New England Plains** or east to the coast through some of Australia's most beautiful national parks. The main access road, the sealed World Heritage drive **Waterfall Way**, travels to Coffs Harbour via hundreds of kilometres of rainforest roads, waterfalls and lookouts. The exceptional **New England National Park**, 85km east, and the several patchwork sections of the **Oxley Wild Rivers** (see p.272), **Guy Fawkes River** and **Cathedral Rock** national parks around it, are full of ancient ferns, towering canopy trees, gorges and spectacular **waterfalls** (although the falls can diminish to a trickle during prolonged dry spells).

The **Wollomombi Falls** are among the highest waterfalls in Australia, plunging 225m into a gorge just over 40km east of Armidale, off the road to Dorrigo. Nearby are the **Chandler Falls**, while **Ebor Falls**, a stunning double-drop of the Guy Fawkes River, can be viewed from platforms just off Waterfall Way, another 40km beyond Wollomombi.

Between Wollomombi and Ebor, **Point Lookout** in the New England National Park offers a truly wonderful panoramic view across the forested ranges – you'd be forgiven for thinking you were in the middle of the Amazon. The road to the lookout is unsealed gravel, but is usually in reasonable condition. The rest of the park is virtually inaccessible wilderness.

ACCOMMODATION

THE WATERFALL WAY

Thungutti campground New England National Park ☏02 6657 2309. Camp under the shade of eucalyptus trees. The Tea Tree Falls walk starts from here, and there are BBQs, drinking water, composting toilets and cold showers on site. $12

Toms Cabins New England National Park ⓦ environment.nsw.gov.au. Basic cabins with bunk beds, a gas cooker and no electricity or drinking water. Bring bedding and cooking equipment. Minimum two-night stay. $50

Glen Innes

GLEN INNES, the next major stop north on the New England Highway, about 100km north of Armidale, is a decent-sized town in a beautiful setting. Although agriculture is still important up here, you begin to see more and more evidence of the gemfields – sapphires are big business as, to a lesser extent, is tin mining. In the centre, on **Grey Street** especially, numerous century-old public buildings and parks have been renovated and spruced up, and there's some fine country architecture, including a couple of large corner pubs with iron-lace verandas. As in Armidale, the autumnal foliage is exceptionally beautiful.

The Land of the Beardies History House

Cnr West Ave & Ferguson St • Mon–Fri 10am–noon & 1–4pm, Sat & Sun 1–4pm • $8 • ⓦ beardieshistoryhouse.info

The Land of the Beardies History House, in the town's first hospital, displays pioneer relics, period-room settings and a reconstructed slab hut. The name alludes to the two hairy stockmen who settled the area in the nineteenth century, and the title is one of which the town is proud.

Australian Standing Stones

Scottish legacy of the original settlers is reflected in the name of the town itself and in many of its streets, which are rendered in both English and Gaelic. The local granite **Australian Standing Stones** at Martins Lookout on Watsons Drive, are based on the Ring of Brodgar in Scotland and honour the "contribution of the Celtic races to Australia's development". The stones are the site of the **Australian Celtic**

THE MYALL CREEK MASSACRE

In the first decades of the nineteenth century, when European settlers started to move up to the highlands and to use Aboriginal-occupied land on the plateau as sheep and cattle pasture, many of the local Aborigines fought back. Time and again bloody skirmishes flared up, though most were never mentioned in pioneer circles and have subsequently been erased from public memory. The **Myall Creek massacre** is one of the few that has found a place in the history of white Australia.

For Aboriginal people, expulsion from the lands of their ancestors amounted to spiritual as well as physical dispossession, and they resisted as best they could: white stockmen staying in huts far away from pioneer townships or homesteads feared for their lives. In 1837 and 1838, Aborigines repeatedly ambushed and killed stockmen near the Gwydir and Namoi rivers. Then, during the absence of the overseer at Myall Creek Station, near present-day Inverell, twelve farm hands organized a raid in retribution, killing 28 Aborigines. In court, the farm hands were acquitted – public opinion saw nothing wrong with their deed, and neither did the jury. The case was later taken up again, however, and seven of the participants in the massacre were sentenced to death on the gallows.

Festival (ⓦaustraliancelticfestival.com) during the first weekend of May, when locals dust off their bagpipes, brave haggis, stage Highland games and see the Celtic slaves take on the Roman legions.

ARRIVAL, INFORMATION AND ACTIVITIES   GLEN INNES

By bus Greyhound buses and NSW TrainLink services stop in town daily en route between Sydney (10hr) and Brisbane (6hr 15min).

Tourist information The visitor information centre (Mon–Fri 9am–5pm, Sat & Sun 9am–3pm; ☎02 6732 2400, ⓦgleninnestourism.com) is at 152 Church St, as the New England Hwy is called as it passes through town. It has a sapphire shop attached and can help book accommodation. You can also buy bags of wash here for

$10, if you want to try your luck looking for gemstones.

Festival Minerama (ⓦminerama.com.au) is a fossicking and gem show held every year on the second weekend in March, and the main draw is the programme of fossicking field trips.

Fossicking Most campsites around Glen Innes offer fossicking opportunities, and there are a number of other sites within easy reach of town (some with picnic facilities); the visitor centre can point you in the right direction.

ACCOMMODATION

Anna Bella Motel 60 Church St ☎02 6732 2688. Run by a friendly Dutch couple, the clean, spacious rooms here are set back from the main highway. Ask for a king if you need more space. Beds are comfy. $96

Glen Rest Tourist Park 9807 New England Hwy ☎02 6732 2413. The only campsite not in town but it's set back from the highway behind what was once a petrol station and offers shady sites. Amenities are clean, the owners friendly and the camp kitchen and TV area well equipped. There's also

fossicking on site. Rates include free (but limited) wi-fi. Un/powered sites $24/32, cabins $79

Great Central Hotel 313 Grey St ☎02 6732 1966, ⓦgreatcentralhotel.com. This historic two-storey building, dating from 1874, offers 14 refurbished rooms – all clean and smartly furnished, but none en suite –above the pub and restaurant. There's a guest lounge and kitchenette, as well as a wide veranda overlooking the main street. The on-site café serves breakfast. No wi-fi. $65

EATING AND DRINKING

The Crofters Cottage Standing Stones. A homely café serving hearty breakfasts, including eggs benedict and a vegetarian option with mushrooms, wilted spinach, roast tomatoes, pesto and avocado. The lunch menu is equally good, with dishes such as coconut-crumbed prawns and soft-shell crab with a pear, walnut and blue cheese salad ($18). There's a good selection of cakes and scones for afternoon tea. Mon–Sun 9am–5pm.

Cuisine Café 305 Grey St. A bright little café with red walls, black furniture and art on the walls. The menu features burgers, schnitzels and seafood, with blackboard

specials like beer-battered perch fillets ($18.50), warm duck salad ($24) and roasted quail with couscous and grilled pears ($24). Takeaway also available. Mon–Sun 8am–2pm.

Bluestill Distillery 375 Furracabad Rd ⓦbluestill.com.au. This distillery, relocated from Young, produces an interesting range of bourbons, whiskies, gins, vodkas and other "country-style" spirits. The distillery offers tastings and retail sales – try the Red Kelpie Dark Rum ($26). Mon–Fri 9am–5.30pm, Sat 9.30am–5pm, Sun 10am–3pm.

Inverell

The area between Glen Innes and **INVERELL**, 67km to the west, is one huge gemfield. Industrial diamonds, topaz, zircons and, during the boom years, eighty percent of the world's sapphires have been mined in the area. The town is still known as "Sapphire City", and though not much mining takes place anymore, you can still watch gems being washed, sorted and cut at local jewellers. If you want to try your own luck, you'll need to contact the **visitor centre** (see below), which can direct you to the designated areas.

ARRIVAL AND INFORMATION   INVERELL

By bus NSW TrainLink services run from Tamworth and Armidale, as well as from Grafton.

Destinations Armidale (weekly on Tues; 1hr 50min); Grafton (3 weekly; 3hr); Tamworth (6 weekly; 3hr 20min).

Tourist information The visitor information centre (Mon–Fri 9am–5pm, Sat & Sun 9am–2pm; ☎02 6728 8161, ⓦinverell.com.au) is on Campbell St.

Tenterfield and around

Less than 20km from the Queensland border, the quiet little town of **TENTERFIELD** marks the northern end of the New England Plateau. From here you can go straight to Ballina on the coast or continue north on the New England Highway. Settled by 61 German families, today Tenterfield honours its Germanic origins with a week-long **beer festival** in the March of odd-numbered years. Tenterfield has a confirmed place in Australian history, being the birthplace of the **Australian Federation**. Its title was earned when the prime minister of New South Wales, Sir Henry Parkes, made his famous Federation speech here in 1889, advocating the union of the Australian colonies; twelve years later the **Commonwealth of Australia** was inaugurated (see p.974). The **Sir Henry Parkes Museum** (Mon–Fri 9am–5pm, Sat & Sun 10am–4pm; $12) recalls the occasion, and you'll still see the federation flag flown around town.

Bald Rock National Park

$8 per vehicle for 24hr

Tenterfield's real attractions lie outside town. **Bald Rock**, 35km to the northeast, is in the national park of the same name and claims to be Australia's second-largest monolith after Uluru, but a grey-granite version, 213m high. You can walk up the northeast side to the summit, from where there are breathtaking panoramic views well into Queensland.

Boonoo Boonoo Falls

The excursion to Bald Rock combines nicely with a visit to the nearby 210m-high **Boonoo Boonoo Falls**, also set in a national park of the same name, which is home to endangered brush-tailed rock wallabies. The road is sealed as far as Bald Rock, but there's an unsealed road (usually passable in a 2WD) branching off before you reach the rock and running for around 12km to the falls. En route to Bald Rock on the left you'll pass **Thunderbolt's Hideout**, the rock shelter and stable of the bushranger Captain Thunderbolt (see p.169). Details are available from the **visitor centre** (see below)

ARRIVAL AND INFORMATION

TENTERFIELD AND AROUND

By bus There are daily Greyhound services to Tenterfield from Brisbane (5hr 10min) and Sydney (11hr 10min), and NSW TrainLink run here from Armidale (2hr 30min).

Tourist information The visitor information centre is at 157 Rouse St (Mon–Fri 9am–4.30pm, Sat 9am–4pm, Sun 10am–2pm; ☏ 02 6736 1082, ⊛ tenterfieldtourism.com.au).

ACCOMMODATION AND EATING

Courtyard Café 203 Rouse St ☏ 02 6736 5792. Tucked away at the back of the Sir Henry Parkes Museum, this sunny café offers a range of wholesome breakfast treats such as house-made granola with yoghurt ($9) and quesadillas ($11.50). The lunch menu includes sliders, burgers and more substantial food like beef lasagne ($15). Mon–Fri 9am–4pm, Sat & Sun 8am–4pm.

Tenterfield Lodge Caravan Park & Guest House 2 Manners St ☏ 02 6736 1477, ⊛ tenterfieldlodge caravanpark.com.au. Set away from the main road, the

caravan park here is grassy and shady with a good choice of sites, and there are also rooms and dorms available in the guesthouse for a two-night minimum stay. Un/powered sites $27/29, cabins $105

Tenterfield Tavern 378 Rouse St ☏ 02 6736 2888, ⊛ tenterfieldtavernmotorinn.com. Large, clean motel rooms set behind a pub. The brown and purple may be a little jarring but the big bathrooms, the microwave and sofa make up for it. Basic breakfast provisions included. $92

The northwest

From Dubbo, the **Newell Highway**, the main route from Melbourne to Brisbane, continues through the wheat plains of the northwest, their relentless flatness relieved by the ancient eroded mountain ranges of the **Warrumbungles**, near Coonabarabran, and **Mount Kaputar**, near Narrabri, with the vast Pillaga Scrub between the two towns. Clear skies and the lack of large towns make this an ideal area for stargazing, and large telescopes stare into space at both **Coonabarabran** and **Narrabri**. The thinly populated northwest is home to a relatively large number of Aboriginal people, particularly in the town of Moree, the area's largest. In 1965 Charles Perkins, an Aboriginal activist, led the **Freedom Ride**, a group of thirty people – mostly university students – who bussed through New South Wales on a mission to root out racism in the state. The biggest victory was in Moree itself when the riders, facing hostile townsfolk, broke the race bar by escorting Aboriginal children into the public swimming pool.

The area with rich black soil that extends from **Gunnedah**, just west of Tamworth, to Walgett is **cotton country**. Beyond Walgett, just off the Castlereagh Highway that runs from Dubbo, is **Lightning Ridge**, a scorching-hot opal-mining town relieved by hot artesian bore baths.

Coonabarabran

Known as the "Astronomy Capital of Australia", the country town of **COONABARABRAN** on the Castlereagh River, 160km north of Dubbo via the Newell Highway, draws people to **gaze at stars** in the clear skies, or for bushwalking and climbing in the spectacular **Warrumbungles** mountain range 35km to the west. In 2013, a severe bushfire swept through the area, burning out 56,000 hectares and razing 56 homes. Although the landscape has largely recovered, some scars are still visible.

Siding Spring Observatory Complex

Tues–Fri 9.30am–4pm • $15 • ⓦ nationalparks.nsw.gov.au

The **Siding Spring Observatory Complex** is perched high above the township on the edge of Warrumbungle National Park. The skies are exceptionally clear out here, due to the dry climate and a lack of pollution and population. The giant 3.9m optical telescope (one of the world's largest) can be viewed close up from an observation gallery, and there's an astronomy exhibition, complemented by hands-on exhibits and a film. You can't actually view the stars at Siding Spring because, as a working observatory, it's closed at night. It opens to the public on one night of the year during October's **Festival of the Stars**, when you can also catch pub talks by astronomers, as well as markets and Coonabarabran's annual racing carnival.

Warrumbungle Observatory

$24 • Bookings are essential, shows cancelled if it rains • ☎ 04 8842 5112

The improbably named Peter Starr, a retired Siding Spring astronomer, offers **stargazing tours** at **Warrumbungle Observatory**. Bring along a digital SLR and he'll take some close-up photos of the moon's lunar landscape as well as stunning astral skies for you.

ARRIVAL AND INFORMATION   COONABARABRAN

By train NSW TrainLink has daily services from Sydney; take the train to Lithgow (daily; 5hr) and then change to a bus.

Tourist information Coonabarabran visitor information centre (daily 9am–5pm; ☎ 02 6849 2144 or ☎ 1800 242 881, ⓦ warrumbungle.nsw.gov.au) is on the Newell Hwy, or John Street as it's called as it passes through town. There's a display of ancient megafauna inside.

ACCOMMODATION AND EATING

All Travellers Motor Inn 23–25 John St ☎ 02 6842 1133, ⓦ alltravellers.com.au. Modern brick-and-timber motel with spacious rooms (one wheelchair-accessible) and a pool. In a good location, quiet and near some decent eating options. Rates include a Continental breakfast. No wi-fi. **$140**

John Oxley Caravan Park 1.5km along the Oxley Hwy ☎ 02 6842 1635, ⓦ johnoxeycvn.net. Shady and relaxing caravan park, one of two in town, with BBQs and a small kiosk. Even if you're not staying you can use its toilets and powerful hot showers for $4. Un/powered sites **$22/28**, cabins **$70**

2

Tastebuds on Dalgarno 3/48 Dalgarno St ☎0431 862 357, ⓦtastebudsondalgarno.com.au. This buzzy space contains a café and a health-food store selling pesticide-free fruits and vegetables. The blackboard menu offers wholesome snacks such as lentil dahl on brown rice and nachos with cauliflower nuggets and salad (both $14.50). Mon–Fri 7.30am–5pm.

WINERIES

Coonandry Wines Some 4km north of town on Dandry Rd ☎02 6842 1649. Boutique local winery that specializes in Chardonnay and Cabernet Sauvignon, and is open for tasting and sales at weekends. Sat & Sun 10am–5pm. **Warrumbungle Wines** 20km northeast of Coonabarabran, South Burloo ☎02 6842 1228, ⓦblowflywines.com. Boasts an eclectic variety of wines under the Blowfly label, including Merlot, Petit Verdot and a Brut Reserve NV sparkling wine. Tastings by appointment only.

Warrumbungle National Park

The rugged **Warrumbungles** are ancient mountains of volcanic origin with jagged cliffs, rocky pinnacles and crags jutting from the western horizon. The dry western plains and the moister environment of the east coast meet at these ranges, with plant and animal species from both habitats coexisting here. **Warrumbungle National Park** ("crooked mountains") was once bordered by three different language groups – the Gamilaroi, the Weilwan and the Kawambarai – and evidence of past Aboriginal habitation here is common, with stone flints used to make tools indicating old campsites. The park is particularly spectacular in spring when wild flowers bloom in the sandstone areas, and resident fauna include four species of kangaroo, plus koalas and a variety of birds including wedgetail eagles, superb blue wrens, eastern spinebills and emus, as well as heaps of dancing butterflies along the trails. Remember to bring plenty of water when walking in the summer and warm clothing in winter, as nights can be very chilly.

Gurianawa Track and White Gum Lookout Walk

The wheelchair-accessible bitumen **Gurianawa Track** makes a short circuit around the centre and overlooks the flats where eastern grey kangaroos gather at dusk. Another good introduction to the park is the short **White Gum Lookout Walk** (1km), with spectacular panoramic views over the ranges that are especially dramatic at sunset.

Grand High Tops Trail

The ultimate challenge – for the reasonably fit only – is the 14.5km (roughly 5hr) **Grand High Tops Trail** along the main ridge and back. The walk begins at Pincham car park and follows the flat floor of Spirey Creek through open forests full of colourful rosellas and parrots, and lizards basking on rocks. As the trail climbs, there are views of the 300m-high Belougery Spire, and more scrambling gets you to the foot of the **Breadknife**, the park's most famous feature, a 2.5m-wide rock flake thrusting 90m up into the sky. From here the main track heads on to the rocky slabs of the Grand High Tops, with tremendous views of most of the surrounding peaks. Experienced walkers could carry on to climb Bluff Mountain and then head west for Mount Exmouth (1205m), the park's highest peak; both are great spots from which to watch the sunrise.

ESSENTIALS   WARRUMBUNGLE NATIONAL PARK

Entry $8 per vehicle for 24hr.

Access There's no public transport to the Warrumbungles, so you'll need your own.

Tourist information The Warrumbungle Visitor Centre (daily 9am–4pm; ☎02 6825 4364, ⓦenvironment .nsw.gov.au) is in the park just off John Renshway Parkway. It houses hands-on displays, can provide detailed maps of walking tracks, and during school holidays runs a range of guided activities including bird- and flower-identification, caving and activities for kids.

Rock climbing Climbers are allowed to climb anywhere except the Breadknife and Chalkers Mountain; permits are required from the visitor centre.

ACCOMMODATION

IN THE PARK

Balor Hut campground Adjacent to the Breadknife ☏ 02 6825 4364. As well as camping spots, *Balor Hut* also has a walkers' hut from the 1950s and visitors can sleep inside on a slab bunk (no bedding or mattress supplied) but booking in advance is essential and the key needs to be picked up from the visitor centre. Camping per person $6

NEAR THE PARK

The Cottage 74 Tibuc Road, Coonabarabran ☏ 0455 112 535, ⓦtibucgardens.com. Nestled in the foothills of the Warrumbungles, this modern, self-contained cottage offers two bedrooms, a fully equipped kitchen, TV and outdoor BBQ. To get online, head to the nearby café, where there's free wi-fi. $140

Barkala Farmstay 2630 Dandry Rd, Coonabarabran ☏ 02 6842 2239, ⓦbarkalafarmstay.com.au. This working Aussie farm and pottery offers a range of accommodation, including cottages, a farmhouse, an old school house, artists' studio and several camping sites. There's an on-site café, but no wi-fi. Unpowered sites $18, doubles $95

The Pilliga Forest

Covering some 1,235,000 acres, the **Pilliga Forest**, a mighty expanse of towering iron barks and white cypress trees, is the largest native inland forest west of the Great Dividing Range and lies about 28km north of Coonabarabran. At first glance it seems like impenetrable scrubland, but delve a little deeper and you'll see emus, other birds and kangaroos. Well worth a visit within the forest are the **Sculptures in the Scrub**, a series of Aboriginal-themed sculptures made from steel, bronze and stone perched over a fantastic gorge along a pleasant walking trail (around 1hr), and the **Sandstone and Salt Caves**, which feature preserved Aboriginal paintings.

INFORMATION   PILLIGA FOREST

Tourist information Before you start out, pick up a detailed forest map from the Pilliga Forest Discovery Centre (Mon–Fri 9am–5pm, Sat & Sun 10am–5pm; ☏ 02 6843 4011), located at 50–58 Wellington St in Baradine, about 28km north of Coonabarabran, and inform them of your plans – there is no mobile phone reception in the forest and it is a vast, uninhabited place with totally unsealed roads. As always, ensure you have plenty of food and water with you, and in the event of a breakdown stay with your vehicle.

Gunnedah and around

On the Oxley Highway, 76km west of Tamworth, **GUNNEDAH** is one of the largest towns in the northwest. It's often referred to as Australia's **koala capital**, and the **visitor centre** has updated information from local spotters on the whereabouts of the town's bears (it even sells "koala kitsch" – ie koala droppings). Otherwise, you have a good

DOROTHEA MACKELLAR

Gunnedah was the inspiration for the Australian poet **Dorothea Mackellar** (1885–1968) and her ode to this drought-stricken land, *My Country*, was penned while staying on her family's property here. The opening stanza is familiar to most Australians, who learn it by rote at school:

I love a sunburnt country
A land of sweeping plains
Of ragged mountain ranges
Of drought and flooding rains…

Today, Dorothea Mackellar lends her name to Gunnedah's nationally recognized poetry award (ⓦdorothea.com.au). A **poets' drive** has been established around town, with plaques at selected points, and it finishes at the quirky **Lyrical Loos** which offer piped poetry and words carved into the back of the door; a more cultural than average call of nature.

chance of seeing the bears on the **Bindea Walking Track**, a 7.4km walk from the visitor centre, or a 4.5km trek through the bush from the car park at **Porcupine's Lookout** in the porcupine reserve, just southeast of the centre.

Water Tower Museum

Sat 10am–2pm, other days by appointment • $5

Directly behind the visitor centre in Anzac Park, the **Water Tower Museum** has three floors of exhibits on the town's indigenous and European settlement history including some of Dorothea Mackellar's childhood dolls, as well as a panoramic viewing deck. The tower was built in 1908 and remained in service until the late 1950s.

Waterways Wildlife Park

7km west of Gunnedah on Mullaley Rd (the Oxley Hwy) • Daily 10am–4pm • $5

The **Waterways Wildlife Park** is a green lakeside spot that makes an inviting break from the highway and is home to tame, strokeable koalas, emus, kangaroos, wallabies, wombats, lizards and possums as well as a variety of beautiful native birds. There are also barbecues here, and it's a good place for a picnic.

ARRIVAL AND INFORMATION

GUNNEDAH AND AROUND

By train A daily NSW TrainLink train stops in Gunnedah Station – in the town centre – on its way from Sydney (6hr 15min) to Moree (2hr 20min).

Tourist information The visitor centre (Mon–Fri 9am–5pm, Sat & Sun 10am–3pm; ☎ 02 6740 2230, ⊛ gunnedah.nsw.gov.au) is in Anzac Park on South St.

ACCOMMODATION

Gunnedah Tourist Caravan Park 51 Henry St, 1km east of town ☎ 02 6742 1372, ⊛ gunnedahcaravanpark .com. A small, quiet caravan park on the edge of town with grassy sites, BBQs and a small shaded pool; sadly, there's no camp kitchen though. Free wi-fi only in the office. Un/powered sites $25/33, cabins $70

Mackellar Motel 342 Conadilly St ☎ 02 6742 6838, ⊛ mackellarmotel.com.au. A central, modern motel with rooms that are clean and large with kitchenettes. The bathrooms are a good size too and some have spa baths. There's also a covered parking area. $179

Narrabri and around

The riverside town of **NARRABRI** is recognized as the commercial centre of cotton growing, and has a large number of parks and green spaces. Unless you are here to work picking or ginning cotton (available from April–May), you are probably in the area to visit the Australia Telescope complex or Mount Kaputar National Park.

Australia Telescope Compact Array

Yarrie Lake Rd, 20km west of Narrabri • Visitor centre daily 8am–4pm, unstaffed • Free

Said to be the most advanced radio telescope in the southern hemisphere, the **Australia Telescope Compact Array** consists of six antennae, five of which move along a 3km railtrack. They detect radiowaves from space, which are then interpreted by scientists from around the world. There is a visitor centre on site with lots of computer models to play with and a film about how the telescope works, as well as a viewing platform.

Mount Kaputar National Park

The other draw around Narrabri is **Mount Kaputar National Park**. The 50km drive into the park to the 1524m-high **lookout** – with views over the vast Pilliga Forest – is steep, narrow and partly unsealed. There are nine marked bushwalking trails in the park, with brochures available from the **NPWS office** in Narrabri (see opposite). The most striking geological feature of the park is **Sawn Rocks**, a basalt formation that looks like a series of organ pipes; it's reached via the northern end of the park on the unsealed road heading to Bingara.

Wee Waa

The town of **WEE WAA**, roughly 40km west of Narrabri, was where the Namoi cotton industry began in the 1960s, and the large cotton "gins" or processing plants are located here. If you can stand the rather raw, dispirited town and the blazing summer heat, you could earn some cash from the abundant **cotton-chipping** work available here in April and May; ask at one of the two pubs on Rose Street, the main drag, and someone will send you in the right direction.

INFORMATION

Tourist information The visitor information centre (Mon–Fri 9am–5pm, Sat & Sun 9am–2pm; ☎ 02 6799 6760, ⍈ visitnarrabri.com.au) is on the Newell Hwy. The

NARRABRI AND AROUND

NPWS office is at 100 Maitland St (Mon–Fri 8.30am–4.30pm; ☎ 02 6792 7300).

ACCOMMODATION

NARRABRI

Crossroads Hotel 170 Maitland St ☎ 02 6792 5592. This long-established pub offers some refurbished one- and two-bedroom apartments – now the swishiest accommodation in town. Rooms come with kitchenettes, cable TV and fridges. Breakfast is available in the restaurant. $143.

MOUNT KAPUTAR NATIONAL PARK

Camping There are a couple of camping spots: *Bark Hut* and *Dawsons Spring* have BBQs, flush toilets, hot showers and drinking water. Unpowered sites per person $6
Dawsons Spring cabins ☎ 02 6792 7300. These cabins sleep a maximum of six and have a bathroom, kitchen and wood stove. Bookings need to be made in advance and there's a two-night minimum stay. $125

Lightning Ridge

The population of **LIGHTNING RIDGE**, 74km north of Walgett on the Castlereagh Highway, is a transient one, where people in their hordes pitch up, lured by the promise of **opal**. Amid this harsh landscape scarred by holes and slag heaps, Lightning Ridge's opal fields are the only place in the world where black opal is found. Against their dark background, these "black" stones display a vivid spectrum of colours, and command top dollar. You can try your luck at finding opals in clearly demarcated **fossicking** areas (in 2007, a tourist unearthed a $20,000 black opal), but don't do it anywhere else, or you may stray onto others' claims and infringements are taken *very* seriously.

Walk-in Mine

Bald Hill • Daily: April–Oct 9am–5pm; Nov–March 9am–3pm • Tours $20

Opal galleries and mines proliferate in town and among them is the **Walk-in Mine**, which offers underground mine tours. Experience underground life, learn more about the local miners and their lives, and be briefed on what to look out for when fossicking. There's also an opal showroom on site.

Chambers of the Black Hand

Three Mile Rd, 5km south of town • Tours at 10am & 3pm, more frequently in winter • Carvings & mine tour $35 • ☎ 02 6829 0221, ⍈ chambersoftheblackhand.com.au

A 100-year-old mine, the **Chambers of the Black Hand** is where owner/miner Ron Canlin has hand-chiselled more than 450 surreal life-size carvings – everything from Egyptian tombs to superheroes – in the mine's soft sandstone walls, and installed an underground opal shop.

Bottle House

60 Opal St • Daily 9am–5pm • $10

The effects of the opal obsession can be seen in the gloriously crazy constructions of the few who have struck it lucky, such as the **Bottle House**, a bizarrely beautiful cottage and dog kennel built entirely from beer and wine bottles set in stone.

2

Artesian Bore Baths

Pandora St • 24hr • Free

Recover after fossicking in the 42°C water of the hot **artesian bore baths** on Pandora Street, which tap into the Great Artesian Basin, an underground lake of fresh water about the size of Queensland.

ARRIVAL AND INFORMATION   LIGHTNING RIDGE

By bus NSW TrainLink runs buses to Lightning Ridge from Dubbo daily (4hr 30min).

Tourist information The visitor information centre (daily 7am–8.30pm; ☎02 6829 1670, ⊛lightningridgeinfo .com.au) is in the Lions Park, on Bill O'Brian Way; ask for the useful *Lightning Ridge and the Walgett Region* brochure. Aboriginal artist Johanna Parker's work can also be viewed and bought here.

Seasonal work Backpackers looking for work have a good chance of finding it off season (Easter to end Oct); Trevor at the Chambers of the Black Hand (see p.283) will help you out.

Festival The four-day Opal and Gem Festival (⊛lightningridgeopalfestival.com.au) in late July sees the population of Lightning Ridge shoot up by a few thousand. There is an opal and gem expo, jewellery design awards and a Fire and Ice Ball.

TOURS

Car Door Tours To explore by yourself, pick up a leaflet at the visitor centre ($1) to follow one of four colour-coded car door trails covering various points of interest, each marked with an original old car door resting in the scrub.

Black Opal Tours ☎02 6829 0368, ⊛blackopaltours .com.au. This three-hour tour includes a free pick up from your accommodation, visits to opal mines, complimentary Devonshire tea, an opal-cutting demonstration and a spot of fossicking. Tours operate daily ($35).

ACCOMMODATION AND EATING

Bruno's Restaurant 38 Morilla St ☎02 6829 4157. A busy and popular place serving a range of Italian dishes, but the wood-fire pizzas ($18–19, large pizza) come highly recommended. There's also takeaway available. Book in advance. Tues–Sun 11.30am–9pm.

Lorne Station Morilla St, 3km from Lightning Ridge, off Opal St ☎02 6829 0253, ⊛lornestation.com. This 10,000-acre property offers a range of accommodation from camping to bunkhouses (linen included), and there are free activities such as pancake breakfasts and singing round the fire. You can fossick in the old river bed or spend some time searching the opal heap. They also offer free walking tours.

No wi-fi. Un/powered sites $20/25, bunkhouses $50

Morilla's Café 2 Morilla St ☎02 6829 0009. A central café that offers toasted sandwiches, wraps, cakes and milkshakes. Sit in a shady spot and relax over a good coffee. Daily 7.30am–4pm.

Wallangulla Motel Morilla St ☎02 6829 0542, ⊛wallangulla.com. Annexed to the bowling club, this is a friendly, central option and you can charge meals at the club to your room. The motel is in two parts, the renovated original section and the new rooms; prices vary. The motel offers clean rooms, a swimming pool, sundeck and internet café. $105

SHOPPING

John Murray Art Gallery 8 Opal St ⊛johnmurrayart .com.au. Murray's intricately detailed images of the town and its residents are on show here, and there's a

wide range of originals, prints and cards for sale. Mon–Fri 9am–5pm, Sat & Sun 9am–2pm.

Back O'Bourke: the Outback

Travelling beyond Dubbo into the northwest corner of New South Wales, the landscape transforms into an endless expanse of largely uninhabited red plain – the quintessential **Australian Outback**. The searing summer heat can make touring uncomfortable from December to February. Bourke, about 370km along the Mitchell Highway, is generally considered the turning point; venture further and you're into the land known as **"Back O'Bourke"** – the back of beyond.

En route to Bourke, the Mitchell passes through **Nyngan**, the geographical centre of New South Wales, where the Barrier Highway heads west for 584 sweltering kilometres, through **Cobar** and **Wilcannia**, to **Broken Hill**.

Bourke and around

BOURKE is mainly known for its remoteness, and this alone is enough to attract tourists; once you've crossed the North Bourke Bridge that spans the Darling River, you're officially "out back". Bourke was a **bustling river port** from the 1860s to the 1930s, and there remain some fine examples of riverboat-era architecture, including the huge reconstructed wharf, from where a track winds along the magnificent, tree-lined river. The Darling River water has seen crops as diverse as cotton, lucerne, citrus, grapes and sorghum successfully grown here despite the 40°C-plus summer heat, while Bourke is also the commercial centre for a vast sheep- and cattle-breeding area.

Bourke has suffered in former years due to prolonged periods of drought, consequently losing one-third of its population (some one thousand people), who moved out of the region to find employment, but **tourism** is helping the town get back on its feet. An ideal way to see how life is lived out here is to stay on an **Outback station**; the visitor centre has details of those that welcome guests.

The **Back O' Bourke Exhibition Centre** on Kidman Way (daily 9am–5pm; $22; ☎02 6872 1321) features interesting and well-thought-out multimedia displays on Outback life within a vast sail-covered building. It's possible to combine a visit here with a paddleboat cruise (see below), and there's a nice café on site.

Mount Gunderbooka

Amid the empty, featureless plains, the elongated **Mount Gunderbooka** (498m), about 70km south of Bourke en route to Cobar, appears all the more striking. Likened to a mini-Uluru, the mountain was of similar cultural significance to the Aboriginal people of the area, with semipermanent waterholes and caves with rock art – contact the **NPWS** in Bourke for details (see below).

ARRIVAL, INFORMATION AND ACTIVITIES — BOURKE AND AROUND

By bus NSW TrainLink buses arrive here from Dubbo four times weekly (4hr 30min).

Tourist information The visitor centre (daily 9am–5pm; ⊛ visitbourke.com) is inside the Back of Bourke Exhibition Centre and can provide hand-drawn mud maps marking places of interest off the beaten track in the surrounding area, though bear in mind that these destinations can be as far as 200km away and lesser-travelled roads little more than dirt tracks. The NPWS office (Mon–Fri 8.30am–4.30pm) is at 51 Oxley St.

Seasonal work The visitor centre can help those interested in harvesting tomatoes, onions and grapes or chipping and picking cotton. July and Aug are really the only months when there's nothing to harvest.

River cruises River cruises are available aboard the old paddleboat *Jandra*, which operates two cruises per day ($16) during the winter months (between Easter and Oct) and one weekday cruise during the summer. Book through the visitor centre.

ACCOMMODATION

Bourke Riverside Motel 3–13 Mitchell St ☎02 6872 2539, ⊛ bourkeriversidemotel.com.au. On the river, this historic hotel has lovely gardens, the owners are very friendly and there are a variety of a/c rooms on offer (some self-contained and some more spacious than others). There's also a pool. $125

Comeroo Camel Station ☎02 6874 7735, ⊛ comeroo. com. This is a unique place to stay: guests can soak in bores (hot artesian pools fed by holes in the ground). Other activities include fishing and watching the local wildlife, which includes

buffalo and ostrich. You can stay in one of the bungalows, pitch a tent or park up in your camper. There are also camel treks on offer. Rate for the bungalow includes breakfast. No wi-fi. Un/powered sites $20/30, bungalows $260

Kidman's Camp Kidman Way, 7km north of Bourke ☎02 6872 1612, ⊛ kidmanscamp.com.au. A great little camping spot with a pool – and fabulous log cabins with porches perfect for stargazing, plus two swimming pools. There are campfire nights organized and a bush entertainer reciting poetry and singing. Un/powered sites $30/34, cabins $139

EATING

Diggers on the Darling 23–25 Sturt St ☎02 6870 1988, ⊛ diggersonthedarling.com.au. The menu at this good-value place near the wharf is wide-ranging for

Bourke and varies from lamb shanks ($26.50) to savoury buttermilk crêpes ($18.90). They have a limited wine list, too. Daily 7am–11pm.

Port of Bourke Hotel 23 Mitchell St ☎02 6872 2544. The place to come for filling pub food such as steak, schnitzel or sausage and mash. Try the local grain-fed steak ($30). The pub has twenty rooms, with shared bathrooms (doubles $90). Tues–Sat noon–2pm & 6.30–8.30pm, Mon 6.30–8.30pm.

The Darling River Run

Adventurous travellers wanting to see a remoter tranche of Outback should consider heading southwest from Bourke on the **Darling River Run** – one of Australia's last great adventures, taking in 829km of Outback history, heritage and landscape, running from Brewarrina near Bourke southwest to Wentworth.

The route is predominantly unsealed and closely follows the east and west banks of the Darling River. When dry it is passable in ordinary vehicles but it always pays to ask local advice about the roads and take spare fuel, water and food.

First stop, 100km southwest of Bourke, is tiny Louth, where there's a river crossing, and **Shindy's Inn** sells diesel and petrol, and has basic accommodation. In early August the population of thirty briefly balloons to around 4000 for the **Louth Races**, along the lines of its more famous Birdsville cousin. You can get a real Outback experience by staying at either **Trilby Station**, 25km downstream, or **Kallara Station**, a further 50km southwest.

At Tilpa, 15km on, there's a bridge over the river and the classic Outback pub, the 1890s **Tilpa Hotel**, with meals and fuel. The 130km-run down to Wilcannia passes **Mount Murchison Station**, on the west side of the river, allegedly once managed by the son of Charles Dickens. From Wilcannia you can follow the river downstream to Menindee (see p.295) and explore the Kinchega National Park before the final 250km run down to Wentworth on the Victorian border.

INFORMATION THE DARLING RIVER RUN

Tourist information The official NSW Tourism website (ⓦvisitnsw.com) has detailed itineraries, touring suggestions and town information. While travelling this way you can just camp beside the river pretty much wherever you want – but it's best to contact the Bourke visitor centre beforehand (see p.285).

ACCOMMODATION

Kallara Station 15min from Tilpa ☎02 6837 3963, ⓦoutbackbeds.com.au/kallara-station. With riverside a/c units, more luxurious lodge rooms, and a camp area for tents and campervans (as well as more secluded spots), this is a good place to get away from it all. Meals are available on request, but there's no wi-fi. Powered sites $5, fisherman's huts $35, doubles $100

Shindy's Inn Wilcannia–Bourke Rd ☎02 6874 7422, ⓦshindysinn.com.au. Powered and unpowered sites, as well as two self-contained cabins on the banks of the river. There's also food on offer here. Un/powered sites $20/25, cabins $90

Tilpa Hotel 1 Darling St ☎02 6837 3928. Rooms with shared bathrooms in an Outback pub, as well as meals (the steak sandwiches are huge) and fuel. For a $2 donation towards the Royal Flying Doctor Service, you can immortalize your name on the pub's tin wall. No wi-fi. $60

Trilby Station ☎02 6874 7420, ⓦtrilbystation .com.au. A 4WD is recommended to reach *Trilby Station*, where there are riverside camping spots, cottages and a bunkhouse with twin rooms. You can self-cater or enjoy the home-cooked food on offer. Ring in advance. Limited wi-fi available. Un/powered sites $23/30, twins $70, cottages $115

Cobar

Since copper was discovered here in 1870, **COBAR**, just under 160km south of Bourke and the first real stop on the Barrier Highway between Nyngan and Broken Hill, has experienced three mining booms. Today, this town of around 7000 people is home to the vast **CSA Copper Mine**, which extracts well over half a million tonnes of copper ore every year, as well as gold and silver mines. Earlier booms resulted in a number of impressive public buildings, among them the 1882 courthouse and the police station, as well as the **Great Western Hotel** on Marshall Street, whose iron-lace verandas are among the longest in the state. Most people only stop here to refuel before the monotonous 260km stretch to Wilcannia; there is, however, a lovely picnic spot in Drummond Park, just off the highway on Linsley Street.

The **Great Cobar Heritage Centre** (Mon–Fri 8.30am–5pm, Sat & Sun 9am–5pm; $12) is attached to the visitor centre on Barrier Hwy (see below) and has some great exhibits on mining, local Aborigines and the colonial social history of the area. Outside, the 1907 train carriage fitted out as a travelling clinic was used until the 1960s by the Far West Children's Health Scheme, which still brings medical assistance to remote communities.

ARRIVAL AND INFORMATION — COBAR

By bus NSW TrainLink operates regular bus service from Dubbo to Cobar (daily; 4hr) with a train connection to Sydney. The bus station is on Marshall St.

Tourist information Cobar Visitor Information Centre (Mon–Fri 8.30am–5pm, Sat & Sun 9am–5pm; ☎02 6836 2448, ⓦcobar.nsw.gov.au) is on the Barrier Hwy.

Staff can provide information on places of interest around Cobar – including the platform with views down into the open-cast gold mine – and advise on Outback bush-stays. If you're headed out to the Mount Grenfell Historic Site (see below), pick up a leaflet from the visitor centre.

ACCOMMODATION

Cobar Caravan Park 101 Barrier Hwy ☎02 6836 2425, ⓦcobarcaravanpark.com.au. This large site has smart cabins and a hundred powered sites surrounded by landscaped gardens. The amenities include a small kiosk, BBQ areas and camp kitchen facilities. Un/powered sites **$33/$35**, cabin **$120**

Cobar Crossroads Motel Cnr Bourke & Louth rds (on the Kidman Way) ☎02 6836 2711, ⓦcobarcrossroadsmotel.com.au. A good budget option with clean, neat rooms and situated only a short distance from town. Good a/c and friendly owners. There's also a saltwater pool. **$110**

Mount Grenfell Historic Site

40km west of Cobar along the Barrier Highway then 32km north along a gravel road • Sunrise to sunset • Free • ⓦenvironment.nsw .gov.au • Be sure to check road conditions at the visitor centre before setting off

Arguably one of the most significant Aboriginal rock-art locations in New South Wales is the **Mount Grenfell Historic Site**. The rocky ridge contains three art sites with more than thirteen hundred motifs – human and animal figures, including the emus that you're still likely to see around the site, plus abstract designs and hand stencils. Older layers are visible beneath the more recent pigments, but there's no way to tell exactly how old the art is. The adjacent semipermanent waterhole explains the significance of the site for the Ngiyampaa people. The signposted **Ngiyampaa Walkabout** (5km return) goes to the top of the ridge with wide views and is well signposted.

Wilcannia

WILCANNIA is 260km west of Cobar, on the Barrier Highway. The former "Queen City of the West" was founded in 1864 and until the early 1900s was a major port on the Darling River, from where produce was transported by paddle steamers and barges down the Darling–Murray river system to Adelaide. Droughts, the advent of the railways and road transport put an end to the river trade, and today it is difficult to imagine a steamer getting anywhere near the place. The only reminders of that prosperous era are the ruins of the docks (although there are plans to rebuild these) and the old lift-up bridge, along with a few impressive public buildings such as the post office, police station, courthouse, Catholic convent and the Council Chambers on Reid Street. Nowadays Wilcannia is a cheerless, boarded-up place, with high unemployment and alcoholism affecting the significant Aboriginal population.

Note that the only fuel stop between Wilcannia and Broken Hill is at the **Little Topar Hotel**, roughly halfway along the 195km stretch of the Barrier Highway.

INFORMATION

Services There's a bank, shop, two motels, a post office and a service station in town, but the fortified pub is only open a couple of hours a day. Meals and drinks are best sought at the golf club on Ross St or the *Courthouse Café & Gallery* on Reid St.

White Cliffs

From Wilcannia, you can head north off the Barrier Highway to the opal fields at **WHITE CLIFFS**, 98km away. Four kangaroo shooters found opals here in 1889 and four thousand miners followed. Besides opals, White Cliffs is famous for its extraordinary summer heat, and many of the two hundred residents **live underground** in "dug-outs". For a few dollars, several people will show you their one-man mining operations, dug-out homes and opal collections, and you can inspect the solar power station that looks like something out of a space odyssey. The big event in White Cliffs is the **Gymkhana and Rodeo** that takes place around April and attracts people from all over the country.

INFORMATION AND TOURS

Tourist information Information is available on Keraro Rd at the White Cliffs General Store (☎08 8091 6611; Mon–Sat 7.30am–7.30pm, Sun 8am–7.30pm) and at the NPWS Paroo–Darling Visitor Centre (Mon–Fri 8.30am–4.30pm, also open some weekends) in the middle of town, which has info on local national parks.

Tours There are several tours to White Cliffs from Broken Hill, including a two-day trip with Tri State Safaris ($1055 including accommodation at the *White Cliffs Underground Motel*, all meals and entrance fees; ☎08 8088 2389, ✆tristate.com.au). As well as being a good café, *Red Earth* (☎08 8091 6900, ✆redearthopal.com) also offers an opal-mine tour daily at 3pm ($20). Bookings are essential.

ACCOMMODATION

White Cliffs Underground Motel 129 Smiths Hill ☎08 8091 6677, ✆undergroundmotel.com.au. This very friendly motel comes with a warren of 32 white-painted rooms (almost all shared-bath, two are above ground) dug into the hillside, an underground bar, and a topside licensed restaurant and outdoor swimming pool. Rates include Continental breakfast. No wi-fi. **$149**

Broken Hill

The ghosts of mining towns that died when the precious minerals ran out are scattered all over Australia. **BROKEN HILL**, on the other hand, has been riding the minerals market roller-coaster continuously since 1888. Its famous "Line of Lode", one of the world's major lead-silver-zinc ore bodies and the city's *raison d'être*, still has a little life left in it yet.

Almost 1200km west of Sydney and about 500km east of Adelaide, this surprisingly gracious Outback mining town – with a population of around 20,000 and a feel and architecture reminiscent of the South Australian capital – manages to create a welcome splash of green in the harsh desert landscape that surrounds it. Extensive revegetation schemes around Broken Hill have created grasslands that, apart from being visually pleasing, help contain the dust that used to make the residents' lives a misery. The city has experienced chronic water shortages over recent years, prompting the state government to spend $500m on a new water pipeline from the Murray River – the project is due for completion by the end of 2018.

Inevitably, life in Broken Hill revolves around the **mines**, and the slag heap towering over the city centre leaves you in no doubt that, above all, this is still a mining town. Since the 1970s, however, it has also evolved into a thriving **arts centre**, thanks to the

---

CHECK YOUR WATCH

Remember to adjust your watch here: Broken Hill operates on **South Australian Central Standard Time**, half an hour behind the rest of New South Wales. All local transport schedules are in CST, but you should always check.

BROKEN HILL

ACCOMMODATION
Caledonian B&B	1
Daydream Motel	7
Ibis Styles	5
The Imperial	2
Lake View Caravan Park	3
Palace Hotel	9
Red Earth Motel	8
Royal Exchange Hotel	6
Tourist Lodge	4

EATING
Alfresco	4
Bell's Milk Bar	5
Noodle & Sushi Bar	2
Sidebar Restaurant	3
Thom, Dick & Harry's	1

DRINKING & NIGHTLIFE
Alma Hotel	5
Broken Hill Musicians Club	4
Mulga Hill Tavern	1
Palace Hotel	3
Red Lush Wine Bar & Cocktail Lounge	2

initiative of the **Brushmen of the Bush**, a painting school comprising local artists Hugh Schulz, Jack Absalom, John Pickup, Eric Minchin and Pro Hart. Diverse talents have been attracted to Broken Hill, and their works are displayed in galleries scattered all over town. Some may be a bit on the tacky side, but others are excellent, and it's well worth devoting some time to gallery browsing.

The CBD and the bulk of town lies to the northwest, while the mostly residential South Broken Hill lies southeast and feels quite separate. The streets – laid out in a grid – are mostly named after chemicals; **Argent Street** (Latin for silver) is the main thoroughfare, with the highest concentration of historic buildings and a really good art gallery.

The city is also a convenient base for touring far-northwest New South Wales and nearby areas in South Australia.

Argent Street
You'll get a pretty good feel for Broken Hill just strolling along broad Argent Street with its grand edifices, century-old pubs with ornate iron verandas and commemorative plaques. The two finest buildings, both from the early 1890s, are near the junction with Chloride Street. The brick **Post Office**, with its large square tower and double-height veranda, still fulfils its original function, while the former **Town Hall** is possibly the finest building on the street, done in South Australian Italianate style with its distinctive, almost minaret-like tower.

Broken Hill Regional Art Gallery
404–408 Argent St • Mon–Fri 10am–5pm, Sat & Sun 11am–4pm • Gold coin donation

The **Broken Hill Regional Art Gallery** is housed in a heritage-listed building and has an excellent representative collection of artists from Broken Hill as well as Australian art in general. Established in 1904, it's the second-oldest gallery in the state – after Sydney's Art Gallery of New South Wales – and has a small collection of nineteenth- and early twentieth-century paintings including works by Sidney Nolan, Margaret Preston, John Olsen and the "Brushmen of the Bush".

The Silver City Art Centre & Mint
66 Chloride St • Daily 10am–4pm • $7.50

Tucked at the back of **The Silver City Art Centre & Mint**, behind the shop and gallery, is a painting by renowned photorealist bird painter Peter Anderson. He spent two solid years working on what is said to be the largest acrylic-on-canvas painting in the world. The vast 100m-long tableau of local desert and scenes features the Sculpture Park, Silverton and the distant Flinders Range.

Railway Mineral & Train Museum
Blende St, diagonally opposite the visitor centre • Daily: Jan & Feb 9am–3pm; March–Dec 10am–3pm • $5

The **Railway Mineral & Train Museum** occupies the former station of a rail service that ran from here to Silverton. A highlight among the old railway carriages and machinery is the sleek, diesel *Silver City Comet*, the first air-conditioned train in the southern hemisphere, which ran from here to Parkes from 1937 until 1989. There's also a small hospital museum, a good section on immigrants to the region, and an extensive mineral collection.

Albert Kerstin Mining & Minerals Museum
Cnr Bromide & Crystal sts • Mon–Fri 10am–4.45pm, Sat & Sun 1–4.45pm • $6

The **Albert Kerstin Mining & Minerals Museum**, housed in a nineteenth-century bond store, looks at Broken Hill's geology, mineralogy and metallurgy. Highlights include a 42kg silver ingot and the spectacular *Silver Tree*, a 68cm figurine wrought of pure silver from the Broken Hill Mines, depicting five Aborigines, a drover on horseback, kangaroos, emus and sheep gathered under a tree.

Line of Lode Miners Memorial
Daily 6am–9pm • Free

Broken Hill grew up around the **Line of Lode**, a strip of mines that runs from northeast to southwest through town, most obviously marked by a 50m-high **slag heap**, a pile of mine waste topped by the Miners Memorial. Drive to the top of the slag heap, enjoy the view from the giant bench and visit the moving **Miners Memorial**, a modern rusted-steel sculpture commemorating the lives of lost miners.

White's Mineral Art and Mining Museum
1 Allendale St, 2km west of the centre off Silverton Rd • Daily 9am–5pm • $7.50

A visit to the bizarre but wonderful **White's Mineral Art and Mining Museum** is the next best thing to going underground, though it occupies part of a suburban house. The art section is pretty extraordinary, consisting mainly of collages of crushed minerals depicting Broken Hill scenes, and at the back there's a convincingly recreated walk-in underground mine. Inside, ex-miner Kevin White gives an entertaining talk, with videos and models, on the history of Broken Hill and its mines, while a shop sells minerals, opals, jewellery and pottery.

Pro Hart Gallery
108 Wyman St • Mon–Sat 9am–5pm, Sun 10am–5pm • $5 • ⊛ prohart.com.au

If you only go to one gallery in Broken Hill, make it the **Pro Hart Gallery**. The gallery showcases the work of Broken Hill miner-turned-artist, Pro Hart, who died in 2006.

Sculptures, etchings and prints typically depict Outback events and people such as race meetings, backyard barbecues and union leaders – look out for the fantastic 10m-long *History of Australia* showing scenes of Aboriginal life before the arrival of Captain Cook, the early pioneers, bushrangers and the founding of Broken Hill. Hart's delightfully chaotic studio has now been moved in its entirety into the gallery, with one of his final iconic dragonfly paintings on the easel. To celebrate the millennium Hart also took his paintbrush to one of his Rolls-Royces, now garaged outside. You can buy some of his work here: a digital print or etching costs from $495, while a small painting will set you back about $950.

The Royal Flying Doctor Service (RFDS)

Broken Hill Airport, 5km south of town • Mon–Fri 9am–5pm, Sat & Sun 10am–3pm • $8.50 • ⓦ flyingdoctor.org.au

The **Royal Flying Doctor Service** offers short, guided tours followed by a film and a chance to look around the museum. In the headquarters you'll first see the radio room where calls from remote places in New South Wales and Queensland are handled, before going out to the hangar to see the aircraft. Since a third of the service's annual budget has to come through fundraising – the rest of the money is from the state and federal governments and means the service provided is free of charge – whatever you spend on the tour and at the souvenir shop here is going to a good cause.

School of the Air

Lane St, 2km north of the centre • Mon–Fri term-time only, tours start 8.15am • Book the day before at the visitor centre • $4.40

The **School of the Air** shows how lessons for children in the Outback were carried out in a transmission area of 1.8 million square kilometres via RFDS two-way radio (these days it's all by webcam). The radio service was established in 1956 to improve education for children in the isolated Outback, and you can still listen to the transmission in a schoolroom surrounded by children's artwork. It will take adults back to their school days, with jolly primary-school teachers hosting singalongs, but the children in the far-flung areas seem to enjoy it.

Living Desert Flora & Fauna Sanctuary

Dawn–dusk • $6 • Cultural Walk Trail 1hr 30min; closes 6pm in summer, 5pm in winter

Ten kilometres northwest of town, 24 square kilometres of the eroded Barrier Ranges desert region has been sectioned off as the **Living Desert Flora & Fauna Sanctuary**, a beautiful area, especially at either end of the day when the wildlife is more active. The **Cultural Walk Trail** (a 2km loop) takes in an Aboriginal quartz quarry, mining claim markers and lots of desert flora (possibly including the lovely red Sturt's desert pea). At the beginning of the walk, an electrified predator-proof fence keeps introduced pests (mainly cats and foxes) out of a large compound now repopulated with threatened species such as yellow-footed rock wallabies, brush-tailed bettongs and bilbies.

The highest hill within the Living Desert is crowned by the **Broken Hill Sculpture Park**, easily the most dramatic of Broken Hill's art exhibits. It's a pleasant fifteen-minute walk up the hill from the Sanctuary car park, or you can drive right up to the car park beside the sculptures. Carved from Wilcannia sandstone boulders, the sculptures are the work of twelve artists who took part in a sculpture symposium in 1993. They were drawn from diverse cultures – two apiece from Mexico and Syria, three from Georgia (in the Caucasus), and five Australians, including two Bathurst Islanders – as reflected in the variety of their works. Antonio Nava Tirado's Aztec-influenced *Bajo El Sol Jaguar* (Under the Jaguar Sun) is particularly fine: the image is recreated everywhere and has become a kind of de facto symbol of Broken Hill.

Everyone comes up to visit the sculptures at sunset; no surprise, since on a clear evening the light can be magical and the rocks glow crimson.

2

ARRIVAL AND DEPARTURE

By plane The airport is 5km south of town but there's no shuttle bus – either catch a taxi (around $20) or arrange to have a rental car waiting (see below).
Destinations Adelaide (2–3 daily; 1hr 10min); Dubbo (Mon–Fri 2 daily, 1 on Sun; 1hr 30min); Mildura (Mon–Sat 1–2 daily; 1hr 25min); Sydney (1–3 daily; 2hr 20min).
By train Great Southern Rail trains (Indian Pacific) from Sydney and Adelaide, and a once-weekly NSW TrainLink train from Sydney, arrive at the train station on Crystal St at the foot of the slag heap.

GETTING AROUND

By bus Murton's City Bus (☎ 08 8087 3311, ⊛ murtons .com.au) runs hourly or half-hourly along four routes through Broken Hill – the visitor centre can provide a combined timetable and route map. Buy a day-ticket for $5 and you can hop-on-hop-off at various attractions around town.
By car Car rental companies include Thrifty at 190 Argent

INFORMATION AND TOURS

Tourist information The visitor centre (daily 8.30am–4pm; ☎ 08 8080 3560, ⊛ brokenhillaustralia .com.au) shares space with the bus station at the corner of Bromide and Blende streets. You can book tours here, pick up information, including a self-guided tour map, and get updates on road conditions. Visit the NPWS office (Mon–Fri 8.30am–4.30pm; ☎ 08 8080 3200) at 183 Argent St for information on the surrounding national parks.
Broken Hill City Sights Tours 51 William St ☎ 08 8087 2484, ⊛ bhoutbacktours.com.au. Offers a twice-daily

ACCOMMODATION

Caledonian B&B 140 Chloride St ☎ 08 8087 1945, ⊛ caledonianbnb.com.au. Five comfortable if cluttered rooms, one en suite and the rest with shared bathrooms. Not for you if you don't like talking in the morning no matter how good the coffee, as breakfast (included) is taken at a communal table. Alternatively, book one of their nearby cottages which sleep up to six. Doubles $89, cottages $145
Daydream Motel 77 Argent St ☎ 08 8088 3033, ⊛ daydream.budgetmotelchain.com.au. A friendly, basic and central motel that's clean and well looked after but beginning to show its age. Breakfast is available on request – order the night before. There are also two cottages available. Doubles $95, cottages $135
Ibis Styles 120 Argent St ☎ 08 8088 4044, ⊛ accorhotels .com. This revamped three-star motel in a central location right near the bus station has stylish rooms with fridge and minibar, and there's a small pool. Fee for wi-fi. $150
★The Imperial 88 Oxide St ☎ 08 8087 7444, ⊛ imperialfineaccommodation.com. This classy

BROKEN HILL

Destinations Adelaide (2 weekly; 9hr 30min); Menindee (weekly; 50min); Sydney (Southern Rail: weekly; 15hr 35min; NSW TrainLink: 1 direct weekly, daily change at Dubbo; 12hr 50min & 15hr 35min).
By bus NSW TrainLink buses arrive here from Dubbo, and Buses R Us (☎ 08 8285 6900, ⊛ busesrus.com.au) runs services from Adelaide and Mildura. Most buses stop at the Tourist and Travellers Centre on the corner of Blende and Bromide streets.
Destinations Adelaide (3 weekly; 7hr); Cobar (daily; 5hr 40min); Dubbo (daily; 9hr 40min); Mildura (2 weekly; 4hr).

St (☎ 08 8088 1928, ⊛ thrifty.com.au), and Hertz opposite at no. 193 Argent St (☎ 08 8087 2719 ⊛ hertz.com.au); both have desks at the airport too, where there's also an Avis (☎ 08 8082 5555, ⊛ avis.com.au).
On a tour Many of the sights are scattered out of town; if you don't have your own vehicle, a tour is really the only solution for getting to them.

tour of Broken Hill ($60) and a popular Sunset Sculpture Symposium Tour ($40) most evenings.
Silvercity Tours 380 Argent St ☎ 08 8087 6956, ⊛ silvercitytours.com.au. Day-trips to Kinchega National Park and Menindee Lakes to watch birdlife and cruise the wetlands. Mon & Wed only. $150.
Tri State Safaris 478 Lane St ☎ 08 8088 2389, ⊛ tristate.com.au. A number of tours, including one-day tours of Mutawintji National Park, and a one-day Kinchega National Park tour that includes Menindee Lake and Kinchega National Park ($230).

four-and-a-half-star property is located in a beautiful old building with a huge veranda. The six spacious rooms (plus a large apartment) have all mod cons, and there's also a kitchenette, free self-serve breakfast, a billiard room, a guest lounge, pool and garden. Doubles $170, apartment $270
Lake View Caravan Park 1 Mann St, 3km northeast ☎ 08 8088 2250, ⊛ lakeviewcaravanpark.com.au. An oldy but a goody, this large site on the edge of town has Outback views, disabled access, a refreshing swimming pool, a kiosk and an array of en-suite cabins and more elaborate two-bedroom cottages. No wi-fi. Un/powered sites $25/35, cabins $80, cottages $130
Palace Hotel 227 Argent St ☎ 08 8088 1699, ⊛ thepalacehotelbrokenhill.com.au. Corner pub with the largest hotel balcony in New South Wales and a profusion of murals on every available surface, including a Botticelli-style *Birth of Venus* (painted by the late Mario, former landlord), which featured to hilarious effect in the

film *Priscilla, Queen of the Desert*. All rooms have a/c and a sink, some are en-suite, and singles are available ($55). Free wi-fi only in en-suite rooms. **$75**

Red Earth Motel 469 Argent St ☏08 8088 5694, ⊛redearthmotel.com.au. A very smart and popular motel, offering a choice of modern studios and two- or three-bed apartments. All rooms have king-size beds, kitchenettes and good bathrooms. Hotel facilities include a heated swimming pool, 24hr reception, guest laundry and BBQ area. **$150**

Royal Exchange Hotel 320 Argent St, cnr of Chloride St ☏08 8087 2308, ⊛royalexchangehotel.com. Plush hotel with lovely Art Deco public areas and en suites with smart furnishings, some with bathtub. It's very central but there's no parking on site. Also home to a popular restaurant. **$130**

Tourist Lodge 100 Argent St ☏08 8088 4575, ⊛thetouristlodge.com.au. Large hostel near the bus terminal – the only backpacker place in town. There's a/c, fridges and TVs in many rooms, a well-equipped, shared kitchen/dining/TV room, laundry facilities, a pool and bikes for rent. Dorms **$55**, doubles **$80**

EATING

Restaurants aren't really Broken Hill's style – if your meal looks like it was trucked a thousand kilometres through a sandstorm to get here, that's because it probably was. There's still the proverbial pub on every corner, and most of them serve **counter meals** where quantity usually prevails over quality. For **grocery** supplies, visit the central IGA on William St (Mon–Fri 8am–6.30pm, Sat 8am–5pm, Sun 9am–3pm), Woolworths in Centro Westside, 1km southwest of the centre (daily 7am–10pm), or Coles on the corner of South Rd and Galena St (daily 7am–10pm).

Alfresco 397 Argent St. Popular place with all-day pavement dining and a large selection of gourmet salads, pastas ($18.50), burgers ($13.50) and pizza ($16.50). The food is fairly standard but prices are reasonable and servings generous. Daily 7am–late.

Bell's Milk Bar 160 Patton St, South Broken Hill ☏08 8087 5380, ⊛milkbar.com.au. This place feels a bit like a 1950s diner and has a rock'n'roll jukebox. They specialize in spiders (soda ice-cream floats), milkshakes and smoothies, with hot waffles ($8.50), apple pie and hot dogs ($4.20) the only food options. There's wi-fi access here. Daily: Jan & Dec 11am–9pm, Feb–Nov 10.30am–5.30pm.

Noodle & Sushi Bar 351 Argent St. Something completely different and a popular local takeaway option, with everything from *nasi goreng* ($10.80) to teriyaki beef with rice ($13.50) and sushi. Daily 11.30am–8.30pm.

Sidebar Restaurant Palace Hotel 227 Argent St ☏08 8088 1699, ⊛thepalacehotelbrokenhill.com.au. Atmospheric restaurant inside the *Palace Hotel*, serving up dishes that are better quality than the average pub food. Alongside the likes of Asian BBQ chicken ($25.50) and Scotch fillet steak ($32.50), there's a decent range of wine and cocktails on offer. Mon–Wed 3–9pm, Thurs–Sat noon–2.30pm & 3–9pm.

Thom, Dick & Harry's 354 Argent St ☏08 8088 7000. This café is also a florist and a homewares shop, with a touch of deli and clothing boutique thrown in. They serve baguettes and sandwiches, sweet treats like honey, ricotta, banana and cinnamon on Turkish bread ($8.90), as well as the city's best coffee. Settle at the big table and attack the pile of magazines. Mon–Thurs 9am–5.30pm, Fri 9am–6pm, Sat 9am–2pm.

DRINKING AND NIGHTLIFE

The city has always been a legendary **drinking hole**, and once had more than seventy hotels. Many pubs have been converted for other uses, but there are still more than twenty licensed establishments and a pub crawl is highly recommended. Numerous clubs often host live entertainment on Fri and Sat nights: just sign yourself in.

Alma Hotel Cnr Hebbard & South sts, South Broken Hill. A local that's good for a drink any time, and the only place with live country music on Sun night. Daily 10am–midnight.

Broken Hill Musicians Club 276 Crystal St. This club has live music on Fri and Sat night from 8.30pm, karaoke on the first Sat of the month and dancing on the second Sat. It was immortalized by Kenneth Cook's 1961 novel (and later film), *Wake in Fright*. Mon–Thurs 10am–midnight, Fri & Sat 10am–1am, Sun 10am–10pm.

Mulga Hill Tavern Cnr Oxide & William sts. This pub has a wide variety of clientele, cold beer and counter meals, as well as an attached bistro. There's also a drive-through bottle shop. Mon–Sat 10am–late, Sun noon–10pm.

Palace Hotel 227 Argent St. Try to make it here on Fri (from 9pm) when it operates Broken Hill's famous *Two Up*, once an illegal back-lane gambling operation. The boys from the bush turn up to bet as much as $200 on one flip of a coin, though $10 or $20 is more common. There is also live music here on Sat, or you can settle on the balcony for a drink and some people watching. Mon–Sat 3pm–late.

Red Lush Wine Bar & Cocktail Lounge The Astra, 393 Argent St. A bit swankier than some of the pubs, this place has guest DJs and serves cocktails and nibbles, plus a range of beers and wines. Daily noon–10pm.

Silverton and around

The semi-ghost town of **SILVERTON** makes a great day out from Broken Hill, but note that there's no **fuel** available here so check your gauge before you set off. If the scene looks vaguely familiar, you've probably seen it before: parts of *Mad Max 2* were shot around here, and the **Silverton Hotel** has appeared as the "Gamulla Hotel" in *Razorback*, "Hotel Australia" in *A Town Like Alice*, and in Aussie gangster movie *Dirty Deeds*. It also seems to star in just about every advertisement – usually beer-related – that features an Outback scene. In the tradition of all Outback pubs, it has its own in-jokes; you'll find out what all the laughter is about if you ask to "take the test" (gold coin donation to charity).

Taking the **Silverton Heritage Trail**, a two-hour stroll around town marked by interpretive signs, is a good way to work up a thirst, though it's far too hot to attempt in the summer.

Horizon Gallery

Layard St • Daily 9am–5pm • ⊛ horizongalleries.com.au

There's a burgeoning **art scene** here, with several galleries to browse through, including **Horizon Gallery**, run by fine local artist Albert Woodroffe and also showing work by some of his peers.

Silverton Gaol Museum

Daily 9.30am–4pm • $4

The 1889 vintage **Silverton Gaol Museum** has a bit of just about everything you could imagine there ever was in Silverton – washboards, typewriters, masonic garb, assay scales and so on. There's also material on Dame Mary Gilmore (pictured on the $10 note), who was assistant teacher here from 1887 to 1889 and later became a noted socialist journalist and poet.

Mad Max Museum

Daily 10am–4pm • $7.50

The **Mad Max Museum** is a fan's haven, a labour of love set up by British man Adrian Bennett who has spent years collecting memorabilia from the film franchise. There are behind-the-scenes photos taken by extras, original and replica vehicles, and mannequins in full costume.

Mundi Mundi Plains Lookout

Beyond Silverton, the sealed road continues 5km north to the **Mundi Mundi Plains Lookout**, where the undulating plateau you have been driving across descends gradually to a vast plain. On clear days you can see the blurred outline of the Boolcoomata Hills, 80km away (the lookout is the spot where, at the end of *Mad Max 2*, Mel Gibson tipped the semi-trailer). A further 5km on there's a picnic area overlooking the **Umberumberka reservoir**, Broken Hill's only source of water until the Menindee Lakes Scheme was set up.

Day Dream Mine

20km northeast of Broken Hill on Silverton Rd then 13km north along an unsealed road • Daily tours at 10am & 11.30am; hourly tours during school holidays • $25

The only opportunity to experience something of what it was like to mine underground is to visit **Day Dream Mine**. Predating the discovery at Broken Hill, the Day Dream operated between 1882 and 1889, and you can don a hard hat and take a guided tour underground to see the old workings where children as young as eight laboured, and catch a glimpse of the silver seam.

ACCOMMODATION AND EATING   **SILVERTON AND AROUND**

Blue Bush Country Cottage Lot 226 ☎ 08 8088 4488. A self-contained cottage, sleeping four, a short distance from Silverton centre. The master bedroom is underground.

Linen is provided, but bring food unless you want to pop back to Broken Hill. No wi-fi. **$100**

Penrose Park ☎ 08 8088 5307. A well-kept campsite

with a tennis court, BBQs, some aviaries and resident goats and sheep. There are bunkhouses that sleep up to eight, and special rates for families. You can use the showers here for a $5 fee if you're a non-resident. No internet access. Un/powered sites $20/$30, bunkhouse (for four) $55

Silverton Tea Rooms Next door to the Mad Max Museum ☎ 08 8088 6601. This licensed café does a great line in home-made country food including stews with damper ($16.90) and a Bushman's burger (pattie between damper with gravy; $9.50). The quandong pie with ice cream ($7.50) is made from a native Australian fruit with a taste somewhere between plum and rhubarb. The other rooms in the house are dedicated to a doll museum and a collection of old bottles. Daily 8am–5.30pm.

Silverton Hotel Silverton St ☎ 08 8088 5313. In the centre of Silverton, this is the iconic hotel that's featured in many films (see opposite). There are cast photos on display inside, and it's a welcoming place with a large beer garden, a circular counter and pub food such as burgers ($9–12) and pie, chips and gravy ($11.50). Mon–Sat 9am–late, Sun 10am–10pm.

Mutawintji National Park

Mutawintji National Park, 130km northeast of Broken Hill in the Byngnano Ranges, has magnificent scenery, with secluded gorges and quiet waterholes attracting a profusion of wildlife. The main highlights of the park are the ancient galleries of **Aboriginal rock art** in the caves and overhangs. The historic site can only be visited by booking a tour (see below) led by qualified indigenous guides. Also worth visiting is the **Mutawintji Cultural Centre**, an amazing multimedia collaboration between indigenous Australians and the National Parks and Wildlife Service, which tells of tribal history and myth in sound and pictures.

More Aboriginal rock art can be seen on a series of walks from the Homestead Creek day-area, ranging from the wheelchair-accessible **Thaaklatjika Mingkana Walk** (800m return; 30min; flat) to the excellent **Byngnano Range Walk** (7.5km loop; 4–5hr; moderate to hard). About 10km southeast, the **Mutawintji Gorge Walk** (6km return; 3hr; easy) is equally good; it heads into one of the park's most picturesque gorges, ending at a peaceful rock pool enclosed by towering, rusty red cliffs.

ESSENTIALS AND ACCOMMODATION   MUTAWINTJI NATIONAL PARK

Access Access to the park is largely on unsealed dirt roads and there's no fuel so fill up before leaving Broken Hill. The road is normally fine for 2WD vehicles, but check locally as the roads can quickly become impassable after even a light rain; bring extra food and water just in case. The Argent St NPWS office in Broken Hill can provide other information (see p.292).

Tours Broken Hill-based Tri State Safaris (☎ 08 8088 2389, ⊕ tristate.com.au) offer one-day tours of Mutawintji National Park (Wed & Sat, $199); tours depart from either Broken Hill or the Mutawintji camping ground. You can also tag along in your own 4WD joining at Broken Hill or at the national park visitor centre ($120).

Homestead Creek Campground Near the Mutawintji historic site ☎ 08 8080 3200. An unpowered camping area among river red gums, with BBQs, hot showers and flush toilets. Suitable for both tents and campervans. Bring drinking water with you. No wi-fi. Ask in the park visitor centre for directions. Unpowered sites per person $6

Kinchega National Park and the Menindee Lakes

From Broken Hill it is a predominantly flat 110km tar-sealed run southeast to the township of Menindee, amid the **Menindee Lakes**, actually a series of flood plains fed by the Darling River. The upper lakes have been harnessed and channelled to provide water for Broken Hill and generally have water in; those downstream within the Kinchega National Park were dry for several years, but are now full thanks to heavy rains. Together they are a major habitat for **waterbirds**; there are over 210 species here in total, including numerous little black cormorants (shags), pelicans, ibis, white egrets and whistling kites. Most of the promo photos you'll see of **Kinchega National Park** show skeletal trees emerging from placid waters silhouetted against a late dusk sky.

The historic and exceptionally well-preserved **Kinchega Woolshed** (found near the visitor centre), on the vast Kinchega Station, was one of the first pastoral settlements in the area when it was established in 1850, and it continued to operate until 1967; you can explore it by following the signposted **woolshed walk**.

2

2

ESSENTIALS

Entry $8 per vehicle for 24hr; bring correct money. Trains from Sydney stop at Menindee on Mon (12hr).

Access Before heading here, check road conditions with Broken Hill NPWS (see p.292): roads are all dirt – fine in a 2WD in the dry season but impassable after rain. If you don't have transport, take a day-trip from Broken Hill with Tri State Safaris and Silvercity Tours (see p.292).

Information 5km west of Menindee into the park is an information shelter where you pay park fees. From here a road heads 10km to a sporadically staffed visitor centre.

Tours Broken Hill-based Tri State Safaris (☎ 08 8088 2389, ⓦ tristate.com.au) offer a one-day Kinchega National Park tour (Tues & Fri, $220) that includes Menindee Lake and Kinchega National Park.

ACCOMMODATION

Darling River Campground River Drive. This is a remote spot so come prepared and bring your own water. Showers are available at the Shearers' Quarters. Check road conditions before coming – the campground can close during heavy rain. No wi-fi. Unpowered sites $12

Shearers' Quarters Woolshed Drive ☎ 08 8080 3560. Six rooms with bunks and a shared kitchen and amenities block. You need to provide your own linen, pillows and towels, and all food etc. Guests must pay a daily vehicle fee ($8) to enter the park. Camping per person $20

Wentworth

Once a thriving river port, **WENTWORTH** was founded in 1859 at the confluence of the Murray and Darling rivers. For over fifty years it was the hub of paddle-steamer traffic between New South Wales, Victoria and South Australia, but in 1903 the railway reached Mildura, 30km southeast in Victoria. Mildura burgeoned at Wentworth's expense and the "two rivers" town is now a sleepy place of around 1500 people. It makes a good base for exploring **Mungo National Park**, and is a pleasant spot to overnight.

Old Wentworth Gaol

Beverly St • Daily 10am–5pm • $8

The National Trust's striking **Old Wentworth Gaol** ranks as the first Australian-designed jail, the work of colonial architect James Barnett who also designed the Sydney Post Office. It was built of handmade bricks in 1879, and ghosts of former prisoners are believed to make the occasional appearance, leaving shadows on pictures taken.

Pioneer World Museum

117 Beverly St • Daily 10am–4pm • $5

Opposite the Old Gaol, **Pioneer World** is a folk museum exhibiting items collected by the Rotary Club that relate to the Aboriginal and European history of the area, and also displays models of extinct megafauna once found hereabouts.

Perry Sandhills

6km north of town along Old Renmark Rd

Perhaps the most interesting thing to do in Wentworth is to drive out to look at the amazing, Sahara-like dunes of the **Perry Sandhills**. Dating back over 40,000 years, these sand dunes have gradually eroded and yielded skeletal remains of megafauna (on display in the Pioneer World Museum; see above) and evidence of local Aboriginal tribes.

ARRIVAL AND INFORMATION

By air Commercial airlines offer a regular service to Mildura Airport, which is 30km from Wentworth. Taxis can be ordered from the terminal (☎ 03 5023 0033).

By bus Buslink (ⓦ buslink.com.au) route #950 runs

from Mildura to Wentworth (4 daily Mon–Fri; 40min).

Tourist information The visitor centre (Mon–Fri 9am–5pm, Sat & Sun 9am–1pm; ☎ 03 5027 5080, ⓦ visitwentworth.com.au) is at 66 Darling St.

ACCOMMODATION

Wentworth Grande Resort 61 Darling St ☎ 03 5027 2225, ⓦ wentworthgranderesort.com.au. An upmarket

hotel in a central location. It's looking a little dated, however, so opt for an upstairs room with a balcony overlooking the

river. There's also a pool on site. Rate includes breakfast. **$99**
Willow Bend Caravan Park Darling St ☎ 03 5027 3213, ⓦ willowbendcaravanpark.com. The best

waterfront choice, this shady site is right near the shops but also at the confluence of the Darling and Murray rivers. No wi-fi. Un/powered sites **$25/28**, cabins **$95**

Lake Victoria

In 1994, ancient Aboriginal graves were discovered at **Lake Victoria**, 65km west of Wentworth, when the partial draining of the lake revealed skeletons buried in deep layers. Some of the estimated ten thousand graves (well known to the Barkindji people) date back six thousand years, in what is believed to be Australia's largest preindustrial burial site, surpassing any such finds in Europe, Asia or North and South America. The site also challenges the premise that Aboriginals were once solely nomadic, suggesting that here at least they lived in semipermanent dwellings around the lake.

Mungo National Park

Mungo National Park, 135km northeast of Wentworth, is most easily reached from the river townships of Wentworth, and Mildura (over the Victorian border about 110km away).

The park is part of the dried-up **Willandra Lakes System**, which contains the longest continuous record of Aboriginal life in Australia, dating back more than forty thousand years. During the last Ice Age the system formed a vast chain of freshwater lakes, teeming with fish and attracting water birds and mammals. Aborigines camped at the shores of the lake to fish and hunt, and buried their dead in the sand dunes. When the lakes started drying out fifteen thousand years ago, Aborigines continued to live near soaks along the old river channel. The park covers most of one of these dry lake beds, and its dominant feature is a long, crescent-shaped dune, at the eastern edge of the lake, commonly referred to as the **Walls of China**.

Nearby, the impressive old **Mungo Woolshed** is open for inspection at any time. From here a 50km loop road heads out across the dry lake bed to the dunes, then around behind them and back through malee scrub to the visitor centre. Many people just drive the first 10km to a car park from where a short boardwalk takes you onto the **Walls of China** dunes. This low dune system barely rises 30m from the level of the lake bed, but it is a dramatic spot especially around dawn and sunset when the otherworldly shapes and ripple patterns glow golden, and kangaroos and goats make their way onto the dunes for meagre pickings. It is a 500m walk to the top of the dunes and views over the other side.

ESSENTIALS · MUNGO NATIONAL PARK

Entry $8 per vehicle for 24hr.

Access Organized tours run from both Wentworth and Mildura, but as long as the roads are dry it's easy enough to drive yourself in an ordinary car. The last 90km to the park are dirt, as are all the roads in the park. Ensure you carry enough food and water for emergencies; mobile phones do not work in the park. Check road conditions before travelling.

Information There's an NPWS office (daily 8.30am–4.30pm; ☎ 03 5021 8900, ⓦ visitmungo.com) on the corner of the Sturt Hwy at Buronga, 3km northeast of Mildura in Victoria, where you can book accommodation in the park. The park's visitor centre (daily 8.30am–4.30pm) is near the southwest entrance.

Tours Aboriginal-owned Harry Nanya Tours (☎ 03 5027 2076, ⓦ harrynanyatours.com.au) is one of the best of the companies running tours to the park.

ACCOMMODATION

None of the accommodation options listed below has mobile phone coverage or wi-fi.

Main Campground 2km from visitor centre ☎ 03 5021 8900. Campground near the park entrance with BBQs and composting toilets. No prebooking. **$12**
Mungo Lodge Arumpo Rd, 3km from visitor centre ☎ 03 5029 7297, ⓦ mungolodge.com.au. Twenty plush, en-suite

a/c cabins (sleeping two–four), with private decks. **$269**
Shearer's Quarters By the visitor centre ☎ 03 5021 8900. Heritage property with rooms sleeping up to six (shared hot showers) and a well-equipped kitchen. Bring your own sheets and towels. **$60**

Coastal Queensland

THE GOLD COAST

Coastal Queensland

Stretching for more than 2500km, from the border with New South Wales to the northernmost tip of the continent at Cape York, Coastal Queensland encapsulates just about everything that lures visitors to Australia. From idyllic backpacker havens to plush luxury resorts, and wave-pummelled surfing beaches to crocodile-infested rivers, the shoreline of Queensland rewards weeks of exploring. Above all else, though, the prime attraction in these parts is the fragile but still astonishing Great Barrier Reef, which parallels the coast for almost its entire length.

3

State capital **Brisbane**, in Queensland's more developed southeastern corner, is a relaxed city with a lively social scene and good work possibilities. The **Gold Coast**, to the south, is Australia's most famous holiday playground. Its reputation was founded on some of the country's best surf, though that now takes second place to a belt of beachfront high-rises, theme parks, and the host of lively bars and nightclubs that surround Surfers Paradise. An hour inland, a chain of national parks, packed with wildlife and stunning views, line the green heights of the **Gold Coast Hinterland**.

North of Brisbane, fruit and vegetable plantations behind the gentle **Sunshine Coast**, overlooked by the spiky, isolated peaks of the **Glass House Mountains**, benefit from rich volcanic soils and a subtropical climate. Down by the ocean, **Noosa** is a fashionable resort town with great surfing. Beyond looms **Fraser Island**, where huge wooded dunes, freshwater lakes and sculpted coloured sands form the backdrop for exciting safaris, while the surrounding waters teem with activity during the annual whale migration.

North of Fraser, as you head **into the tropics**, the humidity and temperature begin to rise. Though an ever-narrowing farming strip still hugs the coast, the Great Dividing Range edges seawards as it progresses north, dry at first, but gradually acquiring a green sward that culminates in the steamy, rainforest-draped scenery around the bustling, backpacker-dominated city of **Cairns**. Along the way are scores of beaches, archipelagos of islands and yet more national parks, some – such as **Hinchinbrook Island** – with superb walking trails. Visitors with work visas can also recharge their bank balances along the way by **fruit and vegetable picking** around the towns of **Bundaberg**, **Bowen**, **Ayr** and **Innisfail**. North of Cairns, beyond the lively little resort hub of **Port Douglas** and the world's oldest rainforest, known as the **Daintree**, you finally come to the savannah of the huge, triangular **Cape York Peninsula**, a sparsely populated setting for a gloriously rugged 4WD adventure.

GREAT BARRIER REEF

Highlights

❶ Brisbane's South Bank The perfect place to while away a sunny Brisbane day, wandering the riverfront parklands from museum to café. **See p.310**

❷ Gold Coast The beaches, bars and theme parks of Australia's prime domestic holiday destination provide raucous thrills around the clock. **See p.325**

❸ Fraser Island Discover the giant dunes and pristine lakes of this beautiful sand island on an action-packed 4WD safari. **See p.350**

❹ Great Barrier Reef Scuba diving is the best way to explore the world's most famous and beautiful coral complexes. **See pp.358–389**

❺ The Whitsundays Lying inside the Great Barrier Reef, the rainforested peaks and long white beaches of the Whitsunday Islands offer some of Australia's most picturesque cruising. **See p.372**

❻ Port Douglas This pocket-sized resort town has great hotels and restaurants, plus easy access to some of the Barrier Reef's finest dive and snorkel sites. **See p.417**

❼ The Daintree The world's oldest rainforest slopes down to breathtaking beaches peppered with facilities for budget travellers. **See p.419**

❽ Four-wheel driving on Cape York The Cape York Peninsula has some of the most challenging 4WD territory in Australia – watch out for crocs on river crossings. **See p.431**

HIGHLIGHTS ARE MARKED ON THE MAP ON P.302

COASTAL QUEENSLAND

HIGHLIGHTS

1. Brisbane's South Bank
2. Gold Coast
3. Fraser Island
4. Great Barrier Reef
5. The Whitsundays
6. Port Douglas
7. The Daintree
8. Four-wheel driving on Cape York

Thursday Island

Bamaga

Branwell Junction

Weipa

KUTINI-PAYAMU (IRON RANGE) NATIONAL PARK

Archer River

CAPE YORK PENINSULA

Coen

Great Barrier Reef

CORAL SEA

RINYIRRU (LAKEFIELD) NATIONAL PARK

Lizard Island

Laura

Lakeland

Cooktown

Cape Tribulation

DAINTREE NATIONAL PARK

Mossman

Chillagoe

Kuranda

Port Douglas

Chillagoe-Mungana Caves NP

Mount Molloy

Palm Cove

Mareeba

Cairns

Atherton

Bartle Frere

Babinda

Paronella Park

Innisfail

Tully

Dunk Island

Mission Beach

GIRRINGUN NATIONAL PARK

Cardwell

Hinchinbrook Island

Ingham

Lucinda

Paluma

Palm Island

Magnetic Island

Townsville

Mount Surprise

Charters Towers

CONTINUED ON RIGHT MAP

0 50 kilometres

CONTINUED ON LEFT MAP

Townsville

Ayr

PACIFIC OCEAN

Bowen

Great Barrier Reef

Proserpine

Airlie Beach

Whitsunday Islands

EUNGELLA NATIONAL PARK

CAPE HILLSBOROUGH NP

Mackay

Charters Towers

Clermont

Emerald

Yeppoon

Rockhampton

Emu Park

Great Keppel Island

Gladstone

Heron Island

Miriam Vale

Lady Musgrave Island

Lady Elliot Island

Agnes Water & 1770

Gin Gin

Bundaberg

Childers

Hervey Bay

Fraser Island

Maryborough

River Heads

Tin Can Bay

Hook Point

Gympie

Rainbow Beach

Eumundi

Noosa

Maleny

Nambour

Woodford

Maroochydore, Mooloolaba

Caloundra

Glass House Mountains

Brisbane

Moreton Island

LAMINGTON NP

North Stradbroke Island

Tamborine Mountain

Gold Coast

SPRINGBROOK NP

Sydney

Toowoomba

Warwick

0 50 kilometres

NATIONAL PARKS IN QUEENSLAND

National parks are run by Queensland's Department of National Parks, Recreation, Sport and Racing (NPRSR). Their excellent **website** (wnprsr.qld.gov.au/parks) has up-to-date information on walking trails, camping, vehicle access, seasonal closures and other topics of interest to hikers, drivers and bushcampers. Unlike other states, all of Queensland's parks are free to enter, but in a few cases hiking or vehicle **permits** must be obtained in advance, either online, over the phone (☎ 13 74 68) or from a Queensland Parks and Wildlife Service office (QPWS locations, opening times and fees are listed on the website). Hiking permits are required for trails on which numbers are restricted, notably Hinchinbrook Island's Thorsborne Trail. You'll need a vehicle permit to take a car across to Bribie Island, Cooloola, Moreton Island or Fraser Island.

CAMPING

It's possible to **camp** in most national parks. Facilities vary a great deal – some campsites have cooking, washing and toilet facilities, while others require you to be totally self-sufficient. Campsite fees are fixed at $5.95 per person per night and usually payable in advance by phone (☎ 13 74 68), online (wnprsr.qld.gov.au/experiences/camping) or at a nearby QPWS office or ranger station. You'll receive a booking number and a printable camping tag (if purchased online). When paying camping fees in advance, you can choose between specific slots – required if you're tackling any of Queensland's Great Walks (wnprsr.qld.gov.au/experiences/great-walks) – or general-purpose credits that allow you to fine-tune your itinerary later.

Offshore, the Tropical Coast is marked by the appearance of the **Great Barrier Reef**, among the most extensive coral complexes in the world. The southern portions, out from Bundaberg and **1770**, are peppered with sand islands or **cays**, while further north beautiful granite islands pepper the inshore waters between the coast and reef, and are covered in thick pine forests and fringed in white sand – the pick are the **Whitsundays** near **Airlie Beach** and **Magnetic Island** off Townsville. Many such islands are accessible on day-trips, though some offer everything from campsites to luxury resorts if you fancy a change of pace. The reef itself can be explored on **boat excursions** ranging up to several days' duration; **scuba divers** are well catered for, though there's plenty of coral within easy snorkelling range of the surface.

As a major tourist destination, Queensland's coast holds a good range of **accommodation**, from budget to upmarket options in most locations. During the Easter and Christmas holidays, though – and even simply at weekends – **room shortages** and price hikes can occur at popular spots, including national parks, so it's worth booking in advance.

As for **weather**, winters are generally dry and pleasant throughout the region, but the summer climate (Dec–April) becomes more oppressive the further north you travel, with the possibility of cyclones bringing torrential rain and devastating storms to the entire Tropical Coast.

Brief history

Long lampooned as being slow and regressive, Queensland is arguably Australia's most **conservative** state. Marked physical and **social divisions** remain between the densely settled, city-orientated southeastern corner and the large rural remainder, dating back to when Queensland separated from New South Wales in 1859, and **Brisbane** was chosen as capital. The city proved an unpopular choice with the northern pioneers, who felt the government was too far away to understand, or even care about, their needs, which centred around the use of Solomon Islanders for labour on the north's **sugar plantations**, a practice that the government equated with slavery, and finally banned in 1872. While demands for further separation, this time between tropical Queensland and the southeast, have continued to this day without ever bearing fruit, the sheer remoteness of the northern settlements led in any case to local self-sufficiency, making Queensland far less homogeneous than the other eastern states.

The darker side of this conservatism has seen Queensland endure more than its fair share of extreme or simply **dirty politics**. During the 1970s and early 1980s, the repressive stranglehold of a strongly conservative National Party government, led by the charismatic and slippery Sir Johannes Bjelke-Petersen (better known as "**Joh**"), did nothing to enhance the state's image.

In recent years, state politics seem to have become more volatile. Immediately after the millennium, Labor's Premier **Peter Beattie** served three successive terms as premier, and was succeeded by his deputy, **Anna Bligh**, who became the state's first elected female premier in 2009. Bligh's popularity briefly spiked following her calm handling of the crises caused by extreme weather events of 2010–11, but Labor suffered a catastrophic defeat in the state elections of 2012, and she was succeeded as premier by the Liberal former Lord Mayor of Brisbane, **Campbell Newman**. The Newman Government swiftly lost support in turn, and Labor returned to power in 2015, under **Annastacia Palaszczuk**.

GETTING AROUND   COASTAL QUEENSLAND

The **rail line** runs north from Brisbane to Cairns and south from Brisbane to Surfers Paradise; incredibly, there's no train between Surfers Paradise and Byron Bay in New South Wales, just a connecting bus. Travelling by **road**, Highway 1 connects Brisbane to Cairns, with frequent long-distance **buses** serving all towns. A few out-of-the-way spots are covered by local transport, but it's well worth renting a car from time to time.

By plane Virgin Australia (☎ 13 67 89, ⓦ virginaustralia .com), Qantas (☎ 13 13 13, ⓦ qantas.com.au), QantasLink and its budget sidekick, Jetstar (☎ 13 15 38, ⓦ jetstar .com), account for almost all commercial domestic flights in Queensland.

By train Queensland Rail (☎ 1800 872 467, ⓦ queenslandrail.com.au) run the modern *Spirit of Queensland* train five times weekly on the 1680km, 24hr journey between Brisbane and Cairns, while *Tilt* trains also make one or two trips each day between Brisbane, Bundaberg (4hr 30min–6hr) and Rockhampton (8hr–10hr 30min).

By bus Both Greyhound (hop-on-hop-off passes available; ☎ 1300 473 946, ⓦ greyhound.com.au) and Premier (☎ 13 34 10, ⓦ premierms.com.au) operate daily buses north from Brisbane to Cairns (29–32hr) and south to Sydney

(15–17hr), stopping at major towns en route. Sunbus (☎ 13 12 30, ⓦ sunbus.com.au) provide local bus connections, especially along the Sunshine Coast and in the Cairns area, while Trans North buses (☎ 07 4095 8644, ⓦ transnorthbus.com) run from Cairns up into the Atherton Tablelands and north to Port Douglas and Cooktown.

By car Queensland's road signs can be infuriatingly confusing, so equip yourself with a good map (those put out by the state automobile association, the RACQ, are the best). Don't expect to average more than 80kph if you're heading all the way north from Brisbane to Cairns on Highway 1. Tailgating seems to be mandatory, while from Bundaberg north you also need to watch out for cane trains that cross roads during the sugar-crushing season (roughly June–Dec); crossings are usually marked by flashing red lights.

Brisbane

Queensland's state capital, and largest city by far, **BRISBANE** has boomed in recent years; taking all its 185 suburbs into account, it's now home to more 2.4 million people. Back in the 1990s, it acquired the nickname **Brisvegas** as a tongue-in-cheek reference to its perceived lack of glamour. These days, though, the term has lost its derogatory edge to become an affectionate tribute to a dynamic and very liveable modern city, and it even received a presidential seal of approval when adopted by the visiting Barrack Obama during the 2014 G20 summit.

While the open sea lies little more than a dozen kilometres east, Brisbane is very much a river city. Its various neighbourhoods spread across successive promontories, defined by the extravagant meanders of the **Brisbane River**, lined with riverfront promenades and gardens, and linked by ferries and footbridges. At its core, the wedge-shaped Central Business District or **CBD** is very much the city's commercial and administrative heart, an Australian Manhattan where the remaining sandstone colonial buildings are increasingly overshadowed by colossal modern skyscrapers. There's a lively restaurant and nightlife scene here, and the lush **Botanic Gardens** tucked into the river bend to the south offer a welcome refuge. The major goal for visitors, though, lies immediately across the river, where the **South Bank Cultural Centre** holds several stunning museums and galleries, and the adjoining **South Bank Parklands** form a verdant riverside playground.

Radiating north from the CBD, Brisbane's urban polish gives way to more residential neighbourhoods like **Spring Hill**, **Fortitude Valley** and **New Farm**, characterized by less conservative shops, accommodation and restaurants, and the aspiring suburbs of **Petrie Terrace** and **Paddington**. Office buildings and one-way streets are encroaching hereabouts too, but the city's roots are reflected in the many high-set, wooden-balconied and tin-roofed Queenslander houses still left standing, often lovingly restored to their original condition.

Across the river, **Kangaroo Point**, crowned by the Story Bridge, is an activity heartland for energetic locals – the cliffs here make a great spot for watching the sun set over the city – while the bohemian, bustling streets of **South Brisbane** and the **West End** tend to feel infinitely more relaxed than their northern counterparts. Further west, there's a blaze of riverside homes at Milton and Toowong, beyond which lies **Mount Coot-tha**.

Brisbane is a fairly easy place to find casual, short-term **employment**, and the healthy, unpredictable social scene tempts many travellers to spend longer here than they had planned. As for exploring further afield, you'll find empty beaches and surf on **North Stradbroke Island** and dolphins around **Moreton Island** – both easy to reach from the city.

Brief history

In 1823, the New South Wales government sent Surveyor General **John Oxley** north to find a suitable site for a new prison colony. The aim was to shift the "worst type of felons" – those who had committed further offences after arriving in Australia – away from Sydney, and thus make transportation "an object of real terror" once more. Sailing into **Moreton Bay**, Oxley was shown a previously unknown river by three shipwrecked convicts who had been living with Aborigines. He explored it briefly, named the river "Brisbane" after the governor, and the next year established a convict settlement at **Redcliffe** on the coast. This was immediately abandoned in favour of better anchorage further upstream, and by the end of 1824 what's now the city centre had become the site of Brisbane Town.

Twenty years on, a land shortage down south persuaded the government to move out the convicts and free up the Moreton Bay area to settlers. Immigrants on government-assisted passages poured in and Brisbane began to shape up as a busy **port** – an unattractive, awkward town of rutted streets and wooden shacks. As the largest regional settlement, Brisbane was the obvious choice as capital of the new state of Queensland on its formation in 1859, though the city's first substantial buildings were constructed only in the late 1860s, after fire had destroyed the original centre and state bankruptcy was averted by Queensland's first gold strikes at Gympie. Even so, development was slow and uneven: new townships were founded around the centre at Fortitude Valley, Kangaroo Point and Breakfast Creek, gradually merging into a city.

After World War II, when **General Douglas MacArthur** used Brisbane as his headquarters to coordinate attacks on Japanese forces throughout the Pacific, Brisbane stagnated, earning a reputation as a dull, underdeveloped backwater – not least during the nineteen-year premiership of **Joh Bjelke-Petersen**, between 1968 and 1987.

Brisbane's recent growth was largely triggered by its hosting of the 1988 **World Expo**, which prompted the transformation of the South Bank in particular. Since then, the skyline of Australia's third city has changed beyond all recognition. The protracted boom in the economy, population and house prices has seen a snazzy redevelopment of the dilapidated Brisbane River foreshore so that it's now home to upmarket apartment blocks, and an influx of big-name, high-end restaurants. Even

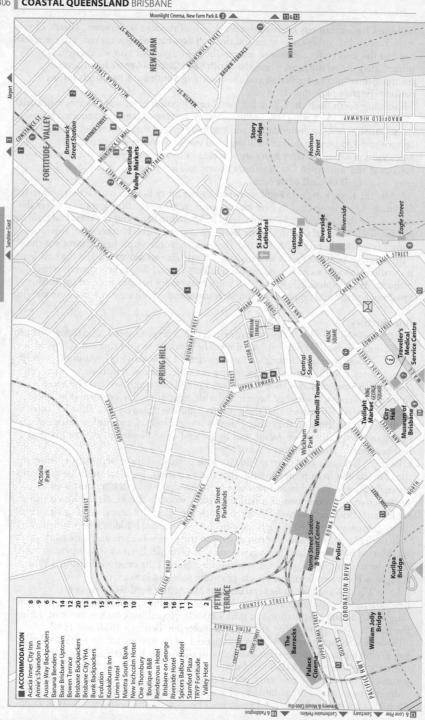

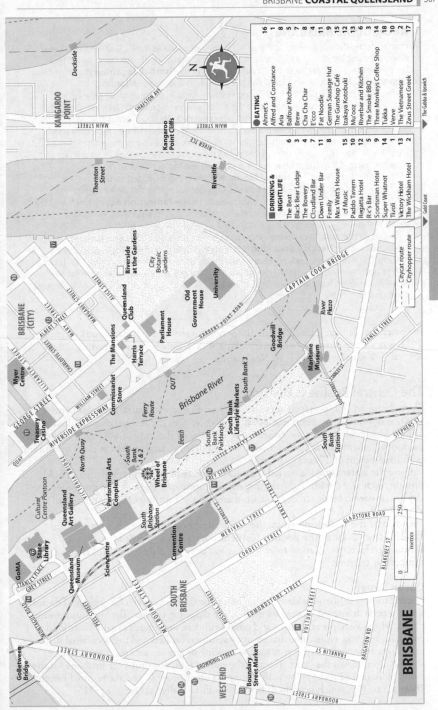

BRISBANE

● EATING

Ahmet's	16
Alfred and Constance	1
Aria	8
Balfour Kitchen	5
Brew	7
Cha Cha Char	8
E'cco	4
Fat Noodle	11
German Sausage Hut	9
The Gunshop Café	15
Izakaya Kotobuki	12
Mu'ooz	13
Riverbar and Kitchen	6
The Smoke BBQ	3
Three Monkeys Coffee Shop	14
Tukka	18
Verve	10
The Vietnamese	2
Zeus Street Greek	17

■ DRINKING & NIGHTLIFE

The Beat	6
Black Bear Lodge	3
The Bowery	4
Cloudland Bar	7
Down Under Bar	11
Family	8
Mex Watt's House of Music	15
Paddo Tavern	10
Regatta Hotel	12
R c's Bar	5
Scortsman Hotel	9
Super Whatnot	14
Tivoli	1
Victory Hotel	13
The Wickham Hotel	2

▶ The Gabba & Ipswich

▶ Gold Coast

- - - - Citycat route
— — Cityhopper route

3

3

> ## ABORIGINAL BRISBANE
>
> Human occupation of the Brisbane area has been dated back at least 22,000 years, to a time when the coast lay 30km further east and what's now North Stradbroke Island would have been an inland hill. These were the traditional lands of the **Turrbal**, **Jagarra** and **Quandamooka** people, who knew the site of modern Brisbane as **Mianjin**.
>
> John Oxley recorded that the local Aborigines were friendly; in the early days, they even rounded up and returned runaways from the settlement. In his orders to Oxley on how to deal with the indigenous peoples, Governor Brisbane conceded, albeit in a roundabout way, that the land belonged to them: "All uncivilized people have wants … when treated justly they acquire many comforts by their union with the more civilized. This justifies our occupation of their lands."
>
> But future governors were not so liberal, and things had soured long before the first squatters moved into the Brisbane area and began leaving out "gifts" of poisoned flour. From 1848 onwards, the infamous **Native Mounted Police** were wielded to "disperse" – a euphemism for exterminate – Queensland's Aborigines. Later in the nineteenth century, survivors from these early days were dispossessed by the **Protection Act** (in force until the 1970s), which saw them rounded up and relocated onto special reserves away from traditional lands.
>
> Around forty thousand people of Aboriginal descent now live in Brisbane. A trace of the past can be seen at the **Nudgee Bora Ring**, 12km north of the centre at Nudgee Waterhole Reserve. The two low mounds here were used for initiation ceremonies for boys until 1860; they're now bare relics, so you may feel it's not worth the trip. More rewarding are the several Aboriginal walking trails at Mount Coot-tha; leaflets from the City Hall information desk explain traditional uses of the area.

the extensive damage caused by the (hopefully) once-in-a-century **floods** of January 2011 was swiftly repaired, with the major visible legacy being the reconstructed Riverside Walkway that leads to New Farm.

The Central Business District

Tucked into an elbow-shaped curve of the river, Brisbane's **Central Business District** (**CBD**) is dominated by gleaming, glassy high-rises, with the few surviving old buildings hidden like jewels among the newer constructions. At the time of writing, three mighty additional behemoths were under construction here, all targeted at the city's maximum permitted height of 274m.

Along the **water's edge**, assorted wharves and piers have been remodelled to hold upscale restaurants, with high-end shops lining upmarket Eagle Street alongside. The city's mainstream **retail** activity is centred around the bustling Queen Street Mall and along Adelaide Street.

Known as the **historic precinct**, the neighbourhood that stretches south from Queen Street as far as the Botanic Gardens boasts some of Brisbane's finest colonial architecture, dating from the earliest days of settlement until the late nineteenth century.

Queen Street

Queen Street is Brisbane's oldest thoroughfare, the stretch between George and Edward streets a **pedestrian mall** flanked by multistorey shopping centres. The area bustles with diners, window-shoppers, tourists and errand-runners, and there's usually some kind of entertainment too: either informal efforts – acrobats, buskers and the occasional soap-box orator – or more organized events such as dancing or jazz sessions on the small stage about halfway down the street. Towards the eastern end, don't miss the **Brisbane Arcade**, a rather glorious 1920s shopping mall that opens off at no. 160, and the restored **Regent Theatre**, no. 167, which now holds Brisbane's official visitor centre (see p.316)

City Hall

King George Square • Daily, hourly guided tours (45min) 10.30am–3.30pm; Clock Tower daily 10.15am–4.45pm, tours every 15min • Free • Reserve on ☎ 07 3339 0845, ⌨ museumofbrisbane.com.au

The open space of **King George Square**, reached by heading north along Albert Street from Queen Street's pedestrian mall, is a popular gathering place for the city's business workers. Free guided tours explore **City Hall**, the stately, columned 1920s structure that dominates the west side of the square and is home to the Museum of Brisbane.

Visitors can also queue to ascend City Hall's 92m **Clock Tower**. Until 1967 this was the city's tallest structure; sadly, the views today tend to look up towards, rather than down over, Brisbane's ever-expanding skyline.

Museum of Brisbane

Level 3, Brisbane City Hall • Daily 10am–5pm • Free • ☎ 07 3339 0800, ⌨ museumofbrisbane.com.au

The **Museum of Brisbane**, upstairs in City Hall, hosts changing exhibitions with a Queensland theme, with an emphasis on work by emerging Brisbane artists. Current hit "One Hundred Percent Brisbane" – the individual stories of a hundred locals – will remain in place until 2019.

Treasury Building

130 William St • ☎ 07 3306 8888, ⌨ treasurybrisbane.com.au

The classical facade of the former **Treasury** occupies an entire block, between Elizabeth and Queen streets. Built in the 1890s, its grandeur reflects the wealth of Queensland's gold mines – most of which were in fact in decline by this point – and served as a slap in the face to New South Wales, which had spitefully withdrawn all financial support from the fledgling state on separation some forty years previously, leaving it bankrupt. The building now holds Brisbane's 24-hour **casino**, incorporating restaurants, bars and some of the city's plushest hotel rooms.

Commissariat Store

115 William St • Tues–Fri 10am–4pm • $7 • Free tours • ☎ 07 3221 4198, ⌨ queenslandhistory.org

Built as a granary by convicts in 1829, using stone cleaved from Kangaroo Point, the **Commissariat Store** is now both an insightful museum and the headquarters of the Royal Historical Society of Queensland. Even after the flooding it sustained in 2011, commemorated in a new exhibition, it's still in considerably better shape than its close contemporary, the Windmill Tower. It also holds scale models of the Moreton Bay Penal Settlement and early Brisbane, but its most famous exhibit remains the gruesome "**Convict Finger**", preserved in a jar and hailing from the former prison on nearby St Helena Island.

Harris Terrace and The Mansions

Further south along George Street (straddling Margaret Street) you pass **Harris Terrace** and **The Mansions**, two of the city centre's last surviving rows of Victorian-era terraced houses, the latter featuring stone cats rendered from New Zealand limestone guarding the parapet corners.

Parliament House

Cnr George & Alice sts • Mon–Fri 9am–4.15pm; tours 1pm, 2pm, 3pm & 4pm when Parliament is not in session, 1pm when it is • Free • ☎ 07 3553 6470, ⌨ parliament.qld.gov.au

Parliament House was built to a design by Charles Tiffin in 1868, in an appealingly compromised French Renaissance style that incorporates shuttered north windows, shaded colonnades and a high, arched roof to allow for the tropical climate. Tours of the grand interior operate more frequently when Parliament is not sitting.

Old Government House

2 George St • Daily except Sat 10am–4pm • Free • ☎ 07 3138 8005, ⓦ ogh.qut.edu.au

Designed by Charles Tiffin, and completed in 1862, **Old Government House** served as the official residence of Queensland's governors and premiers until 1910. The building has been comprehensively restored to its stately, early twentieth-century condition. Amid its magnificent furnishings, virtual exhibits tell the story of its former inhabitants, and there's an interactive panorama of 1870s Brisbane.

Windmill Tower

Flanked by Albert Street and Wickham Terrace, tiny **Wickham Park** sits in the shadow of the grey cone of Brisbane's oldest building, the **Windmill Tower**. Sometimes called the **Observatory**, this cherished landmark was erected by convicts in 1829 to grind corn for the early settlement. After the original wooden sails proved too heavy to turn, it found use as a gallows until being pulled off in 1850. All grinding thereafter was done by treadmill – severe punishment for the convicts who had to work it. After the convict era the building became a signal station, and was used for Australia's first TV broadcast in 1934, but it now stands locked and empty.

City Botanic Gardens

Southeast corner of CBD; enter via Alice St or Gardens Point Rd • Daily 6am–6pm • Tours leave Mon–Sat 11am & 1pm from the rotunda, 100m inside the main Alice St entrance • Free • ☎ 07 3403 2305, ⓦ brisbane.qld.gov.au

Bordered by Alice and George streets as well as the river, Brisbane's **Botanic Gardens** overlook the cliffs of Kangaroo Point. While more of a park than a botanic garden, they provide a generous arrangement of flowers, shrubs, bamboo thickets and green grass for sprawling on.

Walter Hill, who laid out formal gardens in 1855, on what was originally a vegetable patch cultivated by convicts, experimented with local and imported plants to see which would grow well in Queensland's then-untried climate. His more successful efforts include the oversized **bunya pines** around the Edward Street entrance, planted in 1860, and a residual patch of the **rainforest** that once blanketed the area, at the southern end of the park. **Mangroves** along the river, accessible by a **boardwalk**, are another native species more recently protected. Classical music recitals are held in summer on an open-air stage at the southern end of the gardens, beyond which the pedestrian **Goodwill Bridge** crosses the river to South Bank Parklands.

South Bank

Ever since it was transformed to host the World Expo of 1988, Brisbane's **South Bank** has been the obvious goal for city visitors in search of culture, sightseeing or simply a waterside picnic. Lying in fact directly *west* across the river from the CBD, it's most enjoyably reached on foot, via either of two pedestrian footbridges – the curving, convoluted **Kurilpa Bridge** at its northern end, or the **Goodwill Bridge**, which connects with the CBD's southern tip.

The highlight here is the **South Bank Cultural Centre**, a complex of concrete-and-glass buildings between Grey Street and the river that holds the Queensland Museum, Sciencentre, the Queensland Art Gallery, State Library and Gallery of Modern Art (better known as GoMA). Stretching south beside the river from there, the beautifully landscaped **South Bank Parklands** make a lovely spot to unwind, while immediately inland Grey and Little Stanley streets are home to an amazing array of restaurants and cafes.

A short walk further south and west, the **West End** is South Brisbane's answer to Fortitude Valley, where there are no sights as such but a plethora of vintage boutiques, live music venues and yet more **restaurants** and **cafés** strung out along Boundary Street.

THE BRISBANE RIVER

The sluggish, meandering **Brisbane River** is, at four hundred million years old, one of the world's most ancient waterways. Its historic course ran for 344km from Mount Stanley, northwest of the city, to the sea, though it was dammed from 1973 onwards to create Lake Wivenhoe, 80km from central Brisbane. From there it now flows past farmland, into quiet suburbs and through the city before emptying downstream into Moreton Bay. Once an essential trade and transport link with the rest of Australia and the world, it now serves primarily to delineate the many neighbourhoods of the city; though the central stretch is busy with ferries, most of the old wharves and shipyards now lie derelict or buried under parkland.

The river has long had the habit of reasserting its presence through **flooding**. In February 1893 cyclonic rains swelled the flow through downtown Brisbane, carrying off Victoria Bridge and scores of buildings: eyewitness accounts stated that "debris of all descriptions – whole houses, trees, cattle and homes – went floating past". This has since been repeated many times, notably in 1974 when rains from **Cyclone Wanda** completely swamped the centre, swelling the river to a width of 3km at one stage. The completion of the Lake Wivenhoe dam in 1984 gave property developers (and their insurers) the confidence to build some of Brisbane's poshest homes beside the river, notably at Yeronga, Graceville and Chelmer, southwest of the centre. However, the dam couldn't contain the sheer volume of rain that fell in January 2011 and the river burst its banks once again, causing millions of dollars' worth of damage.

3

Queensland Museum

Cnr Grey & Melbourne sts • Daily 9.30am–5pm • Free • ☎ 07 3840 7555, ⓦ qm.qld.gov.au

From the humpback whale family that dangles (in model form) over the walkway outside, the **Queensland Museum** is largely devoted to natural history. Targeted principally at teaching local school kids about their home state, it also makes a good introduction for out-of-towners. The "Lost Creatures" section celebrates long-extinct species unearthed as fossils, including a huge plesiosaur and a reconstruction of Queensland's own *Muttaburrasaurus*, while smaller displays explore the marine environment, particularly turtles.

Upstairs, the Dandiiri Maiwar exhibition focuses on **Aboriginal Queensland**, using photos, accounts by Aboriginal elders and early settlers, and Dreamtime stories, with lots of material on the peoples of the Torres Strait.

Sciencentre

Cnr Grey & Melbourne sts • Daily 9.30am–5pm • $14.50 • ☎ 07 3840 7555, ⓦ sciencentre.qm.qld.gov.au

The **Sciencentre** offers museum visitors the chance to prod and dismantle exhibits rather than simply peer at them through protective glass cases. Hits with the kids include the mind-bending puzzles and illusions in the Body Zone, and the "Thongophone", a set of giant panpipes played by whacking the top with a flip-flop – all good rainy-day fun.

Queensland Art Gallery

Stanley Place • Daily 10am–5pm • Free • ☎ 07 3840 7303, ⓦ qagoma.qld.gov.au

The remit of the excellent **Queensland Art Gallery** extends well beyond Queensland itself, with its collection ranging not only all over Australia but further afield, to include Toulouse Lautrec and Japanese woodblock prints. Everywhen, Everywhere, its opening section, covers Aboriginal art, though the gallery's watercolours by the iconic Albert Namatjira are not always on display. Stand-outs later on include astounding paintings by Sidney Nolan from his series on **Mrs Fraser** (of Fraser Island fame), Ian Fairweather's abstract canvases, and a nineteenth-century **stained-glass window** of a kangaroo hunt. This broad selection traces how Australian art initially aped European tastes and then, during the twentieth century, found its own style in the alienated works of Nolan, Boyd and Whiteley, all of whom were inspired by Australian landscape and legends.

Gallery of Modern Art

Stanley Place • Daily 10am–5pm • Free • ☎ 07 3840 7303, 🖰 qagoma.qld.gov.au

GoMA, the **Gallery of Modern Art**, continues to confirm Brisbane's status as a major international arts centre. A huge, airy space that's ideally suited to contemporary works, the gallery doesn't display a permanent collection, but is instead overhauled each year to host big-name **temporary exhibitions** honouring the likes of Picasso, Warhol, and more recently Anish Kapoor and Cindy Sherman. It also has great views of the river, spanned at this point by the zany Kurilpa Bridge, and the evolving skyline beyond.

The South Bank Parklands

Take the pedestrian Kurilpa or Goodwill bridges; the ferry or City Cat; or the CityTrain to South Bank station

While very much manicured and landscaped rather than wild, the **South Bank Parklands** rank among the nicest parts of the city. Visitors can promenade in the shade of fig trees along the riverfront; **picnic** under rainforest plants and bamboo on lawns lining the banks of shallow, stone-lined "streams" (which are convincing enough to attract large, sunbathing water dragons and birds); or make use of the sandy, artificial **Streets Beach** and accompanying saltwater pool. **Bands** play most Saturday nights, either on the outdoor stage or at the *Plough Inn*, a restored 1885 pub on the cobbled high street, and lots of cafés and restaurants offer alfresco meals in the park itself, complementing the buzzing restaurant strip on Little Stanley Street alongside.

Maritime Museum

412 Stanley St • Daily 9.30am–4.30pm • $16 • ☎ 07 3844 5361, 🖰 maritimemuseum.com.au

Brisbane's rather old-school **Maritime Museum**, next to the Goodwill Bridge at the southern end of the parklands, is well worth a visit. Its pride and joy is a World War II River Class frigate, the *Diamantina*, that's moored in the Heritage-listed dry dock; visitors are free to wander aboard and explore it top to bottom, where there are all sorts of fascinating displays. There's also a separate gallery on terra firma alongside, with displays on such themes as Australian lighthouses, the Mutiny on the Bounty, and "Women and the Sea".

Fortitude Valley and New Farm

While Brisbane's northern neighbourhoods are mainly residential, **Fortitude Valley** – generally known as simply "**the Valley**" – is a tangled mix of shops, restaurants, bars and clubs, comprising Brisbane's unofficial centre of artistic, gastronomic and alcoholic pursuits. An eclectic mix of the gay, the groovy and the grubby, the Valley is mostly focused along partially pedestrianized **Brunswick Street**, which sports a kilometre-long melange of nightclubs, an Irish pub, a compact Chinatown complete with busy restaurants and stores, and a burgeoning European street-café scene. In recent years, the area has been steadily becoming gentrified, with the urban poor making way for hipsters, artists and students, though Brunswick Street itself has largely avoided the yuppies and smarmy wine bars that have descended on parallel **James Street**. It's best at weekends when cafés buzz, live musicians compete for your attention, and a secondhand

---

DRINKS FOR WOMEN: THE REGATTA HOTEL

Though Australian **pubs** still tend towards being **all-male** enclaves, **women** were once legally barred to "protect" them from the corrupting influence of foul language. On April 11, 1965, Merle Thornton (mother of the actress Sigrid Thornton) and her friend Rosalie Bogner chained themselves to the foot rail of the **Regatta Hotel** bar at Toowong in protest. The movement they inspired led to the granting of "the right to drink alongside men" in the mid-1970s. The grand, pink-and-white colonial hotel is on the west bank of the river along Coronation Drive, 2km from the city centre.

market sells arts and crafts in the mall. After dark the Valley's streets can turn somewhat sleazy – if you plan to go any distance on your own after the pubs close, take a taxi.

South of Harcourt Street, Brunswick and James streets plunge into **New Farm**, a leafy low-slung residential suburb that's home to sizeable parklands and a thriving café/foodie scene. You can walk all the way here from the CBD by following the wonderful **Riverside Walkway**, rebuilt in the wake of the 2011 flood and now perched as far as Sydney Street on a stilted boardwalk above the river itself. CityCat ferries keep going beyond Sydney Street to **The Powerhouse**, Brisbane's premier performing-arts venue, in a converted power station at the southern end of **New Farm Park**.

Castlemaine Perkins Brewery: XXXX

185 Milton Rd • 1hr 30min tours Mon–Fri 11am, 12.30pm, 3pm & 5pm; Sat 11am, 11.30am, noon, 12.30pm, 1pm, 1.30pm, 2pm, 3pm & 5pm; closed-toe shoes must be worn • $32 • ☎ 07 3361 7597, ⊛ xxxx.com.au • CityTrain to Milton

The **Castlemaine Perkins Brewery** has been making Queensland's own beer since 1878. Its famous yellow-and-red **XXXX** emblem is part of the Queensland landscape – it's splashed across T-shirts, the roofs of Outback hotels, and the labels of countless discarded bottles and cans littering everything from roadsides to the Great Barrier Reef. For enthusiasts, the adjacent **XXXX Visitor Centre** runs tours that incorporate a one-hour overview of the brewing process followed by free beers in the Ale House afterwards.

Mount Coot-tha

Sir Samuel Griffith Drive • Free • ☎ 07 3369 9922, ⊛ brisbanelookout.com • Bus #471 from Adelaide St (30min)

At the day's end, Brisbanites and tourists alike head up the road to the summit of **Mount Coot-tha** for panoramas of the city and, on a good day, the Moreton Bay islands. Walking tracks from the **Brisbane Lookout** here offer moderate hikes of thirty minutes to an hour through dry gum woodland. They include several **Aboriginal trails**, the best of which branches off the Summit Track, and features informative signs pointing out plants and their uses, and weaves past artwork in the form of rock paintings, tree carvings and etchings. Trail guides are available from the botanic gardens.

Brisbane Botanic Gardens Mount Coot-tha

Mt Coot-tha Rd, Toowong • **Botanic gardens** Daily: Sept–March 8am 5.30pm, April–Aug 8am–5pm; guided walks set off from info kiosk Mon–Sat 11am & 1pm • Free • ☎ 07 3403 2535, ⊛ brisbane.qld.gov.au • **Planetarium** Tues–Fri 10am–4pm, Sat 11am–8.15pm, Sun 11am–4pm; show times vary, see website for schedule • Shows $15.40 • ☎ 07 3403 2578, ⊛ brisbane.qld.gov.au • Bus #471 from Adelaide St (30min)

The lower slopes of **Mount Coot-tha** are the setting for Brisbane's second **botanic gardens**. Sunday picnickers are a common sight in this leafy haven, where careful landscaping and the use of enclosures have created a variety of climates – dry pine and eucalypt groves, a cool subtropical rainforest complete with waterfalls and streams, and the elegant Japanese Gardens with bonsai and fern houses. The steamy **tropical plant dome** contains a pond stocked with lotus lilies and fish, overhung by lush greenery dripping with moisture.

The gardens are also home to the **Sir Thomas Brisbane Planetarium**, where visitors can enjoy unique perspectives of Brisbane's night sky and other aspects of the universe at large, while lying back under its "Cosmic Skydome".

Lone Pine Sanctuary

708 Jesmond Rd, Fig Tree Pocket • Daily 9am–5pm • $36 • ☎ 07 3378 1366, ⊛ koala.net • Bus #445 from Adelaide St (45min) or #430 from Queen St station (40min) to Lone Pine

Lone Pine Sanctuary has been a popular day-trip upstream since opening its gates in 1927. Australian fauna can be seen in its natural state which, in the case of the sanctuary's 130-plus koalas, means being asleep for eighteen hours a day. In nearby cages you'll find other slumbering animals, including Tasmanian devils and fruit bats. Lively sheepdog and raptor demos add welcome animation, and in the outdoor paddock, tolerant wallabies and kangaroos are petted and fed by visitors. For an extra $150 you can follow in the footsteps of famous visitors from Mikhail Gorbachev to Slipknot, and cuddle a koala.

CityCat and other public ferries do not go this far upstream, but Mirimar Cruises do: their **river cruise** (1hr 15min) is highly enjoyable, although the timings mean that if you book the return trip you'll miss some of the shows at the sanctuary.

ARRIVAL AND DEPARTURE   BRISBANE

All long-distance buses and trains end up at Brisbane's **Transit Centre**, on Roma St in the heart of the city (ⓦ brisbanetransitcentre.com.au). The highest of its three levels holds the **bus offices**, a hostel information desk (daily 8am–4pm) and luggage lockers (there are more lockers on the ground floor). The middle floor has fast-food joints, a bar, toilets and showers, a medical centre and ATMs, while on the ground floor is the arrival and departure point for local and interstate **trains** as well as several car-rental companies. **Local buses** depart from street level; **long-distance buses** and **taxis** from Level 3. Most hostelers either meet buses or will pick you up if you call them. You can't always rely on a pick-up late at night, however, when it's best to take a taxi – it's never a good idea to wander around after midnight with your luggage in tow.

BY PLANE
Brisbane Airport The city's airport (ⓦ bne.com.au) stands 9km northeast of the centre, at the end of Kingsford Smith Drive, just off the highway connecting the Gold Coast and the Sunshine Coast. Inconveniently, the domestic and international terminals are 2km apart; they're connected every 10–20min by the free Airport Transfer Bus and also by the Airtrain. Both terminals hold banks, ATMs and luggage-storage lockers ($10–14/24hr).

Flight destinations Adelaide (6 daily; 3hr); Alice Springs (2 weekly; 3hr 30min); Biloela (1 daily; 1hr 15min); Blackall (3 weekly; 2hr); Bundaberg (4 daily; 1hr); Cairns (13 daily; 2hr 30min); Canberra (7 daily; 2hr); Charleville (4 weekly; 2hr); Darwin (3 daily; 4hr 15min); Emerald (4 daily; 1hr 40min); Gladstone (6 daily; 1hr 15min); Hamilton Island (1 daily; 1hr 45min); Hervey Bay (2 daily; 50min); Hobart (1 daily; 2hr 50min); Launceston (5 weekly; 2hr 40min); Longreach (2 weekly; 2hr 25min); Lord Howe Island (1 weekly; 1hr 45min); Mackay (9 daily; 1hr 40min); Melbourne (many daily; 2hr 30min); Mount Isa (2 daily; 2hr 40min); Newcastle (6 daily; 1hr 50min); Norfolk Island (2 weekly; 2hr 20min); Perth (7 daily; 5hr 45min); Proserpine (2 daily; 1hr 50min); Rockhampton (11 daily; 1hr 15min); Roma (2 daily; 1hr 10min); Sydney (many daily; 1hr 40min); Townsville (7 daily; 2hr 10min).

City connections The speedy Airtrain (5.04am–10.04pm; ⓦ airtrain.com.au) connects both airport terminals with central Brisbane, taking 28min to reach the Transit Centre ($17.50 one-way, $33 return). The shared door-to-door shuttle service Con-X-ion ($20 one-way, or $49 to Gold Coast; ☎1300 266 946, ⓦ con-x-ion.com) takes up to 40min but delivers direct to central accommodation or the Transit Centre. Con-X-ion is a better option for the Gold Coast than Airtrain, which does serve Nerang and Varsity

Lakes but skirts the coast by 4km. Taxis into Brisbane from the city cost around $45 for the 30min trip.

BY TRAIN
Trains run up the coast all the way north to Cairns, as well as inland to Charleville and Longreach and south down to Sydney, with a bus connection between Brisbane/Surfers Paradise and Casino in northern New South Wales.

Destinations Ayr (5 weekly; 16hr 30min); Bowen (5 weekly; 15hr); Bundaberg (2–3 daily; 4hr 30min–6hr); Caboolture (2–3 daily; 1hr); Cairns (5 weekly; 24hr); Cardwell (5 weekly; 20hr); Charleville (2 weekly; 17h 30min); Gladstone (6 weekly; 6hr 15min–8hr 45min); Ingham (5 weekly; 19hr); Innisfail (5 weekly; 22hr); Longreach (2 weekly; 24hr); Mackay (5 weekly; 12hr); Proserpine (6 weekly; 14hr); Rockhampton (2–3 daily; 8hr–10hr 30min); Sydney (1 daily; 14hr); Townsville (5 weekly; 17hr 30min); Tully (5 weekly; 21hr).

BY BUS
Con-X-ion (☎1300 266 946, ⓦ con-x-ion.com) run local buses to the Gold and Sunshine coasts. Greyhound run four daily services from Brisbane north to Hervey Bay, of which one continues all the way to Cairns, and four services south via Surfers Paradise to Byron Bay in New South Wales, of which two continue to Sydney. Under the Oz Experience brand (ⓦ ozexperience.com), they sell various hop-on-hop-off passes for travellers heading between Brisbane and Cairns, including multi-night stopovers on Fraser Island and the Whitsundays. Premier's daily Lismore/Sydney service also stops on the Gold Coast. Crisp's Coaches (☎07 4661 8333, ⓦ crisps.com.au) runs daily to the southeastern towns of Warwick, Tenterfield and Moree.

Destinations Agnes Water (2 daily; 11hr); Airlie Beach (2

daily; 18hr); Ayr (2 daily; 23hr); Bowen (2 daily; 19hr); Bundaberg (2 daily; 8–10hr); Burleigh Heads (2 daily; 1hr 40min); Byron Bay (5 daily; 4–5hr); Cairns (1 daily; 29hr); Cardwell (1 daily; 25hr 30min); Childers (2 daily; 8hr); Coolangatta (2 daily; 2hr); Gladstone (1 daily; 11hr); Hervey Bay (4 daily; 6hr 20min); Ingham (1 daily; 25hr); Innisfail (1 daily; 28hr); Mackay (2 daily; 15hr 30min); Mission Beach (1 daily; 27hr); Mooloolaba (2–3 daily; 1hr 40min); Moree (1 daily; 6hr); Noosa (3 daily; 2hr 20min); Rainbow Beach (2 daily; 5hr 20min); Rockhampton (2 daily; 13hr); Surfers Paradise (6 daily; 1hr 15min); Sydney (3 daily; 16hr–17hr 30min); Tenterfield (1 daily; 4hr 10min); Townsville (2 daily; 24hr); Tully (1 daily; 26hr 30min); Warwick (2 daily; 2hr 15min).

GETTING AROUND

All public buses, CityTrain services and Council ferries are operated by **TransLink**, which has an office at the Queen Street Mall visitor centre (Mon–Thurs 9am–5.30pm, Fri 9am–7pm, Sat 9am–5pm, Sun 10–5pm; ☏13 12 30, ⊚translink .com.au) and serves 23 zones extending north to Noosa and south to Coolangatta. All tickets are valid on all services – boat, bus and train. A single cash fare in the central zone is $4.80, while a ride out to Mount Coot-tha in zone 2 costs $5.60. If you make multiple trips, it's cheaper and easier to get a TransLink smartcard, called a **go card**, which you can buy (and top up) in stations and at newsagents and convenience stores (such as 7-Eleven).

By train The electric CityTrain network provides a faster service than the buses, but it's not as frequent or comprehensive. Trains through central Brisbane run every few minutes, but for the more distant suburbs you can wait up to an hour. The last trains leave Central Station on Ann St at about 11.45pm, with later hours on Friday and Saturday nights – timetables are available from ticket offices. You can buy tickets and passes at stations.

By bus Buses (drivers give change) run between around 5am and 11pm, with most travelling via Queen Street Bus Station below the Myer Centre. The free City Loop makes a good way to get around the CBD (Mon–Fri 7am–6pm). The distinctive red buses circle every 15min both clockwise and anticlockwise between Central Station and Botanic Gardens via Queen St Mall and Riverside, with ten stops en route.

By ferry Brisbane's ferries provide a quick, scenic and very enjoyable way to get around the city. There are a couple of regular cross-river ferry connections, but the most useful are the CityCat and free CityHopper services, which run separate routes but share two stops, at North Quay, next to Victoria Bridge near the South Bank Parklands, and at Sydney St in New Farm. CityCat (fares payable on board, or using Translink go cards; daily 5.30am–11.45pm, every 6–30min) travels between the University of Queensland campus in the southwest and Bretts Wharf and Northshore Hamilton,

towards the airport on Kingsford Smith Drive. The bright-red, free CityHopper ferries (daily 6am–midnight, every 30min), stop at the main tourist sights, including the Maritime Museum, Thornton St (for Kangaroo Cliffs) and Sydney St. You can buy go cards, and pick up information, from a waterfront booth at the Riverside Ferry Terminal (daily 9am–5pm; ☏07 3229 7778, ⊚brisbaneferries.com.au).

By car You'll pay around $35 for a single day's car rental; longer terms work out from $26/day, while campervans start at $54/day for long-term rental. Shop around and read conditions before signing; most places will deliver and the minimum age is usually 21. Local outfits include Alpha (☏1300 227 473, ⊚alphacarhire.com.au); Britz (☏1800 331 454, ⊚britz.com.au); East Coast (☏1800 327 826, ⊚eastcoastcarrentals.com.au); and Wicked (☏1800 246 869, ⊚wickedcampers.com.au).

By taxi Yellow Cab Company (☏13 19 24, ⊚yellowcab .com.au) or Black & White Cabs (☏133 222, ⊚blackandwhitecabs.com.au). After dark, taxis cruise round the clubs and hotels.

By bike Maps of the city's many cycle routes are available from visitor centres and libraries. Some hostels also loan bikes. Using Brisbane's CityCycle public bike loan scheme costs from $2 a day, with the first 30min of any hire free; helmets are mandatory (☏1300 229 253, ⊚citycycle.com.au).

BRISBANE FESTIVALS

Anywhere Festival May ⊚anywherefest.com. Two-week jamboree of theatre, cabaret, music and comedy performances, plus exhibitions and architecture tours, all over the city.

Queensland Music Festival July ⊚qmf.org.au. Biennial statewide musical events, staged in odd-numbered years only.

Brisbane Festival September ⊚brisbanefestival.com.au. World-class arts festival with music, theatre, comedy, dance, opera and circus events held across the city.

Brisbane Writers Festival September ⊚bwf.org.au. Four days of talks, readings, workshops and fringe events.

Pride Festival September ⊚brisbanepride.org.au. Month-long celebration of Gay Pride.

Northern Exposure October ⊚brisbears.org.au. Seven days of LGBT-friendly events.

INFORMATION

Tourist information Brisbane's main visitor centre, in the former Regent Theatre at 167 Queen St, offers a huge array of brochures and maps, as well as a ticket office for city tours and attractions (Mon–Thurs 9am–5.30pm, Fri 9am–7pm, Sat 9am–5pm, Sun 10am–5pm; ☎07 3006 6290, Ⓦ visitbrisbane.com.au). Be sure to wander

through to the back to admire the theatre's majestic restored lobby. There are further visitor centres in the Stanley St Plaza on the South Bank (daily 9am–5pm; ☎07 3156 6366), and on Level 2 of the airport's International Terminal (daily 5am–2am; ☎07 3406 3190, Ⓦ southernqueensland.com.au).

TOURS

CITY TOURS

Brisbane Explorer ☎07 9567 8400, Ⓦ theaustralianexplorer.com.au. Hop-on-hop-off narrated sightseeing tours on open-top double-decker buses, looping around the centre and out to Mount Coot-tha. Daily 9am–5.15pm; $70 for 24hr, $120 for 48hr.

Brisbane Greeters ☎07 3156 6364, Ⓦ brisbanegreeters.com.au. Informative 2–4hr city tours, hosted by friendly, in-the-know local volunteers, on foot or bike, and tailored to your tastes: arts, culture, dining, heritage, architecture, sites and attractions. Free; reserve at least three days in advance.

CRUISES

Kookaburra River Queen ☎07 3221 1300, Ⓦ kookaburrariverqueens.com. Restored paddlewheeler offering lunch, dinner and sightseeing cruises from Eagle St Pier. Thurs–Sun, from $49.

Mirimar Cruises ☎0412 749 426, Ⓦ mirimar.com. 1hr 15min cruise to Lone Pine Sanctuary from the Cultural Centre Pontoon. Daily 10am, return trip leaves at 1.45pm; $72 return including Lone Pine entry.

River City Cruises ☎0428 278 473, Ⓦ rivercitycruises.com.au. Round-trip cruises depart from South Bank Parklands Jetty A, and take 1hr 30min to head downstream past the CBD and back again. Daily 10.30am & 12.30pm; $29.

TOURS FROM BRISBANE

The most popular tours from Brisbane are day-trips by bus to Lamington, Tamborine Mountain, Moreton Island, the Sunshine Coast or Gold Coast. Most tour companies also offer transfers from the Gold Coast.

Bushwacker ☎1300 559 355, Ⓦ bushwacker-ecotours.com.au. Excellent day-trips to the Gold Coast Hinterland; expect plenty of wildlife, rainforests, bushtucker and swimming holes ($129).

Cat-o'-Nine-Tails Day-trips and night ghost tours to St Helena Island (see p.322).

Moreton Bay Escapes ☎1300 559 355, Ⓦ moretonbayescapes.com.au. Day-tours with snorkelling and sandboarding ($199) or overnight camping trips to Moreton Island (2 days; $259).

Sunrover Expeditions ☎1800 353 717, Ⓦ sunrover.com.au. Day-trips to Moreton, North Stradbroke and Fraser islands from $140.

ACTIVITIES

Bridge climb Story Bridge Adventure Climb, 170 Main St, Kangaroo Point (☎1300 254 627, Ⓦ sbac.net.au) run dawn, day, night and twilight climbs up Brisbane's iconic Story Bridge from $79; abseiling also available.

Outdoor activities Riverlife, Lower River Terrace, Kangaroo Point (☎07 3891 5766, Ⓦ riverlife.com.au) offer activities ranging from rock climbing Kangaroo Cliffs (Sat & Sun 8.30–10.30am, $55) to kayaking on the Brisbane River (daytime kayak rental from $28 for 1hr 30min; night-time tours Fri & Sat 7pm $59, or $85 with BBQ dinner) and stand up paddleboarding (daily 3–4.30pm; $55).

Sports Queensland's sport is rugby league, and the Broncos' stomping ground is the Suncorp Stadium (40

Castlemaine St, Milton; Ⓦ suncorpstadium.com.au), a 5min walk west of the city, with matches played between March and Sept and the all-important State of Origin series in May or June. The Queensland Reds rugby union team also play at Suncorp stadium between Feb and May. International (including Ashes tests) and domestic cricket matches, and home games of the Brisbane Lions Aussie Rules team are played at The Gabba (411 Vulture St, Woolloongabba; Ⓦ thegabba.com.au), just across the river from downtown, 1.5km southeast of South Bank station. Tickets for sports events are available from Ticketek (Ⓦ ticketek.com.au) or Ticketmaster (Ⓦ ticketmaster.com.au).

ACCOMMODATION

Brisbane's **hostels** are bursting with travelling casual workers, while the luxury boutique **apartments** are often rented long-term by the expanding business and law fraternity. You should **book** at least a week ahead, longer if your visit coincides with the Brisbane Cup horse race in June, the Royal Queensland Show (the "Ekka") in August, or the week-long Brisbane Festival in September. **Prices** at high-end places may drop at weekends and during December and January, when business customers are scarcer and there's competition from the Gold Coast.

CITY CENTRE

Acacia Inner City Inn 413 Upper Edward St ☎ 07 3832 1663, ⓦacaciainn.com. Behind its austere 1940s brick facade, this low-key budget inn offers tiny but very affordable singles and doubles that share bathrooms, plus larger, en-suite family rooms ($110). There's also a guest kitchen. **$95**

Annie's Shandon Inn 405 Upper Edward St ☎ 07 3831 8684, ⓦanniesbrisbane.com. This welcoming family-run B&B, a 5min walk up from the CBD, dates from the late nineteenth century. Some of its old-fashioned but cosy rooms share bathrooms; paying $10 extra gets you en-suite facilities. **$89**

Base Brisbane Uptown 466 George St ☎ 07 3211 2433, ⓦstayatbase.com. Right across from the Transit Centre, with bright air-conditioned dorms (with four to fourteen beds) and doubles, all en suite, 24hr reception, good chill-out areas and a lively ground-floor restaurant/ bar, *The Guilty Rogue*. Dorms **$30**, doubles **$144**

Evolution 18 Tank St ☎ 07 3034 3700, ⓦevolutionapartments.com.au. Gleaming 36-storey tower-block hotel holding fully equipped studios and one- and two-bedroom modern apartments – the best have outstanding river views – plus a heated pool, deck and gym. **$179**

New Inchcolm Hotel 73 Wickham Terrace ☎ 07 3226 8888, ⓦinchcolm.com.au. Exquisitely modernized Art Deco inn, perched on the upper edge of the CBD, with fifty very tasteful, upscale rooms and suites plus a good restaurant and café/bar. **$235**

Rendezvous Hotel Brisbane on George 103 George St ☎ 07 3221 6044, ⓦrendezvoushotels.com. While not especially fancy, these hotel rooms are spacious and comfortable. Some offer partial river views, and there's a small pool and ground-floor café-bar. **$162**

Stamford Plaza Cnr Edward & Margaret sts ☎ 07 3221 1999, ⓦstamford.com.au. High-class landmark hotel, with a grand mix of colonial and modern buildings overlooking the river and botanic gardens, plus a Japanese restaurant, a riverside buffet-style brasserie, and afternoon tea in the lobby. **$350**

SOUTH BRISBANE

Brisbane Backpackers 110 Vulture St, West End ☎ 1800 626 452, ⓦbrisbanebackpackers.com.au. Sociable resort-style backpackers' near Boundary St, with free hourly shuttles into town. Facilities include a bar, smallish kitchen and pool, and there's a job club and free parking. Dorms **$25**, doubles **$120**

Mantra South Bank 161 Grey St, South Bank ☎ 07 5665 4450, ⓦmantra.com.au. Contemporary rooms and apartments, some with balconies, in the heart of the South Bank. There's also a gym and token lap pool. Doubles **$289**, apartments **$334**

Riverside Hotel 20 Montague Rd, South Bank ☎ 07 3846 0577, ⓦriversidehotel.com.au. While undeniably rather basic, these simple hotel rooms and apartments are a bargain for budget-conscious travellers, being so close to the museums and restaurants along the South Bank. Doubles **$157**, apartments **$187**

PETRIE TERRACE AND SPRING HILL

Aussie Way Backpackers 34 Cricket St ☎ 07 3211 3221, ⓦaussiewaybackpackers.com. Hostel with the feel of an inn, housed in a historic colonial-era hotel and offering attractive dorms and doubles plus a veranda and games room and a slightly cramped communal kitchen. Dorms **$24**, doubles **$80**

Banana Benders 118 Petrie Terrace ☎ 07 3367 1157, ⓦbananabenders.com. Small, friendly hostel, 700m west of Roma St station, with a homely, easy-going feel and an established job club that's affiliated with WWOOF. Dorms **$27**, doubles **$78**

★**Brisbane City YHA** 392 Upper Roma St ☎ 07 3236 1004, ⓦyha.com.au. The best option on the backpacker strip – safe, friendly and helpful, with a maximum dorm size of just six beds, plus a great kitchen and a cute rooftop pool. Dorms **$32**, doubles **$96**

Kookaburra Inn 41 Phillips St, Spring Hill ☎ 07 3832 1303, ⓦkookaburra-inn.com.au. *Kookaburra*'s quiet residential locale and homely vibe make it popular with single travellers, older backpackers and long stayers. Rooms are small but spotless, and there's a kitchen and outdoor terraces. **$83**

★**One Thornbury Boutique B&B** 1 Thornbury St, Spring Hill ☎ 07 3839 5334, ⓦonethornbury.com. Very charming B&B set in a timber-frame nineteenth-century cottage, a 10min walk up from the CBD, with seven bright, comfortable en-suite rooms, plus a tropical garden. Breakfast served in the shared lounge. Rates drop for multi-night stays. **$139**

FORTITUDE VALLEY AND NEW FARM

The Valley's accommodation is well placed for clubs but the area can be noisy and seedy late at night. New Farm is a quieter option. Take a direct bus from Adelaide St or the CityTrain to Brunswick St station.

Bowen Terrace 365 Bowen Terrace, New Farm ☎ 07 3254 0458, ⓦbowenterrace.com.au. Quaint singles, doubles and two- to four-bed dorms in a lovely and peaceful old Queenslander, with a communal kitchen, outdoor terrace and pool. Dorms **$36**, doubles **$89**

Bunk Backpackers 21 Gipps St ☎ 1800 682 865, ⓦbunkbrisbane.com.au. Stark from the outside, this warehouse-sized backpackers' is located on a busy crossroads, but good-quality facilities including a pool and hot tub, compensate. Dorms range from the cheapest twenty-bed option to four-bed, mixed en-suite rooms. Dorms **$25**, doubles **$100**

3

Limes Hotel 142 Constance St, Fortitude Valley ☎07 3852 9000, ⓦlimeshotel.com.au. Smart, stylish modern hotel where the rooftop bar has hot tubs and an outdoor movie screen (not surprisingly, it can get noisy). Many of the actual rooms are small, though. $230

Spicers Balfour Hotel 37 Balfour St, New Farm ☎1300 597 540, ⓦspicersgroup.com.au. Boutique hotel that's home to nine plush, if compact, rooms, with Bose music systems, iPod docks and Nespresso machines.

For more space, splash out on a courtyard or terrace room. $279

TRYP Fortitude Valley Hotel 14–20 Constance St, Fortitude Valley ☎07 3319 7888, ⓦtrypbrisbane.com. Arty, post-industrial boutique hotel near all the Fortitude Valley action. The walls have been splashily adorned by local street artists, and there's a bar on the roof plus a popular bistro on the ground floor, while the rooms are comfortable but a bit more generic. $151

EATING

Brisbane's foodie credentials have been improving year upon year. Fortitude Valley has a dense grouping of Asian restaurants (and a fashionable café society) while Boundary St in the West End has more of a European flavour. The **counter meals** offered by many downtown hotels (especially during the week) are the cheapest route to a full stomach – aim for lunch at around noon and dinner between 5 and 6pm – or try one of the scores of central cafés and **food courts** that cater to office workers (there's a good one at Post Office Square).

CITY CENTRE

Aria Eagle St Pier ☎07 3233 2555, ⓦariarestaurant.com. Glitzy, see-and-be-seen restaurant, with great river views and very classy contemporary cuisine. Starters like local Moreton Bay bugs grilled with sea urchin custard, cost around $35–40, while fish or meat mains, given deceptively simple names like "veal" or "duck", average $55. Tasting menus cost $130 for four courses, $175 for seven, with wine pairings available. Mon–Fri 11am–2.30pm & 5.30–10pm, Sat 5–10pm, Sun 5.30–9.30pm.

★**Brew** Lower Burnett Lane ☎07 3211 4242, ⓦbrewcafewinebar.com.au. Tucked down a gritty side alley, this quirky, cellar-like café-cum-bar makes a welcome escape from the shiny corporate feel of the CBD. Besides good strong coffee, the menu (packaged in vintage album sleeves) includes eggs and bagels until 3pm and burgers and tacos all day ($14–17), while in the evening *Brew* becomes more of a bar, with beer and cocktails. No reservations. Mon 7am–4pm, Tues & Wed 7am–10pm, Thurs 7am–1pm, Fri 7am–midnight, Sat 9am–midnight, Sun 9am–4pm.

Cha Cha Char Eagle St Pier ☎07 3211 9944, ⓦchachachar.com.au. With an owner well connected to the beef industry, steak ($37–110) is the obvious option while you enjoy the panoramic views from this opulent riverside spot, but there's plenty of enticing seafood too. Mon–Fri noon–2pm & 6–11pm, Sat & Sun 6–11pm.

E'cco 100 Boundary St ☎07 3831 8344, ⓦeccobistro.com. Celebrated mod-Oz restaurant, with multiple awards and cookbooks to its name, and prices to match. The pan-roasted chicken with smoked eggplant will set you back $36, while the tasting menu (entire table only) costs $89 per person. Tues–Fri noon–2.30pm & 6–9.30pm, Sat 6–9.30pm.

Fat Noodle The Treasury Casino, 130 William St ☎07 3306 8888, ⓦtreasurybrisbane.com.au. Head here for tasty Asian staples, including *laksa*, pad thai and an epic twenty-hour beef broth ($22), all served until late. Mon–Thurs & Sun 11.30am–11pm, Fri & Sat 11.30am–midnight.

German Sausage Hut Burnett Lane ☎07 3210 2447, ⓦgermansausagehut.com.au. Follow your nose up Brisbane's oldest street to this bijou wurst specialist. Bangers and mash with sauerkraut will set you back $12.50, while Friday night there's a pork knuckle fest. Licensed. Tues–Thurs 11am–3pm, Fri 11am–9pm.

Izakaya Kotobuki 93 Albert St ☎07 3061 2152, ⓦsushikotobuki.com.au. Fast-paced, great-value sushi restaurant, steps from Queen St mall in the heart of the CBD. Order via the on-table iPads; set meals start around $14, but with individual dishes from $3.50, it's a chance to try new things – perhaps a skewer of battered octopus? Mon–Fri 11am–2.30pm & 5.30–10pm, Sat noon–4pm & 5.30–10pm.

Riverbar and Kitchen 71 Eagle St ☎07 3211 9120, ⓦriverbarandkitchen.com.au. One of the more reasonably priced riverside restaurants, with breakfast eggs from $18 and lunch and dinner mains from $20. Grab a terrace table, order a beer-battered flathead and chips ($29), along, perhaps, with a speciality cocktail, and watch the ferries go by. Daily 7am–11.30pm.

Verve Metro Arts Building, 109 Edward St ☎07 3221 5691, ⓦvervecafe.com.au. Basement Italian bistro, with funky ambient music and art, dishing up pastas, risottos and enticing blackboard specials such as flash-seared skirt steak. Mains $19–23. Mon–Fri noon–9pm, Sat 5–9pm.

SOUTH BANK AND WEST END

When it comes to eating, South Bank visitors are spoiled for choice. An unbroken succession of restaurants line Grey and Little Stanley streets (many with access from both sides), as well as the Parklands. The West End, too, abounds in options, though for a quick snack at the weekend, the Boundary Street Markets can't be beat (see p.321).

Ahmet's 168 Grey St ☎ 07 3846 6699, ⓦ ahmets.com. Much-loved South Bank fixture, serving Turkish specialities from bread and *pide* through to dessert, with a mixed meze board for two at $19.50, a standard kebab $14.50, and a huge mixed grill $36. Daily 11.30am–3pm & 6–9.30pm.

The Gunshop Café 53 Mollison St ☎ 07 3844 2241, ⓦ thegunshopcafe.com. Housed in, you guessed it, a former gunshop, this exposed brick gastropub is famed for its weekend brunches, which can only be reserved from 12.30pm onwards. They champion local produce; try the stuffed barramundi ($32). Mon–Thurs & Sun 7am–2.30pm, Fri & Sat 7am–2.30pm & 5.30pm–late.

Mu'ooz 54 Mollison St ☎ 07 3844 8378, ⓦ muooz .com.au. Run as a not-for-profit social enterprise, staffed by female refugees, this attractive little West End cottage restaurant devotes itself to African cuisine, from Eritrea in particular. Spicy meat, fish and vegetarian dishes cost $21–24. Mon 5.30–10pm, Wed–Sat 11.30am–3pm & 5.30–10pm.

Three Monkeys Coffee Shop 58 Mollison St ☎ 07 3844 6045. Adorned with a funky assortment of African oddments, this place effortlessly achieves the bohemian atmosphere to which other cafés merely aspire. Tasty coffee and cakes, plus lots of vegetarian options for less than $15. Mon–Thurs 9.30am–11pm, Fri & Sat 9am–11.30pm, Sun 9am–11pm.

★**Tukka** 145B Boundary St ☎ 07 3846 6333, ⓦ tukkarestaurant.com.au. Championing "Advanced Australian Fare", this dinner-only, all-indoor restaurant combines native fruits, seeds, herbs and meats like emu and kangaroo with European-style cooking techniques for an imaginative meal, inspired by Aboriginal bushtucker. Typical mains $30–35. Mon–Thurs & Sun 6–9.30pm, Fri & Sat 6–10.30pm.

Zeus Street Greek 13/14 Little Stanley St ☎ 07 3846 0200, ⓦ zsg.com.au. Queensland's first outlet of this NSW

favourite has been an instant South Bank hit, with its great-value $13 pita bread sandwiches, containing anything from halloumi cheese to soft-shelled crab, and more substantial lamb, pork and chicken grills, still for under $20. Daily 11.30am–9.30pm.

FORTITUDE VALLEY AND NEW FARM

Alfred and Constance 130 Constance St ☎ 07 3251 6500, ⓦ alfredandconstance.com.au. This Fortitude Valley institution sprawls through a cluster of charming old cottages – the restaurant section, extending across a beer garden, serves breakfasts and good pub grub, from $25 cheeseburgers to $35 mains like roast pork and whole grilled fish, and there's also a great tiki bar and a dance club downstairs. Daily 7am–late.

Balfour Kitchen Balfour Hotel, 37 Balfour St ☎ 1300 597 540, ⓦ spicersretreats.com. Popular New Farm rendezvous, set in a venerable Queenslander that's been converted into a boutique hotel, and serving all meals daily, indoors and out on the veranda. Breakfast choices range from $14 to $25; lunch and dinner mains like lamb rump or mushroom tortelloni are $32–36. Mon–Fri 6.30–11am, noon–2.30pm & 5.30–8.30pm, Sat & Sun 7.30–11am, noon–2.30pm & 5.30–8.30pm.

The Smoke BBQ 85 Merthyr Rd ☎ 07 3358 1922, ⓦ thesmokebbq.com.au. American-style barbecue joint, with pavement tables in New Farm's busiest pedestrian area. Lunch bargains include pulled pork, steak or chicken sandwiches for around $17; dinner steaks or ribs cost up to $40. Mon 6–9pm, Tues & Wed 11.30am–2pm & 6–9pm, Thurs–Sat 11.30am–2.30pm & 5.30–9pm.

The Vietnamese 194 Wickham St ☎ 07 3252 4112, ⓦ thevietnameserestaurant.com.au. With an interior as plain as the name over the door, this is no-frills, genuine Vietnamese food – the crispy duck in plum sauce is excellent, and there's good choice for vegetarians too. Almost all mains cost well under $20. Daily 11am–3pm & 5–10pm.

3

LGBT BRISBANE

Brisbane's LGBT crowd revels in a loud and energetic scene that gets better every year. In September the Pride Collective hosts the annual **Pride Festival** (ⓦ brisbanepridefestival.com. au), a varied month-long event with a street march, fair, art exhibitions, a film festival, sports events and general exhibitionism, kicking off with the Pride Festival Opening Gala. Other events to look out for include **Northern Exposure** in October, organized by Brisbears (ⓦ brisbears.org.au).

The **LGBT scene** is largely clustered around the suburbs of Spring Hill, Fortitude Valley, New Valley, New Farm and Paddington. For up-to-the-moment information, listen to the Queer Radio slot on 4ZZZ 102.1FM (Wed 9–11pm, ⓦ 4zzzfm.org.au), read the fortnightly *Qnews* (ⓦ qnews.com.au) or the monthly *Queensland Pride* from LGBT nightclubs, street distributors and coffee shops. Nightlife focuses on *The Wickham Hotel*, *Sportsman Hotel* and *The Beat* (see p.320). Bent Books at 205 Boundary St, West End (ⓦ bentbooks.com.au), is the longest-established LGBT bookshop in Brisbane.

DRINKING AND NIGHTLIFE

Brisbane is a hotbed of musical talent: **bands** and artists such as Savage Garden, Powderfinger, Keith Urban, The Grates and Yves Klein Blue all hail from here. While there are plenty of central places to fire up with a few drinks on Friday and Saturday nights, the big push is out to Fortitude Valley's **bars and clubs**. Live music venues are very fluid and tend to open and close in the blink of an eye; places listed below should be here to stay, but check with music stores such as Rocking Horse, 245 Albert St (ⓦ rockinghorse.net), or have a browse through *Scene* mag (ⓦ scenemagazine.com.au) or *Time Out Brisbane* (ⓦ au.timeout.com/Brisbane) for up-to-the-minute reviews and **listings**. There's no standard charge for club entry, and many places offer free nights and deals.

CITY CENTRE

Down Under Bar 308 Edward St ⓣ07 3166 8000. Hugely popular and often overtly drunken venue for travellers on the ground floor of *Base Central Backpackers*. Mon–Thurs 11am–3am, Fri 11am–5am, Sat 5pm–5am, Sun 5pm–3am.

Super Whatnot 48 Burnett Lane ⓣ07 3210 2343, ⓦ superwhatnot.com. Diminutive little self-styled "laneway bar" that's a haven for alternative types adrift in the CBD, serving craft beers and cocktails, plus a knowing selection of nachos, chilli dogs and burritos. Mon–Thurs 3–11pm, Fri noon–1am, Sat 3pm–1am.

Victory Hotel 127 Edward St ⓣ07 3221 0444, ⓦ thevictory.com.au. Large pub with live entertainment Wed–Sun – especially on the weekly "thirsty Thursday" and braziers in the beer garden to take the chill off in winter. Mon–Wed & Sun 10am–late, Thurs–Sat 10am–5am.

SOUTH BRISBANE

Max Watt's House of Music 125 Boundary St, West End ⓣ1300 843 443, ⓦ maxwatts.com.au/brisbane. Formerly the *Hi-Fi*, this loud live music venue has long been popular with touring bands; check the website for upcoming gigs.

Regatta Hotel 543 Coronation Drive, Toowong ⓣ07 3871 9595, ⓦ regattahotel.com.au. A favourite with Friday evening's after-work crowd, this historic pub with its icon-lace balconies is a relaxed place for a daytime drink. Daily 11.30am–2.30pm & 5–9pm.

PETRIE TERRACE AND SPRING HILL

Paddo Tavern 186 Given Terrace (cnr of Caxton St) ⓣ07 3369 7064, ⓦ thepaddo.com.au. Huge Irish pub with pool tables, music and cheap meals. Live comedy Thurs, Fri & Sat in the *Squeeze Bar* downstairs. Mon, Tues, Thurs & Sun 10am–2am, Wed 10am–1am, Fri & Sat 10am–3am.

Sportsman Hotel 130 Leichhardt St ⓣ07 3831 2892, ⓦ sportsmanhotel.com.au. A gay, lesbian and straight crowd fills the trio of bars across two floors, which have pool tables, pinball, bands, bottle shop and bistro. Fantastic drag nights. Mon–Thurs & Sun 1pm–late, Fri & Sat 1pm–5am.

FORTITUDE VALLEY AND NEW FARM

The Beat 677 Ann St ⓣ07 3852 2661, ⓦ thebeatmegaclub.com.au. Small, crowded and sweaty LGBT club playing thumping techno/dance, with a beer garden where you can take a break and fuel up on bar food. Daily 8pm–5am.

Black Bear Lodge 322 Brunswick St, ⓦ blackbearlodge .com.au. Long famous as the "Troub", this much-loved live music venue, raised above street level, remains a hub for pub-style acoustic or rock, while also putting on DJ nights. Wed, Thurs & Sun 7pm–late, Fri & Sat 5pm–3am.

The Bowery 676 Ann St ⓣ07 3252 0202, ⓦ thebowery .com.au. Sophisticated bar, in the heart of Fortitude Valley, that's perfect for early cocktails or ambient late-night drinks. Tues–Sun 5pm–3am.

Cloudland Bar 641 Ann St ⓣ07 3872 6600, ⓦ katarzyna.com.au. Upmarket cocktail bar (try the rose blossom martini) and events venue (Thurs–Sun) complete with tropical garden, retractable glass roof and futuristic lighting. Their Thurs night "soulsa" shindigs are lots of fun. Tues 5–11pm, Wed & Thurs 3pm–3am, Fri & Sat 11am–5am, Sun 11am–3am.

Family 8 McLachlan St ⓣ07 3852 5000, ⓦ thefamily .com.au. Serious dance venue with three huge floors, where established DJs play everything from house to 1970s funk. Fri–Sun 9pm–5am.

Ric's Bar 321 Brunswick St ⓣ07 3666 0777, ⓦ ricsbar .com.au. Narrow, crowded place presenting a mix of live Aussie bands and DJ-driven techno; chill in the patio out back, complete with fake grass. Mon–Thurs 5pm–3am, Fri 4pm–5am, Sat noon–5am, Sun noon–3am.

Tivoli 52 Costin St ⓣ07 3852 1711, ⓦ thetivoli.net.au. Originally an Art Deco theatre, this century-old landmark is now one of Brisbane's most popular live venues for big-name touring bands and comedians.

Wickham Hotel Cnr Wickham & Alden sts ⓣ07 3852 1301, ⓦ thewickham.com.au. Queensland's most popular LGBT pub, finally reopened after extensive renovations, now boasts a state-of-the-art nightclub on its top floor. Mon–Thurs 10am–2am, Fri 5pm–5am, Sat 9pm–late, Sun 4pm–late.

ENTERTAINMENT

Moonlight Cinema Brisbane Powerhouse, New Farm Park ⓦ moonlight.com.au. Open-air cinema showing current and classic films through the summer; screenings begin at 7pm.

SHOPPING

MARKETS

Boundary Street Markets 137 Boundary St, West End ⓦ boundarystreetmarkets.com.au. A weekend institution in the West End, this colourful collection of food stalls, complemented by crafts vendors and live music, features all the ethnic choices you could hope for, and plenty more besides – German, Tibetan, even Venezuelan. Fri & Sat 4–10pm.

Fortitude Valley Markets Brunswick St Mall, ⓦ fortitudevalleymarkets.com.au. New and secondhand threads, vintage items and food stalls. Sat & Sun 9am–4pm.

South Bank Lifestyle Markets South Bank Parklands, ⓦ collectivemarkets.com.au. Homewares, handicrafts and organic produce for sale, with a family atmosphere. Fri & Sat 10am–9pm, Sun 9am–4pm.

Twilight Market King George Square, in front of City Hall, ⓦ brisstyle.com.au. Hosted one Friday a month, Twilight Market focuses on emerging designers and contemporary handmade crafts. One Fri per month 5–9pm.

Riverside at the Gardens City Botanical Gardens, 147 Alice St. Crafts, clothes, jewellery and leatherwork, plus a mouthwatering assortment of ethnic food stalls. Sun 8am–3pm.

DIRECTORY

Banks Queensland banking hours are Mon–Thurs 9.30am–4pm & Fri 9.30am–5pm; major city branches may be found around Queen and Edward sts.

Consulates Britain, Level 9, 100 Eagle St ☎ 07 3223 3200; Japan, 12 Creek St ☎ 07 3221 5188; Malaysia, Level 8, 239 George St ☎ 07 3210 2833; Papua New Guinea, Level 3, 344 Queens St ☎ 07 3221 7915; Philippines, Unit 2, 269 Abbotsford Rd, Bowen Hill ☎ 07 3252 8215; Thailand, 87 Annerley Rd, Woolloongabba ☎ 07 3846 7771.

Hospitals and medical centres Royal Brisbane, Butterfield St, Herston (☎ 07 3646 8111); Travellers' Medical Service, Level 1, 245 Albert St (Mon–Fri 7am–7pm, Sat 8.30am–5pm, Sun 9.30am–5pm; ☎ 07 3211 3611,

ⓦ travellersmedicalservice.com), for general services, vaccinations and women's health.

Pharmacies Day & Night Pharmacy, Queen St Mall (Mon–Sat 7am–9pm, Sun 8.30am–6pm).

Police Queensland Police Headquarters is opposite the Transit Centre (200 Roma St ☎ 07 3364 3011; emergencies ☎ 000).

Post office 261 Queen St (Mon–Fri 7am–6pm, Sat 10am–1.30pm; ☎ 13 13 18 for poste restante).

Work Brisbane offers fairly good employment prospects if you're not too choosy. Many hostels run effective ad hoc agencies for their guests, or for out-of-town work, try Brisbane's WWOOF office at *Banana Benders*, 118 Petrie Terrace (☎ 07 3367 1165).

Moreton Bay Islands

The shallow waters of **Moreton Bay**, offshore from Brisbane, are famous throughout Australia as the home of the unfortunately named Moreton Bay Bug – actually a small, delicious lobster-like crustacean. The largest of the bay's islands, **Moreton** and **North Stradbroke**, are generously endowed with sand dunes and beaches, and are just far enough from the city to make their beaches accessible but seldom crowded. **St Helena** island is not a place you'd visit for sun and surf, but with prison ruins recalling the convict era it makes an interesting day-trip. In the bay itself, look for dolphins, dugong (sea cows) and **humpback whales**, which pass by in winter en route to their calving grounds up north.

St Helena Island

Small, low and triangular, **St Helena Island**, 8km from the mouth of the Brisbane River, served as a **prison** from the 1850s until the early twentieth century. The government found it particularly useful for political troublemakers, such as the leaders of the 1891 shearers' strike and, with more justice, a couple of slave-trading "Blackbirder" captains.

A tour of the penal settlement, once the "Hell Hole of the South Pacific", leaves you thankful you missed out on the "good old days". Escape attempts (there were only ever three) were deterred by sharks, whose presence was actively encouraged around the island. Evidence of the prisoners' industry and self-sufficiency can still be seen in the stone houses, as well as in the remains of a sugar mill, paddocks, wells, and an ingenious lime kiln built into the shoreline. The Deputy Superintendent's house has been turned into a bare **museum**, displaying a ball and chain lying in a corner and photographs from the prison era. Outside, the two cemeteries have been desecrated: many headstones were carried off as souvenir coffee tables, and the corpses dug up and sold as medical specimens. The remaining stones comprise simple concrete crosses stamped with a number for the prisoners, or inscribed marble tablets for the warders and their children.

ARRIVAL AND DEPARTURE | ST HELENA ISLAND

On a tour Cat-o'-Nine-Tails (☎ 1300 438 787, ⓦ sthelenaisland.com.au) offer day-trips by catamaran. Schedules vary – day-tours including lunch cost $79; evening ghost tours, with theatrical sound-and-light show and dinner, cost $95. Boats leave from the public jetty in Manly, 15km east of Brisbane and a 10min walk from Manly station, which is served by direct trains from Roma St, Central and South Brisbane stations.

Moreton Island

A narrow, 38km-long band of stabilized, partly wooded sand dunes, **Moreton Island** boasts faultless beaches that are distinctly underpopulated for much of the year, and perfect for lounging, surfing or fishing.

If you're planning to stay a while, note that supplies are expensive, so it's best to be self-sufficient. Be very careful swimming in the sea, as the beaches aren't patrolled and there are no shark nets. The worst times to visit are at Christmas and Easter, when a thousand vehicles can crowd onto the island all at once.

Tangalooma

The main arrival point on Moreton Island is **TANGALOOMA** on the west coast, where a set of wrecks were deliberately sunk offshore to create an artificial reef that provides fine **snorkelling** at high tide. The beachfront *Tangalooma Island Resort* here is the only place on the island that has a restaurant and serves cold drinks – tidy dress is required. Island visitors can only access the resort if they book a free day-pass in advance, via ⓦ tangalooma.com. A 3km track heads south to the **desert**, where the dunes are a great place to try **sand-tobogganing**.

East side of the island

With your own vehicle, or a willingness to hike, you can take the 10km track from Tangalooma across to Moreton's more attractive eastern side, where the beach has good **surf** and it's less crowded. Before reaching the eastern coast at **Eagers Creek**, a sandy track branches off north, winding its way to **Mount Tempest**'s 280m peak – the climb to the top is an exhausting 2.5km, but the view is outstanding. Back at Eagers Creek, head 10km north up the beach to find **Blue Lagoon**, the largest of the island's freshwater lakes, only 500m from the beach campsite and adjacent to the smaller, picturesque **Honeyeater Lake**. Dolphins come in close to shore – a practice that Moreton's Aborigines turned to their advantage by using them to chase fish into the shallows.

Bulwer and Kooringal

The tiny settlements at the north and south ends of the island are only accessible from the Tangalooma area by 4WD, often by driving on the beach.

BULWER, on the northwest coast, comprises a cluster of weatherboard "weekenders", holiday homes, a campground and a general store stocking beer. There's road access from here to Cape Moreton Lighthouse at the northern tip of the island, where you can usually spot migrating humpback whales from the cliffs between May and October, as well as sea turtles bobbing in the ocean.

At Moreton's southern tip, tiny **KOORINGAL** is home to the Toulkerrie Oyster Farm (call to visit; ☎ 07 3409 0133) and holds a licensed store offering supplies, as well as holiday units that sleep up to ten.

ARRIVAL AND DEPARTURE

By ferry *Tangalooma Island Resort* operates ferries to the resort from Holt St Wharf, off Kingsford Smith Drive at Pinkenba, 8km out of Brisbane (daily 7am, 10am & 5pm; additional service Fri–Sun 12.30pm; 1hr 15min; $80 return; ☎ 1300 652 250, ⓦ tangalooma.com). Book ahead for transfers from Brisbane and the Gold Coast to the wharf, costing $23/person. Tangalooma also offer a $65 day-trip from Brisbane, which works out cheaper than the ferry ticket alone and includes city transfers as well as land-based activities.

MORETON ISLAND

By barge The huge Micat vehicle and passenger barge crosses to the west-coast wrecks from 14 Howard Smith Drive, Lytton, 22km from Brisbane (schedules vary, usually daily 8.30am; $199–299 return for 4WD and two adults, foot passengers $52 return; ☎ 07 3909 3333, ⓦ moretonislandadventures.com.au).

By car To drive on the island, you need to bring a 4WD across and purchase a one-month permit ($46.45) from ⓦ nprsr.qld.gov.au.

ACCOMMODATION AND EATING

Blue Lagoon Campground Near Blue Lagoon ☎ 13 74 68, ⓦ nprsr.qld.gov.au. Blessed with shady trees, the dunes behind the beach make an ideal place to camp; facilities include water, showers and toilets. **$5.95**

Castaways Bulwer ☎ 07 3909 3333, ⓦ moretonisland adventures.com.au. Colourful, modern and substantial self-contained six-person units just 100m from the beach, plus a store and restaurant that's famous for big breakfasts ($14.50), lazy lunches (fish'n' chips $15) and dinners (Fri & Sat only; mains $24 and up). **$249**

Gutter Bar 21 Kooringal Esplanade, Kooringal ☎ 07 3409 0170, ⓦ thegutterbar.com.au. Cold beer and fresh platters of locally harvested crabs, Moreton Bay bugs and oysters.

Mon–Thurs & Sun 9.30am–4pm, Fri & Sat 9.30am–11pm.

Tangalooma Island Resort ☎ 1300 652 250, ⓦ tangalooma.com.au. A laidback, family-oriented affair with assorted rooms, apartments and holiday villas built around a former whaling station. Casual restaurants dish up fresh seafood, pizzas, burgers and steaks (daily 7am–9pm), while activities include dolphin-feeding cruises ($115), whale-watching ventures (June to mid-Oct; $115), and sand-tobogganing trips ($45). **$199**

The Wrecks Tangalooma ☎ 13 74 68, ⓦ nprsr.qld .gov.au. National Parks campground, with water, showers and toilets, near the barge landing point – permits are available online or from the resort-based ranger. **$5.95**

North Stradbroke Island

North Stradbroke Island is, at 40km long, Moreton Bay's largest and most established island, and has sealed roads and three fully serviced townships. Until recently, much of "**Straddie**" was given over to mining its titanium-rich sands. Most local residents are employees of Consolidated Rutile Ltd, but mining is due to end by 2019. Stradbroke's **diving** is renowned for congregations of the increasingly rare grey nurse shark, along with moray eels, dopey leopard sharks and summertime manta rays.

Dunwich

Unless you need to fuel up or visit the bank, there's little to keep you at **DUNWICH**, Straddie's ferry port. Two sealed roads head out of town, one leading north to Amity and Point Lookout, the other heading east through the island's centre. The latter route passes two lakes, the second and smaller of which, **Blue Lake**, is a national park and source of fresh water for the island's wildlife, which is most visible at dawn.

Main Beach

The route east beyond Blue Lake, crossing the **Eighteen Mile Swamp** to reach **Main Beach** along a causeway, is for 4WDs only. You can **camp** behind the beach anywhere south of the causeway, but be prepared for the mosquitoes that swarm around the mangroves; the southernmost point is an angling and wildlife mecca, with birdlife and kangaroos lounging on the beaches.

Amity

Head north from Dunwich and it's 11km to where the road forks left for a further 6km to **AMITY**, a sleepy place built around a jetty at the island's northwestern point, where there are holiday houses, a café and a store.

Point Lookout

Stay on the road from Dunwich past the Amity turn-off, and another 10km brings you to **POINT LOOKOUT**, at Straddie's northeastern tip. The township spreads out around the island's single-rock headland, overlooking a string of beaches, and is home to fish'n'chip shops, a *gelato* and coffee bar, a store, some cafés and various **places to stay**.

Point Lookout's **beaches** are picturesque, with shallow, protected swimming along the shore. Main and Cylinder beaches are both patrolled and, therefore, crowded during holiday weekends; if you don't mind swimming in unwatched waters, head for the more easterly Deadman's Beach or Frenchman's Bay. The headland above the township offers fine views and the chance to see loggerhead turtles and dolphins; from the boardwalk and walking track around North Gorge to Main Beach you might even see whales.

ARRIVAL AND DEPARTURE   NORTH STRADBROKE ISLAND

By ferry Ferries to Straddie depart Toondah Harbour at Cleveland, which is connected to Cleveland's train station by special red-and-yellow National buses. Stradbroke Ferries carry cars (10–15 daily; foot passengers $20 return, vehicles $110–190; ☎07 3488 5300, ⓦ stradbrokeferries.com.au), while the speedy Stradbroke Flyer only takes foot passengers (10–13 daily; $19 return; ☎07 3286 1964, ⓦ flyer.com.au).

GETTING AROUND AND ACTIVITIES

By bus Local buses meet all ferries (ⓦ stradbrokeisland buses.com.au), and run to Amity and Point Lookout, but not Main Beach.

By car Off-roading through the centre of the island is not advised. Driving on the beach requires a 4WD and a permit ($42.30), obtained from *Straddie Camping* at 1 Juneer St, Dunwich (☎07 3409 9668, ⓦ straddiecamping.com.au).

Activities "Barefoot Dave" at Straddie Kingfisher Tours (☎07 3409 9502, ⓦ straddiekingfishertours.com.au) leads activity tours, such as snorkelling, sandboarding, kayaking and fishing, from $35, plus 4WD island tours from $60.

ACCOMMODATION

Amity Point Camping Ground Amity Point ☎07 3409 9668, ⓦ straddiecamping.com.au. Spacious gum-shaded campground, with an enviable beachfront setting and good facilities, including two sheltered camp kitchens with electric BBQs, plus potential koala sightings. Un/powered sites $31/38, cabins $115

Beach camping Basic beach camping is available at either Main Beach or Flinders Beach, both of which are only accessible with 4WD – only Flinders Beach even has toilets – and must be booked in advance through Straddie Camping (ⓦ straddiecamping.com.au). $24

Manta Lodge YHA 1 Eastcoast Rd, Point Lookout ☎07 3409 8888, ⓦ mantalodge.com.au. Friendly lodge with dorms, simple budget rooms and kitchen facilities. A scuba-diving centre offers PADI courses and day-dives, plus fishing trips, board rental and 4WD tours. Dorms $34, doubles $86

Sea Shanties 9A Cook St, Amity ☎07 3409 7161, ⓦ seashanties.com.au. Smart yet low-key beachfront accommodation in bright, shabby-chic en-suite cabins that sleep four. Bring your own bedding, or hire for a small additional fee. $155

Straddie Views B&B 26 Cumming Parade, Point Lookout ☎07 3409 8875, ⓦ straddieviews.com.au. Top of the range B&B, where each of the spacious suites has its own private courtyard and shares use of an ocean-view deck, plus appealing touches like complimentary port and chocolate; two-night minimum stay. $150

EATING AND DRINKING

Fishes at the Point Point Lookout ☎07 3415 3444, ⓦ fishesatthepoint.com.au. Smart restaurant and takeaway that serves breakfast until 11am, and surf and turf all day (fish'n'chips $18). Daily 8am–8pm.

Tillers Café & Pantry 43–57 Eastcoast Rd, Point Lookout ☎07 3415 3780. Welcoming café, with lots of breakfast options, good pizza and seafood later on, as well as frequent live music at weekends. Daily 6am–9pm.

Seashells Café 21 Ballow St, Amity Point ☎07 3409 7886. Dine on seafood, steaks and pizza from the nice sea-view deck. Special $10 weekday lunches. Licensed. Mon 9am–3pm, Wed–Sat 9am–9pm, Sun 8am–3pm.

The Gold Coast

Beneath a jagged skyline shaped by a veritable forest of high-rise beachfront apartment blocks, the **Gold Coast** is Australia's Miami Beach or Costa del Sol, a striking contrast to Brisbane, which is only an hour to the north. The coast forms a virtually unbroken beach 40km long, from **South Stradbroke Island** past **Surfers Paradise** and **Burleigh Heads** to the New South Wales border at **Coolangatta**. The **beaches** swarm with bathers and board-riders all year round: **surfing** blossomed here in the 1930s, and the key surf beaches at Coolangatta, Burleigh Heads and South Stradbroke still pull daily crowds of veterans and novices.

In recent years, other attractions have sprung up, notably the **club and party scene** centred on Surfers Paradise and Broadbeach, and several action-packed **theme parks**, mostly based around 15km northwest of town. Aggressively superficial, Surfers is hardly the place for peace and quiet, but its sheer brashness can be fun for a couple of days. There's little variation on the beach and nightclub scene, however, and if you anticipate that this may leave you jaded, bored or broke, you're better off avoiding this corner of Queensland altogether.

With around hundred days of sunshine each year, there's little "off season" on the Gold Coast. **Rain** can, however, fall at any time, including midwinter – when it's usually dry in the rest of the state – but even if the crowds do thin out a little, they reappear in time for the **Gold Coast Indy** car race in October and then continue to swell, peaking over Christmas and New Year. The end of the school year in mid-November also heralds the phenomenon that is **Schoolies Week**, when thousands of high-school leavers from across the country ditch exam rooms and flock to Surfers for a few days of hard partying, a rite of passage that causes an annual budget-accommodation crisis.

Don't bring your dogs here illegally, as Amber Heard did to her cost in 2014, when she flew in, pooches in tow, to visit then-husband Johnny Depp during the filming of yet another *Pirates of the Caribbean* movie.

ARRIVAL AND DEPARTURE
THE GOLD COAST

By plane Gold Coast Airport (ⓦ goldcoastairport.com.au) is 22km south of Surfers Paradise at Coolangatta, on the New South Wales border. The Gold Coast Tourist Shuttle (ⓣ 07 5552 2760, ⓦ gcshuttle.com.au) connects the airport with Surfers Paradise for $22 one-way, and also offers a great-value Freedom Pass (valid three to ten days, $79–149), covering return airport transfers, theme park transfers and unlimited use of the Surfside local bus network. Con-X-ion (ⓣ 07 5556 9888, ⓦ con-x-ion.com) offers a door-to-door shuttle service from Gold Coast and Brisbane airports to most Gold Coast hotels, costing $15–49.

By train Both the Airtrain from Brisbane Airport and the CityTrain from central Brisbane stop at Nerang, Robina and Helensvale, which are on the Gold Coast's public bus network, Surfside. Airtrain also offers a rail-plus-road service (Airtrain Connect) from Brisbane Airport to any Gold Coast accommodation for $59 one-way.

By bus While there are no public buses between the Gold Coast and Brisbane (trains being much more convenient), Greyhound's four daily services between Brisbane and Sydney or Byron Bay, or Premier's daily Lismore/Sydney to Brisbane service, all stop en route in the Gold Coast suburbs of Southport, Surfers Paradise and Coolangatta.

GETTING AROUND

By bus Surfside (ⓣ 13 12 30, ⓦ surfside.com.au) operates a frequent, 24hr bus service along the Gold Coast Highway from Tweed Heads and Coolangatta to Surfers Paradise and out to all the theme parks. You can pay fares in cash or by TransLink go card smartcard (see p.315).

By tram The G:Link tram system links Southport with Broadbeach via Surfers (frequent services Mon–Fri 5am–midnight, Sat & Sun 24hr; ⓦ ridetheg.com.au). A single journey costs from $4.80, but it's cheaper to use a TransLink go card (see p.315).

TOURS

Mountain Coach Company ⓣ 14 4967 0510, ⓦ mountaincoach.com.au. Well-priced tours (from $98) to *O'Reilly's* at Lamington, Tamborine Mountain and Springbrook's glow-worm caves.

Mountain Trek Adventures ⓣ 0431 647 030, ⓦ mountaintrekadventures.com.au. Personalized

half- and full-day 4WD nature tours (eight people max) to all Hinterland national parks.
Southern Cross ☎07 5574 5041, ⓦsc4wd.com.au.

Specializing in off-the-beaten-track, upmarket 4WD half- and full-day Hinterland adventures. Transfers to *O'Reilly's Rainforest Retreat* available on request.

Surfers Paradise

Spiritually, if not geographically, **SURFERS PARADISE** is the heart of the Gold Coast, the place where its aims and aspirations are most evident. For the residents, this involves making money by providing services and entertainment for tourists; visitors reciprocate by parting with their cash. All around, and irrespective of what you're doing – sitting on the beach, **partying** in one of the frenetic nightclubs along Orchid or Cavill avenues, shopping for clothes or even finding a bed – the pace is brash and glib; your enjoyment of Surfers will depend largely on how much you appreciate having the party mood rammed down your throat.

Surfers' **beaches** have been attracting tourists for over a century, though the town only started developing along commercial lines during the 1950s, when the first multistorey beachfront apartments were built. The demand for views over the ocean led to ever-higher towers, which began to encroach on the dunes; together with the sheer volume of people attracted here, this has caused **erosion** problems along the entire coast. But none of this really matters. Though Surfers Paradise is a firm tribute to the successful marketing of the ideal Aussie lifestyle as an eternal beach party, most people come here not so much for the sun and sand as simply because everyone else does.

From its dingiest club to its best restaurant, Surfers exudes entertainment, and at times – most notoriously at New Year and Christmas – you can spend 24 hours a day out on the town. Another thing you'll spend is money: the only free venue is the beach, and with so many distractions it can be financial suicide venturing out too early in the day – the city is full of tourists staggering around at noon with terrible hangovers and empty wallets, complaining how expensive their holiday has become. The area around **Orchid Avenue**, and the partly pedestrianized **Cavill Avenue**, is a bustle of activity from early morning – when the first surfers head down to the beach and the shops open – to after midnight, when there's a constant exchange of bodies between the bars and clubs.

Finally, a word of warning: **petty thieves** come to Surfers simply to prey on tourists, especially around Christmas, Easter and Schoolies Week in November – so take common-sense precautions while you're here.

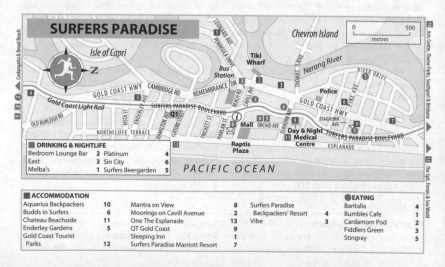

■ DRINKING & NIGHTLIFE			
Bedroom Lounge Bar	2	Platinum	4
East	3	Sin City	6
Melba's	1	Surfers Beergarden	5

■ ACCOMMODATION						
Aquarius Backpackers	10	Mantra on View	8	Surfers Paradise		●EATING	
Budds in Surfers	6	Moorings on Cavill Avenue	2	Backpackers' Resort	4	Baritalia	4
Chateau Beachside	11	One The Esplanade	13	Vibe	3	Bumbles Cafe	1
Enderley Gardens	5	QT Gold Coast	9			Cardamom Pod	2
Gold Coast Tourist		Sleeping Inn	1			Fiddlers Green	3
Parks	12	Surfers Paradise Marriott Resort	7			Stingray	5

SURFING THE GOLD COAST

As locals will tell you, the Gold Coast is home to some of the finest **surfing beaches** in the world. In terms of consistency, this might be true – on any given day there will be good surf somewhere along the coast – with 200m-long sand-bottom point breaks and rideable waves peaking at about 4m in prime conditions.

The coast is known for its **barrels**, particularly during the summer storm season when the winds shift around to the north; in winter the swell is smaller but more reliable, making it easier to learn to surf. A rule of thumb for finding the best surf is to **follow the wind**: head to the north end of the coast when the wind blows from the north and the south when it comes from the south. Generally, you'll find the **best swell** along the southern beaches, and on South Stradbroke Island. With sea temperatures ranging from 26°C in December down to 17°C in June, a 2–3mm wetsuit is adequate. Hard-core surfies come for Christmas and the cyclone season, though spring is usually the busiest time.

As for **general safety**, all beaches as far north as Surfers are patrolled – look for the signs – and while sharks might worry you, more commonplace hostility is likely to come from the local surfies, who form tight-knit cliques with very protective attitudes towards their patches.

Competitions or events take place somewhere along the coast on most weekends, advertised through local surf shops.

SURF SCHOOLS

Get Wet Surf School Seaworld Drive ☎ 1800 438 938, ⓦ getwetsurf.com. Learn to surf at daily 2hr beach or wave pool (at Whitewater World) group sessions for $60/person or privately from $85.

Go Ride A Wave ☎ 07 5526 7077, ⓦ gorideawave .com.au. For expert tuition, tours, gear or advice anywhere on the Gold Coast. Beginners booking in advance pay $65 for a 2hr session. Board rental $45/day.

Surf FX 127 Ferry Rd, Southport ☎ 07 5531 3199, ⓦ surffx.com.au. Lessons in kiteboarding, windsurfing and stand-up paddle surfing, plus equipment rental.

Q1

SkyPoint observation deck Levels 77 & 78, Q1, 9 Hamilton Ave • Mon–Thurs & Sun 7.30am–9pm, Fri & Sat 7.30am–8pm • $24; SkyPoint Climb (1hr 30min) from $74 • ☎ 07 5680 7700, ⓦ skypoint.com.au

While Surfers' tower-block cityscape makes an immediate impression, one building, literally, stands out above all. Occupying an entire block on the highway between Clifford Street and Hamilton Avenue, the 322.5m-tall **Q1** was, when it opened in 2005, the world's tallest residential building (it's currently sixth). You can ride the lift up 77 storeys, or 230m, in 42.7 seconds to the **SkyPoint observation deck** for a drink at the bar and stupendous 360-degree views down over the puny high-rises below, the endless strip of golden sand fringing the sea, and inland as far south as Mount Warning in New South Wales. If you're feeling brave, you can stagger even higher up to the apex of the building on the open-air **SkyPoint Climb**.

The beach

Across the Esplanade, the **beach** is all you could want as a place to recover from your night out; it runs 5km or more north from here via **Main Beach** to **the Spit**, so finding empty sand shouldn't be too difficult. If you're feeling energetic, seek out a game of volleyball or head for the surf: the swell here is good in a northerly wind, but most of the time it's better for boogie-boards.

The Nerang River

Downtown Surfers Paradise consists of a thin ribbon of partially reclaimed land between the ocean and the **Nerang River**, which – as the Broadwater – flows north, parallel with the beach, past **the Spit** and South Stradbroke Island into the choked channels at the bottom end of Moreton Bay. Reclaimed land in the river forms islands whose names reflect the fantasies of their founders – Isle of Capri, Sorrento, Miami Keys – and which have become much-sought-after real estate.

River cruises (see below) let you ogle some of these glitzy properties and take time out from the beach.

Wet 'n' Wild

Pacific Highway, Oxenford, 14km north of Surfers • Daily 10am–5pm • $74 • ☎ 13 33 86, ⊛ wetnwild.com.au

Wet 'n' Wild is an adrenaline-inspired water park that takes some beating on a hot day – the back-breaking Kamikaze and the fully enclosed, dizzying Blackhole alone are worth the entrance fee.

Australian Outback Spectacular

Pacific Highway, Oxenford, 14km north of Surfers (between Wet 'n' Wild and Movie World) • Tues–Sat 7.30pm, plus occasional Sundays (see website) at 12.30pm; doors open 1hr before showtime • $90 • ☎ 13 33 86, ⊛ outbackspectacular.com.au

Although not strictly speaking a theme park, the themed show – "Spirit of the Horse" – at the **Australian Outback Spectacular** gets great reviews. This two-hour evening extravaganza features stunning demonstrations of horsemanship and a cattle roundup, followed by a huge barbecue meal.

Warner Brothers Movie World

Pacific Highway, Oxenford, 14km north of Surfers • Daily 9.30am–5pm • $89 • ☎ 13 33 86, ⊛ movieworld.com.au

Showcasing Hollywood favourites from Superman to Scooby-Doo, **Warner Brothers Movie World** features studio tours, Western shows and stunt demonstrations. Most of its hair-raising rides, such as the Batwing Supershot which catapults riders 60m into the heavens, are themed around Marvel and DC superheroes.

Dreamworld

Pacific Highway, Coomera, 17km north of Surfers • Daily 10am–5pm • $85 • ☎ 07 5588 1111, ⊛ dreamworld.com.au

Home to over forty rides, including five roller coasters, **Dreamworld** is the largest theme park along the Gold Coast, and is notorious as the scene of a tragic incident in 2016, when four visitors died on the Thunder River Rapids attraction. Other sections of the park are devoted to Dreamworks movies like *Shrek* and *Kung Fu Panda*, and there's also a collection of hand-reared tigers in a large enclosure.

ARRIVAL AND DEPARTURE   SURFERS PARADISE

By bus Greyhound and Murrays operate services to and from Brisbane, Byron Bay and beyond from Surfers Paradise Transit Centre, on Beach Rd near the highway, one street down from Cavill Ave. The Transit Centre holds luggage lockers, bus company desks and the Travellers Lounge, where you can make hostel bookings or arrange a free pick-up. Gold Coast Tourist Shuttle ($16–27; ☎ 07 5552 2760, ⊛ gcshuttle.com.au) offers a shared door-to-door service between your hotel, the Gold Coast Airport and all theme parks.

Destinations Brisbane (5 daily; 1hr 30min); Burleigh Heads (every 10min; 30min); Byron Bay (5 daily; 3hr); Coolangatta (every 10min; 1hr); Sydney (5 daily; 15hr 30min).

By ferry Passenger ferries make the 15min crossing between Hope Harbour Marina and *Couran Cove Resort* on South Stradbroke Island, 25km north of Surfers Paradise (3–4 daily; $30 return).

GETTING AROUND

By car East Coast Car Rentals, 80 Ferny Ave ☎ 07 5555 8900, ⊛ eastcoastcarrentals.com.au; Red Back Rentals, 10 Beach Rd ☎ 07 5592 1655, ⊛ redbackrentals.com.au; or SEQ RentACar, 9 Trickett St ☎ 1800 241 346, ⊛ seqrentacar.com.

By taxi Gold Coast Cabs ☎ 13 10 08, ⊛ gccabs.com.au.

INFORMATION AND ACTIVITIES

Tourist information The visitor centre is at 2 Cavill Ave (Mon–Fri 8.30am–5pm, Sat 9am–6pm, Sun 9am–4pm; ☎ 1300 309 440, ⊛ visitgoldcoast.com).

Jet boats Paradise Jet Boating offer hourly white-knuckle jet boat rides on the Nerang River (55min; from $59; ☎ 1300 538 262, ⊛ paradisejetboating.com.au).

River cruises Wyndham Cruises operate excursions of varying lengths on the Nerang River and canals (from $27; ☎ 07 5539 9299, ⊛ wyndhamcruises.com.au).

Services Gold Coast University Hospital is at 1 Hospital Blvd, Southport (☎1300 744 284), while the Amcal Pharmacy at Piazza on The Boulevard, 3221 Surfers Paradise Blvd, stays open 24hr. The post office is in the Centro Centre on Cavill Ave (Mon–Fri 9am–5pm, Sat 9am–12.30pm).

ACCOMMODATION

HOTELS

Mantra on View 22 View Ave ☎07 5665 4416, ⓦmantra.com.au. This good-value hotel is very close to the beach, and features reasonably priced rooms – the rates drop significantly for multi-night stays – plus a pool. $185

★**QT Gold Coast** 7 Staghorn Ave ☎07 5584 1200, ⓦqtgoldcoast.com.au. Taking the Gold Coast in a fresh new direction, this wittily furnished hotel combines old-style surfer chic with a cool urban vibe, and has a great bar, spa and restaurant. $233

Surfers Paradise Marriott Resort 158 Ferny Ave ☎07 5592 9800, ⓦmarriott.com.au. Flash international chain hotel that offers good deals for luxury rooms with great facilities including a spa, a seafood buffet and a teppanyaki restaurant, plus a gorgeous pool and lagoon. $300

★**Vibe** 42 Ferny Ave ☎07 5539 0444, ⓦvibehotels .com.au. Plain from the outside but with a slickly designed interior, a nice riverside pool and spa, this medium-sized hotel is excellent value. Paying a little extra gets you fabulous river views. $116

MOTELS AND APARTMENTS

Chateau Beachside 52 The Esplanade ☎07 5538 1022, ⓦchateaubeachside.com.au. Overlooking the beach from the heart of Surfers, this modern tower block is a great mid-range deal, with good-sized rooms, studios and apartments, as well as a pool and BBQ area. $170

Enderley Gardens 38 Enderley Ave ☎07 5570 1511, ⓦenderleyresort.com.au. Simple but tidy apartments in a low-rise complex that's arranged around a small but pleasant tropical garden and pool. Prices drop the longer you stay. $160

Moorings on Cavill Avenue 63 Cavill Ave ☎07 5538 6711, ⓦmooringsoncavill.com.au. High-rise tower overlooking the Nerang River that holds one- to three-bedroom apartments of differing degrees of luxury, plus a pool, spa and games room; budget-conscious groups can find real bargains. $160

One The Esplanade 1 The Esplanade ☎07 5538 3154, ⓦoneontheesplanade.com.au. Attractive two- and three-bedroom apartments, each with its own balcony offering views north up Surfers Beach, plus a heated saltwater pool, BBQ facilities and direct access to the sand. $195

HOSTELS AND CAMPING

Aquarius Backpackers 44 Queen St, Southport, 5km north of Cavill Ave ☎07 5527 1300, ⓦaquariusback packers.com.au. Offers a tiny TV lounge on each floor, pool and communal kitchen, plus a licensed bar and courtesy bus to and from Surfers. Small four- and six-bed dorms plus private doubles. Dorms $29, doubles $75

Budds in Surfers 6 Pine Ave ☎07 5538 9661, ⓦbuddsinsurfers.com.au. Close to the riverfront Budds Beach, this new independent backpackers' has four- and eight-bed dorms and private doubles, plus a lounge and palm-fringed pool area. Dorms $25, doubles $75

Gold Coast Tourist Parks ☎07 5532 0316, ⓦgoldcoasttouristparks.com.au. The council operates seven well-maintained parks, including ones close to the action at Main Beach and Ocean Beach. Facilities include heated pools; be sure to book ahead. Un/powered sites $41/$45

Sleeping Inn 26 Peninsula Drive ☎07 5592 4455, ⓦsleepinginn.com.au. Budget resort offering apartment-style eight-bed dorms and private rooms with shared or private en-suite bathrooms, and promising a party vibe (there's no bar, so you can BYO). Courtesy bus to Surfers' Transit Centre. Dorms $29, doubles $75

Surfers Paradise Backpackers' Resort 2837 Gold Coast Hwy ☎1800 282 800, ⓦsurfersparadiseback packers.com.au. Modern, sparklingly clean and efficient, with spacious dorms and apartments, plus abundant facilities including spa, pool, sauna, nightclub passes and free laundry. Dorms $27, doubles $74

EATING

There's somewhere to eat wherever you look in Surfers, though few places are particularly memorable. For the best choice of places to eat and drink, head south to Broadbeach or north to Broadwater and Southport. For **supplies**, try the supermarket in the Centro Centre (on Cavill Ave) or the 24hr Night Owl near Trickett St.

Baritalia Chevron Renaissance Centre, Surfers Paradise Blvd at Elkhorn ☎07 5592 4700, ⓦbaritaliagoldcoast.com.au. While this stylish contemporary Italian restaurant is open for all meals daily, it's at its best in the early evening, when its roomy terrace bathes in the glow of the setting sun. Most pasta mains cost $20–30, while lunchtime burgers and paninis start from $11. Daily 8am–late.

Bumbles Cafe 21 River Drive ☎07 5538 6668, ⓦbumblescafe.com. Peaceful riverside café that's a favourite local rendezvous for a leisurely breakfast – try the $18 smoked salmon with mashed avocado – and

3

wholesome lunches of salads, wraps and sandwiches, again mostly under $20. Mon–Wed & Fri–Sun 7am–4pm, Thurs 7am–10pm.

★ **Cardamom Pod** 2685 Gold Coast Hwy, Broadbeach ☏ 0452 218 108, ⓦ cardamompod.com.au. Design-driven restaurant where the delicious home-cooked, Indian-spiced veggie meals change daily, and can be mixed and matched, with typical prices around $20. Daily 11.30am–9.30pm.

Fiddlers Green 39 Cavill Ave ☏ 07 5538 9122, ⓦ fiddlers.com.au. Huge Irish pub with plenty of atmosphere and decent food (served until 9pm) right in the thick of the action, plus live music and a nice front terrace for people-watching. Mains are around $20, but there are loads of daily $10 deals. Daily 10am–3am.

Stingray QT Gold Coast, 7 Staghorn Ave ☏ 07 5584 1200, ⓦ qthotelsandresorts.com. Supercool lounge bar with a tempting menu of contemporary Mexican-inspired dishes (tacos from $8), gourmet burgers, sausages and sandwiches (chorizo hot dog $13), pizzas (from $15) and tasting plates. Until 6pm, they even serve a "Man Tea" including a burger, a pie, a doughnut and a chocolate cigar, for $39. Daily noon–midnight.

DRINKING AND NIGHTLIFE

Apart from the beach, Surfers' **nightclubs** and **bars** – mostly along Orchid Ave – are its reason to be. Initially, particularly if you're staying at a hostel or pick up a free pass somewhere, your choice will probably be dictated by the various **deals** on entry and drinks. The Surfers scene is very youth-orientated; the Gold Coast's more mature crowd makes for Broadbeach. Typical opening times are from 6pm until 3am or later; bars are open daily, and clubs from Thursday to Sunday. Watch out for overpriced club entry/free drinks packages. Sellers work on commission, and entries into most clubs are usually free before 10pm. In addition, the Gold Coast often hosts big **dance parties** and live **music festivals**, usually held at Parklands Showgrounds. Several hostels jointly promote "Big Night Out" (Wed & Sat $30), a mass pub-and-bar-crawl with drinks promotions, party games, free bus transport and VIP entry into four selected clubs.

Bedroom Lounge Bar 26 Orchid Ave ☏ 07 5592 0088, ⓦ bedroomloungebar.com.au. One of the best places on the coast for house and dance, with rotating local and international DJs. Wed–Sun 9pm–5am.

East 88 Surf Parade, Broadbeach ☏ 07 5538 8868, ⓦ east88.com.au. DJs spin R&B and dance tunes at this restaurant, lounge bar and club for grown-ups. Thurs–Sat 6pm–5am, Sun 9pm–5am.

Melba's 46 Cavill Ave ☏ 07 5538 7411, ⓦ melbas.com.au. Large, relatively upmarket nightclub with a colossal, atmospherically lit bar and powerful sound system, plus a noticeably older crowd than the rest of Surfers' clubs. The attached café-restaurant serves light meals daily, and – unusually for Surfers – has pavement tables. Thurs–Sat 9pm–5am.

Platinum 19 Victoria Ave, Broadbeach ☏ 07 5592 4433, ⓦ platinumnightclub.com.au. Chill-out dance club and lounge bar with international DJs. Fri & Sat 9pm–5am.

Sin City 22 Orchid Ave, Surfers ☏ 07 5538 7543, ⓦ sincitynightclub.com.au. DJ sessions and regular weeknight drinks specials guarantee a lively atmosphere in this opulent over-the-top nightclub. Mon–Sat 9pm–5am.

Surfers Beergarden Cavill Ave, opposite Orchid Ave ☏ 07 5570 1322, ⓦ surfersbeergarden.com.au. Excellent live music action, with local and interstate band talent on Thurs–Sun nights. Daily noon–5am.

South Stradbroke Island

South Stradbroke Island is a 20km-long, narrow strip of sand, separated from North Stradbroke Island by the 1896 cyclone. Conservation areas protect much of the island, and its relatively isolated and quiet beaches offer something of an escape from the mainland. There's also some of the coast's finest **surf** to ride along the southeast shore, though local surfies are notoriously protective.

ARRIVAL AND DEPARTURE
SOUTH STRADBROKE ISLAND

By ferry Three to four ferries each day (20min; $30 return) carry guests to the island's one resort, halfway up the west coast at Couran Cove from Hope Harbour Marina, 60 Sickle Ave, Hope Island, which is accessible by road and on Translink rail and bus services from Brisbane. Alternatively, Zane's Water Taxis (☏ 0404 905 970, ⓦ inzanewatertaxis.com.au), operating from Runaway Bay Marina in Hollywell at the north end of the Gold Coast, offer a chartered service for up to twelve passengers to various locations on the island, including Tipplers Passage (around $90 per boat one-way).

ACCOMMODATION

Couran Cove Island Resort ☏ 07 5597 9999, ⓦ courancove.com.au. An environmentally friendly hotel with rooms and self-contained units with marina or wetland views; prices include bikes, kayaks and nature walks. __$210__

Tipplers Hub campsite ☎ 07 5577 2849, ⓦ mystraddie.com.au. Close to McLaren's Landing, this big campsite has permanent Wallaby tents, unpowered sites and gas BBQs, while a licensed kiosk nearby holds a lively café that's open daily. Tents **$76**, unpowered sites **$29**

Burleigh Head National Park

Burleigh Heads, around 7km south of Surfers, consists of a traffic bottleneck where the multilane highway dodges between the beach and a rounded headland; while there can be very good surf here, the rocks make it rough for novices. Seventy years ago, before the bitumen and paving took over, this was all dense eucalypt and vine forest, the last fragment of which survives as **Burleigh Head National Park.**

Geologically, Burleigh Heads stems from the prehistoric eruptions of the Mount Warning volcano, 30km southwest. Lava surfaced through vents, cooling to form tall hexagonal basalt columns that are now mostly tumbled and covered in vines. Rainforest colonized the richer volcanic soils, while stands of red gum grew in weaker sandy loam; along the eastern seafront there's a patch of exposed heathland bordered by groups of pandanus, and a beach along the mouth of Tallebudgera Creek. This diversity is amazing considering the minimal space, but urban encroachment has seriously affected the **wildlife** – though you can still see butterflies, scrub turkeys and sunbathing dragons.

David Fleay Wildlife Park

West Burleigh Rd, West Burleigh • Daily 9am–5pm • $20.80 • ☎ 07 5576 2411, ⓦ fleayswildlife.com.au

The **David Fleay Wildlife Park**, less than 2km inland from Burleigh Heads, is an informal park where boardwalks lead through forest pens and there are plenty of rangers on hand to answer your questions. The late David Fleay was the first person to persuade platypuses to breed in captivity, and the park has a special section devoted to this curious animal, along with crocodiles, koalas, glider possums and plenty of birds. Various guided tours set off through the day, including one through the **nocturnal house** – a chance to see normally somnambulant Australian wildlife in action.

Currumbin Beach

Currumbin Beach, 10km south of Burleigh Heads, is a good, relatively undeveloped stretch of coast between Elephant Rock and Currumbin Point. Given a breeze, there are usually some decent rollers to ride. **Palm Beach**, just north, is more sheltered.

Currumbin Wildlife Sanctuary

28 Tomewin St, Currumbin, just off the Gold Coast Highway • Daily 8am–5pm • $49 • ☎ 07 5534 1266, ⓦ cws.org.au

Currumbin itself is a humdrum development whose main point of interest is **Currumbin Wildlife Sanctuary**. This seventy-acre reserve of forest and water was started in 1946 by Alex Griffiths, who developed it as a native wildlife refuge. There are the usual feeding times (throughout the day) and tame kangaroos, but the park's strongest points are its lively, educational shows and its wildlife hospital, which has large windows looking onto the operating rooms. On Friday evenings, the **Sanctuary Markets** features local and international food stalls, as well as arts and crafts (Fri 4–9pm).

Coolangatta

On the Queensland–New South Wales border 10km south of Currumbin, **COOLANGATTA** merges seamlessly with Tweed Heads (in New South Wales) along Boundary Street. With only a giant concrete plinth just off the main road to mark the border, you'll probably make the crossing between states without realizing it. Unless it's

3

New Year, when everyone takes advantage of the one-hour time difference between the states to celebrate twice, most travellers bypass Coolangatta completely; in doing so, they miss some of the best surf, least crowded beaches and the only place along the Gold Coast that can boast a real "local" community.

Coolangatta is set out one block back from **Greenmount Beach** along **Griffith Street**, where you'll find banks, shops and little in the way of high-density development. Running parallel, and connected by a handful of short streets, **Marine Parade** fronts the shore, the view north over sand and sea ending with the jagged teeth of the skyscrapers on the horizon at Surfers Paradise. The state border runs along Griffith Street and uphill to the east along its continuation, Boundary Street, up to Point Danger at the end of the small peninsula.

At **Point Danger**, the Captain Cook Memorial Lighthouse forms a shrine where pillars enclose a large bronze globe detailing Cook's peregrinations around the southern hemisphere. Twenty-five metres below, surfers in their colourful wetsuits make the most of **Flagstaff Beach**'s swell – at weekends this area is very crowded. Other good spots to **surf** include the area between Point Danger and Kirra Point, to the west (world surfing champion Kelly Slater nominated the latter as his favourite break); Greenmount, which is fairly reliable and a good beach for beginners; and Snapper Rocks and Point Danger, at the end of the peninsula, for the more dedicated – exactly where depends on the wind.

For sun-worshippers, **Coolangatta Beach**, just west of Greenmount, is right in town, but the 6km stretch of sand further west, beyond Kirra Point, is wider, prettier and less crowded.

ARRIVAL AND DEPARTURE

COOLANGATTA

By plane Gold Coast Airport is 3km west of Coolangatta. The Gold Coast Tourist Shuttle (from $22; ☏ 07 5552 2760, ⓦ gcshuttle.com.au) offers a shared door-to-door service between your hotel, the Gold Coast Airport and all theme parks. Book by 7pm for next day pick-up.

Destinations Adelaide (2 daily; 2hr 45min); Auckland (1 daily; 3hr); Cairns (1 daily; 2hr 30min); Hobart (4 weekly; 4hr 35min); Kuala Lumpur (5 weekly; 8hr 30min); Melbourne (12 daily; 2hr 15min); Newcastle (1 daily; 1hr 10min); Perth (5 weekly; 5hr 45min); Sydney (21 daily; 1hr 30min); Tokyo (1 daily; 9hr).

By bus There are two long-distance bus stops: Premier set down in Wharf St, Tweed Heads (inside the NSW time zone), while Greyhound use a bus shelter on Warner St, between Lanham and Chalk streets, Coolangatta (Queensland).

Destinations Brisbane (5 daily; 2hr 30min); Byron Bay (5 daily; 2hr); Surfers Paradise (every 10min; 1hr); Sydney (5 daily; 14hr 30min).

GETTING AROUND

By car Car rental is available at the airport through Alpha Car Hire (from $30/day; ☏ 1300 227 473, ⓦ alphacarhire.com.au).

By taxi Gold Coast Cabs ☏ 13 10 08, ⓦ gccabs.com.au.

INFORMATION AND ACTIVITIES

Services There's a 24hr Night Owl convenience store at the Showcase Shopping Centre on Marine Parade and bigger supermarkets at the main shopping centre on Wharf St, in Tweed Heads.

Surfing All shops have decent secondhand boards for sale, though local boards tend to be too thin and lightweight to use elsewhere. Several companies offer tuition (see box, p.327). For surfing gear, drop by Mt Woodgee at 122 Griffith St (Mon–Fri & Sun 9am–5pm, Sat 8.30am–5pm; ☏ 07 5536 5937) which has loads of surfboards for rent for around $40 a day plus credit card deposit.

ACCOMMODATION

Coolangatta Sands Hostel Cnr McLean & Griffith sts ☏ 07 5536 7472, ⓦ coolangattasandshostel.com.au. Tidy, clean and modern dorms opening onto a fab communal living deck, plus good bathrooms, all above a pub with live music Fri–Sun. Dorms $30, doubles $80

Coolangatta YHA 230 Coolangatta Rd, Bilinga ☏ 07 5536 7644, ⓦ coolangattayha.com. Helpful management and nicely located for the quieter beaches, albeit 4km from the action, out by the airport. Dorms $34, doubles $75

Kirra Beach Tourist Park 10 Charlotte St, Kirra ☏ 07 5667 2740, ⓦ goldcoasttouristparks.com.au. Probably the cheapest bet in the area, 1km west of town, with a pool, cabins sleeping up to four and plenty of space to camp. Un/powered sites $47/57, cabins $138

Komune 146 Marine Parade ☏ 07 5536 6764,

ⓦkomuneresorts.com. Aimed squarely at style-conscious backpackers, this trendy pad has smart shared rooms and apartments, plus a bar dishing out daiquiris to lounge tunes. Also a cinema and weekend pool parties. Dorms $38, doubles $109

Sunset Strip Budget Resort 199 Boundary St ⓣ07 5599 5517, ⓦsunsetstrip.com.au. Classic 1960s-style guesthouse with simple but serviceable rooms and apartments – the latter have a three-night minimum stay – plus parking and a 20m pool. Doubles $77, apartments $275

EATING AND DRINKING

Coolangatta Hotel Cnr Warner St & Marine Parade ⓣ07 5589 6888, ⓦthecoolyhotel.com.au. Pub, restaurant and live music venue that's famed for its legendary "Cooly" Sunday sessions. Pizzas and burgers for under $20, chicken, ribs or fish'n'chips for $20–30. Daily 11am–late.
Coolangatta Surf Club Cnr Marine Parade & Dutton St ⓣ07 5536 4648, ⓦcoolangattasurfclub.com. Fantastic value; dine for under $30 on steaks, seafood and salads, at

tables along an extensive balcony overlooking the sand. Daily 11am–8pm.
O-Sushi 66–70 Marine Parade ⓣ07 5536 5455, ⓦosushi.com.au. This deservedly popular Japanese restaurant is every bit as good for conveyor-belt sushi as its sister branch in Byron Bay, with individual dishes from $5 and speciality rolls and main dishes more like $15–25. Daily 11am–late.

The Gold Coast Hinterland

Starting around 30km inland from the jangling excesses of the shoreline, the **Gold Coast Hinterland** is a mountainous, rainforested plateau that encompasses a series of magnificently wild **national parks**, all packed with scenery, animals and birds. The pick of the bunch is **Green Mountain** at **Lamington National Park**, with atmospheric **hiking trails** through beech forest and a stunning density of birdlife. **Tamborine Mountain**'s less rugged walking tracks and country "villages" also provide a relaxing weekend escape, while the waterfalls of **Springbrook National Park** make for an easy day-trip.

Weather ranges from very wet in summer (when leeches are abundant, and some hiking trails are closed) to fairly cool and dry in winter, though rain is a possibility year-round. If you plan to **hike**, you'll find that trails are well marked, but can be slippery, so bring good footwear. **Accommodation**, which is best booked in advance, is in resorts, motels and campsites; if you're on a tight budget bring a **tent**. You'll need a **fuel stove** if you're camping, as collecting firewood in national parks is forbidden; barbecues and wood are often supplied on sites, however.

ARRIVAL AND GETTING AROUND   THE GOLD COAST HINTERLAND

On a tour You can get here by tour bus from Brisbane (see p.325) or the Gold Coast (see p.316).
By car To explore to any extent you'll need your own

vehicle. If you drive, carry a good road map, as signposts are few and far between – all destinations are reached off the Pacific Highway between Brisbane and the Gold Coast.

Tamborine Mountain

Tamborine Mountain is a volcanic plateau, 40km inland from the Gold Coast as the crow flies, where the remaining pockets of rainforest are interspersed with the little satellite suburbs of northerly **Eagle Heights**, adjoining **North Tamborine** and **Mount Tamborine**, 5km south. Once the haunt of the Wangeriburra people, the forests here were targeted by the timber industry from the late nineteenth century onwards, until locals succeeded in getting the area declared Queensland's **first national park** in 1908. Visits provide a pleasant escape from the city, with a surplus of tearooms, country accommodation and easy walking tracks through accessibly small, jungly stands of timber.

Eagle Heights

EAGLE HEIGHTS, 5km south of Tamborine National Park and the largest settlement in the vicinity, amounts to little more than the 500m strip of **Gallery Road**, lined with cafés and craft showrooms. Worth a look are the pretty **botanic gardens** on Forsythia

Drive, off Long Road (open during daylight hours; free), where small picnic lawns surround a pond overlooked by tall trees.

In the national park itself, the easy **Palm Grove Circuit**, accessed from the picnic area at the end of Palm Grove Avenue, loops for 2.5km through a mix of dry forest, a few small creeks, and a limpid, eerie gloom created by an extensive stand of elegant piccabeen palms. Hidden 20m up in the canopy the elusive wompoo pigeon is often heard but seldom seen, despite its vivid purple and green plumage. You can turn the hike into a longer 4.5km trek, and enjoy spectacular views, by continuing at an obvious junction along the **Jenyn Falls** segment.

North Tamborine

A few kilometres west of Eagle Heights, **NORTH TAMBORINE** holds a visitor centre, a post office, ATMs, fuel stations and yet more cafés. The best walk in North Tamborine is about 1km south down Western Road, where a 3km track slaloms downhill through open scrub and rainforest to **Witches Falls**. The easy walk is more rewarding for the views off the plateau than for the falls themselves, which are only a trickle that disappears over a narrow ledge below the lookout.

You can study the canopy from tip to root by wandering along elevated steel walkways at **Skywalk**, 333 Geissman Drive (daily 9.30am–5pm; $19.50; ☎07 5545 2222, ⊛rainforestskywalk.com.au), including a fantastic cantilevered platform, before following the gravel pathway down through rainforest to serene rock pools.

At 87–91 Beacon Rd, the internationally renowned **Tamborine Mountain Distillery** (Mon–Sat 10am–3pm; $5; ☎07 5545 3452, ⊛tamborinemountaindistillery.com) offers fun tastings of its award-winning vodkas, schnapps and liqueurs laced with anything from sour plum to choc'n'chilli.

Cedar Creek Falls and Lepidozamia National Park

A reliably good swimming spot a couple of kilometres north of North Tamborine along Geissmann Drive (the road to Brisbane) is at **Cedar Creek Falls**, where whitewater tumbles dramatically all year around.

Down near **Mount Tamborine** – which is otherwise purely residential – there's a stand of primitive, slow-growing cycads and a relatively dry climate at **Lepidozamia National Park** on Main Western Road.

ARRIVAL AND INFORMATION

TAMBORINE MOUNTAIN

By car Driving from the coast, turn off the Pacific Highway at Oxenford and follow Route 95 up to Eagle Heights; from Brisbane, turn off the highway at Beenleigh and take Route 92 to North Tamborine.

Tourist information The Tamborine Mountain Visitor Centre is at Doughty Park, North Tamborine (daily 10am–4pm; ☎07 5545 3200, ⊛tamborinemtncc.org.au).

ACCOMMODATION

★**Avocado Sunset** 186 Beacon Rd, North Tamborine ☎07 5545 2365, ⊛avocadosunset.com.au. Four beautifully decorated rooms, full English breakfasts (with black pudding) and a superb sunset deck; bag "Safari" for its four-poster bed, spa bath, log fire and amazing valley views. $195

Pethers Rainforest Retreat 28B Geissman St, North Tamborine ☎07 5545 4577, ⊛pethers.com.au. Very stylish, wooden pole-frame "treehouses" set in landscaped gardens, along with an excellent restaurant and bar. $325

The Polish Place 333 Main Western Rd, North Tamborine ☎07 5545 1603, ⊛polishplace.com.au. This reliable option consists of cosy, timber, fully self-contained chalets with wood-burning stoves, spas and stunning views – plus a Polish restaurant. Checkout isn't until noon. $259

Tall Trees Motel 9 Eagle Heights Rd, North Tamborine ☎07 5545 1242, ⊛talltreesmotel.com.au. Five clean budget rooms, which open onto a pretty lawned garden; there's also a café serving cheap food. $130

Tamborine Mountain Caravan and Camping Thunderbird Park, Mountain Rd, Mount Tamborine ☎07 5545 0034, ⊛tamborine.info. A wooded campground near Cedar Creek and a stone's throw from Thunderbird Park. Un/powered sites $24/32, safari tents $85

Springbrook National Park

At the edge of a plateau along the New South Wales border, **Springbrook National Park** comprises several separate morsels boasting abundant forest, waterfalls, luminous colonies of glow-worms and swimming holes.

Purling Brook Falls

The park's arguable highlight, the 109m **Purling Brook Falls**, are very impressive after rain has swollen the flow; a 4km track zigzags down the escarpment and into the rainforest at the base of the falls before curving beneath the waterfall (expect a soaking from the spray) and going back up the other side. Following a number of recent accidents, access to both the top and the bottom of the falls has been restricted. If you're looking to swim, head instead for the **pools** downstream from the base, picturesquely encircled by lianas and red cedar.

Best of All Lookout

A 10km drive south beyond the falls brings you to the start of a 300m trail to reach the aptly named **Best of All Lookout**, which affords a panoramic vista south to Mount Warning and across the Tweed Valley.

Natural Bridge

Natural Bridge, roughly 24km from the Purling Brook Falls junction, is a dark, damp and hauntingly eerie place, where a collapsed cave ceiling beneath the river bed has created a subterranean waterfall. You can walk in through the original cave mouth some 50m downstream; from the back of the cave the forest outside frames the waterfall and blue plunge pool, surreally lit from above; **glow-worms** illuminate the ceiling at night and their galaxy-like bioluminescence is best seen during the warmer, wetter months of the year (Dec–March). Swimming in Cave Creek is strictly prohibited.

ARRIVAL AND INFORMATION	SPRINGBROOK NATIONAL PARK
By car Turn off the Pacific Highway inland from Burleigh Heads at Mudgeeraba, then follow the twisty road 20km southwest to a junction where Route 99 heads left to Purlingbrook, and Route 97 heads right to Natural Bridge.	**Information** The ranger station at 87 Carricks Rd, Springbrook (Mon–Fri 8am–3.30pm) stocks national park walking maps.

ACCOMMODATION

Settlement Campground Off Carricks Rd ☎13 74 68, ⓦ nprsr.qld.gov.au. The only campsite in the park has toilets and free electric BBQs, but sites aren't very	well shaded and there are no showers. Purling Brook Falls is a short wander away. Advance bookings essential. **$5.95**

Lamington National Park

Lamington National Park occupies the northeastern rim of a vast 1156m-high caldera that centres on Mount Warning, 15km south in New South Wales. An enthralling world of rainforest-flanked rivers, open heathland and ancient eucalypt woods, Lamington is located on a crossover zone between subtropical and temperate climes, and thus home to a staggering variety of plants, animals and birds, with isolated populations of species found nowhere else in the world.

Both the two potential bases for exploring the park, **Binna Burra** on the drier northern edge and **Green Mountains** in the thick of the forest, offer resort and campsite **accommodation**, which must be booked in advance (see p.337). Beechmont and Canungra, further out, are the last proper sources of **supplies**, fuel and cash. Once here, Lamington has to be explored on foot: most of the tracks described below are clearly signposted.

Binna Burra

Binna Burra is a massive tract of highland forest, overlooking the Numinbah Valley from woodland on the crown of Mount Roberts. Of Binna Burra's **walks**, try the 5km **Caves Circuit**, which follows the edge of the Coomera Valley past the white, wind-sculpted Talangai Caves to remains of Aboriginal camps, strands of *Psilotum nudum* (a rootless ancestor of the ferns), and a hillside of strangler fig and red cedar. The **Ships Stern Circuit** (21km; all day) is relatively demanding, with some vertical drop-offs. Key features en route include views of Egg Rock from the precipitous **Bellbird Lookout**, at its most mysterious shrouded in dawn mists, and a stand of majestic 40m-tall box brush trees.

Dave's Creek Circuit (12km; all day) descends into the Kurraragin Valley, crossing bands of rainforest and sclerophyll before emerging onto heathland. Look for tiny clumps of red **sundew** plants along the track, which supplement their nitrogen intake by trapping insects in sticky globules of nectar.

By far the best of the longer tracks is the **Border Track**, a relatively easy 21km, seven-hour path (one-way) through rainforest and beech groves that links Binna Burra with the Green Mountains.

Green Mountains

Green Mountains encapsulates Lamington at its best, a huge spread of cloudforest filled with ancient, moss-covered trees and a mass of wildlife including so many birds that you hardly know where to start looking. The road up from Canungra finally ends at *O'Reilly's Rainforest Retreat*, before which you pass a campsite, picnic ground and a national parks office.

The **birdlife** around *O'Reilly's* is a major attraction. Many species are drawn to the resort's botanical garden: you can't miss the chattering swarms of crimson rosellas mingling with visitors on the lawn, and determined twitchers can clock up over fifty species without entering the forest. The most spectacular is the black and gold regent bowerbird.

Treetop Walk

For exceptional views over the forest canopy, follow the **Treetop Walk** boardwalk beyond *O'Reilly's* to reach a suspended walkway swinging 15m above ground level. A narrow ladder at the halfway anchor climbs to vertigo-inducing mesh platforms 30m up the trunk of a strangler fig, enabling you to see the canopy at eye level. Soaking up the increased sunlight at this height above the forest floor, tree branches become miniature gardens of mosses, ferns and orchids. By night the walkway is the preserve of possums, leaf-tailed geckos and weird stalking insects.

West Canungra Creek Circuit

If you manage only one day-walk at Lamington, make it the exceptional 14km **West Canungra Creek Circuit** (5hr 30min return), which features all the jungle trimmings: fantastic trees, river crossings and countless opportunities to fall off slippery rocks and get soaked. The first hour is dry enough as you tramp downhill past some huge red cedars to **Blue Pool**, a deep, placid waterhole where platypuses are sometimes seen on winter mornings; this makes a good walk in itself. After a dip, head upstream along **Canungra Creek**; the path traverses the river a few times (there are no bridges, but occasionally a fallen tree conveniently spans the water) – yellow or red arrows painted on the rocks show you where to cross. Seasonally, the creek can almost dry up; if the water is more than knee-deep, you shouldn't attempt a crossing and will need to retrace your steps. Follow the creek as far as **Elabana Falls** and **Picnic Rock**, where there's a swimming hole, or bypass the falls; either way, the path climbs back up towards *O'Reilly's*.

Toolona Creek Circuit

The **Toolona Creek Circuit** is an excellent all-day trail (17.5km return; 6hr) via **Box Creek Falls** to the eastern escarpment at **Toolona Lookout**, on the Border Track to Binna

Burra. Rewards include half a dozen waterfalls, dramatic views into New South Wales, and encounters with clumps of moss-covered **Antarctic beech trees**, a Gondwanan relic also found in South America.

ARRIVAL AND INFORMATION   LAMINGTON NATIONAL PARK

By car From Brisbane or the coast, aim for Nerang, inland from Surfers Paradise on the Pacific Highway. From here, Binna Burra is 36km southwest via tiny Beechmont, while Green Mountains is 65km via Canungra.

On a tour If you don't have a car, accommodation might provide a pick-up from the coast, and some tour operators may be willing to take you up one day and pick you up on

another, although you might need to book one of their day-tours to do so.

Information and maps The useful Binna Burra Park Office (Mon–Fri 7.30am–4pm; ☎ 61 13 74 68) and Green Mountains Park Office (Mon–Fri 8am–3.30pm; ☎ 61 13 74 68) can sort you out with walking maps.

ACCOMMODATION

Between February and November, hikers can bush camp at various sites inside the national park. Advance bookings are essential (☎ 13 74 68, ⊛ nprsr.qld.gov.au).

BINNA BURRA

Binna Burra Mountain Lodge Binna Burra Rd, Beechmont ☎07 5533 3622, ⊛binnaburralodge .com.au. Accommodation ranging from wooden twin-share rooms and a campsite with on-site tents (with hot showers) to Heritage-listed log-fired timber cabins dating from the 1930s, and modern studio apartments. There's also a restaurant serving stodgy hikers' fare and a café. Un/powered sites $28/35, safari tents $65, lodge doubles $190

GREEN MOUNTAINS

Cainbable Mountain Lodge Lamington National Park Rd ☎07 5544 9207, ⊛cainbable.com. This trio of self-contained timber chalets, 10km short of O'Reilly's, sleep from four to eight people and have splendid views. Rates

increase at weekends. $120

Green Mountains Campsite At the end of Lamington National Park Rd ☎ 13 74 68, ⊛nprsr.qld .gov.au. An exposed hillside site, not far from O'Reilly's and offering tenting and van sites, toilets and hot showers. $5.95

O'Reilly's Rainforest Retreat Lamington National Park Rd ☎07 5902 4911, ⊛oreillys.com.au. The splendid main house opened as a guesthouse in 1926. The complex has now grown to include suites and villas overlooking parklands and forest, a basic shop, a restaurant and a spa. The O'Reilly family still rule the roost, and there's a packed programme of walks and other activities; although the resort hosts hordes of day-trippers, it's peaceful once they've moved on. $167

The Sunshine Coast

The **Sunshine Coast**, a mild-mannered counterpart to the Gold Coast, stretches north of Brisbane as far as Noosa. The larger towns are rather bland, but there are good beaches and surf at **Maloolaba** and **Maroochydore**, and upmarket beach life at **Noosa**. Though you'll find the **hinterland** far tamer than that behind the Gold Coast, there's striking scenery at the **Glass House Mountains**, and the rolling landscape also holds some lovely laidback hamlets, rife with Devonshire cream teas and weekend markets.

ARRIVAL AND GETTING AROUND   THE SUNSHINE COAST

By plane Sunshine Coast Airport (⊛sunshinecoastai rport.com.au), in Marcoola, 10km north of Maroochydore and 30km south of Noosa, has services to Melbourne (4 daily; 2hr 30min) and Sydney (4 daily; 1hr 45min). Sun Air offer door-to-door shared buses from the airport to all Sunshine Coast suburbs (from $18; ⊛sunair .com.au).

By bus If you don't have your own transport, the easiest way through the area is by bus, either with local transport (Sunbus services cover all main destinations; ☎13 12 30, ⊛sunbus.com.au) or the national long-distance carriers.

By train Brisbane's CityTrain network stops at the Glass House Mountains, Woombye, Nambour and Eumundi, from where there's a connecting local bus to Noosa.

Glass House Mountains National Park

To the Kabi Aborigines, the nine dramatic, isolated pinnacles that jut from a flat plain 75km north of Brisbane – on a clear day, they're visible from the city – are the petrified forms of a family fleeing the incoming tide. Their current name of the **Glass House Mountains**, though, was bestowed by Captain Cook because their conical shape gave them a close resemblance to the furnace stacks of glass factories he'd seen back home in Yorkshire.

The **Glass House Mountains Look Out**, the focal point of the park, is reached by following a clearly signposted road for 15km west of the Bruce Highway. As well as offering great views of the main peaks, it features explanatory displays and an easy 800m walking trail dipping into the forest.

The mountains themselves vary enormously. The very tallest are much too steep for anyone other than professional climbers to attempt, but it's worth hiking up at least one of the easier, more rounded peaks. **Beerburrum**, overlooking the township of the same name, and **Ngungun**, near the Glass House Mountains township, are fairly easy to climb, with well-used tracks that shouldn't take more than two hours return.

ARRIVAL AND INFORMATION   GLASS HOUSE MOUNTAINS NATIONAL PARK

By car The best ways into the area are up along Route 60 via Beerburrum to the Steve Irwin Way or south along Route 6 via Landsborough.

By train The QR CityTrain (☎ 13 12 30, ⍵ translink.com .au) stops at the Glass House Mountains township (19 daily; 1hr 45min) on its services between Brisbane and Nambour.

Tourist information The visitor centre, between Reed St and Steve Irwin Way in Glass House Mountains (daily 9am–4pm; ☎ 1300 847 481) can advise on climbing conditions.

ACCOMMODATION AND EATING

Glass House Mountains Camping Ground Cnr Old Gympie & Mt Beerwah rds ☎ 07 5496 9588, ⍵ ghmc .com.au. The cheapest place to camp close to the park. Facilities are basic, but the sites are shady and the setting very peaceful. POA for power (depends on needs). **$24**

★ **Glass on Glasshouse** 182 Glass House–Woodford Rd ☎ 07 5496 9608, ⍵ glassonglasshouse.com.au. It's worth paying the premium prices for these three self-contained one-bedroom glass-walled cottages, alongside the *Lookout Café*, to enjoy floor-to-ceiling views across bushland towards the jutting peaks of Beerwah and Coonowrin. Each comes with a kitchenette, spa bath and daily breakfast basket. **$295**

Lookout Café 182 Glass House–Woodford Rd ☎ 0498 471 232. Open views over rolling meadows to mounts Beerwah and Coonowrin make this verdant spot, 1km short of the park lookout, a great halt for breakfast (bacon and eggs $12), lunch (mains $12–16) or afternoon tea ($10.50, with scones and jam). Mon–Fri 9am–3pm, Sat & Sun 9am–4pm.

Australia Zoo

Steve Irwin Way • Daily 9am–5pm • $59, ages 3–14 $35 • ☎ 07 5436 2000, ⍵ australiazoo.com.au • Greyhound buses run here from Brisbane (2 daily; 1hr 15min) or Noosa (1 daily; 1hr 35min); also, the QR CityTrain (☎ 13 12 30, ⍵ translink.com.au) stops at Beerwah on its Brisbane–Nambour service (19 daily; 1hr 30min) – the zoo sends a free bus to meet most trains at Beerwah railway station (if there isn't one there, call for a free pick-up)

North of the Glass House Mountains, Route 6, otherwise known as the Steve Irwin Way, continues 10km to the unremarkable town of **Beerwah**, a transit point for **Australia Zoo**. The zoo is famous for the antics of the late zoo director **Steve Irwin**, otherwise known for his "Crocodile Hunter" screen persona. The staff continue his tradition of exuberant exhibitionism (as indeed does his daughter Bindi), and it remains one of Australia's largest and most enjoyable commercial zoos, with plenty of hands-on experience with foreign and native animals.

Caloundra

Despite boasting half a dozen very pleasant **beaches**, the southernmost of the Sunshine Coast towns, **CALOUNDRA**, 90km north of Brisbane, remains relatively

low-key compared to the resorts further north. While it too holds its fair share of towering apartment blocks, its main commercial thoroughfare – tree-lined **Bulcock Street**, a block or so up from the waterfront – still has the feel of an unassuming country community. The closest beaches are Bulcock Beach, just two streets south, and family-friendly Kings Beach, a short walk beyond.

ARRIVAL AND INFORMATION   CALOUNDRA

By train Sunbus #605 links Caloundra with Landsborough railway station, 20km west (frequent; 30min), connected in turn to Brisbane by Translink CityTrains (19 daily; 1hr 30min).

By bus The bus station is on Cooma Terrace, one street south of Bulcock. Sunbus services depart here for Maroochydore via Mooloolaba (every 15–30min; 50min), with onward connections to Noosa. Greyhound connect Caloundra with Brisbane (2 daily; 1hr 30min).

Tourist information The visitor centre is at 7 Caloundra Rd (Mon–Fri 9am–4pm, Sat & Sun 9am–3pm; ☎07 5420 6240, ⓦvisitsunshinecoastvcom.au).

ACCOMMODATION AND EATING

Caloundra Backpackers 84 Omrah Ave ☎07 5499 7655, ⓦcaloundrabackpackers.com.au. Clean, well run, and two minutes from Bulcock Beach. Freebies include surf trips, board rental, Saturday night BBQs and stand-up paddleboards. Can also help find work. Dorms $30, doubles $60

De Lish Fish 8 Levuka Ave, Kings Beach ☎07 5437 0344, ⓦdelishfish.com.au. This top-notch fish'n'chip shop is the pick of a cluster of simple beachfront restaurants, with salt-and-pepper squid for $13 and a sideline in tasty *gelati*. Mon & Wed–Sun 10am–8pm, Tues 10am–3pm.

Golden Beach Holiday Park 9 Onslow St, just off the Esplanade ☎07 5492 4811, ⓦgoldenbeachholidaypark.com.au. The cheapest and friendliest campsite in town. It's seconds from the beach, and also has a number of smart self-contained cabins and motel rooms. Powered sites $39, cabins $140

Rolling Surf Resort 10 Levuka Ave, Kings Beach ☎07 5491 9777, ⓦrollingsurfresort.com.au. Self-catering apartments facing a nice family beach, with one to three bedrooms, sea-view balconies, a good-sized pool and all amenities in easy reach. $265

Mooloolaba

It's at **MOOLOOLABA**, 20km north of Caloundra, where the Sunshine Coast really kicks off as a major tourist destination. This once-sleepy seaside town has made a surprisingly good job of transforming itself into a glitzy modern resort. Across from the high-end boutiques, restaurants and cafés that line its central Esplanade, the oceanfront lawns have been rather beautifully landscaped with pedestrian footpaths (and check out the "Loo with a View"), while the beach itself is long, sandy and excellent for surfing.

The town's sole land-based attraction is **Underwater World** on Parkyn Parade (daily 9am–5pm, last entry at 4pm; $39; ☎07 5458 6226, ⓦunderwaterworld.com.au), with superb views of sharks, turtles and nonchalant freshwater crocodiles staring blankly at you through tunnelled observation windows. If this isn't close enough, you can go scuba diving (from $195) or snorkelling ($81) with the sharks, rays and other fish.

ARRIVAL AND DEPARTURE   MOOLOOLABA

By bus Buses set down on Smith St, just back from shops and restaurants lining the 100m-long, seafront Esplanade. Regular Sunbus services run south to Caloundra (35min) and north to Maroochydore (15min), with connections to Noosa (every 15–30min). Greyhound and Premier buses from/to Brisbane (1hr 40min) stop on Brisbane Rd, adjacent to the Bowling Club.

ACTIVITIES

Diving Sunreef at 110 Brisbane Rd (☎07 5444 5656, ⓦsunreef.com.au) takes qualified divers 15min offshore to where the 133m-long destroyer HMAS *Brisbane*, deliberately sunk as a dive site in 2005, lies in 8 to 28m of water. A two-tank dive costs $240 including all gear. In heavy swell, conditions can be unpleasant; if you're heading north, save your dollars for the *Yongala* (see p.378).

ACCOMMODATION

Kyamba Court Motel 94 Brisbane Rd ☎ 07 5444 0202 ⓦ kyambacourtmotel.com.au. Reasonably priced, clean and spacious motel rooms overlooking a canal, just a short walk from the beach, with pool and shared kitchen facilities. $110

Mooloolaba Backpackers 75 Brisbane Rd ☎ 07 5444 3399, ⓦ mooloolababackpackers.com. Laidback hostel where rates include breakfast, use of bikes, kayaks and boogie boards, and BBQ nights. They'll also help you find seasonal work and print job resumes. Dorms $30, doubles $75

Peninsular 13 Mooloolaba Esplanade ☎ 07 5444 4477, ⓦ peninsular.com.au. Most of these apartments, across from the beach, enjoy superb views of the bay from their private balconies – especially those on the uppermost of the ten floors – and there's a pool and a gym. $270

EATING

Montezuma's Cnr Esplanade & Brisbane Rd ☎ 07 5444 8444, ⓦ montezumas.com.au. This cheap and cheerful Mexican, just back from the sea, is usually packed at weekends. Enchiladas, such as chorizo or chicken, cost $20. Daily 11am–2.30pm & 5–9pm.

★ **Mooloolaba Surf Club** The Esplanade ☎ 07 5444 1300, ⓦ thesurfclub.com.au. Smart café, bar and restaurant that's very much the social hub of town, with the best deals and views around. All gleaming polished wood, thanks to a top-to-bottom makeover, it serves everything from $18.50 Sunday-morning brunch buffets to fish'n'chips or mixed vegetarian plates (both at $20) and $35 T-bone steaks, and has a fabulous oceanfront deck. Daily 7–10am, noon–2pm & 5.30pm–late.

Maroochydore

Given the multilane highway tearing through the middle of town, first impressions of **MAROOCHYDORE**, 3km north of Mooloolaba and 30km south of Noosa, are not immediately enticing. From the centre, though, which stretches beside the Maroochy River just short of the ocean, you only have to continue 1km east to the **Cotton Tree** district to find glorious beaches, where the surf – as usual – is great.

ARRIVAL AND DEPARTURE
MAROOCHYDORE

By train Bus #610 connects Maroochydore with Nambour railway station, 17km west (35min), itself served by Translink CityTrain from Brisbane (19 daily; 1hr 45min).

By bus Greyhound and Premier buses set down beside the visitor centre at the corner of Sixth Ave and Melrose Place. Sunbus services to Noosa (every 30min; 1hr) and Mooloolaba (every 15–30min; 15min) depart from the interchange at Sunshine Plaza.

ACCOMMODATION

Maroochydore Beach Caravan Park Melrose Parade ☎ 07 5443 1167, ⓦ sunshinecoastholidayparks.com.au. Shady sites, tidy one- and two-bedroom villas, BBQ facilities and direct access to a patrolled surf beach, close to the Maroochydore Surf Club. Powered sites $45, villas $155

Space 45 The Esplanade, Cotton Tree ☎ 07 5430 0000, ⓦ spaceholidayapartments.com.au. This comfortable apartment hotel, 1km beyond the centre, ranks among Maroochydore's smarter options, with shared pool, spa and BBQ area. $320

EATING

Boat Shed The Esplanade, Cotton Tree ☎ 07 5443 3808, ⓦ theboatshed.com.au. Lovely seaside spot with a pricey mod-Oz menu; barramundi with *fattoush* salad and cardamom *labna*, for example, costs $37. Daily 11.30am–9pm.

Envy 31 Cotton Tree Parade ☎ 07 5443 8494, ⓦ envycafe .com.au. This café's a good bet for all-day breakfasts (poached eggs on toast $11), plus lunchtime salads, sandwiches, burgers, smoothies and juices. Daily 6am–5pm.

Solbar 12–20 Ocean St ☎ 07 5443 9550, ⓦ solbar .com.au. Hip music venue in central Maroochydore, with sofa-stuffed lounge bar for acoustic acts and a band room out back, plus an all-day coffee bar and restaurant serving $10 daily specials, and pizzas and burgers from $15. Live music Thurs–Sun. Mon 11am–2.30pm, Tues 11am–2.30pm & 5.30pm–late, Wed–Fri 8am–2.30pm & 5.30pm–late, Sat & Sun 8am–late.

The Sunshine Coast hinterland

A two-hour (90km) circuit drive along the Blackall Range from the humdrum farming town of **NAMBOUR**, 15km inland from Maroochydore, takes you into the **Sunshine**

Coast hinterland, a rural idyll reminiscent of Tolkien's Shire, with fields dotted by herds of pied dairy cattle, and occasional long views out to the coast.

Several settlements in these parts – such as **Montville** and **Mapleton** – have dolled themselves up as "villages" and suffer from an overdose of potteries and twee tearooms. It's worth stretching your legs, though, to reach a couple of respectably sized **waterfalls**: Kondalilla, 3km north from Montville towards Nambour, with swimming holes along Obi Obi Creek; and Mapleton Falls, just west of Mapleton, where the river plunges over basalt cliffs.

Big Pineapple

Woombye • Daily 9am–4pm • Free except tours and rides • ☎ 07 5442 3102, ⊕ bigpineapple.com.au • Served by CityTrain from Brisbane (8 daily; 1hr 45min) and frequent Sunbus services from Maroochydore (#610; 20min) via Nambour

Few visitors driving along the main north–south Highway 1 can resist pulling off the highway at **WOOMBYE**, 5km south of Nambour, to gawk at the renowned and ridiculous **Big Pineapple**. Activities here include trips around the adjoining plantation on a cane train and, of course, climbing the fibreglass fruit.

Maleny

With its single street of cafés, ageing hippy population, cooperative supermarket, and short riverside stroll, little **MALENY** has a pleasantly alternative atmosphere. If you have your own vehicle, it's worth making your way up here, 50km from the coast, to visit the **Mary Cairncross Scenic Reserve**, 148 Mountain View Rd (daily 7am–6pm; donation; ☎ 07 5479 6122, ⊕ mary-cairncross.com.au). This small patch of subtropical rainforest is inhabited by snakes, wallabies and plenty of birds, and can be explored on a 2km loop of trails and boardwalks. Both the entrance and the lively on-site café offer fantastic views south over the Glass House Mountains.

ACCOMMODATION AND EATING   MALENY

Lyndon Lodge 3 Benecke Rd ☎ 07 5494 3307, ⊕ lyndonlodge.com.au. Two clean and cosy rooms, and one larger suite, offering superb views, set in attractive gardens and sharing use of a gloriously spacious communal sitting area with the helpful German-Australian owners. **$105**

Maleny Hills Motel 932 Maleny–Montville Rd ☎ 07 5494 2551, ⊕ malenyhills.com.au. This friendly family-run motel, in a rural hillside setting 5km east of town towards Montville, offers bright, light, self-contained rooms, each capable of sleeping up to three and with its own courtyard. **$120**

Maleny Lodge 58 Maple St ☎ 07 5494 2370, ⊕ malenylodge.com.au. Located right in town, this charming century-old Queenslander has been reinvented as a boutique hotel, offering cosy rooms, fluffy towels and scrummy breakfasts. **$244**

Monica's Cafe 43 Maple St ☎ 07 5494 2670, ⊕ monicascafe.com.au. This healthy modern café opens early for coffee and cooked breakfasts, and is the ideal place to pick up a lunchtime snack or sandwich, with burgers costing up to $20. Mon–Fri 6.30am–3pm, Sat & Sun 7am–3pm.

Eumundi

EUMUNDI, just off Highway 1 at the point where Hwy-12 heads down towards the coast at Noosa, 20km northeast, is a pretty rural village that has been almost entirely taken over by the success of its Wednesday and Saturday artisan **markets** (Wed 8am–1.30pm, Sat 7am–2pm; ⊕ eumundimarkets.com.au), reputed to be the biggest and best in Australia. Come on those days, and you can browse dozens of stalls selling local produce, fashion, art and crafts. Eumundi makes an appealing stop-off any day of the week, though, to relish the laidback cafés and secondhand bookstores that line its single broad street.

ARRIVAL AND DEPARTURE   EUMUNDI

By train Eumundi is a stop on the CityTrain line from/to Brisbane (2 daily; 2hr 20min).

By bus Bus #610 (8 services a day on Sat & Sun) links Eumundi with Nambour (20min) and Noosa (30min).

EATING AND NIGHTLIFE

Bohemian Bungalow 69 Memorial Drive ☎07 5442 8679, ⓦbohemianbungalow.com.au. Bright, breezy and very colourful, this bungalow cottage restaurant serves delicious, quirkily named dishes from Eggs Benedict ("Benny & the Jets"; $20) to cumin-rubbed lamb rump ("Bam Bah Lamb"; $34) and king prawn curry ("Gypsy Kings"; $35). Wed & Sun 8–11am & noon–2pm, Thurs & Fri noon–2pm & 5.30–9pm, Sat 7.30–11am, noon–2pm & 5.30–9pm.

Imperial Hotel 80 Memorial Drive ☎07 5442 8811, ⓦimperialhoteleumundi.com.au. The imposing, century-old Queenslander that's Eumandi's principal landmark serves lunch and dinner daily, with burgers and pizzas for around $18, and substantial meat and fish mains for more like $30; has a wonderful wraparound veranda; and it puts on live music from 7pm on Fri & Sat. Daily 10am–late.

Noosa

The Sunshine Coast's most exclusive resort, peppered with multimillion-dollar celebrity residences, **NOOSA** became popular in the 1960s, when the first **surfers** arrived to ride the fierce waves around the beautiful, beach-fringed headland that marks the mouth of the **Noosa River**. These days, it's also a haven for gourmets, beach bums, boating types and conservationists.

Resort activity is most heavily concentrated around **Noosa Heads**, stretched beside a long sandy spit where the river meets the sea. On the headland itself, in the pocket-sized **Noosa National Park**, lovely coastal walks lead through woods, where you've a good chance of seeing **koalas**, to successive sandy coves. South of the park, facing the open ocean, **Sunshine Beach** is a beach suburb with lower prices and pretensions, while to the west, sleepy **Noosaville** stretches beside the placid final reaches of the Noosa River, its waterfront lawns compensating for the lack of a beach.

Noosa Heads

Very much the commercial core of Noosa, **Noosa Heads** centres on **Hastings Street**, a tree-lined boulevard where the high-end shops, apartment blocks and restaurants obscure

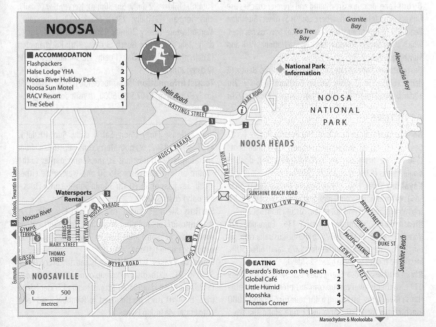

all sight of stunning **Main Beach**, which runs parallel just a few metres away. Thread your way between them to reach a long strip of fine sand that's always busy with families.

Noosa Junction, a far more down-to-earth area of shops, banks and cafés, lies 1km inland along **Sunshine Beach Road**.

Noosa National Park

No visitor should leave Noosa with making at least a brief foray into **Noosa National Park** on the headland itself. A breathtaking array of graded and clearly marked footpaths leads through the mature rainforest and coastal heathlands here, offering tremendous views. Walking routes radiate from the park **visitor centre** at the end of Park Road, which is easily reached by following the line of Hastings Street along the shoreline for roughly 1km. The most obvious destinations are the many fine **beaches**; both Tea Tree Bay and Alexandria Bay ("swimwear optional"), for example, have good sand pounded by unpatrolled surf. Recent **koala** sightings are noted on a blackboard at the visitor centre.

Sunshine Beach

South of the headland and national park, the Pacific coast suburb of **Sunshine Beach** features Noosa's longest and least crowded stretch of sand, plus some of the town's cheapest places to eat and stay.

Noosaville

Noosaville, 3km west of the Noosa Heads action, is a largely residential riverfront district where the restaurant scene has been growing in recent years. In the late afternoon, half of Noosa promenades along **Gympie Terrace** as the sinking sun colours a gentle tableau: mangroves on the opposite shore, pelicans eyeing anglers for scraps and landing clumsily midstream, and everything from cruise boats to windsurfers and kayaks out on the water.

ARRIVAL AND INFORMATION   NOOSA

By bus Long-distance Greyhound and Premier coaches use Noosa's main bus station, where Cooyar St meets Sunshine Beach Rd in Noosa Junction, as do local Sunbus services, which also connect Noosa Heads, Noosa National Park and Sunshine Beach.

Destinations Agnes Water (2 daily; 9hr); Airlie Beach (2 daily; 16hr); Ayr (2 daily; 20hr); Brisbane (6 daily; 2hr 30min); Bundaberg (4 daily; 7hr); Cairns (2 daily; 27hr

30min); Childers (2 daily; 5hr 30min); Hervey Bay (4 daily; 4hr); Ingham (2 daily; 23hr); Mackay (2 daily; 14hr); Maroochydore (every 30min; 15min); Mission Beach (2 daily; 25hr); Rainbow Beach (3 daily; 3hr); Rockhampton (2 daily; 10hr); Tin Can Bay (1 daily; 2hr 30min); Townsville (2 daily; 21hr).

Tourist information The visitor centre is at 61 Hastings St (daily 9am–5pm; ☎ 07 5430 5000, ⓦ visitnoosa.com.au).

ACTIVITIES

Boat rental Pelican Boat Hire, 180 Gympie Terrace (☎ 07 5449 7239, ⓦ pelicanboathire.com.au), have small boats ($40 for the first hour and $20/hr thereafter), double/single kayaks ($15/hr) and SUPs ($30/hr).

Kayaking Kayak Noosa, 194 Gympie Terrace (☎ 07 5455 5651, ⓦ kayaknoosa.com), rent gear and run superb guided trips along the river and out to sea, costing from $60.

Kitesurfing Adventure Sports, 136 Eumundi Rd, Noosaville (☎ 07 5455 6677, ⓦ kitesurfaustralia.com.au) run 2.5hr kitesurfing courses for $275, and offer SUPs, kayak and mountain-bike hire ($25/day).

River cruises Noosa Everglades Discovery (☎ 07 5449 0393, ⓦ thediscoverygroup.com.au) promote enjoyable Noosa River trips, including a 4hr tour for $75 and a BBQ lunch cruise for $110. For a quick ride along the river,

take a Noosa Ferry (Mon–Sat 6 daily, Sun 10 daily; ☎ 07 5449 8442, ⓦ noosaferry.com) upstream from Sheraton Jetty off Hastings St; the 40min journey to the suburb of Tewantin costs $15.50 one-way, while either an all-day pass or a BYO 1hr 30min Sunset cruise (Tues–Sat only) costs $22.50.

Surfing Merrick's Learn to Surf (☎ 0418 787 577, ⓦ learntosurf.com.au) offer board hire, group surf lessons every day at 9am and 1.30pm ($66) and stand-up paddleboarding tuition ($77).

Tours to Fraser Island Fraser Island Discovery (☎ 07 5449 0393, ⓦ thediscoverygroup.com.au) run one-day ($175) and two-day ($369) accommodated Fraser Island trips, by 4WD truck up the coast to Rainbow Beach and onto Fraser via Inskip Point.

ACCOMMODATION

★**Flashpackers** 102 Pacific Ave, Sunshine Beach ☎07 5455 4088, ⓦflashpackersnoosa.com. Superb boutique-style modern hostel with air-conditioned rooms, a lagoon pool, big screen and freebies including surf- and boogie-board use, town shuttle service, and breakfast. Dorms $\overline{\$34}$, doubles $\overline{\$80}$

Halse Lodge YHA 2 Halse Lane, off Noosa Drive, Noosa Heads ☎07 5447 3377, ⓦhalselodge.com.au. Charming 1888 Queenslander with shady balconies, in leafy grounds close to Main Beach. Facilities, including a pub-bistro, are excellent. Attracts all ages. Dorms $\overline{\$29}$, doubles $\overline{\$78}$

Noosa River Holiday Park 4 Russell St, Noosaville ☎07 5449 7050, ⓦnoosaholidayparks.com.au. Large campsite and van park with splendid river views, a 20min walk from the town centre, with its own small shop and shared kitchen facilities. No cabins or villas. Powered sites $\overline{\$45}$

Noosa Sun Motel 131 Gympie Terrace, Noosaville ☎07 5474 0477, ⓦnoosasunmotel.com.au. Simple but clean, spacious, comfortable and especially affordable self-contained motel-style apartments, close to the river – one of the best deals in town. $\overline{\$130}$

RACV Resort 94 Noosa Drive, Noosa Heads ☎07 5341 6300, ⓦracv.com.au. Beautifully located on the edge of pristine wetlands, this very stylish resort offers generously sized studios and apartments, a great pool and attentive service. $\overline{\$215}$

The Sebel 32 Hastings St, Noosa Heads ☎07 5474 6400, ⓦthesebel.com. Luxury apartment hotel arranged around a stylish pool in Noosa's shopping, dining and people-watching district. All units have full kitchens and separate dining area, and there's an on-site gym. $\overline{\$220}$

EATING

Berardo's Bistro on the Beach 49 Hastings St, Noosa Heads ☎07 5448 0888, ⓦberardos.com.au. This hip but casual restaurant, in a prime location right on the sand, is the best place to dine on Main Beach. The mod-Oz menu ranges from "small plates", like a Wagyu burger ($25), up to a $38 steak. Daily 6.30am–11.30am, noon–3.30pm & 5–8.30pm.

Global Café 13 William St, Noosaville ☎075474 1844. Backpacker-friendly café that serves up full breakfasts and a modest selection of globally inspired main meals for around $15, and turns into the liveliest bar around later on. Daily 7–11am & 5–10pm.

★**Little Humid** 235 Gympie Terrace, Noosaville ☎07 5449 9755, ⓦhumid.com.au. This pocket-sized place, spreading onto the pavement, is so popular with in-the-know local foodies that dinner reservations are essential. Menu highlights include spatchcock chicken with stuffed courgette flower, and braised lamb shank, both at $32. Tues 6–9pm, Wed–Sun noon–2pm & 6–9pm.

Mooshka 46 Duke St, Sunshine Beach ☎07 5474 5571, ⓦmooshka.com.au. Colourful and relaxed café-restaurant with a retro-bohemian feel in villagey Sunshine Beach. Wallet-friendly lunch ($19.50 with beer or wine) and daytime specials, plus substantial dinner curries and steaks for more like $34. Daily 10am–midnight.

Thomas Corner 201 Gympie Terrace, Noosaville ☎07 5470 2224, ⓦthomascorner.com.au. Perfect for people-watching, this designer restaurant stands beside Noosaville's main riverfront intersection. The imaginative menu focuses on flavoursome local produce, with plenty of seafood, and meat dishes like star anise braised beef cheek ($34). Mon–Fri 11.30am–9pm, Sat & Sun 8am–9pm (closed Sun pm in winter).

Lakes Cooroibah and Cootharaba

Immediately north of Noosa, a winding 6km stretch of the Noosa River pools into lakes **Cooroibah** and **Cootharaba** as it nears Tewantin. Placid, and fringed with paperbarks and reedbeds, the lakes look their best at dawn before there's any traffic; they're saltwater and average just 1m in depth, subject to tides.

You can **cruise** the lakes from Noosa, or drive up from Tewantin. Turn off the main road onto Werin Street at the school – there is a sign, but it's easy to miss – then turn left again and follow the signposts. Canoes and kayaks can be rented at all the lake townships from around $40 per day.

About 6km along, there's a boat ramp at **Cooroibah township** on Cooroibah's western shore. From there it's 10km by water to Lake Cootharaba, or 17km by road to lakeshore **Boreen Point**, a small community with fuel, a general store and the popular *Apollonian Hotel*. The road runs out another 4km on at **Elanda Point**, from where a footpath leads to Cootharaba's northernmost edge at **Kinaba**, which is, basically a visitor centre (unstaffed) positioned where Kin Kin Creek and the Noosa River spill lazily into the lake through thickets of mangroves, hibiscus and tea trees – the so-called **Everglades**.

A boardwalk from Kinaba continues to a bird hide, and the picnic area here is a former **corroboree ground**, which featured in the saga of Eliza Fraser (see box, p.351).

ACCOMMODATION AND EATING	LAKES COOROIBAH AND COOTHARABA
Apollonian Hotel 19 Laguna St, Boreen Point ☎ 07 5485 3100, ⓦ apollonianhotel.com.au. A low-slung, colonial-era wooden hotel serving cold drinks and pub lunches (meals noon–2pm & 6–8pm). Rooms are in an adjacent restored railway quarters building. Dorms $40, doubles $65	**Boreen Point Campground** The Esplanade, Boreen Point ☎ 07 5485 3244, ⓦ noosaholidayparks.com.au. Small council-run campsite on the shores of Lake Cootharaba with shady sites and adequate facilities. No cabins or units. Un/powered sites $23/$29

The Fraser Coast

A wonderland of giant dunes, dense forests, coloured sands and freshwater lakes, much loved by devotees of fishing and four-wheel driving in particular, the **Fraser Coast** stretches along the shoreline for almost 200km north of Noosa. For once, exploring doesn't have to consist of a macho battle against the elements; it's easy and inexpensive to rent tents and a 4WD and set off in comfort. The main destination is **Fraser Island**, an enormous, elongated and largely forested sand island, which somehow holds ample room to absorb the thousands of tourists who visit each year. On the way there, the small coastal townships of **Rainbow Beach** and **Tin Can Bay** offer a more laidback perspective on the region, with another long strip of beach and the chance to feed wild **dolphins**. While most ferries to Fraser Island depart from the **Hervey Bay** area, further north – a tourist hub that also offers seasonal **whale-watching cruises** – you can also get there from Rainbow Beach.

The abundant fresh water, seafood and vegetation along the Fraser Coast supported a very healthy Aboriginal population; campfires along the beach allowed Matthew Flinders to navigate Fraser Island at night in 1802. Although the area was declared an Aboriginal reserve in the early 1860s, Europeans were soon flocking in, after **gold** was discovered at Gympie in 1867. The gold rush saved the fledgling Queensland from bankruptcy, but ever-increasing white settlement saw the Aboriginal population cleared out, and the area opened up for recreation and logging. Since 2009, the coast has been protected as part of the UNESCO Great Sandy Biosphere Reserve, which extends from Noosa to Bundaberg.

GETTING AROUND	THE FRASER COAST
By car The main route into the area is off Highway 1, 60km north of Noosa at Gympie for Tin Can Bay and Rainbow Beach, or a further 85km north up the highway at Maryborough for Hervey Bay. **By bus** Long-distance buses serve Tin Can Bay and Rainbow Beach daily.	**On a tour** Tours around the region generally run from Noosa, Rainbow Beach and Hervey Bay (the best place to arrange self-drive 4WD expeditions); those from Noosa avoid the highway and instead use 4WD to zip straight up Cooloola's sands from Tewantin to Rainbow Beach, a picturesque 40km run of uninterrupted sand.

Tin Can Bay

TIN CAN BAY, 100km north of Noosa by road, occupies a long wooded spit jutting north into a convoluted inlet. It's a leafy, sprawling place where the main drag, **Tin Can Bay Road**, runs for a couple of kilometres past a small shopping centre, post office and a handful of places to stay and eat before petering out at the Yacht Club. The most likely reason to come here is to see – and even feed – the wild **Indo-Pacific dolphins** that pull in around 8am most mornings at **Norman Point** boat ramp next to *Barnacles* kiosk.

ARRIVAL AND DEPARTURE	TIN CAN BAY
By bus Greyhound buses set down just off the main road in Bream St.	Destinations Brisbane (1 daily; 5hr 45min); Hervey Bay (1 daily; 1hr 25min); Rainbow Beach (1 daily; 35min).

ACCOMMODATION AND EATING

Barnacles Norman Point ☎07 5486 4899, ⊛barnaclesdolphins.com.au. As well as brewing decent coffee and serving good, inexpensive all-day breakfasts and lunches (from $6), this café arranges a daily 8am dolphin-feeding session, charging $5 admission and $5 for fish to give the dolphins. Daily 7am–5pm.

Kingfisher Caravan Park 48 The Esplanade ☎07 5486 4198, ⊛kingfishercaravanpark.com.au. Well-equipped park with the ocean easily accessible to either side, offering nine very comfortable shared-facility cabins as well as camping. Un/powered sites $25/30, cabins $85

Rainbow Beach

RAINBOW BEACH is a very casual knot of streets set just back from a fantastic **beach** facing into **Wide Bay**. The one access road, logically enough called **Rainbow Beach Road**, dead-ends above the surf, at a **shopping centre** holding cafés, a pub and a service station, plus a post office and store. The main recreations here are fishing, surfing and kiteboarding – a moderate southeasterly is almost always blowing – which can be arranged through your accommodation.

You can take a 4WD (when the tide is right) or walk 10km south along Rainbow Beach to the coloured sand cliffs at **Double Island Point**, whose streaks of red, orange and white are caused by minerals leaching down from the clifftop. On the far side of the point lies the rusty frame of the *Cherry Venture* **shipwreck**, beached during a storm in 1973.

ARRIVAL AND DEPARTURE

RAINBOW BEACH

By bus Long-distance buses pull in at Spectrum St, opposite Rainbow's three hostels.
Destinations Brisbane (2 daily; 5hr 30min); Hervey Bay (2 daily; 2hr); Noosa (2 daily; 2hr 45min); Tin Can Bay (1 daily; 35min).

By car Rainbow Beach lies 80km from Gympie and 48km from Tin Can Bay; Rainbow Beach Rd cuts away south from Tin Can Bay Rd 11km short of Tin Can Bay itself.
By ferry Barges connect Inskip Point, 10km north of Rainbow Beach, with Fraser Island (see p.350).

ACTIVITIES

4WD Adventure 4WD Centre, 13 Spectrum St (☎07 5486 3288, ⊛adventurecentre.com.au), rents 4WDs and camping equipment.
Fraser Island Tours Dropbear Adventures (☎04 8733 3606, ⊛dropbearadventures.com.au) run fun tag-along

camping tours from Rainbow Beach and Noosa, hosted by enthusiastic guides and offering ample food, decent vehicles and hot showers (two days, one night for $395; three days, two nights for$465).

ACCOMMODATION AND EATING

Café Jilarty 12 Rainbow Beach Rd ☎07 5486 3277. Friendly all-day café, offering full cooked breakfasts for $10–15, and wraps, salads and fish'n'chips at similar prices – the fresh-caught mackerel is sensational. Daily 6am–8pm.
★ **Debbie's Place** 30 Kurana St ☎07 5486 3506, ⊛rainbowbeachaccommodation.com.au. Spotless white Queenslander, with motel rooms and self-contained one- to three-bed apartments, plus spacious verandas and a nice BBQ terrace. $150
Dingo's Backpacker Resort 18 Spectrum St ☎07 3139 1649, ⊛dingosresort.com. Basic but perfectly adequate party hostel, with a licensed bar, hammock-bedecked "chill-out gazebo", and $6 burger dinners; most guests are

here for their Fraser Island tours, lasting one day ($159) or three days, two nights ($460). Dorms $28, doubles $80
Plantation Bar & Bistro Rainbow Beach Hotel ☎07 5486 3008, ⊛rainbowhotel.com.au. Landmark colonial-style pub, nicely spruced up and serving "pub favourites" including pizzas and burgers for $20, plus lamb cutlets and huge steaks for around $35. Daily 11.30am–2pm & 5.30–8pm.
Rainbow Beach Holiday Village 13 Rainbow Beach Rd ☎07 5486 3222, ⊛rainbowbeachholidayvillage .com. A large tidy park right in the heart of town, holding assorted accommodation options (chalets, villas and studios) and sites. Un/powered sites $41/50, villas $145

Hervey Bay

More a conglomeration of low-key residential – and especially, retirement – suburbs than a tourist destination in its own right, **HERVEY BAY** sprawls along the coast roughly

3

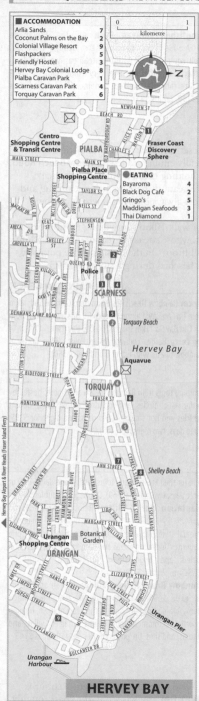

ACCOMMODATION

Arlia Sands	7
Coconut Palms on the Bay	2
Colonial Village Resort	9
Flashpackers	5
Friendly Hostel	8
Hervey Bay Colonial Lodge	8
Pialba Caravan Park	1
Scarness Caravan Park	4
Torquay Caravan Park	6

EATING

Bayaroma	4
Black Dog Café	2
Gringo's	5
Maddigan Seafoods	3
Thai Diamond	1

HERVEY BAY

200km north of Noosa. Though very spread out, it's a straightforward enough place, which most people visit only to catch a ferry to **Fraser Island**, or, in spring, to venture into the bay to spot **whales**.

Pialba is Hervey Bay's commercial centre, an ugly blob of car parks, shopping malls and industrial estates where the road from Maryborough enters town. Around 1km north of there, the **Esplanade** runs east along a wooded foreshore in a pleasant 7km string of motels, cafés and shops, passing successively through the beachfront suburbs of **Scarness** and **Torquay**, and on to beach-less **Urangan** with its protruding pier and boat harbour for whale watching.

At the **Fraser Coast Discovery Sphere** (166 Old Maryborough Rd, Pialba; daily 10am–4pm; $5.50; ☎07 4191 2610, ⊛frasercoastdiscoverysphere.com.au), there's a walk-through display giving you the lowdown on Hervey Bay's whales, dugongs and indigenous Butchella people through a mixture of exhibits, information boards and a twenty-minute audiovisual show.

ARRIVAL AND DEPARTURE
HERVEY BAY

By plane Hervey Bay Airport (☎07 4194 8100, ⊛frasercoastairport.com.au), 5km south of Urangan off the Booral Rd, is used by scheduled services to and from Brisbane and Sydney, as well as charter flights to Fraser Island with Air Fraser Island (☎1300 172 706, ⊛airfraserisland.com.au), and to Lady Elliot Island with Seair Pacific (☎1300 473 247, ⊛seairpacific.com.au). Bay2Dore (☎07 4124 3516, ⊛bay2dore.com.au) offer a door-to-door shuttle bus service between Hervey Bay and the airport from $15 one-way.

By car To reach Hervey Bay from the north–south road, turn off Highway 1 at Maryborough – 150km north of Noosa – and head northeast for 35km on Route 57.

By bus Long-distance buses wind up in Pialba's Transit Centre at the Centro Shopping Complex, off Boat Harbour Drive.

Destinations Airlie Beach (3 daily; 14hr); Brisbane (8 daily; 4–7hr); Cairns (2 daily; 23–27hr); Noosa (3 daily; 4hr 30min); Rockhampton (2 daily; 6hr 15min); Townsville (2 daily; 17hr 30min).

By ferry Passenger ferries and barges to Fraser Island depart River Heads, 18km south of Hervey Bay (see p.353).

GETTING AROUND

By bus Fraser Wide Bay Transit run regular services around and between Hervey Bay, Urangan and Maryborough (daily 5am–7pm; ☎07 4121 4070, ⊛widebaytransit.com.au).

By taxi Hervey Bay Taxi Service ☎13 10 08.

INFORMATION AND ACTIVITIES

Tourist information The visitor centre is at 227 Maryborough–Hervey Bay Rd (daily 9am–5pm; ☎1800 811 728, ⓦ visitfrasercoast.com).

Watersports Aquavue, 415 The Esplanade, Torquay (☎07 4125 5528, ⓦ aquavue.com.au), rent sailing catamarans ($120/3hr), SUPs and kayaks (both $20/hr), and jet skis for tours to Fraser Island (from $250).

TOURS

Guided tours to **Fraser Island** from Hervey Bay range from day-trips starting at around $150, to two- and three-day camping trips ($300/$400). Many options, especially for backpackers, come in the form of guided self-drive tag-along tours, where everyone piles into a convoy of 4WDs and takes their turn at tackling Fraser's terrain – the island's roads are 4WD only (see p.354). Check exactly what you're paying for; cheaper trips might sound attractive but can come with hidden charges, for fuel or food.

Air Fraser Island ☎1300 172 706, ⓦ airfraserisland .com.au. Air tours make a nifty way to see the sights of Fraser, and can work out cheaper than one-day tours. Air Fraser Island offer aerial whale spotting and day-tours to Fraser, including a fly/drive option for $250 that includes 4WD rental to explore Fraser on your own.

Cool Dingo Tours ☎07 4120 3333, ⓦ cooldingotour .com. Fraser Island Tours aimed at the young and adventurous 18–35 crowd, from $360 for one night up to $625 for four nights, including bunk accommodation.

Fraser Explorer Tours ☎07 4194 9222, ⓦ fraserexplorertours.com.au. Day-trips with great vehicles and first-rate guides, plus an excellent BBQ lunch, from $179, plus other options including overnight trips with accommodation at Eurong (from $330).

ACCOMMODATION

Arlia Sands 13–15 Ann St, Torquay ☎07 4125 4360, ⓦ arliasands.com.au. Comfortable, well-equipped apartments sleeping up to four, in a quiet street off the Esplanade – an ideal family option. **$120**

Coconut Palms on the Bay 335 The Esplanade, Scarness ☎07 4124 0200, ⓦ coconutpalmsonthebay .com.au. Small but well-presented apartments, with Balinese-inspired decor and friendly hosts. The tropical landscaped swimming pool adds to the calming atmosphere. **$123**

Colonial Village Resort 820 Boat Harbour Drive, Urangan ☎07 4125 1844, ⓦ colonialvillageresort.com .au. Leafy resort set in extensive gardens within easy reach of Urangan Boat Harbour, and incorporating a YHA hostel. As well as dorms and budget doubles, they also offer everything from camping to deluxe en suites ($90) and five-person cabins ($149). Facilities include a pool, restaurant, pub and tennis courts, plus shuttle pick-up from Pialba (but not Torquay). Dorms **$27**, doubles **$62**

★ **Flashpackers** 195 Torquay Terrace, Torquay ☎07 4124 1366, ⓦ flashpackersherveybay.com. Gleaming brand-new hostel, just back from Torquay Beach, offering four- to eight-bed dorms and en-suite doubles, plus a pool, movie nights, Fraser Island tours, Greyhound pick-ups and town shuttle. Dorms **$26**, doubles **$80**

Friendly Hostel 182 Torquay Rd, Pialba ☎07 4124 4107, ⓦ friendlyhostel.com.au. Relaxed, intimate guesthouse, with comfy dorms (most without bunks), pleasant doubles, family-friendly two-bed apartments, free bike rental and a nice family atmosphere. Dorms **$26**, doubles **$57**, apartments **$150**

Hervey Bay Colonial Lodge 94 Cypress St, Torquay ☎07 4125 1073, ⓦ herveybaycoloniallodge.com.au. Spotless, great-value, modern one- and two-bed self-catering apartments on a peaceful street a block from the waterfront, with a good pool and tour desk. **$95**

Pialba, Scarness & Torquay Beachfront Caravan Parks The Esplanade ☎07 4128 1399, ☎07 4128 1274 & ☎07 4125 1578 ⓦ beachfronttouristparks.com.au. Well-shaded, council-run beachfront caravan parks right by the beach; all locations are also handy for shops and restaurants. Un/powered sites **$32/$39**

EATING

Bayaroma 428 The Esplanade, Torquay ☎07 4125 1515, ⓦ bayaroma.com.au. Popular café that's renowned for its all-day breakfasts – the full works, with a chunky lamb sausage, costs $19.50 – but also serves good-value lunches, with pretty much everything from Thai basil salad to garlic prawns pasta costing under $20. Daily 6am–3.30pm.

Black Dog Café 381 The Esplanade, near Denman Camp Rd, Torquay ☎07 4124 3177, ⓦ theblackdogcafe .com.au. Prominent east-meets-west restaurant at a busy seafront intersection, with loads of outdoor seating. The eclectic menu ranges from $7.50 sushi rolls to $16.50 prawns with wonton noodles and a $37 half-lobster salad. Mon–Sat 8.30am–2pm & 5.45–8.30pm, Sun 8.30am–2pm.

Gringo's 16 Bideford St, Torquay ☎07 4125 1644,

3

3

WHALE WATCHING FROM HERVEY BAY

Humpback whales are among the most exciting marine creatures you can encounter: growing to 16m long and weighing up to 36 tonnes, they make their presence known from a distance by "**breaching**" – making spectacular, crashing leaps out of the water – and expelling jets of spray as they exhale. Before 1952, around ten thousand whales made the annual journey between the Antarctic and the tropics to breed and give birth in shallow coastal waters; a decade later whaling had reduced the population to just two hundred. Now protected, an estimated 25,000 pass along the eastern coast of Australia on their annual migration. Around two-thirds of those enter **Hervey Bay**, making it one of the best places to spot humpbacks in the country.

The **whale-watching season** here lasts from August to November, a little later than northern waters because Fraser Island angles outwards, deflecting the creatures away from the bay as they migrate north, but funnelling them in to the constricted waters when returning south. The town makes the most of their visit with an August **Whale Festival** (w herveybaywhalefestival.com.au), and operators are always searching for new gimmicks to promote day-cruises and flights.

In the early months you're more likely to see mature **bulls**, which, being inquisitive, swim directly under boats and raise their heads out of the water, almost close enough to touch. You may even observe them fighting over mating rights and hear their eerie mating songs; of course you may also see and hear nothing at all. The later part of the season sees **mothers and playful calves** coming into the bay to rest before their great migration south, and is a good time to watch the humpbacks breaching. Whether all this voyeurism disturbs the animals is unclear, but they seem at least tolerant of the attention.

WHALE-WATCHING CRUISES

Cruises last for a morning or a full day and cost around $115 per person. Some boats carry up to 150 passengers without necessarily feeling overcrowded – check the boat size, viewing space, speed of vessel and how many will be going before committing yourself. Breakfast or lunch is usually included. Most boat operators continue to offer cruises outside the whale-watching season and spend four hours searching for dolphins, turtles and – with real luck – dugongs (sea cows) for around $95 per person.

Quick Cat II ☎ 07 4128 9611, w herveybaywhale watch.com.au. Speedy and comparatively small purpose-built catamaran with hydrophones and a large viewing deck. Morning and afternoon departures every day.

Spirit of Hervey Bay ☎ 1800 642 544, w spiritofherveybay.com. Big boats with hydrophones and underwater portals to view the whales if they come close, offering 4hr and 5hr cruises.

Tasman Venture ☎ 1800 620 322, w tasmanventure.com.au. Half-day tours, morning or afternoon, on purpose-built boats equipped with hydrophone, underwater viewing windows, whale-watching platform and whale cam.

w gringos.com.au. Good Mexican with all the usual offerings, spiced to your preference. Even the most expensive steak or seafood mains only cost around $22, and bean fillings make an alternative to meat. Daily 5.30–9pm.

Maddigan Seafoods 401 The Esplanade, Torquay ☎ 07 4128 4202. As you might hope from what's primarily a fishmonger's, this simple takeaway café sells supremely fresh seafood, to enjoy at pavement tables outside. Half a dozen battered mussels for $4.50, and

fish'n'chips made with everything from barramundi to trout, the cheapest option being mackerel for $9.50. Daily 9am–7.30pm.

Thai Diamond 353 The Esplanade, Scarness ☎ 07 4124 4855, w thaidiamondweb.com. Substantial but inexpensive Thai favourites – crispy chicken $16.50, prawn green curry $22 – in an unassuming cafeteria-style setting, with cheerful service. Mon & Tues 5.30–9pm, Wed–Sun 11.30am–2pm & 5.30–9pm.

Fraser Island

A glorious offshore Eden, **Fraser Island** (or K'gari) is the world's largest sand island, measuring 123km from top to bottom. Accreted from two million years' worth of sediments, swept north from New South Wales, it boasts scenery ranging from silent forests and beaches sculpted by wind and surf to crystal-clear streams and dark, tannin-stained lakes. Above all, it remains very much a wilderness, preserved largely because it holds almost no paved roads, just a very limited network of rugged narrow tracks that are only negotiable in **4WD** vehicles.

Fraser Island's colossal scale is best appreciated as you travel the 90km length of its razor-edge east coast. With the sea as a constant, the dunes along the shoreline seem to evolve before your eyes – in places low and soft, elsewhere hard and worn into intriguing canyons. On the beach itself, 4WD vehicles race along the open sands. Progress through the forests of the interior, by contrast, is much slower, creating more subtle impressions of age and permanence – a primal world predating European settlement – that are only brought into question when the view opens suddenly onto a lake. In 1992, the entire island was recognized as a UNESCO **World Heritage Site**, with all but a few pockets of freehold land and the tiny township of Eurong belonging to the Great Sandy National Park.

The east-coast settlements of **Happy Valley** and **Eurong** have stores, telephones, bars and fuel, and there's another well-equipped store with fuel and café at *Frasers at Cathedral Beach*, but no shops or restaurant at *Dilli*. You'll save money by bringing whatever you need with you (including powerful insect repellent).

The west coast

Ferries from the mainland reach Fraser Island at either *Kingfisher Bay Resort* or Wanggoolba Creek on the **west coast**, or **Hook Point** at its southern tip. As the western side of the island is almost entirely inaccessible to vehicles, however, consisting of a mix of mangrove swamp and treacherously soft beaches, arriving passengers invariably head directly inland.

Central Station

Most visitors get their bearings by making a first stop at **Central Station** in the middle of Fraser Island, halfway from Wanggoolba Creek to Eurong on the east coast. This former logging depot, sheltering beneath some monstrous bunya pines, holds little more than a campsite, a telephone and an information hut.

A half-hour stroll from Central Station, along a trail that follows the upper reaches of **Wanggoolba Creek** – a magical, sandy-bottomed stream that's so clear it's hard at first to see the water flowing across the forest floor – brings you to **Pile Valley**, where some astonishing, enormous satinay trees soar 60m into the sky. The ultra-dense timber from these trees, which was used as sidings on the Suez Canal, was what attracted the loggers to Fraser Island; very few satinay now remain.

HOW FRASER ISLAND GOT ITS NAME

To the Kabi Aborigines, **Fraser Island** is **K'gari**, a beautiful woman so taken with the earth that she stayed behind after creation, her eyes becoming lakes that mirrored the sky and teemed with wildlife so that she wouldn't be lonely.

The story behind the European name is far less enchanting. In 1836, survivors of the wreck of the *Stirling Castle*, including the captain's wife **Eliza Fraser**, landed at Waddy Point. Although runaway convicts had already been welcomed into Kabi life, the castaways suffered "dreadful slavery, cruel toil and excruciating tortures". Two months after the death of the captain, Eliza was presented as a prize during a corroboree at Lake Cootharaba, only to be dramatically rescued by former convict John Graham, who had lived with the Kabi and was part of a search party alerted by other survivors from the *Stirling Castle*. While the exact details of Eliza's captivity remain obscure – she produced several conflicting accounts – her role as an "anti-Crusoe" inspired both novelist Patrick White and artist Sidney Nolan.

The southern lakes

Several **lakes** can be reached on foot, along decent unpaved roads, from Central Station. A 9km track leads north to **Lake McKenzie**, the most popular on the island. With its clear, tea-coloured water reflecting a blue sky, this is a wonderful place to spend a day, even if it's often crowded. A long beach of white sand fringes the side you can access, and swimming is irresistible. You can't walk all the way round the lake, though, and neither are you permitted to bring food to the shore – to deter dingoes, you can only picnic in a fenced-off precinct beside the car park.

Of the other nearby lakes, **Birrabeen**, 8km south of Central Station, is largely hemmed in by trees, while **Boomanjin**, perched in a basin above the island's water table 8km further on, is more open. The privately run *Dilli Village* is on the coast not far beyond (see p.355).

The northern interior

The northern reaches of Fraser Island's wooded **interior** make a striking contrast to the busy coast and popular southern lakes, and see relatively few visitors. The name of **Yidney Scrub** may not sound compelling, but it refers to the only major stand of **rainforest** left on the island, where the majestic trees include towering kauri pines.

The road up through Yidney from Happy Valley takes in **Boomerang** and **Allom** lakes on its long route to the east-coast beach near the *Maheno* shipwreck. You can camp at Allom, a small lake surrounded by pines and cycads, and completely different to its flashier southern cousins. Further north, another road heads in from Dundubara township to **Lake Bowarrady**, the island's highest perched lake.

Seventy-Five-Mile Beach

Seventy-Five-Mile Beach runs down the entire eastern shoreline of Fraser Island, washed on one side by the endlessly pounding surf. Assuming you approach the beach from Central Station, you reach it at **Eurong**, a complex of motel accommodation and shop stands. Immediately beyond that, the road simply opens onto the sands. This broad, trackless expanse serves as Fraser's main thoroughfare, with 4WD vehicles hurtling to and fro, pedestrians and anglers hugging the shore, and tents dotting the foredunes.

Lake Wabby

From the beach, 5km north of Eurong, a 2km track leads across sand blows to **Lake Wabby**, a small but deep patch of blue below the dunes with excellent swimming potential. The shifting sands of the easterly **Hammerstone Blow** are slowly engulfing this freshwater lake; in another century it will certainly be gone. It's deceptively shallow, so don't be tempted to dive.

Rainbow Gorge

A short trail runs from the beach between two blows, 16km north of Eurong, through a hot, silent desert landscape where sandblasted trees emerge denuded by their ordeal.

STAYING SAFE ON FRASER

Visitors to Fraser Island need to bear a couple of **safety points** in mind. As there have never been domestic dogs on the island, Fraser's **dingoes** are considered to be Australia's purest strain, and they used to be a common sight. After one killed a child in 2000, however, dingoes that frequented public areas were culled, so you probably won't see many. If you do encounter some, keep your distance, back off rather than run if approached, and – despite their misleadingly scrawny appearance – **don't feed them**, as it's the expectation of hand-outs that makes them aggressive.

You should also be aware that **sharks** and severe **currents** make it too dangerous to venture into the sea. If you want to swim, stick to the freshwater lakes.

Incredibly, a dismal spring seeps water into the valley, eagerly swallowed by the sand; "upstream" are the stubby, eroded red fingers of **Rainbow Gorge**. You can climb up the Kirrar Sandblow for stunning views.

Eli Creek

At picturesque **Eli Creek**, 7km north of Rainbow Gorge, a powerful permanent stream gushes briskly and almost invisibly between verdant banks before spilling into the sea. Sand-filtered, this is Fraser's loveliest **swimming spot**, though the water is always icy cold, and many visitors simply wade or float downstream between the two separate footbridges just back from the beach.

Shortly before Eli Creek, signposted just back from the beach, the tiny settlement of **Happy Valley** offers supplies and accommodation.

The Maheno shipwreck and the Pinnacles

The rusting *Maheno* **shipwreck**, stranded on the beach 7km north of Eli Creek, is all that remains of a former luxury liner, which as a hospital ship made six landings at Gallipoli's Anzac Cove in 1915, and ran aground here in 1935. Now little more than a skeleton, eroded by the elements, it marks the start of a line of multicoloured sand cliffs known as the **Pinnacles**.

From behind the **Dundubara campsite**, 6km further north, a tiring, hot, 4km walk leads up **Wungul Sandblow**, through what feels like the Sahara desert. Turn around at the top though, and the glaring grey dune-scape is set off by distant views of a rich blue sea.

Indian Head and the Champagne Pools

Indian Head, 20km north of Dundubara, is a rare – and pretty tall – rocky outcrop, the anchor around which the island may well have originally formed. The walk to the top is not hard, with rewards on a sunny day likely to include views down into the surf full of dolphins, sharks and other large fish chasing each other. In season you'll certainly see pods of whales too, breaching or just lying on their backs, slapping the water with outstretched fins.

From here the road turns inland before returning to the beach at the **Champagne Pools**, a cluster of shallow, safe swimming pools above the surf line, which marks as far north as vehicles are allowed to travel.

ARRIVAL AND DEPARTURE   FRASER ISLAND

By plane Air Fraser Island (☎1300 172 706, ⓦairfraserisland.com.au) run tours and charter flights from Hervey Bay. Day-trips cost from $150, fly/drive trips including 4WD rental from $250. They also offer 15min scenic flights that take off from Seventy-Five-Mile Beach ($75), one of only two places in the world where passenger aircraft are permitted to land on the beach; the planes simply hang around there all day, touting for passengers.

By ferry from River Heads Fraser Island Barges (☎1300 227 437, ⓦfraserislandferry.com.au) connect River Heads, 18km south of Hervey Bay, with *Kingfisher Bay Resort* (5–6 daily; 50min) and Wanggoolba Creek (3 daily; 30min) on Fraser's west coast. A round trip on either route costs $58 for foot passengers, or $175 per vehicle, including driver and three passengers. The only place you can drive a 2WD vehicle on Fraser Island is at the *Kingfisher Bay Resort* itself, but it can still work out cheaper for resort guests to bring their vehicles than to leave them in Kingfisher's River Heads

car park ($20/$30/$45 for one/two/three nights). There's no public transport to River Heads; a taxi from Hervey Bay costs around $40.

By ferry from Inskip Point Mantaray Barges, 66 Rainbow Beach Rd, Rainbow Beach (☎07 5486 3935, ⓦmantarayfraserislandbarge.com.au) shuttle back and forth on the 10min crossing between Inskip Point, 10km north of Rainbow Beach, and Hook Point on Fraser's south coast. The first barge leaves Inskip Point at 6am and the last departs Fraser at 5.30pm. Only 4WD vehicles are allowed – and it's a difficult landing, not suitable for novice drivers – with a round trip costing $120 for the vehicle and all passengers. No reservations are taken.

On a tour Guided day-trips from Hervey Bay (see p.349) are a good way to whip around the main sights – usually some of the forest, a couple of lakes, and the beach up to the *Maheno* shipwreck or so – but can leave you with barely a glimpse of the island's true wilderness, or its wildlife. Most backpackers' hostels in the region, including those in Rainbow Beach and Noosa, organize day-trips and self-drive camping tours to Fraser Island, usually lasting two to three days; prices are low, but you may have to wait a few days until they've managed to fill a vehicle, and extras like food, bedding and fuel can really bump up the cost.

GETTING AROUND

BY 4WD

To drive on Fraser Island, you must have a 4WD vehicle, plus a permit, which costs $46.65 direct from QPWS (T 13 74 68, W nprsr.qld.gov.au), and is also available through rental companies and tour operators. Seventy-Five-Mile Beach on the east coast serves as the main highway, with access roads running inland to popular spots, and other tracks, always slower than the beach, crisscrossing the interior. Make sure that you pick up a tide timetable from barge operators, as sections of the beach are only reliably negotiable at low tide.

3

4WD RENTAL

Assembling your own group and renting a 4WD to explore Fraser offers more flexibility for experienced drivers, and will probably work out cheaper than taking a tour. Conditions include a minimum driver age of 21 and a $1000 deposit – advertised prices are normally for renting the vehicle only, so tents, food, fuel, and ferry and vehicle permits are extra. Renting a 4WD over three days, expect to pay around $180 per day for two-seaters such as a Suzuki, $205 per day for a five-person Land Rover Defender and around $230 per day for an eight-seater Toyota Landcruiser, including standard 4WD insurance. Note that older ex-army Land Rovers, while mechanically sound, are uncomfortable and best avoided.

Fraser Magic 5 Kruger Court, Urangan, Hervey Bay T 07 4125 6612, W fraser4wdhire.com.au. This company has been around forever, and offers packages including 4WD rental, camping gear, barge transfer and vehicle/camping permits.

Aussie Trax 56 Boat Harbour Drive, Pialba, Hervey Bay T 07 4124 4433, W fraserisland4wd.com.au. Nifty two-person Suzuki Jimnys and larger eight-person Landcruisers, usually rented as part of a package deal that includes barge tickets, vehicle permits, and potentially accommodation at Happy Valley on Fraser Island.

ON FOOT

Walking is an excellent way to see Fraser Island. One established three-day circuit, which requires no special skills beyond endurance and the ability to set up camp before you pass out, runs from Central Station south past lakes Birrabeen and Boomanjin, then up the coast and back to Central Station via lakes Wabby and McKenzie. Highlights include circumnavigating the lakes, chance encounters with goannas and dingoes, and the energetic burst up Wongi Sandblow for sweeping views out to sea. The longer Fraser Island Great Walk, a 90km (or six- to eight-day) inland trek between *Dilli Village* and Happy Valley, takes in Lake McKenzie, Central Station and Lake Wabby.

ACCOMMODATION AND EATING

All Fraser Island **accommodation** must be **booked** in advance, and lies, apart from *Kingfisher Bay Resort*, along the east-coast Seventy-Five-Mile Beach. With a National Parks camping permit (bookings T 13 13 04, W nsrpr.qld.gov.au), you can **camp** anywhere along the eastern foreshore except where signs forbid. If you need tank water, showers, toilets and gas BBQs use the National Park campsites at Central Station, Dundubara and Waddy Point. Lakes Boomanjin and Allom have flushing toilets.

4WD DRIVING ADVICE

Every 4WD rental company on Fraser Island is obliged to protect both itself and its customers by giving a full briefing on the island and **driving practicalities**. General 4WD advice is to lower your **tyre pressure** to around 12psi to increase traction on the sand, but this isn't generally necessary (if you get bogged, however, try it first before panicking). Rain and high tides harden sand surfaces, making driving easier. Most **accidents** involve collisions on blind corners, rolling in soft sand (avoid hard braking or making sudden turns – you don't have to be going very fast for your front wheels to dig in, turning you over), and trying to cross apparently insignificant creeks on the beach at 60kph – 4WDs are not invincible. Don't drive your vehicle into the surf; you'll probably get stuck, and even if you don't, the salt water will rust out the bodywork within days (something rental companies can easily test for, and will charge you for). Exposed "**coffee rocks**" along some areas of the beach can be very tricky to navigate; use inland bypasses where possible. And give **pedestrians** on the beach a wide berth; they can't hear vehicles above the roar of the surf, and won't be aware of your presence until you barrel through from behind.

Cathedrals on Fraser ☎07 4127 9177, ⓦcathedrals
onfraser.com.au. Long-established campsite with fuel, café,
bottle shop and well-stocked store, offering shady sites,
permanent tents (no linen) and self-contained units (the
cheapest share bathrooms). Un/powered sites $\underline{$29/39}$, tents
$\underline{$49}$, units $\underline{$160}$

Dilli Village ☎07 4127 9130. Not far from Lake
Boomanjin, this pretty, dingo-fenced private university-
owned campsite is just 24km north of Hook Point. Un/
powered sites $\underline{$20/25}$, bunkhouses $\underline{$50}$, cabins $\underline{$120}$

Eurong Beach Resort ☎07 4120 9600, ⓦeurong
.com.au. Complex of spacious, if sterile, motel-style rooms
and two-bed apartments at the end of the road from
Central Station, with a buffet restaurant open for all meals
daily (breakfast $10.50 or $19.50; lunch $19.50; dinner
$24.50). $\underline{$114}$

★ **Kingfisher Bay Resort** ☎07 4120 3333,
ⓦkingfisherbay.com. Set in beautiful coastal wetlands
on the west shore, served by direct barges from River
Heads, this ecofriendly, architecturally imaginative resort is
Fraser's most luxurious option. Accommodation is in lodge-
style hotel rooms and self-contained villas, and there are
two excellent restaurants – dinner mains like braised duck
legs with bok choy at the pricier *Seabelle* cost around $40
– as well as a couple of pools and a lively bar. The wild
on-site lagoon offers great birdwatching; the beach (not
safe for swimming) glows at sunset, and numerous
activities and tours are available. $\underline{$126}$

Yidney Rocks Beachfront Units ☎07 4127 9167,
ⓦyidneyrocks.com.au. Great-value self-contained one-
bedroom studios and apartments sleeping up to eight near
Happy Valley, with stunning ocean views and BBQs. $\underline{$220}$

The Southern Reef

North of Fraser Island, and 80km offshore, a cluster of tiny, coral-fringed islands
– **cays**, formed by sand that's carried up the coast by ocean currents and swept out to
sea by Fraser's massive outwards-leaning edge – mark the southernmost tip of
Queensland's mighty **Great Barrier Reef**. Successive coastal settlements such as
Bundaberg, **1770** and **Gladstone** each offer access to a specific cay; whether you go for a
day-trip or an overnight stay in a resort, there's the potential for some excellent **scuba
diving**. Bundaberg – along with the nearby hamlet of **Childers** – also lies at the heart of
a rich sugar cane, fruit and vegetable farming area, and both are popular places to find
short-term crop-picking **work** in the harvest season (April–Sept).

Childers and around

The pretty, one-horse highway town of **CHILDERS** stands 60km north of Hervey Bay.
Heritage-listed Queenslanders lining central Churchill Street include the photogenic
Federal Hotel, a wooden pub built in 1907, and the musty, bottle-filled **Old Pharmacy**
at no. 90 (Mon–Fri 9am–3pm, Sat 9am–1pm; $5; ☎0800 376 359), which is stuffed
with dental equipment, specimen jars and medicine bottles, plus a fearsome-looking
dentist's chair.

In 2000, a disastrous **fire** burned down the old *Palace Backpackers*, killing fifteen
people. The rebuilt site now includes a tasteful, low-key memorial, with a visitor
centre opposite.

Flying High Bird Sanctuary

5km northwest of Childers, where Bruce Highway meets Old Creek Rd in Apple Tree Creek • Daily except Sat 7.30am–5pm, closed on rainy
days • $20 • ☎07 4126 3777

The **Flying High Bird Sanctuary**, 5km up the highway from Childers, is the largest
walk-through aviary in Australia. Expect to see just about every type of Australian
parrot and finch zipping around, squawking, or chewing the furnishings, plus an
owl enclosure.

ARRIVAL AND INFORMATION	CHILDERS AND AROUND

By bus Childers is connected by Greyhound and Premier
buses with Brisbane (5 daily; 5hr 40min) and Cairns (4
daily; 25hr 45min).

Tourist information 72 Churchill St (Mon–Fri
9am–4pm, Sat & Sun 9am–1pm; ☎1300 722 099).

ACCOMMODATION

Childers Oasis Motel 17 Macrossan St ☎ 07 4839 7643, ⓦ childersoasismotel.com. Peaceful, central place to stay, all the quieter for being a block off the highway, with lush gardens, a pool and shared kitchen. **$135**

Bundaberg

The humdrum town of **BUNDABERG**, noteworthy only for its **rum**, stands amid cane fields and fruit farms 50km north of Childers, reached along Isis Hwy off Hwy 1. Its main thoroughfare, **Bourbong Street**, runs parallel to the **Burnett River**, which flows another 15km north to reach the coast at Mon Repos, where **marine turtles** mass in huge numbers every summer to lay their eggs. You can also fly from Bundaberg to **Lady Elliot Island**, a Barrier Reef cay that offers a basic eco-resort and good scuba diving.

Anyone looking for **work** is virtually guaranteed seasonal employment (mostly Feb–Nov) picking avocados, tomatoes, snow peas and courgettes on local farms.

Rum distillery

Whittred St, 2km east of the centre along Bourbong St • Mon–Fri 10am–5pm, Sat & Sun 10am–4pm; hourly tours Mon–Fri 10am–3pm, Sat & Sun 10am–2pm • Self-guided visit $15, tours $25; closed-toe shoes must be worn • ☎ 07 4131 2989, ⓦ bundabergrum.com.au

"**Bundy**", as it's affectionately known, is synonymous with rum throughout Australia. If you believe its advertising pitch, the town's **rum distillery** accounts for half the rum consumed in the country each year. Taking a tour allows fans to wallow in the overpowering pungency of raw molasses and ends, of course, with a free sample – though you probably won't need to drink much after inhaling the fumes in the vat sheds, where electronic devices are prohibited in case a spark ignites the vapour.

Hinkler Hall of Aviation

Bundaberg Botanic Gardens, cnr Mount Perry Rd & Young St • Daily 9am–4pm • $18 • ☎ 07 4130 4400, ⓦ hinklerhallofaviation.com

By flying 1270km from Sydney to Bundaberg in 1921, **Bert Hinkler** set a world record for continuous flight, demonstrating the potential of his flimsy wire-and-canvas Baby Avro for reaching remote areas and thus encouraging the formation of Qantas the following year. The **Hinkler Hall of Aviation** holds replicas of this and all Hinkler's flying

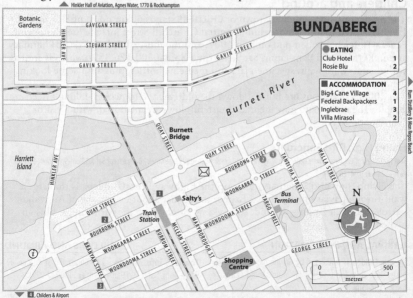

● EATING	
Club Hotel	1
Rosie Blu	2

■ ACCOMMODATION	
Big4 Cane Village	4
Federal Backpackers	1
Inglebrae	3
Villa Mirasol	2

machines, along with photos and simulators. Tickets include a visit to **Hinkler House**, his former English home, transported here in 1983 and rebuilt, brick by brick. Outside the house, landscaped gardens flank ponds where Hinkler was supposedly inspired to design aircraft by watching ibises in flight.

Mon Repos Beach

14km east of Bundaberg • Turtle Encounters Nov to late March 7pm; the beach is otherwise off limits between 6pm and 6am during this period • $11.60 (plus $3 booking fee); book in advance through the Bundaberg Visitor Centre • ☎ 1300 722 099, ⊛ bundabergregion.org • Follow Bourbong St out of Bundaberg towards the port, then look out for small brown signposts to the beach

Once the site of a French telegraph link to New Caledonia, **Mon Repos Beach** is Australia's most accessible **loggerhead turtle rookery**. From October to April, female loggerheads clamber laboriously up the beaches after dark, excavate a pit with their hind flippers above the high-tide mark, and lay around a hundred parchment-shelled eggs. During the eight-week **incubation period**, the ambient temperature of the surrounding sand will determine the sex of the entire clutch; 28.5°C is the changeover point between male and female. On **hatching**, the endearing youngsters stay buried in the nest until after dark, when they dig themselves out en masse and head for the sea. In season, about a dozen turtles lay each night, and watching the young leave the nests and race towards the water like clockwork toys is both comical and touching – your chances of seeing both laying and hatching in one evening are best during January.

ARRIVAL AND INFORMATION   BUNDABERG

By plane Bundaberg Airport, 5km southwest of the centre on the Childers Rd, is served by flights from/to Brisbane (4–6 daily; 50min) and Lady Elliot Island (2 daily; 45min).
By train The train station is on McLean St, 500m west of the centre.
Destinations Ayr (6 weekly; 11hr 30min); Bowen (6 weekly; 10hr); Brisbane (2–3 daily; 4hr 30min–6hr); Caboolture (6 weekly; 4hr); Cairns (5 weekly; 19hr); Cardwell (6 weekly; 15hr 30min); Gladstone (6 weekly; 1hr 45min); Ingham (6 weekly; 14hr 30min); Innisfail (5 weekly; 17hr); Mackay (6 weekly; 7hr 15min); Rockhampton (2–3 daily; 3hr 20min–5hr); Townsville (6 weekly; 12hr 30min).

By bus Long-distance buses set down at the bus terminal at 66 Targo St.
Destinations Agnes Water (2 daily; 1hr 30min); Airlie Beach (3 daily; 10hr 30min); Ayr (3 daily; 14hr); Brisbane (2 daily; 6hr 30min); Cairns (3 daily; 20hr 30min); Childers (4 daily; 50min); Hervey Bay (4 daily; 1hr 45min); Mackay (3 daily; 9hr); Mission Beach (1 daily; 22hr); Noosa (2 daily; 7hr); Rainbow Beach (2 daily; 4hr 30min); Rockhampton (3 daily; 3hr 30min); Townsville (3 daily; 15hr 30min).
Tourist information Bundaberg's visitor centre is at 271 Bourbong St (daily 9am–5pm; ☎ 07 4153 8888, ⊛ bundabergregion.org).

ACCOMMODATION

Big4 Cane Village 94 Twyford St ☎ 07 4155 1022, ⊛ cane-village-holiday-park.qld.big4.com.au. Tidy site for tents, caravans and campervans, southwest of town, with a saltwater pool and close to the Sugarlands mall which holds a bar and cinema. Un/powered sites $35/$40, cabins $115
Federal Backpackers 221 Bourbong St ☎ 07 4153 3711, ⊛ federalbackpackers.com.au. Sadly, none of Bundaberg's many backpackers' hostels has a particularly good reputation; this is probably the best of the bunch, though, and is located in an imposing building on Bundy's busiest street. Dorms $150 per week

★**Inglebrae** 17 Branyan St ☎ 07 4154 4003, ⊛ inglebrae.com. Charming B&B set in a century-old Queenslander, with three immaculate pastel-coloured rooms, deep wraparound verandas, and with friendly hosts. Breakfasts are generous and carafes of port and chocolates lie in wait in each room. $130
Villa Mirasol 225 Bourbong St ☎ 07 4154 4311, ⊛ villa.net.au. One of the nicer motels along Bourbong St, with clean rooms, saltwater pool and BBQ area, lots of attractive Spanish-style tiling and Mexican artefacts, and free breakfast for guests. $145

EATING

Club Hotel 50 Bourbong St ☎ 07 4151 3262, ⊛ clubhotelbundaberg.com.au. The pick of several busy, unsophisticated pubs set in one of Bundaberg's grand old buildings. Locals rave about the $30 steaks, but you can get a good, filling meal for half that. Mon–Thurs & Sun 10am–10pm, Fri & Sat 10am–3am.

Rosie Blu 90 Bourbong St ☎ 07 4151 0957. A popular deli-café offering breakfasts until 11am, plus sandwiches, salads, great coffee, juices and wicked cakes, with home-cooked takeaway meals from $10. Mon–Fri 8.30am–4pm, Sat 8am–1.30pm.

Lady Elliot Island

The southernmost outpost of the Great Barrier Reef, **Lady Elliot Island** is a 2km-square patch of casuarina and pandanus trees stabilizing a bed of coral rubble, sand and – like all the southern cays – plenty of overpoweringly pungent **guano**, courtesy of generations of birds. The elegant **lighthouse** on its west side was built in 1866 after an

---

THE GREAT BARRIER REEF

The **Great Barrier Reef** is to Australia what rolling savannahs and game parks are to Africa. Calling it "another world", as the commonest cliché has it, doesn't begin to describe the feeling of donning mask and fins and coming face to face with its extraordinary animals, shapes and colours. There's so little relationship to life above the surface that the distinctions one usually takes for granted – for example between animal, vegetable and mineral – seem blurred, while the respective roles of observer and observed are constantly inverted as shoals of curious fish follow the human interlopers about.

Extending 2300km north from Lady Elliot Island, off Bundaberg, all the way to New Guinea, the Barrier Reef follows the outer edge of Australia's continental plate, running closer to land as it moves north: while it's 300km to the main body from Gladstone, Cairns is barely 50km from the Reef. Far from being a continuous, unified structure, the Reef consists for most of its length of an intricate maze of individual, disconnected patch reefs, which – especially in the south – may act as anchors for the formation of low sand islands known as **cays**. Continental islands everywhere become ringed by **fringing reefs**, while northern sections form long **ribbons**. All of it, however, was built by one kind of animal: the tiny **coral polyp**. Simple organisms, related to sea anemones, polyps grow together like building blocks to create modular colonies – **corals**. These provide food, shelter and hunting grounds for larger, more mobile species. Around their walls and canyons flows a bewildering assortment of creatures: large rays and turtles "fly" effortlessly by, fish dodge between caves and coral branches, snails sift the sand for edibles, and brightly coloured nudibranchs dance above rocks.

THE REEF IN CRISIS

As has been widely reported, the Barrier Reef is in serious trouble. The biggest long-term threat comes from **climate change**; with ocean temperatures rising the world over, mass **bleaching** events have become ever more frequent. That problem is exacerbated in Queensland by run-off from **agriculture** and **mining**. Any precise statistics will almost certainly have changed by the time you read this, but the current headline figures make grim reading. Half of the Reef's coral cover has gone in the last three decades, and experts believe the Reef may be destroyed altogether in another thirty years. Of its three thousand component reefs, 93 percent have been affected, with the devastation most heavily concentrated north of Cairns.

What's even more shocking than the destruction of the Reef has been the attitude of the Australian government, which, rather than addressing the problem, has chosen instead to devote its efforts to covering it up. In 2016, for example, the government successfully lobbied the UN to delete all mention of the Barrier Reef – and Australia as a whole – from its landmark report on climate change, on the basis that it would damage tourism.

Is the Barrier Reef still worth visiting? Emphatically yes – many regions remain more or less intact, and casual visitors may well not notice anything amiss. For how long that will continue to be true, however, remains to be seen. Check new reports before you visit to discover the current situation – Queensland's boat operators, after all, are hardly likely to alert potential customers to the extent of the damage.

extraordinary number of wrecks on the reef; an average of one vessel per year still manages to come to grief here. Wailing shearwaters and the occasional suicide of lighthouse staff didn't endear Lady Elliot to early visitors, but a low-key **resort** and excellent reef have now turned it into a popular escape.

Shearwaters aside, there's a good deal of **birdlife**; residents include thousands of black noddies and bridled terns, along with much larger frigate birds and a few rare **red-tailed tropicbirds** – a white, gull-like bird with a red beak and wire-like tail – that nest under bushes on the foreshore. Both loggerhead and green **turtles** nest on the beaches too; in a good summer scores lay their eggs here each night.

DIVING AND OTHER WAYS TO SEE THE REEF

Perhaps it's too obvious to mention, but seeing the Great Barrier Reef requires you to do two things: first you have to take a **boat trip** of at least an hour out from the mainland, then once you're there you have to stick your head under the water.

Scuba diving is the best way to explore the Reef up close. If you're happy just to see it once or twice, you don't have to learn to dive – almost all day-trip operators offer so-called **resort dives** or **instructor dives**, typically costing around $80, in which you receive instruction on equipment and safety, and are then closely accompanied by an instructor on the actual dive. Otherwise, **dive courses** are available all along the coast. It takes at least five days to safely cover the course work – three days pool and theory, two days at sea – and get your official C-card. Both the quality of training, and the price, vary enormously; before signing up, ask other divers about specific businesses, and especially whether their main concern seems to be processing as many students in as short a time as possible. **Qualified divers** can save on rental costs by bringing gear along; dive packages usually include tanks and weight belts, but anything else is extra. You need an alternative air source, timer, C-card and log book to dive in Queensland (the last is often ignored, but some places insist, especially for deep or night-time dives).

Snorkelling makes a good alternative to diving: it's very easy to learn, and the most colourful corals and sea creatures tend to be close to the surface. Rental gear nearly always leaks, so it's worth buying your own mask and snorkel. Look for a silicone rubber and toughened glass mask, and ask the staff to help you find a good fit.

If getting wet just isn't for you, try **glass-bottomed boats** or "subs", or even a "helmet dive" which can still turn up everything from sharks to oysters.

REEF HAZARDS

Stories of shark attacks, savage octopuses and giant clams make good press, but are mostly the stuff of fiction. However, a few things are capable of putting a dampener on your holiday, and it makes sense to be careful. The best protection is simply to **look and not touch**, as nothing is actively out to harm you.

Seasickness and **sunburn** are the two most common problems, so take precautions. Coral and shell **cuts** become badly infected if not treated immediately by removing any fragments and dousing with antiseptic. Some corals can also give you a nasty **sting**, but this is more a warning to keep away from something to worry about seriously. Animals to avoid tend to be small. Some dangerous **jellyfish** (see p.42) are found at the Reef during summer – wear a protective Lycra "stinger suit" or full wetsuit with hood. Conical **cone shells** are home to a fish-eating snail armed with a venomous barb that has caused fatalities. Don't pick them up: there is no "safe" end to hold them. Similarly, the shy, small, **blue-ringed octopus** has a fatal bite and should never be handled. **Stonefish** are camouflaged so that they're almost impossible to distinguish from a rock or lump of coral. They spend their days immobile, protected from attack by venomous spines along their back. If you tread on one, you'll end up in hospital. Of the larger animals, **rays** are flattened fish with a sharp tail-spine capable of causing deep wounds – don't swim close over sandy floors where they hide. At the Reef, the most commonly encountered **sharks** are the black-tip and white-tip varieties, and the bottom-dwelling, aptly named carpet shark, or wobbegong – all are inoffensive unless hassled.

Finally, to **minimize damage**, never stand on or hold onto reefs when snorkelling or diving; even if you don't break off branches, you'll certainly crush the delicate polyps.

The main reason visitors come to Lady Elliot, however, is to go **snorkelling** or **scuba diving**: the best dive spots are out from the lighthouse, but check on currents with staff at the resort. You've a good chance of encountering harmless leopard sharks, sea snakes, barracuda, turtles and manta rays wherever you go. Shore dives cost $50 per person, while boat dives are $70 ($90 for night dives), plus gear rental. The Blowhole is a very popular dive site, with a descent into a cavern. Expect to see lion fish, manta shrimp and the unique "gnomefish". The 1998 wreck of the twin-masted yacht *Severance*, a few minutes offshore, is famous for large schools of pellagics.

ARRIVAL AND ACCOMMODATION   LADY ELLIOT ISLAND

On a tour No scheduled boats go to Lady Elliot Island. Whether you visit on a day-trip or stay overnight, you can only get here by air, arranged through *Lady Elliot Island Resort*. Day-tours depart Bundaberg and Hervey Bay airports (from $365) or Brisbane and the Gold Coast airports (from $799); packages include flights, island tour, buffet lunch and guided snorkel trip.

Lady Elliot Island Resort ☎ 1800 072 200, ⓦ ladyelliot .com.au. A refreshingly basic set-up with no mobile phone signal and a pioneering approach to alternative energy – there's an impressive solar power station, and minimal use of air conditioning. Accommodation is in suites with ocean views or "eco hut" safari tents, with rates including breakfast and dinner but not flights. Tents $246, doubles $596

Agnes Water

On the coast 100km north of Bundaberg along the Rosedale road, the tiny settlements of **Agnes Water** and nearby 1770 mark the spot where Captain Cook first set foot in Queensland on May 24, 1770. Attractions in this pretty area include pockets of mangrove, fan palm and paperbark wetlands, and Queensland's northernmost **surf beach**.

Agnes Water consists of a service station, two shopping complexes, several large resort villages, and a few places to eat. The town is fronted by a stunning, sweeping **beach** backed by sand dunes. Delightful coastal walks in the area include the 3km trail from Agnes Headland along the wooded ridge to Springs Beach.

ARRIVAL AND INFORMATION   AGNES WATER

By bus Greyhound buses stop at the Caltex service station on Captain Cook Drive. Premier inconveniently drop passengers at Fingerboard Rd, a 20min walk out of town. Destinations Airlie Beach (2 daily; 11hr); Brisbane (3 daily; 11hr 30min); Bundaberg (3 daily; 1hr 30min); Cairns (2

daily; 20hr 30min); Hervey Bay (3 daily; 4hr).
Tourist information The visitor centre is at 71 Springs Rd (Mon–Fri 9am–5pm, Sat & Sun 9am–4pm; ☎ 07 4974 7557, ⓦ discover1770.com.au).

ACCOMMODATION AND EATING

1770 Getaway 303 Bicentennial Drive ☎ 07 4974 9323, ⓦ 1770getaway.com.au. Nicely designed self-contained lodges with balconies, overlooking lush landscaped gardens. The on-site *Getaway Garden Café* serves hearty daytime snacks daily except Sat, and also opens for dinner, by reservation only, Wed & Sun. Mon,

Tues, Thurs & Fri 8am–2.30pm, Wed & Sun 8am–2.30pm & 6–8pm. $175
Cool Bananas 2 Springs Rd ☎ 07 4974 7660, ⓦ coolbananas.net.au. A well-organized, sociable back-packers' hostel with bright, eight-share dorms and a big lounge. Dorms $28

1770 and around

Smaller than Agnes Water, and occupying the foreshore of a narrow promontory 6km north, **1770** (also called Seventeen Seventy, or Town of 1770) is the launchpad for boats out to **Lady Musgrave Island** and nearby reefs. Windswept Round Hill, at the end of the road, offers exposed walking trails and coastal views. There are few places to stay apart from holiday rentals; most visitors come for **day-trips to the Reef**, local tours, watersports and spectacular sunsets.

Eurimbula National Park, west of 1770 across Round Hill Creek, abounds with birdlife. For 4WD road access, head 10.5km back towards Miriam Vale from Agnes Water.

TOURS
1770 AND AROUND

Amphibious tours Using hot pink amphibious ex-military supply vehicles, LARC, 1770 Marina (☎07 4974 9422, ⊛1770larctours.com.au) offer daily cruises (from $38), and great day-long tours up the Eurimbula coastline, visiting the pristine Bustard Lighthouse (Mon, Wed & Sat; $145).

ACCOMMODATION AND EATING

1770 Camping Ground 578 Captain Cook Drive ☎07 4974 9286, ⊛1770campingground.com.au. Absolute beachfront, and cheaper than the ground at Agnes Water, although sites are closer together. Facilities include a store and bistro. Un/powered sites $35/$39

The Beach Shacks 578 Captain Cook Drive ☎07 4974 9463, ⊛1770beachshacks.com. Four beautifully furnished timber houses facing the 1770 boardwalk and ocean, sleeping two to six. Each has its own private deck, with gas BBQ and outdoor dining area. $198

The Tree 1770 Beach Hotel, 576 Captain Cook Drive ☎07 4974 7446, ⊛1770beachhotel.com.au. All-day meals, served on a long sea-view terrace that's fabulous at sunset; bucket of prawns $30. The hotel runs a courtesy bus from Agnes Water from 6.30pm (book ahead). Mon–Fri 9am–10pm, Sat & Sun 8.30am–11pm.

Lady Musgrave Island

Lady Musgrave Island, the southernmost of the eight tiny coral cays constituting Capricornia Cays National Park, is covered in soft-leaved **pisonia trees** that host the usual throng of roosting birdlife, ringed by a coral wall that forms a large turquoise **lagoon**. Diving inside the lagoon here is safe (no stinger suits are needed year-round) but pretty tame, though snorkelling is good; outside the wall is more exciting.

ARRIVAL AND ACCOMMODATION
LADY MUSGRAVE ISLAND

By boat Lady Musgrave Cruises sail daily to the island from 1770's marina ($180, includes snorkelling, semi-submarine tour and a buffet lunch; ☎07 4974 9077, ⊛lmcruises.com.au); a scuba dive costs an extra $60 (for qualified divers) or $95 (trial dive), including equipment.
Camping Easy, inexpensive access makes Lady Musgrave the best of the southern cays for campers (April–Jan).

There are no facilities at all, so bring absolutely everything you need, including plenty of water (at least five litres day). If you plan a longer stay, arrange for Lady Musgrave Cruises to bring you supplementary provisions. Return transfers to the island will set you back a hefty $450, and you'll also need a camping permit ($5.75; ⊛nprsr.qld.gov.au).

Heron Island

Accessible from the port city of Gladstone, 90km up Highway 1 from the Miriam Vale turn-off, **Heron Island** is the exclusive preserve of well-heeled ecotourists, as it's not open for day-trippers or camping. It's small enough to walk around in an hour, with half the cay occupied by an exclusive **resort** and **research station**, and the rest covered in groves of pandanus, coconuts and shady pisonias.

Heron Island is famous for **diving**; you can literally walk off the beach and into the Reef's maze of coral, or swim along the shallow walls looking for action. The eastern edges of the lagoon are good for snorkelling at any time, but some of the best coral is on the outer reefs, accessible only by boat. A drift along the wall facing Wistari reef to Heron Bommie covers about everything you're likely to encounter. The coral isn't that good but the amount of life is astonishing: tiny boxfish hide under ledges; turtles, cowries, wobbegong, reef sharks, moray eels, butterfly cod and octopuses secrete themselves among the coral; manta rays soar majestically; and larger reef fish gape vacantly as you drift past. The bommie itself makes first-rate **snorkelling**, while the Tenements along the reef's northern edge are good for bigger game, including sharks.

ARRIVAL AND DEPARTURE

HERON ISLAND

By ferry The *Heron Islander* ferry carries passengers to the island from Gladstone Marina, on Bryan Jordan Drive 2km north of central Gladstone (Mon, Wed & Fri–Sun 2pm; $62 one-way). Gladstone's airport is connected with Brisbane (5 daily; 1hr) and Rockhampton (5 weekly; 25min).

By air Australia by Seaplane (bookable through the resort ☎ 1300 863 248) provides air transfers to the island from Gladstone Airport on demand, costing $338 per person one-way, with a minimum of two passengers.

ACCOMMODATION

Heron Island Resort ☎ 1300 863 248, ⓦ heronisland .com. The island's sole accommodation option is excellent, with an array of gorgeous oceanfront rooms and suites and

a restaurant that's open for all meals daily. The outer reef is only accessible on a half-day cruise ($150/person) and a standard dive costs a further $75, or $99 at night. **$320**

Rockhampton

3

Straddling the Tropic of Capricorn, **ROCKHAMPTON** was founded after a false gold rush in 1858 left hundreds of miners stranded at a depot 40km inland on the banks of the sluggish **Fitzroy River**, whereupon their rough camp was adopted by local stockmen as a convenient port. The iron trelliswork and sandstone buildings fronting the river recall the balmy 1890s, when money was pouring in from the prosperous cattle industry and nearby gold and copper mines. Today, Rockhampton feels a bit despondent – the mines have closed, the beef industry is down in the dumps, and the summers, unrelieved by coastal breezes, are appallingly humid. All in all, it's best seen as a springboard for the adjacent Capricorn Coast.

Rockhampton is fairly small and easy to navigate. Services are clustered south of the **Fitzroy Bridge** along Quay and East streets, while the Bruce Highway runs right through town past two pairs of fibreglass bulls (repeatedly "de-balled" by pranksters).

The **Tropic Marker**, as you enter Rockhampton 3km south of the river, is just a spire informing you of your position at 23° 26′ 30″ S, backed by a small visitor centre.

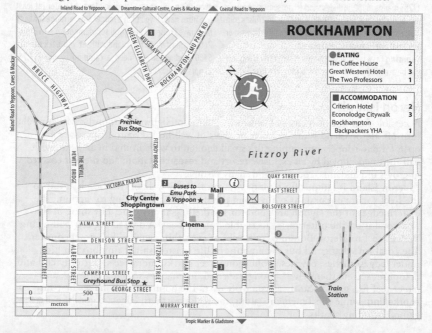

WEATHER IN QUEENSLAND'S TROPICS

Queensland's tropics kick in at Rockhampton. Featuring dry, relatively **cool winters** (June–Aug), the region experiences extremely **humid summers** (Dec–Feb) with torrential rainfall and devastating cyclones – February and March are when the worst systems, such as 2011's Cyclone Yasi, are most likely to hit.

Dreamtime Cultural Centre

Bruce Highway, 6km north of Rockhampton • Mon–Fri 9.30am–3.30pm • $15.50 • Guided tours (included in entry price) 10.30am & 1pm • ☎ 07 4936 1655, ⓦ dreamtimecentre.com.au

For a good introduction to central Queensland's Aboriginal heritage, drop in at the **Dreamtime Cultural Centre**, 6km north of town. Inside, chronological and Dreamtime histories are intermingled, with a broad dissection of the archeology and mythology of Carnarvon Gorge (see p.447). The tour also discusses plant usage and introduces boomerang, dance and didgeridoo skills.

Mount Etna and Capricorn caves

The Caves • **Mount Etna Caves Bat Cleft tour** Dec to mid-Feb Mon, Fri & Sat 5.45pm; 3hr • $10.70 • ☎ 07 4936 0570 • Take a torch and wear durable shoes • **Capricorn Caves** Daily 8.30am–6pm • Tours hourly 9am–4pm; $30 • 2hr Geotour, adventure caving for ages 16 and over $75 • ☎ 07 4934 2883, ⓦ capricorncaves.com.au • Turn off the Bruce Highway 25km north of Rockhampton and follow the brown signs

The limestone hills north of Rockhampton are riddled with a **cave system**, thick with tree roots encased in stone after forcing their way down through rocks, "cave corals" and "frozen waterfalls" – minerals deposited by evaporation after annual floods. The **ghost bat** (Australia's only carnivorous species) and the **little bent-winged bat** – both now endangered – seasonally use the caves for roosts, and you might catch the odd group huddled together on the ceilings, eyes peering down over leaf-shaped noses.

Two sets of caverns are open to the public. The **Mount Etna Caves** are undeveloped but none too extensive; you can explore on your own between March and October or go on a three-hour **Bat Cleft Tour** with a National Parks ranger from December to mid-February (the bats' breeding season) to see little bent-winged bats escaping their roost in Bat Cleft at dusk. The **Capricorn Caves** are rather more impressive and visitor-friendly, with plenty of spotlights illuminating their interiors.

ARRIVAL AND DEPARTURE ROCKHAMPTON

By plane Rockhampton Airport is on Canoona Rd, 4km west of town. Young's buses run between the airport and the city (Mon–Fri 7 daily, 2 on Sat, ⓦ youngsbusservice .com.au; 30min).

Destinations Brisbane (11 daily; 1hr); Gladstone (1 daily; 25min); Mackay (2 daily; 50min); Townsville (6 weekly; 1hr 45min).

By train The train station is on Murray St, 1km south of the centre.

Destinations Ayr (6 weekly; 8hr 30min); Bowen (6 weekly; 7hr); Brisbane (6 weekly; 7hr 30min); Bundaberg (2–3 daily; 3hr 20min–5hr); Caboolture (2–3 daily; 7hr–9hr 30min); Cairns (6 weekly; 16hr); Gladstone (6 weekly; 1hr 15min); Ingham (6 weekly; 11hr 30min); Mackay (6 weekly; 4hr 15min); Proserpine (6 weekly; 6hr 30min); Townsville (6 weekly; 9hr 30min).

By bus Premier buses stop at the Mobil service station just north of the bridge, while Greyhound services depart from the Greyhound ticket counter on George St. Young's buses set off to Emu Park and Yeppoon from the car park in Bolsover St, near William St (ⓦ youngsbusservice.com.au).

Destinations Airlie Beach (3 daily; 7hr 30min); Ayr (4 daily; 10hr); Brisbane (4 daily; 11hr 30min); Bundaberg (3 daily; 3hr 30min); Cairns (4 daily; 17hr 30min); Childers (4 daily; 5hr); Emu Park (5–12 daily; 1hr 15min); Hervey Bay (4 daily; 6hr); Mackay (3 daily; 5hr); Mission Beach (4 daily; 16hr); Noosa (2 daily; 10hr); Townsville (3 daily; 11hr); Yeppoon (5–11 daily; 40min).

INFORMATION

Tourist information The visitor centre is alongside the Tropic of Capricorn Spire, on Gladstone Rd (Mon–Sat 9am–5pm, Sun 9am–3pm; ☎ 07 4922 5339, ⓦ capricornenterprise.com.au).

3

ACCOMMODATION

Criterion Hotel 150 Quay St ☎07 4922 1225, ⓦ thecriterion.com.au. Simple budget rooms and suites, liable to be noisy, above a pub that's home to the popular *Bush Grill* steakhouse, plus smarter modern rooms in a separate motel section. Hotel $75, motel $125

EconoLodge Citywalk 129 William St ☎07 4922 6009, ⓦ econolodgecitywalk.com.au. Exceptionally welcoming budget motel in a peaceful spot not far from restaurants and bars, and offering good, clean, well-equipped rooms plus free laundry. $119

Rockhampton Backpackers YHA 60 MacFarlane St ☎07 4927 5288, ⓦ rockhamptonbackpackers.com.au. Well-maintained YHA backpackers', north of the river, with en-suite cabins as well as dorms and doubles. Dorms $22, doubles $50, cabins $60

EATING

The Coffee House 51 William St ☎07 4927 5722, ⓦ coffeehouse.com.au. Modern Australian café, attached to an apartment hotel, serving good breakfasts and quality bistro dishes from around $20. Mon–Fri 6.30am–8pm, Sat & Sun 8am–2pm & 6–8pm.

★ **Great Western Hotel** Cnr Stanley & Denison sts ☎07 4922 1862, ⓦ greatwesternhotel.com.au. This cavernous landmark pub is renowned for its great steaks and ribs (typically costing $25–35), which you can enjoy beside the huge indoor rodeo arena "out back", where they stage a practice rodeo at 7pm on Wednesdays and Fridays, plus occasional pro events at other times. See the website for schedules of live country music performances. Daily noon–2pm & 6–9pm.

The Two Professors 49 William St ☎07 4927 2301. Top-quality early-morning coffee in a hip urban setting, with gourmet breakfasts followed by burgers and other snacks later on. Mon–Fri 5.30am–5.30pm, Sat 6.30am–3pm, Sun 6.30am–1.30pm.

The Capricorn Coast

Views from the volcanic outcrops overlooking the **Capricorn Coast**, 40km east of Rockhampton, stretch across graziers' estates and pineapple plantations to exposed headlands, estuarine mudflats and the Keppel islands. The coastal townships of **Yeppoon** and **Emu Park**, 20km apart and settled by cattle barons in the 1860s, later became resorts where Rockhampton's elite could escape the summer heat. Today, they retain a pleasantly dated holiday atmosphere, and make much more relaxing places to stay than Rockhampton itself. **Great Keppel Island**, however, accessed from **Rosslyn Bay** just south of Yeppoon, is the major attraction along the coast.

Emu Park

The tranquil, laidback settlement of **EMU PARK** consists of a pleasant sandy beach and breezy hillside covered by scattered Queenslander houses, where the wind howls mournful tunes through the wires of the **Singing Ship**, a quirky monument to Captain Cook.

ARRIVAL AND DEPARTURE   EMU PARK

By bus Young's buses from/to Rockhampton stop on Pattison St, just off Hill St (ⓦ youngsbusservice.com.au). Destinations Rockhampton (5–12 daily; 1hr 15min); Rockhampton Airport (2–5 daily except Sun; 1hr 40min); Rossyln Bay (6–12 daily; 15min); Yeppoon (hourly; 30min).
By car Turn east north of the river in Rockhampton, and it's 50km to Emu Park.

ACCOMMODATION AND EATING

Emu Park Pizza & Pasta 6 Hill St ☎07 4938 7333. Simple BYO restaurant, with a few outdoor tables, selling meat and seafood pizzas from $12, and large plates of pasta or risotto for $14.50. Daily except Wed 10.30am–1.30pm & 4.30–9pm.

★ **Emus Beach Resort** 92 Pattison St ☎07 4939 6111, ⓦ emusbeachresort.com. Friendly, modern backpacker retreat with well-ventilated rooms, cheery bunkless dorms, a pool and a sociable bar. The beach and town are a 5min walk away. Campervans can park here for $5/night. Dorms $26, doubles $85

Endeavour Inn 18–20 Hill St ☎07 4939 6777, ⓦ endeavourinn.com.au. Clean, reasonably priced rooms and suites, some with private balconies, in the heart of town, arrayed around a nice pool. $115

Yeppoon

YEPPOON's quiet handful of streets, 18km north up the coast from Emu Park via **Rosslyn Bay**, face the Keppel islands across a blustery expanse of sand and sea. All services are on **Normanby Street**, at right angles to the seafront Anzac Parade.

ARRIVAL AND DEPARTURE   YEPPOON

By bus Young's buses use a depot on Hill St, parallel with Normanby St (ⓦ youngsbusservice.com.au).
Destinations Rockhampton city (5–11 daily; 40min);

Rockhampton Airport (2–8 daily except Sun; 1hr 10min); Emu Park (hourly; 30min).

ACCOMMODATION

Coast Motel 52 Scenic Hwy ⓣ 07 4930 2325, ⓦ thecoastmotel.com.au. Very smart modern motel, 3km south of the centre, where the crisp, clean rooms and suites have balconies overlooking an excellent pool. **$135**
Coral Inn 14 Maple St ⓣ 07 4939 2925, ⓦ coralinn .com.au. Appealing budget motel, with vibrant, lavishly decorated en-suite rooms (check out the "newspaper" walls

and floors in the bathrooms); there's a pool, sauna, kitchen and pizza oven. **$99**
Poinciana Tourist Park 9 Scenic Hwy ⓣ 07 4939 1601, ⓦ poincianatouristpark.com. Located south of town, this offers well-shaded sites and a saltwater pool. Un/powered sites **$31/$33**, cabins **$75**

EATING AND DRINKING

Flour Cafe 9–11 Normanby St ⓣ 07 4925 0725. Buzzing central café, where the "book" menu features tasty breakfasts and lunches, plus coffee and delicious cakes. Typical mains, like pumpkin with couscous, cost $15–17. Mon–Fri 7am–3pm, Sat 7am–2pm.
The Strand 2 Normanby St ⓣ 07 4939 1301,

ⓦ thestrandyeppoon.com.au. Popular restaurant and bar with sea views. Mains – a gourmet take on pizza, seafood and burgers – cost from $15, with oysters at $36 per dozen, and steaks approaching $40. Mon–Fri 11.30am–2.30pm & 5.30–9pm, Sat & Sun 11.30am–9pm.

Great Keppel Island

Great Keppel is the largest of the eighteen Keppel islands, a windswept hillock covered in casuarinas and ringed by white sand so fine that it squeaks when you walk through it, all surrounded by an invitingly clear blue sea. For the moment, it's a wonderfully peaceful and secluded getaway, though that may change when the long-awaited, repeatedly postponed **redevelopment** of the *Great Keppel Island Resort* finally comes to fruition (for the latest news, see ⓦ gkiresort.com.au).

The two main **beaches** on Great Keppel, Putney and Fisherman's, are absolutely breathtaking. Long Beach, half an hour's walk along a woodland path beyond the resort, is even more secluded, while snorkellers can make the short haul over the dunes at the western end to shallow coral on Monkey Beach. The **middens** (shell mounds) there were left by Woppaburra Aborigines, who were enslaved and forcibly removed to Fraser Island by early settlers.

ARRIVAL AND TOURS   GREAT KEPPEL ISLAND

By ferry Freedom Fast Cats run ferries to Great Keppel (Mon & Tues 10.30am, Wed–Sun 9.15am; $52 return; 30min; ⓣ 07 4933 6888, ⓦ freedomfastcats.com.au) from Rosslyn Bay Harbour, halfway between Yeppoon and Emu Park and served by Young's buses (6–12 daily; ⓦ youngsbusservice.com.au).

Tours Sail Capricornia, based at the Keppel Bay Marina in Rosslyn Bay (ⓣ 0402 102 372, ⓦ sailcapricornia.com.au), offer $125 full-day catamaran cruises, stopping at island beaches and snorkelling spots (gear included), and including a buffet lunch and soft drinks, and also shorter sunset cruises ($55).

ACCOMMODATION AND EATING

Great Keppel Island Holiday Village ⓣ 07 4939 8655, ⓦ gkiholidayvillage.com.au. Self-contained cottages and cabins of assorted sizes, plus safari tents.

Motorized canoes and snorkelling equipment available. Doubles **$100**, safari tents **$110**, cabins **$140**
Island Pizza Esplanade, Fisherman's Beach

☎07 4939 4699. Popular licensed pizza shack that's been going for years (pizzas from $15). A good place for sunset. Daily noon–2pm & 5–8pm.

Svendsens ☎07 4938 3717, �🌐svendsensbeach.com. Sleep in rustic eco-tents, or rent a studio or larger house,

on the island's remote eastern shore. The owner will pick you up by boat from the ferry; he has written books on both snorkelling and bushwalking on Great Keppel, so you're in good hands. BYO provisions. Safari tents $115, studio $150

Mackay and around

The fertile Pioneer Valley, 360km north of Rockhampton along a barely populated but reasonably attractive stretch of Highway 1, makes the **MACKAY** area a welcome break from the largely dry country between Bundaberg and Townsville. Despite violent confrontations with Juipera Aborigines, John Mackay settled here in 1861. Within four years, the city was founded and the first **sugar cane** plantations were established. Sugar remains the main industry, though the **coal mines** out west in the Bowen Basin have forced Mackay to become a service centre, and its dreary motel accommodation is usually full with casual workers and travelling business people.

Mackay's main attraction is its proximity to two attractive and little-visited national parks, seafront Cape Hillsborough and rainforested Eungella. South of the river, though, the easily navigable city centre is dotted with eye-catching 1890s heritage buildings. It's worth dropping in at **Artspace**, 61 Gordon St (Tues–Fri 10am–5pm, Sat & Sun 10am–3pm; donation; ☎07 4961 9722, �🌐artspacemackay.com.au), a contemporary gallery that hosts changing short-term exhibitions of works by local and visiting artists, but few tourists linger in town.

ARRIVAL AND INFORMATION

MACKAY

By plane Mackay Airport (�🌐mackayairport.com) is on East Boundary Rd, 6km south of the centre. Taxis (☎13 10 08) into town cost around $20.

Destinations Brisbane (11 daily; 1hr 25min); Rockhampton (1 daily; 50min); Sydney (1 daily; 2hr 15min); Townsville (3 daily; 1hr).

By train The station is on Connors Rd in Paget, 3km south off Milton St.

Destinations Ayr (6 weekly; 4hr); Bowen (6 weekly; 2hr 30min); Brisbane (6 weekly; 12hr 30min); Bundaberg (6 weekly; 7hr 45min); Caboolture (6 weekly; 12hr); Cairns (6 weekly; 12hr); Proserpine (6 weekly; 1hr 30min);

Rockhampton (6 weekly; 4hr 15min); Townsville (6 weekly; 5hr); Tully (6 weekly; 9hr).

By bus Long-distance buses stop at the Caltex service station, at Tennyson and Victoria streets.

Destinations Airlie Beach (4 daily; 2hr 15min); Ayr (4 daily; 5hr); Brisbane (6 daily; 15hr 30min); Bundaberg (3 daily; 9hr); Cairns (5 daily; 13hr); Hervey Bay (4 daily; 10hr 30min); Ingham (5 daily; 9hr); Mission Beach (4 daily; 10hr 30min); Noosa (2 daily; 14hr); Rainbow Beach (2 daily; 12hr); Rockhampton (4 daily; 5hr); Townsville (5 daily; 6hr 30min).

Tourist information The visitor centre is at 320 Nebo Rd (daily 9am–5pm; ☎1300 130 001, mackayregion.com).

ACCOMMODATION

Gecko's Rest 34 Sydney St ☎07 4944 1230, �🌐geckosrest.com.au. Slightly sterile budget option that's popular with long-stayers, offering compact rooms, laundry facilities and a well-equipped kitchen. Dorms $28, doubles $65

International Lodge Motel 40 Macalister St ☎07 4951 1022, �🌐internationallodge.com.au. Renovated

city-centre motel, with friendly management and bright, attractive and quiet rooms. $130

The Park 284 Farrellys Rd ☎07 4952 1211, �🌐theparkmackay.com.au. Southwest of town, just off the highway, with tidy sites, cabins and self-contained villas in a garden setting. Un/powered sites $29/33, cabins or villas $85

EATING

Oscar's 62 Sydney St ☎07 4944 0173. Great breakfasts from $17, with lots of light options later on, including sandwiches, wraps, quesadillas and salads. Mon–Thurs 7am–5pm, Fri & Sat 7am–9pm, Sun 8am–4pm.

Spice n Flavor 162 Victoria St ☎07 4999 9639,

⍟spicenflavor.com.au. Dependable Indian place, dishing up tasty traditional and fusion curries, including plenty of vegetarian options. Lamb *rogan josh* costs $20. Licensed. Daily 5–9.30pm.

Toong Tong Thai 10 Sydney St ☎07 4957 8051,

ⓦtoongthongthai.com.au. A well-established Asian restaurant serving cheap and cheerful hot and spicy meals. Curries or pad thai from $19, seafood from $25. Takeaway and eat in are available. Mon–Thurs 5–10pm, Fri & Sat 11.30am–2.30pm & 5–10pm.

Farleigh Mill

Armstrong St, Farleigh (10km northwest of Mackay) • Visit on guided tours only; Reeforest run $28 tours during the crushing season, daily June to mid-Dec 8.30am (☎ 07 4959 8360, ⓦ reeforest.com.au) • Closed-toe shoes must be worn

If you've ever wondered how sugar is processed, take an informative guided tour around the still-operational **Farleigh Mill**, built in 1883. You'll see the entire process from the arrival of the sugar cane at the mill to the dispatch of the finished product, with plenty of opportunity to taste sugary samples along the way. Sturdy closed-toe shoes, a long-sleeve shirt (tucked in) and long trousers are essential.

Cape Hillsborough National Park

Cape Hillsborough, 50km north of Mackay, is the site of a pretty beachfront national park that centres on a broad 2km **beach**. Backed by a good picnic area, and framed by the beautifully wooded cliffs of Cape Hillsborough to the north and Andrews Point to the south, the shallow bay is good for swimming outside stinger season.

An enjoyable **walk** heads 2km south from the beach to **Hidden Valley**, a patch of cool, shady forest on a rocky beach where you'll find the outline of an Aboriginal fish trap; keep an eye out for dolphins, turtles and pelicans in the bay.

Starting 500m back up the road towards Mackay, an excellent 1.2km circular trail follows a **boardwalk** through coastal mangroves (bring repellent), then snakes up to a ridge for views out over open gum woodland peppered with grevillias, cycads (see box, p.421) and grass trees (identified by their tall, spear-like flower spike). There's also a huge **midden** up here, left over from Aboriginal shellfish feasts, and plenty of reptiles sunning themselves around the edges of the path.

> ### SUGAR CANE ON THE TROPICAL COAST
>
> Grown in an almost continuous belt between Bundaberg and Mossman, north of Cairns, **sugar cane** is the Tropical Coast's economic pillar of strength. Introduced in the 1860s, the crop subtly undermined the racial ideals of British colonialists when farmers, planning a system along the lines of the southern United States, employed **Kanakas** – Solomon Islanders – to work the plantations. Though only indentured for a few years, and theoretically given wages and passage home when their term expired, Kanakas on plantations suffered greatly from unfamiliar diseases, while the recruiting methods used by "**Blackbirder**" traders were at best dubious and often slipped into wholesale kidnapping. Growing white unemployment and nationalism through the 1880s eventually forced the government to ban blackbirding and repatriate the islanders. Those allowed to stay were joined over the next fifty years by immigrants from Italy and Malta, who mostly settled in the far north, and now form large communities scattered between Mackay and Cairns.
>
> After the cane is planted in November, the land is swiftly covered by a blanket of dusky green. Before cutting, seven months later, the fields have traditionally been fired to burn off leaves and maximize sugar content. The practice is dying out, but **cane fires** still take place, often at dusk, and are as photogenic as they are brief; to be at the right place at the right time, ask at a mill.
>
> Cut cane is transported to the mills along a rambling rail network. The **mills** themselves are incredible structures, with machinery looming out of makeshift walls and giant pipes that belch out steam around the clock. Cane is juiced for raw sugar or molasses, as the market dictates; crushed fibre becomes fuel for the boilers that sustain the process; and ash is returned to the fields as fertilizer.

By car To reach the park, follow signs north off the Bruce Highway 20km north of Mackay. Another partly paved road leaves the highway at Mount Ossa, 79km south of Proserpine. There's no public transport.

Cape Hillsborough Nature Tourist Park 51 Risely Parade ☏ 07 4959 0152, ⓦ capehillsboroughresort.com .au. Rooms, huts and cabins with a back-to-basics feel, beautifully positioned at the southern end of the beach. The cheapest share bathrooms and don't provide linen, but there's a pool and restaurant. Un/powered sites $31/36, doubles $80

Eungella National Park

The magical rainforest and rivers would make **Eungella National Park**, 80km west of Mackay and pronounced "young-g'lla", worth the journey even if you didn't have an excellent chance of seeing a **platypus**. It consists of two separate sections: lowland swimming holes and tropical rainforest at **Finch Hatton Gorge**, and highland rainforest at **Broken River**. The park's isolation has produced several unique species, including the Mackay tulip oak, the Eungella honeyeater and the much-discussed but now extinct **gastric brooding frog**, known for incubating its young in its stomach.

Finch Hatton Gorge

The Eungella road cuts through prime cane country as it runs the length of the Pioneer Valley, past the townships of **Marian** and **Mirani**. The turn-off to **Finch Hatton Gorge** comes 60km out from Mackay, just before Finch Hatton township. The gorge itself lies 12km north of the main road, across several fords – access depends on the season, though generally it's negotiable by all vehicles.

From a picnic area at road's end, graded **walking tracks** ascend through a hot jungle of palms, vines and creepers to where the gorge winds down the side of Mount Dalrymple as a rocky creek pocked with swimming holes. **Araluen Falls**, a beautiful – if icy – pool and cascade 1.5km along, is the perfect place to spend a summer's day. Another 1.5km further up, there's an even prettier cascade at the **Wheel of Fire Falls**, where you can sit up to your neck in the water.

Eungella township

About 15km past Finch Hatton township, the main road makes an unforgettably steep and twisting ascent up the range to **EUNGELLA**. This spread-out hamlet comprises a general store and a couple of cafés. Be prepared for **rain**: Eungella translates as "Land of Cloud".

Broken River

Continue for 5km beyond Eungella, through patches of forest and dairy pasture, and you'll come to a tiny bridge that crosses **BROKEN RIVER** itself. Pretty landscaped picnic grounds on the far side are home to the Platypus Lodge café and the attached, generally unmanned, park **visitor centre**.

Platypus-watching

Paved footpaths follow the riverbank both east and west of the bridge, each ending after roughly 400m at a separate **platypus-watching** platforms. Both enjoy attractive settings, but your best chance of actually spotting a platypus is right under the bridge itself. Platypuses are fiercely territorial little creatures, and the entire stretch of river between the two platforms "belongs" to one small family (of four, at last count). Normally timid, they've become quite tolerant of people here, and although they're more active at night – with sunrise as the optimum moment for sightings – you may see them at any time of day.

The forest

The real star of Broken River is the **forest** itself, which can be explored along hiking trails that branch off into the woods beyond either platform, running parallel to the river. Ancient trees with buttressed roots and immensely high canopies conceal a forest floor of rich rotting timber, ferns, palms and vines. Local cabbage palms, with their straight trunks and crown of large, fringed leaves; huge, scaly-barked Mackay cedar; and tulip oaks are all endemic. It can be difficult to see **animals** in the undergrowth, but the sun-splashed paths attract goannas and snakes, and you'll certainly hear plenty of birds.

ARRIVAL AND DEPARTURE

By car From Mackay, head south down Nebo Road (Hwy 1) to the city limits, then follow signs west along the Peak Downs Highway; if you're coming down the highway from Proserpine, follow signs just south of tiny Kuttabul, 30km north of Mackay.

EUNGELLA NATIONAL PARK

On a tour Reeforest run tours from Mackay that take in both sections of the park including a BBQ lunch and a swim at Finch Hatton Gorge (from $120; Wed & Sun 11am, other days on request; ☎ 07 4959 8360, ☎ reeforest.com.au).

ACTIVITIES

Ziplining Zip through the treetops (and a flying-fox colony) with Forest Flying (☎ 07 4958 3359, ☎ forestflying.com) for as close a view of the forest canopy as you're ever likely to get ($60). Pick-up from *Finch Hatton Gorge Cabins*.

ACCOMMODATION AND EATING

FINCH HATTON GORGE

Finch Hatton Gorge Cabins 730 Gorge Rd ☎ 07 4958 3281, ☎ finchhattongorgecabins.com.au. Self-contained units in tranquil woodland with BBQ facilities, and breakfast and home-cooked meals available. Minimum two-day stay. **$155**

★ **Platypus Bush Camp** Gorge Rd, immediately across the first creek ☎ 07 4958 3204, ☎ bushcamp .net. Camping and basic cabin accommodation: mattress, pillow, amenities and kitchen (for cabins) are supplied; the rest (including food) is up to you. It's an incredibly authentic rainforest experience: you'll see an astonishing array of bird and animal life (including the elusive platypus), sit by a fire under the stars, shower in the rainforest amid fairy-like fireflies, and be lulled to sleep by a gurgling creek. Unpowered sites **$15**, dorms **$25**, cabins **$75**

EUNGELLA TOWNSHIP

Eungella Chalet Chelmer St ☎ 07 4958 4509 ☎ eungellachalet.com.au. The back-lawn beer garden of this popular pub sits just metres away from a 700m drop into the forest, with a fantastic panorama down the valley. Full breakfasts, and burgers and steaks for $17–22. Daily 8–9.30am, noon–2pm & 6–8pm.

BROKEN RIVER

Broken River Bush Camp 600m from the Broken River picnic spot ☎ 13 74 68, ☎ nprsr.qld.gov.au. Set in open bushland just before the bridge, this campground is suitable for motorhomes and caravans as well as tents, but has no water or toilets; campers have to use the park facilities across the river. **$5.95**

★ **Broken River Mountain Resort** Eungella Dam Rd ☎ 07 4958 4000, ☎ brokenrivermr.com.au. A stunning riverside hideaway for nature lovers, a couple of minutes' walk from the platypus-watching area, with good, large motel rooms, a pretty pool, reference library, and free wildlife walks on offer. Possums sport nightly on the veranda of the very good on-site restaurant, where hearty mains cost around $30. **$140**

Fern Flat Camping Area Around 600m west of the bridge ☎ 13 74 68, ☎ nprsr.qld.gov.au. Shady site above the river accessible along an unpaved track. There's a basic loo, although better toilet facilities, a kiosk and gas BBQs are available at the nearby picnic spot. **$5.95**

Platypus Lodge Restaurant 534 Eungella Dam Rd ☎ 07 4958 4785, ☎ platypuslodgerestaurant.com.au. Friendly little café, adjoining the park visitor centre just steps from the river – you can eat right on the bank – and serving all-day breakfasts, plus kangaroo or crocodile burgers for $16 and schnitzel or steak for $18. Wed–Sat 9.30am–3.30pm, Sun 7am–3.30pm.

Airlie Beach and around

Best known as the gateway for visitors heading to and from the breathtaking **Whitsunday Islands**, but also a destination in its own right, **AIRLIE BEACH** stretches along the shores of Pioneer Bay, 150km north of Mackay. Squeezed between the sea and a hillside covered in apartment blocks, it fully deserves its reputation as a party town, but although it's always buzzing with backpackers, it has plenty of fancier accommodation and restaurant options as well.

Despite the name, Airlie Beach only has a couple of scruffy scraps of beach. Instead, the oceanfront lawns have been landscaped to form a free, open-air **lagoon**, fringed with sand and complete with showers, changing rooms, picnic hotplates, benches and emerald expanses of grass. Beyond that lies the deep turquoise bay, dotted with yachts and cruisers and absolutely gorgeous, while local commercial activity is concentrated along **Shute Harbour Road** and the brief **Esplanade**, inland.

Just beyond the east end of town, the gleaming new **Port of Airlie** has become the main ferry port for the Whitsundays. Some excursion boats still operate, however, from both **Shute Harbour** (aka **Shutehaven**), 10km further east beyond Cape Conway National Park, and **Abell Point Marina** in the sprawling community of **Cannonvale**, just around the headland west of Airlie Beach and best reached by a very pleasant boardwalk stroll.

Conway National Park

Stretching inland of Airlie Beach to both east and west, **Conway National Park** preserves a thick expanse of lowland tropical rainforest basking in the shadow of the Conway Range. An easy walking track from a small roadside parking area on Shute Harbour Road, 6.5km east of town, climbs **Mount Rooper** to an observation platform that gazes out towards the white peaks of the Whitsundays, jutting out of the unbelievably blue sea.

Alternatively, drive 5km east up Forestry Road, which leaves Shute Harbour Road 11km west of Airlie Beach, and you'll find yourself at the start of the **Conway Circuit**. A total hike of 27km from here, usually done by camping out for one or two nights en route, would bring you back to Airlie Beach. For a more manageable day-hike in the dense rainforest up here, either take the short **Kingfisher Circuit** (2km), or follow the main trail as far as **Little Impulse Creek**, and then turn back (9km round-trip).

ARRIVAL AND DEPARTURE — AIRLIE BEACH AND AROUND

By plane Whitsunday Coast Airport, 14km south of the workaday sugar town of Proserpine on Laschelles Ave and also known as Proserpine Airport, is the mainland airport serving island visitors, with flights to Brisbane (2 daily; 1hr 30min) and Sydney (3 weekly; 2hr). Whitsunday Transit meets every flight, and charges $20 one-way for the 38km transfer to Airlie Beach, which must be pre-booked. The private airstrip at Whitsunday Airport, 5km east of Airlie (☎07 4946 9180, �🌐whitsundayairport .com), is used by charter flights to and from the islands, and by GSL Aviation (☎07 4946 9097, �🌐gslaviation .com.au), who offer scenic flights as well as on-demand transfers to Hamilton Island.

By train Trains between Cairns (10hr north) and Brisbane (14hr south) stop at Proserpine station, 26km southeast of

Airlie Beach and connected by Whitsunday Transit buses ($16.50 one-way).

By bus Long-distance buses stop at the Heart of the Reef terminal at the Port of Airlie.
Destinations Ayr (6 daily; 3hr 15min); Brisbane (4 daily; 19hr); Bundaberg (3 daily; 12hr 30min); Cairns (4 daily; 10hr); Hervey Bay (4 daily; 14hr); Mackay (5 daily; 2hr 15min); Mission Beach (3 daily; 8hr); Noosa (2 daily; 16hr 45min); Rainbow Beach (2 daily; 15hr); Rockhampton (4 daily; 7hr 30min); Townsville (3 daily; 4hr).

By ferry Ferries go to the Whitsundays (see p.372) from the Port of Airlie (�🌐portofairlie.com.au), as do cruises from Shute Harbour, 10km east, and Abell Point, 1km west.

By car Airlie Beach is 26km east of Highway 1, via a turn-off just north of Proserpine.

GETTING AROUND

By bus Whitsunday Transit (☎07 4946 1800, �🌐whitsundaytransit.com.au) run scheduled buses between Proserpine and Shutehaven, stopping at Cannonvale and Airlie Beach, and also on-demand shuttles

to and from Proserpine's airport and train station.
By car There's very little free parking; leaving your car at the Port of Airlie costs $8/day.
By taxi Whitsunday Taxis ☎ 13 10 08.

INFORMATION AND ACTIVITIES

Tourist information The Whitsunday Region Information Centre is on Hwy 1 in Proserpine (daily 9am–5pm; ☎07 4945 3967). Airlie Beach does not have an

official visitor centre, just lots of private ticket and transport agencies. The National Parks office in Shutehaven sells island camping permits (Mon–Fri 9am–4.30pm;

📞 07 4946 7022, 🖥 nprsr.qld.gov.au).

Kayaking Salty Dog (📞 07 4946 1388, 🖥 saltydog.com.au) rent camping and snorkelling gear, plus kayaks for $50/day, and run excellent guided sea-kayaking expeditions (from $80 for half a day up to $1750 for a six-day camping trip).

Scenic flights Whitsunday Tigermoth Adventures offer scenic tours and stunt flights over the Whitsundays in a vintage Tiger Moth biplane (10min–1hr; $125–360; 📞 07 4946 9111, 🖥 tigermothadventures.com.au); Air Whitsunday Seaplanes run scenic flights over the Whitsundays and Great Barrier Reef in a seaplane (from

$295; 📞 07 4946 9111, 🖥 airwhitsunday.com.au); Helireef offer exhilarating helicopter flights over the islands and reef (from $135; 📞 07 4946 9102, 🖥 helireef.com.au).

Segway Tours Whitsunday Segway Tours run a fantastic rainforest tour in the upper reaches of Conway National Park every morning and an evening boardwalk tour to Abell Point from Airlie Beach each evening, including a stop for tapas ($129/$99; 📞 04 3273 4929, 🖥 whitsundaysegwaytours .com.au).

Skydiving Freefall from 14,000ft with Skydive Airlie Beach (from $284; 📞 07 4946 9115, 🖥 skydiveairliebeach.com.au).

ACCOMMODATION

Airlie Beach Hotel 16 The Esplanade 📞 07 4964 1999, 🖥 airliebeachhotel.com.au. Right at the heart of the Esplanade action, this is one of the smartest places to stay, eat and drink in Airlie; paying a little extra gets you a sea-view balcony. **$195**

Backpackers by the Bay 12 Hermitage Drive 📞 07 4946 7267, 🖥 backpackersbythebay.com. Homely hostel, just up the hill from the centre and with less of a party atmosphere than its neighbours down below. Friendly old-school service, clean four- and eight-bed dorms, a pool, lovely grassy garden, plus a bar and terrace screening outdoor movies. Dorms **$27**, doubles **$83**

Base Airlie Beach 336 Shute Harbour Rd 📞 07 4948 2000, 🖥 stayatbase.com.au. Resort-style party hostel with big en-suite dorms and doubles (some with spa baths), a lagoon-style pool, and a loud bar and nightclub. Dorms **$32**, doubles **$70**

Big4 Airlie Cove Resort and Van Park 2634 Shute Harbour Rd, Jubilee Pocket 📞 07 4946 6727, 🖥 airliecove.com.au. Family resort in lush woodlands 3km east of Airlie, with ample space to camp and a good range of cabins (the cheapest share bathrooms), right up to Bali-style villas. Powered sites **$39**, cabins **$95**, villas **$180**

Coral Point Lodge 54 Harbour Ave, Shute Harbour 📞 07 4946 9500, 🖥 coralpointlodge.com.au. Delightful, light-filled and excellent-value rooms and self-catering apartments, with fabulous views over the Whitsundays. **$150**

Coral Sea Resort 25 Oceanview Ave 📞 07 4946 1300, 🖥 coralsearesort.com. Full-blown resort, in a great location at the headland towards Cannonville, a short walk from central Airlie Beach. All the rooms are very smart – some have ocean views – and there's a good restaurant, private jetty, popular bar and pool area too. **$259**

★ **Kipara** 2614 Shute Harbour Rd, Jubilee Pocket 📞 07 4946 6483, 🖥 kipara.com.au. Wonderfully verdant budget resort, near Conway National Park 1.5km east of the ferry marina, holding simple en-suite doubles plus larger cabins and self-catering family villas, along with a pool, sundeck and two camp kitchens. Doubles **$85**, cabins **$130**, villas **$150**

Water's Edge Resort 4 Golden Orchid Drive 📞 07 4948 4300, 🖥 watersedgewhitsundays.com.au. Spacious, stylish, contemporary one- to three-room apartments, all with island-view balconies, perched on the hillside 100m up from the heart of town and sharing three infinity pools. **$225**

EATING AND DRINKING

For **supplies**, the biggest supermarket is in Cannonvale, though there's a well-stocked food store on Shute Harbour Rd, halfway through Airlie Beach.

Cool LaLa 265 Shute Harbour Rd 📞 07 4948 2405. Friendly Chinese place, a few steps from the lagoon at the western end of town, where the Taiwanese owner serves bubble tea as well as tasty dishes like braised beef cheek or garlic stir-fried chicken, with mains at around $20. Tues–Sat 11am–8.30pm, Sun 11am–4pm.

Denmans 33 Port Drive, Port of Airlie 📞 07 4948 1333. Halfway along the fancy mall that leads to the ferry terminal, this waterfront bar/restaurant serves tapas-style snacks like a delicious $14 grilled kangaroo, more substantial fish'n'chips for around $20, plus sundowner cocktails and every bottled beer you could dream of. Mon & Wed–Fri noon–9pm, Sat & Sun noon–10pm.

★ **Fish D'vine** 303 Shute Harbour Rd 📞 07 4948 0088, 🖥 fishdvine.com.au. Serendipitous combination of specialist rum bar, stocking 450 brands from all over the world, and award-winning seafood café, with exceptionally well-cooked beer-battered fish and chips for $24, plus fish curries and fusion dishes for around £32. Mon–Fri 5pm–late, Sat & Sun 11.30am–10pm.

Magnum's 336 Shute Harbour Rd 📞 07 4946 6188, 🖥 magnumshotel.com.au. In the backpackers' of the same name this loud and proud drinking venue is home to six bars, with self-explanatory names including the buzzing *Beer Garden* and the *Party Bar*, which hosts live touring bands. Daily 10am–3am.

3

3

Mr Bones Shop 263 Shute Harbour Rd ☏ 0413 017 331. Cool café-bar overlooking the lagoon serving breakfast until 4pm and all-day meals, including 12-inch pizzas (from $18) and inventive tapas. Tues–Sat 9am–9pm.

DIRECTORY

Banks NAB and Commonwealth in Airlie Beach.
Doctor 283 Shute Harbour Rd (Mon–Fri 8am–5pm, Sat 9am–5pm; 24hr phoneline ☏ 07 4948 0900).
Pharmacy Airlie Day and Night Pharmacy, 366 Shute Harbour Rd (daily 8am–8pm).

Police 8 Altmann Ave, off Shute Harbour Rd, Cannonvale ☏ 13 14 44.
Post office 226 Shute Harbour Rd, Cannonvale (Mon–Fri 9am–5pm, Sat 9am–12.30pm).

The Whitsunday Islands

Still resembling the granite mountain peaks they used to be, until rising sea levels cut them off from the mainland six thousand years ago, the 74 beautiful **Whitsunday Islands** are the jewels of the Queensland coast. When Captain Cook passed through

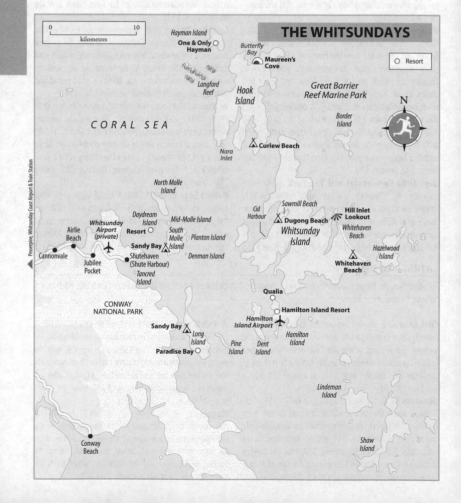

this way in 1770 the islands were seasonally inhabited by the Ngaro Aborigines. Cook proceeded to name the area as a whole after the day of his arrival, and assorted specific locations after his expedition's sponsors. Clad in dense green pine forest, their roughly contoured coastlines etched against the vivid blue water and the surrounding seas bustling with yachts and cruisers, the islands make an unforgettable spectacle.

Although the first resorts opened here in the 1930s, there are currently only a handful in operation, and most of the islands remain undeveloped national parks, with around fifteen of them holding campsites. The few islands left in private hands are largely uninhabited, and predominantly the preserve of local yachties. Many visitors therefore base themselves in **Airlie Beach** (see p.369), and explore the islands on boat excursions and cruises.

Don't miss the chance to go **whale watching** if you're here between June and September, when humpbacks arrive from their Antarctic wintering grounds to give birth and raise their calves before heading south again.

ARRIVAL AND DEPARTURE — THE WHITSUNDAY ISLANDS

3

By ferry Cruise Whitsundays (☎07 4846 7000, ⓦcruisewhitsundays.com.au) run ferries from the Port of Airlie terminal in Airlie Beach to Daydream Island (9 daily, 6.45am–5pm; 30min; $40 one-way) and Hamilton Island (8 daily, 7.15am–3.50pm; 1hr 10min; $61 one-way), and also from Shute Harbour, east of Airlie Beach, to Hamilton Island only (3 daily, 6.30am–4.45pm; 35min; $61 one-way). Other resorts run their own transfers for guests only.

Camping transfers For camping transfers to National Parks campsites on Whitsunday, Hook, Henning, Denman, Planton and South Molle islands, use the Scamper water taxi (☎07 4946 6285, ⓦwhitsundaycamping.com.au). Return drop-offs range from $65–160, and they also rent two-person camping kits ($40 for first night, $20 per night thereafter).

CRUISES

When choosing a **cruise**, it's always worth asking around for the latest word-of-mouth advice on current deals and operators. Check the length of trips carefully – "three days" might mean one full day and two half-days – along with how much time is actually spent cruising and at the destination, and how many other passengers will be on the vessel.

DAY-TRIPS

Day-trips usually offer the chance to experience the thrills of boom-netting – sitting in a large rope hammock stretched above the water at the front of the boat, to catch the full soaking force of the waves – and snorkelling; some, though, concentrate on a single theme, such as whale watching, fishing or lazing on Whitehaven Beach. Most cruises include free pick-up from Airlie Beach hotels.

Cruise Whitsundays ☎07 4846 7000, ⓦcruisewhitsundays.com.au. The island ferry operator also offers day-trips from the Port of Airlie, including a tour that takes you to the beach on Whitehaven Island with stops at Daydream and Hamilton islands ($205), and an excursion out to the permanently tethered Reefworld pontoon, where you can snorkel, and ride over the Great Barrier Reef in a glass-bottomed semi-submersible ($235; diving $99 extra).

Derwent Hunter ☎07 4946 7124, ⓦtallship adventures.com.au. This 30m schooner, now kitted out with timber decking and fittings after years as a research vessel and a film set, visits Langford Reef and/or Bali Hai ($175).

Ocean Rafting ☎07 4946 6848, ⓦoceanrafting.com. Two great-value, action-packed cruises to Whitehaven Beach, on zippy, semi-rigid inflatables that charge through the waves in search of thrills. Both visit Hill Inlet; one allows more time snorkelling, the other more time on the beach ($149, lunch $15). Maximum of 25 passengers.

Whitehaven Express ☎07 4946 1585, ⓦwhitehave nxpress.com.au. Family-orientated trips to Whitsunday Island, including Hill Inlet, a beach BBQ at Whitehaven and snorkel at Manta Ray Bay ($175).

LONGER TRIPS

Multiday cruises cover much the same territory as day-trips but at a slower pace, typically visiting Hook Island via Nara Inlet, then continuing to Whitehaven Beach on Whitsunday, and costing $400–550 for two-night, three-day outings. Several operators give sailing lessons or offer scuba diving for certified divers (rates vary upwards from $75 for a first dive, $40 for subsequent dives).

Anaconda III ☎07 4914 2425, ⓦanacondaiii.com. Large, fantastically comfortable party yacht, taking up to 32 passengers. Relatively expensive, but you do get three full days and three nights aboard, with a full day at Bait Reef (diving available).

Avatar ☎07 4946 6877, ⓦozsail.com.au. Slick, fast 26-passenger trimaran with plenty of room for lounging, offering two nights aboard.

On Ice ☎ 1300 414 419, ⓦ isailwhitsundays.com. Snazzy 46ft catamaran (sleeping 10) for 46hr sails, kitted out with sea scooters, stand-up paddleboards and see-through kayaks.
Southern Cross ☎ 07 4946 4999, ⓦ soxsail.com.au. Company specializing in maxi-yacht racers, offering one- and two-night cruises on high-speed racing yachts.
Waltzing Matilda Whitsundays Sailing Adventures ☎ 07 4940 2000, ⓦ whitsundayssailingadventures.com.au. More modern than most of the tall and vintage-style ships offered by this large operation, this 16m, fourteen-passenger ketch is not that roomy, but has a great atmosphere, and operates three two-day, one-night trips per week.

BAREBOAT CHARTERS

Only experienced sailors should consider a bareboat charter – renting a yacht without a skipper or crew. The average wind speed in the Whitsundays is 15–25 knots, which means serious sailing. Unless you know exactly what you want, it's best to book through an agent. Reliable operators include Whitsunday Rent-a-Yacht (☎ 07 4946 9232, ⓦ rentayacht.com.au) and Queensland Yacht Charters (☎ 07 4946 7400, ⓦ yachtcharters.com .au). Small yachts start at around $500/day; add another $100 or so during holiday seasons.

ACCOMMODATION

Camping If you're planning to use the island campsites, you'll need to arrange transport, then obtain permits from the National Parks office in Shutehaven (see p.370). At most, facilities comprise a pit toilet, picnic tables and rainwater tanks, so take everything you'll need with you, especially insect repellent, a fuel stove (wood fires are prohibited) and drinking water – you can rent gear (tent, stove, esky, etc) from Scamper (☎ 07 4946 6285, ⓦ whitsundaycamping.com.au). If you're staying a

while, you can ask their water taxi to ferry in supplies.
Resorts These sometimes have a higher profile than the islands on which they stand. The cost tends to be beyond most budget travellers' means, but standby deals can slash prices, and polite bargaining is always worth a try. Most also allow day-trippers to use their facilities, an economical way to explore the islands while staying at cheaper Airlie Beach options.

Daydream Island

As the most accessible of the Whitsundays, just half an hour by ferry from the Port of Airlie, **Daydream Island** is the most visited of the islands, and makes an obvious target for a day-trip. Little more than a tiny wooded rise between South Molle and the mainland, it's almost entirely taken over by the eponymous **Daydream Island Resort**. So long as you don't arrive expecting a wilderness experience, it's actually a fun place to spend some time. A narrow coarse-sand **beach** runs the length of its eastern shore, while attractive little **Lovers Cove** at the north end holds some coral to snorkel over. Wild wallabies wander through the resort, and day-trippers are welcome to use facilities like its mini golf course and various bars and cafés.

ARRIVAL AND ACCOMMODATION   DAYDREAM ISLAND

By ferry Cruise Whitsundays (☎ 07 4846 7000, ⓦ cruisewhitsundays.com.au) run regular ferries from the Port of Airlie to Daydream Island (9 daily, 6.45am–5pm; 30min; $40 one-way), many of which continue to Hamilton Island. Several operators also pick up guests from Daydream Island for excursions to the outer Whitsundays.

★**Daydream Island Resort** Daydream Island ☎ 07 3259 2350, ⓦ daydreamisland.com. Ideal for families, this large low-rise resort occupies most of the island, and holds three meandering swimming pools, assorted restaurants and cafés, an outdoor cinema, and a huge open-air Living Reef aquarium that's stocked with reef sharks and manta rays. $380

The Molles islands

South Molle Island was a source of fine-grained stone for Ngaro Aborigines, a unique material for the tools that have been found on other islands and may help in mapping trade routes. A series of fabulous coastal **walking tracks** crisscross the island, including one that leads from behind the nine-hole golf course through gum trees and light forest, encompassing vistas of the islands from the top of Spion Kop and Mount Jeffreys, and on to some quiet beaches at the south end.

Tiny **Planton**, **Tancred** and **Denman** islands, just offshore from South Molle with no facilities and only limited camping at National Parks sites, are about as isolated as you can get in the Whitsundays. All three are surrounded by reef, but beware of strong currents.

ARRIVAL AND ACCOMMODATION   THE MOLLES ISLANDS

By boat Scamper offer drop-offs by boat on South Molle, Planton and Denman islands for $65 return (☎ 07 4946 6285, ⓦ whitsundaycamping.com.au).
Sandy Bay South Molle Island ☎ 13 74 68,

ⓦ nprsr.qld.gov.au. There's good access to the island's walking tracks from this open campsite next to the beach and shaded by casuarinas. **$5.95**

Long Island

Long Island is exactly that, being not much more than a narrow, 10km ribbon almost separated from the mainland forests by a 500m-wide channel. At the time of writing, the signature *Long Island Resort* was closed indefinitely, pending refurbishment. The island's fabulous **beaches** are still there, though, along with looping hikes that lead through the rainforest to **Sandy Bay** and up **Humpy Point**.

3

ARRIVAL AND ACCOMMODATION   LONG ISLAND

By boat There is currently no ferry service to Long Island.
Paradise Bay ☎ 04 1903 0626, ⓦ paradisebay. au. Pure escapism; nine luxury waterfront cabins, superb food (included) and attentive service. You can only get here by helicopter on a 10min scenic flight from Hamilton

Island or Airlie Beach, which costs an additional $760 per bungalow. **$1500**
Sandy Bay Campsite ☎ 13 74 68, ⓦ nprsr.qld.gov.au. Next to a secluded beach, and only accessible with your own boat, this National Park campsite has access to the island's walking tracks. **$5.95**

Hamilton Island

With a large marina, an airstrip, tons of motorized sports and several high-rise apartment towers, **Hamilton Island** is by far the most heavily commercialized of all the islands. Privately owned, its businesses operate under a lease: development includes a waterfront strip facing the marina on the west coast, complete with bank, post office, bakery, nightclub, and restaurants, and a five-minute walk from there, across the island's narrowest point, four hotels that operate under the umbrella of **Hamilton Island Resort**. The twin towers of *Reef View Hotel* loom over **Catseye Beach** here – an enormous expanse at low tide – with dramatic views of Whitsunday Island across the narrow strait.

To explore Hamilton Island, you can rent a motorized dinghy or a golf buggy to ride around the residential roads twisting along the northern peninsula. The best option, though, is the well-used walking track to the 239m-high **Passage Peak**, which offers the finest 360-degree panorama in the Whitsundays.

ARRIVAL AND DEPARTURE   HAMILTON ISLAND

By plane Hamilton Island Airport, also known as Great Barrier Reef Airport (ⓦ hamiltonisland.com.au.airport), has flights to Brisbane (1 daily; 1hr 30min); Cairns (1 daily; 1hr 30min); Melbourne (5 weekly; 3hr); and Sydney (2 daily; 2hr 20min).
By ferry Cruise Whitsundays (☎ 07 4846 7000,

ⓦ cruisewhitsundays.com.au) run ferries to Hamilton from the Port of Airlie terminal (8 daily, 7.15am–3.50pm; 1hr 10min; $61 one-way), and Shute Harbour (3 daily, 6.30am–4.45pm; 35min; $61 one-way), with frequent connections to Daydream Island.

GETTING AROUND

By bus Free shuttle buses run three routes on the island, every 15min 7am–11pm.

By boat You can rent a motorized dinghy from the marina (daily 8.30am–4.30pm; half/full day $145/$235).

3

ACCOMMODATION AND EATING

Hamilton Island Resort ☎13 73 33, ⓦhamiltonisland.com.au. The resort holds four excellent hotels: the individual A-frame cabins of *Palm Bungalows*, the high-rise *Reef View Hotel*, the boutique adult-only *Beach Club*, and the ultra-exclusive *Qualia* (where Taylor Swift stayed on her 2015 visit). $370

Popeyes Takeaway Front St ☎07 4946 9999. Affordable chippie with tables on the terrace beside the marina. Salt and pepper squid costs $10.50. Licensed. Daily 10am–9pm.

Tako Front St ☎07 4946 8032. On an open deck overlooking the marina, this excellent dinner-only Mexican restaurant has some surprising Korean and Japanese influences – *tako* is Japanese for octopus, and they serve a tako taco. The $9 grilled corn starter is great, and so too is the $21 chicken mole plate. Daily 5.30–9pm.

Whitsunday Island

The largest of the islands, National Parks-run **Whitsunday Island**, is also one of the most enjoyable. Its east coast is famed as home to the 5km-long **Whitehaven Beach**, not only the finest in all the islands but often ranked among the very best in all the world, and on the itinerary of just about every cruise boat hereabouts. Blindingly white, and still clean despite the numbers of day-trippers and campers, it's a beautiful spot where there's blissfully little to do. The headland off the southern end of the beach facing Haslewood Island is the best place for snorkelling. On the beach's northern end, a short track winds up to **Hill Inlet Lookout**, where everyone jostles to take the definitive panoramic photo of the dazzling expanse of sand.

Cid Harbour, over on Whitsunday's west side, is a quieter hideaway that lacks a great beach, but instead enjoys a backdrop of giant granite boulders and tropical forests, with several more campsites above coral and pebble shingle. **Dugong Beach** is the nicest, sheltered under the protective arms and buttressed roots of giant trees; from here you can walk along the narrow hill paths to another campsite at Sawmill Beach.

ARRIVAL AND ACCOMMODATION   WHITSUNDAY ISLAND

By boat Several companies offer day-trips to Whitehaven, while Scamper take bush campers there by boat for $105–155 return (☎07 4946 6285, ⓦwhitsundaycamping.com.au).

Dugong Beach ☎13 74 68, ⓦnprsr.qld.gov.au. Campsite beside a pretty beach in a dry rainforest setting, with minimal shelter provided by whispering casuarinas. $5.95

Whitehaven Beach ☎13 74 68, ⓦnprsr.qld.gov.au. Waking up to Whitehaven's dazzling white sands is the major lure for campers here; sites are shaded by vine forest and eucalyptus. $5.95

Hook Island

Directly north of Whitsunday, and pretty similar in appearance, **Hook Island** is the second largest in the group. Its solitary resort hotel having been closed for several years – in theory it's due to be redeveloped, but no willing investors have come forward – it's little visited these days. Day-cruises from Airlie to the snorkelling spots visit the top-rate fringing coral at **Manta Ray Bay**, **Langford Reef** and **Butterfly Bay**, on the northern and northeastern tips of the island – visibility can be poor, but on a good day these sites offer some of the Whitsundays' finest diving.

Occasional cruises also pull into southern **Nara Inlet**, for a look at the **Aboriginal paintings** on the roof of a small cave above a tiny shingle beach. Though not dramatic in scale or design, the art is significant for its net patterns, otherwise found only at central highland sites such as Carnarvon Gorge (see p.447).

ARRIVAL AND ACCOMMODATION   HOOK ISLAND

By boat Scamper take bush campers to Hook Island by boat for $160 return (☎07 4946 6285, ⓦwhitsundaycamping.com.au).

Curlew Beach ☎13 74 68, ⓦnprsr.qld.gov.au. Campsite on one of the island's nicest beaches – sheltered, pretty, backed by rainforest and accessible only with your own vessel or prior arrangement with Scamper. $5.95

Hayman Island

Tiny Hayman Island, off the northwest tip of **Hook Island** and thus the northernmost of the Whitsundays, is home to the island's most exclusive and expensive resort. The sheer cost of staying here is eclipsed by the expense of building the *One & Only* resort in the first place – over $300 million. Public access is restricted to a couple of luxury tour operators, although some cruises and dive-trips stop for a look at the coral off **Blue Pearl Bay** – not actually all that exciting – on the west coast.

ACCOMMODATION   HAYMAN ISLAND

One & Only Hayman Island ☎07 4940 1244, ⓦhayman.com.au. One of the the Whitsundays' most luxurious options, offering rooms, suites and beachfront villas; facilities include an iconic pool, spa and four restaurants. Staff move about through underground tunnels to avoid getting in anyone's way. $620

Bowen

The seafront Hwy 1 settlement of **BOWEN**, 80km northwest of Airlie Beach, was once a candidate to become state capital, but it floundered after the foundation of Townsville. Overlooked and undeveloped ever since, it's a sleepy sort of place, dotted with historic clapboard buildings and offering a certain small-town charm.

Bowen made the perfect location for Baz Luhrmann's 2008 movie, *Australia*. Deluged in red sand, the waterfront stood in for 1940s Darwin, but the entire movie set was destroyed in the filming of a wartime bombing raid, and nothing now remains from the mass Hollywood intrusion. Instead, the main attraction for travellers is the prospect of seasonal **farm work**: Bowen's mangoes and tomatoes are famous throughout Queensland, and a large floating population of itinerant pickers moves into town between April and January.

Bowen's centre overlooks **Edgecumbe Bay**, with shops and services spaced out along broad but empty **Herbert Street**. Attractive **beaches** north of the centre include north-facing **Queens Beach**, which is sheltered, long and has a stinger net for the jellyfish season, but the best is **Horseshoe Bay**, small, and hemmed in by some sizeable boulders, with good waters for a swim or snorkel.

ARRIVAL AND INFORMATION   BOWEN

By train The train station is alongside the highway, 5km west of the centre.
Destinations Ayr (6 weekly; 2hr 15min); Brisbane (6 weekly; 14hr 30min); Bundaberg (6 weekly; 9hr 30min); Caboolture (6 weekly; 13hr 30min); Cairns (6 weekly; 9hr 30min); Mackay (6 weekly; 1hr 30min); Rockhampton (6 weekly; 6hr 30min); Townsville (6 weekly; 3hr 30min).

By bus Long-distance buses stop outside Bowen Travel (☎07 4786 2835), just off Herbert St on Williams St.
Destinations Airlie Beach (4 daily; 1hr); Brisbane (4 daily; 20hr); Cairns (5 daily; 10hr); Hervey Bay (4 daily; 15hr 30min); Mission Beach (4 daily; 8hr); Rockhampton (4 daily; 7hr 30min); Townsville (5 daily; 3hr 45min).

ACCOMMODATION

Bogie River Bush House 13 Normanby Rd, Binbee ☎07 4785 3407, ⓦbushbunks.com. If you're looking for work, try this ranch-style abode, 60km southwest of Bowen towards Collinsville. Budget accommodation is offered at weekly rates to potential farm workers, and should be booked in advance. It doubles as a splendid B&B retreat, with a decent dining room and pool, and guests can go horseriding, fishing, or play with tame wildlife. Dorms $28, doubles $145
Bowen Backpackers Beach end of Herbert St ☎07 4786 3433, ⓦbowenbackpackers.com.au. Long-standing working hostel with adequate rooms and a pool, plus connections with local farms. Sometimes closed Feb–March. Dorms $40
Castle Motor Lodge 6 Don St ☎07 4786 1322, ⓦcastlemotorlodge.com.au. This friendly central motel sports a castle-like facade, and medieval armour festooning the restaurant, along with clean exposed-brick rooms, a pool and a free laundry. $120

EATING

Food Freaks 1 Starboard Drive ☎07 4786 5133. Colourful café by the harbour, dishing out gourmet sandwiches, pasta, burgers and seafood from around $15. Wed–Sun 9.30am–2.30pm.

Jochheims Pies 49 George St ☎07 4786 6600, ⓦjochheimspies.com.au. Look closely in the movie

Australia and you'll see evidence of one or more of these definitive Aussie pies contributing to the curve of Hugh Jackman's belly. Steak and other flavours from $5.15, plus scones, muffins and custard tarts, to eat in the café or take away. Mon–Fri 5.30am–3.30pm, Sat 6am–3pm.

Ayr and around

The towns of **Home Hill** and **Ayr** stand 100km further on up the highway from Bowen, separated by a mill, around 10km of cane fields, and the iron framework of the **Burdekin River Bridge**. This gaping river, a major landmark hereabouts, is still liable to flood during severe wet seasons, despite having to fight its way across three weirs and a dam.

AYR, north of the bridge, is a compact farming town that's another popular stop on the **farm-work** trail. It's also a great place to come **diving**: the *Yongala*, a 109m-long passenger ship that sank with all hands during a cyclone in March 1911, now lies intact and encrusted in coral in 14–28m of water off Ayr. Home to turtles, rays, moray eels and huge schools of barracuda, mackerel and trevally, it makes a staggeringly good wreck dive.

ARRIVAL AND ACTIVITIES

By bus You'll find the bus stop (and all essential services) on the highway, which runs through town as Queen St. Destinations Bowen (6 weekly; 2hr 15min); Brisbane (6 weekly; 16hr 45min); Cairns (6 weekly; 7hr 15min); Townsville (6 weekly; 1hr 15min).

Diving Yongala Dive, 56 Narrah St, Alva Beach (☎07 4783

1519, ⓦyongaladive.com.au) offer two-dive trips, for certified and highly experienced divers only, from $259, including gear rental, and also have their own accommodation. As the wreck is in an exposed location, it's not much fun diving here if the weather is rough.

ACCOMMODATION AND EATING

Ayr Backpackers 54 Wilmington St ☎07 4783 5837, ⓦayrbackpackers.com.au. Working hostel set in two old Queenslanders, 100m from Coles supermarket, with small dorms and a pool. No reservations; first come, first served. Dorms **$160** per week

Burdekin Hotel 204 Queen St ☎07 4783 5419, ⓦtheburdekinhotel.com.au. Renovated central hotel, offering simple accommodation plus good, substantial meals daily, with mains costing around $15 for lunch, more like $20 for dinner. **$60**

Townsville

Regional capital and industrial powerhouse, **TOWNSVILLE** sprawls around a broad spit of land between the craggy humps of Castle Hill and swampy Ross Creek. While most travellers skip town altogether and head straight out to the beaches of laidback **Magnetic Island**, just offshore, the city does have its moments, with its palpable maritime history, active and energetic population, long sea views from the Strand promenade, and the muggy, salty evening air and old pile houses on the surrounding hills, which mark out Townsville as the coast's first real tropical city.

Townsville was **founded** in 1864 by entrepreneurs John Melton Black and Robert Towns, who felt that a settlement was needed for northern stockmen who couldn't reach Bowen when the Burdekin River was in flood. Despite an inferior harbour, the town soon outstripped Bowen in both size and prosperity, its growth accelerated by **gold** finds inland at Ravenswood and Charters Towers. Today, it's the gateway to the far

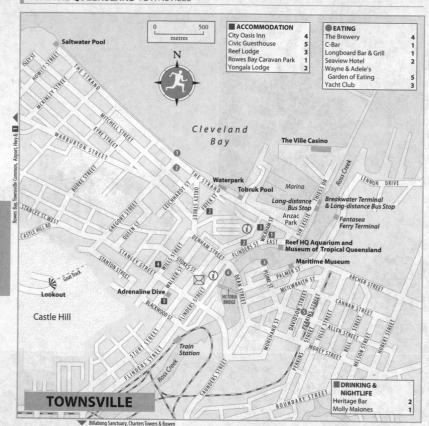

north and transit point for routes west to Mount Isa and the Northern Territory; it's also an important military centre, seat of a university, and home to substantial Torres Strait Islander and Aboriginal communities.

Flinders Street

Ross Creek, flowing towards Cleveland Bay, marks the southern boundary of downtown Townsville. **Flinders Street**, paralleling the river one block north, is the city's main drag, punctuated by the short pedestrian mall of **Flinders Square** shortly before it veers right to run its last 500m as **Flinders Street East**. This final stretch in particular holds some imposing colonial buildings, funded thanks to the nineteenth-century gold mines that lay inland.

In a grand historic edifice at the corner of Flinders and Denham streets, the **Perc Tucker Art Gallery** holds changing exhibitions of local and international art (Mon–Fri 10am–5pm, Sat & Sun 10am–2pm; free). On Sunday mornings, that same block hosts **Cotters Markets**, selling fresh produce, takeaway food and crafts (Sun 8.30am–1pm; ⓦ townsvillerotarymarkets.com.au).

Reef HQ Aquarium

2–68 Flinders St • Daily 9.30am–5pm • $28 • ☎ 07 4750 0800, ⓦ reefhq.com.au

Townsville's showpiece **Reef HQ** centres on a 2.5-million-litre aquarium that's said to be the largest tank in the world that actually contains **living coral**. A federal institution that aims for authenticity and education rather than just entertainment, it's a spectacular place, where you can watch schools of fish drifting over coral, clown fish hiding inside anemones' tentacles and myopic turtles, leopard sharks and even the odd hammerhead cruising past. Separate smaller tanks hold the likes of huge sea snakes, deep-sea nautiluses, seahorses, hideous stonefish (the no-nonsense Latin name for which is *Synanceia Horrida*), and lobsters.

Museum of Tropical Queensland

70–102 Flinders St · Daily 9.30am–5pm · $15 · ☏ 07 4726 0600, ⊛ mtq.qm.qld.gov.au

An innovative building alongside Reef HQ houses the **Museum of Tropical Queensland**, devoted to the Queensland Museum's marine archeology collection. Its pride and joy is

THE BOUNTY AND THE PANDORA

In 1788, the British Admiralty vessel **Bounty** sailed from England to Tahiti, on a mission to collect **breadfruit** seedlings, intended to provide a cheap source of food for Britain's plantation slaves in the West Indies. The stay in Tahiti's mellow climate proved so much better than life aboard the *Bounty*, however, that on the return journey in April 1789 the crew **mutinied**, led by the officer **Fletcher Christian**. Along with eighteen crew who refused to join in the mutiny, **Captain William Bligh** was set adrift in a longboat far out in the Pacific, while the mutineers returned to Tahiti, intending to settle there.

Things didn't go as planned. In an incredible feat of navigation, Bligh and all but one of his companions managed to cross more than 3600 nautical miles of open sea. They reached the Portuguese colony of Timor in June, emaciated but alive, whereupon Bligh lost no time in catching a vessel back to England, arriving there in March 1790. His report led the Admiralty to dispatch the frigate **Pandora** to Tahiti under the cold-hearted **Captain Edwards**, with instructions to bring the mutineers back to London to stand trial.

Meanwhile, Christian and seven of the mutiny's ringleaders – knowing that sooner or later the Admiralty would try to find them – had left Tahiti, along with a group of islanders, and sailed off into the Pacific in the *Bounty*. The fourteen of the *Bounty*'s crew who remained in Tahiti were rounded up when the *Pandora* arrived there in March 1791, and incarcerated in the ship's brig, a 3m-long wooden cell they knew as "**Pandora's Box**".

After a few fruitless months island-hopping in search of the *Bounty*, Captain Edwards headed up the east coast of Australia. On the night of August 29, the *Pandora* hit a northern section of the Great Barrier Reef. The next day, as waves began to break up the vessel, Edwards ordered the longboats to be loaded with supplies and abandoned ship, leaving his prisoners still locked up on board; it was only thanks to one of the crew that ten of them scrambled out as the *Pandora* slid beneath the waves.

In a minor replay of Bligh's voyage, the *Pandora*'s survivors took three weeks to get to Timor in their longboats, and arrived back in England the following year. Edwards was castigated for the heartless treatment of his prisoners, but otherwise held blameless for the wreck. The ten surviving mutineers were court-martialled: four were acquitted, three hanged, and three had their death sentences commuted. Captain Bligh later became Governor of New South Wales, where he suffered another mutiny known as the "**Rum Rebellion**" (see p.972). To add insult to injury, the *Bounty*'s whole project proved a failure; when breadfruit trees were eventually introduced to the West Indies, the slaves refused to eat them.

Seventeen years later, the American vessel *Topaz* stopped mid-Pacific at the isolated rocky fastness of **Pitcairn Island** and, to the amazement of its crew, found it settled by a small colony of English-speaking people. These turned out to be the descendants of the *Bounty* mutineers, along with the last survivor, the elderly **John Adams** (also known as Alexander Smith). Adams told the *Topaz*'s crew that, having settled Pitcairn and burned the *Bounty*, the mutineers had fought with the Tahitian men over the women, and that Christian and all the men – except Adams and three other mutineers – had been killed. The other three had since died, leaving only Adams, the women, and their children on the island. After Adams' death, Pitcairn's population was briefly moved to Norfolk Island in the 1850s (see p.246), though many of their descendants returned and still live on Pitcairn.

a full-sized, cut-away replica – figurehead and all – of the front third of the **Pandora** (see box, p.381), which is also mapped out on the carpet to give a full sense of scale. The accompanying exhibition is wonderful, with detailed displays telling the full story and an astonishing array of artefacts salvaged from the wreck itself, which was discovered in 1977. As well as water jars and bottles, tankards owned by the crew, and the surgeon's pocket watch, it even has the iron and copper fireplace, retrieved intact from the captain's cabin. There's also a fascinating account of the history of diving, while the **Ancient Seas and Reefs** gallery holds fossils finds from Outback Queensland, plus life-sized model dinosaurs.

The Strand

The Strand runs northwest along Cleveland Bay, facing out to Magnetic Island and lined with old houses and fig trees. The busy waterfront strip here is a pretty stretch of palms, beach, shady lawns and free hotplates for picnics, plus cafés, a swimming pool and an excellent **children's water park**; there's also a specially built jetty for fishing. At its eastern end, you'll find the Magnetic Island Breakwater Ferry Terminal, a **marina** (where most dive-trips depart), and a casino.

Castle Hill

A sequence of exposed pink-orange cliffs of which the tallest is 286m high, **Castle Hill** looms over central Townsville. For visitors, it's an obvious vantage point for clear views over the city and out to the distant Hervey Range and Magnetic Island. It's also the target of a nightly horde of sporting locals, who cycle, run or walk up the 3km road to the top, which starts from Stanley Street, itself 1.2km back from the sea via Gregory Street.

Townsville Town Common Conservation Park

On the coast at Pallarenda, 6km north of the centre • Daily 6.30am–6.30pm • Free

The lush, coastal **Townsville Town Common Conservation Park** makes a welcome escape from the city. The Bohle River pools into wetlands below the Many Peaks Range, a habitat perfect for **wildfowl** including the brolga, the stately symbol of the northern marshes, and magpie geese that visit in huge flocks after rain. You need a vehicle to reach the park, but once there you can get about on foot, although a car or bike makes short work of the less interesting tracks between lagoons. Camouflaged **hides** at Long Swamp and Pink Lily Lagoon let you clock up a few of the hundred or more bird species present: egrets stalk frogs around water lilies, ibises and spoonbills strain the water for edibles, and geese honk at each other, undisturbed by the low-flying airport traffic – bring binoculars.

Billabong Sanctuary

Bruce Highway, 17km south of Townsville • Daily 9am–4pm • $35 • ☎ 07 4778 8344, ⓦ billabongsanctuary.com.au

Billabong Sanctuary is a well-kept collection of Australian fauna in an attractive setting. Free-ranging wildlife includes wallabies and flocks of demanding whistling ducks on the prowl for handouts; among animals you'll probably be happier to see caged are saltwater crocs, cassowaries (bred for release into the wild), dingoes, wedge-tailed eagles and snakes. A swimming pool and snack bar make this a fine place to spend a few hours.

| **ARRIVAL AND DEPARTURE** | **TOWNSVILLE** |

By plane Townsville Airport (ⓦ townsvilleairport.com.au) is 5km northwest of town.
Destinations Brisbane (7 daily; 1hr 45min); Cairns (4 daily; 1hr); Darwin (4 weekly; 4hr 45min); Mackay (2 daily; 1hr); Melbourne (5 daily; 3hr); Mount Isa (2 daily except Sat; 1hr 50min); Rockhampton (2 daily; 1hr 30min); Sydney (1 daily; 2hr 30min).

By train The train station, 2km southwest of the centre along Flinders St, is served by local buses and taxis.
Destinations Ayr (4 weekly; 1hr 15min); Bowen (6 weekly; 2hr 30min); Brisbane (6 weekly; 17hr 30min); Caboolture (6 weekly; 17hr); Cairns (6 weekly; 6hr); Cardwell (6 weekly; 2hr 30min); Gladstone (6 weekly; 11hr 15min); Ingham (6 weekly; 1hr 30min); Mackay (6 weekly; 5hr);

Proserpine (6 weekly; 3hr 30min); Rockhampton (6 weekly; 9hr 30min).

By bus Long-distance buses pull in outside the Breakwater Ferry Terminal on the Strand.

Destinations Airlie Beach (5 daily; 4hr); Ayr (4 daily; 1hr); Brisbane (5 daily; 24hr); Bundaberg (4 daily; 15hr 30min); Cairns (5 daily; 6hr); Cardwell (5 daily; 2hr); Childers (4 daily; 18hr); Hervey Bay (5 daily; 19hr); Ingham (5 daily; 1hr 30min); Mackay (5 daily; 6hr 30min); Mission Beach (4

daily; 3hr 30min); Noosa (2 daily; 17hr); Rockhampton (4 daily; 11hr).

By ferry There are frequent passenger ferries to Magnetic Island from the Breakwater Terminal on the Strand (hourly 5.30am–10.30pm, crossing 25min; $32 return; ☎ 07 4726 0800, ⊛ sealinkqld.com.au), and car ferries from Ross St, South Townsville (every 2hr, 5.20am–6.05pm; $193 return for a car and up to four passengers, $26 for pedestrians; ☎ 07 4796 9300, ⊛ fantaseacruisingmagnetic.com.au).

GETTING AROUND

By car Independent, at 257 Ingham Rd (☎ 1800 678 843, ⊛ independentrentals.com.au), rents cars from $40/day.

By taxi There's a stand at Flinders St Mall ☎ 13 10 08.

INFORMATION AND ACTIVITIES

Tourist information The visitor centre is on Flinders Square (Mon–Sat 9am–5pm, Sun 9am–1pm; ☎ 07 4721 3660, ⊛ townsvillenorthqueensland.com.au).

Tours Kookaburra (☎ 0448 794 798, ⊛ kookaburratours .com.au) have many tour options including the city itself ($40), as well as Wallaman Falls, and Charters Towers and Paluma in the rainforest ($125 each).

Diving While Townsville's main attraction for divers is the *Yongala* shipwreck (see p.378), there's also access to the local stretch of the Barrier Reef. Adrenaline (☎ 07 4724 0600, ⊛ adrenalindive.com.au) run courses, day-trips to the *Yongala* and the reef as well as two- and three-night liveaboard trips. Two dives cost $304 including gear. Snorkellers welcome too.

ACCOMMODATION

City Oasis Inn 143 Wills St ☎ 07 4771 4068, ⊛ cityoasis .com.au. Smart motel, 1km inland from the Strand, with spotless budget and executive rooms, a lovely lagoon-style pool and off-street parking. **$108**

★ **Civic Guesthouse** 262 Walker St ☎ 07 4771 5381, ⊛ civicguesthousetownsville.com.au. Tidy backpackers' with a good kitchen, spa pool, lots of outdoor space, and free Greyhound and ferry shuttles. Both dorms and doubles come with or without a/c. Dorms **$22**, doubles **$56**

Reef Lodge 4–6 Wickham St ☎ 07 4721 1112, ⊛ reeflodge.com.au. Friendly and very central hostel, albeit rather cramped, which attracts both travellers and long-stayers working locally. Not a party hostel, but it does

have a great 1960s video arcade. Dorms **$23**, doubles **$61**

Rowes Bay Caravan Park 46 Heatleys Parade, Belgian Gardens ☎ 07 4771 3576, ⊛ rowesbaycp.com.au. Located on the coast, 3km north of the city, with decent amenities and a pool, and offering everything from tent camping to two-bed villas. Un/powered sites **$29/$41**, cabins **$80**, villas **$120**

★ **Yongala Lodge** 11 Fryer St ☎ 07 4772 4633, ⊛ historicyongala.com.au. Charming, rambling and very welcoming 1880s Queenslander, just off the Strand. A good restaurant spreads out from the main building onto a broad veranda, while the spacious rooms are in the motel block behind. **$88**

EATING

The Brewery 252 Flinders St ☎ 07 4724 2999, ⊛ townsvillebrewery.com.au. The cavernous spaces of Townsville's very grand former post office building hold assorted stylish eating and drinking options, including the *Tavern*, which serves $18 burgers and pub grub to go with its craft beers, and the *Malt* restaurant, selling mains like pan-seared salmon or braised short rib for upwards of $30. Mon–Thurs 11.30am–11pm, Fri & Sat 11.30am–midnight.

C-Bar The Strand Headlands, Gregory St ☎ 07 4724 0333, ⊛ cbar.com.au. Spotlighted on the waterfront promenade by palm trees circled with coloured lights, this restaurant/bar has outdoor tables looking out towards Magnetic Island. As well as serving excellent food all day, with dinner mains like prawn coconut *laksa* or crispy

steamed barramundi for $24–28, it's good for anything from a breakfast coffee to a sunset cocktail. Daily 6am–10pm.

Longboard Bar & Grill The Strand Headlands, 80 Gregory St ☎ 07 4724 1234, ⊛ longboardbarandgrill .com. Relaxed seafront restaurant, great for a casual sandwich lunch – the ham-hock "knuckle sandwich" costs $17.50 – or a dinner of fish'n'chips or short ribs for more like $25–30; they also serve pizzas from $16.50 all day. Mon–Sat 11am–3pm & 5.30pm–late, Sun 11am–late.

Seaview Hotel 56 The Strand ☎ 07 4771 5005, ⊛ seaviewhotel.com.au. Lively pub that's the social hub of Townsville's waterfront boulevard, with food served indoors or out in the massive beer garden. Pies, burgers and pizza cost under $20, while steaks range up to $40.

Mon–Thurs 10am–midnight, Fri–Sun 10am–1am.

Wayne & Adele's Garden of Eating 11 Allen St ☎07 4772 2984. Besides a healthy dose of humour, there's a real passion for food in this delightful neighbourhood garden restaurant. Most mains, like the Chinese-style shredded duck or the grilled kangaroo fillet, cost $35–40, and also come as starters for half the price. BYO wine. Mon &

Thurs–Sat 6.30–11pm, Sun noon–3pm.

Yacht Club 1 Plume St, South Townsville ☎07 4772 1992, ⓦtownsvilleyachtclub.com.au. Hearty, bistro-style meals including prawns, calamari, oysters and grills ($16–32), with great views from the waterfront deck. Live music on Fridays. Mon–Thurs noon–2.30pm & 5.30–8.30pm, Fri & Sat noon–8.30pm, Sun 8am–10.30am & noon–8.30pm.

DRINKING AND NIGHTLIFE

Heritage Bar 137 Flinders St East ☎07 4771 2799, ⓦtheheritagetownsville.com. Fashionable wine bar, spreading out across pavement tables, serving bar snacks and cocktails, and playing lively music till 2am. Tues–Thurs 5pm–late, Fri 4pm–2am, Sat 5pm–2am.

Molly Malones 87 Flinders St East ☎07 4771 3428, ⓦmollymalonesirishpub.com.au. Irish bar with stout on tap, four separate bars plus pavement tables, and live bands Tues & Thurs–Sat. Mon–Wed 11.30am–midnight, Thurs 11.30am–2am, Fri 11.30am–5am, Sat 5pm–5am.

Magnetic Island

A beautiful, triangular granite core 12km off Townsville, **Magnetic Island** was named by Captain Cook in 1770, after his compass played up as he sailed past. Small enough to drive around in half a day, but large enough to harbour several small settlements, it has a lot to offer visitors: lounging on a beach, swimming over coral, bouncing in a Moke from one roadside lookout to the next, and enjoying the sea breeze and the island's vivid colours. Accommodation and transfer costs are considerably lower than on many of Queensland's other islands, while if you've ever wanted to see a **koala** in the wild, this could be your chance – they're often spotted wedged into the gum trees of the island's northeast corner.

Seen from the sea, the island's apex, **Mount Cook**, hovers above eucalypt woods variegated with patches of darker green vine forest. The north and east coasts are pinched into shallow **sandy bays** punctuated by granite headlands and coral reefs, while the western part is flatter and edged with mangroves. A little less than half the island is national park, with the settlements of **Picnic Bay**, **Nelly Bay**, **Arcadia** and **Horseshoe Bay** dotted along the east coast. With shops and supplies available, there's no need to bring anything with you.

Nelly Bay

Home to a modern marina complex as well as the island's ferry terminal, the thriving east-coast community of **NELLY BAY** comprises a sprawl of houses fronted by a good beach, with a little reef some way out. Two streets back there's a shopping complex with a supermarket and a couple of places to eat, while a 2km **walking track** leads to Arcadia. It can be hot work – start early and take plenty of water.

Arcadia

Just 2km northeast of Nelly Bay along the coast, **ARCADIA** surrounds Geoffrey Bay, and is home to the brilliant *Stage Door Theatre Restaurant* (see p.386). At Arcadia's northern end, the perfect swimming beach of **Alma Bay** is hemmed in by cliffs and boulders; there's good snorkelling over the coral just offshore. Further short **walking tracks** lead from the end of Cook Road towards Mount Cook and up to Sphinx Lookout, for sea views. Look out for the diminutive island **rock wallaby** near Arcadia's jetty at dawn or dusk.

North of Arcadia

North of Arcadia the road forks. The right branch (prohibited to rental vehicles) leads via tiny, exquisitely pretty **Florence Bay** to Radical Bay, while the main road carries on to

Horseshoe. Leave your car at this junction and continue uphill on foot to **the Forts**, built during World War II to protect Townsville from Japanese attack. The track climbs gently for 1.5km through gum-tree scenery to gun emplacements (now just deserted blockhouses), set one above the other among granite boulders and pine trees. The best views come from the slit windows at the command centre, right at the pinnacle of the hill, while the woods below the Forts offer a great chance of seeing **koalas**, introduced here in 1930.

Horseshoe Bay and around

The road ends in the north at **HORSESHOE BAY** on Magnetic Island's longest and busiest beach, half of which is developed and half of which remains blissfully secluded, with views north beyond the bobbing yachts to distant Palm Island. Good for swimming most of the year, the beach is backed by cafés and is a great place for activities. The cluster of shops at the road's eastern end features a general store and bakery, and there's a decent craft market on the last Sunday of every month.

Set 500m back from the bay on Horseshoe Bay Rd, the small hands-on **Bungalow Bay Koala Village** (daily tours at 10am, noon & 2.30pm; $29; ☎07 4778 5577, ⓦbungalowbay .com.au) is a wildlife park where on a ranger-led tour you can stroke crocs, handle lizards, meet cockatoos and have a cuddle (and a photo, of course) with a koala.

From Horseshoe's eastern headland, **walking tracks** take around half an hour to reach Radical Bay by way of lovely **Balding Bay**; you can spend a perfect day here snorkelling around the coral gardens just offshore and cooking on the hotplate provided. **Radical Bay** itself is another pretty spot; half a kilometre of sandy beach sandwiched between two huge, pine-covered granite fists.

Picnic Bay

Set on Magnetic Island's southernmost tip, at the end of the sealed road, the tiny settlement of **PICNIC BAY** is a languid spot. Well shaded by surrounding gum woodland and beachfront fig trees, it faces a nice beach with views back towards Townsville. The wooden pier protruding over the ocean was the island's ferry terminal until Nelly Bay took over. Aside from beachcomb, there's little to do here.

ARRIVAL AND DEPARTURE

MAGNETIC ISLAND

By ferry Magnetic Island's ferry terminal is in Nelly Bay. Sealink run passenger ferries from the Breakwater Terminal at the east end of the Strand in Townsville (hourly 5.30am–10.30pm, crossing 25min; $32 return; ☎07 4726 0800, ⓦsealinkqld.com.au). Fantasea car ferries leave from Ross St, South Townsville (every 2hr, 5.20am–6.05pm; $193 return for a car and up to four passengers, $26 for pedestrians; ☎07 4796 9300, ⓦfantaseacruisingmagnetic.com.au). It costs $8/24hr to leave your vehicle at Sealink's Townsville terminal, while parking is free at the Fantasea terminal.

GETTING AROUND

By bus Sunbus (☎07 4778 5130, ⓦsunbus.com.au) meets all ferries and runs between Picnic Bay and Horseshoe Bay more or less hourly between 5.55am and 9.10pm, with services until 11.40pm at weekends; a $7.50 day-pass allows unlimited travel.

By car or Mini Moke The island has 35km of road, including a dirt track to West Point and a sealed stretch between Picnic and Horseshoe bays. Tropical Topless Nelly Bay rent fun Mini Mokes and pink Daihatsu open-top minicars (from $75/day ☎07 4758 1111, ⓦmiwheels .com.au). Tropical Palms Picnic Bay rent 4WDs for accessing remote beaches (from $90/day; ☎07 4778 5076, ⓦtpmi .com.au).

By bike Fish'n N Fuel'n rent out bicycles from a couple of locations (from $20/6hr; ☎07 4778 5126, ⓦfishnnfueln .com.au).

ACTIVITIES

Most lodgings on the island rent snorkelling gear, bikes, and watersports equipment, and can make tour bookings for you.

Diving Relatively murky waters mean that Magnetic Island is not the most dramatic place to learn to dive, but with easy shore access it's very cheap. PADI courses with

Pleasure Divers start at $349 (☎07 4778 5788, ⓦpleasuredivers.com.au)– and on a good day there's some fair coral, a couple of small shipwrecks and decent fish life. They also offer snorkelling tours and take experienced divers to the *Yongala* (see p.378).

Horseriding Horseshoe Bay Ranch offer scenic rides through the bush and into the sea for a swim ($120/2hr; ☎07 4778 5109, ⓦhorseshoebayranch.com.au).

Island tours Tropicana Tours run day-long island tours from Nelly Bay in a stretch 4WD ($198; ☎07 4758 1800, ⓦtropicanatours.com.au). The cost seems steep, but you'll be very well fed and looked after, and see just about every beach and bay.

Watersports Beachfront operators in Horseshoe Bay rent out jet skis, kayaks, surf skis and boats, and provide joy-rides on inflated tubes and water skis.

ACCOMMODATION

Arcadia Beach Guest House 27 Marine Parade, Arcadia ☎07 4778 5668, ⓦarcadiabeachguesthouse .com.au. Nautically themed accommodation with a slightly quirky touch, from basic dorms to comfortable suites. They rent small 4WDs, but might even pick you up from the ferry in a Rolls Royce. Dorms $35, safari tents $64, doubles $85

Base 1 Nelly Bay Rd, Nelly Bay ☎1800 242 273, ⓦstayatbase.com. Large, modern beachside backpackers' with a pool and a very lively atmosphere, especially on full moon party nights. Dorms $32, female-only dorm $38, doubles $80

Beachside Palms 7 Esplanade, Nelly Bay ☎04 1966 0078, ⓦmagnetic-island-qld.com.au. Four clean and spacious apartments facing the beach, with a pleasant solar-heated pool. $120

★ **Bungalow Bay Koala Village** 40 Horseshoe Bay Rd, Horseshoe Bay ☎07 4778 5577, ⓦbungalowbay .com.au. Quiet retreat with cute cabins in a large wooded setting, a 10min walk from the beach adjoining the wildlife park (see p.385), with pool, restaurant, large kitchen and a campsite. YHA discounts. Un/powered sites $32/40, dorms $30, bungalows $95

Sails 13–15 Pacific Drive, Horseshoe Bay ☎07 4778 5117, ⓦsailsonhorseshoe.com.au. Pleasant apartments at the quiet end of the bay, with a full range of amenities, including a pool and outdoor BBQ area. $170

Tropical Palms 34 Picnic St, Picnic Bay ☎07 4778 5076, ⓦtropicalpalmsinn.com.au. Low-key guesthouse, one street back from the beach, where all the simply furnished, garden-set rooms have kitchenettes. The property also rents 4WDs and has a good pool. $120

EATING AND DRINKING

★ **Stage Door Theatre Restaurant** 5 Hayles Ave, Arcadia ☎07 4758 5448, ⓦstagedoortheatre.com .au. Three-course set meals ($85) serenaded by a hilarious cabaret show featuring plenty of comedy impersonations, glitzy outfits and songs. Book ahead. Fri & Sat 6.45pm.

Barefoot 5 Pacific Drive, Horseshoe Bay ☎07 4758 1170, ⓦbarefootartfoodwine.com.au. Art gallery and restaurant with a relaxed beachhouse vibe; mains like green curry or pork belly from $25, and plenty of lunch specials. Mon & Thurs–Sun 11.30am–3pm &

5.30–9pm.

Man Friday 37 Warboys St, Nelly Bay ☎07 4778 5658. Quirky BYO restaurant, with old-school Mexican dishes (most mains $22–36), a fun vibe and wildlife – possums, bats and geckos – to watch between courses. Mon & Wed–Sun 6–9pm.

Marlin Bar 3 Pacific Drive, Horseshoe Bay ☎07 4758 1588. Popular pub with cheap steaks, several beers on tap and cocktails by the jug. Live music Sun evening. Mon–Fri 11am–midnight, Sat & Sun 8am–midnight.

North of Townsville

Just an hour north of Townsville the arid landscape that has predominated since Bundaberg transforms into dark green plateaus shrouded in cloud. There's superlative scenery at **Wallaman Falls**, inland from **Ingham**, and also near Cairns as the slopes of the coastal mountains rise up to front the **Bellenden Ker Range**. Forests here once formed a continuous belt, and though logging has thinned them to a disjointed necklace of national parks, almost every side track off the highway still seems to lead to a waterhole or falls surrounded by jungle – this is where it really pays to have your own vehicle. There are also **islands** to explore, including the wilds of **Hinchinbrook**, as well as the **Mission Beach** area between **Tully** and **Innisfail**, where you might find regular work on fruit plantations or further opportunities to slump on the sand.

Little Crystal Creek

Halfway to Paluma, a solid stone bridge, built by relief labour during the Great Depression of the 1930s, spans **Little Crystal Creek**. Picnic tables and barbecue hotplates stand by the road, and there are deep swimming holes overshadowed by rainforest just up from the bridge. Large, metallic-blue **Ulysses butterflies** bob around the canopy, but do not underestimate the danger here; visitors have drowned in the strong currents.

Paluma

The climate begins to shift 60km north of Townsville, where the Mount Spec road turns west off the highway and climbs a crooked, stunning 21km into the hills to reach **PALUMA** township, a handful of weatherboard cottages in the rainforest at the top of the range. A couple of short **walking tracks** from the town – the longest, a ridgetop track to Witt's Lookout, is 2km – lead you into the gloom. Keep your eyes open for **chowchillas**, plump little birds with a dark body and white front, which forage by kicking the leaf litter sideways. You'll also hear whipbirds and the snarls of the black-and-blue **Victoria riflebird**, a bird of paradise – they're fairly common in highland rainforest between here and the Atherton Tablelands, but elusive.

ACCOMMODATION AND EATING   PALUMA

Hidden Valley Cabins Running River, 24km west of Paluma on a dirt road ☎07 4770 8088, ⓦhiddenvalleycabins.com.au. This carbon-neutral, solar-powered site offers rustic en-suite cabins or rooms with shared bathrooms, plus a restaurant open for all meals daily – dinner mains cost around $30 – and a pool. Activities include nature walks and platypus safaris. **$89**

Paluma Rainforest Inn 1 Mt Spec Rd ☎07 4770 8688, ⓦrainforestinnpaluma.com. Primarily a restaurant serving lunchtime pizza, wraps and salads (for around $20), though there are half a dozen comfy motel-style rooms at the back ($125). Mon, Fri & Sat 10.30am–3.30pm, Sun 8.30am–3.30pm.

Jourama Falls

North of Paluma on the coastal highway, you pass the **Frosty Mango roadhouse**, before you come to the sign pointing west to **Jourama Falls**. From the low-key **National Parks campsite** at the end of the 6km part-asphalt road to the falls, an hour-long walking track follows chains across the rocky river bed to swimming holes surrounded by gigantic granite boulders and cliffs. The trail finally winds up at the falls themselves – impressive in full flood but fairly insignificant by the end of the dry season.

ACCOMMODATION AND EATING   JOURAMA FALLS

Jourama Falls ☎13 74 68, ⓦnprsr.qld.gov.au. Set among gum and wattle bushland peppered with huge cycads (see box, p.421), this simple campsite has toilets, cold showers and BBQs. **$5.95**

Ingham

Home to Australia's largest Italian community, the small town of **INGHAM**, 110km north of Townsville, is well placed for trips inland to **Girringun National Park** and also gives access to the tiny port of **Lucinda**, the southern terminus for ferries to Hinchinbrook Island (see p.389). There's pasta and wine galore during August's annual **Australian Italian Festival** (ⓦaustralianitalianfestival.com.au), but the town is better known for events surrounding the former Day Dawn Hotel (now *Lee's Hotel*) on Lannercost Street, the legendary "**Pub with No Beer**". During World War II, Ingham was the first stop for servicemen heading north from Townsville, and in 1941 they drank the bar dry, a momentous occasion recorded by local poet Dan Sheahan. The poem was later incorporated into a Slim Dusty song, written at the *Taylors Arm* in New

South Wales, the other hostelry that markets itself as "the original Pub with no Beer".

The highway curves through town as Herbert Street, though most services are located along **Lannercost Street**, slightly west. If you've an hour or so to kill, enjoy a nice easy **walk** around the well-signposted **TYTO Wetlands** on the southern outskirts (Mon–Fri 9am–5pm, Sat & Sun 9am–4pm; free; ☎07 4776 4850, ☻tyto.com.au).

ARRIVAL AND DEPARTURE
INGHAM

By train Trains stop 1km east of town on Lynch St. Destinations Ayr (6 weekly; 3hr); Bowen (6 weekly; 4hr 30min); Brisbane (6 weekly; 20hr); Caboolture (6 weekly; 19hr); Cairns (6 weekly; 4hr 30min); Cardwell (6 weekly; 1hr); Innisfail (6 weekly; 3hr); Mackay (6 weekly; 7hr); Proserpine (6 weekly; 5hr); Rockhampton (6 weekly; 11hr 30min); Townsville (6 weekly; 1hr 30min); Tully (6 weekly; 1hr 45min).

By bus Long-distance buses stop where the Southern Highway meets Lannercost St (opposite Kelly Theatre).

Ingham Travel run buses to Townsville, via Lucinda, for the Hinchinbrook Island ferry, and Cardwell (Mon–Fri 3 daily, Sat & Sun 1 daily, reservations essential; ☎07 4776 5666, ☻inghamtravel.com.au).

By car The route to Girringun National Park along Highway 1 is well marked. For Mount Fox and Wallaman Falls, turn west down Lannercost St and follow the Trebonne road (lucidly signposted "This road is not Route 1"). For Lucinda, follow signs from the centre for Forest Beach and Halifax.

ACCOMMODATION

Palm Tree Caravan Park 49450 Bruce Hwy ☎07 4776 2403, ☻palmtreecaravanpark.com.au. Friendly owners and shady sites, plus en-suite and shared-bath cabins, 3km south of town next to a rumbling train track. Un/powered sites $26/$32, cabins $90

Tropixx Motel 45 Cooper St ☎07 4776 0000, ☻tropixx .com.au. Crisp modern rooms and suites next to the TYTO Wetlands Centre, plus a tiny pool and restaurant. $145

EATING

Casa Pasta 108 Lannercost St ☎07 4776 2520, ☻casapasta.net.au. Good-value lunch spot where you pick a pasta and then select a delicious home-made sauce; try the chicken and cracked pepper ravioli ($14). Daily 11am–1.30pm.

Lee's 58 Lannercost St ☎07 4776 1577, ☻leeshotel. com.au. The food in this iconic hotel's Art Deco-style restaurant is unremarkable, but there's always a $12 lunch special, and at least the bar hasn't run out of beer since the 1940s. Mon–Sat 11.30am–2pm & 6–8pm.

Mick's Bread Kitchen 1 Authurs St ☎07 4776 3932. Cheery bakery on the northern edge of town, with a great array of savoury and sweet pies from $5, and a couple of pavement tables. Mon–Fri 6am–5.30pm, Sat 6am–1pm.

Girringun National Park

Several distinct wilderness areas west of Ingham collectively form **Girringun National Park**, named after a mythical Aboriginal storyteller from the region. Highlights include the trek up Mount Fox and the 268m Wallaman Falls.

Mount Fox

A rocky, unmarked path climbs from the base of **Mount Fox**, a dormant volcano that last erupted 100,000 years ago, to the crater rim. Leading through scanty eucalypt forest to reveal views of the Kangaroo Hills, it's hot work, so start early and allow a good hour and a half to get up and down. The crater itself is only about 10m deep, tangled in vine forest and home to the Sharman's rock wallaby, easy to identify by the black tip on its tail.

Wallaman Falls

The Djyinda Trail starts at the lookout facing **Wallaman Falls** – Australia's highest waterfall – which cascade in a thin ribbon over the sheer cliffs of the plateau. You can't access the lip of the falls, but a narrow and slippery path descends towards the plunge pool. If you're staying the night, walk from the campsite along the adjacent stretch of **Stoney Creek** at dawn or late afternoon for a chance to spot platypuses.

ARRIVAL AND ACCOMMODATION
GIRRINGUN NATIONAL PARK

By car The road west of Ingham divides 20km along at Trebonne. Stone River Rd heads another 55km southwest across cattle country to the foot of Mount Fox; the final 2km are dirt and can be unstable. The other route runs along a mostly sealed road up the tight and twisting range towards Wallaman Falls. Tunnelling through thick rainforest along

the ridge, the road reaches the campsite, and the picnic area at the falls lookout, after 31km.

Wallaman Falls 13 74 68, ⓦnprsr.qld.gov.au. A pretty but bettong-infested National Parks campsite adjacent to Stony Creek with cold showers, gas BBQ and running water. $5.95

Cardwell

The modest little town of **CARDWELL**, 50km north of Ingham, consists of a quiet 2km string of shops and cafés on one side of the highway, with the sea on the other. A popular destination for yachting enthusiasts, it's made attractive by the outline of **Hinchinbrook Island**, which hovers just offshore, so close that it almost seems to be part of the mainland. Access to the island is the main reason to stop here, though you can also buy very cheap **lychees** from roadside stalls in December. Cardwell's banks, the post office, supermarket and hotels are all near or south of the **old jetty**.

The council-run **Rainforest and Reef Centre**, just north of the jetty at 142 Victoria St (Mon–Fri 8.30am–5pm, Sat & Sun 9am–1pm; free; ☎07 4066 8601, ⓦgreatgreenwaytourism.com), has a walk-through rainforest and mangrove display, and holds a useful **visitor centre** where you can book national park camping permits and find out about getting to Hinchinbrook Island.

ARRIVAL AND DEPARTURE
CARDWELL

By train The train station is on Bowen St. Tilt and Sunlander services run six times a week in each direction between Brisbane (21hr) and Cairns (4hr); stops include Townsville (2hr 15min) and Proserpine (4hr).

By bus Long-distance buses pull up beside the BP service station on Brasenose St. Greyhound and Premier buses stop here four to five times a day on their journey between

Brisbane (27hr 30min) and Cairns (2hr 15min); local connections include Ingham (1hr 30min), Mission Beach (1hr) and Townsville (3hr).

By ferry Hinchinbrook Island Cruises provide access to Hinchinbrook Island ($190 return; ☎04 9933 5383, ⓦhinchinbrookislandcruises.com.au) from Cardwell.

ACCOMMODATION AND EATING

Annie's Kitchen 107 Victoria St ☎07 4066 8818, ⓦannieskitchen.com.au. The pick of Cardwell's roadside cafés, serving well-priced fish'n'chips with lovely sea views. Mon 8am–3pm, Tues–Sun 8am–7.30pm.

Cardwell Beachcomber Motel and Tourist Park 43A Marine Parade ☎07 4066 8550, ⓦcardwellbeachcomber.com.au. Contemporary motel rooms and en-suite cabins facing the sea, along with a palm-studded campground and a decent restaurant that's open for breakfast and dinner daily. Un/powered sites

$29/$38, doubles $98, cabins $120

Cardwell Beachfront Motel 1 Scott St ☎07 4066 8776, ⓦcardwellbeachmotel.net. Simple but beautifully maintained units, some self-contained, enjoying superb sea and island views. $99

Kookaburra Holiday Park 175 Bruce Hwy ☎07 4066 8648, ⓦkookaburraholidaypark.com.au. Central park offering camping and motel rooms as well as dorms, and they can help backpackers find farm work. Powered sites $34, dorms $32, cabins $68

Hinchinbrook Island

Across the channel from Cardwell, **Hinchinbrook Island** looms huge and green, with mangroves rising to forest along the mountain range that forms its spine, peaking at **Mount Bowen**. The island's drier east side, hidden behind the mountains, holds long beaches separated by headlands and the occasional sluggish creek. This is Bandjin Aboriginal land; early Europeans reported the people as friendly, but attitudes later changed and nineteenth-century "dispersals" had the same effect here as elsewhere. The island was never subsequently occupied, and apart from a single resort (currently closed), Hinchinbrook remains much as it was two hundred years ago.

The Thorsborne Trail

Today, Hinchinbrook Island's main attraction is the superb **Thorsborne Trail**, a moderately demanding hiking track along the east coast, taking in forests, mangroves, waterfalls and beaches. At 32km, it's manageable in two days, though at that pace you won't see much; allow yourself at least three nights on the island. **Trailheads** are at **Ramsay Bay** in the north and **George Point** in the south, and the route is marked with orange triangles (north to south), or yellow triangles. The north–south route detailed below is considered slightly more forgiving, as it eases into ascents.

Day one

From Ramsay Bay, the trail winds its way in the first couple of hours to **Nina Bay**, along a fantastic stretch of coast with rainforest sweeping right down to the sand and Mount Bowen and Nina Peak as a backdrop. If long bushwalks don't appeal, you could spend a few days camped at the forest edge at Nina instead; a creek at the southern end provides drinking water, while Nina Peak can be climbed in an hour or so. Otherwise, continue beyond a small cliff at the southern end of Nina, and walk for another two hours through a pine forest to reach the campground at **Little Ramsay Bay** (drinking water from Warrawilla Creek).

3

Day two

Moving on, you scramble over boulders at the far end of the beach before crossing another creek (at low tide, as it gets fairly deep) and entering the forest beyond. From here to the next camp at **Zoe Bay** takes around five hours, following creek beds through lowland casuarina woods and rainforest, before exiting onto the beach near Cypress Pine waterhole. A clearing and pit toilets at the southern end of Zoe Bay mark the **campsite** – check with the National Parks service about the safest areas to camp, as **crocodiles** have been seen here. Be sure to bring insect repellent.

Day three

Next day, take the path to the base of **Zoe Falls** – where the fabulous waterhole is not safe for swimming – then struggle straight up beside them to the clifftop, for tremendous vistas. Across the river, forest and heathland alternate: the hardest part is crossing **Diamantina Creek** – a fast-flowing river with huge, slippery granite boulders. **Mulligan Falls**, where there's a campground, not much further on, is the last source of fresh water, with several rock ledges for sunbathing around a pool full of curious fish – stay off the dangerously slippery rocks above the falls. Zoe to Mulligan takes around four hours, and from here to George Point is only a couple more if you push it, though the falls are a better place to camp and give you the chance to backtrack a little to take a look at the beachside lagoon at **Sunken Reef Bay**.

Day four

The last leg to **George Point** is the least interesting section of the trail: rainforest replaces the highland trees around the falls as the path crosses a final creek before arriving at unattractive Mulligan Bay. The campsite at George Point has a table and toilet, but there's no fresh water, nothing to see except Lucinda's sugar terminal, and little to do except wait for your ferry.

ARRIVAL AND DEPARTURE — HINCHINBROOK ISLAND

By boat Hinchinbrook Island Cruises ferry hikers to Ramsay and George Point, at either end of the Thorsborne Trail ($190 return; ☎ 04 9933 5383, ⓦ hinchinbrookislandcruises.com.au), from either Cardwell or Lucinda (near Ingham). They also offer an excellent day-trip to Ramsay Bay and Zoe Bay, cruising after dugong and stopping for beach, waterfall and rainforest walks ($150 from Cardwell, $120 from Lucinda). Bus transfers between Lucinda and Cardwell (from $40) can be booked at Cardwell's visitor centre.

HIKING THE THORSBORNE TRAIL

Book your campsites well in **advance**, at ⓦnprsr.qld.gov.au (where you can also read current warnings and download a trail map). Only forty walkers are permitted on the trail at a time, so it's usually booked solid, especially during school holidays. Once you've got this sorted, book your ferry transfers (see opposite).

The drier winter months (June–Oct) provide optimum hiking **conditions**, though it can rain throughout the year.

Hiking **essentials** include water-resistant footgear, pack and tent, a lightweight raincoat and insect repellent. Wood fires are prohibited, so bring a fuel stove. *Kookaburra Holiday Park* in Cardwell (see p.389) rents out camping gear. You'll need to be completely self-sufficient and carry four litres of water per day. Although streams with drinking water are fairly evenly distributed, they might be dry by the end of winter, or only flowing upstream from the beach – collect from flowing sources only.

As for **wildlife**, you need to beware of crocodiles in lowland creek systems. Less worrying are the white-tailed rats and marsupial mice that will gnaw through tents to reach food; there are metal food stores at campsites, though hanging anything edible from a branch may foil their attempts.

3

ACCOMMODATION

Camping ⓣ 13 74 68, ⓦ nprsr.qld.gov.au. There are seven National Parks campgrounds along the Thorsborne Trail, facilitated with pit toilets. All operate a two-night maximum stay except *Mulligan Falls* where you can only stay one night. Campsites must be booked well in advance. **$5.95**

Hinchinbrook Island Wilderness Resort The *Hinchinbrook Island Wilderness Resort* was badly damaged by Cyclone Yasi in 2011, and has remained closed ever since; check ⓦ porthinchinbrook.com.au/island-resort for updates.

Tully

TULLY lies to the left of the highway 45km north of Cardwell, on the slopes of **Mount Tyson**, whose 450cm annual rainfall is the highest in Australia. Chinese settlers pioneered banana plantations here a century ago, and it's now a stopover for **whitewater-rafting** day-trips out of Cairns and Mission Beach on the fierce and reliable **Tully River**, 45km inland. Otherwise the town is nothing special, a triangle of narrow streets with cultivated lawns and flower beds backing onto roaring jungle at the end of Brannigan Street, a constant reminder of the colonists' struggle to keep chaos at bay.

ARRIVAL AND ACCOMMODATION   TULLY

By bus Long-distance buses set down at the Banyan Park Transit Centre on Butler St. Greyhound and Premier buses stop here four to five times a day on their journey between Brisbane (28hr) and Cairns (2hr 45min); local connections include Cardwell (30min), Mission Beach (30min) and Townsville (3hr 35min).

Banana Barracks 50 Butler St ⓣ 07 4068 0455,

ⓦ bananabarracks.com. Organized hostel, with good farm-work connections for travellers, plus weekend beach-trips and BBQs. Dorms **$135** per week

Mount Tyson Hotel 23 Butler St ⓣ 07 4069 1088, ⓦ mttysonhotel.com.au. Small singles and doubles above Tully's atmospheric "bottom pub" (the lower of the two main-street pubs), plus a decent restaurant. **$105**

Mission Beach and around

A couple of kilometres north of Tully, a loop road branches east off the Bruce Highway and runs 18km through cane fields and patches of rainforest to **Mission Beach**, the collective name for four peaceful hamlets strung out along a 14km stretch of sand. The coastal forest is home to the largest surviving **cassowary** population in Australia.

The area owes its name to the Hull River Mission, destroyed by a savage **cyclone** in 1918. Similarly devastating cyclones returned in 2006 (Larry) and 2011 (Yasi), stripping the rainforest canopy and flattening farms between here and Cairns.

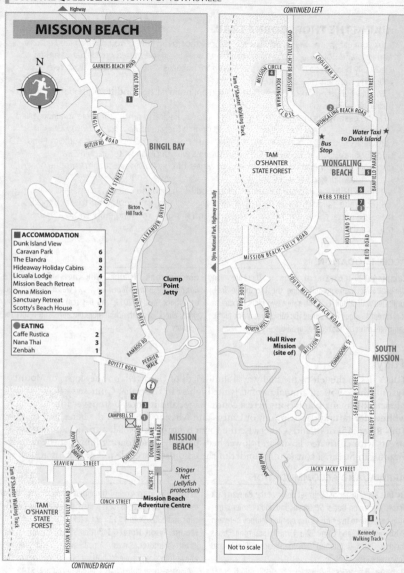

MISSION BEACH

ACCOMMODATION

Dunk Island View	
Caravan Park	6
The Elandra	8
Hideaway Holiday Cabins	2
Licuala Lodge	4
Mission Beach Retreat	3
Onna Mission	5
Sanctuary Retreat	1
Scotty's Beach House	7

EATING

Caffe Rustica	2
Nana Thai	3
Zenbah	1

South Mission

Right down at the bottom end of the beach, **SOUTH MISSION** is a quiet, mostly residential spot, with a long clean beach. A monument marks the original site of the **Hull River Mission** on Mission Drive, off the main road; after the 1918 cyclone, the mission was relocated to safer surroundings on Palm Island. At the end of beachfront Kennedy Esplanade, the **Kennedy Walking Track** weaves through coastal swamp and forest for a couple of hours to the spot where Edmund Kennedy originally landed near the mouth of the Hull River. It's a good place to spot coastal birdlife and, quite likely, crocodiles.

Wongaling Beach

WONGALING BEACH, 4km north of South Mission, is a slowly expanding settlement based around a shopping centre, a scattering of places to stay and eat, and Mission's only **pub**. During the day skydivers can be spotted gently descending onto the beach.

Mission Beach

MISSION BEACH itself, a further 4km from Wongaling Beach, consists of a cluster of shops, boutiques, restaurants, banks and a post office one block back from the beach on Porter Promenade. You can walk here from Wongaling via a 6km walking track that weaves through **Tam O'Shanter State Forest**, a dense maze of muddy creeks, vine thickets and stands of licuala palms (identified by their frilly, saucer-shaped leaves). There's a decent chance of seeing **cassowaries** here, perhaps leading their knee-high, striped chicks through the undergrowth.

Djiru National Park, 4km directly inland from Mission Beach, also offers some excellent short hiking trails, again passing through prime cassowary habitat. The **Lacey Creek Walk**, for example, is a half-hour, 1.5km loop which threads back and forth across pretty Lacey Creek.

To learn more about cassowaries, drop into the **C4 Environmental Centre** on Porter Parade (Mon–Fri 9am–5pm; free), which has displays on the local habitat, along with a nursery growing seeds collected from cassowary droppings, with the aim of safeguarding the food supply for future generations of the giant bird.

Bingal Bay

Continuing 6km north of Mission township past **Clump Point** – a black basalt outcrop with views south down the beach sitting above **Clump Point Jetty** – the road winds along the coast to sleepy **BINGIL BAY**. Just before, there's a parking bay on the roadside for the excellent **Bicton Hill track**, a 4km hilly walk through wet tropical forest where encounters with cassowaries are again a definite possibility. From here, the road continues inland alongside the **Clump Mountain National Park** and back to the main highway.

ARRIVAL AND DEPARTURE
MISSION BEACH AND AROUND

By bus Long-distance buses set down by the Big Cassowary on the approach to Wongaling Beach. Greyhound and Premier buses stop here three times a day en route between Brisbane (29hr) and Cairns (2hr 15min); useful connections include Airlie Beach (7hr), Cardwell (1hr), Townsville (3hr 45min) and Tully (30min).

GETTING AROUND

By bus Mission Link buses run the length of the Mission Beach area (7 daily), with two services continuing to Tully (☎ 04 7458 0000, ⓦ missionlink.com.au).

By taxi Mission Beach Taxi ☎ 04 4812 5984, ⓦ missionbeachtaxi.com.au.

By bike Mission Beach Bike Hire, at 71 Banfield Parade, Wongaling Beach (daily 9am–5pm; ☎ 07 4068 8310, ⓦ missionbeachbikehire.com), rent bikes for $15/day.

CASSOWARIES

Aside from the lure of the beach, Mission's forests are a reliable place to spot **cassowaries**, a blue-headed and bone-crested rainforest version of the emu, whose survival is being threatened as their habitat is carved up. Estimates suggest that there are only a couple of thousand birds left in tropical Queensland (though they are also found in New Guinea and parts of Indonesia). Many larger trees rely on the cassowary to eat their fruit and distribute their seeds, meaning that the very make-up of the forest hinges on the presence of the bird. Unlike the emu, cassowaries are not at all timid and may attack if they feel threatened. They have savage claws, so if you see one, remain quiet and keep a safe distance.

INFORMATION AND ACTIVITIES

Tourist information The visitor centre is on Porter Promenade (Mon–Sat 9am–5pm, Sun 10am–2pm; ☎ 07 4068 7099, ⓦ missionbeachtourism.com).

Cruises Fozzy's 3hr tours with Mission Beach Dunk Island Water Taxi, Wongaling Beach (Mon, Wed & Fri 12.30pm; $50; ☎ 07 4068 8310, ⓦ missionbeachwatertaxi.com) cruise to Timara, Kumboola and Bedarra islands, with witty commentary and time to relax on a secret beach.

Kayaking Kayaking trips with Coral Sea Kayaking (☎ 07 4068 9154, ⓦ coralseakayaking.com) range from Dunk Island day-tours ($136) to a seven-day Hinchinbrook Island expedition ($2090).

Rafting Good-value small-group rafting trips down the Tully River can be arranged with Raging Thunder (☎ 07 4030 7900, ⓦ ragingthunder.com.au) – a full day costs $159 plus a $30 levy but it's worth forking out an extra $36 for the "Xtreme" package, to guarantee that you're first on the river and not caught up in a conveyor belt of rafts.

Skydiving Skydive Mission offer skydiving from 4200m ($334; ☎ 1300 663 634, ⓦ jumpthebeach.com.au).

Tours Ingan Tours run indigenous rainforest walks and river tours, including superb half-day kayaks down the crystal-clear Bulgan Creek, with easy rapids and lots of birds ($10; ☎ 1300 728 067, ⓦ ingan.com.au).

ACCOMMODATION

SOUTH MISSION

The Elandra Explorer Drive ☎ 07 4068 8154, ⓦ elandraresorts.com. Posh, hugely luxurious resort where guests get to enjoy a superb pool, cliffside gardens and attractive rooms decorated with quirky touches of ethnic art. **$710**

WONGALING BEACH

Dunk Island View Caravan Park 21–35 Webb Rd ☎ 07 4068 8248, ⓦ dunkislandviewcaravanpark.com. Top spot 50m from the beach, with minimal shade but clean amenities, including a simple café and a little pool. Un/powered sites **$32/$42**, units **$105**

Onna Mission 27 Banfield Parade ☎ 07 4068 9920, ⓦ onnamission.com. This spacious, fully self-contained two-bedroom apartment, sleeping up to five, is right beside the sea, and superb value. You can take just one bedroom and still have the house to yourselves. Facilities include a BBQ terrace and kids' splash pool. One bedroom **$145**, two bedrooms **$175**

Scotty's Beach House 167 Reid Ave ☎ 1800 665 567, ⓦ scottysbeachhouse.com.au. Popular backpackers' with a big bowl, clean dorms, upbeat vibe and super-friendly, old-school service. Campers can park out back for $10 per person. Weekly rates are also available. Dorms **$24**, doubles **$71**

MISSION BEACH

Eco Village Clump Point Rd ☎ 07 4068 7534,

ⓦ ecovillage.com.au. Not particularly ecofriendly, but with cosy rooms set among pandanus and nutmeg trees, just back from a pretty beach. **$130**

Hideaway Holiday Cabins 58–60 Porter Promenade ☎ 07 4068 7104, ⓦ missionbeachhideaway.com.au. Palm-shaded sites plus spruce cabins and villas, just steps from the beach. Un/powered sites **$33/39**, cabins **$89**, villa **$125**

Licuala Lodge 11 Mission Circle ☎ 07 4068 8194, ⓦ licualalodge.com.au. Delightful tropical-style B&B with airy wooden verandas and traditional, high-ceilinged interiors. The landscaped garden and pool are gorgeous, while the huge breakfast will keep you going all day. **$135**

Mission Beach Retreat 49 Porter Promenade ☎ 07 4088 6229, ⓦ missionbeachretreat.com.au. Laidback backpacker pad, conveniently located for the shops and beach, with a small pool. Dorms **$22**, doubles **$56**

BINGIL BAY

★**Sanctuary Retreat** 72 Holt Rd ☎ 07 4088 6064, ⓦ sanctuaryretreat.com.au. Outstanding ecolodge set in fifty acres of thick, steep rainforest that harbours abundant wildlife, including cassowaries. Huts are stilted (and walled with fine netting, so you wake up enveloped by greenery), while cabins have verandas; there's also a bar, pool, yoga lessons and great-value food. Huts **$75**, cabins **$170**

EATING

WONGALING

Caffe Rustica 24 Wongaling Beach Rd ☎ 07 4068 9111, ⓦ caffe-rustica.com.au. Authentic pasta and pizzas from $16, including gourmet options with toppings like black tiger prawns. Wed–Sat 5–9pm, Sun 10am–9pm.

Nana Thai 165 Reid Rd ☎ 07 4068 9101. Steaming soups, fried rice and fragrant Thai curries, including a delicious beef massaman ($20), accompanied by Dunk Island views. BYO. Tues–Sun 5–8.30pm.

MISSION BEACH

Zenbah 39 Porter Parade ☎ 07 4088 6040. Fun and friendly restaurant-bar, open pretty much around the clock, and dishing up reasonably priced pasta, salad and pizza, plus seafood and steaks for up to $30, and backpacker specials from $12. Live music and DJs at weekends. Mon 7am–4pm, Tues–Thurs & Sun 7am–10.30pm, Fri & Sat 7am–1am.

Dunk Island

In 1898 Edmund Banfield, a Townsville journalist who had been given only weeks to live, waded ashore on **Dunk Island**, just off Wongaling Beach. He spent his remaining years – 25 of them – as Dunk's first European resident, crediting his unanticipated longevity to the relaxed island life. A tiny version of Hinchinbrook, at a mere 5km long, and part of the Greater Family group of islands, Dunk Island is much easier to reach from the mainland; the crossing takes just ten minutes. While the luxurious *Dunk Island Resort* has still not reopened after being devastated by Cyclone Yasi in 2011, ferry services and campgrounds are operating as usual.

Before falling victim to lethargy, walk northeast of the spit, passing Banfield's grave, to join a circuit of the island's west coast. The full 7km **trail** up 271m **Mount Kootaloo**, down to Palm Valley and back along the coast is a three-hour rainforest trek, best tackled clockwise. You'll see green pigeons and yellow-footed scrubfowl foraging in leaf litter, as well as vines, trunkless palms and, from the peak, a vivid blue sea dotted with hunchback islands.

ARRIVAL AND ACCOMMODATION DUNK ISLAND

By boat Mission Beach Dunk Island Water Taxi run ferries between Wongaling Beach and Dunk Island (daily 9am, 10am & 11am; $35 return; ☎07 4068 8310, ⊛ missionbeachwatertaxi.com)

Dunk Island Camping Area ☎0417 873 390. A stone's throw from the jetty and near the beach, this shady campground has toilets, showers and drinking water, and is the starting point for several walking tracks. **$5.95**

Paronella Park

1671 Japoonvale Rd • Daily 9am–7.30pm • $40 • ☎07 4065 0000, ⊛ paronellapark.com.au

Tiny **Silkwood**, on the highway 24km northwest of Mission Beach, marks the turn inland for the 23km run through cane fields to **Paronella Park**. This extraordinary estate was laid out in 1929 by **José Paronella**, a Spanish immigrant who constructed a **castle**, complete with florid staircases, water features and avenues of exotic kauri pines, among the tropical forests. Reclaimed from the jungle and restored during the 1990s, it now forms a splendidly romantic theme park, with half-ruined buildings artfully part-covered in undergrowth, lush gardens and arrays of tinkling fountains – all gravity-fed from the adjacent Mena Creek. A former walk-through aquarium has become the roost of endangered little bent-winged bats, and native vegetation includes a bamboo forest and dozens of *angiopteris* ferns, rare elsewhere. Admission includes a 45-minute guided **storytelling tour** and an evening **light show**, as well as a **botanical walk**, so you'll need a few hours to do the place justice. Tickets entitle campers to one free night in the park's campsite.

ACCOMMODATION AND EATING — PARONELLA PARK

Mena Creek Hotel 1 Mena Creek Rd ☎07 4065 3201, ⊛ menacreekhotel.com.au. Surrounded by a long veranda, this orange Queenslander, a 5min walk from the park, offers simple rooms as well as a good restaurant open for lunch and dinner daily, and serving the likes of steak

sarnies and home-made burgers. **$75**
Paronella Park 1671 Japoonvale Rd ☎07 4065 0000, ⊛ paronellapark.com.au. Staying in the park's smart and well-shaded little cabins enables you to explore the place after dark. **$90**

Innisfail

The Paronella Park road and highway converge at **INNISFAIL**, a small but busy town on the Johnstone River that's a good spot to find work **picking bananas**. Innisfail serves as a reminder that modern Australia was not built by the British alone: there's a sizeable **Italian community** here, represented by the handful of delicatessens displaying herb sausages and fresh pasta along central Edith Street. The tiny red **Lit Sin Gong temple** on Owen Street (and the huge longan tree next to it) was established in the 1880s by migrant workers from southern China, who cleared scrub and created market gardens here. More recently, many of Innisfail's banana plantations have been bought up by Hmong immigrants from Vietnam.

ARRIVAL AND ACCOMMODATION INNISFAIL

By bus Long-distance buses that set down at the Bus Centre, by King George Park, include Greyhound and Premier buses en route (4–5 times daily) between Brisbane (30hr) and Cairns (1hr 15min); connections include Airlie Beach (10hr), Cardwell (2hr), Townsville (4hr 45min) and Tully (30min).

Black Marlin Motel 26 Glady St ☎ 07 4061 2533, ⓦ blackmarlinmotel.com. Small motel just off the highway in the heart of town, where the simple rooms abound in attentive and thoughtful touches, like decorative glass and extra-fluffy towels. $125

The Bellenden Ker Range

Just north of Innisfail, the Palmerston Highway turns off Highway 1 and climbs towards the southern end of the Atherton Tablelands (see p.407). Around the same point, you start to see the **Bellenden Ker Range**, which dominates the remaining 80km to Cairns and includes Queensland's highest mountain, the 1600m **Bartle Frere**.

The 15km, two-day return climb through **Wooroonooran National Park** to the **summit** is within the reach of any fit, well-prepared bushwalker; check the National Parks website, though, for details of closures and routes (ⓦnprsr.qld.gov.au). To access the **Bartle Frere summit trail**, leave the highway 19km north of Ingham at one-house **Pawngilly**, and continue for 8km via Bartle Frere township. **Josephine Falls**, where the track begins, is renowned for its enclosed jungle water slides, but they can be extremely dangerous; a British tourist was swept to his death here in 2016. Beyond the falls, the trail is marked with orange triangles and passes through rainforest, over large granite boulders and out onto moorland with wind-stunted vegetation. Much of the summit is blinded by scrub and usually cloaked in rain, but there are great views of the Tablelands and coast during the ascent.

Further along the highway, a detour at **BABINDA** township – dwarfed by a huge sugar mill – leads to another waterhole 7km inland at **the Boulders**, where an arm of Babinda Creek forms a wide pool before spilling down over house-sized granite slabs. Cool and relatively shallow, the pale blue waterhole is an excellent place to swim, though once again several deaths have resulted from subtle undertows dragging people over the falls. Be very careful and stay well clear of the falls side of the waterhole. You can **camp** here for free.

On to Cairns

From **Gordonvale**, near the end of the Bellenden range – the place where the notorious **cane toad** was introduced to Australia (see box, p.987) –the tortuous Gillies Highway climbs from the coast to lakes Barrine and Eacham on the Atherton Tablelands. **Walsh's Pyramid**, a natural formation marking the turn-off, really does look like an overgrown version of its Egyptian counterpart. Alternatively, the final section of Highway 1 carries you from here to Cairns in half an hour.

Cairns

For visitors arriving from coastal Queensland's lower-key communities, the sprawling city of **CAIRNS** can come as a bit of a shock. The major base for trips to the **Great Barrier Reef**, it's very much dominated by tourism, and by youthful, partying backpackers in particular. With its attractive waterfront, though, backed by bustling streets of restaurants and cafés, it still makes a likeable and lively base, whether your interests lies in exploring the reef or venturing into the rainforest nearby.

Brief history

Cairns was originally pegged out over the site of a sea-slug **fishing camp**, after gold deposits were found further north in 1876. It was the tin and timber resources of the Atherton Tablelands, however, that enabled the town to stay ahead of neighbouring Port Douglas (see p.417), and its **harbour** is still the epicentre of the fish and prawn industries of northern Queensland. **Tourism** began modestly when marlin fishing became popular after World War II, then snowballed with the "discovery" of the reef in the 1970s. As a result, high-profile development has long since overshadowed the unspoiled, lazy tropical atmosphere that everyone originally came to Cairns to enjoy.

The Esplanade

Cairns' seafront **Esplanade** is packed through the day and into the night with visitors cruising between accommodation, shops and restaurants. Grabbing an early-morning coffee here, you'll witness a quintessentially Cairns scene: fig trees (home to a colony of endangered flying foxes) framing the waterfront, with trawlers, cruise boats and seaplanes bobbing at anchor in the harbour.

In the absence of a natural beach on these tidal flats, the Esplanade focuses instead on a well-planned **artificial beach**, enclosing a hugely popular landscaped swimming lagoon. From the 3km pedestrian walkway that hugs the shoreline, you can watch pelicans lazing in the sun and other smaller birds feeding in the shallows; identification panels help you pick out a tern from a shearwater, and there's an excellent **skateboard park** up to the north, towards the hospital. In the opposite direction, east of the

3

CAIRNS

■ DRINKING & NIGHTLIFE	
Buddha Bar	2
Gilligans	5
The Pier Bar & Grill	1
PJ O'Brien's	4
Saloon Bar	3

● EATING	
Bayleaf Balinese	1
Caffeind	5
Corea Corea	6
Dundee's	4
Ganbaranba	7
Green Ant Cantina	9
Meldrums	8
Perrottas at the Gallery	2
Woolshed	3

■ ACCOMMODATION	
Cairns Central YHA	10
Cairns Coconut Holiday Resort	14
Cairns Holiday Park	2
Calypso Inn	1
Dreamtime Travellers Rest	9
Hides Hotel	7
Il Centro	12
Inn Cairns	8
Mantra Esplanade	5
Northern Greenhouse	6
Royal Harbour	4
Shangri-la	3
Travellers Oasis	11
Tropic Days	13

lagoon, the **Reef Fleet Terminal** has booking desks for most Barrier Reef day-cruises, while **Marlin Wharf** is lined with pricey restaurants.

The Esplanade's central **night market** (daily 5pm–late) runs through to Abbott Street and has a mix of fast-food courts, $10 massage stalls, trendy tack and good-quality souvenirs, plus a great location near plenty of bars.

Cairns Museum

13 Grafton St • Mon–Sat 10am–4pm • $5 • ☎ 07 4051 5582, ⊛ cairnsmuseum.org.au

The prestigious **Cairns Museum** was closed for a major overhaul when this book was researched, but should have reopened by the time you read this. Assuming it remains as good as ever, expect an excellent introduction to the region's heritage, using photos and artefacts to explore such topics as maritime history, the Tjapukai and Bama Aborigines of the Tablelands, and the role played by the Chinese in the city and the Palmer goldfields.

Cairns Regional Gallery

Cnr Abbot & Shields sts • Mon–Fri 9am–5pm, Sat 10am–5pm, Sun 10am–2pm • $5 • ☎ 07 4046 4800, ⊛ cairnsregionalgallery.com.au

The **Cairns Regional Gallery**, set just a few steps back from the Esplanade, is a stimulating – and, it has to be said, refreshingly air-conditioned – space that stages challenging temporary exhibitions. Shows generally explore local themes, both historical and contemporary, and there's also a good little shop.

Rusty's Markets

Between Grafton and Sheridan sts • Fri & Sat 5am–6pm, Sun 5am–3pm

The 180 or so stalls at **Rusty's Markets** exhibit a fantastic range of local produce from crafts to herbs, tropical fruit and veg, coffee, fish and fashion. From noon onwards on Sunday, you can find excellent deals on surplus stock.

Cairns Wildlife Dome

35–41 Wharf St • Daily 9am–6pm • $24, plus fees for extra activities • ☎ 07 4031 7250, ⊛ cairnszoom.com.au

Curving atop the city's **casino**, facing the lagoons at the end of the Esplanade, the **Cairns Wildlife Dome** holds a small zoo whose caged birds and reptiles enjoy some of the best views in town. It's also home to ZOOm, a network of high ropes and ziplines, including a wire that skims across a crocodile enclosure.

Flecker Botanical Gardens

Off Collins Ave, west of the northern end of Sheridan St • Daily 7.30am–5.30pm • Free guided walks Mon–Fri 10am • Bus #131 from City Mall

The wonderful **Flecker Botanic Gardens**, 5km northwest of central Cairns, are home to four thousand tropical species from across the globe, including bamboo, palms, orchids, bromeliads and ferns. Star attractions include the rare titan arum or stinking "corpse flower", although you'd be lucky to see one in bloom.

Mount Whitfield Regional Park

Off Collins Ave • Bus #131 from City Mall

The forested **Mount Whitfield Regional Park**, behind the Flecker Botanical Gardens northwest of the centre, offers three good **walking trails**. The shortest, marked by red arrows, winds up through the rainforest for superb city views; the round-trip hike takes about an hour. The park is a refuge for wildlife and its cool, tranquil rainforest is even dense enough for wallabies.

Mangrove Boardwalk

Two separate routes lead along the **Mangrove Boardwalk** on the airport approach road, proffering glimpses of different species of mangrove trees, as well as birds, mudskippers and red-clawed, asymmetric fiddler crabs. Bring insect repellent, or you'll end up giving the bugs a free lunch.

ARRIVAL AND DEPARTURE

By plane Cairns Airport (w cairnsairport.com.au) is 6km north of central Cairns along Lake St and the Cook Highway. Sun Palm (t 07 4099 1191, w sunpalmtransport.com.au) run the Airport Connect bus to and from Sheridan St in town ($4 one-way) and also shuttle buses to accommodation in Cairns ($15 one-way) and Port Douglas ($33). Taxis into town cost around $30.

Destinations Adelaide (6 weekly; 3hr 15min); Alice Springs (1 daily; 2hr 30min); Auckland (5 weekly; 4hr 30min); Bamaga (5 weekly; 2hr); Brisbane (12 daily; 2hr); Coen (2 weekly; 1hr 15min); Cooktown (1–3 daily except Sunday; 45min); Darwin (3 weekly; 2hr); Hamilton Island (1 daily; 1hr 30min); Horn Island (2 daily; 2hr 10min); Lizard Island (1 daily; 1hr); Melbourne (6 daily; 3hr 20min); Mount Isa (5 weekly; 2hr); Perth (4 weekly; 5hr); Sydney (8 daily; 3hr); Townsville (3 daily; 1hr); Uluru (1 daily; 3hr); Weipa (1 daily; 1hr 40min).

By train The train station is 750m inland from the main drag, beneath the Cairns Central shopping centre between Bunda and McLeod streets. Queensland Rail (t 13 16 17, w qr.com.au) trains head south to Brisbane and up to Kuranda on the Atherton Tablelands while *The Savannahlander* (t 07 4053 6848, w savannahlander .com.au) runs west to Forsayth in the Gulf region.

Destinations Ayr (6 weekly; 7hr 30min); Bowen (6 weekly; 9hr); Brisbane (6 weekly; 24hr); Bundaberg (6 weekly; 19hr); Cardwell (6 weekly; 3hr 30min); Gladstone (6 weekly; 17hr 30min); Ingham (6 weekly; 4hr 30min); Innisfail (6 weekly; 2hr); Kuranda (2 daily; 1hr 45min); Mackay (6 weekly; 11hr 15min); Proserpine (6 weekly; 9hr 30min); Rockhampton (6 weekly; 16hr); Townsville (6 weekly; 6hr); Tully (6 weekly; 3hr).

By bus Long-distance Greyhound buses set down at the Reef Fleet Terminal, while Premier set down at the train station. Trans North (t 07 4095 8644, w transnorthbus .com) run daily buses to several Atherton Tablelands towns from the bays below the Cairns Central shopping centre; buy tickets on board. Country Road Coachlines (t 07 4045 2794, w cooktownandcapeyork.com) go to Cooktown via Port Douglas and Cape Tribulation, or Mareeba and Lakeland Downs, from bay 16 at the Reef Fleet Terminal. Port Douglas Bus (t 07 4099 5665, w portdouglasbus .com) also connect Cairns with Port Douglas, while Sun Palm Coaches offer a door-to-door service to Port Douglas, via the airport (t 07 4099 1191, w sunpalmtransport .com.au).

Destinations Airlie Beach (4 daily; 11hr); Atherton (1–3 daily; 1hr 45min); Ayr (4 daily; 7hr 30min); Brisbane (4 daily; 28hr 30min); Bundaberg (3 daily; 20hr 30min); Cape Tribulation (2 daily; 3hr); Cardwell (5 daily; 3hr); Childers (4 daily; 23hr); Cooktown (up to 6 weekly; 5hr via inland route or 6hr 30min via Cape Trib); Hervey Bay (4 daily; 24hr); Ingham (5 daily; 3hr 30min); Innisfail (5 daily; 1hr 15min); Kuranda (1–3 daily; 30min); Mackay (4 daily; 13hr); Mission Beach (4 daily; 2hr 30min); Noosa (2 daily; 27hr 30min); Port Douglas (15 daily; 1hr 30min); Rainbow Beach (2 daily; 26hr); Rockhampton (4 daily; 17hr 30min); Townsville (5 daily; 6hr); Tully (5 daily; 2hr 45min).

Travel agents Downtown Cairns holds dozens of agencies that specialize in making onward travel arrangements of all kinds. Recommended agents include Flight Centre, 24 Spence St (t 1300 358 508, w flightcentre.com.au), and Happy Travels, 4–7 Grafton St (t 07 4031 6337, w happytravels.com.au).

GETTING AROUND

By bus Sunbus services from the Transit Mall on Lake St go all over town, and as far up the Northern Beaches as Palm Cove; daily, weekly and monthly passes are available (t 07 4057 7411, w sunbus.com.au).

By car Car rental rates start at around $35 plus insurance for a runaround, discounted for long rentals; 4WD vehicles cost more like $165/day. The international chains are represented at the airport, while local agencies include A1 Car Rental, 141 Lake St (t 07 4031 1326, w a1carrentalcairns.com.au);

Minicar Rentals, 150 Sheridan St (t 07 4051 6288, w minicarrentals.com.au); and Travellers Autobarn, 123 Bunda St (secondhand vehicles available for sale; t 07 4041 3722, w travellers-autobarn.com).

By taxi The main taxi rank is on Lake St, west of City Place (t 13 10 08, w cairnstaxi.com.au).

By bike Cairns Scooter & Bicycle Hire, 47 Shields St (t 07 4031 3444, cairnsbicyclehire.com.au), rent bicycles from $10/24hr, scooters from $90/24hr.

INFORMATION

Tourist information Cairns' friendly visitor centre is at 51 Esplanade (Mon–Fri 8.30am–6pm, Sat & Sun 10am–6pm;

t 07 4041 3588, w cairns-greatbarrierreef.org.au).

3

TOURS

Bear in mind that while most day-tours will set you back at least $85 per person, it costs as little as $35 per day to rent a small car, plus fuel and insurance – though of course you'll miss out on a tour guide's local knowledge. **Day-trips** generally head either to the Atherton Tablelands, where the focus is on waterfalls and wildlife; or to Cape Tribulation and the Daintree, including a stop at Mossman Gorge and a crocodile cruise. Cairns Discount Tours (☎07 4055 7158, ⓦcairnsdiscounttours.com.au) specializes in **last-minute deals** and is highly recommended for its honest approach and comprehensive knowledge of local tour options.

Adventure North ☎07 4028 3376, ⓦadventure northaustralia.com. Specializes in cultural journeys to Cooktown, taking in Aboriginal sites, including a two-day fly-drive trip taking in the Rainbow Serpent ($739).
Barefoot Tours ☎07 4032 4525, ⓦbarefoottours .com.au. Thrills'n'spills day-trips up to the lakes, waterfalls and natural wonders of the Tablelands ($105).
Billy Tea Safaris ☎07 4032 0077, ⓦbillytea.com.au. Day-tours to Chillagoe Caves and Mareeba Wetlands ($230) and Cape Trib, visiting Emmagen Creek ($220).
Cape Trib Connections ☎07 4032 0500, ⓦcapetribconnections.com. Trips to the Atherton

Tablelands ($89, no lunch), plus day-trips ($139) and multi-night packages to Cape Trib.
Daintree Air Services ☎07 4034 9300, ⓦdaintreeair .com.au. An hour's flight over the reef for $190, and day-trips up to Lizard Island or Cape York.
Trek North Safaris ☎07 4041 4333, ⓦtreknorth .com.au. One-day small-group 4WD tours to Cape Trib and the Daintree ($190).
Uncle Brian's Tours ☎07 4033 6575, ⓦunclebrian .com.au. Brilliant day-trips to the Atherton Tablelands ($119).

ACTIVITIES

Birdwatching Both Wild Watch (☎07 4097 7408, ⓦwildwatch.com.au) and Cassowary Tours (☎07 4093 7318, ⓦcassowarytours.com.au) offer specialized birding trips, and can put together week-long packages to the Tablelands and Cape York.
Bicycle tours Dan's Mountain Biking organize moderate to extreme off-road biking tours around Cairns and Cape Tribulation ($95–185; ☎07 4032 0066, ⓦdansmountainbiking.com.au).
Bungee jumping A 50m purpose-built platform surrounded by rainforest is tucked into the hills off the coastal highway 8km north of Cairns; contact AJ Hackett ($169; ☎07 4057 7188, ⓦcairns.ajhackett.com). Check the website for package deals with other extreme-sport operators.
Cruising Seaswift accommodates passengers on five-night cruises to the tip of Cape York aboard its weekly cargo ship, MV *Trinity Bay*; rates include buffet meals and snacks, and passengers can disembark and explore during stops at Horn and Thursday islands (departs Fri; from $800 per person; ☎07 4034 1234, ⓦseaswift.com.au).

Diving and snorkelling Many operators offer trips to the Great Barrier Reef (see box, pp.404–405).
Hot-air ballooning Scenic early-morning hot-air ballooning flights over the Atherton Tablelands are available through Raging Thunder (from $250 for 30min, including transfers; ☎07 4030 7990, ⓦragingthunder.com.au).
Whitewater rafting Rafting the dependable Tully River near Tully, or the slightly less turbulent Barron River behind Cairns, is wild fun. It's a conveyor-belt business, though: as you pick yourself out of the river, the raft is dragged back for the next busload. A "day" gets you around five hours' rafting, a "half-day" about two. Day-trips with agents like Raging Thunder (☎07 4030 7990, ⓦragingthunder.com .au) or RnR (☎07 4041 9444, ⓦraft.com.au) cost $133–189.
Wildlife spotting Tours focusing on the platypuses, tree kangaroos and rare possums of the Atherton Tablelands are run by Wait-a-While Tours (☎04 2908 3338, ⓦwaitawhile .com.au) and Wild Watch (☎07 4097 7408, ⓦwildwatch .com.au); expect to pay around $200 for an afternoon-to-night excursion.

ACCOMMODATION

HOTELS, MOTELS AND GUESTHOUSES

Hides Hotel 87 Lake St ☎07 4051 1266, ⓦhideshotel .com.au. Very central, convenient and affordable, with long corridors of basic but acceptable rooms (a few singles), the cheapest sharing bathrooms. **$75**
Il Centro 26–30 Sheridan St ☎07 4031 6699, ⓦilcentro com.au. Modern and fairly spacious one-bedroom apartments with either pool or street views. **$133**
Inn Cairns 71 Lake St ☎07 4041 2350,

ⓦinncairns.com.au. Small but smart apartments slap in the centre of town, with kitchenettes and private balconies, as well as a pool, BBQ area and rooftop views out to sea. **$145**
Mantra Esplanade 53–57 Esplanade ☎07 4046 4141, ⓦmantraesplanadecairns.com.au. Plush high-rise hotel, in a prime location close to restaurants, shops and the "beach", and offering apartments as well as rooms – all have balconies – plus a great pool. The staff are exceptionally helpful. **$175**

Royal Harbour 73–75 Esplanade ☎07 5655 4408, ⓦbreakfree.com.au/royal-harbour. Comfortable modern apartment block with sea views. For such a prime location, it feels surprisingly secluded. $185

Shangri-La Pierpoint Rd ☎07 4031 1411, ⓦshangri-la .com/cairns. Luxurious waterfront hotel with sleek contemporary styling and immaculate service, plus a great pool and top-class restaurants and bars. $200

HOSTELS AND CAMPSITES

Cairns Central YHA 20–26 McLeod St ☎07 4051 0772, ⓦyha.com.au. Large, friendly and well-kept hostel with good security and a cool pool. Lots of doubles and some family rooms. Dorms $24, doubles $71

Cairns Coconut Holiday Resort 23–51 Anderson Rd ☎07 4088 1533, ⓦcoconut.com.au. Well-run family-oriented resort, beside Bruce Highway 8km southwest of the centre, with two great pools, amenities like minigolf and outdoor movie screenings, and comfortable en-suite cabins as well as camping. Powered sites $49, cabins $140

Cairns Holiday Park 12–30 Little St ☎07 4051 1467, ⓦcairnsholidaypark.com.au. The closest official campsite to central Cairns, holding tents and van sites plus cabins and studios, with good amenities and a pool. Un/powered sites $38/$51, cabins $76, studios $106

Calypso Inn 5–9 Digger St ☎07 4031 0910, ⓦcalypsobackpackers.com. Long-standing backpackers', a couple of blocks off the Esplanade 2km north of the centre, home to the lively *Zanzibar*, with helpful staff and free buses into town. Dorms $22, doubles $60

★**Dreamtime Travellers Rest** 189 Bunda St ☎07 4031 6753, ⓦdreamtimehostel.com. Cute and friendly hostel accommodation in three neighbouring Queenslanders, with a keen owner, right by the railway station a 10min walk from the waterfront. Dorms $26, doubles $60

Northern Greenhouse 117 Grafton St ☎07 4047 7200, ⓦnortherngreenhouse.com.au. Classy, non-party backpackers' in a convenient central location, with spotless dorms and apartments arranged around a pool, and spacious common areas. Dorms $30, apartments $95

Travellers Oasis 8 Scott St ☎07 4052 1377, ⓦtravoasis.com.au. Welcoming hostel in a gorgeous old Queenslander, with small dorms and comfortable double rooms, some of which have private balconies. Dorms $28, doubles $68

Tropic Days 28 Bunting St ☎07 4041 1521, ⓦtropicdays .com.au. Excellent hostel, inland from the station, with a pool, nice gardens (with room to camp), colourful rooms (with shared bathrooms), fab Aussie BBQs, hourly courtesy buses into town, and a highly sociable atmosphere. Unpowered sites $28, dorms $26, doubles $64

EATING

Bayleaf Balinese Cnr Lake & Gatton sts ☎07 4051 4622, ⓦbayvillage.com.au/bayleaf. Top-notch Balinese food, in an intimate atmosphere, with good service; typical main dishes like beef braised in coconut milk cost around $25, while the *rijstafel* set menu, for groups to share, is $49/person. Mon–Fri 6.30–9.30am, noon–2pm & 6–9pm, Sat & Sun 6.30–9.30am & 6–9pm.

Caffiend 78 Grafton St ☎07 4051 5522, ⓦcaffiend .com.au. Classy little coffee place, tucked down an alley and decorated with local artworks. Most of the food, from breakfast favourites like smashed avocado on sourdough to lunch specials like coffee-imbued beef tacos, costs $15–20. Tues–Sat 7.30am–3pm, Sun 8am–2pm.

★**Corea Corea** 1st Floor Orchid Plaza, 78 Abbott St ☎07 4031 6655. Don't be put off by the run-of-the-mill setting, in a mall food court. This simple Korean counter serves up tasty meals at great prices (up to $17); the $15 sizzling BBQ pork pot is more than enough for two. Mon–Fri 11am–4pm & 6–9pm, Sat & Sun noon–4pm & 6–9pm.

Dundee's 1 Marlin Parade ☎07 4051 0399, ⓦdundees .com.au. The pick of the dozen or so similar upmarket restaurants, with indoor/outdoor seating, along the waterfront. The contemporary Australian menu has steak or seafood mains for around $40, specialities like kangaroo loin or satay for around $32, and a mixed bushtucker sampler for $40. Daily 11.30am–2.30pm & 5.30–9pm.

★**Ganbaranba** 12/20 Spence St ☎07 4031 2522. Busy hole-in-the-wall Japanese diner that styles itself a "Noodle Colosseum" and serves excellent soups and noodle dishes for $10–13, including fabulous *ebisu* salt ramen topped with prawns and infused with prawn oil. No reservations, and no cash. Daily 11.30am–2.30pm & 5–8.30pm.

Green Ant Cantina 183 Bunda St ☎07 4041 5061, ⓦgreenantcantina.com. Part Mexican cantina, part brewpub, with live bands at weekends and cheap, cheerful and tasty evening meals such as 'roo burgers for $20, fajitas for $29, and super-hot "Wings of Death" chicken wings for $16. Tues–Sat 4pm–midnight.

Meldrums 97 Grafton St ☎07 4051 8333. A true Cairns institution, this old-fashioned pie shop sells a fine array of savoury pies, with macadamia chicken and tuna mornay as well as sorts of steaks, for $6, and has lots of indoor tables. Mon–Fri 7am–4pm, Sat 6.30am–2.30pm.

Perrottas at the Gallery 38 Abbott St ☎07 4031 5899, ⓦperrottasatg.com. Relaxed Italian-style bistro, spreading across a large and very pleasant streetside veranda next door to the Regional Art Gallery, and offering discounts for gallery visitors. Lunch and dinner mains range from burgers or meatballs for under $20 up to almost $40 for rich steak, lamb or seafood dishes. Daily 6.30am–3pm & 5.30–10pm.

3

Woolshed 24 Shields St ☎07 4031 6304, ⓦthewoolshed.com.au. Raucous bar and budget diner beloved of backpackers, serving huge and inexpensive meals. There's a $10 daily special, and most dishes cost well under $20 – though a rump steak will set you back $26 – plus beer by the jug, themed nights and nonstop party fever. Mon–Thurs & Sun 11.30am–3am, Fri & Sat 11.30am–5am.

DRINKING AND NIGHTLIFE

Cairns has a thriving pub and club culture. **Clubs** open around 6pm, and typically charge $5 entry for the bar and disco, more if there's a band playing. Many **pubs** also feature live music once a week; for indigenous sounds, try to catch one of the city's Torres Strait Islander performers. Petty crime can be a problem after dark: don't make yourself an obvious target.

Buddha Bar 59 The Esplanade ☎07 4051 1550. Ambient lounge bar geared towards over-25s; a decent place to chat with your mates, with live chill-out music. Cocktails $15. Thurs–Sat 7pm–2am.

Gilligans 57–89 Grafton St, ⓦgilligans.com.au. Attached to the massive backpackers', this is Cairns' most frenetic nightspot, with beer pong, jelly wrestling and wet T-shirt contests. Nightly DJs, and live bands Thurs–Tues. Entry $10 Fri & Sat nights. Daily noon–5am.

The Pier Bar & Grill 1 Pier Point Rd ☎07 4031 4677, ⓦthepierbar.com.au. Locals flock to the deck of this lively pub for the daily 5–7pm happy hour. Live music and $5 pizzas served all day Sunday. Daily 11.30am–late.

PJ O'Brien's 87 Lake St ☎07 4031 5333, ⓦpjobriens .com.au. This Irish bar attracts a mix of locals and tourists, and hosts big-name Queensland indie band nights. Happy hour 9–10pm. Daily 11am–3am.

Saloon Bar Woolshed, 22 Shields St ☎07 4031 6304, ⓦthewoolshed.com.au. Cavernous venue attracting backpackers through drinks specials and Friday- and Saturday-night house and trance, with guest DJs after 11pm. Mon–Thurs & Sun 7pm–3am, Fri & Sat 7pm–5am.

DIRECTORY

Banks and exchange Banks are concentrated around the intersection of Shields and Abbott streets, and in Cairns Central. Bureaux de change on the Esplanade offer poor value.

Camping equipment Adventure Equipment, 133 Grafton St (☎07 4031 2669, ⓦadventurequip.com.au), stocks and rents all types of outdoor gear, including kayaks.

Hospitals and medical centre Cairns Medical Centre, cnr Florence & Grafton sts (☎07 4052 1119), is open 24hr. Hospitals include Base Hospital, 165 Esplanade (☎07 4226 0000), and Cairns Private Hospital, cnr Upward & Lake sts (☎07 4052 5200, ⓦcairnsprivate.com.au).

Pharmacy Cairns Apothecary, cnr Grafton & Florence sts (daily 7am–11pm; ☎07 4031 8411, ⓦcairnsapothecary.com).

Police 5 Sheridan St ☎07 4030 7000.

Post office 115 Abbott St (daily 9am–9pm).

Work Backpacker contact points along Shields St, and individual hostels, may be able to help with finding WWOOF placements on the Atherton Tablelands.

The Reef off Cairns

Almost everyone who comes to Cairns is here to see the **Great Barrier Reef**, and with so many cruise or dive options available, choosing one can be daunting. You'll hear a lot of chat about the **inner reef** (closer to the coast, and visited by slower boats), the **outer reef** (closest to the open sea and the target of most speedy operators) and **fringing reef** (surrounding Fitzroy and Green islands), but the coral and fishlife at any of them can be either excellent or tragic. The state of Cairns' **coral** is the subject of much debate: years of agricultural run-off and recent **coral-bleaching** events – not to mention the sheer number of visitors – have had a visibly detrimental effect in the most-visited areas, though remoter sections tend to be in better condition. That said, almost everywhere teems with marine life, ranging from tiny gobies to squid, turtles and big pelagic fish – only seasoned divers might come away disappointed.

Reef Teach

Mainstreet Arcade, 85 Lake St, Cairns • Tues–Sat 6.30pm • 2hr • $23 • ☎07 4031 7794, ⓦreefteach.com.au

Before you go to the Reef – or even if you're not planning to go – take in the superb two-hour **Reef Teach** multimedia and interactive show, which is arguably the most worthwhile thing you can do in Cairns. The marine biologists here provide more essential background than any dive school or tour operator has the time to impart.

Inner reef

Most Barrier Reef day-cruises visit sites on the **inner reef**, where heavy day-tripping means that you'll probably share the experience with several other boatloads of passengers, with scores of divers in the water at once. On a good day, snorkelling over shallow outcrops is enjoyable; going deeper, the coral shows more damage, but there's still plenty of patchily distributed marine life to be seen, and turtles are a common sight.

Michaelmas Cay, a small, vegetated crescent of sand presents a twin attraction; over thirty thousand sooty, common and crested terns roost on the island (which on the downside covers much of it in bird guano), while giant clams, sweetlips and reef sharks can be found in the surrounding waters. Both Michaelmas, and nearby Upolu Reef, are often included in dive- or reef-trip packages that also visit outer reef sites.

Outer reef

Of the more northerly sites on the **outer reef**, **Hastings Reef** is famed for its coral pinnacles, swim-throughs, and schools of cod, trout and sweetlips, with sea stars and snails gracing the sand beneath. Another favourite, **Norman Reef**, tends to have very clear water, and some sites here preserve decent coral gardens where the abundant marine life includes resident moray eels, giant clams and bulky Napoleon Maori wrasse. Popular reefs visited further south include Flynn, Milln, Thetford and Moore.

Multiday cruises

It can take up to two hours to reach some of the outer reef sites, so it's worth considering staying overnight on a **liveaboard**. These venture further from Cairns into two areas, either a circuit north to the Cod Hole and Ribbon reefs, or straight out into the Coral Sea.

The **Cod Hole**, near Lizard Island, has no coral but is justifiably famous for the mobs of hulking potato cod that rise from the depths to receive handouts; currents are strong, but having these monsters come close enough to cuddle is awesome. **The Ribbons** are a 200km string boasting relatively pristine locations and good visibility. The **Coral Sea** sites are isolated, vertically walled reefs some distance out from the main structure, and require a three-day trip or longer. They are surrounded by open water teeming with seasonal bundles of pelagic species including mantas, turtles and minke whales. The most-visited Coral Sea site is **Osprey** reef, whose **North Horn** dive site is teeming with sharks, including powerful silvertips and greys.

Green Island

Tiny and sandy, **Green Island** is the easiest of any of the Barrier Reef's coral cays to reach, making it an accessible, if expensive, day-trip from Cairns. This, combined with the island's size, means that it can be difficult to escape other visitors, but you only need to put on some fins, strap on a tank, or go for a cruise in a glass-bottom boat to see plentiful coral, fish and turtles. Day-trippers on a budget should bring their own lunches, as the resort's restaurant is pricey.

| **ARRIVAL AND ACCOMMODATION** | **GREEN ISLAND** |

By boat Day-trips to Green Island from Cairns' Reef Fleet Terminal are offered by Big Cat (9am, 11am & 1pm; ☏07 4051 0444, ⓦgreenisland.com.au) and Great Adventures (8.30am, 10.30am & 1pm; ☏07 4044 9944, ⓦgreatadventures.com.au). Both charge $90 return, with rates including snorkelling gear or a glass-bottom boat tour, but no lunch; potential extras include diving, parasailing and scenic flights. Ocean Free (☏07 4052 1111,

ⓦoceanfree.com.au) run sailing tours to Green Island with offshore snorkelling at Pinnacle Reef, departing from the Marlin Marina at 8am ($195).

Green Island Resort ☏07 4031 3300, ⓦgreenislandresort.com.au. Luxury resort where the five-star rooms attract long-term guests; there are dining outlets and a pool open to day-trippers, plus lots of sand to laze on. Rates include boat transfers. __$375__

Fitzroy Island

Fitzroy Island is a small rugged continental island covered in tropical forest that stands just 35km southeast of Cairns and a mere 4km off the Yarrabah Peninsula, and is home to the upmarket *Fitzroy Island Resort*. You can visit as a day-tripper, and away from the manicured beach fronting the resort there are some worthwhile walks through highland greenery, notably the two-hour trek to the Lighthouse for excellent views.

ARRIVAL AND ACCOMMODATION

FITZROY ISLAND

By boat Boats depart from the Reef Fleet Terminal in Cairns. Fitzroy Island Resort Fast Cat provides a straightforward ferry service (8am, 11am & 1.30pm; $78 return), while Raging Thunder runs snorkelling day-trips including lunch (9am; $105; ☎ 07 4030 7990, ⓦ ragingthunder.com.au).

Fitzroy Island Resort ☎ 07 4044 6700, ⓦ fitzroyisland .com. A sizeable resort with comfortable suites, cabins and apartments, plus a pool, restaurants, spa, dive centre and small store. They also manage the pleasant National Parks campsite nearby. Unpowered sites $34, suites $185

3

CHOOSING A DIVE OPERATOR

Vessels that carry passengers to the Barrier Reef range from old trawlers to racing yachts and high-speed cruisers; **cruises** and **dive-trips** last from a day to over a week. All day-trip operators have **ticket desks** at, and depart from, the **Reef Fleet Terminal** at the end of Spence Street in Cairns; you can also **book** through an agent, but either way you should make reservations at least a day in advance. One way to choose the right boat is simply to consider the **price**. You get what you pay for, so small, cramped, slow tubs are the cheapest, while roomy, faster catamarans – some venturing to activity-packed pontoons – cost more. To narrow things down further, find out which serves the best **food**.

The **reef cruises** and **diving** listings given below are not mutually exclusive – most outfits offer diving (prices vary wildly – you'll pay anything from $85–245 for two dives including gear), snorkelling (usually free) or just plain old sailing. **Prices** can come down by as much as thirty percent during the low seasons (Feb–April & Nov). Dive schools usually run trips in their own boats, primarily to take students on their certification dives – **experienced divers** may want to avoid these, and should always make their qualifications known to onboard dive staff, who might then be able to arrange something a bit more adventurous. Beware of "**expenses only**" boat trips – there's often a catch. If in doubt, ask a booking office in town if you're dealing with an authorized, registered operator.

SAILING BOAT CRUISES

Day-trips cost around $130–210.

Falla ☎ 04 5842 6005, ⓦ fallareeftrips.com. Reasonably priced day-cruises aboard a 1950s Aussie timber pearl lugger, which makes leisurely visits to two reef locations, including shallow Upolu Cay.

Ocean Spirit Cruises ☎ 07 4044 9944, ⓦ oceanspirit.com.au. This large vessel, which holds well over a hundred passengers, sails out to Michaelmas Cay and motors back, ensuring adequate time on the Reef. The presentation is great.

Passions of Paradise ☎ 07 4041 1600, ⓦ passions .com.au. Popular with backpackers, this roomy and very stable sail-catamaran cruises out to Paradise Reef and Michaelmas Cay. Great value.

POWER CRUISERS

Day-trips range from $150 to $250. Some companies cruise out to their own pontoons, which offer stable moorings ideal for families, plus toilet facilities and underwater viewing chambers where you can get as

wet or stay as dry as you like; dive, snorkel, jump in a glass-bottom boat or semi-submersible vessel, or walk underwater on a "helmet" dive. You can also take a 10min helicopter reef flight from all pontoons, or fly in or out one-way by air.

Evolution ☎ 07 4052 8300, ⓦ downunderdive .com.au. Speedy vessel which runs out to the outer Norman and Hastings reefs; comfortable boat, great crew and fantastic BBQ lunch.

Great Adventures ☎ 07 4044 9944, ⓦ greatadventures.com.au. Trips on a large, fast catamaran to a private reef pontoon, with the option of stopping off at Green Island.

Reef Magic ☎ 07 4031 1588, ⓦ reefmagiccruises .com. Speedy catamaran, which spends five hours at the Marine World pontoon, on the outer reef, for snorkelling, diving and glass-bottom-boat trips.

Sunlover Cruises ☎ 07 4050 1333, ⓦ sunlover .com.au. Fast catamaran to a private pontoon at Moore Reef where you spend four hours exploring the outer reef.

Cairns' Northern Beaches

Cairns' quieter, sandy **Northern Beaches**, lying off the highway north of the airport, offer a slower pace than the city, while still being close enough for easy access – all but distant Ellis are on bus routes.

Holloways Beach and Yorkeys Knob

From Cairns' City Mall, bus #120 goes to Holloways Beach, and #113 to Yorkey's Knob

HOLLOWAYS BEACH, 8km north of Cairns, is a string of suburban streets fronting a long strip of sand, quiet but for the airport to the south; **YORKEYS KNOB**, 2km further up the highway and away from the airport noise, is one of Australia's best **kitesurfing** beaches.

DIVING DAY-TRIPS

Expect to pay $200–300 for two dives, gear rental, food and drink; a third dive generally costs around $25 extra. **MV Reef-Kist** ☎07 4051 0294, ⓦcairnsdive .com.au. Budget dive and snorkel operator visiting Moore and Thetford reefs via Fitzroy Island on a modern 17.5m catamaran.

Reef Quest ☎07 4046 7333, ⓦdiversden.com.au. Stable, well-equipped catamaran visiting Norma, Saxon and Hastings outer reef sites, with the option of diving three times in the day. Good value.

Seastar ☎07 4041 6218, ⓦseastarcruises.com.au. Long-established family business with permits for some of the best sections of Hastings Reef and Michaelmas Cay, and a no-crowds policy (max 35 passengers).

Silverswift ☎07 4044 9944, ⓦsilverseries.com.au. Large, speedy 29m catamaran visiting Flynn, Pellowe, Milln and/or Thetford outer reef sites, with time to get in three dives if you want.

Tusa ☎07 4047 9100, ⓦtusadive.com. Snazzy purpose-built vessel holding a maximum of sixty passengers, with visiting three out of a potential sixteen dive sites on its daily itineraries.

LIVEABOARD DIVE-TRIPS

Liveaboard trips last from one night (for snorkelling, cruising or diving) to over a week (for experienced divers), and typically cover the best reefs: you'll get longer in the water, visit a greater variety of sites, and also have the opportunity for some night diving. And, of course, you don't have to pay for accommodation on the mainland while you're out at sea. Prices vary seasonally, ranging from $500 for overnight trips, $650 for three days and up to $3600 for a week, with cheaper rates Feb– June. All costs generally include berth and meals, with dives typically included for longer voyages, but not gear rental. For further information, contact Diversion Dive Travel (☎07 4039 0200, ⓦdiversiondivetravel.com.au).

Coral Sea Dreaming ☎07 4229 9000, ⓦcoralseadreaming.com.au. Two-day snorkelling and diving trips to Flynn, Milin and Thetford reefs on a 16m steel ketch sleeping up to eighteen.

Mike Ball ☎07 4053 0500, ⓦmikeball.com. Luxury diving with one of Queensland's best-equipped and longest-running operations; venues include the Cod Hole and Coral Sea sites, with most trips including dives with minke whales.

Spirit of Freedom ☎07 4047 9150, ⓦspiritoffreedom.com.au. Huge 37m vessel with superlative facilities, sailing to Cod Hole, the Ribbons and Coral Sea.

Rum Runner ☎07 4041 1054, ⓦrumrunnercairns .com.au. Budget motor schooner, sleeping sixteen in basic shared cabins, offering 24hr outer reef trips and affordable three-day Coral Sea expeditions.

DIVE SCHOOLS

Training standards in Cairns are uniformly sound, but it's worth asking around as to what each dive school offers. You'll pay around $480–575 for a budget Open-Water Certification course, diving lesser reefs while training and returning to Cairns each night; and $650–850 for a four- or five-day course using better sites and staying on a liveaboard at the reef for a couple of days doing your certification. The following dive schools are well established and have solid reputations, and offer one-day as well as longer liveaboard trips. Certification dives are either made north at Norman, Hastings and Saxon reefs, or south at Flynn, Moore and Tetford.

CDC 121 Abbott St ☎07 4051 0294, ⓦcairnsdive.com.au.

Deep Sea Divers Den 319 Draper St ☎07 4046 7333, ⓦdiversden.com.au.

Down Under Dive 287 Draper St ☎07 4052 8300, ⓦdownunderdive.com.au.

Pro-Dive 116 Spence St ☎07 4031 5255, ⓦprodivecairns.com.

3

Tjapukai Aboriginal Cultural Park

Captain Cook Hwy, Smithfield • Daily 9am–5pm • 2hr night performance 7.30pm • Day admission $56, night $111 • ☎ 07 4042 9999, ⓦ tjapukai.com.au • Return transfers $27

The township of **Smithfield**, 12km north of Cairns, marks the starting point of the Kennedy Highway's ascent to Kuranda, in the Atherton Tablelands. Shortly before, a large complex on the roadside houses both the **Kuranda Skyrail** cable-car terminus (see p.410) and the **Tjapukai Aboriginal Cultural Park**. The park's hefty admission price isn't bad value, as it includes entry to boomerang and didgeridoo displays, a fine museum, and three separate theatre shows featuring Dreamtime tales and dancing; it's not eye-opening stuff, but does offer a light-hearted and entertaining introduction to Aboriginal culture.

Trinity Beach and Palm Cove

Buses #110 or #111 from Cairns' City Mall go to Trinity Beach, Kewarra and Palm Cove

The more developed and upmarket tourist areas of **TRINITY BEACH** and **PALM COVE**, north along Captain Cook Highway from Smithfield, feature spotlessly clean, palm-fringed beaches and lots of luxury holiday apartments, beach resorts, cafés, boutique shops, restaurants and watersports. You can expect to pay well over $200 per night at the resorts here, with minimum stays enforced during the high seasons.

Ellis Beach

If you want to really escape for a few days, you couldn't ask for a finer place to unwind than **ELLIS BEACH**, thirty minutes north of Cairns en route to Port Douglas (and unfortunately beyond the reach of bus services). Apart from the popular *Ellis Beach Bungalows*, there's really nothing more than an endless strip of sand and coastal belt of trees.

ACTIVITIES
CAIRNS' NORTHERN BEACHES

Kitesurfing Kiterite, 471 Varley St, Yorkey's Knob (☎ 07 4055 7918, ⓦ kiterite.com.au), offer introductory kitesurfing lessons for $79/hr or two-day courses for $499.

ACCOMMODATION AND EATING

HOLLOWAYS BEACH

Strait on the Beach 100 Oleander St ☎ 07 4055 9616. Café serving up *focaccia*, burgers and fish'n'chips – typical mains $15–20 – with great views from its shaded terrace, and live music on Sunday afternoons. Daily 7.30am–8.30pm.

YORKEYS KNOB

Driftaways Yorkeys Knob Boating Club, 25 Buckley St ☎ 074055 7711, ⓦ ykbc.com.au. You can dine all day at the popular and picturesque marina; dinner mains start at $15, and on Saturdays you can get a dozen oysters for $12. Mon noon–3pm & 6–9pm, Tues–Sat noon–9pm, Sun 8–10.30am & noon–9pm.

★ **Villa Marine** 8 Rutherford St ☎ 07 4055 7158, ⓦ villamarine.com.au. Spacious apartments of varying degrees of luxury, dotted with funky artefacts from the Torres Islands and set 50m back from the beach beside a cool patch of rainforest. The manager is a mine of useful information about things to see and do in Cairns. $139

TRINITY BEACH AND PALM COVE

Reef House Resort & Spa 99 Williams Esplanade ☎ 07 4080 2600, ⓦ reefhouse.com.au. This colonially inspired hotel is one of Palm Cove's more atmospheric resorts, with assorted pools and terraces, gleaming hardwood floors in rooms and suites, and two restaurants. $240

Kewarra Beach Resort 8 Kewarra St ☎ 07 4058 4000, ⓦ kewarra.com. A scattering of gorgeous suites and bungalows tucked away in secluded rainforest on the quietest stretch of beach. $299

ELLIS BEACH

★ **Ellis Beach Bungalows** Captain Cook Hwy ☎ 07 4055 3538, ⓦ ellisbeach.com. A tidy resort with self-contained bungalows, cabins (shared facilities) and nice shady campsites, some right by the beach; it's popular with repeat guests, so it pays to book ahead. Un/powered sites $34/41, cabins $115, bungalows $170.

The Atherton Tablelands

The **Atherton Tablelands**, the highlands behind Cairns, are named after **John Atherton**, who made the tin deposits at Herberton accessible by opening a route to the coast in 1877. Most of the dense forest that originally covered these highlands was felled for timber, and the cleared patches given over to dairy cattle, tobacco and grain. While the pockets of forest that remain are magnificent, it's the area's understated beauty that draws most visitors today, and though **Kuranda** pulls in tour parties from the coast,

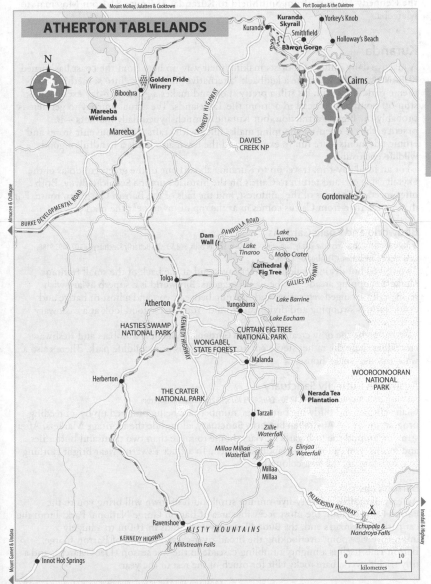

ATHERTON TABLELANDS

3

N

Mount Molloy, Julatten & Cooktown

Port Douglas & the Daintree

Kuranda
Kuranda
Skyrail
Smithfield
Barron Gorge

Yorky's Knob
Holloway's Beach

Cairns

Golden Pride
Winery
Biboohra

Mareeba
Wetlands
Mareeba

Kennedy Highway

DAVIES
CREEK NP

Gordonvale

Almaden & Chillagoe

Burke Developmental Road

Danbulla Road

Dam
Wall

Lake
Tinaroo

Lake
Euramo

Mobo Crater

Cathedral
Fig Tree

Gillies Highway

Tolga

Atherton

Yungaburra

Lake Barrine

Lake Eacham

HASTIES SWAMP
NATIONAL PARK

CURTAIN FIG TREE
NATIONAL PARK

WONGABEL
STATE FOREST

Kennedy Highway

Malanda

WOOROONOORAN
NATIONAL
PARK

Herberton

THE CRATER
NATIONAL PARK

Nerada Tea
Plantation

Tarzali

Zillie
Waterfall

Millaa Millaa
Waterfall

Elinjaa
Waterfall

Millaa
Millaa

Palmerston Highway

Ravenshoe

MISTY MOUNTAINS

Kennedy Highway

Millstream Falls

Innot Hot Springs

Mount Garnet & Undara

Tchupala &
Nandroya Falls

Innisfail & highway

0   10
kilometres

there are several quieter national parks brimming with rare species. You could spend days here, driving or hiking through rainforest to crater lakes and endless small waterfalls, or simply camp out for a night and search for wildlife with a torch. For a contrast, consider a trip west to the mining town of **Chillagoe** (see p.412), whose dust, limestone caves and Aboriginal art place it firmly in the Outback.

Numerous tours set off into the Tablelands from Cairns (see p.400), but to explore properly you really need your own vehicle. Drivers can access the region along the Palmerston Highway from Innisfail; the twisty Gillies Highway from Gordonvale; the Kennedy Highway from Smithfield to Kuranda; or Route 81 from Mossman to Mareeba.

Kuranda

A massive daily influx of tourists making their way up here from the coast has turned **KURANDA**, which was once a laidback "alternative" hill village, into something of a theme park. That said, it's still a pretty spot, and makes a good half-day excursion or stop-off point as you head to or from the Tablelands. The actual journey to get here is probably the biggest attraction, but Kuranda's much-hyped daily **markets** – in practice, they're open-air shopping malls, filled with crafts stalls, souvenir stores and ethnic oddments – are fun to explore, and the town also holds a handful of good **wildlife** enclosures.

For an ideal day-trip, travel up to Kuranda aboard one of the green gondolas of the **Skyrail** cable car, and return to Cairns on the historic **Kuranda Scenic Railway**. Both offer spectacular views of the rainforest, and the falls of the Barron Gorge, en route. For drivers, the road from Cairns comes in at the top of town, near the markets.

Birdworld and Koala Gardens

Heritage Markets, Rob Veivers Drive • Daily 9am–4pm • $18 each, $31 for both, $48.50 with Butterfly Sanctuary • ☎ 07 4093 9188, Ⓦ birdworldkuranda.com, Ⓦ koalagardens.com

Two linked but distinct wildlife attractions stand at the back of the small **Heritage Markets** shopping arcade. As the name suggests, **Birdworld** is a superb aviary with realistically arranged vegetation and nothing between you and a host of native and exotic rarities swooping and diving all around. You'll get a good look at a cassowary here too.

Koalas aren't the only creature at **Koala Gardens**: wallabies, wombats and freshwater crocodiles share the rather sterile environment at this mini wildlife park. There's also a walk-through snake house.

Australian Butterfly Sanctuary

Rob Veivers Drive • Daily 9.45am–4pm • $19.50 • ☎ 07 4093 7575, Ⓦ australianbutterflies.com

Giant Ulysses and birdwing butterflies' numbers are being pumped up by a breeding programme at the **Australian Butterfly Sanctuary**, alongside the Heritage Markets. After strolling around the lush garden aviary, home to more than two thousand butterflies and moths, you can visit the laboratory itself. To attract a swarm, wear bright clothing (red or white are the best colours).

Barron Falls

An easy 3km drive or forty-five-minute stroll south of town will bring you to the **Barron Falls Lookout**, the most accessible area of Barron Gorge National Park. From the car park at the road's end, the **Budadji canopy walk** leads in 100m to a hugely impressive viewpoint overlooking the broad river-carved canyon of Barron Gorge. Barron Falls itself is a mighty tumbling cascade in the wet season (Dec–March), and a tiny trickle over a bare rocky cliff for much of the rest of the year.

Beyond the lookout, the rainforest boardwalk drops down 650m to reach Barron Falls Station, where trains on the **Kuranda Scenic Railway** stop briefly to give passengers the chance to enjoy the views from an even more dramatic trackside lookout. On the far side of the gorge, you'll be able to see the little **Skyrail** cars swinging along over the treetops.

RainForeStation

Kennedy Hwy • Daily 9am–4pm • $47 • ☎ 07 4085 5008, ⓦ rainforest.com.au

Across the Barron River west of town, **RainForeStation** is a wildlife park that offers a taste of Pamagirri Aboriginal culture as well as guided boardwalks and rainforest and river tours in a World War II amphibious army duck. The wildlife area is home to koalas, Tasmanian devils and a giant 5m saltwater crocodile tastefully known as "Jack the Ripper".

ARRIVAL AND DEPARTURE   KURANDA

Kuranda's train and Skyrail stations stand at the foot of Condoo St, 500m south of Rob Veivers Drive, the town's main commercial street.

By bus Trans North buses (2–3 daily; ☎ 07 4095 8644, ⓦ transnorthbus.com) connect Kuranda with Cairns Central (40min), Mareeba (45min), and Atherton (1hr 15min); three times weekly, buses continue all the way west to Karumba in the Gulf (Mon, Wed & Fri 7.05am; 10hr 30min). John's Kuranda Bus also travels between Kuranda and Cairns three times daily (☎ 04 1877 2953).

By cable car The exhilarating Kuranda Skyrail carries passengers for 7.5km between Smithfield's Caravonica Station, 12km north of Cairns, and Kuranda, dangling over dramatic rainforest scenery with spectacular views of

Barron Gorge ($50 one-way, from $75 return; allow 1hr 30min each way, with stops; fares include transfers from Cairns ☎ 07 4035 5555, ⓦ skyrail.com.au). All sorts of packages are available, including day-trips that travel to Kuranda on the Skyrail in the morning and return to Cairns by rail in the afternoon (from $109.50), or that combine the Skyrail ride with the Tjapukai Aboriginal Cultural Park (see p.406) and/or the various wildlife attractions in Kuranda.

By scenic railway Kuranda Scenic Railway ($49 one-way, $79 return; 2hr; ☎ 07 4036 9333, ⓦ ksr.com.au) travels between Cairns and Kuranda twice each day, winding through rainforest and alongside the Barron Gorge, where passengers disembark for a photo opportunity. Both trains leave Cairns in the morning, and return from Kuranda in the afternoon.

INFORMATION AND ACTIVITIES

Tourist information Kuranda's helpful visitor centre is in Centenary Park, at the top of Condoo St (daily 10am–4pm; ☎ 07 4093 9311, ⓦ kuranda.org).
Cruises Kuranda Riverboat offers 45min cruises from its

jetty beyond the railway station, reached via a bridge over the platform (5 daily; $18; ☎ 04 1215 9212, ⓦ kurandariverboat.com.au).

ACCOMMODATION AND EATING

Frogs Heritage Markets, Rob Veivers Drive ☎ 07 4093 8952, ⓦ frogsrestaurant.com.au. Breezy open-air restaurant, within appealing earshot of Birdworld, and serving an extensive menu of $13–17 burgers, pizzas and salads, plus a daily curry special, like the tasty chickpea and spinach option, for $15, and steaks for around $25. Daily 9am–3.30pm.
Kuranda Hotel Motel 2–4 Arara St ☎ 07 4093 7206,

ⓦ kurandahotel.com.au. Kuranda's village pub, with an Irish-themed bar, a tea terrace and rather basic motel rooms out the back. $120
Petit Café Original Rainforest Markets ☎ 04 2179 9131. Tucked into a little alleyway, this hidden gem serves up organic, gluten-free sweet and savoury crêpes from $11, with fillings such as kangaroo prosciutto and macadamia pesto, plus an $18, all-day breakfast. Daily 8am–3pm.

Mareeba and around

West of Kuranda, rainforest quickly gives way to dry woodland and tobacco plantations, quite a change from the coast's greenery. **MAREEBA**, 35km along, is a quiet place and the Tablelands' oldest town, founded in the 1900s after the area was opened up for **tobacco** farming. There's not much to do here, the main attraction being the wetlands north of town.

Shops and banks can be found on Byrnes Street, with the **visitor centre** about 1km south of town along the Atherton road. The town can be seedy **after dark**, with plenty of drunks staggering around even early on.

Coffee Works

136 Mason St • Daily 9am–4pm, last tour 3pm • Admission free; tours $19 • ☎ 1800 355 526, ⓦ coffeeworks.com.au

Occupying a huge, ramshackle tin-roofed shed at the southern end of town, **Coffee Works** is a commercial coffee-roasting facility that holds a courtyard café (serving food until 2pm daily) and gift store. Pay for a tour of its facilities, and you'll see an impressive coffee museum and get the chance to taste numerous varieties of coffee, tea and chocolate.

Golden Pride Winery

227 Bilwon Rd, Biboohra, off the highway 10km north of Mareemba • Daily 9am–5.30pm • ☎ 07 4093 2750, ⓦ goldendrop.com.au

Fruit plantations are a profitable business in the Tablelands. **Golden Pride Winery** is typical of several farms that have branched out into producing **tropical fruit wine**, and opened their cellar doors so that visitors can sample the likes of mango wine, coffee liqueur and banana brandy.

Mareeba Wetlands

Pickford Road, 6km west of Biboohra, and 13km northwest of Mareeba • April–Dec daily 8.30am–4.30pm, closed Jan–March • ☎ 07 4093 2514, ⓦ mareebawetlands.org

Not far west of Biboohra, the **Mareeba Wetlands** is a stunning five-thousand-acre reserve of tropical savannah woodlands with grass-fringed lagoons that attract seasonal flocks of brolgas, jabiru storks and black cockatoos, along with resident wallabies and goannas. The wetlands are also part of a breeding programme for rainbow-coloured **Gouldian finches**, a formerly common bird now virtually extinct in the wild, but which you can see in the aviary next to the interpretation centre at pretty Clancy's Lagoon; here you can also rent canoes, join an eco-boat cruise, sunrise or sunset safari, and pick up self-guided walking trail maps.

ARRIVAL AND INFORMATION

By bus Trans North buses (2–3 daily) connect Mareeba with Kuranda (45min), Cairns Central (2hr), and Atherton (30min); three times weekly, buses continue west to Karumba in the Gulf (Mon, Wed & Fri 7.40am; 9hr 50min).

MAREEBA AND AROUND

Tourist information Mareeba Heritage Museum and Visitor Centre, 1km south of the centre at 345 Byrnes St (daily 9am–5pm; ☎ 07 4092 5674).

ACCOMMODATION

Granite Gorge Nature Park 332 Paglieto Rd ☎ 07 4093 2259, ⓦ granitegorge.com.au. This scenic private park, 12km west of town, is the best place to camp near Mareeba. Sightings of rock wallabies are almost guaranteed. Un/powered sites $28/$32, tents $65, cabins $95

Jabiru Safari Lodge Mareeba Wetlands ☎ 07 4093 2514, ⓦ jabirusafarilodge.com.au. Safari-style en-suite

---

BIRDING ON THE TABLELANDS

The northern end of the Atherton Tablelands, sloping downhill between Mareeba and Mossman, encompasses a broad range of habitats, from dry gum woodland to highland rainforest, open farmland, lowland wetlands and the coast. This is therefore one of the richest areas for **birding** in Australia, with over 350 species recorded, including thirteen endemics. Several places along the Mareeba–Mossman road have set up as **birdwatchers' retreats**, and can fill you in on places where you can improve your tallies.

★**Kingfisher Park Birdwatchers Lodge** Mount Kooyong Rd, Julatten ☎ 07 4094 1263, ⓦ birdwatchers.com.au. This simple lodge, 50km north of Mareeba via Mount Molloy, has clued-up owners, a choice of bunkhouse rooms with shared bathrooms or en-suite units, and guided walks. The retreat is within striking distance of fabled (in birding circles at least) Mount Lewis, and features in Sean Dooley's book *The Big Twitch*, a humorous insight into the obsessive world of serious birdwatching. Un/powered sites $40/45, bunkhouse rooms $75, units $170

tented cabins, the more expensive with secluded spa baths, set in open savannah woodland. **$218**
Jackaroo Motel 340 Byrnes St ☎07 4092 2677, ⓦjackaroomotel.com. Mareeba's best-value accommodation option, adjacent to the visitor centre and offering comfortable motel rooms and a small pool. **$140**

Chillagoe

The remote settlement of **CHILLAGOE**, 140km west of Mareeba, dates from 1887, when enough copper ore was discovered to keep a smelter running until the 1950s. These days, a gold mine another 16km west at Mungana seems to keep the place ticking over. Red dust, hillocks, a service station, a general store and a single, short street of oversized hotels complete the picture.

Chillagoe-Mungana Caves National Park

Park HQ The Hub, 21–23 Queen St • Daily 8am–3.30pm • One cave tour $25.45, two tours $40.35, three $50.70 • ☎07 4094 7111, ⓦnprsr.qld.gov.au

The main reason to come to Chillagoe is to visit **caves** that have been hollowed by rain into the ancient limestone hillocks hereabouts, collectively protected in **Chillagoe-Mungana Caves National Park**. Daily guided tours, all of which involve climbing and descending several hundred steep steps, lead small groups through each of the three most interesting caves. Call ahead, or drop in at the Hub in Chillagoe, which is also the place to buy tickets, to check that the tours are running – during the wet season, they often aren't.

Tours of both **Donna Cave** (9am; 1hr) and **Trezkinn Cave** (11am; 30–45min) start from the Donna Cave car park, 1.8km southeast of Chillagoe, while the car park for **Royal Arch Cave** (1.30pm; 1hr 30min) is 6km southwest of town. All are filled with natural formations, including a few large **stalagmites**. Wildlife here includes grey swiftlets and agile pythons, which somehow manage to catch bats on the wing. Along the various footpaths that lead through grassland between the caves, many of which are half-buried in the scrub, you can hope to spot echidnas, kangaroos, black cockatoos and frogmouths, the last being odd birds whose name fits them perfectly.

Balancing Rock, also accessible from the Donna Cave car park, offers panoramic views, with Chillagoe hidden by low trees, while obscure Aboriginal paintings and engravings have been found near **the Archways**, west at Mungana.

ARRIVAL AND DEPARTURE   CHILLAGOE

By bus Chillagoe Bus Service runs a 7.30am service to Mareeba on Mon, Wed & Fri; the same bus returns from Mareeba at 1pm Mon & Fri, and 11.30am on Wed (1hr 30min; ☎07 4094 7155, ⓦcoel.com.au).
By car The 140km road from Mareeba to Chillagoe is

sealed except for 16km of corrugated gravel, which poses no real problem during the dry season. West beyond Chillagoe, it continues 500km to Karumba and the Gulf of Carpentaria (see p.475), but it doesn't improve, and there's little fuel or help along the way.

ACCOMMODATION

Chillagoe Cabins Queen St ☎07 4094 7206, ⓦchillagoe .com. Self-contained cottages designed to resemble early nineteenth-century miners' huts, each with kitchenette and private courtyard, plus a pool, BBQ area and restaurant. **$150**
Chillagoe Observatory & Ecolodge Hospital Ave

☎07 4094 7155, ⓦcoel.com.au. Shared-bath private rooms, family units, two separate camping areas – one well-shaded and close to shared amenities, the other much more rustic – and a mini observatory for stargazing. Un/powered sites **$20/$24**, doubles **$60**

Atherton

In a rather bland setting 30km south of Mareeba, and centrally placed for forays to most of the area's attractions, **ATHERTON** is the largest town in the Tablelands. It was founded in part by Chinese miners who settled here in the 1880s after being chased off the goldfields.

The corrugated-iron **Hou Wang Temple**, 2km south of the centre at 86 Herberton Rd (Wed–Sun 11am–4pm; $10; ☎07 4091 6945, ⓦhouwang.org.au) is the last building to survive from Atherton's old **Chinatown**, a once-busy enclave of market gardens and homes abandoned after the government gave the land to returning World War I servicemen. The temple was restored in 2000, with an accompanying museum full of photographs and artefacts found on site.

You can spot local **birdlife** at **Hasties Swamp**, a big waterhole and two-storey observation hide 5km south of town. While nothing astounding, it's a peaceful place populated by magpie geese, pink-eared ducks, swamp hens and assorted marsh tiggets.

ARRIVAL AND INFORMATION ATHERTON

By bus Trans North buses (2–3 daily) connect Atherton with Cairns Central (2hr 30min) by way of Kuranda (1hr 15min) and Mareeba (30min); three weekly buses continue west to Karumba in the Gulf (Mon, Wed & Fri 8.20am; 9hr 10min).

Tourist information The visitor centre is at the town's central intersection, where Main and Silo roads meet (daily 9am–5pm; ☎07 4091 4222, ⓦitablelands .com.au).

ACCOMMODATION AND EATING

Big4 Atherton Woodlands Tourist Park 141 Herberton Rd ☎07 4091 1407, ⓦwoodlandscp.com. au. Green and spacious sites, at the edge of town. Un/powered sites $30/$40, cabins $135
Barron Valley Hotel 53 Main St ☎07 4091 1222, ⓦbvhotel.com.au. This rather splendid Art Deco hotel is the town's chief landmark, and holds some fascinating

displays on its role during World War II, as well as a restaurant and plain but decent guest rooms, the cheapest of which share bathrooms. $60
Pagoda Chinese Restaurant 102 Maunds Rd ☎07 4091 4555. Popular restaurant that serves up Atherton's most reliable Chinese food; the sizzling beef's the star. Daily 12.30–2.30pm & 6–9pm.

Lake Tinaroo

From the village of **Tolga**, 5km north of Atherton, a turn-off leads northeast to **Lake Tinaroo**, a convoluted reservoir that was created by pooling the headwaters of the Barron River. After 15km, on reaching the dam wall, the bitumen turns to gravel, and circulates for 25km around the lake, passing five very cheap campsites on the north shore before cutting deep into native forests, and eventually reaching the Gillies Highway, 15km east of Yungaburra. It's worth stopping along the way for the short walks to bright-green **Mobo Crater**, spooky **Lake Euramo**, and the **Cathedral Fig**, a giant tree some 50m tall and 43m around the base; the thick mass of tendrils supporting the crown has fused together like molten wax.

ACTIVITIES AND ACCOMMODATION LAKE TINAROO

Kayaking You can rent kayaks from *Lake Tinaroo Holiday Park* for $50/day.
Lake Tinaroo Holiday Park Tinaroo Falls Dam Rd ☎07 4095 8232, ⓦlaketinarooholidaypark.com.au.

Near the Tinaroo Dam, with shady sites, basic cabins and waterfront villas. Late Sunday checkouts (till 4pm) cost just $1 extra. Un/powered sites $27/37, cabins $90, villas $135

Yungaburra and around

Just 13km east of Atherton at the start of the Gillies Highway to Gordonvale, the delightfully pretty village of **YUNGABURRA** consists of the old wooden *Lake Eacham Hotel*, a store, a handful of quaint houses – many Heritage-listed, dating back to 1910 – and some of the Tableland's best restaurants. An excellent base from which to explore the Tablelands and surrounding lakes, it's also the venue for a huge **market** held on the last Saturday of each month.

Prime local places to spot wildlife include the **platypus-viewing platform** by the Peterson Creek, near the river where the road (Gillies Highway) from Atherton comes into town. Take the 2km walking track from the car park here, which leads under the bridge and beside the river to another viewing platform and further opportunities to see platypus; if you're lucky, you might also sight a rare tree kangaroo.

Curtain Fig Tree National Park

It's not often that a single tree gets a national park to itself, but the **Curtain Fig Tree**, 2km southwest of town along Fig Tree Boulevard, truly deserves the accolade. The 39m base of this astonishingly large parasitic strangler fig is entirely overhung by a stringy mass of aerial roots – a "curtain" – drooping off the higher branches. A timber boardwalk encircles the tree, allowing you to survey the strangler from all angles.

The crater lakes

A couple of superb **crater lakes**, or "maars", are located immediately east of Yungaburra, at the top of the Gillies Highway down to Gordonvale. Blue, still discs, encircled by thick rainforest, they're thought to be around 60m deep and more than 10,000 years old. Local Aboriginal stories that describe them as appearing suddenly, in a single day, agree with the modern theories of geologists.

Lake Eacham

Lake Eacham is 6km out of town, signposted south off the highway. Once you get away from the extensive lakefront parking and picnic area, where visitors **swim** from a broad platform, launch themselves into the water in **kayaks**, or simply cook barbecue lunches, you can follow a peaceful 4km **footpath** around the entire circumference. It's a great walk, even though for almost its entire length, the trail remains well above the water level, with only occasional glimpses of the lake and no access to the shore. In theory, though, you might spot an inoffensive **amethystine python** – Australia's largest snake – sunning itself down by the water.

Lake Barrine

Access to **Lake Barrine**, 10km northeast of Yungaburra, is dominated by a venerable old tearoom. A **cruise boat** sets off from the quay alongside to spend an hour circuiting the lake (daily 9.30am, 11.30am & 1.30pm; $16). To escape the crowds, head for the two enormous kauri pines that mark the start of an underused 6km **walking track** around the lake; keep your eyes peeled for spiky-headed water dragons, hordes of musky rat-kangaroos, which look exactly as you'd expect them to, as well, potentially, as more pythons.

INFORMATION AND TOURS

Tourist information The visitor centre is in Maud Kehoe Park in the centre of Yungaburra (Mon–Sat 9am–5pm, Sun 10am–4pm; ☎07 4095 2416, ⓦyungaburra.com).
Alan's Wildlife Tours ☎07 4095 3784, ⓦalanswildlifetours.com.au. Experienced wildlife

YUNGABURRA AND AROUND

enthusiast Alan Gillanders can help you spot some of the rarer nocturnal marsupials around town on a private 2hr nocturnal spotlighting tour (from $80 for two). He also runs half- and full-day birding trips and wildlife tours.

ACCOMMODATION

YUNGABURRA

Eden House Retreat 20 Gillies Hwy ☎07 4089 7000, ⓦedenhouse.com.au. Stylish hotel with cosy garden cottages and modern villas, plus an inviting mountain spa. There's also a good restaurant, *Obi's*, open Wed–Sun only. Rates include a breakfast hamper. **$155**
Kookaburra Lodge 3 Eacham Rd ☎07 4095 3222, ⓦkookaburra-lodge.com. Great value-for-money motel rooms opening onto a lovely garden, with a BBQ deck for sizzling your own steaks. **$95**
Mt Quincan Crater Retreat Hunt Rd ☎07 4095 2255, ⓦmtquincan.com.au. For a romantic weekend, these secluded wooden-pole houses overlooking an extinct

volcano crater, 8km southeast of Yungaburra, are absolutely unbeatable – and offer a good chance of spotting tree kangaroos. No kids. **$298**
★**On the Wallaby** 37 Eacham Rd ☎07 4095 2031, ⓦonthewallaby.com. This welcoming pine-and-slate lodge is an excellent budget option. Daily canoe, bike and wildlife-spotting trips ($40), and bike rental for $20/day. Camping **$20**, dorms **$25**, doubles **$60**

LAKE EACHAM

Chambers Wildlife Rainforest Lodges Eacham Close ☎07 4095 3754, ⓦrainforest-australia.com. Self-contained one- or three-bedroom lodges, each with full kitchen facilities, plus a platform for nocturnal wildlife viewing. Minimum three-night stay. $130

Crater Lake Rainforest Cottages 17 Eacham Close ☎ 07 4095 2322, ⓦ craterlakes.com.au. Cosy and stylish

timber stand-alone cabins, set in a forest clearing. Decorated to themes ranging from Tuscany to Bali, they're quite idyllic. $250

EATING

YUNGABURRA

Flynn's 17 Eacham Rd ☎ 07 4095 2235, ⓦ flynnsyungaburra.com. Excellent Mediterranean bistro food in pleasant surroundings. All main dishes, from braised ox cheek to prawns with linguini, cost $30. Mon, Tues & Sat 11am–2pm & 5.30–10pm, Fri 5.30–10pm, Sun 11am–2pm.

Spencer & Murphy Booksellers The Mews ☎ 07 4095 2123. A cavernous, old-school secondhand bookshop where you can buy a cuppa ($4) and a cake ($5), and browse an enormous selection of novels, travel guides and local interest books; heaven for bookworms. Mon, Tues & Thurs–Sat 10am–5pm, Sun 10am–4pm.

Whistle Stop Cafe 36 Cedar St ☎ 07 4088 1593. This

cool cottage, with pavement tables and a more secluded and well-shaded garden, is a great place to stop off for home-made pies, lunch specials like quiche and salad for $12, or simply tea and a scone for $4. Be sure to try a delicious $6 Tuscany chocolate cake. Mon–Fri 8.30am–3pm, Sat 7.30am–2pm, Sun 8.30am–noon.

LAKE BARRINE

Tea House Gillies Hwy, Lake Barrine ☎ 07 4095 3847, ⓦ lakebarrine.com.au. Perched above the lake, this 80-year-old teashop serves Devonshire cream teas and full-scale meals, with daily specials such as salmon with mac nuts for $18–22. Mon–Fri 9am–4pm, Sat & Sun 8.30am–4pm.

The Southern Tablelands

The Kennedy Highway continues 80km down from Atherton to **Ravenshoe**, the highlands' southernmost town. Along the way, you can find easy walking tracks at, first, **Wongabel State Forest** and then at the **Crater** at Mount Hypipamee, a 56m vertical rift formed by volcanic gases blowing through fractured granite that's now filled with deep, weed-covered water. There are picnic tables here but camping is prohibited.

Herberton

An alternative road south from Atherton circles west via **HERBERTON**, a quaint, one-time timber town with a sprawling open-air museum, Herberton Historic Village. During the 1880s thirty thousand people lived here – a century before Cairns' population numbered that many – and the towns was served by a railway from Atherton.

Herberton Historic Village

6 Broadway • Daily: mid-March to mid-Oct & late Dec to late Jan 9am–5pm, otherwise 9am–4pm; last entry 1hr 30min before closing • $28 • ☎ 07 4092 2002, ⓦ historicvillageherberton.com.au

More than fifty restored period buildings, including a chemist, schoolhouse and music shop stuffed to the brim with delightful period memorabilia and unique Aussie collectibles are recreated at **Herberton Historic Village**. Check out the gleaming penny-farthing in the Coach House. There are live demos and steam engines some weekends.

ARRIVAL AND DEPARTURE   HERBERTON

By bus Trans North buses stop outside Herberton News on Grace St en route to Cairns (Tues, Thurs & Sun 3.20pm; 2hr

10min) and Karumba (Mon, Wed & Fri 8.35am; 9hr).

Ravenshoe

RAVENSHOE is noteworthy as home to the *Tully Falls Hotel*, Queensland's highest pub, and **Millstream Falls**, Australia's broadest waterfall, 5km southwest. For many years, a **steam railway** has operated here too. At the time of writing, it was closed down, pending approval to resume services; check ⓦ ravenshoesteamrailway.webs.com to find whether it's once more offering Sunday excursions to the tiny siding of Tumoulin, Queensland's highest train station.

ARRIVAL AND INFORMATION

By bus Trans North buses stop at the *Tall Timbers Roadhouse* on the Kennedy Hwy en route to Cairns (Tues, Thurs & Sun 2.50pm; 2hr 40min) and Karumba (Mon, Wed & Fri 9.45am; 7hr 45min).

Tourist information Ravenshoe Visitor Centre, 24 Moore St (daily 9am–5pm; ☎ 07 4097 7700).

ACCOMMODATION AND EATING

Chilverton Cottages 12028 Kennedy Hwy ☎ 07 4097 6785, ⓦ chilvertoncottages.com.au. Comfortable apartments and cottages within the rainforest, with a day-spa and restaurant that's open to nonguests and serves all meals daily, including afternoon tea; the three-course dinner menu costs $80. **$250**

The Club Hotel 45 Grigg St ☎ 07 4097 6136, ⓦ clubhotelravenshoe.com. Popular pub serving excellent, freshly cooked meals; hits include thick steak burgers and slow-braised lamb. Specials from $13. Daily noon–2pm & 6–8pm.

The Pond Cottage 844 Tully Falls Rd ☎ 07 4097 7189, ⓦ bnbnq.com.au/pondcottage. Cute self-contained cottage (sleeps five) overlooking platypus ponds, with daily breakfast hampers and bubbly on arrival. **$230**

3

Malanda

MALANDA, 25km southeast of Atherton, is home to a **dairy** that provides milk and cheese for the whole of Queensland's far north, plus most of the Northern Territory and even New Guinea.

At **Malanda Falls**, 1km up the highway towards Atherton, an excellent visitor centre (daily 9am–4.30pm; ☎ 07 4096 6957, ⓦ malandafalls.com) gives a rundown of the geology, wildlife, and Aboriginal and settler history of the Tablelands. There's also a roadside swimming hole, and a couple of short but enjoyable rainforest trails.

ACCOMMODATION

Canopy Treehouses Hogan Rd ☎ 07 4096 5364, ⓦ canopytreehouses.com.au. This superlative complex, 12km south of Malanda via Tarzali, consists of wooden pole-frame lodges set among a hundred acres of thick, wildlife-packed rainforest. Minimum two nights. **$349**

Malanda Hotel 12 English St ☎ 07 4096 5488. Built in 1911 to sleep three hundred people, this cavernous hotel claims to be the largest wooden building in the southern hemisphere. As well as offering basic but characterful rooms on the first floor, it's full of old furnishings and has an excellent restaurant. **$75**

Nerada Tea Plantation

933 Glen Allyn Rd, 11km southeast of Malanda • Mon–Fri 9am–4pm, closed Feb • Free • ☎ 07 4096 8328, ⓦ neradatea.com.au

The fields of the **Nerada Tea Plantation** – Australia's largest – spread across idyllically verdant countryside in the back roads east of Malanda. Although you can take a tour to watch the sorting and packing process in their tin-roof factory, the real reason to come here is to catch an almost certain sighting of the resident colony of **tree kangaroos**. So long as you buy a few packets of tea, or better still a $7 **cream tea**, complete with scones and jam, in the on-site café/store, helpful staff are happy to point out in which of the nearby trees the elsewhere elusive creatures happen to be spending the day.

Millaa Millaa

MILLAA MILLAA, 20km south of Malanda, is a quiet, 500m-long street with the usual hotel and general store. A waterfall circuit starts 2km east, along a 15km road that passes three small cascades. The most famous, **Millaa Millaa Falls** – as seen in the video for Peter André's *Mysterious Girl*, no less – is a magnificent curtain of water, tumbling evenly into a pristine plunge pool that's home to elusive platypus. It's a great spot for a dip, with changing rooms, but come early to beat the tour-bus crowds.

ACCOMMODATION

Henrietta Creek Campsite Palmerston Hwy ☎ 13 74 68, ⓦ nprsr.qld.gov.au. Grassy sites shaded by rainforest beside Henrietta Creek, 12km southeast of Millaa Milla town, with basic toilets and BBQs. **$5.95**

Port Douglas

Once a quaint fishing village, **PORT DOUGLAS**, has in recent years transformed itself into an upscale, in-the-know alternative to Cairns, its main street thronging with well-heeled visitors strolling between fancy restaurants and pricey boutiques. While the sheer scale of development can come as a shock, though, it's still a great place to spend a few days, and every bit as good as Cairns as a base for a rainforest adventure or Barrier-Reef dive-trip.

The prime attraction is idyllic **Four Mile Beach**. Stretching south from the east side of town, it's a wonderful expanse of sand, perfect for playing, hiking or jogging year-round, though the presence of jellyfish means that in winter you can only swim within a small netted area.

Port Douglas's main commercial drag, **Macrossan Street**, runs between Four Mile Beach and **Anzac Park**, scene of a Sunday-morning **market** that's good for fruit, veggies and souvenirs. A small grid of leafy streets lies below Macrossan, with the busy **marina** just south of the park. Just north of the park, near its small jetty, the whitewashed timber church of **St Mary's by the Sea** was built after the 1911 cyclone swept away its predecessor. Out to sea, the vegetated sand cays known as **the Low Isles** make a good day-trip, with fine snorkelling, a lighthouse and an interpretive centre.

3

ARRIVAL AND INFORMATION   PORT DOUGLAS

By bus Port Douglas Bus operate regular services between Cairns and Port Douglas via Cairns Airport (📞 07 4099 5665, 🌐 portdouglasbus.com), while Sun Palm Coaches offer a door-to-door service from Cairns or the airport (📞 07 4099 1191, 🌐 sunpalmtransport.com.au). Trans North buses stop at Port Douglas en route between Cairns and Mossman, Cape Tribulation and Cooktown (3 weekly; 📞 07 4045 8644, 🌐 transnorthbus.com).
Destinations Cairns (15 daily; 1hr 30min); Cape Tribulation (4 weekly; 2hr 45min); Cooktown (4 weekly; 5hr 30min);

Mossman (3 daily; 20min).
By car Port Douglas is an hour's drive north from Cairns, and stands 5km north of the stunning Captain Cook Hwy, which continues north towards Mossman and Cape Tribulation.
Tourist information There is no council-run visitor centre; of the many private agencies, Port Douglas Visitor Centre at 23 Macrossan St (daily 8.30am–7pm; 📞 07 4099 5599, 🌐 infoportdouglas.com.au) is especially useful for arranging local tours and transport.

ACTIVITIES

BIKE RENTAL
Port Douglas Bike Hire 3 Warner St 📞 07 4099 5799, 🌐 portdouglasbikehire.com. From $20/day; open Mon–Fri 9am–5pm, Sat & Sun 7am–3pm.

WATERSPORTS
Wind Swell 📞 04 2749 8042, 🌐 windswell.com.au. Kitesurfing lessons for $240, SUP tours from $50.

TOURS
Back Country Bliss 📞 07 4099 3677, 🌐 backcountrybliss.com.au. Excellent outfit, specializing in active guided tours, including river drift snorkelling in a pristine rainforest creek ($99) and 3hr night mountain biking ($120).

SAILING AND REEF TRIPS
Day-trips range from $195 to $270; sailing boats make for the idyllic coral cays of the Low Isles, while most reef trips head to Agincourt Reef. Dwarf minke whales pass by May–Aug; some operators allow you to swim with them. Diving

is usually not included; expect to pay $70–150 for two dives and gear. For a free sunset sail (over-16s only), head to the Port Douglas Yacht Club, on Spinmaker Close, at 4pm on Wednesday.
Aquarius 📞 07 4099 6999, 🌐 tropicaljourneys.com. Snorkel-only cruises to the Low Isles and $60 sunset cruises on a 23-passenger sailing cat.
Quicksilver 📞 07 4087 2100, 🌐 quicksilver-cruises.com, 🌐 poseidon-cruises.com.au, 🌐 wavedancerlowisles.com. Port Douglas's major cruise operator offers cruises on several different vessels, to suit different tastes. The flagship *Quicksilver* vessels are large and very comfortable catamarans that dock at a stable pontoon mooring on the outer Agincourt Reef, for snorkelling and, for an additional fee, diving. *Poseidon* is a 24m catamaran dedicated to diving, which visits up to three out of a range of sixteen dive sites each day, while *Wavedancer* is an elegant sailing cat that heads out to the Low Isles for a day of family-friendly sunshine and snorkelling.
Sailaway 📞 07 4099 4200, 🌐 sailawayportdouglas .com. Large French-built sailing cat which cruises out to

the Low Isles and moors for 5hr, and also offers a $60 sunset cruise.

Silversonic ☎07 4044 9944, ⊛silverseries.com.au. High-speed 29m catamaran visiting up to three different Agincourt ribbon reef sites for 5hr of snorkelling and diving.

Wavelength ☎07 4099 5031, ⊛wavelength.com.au. Small and personal snorkelling tours for up to thirty passengers, mooring at Opal, St Crispins and Tongue reefs.

ACCOMMODATION

Dougies 111 Davidson St ☎07 4099 6200, ⊛dougies .com.au. Well-established backpackers', complete with hammocks and pool, beside the highway 1.5km south of the centre. There's camping space in the gardens, as well as four- and seven-bed dorms and private shared-bath rooms. Camping **$25**, dorms **$30**, doubles **$80**

Lazy Lizard Motor Inn 121 Davidson St ☎07 4099 5900, ⊛dougies.com.au. If you're looking for a clean, simple place to sleep, this single-storey motel south of the centre, affiliated with Best Western, offers some of the best-value rooms around. Rates rise at weekends. **$120**

Palm Villas 40 Warner St ☎07 4099 4822, ⊛palmvillas.com.au. Comfortable one-bedroom apartments close to town with friendly, helpful management. No minimum stay. **$160**

Pandanus Tourist Park 97–107 Davidson St ☎07 4099 5944, ⊛pandanuscp.com.au. Good facilities, including a gleaming camp kitchen, leafy environs and a pool, 1km south of town. Un/powered sites **$38/$45**, cabin **$125**

★**Pink Flamingo** 115 Davidson St ☎07 4099 6622, ⊛pinkflamingo.com.au. This gay-owned, adults-only oasis a 20min walk south of the centre is Port Douglas' most intimate accommodation; its kitchenette studios and spacious villas with outdoor showers all share a lovely pool. Studios **$145**, villas **$205**

Port Douglas B&B 59 Reef St, Four Mile Beach ☎07 4099 3324, ⊛portdouglasbb.com. Cosy two-room garden B&B, with kind hosts, amazing tropical breakfasts and a nice pool, 5km south of the centre and just 50m from beautiful Four Mile Beach. **$150**

QT Resort 87–109 Port Douglas Rd ☎07 4099 8900, ⊛qtportdouglas.com.au. With a Hamptons meets *Mad Men* fit-out, this chic boutique hotel, 3km from the centre, boasts sleek digs (spa rooms are the quietest), a meandering pool, spa and in the winter, an outdoor cinema. There's also an excellent restaurant and bar. **$308**

EATING

The Beach Shack 29 Barrier St, Four Mile Beach ☎07 4099 1100, ⊛the-beach-shack.com.au. Lively haunt, 4km out of town via the main highway, and 50m back from the south end of the beach. The main emphasis is on wood-fired pizzas, usually from $20, but only $10 in the lounge on Sat, and wicked mojitos, but they also serve good curries and seafood specials costing up to $30. Daily 5.30–10pm.

Mango Jam Café 24 Macrossan St ☎07 4099 4611, ⊛mangojam.com.au. Big, busy, all-day family restaurant, wide open to the street, which sets out to find something for everyone, with wood-fired pizzas of every imaginable flavour from around $15, plus burgers, curries, and hearty mains like BBQ ribs or grilled salmon for up to $35. Daily 7.30am–10pm.

Salsa Bar and Grill 26 Wharf St ☎07 4099 4922, ⊛salsaportdouglas.com.au. This light, breezy mod-Oz restaurant has a devoted local following, thanks to its imaginative menu of Asian-influenced meat and seafood dishes – typically costing $20–30 for lunch, $30–40 in the

evening –and excellent wine list. Daily noon–3pm & 5.30–10pm.

Under Wraps 22 Macrossan St ☎07 4099 5792, ⊛under-wraps.com.au. Great salad, sandwich and breakfast bar, displaying numerous fresh options for pic 'n' mixing, plus juices and meals such as $9 lentil burgers and $12 Thai green curry. Daily 8am–4pm.

★**Watergate** 31 Macrossan St ☎07 4099 5844, ⊛watergateportdouglas.com.au. Port Douglas' most romantic restaurant is rather hidden away, so after dark there's generally someone posted on Macrossan St to point you towards their garden dining area, lit by flaming torches. Expect to pay special-occasion prices – well over $30 for dinner – for mod-Oz dishes like kangaroo loin or spiced yellowfin tuna. Daily noon–2.30pm & 5.30–10pm.

Whileaway Bookshop & Cafe 43 Macrossan St ☎07 4099 4066. Pick up a coffee or snack from the counter, then sit out at the pavement tables or browse among a fine selection of new books. Daily 7am–6pm.

DRINKING AND NIGHTLIFE

Court House Hotel Cnr Wharf & Macrossan sts ☎07 4099 5181, ⊛courthousehotelportdouglas.com.au. This great big pub has been here forever – well, since 1878 – and still oozes local atmosphere, making it a great place for an evening drink. Daily 11.30am–11pm.

The Iron Bar 5 Macrossan St ☎07 4099 4776, ⊛ironbarportdouglas.com.au. Huge, vibrant pub with rough-cut timber furniture, surf 'n' turf menu (mains $22–40), and daily cane toad racing at 8.30pm. Daily 11am–midnight.

The Daintree

Remarkable not only as Australia's largest expanse of **tropical rainforest**, but the oldest to survive anywhere in the world, the extraordinary **Daintree** stretches uninterrupted for 1200 square kilometres between the Daintree and Bloomfield rivers. The sheer diversity of its flora and fauna is astonishing; home to as many as thirteen different ecosystems, this is among the most complex rainforest structures on earth.

World Heritage listing hasn't spared the Daintree from development, however: roads are being surfaced, land has been subdivided, and tourism facilities seem to increase year after year. While this may undermine its wild and remote brochure image, and disappoint some visitors, the majestic forest still descends thick and dark right to the sea around **Cape Tribulation**, and you can explore paths through the jungle leading to pristine waterholes, climb velveteen peaks, watch for wildlife, or just rest on the beach.

Although the Daintree holds several **accommodation** possibilities, targeted especially towards budget backpackers, most visitors simply visit for the day, whether on a guided tour or in a private vehicle. While the Daintree proper only begins once you've taken the **ferry** across to the north side of the Daintree River, most itineraries also take in one or both of the towns south of the river – **Daintree** itself, and sleepy Mossman, home to the dramatic **Mossman Gorge**.

Mossman Gorge

3km west of Mossman, 22km northwest of Port Douglas • Daily 8am–6pm • Shuttle buses from visitor centre $9/day • ☏ 07 4099 7000, ⓦ mossmangorge.com • Port Douglas Bus runs day-trips to the gorge ($29 from Port Douglas, $92 from Cairns; ☏ 07 4099 5665, ⓦ portdouglasbus.com)

The sedate little sugar town of **MOSSMAN**, up the highway 20km northwest of Port Douglas is noteworthy solely as home to the **Mossman Gorge**, immediately west. The gorge conforms to everything you'd hope for from a rainforest river, with boulder-strewn flow and crystal-clear pools that are wonderful for messing around in on a quiet day. Unfortunately, though, it attracts

THE DAINTREE

Bloomfield Track to Wujal Wujal, Rossville Ayton, ▲ Lion's Den & Cooktown

N

● **EATING**
Cassowary Café	1
Daintree Ice Cream Co	5
Mason's Café	4
On The Turps	3
Whet	2

■ **ACCOMMODATION**
Cape Trib Beach House	1
Cape Tribulation Camping	5
Coral Sea Views B&B	8
Crocodylus Village	9
Daintree Ecolodge	11
Epiphyte B&B	10
Ferntree Rainforest Resort	3
Heritage Lodge & Spa	6
Lync-Haven	7
PK's Jungle Village	2
Rainforest Hideaway B&B	4

Emmagen Creek
Emmagen Beach
Cape Tribulation
Kulki
Black Mountain
Bat House
Myall Beach
DAINTREE NATIONAL PARK
Cape Trib Store
Dubuji Boardwalk
Coconut Beach
National Parks Campsite
Noah Creek
Noah Beach
Marrdja Botanical Walk
Thornton Beach
Mount Emmett
Alexandra Bay
Cooper Creek Tea Plantation
Bailey Point
Bailey Hill
Airstrip
BUCHANAN CREEK RD
Cow Bay
Daintree Discovery Centre
Jindalba Boardwalk
Mount Alexandra
Ferry Crossing
DIRT ROAD
Daintree River
Cape Kimberley
0 25 kilometres
Mossman

3

streams of tour buses in peak season. All access is via the Mossman Gorge Centre, which holds a café, shop and indigenous art gallery. From there, frequent shuttle buses carry visitors to and from the gorge itself, where **walking trails** of varying lengths allow you to escape the crowds.

The **Kuku Yalanji**, the local Aboriginal community, lead small groups on informative **Dreamtime Gorge Walks** from the visitor centre, explaining their affinity with their tropical environment, demonstrating local plant usage and identifying sources of indigenous bush food (daily 10am, 11am & 3pm; 1hr 30min; $62).

Daintree and the Daintree River

North of Mossman, forested peaks start to loom on the skyline ahead, shrouded in halos of mist. There's still one final hurdle to cross before you reach the Daintree itself: the **Daintree River Ferry**, 30km north of Mossman, a simple platform that's attached to a cable and towed across the river (daily 6am–midnight; cars/motorbikes $25/$10). It shuttles back and forth every fifteen minutes or so, but it only carries 25 vehicles per trip, so you can expect to wait at peak times.

Alternatively, a 10km detour northwest off the highway shortly before the ferry crossing will bring you to **DAINTREE** township. This former timber camp is now little more than one big pub, a general store and a campsite, only worth visiting to join a bird- and crocodile-spotting nature cruise.

TOURS   **DAINTREE**

Daintree Boatman Nature Tours ☏ 04 1765 1929, ⓦ daintreerivertours.com.au. Exceptional dawn birding tours, from Daintree Village Jetty (2hr; $60).

Solar Whisper ☏ 07 4098 7131, ⓦ solarwhisper.com. Cruises in a quiet solar-powered boat, with on-board croc-cam, starting 400m before the ferry (6 daily; 1hr; $28).

ACCOMMODATION AND EATING

Daintree Ecolodge 3189 Mossman–Daintree Rd ☏ 07 4098 6100, ⓦ daintree-ecolodge.com.au. Luxury resort in a spectacular location; rooms are "tree houses" and facilities include a spa. Its beautiful lagoon-side

Julaymba restaurant, open daily for all meals, prepares interesting dishes using rainforest ingredients like red claw and lemon myrtle, with dinner mains costing around $32. **$345**

The Cape Tribulation road

Once across the Daintree River, you enter **Daintree National Park**, and set off along the 35km scenic drive to the tiny settlement of **Cape Tribulation**, where the sealed road ends. As you head north, be sure to take the time to enjoy at least one of the park's four free-access **boardwalks**, signposted off the beach side of the highway and offering easy but exhilarating short hikes through the rainforest and/or mangrove swamps. Be very careful on the **beaches**, though; the waters hereabouts are home to predatory saltwater **crocodiles**.

Daintree Discovery Centre

Tulip Oak Rd, 9km northeast of ferry • Daily 8.30am–5pm • $32 • ☏ 07 4098 9171, ⓦ discoverthedaintree.com

Although it's undeniably expensive, the **Daintree Discovery Centre** makes a worthy introduction to the region. The centrepiece here is a 27m-tall tower that enables you to inspect the rainforest from five separate levels, culminating in great views over the top of the canopy. There's a chance you might spot a cassowary or amethystine python, but even if you don't, the informative displays on flora and wildlife, along with assorted caged reptiles, should keep you interested.

Jindalba Boardwalk and Cow Bay

The **Jindalba Boardwalk**, at the dead end of Tulip Oak Rd 500m beyond the Daintree Discovery Centre, offers a choice of two routes along a wooden walkway that criss crosses streams as it undulates through the forest. The 700m circuit only takes around fifteen minutes, while the 2.7km alternative is steeper and a bit more demanding.

The Daintree's first access to the sea comes slightly further north, at **Cow Bay**, reached via the 6km Buchanan Creek Road. The spectacular **beach** here was known to local Aborigines as Kaba Kada, which means "rain a lot".

Thornton Beach and Noah Beach

North of Cow Bay, the Cape Tribulation road passes various restaurants and commercial attractions, then crosses **Cooper Creek** and approaches the coast for the first time. Sandy Thornton Beach, notorious as the spot where a night-swimming visitor was snatched by a crocodile in 2016, is another huge expanse of sand, and has its own small café.

Another 5km on, the concrete paths and boardwalks of the wonderful, 1.2km **Marrdja Botanical Walk** follow Noah Creek through a mixture of forest and mangroves almost, but not quite, to the river mouth on **Noah Beach**. Look for spiky lawyer cane, lianas twisted into corkscrew shapes where they once surrounded a tree, and the spherical pods of the cannonball mangrove – dried and dismembered, they were used as puzzles by Aboriginal peoples, the object being to fit the irregular segments back together.

Myall Beach and Cape Tribulation

North of Noah Beach, near the **Cape Trib Store** café-cum-grocery (daily 8.30am–5.30pm), a short road opposite a natural swimming hole heads through thick forest to the southern end of **Myall Beach**. Plants close in again a couple of kilometres up the main road at **Dubuji Boardwalk**, a 1.2km-long replay of Marrdja, though with a greater range of forests. A spur trail off the main route leads to the gorgeous, powdery white sand of the beach's central portion.

Cape Tribulation, marking the northern end of Myall Beach, was named when Captain Cook's vessel hit a reef offshore in June 1770. A small settlement, also known as Cape Tribulation, now straddles the highway at the foot of the steep, forested slopes of the inland hill that Cook dubbed **Mount Sorrow**. Visit the **Bat House** here, part of the Austrop Tropical Research Foundation, to handle tame, orphaned flying foxes (Tues–Sun 10.30am–3.30pm; $5; austrop.org.au).

Another short spur road leads to the beach on the northern flanks of the cape. Parking at the end enables you to follow the short but hugely enjoyable **Kulki** trail, which heads right for 350m, climbing parallel to the beach, to reach a viewpoint perched above the mangroves and facing north up the Cape York coastline. Along the way, you may see brilliantly coloured pittas (small, tailless birds with a buff chest, green back and black-and-rust heads) bouncing around in the leaf litter, or spot a crocodile sunning itself on the sands below. You can walk back along the beach itself.

The paved portion of the highway finally comes to an end at the *Beach House* backpackers' resort, 1.5km north.

CYCADS

Living relics from the age of dinosaurs, **cycads** are extremely slow-growing, fire-resistant plants found throughout the tropics, with tough, palm-like fronds. Female plants produce large **cones** that break up into bright orange segments, each containing a seed; these are eaten (and thus distributed) by emus and other creatures. Despite being highly toxic to humans – almost every early Australian explorer made himself violently ill trying them – these seeds were a staple of Aborigines, who detoxified flour made from the nuts by prolonged washing. They also applied "fire-stick farming" techniques, encouraging groves to grow and seed by annual burning.

ARRIVAL AND DEPARTURE

By bus Weather permitting, Trans North run 4WD buses (3 weekly) all the way up Cape Tribulation Rd to Cooktown

ACTIVITIES

Cruises Cape Tribulation Wilderness run croc-spotting cruises up Cooper Creek along pristine mangrove estuaries (1hr cruise $30, 6hr cruise and walk $130; ☎ 04 5773 1000, ⍟ capetribcruises.com).

Snorkelling Ocean Safari offer awesome half-day tours from Myall Beach, aboard zippy inflatables that take just

THE CAPE TRIBULATION ROAD

from Cairns (5hr 50min) and Port Douglas (4hr 40min).

25min to reach two pristine Barrier-Reef snorkel sites ($139; ☎ 07 4098 0006, ⍟ oceansafari.com.au).

Ziplining Glide across flying fox ziplines, 19m up over the rainforest canopy, with Jungle Surfing Tours ($95; ☎ 07 4098 0043, ⍟ junglesurfing.com.au).

ACCOMMODATION

COW BAY

★ **Coral Sea Views B&B** Mahogany Rd ☎ 07 4098 9058, ⍟ coralseaviews.com.au. Two cute cabins secreted high on a hill with dazzling sea, valley and rainforest views; each comes with a queen bed, bathroom and open-sided lounge deck with hammocks. Shared kitchen and lovely pool. $160

Crocodylus Village Buchanan Creek Rd ☎ 07 4098 9166, ⍟ daintreecrocodylus.com.au. Basic, off-the-grid dorms and rooms amid dense rainforest, with inexpensive meals and lots of activities on offer including night walks, horseriding and overnight kayak trips to Snapper Island ($299). Dorms $25, doubles $75

Epiphyte B&B 22 Silkwood Rd ☎ 07 4098 9039, ⍟ rainforestbb.com. Laidback B&B with views to Thornton's Peak from the front veranda, and offering four well-priced rooms plus a secluded honeymoon cabin. Doubles $110, cabins $150

Lync-Haven Lot 44, Cape Tribulation Rd ☎ 07 4098 9155, ⍟ lynchaven.com.au. Nice tidy units backing onto a wallaby enclosure, plus well-shaded tropical camping spots, with use of kitchen and laundry. The on-site café/bar is open daily for all meals, with fish'n'chips $25, steaks $30. Un/powered sites $28/$32, doubles $150

THORNTON BEACH AND NOAH BEACH

Heritage Lodge & Spa 32 Turpentine Rd ☎ 07 4098 9321, ⍟ heritagelodge.net.au. Cosy, classy little resort, tucked 1km inland off the highway just back from Thornton Beach, and offering twenty comfortable cabins, some family-sized, with private balconies. The views of Cooper Creek, and its wildlife, are especially good from the *On The Turps* restaurant, open for all meals and serving kangaroo fillet for $37. $330

MYALL BEACH AND CAPE TRIBULATION

Cape Trib Beach House 152 Rykers Rd ☎ 07 4098 0030, ⍟ capetribbeach.com.au. Set in the coastal forest at the end of the paved road, this ramshackle collection of timber cabins and small bunkhouses are dotted down a pedestrian lane that drops right down to the beach. Accommodation is rustic and simple, but the setting is utterly superb. There's a pool and communal kitchen, while the large and lively restaurant/bar *Tides* is at beach level, with chairs out on the sand. Dorms $29, doubles $150

Cape Tribulation Camping Lot 11, Cape Tribulation Rd ☎ 07 4098 0077, ⍟ capetribcamping.com.au. Superb location, behind Myall Beach, with a big lawn and grassy sites, though those near the bar often get noisy. Wood-fired pizzas are available most nights and you can rent kayaks for $100/day. Un/powered sites $30/$40

Ferntree Rainforest Resort Camelot Close ☎ 07 4098 0000, ⍟ ferntreerainforestlodge.com.au. Budget dorms and lovely timber-frame cottages, plus two pools and a bar. The pleasant *Cassowary Café* is open for breakfast and dinner only, with dinner mains like seafood paella for around $25. Dorms $28, cabins $130

PK's Jungle Village PMB 7, Cape Tribulation Rd ☎ 07 4098 0040, ⍟ pksjunglevillage.com.au. Large and well-kept budget resort just off Myall Beach, with five- to eight-bed dorms, basic doubles, cabins and camping, plus a pool, all-day restaurant, and the laidback *Jungle Bar*, which has a pool table and games. Unpowered sites $30, dorms $25, doubles $70, cabins $95

Rainforest Hideaway B&B Camelot Close ☎ 07 4098 0108, ⍟ rainforesthideaway.com. Comfy but rustic wooden cabins, nestling amid rainforest that's dotted with sculptures, set 200m up in the hills. $135

EATING

In addition to the following places, many of the accommodation options listed above have appealing on-site **restaurants**, including *Lync-Haven*, *Heritage Lodge & Spa*, *Cape Trib Beach House*, *Ferntree Rainforest Resort* and *PK's Jungle Village*.

COW BAY

Daintree Ice Cream Co Lot 100, Cape Tribulation Rd

☎ 07 4098 9114. Utterly sublime ice cream/*gelato*, using exotic fruits from the orchard alongside, where home-grown fruits like the notorious strong-smelling durian are on display: $6.50 will get you three scoops of the day's chosen flavours. Daily 11am–5pm.

MYALL BEACH AND CAPE TRIBULATION
Mason's Café 3781 Cape Tribulation Rd ☎07 4098 0070, ⓦmasonstours.com.au. Simple lunch spot, adjoining a store and tour-company office, with its own

glorious swimming hole. The menu ranges through chicken, fish and meat, with buffalo, kangaroo or croc burgers at $15. Daily 11am–3.30pm.
Whet Lot 1, Cape Tribulation Rd ☎07 4098 0007, ⓦwhet .net.au. Café-bar with small menu of mod-Oz gourmet food; try the garlic and kaffir-lime tiger prawns steamed in fresh coconut ($29). Watching a movie in the cinema lounge upstairs costs $10–15. Daily 11am–4pm & 6–8.30pm.

The Bloomfield Track

The unpaved **Bloomfield Track** stretches north for 80km from Cape Tribulation, until it meets the Cooktown Road at Black Mountain. Even at the best of times, the going is so rough and rutted that it can only be tackled using 4WD; after rain, it becomes completely impassable.

The southern section of the Bloomfield Track makes the most exciting drive, all virgin rainforest and drastic gradients. The halfway point comes at the tidal **Bloomfield River**, which has to be crossed at low water. Beyond the **Wujal Wujal Aboriginal community** on the north side, the road flattens out towards Rossville, before reaching the famous *Lions Den* pub at Helenvale near **Black Mountain** (see below), half an hour south of Cooktown.

ARRIVAL AND TOURS	THE BLOOMFIELD TRACK
By bus Weather permitting, Trans North run 4WD buses up the Bloomfield Track to Cooktown from Cairns (3 weekly; 5hr 15min).	**4WD tours** Darcy of Daintree offer small and personal 4WD tours from Cape Tribulation (Bloomfield Falls half-day $146, Cooktown full-day $265; ☎07 4097 9180, ⓦdarcyofdaintree.com.au)

ACCOMMODATION AND EATING

Bloomfield Beach Camp 20 Bloomfield Rd, Ayton ☎07 4060 8207, ⓦbloomfieldbeach.com.au. Formerly known as *Haley's*, and accessible on a paved road from the north, this attractive waterfront resort offers plentiful camping space, basic cabins with shared bathrooms, and a separate two-bedroom cottage ($160), plus a licensed restaurant. Camping __$25__, cabins __$85__
Lions Den 398 Shipton Flats Rd, Helenvale ☎07 4060

3911, ⓦlionsdenhotel.com.au. Accessible on paved road from the Cooktown end of the Bloomfield Track, this landmark pub dates from 1875. During the day, it plays up its eccentric past for tourists, but at night it's a wonderfully evocative spot, from the iron sheeting and beam decor to the nasty exhibits in glass bottles on the piano. They serve average pizzas and better steaks (around $25), and there's also a lovely campsite. Un/powered sites __$24/28__, doubles __$65__, safari tents __$80__

The Cape York Peninsula and Torres Strait Islands

The **Cape York Peninsula** points north towards the Torres Strait and New Guinea. Tackling the rugged tracks and hectic river crossings on the "Trip To The Tip" is an adventure in itself, as well as a way to reach **Australia's northernmost point** and the communities at **Bamaga** and **Thursday Island**, so different from anywhere else in Australia that they could easily be in another country. But it's not all four-wheel driving across the savannah: during the dry season the historic settlement of **Cooktown**, the wetlands at **Lakefield National Park** and the Aboriginal sites near **Laura** are only a day's journey from Cairns in any decent vehicle. Given longer, you might get as far as the mining company town of **Weipa**, but go no further unless you have an off-road vehicle.

Thousands make the overland journey between May and October, but while a **breakdown** won't necessarily leave you stranded, towing and/or repairs can be extraordinarily expensive. **Bikers** should travel in groups and have off-roading experience.

Mobile signal is almost nonexistent (tree trunks or termite mounds are often graffitied to identify locations with mobile signal), so consider renting a satellite phone.

You'll find a few roadhouses (with rooms) and motels along the way, but north of Weipa **accommodation** is mostly limited to camping, and if you head right to the Tip you'll have to spend at least one night in the bush. Settlements also supply meals and provisions, but there won't be much on offer, so take all you can carry. Don't turn bush campsites into rubbish dumps: take bin liners and remove all your garbage.

Estuarine crocodiles are present throughout the Cape: read the warning under "Wildlife dangers" in Basics (see p.52). There are few **banks**, so take plenty of cash

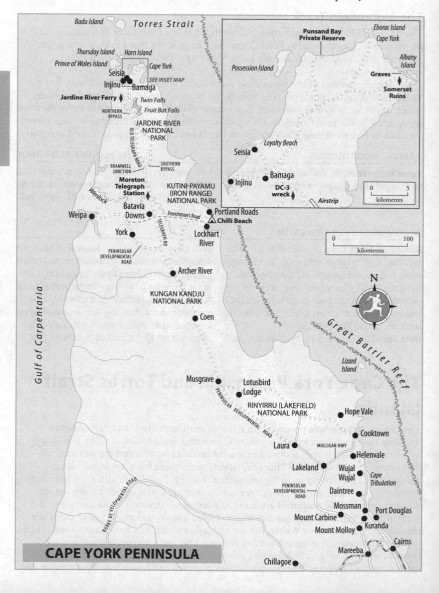

CAPE YORK PENINSULA

– most roadhouses accept plastic. The RACQ (🌐racq.com) has up-to-date information on road conditions; you'll find general tips on off-road driving in Basics (see p.52).

GETTING AROUND   THE CAPE YORK PENINSULA AND TORRES STRAIT ISLANDS

By public transport Trans North buses (3 weekly; ☎07 4045 8644, 🌐transnorthbus.com) connect Cooktown with Cairns (5hr 15min) and Port Douglas (4hr 40min). It's also possible to cruise from Cairns up to Bamaga, Horn Island and Thursday Island (see p.400). Airlines serving the Cape from Cairns include QantasLink (see p.399) and Skytrans (☎1300 759 872, 🌐skytrans .com.au).

By car Captain Billy's in Cairns (☎07 4041 2191, 🌐captainbilly4wdhire.com.au) rents self-drive 4WD vehicles, and also offers tag-along tours using 4WD Toyota Landcruiser campers; sixteen-day expeditions cost from $3500, including standard insurance.

On a tour Several companies, including Heritage Tours (☎07 4054 7750, 🌐heritagetours.com.au) and Oz Tours (☎07 4055 9535, 🌐oztours.com.au), organize trips to the Tip by 4WD, plane and boat; all-inclusive prices start from $2500 for a week-long trip, and rise according to the level of comfort offered. Groups are small and tours only operate in the "Dry" (May to October).

The inland road to Cooktown

Not as pretty as the coastal Bloomfield Track but considerably easier, the 260km inland road to Cooktown and points north leaves the Cook Highway just south of Mossman and climbs to the drier scrub at **Mount Carbine**, a former tungsten mine. Next stop is **Lakeland**, where the Peninsula Developmental Road branches off towards Laura. The road to Cooktown heads east, past cataracts at the **Annan River Gorge**, and the mysterious **Black Mountain**, two huge dark piles of lichen-covered granite boulders looming above the road. Aborigines describe the formation as the result of a building competition between two rivals fighting over a girl, and tell of people wandering into the eerie, whistling caverns, never to return.

At this point, it's worth making the 4km detour south along the initial paved section of the Bloomfield Track to the *Lions Den* at **Helenvale** (see p.423). Anyone with a 4WD vehicle can continue all the way to Cape Tribulation (see p.420). Back on the main road, it's another twenty minutes to Cooktown, passing the birdlife-filled waterholes of **Keatings Lagoon Conservation Park** 5km short of town.

ACCOMMODATION AND EATING   THE INLAND ROAD TO COOKTOWN

Lakeland Hotel/Motel Lakeland ☎07 4060 2142. The obvious place for a meal or overnight break on the long drive to Cooktown, this sprawling pub serves a simple menu of burgers and steaks, with a seafood basket for $18, and also has basic rooms. **$70**

Cooktown

Modern **COOKTOWN**, laid out in 1873 when **gold** was discovered southwest on the Palmer River, stands beside the natural harbour where Captain Cook sought refuge a century earlier after the *Endeavour* had almost foundered at Cape Tribulation to the south. Cook spent two months here in 1770, repairing his vessel at the mouth of what's now the **Endeavour River**, observing the "Genius, Temper, Disposition and Number of the Natives" and – legend has it – naming the kangaroo after an Aboriginal word for "I don't know".

Cooktown prospered during the **Gold Rush**, its main street alive with hotels and its busy port doing brisk trade with Asia through thousands of Chinese prospectors and merchants. By 1910, though, the reserves were exhausted and Cooktown was on the decline. Today, it makes a pleasant, tranquil place for a wander or a couple of days' stay. The main drag, Charlotte Street, is neat but quiet, good for random wandering past the old wharves and **Endeavour Park**, the site of Cook's landing, now graced by a statue of the great navigator. If your visit coincides with Cooktown's **Discovery Festival**, spread over three days in June, you can see a re-enactment of his landing, wooden boat, redcoats, muskets and all (🌐cooktowndiscovery.com).

3

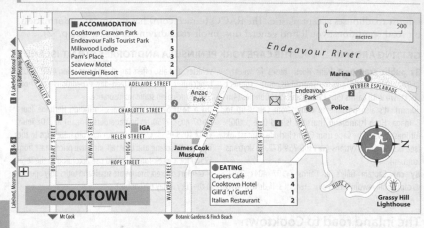

3

James Cook Museum

50 Helen St • Daily: Feb 10am–1pm, March & Nov–Jan 9.30am–4pm, April–Oct 9.30am–4pm • $10 • ☎ 07 4069 5386, ⓦ nationaltrust.org.au

Perched a block up from the sea in a former convent, with great views from its top floor, the **James Cook Museum** holds one astonishing artefact: the original anchor from the *Endeavour*, recovered from the reef twelve miles offshore in 1971. You can also inspect the stump of the tree to which the ship was tethered here in Cooktown; spears and boomerangs of the local Guugu Yimithirr people; photos of the Sisters of Mercy, who once occupied this building; and some brass-band instruments damaged by roosting bats.

Grassy Hill Lighthouse and Mount Cook

An easy 1km drive or a breathless steep walk up Hope Street at the north end of town will bring you to the stubby little red-and-white **Grassy Hill Lighthouse**. Captain Cook climbed to this spot on his first day in the area, and described what he saw as "a very indifferent prospect". To modern eyes, though, the view seems spectacular, across the curved river, up the coast, and inland toward the mountains.

A much tougher four-hour return hike on meagre paths from the southeast corner of town leads through thick forest to the summit of **Mount Cook**.

ARRIVAL AND DEPARTURE   COOKTOWN

By bus Trans North buses connect Cooktown with Cairns (5hr 15min) and Port Douglas (4hr 40min), both along the coastal road via Cape Tribulation and the Bloomfield Track, and inland via Mount Molloy and Lakeland (3 weekly; ☎ 07 4045 8644, ⓦ transnorthbus.com).

INFORMATION AND TOURS

Tourist information Cooktown doesn't have a visitor centre, but you can get advice and brochures at the James Cook Museum.

Tours Guurrbi Tours' charismatic Aboriginal elder Willie Gordon leads tours of ancient rock-art sites along the Endeavour Valley (2hr $100, 4hr $135; ☎ 07 4069 6043, ⓦ guurrbitours.com).

ACCOMMODATION

Cooktown Caravan Park 14–16 Hope St ☎ 07 4069 5536, ⓦ cooktowncaravanpark.com. Sandfly-free campsite below Mount Cook, with low rates. There's no camp kitchen, but they do have BBQs. Un/powered sites **$30/$37**

Endeavour Falls Tourist Park ☎ 07 4069 5431, ⓦ endeavourfallstouristpark.com.au. Lovely forested spot, 32km northwest of town towards Rinyirru National Park and accessible via 4WD only, with shady sites and cabins. As well as the nearby waterfall, there's a swimming hole – but check with the friendly owners that it's croc-free. Un/powered sites **$30/34**, units **$120**

Milkwood Lodge Annan Rd ☎ 07 4069 5007, ⓦ milkwoodlodge.com. Six old-fashioned cabins, off the main road 2km out of town and surrounded by greenery, with lovely valley views. **$145**

Pam's Place Charlotte St ☎07 4069 5166, ⓦcooktownhostel.com. The best bet for budget beds, also known as Cooktown Motel, and offering bright shared or private rooms, plus smarter motel units behind. Dorms **$30**, doubles **$60**, motel units **$95**

Seaview Motel 178 Charlotte St ☎07 4069 5377, ⓦcooktownseaviewmotel.com.au. Good-value hillside motel overlooking the wharf; rooms vary in comfort, but all have views and en-suite facilities. **$95**

Sovereign Resort 128 Charlotte St ☎07 4043 0500, ⓦsovereignresort.com.au. Cooktown's most luxurious option, housed in a rather splendid Queenslander, holds bright modern rooms and suites and a fancy mod-Oz restaurant where dinner mains like emu rump cost up to $40. **$180**

EATING

Capers Café 160 Charlotte St ☎07 4069 5737. The go-to place for big breakfasts and fab coffee, opening onto a nice breezy deck overlooking Endeavour Park. Mon–Fri 7am–2pm, Sat 7am–noon.

Cooktown Hotel 96 Charlotte St ☎07 4069 5308. Also known as the *Top Pub*, this is a great spot for a drink, while its dining room, the *Endeavour River Grill*, serves burgers and pizzas for under $20, plus steaks and seafood for more like $30. Daily 10am–midnight.

Gill'd 'n' Gutt'd Fisherman's Wharf ☎07 4069 5863. Takeaway serving excellent fish'n'chips, best munched from a bench in nearby Endeavour Park at sunset. Daily 11.30am–9pm.

Italian Restaurant 95 Charlotte St ☎07 4069 6338, ⓦtheitalianrestaurantcooktown.weebly.com. Friendly, open-air licensed restaurant, where the Sicilian chef prepares delicious pizzas, pasta dishes, and risottos, for $20–30. Tues–Sat 4–9.30pm.

Rinyirru (Lakefield) National Park

Fifty thousand square kilometres of savannah and riverine flood plain, **Rinyirru National Park** – formerly known as Lakefield National Park – is located 170km northwest of Cooktown. If you have 4WD, you can get here directly by heading to Hope Vale, and then following the Battle Camp road. Without 4WD, you'd have to head back southwest to Lakeland, and turn north there, for a total drive of 227km.

Ideally you'd spend at least a week here, but even a single night will give you a feel for the Cape's most accessible wilderness area. Apart from the **Old Laura Homestead** – built between 1892 and 1940 and standing abandoned in the scrub on the **Laura River** – the park's pleasures revolve around outdoor pursuits, fishing and exploring lagoons for wildlife. Thanks to Rinyirru's **crocodile-conservation** programme, you may see both fresh- and saltwater types; birdlife is plentiful and lots of kangaroos put in an appearance. **Magnetic ant hills** are a common landmark: the ants build these flattened towers aligned north to south to prevent overheating in the midday sun.

ESSENTIALS   RINYIRRU NATIONAL PARK

Opening times The park is closed Dec–April.

Access 4WD vehicles are strongly recommended for all routes, though lesser vehicles can usually manage the rough 170km track through the park between Laura and *Musgrave Roadhouse* if there hasn't been any rain for a good while.

Camping Permits for the park's 24 campgrounds must be booked in advance, either online at ⓦnprsr.qld.gov.au or

at the ranger stations at New Laura (☎07 4060 3260), 50km north of Laura at the southern end of the park; Lakefield (☎07 4060 3271), 30km further on at the centre of the park; or Cooktown (☎07 4097 5777). The pick are *Kalpowar Crossing* (near Lakefield ranger base, with showers and toilets), *Six Mile Waterhole*, 15km south of Lakefield ranger station, and *Hann Crossing* (with hybrid toilets), towards the north of the park.

Lizard Island

One of Australia's most isolated resorts, **Lizard Island** is a granite rise covered in stunted trees and heath, 90km north of Cooktown and 30km offshore within sight of the outer reef. **Divers** have long raved about the fringing coral here, but the reef locally has suffered serious bleaching in recent years. Lizard Island tends to feature so prominently in reports of reef damage partly because it's home to a major research centre, but if you're considering coming here to dive, you should check the current situation.

Shell middens show the island to have been regularly visited by Aboriginal peoples, but it was uninhabited when **Robert Watson** built a cottage and started a sea-slug processing operation here in the 1870s, accompanied by his wife **Mary** and two Chinese servants. Aborigines attacked the house while Robert was at sea in 1881, killing one of the Chinese and forcing Mary, her baby and the other servant, Ah Sam, to flee in a water tank; they paddled west for five days before dying of thirst.

ARRIVAL AND DEPARTURE   LIZARD ISLAND

By plane The only regular access is on flights from Cairns with either Hinterland Aviation ($498 return; ☎ 07 4040 1333, ⊚ hinterlandaviation.com.au), which provides transfers for those staying on the island, or a day-tour with Daintree Air Services ($225; ☎ 07 4034 9300, ⊚ daintreeair .com.au), with snorkelling and guided walks.

ACCOMMODATION

Lizard Island Resort ☎ 1300 731 551, ⊚ lizardisland .com.au. This is the island's only lodge, a swish but ultra-expensive resort with diving facilities, a bar, a restaurant and a string of awards. Full board. **$1456**

Watsons Beach campsite 1.2km from the airstrip ☎ 13 74 68, ⊚ nprsr.qld.gov.au. Facilities include toilets and gas barbecues. Campers should be self-sufficient in food, as the resort is off-limits to nonguests. However, its staff bar, *Marlin Bar*, is open twice weekly and welcomes campers. **$5.95**

Laura

North of Lakeland, the Peninsular Developmental Road is sealed as far as **LAURA**, 60km along. Both the store-cum-post-office and the café-cum-fuel-station *Laura Roadhouse* here support the two-day **Aboriginal Dance Festival** (⊚ lauradancefestival .com), an electrifying assertion of Aboriginal identity celebrated in June of odd-numbered years, while there's a rodeo and horseracing festival every July.

Split Rock

Most visitors to Laura are here to see the fascinating **Aboriginal art** that adorns the sandstone caves and ridges at **Split Rock**, 12km south of town, which has been ranked by UNESCO among the world's finest rock-art sites. It takes about twenty minutes to walk up, and another twenty to return. Paintings depict animals, humans and startling spirit figures associated with sorcery: spidery, frightening **Quinkan** with pendulous earlobes, and dumpy **Anurra**, often with their legs twisted upwards. Other sites show scenes from post-contact life, depicting horses, rifles and clothed figures; some caves here were probably in use until the 1930s.

The **Quinkan and Regional Cultural Centre** (late March to early Dec; daily, irregular hours; $5; ☎ 07 4060 3457, ⊚ quinkancc.com.au) organizes excellent guided rock-art **tours**, essential for anyone keen to understand its significance, and can tell you about upcoming dance festivals.

ACCOMMODATION AND EATING   LAURA

Laura Roadhouse ☎ 07 4060 3440. This lonesome outpost offers home-cooked meals and occasional pizza (daily 6am–8pm), and takes bookings for the adjoining campground (shower and toilet facilities). Un/powered sites **$20/$24**

Laura to Archer River

Following the main road, the 310km between Laura and Archer River passes in a haze of dust, jolts and **roadhouses** supplying fuel, food, beds and drink. First on the list is the **Hann River Roadhouse**, 75km north of Laura, where there's food and fuel. At **Musgrave**, a converted homestead 62km further on, the track from Rinyirru National Park joins the Peninsular Developmental Road. The next two hours, to **COEN** 108km on, are a wild roller-coaster ride – watch out for "Dip" signs warning of monster gullies. Coen's **main store** handles camping, provisions, fuel and post-office business, and has credit card (EFTPOS) facilities.

Then it's 65km to the friendly **Archer River Roadhouse**, which has facilities for emergency cash, and the last reliable **fuel** on the main Cape York road before Bramwell Junction, 170km away. Routes beyond diverge east to Iron Range (143km) and west to Weipa (195km).

ACCOMMODATION AND EATING   LAURA TO ARCHER RIVER

Archer River Roadhouse Archer River ☏ 07 4060 3266. Friendly roadhouse serving up cool drinks and mighty "Archer burgers", with an acceptable campsite as well as overpriced units close to the river bed. Closed Jan–April. Camping $20, units $150

Exchange Hotel Regent St, Coen ☏ 07 4060 1133, ⓦ coencapeyork.com.au. Adequate rooms, pub lunches and dinners, and a bar full of cooling drinks. Camping $30, doubles $100

Homestead Guest House 37 Regent St, Coen ☏ 07 4060 1157, ⓦ coenguesthouse.com.au. Eleven clean but very simple single and double motel-style rooms, sharing bathrooms, BBQ and a communal kitchen and lounge. $100

Lotusbird Lodge Marina Plains Rd, 28km east of Musgrave ☏ 07 4060 3400, ⓦ lotusbird.com.au. Birders in particular love these ten spacious wooden cottages on the western boundary of Rinyirru National Park, whose balconies overlook a billabong. Closed Dec–April. Full board. $600

Kutini-Payamu (Iron Range) National Park

Australia holds nothing else quite like the magnificent jungle at **Kutini-Payamu (Iron Range) National Park**, a relic of the Ice Age link to New Guinea that's home to fauna found nowhere else on the continent – the nocturnal **green python** and brilliant blue-and-red **eclectus parrot** are the best-known species. Follow the 4WD-only road that heads east 35km north of Archer River, and after 110km, or one and a half hours, you'll reach a clearing where the army simulated a nuclear strike in the 1960s – fortunately using ton of conventional explosives instead of the real thing. Turning right here takes you past the **ranger station** to **Lockhart River**, an east-coast Aboriginal mission and fishing beach where supplies and fuel are sold during weekday trading hours, and until noon on Saturdays. The road left passes three bush campsites near the Claudie River and Gordon's Creek crossings, before winding up at **Portland Roads** and the remains of a harbour used by US forces in World War II – there are a few houses and beach **accommodation** here, a store and café. There's further **bush camping** at popular **Chilli Beach**, 21km southwest, a perpetually blustery, yet pretty tropical setting backed by forest and coconut palms.

INFORMATION AND ACCOMMODATION   KUTINI-PAYAMU NATIONAL PARK

Information Contact the ranger station for details on campsite permits and park walking tracks (☏ 07 4060 7170). **Chilli Beach campsite** ☏ 13 74 68, ⓦ nprsr.qld.gov.au. Idyllic spot, shaded by coconut palms, that's prone to gusts – find a scrubby site to shield yourself from the wind. $5.95 **Portland House** Lot 10, Portland Rd ☏ 07 4060 7193, ⓦ portlandhouse.com.au. This homely

self-contained beach house sleeps up to twelve, comes with a wood-fired pizza oven and gazes over the Coral Sea. Each person $95

Rainforest, Cooks Hut & Gordon Creek bush camps ☏ 13 74 68, ⓦ nprsr.qld.gov.au. Small bush camps between the Claudie River and Gordon Creek's crossings; only Cooks Hut has toilets. $5.95

Weipa

From a fork in the main Cape York road 15km northwest of the Kutini-Payamu turn-off, a total of 50km north of Archer River, the Telegraph Road spikes north, onwards up the Cape, while the Peninsular Developmental Road curves northwest for 146km to the kaolin and bauxite mining town of **WEIPA** on the west coast.

The Weipa region was among the first places in Australia to be described by Europeans. Willem Janszoon encountered "savage, cruel blacks" here in 1606, and his report was later reiterated by Jan Carstensz, who found nothing of interest and sailed off to chart the Gulf of Carpentaria instead. Apart from a mission built at **Mappoon** in the nineteenth century, little changed until aluminium ore was first mined here in the 1950s, and Comalco built the town.

All traffic in Weipa avoids the restricted areas, and gives way to the colossal yellow mining trucks. The town consists largely of company housing, but does offer long-forgotten luxuries: you can pick up **vehicle spares** at the auto wreckers and service station on the way into town, and there's a **supermarket** and post office in front of *Weipa Camping Ground*.

ARRIVAL AND DEPARTURE — WEIPA

By plane Flights from Cairns to Weipa's airstrip, 7km southeast of town, are operated by QantasLink (daily) and Skytrans (Mon–Fri). For a taxi, call ⓣ 07 4069 7540.

By car Heading north, you can save yourself a bit of driving by turning onto the rough easterly track at York, 74km along the Peninsular Developmental Road from Weipa, to rejoin the Cape York road after 39km at Batavia Downs.

ACCOMMODATION

3

Albatross Bay Resort 10 Duyfken Crescent ⓣ 07 4090 6666, ⓦ albatrossbayresort.com.au. Plain but tidy rooms and a great restaurant/bar, *Bauxite Bill's*, whose deck looks out over the western sea. $165

Weipa Caravan Park and Camping Ground Kerr Point Rd ⓣ 07 4069 7871, ⓦ campweipa.com.au. Large seaside campsite with hot showers, a pool and laundry, where you can unwind and swap tales about the rigours of the trip. There's also a comfortable lodge, and they run mine and town tours (2hr 30min; $40). Un/powered sites $30/35, cabins $100, doubles $170

North of the Wenlock River

The bridge across the seasonally deep, fast-flowing **Wenlock River**, at Moreton Telegraph Station, an hour north of the southern Weipa junction on the main Cape road, marks the start of the most challenging part of the journey north, with road conditions changing every wet season. At **Bramwell Junction** – 42km further on, with fuel, food and camping – the road divides. Two alternative routes continue up the Cape: the notorious Old Telegraph Road, and the easier, well-maintained Southern and Northern bypass roads.

Old Telegraph Road

Die-hards head straight on from Bramwell Junction along the heavily rutted **Old Telegraph Road**, which involves some challenging **creek crossings: Bertie's** potholes are large enough to submerge an entire vehicle; the 3m vertical clay banks at **Gunshot**, where dozens wipe out every season, are a real test of skill (use low range first, and keep your foot off the brake); and the north exit at **Cockatoo** is deceptively sandy.

The Old Telegraph Track rejoins the bypass briefly after 63km before ploughing on past beautiful clear green water and basalt formations at **Twin Falls**' safe swimming holes, through the deep **Nolans Brook**, before reaching the 100m-wide **Jardine River** – the likelihood of crocodiles here only adds to the risks. As you move on, the old road continues through the river but few attempt this perilous crossing; instead, head back south 35km to join the northern bypass road for the **Jardine River Ferry**.

Southern and Northern bypass roads

If you're at all unsure of your driving skills, take the much longer, but well-maintained **Southern** and **Northern bypass roads** from Bramwell, consisting of 200km of loose gravel, bulldust and shocking corrugations. The southern bypass initially heads northeast, then turns back west to join the Old Telegraph Road after 110km. Travelling north for another 9km brings you to the junction with Fruit Bat Falls, where the northern bypass diverges west for the final 53km haul to the **Jardine River Ferry** crossing (daily 8am–noon & 1–4pm; $99 return; ⓣ 07 4090 4100). Beyond the river, the last hour to Bamaga passes near the remains of a **DC-3** that crashed just short of the airstrip in 1945.

Bamaga and around

A community of stilt houses and banana palms founded by Saibai islanders in 1946, **BAMAGA** owes nothing to the rest of Australia's suburban values. It's the most-equipped town this far north; around the intersection you'll find a workshop and **service station** selling fuel (Mon, Sat & Sun 6.30am–7.30pm, Tues & Wed 6.30am–8pm, Thurs & Fri 6.30am–8.30pm), a hotel, a welcome **supermarket**, an ATM, a tavern, a swimming pool, telephones, a café and post office.

Turning right past the shopping centre, you come to the coast at **SEISIA** (Red Island Point), which holds another fuel station (dishing up locally famed "Silver's Hotdogs") and a well-stocked supermarket with ATM machine, both open daily.

ARRIVAL AND DEPARTURE   BAMAGA AND AROUND

By plane Skytrans fly from Cairns to Bamuga's Northern Peninsular Airport, 12km southeast of town (Mon–Fri only; ☎ 1300 759 872, ⍟ skytrans.com.au). Most accommodation can arrange pick-up (around $35).

By ferry Ferries connect Seisia with Thursday Island (see p.432).

ACCOMMODATION AND EATING

Cape York Peninsula Lodge Cnr Lui & Adidi sts, Bamaga ☎ 07 4069 3050, ⍟ resortbamaga.com.au. Expensive resort in the town centre, holding en-suite rooms and cabins, a licensed restaurant and a pool. **$305**

Seisia Holiday Park 6 Koraba Rd, Seisia ☎ 07 4203 0992, ⍟ seisiaholidaypark.com. Great camping ground under palms near the jetty, with showers and laundry, plus booking for tours, fishing safaris and boat rental. The on-site fish'n'chip shop, *Island Breeze*, is excellent. Un/powered sites **$24/40**, lodges **$125**, cottage **$235**

Cape York

From Seisia, head 17km north to a road junction, then bear left for 11km to the idyllic beach at **Punsand Bay**, where there's a comfortable campsite. Around here you might spot the rare **palm cockatoo**, a huge, crested black parrot with a curved bill. You could spend a day recuperating on the beach, or return to the junction and take the 17km road to its very end at the **tip of Cape York**, past the Somerset fork. Follow the footpath through vine forest onto a rocky, barren headland and down to a turbulent sea opposite the lighthouse on Eborac Island, where a sign concreted into an oil drum marks the tip of mainland Australia.

ACCOMMODATION   CAPE YORK

Cape York Camping Punsand Bay ☎ 07 4069 1722, ⍟ punsand.com.au. A just reward for the trials of the journey, prettily situated beside the beach 5km west of the tip, with a licensed pizza restaurant, pool and store selling basic provisions. Un/powered sites **$34/50**, cabins **$150**, safari tents **$210**

CROSSING CREEKS BY 4WD

While Cape York's **crocodiles** make the standard 4WD procedure of walking creek crossings before driving them potentially dangerous, wherever possible you should make some effort to gauge the depth of the water and find the best route. *Never* blindly follow others across. Make sure all **rescue equipment** – shovel, winch, rope, etc – is easy to reach, outside the vehicle. **Electrics** on petrol engines need to be waterproofed. On deep crossings, block off air inlets to prevent water entering the engine, slacken off the fan belt and cover the radiator grille with a tarpaulin; this diverts water around the engine as long as the vehicle is moving. Select an appropriate **gear** (changing in midstream lets water into the clutch), drive through at walking speed, and clear the opposite embankment before stopping again. In deep water, there's a chance the vehicle might float slightly, and get pushed off-track by the current – though there's not much you can do about this. If you **stall**, switch off the ignition immediately, exit through windows, disconnect the battery (a short might restart the engine) and winch out. Don't restart the vehicle until you're sure that water hasn't been sucked in through the air filter – which would destroy the engine.

Somerset

Established on government orders in 1864, to balance the French naval station in New Caledonia, **SOMERSET** is known for one of its first settlers, **Frank Jardine**, whose legendary exploits assume larger-than-life proportions (fearless pioneer to some, brutal colonialist to others). Envisaged as a second Singapore, Somerset never amounted to more than a military outpost, and in 1877, after the pearling trade in the Torres Strait erupted into lawlessness, the settlement was abandoned in favour of a seat of government closer to the problem at Thursday Island.

Only a few cannons, machine parts and mango trees now testify to Somerset's former inhabitants; the buildings succumbed to white ants or were moved long ago. Frank and his wife Sana are buried on the beach directly below (standing up, say locals), next to a **Chinese cemetery** and traces of a jetty into the Adolphus Channel. Dogged exploration of the dense undergrowth above the beach to the left will uncover remains of a **sentry post** and a cave with stick-figure paintings, presumably Aboriginal.

The Torres Strait

Just a short boat ride beyond Cape York, little **Thursday Island** is the administrative centre for the dozens of other populated specks of land that lie scattered across the 200km-wide **Torres Strait**, which separates Australia from New Guinea. It offers a fascinating glimpse into an all-but-forgotten corner of Australia, and one in which the inhabitants, the **Torres Strait Islanders**, have a very different world view from the country's white population.

The strait is named after **Luís Vaez de Torres**, who navigated its waters in 1606. **Pearling** (for mother-of-pearl) was the main source of employment here until after World War II, when the advent of plastics saw the industry collapse and a mass migration of islanders to the Australian mainland. Those who chose to stay formed a movement to establish an Islander Nation, which bore its first fruit in 1992, when the **Mabo Decision** acknowledged the Merriam as traditional owners of easterly Murray Island, and thereby set a precedent for mainland Aboriginal claims.

Thursday Island

A mere three-square-kilometre dot, tiny **Thursday Island** wears a few aliases. Known simply as "TI" in day-to-day use, it was coined "Sink of the Pacific" for the various peoples who passed through in pearling days, and the local tag is Waiben or (very loosely) "Thirsty Island" – once a reference to the availability of drinking water and now a laconic aside on local beer consumption. The pace of life is languid, and only for events like Christmas, when wall-to-wall aluminium punts from neighbouring islands make the harbour look like a maritime supermarket car park, do things liven up. Other chances to catch Thursday in carnival spirit include the annual **Coming of the Light festivities** on July 1, and the full-bore **Island of Origin** rugby league matches later in the same month – in one year 25 players were hospitalized, and another killed.

In town there are traces of the **old Chinatown** district around Milman Street, and a reminder of Queensland's worst shipping disaster in the **Quetta Memorial Church**, way down Douglas Street, which was built after the ship hit an uncharted rock in the straits in 1890 and went down with virtually all the Europeans on board. The Aplin Road **cemetery**, where two of the victims are buried, has tiled Islander tombs and depressing numbers of **Japanese graves**, all victims of pearl diving a century ago. As a by-product of the industry, Japanese crews had accurately mapped the strait before World War II and it's no coincidence that the airstrip was **bombed** when hostilities were declared in 1942; fortifications are still in place on Thursday's east coast. Bunkers and naval cannon at the hilltop **Green Hill Fort** on the opposite side date from the 1890s and its underground tunnels are now home to the small Torres Straits Historical Museum (opens for tour groups or by appointment – check with Peddell's). The panoramic views from Green Hill across the vivid turquoise straits and neighbouring islands are well worth the blustery trek to the top.

The climate-controlled **Gab Titui Cultural Centre** across from the ferry terminal on the corner of Blackall Street and Victoria Parade (Mon–Sat 10am–3pm; free; ⓦgabtitui .com.au) provides an interesting insight into island affairs, holds exhibitions by local indigenous artists, and stages cultural performances.

3

ARRIVAL AND INFORMATION THURSDAY ISLAND

By boat Peddell's run a ferry service from Seisia (June–Sept 2 daily except Sun; Oct–May 2 on Mon, Wed & Fri only; $58 one-way; 1hr; ☎07 4069 1551, ⓦpeddellsferry .com.au). It's also possible to cruise up to Thursday Island aboard the *Trinity Bay* cargo ship (see p.400).
Services Thursday's wharf sits below the colonial-style Customs House. Douglas St, a minute away in the town

centre, holds a post office with payphones, an NAB bank (with ATM) and two hotels.
Tours Peddell's (see above) meet incoming ferries for an informative 1hr 30min island tour ($32), and offer 4WD day-tours to Cape York and the tip, and a more comprehensive day-trip from Seisia to both Thursday and Horn islands.

ACCOMMODATION AND EATING

Bernie's Kai Kai Bar 34 Victoria Parade. Not a bar, but a waterfront bakery famed for its tasty crayfish pies, which sell out fast. Try the chilli version ($8). Mon–Fri 6am–2pm.
Grand Hotel 6 Victoria Parade ☎07 4069 1557, ⓦgrandhotelti.com. A few minutes' walk from the jetty, the *Grand* has decent rooms (some without windows), plus a restaurant open Mon–Fri only, and a licensed bar. **$190**

Jardine Motel Cnr Victoria Parade & Normanby St ☎07 4069 1555. Thursday's most upmarket option with a mixed bag of rooms, including cheaper ones in a lodge out back. **$220**
Torres Strait Hotel Cnr Douglas & Normanby sts ☎07 4069 1141. The "top pub" has a lovely front deck where you can sip cold beers and fill up on pub grub (lunch $12 specials). Food noon–2pm & 6–8pm.

Horn Island

A fifteen-minute ferry ride from Thursday Island, **Horn Island** is a larger chunk of land that's surrounded by mangroves and coral, the site of an open-cut gold mine and the **regional airport**. During World War II Horn Island housed an advanced operational airbase and over five thousand servicemen; the Japanese bombed it several times.

The **Torres Strait Heritage Museum** (Mon–Sat 10am–4pm; $7; ⓦtorresstraitheritage .com) is stocked with memorabilia relating to the pearling industry, World War II, and local myths and legends. "In their steps" tour uses the stories of former veterans to illuminate the island's war years.

ARRIVAL AND DEPARTURE HORN ISLAND

By plane QantasLink flies from Cairns direct to Horn Island (2 daily; 1hr 45min, ⓦqantas.com.au).
By ferry Frequent ferries connect Thursday and Horn

islands (7–12 daily; $10 one-way, $23 with airport shuttle; ☎1300 664 875, ⓦtiferry.com.au).

ACCOMMODATION

Gateway Torres Strait Resort 24 Outie St ☎07 4069 2222, ⓦtorresstrait.com.au. Home to the Torres Strait

Heritage Museum, this dated resort has average rooms, a pool, bar and buffet meals. **$196**

Outback Queensland

UNDARA LAVA TUBES

Outback Queensland

Outback Queensland, the vast area west of the more populated and tourist-oriented coast, is a dramatic change from the state's lush, wet tropics. Tenacious farming communities are also concentrated in the relatively fertile highlands along the Great Dividing Range, and while generally too green and not remote enough to be strictly considered "outback", it's also far from the main tourist routes. On the far side of the Range, expansive, empty plains slide over a hot horizon into the fringes of South Australia and the Northern Territory. But opportunities for exploration are immense, with gemstones, fossils, waterholes and Aboriginal art in abundance. The region has also produced two of Australia's best-known icons: Qantas and the song *Waltzing Matilda*, first performed by the poet and writer "Banjo" Paterson in Winton in 1895.

Summers can hamper or prohibit travel in Outback Queensland, due to searing temperatures and violent **flash floods** that isolate some areas (especially in the Channel Country on the far side of the Great Dividing Range) sometimes for days or weeks on end. Even settlements on higher ground see little mercy from the rage of tropical storms; heavy rain in January 2011 lashed southeast Queensland, the floodwaters sweeping destructively through the city of Toowoomba and down into the Lockyer Valley on its way to Brisbane, resulting in devastation of property and a significant loss of life.

As a result of these tropical deluges, many tour companies, visitor centres and motels close between November and March, or at least during January and February. But it's not all bad news – this water (scarce at other times of the year) revives dormant seeds and fast-growing desert flowers. During **winter**, expect hot days and cool, star-filled nights.

GETTING AROUND   OUTBACK QUEENSLAND

BY PUBLIC TRANSPORT

Trains and buses, as well as planes, serve Outback Queensland's major towns (if infrequently). Choosing where to go is usually determined by the most convenient starting point. Main roads and trains head west from the coast at Brisbane, Rockhampton, Townsville and Cairns; buses from Brisbane, Cairns and Townsville cross Outback Queensland as they head interstate, but otherwise public transport is poor.
By bus Greyhound (☎ 1300 473 946, ⓦ greyhound.com.au) offers the most extensive service to Queensland's more remote towns; Trans North (☎ 07 4095 8644, ⓦ transnorthbus.com) operates in the far north, from Cairns to Karumba; Crisps Coaches (☎ 07 4661 8333, ⓦ crisps.com.au) runs from Brisbane west to Toowoomba, Warwick and Stanthorpe.
By train The main rail operator in the region is Queensland Rail (☎ 1800 872 467, ⓦ queenslandrailtravel.com.au),

which runs three long-distance trains to outback regions. They are The Inlander (Townsville–Mount Isa), Spirit of the Outback (Brisbane–Rockhampton–Longreach) and The Westlander (Brisbane–Charleville).
By plane QantasLink (ⓦ qantas.com.au), Virgin Australia (ⓦ virginaustralia.com) and Regional Express (ⓦ rex .com.au) operate domestic flights several times a day to regional airports including Longreach, Mount Isa, Charleville, Cunnamulla, Cloncurry, Emerald and Birdsville.

BY CAR

Your vehicle must be well maintained and you should carry essential spares, as even main centres often lack replacement parts. A number of sealed roads are single-vehicle width – pull over to let traffic pass or overtake, and pull off completely to give way to the gigantic road trains.

KARUMBA BEACH AT SUNSET

Highlights

❶ Carnarvon Gorge Hike through the verdant Carnarvon Gorge in Queensland's Central Highlands to reach ancient Aboriginal art sites. **See p.447**

❷ Longreach Visit the Stockman's Hall of Fame museum for an insightful look into life in the Outback, or walk on the wing of a Boeing 747 in Qantas' thriving birthplace. **See p.460**

❸ Winton Unravel the yarns and legends behind Australia's favourite song, Waltzing Matilda, in this archetypal frontier town, which also lies within striking distance of the dinosaur remains at Lark Quarry. **See p.462**

❹ Boulia Spot the mysterious Min Min lights in the Channel Country around Boulia or at this rustic town's automated sound-and-light show. **See p.464**

❺ Undara Explore Undara's massive, contorted lava tubes, formed by a 190,000-year-old volcanic eruption. **See p.476**

❻ Karumba Savour prized barramundi and watch incredible sunsets over the Gulf of Carpentaria at this far-flung fishing town. **See p.479**

HIGHLIGHTS ARE MARKED ON THE MAP ON P.438

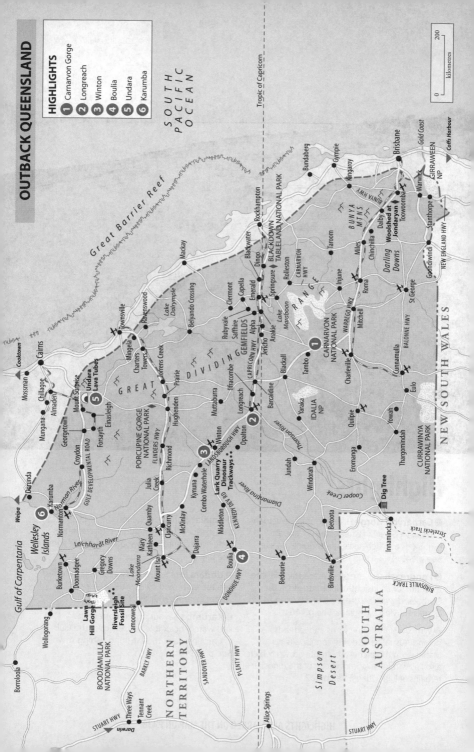

OUTBACK QUEENSLAND

HIGHLIGHTS

1. Carnarvon Gorge
2. Longreach
3. Winton
4. Boulia
5. Undara
6. Karumba

SOUTH PACIFIC OCEAN

Tropic of Capricorn

Great Barrier Reef

0 — 200 kilometres

Cooktown
Mossman
Cairns
Chillagoe
Almaden
Mungana
Georgetown
Croydon
Forsyth
Einasleigh
Mount Surprise
5 Undara Lava Tubes
GREAT DIVIDING RANGE
Georgetown
GULF DEVELOPMENTAL ROAD
PORCUPINE GORGE NATIONAL PARK

Townsville
Mingela
Charters Towers
Ravenswood
Lake Dalrymple
Mackay
Torrens Creek
Prairie
Hughenden
FLINDERS HWY
Richmond
Julia Creek
Kynuna
Combo Waterhole
Middleton
Lark Quarry Dinosaur Trackways
3 Winton
LANDSBOROUGH HWY
Opalton

Belyando Crossing
Clermont
Capella
Emerald
Blackwater
Dingo
BLACKDOWN TABLELAND NATIONAL PARK
Rockhampton
Bundaberg
Gympie
Brisbane
Gold Coast
Coffs Harbour

Rubyvale
Saffire
GEMFIELDS
Alpha
Jericho
CAPRICORN HWY
Anakie
Lake Maraboon
Springsure
Rolleston
CARNARVON HWY
Tambo
Blackall
Barcaldine
2 Longreach
Ilfracombe
Muttaburra
1
CARNARVON NATIONAL PARK
Injune
Tiaroom
Miles
Chinchilla
BUNYA MTNS
Dalby
Woolshed at Jondaryan
Toowoomba
Kingaroy
BUNYA HWY

Yaraka
IDALIA NP
Thomson River
Charleville
Mitchell
Roma
WARREGO HWY
St George
Goondiwindi
NEW ENGLAND HWY
Warwick
Stanthorpe
GIRRAWEEN NP

Cunnamulla
Quilpie
Eromanga
Windorah
Jundah
Cooper Creek
Yowah
Thargomindah
Eulo
BALONNE HWY
CURRAWINYA NATIONAL PARK

NEW SOUTH WALES

Dig Tree
Betoota
Innamincka
Stzelecki Track

Birdsville
Bedourie
4 Boulia
Diamantina River
DONOHUE HWY
KENNEDY DEV HWY

SIMPSON DESERT
SOUTH AUSTRALIA
BIRDSVILLE TRACK

Dajarra
Mount Isa
Cloncurry
McKinlay
Kynuna
Mary Kathleen
Quamby
Lake Moondarra
Gregory Downs
Camooweal
Burketown
Doomadgee

Gulf of Carpentaria
Karumba
Normanton
Norman River
Leichhardt River
6 Karumba
Weipa
Wellesley Islands

Lawn Hill Gorge
Riversleigh Fossil Site
BOODJAMULLA NATIONAL PARK
Wollogorang
Borroloola

NORTHERN TERRITORY
BARKLY HWY
SANDOVER HWY
PLENTY HWY
STUART HWY
Three Ways
Tennant Creek
Alice Springs
Darwin

Brisbane to Cooper Creek and Birdsville

The thousand-plus-kilometre haul from the coast to Queensland's remote southwestern corner dumps you tired and dusty on the South Australian border, with some exciting routes down the Birdsville and Strzelecki tracks or through the hostile red barrier of the Simpson Desert beyond. After crossing the fertile disc of the **Darling Downs**, the country withers and dries, marooning communities in isolation and hardship. However, detour north through Queensland's **Central Highlands** and you'll find forested gorges and the Aboriginal sites at **Carnarvon National Park** – worth the journey alone. Continuing west, there are two ultimate targets: the outpost of **Birdsville**, with its annual horseraces, and the **Dig Tree** at Nappa Merrie on **Cooper Creek**, monument to the Burke and Wills tragedy (see box, p.451).

GETTING AROUND	BRISBANE TO COOPER CREEK AND BIRDSVILLE
By train The *Westlander* train runs from Brisbane to Charleville twice weekly (Tues & Thurs 7.15pm; 17hr; no sleeper carriages). **By bus** Greyhound buses will get you as far west as Roma. **By car** From Brisbane, the most practical route is the Warrego Highway, through Toowoomba, Roma and Charleville towards Quilpie. Roma is the jumping-off point	for the highlands, and from Quilpie there are partly unsurfaced roads to Birdsville and the Dig Tree. Alternatively, the southern Cunningham Highway runs via Warwick to Goondiwindi, from where you can continue east to Cunnamulla (the terminus for buses in this direction) via St George. Heading beyond Cunnamulla to the Dig Tree, the road via Noccundra is sealed up to the Naccowlah Oil Field.

The Darling Downs

4

The **Darling Downs**, a broad spread of prime agricultural land first explored by **Ludwig Leichhardt** in the 1840s, sprawls westwards from the back of the Great Dividing Range behind Brisbane. Settlements along the main roads are mostly farming centres, though solid stone architecture lends some sense of history to the gateway towns of **Toowoomba** and **Warwick**. A bigger draw is the scenery along the Downs' fringes, particularly the **Bunya Mountains** between Toowoomba and Kingaroy in the north, and around the southeasterly **Granite Belt** where there are some superb wineries and possibilities for **farm work**. The flat grasslands provide evidence of Aboriginal custodial practices: created by controlled burning designed to clear woodland and increase grazing land for game, which perfectly suited European pastoral needs. The Downs are fertile black soil plains, with stud farms, dairy, cotton, wool and cereal farming all flourishing at one time or another.

From Brisbane, the Warrego Highway climbs a steep escarpment to Toowoomba and the central downs (as do long-distance **buses**), while the Cunningham Highway cuts through Cunningham's Gap to Warwick and the south.

Toowoomba

TOOWOOMBA, 160km west of Brisbane, is a stately university city perched on the edge of a 600m escarpment, with stylish houses and a blaze of late nineteenth-century sandstone architecture along its central Main and Ruthven streets. In spite of its elevation, the city was one of the worst affected settlements in Queensland's 2011 floods when a wall of water swept through town, effectively splitting it in two. The raging torrent – caused by 36 hours of torrential rain – killed nine people here and devastated homes, businesses and infrastructure. Toowoomba's ensuing revival kick-started a trend for vibrant street art, which can be seen all over town – check out Neil Street, Duggan Street, Club Lane and Margaret Street (between Ruthven and Victoria sts). Known as "the Garden City", Toowoomba is home to several public

Full details of Queensland's **national parks** are given in Chapter Three.

gardens which are at their finest during September's **Carnival of Flowers festival**. Downtown Toowoomba is a compact area based around the intersection of **Ruthven Street**, which runs north to south, and **Margaret Street**, also known as "Eat Street" for its plethora of cafés and restaurants.

Cobb & Co. Museum

27 Lindsay St • Daily 10am–4pm • $12.50 • Guided tours (included in entry fee) daily 10.30am and 2.30pm • ☎ 07 4659 4900; ⓦ cobbandco.qm.qld.gov.au

Toowoomba's prime attraction is the **Cobb & Co. Museum**, 500m northeast of the centre across spacious Queens Park. The museum's spectacular National Carriage Gallery recalls the period from the 1860s to 1924, when intrepid coachmen bounced across the Outback delivering mail and passengers. Aside from an impressive interactive assembly of these vehicles, the museum also houses a remarkable collection of Aboriginal artefacts, an art gallery, a working smithy, and a factory where you can watch working tradesmen or have a go yourself.

Ju Raku En

Next to the University of Southern Queensland's northern car park, Ring Road West (off Baker St) • Daily 6am–dusk • Free

Covering twelve tranquil acres, **Ju Raku En** (the name roughly means "to enjoy peace and longevity in a public place") is one of Australia's largest Japanese gardens, featuring more than 230 species of trees and plants, plus streams, waterfalls, lakes, lawns, pavilions and pergolas.

Picnic Point

164 Tourist Rd, 2.5km east of central Toowoomba

Splendid views of the escarpment unfold from the parkland of **Picnic Point**, a few kilometres outside Toowoomba, as do several bushwalking tracks ranging from 850m to 5.3km in length. There's also a café.

ARRIVAL AND INFORMATION
TOOWOOMBA

By plane Toowoomba's gleaming new airport, rather confusingly called Brisbane West Wellcamp Airport (ⓦ wellcamp.com.au), opened in 2015; it's around 15km out of town on the Toowoomba–Cecil Plains Rd. QantasLink (☎ 013 13 13, ⓦ qantas.com.au), Air North (☎ 1800 627 474, ⓦ airnorth.com.au) and Regional Express (☎ 13 17 13, ⓦ rex.com.au) operate flights from here. Peters Airport Shuttle Service (☎ 1300 602 902, ⓦ peterscoaches .com.au) runs a door-to-door pick-up/drop-off service ($28 one-way) servicing all flights.

Destinations Bedourie (2 weekly; 6hr 25min); Birdsville (2 weekly; 5hr 30min); Boulia (2 weekly; 7hr 15min); Brisbane (4 weekly; 40min); Cairns (3 weekly; 2hr 15min); Charleville (2 weekly; 1hr 40min); Cunnamulla (2 weekly; 2hr 15min); Melbourne (1–2 daily; 2hr 10min); Quilpie (2 weekly; 2hr 45min); St George (2 weekly; 1hr); Sydney (1–3 daily; 1hr 40min); Townsville (3 weekly; 1hr 55min).

By train The station, on Railway St, 500m northwest of the bus station, is served by *The Westlander* (ⓦ queenslandrailtravel.com.au).

Destinations Brisbane (2 weekly; 3hr 50min); Charleville (2 weekly; 12hr 20min); Mitchell (2 weekly; 8hr 30min); Roma (2 weekly; 6hr 40min).

By bus The bus station, on Neil St, is served by Crisps Coaches (☎ 07 4661 8333, ⓦ crisps.com.au), Greyhound (☎ 1300 473 946, ⓦ greyhound.com.au) and Murrays Coaches (☎ 013 22 51, ⓦ murrays.com.au).

Destinations Brisbane (13–19 daily; 2hr); Roma (2 daily; 5hr 30min); Stanthorpe (1–3 daily; 2hr 50min); Warwick (1–4 daily; 1hr 15min).

Tourist information The visitor centre (daily 9am–5pm; ☎ 1800 331 1155, ⓦ southernqueenslandcountry.com.au) is on James St, east off Ruthven St.

ACCOMMODATION, EATING AND DRINKING

★**Fitzy's** 153 Margaret St ☎ 07 4631 3700, ⓦ fitzys .com. Atmospheric grand old pub, with a swish modern bar at the front and a large restaurant with indoor and outdoor dining at the back. Brick walls, ornately tiled floors and good service add up to a good night out. Tapas rules in the

bar ($12–15), while main courses in the restaurant include pub staples such as braised beef and onion pie, or slow-cooked lamb shanks. Mains from $23. Live music on Sat nights. Daily noon–2.30pm and 6pm–late.

GPO Bar & Café 140 Margaret St ☎ 07 4659 9240,

ⓦbit.ly/GPObarcafe. A popular spot for breakfast, this cheerful café has all the usual menu items – including eggs benedict and sweetcorn fritters – and a lunch menu of simple salads and pastas. Good for an early dinner, too, with dishes such as pork cutlet with mash and asparagus puree, or grilled salmon with hot Thai lime dressing (mains from $17). Daily 6.30am–8.30pm.

★ **Quest Toowoomba** 133 Margaret St ☎07 4690 2222, ⓦquestapartments.com.au. This is one of the best places to stay in town – a stylish and comfortable modern apartment hotel, configured inside the shell of a beautiful old brick church. There are 74 smart studios and one-, two- and three-bedroom apartments. Most apartments have balconies. Facilities include a laundry service and gym. **$199**

Vacy Hall 135 Russell St ☎07 4639 2055, ⓦfacebook.com/vacyhall. This grand homestead, Toowoomba's only heritage-listed accommodation, lies in the heart of the city. Built in 1899, it has seven rooms (although a couple are tiny), which all open to a wraparound veranda. Filled with antiques and collectables, it's a romantic getaway. Every room has a fireplace, but be warned: there's a $25 cleaning charge if you use it. **$160**

Kingaroy

KINGAROY is a thriving town in the heart of peanut country on the fringes of the downs, 120km north of Toowoomba. A cluster of peanut silos in the middle of town aptly symbolizes the fame Kingaroy owes to the late **Sir Johannes Bjelke-Petersen** – better known simply as "Joh" – who farmed nuts here before becoming Queensland Premier in 1968, an office he held for nineteen years. His wife Flo also attained fame with her iconic pumpkin scone recipe. Joh died in 2005, but remains in no danger of obscurity, with a dam, bridge, road and sports ground named after him, and his catchphrase "Don't you worry about that" still in use.

Bethany

218 Petersen Drive • Late Feb–Nov guided tours Wed & Sat 2pm (1hr 30min) • $12.50, booking essential • ☎07 4162 7046, ⓦbethany.net.au

The Bjelke-Petersen family farm, **Bethany**, just south of town, is now run by Joh and Flo's son John and his wife Karyn, and can be visited on a prearranged guided tour. The tour includes Sir Joh's gravesite and an afternoon tea of pumpkin scones. It's also possible to stay in one of the cottages (see below) on the property,

INFORMATION

Tourist information The visitor centre (Mon–Fri 9am–4.30pm, Sat 10am–2pm, Sun 10am–4pm; ☎07 4189 917262 6272, ⓦtourism.southburnett.com.au), opposite the peanut silos on Haly St, has a food and wine trail map, and screens short films on how peanuts are grown and harvested.

ACCOMMODATION AND EATING

Bethany Cottages Petersen Drive ☎07 4162 7046, ⓦbethany.net.au. These four attractive, self-contained cottages on the Bjelke-Petersen property are a good option for families, groups or anyone after a bit of peace and quiet. Each one sleeps up to four, and has its own fireplace. Rates include a light breakfast. **$140**

★ **Cassis** Hayens and Shellbachs Rds, Booie ☎07 4162 3465, ⓦcassisrestaurant.com.au. The bell tower on this unusual building, around 7km from the centre of Kingaroy, is a good landmark. The menu changes frequently, but might include dishes such as seafood chowder, slow-cooked shoulder of lamb, or pan-roasted mackerel fillet. Mains $18–34. Wed–Sat 10am–10pm, Sun 10am–5pm.

★ **Deshons Retreat** 164 Haydens Rd ☎07 4163 6688, ⓦdeshons.com.au. Accommodation here is made up of two bright and comfortable luxury retreats (cabin is too plain a word), colour themed throughout – one yellow, one purple. Each contains a king-size bed, kitchenette, large bathtub and all the trimmings. There's a fireplace for cool mountain nights, and plenty of rugs and cushions. Limited mobile phone or TV reception (but free wi-fi). You'll even get a welcome from the owners' big black Labrador. Rates

4

NINETY PERCENT NUTTY

Native to South America, **peanuts** were introduced to Australia during the gold rush of the 1800s. A legume, rather than a nut, they grow underground, taking about five months to cultivate. Around ninety percent of Australia's annual crop of about 60,000 tonnes is grown in and around Kingaroy, which has the country's largest peanut processing plant and is known as the "Peanut Capital of Australia".

include a generous Continental breakfast. **$250**

The Peanut Van 77 Kingaroy St ☎07 4163 6444, ⍈peanutvan.com.au. Get in touch with what Kingaroy is all about by stopping at *The Peanut Van*, which sells over twenty flavours of boiled and roasted nuts – from chilli-and-lime to wasabi or plain beer nuts. ($3.50/100g). Daily 8.30am–5pm.

Taste South Burnett 36 Alford St (down the laneway) ☎07 4162 8222, ⍈tastesouthburnett.com.au. This café-deli is a one-stop-shop showcasing the region's best culinary offerings, including wine, fudge, liqueurs and cheese, plus snacks and light lunches ($10). Tues–Fri 11am–5.30pm, Sat 10am–4pm.

Bunya Mountains

The ranger's office (daily 2–4pm; ☎07 4668 3127) is in the hamlet of Dandabah, which sits next to the national park

Southwest of Kingaroy, a 60km section of road twists through the **Bunya Mountains** before reaching Dalby, back on the Warrego Highway. Among the mountains' greenery and clusters of unlikely flowers are enormous **bunya pines**, once a valuable seasonal food source for local Aborigines, who would put aside tribal feuds to meet and feast on the bunya nuts every few years. Despite prolific logging in the years before they were awarded national park status in 1908, the Bunya Mountains still retain the world's largest stand of ancient bunya pines, along with orange-flowering silky oaks and age-old **grass trees**, with their 3m-high, spear-like flower heads.

The mountains are cooler than the plains below and seriously cold in winter. Up to 30km of walking tracks between the three campsites lead through the forest to orchid-covered lookouts and waterfalls – **satin bowerbirds** and **paradise riflebirds**, with their deep blue-black plumage and long curved beaks, are both fairly common here.

ACCOMMODATION   THE BUNYA MOUNTAINS

Campsites ⍈parks.nprsr.qld.gov.au. Two areas along the road at Burton's Well and Westcott make for good bush camping, with another site at the hamlet of Dandabah, where you are likely to share the space with wallabies. Advance booking is essential, as permits cannot be issued on arrival. Permits per person **$6.15**

Bunya Mountains Accommodation Centre ☎07 4668 3126, ⍈bunyamountains.com.au. You can rent a chalet – from a selection of around thirty – through this company. Minimum stays of three or four nights required during busy periods. Chalets **$110**

The Bunyas Bunya Ave ☎07 4668 3131, ⍈thebunyas .com.au. A peaceful spot, 200m from the park entrance,

with simple newly refurbished units with kitchenette, each sleeping two to four, and more appealing three-bedroom chalets. There's an on-site general store, café and restaurant. Discounts available if you stay two or more nights. Unit **$125**, chalets **$210**

★**Godshill** 29 Lilypilly Place ☎07 5641 0225, ⍈godshill.com.au. This large, modern house, renovated in 2015, has several wings that can be individually booked. It's surrounded by rainforest and Bunya pines, while wallabies roam the lawn and king parrots nestle in the trees. The studio cottage and West Wing are both designed for couples, while the lodge sleeps up to ten. **$190**

Warwick and around

Around 85km south of Toowoomba, **WARWICK** makes a fine base for exploring the surrounding region. Services centre on Grafton and Palmerin streets, where sandstone buildings date back to the time when Warwick graziers competed fiercely with Toowoomba's merchants to establish the Darling Downs' premier settlement. Warwick, with a population of around 13,000, sits beside the **Condamine River**, which later joins the Murray/Darling river system, Australia's longest.

Queen Mary Falls

At **Queen Mary Falls**, 43km east of Warwick beyond Killarney, a tributary exits the forest and plunges off the top of a plateau. A 2km-long track climbs to the escarpment at the head of the falls from the road, with a kiosk, accommodation and lunches available at *Queen Mary Falls Caravan Park* (see opposite); you'll need your own transport to get here.

ARRIVAL AND INFORMATION   WARWICK AND AROUND

By bus Greyhound buses (⍈greyhound.com.au) and Crisps Coaches (⍈crisps.com.au) arrive and depart from

Grafton St in the centre.

Destinations Brisbane (1–2 daily; 2hr 15min); Stanthorpe

(1–2 daily; 45min); Toowoomba (2–3 daily; 1hr 15min).
Tourist information The visitor centre is on Albion St near the library (Mon–Fri 9am–5pm, Sat & Sun 10am–1pm; ☎ 07 4661 3122, ⓦ southerndownsandgranitebelt.com.au).

Festivals Catch bucking broncos and steer wrestling at the October rodeo (ⓦ warwickshowandrodeo.com.au). In July, knitters kit out the town's trees for the quirky Jumpers and Jazz Festival (ⓦ jumpersandjazz.com).

ACCOMMODATION

Country Rose Motel 2 Palmer Ave ☎ 07 4661 7700, ⓦ countryrosemotel.com. Small, friendly motel in a quiet location. Comfortable en-suite rooms each have a kitchenette, and there's an outdoor saltwater pool and BBQ area. **$100**

Kahler's Oasis Caravan Park 98 Wallace St ☎ 07 4661 2874, ⓦ big4.com.au. Choose from caravan sites or cabins (either shared or en-suite bathrooms) at this appealing park, 1km south of the town centre, with a pool. Un/powered site **$31/$35**, cabins **$99**

Queen Mary Falls Caravan Park Spring Creek Rd ☎ 07 4664 7151, ⓦ queenmaryfallscaravanpark.com .au. In a peaceful location close to the falls, this award-winning park is a decent option, with reliable accommodation and an on-site café serving snacks, lunches and home-made cakes. You can hand-feed the colourful king parrots and crimson rosellas, and there are a number of walking routes. Un/powered site **$30/$35**, cabins **$95**

Stanthorpe

The southeastern edge of the Darling Downs along the New South Wales border is known as Queensland's **Granite Belt**, a major wine- and fruit-producing area, which regularly records the state's **coldest temperatures**, dropping well below freezing on winter nights.

Sixty kilometres south of Warwick along the New England Highway, **STANTHORPE** was founded in the 1880s around a tin-mining operation on Quart Pot Creek, but really took off in the 1940s after Italian migrants started up the fruit farms, and wineries now throng the region. In season there are plenty of opportunities for **fruit-picking work**.

4

ARRIVAL AND DEPARTURE

STANTHORPE

By bus Crisps Coaches (☎ 07 4681 2299, ⓦ crispscoaches. com.au) arrive and depart from 12–14 Davadi St; Greyhound services (☎ 1300 473 946, ⓦ greyhound.com. au) call in at the Shell service station.

Destinations Brisbane (3–4 daily; 3hr 25min–4hr 40min); Toowoomba (2–3 daily except Sat; 2hr 50min); Warwick (2–3 daily except Sat; 50min).

INFORMATION AND TOURS

Tourist information Stanthorpe's visitor centre (daily 9am–4pm; ☎ 1800 762 665, ⓦ granitebeltwinecountry .com.au) overlooks the river just south of the centre on Leslie Parade. You can pick up a full list of traditional and emerging "alternative" wineries here, and staff can book B&B accommodation and organize permits ($7.50/month) to fossick for semiprecious topaz, 13km northwest at Swiper's Gully.

Farm work Grape-picking season is Jan–April, and fruit harvesting Oct–May. Check out the Australian Harvest Trail website (ⓦ jobsearch.gov.au/job/search/harvest) for more information on farm work.

Tours Several companies, among them Granite Highlands Maxi Tours (☎ 07 4681 3969, ⓦ maxitours.com.au) and Filippo's (☎ 07 4681 3130, ⓦ filippostours.com.au), run half- or full-day vineyard and brewery tours (from $75).

ACCOMMODATION AND EATING

Anna's Restaurant Cnr Wallengarra Rd and O'Mara Terrace ☎ 07 4681 1265, ⓦ annas.com.au. Long-established Italian restaurant set in a romantic Queenslander timber house with log fires and alfresco tables. The menu runs from "mama's own recipe" lasagne and saltimbocca to cannoli and panna cotta (mains $19–30). Tues–Thurs 6–9.30pm, Fri & Sat 6.30–10pm.

Stannum Lodge Motor Inn Wallangarra Rd ☎ 07 4681 2000, ⓦ stannumlodge.com.au. This small well-run motel, surrounded by pretty landscaped gardens, has a

good range of facilities – a saltwater swimming pool, restaurant, tour desk and free wi-fi access – and 12 comfortable en-suite rooms. **$130**

Top of the Town Tourist Park 10 High St ☎ 07 4681 4888, ⓦ topoftown.com.au. Located 2km north of Stanthorpe's town centre and surrounded by bushland, *Top of the Town* has an extensive range of accommodation options, including caravan sites, bungalows and smarter motel-style rooms, and also boasts a pool, games room and restaurant. Powered sites **$48**, bungalows **$110**, cabins **$120**, motel-style rooms **$125**

SHOPPING

Market in the Mountains The Showgrounds, High St Ⓦ marketinthemountains.org. At this fortnightly market, local producers sell delectable preserves, jams, crafts and more. Every second Sun 8am–noon.

Girraween National Park

The granite hills around Stanthorpe are exposed as fantastic monoliths at **Girraween National Park**, where you have the chance of seeing small, shy, active **sugar gliders** just after dark.

With more energy than skill, you can climb several of the giant hills with little risk, as long as rain hasn't made them dangerously slippery; trails are well marked and **free maps** are available from the visitor centre. The **Castle Rock** track (2hr return) initially follows a gentle incline past lichen-covered boulders to a thin ledge above the campsite. Follow this around to the north side and clamber to the top for superb views of the Pyramids, the Sphinx and Mount Norman, the park's 1267m apex, poking rudely out of the woods.

It's a further forty minutes' walk from the *Castle Rock* campsite to the Sphinx and Turtle Rock. **Sphinx** is a broad pillar topped by a boulder, while **Turtle Rock**'s more conventional shape means a scramble. Then, on the final stretch, there are no handholds to the top of the completely bald **South Pyramid** (2hr return from Castle Rock). At the top is Balancing Rock, a precariously teetering oval boulder. From here you can gaze across to the unscaleable North Pyramid.

ARRIVAL AND INFORMATION   GIRRAWEEN NATIONAL PARK

By car The park is accessed by a turn-off 26km south of Stanthorpe down the New England Highway. From here it's another 9km to the visitor information centre.

Information The visitor information centre is open daily 9am–5pm (☎ 07 4684 5157, Ⓦ nprsr.qld.gov.au). Free walking trail maps are available here, or can be downloaded from the website.

ACCOMMODATION

Castle Rock and Bald Rock Creek campsites ☎ 13 74 68, Ⓦ parks.nprsr.qld.gov.au. Both of these sites are easily accessible from the visitor information centre and have toilets, hot showers and BBQs. *Castle Rock* is better suited to those with caravans. Bush camping is also possible at seven sites in the park, but is suitable only for experienced campers, who need to be fully self-sufficient (see website for more details). Booking well in advance is essential (up to 12 months ahead) for all camping. Per person $6.15

The Central Downs and around

The journey northwest across the **Central Downs** from Toowoomba to Roma is unexciting, so it's worth popping into the Woolshed at Jondaryan for a break. Stops over the next 200km include Dalby, Chinchilla and Miles – rural centres largely devoid of attractions but with services and places to stay. One worthwhile stop, however, is *Possum Park* (see below), some 20km north of Miles.

Woolshed at Jondaryan

Jondaryan, 45km northwest of Toowoomba • Daily 8.30am–4.30pm • $10 • ☎ 07 4692 2229, Ⓦ jondaryanwoolshed.com.au

The **Jondaryan Woolshed**'s collection of mostly re-sited old buildings gives a glimpse of old-time life on the downs: exhibits include a document dating from 1880 itemizing the schoolmistress's tasks – including splinting broken legs, wallpapering buildings to keep out snakes and fighting off swagmen hoping to bunk in the schoolhouse. There are machinery displays and an animal nursery, as well as various accommodation options and a café.

ACCOMMODATION   THE CENTRAL DOWNS AND AROUND

Possum Park 20km north of Miles ☎ 07 4627 1651, Ⓦ possumpark.com.au. Based on what was once a top-secret World War II ammunition dump, *Possum Park* provides atmospheric accommodation in renovated bunkers and troop train carriages; there are also caravan and tent sites. A family "igloo" sleeps up to eight. You'll need your own vehicle to get here, and your own food to stay. Powered sites $25, train carriage/bunkers $90

Woolshed at Jondaryan 264 Jondaryan Evanslea Rd, ☎ 07 4692 2229, ⓦ jondaryanwoolshed.com.au. The exhaustive range of accommodation here, suitable for

travellers of all budgets, includes caravan sites, rustic shearers' quarters (sleeping five) and self-contained cottages (sleeping two to six). Guests get free admission to the museum. Un/powered sites $22.50/$28.50, shearers' quarters $55, cottages $110

Roma

ROMA, 140km west of Miles, thrives on farming, supplemented by **oil and gas** fields. Not long after it was settled in 1862, Roma was the venue for the 1871 trial of the audacious **Captain Starlight** (aka Harry Redford), who stole a thousand head of cattle from a nearby property and drove them down through the South Australian deserts to Adelaide to sell. An unusual white bull in the herd was recognized and Redford arrested, but his pioneering of a new stock route won such popular approval that the judge refused to convict him. It's still cattle country, and, every Tuesday and Thursday from 8am, the auction action is at Australia's largest **cattle saleyards**, on the Warrego Highway. Free tours of the Roma saleyards are run from 8.30am every Tuesday (and on Thurs April–Oct). Contact the visitor centre (☎ 07 4622 8676) for more information.

Roma's wide main streets are lined with **bottle trees** (not only bottle-shaped but also full of moisture), planted in 1920 as a World War I commemoration, and lent a slightly dated air by the iron decorations and wraparound balconies of its hotels. Most of the shops, banks and businesses are one block north of Bowen Street, on parallel McDowall Street.

Big Rig

Bowen St • Daily 9am–5pm • $12, nightly show $10 • ☎ 07 4622 4355, ⓦ bigrig.net.au

On the eastern edge of town is the **Big Rig**, originally a drilling tower, left as a monument to the oil boom of the 1920s and now a multimillion-dollar complex exploring the history of Australia's oil and gas industry. The rig also doubles as the town's visitor centre.

ARRIVAL AND DEPARTURE

ROMA

By plane The airport, 3km north of town, is served by Qantas (ⓦ qantas.com.au) and its subsidiaries.
Destinations Brisbane (2–3 daily; 1hr); Charleville (3 weekly; 45min).

By train Roma's train station, one block south of the highway off Station St, is served by *The Westlander*.
Destinations Brisbane (2 weekly; 12hr); Charleville (2 weekly; 5hr 20min); Mitchell (2 weekly; 1hr 50min); Toowoomba (2 weekly; 7hr 20min).

By bus Greyhound buses pull up at the stop outside Roma

Motors on Arthur St.
Destinations Barcaldine (daily; 9hr 5min); Blackall (daily; 7hr 5min); Brisbane (daily; 7hr 30min); Charleville (daily; 3hr 50min); Cloncurry (daily; 17hr 30min); Longreach (daily; 10hr 20min); Mitchell (daily; 1hr); Mount Isa (daily; 18hr 50min); Toowoomba (daily; 5hr); Winton (daily; 13hr).
By car The Northern Rd (take Quintin St from the town centre) heads towards Carnarvon National Park; otherwise, the next stops west along the highway are Mitchell and Charleville.

INFORMATION

Tourist information The Roma visitor centre (Mon–Fri 8.30am–5pm, Sat & Sun 9am–5pm; ☎ 07 4622 8676, ⓦ outbackqueensland.com.au) is located at the Big Rig on Bowen St at the eastern edge of town (see above).

Festivals The town's biggest annual shindig is Easter in the Country (ⓦ easterinthecountryroma.com.au): six days of entertainment including billy-cart races, a bush poets' breakfast, wife-carrying contest and a rodeo and bull-ride.

ACCOMMODATION AND EATING

Big Rig Top Tourist Park 4 McDowall St ☎ 07 4622 2538, ⓦ bigrig.net.au. Close to the Big Rig, 500m from the town centre, this caravan park has bright, modern cabins (shared bathrooms), more comfy "house" rooms and caravan sites. Powered sites $36, cabins $75, doubles $92

Starlight Motor Inn 20B Bowen St ☎ 07 4622 2666, ⓦ starlightroma.com. This brick motel is a comfortable if unexciting place to stay, with standard rooms – each with a/c, TVs, private bathrooms, and tea- and coffee-making facilities. $140

4

Mitchell

MITCHELL is a delightful, single-street highway town 88km west of Roma beside the Maranoa River. Like Roma, Mitchell has its local outlaw legend; the protagonists this time were the two **Kenniff Brothers**, who raided the district for cattle and horses in the early 1900s. After killing a policeman during one arrest attempt, they were finally ambushed south of town.

Great Artesian Spa

Cambridge St • April–Sept 8am–6pm, Oct–March 8–11.30am & 2–6pm • $8 • ☎ 07 4624 6923

There are two reasons to pass through Mitchell – either to follow the 200km track north to **Mount Moffat** in Carnarvon National Park, or to take a dip in the town's hot springs at the **Great Artesian Spa**. They have been channelled into two open-air swimming pools and a spa in the grounds of the old courthouse – they're good, steamy fun on a cold winter's morning.

ARRIVAL AND DEPARTURE   MITCHELL

By train The train station, 500m from the old courthouse at the western side of town, is served by *The Westlander*. Destinations Brisbane (2 weekly; 12hr 50min); Charleville (2 weekly; 3hr 40min); Roma (2 weekly; 1hr 40min); Toowoomba (2 weekly; 10hr).

By bus Bus Queensland (🔾 busqld.com.au) services stop outside the Mitchell Newsagency on the corner of Cambridge and Alice streets. Destinations Brisbane (daily; 9hr); Charleville (daily; 2hr 40min); Roma (daily; 1hr); Toowoomba (daily; 6hr 35min).

ACCOMMODATION

Major Mitchell Caravan Park Beside the Maranoa River ☎ 07 4623 6600, 🔾 majormitchellcaravanpark .com.au. In a serene riverside setting at the eastern end of town, 100m from the artesian spa, this friendly place has regular pancake breakfasts, poetry performances and karaoke nights. Un/powered sites $20/$30, cabins $100

Carnarvon National Park

North of Roma and Mitchell, Queensland's Central Highlands consist of a broad band of weathered sandstone plateaus, thickly wooded and spectacularly sculpted into sheer cliffs and pinnacles. It's an extraordinarily primeval landscape, and one still visibly central to Aboriginal culture, as the highlands were relatively unscathed by European colonization. Covering a huge slice of the region, the fragmented sections of **Carnarvon National Park** include **Carnarvon Gorge** and **Mount Moffatt**: Carnarvon Gorge has the highest concentration of Aboriginal art and arguably the best scenery, while Mount

BOOMERANGS

Curved **throwing sticks** were once found throughout the world. Several were discovered in Tutankhamun's tomb, Hopi Native Americans once used them, and a 23,000-year-old example made from mammoth ivory was found in Poland. Since that time, the invention of the bow and arrow superseded what Aborigines call a **boomerang** or *karli*, but their innovation of a stick that returns has kept the boomerang alive, not least in people's imaginations – they were originally used as children's toys but were then modified into decoys for hunting wildfowl. The non-returning types depicted in Carnarvon Gorge show how sophisticated they became as **hunting weapons**.

Usually made from tough acacia wood, some are hooked like a pick, while others are designed to cartwheel along the ground to break the legs of game, which can then be easily tracked and killed. At Carnarvon Gorge, the long, gently curved boomerangs stencilled on the walls in pairs are not repetitions but portraits of two weapons with identical flight paths; if the first missed through a gust of wind, for instance, the user could immediately throw the second, correcting his aim for the conditions. Besides hunting, the boomerang was also used for **digging**, **levering** or **cutting**, as well as for **musical or ceremonial accompaniment**, when pairs would be banged together.

Moffatt is harder to reach but wilder – you can't drive directly between the two sections, though it's possible to hike with the rangers' consent.

Carnarvon Gorge

The creek's journey between the vertical faces of the **Carnarvon Gorge** has created some magical scenery, where low cloud often blends with the cliffs, making them appear infinitely tall. Before setting off between them, scale **Boolimba Bluff** from the *Takarakka* resort site (see p.448) for a rare chance to see the gorge system from above; the views from the "Roof of Queensland" make the tiring 3.2km track to the top worth the effort.

The superb **day-walk** (19km return from the ranger station) into the gorge features several intriguing side gorges. The best of these contain the **Moss Garden** (3.5km), a vibrant green carpet of liverworts and ferns lapping up a spring as it seeps through the rock face, and **Alijon Falls** (5km), which conceal the enchanting Wards Canyon, where a remnant group of *angiopteris* ferns hangs close to extinction in front of a second waterfall and gorge, complete with bats and red river stones.

Aboriginal art sites

Carnarvon's two major **Aboriginal art sites** are the Art Gallery (5.4km) and Cathedral Cave (at the end of the trail, 9.3km from the *Takarakka* campsite), both on the gorge track, though if you keep your eyes open you'll spot plenty more. The **Art Gallery** is one of Queensland's most documented Aboriginal art sites, though the paintings themselves remain enigmatic. Symbols include kangaroo, emu and human tracks; a long, wavy line here might represent the rainbow serpent, shaper of many Aboriginal landscapes. Overlaying the engravings are hundreds of coloured stencils, made by placing an object against the wall and spraying it with a mixture of ochre and water held in the mouth.

In addition to adults' and children's hands there are also artefacts, boomerangs and complex crosses formed by four arms, while goannas and mysterious net patterns at the near end of the wall have been painted with a stick. **Cathedral Cave** is larger, with an even greater range of designs, including seashell pendant stencils – proof that trade networks reached from here to the sea – and engravings of animal tracks and emu eggs.

Mount Moffatt

Mount Moffatt is part of an open landscape of ridges and lightly wooded grassland, at the top of a plateau to the west of Carnarvon Gorge. It was here that the Kenniff Brothers (see opposite) murdered a policeman and station manager in 1902, events that were to lead to their being run to ground by a group of vigilantes. In 1960, archeological excavations at their hideout, **Kenniff Cave** (closed due to instability), were the first to establish that Aboriginal occupation of Australia predated the last Ice Age.

Mount Moffatt's attractions spread out over an extensive area. At the park's southern entrance, the **Chimneys** area has some interesting sandstone pinnacles and alcoves that once housed bark burial cylinders. Around 6km on, the road forks and the right track continues 10km to the ranger station. The left track runs 6km past *Dargonelly* campsite to **Marlong Arch**, a sandstone formation decorated with handprints and engravings. Five kilometres northeast from here, a trail leads to **Kookaburra Cave**, named after a weathered, bird-shaped hand stencil. A further 5km beyond the cave is **Marlong Plain**, a pretty expanse of blue grass surrounded by peaks, and another sandstone tower known as **Lot's Wife**. Ten kilometres north of Marlong Plain, a lesser track leads to several sites associated with the Kenniff legend, including the murder scene, and the rock where they are believed to have burned the evidence. Finally, for pure scenery, head 15km due east of Marlong Plain to the **Mahogany Forest**, a stand of giant stringy-bark trees.

ARRIVAL AND DEPARTURE

BY CAR

As there's no public transport to any section of the park (and no overnight tours), you'll need your own vehicle: access to the gorge is from Roma to the south, or Emerald to the north, and to Mount Moffatt from Roma or Mitchell. All these roads involve long stretches of dirt, making them impassable even in a 4WD after heavy rain (most likely Nov–May). Always carry extra rations in case you get stranded and – unless you're desperately short of supplies – stay put in wet weather so you don't churn the road up and make it harder to use. Although the park perimeter can be reached in 2WD vehicles in dry conditions, you'll need a high-clearance 4WD to get around once inside. As there is no fuel or supplies of any kind available in the park, make sure you fill up in Injune, Rolleston or Mitchell.

To Carnarvon Gorge The Carnarvon Gorge Development (access) Rd (sealed except for the final 15km) is reached off the Carnarvon Hwy at Wyseby between Roma (201km) and Emerald (196km), from where it runs 45km west, past views of the Consuelo Tableland standing out magnificently above dark forests, to the park's edge at the mouth of the gorge.

To Mount Moffatt Access to this area of the park is direct from Mitchell (220km), or from Roma (245km) via the small town of Injune (160km).

CARNARVON NATIONAL PARK

INFORMATION

Summer temperatures often reach 40°C, while winter nights can be below freezing. Gathering firewood is prohibited inside the park, so stop on the way in or bring a gas stove. For information and campsite bookings visit ⓦ nprsr.qld.gov.au.

Visitor centres The visitor centre at Carnarvon Gorge (daily 8am–5pm; ☏ 07 4984 4505) has an orientation model of the gorge, maps and a library. Injune also has a helpful visitor centre (daily 9am–5pm; ☏ 07 4626 0503, ⓦ visitinjune .com.au) on the highway (here called Hutton St, Injune). The Mount Moffatt ranger station (generally daily 9am–5pm; ☏ 07 4626 3581) 16km from the southern entrance to the park, has maps of the area and can help you plan bushwalking.

Tours Guided tours of the park, including night-time wildlife-spotting tours, can be booked with Australian Nature Guides (from $25; ☏ 07 4984 3334) at the Injune visitor centre.

ACCOMMODATION

Camping Year-round camping is available at Big Bend (ⓦ parks.nprsr.qld.gov.au), reached by a 9.7km walk from the visitor centre. Camping near the visitor area is available only during Queensland winter and spring school holidays and over Easter, but competition for sites is tough; book as far ahead as possible to get one of these prime spots. **$6.15**

Carnarvon Gorge Wilderness Lodge 4043 O'Briens Rd (3km before the visitor centre) ☏ 07 4984 4503, ⓦ carnarvon-gorge.com. These "safari-style" cabins, each with their own veranda, tea- and coffee-making facilities and fridge, are fine choices for anyone seeking peace. There's also a restaurant (no cooking facilities are available), a saltwater swimming pool and laundry. Book well in advance. **$220**

Takarakka Bush Resort 4km before the Carnarvon Gorge visitor centre ☏ 07 4984 4535, ⓦ takarakka.com.au. This creekside camp, set in ninety acres of bush, has caravan sites, fixed safari-style "taka" tents, and en-suite cabins, for those who want something a little more solid. There's a general store and regular spit-roast BBQs during the high season. Un/powered sites **$38/$45**, safari tents **$95**, cabins **$165**

Charleville

The last place of any size on the journey west from Roma is **CHARLEVILLE**, a busy country town whose broad streets and shaded pavements are flanked by some solid buildings constructed when the town was a droving centre and staging post for Cobb & Co. It's well known for its **contradictory weather** – in November 1947 a hot summer afternoon was interrupted for twenty minutes as a blast of massive hailstones stripped trees, smashed windows and roofs and killed poultry. In 1990 the town centre was struck by 5m-deep floodwaters from the Warrego River, requiring mass evacuation – a dramatic end to years of drought. The town's small hub centres on the intersection of Wills and Galatea streets.

Charleville Bilby Experience

Historic Charleville Railway Station, King St • April–Oct Tues–Sat 11am–6pm; Bilby Experience tour daily 5pm (1hr); Up Close and Personal Encounter Tues–Sat 12.30pm (1hr) • Free; Bilby Experience tour $10; Up Close and Personal Encounter $25 • ☏ 07 4654 7771, ⓦ savethebilbyfund.com

The **Charleville Bilby Experience** is dedicated to studying and breeding populations of the vulnerable (nationally) and endangered (in Queensland) **bilby**, which, with its long ears and nose, looks like a cross between a rabbit and a bandicoot. Learn more about these absurdly cute nocturnal marsupials, and the work of the volunteers who ensure their survival through the Bilby Experience tour or the Up Close and Personal Encounter.

Cosmos Centre and Observatory

1 Milky Way (off Qantas Drive) • April–Oct daily 10.30am–4pm, night shows daily 6.30pm & 7.30pm; Nov–March Mon–Sat 10am–4pm, night shows Mon, Wed & Fri 8.30pm • Day/night sessions $10/$28 • Booking essential on ☎ 07 4654 7771, ⓦ cosmoscentre.com

The lack of industrial light and pollution, combined with a low horizon, makes Charleville's location ideal for stargazing. The excellent **Cosmos Centre and Observatory**, 3km south of town, enables you to observe the spectacular night sky through powerful **Meade telescopes**. During daylight hours, the centre has interactive displays and films explaining the history of astronomy and the formation of the universe.

ARRIVAL AND INFORMATION   CHARLEVILLE

By plane The airport, 1km south of town, is served by Qantas (ⓦ qantas.com.au) and Regional Express (ⓦ rex.com) to Bedourie, Birdsville, Boulia, Brisbane, Mount Isa, Quilpie, Roma, Toowoomba (Brisbane West Wellcamp) and Windorah. Destinations Bedourie (2 weekly; 4hr 20min); Birdsville (2 weekly; 3hr 30min); Boulia (2 weekly; 6hr 15min); Brisbane (daily; 1hr 45min on Qantas, 2hr 35min on Rex); Mount Isa (2 weekly; 7hr 15min); Quilpie (2 weekly; 45min); Roma (3 weekly; 50min); Toowoomba (2 weekly; 1hr 35min); Windorah (2 weekly; 1hr 50min).

By train *The Westlander* arrives and departs from the railway station on the corner of Wills and King streets. Destinations Brisbane (2 weekly; 17hr); Mitchell (2 weekly; 3hr 30min); Roma (2 weekly; 5hr 20min);

Toowoomba (2 weekly; 12hr 45min).

By bus Bus Queensland (☎ 1300 287 537, ⓦ busqld.com.au) runs a daily service between Charleville and Brisbane, a trip of about 11 hours. Buses arrive and depart from the Charleville railway station on the Mitchell Highway (Wills Street).

By car From Charleville, sealed roads head north to Blackall and Longreach, south via Cunnamulla to Bourke, and further west to Quilpie.

Tourist information The excellent visitor centre is situated within the Cosmos Centre and Observatory at 1 Milky Way (April to mid-Oct Mon–Fri 9am–5pm, Sat & Sun 10am–5pm; mid-Oct to March Mon–Sat 10am–5pm; ☎ 07 4654 7771).

Services Banks and shops are on Wills St, and the post office (Mon–Fri 9am–5pm) is on Alfred St.

ACCOMMODATION AND EATING

Bailey Bar Caravan Park 196 King St ☎ 07 4654 1744, ⓦ charlevillebaileybar.com.au. The welcoming owners of this pleasant caravan park – which has powered sites and comfy cabins – stage regular BBQs and bush activities such as "yabby races". Powered site **$37**, cabin **$105**
The Rocks Motel 74 Wills St ☎ 07 4654 2888,

ⓦ rocksmotel.com.au. The newest motel in Charleville, this modern Outback-style place in a convenient location across the street from the railway station, has a smart restaurant that is open daily for breakfast (7–9.30am), lunch (noon–2pm) and dinner (6–8.30pm), and swimming pool. All rooms have a veranda out the front. **$155**

Cunnamulla and into the west

Cunnamulla Fella Centre Jane St (Mon–Fri 9am–4.30pm, May–Oct also Sat & Sun 10am–2pm; ☎ 07 4655 8470, ⓦ paroo.info)

A trucking stop 200km south of Charleville on the long run down the Mitchell Highway to Bourke in New South Wales, the isolated town of **CUNNAMULLA** comprises a handful of service stations and motels, and is a good base for visiting the Yowah Opal Field and Currawinya National Park.

The **Cunnamulla Fella Centre** houses the **visitor centre**, a local history **museum**, performing arts centre, and the superb **Outback Dreaming Art Gallery**. Among its attractions is the Artesian Time Tunnel, which traces the evolution of the artesian basin on which the town sits back to the age of the dinosaurs, a hundred million years ago.

Yowah Opal Fields

Cunnamulla's council offices can arrange a **fossicking licence** (see box, p.456) if you're planning to head 160km northwest to the **Yowah Opal Fields**, where shallow deposits yield much-sought-after Yowah Nuts. At the fields, beware of vertical shafts – always look where you're going and never step backwards. Yowah has fuel and a caravan park.

Currawinya National Park

Ranger station ☎ 07 4655 4001, ⓦ nprsr.qld.gov.au/parks/currawinya

If you have a 4WD, venturing 170km southwest of Cunnamulla brings you to **Currawinya National Park**, home to the highly endangered **bilby** (see p. 449). Feral cats, rabbits and grazing cattle have brought the bilby close to extinction, but a **fence** at Currawinya keeps these pests out, allowing the bilby population – reintroduced from Charleville's National Parks Centre – to prosper. You can camp at Currawinya, but check on road conditions with the Currawinya ranger station first. Past Currawinya is the tiny border town of **Hungerford**, where you can stock up on fuel and groceries. From here it's a 210km run southeast on a gravel road to Bourke.

INFORMATION   CUNNAMULLA AND INTO THE WEST

Tourist information The helpful visitor centre (Mon–Fri 9am–4.30pm, May–Oct also Sat & Sun 10am–2pm; ☎ 07 4655 8470, ⓦ paroo.info) is part of the Cunnamulla Fella Centre on Jane St.

Festival The Cunnamulla Fella Festival, famed for rodeo, bush poetry and live music, takes place each Aug.

Fossiking The Paroo Shire Council offices (cnr Stockyard & Louise sts; Mon–Fri 9am–5pm; ☎ 07 4655 8400) can arrange a fossicking licence ($7.50/month).

ACCOMMODATION

Cunnamulla Tourist Park 65 Watson St ☎ 07 4655 1421, ⓦ cunnamullapark.com. Accommodation is tight year-round in Cunnamulla, and what is available is pretty basic. This caravan park, located in the east of town, is fine for a night. It offers free BBQs, a small kiosk, coin-operated washing machines and a simple kitchen area. Powered sites $32, cabins $105

Quilpie and the road to the Dig Tree

A sealed road leads 200km west of Charleville to **QUILPIE**, a compact, dusty farming community with a handful of amenities including a supermarket, petrol station and bakery.

A **map** is essential if you plan to follow the 490km, partly unsealed **road from Quilpie to the Dig Tree** at Nappa Merrie, just 30km from the South Australian border. Fuel up at **EROMANGA**, famed for being the furthest town from the ocean in Australia – no small claim on this vast continent. From here you head across stony plains above the huge gas and oil reserves of the **Cooper Basin**, past the Durham Downs cattle station, to the Dig Tree on **Cooper Creek**. The creek itself also achieved fame through references in the works of poet A.B. "Banjo" Paterson.

The site of Burke and Wills' **stockade** (see box opposite), Depot Camp 65, is on a beautiful shaded riverbank alive with pelicans and parrots – it's hard to believe that anyone could have starved to death nearby. The **Dig Tree** is still standing and protected by a walkway, but the three original blaze marks reading "BLXV, DIG 3FT NW, DEC 6 60-APR 21 61" have been cemented over to keep the tree alive. Burke's face was carved into the tree on the right by John Dickins in 1898, and is still clearly visible.

Pressing on, you'll be relieved to know that it's only 50km to **Innamincka**'s pub (see p.725), at the top of the Strzelecki Track in South Australia.

ARRIVAL AND INFORMATION   QUILPIE AND THE ROAD TO THE DIG TREE

By plane Quilpie airport, just west of town, is served by Regional Express (ⓦ rex.com.au) services.
Destinations Bedourie (2 weekly; 3hr 20min); Birdsville (2 weekly; 2hr 25min); Boulia (2 weekly; 3hr 45min); Brisbane (2 weekly; 3hr 30min); Charleville (2 weekly; 45min); Mount Isa (2 weekly; 5hr 10min); Toowoomba (2 weekly;

2hr 40min); Windorah (2 weekly; 45min).

Tourist information Quilpie's tourist office, 51 Brolga St (Mon–Fri 8am–5pm, April–Sept also Sat & Sun 10am–4.30pm; ☎ 07 4656 0540, ⓦ visitquilpieshire.com), can help with accommodation bookings and info on the local area.

THE BURKE AND WILLS SAGA

In 1860, the government of Victoria, then Australia's richest state, decided to sponsor an expedition to make the first south-to-north **crossing** of the continent to the Gulf of Carpentaria. Eighteen men, twenty camels (shipped, along with their handlers, from Asia) and more than twenty tonnes of provisions left Melbourne in August, led by **Robert O'Hara Burke** and **William John Wills**. It didn't take long for the leaders' personalities to cause problems, and by December, Burke had impatiently left the bulk of the expedition and supplies lagging behind, and raced ahead with a handful of men to establish a base camp on **Cooper Creek**. When Wills and the rest arrived, they built a stockade before the two leaders started north again, along with two other members of their team (Gray and King), six camels, a couple of horses and food for three months. Four men remained at camp, led by William Brahe, waiting for the rest of the expedition to catch up. In fact, most of the supplies and camels were dithering halfway between Melbourne and Cooper Creek, unsure of what to do next.

As neither Burke nor Wills kept a regular diary, few details of the **"rush to the Gulf"** are known. Aborigines saw them following the Corella River into the Gulf, where they found that vast salt marshes lay between them and the sea. Disappointed, they left the banks of the Bynoe (near present-day Normanton) on February 11, 1861, and headed back south. Their progress slowed by the wet season, they killed and ate the camels and horses as their food ran out. Gray died after being beaten by Burke for stealing flour; remorse was heightened when they staggered into the Cooper Creek stockade on April 21 to find that, having already waited an extra month for them to return, Brahe had decamped that morning. They found supplies buried under a tree marked **"Dig"**, but failed to change the sign when they moved on, which meant that when the first rescue teams arrived on the scene, they assumed the explorers had never returned from the Gulf. Trying to walk south, the three reached the Innamincka area, where Aborigines fed them fish and seeds, but by the time rescuers tracked them down in September, only King was still alive. The full, sad tale of their trek is expertly told by Alan Moorehead in his classic account *Cooper's Creek*, which is well worth tracking down (see p.995).

ACCOMMODATION

Channel Country Tourist Park & Spas 21 Chipu St, Quilpie ☏07 4656 2087, ☻bit.ly/cannelcountry. A natural spa thanks to the area's hot artesian water is the highlight of this caravan park, which provides reliable accommodation and info on the local area. Breakfast supplies are available on site year-round, and other meals in the high season. Un/powered sites $26/$33, cabins $115

Quilpie to Birdsville

Depth markers en route from **Quilpie to Birdsville** give an idea of how saturated this **Channel Country** becomes after rainfall – always check forecasts before setting out. First stop is **WINDORAH** – famed for its rippling red sand hills 10km west of town – with a clutch of buildings offering fuel, a post office and a general store. Windorah is the last place with **fuel** before Birdsville, 385km west along a mostly unsealed road. Heading northeast via Jundah, the road is sealed all the way to Longreach.

Betoota

The ruins of the *John Costello* hotel – also known as *"The J.C."* – lie 80km west of Windora, while another 140km brings you to more remains at **Betoota**, whose only building, the 1880s-built *Betoota Hotel*, was in business until 1997, when this was Australia's smallest town (population 1). Despite its isolation, Betoota comes alive on the last weekend in August when crowds gather for its annual horseracing event, the **Betoota Races** (☻betootaraces.com), held a week before the famous Birdsville Races (see p.47). Beyond here the country turns into a rocky, silent plain, with circling crows and wedge-tailed eagles the only signs of life. Driving can be hazardous here, but with care (and good luck) the Diamantina River and Birdsville are just three hours away.

INFORMATION

Tourist information Windorah's visitor centre is on Maryborough St (April–Oct daily 8.30am–5pm;

Nov–March Mon–Fri 8.30am–5pm; ☎07 4656 3063, Ⓦbarcoo.qld.gov.au).

ACCOMMODATION AND EATING

Western Star Hotel 15 Albert St, Windorah ☎07 4656 3166, Ⓦwesternstarhotel.com.au. This appealing hotel is hard to resist for a cold drink, meal (restaurant open daily 7am–8pm) and a look at its collection of old photos. It also provides economical accommodation in basic "hotel" rooms with shared bathrooms, and smarter "motel" en suites. There's also camping on the pub's back lawn, for the price of a gold coin (a dollar or two) donation to the Royal Flying Doctor Service. Hotel $95, motel $150

Birdsville and around

Legendary for its **horseracing** during the first weekend of September (see p.47), when up to eight thousand beer-swilling spectators pack out the dusty little settlement, **BIRDSVILLE** is at other times merely a far-flung handful of buildings where only the hotel and roadhouses seem to be doing business. But unless you've flown in, you'll probably be glad simply to have arrived intact.

About 12km north on the Bedourie Road, some slow-growing, old and very rare **Waddi trees** stand about 5m tall and resemble sparse conifers wrapped in prickly feather boas with warped, circular seed pods; the wind blowing through the needles makes an eerie noise, like the roar of a distant fire.

Big Red

38km west of Birdsville • Two-wheel-drive vehicles can often reach the base with care – check conditions before setting off

For a dramatic sight, head west of Birdsville to **Big Red**, the desert's largest dune, at the start of the Simpson Desert crossing. It's worth the journey to see the dunes, flood plains and stony gibber country (red desert, covered with loose stone) on the way.

ARRIVAL AND INFORMATION

By plane The airport, off Graham St, northwest of Birdsville town centre, is served by Regional Express (Ⓦrex. com.au). Extra flights from Brisbane are scheduled for the Birdsville Races in early Sept.
Destinations Bedourie (2 weekly; 40min); Boulia (2 weekly; 1hr 30min); Brisbane (2 weekly; 5hr 25min); Mount Isa (2 weekly; 2hr 30min); Quilpie (2 weekly; 2hr 25 min); Toowoomba (2 weekly; 5hr 25 min); Windorah (2 weekly; 1hr).

Services The Birdsville Roadhouse on Frew St (daily 8am–6pm; ☎07 4656 3226, Ⓦbirdsvilleroadhouse .com.au) has a general store selling groceries, souvenirs and more. It also sells fuel, and staff will even do mechanical repairs if you need them.

INFORMATION

Tourist information The Wirrarri Visitor Information Centre (March–Oct Mon–Fri 9am–5pm, Sat & Sun 10am–4.30pm; Nov–Feb Mon–Fri 8.30am–4.30pm; ☎07 4656 3300, Ⓦthediamantina.com.au) at 29 Burt St will give you the lowdown on the state of the various Outback tracks. Staff can also direct you to another tree blazed by Burke and Wills across the Diamantina, otherwise hard to locate among the scrub, or to attractions in town such as the stone shell of the original 1923 Australian Inland Mission.

Festival For more on the Birdsville Races race weekend – alcohol and horses, in that order (the Birdsville Hotel trades over 50,000 cans of beer in just two nights) – check out Ⓦbirdsvilleraces.com.

ACCOMMODATION AND EATING

Birdsville Caravan Park Florence St ☎07 4656 3214, Ⓦbirdsvillecaravanpark.com. This friendly place, set on the banks of the Diamantina billabong, is a good place to stay for a night, with caravan sites, motel-style rooms and cabins. Advanced booking recommended. Un/powered sites $30/$37, doubles $90, cabins $130

Birdsville Hotel Florence St ☎07 4656 3244, Ⓦtheoutback.com.au. Given the lack of alternatives, be sure to book ahead for the comfy accommodation at this iconic, award-winning hotel. It also has a great bar-restaurant with regular roasts, BBQs and buffets, plus a "seven-course takeaway" – a pie and six-pack. $165

Beyond Birdsville

North of Birdsville, the next substantial settlement, **Mount Isa**, is a lonely 700km further on, and fuel is available about every 200km.

Bedourie, 190km to the north, is well worth a stopover for its pool, artesian spa and hotel (see below). Those heading **west across the Simpson Desert** to Dalhousie Springs in South Australia need a Desert Parks Pass (see below). Feasible in any sound vehicle during a dry winter, the 520km **Birdsville Track** descends to Marree in South Australia (see p.727).

INFORMATION	BEYOND BIRDSVILLE

Permits The Desert Parks Pass ($150) is available online at ⓦ environment.sa.gov.au or from Wirrarri Information Centre in Birdsville (see opposite).

ACCOMMODATION	

Royal Hotel Herbert St, Bedourie ⓣ 07 4746 1201, ⓦ bedouriehotel.com. This atmospheric hotel, built of adobe bricks in 1886, provides cosy en-suite rooms, hearty "Outback dining" – such as colossal T-bone steaks washed down with cold beer – and a welcoming atmosphere, whether you are staying here or not. It's open daily from 10am. **$88**

Rockhampton to Winton

West from Rockhampton, the Capricorn and Landsborough highways traverse the heart of **central Queensland** to Winton and ultimately Mount Isa. There's a lot to see here – just a couple of hours from the coast you'll find magical scenery atop the forested, sandstone plateau of the **Blackdown Tableland National Park**, while the town of **Emerald** offers seasonal farm work, and is a gateway to **The Gemfields**' sapphire mines. Continue inland for both **Barcaldine** and **Longreach**, which are historically significant towns, while further west, **Winton** sits surrounded by a timeless, harsh orange landscape, with access to remote bush imprinted with dinosaur footprints at **Lark Quarry**.

4

GETTING AROUND	ROCKHAMPTON TO WINTON

By train The twice-weekly *Spirit of the Outback* train (ⓦ queenslandrailtravel.com.au) travels north from Brisbane to Rockhampton and then west to Longreach. It leaves Brisbane on Tues at 6.10pm and Sat at 1.55pm, and takes around 25hr for the full journey. The return trip leaves Longreach at 10am Mon & Thurs.

By bus Greyhound (ⓦ greyhound.com.au) connects Rockhampton with Barcaldine (2 weekly; 8hr 10min) and Longreach (2 weekly; 9hr 20min), from either of which you can pick up a Bus Queensland (ⓦ busqld.com.au) service to Winton on its Brisbane–Mount Isa run (2hr 50min from Longreach, 4hr from Barcaldine).

Blackdown Tableland National Park

As you move inland, the coastal humidity is left behind and the undulating landscape becomes baked instead of steamed. The highway loops over hills, running straight for many kilometres then surprising you with a bend. Gradually, the **Blackdown Tableland National Park** emerges from the horizon, dominating the landscape by the time you reach tiny Dingo, 150km from Rockhampton.

Sitting at 600m above the heat haze of the highway, the gum forests, waterfalls and escarpments of the national park are a delight. A 20km sealed **access road** is signposted on the highway 11km west of Dingo, and runs flat through open scrub to the base of the range. Views over a haze of eucalyptus woodland are generally blocked by the thicker forest at the top of the plateau, but at **Horseshoe Lookout** there's a fabulous view north and, after rain, **Two Mile Falls** rockets over the edge of the cliffs. From here the road runs past **Munall campground** (see p.454). At night, the air fills with the sharp scent of woodsmoke, and the occasional dingo howls in the distance – with a torch, you might see **greater gliders** or the more active brushtail possum.

Walks in the park

Walks in the park include short marked trails from the campsite to **Officers Pocket**, a moist amphitheatre of ferns and palms with the facing cliffs picked out yellow and white in the late afternoon; and a circuit track along **Mimosa Creek**, past remains of cattle pens and stock huts to some beautifully clear, ochre stencils of hands and weapons made by the Gungaloo people over a century ago.

Rainbow Waters

At the end of the vehicle track, 6km past the turn off to Munall campground

Blackdown's finest scenery is at **Rainbow Waters**. These falls are surrounded by eerie gum forest and are at their glorious best around dawn; from the lookout above you can spy on birds in the rainforest below and hear the explosive thumps of rock wallabies tearing across ledges hardly big enough for a mouse. A long staircase descends into a cool world of spring-fed gardens, ending on a large shelf where the falls spray from above into a wide pool of beautifully clear but paralysingly cold water.

ARRIVAL AND INFORMATION   BLACKDOWN TABLELANDS

By car There's no public transport into the park, so you will need your own vehicle. Some parts of the park (including the campground) are accessible by 2WD, but a 4WD is essential for the scenic Loop Road.

Climate Temperatures can reach 40°C on summer days, and drop below zero on winter nights.

ACCOMMODATION

Munall campground 8km beyond the park entrance ❶ 13 74 68, ⓦ parks.nprsr.qld.gov.au. This excellent spot is shaded by massive stringy-bark trees, with toilets, fire pits and a creek to bathe in; there's no water so bring plenty with you. Watch out for currawongs (crows) that raid unattended tables, tents and cars for anything, edible or not. Advance bookings essential. Per person **$5.95**

Emerald

The highway west of Dingo crosses the lower reaches of the **Bowen Basin coalfields** into cotton country, signalled by fluffy white tailings along the roadside. Despite its proximity to the Gemfield towns of Sapphire and Rubyvale, **EMERALD**, 125km along, was named by a surveyor who passed through after heavy rains had greened the landscape. A dormitory town for nearby coal mines, at the junction of routes north to Mackay and south to Carnarvon Gorge, Emerald's rich soil supports sunflowers, citrus trees, grapevines, lychees and rock melons, all of which attract swarms of seasonal **fruit-pickers**. Most essential services are on the Capricorn Highway, here called **Clermont Street**, including the town's landmark railway station, built at the turn of the twentieth century.

ARRIVAL AND DEPARTURE   EMERALD

By plane The airport, 6km south of the town centre, is served by Qantas (ⓦ qantas.com.au) and Virgin Australia (ⓦ virginaustralia.com).
Destination Brisbane (2–6 daily; 1hr 30min).

By train The twice-weekly *Spirit of the Outback* (ⓦ queenslandrailtravel.com.au) travels north from Brisbane to Rockhampton and then west to Longreach, stopping at Emerald. It leaves Brisbane Tues at 6.10pm and Sat at 1.55pm, arriving at Emerald at 9.30am on Wed and 5.52am on Sun.

Destinations Barcaldine (2 weekly; 7hr 10min); Brisbane (2 weekly; 16hr 25min); Longreach (2 weekly; 9hr 45min); Rockhampton (2 weekly; 4hr 50min).

By bus Greyhound coaches (ⓦ greyhound.com.au) arrive and depart from the train station.
Destinations Barcaldine (2 weekly; 3hr 35min); Blackwater (daily; 55min); Dingo (daily; 2hr 30min); Longreach (2 weekly; 5hr); Rockhampton (daily; 3hr 45min).

INFORMATION

Tourist information At the west end of Clermont St, the visitor centre (Mon–Fri 9.30am–4.30pm, Sat & Sun 10am–3pm; ❶ 07 4982 4142, ⓦ capricornholidays.com.au) sits in a shady park in front of the world's largest Van Gogh sunflower print, mounted on a giant easel.

ACCOMMODATION

Due to a steady influx of workers, accommodation is tight year-round (particularly midweek), especially during the April harvest or November cotton-chipping season.

Lake Maraboon Holiday Village Cnr of Fairbairn Dam Access & Selma Rd ☎ 07 4982 3677, ⓦ lakemaraboon holidayvillage.com.au. Lying 18km southwest of town, this park has serene sites and cabins overlooking a meandering lake three times the size of Sydney Harbour – it's stunning at sunset. Facilities include a restaurant, picnic spots, camp kitchens, pool, free BBQs and kayak and boat hire. Un/powered sites **$22/$32**, cabins **$99**

Emerald Explorers Inn Gregory Highway ☎ 07 4982 2822, ⓦ emeraldexplorersinn.com.au. At the edge of town, the *Emerald Explorers Inn* provides comfortable well-appointed rooms (some with spa baths), a licensed restaurant and a saltwater swimming pool, all within walking distance of the main shopping centre. **$129**

Springsure and around

Carnarvon Gorge (see p.447) lies 250km or so south of Emerald via the town of **SPRINGSURE**, which is set below the weathered orange cliffs of Mount Zamia, also known as the Virgin Rock – though weathering means you can no longer see the likeness of the Madonna and Child. It's 70km from Springsure to Rolleston, the last source of fuel and supplies before Carnarvon Gorge.

Old Rainworth Fort & Heritage Complex

10km southwest of Springsure • March–Nov daily except Thurs 9am–2pm, Sat & Sun 9am–5pm • $8 • ☎ 07 4984 1964

The **Rainworth Fort & Heritage Complex** is a squat stockade of basalt blocks and corrugated iron built by settlers in 1862 after "**the Wills Massacre**", when on October 17, 1861, Kari Aboriginal forces stormed Cullin-la-ringo station and killed nineteen people in apparent retaliation for the slaughter of a dozen Aborigines by a local squatter. Despite its name, the fort was designed to securely store supplies from potential invaders rather than safeguard people, and its design was unique at the time. Sharing the fort's serene situation are the relocated Cairdbeign School and Homestead, each of which dates back to the nineteenth century and beautifully displays relics of the period.

| ACCOMMODATION | SPRINGSURE AND AROUND |

Overlander Motel 10 Eclipse St ☎ 07 4984 1888, ⓦ springsureoverlandermotel.com.au. If you wind up in Springsure for the night, try this motel, which has 40 decent en-suite rooms with a/c, TVs and DVD players. There's a licensed restaurant on site and undercover parking to keep your car shaded in the Outback heat. **$125**

The Gemfields

The hot, sparse, rubble-covered country an hour west of Emerald masks one of the world's richest **sapphire fields** and, with hard work, the chances of finding some are good – though you're unlikely to get rich. The closest fields to Emerald (and the best-geared for beginners) are **Sapphire** and **Rubyvale**.

Sapphire

The well-worked country around **SAPPHIRE** looks like a war zone, with mine remnants scarring the countryside. There's not much here except a post office, and the houses are scattered along the road and a section of Retreat Creek, where the first gems were found.

Rubyvale

Miner's Heritage: 97 Heritage Rd • Daily: April–Sept 9am–5pm; Oct–March 9am–3pm • 35min mine tours $20 • ☎ 07 4985 4444, ⓦ minersheritage.com.au

The town of **RUBYVALE** has several shops, service stations, a pub and a few exhibition mines to tour. The most popular is **Miner's Heritage**, which was opened as a working

4

GEM MINING

Gems were first discovered in 1870 near Anakie, but until Thai buyers came onto the scene a century later, operations were low-key; even today there are still solo fossickers making a living from their claims. Formed by prehistoric volcanic actions and later dispersed along waterways and covered by sediment, the **zircons**, **rubies** and especially **sapphires** found here lie in a layer of gravel above the clay base of ancient river beds. This layer can be as far as 15m down, so gullies and dry rivers, where nature has already done some of the excavation work, are good places to start digging.

SPECKING AND FOSSICKING

Looking for surface gems, or **specking**, is best after rain, when a trained eye can see the stones sparkle in the mud. It's erratic but certainly easier than the alternative – **fossicking** – which requires a pick, shovel, sieve, washtub full of water and a canvas sack before even starting (this gear can be rented at all of the fields). Cut and polished, local zircons are pale yellow, sapphires pale green or yellow to deep blue, and rubies are light pink, but when they're covered in mud it's hard to tell them from gravel, which is where the washing comes in: the wet gems glitter like fragments of coloured glass.

You have to be extremely enthusiastic to spend a summer on the fields, as the mercury soars, topsoil erodes and everything becomes coated in dust. The first rains bring floods as the sunbaked ground sheds water, and if you're here at this time you'll be treated to the sight of locals specking in the rain, shuffling around dressed in Akubra hats and long Drizabone raincoats. Conditions are best (and hence the fields busiest) as soon after the wet season as possible (around May), when the ground is soft and fresh pickings have been uncovered.

GEM PARKS AND MINE TOURS

If this all seems like too much hard work, try a **gem park** such as Pat's Gem Tourist Fossicking Park (☎ 07 4985 4544), just outside Sapphire, where they've done the digging for you and supply a bucket of wash along with all the necessary gear (around $10–15). All you have to do is sieve the wash, flip it onto the canvas and check it for stones. There's certainly an art to sieving and flipping, but visitors frequently do find stones. Alternatively, Pat's sells bags for $15 that include among the wash a sapphire ready for faceting (cutting). Gem parks can also value and cut stones for you. For a break from the business end of a pick, take a **mine tour** (see below) and see if the professionals fare any better. In some ways they do – the chilled air 5m down is wonderful – but the main difference is one of scale; the method and intent are the same.

FOSSICKING LICENCES

If you're keen to hunt for gems, you'll need a **fossicker's licence**, available from shops and gem parks, which allows digging in areas set aside for the purpose or on no-man's-land. The $7.50 licence is valid for one month and gives you the right only to keep what you find and to camp at fossicking grounds.

---

sapphire mine in 1982. You can go on a guided tour and try your hand at fossicking – if you don't find anything of value, there's always the gift shop.

ARRIVAL AND INFORMATION
THE GEMFIELDS

By car The (sealed) turn-off to both Sapphire and Rubyvale is off the Capricorn Highway about 43km west of Emerald; from here, Sapphire is 11km north and Rubyvale a further 7km north.

Festivals You'll hear plenty of tall stories during the annual Gemfest (☎ gemfest.com.au), held in Aug at the Allen King Memorial Park in Anakie (just opposite the turn-off from the Capricorn Highway to Sapphire and Rubyvale).

ACCOMMODATION

Blue Gem Tourist Park On the banks of Retreat Creek, Sapphire ☎ 07 4985 4162, ☎ bluegemtouristpark.com .au. About 30 minutes drive west of Emerald, this caravan park has adequate caravan sites and cabins (with either shared or en-suite bathrooms). However, the best

accommodation here is a converted 1922 railway carriage, complete with kitchen and en-suite bathroom. There's also a store selling basic supplies and (fast) food. Un/powered site $26/$31, cabins $75, railway carriage $120
Rubyvale Motel & Holiday Units 35 Heritage Rd,

Rubyvale ☏ 07 4985 4518, ⊛ rubyvaleholiday.com.au. This complex has a mix of standard motel rooms and larger self-contained one or two-bedroom apartment "units", as well as a shaded pool, jewellery shop, and – rather surprisingly – a small observatory ($32 for stargazing tours; no under-16s). Doubles **$130**, apartments **$152**

Over the Range to Winton

Vistas from the rounded sandstone boulders at the top of the Great Dividing Range reveal a dead flat country beyond. Rivers flow to the Gulf of Carpentaria or towards the great dry lakes of South Australia, while sealed roads run north to Clermont and south to Charleville. You'll notice an increase in temperature as flies appear from nowhere, tumbleweeds pile up against fences and trees never seem closer than the horizon. **Sheep** dominate these parts, though there are some cattle and even a few people out here. The next stops on the road or rail line before Barcaldine ("Barcy" to the locals) are the townships of **Alpha** where you can find fuel and a café, and **Jericho**, one of the last places in Queensland with a drive-in cinema (daily evening shows of recent releases).

Barcaldine

It was near **BARCALDINE**, 300km west of Emerald, during the 1885 drought, that geologists first tapped Queensland's **artesian water**, revolutionizing Outback development. The town further secured its place in history during the 1891 **shearers' strike**, which – though a failure itself – ultimately led to the formation of the **Australian Labor Party**.

The Tree of Knowledge

Oak St • ⊛ treeofknowledge.com.au

A lone eucalyptus "ghost gum" – so called for its stark white trunk – was a rallying point for the striking shearers in 1891, and became an icon of Australia's labour movement. It was included on the National Heritage List in 2006, but later that year was poisoned and died. Its stump and root ball have been preserved as part of a controversial multimillion-dollar monument, **The Tree of Knowledge**, shaded by a veil of more than four thousand hanging charred timbers, topped by a sparkling glass roof. At night it is lit to great effect. You'll either love it, or hate it. Under it is a granite sculpture, resembling the tips of a pair of shears, which forms a memorial to shearers arrested during the strike.

Australian Workers' Heritage Centre

94 Ash St • Mon–Sat 9am–5pm, Sun 10am–4pm • $17 • ☏ 07 4651 2422, ⊛ australianworkersheritagecentre.com.au

You'll struggle to miss the **Australian Workers' Heritage Centre**, underneath a massive yellow-and-blue marquee. It has an expanding collection of displays that concentrates on the history of the workers' movement after the shearers' strike. There is also film footage, artefacts and plenty of sepia-tinted photos, covering themes including Outback women and Aboriginal stockmen.

ARRIVAL AND DEPARTURE

BARCALDINE

By plane The airport, on Myall St, just west of the town centre, is served by Qantas (⊛ qantas.com.au) and its subsidiaries.
Destination Brisbane (3 weekly; 2hr); Longreach (1 weekly; 30min).
By train The railway station, on Oak St, is served by the Spirit of the Outback (⊛ queenslandrailtravel.com.au).
Destinations Emerald (2 weekly; 6hr 15min); Longreach (2 weekly; 2hr 10min); Rockhampton (2 weekly; 11hr 20min).
By bus Greyhound (⊛ greyhound.com.au) calls in at Barcaldine on its Rockhampton–Longreach run. The bus stops at the Choice Roadhouse, at Box Street, on the Capricorn Hwy.
Destinations Emerald (2 weekly; 3hr 25 min); Longreach (2 weekly; 1hr 25min); Rockhampton (2 weekly; 7hr 30min).

INFORMATION AND TOURS

Tourist information The visitor centre (April–Nov daily 8.15am–4.30pm; Dec–March closed Sat & Sun; ☏ 07 4651 1724, ⊛ barcaldinerc.qld.gov.au) is at 149 Oak St (on the highway).

Tours For a closer look at Outback caves, waterholes and Aboriginal art – much of it on private property – with a tall tale or two thrown in, contact Tom Lockie at Artesian Country Tours (☎07 4651 2211, ⓦartesiancountrytours .com.au); the day-long "Aramac & Gracevale" tour ($145 including lunch) is highly recommended.

ACCOMMODATION AND EATING

Barcaldine Tourist & Caravan Park 51–65 Box St ☎07 4651 6066, ⓦbarcaldinetouristpark.com.au. Popular with campers and caravanners, this is also a good option for those who prefer a bit more comfort, which can be found in the en-suite cabins. It's easy to see why, especially when you factor in the free billy tea and damper in the afternoons during high season (May–Sept). Un/powered sites $22/$29, cabins $80

Ironbark Inn Motel 72 Box St ☎07 4651 2311, ⓦironbarkmotel.com.au. The corrugated-iron-roofed *Ironbark Inn* is a typical Outback-style motel, with reasonable if rather old-fashioned rooms and cabins, an outdoor pool, and the attached *3Ls* bar-steakhouse ("liars, larrikins and legends" – and everyone else – welcome daily 6–9pm. Cabins $95, doubles $120

Blackall and around

A one-hour drive south of Barcaldine on the Landsborough Highway takes you to the small town of **BLACKALL**, which sits on the banks of the often dry (but occasionally 5m-deep) Barcoo River. The famous **black stump**, a surveying point used in pinpointing Queensland's borders in the nineteenth century, is on Thistle Street near the school. The original stump has been replaced by a more interesting (if less blackened) fossilized one. In Aussie parlance, anything east of here is "this side of the black stump", while anything west is "beyond the black stump", another term for Outback remoteness.

Shamrock Street, shaded by palms and bottle trees, is the main road on which you'll find banks, supplies, the visitor centre and a few places to eat.

Woolscour

Evora Rd, 4km north of the town centre • Guided tours daily on the hour every hour, 9am–4pm • $16 • ☎07 4657 6042, ⓦblackallwoolscour.jimdo.com

In 1892, in the merino country surrounding Blackall, **Jackie Howe** fleeced 321 sheep in under eight hours using hand shears, a still unbroken record. You can learn more about the area's merino wool heritage at the steam-driven **Woolscour** (Australia's last remaining steam-operated plant where the freshly sheared fleeces are vigorously washed and cleaned), which was built in 1908 and was in commercial operation for seventy years.

ARRIVAL AND INFORMATION

By bus Bus Queensland (ⓦbusqld.com.au) services between Brisbane and Mount Isa stop off at the BP station, 10 Shamrock St.
Destinations Barcaldine (daily; 1hr 25min); Brisbane (daily; 14hr 50min); Charleville (daily; 4hr); Longreach (daily; 2hr 20min); Mount Isa (daily; 11hr); Toowoomba

(daily; 6hr 35min); Winton (daily; 4hr 30min).
Tourist information The visitor centre is at Ram Park, 145A Shamrock St (Mon–Fri 9am–5pm, Sat & Sun variable: March–April & Sept–Oct Sat 9am–noon, May–Aug Sat 9am–noon & 1–4pm, April–Oct Sun 10am–1pm); ☎07 4657 4637, ⓦblackalltambotourism.com.au).

ACCOMMODATION

Blackall Caravan Park 53 Garden St ☎07 4657 4816, ⓦblackallcaravanpark.com.au. A 10min walk from the town centre, this caravan park has a general store, regular country music performances, billy tea and damper in the afternoons, and a huge campfire perfect for swapping stories in the evenings. Un/powered sites $27/$32, cabins $115

Ilfracombe

On the Landsborough Highway between Barcaldine and Longreach, 80km west of the former and just 27km east of the latter, **ILFRACOMBE** essentially forms a living museum. The main drag comprises the "Machinery Mile", with pastoral machinery,

vehicles and farming equipment lined up next to the highway. Also here are an artesian spa in the town's Memorial Park, Australia's biggest bottle collection at Hilton's Bottles, and a hundred-year-old homestead.

ACCOMMODATION AND EATING   ILFRACOMBE

Wellshot Hotel 20 Main Ave ☎07 4658 2106, ⓦwellshothotel.com.au. The iconic *Wellshot Hotel* is the town's centrepiece, boasting an array of local memorabilia (including some evocative old photos), ice-cold beer and daily meals at lunch (noon–2pm) and dinner (6–8.30pm), plus brunch on Sun. Expect pub grub – burgers, steak sandwiches, steaks and salad – with some home-style desserts at dinner (apple pie and whipped cream, anyone?). Eight basic rooms have a/c and shared bathrooms. $60

Longreach

Unlike many other western towns, **LONGREACH**, 110km west of Barcaldine and right on the Tropic of Capricorn, is more than surviving. The lynchpin for this is the ambitious Australian Stockman's Hall of Fame and Outback Heritage Centre (usually just known throughout Queensland as the less tongue-tangling "Hall of Fame"), but the town was also one of the first to realize the potential of tapping Queensland's artesian water reserves for stock farming, and was the original headquarters of **Qantas** (see box below). Longreach's main drag is south off the highway along **Eagle Street**, where you'll find hotels, cafés, banks, a cinema and a supermarket.

Australian Stockman's Hall of Fame and Outback Heritage Centre

Just off the highway 2km north of the town centre • **Museum** Daily 9am–5pm • $32 • **Stockman's Show** April–Oct Tues–Sun 11am • $25 • ☎07 4658 2166, ⓦoutbackheritage.com.au

The **Australian Stockman's Hall of Fame and Outback Heritage Centre** is a masterpiece not just in architectural design – it's a blend of aircraft hangar and cathedral – but in being an encyclopedia of the Outback. Displays unashamedly romance the Outback through film footage, multimedia presentations, photographs and exhibits. History starts in the Dreamtime and moves on to early European explorers and pioneers (including a large section on women in the Outback), before ending with personal accounts of life in the bush. There's also an art gallery, a café and the exciting **Outback Stockman's Show**, where third-generation horse-breaker and stockman-famed drover Lachie Cossor heads a team of performing horses and cattle dogs. Allow at least half a day to take it all in.

Qantas Founders Museum

On the highway, opposite the Hall of Fame • Daily 9am–5pm (Dec–March till 4pm); tours 9.30am, 11am, 1pm & 2.30pm • $28 (return pass for another day free, if requested); combined with tour $63 (book ahead); wing walk tour $65 (on top of entrance fee) at 11am, 12.30pm & 2.30pm; flight simulator session $25 • ☎07 4658 3737, ⓦqfom.com.au

The **Qantas Founders Museum**'s prized possessions are a decommissioned Qantas jumbo jet and a restored 1950s Boeing 707, Australia's (and Qantas's) inaugural registered passenger jet. Each can be viewed on various guided tours, including a 747 "wing walk" tour, during which you take a stroll along the wing of a (grounded) 747 jumbo jet. An

---

QANTAS

Though **Qantas** (the Queensland and Northern Territories Aerial Services) was founded in Winton in 1920, the first joy-flights and taxi service actually flew from Longreach in 1921, pioneered by Hudson Fysh and Paul McGinness. Their idea – that an airline could play an important role by carrying mail and passengers, dropping supplies to remote districts and providing an emergency link into the Outback – inspired other projects such as the Royal Flying Doctor Service. Though the company's headquarters moved to Brisbane in 1930, Qantas maintained its offices at Longreach until after World War II – during the war US Flying Fortresses were stationed here – by which time both the company and its planes had outgrown the town.

original 1922 hangar forms part of the exhibition, which also includes interactive displays, classic advertising posters and cabin staff uniforms from days gone by. There's also a flight simulator. Allow at least half a day – and if you're an aviation buff and want to come back, request a free return pass for another day.

Kinnon & Co

128 Eagle St • **Shop** Mon–Fri 8.30am–5pm, Sat 9am–1pm • **Free Stagecoach rides** Mid-March to Oct Mon–Fri from 7.30am; 1hr • $74, bookings essential • **Tent Show** Mon–Fri at noon • $15 • **Combined experience** 4hr • $94 ⊙ 07 4658 1776, ⓦ kinnonandco.com.au

The family-run enterprise of **Kinnon & Co** encompasses a range of different experiences, including stagecoach rides (including a gallop through the bush), the **Station Store** emporium (with café), which sells quality Outback crafts and clothing, and an old-time **Tent Show** (with animals, stockmen and live theatre). You can opt for a combined experience which includes a stagecoach ride and Tent Show, plus "smoko" morning tea and an Australian classic movie. Kinnon & Co also act as a booking agent for other local attractions.

ARRIVAL AND DEPARTURE

By plane The airport (ⓦ longreachairport.com.au) is off the highway directly behind the Qantas museum. It's served by Qantas from Brisbane and Regional Express from Townsville.
Destinations Brisbane (daily; 1hr 55min); Townsville (daily; 2hr 30min).

By train The railway station, at the junction of Galah St and the highway, is served by the *Spirit of the Outback*

(ⓦ queenslandrailtravel.com.au).
Destinations Barcaldine (2 weekly; 2hr 10min); Brisbane (2 weekly; 23hr); Emerald (2 weekly; 9hr 20min); Rockhampton (2 weekly; 12hr 10min).

By bus Greyhound (ⓦ greyhound.com.au) buses arrive and depart from Duck St (opposite *Commercial Hotel*).
Destinations Barcaldine (2 weekly; 1hr 25min); Emerald (2 weekly; 5hr); Rockhampton (2 weekly; 9hr).

INFORMATION AND TOURS

Tourist information The visitor centre (cnr Eagle & Duck sts; Mon–Fri 9.30am–4.45pm; ☎ 07 4658 4150, ⓦ longreachtourism.com.au) is in a replica of Qantas's original office.

Tours Alan Smith ("Smithy") and his wife Sue run the well-established Outback Aussie Tours (☎ 07 4658 3000,

ⓦ outbackaussietours.com.au). They offer a wide range of tours in and around Longreach and further afield, including sunset cruises on the Thomson River (4hr; $99 including dinner), dinner shows (3hr; $79), day-trips to Winton ($199) and more.

ACCOMMODATION AND EATING

★ **Albert Park Motor Inn** Cnr Ilfracombe & Stork roads ☎ 07 4658 2411, ⓦ longreachaccommodation .com. This large motel has spacious and well-equipped rooms, plus an outdoor pool and a decent restaurant. It's a brisk 25min walk from the town centre, but close to the Hall of Fame and Qantas Founders Museum. They operate a courtesy transfer bus to the train station and airport. $139

Apex Riverside Park Campsite 5km west of town ☎ 07 4658 4150, ⓦ longreachtourism.com.au. Located in a park next to the Thomson River and run by the local council, this unpowered campsite has toilets and a BBQ area, but no showers. Four-night maximum stay; bring all equipment with you. Pay the per-car fee at the information centre. Camping $3

The Lazy Sheep 120A Eagle St ☎ 07 4658 0591. This deli-café is a good spot for breakfast or lunch, with a more inventive menu than most. Dishes ($7.50–15) include sandwiches, wraps, omelettes and soups, plus coffee and

cakes. Try the salad of the day, such as couscous and greens with Moroccan spices. Mon–Fri 8am–2.30pm, Sat 9am–1.30pm.

Longreach Motor Inn 84 Galah St ☎ 07 4658 2322, ⓦ longreachmotorinn.com.au. This friendly, centrally located motel is a good choice. Rooms are smart and comfortable, there's a palm-shaded pool, and a very good on-site restaurant, *Harry's*. Family rooms and two-bedroom suites offer more space. Doubles $130 family room $175 suites $230

Longreach Tourist Park 12 Thrush Rd ☎ 07 4658 1781, ⓦ longreachtouristpark.com.au. Located around 2km from the town centre, not far from the Hall of Fame and the Qantas Founders Museum, *Longreach Tourist Park* is one of the town's more economical options, with a mix of caravan sites and cabins, plus a decent restaurant, open for dinner May–Oct (closed Tues), and offering live music and entertainment most nights. Un/powered sites $28/37, cabins $115

LONGREACH

4

Winton and around

A 180km-long run northwest from Longreach across the barren Mitchell Plains, **WINTON** is a real frontier town where dust devils blow tumbleweeds down the streets – a fitting backdrop for the 1800s-set film *The Proposition* (2004), written by Nick Cave. As Queensland's largest cattle-trucking depot, Winton has a constant stream of road trains rumbling through, and a fair swag of history: **Waltzing Matilda** premiered at the *North Gregory Hotel* (see opposite), and Qantas was founded here in 1920. The surrounding country is an eerie world of windswept plains and eroded **jump-ups** (flat-topped hills layered in orange, grey and red dust), **opal deposits** and **dinosaur footprints**.

Winton's premier tourist attraction, the **Waltzing Matilda Centre** (w matildacentre .com.au), burnt to the ground in 2015, delivering what the mayor termed "a kick in the guts" to the town. However, some of the artefacts in the museum have been recovered, and a fund established to rebuild it, with the aim to reopen it before the end of 2017. A surviving part of it, the **Qantilda Museum** (see opposite), has reopened.

Australian Age of Dinosaurs

Dinosaur Drive, 25km south of Winton • April–Sept daily 8.30am–5pm, Oct–March closed Sun; tours daily 9am, 11am, 1pm & 3pm • $33; free with Dinopass (see opposite); two-day fossil-preparing packages are available ($164 single, cheaper if there are two of you) • ☎ 07 4657 0078, w australianageofdinosaurs.com • The last 12km of the road from Winton is unsealed

The **Australian Age of Dinosaurs** is spectacularly sited on a red mesa plateau 25km south of Winton. It's home to the world's largest collection of Australian dinosaur fossils, which are examined on the interpretive guided tours. You can watch as skilled technicians painstakingly prise million-year-old bones from their rocky tombs – and if you have a couple of days to spare, you can get your hands dirty by learning how to prepare fossils in the laboratory and volunteering some time to the work. This whole place is a fascinating experience, and kids will love the animated recreations of two "local" dinosaurs, Banjo and Matilda.

Corfield & Fitzmaurice building

Elderslie St • March & Nov to mid-Dec Mon–Fri 10am–4pm; April–Oct Mon–Fri 9am–5pm, Sat 9am–1pm, Sun 11am–3pm • $5 • ☎ 07 4657 1466

Next to the *North Gregory Hotel* (see opposite) is the immense, wooden **Corfield & Fitzmaurice building**, which opened as a general store in 1916 and now houses a vast collection of rocks and fossils from around the world, including a life-size diorama of the Lark Quarry dinosaurs, as well as displays about opal mining and the wool industry.

WALTZING MATILDA

The first public performance of **"Banjo" Paterson**'s ballad **Waltzing Matilda** was held in April 1895 at Winton's *North Gregory Hotel*, and has stirred up gossip and speculation ever since. Legend has it that **Christina MacPherson** told Paterson the tale of a swagman's brush with the law at the Combo Waterhole, near Kynuna, while the poet was staying with her family at nearby Dagwood Station. Christina wrote the music to the ballad, a collaboration which so incensed Paterson's fiancée, Sarah Riley, that she broke off their engagement. (Neither woman ever married.)

While a straightforward "translation" of the poem is easy enough – "Waltzing Matilda" was contemporary slang for tramping (carrying a bedroll or swag from place to place), "jumbuck" was slang for sheep, and "squatters" refers to landowners – there is some contention as to what the poem actually describes. The most obvious interpretation is of a poor tramp, hounded to death by the law, but first drafts of the poem suggest that Paterson – generally known as a romantic rather than a social commentator – originally wrote the piece about the arrest of a union leader during the shearers' strike.

Either version would account for its popularity – it was one of four songs Australians voted to become the national anthem in 1977, coming in second, and Aussies readily identify with an underdog who dares to confront the system.

Qantilda Museum

50 Elderslie St • Daily 9am–4pm • $10 • ☎ 07 4657 1466

The only part of the Waltzing Matilda Centre to survive the fire in 2015, the **Qantilda Museum** includes Christina MacPherson's cottage (see box opposite), a collection of machinery and horse-drawn vehicles, a steam train, and displays about Winton's wool industry in an old shearing shed.

Lark Quarry Dinosaur Trackways

120km southwest of Winton along an unsealed road (2hr; check with tourist office about road conditions) • Daily guided tours 10am, noon & 2pm (book at tourist office) • $12; free with Dinopass (see below) • ⓦ dinosaurtrackways.com.au

You may need to dodge kamikaze kangaroos and patches of bulldust on the way to **Lark Quarry Dinosaur Trackways**, 120km southwest of Winton. It's not surprising to find **dinosaur** remains here: the place looks prehistoric, surrounded by stubby hills where stunted trees and tufts of grass tussle with rocks for space. Some 95 million years ago a carnivorous dinosaur chased a group of turkey-sized herbivores to a rock face where it caught and killed one as the others fled. Over **three thousand footprints** have been found recording these few seconds of action, excavated in the 1970s and now protected within a temperature-controlled building. Indentations left by small, amazingly sharp, three-clawed feet – some very light as the prey panicked and ran on tiptoe – stream in all directions beside a raised boardwalk, while those left by the larger predator go only one way.

ARRIVAL AND DEPARTURE

By bus Bus Queensland (ⓦ busqld.com.au) buses depart from Elderslie St once daily in each direction towards Mount Isa and Brisbane.
Destinations Barcaldine (daily; 3hr 15min); Blackall (daily;

WINTON AND AROUND

4hr 30min); Brisbane (daily; 18hr); Charleville (daily; 8hr 35min); Cloncurry (daily; 3hr 45min); Longreach (daily; 2hr); Mount Isa (daily; 5hr 45min).

INFORMATION

Tourist information The tourist office is at 73 Elderslie St, at the Gift & Gem Centre (April–Sept daily 9am–5pm; Oct–March Mon–Fri 9am–5pm, Sat & Sun 9am–3pm; ☎ 07 4657 1466, ⓦ experiencewinton.com.au). You can book local tours (including to Carisbrook Station and Lark Quarry Dinosaur Trackways) here, and buy the Dinopass ($65) for discounted entry to Lark Quarry, the Australian

Age of Dinosaurs, Kronosaurus Korner in Richmond (see p.468) and the Flinders Discovery Centre in Hughenden (see p.467).
Fossicking Staff at the tourist office can offer up-to-date advice on travelling the 125km of unsealed road south to Opalton to fossick for semiprecious stones, though to go there you must be entirely self-sufficient.

ACCOMMODATION AND EATING

Banjos Overnight & Holiday Units 78 Manuka St ☎ 07 4657 1213, ⓦ facebook.com/Banjos-Over-nigh t-Holiday-Units. Around 700m north of Elderslie St, this neat and tidy place offers no-nonsense rooms with attached bathrooms, a/c, microwaves, hobs and cooking utensils. There's also a small pool and a BBQ area. $134
Boulder Opal Motor Inn 16 Elderslie St ☎ 07 4657 1211, ⓦ boulderopalmotorinn.com.au. Roomy accommodation in clean and pleasant – if fairly standard – a/c motel rooms. Adjoining rooms are a good option for

families, and there's a swimming pool, BBQs, and a good restaurant. $138
★**North Gregory Hotel** 67 Elderslie St ☎ 07 4657 0647, ⓦ northgregoryhotel.com. Although the decor is a little dated, this is easily the most charming and character-filled place to stay in town, with a range of clean and simple rooms (some with shared bathrooms, others en suite), a restaurant (daily specials $12–15, with a menu featuring local produce including lamb, beef and Queensland seafood), and a bar and café. $120

ENTERTAINMENT

Cinema On Wed evenings April–Sept, treat yourself to a session in Winton's Royal Open Air Theatre, complete with canvas seats and original projector, at the corner of Elderslie and Cobb streets, behind the Wookatook store. Check what's on at the visitor centre (see above).

Festivals Every Sept Winton stages the five-day Outback Festival, (ⓦ outbackfestival.com.au) which features rodeo and bush poetry events. In late June/early July, Winton's Royal Open Air Theatre is the venue for the ten-day Vision Splendid Outback Film Festival ($10; ⓦ visionsplendidfilmfest.com).

North of Winton

Some 165km **north of Winton** lies the shaded, muddy **Combo Waterhole**, 8km (unsealed) off the road, which is allegedly the billabong mentioned in *Waltzing Matilda*. A shade further on, **KYNUNA**'s low-slung *Blue Heeler Hotel* was another of the first places where the song was performed. Definitely worth a stop, this atmospheric pub has plenty of memorabilia (write your name on the walls along with other travellers) and you might even see the dancing brolgas that fly in on a daily basis. You might recognize the single-storey *Walkabout Creek Hotel* at **MCKINLAY**, 75km past Kynuna, as the rowdy Outback pub in the film *Crocodile Dundee*. It's quieter these days, but worth a look.

Boulia

West of Winton, it's a sealed road 366km to **BOULIA** along one of the most beautiful and surprisingly varied stretches of scenery in Queensland's Outback, alternating between endless plains, lush creeks and blood-red hills. Boulia is best known for its enigmatic **Min Min Light**, an eerie, unexplained car-headlamp-like light reputedly seen in the bush at night.

Min Min Encounter Centre

Herbert St • Mon–Fri 8.45am–5pm, Sat & Sun 9am–5pm (Sat & Sun till 1pm Oct–March) • $20 • ☎ 07 4746 3386, ⊛ boulia.qld.gov.au

If you don't see the real Min Min Light (locals maintain "you don't go looking for it, it comes looking for you"), drop into the **Min Min Encounter Centre** for a 45-minute sound-and-light show where you're directed through a series of rooms to meet automated characters depicting real-life locals, describing their close personal encounters with the lights. Spooky.

Stonehouse Museum

Cnr of Pituri & Hamilton sts • April–Sept Mon–Fri 8.30am–5pm, Sat & Sun 10am–2pm • $12 • ☎ 07 4746 3386, ⊛ boulia.qld.gov.au

The **Stonehouse Museum** was one of the first homes to be built in western Queensland, constructed in 1884 out of local stone bonded with limestone, gidyea ash and sand. Today it's a small but interesting museum featuring rare Aboriginal artefacts and lots of marine fossils.

ARRIVAL AND DEPARTURE   BOULIA

By plane The airport, on Herbert St, west of the centre, is served by Regional Express (⊛ rex.com.au).
Destinations Bedourie (2 weekly; 40min); Mount Isa (2 weekly; 35min).
By car If you're driving from Winton, you can stop at the fuel station 163km west of Winton at Middleton's combined pub/general store. From Boulia, Mount Isa is 303km north on sealed roads and Birdsville is 400km south on an unsealed road. If you're really enjoying the ride, Alice Springs is 814km west on the Donohue and Plenty "highways" – a long stretch of dust and gravel. Be sure to fuel up in Boulia if you're heading that way, as the next chance is 467km west in Jervois in the NT.

INFORMATION

Tourist information Boulia's visitor centre (Herbert St; April–Sept Mon–Fri 8.45am–5pm, Sat & Sun 9am–5pm (Sat & Sun till 1pm Oct–March); ☎ 07 4746 3386, ⊛ boulia .qld.gov.au) is at the Min Min Encounter Centre.

Festivals Families flock to Boulia for the July camel races (⊛ bouliacamelraces.com.au); camping at the rodeo grounds is free up to one week beforehand and during the three-day event, which also features live bands.

CAMELS IN THE OUTBACK

Camels were introduced to the Australian deserts in the 1800s, as an aid to European explorers opening up the inland areas of the continent. Later set free, they bred prolifically, and there are now estimated to be more than 300,000 feral camels in the whole country, most of them in central Australia. Culling is carried out, but is controversial. Australia also now exports camels to the Middle East. And in some Outback restaurants, you might even find camel on the menu.

ACCOMMODATION

Desert Sands Motel 50 Herbert St ☎ 07 4746 3000, ⊚ desertsandsmotel.com.au. The pick of the town's (admittedly limited range of) accommodation options, the *Desert Sands Motel* is a quiet place with a dozen functional en-suite rooms, welcoming owners, and pleasant, shady gardens. **$142**

Townsville to the Territory

All the major settlements along the 1000km stretch between Townsville and the Northern Territory border are **mining** towns, spaced so far apart that precise names are redundant: **Mount Isa** becomes "the Isa", **Cloncurry** "the Curry", and **Charters Towers** "the Towers". It's a shame that most people see this vast area as something to be crossed as quickly as possible – even if time is limited, Charters Towers' century-old feel and Mount Isa's strange setting are worth a stopover. With the freedom of your own vehicle you can explore the scenic **Porcupine Gorge National Park**, which is a great place to swim, and the spectacular oasis of **Lawn Hill Gorge**.

GETTING AROUND   TOWNSVILLE TO THE TERRITORY

By public transport The main route into the Territory is along the Flinders and Barkly highways – covered twice a week by Greyhound buses heading to Alice Springs – and there's also *The Inlander* train, twice-weekly between Townsville and Mount Isa.

Gold country

Two hours west of the coast, the dry scrub at the heights of the inland range at the community of **Mingela** once covered seams of ore that had the streets of both **Charters Towers** and **Ravenswood** bustling with lucky-strike miners. Those times are long gone – though gold is still extracted from old tailings or sporadically panned from the creek beds – and the towns have survived at opposite extremes: connected by road and rail to Townsville, Charters Towers became a busy rural centre, while Ravenswood, half an hour south of Mingela, was just too far off the track, and today is almost a ghost town.

Ravenswood

The wind blows dust and dried grass around the streets between the mine shafts and lonely old buildings of **RAVENSWOOD**, and some are sealed 50km south off the main highway. Gold was discovered here in 1868, and within two years there were seven hundred miners on Elphinstone Creek. The main attraction is to wander among the restored buildings, notably the still-trading *Railway* and *Imperial* hotels, and stroll up to the hilltop lookout.

ACCOMMODATION AND EATING   RAVENSWOOD

★ **Imperial Hotel** Macrossan St ☎ 07 4770 2131. One of the best Edwardian buildings in town, the wonderfully atmospheric *Imperial* has been carefully restored and still has its original wood panelling. The antique-filled bar is a fine place for a drink or a meal, and you can stay the night in one of the charming rooms (shared bathrooms). **$80**

Charters Towers

Once Queensland's second-largest city, and often referred to in its heyday simply as "the World", **CHARTERS TOWERS** is a showcase of colonial-era architecture. An Aboriginal boy named **Jupiter Mosman** found gold here in 1871, and within twelve months three thousand prospectors had stripped the landscape of trees and covered it with shafts, chimneys and crushing mills. At first, little money was reinvested – the **cemetery** is a sad record of cholera and typhoid outbreaks from poor sanitation – but by 1900, despite diminishing returns, Charters Towers had become a prosperous centre. There's been minimal change since, and the population, now mainly sustained

4

by cattle farming, sits at around 8500, about a third of what it was in the town's heyday. Don't be surprised if you hear local wags refer to the place as "Charlie's Trousers" (for no reason other than that it's a silly rhyme).

In the city centre, Gill and Mosman streets are shaded by old wooden arcades, and numerous spruce old buildings include the headquarters of one of Queensland's oldest surviving newspapers, *Northern Miner*, and the classically elegant post office and **World Theatre**. Shops, art galleries and cafés now line the glass-roofed courtyard of the former **Stock Exchange**, and the solid facade at the adjacent **town hall** betrays its original purpose as a bank, which stored gold bars smelted locally.

Zara Clark Museum

36 Mosman St • Daily 10am–2pm • $5 • ☎ 07 4787 3672, ⍟ nationaltrust.org.au/places/zara-clark-museum

Housed in a late Victorian building, which was once a general store, the **Zara Clark Museum** has an absorbing jumble of everything from old wagons to a set of silver tongs for eating frogs' legs, as well as local mining, transport and medical exhibits.

The Miner's Cottage

26 Deane St • By prior arrangement only; check at the visitor centre (see opposite) • $5; gold panning $11 • ☎ 07 4787 4021, ⍟ theminerscottage.com.au

The Miner's Cottage is a typical nineteenth-century timber-framed worker's house jam-packed with a private collection of period artefacts and mining, sadly now only accessible for visitors by prior arrangement. The welcoming and informative host will explain how to pan for gold, before showing guests how to try it themselves.

Lissner Park

Off Bridge St, east of the centre

There's plenty of shade under giant bat-inhabited fig trees at **Lissner Park**, whose Boer War memorial recalls stories of **Breaker Morant** – a local soldier and poet executed by the British after shooting a prisoner, who has, thanks to several books and a 1980 feature film, become an Australian folk hero.

Venus Gold Battery

4km out of town on Millchester Rd • Guided tours (1hr 15min): June–Oct daily 10am and also Mon, Wed, Fri 11.45am & 2.30pm, Sat 11.45am; Nov–May Mon, Wed, Fri, Sat 10am • $15 • ☎ 07 4561 5533, ⍟ historytoursaustralia.com.au

The **Venus Gold Battery** is a fascinating illustration of the monumental efforts needed to separate gold from rock. Abandoned in 1972 after a century of operations, the battery is a huge, gloomy temple to the past, its discarded machinery testament to the fact that this was once a sweatbox filled with noxious mercury fumes and the noise of huge hammers smashing ore into manageable pieces. Highlights of the tours include two holographic film presentations that bring the mill to life.

Texas Longhorn Wagon Tours & Safaris

441 Urdera Rd, Leahton Park, 8km north of town • **Safari** May–late Sept Mon, Tues, Thurs & Fri 8.30am, booking essential • $55 • **Wagon tour** May–late Sept Wed & Sun 9.30am; 3hr • $75 • ☎ 0474 561 122, ⍟ texaslonghorn.com.au

It's worth heading out to Leahton Park, home of the **Texas Longhorn Wagon Tours & Safaris**, where you can see the country's largest herd of purebred Texas Longhorns from the vantage point of wagons pulled by Percheron draught horses. As well as the safari, there's a bi-weekly option for a longer wagon tour including morning tea and saddlery demos. Tours operate only between May and late September.

ARRIVAL AND INFORMATION   CHARTERS TOWERS

By train The railway station, on Enterprise Rd, is served by *The Inlander* (⍟ queenslandrailtravel.com.au). **Destinations** Cloncurry (2 weekly; 13hr 20min); Hughenden (2 weekly; 4hr 25min); Mount Isa (2 weekly; 18hr); Richmond (2 weekly; 7hr); Townsville (2 weekly; 3hr).

By bus Greyhound (ⓦ greyhound.com.au) buses pull in by the Woolworths service station on Gill St.

Destinations Cloncurry (2 weekly 7hr); Hughenden (2 weekly; 3hr); Mount Isa (2 weekly; 10hr); Richmond (2 weekly; 5hr); Townsville (2 weekly; 1hr 40min).

Tourist information The helpful visitor centre is at 74 Mosman St (daily 9am–5pm; ☎07 4761 5533, ⓦ charterstowers.qld.gov.au).

ACCOMMODATION AND EATING

Dalrymple Cabin & Van Park 24 Dalrymple Rd (Lynd Hwy) ☎07 4787 1121, ⓦ dalrymplevanpark.com.au. Overlooking the golf course, 1.5km north of the city centre, this caravan park has well-spaced, shady sites, cabins (shared and en-suite bathrooms), two-bedroom motel units, a saltwater swimming pool and a sauna. Un/powered sites $25/$33, cabins $105, double $140

Irish Molly's Bar and Grill 120 Gill St ☎07 4787 1187, ⓦ facebook.com/irishmollyhotel. A lively spot for a no-nonsense meal – think steaks with a choice of sauces and fish and chips – and a drink (they even have Guinness on tap). Good-value specials for around $15, and there's live music on Fri nights. Daily noon–2pm & 6–8pm.

★ **Royal Private Hotel** 100 Mosman St ☎07 4787 8688, ⓦ royalprivate-hotel.com. This family-run, centrally located grand hotel (built in 1888) is excellent value for money, with spick-and-span budget rooms with shared bathroom facilities; more elaborate larger rooms have en suites. There's plenty of communal space and a kitchen for guests to use, plus a kitsch indoor "fairy garden". $65

Hughenden and around

HUGHENDEN, 245km west of Charters Towers along the highway, comprises little more than a dozen wide streets, a supermarket, a couple of hotels and some banks. Eight kilometres south of town, **Mount Walker** rises 152m above the pancake-flat black soil plains, offering a 360-degree panorama of the district – especially photogenic at sunset. The road is sealed till the turn-off, then again to the summit's six lookout points.

Flinders Discovery Centre

37 Gray St • March–Oct daily 9am–5pm; Nov–Feb Mon–Fri 9am–5pm, Sat & Sun 9am–1pm • $5; free with Dinopass (see p.463) • ☎07 4741 2970, ⓦ visithughenden.com.au

Hughenden's main draw for visitors is the **Flinders Discovery Centre**, which focuses on the swamp-dwelling **Muttaburrasaurus**, which lived in the early Cretaceous period around a hundred million years ago. Its bones were found south of town in 1963 and assembled into a 7m-long skeleton (now known as "Hughie").

Porcupine Gorge National Park

63km north of Hughenden along the partially surfaced Kennedy Developmental Rd

Porcupine Gorge National Park is best seen at the start of the dry season (May–July) before the **Flinders River** stops flowing, when good swimming holes, richly coloured cliffs, flowering bottlebrush and banksia trees reward the effort of getting here.

Look for wallabies on the walk into the gorge, which leads down steps from the campsite and becomes an increasingly steep, rough path carpeted in loose stones. The white river bed, sculpted by water, curves into a pool below the orange, yellow and white bands of **Pyramid Rock**. This is the bush at its best – sandstone glowing in the afternoon sun against a deep-blue sky, with wildlife calls echoing along the gorge as its stony shadow creeps over distant woods.

ARRIVAL AND INFORMATION   HUGHENDEN AND AROUND

By train Hughenden's railway station, off Resolution St, is served by The Inlander (ⓦ queenslandrailtravel.com.au). Destinations Charters Towers (2 weekly; 4hr 20min); Cloncurry (2 weekly; 8hr 40min); Mount Isa (2 weekly; 12hr 50min); Richmond (2 weekly; 2hr 35min); Townsville (2 weekly; 7hr 30min).

By bus Greyhound (ⓦ greyhound.com.au) buses pull into the Lights on the Hill Roadhouse on the Flinders Highway. Destinations Charters Towers (2 weekly; 2hr 55min); Richmond (2 weekly; 1hr 25min); Townsville (2 weekly; 4hr 35min).

Tourist information Hughenden's visitor centre is at 37 Gray St, in the Discovery Centre, (daily 9am–5pm; ☎07 4741 2970, ⓦ visithughenden.com.au).

ACCOMMODATION AND EATING

HUGHENDEN

FJ Holden Café 55 Brodie St ☎ 07 4741 0254. Named after a classic range of Australian cars, this cheerful 1950s-style diner is decked out with gingham tablecloths and Elvis memorabilia. The menu features everything from whopping great burgers to chai lattes. Drinks from $3.50. Mon–Sat 8am–8pm.

Hughenden Allen Terry Caravan Park 2 Resolution St ☎ 07 4741 1190, ⊛ hughendenvanpark.com.au. Located next to the town's 35m swimming pool, this caravan park has well-spaced, grassy sites and self-contained, a/c, en-suite cabins for those wanting a little more comfort. Un/powered sites $20/$28, cabins $80

PORCUPINE GORGE

Pyramid Campground 11km along the access road ☎ 13 74 68, ⊛ parks.nprsr.qld.gov.au. Perched at the top of the gorge, this campsite has 22 sites for caravans and campers, composting toilets and limited cold water for washing. Bring all your gear (including stoves, food and drinking water) with you. Camping permits are required (book online). Permits per person $6.10

Richmond

A 115km journey west of Hughenden along the highway brings you to the small town of **RICHMOND** on the banks of the Flinders River, one of Queensland's longest. One of its major attractions is **Lake Fred Tritton**, named after a former mayor, which is popular for fishing, swimming and water-skiing.

Kronosaurus Korner museum

91 Goldring St • April–Oct daily 8.30am–5pm; Nov–March Mon–Fri 8.30am–4pm, Sat & Sun 8.30am–2.30pm • $20; free with Dinopass (see p.463) • ☎ 07 4741 3429, ⊛ kronosauruskorner.com.au

The **Kronosaurus Korner museum** displays the fossils of hundred-million-year-old fish, long-necked elasmosaurs, and models of a "**kronosaurus Queenslandius**" excavated in the 1920s by a team from Harvard University and now on show in the US. Pride of the collection is a complete skeleton of a seal-like **pliosaur**, from the Cretaceous period a hundred million years ago – the most intact vertebrate fossil ever found in Australia – and the **minmi ankylosaur**, with its armour-plated hide. Look for the big blue-and-white kronosaurus outside; the museum doubles as a visitor centre, there's also a café and bakery.

ARRIVAL AND INFORMATION

By train The railway station on Middleton St is served by *The Inlander* (⊛ queenslandrail.com).
Destinations Charters Towers (2 weekly; 7hr); Cloncurry (2 weekly; 6hr 15min); Hughenden (2 weekly; 2hr 15min); Mount Isa (2 weekly; 9hr 50min); Townsville (2 weekly; 10hr 5min).
By bus Greyhound (⊛ greyhound.com.au) buses arrive and depart from Kronosaurus Korner.

Destinations Charters Towers (2 weekly; 4hr 55min); Cloncurry (2 weekly; 3hr); Hughenden (2 weekly; 1hr 25min); Mount Isa (2 weekly; 5hr); Townsville (2 weekly; 6hr 35min).
Tourist information The visitor centre is at Kronosaurus Korner, 91 Goldring St (April–Oct daily 8.30am–5pm; Nov–March Mon–Fri 8.30am–4pm, Sat & Sun 8.30am–2.30pm; ☎ 07 4741 3429, ⊛ kronosauruskorner .com.au).

ACCOMMODATION

Lake View Caravan Park Goldring St ☎ 07 4741 3772, ⊛ richmondlakeviewcaravanpark.com.au. Close to Kronosaurus Korner and overlooking Lake Tritton, this is the best place to stay in town, with caravans, basic bunkhouses, and more comfortable en-suite cabins. Un/powered sites $20/$28, bunkhouses $70, cabins $95

Julia Creek

JULIA CREEK, a 149km drive west of Richmond along the main highway, is home to the endangered **fat-tailed dunnart**, a nocturnal, insect-eating, mouse-like marsupial measuring just 10–12cm. You can see two of them going about their business and learn about them at the live exhibit called Beneath the Creek in the information centre (see opposite). However, the town is best known for April's quirky three-day **Dirt n Dust Festival** (⊛ dirtndust.com) which combines serious sporting competitions such as horseracing and a triathlon with more offbeat events such as bog snorkelling – an artificial bog is dug out of the dry soil for the occasion.

ARRIVAL AND INFORMATION   JULIA CREEK

By train The railway station at the south end of Julia St is served by *The Inlander* (⚙ queenslandrailtravel.com.au). Destinations Charters Towers (2 weekly; 10hr); Cloncurry (2 weekly; 2hr 50min); Hughenden (2 weekly; 5hr 30min); Mount Isa (2 weekly; 7hr 25min); Townsville (2 weekly; 13hr 10min).

By bus Greyhound (⚙ greyhound.com.au) buses arrive and depart from the rest area opposite Julia Creek News on Burke St.

Destinations Charters Towers (2 weekly; 6hr 35min); Cloncurry (2 weekly; 1hr 25min); Hughenden (2 weekly; 3hr); Mount Isa (2 weekly; 2 hr 45min); Townsville (2 weekly; 8hr 15min).

Tourist information The town's visitor centre (April–Sept Mon–Fri 8.30am–5pm, Sat & Sun 9am–noon; Oct–March Mon–Fri 8.30am–5pm; ☎ 07 4746 7690, ⚙ atthecreek.com.au) is on the corner of Julia and Burke streets. The fat-tailed dunnart exhibition costs $3.

ACCOMMODATION AND EATING

Julia Creek Caravan Park Old Normanton Rd ☎ 07 4746 7108, ⚙ jccaravanpark.com.au. Backing onto Julia Creek itself and a good spot for fishing and nature walks, this caravan park has low-cost sites, cabins (shared and en-suite bathrooms), a TV lounge and a pool. In high season (April–Sept) they offer $15 home-cooked two-course meals, prepared by volunteers from a local service club. Un/powered site <u>$20/$24</u>, cabin <u>$60</u>

Cloncurry

CLONCURRY, 137km west of Julia Creek, is caught between two landscapes, where the flat eastern plains rise to a rough and rocky plateau. Given that Cloncurry is one of the hottest places in Australia, you can be assured of a warm welcome: average summer highs are between 36°C and 38.5°C (still nowhere near the record high of 46.9°C, hit in December 2012). Cloncurry offers glimpses into the **mining history** that permeates the whole stretch west to larger Mount Isa. Copper was discovered here in 1867, but as the town lacked a rail link to the coast until 1908, profits were eroded by the necessity of transporting the ore by camel to Normanton. The highway runs through town as **McIlwraith Street** east of the railway line, and **Ramsay Street** to the west.

Mary Kathleen Memorial Park Museum

McIlwraith St • Nov–April Mon–Fri 8.30am–4.30pm, Sat & Sun 9am–2pm; May–Oct Mon–Fri 8am–4.30pm, Sat & Sun 9am–4.30pm • Entry by donation • ☎ 07 4742 1361, ⚙ cloncurry.qld.gov.au

Buildings at the **Mary Kathleen Memorial Park Museum** were salvaged from the short-lived town of Mary Kathleen (see p.470). The museum is primarily of geological interest, a comprehensive catalogue of local ores, fossils and gemstones arranged in long cases, though Aboriginal tools and Burke's water bottle add historical depth. The complex is also home to the town's visitor centre.

John Flynn Place

Cnr King & Daintree sts • May–Sept Mon–Fri 9am–4pm, Sat & Sun 9am–3pm; Oct–April Mon–Fri 9am–4pm • Admission by donation • ☎ 07 4742 2778, ⚙ johnflynnplace.com.au

Cloncurry's isolation inspired the formation of the Royal Flying Doctor Service, and **John Flynn Place** is a monument to the man who pioneered the use of radio and plane to provide a "mantle of safety over the Outback". The exhibition explains how ideas progressed with technology, from pedal-powered radios to assistance from the young Qantas, resulting in the opening of the first Flying Doctor base in Cloncurry in 1928.

The Chinese and Afghanistan cemeteries

Chinese Cemetery: off Isley St • Afghanistan Cemetery: north end of Henry St

A different aspect of Cloncurry's past is evident in the cemeteries on the outskirts of town. To the south of the highway, before you cross the creek on the way to Mount Isa, is the **Chinese Cemetery**. Here a hundred plots recall a brief nineteenth-century gold rush when the harsh conditions took a terrible toll on Chinese prospectors. At the north end of Henry Street the unnamed graves at the **Afghanistan Cemetery** are all aligned with Mecca. Afghanis were vital to Cloncurry's survival before the coming of the railway, organizing camel trains that carried the ore to Normanton from where it was shipped to Europe.

ARRIVAL AND INFORMATION
CLONCURRY

By train The railway station off Daintree St is served by *The Inlander* (ⓦ queenslandrailtravel.com.au).
Destinations Charters Towers (2 weekly; 13hr 15min); Hughenden (2 weekly; 8hr 55min); Mount Isa (2 weekly; 4hr 15min); Townsville (2 weekly; 16hr 25min).
By bus Greyhound (ⓦ greyhound.com.au) buses arrive and depart from Cloncurry Agencies at 45 Ramsay St.
Destinations Hughenden (2 weekly; 4hr 30min); Julia Creek (2 weekly; 1hr 25min); Mount Isa (2 weekly; 1hr 50min); Richmond (42 weekly; 3hr); Townsville (2 weekly; 9hr 40min).

Tourist information The town's Cloncurry Unearthed visitor centre (Nov–April Mon–Fri 8.30am–4.30pm, Sat & Sun 9am–2pm; May–Oct Mon–Fri 8am–4.30pm, Sat & Sun 9am–4.30pm; ☎ 07 4742 1361, ⓦ cloncurry.qld. gov.au) is at the Mary Kathleen Memorial Park Museum on McIlwraith St. Staff can advise on where to go bush-bashing for gemstones and furnish you with a fossicking licence.
Services Most services – banks, supermarket, half-dozen bars and a post office (Mon–Fri 9am–5pm, Sat 9am–1pm) – are along Ramsay St or the grid of streets immediately north.

ACCOMMODATION AND EATING

Cloncurry Caravan Park Oasis McIlwraith St ☎ 07 4742 1313, ⓦ cloncurrycaravanparkoasis.com.au. The best caravan park in Cloncurry, with camping sites, thirteen cabins (five without en-suites) and a saltwater pool to cool off in. Un/powered sites $22/$30, cabins $50

★**Gidgee Inn** McIlwraith St ☎ 07 4742 1599, ⓦ gidgeeinn.com.au. This eco-conscious motel, named after a local tree and with distinctive red "rammed earth" walls, is a step up in quality, with spacious en suites and a good restaurant (Mon–Sat 6–8.30pm) specializing in char-grilled steaks. $165

North from Cloncurry

The (sealed) Burke Developmental Road heads 380km **north from Cloncurry** past forests of termite mounds and kapok trees to Normanton (see p.479). The tiny settlement of **Quamby** is about 46km north of Cloncurry and the **Burke and Wills Roadhouse** another 137km beyond it. Aside from being a welcome break in the journey, with fuel pumps and a bar, the roadhouse also marks the turning west on a sealed road to Gregory Downs, gateway to the oasis of Boodjamulla (Lawn Hill) National Park.

West to Mount Isa

The rough country between Cloncurry and Mount Isa, 118km along the highway, is evidence of ancient upheavals that shattered the landscape and created the region's extensive mineral deposits. While the highway continues to Mount Isa past the **Burke and Wills monument** and the Kalkadoon/Mitakoodi **tribal boundary** at Corella Creek, forays into the bush uncover remains of less fortunate mining settlements.

Mary Kathleen
About 2km off Barkly Highway (on an unsealed road normally reachable in a 2WD in dry conditions)
About midway between Cloncurry and Mount Isa, is **KATHLEEN**, where uranium was found in 1954. The two-street town was built in 1956 and completely dismantled in 1982 when export restrictions halted mining; only the floors of the garages have been preserved.

Mount Isa

As the only place of consequence for 700km in any direction, the industrial smokestacks, concrete paving and sterile hills of **MOUNT ISA** assume strange oasis-like qualities on arrival; it's a shock to see that the mine is right in the heart of the city. There are a number of things to peak visitors' interest before heading on: unusual **museums**, local **mine tours**, Australia's **largest rodeo** every August, and simply the fascinating way the town has grown around the mine. 3One of the world's largest cities in terms of surface area – its administrative boundaries stretch halfway to Cloncurry and all the way to Camooweal – Mount Isa sits astride a wealth of zinc, silver, lead and copper. The city's founding father was **John Campbell Miles**, who discovered **ore** in 1923, established **Mount Isa Mines** the next year and began commercial mining in 1925 (see box, p.472).

West of the often-dry Leichhardt River, **Mount Isa Mines**, with its two huge chimneys illuminated at night, is the city's major landmark; the **City Lookout** on Hilary Street gives an excellent view. The Barkly Highway runs through town as Marian and Grace streets, with the city centre immediately south of the latter between Simpson and West streets; the highway then crosses the river and joins the road to Camooweal in front of Mount Isa Mines.

Isa Experience Gallery

Outback at Isa Centre, Marian St • Daily 8.30am–5pm • $20 • ☏ 07 4749 1555, ⓦ mietv.com.au

The history of the region is explored in the **Isa Experience Gallery**. The ground floor consists of a series of informative multimedia displays examining early prehistoric life, indigenous culture and the development of Mount Isa as a centre of mining activity, while the theatre on the upper level shows a poignant film focusing on the personalities who fostered the city's multinational community over the years.

Riversleigh Fossil Centre

Outback at Isa Centre, Marian St • Daily 8.30am–5pm • $12 • Laboratory tours (included in the admission) Mon–Fri 10am & 2pm • ☏ 07 4749 1555, ⓦ mietv.com.au

The **Riversleigh Fossils Centre** gives an excellent insight into how paleontologists working at the Riversleigh Fossil Site have discovered an incredible record

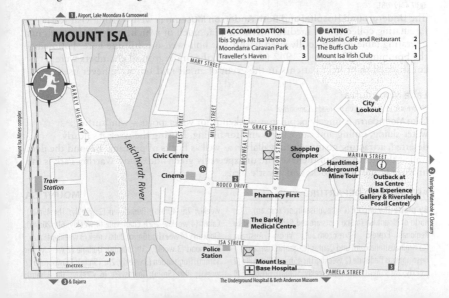

> ## MOUNT ISA MINES COMPLEX
>
> The **Mount Isa Mines complex**, owned since 2013 by multinational mining giant Glencore, is a land of trundling yellow mine trucks, mountains of slag, intense activity and kilometres of noisy vibrating pipelines. Copper, silver, lead and zinc deposits are mined almost 2km down by a workforce of four thousand; the rock is roughly crushed and hoisted to the surface before undergoing a second crushing, grinding and washing in flotation tanks, to separate ore from waste. Zinc is sold as it is, copper is smelted into ingots and transported to Townsville for refining, while four-tonne ingots of lead and silver mix are sent to England to be separated.

of the marsupial and mammalian evolution and environmental change that occurred between ten thousand and twenty million years ago. Imaginative, life-sized dioramas and an informative video recreate the region at a time when it was a lush wetland, populated by ancestral platypus and koalas, giant snakes and emus, carnivorous kangaroos and the enigmatic "thingadonta" (so called by researchers because it was unlike anything they'd seen before). Officially, this strange creature is now known as Yalkaparidon coheni. You can also visit the **laboratory** out the back, where fossils are prepared by soaking boulders collected at Riversleigh in weak acid, dissolving the rock to leave bones, beaks and teeth intact.

Hard Times Underground Mine Tour

Next to the Outback at Isa Centre, Marian St • 2.5hr tours run daily (book ahead; check with the centre for times) • $76; not suitable for children under 7 • ☎ 07 4749 1555, ⊛ mietv.com.au

Mount Isa's working mines are not accessible to the general public. However, you can get a vivid taste of what it's like beneath the surface by taking the miner-led **Hard Times Underground Mine Tour**. Visitors are equipped with full protective gear, including hard helmet and torch, before descending into the 1.2km of tunnels that make up the specially constructed mine. Guides are former miners.

Underground Hospital and Beth Anderson Museum

Joan St (at Spence St, near Mount Isa Base Hospital) • April–Sept daily 10am–2pm; Oct–March by appointment • $10 • ☎ 07 4749 0281

The **Underground Hospital and Beth Anderson Museum** is well worth a visit for its fascinating collection of medical memorabilia, much of which, including an original operating table, is still coolly sited within the hollowed-out hillside here. Following the bombing of Darwin in 1942 (see p.515), the underground chambers were constructed to protect patients in the event of an air raid but were never used.

Lake Moondarra

20km north of Mount Isa, on the road to Camooweal

Lake Moondarra is hugely popular at weekends for watersports – windsurfing, water-skiing, sailing and canoeing – and for fishing. During the week it's nearly deserted, attracting goannas and wallabies as well as flocks of pelicans. Beyond the dam wall at the north end of the lake, the unexpectedly green and shady Warrina Park is the unlikely home of peacocks and apostle birds.

ARRIVAL AND DEPARTURE   MOUNT ISA

By plane The airport (⊛ mountisaairport.com.au), 7km north of Mount Isa (a taxi costs around $35), is served by Regional Express (⊛ rex.com.au), Virgin Australia (⊛ virginaustralia.com) and Qantas (⊛ qantas.com.au). Destinations Bedourie (2 weekly; 1hr 45min); Birdsville (2 weekly; 2hr 35min); Boulia (2 weekly; 50min); Brisbane (9 weekly; 2hr 40min); Burketown (2 weekly; 1hr 45min); Cairns (4 weekly; 2hr); Charleville (4 weekly; 6hr 20min); Cloncurry (4 weekly; 30min); Julia Creek (3 weekly; 45min); Richmond (3 weekly; 1hr 30min); Quilipie (2 weekly; 5hr 15min); Hughenden (3 weekly; 2hr 15min); Toowoomba (2 weekly; 8hr 15min); Townsville (6 weekly; 1hr 35min);

Windorah (2 weekly; 3hr 50min).

By train The railway station, on Station St in front of Mount Isa Mines, is served by *The Inlander* (ⓦqueenslandrailtravel.com.au).

Destinations Charters Towers (2 weekly; 17hr); Cloncurry (2 weekly; 4hr 15min); Hughenden (2 weekly; 12hr 50min); Julia Creek (2 weekly; 7hr 25min); Richmond (2 weekly; 9hr 50min); Townsville (2 weekly; 21hr).

By bus Both Greyhound (ⓦgreyhound.com.au) and Bus Queensland (ⓦbusqld.com.au) pull in at the Outback at Isa Centre on Marian St.

Destinations Barcaldine (daily; 9hr 45min); Blackall (daily;

11hr 10min); Brisbane (1–2 daily; 26hr 10min); Charleville (daily, 15hr 5min); Charters Towers (2 weekly; 10hr); Cloncurry (1–2 daily; 1hr 20min); Hughenden (2 weekly; 6hr 25min); Julia Creek (2 weekly; 3hr 15min); Longreach (daily; 8hr 30min); Mitchell (daily; 17hr 45min); Richmond (2 weekly; 6hr 40min); Roma (daily; 18hr 50min); Toowoomba (daily; 23hr 50min); Townsville (2 weekly; 11hr 45min); Winton (daily; 5hr 50min).

By car From Mount Isa it's a monotonous 200km to Camooweal and the fringes of the black soil Barkly Tablelands, and over twice that to Boodjamulla. Several car rental firms have offices at the airport.

INFORMATION

Tourist information The excellent visitor centre is in the Outback at Isa Centre on Marian St (daily 8.30am–5pm; ☎07 4749 1555, ⓦmietv.com.au). It offers a range of

excursions, including two- to three-day trips to Boodjamulla National Park (from $795).

ACCOMMODATION

The mining boom has seen rents skyrocket, and this, combined with the town's role as a staging post for interstate travellers, means accommodation is surprisingly expensive and in short supply.

★**Ibis Styles Mt Isa Verona** Cnr Rodeo Drive & Camooweal St ☎07 4743 3024, ⓦibis.com. A reliable mid-range hotel with a few colourful quirks to it, bang in the centre of town, providing welcoming service, pool, restaurant, and well-equipped and spacious en suites with a/c, flat-screen TV, bathtub, and loungers. Rates include breakfast. $130

Moondarra Caravan Park 2 Moondarra Drive, 4km north of the city off Camooweal Rd ☎07 4743 9780, ⓦmoondarracaravanpark.weebly.com. The best bet for caravanners, the *Moondarra Caravan Park* is in a

picturesque location beside a shady bird-filled creek, and offers a saltwater swimming pool, basic bunkhouses and en-suite cabins. Un/powered sites $32/35, bunkhouses $50, cabins $80

Traveller's Haven Cnr Pamela & Spence sts ☎07 4743 0313, ⓦtravellershaven.com.au. *Traveller's Haven* is Mount Isa's only real backpacker option, a 10min walk from the centre, offering decent three- to five-bed dorms and private rooms, plus a pool, communal kitchen and TV lounge. Dorms $30, doubles $75

EATING AND DRINKING

Abyssinia Café Restaurant Townview Motel, 103 Marian St ☎07 4743 3328. Run by an Ethiopian chef who moved to the town with her Australian miner husband, this restaurant only has a couple of Ethiopian dishes on the menu, including *wot* (a thick, spicy stew) and *injera* (unleavened bread), though there are also some tasty Indian and Malaysian options (mains $25–35). Alcohol available. Daily 6am–9pm.

The Buffs Club Cnr Grace & Simpson sts ☎07 4743 2365, ⓦbuffs.com.au. *The Buffs* (for buffalo), is the best all-rounder in town, with a complex containing a restaurant, café, bar, bottle shop, and dozens of poker machines. The menu is firmly weighted towards carnivores, with steaks,

chicken, pizzas, a few pasta dishes and the odd curry (most mains $18–30, steaks $25–52). It offers a free courtesy bus if you're staying outside the centre. Mon–Fri 8am–3am, Sat & Sun 7.30am–3am; restaurant daily 11.30am–2pm & 6–9pm, Sat & Sun also 7.30–11.30am.

Mount Isa Irish Club Nineteenth Ave, 2km south of the centre ☎07 4743 2577, ⓦtheirishclub.com.au. Similar in style to *The Buffs* but with a more Celtic feel, this restaurant-bar-club-coffee shop has a good selection of daily specials, including a Sun eve roast (around $15). It also has a free courtesy bus service. Mon–Thurs & Sun 10am–2am, Fri & Sat 10am–3am; restaurant Mon–Thurs 7–9pm, Fri–Sun 6–9pm.

Boodjamulla National Park

West of Mount Isa, off the Barkly Highway, **Boodjamulla National Park** is hidden from the rest of the world by the Constance Range. Suddenly, the park's red sandstone walls and splash of tropical greenery are revealed. There's little warning of this change in scenery; within moments, a land that barely supports scattered herds of cattle is exchanged for palm forests and creeks teeming with wildlife. There are two sections to the park, **Riversleigh Fossil Site** and **Lawn Hill Gorge**, both highly worthwhile.

Gregory Downs

The gateway to the area, **GREGORY DOWNS**, is a tiny community where the pub is the local hub. Each May Day weekend, there's a wild **canoe race** down the Gregory River behind the hotel, beside which is a beautiful sandy shore where you can camp for free (toilets and showers available in town). From here, Lawn Hill Gorge is 76km west along a decent gravel road.

Riversleigh Fossil Site

Around 110km north of Camooweal, the World Heritage **Riversleigh Fossil Site** was once cloaked in rainforest supporting many ancestral forms of Australian fauna. The road from Camooweal to Riversleigh crosses the Gregory River three times around **Riversleigh Fossil Site**, offering sudden patches of shady green and cool air in an otherwise hostile landscape. Camping is not allowed at Riversleigh; the nearest place is at Lawn Hill Gorge.

Riversleigh's **fossil finds** cover a period from twenty million to just ten thousand years ago, a staggering range for a single site, and one that details the transitional period from Australia's climatic heyday to its current parched state. Riversleigh may ultimately produce a fossil record of evolutionary change for an entire ecosystem, but don't expect to see much *in situ* as the fossils are trapped in limestone boulders which have to be carefully blasted out and treated with acid to release their contents. A roadside shelter houses a map of the landscape while fossil sites – comprising entombed bones and teeth – surround the rocky outcrop behind, linked by marked pathways highlighted by illustrated interpretation boards.

Lawn Hill Gorge

When **Lawn Hill Creek** started carving its 40m-deep gorge the region was still a tropical wetland, but as the climate began to dry out, vegetation retreated to a handful of moist, isolated pockets. Animals were drawn to creeks and waterholes and people followed the game – middens and art detail an **Aboriginal culture** at least seventeen thousand years old. The National Parks **campsite** occupies a tamed edge of the creek at the mouth of the gorge. An easy hour's paddle over calm green water takes you from the National Parks campsite between the stark, vertical cliffs of the **Middle Gorge** to **Indari Falls**, a wonderfully refreshing swimming spot with a ramp so you can carry your gear down. Beyond here the creek alternates between calm ponds and slack channels choked with vegetation before slowing to a trickle under the rock faces of the **Upper Gorge**. You'll see plenty of birds – egrets, bitterns and kites – though **freshwater crocodiles** are harder to spot. Since visitor numbers have increased, this timid reptile has retreated to the **Lower Gorge**, a sluggish tract edged in water lilies and forest where goannas lounge during the day and rare purple-crowned fairy wrens forage in pandanus leaves. The rocks along the banks of the Lower Gorge – reached on a short walking track from the campsite – are daubed with designs relating to the **Dingo Dreaming**, a reminder of the sanctity of the gorge to the Waanyi people.

In the creek itself are turtles, shockingly large catfish, and sharp-eyed **archer fish** that spit jets of water at insects above the surface. Just how isolated all this is becomes clear from the flat top of the **Island Stack**, a twenty-minute walk from the camp. A pre-dawn hike up the steep sides gives you a commanding view of the sun creeping into the gorge, highlighting orange walls against green palm-tops, which hug the river through a flat, undernourished country.

ARRIVAL AND DEPARTURE

By car If you're making for either Riversleigh Fossil Site or Lawn Hill Gorge, ensure you have a campsite booked and check the latest road conditions (☎13 19 05, ☺racq .com.au) before setting out. The unsealed route to Riversleigh is generally 4WD only (or sometimes even

ACCOMMODATION

★**Adel's Grove** 5km from the gorge ☎07 4748 5502, ☺adelsgrove.com.au. Founded as a miner's homestead, and then turned into a botanical garden, this eighty-acre site is an appealing place to stay, with caravan sites, pre-erected safari-style tents, cabins (some with en-suite bathrooms), and bunkhouse rooms (sleeping six). There's a shop, meals are available, and canoes can be rented. Advanced bookings essential. Unpowered sites **$36**, safari

BOODJAMULLA NATIONAL PARK

closed altogether), but the Lawn Hill road via the *Gregory Downs Roadhouse*, while also unsealed, is fine for most cars if it's dry. The two sections of the park are linked by a 70km track, which is sometimes closed or 4WD only. Wherever you're driving from, make sure you fuel up.

tents **$155**, bunkhouse **$160** cabins **$170**
Lawn Hill Gorge 4km from the park entrance ☎13 74 68, ☺parks.nprsr.qld.gov.au. This National Parks campsite occupies a tamed edge of the creek close to the mouth of the gorge. Tank water, flushing toilets and cold showers are the only facilities available. Bookings (especially March–Oct) should be made well in advance. **$5.95** per person

The Gulf of Carpentaria

The great savannahland of the **Gulf of Carpentaria** – described by the Dutch explorer Jan Carstensz as being full of hostile tribes – were ignored for centuries after his 1623 visit, except by Indonesians gathering sea slugs to sell to the Chinese. Interest in its potential, however, was stirred in 1841 by **John Lort Stokes**, a lieutenant on the *Beagle* (which had been graced by a young Charles Darwin on an earlier voyage), who absurdly described the coast as "Plains of Promise".

It took Burke and Wills' awful 1861 trek to discover that the land here was deficient in nutrients and that the black soil became a quagmire during the wet season. Too difficult to develop, the region hung in limbo as settlements sprang up, staggered on for a while, then disappeared – even today few places could be described as thriving communities. Not that this should put you off visiting – with few real destinations but plenty to see, the Gulf is perfect for those who just like to travel. On your way from Cairns, don't miss the awesome lava tubes at **Undara**, while further afield there are **gemstones** to be fossicked, the coast's birdlife and exciting **barramundi fishing** to enjoy, as well as the Gulf's extraordinary sunsets and sheer remoteness to savour.

ESSENTIALS

Tourist information Visitors to the Gulf need to be reasonably self-sufficient, as there are few banks, and accommodation is limited to campsites or pricey motels. For information before you go, contact Savannah Guides (☺savannah-guides.com.au), a respected network of tour guides who manage many of the regional reserves.

GULF OF CARPENTARIA

Dangers It's possible that you will come face to face with the Gulf's two crocodile species. Locals stress that the only place you're safe in the water is the shower, so habitually check swimming pools before plunging in, as these amphibians often wander. Stay away from the edges of waterways at all times. Also be sure to bring plenty of insect repellent.

GETTING AROUND

The main route through the region is along the sealed, 580km-long Gulf Developmental Rd (also part of the Savannah Way touring route) west off the Atherton Tablelands. If you want to travel further afield, you'll need your own vehicle. Alternatively, you could join a safari from Cairns or board one of the tourist trains that still operate in the region.

BY TRAIN

The Savannahlander (☎07 4053 6848, ☺savannahlander.com.au) train service runs every Wed morning (March–Dec) from Cairns to Almaden on the

Chillagoe road, where it overnights before continuing via Mount Surprise, with a coach return to Cairns. There's a range of ticket options, starting with a $50 half-day trip between Forsayth and Einasleigh. The train travels at a snail's pace, hauling over rickety bridges in carriages with corrugated-iron ceilings and wooden panelling – a pastiche of Outback iconography. Tour packages and basic train-only fares ($245 for the full return journey) can all be booked online.

The Gulflander (⊙ 07 4036 9333, ⊛ gulflander.com.au) train runs once a week each way along an isolated stretch of line between Croydon and Normanton, a journey that takes a mere 4hr. The train departs Croydon on Thurs at 8.30am and Normanton on Wed at 8.30am ($69 single, $115 return), though you can also come back the same day by bus (see below). Special services to Critters Camp (2hr each way, $49 return) run irregularly May–Sept (enquire at the Normanton Railway Station).

BY BUS

The route along the Gulf Developmental Rd to Normanton and then north to Karumba is covered from Cairns by Trans North (⊙ 07 4095 8644, ⊛ transnorthbus.com.au) three times a week in each direction. It's an 11hr journey from Cairns, and costs $156. From Normanton to Karumba takes only 55min and costs $12.20.

BY CAR

Be warned that wet-season flooding (possible Dec–April) can cut main roads and isolate areas of the Gulf for weeks at a time. You shouldn't venture far off-road without a 4WD at any time.

ON A TOUR

If you'd prefer to traverse the region accompanied, try Heritage Tours (⊙ 07 4054 7750, ⊛ heritagetours.com.au), who offer excellent tours in this part of Outback Queensland. Nine-night 4WD safaris, staying in a mix of safari tents and motels, with most meals included, are priced from $3795 (twin share).

Undara Lava Tubes

The **Undara Lava Tubes** are astounding, massive subterranean tunnels running in broken chambers for up to 160km beneath the scrub – most weren't even uncovered until the 1980s, although tool sites around the cave mouths show that local Aboriginal groups knew of their existence. The tubes were created 190,000 years ago after lava flowing from the now-extinct **Undara volcano** followed rivers and gullies as it snaked northwest towards the Gulf. Away from the cone, the surface of these lava rivers hardened, forming insulating tubes that kept the lava inside in a liquid state and allowed it to run until the tubes were drained. Today, thick vegetation and soil have completely covered the tubes, and they'd still be hidden if some of their ceilings hadn't collapsed, creating a way in. These **entrance caves** are decked in rubble and remnant pockets of thick prehistoric vegetation quite out of place among the dry scrub on the surface.

Once **inside**, you'll find that the scale of the tubes is immense. Up to 19m high, their glazed walls bear evidence of the terrible forces that created them – coil patterns and ledges formed by cooling lava, whirlpools where lava forged its way through rock from other flows, and "stalactites" made when solidifying lava dribbled from the ceiling. Some end in lakes, while others are blocked by lava plugs. Animal tracks in the dust indicate the regular passage of kangaroos, snakes and invertebrates, but the overall scale of the tubes tends to deaden any sounds or signs of life. Four species of microbat use some of the tubes as a maternity chamber, emerging at night en masse to feed – up to 150,000 at a time. Lying in wait (though harmless to humans) are brown tree snakes, commonly known as night tigers, which dangle from the treetops.

ARRIVAL AND TOURS

UNDARA LAVA TUBES

By bus Trans North (⊛ transnorthbus.com.au) buses drop off at the Gulf Developmental Rd junction, and the Undara Experience (see below) can pick you up if forewarned. Undara Experience also runs coaches from Cairns.

Destinations Cairns (3 weekly; 4hr 25min); Croydon (3 weekly; 3hr 30min); Karumba (3 weekly; 6hr 35min); Mount Surprise (3 weekly; 25min); Normanton (3 weekly; 5hr 40min).

By car Undara is 275km southwest of Cairns and 390km northwest from Townsville, on the Savannah Way.

Tours Access to the lava tunnels themselves is only allowed on a Savannah Guides-led tour, which you can book at the Undara Experience (⊙ 07 4097 1900, ⊛ undara.com.au). The main tour (from $58) takes you through some of the tubes and delivers an intimate rundown on local geology, flora, fauna and history. Sunset tours ($60) include the flight of the microbats.

ACCOMMODATION

★ **Undara Experience** Savannah Way ☎ 07 4097 1900, ⓦ undara.com.au. A bar and an excellent restaurant accompany a range of accommodation options here, including eleven restored, early 1900s railway carriages with beautiful original features such as leather seats, pull-down stainless-steel handbasins and polished timber fittings. There's a pool, and you'll find plenty of other activities, including sunset wildlife-spotting tours and numerous self-guided walks. Un/powered sites $30/$37, swag tents $75, railway carriages $175, pioneer huts $187

Mount Surprise and around

Aside from being a stop for the *Savannahlander* **train**, there's little more to **MOUNT SURPRISE**, 40km north of Undara, than a service station, a hotel and a couple of caravan parks. Beyond Mount Surprise, the Gulf Developmental Road – sealed, but among the worst in Queensland for stray cattle – crosses **the Wall**, where expanding gases in a blocked subterranean lava tube forced the ground above it up 20m into a long ridge.

O'Briens Creek Topaz Field

The area's main attraction lies a bumpy 40km north of Mount Surprise at **O'Briens Creek Topaz Field** and its waterhole known as **the Oasis** (check road conditions before departing). You'll need a fossicker's licence to search for gems – you can pick one up from *Mount Surprise Gems* (see below).

ARRIVAL AND INFORMATION · MOUNT SURPRISE

By train The *Savannahlander* (ⓦ savannahlander.com.au) passes through Mount Surprise (see p.475).

By bus Trans North (ⓦ transnorthbus.com.au) buses between Cairns and Karumba pass through town.
Destinations Cairns (3 weekly; 5hr); Croydon (3 weekly; 2hr 30min); Karumba (3 weekly; 5hr 25min); Undara (3 weekly; 25min).

By car Check road conditions at ⓦ racq.com.au or call ☎ 07 13 19 05.

Fossicking *Mount Surprise Gems* (Garland St, Mount Surprise; ☎ 07 4062 3055, ⓦ thegemden.com.au) is a shop and café that sells fossicker's licences ($7.50) and rents out fossicking equipment ($30/day).

ACCOMMODATION

Bedrock Village Caravan Park Garnet St ☎ 07 4062 3193, ⓦ bedrockvillage.com.au. This is a friendly place – with a nod to the Flintstones – and offers decent sites and cabins. The owner here is a registered Savannah Guide and runs tours to Undara (see opposite) from $82. Un/powered sites $24/$28, cabins $85

Georgetown

On the Gulf Developmental Road, about 90km west of Mount Surprise, **GEORGETOWN** is a diminutive but nonetheless lively little place, home to several places to stay, and with shops and pubs strung out along the main street. The area around Georgetown has a reputation as a good place to fossick for **gold nuggets**.

ARRIVAL AND INFORMATION · GEORGETOWN

By bus Trans North (ⓦ transnorthbus.com.au) buses between Cairns and Karumba pass through Georgetown.
Destinations Cairns (3 weekly; 6hr 35min); Croydon (3 weekly; 1hr 30min); Karumba (3 weekly; 3hr 25min); Mount Surprise (3 weekly; 1hr); Undara (3 weekly; 2hr 10min).

Tourist information The Terrestrial Centre on Low St (April–Sept daily 8am–5pm; Oct–March Mon–Fri 8.30am–4.30pm; ☎ 07 4062 1485, ⓦ etheridge.qld.gov.au/terrestrial) acts as a visitor centre.

ACCOMMODATION

Latara Motel Gulf Development Rd ☎ 07 4062 1190, ⓦ georgetownaccommodation.com. Set amid seven acres of bushland, the *Latara Motel* has basic en-suite rooms with TVs, fridges and tea- and coffee-making facilities, as well as a pool and restaurant-bar. $140

4

Cobbold Gorge

Forty kilometres south of Georgetown along a partly gravelled road is **FORSAYTH**, terminus for the *Savannahlander* train and the last place to stock up before heading into the bush to two unusual locations: **Agate Creek** (2hr south in a 4WD through the scrub), where fossickers scour the creek banks after each wet season for these semiprecious stones, and **Cobbold Gorge**, 50km south of Forsayth on a passable dirt road. An attractive oasis inhabited by freshwater crocodiles and crayfish, the gorge is surrounded by baking-hot sandstone country. Located on Robin Hood cattle station, it's owned by the Terry family, who run tours (see below).

ARRIVAL AND TOURS   COBBOLD GORGE

By train *The Savannahlander* (ⓦsavannahlander.com.au) travels between Forsayth and Cairns (see p.475), and runs trips to the gorge from Forsayth.
Destinations from Forsayth Cairns (1 weekly; 2 days); Mount Surprise (1 weekly; 5hr 15min).

Tours Between April and Oct, Savannah Guides runs 3hr boat tours of the gorge ($95), scenic helicopter flights ($139 per person/15min), and full-day tours of the gorge and surrounding region ($160).

ACCOMMODATION

Cobbold Village Agate Creek Rd ☎07 4062 5470, ⓦcobboldgorge.com.au. As well as caravan sites and en-suite cabins (the latter come with a/c, TVs and kitchenettes), this resort/village on Robin Hood cattle station has a restaurant and coffee shop and a pool to cool off in. Savannah Guides run tours from here. Un/powered sites $28/$38, cabins $120

Croydon

CROYDON, 150km west of Georgetown along the Gulf Developmental Road, was the site of Queensland's **last major gold rush** after two station hands found nuggets in a fence-post hole in 1885. Within five years the **railway** was built, carrying up to two hundred passengers a week, and lucky miners whooped it up at Croydon's 36 hotels (only one survives today), before chaotic management brought operations to a close in 1900. Today the place feels frozen in time, with most of its elegant buildings predating 1920. Several of these now form the core of the heritage precinct, including the general store and the restored old courthouse with their original fittings; it's free to wander inside.

Lake Belmore

4km north of town along a sealed road

The highlight of the local area is **Lake Belmore**, a great spot for a picnic (free electric barbecues are available) or a spot of barra fishing. Some locals swim here, though be warned: there are freshwater crocodiles about; camping is prohibited. En route to/from Croydon you'll pass the stunning Diehm's Lookout.

ARRIVAL AND INFORMATION   CROYDON

By train The weekly *Gulflander* (ⓦgulflander.com.au) terminates at the station on Helen St.
Destination Normanton (1 weekly; 5hr).
By bus Trans North (ⓦtransnorthbus.com.au) buses pass through town en route between Cairns and Karumba.
Destinations Cairns (3 weekly; 8hr 5min); Georgetown (3 weekly; 1hr 30min); Karumba (3 weekly; 2hr 35min);

Mount Surprise (3 weekly; 2hr 30min); Normanton (3 weekly; 2hr).
Tourist information The friendly "True Blue" visitor centre on Samwell St (April–Nov daily 9am–4.30pm; Dec–March closed Sat & Sun; ☎07 4748 7152, ⓦcroydon .qld.gov.au) has a self-guided walking tour leaflet and can provide directions to other scattered relics, as well as to Lake Belmore.

ACCOMMODATION

Croydon Caravan Park Brown St ☎ 07 4745 6238. The well-shaded *Croydon Caravan Park*, on the Georgetown side of town, is a good place to stop for the night, with sites and cabins, plus a pool and a book exchange. Un/powered sites $20/$30, cabins $100

Normanton

Founded on the flat, gritty banks of the Norman River in 1868, **NORMANTON** was once the Gulf's main port, connected to the Croydon goldfield by rail and Cloncurry's copper mines by camel train. Normanton's fortunes declined along with regional mineral deposits, and today there's only a sparse collection of stores and service stations, with shop awnings and a handful of trees providing scant shade. A worthy survivor of former times is the beautiful timber **Burns Philp Store**, built in the 1880s, which covers almost an acre and remains upright despite the attentions of over a century's worth of termites. It now houses the library, along with the visitor centre.

ARRIVAL AND DEPARTURE   NORMANTON

By plane The airport, southwest of the centre off Airport Rd, is served by Regional Express (⊛ rex.com.au).
Destinations Cairns (4 weekly; 1hr 30min).
By train Normanton's historic railway station, on Matilda St and adorned with ferns and greenery, is served by the *Gulflander* (see p.476; ⊛ gulflander.com.au).
Destination Croydon (1 weekly; 5hr).
By bus Trans North (⊛ transnorthbus.com.au) buses pass through town en route between Karumba and Cairns.
Destinations Cairns (3 weekly; 10hr 5min); Croydon (3 weekly; 1hr 40min); Karumba (3 weekly; 55min); Mount Surprise (3 weekly; 4hr 30min).
By car Karumba lies 70km north on a sealed road; Cloncurry is 400km south via the *Burke and Wills Roadhouse*; Burketown is 226km west on a partially unsealed and often dusty road.

INFORMATION

Tourist information The visitor centre (April–Sept Mon–Fri 9am–4.30pm, Sat & Sun 10am–3pm; Oct–March Mon–Fri 9.30am–4pm; ☎ 07 4747 8444, ⊛ carpentaria .qld.gov.au) is in the Burns Philp Store, corner of Caroline and Landsborough sts. Pick up a self-guided walking-trail leaflet of the town's historical points of interest.

ACCOMMODATION

Gulfland Motel and Caravan Park 11 Landsborough St ☎ 07 4745 1290, ⊛ gulflandmotelandcaravanpark .com. As well as powered sites shaded by mango and palm trees, rather old-fashioned motel rooms are on offer here. Facilities include a pool, restaurant, BBQ area, book swap, and laundry. Un/powered sites $20/$26, doubles $115

Normanton Tourist Park 14 Brown St ☎ 07 4745 1121, ⊛ normantontouristpark.com.au. In the centre of town, this park has shady caravan sites and self-contained (but very compact), en-suite cabins, as well as an artesian spa and a large pool. Un/powered sites $24/$33, cabins $110

Karumba

Reached from Normanton along a 70km sealed stretch of cracked, burning saltpan, patrolled by saurus cranes and jabiru storks, **KARUMBA** sits near the mouth of the Norman River. The town mostly survives on prawn trawling and fishing, and live cattle exports to Asia.

Central Karumba is along Yappar Street on the Norman River's south bank, with a supermarket, café, post office, and a smattering of places to stay. **Karumba Point**, 10km downstream, overlooks mudflats and mangroves along the river mouth where it meets the Gulf's open seas. It's the nicer of the two areas and has more places to stay.

4

Barramundi Discovery Centre

Yappar St, 2km outside town along the river • **Shop** Mon–Fri 9am–3.30pm, Sat & Sun 9am–noon • Free • **Tour** April–Sept Mon–Fri 10.30am & 1.30pm, Sat & Sun 9.30am; 1hr • $12.50 • ☏ 07 4745 9359

Declining stocks of barramundi in the Gulf have inspired the opening of the **Barramundi Discovery Centre**, which raises fish for release into the wild. During the tour, you have the chance to hand-feed the fish and learn about their regeneration.

ARRIVAL AND DEPARTURE

By bus Trans North (ⓦ transnorthbus.com.au) buses arrive and depart from outside *Ash's Holiday Units* at 21 Palmer St, Karumba Point.

Destinations Cairns (3 weekly; 11hr); Croydon (3 weekly; 2hr 35min); Mount Surprise (3 weekly; 5hr 25min); Normanton (3 weekly; 55min).

INFORMATION AND ACTIVITIES

Tourist information The visitor centre (April–Sept Mon–Fri 9am–4.30pm, Sat & Sun 10am–3pm; Oct–March Mon–Fri 9.30am–4pm; ☏ 07 4745 9582, ⓦ carpentaria.qld.gov .au) is in the library, 154 Walker St, as you enter town.
Fishing and cruises If you want to go fishing or on a sunset wildlife-spotting cruise (from $55) call Kerry D Fishing (☏ 07 4745 9275, ⓦ kerrydfishing.com.au), Kathryn M Fishing Charters (☏ 07 4745 9449 ⓦ kathrynm .com.au) or Ferryman River Cruises (☏ 07 4745 9155, ⓦ ferryman.net.au).

ACCOMMODATION, EATING AND DRINKING

★ **End of the Road Motel** Palmer St, Karumba Point ☏ 07 4745 9599, ⓦ endoftheroadmotel.com.au. The smartest option in town, the award-winning *End of the Road Motel* has bright and spacious en suites and apartments opening directly onto the waterfront, plus a pool and all mod-cons, including hairdryers and DVD players. $165
Karumba Point Sunset Caravan Park Cnr Yapper St & Massey Drive ☏ 07 4745 9277, ⓦ sunsetcp.com.au. A short walk from town, this caravan park is a solid choice, offering both cabins (with either shared or private bathrooms), as well as sites and a pool. Un/powered sites $37/$43, cabins $127
★ **Sunset Tavern** Palmer St, Karumba Point ☏ 07 4745 9183. A popular local pub, right on the waterfront, this is the perfect spot for a cold beer or glass of wine ($6–12) while watching the sun set across the Gulf. Generous servings of good pub grub, including super-fresh barra and mud crabs, are on offer too. Main courses, such as fish'n'chips or steak with salad, are around $30, or you could splash out and have the enormous seafood platter ($100). Daily 10am–midnight.

Burketown

Set on the Albert River some 230km west of Normanton, via the site of Burke and Wills' northernmost camp near the Bynoe River, **BURKETOWN** balances on the dusty frontier between grassland and the Gulf's 30km-deep coastal flats. Another Gulf fishing hotspot, it's renowned for the spectacular Morning Glory rolling cloud formations that appear in the early morning from late September to early November. The **Morning Glory Festival** (ⓦ morninggloryfestival.com.au) celebrates this natural phenomenon each September. The lack of sealed roads into town makes Burketown something of an outpost (the closest sealed road extends as far as Gregory Downs, 117km to the south; see p.474), but you'll find a good range of facilities including a modern pub and a hot artesian spring.

ARRIVAL AND INFORMATION

By plane If you don't have your own vehicle, the only option is to fly with Regional Express (ⓦ rex.com.au). The airport is 2km southwest of town.
Destinations Cairns (2 weekly; 3hr 30min); Mount Isa (2 weekly; 1hr 45min); Normanton (2 weekly; 1hr 50min).
Tourist information The visitor centre (April–Oct daily 8.30am–4.30pm; ☏ 07 4745 5111, ⓦ burke.qld.gov.au) is on the corner of Musgrave and Burke sts in the old post office building.
Services There's a general store on Beames St, and a post office (Sloman St; Mon–Fri 9am–5pm, Sat 9am–noon). *The Tirranna Springs Roadhouse*, 27km west of town, is the nearest place to get fuel.

ACCOMMODATION AND EATING

Burketown Caravan Park Slomen St ☎07 4745 5118, ⓦburketowncaravanpark.net.au. A welcoming place for travellers, with decent powered sites, basic rooms and larger cabins (the latter have shared or private bathrooms). Basic groceries are available on site, as is fishing gear if you prefer to catch your own dinner. Powered sites $35, doubles $80, cabins $96

Burketown Pub Beames St ☎07 4745 5104, ⓦburketownpub.com. Built in 2013 to replace the historic old pub that burnt down the year before, the Burketown Pub is one of a handful of places to eat in this small town. It's got two bars, a dining room, pool tables, and a beer garden. Burgers, sandwiches and fish and chips are on the menu for lunch, while for dinner there are steaks, local grilled barramundi, seafood baskets, lasagne and more (mains $25–30). Mon, Tues & Sun 11am–late, Wed–Sat 10am–late.

The Hell's Gate Track

If you have a 4WD and want to head into the Northern Territory, drive 170km west from Burketown via the Aboriginal settlement of **Doomadgee** to the **Hell's Gate Roadhouse**, 50km from the NT. As you continue the drive west through pandanus-frilled waterholes and anthill-strewn landscapes, you're rewarded with glimpses of plentiful wildlife and even saltwater crocs. The road on from Hell's Gate improves inside the Territory, and once there you shouldn't have any trouble reaching **Borroloola**, 266km up the track.

4

Northern Territory

ULURU

5

Northern Territory

For most Australians the Northern Territory – known simply as "the Territory" or "NT" – embodies the antithesis of the country's cushy suburban seaboard. The name conjures up a distant frontier province – and to some extent that's still the case. Even today, just over one percent of Australians inhabit an area covering a fifth of the continent. This partly explains why the NT has never achieved full statehood – though there is increasing political momentum behind making the step up. Territorians love to emphasize the extremes of climate, distance and isolation that mould their temperaments and accentuate their tough, maverick image as outsiders in a land of "southerners". Beneath the grizzled clichés, you'll unearth a potent, unforgettable travel destination that offers stark desert landscapes, rivers packed with giant crocodiles, seemingly endless roads and ancient rock art. And that's without mentioning the vibrant, multicultural city of Darwin and the world's most famous rock formation, Uluru (Ayers Rock), set in an outstanding national park.

The small, sultry city of **Darwin**, the Territory's capital, is closer to Bali than Sydney, with an unhurried tempo that regularly waylays travellers. Its location makes it the natural base for explorations around the **Top End**, as tropical NT is known. Most visitors make a beeline for the nearby natural attractions, notably the photogenic swimming holes of **Litchfield National Park** and the UNESCO World Heritage-listed, Aboriginal-managed **Kakadu National Park**, with its astonishing array of ancient rock art sites, waterways and wildlife: if croc-spotting's a priority, you're unlikely to leave disappointed. **Arnhem Land**, east of Kakadu, is Aboriginal land, requiring a permit to enter: some Darwinites think nothing of getting a permit every weekend to go fishing, but if you don't want to go it alone, certain tours are authorized to visit the spectacular wilderness of scattered indigenous communities.

Around 100km south of Kakadu, the main attraction near the town of **Katherine** is the magnificent gorge complex within **Nitmiluk National Park**. As you continue south, a dip in **Mataranka**'s thermal pools and some colourful "bush pubs" are the highlights of the 670km to **Tennant Creek**, by which time you've left the Top End's savannah woodland and wetlands to travel through pastoral tablelands. The Stuart Highway continues to spool southwards, passing the rotund boulders of the **Devil's Marbles** and rolling on into the deserts surrounding **Alice Springs**. By no means the dusty Outback town many expect, Alice is an enjoyable base from which to learn about the Aboriginal

FOUR-WHEEL DRIVING IN THE RED CENTRE

Highlights

❶ Darwin NT's youthful and exuberant capital city boasts an excellent range of heritage and wildlife attractions, plus great Southeast Asian cuisine. **See p.487**

❷ Aboriginal culture Get a taste of 40,000 years of indigenous Australian culture on an indigenous-run tour. **See p.489**

❸ Kakadu National Park Australia's largest national park has some fascinating ancient rock art and an extraordinary diversity of flora and fauna. **See p.502**

❹ Top End crocs The Territory is proud of its big, scary saltwater crocs and there are many

opportunities to see them in the wild. **See p.503**

❺ Nitmiluk Gorge Cruise or canoe beneath the ochre walls of this spectacular gorge system. **See p.519**

❻ Four-wheel driving in the Red Centre Hop into a 4WD to explore the network of dirt tracks that radiate outwards from Alice Springs. **See p.545**

❼ Uluru One of the world's natural wonders, Uluru (Ayers Rock) has an elemental presence that emphatically transcends all the hype. **See p.547**

HIGHLIGHTS ARE MARKED ON THE MAP ON P.486

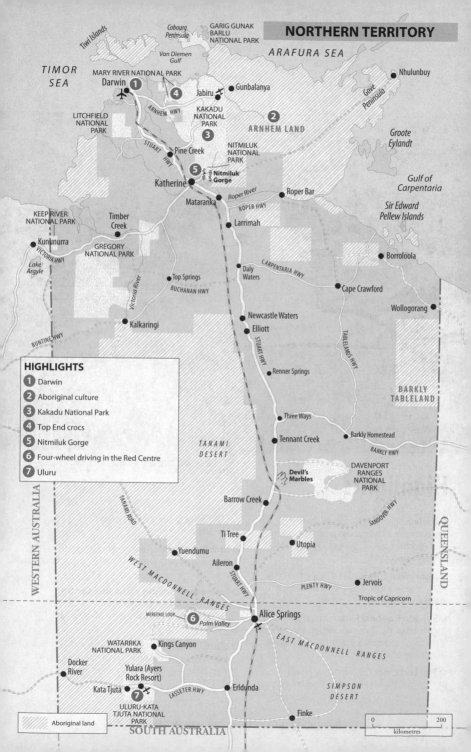

communities of the Western Desert and explore the region's natural wonders, of which the stupendous monolith, **Uluru (Ayers Rock)** – 450km to the southwest – is just one of many. The **West MacDonnell Ranges**, a series of rugged ridges cut at intervals by slender chasms and huge gorges, start on Alice Springs' western doorstep. On the other side of town, the **East MacDonnells** are less visited but no less appealing, while the remote tracks of the **Simpson Desert** to the south attract intrepid off-roaders. To the west, lush **Palm Valley** is accessible via a rough 4WD route and linked to the yawning chasm of **Kings Canyon** via a dirt track, the **Mereenie Loop**. These sights combined make for a memorable Outback tour. Renting a 4WD is recommended to get the most out of the trip; there are many interesting off-road tracks (see box, p.545).

GETTING AROUND NORTHERN TERRITORY

By plane Regular flights connect Darwin, Alice Springs and Yulara (gateway to Uluru).

By train The luxury *Ghan* train (see box, p.534) connects Darwin and Adelaide, calling at Katherine, Alice Springs and (on certain services) Coober Pedy.

By bus Greyhound covers the NT's major settlements, linking Darwin, Katherine, Tennant Creek, Alice Springs and smaller Stuart Highway stop-offs, as well as Kakadu to the east and Timber Creek to the west.

By car It's possible to cover the majority of the NT's key sights in a 2WD vehicle, the only hindrance being the extreme distances involved. For those keen to leave the bitumen behind, there's a huge network of 4WD tracks.

Darwin and around

Despite its modest size, torrid climate and often traumatic history, **DARWIN** is young, vibrant and cosmopolitan, a mood illustrated as much by Mitchell Street's buzzing bars as the runners and cyclists making the most of the tropical parks and waterfront suburbs. Travellers accustomed to the all-enveloping conurbations of the east coast can initially be underwhelmed by its low-rise, laidback mood, but Darwin more than

---

TOP END WEATHER

There is a certain amount of misunderstanding about the Top End's **tropical climate**, usually summed up as the hot and humid "Dry" and the hotter and very humid "Wet". Give or take a couple of weeks either way, this is the pattern: the **Dry** begins in April when rains stop and humidity decreases – although this always remains high, whatever the season. The bush is at its greenest, and engorged waterfalls pound the base of the escarpments, although it may take a couple of months for vehicle access to be restored to all far-flung tracks. From April until October skies are generally cloud-free, with daily temperatures reliably peaking in the low thirties centigrade, though June and July nights might cool down to 10°C.

From October until December temperatures and humidity begin to rise during the **Build Up**. Clouds accumulate to discharge brief showers, and it's a time of year when the weak-willed or insufficiently drunk can flip out and "go troppo" as the unbearable heat, humidity and dysfunctional air conditioning push people over the edge. Around November storms can still be frustratingly dry but often give rise to spectacular lightning shows. Only when the monsoonal **Wet** season commences at the turn of the year do the daily afternoon storms rejuvenate and saturate the land. This cycle lasts for two months or so and is much more tolerable than you might expect, with a daily thunderous downpour cooling things down from the mid- to low thirties.

Cyclones occur most commonly at either end of the Wet and can dump 30cm of rain in as many hours, with winds of up to 300kph. Frequent updates on the erratic path and intensity of these tropical depressions are given on the radio, so most people are prepared when a storm hits. Some fizzle out or head back out to sea; others can intensify and zigzag across the land, most infamously in the form of 1974's Cyclone Tracy, which pulverized Darwin.

And if further proof were needed that the Top End's weather patterns warrant more distinction than merely Wet and Dry, know that the region's Aboriginal groups traditionally recognize no fewer than six distinct seasons.

5

matches its billing as one of the fastest-growing cities in Australia, and its population of over 136,000 accommodates a jumble of different ethnic backgrounds. To fully appreciate Darwin you should allow a minimum of three days to absorb its heritage buildings and wildlife attractions, visit the gleaming new waterfront quarter, sample some excellent Southeast Asian cuisine, and enjoy the lively nightlife.

Day-trips from Darwin include the ever-popular Litchfield National Park as well as the Aboriginal-owned Tiwi Islands, a thirty-minute flight from town. Crocodylus Park, on the city's edge, makes for a full day out when combined with the excellent Territory Wildlife Park (see p.494). On paper, Kakadu is another day-trip option, but to appreciate it properly you'll need longer, possibly on a tour (see p.495).

Brief history

Setting up a colonial settlement on Australia's remote northern shores was never going to be easy, and it took four abortive attempts in various locations over 45 years before **Darwin** (originally called Palmerston) was established in 1869 by the new South Australian state keen to exploit its recently acquired "northern territory". The early colonists' aim was to pre-empt foreign occupation and create a trading post – a "new Singapore" for the British Empire.

Things got off to a promising start with the 1872 arrival of the **Overland Telegraph Line (OTL)**, following the route pioneered by explorer **John McDouall Stuart** in 1862 that finally linked Australia with the rest of the world. **Gold** was discovered at Pine Creek while pylons were being erected for the OTL, prompting a gold rush and construction of a southbound railway. After the gold rush ran its course, a cyclone flattened the depressed town in 1897, but by 1911, when Darwin adopted its present name (a legacy of Charles Darwin's former ship, the *Beagle*, having laid anchor here in 1839), the rough-and-ready frontier outpost had grown into a small government centre, servicing the mines and properties of the Top End. Yet even by 1937, after being razed by a second cyclone, the town had a population of just 1500.

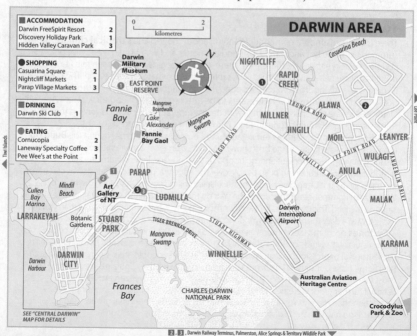

DARWIN AREA

■ ACCOMMODATION	
Darwin FreeSpirit Resort	2
Discovery Holiday Park	1
Hidden Valley Caravan Park	3

● SHOPPING	
Casuarina Square	2
Nightcliff Markets	1
Parap Village Markets	3

■ DRINKING	
Darwin Ski Club	1

● EATING	
Cornucopia	2
Laneway Specialty Coffee	3
Pee Wee's at the Point	1

SEE "CENTRAL DARWIN" MAP FOR DETAILS

2 , 3 , Darwin Railway Terminus, Palmerston, Alice Springs & Territory Wildlife Park

ABORIGINAL PEOPLE AND TOURISM

More than a quarter of the NT's population are Aborigines, a far higher proportion than anywhere else in Australia, and half of the Territory is once again **Aboriginal-owned land**, returned after protracted land claims. As a tourist, however, meeting Aboriginal people and getting to know them can be difficult. Excepting the national parks, most Aboriginal land is out of bounds to visitors without a **permit** or invitation, and most communities and outstations, where the majority of Aboriginal people live, are remote even by Territory standards.

There's a tendency for outsiders to think of "Aborigines" as a single mass of people, overlooking the fact that dozens of culturally distinct indigenous groups have traditionally inhabited the NT region. But it's true, sadly, that the most visible Aboriginal people in places like Darwin and Alice Springs are those living rough, a sad sight that shows little sign of changing. Likewise, the extent of certain social problems – notably alcoholism – is also clearly apparent.

These issues are real but far from all-defining, and for those interested in getting to the heart of the enigmatic Australian Outback and meeting indigenous Australians, the NT provides an introduction to a land that's sustained fascinating and complex cultures for at least forty thousand years. Many Aborigines have a new-found pride in their heritage and identity, demonstrated in superb museums, successful tourism **projects** and a flowering of indigenous art, media, music and literature.

The most meaningful contact for the short-term visitor is likely to be from an **indigenous tour** guide, a knowledgeable non-Aboriginal guide, or a visit to a festival (see box, p.511). Try to choose Aboriginal-owned tour providers, for example Northern Territory Indigenous Tours (see p.496). Keep in mind that most tours will only scrape the surface of a complex way of life – secrecy is one of the pillars that supports traditional society, so what you'll probably learn is a watered-down version. But if you're keen to learn about the meaning of the country for Aborigines, about languages, bushtucker, bush medicine and Dreamtime stories, these tours can be enriching.

During World War II, the threat of a Japanese invasion led to the evacuation of women and children from Darwin, which occupied a key defensive location for the Allies. The city was subsequently destroyed by **Japanese air raids**, which killed hundreds – information that was suppressed at the time. Coupled with the urgent need to get troops to the war zone, the fear of invasion also resulted in the swift construction of the **Stuart Highway**, the first reliable land link between Darwin and the rest of Australia.

After the war Darwin was rebuilt, and three decades of prosperity followed until Christmas Eve 1974, when **Cyclone Tracy** rolled in overnight and devastated the city. Despite the relatively low death toll of 66, Tracy marked the end of old Darwin, psychologically as well as architecturally, and most of the population was evacuated before the hasty rebuilding process began. In recent decades links with Asia, and an influx of Aussies seeking warmer weather and a slower pace of life, have transformed the city into a vibrant multicultural destination. In 2004 tourism and the mining industry were boosted by the completion of the **Darwin rail link** with Alice Springs (and Adelaide). More recently, the billion-dollar **waterfront regeneration** project and the discovery of vast amounts of natural gas offshore have attracted more migrants and money.

The modern city spreads north from the end of a stubby peninsula where a settlement was originally established on the lands of the Larrakia Aborigines. For the visitor most of the action lies between the Waterfront Area and East Point, 9km to the north.

Parliament House

Mitchell St • Mon–Fri 8am–6pm, Sat & Sun 9am–6pm • **Tours** Feb–Nov Sat 9am & 11am, May–Sept also Wed 10.30am • 1hr 30min • Free • **State Library** Tues–Fri 10am–5pm, Sat & Sun 1–5pm • Free • ☎ 08 8946 1434 or ☎ 08 8946 1430, ⊛ nt.gov.au

The strikingly modern **Parliament House** makes a good starting point for your wanderings. It's certainly the grandest building in the Territory, and imaginatively

5

designed too – note the bomb-tail styling at the top of the exterior corner pillars, allegedly a nod to Darwin's wartime woes. Inside, past the airport-style security, you'll find the foyer beautifully airy and full of little Territorian details, from the original NT crest to a desert flower mosaic. In the main reception hall, a plaque on the floor pinpoints where a Japanese bomb fell during the air raids of 1942. You can also access the **State Library** (also known as the Northern Territory Library) here and take in the views at the *Speaker's Corner Café* (see p.498).

The Heritage Trail

Cyclones, air raids and termites have destroyed many of Darwin's old buildings, although a few architectural gems have survived. A short walk from Parliament House, the restored **Government House** was rebuilt in the 1870s after the original residence was devoured by white ants. Its cream corrugated roof and potted palms make it a fine example of an elegant, tropical building, and it remains the official residence of the Administrator of the NT.

At the end of Smith Street are the poignant ruins of **Palmerston Town Hall**, built in 1883 and destroyed by Cyclone Tracy. It is occasionally used as a location for outdoor performances by the Darwin Theatre Company, which is based in the atmospheric 1885 **Brown's Mart Theatre** opposite. The park adjoining Brown's Mart marks the location of the former Chinatown, destroyed during World War II air raids. At the beginning of the twentieth century, the industrious Chinese outnumbered Europeans three to one in the Top End, and were involved in everything from building the Pine Creek railroad to running market gardens. Turning up Bennett Street then left onto Woods Street, you'll find the serene, incense-fragranced **Chinese Temple** (daily 8am–4pm; free), another post-Tracy restoration, employing the altar and statues from the 1887 original. It has a small museum of Chinese heritage in the NT (Tues–Sun 10am–2pm). A little further up Woods Street, turn left onto Knuckey Street and head towards the Esplanade for the former **Old Admiralty House**, a tropical 1920s stilted house that survived cyclones and air raids. Recently renovated, it now houses *Char* restaurant (see p.497). Opposite, the 1925 stone **Lyons Cottage** (Mon–Fri 9am–5pm, Sat & Sun 9am–2pm; free) was built to house the Darwin Cable Company staff, but now holds a museum of Darwin's early history and a not-for-profit Aboriginal retail outlet.

Crocosaurus Cove

58 Mitchell St • Daily 9am–6pm (last admission 5pm); croc-feeding shows 11.30am & 2.30pm • $35; Cage of Death $165pp, $125pp for two; behind-the-scenes "Big Croc Feed" tour $79 per person • ☎ 08 8981 7522, ⓦ crocosauruscove.com.au

One of the city's biggest attractions, devoted to the region's toothy, scaly poster-boys, **Crocosaurus Cove** boasts some of the largest captive saltwater crocs in the world, housed in open-air tanks. The centrepiece is the "Cage of Death" experience, in which grinning tourists are lowered into croc enclosures inside a clear perspex box. The crocs themselves often need coaxing to move – not an altogether edifying spectacle. There are twice-daily feeding shows, and you'll get the chance to handle baby freshwater crocs.

The Esplanade

The leafy Bicentennial Park lawns along the **Esplanade** make for a pleasant stroll. You'll see panels of inlaid tiles along the walkway, each bearing a name, in recognition of two hundred "Remarkable Territorians". Those chosen range from drovers and dancers to cameleers and railwaymen, giving a taste of the Territory's storied past. Further along, cast your eyes down Daly Street: this is the road that becomes the Stuart Highway, and from here it's a cool 2722km run to Port Augusta in South Australia.

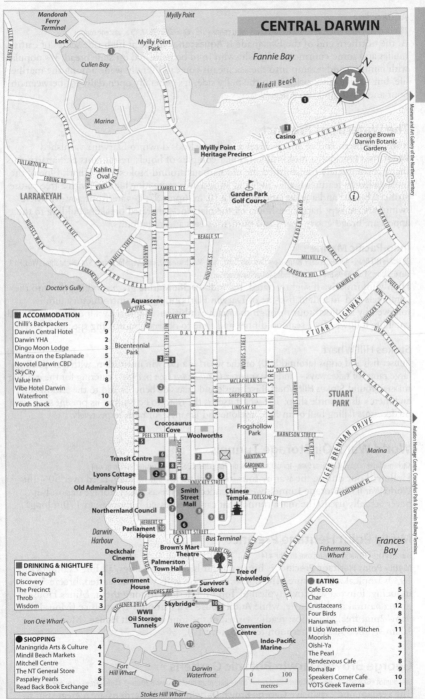

CENTRAL DARWIN

ACCOMMODATION

Chilli's Backpackers	7
Darwin Central Hotel	9
Darwin YHA	2
Dingo Moon Lodge	3
Mantra on the Esplanade	5
Novotel Darwin CBD	4
SkyCity	1
Value Inn	8
Vibe Hotel Darwin	
Waterfront	10
Youth Shack	6

DRINKING & NIGHTLIFE

The Cavenagh	4
Discovery	1
The Precinct	5
Throb	2
Wisdom	3

SHOPPING

Maningrida Arts & Culture	4
Mindil Beach Markets	1
Mitchell Centre	2
The NT General Store	3
Paspaley Pearls	6
Read Back Book Exchange	5

EATING

Cafe Eco	5
Char	6
Crustaceans	12
Four Birds	8
Hanuman	2
Il Lido Waterfront Kitchen	11
Moorish	4
Oishi-Ya	3
The Pearl	7
Rendezvous Cafe	8
Roma Bar	9
Speakers Corner Cafe	10
YOTS Greek Taverna	1

5

Aquascene

28 Doctors Gully Road · Tide-dependent feeding hours listed online · $15 · ☎ 08 8981 7837, ⓦ aquascene.com.au

At the northern end of the Esplanade is **Aquascene**, where at high tide scores of catfish, mullet and some enormous milkfish swim in to be hand-fed on stale bread. It's popular with families, and a ramp into the sea means you can literally wade among the marine life, but the entrance price is on the hefty side. It's generally open daily for between an hour and a half and three hours.

The Waterfront Precinct

At the southern end of Smith Street a walkway leads down to Darwin's varnished **Waterfront Precinct**, a multimillion-dollar complex of hotels, restaurants and apartments that has completely transformed the old harbour around Stokes Hill Wharf. One of the most welcome features is the croc- and stinger-free **recreation lagoon** (with a free-to-use artificial beach) and a **wave lagoon** (daily 10am–6pm; $7; ⓦ waterfront.gov.nt) where swimmers are kept happy for hours by the machine-generated breakers. Adding to the appeal are broad grassy lawns and numerous bars and restaurants.

Indo-Pacific Marine

29 Stokes Hill Road · April–Oct daily 10am–4pm (last tour 3pm); Nov–March variable, call ahead for times · $24 · Night shows Wed, Fri & Sun 6.30pm; $120 · ☎ 08 8981 1294, ⓦ indopacificmarine.com.au

Highly informative if slightly dated, the **Indo-Pacific Marine** gives good insight into the coral reefs and attendant fish-life of Darwin Harbour. A short introductory film is followed by a guided tour through the main exhibition. Night shows focus on nocturnal coral life followed by a seafood dinner and time to observe fluorescing species.

Stokes Hill Wharf

Sunset fish and chips (around $20) on the wharf is a Darwin institution, with a surprisingly large range of takeaways – and the smarter *Crustaceans* (see p.498) – catering for the evening masses around **Stokes Hill Wharf**. Live music and quayside benches add to the atmosphere, and there's also a bottle shop. The wharf itself is the third to be built in its present spot, its predecessors falling foul of an 1897 cyclone and Japanese air raids respectively.

World War II Oil Storage Tunnels

Kitchener Drive · Daily: May–Sept 9am–4pm; Oct–April 9am–1pm, closed Dec · $8 · ⓦ waterfront.nt.gov.au

Hollowed out during the war by four hundred men – all of them aged over 50 – the **World War II Oil Storage Tunnels** were intended to serve as a fuel storage depot, but never actually used. The main tunnel that can be accessed is more than 170m long.

Myilly Point Heritage Precinct

Burnett Place · ⓦ nationaltrustnt.com.au · Bus #14

Myilly Point Heritage Precinct is home to four historic buildings, all fine examples of 1930s tropical architecture. The houses are set on stilts with the slatted, breeze-inducing, louvred windows typical of Top End design. Among them, Mines House is now a natural health centre, while **Audit House** is a National Trust office (Mon–Fri 9am–2pm; free). The most readily visited of the four is **Burnett House** (Mon–Sat 10am–1pm; $5; Sun afternoon tea 3–5pm; $10).

George Brown Darwin Botanic Gardens

Geranium St · Gates daily 7am–7pm; orientation centre 8am–4pm; plant display house 8.30am–3.30pm · Free · ⓦ nt.gov.au

The verdant and expansive **George Brown Darwin Botanic Gardens** are a great spot to while away an hour or two wandering under shady palms and eucalypts and reading about indigenous uses for plants. Among other points of interest, the gardens also have a wooden Wesleyan church, the NT's oldest church building, which originally stood in the city centre and is now home to a café.

Museum and Art Gallery of the Northern Territory

19 Conacher St • Mon–Fri 9am–5pm, Sat & Sun 10am–5pm • Free • ☎ 08 8999 8264, ⓦ magnt.nt.gov.au • Bus #6

The NT's excellent showpiece museum features an absorbing Gallery of Indigenous Art, with burial poles from the Tiwi Islands and cross-hatch-style artworks from the Top End. Other highlights at the **Museum and Art Gallery of the Northern Territory** include the sobering Cyclone Tracy exhibition commemorating Darwin's tragic destruction on Christmas Eve 1974, and the hangar-like Maritime Gallery housing various historic craft including pearl luggers, Polynesian outriggers and dugout canoes. Elsewhere there are stuffed examples of everything that flies, swims, hops, skips or jumps in the Territory, including Sweetheart, a colossal stuffed 5.1m crocodile that was 50 years old and weighed 780kg when caught in 1979.

East Point Reserve

East Point Road • Open 24hr, no camping • Free

A 200-hectare recreational reserve on a spit of land some 5km north of the city centre, the **East Point Reserve** offers a swimming lake, playgrounds, bike lanes, barbecues and two hiking tracks (a 3km-return mangrove boardwalk and a 2.7km monsoon forest walk). It's home to around six hundred wallabies, best seen late in the day, and is also a splendid spot to observe the hues of Darwin's sunsets; if driving, watch out for the wildlife on the way back.

Darwin Military Museum

Alec Fong Lim Drive, East Point • Daily 9.30am–5pm • $18 • ☎ 08 8981 9702, ⓦ darwinmilitarymuseum.com.au

This engaging museum, formerly a wartime command post, has been made more absorbing by the 2012 opening of a multimillion-dollar Defence of Darwin exhibition, which features a special-effects-packed short film about the Japanese bombardment of the city during World War II. The war features heavily in the rest of the **Darwin Military Museum**, alongside Australia's role in other conflicts, like the Vietnam War. There is fascinating archival footage and displays of uniform and memorabilia, while in the grounds a collection of engines, vehicles and guns rusts away.

Fannie Bay Gaol

East Point Road • Daily 10am–3pm • Free • ☎ 08 8999 8290, ⓦ magnt.net.au • Bus #4 or #6

A working prison from 1883 to 1979, the bleakly atmospheric **Fannie Bay Gaol** showcases the near-undamaged features of a tropical, medium-security lock-up. Lengthy information panels add poignancy to the empty cells and buildings, one of which still contains a used gallows crossbar.

Australian Aviation Heritage Centre

557 Stuart Highway, 10km from the city centre • Daily 9am–5pm • $14 • ☎ 08 8947 2145, ⓦ darwinsairwar.com.au • Bus #5 or #8

In a hangar on the southeastern edge of the airport, the fascinating **Australian Aviation Heritage Centre** is dominated by the huge bulk of a B-52 bomber on loan from the US Air Force, along with an F-111 which saw combat in Vietnam and

5

many other aircraft, together describing the story of civil and military aviation in the region.

Crocodylus Park

815 McMillans Rd • Daily 9am–5pm; tours & croc feeding 10am, noon, 2pm & 4pm • $40 • ☎ 08 8922 4500, ⓦ crocodyluspark.com • Bus #5 or #9

Battling with Crocosaurus Cove for your croc dollar, out-of-town **Crocodylus Park** is worth visiting for a rather more considered look at these reptiles. The four-times-daily guided feeding tours are worth catching, particularly if you're with kids. There's a menagerie of other Aussie wildlife too, as well as some slightly incongruous big cats and South American primates.

Territory Wildlife Park

Cox Peninsula Rd • Daily 9am–5pm, last admission 4pm • $32 • ☎ 08 8988 7200, ⓦ www.territorywildlifepark.com.au

Fifty kilometres south of Darwin is the excellent, gimmick-free **Territory Wildlife Park**, where you can easily spend half a day wandering through a variety of Territorian habitats, including huge aviaries, nocturnal houses and walk-through aquariums. The entry fee includes free rides on the circulating train to different habitats, saving trudging along the 4km roadway in the sticky heat.

ARRIVAL AND DEPARTURE   DARWIN

Given the proximity of Indonesia, Darwin is the cheapest place from which to leave Australia. On the other hand, it's a long way from anywhere in the country – the bus journey from Townsville, in Queensland, lasts a gruelling 34 hours (and takes even longer going the other way); from Sydney, Melbourne or Perth, you're better off flying.

By plane Darwin International Airport (ⓦ darwinairport .com.au) is 13km northeast of the Central Business District (CBD); shuttle buses (☎ 08 8983 0577, ⓦ metrominibus .com.au; $18) meet international and domestic flights and drop passengers at major hotels and the Transit Centre behind 69 Mitchell St; a taxi (Darwin Radio Cars; ☎ 13 10 08) to town from the airport costs about $30 (slightly more at weekends). Flight Centre (Mon–Thurs 9am–5.30pm, Fri 9am–7pm, Sat 9am–5pm, Sun 10am–3pm; ☎ 1300 514 460, ⓦ flightcentre.com.au) in the Mitchell Centre can organize overseas flights and visits to Bali, Phuket and elsewhere.
Destinations Adelaide (3 daily; 3hr 35min); Alice Springs (3 daily; 2hr); Brisbane (5 daily; 4hr); Cairns (1–2 daily; 2hr 25min); Denpasar, Bali (2–3 daily); Dili, East Timor (1–2 daily); Kununurra (1 daily; 1hr); Manila, Philippines (4

weekly); Melbourne (3 daily; 4hr 10min); Perth (2–3 daily; 3hr 50min); Singapore (1–2 daily); Sydney (3–4 daily; 4hr 20min).
By train The famous *Ghan* (see box, p.534) arrives on Tuesdays at 5.30pm at the Darwin Passenger Rail Terminal 15km south of town.
Destinations Adelaide (Wed; 49hr 30min–74hr 50min); Alice Springs (Wed; 23hr 10min–24hr); Coober Pedy (Wed, May–Oct only; 47hr); Katherine (Wed; 3hr 40min).
By bus Greyhound buses (☎ 08 8981 8700, ⓦ greyhound .com.au) arrive and depart from the bus terminal on Harry Chan Avenue.
Destinations Alice Springs (1 daily; 21hr 35min); Broome (Sun–Fri; 23hr 45min); Jabiru (3 weekly; 3hr 45min); Katherine (2 daily; 3hr 50min); Kununurra (Sun–Fri; 9hr); Tennant Creek (1 daily; 14hr 10min).

GETTING AROUND

By bus The city's inexpensive bus service ($3 ticket valid for 3hr; $7 ticket valid all day; tickets can be bought when boarding or at main interchanges) takes you to most corners of Darwin. Services operate daily from around 6.30am to 10pm, with some routes running later on Friday and Saturday. The bus terminal (☎ 08 8936 4007) is on Harry Chan Ave, at the bottom of Cavenagh St, with a major interchange at Casuarina Shopping Centre in the suburbs. Full timetables and route maps are available at

the visitor centre.
By car Several local car rental outfits do battle around town, with prices starting from as little as $40 a day for an economy car, plus mileage: Britz 4WDs and campervans, 17 Bombing Rd (☎ 08 8981 2081, ⓦ britz.com.au); Europcar, 77 Cavenagh St (☎ 08 8941 0300, ⓦ europcar.com.au); Thrifty Rental Cars, 64 Stuart Hwy (☎ 08 8924 0000, ⓦ thrifty.com.au); Travellers Autobarn, 13 Daly St (☎ 08 8941 7700, ⓦ travellers-autobarn.com.au).

By scooter Given the heat and humidity you might be tempted to travel by scooter; you can rent them from The Scooter Shop at 9 Daly St from $70/day for a 50cc, $100 for a 300cc (☎ 08 8941 2434, ⓦ thescootershop.com.au).

By bike For cycle rental try The Scooter Shop (see above; $25/day). There's also the Spinway scheme (ⓦ spinwaynt. com.au), similar, though much smaller in scale, to the bike hire schemes in London and Paris. You just swipe your credit/debit card and collect a bike from one of several stations around Darwin, including beside the visitor centre ($11/hr, $28/4hr, $38/24hr).

By taxi Taxis work out at around $2 per kilometre but there are few cruising around: book one from Darwin Radio Taxis on ☎ 13 10 08.

INFORMATION

Tourist information Five minutes' walk from the Mitchell Street Transit Centre (Cnr Bennett & Smith sts) the helpful Tourism Top End visitor centre (Mon–Fri 8.30am–5pm, Sat & Sun 9am–3pm; ☎ 1300 138 886, ⓦ tourismtopend.com.au) has plenty of information on the city and the surrounding area.

Newspapers & magazines The free Info glossies, *This Week in Darwin* and *Destination Darwin and the Top End*, can be picked up around town and are handy for their maps, bus routes and tour times. For a more entertaining read have a flick through the daily *NT News* (ⓦ ntnews. com.au), the local tabloid, known for its often lurid stories.

Festivals The onset of the Dry season sees an upsurge in activity as the city shakes off the languor of the Wet. As well as the long-standing Royal Darwin Show (ⓦ darwinshow.com.au), which is part agricultural fair, part community knees-up, the city also plays host to theatre, cabaret, music, movies and workshops around the city for August's 18-day Darwin Festival (ⓦ darwinfestival.org.au). A month earlier, Territory Day on July 1 is marked by fireworks on Mindil Beach, also the setting for the famous and eccentric Beer Can Regatta (ⓦ beercanregatta.org.au) – wacky boat races in craft made from beer cans.

TOURS

CITY TOURS

Darwin Explorer ☎ 0416 140 903, ⓦ darwinexplorer .com.au. This hop-on-hop-off bus service takes in ten key sites around Darwin. Tickets ($40/60) are valid for 24/48 hours.

Darwin Walking Tours ☎ 08 8981 0227, ⓦ darwinwalkingtours.com. Take a "guided heritage tour" on foot, under the watch of an experienced local guide. Good for a historical overview. Daily 2hr tours; $50.

Duckabout Tours ☎ 1300 382 522, ⓦ duckabout.com. au. Amphibious vehicles that quickly cover the main sights before plunging into the harbour. Short tours last 1hr 15min; 2hr sunset tours also available ($38/$57).

Tour Tub ☎ 08 8985 6322, ⓦ tourtub.com.au. The Tour Tub minibus offers a 5hr tour taking in the city's main attractions (entry to several of which are included in the price; $110).

CRUISES

Boats depart from the waterfront quarter or Cullen Bay. Cruises can be booked through the operators below or at the visitor centre.

Cape Adieu ☎ 0439 893 939, ⓦ capeadieu.com.au. Sunset cruise departing from the waterfront quarter, including a seafood dinner (departs daily 5pm from April–Nov; 3hr; $99; cruise-only price $49).

Sea Darwin ☎ 1300 065 022, ⓦ seadarwin.com. Four different eco-cruises to choose from, including an 8hr voyage to watch turtles nesting (April–Sept; $250).

Spirit of Darwin ☎ 0417 381 977, ⓦ spiritofdarwin .com.au. A more economical option from Stokes Hill Wharf

with a licensed bar on board. There's a sunset cruise at 5.30pm ($65; $95 with dinner).

Streeter ☎ 0448 675 824, ⓦ streetercruises.com.au. Sunset boat tour setting sail from the waterfront quarter on a historic pearl lugger. BYO and licensed. Departs daily 5.20pm from April–Dec; 2hr 10min; $60.

FISHING

Fish Darwin ☎ 08 8985 5898, ⓦ fishdarwin.com.au. Locally owned operation with 4hr fishing trips for $140 per person, plus several longer options.

Helifish ☎ 0408 872 212, ⓦ helifish.com.au. Various heli-fishing trips and tours, the most popular of which is the full-day option from $1100 per person. Expect barra aplenty.

TOURS AROUND THE TOP END

Darwin is a great base for trips into the surrounding area. Kakadu is a must-do, but if you only have a day, Litchfield Park is nearer. Kakadu tour operators offer one- to five-day tours, including possible excursions into Arnhem Land (see p.510) or a return via Litchfield; the one-day tours are rushed. The tours themselves vary from backpacker jaunts to those aimed at more mature travellers.

AAT Kings ☎ 1300 228 546, ⓦ aatkings.com.au. Professionally run outings across the Top End, including various Kakadu itineraries and an Arnhem Land option, plus a Darwin city tour (from $95). Well suited to older visitors.

Adventure Tours ☎ 1300 654 604, ⓦ adventuretours .com.au. Offers a number of 2- and 3-day tours around Kakadu, Katherine and Litchfield with a maximum group

5

size of 16. A 3-day trip combing Litchfield and Kakadu costs from $570.

Experience the Wild ☎08 8932 7011, ⓦexperiencethewild.com.au. Runs birdwatching and 4WD nature tours (from $245) around Darwin and surrounds. The guides are passionate and know their stuff.

Kakadu Dreams ☎1800 813 266, ⓦkakadudreams .com.au. Fun, low-cost tours in packed 4WDs, aimed at a young crowd. Two-day Kakadu tours from $350 (plus park fees).

★ **Northern Territory Indigenous Tours** ☎1300 921 188, ⓦntitours.com.au. Luxury indigenous operator providing pricey but much recommended day, multiday and private charter options (from $249), with high-class food and accommodation. Also runs wet-season tours.

Original Jumping Crocodile Cruises ☎08 8988 8144, ⓦjumpingcrocodilecruises.com.au. There are numerous Adelaide River "jumping croc" cruises – this is indeed the original. The spectacle involves enticing wild saltwater crocs to surge out of the water to snap at bony offal on a string. The cruise costs $55 and departs daily at 9am, 10am, 11am, 1pm, 2pm & 3pm. Timetables can change from Nov–Feb.

Outback Float Plane Adventures ☎08 8981 4881, ⓦoutbackfloatplanes.com.au. If you're looking to splurge on a memorable day-tour, this company offers several floatplane and helicopter trips (from $795).

Top End Tandems ☎0417 190 140, ⓦtopendtandems .com.au. Tandem skydiving above the city and its beaches, with 8000ft dives from $380 per person and 12,000ft dives from $420 per person.

ACCOMMODATION

Rates in the town's apartments and more expensive hotels can drop by half during the Wet (Oct–April). Prices below are for high season (May–Sept).

HOTELS AND APARTMENTS

Most accommodation is in the city centre, with a stack of properties along the Esplanade offering sea views. If you're looking to self-cater, you'll find some first-rate serviced apartments. Note: rooms can be notoriously difficult to find if your stay coincides with big cultural or sporting events.

Darwin Central Hotel 21 Knuckey St ☎08 8944 9000, ⓦdarwincentral.com.au; map p.491. With a Knuckey Street location that's hard to beat, this is a good-value, upper-mid-range option. En suites are well equipped and comfortable, though rather unimaginatively decorated. Facilities are limited: there's a small plunge pool, a restaurant and not a great deal else. Good off-season/internet rates. **$145**

Mantra on the Esplanade 88 The Esplanade ☎08 8943 4333, ⓦmantra.com.au; map p.491. Attracting more of a holiday clientele than the other Mantra property in Darwin, this is a clean, classy hotel with a pool and a handy location directly in front of the Transit Centre. **$229**

Novotel Darwin CBD 100 The Esplanade ☎08 8941 0755, ⓦnovotel.com; map p.491. In an enviable seafront location, this well-run hotel has a soaring atrium filled with vines and palms, and a range of spacious, very comfortable en suites (those at the front on the top floors have great views). Facilities include a good restaurant, bar and an outdoor pool; guests can also use a nearby gym for free. **$185**

SkyCity Gilruth Ave, The Gardens ☎08 8943 8888, ⓦskycitydarwin.com.au; map p.491; bus #4. Five-star hotel, known primarily for its casino and location adjoining Mindil Beach Markets. It has a newer wing of resort-style guestrooms; other plus points are beachfront gardens, an infinity pool and one of the city's top restaurants, *Evoo*. **$199**

Vibe Hotel Darwin Waterfront 7 Kitchener Drive

☎08 8982 9998, ⓦtfehotels.com; map p.491. Boasting a great location in the Waterfront Precinct, this top-notch hotel has swish, modern en suites, and a wide range of facilities including an indoor pool, gym, restaurant and bar. Good online deals. **$189**

BUDGET ACCOMMODATION

With a few exceptions, Darwin's hostels are not particularly high quality. Most are found along Mitchell Street, doubling up as poolside bars and travel agencies. The one-time practice of only turning on air conditioning at night has largely stopped, but it's still worth checking at time of booking. Most charge for wi-fi.

Chilli's Backpackers 69A Mitchell St ☎08 8941 9722, ⓦchillis.com; map p.491. Popular, though slightly institutional, backpacker joint with a high-roofed deck looking out over Mitchell Street and, out back, a deck with two whirlpool jacuzzis (the water's cool, mercifully). There's a free basic breakfast, and guests can also use facilities at adjacent property *Youth Shack* (see opposite). Dorms **$30**, doubles **$90**

★ **Darwin YHA** 97 Mitchell St ☎08 8981 5385, ⓦyha .com.au; map p.491. Located in a converted motel on a quieter stretch of Mitchell Street, Darwin's YHA is clean, well-run and more peaceful than some of its competitors. Accommodation is in four- to six-bed dorms (single-sex and mixed available) and private rooms with en suites. There's a pool, kitchen and range of free events, including yoga classes and BBQs. Dorms **$34**, doubles **$128.50**

Dingo Moon Lodge 88 Mitchell St ☎08 8941 3444, ⓦdingomoonlodge.com; map p.491. An increasingly popular alternative to the big boys farther along Mitchell St. It's quiet, professionally run and has an extensive breakfast included in the price. There's free laundry too, as well as the obligatory swimming pool. Four-, six- and eight-bed dorms and private rooms are available. Dorms $34.50, doubles $102.50

Value Inn 50 Mitchell St ☎08 8981 4733, ⓦvalueinn .com.au; map p.491. No-frills motel with a plum – though rather noisy – location on Mitchell Street. Rooms are cramped, but have a/c, fridges and a double and a single bed – groups of up to three are accepted. En-suite rooms are also available. Guests have access to the nearby *Melaleuca* hostel's pools and bar areas. $105

Youth Shack 69 Mitchell St ☎1300 793 302, ⓦyouthshack.com.au; map p.491. Sister hostel to *Chilli's* (see p.491), *Youth Shack* draws a young, geed-up party crowd with its pumping music and poolside *Batji Bar*, which runs themed nights and, in high season, regular barbecues. The rooms and dorms, however, are poky, and you need to pay a deposit to use the kitchen equipment. There's a tour desk, and the notice board is useful for secondhand vehicles. It's also home to Job Shack (☎08 8923 9774), a backpacker employment agency. Dorms $30, doubles $90

CAMPING AND CARAVAN PARKS

The following are all 7–18km from the city centre. Buses #5 and #8 run here from the central bus terminal.

Darwin FreeSpirit Resort 901 Stuart Hwy ☎08 8935 0888, ⓦdarwinfreespiritresort.com.au; map p.488. Relaxed, family-friendly resort with a wide range of cabins, villas and campsites with shade and privacy. Facilities include three pools, playground and restaurants. Standard cabins $99, poolside villas $170, un/powered sites $45/52

Discovery Holiday Park 11 Farrell Crescent, Winnellie ☎08 8984 3330, ⓦdiscoveryholidayparks.com.au; map p.488. Formerly known as *Shady Glen*, this park's rooms, cabins and campsites draw mixed reviews, but it is in a convenient location, a 10min drive from the city centre. Doubles $148, cabins $170, powered sites $49

Hidden Valley Caravan Park 25 Hidden Valley Rd, Berrimah ☎08 8984 2888, ⓦhiddenvalleytouristpark .com.au; map p.488. Set in tropical gardens, this tidy caravan park has a pool, café and tour desk, and offers cabins, various types of villa and spacious if rather pricey camping sites. Cabins $120, family villas $195, powered sites $50

EATING

Darwin has a surprisingly sophisticated restaurant scene, with a particularly good range of Asian – most notably Southeast Asian – joints. Indeed, *laksa* (a tasty noodle soup) is arguably the city's signature dish. Also look out for seafood, particularly **barramundi**, a sweet-tasting fighting fish which is near inescapable on the city's menus. The Darwin Foodies (ⓦdarwinfoodies. com) blog is a good place to find the latest restaurant reviews. Local favourites can often fill up, so try to book ahead.

CITY CENTRE AND MINDIL BEACH AREA

Café Eco 12 Knuckey St ☎04 7716 7530, ⓦfacebook .com/cafeecodarwin; map p.491. If you've overindulged the night before, this is the spot to recover the morning after, with an extensive range of juices, smoothies and protein shakes ($6–9), plus salads, wraps and – slightly out of keeping with the healthy-eating ethos – burgers. Mon–Fri 6am–3.30pm, Sat 7.30am–4pm, Sun 8am–3pm.

Char Cnr Esplanade & Knuckey St ☎08 8981 4544, ⓦchardarwin.com.au; map p.491. Occupying the handsome prewar architecture of Admiralty House, this classy bar and restaurant has alfresco seating out the front and mod-Oz cuisine on the menu. It's mainly known for its

steaks ($49–68) but also serves up strong seafood dishes such as seared NT barra with a saffron veloute ($42). Sat–Tues 6–11pm, Wed–Fri noon–11pm.

Cornucopia Museum & Art Gallery of the NT, 19 Conacher St ☎08 8941 9009, ⓦcornucopiacafe .com.au; map p.488; bus #6. Housed within the NT's showpiece museum, this café is well worth factoring into a visit. There's a beautiful terrace with a sea view. Alongside quality burgers and seafood, there's an all-day breakfast menu with items like eggs Benedict ($18) and croque madame ($16). Mon–Fri 9am–5pm, Sat–Sun 8am–5pm.

★**Four Birds** 2 Star Village, 32 Smith St ☎04 0872 9708, ⓦbit.ly/fourbirds; map p.491. Charming little café

AUSTRALIA'S GATEWAY TO ASIA

Closer to Indonesia than Sydney, Darwin is known as **Australia's gateway to Asia**, with extensive trade links and an incredibly diverse population featuring over 60 different nationalities. In recent years the city's Southeast Asian communities, in particular, have stamped a real mark on the eating-out scene to such an extent that *laksa* – a tasty pan-Southeast Asian noodle soup – has become a fixture in cafés, restaurants and streetfood stalls. The best places to sample food from Southeast Asia – and beyond – are at the lively Mindil Beach (see p.499) and Parap Village (see p.500) markets, where you can find everything from authentic Vietnamese *pho* to crocodile tail sushi.

5

with a good line in coffee ($3.50–4.50) and breakfast, brunch and lunch options, which range from the healthy – like "smashed" avocado on sourdough toast– to the decadent – like the "breakfast burgers". If you've got a sweet tooth, try the Nutella *affogato*. Mon–Fri 7am–3pm, Sat 8am–2pm.

★**Hanuman** 93 Mitchell St ☎08 8941 3500, ⓦhanuman.com.au; map p.491. Understandably popular by virtue of its delicious Indian, Nyonya and Thai dishes. The signature poached Hanuman oysters ($19.50) are a must – other recommended options are the Goan prawn curry ($36) and the butter chicken ($29), a house speciality. If you can't get a table, note that they offer a takeaway service. Mon–Fri noon–2.30pm & 6–10pm, Sat & Sun 6–10pm.

Moorish 37 Knuckey St ☎08 8981 0010, ⓦmoorishcafe.com.au; map p.491. The Spanish and North African-inspired tapas at this award-winning restaurant are great – try the Berber-spiced kangaroo with tomato jam ($8.50). For something more substantial, choose the tagine of the day ($31.50) or the dukkah-crusted fillet of beef ($44.50). Good wine list, too. Tues–Fri 10am–2.30pm & 6–10pm, Sat 9am–10pm.

Oishi-Ya Mitchell Centre (street-facing) ☎08 8942 2906; map p.491. An unassuming Japanese restaurant pulling in a steady stream of patrons thanks to a well-priced menu. Try a bento box ($17.50–21.50) or, if the NT's temperatures aren't quite extreme enough for your tastes, a spicy ramen ($14.90–15.90). Takeaway available. Daily 11.30am–2am.

The Pearl Victoria Arcade, 27 Smith St ☎04 3582 1648, ⓦthepearl.com.au; map p.491. This award-winning bistro, tucked away in the Victoria Arcade, is one of the best places to eat in town, with an ever-changing menu (6-course fixed menu $70; mains $28–40) that draws inspiration from around the world. It's also good for an afternoon coffee or a pre-dinner cocktail. Tues–Thurs 3pm–midnight, Fri 8am–midnight, Sat 8.30am–midnight, Sun 8.30am–2pm.

Rendezvous Cafe 6 Star Village, 32 Smith St ☎08 8981 9231, ⓦrendezvouscafedarwin.com.au; map p.491. At first glance this canteen seems eminently missable: cramped wooden tables covered with plastic crowd a plain, rather stark dining room. But the Malaysian-Thai food here is the real deal. *Laksa* ($12–15) is the house speciality – try the barbecued pork, and ask for extra chilli to cut through the creamy coconut milk – but the *tom yum* soup, *gado gado* (mixed vegetables in a peanut sauce) and red, yellow, green and *rendang* curries are all worth a look too. Mon, Tues & Sat 10.30am–2.30pm, Wed–Fri 10.30am–2.30pm & 5–9pm.

Roma Bar 9–11 Cavenagh St ☎08 8981 6729, ⓦromabar.com.au; map p.491. A favourite meeting spot for Darwin caffeine addicts since 1973. There's proper coffee ($4–5.50) and a good all-day breakfast menu – try the coconut bread with lemon curd ($10.50). The takeaway "plane boxes" are great if you've got a long journey coming up. Mon–Fri 7am–3pm, Sat 8am–2pm, Sun 8am–1pm.

Speakers Corner Café Parliament House ☎08 8946 1439, ⓦkarensheldoncatering.com; map p.491. Home to arguably the best terrace in town – namely Parliament House's manicured back lawn, with a sweeping view over Port Darwin – the café stocks a more-than-passable range of cakes, sandwiches and mains ($12–18). Mon–Fri 7.30am–4pm.

THE WATERFRONT AREA

Crustaceans Stokes Hill Wharf ☎08 8981 8658, ⓦcrustaceans.net.au; map p.491. *Crustaceans* has the classiest menu on Stokes Hill Wharf, offering all-Aussie seafood such as garlic prawns ($14.90) and grilled Moreton Bay bugs ($38.90). It's located at the far end of the wharf. Daily 5.30pm–late.

Il Lido Waterfront Kitchen Wharf One, Darwin Waterfront ☎08 8941 0900, ⓦillidodarwin.com.au; map p.491. Sleekly designed mod-Oz restaurant with lovely views over the harbour. Wood-fired pizzas (from $25) are the order of the day here: if you are in a group – or just have a huge appetite – go for the metre-long one. Sun–Thurs noon–10pm, Fri–Sat noon–2am.

CULLEN BAY MARINA AND EAST POINT RESERVE

Pee Wee's at the Point 5775 Alec Fong Lim Drive ☎08 8981 6868, ⓦpeewees.com.au; map p.488. Despite the playful name, Pee Wee's is a serious restaurant, regularly named the best in Darwin. While the food is excellent – think coconut-crusted crocodile tail, hot and sour pork cheek and venison striploin steak – prices are steep (mains $41–68). The setting, inside the East Point Nature Reserve, is lovely. Daily 5.30pm–late.

YOTS Greek Taverna 54 Marina Blvd ☎08 8981 4433, ⓦwww.yots.com.au; map p.491; bus #14. This sizeable restaurant overlooking the marina does great home-style Greek food. Try the souvlaki lamb or chicken skewers ($33) or get a blast of the ocean with the prawns *saganaki* ($34.50). There's a large terrace. May–Sept Tues–Sun 11am–11pm; Oct–April Tues–Sun 3–11pm.

PARAP

Laneway Specialty Coffee 4/1 Vickers St ☎08 8941 4511, ⓦfacebook.com/lanewayspecialtycoffee; map p.488. Located in the fast-developing "Parap Village", this hip café serves top-notch coffee ($4–5), breakfast, brunches and lunches: the burgers, sourdough bread and doughnuts are among the highlights. Mon–Fri 7am–4pm, Sat 7.30am–4pm, Sun 8am–2.30pm.

DRINKING AND NIGHTLIFE

Darwin's alcohol consumption is notoriously high and weekends get lively. The hub is **Mitchell Street**, where a cluster of bars compete for trade with happy hours, big-screen sport and live music and DJs. For a more sedate evening head to the Waterfront Quarter or catch a movie under the stars (see below). There's no mass-market NT-brewed beer, but for the ultimate hangover cure, try a Pauls Iced Coffee (which is only sold in the Territory).

BARS AND PUBS

The Cavenagh Cavenagh St ☎08 8941 6383, ⓦthecavenagh.com; map p.491. Affectionately known as "the Cav", this bar-restaurant has a large terrace and a convivial atmosphere. Its Saturday evening Brazilian BBQ is consistently popular. *The Cav* is technically a hotel too, although rooms are invariably taken up by locally contracted workers. Daily 6.30am–late.

Darwin Ski Club Conacher St, Fannie Bay ☎08 8981 6630, ⓦdarwinskiclub.com.au; map p.488; bus #6. In-the-know locals head out to this amicable beachside water-ski club opposite the NT Museum – it's great at sunset and boasts a large outdoor screen for big sporting events. Tourists are welcome (you can sign in on arrival) and there's live music every Fri & Sun. Daily noon–late.

★**The Precinct** 7 Kitchener Drive, Darwin Waterfront ☎08 8941 9000, ⓦtheprecincttavern.com.au; map p.491. The big draw here is the range of 44 draft beers and ciders, the vast majority of them Australian. If you're stuck for choice, try the four-drink tasting tray ($12). Sun–Thurs 10am–late, Fri–Sat 10am–2am.

Wisdom 48 Mitchell St ☎08 8941 4866, ⓦwisdombar.com.au; map p.491. Among the best on Mitchell St, with a pleasant beer garden set under a shady tree and live music every night. There are some fifty beers to sample – try them all and qualify for a "Wall of Wisdom" lifetime ten-percent discount. Decent pub grub too, with plenty of nightly offers, plus a $12.50 special lunch menu. Daily 9am–2am.

CLUBS

Discovery 89 Mitchell St ☎08 8942 3300, ⓦdiscoverydarwin.com.au; map p.491. On Saturday nights it can seem as if the whole of Darwin is in *Discovery*. There are three floors, seven bars and a welter of musical styles (though all tend towards the commercial). Fri 10pm–4am, Sat 9pm–4am.

Throb Level 1, 64 Smith St ☎08 8942 3435, ⓦthrobnightclub.com.au; map p.491. Darwin's pre-eminent gay club, *Throb* has nightly DJs, drag queens and regular theme nights. Check the Facebook page (ⓦfacebook.com/throbnightclub) to see what's on when you're in town. Fri & Sat 11pm–4am.

ENTERTAINMENT

To find out what's on, check out the excellent monthly *Off the Leash* (ⓦofftheleash.net.au) magazine.

Birch Carroll & Coyle Cinema (BCC) Cnr Mitchell & Briggs sts ☎08 8981 5999, ⓦeventcinemas.com.au; map p.491. Opposite the Entertainment Centre, this multi-screen cinema shows all the latest big releases. Tickets $20. Daily 10.30am–midnight.

Darwin Entertainment Centre 93 Mitchell St ☎08 8980 3333, ⓦyourcentre.com.au; map p.491. Has a full cultural programme, from touring pop stars and string quartets to theatre, comedy, musicals, jazz and blues.

Deckchair Cinema Cnr Esplanade below Parliament House ⓦdeckchaircinema.com.au; map p.491. The open-air Deckchair Cinema shows a mix of home-grown, art-house and cult classic movies. Snacks and drinks, including wine and beer, are all available. Films start at 7.30pm. Tickets $16. Closed Dec–March.

SHOPPING

Casuarina Square 247 Trower Road ☎08 8920 2345, ⓦcasuarinasquare.com.au; map p.488; bus #4 or #10 (35min). A large-scale shopping centre in the suburbs 10km north of the centre. Offers over two hundred retailers, cafés, restaurants and a 3D cinema. Mon–Thurs 9am–5.30pm, Fri 9am–9pm, Sat 9am–5pm, Sun 10am–3pm.

Maningrida Arts & Culture 1/32 Mitchell St ☎08 8981 4122, ⓦmaningrida.com; map p.491. A great option for those in search of indigenous art, this smart Aboriginal-owned store showcases work from an Arnhem Land community. Mon–Fri 9am–2pm, Sat 9am–1pm.

Mindil Beach Markets ☎08 8981 3454, ⓦmindil.com.au; map p.491; 3km walk from town or a short bus journey (#4 or #6) from the centre. This well-known market attracts locals who unpack their eskies and fold-up furniture and settle in on the sand for the sunset. There are sizzling food stands, mostly Asian, while stalls sell handicrafts and Aboriginal art, and performers add to the atmosphere. The Thursday market is larger than Sunday's. Thurs 5–10pm, Sun 4–9pm (later April–Oct).

Mitchell Centre 55–59 Mitchell St ☎08 8981 5688, ⓦmitchellcentre.com.au; map p.491. The most central shopping centre, with a large branch of Coles (open earlier

5

and later than rest of centre, daily 6am–10pm), a pharmacy, mobile phone stores and a couple of bakeries and cafés. Mon–Thurs 9am–6pm, Fri 9am–8pm, Sat 9am–4pm, Sun 10am–3pm.

Nightcliff Markets Pavonia Way, Nightcliff ☎ 0414 368 773, ⊛ nightcliffmarkets.com.au; map p.488; bus #4. Ideal for a Sunday morning mooch, with brunch, coffee and smoothie stalls alongside arts and crafts stands. There's usually live music too. Sun 6am–2pm year-round.

The NT General Store 42 Cavenagh St ☎ 08 8981 8242, ⊛ thentgeneralstore.com.au; map p.491. Has everything you need for going out into the bush, from a new pair of boots to mosquito nets, eskies and swags. Mon–Wed 8.30am–5.30pm, Thurs & Fri 8.30am–6pm, Sat 8.30am–1pm.

Parap Village Markets Around Parap Shopping Village on Parap Rd ☎ 08 8942 0805, ⊛ parapvillage.com.au;

map p.488; bus #6. Expect Asian food stalls, crafts, jewellery, vintage and handmade clothes and knick-knacks. It's been running here on Saturdays since the early 1980s, and remains good for a blast of Territory atmosphere. Free shuttle buses (hourly 7.30–11.30am) run to and from the Transit Centre. Sat 8am–2pm year-round.

Paspaley Pearls 27 Smith St Mall ☎ 08 8930 4500, ⊛ paspaley.com; map p.491. Darwin's historical association with South Sea pearling makes it the base of Paspaley, Australia's biggest pearling company, whose suitably swish boutique sells necklaces, rings and other adornments. Mon–Fri 9.30am–5pm, Sat 10am–3pm, Sun 10am–1pm.

Read Back Book Exchange 32 Smith St Mall ☎ 08 8981 8885; map p.491. A good bet for secondhand paperback thrillers and Outback literature. It also stocks some Asian travel guidebooks. Mon–Fri 9am–5pm, Sat–Sun 10am–2pm.

DIRECTORY

Banks The major banks are in or near Smith St Mall (many are clustered on Smith St close to Woolworths) and have 24hr ATMs.

Consulate Indonesia, 20 Harry Chan Ave (Mon–Fri 9am–1pm & 2–4.30pm; ☎ 08 8943 0200, ⊛ darwin. kemlu.go.id).

Hospital Royal Darwin Hospital, 105 Rocklands Dr, Casuarina (☎ 08 8922 8888, ⊛ health.nt.gov.au).

Internet access Free wi-fi and terminals are available at the NT Library within Parliament House (Mon–Fri 10am–5pm, Sat & Sun 1–5pm); there's also free wi-fi in Smith St Mall and on some buses. Otherwise all hostels

---

BUYING AND PLAYING A DIDGERIDOO

Authentic didges are created from termite-hollowed branches of stringybark, woollybark and bloodwood trees that are indigenous from the Gulf to the Kimberley. They're most commonly associated with Arnhem Land, where they were introduced between 1500 and 2000 years ago and are properly called *yidaka* or *molo* by the Yolngu people of that region. "**Didgeridoo**" is an Anglicized name relating to the sound produced.

Tiny bamboo and even painted pocket didges have found their way onto the market, but a real didge is a natural tube of wood with a rough interior. Painted versions haven't necessarily got any symbolic meaning; plain ones can look less tacky and are less expensive. Branches being what they are, every didge is different, but if you're considering playing it rather than hanging it over the fireplace, aim for one around 1.3m in length with a 30–40mm diameter mouthpiece. The bend doesn't affect the sound, but the length, tapering and wall thickness (ideally between 5mm and 10mm) do. Avoid cumbersome, thick-walled items that get in the way of your face and sound flat. For authentic didges visit the workshop run by Richard Williams (⊛ 21firstst.com), based at *Coco's* in Katherine (see p.518). Sounds of Starlight in Alice Springs (see p.537) also has an extensive range.

The key to making the right sound is to hum while letting your pressed lips flap, or vibrate, with the right pressure behind them – it's easier using the side of your mouth. The tricky bit – beyond the ability of most beginners – is to master circular breathing; this entails refilling your lungs through your nose while maintaining the sound from your lips with air squeezed from your cheeks. A good way to get your head round this concept is to blow or "squirt" bubbles into a glass of water with a straw, while simultaneously inhaling through the nose. Most shops that sell didges also have CDs and "how to" booklets.

Some Aboriginal communities forbid **women** to play the didge – as actress Nicole Kidman found out after she played one on German television to promote the film *Australia*. Besides being criticized for cultural insensitivity, Kidman was later informed that some Aboriginal groups believe that playing it makes women infertile.

offer paid-for access, usually through Global Gossip (24hr wi-fi cards $5).

Permits for Aboriginal Land Northern Land Council, 45 Mitchell St (Mon–Fri 8am–4.50pm; ☎ 08 8920 5100, ⊛ nlc.org.au).

Pharmacy Pharmasave Mitchell Centre Pharmacy, Shop 4 Mitchell Centre (Mon–Fri 8.30am–6pm, Sat 9am–5pm, Sun 10am–3pm; ☎ 08 8981 4442).

Police 55 Mitchell St, entrance on Knuckey St (open 24hr; ☎ 08 8901 0208, ☎ 13 14 44 for police assistance, ☎ 000 for emergencies).

Post office 48 Cavenagh St, cnr Edmunds St (Mon–Fri 9am–5pm, Sat 9am–12.30pm; poste restante Mon–Fri only).

Swimming Apart from the wave and swimming lagoon at the Waterfront, the most central choice is the 50m pool at Ross Smith Ave, Parap (Mon–Fri 6am–7.30pm, Sat 8am–6pm, Sun 10am–6pm; ☎ 08 8981 2662; bus #4 or #10 from the city centre). It's chilled in the wet season. Or try Lake Alexander at East Point.

Vaccinations If you're travelling on to Southeast Asia and need vaccinations, try the Cavenagh Medical Centre, 50 Woods St (☎ 08 8981 8566, ⊛ cavmed.com.au).

The Tiwi Islands

Bathurst and Melville islands, 80km north of Darwin, are known as the **Tiwi Islands**, home to the Tiwi Aborigines, who are famous for their unique arts and crafts and a love of Aussie Rules football. The Tiwi had limited contact with Aboriginal mainland tribes until the nineteenth century and speak their own language. Tiwi hostility towards intruders doubtless hastened the failure of **Fort Dundas** on Melville Island, Britain's first north Australian outpost, which survived for just five years until 1829. The Tiwi word for white men, *murantani* or "hot, red face", probably originates from this time. In 1912 a Catholic mission was established in Nguiu on Bathurst, which forms the focal point for most visits.

ARRIVAL AND INFORMATION   THE TIWI ISLANDS

By ferry A Sealink ferry service (☎ 1300 130 679, ⊛ sealinknt.com.au) runs between Darwin's Cullen Bay and Wurramiyanga on Bathurst Island (April–Dec 16 Thurs & Fri 8am, returns 5.45pm; $105 return). Voyages take approximately 2hr. Further services are laid on specifically for sports fans keen to attend Tiwi Bombers (Aussie Rules) games on the island – the Sealink website gives full details.

Tours Sealink also runs walking tours ($335 including ferry tickets), which feature a local guide, museum visit, art workshop and lunch. AAT Kings (see p.495) runs similar, though less comprehensive minibus tours ($285, including ferry tickets; $569 with flights, rather than a ferry crossing).

Permits If you're travelling independently, you'll need a visitor permit (free), which are available online from the Tiwi Land Council (⊛ permits.tiwilandcouncil.com).

ACCOMMODATION

Camping Unless you want to stay at one of the eye-wateringly expensive sport-fishing lodges (for example ⊛ tiwiadventures.com.au), your only option is to camp at one of two basic sites – Cape Point and Robertson Creek

– both on Melville Island ($20pp; ☎ 08 8970 9397, ⊛ permits.tiwilandcouncil.com). However, they are difficult to reach without your own transport, and are predominantly used by fishing enthusiasts on organized trips.

The Arnhem Highway

The **Arnhem Highway**, which runs east to Kakadu, parts company with the main southbound Stuart Highway 25km south of Darwin. About 5km along the Arnhem Highway you'll pass Humpty Doo, a small mango-growing community, home to a popular Outback-style pub.

Fogg Dam Conservation Reserve

Open all year, the lush **Fogg Dam Conservation Reserve** is part of the Adelaide River catchment – the dam itself is a legacy of a postwar attempt at rice growing. Driving across the barrage you'll quickly spot jacanas, egrets and geese, and possibly one of the countless pythons that feed on the water rats, goannas and wallabies. It is the first bit of wetland on the arid drive out of Darwin, and all the more pleasant if you do the 2.2km-return Woodlands-to-Waterlily Walk along a boardwalk through the mangrove

5

forests fringing the lagoon. Across the dam wall there are wonderful views from the Pandanus Lookout (2.5km return). Don't leave the boardwalks and stay clear of the water's edge, as there are saltwater crocs here.

Window on the Wetlands Visitor Centre
Just off the Arnhem Highway • Daily 8am–7pm • Free

Looming above the Arnhem Highway is the distinctive observation platform of the **Windows on the Wetlands Visitors Centre**, which overlooks the Adelaide River flood plain from the top of Beatrice Hill. To the local indigenous Limilngan-Wulna people, the hill represents "turtle dreaming". On the top floor are interactive displays describing the surrounding ecology and seasons, as well as binoculars to admire the rich birdlife. During the Dry there are nature talks twice daily on Saturday and Sunday.

Mary River National Park

Mary River's attractions aren't as spectacular as Kakadu's, but the national park offers a chance to explore Australia's largest wetland expanse and get as close as you dare to huge crocs. Rod Ansell, the real-life inspiration for Paul Hogan's "**Crocodile Dundee**", ran a cattle station here before meeting a tragic end following a drug-induced psychotic episode.

Experienced off-road drivers with a 4WD can try the 32km **Wildman Track** (dry season only), a bumpy drive along a little-used trail amid hopping marsupials, flocks of birds and crocs cruising among the lilies at Connellan Lagoon.

ARRIVAL AND INFORMATION   MARY RIVER NATIONAL PARK

By car The park is 150km east of Darwin, down a turn-off clearly marked along the Arnhem Highway. The area is best negotiated in a 4WD – many of its driving tracks are unsealed, and from Oct–April flooding can lead to road closures. There's no public transport.

Information Before leaving Darwin, pick up an up-to-date copy of the park factsheet from the visitor centre or download it from ⓦ nt.gov.au. It gives details of a few short walks, as well as camping and driving options.

ACCOMMODATION

There are basic camping areas available in the park at **Couzens Lookout**, great for sunset viewing, and further north at **Shady Camp**, a popular fishing spot.

Mary River Wilderness Retreat Arnhem Hwy ⊕08 8978 8877, ⓦ maryriverretreat.com.au. Only 110km from Darwin with a location on the Arnhem Highway, this 900-acre park gives the prime opportunity to enjoy the Mary River's birdlife and billabongs. It has a small pool and various categories of bungalow, as well as a campsite. Pool bungalows **$240**, bush bungalows **$160**, un/powered sites **$24/38**
Point Stuart Wilderness Lodge Off Point Stuart Rd ⊕08 8978 8914, ⓦ pointstuart.com.au. Only reachable via a 7km unsealed road, this friendly retreat offers a mix of

lodge-style and more standard rooms, plus safari tents and caravan sites. Staff can arrange fishing safaris and wetland cruises. Powered sites per person **$17.50**, tents per person **$25**, doubles **$130**, lodge rooms **$195**
Wildman Wilderness Lodgev Off Point Stuart Rd ⊕08 8978 8955, ⓦ wildmanwildernesslodge.com.au. Small-scale and luxurious, this is one of the Top End's most memorable places to stay. It has picked up a number of awards thanks to an ecofriendly approach, swish safari tents and cabins, and excellent private tours. Cabins **$769**, safari tents **$615**

Kakadu National Park

Some 150km east of Darwin lies **KAKADU NATIONAL PARK**, one of the most spectacular and varied wilderness areas in Australia, and World Heritage-listed for both its natural and cultural riches. The area's traditional owners are the Bininj and the Mungguy peoples, who jointly manage the park with the Australian government.

Covering more than 20,000 square kilometres, Kakadu is a challenging place to appreciate in a short visit; aim to allow a minimum of **three days**, and consider renting a 4WD or joining a 4WD tour. Try also to factor in a river cruise to get to more remote areas. The **dry season months** are the most popular times to visit, with little or no rain, acceptable humidity and temperatures, and conspicuous wildlife. Towards the end of the Dry, birdlife congregates around the shrinking waterholes, while November's rising temperatures and epic electrical storms herald the onset of the Wet. To visit Kakadu during the **Wet**, when the area gets up to 1600mm of torrential rainfall between December and March, or the early Dry is, many argue, to see it at its best. While some major sights are inaccessible and the wildlife dispersed, the waterfalls are in full flow and the land possesses a verdant splendour.

You could easily spend a week visiting all the spots detailed below, ideally followed by a return visit six months later to observe the seasonal changes. All the places below are reached off either the Arnhem or Kakadu highways. Most roads are accessible to 2WDs, except where indicated; 4WD tracks are closed during the Wet when even the highways can be underwater at times.

Jabiru

JABIRU was originally built to serve Kakadu's uranium-mining leases before the park was established. The small town is now populated by mineworkers, park employees and Aboriginal organizations and, apart from **accommodation**, offers a range of **services** to tourists (see p.507). You'll also find a 50-metre swimming pool (June–Sept daily noon–6.30pm, Oct–May Mon, Wed & Fri noon–6.30pm, Tues & Thurs 6–8am & noon–6.30pm, Sat 9am–6.30pm; $5), the only year-round safe public swimming spot in Kakadu.

Ubirr

43km north of Jabiru • Dry season 8.30am–sunset; Wet season 2pm–sunset

Ubirr is a site renowned for its ancient **rock art**. A 1km circular walking track takes you by five impressive rock galleries that illustrate the rich food resources of the wetlands. Fish, mussels, lizards, marsupials and the now-extinct Tasmanian tiger (thylacine) are depicted, as well as stick-like Mimi spirits, the first Creation Ancestors to be painted on

---

KAKADU'S WILDLIFE

Kakadu encompass a huge range of **habitats**, from sandstone escarpments topped with heathland to savannah woodlands, wetlands and tidal mangroves, all changing throughout the seasons. Within these habitats an extraordinary diversity of **wildlife** thrives, including 2000 different plants, more than 10,000 species of insect, 68 mammals and 120 different reptiles, including thousands of crocodiles (the park's main watercourse, the **South Alligator River**, was misnamed after the prolific croc population on its banks). You'll also find a third of Australia's bird species within Kakadu, including the elegant jabiru (black-necked stork), the similarly large brolga, with its curious courting dance, and white-breasted sea eagles, as well as galahs and magpie geese by the thousand. Mammals include kangaroos, wallabies, wallaroos, 26 species of bat and dingoes.

With so many interdependent ecosystems, maintaining the park's natural balance is a full-time job. **Burning off** has long been recognized as a technique of land management by Aborigines who have a safe, effective process that involves lighting small, controllable fires in a patchwork quilt-like pattern to stimulate new plant growth. Today, rangers imitate these age-old practices, burning off the drying speargrass during Yegge, the indigenous "cool weather time" season from May to June. Managing **introduced species**, from water buffalo to troublesome grasses and cane toads, is also a major priority in order to preserve the park's environment.

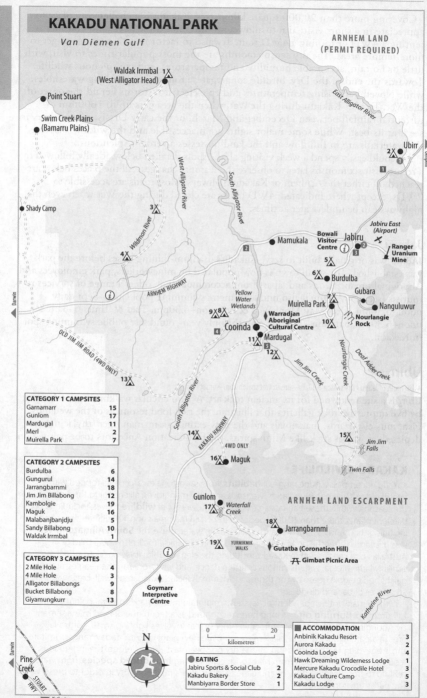

KAKADU NATIONAL PARK

Van Diemen Gulf

ARNHEM LAND (PERMIT REQUIRED)

Waldak Irrmbal **1** (West Alligator Head)

Point Stuart

Swim Creek Plains (Bamarru Plains)

Shady Camp

West Alligator River

South Alligator River

East Alligator River

Oenpelli

Ubirr **2** **1**

Wildman River

Darwin

3

4

ARNHEM HIGHWAY

Mamukala

2

Bowali Visitor Centre

Jabiru

Jabiru East (Airport)

Ranger Uranium Mine

5

6 Burdulba

Gubara

Muirella Park **7**

Nanguluwur

9 **8**

Yellow Water Wetlands

Cooinda

Warradjan Aboriginal Cultural Centre

10

Nourlangie Rock

4

11 Mardugal

5

12

Jim Jim Creek

Nourlangie Creek

Deaf Adder Creek

OLD JIM JIM ROAD (4WD ONLY)

13

KAKADU HIGHWAY

South Alligator River

14

4WD ONLY

15

Jim Jim Falls

Twin Falls

16 Maguk

ARNHEM LAND ESCARPMENT

Gunlom

17 *Waterfall Creek*

18

Jarrangbarnmi

19 YURMIKMIK WALKS

Gutatba (Coronation Hill)

Gimbat Picnic Area

Goymarr Interpretive Centre

Darwin

Pine Creek

STUART HWY

Katherine

Katherine River

CATEGORY 1 CAMPSITES

Garnamarr	15
Gunlom	17
Mardugal	11
Merl	2
Muirella Park	7

CATEGORY 2 CAMPSITES

Burdulba	6
Gungurul	14
Jarrangbarnmi	18
Jim Jim Billabong	12
Kambolgie	19
Maguk	16
Malabanjbanjdju	5
Sandy Billabong	10
Waldak Irrmbal	1

CATEGORY 3 CAMPSITES

2 Mile Hole	4
4 Mile Hole	3
Alligator Billabongs	9
Bucket Billabong	8
Giyamungkurr	13

0   20
kilometres

N

● **EATING**

Jabiru Sports & Social Club	2
Kakadu Bakery	2
Manbiyarra Border Store	1

■ **ACCOMMODATION**

Anbinik Kakadu Resort	3
Aurora Kakadu	2
Cooinda Lodge	4
Hawk Dreaming Wilderness Lodge	1
Mercure Kakadu Crocodile Hotel	3
Kakadu Culture Camp	5
Kakadu Lodge	3

the rocks. A moderate 250m clamber up the rocky escarpment brings you to a **lookout** offering one of the park's most beautiful views (especially at sunset) across the Nardab flood plain and the East Alligator River to the rocky outcrops of Arnhem Land. During the dry season, rangers at Ubirr give daily talks on Aboriginal art and culture – you'll find full info at the Bowali Visitor Centre (see p.507). There are several walks in the area including the 6.5km circular **sandstone and river bushwalk** (dry season only) along the East Alligator River, one of the few longish walks in the park.

Nourlangie Rock Area

Dawn–sunset

Nourlangie Rock, one of Kakadu's most accessible and most visited sites, is 31km south of the Park HQ. Here, the protected **Anbangbang Shelter** has preserved evidence of occupation stretching back twenty thousand years; dimples on boulders show where ochre was ground and then mixed with blood for painting. Nearby, the paintings at the **Anbangbang Gallery** depict the dramatic figures of Nabulwinjbulwinj, Namarrgon (the Lightning Man) and his wife Barrginj. Unusually vivid, they were in fact repainted (a traditional and sometimes ritual practice) in the 1960s over similar faded designs.

Barrk Sandstone Walk

The **lookout** over the Arnhem Land escarpment, traditionally recognized as the home of Namarrgon, marks the beginning of the 12km **Barrk Sandstone Walk** – a rugged six- to eight-hour trek through Nourlangie Rock's back country. The trail is marked, should not be undertaken lightly, and is best started in the cool of daybreak.

Nanguluwur and Nawurlandja

Other signposted walks include **Nanguluwur**, a 3.4km return walk from Nourlangie car park to a fascinating art site featuring images from the "contact period" when Aborigines first encountered explorers and settlers. A short distance to the west, meanwhile, **Nawurlandja Lookout** has views onto the imposing hulk of Nourlangie Rock itself, which looms over **Anbangbang Billabong**. During the Dry, a 2.5km, one-hour return track circles the billabong.

Gubara Pools Walk

Almost halfway along Nourlangie road toward the Arnhem Highway, a 9km 4WD track to the right leads to the starting point of the dry-season-only 6km, four-hour return **Gubara Pools Walk**, which takes you to a string of small pools along a palm-shaded creek. Check on accessibility and crocs, particularly during the Wet, before heading out. Swimming is very much at your own risk (see box, p.510).

ABORIGINAL ROCK ART

More than five thousand known **Aboriginal art sites** cover the walls of Kakadu's caves and sheltered outcrops, ranging in age from just 30 years old to more than 20,000. Most of the art sites are of spiritual significance to Aborigines who live in the park, and only a few locations, such as Ubirr and Nourlangie, can be visited by tourists. The paintings incorporate a variety of styles, from handprints to detailed "X-ray" depictions of animals and fish from the rich **Estuarine period** of six thousand years ago. At this time, rising sea levels are thought to have submerged the land bridge by which Aborigines crossed into Australia. It's not unusual to see paintings from successive eras on one wall. **Contact period** images of seventeenth-century Macassar fishing *praus* and larger European schooners might be superimposed over depictions of ancient Mimi spirits or creation ancestors. For the indigenous people, the art sites are *djang* (dreaming places), depicting Dreamtime stories, and the images serve as prompts to communicate valuable lessons that are still passed down from generation to generation.

5

Jim Jim Falls and Twin Falls

Allow a full day to visit these two dramatic waterfalls 100km south of Jabiru, accessed by a bumpy four-hour return drive from the Kakadu Highway along a 60km 4WD-only track, open 6.30am to 8.30pm (dry season only). Alternatively, visit with an operator from Darwin or Jabiru.

Jim Jim Falls plunge 150m off the escarpment and can be viewed on a scenic flight in the Wet or from the ground when they're reopened around June; the falls stop flowing around August. The rocky trail to the plunge pool at the base may only be 1km long, but you need to be in good shape as the rocks are hard going, and although the track runs beside a pool, it's like an oven within the canyon walls from September to November. Swim at your own risk. A steepish 1km track leads to the spectacular Budjmi Lookout at the top of the cliffs – again, be prepared for a moderate slog.

Twin Falls is a sandy 10km drive from Jim Jim, involving a creek crossing, which, even in a high-clearance 4WD (ensure it comes with a snorkel), you'll need to take cautiously. From the car park, you'll need to take the Twin Falls Gorge Boat Shuttle ($15pp, tickets sold at Bowali Visitor Centre, Twin Falls and some commercial outlets), which ferries you up the gorge where a stroll along a boardwalk takes you to the waterhole (no swimming). There's a 3km hike up to the top: once there, you can look over the falls and, providing they have been cleared of crocs, swim in natural pools along the creek.

Yellow Water Wetlands

As Jim Jim Creek meanders into the flood plains close to Cooinda, 50km southwest of Jabiru, it forms the inland lagoon of **Yellow Water**. From the car park, a short walk leads along the edge of the billabong from where highly recommended **cruises** weave through the lushly vegetated waterways, stopping periodically to view abundant birdlife and bank-basking crocs.

Warradjan Aboriginal Cultural Centre

Cooinda access road • Daily 9am–5pm; reduced hours during the wet season • Free • ☎ 08 8979 0051

The turtle-shaped **Warradjan Aboriginal Cultural Centre** offers an impactful interpretive display on the culture and lore of the local Aborigines that definitely warrants an hour or so of your time. Don't be surprised to see certain individuals' names or photographs covered up – it's a form of respect for the recently deceased. There is also a good gift shop.

Maguk

The 12km corrugated 4WD track to **Maguk** (also known as Barramundi Gorge) leaves Kakadu Highway 53km southwest of Cooinda. A 1km path from the car park runs alongside the creek to a lovely tranquil waterhole. The top of the waterfall and more rock pools can be reached by an unsigned clamber up the tree roots to the right of the falls. Saltwater crocs have been found here in recent years, so ensure that you check the status of croc surveys before swimming (see box, p.510).

Gunlom

Gunlom (also known as Waterfall Creek) is accessed by an unsealed gravel road 37km off the Kakadu Highway close to the park's southwestern exit; at the T-junction after 26km, turn left. Although the falls don't flow all year, it's a lovely paperbark-shaded place, and as you can camp here it's worth the diversion. The steep 2km climb to the top of the falls reveals still more pools and an outspread view of southern Kakadu.

A right turn at the 26km junction leads to the shady Gimbat Picnic Area near Guratba or Coronation Hill, the site of a former uranium mine: to local Jawoyn Aborigines this area is traditionally "Sickness Country", suggesting that even in its natural state, uranium,

KAKADU'S YELLOW GOLD

The land around Kakadu's border with Arnhem Land contains fifteen percent of the world's known **uranium reserves**, and mining and refining the ore produces millions of dollars in royalties for the park's traditional owners (not to mention making a pretty penny for the mining company itself, Energy Resources of Australia, whose major shareholder is multinational Rio Tinto). Environmentalists have long campaigned against mining in the park, arguing that it's impossible to contain the low-level radioactive waste produced. There have been more than 150 **leaks** and spills at the Ranger Uranium Mine near Jabiru since it opened in 1981, and the vast open pit (surrounded by, but technically separate from, the national park) certainly makes for a sight deeply incompatible with the park itself. Indeed, there was a million-litre radioactive spill in 2013, though it was contained before it could leak into the park. Until recently it was possible to take guided tours of the mine, although these were halted after a transition began from open-cut mining to underground exploration.

Energy Resources Australia stopped mining in 2012, and must rehabilitate the area by 2026.

along with other toxic minerals found in the area, has proved harmful to humans. About 7km before Gimbat, a turn-off to the left takes you along a 9km 4WD-only track (inaccessible during the Wet) to **Jarrangbarnmi** and **Koolpin Creek**. As the number of daily visitors is limited, you'll need to organize a permit beforehand (preferably at least a week in advance) through Kakadu's Permits Officer (☏08 8938 1140, ⓦenvironment.gov.au).

ARRIVAL AND DEPARTURE
KAKADU NATIONAL PARK

By bus Greyhound operates buses between Darwin and Jabiru (Mon, Wed & Fri; 3hr 45min, departing Darwin 8.30am, departing Jabiru 1.30pm).

By car Unless you're renting a 4WD, it's well worth considering taking a 4WD tour from Jabiru, Darwin (see p.495) or Katherine (see p.518). That said, 2WD vehicles can still reach many of Kakadu's key points of interest. Most park visitors arrive via the Arnhem Highway from Darwin,

but you can also access the park from the south via the sealed Kakadu Highway, which runs from Pine Creek to Jabiru via Cooinda. The unsealed 4WD-only Old Jim Jim Road offers a more adventurous route from the west, linking up with the Arnhem Highway.

On a tour With planning, you can take in Kakadu's (and Arnhem Land's) highlights on day-tours from Jabiru, Cooinda and Darwin.

INFORMATION

Passes To visit Kakadu you need to buy a Park Pass (April–Oct $40 valid for 7 days, rest of year $25 valid for 14 days) from Tourism Top End in Darwin (see p.495), at the Bowali Visitor Centre or online (ⓦparksaustralia.gov.au/kakadu).

Tourist information The Bowali Visitor Centre (daily 8am–5pm; ☏08 8938 1120) near Jabiru provides displays and a huge range of information on the park. It also has a pleasant café (daily 9am–5pm). Make sure you pick up the excellent *Kakadu Visitor Guide* (also available online: ⓦkakadu.com.au) with helpful maps, itineraries and notes on all activities. If you want a more detailed map, try the HEMA 1:400,000 *Kakadu National Park*. Check ⓦkakadu .com.au/access for updates on accessibility. Elsewhere in the park, the Manbiyarra Border Store (daily 8am–8pm; ☏08 8979 2474) on Oenpelli Road near Ubirr stocks some local books and takes some tour reservations.

Services Jabiru has a range of services, all within walking distance of each other and the town's hotels. There's a tour booking office at Jabiru Tourist Centre (☏08 8979 2548), a branch of the Northern Lands Council to obtain Arnhem Land permits (☏08 8938 3000; Mon–Fri 8am–4.15pm), a reasonably big IGA supermarket (Mon–Wed & Fri 9am–5.30pm, Thurs 9am–8pm, Sat 9am–3pm, Sun 9am–1pm), café (Mon–Fri 8am–6pm, Sat 8am–noon), a post office (Mon–Fri 9am–5pm, Sat 9am–noon; ☏08 8979 2020) and a Westpac bank (☏08 8938 1000; Mon–Fri 10am–4pm) with 24hr ATM. You'll also find the police (☏08 8979 2122), a health clinic (Mon & Wed 9am–noon & 1–4pm, Tues & Fri 8am–noon & 1–4pm, Thurs 8am–noon; ☏08 8979 2018; phone number also good for after-hours emergencies) and a swimming pool (see p.503).

TOURS

Ayal Aboriginal Tours ☏08 8979 0483, ⓦayalkakadu .com.au. Run by experienced former park ranger Victor Cooper, who offers highly recommended 6hr dry season

tours ($220) taking in Ubirr, the East Alligator River, the Mamukala wetlands and the Bowali Visitor Centre, generally departing around 8am. He's also planning tours

5

of the little-visited Kapalga region, where he grew up.

Guluyambi Cultural Cruise ☎1800 895 179, ⓦkakaduculturaltours.com.au. A local Aboriginal guide takes you upstream along the East Alligator River to view the rocky escarpment while pointing out crocs and birdlife on the water. You get the chance to set foot, briefly, on Arnhem Land and enjoy a demonstration of some canny bush trickery. The combination of Aboriginal insight and lush scenery makes it a special experience. Daily May–Nov, 9am, 11am, 1pm & 3pm; 1hr 45min; $76, bookings online or at Manbiyarra Border Store (see p.507).

Kakadu Air ☎1800 089 113, ⓦkakaduair.com.au. Operates out of the airstrip 6km east of Jabiru, offering various scenic flights along the escarpment and wetlands.

For waterfall viewing, the 1hr flight is a great option in the Wet (30min fixed-wing flight $150; 1hr fixed-wing flight $250; 20min helicopter flight $230).

Scenic Flight Company 7 Lakeside Drive, Jabiru ☎08 8979 3432, ⓦscenicflight.com.au. Another airborne option, with a 1hr plane flight for $240pp and a 30min trip for $140pp.

★**Yellow Water Cruises** ☎08 8979 1500, ⓦkakadutourism.com. Superb cruises, with informative guides pointing out local flora and fauna in a dramatic setting. During the Dry, expect crocs aplenty. The early morning cruises catch the lagoon and wildlife at their best, although the heat-of-the-day tours are still very worthwhile. Six daily in dry season, four daily in wet season ($72–99); book in advance.

ACCOMMODATION

Most accommodation is at **Jabiru** or **Cooinda**. At the time of writing, Kakadu Cultural Tours (ⓦkakaduculturaltours.com) was planning to open a backpacker-focused hostel at the Manbuyarra Border Store (see p.507); check out the latest online. The park also has over twenty **campsites**: those in category one ($15pp, paid at campsite) are managed and offer good facilities; those in category two ($6pp; paid into collection box) are referred to as "bush campgrounds" and offer basic facilities; those in category three are free, no-frills sites. Bookings are not possible – it's first-come, first-served – and many are only accessible and open during the Dry. For comprehensive campsite listings check at Bowali Visitor Centre or go to ⓦkakadu.com.au/ticket.html.

Anbinik Kakadu Resort Just off Jabiru Dr, 800m from the Arnhem Hwy, Jabiru ☎08 8979 3144, ⓦkakadu .net.au. The award-winning Anbinik provides good value (at least for Jabiru) accommodation in cabins, rooms, "bush bungalows" (rustic huts with private or shared bathrooms) and caravan sites, plus a pool and laundry facilities. Cabins $250, doubles $150, bush bungalows $125, powered sites $42

Aurora Kakadu Arnhem Hwy, 2.5km west of South Alligator Bridge ☎08 8979 0166, ⓦauroraresorts .com.au. Appealing, carefully landscaped resort with a restaurant, bar and central pool area visited by birds and wallabies. There are large standard and smart superior rooms with terraces overlooking the lawns. $205

Cooinda Lodge 1 Kakadu Highway, Cooinda ☎08 8979 1500, ⓦkakadutourism.com. An attractive lodge next to the Yellow Water Billabong with the feel of a village: there are spacious en suites, permanent tents (with shared bathrooms), caravan sites, a large pool and a restaurant, plus a private airstrip, should you wish to fly in. Doubles $289, tents $160, powered sites $46

Mercure Kakadu Crocodile Hotel 1 Flinders St, Jabiru ☎08 8979 9000, ⓦmercure.com. Commonly known as the "Croc", this ambitiously designed crocodile-shaped hotel is the most comfortable option in the region. The en suites were

being revamped at the time of research to give them a more contemporary feel (the comfy loungers are highlights). There's also a shady pool, a restaurant-bar and displays of local art – and often artists-in-residence – in the lobby area. $279

Hawk Dreaming Wilderness Lodge Cannon Hill, near Ubirr ☎1800 895 179, ⓦkakaduculturaltours.com.au. Made up of a dozen twin-tented cabins, this lodge draws plaudits for its away-from-it-all location. It's not as luxurious as the price tag might suggest, but it's a special spot nonetheless. Rates include breakfast, dinner and a rock art sunset tour. $289 per person

Kakadu Culture Camp Bowali Creek ☎0428 792 048, ⓦfacebook.com/kakaduculturecamp. This multi-award-winning retreat places emphasis on learning about Aboriginal culture, but caters mainly for special-interest groups. It was closed at the time of research, but is due to reopen in mid-2017, when it is likely to be one of the more budget-friendly options in the region. Check its Facebook page for updates.

Kakadu Lodge Jabiru Drive, Jabiru ☎08 8979 2422, ⓦauroraresorts.com.au. The inviting pool is the highlight of this resort hotel, which has a decent – though unexciting – selection of rooms and cabins (the latter have shared bathrooms), plus a caravan site and a reasonable (for Jabiru) restaurant. Cabins $240, doubles $149

EATING

If you're not self-catering or eating at one of the pricey resort restaurants, there are slim pickings for meals out. As well as the three options here, the *Jabiru Golf Club* is a further alternative.

5

Jabiru Sports & Social Club 27 Lakeside Drive, Jabiru ☎ 08 8979 2326, �🌐 jabirusportsandsocialclub .com.au. The club exists mainly for local miners and their families, but guests are welcome to sign in (bring photo ID) and eat and drink (there are standards like pies, fish and chips, and so on for around $25). There's a bar area with enormous panel fans and a more formal dining space. Restaurant Mon–Sat 6–8.30pm, Sun noon– 2pm & 6–8.30pm; bar Mon 2–11pm, Tues–Fri noon– 11pm, Sat–Sun 11am–11pm.

Kakadu Bakery Gregory Place, Jabiru ☎ 08 8979 2320. The best value option in Jabiru – short of self-catering – this little bakery has a good selection of bread, cakes and pies. It also serves breakfast options and light meals (around $15) like pizzas and burgers to take away. Nothing fancy, but at least it won't break the bank. Mon–Fri 6.30am–4pm, Sat 6.30am–3pm, Sun 8am–3pm (closed Sun in wet season).

Manbiyarra Border Store Oenpelli Road, near the East Alligator River ☎ 08 8979 2474. One of the owners is originally from Thailand, and an accomplished cook to boot, which makes *Manbiyarra* a better choice than might be assumed. Counter meals include *tom yum* soup, pad thai and red, yellow and green curries (mains around $25). Takeaway also available. Mon 8.30am–5pm, Tues–Sun 8.30am–8pm (dry season only).

Arnhem Land

Pristine **ARNHEM LAND** is geographically the continuation of Kakadu eastwards to the Gulf of Carpentaria, but without the infrastructure and picnic areas. Never colonized and too rough to graze, the 91,000-square-kilometre wilderness was designated an Aboriginal reserve in 1931 and has remained in Aboriginal hands since that time. In 1963 the Yirrkala of northwestern Arnhem Land appealed against the proposed mining of bauxite on their land. It was the first protest of its kind and included the presentation of sacred artefacts and a petition in the form of a bark painting to the government in Canberra. Their actions brought the issue of Aboriginal land rights to the public eye, paving the way for subsequent successful land claims in the Territory.

Independent tourists are not allowed to visit Arnhem Land without a **permit**, and the twelve thousand Aborigines who live here prefer it that way. Little disturbed for more then forty thousand years, Arnhem Land, like Kakadu, holds thousands of rock art sites and burial grounds, wild coastline, rivers teeming with fish, stunning stone escarpments, monsoon forests, savannah woodlands and abundant wildlife. In recent

---

BE CROCWISE!

There are an estimated 90,000 estuarine or **saltwater crocodiles** in the Top End, far more than other tropical areas of Australia, and they continue to present a real danger to humans. "Salties", not to be confused with the smaller and much less threatening "freshies" (freshwater or Johnston crocodiles), can live in both salt and fresh water and grow up to 6m long. They have superb hearing, can see in the dark (and underwater) and are able to stay submerged for over an hour waiting for dinner to walk by.

Most crocodile-infested waters are already well signposted, with two types of **warning signs** essentially saying "don't swim here" or "swim at your own risk". Those who ignore this advice (more often locals than tourists) run the risk of becoming a statistic. One such statistic was a 23-year-old female German backpacker who was killed by a 4.5m saltie in 2002 at Kakadu, after her tour guide, ignoring the warning signs, took his group for a midnight swim near Nourlangie Rock. More recently, a Darwin IT worker met an inopportune end when swimming in the Mary River in 2013, and a fisherman was killed in Kakadu after a croc snatched him from his boat in 2014. So far, the Territory Government has resisted the idea of culling, relying on a policy of education and removing "problem crocodiles". Its **"crocwise"** campaign (�🌐 nt.gov.au/becrocwise) includes the following advice:

- Only swim in designated safe swimming areas and obey all crocodile warning signs.
- Always stand a minimum of 5m from the water's edge when fishing and camp a minimum of 50m away.
- Never prepare food or wash dishes at the water's edge; dispose of all food scraps and waste away from campsites.

ABORIGINAL FESTIVALS

Attending an **Aboriginal festival** is a memorable experience. Below are some of the best, and most memorable, in the Territory. They are almost exclusively alcohol-free.

Ngukurr (June; ⓦ katherineregionalarts.org.au) A three-day festival at a remote community on the Roper Highway, incorporating everything from footy matches and craft workshops to hip-hop competitions and family activities. No charge.

Barunga (June; ⓦ barungafestival.com.au) One of the best known of the NT's indigenous festivals, with a focus on music, sport and culture. Eighty kilometres southeast of Katherine. Three-day tickets $50, including camping fees.

Walking with Spirits (July; ⓦ djilpinarts.org.au) Held by the Wugularr community in SW Arnhem Land, sharing songs, dance, stories and music in a spectacular waterside setting. 4WD recommended for access. Tickets $50.

Walaman Cultural Festival (July; ⓦ katherineregionalarts.org.au) A colourful celebration involving workshops, traditional dancing, bush games and fire sculptures. Takes place in Bulman, 400km southeast of Darwin. No charge for tickets, all welcome. Camping $12 per night.

Garma (August; ⓦ garma.com.au) Rightly famed and hugely popular, drawing large numbers of non-indigenous visitors to the Gove Peninsula to immerse themselves in the music, ceremonies and bushcraft of the "First Australians". Tickets $1815.

years, the mystique of this "forbidden land" has proved a profitable source of income for Arnhem Land's more accessible communities, and tours, particularly to the areas adjacent to Kakadu, are now offered in partnership with a select few operators.

Injalak Arts and Crafts Centre

15km from the East Alligator River crossing • Mon–Fri 8.30am–5pm, Sat 9am–2pm • Free • ☎ 08 8979 0190 or ☎ 1800 334 944 to pre-arrange an interpreter, ⓦ injalak.com

At the **Injalak Arts and Crafts Centre** in **Gunbalanya** (Oenpelli) at Ubirr's Border Store, you can talk to artists and purchase works. The back of the centre looks over a billabong onto the rocky Injaluk Hill, a remarkable site which can be visited on a guided 2.5hr walk (three times daily except Sun, dry season only; $110; bookings through website).

Nhulunbuy

The major settlement in Arnhem Land is **NHULUNBUY** on the **Gove Peninsula**, in the northeast corner, which boasts sublime white-sand beaches and aquamarine water. On the northwest corner, the Cobourg Peninsula is one of Australia's finest fishing spots (best appreciated by boat), and home to the **Garig Gunak Barlu National Park** (permit $232.10 per vehicle for overnight stays, book at least six weeks in advance), a paradise for birdwatchers.

INFORMATION AND TOURS   ARNHEM LAND

For more information on Arnhem Land permits (from $15) and application forms visit the website of the Dhimurru Aboriginal Corporation (ⓦ dhimurru.com.au). Alcohol is not allowed to be brought in to the region. The operators below tend to agree on exclusive access to particular sites, although there's nothing to stop travellers visiting them independently.

★ **Arnhemlander** ☎ 1800 525 238, ⓦ kakaducultural tours.com.au. This well-organized day-trip takes in the region's fascinating culture, heritage and landscape, incorporating a visit to Injalak, several rock art sites, an overview of local cultural beliefs, lunch by a billabong and

the chance to take in some memorable views ($269). Highly recommended.

Davidson's Arnhemland Safaris ☎ 08 8979 0413, ⓦ arnhemland-safaris.com. Top-notch Arnhem Land operator with a beautiful lodge (and its own airstrip) in the

5

rugged Mount Borradaile area. Package deals from $750 include a night's accommodation, all meals, tours and activities including barramundi fishing. Flights from Darwin/Jabiru $550/250pp each way.

★ **Lords Safaris** ☎ 08 8948 2200, ⓦ lords-safaris.com. Award-winning Arnhem Land operator Sab Lord grew up with the traditional owners, as is evident from his intimate knowledge of the land, people and culture, his use of indigenous guides and the access he and his staff are granted on their small-group 4WD tours. One-day trip $240 from Jabiru, $270 from Darwin, May–Oct only.

Nomad Tours ☎ 08 8987 8085, ⓦ banubanu.com.

Fishing specialists running tours to Bremer Island near Nhulunbuy on the Gove Peninsula. They operate an ecowilderness retreat on the island in partnership with the traditional owners. Boat transfers from Nhulunbuy are $160pp; air transfers can also be arranged. Accommodation from $336pp (minimum two-night booking; full board). Fishing trips charged separately (full-day $380pp, half-day $250pp).

Venture North ☎ 08 8927 5500, ⓦ venturenorth.com.au. Offers a couple of multiday trips through Arnhem Land and the Cobourg Peninsula, most notably a four-day itinerary leaving Jabiru on Tues and Fri in the dry season, which includes three nights at a coastal camp ($2690).

Along the Stuart Highway

South of Darwin, the **Stuart Highway** passes old mining outposts and overgrown, but still commemorated, World War II airstrips. The highway itself snakes all the way down to South Australia, but along its most northern stretch are a number of attractions that can be visited either as excursions from Darwin or as diversions on the journey to Katherine, 320km to the south.

Litchfield National Park

"Kaka-don't, Litchfield-do" is an oversimplified quip expressing many Darwin residents' preference for **LITCHFIELD NATIONAL PARK** over its much larger near-neighbour. Situated just 100km south of Darwin, and roughly 16km west of the Stuart Highway, the park encompasses the Tabletop Range, a spring-fringed plateau from which several easily accessible **waterfalls** gush into swimming holes. The whole park is a laidback destination, great for bushwalking and lingering nature appreciation, without the hassle of long drives, permits or 4WDs. It offers comparatively little in the way of visible Aboriginal culture, but if you're after a relaxed day or two in striking surrounds, it's ideal. Pay attention to the signs warning of **crocodiles** (see box, p.510).

THE INDEFATIGABLE MR STUART

If one man can be said to have put Northern Territory on the map it is **John McDouall Stuart** (1815–66). A diminutive Scottish surveyor with unlimited reserves of flinty perseverance, he led no fewer than six expeditions into the Red Centre, never losing a man in the process. For the early British colonists the Territory was essentially *terra incognita*, a land of scorching desert that attracted only those willing to search for gold or ever-elusive grazing lands. However, in the late 1850s the need for a telegraph line to link Australia's southern colonies to the rest of the Empire saw serious attention turn north. The government of South Australia offered £2000 to any man who could find a suitable route through to the north coast from where the line would be connected undersea to Java.

Stuart was experienced, having already charted vast expanses of the desert by travelling light and relying on an uncanny ability to find water. He set out from Adelaide in 1861 leading a party of ten men on an expedition that would take a gruelling nine months to find a way through to the Top End. Along the way he suffered terribly from scurvy, was attacked by boomerang-wielding Aborigines, and had to be carried on a stretcher for the last few kilometres. On July 24, 1862, they finally reached their goal at Chambers Bay. Stuart's journal records that when one of his men exclaimed "The Sea!", they were so astonished that he had to repeat himself, after which they gave "three long and hearty cheers". Though he returned a hero to Adelaide, Stuart's exertions had taken their toll and he died just four years later back in the UK.

5

THE TOP END

Black Point

Port Essington

GARIG GUNAK
BARLU NATIONAL
PARK

Cobourg Peninsula

Tiwi
Islands

Bathurst
Island

Melville Island

Nguiu

Van Diemen Gulf

DJUKBINJ
NATIONAL
PARK

West
Alligator
Head

Beagle Gulf

Gunn Point

Point
Stuart

South Alligator River

Darwin

Mandorah

Humpty
Doo

Fogg
Dam

Adelaide River

MARY RIVER
NATIONAL
PARK

Jabiru

Cox
Peninsula

Window on the
Wetlands
Visitor Centre

DJUKBINJ
NATIONAL
PARK

ARNHEM HIGHWAY

**Territory Wildlife
Park**

ADELAIDE
RIVER
CROSSING

JIM JIM ROAD

**Berry Springs
Nature Park**

LITCHFIELD
PARK ROAD

Mary River

KAKADU
NATIONAL
PARK

*Wangi
Falls*

Batchelor

Adelaide River

LITCHFIELD
NATIONAL PARK

STUART HIGHWAY

*Robin
Falls*

KAKADU HIGHWAY

Hayes Creek

**Douglas Hot Springs
& Butterfly Gorge**

Pine Creek

NITMILUK
NATIONAL
PARK

Daly River

OOLLOO
CROSSING

Daly River

**Umbrawarra
Gorge**

Edith Falls

**Nitmiluk
(Katherine)
Gorge**

N

Katherine

Aboriginal land

**Cutta Cutta
Caves**

0   50

kilometres

Katherine River

VICTORIA HWY

▼ Western Australia

Batchelor

Lush, leafy **BATCHELOR** – 8km west of the Stuart Highway – was originally built to serve
the postwar rush to mine uranium at nearby Rum Jungle. In the 1980s, when large-scale
mining had ceased, the establishment of Litchfield as a national park gave the town a new
lease of life. It still has spots of heritage interest, and there's been ongoing work for years
on the volunteer-project Batchelor Museum (call ahead of time to check hours; ☎08
8976 7006, ⑩batchelormuseum.org.au). Try to pick up **information** on Litchfield's sights

5

and bushwalks from the occasionally manned visitor centre (daily 8.30am–5pm) on Tarkarri Road, although the range of free-to-take literature isn't vast. The general store opposite the visitor centre is a good place to pose any questions on local attractions.

Along Litchfield Park Road

Heading into the park from Batchelor you'll pass red-dirt plains dotted with tombstone-like **termite mounds**, varying in shape and size, with some up to 4m high. A signed lay-by gives the chance for a closer look at the "magnetic" or "meridian" variety, mind-boggling flattened slabs aligned north to south to regulate internal temperature. The first chance for a splash is at the **Buley Rock Holes**, a string of easily accessible rock pools with basic camping nearby. They're great for a wallow, but can get crowded. From here, both the road and a 3km trail follow the Buley Creek to **Florence Falls**, one of the park's natural highlights. A cantilevered lookout surveys the twin 20m falls from above the treetops, from where a stairway drops right down to the shady plunge pool where it's possible to swim.

Back on the Litchfield Park Road (the main sealed road in the park linking all the most visited spots), a turn-off south leads to the dry-season-only 4WD track to the **Lost City**, a jumble of unusually weathered sandstone columns. Back on the main park road the birdlife-rich but relatively undramatic Tabletop Swamp is followed soon after by **Tolmer Falls**, 450m from the road, arguably the park's most photogenic waterfall. There's no access to the bottom of the falls. From **Green Ant Creek** a one-hour return walk leads through pockets of rainforest to the top of the **Tjaetaba Falls**, with an uncrowded pool to cool off in right on the lip of the cascade.

Wangi Falls

Packed out at weekends and during school holidays, **Wangi Falls**, 1.6km from the main road, on the west side of the park, has easy access past tree-shaded lawns, picnic tables and a café (daily 9am–5pm) to an enormous natural swimming hole. Near the base of the main cascade is a sun-warmed plunge pool that can be climbed into. (Swimming halts in the Wet when undertows develop and crocs lurk.) A trail leads through a rainforest boardwalk up over the falls and down the other side via a **lookout** – a good way to work off lunch.

Past Wangi is the park's main accommodation option, *Litchfield Safari Camp*, and further along the main road you'll find peaceful bushwalking and swimming options at **Cascades** and, down a dirt track, an interesting heritage wander at **Bamboo Creek Tin Mine**.

The Reynolds River Track

Near Green Ant Creek, the high-clearance 4WD-only **Reynolds River Track** leads 44km south out of the park to the sealed Daly River Road. The half-metre-deep creek crossing near the start of the track is a sign of things to come, with a particularly sandy section before Surprise Creek Falls, and some steep drops into deep creek crossings. The track (closed during the Wet and after any rain) passes huge termite mounds and verdant woodland.

A few kilometres after the start of the track is a turn-off left (sometimes closed) to the spooky, abandoned **Blyth Homestead**. Back on the main track, you soon reach a turn-off leading in a couple of kilometres to **Tjaynera Falls** campsite (also known as Sandy Creek). From the campsite car park it's a 1.7km walk to the falls above a large plunge pool. At the Tjaynera turn-off, on the main track, take note of the sign warning that 4WDs should have a raised air intake to cross the Reynolds River, 6km beyond. **Surprise Creek Falls** (with camping), about 20km further on, is the highlight along the track. From this point it's about a twenty-minute drive, over a few more humps, to Daly River Road.

| **ARRIVAL AND DEPARTURE** | **LITCHFIELD NATIONAL PARK** |

By car A common approach is along the sealed road via Batchelor. Alternatively, from Darwin you can take Cox Peninsula Road (but this route involves 40km of gravel road), and exit via Batchelor to the east or, with a 4WD,

leave to the south via the Reynolds River Track.
On a tour Organized tours are the only way to see the park without your own transport.

ACCOMMODATION

There are several **accommodation** options in and around the Batchelor area, but choose your time and place carefully, especially at weekends in the Dry, when Litchfield draws sizeable crowds. Camping within the park itself is available at Wangi Falls, Buley Rockhole, Florence Falls and along Walker Creek, as well as a handful of 4WD-only locations.

Banyan Tree Caravan Park Litchfield Park Road ☎ 08 8976 0330, ⓦ banyan-tree.com.au. Nicely located between Batchelor and Litchfield itself, this likeable place has chalets, cabins and budget rooms, as well as van sites and a pool. There's a free BBQ on Mon, Wed and Fri in the Dry. Cabins/chalets $130, doubles $65, un/powered sites per person $12/29

Batchelor Butterfly Farm 8 Meneling Rd ☎ 08 8976 0110, ⓦ butterflyfarm.net.au. A resort-cum-menagerie run by part-English owner Chris, who keeps ducks, fish, bunnies and guinea pigs, as well as an enclosure's-worth of butterflies (tours daily 9am–4pm; $12 entry for nonguests). Accommodation is in colourfully decorated bungalows. $160

Litchfield Safari Camp Litchfield Park Road ☎ 08 8978 2185, ⓦ litchfieldsafaricamp.com.au. An agreeable enough option situated a kilometre down an unsealed road along the western edge of the park, ideally placed for Wangi Falls. A café serves simple food. Un/powered sites $25/35, safari tents with en suite $150, backpacker tents $30

Litchfield Tourist Park Litchfield Park Road ☎ 08 8976 0070, ⓦ litchfieldtouristpark.com.au. Almost adjacent to the *Banyan Tree*, Litchfield Tourist Park has good facilities including a licensed bar, internet access and various room types. Cabins $141, bunkhouses $79, powered sites $37

Rum Jungle Bungalows 10 Meneling Rd ☎ 08 8976 0555, ⓦ rumjunglebungalows.com.au. Located in Batchelor, these Asian-inspired bungalow-style rooms come with their own private veranda and "breakfast nook" featuring a kettle, toaster and fridge – ingredients for a Continental breakfast are provided for your first morning. There's also a leafy garden, pool and barbecue facilities $160

Adelaide River and around

Established during the construction of the Overland Telegraph Line, the town of **ADELAIDE RIVER** was the supply head for Darwin's defence during World War II and consequently suffered sporadic Japanese bombing. The town is best known for its **war cemetery**, where many of the victims of the Top End air raids are buried. Officially, 243 people died as a result of the eighteen months of Japanese bombing, which began in February 1942, but the cemetery also houses many others who perished in the war years.

Just south of town, the old highway forks west along a rolling 75km scenic drive before rejoining the main road at Hayes Creek roadhouse. After the first 17km on this route you'll come to the turn-off for **Robin Falls**, a pretty little cascade reached after a ten-minute scramble up the creek bed from the car park. Seventeen kilometres south of the Robin Falls turn-off, a sealed road leads to the **Daly River** community (passing a southern entrance into Litchfield Park; 4WD only), a dead end favoured by barra fishermen; beyond is Aboriginal land.

ACCOMMODATION   ADELAIDE RIVER AND AROUND

Adelaide River Inn 106 Stuart Highway ☎ 08 8976 7047, ⓦ adelaideriverinn.com.au. A pleasant roadside inn that also has rooms, cabins and camping spaces. The bar plays host to the (now stuffed) water buffalo that starred in *Crocodile Dundee*. Cabins $140, doubles $85, un/powered sites $18/28

Pine Creek

From Pine Creek it's 200km along the sealed Kakadu Highway to Jabiru, in the heart of Kakadu National Park (see p.502).

Site of the Territory's first gold rush, **PINE CREEK**, 230km from Darwin, is one of the Territory's oldest towns and has managed to hang on to an unreconstructed charm despite (or perhaps because of) its low tourist status. Gold was discovered here in 1871 when holes were dug for the Overland Telegraph Line. Unfortunately, the ore was in the rock, rather than the river beds. This required laborious crushing, which was too much like hard work for most of the newly arrived prospectors. The subsequent labour shortage was solved by importing Chinese workers until fears of Asian dominance led to Chinese immigration being banned in 1888. Ah Toys general store on Main Terrace is today run by the fifth-generation descendants of its original Chinese owner.

Around the town are various time-worn buildings, such as the 1889 **Old Playford Hotel** and **Old Bakery**. The **Miners Park**, at the northern end of town, displays crude mining hardware from more than a century ago, and there's a small **museum** (April–Sept Mon–Fri 11am–5pm, Sat 11am–1pm, Oct–March Mon–Fri 1–5pm; ☎08 8981 2848; $2) on Railway Terrace. Elsewhere, a lookout over town is accessible by car up a steep lane, and gives a worthwhile view of a large open-mining pit, now water-filled.

ACCOMMODATION **PINE CREEK**

Lazy Lizard Caravan Park 299 Millar Terrace ☎08 8976 1019, ⓦlazylizardpinecreek.com.au. Pine Creek has a handful of places to stay, including this well-run caravan park, which has a tavern, a bistro and plenty of birdlife. The park also sells quality indigenous works by a local artist. Cabins **$120**, dorms **$30**, un/powered sites **$18/30**

Edith Falls

Down the Stuart Highway, 91km south of Pine Creek, a turn-off leads 18km east to **Edith Falls** (Leliyn), part of Nitmiluk National Park (see p.519). Edith Falls is popular on weekends, with a campsite ($6.60pp honesty box) with barbecue and toilet facilities and a small waterfall at the back of a large plunge pool. To get away from the crowds you can take a leisurely half-hour walk round to the secluded upper pools, or carry on to Sweetwater Pool (a further 9km return).

Katherine and around

The small town of **KATHERINE**, 317km south of Darwin, is a worthwhile stopover, primarily for a side trip to the dramatic **Nitmiluk Gorge** (formerly Katherine Gorge) or to strike out along the epic **Victoria Highway** to Western Australia. The fast-flowing **Katherine River**, which runs through the gorge and town, must have been a sight for explorer John McDouall Stuart's sore eyes as he struggled north in 1862. Having got this far, he named the river after a benefactor's daughter, and within ten years the completion of the Overland Telegraph Line (OTL) encouraged European settlement, as drovers and prospectors converged on the first reliable water north of the Davenport Ranges. In 1926 a narrow-gauge railway line linked Katherine with Darwin and the former was established on the present site.

Katherine is essentially a "one-street" place, though in January 1998 when the river rose to 22m and broke its banks that street found itself under 2m of water – a crocodile was even spotted cruising lazily past the semi-submerged Woolworths.

The Stuart Highway becomes **Katherine Terrace**, the main street, as it passes through town. Along it lie most of the shops and services, while sprinkled around the centre are several excellent Aboriginal arts and crafts galleries. Katherine can be a good place to pick up **casual work** at the surrounding stations and market gardens (most readily during the main Nov–Dec mango season).

Katherine Outback Heritage Museum

Gorge Road • **Museum** Daily 9am–4pm • $10 • ☎08 8972 3945, ⓦkatherinemuseum.com • **Stockman's Camp Tucker Night** 5 weekly; call ahead for precise dates • $75 food & entertainment only, BYO alcohol • ☎0427 112 806, ⓦmarksiescamptucker.com.au

For some local history head 3km up Giles Street to the history-buff-friendly **Katherine Outback Heritage Museum**. On site are myriad displays on Katherine's pioneering past, from the 1870s through to the mid-twentieth century. A smart new gallery opened in 2013, dominated by a 1930s Gypsy Moth plane used by Dr Clyde Fenton, the NT's first flying doctor. Three nights each week the grounds play host to **Stockman's Camp**

5

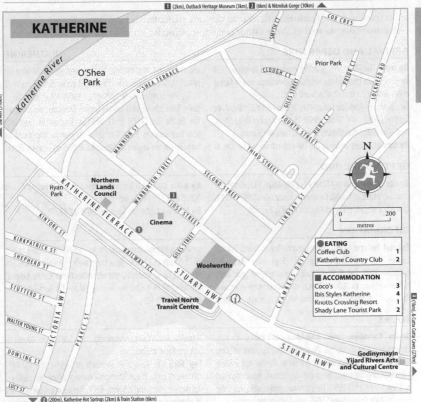

KATHERINE

COX CRES

SMITH TCE

O'Shea
Park

Prior Park

CLOUGH CT

PRIOR CT

LOCKHEED RD

O'SHEA TERRACE

GILES STREET

Darwin (310km) ◀

Katherine River

FOURTH STREET

HUNT CT

MANNION ST

THIRD STREET

N

WARBURTON STREET

SECOND STREET

LINDSAY ST

Northern
Lands
Council

Ryan
Park

KATHERINE TERRACE

FIRST STREET

3

Cinema

0   200
metres

KINTORE ST

GILES STREET

KIRKPATRICK ST

RAILWAY TCE

SHEPHERD ST

STUART HWY

Woolworths

CHAMBERS DRIVE

● **EATING**
Coffee Club   1
Katherine Country Club   2

STUTTERD ST

VICTORIA HWY

PEARCE ST

WALTER YOUNG ST

**Travel North
Transit Centre**

■ **ACCOMMODATION**
Coco's   3
Ibis Styles Katherine   4
Knotts Crossing Resort   1
Shady Lane Tourist Park   2

(1km), & Cutta Cutta Caves (27km) ▶

DOWLING ST

STUART HWY

LUCY ST

**Godinymayin
Yijard Rivers Arts
and Cultural Centre**

Tucker Nights, where you can try the tucker typical of a stockman's camp, including roo fillets, coal-fired veggies, damper and billy tea, and be entertained by campfire yarns.

Katherine Hot Springs

The crystal-clear waters of **Katherine Hot Springs**, a five-minute drive from the centre, accessed by the Victoria Highway or Riverbank Drive, are worth an hour's soak, although they don't quite compare to those in Mataranka. They're free, and the grassy banks are great for a picnic.

Godinymayin Yijard Rivers Arts & Cultural Centre

Stuart Highway • Tues–Fri 10am–5pm, Sat 10am–3pm • ☎ 08 8972 3751, ⬡ gyracc.org.au
A few hundred metres south of town along the Stuart Highway, the absorbing **Godinymayin Yijard Rivers Arts & Cultural Centre** holds regularly changing exhibitions of local art and photography. It gives equal weight to indigenous and non-indigenous culture, and also hosts various music and theatre events.

Cutta Cutta Caves

27km south of town • Guided tours hourly 9–11am & 1–3pm daily (sometimes flooded in the Wet) • $19, cash only • ☎ 1300 146 743, ⬡ nitmiluktours.com.au
Cutta Cutta Caves can only be visited on guided tours. The two caves display

5

subterranean karst features as diverse as they are delicate, and are home to rare orange horseshoe bats, as well as some rather alarming stalactite-climbing brown snakes.

ARRIVAL AND DEPARTURE
KATHERINE

By train The *Ghan* arrives at the modern rail terminal 7km west of town from where shuttle buses (included in fares) meet arrivals; a taxi costs around $20.
Destinations Adelaide (Wed; 41hr 10min–68hr 25min); Alice Springs (Wed; 14hr 50min–18hr 15min); Coober Pedy (Wed, Aug–Oct only; 38hr 40min); Darwin (Tues; 4hr 30min).
By bus All buses arrive at the Travelnorth Transit Centre, at

the south end of Katherine Terrace, next to the 24-hour BP petrol station. There are Greyhound services to Darwin (2 daily; 3hr 50min), Alice Springs (1 daily; 16hr); Broome (1 daily; 18hr 30min, also calls at Timber Creek and Kununurra). The Bodhi Bus (☎08 8971 0774, ☜thebodhibus.com.au) also has services from Katherine to remote communities throughout the region and beyond, including Tennant Creek.

GETTING AROUND

By car To rent a car try Thrifty (☎1800 626 515, ☜thrifty. com.au, office at Transit Centre) or Hertz (☎08 8971 1111, ☜hertz.com.au, office at *Knotts Crossing Resort*).

By bike Bikes can be rented from *Knotts Crossing Resort* (☎08 8972 2511, $20/day).
By taxi Try Katherine Taxis (☎08 8972 1777).

INFORMATION

Tourist information Opposite the Travel North Transit Centre is the visitor centre (Sept–May Mon–Fri 8.30am–5pm, Sat & Sun 10am–2pm, rest of year daily 8.30am–5pm; ☎1800 653 142, ☜visitkatherine.com.au). For more detailed information on local national parks

including Nitmiluk visit the Parks and Wildlife office (☎08 8973 8888) at 32 Giles St, a short walk from the centre. For Arnhem Land permits, there's a Northern Lands Council Office at 5/29 Katherine Terrace (Mon–Fri 8am–4.30pm; ☎1800 653 142).

TOURS

Gecko Canoeing and Trekking ☎1800 634 319, ☜geckocanoeing.com.au. Award-winning operator offering relaxed one- to six-day canoeing trips on the Katherine River. The most popular trip is the three-day option, departing Wed and Sun May–Oct ($1090). They also run guided treks along the five-day Jatbula Trail from $1695, plus birdwatching trips.
Katherine Aviation ☎08 8971 1277, ☜katherine aviation.com.au. Scenic flights in light aircraft over

Nitmiluk, Edith Falls and Kakadu, from $285pp for 40min to $815pp for 4hr/5hr.
Top Didj Cnr Gorge & Jaensch rds ☎08 8971 2751, ☜topdidj.com. These Aboriginal cultural experiences (May–Oct daily 9.30am and 2.30pm; $70) offer a fun couple of hours of didgeridoo playing, painting, spear-throwing and fire-lighting. There is also a small art gallery (April–Oct daily 9am–5pm; Nov–March open by appointment; free).

ACCOMMODATION

Coco's 21 First St ☎08 8971 2889, ✉coco21firstst @yahoo.com. An old-fashioned backpackers' with chickens clucking about, acoustic guitars lying around and an interesting mix of travellers, some seasonal workers and a few long-distance cyclists for whom *Coco's* is a well-known stop. The place also attracts didgeridoo aficionados – the owner, Richard Williams (aka "Coco"), is an expert on the instrument and sells prized examples at the on-site shop. Dorms $35, camping $20
Ibis Styles Katherine Stuart Hwy ☎08 8972 1744, ☜ibis.com. Sprawling hotel complex set in lush gardens at the southern end of town. The rooms are standard-issue but spacious and comfortable. There's also a pool, bar and restaurant. Continental breakfast and some internet included. $130

Knotts Crossing Resort Cnr Giles & Cameron sts ☎08 8972 2511, ☜knottscrossing.com.au. An award-winning tourist park with accommodation options for all budgets, a full range of facilities (two pools, spa, wi-fi, restaurant, ATM, travel agency, etc) and an appealing atmosphere. Suites $165, cabins $115, un/powered sites $28/47
Shady Lane Tourist Park 257 Gorge Rd ☎1800 043 043, ☜shadylanetouristpark.com.au. This caravan park is certainly shady (in a good way) and yes, it's down a lane, located far enough outside of town to guarantee a quiet stay. It's a short walk from the river too. You'll find a range of tropical-style en-suite cabins on stilts, a nice pool and powered sites. Cabins $180, powered sites $45

EATING

Eating out in Katherine is nothing to get excited about. There are several cafés and fast-food places, as well as a sprinkling of hotel restaurants. In the evenings, the Stockman's Camp Tucker Night (see p.516) at the Outback Heritage Museum is a good bet.

Coffee Club 23 Katherine Terrace ☎08 8972 3990, ⓦ coffeeclub.com.au. This reliable chain has cafés across Australia and provides a decent option for a feed. The menu offers a large all-day breakfast alongside various sandwiches, wraps and salads ($15–30). Mon–Fri 6.30am–4.30pm, Sat–Sun 7am–3pm.

Katherine Country Club 40 Pearce St ☎08 8972 1276, ⓦ katherinecountryclub.com.au. A sociable NT country club complete with nine-hole golf course ($15/9 holes, $20/18 holes) and some filling Aussie menu options, plus an all-you-can-eat buffet breakfast on Sun (7–10am $16). Visitors need to sign in. Mon 11.30am–2pm & 6–8.30pm, Tues–Fri 11.30am–2pm & 6–9pm, Sat 11am–2.30pm & 6–9pm, Sun 11am–2.30pm & 6–8.30pm.

Nitmiluk National Park

The magnificent 12km **Nitmiluk Gorge**, carved by the Katherine River through the Arnhem Land plateau, is the centrepiece of the **Nitmiluk National Park**. The river, hemmed in by sheer ochre cliffs, makes for a spectacular **cruise** or canoeing trip (there are, in fact, thirteen gorges split by sections of rapids). Nitmiluk also has eight marked **walking trails**, including the renowned 36km Jatbula Trail. The local Jawoyn (pronounced jar-wen) people own the park's accommodation options and also run Nitmiluk Tours (see below), which organizes visitor activities in the park.

ARRIVAL AND DEPARTURE | NITMILUK NATIONAL PARK

By bus Nitmiluk Tours (☎1300 146 743, ⓦ nitmiluktours .com.au) runs shuttle buses ($30) from April to September covering the 30km between Katherine and the gorge. Although they were running at the time of research, the shuttles have been suspended in the past, so it is worth checking the website ahead of your visit. Taxis (around $100) are also available.

INFORMATION AND TOURS

Tourist information The visitor centre at the gorge (July–Aug daily 6.30am–5.30pm, Sept–June daily 8am–5pm) has an interpretive display on the Jawoyn and the park's geology, flora and fauna, and a tour desk with information and maps detailing walking trails. There's also a café and gift shop. As you sit on the terrace overlooking the river, consider that in January 1998 you would have been under a metre of water.

Nitmiluk Tours ☎1300 146 743, ⓦnitmiluktours. com.au. Offers various cruises and scenic flights, all of which can be arranged from the visitor centre or online. There are four gorge cruises: the 2hr dawn cruise ($90;

May–Oct) departs at 7am daily, when the light has a gorgeous clarity; 2hr daytime cruises ($87; April–Oct) are a good bet for a standard overview of the area's scenery and culture; the 4hr daytime cruise ($124.50; April–Aug) travels further into the gorge system; and the 3.5hr sunset dinner cruise takes in the sunset-flamed rocks of the first two gorges as well as a high-quality three-course meal ($159.50; late April–Oct). All cruises are subject to river conditions. The scenic helicopter flights up the gorge start from $99 per person for ten minutes and run all year – it's a magnificent sight from the air.

ACTIVITIES

Swimming There is relatively safe swimming in the dry season, although the gorges are closed to swimmers and canoeists between December and April. Rangers remove saltwater crocs at the start of the dry season, although you may well see freshies basking on the banks. They're said to be harmless if undisturbed, but don't enter nesting sites.

Canoeing Paddling up the gorge is exhilarating, if sometimes exhausting, especially against the breeze. Don't expect to reach the thirteenth gorge in a day. Nitmiluk Tours rent single/double canoes for $57/41.50 per person for 4hr, $77.50/61 per person for 8hr, and $140/83 per person for overnight hire. It's well worth doing at least a full day, which gives time to paddle the spectacular second gorge. Book well ahead in peak season. A deposit of $50 per canoe is required and, for overnight trips, a permit ($3.30). You'll need to provide your own camping equipment. Expect long

sections of canoe-carrying over boulders and successively shorter sections of water as you progress up the gorges. Canoeing is best done early in the Dry, when small waterfalls run off cliff walls and the water level is still high enough to reduce the length of the walking sections.

Hiking The Southern Walks information sheet (available at the visitor centre) details seven marked trails (from the 1.8km/1hr climb to the lookout above the cruise jetty to the 39km/2–3 days Jawoyn Valley hike), while the Jatbula Trail information sheet has basic information on the 58km walk to Edith Falls, usually closed Oct–May, which takes four to five days and has a 15-hiker limit per day, so book well in advance. You need to register with the rangers for any overnight walks, as well as book the ferry crossing and return bus service and provide a $50 refundable deposit.

5

ACCOMMODATION

★ **Cicada Lodge** ☎ 1300 146 743, ⓦ cicadalodge.com.au. Adjacent to the *Nitmiluk National Park Campground & Chalets* (see below) – but a world away in terms of comfort – is this luxurious, award-winning, Jawoyn-owned lodge. You'll find smooth service, a stylish pool area and large, spotless rooms. The food is similarly excellent, and it is a great place for a splurge. __$616__

Nitmiluk National Park Campground & Chalets ☎ 1300 146 743, ⓦ nitmiluktours.com.au. There are various types of accommodation near the visitor centre at this shady campsite. All have access to the large swimming pool and there are plenty of barbecue sites (a fact not lost on the wallabies that pop by for scraps). The backpacker rents include linen, a pancake breakfast and takeaway dinner – there are also smarter safari tents – while the chalets have TV, kitchen and wi-fi. Unpowered sites per person __$16.50__, powered sites __$47.50__, backpacker tents __$143__, safari tents __$159__, chalets __$218__

The Victoria Highway to Western Australia

The **Victoria Highway** stretches for 510km southwest of Katherine to Kununurra in Western Australia. The two pit stops on the long journey west are the *Victoria River Roadhouse*, 194km west of Katherine, access point for the eastern sector of the remote and wild **Gregory National Park**, and **Timber Creek**, another 91km along the highway, near the entrance to the park's western sector. More accessible and also worth a diversion is the **Keep River National Park**, just before the Western Australia border.

South of the highway, between Gregory and Keep River national parks, is the legendary **Victoria River Downs (VRD)** station, once the country's biggest cattle station and the base of Australia's biggest heli-mustering outfit (☎ 08 8975 0777, ⓦ heli-musternt.com.au).

Timber Creek

TIMBER CREEK, almost 300km west of Katherine, makes a welcome break on the long run to Kununurra. In 1856, the explorer Augustus Gregory's ship ran aground on the Victoria River and, forced to make repairs, Timber Creek was born, an inland port to serve the vast pastoral properties then being established throughout the region. This remote outpost was soon the scene of bitter disputes between Aborigines and the settlers, and in 1898 a **police station** was set up in a hut at Timber Creek, staffed by two officers and an Aboriginal tracker whose task was to patrol an area the size of Tasmania. The old police station precinct is now a National Trust-owned **museum** (April–Aug Mon–Fri 10am–noon; $3), and gives a pithy historical commentary on the region illustrated with relics from the pioneer days.

INFORMATION   TIMBER CREEK

Tourist information Try the Victoria River Cruise office's Croc Stock Shop (Mon–Sat 8am–4pm; ☎ 0427 750 731, ⓦ victoriarivercruise.com), from where you can also book a sunset cruise ($95).

Services Buy food and other goods at Fogarty's Store, attached to the *Timber Creek Hotel*.

ACCOMMODATION

Timber Creek Hotel & Circle F Caravan Park ☎ 08 8975 0722, ⓦ timbercreekhotel.com.au. A roadhouse set-up with basic accommodation, fuel and food, as well as a daily croc-feeding session during the Dry at 5pm from the bridge at the back of the place. Un/powered sites __$27/30__, doubles __$110__

Gregory National Park

Gregory National Park (also known as Judbarra), the Territory's second-largest reserve, exhibits striking sandstone escarpments, deep dramatic gorges and limestone hills. With a 4WD and the right gear, you can explore plenty of remote Outback tracks and do a spot of bush camping.

Accessible from the Victoria Highway, 2km west of *Victoria River Roadhouse* in the eastern sector, the steep 3km return **Escarpment Walk** boasts breathtaking vistas of the surrounding red escarpments and picturesque valley.

In the western sector, the park's main attraction, **Limestone Gorge**, can only be reached by high-clearance 4WD along a corrugated track 48km south of the highway. The 1.8km Limestone Ridge Loop Walk winds through a stunning karst landscape that affords magnificent views of the valley and East Baines River. There's a campsite, and while you can swim in the billabong, you can only fish the river. The historic Bullita Homestead and stockyards are 9km south of the Limestone Gorge turn-off.

The one-way 70km **Bullita Stockroute** is a looped track to the west of the main access road, following an old stock route. The eight-hour drive involves a couple of challenging river crossings and crawling over extremely rocky terrain. It's vital to assess conditions before attempting the route (check on ☎ 1800 246 199, ⦿ ntlis.nt.gov.au/ roadreport, or call the local Parks & Wildlife Office (see below). For avid off-roaders, this is 4WD paradise; **camping** is permitted at designated spots along the way.

ARRIVAL AND INFORMATION   GREGORY NATIONAL PARK

By car The park is accessible during the Dry, from May to November. At other times, roads may be closed due to flooding. To make the most of the park you'll need a high-clearance 4WD vehicle with snorkel, spare tyres, and lots of fuel, food and water.

Tourist information Stop at the Parks & Wildlife office at Timber Creek (turn right just before Watch Creek, west of town; ☎ 08 8975 0888) to get a map and information about 4WD tracks, walks and camping, check road conditions, and to register your trip plans.

Keep River National Park

West of Timber Creek, the land flattens out into the evocatively named **Whirlwind Plains**, where the East and West Baines rivers frequently flood the Victoria Highway in the Wet. **Keep River National Park** lies just before the Western Australia border, 185km from Timber Creek. The corrugated gravel roads are accessible to 2WDs, although they are often closed due to flooding from November to April. It's an easily explored park, teeming with wallabies and birds, and boasting colossal domed rocks and Aboriginal art sites, the best of which is **Nganalam**, 24km from the park entrance. Marked walking trails start from the two **campsites**, *Gurrandalng*, 18km from the park entrance, and *Jarnem*, 31km.

INFORMATION   KEEP RIVER NATIONAL PARK

Tourist information Call into the Cockatoo Lagoon Information Centre (☎ 08 9167 8827), 3km from the highway, for information on road conditions. If continuing into WA, eat or discard any fresh produce or honey before you get to the border as there are restrictions on what you can take in.

South to Alice Springs

The 1100km south from Katherine down "**the Track**", as the Stuart Highway is known, to Alice Springs, is something of a no-man's-land for travellers – taken up by a sparsely populated, flat, arid plain rolling all the way to the Red Centre. The bleak landscape can provoke a slight anxiety when looking at the fuel gauge (see box, p.523). If you really have to drive straight through, allow a good twelve hours, though it makes sense to break the journey at **Mataranka** to visit the hot springs and overnight further south at **Tennant Creek**. Avoid driving in the dark, as there's a strong likelihood of hitting kangaroos or dozy cattle, which often wander across the road.

West of the Track, the vast Aboriginal lands of the Warlpiri and neighbouring groups occupy just about the entire **Tanami Desert**, while to the east are the grasslands of the **Barkly Tableland**, a dramatic drought-affected pastoral region extending north to the seldom-visited coast of the **Gulf of Carpentaria**.

5

Mataranka and around

The tiny town of **MATARANKA** – just over 100km from Katherine – is the capital of "Never Never" country, named after Jeannie Gunn's 1908 novel about a pioneering woman's life, and set in the area, *We of the Never Never*. Nearby, the hot springs of **Elsey National Park**, **Mataranka Homestead** and the freshwater wetlands of the **Roper River** lure passing travellers from May to September. You'll find accommodation, fuel, a supermarket and local museum (Mon–Fri 9am–4pm; $3) on Roper Terrace (Stuart Highway).

Elsey National Park

The main attractions in the 4000-acre **Elsey National Park** are the natural springs that feed the Roper River. Set amid tropical woodlands off Martins Road, 2km northeast of Mataranka, the swampy pools of **Bitter Springs** have lukewarm minty-blue mineral waters, in which you can swim and drift with the current. There are picnic areas and toilets at the springs, plus a short nature walk with signboards detailing the local geology and wildlife.

The clear 34°C waters of **Rainbow Springs** and Mataranka Thermal Pool, adjoining *Mataranka Homestead Tourist Resort*, 6km east of town off Homestead Road, make for another refreshing pit stop. The sandy-bottomed pool is surrounded by palm woodlands.

Mataranka Homestead

Established in 1916 as an experimental sheep and cattle station, **Mataranka Homestead** is a fine example of tropical Top End architecture. Sitting across the car park from the homestead itself is the fascinating Elsey Homestead replica, built for the 1982 film *We of the Never Never*, which has a free daily screening at noon at the *Mataranka Homestead Tourist Resort*.

ACCOMMODATION
MATARANKA AND AROUND

Bitter Springs Cabins 255 Martin Rd, Bitter Springs ☎ 08 8975 4838, ⓦ bittersprings cabins.com.au. Formerly *Mataranka Cabins*, these attractive cabins and camping are set by the river, a 500m walk to Bitter Springs. Guests can fish for barramundi, and rare goshawks nest nearby. Cabins $\underline{130}$, un/powered sites $\underline{30/35}$

Mataranka Homestead Tourist Resort Homestead Rd ☎ 08 8975 4544, ⓦ matarankahomestead.com.au. Perfectly located for a dip in Rainbow Springs (open to non-guests). Accommodation includes basic motel rooms, self-catering cabins and a campsite. There's live music most nights, and canoes to rent. Cabin $\underline{115}$, doubles $\underline{89}$, un/powered sites $\underline{26/30}$

Territory Manor 51 Martin Rd ☎ 08 8975 4516, ⓦ matarankamotel.com. Set in leafy grounds with a swimming pool and twice-daily barramundi-feeding shows (9.30am and 1pm). There's a restaurant, and occasional evening entertainment. Doubles $\underline{120}$, unpowered sites per person $\underline{15}$, powered sites $\underline{30}$.

The Roper Highway

During the Dry, experienced off-roaders with a 4WD (and spare tyres) can take the **Roper Highway**, south of Mataranka, east for 185km (the single-lane bitumen ends at around 130km) to the remote **ROPER BAR** community where the *Roper Bar Store* has food, fuel and some accommodation. Take care crossing the causeway. If you're planning on taking the 4WD Nathan River Road from here to **Borroloola**, 362km away (see p.524), for some fishing, stock up on food, water and fuel as there's nothing on the way.

INFORMATION
THE ROPER HIGHWAY

Services *Roper Bar Store* (Mon–Sat 9am–6pm, Sun 1–6pm, essential to call ahead; ☎ 08 8975 4636, ⓦ roperbar.com.au) has food, fuel, fishing gear and some accommodation. It doesn't sell alcohol.

WHERE TO STOP FOR FUEL

Given the distances involved when driving the Stuart Highway, it pays to know where you can **refuel** en route. Prepare yourself too for the fact that fuel gets more **expensive** as you reach more remote areas. The price per litre at Kings Canyon can be some forty percent higher than at Katherine. The figures below are for southbound travel on sealed roads and note the distance from the previous fuel stop.

Katherine to Erldunda (Lasseter Highway turn-off): Mataranka (106km), *Hi-Way Inn*/Daly Waters (167km), Dunmarra (48km), Elliott (104km), Renner Springs (92km), Threeways (24km), Tennant Creek (115km), Wauchope (18km), Wycliffe Well (92km), Barrow Creek (90km), Ti Tree (59km), Aileron (130km), Alice Springs (95km), Stuarts Well (107km), Erldunda (73km).

Erldunda to Yulara (*Ayers Rock Resort*): Curtin Springs (160km), Yulara (84km).

Erldunda to Kings Canyon (*Kings Creek Station* (179km), *Kings Canyon Resort* (34km).

Larrimah

LARRIMAH, 72km south of Mataranka, was where the old Darwin railway terminated until 1976 when it closed for good following Cyclone Tracy. Up until then, it had been a busy road–rail terminus, receiving goods brought up from Alice Springs. Now it's just a fuel stop on the highway with a bit more history than most.

ACCOMMODATION AND EATING   LARRIMAH

Larrimah Wayside Inn Mahoney St ☎08 8975 9931, ✉la.pub@telstra.com. Also known as the *Pink Panther Pub* (and boasting the garish paint job to match), with simple food and scruffy accommodation as well as a free "zoo" and a surprisingly good museum (24hr; free) in an old repeater station. No fuel. Doubles $70, un/powered sites per person $10/12.50

Daly Waters

Another 89km south brings you to **DALY WATERS**, 3km off the highway and site of Australia's first international airstrip. Today's focal point is *The Daly Waters Pub* (see below), here since the 1930s and originally a supply point for drovers. It's laden with memorabilia, including money and IDs stuck to the bar and underwear hanging from the ceilings: you're welcome to contribute. In its earliest days, when Qantas's Singapore flights refuelled here, world-class aviators would pop in for a cold one.

Just 2km further along the Stuart Highway, at the *Hi-Way Inn Roadhouse*, the turn-off to the **Carpentaria Highway** heads east to Cape Crawford, 270km away, and Borroloola, 414km (see p.524). Further down the Track, a few kilometres before *Dunmarra Roadhouse*, there's a turn-off west to the **Buchanan Highway** and, 182km later, *Top Springs Roadhouse*, where you can link with roads leading on into WA.

ACCOMMODATION   DALY WATERS

Daly Waters Pub Stuart St ☎08 8975 9927, ⓦdalywaterspub.com. A hugely popular stop-off for Australia's legions of road-tripping "grey nomads", who make the most of the bawdily patriotic on-stage entertainment (nightly from 5.30pm in high season). There's a big, usually busy, caravan site out the back, and the daily beef-and-barra BBQ (6–8.30pm) is a further draw. A memorable place. Cabins $135, doubles $75, un/powered sites per person $9/16

Cape Crawford

Remote **Cape Crawford**, bizarrely sited well over 100km away from the sea, is the gateway to the spectacular, towering sandstone rock formations of the **Lost City**. The settlement itself is named after Lindsay Crawford, a cattle drover of the 1880s who was one of the first to discover the site.

Heartbreak Hotel Cnr Carpentaria & Tablelands hwys ☎ 08 8975 9928. An authentic NT accommodation experience, not so much for its unremarkable rooms as for the remarkable region it sits in. Twin rooms $90, un/powered sites $10/30

Borroloola

Situated on the croc-infested **McArthur River**, **BORROLOOLA** is a rough Aboriginal welfare town mainly of interest as a pit stop for 4WD drivers and for **fishing** fanatics who visit for the fabled barramundi. It does, however, have a colourful **history**. Explorers Leichhardt and Gregory passed through in the mid-nineteenth century, reporting good pasture, and cattle drovers followed. By the early 1880s, Borroloola was a wild outpost that even missionaries avoided, and when the stock route dried up soon afterwards only a handful of settlers remained, leaving local Aboriginal groups to reclaim the area. The only original building to have survived punch-ups, termites and floods is the **Old Police Station** (May–Sept Mon–Fri 10am–4pm; $5), now a museum documenting Borroloola's early history.

By car Borroloola is accessible from the west via the Carpentaria Highway and Cape Crawford, and from the east from *Hell's Gate Roadhouse* in Queensland (see p.481) via the unsealed Savannah Way, a route that can be challenging, and impassable during the Wet, and is best attempted by high-clearance 4WD.

Savannah Way Motel Robinson Rd ☎ 08 8975 8883, ⓦ savannahwaymotel.com.au. Doubling as a car and boat rental outlet, the *Savannah Way Motel* has a range of rooms and cabins (some of the latter have kitchenettes) in a garden setting. Doubles $80, cabins $120

Newcastle Waters

Further down the Track, there's a turn-off west, 4km, to **NEWCASTLE WATERS**. A handful of people still live here in what was once a thriving droving township, but it's been largely abandoned. Visitors can wander a slightly creepy old hotel and general store.

Elliott and around

Around 30km south of Newcastle Waters, **ELLIOTT** has a couple of roadhouses and a few shops serving the Jingili Aboriginal community, but there's little reason to linger other than to refuel.

As you head south from here, the trees that dotted the landscape start to recede into low-lying mallee scrubland as you approach Central Australia. Worth a quick look if you're ticking off bush pubs, **Renner Springs** is plastered with eccentric knick-knacks and has excellent home-baked bread and pies.

Banka Banka Station Stuart Hwy ☎ 08 8964 4511. Open year-round, this working cattle station has a bit more character than many of the other Stuart Highway stop-offs. It's about 70km north of Three Ways. Unpowered sites per person $10

Three Ways and around

On the way to **THREE WAYS** (where there's a roadhouse and not much more) watch out for the turn-off to **Attack Creek Memorial** where explorer Stuart was repelled by Aborigines on one of his expeditions. From Three Ways, the **Barkly Highway** heads east to Camooweal, Mount Isa and Townsville in Queensland; at 187km you'll hit *Barkly*

Homestead (☎08 8964 4549, ⊛barklyhomestead.com.au), which has the usual services. From here, the single-lane **Tablelands Highway** offers a narrow bitumen route to Cape Crawford (see p.523).

Tennant Creek

With its handful of shops, restaurants and sights, including an excellent Aboriginal cultural centre, **TENNANT CREEK**, 26km south of Three Ways, remains the best stopover on the long haul between Katherine (669km north) and Alice Springs (507km south). At the heart of the Barkly Region, Tennant is a hub for the mining and beef industries and the surrounding area is home to the NT's oldest, and some of the world's biggest, cattle stations.

Sadly, Tennant also has a dark side, with social problems and alcohol-related issues blighting sections of the Aboriginal community which makes up close to half the town's population of around 3000. It can feel edgy when venturing out at night – taxis are a good idea if you're taking more than a short walk – but the small town has for decades made efforts to shake off its reputation, and it deserves to be visited with an open mind.

John McDouall Stuart came through Tennant Creek in the early 1860s, followed by the Overland Telegraph Line ten years later. Pastoralists and prospectors arrived from the south and east, and in 1933 it was the site of Australia's last major **gold rush**. Mining corporations continue to exploit the rich deposits here, with mineral exploration the most important industry alongside beef. The Stuart Highway becomes Paterson Street, the town's main drag, as you enter Tennant.

Battery Hill Mining Centre

Peko Road • Daily 9am–5pm • Museum only $7, Gold Stamp Battery Tour (Mon–Fri 10.30am) $25, including entrance to the museum • ☎08 8962 1281

The scale of the 1930s gold rush was significant; for a year the equivalent of around a million dollars of gold was extracted from Tennant each day. The **Battery Hill Mining Centre** traces this remarkable history through its on-site museum, which houses an impressive minerals collection as well as a colourful account of the region's social history in the fascinating Freedom, Fortitude and Flies exhibition. Out the back, daily weekday tours give the chance to find out more about the old stamp battery (crushing machinery).

Nyinkka Nyunyu Cultural Centre

Paterson Street • May–Sept Mon–Sat 8am–6pm, Sun 10am–2pm; Oct–April Mon–Fri 9am–5pm, Sat & Sun 10am–2pm • $15 with self-guided audio tour • ☎08 8962 2699, ⊛nyinkkanyunyu.com.au

At the southern end of Paterson Street, the **Nyinkka Nyunyu Cultural Centre** gives a revealing insight into the local indigenous Warumungu people, with innovative displays on their involvement in the cattle and mining histories, and on land claims and bushtucker, including films of Warumungu talking about their experiences.

Bill Allen Lookout

Not far from the Battery Hill Mining Centre, the **Bill Allen Lookout** is easily accessed and it provides an impressive sweep of the surrounding region, offering up a sense of the town's isolation and the mind-blowingly large terrain covered by Stuart and his ilk.

Telegraph Station

If you have your own vehicle, the beautiful old **Telegraph Station**, located 11km north of Tennant Creek, is well worth a quick look. Pick up the keys from the visitor centre or the *Outback Caravan Park* (you have to leave a $20 deposit in both cases).

5

ARRIVAL AND INFORMATION

By bus Greyhound buses stop at the Transit Centre (opposite *Jackson's Bar* on Paterson Street). As both north- and southbound buses come through at ungodly hours, you should arrange with your accommodation to pick you up or book a taxi. Buses (1 daily in either direction) then depart north towards Darwin at 3.15am (14hr) and south towards Alice at 3.10am (6hr).

The Bodhi Bus (☎ 08 8971 0774, ⊛ thebodhibus.com.au) also has services to/from Katherine and remote communities throughout the region.

Tourist information The helpful visitor centre is at Battery Hill Mining Centre (daily 9am–5.30pm; ☎ 1800 500 879, ⊛ barklytourism.com.au), 1.5km east along Peko Road.

ACCOMMODATION

There are motels at each end of town and one in the middle, but book ahead as they fill up quickly.

ElDorado Motor Inn Paterson St ☎ 08 8962 2402, ⊛ eldoradomotorinn.com.au. One of the more comfortable accommodation options, this motel is located at the north end of town, and has a decent licensed restaurant (offering 30 types of schnitzel) and small pool. Triples and family rooms as well as doubles. $150

Outback Caravan Park 71 Peko Road ☎ 08 8962 2459. The better of Tennant Creek's two tourist parks (although this isn't a ringing endorsement), shaded under tall trees

and offering a pool, licensed café and small shop. Cabins $115, un/powered sites $27/36

Tourists Rest VIP Hostel Leichhardt St ☎ 08 8962 2719, ⊛ touristrest.com.au. The only hostel in town. Plus points: 24hr check-in, pool, kitchen, tour desk and free pick-ups from the bus stop. Minus points: the dorms and private rooms are worn and the bathrooms pretty basic. Dorms $30, doubles $65

EATING

Taste of Asia Sporties Club, cnr Ambrose & Stuart sts ☎ 08 8962 3330. Asian option (dishes $15–35) at the sports club – staff recommend the chicken chow mein. Standard Aussie pub grub is also available in the club. And if you join spectators at the keenly contested Sat afternoon AFL games held here, it can be a rewarding way of seeing a

different side to the local indigenous community. Mon–Sat 6–9pm.

Woks Up 108 Paterson St ☎ 08 8962 3888. A cheerful Chinese restaurant on the main drag, with standard dishes ($15–30) such as sweet-and-sour squid and chicken chop suey. Takeaway also available. Daily 5pm–late.

Davenport Ranges National Park

Eighty-seven kilometres south of Tennant Creek, a sign points east towards the **Davenport Ranges National Park**. Here, a 4WD track runs east along the north side of the ranges and then south some 160km to Old Police Station Waterhole before looping back west along the rougher but scenically more interesting southern side, passing a couple of waterholes, station homesteads and outstations. While you could do the loop (approximately 315km in total) with a stop for swimming and lunch in a day, an overnight camp at the Waterhole is more fun. The only problem is that you'll emerge 63km further down the Stuart Highway and will have to backtrack 46km to see the Devil's Marbles; alternatively, see them in the morning (when the light is better anyway) before heading to the Davenports. Get info from Tennant Creek's visitor centre and ensure you have sufficient provisions.

The Devil's Marbles

Just off the highway about 130km south of Tennant Creek, the marvellous **Devil's Marbles** are worth an hour or so of your time. Genuine geological oddities, the boulders are spectacular at sunrise and sunset, when they positively glow in the low-angled light. During the day, expect a steady stream of visitors striking elaborate between-rock poses for photos. The local Warumungu people believe the Marbles are the eggs of the Rainbow Serpent.

ACCOMMODATION

Camping There's a basic campsite here (there are no toilets, no showers, etc) which is well worth staying at if

you want to catch the Marbles at dusk or dawn. Payment is on an honesty system. $3.30 per person

Wauchope Hotel Stuart Hwy ☎08 8964 1963, ⓦwauchopehotel.com.au. An 8km drive south of the Devil's Marbles, this 1930s pub and roadhouse at Wauchope (pronounced "Walkup") has rooms sleeping one to four, as well as cabins, camping and a basic restaurant. One to two person rooms $70, two to four person rooms $130, two to four person cabins $160, un/powered sites $10/30

Wycliffe Well Holiday Park Stuart Hwy ☎08 8964 1966, ⓦwycliffe.com.au. Wycliffe Well Holiday Park, aka "the UFO capital of Australia", stands as one of the Stuart Highway's most unusual campsites-cum-roadhouses. There's a landing pad on the forecourt ("earthlings also welcome"), an emu enclosure, and scores of newspaper articles inside attesting to the regular sightings of UFOs. One theory is that spottings have been related to the eerie Aboriginal "Min Min Light" (see p.464). There's a good campsite, with cabins and a café. Doubles $130, cabins $70, un/powered sites $35/36

Barrow Creek

Some 90km beyond the Devil's Marbles, **BARROW CREEK** has a chilling history. In 1874 ninety Kaytetye people were slaughtered here in reprisal for the killing of two white settlers whose graves are in the forecourt. In 1928 a police-led posse set out from Barrow Creek following the killing of a white dingo-trapper by Aborigines. More than seventy were killed at Coniston Station, 100km away, the last known **massacre** of indigenous Australians.

In 2001, a few kilometres down the highway from Barrow Creek, British tourist **Peter Falconio** was murdered (although his body was never found) and his girlfriend Joanne Lees abducted by drug-runner Bradley John Murdoch; the case inspired horror film *Wolf Creek*.

ACCOMMODATION   BARROW CREEK

Barrow Creek Hotel Stuart Hwy ☎08 8956 9753, ⓔbarrowcreekpub@bigpond.com. If you're up for staying, this 1926 pub is as quirky as they come, its walls daubed in coarse humour and foreign banknotes. It was once an Overland Telegraph Line outpost, and has simple, no-frills rooms and an exposed campground. Doubles $75, powered sites $20

Ti Tree

After spying Central Mount Stuart away to the west, you'll come to **TI TREE**, an Aboriginal community close to the middle of the continent. There's a bog-standard roadhouse, but of more interest is **Red Centre Farm** (daily 9am–7pm; ☎08 8956 9828), 12km further south, where you can buy delicious mango ice cream, as well as jam, chutney and (very sweet) wine.

Aileron

Another 58km south, **AILERON** is the last fuel stop before Alice Springs, 132km away. It's also home to a 17m hilltop statue of the Anmatjere Man – a memorial to Charlie Quartpot, a rainmaker who lived in the area – and, at ground level, a similarly proportioned woman and child. The adjacent Anmatjere Art Gallery (hours vary, usually daily 9am–5pm) has some excellent indigenous works at good prices.

ACCOMMODATION   AILERON

Aileron Roadhouse Stuart Hwy ☎08 8956 9703, ⓦaileronroadhouse.com.au. Expect an unvarnished Aussie welcome at the *Aileron Roadhouse*, where there's pub grub at the *Glen Maggie Bar*, camping, dorms and rooms. Doubles $130, camping (un/powered same price) $12

The Plenty and Sandover highways

Before embarking, check the latest conditions online at ⓦntlis.nt.gov.au/roadreport or phone ☎1800 246 199

Towards Alice Springs, the land begins to crumple as you near the MacDonnell Ranges. The **Plenty and Sandover highways**, which run off the Stuart Highway 66km south of Aileron, head northeast to Queensland through the scenic Harts and Jervois ranges.

5

After the first sealed 145km, the Plenty becomes a dirt track, deteriorating after Jervois homestead into large ruts and bulldust and continuing to the NT–Queensland border, where it's called the Donohue Highway. After the first 30km of sealed road, the more remote Sandover is a dirt track for the remaining 520km, still with only one fuel supply en route at Arlparra Store. These routes are susceptible to flooding, impassable after rain, and prone to washouts, remaining shut for months at a time until repaired and graded. They should only be attempted by experienced off-road drivers in a high-clearance 4WD with plenty of spare fuel, food, water and tyres. Unbelievably, road trains use these tracks (particularly Plenty), so take care.

ACCOMMODATION   PLENTY HIGHWAY

Gemtree Caravan Park Plenty Hwy ☎ 08 8956 9855, ⓦ gemtree.com.au. Sitting 140km northeast of Alice (on sealed roads), this likeable spot has fossicking tours, a bar, set-menu dinners and regular free entertainment. As well as caravan sites and cabins, there are some basic singles ($50). Cabins $85, un/powered sites $25/32

The Tanami Road

Before embarking, check the latest conditions online at ⓦ ntlis.nt.gov.au/roadreport or phone ☎ 1800 246 199

Twenty kilometres north of Alice Springs, the legendary **Tanami Road** leads 1055km northwest to Halls Creek in Western Australia. The 4WD-recommended road is sealed for the first 188km to *Tilmouth Roadhouse*, after which it's a corrugated dirt road, parts of which are in a severely bad state following heavy use from mining trucks. There's ongoing pressure for the road to be upgraded. If you're heading from Alice Springs to Purnululu (see p.489), the Tanami is quicker than the bitumen via Katherine.

Alice Springs and around

The bright, clear desert air of **ALICE SPRINGS** is a welcome relief after a long drive south from the languid, tropical north down the Stuart Highway. Home to almost 29,000 people, the town has some interesting sights, notably the wonderful **Araluen Arts Centre** and the out-of-town **Desert Park**, and a couple of nights is the minimum you should budget for. Timing your visit with one of Alice Springs' quirky festivals, which include everything from dry river-bed regattas to the Camel Cup, is also worth considering.

The centre occupies a compact area between the Stuart Highway and Leichhardt Terrace, along the almost perennially dry Todd River, bordered to the north and south by Wills Terrace and Stott Terrace respectively. Bisecting this rectangle is **Todd**

THE RED CENTRE: WHEN TO GO AND WHAT TO TAKE

The aridity of the Centre results in seasonal extremes of temperature. In the midwinter months of July and August the weather is lovely and the light clear, although **freezing nights**, especially around Uluru, are not uncommon. In December and January the temperature can reach 40°C by 10am and not drop below 30°C all night. The transitional seasons of autumn (April–June) and spring (Sept & Oct) are the best times to explore the region in comfort, although in spring there's the chance of rain. While you may encounter floods and road closures, rain can transform the desert into a green garden with sprouting wild flowers, though generally it's the **midsummer storms** that bring the most rain.

Out here a **wide-brimmed hat** is not so much a fashion accessory as a lifesaver, keeping your head and face in permanent shadow. A head net is also highly advisable – the flies can be maddening during the day, especially at Uluru. All walks require a **water bottle** and lashings of **sun block**. Australia's venomous (but rarely seen) snakes, rocky paths and the prickly spinifex grass that covers a fifth of the continent make a pair of **covered shoes or boots** essential too.

Mall, a pedestrian thoroughfare lined with cafés and galleries. Get an overview of Alice's setting by nipping up **Anzac Hill** (off Wills Terrace) for 360-degree views over the town and the MacDonnell Ranges. Note that Alice Springs isn't the safest place for a long wander at night, so it's best to take a taxi after dark.

Brief history

The area has been inhabited for at least forty thousand years by the Arrernte (also known as Aranda), who moved between reliable water sources along the MacDonnell

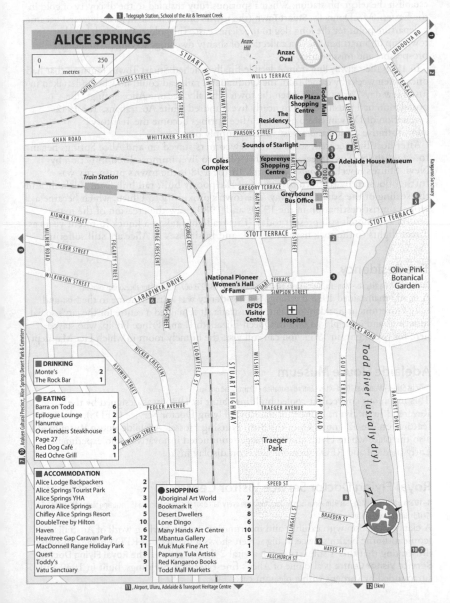

ALICE SPRINGS

0 — 250
metres

DRINKING
Monte's	2
The Rock Bar	1

EATING
Barra on Todd	6
Epilogue Lounge	2
Hanuman	7
Overlanders Steakhouse	5
Page 27	4
Red Dog Café	3
Red Ochre Grill	1

ACCOMMODATION
Alice Lodge Backpackers	2
Alice Springs Tourist Park	7
Alice Springs YHA	3
Aurora Alice Springs	4
Chifley Alice Springs Resort	5
DoubleTree by Hilton	6
Haven	6
Heavitree Gap Caravan Park	12
MacDonnell Range Holiday Park	11
Quest	8
Toddy's	9
Vatu Sanctuary	1

SHOPPING
Aboriginal Art World	7
Bookmark It	9
Desert Dwellers	8
Lone Dingo	6
Many Hands Art Centre	10
Mbantua Gallery	5
Muk Muk Fine Art	1
Papunya Tula Artists	3
Red Kangaroo Books	4
Todd Mall Markets	2

Map labels: Telegraph Station, School of the Air & Tennant Creek; Anzac Hill; Anzac Oval; STUART HIGHWAY; WILLS TERRACE; UNDOOLYA RD; STUART TERRACE; SMITH ST; STOKES STREET; COLSON STREET; RAILWAY TERRACE; Alice Plaza Shopping Centre; Cinema; Todd Mall; LEICHHARDT TERRACE; The Residency; GHAN ROAD; WHITTAKER STREET; PARSONS STREET; Sounds of Starlight; Adelaide House Museum; Kangaroo Sanctuary; Coles Complex; Yeperenye Shopping Centre; Train Station; BATH STREET; GREGORY TERRACE; Greyhound Bus Office; HARTLEY ST; TODD ST; KIDMAN STREET; GEORGE CRESCENT; GEORGE CRES; MILNER ROAD; ELDER STREET; FOGARTY STREET; STOTT TERRACE; WILKINSON STREET; LARAPINTA DRIVE; HONG STREET; National Pioneer Women's Hall of Fame; TERRACE; SIMPSON STREET; Olive Pink Botanical Garden; RFDS Visitor Centre; Hospital; TUNCKS ROAD; Todd River (usually dry); NICKER CRESCENT; BLOOMFIELD ST; ASHWIN STREET; STUART HIGHWAY; WILSHIRE ST; SOUTH TERRACE; BARRETT DRIVE; PEDLER AVENUE; TRAEGER AVENUE; GAP ROAD; NEWLAND STREET; Traeger Park; SPEED ST; BALLINGALL ST; BRAEDEN ST; HAYES ST; ALLCHURCH ST; Araluen Cultural Precinct, Alice Springs Desert Park & Cemetery; Airport, Uluru, Adelaide & Transport Heritage Centre; (3km)

5

Ranges. But, as elsewhere in the Territory, it was only the arrival of the Overland Telegraph Line in the 1870s that led to a permanent settlement here. It was **Charles Todd**, then South Australia's Superintendent of Telegraphs, who saw the need to link South Australia with the Top End, which in turn would give a link to Asia and, ultimately, the rest of the empire. The town's river and its tributary carry his name, while the "spring" (actually a billabong) and town are named after his wife, Alice.

With repeater stations needed every 250km from Adelaide to Darwin to boost the OTL signal, the billabong north of today's town was chosen as the spot at which to establish the telegraph station. When a spurious ruby rush led to the discovery of gold in the Eastern MacDonnells, **Stuart Town** (the town's official name in its early years) became a departure point for the long slog to the riches east. The gold rush fizzled, but the township of Stuart remained, a collection of shanty dwellings serving pastoralists, prospectors and missionaries.

In 1929 the **railway line** from Adelaide finally reached Stuart Town. Journeys that had once taken weeks by camel from the Oodnadatta railhead could now be undertaken in just a few days, so by 1933, when the town officially became Alice Springs, the population had mushroomed to nearly five hundred white Australians. The 1942 evacuation of Darwin (see p.642) saw Alice Springs become the Territory's administrative capital and a busy military supply base.

After hostilities ceased, some of the newcomers stayed on and Alice Springs began to establish itself as a pleasant if quirky place to live, immortalized in fiction by Nevil Shute's novel, *A Town Like Alice*. In the 1980s the town's prosperity was further boosted by the reconstruction of the poorly built rail link from Adelaide and the sealing of the Stuart Highway. The town's proximity to Uluru, which became a global tourist destination in the 1970s and 1980s, saw the creation of the many resorts and motels still present today. This trade has taken a knock in recent years as direct flights to the rock have increased, and businesses in Alice are still suffering.

The Residency

Cnr Parsons & Hartley sts • Mon–Fri 10am–3pm • Entry by donation • ☎ 08 8953 6073, ⓦ heritagealicesprings.com.au

A neatly maintained 1928 dwelling, **The Residency** was initially home to the first and only Government Resident of Central Australia. It remained a centre for the city's social functions and once played host to Queen Elizabeth II and Prince Philip, who stayed here for two nights in 1963. You can still visit the homely room in which Her Maj slept.

Adelaide House Museum

Parsons Street • Mon–Sat 10am–4pm • Entry by donation • ⓦ flynntrail.org.au

This ingenious convection-cooled building, built in 1926, was designed by the Reverend John Flynn, founder of the Royal Flying Doctor Service (RFDS), who now features on the $20 note. Once the Bush Nursing Hostel, **Adelaide House Museum** was also the place where Flynn and Alf Traeger conducted innovative radio experiments. Early medical and RFDS memorabilia is on display inside.

Royal Flying Doctor Service Visitor Centre

8–10 Stuart Terrace • Mon–Sat 9am–5pm, Sun 1–5pm; tours run every half hour (last tour 4pm) • $15 (including tour) • ☎ 08 8958 8411, ⓦ rfdsalicesprings.com.au

A classy attraction with exhibits and information on the sterling work of Australia's iconic airborne health service. A big screen shows a live feed of RFDS plane call-outs, illustrating that this is still very much a vital 24hr operation. The **Royal Flying Doctor Service Visitor Centre** is also one of Alice's finest heritage buildings, built in 1939 and surrounded by gardens with a pleasant café.

National Pioneer Women's Hall of Fame

2 Stuart Terrace • Daily 10am–5pm, closed Jan • $10 • ☎ 08 8952 9006, ⓦ pioneerwomen.com.au

Located within the walls of the Old Alice Springs Gaol, the **National Pioneer Women's Hall of Fame** is a stirring exhibition detailing the achievements of admirable women such as Molly Clark, an archetypal Outback "battler" who was a proud exponent of equal gender recognition.

Olive Pink Botanical Garden

Tuncks Road • Daily 8am–6pm • Entry by donation • ☎ 08 8952 2154, ⓦ opbg.com.au

A famed activist for Aboriginal rights in the mid-twentieth century, local lady Olive Pink also found time to collect native flora from the surrounding area. Some five hundred species are identified along pathways winding through the **Olive Pink Botanical Garden**, which was founded more than fifty years ago. There's a good café here too.

The Telegraph Station

Herbert Heritage Dr • Daily 8am–9pm (for reserve), 9am–5pm (for historical precinct) • $13.75 (free for reserve) • ☎ 08 8952 3993, ⓦ alicespringstelegraphstation.com.au

The atmospheric buildings of the restored old **Telegraph Station** are tucked in the hills 4km north of the centre, accessible by car from the Stuart Highway or by foot/bike along a 3km riverside walk from Wills Terrace. It's the original site of European settlement in the area, and the best preserved of Australia's dozen Overland Telegraph Line stations. The lawned area is a popular picnic spot, with waterholes for swimming.

School of the Air

80 Head St • Mon–Sat 8.30am–4.30pm, Sun 1–4.30pm • $7.50 • ☎ 08 8951 6834, ⓦ assoa.nt.edu.au • Bus #100 or #101

This famous Outback institution, "the largest classroom in the world", serves an area of 1.3m square kilometres – ten times the size of England – educating children living on remote stations using broadband satellite technology (it employed radio in former times). If you're visiting the **School of the Air** in term-time between 8.30am and 2.30pm, there's a good chance of watching a live lesson.

Araluen Cultural Precinct

61 Larapinta Dr • Mon–Fri 10am–4pm, Sat & Sun 11am–4pm • $15 • ☎ 08 8951 1120, ⓦ araluenartscentre.nt.gov.au • Bus #400 or #401

About 2km from town, the **Araluen Cultural Precinct** combines a range of must-see attractions focused around the **Aruluen Arts Centre**. The main highlights are the stylish **art galleries**, showing paintings from the wonderful Albert Namatjira Collection, the Hermannsburg School and early Papunya art, as well as contemporary exhibitions. Close by, the excellent **Museum of Central Australia** traces the evolution of the area and has an impressive wildlife display. In the same rammed-earth building, an exhibit commemorates the life and work of Aboriginal researcher T.G.H. Strehlow. Also within the Precinct, the **Central Australian Aviation Museum**, located in the Old Connellan Hangar, houses many of the aircraft in which Outback plane travel was pioneered.

Alice Springs Memorial Cemetery

Memorial Dr • Daily 6.30am–6.30pm

The interesting **Alice Springs Memorial Cemetery** includes the graves of the pioneer aviator Eddie Connellan, as well as artist Albert Namatjira and gold prospector Harold Lasseter. There is also a special section for Afghan cameleers, who functioned as the Outback's transportation system in the late nineteenth and early twentieth centuries.

5

Alice Springs Desert Park

6km outside town • Daily 7.30am–6pm, last admission 4.30pm • $32 • ☎ 08 8951 8788, ⓦ alicespringsdesertpark.com.au • No direct public transport; buses #400 & #401 get you as far as Albrecht Dr from where it's a 20–25min walk; Alice Wanderer (see p.534) offers transfers from town at 8am, 11.30am and 2pm, returning noon, 2.30pm and 4.30pm (from $38, including entry); taxi around $25 one-way

Alice Springs Desert Park is the town's premier attraction, with a thoughtful and imaginative design featuring several of the Territory's natural environments. Allow two hours for the self-guided walk through the creek, sand dune and woodland habitats, more if you're planning on enjoying the entertaining presentations, such as the Birds of Prey show. Among the highlights are the various aviaries and the large **nocturnal house** where everything from lethal-looking scorpions to cute, rabbit-eared bilbies can be seen scurrying around in artificial moonlight. An hour-long nocturnal tour (April–Oct 7.30pm, Nov–March 8pm) gives the chance to explore the park by headlamp.

Alice Springs Transport Heritage Centre

1 Norris Bell Dr • Daily 9am–5pm • The Old Ghan Museum $12, NRT Hall of Fame $15 • ⓦ roadtransporthall.com

About 10km south of town, the **Alice Springs Transport Heritage Centre** at MacDonnell Siding is home to the **Old Ghan Museum** and original *Ghan* carriages, as well as the **National Road Transport Hall of Fame**, which features a collection of old vehicles, including the first road trains used to slog up to Darwin during the 1930s at 30kph. The whole place has a rambling, old-time sparkle to it, and there's a lovely tearoom.

Kangaroo Sanctuary

15km outside Alice Springs • 2.5hr sunset tours Feb–Nov Wed–Fri • $85, including transfers from Alice • ☎ 08 8965 0038, ⓦ kangaroosanctuary.com

Run by Chris "Brolga" Barnes – star of BBC's *Kangaroo Dundee* programmes – the 188-acre **Kangaroo Sanctuary** is home to a mob of red kangaroos, many of them rescued as orphans after their mothers were hit by cars. Brolga is an engaging guide, and the roos are by turns entertaining and cute. You even get the chance to cuddle a joey. Access is by tour only.

ARRIVAL AND INFORMATION

ALICE SPRINGS

By plane The airport (ⓦ alicespringsairport.com.au) is 14km south of town. Shuttle services ($16; ☎ 08 8952 2111, ⓦ alicewanderer.com.au) meet incoming flights; taxis cost around $45.

Destinations Ayers Rock (1 daily; 55min); Adelaide (1 daily; 1hr 55min); Cairns (1 daily; 1hr 55min); Darwin (2–3 daily; 2hr); Melbourne (1 daily; 2hr 35min); Perth (1 daily; 3hr 25min); Sydney (1–2 daily; 2hr 45min).

By train The train station – open only when *Ghan* trains are due to arrive – is on George Crescent, just off Larapinta Drive, about a fifteen-minute walk ($10 by taxi) from the centre.

Destinations Adelaide (Thurs; 23hr 15min–39hr 5min;

Coober Pedy (Thurs, May–Oct only; 11hr 15min); Darwin (Mon; 23hr 30min); Katherine (Mon; 15hr).

By bus Buses arrive and depart from the Greyhound booking office at 2/76 Todd Street.

Destinations Towards Adelaide (1 daily, departs 10.30am; 8hr to Coober Pedy; 20hr to Adelaide); towards Darwin (1 daily, departs 7.15pm; 6hr 35min to Tennant Creek; 16hr 25min to Katherine; 22hr 5min to Darwin).

Tourist information The helpful visitor centre (Mon–Fri 8.30am–5pm, Sat & Sun 9.30am–4pm; ☎ 08 8952 5800 or ☎ 1800 645 199, ⓦ discovercentralaustralia.com) is at the corner of Todd Mall and Parsons St.

GETTING AROUND

By bus The main terminus/interchange for the local bus network (all tickets $3) is on the corner of Gregory Terrace and Railway Terrace; timetables are available from the visitor centre or ⓦ transport.nt.gov.au/public/bus/alice.

By car For vehicle rental, Thrifty (☎ 08 8952 9999, ⓦ thrifty.com.au) has a branch at the corner of Hartley St and Stott Terrace; Britz (☎ 08 8952 8814, ⓦ britz.com.au)

is on the Stuart Hwy at the northern edge of the city and locally owned Alice Camp'n'Drive (☎ 08 8952 0098, ⓦ alicecampndrive.com) is at 76 Hartley St.

By bike Outback Cycling (☎ 0439 860 735, ⓦ outbackcycling .com) offers rentals from three hostels (YHA, *Annie's Place* and *Toddy's*) and the *DoubleTree* hotel from $45/day, plus guided tours. There's an enjoyable 17km sealed cycle track

CLOCKWISE FROM TOP SALTWATER CROCODILE (P.510); CULLEN BAY MARINA, DARWIN (P.487); DIGERIDOOS FOR SALE IN DARWIN (P.500) >

5

through the bush to Simpson's Gap, starting at Flynn's Grave, 7km west of town on Larapinta Drive.

By taxi The main taxi rank is at the river end of Gregory Terrace; call ☎ 08 8952 1877 to book in advance.

TOURS

A large number of **tour operators** offer adventure, cultural or historic tours throughout the area, best booked directly, or at one of the travel shops around the corners of Todd Street and Gregory Terrace. Though Uluru could be visited from Alice in a long day, you'll get much more from a two- to three-day tour, ideally incorporating Kings Canyon.

ALICE AND AROUND

Emu Run Tours ☎ 1800 687 220, ⊛ emurun.com.au. Runs day-tours out to the West MacDonnell Ranges, leaving Alice at 7.45am ($119). Also has various options to Uluru and Kings Canyon.

Jukurrpa Bikes ☎ 08 8953 7039, ⊛ jungala.com.au. Indigenous-operated half-day mountain-bike tours to cultural sites ($110). The same company also runs day-long Larapinta culture treks (8am–4pm; $225).

Outback Ballooning ☎ 08 8952 8723, ⊛ outbackballooning.com.au. Alice Springs is Australia's ballooning capital and this excellent operator will take you up, up and away – and back down for a champagne breakfast in the desert ($295 for 30min flight, $390 for 1hr).

Outback Quad Adventures ☎ 08 8953 0697, ⊛ oqa.com.au. Fun quad-bike rides on a cattle station close to town using automatic machines: all you have to do is turn the throttle and steer (from $138 for a 2.5hr tour). Dress for extreme dust.

Pyndan Camel Tracks ☎ 0416 170 164, ⊛ cameltracks.com. Join "Camel Man" Marcus Williams for fun one-hour ($70) camel rides in the Ilparpa Valley, a fifteen-minute drive from Alice; transfers included in the price.

RT Tours ☎ 08 8952 0327, ⊛ rttoursaustralia.com.au. Aboriginal chef Bob Taylor takes guests out to an authentic bush site in the West MacDonnells for a dining experience with a difference. Lunch costs $150, dinner is $160pp.

ULURU TOURS

Intrepid Travel ☎ 1300 018 871, ⊛ intrepidtravel.com. Professional operation offering camping and accommodated tours through the West MacDonnells, to Kings Canyon and Uluru, using comfortable minibuses. The longer tours are the best value.

The Rock Tour ☎ 1800 246 345, ⊛ therocktour.com.au. A hugely popular three-day, two-night bus jaunt taking in Uluru, Kata Tjuta and Kings Canyon. Departs daily 6am; $375 including park fee.

Mulga Tours ☎ 1800 359 089, ⊛ mulgas.com.au. Cheap and cheerful three-day Rock tours sleeping in swags ($390 including park fee, meals and camel ride).

Alice Wanderer ☎ 1800 722 111, ⊛ alicewanderer.com.au. If you can only spare a day to take in Uluru and Kata Tjuta, this is one of your options. Also two-day tours via Kings Canyon.

Wayoutback ☎ 08 8300 4900, ⊛ wayoutback.com.au. Long-established specialists offering assorted three- to five-day Rock and Canyon tours, including the four-day 4WD "wallaby dreaming safari" ($995), which also takes in the West Macs.

THE GHAN

These days a rail adventure of international renown, **The Ghan** – the train service which travels year-round between Adelaide and Darwin – is remarkable for several reasons, not least the fact that it exists at all. Work first started on a rail line that would join the two cities in 1877, but poor engineering practices coupled with a flimsy understanding of seasonal rains meant decades of failed attempts. The service takes its name from the "Afghan" cameleers who had nailed Outback travel rather more effectively (while some were from Afghanistan, most came from across what is now India, Pakistan, Iran and Turkey).

A workable stretch of track from Adelaide to Alice Springs was in place from the 1930s, although it wasn't until as recently as 2004 that it finally reached Darwin. It's a blessing that it now does. There are two types of ticket available, both of which grant you a smart private cabin, indulgent food and drinks, a range of off-train tours and an overriding sense of rail travel as it should be: **Gold Service** (Adelaide–Darwin $2599 for twin cabin, Alice–Darwin $1419) and **Platinum Service** (Adelaide–Darwin $3989, Alice–Darwin $2749). These are high-season fares; cheaper options are available Dec–Jan. If you've got more time, opt for the Ghan Expedition (May–Oct; platinum $5239, gold $3499), an extended three-night, four-day journey from Darwin to Adelaide that also takes in Coober Pedy (see p.715) and a range of other activities.

Whatever class you travel in, *The Ghan* (☎ 1800 703 357, ⊛ gsr.com.au) is one of the world's great railway journeys, and is highly recommended.

ACCOMMODATION

There are decent **accommodation** options scattered across the town, on both sides of the Todd River. Booking ahead is advisable during the winter school holidays (June & July) and events like the biennial Masters Games in October (even-numbered years).

HOTELS, MOTELS AND RESORTS

Aurora Alice Springs 11 Leichhardt Terrace ☏ 08 8950 6666, ☉ auroraresorts.com.au. This reliable four-star has a good central location. Rooms are large (though have thin walls) – most "executive" and "deluxe" options ($127/143) also have balconies/patios – and there's covered parking and a pool. It's also home to the *Red Ochre Grill* (see p.536). Go online for the best rates. $111

Chifley Alice Springs Resort 34 Stott Terrace ☏ 08 8951 4545, ☉ chifleyhotels.com. Just over the river, this four-and-a-half-star has stylish, spacious rooms centred around a lagoon-style pool with a summer-only swim-up bar. The low-rise architecture gives it a pleasant, oasis-like feel. You can also eat here at the fine *Barra-on-Todd* restaurant (see p.536). $139

DoubleTree by Hilton 82 Barrett Drive ☏ 08 8950 8000, ☉ doubletree.com. This very comfortable chain hotel covers a vast area and is partly powered by the large solar panels on the roof. It has a huge pool and boasts the superb *Hanuman* restaurant (see p.536), which is useful as it's a fair distance to town. $160

Quest 9–10 South Terrace ☏ 08 8959 0000, ☉ questapartments.com.au. Sleek, contemporary studios (with kitchenettes) and apartments (with kitchens and washing machines) are on offer here, and there's a small outdoor pool. Reception staff are friendly and full of ideas on how to enjoy your stay. Free wi-fi. Call direct for good advance rates. Studios $190, apartments $238

★ **Vatu Sanctuary** 18 Knuckey Avenue ☏ 0417 274 431, ☉ vatusanctuary.com.au. Set in the northern suburb of Braitling, this gem of a find makes up in arty character what it lacks in a central location. Choose from six creatively designed apartments, each exquisite in their own way. Minimum stay two to seven nights depending on which apartment you choose; the longer you stay the lower the nightly rate. $250

HOSTELS

Alice Lodge Backpackers 4 Mueller St ☏ 08 8953 1975 or ☏ 1800 351 925, ☉ alicelodge.com.au. Based in a converted house on a quiet residential street on the east side of the river, this hostel is a perennial backpacker favourite with decent dorms and (tiny) private rooms. Closer to the centre than it seems, there's a shady garden area and pool. Breakfast, internet and pick-ups included. Dorms $30, doubles $74

Alice Springs YHA Cnr Leichhardt Terrace & Parsons St ☏ 08 8952 8855, ☉ yha.com.au. Set in a historic Art Deco cinema building, this hostel is the most central in town, with a small pool and good-sized kitchen. It still screens nightly movies, and the four- to sixteen-bed dorms, private rooms and communal bathrooms are all well maintained. The downside is a lack of parking – try to avoid leaving your car by the river as theft is common. Dorms $23.50, doubles $78

Haven 3 Larapinta Drive ☏ 08 8952 4663, ☉ alicehaven. com.au. Set in a utilitarian former motel with secure off-street parking, bar and small pool. It's popular with groups, with plenty of space to chill out with a laptop or knock up a meal in the kitchen. All the four- to eight-bed dorms are en suite though those near communal areas can be noisy. Free breakfast. Dorms $28, doubles $95

Toddy's 41 Gap Rd ☏ 08 8952 1322, ☉ toddys.com.au. Long-established mega-hostel with a huge range of dorms, motel-style rooms and two pools. There's a lively bar, now serving food, which makes up for the location, a 20min hike from the town centre. Free breakfast and wi-fi. Dorms $29.50, doubles $105

CAMPSITES

Alice Springs Tourist Park Opposite Araluen Centre, Larapinta Drive ☏ 1300 823 404, ☉ alicespringstouristpark.com.au. Formerly known as

---

FESTIVALS IN ALICE SPRINGS

Most of the events calendar is squeezed into the cooler months, starting with the **Bangtail Muster** (cattle round-up) on the first Monday in May, followed by May's **Heritage Week** celebrating Alice Springs' history, a lively parade of silliness. In late June, the **Alice Springs Beanie Festival** (☉ beaniefest.org), probably the world's largest hat-related festival, takes over the Araluen Arts Centre with colourful designs produced by Aboriginal women. The **Camel Cup** races (☉ camelcup.com.au) in mid-July are the biggest of their kind in Australia, and end with a huge fireworks display. The rodeo season also hits Alice Springs at around this time, while the town's most famous event, the wacky **Henley-on-Todd Regatta**, kicks off at the end of August (☉ henleyontodd.com.au) when bottomless boats and other contraptions are run down the dry river bed.

5

the Stuart Caravan Park, this is the most central caravan park, situated around 2km west of town. The accommodation options are good value, the site is child-friendly and facilities include a pool, minimart, ATM and laundry. Un/powered sites $34/39, cabins $85
Heavitree Gap Caravan Park Palm Circuit ☎08 8950 4444, ⓦauroraresorts.com.au. This good-value three-star at the southern gap in the MacDonnell Ranges best suits self-drivers, although there are four daily shuttle buses into town. There's a nice pool, BBQs,

wallaby feeding at dusk and a tavern. Lodge rooms $100, bunkhouses (for up to six) $140, un/powered sites $26/34
MacDonnell Range Holiday Park Palm Place ☎08 8952 6111, ⓦmacrange.com.au. Family-friendly camping, rooms and cabins with all mod cons in a leafy setting on the south edge of town. Entertainment most nights including stargazing and music; free pancake breakfast on Sun. Un/powered sites $42/48, cabins $150

EATING

There are plenty of good places to **eat** in Alice Springs. Todd Mall boasts a handful of **cafés and restaurants** with outdoor seating. **Nightlife** is fairly low-key, though Friday and Saturday nights get lively; doormen and regular police patrols keep things from getting too hairy but it's safest to get a taxi back to your accommodation if you have more than a five-minute walk. The twice-weekly *Centralian Advocate* (ⓦntnews.com.au) carries details of live music and other entertainment.

CAFÉS

★Page 27 Fan Arcade, Todd St Mall ☎08 8952 0191. With its retro decor, inventive menus (try the parmesan-and-herb crumbed aubergine wrap for $15.90), buzzy, alternative vibe, and the best coffee in town, this hip café would be equally at home in inner-city Sydney or Melbourne. Tues–Fri 7.30am–2.30pm, Sat & Sun 8am–2pm.
Red Dog Café 62 Todd Mall ☎04 5117 5130. A popular spot for travellers and locals alike, *Red Dog* serves up fine breakfasts, snacks, lunches ($15–20) and coffee in the sunshine at one of the tables on the mall. If you're hungry, go for the all-day Big Bushman's Breakfast ($17). Daily 7.30am–5pm.

RESTAURANTS

Barra on Todd Chifley Alice Springs Resort, 34 Stott Terrace ☎08 8952 3523, ⓦsilverneedlehotels.com. The speciality of the mod-Oz menu at this smart hotel bistro is seafood, with a score of different barramundi dishes, including Sichuan-style barra (mains around $30). Daily 6–10am, 11.30am–5.30pm & 6pm–late.
Epilogue Lounge 58 Todd Mall ☎08 8953 4206, ⓦfacebook.com/epiloguelounge. Popular restaurant-bar with a mix of sandwiches, burgers, tapas (all from $10 upwards) and good coffee. There's also regular live music, DJs, open-mic nights, salsa dancing and film screenings:

check its Facebook page to see what's on. Sun–Mon 8am–3pm, Wed–Sat 8am–11.30pm.
★Hanuman DoubleTree by Hilton, 82 Barrett Drive ☎08 8953 7188, ⓦhanuman.com.au. The Alice outpost of a Darwin favourite (see p.498), *Hanuman* is a stylishly lit Asian restaurant, specializing in Thai, Nonya and Indian and serving up a combination of spicy classics (red and green curries $24.50–27) alongside more contemporary dishes (lemongrass, basil, ginger and chilli-spiked oysters $19). Daily noon–2.30pm & 6–10.30pm.
Overlanders Steakhouse 72 Hartley St ☎08 8952 2159, ⓦoverlanders.com.au. A carnivorous institution renowned for the "drovers blowout", a huge Territorian meat plate, featuring barramundi, crocodile, camel, buffalo, kangaroo and beef, served with soup, damper and pavlova. More modest – but still sizeable – mains ($30–42) include "Roo burger" and lamb shanks. There are also some veggie options. Daily 6pm–late.
Red Ochre Grill 57 Todd Mall ☎08 8952 9614, ⓦredochrealice.com.au. This bright bistro has a pleasant patio from which to watch the world wander by while enjoying the pricey bushtucker-inspired mod-Oz dishes and "Outback tapas" ($10–20 for the latter), such as camel and date sausages, saltbush and yam fritters, and smoked kangaroo salad. Daily 6.30am–late.

DRINKING

★Monte's 95 Todd Street ☎0409 697 937, ⓦmontes.net.au. A riotously loveable pub with a kind of twisted fairground theme. The eccentric decor includes disco balls, carnival horses and swings, but just as notable are the craft beers and gourmet burgers ($20–30). Check out the Facebook page (ⓦfacebook.com/Monteslounge) to find out what bands/DJs are playing when you're in town.

Wed–Sun 2pm–late.
The Rock Bar 78 Todd Street ☎08 8953 8280, ⓦfacebook.com/therockbaralicesprings. A hit with backpackers, thanks to nightly live music, sport on the big screen, a deck area outside, decent pub grub (from $15) and the fact that it stays open later than most. Daily noon–2am.

ENTERTAINMENT

Theatre and cinema The Araluen Cultural Precinct (see p.531) has a 500-seat theatre with a programme of plays, music and dance as well as an art-house cinema. For mainstream flicks there's the centrally located cinema (☗ alicespringscinema.com.au; tickets $18.50, Tues $12.50) at the top of Todd Mall.

Sounds of Starlight The Sounds of Starlight Theatre at 40 Todd Mall has 1hr 30min didgeridoo shows (April–Nov Tues, Fri & Sat 8pm; $30, $85 with dinner; ☎ 08 8953 0826, ☗ soundsofstarlight.com) featuring local didgeridoo impresario Andrew Langford and friends. He also runs workshops (Mon–Fri 11–11.30am; $10).

SHOPPING

Alice Springs is Australia's foremost **Aboriginal art and crafts** centre and Todd Mall is full of galleries. The most popular artworks are **dot paintings**, which derive from the temporary sand paintings once used to pass on sacred knowledge during ceremonies. While serious collectors pay hundreds of thousands of dollars for top-name artists, you can pick up finely crafted art for well under $1000. Always buy from dealers who have relationships directly with the artist (we've recommended galleries on below). Souvenir shops sell far cheaper paintings from around $30, although such pieces are purely decorative. The more you spend, the more chance there is of getting a discount, shipping and insurance included. Reputable galleries should provide certificates or labels of authenticity with each artwork. The government has established a "fair trade" style **Indigenous Art Code** (☗ indigenousartcode.org), but while its aims are laudable, the royalty scheme has received much criticism from artists and dealers who claim it is too bureaucratic and favours established artists.

ABORIGINAL ART

Aboriginal Art World 89 Todd Mall ☎ 08 8952 7788, ☗ aboriginalartworld.com.au. One of the leading authorities on Aboriginal art, this gallery funds the development of many artists. Prices range from the low hundreds to tens of thousands. Mon–Fri 9am–5pm, Sat 9am–4pm, Sun 9am–3pm.

Many Hands Art Centre 29 Wilkinson St ☎ 08 8950 0908, ☗ ngurart.com.au. This long-established Arrernte art centre is a good place to witness artists at work (Mon–Thurs 10am–3pm). Mon–Fri 9am–5pm.

Mbantua Gallery 64 Todd Mall ☎ 08 8952 5571, ☗ www.mbantua.com.au. As well as selling works, this gallery has a free museum at the back of the store with displays on bushtucker, weapons, traditional handicrafts and paintings. Nov–April Mon–Fri 9am–6pm, Sat 10am–2pm; rest of year Mon–Fri 9am–6pm, Sat 9am–4pm, Sun 10am–2pm.

★ **Muk Muk Fine Art** 14 Lindsay Ave ☎ 08 8953 6333. A superb gallery based in an old butchers' store on the east side of town. Showcases works from Utopia and Central and Western deserts, alongside contemporary Australian art. Mon–Fri 10am–6pm, Sat 10am–2pm.

★ **Papunya Tula Artists** 63 Todd Mall ☎ 08 8952 4731, ☗ papunyatula.com.au. This well-respected

community-owned gallery sells works from the Papunya Tula Artists, the founders of the Central and Western Desert Art Movement. Mon–Fri 9am–5pm, Sat 10am–2pm.

OTHER SHOPS

Books and maps Red Kangaroo Books, 79 Todd Mall (Mon–Fri 9am–5.30pm, Sat & Sun 9am–3pm; ☎ 08 8953 2137, ☗ redkangaroobooks.com), is good for Australian literature. Bookmark It (113 Todd St; Mon–Fri 10am–5pm, Sat 10am–1pm) has secondhand novels and a few travel guides.

Camping supplies Desert Dwellers at 38 Elder St (Jan–Feb 9am–3pm, Sat 9am–1pm, rest of year Mon–Fri 9am–5pm, Sat–Sun 10am–2pm; ☎ 08 8953 2137, ☗ desertdwellers.com.au), and Lone Dingo Adventure on Todd Mall (Mon–Fri 9am–5.30pm, Sat 9am–4pm, Sun 10am–3pm; ☎ 08 8953 3866, ☗ lonedingo.com.au) are both recommended.

Supermarket Coles (Mon–Fri 6am–11pm, Sat–Sun 6am–10pm; ☎ 08 8952 5166, ☗ coles.com.au), on the corner of Bath St and Gregory Terrace, is centrally located and well sized (daily 6am–midnight).

Market Todd Mall Markets (☗ toddmallmarkets.com.au) are held every second Sunday from 9am–1pm (9am–2pm in July).

DIRECTORY

Hospital Alice Springs Hospitel, Gap Rd ☎ 08 8951 7777.
Internet access There's free wi-fi along Todd Mall. Otherwise, try the terminals at the library at cnr Leichhardt Terrace & Gregory Terrace.
Permits for Aboriginal land Central Land Council, 27 Stuart Hwy (☎ 08 8951 6211, ☗ clc.org.au). For the WA section of the Great Central Rd, get your permit from the

Ngaanyatjarra Council, 6/58 Head St (☎ 08 8950 1711, ☗ ngaanyatjarra.org.au). You can get over-the-counter permits ($5) for the Mereenie Loop from the visitor centre.
Police 6 Parsons St (☎ 08 8951 8888 or ☎ 131 144).
Post office 31–33 Hartley St (Mon–Fri 8.15am–5pm; ☎ 0870 131 318).

5 The MacDonnell Ranges

The **MacDonnell Ranges** are among the longest of the parallel ridge systems that corrugate the Centre's landscape. Their east–west axis, passing through Alice Springs, is broken by a myriad of gaps carved through the ranges during better-watered epochs. It is these striking ruptures, along with the grandeur and colours of the rugged landscape – particularly west of Alice Springs – that make a few days spent in the MacDonnells so worthwhile. The expansive **West MacDonnells** (or West Macs) are best appreciated with at least one overnight stay (see p.542), while the often-overlooked **East MacDonnells** are a better bet if your time is limited. Both can be visited as part of a tour (see p.534) or with your own vehicle – a 4WD is recommended to get the most out of a visit, as some of the best spots are along corrugated dirt tracks. Take heed of **off-road driving advice** (see box, p.34).

The West MacDonnells

Most of the ranges west of Alice are now part of the **West MacDonnells National Park**. The **route** described below follows an anticlockwise loop out along Larapinta Drive, then north along Namatjira Drive to *Glen Helen Homestead Lodge* (see p.542), a short while after which a 110km partly dirt road takes you south past Gosses Bluff to the Mereenie Loop and turn-off (east) for Palm Valley and Hermannsburg, and back to Alice Springs. A total distance of 370km, it can be slow-going depending on the condition of the road after Glen Helen and the Mereenie Loop, which is prone to flash flooding in rain and can be closed for weeks after. The Mereenie Loop (which is not part of the national park) passes through **Aboriginal land**; get a permit from the Alice Springs visitor centre and check road conditions; do not attempt the route if rain is forecast.

Simpsons Gap
18km west of Alice Springs • Daily 5am–8pm • Free

Simpsons Gap is the nearest and most popular of the West MacDonnells' gaps, where a sandy river bed lined with red and ghost gums leads up to a small pool. It's a beautiful spot. Black-footed rock wallabies live on the cliffs and there's a **ranger station** (daily 8am–5pm) with plenty of visitor info. You can cycle here along a 17km bike track. The first stage of the **Larapinta Trail** also ends here – a 24km walk from the Telegraph Station in Alice Springs.

Standley Chasm
50km outside Alice Springs • Daily 8am–5pm • $12 • ☎ 08 8956 7440, ⊕ standleychasm.com.au

Situated on Iwupataka Aboriginal land 50km from Alice Springs, **Standley Chasm** is another much-frequented stop-off. It's privately owned, hence the entrance fee. An uneven walk along the cycad palm-lined river bed leads to a narrow 50m-long chasm formed by the erosion of softer rock that once lay between the red-quartzite walls. Between 11.30am and 1pm the 80m-high walls blaze golden red from the overhead sun – it can get busy. There is a campsite (see p.543), café and souvenir shop.

Along Namatjira Drive

Another 6km along Larapinta Drive, **Namatjira Drive** turns north amid the West MacDonnell Ranges. Continuing on Larapinta brings you to Hermannsburg and Palm Valley (see p.542). Along Namatjira Drive, a scenic 42km ahead is **Ellery Creek Big Hole** (barbecues, toilets and camping, $5 per person), the biggest waterhole in the area. If you catch it without a visiting tour group, it's shimmeringly peaceful and a spectacular spot to picnic (and take a dip if you can stand the cold water). Eleven kilometres to the west a rutted 3km turn-off leads to handsome **Serpentine Gorge** (toilets but no camping), where you can do a half-hour walk into the gorge or climb up to a lookout with one of the best views in the entire region. The Arrernte believe the pool in the gorge itself is the home of a

THE LARAPINTA TRAIL

A wonderful way to experience the West MacDonnells is to trek the long-distance **Larapinta Trail**, which follows the ranges, beginning at the Telegraph Station north of Alice Springs and ending 223km to the west on the 1347m Mount Sonder summit. The walk is divided into around a dozen sections, but these don't necessarily delineate a day's walk. Trailside water tanks are situated no more than two days' walk or 30km apart. The more impressive and more arduous sections are near town. Section two from Simpsons Gap to Jay Creek is 25km long – an overnight stop is advised – while the next section is a short but hard 14km to Standley Chasm with 350m of climbing. Pre-check weather conditions – it's best tackled between April and October when the temperatures are lower. You can print basic trail guides from the NT government website (visit ⓦ nt.gov.au, search for "larapinta" and then click on the "Sections of the Larapinta Trail" link) or, better, buy the comprehensive Larapinta Trail information pack ($38, plus postage; see ⓦ NT.gov.au for more information), which includes waterproof trail maps and notes. For those walkers looking for a touch of Larapinta comfort, it's possible to make use of rather stylish semi-permanent campsites through World Expeditions (ⓦ worldexpeditions .com). Alice Wanderer (☏ 08 8952 2111, ⓦ larapIntatransfers.com.au) offers transfers ($90–155pp) between Alice Springs and various points on the Larapinta Trail.

serpent, and even today they visit the place reluctantly and never enter the water. Further down Namatjira Drive, a tough track leads to the **Serpentine Chalet** bush-camping area, which has pitches amid the rather arid bushland. It's recommended as 4WD-only.

The **Ochre Pits**, signposted off Namatjira Drive, make an interesting diversion. Ochre was a highly valued trading commodity and is still used by the Arrernte for ceremonial purposes. From here there's a walk to **Inarlanga Pass** (a narrow gorge on the Larapinta Trail) and an enjoyable two-hour hike along rounded ridges and through wooded valleys.

Fourteen kilometres further west, the imposing **Ormiston Gorge** has barbecues, a kiosk, staffed ranger station (☏ 08 8956 7799) and camping (see p.542). It's one of the most magnificent and easily accessible spots in the West MacDonnells. The short ascent up to **Gum Tree Lookout** (the walk continues down into the gorge) gives a superlative view over the 250m-high gorge walls rising from the pools below. The 7km, three-hour **Pound Walk** includes some rock hopping, while longer overnight walks can be undertaken by those properly equipped.

Glen Helen Gorge

Just west of Ormiston is **Glen Helen Gorge**, another wide chasm with a perennial reed-fringed waterhole in the bed of the ancient **Finke River**, which is thought to have flowed along roughly the same course for more than 100 million years. If you're heading towards Kings Canyon along the 4WD-only **Mereenie Loop** (see box, p.545), buy your permit here ($5) if you didn't get it in town.

If you intend to complete the loop, note that it's about 107km to Hermannsburg along a mostly dirt track (a small section is sealed), and another 126km east along Larapinta Drive to Alice Springs. Check road conditions as the track is subject to flash flooding after rain and can be closed for weeks at a time.

Redbank Gorge

Shortly after leaving Glen Helen you'll reach a lookout to **Mount Sonder**, well worth getting to early in the morning. The mountain, said by Aboriginals to be a pregnant woman lying on her back, is featured in many of Albert Namatjira's best-known paintings. **Redbank Gorge** turn-off is 25km from Glen Helen; continue a further 5km (unsealed) to reach the car park. On the way you'll pass the *Woodland* and the more exposed *Ridgetop* **campsites**. From the car park a strenuous eight-hour return hike leads to the summit of Mount Sonder, though most visitors settle for the 2km hike to Redbank Gorge itself. The narrowest cleft in the West MacDonnells, Redbank is never warmed by direct sunlight and, anytime outside the height of summer, exploring its freezing string of rock pools is for the hardy only.

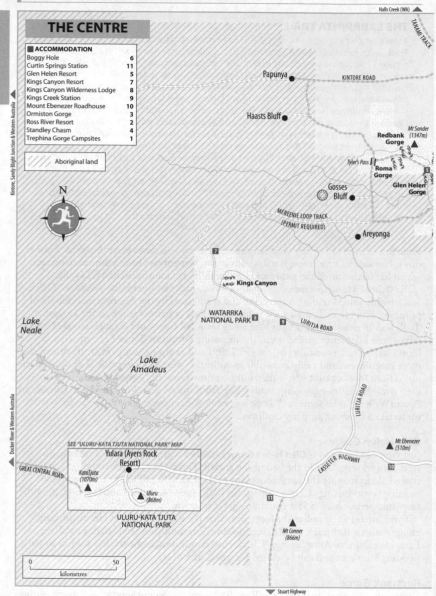

Halls Creek (WA)

THE CENTRE

ACCOMMODATION	
Boggy Hole	6
Curtin Springs Station	11
Glen Helen Resort	5
Kings Canyon Resort	7
Kings Canyon Wilderness Lodge	8
Kings Creek Station	9
Mount Ebenezer Roadhouse	10
Ormiston Gorge	3
Ross River Resort	2
Standley Chasm	4
Trephina Gorge Campsites	1

Aboriginal land

N

TANAMI TRACK

Papunya
KINTORE ROAD

Haasts Bluff

Mt Sonder (1347m)
Redbank Gorge

Tyler's Pass
Roma Gorge

Glen Helen Gorge

Gosses Bluff

MEREENIE LOOP TRACK
(PERMIT REQUIRED)

Areyonga

Kings Canyon

WATARRKA NATIONAL PARK

LURITJA ROAD

Lake Neale

Lake Amadeus

LURITJA ROAD

Mt Ebenezer (510m)

SEE "ULURU-KATA TJUTA NATIONAL PARK" MAP

Yulara (Ayers Rock Resort)

Kata Tjuta (1070m)

Uluru (868m)

GREAT CENTRAL ROAD

LASSETER HIGHWAY

ULURU-KATA TJUTA NATIONAL PARK

Mt Conner (866m)

0   50
kilometres

Stuart Highway

Kintore, Sandy Bligh Junction & Western Australia

Docker River & Western Australia

Gosses Bluff

After passing the Haasts Bluff and Papunya turn-off to your right (these tracks eventually lead north to the Tanami Track), the turning to **Tyler's Pass Lookout** is 13km away. Further along is another junction, where you can drive down a sandy 4WD-only track leading to the **Tnorala (Gosses Bluff) Conservation Reserve**, an extraordinary 2km-wide crater created by a meteorite impact 140 million years ago. A good way to appreciate the wonder of it all is to scramble up to the rim; there's no path, though it's less steep on the outside slope.

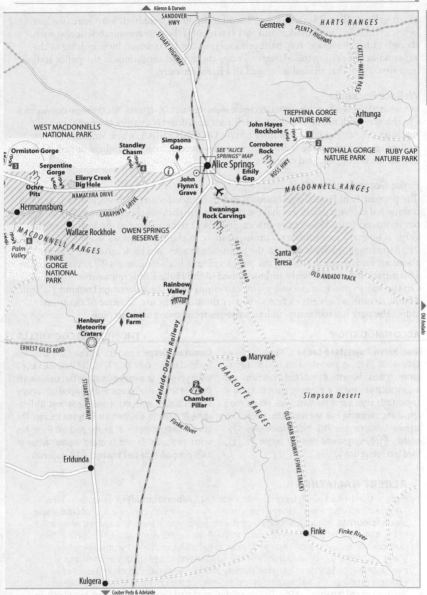

South of the bluff, you reach the Hermannsburg–Mereenie Loop junction. Left leads to Palm Valley, Hermannsburg and Alice Springs; right to Kings Canyon (see p.546).

Hermannsburg

Now an indigenous township, **HERMANNSBURG**, 125km west of Alice Springs, was the first mission in the Northern Territory, established by the Lutherans in 1877. You can visit the original eighteen mission buildings and church at the **Historic Precinct** (daily 9am–5pm; ☎08 8956 7402; $10), one of which has been converted into tearooms and

5

an art gallery. Albert Namatjira and Theodor Strehlow were both born here (see box below). There is a supermarket and fuel (cash only), but no accommodation as such, though rather desperate, very basic self-catering can be arranged by enquiring at the supermarket; if driving the Mereenie Loop, check road conditions at the police station here first. Note that alcohol is banned in Hermannsburg.

Wallace Rockhole

Tours: rock art $12 per person; dot-painting workshop $25; camping: un/powered sites $10/20 • ☎ 08 8956 7993, ⓦ wallacerockholetours.com.au

On the way back to Alice Springs, you'll pass the **Albert Namatjira Memorial** before reaching the Aboriginal community of **WALLACE ROCKHOLE**, where various tours can be arranged – prebooking is essential, and they need sufficient numbers to run. There's also an art centre, fuel and camping.

Finke Gorge National Park

The popularity of **Finke Gorge National Park** is founded on its prehistoric cycads and the unique red cabbage palms that have survived in the park's sheltered **Palm Valley** for over ten thousand years. Despite the challenging 4WD track leading to the lush valley, the gorge is on every tour itinerary – unsurprisingly, as the 1hr Arankaia Walk and longer 2hr Mpulungkinya Walk through the palm-filled valley and back across the plateau above are both magical. Visiting the park requires a high-clearance 4WD, as most of the 16km track follows the sandy and rocky bed of the Finke River, impassable after rain. On the way in or out of the valley, you can climb up to the **Kalarranga Lookout** (1.5km, 45min return), which gives a fine view over the amphitheatre, a cirque of sandstone cliffs. The park has barbecues, toilets, solar-heated showers and camping.

ACCOMMODATION

THE WEST MACDONNELLS

Glen Helen Homestead Lodge 1 Namatjira Drive ☎ 08 8956 7489, ⓦ glenhelen.com.au. This former cattle station homestead has fuel, camping and accommodation, and is a charming place to spend a comfortable night out in the West Macs, with a good restaurant, swimming hole and warm atmosphere. Can arrange helicopter and 4WD trips. Bunkhouses $35, doubles $160, un/powered sites per person $12/15, fixed tents per person $20

Ormiston Gorge Campsite signed turn-off from Larapinta Drive ☎ 08 8956 7799. The West Macs aren't lacking in park-run campsites, but one that stands out is *Ormiston Gorge*, chiefly because it's a logical spot to stop after a full day's exploration from Alice Springs. It's first-come, first-served, and there are BBQs and showers. The basic *Ridgetop* campsite at nearby Redbank Gorge has better views, but Ormiston's grants on-foot access to what is arguably the park highlight. $10 per person

ALBERT NAMATJIRA

Born on the Hermannsburg Lutheran mission in 1902, **Albert Namatjira**, a member of the Arrernte tribe, was the first of the Hermannsburg mission's much-copied school of **landscape watercolourists**. Although lacking much painting experience, Namatjira assisted white artist Rex Battarbee on his painting expeditions through the Central Australian deserts in the 1930s during which his talent soon became obvious to Battarbee, who later became Namatjira's agent. Like all NT Aborigines at that time, Namatjira was forbidden to buy alcohol, stay overnight in Alice Springs or leave the Territory without permission. At the insistence of southern do-gooders – and against his wishes – he was the first Aborigine to be awarded **Australian citizenship**, in 1956. This meant he could travel without limitations, but needed a permit to visit his own family on Aboriginal reserves. Following the success of his first exhibition in Melbourne, he became a reluctant celebrity, compelled under Aboriginal tradition to share his wealth with his extended family. A shy and modest man, he died in 1959 following a sordid conviction and short imprisonment for supplying alcohol to fellow Aborigines.

Critics could never make up their minds about his work, but his popular appeal was undoubted: today his paintings remain among the most valuable examples of Australia's artistic preoccupation with its landscape. Sadly, the Twin Ghost Gums in the West MacDonnell Ranges, which featured in some of his most famous works, were destroyed in a suspected arson case in 2013.

Standley Chasm Signed turn-off from Larapinta Drive ⊙ 08 8956 7440, ⬤ standleychasm.com.au. The owners offer a variety of campsites in the bush around the chasm itself, including one reserved exclusively for Larapinta Trail walkers. The camping fee includes entry to the chasm. Camping per person $20

The East MacDonnells

Heading out of Alice Springs through **Heavitree Gap** and along the **Ross Highway** you soon reach tranquil **Emily Gap**, Alice Springs' nearest waterhole, 10km from town. This is one of the most significant Arrernte sacred sites, being the birthplace of the ancestral Caterpillar beings who formed the surrounding landscape. There are some interesting stylized depictions of the caterpillars on the far side of a natural pool; and again at the equally peaceful **Jessie Gap**, a little further east. **Corroboree Rock**, 47km east of Alice Springs, is an unusual, fin-like outcrop of limestone with an altar-like platform and two crevices piercing the fin. The rock was once a repository for sacred objects and a site of initiation ceremonies, or *corroborees*.

Trephina Gorge Nature Park

Just 85km from Alice Springs, **Trephina Gorge Nature Park** is one of the most satisfying destinations in the East MacDonnell Ranges, offering superb scenery and a selection of enjoyable walks. The gorge itself is perhaps the most impressive spot in the eastern part of the range, a sheer-sided sandy ravine whose golden-red walls support slender, white-barked ghost gums and a small natural pool, while huge river red gums grow in the bed providing welcome shade. There are excellent **campsites** (see p.544) and two enjoyable walks, the Gorge and Panorama, both taking about 1hr return. **John Hayes Rockhole** is actually a series of pools linked by waterfalls through a canyon. The rockhole can be reached either along a rocky 4km track requiring a high-clearance 4WD or by a four-hour hike from Trephina Gorge. Once there, the ninety-minute Chain of Pools walk runs above the pools before meandering down to the waterhole. Alternatively, the lower pools are accessible on a ten-minute walk from the car park. There's a ranger station in the gorge (⊙08 8956 9765) which can be contacted in case of emergency.

Arltunga

Five kilometres beyond Trephina Gorge is the turn-off northeast to a gravel road leading 33km to **Arltunga Historical Reserve**, the site of Central Australia's first official town, the gold rush outpost of Arltunga. Allow plenty of time to get here as driving conditions vary depending on whether the road has been graded or not. There's an exhibit on the mining era at the **visitor centre** (daily 8am–5pm), where you can pick up an *Explore Arltunga* brochure with details on the old Post Office, Blacksmith Shop and Police Station. The best picnic spots are at the visitor centre and Police Station.

Gold was discovered here in 1888, but Arltunga was never a particularly rich field and remains yet another abandoned testament to pioneer optimism. With a high-clearance 4WD it's possible to continue on to Ruby Gap (see below) or north over the ranges along the Binns Track to the Plenty Highway (see p.527).

N'Dhala Gorge Nature Park

Further along the Ross Highway is the *Ross River Resort* (see p.544), located at the historic 1890s Loves Creek Homestead. Just before the resort a right turn leads along an 11km track to **N'Dhala Gorge Nature Park**. A high-clearance 4WD is required to negotiate the rough track and wide, sandy river beds. The gorge is home to various **Aboriginal rock engravings**, which can be appreciated on the 90min return Gorge Walk.

Ruby Gap Nature Park and Glen Annie Gorge

From Arltunga, there's a rough 47km high-clearance 4WD-only track (impassable after rain) along the sandy bed of the Hale River to Ruby Gap and Glen Annie Gorge (see box, p.545).

5

Both are beautiful and wild places. Back in 1885, the explorer Lindsay discovered "rubies" while in the process of digging for water, thereby initiating the customary rush for what turned out to be garnets. Once at **Ruby Gap** (no facilities although camping permitted), the drive gets even more challenging, and after 5km you need to leave your vehicle for the final 2km walk to **Glen Annie Gorge**. At day's end, even with the flies handing over to the mozzies, it's one of the most tranquil places you'll find in Central Australia.

ACCOMMODATION   THE EAST MACDONNELLS

Ross River Resort Ross Hwy ☎08 8956 9711 or ☎1800 241 711, ⓦrossriverresort.com.au. Located at the historic 1890s Loves Creek Homestead, the Ross River Resort has a range of accommodation options, plus fuel, a few self-guided walking tracks, bar meals and fire pits. Cabins $130, bunkhouses $35, un/powered sites $25/32

Trephina Gorge Campsites Ross Hwy ☎08 8956 9765. Camping areas don't come much more perfectly situated than the two spacious grounds (*Gorge* and *Bluff*) at Trephina Gorge, both loomed over by walls of ochre rock. Drinking water and pit toilets provided. Camping per person $3.30

The Old South Road and the northern Simpson Desert

Just 14km out of Alice Springs, shortly after the airport turn-off, a sign indicates "Chambers Pillar (4WD)". This is the **Old South Road**, which follows the abandoned course of the *Ghan* and original Overland Telegraph Line to Adelaide; these days, the sandy route has become part of the Old Ghan Heritage Trail, which takes adventurous off-roaders all the way to South Australia. If you're not an experienced off-road driver, some full-day tours from Alice Springs (see p.534) include Chambers Pillar.

Rainfall permitting, ordinary cars can normally cover the 35km to **Ewaninga Rock Carvings**, a jumble of rocks by a small claypan that is a sacred Aboriginal Rain Dreaming site, but after the store at **MARYVALE** (also known as Titjikala; has shop and fuel) you'll need a 4WD and to be in the mood for a thorough shaking until Charlotte Ranges. After the ranges there are sand ridges all the way to **Chambers Pillar** (camping), a historic dead end, 165km from Alice Springs. Named by Stuart after one of his benefactors, the 50m-high sandstone pillar was used as a landmark by early overlanders heading up from the railhead at Oodnadatta, SA. The plinth is carved with their names as well as those of many others, and can be seen from the platform at the pillar's base.

South to Kings Canyon and Uluru

Stunning **Kings Canyon** in Watarrka National Park, southwest of Alice Springs, is accessible by three different routes. Most take the circuitous four-hour 450km journey south from Alice Springs on the Stuart Highway, then west on the Lasseter Highway (which continues on to Uluru), then north on the Luritja Road. Alternatively, a couple of 4WD routes, the Mereenie Loop (see box opposite) and the Ernest Giles Road off the Stuart Highway, also access the park.

If you're not self-driving, most **tours** of two days or more departing from Alice Springs include Kings Canyon on their itineraries, en route to or from *Ayers Rock Resort*. There are also daily bus transfers, with guided commentary, between *Ayers Rock Resort* and Kings Canyon with AAT Kings (see p.495), with onward connections to Alice Springs.

The Stuart Highway to Kings Canyon

Most drivers do the Alice Springs-to-Kings-Canyon journey in a single stint, but if you are looking for some diversions en route and have a sturdy enough vehicle, there are a number of rewarding options, including the Henbury Meteorite Craters (see p.546).

SOME 4WD TRACKS IN THE CENTRE

Renting a 4WD for a few days of off-road driving can get you to some beautiful corners of the central deserts. Below are some **4WD-only** routes close to Alice Springs. Read the advice and carry the gear recommended in Basics (see p.34). The Alice Springs Visitor Centre can provide maps and information on **road conditions** (☎ 1800 246 199, ⓦ ntlis .nt.gov.au/roadreport). Beginners should also consider taking a **4WD course** such as those offered by Train Safe NT (☎ 04 3518 2042, ⓦ trainsafe.net), which offers classes in Alice Springs and Darwin. Also make sure you are appropriately equipped for travelling in remote areas, with plenty of food and water, tow ropes, a second spare tyre and spare jerry cans. All rental agents in the Alice Springs "Getting around" section (see p.532) can arrange 4WDs.

MEREENIE LOOP TRACK

The main appeal of the 195km **Mereenie Loop**, linking Hermannsburg with Kings Canyon (allow 3–4hr), is that it avoids backtracking on the usual "Canyon and Rock" tour. It is a stunning drive with plenty of desert oaks, river crossings, wild horses, donkeys and dingoes. The corrugations can be fearsome; don't even think about the trip if rain is forecast as it's prone to flash flooding and inaccessible after rain. Obtain a permit at Alice Springs Visitor Centre, Glen Helen or Kings Canyon. Note that you're not allowed to stop (except at the official "Jump-Up" lookout area, close to Kings Canyon) or camp.

FINKE RIVER ROUTE

With a day to spare and experience with a 4WD, following the Finke river bed from **Hermannsburg** down to the **Ernest Giles Road** offers an adventurous alternative to the highway and saves some backtracking. Rewards include stark gorge scenery, a reliable waterhole and the likelihood that you'll have it all to yourself. Before you set off, check the road conditions.

The 100km **Finke River Route** starts immediately south of Hermannsburg. After 10km of corrugated road you descend into the river bed. From here on driving is slow, along a pair of sandy or pebbly ruts – you should deflate your tyres to at least 25psi/1.7bar and keep in the ruts to minimize the risk of getting stuck. There's just one designated campsite en route, **Boggy Hole**, which looks out from beneath river red gums to permanent reed-fringed waterholes.

Beyond, the track crisscrosses rather than follows the river bed before taking a roller-coaster ride to the Giles Road across some low dunes thinly wooded with desert oaks – beware of oncoming traffic on blind crests. Boggy Hole to the Giles Road is 65km, so allow three hours.

ARLTUNGA TO RUBY GAP

Call the **Arltunga Ranger Station** (☎ 08 8956 9770), 101km east of Alice Springs, for the latest track conditions for this scenic, if bumpy, 47km drive (allow 2hr) through the Eastern ranges. It includes some steep creek crossings until you reach the sandy river bed of the Hale and the **Ruby Gap Nature Park**. From here, keep to the sandy ruts and inch carefully over the rocks for 5km, at which point you'll need to stop and walk the last 2km to **Glen Annie Gorge**.

CATTLEWATER PASS

Another challenging track (impassable after the rain) heads north from Arltunga past Claraville Station and up over the Harts Ranges through **Cattlewater Pass** to the Plenty Highway, 56km or three hours from Arltunga. It's a scenic way of returning to Alice Springs from Arltunga and you're bound to see some hopping marsupials along the way, but ensure you allow plenty of time, as it's slow going in places.

OWEN SPRINGS TRACK

A great option for those who want to combine 4WD touring with the region's pioneering history. It's a sandy but relatively short undertaking, running for 50km and forming a through-route from Larapinta Drive (50km west of Alice) to the Stuart Highway (66km south of Alice). Highlights along the **Owen Springs Track** include old Aboriginal stockmen's quarters and a log-hut homestead. There's a detailed self-drive info sheet available online (ⓦ parksandwildlife.nt.gov.au) or from the Simpsons Gap ranger station.

5

Rainbow Valley

Around 75km along the Stuart Highway from Alice Springs, the turn-off east to **Rainbow Valley** (4WD officially "recommended but not essential"; basic camping) follows a 22km dirt track (some of which is very sandy) to the "valley", a much-photographed outcrop set behind claypans said to produce rainbows following rain. What you are more likely to see is the spectacular way the sunset catches the red-stained walls. This is a wild place to spend the night, best followed in the morning by a climb up the crag.

Henbury Meteorite Craters

Back on the Stuart Highway, the next turn-off west is the Ernest Giles Road for Kings Canyon, a strictly 4WD-only road, inaccessible after rain and closed for long periods. Not far along this track is the turn-off to **Henbury Meteorite Craters**, twelve depressions, ranging in size from 2m to 180m in diameter, caused by an extraterrestrial shower 4700 years ago. A walk with interpretive signs winds among the craters. There's camping, as well as barbecues and toilets.

Kings Creek Station

ⓘ 08 8956 7474, ⓦ kingscreekstation.com.au

Some 35km before Kings Canyon itself, you'll pass the friendly **Kings Creek Station**, a working cattle/camel station that runs various activities. Take your pick from quad biking ($100/hr), helicopter flights ($60/5min) and camel rides ($8/5min, $55 for a sunset safari). There's also a shop/café and fuel. A portion of all money goes to an indigenous children's charity founded by the station owners.

ACCOMMODATION	KINGS CREEK STATION

Kings Creek Station Luritja Rd ⓘ 08 8956 7474, ⓦ kingscreekstation.com.au. The station has some decent accommodation options, with permanent safari cabins sleeping two people as well as powered and unpowered sites on offer. For a night to remember, you can also arrange to be choppered out to a remote campsite (from $424pp inc helicopter flights, swags, camp cook, meals). Cabins $180, un/powered sites per person $21.50/24.50

Kings Canyon (Watarrka National Park)

As you cross the boundary of the **Watarrka National Park**, you'll see the turn-off to **Kathleen Springs**, where a walk (90min return) takes you to a sacred Aboriginal waterhole. Once used to corral livestock, it's now a good place to catch sight of colourful birdlife.

Another twenty minutes' drive down the road is the majestic **KINGS CANYON** itself, part of the magnificent George Gill Range. The big attraction is the three- to four-hour, 6km **Rim Walk** up and around the canyon, its scintillating views and complex natural history making it one of the region's best hikes. **Early morning** is the most popular time – if you don't mind missing the sunrise, you might have the place to yourself in the late afternoon when the light is better, but avoid the heat of the middle of the day. The walk actually gets closed if temperatures are forecast to peak above 36°C (most commonly in January or February).

Undertaken in a now mandatory clockwise direction, the walk starts with a well-constructed stepped ascent (the toughest part of the walk), after which the trail leads through a maze of sandstone domes, known as the **Lost City**, where interpretive boards fill you in on the geology and botany. About halfway along, you clamber down into a cool, palm-filled chasm known as the **Garden of Eden**. Coming up the far side, there's an easily missed detour downstream to a shady **pool** where you can swim. From here you get a blockbuster **view** of the sunlit south wall and the canyon below. Returning to the staircase, the walk comes to the very edge of the south wall and then descends gently to the car park. For a different perspective, the easy 2km return walk along the canyon bottom is also worthwhile.

ACCOMMODATION — KINGS CANYON

Kings Canyon Resort Luritja Rd ☎ 1800 837 168, ⓦ kingscanyonresort.com.au. The nearest accommodation to the canyon (just 10km distant), *Kings Canyon Resort* has a range of options including deluxe spa rooms with decks overlooking bushland, lodge rooms, en-suite doubles and a grassy campsite (which, ironically, has the best view of the lot). There's a pool, wi-fi, three restaurants (the smart *Carmichaels*, the lower-key *Desert Oaks Bistro* and the lively *Outback BBQ & Grill*, which has live music May–Oct), the *Thirsty Dingo* bar, a service station/minimart, kitchen and washing facilities, and a great sunset-viewing platform. It also offers guided hikes, quad bikes, bike rental, helicopter tours, birdwatching and the romantic "Under a Desert Moon" dining experience, a four-course meal with glass of bubbles ($149pp) served around a fire. Spa rooms $380, en-suite rooms $287, lodge rooms $149, un/powered sites per person $20/25

Kings Canyon Wilderness Lodge Luritja Rd ☎ 1800 891 121, ⓦ aptouring.com.au. Located east of Kings Canyon, but accessible from Luritja Rd, this lodge is open only to self-drivers and special groups. It boasts luxury tented cabins, good food and a telescope for stargazing. Rates include dinner and breakfast. $376

The Lasseter Highway

It's 177km from Alice Springs to **Erldunda**, a busy roadhouse on the Stuart Highway, from where the **Lasseter Highway** heads to *Ayers Rock Resort*, 268km to the west. After 56km is *Mount Ebenezer Roadhouse* and later the turning for the **Luritja Road**, which leads 168km up to Kings Canyon. The next thing to catch your eye will be the flat-topped mesa of **Mount Conner**, from a distance regularly mistaken for Uluru. You-know-what is now only 106km away.

ACCOMMODATION — THE LASSETER HIGHWAY

Curtin Springs Station Lasseter Highway, 11km west of Mount Conner ☎ 08 8956 2906, ⓦ curtinsprings.com. Good-value accommodation, including free unpowered camping sites ($3 charge for showers), snug budget rooms and more comfortable en-suite rooms (including some that sleep up to seven). There's a reasonably priced restaurant (breakfast, lunch & dinner daily), as well as a bar, shop, fuel and station tours. Powered sites $40, doubles $130

Mount Ebenezer Roadhouse Lasseter Highway, 212km west of Ayers Rock Resort ☎ 08 8956 2904, ⓦ www.mtebenezer.com.au. Recently reopened, this roadhouse has a collection of neat en-suite rooms, as well as a caravan park, restaurant, bar with well-stocked juke box, fuel and an interesting Aboriginal art gallery and shop. Un/powered sites per person $5/25, doubles $120

Uluru and around

Uluru–Kata Tjuta National Park encompasses **Uluru** (Ayers Rock) and **Kata Tjuta** (once known as the **Olgas**). If you're wondering whether all the hype is worth it, the answer is, emphatically, yes. The Rock, its textures, colours and not least its elemental presence, is without question one of the world's natural wonders. While overt commercialization has been controlled within the park, designated a World Heritage Site by UNESCO in 1987, it's impossible to avoid other tourists, but this shouldn't affect your experience.

In many ways just as spellbinding, Kata Tjuta (meaning "Many Heads") lies 45km west from the park entry station. A cluster of rounded domes divided by narrow chasms and valleys, it is geologically quite distinct from Uluru and makes for a stunning early-morning hike spotting rock wallabies along the way.

Yulara (Ayers Rock Resort)

The purpose-built **AYERS ROCK RESORT** at the township of **YULARA** is far from the eyesore it could have been. Low-impact, and environmentally aware, the resort was ahead of its time when it was built between 1983 and 1990, keeping building heights below the adjacent landscape, carefully recycling water and using solar-powered electricity. Everything branches off a central ring road, Yulara Drive: within this ring the natural bushland is crisscrossed with walking tracks and several lookouts.

ARRIVAL AND GETTING AROUND

YULARA (AYERS ROCK RESORT)

By plane Ayers Rock Airport (also known as Connellan Airport) is 6km from Yulara. Qantas, Jetstar and Virgin Australia offer direct flights from Sydney, Melbourne, Cairns and Alice Springs. All incoming flights are met by a free shuttle bus to *Ayers Rock Resort* (10min) or a 4WD for those heading to *Longitude 131°*.

Destinations Alice Springs (1 daily; 55min); Cairns (1 daily; 2h 45min); Melbourne (5 weekly; 2hr); Sydney (1–2 daily; 3hr 35min).

By bus Bus transfers from Alice Springs (5hr 30min–7hr) and Kings Canyon (3hr 30min) are run by companies like AAT Kings

(☏ 1300 228 546, ⓦ aatkings.com), Gray Line (☏ 1300 858 687, ⓦ grayline.com.au) and Emu Run (☏ 1800 687 220, ⓦ emurun.com.au) – the latter, popular with backpackers, is generally the cheapest option. Greyhound buses do not run here. A free shuttle bus circulates around Yulara Drive (daily 10.30–12.30am; roughly every 20min).

By car Many visitors choose to self-drive from Alice Springs along the Lasseter Highway (see p.547). Vehicle rental is available at Ayers Rock itself from Hertz (☏ 08 8956 2244), Avis (☏ 08 8956 2266) and Thrifty (☏ 08 8956 2030); all have counters in the Tours and Information Centre (see below).

INFORMATION

Tourist information There's a Tours and Information Centre (daily 8am–7pm; ☏ 08 8957 7324, ⓦ ayersrockresort .com.au/facilities) where you can pick up info, rent a car and book from a wide range of tours and activities.

Services In the Shopping Centre, the hub of the resort, you'll find a post office (Mon–Fri 9am–5pm, Sat

9am–noon), supermarket (daily 8am–9pm), newsagent, cafés, restaurants and an ANZ bank (Mon–Thurs 10am–3pm, Fri 10am–4pm) with an ATM. In case of emergencies, there's the Yulara Medical Centre (Mon–Fri 9am–noon & 1–4pm; ☏ 08 8956 2286), as well as fire and police stations near the campsite on Yulara Drive.

TOURS AND ACTIVITIES

All tours except the ranger-guided walks and Uluru Aboriginal Tours can be booked at your hotel desk or at the **Tours and Information Centre** in the Shopping Centre at the resort; note that some do not include the $25 park entry fee, so you need to have your permit with you. In addition to the options listed below, there is an ever-changing range of free activities around the resort – from nature walks to cultural shows. Drop in at the Tours and Information Centre to find out what's on during your visit.

Ayers Rock Scenic Flights ☏ 08 8956 2345, ⓦ ayersrockresort.com.au. Runs a lengthy roster of scenic flights in high-wing aircraft and helicopters (from $115), plus tandem skydives ($399).

Outback Sky Journeys ⓦ ayersrockresort.com.au. Given the absence of artificial light, the skies above Uluru are wonderful for stargazing. There are a couple of tours (from $46; book at the Tours and Information Centre or via your hotel), including one aimed at children. The Astro Hub (daily noon–3pm; free) at the Outback Pioneer Hotel & Lodge also offers several free astronomy-related activities.

Desert Awakenings ☏ 08 8957 7524, ⓦ ayersrockresort.com.au. Small-group breakfast tours to Uluru, travelling away from the crowds along 4WD tracks: $185 including bush breakfast.

Professional Helicopter Services ☏ 08 8956 2003, ⓦ phs.com.au. Fifteen-minute helicopter rides over the Rock ($150), with longer options such as one covering Uluru and Kata Tjuta (30min; $285).

Ranger-guided walks Free walks along part of the base of Uluru, looking at the history and traditions associated with the Rock. Book at the Uluru–Kata Tjuta Cultural Centre (see p.550).

SEIT Tours ☏ 08 8956 3156, ⓦ seitoutbackaustralia .com.au. Runs 4WD excursion to Mt Conner, with 3-course dinner, for $265. Also offers various small-group tours in and around the park.

★Sounds of Silence Secret desert location ⓦ ayersrockresort.com.au. If you fancy sunset champers and canapés overlooking Uluru followed by a white tablecloth dinner under the stars, then sign up for this pricey ($195pp) though worthwhile experience. The buffet meal is decent enough but the stargazing talk afterwards is the real highlight. Buses pick up from the hotels 1hr before sunset. Tali Wiru (also ⓦ ayersrockresort.com.au) is similar, but even more exclusive (and pricey; $325pp), taking place on a sand dune and featuring storytelling and a didgeridoo performance.

Uluru Aboriginal Tours ☏ 0447 878 851, ⓦ uluruaboriginaltours.com.au. Little-marketed, indigenous-run outfit offering a 90min cultural tour for $45. Find out more at the Walkatjara art centre (see p.550) at the Uluru–Kata Tjuta Cultural Centre.

Uluru Camel Farm and Tours ☏ 08 8956 3333, ⓦ ulurucameltours.com.au. Based on "Australia's largest camel farm" (daily April–Oct 9am–3pm, Nov–March 9am–1pm; free), this outfit operates sunrise and sunset camel rides (both $129), plus a 45min "Camel Express" tour ($80). The farm is a couple of kilometres south of the resort – ask the shuttle bus driver to drop you off.

Uluru Motorcycle Tours ☏ 08 8956 2019, ⓦ ulurucycles .com. Pillion rides round the Rock and Kata Tjuta on the back of a Harley-Davidson. Sunrise and sunset tours available (Uluru, 1hr 30min, $199; Kata Tjuta, 2hr, $249).

ACCOMMODATION

The resort is managed by the Voyages Group (⌾ voyages.com.au), which has the monopoly on all accommodation. You'll find everything from five-star luxury to dorms and campsites. Prices are high across the board, more on a par with Sydney and Melbourne than Alice Springs, although they can drop by twenty percent outside of the peak July-to-October season, and in the smarter hotels there's often a discount for stays of more than one night. No matter what the season, **book ahead**, because the constant flow of tour groups from all over the world fills the hotels quickly, while the campsite overflows during winter and school holidays. All the places below can be booked **online** at ⌾ ayersrockresort.com.au, and with the exception of *Longitude 131°*, are situated off Yulara Drive.

Ayers Rock Campground ☎08 8957 7001, ⌾ayersrockresort.com.au. Offers BBQs, a small shop and a pool, and does its best to keep the sites grassy for tents. Has various lookouts and claims to be one of the largest sites in the southern hemisphere. Cabins (sleeping up to six) $160, un/powered sites $40/49

Desert Gardens Hotel ☎08 8957 7714, ⌾ayersrockresort.com.au. Comfortable four-star hotel with a vast light-filled lobby and one of the resort's best restaurants, the *Argnuli Grill* (see below). The spacious rooms (some with views of Uluru) are set around a pleasant courtyard garden with pool. $385

Emu Walk Apartments ☎08 8957 7714, ⌾ayersrockresort.com.au. These spacious, though expensive, one- and two-bed apartments, located close to the Shopping Centre, come with a fully equipped kitchen, lounge and small balcony or terrace. A good option for families or groups. $475

Longitude 131° ☎08 8957 7131, ⌾longitude131 .com.au. Located well away from the rest of the resort, this deeply luxurious eco-retreat recently played host to Prince William and Kate Middleton. It has just fifteen safari-style tents (with king-sized beds, en-suite bathrooms and private terraces) hidden among the desert dunes close to Uluru. There's a spa, and rates include meals, drinks and tours. Minimum two-night stay. $1350

Outback Pioneer Hotel & Lodge ☎08 8957 7605, ⌾ayersrockresort.com.au. This budget (for Yulara at least) option is a 15min walk from the Shopping Centre. There are vast twenty-bed single-sex dorms, mixed four-bed dorms, budget rooms and en-suite "hotel" rooms. None of them are particularly comfortable. On the plus side, there are good facilities including a pool, various eateries, a camp kitchen, a bar with live music and the resort's only bottle shop. Dorms $38, doubles $225

Sails in the Desert Hotel ☎08 8957 7417, ⌾ayersrockresort.com.au. This five-star hotel takes its name from the large sun-reflecting sails on its roof. Expect fluffy bathrobes, plump pillows and designer bathrooms – some rooms come with large sun terraces with jacuzzi. There's also a spa (open to non-guests), a fine-dining restaurant, Aboriginal art gallery and a leafy pool area. $476

EATING

There are numerous **restaurants** and **cafés** dotted around the resort; all are overpriced. During the high season, wherever you decide to eat, it's a good idea to book a table for dinner. Self-caterers can stock up with essentials at the supermarket in the Shopping Centre. The sole liquor store is the bottle shop at the *Outback Pioneer Lodge*.

Argnuli Grill Desert Gardens Hotel ☎08 8957 7705. Large, buzzy hotel restaurant popular with families. The menu has tempting dishes like herb-and-pistachio-crusted rack of lamb ($43) and baked snapper ($41), as well as an array of steaks. Daily 6.30–9.30pm (the adjacent lobby bar is open for lunch 11.30am–4pm).

Ayers Wok Shopping Square. Tucked away in a corner beside *Gecko's*, this amusingly named takeaway dishes up construct-your-own stir-fries ($16): choose rice or noodles, a protein and a sauce/style (pad thai, sweet and sour, etc). Daily noon–2pm & 5.30–8.30pm.

Bough House Restaurant Outback Pioneer Hotel & Lodge ☎08 8957 7605. This low-key place offers a dinner buffet (two courses $38, three courses $43) laden with traditional Aussie favourites like barra and steak. Nearby, you'll find the *Pioneer BBQ* where you can buy various cuts of meats to cook (6–9pm; $26–29 including an unlimited salad bar), and a kiosk selling takeaway burgers, fish and chips, etc

($12–15). Daily 6.30–10.30am & May–Oct 6–9.30pm.

Gecko's Shopping Square. A laidback bistro and bar serving up Mediterranean-style dishes, including reasonable pasta ($19–26) and wood-fired pizza ($22–28), along with steaks, ribs, burgers and fish and chips. There are also daily drink-and-food combo offers. Daily noon–2.30pm & 5.30–9pm.

Kulata Academy Café Shopping Square. Head here for an inexpensive (by Yulara standards) sandwich, baguette or pie (all $5.50–9.50) for lunch, or a coffee and a cake. The young staff members are trainees from the local National Indigenous Training Academy. Daily 8am–5pm.

Ilkari Sails in the Desert ☎08 8957 7888, ⌾ayersrockresort.com.au. Probably the fanciest of the resort's restaurants – with prices to match – serving up innovative contemporary Australian cuisine (mains around $40). Expect to see dishes such as Wagyu steak and pan-fried barramundi. Daily 7–10pm.

5

Uluru–Kata Tjuta National Park

Dec–Feb 5am–9pm, March 5.30am–8.30pm, April 5.30am–8pm, May 6am–7.30pm, June–July 6.30am–7.30pm, Aug 6am–7.30pm, Sept 5.30am–7.30pm, Oct 5am–8pm, Nov 5am–8.30pm • $25, $12.50 for 5–15 year olds

The entry fee for **ULURU–KATA TJUTA NATIONAL PARK** allows unlimited access for up to three days, though it's easily extendable (an annual pass is just $32.50). Besides the two major sites of Uluru and Kata Tjuta, the park incorporates the closed Aboriginal community of Mutujulu, near the base of the Rock, the site of the original caravan park before the resort was built. More than 400,000 tourists visit the park every year, and as many come in tour-bus groups, the place can sometimes feel crowded.

As the park is on Aboriginal land, you can't go anywhere other than Uluru, Kata Tjuta, the Cultural Centre, and the few roads and paths linking them.

Brief history

It is thought that Aboriginal people arrived at Uluru more than 20,000 years ago, having occupied the Centre more than 10,000 years earlier. They survived in this semi-arid environment in small mobile groups, moving from one waterhole to another. Water was their most valued resource, and so any site like Uluru or Kata Tjuta that had permanent waterholes and attracted game was of vital practical – and therefore religious – significance.

The first European to set eyes on Uluru was the explorer Ernest Giles, in 1872, but it was a year later that William Gosse followed his Afghan guide up the Rock and thereby made the first ascent by a European, naming it **Ayers Rock** after a South Australian politician. With white settlement of the Centre and the introduction of cattle came the relocation of its occupants from their traditional lands.

The first **tourists** visited the Rock in 1936, and in 1958 the national park was excised from what was then an Aboriginal reserve. By the early 1970s the tourist facilities in the park were failing to cope and the purpose-built township and resort of Yulara was conceived and completed within a decade. At the same time the traditional custodians of Uluru began to protest about the desecration of their sacred sites by tourists, who at that time could roam anywhere. After a long land claim the park was subsequently returned with much flourish to the Yankunytjatjara and Pitjantjatjara peoples in 1985, on condition that it was leased straight back to the Department of Environment and Heritage, which now jointly manages the park with the Anangu.

Uluru–Kata Tjuta Cultural Centre

Daily 7am–6pm • Free • ☎ 08 8956 1128, ⊛ parksaustralia.gov.au/uluru

The striking **Uluru–Kata Tjuta Cultural Centre**, 1km before the Rock, is a destination in itself. Inside, a compelling exhibition covers aspects of traditional indigenous life, Dreaming stories related to Uluru, land care and bushtucker know-how. The centre also houses a café, souvenir shop and two galleries: allow at least an hour to look around.

While you're here, drop by the National Parks **information desk** to pick up the informative *Park Notes* on various topics. The park is home to more than 400 plant species, 25 native mammals, 178 different birds and no fewer than 72 species of reptile, and features subtly diverse habitats ranging from spinifex-covered sand hills to desert oak woodlands.

Of the two galleries, Maruku (daily 7.30am–5.30pm; ☎ 08 8956 2153, ⊛ maruku .com.au) specializes in rustic handicrafts from the Central and Western deserts, such as boomerangs, spears and music sticks, while Walkatjara Art Uluru (daily 8am–4pm; ☎ 08 8956 2537, ⊛ desart.com.au) sells fine paintings from talented local artists, some of whom have exhibited at Australia's best museums and galleries. You can walk the easy 2km from the Cultural Centre to the west face of the Rock along the **Liru Walk**.

Climbing Uluru

Although it is not illegal, climbing Uluru is a controversial issue. An unequivocal statement on a large sign at the base sums up the sentiments of the Anangu: "Please

ULURU-KATA TJUTA NATIONAL PARK

don't climb." Uluru is a sacred site for the Anangu, and the climbing route is associated with traditional religious ceremonies. They also feel a duty to safeguard visitors, and feel personally responsible when tourists die or hurt themselves (36 people have lost their lives climbing the rock and many more have been injured or required rescuing).

The strength of feeling was highlighted in 2015 when a local activist cut the path's chain-link fence in a high-profile protest. Many people visit Uluru with the intention of climbing only to change heart after learning more about the Anangu's long and complex relationship with the site.

Despite this, a minority of tourists still attempt the hour-long hike up to the summit, though numbers have steadily fallen over the last decade. If you plan to climb, note that it is tough going and potentially dangerous, thanks to strong winds and sheer drops. If you're at all unfit or nervous about heights, do not attempt it. Wear a tightly secured hat and walking boots, take plenty of water, and do not urinate or drop litter along the route. Make sure you also stick to the designated trail – in 2016 three hikers sparked an 11-hour rescue mission after leaving the path and getting stuck in a crevice.

The climb is regularly closed during high winds or by 8am if the temperature that day is expected to exceed 36°C. Between Aug/Sept and April/May it gets windy; Nov–Jan is the hottest period when temperatures can hover around or above 40°C; and January–March is wet, when the annual average of 300mm of rain can fall in the park (though this figure is extremely variable); it can also rain during the build-up and lightning season from late November. Daily weather forecasts are posted at the resort.

ULURU GEOLOGY

The reason Uluru rises so dramatically from the surrounding plain is because it is a **monolith** – that is, a single piece of rock, with most of its bulk hidden below ground like an iceberg. With few cracks to be exploited by weathering, and the layers of very hard, coarse-grained **sandstone** (or arkose) tilted to a near-vertical plane, the Rock has resisted the denudation of the landscape surrounding it. However, wind and rain have had their effects. During storms, brief, but spectacular, waterfalls stream down the rock forming dirty channels. In places, the surface of the monolith has peeled or worn away, producing bizarre features and many caves, most out of bounds but some accessible on the walking trails. The striking orangey-red hue is actually superficial, the result of oxidation ("rusting") of the normally grey sandstone that can still be seen in some nooks and caves.

5

Kuniya Walk

Far less strenuous that climbing Uluru, no less satisfying and certainly more in keeping with the spirit of the place, are the **walks** one can take along the base of the rock. At the very least, the 1km **Kuniya Walk** from the Kuniya car park to **Mutitjulu Waterhole**, a perennial pool, rock-art site and scene of epic ancestral clashes, is recommended.

Mala Walk

1.5hr ranger-guided Mala walks daily 8am Oct–April, 10am rest of year • Free • Meet at the Mala car park

Departing from the Mala car park, the 2km **Mala Walk** to **Kantju Gorge** is even better, passing unusually eroded caves, more rock art, as well as pools shaded by groves of desert oaks, ending at the huge cliff above Kantju Gorge itself.

Base Walk

Best of all is the 9.8km **Base Walk** around the Rock, which takes three to four hours, including time for nosing about. It offers a closer look at sacred Anangu sites (many of which cannot be photographed – heed any notices), as well as a chance to appreciate the extraordinary textural variations and surface features. Remember, though, to take plenty of water, a hat and appropriate footwear.

Kata Tjuta

The "Many Heads", as **Kata Tjuta** – formerly the **Olgas** – translates from the local Aboriginal languages, are situated 53km from the resort at Yulara. This remarkable formation may have once been a monolith ten times the size of Uluru, but has since been carved by aeons of weathering into 36 "monstrous domes", to use explorer Ernest Giles' words, each smooth, rounded mass divided by slender chasms or broader valleys. The composition of Kata Tjuta – markedly different from Uluru's fine-grained rock – can be clearly seen in the massive, sometimes sheared, boulders set in a **conglomerate** of sandstone cement. Access to this fascinating maze is unfortunately limited to just two walks, in part because of earlier problems with overambitious tourists, but also because the east of Kata Tjuta is a site sacred to Anangu men.

The first of the permitted walks, the 2.6km **Walpa Gorge Walk**, involves an easy stroll into the dramatic dead-end chasm flanking Mount Olga (which, at 1070m, is the highest point in the massif). Keep an eye out for hill kangaroos. Better still is the **Valley**

ABORIGINAL PEOPLE IN THE RED CENTRE

The Red Centre includes the lands inhabited by the "**Anangu**", which simply means "Aboriginal people" in the languages of the Western Desert. Tribes include the Arrernte from the Alice Springs area, Luritja from the Papunya area, the Pitjantjatjara from the region stretching from Uluru/Yulara to Docker River, and the Yankunytjatjara and Antakarinja, from the areas in between. Notwithstanding massacres as late as 1928, the Aborigines of the central deserts were fortunate in being among the last to come into **contact** with white settlers, by which time the exterminations of the nineteenth century had passed and anthropologists like Ted Strehlow were busy recording the "dying race". However, their isolation is thought to have made adjustment to modern life more challenging for them than for Aborigines of the northern coast.

At the centre of Anangu life and society is the concept of **Tjukurpa**, sometimes translated as "Dreamtime". It's a complex concept that encompasses the past, present and future; the creation period when the **ancestral beings** (*Tjukaritja*) created the world; the relationship between people, plants, animals and the land; and the knowledge of how these relationships formed, what their meaning was, and how they should be maintained through daily life and ceremony. In Aboriginal society their stories (which can sound simplistic when related to tourists) acquire more complex meanings as an individual's level of knowledge increases with successive initiations. Read the interpretive signs at the base of the Rock to learn about *Tjukaritja* such as the *Mala* (rufous hare wallaby), *Liru* (venomous snake) and *Kuniya* (python).

of the Winds Walk, a 7.5km loop that takes about three hours, the first part of which is a 2km climb to the **Karu Lookout** – suffice to say it's worth the effort. This is as much as you can see of Kata Tjuta's interior. The longer stretch from Karu Lookout onwards is closed at 11am if temperatures are forecast at 36°C or higher.

ARRIVAL AND GETTING AROUND ULURU–KATA TJUTA NATIONAL PARK

By bus If you're not on a tour and don't have your own vehicle, catch the Uluru Express (☎08 8956 2152, ⓦuluruexpress.com.au) minibus, which shuttles you from your accommodation to Uluru and/or Kata Tjuta (from $60–95 for a sunrise, daytime or sunset return trip, $220 for a two-day pass, $250 for a three-day pass).

By bike If you fancy cycling the 15km pathway around the base of Uluru, hire a bike from Outback Cycling ($45/3hr; children's bikes, toddler seats and tag-alongs also available; ☎04 3791 7018, ⓦoutbackcycling.com) at the Uluru–Kata Tjuta Cultural Centre.

The Great Central Road

From Kata Tjuta the mostly unsealed **Great Central Road** leads west over 1100km to Laverton, in Western Australia. The track forms part of the longer Outback Way (ⓦoutbackway.org.au), which also stretches east to Queensland. As long as you don't get caught in a storm (check weather forecasts and do not attempt the route if rain is predicted), a 4WD is recommended, but the usual precautions for driving on dirt roads apply (see p.34).

Because the track passes through remote communities, and goes cross-border, you'll need two sets of transit permits (see below). There are four accommodation options en route, roughly at 200km intervals. From Tjukayirla it's another 305km to Laverton, from where sealed roads lead on to Leonora and Kalgoorlie.

INFORMATION THE GREAT CENTRAL ROAD

Permits Transit permits (free) are needed to travel in both the NT and WA sections, available over the counter in Alice Springs and Perth or online from ⓦclc.org.au and ⓦdaa.

wa.gov.au. Both permits are for a direct transit only.
Foodstuffs Note that you cannot bring foodstuffs, plants etc. from NT to WA (quarantine bins are provided at Laverton).

ACCOMMODATION

All roadhouses offer basic **accommodation** (try to book ahead) and supply diesel and **opal**, an unleaded petrol substitute (as in several other parts of the NT, regular gasoline is restricted owing to the problem of petrol sniffing in remote Aboriginal communities).

Docker River Campsite 227km from Yulara ☎08 8955 8245. Well signposted on the left as you drive west, this basic, community-maintained campsite has toilets, cold showers and an honesty payment system. Good for sunset viewing.
Warakurna Roadhouse 98km from Docker River ☎08 8956 7344, ⓦwarakurnaroadhouse.com.au. A dirt-track roadhouse with fuel, takeaway food, small store, rooms (including some basic dorm-style options aimed at backpackers) and drive-through camping sites. Dorms $40, doubles $165, un/powered sites per person $10/12
Warburton Roadhouse 230km from Warakurna ☎08 8956 7656, ⓦwarburtonroadhouse.com.au. Offers

respite from the desert highway in the form of accommodation (including some economical singles from $100) and meals, with a good Aboriginal art gallery (Mon–Fri 8.30am–4pm) giving further reason to stop off. Doubles $170, camping per person $15
Tjukayirla Roadhouse 245km from Warburton ☎08 9037 1108, ⓦtjukayirlaroadhouse.com.au. Sitting 305km before Laverton, this roadhouse has camping options as well as "backpacker rooms" with shared bathrooms, plus smarter en-suite options (the latter from $160). Prides itself on its food, particularly its burgers. Doubles $120, un/powered sites $15/20

Western Australia

PURNULULU NATIONAL PARK

Western Australia

Western Australia (WA) covers a third of the Australian continent, yet it has just 2.6 million residents. Conscious of its isolation from the more populous eastern states – or indeed anywhere else – WA has a strong sense of its own identity and a community that is very proud to call it their home. And well they should be. Western Australia offers an enticing mix of Outback grandeur, glorious coastal scenery and laidback living, and is attracting increasing numbers of tourists keen to break away from "the East", as the rest of the country is known in these parts, in search of the real Australia.

Perth, the state's capital and where most of Western Australia's population is based, retains the leisure-oriented vitality of a young city, while the atmospheric port of **Fremantle**, really just a suburb, resonates with a youthful and somewhat boisterous charm. Both have seen extensive redevelopment in recent years and have never been more enticing. South of Perth, the wooded hills and trickling streams of the **Southwest** support the state's most celebrated wine-growing region **Margaret River**, while the giant **eucalyptus forests** around **Pemberton** provide numerous opportunities for hiking and generally getting to grips with nature. East of the forests is the state's intensively farmed **wheat belt**, an interminable man-made prairie struggling against the saline soils it has created. Along the Southern Ocean's stunning storm-washed coastline, **Albany** is the primary settlement; the dramatic granite peaks of the **Stirling Ranges** just visible from its hilltops are among the most botanically diverse habitats on the planet. Further east, past the beautifully sited coastal town of **Esperance** on the edge of the Great Australian Bight, is the **Nullarbor Plain**, while inland are the **Eastern Goldfields** around Kalgoorlie-Boulder, the largest central urban area in this region and a hardy survivor of the century-old mineral boom on which WA's prosperity is still firmly based.

While the temperate southwest of WA has been tamed by increasing urbanization, the north of the state is where you'll discover the raw appeal of the **Outback**. The virtually unpopulated inland deserts are blanketed with spinifex and support remote Aboriginal and mining communities, while the west coast's winds abate once you venture into the tropics north of **Shark Bay**, home of the friendly dolphins at **Monkey Mia**. From here, the mineral-rich **Pilbara** region fills the state's northwest shoulder, with the dramatic gorges of the **Karijini National Park** at its core. An unmissable attraction on the state's central coast – aka the Coral Coast – is the unspoiled and easily accessible

WHALE SHARK, NINGALOO MARINE PARK

Highlights

❶ Fremantle Eclectic, energetic and full of charm – make Freo your first port of call and slip into the sun-drenched WA lifestyle. **See p.570**

❷ Margaret River One of Australia's leading regions for food and wine, Margaret River is the best place in the state to indulge. See p.585

❸ Tall Timber Country Hike or cycle forest tracks, paddle the Blackwood River or drive among magnificent karri forests. See p.589

❹ Shark Bay The friendly Monkey Mia dolphins are still top of everyone's list, but there's much more to this incredibly biodiverse region. **See p.613**

❺ Ningaloo Marine Park Enjoy superlative snorkelling and diving – plus new humpback whale swimming tours – at the "barrier reef without the barriers". See p.622

❻ Karijini National Park Experience exhilarating camping and canyoning in gorgeously gorge-ridden Karijini. See p.625

❼ The Kimberley The stunning, untamed Kimberley is the country's last frontier and a backdrop to real adventure. See p.630

❽ Purnululu National Park Accessible only by 4WD or air, the striped beehive domes and narrow gorges of the Bungle Bungle massif make the trek worthwhile. See p.642

HIGHLIGHTS ARE MARKED ON THE MAP ON P.558

Ningaloo Reef, the world's largest fringing reef; those in the know rate it more highly than Queensland's attention-grabbing Great Barrier Reef.

Northeast of the Pilbara, the **Kimberley** is regarded as Australia's last frontier. **Broome**, once the world's pearling capital, is a beacon of civilization in this hard-won cattle country, while adventurous travellers fall in love with the stirring, dusty scenery around **Cape Leveque** and the **Gibb River Road**. The region's convoluted, barely accessible coasts are washed by huge tides and occupied only by secluded pearling operations, a handful

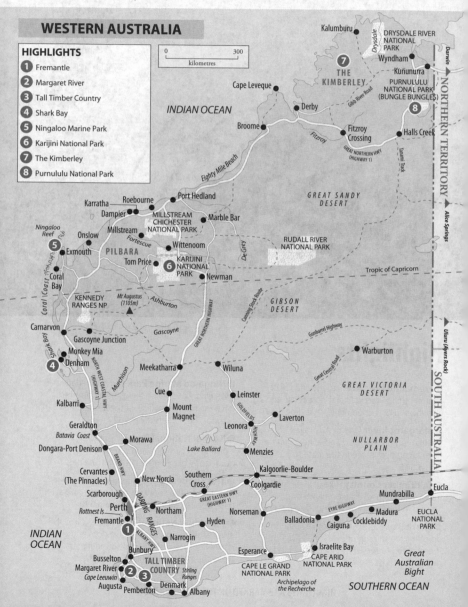

WESTERN AUSTRALIA

HIGHLIGHTS

1. Fremantle
2. Margaret River
3. Tall Timber Country
4. Shark Bay
5. Ningaloo Marine Park
6. Karijini National Park
7. The Kimberley
8. Purnululu National Park

0   300
kilometres

THE CLIMATE

WA's **climate** is a seasonal mix of temperate, arid and tropical. **Winters** are cool in the south and wet in the southwest corner, while at this time of year the far north basks in daily temperatures of around 30°C, with no rain and tolerable humidity: this is the tropical dry season. Come the **summer**, the wet season or "Wet" (Dec–April) renders the Kimberley lush but inaccessible, while the rest of the state, particularly inland areas, crackles in the heat, with temperatures frequently climbing above 40°C. The southern coast is the only retreat for the heat-struck; the southwest coast is cooled by dependable afternoon sea breezes, known in Perth as the "Fremantle Doctor".

6

of Aboriginal communities, a couple of luxury retreats, and crocodiles. On the way to the Northern Territory border is **Purnululu National Park**, home to the surreal **Bungle Bungle massif** – one of Australia's greatest natural wonders.

Brief history

Aborigines had lived in WA for at least forty thousand years by the time the seventeenth-century traders of the **Dutch East India Company** began wrecking themselves on the west coast mid-journey to the Dutch East Indies (modern-day Indonesia), where they sought valuable spices. While some dispute remains about the first foreigner to see Australia, with French, Portuguese and Chinese explorers all laying a claim, it can safely be said that Dutch mariner **Dirk Hartog** was the first European to set foot on Western Australian soil, leaving an inscribed pewter plate on the island off Shark Bay that now bears his name, in 1616. For the next two hundred years, however, WA's barren lands remained – commercially at least – uninspiring to European colonists.

France's interest in Australia's southwest corner at the beginning of the nineteenth century led the **British** to hastily claim the unknown western part of the continent in 1826, establishing **Fredricktown** (Albany) on the south coast; the **Swan River Colony**, today's Perth, followed three years later. The **new colony** initially rejected convict labour and as a result struggled desperately in its early years, but it had the familiar effect on an Aboriginal population that was at best misunderstood and at worst annihilated.

Economic problems continued for the settlers until stalwart explorers in the mid-nineteenth century opened up the country's interior, leading to the gold rushes of the 1890s that propelled the colony into autonomous statehood by the time of Australian federation in 1901. This **autonomy**, and growing antipathy towards the eastern states, led to a move to secede in the depressed 1930s, when WA felt that the rest of the country was dragging it down – an attitude that persists today. However, following World War II the whole of white Australia – and especially WA – began to thrive, making money first from wool and later from huge iron ore and offshore gas discoveries that continue to form the basis of the state's wealth. Meanwhile, most of WA's seventy thousand Aborigines continue to live in desperately poor and remote communities, as if in another country.

GETTING AROUND

Travellers never fail to underestimate the **massive distances** in WA. If you hope to explore any significant part of the state's more than 2.5 million square kilometres, and in particular the remote Northwest, your own vehicle is essential, although you can still get to many interesting places by combining local tours with buses (see p.560).

By plane Flights into and out of Perth and around WA are operated mostly by Qantas (ⓦqantas.com), with some useful Virgin Australia (ⓦvirginaustralia.com) and Airnorth (ⓦairnorth.com.au) routes too.

TIME IN WA

Keep in mind that Western Australia is one and a half hours behind the Northern Territory and South Australia and two hours behind the other eastern states. Unlike some states, it does not operate **daylight savings** in summer.

By bus For those without a car, the rigid schedules and butt-numbing nature of long-distance bus travel require a certain equanimity. The main state bus operator is Transwa (☏ 1300 662 205, ⓦ transwa.wa.gov.au), with other services provided by Greyhound (☏ 1300 473 946, ⓦ greyhound.com.au); Integrity Coachlines (☏ 08 9274 7464, ⓦ integritycoachlines.com.au); and South West Coach Lines (☏ 08 9261 7600, ⓦ southwestcoachlines.com.au).

By tour bus Several tour buses ply the entire length of the WA coast, from Perth to Broome, the most popular of which is Adventure Tours (☏ 03 8102 7800, ⓦ adventuretours.com.au).

Perth

Western Australia's youthful capital city **PERTH** is home to more than 1.8 million people and has a reputation for endless sunshine and an easy-going lifestyle. After work, it's typical for people to go surfing, sailing, swimming or fire up a barbie somewhere on the shores of the Swan River, which forms a broad lagoon through the city and is ideal for recreation and sport. This enviable social life partly explains Perthites' contented detachment from the rest of the country. Another factor is simply the physical distance: Perth is Australia's (and, many say, the world's) most isolated city, almost 4000km from Sydney by road, a four-hour flight from the east coast and in a different time zone (Western Standard Time) to the rest of the country. People here love to go their own way, sparking plenty of entrepreneurial projects and small businesses.

The state's recent mining boom has also sparked one of the largest building projects ever seen in the city and numerous redevelopments were in progress at the time of writing. The Central Business District (CBD) is undergoing something of a renaissance as more international companies set up shop here (particularly Chinese and Indian firms), while the area between the city and Northbridge is currently being completely revamped, with the previously above-ground train line being buried beneath an area of plazas, including a new major public space called Yagan Square, to be completed sometime in 2017.

Just north of the CBD, **Northbridge** is perhaps Perth's most notorious suburb, with an other-side-of-the-tracks feel and a vibrant, intoxicating nightlife – it is also the centre for Perth's Asian community. Due to years of CBD neglect (and harsh liquor licensing) much of the city's daily life continues to take place in its outer reaches, with the inner west suburbs of **Leederville** and **Subiaco** boasting boutiques, cafés, restaurants and pubs galore.

The CBD

Perth has some wonderful examples of colonial and Federation-era architecture dotted around the city centre, providing an interesting contrast to the thrusting modern skyscrapers that characterize the skyline here – and are going up in increasing numbers. The core of the **CBD**, including **Hay Street**, **Murray Street** and **St Georges Terrace** along with the laneways between them, is gradually developing from a quiet business and shopping district into a vibrant downtown area, with many of the most interesting buildings finding new life as restaurants and bars – there is always somewhere new to check out.

William Street cuts through the centre of the CBD before running north over the railway at **Horseshoe Bridge** and on into the pubs, clubs and Asian eating places of Northbridge. Barrack Street, just east of William Street and bordering the Hay and Murray Street malls, runs south to the **Barrack Street Jetty** and **Elizabeth Quay** on the Swan River.

Swan Bell Tower

Barrack Square, Riverside Drive • Daily 10am–3.45pm (last entry) • $14 • Demonstrations generally Mon–Sat between 10.30am and 2.30pm, ringing Sun, Mon & Thurs noon–1pm • ☏ 08 6210 0444, ⓦ swanbells.com.au

This distinctive tower on the waterfront houses the bells of London's St-Martin-in-the-Fields Church, presented to WA on the 1988 bicentenary, and is the only place in the world where you can watch 16 bells being rung simultaneously. The eighteenth-century

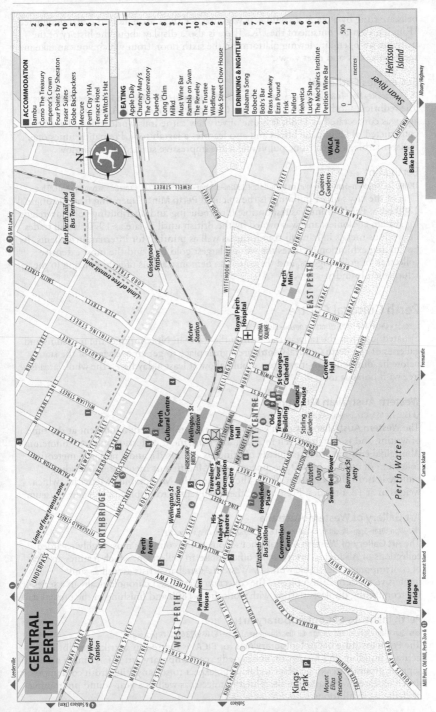

CENTRAL PERTH

■ ACCOMMODATION	
Bambu	2
Como The Treasury	9
Emperor's Crown	3
Four Points by Sheraton	4
Fraser Suites	10
Globe Backpackers	5
Mercure	8
Perth City YHA	6
Terrace Hotel	7
The Witch's Hat	1

● EATING	
Apple Daily	7
Chutney Mary's	4
The Conservatory	6
Duende	1
Long Chim	8
Milkd	3
Must Wine Bar	2
Rambla on Swan	11
The Reveley	7
The Trustee	9
Wildflower	9
Wok Street Chow House	5

■ DRINKING & NIGHTLIFE	
Alabama Song	5
Bobeche	7
Bob's Bar	7
Brass Monkey	4
Ezra Pound	2
Frisk	1
Halford	8
Helvetica	6
Lucky Shag	10
The Mechanics Institute	3
Petition Wine Bar	9

bells are rung by a team of volunteers who practice their art here in the first designated "Ringing Centre" outside of the UK. There is also a display about the history of the bells and an open-air viewing platform on the sixth floor, from which you can take in spectacular city and river views.

6

St Georges Cathedral

38 St Georges Tce • Mon–Fri & Sun 7am–6pm, Sat 7am–5pm (till 5.30pm in winter) • Free • ☎ 08 9325 5766, ⊛ perthcathedral.org

The redbrick, Gothic Revival **St Georges Cathedral** is WA's main Anglican cathedral and was consecrated in 1888. It is one of very few cathedrals worldwide to have been constructed of handmade bricks and also features a jarrah roof, Fremantle limestone, Italian marble, a Caen stone pulpit and some impressive stained-glass windows.

Perth Mint

310 Hay St • Daily 9am–5pm • $19 • Tours on the half-hour 9.30am–3.30pm • ☎ 08 9421 7222, ⊛ perthmint.com.au • Red CAT bus

One of the city's finest buildings is the splendid **Perth Mint**. Operating from its original 1899 base, Perth's mint was responsible for producing and distributing gold sovereigns for Britain's colonies, and was owned by the British until as late as 1970. It still trades in precious metals in bar and coin form, as well as minting for international clients. Its fascinating exhibition includes the world's largest gold bars and the most extensive collection of gold nuggets, and there are also demonstrations of gold pouring in the refurbished foundry.

Perth Cultural Centre

James St • ☎ 08 6557 0700, ⊛ mra.wa.gov.au • Blue CAT bus

Situated just over the railway tracks from the CBD in Northbridge, the museums and galleries of the **Perth Cultural Centre** are a great place to get an overview of the state before heading out into it and you should allow at least a day here. The whole area is a free wi-fi hotspot too.

Western Australian Museum

☎ 1300 134 081, ⊛ museum.wa.gov.au

The **Western Australian Museum** was closed for a complete redevelopment at the time of writing and is due to reopen in 2020. The permanent collection includes numerous Aboriginal cultural artefacts, plenty of minerals and fossils, and a fantastic meteorite collection of around 14,000 specimens from 750 different meteorites, including hundreds from the Nullarbor Plain. The largest is the Mundrabilla Meteorite, which weighs in at 12.4 tonnes. Presumably, these will return to display in the new museum.

Art Gallery of Western Australia

Wed–Mon 10am–5pm • Voluntary donation • ☎ 08 9492 6600, ⊛ artgallery.wa.gov.au

The **Art Gallery of Western Australia** houses one of the country's most highly regarded collections of Aboriginal art, plus the official state art collection, which features an array of contemporary and classic works by Western Australian artists as well as some impressive modern British pieces. The collection is arranged chronologically in a series of interconnecting displays, starting with works from 1800 and finishing in the present day.

Perth Institute of Contemporary Arts

Tues–Sun 10am–5pm (closed during exhibition changeovers) • Free • ☎ 08 9228 6300, ⊛ pica.org.au

The **Perth Institute of Contemporary Arts** (or **PICA**) is housed in a striking redbrick heritage building and focuses on cutting-edge contemporary art. PICA's main aim is to support ground-breaking artists and you can expect to see anything from contemporary dance to state-of-the-art interdisciplinary projects, as well as a year-round programme of changing exhibitions.

Kings Park

Fraser Ave • Visitor centre daily 9.30am–4pm • Free • ☏ 08 9480 3600, ⓦ bgpa.wa.gov.au/kings-park • Bus #37 from St Georges Tce

The five-square-kilometre expanse of **Kings Park**, two-thirds of which is native bushland, is situated 2km west of the centre. Created with great foresight in 1872, this is Perth's most popular attraction and its sweeping parklands are flooded with locals on weekends, enjoying picnics and barbecues, and jogging and playing sports.

There are numerous walking trails and bike tracks throughout; pick up maps at the **visitor centre** next to the car park or join one of the free guided walks, which start here at 10am, noon and 2pm.

6

Botanic Garden

Daily 9am–5pm • Voluntary donation • ⓦ bgpa.wa.gov.au

The **Botanic Garden** opened in 1965 and is a showcase for Western Australia's unique flora – the state has half of Australia's 25,000 species, most of which aren't found anywhere else on earth.

The elevated **Lotterywest Federation Walkway** runs from the garden's entrance for 620 metres, gradually rising in height until you are some sixteen metres up in the forest canopy looking down on marri, karri, tingle and jarrah trees. The highlight is a spectacular glass-walled bridge with sweeping views of the park and the Swan River. The walkway is wheelchair accessible and includes artworks by the local indigenous Nyoongar people.

Perth Zoo

20 Labouchere Rd, South Perth • Daily 9am–5pm (including all holidays) • $29 • ☏ 08 9474 0444, ⓦ perthzoo.com.au • Buses #30 & #31 run from the CBD

Perth Zoo offers an introduction to Australia's famous wildlife, as well as the chance to see animals from around the world. If you won't be getting the chance to explore the bush and meet Aussie animals in the wild, then this is a good place to get your fix of kangaroos and koalas. Take the Australian Bushwalk trail (1hr; free) to see these as well as penguins, crocodiles, emus, echidnas, wombats and other native animals. There are also wildlife tours by "Zebra Car" ($5) and the chance to feed a giraffe ($10 per person).

ARRIVAL AND DEPARTURE   PERTH

BY PLANE

Perth's airport (☏ 08 9478 8888, ⓦ perthairport .com.au) is located to the east of the city centre and is divided into four terminals. T1 is the terminal for all international flights; T2, T3 and T4 are domestic terminals. There's a free transfer bus between terminals 24 hours a day. All major WA towns and cities are served by flights from Perth, with Qantas (ⓦ qantas.com.au) and Virgin Australia (ⓦ virginaustralia.com) offering the greatest number of services and AirNorth (airnorth.com. au) and Rex (rex.com.au) filling in some gaps.

Destinations Adelaide (2–5 daily; 2hr 50min); Albany (1–4 daily; 1hr 10min); Alice Springs (daily; 2hr 40min); Brisbane (2–5 daily; 4hr 20min); Broome (2–4 daily; 2hr 30min); Darwin (2–3 daily; 3hr 30min); Esperance (2–4 daily; 1hr 35min); Exmouth (1–2 daily; 1hr 55min–2hr 45min); Geraldton (1–4 daily; 1hr); Karratha (5–15 daily; 2hr); Kununurra (4 weekly; 3hr 10min); Melbourne (up to 16 daily; 3hr 30min); Port Hedland (3–6 daily; 2hr 5min); Sydney (10–13 daily; 4hr 10min).

GETTING INTO TOWN

Buses The Perth Connect shuttle bus ($15 one-way; ☏ 08 9277 4666, ⓦ perthairportconnect.com.au) picks up at T3 and takes you to your accommodation in the city centre. There's no need to book in advance. From T1 and T2 you can also catch Transperth bus #380 (☏ 13 62 13 or 08 9428 1900 from outside Perth, ⓦ transperth.wa.gov.au) to the Elizabeth Quay Bus Station in the city centre, running every 30–60 minutes. Routes #37 and #40 also run from T3 and T4 to the Elizabeth Quay Bus Station (all three routes airport to CBD $4.50).

Taxis There are taxi ranks at all of the airport terminals. A trip by taxi from the airport to the CBD costs around $40; to Fremantle it's at least $60. Some drivers will ask you to pay in advance and there is an additional $2 airport fee, which goes towards improving infrastructure.

BY TRAIN

Interstate trains terminate at and depart from the East Perth Rail and Bus Terminal, three train stops east of the central Transperth train station on Wellington Street.

6

DRIVING HIGHWAY 1

The 4400km drive up Highway 1 from Perth to Broome, across the Kimberley and on to Darwin in the Northern Territory, is one of Australia's great road journeys. Contrary perhaps to expectations, the **Batavia** and **Coral** coasts, **Central Midlands** region, the **Pilbara** and the **Kimberley** all have distinct personalities that become evident as you rack up the kilometres. On some days it'll seem like all you've seen are road trains, road kill and roadhouses, but to compensate there are innumerable places en route whose beauty will take your breath away, and even more that give an insight into Australia that you rarely get on the east coast.

If any single trip across Australia benefits from independent mobility it's this one: a car will allow you to explore intimately and linger indefinitely. If you want to discover the wayside attractions, allow at least four to five weeks for the journey from Perth to Darwin. Three weeks will whizz you through the highlights; anything less and you may as well fly. Highway 1 is sealed all the way, but to really experience northern WA you'll need to get off the beaten track and explore, as towns en route are almost without exception lacking in charm. A glance at a map shows the long distances between roadhouses, let alone settlements; carry plenty of water, always plan your next petrol stop and make sure that your vehicle is in sound condition, particularly the tyres and the cooling system, both of which will be working hard. Carry at least one spare tyre and take out adequate insurance.

Transwa's Prospector service (transwa.wa.gov.au) runs from Perth to Kalgoorlie, while the Australind runs to Bunbury. The Indian Pacific (ⓦ greatsouthernrail.com.au) runs from Perth to Kalgoorlie-Boulder, then on across the Nullarbor Plain on the world's longest straight piece of track (480km) to Adelaide, Broken Hill and Sydney.

Destinations Adelaide (weekly; 45hr); Broken Hill (weekly; 57hr); Bunbury (2 daily; 2hr 30min); Kalgoorlie (Prospector 1–2 daily; 7hr; Indian Pacific weekly; 11hr); Sydney (weekly; 73hr).

BY BUS

Interstate buses as well as most Transwa services to rural WA use the East Perth Rail and Bus Terminal. The Wellington Street bus station is used for suburban services, while the Elizabeth Quay Busport on Mill Street by the Perth Convention Centre is the terminus for several major bus services including some serving Fremantle. Some South West Coach Lines services (ⓦ southwestcoachlines.com.au) also call at the airport on the way out of Perth.

Integrity Coachlines ⓞ 08 9274 7464, ⓦ integritycoachlines.com.au. Integrity buses run from Perth up the coast to Broome twice a week, leaving from the Wellington Street station on Tuesday and Thursday evenings (9.30pm). This service calls at numerous stops including Cervantes (2hr 50min), Dongara (5hr), Geraldton (6hr 10min), Carnarvon (11hr 30min), Coral Bay (14hr

30min), Exmouth (16hr 40min), Karratha (24hr 30min), Port Hedland (28hr 15min) and finally Broome (34hr 45min). There is also a faster service to Port Hedland, which leaves on Tuesday evenings, also from Wellington Street, and runs up the inland Great Northern Highway calling at stops including New Norcia (1hr 55min), Newman (16hr 5min) and Port Hedland (22hr).

Transwa ⓞ 1300 662 205, ⓦ transwa.wa.gov.au. Transwa buses run from East Perth to destinations including Albany (1–2 daily; from 6hr); Augusta (1–2 daily; 5hr 30min); Bunbury (1–2 daily; 2hr 30min); Esperance (6 weekly; 10hr); Geraldton (2 daily; 6hr–8hr 30min); Hyden (for Wave Rock; weekly; 4hr 40min); Kalbarri (3 weekly; 8hr 30min); and Pemberton (3 weekly; 7hr 30min).

South West Coach Lines ⓞ 08 9261 7600, ⓦ southwestcoachlines.com.au. Bunbury (3–9 daily; 2hr 45min), Busselton (2–8 daily; 3hr 45min); Dunsborough (daily; 4hr 15min) and Margaret River (2 daily; 4hr 30min).

BY CAR

Travellers Auto Barn 365 Newcastle St, Northbridge ⓞ 1800 674 374, ⓦ travellers-autobarn.com.au. A well-respected company with offices throughout the country. Prices start from $45/day for a compact car, $59/day for a camper. Cars and campers can also be bought here with guaranteed buy-back at the end of your trip.

GETTING AROUND

USING THE TRANSPORT SYSTEM

Zones Both of Perth's central bus stations, as well as the local train stations' stops on either side of the main Wellington Street train station, are within the Free Transit Zone, or FTZ. Most buses passing through the FTZ offer free travel within it, as do the snazzy CAT (Central Area Transit) buses

serving the city centre. Outside the Free Transit Zone, Perth is divided into nine concentric areas – zones 1 and 2 are the most useful to visitors, incorporating Fremantle, the northern beaches and the Swan Valley, as well as the airport (zone 2).

Tickets If you're travelling beyond the FTZ, tickets are available from bus and ferry drivers or the vending machines at all (mostly unstaffed) train stations. Tickets are valid on all Transperth buses, trains and ferries for either two or three hours' unlimited travel within the specified zones (two hours for journeys up to 4 zones; three hours for journeys covering 5 to 9 zones). All-zone day-passes ($12.10) are also available and are valid on all Transperth services after 9am on weekdays, all day on weekends.

BY BUS
Bus stations The city centre has two suburban bus stations, Wellington Street (information office Mon–Fri 7am–6.30pm, Sat 7am–6pm, Sun 8.30am–6pm; ☎13 62 13) next to the central train station and the Elizabeth Quay Busport (information office Mon–Fri 7.30am–5.30pm, Sat 10am–2pm, Sun noon–4pm; ☎13 62 13), ten minutes' walk south at the bottom of Mill Street, which caters mostly for services south of the river.

CAT buses You can board the CAT buses, run by Transperth (☎ transperth.wa.gov.au, ☎13 62 13), at special CAT stops to take you along two circular routes, with a third route, the Yellow CAT, running up and down Wellington Street to East Perth. Press a button at the bus stops and a voice tells you when the next bus is due. The Blue CAT runs from Barrack Street Jetty along the Foreshore and up Mounts Bay Road to Barrack Street and Aberdeen Street, and then down William Street and over Horseshoe Bridge back to the river, while the Red CAT runs along the non-pedestrianized parts of Hay and Murray streets. All routes run daily from early morning until early evening, with intervals of fifteen minutes at most. The Blue CAT also runs until 1am Fridays and Saturdays.

BY TRAIN
Perth has an excellent underground and suburban train network, with lines running out to the suburbs from the main Perth train station on Wellington Street. There are five main lines: to Armadale, to Midland in the Swan Valley, to the northern coastal suburbs, to Fremantle and to Mandurah. All terminate at Perth station on Wellington Street.

BY BIKE
Perth has a comprehensive and far-reaching network of cycle lanes, which spread out to the suburbs and make cycling a pleasant and viable option. Bicycling Western Australia (☎08 6336 9696, ☎ bwa.org.au) can provide more information.

Bike rental About Bike Hire, based near the car park in the Point Fraser Reserve, at the eastern end of Riverside Drive (Nov–March daily 9am–5pm; April weekdays 9am–5pm, weekends 8am–6pm; May–Oct weekdays 9am–5pm, weekends 8am–5pm; ☎08 9221 2665, ☎ aboutbikehire.com.au), offers hybrid, mountain, road racing, touring and tandem bikes to rent from $10/hr or $24/day.

BY TAXI
Swan Taxis ☎13 13 30, ☎ swantaxis.com.au. Perth's reliable local taxis can be flagged down on the street or booked in advance by telephone.

Uber ☎ uber.com/cities/perth. The Uber taxi-ordering app is available in Perth.

INFORMATION & TOURS

City Sightseeing ☎08 9203 8882, ☎ citysightseeingperth.com. The City Sightseeing bus ($32 for a 24-hour ticket) calls at all the main attractions several times daily and tickets allow you to hop on and off.

Food Loose ☎ foodloosetours.com.au. A food tour with a side order of local history, Foodloose offers enlightening walks around Fremantle, Northbridge and the backstreets of the city, hitting plenty of great off-the-beaten-track places to eat. Tickets cost $41.75 not including food (budget another $25–30 for this).

Two Feet and a Heartbeat ☎1800 459 388, ☎ twofeet.com.au. These guys really know Perth and their walking tours of the CBD and Fremantle (from $35) are sure to enlighten even locals. The popular Eat Drink Walk ($55) three-hour evening tour takes in a selection of the city's best small bars and is a great introduction to Perth's ever-expanding nightlife scene.

Visitor centre The main visitor centre on William Street (Mon–Fri 9am–5.30pm, Sat 9.30am–4.30pm, Sun 11am–4.30pm; ☎1800 812 808, ☎ westernaustralia.com) has numerous free city guides and maps, tour information and state-wide promotional videos.

ACCOMMODATION

There's a full range of accommodation around the centre of Perth, from backpackers' hostels to luxury hotels and serviced apartments, with most places conveniently close to, or even right in, the city centre. Self-contained apartments can be great value for groups and families. The nearest campsites are 7km from the city.

HOTELS AND SELF-CONTAINED APARTMENTS

★**Como The Treasury**, 1 Cathedral Avenue ☎08 6168 7888, ☎ comohotels.com/thetreasury. The nineteenth-century States buildings have finally emerged from redevelopment as the city's leading five-star hotel. Soaring ceilings and brilliant white columns give a sense of space as soon as you enter the *Como* and the rooms are splendid – some have freestanding bathtubs. There's also an indoor pool with city views. $595.

6

TOURS FROM PERTH

Commercial ferry operators are all based at **Barrack St Jetty** and offer cruises up and down the Swan River, to Fremantle in one direction and the Swan Valley in the other. Bus and 4WD tours also leave daily in all directions from Perth, with popular destinations including the peculiar Pinnacles, near Cervantes, the wineries of the Upper Swan Valley, New Norcia, Wave Rock and even the Tree Top Walk near Walpole – the last two entailing a long day on a bus. A number of tour operators also specialize in Rottnest Island (see p.574) and the Swan Valley (see p.577).

For the **Southwest**, overnight tours are better: a three-night trip will typically pack in all the highlights in a loop via Albany. North of Perth the west-coast hotspots after the Pinnacles are Kalbarri, Shark Bay and then Coral Bay on Ningaloo Reef, with four days or more being a good relaxed pace for the trip up. From here some tours shoot straight back down to Perth; others head inland to Karijini National Park in the Pilbara, something that's well worth the effort if you've come this far north, though it's not generally accessible during the wet season (Nov–May). In the Northwest, there are many companies specializing in tours of the Kimberley (see box, p.636).

BOAT TRIPS AND CRUISES

Captain Cook Cruises ☎08 9325 3341, ⓦcaptaincookcruises.com.au. Offers a whole range of tours on the Swan River including wine cruises up the Swan Valley ($111–169), trips to Fremantle (from $30 one-way and $40 return) and Perth's longest-running dinner cruise (from $128), as well as a new Beer Cruise ($149) to Fremantle for a walking tour of the top craft beer bars.

GoBoats ⓦgoboatperth.com.au. New self-drive boat hire on the Swan River. No skipper experience is required and boats can take up to eight people. From $190 for two hours.

Golden Sun Cruises ☎08 9325 9916, ⓦgoldensuncruises.com.au. Cruises upriver to visit the National Trust property at Tranby House, historic Guildford and the Swan Valley wineries (from $52). Also downriver cruises to Fremantle (from $15).

Little Ferry Company ☎04 8877 7088, ⓦlittleferryco.com.au. Perth's newest cruise is also its shortest, a simple hop up the river from Elizabeth Quay to Claisebrook Cove in East Perth. The skipper gives a commentary en route and there are five ferries a day in each direction; $10 single, $18 return.

Oceanic Cruises ☎08 9325 1191, ⓦoceaniccruises.com.au. Two-hour whale-watching adventures on which sightings are guaranteed or your next tour is free (mid-Sept to early Dec), leaving from Fremantle ($65) and Perth ($75). Boats have large viewing decks and an interpretive DVD.

Rottnest Fast Ferries ☎08 9246 1039, ⓦrottnestfastferries.com.au. No longer just going to Rottnest (see p.574), Rottnest Fast Ferries also run a 1.5hr Coastal Cruise up the Sunset Coast north of Perth for views back to the city's white-sand beaches as well as out to the Indian Ocean ($30, Jan–April only).

DAY-TRIPS AND OVERNIGHT TOURS

Adams Pinnacle Tours ☎08 6270 6060, ⓦadamspinnacletours.com.au. Half- and full-day tours plus short breaks of two to four days around southwest WA or up the coast to the Pinnacles and beyond. The half-day Morning Perth & Fremantle City Explorer starts at $65, the full-day Pinnacles, New Norcia and Wildflowers (when in season) costs from $215, and the three-day break to the Pinnacles, Kalbarri and Monkey Mia starts from $1198.

Adventure Tours ☎03 8102 7800, ⓦadventuretours.com.au. Offers numerous itineraries including tours up the coast to Exmouth, Broome and Darwin and a loop around the Southwest taking in Esperance, the Stirling Ranges and Margaret River. The six-day loop around the Southwest costs from $450; the ten-day one-way tour to Broome from £880.

Explore Tours ☎1300 135 752, ⓦexploretoursperth.com.au. Day-trips from Perth out to highlights such as The Pinnacles (from $159), Penguin Island (from $179) and Wave Rock ($185). Also wild-flower tours when in season (from $159). Be prepared for a long day – some tours run for up to 13 hours.

Red Earth Safaris ☎08 9279 9011 or ☎1800 501 968, ⓦredearthsafaris.com.au. One-way and return tours to Exmouth. The northbound journey takes six days and includes the Pinnacles, Kalbarri, Monkey Mia and Coral Bay; the southbound return is a speedy hop done over just two days. One-way $200 southbound, $785 northbound; return (eight days) $985.

Western Travel Bug ☎08 9486 4222, ⓦtravelbug.com.au. Packed full-day tours to the Pinnacles, Wave Rock, Margaret River, the Swan Valley or Mandurah (all $185) plus multiday trips around the Southwest or up the coast (from $490).

Four Points by Sheraton 707 Wellington St ☎ 08 9327 7000, ⓦ fourpoints.com/perth. Located just opposite the Perth Arena, this hotel is a popular choice for concert-goers. Staff are friendly and welcoming and the rooms are spacious, bright and modern. **$200**

Fraser Suites 10 Adelaide Tce, East Perth ☎ 08 9261 0000, ⓦ perth.frasershospitality.com. Stylish and chic, this is a great choice for a CBD base. Apartments feature glorious city views and every possible facility you could ask for, from an open-plan kitchen and dining area to iPod docks and wi-fi. There's a swimming pool and 24-hour gym too. **$175**

Mercure 10 Irwin St ☎ 08 9326 7000, ⓦ mercure perth.com.au. Although the rooms here are slightly dated (the bathrooms could do with an update) they are spacious, with a separate seating area and dedicated workspace. Breakfast is served in the ground-floor restaurant and there's a rooftop swimming pool. **$206**

Terrace Hotel 237 St Georges Tce ☎ 08 9214 4444, ⓦ terracehotelperth.com.au. Housed in a Heritage-listed building in the centre of the CBD, this slick boutique hotel has fifteen stylish suites. The bathrooms are truly opulent, with standalone baths, rainfall showers and double sinks, and there's a range of in-room technology, from an iPad to AppleTV. **$229**

HOSTELS

The majority of Perth's backpackers' are located in Northbridge, where a variety of converted hotels and houses have been turned into sociable dens for working holiday-makers and travellers. Northbridge has few free on-street daytime parking spots, but off-street parking is available at some accommodation as indicated below. The keener establishments meet incoming trains and buses at East Perth Rail and Bus Station and will also collect you from the airports, though a two-night minimum stay may be required.

CITY CENTRE

Globe Backpackers 561 Wellington St at Queen St ☎ 08 9321 4080, ⓦ globebackpackers.com.au. About as central as you can get, with a fully equipped kitchen, sociable outdoor eating area, TV rooms and internet access. Dorms range from four to twenty beds, some en suite and some female only. Dorms **$23**, doubles **$79**

★ **Perth City YHA** 300 Wellington St ☎ 08 9287 3333, ⓦ yha.com.au. This stylish, renovated 1940s heritage building is close to everything, including, unfortunately, the train line (bring earplugs). Facilities are top-notch though, including spacious lounge areas, internet facilities, well-equipped kitchens and dining areas, on-site bar/café and a small outdoor pool. Often fills up so booking is essential. Dorms **$29**, doubles **$79**

NORTHBRIDGE

Bambu 75 Aberdeen St ☎ 08 9228 2909, ⓦ bambubackpackersperth.com. This renovated former warehouse and self-styled "boutique" hostel is decked out with Asian arts and crafts. It's extremely comfortable but with its weekend club nights and mood lighting, it's one for travellers who like to party. Complimentary breakfast. Dorms **$24**, doubles **$60**

Emperor's Crown 85 Stirling St ☎ 08 9227 1400, ⓦ emperorscrown.com.au. Outstanding flashpacker hostel, with a clean, modern interior, plasma-screen TV/DVD in the lounge and a fully equipped kitchen. Four-bed dorms and several double or triple configurations, some with en suite. Limited free parking. Dorms **$23**, doubles **$80**

The Witch's Hat 148 Palmerston St ☎ 08 9228 4228 or ☎ 1800 818 358, ⓦ witchs-hat.com. Exceptionally well-managed hostel located in a beautiful heritage building in a residential area northeast of Northbridge, with a real home-from-home feel. There are comfy communal areas and a BBQ, air conditioning in the evenings, plus free parking, job and tour services, and friendly staff. Dorms **$27**, doubles **$75**

EATING

Perth is blessed with a great food scene – and it's improving all the time. You'll find plenty of cafés and restaurants in the CBD, Northbridge (especially on James and William streets, the latter a real Asian eat street), nearby at Mount Lawley, at Leederville in the inner-west, at Subiaco, close to Kings Park, and especially in Fremantle (see p.573). If you're on a tight budget, try the food courts in the CBD and Northbridge, including the predominantly Asian *Old Shanghai* on James Street, Enex 100 off the Hay Street Mall and the Carillon off Murray Street Mall, where you'll find outlets including Red Rooster, Subway, Hungry Jacks and various Asian places. A main dish at any of these will give you change from $10.

THE CENTRE AND NORTHBRIDGE

Apple Daily Brookfield Place, CBD ☎ 08 6282 0000, ⓦ printhall.com.au. On the first floor of the Print Hall, Apple Daily is an Asian-style "eating house" where a young crowd sit in dark and atmospheric booths to order street food and sharers. Salt and pepper soft-shell crab is $26,

four roast duck buns $28. Mon–Fri 11.30am–midnight, Sat 4pm–midnight.

The Conservatory 356 Murray St, CBD ☎ 08 9481 1960, ⓦ theconservatory.net.au. This rooftop bar and restaurant has a retractable roof to take advantage of sunny days and the panoramic city views. All fish and

6

meats are sourced locally in southwestern Australia. Mains include roasted spiced chicken breast ($19.50) and local fresh grilled fish ($23). A burger is just $13.Wed–Thurs 4.30pm–1am, Fri & Sat noon–3am.

Long Chim Cnr St Georges Tce and Barrack St, CBD ☎08 6168 7775, ☜longchimperth.com. An authentic Thai street-food restaurant with a Bangkok chef has landed in Perth's Cathedral Square precinct. Single dishes and sharing plates range from bean curd *laksa* ($26) to barramundi curry ($45). The bar menu is inventive too, with Thai-inspired cocktails sitting alongside local craft beers. Daily midday–late.

Rambla on Swan 85 South Perth Esplanade, South Perth, ☎08 9367 2845, ☜ramblaonswan.com.au. Funky riverside restaurant serving simple, modern dishes such as oysters, beef carpaccio and Carnarvon prawn spaghetti ($40) with a view of the Swan River. Tues–Sun 11.30am–late.

The Reveley Elizabeth Quay, CBD ☎08 6314 1350, ☜thereveleybar.com.au. Only the very best of WA's seafood makes it onto the menu here, from Exmouth cod fillet to Fremantle tuna. There are local oysters too (half dozen $24) and Wagyu beef raised in Margaret River ($44). Mains start at $36 and you'll get a view out over the shiny new Elizabeth Quay district. Daily lunch and dinner.

★The Trustee 133 St Georges Tce, CBD ☎08 6323 3000, ☜thetrustee.com.au. This popular basement bar and bistro believes in nose-to-tail dining and serves a wide range of tasty meat dishes including bone marrow and beef cheek. If there are two of you, go for the chateaubriand, served with fat chips, bourguignon mushrooms and béarnaise sauce ($120). There's seafood too, including oysters and whole marron. Mon–Fri noon–late, Sat 5.30pm–midnight.

Wildflower 1 Cathedral Avenue, CBD ☎08 6168 7855, ☜wildflowerperth.com.au. Fine dining on the rooftop of Perth's best hotel, the *Como* (see p.565). Take in views of the Swan River as you feast on seasonal cuisine with a WA slant – think Shark Bay scallops, dry aged duck from Wagin, and Dorper lamb (mains from $36). The five-course

tasting menu is $145 per person, a two-course lunch menu $65 (Tues to Thurs only). Worth a splurge and the kind of place to dine on your first or last night in Oz. Tues–Fri lunch and dinner, Sat dinner.

Wok Street Chow House 47 Lake Street, Northbridge ☎08 9328 9883, ☜wokst.com.au. Sharing plates from Thailand arrive at your table whenever they're ready. Everything is tasty and fresh and prices are reasonable. Wok dishes from $14, bigger sharers from $26. Tues–Sat 5pm–late.

THE INNER SUBURBS

Chutney Mary's 67 Rokeby Rd, Subiaco ☎08 9381 2099, ☜chutneymarys.com.au. This funky Indian place serves up authentic, fiery Indian cuisine (traditional and fusion) to a loyal local crowd. Chicken tikka masala is $25, masala scallops $26. There's a decent wine list too, or you can BYO Mon–Wed for $7.50. Mon–Sat noon–2.30pm & 5.30–10.15pm, Sun 5.30–10.15pm.

Duendé 662 Newcastle St, Leederville ☎08 9228 0123, ☜duende.com.au. At Perth's best Spanish joint, you can expect traditional tapas (from $4) alongside more creative contemporary versions of classics. Affordable prices (octopus or meatballs for $17) and great wines by the glass too. Mon–Thurs noon–late, Fri 7.30am–late, Sat–Sun 8.30am–late.

Milkd 32 Angove St, North Perth ☎08 9228 8867, ☜milkd.com.au. You're sure to see a line of locals at this funky coffee bar where all things caffeinated are taken very seriously. There are also delicious sandwiches and breakfasts (toasted banana bread $6). Other branches in Subiaco (Denis St) and Maylands (8th Avenue). Sandwiches, such as a Rueben on rye or roast chicken $12.90. Daily 6.30am–6pm.

Must Wine Bar 519 Beaufort St, Highgate ☎08 9328 8255, ☜must.com.au. One of Perth's hippest spots is a fine-diner, casual eatery and bar all in one. The meals in the Parisian-style brasserie are French classics with a twist, using fantastic fresh local produce. Confit duck leg is $38. Daily noon–midnight.

DRINKING AND NIGHTLIFE

Northbridge and Fremantle (see p.570) are the focal points for after-dark action, with plenty of pubs, bars and clubs between them, but the nightlife scene in the CBD has improved markedly in recent years. Thanks to a relaxation of the liquor laws, a wide variety of small bars has opened up – and should not be missed. The free weekly *X Press* magazine (☜xpressmag.com.au) has comprehensive movie, music and club listings, while the weekly community paper *Out in Perth* (☜outinperth.com) can give you the lowdown on the LGBT scene. Both are available at various boutiques, music stores, cafés, bars and pubs.

Alabama Song Rear of 232 William St, Northbridge, ☜facebook.com/alabamasongbar. Perth's home of all things honky tonk is this Americana-themed bar with some 120 different American whiskys and plenty of local craft beer. Mon–Sat 6pm–late, Sun 8pm–late.

Bobeche Brookfield Place, CBD ☎08 9226 5596,

☜bobeche.com.au. This moody basement bar has a speakeasy style and serves an enticing range of inventive cocktails. There's also an extensive spirits list with a great range of whiskies. Mon–Thurs 4pm–midnight, Fri–Sat 4pm–2am (last entry 1am).

Bob's Bar Brookfield Place, CBD ☎08 6282 0000,

ⓦprinthall.com.au/bobs-bar. This rooftop bar is named after ex-prime minister Bob Hawke and is reached by a newspaper-lined staircase – this used to be the West Australian printing press and the neon sign is still in evidence. There are numerous beers on draft, an extensive wine list and several "civilized beverages of large proportion" for groups. Mon–Thurs 4pm–midnight, Fri–Sat noon–late.

Brass Monkey Cnr William & James sts, Northbridge ⓣ08 9227 9596, ⓦthebrassmonkey.com.au. Enduringly popular pub with a buzzy atmosphere in the heart of Northbridge. Serves a great range of local beers and hosts regular live gigs and themed nights, including burlesque. There's also a rooftop bar, with large TVs showing live sports. Mon & Tues 11am–midnight, Wed & Thurs 11am–1am, Fri & Sat 11am–2am, Sun 10am–midnight.

Ezra Pound 189 William St, Northbridge ⓣ0415 757666, ⓦepbar.com.au. Tucked away on a laneway in Northbridge, this is one of Perth's hippest bars, with a Prohibition theme and professionally mixed drinks. The low-key vibe makes it great for a relaxed no-nonsense tipple. Tues–Sat 3pm–midnight, Sun 1–10pm.

Frisk 103 Francis St, Northbridge ⓦfrisksmallbar .com.au. Small bar located slightly off the main drag and serving a full range of drinks, including dozens of different gins, a wide range of whiskies and an ever-changing range of draft beers. There's a pleasant area of wooden bench seating and small tables outside too – and great coffee. Tues–Sat 3pm–midnight, Sun 2–11pm.

Halford Hay St & Cathedral Avenue, CBD ⓣ08 9325 4006, ⓦhalfordbar.com.au. Tucked away in the Safe Room of the 1897 Titles Building, this brooding bar is all decadence, from the marble and velvet decor to the classically strong cocktails (martinis and juleps, no

mojitos here). Sun–Wed 4pm–midnight, Thurs–Sat 4pm–2am.

Helvetica Rear of 101 St Georges Tce, CBD ⓣ08 9321 4422, ⓦhelveticabar.com. Hidden down an unassuming alleyway, this hip whisky joint serves inventive cocktails and local beers, plus a wide range of whiskies available both by the glass and by the bottle (which they'll put your name on and keep behind the bar for you). Mon–Thurs 3pm–midnight, Fri noon–1am (last entry 12.30am), Sat 6pm–1am (last entry 12.30am).

Lucky Shag Barrack St Jetty, CBD ⓣ08 9221 6011, ⓦluckyshagbar.com.au. The tables on the wooden boardwalk overlooking the Swan River here are a wonderful place to be for sunset or on a sunny afternoon. There's live music most evenings. Mon–Thurs 11am–11pm, Fri & Sat 11am–midnight, Sun 11am–10pm.

The Mechanics Institute Rear of 222 William St, Northbridge ⓣ08 9228 4189, ⓦmechanicsinstitutebar .com.au. Located on a laneway around the back of William Street, this hip bar attracts the locals in large numbers every day of the week. Settle into one of the comfy reclaimed chairs inside or take a seat on the terrace with its city views and order a cocktail – the gin mule is especially good. A range of beers is also available, including bottles from Swan Valley's Feral Brewery. Mon–Sat noon–midnight, Sun noon–late.

Petition Wine Bar Cnr Barrack St & St Georges Tce, CBD ⓣ08 6168 7771, ⓦpetitionperth.com/wine. Think you know your wines? Test yourself at this highly knowledgeable (but very friendly) wine bar, home to an ever-changing array of local and international wines by the glass including some from lesser-known WA regions such as Denmark and Great Southern. Daily noon–late.

PERFORMING ARTS

Perth is fast shaking off its reputation as something of a cultural desert, with several different venues in the CBD offering high-quality performances of everything from opera to ballet, classical music to cutting-edge hip-hop. The addition of the Perth Arena has made the city an attractive stop on any international artist's Australian tour and big-name acts frequently play here.

Perth Arena 700 Wellington St ⓣ08 6365 0700, ⓦpertharena.com.au. Perth's multipurpose venue, located in the heart of the CBD, hosts big-name concerts and shows from international artists (Elton John, Pink, Cirque du Soleil) as well as sports events.

Perth Concert Hall St Georges Tce ⓣ08 9231 9900, ⓦperthconcerthall.com.au. The acclaimed Western Australian Symphony Orchestra plays at the stunning Perth Concert Hall, which was built in the 1970s and is said to have some of the best acoustics in Australia.

FESTIVALS IN PERTH

The city's huge **Fringe World** festival (ⓦfringeworld.com.au) brings all manner of arts and cultural events to the city in summer, including circus, cabaret and comedy, as well as dance, music and film. It even owns its own spiegeltent.

Eat Drink Perth (ⓦvisitperthcity.com/eatdrinkperth) takes place every March/April and highlights the best places to eat, with tours, markets and masterclasses taking place around Perth and Fremantle.

His Majesty's Theatre Cnr of King & Hay streets ☎ 08 9265 0900, ⊛ ptt.wa.gov.au/venues/his-majestys-theatre. The splendidly restored His Majesty's Theatre (affectionately known as "The Maj") is the only remaining working Edwardian theatre in Australia. The West Australian Ballet and West Australia Opera perform here.

DIRECTORY

Hospitals Royal Perth Hospital, Wellington St ☎ 08 9224 2244; Fremantle Hospital, Alma St ☎ 08 9431 3333.
Internet access Perth is well equipped with wi-fi access, with most bars and restaurants offering it free of charge. There is also free wi-fi in all areas of the Cultural Centre, and the State Library (☎ 08 9427 3111) has computers you can book by the hour for free.
Police ☎ 13 14 44 (000 for emergencies only).
Post office 7 Forrest Place (Mon–Fri 8.30am–5pm, Sat 9am–12.30pm; ⊛ auspost.com.au).

Around Perth

For excursions beyond central Perth, the port of **Fremantle**, at the mouth of the Swan River, should not be overlooked, nor should a trip over to **Rottnest Island**, a ninety-minute ferry ride from the city. It is also well worth the short trip out to Hillary's Boat Harbour to visit the **Aquarium of Western Australia**. Perth's **beaches** form a near-unbroken line north of Fremantle, just a short train or bus ride from the centre, with **Cottesloe** and **Scarborough** the top picks. With your own vehicle you can escape to the **Upper Swan Valley** wineries and the **national parks** inland, which run parallel to the coast and atop the **Darling Ranges**, where patchily forested hills, just half an hour's drive east of the city, offer a network of scenic drives and marked walking trails among the jarrah woodlands. Further afield, the monastic community of **New Norcia** can make a satisfying day-trip.

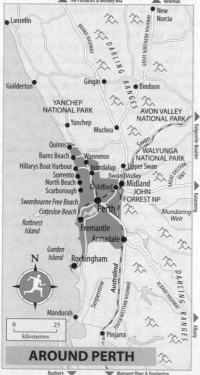

AROUND PERTH

Fremantle

Although long since merged into the metropolitan area's suburban sprawl, Perth's port of **FREMANTLE** – "Freo" – retains a character altogether different from the city centre. It's small enough to keep its energy focused, with a real working harbour and busy yacht marina, and it has an eclectic, arty ambience without too many upmarket pretensions. An increasing number of small bars are opening up and drawing the hipsters in, too. The town attracts people for its famed weekend **markets** (worth planning your visit around) and café-lined "Cappuccino Strip" or **South Terrace**, where funky boutiques are also found. It's worth noting that in the heat of summer Fremantle is often a breezy 5°C cooler than Perth, a mere half an hour away by train.

Exploring Fremantle on foot, with plenty of streetside café breaks, is the most agreeable way of visiting the town's compactly grouped sights. If you want to tick off all of them, start your appraisal on the east side before moving down to the ocean to end up at the **Fishing Boat Harbour**, ready for a sunset seafood dinner.

Fremantle Prison
The Terrace, end of William St • Daily 10am–5pm (tours half-hourly), plus Wed & Fri eves • Day-tour $20; Torchlight Tour $26; Tunnel Tour $60; all-tours pass $100 • ☎ 08 9336 9200, ⓦ fremantleprison.com

Built by convicts and first housing prisoners in 1852, Fremantle's hillside **prison complex** was only decommissioned in 1991. For most of its life the prison held the very highest security prisoners, in surroundings that were almost constantly criticized for their bleakness – it is said that after closing it took two and a half years to get rid of the smell.

The excellent **Doing Time tour**, sometimes guided by ex-wardens, takes you around the main building and the outlying courtyards. You'll see cells from various periods in the prison's history, including that of Aboriginal prisoner Peter Irwin Cameron, who dot-painted his entire cell. There are numerous other tours, including torchlit tours on Wednesday and Friday evenings, and a two-and-a-half-hour tour of the tunnels beneath the prison, where prisoners worked. The prison is also now home to a YHA hostel (see p.573).

6

Fremantle Markets
Cnr Henderson St & South Terrace • Fri 8am–8pm, Sat & Sun 8am–6pm • ☎ 08 9335 2515, ⓦ fremantlemarkets.com.au

The cheery **Fremantle Markets** include a fruit and veg market, and a more tourist-focused section crammed with stalls selling souvenirs, arts and crafts and New Age paraphernalia. The buskers who play here are said to be some of the city's best.

Round House
Arthur Head • Daily 10.30am–3.30pm • Donation • ☎ 08 9336 6897, ⓦ fremantleroundhouse.com.au

The **Round House** is WA's oldest building and the state's original jail. It opened in 1831, just eighteen months after settlement and, although threatened with demolition in the 1920s, today boasts fine views of the headland, sea and town. The cannon is fired daily at 1pm.

Western Australian Maritime Museum
Victoria Quay • Daily 9.30am–5pm • $15 entry; $15 for access to submarine (bookings advised); $25 combined ticket • ☎ 1300 134 081, ⓦ museum.wa.gov.au/museums/maritime

The striking **Western Australian Maritime Museum** covers just about every nautical aspect of WA, with displays on fishing, whaling, pearling and trade across the Indian Ocean. Pride of place goes to the glossy-hulled *Australia II* yacht, which won the America's Cup several times, while a series of hands-on exhibits, including the SS *Perth*'s expansion steam engine, gives visitors a greater appreciation of the intricacies of seafaring. The **submarine** *Ovens* is round the back.

E-Shed markets
Victoria Quay • Fri–Sun & public holidays 9am–5pm; food court open until 8pm • ⓦ eshedmarkets.net.au

The lively **E-Shed markets** are located in a historic warehouse building on the waterside and are worth a quick look, especially for their budget food stalls. There's also free wi-fi here during trading hours. Nearby, outside the Fremantle Port Authority (FPA) building at the end of Phillimore Street, there's a **statue** to C.Y. O'Connor, who masterminded the rebuilding of the docks in the 1890s, as well as the construction of the vital water pipeline to Kalgoorlie.

Shipwreck Galleries
Cliff St • Daily 9.30am–5pm • Suggested $5 donation • ☎ 1300 134 081 ⓦ museum.wa.gov.au/museums/shipwrecks

The **Shipwreck Galleries** tell the compelling stories of the myriad vessels lost on WA's treacherous coast. The centrepiece is the *Batavia*, the Dutch East Indiaman wrecked off present-day Geraldton in 1629. The exhibit includes the ship's reconstructed stern, a stone portico bound for the Dutch East India Company's unfinished fort at Batavia

FREMANTLE

● **EATING**

The Attic	3
Bathers Beach House	5
Bib and Tucker	1
Cicerello's	6
Gino's	4
Kazoomies	2
Little Creatures	7

■ **ACCOMMODATION**

Fremantle Prison YHA	2
Fremantle Village Caravan Park	7
Hougoumont	4
Norfolk Hotel	5
Old Fire Station Backpackers	1
Sundancer Backpacker Resort	3
Terrace Central B&B	6

■ **DRINKING & NIGHTLIFE**

Left Bank Bar & Café	1
Metropolis	3
Sail & Anchor	4
Strange Company	5
Sweetwater Rooftop	2
Whisper Wine Bar	6

(modern-day Jakarta), numerous corroded artefacts, and a fascinating film about the extraordinary drama of the wrecking (and subsequent salvage) of the ship.

Fishing Boat Harbour

Mews Rd · ⓦ fremantlefishingboatharbour.com

Across the railway tracks from the town centre is the appealing but very busy **Fishing Boat Harbour**. This remains a working harbour but is predominantly now a place to dine, with numerous restaurants selling fish and chips lining the boardwalks and presided over by seagulls.

ARRIVAL AND DEPARTURE
FREMANTLE

By plane If you're coming straight from Perth Airport, a taxi to Fremantle will take approximately 50min and set you back around $60.

By train Fremantle Station is located at the top end of Market St, five minutes' walk north of the town centre; trains to Fremantle leave Perth city centre at least every fifteen minutes.

By bus Routes #103 and #107 from Wellington St bus station and #106 and #111 from the Elizabeth Quay Busport, both in Perth, call in at Fremantle Station.

By ferry Ferries to Rottnest and Perth leave from the wharfside C-Shed, which is five minutes' walk from the station along Phillimore St.

GETTING AROUND AND INFORMATION

By bus The bright-orange Fremantle CAT bus (Mon–Thurs 7.30am–6.15pm, Fri 7.30am–7.45pm, Sat, Sun & holidays 10am–6.15pm, ⓦ transperth.wa.gov.au) is a free service running approximately every 15 minutes from Fremantle

Station to Douro Road (the Blue CAT) and from the Maritime Museum to Ord Street (the Red CAT).

By tram The Fremantle Tram offers informative commentaries on its hop-on-hop-off tours (daily at various times from 9.45am to around 3pm; from $25; ☎ 08 9473 0331, ⓦ fremantletrams.com.au), and departs from several different locations including the station, the harbour and outside the town hall.

Tourist information The busy visitor centre is next to the Town Hall on Kings Square (Mon–Fri 9am–5pm, Sat 9am–4pm, Sun 10am–4pm; ☎ 08 9431 7878, ⓦ visitfremantle.com.au).

6

ACCOMMODATION

Fremantle Prison YHA 6A The Terrace ☎ 08 9433 4305, ⓦ yha.com.au. Take your chance to stay in a World Heritage-listed building, sleeping in former prison cells or the more modern dorms and doubles at this shiny new YHA outpost in Fremantle. There's a games room, garden and parking too. Dorms $26, doubles $76

Fremantle Village Caravan Park 25 Cockburn Rd, South Fremantle ☎ 08 9430 4866, ⓦ fremantlevillage .com.au. The nearest campsite to the centre of town, with a range of on-site cabins and motel units. There are also two camp kitchens and free gas BBQs. Powered sites $43, cabins $135

Hougoumont 15 Bannister St ☎ 08 6160 6800, ⓦ hougoumonthotel.com. Funky, modern hotel with small rooms best suited to those on shorter breaks without too much luggage. All the essentials are here though: decent showers, a/c, tea/coffee facilities and a fridge. You'll need to head across the street to *The Attic* for breakfast (not included). $189

Norfolk Hotel 47 South Terrace ☎ 08 9335 5405, ⓦ norfolkhotel.com.au. Centrally located pub accommodation with mostly en-suite rooms plus a few budget options, all with kettle, TV and fridge. Quiet despite bands playing Thurs–Sat in the basement. $120

Old Fire Station Backpackers 18 Phillimore St ☎ 08 9430 5454, ⓦ old-firestation.net. Just 100m from the station, this sprawling hostel has a huge common room, an outdoor cinema area and free use of a pool table, table tennis table, Nintendo Wii and Sony PS4. Private rooms have TV and fridge. Dorms $28, doubles $75

Sundancer Backpacker Resort 80 High St ☎ 08 9336 6080 or ☎ 1800 061 144, ⓦ sundancerbackpackers.com. Fremantle's designated party hostel has an outdoor pool, beer garden and bar with various drink specials. Free satellite TV, luggage storage and tea and coffee. Dorms $28, doubles $80

Terrace Central B&B 79–85 South Terrace ☎ 08 9335 6600, ⓦ terracecentral.com.au. Located at the centre of the action in a heritage building, this friendly B&B has cosy, refurbished en-suite doubles with a/c, fridge, tea & coffee facilities and TV/DVD. Free breakfast. $240

EATING

The Attic 16A Bannister St, ☎ 04 3175 0800, ⓦ theatticfremantle.com.au. Two-level café with street seating and an airy upstairs space serving inventive breakfasts such as *shakshouka* (Tunisian-style poached eggs) and smashed avocado with toasted black quinoa ($16). Good smoothies too. Tues–Sun 7am–3pm.

Bathers Beach House 47 Mews Road, ☎ 08 9335 2911, ⓦ bathersbeachhouse.com.au. This laidback restaurant and beach bar is said to be the first place in Australia to serve alcohol on the beach – direct to your lounger. The dinner menu starts with oysters and includes a delicious charred wagyu rump ($42) and crispy skin barramundi ($38). Daily 11am–late.

★ **Bib and Tucker** 18 Leighton Beach Blvd, ☎ 08 9433 2147, ⓦ bibandtucker.net.au Quite simply the best place to eat in the Fremantle area. The menu is inventive mod Oz and the view is uninterrupted sand and sea – the perfect combination. Almost all produce used is Australian – from Fremantle mushrooms to Clarence River prawns. There's an interesting list of pizzas too, and plenty of WA wines by the glass. Mains are from $30–40. Daily breakfast 7am–11am, lunch noon–3pm and Wed–Sun dinner 5.30–9pm.

Cicerello's 44 Mews Rd ☎ 08 9335 1911, ⓦ cicerellos .com.au. Hugely popular casual seafood joint right on the harbour, with tables on the wooden boardwalk. Seafood platters are a good deal if there are a few of you, while

traditional fish and chips go for $14.60. Daily 10am–late.

Gino's 1 South Terrace ☎ 08 9336 1464, ⓦ ginoscafe .com.au. This enduringly popular and unpretentious pavement café serves great coffee and cakes, paninis for lunch and traditional handmade pastas (around $25) for dinner. A good spot for breakfast too, with everything from Bircher muesli to eggs Benedict on the menu. Service can be a little gruff but the outdoor terrace is the place to sit in Fremantle by night. Daily 7am–10.30pm.

★ **Kazoomies** E-Shed Markets, ☎ 04 0183 9058, ⓦ nimrodkazoom.com. Crowd-funded and ethical in all it does (they donate lots of food to OzHarvest, which feeds those in need), this locally loved café has views over the port and a creative menu of breakfasts and Latin and North African tapas from passionate chef Nimrod Kazoom. The ultimate feel-good food. Try the Fal-waffle, which has poached eggs on a falafel-based waffle ($24). Fri–Sun 9am–3pm.

Little Creatures 40 Mews Rd ☎ 08 6215 1000, ⓦ littlecreatures.com.au. Sit amid towering vats of fermenting ale in this atmospheric old aircraft hangar, and enjoy wood-fired pizzas with toppings such as harissa-spiced lamb ($23) or garlic chilli prawns, red pepper and salsa verde ($24) that wash down nicely with one of *Little Creatures'* own delicious ales. There are also tables outside overlooking the water. Mon–Fri 10am–late, Sat 9am–late, Sun 9am–11pm.

6

DRINKING AND NIGHTLIFE

Left Bank Bar & Café 15 Riverside Rd ☎ 08 9319 1315, ⓦ leftbank.com.au. A beautifully renovated nineteenth-century house on the Swan River in East Freo that gets packed on sunny weekends and has a courtyard overlooking the river. Serves everything from breakfast (Left Bank Benedict $16) right through to beers and wines, many of which are local. Mon–Thurs 7am–9pm, Fri–Sat noon–10pm, Sun noon–9pm.

Metropolis 58 South Tce ☎ 08 9336 1880, ⓦ metropolisfremantle.com.au. This live-music venue and nightclub offers a choice of bars and dance floors and is one of Fremantle's liveliest nights out. Students fill the place on Frat House Fridays, while Saturday sees WA's best DJs take to the decks. There's also live music some weeknights. Fri & Sat 9pm–late, selected weeknights from 7.30pm or 8pm.

Sail & Anchor 64 South Tce ☎ 08 9431 1666, ⓦ sailandanchor.com.au. This local favourite serves an ever-changing variety of craft beers, and its bars, downstairs and upstairs on the veranda, are the place for a late-afternoon weekend drink. If you're craving a proper pint, this is the place to come – there are three traditional hand pumps. Mon & Tues 10am–11pm, Wed & Thurs 10am–midnight, Fri & Sat 10am–1am, Sun 10am–10pm.

Strange Company 5 Nairn St ☎ 08 9431 7373, ⓦ strangecompany.com.au With knowledgeable bar staff and an impressive line-up of bottles behind the counter, this is the best place in Fremantle for a serious drink – be that local gin or Scottish whisky. Attracts an older, laidback crowd and gets busy later in the week. Mon–Thurs 4pm–late, Fri–Sun noon–late.

Sweetwater Rooftop 1 Silas St ☎ 08 9387 0888, ⓦ sweetwaterbar.com.au. The tagline "avant-garde Bohemia meets Asia" might be a bit of a stretch, but this hip new bar on the rooftop of the Richmond Quarter is certainly the place to see and be seen. The cocktail list is inventive and there's plenty of craft beer and Aussie wine. Wed–Sat noon–late, Sun noon–10pm.

★ **Whisper Wine Bar** 1/15 Essex St, ☎ 08 9335 7632, ⓦ whisperwinebar.com.au. Run by former Parisien Thierry Rodari, this cute little wine bar based in a restored nineteenth-century flour mill has Freo's best wine selection and dreamy baguettes – a proper taste of France. Wed–Sun noon–late.

Rottnest Island

Eighteen kilometres west of Fremantle, **Rottnest Island** was so named by seventeenth-century Dutch mariners who mistook its unique, indigenous **quokkas**, beaver-like marsupials, for rats. Today, following an ignominious period as a brutal Aboriginal penal colony in the nineteenth century, Rottnest's sweeping sandy beaches and brilliant turquoise waters make it a popular holiday destination, easily accessible from Perth or Fremantle by ferry and – at the very least – a great place for a fun day out.

The island, inevitably abbreviated to "Rotto", is 11km long and less than half as wide, with a historic chocolate-box settlement of charming **colonial houses**, a small shopping mall and local amenities including a cinema, police station and nurse's post, stretching along the sheltered Thompson Bay on the eastern side. West of the settlement, past **Bathurst Lighthouse**, a low heathland of salt lakes meets the coastline, which boasts twenty clear scalloped bays, 63 small beaches, and fascinating offshore reefs ending at the "West End", as the seaward "tail" of the island is known.

The diving and snorkelling are quite unlike anywhere on the adjacent mainland – at Little Salmon Bay and Parker Point on the south coast, there's even a **snorkel trail** with underwater plaques describing the surroundings, while Porpoise Bay is home to underwater shipwreck *The Shark*.

ARRIVAL AND DEPARTURE ROTTNEST ISLAND

By plane You can fly to Rotto in less than fifteen minutes from Jandakot Airport, about 20km south of Perth, with Rottnest Air Taxi (☎ 04 1126 4547, ⓦ rottnest.de; from $380 return for three passengers, $480 for five). Rottnest Airport is 800m from the settlement, and there's a regular shuttle bus service (free to accommodation guests).

By ferry Ferries to Rottnest Island are operated by Rottnest Express (☎ 1300 467 688, ⓦ rottnestexpress.com.au) and Rottnest Fast Ferries (☎ 08 9246 1039, ⓦ rottnestfastferries.com.au). Daily services with Rottnest Express depart from Perth's Barrack Street Jetty just south of the CBD and the B-Shed in Fremantle, costing $79 for same-day return from Freo, $99 from Perth – including the island admission fee. The trip from Perth takes about two hours but it's less than thirty minutes from Fremantle – to make the most of your day aim to board at the latter. Ferries arrive at the jetty in Thomson Bay right in front of the island's visitor centre. Rottnest Fast Ferries operate from Hillarys Boat Harbour, a 25min drive north of Perth CBD, so are only really convenient if you're staying out that way and have your own transport. Prices start from $85.80 including the admission fee.

Admission fee There is an island admission fee (day visitor $18; overnight stays $23.50) which is included in the price of your ferry ticket or air transfer.

GETTING AROUND

By bus The hourly hop-on-hop-off Island Explorer bus service (daily 8.45am–5.15pm; $20 day-ticket) circles the main body of the island, while the accommodation areas are served by free shuttle buses until 6pm Sun–Thurs and 8pm Fri & Sat.

By train You can take a train ride from the settlement's small train station up to Oliver Hill (two trips daily; $20).

By bike Motorized traffic on the island is virtually nonexistent, a real treat that makes cycling from bay to sparkling bay a great way to spend a relaxing day. Rottnest Island Pedal and Flipper (daily, hours vary seasonally; from $30/day including helmet and lock, photo ID required; ☎08 9292 5105, ⓦrottnestisland .com/pedalandflipper) behind the *Hotel Rottnest* (see below) has more than 1300 bikes for rent and well-trained, helpful staff. You can hire snorkels here too ($20/day). Bikes are also available from Rottnest Express and can be booked as part of your ferry ticket.

INFORMATION AND TOURS

Tourist information The visitor centre (Thomson Bay, Sat–Thurs 7.30am–5pm or until 6pm in summer, Fri until 7pm or 7.30pm in summer; ☎08 9432 9300, ⓦrottnestisland.com) has maps and bus timetables and also serves as a post office. Free daily walking tours run by Rottnest Voluntary Guides (ⓦrvga.asn.au) start at the Salt Store building behind the visitor centre.

Rottnest Express ☎1300 467 688, ⓦrottnest express.com.au. Cruises from both Perth and Fremantle daily, plus bike rental, lunch deals and tour packages. From $99 for Fremantle departures, $119 for Perth, including island admission fee and bike and snorkel hire for the duration of your visit to the island. Rottnest Express also offers the Rottnest Adventure Tour (mid Sept–late April, from $132 including ferry), a thrilling roller-coaster ride in a rigid inflatable boat that circumnavigates the island at breakneck speed, slowing to spot New Zealand fur seals (at Cathedral Rocks), dolphins, sea birds and humpback whales (when in season, Sept–Nov).

Rottnest Fast Ferries ☎08 9246 1039, ⓦrottnestfastferries.com.au. Day-packages departing from Hillarys Boat Harbour, a short drive north of Perth. From $105.50 for ferry and bike hire.

ACCOMMODATION

Although well attuned to the demands of its daily stream of visitors (the island receives over 500,000 of them a year), Rotto gets packed out during school summer holidays, throughout Schoolies Week (late Nov/early Dec, when high school graduates have a week off post-exams) and around Christmas and New Year when accommodation is booked months ahead. All accommodation is centrally managed and can be booked online (ⓦbookings.rottnestislandonline.com) or via the central reservations number (☎08 9432 9111, Mon–Fri 8.30am–5pm). Most visitors to the island stay in one of the numerous self-contained units, which sleep between four and eight people and have fully equipped kitchens and all linens included. At the time of writing a new glamping site was being constructed, due to open in early 2017.

Hotel Rottnest 1 Bedford Ave ☎08 9292 5011, ⓦhotelrottnest.com.au. Located a five-minute walk from the visitor centre and on the beachfront at Thomsons Bay, the historic *Hotel Rottnest* is where the governor of WA used to stay each summer. Now a luxury hotel, it has chic contemporary rooms, some with sea views and private courtyards. $159

Karma Rottnest Kitson St ☎1300 7688 6378, ⓦkarmagroup.com. Some basic and some high-quality apartments arranged resort-style around a pool. Premium rooms have been recently refurbished and are worth the splurge, with private balconies overlooking the lake. *Riva* on-site restaurant serves wood-fired pizzas. $190

Rottnest Hostel Kingstown ⓦrottnestisland.com.

The budget end of the market is dominated by *Rottnest Hostel*, which has 50 beds in single and family rooms plus a fully equipped kitchen and TV lounge. Linens are provided but you will need to bring your own towels. Bathrooms are communal. Alcohol is not permitted. Single rooms $52, family rooms $114

Thomson Bay Camping Area Kingsway Hwy ☎08 9432 9111, ⓦrottnestisland.com. There is only one designated campsite on the island, behind the Caroline Thomson Cabins in the Thomson Bay area. Sites are partly shaded and no open fires or generators are permitted. There is an ablutions block, water tap, lighting and some BBQs. A maximum of six people are allowed on any one site. $36

6

EATING AND DRINKING

Hotel Rottnest 1 Bedford Ave ⊕08 9292 5011, ⓦhotelrottnest.com.au. Take a seat in the large alfresco dining area for delicious mod-Oz dishes, from fresh seafood, steaks and salads to handmade pizzas. Try the local market fish ($35) or 18hr braised arkady lamb shoulder ($33). There's a good wine list too. Daily noon–late.

Aquarium of Western Australia

91 Southside Drive, Hillarys Boat Harbour • Daily 10am–5pm • $30 • ⊕08 9447 7500, ⓦaqwa.com.au

At Hillarys Boat Harbour, about 20km north of the city, is the **Aquarium of Western Australia**. This is the country's largest aquarium and is well worth a visit to get an overview of WA's fascinating marine life – and to get a sense of what lies ahead if you're planning to get out on the water while you're here. The most exciting bit is the large underwater tunnel where sharks, turtles and vast stingrays float overhead as you pass through on a moving walkway. If you're travelling with kids, you should consider the aquarium an unmissable stop on your Perth itinerary. You can also dive or snorkel with the sharks ($159 including entry).

Perth's beaches

Perth's closest beaches extend along the **Sunset Coast**, 30km of near-unbroken sand and coastal suburbs stretching north of the Swan River, bordered by the Indian Ocean and cooled by afternoon sea breezes. Two of the most popular are Cottesloe Beach and Scarborough. There are also tiny inshore beaches worth a look along the **Swan River** at Crawley, Nedlands, Peppermint Grove and Mosman Bay on the north shore, and Como, Canning Bridge and Applecross on the south shore, which are calm and safe for children, and make wonderful picnic spots.

Cottesloe Beach and Swanbourne Free Beach

Cottesloe Beach, 7km north of Fremantle, is the most popular city beach, with safe swimming. There are ice-cream vendors, cafés and watercraft-rental outlets aplenty, all just a ten-minute walk from Cottesloe train station. Two kilometres north of Cottesloe, **Swanbourne Free Beach** – cut off by army land in both directions but accessible from the road – has Perth's only nude bathing.

Scarborough

About 14km north of Perth, **Scarborough** is a coastal suburb where living the Aussie dream is a daily reality. Here you'll see joggers on the beach at dawn, parents with pushchairs on the boardwalk at lunchtime and surfers in the ocean at dusk. There is plenty of apartment-style accommodation here and it's a pleasant place to relax for a few days, or to combine the beachside lifestyle with easy access to the city, just a 15-minute drive away. The entire foreshore was under redevelopment at the time of writing, with completion slated for 2017. Expect a freshwater alfresco swimming pool and plenty of new restaurants, bars and shops.

North of **Scarborough** the surf and currents are more suited to wave-riding and experienced swimmers, though with fewer beachside facilities, crowds are reduced.

ARRIVAL AND DEPARTURE
PERTH'S BEACHES

By train Transperth trains on the Fremantle line call at Cottesloe station, running every 10–15min from Perth's Wellington St station at peak times and taking about 20min.

By bus Buses to Scarborough Beach run from Perth's Wellington Street station every 15min at peak times. The journey takes about 45min.

ACCOMMODATION AND EATING

Cottesloe Beach Hotel 104 Marine Parade, Cottesloe Beach ⊕08 9383 1100, ⓦcottesloebeach hotel.com.au. Well-located hotel on the seafront with simple, modern rooms complete with en-suite bathrooms, flat-screen TV, free wi-fi, minibar and tea- and coffee-making facilities. Some rooms have large balconies overlooking the Indian Ocean – perfect for sunsets. The sophisticated beer-garden-style restaurant, *The Beach Club*, has plenty of cosy corners and a laidback atmosphere. Try the WA snapper and chips ($26) or the slow-braised short ribs ($28). There are also wood-fired pizzas from $19. **$200**

Matisse Beach Club 148 The Esplanade, Scarborough ☎08 9245 2000, ⓦmatissebeachclub .com.au. Miami-style beach club with indoor and outdoor pools to lounge beside and a series of (pricey) cabanas offering bottle service. The restaurant area serves decent seafood and steak dishes, plus a quality line-up of WA wines. Give the cocktails a wide berth though – sugar features far too strongly. Free entry to the beach club. Sun–Thurs 11am–midnight, Fri–Sat 11am–1am.

Seashells 178 The Esplanade, Scarborough ☎08 9341 6644, ⓦseashells.com.au. Spacious one-, two- and three-bedroom apartments with fully equipped kitchens, a dining area, lounge, laundry and separate bedrooms. Superior apartments feature balconies with 180-degree sea views – the perfect place to watch the coastline's famous blazing sunsets. There's also a small and shady outdoor pool and plenty of free parking. It's all in need of an update though, with furnishings a little rough around the edges. **$245**

The Squire's Fortune 148 The Esplanade, Scarborough ☎08 9245 1200, ⓦjamessquire .com.au. Contemporary and reasonably stylish pub-style bar serving James Squire beers and a decent wine list, along with some local tipples. Mon–Sat 11am–late, Sun 11am–10pm.

The Swan Valley

Dating back to the earliest years of the colony, **GUILDFORD**, a twenty-minute drive up the Swan River from Perth, is a historic town with several Federation-era grand hotels, a number of historic buildings, antique shops and cafés. The town serves as a gateway for the **SWAN VALLEY** – WA's oldest wine-growing region.

The Swan Valley makes for a pleasant day's **wine tasting** and, being within such easy reach of Perth CBD (roughly 25min by car), is an attractive rival to the more famous Margaret River region several hours' drive to the south. Two main roads run through the valley from Guildford – West Swan Road and the Great Northern Highway. These run either side of the Swan River and pretty much mark the extent of the fertile land – everything between river and road is ripe for grape-growing and this strip is where you will find all the major wineries.

ARRIVAL AND INFORMATION   **THE SWAN VALLEY**

By train Transperth trains (☎13 62 13, ⓦtransperth .wa.gov.au) on the Midland line run from Perth's Wellington St station to Guildford every 15min at peak times. Journey time is 20min.

Tourist information The visitor centre, cnr Swan & Meadow sts in Guildford (daily 9am–4pm; ☎08 9207 8899, ⓦswanvalley.com.au), stocks the useful free Swan Valley Food and Wine Trail Map.

SWAN VALLEY WINERIES

Houghton 148 Dale Rd, Middle Swan ☎08 9274 9540, ⓦhoughton-wines.com.au. This was one of the first vineyards on the Swan and it shows in the quality of the wines. Chenin Blanc, Chardonnay and Verdelho are grown here, with Cabernet Sauvignon and Malbec brought up from Margaret River to make some cracking reds too. There's a small museum, art gallery and café on site, plus free tastings. Daily 10am–5pm.

Sandalford 3210 West Swan Rd, Caversham ☎08 9374 9374, ⓦsandalford.com. Along with Houghton's, this is the valley's biggest name, with a range of wines that run the gamut from classy whites to rich reds. You can also do a winery tour for $25 (noon daily). Tastings from $2.50. Daily 10am–5pm.

Sittella 100 Barratt St, Herne Hill ☎08 9296 2600, ⓦsittella.com.au. Don't know much about wine? Make Sittella your first port of call for a tasting with Shannon – one of the most knowledgeable cellar door managers you are likely to ever meet. Enjoy a free tasting (don't miss the sparkling wines) and stay for lunch in the classy restaurant, where the full range of wines are served to wash down the steak and seafood. Tues–Sun noon–4pm (morning coffee from 10am).

6

TOURS

Captain Cook Cruises ☎08 9325 3341, ⓦcaptain cookcruises.com.au. Cruise to the upper reaches of the Swan Valley on this full-day tour ($169), which includes a behind the scenes visit, tasting and gourmet lunch at Sandalford Estate – one of the valley's leading wineries. A dessert buffet and afternoon tea are served on the return cruise and there's live entertainment too.

Out and About Wine Tours ☎08 9377 3376, ⓦoutandabouttours.com.au. A range of Swan Valley tours ($85–149), including the original Winery Experience, which visits a range of vineyards from the small, family-run boutique wineries to the large well-known estates. A half-day tour and a twilight tour are also available.

Swan Valley Tours ☎08 9274 1199, ⓦsvtours .com.au. Six different daily tours of the Swan Valley, from the half-day coach tour Afternoon Delights, with tastings at three wineries and a brewery, to a full-day cruise up and back from Perth with numerous winery visits, lunch and a chocolate tasting ($70–169).

ACCOMMODATION AND EATING

Novotel Vines Resort Verdelho Drive, The Vines ☎08 9297 3000, ⓦvines.com.au. This stylish resort overlooking the golf course offers spacious rooms with lounge area, tea- and coffee-making facilities, large modern bathroom and a dressing area. Many of the balconies have views over the golf course and the hotel's small vineyard. The outdoor pool area is equipped with sun loungers and a spa bath. Internet access is available for a fee. *Muscat's*, the resort's upmarket yet unstuffy restaurant, features fresh Aussie produce such as King Island salmon and lamb rump (both $38). The wine list is almost exclusively Australian with plenty of WA wines by the glass too. **$175**

Rose and Crown 105 Swan St, Guildford ☎08 9347 8100, ⓦrosecrown.com.au. This historic pub was built in 1841, which makes it the oldest in the state. Inside, you'll find a boutique-style bar and restaurant which rambles from upscale bar (*The Posh Convict*) to formal restaurant with open fireplaces (the *1841*). There's also a garden. Beef and Guinness pie is $23, pork belly $39. Food served daily noon–3pm and 6–9pm.

New Norcia

One of WA's most unusual architectural sights is **NEW NORCIA**, a monastic community dating from the nineteenth century, 130km northeast of Perth. This unexpected collection of Spanish-inspired buildings in the Australian bush is part of a community founded by Benedictine monks in 1846 with the aim of converting the local Aborigines to Christianity. A 2km self-guided New Norcia **heritage trail** begins at the *New Norcia Hotel* (see p.580) and takes you on a circuit past the community's impressive buildings, but if you want access to all of them, you'll need to take the museum's guided tour (daily 11am & 1.30pm, $15).

The two most ornate buildings in the community are on either side of the cemetery, **St Gertrude's Residence for Girls** and **St Ildephonsus College for Boys** (both open only for tours). Among other buildings, you can visit the **Flour Mills** (arrange at the visitor centre) and the Abbey Church – both relatively ordinary in comparison. Should you wish to, you can join the monks in prayer at Mass times (Mon–Sat 7.30am, Sun 9am) or pray in private in the chapel (six times daily; ask at the visitor centre). You'll find the famous wood-fired **bread** made at the mills here in Perth's best restaurants, while the **gift shop** sells bottles of the Abbey's wine, port and Muscat, along with candles, chocolates and crafts made on site.

New Norcia Museum

Daily 9.30am–4.30pm • Museum only $12.50, ticket with tour $25 • ⓦnewnorcia.wa.edu.au

The community's welcoming museum explains the Benedictines' motivation in coming here, tells the story of the town's time as an Aboriginal mission and displays a fine collection of religious and contemporary Australian art.

By bus New Norcia is served four times a week by Transwa's (ⓦtranswa.wa.gov.au) rural bus service from East Perth to the roadhouse.

By car It's an easy two-hour drive on the Great Northern Highway from Perth.

Tourist information The museum also functions as the visitor centre and is the point from which all town tours leave.

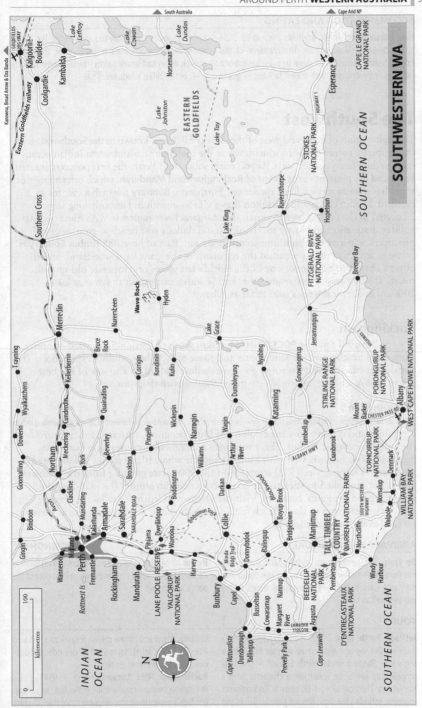

SOUTHWESTERN WA

6

INDIAN OCEAN

SOUTHERN OCEAN

South Australia

Cape Arid NP

0   100
kilometres

N

Rottnest Is

Cape Naturaliste
Cape Leeuwin

GOLDFIELDS HIGHWAY
Kanowna, Broad Arrow & Ora Banda
Eastern Goldfields railway

Lake Lefroy
Lake Cowan
Lake Dundas

Kalgoorlie
Boulder
Kambalda
Coolgardie

Norseman

CAPE LE GRAND NATIONAL PARK

Esperance

HIGHWAY 1

STOKES NATIONAL PARK

SOUTHERN OCEAN

Lake Johnston

EASTERN GOLDFIELDS

Lake Toy

Southern Cross

Lake King

Ravensthorpe

Hopetoun

FITZGERALD RIVER NATIONAL PARK

Bremer Bay

Merredin

Wave Rock

Hyden

Lake Grace

Trayning
Wyalkatchem
Dowerin
Goomalling

Kellerberrin
Cunderdin
Meckering
Northam

Bruce Rock
Corrigin
Kondinin
Kulin

Narembeen

Nyabing

Dumbleyung

Gnowangerup

Jerramungup

HIGHWAY 1

STIRLING RANGE NATIONAL PARK

Mount Barker

PORONGURUP NATIONAL PARK

Albany

CHESTER PASS RD

WEST CAPE HOWE NATIONAL PARK

York
Beverley
Quairading
Wickepin
Pingelly

Brookton
Williams
Narrogin
Wagin
Katanning

Tambellup
Cranbrook

ALBANY HWY

TORNDIRRUP NATIONAL PARK

Denmark

WILLIAM BAY NATIONAL PARK

Clackline
Mundaring
Kalamunda
Armadale
Sawyers Valley
Sarahdale

SARAHDALE ROAD

Bindoon
Gingin
Wanneroo
Midland
Perth
Fremantle
Rockingham
Mandurah

Pinjarra
Waroona

LANE POOLE RESERVE
YALGORUP NATIONAL PARK

Dwellingup

Boddington

Darkan

Collie

Harvey

Minda Bidji Trail

Bibbulmun Track

Blackwood

Boyup Brook

Bridgetown

Balingup
Donnybrook
Nannup

Manjimup

SOUTH WESTERN HIGHWAY

TALL TIMBER COUNTRY

WARREN NATIONAL PARK

Northcliffe

Nornalup
Walpole

Bunbury
Capel
Busselton
Margaret River
Cowaramup
Augusta

BUSSELL HIGHWAY

BEEDELUP NATIONAL PARK

Pemberton

D'ENTRECASTEAUX NATIONAL PARK

Windy Harbour

Dunsborough
Yallingup
Prevelly Park

Avon

ACCOMMODATION AND EATING

New Norcia Hotel Great Northern Hwy ☎ 08 9654 8034, ⊚ newnorcia.wa.edu.au. The grandeur of this colossal historic building is let down by poky, basic rooms with no air conditioning and shared facilities – you're better off visiting on a day-trip from Perth. The hotel's restaurant is the only place to eat in town, though the menu is dreary and service patchy (chicken parma $25). No wi-fi, but breakfast is included. **$100**

6 The Southwest

The region south of Perth and west of the Albany Highway, known as **the Southwest**, is the temperate corner of the continent, where the cool Southern and warm Indian oceans meet to drop heavy winter rains. As you travel south from Perth, the first points of interest lie around the pleasant resort towns of **Rockingham** and **Mandurah**, which offer a range of water-based tours and wildlife experiences. Further on, **Bunbury** is worth a visit for its excellent dolphin centre and **Busselton** draws visitors in with its famously long jetty.

Located in the far southwest corner, the **Margaret River region** is WA's most popular holiday destination and justly so, thanks to its fabulous surf beaches, gourmet food producers, wineries and boutique accommodation. East of here, **Tall Timber Country** is home to attractive towns set amid the remnants of the giant karri woodland, and it offers a chance to experience one of the world's last pieces of temperate old-growth forest. The best way to get around this area is with a car; expect to cover at least 2000km in a typical week's tour as far as Albany.

Rockingham

The small coastal town of **ROCKINGHAM**, 40km south of Perth, offers award-winning white-sand beaches, walks, watersports and some of WA's best wildlife experiences. The Shoalwater Marine Park has some good snorkelling and this is also one of the best places in WA – if not the world – to go swimming with dolphins.

Penguin Island

Shoalwater Bay • Daily Sept–June; ferries depart hourly 9am–3pm • Ferry only $12, ferry and penguin feeding $19.50 • ⊚ penguinisland.com.au

Penguin Island is home to a large colony of Little penguins, who make their burrows in the sand beneath the bushes. There was once accommodation over here but these fragile birds do not mix well with humans and the whole island is now a designated sanctuary. A ferry service ($23) operates on the 900-metre crossing from the mainland and visitors are asked to stick to the boardwalks that run around the island to avoid destroying the penguins' burrows. Visit the Discovery Centre for talks and feeding sessions or head over to Back Beach for a day on the sands – bring a picnic, as there is no food available on the island.

ARRIVAL AND DEPARTURE   ROCKINGHAM

By train Transperth trains (⊚ transperth.wa.gov.au) run from Perth to Rockingham on the Mandurah line daily with trains every 10–15min at peak times, taking just over half an hour.

By bus It's possible to take Transperth buses from Perth to Rockingham, but you'll need to change at least once so the train is a better bet.

TOURS

JetPack Perth ☎ 0452 500 550, ⊚ jetpack-perth .com.au. Get wet and get a smile on your face with a Jetpack or Flyboard session with Edward – you'll be propelled up above the water like a character from a Marvel film. There are also jet-ski tours of Rockingham's shoreline, including the short run out past Garden Island to Carnac Island and its seal colony. Jetpack and Flyboard from $135 each, jet-ski tours $210 for one rider, $260 for two riders (on the same jet ski).

Rockingham Wild Encounters ☎ 08 9591 1333, ⊚ dolphins.com.au. Local wildlife enthusiast Terry set up this highly professional tour company more than 25 years ago when he started paddling out to gain the trust of a local pod of dolphins. Now the company offers some of the best dolphin swimming tours in Australia, with a 99 percent success rate (Sept–June; $205). If you don't get to swim with the dolphins on your tour, you can return again for free. Pick-up from Perth hotels available. Rockingham Wild Encounters also operate the ferry over to Penguin Island ($23). During the winter (June–Sept) you can join the Seal Island Wildlife Cruise, which gets you out on the water to spot dolphins, seals and sea birds ($25).

EATING AND DRINKING

Pengo's Café 153 Arcadia Drive (cnr Penguin Rd), Shoalwater ☏08 9592 6100, ⊛penguinisland .com.au. Simple meals served from what has to be the state's best kiosk, with sheltered picnic tables at which to eat your snapper and chips ($18) or spicy squid ($15.50). Gluten-free options and great coffee and cakes available too. Mon–Sun 8am–4.30pm.

Mandurah and around

A pleasant resort town just 70km south of Perth, **MANDURAH** is located on a narrow bridge of land between the Indian Ocean and the Peel Inlet, making it a good place for waterborne activities. The town itself is pleasant if unexciting, but along the waterfront you'll find a boardwalk with a range of restaurants and bars, along with some high-quality accommodation.

Yalgorup National Park

Just half an hour's drive south of the town along the Old Coast Road, the small **Yalgorup National Park** offers the most accessible area of thrombolites in WA. These ancient life forms are essentially "living rocks" and are the predecessors of all life on earth. Wonder at the sheer unlikeliness of it all on the boardwalk, which takes you a couple of hundred metres out over the waters of Lake Clifton to view them (allow fifteen minutes).

Lane Poole Reserve

About 45km (and a forty-minute drive) east of Mandurah, the **Lane Poole Reserve** is transected by the meandering Murray River as well as the Bibbulman Track and Munda Biddi trail (see box, p.589), and is a pleasant place for a stroll through the ancient forest that covers much of southwest WA. Although long popular with Perth residents (the city is just 100km away), the park saw few visitors from further afield until the 2016 opening of the Trees Adventure treetop high ropes course (⊛treesadventure.com.au), which runs through the pine and jarrah trees of *Nanga Mill Campground* ($45 for two hours on the course).

ARRIVAL AND DEPARTURE

MANDURAH AND AROUND

By train Transperth trains (⊛transperth.wa.gov.au) run from Perth to Mandurah, the terminus of the Mandurah line, daily with trains every 10–15min at peak times and taking under 20 minutes.

By bus Although it's possible to get Transperth buses from Perth to Mandurah, you'll need to change more than once so the train is a better bet.

TOURS

Mandurah Cruises Mandurah Tce ☏08 9581 1242, ⊛mandurahcruises.com.au. One-hour cruises on the Peel Inlet to see the bottlenose dolphins that live in the waters here. Board a lunchtime cruise (12pm or 1pm) and you can order fish and chips (for an extra $12) to enjoy while you float past some highly impressive – and highly expensive – waterfront homes. From Nov–April there are also crabbing tours where you can try your hand at "scooping" for Mandurah's famous crabs in the shallow waters of the Inlet. Includes a BBQ lunch of – you've guessed it – crab. Dolphin cruise $28, crabbing $150.

ACCOMMODATION AND EATING

Seashells Mandurah 16 Dolphin Drive ☏08 9550 3000, ⊛seashells.com.au. Gorgeous modern apartments with fully equipped kitchens, laundry facilities, comfy lounges and bathrooms complete with spa bath. Many of the apartments and villas have stonking sea views (some villas are right on the beachfront) and the pool terrace leads straight out onto the beach. The location is handy too, within a five-minute walk of the boat tours departure point and the boardwalk with its cafés, bars and restaurants. $216

Stage Door Waterfront Restaurant The Mandurah Boardwalk, ☎08 9586 3733, ⍉thestagedoor .com.au. Simple café-restaurant in the Performing Arts

Centre serving everything from whole baby snapper ($30) to Sunday roasts ($23 including a glass of wine). Come at lunchtime for the $15 specials. Guests staying at Seashells Mandurah get their second main meal at half-price (with proof of stay). Mon–Sat 10am–9pm, Sun 8am–9pm.

6 Bunbury

Described as the capital of the Southwest, **BUNBURY** is clearly prosperous and content, yet not the sort of place you'd generally cross oceans to see. A day's dallying here on the way south offers a chance to commune with **dolphins**, found around The Cut on Leschenault Inlet.

Bunbury Dolphin Discovery Centre

Daily Oct–April 8am–4pm; May 8am–2pm; June–Sept 9am–2pm • $10 • ☎08 9791 3088, ⍉dolphindiscovery.com.au

The Interaction Zone in front of the centre at the beach off Koombana Drive is a reliable place to see bottlenose dolphins, a pod of which visits more or less daily. The centre itself offers educational resources including an aquarium and a state-of-the-art 360-degree digital "dolphinarium" where three short stories about dolphins are screened.

ARRIVAL AND DEPARTURE   BUNBURY

By train Transwa's (⍉transwa.wa.gov.au) Australind runs twice daily from Perth (approx 2hr 30min) to the train station, 3km from the centre, from where shuttle buses trundle into the town centre.

By bus Daily South West Coach Lines (☎08 9753 7700, ⍉southwestcoachlines.com.au) bus services from Perth's Elizabeth Quay Busport (taking approx 3hr) drop

off at the Central Bus Station on Carmody Place in the centre of town.

Destinations Albany (1–2 daily; 5hr 30min); Augusta (1–2 daily; 2hr 30min); Busselton (4 daily; 45min); Dunsborough (daily; 1hr 15min); Margaret River (1–2 daily; 2hr); Nannup (3 weekly; 4hr 5min); Pemberton (3 weekly; 4hr 35min); Yallingup (daily; 1hr 20min).

INFORMATION AND TOURS

Tourist information The visitor centre (Mon–Fri 9am–5pm, Sat 9.30am–4.30pm, Sun 10am–2pm; ☎08 9792 7205, ⍉visitbunbury.com.au) is in the old railway station on Carmody Place.

Tours The Bunbury Dolphin Discovery Centre (see above) offers eco-cruises ($49) as well as swims with wild bottlenose dolphins ($165) in Koombana Bay, with a marine biologist as your guide.

ACCOMMODATION AND EATING

Dolphin Retreat YHA 14 Wellington St ☎08 9792 4690, ⍉dolphinretreatbunbury.com.au. This clean and welcoming hostel is close to everything and can help you with finding work. Rates include free linens, breakfast and parking, and there are regular movie nights, a pool table and table tennis. There are some family rooms, sleeping up to five. Dorms $24, doubles $73

Mantra Bunbury 1 Holman St ☎08 9721 0100, ⍉mantra.com.au. There is plenty of accommodation in and around town, but by far the most luxurious is Mantra Bunbury in the Heritage-listed Silos precinct. Here you'll find stylish, modern suites with water views and vast bathrooms, an indoor pool and day-spa, and fascinating displays on the building's history, plus

the city's best restaurant, Silos, which serves up inventive mod-Oz dishes such as beef carpaccio with pea purée. $159

Rose Hotel Victoria St ☎08 9721 4533, ⍉rosehotel .com.au. The historic 1865 Rose Hotel is located in the heart of the CBD and has surprisingly modern motel-style units with twin beds, en-suite bathrooms, air conditioning and secure parking. $120

Wander Inn 16 Clifton St ☎1800 039 032, ⍉bunbury backpackers.com.au. Pleasant, laidback place off Victoria Street (the main road), with brightly coloured dorms and bathrooms, a laundry room and pleasant backyard area. There's also a free daily breakfast, coffee and cake, and help finding work. Stay for four or more nights to save 15 percent. Dorms $27, doubles $69

6

Busselton

Named after a prominent pioneering family, **BUSSELTON** is a sprawling holiday town with sheltered white-sand beaches that make it a popular resort. The main reason to visit though is to take the 1.8-km journey out into Geographe Bay on the Busselton Jetty.

Busselton Jetty

Jetty Daily 24 hours • $3 • **Train** Daily 9am–5pm • $12 (return, including day-pass) • ☎ 08 9754 0900, ⓦ busseltonjetty.com.au

The longest timber-piled jetty in the southern hemisphere. The jetty was part of a working port for more than a century, before it finally closed in 1973 and fell into disrepair once government maintenance ceased. In 1978, residents of Busselton formed a community group to save the jetty and raised the funds to restore it. It reopened in 2011 and is now a pleasant place for a stroll out over the water.

Underwater Observatory

Daily 9am–4pm • $33 (including tour, train and jetty day-pass) • ⓦ busseltonjetty.com.au

At the Jetty's far end is the Underwater Observatory, which allows visitors to see the 300-odd species of marine life that have made the artificial reef the jetty has created their home. Those keen to see more can also do the new undersea walk where you don a helmet to walk underwater and check out the fish and corals ($165; ☎ 1800 994 210, ⓦ divebusseltonjetty.com.au).

ARRIVAL AND INFORMATION   BUSSELTON

By bus South West Coach Lines (ⓦ southwestcoachlines.com.au) offers three daily bus services from Perth to Busselton, via Bunbury.
Destinations Bunbury (3 daily; 1hr); Dunsborough (2 daily; 25min); Margaret River (1 daily; 40min); Perth (3 daily; 3hr 5min).

Tourist information The visitor centre on the Foreshore (Mon–Fri 9am–5pm, Sat & Sun 9.30am–4.30pm; ☎ 08 9752 5800, ⓦ margaretriver.com) has lots of information on accommodation, restaurants, beaches, wineries and other nearby attractions.

Dunsborough and around

Out of Busselton the highway turns south towards Margaret River, though continuing west brings you to the pleasant surfy town of **DUNSBOROUGH**, 23km from Busselton, which is a good base for exploring the region. **Cape Naturaliste**, 14km northwest of the resort, is the less impressive of the two capes that define the Margaret River region (the other is Cape Leeuwin, see p.586). You can visit its truncated **lighthouse** (tours every 30min daily 9.30am–4.30pm; $14) and explore secluded beaches and coves on the way.

ARRIVAL AND DEPARTURE   DUNSBOROUGH AND AROUND

By bus South West Coach Lines (ⓦ southwestcoachlines.com.au) offers a daily bus service (4hr 15min) from Perth

Elizabeth Quay Busport, dropping off at the visitor centre and calling at Bunbury and Busselton en route.

INFORMATION AND ACTIVITIES

Tourist information The well-equipped visitor centre, at the Dunn Bay Centre (Mon–Fri 9am–5pm, Sat & Sun 9.30am–4.30pm; ☎ 08 9755 3517, ⓦ margaretriver.com), offers accommodation- and tour-booking services.
Surfing Surfboard rental is available at Yahoo Surfboards (☎ 08 9756 8336, ⓦ yahoosurfboards.com.au), at 222

Naturaliste Terrace, for $30 per half-day or $50 a day.
Jet boating Jet Adventures (☎ 1300 325 115, ⓦ jetadventures.com.au) run exhilarating jet boat rides from Quinadalup beach to check out nearby secluded bays at breakneck speed. Tours run four times weekly, last 30min and cost $69.

ACCOMMODATION AND EATING

Bunker's Beach Café Farm Break Lane ☎ 08 9756 8284, ⓦ bunkersbeachcafe.com.au. Located in a sublime seaside location nestled in the dunes, this independent

café overlooking the ocean serves healthy breakfasts (from $10), local seafood (fish of the day is $38) and home-made cakes. Fri–Tues 8.30am–4pm.

Dunsborough Beach Lodge 13 Dunn Bay Rd ☎08 9756 7144, ⓦdunsboroughbeachlodge.com.au. In town, just 100m from the water, this hostel has clean dorm rooms (some en-suite), private doubles and a big sunny balcony. They also hire out surfboards, bikes and snorkelling gear and there's a pool room. Wi-fi isn't free, though ($2/hour, $5/24hrs). Dorms $\overline{45}$, doubles $\overline{53}$

Lanterns Retreat 16 Newberry Rd ☎08 9756 7542, ⓦlanternsretreat.com.au. This luxurious, old-fashioned B&B has a range of comfortable suites with king-size beds. Some rooms have private balconies or verandas; all have TVs, fridges, microwaves and air conditioning. The large cottage gardens are a fantastic place to relax and there's also a guest lounge with complimentary port and chocolates in the evenings – and a log fire in winter. $\overline{235}$

6

Margaret River region

The **Margaret River region** is WA's premier holiday destination, with sweeping beaches and ancient caves to explore as well as superb wineries, choice restaurants and snug

---

MARGARET RIVER WINE

Margaret River is a relatively new **wine region** – the first significant vine planting took place here in the late 1960s – but it has quickly established itself as one of Australia's biggest wine-growing names. There are more than 200 producers in the region, the bulk of which are located in a 100km-long stretch of land between the Bussell Highway and the Indian Ocean, though technically the region extends further east to the line of longitude known as Gladstones Line. Most of the wineries are **boutique** producers making relatively small quantities and selling only at the cellar door – visiting is a great opportunity to try something new and unusual.

The Margaret River region has a reasonably cool, maritime climate with plenty of summer sunshine and very little rain during the grapes' ripening season – in Bordeaux such conditions would produce a great year. Consequently many of the **Bordeaux** grape varieties grow very well here, including Cabernet Sauvignon, Merlot, Semillon and Sauvignon Blanc. You will see Margaret River SBS (a Sauvignon Blanc–Semillon blend) on menus up and down the state, as well as overseas – it's reliably good. Great Chardonnays and Cabernet Merlot blends are also standouts from the region.

Wineries in Margaret River do not charge for tastings and you'll pretty much always find a friendly welcome and unpretentious atmosphere. Don't be scared to ask questions – these are passionate winemakers keen to share.

★**Arimia** 242 Quininup Rd, Yallingup ☎08 9755 2528, ⓦarimia.com.au. Cam, at the cellar door here, is about the friendliest and most knowledgable wine-lover in Margaret River and will guide you through a tasting of this winery's unusual range, which includes a Verdelho and a Zinfandel. Daily 10am–5pm.

★**Leeuwin Estate** Stevens Rd, Margaret River ☎08 9759 0000, ⓦleeuwinestate.com.au. Leeuwin is one of Margaret River's big hitters, with a long-standing pedigree of producing award-winning wines. A tasting here is not to be missed; Leeuwin offers an extensive free tasting at its classy cellar door, and there's a balcony restaurant and regular outdoor concerts here to boot. Cellar door daily 10am–5pm; restaurant daily for lunch plus Sat for dinner.

Vasse Felix Cnr Caves Rd and Tom Cullity Drive, Cowaramup ☎08 9756 5000, ⓦvassefelix.com.au. Margaret River's oldest winery has a welcoming cellar door and a fabulous restaurant (see p.589) with panoramic views of the vineyards. The range of wines produced here is focused on classic Margaret River grape

varieties, meaning all wines are excellent, especially the Heytesbury. Cellar door daily 10am–5pm; restaurant Mon–Fri noon–3pm, Sat & Sun noon–4pm.

Watershed Premium Wines Cnr Bussell Hwy & Darch Rd, Margaret River ☎08 9758 8633, ⓦwatershedwines.com.au. Modern winery offering tastings of their range of highly regarded wines, which includes the fabulous Senses Shiraz. The restaurant serves an inventive menu of fresh seafood and steaks, from Exmouth prawns ($21) to slow-cooked beef cheek ($39). Cellar door daily 10am–5pm; restaurant daily noon–4.30pm.

Wills Domain Cnr Abbey Farm & Brash Rds, Yallingup ☎08 9755 2327, ⓦwillsdomain.com.au. The cellar door of this family-owned and operated winery is a friendly place for a relaxed wine tasting. The restaurant serves mod-Oz cuisine with a twist, such as a starter of grilled marron with preserved-onion congee and kombu ($23), and a main course of Wagin duck with kohlrabi, quince and Japanese mustard ($38). Daily 10am–5pm; restaurant daily noon–3.30pm.

CAPE TO CAPE TRACK

Hikers may want to consider the 135km coastal walk from Cape Leeuwin to Cape Naturaliste, known as the **Cape to Cape Track**, which can be tackled in one go or in smaller segments. It takes 7–10 days to walk in its entirety, but if you can't face that it's still well worth including a short section in your visit here to take in the lovely coastal views and look out for whales. For more information check out the Friends of the Cape to Cape Track online at ⓦ capetocapetrack.com.au.

6

hideaways. There's plenty to see, do, taste and spend your money on here and the area is well worth a few days of your time.

The town of **Margaret River** itself gets busy at weekends and throughout the summer with surfers, tourists and gastronomes escaping from Perth and the east-coast cities, and many make it their base for wine tasting by day and fine dining by night. Though you may not want to stay here if it's beach or rural bliss you're seeking (and the wineries are all out of town anyway), you'll still find Margaret River handy for shopping, eating out and browsing for art, crafts and gourmet goodies. The area surrounding it warrants several days' exploration and stands up well to repeat visits, with new ventures opening up all the time.

Limestone caves

Lake Cave and Jewel Cave tours every hour daily 9.30am–3.30pm; Mammoth Cave daily 9am–4pm; Ngilgi Cave semi-guided tours every 30min daily 9.30am–4pm • $22.50 per cave; pass for all four $67 • ☎ 08 9757 7411, ⓦ margaretriver.com

A band of limestone passing through the cape has created hundreds of caves around the Margaret River area, four of which are open to the public. Lake and Jewel caves can only be seen on a guided tour to avoid damage and accidents, and the shuffling crowds detract somewhat from the cavernous spectacle (tours last 55min). All the caves are fairly humid and include some long, stepped ascents, with temperatures around 17°C. Note that lighting is dim in all caves.

Jewel Cave is the best and features extraordinary formations such as 5m-high "helictites" (delicate, straw-like formations) protected by breeze-proof doors, while a collapsed cavern overgrown with huge karri trees marks the impressive entrance to **Lake Cave**, where a unique "suspended table" hangs over the subterranean lake. **Mammoth Cave** is a large cavern with easy access but is the least impressive.

Ngilgi Cave has plenty of nooks to explore and delicate features to admire, including numerous stalactites, stalagmites and shawl formations. It features in an Aboriginal legend that tells of the battle between evil spirit Wolgine and good spirit Ngilgi, for whom it is named.

Cape Leeuwin

Cape Leeuwin at the far end of the Bussell Highway is well worth the journey this far south, with its windswept "land's end" feel – especially on a moody day. A Dutch captain named the cape after his ship in 1622, and English Captain Matthew Flinders began the onerous task of mapping Australia's coast right here in 1801. From the top of Cape Leeuwin Lighthouse, mainland Australia's tallest **lighthouse** (daily 8.45am–5pm; tours every 30min 9am–4.30pm; $40; ⓦ margaretriver.com), which opened in 1896 and is still operational, you can contemplate Australia's most treacherous reef and your own location – at the meeting of the Southern and Indian oceans. Nearby, an **old water wheel**, originally constructed for the lighthouse builders, is petrified in salt.

ARRIVAL AND INFORMATION   MARGARET RIVER

By bus South West Coach Lines buses (ⓦ southwestcoachlines .com.au) run to Margaret River daily from Perth's Elizabeth Quay Busport via Bunbury and Busselton.

Tourist information The visitor centre (daily 9am–5pm;

☎ 08 9780 5911, ⓦ margaretriver.com) on the Bussell Highway can book accommodation, transport and winery tours. Grab the essential, and free, Margaret River Map and Guide, which pinpoints all wineries, from here.

TOURS AND ACTIVITIES

Although distances between attractions can be fairly large, Margaret River is not a place to drive yourself, with too many tempting wines on offer at every turn. Wine-tasting tours are operated by numerous companies, and there are plenty of other ways to enjoy the area.

Bushtucker River & Wine Tours ☎08 9757 9084, **w** bushtuckertours.com. The full-day Winery and Brewery Tour visits numerous wineries, a brewery and several local food producers including the chocolate factory ($95 with a winery lunch). Canoe and cave tours also available ($95–155).

Cheers ☎08 9757 2270, **w** cheerstours.com. A full day of touring wineries and vineyards by air-conditioned bus, plus visits to key food producers including chocolate and cheese factories. Lunch at one of the region's top winery restaurants is included in the price ($90).

The Flying Corkscrew ☎0403 847 607, **w** flyingcork screw.com.au. Billing itself as "a long lunch like no other", this new tour goes behind the scenes at two boutique wineries before visiting one of the area's leading vineyards (choose from names such as Vasse Felix, Voyager and Wills Domain) for a long, languid lunch with matching wines. You can arrive by helicopter (after a 15min ride along the coast) to really add a touch of glamour. Without helicopter ride from $249, with helicopter ride from $499.

★ Margaret River Discovery Company ☎0439 910 064, **w** margaretriverdiscovery.com.au. The best operator in town, the Margaret River Discovery Company offers tours "for people who don't do tours". The Discovery Tour is limited to only six guests and lets you canoe along the river, explore the national parks and Cape to Cape Track, and enjoy a gourmet lunch at the Fraser Gallop estate (not otherwise open to the public), while the Best of the Best Wine Tour goes behind the scenes at some of the area's top wineries ($208; quote "Rough Guide" or check online for a special rate of $188).

Margaret River Surf School ☎0401 616 200, **w** margaretriversurfschool.com. Learn to surf at this nationally accredited surf school. Lessons are normally held at Redgate Beach, a beautiful spot about 15 minutes from Margaret River town. Daily two-hour group lessons $50; private group lessons from $70.

Margaret River with Neil McLeod ☎08 9757 2747, **w** toursmargaretriver.com.au. Whole-day and afternoon winery and brewery tours with personalized wine tastings and lunch included. You'll also get chocolate, cheese and olive oil tastings. Half-day $99, full-day $115.

Wine For Dudes ☎0427 774 994, **w** winefordudes .com. Laidback full-day tour including an exclusive wine blending session, and visits to a brewery and two different food producers, as well as a gourmet lunch ($105).

ACCOMMODATION

Bridgefield 73 Bussell Hwy **☎**08 9757 2013, **w** bridgefield.com.au. This historic guesthouse (the oldest in the area) on the edge of town has charming antique rooms and plenty of character. The price includes breakfast and there's a lovely teahouse. Note that reception is at *Adamsons Riverside Accommodation* on the corner of Bussell Highway and Higgins Street, Margaret River. **$110**

MARGARET RIVER BREWERIES

Different from the wineries, the **breweries** in Margaret River charge for a tasting, usually as a paddle of between four and eight varieties. The atmosphere is more pub-style, with beers ordered at the bar and drunk at private tables. Don't expect as much variety here as there is with wine – the beers are all quaffable without being anything to get too excited about.

Brewhouse Margaret River 35 Bussell Hwy, Margaret River, **☎**08 9757 2614, **w** brewhousemargaretriver.com.au. Modern, breezy brewery on the edge of Margaret River town (within walking distance) serving a wide and very good range of different lagers, ales and ciders. Three tasters $10. Mon–Wed 11am–5pm, Thurs–Sat 11am–7pm, Sun 11am–10pm.

Cheeky Monkey 4259 Caves Rd, Wilyabrup, **☎**08 9755 5555, **w** cheekymonkeybrewery.com.au. Lively brewery in a beautiful setting, with log fires in winter. Good range of different beers, with six tasters for $16. Daily 10am–6pm, lunch 11.30am–3.30pm (pizzas until 5pm).

Eagle Bay Brewing Company Eagle Bay Rd, Eagle Bay, **☎**08 9755 3554, **w** eaglebaybrewery.com.au. One of the region's more established names, this brewery and restaurant sits in rolling countryside with views down to the distant ocean. A good lunch stop, with mains such as a fish burger ($24) and prawn, bacon and sweetcorn chowder ($30). Taste six beers (with large servings) for $16 – probably the best-value beer tasting in the region. Daily 11am–5pm, plus Fri 7–11pm and Sat 7pm–midnight.

6

Cape Lodge 3341 Caves Rd ☎08 9755 6311, Ⓦcapelodge.com.au. This is the quintessential Margaret River boutique hotel and a popular foodie destination, with the region's finest restaurant on site. Rooms are vast and extremely well equipped, and there's a swimming pool, tennis court and complimentary daily tasting of the wines made on site. Upgrade to a spa suite for a large balcony overlooking the lake. **$475**

Central Avenue Apartments 1 Charles West Ave ☎08 9758 7025, Ⓦcentralavenue.com.au. These airy, contemporary apartments have enormous balconies and are centrally located – ideal for wine tasting by day and dining in town by night. One- and two-bedroom apartments are available and all have fully equipped kitchens. Wi-fi available for a fee. **$275**

★**Injidup Spa Retreat** 31 Cape Clairault Rd, Yallingup ☎08 9750 1300, Ⓦinjidupsparetreat.com.au. Fabulous adults-only resort with opulent two-bedroom villas offering every conceivable convenience – from private plunge pool and BBQ to breakfast hamper and in-room meals. The on-site spa will have you walking on air and the Cape to Cape track runs right outside. **$650**

Margaret River Backpackers 66 Town View Tce ☎08 9757 9572, Ⓦmargaretriverbackpackers.com.au. Jointly managed with Margaret River Lodge (see below), this smart and fairly new "working" hostel is located slap-bang in the town centre, and offers a jobs desk and free transport to local beaches and the vineyards (for work). Dorms **$30**

Margaret River Hotel 125 Bussell Hwy ☎08 9757 2655, Ⓦmargaretriverhotel.com.au. Large country pub in the heart of town, with spacious heritage-style rooms, some with spa bath and open fireplace. All rooms have tea/coffee facilities. **$110**

Margaret River Lodge 220 Railway Tce ☎08 9757 9532, Ⓦmargaretriverbackpackers.com.au. Jointly managed with Margaret River Backpackers (see above), this huge YHA resort-style hostel is based in a bushland setting 1.5km southwest of town, with a pool, arcade games and bike rental. Pay for six nights and get the next one free. Dorms **$30**, doubles **$76**

Riverview Tourist Park 8 Wilmott Ave ☎08 9757 2270 or ☎1300 666 105, Ⓦriverviewtouristpark.com. Powered camping sites (some en-suite) and a range of basic and more deluxe cabins in a picturesque setting on the river, 800m from town. Powered sites **$30**, cabins **$110**

Seashells Yallingup Yallingup Beach Rd, off Caves Rd ☎08 9750 1500, Ⓦseashells.com.au. Light and airy apartments with all the facilities you could possibly want, including a full kitchen, private laundry and free in-house movies. The *Caves House Hotel* on the same site serves pub meals and more upmarket fare in its attached restaurant. **$186**

Smiths Beach Resort 67 Smiths Beach Rd, Yallingup ☎08 9750 1200, Ⓦsmithsbeachresort.com.au. Comfortable private villas with full kitchens and sea views as well as private undercover parking and luxurious bathrooms with tubs. The on-site restaurant, *Lamont's*, is one of the region's best too (see below). **$350**

EATING AND DRINKING

Despite Perth's recent renaissance, Margaret River remains the place in WA (if not Australia) for cracking food and wine, and if you can afford to splash out anywhere, make sure you do it here. The countryside surrounding Margaret River is dotted with truly outstanding **restaurants** attached to wineries (see box, p.585), many serving delicious **local produce**. Aside from formal dining, there are also numerous local producers offering tastings right from the factory or farmhouse door. Note that most winery restaurants only serve lunch. For dinner, the restaurants in town are your best option; most are on the main road, the Bussell Highway.

Cape Lodge Restaurant Caves Rd ☎08 9755 6311, Ⓦcapelodge.com.au. The region's best restaurant, with a daily changing menu featuring high-quality WA produce. Sit looking out over the lake or beside the log fire and dive into the tasting menu ($160), which is backed up with wine pairings from the region. Dishes can include Exmouth snapper and Chestnut Grove pork belly. Reservations are essential as tables are limited. Daily 7.30–10am for breakfast and from 6pm for dinner.

★**Lamont's Smiths Beach** 67 Smiths Beach Rd, Yallingup, ☎08 9757 1299, Ⓦlamonts.com.au. WA's very best produce makes it onto the menu here, including local crayfish and Exmouth prawns ($22.50) as well as plenty of fresh veggies and a great Angus eye fillet ($41.50). *Lamont's* also produce their own wine – ask for recommendations that match your food order. Don't miss the chocolate oblivion for

dessert – probably among the top desserts in the state. Daily breakfast, lunch and dinner; closed Tuesday and Wednesday lunch and dinner in winter.

Morries 149 Bussell Hwy ☎08 9758 8280, Ⓦmorries.com.au. This is the sort of place you can pop in for breakfast, spend an hour or two over lunch or catch up with mates over a few glasses of local wine come nightfall. Service is low-key and friendly, while the daily lunch specials menu ($25 including a drink) features dishes such as beetroot gnocchi and prawn and chorizo tagliatelle. Daily noon–late.

Settler's Tavern 114 Bussell Hwy ☎08 9757 2398, Ⓦsettlerstavern.com. Simple Aussie tavern (affectionately known as "The Tav") serving up all the staples at some of Margaret River's most affordable prices. Chicken parma is $28, fish and chips $22. There's also a separate gluten-free menu. Regular live music and English football on TV.

THE BIBBULMUN TRACK AND MUNDA BIDDI TRAIL

The Tall Timber region is a paradise for anyone who likes to travel on two feet or two wheels. For walkers, the **Bibbulmun Track** has established itself as one of the great rites of passage. Stretching almost 1000km from Kalamunda in the Perth Hills to Albany (see p.592) on the south coast, it passes through some of the Southwest's most remote areas, winding amid towering karri and tingle forests, ranging over granite hills and clinging to the spectacular coastline. Walkers can stroll sections or tackle the track in its entirety over an epic eight-week adventure. There are 48 bushwalker campsites en route, as well as numerous small towns for those who like a little more comfort.

The **Munda Biddi Cycle Trail** runs for approximately 1000km from Mundaring through the heart of the forest to Albany and can be completed in one (very long) stretch or picked up at one of the picturesque ex-logging towns along the way. Some sections are challenging but experienced cyclists will love whizzing along the forest floor and dodging ancient jarrah trees. Nights are spent in one of the free purpose-built (but very basic) huts located every 35–40km or in atmospheric B&Bs along the route.

For more information contact the Bibbulmun Track Foundation (☎08 9481 0551, ⓦbibbulmun track.org.au) or the Munda Biddi Trail Foundation (☎08 6336 9699, ⓦmundabiddi.org.au).

6

Mon–Fri 11am–midnight, Sat 10am–midnight, Sun 11am–10pm, food served daily noon–8.30pm.

Vasse Felix Cnr Caves Rd and Tom Cullity Dr, Cowaramup ☎08 9756 5000, ⓦvassefelix.com.au. One of the region's standout restaurants, with creative dishes using local produce and plenty of seasonal vegetables. Try the barramundi with Jerusalem archichoke, macadamia and mussels ($39). An extensive list of Vasse Felix wines is also served here, even when they have sold out at the cellar door, and the view is of the vineyards. Daily 10am–3pm.

Tall Timber Country

Sandwiched between the popular tourist areas of the Margaret River region and Albany's dramatic coast, the forests of the so-called **Tall Timber Country** are some of WA's greatest sights. Along with the sinuous **Blackwood River**, which is ideal for sedate canoeing, especially downstream of Nannup (see below), the highlight of the region is the brooding majesty of the **karri forests**, famed not so much for their arboreal gimmicks – of which the **Gloucester Tree** near Pemberton is the best known – as for the raw, elemental nature of the unique wooded environment. The breathtaking **Tree Top Walk** near the peaceful village of **Walpole** provides a unique view on this primeval forest. Check out ⓦsouthernforests.com.au for further details on this area.

The Blackwood River Valley

The northern part of the forest country is watered by the **Blackwood River** and divided by scenic roads that link the riverside mill towns. Once an insular loggers' town, in the late hippy era **NANNUP** was compared to New South Wales' Nimbin (see p.238). These days Nannup, 60km southeast of Busselton, is an idyllic and little-visited settlement of wooden cabins nestled quietly amid forested hills.

From Nannup, a **scenic drive** winds 41km northeast along the river to unremarkable Balingup, while the tree-lined Brockman Highway heads east 46km to historic mill town **BRIDGETOWN**. This is the only Heritage-listed town in Southwest WA, with an attractive church dating from 1911, an old jail, post office and railway station.

ARRIVAL AND INFORMATION

BLACKWOOD RIVER VALLEY

By bus Transwa buses (ⓦtranswa.wa.gov.au) run to Bridgetown twice a week (4.5 hours) and Nannup three times a week (6.5 hours) from East Perth. All services travel via Bunbury.

Tourist information Nannup's visitor centre, inside *A Taste of Nannup* on Warren Rd (daily 10am–4pm; ☎08 9756 0050, ⓦeverythingnannup.com.au), can help with local accommodation and advice. The busy visitor centre in Bridgetown is on the main Hampton St (Mon–Fri 9am–5pm, Sat 10am–3pm, Sun 10am–1pm; ☎08 9761 1740, ⓦbridgetown.com.au).

6

ACTIVITIES

Canoeing If not walking or cycling, then a great way to enjoy the region is by canoe. Blackwood Canoeing (☎ 08 9756 1209, ⓦ blackwoodrivercanoeing.com) offers self-guided, fully supported two- to five-day trips on the lower Blackwood River, starting 27km south of Nannup (from $35/day), and offers a pick-up service from town. That said, you can simply paddle around for a day or even just an hour or two ($25 for a day).

ACCOMMODATION AND EATING

Blue House Barrabup Rd, Nannup ☎ 08 9756 3091, ⓦ facebook.com/bluehousenannup. This friendly three-room bed and breakfast has superb breakfasts and a communal veranda overlooking the surrounding woodland. One room is en-suite with north-facing views over the valley; the other two share a bathroom and look out over the lavender, where numerous blue wrens make their home. **$95**

Bridgetown Hotel 157 Hampton St, Bridgetown ☎ 08 9761 1034, ⓦ bridgetownhotel.com.au. Restored 1920s hotel with eight spacious, contemporary spa suites opening onto a wide veranda overlooking the historic town centre. There is also a restaurant (pizzas from $15, steaks from $35.00) and beer garden. **$165**

Holberry House 14 Grange Rd, Nannup ☎ 08 9756 1276, ⓦ holberryhouse.com. English manor-style rooms (one with a spa bath) in lovely large gardens. There's a guest lounge with reading nook and there is also an outdoor swimming pool. Breakfast is available for $14 per person. **$165**

Manjimup

Thirty-seven kilometres south of Bridgetown, **MANJIMUP** is the region's commercial centre, and known for its truffles, which can be tasted and purchased at The Wine & Truffle Co. (see below). The **visitor centre** on Giblett St has loads of information and maps detailing local bushwalks and attractions, including a 600-year-old **King Jarrah tree** 3km from town. Some 10km south of town you can climb the **Diamond Tree Lookout** at the top of a 51m karri tree, while about 20km from Manjimup there's a **100-Year-Old Forest**. **One Tree Bridge**, made from a single karri tree felled to cross the Donnelly River in 1904, and the magnificent **Four Aces**, a quartet of huge 230-year-old karri trees standing in a row, are accessible from Graphite Road.

ARRIVAL AND INFORMATION

MANJIMUP

By bus Transwa buses (ⓦ transwa.wa.gov.au) run to Manjimup from Perth's Elizabeth Quay Busport daily Mon–Fri, via Bunbury (4hr 45min).

Tourist information Giblett St (daily 9am–5pm; ☎ 08 9771 1831, ⓦ manjimupwa.com).

EATING

The Wine & Truffle Co. Seven Day Rd ☎ 08 9777 2474, ⓦ wineandtruffle.com.au. Taste Truffle Hill wines and Perigord truffles at this gourmet food producer's cellar door. The on-site *Truffle Kitchen* serves up simple lunches such as seafood ravioli with truffle ($35) and beef and confit duck with truffle mash ($38). Cellar door daily 10am–4pm, café 10am–3pm.

Pemberton and around

The quaint town of **PEMBERTON** makes a central base, for Tall Timber touring, with enough craft shops, galleries, wineries and gourmet destinations to keep you occupied for a while. Call into the **Pemberton Discovery Centre** at the visitor centre (daily 9am–5pm; $1 donation) for a detailed explanation of the area's fauna and wildlife. A fun way of enjoying the surrounding forest is to take the **tram** (Mon–Sat 10.45am & 2pm; 1hr 45min return; $28; ☎ 08 9776 1322, ⓦ pemtram.com.au) from Pemberton to Warren Bridge. The diesel tram rattles noisily along the old logging railway, over timber bridges spanning tiny creeks, visiting the **Cascades**, a local beauty spot also accessible by road.

The most popular attraction is the **Gloucester Tree** (DpaW fee), 3km out of town. At 60m, it's said to be the world's tallest fire-lookout tree and its platform is accessible by climbing a terrifying spiral of horizontal stakes. Only a small proportion of people actually climb to the platform – these being people with courage to spare and no fear of heights.

The surrounding countryside is crisscrossed with peaceful walking trails and enchanting forest drives venturing deep into the karri woodlands. From **Beedelup National Park** (DPaW fee) on the Vasse Highway 20km west of town, there's a short walk to lovely **Beedelup Falls**, while the drive through the native karri forests of the **Warren National Park** (DPaW fee), around 10km southwest of town, will leave you in awe of these colossal trees. The specially signed 86km **Karri Forest Explorer** is a scenic drive that winds past many of the above attractions on a mixture of dirt and sealed roads.

6

ARRIVAL AND INFORMATION

By bus Transwa buses (wtranswa.wa.gov.au) run to Pemberton three times a week from Perth's Elizabeth Quay Busport via Bunbury, arriving at the visitor centre seven and a half hours later.

Tourist information Stop at the visitor centre (daily

PEMBERTON AND AROUND

9am–5pm; ☎08 9776 1133, wpembertonvisitor.com.au), halfway up the hill on Brockman St, to pick up a free map and information on activities, local tours and walking trails in the area, including the Bibbulmun Track.

TOURS AND ACTIVITIES

Pemberton Discovery Tours ☎08 9776 0484, wpembertondiscoverytours.com.au. Pemberton Discovery Tours has day-trips ($115–185) around the southern forests and to the spectacular D'Entrecasteaux dunes, as well as to see the wild flowers when in season (roughly Sept–Nov).

Pemberton Hiking and Canoeing ☎08 9776 1559, whikingandcanoeing.com.au. Offers half-day and full-day tours through Warren National Park, including canoeing trips on the Warren River and full moon walks through the karri and jarrah forest ($50–100).

ACCOMMODATION AND EATING

Jarrah Jacks Brewery 64 Kemp Rd ☎08 9776 1333, wjarrahjacks.com.au. Taste local, hand-brewed beers along with dishes that are a cut above the usual café fare. Try the Fisherman's Dinghyplatter, with local marron, WA prawns, scallops and Tasmanian salmon ($31). Thurs–Sun 11am–5pm.

Old Picture Theatre Cnr Ellis & Guppy sts ☎08 9776 1513, woldpicturetheatre.com.au. A quirky option, the distinct apartments are housed in the old picture theatre, built in 1929. Rooms have polished jarrah floors, fully equipped kitchens and large, comfortable living areas. **$170**

Pemberton YHA 7 Brockman St ☎08 9776 1105, wyha.com.au. This YHA hostel is centrally located, within easy walking distance of the town centre, and has

single, twin and queen rooms as well as dorms. There are several outdoor seating areas and a BBQ. Dorms **$33**, doubles **$70**

Pemberton Caravan Park Pumphill Rd ☎08 9776 1800, wpembertonpark.com.au. This large site under the canopy of the karri forest has numerous powered and unpowered sites plus a range of cabins, from basic timber ones with simple kitchens to en-suite bungalows sleeping up to five. Camping **$48**, cabins **$80**

Warren River Resort 713 Pemberton Northcliffe Rd ☎08 9776 1400, wwarrenriverresort.com.au. Two- and three-bedroom cottages in a tranquil forest environment. All cottages are fully self-contained with laundry facilities and undercover gas BBQs, and there's also a swimming pool. **$190**

Walpole

From Pemberton, the **South Western Highway** continues its scenic run 120km southeast through more colossal forests to **WALPOLE**, the hub of many scenic drives to towering forests, oceanic lookouts and sheltered inlets. Surrounding Walpole, the forest of massive tingle and karri trees that make up the **Valley of the Giants** is best known for its **Tree Top Walk** (daily 9am–5pm, last entry 4.15pm; $21; ☎08 9840 8263, wvalleyofthegiants.com.au), a 600m walkway (accessible to wheelchairs) among the tingle-tree crowns, 40m above the ground, which opens up a whole new world to those brave enough to explore it. Beneath, the **Ancient Empire Walkway** (same hours, free) winds across the forest floor, passing through the centre of a tree almost large enough to drive through.

ARRIVAL AND INFORMATION

WALPOLE

By bus Transwa (wtranswa.wa.gov.au) buses run to Walpole from Bunbury five times a week (4hrs 30min), dropping off at the visitor centre.

Tourist information The Walpole-Nornalup visitor centre is at Pioneer Park on the South Coast Hwy (Mon–Fri 9am–5pm, Sat & Sun 9am–4pm; ☎08 9840 1111, wwalpole.com.au).

ACCOMMODATION

Tingle All Over YHA 60 Nockolds St ☎08 9840 1041, wyha.com.au. Situated at the west end of town, this comfortable hostel has a wood fire in the lounge (a must in winter) and owns an enormous chess set (the pieces are around 60cm tall). Rooms are well kept and modern, and there's a spacious kitchen and free tea and coffee too. Dorms $31.50, doubles $73.50

Walpole Lodge Cnr Pier St & Park Ave ☎08 9840 1244, wwalpolelodge.com.au. Popular with walkers, this hostel has a relaxed atmosphere and mixed and female dorms, as well as private rooms with shared and en-suite bathrooms. There's a full kitchen, guest lounge and a pool table. Dorms $27, doubles $65

Albany and around

Alternating sheltered bays and rounded granite headlands make up the **southern coast**, or "Great Southern", around **Albany**, 410km from Perth. The temperate climate and changeable weather here create a rural Antipodean–English idyll unknown in the rest of WA. The site of the region's original settlement, nowadays it's an appealing area of wineries, arts and crafts galleries and fine restaurants. The town of Albany itself is an agricultural centre and holiday destination, while an hour's drive north lie the burgeoning winemaking region of Mount Barker, the ancient granite highlands of the **Porongurups** and the impressive thousand-metre-high **Stirling Ranges**. While Perth's radial **bus services** to the main centres run on a fairly frequent basis, moving around by bus requires considerable planning to avoid inconvenient delays. Consequently the area is best explored by car.

Albany

In 1826, three years before the establishment of the Swan River Colony, the British sent Major Lockyer and a team of hopeful colonists from Sydney to settle Albany's strategic **harbour**, where they built the Princess Royal Fortress. It was a hasty pre-emptive response to French exploration of Australia's Southwest, and the small colony, originally called Frederickstown, was allowed to grow at a natural pace. Prior to the establishment of Fremantle Harbour in the 1890s, **ALBANY**'s huge natural harbour was a key port on the route between England and Botany Bay: a coaling station in the age of steamers. It was also the last of Australia that many Anzacs saw on their way to Gallipoli in 1914.

Now serving the southern farming belt, Albany has also become one of the Southwest's main holiday areas. Its attractions are spread between the **Foreshore** – where the original settlers set up camp – the calm white-sand beaches around Middleton Beach, the town's central beach, and Emu Point on the still waters of Oyster Harbour. To get a good view on things, climb up to one of Albany's two lookouts. The curious tower on top of **Mount Melville Lookout**, off Serpentine Road, is colloquially known as "the spark plug" and offers good seaward vistas, while **Mount Clarence Lookout**, up Marine Drive, has an Anzac memorial, from which, on a clear day, you can see the Stirling Ranges, 80km north. **Middleton Beach** is best first thing, when you may even have the sweeping sands to yourself. This is a decent spot for a swim, though Torndirrup National Park (see p.596) is far superior.

Amity

Albany Historical Precinct, off Princess Royal Drive • Daily 9.30am–4pm • $5 • ⓦ historicalbany.com.au

On the Foreshore, there's a replica of the *Amity*, the brig that landed its sixty-odd settlers here on Christmas Day 1826, after six weeks at sea. The self-guided audio tour takes visitors around the ship and below deck, giving a good sense of life on board, and explains the impact these first European settlers had on the local community.

Albany Convict Gaol & Museum

Museum Stirling Tce (cnr Parade St) • Daily 10am–4pm • $5 • ☎ 08 9841 6174, ⓦ historicalbany.com.au • **Night tours** Daily 7.45pm by arrangement • $20 • ☎ 08 9841 3180, ⓦ jjtoursalbany.com

The **Old Gaol & Convict Museum**, built in 1852, is an early surviving relic of colonization in the area and features displays on the conditions in the prison and stories of the inmates. Atmospheric night tours by torchlight are offered by JJ Tours and involve an element of theatrics that will delight all ages, plus the chance to experience the spooky "black hole" cell.

Western Australian Museum – Albany

Residency Rd • Wed noon–7pm, Thurs–Tues 10am–4.30pm • Suggested donation $5 • ☎ 1300 134 081, ⓦ museum.wa.gov.au

This museum is one of the best in the state, with fascinating displays on both the Aboriginal and European history of the area. Members of Albany's indigenous Noongar community were involved in the development of the museum, and local resident Larry tells stories and runs regular workshops on subjects such as tool-making and bushtucker.

National ANZAC Centre

7 Forts Rd • Daily 9am–5pm, last admission 4pm • $24 • ☎ 08 9841 9333, ⓦ nationalanzaccentre.com.au

The **National ANZAC Centre** opened in 2014 and is dedicated to the Australians and New Zealanders who left from Albany to fight in World War I. It's a moving place to visit, with personal stories interwoven with historical facts to tell the story of the Great War, from recruitment through to the after-effects.

The centre is part of the **Albany Heritage Park**, which also incorporates **Princess Royal Fortress**, which dates from 1893 and was the first federal defence of Australia. Today this is one of the country's best outdoor military museums and boasts restored shore batteries, armouries and barracks, plus an impressive collection of naval guns and torpedoes. The Convoy Lookout at the top of Mount Adelaide has a cracking view over King George Sound.

Old Farm Strawberry Hill

Middleton Rd • Daily 10am–4pm • Donation • ☎ 08 9841 3735, ⓦ nationaltrust.org.au

Towards Middleton Beach along Middleton Road is the **Old Farm Strawberry Hill**. Reminiscent of an English cottage, the farm (WA's first) provided settlers with locally grown produce, while the building (from 1836) once housed the visiting Governor Stirling. The fascinating displays describe early life in the town and the mature gardens are a lovely place for a stroll.

ARRIVAL AND DEPARTURE   ALBANY

By plane Regional Express (☎ 13 17 13, ⓦ rex.com.au) has 1–4 flights daily from Perth to Albany. The airport is 12km north of Albany on the Albany Highway. There's no public transport from the city, but a taxi from the airport to Albany costs around $35.

By bus Transwa (ⓦ transwa.wa.gov.au) buses depart from Perth for Albany at least daily, either directly down the Albany Highway (6hr) or via Bunbury and Tall Timber Country (around 9hr). Albany can also be reached by bus from Esperance (see p.598) on Thursdays (6hr 30min), and the return journey runs on Wednesdays; in both directions you'll need to change at Hopetoun general store. All regional buses arrive at the visitor centre.

6

Destinations Bunbury (daily; 6hr); Denmark (daily; 45min); Esperance (weekly; 6hr 30min); Northcliffe (daily; 2hr 30min); Pemberton (daily; 3hr 20min); Perth (1–2 daily; from 7hr); Walpole (daily; 1hr 45min).

GETTING AROUND

By bus TransAlbany (timetables at the visitor centre and ⓦpta.wa.gov.au) provides in-town public transport: the #803 route between Peels Place in the centre of town and Middleton Beach/Emu Point is particularly useful (Mon–Fri 8.45am–3.10pm, Sat to Middleton Beach only 10.30am–1.20pm).

By car For car rental try Albany Truck and Car Hire at 376 Albany Hwy (from $40/day, 100km and RAC roadside assistance included; ☎08 9841 8150 or ☎0427 418 150, ⓦalbanytruckandcarhire.com.au).

By bike Albany Bicycle Hire (☎08 9842 2468, ⓦalbanybicyclehire.webs.com) has a range of bikes from $25/day.

By taxi Amity Taxis (☎08 9844 4444).

INFORMATION

Tourist information The visitor centre, housed in the old railway station at 55 Proudlove Parade (Mon–Fri 9am–5pm, Sat–Sun and holidays 9am–1.30pm; ☎08 9841 9290, ⓦamazingalbany.com), dispenses handy free local and regional maps and brochures detailing walking itineraries and cycling routes.

Department of Parks and Wildlife The DpaW office, at 120 Albany Hwy (Mon–Fri 8am–5pm; ☎08 9842 4500), provides information on parks, birdwatching and walking (including the Bibbulmun Track). Passes for WA national parks (see box below) are also sold here.

TOURS

Albany Ocean Adventures ☎0428 429 876, ⓦwhales .com.au. Whale watching (twice daily, July–Oct only) to see humpbacks ($88), with a sighting guarantee.

Busy Blue Bus ☎08 9842 2133, ⓦbusybluebus .com.au. Wide range of day-tours, including the history and highlights of Albany (Mon & Wed 9am, $99) and to the Porongurups (Sun 9.30am, $135; see p.597).

JJ Tours ☎08 9841 3180, ⓦjjtoursalbany.com. Fascinating two-hour walking tours of the main historic sights (Mon–Sat 10am; $20) as well as a night tour of the jail (see p.593).

ACCOMMODATION

Several **guesthouses** and **B&Bs** are situated along Stirling Terrace, a block from the harbour; there are also motels, self-contained units, and caravan and camping grounds in the Middleton Bay area, 3km east of the centre.

Albany Backpackers Cnr Stirling Tce & Spencer St ☎1800 260 130, ⓦalbanybackpackers.com.au. One of Albany's oldest buildings: a warren of corridors and rooms with murals at every turn, plenty of amenities, and a good atmosphere. There's free parking, breakfast is included and on Sundays there's free coffee and cake during the day. Dorms $27, doubles $69

Bayview Lodge 49 Duke St ☎08 9842 3388, ⓦbayviewbackpackers.com.au. Old wooden building with charm, five minutes' walk from the centre. There are dorms sleeping four and six, plus doubles, twins and family rooms. There's a BBQ, open fireplace and large kitchen too. Dorms $30, doubles $78

The Beach House at Bayside 33 Barry Court, Bayside Links ☎08 9844 8844, ⓦthebeachhouseat bayside.com.au. Nestled just beyond the dunes of

---

NATIONAL PARK ENTRY FEES

DPaW (the state government's Department of Parks and Wildlife) maintains WA's parks, and to enter most of them you'll need to pay an entry fee or buy a pass. The DPaW website (ⓦdpaw .wa.gov.au) can provide information about all passes, which you can also buy online, as well as useful details on all of WA's national parks. You can also obtain a pass from the entry station (often unattended), local DPaW offices and some visitor centres. Note that fees only apply if arriving by vehicle; walking or cycling in is free. Camping in a national park attracts an additional fee ($7–18, depending on the facilities/location).

Day Entry Pass $12 per vehicle (and up to 12 people). For any number of WA parks visited in one day; particularly useful in the Southwest where parks are close together.

Holiday Pass $44 per vehicle (and up to 12 people); allows entry into all WA parks for four weeks.

Annual All Parks Pass $88 per vehicle (and up to 12 people); allows entry into all WA parks for one year.

Middleton Beach, this luxury hotel has plush rooms and suites as well as double-storey Garden Suites. All rooms have air conditioning, tea- & coffee-making facilities and flat-screen TVs. The lounge has a DVD library and a log fire in winter. In summer you'll want to sit outside in the pleasant courtyard. Included extras range from airport transfers to breakfast, afternoon tea and nightly port. $280

Emu Beach Emu Point ☎08 9844 1147 or ☎1800 984 411, ⓦemubeach.com. As well as having the beach on its doorstep, this bright and breezy campsite has free BBQs, a camp kitchen, laundry facilities and minigolf. There's a shop on site too as well as a range of chalets sleeping up to six.

Un/powered sites $30/40, chalets $141

Middleton Beach 28 Flinders Parade, Middleton Beach ☎1800 644 674, ⓦholidayalbany.com.au. Right on the beach, this swish holiday park boasts an outdoor solar-heated swimming pool, indoor spa, BBQ areas, camp kitchens, a laundry and mini movie theatre. Un/powered sites $81, en-suite powered sites $111, cabin $210

My Place Colonial Accommodation 47–61 Grey St East ☎08 9842 3242, ⓦmyplace.com.au. Has a variety of charming options, from renovated, fully self-contained historic cottages to modern units and apartments, most with kitchens. There's free off-street parking for each unit. $149

EATING

Albany shares the rest of the Southwest's laudable preoccupation with quality eating. **Food markets** are big here and great for picnic supplies.

RESTAURANTS

Dylans 82 Stirling Tce ☎08 9841 8720, ⓦdylans .com.au. This popular place does breakfasts, burgers and pancakes to eat in or take away. Call in early for eggs hollandaise (from $12.50) or pick up a burger for $15. Tues–Sat 7am–late, Sun 8am–4pm.

Lime 303 Dog Rock Motel, 303 Middleton Rd ☎08 9841 1400, ⓦdogrockmotel.com.au/lime-303. A local favourite, this chic restaurant serves creative, mod-Oz and Med-inspired cuisine. Try the fish of the day served with chips ($33) or the steak with wok-fried veggies ($36). Daily 5–9pm.

The Squid Shack Boat Ramp, Emu Point ☎08 9844 9771. This local institution with outdoor tables is the spot for the freshest takeaway seafood. Fish and chips is $12. Wed–Sun & holidays 11am–7pm.

MARKETS

Albany Farmers Market Collie St ⓦalbanyfarmers market.com.au. Fresh seasonal produce with that just-picked taste. Sat 8am–noon.

Boat Shed Markets Albany Boatshed, Princess Royal Drive ⓦalbanyboatshedmarkets.com. Local growers sell their wares on the waterfront. Sun 10am–1pm

Denmark

DENMARK, set on the river of the same name and ranged along the shores of Wilson Inlet, is a quaint little country town and a pleasant spot to enjoy lunch or a boat ride up the river. Just outside the inlet's mouth is **Ocean Beach** (accessible via Ocean Beach Rd), with spectacular views across broad Ratcliffe Bay, where the swells sweep in to create good **surfing** conditions for learners. Denmark is also an up-and-coming **wine** region and there are several **wineries** close to town.

ARRIVAL AND INFORMATION

DENMARK

By bus Transwa (ⓦtranswa.wa.gov.au) buses run to Denmark from Bunbury five times a week (5hrs 30min), dropping off on Hollings Rd in the town centre.

Tourist information Denmark's visitor centre, 73 South Coast Hwy, on the corner of Ocean Beach Rd (Mon–Sun 9am–5pm; ☎08 9848 2055, ⓦdenmark.com.au), can advise on the myriad places to stay in the vicinity and book on your behalf.

ACTIVITIES

Surfing Mike Neunuebel's well-regarded South Coast Surfing (☎08 9848 2057 or ☎0401 349 854, ⓦsouthcoastsurfinglessons.com) offers one-to-one lessons and group sessions (2hr; $60–90), plus gear rental.

ACCOMMODATION

Blue Wren Travellers' Rest YHA 17 Price St ☎08 9848 3300, ⓦdenmarkbluewren.com.au. Laidback hostel in the heart of town with just twenty beds – and one huge dining table to encourage a community feeling. Bike hire, laundry and a wood fire in winter. Dorms $40, doubles $100

6

Denmark Waterfront 63 Inlet Drive ☎ 08 9848 1147, ⓦ denmarkwaterfront.com.au. Well-equipped two-storey timber units, some with water views and spa baths, all with en-suite bathrooms, TV/DVD and tea-/coffee-making facilities. Plenty of parking. **$110**

EATING AND DRINKING

RESTAURANTS
Bibbulmun Café South Coast Hwy ☎ 08 9848 1289, ⓦ facebook.com/bibbulmuncafe. This bustling café serves a range of hearty breakfasts, a selection of sandwiches for lunch (from $12) and top coffee. A great place to start the day, with a relaxing atmosphere.

The Denmark Tavern South Coast Hwy ☎ 08 9848 2206, ⓦ thedenmarktavern.com.au. The town's tavern may not appear immediately enticing but it is the best place in town for a drink, with a pleasant terrace overlooking the river. The food is decent too, with mains such as macadamia and cranberry-crusted barramundi ($32) and beer-battered fish and chips ($25). Mon–Sat 10.30am–midnight, Sun 11am–10pm.

Pepper & Salt Restaurant Cnr South Coast Hwy & Myers Rd ☎ 08 9848 3053, ⓦ pepperandsalt.com.au. The foodie favourite is the fabulous *Pepper & Salt Restaurant* at Forest Hill. Run by Aussie chef Silas Masih, the ever-changing menu features fresh fish and locally raised beef as well as a range of delicious desserts and, of course, a cracking selection of wines. Beef eye fillet is $44, Silas' chilli crab $24. Thurs–Sun lunch from noon, Fri also dinner from 6pm.

WINERIES
Castelli Estate 390 Mount Shadforth Rd, ☎ 08 9848 3174, ⓦ castelliestate.com.au. This winery in an idyllic setting is fast becoming known as one of the region's best. There's wine tasting at the cellar door, while the bistro, with its lovely outdoor terrace, serves mod-Oz dishes such as "beef and reef" (scotch fillet served with king prawns and scallops, $42). Cellar door daily 10am–3pm, bistro daily 10am–10pm.

The Lake House 106 Turner Rd ☎ 08 9848 2444, ⓦ lakehousedenmark.com.au. Offers complimentary tastings of their award-winning wines, which are organized into three ranges – "He Said She Said", the Lake House Denmark Series and the Premium Reserve Range. The restaurant serves organic set-menu lunches in a tranquil lakeside setting (from $48 per person, minimum of two people). Daily 10am–5pm.

Torndirrup National Park

20km southwest of Albany • DPaW fee (see box, p.594) • ☎ 08 9842 4500, ⓦ dpaw.wa.gov.au

Frenchman Bay Road leads onto a peninsula incorporating the **Torndirrup National Park**, where there are stunning beaches, lookouts and other natural attractions. The first turn-off is to the **Wind Farm** where a ridgetop boardwalk allows close-up views of the windmills and stunning coastal vistas. After this, **the Gap** and **Natural Bridge** are the first attractions worth visiting, but take care as this area has claimed several lives with people slipping or getting dragged into the sea by **king waves**, immense waves that are indistinguishable in the swell. From the car park, a path leads down to the sloping granite shoreline of **Cable Beach**.

Further along, the views from Stony Hill (an old watchtower) and Misery Beach are worth a look. Nearby, a track leads to the summit of **Isthmus Hill** (1km), which in spring passes varieties of orchids on the way. A bracing **walk** (around 4km) leads from the summit, culminating at Bald Head on the tip of the Flinders Peninsula. If you continue along Frenchman Bay Road beyond the park, you'll arrive at pretty, sheltered **Frenchman Bay** on Princess Royal Harbour, a sublime spot for a swim.

Historic Whaling Station

20km south of Albany on Frenchman Bay Rd • Daily 9am–5pm • $29 • Tours on the hour 10am–3pm • ☎ 08 9844 4021, ⓦ discoverybay .com.au/historic-whaling-station

The site of Australia's last whaling station, which closed in 1978, is now an engaging museum dedicated to the world's biggest creatures, once hunted to near extinction. The informative hour-long **tours** explain Australia's role in ending the hunting, though not before describing the process of dismembering and boiling down the whale blubber and bones, and displaying the machinery that did the job. Don't miss seeing the towering *Cheyne IV* whale chaser beached in the middle of the complex.

Porongurup National Park

52km north of Albany along Chester Pass Rd • DPaW fee (see box, p.594) • ☎ 08 9853 1095, ⓦ dpaw.wa.gov.au

The granite hills comprising the **Porongurup National Park** are often described as "among the oldest rocks on earth" and encompass a dozen wooded peaks, whose protruding bald summits are over 600m high. The 15km-long ridge catches coastal moisture to support its karri forests, thereby leaving the loftier Stirlings to the north dry and treeless.

Once at the park, most people are happy to do no more than take the five-minute stroll to **Tree in a Rock**, a natural oddity near the park's northern entrance. However, if you want to get your teeth into a good walk, head up the marked trail to **Devil's Slide** (671m) and return via Nancy and Hayward peaks; the full route warrants at least half a day. **Balancing Rock**, at the eastern end, can be reached in 45 minutes from the car park, and there's a cage on the exposed outcrop of **Castle Rock** providing safe viewing.

Stirling Range National Park

North of Albany looms the **Stirling Range National Park**, where the distinctive profile of Bluff Knoll will, if you're lucky, emerge from the cloudbanks often obscuring its summit. Avid hill-walkers could spend a few days "peak bagging" here and come away well satisfied; the Stirlings are WA's best – if not only – mountain-walking zone, with as many as five peaks over 1000m. Be aware, however, that the area can experience blizzards as late as October. **Bluff Knoll** (1095m), the park's highest and most popular ascent, has a well-built path involving a three-hour return slog (2hr up, 1hr back). Like much of the area, the floral biodiversity in the Range is exceptional.

The unsealed 45km Stirling Range **scenic drive** winds amid the peaks to Red Gum Pass in the west, where you can turn around and go back the same way (with superior views). Halfway along the drive, **Talyuberlup** (800m) is a short ascent, with great vistas at the top, while **Toolbrunup Peak** (1052m), accessed by a track next to the park campsite, is a steep, 4km, three-hour trip, with some exposed scrambling near the summit. Many other **trails** wander between the peaks and link up into overnight walks.

ARRIVAL AND INFORMATION   STIRLING RANGE NATIONAL PARK

By car The Chester Pass Road enters the national park from the south, just under 100km north of Albany.

Tourist information If you are planning to head off walking into the mountains, check conditions and pick up a brochure from the DPaW office at Albany first for directions. You can also buy a DPaW pass or pay the fee while you're there (see box, p.594).

ACCOMMODATION

The Lily 9793 Chester Pass Rd ☎ 08 9827 9205 or ☎ 1800 980 002, ⓦ thelily.com.au. Ten kilometres north of the Bluff Knoll turn-off is *The Lily*, which offers a charming touch of Holland in the middle of nowhere. Look out for the sixteenth-century replica windmill (which is operational), and prepare yourself for incredibly good food, quaint Dutch cottages and Dutch bicycle-riding owners. You can even stay in a 144 Dakota airplane ($259). **$159**

Moingup Springs Campground Chester Pass Rd. This campsite is the only one in the Stirling Range National Park. It is very basic, with no power or drinking water available. There are gas BBQs, toilets and picnic tables. Operates on a first come, first served basis – no bookings. Camping per person **$10**

Mount Trio Bush Camp Ground & Caravan Park 4580 Salt River Rd ☎ 08 9827 9270, ⓦ mounttrio.com.au. Pick your own site to set up camp at this friendly campground. There's a bush kitchen with free gas BBQs, a communal fridge/freezer, microwave, toaster and kettle, plus hot showers and flushing toilets. There's also a games room with a table tennis table. Un/powered sites per person **$14/25**

Stirling Range Retreat 8639 Chester Pass Road ☎ 08 9827 9229, ⓦ stirlingrange.com.au. This campsite has a range of comfortable accommodation options including cabins and motel-style rooms (from $155). There are gorgeous views of the mountains and plenty of opportunities for hikes. Unpowered sites per person **$16**, powered sites **$36** (up to two people), cabins **$145**

Esperance and around

Few places in Australia have coastal scenery as surreally beautiful as **Esperance**, some 720km southeast of Perth and at the western end of the **Archipelago of the Recherche** – also known as the **Bay of Isles**. The archipelago's string of haze-softened granite isles, bobbing in the inky blue Southern Ocean, makes for a captivating seascape and the mild summer weather (rarely exceeding 30°C), abundant fishing opportunities and surrounding national parks ensure that the town is a popular destination for heat-sensitive holiday-makers.

The hundred-odd islands of the Archipelago of the Recherche are home mostly to seals, feral goats and sea birds, while dolphins can be spotted offshore and southern right whales migrate past en route to the Antarctic in spring. Around 50km east of Esperance is **Cape Le Grand National Park**, and a further 70km the more remote **Cape Arid National Park** (DPaW fee), on the edge of the Great Australian Bight. Care should be taken all along this coastline, as unpredictable **king waves** frequently sweep the unwary away from exposed, rocky shores.

Esperance

After prospering briefly as a supply port during the heyday of the Eastern Goldfields, **ESPERANCE** was revived in the 1960s as a farming and holiday centre. It makes an ideal base from which to explore the south coast's dazzling beaches and storm-washed headlands, and the town boasts a laidback charm that's extremely appealing – you may end up staying here longer than you had planned to.

Dempster Street is the town's main road, where you'll find the visitor centre and the various tourist-oriented shops, cafés, art galleries and crafts stores housed in a dozen historic bungalows known as the **Museum Village**. The **Esperance Museum**, in the historic railway goods shed on James Street (daily 1.30–4.30pm or by appointment; $8; ⓦ esperancemuseum.com.au), is a good repository of local memorabilia and very proud of its display on the Skylab satellite. The Skylab disintegrated over Esperance in 1979 and NASA was reputedly fined $400 for littering.

Great Ocean Drive

Heading west from Esperance, the scenic 40km **Great Ocean Drive** takes in numerous beaches then loops inland and back towards town. Travelling clockwise, stop first at the **Rotary Lookout** to climb the metal tower for 360-degree views of the captivating seascape (there are also two short walking trails here), before continuing to the turquoise waters and white sands of **West Beach**, windswept **Salmon Beach** and **Fourth Beach**. The idyllic **Twilight Beach** is up next, and is the prettiest spot of all. From here settle in for more windswept grandeur (and a nudist beach) at **Observatory Point**, and views of the windfarm above **Nine Mile Beach**, before the road turns inland towards **Pink Lake**. This is one of many lakes between here and Merredin, sometimes so-coloured by salt-tolerant algae, whose seafaring cousins give the coastline its enchanting turquoise hue.

ARRIVAL AND DEPARTURE ESPERANCE

By plane Regional Express (ⓣ 13 17 13, ⓦ rex.com.au) has 1–4 daily flights (around 90min) from Perth to Esperance. The airport is 23km north of Esperance near Gibson. There's no public transport from the city, though a taxi with Esperance Taxi Services (ⓣ 08 9071 1782) costs around $50.

By bus You can get to Esperance on Transwa bus services (ⓦ transwa.wa.gov.au) from Perth (daily except Sat; 10hr), Kalgoorlie (Mon, Wed & Fri; 5hr) and Albany (Wed; 6hr 30min). There are also services to Hyden, for Wave Rock (Thurs; 5hr). All services stop in the town centre at the Dempster St bus shelter.

By car Driving to Esperance is straightforward and somewhat dull; from Perth along the South Coast Highway it's eight and a half hours, while Highway 1 takes you to Esperance from Albany in five hours and from Kalgoorlie in four.

INFORMATION AND TOURS

Tourist information The visitor centre is in the Museum Village on Dempster St (Mon, Tues & Thurs 9am–5pm, Wed & Fri 8am–5pm; Sat 9am–4pm, June–Aug till 2pm; Sun 9am–2pm, June–Aug till noon; ☎ 08 9083 1555 or ☎ 1300 66 44 55, ⓦ visitesperance.com) and can book Transwa buses and trains for you. The DPaW office, Dempster St (☎ 08 9083 2100), provides information and sells passes (see box, p.594) for all WA national parks.

Cruises Esperance Island Cruises, 71 The Esplanade (☎ 08 9071 5757, ⓦ esperancecruises.com.au), offers daily half-day and full-day wildlife cruises in the Bay of Isles ($120–185).

Tours Aborigine-operated Kepa Kurl (☎ 08 9072 1688, ⓦ kepakurl.com.au) offers an excellent and engaging series of tours, which include rock-art viewing, indigenous stories and bushtucker in Cape Le Grand/Frenchman Peak and Mount Ridley. Tours include a bushtucker tasting ($105).

6

ACCOMMODATION

Esperance B&B By the Sea 72 Stewart St ☎ 08 9071 5640, ⓦ esperancebb.com. A contemporary beach house B&B with panoramic sea views from all rooms and a comfy, homely feel. The guest living room has a TV and DVD player and there's access to a microwave and fridge, plus a lovely outdoor dining terrace. $180

Esperance Clearwater Motel Apartments 1A William St ☎ 08 9071 3587, ⓦ clearwatermotel.com.au. Recently refurbished, chic apartments partly set in the historic old hospital. Rooms have king-sized beds, kitchenettes, en-suite bathrooms and balconies. Some apartments also have spas, BBQ decks and ocean views. $140

Esperance YHA 299 Goldfields Rd ☎ 08 9071 1040,

ⓦ yha.com.au. Backpacker hostel just 20m from the seafront offering pick-ups, bikes and a huge kitchen. There's also an open fireplace for colder days and plenty of parking as well as some triples and family rooms. Dorms $31, doubles $71

Tranquil Retreat Tranquil Drive, Windabout ☎ 08 9071 5392, ⓦ tranquilretreat.com.au. Luxury B&B with a traditional feel a short drive east of the centre. There are two shared lounges – the upstairs one has wraparound views of the serene local countryside. Dinner can be arranged on request and there are complimentary breakfasts, cakes, cookies, chocolates and port. $170

EATING AND DRINKING

Coffee Cat The Esplanade ☎ 04 2930 1066. This coffee van pulls up in the jetty car park daily and serves up quality takeaway coffees for the locals to sip while lounging around in the sun and socializing. Cash only. Mon–Fri 7am–2pm.

Loose Goose 9A Andrew St ☎ 08 9071 2320, ⓦ loosegooseesperance.com.au. For a creative mod-Oz meal head to this family-run favourite, which serves up local produce including all-Aussie fresh seafood on its fixed-price menus (from $45.50 per person). Tues–Sat 4pm–midnight.

The Pier Hotel The Esplanade ☎ 08 9071 1777, ⓦ thepierhotelesperance.com. Affordable counter meals

such as chicken parmigiana and barramundi plus a range of wood-fired pizzas (from $17). The *Saloon Bar* has TVs showing live sports; the nightclub here is the only one in town. Bar: Mon–Wed 9am–midnight, Thurs–Sat 9am–late, Sun 9am–midnight. Food served daily 11.30am–2pm & 5.30–9pm.

Taylors Beach Bar Taylor St Jetty, ☎ 08 9071 4317. The best spot in town for food with a view, this simple but friendly café serves breakfast, brunch and some fabulous seafood (tasting plate of chilli mussels and garlic mushrooms $25). There's live music on Sunday afternoons too. Wed–Sun 8am–10pm.

Cape Le Grand National Park

50km southeast of Esperance • DPaW fee • ☎ 08 9842 4500, ⓦ dpaw.wa.gov.au

If you've made it as far as Esperance, a visit to **Cape Le Grand National Park** is well worth the expense of renting a car or taking a tour. It's essentially a climb up a hill and a beach-hop, but on a good day they're the kind of beaches you'll want to roll up and take home with you.

It's an easy 1hr 10min drive to the park (though the last 5km are on a single-track road) and, once inside, the sealed road in leads straight down to picturesque **Le Grand Beach**. A left turn-off into the rest of the park takes you to a T-junction: fork right for the perfect sheltered cove **Hellfire Bay**, left for the car park for **Frenchman Peak**. The climb to the peak's summit (262m; allow 2hr) is not as hard as it looks, if you have a sturdy pair of shoes, and warrants the exertion. The secret of its distinctive, hooked crest is an unexpected hole near the top, which frames an impressive view out to sea and back over the national park.

The **Le Grand Coastal Trail** (sturdy shoes required; 15km; 8hr) links the beaches along the park's coast, beginning at Le Grand Beach and calling in at **Hellfire Bay**, the gorgeously secluded **Thistle Cove** and lovely **Lucky Bay** – where you'll find kangaroos on the sand, great camping facilities ($10pp; ⓦparkstay.dpaw.wa.gov.au), sheltered swimming and wonderful ocean colours – before finishing at pleasant **Rossiter Bay**. This last stretch is also served by unsealed road.

6

Wave Rock

Wave Rock Rd, Hyden · $10 parking fee · ☎ 08 9880 5022, ⓦ waverock.com.au

WA's best-known natural oddity is the striking **Wave Rock**, about a four-hour drive north through the Wheatlands from Esperance (or the same from Albany) and 4km from the tiny farming settlement of Hyden. At 14m high and 110m long, the granite formation resembles a breaking wave, an impression enhanced by the vertical water stains running down the overhanging face. From the base of the rock a marked twenty-minute walking trail leads to another outcrop, Hippo's Yawn.

ARRIVAL AND TOURS

WAVE ROCK

By bus There's a weekly Transwa service (ⓦtranswa .wa.gov.au) from East Perth to Hyden (Tues; 5hr).

Tours If you can't face the drive, Western Travel Bug offers full-day tours three times a week from Perth (departs 7am

Tues, Thurs & Sat, returns 5.30pm; $185, including meals and entrance fees; ⓦtravelbug.com.au), which takes in a couple of other sights along the way, including the wild flowers when in season (Aug–Oct).

ACCOMMODATION AND EATING

Tressie's Museum and Caravan Park Karlgarin, 17km west of Hyden ☎ 08 9889 5043. This caravan park has a grassed tent area and modern facilities including a decent camper's kitchen with communal fridge, plus BBQ and laundry facilities. There are also some basic cabins and a two-bedroom chalet. Un/powered sites $23/27, cabins $60, chalets $115

Wave Rock Motel 2 Lynch Street ☎ 08 9880 5052, ⓦ waverock.com.au. Simple and slightly dated motel with standard and "executive" rooms, which have spa baths and private courtyards. There's a guest lounge with open fireplace and baby grand piano plus a solar-heated swimming pool in the gardens. $150

The Eastern Goldfields

Six hundred kilometres east of Perth, at the end of the **Great Eastern Highway**, are the **Eastern Goldfields**, a fascinating region replete with historic sights. In the late nineteenth century, gold was found here in what still remains one of the world's richest gold-producing regions, and boom towns, boasting grand public buildings, multiple hotels and a vast periphery of hovels, would spring up and collapse in the time it took to extract any ore. Many of these ornate buildings exist today as ghostly relics – a photographer's dream.

In 1894 the railway from Perth reached the town of **Southern Cross**, just as big finds turned the rush into a national stampede. Although this huge influx of people made the region one of the state's most multicultural, it also accentuated the water shortage, dealt with finally when a pipeline reached Kalgoorlie in 1903. Around this time many of the smaller gold towns were already in decline, but the Goldfields' wealth and boost in population gave WA the economic autonomy it sought in its claim for statehood in 1901.

In the years preceding the gold rush, the area was briefly one of the world's richest sources of **sandalwood**, an aromatic wood greatly prized throughout Asia for joss sticks. Exacerbating the inevitable over-cutting was the gold rush's demand for timber to prop up shafts, or to fire the pre-pipeline water desalinators. Today the region is a pit-scarred and prematurely desertified landscape, dotted with the scavenged vestiges of past settlements, while at its core the **Super Pit** gold mine in Kalgoorlie (see p.602) gets wider and deeper every year.

Kalgoorlie–Boulder

From whichever direction you approach **KALGOORLIE** – the bustling gold capital of Australia, municipally merged but still fervently distinct from **Boulder** – it comes as a surprise after hundreds of kilometres of desolation. In 1893 **Paddy Hannan** and his mates, Tom Flanagan and Dan O'Shea, brought renewed meaning to the expression "the luck of the Irish" when a lame horse forced them to camp by the tree which still stands at the top of Egan Street in Kalgoorlie. With their instincts highly attuned after eight months of prospecting around Coolgardie, they soon found **gold** all around them, and as the first on the scene enjoyed the unusually easy pickings of surface gold. Ten years later, when the desperately needed water pipeline finally gushed into the Mount Charlotte Reservoir, Kalgoorlie was already the established heart of WA's rapidly growing mineral-based prosperity. As the sole survivor of the original rush, and revitalized by the 1960s nickel boom, Kalgoorlie has benefited from new technology that has largely dispensed with slow and dangerous underground mining. Instead, the fabulously rich "**Golden Mile**" reef east of town, near Boulder, is being excavated around the clock, creating a colossal hole, the open-cast "Super Pit" (see p.602), which is still going strong and grows larger every day – the great hole in the landscape is an incredible sight.

Questa Casa

133 Hay St • Tours daily 3pm; 1hr 15 min • $25; 18+ only, book at the visitor centre or pay on arrival • ☎ 08 9021 4897, ⓦ questacasa.com

Tours at **Questa Casa**, Australia's oldest brothel at over 100 years, are led by Madam Carmel who has a no-nonsense approach and a natural storytelling ability. Hearing her tales of girls coining it in, clients kicking the bucket and marriages forged in the brothels here is an unmissable part of a visit to Kalgoorlie and one of the best-value tours in the state.

Hannan Street

Hannan Street is one of Kalgoorlie's finest sights, with superbly restored **Federation-era architecture**, imposing public buildings and flamboyant hotel facades. Pick up the self-guided audio tour ($10) at the visitor centre to discover the stories behind some of the town's grandest buildings – it's only when you stop to reflect that this is a remote, century-old town in the Western Australia desert that the stunning wealth of the still-continuing boom years is brought home. You're welcome to inspect the grandiose interior of the **town hall** (Mon–Fri 8.30am–5pm, free tours Wed 1.30pm). Outside is the replica of a bronze **statue** of Paddy himself.

PROSTITUTION IN KALGOORLIE

Prostitution has long been legal in WA and due to Kalgoorlie's perceived "special needs" (a large male population in need of a "safety valve" and significant lack of females), the high rates paid here saw willing women flock to the town. Until 1994, a "containment" policy meant that prostitutes were not allowed to live in the community nor go "where people gathered", effectively confining them to the one-street red-light district of **Hay Street**. Now, with containment lifted, the street's appeal has diminished, prostitutes have flooded in in larger numbers, prices have dropped and almost all the brothels have closed. Just two remain, one of which offers **brothel tours** (see above).

6

Western Australian Museum

Hannan St • Daily 10am–4.30pm • Suggested donation $5 • Ⓦ museum.wa.gov.au

The **Western Australian Museum** is located right next to the spot where Paddy and his crew found their first, auspicious nuggets. Get an overview of the area in the galleries here, which feature displays on Aboriginal and mining history, and take the lift up to the top of the red 33m-high Ivanhoe Headframe where the viewing platform boasts 360-degree views of the city and its mines.

Hannan's North Tourist Mine

Goldfields Hwy • Sun–Fri 9am–4pm (last admission 3.30pm) • $10 • ☎ 08 9093 3488, Ⓦ hannansnorth.com.au

Hannan's North Tourist Mine is based on the site of Paddy Hannan's original lease and was a working mine until 1952. Today it is home to a reconstruction of what the old mine might have been like and offers visitors the chance to clamber aboard a vast digger and to try their hand at gold panning, as well as experience a modern underground refuge chamber that can keep up to twelve people alive for 72 hours.

Super Pit Lookout

Outram Street, Boulder • Daily 7am–7pm • Ⓦ superpit.com.au

The astonishing **Super Pit Lookout**, a short drive along the Goldfields Highway from the town, is an absolute must – and no words can quite prepare you for the sheer scale of it all. Here a crude lookout shelter contains information about the history of gold mining in the area and the current operations, but the real attraction is the pit itself, which dominates the landscape from your feet to the horizon. Phone the KCGM Public Interaction Line (☎ 08 9022 1100) to find out when a blast is scheduled and watch the earth quite literally being moved in search of gold.

ARRIVAL AND DEPARTURE

KALGOORLIE–BOULDER

By plane You can fly to Kalgoorlie from Perth with Qantas and Virgin Australia; the airport (☎ 08 9093 3436) is just 7km from the city centre and there are flights at least once a day.

By train Transwa's Prospector train (Ⓦ transwa.wa.gov. au) travels between Perth and Kalgoorlie daily (7hr, note that the buffet car accepts cash only). The Indian Pacific (Ⓦ greatsouthernrail.com.au) runs from Kalgoorlie on to Adelaide (31hr), Broken Hill (43hr) and Sydney (59hr) once a week, crossing the Nullarbor Plain on the world's longest

straight piece of track (480km). Kalgoorlie Taxis (☎ 08 9091 5233) meet the trains and will be your best bet if you have heavy bags ($8–10).

By bus Transwa buses arrive from Esperance on Wednesday, Friday and Sunday (returning Mon, Wed & Fri; 5hr), dropping off at the railway station and calling at Coolgardie en route.

By car It's a six-hour drive from Perth on the Great Eastern Highway; the journey north from Esperance on Highways 1 and 94 takes 4hr 45min.

INFORMATION AND TOURS

Tourist information Kalgoorlie's informative visitor centre, at 316 Hannan St (Mon–Fri 8.30am–5pm, Sat & Sun and holidays 9am–2pm; ☎ 08 9021 1966, Ⓦ kalgoorlietourism.com), stocks maps, books tours and supplies timetables for the frequent local TransGoldfields (☎ 08 9021 2655) bus service between Kalgoorlie and Boulder and Hannans (Mon–Fri 7am–6pm, Sat limited service).

Tours Kalgoorlie Tours at 250 Hannan St runs Super Pit Tours (Mon–Sat 9.30am, 2hr 30min; $70; ☎ 1800 620 441, Ⓦ kalgoorlietours.com), the only tour that goes into the Super Pit's operations. Don high-vis jackets and safety goggles to visit internal viewing platforms and old mine shafts and see the vast dumptrucks in action. Enclosed shoes, long sleeves and long trousers must be worn and you may have to undergo a breathalyser test.

ACCOMMODATION

Kalgoorlie Backpackers 166 Hay St ☎ 08 9091 1482, Ⓦ kalgoorliebackpackers.com.au. Based in a former brothel, with a big kitchen, dorms and private rooms, as well as a large swimming pool, BBQ area and table tennis and pool tables. Dorms $33, doubles $85

Palace Hotel 137 Hannan St ☎ 08 9021 2788, Ⓦ palacehotel.com.au. Beautiful old building slap-bang in the centre of town with an assortment of accommodation of varying quality. Rooms run the gamut from cheaper, old-style backpacker doubles which share bathroom facilities to standard refurbished en suites and more expensive, more attractive doubles with private balconies. Some rooms are across the street at the *Australia Hotel*. $75

Rydges Kalgoorlie 21 Davidson St ☎08 9080 0800, ⓦrydges.com. It's about a 30min walk from this comfortable hotel to the town centre but it's worth it for the peace and quiet and the garden villa feel. Rooms are stylish with floor-to-ceiling windows and there are indoor

and outdoor pools plus a restaurant and spa. Free parking and a 24hr reception. $166

YHA Golddust Backpackers 192 Hay St ☎08 9091 3737, ⓦyha.com.au. Purpose-built hostel with a/c and a swimming pool for summer and a cosy wood fire for winter. There are bikes to borrow, a TV room and internet access but be aware that many of those staying here are miners working in the area and that consequently the atmosphere can be a little rowdy. Dorms $33

EATING AND DRINKING

Balcony Bar and Restaurant Palace Hotel 137 Hannan St ☎08 9021 2788, ⓦpalacehotel.com.au. This historic hotel has a simple interior dining room and a pleasant wraparound balcony (heated in winter) for drinks and dining. The menu features all the mod-Oz classics, from cirus and almond-crusted barramundi ($38) to crispy duck ($42). The wine list has some good WA varieties. Bar open daily from 4pm, dinner from 5pm.

Blue Monkey 418 Hannan St ☎08 9091 3833, ⓦbluemonkeyrestaurant.com.au. This bright and breezy restaurant may not have the character of the pub balconies, but the food is high quality and the atmosphere quieter – and more family friendly. Barramundi from the Kimberley is $36, surf and turf $44. Mon–Fri 6–10am & 6–8.30pm, Sat & Sun 6–11am & 6–8.30pm.

Paddy's The Exchange Hotel 135 Hannah St ☎08 9021 2833, ⓦexchangekalgoorlie.com.au. This grand old hotel in the centre of town has been one of Kal's liveliest pubs for more than a century. Today *The Exchange* offers

balcony dining at *Paddy's* (chicken parma $29), raucous drinking and live music seven nights a week, but has been recently refurbished, giving it a classier edge. Daily 11am–midnight, food served daily 11am–9pm.

Top End Thai 71 Hannan St ☎08 9021 4286. Decent Aussie-style Thai restaurant with all the usual suspects on the menu including beef in oyster sauce, tempura king prawns and pad thai ($22). This is also one of the best-value restaurants in town and a good choice if you would rather avoid the hotel bars. Tues–Sun 11am–2pm and 5–9pm.

The York 259 Hannan St ☎08 9021 2337, ⓦyorkhotel.com.au. Proper Aussie sports bar with a friendly but blokey feel. There are several Australian beers on tap and a decent wine list (though reds by the glass are lacking) plus an open fire in winter, TVs on the walls, a pool table and a dart board that sees plenty of action. This is not a late-night venue, sometimes closing earlier than advertised, and is a good choice for a quieter drink. Mon–Sat 11am–midnight.

Coolgardie

Quiet **Coolgardie** was the original gold-rush settlement and there is much evidence of the town's importance, from its historic buildings to the grand sweep of Bayley Street – wide enough to turn around a camel train. At its peak, the town had 23 hotels, three breweries and seven newspapers serving a population ten times greater than its present one thousand. Check out the map outside the Pharmaceutical Museum for an index of the 155 historical markers spread around the area, which tell the story of this fascinating ghost town.

Goldfields Exhibition Museum

62 Bayley St • Mon–Fri 9am–4pm, Sat & Sun 10am–3pm • $4 (combined ticket with Pharmacy Museum) • ⓦgoldfieldstourism.com.au

The grand **Mining Warden's Court Building** on Bayley Street is home to the town's **visitor centre** (Mon–Fri 9am–4pm, Sat & Sun 10am–3pm; ☎08 9026 6090). The **Goldfields Exhibition Museum** here contains one of WA's most comprehensive displays on the gold rush and its impact. You'll find recreations of mining camps and workers' homes and have the chance to peak inside the old courtroom.

Pharmacy Museum

Bayley St • Daily 9am–5pm • $4 (combined ticket with Goldfields Exhibition Museum)

Inside the old drill hall, the fascinating **Pharmacy Museum** displays a collection of eighteenth-, nineteenth- and early twentieth-century medicines, dental tools and cool retro posters. It offers an interesting – and somewhat gruesome – insight into

6

THE WORLD'S LONGEST GOLF COURSE: NULLARBOR LINKS

The tedious journey across the Nullarbor was made a little more bearable in 2009 with the launch of the **Nullarbor Links** (ⓦ nullarborlinks.com), an eighteen-hole, par 72 golf course that stretches 1365km from Kalgoorlie to Ceduna in South Australia. Each town or roadhouse along the route features one or two holes with a tee, a somewhat rugged Outback-style natural terrain fairway and a green. Score cards can be purchased at Kalgoorlie Golf Course (where the first two holes are located), and the visitor centres at Kalgoorlie (see p.602), Ceduna (see p.711) and Norseman (see opposite), and must be stamped at each hole. Clubs can be rented at each hole for $5 (extra deposit required) and golfers completing the course receive a free certificate in either Kalgoorlie or Ceduna.

---

historical medical practices and is considered to be one of the best pharmaceutical displays in Australia.

Ben Prior's Open-Air Museum

Bayley St • Daily • Free

Behind a picket fence in the centre of town stands the **Ben Prior's Open-Air Museum**. The museum was set up by Prior, an avid collector who owned a garage, Volkswagen dealership and gold mine – hence the array of motoring and mining memorabilia you can see here today.

Warden Finnerty's Residence

McKenzie St • Daily except Wed 11am–4pm • $4 • ☎ 08 9026 6028 • ⓦ nationaltrust.org.au

Warden Finnerty's unenviable job was to set the ground rules for mining at the height of the rush. His stone house built in 1895 on McKenzie Street has been finely restored. Next to it is the Aboriginal waterhole, after which Finnerty is said to have named the town. Call ahead or check at the visitors centre (see p.603) to check that the property is open.

The Eyre Highway to South Australia

South of Kalgoorlie the Great Eastern Highway runs 190km to Norseman, at the western end of the **Eyre Highway**. The highway is named after the explorer Edward John Eyre who crossed the southern edge of the continent in 1841, a gruelling eight-month trek that would have cost him his life but for the Aborigines who helped him locate water. Eyre crawled into Albany on his last legs but set the route for future crossings, the telegraph lines and the highway.

If you're heading east on the Eyre Highway from Norseman, it's about 700km to the South Australian border and another 470km from there to Ceduna. This is the legendary **Nullarbor Plain**, where a flat, arid and famously monotonous landscape stretches away from the road on both sides, with barely a tree to break it up (*nullarbor* means "no trees" in Latin). Once this comes to an end at Ceduna, there is still a featureless 775km before you reach Adelaide.

Although the longest stretch without fuel is only 200km, do not underestimate the rigours of the journey on your vehicle. Carry reserves of fuel and water, take rests every few hours and don't drive at dawn or dusk when kangaroos are crossing the road to feed. There's a quarantine checkpoint at the **border** where a large range of prohibited animal and vegetable goods must be discarded.

Norseman

NORSEMAN was named after a prospector's horse that kicked up a large nugget in 1894 – a genuine case of lucky horseshoes. A bronze effigy of the nag now stands proudly on the corner of Roberts and Ramsay streets. Arrivals from South Australia may be eager to pick up their "I've crossed the Nullarbor" certificate from the **visitor centre**.

The Nullarbor Plain

The **Nullarbor Plain** is the world's largest single piece of limestone, covering an area of some 200,000 square kilometres, and crossing it is mind-bendingly dull. That said, there are a few very worthwhile viewpoints along the southern side of the road, where the arid landscape ends rather suddenly at the Great Australian Bight – there is nothing between here and Antarctica.

Facilities along the route are limited. **BALLADONIA**, 191km east of Norseman, has the *Balladonia Hotel Motel*. Some 246km of virtually dead-straight road further along, you reach **COCKLEBIDDY**, which has a motel, while **MADURA**, 83km east, is halfway between Perth and Adelaide (if you're still counting), and has rooms and caravan sites. **MUNDRABILLA**, 115km further on, also has a motel and campsite.

Eucla

EUCLA, just 13km from South Australia, was re-established up on the escarpment after sand dunes engulfed the original settlement by the sea. Down near the ocean, the old telegraph and weather station, 4km away, is still visible above the sands, an eerie sight well worth a look. South of town is the **Eucla National Park** (DpaW fee), where the coastal cliffs extend east for 290km along the coast of South Australia. There are motel units and caravan-camping sites at the *Eucla Amber Motor Hotel* (see below), or right on the border with South Australia at the *Border Village* (see p.712).

INFORMATION

Tourist information The Norseman visitor centre (Mon–Fri 9am–5pm, Sat 9am–noon & 1–4pm, Sun 9.30am–4pm; ☎08 9039 1071, ⓦnorseman.info) is in

THE EYRE HIGHWAY TO SOUTH AUSTRALIA

Welcome Park, where there are also public toilets. For further information on the Nullarbor Plain, visit ⓦnullarbornet.com.au.

ACCOMMODATION AND EATING

Balladonia Hotel Motel Balladonia ☎08 9039 3453, ⓦballadoniahotelmotel.com.au. This pleasant hotel has a range of rooms with en-suite bathrooms, air conditioning and TVs, plus a restaurant serving all the usuals. Chicken parma is $26.90, fish of the day $28.90. The caravan park has dozens of sites plus a campers' kitchen and BBQ area. Powered sites $30, doubles $140

Eucla Amber Motor Hotel Eucla-Reid Rd, Eucla ☎08 9039 3468. There are simple hotel rooms, motel units and a few "executive rooms", as well as powered caravan sites and unpowered tent sites. Un/powered sites $15/20, doubles $70

Madura Roadhouse Eyre Highway, Madura ☎08 9039 3464. One of the best choices for accommodation along the Nullarbor, the *Madura Roadhouse* has budget rooms for backpackers plus some nicer motel rooms. There is also a campsite and an outdoor swimming pool, plus a licensed restaurant. Un/powered sites $20/25, doubles $80

Mundrabilla Roadhouse Eyre Hwy, Mundrabilla ☎08 9039 3465. The roadhouse in Mundrabilla has 10 simple en-suite motel units with fridges and TVs, plus powered and unpowered sites for caravans and tents. The bar here has a pool table and simple meals. Un/powered sites $15/20, doubles $85

The Railway Motel & Inn Roberts St, Norseman ☎08 9039 0003, ⓦtherailwaynorseman.com.au. This renovated Art Deco hotel has functional budget rooms suitable for backpackers, simple en-suite motel rooms and nicer spa suites. There's also a comfortable guest lounge, a pool table, gym and shared kitchen as well as a coin-operated laundry. $90

Wedgetail Inn Eyre Hwy, Cocklebiddy ☎08 9039 3462. This friendly roadhouse has a wide range of motel-style units, including singles, doubles, triples and family rooms sleeping up to six people. There is also a simple campsite, a licensed restaurant and a bar with a pool table. Un/powered sites $20/25, doubles $125

6

The Batavia Coast

The Batavia Coast's moniker comes from the Dutch East India Company's ship the *Batavia*, which was wrecked off the **Houtman Abrolhos** islands, 80km west of Geraldton, in 1629 – just one of many ships wrecked in this area (see box, p.610). If you're travelling north up this coastline from Perth, the first obligatory stop is **Nambung National Park** where the weird and wonderful **Pinnacles** are one of WA's must-sees. Avoid the dreary Brand Highway in favour of the more scenic Indian Ocean Drive to reach the Pinnacles in around two and a half hours, making a (long) day-trip from Perth a possibility. Alternatively, stop over in the windswept crayfishing town of **Cervantes**.

Geraldton is the Batavia Coast's administrative centre and a decent place to stock up for the onward journey, while further north the attractive seaside resort of **Kalbarri** is an enticing place to spend a day or two. Historic **Greenough** also makes a worthwhile stopover.

The Pinnacles and around

From Indian Ocean Drive, an entry road (look out for emus and kangaroos) leads into **Nambung National Park** (DPaW fee). The **Pinnacles** are the park's main attraction: this spread of 3m-high limestone columns was originally formed underground and has since been exhumed from the sands, like a terracotta army, by the perennial southwesterlies.

The park entrance leads to the 3km Pinnacles Drive, which winds among the pillars and offers parking bays at frequent intervals. Don't miss the extra loop to the left just past the main lookout; you'll skip around a third of the park if you do. Make sure that you spend some time wandering around this eerie expanse and getting in amid the atmospheric landscape – seeing it from the car just doesn't measure up.

Cervantes

For those wanting to see the Pinnacles, a stop in **Cervantes** (around 29km from the park entrance) was almost essential before the Indian Ocean Drive opened. Today, the easier access from Perth renders it unnecessary but it remains a pleasant place to stop, and if you do decide to stay there are several sound accommodation options and an array of pleasant sandy **beaches**. There is also a small visitor centre on the main strip here, along with a bottle shop, fish-and-chip shop and small general store.

ARRIVAL AND DEPARTURE · THE PINNACLES AND AROUND

By bus Integrity (ⓦintegritycoachlines.com.au) buses on the Perth–Broome run stop at the post office in Cervantes twice a week in each direction, though not at very civilized times of day and on request only (12.20am on the way north and 4.05am on the way south). There is no public transport to the national park; bring your own vehicle or take a tour from Perth.

INFORMATION AND TOURS

Tourist information The Pinnacles Desert Discovery Centre (daily 9.30am–4.30pm; ☏08 9652 7913) at the main car park at the Pinnacles explains the geology on show, but falls a little short in terms of its explanation. In Cervantes, the post office on Cadiz St houses the small visitor centre (Mon–Sat 9am–5.30pm, Sun 9am–5pm; ☏08 9652 7700, ⓦvisitpinnaclescountry.com.au), which has scant information beyond a list of things to do in the area.

Tours Most day-tours from Perth arrive around noon, and then miss the evening sun's long shadows, which add still further to the Pinnacles' photogenic qualities. Still, if you're keen to see them and can only spare the day, consider Western Travel Bug (☏08 9486 4222, ⓦtravelbug.com.au), which has a day-trip on Tuesdays, Thursdays and Saturdays, departing Perth at 7am and returning at 5.30pm for $185.

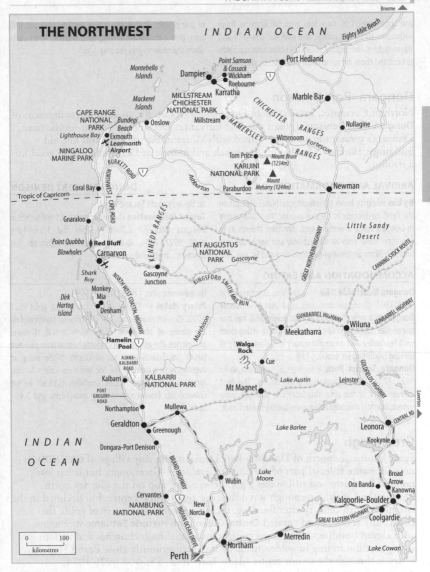

THE NORTHWEST

6

ACCOMMODATION AND EATING

Cervantes Lodge and Pinnacles Beach Backpackers
91 Seville St ☎ 08 9652 7377 or ☎ 1800 245 232,
ⓦ cervanteslodge.com.au. This shared building offers a
good range of accommodation. The rooms are a bit bland,
but the friendly owners, characterful lounge area and
superbly equipped communal kitchen make this a real home
from home. The wi-fi is expensive at $1 for 10min. Dorms
$33, doubles $90

Pinnacles Caravan Park 35 Aragon St ☎ 08 9652 7060,
ⓦ pinnaclespark.com.au. A fairly standard site right by the
beach, with some excellent wooded pitches for campers and
the usual rows of cabins (with communal bathrooms)
further back. Un/powered sites $33/38, cabins $75
Pinnacles Edge Resort 7 Aragon St ☎ 08 9652 7788,
ⓦ pinnaclesedgeresort.com.au. By far the best place to
stay in the area. The self-contained units are well equipped

and large enough to move into, with full kitchens, huge bathrooms and a vast lounge area with flat-screen TV and stereo system. The slightly pricier spa suites have spa baths to boot and there are some larger apartments, sleeping up to five people. There's also a nice outdoor pool and BBQ area, plus a restaurant serving fresh seafood. Rates come down the more nights you stay. $195

Dongara–Port Denison

North of Cervantes, Indian Ocean Drive continues up the coast to the twin towns of **Dongara–Port Denison**, 130km north of Cervantes. Set slightly back from the coast, Dongara's pleasant main street is lined with Moreton Bay fig trees and fine old buildings; 1km or so further on, the beach and marina at Denison are both good for a stroll.

ARRIVAL AND INFORMATION

DONGARA–PORT DENISON

By bus Integrity buses (ⓦintegritycoachlines.com.au) on the Perth-to-Broome route stop outside the visitor centre in Dongara twice a week in each direction, though as in Cervantes these stop on request only and not at sociable hours (2.30am on the way north on Wed and Fri and 2am on the way south Sat and Mon).

Tourist information The visitor centre at 9 Waldeck St in Dongara (Mon–Fri 8.30am–4.30pm, Sat 10am–1pm; ☎08 9927 1404, ⓦdongaraportdenison.com.au) has brochures, maps and souvenirs.

ACCOMMODATION AND EATING

Dongara Beachside B&B 4 Swan View, Dongara ☎08 9927 1307, ⓦdongarabnb.com.au. A 2km drive outside Dongara in a peaceful location, this bright B&B has one queen-size double and one twin plus a guest sitting room with tea/coffee and a complimentary breakfast. Plenty of parking (including for boats). $130

Dongara Tourist Park 8 George St, Denison ☎08 9927 1210, ⓦdongaratouristpark.com.au. The best caravan park in the area, this leafy site also has some superb, brightly coloured cabins overlooking South Beach. Un/powered sites $26/37, cabins $99

Priory Hotel 11 St Dominics Rd, Dongara ☎08 9927 1090, ⓦprioryhotel.com.au. This colonial-style hotel on the banks of the Irwin River offers a real all-round experience. The assortment of rooms here all have polished jarrah floorboards and lots of charm. While away an evening with a drink in the bar and then have a famous (once award-winning) steak sandwich ($19.50) in the *Colonial Bar* (meals served daily noon–2pm and 5.45–8pm). $70

Greenough

Forty kilometres north of Dongara–Port Denison, the tiny village of **GREENOUGH** is now (in name at least) part of the city of Geraldton–Greenough, but it has lost none of its charm and still makes a good overnight stop on the journey north. During the 1860s, Greenough was a thriving agricultural centre, but declined in the late nineteenth century after flooding, cyclones and the discovery of gold. The beautifully restored and curated **Central Greenough Historic Settlement** remains, with eleven buildings including a courthouse, social hall, churches and various cottages still standing in golden fields by the incongruously close Brand Highway. Entry is through the visitor centre (daily 9am–4pm; $5; ☎08 9926 1084, ⓦcentralgreenough.com).

Call in also to the **Pioneer Museum** (daily 10am–4pm; $4.50; ☎08 9921 3999), home to the Maley family from 1862 to 1932 and almost entirely unchanged. Around the village you'll also notice Greenough's strange **leaning trees** – some bent almost flat against the ground by the prevailing salt-laden winds. A couple of lookouts off the highway provide photo opportunities.

ARRIVAL AND INFORMATION

GREENOUGH

By car Greenough is a 4hr 15min drive up Highway 1 from Perth and a 20-minute drive south of Geraldton (see opposite).

Tourist information Visitor centre (daily 9am–4pm; ☎08 9926 1084, ⓦgeraldtonvisitorcentre.com.au).

ACCOMMODATION AND EATING

Central Greenough Café Brand Hwy ☎ 08 9926 1084, Ⓦ centralgreenough.com. The visitor centre houses a surprisingly classy, airy café serving breakfast, delicious light lunches and cracking caramel slices. Mon–Fri 9am–4pm, Sun 8am–4pm.

Hampton Arms 338 Company Rd ☎ 08 9926 1057, Ⓦ hamptonarms.com.au. This cute English-style pub has lots of nooks and crannies to explore, a secondhand bookshop, plus light lunches, rooms and dinner on request. Fish and chips is $24.50, chicken parma $28.50. Rooms are simply furnished but comfortable and rates include breakfast. $95

Geraldton

GERALDTON is situated in the middle of the **Batavia Coast**, 430km north of Perth and just 25km beyond Greenough. Now officially called Geraldton–Greenough after the 2007 amalgamation with its neighbour, it's a slightly more bustling place than many towns further north, though you'll still find some services disappointingly lacking – supermarkets are all closed on Sundays.

Geraldton's main drag, Marine Terrace, is lined with shops and restaurants. The next block over is Foreshore Drive, with the family-friendly Town Beach at its centre, and a **marina** complex full of swanky boats at its eastern end. West of town, beyond the harbour and **Fisherman's Wharf**, are good beaches and a striking red-and-white-striped lighthouse at **Point Moore**. Fresh seafood can be bought at the wharf, although for kite-surfers and adrenaline junkies the real attraction at this end of town is the blustery beach at the point.

Looming over the city on the corner of George and Victoria streets is the **HMAS Sydney memorial**, a rather grandiose domed monument to the lost ship. It's in urgent need of an information update since the wreck was discovered off Steep Point near Shark Bay in 2008, solving a mystery that has taxed Australians and conspiracy theorists since World War II. There are great views out to sea from here and daily 30-minute tours from the car park (10.30am; donation).

St Francis Xavier Cathedral

Cathedral Ave • Tours Mon & Fri 10am and Wed 4pm • $5 donation

On Cathedral Avenue, **St Francis Xavier Cathedral**, completed in 1938, is the crowning glory of Monsignor John Hawes' career – have a peek inside to see the bright stained-glass windows and striking orange-and-grey-striped interior. Combining the unlikely professions of architect and priest, Hawes' distinctive hand can be seen in numerous other churches and religious buildings in the area. You can buy a **Monsignor John Hawes Heritage Trail** leaflet at the visitor centre – the self-drive trail takes a good three days.

Western Australian Museum Geraldton

1 Museum Place • Daily 9.30am–4pm • Suggested donation $5 • ☎ 1300 134 081, Ⓦ museum.wa.gov.au

It's easy to get engrossed in the **Western Australian Museum Geraldton**, down near the marina. Covering regional flora and fauna, Dreamtime stories and Aboriginal history, it also has a room dedicated to the moving story of the HMAS *Sydney* (see box, p.610). The Shipwrecks Gallery focuses on earlier wrecks around the Batavia Coast, including the Dutch East India Company ships the *Batavia* and the *Zuytdorp* and features artefacts from both shipwrecks, including clay pipes, silver coins, cannons, the original *Batavia* stone portico and numerous other relics.

City of Greater Geraldton Regional Art Gallery

24 Chapman Rd • Mon–Sat 10am–4pm • Free, but donations appreciated • ☎ 08 9964 7170, Ⓦ artgallery.cgg.wa.gov.au

This excellent regional gallery is part of the Art Gallery of Western Australia, based in Perth, and hosts local, national and international exhibitions. The City of Greater

6

SHIPS AND SHIPWRECKS

This stretch of coast is awash with maritime history. The seventeenth and eighteenth centuries were notable for the wrecking of numerous Dutch East India Company ships, including the *Batavia* in 1629, and the *Zuytdorp* in 1710. The **Batavia**'s story is especially compelling: the ship set sail from Amsterdam in 1628 for the Dutch East Indies, laden with silver and other goodies to trade for precious spices on arrival. During the journey, merchants Adriaene Jacobsz and Jeronimus Cornelisz hatched a plan to hijack the ship and effect a mutiny, allowing them to steal the booty on board and start a new life somewhere. After Jacobsz deliberately steered the ship off course, the *Batavia* struck a reef close to the Houtman Abrolhos islands. Most passengers managed to get ashore, but on finding no fresh water Captain François Pelsaert, Jacobsz and other crew members set off to find help, eventually arriving at Batavia (modern-day Jakarta) 33 days later. Pelsaert was given a new ship with which to rescue those left on the island, but on his return found that Cornelisz had unleashed a bloody mutiny, killing 125 survivors. The wreck of the *Batavia* was salvaged in the 1970s, with many of the items on board now displayed in museums in **Geraldton** and **Fremantle**.

In the 1920s the remains of a castaway's camp were discovered on the clifftops between Kalbarri and Shark Bay, subsequently named the Zuytdorp Cliffs. The fate of the **Zuytdorp** survivors had been a 300-year-old mystery until a rare disease endemic among seventeenth-century Afrikaaners (ships en route to the Dutch East Indies routinely stopped in South Africa to stock up on provisions) was discovered in local Aborigines, which suggests that some of the castaways survived long enough to pass the gene on. Recent research has discredited this idea, but controversy surrounding the wreck remains, with various locals claiming its discovery between the 1920s and 1960s, and accusations of looting rife.

In modern times, the ship that has most interested WA is the **HMAS Sydney**, whose success in the early years of World War II was the source of much national pride. It was sunk in mysterious circumstances off the West Australian coast in 1941, after a confrontation with the *Kormoran*, a German merchant trader disguised as a Dutch ship. After decades of searching (and a bill of some $3.5 million), the ship was found 200km off Steep Point near Shark Bay on March 16, 2008, 22km away from the *Kormoran*. It made front-page news in Australia and finally granted some peace to the families of the 645-strong crew who were lost.

Geraldton Collection of 404 pieces is on permanent display here and includes some 90 drawings of the Geraldton area by local artist Elizabeth Durack.

ARRIVAL AND DEPARTURE
GERALDTON

By bus Integrity buses (ⓦ integritycoachlines.com.au) on the Perth–Broome line (twice weekly in each direction) and Transwa buses (ⓦ transwa.wa.gov.au) from Perth pull in at the old train station just down the road from the visitor centre.

Destinations Broome (2 weekly; 28hr 30min); Kalbarri (daily; 2hr 20min); Meekatharra (2 weekly; 7hr); New Norcia (3 weekly; 5hr); Perth (2 daily; 6hr–8hr 30min).

INFORMATION AND TOURS

Tourist information The helpful visitor centre on Marine Terrace (Mon–Fri 9am–5pm, Sat & Sun 9am–1pm; ☎ 08 9956 6674, ⓦ visitgeraldton.com.au), can help with

accommodation and tour bookings.

Tours Spectacular scenic flights and tours to Houtman Abrolhos (see opposite) depart from Geraldton.

ACCOMMODATION

Belair Gardens Tourist Park 463 Marine Tce ☎ 08 9921 1997 or ☎ 1800 240 938, ⓦ belairgardenscaravanpark .com.au. Small, slightly cramped site but with good facilities including a campers' kitchen and pool, and well situated next to beautiful Point Moore beach and lighthouse. Un/powered sites $30/34, chalets $110

Broadwater Mariner Resort 298 Chapman Rd ☎ 08 9965 9100 or ☎ 1800 181 480, ⓦ mariner.broadwaters. com.au. Lovely resort-style hotel arranged around a large

pool and BBQ area. Apartments have fully equipped kitchens complete with dishwasher and oven, two flat-screen TVs in the living area and bedroom and a separate bathroom. The smaller studios are much less expensive (from $185). $225

★ **Foreshore Backpackers** 172 Marine Tce ☎ 08 9921 3275, ⓦ foreshorebackpackers.com.au. Beautiful, rambling house right in the centre of town. Has great rooms with polished floorboards, retro furniture and potted plants, a funky lounge and a relaxed spirit imbued by the friendly young owner. Pick-ups from the bus station on request, and room rates come down if you stay more than one night. Dorms $35, doubles $75

Mantra 221 Foreshore Drive ☏08 9956 1300,

ⓦmantra.com.au. Down on the Foreshore, this stylish apartment hotel has a spa and pool area but is just 500m from the beach. Apartments (with one, two or three bedrooms) have full kitchens, a lounge and dining area and a laundry. Some also have harbour views. $199

EATING, DRINKING AND NIGHTLIFE

The Camel Bar 20 Chapman Road, ☏08 9965 5500, ⓦfacebook.com/thecamelbargeraldton. Proper Aussie tavern, popular with a young crowd who come for the poker, beers (there are more than 50 of them) and live music. Sun–Thurs 11am–10pm, Fri & Sat 11am–1am.

Freemasons Hotel 79 Marine Tce ☏08 9964 3457, ⓦthefreemasonshotel.wixsite.com/home. This lively pub often hosts live music and comedy and serves huge portions of pub food such as chicken parmigiana for $22 and burgers from $16. The wine list is Aussie-focused too. Mon–Tues 5.30–9pm, Wed & Thurs 11am–3pm & 5.30–9pm, Fri–Sun 11am–10pm.

The Provincial 167 Marine Tce ☏08 9964 1887. Great place for any-time-of-day eating with an extensive menu of breakfasts, local seafood lunches and delicious wood-fired pizzas (from $14). Lively in the evenings for

drinks too. Tues–Sat 4.30pm–midnight.

The Salt Dish 35 Marine Tce ☏08 9964 6030, ⓦfacebook.com/saltdishcafe. This cute and friendly café serves great coffees and cakes by day and a set menu of dishes such as pulled beef and crispy skinned barramundi by night (two courses $55). Gluten-free options available. Mon–Thurs 7am–4pm, Fri 7am–4pm & 6–11pm, Sat 6–11pm.

Skeetas 219 Foreshore Drive ☏08 9964 1619, ⓦskeetas.com.au. Bag a table on the seafront terrace and opt for the all-day menu's tasty seafood, which includes the catch of the day and local rock lobster ($45; 24hrs notice required). Meat and vegetarian dishes also available. Daily 11.30am–2.30pm & 5.30–9.30pm.

Houtman Abrolhos islands

Geraldton is the departure point for flights and boat trips to the **Houtman Abrolhos islands**, 60km offshore, and the cause of many a historic shipwreck. The 122 islands, spread over more than 100km, are renowned for their spectacular coral gardens and large breeding colonies of sea birds. There's no accommodation on the Abrolhos, but several companies offer scenic flights and some land on the islands for lunch and snorkelling; expect to pay upwards of $200.

TOURS	HOUTMAN ABROLHOS ISLANDS

Geraldton Air Charters ☏08 9923 3434, ⓦgeraldton aircharter.com.au. Short scenic tours over the islands, some with a landing for morning or afternoon tea ($215–260). Also half-day and full-day tours including snorkelling (equipment provided) and nature walks.

Kalbarri Scenic Flights ☏08 9937 1130, ⓦkalbarriair charter.com.au. A five-hour tour of the islands taking off from Kalbarri and including snorkelling, walking and refreshments ($255).

Kalbarri and around

Idyllic **KALBARRI** is one of the best of the west coast's resorts. With the dramatic scenery of Kalbarri National Park on its doorstep, it's a refreshing place to spend a day or so, with a good range of affordable quality accommodation and a host of activities on offer. Situated on the mouth of the Murchison River nearly 600km north of Perth, the town can be accessed via the coastal Port Gregory Road, which leaves Highway 1 at Northampton (105km), or from Ajana–Kalbarri Road, which heads west off the highway just north of Binnu (65km).

Entering Kalbarri via Ajana–Kalbarri Road, you can see exactly why its setting is so unique; rugged, gorge-scarred bush slides unexpectedly quickly into the mouth of the Murchison River, offering stunning views as you approach the town. The settlement itself is conveniently laid out along Grey Street, which runs from the **marina** along the river all the way to **Chinaman's Rock**, where big rollers break over the reef at the river mouth; just below the rock is the family-friendly **Chinaman's Beach**. The town's unmissable main attraction is the daily free **pelican feeding** (8.45am) on the Foreshore, which includes a discussion of these magnificent birds and the chance to throw fish into an enthusiastic gaggle of them.

Kalbarri National Park

Off Ajana–Kalbarri Rd • DPaW fee (see box, p.594) • ☎ 08 9937 1140, ⊕ dpaw.wa.gov.au

Kalbarri National Park has two distinct sections: the **coastal gorges** just south of Kalbarri, and the serpentine **river gorges** of the upper Murchison River to the east. It's typically ten degrees hotter in the river gorges than in Kalbarri, so take the necessary precautions.

Eleven kilometres east of Kalbarri on the Ajana–Kalbarri Road, a corrugated, wild-flower-flanked track turns north for 20km to the **river gorges** along the Murchison River, before reaching a T-junction where you can go a further 6km north to **Nature's Window** and **The Loop**, or 5km south to **Z Bend**. From the right-hand northern car park, a short track leads to Nature's Window, for superlative 360-degree views through the rock formation that forms the viewpoint. From here, you can continue on The Loop walk (8km; 3hr return; moderate) around a horseshoe bend in the Murchison River; if the heat or laziness prevails note that there's a lookout over The Loop at the left-hand car park. To the south, Z Bend lookout gives a real sense of how the river has shaped the land here, and the small birds zigzagging the gorge far below put its great size into perspective. From here, you can continue on a walk into the gorge itself (2.5km; 2hr return; moderate with some steep sections).

Back on Ajana–Kalbarri Road heading east, you come to the turn-off for Hawks Head and Ross Graham lookouts, both a few kilometres off the road, with river access at the latter; the views here are less impressive but worth a quick look.

At the time of writing a new Skywalk was being planned at the Inyaka Wookai Watju site on the West Loop. This promises two 100-metre-high walkways out over the gorge's rim and is planned to open in 2017.

ARRIVAL AND INFORMATION

KALBARRI AND AROUND

By bus The Transwa bus (⊕ transwa.wa.gov.au) from Perth pulls into town at 5pm Mon, Wed and Fri, stopping in the centre and at the visitor centre.

Tourist information The visitor centre is on the foreshore at Grey St (Mon–Sat 9am–5pm, Sun 9am–5pm, until 1pm in winter); ☎ 08 9937 1104, ⊕ kalbarriwa.info).

ACTIVITIES

Abseiling Abseil ($90) into the gorges of Kalbarri National Park with Kalbarri Abseil (☎ 08 9937 1618, ⊕ kalbarriabseil. com) on the half-day adventure tour.

Boat hire Various vessels from paddleboats and kayaks to powerboats can be rented for trips upriver with Kalbarri Boat Hire on Grey St (☎ 08 9937 1245, ⊕ kalbarriboathire.com). Prices start at $15/hour for a kayak, $60 for a dinghy. The outfit also runs half-day canoe safaris ($70, breakfast or lunch included).

Flights Kalbarri Scenic Flights (☎ 08 9390 0999, ⊕ kalbarriaircharter.com.au) offers six different scenic flights out of Kalbarri (from $84), from the short but spectacular Coastal Cliffs run (20min) to a six-hour visit to Monkey Mia or

full-day tour to the Houtman Abrolhos islands (see p.611).

Horseriding Big River Ranch (☎ 08 9937 1214, ⊕ bigriverranch.net) offers horseriding for beginners and experts in beautiful bush just 2km east of town on the Ajana–Kalbarri Rd. Tours run at 9am and 3pm daily ($85) and include an hour and a half in the saddle plus half an hour for preparation.

Sandboarding One of the most fun things you can do in Kalbarri — learn to surf the sand dunes, including the 8km-high "Superbowl" sand crater. Try it out with Kalbarri Sandboarding (☎ 08 9937 2377, ⊕ sandboardingaustralia. com.au). Morning tea is included but not lunch; bring your own ($80–95).

ACCOMMODATION

Anchorage Caravan Park Anchorage Lane ☎ 08 9937 1181, ⊕ kalbarrianchorage.com.au. A short walk from the centre at the marina end of town. Great pitches with tranquil river views, lots of shade, a good pool and a communal BBQ (Thurs). There are basic cabins too, some

with bathrooms. Powered sites $40, cabins $80

Blue Ocean Villas Auger St ☎ 1800 165 146, ⊕ blueoceanvillas.com.au. Six light, spacious two-bed apartments that are the size of a standard suburban house — the pick of the many apartments in Kalbarri in this price bracket. There's a small pool too. Seven-night minimum stay in peak season. $225

Gecko Lodge 9 Glass St ☎08 9937 1900, ⓦgeckolodgekalbarri.com.au. This stylish, modern B&B stands out amid the bland apartments and resorts in Kalbarri. A short walk from town, it has five supremely comfortable rooms and a nice pool. Nothing is too much trouble for guests, and afternoon tea as well as evening choccies and port are included. Rooms range from king and queen suites, some with two-person spa tubs, to the penthouse luxury apartment with separate kitchen and lounge. Adults only. $195

Kalbarri Backpackers 51 Mortimer St ☎08 9937 1430, ⓦyha.com.au. Clean and spacious if not overly atmospheric, with large, bright dorms, a pool and free snorkel and boogie-board rental. Bike rental Is also available and they'll drop you in the coastal section of the national park so you can cycle back. Dorms $26

Kalbarri Edge Resort 22 Porter St ☎08 9937 0000 or ☎1800 286 155, ⓦkalbarriedge.com.au. Generously proportioned and superbly well-equipped studios and apartments located in the heart of town and arranged around a pool. All rooms have deluxe bathrooms, wi-fi and flat-screen TVs; spa suites and apartments have a spa bath, large kitchens, private balconies with BBQs and their own laundry facilities. The on-site restaurant, *Edge*, specializes in local seafood and there's oversized chess by the pool. Studios $145, spa suites $160

Pelican Shore Villas Cnr Grey & Kaiber Sts ☎08 9937 1708 or ☎1800 671 708, ⓦpelicanshorevillas.com.au. The nicest of the many resort-style places in town – the spacious, well-kept apartments are centred around a pleasant pool, and the latticed verandas and many pot plants give it a cheery, welcoming air. Pricier rooms have ocean views. $196

EATING AND DRINKING

Black Rock Café 80 Grey St ☎08 9937 1062, ⓦblackrockcafe.com.au. Great pancake stacks for breakfast, gourmet salads for lunch and mod-Oz mains in the evening, including local crayfish and steak ($36). Licensed or BYO wine only ($6 corkage). Tues–Fri 5.30–9pm, Sat & Sun 7–11am and 5.30–9pm.

★ **Finlay's Fish BBQ** Magee Crescent ☎08 9937 1260, ⓦfinlaysfreshfishbbq.com. Don't leave Kalbarri without checking out this unique place. Choose from the bewildering array of seafood chalked up on the huge blackboard, and munch on fresh damper (wrapped in newspaper and served with your very own tub of butter) until your perfectly cooked fish ($35) comes off the BBQ. The guiding principles in this unusual indoor/outdoor setting are BYO and DIY; songs around the campfire and a nightly charity raffle add to the warm vibes. No corkage. Daily from 5pm.

Pelican's Café 94–96 Grey St ☎04 5813 2217. Stunning views over the Kalbarri waterfront and simple fresh meals, all also available to take away. The steak burger is $17. Fully licenced so no BYO. Desserts are especially good. Tues–Sat 8.30am–3pm and 6–9.30pm, Sun 8.30am–3pm.

The Coral Coast

The beautiful Coral Coast stretches from **Shark Bay**, an ecological and evolutionary hotspot of the highest order, up to the arid spike of land on which **Exmouth** and **Coral Bay** rest. People head here to see the stunning 260km **Ningaloo Reef** that fringes the western edge of the peninsula, never more than 7km offshore and in places accessible right from the beach. Increasing numbers head to the tiny, laidback resort of Coral Bay at the southern end of the reef, rather than basing themselves in sterile Exmouth, near the tip of the peninsula.

Aside from viewing the reef, people flock here for the rare opportunity to swim with the world's largest fish, the **whale shark** (see box, p.619), which feeds in the area between April and July each year, as well as with humpback whales. In between Shark Bay and Exmouth is **Carnarvon**, a good base for exploring the exhilarating 4WD track north to *Gnaraloo Station* (see p.618), past wild beaches and tumultuous seas.

Shark Bay

Shark Bay is the name given to the two prongs of land and their corresponding lagoons situated west of *Overlander Roadhouse* on Highway 1. **Denham**, the only settlement, is on the western side of the eastern Peron Peninsula, while at **Monkey Mia** on the sheltered eastern side, bottlenose dolphins have been coming up to the beach almost daily since the 1960s. Shark Bay was **World Heritage** listed in 1991; this remarkable place qualifies

6

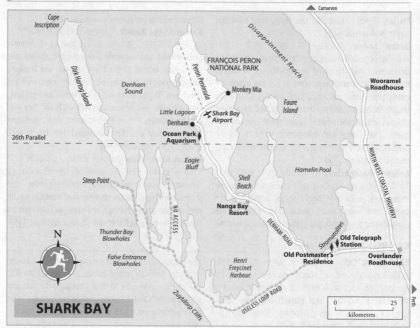

SHARK BAY

under no fewer than four of UNESCO's "natural" criteria. Note that fresh water is very precious in the Shark Bay area: salty bore water is used as much as possible.

Ocean Park Aquarium

1 Ocean Park Rd • Tours daily 9am–5pm • $25 • ☎ 08 9948 1765, ⓦ oceanpark.com.au

This world-class aquarium offers a good introduction to the marine life of Shark Bay, allowing visitors to see baby sea turtles, stingrays and sharks on the obligatory guided tour, which is led by a marine biologist. Every tour includes shark feeding and those feeling brave can sign up for the Shark Dive Experience (from $200), which lets you scuba with the sharks in the aquarium's lagoon.

Western peninsula

The **western peninsula**, accessed by Useless Loop Road 43km west of the *Overlander*, ends at **Steep Point**, mainland Australia's westernmost spot. There's much to see en route, including blowholes, sheltered white beaches and the endless Zuytdorp Cliffs – a 4WD is required, and you'll need to be able to deflate and re-inflate your tyres to make it over some soft dunes. There are no facilities at all down this peninsula, so come prepared – call the ranger (☎ 08 9948 3993, ⓦ steeppoint.com.au) ahead of arrival for instructions.

Dirk Hartog Island

March–Oct • ☎ 08 9948 1211, ⓦ dirkhartogisland.com

South Passage separates Steep Point from **Dirk Hartog Island**, which offers good snorkelling, scuba diving, fishing and walking, as well as the unique experience that is setting foot on Cape Inscription, where Dutch captain Dirk Hartog left an inscribed plate in 1616. The *Eco Lodge* (see p.616) is the only accommodation on the island and transport is arranged through them on booking. There are air transfers from Shark Bay airport, boat transfers from Denham and a landing barge for 4WD vehicles. If you want to explore the island fully, you'll need to bring your own 4WD and use the barge.

Hamelin Pool

From the North West Coastal Highway, a road leads 5km north to the **Old Telegraph Station**, **Old Postmaster's Residence** and **Hamelin Pool**. The pool is home to a community of **stromatolites**, colonies of sediment-trapping algae that are direct descendants of the earth's earliest life forms, dating back over three billion years – you'll find similar examples only in the Bahamas and the Persian Gulf. It is their ancestors we can thank for diligently oxygenating the earth's atmosphere, which eventually led to more complex life forms. Viewed from a boardwalk behind the Old Postmaster's Residence, the examples in Hamelin Pool flourish because no predators can handle the pool's hyper-saline water. The Old Postmaster's Residence houses a café and you can enquire here about camping, as well as tours of the Old Telegraph Station opposite.

6

Shell Beach

Heading out onto the Peron Peninsula towards Denham, you'll pass *Nanga Bay Resort* (see p.616) on the left. Across the isthmus is stunning **Shell Beach**, composed entirely of millions of tiny bivalve cardiid cockle shells – one of only two such beaches in the world. The shells lie up to 10m deep, and have consolidated under their own weight. The mass is cut into blocks to restore local buildings – you can see the shell brick quarry in Shark Bay at Hamelin Pool.

Eagle Bluff

Twenty kilometres before Denham, **Eagle Bluff** is an impressive clifftop lookout with views of Dirk Hartog Island. The shallow green waters of Denham Sound and Henri Freycinet Harbour, below the bluff, are perfect for spotting dolphins, manta rays and even dugongs – some ten to twelve thousand, or around ten percent of the world's dugong population, live in Shark Bay, attracted here by the plentiful supply of their favourite snack, sea grass.

Denham

A small ex-pearling town and holiday resort, **DENHAM** is arranged along the breezy seafront Knight Terrace and has more amenities than the resort at Monkey Mia (see p.616), with its main strip hosting a couple of small **supermarkets** and a petrol station.

The **Shark Bay Discovery Centre and Visitor Centre** on Knight Terrace (Mon–Fri 9am–5pm, Sat & Sun 10am–4pm; $11 for discovery centre; ☎08 9948 1590, ⓦsharkbayvisit.com.au) is well worth an hour of your time. This innovative facility about all things Shark Bay has displays arranged geographically on the floor, creating a 3D multimedia map of the area.

Four kilometres out of Denham along Monkey Mia Road is **Little Lagoon**, which is filled with clear turquoise waters and fringed by a narrow strip of white sand; when the wind gets up here it's ideal for windsurfing (though you have to bring your own equipment).

François Peron National Park

DPaW fee (see box, p.594) • ☎08 9948 1208, ⓦdpaw.wa.gov.au

Just past Little Lagoon is the access way for **François Peron National Park**, at the northern tip of the peninsula. Named after the naturalist on *Le Geographe*, which sailed past in 1801, the park's clear waters, red dunes and sandy beaches are entrancing, while marine wildlife can be spotted from **Cape Peron**, and the fishing opportunities are second to none. **Peron Homestead**, a former sheep station, is just 8km off the Denham–Monkey Mia road and usually accessible by 2WD – the hot tub of artesian water here is great for any aches and pains acquired on your travels. The park is also paradise for four-wheel drivers – a sturdy high-clearance vehicle is needed to go beyond the homestead. There's no drinking water or fuel here; make sure you have enough of both for the 130km return trip to Denham from the park.

6

Monkey Mia

DPaW day-fee $12pp, month $18 (park passes do not apply)

After all the hype, you might be surprised to find that **Monkey Mia** is just a resort and a jetty by a pretty beach. It's to this beach that scores of people flock to see the almost daily visits by between five and ten adult female **dolphins** and their attendant calves, all known by name. Get here at 7.30am to watch the first feeding at around 8am. There are usually another two feeds per day, always before noon, to encourage the dolphins to spend the afternoon foraging for food in the bay – these two later feeds can be a better option if you don't want to fight your way through the excitable crowds standing in the shallows.

ARRIVAL AND INFORMATION

SHARK BAY

By plane Skippers (☎ 1300 729 924, ✆ skippers.com.au) fly to Shark Bay airport from Perth five times a week, returning via Carnarvon.

By bus Integrity buses (✆ integritycoachlines.com.au) on the Perth–Exmouth route stop at *Overlander Roadhouse* twice weekly (Wed and Fri), where they are met by shuttle

services on to Denham and Monkey Mia – contact Shark Bay Shuttle to arrange (☎ 08 9948 3032).

Tourist information The visitor information centre is within the Shark Bay Discovery Centre on Knight Terrace in Denham (Mon–Fri 9am–5pm, Sat & Sun 10am–4pm; ☎ 08 9948 1590, ✆ sharkbayvisit.com.au).

TOURS

Shark Bay is a hub for tours and activities. Many excursions are based in or depart from Monkey Mia; check when you book and note that pick-ups are often available. With luck, on most water-based tours you'll see plenty of marine life, including dolphins, rays and dugongs.

Monkey Mia Wildsights ☎ 08 9948 1481 or ☎ 1800 241 481, ✆ monkeymiawildsights.com.au. Offers 4WD tours around François Peron National Park (8hr; $195) and three-hour wildlife cruises to see bottlenose dolphins, green turtles and loggerhead turtles plus dugong and stingrays in season ($99).

Perfect Nature Cruises ☎ 08 9948 1446 or ☎ 1800 030 427, ✆ monkey-mia.net. Gentle cruises along the coastline

of François Peron national park aboard the catamaran *Aristocat 2* with the added thrill of boom-netting ($249).

Shark Bay Scenic Flights ☎ 08 9948 1773, ✆ sharkbayair.com.au. Scenic flights over the area ranging from a 15min flight over Monkey Mia and the Peron Homestead ($59), to flights over the Zuytdorp Cliffs and full-day trips up to Coral Bay and inland to Mount Augustus ($755 including lunch).

ACCOMMODATION AND EATING

DIRK HARTOG ISLAND

Eco Lodge The Homestead ☎ 08 9948 1211, ✆ dirkhartogisland.com. Get away from it all on Dirk Hartog Island and stay in the original limestone shearers' quarters. Ocean rooms have a double and a single bed and are en-suite. The Ocean Villa sleeps up to seven people and has three bedrooms and a living area with kitchenette. It's also possible to camp (from $19). $435

HAMELIN POOL AND AROUND

Nanga Bay Resort Nanga Bay ☎ 08 9948 3992, ✆ nangabayresort.com.au. Laidback park on Nanga Bay with a wide selection of accommodation, including sites, dorms, motel rooms, cabins and villas. There's an outdoor swimming pool, restaurant, bottle shop and boat ramp too. Un/powered sites $25/30, doubles $165, cabins $90

DENHAM

Bay Lodge Knight Tce ☎ 08 9948 1278 or 1800 812 780, ✆ baylodge.info. A fairly ramshackle but homely

backpackers', with a scattering of random furniture, a large outdoor communal kitchen and a sun-baked pool area. There's a free shuttle to Monkey Mia and free airport transfers too. Dorms $30, doubles $80, motel units $110

Old Pearler Knight Tce ☎ 08 9948 1373. This adorable little restaurant is made from local shell block and has an interior straight out of rural France. The menu focuses on seafood with garlic prawns and chilli squid $17. Daily 5–9pm.

Seaside Tourist Village Knight Tce ☎ 08 9948 1242, ✆ sharkbayfun.com. The best of Denham's three caravan parks, opening onto a small beach and with pleasant wooded pitches – the ground is very hard though, so tent campers may struggle. Un/powered sites $36.50/45, cabins $100, villas $160

Tradewinds Holiday Village Knight Tce ☎ 08 9948 1222, ✆ tradewindsdenham.com.au. Comfortable and welcoming apartment complex, run by the lovely Fay and Trevor. The self-contained one- and two-bed apartments

6

are great value and have more kitchen equipment than most homes – not to mention gorgeous ocean views. **$145**

MONKEY MIA

Monkey Mia Dolphin Resort ☎ 08 9948 1320 or ☎ 1800 653 611, ⓦ monkeymia.com.au. Arranged along the beautiful beach to the left of the dolphin interaction zone, this resort is the only place to stay in Monkey Mia. It's quite basic by resort standards, though its isolated location should make you more than grateful for its comfortable rooms, counter meals and small pool. Staying in a beachfront unit here is a real treat and there are few better experiences than strolling across the sand for a sunset swim with the dolphins or eating on your terrace as an emu wanders past. Dorms **$35**, doubles **$260**

Carnarvon and around

CARNARVON is a service town for prawning fleets and the sheep stations of the Upper Gascoyne region, located just over 900km from Perth and 200km north of the turn-off to Shark Bay. The town also supports a large agricultural zone, thanks to the superficially dry Gascoyne River's retrievable subterranean water, and is popular with fruit pickers. The town has had a bad reputation in the past due to its proclivity for drunken violence, but it's actually a pretty easy-going place to stock up and spend a night, and those expecting a brawl will most likely be disappointed.

A pleasant hour or two can be spent moseying around Carnarvon's **Heritage Precinct** on Babbage Island (free; ⓦ carnarvonheritage.com.au), which is reached from the end of Robinson Street, the main strip, via a footbridge and old railway track. The precinct contains a number of gentle things to do, including a trip along the One Mile Jetty on foot (daily, $5) or aboard the tiny *Coffee Pot* train (April–Nov daily 9am–4pm; $10); the Lighthouse Keeper's Cottage Museum (daily 10am–1pm; donation), an eclectic range of old vehicles; and the water-tower lookout, for 360-degree views of the town and Gascoyne River.

ARRIVAL AND INFORMATION

CARNARVON

By plane Skippers (☎ 1300 729 924, ⓦ skippers.com.au) fly to Carnarvon airport from Perth once or twice daily, sometimes via Monkey Mia.

By bus Integrity buses (ⓦ integritycoachlines.com.au) on the Perth–Exmouth route arrive at the visitor centre on Wednesday and Friday mornings on their way north, and Friday and Sunday afternoons on the route south.

Tourist information Carnarvon's helpful visitor centre is in the Civic Centre, cnr Robinson St & Camel Lane (Mon–Fri 9am–5pm, Sat & Sun 9am–noon, closed Sundays Nov–April; ☎ 08 9941 1146, ⓦ carnarvon.org.au).

ACCOMMODATION AND EATING

Best Western Hospitality Inn 6 West St ☎ 08 9941 1600, ⓦ carnarvon.wa.hospitalityinns.com.au. Standard motel rooms with rather dated decor arranged around a nice pool. There's also a free guest laundry, BBQ facilities and plenty of free parking. **$159**

Coral Coast Tourist Park 108 Robinson St ☎ 08 9941 1438, ⓦ coralcoasttouristpark.com.au. Large grassy campsites as well as a range of cabins to suit all budgets, all with kitchenettes and some with en-suite bathrooms. There's also a camper's kitchen and a laundry. Powered sites **$43**, en-suite sites **$52**, cabins **$99**

North to Gnaraloo Station

The awe-inspiring 150km run up to *Gnaraloo Station* is best done in one go. Starting 24km north of town, the sealed Blowholes Road heads 41km west to a T-junction with a sign bearing the legend "King Waves Kill"; take note before viewing the **Blowholes** at Point Quobba, just to the left. On all but the calmest days, incoming waves compress air through vents in the craggy coastline and erupt noisily up to 20m into the air. The road north from here is unsealed and a 4WD is required. Continuing over a couple of private roads belonging to the Dampier Saltworks (watch out for road trains), you'll come to a signed turn-off which heads down a rocky track to spectacular **Red Bluff**, a broad sweep of white sand with some of the craziest surf you'll ever see.

Departing Red Bluff, you move on to windy, sun-bleached *Gnaraloo Station*. You'll pass a stunning lagoon-side camping spot at **Three Mile Camp** before you reach the homestead, which boasts enticing, ramshackle accommodation, world-class wave-sailing and mesmerizing views. Seven kilometres beyond the homestead are the turquoise waters of deserted, tranquil **Gnaraloo Bay**, perfect for snorkelling and a spot of skinny-dipping.

ACCOMMODATION

NORTH TO GNARALOO STATION

Gnaraloo Homestead ☎ 08 9315 4809, ⓦ gnaraloo .com.au. A slightly mind-boggling range of accommodation is available at this homestead, including swag shelters, dorm-style group accommodation and basic cabins in all shapes and sizes. Some are en-suite, others share ablutions blocks. Unpowered sites per person **$20**, dorms (for four people) **$150**, cabins **$120**

Quobba Station ☎ 08 9948 5098, ⓦ quobba.com.au. A variety of accommodation on an old sheep station, including dorm beds in the Shearers Quarters, shacks with kitchens, diners, communal bathrooms and power from the generator (9/10 hours a day), and powered campsites. Un/ powered sites per person **$13/16**, dorms **$27**, shacks per person **$37** (minimum two people)

Coral Bay

The Northwest Cape Road, turning a few kilometres past *Minilya Roadhouse* 140km north of Carnarvon, leads to beautiful **CORAL BAY**, an idyllic spot from which to enjoy Ningaloo Reef. The tiny, laidback community stretches for little more than 200m along each side of the main road and the stunning sandy beach is the town's defining feature. Just north of town, reef sharks gather in season (Oct–March) at Skeleton Beach, while just south there's good snorkelling at Purdy Point and beach-lounging spots on Paradise Beach. Hot, salty bore water and a lack of available land have kept tourism fairly low-key, and the resort remains far less developed than the other gateway to the reef, Exmouth (see p.620).

ARRIVAL AND DEPARTURE

CORAL BAY

By bus Integrity buses (ⓦ integritycoachlines.com.au) on the twice-weekly Perth–Broome route call at the *Ningaloo*

Club (Wed and Fri northbound, Fri and Sun southbound).

SWIMMING WITH WHALE SHARKS AND HUMPBACKS

There are few experiences in life more memorable than swimming with a whale shark, the world's largest fish, and Ningaloo is one of only a limited number of places worldwide where they appear with any regularity – and in easily accessible waters.

It is the mass spawning of more than 200 species of coral every March or April that brings the whale sharks here and sightings are common until July. Interaction with these gentle giants (the juvenile males seen here can measure up to 12 metres long) is strictly regulated, with only one boat allowed to operate within the exclusive contact zone of 250 metres around each whale shark at any one time and just 10 swimmers in the water at once. This keeps both the whale shark itself and your interaction with it calm and relaxed – you won't be surrounded by too many other people. You will need to be a competent swimmer and can expect to be in and out of the water all day.

Nothing can prepare you for the utter delight of swimming alongside a fish the size of a bus, and with your eyes and ears in the water all else is blocked out until you emerge from this otherworldly experience. If you are in Exmouth during whale shark season this is absolutely not to be missed.

Note too that as of 2016 humpback whale swimming tours are also available. At the time of writing this was a fledgling operation in its first season, so it's best to check with the operators for more details.

TOUR OPERATORS

There are numerous tour operators running trips out from Exmouth (see p.621) and a few based in Coral Bay too (see p.620). Some have their own spotter planes to increase the likelihood of finding a whale shark and all will equip you with masks, snorkel and fins, plus a wetsuit.

6

TOURS AND ACTIVITIES

Coastal Adventure Tours ☎08 9948 5190, ⓦcoralbaytours.com.au. Offers short sailing trips by catamaran, as well as snorkelling, quad biking and manta ray viewing tours and a range of combo packages. Tours run daily and last from a few hours to a full day ($75–210) and you can combine several over multiple days too.

Coral Bay Ecotours ☎08 9942 5885, ⓦcoralbayecotours.com.au. Glass-bottomed boat tours and snorkelling plus a range of all-terrain vehicle trips on the beach are offered year-round, plus there are whale shark and humpback swimming tours ($41–395) in season, roughly Aug–Oct. The full-day Marine Ecotour goes in search of manta rays to swim with ($175).

Ningaloo Experience ☎08 9942 5877, ⓦningaloo experience.com. Ecofriendly wildlife excursions by small boat, including tours through the turtle grounds plus whale shark and humpback swims when in season. The half-day Outer Reef Experience is a good option for seeing everything from manta rays to humpbacks. Tours range from $75 to $395 and there are fishing charters too.

★**Sail Ningaloo** ☎1800 197 194, ⓦsailningaloo .com.au. Luke and Lannie run all-inclusive sailing holidays on board a luxurious catamaran, *Shore Thing*, for a maximum of ten guests. Activities include snorkelling, diving, kayaking and fishing. The catamaran's design means it can get into shallow reef lagoons and the remote reaches of Ningaloo to which few have access. You're sure to see plenty of marine life on this tour – and the food is superb too. From $1700 for a three-day tour.

ACCOMMODATION

Bayview Coral Bay Robinson St ☎08 9385 6655, ⓦcoralbaywa.com. This campsite-turned-resort has pleasant sandy pitches, a pool and tennis courts. There are also cabins, chalets and villas, all with kitchens and air conditioning. Un/powered sites $41/46, cabins $130

Bullara Station Minilya Exmouth Rd ☎08 9942 5938, ⓦbullara-station.com.au. Out of town on the highway, this working cattle and sheep station is a great choice for those seeking to combine the reef with an authentic Outback experience. There are unpowered campsites plus a range of cheery, comfortable rooms in the Shearer's Lodge, which share the outdoor bathroom. There's also a communal fire pit, basic camp kitchen and the *Bull Bar* dining area. Un/powered sites per person $14/24, doubles $140

Ningaloo Club Robinson St, Coral Bay ☎08 9385 6655 (advance room bookings), ☎08 9948 5100 (dorm bookings and this week's availability), ⓦningalooclub .com. This cheery, purpose-built hostel has dorms sleeping from four to ten and double rooms, some of which are en-suite. Facilities include table tennis and a pool table. There's also a central courtyard around a pool. Dorms $29, doubles $95

Ningaloo Reef Resort Robinson St ☎08 9942 5934 or ☎1800 795 522, ⓦningalooreefresort.com.au. This is a lively resort of motel units and apartments popular with young travellers. Rooms are of a good standard, with air conditioning, kitchenettes, TVs and decent bathrooms, and there's a nice swimming pool with views of the beach. The bar has a pleasant outdoor courtyard, which is perfect for enjoying laidback evenings. $220

EATING AND DRINKING

Bill's on the Ningaloo Reef Robinson St ☎08 9385 6655. The best of a limited bunch of places to eat is this pub, which is a cut above the rest. Simple, seafood-focused meals such as fish and chips, oysters, Exmouth prawns and fish curry start at $18. There's live music most evenings too. Daily from 11am.

Fin's Café People's Park Shopping Village, Robinson St ☎08 9942 5900. This popular café serves breakfast and lunch but is particularly busy in the evenings when dinner is served on a terrace strewn with fairy lights. The menu has an international flavour and dishes include smoked kangaroo ($34). Daily 8am–9pm.

Shades Ningaloo Reef Resort, Robinson St ☎08 9942 5934. The on-site café at *Ningaloo Reef Resort* serves up a menu of simple meals including burgers, salads and local fish including Exmouth prawn skewers ($28) and grilled local snapper ($37). Daily 7.30am–9pm.

Exmouth

EXMOUTH is a purpose-built community, created in 1967 as a support centre for the former joint Australian–US Navy Communications Station. Consequently, the town itself has little of interest to visitors, but it is an excellent base for both the Cape Range National Park and the wonderful Ningaloo Marine Park, both located around the North West Cape from the town, on the western coast. To explore the area beyond Exmouth, you really need your own vehicle, but there are also plenty of tours departing from here.

Bundegi Beach

Heading north out of town past Yardie Creek Road (the turn-off for Cape Range and Ningaloo) and the navy base you come to **Bundegi Beach**, set right below some ugly navy antennae. It's still nicer than the town beaches, though, and there's a dark platform of **coral** a couple of hundred metres offshore, so bring a snorkel.

Lighthouse Bay

A turn-off from Yardie Creek Road leads to **Lighthouse Bay** and the wreck of the SS *Mildura* cattle ship, which clipped the reef in 1907 during a cyclone. Visit at low tide to see its vast hulk lying marooned in the waters just offshore – it was used for Allied bombing practice during World War II. At the very tip of the cape, on a headland watching over it all, is **Vlamingh Head Lighthouse**, built in 1912. The lookout here offers sweeping views of the surrounding area and of the Muiron Islands to the northeast. This is an especially popular sunset spot but it also has the distinction of being one of the few places in Australia where you can watch the sun both rise and set.

6

ARRIVAL AND INFORMATION EXMOUTH

By plane There are daily flights to Learmonth airport from Perth with Qantas (ⓦqantas.com.au). The airport is 36km from Exmouth; Exmouth Bus Charter buses (ⓣ08 9949 4623, ⓦexmouthbuscharters.com.au) meet all incoming flights and will drop you at your accommodation. Coral Coast Tours (ⓣ0427 180 568, ⓦcoralcoasttours.com.au) will take you to Coral Bay. Book in advance. All the main car-hire companies are also represented here.
By bus Integrity buses (ⓦintegritycoachlines.com.au)

heading from Perth to Broome (or vice versa) pull in at the visitor centre in the middle of town (Wed and Fri northbound, Fri and Sun southbound).
Tourist information The visitor centre (daily 9am–5pm, Nov–March Sun only until 1pm; ⓣ08 9949 1176, ⓦexmouthwa.com.au) is on Murat Rd opposite *Ningaloo Caravan Holiday Resort* (see p.622), and can book accommodation and tours. The DPaW office is on Nimitz St (Mon–Fri 8am–5pm; ⓣ08 9947 8000).

TOURS AND ACTIVITIES

There are plenty of trips you can take from Exmouth, notably swimming with whale sharks from April through July (see box, p.619). Expect to pay around $400 to get up close to these gentle giants, and make sure you have enough time to wait around for sightings. Tours can be booked direct, through the visitor centre or at most accommodation.

Capricorn Sea Kayaking ⓣ0427 485 123, ⓦcapricornseakayaking.com.au. Half-day, full-day and multiday tours that combine sea-kayaking and snorkelling on the reef ($99–1750; April–Oct). On multiday tours accommodation is at a base camp and all gear is provided.
Ningaloo Ecology Cruises ⓣ08 9949 2255, ⓦglassbottomboat.com.au. Super-enthusiastic Alek takes groups of snorkellers out onto the reef in a glass-bottomed boat for four and a half hours of coral viewing ($80), explaining the ecology of the area and pointing out tropical fish, turtles and sharks along the way. Don't ask him for his tiger shark story until you're safely on the boat back to shore.
Ningaloo Whale Sharks ⓣ1800 994 210, ⓦningaloowhalesharks.com. A range of short diving and snorkelling tours, including diving at the Exmouth Navy Pier and swimming with whale sharks and humpback

whales when in season ($70–390). There are also accredited training courses in everything from scuba diving to night diving and underwater photography.
★**Ocean Eco Adventures** ⓣ08 9949 1208, ⓦoceanecoadventures.com.au. Thanks to their exclusive spotter plane, whale shark sightings on Ocean Eco Adventures' one-day tours ($410) are almost guaranteed. You'll be in and out of the water with them, as well as manta rays, turtles and other marine life. A DVD of your experience is included and lunch is a feast of local gourmet produce including fresh Exmouth prawns.
Three Islands Whale Shark Dive ⓣ08 9949 1994, ⓦwhalesharkdive.com. This passionate company focuses on memorable whale shark snorkel tours with experienced skippers ($385; March–July). A videographer records your day and a complimentary DVD is included.

ACCOMMODATION

Exmouth Cape Holiday Park 3 Truscott Crescent ⓣ1800 871 570, ⓦbig4.com.au. This site, 1.5km south of town, boasts a great campers' kitchen, spotless amenities, an average pool and large shady pitches,

though unpowered sites are stuffed into an unshaded corner. Cabins and units range from basic and bathroomless to deluxe en suites. Un/powered sites $38/53, cabins $131

6

Ningaloo Caravan and Holiday Resort Murat Rd ☎ 08 9949 2377, ⊛ exmouthresort.com. A similar standard to *Exmouth Cape* but with a better pool, nicer unpowered sites and a separate backpackers' known as *Winston's*. Backpacker rooms are good and chalets pleasant and very clean, with wicker furniture and decent kitchens. It is a large site, so can feel empty in low season. Un/powered sites $30/32, doubles $84, chalets $205

★ **Novotel Ningaloo Resort** Madaffari Drive, Marina ☎ 08 9949 0000, ⊛ novotelningaloo.com.au. In a spectacular setting overlooking Sunrise Beach on the outskirts of town, this chic resort hotel has a large outdoor swimming pool and Exmouth's best restaurant (see below).

Rooms have large private balconies (some with sea views), vast beds and opulent bathrooms complete with spa baths – pull back the shutters and you can even watch TV in the bath. $295

Potshot Hotel Resort Murat Rd ☎ 08 9949 1200, ⊛ potshotresort.com and ⊛ yha.com.au. Sprawling resort at the top end of town, with standard en-suite dorms, a scruffy lounge and a good outdoor communal area in the backpackers' section. There are also simple motel-style rooms and self-contained apartments with kitchens, as well as a swimming pool, bottle shop, restaurant and *The Vance Bar* (see below). Discounts for multi-night stays. Dorms $36, backpacker rooms $88, apartments $245

EATING AND DRINKING

There are the usual takeaways, cafés and a bog-standard Chinese restaurant in the shopping centre near Maidstone Crescent, which also has a decent-sized IGA supermarket.

The Bbqfather Murat Rd ☎ 08 9949 4905, ⊛ thebbqfather.com.au. Run by husband and wife team Sabrina and Salvatore, *The Bbqfather* has an attractive outdoor dining terrace and offers home-made Italian food, as well as abundant local seafood and BBQs. Chicken parma is $28, brisket $25. Daily 6–9pm.

Mantaray's Novotel Ningaloo Resort, Madaffari Drive, Marina ☎ 08 9949 0000, ⊛ novotelningaloo.com.au. The town's top pick by a long stretch; mains start at $26 but for that you can expect the likes of fresh Exmouth prawns cooked in garlic ($39) and perfectly grilled eye fillet steak ($43) served in classy surroundings either inside or out by the pool. Try the soft-shell crab to start ($24) and don't miss the oysters. An abundant buffet breakfast is also served. Daily 6.30am–late.

The Vance Bar Potshot Hotel Resort, Murat Rd ☎ 08 9949 1200, ⊛ potshotresort.com. The large bar at the *Potshot Resort* (known to locals as "the Potty"), *The Vance* was named after the cyclone that destroyed it in 1999 and has pool tables and a jukebox. There's also a larger back section with an outdoor terrace that becomes a nightclub on Fridays and Saturdays. This is the best place in town for a drink and has a raucous but fun atmosphere. Daily 10am–midnight.

Whalers Restaurant Kennedy St ☎ 08 9949 2416, ⊛ whalersrestaurant.com.au. This laidback restaurant serves up tasty food with a local vibe, including Exmouth prawns, WA mussels and kangaroo loin. Fish of the day comes beer-battered for $29; seafood spaghetti is $38. Daily from 5.30pm.

Cape Range National Park and Ningaloo Marine Park

The waters offshore of the **Cape Range National Park** are truly enticing. Part of the **Ningaloo Marine Park** (see box below), the area harbours all manner of marinelife and offers the chance to swim with humpback whales, whale sharks and manta rays. Spend time reclining on sublime white-sand beaches or taking a dip in the pristine bays and lagoons.

NINGALOO MARINE PARK

Ningaloo Marine Park protects **Ningaloo Reef**, the world's largest fringing reef and Australia's most accessible – simply step off the white sands of the beach and float over the coral gardens. Ningaloo Reef runs for 300 kilometres from Bundegi Reef in the Exmouth gulf, along the shores of Cape Range National Park and all the way down to Red Bluff (see p.618), just north of Carnarvon. It extends for some 10 nautical miles out to sea and covers more than 5000 square kilometres of ocean. It is the proximity of the continental shelf that gives this marine park such a stunning variety of marine life: more than 700 species of fish and 250 species of coral have been recorded here, attracting migrating humpback whales and whale sharks, plus numerous turtles, reef sharks and rays. There are few better places in Australia – if not the world – for snorkelling to see marine life.

Turquoise Bay and the Oyster Stacks

One of the best spots for snorkelling along the Cape coast is **Turquoise Bay**, where the so-called "drift snorkel" floats you across 200m of colourful coral: drop your clothes by the sand bar, enter the water at the southern end of the beach and hop out in time to pick up your clothes. This should only be attempted at low- to mid-tide by competent swimmers due to the strong currents and you must not swim past the sand bar.

Another prime snorkelling site is at **Oyster Stacks** slightly further south, where legions of colourful fish huddle under the archways created by several shelly protrusions – the coral is so close to the surface here that you can only snorkel at high tide.

6

Yardie Creek

The final stop in the park for most will be **Yardie Creek**, approximately 91km in total from Exmouth without detours. Walks from Yardie Creek include a gentle nature trail (1.2km return; 40min) along the edge of the creek, which leads into the surprisingly steep gorge trail (2km return total; 2hr). This is a fantastic place to spot rock wallabies, camouflaged in the craggy cliffs.

ARRIVAL AND INFORMATION
CAPE RANGE NATIONAL PARK

By car The park entry station is located on Yardie Creek Road, about a 35-minute drive round the cape from Exmouth. You'll need your own car or a tour here.

Tourist information You'll need to pay a DPaW fee (see box, p.594) for access to the park. The Milyering Visitor Centre, just after the T-Bone Bay turn-off (daily 9am–3.45pm; ☎08 9949 2808), has displays on the parks and tide times. Book the Yardie Creek boat cruise here (daily 11am & 12.30pm; 1hr 15min; $35, ⓦ yardiecreekboattours.com.au).

ACCOMMODATION

Camping Numerous idyllic camping spots line the coast: the best are at *Osprey Bay*, with swimming in the milky waters of adjacent Sandy Bay and good vantage points for sunsets or whale watching; and *Ned's Camp*, where there's a lovely sandy beach. You can't book ahead for any of the campsites in the park, which have toilets but no other facilities. Check availability at the park entrance or the DPaW in Exmouth (see p.621), and pay the fee ($10pp) at the park entrance or to the campsite host where available.

★**Sal Salis Ningaloo Reef** Yardie Creek Road ☎08 9949 1776, ⓦ salsalis.com.au. "Camping" doesn't get more luxurious than this. *Sal Salis Ningaloo Resort* is an exclusive safari camp of luxury tents hidden in the white dunes near Mandu Mandu Gorge. The "tents" are more like canvas five-star hotel rooms, with handmade jarrah beds, 500-threadcount sheets and solar-heated showers. The ecofriendly philosophy means that there is no electricity for guest use and a limited amount of water issued per person per day, but the lush sunsets, contemporary Australian cuisine and roaming wildlife make for a stay to remember. There are excellent guided snorkels, swims and walks, all tailored to suit your needs – including whale shark and humpback whale swims ($500). Two-night minimum stay. $1500

The Central Midlands – inland to the Pilbara

About 1000km north of Perth are the ancient, mineral-rich highlands of the **Pilbara**, an area that includes Mount Meharry, at 1249m the highest point in WA. The world's richest surface deposits of **iron ore** were mined here in the 1950s and rich discoveries of ore, crude oil, natural gas and salt continue to be made as private railroads cart the booty to the coast for export to the hungry markets in Japan and China. As a result, company towns such as **Tom Price** and **Newman** abound, offering little to travellers except mine tours and overpriced accommodation. While the Pilbara is unquestionably the economic powerhouse of the state (and indeed the nation), the unquenchable growth of the mining industries has had knock-on effects throughout the region. Chronic housing shortages plague many towns, **Karratha** and **Port Hedland** in particular, and hotels and hostels are often bought up by companies desperate to house their staff, though the recent slowdown in the mining industry has abated this somewhat, with prices falling across the area. Surrounding the huge open-cast mine sites are vast, arid pastoral stations, recovering from or surrendering to overgrazing. In the middle of all this environmental chaos **Karijini National Park** serenely remains, safeguarding some of Australia's most spectacular and timeless natural scenery. Up the coast, **Cossack** and **Point Samson** offer respite from the relentless heat and mining mentality.

The Great Northern Highway

6

Apart from the passage through the Hamersley Ranges north of Newman, scenically there's little to commend the **Great Northern Highway**'s 1649km inland section from Perth to Port Hedland. But like the famed Nullarbor, the monotony can have its own fascination as you pass from the wooded farmlands northward into ever more marginal sheep country, until the only viable commodity is the mineral riches below ground.

Cue

Among the half-dozen surviving towns along this inland route, semi-abandoned **CUE**, 659km north of Perth, retains some character from the gold-rush era and is a good place to stretch your legs. The **visitor centre** on the main strip, Austin Street, has information on the Cue Heritage Trail and sights around town, including the Aboriginal rock paintings at **Walga Rock**, 48km west of town.

Meekatharra

North of Cue the landscape outruns the south's rain-bearing fronts, scrub replaces the trees, and games of "count the roadkill" reach high double figures. **MEEKATHARRA**, 115km to the north, is a mining and pastoral centre with some century-old **hotels** such as the *Royal Mail Hotel* (see opposite) offering decent accommodation and food. From "Meeka", as it's known, continuing north on the Great Northern Highway you'll see a road sign marking the **26th parallel**, welcoming you to the fabled "Nor'west".

Newman

NEWMAN, 422km north of Meeka, is a company town built to serve BHP Billiton's **Mount Whaleback Mine**, a 5.5km-long open-cut iron ore mine that will eventually reach 0.5km deep. Besides stocking up at the Woolworths supermarket, the **mine tours** are the only reason you'd want to stop here (9.30am: May–Sept Mon–Sun; Oct–April Mon–Fri; 1hr 30min; long-sleeved shirt, trousers and enclosed shoes required as well as drinking water; $30, four people minimum; book at the visitor centre). The tours clearly demonstrate the scale and astonishing simplicity of the operation, as **Mount Whaleback** is gradually turned inside out and shipped to Asia.

Marble Bar

From Newman, a dirt road leads north for 300km through the scenic east Pilbara to **Nullagine** and **MARBLE BAR**. The latter, linked to Port Hedland by a sealed road, became known as Australia's hottest town after clocking up 160 consecutive days over 37.8°C (100°F) in 1923 and 1924. This is the sole reason many visitors come to "the Bar", misnamed after a nearby colourful bar of jasper (similar to quartz).

GETTING AROUND AND INFORMATION   **THE GREAT NORTHERN HIGHWAY**

By bus Integrity buses (ⓦ integritycoachlines.com.au) make the 22hr journey between Perth and Port Hedland once a week, heading north on Tuesday nights (arriving Wednesday evening) and south on Fridays and Sundays (arriving first thing Saturday and Monday morning). The coaches are reasonably comfortable and tickets allow unlimited stopovers en route. Fares start from $274 each way.

Tourist information There's a visitor centre in Cue on Austin St (Mon–Fri 9am–4pm; ☎08 9963 8600, ⓦ cue. wa.gov.au) and another in Newman, cnr Fortescue Ave & Newman Drive (Mon–Fri 9am–5pm, Sat & Sun 10am–4pm; ☎08 9175 2888, ⓦ newman.org.au).

ACCOMMODATION

Capricorn Village Great Northern Hwy, Newman ☏ 08 9175 1535, ⊛capricornvillagenewman.com.au. Simple rooms in a modern motel-style building looking out onto a lush green lawn. Outdoor pool, tennis and golf plus laundry facilities and a 24hr fuel station and convenience store make this a great base. Also home to the *Capricorn Bar and Grill*, for delicious steaks and other hearty meat dishes (kangaroo fillet $32). $115

Queen of the Murchison Hotel 10 Austin St, Cue ☏ 08 9963 1625, ⊛queenofthemurchisonhotel.com. This bed and breakfast was formerly a hotel, built in 1938, and has a historic interior featuring high ceilings and plenty of jarrah wood. Rooms are simple with shared bathrooms and there is plenty of outdoor space and secure parking. They also serve meals, taken around the log fire in winter, and have a

collection of exotic birds and vintage motorcycles. $125

Royal Mail Hotel Main St, Meekatharra ☏ 08 9981 1148, ⊛royalmailhotel.com.au. This historic hotel was established in 1899 and has a variety of single, double and family-sized self-contained motel rooms with en-suite bathrooms, air conditioning, TV and fridge. Lunch and dinner are served daily in the bar (until 8.30pm) and there's an attractive beer garden. Secure parking is also available. $125

Seasons Hotel Newman Drive, Newman ☏ 08 9177 8666, ⊛seasonshotel.com.au. The reasonably upmarket *Seasons Hotel* has comfortable rooms with private bathrooms, TVs, fridges and air conditioning. Some rooms have kitchenettes and there's a swimming pool and cocktail bar. The hotel restaurant serves dinner daily, until 9pm (8.30pm Sun). $170

Karijini National Park

DPaW fee (see box, p.594) • ⊛ dpaw.wa.gov.au

Karijini National Park is WA's second-largest protected area, with spectacular, accessible gorges in the north and a vast unvisited section to the south, separated roughly by Karijini Drive, the southernmost of the two roads running through the park. Travellers rave about the nerve-jangling walks, timeless scenery and sparkling waterholes here, and are often taken aback at the lush, spinifex-covered hills and proliferation of white-trunked snappy gums that sprout from the blood-red rock, distinguishing the Pilbara from the better-known but drier Kimberley, especially in July and August (the busiest months).

The **gorges** themselves cut through the north-facing escarpment of the Hamersley Ranges and all offer spectacular views as well as a range of **graded walks** through their interiors. There are scores of superlative **swimming holes** in the park too, but they tend to be situated deep in the gorges, and are rarely less than absolutely freezing, even on the hottest days.

Karijini Drive is sealed, but the northern Banjima Drive, which runs between the gorges, is predominantly corrugated dirt. Barring adverse weather, the park remains accessible for all vehicles throughout the year, although 2WD may find things a little bumpy. The gorges get extremely hot between November and April, making the winter the best time to visit, and **flash floods** are reasonably common so keep an eye on the weather forecast. Check your watch too – ascending out of the gorges in anything less than full daylight is a definite no-no.

The park has a western entrance, accessed from Highway 1 via Tom Price, and an eastern entrance, accessed via the Great Northern Highway from Newman in the south

---

GRADED WALKS

Across Australia, all walking routes are marked as being in one of six different classes. Classes 1–3 can be completed comfortably by most, Class 4 requires a reasonable level of fitness, while Class 5 tend to be exhilarating semi-Indiana-Jones-style adventures. Class 6 requires you to either be a qualified rock-climber and abseiler with all the necessary equipment, or on a guided tour.

While lesser trails are not uniformly well marked, the "**Trail Risk**" signs certainly are, and will warn you if you're about to venture into a Class 6 area. Injuries are common in Karijini National Park, and fatalities do occur, so think carefully about which trail your level of fitness will allow you to complete comfortably, and wear solid walking sandals – on many walks a small slip could see you plunge a fair distance down a gorge face.

or Port Hedland to the north. Whichever way you enter, make sure you fill up at the last available fuel station as **driving distances** in the park tend to be underestimated; count on doing around 250km. There's limited food and drinking water in the park, so it's best to bring your own just in case.

Visitor centre

Daily: April–Oct 9am–4pm; Nov–March 10am–noon • ☎ 08 9189 8121

Around 30km from the Karijini Drive turn-off on the Great Northern Highway is the park's eastern entrance; a further 10km down Banjima Drive brings you to the **visitor centre**. The design of the building represents a goanna moving through the country; inside are some great displays on Karijini's plants, animals and people, and some better-than-nothing maps.

The eastern gorges

Backtracking slightly from the visitor centre, a road leads 10km east to the Dales Gorge area, first passing the basic **Dales Campground** (see opposite). Slightly further on are the Fortescue Falls and Dales Day Use Area car parks, linked by an easy pathway along the gorge rim and a more scrambly one over boulders and through water along the gorge floor. Together, the pathways create a memorable walk (3km return to either car park; 3–4hr; Class 2–4), passing various lookouts and idyllic swimming spots at the stepped **Fortescue Falls** and tranquil **Circular and Fern pools**, where the rusty gorge walls soar overhead. Alternatively, you can drive your vehicle to either car park and just complete shorter sections.

The central gorges

Continuing west of the visitor centre, Banjima Drive turns to dirt and you soon reach a turn-off leading north to **Kalamina Gorge**, with a stream-side walk (3km; 3hr return; Class 3) and swimming at Rock Arch Pool. Back on Banjima Drive, the next turn-off leads to two impressive lookouts: the first onto the tiered amphitheatre of **Joffre Falls** (usually just a trickle) and **Joffre Gorge**, and the second over **Knox Gorge**; there are walks into both gorges from the corresponding lookout (2–3km; 2–3hr return; Class 4).

If you return to Banjima Drive, the next turning north brings you to *Karijini Eco Retreat* (see opposite), owned by the Gumala Aboriginal Corporation. Continuing down the same turn-off, the road ends at Weano Day Use Area car park. A short stroll away, Red, Hancock, Joffre and Weano gorges come together spectacularly at **Oxer Lookout**, the park's big draw-card, with the only slightly less striking **Junction Pool Lookout** right next door.

Mount Bruce

Continuing west along Bunjima Drive, the road snakes across the roof of the Pilbara to the park's western entrance, rejoining Karijini Drive which links Tom Price in the west and the Great Northern Highway in the east. Overlooking the junction is **Mount Bruce**, at 1235m WA's second-highest peak and climbable along a 9km path. Shorter trails from the same car park climb to Marandoo View, a lookout surveying Rio Tinto's iron-ore-producing Marandoo Mine. You can book tours of the mine at the visitor centre in Tom Price (see below).

Tom Price

TOM PRICE, 55km west of the park entrance, is the best base for exploring Karijini. The neat company town is named after Thomas Moore Price, an employee of the American company Kaiser Steel, who convinced mining companies that having a dig around the area might be worth their while.

ARRIVAL AND INFORMATION

By car Unless you're on a tour, you'll need your own vehicle to visit Karijini; there is no public transport. Be sure to fill up just before entering the park.

Tourist information There's a visitor centre on Central Road in Tom Price (April–Oct Mon–Fri 8.30am–5pm, Sat & Sun 8.30am–12.30pm; Nov–March Mon–Fri 8.30am–5pm,

Sat 8.30am–12.30pm; ☎ 08 9188 5488, ⊛ tomprice.org.au), which can book accommodation and tours of Rio Tinto's open-cut iron-ore mine (daily 10am subject to minimum numbers; enclosed shoes required; 1hr 30min; $33). There's also a visitor centre in the park (see opposite).

6

TOURS

Lestok Tours ☎ 08 9189 2032, ⊛ lestoktours.com.au. Full-day tour by coach ($180) with pick-up from Tom Price or Karijini Eco Retreat. Includes a guided walk through Weano Gorge and Handrail Pool, plus plenty of stops at lookouts, a swim at Fern Pool and lunch.

West Oz Active ☎ 04 3891 3713, ⊛ westozactive .com.au. West Oz Active Adventure Tours are the only company running tours right down into the Karijini gorges (March–Oct only; $285). The gorge trips include hiking, swimming, climbing, jumping, sliding, traversing and abseiling and are not for the faint-hearted.

ACCOMMODATION

Dales Campground Dales Gorge area. This basic campground has toilets, water, and gas barbecues. There are showers you can use at the visitor centre and generators are permitted in some areas. Regularly full in high season so calling ahead is advisable. $10 per person

Karijini Eco Retreat Central gorges ☎ 08 9425 5591, ⊛ karijiniecoretreat.com.au. Accommodation is in safari-style, en-suite eco-tents which feature proper beds, electric lighting and a hot shower. Guests can use the shared bush kitchens or eat in the outdoor restaurant

and bar. Campers can pitch up at one of the numerous unpowered sites. Unpowered sites $20, en-suite eco-tents $315

Tom Price Tourist Park Nameless Valley Drive ☎ 08 9189 1515, ⊛ tompricetouristpark.com.au. Nestled below Mount Nameless this friendly campsite has a range of accommodation from sheltered campsites to open-plan cabins and deluxe chalets with full kitchens. There's also a small swimming pool. Un/powered sites $16/21, dorms $50, cabins $195

Up the coast to Broome

It's around 380km from the Burkett Road turn-off (for Exmouth) to the industrial twin towns of **DAMPIER** and **KARRATHA**, with just a few roadhouses to break the journey. Further up the coast there's only **Port Hedland** to look forward to, although wily travellers will bypass this less-than-charming town, and break the drive to Broome at **Eighty Mile Beach** instead.

Dampier and Karratha

The two young towns of **Dampier** and **Karratha** make up the Northwest's biggest industrial centre. Dampier is home to one of the country's busiest ports, shipping iron ore and liquefied natural gas around the globe in vast quantities, while rapidly growing Karratha, 20km east, was established in 1968 when space ran out around Dampier. The town grew dramatically when the **North West Shelf Natural Gas Project** got underway in the early 1980s, collecting gas from offshore platforms for production at the Karratha Gas Plant – the project contributes about 65 percent of WA's domestic gas.

After travelling in rural WA, arriving in Karratha is like entering another world, with its lines of white industry utes, teeming throngs of mine workers and a range of shops not seen since Perth. It's useful for stocking up, but has precious little to detain the passing traveller – Dampier has even less to offer.

ARRIVAL AND INFORMATION

By plane Karratha's airport (☎ 08 9143 1366, ⊛ karrathaairport.com.au) is WA's second busiest, handling hundreds of thousands of fly-in-fly-out (FIFO) workers every year; a new terminal made it a far more pleasant

airport when it opened in 2015. Qantas (⊛ qantas.com.au) and Virgin Australia (⊛ virginaustralia.com.au) both fly here from Perth multiple times daily.

By bus Integrity buses (⊛ integritycoachlines.com.au)

on the Perth–Broome route stop at Karratha Visitor Centre twice a week in each direction (Wed and Fri northbound, Fri and Sun southbound). A community bus (ⓦkarratha.wa.gov.au/community-bus) also runs between Dampier and Point Samson on Tuesdays, Saturdays and Sundays, calling at Karratha, Roebourne and Wickham along the way.

By car All the major car rental companies are represented at Karratha airport.

Tourist information Karratha's visitor centre is on De Witt Rd (Mon–Fri 8.30am–4.30pm, Sat & Sun 9am–2pm; ☎08 9144 4600, ⓦkarrathavisitorcentre .com.au), the main access road off Highway 1, and can book various tours.

6

ACCOMMODATION

There are major accommodation shortages in Karratha as a result of the mining boom – don't show up without a booking. The number of workers requiring accommodation in town has had an equally negative effect on prices, and rooms here are some of the most expensive in the state, as well as some of the most basic.

Best Western 27 Warambie Rd ☎08 9143 9888, ⓦbestwesternkarratha.com.au. Right in the centre of town, this chain motel has studios and one- and two-bedroom apartments plus a nice pool and decent restaurant. All the bedrooms have microwaves so you can self-cater if you want to. **$280**

Discovery Parks – Pilbara Rosemary Rd on the way to Dampier ☎08 9185 1855 or ☎1800 451 855, ⓦbig4 .com.au. Shaded sites for camping (some en-suite) and modern cabins plus a camp kitchen, swimming pool, playground and games room. Powered sites **$38**, cabins **$129**, units **$159**

Ibis Styles Karratha 35–45 Searipple Rd ☎08 9159 1000, ⓦibis.com. This smart, modern hotel has simple rooms with en-suite bathrooms, tea-/coffee-making facilities and satellite TV. There is also an outdoor swimming pool, a bar and free Continental breakfast. Wi-fi is available for a fee. **$209**

Karratha International Cnr Hillview & Millstream rds ☎08 9187 3333, ⓦkarrathainternational.com.au. This upmarket hotel's spacious rooms have a fresh feel and modern bathrooms. There's an attractive outdoor pool area, complete with poolside bar, as well as a poolside restaurant **$229**

Roebourne and around

Established in 1866 and once regarded as the capital of the Northwest, **ROEBOURNE**, 40km east of Karratha on Highway 1, is the oldest surviving settlement in the Pilbara. Now home to local Aboriginal people displaced by pastoral settlement, Roebourne feels just as much a ghost town as formally abandoned Cossack down the road (see below).

The **visitor centre** and **museum** (Mon–Fri 9am–4pm, Sat–Sun 9am–3pm; Nov–April Mon–Fri 9am–3pm; ☎08 9182 1060) are housed in the **Old Gaol** on Queen Street, a fine example of nineteenth-century English penal architecture. The majority of prisoners here were indigenous folk who had offended against their sheep station "owners". The prison was closed in 1924 but astonishingly (given the conditions) was reopened in 1975 and pressed into active service once more until 1984. Other nineteenth-century institutional buildings are dotted around town, along with a couple of indigenous art galleries, the best of which is **Yinjaa-Barni Art Centre** (irregular hours; ☎08 9182 1959, ⓦyinjaa-barni.com.au), located in Old Dalgety House at 3 Roe St.

Cossack

From Roebourne, the Roebourne–Point Samson Road leads north a few kilometres to Wickham and Point Samson (see opposite), after passing a turn-off right to **COSSACK**, originally Roebourne's port and well worth a visit. Cossack used to be quite the little town, with stores, boarding houses and Japanese brothels lining the streets to cater for the Asian pearlers, prospectors and pastoralists who all passed through in the late nineteenth century. But by the end of the century the port began silting up: by the 1950s, Cossack was abandoned and to this day can feel quite eerie if you're the only one prowling the streets.

What's left of this historic ghost town has been finely restored, with interpretive signs filling you in on its origins and history – five buildings remain (open in daylight hours; honesty box), along with a number of ruins and **cemeteries**. At the end of the town, **Readers Head Lookout** offers fine 360-degree views over **Settlers Beach** just below, Point Samson and Jarman Island and Lighthouse.

6

Point Samson

Close to the end of the small peninsula that runs just north of Roebourne is **POINT SAMSON**, a tranquil fishing port that's popular with retirees and local workers on holiday. East of town is pretty **Honeymoon Cove**, which has good swimming at high tide.

ARRIVAL AND DEPARTURE

ROEBOURNE AND AROUND

By bus Integrity buses (ⓦ integritycoachlines.com.au) on the Perth–Broome route stop opposite the *Victoria Hotel* on Roe St in Roebourne twice weekly (Wed & Fri northbound, Fri & Sun southbound).

ACCOMMODATION AND EATING

Point Samson Resort Samson Rd ☎ 08 9187 1052, ⓦ pointsamson.com. Large, self-contained studios and suites arranged around the landscaped grounds. All have kitchenettes with microwaves and there's a complimentary guest laundry and gym. The spa suites have double deluxe spa baths. $300

Samson Beach Chalets 44 Bartley Court ☎ 08 9187 0202, ⓦ samsonbeach.com.au. Deluxe, architect-designed chalets sleeping from two to ten. All have fridges and microwaves, bigger units have full kitchens and there's a large outdoor pool with deck chairs. There's a caravan park here too, with modern ablutions blocks and a laundry. Powered sites $39, doubles $280

Samson Beach Tavern 44 Bartley Court ☎ 08 9187

1503, ⓦ samsonbeach.com.au/tavern. This lively bar at the *Samson Beach Chalets* resort is the best place to head for a cold beer or glass of WA wine. There are two pool tables and an attractive outdoor terrace. The dinner menu is decent too, with classics like chicken parma ($26) and plenty of fish dishes (salt and pepper squid $16.50). Mon–Sat 11.30am–midnight, Sun 11.30am–10pm (food served until 8pm).

Tata's Restaurant Point Samson Resort, Samson Rd ☎ 08 9187 1052, ⓦ pointsamson.com. Minimalist restaurant serving the best food in town. It's all about the seafood here, so start with Esperance scallops ($22) or oysters ($22 for four) before moving on to the saltwater barramundi ($28). Wed–Sat from 5.30pm.

Port Hedland

Approaching **PORT HEDLAND**, 200km east of Roebourne, you'll spot the dazzlingly white stockpile of industrial salt at the Dampier Salt Works, an only mildly interesting sight that is nonetheless about as good as "BHP Billiton-town" gets in the way of tourist attractions. The main strip is Wedge Street, but most of the useful **shops** including Woolworths are at the Boulevard Shopping Centre on nearby Anderson Street. After stocking up, make a visit to the **Courthouse Gallery** (Mon–Fri 9am–4.30pm, Sat & Sun 9am–2pm; ⓦ courthousegallery.com.au) on Edgar Street, an incongruously classy art space hosting good temporary exhibitions.

ARRIVAL AND INFORMATION

PORT HEDLAND

By plane Port Hedland's airport (☎ 08 9160 0500, ⓦ porthedlandairport.com.au) is on the Great Northern Highway about a 7min drive from the town centre. Both Qantas (ⓦ qantas.com.au) and Virgin Australia (ⓦ virginaustralia.com.au) offer regular flights from Perth.

By bus Integrity buses (ⓦ integritycoachlines.com.au)

pull in at the visitor centre twice a week in each direction (Wed & Fri northbound, Fri & Sun southbound).

Tourist information The visitor centre, on Wedge St (Mon–Fri 9am–5pm, Sat & Sun 9am–2pm; ☎ 08 9173 1711, ⓦ visitporthedland.com), can organize tours of the BHP Billiton iron-ore mine (Tues & Thurs 1pm; 45min; $45).

ACCOMMODATION AND EATING

Best Western Hospitality Inn Webster St ☎ 08 9173 1044, ⓦ porthedland.wa.hospitalityinns. com.au. Comfortable but unexciting motel rooms with queen-sized beds, lounge area, minibar, fridge and tea-/coffee-making facilities. Decent outdoor pool too. $159

Discovery Parks – Port Hedland 2 Taylor St ☎ 1800 459 999, ⓦ big4.com.au. Shaded powered campsites, and a range of economical cabins and motel rooms. There's also a swimming pool, playground and games room. Powered sites $38, budget doubles $49, cabins $169

Port Hedland to Broome

The 600km drive northeast from Port Hedland to Broome is one of world-class boredom, a dreary plain of spinifex and mulga marking the northern edge of the **Great Sandy Desert**, broken only by a couple of roadhouses and the pleasant *Eighty Mile*

6

TRAVELLING IN THE NORTHWEST

The best time to visit the Kimberley is from **June to September**, the coolest months, as by late September the heat is already building up. Night comes early and fast in the Northwest – most visitors adapt to a routine of rising with the sun (often the best time to get some driving done) and retiring soon after sunset. Temperatures can stay stifling into the early hours, so a **4WD** and a **mozzie dome** can be preferable to a campervan in these parts – make sure you erect tents and insect domes well away from waterholes in crocodile country.

If you undertake a trip in the Northwest during **the Wet** (Jan–March), expect very high temperatures, humidity and huge amounts of **rain**, with associated flooding and disruption. **Cyclones** are an annual threat to coastal communities between Exmouth and Broome from November to April – acquaint yourself with the safety advice in each town during this time. Following weather damage, roads and bridges on Highway 1 are repaired amazingly quickly, but back roads can be closed for weeks – keep up to date with road conditions and closures at ranger stations, visitor centres, roadhouses and ⓦexploroz.com.

Beach Caravan Park (see below) around the halfway point. Despite Highway 1's proximity to the ocean, this is one of few points on the drive with beach access.

ACCOMMODATION   **PORT HEDLAND TO BROOME**

Eighty Mile Beach Caravan Park Great Northern Hwy ⓣ08 9176 5941, ⓦ eightymilebeach.com.au. Lawned caravan sites with five ablutions blocks, plus ten

self-contained en-suite cabins with open-plan kitchen-dining areas. Each cabin has a gas BBQ and outdoor seating area. Un/powered sites $35/45, cabins $190

The Kimberley

A region of red dust, endless skies, stunning sunsets, big rivers and huge gorges, the **Kimberley** is often romantically described as Australia's last frontier. It's a wilderness dotted with barely viable cattle stations, isolated Aboriginal communities and, increasingly, vast tracts of Aboriginal land, all edged with a ragged, tide-swept coastline inhabited chiefly by crocodiles, secluded pearling operations and a couple of exclusive, fly-in getaways. The land is king here, with devoted locals making annual pilgrimages to their favourite spots armed with only a swag and an esky in the Dry, before retreating in the Wet. When the dry season sets in around April, tourism in the Kimberley gradually comes back to life, with **tours** running mainly between thriving **Broome** and **Kununurra** along the iconic **Gibb River Road**, or down to the mysterious **Bungle Bungles**, south on Highway 1 near Halls Creek. Adventurous travellers are increasingly heading for the stirring scenery around **Cape Leveque** and **Mitchell River National Park**: the many warnings that accompany journeys to these parts can be daunting, but armed with a good 4WD and a dash of Outback knowledge you should be fine. Greyhound buses do ply the **Great Northern Highway** between Broome and Darwin (see p.624), but to see this area properly you either need your own vehicle or to join a tour.

Broome and around

"Slip into Broometime" is a well-worn aphorism that captures the tropical charm of **BROOME**, clinging to the peninsula overhanging Roebuck Bay. This is the western reach of the rugged and remote Kimberley and despite Broome's numerous tourist facilities something of a "Wild West" air prevails. It's a good 2000km from here to the nearest city of any size and the town has more in common with the deepest Outback than it does with downtown Perth.

Broome began its life as a pearling town. Easily collected pearl shell heaped along nearby Eighty Mile Beach led to the northwestern "**pearl rush**" of the 1880s, initially

6

THE KIMBERLEY

ACCOMMODATION
Bungle Bungles Safari Camp	13
Drysdale River Station	3
Emma Gorge at El Questro	4
Home Valley Station	2
Kalumburu Mission	1
Kooljaman Resort	6
Kurrajong Camp	12
Lombadina	8
Mornington Wilderness Camp	16
Mount Barnett Roadhouse	9
Mount Elizabeth Station	5
Nature's Hideaway	7
Silent Grove Campground	10
The Station at El Questro	4
Walardi Camp	14
Warmun Roadhouse	11
Windjana Gorge campground	15

Aboriginal land

N

0 ——— 100
kilometres

enabled by the enslaved Aborigines. Later, indentured workers from Asia sought the shell in ever-greater depths below the waves, and Broome originated as a camp on sheltered Roebuck Bay where the pearl luggers laid up during the cyclone season.

After a violent and raucous beginning, the port finally achieved prosperity thanks to the nacre-lined oyster shells, or **mother-of-pearl**. By 1910, eighty percent of the world's pearl shell came from Broome, and a rich ethnic mix and a rigidly racially stratified society had developed here. Each season one in five divers died, several more became paralysed and, as Broome's cemeteries steadily filled, only one shell in five thousand produced a perfect example of the silvery pearls unique to this area.

Stagnation then rebuilding followed both world wars, after the second of which the Japanese – masters in the secret art of pearl culturing – warily returned and invested in pearl-farming ventures. Things improved with the sealing of the coastal highway from Perth in the early 1980s and the philanthropic interest of English businessman Alistair McAlpine, who led the old town's tasteful development and refurbishment, using its oriental mystique and pearling history as inspiration. Today a mining boom is well underway and Broome is expected to double in population in the next twenty years.

Chinatown

Broome originally flourished around the old port area – centred on Carnarvon Street and bordered by Short Street, Napier Terrace and Dampier Terrace – known as **Chinatown**. This old quarter's original buildings have gradually been reconstructed along oriental lines – with corrugated iron, latticework and old verandas the prominent architectural features – but nowadays feel a little "Disneyfied". Pearl showrooms, cafés, art galleries and boutiques occupy most of the buildings. Some of the best places to see art are the classy Gecko Gallery and the attractively ramshackle Short Street Gallery, both on Short Street, while Paspaley Pearls, over the road, sells quality jewellery from one of Australia's most prestigious pearling families. At the end of Short Street, **Paspaley Plaza Shopping Centre** houses supermarkets, pharmacies and the post office.

Sun Pictures

Carnarvon St • Tickets for screenings $17 • Tours daily 10.30am & 1pm; $5 • ☎ 08 9192 1077, ⓦ broomemovies.com.au

This outdoor garden cinema in the heart of Chinatown is the world's oldest and a uniquely "Broometime" experience. Watch the latest movies from a deckchair while mosquitoes nibble your ankles and the odd light aircraft comes in low across the screen. Screenings take place every evening, with the schedule announced each Thursday. During the day you can visit the shop or take a tour around the virtually unchanged interior to see photographs showing the segregated seating order of the bad old days.

Pearl Luggers

Short St • Daily 9am–5pm • Free • Tours daily 9am, 11am, 1pm & 3pm; $25 • ☎ 08 9192 0022, ⓦ pearlluggers.com.au

At the eastern end of Short Street is **Streeter's Jetty** and **Pearl Luggers**, a free exposition of Broome's pearling heritage, with a couple of dry-docked luggers and informative one-hour tours, which include a taste of pearl meat and serve as an excellent introduction to this pearling town. This is a good option if you don't have time to head out to Willie Creek Pearl Farm (see p.635), which is owned by the same people.

Broome Museum

Robinson St • June–Sept Mon–Fri 10am–4pm, Sat & Sun 10am–1pm; Oct–May daily 10am–1pm • $6 • ☎ 08 9192 2075, ⓦ broomemuseum.org.au

The former Customs House on Robinson Street is now home to **Broome Museum**, an interesting little place that deserves a more prominent position in town. Displays outline Broome's pearling history, with evocative photographs and an old diving suit doing much to highlight the perils that faced divers.

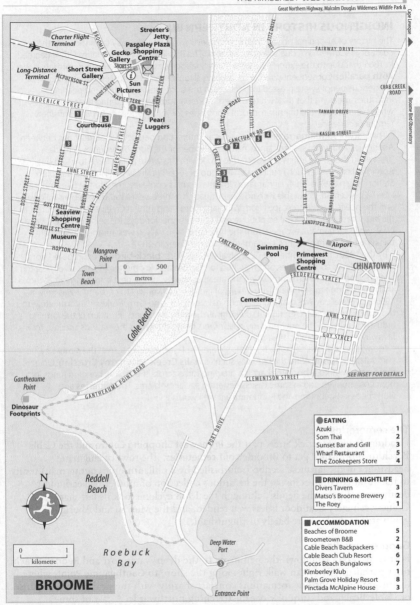

BROOME

Cape Leveque

Broome Bird Observatory

● EATING

Azuki	1
Som Thai	2
Sunset Bar and Grill	3
Wharf Restaurant	5
The Zookeepers Store	4

■ DRINKING & NIGHTLIFE

Divers Tavern	3
Matso's Broome Brewery	2
The Roey	1

■ ACCOMMODATION

Beaches of Broome	5
Broometown B&B	2
Cable Beach Backpackers	4
Cable Beach Club Resort	6
Cocos Beach Bungalows	7
Kimberley Klub	1
Palm Grove Holiday Resort	8
Pinctada McAlpine House	3

SEE INSET FOR DETAILS

Town Beach

The old **Pioneer Cemetery** overlooks **Town Beach**, the nearest sand to the town centre but some way short of Cable Beach's glorious expanses. This is a good vantage point for observing the "**Staircase to the Moon**", the reflections of the full moon rising over the mudflats, which occur at very low tides a few nights a month between March and October. Broome capitalizes on the phenomenon with night markets – dates and times can be obtained from the visitor centre.

6

INDIGENOUS HISTORY IN NORTHERN WA

The history of Aboriginal people in Australia's northwest differs greatly from those on the east coast or in southern WA due to a colonial quirk. The British Colonial Secretaries Office decreed in 1865 that due to the extreme heat no convict labour was to be used further north than the **26th parallel**. Consequently, rather than being slaughtered as on the east coast, local indigenous people were pressed into service in the burgeoning pastoral and pearling industries, meaning that their white "owners" were paradoxically depleting their workforces whenever they wanted to imprison local Aborigines for minor offences (an unsurprisingly regular occurrence).

The story of **Jandamarra** or "Pigeon" gives an interesting perspective on relations between Aborigines and white settlers. Jandamarra, a member of the Bunuba group, was made a "tracker" in the 1890s, and was expected to work with the white police force to weed out Aboriginal criminals. When rounding up a group of such "criminals" at Lillimooloora Police Station (see p.646) in 1894, Jandamarra's loyalties to his people returned to the fore, and he killed a policeman, Constable Richardson, instigating a three-year "war" between his followers and the police force. His escapes from Windjana Gorge and Tunnel Creek entered folklore – in the latter case the police staked out one end of the tunnel for days, in the belief that it was a cave, while Jandamarra escaped from the other end. Ironically, it was another Aboriginal tracker who caught and shot Jandamarra at Tunnel Creek in 1897.

By the 1880s, huge numbers of Aboriginal people were **"black-birded"**, or uprooted from their traditional communities, and marched for hundreds of kilometres to pastoral or pearling stations. With pastoralism dominating the area's economy for the next hundred years, it took a shamefully long time for the mistreatment of indigenous workers to end, and it was only in 1966 that equal pay was granted to Aboriginal stockmen and farm workers. Unfortunately, this did not bring an end to Aboriginal suffering, as the increased mechanization of the farming industry resulted in the now-unwanted labourers being driven off the stations and into towns far away from their traditional land.

Today, the harsh realities of indigenous life are displayed at every turn in the Kimberley, particularly in towns along the highway such as **Halls Creek** and **Fitzroy Crossing**. On a more positive note, **Aboriginal art** is a growing force across the region, bringing funds into poor communities and in some cases alleviating social problems. The **galleries** and workshops in Roebourne and Kununurra are well worth a visit.

The cemeteries

Heading down Frederick Street past the **Primewest Shopping Centre** and the Cable Beach turn-off, you'll get to Broome's old **cemeteries**. The rows of enigmatic headstones in the Japanese section (refurbished by a philanthropic countryman) testify to the hundreds of lives lost in the hazardous collection of mother-of-pearl; most deaths were due to "the bends", although the 1908 cyclone took its fair share. The Chinese cemetery next door is less well tended, and the Muslim and Aboriginal graveyards at the back are barely distinguishable.

Gantheaume Point

Port Drive takes you down the peninsula to the deep-water port and **Reddell Beach**; tides permitting, you can walk right along the shore to **Gantheaume Point**, where the bright red sandstone formations contrast sharply with the pearly white expanse of Cable Beach and turquoise ocean stretching northwards. A cast of some 130-million-year-old **dinosaur footprints** is set in the rocks here – the originals are out to sea and visible at very low tides, one of nine different dinosaur classifications whose footprints have been fossilized on the stretch between Broome and Cape Leveque.

Cable Beach

Named after the nineteenth-century telegraph cable from Singapore that came ashore here, **Cable Beach** extends for an immaculate 22km north of Gantheaume

Point to Willie Creek. This is where much of Broome's recent development has taken place, with five-star resorts, boutiques, bars and restaurants lining the streets around the coast. Patrolled swimming is available in front of the *Cable Beach Club Resort* in season (stingers are a danger Nov–March), with no cars, dogs or nudity allowed. To get rid of the white bits, go instead to the nude-sunbathing area north of the rocks, from where 4WD vehicles can head all the way up to Willie Creek.

6

Malcolm Douglas Wilderness Wildlife Park

Broome Rd, 16km from Broome • Daily 2–5pm • $35 • Tours daily 3pm • Free • ⊛ malcolmdouglas.com.au/wildernesspark.html

Enter the **Malcolm Douglas Wilderness Wildlife Park** through the jaws of a giant fibreglass "saltie" and see dingoes, kangaroos, wallabies and emus – plus scores of saltwater crocodiles. The crocs you'll see here have all been relocated from the wild after terrorizing various Outback communities.

Broome Bird Observatory

Crab Creek Rd • Donation • ☎ 08 9193 5600, ⊛ broomebirdobservatory.com

Leaving Broome, Crab Creek Road branches off the highway around 10km north of town, leading 15km southeast down a corrugated dirt road (4WD recommended) to the tranquil **Broome Bird Observatory**, on the shores of Roebuck Bay. The rich mudflats around the observatory are one of the top global spots for shorebirds, with over 150,000 visiting during the Wet. The centre runs a variety of twitcher tours and courses (from $70). Pick-ups from Broome are available for those booked on tours ($45 return per person).

Willie Creek Pearl Farm

Willie Creek Rd • Tours 8am–4.15pm • $65; with coach pick-up in town $105; with helicopter pick-up $195; booking essential • ☎ 08 9192 0000, ⊛ williecreekpearls.com.au

About 30km up the coast from Broome is **Willie Creek Pearl Farm**, a popular day-tour and the only Kimberley pearl farm easily accessible to the public – the pearls cultivated here are among the finest and biggest in the world. The tour includes a talk on the pearl-farming process, and a boat trip on the beautiful Willie Creek to inspect the racks of seeded oysters, which build up layers of pearlescent nacre as they feed off the tidal nutrients – a process that takes half the normal time. You can take the coach tour, which picks up in Broome, or self-drive, taking the Beagle Bay–Broome road north before turning west on the unsealed Manari Road and Willie Creek Road. A 4WD is required and the journey takes about 1hr 15min.

ARRIVAL AND DEPARTURE

BROOME AND AROUND

BY PLANE

The airport (☎ 08 9194 0600, ⊛ broomeair.com.au) on Macpherson Rd is so centrally located – just over 1km from Chinatown – that planes fly disturbingly low over town. There is no public transport from the terminal, but a taxi to either Chinatown or Old Broome will only set you back around $10.

Destinations Darwin (daily; 2hr 35min); Kununurra (daily; 1hr 10min); Melbourne (3 weekly; 3hr 55min); Perth (4–6 daily; 2hr 40min); Sydney (2 weekly; 4hr 10min).

BY BUS

All long-distance buses pull in at the busy visitor centre on the highway just before town.

Broome to Darwin Greyhound buses (☎ 1300 473 946, ⊛ greyhound.com.au) run from Broome to Darwin once a day (except Sun), stopping at Derby (2hr 30min); Fitzroy Crossing (5hr 55min); Halls Creek (9hr 10min); and Kununurra (13hr 30min), before continuing through the NT to Darwin (27hr 30min). The reverse service also runs once a day (not Sat), arriving early in the morning.

Broome to Perth Integrity Coach Lines (☎ 08 9574 6707, ⊛ integritycoachlines.com.au) operate a service from Broome to Perth twice a week (departs Broome Thurs & Sat 8pm; arrives Perth Sat & Mon 7am; 35hr). The service from Perth also runs twice weekly (departs Perth Tues & Thurs, arrives Broome Thurs & Sat 8.15am; 34hr 45min).

6

GETTING AROUND

By bus The town's useful bus service ($4 per ride, day-pass $10; 10 rides $34; ☎ 08 9193 6585, ⓦ broomebus.com.au) runs hourly between Old Broome and Cable Beach via Chinatown from early morning to early evening, with more frequent services from May to mid-October.

By bike Broome Cycles (☎ 08 9192 1871, ⓦ broomecycles .com.au) has two outlets – one in town at 2 Hamersley St and another on Cable Beach Rd (May–Oct only). A range of bikes for rent (including tandems) from $24/day, plus $50 deposit. Helmets and locks included; photo ID required.

By car Besides the big names with desks at the airport, Broome Broome Car Rentals at 15 Napier Terrace in Chinatown (☎ 08 9192 2210, ⓦ broomebroome.com.au) has a range of vehicles including 4WDs from $40/day, and will meet you at the airport, while Wicked at 31 Clementson St (☎ 1800 246 869, ⓦ wickedcampers .com.au) rents out five-seater 4WD campers and jeeps from around $100/day.

By taxi ☎ 08 9192 1133 or ☎ 13 10 08 within Broome, ⓦ broometaxis.com.au.

INFORMATION

Tourist information The visitor centre (wet season: Mon–Fri 8.30am–4pm, Sat & Sun 9am–noon; dry season: Mon–Fri 8.30am–5pm, Sat & Sun 8.30am–4.30pm; ☎ 08 9195 2200, ⓦ broomevisitorcentre.com.au) is on Hamersley Street, on the first roundabout as you enter the town. Staff here can book accommodation and places on Broome's many tours.

Festivals The vast Shinju Matsuri (ⓦ shinjumatsuri.com. au) takes place over ten days every September, and celebrates Broome's ethnic diversity and the pearl that created it. It starts with a lively opening ceremony, includes float parades, carnivals and cultural events, and finishes up with a huge fireworks display. The town can get packed out for the Shinju, so book your accommodation in advance. It's also worth timing your visit to coincide with A Taste of Broome (ⓦ facebook.com/tastebroome), held one Friday a month May–Sept and promoting the area's indigenous community through arts and food.

TOURS OF THE KIMBERLEY

Travelling from Broome to Kununurra or Darwin on an organized tour is a great way to see the remote Kimberley without the pressures associated with taking your own vehicle. Most companies offer return tours from Broome and Kununurra, as well as one-way trips running both east and west, so select the one that best fits your schedule.

Adventure Wild Broome ☎ 1800 359 008, ⓦ adventurewild.com.au. Extensive tours from Broome to Darwin, Kununurra or back to Broome, most of which travel along the Gibb River Road ($1450–3700). Accommodation is "premium camping" and there are two hosts and a maximum of sixteen guests on each tour.

Australian Adventure Travel ☎ 08 9248 2355 or ☎ 1800 621 625, ⓦ australianadventuretravel.com. Full range of tours, from two to fourteen days in length, visiting the Gibb River Road, the Bungle Bungles and the Mitchell Plateau ($550–2995). All accommodation is camping in two-person tents. Single supplements apply. Departures from Broome, Kununurra and Exmouth, as well as Perth.

Aviair Kununurra ☎ 08 9169 1300 or ☎ 1800 095 500, ⓦ aviair.com.au. Scenic flights over Lake Kununurra, the Argyle Diamond Mine and the Bungle Bungles, plus fly-drive trips into the Bungles and flights from the park ($399–1849). Also Mitchell Falls flight and 4WD combos. Pick-ups and drop-offs at El Questro on the eastern section of the Gibb River Road are also available.

East Kimberley Tours Kununurra ☎ 08 9168 2213, ⓦ eastkimberleytours.com.au. Long-established operator offering tours to the Argyle Diamond Mine and the Bungle Bungles that fly out from Kununurra to stay in the comfortable *Bungle Bungles Bushcamp* ($790–2295). Self-drive option also available, including accommodation at the camp.

Kimberley Wild Expeditions Australia Broome ☎ 08 9193 7778, ⓦ kimberleywild.com.au. Based in Broome, this friendly tour company is a one-stop shop for tours of the Kimberley. Short breaks and adventures range from the two-day Kimberley Gorges Escape ($525), which takes in Windjana Gorge and Tunnel Creek, to the 14-day Broome–Darwin (or vice versa) tour, which includes everything from the Gibb River Road to the Bungle Bungles ($3995). Tour guides are professional, experienced and passionate, and group sizes are kept small.

Kingfisher Tours Kununurra ☎ 08 9168 1333, ⓦ kingfishertours.net. Scenic flights by fixed-wing Cessna over Lake Argyle, the Mitchell Plateau, the Kimberley coast, the Cockburn Ranges and the Bungle Bungles ($245–975). Longer tours include a stop for refreshments. Transfers to/from remote accommodation can also be arranged.

TOURS AND ACTIVITIES

Broome's growing popularity means that there's no shortage of things to do. There are too many activities and tours on offer to do justice to here: suffice to say they include helicopter and hot-air balloon rides, whale watching, skydiving, scenic flights and cruises and indigenous cultural tours – ask at the visitor centre for operators and contact details. The classic Broome activity, the **sunset camel ride** down Cable Beach, is offered by several different operators from around $85. Numerous operators also run multiday tours to Cape Leveque (see p.639) and up the Gibb River Road as far as Darwin, NT (see p.645). Note that most tours from Broome only operate in the Dry.

ACCOMMODATION

6

Most hotels are situated just to the south of Chinatown in Old Broome, with pricey self-contained **apartments** and **resorts** around Cable Beach. Prices across the board are relatively expensive, although bargains can be picked up if you can tolerate the heat and humidity during the Wet, particularly at the high-end resorts where prices often halve. There are also numerous caravan parks and backpackers' in town.

HOTELS, B&BS AND RESORTS

Broometown B&B 15 Stewart St ☎08 9192 2006, ⓦ broometown.com.au. Boutique B&B with only three rooms and correspondingly high levels of service. The rooms are arranged around a small pool and open-air lounge where breakfast is served daily. All rooms have a comfortable seating area, desk space and fridge. Your hosts Toni and Richard have lived in Broome for some 20 years and are a fountain of knowledge and advice. Rates drop like a stone in the Wet. **$225**

Cable Beach Club Resort Cable Beach Rd ☎08 9192 0400 or ☎1800 199 099, ⓦ cablebeachclub.com. This beautifully landscaped five-star hotel is the original Broome resort and remains the only one right on Cable Beach. Designed to reflect the area's history, the architecture is unmistakeably tropical and guests can choose from a range of plush rooms, villas and bungalows set amid mature botanical gardens. There are two swimming pools (one for adults only), four restaurants and a meditative Buddha sanctuary, plus the fantastic Chahoya Spa. **$249**

Cocos Beach Bungalows 6 Sanctuary Rd ☎08 9193 7546, ⓦ cocosbeachbungalows.com. This small resort of just eight deluxe bungalows (two- and three-bedroom) has a sizeable outdoor pool set in tropical gardens, off-street parking and an outdoor spa and is a short walk from Cable Beach. **$410**

Pinctada McAlpine House 55 Herbert St ☎1800 746 282, ⓦ mcalpinehouse.com. A stunning, intimate guesthouse with attentive staff. The library, lush grounds, cushioned lounging areas and gourmet breakfasts

encourage relaxation and socializing. **$259**

HOSTELS AND CARAVAN PARKS

Beaches of Broome 4 Sanctuary Rd ☎08 9192 6665 or ☎1300 881 031, ⓦ beachesofbroome.com.au. "Flashpacker" accommodation with flawless, smart facilities that would put many hotels to shame, perhaps at the expense of the hostel spirit – the clientele are a slightly weird mix of students and retired couples. Note that some rooms are fan-cooled. Dorms **$37**, doubles **$140**

Cable Beach Backpackers 12 Sanctuary Rd ☎08 9193 5511 or ☎1800 655 011, ⓦ cablebeachbackpackers. com. Everything looks a little "pre-loved", but once you're ensconced in a hammock by the pool you won't care. Laid-back atmosphere with lots of activities and a free airport bus. Not all rooms have a/c. Dorms **$22**, doubles **$80**

Kimberley Klub 62 Frederick St ☎08 9192 3233 or ☎1800 004 345, ⓦ kimberleyklub.com. Rated four-star by the YHA, this backpackers' is run by friendly, enthusiastic staff. Good-quality rooms surround a breezy, slightly manic communal area with a good pool, bar, ping-pong, "beach" volleyball and a novel, round pool table – there's always something going on. Doubles in particular are above the usual backpacker standard. Dorms **$25**, doubles **$110**

Palm Grove Holiday Resort Cnr Murray & Cable Beach rds ☎08 9192 3336 or ☎1800 803 336, ⓦ palmgrove .com.au. Excellent campsite with a good pool, covered campers' kitchen and decent cabins with kitchenettes and verandas. The unpowered sites are a bit cramped. Un/powered sites **$35/38**, cabins **$175**

EATING

Azuki 15 Napier Tce ☎08 9193 7211 ⓦ facebook.com/ azukijapanesefusion. Cute, modern Japanese fusion restaurant serving excellent bento boxes ($28) plus everything from teriyaki to sashimi. There's a lovely terrace for dining alfresco and Asian breakfasts are also served. Mon–Fri 7.30am–3pm.

Som Thai 5 Napier Tce ☎08 9192 6186, ⓦ somthairestaurant.com. All the usual suspects such as

sweet and sour pork ($25) and chicken and cashew nuts ($24) are served both in the restaurant and to take away. BYO wine. Daily 11am–2pm & 4.30–10pm.

Sunset Bar and Grill Cable Beach Club Resort, Cable Beach Rd ☎08 9192 0400, ⓦ cablebeachclub.com. This is the place to watch the sunset with a range of grills served up on the terrace overlooking Cable Beach. The Margaret River sirloin is $42; WA lamb back strap $41. The buffet

6

THE BOAB – SYMBOL OF THE KIMBERLEY

East of Derby you'll start to notice the region's distinctive **boab** trees, their bulbous trunks and spindly branches creating startling silhouettes. As much a symbol of the Kimberley as cattle stations and deep red sunsets, it's widely believed that seeds from the African **baobab** – the common name of the genus *Adansonia* and of which the Australian name is a contraction – arrived in the Kimberley by sea from Africa thousands of years ago, gradually evolving into this distinct species.

The trees' huge size enabled their most dubious function as temporary prisons for local Aboriginal people. The most notorious example of a **prison tree**, located about 7km south of Derby on the Derby Highway, held indigenous people kidnapped in the mid- to late nineteenth century from the Fitzroy Crossing and Halls Creek areas. Today, you'll see carved **boab nuts** sold as homewares across the Kimberley, the intricate patterns worked into the flesh by Aboriginal artists. At the beginning of the rainy season the tree produces flowers and fruit, foretelling the beginning of the Wet. Aboriginal people also chew the bark for water – the huge trunks can hold up to 120,000 litres.

breakfast is good value, with a full range of cooked breakfasts as well as fresh fruit and pastries. Daily 6.30–10.30am & 5.30–9pm.

Wharf Restaurant 401 Port Drive ☎08 9192 5700. Fresh local seafood from classic fish and chips ($25) to flavoursome chilli sand crab ($59.80). The oysters are particularly good and the atmosphere here is relaxed, with orders taken at the counter and the food served alfresco

overlooking Roebuck Bay – there aren't many better views in Broome. Takeaway also available. Daily 11am–10pm.

The Zookeepers Store 2 Challenor Drive ☎08 9192 0015, ⓦzks.com.au. Broome's best brunch spot, serving everything from kronuts (made here, $6.50) to courgette fritters ($19). Great coffee too. Daily from 7am for breakfast and noon for lunch, also Thurs–Mon 5pm–late.

DRINKING & NIGHTLIFE

Divers Tavern Cable Beach Rd ☎08 9192 6060, ⓦdiverstavern.com.au. Large pub and bistro with a surrounding terrace that's actually quite pleasant. Big-name bands sometimes play here – check the website for listings. Mon–Sat 11am–midnight.

Matso's Broome Brewery Cnr Hamersley & Carnarvon sts ☎08 9192 7751, ⓦmatsos.com.au. A bona fide Broome institution. The famous Monsoonal Blonde and Ginger beers can be gulped down on the colonial-style veranda, or at a squashy couch in the fanned interior. Great food served all day

– from breakfast through to a detox salad for lunch ($20) and scotch fillet ($38) in the evening. Daily 7am–late.

The Roey Carnarvon St ☎ 08 9192 1221 ⓦroey .com.au. *The Roey* incorporates *Pearlers Bar* and *JC's* restaurant, which has a decent beer garden, and *Oasis Bar*, a larger outdoor space with a stage for live music and plenty of room for happy-hour carousing. Depending on your views about an international panel of women, white T-shirts and water, you might want to attend/stay away on Thursday evenings as appropriate. Daily 11am–late.

The Dampier Peninsula

Surrounded by the Indian Ocean, the beautiful Dampier Peninsula, with its pristine, deserted beaches, dusty red cliffs and mind-altering sunsets, is slowly opening up to low-key tourism. Indigenous cultural experiences at communities such as Beagle Bay (see opposite) and Lombadina (see opposite) now tend to be as much a highlight as the stunning scenery for many visitors. Take Manari Road north from Broome for a tour of the northern beaches, or go the whole hog on the stunning Broome–Cape Leveque Road to the peninsula's far northern point.

The northern beaches

Heading north from Broome along Manari Road past the Willie Creek Pearl Farm, you'll find isolated **bushcamping** along the "northern beaches" on the southwest side of the Dampier Peninsula. If you're travelling independently, be well prepared as there are no facilities whatsoever. The first of the beaches is **Barred Creek**, followed by **Quondong Point** and **Price Point**. The road can get pretty slippery after only a small amount of rain, and continuing beyond **Coulomb Point**, 78km from Broome, will be beyond most vehicles – and drivers.

To Cape Leveque

The first stop on the Broome–Cape Leveque road is the Aboriginal community of **Beagle Bay**, 125km from Broome. The highlight here is the **Sacred Heart Church** built by German missionaries in 1917, a beautiful building with an unusual altar decorated with mother-of-pearl – pay the $5 entry fee when announcing your arrival at the community office. After Beagle Bay the track to Cape Leveque gets narrower and sandier and after a further 20km you'll reach the turn-off leading after 33km to *Nature's Hideaway* at **Middle Lagoon**, a lovely white-sand cove with camping, good swimming and snorkelling. Backtracking to the main road, a further 48km takes you to the community of **Lombadina**, another ex-mission settlement where you'll now find well-equipped accommodation, a range of water- and land-based tours (see below) and a beautiful wide bay. The road ends at spectacular **Cape Leveque**, 220km from Broome at the very tip of the peninsula.

GETTING AROUND AND INFORMATION

Getting around It's best to arm yourself with a solidly built 4WD rental – try Wicked (ⓦ wicked4x4rentals.com) or Britz (ⓦ britz.com.au). Alternatively, join a tour for the corrugated 220km track to Cape Leveque – note that access can be restricted in the Wet.

Permits No permit is required to travel along the Cape Leveque Road, but advance permits are required to visit Beagle Bay and Bardi (One Arm Point); apply online at ⓦ www.daa.wa.gov.au/land/entry-permits or call ☎ 1300 651 077. Even with a permit, phone ahead and announce your arrival at each community, and make sure you stick to

THE DAMPIER PENINSULA

public roads when driving on the peninsula – some communities here don't want to be disturbed.

Services Limited supplies are available from the stores at Beagle Bay, Lombadina, Djarindjin, Ardyaloon and Kooljaman on weekdays and Saturday mornings. All but Kooljaman also have fuel. Some places accept credit and debit cards but many operators accept only cash so carry plenty – don't rely on regular ATMs out here. There's no free camping along the road or in any communities, and all accommodation must be booked in advance; check with your host whether you can BYO alcohol.

TOURS

Adams Pinnacle Tours ☎ 08 6270 6060, ⓦ adams pinnacletours.com.au. Full-day tour from Broome to the Cape and Sacred Heart Church at the Beagle Bay Aboriginal Community and Cygnet Bay Pearl Farm, including a swim at Kooljaman ($269 or $499 with scenic flight back to Broome). **Kimberley Wild Expeditions** ☎ 08 9193 7778, ⓦ kimberleywild.com.au. High-quality two-day tours up

the Dampier Peninsula to Cape Leveque, calling in at the Beagle Bay Aboriginal Community and Cygnet Bay Pearl Farm ($795). **Lombadina Indigenous Tours** ☎ 08 9192 4936, ⓦ lombadina.com. A range of experiences is on offer at Lombadina, from mud crabbing in the tidal estuary ($110) to kayaking out to the reef offshore ($80).

ACCOMMODATION

Kooljaman Resort Cape Leveque ☎ 08 9192 4970, ⓦ kooljaman.com.au. This is the original Dampier Peninsula resort, with accommodation ranging from camping and beach shelters to luxury stilted tents overlooking the ocean. The restaurant is open daily for lunch and dinner from April to mid-October, or you can use the "Bush Butler" service if you can't drag yourself from your room. Entry fees apply if not staying overnight. Un/powered sites $40/45, beach shelters $100, cabins $155

Lombadina ☎ 08 9192 4936, ⓦ lombadina.com. The Lombadina community has a range of accommodation, from single and double rooms with shared facilities to self-contained cabins and apartments sleeping up to five. There's a simple shop and a bakery on site. Doubles $170, cabins $220 **Nature's Hideaway** Middle Lagoon ☎ 08 9192 4002, ⓦ middlelagoon.com.au. A lovely white-sand cove with campsites and self-contained beach cabins (sleeping four or five) with kitchenette, campfire and BBQ. Unpowered sites $20, cabins $150

Derby to Kununurra – the Great Northern Highway

There are two routes from Derby to Kununurra: the Gibb River Road (see p.645) and the Great Northern Highway, which passes through **Fitzroy Crossing** and **Halls Creek** before you come to the access road to **Purnululu National Park** (the Bungle Bungles). Most visitors will do one or the other, although the Bungle Bungles (the only real attraction down this wearying stretch of Highway 1) are close enough to Kununurra (just) to be accessed on an overnight trip.

Derby

Situated 220km northeast of Broome, and 42km north of Highway 1 on a spur of land jutting into the mudflats of King Sound, **DERBY** (pronounced "dur-bee") is a neat, industrious little town and a centre for local Aboriginal communities, which make up around fifty percent of the population. One of the few sights in town is the **old gaol** on the corner of Loch and Hensman streets, where rusting ruins and interpretive boards highlight the horrifying treatment of local indigenous people at the hands of pastoralists and the police; there's a similarly strong sense of history at the **Boab Prison Tree** (see box, p.638) 7km to the south.

Mowanjum Art and Cultural Centre

Daily April–Sept • ☏ 08 9191 1008, ⓦ mowanjumarts.com

Four kilometres down the Gibb River Road, whose western entrance is just south of town, is the much-recommended **Mowanjum Art and Cultural Centre**. The building's architecture celebrates the spirit of the Wandjina, the supreme spirit for the Worora, Ngarinyin and Wunumbul people of the Mowanjum community, and houses a gallery, art studio, outdoor performance space and museum.

ARRIVAL AND INFORMATION   DERBY

By bus Greyhound buses (ⓦ greyhound.com.au) on the Broome–Darwin route arrive at the visitor centre six days a week.

Tourist information The visitor centre is at 30 Loch St (Oct–March Mon–Fri 9am–4pm, Sat 9am–noon; April, May & Sept Mon–Fri 8.30am–4pm, Sat & Sun 9am–1pm; June–Aug Mon–Fri 8.30am–4.30pm, Sat & Sun 9am–3pm; ☏ 1800 621 426, ⓦ derbytourism.com.au).

Services Woolworths supermarket is on the highway just north of town.

TOURS

A scenic flight or cruise to see the impressive West Kimberley coastline and Buccaneer Archipelago is a must, and cheaper than doing the same trips from Broome. The main attraction is the Horizontal Waterfalls, where huge tides rage through a tiny gap in the cliffs in Talbot Bay, one of many small inlets on this rugged shoreline. Other tour operators covering the Kimberley have trips to and scenic flights over this section of coastline as well (see box, p.636).

Derby Bus Service ☏ 08 9193 1550, ⓦ derbybus .com.au. Excellent-value day-trip to the spectacular Windjana Gorge and Tunnel Creek national parks, plus a visit to Lillimooloora Police Station ($195). Lunch plus morning and afternoon tea are provided.

Horizontal Falls Adventure Tours ☏ 08 9192 1172 ⓦ horizontalfallsadventures.com.au. These specialists in the Horizontal Waterfalls offer half-day, full-day and overnight tours by boat and seaplane ($695–845). Departures from Broome and Derby.

ACCOMMODATION AND EATING

Derby Lodge Clarendon St ☏ 08 9193 2924, ⓦ derbylodge.com.au. Twin and family motel-style rooms, some with en-suite facilities. All rooms have air conditioning, TV and fridge and there's a laundry, BBQ area and plenty of parking. Also self-contained apartments with air conditioning, kitchenette and balcony. Motel rooms $160, apartments $210

King Sound Resort Loch St ☏ 08 9193 1044, ⓦ kingsoundresort.com.au. In the heart of town, this laidback resort has simple rooms, including some bunk rooms for backpackers ($40), an outdoor pool and a guest laundry, as well as a restaurant serving everything from locally caught barramundi ($23) to T-bone steak ($28). $200

Fitzroy Crossing

Since the pastoral expansion into the Kimberley in the late nineteenth century, **FITZROY CROSSING** has been a rest stop for travellers and a crucial crossing over the ever-flooding Fitzroy River. The run-off is second only to the Amazon during flood peaks, at which time two cubic kilometres of water a minute surge under the road bridge, gushing out across a forty-kilometre-wide flood plain before disgorging into King Sound. Today, Fitzroy Crossing is a fairly desolate welfare town serving the Aboriginal communities strung out along the Fitzroy Valley, but it's still a better overnight option than Halls Creek (see below).

ARRIVAL AND INFORMATION	FITZROY CROSSING

By car Fitzroy Crossing is a four-hour drive from Broome along Highway 1, a distance of 400km. Highway 1 continues on to Halls Creek and Kununurra.

Tourist information The visitor centre is on Flynn Drive by the roadhouse (Mon–Fri 8.30am–4.30pm, April–Sept also Sat 9am–1pm; ☏ 08 9191 5355).

Services There's an IGA supermarket with limited stock on Forrest Rd.

ACCOMMODATION AND EATING

Crossing Inn Skuthorpe Rd ☏ 08 9191 5080, ⓦ crossinginn.com.au. The most memorable experience in town is a few drinks or some pub food at the atmospheric, century-old *Crossing Inn*, a true-blue Outback pub with a small art gallery, rooms and camping in a natural bush setting. It can get fairly raucous on Thursdays – pay day. Rooms have river or garden views, air conditioning, TV, secure parking and en-suite bathrooms, breakfast is also included with all hotel rooms. Unpowered sites $16pp, powered sites $39 for two, doubles $179

Fitzroy River Lodge On the highway just east of the bridge ☏ 08 9191 5141, ⓦ fitzroyriverlodge.com.au. This lush, sprawling oasis in dusty Fitzroy Crossing has lodges on stilts (to avoid flooding – only an issue Dec–March), smart motel-style rooms and less smart apartments, en-suite safari tents, acres of camping space and excellent facilities including a pool, restaurants and a bar. Bookings are not taken for the campsite – simply turn up. Un/powered sites $30/35, safari tents $180, doubles $230

Geikie Gorge National Park

The 5km **Geikie Gorge**, one of the three Devonian Reef national parks (see p.646), is accessed from Fitzroy Crossing via Forrest Road (Dec–March restricted access), an 18km trip. This mighty gorge carved by the Fitzroy River is best seen by boat between May and October. Watermarks on the gorge walls clearly show how high the river can rise, while below the surface freshwater crocodiles jostle with freshwater-adapted stingrays and sawfish. **Walking trails** lead along the forested western banks, which are dotted with picnic sites and barbecues. The park is normally closed in the Wet, and camping is prohibited.

TOURS

Darngku Heritage Cruises ☏ 08 9191 5552, ⓦ darngku.com.au. Half-day tours by boat through Geikie Gorge ($175), including visits to indigenous sites and the telling of Dreamtime stories. Don't forget to take a hat, as boats are unshaded.

Halls Creek and around

Further down the Great Northern Highway is **HALLS CREEK**, 289km east of Fitzroy Crossing. The gold rush of 1885 took place in the hills 17km south of town; in less than four years thousands of prospectors exhausted the area's potential before stampeding off to Kalgoorlie. Nowadays new diamond mines are opening up, but Halls Creek itself remains a pretty desperate Aboriginal welfare town; wise travellers will fuel up and move on. Note also that this is not the place to break for a meal: with only weekly deliveries, fresh food can be scarce in the shops and the takeaway food on offer from the roadhouses is abysmal.

There are a few attractions south of town down Duncan Road for those with their own transport, including the interesting ruins of **Old Halls Creek**; China Wall, a block-like outcrop of quartzite rising from the hillside; swimming holes at Caroline and Palm springs; and finally Saw Tooth Gorge, 45km out of town. All bar the final creek crossing just before the gorge are manageable in a 2WD during the Dry.

Sixteen kilometres west of town, the **Tanami Track** heads south past **Wolfe Creek National Park** (where a 50,000-ton meteorite crash-landed around 300,000 years ago, making an impressively large crater) on its way to Alice Springs, a remote road for hardened Outbackers only. The brutal Australian horror film *Wolf Creek* (2005) has led many travellers to approach the area with trepidation.

ARRIVAL AND INFORMATION
HALLS CREEK

By car Highway 1 links Halls Creek to Fitzroy Crossing in one direction (300km, or three hours' drive, west) and to Kununurra in the other (350km, or four hours' drive, north).

Tourist information Visitor centre (2 Halls St; Mon–Fri 7am–5pm; ☎1800 877 423, ⓦhallscreektourism .com.au).

ACCOMMODATION

Kimberley Hotel 2 Roberta Avenue ☎08 9168 6101, ⓦkimberleyhotel.com.au. Simple, modern rooms and apartments with air conditioning, flat-screen TVs and free movies. Some rooms have small balconies with attractive views and there's a pleasant outdoor pool and dining area. Doubles $219, apartments $350

Purnululu National Park (Bungle Bungles)
April–Nov depending on the weather • DPaW fee (see box, p.594)

The spectacular **Bungle Bungle** massif, seldom referred to by its official name, the **Purnululu National Park**, is one of Australia's greatest natural wonders – an area of red and black striped domes, knobbly dry creek beds and soaring chasms. The nickname is believed to be a misspelling of the common Kimberley grass, Bundle Bundle, while "Purnululu" means "sandstone" in the local Kija tongue.

A couple of days spent exploring the park's domes, chasms and gorges is well worth the effort (or expense, if you're taking a tour). There are numerous marked trails to enjoy, as listed below; the rest of the park is currently inaccessible, the northeast being the **ancestral burial grounds** of the Djaru and Gidja people.

Entering the park

Because of the need to protect the fragile rock formations from mass tourism, and the rough access road from the Great Northern Highway, 52km south of Warmun/Turkey Creek, entry is strictly limited to 4WDs, with all tow vehicles prohibited. Your last chance to buy supplies is at the *Warmun Roadhouse* (see p.644). It can get stiflingly hot in the Bungles, with temperatures soaring well over 40°C from September onwards. Make sure you carry water, use sunblock and wear a hat on all walks.

From the highway it's a reasonably straightforward 53km dirt-road drive through pastoral station land to the **visitor centre**. Here you can pick up park maps and book your campsite. The centre sells only souvenirs; bring all the food, fuel and water you need unless you're coming with a tour group. Take it easy on the road in as the track is winding and corrugated – expect the journey to take from two to three hours. There are usually at least three creek crossings and frequent heavily rutted sections; high clearance is a must.

Northern walks

From the visitor centre it is 15km north to The Bloodwoods car park, the trailhead for several excellent short walks (allow 25min). The walk into **Echidna Chasm** (2km; 1hr return; moderate) takes you deep into the soaring, maze-like incision, which opens up into a small amphitheatre at the end. Time your walk to be in the amphitheatre at midday when the sun enters the chasm and you can see the colours in the rock to their best advantage. On the way out, make sure you check out the view over the Osmond Ranges and Osmond Creek from **Osmond Lookout**; the creek is the only permanent source of water in the park, and was historically used by Aboriginal groups as a travel pathway. The **Mini Palms** walk (4.4km; 2–3hr return; moderate) runs along a creek bed then squeezes through tiny gaps between boulders, before ascending to a viewing platform and finally a palm-filled amphitheatre. Along the walk you can see tufts of palms clinging to the rock walls hundreds of metres above you; the scale of the clefts is emphasized when you realize that the palms can be up to 20m high.

Southern walks

On the south side of the park, 27km from the visitor centre, is Piccaninny car park (allow 45min). This is the area of the park where you will find the more classic Bungle vistas and should be your preferred destination if time is short. From the car park, the short **Domes Walk** (700m; 30min; easy) leads you among the bungles on the way to the walk into **Cathedral Gorge** (3km; 1–2hr return; moderate), an awe-inspiring overhanging amphitheatre with stunning acoustics and a seasonal pool whose rippled reflections flicker across the roof above. The nearby **Piccaninny Creek Lookout** trail (2.8km return; 1hr; moderate) follows the undulating creek bed before climbing up to the viewpoint itself, where you will find some of the best views in the park, with domes stretching as far as the eye can see.

Kungkalanayi Lookout

Just 3km north of the visitor centre, **Kungkalanayi Lookout** is the best place in the park to watch the sunset. It is a steep climb up to the ridge from the car park; your reward is a sweeping view in all directions over this monumental land. If you plan to hang around long after sunset, bring a torch as it gets dark quickly and there is no lighting to see you on your way back to the car park.

INFORMATION AND TOURS	PURNULULU NATIONAL PARK (BUNGLE BUNGLES)

Tourist information Visitor centre (52km off Highway 1; early April to mid-Oct daily 8am–noon & 1–4.30pm; ☎ 08 9168 7300, ⊛ dpaw.wa.gov.au).

Airplane flights Scenic flights are available over the Bungles. If you don't want to drive into the park you can take a fixed-wing aircraft tour from Kununurra (see p.644).

Helicopter flights There are exhilarating helicopter flights from the park's Bellburn Airstrip just south of

Walardi Camp (April–Oct; 18–48min; from $269; ☎ 08 9166 9300, ⊛ helispirit.com.au). The helicopters are permitted to fly much lower – if you've ever wanted to fly in a chopper you won't be disappointed. The tours available from Broome and Kununurra, which often involve flying to the airstrip and then being driven around in a 4WD, offer the best of both worlds.

ACCOMMODATION

Bungle Bungles Safari Camp On the north side of the park, 7km from the visitor centre ⊛ bunglesafaricamp .com.au. The best accommodation in the park, with private eco-safari tents, hot showers, flushable toilets and a fully equipped camp kitchen. The dining area has stunning views of the Bungles massif. Only bookable as part of a tour with Kimberley Wild (see box, p.636).

Kurrajong Camp On the north side of the park, 7km from the visitor centre. Very basic campsite with room for 100 vehicles (4WD only). Toilets, picnic tables, fireplaces and limited wood for cooking are provided. Bore water

– which should be boiled before drinking – is available from the taps. No generators permitted. Pay camping fee at visitor centre. **$10** per person

Walardi Camp On the south side of the park 12km from the visitor centre. This is the better-laid-out of the two campsites, arranged into generator and non-generator areas. There are picnic tables at some sites and fireplaces and limited wood for cooking are provided. There are toilets and bore water, which should be boiled before drinking. Pay camping fee at visitor centre. Camping per person **$12**

LAKE ARGYLE

Thirty-five kilometres east of Kununurra on the Victoria Highway, a sealed road of the same distance leads to vast, scenic **Lake Argyle**. When the **Argyle Dam** was completed in 1972, the Ord River managed to fill the lake in just one wet season. Along with the neighbouring Victoria and the Fitzroy, these rivers account for a third of Australia's freshwater run-off and plans are often mooted to pipe it south where it's needed. Creating the lake was an engineer's dream: only a small defile needed damming to back up a shallow lake covering up to two thousand square kilometres. Since that time the fish population has grown to support commercial fishing, as well as numerous birds and crocodiles, both saltwater and freshwater.

6

Warmun Roadhouse Great Northern Highway, Warmun ☎ 08 9168 7882, �🌐 warmunroadhouse.com. This is "the gateway to the Bungle Bungles" and your last chance to buy food and fuel before entering the national park. There is also simple motel accommodation and some self-contained units, plus shaded camping and caravan sites and an outdoor swimming pool. Un/powered caravan sites $30/35, tent sites $15, doubles $150

Kununurra

Thriving **KUNUNURRA** is the Kimberley's youngest town, built in the early 1960s to serve the **Ord River Irrigation Project**, fed by Lake Kununurra. The Diversion Dam Wall to the west of town created this lake, essentially the bloated Ord River.

Fifty kilometres upstream is the bigger Argyle Dam Wall, built in 1971 to ensure a year-round flow to the project, which in turn created **Lake Argyle**, the world's largest man-made body of water and the home of an estimated twenty-five thousand crocodiles. Enhanced by the copious amounts of nearby fresh water, which lends itself to recreational use, Kununurra escapes the listless feel of older Kimberley towns. Easy-to-produce sugar cane has become the most viable crop, along with more labour-intensive watermelons and other produce, offering steady opportunities for **farm work** – see the backpackers' notice boards. Cattle-station work is often available as well.

There are some excellent **art galleries** in the centre of town (see opposite) and **Kelly's Knob**, a small hill behind town, is a popular place to watch the sun go down. Kununurra is also the best jumping-off point for tours of the Bungle Bungles and the Gibb River Road.

A couple of kilometres east of town is Hidden Valley or **Mirima National Park** (DPaW fee), a sandstone range of "mini-bungles" with some fun short trails. Take the Lookout Walk (800m; 30min; moderate) to the top of the range for views over the Ord Valley.

North of town on Weaber Plains Road, the **Hoochery** produces the infamous Ord River Rum, the only rum produced in WA and probably none the better for the lack of competition. There are daily tours around the distillery (11am and 2pm; $14; �🌐 hoochery.com.au), which explain the process of rum-making and include a free sample.

ARRIVAL AND INFORMATION   KUNUNURRA

By bus Greyhound buses (�🌐 greyhound.com.au) on the Broome–Darwin route pull in outside the BP Roadhouse on Messmate Way. Buses to Darwin (12hr 30min) depart daily at 9am except Sundays; buses to Broome (13hr) depart daily at 5.40pm except Saturdays.
Tourist information The visitor centre, on Coolibah Drive (Peak season Mon–Fri 8am–5pm, Sat & Sun

9am–4pm, off season Mon–Fri 9am–4pm; ☎ 1800 586 868, �🌐 visitkununurra.com), sells national park passes and has plenty of information on local attractions, and travel on to Broome and Darwin and the Gibb River Road.
Services There is a large Coles supermarket on Konkerberry Drive, where you should stock up if you're heading out into the Outback.

TOURS

Kununurra is an excellent base from which to visit the Bungle Bungles and the East Kimberley. Regional tour operators also offer tours of the area (see box, p.636). Many of the outfits operating out of Broome also run return or one-way tours from Kununurra and a number of local operators organize cruises and other activities centred on the lake and Ord River.

Go Wild Adventure Tours ☎ 1300 663 369, �🌐 gowild .com.au. Self-guided one- to three-day "eco-noeing" trips by Canadian canoe along the Ord River, stopping at eco-campsites along the route ($220). All camping and cooking gear is included.
Kimberley Outback Tours ☎ 1300 286 453, �🌐 kimberleyoutbacktours.com. A full-day cruise on Lake Argyle, with lunch and ending with sunset on the lake ($120).
Lake Argyle Cruises ☎ 08 9168 7687, �🌐 lakeargyle cruises.com. Morning, sunset and half-day boat trips on

the lake, which explore the rugged northern shoreline ($70–185). Half-day cruises include a stop on a remote island and fossicking for "zebra rock". Departures from Kununurra and Lake Argyle. Also dinghy hire for those with a Skipper's Licence (half-day $125, full-day $200).
Triple J Tours ☎ 08 9168 2682, �🌐 triplejtours.net.au. One-way cruises (with bus travel on either the outward or return leg) up the Ord River to Lake Argyle, with a visit to the historic Durack Homestead Museum ($180). You can also add a 30min scenic flight above the Bungle Bungles to your tour ($529).

ACCOMMODATION

Freshwater East Kimberley Apartments 19 Victoria Hwy ☎ 1300 729 267, ⓦ freshwaterapartments.net.au. Kununurra's classiest self-catering option, with studio rooms and one- two- and three-bedroom apartments, a smart swimming pool and tropical gardens. Some rooms have a private outdoor shower, all have dedicated parking, kitchenette and balcony. Complimentary airport pick-ups on request. **$224**

Ibis Styles Messmate Way ☎ 08 9168 4000, ⓦ ibis .com. Recently refurbished motel-style accommodation. Rooms have air conditioning, television and en-suite bathrooms and there's a central swimming pool and useful laundry room. **$153**

Kimberley Croc Backpackers 120 Konkerberry Drive ☎ 08 9168 2702, ⓦ klmberleycroc.com.au. In the centre of town, *Kimberley Croc* hostel has a nice pool, standard dorms and a great kitchen, with lots of outdoor areas and some long-term rooms for workers. Dorms **$31**, doubles **$110**

Kimberley Grande 20 Victoria Hwy ☎ 08 9166 5688,

ⓦ thekimberleygrande.com.au. Smart, resort-style accommodation, with a pool and a couple of restaurants on site. Rooms are spacious and contemporary with all the usual facilities plus either a terrace or a veranda. Spa suites also feature a spa bath and some rooms have attractive pool views. **$231**

Kimberleyland On Lakeview Drive, just south of town ☎ 08 9168 1280 or ☎ 1800 681 280, ⓦ kimberleyland.com.au. Perched on the edge of Lake Kununurra overlooking a glowing red monolith, this is a lovely, peaceful spot to camp. Un/powered sites **$35/45**, cabins **$160**

Lake Argyle Resort Lake Argyle Rd ☎ 08 9168 7777, ⓦ lakeargyle.com. At the end of the sealed road, *Lake Argyle Resort* has campsites on the shores of the lake, safari-style tent cabins, standard cabins, one- and two-bedroom lake-view units and a four-bedroom Grand Villa that sleeps up to 10. There's also a shop, bistro, laundry facilities and a jaw-dropping infinity swimming pool. Un/powered sites **$35/44**, cabins **$259**

EATING AND DRINKING

Hotel Kununurra 37 Messmate Way ☎ 08 9168 0400, ⓦ hotelkununurra.com.au. This traditional Aussie pub has a buzzy atmosphere most evenings and serves simple meals such as chicken parmigiana ($25.50). There is seating both inside and out and the numerous flat-screen TVs make this a great place to watch sports. There are several different Matso's beers (brewed in Broome) on tap. Daily 11am–late.

Pumphouse Restaurant Lakeview Drive ☎ 08 9169 3222, ⓦ thepumphouserestaurant.com. The town's standout spot is the *Pumphouse Restaurant* overlooking Lake Kununurra, where you can take in the gorgeous sunsets from the veranda over a glass of WA's finest, and indulge in gourmet pub food in the industrial interior. Main courses run from $32–42. Tues–Fri from 4.30pm, Sat & Sun from 8am. Dinner served until 7.30pm (7pm Sundays).

SHOPPING

Artlandish Aboriginal Art Gallery 10 Papuana St ☎ 08 9168 1881 or ☎ 1300 362 551, ⓦ aboriginalartshop.com. This well-established art

gallery sells high-quality paintings by local Aboriginal artists in traditional ochres and newer, brighter acrylics. Mon–Fri 9am–4.30pm, Sat 9am–1pm.

The Gibb River Road and the northern Kimberley

To cross the expansive northern Kimberley, the alternative to the quick yet uninspiring Great Northern Highway (see p.639) is the epic **Gibb River Road** (**GRR**). Originally built to transport beef out of the central Kimberley cattle stations to Wyndham and Derby, the "Gibb" cuts through the region's heart, offering a vivid slice of this vast and rugged expanse. It's 670km from its western end just south of Derby to its eastern end between Kununurra and Wyndham, 230km shorter than the Great Northern Highway. Although some people have mistaken it as such, the Gibb is no short cut, with corrugations and punctures guaranteed – heed the advice on off-highway driving (see p.34). Accessed from the Gibb, the even more remote **Kalumburu Road** leads to the increasingly popular **Mitchell River National Park**.

As a scenic drive in itself the Gibb is very satisfying, but it's the wayside attractions that make this route what it is – the homesteads, gorges and pools here are almost uniformly spectacular, and offer a real glimpse of Outback Australia.

If you're traversing the GRR west to east and want to spare your car the full ordeal, turn back at Manning Gorge and head down to the highway via Windjana Gorge – the best and most accessible gorges are along the western half of the GRR. If you just want a taste of the Gibb, it's possible to visit **Windjana Gorge** and **Tunnel Creek** national parks in a day from Derby or Fitzroy Crossing; this snippet is just about doable in a solid 2WD in the Dry. Otherwise, a sturdy **4WD** that you know how to maintain is a must – at the very least carry two spare tyres.

Windjana Gorge National Park

21km south of the Gibb River Rd • DPaW fee (see box, p.594) • ⓦ dpaw.wa.gov.au

A turn-off south from the Gibb River Road, 124km from Derby, leads to the towering ramparts of **Windjana Gorge**. Much of the landscape here and around Tunnel Creek is a remnant of the **Devonian Reef**, a large barrier reef that grew around the then-submerged Kimberley plateau 350 million years ago. A walking trail leads into the spectacular gorge, where freshwater crocodiles sun themselves in the afternoon at a small permanent pool, and fruit-bat-filled paperbark and Leichhardt trees line the riverbanks. Look out also for the striped archerfish, which kills insects by spitting jets of water at them. Three kilometres east of the gorge are the ruins of **Lillimooloora Police Station**, where Constable Richardson died after an altercation with his Aboriginal tracker Jandamarra or "Pigeon" (see box, p.634).

Tunnel Creek National Park

DPaW fee (see box, p.594) • ⓦ dpaw.wa.gov.au

It's a further 37km south of Windjana Gorge to fun **Tunnel Creek National Park**, where the creek has burrowed its way under the range, creating a 750m tunnel hung with fruit bats. Although the collapsed roof illuminates the cavern halfway, the wade through the progressively deeper and colder water to the other end still takes some nerve, especially with the golden eyes of freshwater crocs following your progress from the side of the pool – they shouldn't bother you, though. You'll need a torch and sturdy shoes that you don't mind getting soaked. Moving into the Wet, around November, check **weather conditions** at Fitzroy Crossing, as the tunnel can fill quickly if the Fitzroy River receives a lot of water.

The western Gibb River Road

The GRR winds its way through the impressive **King Leopold** and **Napier ranges** in the King Leopold Ranges Conservation Park (DPaW fee), passing, at 133km from Derby, a famous rock bearing more than a little resemblance to Queen Victoria.

At 196km is the access road for **Lennard River Gorge**, a dramatic cleft carved through tiers of tilted rock, just 8km south of the GRR in the middle of the King Leopold Ranges. You may find it quicker to walk the last 2km, which are very rough in parts. At 219km is the access track north to popular **Bell Gorge** (29km from the GRR; $10 per vehicle entrance fee). This is the loveliest gorge along the GRR, with a pretty swimming hole, and there's camping at *Silent Grove* (see p.648).

Back on the GRR, the **Imintji Store** is 227km from Derby but was closed at the time of writing. It was hoped it would reopen soon, selling diesel fuel, ice and groceries, as

---

DRIVING THE GIBB RIVER ROAD

Travelling along the Gibb River Road is not as strenuous as you may have been led to believe, but is still not to be undertaken lightly. Don't even think about attempting it in anything less than a sturdy 4WD and make sure you have enough **food and water** for several extra days, and around twenty litres of spare **fuel**, in case of emergencies. Some basic mechanical knowledge will get you a long way, but in the event of a breakdown everybody will stop to help. A real sense of camaraderie exists as you make your way along this popular route with the other travellers hardy enough to have embarked on this adventure without a tour guide. Driving up the Kalumburu Road requires some 4WD experience and should only be attempted by the confident.

well as carrying out basic vehicle repairs, but check locally for an update and don't rely on it being open.

Continue on, 253km from Derby, and a long 82km detour south over some creeks brings you to enjoyable *Mornington Wilderness Camp* (see p.648). From here, you can access the impressive **Sir John Gorge**, which has broad pools ideal for swimming – exploring upstream leads you to even greater grandeur.

Charnley River Station is 43km north of the GRR, 257km along the road from Derby. Continuing down the GRR for 35km you reach **Galvans Gorge** (700m), the most accessible of all the GRR's gorges.

At 305km, *Mount Barnett Roadhouse* (see p.648) serves food and carries **fuel** and some supplies. Camping is permitted behind the roadhouse by Manning River, where a 5km trail leads to **Manning Gorge**, with a large swimming hole and a pretty waterfall. Another 29km down the GRR is **Barnett River Gorge** (5km north of GRR), with swimming in a billabong.

At 340km from Derby and 365km from Kununurra, *Mount Elizabeth Station* is about halfway along the GRR, about 30km north, and offers accommodation (see p.648). At 406km you reach the turn-off for the Kalumburu Road before crossing the Durack River.

The Northern Kimberley: up Kalumburu Road

Though a common-enough destination in the Dry, the Northern Kimberley is a very **remote** region where a well-equipped 4WD and Outback skills are essential.

Heading north at the Kalumburu Road junction, midway along the Gibb River Road, you'll come to *Drysdale River Station* after 59km (see p.649), which has accommodation and **fuel** (no LPG). The beautiful, four-tiered **Mitchell Falls**, on the Mitchell Plateau, are the main attraction here, and the reason most people take on the Kalumburu Road – this once remote spot is getting less so by the year and is now a national park.

Take the left turn-off from the Kalumburu Road, 160km north of the GRR, and head 80km west over **King Edward River** to the falls; the turn-off is extremely rough and takes up to four hours one-way. From the Mitchell Falls car park it's a tough 3km walk (4–6hr return) northwest to the falls themselves (passing Little and Big Merten's Falls on the way). You can swim in the upper pools of the main falls, or arrange a scenic flight or a six-minute lift back to the car park via helicopter with Aviair (see box, p.636).

Kalumburu

Continue along the Kalumburu Road from the Mitchell Falls turn-off, 267km after the GRR junction, for **Kalumburu**, an Aboriginal community with a languorous feel. As well as being able to get (expensive) **fuel** and basics at the store here (☎08 9161 4333; Mon–Fri 7.30–11.30am & 1.30–4pm), you can visit the **mission** (Tues, Thurs & Fri 8.30–10.30am; $10) set up in the nineteenth century by Benedictine monks. Kalumburu is a completely dry community, so don't bring any alcohol.

The eastern Gibb River Road

The eastern section of the Gibb River Road has less to detain you than the western section, but more options for stopovers, with a range of homesteads and stations offering accommodation and activities.

There are a few places worth stopping at on *Home Valley Station*, which is half the size of Belgium and runs both sides of the GRR. At 627km from Derby, the **Bindoola Falls Trail** is an easy stroll to a lookout over the rugged cliff edge to the falls beyond; at 642km, pull off into the lookout area for **panoramic views** of the Cockburn Ranges, Cambridge Gulf and Pentecost River. At 643km (and just 120km from Kununurra) is the *Home Valley Station* homestead itself (see p.649), with accommodation, horseriding, cattle mustering, hikes, fishing and station tours.

6

After another 9km you will cross the Pentecost River, an experience in itself as you grit your teeth and drive headlong through the waters, knowing that saltwater crocs lurk nearby. Crossing this feels a little like crossing the finish line, with just 24km remaining between you and the bitumen, at 626km. This is also the turn-off for **El Questro Wilderness Park** (25km south of the GRR), where you'll find both luxury accommodation and campsites (see opposite) and a range of tours including barramundi fishing, horse trekking and helicopter flights.

Don't miss a final stop at **Emma Gorge**. Said to be the GRR's most beautiful gorge, it's all dripping palm fronds, deep red cliffs and waterholes along the 1.6km trail to a glorious swimming hole and waterfall. There are no crocs here and there are few more picturesque places for a dip. Allow two hours for the return hike, including a swim, and wear sturdy shoes.

From here it is a further 23km to the Great Northern Highway junction; turn right for Kununurra (52km) or left for Wyndham (48km).

INFORMATION   THE GIBB RIVER ROAD AND NORTHERN KIMBERLEY

Information A comprehensive and annually updated *Travellers Guide to the Inland Kimberley and Mitchell Plateau* ($5) is available at local visitor centres and is worth picking up.

Permits To visit Kalumburu, you'll need to buy a one-week vehicle permit on arrival from the community office, if there's anyone there ($50, ☏ 08 9161 4300); you'll also need to get another (free) permit in advance from the Department of Aboriginal Affairs (☏ 08 9235 8000 in Perth, ☏ 08 9168 2550 in Kununurra, ⊛ daa.wa.gov.au).

Scenic flights Aviair (see box, p.636) flies helicopters and arranges scenic flights to Mitchell Falls (May–Sept; from $995).

ACCOMMODATION AND EATING

Camping is only allowed in designated **campsites**, and camping fees of around $10 per person always apply. All campsites have bush toilets, drinking water and showers – some also have gas barbecues and other facilities. Many roads, gorges, services and accommodation are closed in the Wet from around November to March – always check conditions and opening dates before you set out and book accommodation in advance where possible. It's best to visit at the start of the **Dry**, when the land is lush from the rains and rivers are full. All accommodation is marked on The Kimberley map (see p.631).

THE DEVONIAN REEF NATIONAL PARKS

Windjana Gorge Campground Windjana Gorge National Park, 124km from Derby; 21km off the GRR ⊛ dpaw.wa.gov.au. DPaW-operated campsite with generator and non-generator sites, flushing toilets, hot showers, fire rings with limited wood for cooking, picnic tables and rubbish bins. Untreated bore water is available and can be drunk if boiled first. $12 per person

THE WESTERN GIBB RIVER ROAD

Mornington Wilderness Camp 253km from Derby; 82km off the GRR ☏ 08 9380 9633, ⊛ australianwildlife .org. A former station that has been bought out by a conservation organization aiming to preserve native fauna. The camp now boasts creekside camping, en-suite safari tents with private verandas (and breakfast, lunch hampers and dinner) as well as a bar and restaurant. $25 per vehicle. Open May–Oct. Unpowered sites per person $20, safari tents per person $300

Mount Barnett Roadhouse 305km from Derby, 360km from Kununurra ☏ 08 9191 7007. Fuel (both diesel and unleaded) is available here and there's a telephone and limited camping and food supplies too. It's not a bad stop for lunch, and offers basic hot food such as fish and chips (May–Oct daily 8am–5pm; Nov–April Mon–Sat 8am–noon & 2–4pm). Camping is permitted behind the roadhouse by the Manning River. Unpowered sites per person $12

Mount Elizabeth Station 340km from Derby, 365km from Kununurra; 30km off the GRR ☏ 08 9191 464. Camp amid shady gum trees with wallabies grazing nearby or book a room in the homestead. The campsite has an amenity block with hot showers, flushing toilets and drinking water plus a BBQ with plenty of firewood supplied. Rooms in the homestead share bathroom facilities, but the rate includes an evening meal. Bookings not required to camp. May–Oct only. Unpowered sites per person $18, doubles $390

Silent Grove Campground King Leopold Range Conservation Park, 219km from Derby; 29km off the GRR ⊛ dpaw.wa.gov.au. First come, first served campsite operated by DPaW. Facilities include flushing toilets, hot showers, fire rings with limited firewood for cooking and picnic tables. Taps of untreated bore water are available and this should be boiled before drinking. Generator and non-generator areas available. Unpowered sites per person $12

THE EASTERN GIBB RIVER ROAD

Emma Gorge at El Questro El Questro Wilderness Park, 624km from Derby, 110km from Kununurra; 25km off the GRR ⓦelquestro.com.au. Safari-style tented cabins with en-suite bathrooms, sleeping up to four people. This is "glamping" at its best, with comfortable beds, an outdoor swimming pool and on-site restaurant with retractable roof for dining under the stars. **$298**

★ **Home Valley Station** 643km from Derby, 120km from Kununurra; 1.5km off the GRR ☎02 8296 8010, ⓦhvstation.com.au. This fantastic homestead offers a full range of accommodation, from campsites right through to the luxurious "Grass Castles" complete with opulent en-suite bathrooms and private balconies with idyllic creek views. There is a real cattle station feel to everything from the decor to the dining and you could easily spend several days here. There are two swimming pools, numerous walking trails and an excellent restaurant and bar with live music, not to mention the chance to try your hand at cattle mustering. Unpowered sites per person **$17**, doubles **$240**

The Station at El Questro El Questro Wilderness Park, 624km from Derby, 110km from Kununurra; 25km off the GRR ⓦelquestro.com.au. Camping is available here, in either the central Black Cockatoo site close to the shared toilets, showers and laundry, or in private riverside sites along the Pentecost about 10 minutes' drive away. There are also self-contained bungalows with garden or river views, some with private balconies. All rooms have en-suite bathrooms, a/c and fridges. The station is also home to the *Steakhouse Restaurant* and *Swinging Arm* bar (with wi-fi access) and it's a short stroll to a peaceful swimming hole. April–October only. Unpowered sites per person **$20**, powered sites **$42**, doubles **$329**

THE NORTHERN KIMBERLEY

Drysdale River Station Kalumburu Road ☎08 9161 4326, ⓦdrysdaleriver.com.au. Camping at two sites with ablutions block and laundry facilities. There's also an excellent bar and beer garden, meals and scenic flights over Mitchell Falls and King Cascades (from $450). May–Oct only. **$150**

Kalumburu Mission Kalumburu ☎08 9161 4333, ⓦkalumburumission.org.au. Simple double and single dongas (transportable buildings) with self-contained kitchens and air conditioning, plus a range of powered and unpowered campsites. There are also laundry facilities. Un/powered sites **$40/52**, dongas **$175**

6

South Australia

THE FLINDERS RANGES

South Australia

South Australia, the driest state of the driest continent, is split into two distinct halves. The long-settled southern part, watered by the Murray River, with Adelaide as its cosmopolitan centre, has a Mediterranean climate, is tremendously fertile and has been thoroughly tamed. The northern half is arid and depopulated, and as you head further north the temperature heats up to such an extreme that by the time you get to Coober Pedy, people are living underground to escape the searing summer temperatures.

7

Many of the highlights of southeastern South Australia lie within three hours' drive of Adelaide. Food and especially **wine** are among the area's chief pleasures: this is prime grape-growing and winemaking country. As well as vineyards, the **Fleurieu Peninsula**, just south of Adelaide, has a string of fine beaches, while nearby **Kangaroo Island** is a wonderful place to see Australian wildlife at its unfettered best. Facing Adelaide across the Investigator Strait, the **Yorke Peninsula** is primarily an agricultural area, preserving a copper-mining history and offering excellent fishing. The superb wineries of the **Barossa Valley**, originally settled by German-speaking immigrants in the nineteenth century, are only an hour from Adelaide on the **Sturt Highway**, the main road to Sydney. Following the southeast coast along the **Princes Highway**, you can head towards Melbourne via the extensive coastal Coorong lagoon system and enjoyable seaside towns such as Robe, before exiting the state at **Mount Gambier**, with its deep-blue crater lakes. The inland trawl via the **Dukes Highway** is faster but less interesting. Head north from Adelaide and there are old copper-mining towns to explore at **Kapunda** and **Burra**, the area known as the mid-north, which also encompasses the **Clare Valley**, another wonderful wine region, famous for its Rieslings.

In contrast with the gentle and cultured southeast, the remainder of South Australia – with the exception of the relatively refined **Eyre Peninsula** and its scenic west coast – is unremittingly harsh **desert**, a naked country of vast horizons, salt lakes, glazed gibber plains and ancient mountain ranges. Although it's tempting to scud over the forbidding distances quickly, you'll miss the essence of this introspective and subtle landscape by hurrying. For every predictable, monotonous highway there's a dirt alternative, which may be physically draining but gets you closer to this precarious environment. The folded red rocks of the central **Flinders Ranges** and Coober Pedy's postapocalyptic scenery are on most agendas and could be worked into a sizeable circuit. Making the most of the journey is what counts here, though – the fabled routes to **Oodnadatta**, **Birdsville** and **Innamincka** are still real adventures.

WELCOME SIGN AT COOBER PEDY

Highlights

❶ **Barossa Valley** A day-trip from Adelaide, the Barossa Valley is home to some of Australia's finest wineries. **See p.676**

❷ **Kangaroo Island** Spectacular scenery and wildlife are found across Australia's third-largest island. **See p.688**

❸ **Murray River** Stay in a houseboat on the beautiful Murray River, lined with majestic river red gums. **See p.700**

❹ **The Eyre Peninsula** Stay here for ocean-fresh seafood, pristine surf beaches and wildlife encounters – including cage shark diving. **See p.708**

❺ **The Nullarbor Plain** Drive or catch a train across the plain and appreciate just how vast Australia actually is. **See p.712**

❻ **Coober Pedy** Gape at the underground homes of the residents of scorching Coober Pedy. **See p.715**

❼ **Wilpena Pound** The main attraction of the Flinders Ranges National Park is the enormous natural basin of Wilpena Pound. **See p.722**

❽ **Lake Eyre** This salt lake periodically fills with water, creating a dramatic inland sea. **See p.726**

❾ **The Strzelecki, Birdsville and Oodnadatta tracks** Fill up your tank and head off into the Outback on one of Australia's fabled journeys. **See p.725 & p.727**

HIGHLIGHTS ARE MARKED ON THE MAP ON P.654

Rail and road routes converge in Adelaide before the long, cross-country route hauls west to Perth via Port Augusta on the *Indian Pacific* train, or north to Alice Springs and Darwin on the *Ghan* – two of Australia's great train journeys.

Brief history

The coast of South Australia was first explored by the **Dutch** in 1627. In 1792 the French explorer Bruni d'Entrecasteaux sailed along the Great Australian Bight before heading to southern Tasmania, and in 1802 the Englishman Matthew Flinders thoroughly charted the coast. The most important expedition, though – and the one that led to the foundation of a colony here – was **Captain Charles Sturt**'s 1830 navigation of the Murray River, from its source in New South Wales to its mouth in South Australia. In 1836, **Governor John Hindmarsh** landed at Holdfast Bay – now the

HIGHLIGHTS
1. Barossa Valley
2. Kangaroo Island
3. Murray River
4. The Eyre Peninsula
5. The Nullarbor Plain
6. Coober Pedy
7. Wilpena Pound
8. Lake Eyre
9. The Strzelecki, Birdsville and Oodnadatta tracks

SOUTH AUSTRALIA

Adelaide beachside suburb of Glenelg – with the first settlers, and the next year Colonel William Light planned the spacious, attractive city of Adelaide, with broad streets and plenty of parks and squares.

Early problems caused by the harsh, dry climate and financial incompetence (the colony went bankrupt in 1841) were eased by the discovery of substantial reserves of **copper**. The population of Adelaide boomed over the following decades, while the state's tradition of civil and religious **libertarianism** that was guaranteed to the early settlers continued; in 1894, South Australia's women were the first in the world to be permitted to stand for parliament and the third in the world to gain the vote (after the Isle of Man and New Zealand). The depressions and recessions of the interwar period hit South Australia hard, but the situation eased following World War II when new immigrants arrived, mostly from Europe, boosting industry and injecting fresh life into the state.

South Australia had an important, though controversial, role during the early years of the Cold War. In 1947 an Anglo-Australian project founded the Woomera rocket range, site of British-run atomic bomb tests in 1950. The Woomera area later became part of the US space programme, and in 1947 launched Australia's first satellite.

7

Aboriginal South Australia

When European settlers arrived in 1836, South Australia was home to as many as fifty distinct **Aboriginal groups**, with a population estimated at fifteen thousand. Three distinct cultural regions existed: the Western Desert, the Central Lakes, and the Murray and southeast region. It was the people of the comparatively well-watered southeast who felt the full impact of white settlement, and those who survived were shunted onto missions controlled by the government. Some Aboriginal people have clung tenaciously to their way of life in the Western Desert, where they have gained title to some of their land, but most now live south of Port Augusta, many in Adelaide.

Adelaide

ADELAIDE is a gracious city and an easy place to live, and despite its population of just over 1.3 million, it never feels crowded. It's a pretty place, laid out on either side of the **Torrens River**, ringed with a green belt of parks and set against the rolling hills of the **Mount Lofty Ranges**. During the hot, dry summer the parklands are kept green by irrigation from the waters of the Murray River, upon which the city depends, though there's always a sense that the rawness of the Outback is waiting to take over.

The original occupants of the Adelaide plains were the **Kaurna people**, whose traditional way of life was destroyed within twenty years of European settlement. After a long struggle with Governor John Hindmarsh, who wanted to build the city around a harbour, the colony's surveyor-general, Colonel William Light, got his wish for an inland city with a strong connection to the river, formed around wide and spacious avenues and squares.

Postwar **immigration** provided the final element missing from Light's plan for the city: the human one. **Italians** now make up the city's biggest non-Anglo cultural group, and in summer Mediterranean-style alfresco eating and drinking lend the city a vaguely European air. Not surprisingly, one of Adelaide's chief delights is its **food and wine**, with South Australian vintages in every cellar, and restaurants and cafés as varied as those in Sydney and Melbourne.

Adelaide may not be an obvious destination in itself, but its free-and-easy lifestyle and liberal traditions make it a fine place for a relaxed break on your way up to the Northern Territory or across to Western Australia.

ADELAIDE

N

North Adelaide

NORTH ADELAIDE

St Peter's Cathedral

Montefiore Park

Adelaide Oval

Brougham Gardens

Adelaide Zoo

Adelaide Festival Centre

Government House

Migration Museum

Adelaide Botanic Garden

Art Gallery of South Australia

National Wine Centre

Parliament House

Elder Park

University of Adelaide

University of SA

Casino

Adelaide Train Station

State Library

South Australian Museum

Ayers House

Nexus Arts Centre

Hindley Street

Rundle Mall

Rundle Street

KENT TOWN

State History Centre

Town Hall & Treasury Building

Tandanya

Backpacker Centre

Central Bus Station

Victoria Sq

Central Market

Rymill Park

Adelaide Parklands Terminal

KESWICK

WAYVILLE

Tram to Glenelg

Adelaide Hills

■ DRINKING & NIGHTLIFE	
Apothecary 1878	4
Casablabla	9
Clever Little Tailor	11
Edinburgh Castle	13
Enigma Bar	8
Exeter Hotel	6
Governor Hindmarsh	2
Hains & Co	12
Jack Ruby	14
Mars Bar	15
Mary's Poppin	5
Rhino Room	3
Royal Oak Hotel	1
Udaberri	10
Wheatsheaf	7

0 — 500 metres

—— Tramline

■ ACCOMMODATION			
Adelaide Backpackers Inn	20	Fire Station Inn	2
Adelaide Beachfront Discovery Park	19	The Franklin Boutique Hotel	13
Adelaide Central YHA	12	Glenelg Beach Hostel	22
Adina Apartment Hotel Adelaide Treasury	14	Hilton Adelaide	17
Big4 Adelaide Shores Caravan Park	19	Majestic Minima Hotel	4
Crowne Plaza	10	Majestic Old Lion Apartments	5
Backpack Oz	16	Majestic Roof Garden Hotel	11
Buxton Manor	3	Mayfair Hotel	9
Clarion Soho	15	Mercure Grosvenor	10
		Norwood Apartments	6/18
		Oaks Horizons	7
		Oaks Plaza Pier Hotel	21
		Seawall Apartments	23

● EATING						● SHOPPING	
The Archer	4	Jasmin	20	Osteria Oggi	18	Adelaide Booksellers	2
Chianti	27	Kings Head Pub	28	Peel Street	16	Better World Arts	4
Coffee Branch	17	The Lion Hotel	8	Perryman's Artisan Bakery	1	Central Market Books	4
Earl of Aberdeen	26	Lucia's Pizza Bar	22	Please Say Please	19	Dymocks	1
Estia	12	Madame Hanoi	9	Sean's Kitchen	10	Tandanya	3
Europa	30	Mandoo	11	Star of Siam	24		
Gaucho's	23	Marrakech	2	The Store	7		
Gilbert Street Hotel	29	Monsoon	5	T-chow	21		
Gin Long Canteen	6	NOLA	15	UR Caffe	3		
Hotel Wright Street	25	Nonna Mallozzi	13	Zest Cafe	31		
		Orana	14				

Adelaide Botanic Garden

North Terrace • Mon–Fri 7.15am–dusk, Sat & Sun 9am–dusk • Free • Bicentennial Conservatory daily 10am–4pm, summer until 5pm • Visitor centre daily 10am–4pm; free tours at 10.30am • ☏ 08 8222 9311, ⊕ botanicgardens.sa.gov.au

The main entrance to the impressive **Adelaide Botanic Garden** is at the eastern extremity of the tree-lined North Terrace. Opened in 1857, these lovely gardens boast ponds, fountains, wisteria arbours, statues and heritage buildings just like a classic

ORIENTATION

Adelaide's city centre is laid out on a strict grid plan surrounded by parkland, and virtually every building, public or domestic, is made of **stone**. At the heart of the grid is **Victoria Square**, and each city quarter is centred on its own smaller square. **North Terrace** is the cultural precinct, home to the major museums, two universities and the state library. **Hindley Street** is the focus of Adelaide's more boisterous nightlife, while most of the city's cool, small bars are concentrated around the Peel Street and Leigh Street laneways. **Rundle Mall**, Adelaide's main shopping area, was given a major facelift in 2015, with new street furniture, paving and market stalls. The **East End**, a five-minute walk from the mall, offers quirkier design stores, cafés and art-house cinemas. West of Victoria Square between **Grote** and **Gouger** streets is the vibrant **Central Market** and **Chinatown**. The **Torrens River** flows to the north of North Terrace, with the Botanic Garden and zoo set on its south bank. Three main roads cross the river to the distinctive colonial architecture and café culture of **North Adelaide**.

English-style garden, but with plenty of native trees too. The elegant glass-and-wrought-iron **Palm House**, completed in 1877, was based on a similar building in Germany and used to display tropical plant species, a role now taken over by the stunning **Bicentennial Conservatory**. This, the largest glasshouse in Australia, houses a complete tropical rainforest environment with its own computer-controlled cloud-making system. Other attractions include a fragrant herb garden, a rose garden and the **Santos Museum of Economic Beauty**, an eccentric nineteenth-century botanical collection showcasing rare plants and papier-mâché models of fruit and funghi dating back 130 years. Other facilities include a visitor centre, which contains a small shop selling souvenirs and books, a small café with a terrace and an upmarket restaurant.

National Wine Centre

Cnr Hackney & Botanic rds • Mon–Fri 8am–9pm, Sat & Sun 9am–9pm • Free • Free tours daily at 11.30am • ☎ 08 8313 3355, ⓦ wineaustralia.com.au

In the southeast corner of the Botanic Gardens is the eye-catching **National Wine Centre**, which takes visitors on a journey through the winemaking process, with the focus firmly on the industry in Australia. Free wine tastings are held at the centre every Friday (from 4.30pm), and you can also join a "Meet The Maker" master class ($25) later in the evening, but these sessions must be booked in advance. Visitors can also book a guided tour of the centre or one of the many wine-tasting experiences; their bar, *Uncorked*, serves 120 different wines by the glass; bar snacks and larger meals are also available.

Ayers House

288 North Terrace • Tues–Sun 10am–5pm • $8 • ☎ 08 8224 0666, ⓦ ayreshouse.com

The National Trust-owned **Ayers House** was home to the politician Henry Ayers, premier of South Australia seven times between 1855 and 1897 and after whom the Rock (now called Uluru) was named. The building began as a small brick dwelling in 1845 – the fine bluestone mansion you now see is the result of thirty years of extensions – and inside, it's elaborately decorated in late nineteenth-century style, with portraits of the Ayers family.

University of Adelaide

North Terrace • Conservatorium of Music Concerts Fri 1.10pm during term-time; $7; ☎ 08 8313 5208, ⓦ music.adelaide.edu.au

Between Frome Road and Kintore Avenue, a city block of North Terrace is occupied by the **University of Adelaide**, along with the art gallery, museum and state library. The university was established in 1874 and began to admit women right from its founding – another example of South Australia's advanced social thinking. The grounds are pleasant to stroll through: along North Terrace are **Bonython Hall**, built in 1936 in a vaguely medieval style, and **Elder Hall**, an early twentieth-century Gothic-Florentine design now occupied by the **Conservatorium of Music**.

Art Gallery of South Australia

North Terrace • Daily 10am–5pm • Free • Tours daily 11am & 2pm • Lunchtime talks daily 12.30pm • ☎ 08 8207 7000, ⊛ artgallery.sa.gov.au

Overbearing Victorian busts of the upright founders of Adelaide line the strip between Bonython Hall and Kintore Avenue until you reach the **Art Gallery of South Australia**, established in 1881. The gallery has an impressive collection of **Aboriginal art**, including many nontraditional works with overtly political content; major works by the **Western Desert school** of Aboriginal artists are on permanent display in Gallery 7. There's a fine selection of colonial art, too, and it's interesting to trace the development of Australian art from its European-inspired beginnings up to the point where the influence of the local, lighter colours and landscape begin to take over. The collection of twentieth-century Australian art includes works by Sidney Nolan, Margaret Preston and Grace Cossington-Smith. There's also a large collection of twentieth-century **British art**, including paintings by Roger Fry and Vanessa Bell. The gallery has an excellent gift shop and coffee shop too.

South Australian Museum

North Terrace • Daily 10am–5pm • Free • Free tours Mon–Fri 11am, Sat & Sun 2pm & 3pm • ☎ 08 8207 7500, ⊛ samuseum.sa.gov.au

A huge whale skeleton guards the foyer of the **South Australian Museum**, whose east wing houses the engrossing **Australian Aboriginal Cultures Gallery**, home to the world's largest collection of Aboriginal artefacts. Among the exhibits are a 10,000-year-old boomerang and the *Yanardilyi (Cockatoo Creek) Jukurrpa*, a huge painting by a collection of artists from across the continent recalling four important Dreaming stories.

The west wing focuses on **natural history** and **geology**, including an extensive collection of minerals from around the world. There's also a permanent exhibition on local geologist **Sir Douglas Mawson** (1882–1958), who was commissioned by the museum to explore much of Australia in the early 1900s and who undertook the historic Australasian Antarctic Expedition in 1911. Some of the animals he brought back from this expedition are still on display, along with others from around Australia. The **fossil gallery** includes a skeleton of *Diprotodon*, the largest marsupial ever to walk the earth, plus the Normandy Nugget (at the east wing entrance on the ground floor), the second-largest gold nugget in the world, weighing 26kg.

Migration Museum

82 Kintore Ave, just off North Terrace • Mon–Fri 10am–5pm, Sat & Sun 1–5pm • Free • ☎ 08 8207 7580, ⊛ history.sa.gov.au

The **Migration Museum** takes you on a journey from port to settlement in the company of South Australia's settlers, through innovative, interactive displays and reconstructions – the "White Australia Walk" has a push-button questionnaire to allow you to see if

> ### ADELAIDE ARCHITECTURE
>
> Adelaide suffered numerous economic setbacks and built up its wealth slowly, and its well-preserved **Victorian architecture** has a reassuring permanence quite unlike the over-the-top style of 1850s Melbourne, with its grandiose municipal buildings funded by easy gold-rush money. The bourgeois solidity of Adelaide's streets is enhanced by the fact that virtually every building, public or domestic, is made of **stone**, whether sandstone, bluestone, South Australian freestone or slate.

you would have been allowed to immigrate under the guidelines of the White Australia policy, which was in force from 1901 to 1958.

The government buildings

North Terrace

Government House, Adelaide's oldest public building, was completed in 1855: every governor except the first has lived here. Across King William Road, two parliament houses, the old and the new, compete for space. The current **Parliament House**, begun in 1889, wasn't finished until 1939 because of a dispute over a dome, and while there's still no dome (and only half a coat of arms), it's a stately building all the same, with a facade of marble columns. Alongside is the modest **Old Parliament House** (closed to the public), built between 1855 and 1876.

Adelaide Festival Centre

7

Festival Drive, off King William St • ☎ 08 8216 8600, ⓦ adelaidefestivalcentre.com.au

Completed in 1973, the **Adelaide Festival Centre** was Australia's first purpose-built arts centre. The building, which overlooks the Torrens, consists of two geometric constructions in concrete, steel and smoked glass. The centre hosts a wide range of performances, including opera, ballet, comedy, musicals and rock music and is a major venue for the Adelaide Festival (see box, p.672). Plans are currently being finalized for a major overhaul of the entire site to bring the venue into the twenty-first century, so expect plenty of scaffolding and building work, though it will continue to operate as normal in the meantime.

Elder Park

Verdant **Elder Park** sits on the banks of the river, with a stunning fountain and the chance to spot black swans. Popeye Cruises sail up to the zoo from the jetty on Jolley's Lane (June–Aug Mon–Fri 10am–3pm, Sat & Sun 10am–4pm hourly; Sept–May daily 10am–4pm hourly; $15 return; ☎ 0400 596 065, ⓦ thepopeye.com.au). You can also rent paddleboats on the wharf near the Festival Centre.

Adelaide Zoo

Frome Rd • Daily 9.30am–5pm • $34.50 • Panda and Friends tour Wed–Sun 8.30–11am; $130, bookings essential • ☎ 08 8267 3255, ⓦ zoossa.com.au

Opened in 1883, **Adelaide Zoo** is the country's second oldest (after Melbourne's), full of century-old European and native trees, and well-preserved Victorian architecture, including the **Elephant House**, built in 1900 in the style of an Indian temple. The zoo is best known for its two giant pandas, Wang Wang and Fu Ni, the only breeding pair of these animals in the Southern Hemisphere. The zoo has a good selection of native and exotic species and visitors have the opportunity to feed, hold and pat some of the more docile animals. Wild Night Sleepovers, which include an evening safari, barbecue dinner and animal encounters, are also available. Access to the zoo is via a pleasant riverbank walk or by joining Popeye Cruises (see above), which arrive at a jetty close to the main zoo entrance.

King William Street

Adelaide's main thoroughfare, **King William Street**, is lined with imposing civic buildings and always crowded with traffic. Look out for the **Edmund Wright House** at no. 59, whose elaborate Renaissance-style facade is one of Adelaide's most flamboyant.

On the other side of the street a couple of blocks south is the **Town Hall** (1866), another of Edmund Wright's Italianate designs. The **General Post Office**, on the corner of Franklin Street, is yet another portentous Victorian edifice, this time with a central clock tower: look inside at the main hall with its decorative roof lantern framed by opaque skylights. Opposite, on the corner of Flinders Street, the **Old Treasury Building** retains its beautiful facade, although it now houses the Adina hotel (see p.665). Midway down King William Street, pleasant **Victoria Square** is home to the **Catholic Cathedral of St Francis Xavier**, which dates back to 1856, and the imposing **Supreme Court**, which stands on the corner of Gouger Street.

Central Market

44–60 Gouger St • Tues 7am–5.30pm, Wed & Thurs 9am–5.30pm, Fri 7am–9pm, Sat 7am–3pm • ⓦ adelaidecentralmarket.com.au

The covered **Central Market** has been a well-loved feature of Adelaide for 140 years, home to eighty specialist stores selling everything from organic fruit and vegetables to smoked meats, artisan cheeses, olive oils and sourdough bread. A walking tour (ⓦ centralmarkettour.com.au) with local food personality Mark Gleeson is the best introduction to the market. Wander outside onto Gouger for cheap and cheerful Asian food, mainly Thai, Chinese and Korean, and expect a crowd on Friday evenings.

Rundle Mall and Rundle Street

The main shopping area in the central business district is the pedestrianized **Rundle Mall**, which manages to be bustling yet relaxed, enhanced by trees, benches, alfresco cafés, fruit and flower stalls, and usually a busker or two. The two main shopping centres are the **Myer Centre**, with over 120 specialist stores spread over five floors, and the **Adelaide Central Plaza**, dominated by the **David Jones** department store, which has a decent food hall in the basement. Towards the east end of the mall is the decorative **Adelaide Arcade** and the **Regent Theatre**. By night, Rundle Mall is quiet, a strange contrast to Hindley and Rundle streets on either side, which really come to life after dark.

East of the junction with Pulteney Street, Rundle Mall turns into the unpedestrianized **Rundle Street**. The street was once the home of Adelaide's wholesale fruit and vegetable market, but was later appropriated by the alternative and arty, and by university students from the nearby campuses on North Terrace (see p.657). It's now home to dozens of **cafés and restaurants**, many of them with alfresco seating, several slick wine bars and some popular pubs. Ebenezer Place, which runs parallel to Rundle Street, is a bustling precinct with a number of design stores, jewellers, good cafés, wine merchants and quirky bars.

Tandanya: the National Aboriginal Cultural Institute

253 Grenfell St • Daily 9.30am–4.30pm • Free • ⓣ 088224 3200, ⓦ tandanya.com.au

Situated opposite the classic old market buildings, the **Tandanya** cultural centre is managed by the Kaurna people, the traditional owners of the Adelaide plains area. Its main focus is the visual arts, with a permanent exhibition that includes political pieces confronting difficult subjects, such as black deaths in custody and the "Stolen Generation". There are also displays on Dreamtime stories, history and contemporary Aboriginal writing. Occasional **didgeridoo and dance performances** are staged in the 160-seat auditorium and the gift shop (see p.672) is an excellent place for high-quality souvenirs.

North Adelaide

A fifteen-minute walk from the city centre up King William Road, or via a spectacular new pedestrian bridge across the Torrens, **NORTH ADELAIDE** is one of the most attractive parts of the city. Its leafy streets are lined with stately mansions, bluestone cottages and other architectural gems such as **St Peter's Cathedral**, built in 1869 in the French Gothic Revival style. There are several green spaces, including **Brougham Gardens** and **Montefiore Park**, and a burgeoning café, restaurant and pub scene on **Melbourne and O'Connell streets**. Numerous buses travel to North Adelaide, including the free Adelaide Connector bus (see p.664).

Adelaide Oval

War Memorial Drive, North Adelaide • Bradman Collection daily 9am–4pm • Free • Guided tours Mon–Fri 10am, 11am & 2pm, Sat & Sun 10am, 11am, 1pm & 2pm • $22 • ☏ 08 8300 3800 or ☏ 08 8305 4700 (tours), ⓦ adelaideoval.com.au • RoofClimb daily $99 daytime/$109 twilight • ☏ 08 8331 522, ⓦ roofclimb.com.au

The **Adelaide Oval**, with its impressive scalloped roofline and massive stands, is one of the city's major attractions. Although best known as a venue for Test cricket, the oval also hosts many other sporting fixtures, including Australian Rules Football, rugby union and soccer, and big name rock concerts. Excellent guided tours of the oval are available every day and it's also possible to get a bird's-eye view of the structure with a RoofClimb experience, which takes visitors onto the roof of the Western and Riverbank stadiums. Cricket fans should explore the Bradman Collection, a contemporary museum space dedicated to the world's most famous batsman and which contains historic items from his personal archive.

Jeffcott Street and around

North Adelaide's best range of early **colonial architecture** lies along **Jeffcott Street**, to the northwest of the oval. Just south in Montefiore Park is **Light's Vision**, a bronze statue of Colonel William Light pointing proudly to the city he designed. On Jeffcott Street itself is the neo-Gothic 1890 mansion **Carclew**, with its round turret, and the **Lutheran Theological College**, a fine bluestone and redbrick building with a clock tower and cast-iron decoration. Halfway up the street, on peaceful **Wellington Square**, lies the pretty 1851 *Wellington Hotel*, complete with its original wooden balcony. Turning into tree-lined **Gover Street** you'll find rows of simple bluestone cottages; in contrast, **Barton Terrace West**, two blocks north, has grand homes facing parklands.

The suburbs

Adelaide's **suburbs** spread a long way, and though they remain little visited, some – such as **Unley** and **Thebarton** – have plenty of local character. Further north, **Port Adelaide** has some excellent museums to set off its dockside atmosphere. West of the city lies a string of beaches, from **Henley** via **Glenelg** to **Brighton**, sheltered by the Gulf St Vincent.

Thebarton

West of the city • Buses #110–113 run from the city centre

The semi-industrial suburb of **Thebarton**, to the city's west, is emerging as one of Adelaide's foodie hubs. It's most famous resident is *The Wheatsheaf Hotel* (see p.670), a shabby old pub which serves up an astonishing range of craft beers and malt whiskies alongside live music. A newer arrival is the Brickworks Marketplace (Cnr Ashwin Parade and South Rd, Torrensville), a compact shopping centre with gift shops, gourmet food outlets and some good-value Asian cafés.

Unley

Just south of the city • Buses #190–200 and #202 run here from the city centre

Immediately south of the city is the prosperous suburb of Unley, which is well known for its antique shops and expensive boutiques. Unley Road, which runs through the centre of the area, is a particularly good hunting ground for shoppers, and also has plenty of good cafés and restaurants. King William Road, in nearby Hyde Park, offers upmarket fashion boutiques, jewellery shops and cheerful places to eat.

Port Adelaide

Northwest of Adelaide • Buses #230 and #150 run from the city centre; trains from Adelaide Railway Station

The unfortunate early settlers had to wade through swamps when they arrived at Port Misery, but thanks to William Light's visionary flair, **Port Adelaide** became the primary gateway to the state. Established not far from Port Misery in 1840, the new port soon become a substantial shipping area with solid stone warehouses, wharves and a host of pubs. The area bounded by Nelson, St Vincent and Todd streets and McLaren Parade is a well-preserved nineteenth-century streetscape; several ships' chandlers and shipping agents show that it's still a living port, a fact confirmed by the many corner pubs still in business. The **visitor centre** (see p.664) has some great self-guided walking tours.

The best day to visit is Sunday or public-holiday Mondays, when the **Sunday Markets** take over a large waterfront warehouse near the Port Adelaide Lighthouse on Queens Wharf. Specializing in books and bric-a-brac, the market adds life to the waterfront.

South Australian Maritime Museum

126 Lipson St • Daily 10am–5pm • $10 • Lighthouse Mon–Fri 10am–2pm, Sun 10am–2pm • ☏ 08 8207 6255, ⓦ maritime.history.sa.gov.au

Port Adelaide's quaint metal **lighthouse**, dating from 1869, can be seen as part of a visit to the **South Australian Maritime Museum**, located in the old Bond Store. The pick of Port Adelaide's several museums, its temporary and permanent exhibitions document South Australia's strong connection with the sea.

National Railway Museum

76 Lipson St • Daily 10am–4.30pm • $12 • ☏ 08 8341 1690, ⓦ natrailmuseum.org.au

The **National Railway Museum** is a trainspotter's delight and brilliant if you are travelling with children, with a collection of over twenty steam and diesel locomotives. There are also thematic displays charting the history of the railways in South Australia and the country as a whole. The museum also operates a tourist train service (see below).

Semaphore

Just west of Port Adelaide • Bus #33 from Port Adelaide

Semaphore, with its picturesque jetty and many grand heritage buildings, is an old-school beachside destination, popular with families and the **gay and lesbian** community. The main street, Semaphore Road, offers an eclectic range of historic buildings, junk shops, New Age boutiques, bookstores and a historic cinema. In the summer, on Sundays, bank holidays and school holidays, the National Railway Museum (see above) runs a **steam train** between the jetty and **Fort Glanville** (359 Military Rd; ☏0413 469 344, ⓦfortglanville.com.au). The fort is the only complete example of many that were built in Australia in the mid-nineteenth century, when fear of Russian invasion reached hysterical heights after the Crimean War. Tours are run once a week (Tues 9am–2pm; $4) and re-enactments once a month (Sept–May on the third Sat of the month, 1–4.30pm; $20).

Grange and Henley beaches

South of Semaphore • Bus #G1 and trains run from the city centre to Grange • Buses #H30, #287 and #H32 run from the city centre to Henley Beach

Grange Beach is a popular summer spot with families, windsurfers and paddleboarders. The beach offers a busy waterfront pub, an outdoor café and a fully restored wooden pier; stand up paddleboards can be hired nearby. **Henley Beach**, further south, is much busier, especially on weekends, attracting families, teenagers and beach joggers. The newly revamped **Henley Square** has a good range of cafés, pubs, restaurants and *gelato* bars – and new changing rooms and showers.

Glenelg

11km southwest of Adelaide • Regular trams (25min) run from Victoria Square

The most popular and easily accessible of Adelaide's beaches is **Glenelg**, site of the landing of **Governor John Hindmarsh** and the first colonists on Holdfast Bay; the **Old Gum Tree** where he read the proclamation establishing the government of the colony still stands on McFarlane Street, and there's a re-enactment here every year on Proclamation Day (Dec 28).

Holiday-makers have been parading along the seaside promenade for over 160 years and Glenelg still has the atmosphere of a busy holiday town, even in the off season. **Jetty Road**, the main drag, is crowded with casual places to eat (most notably fish and chip shops), while **Marina Pier** at the northern end of Holdfast Promenade is home to bars, cafés and restaurants. There's lots of **accommodation** and a useful visitor centre too.

Moseley Square is dominated by the **Glenelg Town Hall** and a clock tower, while opposite the imposing seafront is *Stamford Grand Hotel*, which is crowded with drinkers on Sunday, when Glenelg is at its most vibrant. From Moseley Square, the old jetty juts out into the bay, and in summer the beach is crowded with people swimming; it's a popular windsurfing spot year-round.

7

Bay Discovery Centre

Glenelg Town Hall, Moseley Square • Daily 10am–3pm • Free; donation appreciated • ☎ 08 8179 9508

Glenelg Town Hall is home to the **Bay Discovery Centre**, a wonderful social history museum documenting stories of life by the sea through the use of multimedia and archival images, and covering everything from old seaside amusements from the 1930s to changing beach fashions.

ARRIVAL AND DEPARTURE | ADELAIDE

BY PLANE

The airport (ⓦ adelaideairport.com.au), 7km southwest from the centre, is modern and well equipped and has a currency exchange, car-rental desks and information booth. In addition to the domestic destinations (linked by direct flights) listed below, the airport also has services to a growing number of international cities. Regional Express (☎ 13 17 13, ⓦ rex.com.au) flies to Kangaroo Island (Kingscote) as well as a range of regional destinations including Broken Hill, Ceduna, Mount Gambier, Port Lincoln, Whyalla and Coober Pedy. Virgin Australia (☎ 13 67 89, ⓦ virginaustralia.com) flies to major cities countrywide, as does Qantas (☎ 13 13 13, ⓦ qantas.com.au) and its subsidiary Jetstar (☎ 13 15 38, ⓦ jetstar.com.au). Tiger Airways (☎ 03 9335 3033, ⓦ tigerairways.com.au) flies to Sydney, Brisbane and Melbourne.

Destinations Brisbane (4 daily; 2hr 20min); Broken Hill (2 daily except Sat; 1hr 15min); Cairns (daily; 3hr 5min); Ceduna (2 daily; 1hr 30min); Coober Pedy (daily except Sat; 2hr); Darwin (daily; 3hr 40min); Gold Coast (daily; 2hr 20min); Kingscote, Kangaroo Island (2–4 daily; 35min); Melbourne (5 daily; 1hr 20min); Mildura (daily except Sat; 1hr 35min); Mount Gambier (4 daily; 1hr 10min); Perth (2–3 daily; 3hr 30min); Port Lincoln (5–8 daily; 50min); Sydney (5 daily; 1hr 50min); Whyalla (1–7 daily; 50min).

Bus services The airport is served by Adelaide Metro JetBus (#J1, #J3, #J7 and #J8; daily 5.03am–11.35pm; $3.30–5.20; ☎ 1300 311 108, ⓦ adelaidemetro.com.au) and JetExpress services (#J1X; daily 5.03am–11.35pm; $3.30–5.20; ☎ 1300 311 108, ⓦ adelaidemetro.com.au), which serve over twenty hotels in the city, along Currie, Grenfell and Pulteney streets, while JetBus also runs to Jetty Road in Glenelg. The privately owned Northern Flyer shuttle bus (Mon–Fri 6am–9pm, Sat 6am–6pm, Sun 6am–5pm; $10; ☎ 0433 533 718, ⓦ northernflyer .com.au) offers a door-to-door service within the Central Business District.

Taxis A taxi from the airport costs around $35 to the city; Uber also operate in Adelaide (you'll need to download the app).

BY TRAIN

Interstate trains arrive/depart from Adelaide Parklands Terminal, west of the city centre off the Anzac Highway (not the more central Adelaide Railway Station). There are three options: the *Overlander* to Melbourne, the *Ghan* to Darwin via Alice Springs, and the *Indian Pacific*, which runs east to Sydney and west to Perth. Tickets can be booked through Great Southern Rail (☎ 1800 703 357, ⓦ greatsouthernrail .com.au). A taxi into the centre costs $20–25.

Destinations Alice Springs (1–2 weekly; 25hr 25min); Darwin (1–2 weekly; 53hr 10min); Katherine (1–2 weekly; 44hr 40min); Melbourne (2 weekly; 11hr 5min); Perth (1–2 weekly; 38hr 30min); Sydney (1–2 weekly; 24hr 10min).

BY BUS

Most long-distance buses leave from the Central Bus Station on Franklin St. Tickets can be purchased at the Central Bus Station. For route maps and timetables of bus services throughout South Australia, visit the South Australian Visitor Information Centre (see below), or see ⓦ bussa.com.au.

Interstate services Greyhound Australia (☎ 1300 473 946, ⓦ greyhound.com.au) has an extensive nationwide service that includes Alice Springs in its destinations. Firefly Express (☎ 1300 730 740, ⓦ fireflyexpress.com.au) runs to Melbourne, with connections to Sydney.

South Australia services State services are dominated by Premier Stateliner Coach Service (☎ 08 8415 5555, ⓦ premierstateliner.com.au), which goes to the Riverland, Whyalla, Port Lincoln, Ceduna, the Fleurieu Peninsula and to Mount Gambier either inland or along the coast. LinkSA (☎ 08 8532 2633, ⓦ linksa.com.au) stops at the main towns in the Barossa Valley en route to Angaston, and travels to Murray Bridge via Mannum and Meningie, and to Pinnaroo via Murray Bridge. Yorke Peninsula Coaches (☎ 08 8821 2755, ⓦ ypcoaches.com.au) runs from Adelaide to Yorketown down the east coast via Ardrossan, Port Vincent and Edithburgh, and down the centre via Maitland and Minlaton, as well as the Clare Valley, Burra and Peterborough. Buses R Us (☎ 08 8285 6900, ⓦ busesrus .com.au) has buses to Broken Hill.

Destinations Alice Springs (daily; 20hr 30min); Barossa Valley (2–9 daily; 2hr); Broken Hill (5 weekly; 7hr 10min); Canberra (daily; 15hr 15min); Ceduna (3 weekly; 11hr 15min); Coober Pedy (daily; 11hr 15min); Loxton (daily except Sat; 3hr 45min); McLaren Vale (1–3 daily; 50min); Melbourne (2 daily; 10hr 30min–12hr); Mount Gambier (1–2 daily; 6hr 15min–6hr 55min); Port Augusta (2–5 daily; 3hr 45min); Port Lincoln (daily Sun–Fri; 9hr 50min); Renmark (1–2 daily; 4hr); Sydney (4 weekly; 20hr 30min); Whyalla (2–4 daily; 6hr 10min); Yorke Peninsula (2–3 daily; 3–3hr 40min).

INFORMATION

South Australian Visitor Information Centre The main government information office is located in James Place, just off Rundle Mall, in the centre of Adelaide (Mon–Fri 9am–5pm, Sat & Sun 10am–4pm; ☎ 1300 588 140, ⓦ adelaidecitycouncil.com). It has helpful staff and masses of general information, including excellent free touring guides and maps of Adelaide and the state. You can also purchase a discount booklet if you plan to do a lot of sightseeing.

TOURS AND ACTIVITIES

Adelaide Sightseeing Central Bus Station ☎ 08 8413 6199, ⓦ adelaidesightseeing.com.au. Offers the City Highlights Tour (daily 9.30am; 3hr; $66) covering the city, Glenelg and a stop at Haigh's chocolate factory, and others taking in the Barossa Valley, Kangaroo Island, the Fleurieu Peninsula and Flinders Ranges.

Adventure Kayaking Port Adelaide ☎ 08 8295 8812, ⓦ adventurekayak.com.au. Rents kayaks ($40/day) and runs kayaking trips (from $70) from Torrens Island north of the city to see Port River dolphins and the ship graveyards.

Barossa Daimler Tours 503 Rosedale Road, Barossa Valley ☎ 08 8524 9047, ⓦ barossadaimlertours.com. au. Using vintage Daimler cars, this small company offers bespoke wine tours of the Adelaide Hills, McLaren Vale, the Clare Valley and Barossa Valley (full-day tours from $425 for two people; city pick-ups extra).

Groovy Grape Getaways 10 Bacon St, Hindmarsh ☎ 1800 067 025, ⓦ groovygrape.com.au. Popular with backpackers, the Groovy Grape people offer several tours from Adelaide including to Kangaroo Island (2 days; $435 all-inclusive) and a tour to Alice Springs via the Flinders Ranges (6 days; $795 all-inclusive). Its Barossa day-trip visits four wineries and includes lunch ($99).

Off Piste 4WD Tours McLaren Vale ☎ 0423 725 409, ⓦ offpistetours.com.au. Local guide and winemaker Ben Neville offers a number of handcrafted tours around the Fleurieu Peninsula, showcasing the region's rugged beauty and its talented winemakers and brewers. All-day tours from $299, including city hotel pick-ups.

GETTING AROUND

The city centre is compact and flat, making walking an easy option, but if the heat becomes too much use the network of buses, trams and suburban trains to get around.

FREE BUSES AND TRAMS

The free Adelaide Connector bus service handily circles the city centre and North Adelaide; #99C (every 30min: Mon–Thurs, Sat & Sun 7am–8pm, Fri 7.30am–9.48pm) travels clockwise and #99A (every 30min: Mon–Thurs 7am–7.15pm, Fri early–9.15pm) anticlockwise. There's also a free tram service within central Adelaide running between South Terrace and the Adelaide Entertainment Centre (Mon–Fri 5.15am–11.57pm every 5–20min, Sat & Sun 6.45am–11.57pm every 15–20min) and back again (Mon–Fri 5.50am–12.37am every 5–20min, Sat & Sun 7.25am–12.37pm every 15–20min). For more information call ☎ 1300 311 108 or visit ⓦ adelaidemetro.com.au

ADELAIDE METRO SYSTEM

Adelaide Metro buses and trains run from around 5.30am until about 11.30pm, with reduced services at night and on weekends, while the After Midnight night-bus service operates Saturday nights (around 12.30–5am). The O-Bahn is a fast-track bus that runs on concrete tracks through scenic Torrens Linear Park, between the city (Grenfell St) and Tea Tree Plaza in Modbury, 12km northeast. Suburban train lines run from Adelaide Railway Station to Belair, Gawler, Grange, Osborn, Outer Harbour, Seaford and Tonsley. The tram to Glenelg (every 15–20min; 30min) leaves from King William Street near the junction with Rundle Mall.

Information Tickets, information and free timetables can be found at Adelaide Metro Info Centre, cnr King William & Currie sts (Mon–Fri 8am–6pm, Sat 9am–5pm, Sun 11am–4pm; ⓦ adelaidemetro.com.au). You can also get transport information on the InfoLine ☎ 1300 311 108.

Tickets Metro system tickets come in single-trip, multi-trip and day-trip permutations, and can be used on buses, trains and the tram; one ticket will cover you if you need to use more than one form of transport for a single journey. Single tickets range in price from $3.30 to $5.20, depending on the time of day, and are valid for two hours. You can buy single-journey tickets from machines on board buses and trams, as well as from train-station ticket offices and the Adelaide Metro Info Centre (see above). The Three-Day Visitor Pass ($26.50) and 28-Day Pass ($119.80) are the best-value options if you'll be making a lot of use of public transport. These can be bought from the Adelaide Metro Info Centre, train stations, post offices and some newsagents – look for the Metroticket sign.

CYCLING

Cycling is a popular alternative to public transport: the wide streets and level surfaces make riding a breeze, and there are several good cycling routes – including the Torrens Linear Park track, which runs from the ocean to the Hills. Adelaide City Council provides free daily bike rental, including helmet and lock, with collection points across the city centre. Bike SA, 111 Franklin St (☎ 08 8168 9999, ⓦ bikesa.asn.au), has an overview of all cycling routes and maps, and also offers bikes for longer-term rental.

CAR RENTAL

Avis (☎ 13 63 33, ⓦ avis.com.au), Hertz (☎ 13 30 39, ⓦ hertz.com.au) and Thrifty (☎ 1300 962 142, ⓦ thrifty .com.au) have desks at the airport. Older, cheaper cars can be obtained from Cut Price Car Rentals (cnr South Rd & Sir Donald Bradman Drive; ☎ 08 8443 7788, ⓦ cutprice .com.au), which also does one-way rentals and buy-backs. Britz Campervan, Car and 4WD Rentals (376 Sir Donald Bradman Drive; ☎ 08 8234 4701, ⓦ britz.com.au) has a full range of campervans.

TAXIS

Adelaide cabs do not pick up on the street, so you'll need to find a cab rank. The three standard taxi companies are Adelaide Independent Taxis (☎ 13 22 11), Suburban Taxis (☎ 13 10 08) and Yellow Cabs (☎ 13 22 27) are below standard, with old cabs and geographically challenged drivers. A number of fare-sharing services, such as UberX, are now licensed to operate in Adelaide; download the Uber app to make use of these.

7

ACCOMMODATION

Adelaide has a good choice of budget and mid-range accommodation; you will need to book well in advance if planning to visit from January to March, when the city hosts a number of high-profile events including **Womadelaide** and the **Adelaide Festival**. Most of the backpacker hostels are located on Waymouth St or near the Central Bus Station on Franklin St.

CITY CENTRE

HOTELS AND APARTMENTS

Adina Apartment Hotel Adelaide Treasury 2 Flinders St ☎ 08 8112 0000, ⓦ tfehotels.com. This stylish apartment hotel occupies the former state treasury building on Victoria Square and is packed with appealing facilities, including a lap pool, cocktail bar and gymnasium. The 79 rooms range from modest studios to more elaborate apartments, all tastefully decorated and equipped with kitchens. Wi-fi is only free for the first 24 hours. **$185**

Clarion Soho 264 Flinders St ☎ 08 8412 5600, ⓦ clarionhotelsoho.com.au. This boutique hotel has stylish rooms with chic Italian-style furniture, LCD televisions and iPod docking stations. There's a pool upstairs and a cute bistro downstairs. **$119**

Crowne Plaza 16 Hindmarsh Square ☎ 08 8206 8888, ⓦ crowneplazaadelaide.com.au. A well-established mid-range hotel with spacious rooms, a cocktail bar, heated swimming pool and gym, located in the trendy East End quarter. **$136**

★**The Franklin Boutique Hotel** 92 Franklin Street ☎ 08 8410 0036, ⓦ thefranklinhotel.com.au. The upper floor of this classic Aussie pub has been transformed into seven arty yet superbly comfortable guest rooms, each kitted out with flat-screen TVs, Nespresso machines, iPod docks, small fridges and modern bathrooms. The restaurant downstairs serves excellent local cuisine. **$150**

Hilton Adelaide 233 Victoria Square ☎ 08 8217 2000, ⓦ hilton.com. Although one of the city's older five-star properties, the *Hilton* has been given a tasteful makeover and now offers contemporary rooms, a swimming pool, tour desk, New York-style grill and two cocktail bars. Wi-fi not inlcuded. **$175**

7

Majestic Roof Garden Hotel 55 Frome St ⊕08 8100 4400, ⊛majestichotels.com.au. One of Adelaide's most popular mid-priced hotels, offering comfortable if fairly bland rooms, a fitness centre, small restaurant and a cocktail bar. The hotel's strongest selling point is the central location. $\overline{\$155}$

★**Mayfair Hotel** 45 King William Street ⊕08 8210 8888, ⊛mayfairhotel.com.au. Opened in 2015, the *Mayfair* is the city's most glamorous and contemporary five-star hotel, with lots of personality, stylish, well-appointed rooms, a good restaurant and a sexy rooftop cocktail bar. The rooms come with huge flat-screen TVs and luxurious bathrooms. $\overline{\$249}$

Mercure Grosvenor 125 North Terrace ⊕08 8407 8888, ⊛mercuregrosvenorhotel.com.au. If you are looking for a clean, affordable hotel on Adelaide's premier boulevard then this fits the bill. Rooms are on the smallish side and lack personality, but the staff are very friendly and the location is ideal. Facilities include a fitness centre, a bar and cheerful restaurant. Wi-fi not included. $\overline{\$145}$

Oaks Horizons 104 North Terrace ⊕08 8210 8000, ⊛theoaksgroup.com.au. These modern and spacious self-catering apartments come with kitchens, washing machines and balconies – those on the upper floors have great city or river views – and facilities include a pool, spa and gym. Choose from one-bedroom to two-bedroom formats. Some of the larger apartments have verandas. Limited wi-fi included. $\overline{\$137}$

HOSTELS

Adelaide Backpackers Inn 112 Carrington St ⊕08 8223 1771, ⊛abpi.com.au. This well-run hostel offers clean, modern dorms in a variety of formats, from three to six bedrooms. Guests can make use of a lounge room, kitchen, tour booking desk, laundry, free bike hire and an outdoor courtyard with BBQ. $\overline{\$25}$

Adelaide Central YHA 135 Waymouth St ⊕08 8414 3010, ⊛yha.com.au. Adelaide's top hostel has a convenient central location, efficient staff, modern facilities (including a well-equipped kitchen and a large laundry), plenty of communal space, a sociable atmosphere, tour bookings and even free pancakes for breakfast. The dorms and private rooms, meanwhile, are all comfortable and clean. Dorms $\overline{\$27}$, doubles $\overline{\$88}$

Backpack Oz 144 Wakefield St ⊕08 8223 3551, ⊛backpackoz.com.au. Converted from a nineteenth-century hotel, this award-winning hostel has light, spacious rooms, dorms (4-, 6- and 12-bed) and an attached guesthouse with private rooms. There's a comfortable common room plus a laundry, small kitchen and licensed bar. Free pick-ups from bus or train, and a basic breakfast is included. Tour bookings available. Dorms $\overline{\$24}$, doubles $\overline{\$70}$

NORTH ADELAIDE AND KENT TOWN

To the immediate north and east of the city, within walking distance of the centre, the inner suburbs of North Adelaide

and Kent Town offer some pleasant, central accommodation options among leafy, café-lined streets. The North Adelaide Heritage Group (NAHG; ⊛adelaideheritage.com.au) has some of the most memorable places to stay in this part of Adelaide, including *Fire Station Inn* and *Buxton Manor*.

Buxton Manor 67–75 Buxton St, North Adelaide ⊕08 8267 2020, ⊛adelaideheritage.com. This beautiful NAHG property is a 1908 mansion built in the Arts and Crafts style and surrounded by half an acre of gardens. Staying in one of the lavish suites here – each decorated with period antiques and with self-catering facilities – is like stepping back in time. Minimum two-night stay. $\overline{\$250}$

Fire Station Inn 80 Tynte St, North Adelaide ⊕08 8267 2020, ⊛adelaideheritage.com. Another NAHG property, this historic building was built as a shop in 1866 and then converted into a fire station – the first in Adelaide – in 1904. There are three immaculate rooms, most notably the Fire Engine suite, which contains its own 1942 fire engine and a fireman's pole. Truly unique. $\overline{\$285}$

Majestic Minima Hotel 146 Melbourne St, North Adelaide ⊕08 8334 7766, ⊛majestichotels.com.au. This chic, contemporary self-check-in hotel (there are no staff on site) boasts compact, stylish rooms with pop art murals and minuscule bathrooms. There's also laundry facilities, parking and a modest rooftop area with good street views. Rates include Continental breakfast provisions. $\overline{\$105}$

Majestic Old Lion Apartments 9 Jerningham St, North Adelaide ⊕08 8334 7799, ⊛oldlionapartments .com.au. Set around a leafy landscaped courtyard, these spacious suites and apartments can accommodate up to seven people and have kitchens and laundry facilities, making them ideal for long stays. There is a similar collection of apartments under the same management on nearby Tynte St. Rates include breakfast provisions; check online for the best prices. $\overline{\$171}$

Norwood Apartments 7 Wakefield St, Kent Town ⊕088338 6555, ⊛norwoodapartments.com.au. This company offers a number of modern apartments and heritage cottages in Norwood and nearby Kent Town, boasting one or two bedrooms. All come with kitchens, laundries and car parking – some have gardens. Two-night minimum stay. $\overline{\$160}$

GLENELG

The seaside suburb of Glenelg and the nearby beach resorts, about half an hour away from Adelaide by public transport, are good alternatives to the city centre, with plenty of self-catering apartments and one of Adelaide's liveliest hostels.

Glenelg Beach Hostel 1–7 Moseley St ⊕08 8376 0007, ⊛glenelgbeachhostel.com.au. Award-winning hostel near the beach, in a beautiful 1870s building with high ceilings and verandas. Lots of doubles as well as dorms (5- and 6- bed, no bunks). Facilities include a communal kitchen, laundry, free tea and coffee equipment, common room and newly refurbished bar and beer garden. DJs perform most weekends, and breakfast is included. Dorms $28, doubles $80

Oaks Plaza Pier Hotel 16 Holdfast Promenade ☎ 08 8350 6688, �🌐 theoaksgroup.com.au. The sleek contemporary suites here come with private balconies affording unspoilt ocean or park views and have all the facilities you'd expect in a four-star hotel, including a pool, gym, spa and sauna, but not a great deal of character. $149

Seawall Apartments 21–25 South Esplanade ☎ 08 8295 1197, �🌐 seawallapartments.com.au. These chic self-contained apartments (with one to four bedrooms) face the ocean and are spread across several grand old buildings. Each one oozes charm, and if you book online you can score a good deal. $159

CAMPING AND CARAVAN PARKS

All caravan parks need to be booked well ahead of time during school holidays, especially summer.

Adelaide Beachfront Discovery Park 349 Military Rd, Semaphore Park ☎ 08 8449 7726, ⌐ discoveryholidayparks.com.au. In a lovely seaside location with a swimming pool and playground, this park has sites, cabins, studios and smarter and more spacious villas (both cabins and villas sleep up to six). Powered sites $38, cabins $99, studios $139

BIG4 Adelaide Shores Caravan Park 1 Military Rd, West Beach ☎ 08 8355 7320, ⌐ adelaideshores .com.au; bus #J1 or #J2 from Currie St in central Adelaide, Glenelg, or airport. A wonderful beachfront option that's perfect for young families, with a lagoon pool, games room, trampolines, a BBQ, laundry and a café. Accommodation options include sites, "eco tents" (sturdy tents with beds), and cabins. Powered sites $40, eco tents & cabins $109

EATING

Eating out is a local obsession in Adelaide, and with one of the nation's highest ratios of restaurants per capita you never have to look far for a great feed. One of the city's most popular places for a meal is **Gouger Street** – many of the restaurants have outdoor tables and are at their busiest on Friday night, when the nearby Central Market stays open until 9pm. **Moonta Street**, right next to Central Market, is the home of Adelaide's small Chinatown, and has several Chinese restaurants and supermarkets, as well as an excellent multi-cuisine food hall. **Hutt Street**, on the eastern edge of the city, has a string of fine Italian restaurants and cheaper Asian places. It's also a good place to go for breakfast. Café society is based around Rundle Street in the city's East End, Melbourne Street in North Adelaide and King William Road in Hyde Park.

CITY CENTRE

CAFÉS AND CARTS

Coffee Branch 32 Leigh St ☎ 0451 661 980, ⌐ coffeebranch.com. Some of the finest coffee (from $3.50) in the city is served at this cool Leigh Street joint, which has bicycles hanging from the walls as decoration, plus a few outdoor tables. There's also a small selection of tempting cakes, pastries, tarts and sandwiches. Mon–Fri 7am–4pm.

Nonna Mallozzi Pasta e Panini 22 Peel Street ☎ 0451 661 980. Scottish-born chef Jock Zonfrillo, who also runs *Orana* (see p.668), is the man behind this bright blue food truck, which serves authentic Italian pasta ($12) and panini ($9), plus *gelato*, coffee and great breakfasts. Mon–Fri 8am–5pm.

Please Say Please 50 Grenfell St ☎ 0418 636 175, ⌐ pleasesayplease.com.au. This modest-looking coffee shop has built a cult following for its consistently good coffee and tasty treats. Aside from the espresso and cold-press coffee, they also serve toasted sandwiches ($8), gluten-free muesli ($8) and chai porridge ($9). Mon–Fri 7am–4pm.

PUBS

Earl of Aberdeen 316 Pulteney St, Hindmarsh Square ☎ 08 8223 6433, ⌐ coopersalehouse.net. Set in a gazebo dripping with greenery, and a popular spot to watch the rugby, this place serves huge portions of moderately priced, imaginatively cooked pasta, steak, fish and kangaroo, plus wood-fired pizza (mains $24–32). Attentive service too, and twenty different beers on tap. Sun–Thurs 11am–midnight, Fri & Sat 11am–1am.

Gilbert Street Hotel 88 Gilbert St ☎ 08 8231 9909, ⌐ gilbertsthotel.com.au. Located on Adelaide's southern fringe, this popular corner hotel offers a convivial atmosphere, superior pub food and a quirky (and sunny) beer garden. The handsome front bar serves a good range of craft beers on tap, plus a decent selection of affordable local wines. Thursday is Buffalo wings night. Mon–Thurs 10am–11pm, Fri & Sat 10am–2am, Sun 11am–10pm.

★ **Hotel Wright Street** 88 Wright St ☎ 08 8211 8000, ⌐ hotelwrightstreet.com.au. Adelaide's original gastropub, a short walk from Victoria Square, is still pretty cool, with a funky fit-out, smart bar food, live music and plenty of good ales, ciders and boutique wine by the glass. This is a great place for lunch, with robust dishes such as ale-battered flathead ($29), pea and ham gnocchi ($28) and chimichurri scotch fillet ($33). Daily 10am–late.

Kings Head Pub 357 King William St ☎ 08 8212 6657, ⌐ thekingsbardining.com. Iconic pub with a refurbished bar and restaurant featuring exclusively South Australian produce. Try the surprisingly delicious pie floater ($22) – an Adelaide tradition – with a gourmet spin. Live entertainment Wed–Sun evenings, and daily lunch specials for around $12. Daily 11am–midnight.

7

7

RESTAURANTS

Chianti 160 Hutt St ☎08 8232 7955, ⓦchianticlassico .com.au. You're in for a special experience at this rustic-chic Italian restaurant, a local favourite with Adelaide's Italian-Australian community, run by a warm and welcoming family. Let the staff guide you through the seasonal menu which includes dishes such as *risotto con frattaglie* ($32.90) and *coniglio al forno* ($39.90), or come here for the city's best breakfast. Daily 7.30am–10.30pm.

Gaucho's 91 Gouger St ☎08 8231 2299, ⓦgauchos .com.au. Book ahead for this popular Argentine place, which serves some of the best steaks in town ($38–53). The meat, which includes grain-fed fillet, porterhouse and T-bone, is sourced from the best cattle farms in Australia, and there's also a good choice of seafood dishes and salads for non-carnivores. Mon–Fri 11.30am–3pm & 5.30–11pm, Sat & Sun 5.30–11pm.

Jasmin 31 Hindmarsh Square ☎08 8223 7837, ⓦjasmin.com.au. The menu at this highly regarded North Indian restaurant may not be the most adventurous, but the food (mains $20.50–26.50) is delicious, particularly the tandoori dishes. Tues, Wed & Sat 5.30–10.30pm, Thurs & Fri noon–2.30pm & 5.30–10.30pm.

Lucia's Pizza Bar Shop 1–2 Western Mall, Central Market ☎08 8231 2303, ⓦlucias.com.au. *Lucia's* has been serving the people of Adelaide authentic espresso and scrumptious Italian staples (pizza and pasta $7.50–12) for over 55 years. Alongside the original café, the family has opened a very smart delicatessen, selling pasta sauces, olive oils, freshly baked breads and other delights. Mon–Thurs 7am–5pm, Fri 7am–8.30pm, Sat 7am–3pm.

Madame Hanoi North Terrace ☎08 8218 4166, ⓦmadamehanoi.com.au. Opened in 2015, this Franco-Vietnamese restaurant and bar has been a breath of fresh air in Adelaide. The restaurant, part of the Casino complex, is beautifully decorated with sepia photographs, old posters and giant iron lanterns, while the food is fresh and inventive, featuring plenty of Vietnamese standards, such as peppered shaking beef ($28.60) and crispy pork belly ($39.30), all given a modern twist. Mon–Fri 7.30am–late, Sat & Sun 11am–late.

Mandoo 23 Bank St ☎08 8231 3303. This small Korean canteen specializes in dumplings – pork, chicken, vegetable or *kimchi*, steamed or fried ($12–13) – which provide a surprisingly substantial, low-cost meal. They also do hotpots ($43–57), large enough to feed several people. Mon–Fri 11.30am–9pm, Sat noon–9pm.

NOLA Craft Beer & Whisky 293–295 Rundle St ⓦnolaadelaide.com. Adelaide has flirted with soul food before, but the guys banging the saucepans here have nailed it – the menu includes favourites like fried green tomatoes, gumbo, collard greens and jambalaya. Share plates range from $10. They also serve a fantastic selection of craft beers and whiskies, and wine by the glass.

Tues–Thurs noon–midnight, Fri & Sat noon–2pm, Sun noon–midnight.

Orana 285 Rundle Street ☎08 8232 3444, ⓦrestaurantorana. A culinary journey in the company of chef Jock Zonfrillo, rather than a passive eating experience, this multi-course degustation menu ($175 for 20 courses) includes foraged foods, bush tucker and many other wonders. Tues–Thurs & Sat 6–8pm, Fri noon–1.30pm.

★**Osteria Oggi** 76 Pirie Street ☎08 8359 2525, ⓦosteriaoggi.com.au. In a word, brilliant. This boisterous Italian restaurant is right on the money, with carefully prepared dishes, an impressive wine list and sharp, attentive service. Perfect for lunch or dinner. The menu ranges from small plates, such as cured swordfish ($22), to home-made pasta and gnocchi ($21–27) and braised rabbit ($28). Mon–Sat 11.30am–late.

Peel Street 9 Peel St ☎08 8231 8887, ⓦpeelst.com.au. One of the city's most celebrated restaurants, *Peel Street* is constantly changing and experimenting with its menu: chef Jordan Theodorus is known for his bold flavours and eclectic style. The menu might include dishes such as banana blossom chicken, Middle Eastern baked eggs and harissa-roasted spatchcock. The tasting menu ($65) is good value. Mon–Tues 7.30am–5pm, Wed–Fri 7.30am–11pm, Sat 6–11pm.

Sean's Kitchen Station Road ☎08 8218 4244, ⓦadelaidecasino.com.au. Yorkshire-born Sean Connolly has been influenced by New York and Spain in this funky but still upmarket restaurant, which is part of the Casino complex, along with *Madame Hanoi*. Expect ocean-fresh seafood ($26–39), *jamon* and great steaks ($36–44). Daily 11am–late.

Star of Siam 67 Gouger St ☎08 8231 3527, ⓦstarofsiam-adealide.com.au. This popular Thai restaurant has been going strong for over 25 years thanks to its excellent, reasonably priced menu (mains $16.80–$32.80), including a good range of vegetarian dishes. Mon–Thurs noon–2.30pm & 5.30–9.30pm, Fri noon–2.30pm & 5.30–10pm, Sat 5.30–10pm.

T-chow 68 Moonta St ☎08 8410 1413, ⓦtchow.com. au. This enormously popular Chinese restaurant serves Teochew regional specialities such as tender duck and green-peppercorn chicken, as well as more classic Cantonese fare. The decor isn't great but the food is. Mains $13.80–30. BYO. Daily 11am–3pm & 5–11pm.

NORTH ADELAIDE AND UNLEY

CAFÉS AND BAKERIES

Perryman's Artisan Bakery 54 Tynte St, North Adelaide ☎08 8267 2766, ⓦperrymansbakery.com. There's been a bakery at 54 Tynte St since the early 1850s, when it was set up by a German immigrant, whose influence is still apparent in the delicious apple streusel (a cake with a crumble topping) and gingerbread men. The pies (sweet and savoury) are also some of the best in Adelaide. Cakes and pastries from $2.50. Mon–Fri 8am–5pm, Sat 9am–3pm.

The Store Level 1, 157 Melbourne St, North Adelaide ☎08 8361 6999, ⓦ thestore.com.au. A gourmet deli, corner store and café rolled into one, with plenty of outdoor tables and a tasty menu: breakfast options include buttermilk pancakes and Bircher muesli, while for lunch and dinner (mains $16–32) there's everything from soup to *saltimbocca*. Daily 7am–10/11pm.

UR Caffe 117 Melbourne St, North Adelaide ☎08 8267 3553, ⓦ urcaffe.com. This popular local café is the ideal place for a lazy brunch, serving wholesome food and consistently good coffee. The menu ($5.50–18.50) ranges from the healthy, such as fruit salad and muesli, to indulgent treats like Omega X (smoked salmon with scrambled eggs, asparagus, shaved radish and spicy coconut sauce) or a brioche bun with chorizo, fried egg, rocket and hot tomato sauce. Tues–Fri 7.30am–3.30pm, Sat & Sun 8am–3.30pm.

RESTAURANTS

The Archer 60 O'Connell St, North Adelaide ☎08 8361 9300, ⓦ archerhotel.com.au. Head to this Victorian-era hotel on the main drag for no-frills pub food. *The Archer* serves great-value meals throughout the day (from $13), alongside a decent range of craft beers and good ciders. Mon–Thurs & Sun 11am–midnight, Fri & Sat 11am–2am.

Gin Long Canteen 42 O'Connell St, North Adelaide ☎08 7120 2897, ⓦ ginlongcanteen.com.au. This modern Asian diner offers delicious flavours, quick service and very reasonable prices in one of the more affluent parts of Adelaide. Choose from small dishes like a lobster slider ($12) or more substantial options such as lychee duck curry ($26). Tues–Fri noon–2.30pm & 5.30–9.30pm, Sat 5.30–10.30pm.

The Lion Hotel 135 Melbourne St, North Adelaide ☎08 8367 0222, ⓦ thelionhotel.com. Multi-award-winning restaurant and pub occupying the site of the historic 1870s Lion Brewery. The restaurant offers fine dining in the European tradition with creations such as black truffle risotto ($32.90) and duck breast with Boudin

blanc sausage, kohlrabi and burnt onion custard ($38.90). For something a little more casual, order a chicken schnitzel ($18.90) or beef burger ($19.90), across the bar. Daily 8am–midnight.

Marrakech Restaurant 91 O'Connell St, North Adelaide ☎08 8361 9696, ⓦ marrakechrestaurant .com.au. Formerly located in Hyde Park, this local favourite brings the flavours of North Africa to the city. The signature dish is the Afrah Tagine (lamb cooked with cinnamon, honey, prunes and roasted almond), and mains start from $26. Tues–Sun 6pm–midnight.

Monsoon 135 Melbourne St, North Adelaide ☎08 8267 3822, ⓦ monsoonind.com. Although the food is not the most exciting, the good-value lunch specials make *Monsoon* a decent option. The focus is on North Indian cuisine, though there are a few South Indian options like *masala dosas* (thin, crispy pancakes filled with a potato curry). Mains $16–30. Daily 11.30am–10.30pm.

BEACH SUBURBS

CAFÉS AND RESTAURANTS

Estia Henley Square, Henley Beach ☎08 8353 2875, ⓦ estia.com.au. This award-winning modern Greek-Australian restaurant is steps from the beach, but most patrons are too focused on the food, including delicious meze ($7–22 per dish), to worry about the wonderful beach views nearby. Book ahead. Tues–Sun noon–3.30pm & 6–10pm.

Europa 12–14 Jetty Rd, Glenelg ☎08 8376 3995, ⓦ europaatthebay.eatout-adelaide.com.au. This popular espresso bar and casual diner boasts a stylish contemporary interior and a menu dominated by pasta, pizza and risotto, but the main reason locals drop in is for the authentic Italian coffee. Mains $14–31. Daily 7am–10/11pm.

Zest Café Gallery 2A Sussex St, off Jetty Rd, Glenelg ☎08 8295 3599, ⓦ zestcafe.eatout-adelaide.com.au. This little side-street café/gallery does tasty all-day breakfast ($4–14), lunch and light snacks along with great coffee and a laid-back atmosphere. The cosy courtyard is perfect for a relaxing brunch with the morning paper. Mon–Sat 7.30am–5.30pm, Sun 8.30am–5pm.

7

WHAT'S ON

Adelaide is a lively little city with something going on somewhere every night of the week, from live bands and dance clubs to art-house film and avant-garde theatre. To find out **what's on**, check out *The Guide* in Thursday's *Advertiser*, which has film and theatre listings and reviews. There's also a thriving **free press**. *The Adelaide Review* (ⓦ adelaidereview.com.au) is a monthly newspaper, which covers the visual and performing arts, dance, film, literature, history, wine and food, while *CityMag* (ⓦ citymag.indaily.com.au), a quarterly freesheet, covers much of the same ground but is aimed at the city's hipster/student population. Both publications are available in cafés, bars and other outlets. Online food, style and design magazine *Broadsheet* (ⓦ broadsheet.com.au/Adelaide) provides some useful tips about where to eat, dance and be seen in this southern metropolis.

DRINKING AND NIGHTLIFE

At night, the two spots to head for are Rundle Street, which boasts popular pubs and bars teeming with young hipsters and arty university students, or grittier Hindley Street, where you'll find several funky clubs and live-music venues east of Morphett Street catering for the nearby university crowd. Leigh and Peel streets are both packed with interesting small bars, some very well hidden.

PUBS AND BARS

Apothecary 1878 118 Hindley St ☎ 08 8212 9099, ⓦ theapothecary1878.com.au. One of the coolest venues in town, this atmospheric multilevel wine bar oozes the decadence of a nineteenth-century French salon. Apart from an impressive list of boutique wines (from $14/glass), this bar also serves delicious food – try the chef's tasting menu ($48) – in the downstairs cellar. Daily 5pm–late.

Clever Little Tailor 19 Peel St ☎ 0407 111 857. One of the city's original laneway bars, *Clever Little Tailor* channels the spirit of Paris to deliver an appealing old-world atmosphere paired with a contemporary drinks list. There's always an interesting crowd, so find a perch and settle in for a couple of hours. Cocktails from $16. Mon–Sat 4pm–midnight.

Exeter Hotel 246 Rundle St ☎ 08 8223 2623, ⓦ theexeter.com.au. This spacious old pub with an iron-lace balcony is a long-established hangout for Adelaide's artists, writers and students, yet remains totally unpretentious. Good meals served (the curries are worth a look); music nightly; beer from $7. Mon–Sat 8am–2am, Sun 8am–noon.

Hains & Co 22 Gilbert Place ☎ 08 8410 7088, ⓦ hainsco .com.au. This stylish laneway bar is one of around sixty such establishments which have mushroomed in the city since the licensing laws were relaxed. While some are aimed at art students and hipsters, *Hains & Co* attracts older, discerning drinkers with its good choice of cocktails ($18), wine by the glass (from $11) and craft beers. Tues–Fri & Sun 4pm–late, Sat 6pm–late.

★**Jack Ruby** 88 King William Street ☎ 08 8231 5795, ⓦ jackruby.com.au. Hidden away in a moody basement space on Adelaide's busiest street, this is a real gem, with a stunning range of well-mixed cocktails ($18), draught beer and some interesting wines. The food is pure Americana circa 1960. Daily 4pm–2am.

Udaberri 11 Leigh St ☎ 08 8410 5733, ⓦ udaberri .com.au. Another one of Adelaide's original small bars, *Udaberri* focuses on *pintxos* (bar snacks popular in the Basque country of Spain – the cheese and *jamon* here are particularly good) and a diverse and inventive beer and wine list (wine by the glass from $8). Arrive early as it gets packed. Mon–Fri 4pm–1am, Sat & Sun 6pm–12am.

Wheatsheaf 39 George St ☎ 08 8443 4546, ⓦ wheatsheafhotel.com. The gay-friendly *Wheaty* attracts a good mix of students, craft-beer aficionados and music lovers; the pub hosts blues, R&B and gypsy bands. Beer from $9, whisky from $13. Most gigs are free. Mon–Fri 11am–midnight, Sat noon–midnight, Sun noon–9pm.

CLUBS AND LIVE MUSIC

Casablabla 12 Leigh St ☎ 08 8231 3939, ⓦ casablabla .com. Billing itself as a "multicultural tapas lounge bar", *Casablabla* is a hip venue for eating, drinking and dancing, with an eclectic range of live acts and events – from flamenco to limbo. Beer $6.50–14, cocktails $17. Tues–Thurs 3.30pm–12.30am, Fri noon–3am, Sat 5pm–4am.

Edinburgh Castle 233 Currie St ☎ 08 8231 1435, ⓦ edinburghcastlehotel.com. One of Adelaide's oldest pubs, the *Edinburgh Castle* also hosts a busy programme of live music and DJs, including indie bands and fresh local talent. Beers from $6, and there's a $10 lunchtime menu. Mon–Thurs & Sat 11am–12am, Fri 11am–5am.

Enigma Bar 173 Hindley St ☎ 08 8212 2313, ⓦ enigmabar.com.au. Cool live-music venue for a young alternative crowd – expect anything from goth and metal to indie and hip-hop. The bar spills out into the street at weekends, with either a DJ or live music upstairs. Fri & Sat 8am–12am.

Governor Hindmarsh 59 Port Rd, Hindmarsh ☎ 08 8340 0744, ⓦ thegov.com.au. *The Gov*, as this local institution is affectionately known, is one of Adelaide's leading music venues and hosts a broad range of live acts, stand-up comedy and cabaret. Mon–Fri 11am–midnight, Sat noon–2am.

Rhino Room 13 Frome St ☎ 08 8227 1611, ⓦ rhinoroom.com.au. Alternative club venue with an intimate lounge atmosphere hosting regular live music and theme parties; it's also one of the city's top comedy venues attracting Australian and international stand-ups. Mon, Thurs & Fri 7.30pm–late, Sat 5pm–3am.

Royal Oak Hotel 123 O'Connell St, North Adelaide ☎ 08 8267 2488, ⓦ royaloakhotel.com.au. Popular North Adelaide bar and restaurant with arty decor and a young crowd. Live music most nights (check the website to see who's playing). Mon 11am–12.30pm, Tues–Fri 11am–1.30am, Sat 8am–1.30am, Sun 8am–12.30am.

FILM

In the summer, you can watch films outdoors at the Moonlight Cinema (ⓦ moonlight.com.au) in the Botanic Gardens. If you're visiting in late February/early March in an odd-numbered year, check out the Adelaide Film Festival (ⓦ adelaidefilmfestival.org).

GAY AND LESBIAN ADELAIDE

South Australia was the first state to legalize gay sex and remains one of the most tolerant of lesbian and gay lifestyles, although Adelaide's gay scene remains more modest than Sydney's or Melbourne's. The beach suburb of Semaphore (see p.662) is also a hub of activity for the gay and lesbian community. To find out where the action is, pick up a copy of *Blaze* (see below).

FESTIVALS

Apart from the city's more mainstream annual festivals, there are a few strictly gay and lesbian fiestas.

Feast ☎ 08 8463 0684, ⓦ feast.org.au. The biggest and best gay and lesbian festival, Feast runs for three weeks in October and November. Events include theatre, music, visual art, literature, dance cabaret and historical walks, plus a Gay and Lesbian Film Festival at the Mercury Cinema (see below). The festival culminates in Picnic in the Park, an outdoor celebration in the parklands that surround central Adelaide, which includes a very camp dog show.

USEFUL ORGANIZATIONS AND PUBLICATIONS

Blaze 213 Franklin St ⓦ gaynewsnetwork .com.au. A monthly lifestyle magazine for the LGBTQ communities, the publication covers news, fashion, entertainment and social issues, and is free from venues and bookshops.

Gay And Lesbian Tourism Australia ⓦ galta.com. au. Provides listings for tourism operators in Australia

where gay and lesbian travellers are specifically welcomed.

Same Same ⓦ samesame.com.au. Australia's leading gay and lesbian community and lifestyle website, with up-to-date forums and notice boards.

GAY AND LESBIAN BARS

In addition to the below, the *Wheatsheaf* (see opposite) is a very popular, gay-friendly venue.

Mars Bar 120 Gouger St ☎ 08 8231 9639, ⓦ themarsbar.com.au. This Adelaide institution has been around for years and hosts drag acts for a big, friendly mixed crowd. The musical focus is on pop and dance tunes, and the inexpensive drinks ensure a raucous atmosphere. Fri & Sat 9pm–5am.

Mary's Poppin 5 Synagogue Place ⓦ maryspoppin.com. Launched in mid-2016 under the tagline "unremixed, untainted and unashamed", Adelaide's newest gay venue boasts a great cocktail list, nonstop dance music, stripper poles, a "selfie room" and the occasional drag show. Thurs–Sat 8pm–late.

Capri 141 Goodwood Rd, Goodwood ☎ 08 8272 1177, ⓦ capri.org.au. Alternative and arty films complete with pre-show Wurlitzer organ on Tues, Fri and Sat evenings. Take the tram to Glenelg to get here.

Mercury Cinema Lion Arts Centre, 13 Morphett St ☎ 08 8410 1934, ⓦ mercurycinema.org.au. A wonderful

art-house cinema, based in the Lion Arts Centre, showing shorts, and independent and foreign films.

Palace Nova Eastend Cinemas 250–251 Rundle St ☎ 08 8232 3434, ⓦ palacecinemas.com.au. Alternative venue showing foreign-language and art-house films plus other new releases. Discounts for students and backpackers.

THEATRE AND THE PERFORMING ARTS

Adelaide Festival Centre Festival Drive, off King William Rd ☎ 08 8216 8600, ⓦ adelaidefestivalcentre .com.au. The city's biggest cultural venue, with three stages hosting mainstream and experimental theatre, ballet, opera, contemporary dance, comedy and cabaret.

Adelaide Town Hall 128 King William St ☎ 08 8203 7590, ⓦ adelaidetownhall.com.au. The stately town hall is an atmospheric venue for regular classical music concerts, often performed by the Adelaide Symphony Orchestra.

Elder Hall University of Adelaide, North Terrace

☎ 08 8313 5995, ⓦ music.adelaide.edu.au. The Conservatorium of Music, part of the University of Adelaide, is one of the country's foremost classical music institutions. It hosts regular lunchtime and evening concerts in Elder Hall.

Nexus Arts Centre Cnr Morphett St & North Terrace ☎ 08 8212 4276, ⓦ nexusarts.org.au This multi-discipline arts centre has a varied programme of indigenous music and dance, alongside artists from Africa, India and elsewhere. The space also hosts live jazz, stand-up comedy and cabaret performances.

SHOPPING

You can find most things you'll need on the pedestrianized Rundle Mall (see p.660), which boasts several department stores, and a handy Woolworths. For alternative and retro fashion, head to the city's funkier **East End** (around Rundle Street and Ebenezer Place).

ADELAIDE'S ARTS FESTIVALS

The huge **Adelaide Festival of Arts** (Ⓦadelaidefestival.com.au), which takes over the city for around two weeks each March, attracts an extraordinary range of international and Australian theatre companies, performers, musicians, writers and artists. The festival began in 1960 and has been based at the purpose-built Festival Centre (see p.659) since 1973. In addition, free outdoor concerts, opera and films are held outside the Festival Centre and at various other locations during the period, while other venues around town host an Artists' Week, Writers' Week and a small film festival.

The edgier **Fringe Festival** (Ⓦadelaidefringe.com.au) grew up around the main Adelaide festival to become the country's largest arts event and, for many, the highlight of the festival calendar. Now a stand-alone annual event, it begins with a wild street parade on Rundle Street followed by over three weeks of free outdoor shows and activities, bands, cabaret and comedy at venues all over town, while full use is made of the 24-hour licensing laws.

The **Womadelaide** (Ⓦwomadelaide.com.au) world-music weekend began in 1992 as part of the Arts Festival but has now developed its own separate identity, attracting tens of thousands of people annually. Held in early March in the Botanic Park – with seven stages, workshop areas, multicultural food stalls and visual arts – it's a great place to hear some of Australia's local talent, as well as internationally acclaimed world-music artists from around the globe.

ABORIGINAL ART AND CRAFTS

Better World Arts Central Market ☎08 7225 7047, Ⓦbetterworldarts.com.au. This shop stocks an excellent selection of Aboriginal art and crafts, including paintings, jewellery, rugs, scarves, bags, cushion covers and tableware. There's another branch in Port Adelaide. Mon–Thurs 9am–4.30pm, Fri 9am–7pm, Sat 9.30am–2pm.

Tandanya 253 Grenfell St ☎08 8224 3200, Ⓦtandanya.com.au. Inside the cultural centre of the same name (see p.660), this shop has the widest range of quality Aboriginal artwork and artefacts in South Australia, as well as books and music. Mon–Sat 9.30am–4.30pm.

BOOKS

Adelaide Booksellers 12 Twin St, just off Rundle Mall ☎08 8410 0216, Ⓦadelaidebooksellers.com.au. This centrally located, basement shop has a good range of secondhand fiction and nonfiction, as well as a selection of significantly more expensive antiquarian and out-of-print titles. Mon–Fri 9.30am–5.30pm, Sat 10am–3pm.

Central Market Books Central Market, near the Grote St entrance ☎0419 816 778. Excellent secondhand bookshop in the Central Market selling (and exchanging) everything from comics to classic fiction. Tues 7am–5.30pm, Wed & Thurs 9am–5.30pm, Fri 7am–9pm, Sat 7am–3pm.

Dymocks 135 Rundle Mall ☎08 8223 5380, Ⓦdymocks .com.au. Part of a national bookstore chain, this subterranean space sells a wide range of contemporary fiction and non-fiction, and also has a good selection of travel guides, food, art and military history books. Mon–Thurs 9am–6pm, Fri 9am–9pm, Sat 9am–5.30pm, Sun 11am–5pm.

DIRECTORY

Banks and foreign exchange All the major banks are located on King William St, and ATMs are ubiquitous. Exchange services are available at the international airport, American Express (Shop 32, Rundle Mall; Mon–Fri 9am–5pm, Sat 9am–noon; ☎1300 139 060, Ⓦamericanexpress.com) and Travelex (4 Rundle Mall; Mon–Fri 8.30am–6pm, Sat 9am–3pm, Sun 12am–5pm; ☎08 8231 6977, Ⓦtravelex.com.au); the latter has several outlets in the city, plus branches at the airport and Glenelg.

Camping equipment Paddy Pallin (228 Rundle St; Mon–Thurs 9am–5.30pm, Fri 9am–9pm, Sat 9am–5pm, Sun 11am–5pm; ☎1800 039 343, Ⓦpaddypallin.com.au) sells a range of high-quality camping and outdoor gear.

Hospitals and dentists Royal Adelaide Hospital, North Terrace (☎08 8222 4000); Dental Hospital, Frome Road (☎08 8222 8222).

Laundry Melbourne Street Laundromat, 80 Melbourne St, North Adelaide (☎08 7127 4854; open 24 hours).

Left luggage Adelaide Central Bus Station, 85 Franklin Street (☎08 8203 7203).

Maps The Map Shop, 6–10 Peel St, between Hindley and Currie sts (Mon–Fri 9.30am–5pm, Sat 9am–12.30pm; ☎08 8231 2033, Ⓦmapshop.net.au), has the largest range of local and state maps. If you're a member of an affiliated overseas automobile association, you can get free regional maps and advice on road conditions from the Royal Automobile Association, 41 Hindmarsh Square (☎08 8202 4600, Ⓦraa.com.au).

Pharmacy Midnight Pharmacy, 198 Wakefield St (daily 8am–midnight; ☎08 8232 4445).

Police For emergencies call ☎000.

Post office GPO, 141 King William St, cnr of Franklin St

(Mon–Fri 8am–6pm, Sat 8.30am–noon); for poste restante use Adelaide GPO, SA 5000.

Travellers with disabilities The Disability Information and Resource Centre is at 195 Gilles St (☎08 8236 0555, ⓦdircsa.com.au).

Work Workstay (ⓦworkstay.com.au) operates an online jobs board which is ideal if you are looking for casual work in South Australia. Backpacker Jobs Adelaide (ⓦbackpackerjobboard.com.au/jobs-in/adelaide) offers a similar service aimed specifically at backpackers. Job-seekers and employers can place free ads in the Adelaide Exchange (ⓦadelaideexchange.com.au).

Around Adelaide

Escaping Adelaide for a day or two is easy and enjoyable. Close at hand are the **Adelaide Hills**, southeast of the city, which are popular for weekend outings and have numerous small national and conservation parks. To the south, the **Fleurieu Peninsula** extends towards Cape Jervis and has plenty of fine beaches and around fifty wineries at McLaren Vale.

If wine is your priority, head for McLaren Vale first, then the **Barossa Valley**, Australia's premier wine-producing region, with another sixty or so excellent wineries within 70km of Adelaide. The valley is easily visited in a day from the city, but is also a great place to chill out for a few days. The **Yorke Peninsula**, across the gulf from Adelaide, is often ignored by foreigners, though many locals holiday here: as well as the wonderful beaches, it's home to the remains of an old copper-mining industry and an excellent national park.

The Adelaide Hills

The beautiful **Adelaide Hills** are the section of the **Mount Lofty Ranges** that run closest to the city. Many people have set up home in the hills to take advantage of the cooler air, and there are some grand old summer houses here as well as sleek contemporary weekenders. You can access the towns and some stunning walks via short bus or train rides from Adelaide, but having your own car opens up a lot more of the area, notably the Torrens River Gorge. Leaving the city by Glen Osmond Road you join the **South Eastern Freeway**, the main road to Melbourne – there's an old tollhouse not far out of the city at Urrbrae and several fine old coaching hotels.

The **Heysen Trail** (see box, p.684), a long-distance walk from Cape Jervis to Parachilna Gorge, cuts across the hills, with four quaint YHA hostels along it; most are run on a limited-access basis and you'll have to pick the key up first from the office at the *Adelaide Central YHA* (see p.666).

ACCOMMODATION	ADELAIDE HILLS

B&Bs and guesthouses are plentiful in the hills, and the **visitor centre** in Hahndorf (see p.675) can help, or try **Adelaide Hills Country Cottages** (ⓦahcc.com.au). The **South Australia B&B and Farmstay Association** (ⓦbandbfsa .com.au) and Stayz Accommodation (ⓦstayz.com.au) are both useful sources of information, with the latter offering competitive online rates for properties across South Australia.

Cleland Wildlife Park

365 Mount Lofty Rd, Crafers about 18km southeast of Adelaide • Daily 9.30am–5pm, no entry after 4.30pm • $22 • ☎08 8339 2444, ⓦenvironment.sa.gov.au • Frequent buses #823, #864 and #864F from Adelaide (20min)

Mount Lofty Summit (710m), the highest point of the range, is actually part of the **Cleland Wildlife Park**. Here you can cuddle a koala and wander freely among kangaroos, wallabies and emus. There are several good walking trails through native bush leading from the park into the surrounding Cleland Conservation Area.

Morialta Conservation Park

Morialta Falls Rd, Woodforde, 10km north of Adelaide • Daily 8.30am–sunset • $5/vehicle • ☎08 8336 0901, ⓦenvironment.sa.gov.au • Bus #H30S from Adelaide to Rostrevor (25min), from where it's a 30min walk to the park

The **Morialta Conservation Park** is home to several seasonal waterfalls and numerous

7

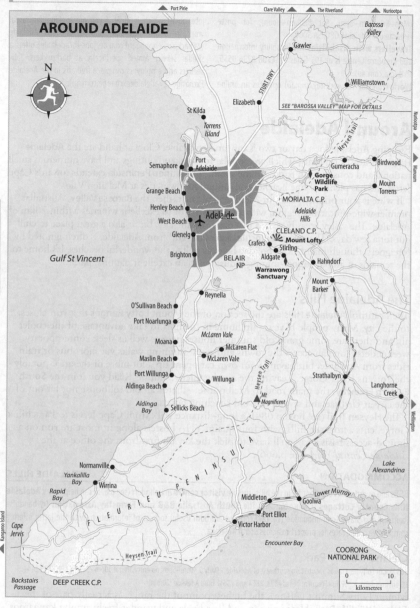

AROUND ADELAIDE

outlooks offering views of the Adelaide plains. From the entrance it's a 1.5km bushwalk to a lovely waterfall or a 7.3km hike to Three Falls Grand for stunning gorges and cataracts.

Belair National Park

Upper Sturt Rd, Belair, 13km southeast of Adelaide • Daily 8am–sunset • $12/vehicle • ☎ 08 8278 5477, ⓦ environment.sa.gov.au • Trains from Adelaide Railway Station (every 30min; 35min)

South of Crafers, virtually in the southern suburbs of Adelaide, is **Belair National Park**, South Australia's first national park (it dates back to 1891). Getting there by train is half the pleasure – the track winds upwards through tunnels and valleys with views of Adelaide and Gulf St Vincent. From Belair Station, steps lead to the valley and the grassy recreation grounds and kiosk. With its joggers, tennis courts, man-made lake, hedge maze and **Old Government House** (Sun 1–4pm; free), a residence built in 1859 as a summer retreat for the governor, this seems more like a garden than a national park, though there are also some more secluded bush trails through gum forest.

Hahndorf

HAHNDORF, 28km southeast of Adelaide, is the most touristy destination in the hills, and gets crowded at weekends. Founded in 1839, it's Australia's oldest **German settlement** and still has the look of a nineteenth-century village. The faux Bavarian restaurants and coffee houses, crafts, antique and gift shops are thoroughly commercial, but it's still enjoyable, especially in autumn when the chestnuts and elms lining the main street have turned golden. The town is basically one street and all the buildings have blue plaques recounting their history.

Hahndorf Academy

68 Main St • Daily 10am–5pm • Free • ☎ 08 8388 7250, ⍵ hahndorfacademy.org.au

The **Hahndorf Academy** is a working artist's studio with a small collection of photographs, prints, displays and well-written interpretive boards that shed light on the lives of early German-speaking settlers, plus a few sketches by the town's most famous resident and one of Australia's best-known artists, **Hans Heysen**, who settled here in 1908.

The Cedars

Heysen Rd, 2.5km northwest of the village • Tues–Sun 10am–4.30pm • Tours usually Tues–Sun: Sept–May 11am, 1pm & 3pm; June–Aug 11am & 2pm • $10 • ☎ 08 8563 2198, ⍵ hansheysen.com.au

Hahndorf's most comprehensive collection of the paintings of acclaimed landscape artist Sir Hans Heysen are on display at his old home, **The Cedars**, which is still maintained by the Heysen family. There are pleasant gardens to explore, and you can also visit the studio of Heysen's daughter Nora, a prize-winning artist in her own right. Guided tours take visitors to parts of the house normally closed to the public.

ARRIVAL AND INFORMATION   **HAHNDORF**

By bus From Adelaide (every 30min; 50min).

Tourist information Adelaide Hills visitor centre, 68

Main St (Mon–Fri 9am–5pm, Sat & Sun 10am–4pm; ☎ 08 8388 1185, ⍵ adelaidehills.org.au).

WINERIES IN THE HILLS

Located less than thirty minutes' drive from the city, the Adelaide Hills' **wineries** may not be as famous as those in the neighbouring Barossa Valley, but they are gaining popularity and are definitely worth a trip. The cool weather (this is the coolest wine-growing region on mainland Australia) contributes to wonderful Sauvignon Blancs and fresh Chardonnays and you can even expect a superb cool-climate Shiraz.

Hahndorf Hill Winery 38 Pains Rd, Hahndorf ☎ 08 8388 7512, ⍵ hahndorfhillwinery.com.au. This family-run winery produces classic Adelaide Hills varietals, such as Pinot Grigio and Shiraz, but is better known for its pioneering work with the Austrian grape varieties of Grüner Veltliner, Zweigelt and Blaufränkisch. Come for lunch or its signature CocoVino experience (daily 10am–3pm; $30; book in advance), which matches premium estate wines with the world's best chocolates. Daily 10am–5pm.

Shaw+Smith 136 Jones Rd, Balhannah ☎ 08 8398 0500, ⍵ shawandsmith.com.au. A wine tasting at this modern steel and glass winery is one of the must-do experiences in the Adelaide Hills. They produce highly acclaimed cool-climate Pinots, Shiraz, Sauvignons and Chardonnays. Daily 11am–5pm.

7

EATING AND DRINKING

Hahndorf Inn Hotel 35 Main St, Hahndorf ☎ 08 8388 7063, ⊛hahndorfinn.com.au. For a glass of authentic locally brewed pilsner, some hearty German food (including a metre-long *bratwurst*; $45), and serving staff in traditional dress, head to the popular *Hahndorf Inn Hotel*. Daily 10.30am–late.

★**Udder Delights** 91A Main St ☎ 08 8388 1588, ⊛udderdelights.com.au. This combined cheese factory and café offers a range of delicious lunchtime treats, such as cheese boards featuring salami, smoked salmon, pâté and pickles (from $14.50), plus larger boards to share, including the café's own version of the Ploughman's Lunch ($33). *Udder Delights* hosts cheese-making classes ($185) and deluxe high teas ($45) in the sunny café; both require bookings. Daily 9am–5pm.

Torrens River Gorge

North of Hahndorf in the upper valley is the 27km Gorge Scenic Drive beside the **Torrens River Gorge**, one of the loveliest areas in the Adelaide Hills. You'll need a car: take the Gorge Road off the A11 from Adelaide, a few kilometres past the suburb of Campbelltown. Just before you reach Cudlee Creek is the **Gorge Wildlife Park** (Redden Drive; daily 9am–5pm; $15; ☎08 8389 2206, ⊛gorgewildlifepark.com.au), a fourteen-acre private park and home to an array of animals including snakes, dingoes and, of course, koalas (cuddling at 11.30am, 1.30pm & 3.30pm).

At Cudlee Creek, the drive turns southwest away from the river and passes through picturesque valleys and vineyards to Mount Torrens. If you want to stick with the river, turn north before Cudlee Creek towards the Chain of Ponds, where the road connects after a few kilometres to the equally stunning Torrens Valley Scenic Drive. Just east of here is the town of Gumeracha, where you'll find the **Toy Factory** (Kenton Valley Rd; daily 9am–5pm; free; ☎08 8389 1085, ⊛thebigrockinghorse.com.au), with its colossal 18m-high rocking horse, the largest in the world ($2 to climb it). The factory sells a wide range of handcrafted wooden toys, including, of course, miniature rocking horses. At the eastern end of the Torrens Valley Scenic Drive is the small township of Birdwood and the impressive **National Motor Museum** (Shannon St; daily 10am–5pm; $12; ☎08 8568 4000, ⊛history.sa.gov.au/motor), home to Australia's largest collection of veteran, vintage and classic cars, trucks and motorcycles.

The Barossa Valley

The **Barossa Valley**, only an hour's drive from Adelaide, produces internationally acclaimed wines and is the largest premium-wine producer in Australia. Small stone **Lutheran churches** dot the valley, which was settled in the 1840s by German-speaking Lutherans fleeing from religious persecution: by 1847 over 2500 Silesian immigrants had arrived and after the 1848 revolution more poured in. German continued to be spoken in the area until World War I, when the language was frowned upon and German place names were changed by an act of parliament. The towns, however – most notably Tanunda – still remain German in character, and the valley is well worth visiting for the **vineyards**, wineries, bakeries and butcher's shops, where old German recipes have been handed down through generations. With around eight hundred thousand visitors each year, the valley can seem thoroughly touristy and traffic-laden if you whizz through it quickly, but the peaceful back roads are more interesting, with a number of small, family-owned wineries to explore.

The first vines were planted in 1847 at the Orlando vineyards, an estate that is still a big producer. There are now over sixty **wineries** with cellar doors, from multinationals to tiny family-owned producers. Because of the variety of soil and climate, the Barossa seems able to produce a wide range of wine types of consistently high quality; the white Rieslings are among the best. The region has a typically Mediterranean climate, with dry summers and mild winters; the best time to visit is autumn (March–May), when the vines turn russet and golden and the harvest has begun in earnest. Much of the grape picking is still done by hand and work is available from February.

OPPOSITE THE BAROSSA VALLEY >

7

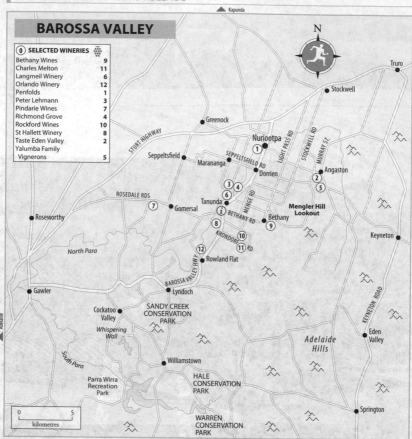

Lyndoch

Settled in 1839, **LYNDOCH** is one of the oldest towns in South Australia, and although vineyards were established from the outset, the primary activity until 1896 was the growing of wheat, until someone had the bright idea of converting a flour mill into a winery. Today there are ten wineries in the immediate Lyndoch area, from some of the smallest to one of the largest in the Barossa, all still family-owned. **Kies Family Wines** (Lot 2 Barossa Valley Way; daily 9.30am–4.30pm; ☎08 8524 4110, ⊛kieswines.com.au) provides free, informal tourist information; its wine-tasting cellars are in the same building.

Orlando Winery/Jacob's Creek

Northeast of the Whispering Wall, 4km along the Barossa Valley Highway, the village of Rowland Flat is dominated by the **Orlando Winery** complex, the oldest winery in the valley and home of some of Australia's best-known wines, sold under the **Jacob's Creek** label.

Johann Gramp planted the first commercial vines at nearby Jacob's Creek in 1847, and forty years later his son expanded the winery and moved it to Rowland Flat. The **Jacob's Creek visitor centre** (daily 10am–5pm; ☎08 8521 3000, ⊛jacobscreek .com), located on the banks of Jacob's Creek itself, has a tasting centre, a good restaurant, and a gallery that includes information on production techniques and the history of the area.

Bethany

BETHANY was the first German settlement in the Barossa. The land is still laid out in the eighteenth-century Hufendorf style, with long, narrow farming strips stretching out behind the cottages, and the creek running through each property. Pretty gardens set off the old stone cottages, which remain well cared for. At dusk each Saturday the bell tolls at **Herberge Christi Church**, keeping up a tradition to mark the end of the working week, and Bethany – without even a pub or a shop – retains its peaceful, rural village feel.

Tanunda

TANUNDA is the Barossa's most quintessentially German town. The tree-lined main drag, Murray **Street**, boasts several beautiful old stone buildings, such as the old Schulz Roller Mills, and a traditional bakery, *Apex*, selling German breads and cakes. There's a more authentic atmosphere in the narrow streets on the western side of town, towards the river. Here, **Goat Square** was the site of the first town market and is bordered by the original cottages; the early market is re-enacted during the Vintage Festival (see p.681).

7

BAROSSA WINERIES

While there is a mind-boggling array of wineries in the Barossa Valley, this selection should start you off on a good footing.

Bethany Wines 378 Bethany Rd, Bethany ☎ 08 8563 2086, ⓦ bethany.com.au. A hillside winery set in an old quarry, with views over the village; the Schrapel family have grown grapes here since 1852 and produce consistently good wines. Very good reds (the Shiraz is outstanding) and a decent Semillon. Mon–Sat 10am–5pm, Sun 1–5pm.

Langmeil Winery Langmeil Rd, near Tanunda ☎ 08 8563 2595, ⓦ langmeilwinery.com.au. This was the original Langmeil village, built in the 1840s; the little vineyard you can see from the tasting area was planted in 1843, and prints of nineteenth-century photos document the local industry. An outstanding winery with excellent reds, particularly the Shiraz – try the increasingly popular sparkling variety. Daily 10.30am–4.30pm.

Peter Lehmann Wines Para Rd, near Tanunda ☎ 08 8565 9500, ⓦ peterlehmannwines.com. A pleasant spot for a picnic as well as a tasting, with some excellent varieties such as the Eden Valley Riesling and the more expensive Stonewall Shiraz. The wines satisfy several price points and palates. Mon–Fri 9.30am–5pm, Sat & Sun 10.30am–4.30pm.

Pindarie Wines 946 Rosedale Rd, Tanunda ☎ 08 8524 9019, ⓦ pindarie.com.au. One of the valley's newer cellar doors, *Pindarie* offers some interesting alternative blends. Set on the western ridge of the Barossa, the family-friendly restaurant and gorgeous heritage function space offer stunning views. Mon–Fri 11am–4pm, Sat & Sun 11am–5pm.

Richmond Grove Para Rd, near Tanunda ☎ 08 8563 7303, ⓦ richmondgrovewines.com. Large, historic winery with a lovely picnic area alongside the North Para River. It's a big producer, sourcing grapes widely, and does a decent Watervale Riesling. Daily 10.30am–4.30pm.

Rockford Wines Krondorf Rd, Tanunda ☎ 1800 088 818, ⓦ rockfordwines.com.au. This excellent winery, established by local celebrity Robert O'Callaghan, produces delicious wines using traditional wine-making techniques. The wines are highly prized in Australia, so snap up a bottle of Basket Press Shiraz, Alicante Bouschet, Moppa Springs or Eden Valley Riesling at the cellar door. Daily 11am–5pm.

St Hallett Winery St Hallet Rd, Tanunda ☎ 08 853 7000, ⓦ sthallett.com.au. Now owned by the giant Lion Nathan conglomerate, this medium-size producer continues to make wine of great quality and is especially famous for its intense, flavourful reds, such as Old Block Shiraz which is sourced from vines 80–100 years old. Daily 10am–5pm.

Taste Eden Valley 6–8 Washington St, Angaston ☎ 08 8564 2435, ⓦ tasteedenvalley.com.au. Ten boutique Eden Valley wineries (an area internationally renowned for its Rieslings and cool-climate reds) are represented in this intimate family-kitchen-like setting. The friendly and knowledgeable staff can walk you through the wines, many of which are available only at the cellar door. Daily 10am–5pm.

Yalumba Family Vignerons Eden Valley Rd, Angaston ☎ 08 8561 3200, ⓦ yalumba.com. Largest and oldest family-operated Barossa winery, established in 1849, set in a lovely old château surrounded by manicured gardens. The complex includes a busy wine room, vast underground cellar and a working cooperage. Daily 10am–5pm.

JACK BOBRIDGE TRACK

The Barossa's newest outdoor attraction, the **Jack Bobridge Track** is a dedicated 27-kilometre walking and cycling route that links the townships of Gawler and Tanunda, via some excellent cellar doors, including St Hallett, Kellermeister, Creed Wines and Jacob's Creek. Contact Barossa Information Centre (66–68 Murray Street, Tanunda, ☎ 08 8563 0600, ⒲ barossa.com) about maps, picnic spots and bicycle hire.

Many wineries dot the town's perimeter, including Peter Lehmann, Richmond Grove, Langmeil and Rolf Binder, all of which operate cellar doors.

Mengler's Hill Lookout

Mengler's Hill Lookout, east of Tanunda along Basedow Road and then the Mengler's Hill Road Scenic Drive, provides an unmatched view of the valley and its vineyards: there's a **sculpture garden** with white marble sculptures on the slopes below, and at night you can see the lights of Adelaide.

Seppeltsfield

Off the Barossa Valley Hwy, 4km northwest of Tanunda • Heritage tours daily 11.30am & 3.30pm, booking necessary • $15 • Fortified wine and canapé tastings Mon–Fri 10.30am & 4pm (from $35) • ☎ 08 8568 6200, ⓦseppeltsfield.com.au

SEPPELTSFIELD must be, visually at least, the most spectacular of the wineries. During the Great Depression the Seppelt family paid their workers in food to plant an avenue of date palms from Marananga to Seppeltsfield; on a hill halfway along the palm-lined avenue stands the Seppelt **family mausoleum**, resting place of the male members of the family. The estate itself was founded in 1851 when Joseph Seppelt, a wealthy merchant, arrived from Silesia with his workers: he turned to winemaking when his tobacco crop failed, establishing the largest winery in the colony, with everything from a port-maturation cellar to a distillery, vinegar factory and brandy bond store. The winery has been refurbished with a new cellar door, excellent dining room (*Fino*) and a private art gallery and shop. The winery is best known for its aged Tawny Port, with consecutive vintages dating back to 1878; it's possible to sample a vintage tawny from your birth year ($60), directly from the barrel in the famous Centennial Cellar.

Nuriootpa

Just 7km from Tanunda, **NURIOOTPA** is the valley's commercial centre: as the place where local Aborigines gathered to barter, it takes its name from the word for "meeting place". The town is dominated by **Penfolds**, the Barossa's largest winery and famous for producing Australia's most collectable wine, Penfolds Grange.

Angaston

ANGASTON, southeast of Nuriootpa, is a pretty little town situated in the Barossa Ranges, an area of predominantly grazing land, red gums and rolling hills, although a few of the Barossa's oldest winemakers have been here for more than a century. This is the side of the Barossa that attracted the British pioneers, including George Fife Angas, the Scotsman after whom the town is named.

ARRIVAL AND DEPARTURE   BAROSSA VALLEY

By bus LinkSA runs several buses (2–9 daily) between Adelaide and destinations in the valley including Angaston (2hr 10min), Lyndoch (1hr 10min), Nuriootpa (1hr 35min), Rowland Flat (1hr 15min) and Tanunda (1hr 20min).

By bike If you're cycling, you might want to consider taking your bike on the train to Gawler (every 30min from Adelaide; 1hr), 14km west of Lyndoch. From Gawler you can join the Jack Bobridge Track (see box above) which runs all the way to Tanunda; there is a second cycleway from Tanunda and Nuriootpa. Bike rental is available from Barossa Bike Hire (ⓦ barossabikehire.com.au; $35/day) in Nuriootpa; Jacob's Creek Visitor Centre in Rowland Flat (ⓦ jacobscreek.com.au) also has good bikes for hire and picnic baskets at reasonable prices.

INFORMATION

Tourist information For a good introduction to the region, head to the Barossa Visitor Information Centre, 66–68 Murray St, Tanunda (Mon–Fri 9am–5pm, Sat & Sun 10am–4pm; ☎08 8563 0600, ⓦbarossa.com).

Festivals The week-long Barossa Vintage (the oldest wine festival in Australia) is held in odd-numbered years starting on Easter Saturday (☎08 8563 0600, ⓦbarossavintagefestival.com.au).

ACCOMMODATION

Barossa Brauhaus Hotel 41 Murray St, Angaston ☎08 8564 2014, ⓦbarossabrauhaus.com.au. Basic and inexpensive rooms (shared bathrooms only) in a centrally located, historic pub, which was first licensed in 1849 and serves a hearty menu of pub grub. Rates include Continental breakfast. **$70**

Blickinstal Vineyard Retreat Rifle Range Rd, Tanunda ☎08 8563 2716, ⓦblickinstal.com.au. Great views over the valley from this six-suite B&B nestled peacefully in the foothills of the Barossa, a five-minute drive from Tanunda. All units are self-contained and a four-course breakfast and afternoon tea are included. **$170**

Discovery Parks Barossa Valley Barossa Valley Way, Tanunda ☎08 8563 2784, ⓦdiscoveryholidayparks .com.au. Set in parkland among beautiful waratah trees, this park caters for families, and has a heated swimming pool, a playground and an inflatable trampoline. There's a wide range of accommodation options, from caravan sites to wooden cabins and spacious cottages. Un/powered sites **$30/35**, cabins **$144**

Langmeil Cottages Langmeil Rd, Tanunda ☎0408 089 722, ⓦlangmeilcottages.com. This German-style stone cottage in a tranquil setting has a spa, sauna, pool and laundry facilities. Each of the suites is a good size and comes with its own kitchenette. Extras include champagne and chocolates on arrival, breakfast provisions and free bicycle use. **$195**

Lawley Farm Krondorf Rd, south of Tanunda ☎08 8563 2141, ⓦlawleyfarm.com.au. Full of charm, this collection of restored, historic stone cottage, barn and stables, shaded by peppertrees, is within walking distance of several wineries. Fresh flowers, fruit baskets and complimentary port, as well as breakfast provisions, are provided. **$175**

The Louise Seppeltsfield Rd, Marananga ☎08 8562 2722, ⓦthelouise.com.au. The opulent rooms at this intimate boutique hotel have private terraces and all the mod cons you can imagine, from BOSE sound systems to espresso machines. The most expensive suites even have outdoor showers. The property includes an award-winning restaurant, swimming pool and delightful outdoor terrace. Rates includes Continental breakfast. **$545**

Lyndoch Hill 1221 Barossa Way, Lyndoch ☎08 8524 4268, ⓦlyndochhill.com. This beautiful winery, complete with a function centre, ornamental rose garden, restaurant and swimming pool, offers the best-value accommodation in the Barossa. The 34 motel-style rooms are clean, well-equipped and peaceful – some have their own balconies. **$139**

★Novotel Barossa Valley Resort Golf Links Rd, Rowland Flat ☎08 8524 0000, ⓦnovotelbarossa .com.au. A great choice if you're after the comfort, style and amenities of a resort. Rooms are spacious, light and modern, while facilities include a restaurant, day-spa, outdoor swimming pool and access to an eighteen-hole golf course. Breakfast included. **$169**

Seppeltsfield Vineyard Cottage Gerald Roberts Rd, Seppeltsfield ☎08 8563 4059, ⓦseppeltsfieldvineyard cottage.com.au. It doesn't get more exclusive than this, with an entire elegant German settler's cottage all to yourself, and wonderful views over the valley from the bathtub. Rates include breakfast provisions and there's a two-night minimum stay. **$690**

Tanunda Hotel 51 Murray St, Tanunda ☎08 8563 2030, ⓦtanundapub.com. This hotel was built from local stone and marble in 1845, with Edwardian additions and decor. It offers a mix of budget rooms with TV, a/c, fridge, tea- and coffee-making facilities (private bathrooms cost $10 extra), and much more stylish, self-contained studio apartments in a separate annex. Doubles **$80**, apartments **$200**

EATING AND DRINKING

1918 Bistro and Grill 94 Murray St, Tanunda ☎08 8563 0405, ⓦ1918.com.au. The focus of this fine restaurant is on hearty rustic fare, such as pork belly and free range duck, using the freshest Australian ingredients (mains $30–38). Dine outside on the shady veranda, or inside the atmospheric old house, built in 1918. Daily noon–2.30pm & 6.30–9pm.

Appellation Seppeltsfield Rd, Marananga ☎08 8562 4144, ⓦthelouise.com.au. One of Australia's finest regional dining rooms, *Appellation* (part of *The Louise*, see above) enjoys an enviable reputation for its astonishing culinary creations showcasing the freshest local produce – including herbs and vegetables from their own garden. The restaurant offers a four-course degustation which changes with the seasons ($120, plus $60 for paired wines). Book well in advance. Daily 6.30–9pm.

Barossa Wurst Haus and Bakery 86A Murray St, Tanunda T08 8563 3598. Specializing in traditional Barossa *Mettwurst* (German sausage) and other German delights, this delicatessen offers tasty great-value snacks

7

(from $4), cakes, pastries, breakfasts and lunches. Mon–Wed 9am–4pm, Thurs & Fri 10am–4pm, Sat & Sun 9am–4pm.

★**Hentley Farm** Cnr Gerald Roberts and Jenke roads, Seppeltsfield ☎08 8562 8427, ⓦhentleyfarm.com.au. Housed in a low-slung farm building, this cutting-edge restaurant is the number one culinary experience in the Barossa. Choose from a four-course or seven-course degustation menu ($105/$180) bursting with interesting dishes, such as puffed wild rice with trevally ceviche and marron (freshwater crayfish) tail with duck-liver parfait. The award-winning dining room is part of an equally successful winery of the same name – the atmospheric cellar door is right next door. Reservations essential. Thurs & Sun noon–2.30pm, Fri & Sat noon–2.30pm & 6–9.30pm.

Lyndoch Bakery & Restaurant Barossa Valley Hwy, Lyndoch ☎08 8524 4422, ⓦlyndochbakery.com.au. One of the best German bakeries in the Barossa Valley, with an adjoining licensed restaurant that serves hearty, moderately priced traditional dishes (including a vast Rhineland mixed grill for $25.90). Daily 10am–3pm.

Maggie's Farm Shop Pheasant Farm Rd, Nuriootpa ☎08 8562 4477, ⓦmaggiebeer.com.au. The shopfront and restaurant of South Australia's much-loved food author, TV cook and restaurateur, Maggie Beer. Here you can buy from Maggie's line of speciality gourmet foods, including pheasant farm pâté and quince paste, or dine on the finest seasonal produce such as Maggie's celebrated pheasant farm terrine ($20). Gourmet picnic baskets are also available ($16) if you want to keep moving. Daily 10.30am–5pm.

Nosh Barossa 78 Murray St, Tanunda ☎0428 817 029. This funky little café/patisserie on Tanunda's main street serves delectable light meals made from quality local produce – try the gourmet Barossa pies – plus gluten-free dishes and great organic coffee (from $3.50). Mon–Fri 7.30am–4pm, Sat 8.30am–4pm, Sun 2.30–4pm.

Salters Kitchen Nuriootpa Rd, Angaston ☎08 8561 0200. Elegant bistro serving delicious Modern Australian food, paired with wines from the historic Saltram winery to which the restaurant belongs. The dining room adjoins the cellar door so you can begin with some wine tasting. Live music Sun. Book ahead in summer. Daily 10am–5pm.

The Yorke Peninsula

Just ninety minutes' drive from Adelaide, the Yorke Peninsula offers a peaceful weekend break as well as good **fishing** and **surfing**. The north proudly upholds its **Cornish heritage** with the three towns of the Copper Triangle or "**Little Cornwall**" – Kadina, Wallaroo and Moonta – hosting the Kernewek Lowender (Cornish Festival) over a long weekend in May during odd-numbered years.

Edithburgh

The east-coast ports of Ardrossan, Port Vincent and Edithburgh are all pleasant to visit, but **EDITHBURGH** offers the most facilities. There's a tidal swimming pool set in a rocky cove, and from Troubridge Hill you can see across to the 1850s lighthouse on Troubridge Island and as far as the Fleurieu Peninsula.

Innes National Park

At the tip of the peninsula • $10/vehicle • ☎08 8854 3200, ⓦenvironment.sa.gov.au

At the tip of the peninsula lies the **Innes National Park**, with its contrasting coastline of rough cliffs, beach and sand dunes, and its interior of mallee scrub. The park is untouched except for the ruins of the gypsum-mining town of **Inneston**, near Stenhouse Bay, and there are several campsites and cabins in which to stay. **Pondalowie Bay** has some of the best **surf** in the state; there are several other good surfing spots around the park and north towards Corny Point. Other more sheltered coves and bays are good for **snorkelling**, with shallow reef areas of colourful marine life, while on land you might see emus, western grey kangaroos, pygmy possums and mallee fowl.

ARRIVAL AND INFORMATION | THE YORKE PENINSULA

By bus Yorke Peninsula Coaches (☎08 8821 2755, ⓦypcoaches.com.au) runs buses from Adelaide to Ardrossan (daily except Tues & Thurs; 2hr 50min), Edithburgh (daily except Tues & Thurs; 3hr 40min), Kadina (1–2 daily; 2hr 20min), Moonta (daily; 3hr 10min), Port Vincent (daily except Tues & Thurs; 3hr 5min) and Wallaroo (1–2 daily; 2hr 50min). There are no buses to Innes National Park.

By ferry Sea SA ferries link Wallaroo on the Yorke Peninsula to Lucky Bay on the Eyre Peninsula (see p.708).

The ferry cuts 350km off the drive via Port Augusta (1–2 daily; one-way fares: passenger $35, cars $140; ☏ 08 8823 0777, ⓦ seasa.com.au).

Tourist information There is a visitor centre in Kadina at 50 Moonta Rd (Mon–Fri 9am–5pm, Sat & Sun 10am–4pm; ☏ 08 8821 2333, ⓦ coppercoast.sa.gov.au).

ACCOMMODATION

Edithburgh Caravan Park O'Halloran Parade, Edithburgh ☏ 08 8852 6065, ⓦ edithburghcaravanpark .com.au. On the foreshore, this place has caravan sites and a range of cabins – all are fully equipped and the more expensive options also boast sea views. Un/powered sites $32/36, cabins $100

★**Redwing Farmstay** 22 Pipeline Road, Weetulta ☏ 0408 252 128, ⓦ redwingfarmstay.com.au. Set on a working farm just outside Moonta, this property offers two accommodation options: a converted 1860s stone cottage and a more modern barn. Both are tastefully decorated and well equipped. Breakfast hampers available for an additional fee. $165

Troubridge Island Lighthouse Troubridge Island ☏ 08 8852 6290. Atmospheric accommodation is available in this lighthouse-keeper's cottage, which dates back to the 1850s and sleeps up to ten people. If you stay here, you'll have the whole island to yourself. Rates include transfers, but you'll need to bring your own food. $360

The Fleurieu Peninsula

The **Fleurieu Peninsula**, thirty minutes south of Adelaide by car, is bounded by Gulf St Vincent to the west and the Southern Ocean to the south, the two connected by the Backstairs Passage at **Cape Jervis** (where ferries leave for Kangaroo Island; see p.688). There are fine beaches on both coasts and more wineries inland in the rolling **McLaren Vale** region. It's a picturesque area: many of the towns were settled from the 1830s, and there's a lot of colonial architecture, much of it now housing restaurants or B&Bs.

GETTING AROUND
FLEURIEU PENINSULA

By train SteamRanger Heritage Railway (☏ 1300 655 991, ⓦ steamrangerheritagerailway.org.au) runs a number of steam- and diesel-hauled tourist services along the railway line running from Mt Barker in the Adelaide Hills to Victor Harbor on the coast. The *Southern Encounter* runs on the first and third Sunday of the month June–November from Mt Barker to Victor Harbor via Strathalbyn, Goolwa and Port Elliot and back (departs Mt Barker at 10am, returns from Victor Harbor 3.45pm; 2hr 20min–2hr 45min one way; $71 return). The *Highlander* covers the same route from Mt Barker on the second Sunday of the month (July–Nov), but turns back at Strathalbyn one hour into the journey. The steam-powered *Cockle Train* runs on an otherwise disused line along the coast between Goolwa and Victor Harbor, via Port Elliot, and back on Wednesdays and Sundays throughout the year and all week during the school holidays (exact times vary – check the website for full details).

On foot For walkers, the Heysen Trail (see box, p.684) starts at the southern tip of the peninsula at Cape Jervis and winds across the hilly countryside north to the Adelaide Hills and beyond to the Flinders Ranges. Although the trail is meant for long-distance walking, there are a number of well-signposted short walks along the way, including the 3.5km Deep Creek Waterfall Trail, just east of Cape Jervis with its wild coastal scenery. The Heysen Trail also passes through the Mount Magnificent Conservation Park, which contains a number of shorter walks offering excellent panoramic views.

On a tour Adelaide Sightseeing Tours (see p.664) runs tours ($144) to the area, visiting Goolwa, Victor Harbor and McLaren Vale.

CYCLING ACROSS THE FLEURIEU PENINSULA

The Fleurieu Peninsula is a good place to cycle. The 24km **Encounter Bikeway** follows a scenic 30km stretch of coast between **Victor Harbor** and **Goolwa**. Parts of the route are on-road and slightly inland, but mostly it follows the coastline and is for cyclists and walkers only. The return trip can be completed comfortably in a day; the most scenic – and hilliest – section is between Dump Beach in Victor Harbor and the town of Port Elliot. Unfortunately, there's no bike rental available in Goolwa, but on Sundays you can take your bike on the *Cockle Train* (see p.686) between Victor Harbor and Goolwa and cycle back.

7

THE HEYSEN TRAIL

The spectacular **Heysen Trail** is Australia's longest dedicated walking trail, spanning a 1200km route between **Cape Jervis** and **Parachilna Gorge**. En route it takes in the Fleurieu Peninsula, the Mount Lofty Ranges, Mount Bryan, and the Flinders Ranges. Walking the full trail, which is open May to November, takes around sixty days, but there are countless shorter strolls, day-hikes and multiday options. For more information, including maps, contact the **Friends of Heysen Trail**, which has an office and shop in Adelaide (Suite 212, 33 Pirie St; Mon–Fri 10.30am–2.30pm; ☎08 8212 6299, ⓦheysentrail.asn.au).

McLaren Vale

The wineries of **McLaren Vale**, in the northwest of the peninsula, are virtually in Adelaide, as the suburban fringes of the city now push right up to Reynella, where the first vineyards were planted in 1838. There are still several wineries in Reynella (including Hardy's), but the largest concentration is around the small town of **MCLAREN VALE**, which has about fifty wineries, mostly small and family run. Numerous B&Bs and restaurants cater for the wine-buff weekend crowd.

ARRIVAL AND INFORMATION

By bus LinkSA (☎08 8532 2633, ⓦlinksa.com.au) operates a daily service between Adelaide and Goolwa via Victor Harbor, Port Elliot and Middleton (1–3 daily; 2hr 10min).

Tourist information The McLaren Vale and Fleurieu

MCLAREN VALE

Visitor Information Centre, on Main St, about 2km from the centre of McLaren Vale township (daily 9am–5pm; ☎08/8323 9944, ⓦmclarenvale.info), has information on the area's wineries, and staff can also book accommodation.

ACCOMMODATION

3 Divas 42 Caffery St ☎08 8323 9806, ⓦwinedivatours .com.au. These two luxurious cottages are within walking distance of the town centre: the charming Marlene is a log chalet with views of the vineyards, while the romantic Moscato is a restored 1850s stone building. Rates include breakfast supplies. **$250**

Lakeside Caravan Park Field St ☎08 8323 9255, ⓦmclarenvale.net. For campers and budget travellers, the *Lakeside Caravan Park* is the best bet, with sites and cabins, plus a scenic setting, swimming pool and tennis

and volleyball courts. Un/powered sites **$30/$35**, cabins **$130**

★**The Vineyard Retreat** 165 Whitings Rd, Blewitt Springs ☎0420 370 310, ⓦthevineyardmv.com.au. Located at the northern end of McLaren Vale, this property consists of four self-contained luxury villas surrounded by lush vineyards. The contemporary villas are equipped with wood-burning heaters, modern kitchens, BBQs and flat-screen TVs; some have private verandas. A daily breakfast hamper is included in the rates. **$375**

EATING AND DRINKING

The Barn Bistro Corner of Main and Chalk Hill rds ☎08 8323 8618, ⓦthebarnbistro.com.au. This much-loved restaurant serves a good selection of regional dishes, such as pan-seared ocean trout ($33) and chargrilled kangaroo fillet ($34), accompanied by lovely local wines. The desserts are particularly good – try the Eton Mess ($14). Mon–Thurs 5–9pm, Fri–Sun noon–3pm & 5–9pm.

Blessed Cheese 150 Main Rd ☎08 8323 7958, ⓦblessedcheese.com.au. For a relaxed breakfast or lunch

($10.50–18), try the wonderfully named *Blessed Cheese*, where, aside from the divine dairy products, you can sample locally grown olives and great coffee. Daily 8am–4pm.

d'Arry's Verandah d'Arenberg Winery ☎08 8329 4848, ⓦdarenberg.com.au. The most famous restaurant in the area, dishing up sublime plates of exquisitely prepared regional produce – try the Sri Lankan duck curry or the slow-roasted pork belly (mains $34–40; degustation menu $95). Daily noon–4pm.

Gulf St Vincent beaches

A series of superb swimming beaches, known as the **Wine Coast**, runs along the Gulf St Vincent shore roughly parallel to McLaren Vale, from **O'Sullivan Beach** down to **Sellicks Beach**. All are easily accessible from Adelaide on public transport. The main town is **PORT NOARLUNGA**, surrounded by steep cliffs and sand hills. Its jetty is popular with anglers and with wetsuit-clad teenagers who dive from it; at low tide a natural reef is exposed. Lifesavers patrol the beaches, and you can rent surf gear. **Moana**, two beaches south, has fairly tame surf that's perfect for novices. The southern end of **Maslins Beach**, south again, became Australia's first legal nude beach in 1975. The wide, isolated beach is reached by a long, steep walking track down the cliffs from the Tait Road car park, deterring all but the committed naturist. **Port Willunga**, the next stop down, offers interesting diving around the wreck of the *Star of Greece*, while just further south is **Aldinga Beach**. On **Sellicks Beach** those with their own car can drive along 6km of firm sand.

ARRIVAL AND ACCOMMODATION

GULF ST VINCENT BEACHES

By train Frequent trains run from Adelaide Railway Station to Noarlunga (every 30min; 40min).

By bus From Adelaide, buses #N3, #N4 and #N5 run to Noarlunga (every 20min; 40min) via several beaches. You can reach Aldinga Beach via one of Sealink's Adelaide–Cape Jervis buses (2 daily; around 1hr 10min); from here there's a connecting bus (#750) to Sellicks Beach.

By ferry Ferries for Kangaroo Island (see p.688) depart

from Cape Jervis, 30km south of Normanville.

Jetty Caravan Park 34 Jetty War, Normanville ☏ 08 8558 2038, ⓦ jettycaravanparknormanville.com.au. A well-equipped campsite close to the beach and a short walk from town. It has powered and unpowered sites, comfortable cabins, a games room and tennis courts. No wi-fi. Un/powered sites <u>$32/$40</u>, cabins <u>$115</u>

7

Victor Harbor

The historic holiday town of **VICTOR HARBOR**, on Encounter Bay, is experiencing a renaissance, thanks principally to whales and penguins. After a decline in the numbers of **southern right whales** due to a long history of whaling in the area, the population is starting to recover, and in recent years there have been regular sightings of hundreds of calves each year enjoying the calm waters.

South Australian Whale Centre

Railway Terrace • Daily 10.30am–5pm • $9 • ☏ 08 8551 0750, ⓦ sawhalecentre.com.au

A Heritage-listed former railway goods shed now houses the **South Australian Whale Centre**, with excellent interpretive displays, exhibits and screenings on whaling and the

---

MCLAREN VALE WINERIES

Listed below are six favourites from a wide choice of excellent wineries.

Chapel Hill Chapel Hill Rd, adjacent to the Onkaparinga Gorge ☏ 08 8323 8429, ⓦ chapelhillwine.com.au. A small but very civilized winery in an old stone chapel with nice views over the vineyards. Daily 11am–5pm.

d'Arenberg Osborn Road ☏ 08 8329 4888, ⓦ darenberg.com.au. A family winery set up in 1928, known for its prize-winning reds and restaurant (see opposite). Look out for the snazzy cellar door in the shape of a giant glass cube, which dominates the surrounding landscape. Daily 10am–5pm.

Kay Brothers Amery Wines Kays Rd ☏ 08 8323 8201, ⓦ kaybrothersamerywines.com. A wonderful family winery established in 1890; old photos of the Kays and the surrounding area cover the oak casks containing port. It's renowned for its Block 6 Shiraz from vines planted in 1892 (it tends to sell out quickly). The winery also has a picnic area set amid towering gum trees. Mon–Fri 9am–5pm, Sat & Sun 11am–5pm.

Lloyd Brothers Wine & Olive Company 34 Warners Rd ☏ 08 8323 8792, ⓦ lloydbrothers.com.au.

Third-generation vignerons producing some of the finest hand-picked Shiraz wines in the region. The cellar door also has a large selection of top-notch olives and olive products from the on-site grove – one of the oldest commercial olive groves in Australia. The Kalamata mustard is fantastic. Daily 11am–5pm.

Oxenberry Farm Wines 24–26 Kangarilla Rd ☏ 08 8323 0188, ⓦ oxenberry.com.au. Small, historic cellar door with a relaxed atmosphere and lovely views across the surrounding vineyards and wetlands. It shares its premises with the award-winning Bracegirdle's House of Fine Chocolate and there's charming accommodation in a restored 1940s cedar cottage ($177.50, with a two-night minimum stay). Mon–Fri 10am–4pm, Sat 10am–4.30pm, Sun 11am–4.30pm.

Wirra Wirra McMurtie Rd ☏ 08 8323 8414, ⓦ wirrawirra.com. A large, classic ironstone building provides the setting for an impressive range of reds (especially Shiraz) and whites (try the Chardonnay). Mon–Sat 10am–5pm, Sun 11am–5pm.

natural history of whales, dolphins and the marine environment. The centre also acts as a monitoring station, locating and tracking whales, and confirming sightings, most likely between May and October. Call the **Whale Information Hotline** (☎ 1900 942 537) if you spot a whale, or for information on where you can see them.

Granite Island Recreation Park
Across the causeway from the esplanade • Penguin walks daily at dusk (1hr) • $15, bookings essential • ☎ 08 8551 0777, ⓦ holidayatvictorharbor.com.au

A short walk or horse-drawn tram ride over a wooden causeway brings the visitor to **Granite Island** Recreation Park. Run by National Parks, the island offers self-guided nature walks, whale spotting and fishing from the breakwater. But the island is best known for its colony of Little penguins though, sadly, numbers have dwindled over recent years. The best time to see them is at dusk, on one of the ranger-led penguin walks organized by the Victor Harbor Visitor Centre (see below; weather dependent, bookings essential). Getting to the island is half the fun – you can walk across the 600m causeway, or take a traditional holiday ride with the Victor Harbor Horse Tram (daily 10.30am–3.30pm; $9 return).

ARRIVAL AND DEPARTURE
VICTOR HARBOR

By bus Victor Harbor is served by LinkSA (☎ 08 8532 2633, ⓦ linksa.com.au) buses that run between Adelaide and Goolwa.

Destinations Adelaide (1–3 daily; 1hr 45min); Goolwa (1–3 daily; 30min); Middleton (1–3 daily; 20min); Port Elliot (1–3 daily; 15min).

By train Both the *Cockle Train* and the *Southern Encounter*, run by SteamRanger (see p.683), serve Victor Harbor. The station is on Railway Terrace, near the esplanade.

Destinations Goolwa (30min one-way; $29 return); Mt Barker (2hr 45min one-way; $71 return); Port Elliot (15min one-way; $10.50 return).

By bike The Encounter Bikeway (see box, p.683) links Victor Harbor and Goolwa.

INFORMATION AND TOURS

Tourist information The Victor Harbor Visitor Centre, next to the causeway (daily 9am–5pm; ☎ 08 8551 0777, ⓦ tourismvictorharbor.com.au), can help with tour bookings and accommodation.

Tours The Big Duck (book via the Whale Centre or the tourist office; ☎ 0405 125 312, ⓦ thebigduck.com.au) runs whale-spotting trips in the winter ($60), and general wildlife-watching tours ($60) and trips to Seal Island ($60), beyond Granite Island, year-round.

Bike rental Mountain-bike rental is available at Victor Harbor Cycle & Skate, 73 Victoria St (☎ 08 8552 1417, ⓦ victorharborcycles.com; Mon & Wed–Fri 9am–5pm, Sat 10am–3pm, Sun 11am–3pm; $40/day).

ACCOMMODATION AND EATING

Anchorage 21 Flinders Parade ☎ 08 8552 5970, ⓦ anchorageseafronthotel.com. The best place to stay and eat is the *Anchorage*, a lovingly restored beachfront pub dating back to 1905, when it was one of the earliest guesthouses in Victor Harbor. It has attractive en-suite rooms, some with balconies and sea views, plus an excellent café and restaurant specializing in seafood. **$85**

The Original Victor Harbor Fish Shop 20 Ocean St ☎ 08 8552 1273, ⓦ originalvictorharborfishshop.com.au. This award-winning fish-and-chip shop, close to the beach, has been grilling and deep-frying since 1927. Expect to pay around $15 for a good feed. Eat in or takeaway. Daily noon–7.30pm.

Nino's 17 Albert Place ☎ 08 8552 3501, ⓦ ninoscafe .com.au. The place to be if you're after Italian food, where you can plough into some generous portions of pasta, authentic pizza and home-made *gelato*. Mains $24.50–38. Daily 9am–9pm.

Port Elliot and around

PORT ELLIOT, just 5km east of Victor Harbor, is a pleasant little town with good coastal walks along the cliffs at Freeman Knob, an attractive sandy beach at Horseshoe Bay and, during the winter, good whale-spotting opportunities. You can also explore the coastal Encounter Bikeway (see box, p.683); numerous places rent out bikes.

Middleton

The village of **MIDDLETON**, a five-minute drive from Port Elliot, is a top surfing spot with a number of well-regarded surf schools. For experienced surfers, the nearby Waitpinga, Parsons and Chiton beaches offer more thrills.

ARRIVAL AND DEPARTURE   PORT ELLIOT AND AROUND

By Bus Port Elliot is served by LinkSA (☎08 8532 2633, Ⓦ linksa.com.au) buses that run between Adelaide and Goolwa. They also stop in Middleton.

Destinations Adelaide (1–3 daily; 2hr); Goolwa (1–3 daily; 15min); Middleton (1–3 daily; 8min); Victor Harbor (1–3 daily; 10min).

By train Both the *Cockle Train* and the *Southern Encounter*, run by SteamRanger (see p.683), serve Port Elliot. The railway station is just off The Strand. The *Cockle Train* will stop at Middleton on request.

Destinations Goolwa (15min one-way; $18.50 return); Mt Baker (2hr 10min–2hr 35min one-way; return $65); Victor Harbor (15min one-way; $10.50 return).

ACTIVITIES

Surfing lessons and equipment rental Surf and Sun (☎1800 786 386, Ⓦ surfandsun.com.au) and Surf Culture (☎08 8327 2802, Ⓦ surfcultureaustralia.com.au), both on Ocean Parade in Middleton, have good reputations. Both offer a long list of programmes, from beginner lessons to surf camps and personal training, and include wetsuit and board rental in the price; rates start at $55 for a two-hour group lesson. They also hire out equipment.

ACCOMMODATION AND EATING

Flying Fish 1 The Foreshore ☎08 8554 3504, Ⓦ flyingfishcafe.com.au. This restaurant overlooks the bay and offers fish, seafood and meat dishes. Although the prices are reasonable (mains $24–36), service and quality is pretty inconsistent. For a less expensive option, head next door to the attached café for fish and chips ($15). Restaurant daily noon–3pm, Fri & Sat 6–8pm (longer hours in summer); café daily 9am–4pm.

★**Hotel Elliot** 35 The Strand ☎08 8554 2218, Ⓦ hotelelliot.com.au. Apart from being the social hub of the village, especially in summer, this renovated pub also serves the best food in town. Expect upmarket pub food, such as prosciutto-wrapped pork fillet, and salt and pepper squid. Mains from $20. Daily noon–2pm & 5.30–8.30pm.

Port Elliot Bakery 31 North Terrace ☎08 8554 2475, Ⓦ portelliotbakery.com. There's been a bakery on this site for over 100 years, and the original wood-fired oven is still in use, producing everything from steak pies and Cornish pasties to éclairs and finger buns. Pies from $3.50. Daily 7am–5.30pm.

★**Port Elliot Beach House YHA** 13 The Strand ☎08 8554 1885, Ⓦ yha.com.au. The best-value accommodation in town is this tranquil hostel housed in a lovely old building with great sea views. The dorms and private rooms are modern and comfortable, there's an ample lounge with an open fire, TV room, kitchen, and even a veggie patch out back from which guests can help themselves. You can also rent bikes here. Book in advance. Dorms $27, doubles $82

Port Elliot Holiday Park Just off the Victor Harbor–Goolwa Rd ☎08 8554 2134, Ⓦ portelliotholidaypark.com.au. Overlooking Horseshoe Bay, the award-winning *Port Elliot Holiday Park* is a popular spot to park a caravan, though it also has a range of cabins and cottages too. Powered sites $35, cabins $90, cottages $150

Goolwa

GOOLWA lies 14km east of Port Elliot, and 12km upstream from the ever-shifting sand bar at the mouth of the Murray River. Boaties love its position adjacent to vast **Lake Alexandrina**, with easy access to the **Coorong** (see p.694) and the ocean. Although it's so close to the coast, Goolwa feels like a real river town.

ARRIVAL AND DEPARTURE   GOOLWA

By bus Goolwa is served by LinkSA buses from Adelaide.

Destinations Adelaide (1–3 daily; 2hr 15min); Middleton (1–3 daily; 10min); Port Elliot (1–3 daily; 15min); Victor Harbor (1–3 daily; 30min).

By train Both the *Cockle Train* and the *Southern Encounter*, run by SteamRanger (see p.683), serve Goolwa. The railway station is on Dunbar Rd.

Destinations Mt Baker (2hr 10min one-way; $54 return); Port Elliot (20min one-way; $18.50 return); Victor Harbor (30min one-way; $29 return).

7

INFORMATION AND CRUISES

Tourist information The helpful Goolwa Visitor Information Centre is at 4 Goolwa Terrace (Mon–Fri 9am–5pm, Sat & Sun 10am–4pm; ☎ 1300 466 592, ⓦ alexandrina.sa.gov.au).
Cruises Spirit of the Coorong Cruises (☎ 08 8555 2203, ⓦ coorongcruises.com.au) run a range of trips to the mouth of the Murray River and into the Coorong National Park to the dune-covered Younghusband Peninsula (see p.694), where passengers can alight and walk to the Southern Ocean (2–6hr; $40–110; transfer to/from Adelaide also available).

ACCOMMODATION AND EATING

The Australasian Circa 1858 1 Porter Street, Goolwa ☎ 08 8555 1088, ⓦ australasian1858.com. The region's most exclusive accommodation marries colonial history with Asian food and design. There's a choice of five immaculate suites, each with a distinct look and feel. Two-night booking required. Rates include gourmet breakfast. $395

★ **Birks Harbor** 138 Liverpool Rd ☎ 08 8555 0338; ⓦ birksharbor.com.au. This classy establishment, 1km outside town, offers lovely riverside accommodation in a historic property, including a converted boat shed overlooking the river. Facilities include a swimming pool, terraced garden and BBQ. Two-night minimum stay.

Gourmet breakfast basket included. $325
Bombora Goolwa Beach Rd ☎ 08 8555 5396, ⓦ bomboragoolwa.com. The menu at this beachfront café-restaurant features filled baguettes, burgers, seafood and a changing list of specials ($12–28), plus some tasty breakfast options. Closed May 24 to July 7. Fri–Mon 8am–5pm.
Goolwa Heritage Cottages ☎ 0433 571 927, ⓦ goolwaheritagecottages.com. Choose between two self-catering heritage buildings: Joseph's Cottage and Jackling Cottage. Both have been fully renovated and offer modern kitchens and bathrooms, and breakfast supplies are provided. Two-night minimum stay. $192

Strathalbyn

The pretty town of **STRATHALBYN** sits among rolling hills 25km north of Goolwa, an hour's drive from Adelaide. Settled in 1839 by Scottish immigrants, the historic town is the market centre for the surrounding farming community, but is also renowned for its antique shops, Heritage-listed buildings and serene atmosphere.

ARRIVAL AND INFORMATION

By bus The only regular public transport is bus #852, which runs to/from Mt Barker (Mon–Fri 5 daily; 30min), which is linked to Adelaide by bus (every 15–30min; 1hr).
By train Both the *Southern Encounter* and the *Highlander*, run by SteamRanger (see p.683), serve Strathalbyn. The *Southern Encounter* departs on the first and third Sunday at 10.52am for Victor Harbor (1hr 53min) and at 5.17pm for Mt Barker (48min); $35–49. The *Highlander* runs on the second Sunday of each month (June–Nov), departing Mt Barker at 10.30am and returning from Strathalbyn at 2pm (50min each way; $34 return). The station is at 20 South Terrace.

Tourist information The visitor centre is at the Railway Station at 20 South Terrace (Mon–Fri 9am–5pm, Sat & Sun 10am–4pm; ☎ 1300 007 842, ⓦ visitalexandrina.com); you can pick up a self-guided walking-tour brochure, among other bits of information.
Events Strathalbyn comes alive during its irregular but well-publicized horseracing meetings and for a few traditional festivals: an antiques fair held on the third weekend of August, and an agricultural show and duck race in November.

ACCOMMODATION AND EATING

Argus House Patisserie Café 33 Commercial Rd ☎ 08 8536 3236, ⓦ argushouse.wordpress.com. Award-winning pies – varieties include lamb *rogan josh* and lentil and sweet potato – are the order of the day at this charming café, which overlooks the park and also sells home-made cakes, tarts and biscuits. Dishes $10–15. Daily 8am–5pm.

Victoria Hotel 16 Albyn Terrace ☎ 08 8536 2202, ⓦ victoriahotelstrathalbyn.com.au. Housed in an 1865 bluestone building, the *Victoria Hotel* has modern, refurbished en-suite rooms, a popular restaurant and a well-stocked bar. Continental breakfast included. $125

Kangaroo Island

As you head towards **Cape Jervis** along the west coast of the Fleurieu Peninsula, **KANGAROO ISLAND** (or KI), only 13km offshore, first appears behind a vale of rolling hills. Once you're on the island, its size and lack of development leave a strong

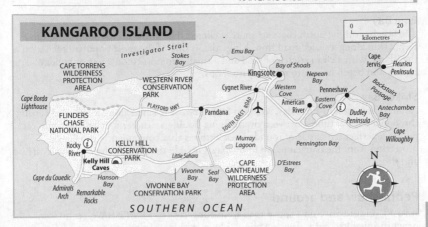

impression. This is Australia's **third-largest island** (after Tasmania and Melville Island), with 450km of spectacular, wild coastline and a multitude of wildlife including kangaroos, koalas, echidnas, platypuses, Little penguins, fur seals, Australian sea lions and, in passing, southern right whales.

To see Kangaroo Island properly you'll need at least three days, though most people only visit the major south-coast attractions – Seal Bay, Little Sahara, Remarkable Rocks and **Flinders Chase National Park**. Although promoted as South Australia's premier tourism destination it's still unspoilt; only in the peak holiday period (Christmas to the end of Jan, when most of the accommodation is booked up) does it feel busy. Once out of the island's few small towns, there's little sign of human presence to break the long, straight roads that run through undulating fields, dense gum forests and mallee scrub. There's often a strong wind off the Southern Ocean, so bring something warm whatever the season, and take care when swimming – there are strong rips on many beaches. **Safe swimming spots** include Hog Bay and Antechamber Bay, both near Penneshaw; Emu Bay, northwest of Kingscote; Stokes Bay, further west; and Vivonne Bay, on the south side of the island.

Coming by ferry you'll arrive at Kangaroo Island's eastern end, at the small settlement of **Penneshaw**. The airport is a little further west in **Cygnet River** near **Kingscote**, the island's administrative centre and South Australia's second-oldest colonial settlement, though little remains to show for it. Between Penneshaw and Kingscote, sheltered **American River** is another good base. From here, the Playford Highway and South Coast Road branch out to traverse the island, entering Flinders Chase National Park from the north and south respectively. The national park and surrounding wilderness protection area cover the entire western end of the island.

Kingscote and the north coast

With banks, shops, a hospital, library and the only high school, **KINGSCOTE** is the island's main town. The coast here has been the scene of several shipwrecks – interpretive boards on the foreshore provide details. For more history, you can walk north along the Esplanade to the **Reeves Point Historic Site**, where boards commemorate the South Australia Company's first landing of settlers in July 1836, before they headed off to establish nearby Adelaide. Less than 1km up the hill above on Centenary Road is **Hope Cottage Folk Museum**, which is based in the restored 1850s home of a pioneering family, the Calnans (Jan daily 10am–4pm; Feb–July & Sept–Dec daily 1–4pm; Aug Sat 1–4pm; $5; ⊛hopecottagemuseum.com). It provides an insight into what life was like during the mid-1800s, and has exhibits depicting the history of the island.

Emu Bay

The beaches on the north coast are more sheltered than those on the south, and Emu Bay, 21km along a sealed road from Kingscote, is one of the most popular beaches on the island, with a clean stretch of sand and a small penguin colony, lots of holiday homes and beach houses to rent, but no shops.

Stokes Bay

About 30km west of Emu Bay, secluded **Stokes Bay** is reached along a dirt road passing through a natural tunnel between overhanging boulders. There's a delightful, calm rock pool – a perfect semicircle of rounded black stones that conveniently provides protection from the dangerous rip in the bay. Outside the tunnel, there's a small café and shop.

Penneshaw and around

It's a 45-minute drive on a sealed road from Kingscote to **PENNESHAW**, set on low, penguin-inhabited cliffs. This is a popular base, with comfortable accommodation and plenty of places to eat. Penneshaw's crescent of sandy beach at Hog Bay curves from the rocks below the wharf, where the ferries come in, around to a wooded headland. The bay provides safe **swimming** and a shady shelter on the sand. **Antechamber Bay**, 10km southeast of Penneshaw, also has good, safe swimming, as does **American Beach**, southwest of Penneshaw.

Penneshaw Penguin Centre

Cnr Middle & Bay terraces • Daily: May–Sept 6–9.30pm; Oct–Jan & mid-Feb–April 8–10.30pm • $13 • ☎ 08 8553 7407

The viewing platforms at the **Penneshaw Penguin Centre** allow you to get close-up sightings of Little penguins in the wild. You can see the birds year-round (especially at dusk, when they return to their cliffside burrows after feeding) but the best time to visit is from autumn through to spring.

Cape Willoughby Lighthouse

10km southeast of Penneshaw • Daily 9am–3.30pm • $3 • Guided tours Thurs–Mon 11.30am, 12.30pm & 3pm; $16 • ☎ 08 8553 4444, ⊕ environment.sa.gov.au

At the eastern end of the island, accessed via an unsealed dusty road from Penneshaw, is the **Cape Willoughby Lighthouse**, which is the oldest in Australia, dating back to 1852. You can stay in the sandstone cottages of the original keepers (see p.693). To learn more about life as a nineteenth-century lighthouse keeper on Kangaroo Island, join a guided tour led by one of the park rangers.

Prospect Hill

Around 20km west of Penneshaw

The Dudley Peninsula, on which Penneshaw stands, is attached to the rest of the island by a narrow neck of sand; at the isthmus 512 steps lead up to **Prospect Hill** (Mount Thisby), a 99m hill of sand with views across to the mainland, to Hungry Beach, Pelican Lagoon and American River on the island's north coast, and in the opposite direction to Pennington Bay.

American River

Facing Penneshaw across Eastern Cove, **American River** is actually a sheltered bay where many small fishing boats moor, aiming to catch some of its abundant King George whiting. It's a peaceful place to stay (see p.693), with a concentration of accommodation along the hilly shoreline, plus a bank, post office, shops (including an IGA supermarket) and pubs.

The south coast

There are several conservation parks strung out along the exposed south coast of KI. The largest is **Cape Gantheaume**, an area of low mallee scrub supporting prolific birdlife around Murray Lagoon, the largest freshwater lagoon on the island.

Seal Bay Conservation Park

Seal Bay Rd • Daily 9am–5pm; school holidays 9am–6pm • Boardwalk access $16, guided tour $35 • ☎ 08 8553 4463, Ⓦ environment .sa.gov.au

The **Seal Bay Conservation Park** is home to hundreds of Australian sea lions, one of the largest breeding populations in Australia. They are fairly tolerant of humans and you can walk quietly among the colony on the beach on a guided tour or view them from a boardwalk if you visit independently.

Raptor Domain

Corner of Seal Bay & South Coast rds • Birds of prey show daily 11.30am & 2.30pm, $18 • Reptile show daily 1pm, $12 • ☎ 08 8559 5108, Ⓦ kangarooislandbirdsofprey.com.au

Raptor Domain, home to rescued eagles, owls, kookaburras, falcons, kestrels and many others, stages fascinating displays of the birds of prey, as well as the interactive "Fang-Tastic" reptile show featuring lizards and snakes.

Little Sahara and Vivonne Bay

West of Seal Bay

Little Sahara comprises a series of perfect white-sand dunes rising out of mallee scrub. This area is a great place to go sandboarding and tobogganing; you can rent equipment in nearby **Vivonne Bay**, one of Australia's best beaches, with a long, sandy strip and bush setting. It's generally safe to swim near the jetty or boat ramp or in the Harriet River, but Vivonne Bay itself has a dangerous undertow. There's a campsite nearby.

Kelly Hill Caves

West of Vivonne Bay • Daily 10.15am–4.30pm • $18 • Adventure caving tours $70 • ☎ 08 8559 7373, Ⓦ environment.sa.gov.au

The main features of the Kelly Hill Conservation Park are the **Kelly Hill Caves**, extensive limestone cave formations. Tours explore the largest cave – not the usual damp, bat-filled cavern, but very dry, with a constant temperature of 16°C. Adventure caving tours of the other three caves are also available. In addition, the (18km return) **Hanson Bay Trail** runs from the caves to the sea, passing freshwater lagoons and dune systems: allow at least eight hours, or longer if you'll be tempted to stop for a swim.

Flinders Chase National Park

Western end of Kangaroo Island • Daily 24hr • One-day pass $11, two-day pass $16 • **Cape Borda Visitor Centre** Mon, Tues & Fri–Sun 9am–5pm • **Lighthouse** $3; guided lighthouse tours 11am, 12.30pm & 2pm; $16 • ☎ 08 8553 4465, Ⓦ environment.sa.gov.au

Flinders Chase National Park, Kangaroo Island's largest, occupies the entire western end of the island. The **visitor centre** is surrounded by open grasslands where large numbers of kangaroos and wallabies graze. Koala signs lead to a glade of trees where you can see the creatures swaying overhead, within binocular range. Follow the **Platypus Waterhole Walk** for 3km to a platypus-viewing area, but be warned that to get a glimpse of the creatures requires endless patience. The winding sealed road through the park will take you to its most spectacular features: the huge, weirdly shaped, rust-coloured **Remarkable Rocks** on Kirkpatrick Point, and the impressive natural formation of **Admirals Arch**, where hundreds of New Zealand fur seals bask around the rocks. At the northern corner of the park, you can go on a guided tour of the 1858 **Cape Borda Lighthouse**.

The main camping area is at Rocky River, and there are various cottages throughout the park and several other good places to stay nearby along the South Coast Road (see opposite). By staying at this end of the island you'll also see the spectacular coastal sights at their best – particularly Remarkable Rocks, which turn a deep orange with the setting and rising sun.

ARRIVAL AND DEPARTURE

KANGAROO ISLAND

BY PLANE

Regional Express (☎13 17 13, ⍟rex.com.au) flies from Adelaide to Kingscote Airport (actually closer to Cygnet River) on Kangaroo Island (1–4 daily; 35min; from $129 one-way). Kangaroo Island Transfers (☎0427 887 575, ⍟kitransfers.com.au) offer a bus service from the airport to Kingscote and beyond, with fares starting from $70 (bookings essential).

BY FERRY

Kangaroo Island SeaLink ferries (☎13 13 01, ⍟sealink .com.au) ply the Backstairs Passage from Cape Jervis to Penneshaw – often a rough journey, but mercifully short (at least two sailings per day year-round and up to seven during peak holiday periods; 45min; passenger $98 return, car $196 return, motorbike $66 return, surfboard/windsurfer/bicycle $22 return).

Connections SeaLink Coach Services connect Adelaide to Cape Jervis ferry terminal (2 daily; 2hr; $56 return) and, less frequently, Goolwa to Cape Jervis (Tues, Thurs & Sun daily; 1hr 45min; $76) and Victor Harbor (daily Tues, Thurs & Sun daily; 1hr 25min; $76). At Penneshaw, connecting SeaLink buses run to American River (around 40min; $33 return) and Kingscote (around 1hr; $39 return); they need to be booked in advance. Penneshaw's SeaLink office is at 7 North Terrace (daily 8am–7pm; ☎08 8202 8688).

GETTING AROUND

Most visitors either bring their own vehicle to KI or hire one when they arrive. Rental cars are available from Budget and Hertz (see below). The local council is currently trialling a special shuttle service for visitors called the Rockhopper (fares from $10; ☎08 8553 4500, ⍟kangarooisland .sa.gov.au/rockhopper), covering Penneshaw, American River, Kingscote, Cygnet River Parndana and Vivonne Bay, but it only operates on Tuesdays, Wednesdays and Fridays. Call ahead to check that it's still running.

BY CAR

Roads to most major attractions are bitumen-sealed, including the scenic 80km South Coast Road from Cygnet River to the Flinders Chase National Park, Remarkable Rocks and Admirals Arch. The main route is the Playford Highway, running from Kingscote through Cygnet River and Parndana to the western tip of the island at Cape Borda; the last part of the highway along the northern edge of Flinders Chase National Park is not sealed and can be rough. At the eastern end of the highway, sealed roads feed off to the airport, Emu Bay, American River and Penneshaw. Driving at night on all roads is best avoided due to the high risk of collision with nocturnal animals; you'll see animal remains alongside the road at depressingly short intervals.

Car rental There are two car rental firms: Budget (☎08 8553 3133, ⍟budget.com.au) and Hertz (☎08 8553 9144, ⍟hertz.com.au). Both have a desk at the airport and additional outlets in Kingscote; Budget can also be found at the Penneshaw Ferry Terminal. Prices range from $91/day for a small car, to $148/day for 4WDs; always book ahead and check whether your insurance covers you to drive on unsealed roads or at night.

BY BIKE

The main roads are all good for cycling, but can get busy during the summer school holidays. There are no bike shops on the island, so you will need to bring your own across on the ferry (see above).

INFORMATION

Tourist information The Kangaroo Island Gateway Visitor Information Centre, at the edge of Penneshaw on the main road to Kingscote (Mon–Fri 9am–5pm, Sat & Sun 10am–4pm; ☎08 8553 1185, ⍟tourkangarooisland .com.au), has an interpretive display on the island's history, geology and ecology and can book tours and accommodation across the island.

Tickets and passes Many of the national or conservation parks on the island charge entry fees and extras for guided tours. However, a one-year Kangaroo Island Tour Pass ($70) gives you unlimited access to all parks and most tours (except for camping, Seal Bay's pre-sunset tour, and adventure caving), and is worth it if you're here for a while. Passes can be bought from the parks themselves, from the Department of Environment, Water and Natural Resources (DEWNR) office at 37 Dauncey St, Kingscote (Mon–Fri 8.45am–5pm; ☎08 8553 4444, ⍟environment.sa.gov.au), or from the Kangaroo Island Gateway visitor centre (see above).

TOURS

Exceptional Kangaroo Island 1139 Playford Hwy, Cygnet River ☎08 8553 9119, ⍟exceptionalkangarooisland.com. Led by award-winning guide Craig Wickham and his wife Janet,

Exceptional KI offers small group 4WD tours with an emphasis on fine food, wine and accommodation as well as nature (one-day tour from $399). Private tours and multi-day packages are also available.

Kangaroo Island Dive and Adventure 15 Kingscote Terrace, Kingscote ☎ 08 8553 3169, ⓦ kangarooisland diveandadventures.com.au. Dive-tour operator offering three-day PADI Open Water dive course and certification ($1095), as well as guided shore dives ($695).

Surf and Sun 44 Victor Harbor–Goolwa Rd, Middleton ☎ 1800 786 386, ⓦ surfandsun.com.au. Budget tours from Adelaide covering all the main sights and activities (two days $425). Cost includes overnight accommodation, park fees, Seal Bay tour and most meals.

Wallaby Bob Baudin Beach, 10km east of Penneshaw on the road to Kingscote ☎ 08 8553 1032, ⓦ wallabybobs.com.au. Local character Wallaby Bob offers unique fishing tours and charters from Baudin Beach (night-fishing tours from $40). He also hires out fishing gear, runabouts and kayaks.

ACCOMMODATION

KINGSCOTE

Kangaroo Island Seaside Inn 7 Cygnet Rd ☎ 08 8553 2707, ⓦ kiseasideinn.com.au. All the well-equipped en suites at this smart motel have views of Nepean Bay, as well as a/c, TVs, and tea- and coffee-making facilities; the most expensive ones (around $166) have spa baths. There's also an on-site restaurant. $126

Kingscote Nepean Bay Tourist Park Brownlow Beach ☎ 08 8553 2394, ⓦ kingscotetouristpark.com. au. If you've brought a caravan with you to KI, or are looking for a lower-cost room, this park 3km outside town is a decent choice, with a range of accommodation options. Un/powered sites $34/40, cabins $90

PENNESHAW

Kangaroo Island Seafront Hotel 49 North Terrace ☎ 1800 624 624, ⓦ seafront.com.au. This friendly hotel is set in landscaped gardens and offers a range of rooms and villas, as well as a heated pool, spa, sauna and restaurant. Good-value deals available online. $165

Kangaroo Island YHA 33 Middle Terrace ☎ 08 8553 1344, ⓦ yha.com.au. The best hostel on the island, located just 100m from the ferry terminal. It has comfortable dorms and private rooms, and a wide range of economical tours on offer. Dorms $22, doubles $59

Thomas Cottage and Seymour Cottage Cape Willoughby ☎ 08 8553 4410, ⓦ environment.sa .com.au. These heritage-listed lighthouse-keepers' cottages are the most atmospheric places to stay in the area. Dating back to 1927, but now fully refurbished, they each sleep up to eight people. No wi-fi. $225

AMERICAN RIVER

Mercure Kangaroo Island Scenic Dr ☎ 08 8553 7053, ⓦ mercure.com. Although it dates from the 1980s, this is still one of KI's better hotels, with spacious rooms and plenty of facilities, including an outdoor swimming pool, tennis court, kayaks and a smart restaurant. $171

Wanderers Rest Bayview Rd ☎ 08 8553 7140, ⓦ wanderersrest.com.au. Perched high on a hill, this old-fashioned guesthouse has comfortable – though pricey – en-suite rooms, each with its own balcony facing the sea, as well as a quality seafood restaurant. $236

THE SOUTH COAST

Hanson Bay Cabins Just west of the Kelly Hill Conservation Park ☎ 08 8559 7344, ⓦ hansonbay .com.au. Located in a secluded wildlife sanctuary (kangaroos and koalas are easy to spot here), these self-contained log cabins and (more expensive) modern cabins overlook Hanson Bay. The sanctuary has a café and the surrounding bushland is crisscrossed with excellent walking trails. No wi-fi. $180

FLINDERS CHASE NATIONAL PARK

Flinders Chase cottages Various locations in the park ☎ 08 8553 4490, ⓦ environment.sa.com.au. The national park has a range of historic cottages for rent in a variety of locations, including spacious lighthouse-keepers' cottages (two-night minimum stay) at Cape de Couedic, and a simple postman's cottage and a two-bedroom homestead at Rocky River. Prices vary according to property size. $75

Rocky River campsite Near the visitor centre ☎ 08 8553 4490, ⓦ environment.sa.com.au. Surrounded by eucalyptus trees, Rocky River is the largest of the park's four campsites, with 22 sites, toilets, hot showers, gas-powered barbecues and picnic tables. Bring all your gear with you. Camping $10.50 per person, caravan $29

★**Southern Ocean Lodge** West of Kelly Hill Conservation Park ☎ 08 8559 7347, ⓦ southernoceanlodge.com.au. Spectacularly set on a headland overlooking the sea, the ecofriendly Southern Ocean Lodge is the most luxurious place to stay on Kangaroo Island, with a spa and stylish, spacious contemporary suites, lounge and bar, superb restaurant, and loads of guided activities, including bushwalks and food- and art-themed island tours. Rates include full board, activities and transfers. $2200

Western KI Caravan Park West of Kelly Hill Conservation Park ☎ 08 8559 7201, ⓦ westernki .com.au. This caravan park is located in a wildlife reserve, where you can set up under tall gum trees and spot koalas. There are camping and caravan sites, plus a collection of cosy log cabins. Facilities include a camp kitchen, laundry, shop and liquor outlet. No wi-fi. Un/powered sites $30/$35, cabins $150

7

EATING AND DRINKING

Dudley Cellar Door 1153 Willoughby Rd, Cuttlefish Bay ⊙08 8553 1333, ⊚dudleywines.com.au. Apart from the glorious ocean views, this cellar door also offers the best wine-tasting experience on the island. Relax on the terrace with a tasty all-day platter or come for lunch when the kitchen serves up fresh ciabatta rolls ($4) and gourmet pizza ($27–32). Daily 10am–5pm.

Fish of Penneshaw 43 North Terrace, Penneshaw ⊙0439 803 843. This chippy offers a good range of local seafood ($15–30), including lobster, whiting and oysters, plus decent fish and chips. A spin-off business, *2 Birds & A Squid*, will deliver restaurant-quality meals, such as grilled halloumi ($20) and wild fennel risotto ($28), to your holiday accommodation; book using the same phone number. Both operations are closed in winter. Daily 4.30–8.30pm.

Rockpool Café North Coast Rd, Stokes Bay ⊙08 8559 2277. Grab an outdoor table at this cute seafood kiosk. Apart from ocean-fresh fish, prawns, calamari and other seafood, they also serve a good selection of pasta, and they're fully licensed. Mains $15–28. Closed in winter. Daily 11am–5pm.

The southeast

7

Most travellers en route between Adelaide and Melbourne pass through southeast South Australia as quickly as possible, which is a shame, as the coastal route offers wild, pristine beaches and tranquil fishing villages, while inland there are a couple of brilliant wine regions.

From Tailem Bend, just beyond Murray Bridge some 85km out of Adelaide, three highways branch out. The northernmost, the **Mallee Highway,** is the quintessential road to nowhere, leading through the sleepy settlements of Lameroo and Pinnaroo to the insignificant town of Ouyen in Victoria's mallee country (see p.850). The second, the **Dukes Highway**, offers a fast but boring route to Melbourne via the South Australian mallee scrub and farming towns of **Keith** and **Bordertown**, before continuing in Victoria as the Western Highway across the monotonous Wimmera (see p.849). It is, however, well worth breaking your journey to visit the **Coonawarra** and **Naracoorte**, in between the Dukes Highway and the coastal route: the former is a tiny wine-producing area that makes some of the country's finest **cabernet sauvignon**; the latter is a fair-sized town with a freshwater lagoon system that attracts prolific birdlife, and a conservation park with impressive World Heritage-listed caves.

The third option, the **Princes Highway** (Highway 1), is much less direct but far more interesting. It follows the extensive coastal lagoon system of the **Coorong** to **Kingston SE**, and then runs a short way inland to the lake craters of **Mount Gambier** before crossing into Victoria. There's another possible route on this last stretch, the **Southern Ports Highway**, which sticks closer to the coast, plus a potential detour along the Riddoch Highway into the scenic Coonawarra wine region.

GETTING AROUND
THE SOUTHEAST

By bus Premier Stateliner (⊙08 8415 5555, ⊚premierstateliner.com.au) buses serve two routes between Adelaide and Mount Gambier: one inland via Keith, Bordertown, Naracoorte, Coonawarra and Penola; the other along the coast via Meningie, Kingston SE, Robe and Millicent. There's further information on getting around the region on the southeast's visitor information website (⊚thelimestonecoast.com).

Coorong National Park

From Tailem Bend, the Princes Highway skirts Lake Alexandrina and the freshwater Lake Albert before passing the edge of the **Coorong National Park**. The coastal saline lagoon system of the Coorong (from the Aboriginal "Karangk", meaning long neck) is separated from the sea for over 100km by the high sand dunes of the **Younghusband Peninsula**. This is the state's most prolific **pelican breeding ground**, and an excellent place to observe these awkward yet graceful birds – there's a shelter with seating and a telescope focused on the small islands where some birds breed at **Jacks Point**, 3km north of Policemans Point on the Princes Highway.

If you're passing by, park your car at the 42-Mile Crossing information area and walk 1km along a sandy 4WD track for **great views** of the sand dunes and the wild Southern Ocean. This track runs alongside the beach all the way up the peninsula to Barkers Knoll and down to Kingston SE, with camping along the way. If you want to stay in more comfort, you'll find plenty of motels at the popular, if dull, fishing centre of **Meningie**, by Lake Albert.

Camp Coorong

10km south of Meningie • Museum Mon–Fri 10am–5pm • Free • ☏ 08 8575 1557, ⓦ ngarrindjeri.com

The **Ngarrindjeri Aborigines** were once one of the largest groups in South Australia, occupying the land around the Coorong and the lower Murray River and lakes. **Camp Coorong**, run by the Ngarrindjeri Lands and Progress Association, details their heritage and culture through cultural programmes and a range of activities, from candlelit bushwalks to basket-weaving. There's a fascinating museum, and you can camp here or stay in the well-fitted-out cabins (see below).

ARRIVAL, INFORMATION AND ACCOMMODATION — COORONG NATIONAL PARK

By boat If you don't have your own transport, you can get to the park on a half-day cruise from Goolwa (see p.68).

Tourist information National Parks South Australia (☏ 08 8575 1200, ⓦ environment.sa.gov.au) does not have an office in the Coorong but has plenty of online information about the wildlife, tours, camping permits and indigenous history, plus maps and downloadable brochures.

Coorong National Park campsites Numerous locations inside the park ☏ 08 8735 1177,

ⓦ envrionment.sa.gov.au. There are ten different campsites inside the park with shelters, BBQs, toilets, running water and marked walking trails. The Coorong is also good for beach camping; with a permit you can camp anywhere along the beach, but cars must be parked in designated places and you must bring your own drinking water, which can be collected outside the seldom-manned Salt Creek ranger station on the edge of the park. Unpowered sites __$15__

Robe

The quaint seaside community of **ROBE**, on the south side of Guichen Bay, 44km from Kingston, was one of South Australia's first settlements, established as a deep-water port in 1847. After 1857, over sixteen thousand Chinese landed here and walked to the goldfields, 400km away, to avoid the poll tax levied in Victoria. As trade declined and the highway bypassed the town, Robe managed to maintain both dignity and a low-key charm, and during the busy summer period the population of fewer than eight hundred expands to over eleven thousand. Summer is also the season for **crayfishing**, Robe's major industry.

ARRIVAL AND INFORMATION — ROBE

By bus Premier Stateliner buses pass through Robe; they call in at the Mobil service station at the end of Main Rd.
Destinations Adelaide (5 weekly; 4hr 30min); Kingston SE (5 weekly; 30min); Mount Gambier (5 weekly; 1hr 40min).

Tourist information Robe's Visitor Information Centre is on Mundy Tce (Mon–Fri 9am–5pm, Sat & Sun 10am–4pm; ☏ 08 8768 2463, ⓦ robe.com.au); it has walking and driving maps, and free internet access.

ACCOMMODATION AND EATING

Caledonian Inn 1 Victoria St ☏ 08 8768 2029, ⓦ caledonian.net.au. This ivy-covered building, known locally as "The Cally", wouldn't look out of place in an English village. It offers atmospheric B&B rooms and serves robust pub food, such as pork cutlet and premium scotch fillet (mains $24–30). Daily 11am–3pm & 6–10pm. __$100__

Sails Restaurant 2 Victoria St ☏ 08 8768 1954, ⓦ sailsrobe.com.au. The most stylish place in town, serving up locally caught lobster and seafood ($28–40).

The food is fairly traditional but consistently good. It gets busy, so you'll need to book a table for dinner in summer. Daily noon–8.30pm.

Sea Vu Caravan Park 1 Squire Drive ☏ 08 8768 2273, ⓦ robeseavu.com. This family-run operation, located next to a beach, is the pick of the four caravan parks around town, with spick and span cabins. Facilities include a camp kitchen, laundry and children's playground. Limited wi-fi available. Sites __$58__, cabins __$170__

7

Beachport

The former whaling port of **BEACHPORT** boasts one of the longest jetties in Australia and many lobster-fishing boats at anchor on Rivoli Bay. Around 1.5km west of the town centre is the Pool of Siloam, a swimming spot reputed to be seven times saltier than the sea.

ARRIVAL, INFORMATION AND ACCOMMODATION   BEACHPORT

By bus Premier Stateliner buses pass through Beachport, stopping off at Jarmo's Automotives on Railway Terrace. Destinations Adelaide (3 weekly; 5hr 10min); Mount Gambier (3 weekly; 1hr 5min); Robe (3 weekly; 30min).
Tourist information The helpful Beachport Visitor Information Centre on Millicent Rd (Mon–Fri 9am–5pm, Sat & Sun 10am–4pm; ☏ 08 8735 8029, ⌨ wattlerange.sa.gov.au)

can provide information on the region including a self-drive map that will show you the way to the Pool of Siloam.
Bompas 3 Railway Terrace ☏ 08 8735 8333, ⌨ bompas .com.au. Overlooking the bay, this historic pub offers a small number of double and queen-size rooms, some with en-suite bathrooms and balconies. Downstairs is a buzzy bar and a restaurant serving mod Oz dishes. $60

7 Canunda National Park

Continue southeast on Southern Ports Highway from Beachport and you'll find several turn-offs to **Canunda National Park**, which has giant sand dunes, signposted coastal walking trails, an abundance of birdlife and camping facilities. The best place from which to explore the park is Southend, but there's also access to the park near historic **Millicent**, 15km to the south, where the Southern Ports Highway rejoins the Princes Highway.

INFORMATION

Tourist information There's a visitor centre at 1 Mount Gambier Rd in Millicent (Mon–Fri 9am–5pm; ☏ 08 8733

0904) with information on the park, local drives, walks and accommodation.

Mount Gambier

Set close to the border with Victoria, **MOUNT GAMBIER** is the southeast's commercial centre and South Australia's second most populous city. The city sprawls up the slopes of an extinct volcano whose three craters – each with its own lake surrounded by heavily wooded slopes and filled from underground waterways – are perfect for subterranean diving.

Blue Lake

Around 2km south of the city centre • Free • **Aquifer Tours** Daily on the hour (45min): Nov–Jan 9am–5pm; Feb–May, Sept & Oct 9am–2pm; June–Aug 9am–noon • $10 • ☏ 08 8723 1199, ⌨ aquifertours.com

The **Blue Lake** is the largest and most stunning of Mount Gambier's three volcanic craters at up to 70m deep and 5km in circumference. From November to March it's a mesmerizing cobalt blue, reverting to a moody steel blue in the colder months. There are lookout spots and a scenic drive around the lake. Guided tours around the crater are offered by Aquifer Tours.

Valley Lake Wildlife Park

Northeast of the Blue Lake • Daily 7am–dusk • Free

Mount Gambier's second-largest crater holds Valley Lake and a **wildlife park**, where indigenous animals range free amid native flora; there are also lookouts, walking trails and boardwalks, plus free barbecues and picnic area.

Cave Gardens

38 Commercial St East • Free

The centrepiece of Mount Gambier is **Cave Gardens**, a shady park surrounding a deep limestone cavern with a flight of steps leading some way down; the stream that runs into it eventually filters into the Blue Lake.

Riddoch Art Gallery

1 Bay Rd • Mon & Wed–Fri 10am–5pm, Sat–Sun 11am–3pm • Free • ☎ 08 8723 9566, ⓦ riddochartgallery.org.au

Fronting the Cave Gardens, close to the former Town Hall, is the **Riddoch Art Gallery**, one of the best public galleries in regional South Australia. Here the focus is on the impressive Rodney Gooch collection of Aboriginal art from the Utopia region of the Northern Territory.

ARRIVAL AND INFORMATION

By Bus V/Line (☎ 1800 800 007, ⓦ vline.com.au) has daily bus services to Portland and Warrnambool, where they connect with train services to Melbourne, while Premier Stateliner runs to Adelaide; buses arrive/depart from the Lady Nelson Victory and Discovery Centre.
Destinations Adelaide (1–2 daily; 6hr 15min–6hr 55min); Beachport (5 weekly; 1hr 5min); Portland (1–2 daily; 1hr 55min); Robe (5 weekly; 40min);

MOUNT GAMBIER

Warrnambool (1–2 daily; 3hr 25min).
Tourist information The Lady Nelson Victory and Discovery Centre on Jubilee Highway East (Mon–Fri 9am–5pm, Sat & Sun 10am–4pm; ☎ 08 8724 9750) has an excellent exhibition exploring the ecology, geology and history of Mount Gambier and doubles up as a visitor centre. It also offers free internet access.

ACTIVITIES

Diving You can dive here in limestone waterways under the city, though you'll need a CDAA (Cave Divers Association of Australia) qualification to do so. Contact the DEWNR at 11 Helen St (☎ 08 8735 1177, ⓦ environment.sa.gov.au/parks) for information and permits for diving and snorkelling in Piccaninnie Ponds Conservation Park and Ewans Pond

Conservation Park, both south of Mount Gambier near Port Macdonnell. At Piccaninnie Ponds, a deep chasm with white limestone walls contains clear water that is filtered underground from the Blue Lake – apparently taking an astonishing five hundred years to get here.

ACCOMMODATION

The Barn 747 Glenelg River Rd ☎ 08 8726 9999, ⓦ barn.com.au. *The Barn* is Mount Gambier's top hotel, with friendly owners, stylish well-equipped guest rooms, five acres of landscaped gardens, and one of the finest restaurants in the region, the *Barn Steakhouse* (see below). **$140**
The Mount Gambier Hotel 2 Commercial St West ☎ 08 8725 0611, ⓦ matthewshotels.com.au. This centrally located hotel has rather old-fashioned albeit spacious en-suite rooms, plus a popular restaurant and bar

downstairs with live music and DJs on weekends. **$130**
The Old Mount Gambier Gaol 25 Margaret St ☎ 08 8723 0032, ⓦ theoldmountgambiergaol.com.au. If you fancy a night in the slammer, head over to the city's former jail, which was built in 1866 and is now a Heritage-listed building: the last inmates left in 1995. Accommodation ranges from ex-prison cells to former offices and a staff cottage, and there are dorm rooms available, too. Guests have the use of a bar, lounge area, tennis court, BBQ and free wi-fi. Dorms **$30**, doubles **$100**

EATING AND DRINKING

The Barn Steakhouse 747 Glenelg River Rd ☎ 08 8726 9999, ⓦ barn.com.au. This impressive steakhouse serves cuts of beef from local, grass-fed Hereford cows and Wagyu sirloin from Mayura Station ($34.50–85). They also have an impressive wine cellar. Worth a splurge. Daily 6.30–10pm.

Wild Ginger 17 Commercial St West ☎ 08 8723 6264, ⓦ wildginger.com.au. *Wild Ginger* has a menu of tasty Thai and pan-Asian soups, stir-fries, curries and salads ($17.90–25.90); highlights include the beef *rendang* and barra in a *penang* curry sauce. Tues–Fri 11.30am–2pm & 5.30pm–late, Sat & Sun 5.30pm–late.

The Coonawarra wine region

Directly north of Mount Gambier, the Riddoch Highway heads through the lovely, low-key **Coonawarra wine region**, and past some World Heritage-listed caves at **Naracoorte**, eventually linking up with the Dukes Highway at Keith. Most wineries are located on a 90km stretch of highway between **Penola** and Padthaway. The region is renowned for the quality of its reds, which have been compared to those of Bordeaux; the soil and drainage are ideal, classic Terra Rossa over limestone, and the climate is perfect – as the weather is not really variable from year to year, the wines are consistently good.

Penola

Twenty-two kilometres north of Mount Gambier, **PENOLA**, gateway to the Coonawarra wine region, is a simple but dignified country town with well-preserved nineteenth-century architecture. Beside the 1857 Cobb & Co. booking office on the corner of Portland Street and Petticoat Lane, the 1860s Woods-MacKillop Schoolhouse is a world away from the sleek, modern **Mary MacKillop Interpretive Centre** next door (daily 10am–4pm; $5; ☎08 8737 2092, ⓦmackilloppenola.org.au). Sister Mary MacKillop (1842–1909) was Penola's most famous resident, and Australia's first saint – canonized by Pope Benedict at St Peter's Basilica in Rome in October 2010. MacKillop set up a school, established her own teaching method and, with Father Julian Tennyson Woods, co-founded the Sisters of St Joseph of the Sacred Heart, a charitable teaching order that spread throughout Australia and New Zealand. Episodes of alleged disobedience and excommunication give her story a certain drama – there's an informative display in the centre, with Barbie-doll lookalike "nuns on the run" and dressed-up dummies in the original schoolroom. Across the fields stand the National Trust-listed cottages of **Petticoat Lane**, where many of Mary's poverty-stricken students lived.

Naracoorte Caves

Midway between Penola and Padthaway • Daily 9am–5pm • $9–30 depending on how many caves you want to visit • Wonambi Fossil Centre $13 • Adventure caving tours $60–100 • ☎08 8760 1201, ⓦenvironment.sa.gov.au

The **Naracoorte Caves Conservation Park** protects a World Heritage-listed system of limestone caves. Your first point of call should be the **Wonambi Fossil Centre**, where you can book tours to the caves below. The centre gives an insight into the area's archeological significance – important fossils of extinct Pleistocene megafauna, including giant kangaroos and wombats, were discovered here in the Victoria Fossil Cave in 1969. You can guide yourself through the **Wet Cave**, named after the very wet chamber at its deepest part; an automatic lighting system switches on as you walk through. A walking trail from here leads to another notable feature, the **Bat Cave**, where you can see bats inside a cave with the help of infrared remote-control cameras.

The other caves are spread out over the conservation park: **Alexandra Cave** has the prettiest limestone formations, while **Victoria Fossil Cave** is, not surprisingly, popular for its fossils.

ARRIVAL AND INFORMATION

By bus Premier Stateliner stops at Penola's visitor centre on its once-daily Adelaide–Mount Gambier inland service. The same service also stops at Naracoorte.

Destinations Adelaide (daily; 5hr 40min); Mount Gambier (daily; 40min–1hr 15min); Naracoorte (daily; 45min).

Tourist information The Penola Coonawarra Visitor Information Centre is in the historic John Riddoch Centre (Mon–Fri 9am–5pm, Sat & Sun 10am–4pm; ☎08 8737 2855, ⓦwattlerange.sa.gov.au), at 27 Arthur St, which

THE COONAWARRA WINE REGION

houses a display on this Coonawarra pioneer. Grab a copy of the *Coonawarra: Australia's Other Red Centre* map, which marks out the region's wineries, and the *Walk with History* map identifying Penola's rich historic architecture. It's also a good source of info on the wine region (ⓦcoonawarra.org).

Tours Penola Coonawarra Tour Services (☎08 8733 2422) offers restaurant transfers and winery tours around the area.

ACCOMMODATION

Penola is a good base for touring the local wineries, but if you like the idea of having them right on your doorstep, look for accommodation in and around Coonawarra Township. Coonawarra Country Cottages (ⓦcoonawarracottages.com.au) has a number of options.

NARACOORTE

Naracoorte Hotel Motel 73 Ormerod St ☎08 8762 2400, ⓦnaracoortehotel.com.au. A solid, if unremarkable option for budget and mid-range travellers alike, offering basic hotel rooms with shared facilities and

smarter motel rooms, as well as a bistro, front bar and bottle shop. $60

Wirreanda Bunkhouse Naracoorte Caves Conservation Park ☎08 8762 2340, ⓦenvironment .sa.gov.au. Close to the caves, this bunkhouse provides dorm-style accommodation, and there are also ten caravan sites at the nearby campsite with hot showers, laundry facilities and rainwater available. Un/powered sites $29/$31, dorms $22

PENOLA

Heyward's Royal Oak Hotel 31 Church St ☎08 8737 2322, ⓦheywardshotel.com.au. This friendly, National Trust-listed hotel is a focal point for the Penola community. It has double rooms with four-poster beds, a few twin rooms, and a lively pub, pleasant beer garden and restaurant. $99

EATING AND DRINKING

Pipers of Penola 58 Riddoch St, Penola ☎08 8737 3999, ⓦpipersofpenola.com.au. The superb Pipers of Penola serves up creative contemporary cuisine, such as blackened steamed pork cheek, Szechuan wood-roasted duck and seared kingfish with soba noodles, in elegant surroundings. The cheese selection is excellent. Mains $32–38. Tues–Sat 6–9.30pm.

A Must@Coonawarra 126 Church St ☎08 8737 3444, ⓦmustcoonawarra.com.au. This ambitious property offers a range of contemporary, ecofriendly apartments and studios, each equipped with the latest mod cons, such as spa baths, DVD players and flat-screen TVs. Rates include breakfast. $169

Penola Caravan Park 2 South Terrace ☎08 8737 2381, ⓦpenolacaravanpark.com.au. This quiet little caravan park, on the edge of town, is one of the more economical places to stay in Penola, with a collection of en-suite cabins and camping sites. Facilities include laundry and BBQs. Powered sites $38, cabins $130

Upstairs at Hollick Ravenswood Lane, Coonawarra Township ☎08 8737 2752, ⓦhollick.com. Overlooking the vineyards at the Hollick Winery, this restaurant serves up carefully prepared dishes ($32–39) based on the freshest of regional produce, accompanied by wines made from grapes grown on the estate. Wed–Sun noon–2.30pm.

7

The Riverland

The Riverland is the name given to the long irrigated strip on either side of the **Murray River** as it meanders for 300km from Blanchetown to Renmark near the Victorian border. The Riverland's deep red-orange alluvial soil – helped by extensive irrigation – is very fertile, making the area the state's major supplier of oranges, stone fruit and grapes. Fruit stalls along the roadsides add to the impression of a year-long harvest, and if you're after **fruit-picking** work it's an excellent place to start; contact the Harvest Trail service (see p.53). The area is also a major **wine-producing** region, though the high-tech wineries here mainly make mass-produced wines for casks and export. Alongside the big-name brands, however, you'll find some boutique operations that are worth visiting; craft breweries are a more recent addition. The **Sturt Highway**, the major route between Adelaide and Sydney, passes straight through the Riverland and Premier Stateliner (see p.664) runs a bus service along it.

Blanchetown

Tiny **BLANCHETOWN**, 130km east of Adelaide, is the first Riverland town and the starting point of the Murray's lock and weir system, which helps maintain the river at a constant height between the town and Wentworth in New South Wales. Eleven kilometres west of town, the **Brookfield Conservation Park** (daily 7am–sunset; free; ☎08 8580 1800, ⓦenvironment.sa.gov.au), a gift to South Australia from the Chicago Zoological Society, is home to the endangered **southern hairy-nosed wombat**, as well as birdlife that includes the rare stone curlew, ground cuckoo shrikes and Australian owlet nightjars.

Morgan

MORGAN is one of the most attractive of the Riverland towns. You can wander through the riverfront park, past the old train station and the stationmaster's building, and up onto the wharves overlooking moored houseboats on the river to bushland beyond. The well-preserved nineteenth-century streetscape of Railway Terrace, the main street, sits above the old railway line and wharf, dominated by the huge Landseer shipping warehouse. You'll need your own vehicle to visit Morgan.

Barmera and around

Almost 100km east of Morgan, on the shores of Lake Bonney, is **BARMERA**. At **Pelican Point**, on the lake's western shore, there's an official **nudist beach**, while every June, the **South Australian Country Music Festival and Awards** are held in the lovely old Bonney Theatre. Just under 16km northwest of Barmera, you pass a bend in the river dubbed **Overland Corner**, the former crossing point for the overland cattle trade heading to New South Wales. Built in 1859, the charming National Trust-protected **Overland Corner Hotel** is now a museum, but it still serves food and drink (Tues–Thurs & Sun 11am–8pm, Fri & Sat 11am–8pm; ☎08 8588 7021). Note the marks indicating the level of the 1956 flood, which are practically up to the roof. You can pick up a leaflet here detailing a walk to some old Aboriginal campsites nearby.

7

THE MURRAY RIVER

The **Murray River** is Australia's Mississippi – or so the American author Mark Twain declared when he saw it in the early 1900s. It's a fraction of the size of the American river, but in a country of seasonal, intermittent streams it counts as a major waterway. Fed by melting snow from the Snowy Mountains, as well as by the Murrumbidgee and Darling rivers, the Murray flows through the arid plains, reaching the Southern Ocean southeast of Adelaide near Goolwa. With the Darling and its tributaries, it makes up one of the biggest and longest watercourses in the world, giving life to Australia's most important agricultural region, the Murray–Darling basin. Almost half of South Australia's water comes from the Murray; even far-off Woomera in the Outback relies on it.

Historically, the Riverland was densely populated by various Aboriginal peoples who navigated the river in bark canoes, the bark being cut from river red gums in a single perfect piece – many trees along the river still bear the scars. The Ngarrindjeri people's Dreamtime story of the river's creation explains how Ngurunderi travelled down the Murray, looking for his runaway wives. The Murray was then just a small stream, but, as Ngurunderi searched, a giant Murray cod surged ahead of him, widening the river with swipes of its tail. Ngurunderi tried to spear the fish, which he chased to the ocean, and the thrashing cod carved out the pattern of the Murray River during the chase.

CRUISES

The best way to appreciate the beauty of the Murray is from the water itself. Several old paddle steamers and a variety of other craft still cruise the Murray for pleasure. The *PS Industry* is one of the few wood-fuelled paddle steamers left on the Murray, and cruises on the first Sunday of the month (1hr 30min; 11am & 1.30pm; $20; bookings through the Renmark visitor centre, see opposite). Murray River Cruises (☎1800 994 620, ⓦmurrayrivercruises.com.au) has a range of two- to seven-day cruises (from $787), many of which start from the lower river town of Mannum, an hour's drive east of Adelaide. Other cruises from Mannum can be booked through the visitor centre, 67 Randell St (☎1300 626 686, ⓦmurrayriver.com.au).

CANOEING AND KAYAKING

The enthusiastic adventure company Canoe Adventures (☎0421 167 645, ⓦcanoeadventure.com.au), based in Berri, offers guided tours, overnight canoe adventures and kayak hire. Short, two-hour tours of the wetlands cost $65, while full-day tours cost $140. Prices include canoe, paddles and lifejackets.

HOUSEBOATS

Renting a houseboat is a relaxing and enjoyable alternative, available in most towns on the river. All you need is a driving licence, and the cost isn't astronomical if you get a group of people together and avoid the peak holiday seasons. A week in an eight-berth houseboat in the high season should cost around $3500–6000. Contact Oz Houseboats (☎08 8365 7776, ⓦozhouseboats.com.au) for details and reservations.

Loxton

South of Lake Bonney, the Murray makes another large loop away from the Sturt Highway, bypassing **Barmera** and twisting instead through **LOXTON**, a quiet town surrounded by some of South Australia's most productive agricultural land. The riverside **Loxton Historical Village**, on Allen Hosking Drive (daily 10am–4pm; $13.50; ☎08 8584 7194, ⓦthevillageloxton.com.au), is a charming (if slightly kitsch) replica of an early twentieth-century Riverland town with a historic main street featuring a bakery, bank, blacksmith, school, farm, and railway station.

Berri

A **Big Orange** sets the scene in **BERRI**, announcing the fact that this is the town where the trademark orange juice comes from, and many travellers are drawn here between October and April by the prospect of fruit-picking work. The river is the main attraction, of course, with scenic river walks above coloured sandstone cliffs.

7

Murray River National Park

Opposite Loxton; road access via the Sturt Highway from Berri • Daily 24hr • Free • ☎ 08 8595 2111, ⓦenvironment.sa.gov.au

The **Murray River National Park (Katarapko)** is where Katarapko Creek and the Murray have cut deep channels and lagoons, creating an island. There is road access to both Katarapko and Lyrup Flats, but you will need a boat to visit Bulyong Island – kayaks are available from Canoe Adventures in Berri (see box opposite).

Renmark

RENMARK, on a bend of the Murray 254km from Adelaide, is the last major town before the Victorian border. As with the other Riverland towns, the main attraction of Renmark is the river and its surrounding wetlands. There's not a great deal to see in the town apart from **Olivewood Estate**, a National Trust property, on the corner of Renmark Avenue and 21st Street (Tues 2–4pm; Thurs–Mon 10am–4pm; $5; ☎08 8585 6175), which is the former home of the Chaffey brothers, the Canadians who pioneered the irrigation and settlement of the Murray region. A palm-lined drive leads through a citrus orchard and olive trees to the house, which is a strange hybrid of Canadian log cabin and Australian lean-to. The attached museum is the usual hotchpotch of local memorabilia, unrelated to the Chaffeys or their ambitious irrigation project.

ARRIVAL AND DEPARTURE   THE RIVERLAND

By bus Premier Stateliner runs a bus service from Adelaide to Renmark via Blanchetown, Waikerie, Barmera, Berri and Loxton. The bus pulls up outside the visitor centre in each town, apart from in Blanchetown where it stops at the BP service station.

Destinations from Adelaide to: Barmera (1–2 daily; 3hr 20min); Berri (1–2 daily; 3hr 40min); Blanchetown (1–3 daily; 2hr); Loxton (daily except Sat; 3hr 45min); Renmark (1–2 daily; 4hr).

INFORMATION

Barmera The visitor information centre is at the shopping centre on Barwell Ave (Mon–Fri 9am–4pm, Sat & Sun 10am–1pm; ☎08 8588 2289, ⓦbarmeratourism.com.au).
Berri The visitor information centre is on Riverview Drive (Mon–Fri 9am–5.15pm, Sat 9am–noon, Sun 10am–1pm; ☎08 8582 5511, ⓦberribarmera.sa.gov.au).
Loxton The visitor information centre is on Bookpurnong

Terrace (Mon–Fri 9am–5pm, Sat 9am–4pm, Sun 10am–4pm; ☎ 08 8584 8071, ⓦvisitloxton.com.au).
Renmark The riverfront Renmark Paringa visitor information centre at 84 Murray Ave (Mon–Fri 9am–5pm, Sat 9am–4pm, Sun 10am–4pm; ☎08 8586 6704, ⓦvisitrenmark.com) can book river cruises (see box opposite).

ACCOMMODATION AND EATING

BARMERA

★**Banrock Station** Holmes Rd ☎08 8583 0299, ⓦbanrockstation.com.au. Apart from producing award-winning wines, this winery is also a conservation park and runs an excellent dining room serving rustic dishes, such as slow-braised pork belly ($27.50) and Tasmanian salmon with pickled beetroot ($28.50). Also offers cooked breakfast and afternoon tea. Guided tours of the restored wetlands available. Daily 9am–4pm.

Barmera Lake Resort Motel Lakeside Drive ☎08 8588 2555, ⓦbarmeralakeresortmotel.com.au. If you don't fancy staying at the nudist resort at Pelican Point, the best bet for fully clothed accommodation is at this motel overlooking the lake, which has good-value rooms, a swimming pool, tennis court and a café/bar. $90

BERRI

Berri Backpackers Old Sturt Highway, 1km outside town ☎08 8582 3144, ⓦberribackpackers.com.au. This quirky hostel is the place to stay if you're fruit picking, but is incredibly popular, so book ahead. Amenities include a sauna, swimming pool, gym, tennis and volleyball courts, plus Balinese-style tree houses, tepees, charming shacks and friendly staff. $35

Berri Hotel Riverview Drive ☎08 8582 1411, ⓦberriresorthotel.com.au. The *Berri Resort Hotel* is a huge riverfront hotel with a swimming pool, tennis courts, good food and a café with great river views. The rooms range from budget options with shared bathrooms to spacious en suites with king-sized beds. $87

Mallee Fowl Restaurant 19042 Sturt Highway, 4km west of Berri ☎08 8582 2096, ⓦmalleefowlrestaurant.com. This barn-like restaurant serves excellent BBQ-style meals – such as T-bone steaks, barramundi with dill and caper sauce, kangaroo fillet with port and mushroom sauce – in a busy and kitsch setting full of Australiana. Mains $22–36. Book ahead. Fri & Sat 6–10pm.

BLANCHETOWN

Salter's Station 72 Paisley Rd ☎08 8540 5023, ⓦsalterstation.com.au. An unusual guesthouse in a renovated 1950s Mobil service station, close to the Murray River and next door to the Burk Salter winery (a free bottle of wine awaits you in your room). The owners also run "wine and wetlands" tours in a vintage 1927 truck. $140

LOXTON

Loxton Community Hotel-Motel 45 East Terrace ☎08 8584 7266, ⓦloxtonhotel.com.au. The most comfortable place to stay in town, with a range of simple hotel rooms with shared facilities and en-suite motel rooms, the best of which have views of the river. There's also a swimming pool, bar and restaurant. $140

MORGAN

Morgan Riverside Caravan Park Main Rd ☎08 8540 2207, ⓦmorganriversidecaravanpark.com.au. In a great spot right by the Murray River, this caravan park has modern sites and cabins, and a wide range of facilities including a pool, shop, minigolf course, playground, and canoes for hire. Un/powered sites $25/32, cabins $85

RENMARK

Renmark Hotel Murray Ave ☎08 8586 6755, ⓦrenmarkhotel.com.au. The landmark *Renmark Hotel*, overlooking the river, was built in 1897 and given its current facade in the 1930s. Accommodation ranges from spa hotel rooms to more basic motel rooms, some with river views. Facilities include a swimming pool, games room, off-street parking and restaurant. $110

Big4 Renmark Riverfront Holiday Park Patey Drive, 2km east of town ☎08 8586 8111, ⓦbig4renmark.com.au. In an idyllic setting outside town, this award-winning park spreads across 1km of riverfront, offering a good choice of camping sites, cabins and more spacious villas. There's a general store, tennis court, adventure playground, laundry and a well-equipped kitchen. Un/powered sites $43/$48, cabins $98, villas $165

★**Wilkdadene Woolshed Brewery** 65 Wilkinson Road, Murtho ☎08 8595 8188, ⓦaboverenmark.com.au. This microbrewery, located in a historic 100-year-old shearing shed on the banks of the Murray, is an idyllic place to break your journey, with fine river views from the old wooden deck, plus tasting trays ($15 for four beers) and guided tours of the brewery available. Daily 11am–5pm

The mid-north

Stretching north of Adelaide up to Port Augusta and the south Flinders Ranges is the fertile agricultural region known as the **mid-north**. The gateway to the region is the town of **Kapunda**, 16km northwest of Nuriootpa in the Barossa Valley (see p.680), which became Australia's first mining town when copper was discovered here in 1842. Kapunda can also be reached as a short detour from the **Barrier Highway** en route to Broken Hill in New South Wales, a route that continues through the larger mining town of **Burra**, and close to Peterborough, the self-proclaimed "frontier to the Outback". The centre of the mid-north's wine area, **Clare**, is 45km southwest of Burra on the Main North Road, the alternative route to Port Augusta.

GETTING AROUND   THE MID-NORTH

Getting around the area by bus is problematic – while most of the major towns have transport links to Adelaide, there are few buses between towns, however close they might be to each other. The Mid North Passenger Network (☎ 08 8842 1677, ⓦ passengernetwork.com.au) operates a community bus service between Burra, Clare, Riverton, Mintaro and other destinations, while LinkSA (☎ 08 8532 2633, ⓦ linksa.com.au) runs buses from Kapunda to Evanston and Tununda to Eudunda.

Kapunda

As you head to **KAPUNDA** from the Barossa, the landscape changes, as vineyards are replaced by crops and grazing sheep. The discovery of **copper** here (and in Burra) in the 1840s put the region at the vanguard of Australia's mining boom, attracting huge numbers of Cornish miners; today as you come into town, you're greeted by a colossal sculpture of a Cornish miner entitled *Map Kernow*, "Son of Cornwall". However, the boom ended as suddenly as it began, as resources were exhausted – mining finished at Kapunda in 1878.

A place that once had its own daily newspaper, eleven hotels and a busy train station is now little more than a picturesque rural town, though it supports a thriving community of painters and other artists, who open their studios to the public. Many of the original buildings have survived, so it's worth taking the self-guided heritage walk (maps from the visitor centre), which includes the old mine site.

ARRIVAL AND INFORMATION   KAPUNDA

By bus LinkSA has weekday buses between Kapunda and Gawler (Mon–Fri 2 daily; 30min), which is connected to Adelaide by regular buses and trains.

Tourist information The Kapunda Visitor Centre, 51–53 Main St (Mon–Fri 9am–5pm, Sat & Sun 10am–4pm; ☎ 1300 770 301, ⓦ light.sa.gov.au/vic) can provide information on the local heritage trail, accommodation and other attractions; there's also a museum in the basement.

Events The best time to visit Kapunda is during the Celtic festival (usually held in mid-Oct), when Celtic music, bush and folk bands feature at the town's pubs.

ACCOMMODATION AND EATING

Ford House 80 Main St ☎ 08 8566 3341. A B&B and café in a beautiful bluestone building that dates back to the 1860s. There are just three rooms, all en suite, and the café is a good spot for breakfast, lunch or afternoon tea. The menu includes sandwiches, hot dogs and home-made cakes (tea and scones $8). Mon–Sat 9am–4pm. **$160**

Kapunda Tourist Park Montefiore St ☎ 08 8566 2094, ⓦ kapundatouristpark.com. This scenic caravan park, with its own kangaroos and emus, is an ideal place to break your journey. Facilities include a guest laundry, playground and electric BBQs. Camping and bush cabins available. Un/powered sites **$22/$28**, cabins **$120**

Burra

In 1851 the "Monster Mine" at **BURRA** was the largest in Australia, producing five percent of the world's copper and creating fabulous wealth. However, when the mines closed in 1877, Burra became a service centre for the surrounding farming community, and nowadays takes advantage of its heritage to attract visitors. Plenty of money has been spent restoring and beautifying the place, and it's now a popular weekend escape between March and November, before it gets too hot. The mine is in the northern part of town, while the southern section has the shopping centre, based around Market Street.

Burra Heritage Trail

Eight sites around town; 11km circuit • Burra Heritage Passport $30, available from the visitor centre

The visitor centre issues the Burra Heritage Passport to people driving the **Burra Heritage Trail** and a key giving access to eight sites en route. Head north along Market Street and the trail takes you to the **Burra Monster Mine** site, where there are extensive remains and interpretive walking trails. Other sites in the northern section of the town include the **Bon Accord Mine Complex**, **old police lock-up and stables**, **Redruth Gaol**, and **Hampton**, a now-deserted private township in the style of an English village. Back in the main part of the town, the pass gets you entry to sites including the **Unicorn Brewery Cellars** (dating back to 1873) and the two remaining miners' dugouts: by 1851, because of a housing shortage, nearly two thousand people were living in homes clawed out of the soft clay along Burra Creek.

ARRIVAL AND INFORMATION · BURRA

By bus Yorke Peninsula Coaches (☎08 8821 2755, ⊛ypcoaches.com.au) operates a weekly service (on Wednesdays) from Adelaide to Burra (3hr 15min), with more frequent services to other destinations in the mid-north, such as Clare (1–3 weekly; 2hr 45min), Auburn (1–3 weekly; 2hr 5min) and Watervale (1–3 weekly; 2hr 25min).

Tourist information The visitor information centre is on Market Square (daily 9am–5pm; ☎08 8892 2154, ⊛visitburra.com).

ACCOMMODATION & EATING

Burra Caravan Park 12 Bridge Terrace ☎08 8892 2442, ⊛burravisitorcentre.com. Located in a pretty spot beside the creek, a couple of minutes' walk from the centre of town, this small caravan park has 38 camping sites, a modern ablution block and BBQs. Un/powered sites $20/30

La Pecora Nera (The Black Sheep) 3 Upper Thames Street, Burra ☎0400 516 896, ⊛blacksheepburra.com. Burra's hottest culinary destination offers authentic Italian wood-fired pizzas ($15–20) that showcase fresh local vegetables, free-range chicken and smoked meats. The menu also includes pasta, salads and meat dishes. Wed–Sun noon–1.30pm, Wed & Thurs 5.30–7.30pm, Fri & Sat 5.50–9pm, Sun 5.30–7pm.

The Clare Valley

In the cool uplands of the **North Mount Lofty Ranges**, the **Clare Valley** is really a series of gum-fringed ridges and valleys running roughly 30km north from **Auburn** to the main township of **Clare**, on either side of Main North Road. The wine industry in the valley was pioneered by Jesuit priests at **Sevenhill** in the 1850s. There's no tourist overkill here: coach tours are not encouraged, and because it's a small area with just over **forty cellar doors**, you can learn a lot about the local styles of wine (the valley is especially recognized for its fine Rieslings). You'll often get personal treatment too, with the winemaker presiding. Several sheep stations can be visited among beautiful historic villages, well-preserved mansions, quaint old pubs, and there's plenty of atmospheric accommodation, as well as numerous superb restaurants attached to wineries.

Auburn to Watervale

Heading north through the valley, the first settlement you come to is the small village of **AUBURN**, 120km from Adelaide, which began life as a halfway resting point for wagons carrying copper ore from Burra to Port Adelaide. The next small villages, **LEASINGHAM** and, 2km north, **WATERVALE**, have several wineries.

Mintaro to Sevenhill

East of Leasingham is **MINTARO**, a village whose tree-lined streets and cottages are beautifully preserved from the 1850s. There's no general store or petrol supply here; the emphasis is on atmospheric cottage accommodation, which is popular with Adelaide weekenders. Heading northwest from Mintaro to the village of **SEVENHILL** takes you through the rolling hills of the Polish Hill River area. Sevenhill is home to

CLARE VALLEY WINERIES

Crabtree North Terrace, Watervale ☎ 08 8843 0069, ⓦ crabtreewines.com.au. The pick of the four wineries at Waterville, and one of the most enjoyable to visit in the valley. Daily 10.30am–4.30pm.

Eldredge Vineyards Spring Gully Rd, Spring Gully ☎ 08 8842 3086, ⓦ eldredge.com.au. Located in a small farmhouse fronting a dam, with a good restaurant. Daily 11am–5pm.

Jim Barry Main North Rd, Clare ☎ 08 8842 2261, ⓦ jimbarry.com. A friendly, family-run place founded by a pioneer winemaker, home to the Clare's most robust reds. Mon–Fri 9am–5pm, Sat 11am–5pm, Sun 11am–4pm.

Knappstein Winery & Brewery 2 Pioneer Ave, Clare ☎ 08 8841 2100, ⓦ knappstein.com.au. Beer has been brewed on this site since 1878 (initially to slate the thirst of miners), but Knappstein is principally a winemaker, producing high-quality reds, whites and rosés. Its best-selling German-style lager is a more recent addition. Mon–Fri 9am–5pm, Sat & Sun 11am–4pm.

O'Leary Walker Wines Main Rd, Leasingham ☎ 08 8843 0022, ⓦ olearywalkerwines.com. Respected smaller winery producing an impressive range of Rieslings, Chardonnays, Cabernet Sauvignons and blends. The cellar door is one of the most congenial in the valley. The company also sources grapes from the Adelaide Hills. Daily 10am–4pm.

Paulett Wines Sevenhill–Mintaro Rd, Polish Hill River ☎ 08 8843 4328, ⓦ paulettwines.com.au. This winery, which has fabulous views, produces classic Polish Hills Riesling, plus reds, sparkling wines and its own beer. The property includes a sensory Australian bush garden and delightful vineyard café. Daily 10am–5pm.

Reilly's Wines Cnr Hill St & Leasingham Rd, Mintaro ☎ 08 8843 9013, ⓦ reillyswines.com.au. The winery, housed in an 1856 stone cottage, is one of the region's most atmospheric, and includes a cellar door, restaurant and heritage B&B accommodation. Daily 10am–4pm.

Sevenhill Cellars College Rd, Sevenhill ☎ 08 8843 4222, ⓦ sevenhill.com.au. Founded in 1851 by the Jesuits to make sacramental wine, this delightful old winery now makes a range of traditional table wines, such as Riesling and Cabernet Sauvignon, alongside more contemporary styles. Daily 10am–5pm.

Skillogalee Winery Trevarrick Rd, Sevenhill ☎ 08 8843 4311, ⓦ skillogalee.com. This family-owned winery makes some of the Clare's most sought-after wines (including basket-pressed Shiraz), but also serves the best food for miles around. Drop in for a wine tasting, but make sure that you stay for lunch. Daily 7.30am–5pm.

7

the valley's oldest winery, *Sevenhill Cellars* (see box above). Just beyond is the Spring Gully Conservation Park, which has the last remnant of red stringybark forest in South Australia. There are steep gullies, waterfalls, wildlife and, in spring, lovely wild flowers.

Clare

CLARE itself is a surprisingly ordinary town, compared to its more historic-looking neighbours, with most of its cafés and shops clustered along the main street. But thanks to the popular Riesling Trail, Clare is slowly changing, with a number of smart new restaurants and gourmet food outlets catering for weekend visitors from the city.

ARRIVAL AND GETTING AROUND
THE CLARE VALLEY

By bus Yorke Peninsula Coaches (☎ 08 8821 2755, ⓦ ypcoaches.com.au) operates services from Adelaide to Clare (4 weekly; 2hr 45min), plus other nearby towns and settlements in the Valley.

By bike Between Clare and Auburn, the old railway line has been transformed into the Riesling Trail, a 27km cycle path; to cycle one-way takes about two hours. Mountain bikes can be rented from Clare Valley Cycle Hire, 32 Victoria Rd, Clare ($30/day; ☎ 0418 802 077, ⓦ clarevalleycyclehire .com.au), which will deliver to anywhere in the valley.

INFORMATION

Tourist information The Clare Valley Wine, Food & Tourism Centre, 8 Spring Gully Rd (daily 9am–5pm; ☎ 08 8842 2131, ⓦ clarevalley.com.au), stocks an excellent free visitors' guide and can book accommodation and restaurants, many of them in wineries.

Events The region's calendar is crammed for most of the year but the biggest event is the Clare Valley Gourmet Weekend, held in May at local wineries.

ACCOMMODATION AND EATING

Bungaree Station Main Road North, 12km north of Clare ☎ 08 8842 2677, ⓦ bungareestation.com.au. The pick of the local farmstays is *Bungaree Station*, a working merino station. One of the oldest properties in the district, it has a range of accommodation, including shearer's quarters, council chambers and the manager's house, which are all decorated in the rustic style. Rates include breakfast and vary widely according to accommodation. No wi-fi. **$198**

Clare Caravan Park Main Road North, 4km south of Clare ☎ 08 8842 2724, ⓦ discoveryholidaypark.com.au. Although some way outside town, this caravan park is a reliable and economical choice, with a range of sites and self-contained cabins, plus a pool, shop and bike hire. Un/powered sites **$24/$35**, cabins **$99**

Dennis Cottage St Vincent St, Auburn ☎ 08 8843 0048, ⓦ denniscottage.com.au. The luxurious *Dennis Cottage* has bags of charm, a spa, and paraphernalia associated with C.J. Dennis, the popular poet who was born here in 1876. Breakfast provisions included, but no wi-fi. **$300**

Skillogalee House Trevarrick Rd ☎ 08 8843 4311, ⓦ skillogalee.com.au. This restored farmhouse, owned by the winery of the same name, offers three large bedrooms, a sitting room, well-equipped kitchen-dining room and a shady patio with BBQ – perfect for a family. Rate includes breakfast provisions. **$390**.

Terroir Auburn Main 20 North Road, Auburn ☎ 08 8849 2509, ⓦ terroirauburn.com.au. Housed in a wonderful old shop in the main street, *Terroir* sources the bulk of its produce from a 100-mile radius. The seasonal menu is modern and fairly global in its influences, with mains such as pan-fried halloumi ($21), confit duck leg ($35) and salt and pepper rabbit ($22). Wed & Thurs 6–8.30pm, Fri & Sat noon–2pm & 6–8pm, Sun noon–2pm.

Thorn Park By The Vines Quarry Road, Sevenhill ☎ 08 8843 4304, ⓦ thornpark.com.au. This elegant property, surrounded by vineyards and natural bushland, is the perfect romantic retreat. The three guest rooms are sophisticated and beautiful, and the hospitality faultless. A full cooked breakfast is included. Two-night minimum stay. **$425**

Port Augusta

How you see **PORT AUGUSTA** depends on where you've come from. If you're arriving from the Outback, the town's trees, shops and hotels can be a real thrill, but compared with the southeast of the state, there's little particularly exciting here. Its role as a transport hub has ensured the town's continued survival, while recent developments have made the foreshore area with its city beach more attractive. In addition, there are a couple of brilliant sights to see in town and some good **bushwalking** country around Mount Remarkable (see p.718), at the tail end of the Flinders Ranges.

Port Augusta sits at the tip of the Spencer Gulf, with the Outback all around. Despite the name, the docks closed long ago, while the power station and railways were drastically scaled down during the 1980s. The centre of town overlooks the east side of the **Spencer Gulf**, more like a river where it divides the town. Shops, banks and the post office are clustered along narrow **Commercial Road**. During summer, you should make the most of the **swimming beach** at the end of Young Street or escape the dust and heat at the attractive foreshore – the old wooden pile crossing, now a footbridge, and a 100-year-old jetty, all that remains of the port, make good perches for fishing and there are barbecue facilities and swimming pontoons in the water.

Wadlata Outback Centre

41 Flinders Terrace • Mon–Fri 9am–5.30pm, Sat & Sun 10am–4pm • $20.50 • ☎ 08 8641 9193, ⓦ wadlata.sa.gov.au

The superb **Wadlata Outback Centre** is dedicated to the Outback and its characters, covering everything from the indigenous people's deep relationship to the land to the explorers who opened up the unforgiving country. There's an impressive use of multimedia and audiovisual technology, and lots of interactive elements to keep you amused (it's wonderful for families). Allow a couple of hours to do the place justice; they'll give you a "pass out" if you want to return later. There's also a café, gift shop and the town's visitor centre (see p.708).

> ## TRAVELLING AROUND THE SOUTH AUSTRALIAN OUTBACK
>
> When travelling through the Outback, **water** is vital: with few exceptions, lakes and waterways are dry or highly saline, and most Outback deaths are related to dehydration or heatstroke – bikers seem particularly prone. As always, stay with your vehicle if you break down. Summer temperatures can be lethally hot, and winters pleasant during the day and subzero at night; rain can fall at any time of year, but is most likely to do so between January and May. Many roadhouses and fuel pumps take credit and/or debit cards, but it's essential to carry cash as well.
>
> To find out about **road conditions** in the Outback, call ☎ 1300 361 033 or visit the South Australia Transport website (♨ transport.sa.gov.au). If you're not driving, it is possible to travel through the region by bus services run by Greyhound (☎ 1300 473 946, ♨ greyhound.com.au) and Premier Stateliner (☎ 08 8415 5555, ♨ premierstateliner.com.au). Flying can save you a lot of time and energy; Regional Express (☎ 13 17 13, ♨ rex.com.au) is the most useful carrier in the area.
>
> ### MAPS
>
> RAA road **maps** are good but lack topographical information, so if you're spending any time in the north, pick up the excellent Westprint Heritage maps and the Gregory's 4WD maps. Hikers traversing the Flinders on the **Heysen Trail** (see box, p.684) need topographic maps of each section and advice from the nearest DEWNR office. Conditions of minor roads are so variable that maps seldom do more than indicate the surface type; local police and roadhouses will have current information.
>
> ### PERMITS
>
> A **Desert Parks Pass** is required for legal entry into Innamincka Regional Reserve, Lake Eyre National Park, Witjira National Park and the Simpson Desert Conservation Park and Regional Reserve: $160 per vehicle allows unlimited access to all of them and use of campsites for twelve months, with copies of the detailed *DEWNR Desert Parks Handbook* and a map thrown in. Passes are available from agencies throughout the north, can be purchased online (♨ environment.sa.gov.au/parks; allow seven days), or bought at the **Port Augusta visitor centre** (see p.708).

Homestead Park Pioneer Museum

Elsie St, behind *McDonald's* • Mon–Fri 9am–noon, Sat & Sun 10am–4pm • $3 • ☎ 08 8642 2035

This small museum provides an insight into the day-to-day lives of South Australia's early European settlers. Its centrepiece is a 140-year-old log homestead that was moved here from Yudnapinna Station, 100km away. The complex includes a buggy shed, with two 1920s carriages, and an original blacksmith's shop with machinery.

Australian Arid Lands Botanic Garden

Stuart Highway • Mon–Fri 9am–5pm, Sat & Sun 10am–4pm • Free • Tours Mon–Fri 10am • $7.95 • ☎ 08 8641 9116, ♨ aalbg.sa.gov.au

Flanking the north side of town is the stunning **Australian Arid Lands Botanic Garden**, a showcase and research centre for native Australian desert flora with 12km of self-guided walking trails and bird hides; it's well worth taking one of the weekday tours. The rain-gathering, solar-powered information centre, shop and café underline the ideals of the garden as an ongoing ecological project.

ARRIVAL AND DEPARTURE   PORT AUGUSTA

By plane The airport, on Old Whyalla Rd, 5km west of the centre, is served by Sharp Airlines (☎ 1300 556 694, ♨ sharpairlines.com), who operate flights to Adelaide (Mon–Fri 2 daily; 55min).

By bus The bus terminal is at 21 Mackay St (☎ 08 8642 5055) and is served by Greyhound from Adelaide to Alice Springs and Premier Stateliner from Adelaide to Whyalla and Ceduna.

Destinations Adelaide (2–5 daily; 3hr 45min); Alice Springs (daily; 15hr 40min); Ceduna (daily; 6hr 25min); Coober Pedy (daily; 6hr 25min); Mambray Creek for Mount Remarkable (2–3 daily; 30min); Port Lincoln (Mon–Sat; 5hr 15min); Whyalla (Mon–Sat; 55min).

By car Cars can be rented from Budget on the corner of McKay and Young streets (☎ 08 8642 6040, ♨ budget.com.au); they also have a branch at the airport.

INFORMATION

Tourist information The chief source of information is the very helpful visitor centre in the Wadlata Outback Centre, at 41 Flinders Terrace (Mon–Fri 9am–5.30pm, Sat & Sun 10am–4pm; ☎08 8641 9194), where you can pick up a brochure detailing a self-guided heritage walk, book tours including scenic flights, fishing expeditions, whale- and dolphin-watching cruises, 4WD tours, camel rides and sheep station experiences, and get your tickets for the Pichi Richi Railway (see p.721). If you need maps and information beyond what's available at the Outback Centre, visit the helpful DEWNR at 9 Mackay St (Mon–Fri 9am–5pm; ☎08 8648 5328, ⓦenvironment.sa.gov.au) where you can pick up park info, maps and passes. The RAA, at 7 Caroona Rd (Mon–Fri 8.30am–5pm; ☎08 8642 2576, ⓦraa.com.au), provides very good road maps to members.

ACCOMMODATION AND EATING

Big 4 Caravan Park Junction of the Eyre and Stuart hwys ☎08 8642 2974, ⓦbig4.com.au. One of the closest caravan parks to town, with extensive grounds that feature a pool, TV room, camp kitchen, shop and range of accommodation options – from camping sites to cabins. Un/powered sites __$34/$39__, cabins __$119__

Hannahville Hotel 30 Gibson St ☎08 8642 2921, ⓦhannahvillehotel.com.au. If you're after hearty, no-nonsense pub grub, this hotel delivers the goods with steaks, seafood and schnitzels ($19–32), plus cooked breakfasts ($10.50–14.50) at the weekends. Mon–Wed & Sun noon–2pm & 6–8pm, Thurs–Sat noon–2pm & 6–8.30pm.

Majestic Oasis Apartments Maryatt St ☎08 8648 9000, ⓦoasisportaugusta.com.au. The smartest accommodation in Port Augusta, this property offers 75 fully equipped apartments, with landscaped gardens, a pool, tour desk and beach access. __$149__

★ **Standpipe Golf Motor Inn** Daw St ☎08 8642 4033, ⓦstandpipe.com.au. This impressive hotel has fifty refurbished rooms, suites and self-contained apartments. The property includes an eighteen-hole golf course, outdoor swimming pool, manicured gardens and the best Indian restaurant for miles around. __$135__

The west

West of Port Augusta the Eyre Highway runs 950km to the border of Western Australia; the journey can be made more interesting by taking a detour around the coast of the **Eyre Peninsula**, which has sandy white beaches, aquamarine sea, excellent fishing, and **Australia's finest seafood**. Once past **Ceduna**, on the eastern edge of the **Nullarbor Plain**, there's little beyond you and the desert. The *Indian Pacific* **train** traverses the Nullarbor further inland, through even more extreme desolation.

The Eyre Peninsula

Long appreciated by Adelaidians as an antidote to city stress, the Eyre Peninsula's broad triangle is protected by the **Gawler** Ranges from the arid climate further north. The area was first farmed in the 1880s, fishing communities sprang up at regular intervals, and iron ore was discovered around 1900 near Whyalla. The drive around the coast passes stunning scenery and superlative **surfing** and **beach fishing**, especially where the Great Australian Bight's elemental weather hammers into the western shore.

Whyalla

For over 100 years, **WHYALLA** has been the state's headquarters of heavy industry, with smelters, steel mills and shipyards dominating the landscape. However, the last steel producer, Arrium, went into voluntary administration in early 2016 and at the time of writing was due to close unless new investors could be found; how this will affect the town remains to be seen. But don't be fooled by the industrial skyline: this resilient little town offers plenty for the visitor, with a good selection of museums, art galleries and places to eat. Many of the original buildings, such as the post office, banks and hotels, can be found around the junction with Forsyth and Patterson streets. The city's newest attraction is a foreshore development which includes landscaped gardens, a boardwalk, safe swimming beach and marina.

The east coast

Beyond Whyalla, the **east coast** is an unassuming string of sheltered beaches and fishing villages, many with attractive historic architecture, nestled beneath towering grain silos – the sort of places you could drive through without a second glance or else get waylaid beachcombing for a week. Cowell is known for its King George whiting and as the world's largest source of black "nephrite" jade, though not much of it is in evidence, since it's largely exported uncut. **Arno Bay**, **Port Neill** and the larger **Tumby Bay** all boast clean, quiet beaches, good fishing and decent accommodation.

Port Lincoln

Australia's seafood capital and largest fishing port, built on a hillside above Boston Bay, **PORT LINCOLN** has the liveliest atmosphere on the peninsula. The town's harbour bobs with trawlers, and the main seafront streets of Tasman Terrace and Liverpool Street are full of cafés, restaurants and big old Aussie pubs.

The seafood farmed or caught wild in the oceans around Port Lincoln is considered to be the country's finest, earning the town and state hundreds of millions of dollars a year. For tourists the main appeal is the chance to go on shark cage-diving tours: the sea off Lincoln is one of the few places in the world where you can cage-dive with **great white sharks** (footage for *Jaws* was filmed here).

7

ARRIVAL AND DEPARTURE
PORT LINCOLN

By plane The airport, 7km north of the centre of Port Lincoln, is served by Regional Express flights to Adelaide (5–8 daily; 50min).
By bus Premier Stateliner buses arrive at and depart from

20 Lewis St, near the seafront.
Destinations Adelaide (daily except Sat; 9hr 50min); Port Augusta (daily except Sat; 4hr 45min).

INFORMATION AND ACTIVITIES

Tourist information The tourist office, Visit Port Lincoln, is at 3 Adelaide Place (Mon–Sat 9am–5pm, Sun 10am–4pm; ☎08 8621 2399, ⓦvisitportlincoln.net), a short walk from where Premier Stateliner buses terminate. They can book fishing trips, wildlife-spotting cruises, boat charters, kitesurfing and farmstays.
Cage-diving and wildlife swims If you want to go cage-diving with great white sharks (around $495) or swim with sea lions ($190) contact Calypso Star Charter Tours (3/10 South Quay Blvd; ☎08 8682 3939,

ⓦsharkcagediving.com.au) or Adventure Bay Charters (2 Jubilee Drive; ☎08 8682 2979, ⓦadventurebaycharters.com).
Fishing Get tackle and bait from Spot On (Mon–Fri 8.30am–5.30pm, Sat & Sun 8am–4pm; ☎08 8683 0021, ⓦspotonfishing.com.au), at 39 Tasman Terrace, where the friendly staff will provide directions to the best fishing and camping spots. Or you could simply fish off the town jetty.

ACCOMMODATION AND EATING

★**Del Giorno's** 80 Tasman Terrace ☎08 8683 0577, ⓦdelgiornos.com.au. This award-winning restaurant serves good pizza and pasta, but the seafood – including bluefin tuna, kingfish and oysters from nearby Coffin Bay – is the star of the show. Mains $18–33. Mon–Sat 7.30am–9pm, Sun 8.30am–9pm.
Port Lincoln Hotel 1 Lincoln Highway ☎1300 766 100, ⓦportlincolnhotel.com.au. The region's most impressive hotel has wanderful harbour views, spacious modern rooms and a good restaurant (specializing in local seafood), plus a bar, fitness centre and an outdoor swimming pool. **$139**
Port Lincoln Tourist Park 11 Hindmarsh St ☎08 8621 4444, ⓦportlincolntouristpark.com.au. At the far end of

the highway, this recently revamped caravan park has a great location, with its own small beach and jetty, free BBQs and super-helpful staff. In addition to powered and unpowered sites, there are also holiday units and cabins on offer. Un/powered sites **$25/$32**, holiday units **$125**, cabins **$140**
Port Lincoln YHA 24–26 London St ☎08 8682 3605, ⓦyha.com.au. This modern hostel is the best backpacker option in town, with clean dorms and private rooms, a café/bar, ample communal space, tour booking facilities, and even a replica cage and great white shark, just to get you in the mood. Dorms **$22**, doubles **$72**

Lincoln National Park

13km southwest of Port Lincoln • Daily 24hr • $11 per vehicle • Camping per person $6 (bring your own gear) • Pay entry and camping fees at Port Lincoln's tourist office (see p.709) • ☎ 1300 788 378, ⓦ visitportlincoln.net

A short drive from Port Lincoln is the wild and unspoilt **Lincoln National Park**, which covers a rough peninsula of sandy coves, steep cliffs and mallee scrub, home to the discreet rock parrot. The tourist office in Port Lincoln (see p.709) can supply maps and advice on road conditions.

Whalers Way

32km south of Port Lincoln • No fixed opening times • $30 • Free bush camping with toilets, picnic tables and gas barbecues (bring your own gear) • Pay entry fee and collect a key from Port Lincoln's tourist office (see p.709) • ☎ 1300 788 378, ⓦ visitportlincoln.net

Whalers Way is a privately owned stretch of road to some of the coast's most ruggedly beautiful landscapes, including Cape Carnot and Cape Wiles. The name Whalers Way derives from the whaling station that once operated at Cape Wiles – its relics are stacked up around the gate – where you can spot fur seals, kangaroos and emus. The power of the Southern Ocean is memorably demonstrated at Cape Carnot, in the southern section, where giant waves and frosty blue surf force their way through blowholes that sigh as they erupt in sync with the swell.

Coffin Bay

The picturesque setting of the town of **COFFIN BAY**, 50km west of Port Lincoln (you'll need your own wheels to get here), is home to Australia's finest oysters. A stroll along the coastal "Oyster Walk" takes you past old fishermen's shacks, now mostly summer houses, and reveals a wealth of bird- and plant life – a taste of the national park just to the west.

Coffin Bay National Park comprises a landscape of dunes and salt marsh, mostly accessible only by 4WD, though parts are open to other types of vehicle ($10 per vehicle; camping $6 per person; before arriving fill in a form at the Port Lincoln tourist office, see p.709). Come here for the sense of isolation, the sand sculptures at Sensation and Mullalong beaches, and some great fishing The semicircular stone walls on the northern shore are **Aboriginal fish traps** – fish were chased in at high tide and then the gaps in the side blocked with nets as the water receded.

TOURS AND ACCOMMODATION   COFFIN BAY

Tours Goin' Off Safaris (☎ 0428 877 488, ⓦ goinoffsafaris .com.au) offer specially designed tours of Coffin Bay and Port Lincoln, showcasing the region's best seafood, scenic locations and native wildlife. Chief guide David "Lunch" Doudle offers many other options, including underwater adventures and hunt and gather safaris. Full-day tours from $185.

Coffin Bay Caravan Park 91 Esplanade ☎ 08 8685 4170, ⓦ coffinbaycaravanpark.com.au. This large caravan park, which covers 12 hectares, offers shady lawns, a laundry, babies' changing room, kitchen, children's playground and BBQs, and cabins and villas alongside 130 campsites. No wi-fi. Un/powered sites __$24/$33__, cabins __$75__, villas __$120__

The west coast

To catch the best of the west coast and the townships along the way, you'll need to detour off the main road between Coffin Bay and Ceduna. The region's coastal communities are a mix of fishermen, farmers and surfies who come to ride the endless succession of strong, 100m-high crests rolling into Waterloo Bay at **Elliston**, one of the state's most highly regarded **surf beaches**. The 12km Great Ocean Tourist Drive from Elliston is a worthwhile detour; it's filled with stunning ocean views and quirky clifftop sculptures.

North of Elliston, just before Venus Bay, rocks have been hollowed by the sea to form the impressive **Talia Caves** – a tribute to the might of the ocean in these parts. To the north again, if you turn to the coast about 20km north of Port Kenny, you pass the striking **Murphy's Haystacks**, a group of low granite monoliths that look like giant mushrooms. Make a small detour to Baird Bay where you can swim with both Australian sea lions and bottlenose dolphins (through Baird Bay Ocean Eco Experience ☎08 8626 5017, ⦿bairdbay.com; $160) in the pristine waters of this sheltered bay.

At **Point Labatt** you can see mainland Australia's only colony of fur seals. Then it's back to the highway at **Streaky Bay** – the only place on the west coast that has a real town centre – and then to drier country as you approach Ceduna and the Nullarbor.

Gawler Ranges

Eerily quiet Iron Knob is the start of forays along dirt tracks into the **Gawler Ranges**, before you rejoin the highway at Wirrulla. While you might not need a 4WD, be aware that it's a remote area that requires advance preparation and advice from the Department of Environment, Water and Natural Resources (⦿environment.sa.gov.au). The ranges are low, rounded volcanic ridges coloured orange by dust, with occasional speckled boulders poking through a thin grass cover, and it's worth walking up one of the peaks for a closer look.

The track into the ranges passes **Lake Gairdner**, largest of the Gawler's **salt lakes**, with the ruins of Pondanna Homestead on a lonely plain at its southern end.

ACCOMMODATION	GAWLER RANGES
Mount Ive Station 135km west of Iron Knob ☎08 8648 1817, ⦿mtive.com.au. Right in the heart of the Gawler Ranges, this sheep station has fuel, information and accommodation in basic rooms (shearers' quarters),	plus camping sites, but don't turn up unannounced and you'll need to bring your own food. Un/powered sites $20/$28, doubles $65

Ceduna

You know where you are in **CEDUNA**: a large signpost in the centre gives distances to everywhere between Perth and Port Augusta, and depending on which direction you're travelling in, this is either the first or last bit of civilization you've seen or will see in a while after or before crossing the Nullarbor. Either way, it's the place to break up the trip and there's no lack of caravan parks, banks or service stations. Ensure that you leave with a full tank of fuel: it's a punishing 1200km west from here to the next town of any note.

Don't miss **Tjutjuna Arts** (cnr Eyre Hwy & Kuhlmann St; Mon–Fri 9am–5pm; free; ☎08 8625 2487,⦿tjutjunaarts.com.au), a resource centre where you can see Aboriginal artists at work, or buy a painting or a handmade boomerang from the small gallery. The centre also houses a language school that is helping to preserve indigenous languages from the desert.

ARRIVAL AND DEPARTURE	CEDUNA
By plane The airport, 3km from the town centre on the eastern edge of town, is served by Regional Express flights to Adelaide (2 daily; 1hr 30min). **By bus** Premier Stateliner buses run between Ceduna and	Adelaide via Port Augusta; buses arrive/depart from outside Autopro at 19/21 McKenzie St. Destinations Adelaide (3 weekly; 11hr 45min); Port Augusta (3 weekly; 6hr 25min).

INFORMATION AND TOURS	
Tourist information The helpful visitor information centre at 58 Poynton St (Mon–Fri 9am–5.30pm, Sat & Sun 9.30am–5pm; ☎08 8625 3343, ⦿cedunatourism.com.au) and the DEWNR, on McKenzie St (Mon–Fri 9am–5pm; ☎08 8625 3144, ⦿environment.sa.gov.au), have info on	the Nullarbor's attractions. **Tours** Ceduna Tours (☎08 8625 2564, ⦿cedunaboatcharter.com.au) runs trips into the area, visiting the Gawler Ranges and Head of the Bight Whale Sanctuary, plus fishing and diving charters.

ACCOMMODATION AND EATING	
Foreshore Hotel-Motel 32 O'Loughlin Terrace ☎08 8625 2008, ⦿cedunahotel.com.au. Overlooking the sea, the community-owned *Foreshore Hotel-Motel* has 57 very	comfortable rooms and suites, most with ocean views, plus a popular bistro and well-stocked front bar. Continental breakfast included. $150

7

The Nullarbor Plain

Nullarbor, from the Latin "Nullus Arbor" or "treeless", is an apt description of the plain, which stretches flat and infertile for over 1200km across the Great Australian Bight. Taking the **train** brings you closer to the dead heart than the **road** does, which allows some breaks in the monotony of the journey to scan the sea for southern right whales, or playing a few holes of golf on the Nullarbor Links (ⓦ nullarborlinks.com) – an eighteen-hole, par-72 golf course between Ceduna and Kalgoorlie in Western Australia. At 1365km, it's the world's longest and arguably the most unusual golf course.

From Ceduna to the Western Australian border it's 480km, which you can easily cover in under five hours; the Dalí-esque fridges standing along the highway in the early stages of the drive are actually makeshift post boxes for remote properties.

Cactus Beach/Point Sinclair

The last chance to catch some **waves** is at **Cactus Beach/Point Sinclair** south of the small town of Penong, about 75km west of Ceduna, where the excellent waves lure surfers from all over the world. Even for non-surfers it's worth the drive (closed after rain) through white dunes, green shrubbery and blue lagoons to watch the extraordinary wave formations.

Head of the Bight

Down a 13km dirt road, 290km west of Ceduna • Daily: June–Oct 8am–5pm; Nov–May 8.30am–4pm • June–Oct $15; Nov–May $7 • ☎ 08 8625 6201

The **Head of the Bight** and its sleek **Interpretive Centre** on Yalata Aboriginal lands is the best place to see southern right whales as they migrate along the coast here between June and October. It's a stirring setting, with the dramatic cliffs plunging to the sea – you can't help feeling that this is how early cartographers must have envisaged the edge of the world. Twenty minutes on from the turn-off is the *Nullarbor Roadhouse* (see below), which is the last place to get fuel before Border Village (see below). Just beyond, one of the famous triple yellow signs warning of camels, wombats and kangaroos on the highway marks the beginning of the treeless run.

Koonalda Cave

Just north of the *Nullarbor Roadhouse*

Curiously enough for a land with minimal rainfall, the Nullarbor is undermined by partially flooded limestone **caverns**. From the outside, **Koonalda Cave** is a large hole with fruit trees growing in the mouth; inside, a tremendously deep network of tunnels leads to an underground lake, the shafts grooved by fingers being dragged over their soft walls. Although the patterns, which date back 22,000 years, are clearly deliberate, their meaning is unknown. Note that you can look around the entrance on your own (bring a flashlight), but it's not advisable to wander too deep into the cave.

Border Village and on to Western Australia

187km west of *Nullarbor Roadhouse*

Border Village (see below) is the best roadhouse along the route. **Eucla** (see p.605) and the rest of the Nullarbor lie 16km over the border in Western Australia on a noticeably worse road and in a considerably earlier time zone. You need to discard any fruit, vegetables and honey before you reach the quarantine checkpoint at the border.

ACCOMMODATION AND EATING | THE NULLARBOR PLAIN

Border Village 12km east of Eucla and 187km west of Nullarbor Roadhouse ☎ 08 9039 3474. This roadhouse has good accommodation options – caravan sites, dorms, cabins and private rooms – plus a restaurant, shop and a petrol station, as well as a natty fibreglass kangaroo in the car park. Un/powered sites $15/$25, dorms $6, doubles $130, cabins $170

Nullarbor Roadhouse Just beyond the Head of the Bight ☎ 08 8625 6271. This lonely roadhouse has adequate budget and smarter motel rooms, as well as caravan sites, a restaurant and a petrol station. Un/powered sites $20/$30, backpacker doubles $55, motel doubles $139

CLOCKWISE FROM TOP COASTLINE AT HANSON BAY, KANGAROO ISLAND (P.691); LAKE EYRE (P.726); PELICAN, KANGAROO ISLAND (P.688) >

The Stuart Highway: Woomera and beyond

North of Port Augusta, the Stuart Highway and the *New Ghan* railway line travel through progressively drier scenery to the Northern Territory. The first place of any consequence is the town of Woomera, from where you can visit the mining centres of Roxby Downs and Andamooka, and the salt flat of Lake Torrens; you'll need your own vehicle to visit these three destinations. Northwest of Woomera, the Stuart Highway heads up to the isolated, iconic settlement of Coober Pedy.

Woomera

WOOMERA is an uncharismatic but well-appointed barracks town two hours beyond Port Augusta. The town is synonymous with two things: the NASA deep tracking station that operated here in the 1960s, and its harsh **detention centre**, which housed political asylum seekers before public pressure brought about its closure in 2003. The whole town was actually closed to the public until 1982, as it sits at the southeast corner of the 500km corridor of the **Woomera Prohibited Area**, the largest land-based missile and rocket range in the world, and the site in the 1950s of the British-run **atomic bomb tests**, from which contaminated dust is still being scraped up and vitrified. The mostly military **Heritage Centre and Museum**, at the corner of Dewrang and Banool avenues (daily 9am–5pm; free; ☎08 8673 7042), contains models, rocket relics and plenty of pictures detailing the European Launcher Development Organisation's efforts to launch the Europa rocket here in the 1960s. It is also home to the visitor centre (see below).

ARRIVAL AND INFORMATION

By bus Greyhound buses travelling on the Stuart Highway don't go into Woomera but will drop you off at the roadhouse at Pimba, 7km away.

Destinations from Pimba Adelaide (daily; 6hr 45min); Alice Springs (daily; 13hr 15min); Coober Pedy (daily; 4hr 15min); Port Augusta (daily; 1hr 55min).

Tourist information There is a visitor centre at the Heritage Centre and Museum (cnr Dewrang & Banool aves; daily 9am–5pm; ☎08 8673 7042).

ACCOMMODATION AND EATING

Eldo Hotel Kotera Cresent ☎08 8673 7867. This 1970s relic, one of only two places to stay in Woomera, has a rather stylish-looking restaurant (with decent food), but drab, poorly maintained rooms that are rapidly going to seed. No wi-fi. Restaurant daily 6.30–8.30pm. $113

Woomera Travellers Village & Caravan Park Pimba Rd ☎08 8673 7800, ⌨woomera.com. This welcoming caravan park/motel has acceptable-for-a-night pitches, dorms, cabins and en-suite rooms. Facilities include a licensed bar, camp kitchen and coin-operated laundry. Un/powered sites $20/$25, dorms $45, cabins $85, doubles $95

Andamooka

ANDAMOOKA is an opal-mining shantytown of block and scrap-iron construction whose red-earth high street becomes a river after rain. The soil proved to be too loose for the underground homes that became *de rigueur* at Coober Pedy (see opposite), but mud lean-tos, built in the 1930s, are still standing opposite the post office. **Facilities** include a petrol station, a supermarket, pubs and a restaurant. If you fancy your luck "noodling", head to **German Gully**; opals here are more vivid than those at Coober Pedy.

Lake Torrens

A thirty-minute 4WD ride away from Andamooka is **Lake Torrens**, a sickle-shaped salt lake related to the Acraman meteorite (see box, p.720) that gets popular with birdwatchers in wet years. The lake is also renowned in paleontological circles for traces of the 630-million-year-old **Ediacaran fauna**, the earliest-known evidence of animal life anywhere on the planet, first found in Australia and possibly wiped out by the meteorite. Delicate fossil impressions of jellyfish and obscure organisms are preserved in layered rock; the South Australian Museum in Adelaide (see p.658) has an extensive selection, but rarely issues directions to the site, which has been plundered since its discovery by the geologist Reg Sprigg back in 1946.

Coober Pedy

COOBER PEDY is the most enduring symbol of the harshness of Australia's Outback and the determination of those who live there. It's a place where the terrain and temperatures are so extreme that homes – and even churches – have been built underground, yet it has managed to attract thousands of opal prospectors. In a virtually waterless desert 380km from Woomera, 845km from Adelaide, and considerably further from anywhere else, the most remarkable thing about the town – whose name stems from an Aboriginal phrase meaning "white man's burrow" – is that it exists at all. **Opal** was discovered by William Hutchison on a gold-prospecting expedition to the Stuart Range in February 1915, and the town itself dates from the end of World War I, when returning servicemen headed for the fields to try their luck, using their trench-digging skills to construct underground dwellings.

In summer Coober Pedy is seriously depopulated, but, if you can handle the intense heat, it's a good time to look for bargain opal purchases – though not to scratch around for them yourself: gem hunting is better reserved for the "cooler" winter months. At the start of the year, spectacular **dust storms** often enclose the town in an abrasive orange twilight for hours. Coober Pedy has a bit of a reputation as a **rowdy** township. This is not really surprising considering the extreme climate, alcohol problems, access to explosives and open mineshafts to fall down.

The local scenery might be familiar to you if you're a film fan, as it was used to great effect in *Mad Max 3*, among other films. There's not much to it, just an arid plain disturbed by conical pink mullock (slag) heaps, and dotted with clusters of trucks and home-made contraptions, and **warning signs** alerting you to treacherously invisible, unfenced 30m shafts. Be very careful where you tread: even if you have transport, the safest way to explore is to take a tour, follow a map, then return on your own.

The Big Winch Lookout

Italian Club Rd, east of Hutchison St • No fixed opening times • Free

The **Big Winch Lookout** in the centre gives a grandstand view of the mix of low houses and hills pocked with ventilation shafts. The welded metal "tree" up here was assembled before any real ones grew in the area, though in the last few years there have been some attempts to encourage greenery with recycled waste water.

Old Timers Mine

Crowders Gully Rd, east of Hutchison St • Daily 9am–5pm • $15 • ☏ 08 8672 5555, ⓦ oldtimersmine.com

This opal mine opened in 1916 and has now been turned into an award-winning museum, the **Old Timers Mine**. You can walk through some of the historic mines, learn about opals, visit some original underground homes, and watch demonstrations.

Umoona Opal Mine and Museum

Hutchison St • Daily 8am–6pm • Museum free; tours of the mine and underground homes $10 • Tours daily 10am, 2pm & 4pm • ☏ 08 8672 5288, ⓦ umoonaopalmine.com.au

Another mine that has been turned into a museum, the **Umoona Opal Mine and Museum** offers guided tours through an old mine and around an underground

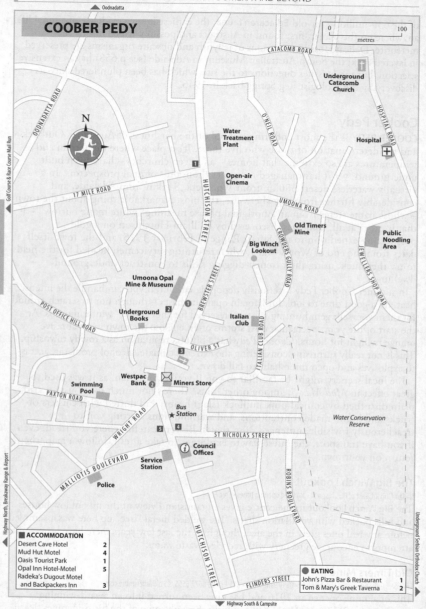

COOBER PEDY

▲ Oodnadatta

CATACOMB ROAD

Underground
Catacomb
Church

Hospital

OODNADATTA ROAD

O'NEIL ROAD

HOSPITAL ROAD

N

Golf Course & Race Course Mail Run

Water
Treatment
Plant

17 MILE ROAD

Open-air
Cinema

UMOONA ROAD

HUTCHISON STREET

Old Timers
Mine

Public
Noodling
Area

Big Winch
Lookout

CROWDERS GULLY ROAD

JEWELLERS SHOP ROAD

Umoona Opal
Mine & Museum

BREWSTER STREET

Underground
Books

POST OFFICE HILL ROAD

Italian
Club

OLIVER ST

ITALIAN CLUB ROAD

Water Conservation
Reserve

Westpac
Bank

Miners Store

Swimming
Pool

PAXTON ROAD

Bus
Station

WRIGHT ROAD

St NICHOLAS STREET

Council
Offices

ROBINS BOULEVARD

MALLIOTIS BOULEVARD

Service
Station

Police

Highway North, Breakaway Range & Airport

HUTCHISON STREET

FLINDERS STREET

▼ Highway South & Campsite

Underground Serbian Orthodox Church

0   100
metres

■ **ACCOMMODATION**
Desert Cave Hotel	2
Mud Hut Motel	4
Oasis Tourist Park	1
Opal Inn Hotel-Motel	5
Radeka's Dugout Motel and Backpackers Inn	3

● **EATING**
John's Pizza Bar & Restaurant	1
Tom & Mary's Greek Taverna	2

home. Visitors can watch opal cutting and polishing, and a documentary on opal-mining.

Breakaway Range
Past the diggings, the stunning **Breakaway Range** consists of a brightly coloured plateau off the highway about 11km north of town, with good views, close-ups of the hostile terrain, and bushwalking through two-hundred-year-old stands of mulga.

FINDING AND BUYING AN OPAL

Opal is composed of fragile layers of silica and derives its colour from the refraction of light – characteristics that preclude the use of heavy mining machinery, as one false blow would break the matrix and destroy the colour. Deposits are patchy and located by trial and error: the last big strikes at Coober Pedy petered out in the 1970s, and though bits and pieces are still found – including an exceptional opalized fossil skeleton of a pliosaur (the reptilian equivalent of a seal) in 1983 – it's anybody's guess as to the location of other major seams (indeed, there may not be any at all).

Unless you're serious (in which case you'll have to buy a Miner's Permit from the Mines Department to peg your 50m-by-50m claim), the easiest way to find something is by noodling over someone's **diggings** – ask the owner first. An area on the corner of Jewellers Shop and Umoona roads has been set aside as a safe area for tourists to poke about freely without danger of finding open mineshafts. Miners use ultraviolet lamps to separate opal from potch (worthless grey opal), so you're unlikely to find anything stunning – but look out for shell fossils and small chips.

The best time to buy opal is outside the tourist season, but with about fifty dealers in town, it's up to you to find the right stone; reputable sources give full written guarantees.

7

ARRIVAL AND DEPARTURE   COOBER PEDY

By plane The airport, around 3km southwest of the centre, is served by Regional Express flights to Adelaide (2 daily except Sat; 1hr 55min); organize a pick-up with your hotel.
By bus Greyhound buses travelling between Adelaide and Alice Springs call in at the small bus station on Hutchison St.
Destinations Adelaide (daily; 11hr 15min); Alice Springs (daily; 8hr 40min); Port Augusta (daily; 6hr 15min).

INFORMATION AND TOURS

Tourist information The visitor information centre (Mon–Fri 8.30am–5pm, Sat & Sun 10am–1pm; ☎1800 637 076, ⓦ opalcapitaloftheworld.com.au) is in the District Council on Hutchison St.
Radeka Downunder 1 Oliver St ☎08 8672 5223, ⓦ radekadownunder.com.au. Apart from its underground accommodation (see p.718), Radeka Downunder also runs one of the best tours in town, a four-hour Desert Breakaways Tour (daily 1pm; $65), which includes visits to the opal fields, mine, church, Dog Fence and Breakaways Scenic Reserve. Range.
Coober Pedy Mail Run Tour ☎08 8672 5226, ⓦ mailruntour.com. If you want to get to Oodnadatta and don't have your own vehicle, note that the direct 200km dirt road from Coober Pedy across the pan of Giddi-Gidna (the Moon Plain) is covered by the Mail Run Tour ($195). The service departs from Underground Books (see p.718) and follows a 12-hour triangular route to William Creek and Oodnadatta every Monday (anticlockwise) and Thursday (clockwise), departing at 9am.

ACCOMMODATION

Finding somewhere to stay can be challenging during the cooler months, although you shouldn't have problems in summer. While not all accommodation is subterranean, it's worth spending at least one night in the naturally cooled tunnels for the experience.

Desert Cave Hotel Hutchison St ☎08 8672 5688, ⓦ desertcave.com.au. The below- or above-ground four-star accommodation is expensive for what it is, but the hotel does have a swimming pool, museum, restaurant, café and bar. Scenic flights, tours and car rental can be arranged. **$259**
Mud Hut Motel St Nicholas St ☎08 8672 3003, ⓦ mudhutmotel.com.au. The very welcoming *Mud Hut Motel* is the best-value accommodation in Coober Pedy. The bare, rammed-earth construction of this well-furnished place gives a flavour of the subterranean without losing out on daylight. **$148**

Oasis Tourist Park Hutchison St ☎08 8672 5169, ⓦ big4cooberpedy.com.au. Unappealingly situated opposite the water-treatment plant, this park is nevertheless a decent option, with a range of caravan sites as well as spacious, a/c cabins and budget rooms. Un/powered sites **$30/$37**, doubles **$63**, cabins **$86**
Opal Inn Hotel-Motel Hutchison St ☎08 8672 5054, ⓦ opalinn.com.au. This hotel-motel-caravan park-campsite has something for everyone, though it is not the most exciting place in town. It also has a restaurant, bar and bottle shop, and also offers tour bookings. Un/powered sites **$22/$31**, doubles **$80**

Radeka Dugout Motel & Backpackers Inn 1 Oliver St ☎ 08 8672 5223, ⚲ radekadownunder.com.au. The best budget option in town. Downstairs, snaking tunnels have alcoves holding from two to six beds, with well-appointed kitchen and toilets; upstairs a bar and pool table provide evening entertainment. Free wi-fi available in public areas. Dorms $40, doubles $85

EATING

John's Pizza Bar & Restaurant Hutchison St ☎ 08 8672 5561. One of the most popular places in town, specializing in pizza ($12–31), pastas and grills. Portions are on the large side, though the quality is hit and miss. Those with adventurous palates can try the Bush Tucker Mix Grill, which features crocodile and kangaroo steaks, emu sausage and wallaby shank. Daily 9am–10pm.

Tom & Mary's Greek Taverna Hutchison St ☎ 08 8672 5622. This restaurant reflects Coober Pedy's significant Greek community, serving up meze ($4.50–15), lamb and chicken souvlaki, moussaka and desserts like baklava, as well as steaks, seafood and a few pasta dishes. Mains $17–32. Mon–Sat 6–9pm.

DIRECTORY

Books and maps Underground Books (Mon–Fri 8.30am–5pm, Sat 10am–4pm; ☎ 08 8672 5558), on Post Office Hill Rd opposite the Mobil service station, stocks a good selection of local books and maps.
Cinema The drive-in, open-air cinema, cnr Hutchison & Umoona sts, regularly screens films – ask at the visitor centre to find out what's playing.
Hospital The hospital is on Hospital Rd at the north end of town (☎ 08 8672 5009).
Swimming pool The pool at the school on Paxton Rd provides a welcome chance to cool down; check the opening hours at the visitor centre.
Post office and bank The Miners Store supermarket on Hutchison St (Mon–Fri 9am–5pm; ☎ 08 8672 5051) is also the post office, pharmacy and Commonwealth Bank agent (there's a Westpac branch opposite).

Marla and beyond

The Stuart Highway extends 350km north from Coober Pedy to the state border. From **Marla** township (where there's a shop, post office and a bank) you could head east to Oodnadatta across the **Painted Desert** at Arkaringa Hills, a larger version of the Breakaway Range, or 35km west into Aboriginal land to the state's newest opal strike at Mintabie – seek permission from Marla's police (☎ 08 8670 7020). If you don't have your own transport, you can still reach Oodnadatta on the **Mail Run Tour** (see p.717).

The Flinders Ranges and northeast

Recognized as one of Australia's oldest natural landscapes, the rugged peaks and tranquil bush scenery of the Flinders Ranges stretch over a distance of 400km from Port Pirie, 220km north of Adelaide, to Lake Callabonna in the far northeast of the state.

From **Mount Remarkable National Park** and the picturesque town of **Melrose** in the southern Ranges, the roads bear west to the hub of Port Augusta or north to the quaint villages of **Quorn** and **Hawker** from where you can take an adventurous route through the spectacular **Ikara-Flinders Ranges National Park** to the off-the-beaten-track settlement of **Blinman** in the **Northern Flinders**. From here it's 200km of dirt road to the **Gammon Ranges** from where you can carry on to the isolated **Strzelecki Track** and the far-flung settlement of **Innamincka**, or head back to the highway to the Outback town of **Marree**.

Mount Remarkable National Park

Mount Remarkable National Park, located in the Southern Flinders Ranges, offers a good range of flora and fauna, including yellow-footed rock wallabies and several threated species of native orchid. The 16,000 hectares includes a number of ancient geological features, such as The Narrows, The Terraces, Alligator Gorge and Gibraltar Rocks, near Melrose. The park is encircled by a ring road that runs via Wilmington, **Melrose** and Port Germein, then up to **Mambray Creek** and **Mount Cavern**, with connecting tracks running to **Alligator Gorge**. If time is short, there are easy walks in Alligator Gorge, while the Mount Cavern circuit is considerably harder – both make good day-trips from Port Augusta.

Alligator Gorge

The 13km road (turn-off 1km south of Wilmington) to **Alligator Gorge** ends at a car park and picnic area perched on a spur above two bush campsites at Teal and Eaglehawk dams. Stairs descend into the gorge, with several **walking** options once you reach the gorge floor, including a 2km, ninety-minute loop taking you along the rocky bed of Alligator Creek and through "the narrows" in spectacular Alligator Gorge, a tight red canyon alive with frog calls, moss gardens and echoes. Although it sometimes gets flooded, there are usually enough stepping stones to avoid wet feet. The path returns to the car park via Blue Gum Flat picnic area. A 9km, four-hour loop follows Alligator Creek upstream beyond the rippled Terraces (the remains of a fossilized lake shore), returning along a park management track and walking trail to the car park. For longer hikes down to Mambray Creek you'll need maps and approval from the Natural Resource Centre in Clare (2/17 Lennon St; ☎08 8841 3400, ⓦnaturalresources.sa.gov.au).

ARRIVAL AND INFORMATION

MOUNT REMARKABLE NATIONAL PARK

By bus Premier Stateliner buses travel between Port Augusta and Mambray Creek (2–3 daily; 30min) and Wilmington (1–3 daily; 15min).
Opening times and fees The park is open daily 24hr,

though may be closed if there is a high risk of fire – check conditions first with the park office (☎08 8634 7068, ⓦenvironment.sa.gov.au).

ACCOMMODATION

Mambray Creek campsite Book online with National Parks South Australia ⓦenvironment.sa.gov.au. This well-established campground is suitable for caravans, camper trailers and other large vehicles. Facilities include

toilets, heated showers, baby changing rooms and communal fireplaces. Park entry fees ($10 per vehicle) also apply. Camping per person $20, cabins $65

Melrose

The historic buildings of the tranquil former 1840s copper-mining town of **MELROSE** have been painstakingly restored. The oldest town in the Flinders, Melrose is home to Rock the Mount (ⓦremarkablefestivals.com.au), a popular country music and ute muster festival held in April. The summit of **Mount Remarkable**, with its panoramic views of Willochra Plain and the Spencer Gulf, can be reached on foot in a five-hour hike (12.5km) via the Heysen Trail (see box, p.684), starting from the War Memorial Monument behind Melrose campsite. You'll need your own vehicle to get here.

ACCOMMODATION

MELROSE

Bluey Blundstone's Blacksmith Shop Stuart St ☎08 8666 2173. B&B accommodation is provided here in a cottage, barn and blacksmith shop, which has been carefully restored to its original 1865 condition. When the proprietor isn't producing decorative wrought-ironwork he serves cakes in the attached coffee shop. No wi-fi. $110

North Star Hotel Nott St ☎08 8666 2110, ⓦnorthstarhotel.com.au. This boutique hotel has a funky café-restaurant-bar, quality live entertainment, and a wide range of stylish rooms (including a few quirky cottages mounted on old truck beds). Rates include Continental breakfast but not wi-fi. Restaurant daily noon–2pm & 6–8pm. $150

From Quorn to Hawker

Some 60km north of Melrose along Main North Road is the settlement of **QUORN**, whose wide streets, big old pubs, and historic stone buildings offer a last taste of the pastoral south before the austerities of the Outback set in. A warning: avoid the town in January and February, the hottest part of the year, when the locals shut shop and head to the beach and the place is a ghost town.

Best known for the **Pichi Richi Railway**, Quorn was a major rail centre until the line was re-routed through Port Augusta in the 1950s. Enthusiasts restored the service twenty years later and started taking passengers on the haul to Port Augusta through the **Pichi Richi Pass** – whose name has been variously attributed to a medicinal herb or an Aboriginal word for "gorge". It makes a relaxing and mildly scenic journey.

The road to Hawker

7

There's great bushwalking off the back road to Hawker along a string of ridges and cliffs, outrunners from the main body of the central Flinders Ranges. Ten kilometres northwest of Quorn is **The Dutchmans Stern**, a five-hour, 10.5km hike for the reasonably fit from the car park to various lookouts. Less dedicated walkers will find the 5.2km **Warren gorge** loop an easier option; easily completed in 2–3 hours, it's also the best place to spot the rare and ravishingly pretty **yellow-footed rock wallaby**, with its bushy, ringed tail and yellow paws. Closer to Hawker, it's also worth taking in the well-preserved remains of **Kanyaka Homestead**, abandoned after a drought in the 1880s, and **Yourambulla Cave**, which has some unusual charcoal symbols in a high overhang, reached by a ladder. Both are signposted from the road.

Hawker

HAWKER, some 100km from Port Augusta, is somewhere to fuel up, make use of the last banks and shops, and have a hearty meal at the *Old Ghan Restaurant* (see opposite). Note that, like Quorn, the town practically closes down in January and February, the hottest part of the year. From here, you'll have to decide whether to press on into the Flinders Ranges and the northeast or continue following the former Ghan line north towards Marree; the bitumen on the latter route extends past the Leigh Creek coalfields to Lyndhurst, at the start of the Strzelecki Track.

INFORMATION AND TOURS — FROM QUORN TO HAWKER

Tourist information The Flinders Ranges Visitors Information Centre in Quorn is at 3 Seventh St (Mon–Fri 9am–5pm; ☎08 8648 6419, ⓦfrc.sa.gov.au), and can provide you with a self-guided walking tour of Old Quorn, book 4WD and camel tours, and has heaps of information on the entire region.

Tours Port Augusta-based Gulf Getaways (☎08 8642 6827, ⓦgulfgetaways.com.au) operates a range of coach tours into the Flinders Ranges, Clare Valley and Port Lincoln.

THE ACRAMAN METEORITE

In the mid-1980s a band of red earth from 600-million-year-old deposits in the Flinders Ranges was bafflingly identified as coming from the Gawler Ranges, 400km away. Investigations and satellite mapping suggested that 35km-wide **Lake Acraman** in the Gawler Ranges was an eroded meteorite crater, while Lake Gairdner and fragmented saltpans (such as Lake Torrens; see p.714) further east were set in ripples caused by the force of the strike. Estimates suggest that to have created such a crater the **meteorite** must have been 4km across; the mystery band in the Flinders Ranges was dust settling after impact. Though there is fossil evidence of animal life prior to this event – notably the *Ediacaran* fauna – recent research indicates that the Acraman meteorite may well have killed it all. It's certainly true that the ancestors of almost all species living today evolved after this impact.

Tourist train The Pichi Richi Railway ($82 return; ☎ 1800 777 245, ⓦ pichirichirailway.org.au) runs between Quorn and Port Augusta (1hr 40min) on Saturdays between June and October; check the latest timetable online. Half-day tours and other novelty rides, such as the Barwell Bull, are also available.

ACCOMMODATION AND EATING

HAWKER
Flinders Ranges Accommodation Booking Service Cnr Cradock & Wilpena rds ☎ 1800 777 880, ⓦ frabs.com.au. This outfit can arrange self-catering accommodation in and around Hawker, on Outback stations, and in shearers' quarters, cottages and huts.

Old Ghan Restaurant Hawker Railway Station ☎ 08 8648 4176. The town's railway station (built in 1884) has been turned into a restaurant, and you can dine on the platform or in the ladies' dining room (mains $20–30). Closed mid-Jan to mid-Feb. Wed–Sat 5.30–8pm.

QUORN
Austral Inn Hotel 16 Railway Terrace ☎ 08 8648 6017,

ⓦ australinn.info. Established in 1878, *The Austral* is the most agreeable hotel in town, with a pleasant renovated bar and restaurant (serving good-value, mod-Oz, bush-inspired dishes), smart rooms at the pub, and more basic rooms in the motel section. Additional charge for wi-fi. $115

Quorn Caravan Park 8 Silo Rd ☎ 08 8648 6206, ⓦ quorncaravanpark.com.au. This ecofriendly caravan park has a lovely garden setting, well-maintained sites, low-cost bunkhouses (basic rooms) and comfortable cabins, and helpful staff who are good sources of local info. Free wi-fi available at the office. Un/powered sites $35/$50, bunkhouses per person $40, cabins $110

Ikara-Flinders Ranges National Park

The procession of glowing red mountains at **Ikara-Flinders Ranges National Park**, folded and crumpled with age, produces some of the Outback's most spectacular and timeless scenery, rising from flat scrub to form abrupt escarpments, gorges and the famous elevated basin of **Wilpena Pound**, a colossal crater rim rising from the plains. The contrast between sky and ranges is softened by native cypresses and river red gums; and in spring the land is burnished by **wild flowers** of all colours and there are more kangaroos than you can count. Bushwalkers, photographers and painters flock here in their hundreds, but with a system of graded **walking tracks** ranging in length from a few minutes to several days – not to mention roads of varying quality – the park is busy without being crowded. Most tracks lead into Wilpena Pound, though you can also pick up the Heysen Trail (see box, p.684) and follow it north from Wilpena for a couple of days around the ABC Range to **Aroona Ruins** on the northern edge of the park.

Hiking is restricted to the cooler winter months between May and October, due to significant bushfire danger and summer temperatures that often exceed 40°C. Don't underestimate conditions for even short excursions: you'll need good footwear, a hat, sunscreen and **water** – at least a litre per hour is recommended. Note that the weather is very changeable; wind-driven rain can be a menace along the ridges, especially for campers, and heavy downpours cause roads to be closed (check conditions on ☎ 1300 361 033).

> ## FLINDERS DREAMING AND GEOLOGY
> The almost tangible spirit of the Flinders Ranges is reflected in the wealth of Adnyamathanha ("hill people") legends associated with them. Perhaps more obvious here than anywhere else in Australia is the connection between landscapes and **Dreamtime stories**, which recount how scenery was created by animal or human action – though, as Dreamtime spirits took several forms, this distinction is often blurred. A central character is Akurra, a gigantic serpent (or serpents) who guards waterholes and formed the Flinders' contours by wriggling north to drink dry the huge salt lakes of Frome and Callabonna. You may well prefer the Aboriginal legends to the complexities of geology illustrated on boards placed at intervals along the Brachina Gorge track, which explain how movements of the "Adelaide Geosyncline" brought about the changes in scenery over hundreds of millions of years.

Wilpena Pound

Nestling up against the edge of Wilpena Pound, **WILPENA** is a good place to orient yourself for a range of accommodation, fuel and food. **Wilpena Pound**'s two main walks are the **Hills Homestead Walk** (6.6km, 2hr) and the **Wangara Lookout Walk** (7.8km, 3hr), both starting at the visitor centre. Consult the visitor centre before attempting the less publicized full-day hikes to **St Mary's Peak** on the rim, and **Edowie Gorge** inside the pound, or any **overnight** trips.

The walk to Hill's Homestead

The walk to **Hill's Homestead** across the pound's flat, grassy bowl takes you to a restored stone homestead, part of the pound's early experimentation with sheep farming. From here you can follow the track northwest to **Cooinda Camp** (register at the Wilpena visitor centre, before you leave; see opposite), about four hours from Wilpena. Assuming you left early, there should be time to pitch a tent and spend the rest of the day following the creek upstream past **Malloga Falls** to **Glenora Falls** (generally flowing May–Sept) and taking in the views of Edowie Gorge before returning to Cooinda. Next morning, you could do the steep climb to **Tanderra Saddle** below the peak, followed by the last burst up to the summit of St Mary's Peak itself. The effort is rewarded by unequalled views west to Lake Torrens and north along the length of the ABC Ranges towards Parachilna; on exceptional mornings the peak stands proud of low cloud inside the pound. The direct descent from the saddle back to Wilpena is initially steep, but shouldn't take more than four hours.

Other walks

Shorter routes from Wilpena lead up **Mount Ohlssen Bagge** (4hr) and **Wangara Lookout** (3hr) for lower vistas of the pound floor, and southwest across the pound to **Bridle Gap** (6hr) following the Heysen Trail's red markers. Things to look out for are wallabies, emus and parrots inside the pound, and cauliflower-shaped fossil **stromatolites** – algal corals – on the Mount Ohlssen Bagge route, similar to those still living at Hamelin Pool in Western Australia (see p.615).

Arkaroo Rock

Two **Aboriginal galleries** worth seeing (although erosion and contact have damaged the paintings) are Arkaroo Rock and Sacred Canyon, cultural heritage sites, 20km from Wilpena. **Arkaroo** is off the main road towards Rawnsley Park Station and involves a ninety-minute walk up the outside of Wilpena Pound to see mesh-protected rock faces covered in symbols relating to an initiation ceremony and the pound's formation, some dating back six thousand years. Snake patterns depict St Mary's Peak as the head of a male Akurra (the Dreamtime snake) coiled round the pound.

Sacred Canyon

To reach **Sacred Canyon**, briefly take the road from Wilpena into the north of the park, past the **Cazneaux Tree** – a river red gum made famous by Harold Cazneaux's prize-winning 1930 photograph *Spirit of Endurance* – before turning right and following a bumpy track to its end. Rock-hop up the narrow, shattered gorge to clusters of painted swirls covered in a sooty patina and clearer, engraved emu prints and geometric patterns; the best examples are around the second cascade.

Bunyeroo and Brachina gorges

The main road through the park heads straight out to Blinman, but another track detours to **Bunyeroo and Brachina gorges** on the western limits. The gorges make good campsites: you have to walk into Bunyeroo but the track passes through Brachina on its way to the surfaced Hawker-to-Marree road.

INFORMATION

Opening times and entry fees The park is open daily 24hr; there's a $10/vehicle entry fee. There's also a $7/person fee if you want a self-guided tour of the Old Wilpena Station, a restored cattle station close to the *Wilpena Pound Resort*.

Road conditions Rain can be heavy and can close roads at short notice; check conditions by calling ☎ 1300 361 033.

Tourist information The visitor centre (daily 8am–5pm; ☎ 08 8648 0048, ⓦ environment.sa.gov.au) at *Wilpena*

IKARA-FLINDERS RANGES NATIONAL PARK

Pound Resort (see below) offers booklets, maps and the latest information on routes; you're recommended to log out and in with them on any walk exceeding three hours.

Tours There's currently no public transport to/from the national park, but a number of travel agencies offer tours from Adelaide or Port Augusta including Gulf Getaways (☎ 08 8642 6827, ⓦ gulfgetaways.com.au) and Genesis Tour & Charter (☎ 08 8552 4000, ⓦ genesistours.com.au).

ACCOMMODATION AND EATING

If you're planning to camp at one of the park's various sites ($13; see ⓦ environment.sa.gov.au for details), a waterproof tent, ground mat and fuel stove are essential.

★**Arkaba Homestead** Wilpena Road, near Hawker ☎ 08 8648 4195, ⓦ arkabastation. This sprawling 60,000-acre property is currently being transformed into a private conservation park and brims with native wildlife. The old homestead offers luxurious accommodation in five elegant suites, and there's a resident chef and large roster of ecotours, including a superb four-day walk ($2150). Rates includes all meals, drinks and short walks and tours, but there's no wi-fi. $930

Rawnsley Park Station Wilpena Rd, about 30km north of Hawker ☎ 08 8648 0030, ⓦ rawnsleypark.com.au. This historic sheep station offers a wide range of accommodation, from luxury self-contained eco-villas and homestead rooms to more basic cabins. A family-run property, it is located below Rawnsley Bluff, overlooking the southern side of Wilpena Pound. Facilities include a licensed

shop, swimming pool and a really excellent restaurant housed in the old shearing shed; in addition, a wide range of 4WD tours, hikes and mountain-bike adventures are available. Wi-fi only at the homestead. Powered sites $35, cabins $95, eco-villas $410, doubles $550

Wilpena Pound Resort Wilpena Rd, at the end of the sealed road to Wilpena Pound ☎ 08 8648 0004 ⓦ wilpenapound.com.au. Once a pioneer of upmarket holiday accommodation in the Flinders, this 1980s complex looks a little tired today, but still offers good quality motel-style rooms, plus some luxury safari tents at the separate *Ikara* complex. The restaurant is surprisingly good, and the bar and pool always packed. The activities desk can arrange guided tours, scenic flights and other adventures. Free wi-fi at the resort, but not *Ikara*; the service is patchy. Un/powered sites $25/$37, doubles $210, safari tents $343

The Northern Flinders

North of Ikara-Flinders Ranges National Park the Wilpena–Blinman road passes through a low group of hills, which are thin in timber but still swarming with wallabies, emus and galahs, to the scenic town of **Blinman**. West of Blinman is the similarly appealing **Parachilna**, a tiny Outback settlement next to the railway line, while north are two little-visited sites of great Aboriginal significance, Chambers Gorge and Big Moro. Further north of here, the Flinders end dramatically with the **Gammon Ranges**. You really need your own vehicle to explore the area properly. Local operator Fargher Air (ⓦ fargherair.com.au) offers air safaris to Lake Eyre, Coopers Creek, Birdsville, Wilpena Pound and the Gammon Ranges.

Blinman and around

Set against a stunning hilly landscape, historic **BLINMAN**, established in 1859, comprises a handful of charming old houses with well-tended gardens, fuel, and the 1869 *Blinman Hotel*. The main track winds west through beautiful Parachilna Gorge, where you could stay at *Angorichina Tourist Village* (see p.724) .The track meets the Hawker–Marree road at characterful **Parachilna**, where there's wonderful bushtucker-inspired cuisine and smart rooms at the atmospheric *Prairie Hotel* (see p.724); 4WD tours and scenic flights can also be arranged. The route into the Northern Flinders lies east, joining up with the direct road from Wilpena and then running north to the **Gammon Ranges National Park** and Arkaroola.

7

Angorichina Tourist Village Off Barndioota Rd, Parachilna Gorge ☎08 8648 4842, ⓦangorichina village.com.au. Though not the best option if you're fussy about creature comforts, *Angorichina Tourist Village* offers a range of basic accommodation and a dirt campsite, plus a shop and bike hire. Unpowered sites $26, cabins $130

Blinman Hotel Main St, Blinman ☎08 8648 4867. The *Blinman Hotel*, which dates back to 1869, has simple rooms with a few period features, plus a log fire, a games room and a pool. There's good food – from pizzas and kebabs to steaks and seafood – available too. No wi-fi. $80

★ **Prairie Hotel** Cnr High St & West Terrace, Parachilna ☎08 8648 4844, ⓦprairiehotel.com.au. Celebrated for its authentic front bar and "feral cuisine" (think camel, kangaroo, emu, etc), the *Prairie* also offers the region's best hotel accommodation. Numerous film stars, including Kate Winslet and Harvey Keitel, have stayed here. The hotel has a number of modern, well-equipped Heritage Rooms – all of them tastefully decorated – while more budget options include basics rooms and a small number of campsites. Hotel staff can advise you about 4WD tours and scenic flights. Limited wi-fi. Un/powered sites $21/$35, doubles $80, Heritage Rooms $195

Chambers Gorge

On the road to the Gammon Ranges, which runs east from Blinman, is the remote and little-visited site of **Chambers Gorge**, worth every groan and twang of your vehicle springs for their stark beauty and Aboriginal significance. In a Dreamtime story, Yuduyudulya, the Fairy Wren spirit, threw a boomerang that split Mount Chambers' eastern end and then circled back to form the crown. An indistinct left fork before the gorge leads to a dense gallery of **pecked engravings**; most are circles, though a goanna stands out clearly on the right, facing the main body of art. Chambers Gorge itself is huge and silent, the broad stony entrance guarded by high, perpendicular cliffs and brilliant green waterholes that would take days to explore properly.

The 10km access track east into **Chambers Gorge** (28km after Wirrealpa) is decidedly dodgy after rain when you'll need a 4WD, but at other times 2WD vehicles should – with care – reach the natural campsite at the foot of **Mount Chambers**, within twenty minutes' walk of the gorge mouth.

Big Moro

Big Moro, 60km on from the Mount Chambers junction, is sacred to the Adnyamathanha as the residence of an Akurra (the Dreamtime snake). The creek trickles through a crumbling gorge into two clear green pools, while limestone outcrops on the south side conceal miniature caves. The gorge lies west down an exceptionally tortuous 15km 4WD track opposite **Wertaloona Station**, 60km from the Mount Chambers junction. Pay attention to any signs and leave the three gates as you found them.

The Gammon Ranges

Arid and bald, the **Gammon Ranges** are the Flinders' last fling, a vicious flurry of compressed folds plunging abruptly onto the northern plains. Balcanoona is the DEWNR headquarters for the otherwise undeveloped **Gammon Ranges National Park**. There are two ways to experience the area: either carry on to the resort at Arkaroola (outside the park; see opposite), or take the road west across the park through **Italowie Gorge** to Copley on the Hawker–Marree road. The steep red walls of the gorge are home to iga – native orange trees that symbolize the Adnyamathanha.

Scene of Australia's most recent volcanic activity, the area is a geologist's dream: **Paralana Hot Springs** (2hr away from Arkaroola on a rough 4WD track) bubble out radioactive radon gas, and walks into the shattered hills surrounding the resort turn up fossils and semiprecious minerals. According to Aboriginal legend, the springs mark the site where a Dreamtime warrior extinguished his fire stick after using it to kill a rival. The area is so rugged that conventional mining isn't really a profitable venture – drilling rigs are airlifted in, then ferried around on the lower half of a Chieftain tank.

By car High-clearance 4WD vehicles with experienced off-road drivers behind the wheel can continue directly north from the Gammon Ranges to join the Strzelecki Track at Mount Hopeless, a little under half the distance to Innamincka. If you're unsure, note that the track can also be reached via Lyndhurst on the Hawker–Marree road, but this involves a 300km detour from Arkaroola.

Arkaroola Resort and Wilderness Sanctuary On

the northern edge of the park **☎**08 8648 4848, **ⓦ**arkaroola.com.au. This award-winning, ecofriendly resort has an array of accommodation choices, plus an atmospheric restaurant, bar, swimming pool, shop and fuel. They also offer a range of tours, including guided walks ($120), 4WD trips ($155) and scenic flights (from $175). Un/powered sites $25/$33, doubles $40, cottages $85

The Strzelecki Track

The 460km **Strzelecki Track** between Lyndhurst and Innamincka is the least interesting of the Outback tracks, offering little variety in scenery and some rough-as-guts sections of heavily corrugated, single-lane track that can be treacherous after rain; it's restricted to 4WD vehicles by the state's Road Transport Authority.

You need to be completely self-sufficient and carry plenty of water, food and extra fuel. Start at Lyndhurst by filling the tank – the next **fuel** is at the other end of the track. The drive first takes you past the northern tip of the Flinders Ranges; once you pass them, the journey becomes flat and pretty dull.

Around 190km from Lyndhurst, the road from Arkaroola connects within sight of **Mount Hopeless** (a pathetic hill, appropriately named); the next place to stop and perhaps camp is at the hot outflow from **Montecollina Bore**, 30km on. From here the scenery improves slightly as the road runs between dunes, and it's hard to resist leaving footprints along one of the pristine red crests.

At **Strzelecki Crossing** there's a fork in the road: to the east is **Cameron Corner**, where there's a store with fuel, a small bar and a campsite; and to the north, Innamincka via Moomba. Within an hour you've crossed into the **Innamincka Regional Reserve** and are approaching Innamincka's charms.

Innamincka

Cooper Creek, which runs through Innamincka, is best known for the misadventures of explorers Burke and Wills, who ended their tragic 1861 expedition by dying here (see box, p.451). **INNAMINCKA** was later founded on much the same spot before the town was abandoned in 1952. Now the area falls within the three-million-acre **Innamincka Regional Reserve and Coongie Lakes National Park** and the increase in popularity of recreational four-wheel driving has led to a renaissance. With a vehicle you could strike out 20km west to **Wills' grave** or 8km east to where **Burke** was buried (both bodies were removed to Adelaide in 1862). Another 8km beyond Burke's cairn is **Cullyamurra waterhole**, the largest permanent body of water in central Australia, and a footpath to rock engravings of crosses, rainbow patterns and bird tracks. If the roads are open, you can also tackle the 110km 4WD track north to the shallow **Coongie Lakes**, where you can swim and watch the abundant birdlife. A five-hour drive east of Innamincka will bring you to the famous Dig Tree, an important site associated with the ill-fated Burke and Wills expedition; eight hours beyond this is Quilpie (see p.450), across the Queensland border.

Permits If you're heading for Innamincka, you'll need to apply in advance for a Desert Parks Pass (**☎**08 8648 5328, **ⓦ**environment.sa.gov.au/parks), which costs $150 per vehicle, and is valid for one year for entry to a range of desert parks.

Cameron Corner Store Cameron Corner **☎**08 8091

3333. This lonely store sits at the edge of three states – South Australia, New South Wales and Queensland. It has a bar, simple rooms with shared facilities and a (basic) campsite. It also sells fuel. Mon–Fri 9am–6pm. Unpowered sites $25, doubles $78

Innamincka Trading Post South Terrace, Innamincka

08 8675 9900, innaminckatp.com.au. The better of this tiny town's two accommodation options, *Innamincka Trading Post* has simple, a/c, en-suite cabins (some with two bedrooms). They also offer an extensive range of supplies and services including fuel, groceries and laundry facilities. **$150**

The far north: Marree and beyond

The highlight of this region is Lake Eyre, a vast, awe-inspiring salt flat. Marree is the closest settlement and the starting point for two epic journeys: the Birdsville and Oodnadatta tracks. There's no public transport in this region, so you'll need your own vehicle.

Marree

MARREE consists of a collection of battered houses that somehow outlived the *Old Ghan*'s demise in 1980, leaving carriages to rust on sidings and rails to be used for tethering posts outside the wonderful big old pub. Although it was first a camel depot, then a staging post for the overland telegraph line, and finally the point where the rail line skirted northwest around **Lake Eyre**, today all traffic comes by road and is bound for the **Birdsville Track** into Queensland or the **Oodnadatta Track**, which follows the former train route to Oodnadatta and beyond into the Northern Territory or **Simpson Desert**.

ACCOMMODATION   MARREE

The Marree Hotel Railway Terrace South 08 8675 8344, marreehotel.com.au. This historic hotel, which first opened its doors in 1883, offers twelve refurbished older-style hotel rooms (with shared bathrooms), 56 newer en-suite motel units and a free campsite. Facilities include a beer garden, swimming pool and an ATM, and tours to Cooper Creek and Witchelina Nature Reserve leave from here. Hotel/motel rates include a free Continental breakfast and wi-fi is available for an additional fee. Sites free, doubles **$120**

Lake Eyre

Lake Eyre is a massive and eerily desolate salt lake caught between the Simpson and Strzelecki deserts in a region where the annual evaporation rate is thirty times greater than the rainfall. Most years a little water trickles into the lake from its million-square-kilometre catchment area, which extends well into central Queensland and the Northern Territory. However, in 2009, 2010, 2011 and 2015 major floods in Queensland and New South Wales filled the basin, transforming it into a massive inland sea. A hypnotic, glaring **salt crust** usually covers the southern bays, creating a mysterious landscape whose harsh surrounds are paved by shiny gibber stones and walled by red dunes – in 1964 the crust was thick enough to be used as a range for Sir Donald Campbell's successful crack at the world land-speed record.

Some **wildlife** also manages to get by in the incredible emptiness. The resident Lake Eyre dragon is a diminutive, spotted grey lizard often seen skimming over the crust, and the rare flooding attracts dense flocks of birds, wakes the plump water-holding frog from hibernation and causes plants to burst into colour.

Timber at the lake is sparse and protected, which means that there's little shade and no firewood. There's no one to help you if something goes wrong, so don't drive on the lake's crust – should you fall through, it's impossible to extricate your vehicle from the grey slush below. This isn't a place to wander off to unprepared, but if you wish to grasp the vastness and emptiness of the state, don't miss it.

ARRIVAL AND INFORMATION   LAKE EYRE

Lake Eyre (also known as Kati Thanda) is a national park (daily 24hr) and you'll need to buy a Desert Parks Pass beforehand from the Natural Resource Centre in Port Augusta (08 8648 5300, environment.sa.gov.au).

By plane Several companies offer scenic flights over the lake, from Coober Pedy, Marree and William Creek, which can be booked at visitor centres, including Wrights Air ($260/person; ⓦ wrightsair.com.au), departing from William Creek.
By car You can reach the shore 95km north of Marree to Level Post Bay via Muloorina Station. It's an isolated area

and only high-clearance 4WDs are permitted. You'll need to be self-sufficient, with plenty of fuel, food and water; a satellite phone is also recommended. Before you leave, check the road conditions on the Department of Planning, Transport and Infrastructure website (ⓦ dpti.sa.gov.au/OutbackRoads).

The Birdsville Track

Tearing north from Marree, the distant tips of the Flinders Ranges dip below the horizon behind, leaving you on a bare plain with the road as the only feature. Look for the **MV Tom Brennan**, a vessel donated to the area in 1949 to ferry stock around during floods, but now bearing an absurd resemblance to a large grey bathtub. Before the halfway house at Mungerannie Gap, a scenic variation is offered by the **Natterannie Sandhills** (150km). The *Mungerannie Hotel* provides the only services on the track (see below). In a 4WD you can head west from the roadhouse to **Kalamurina campsite** near Cowarie Homestead (58km) for the thrill of desert fishing on Warburton Creek.

Back on the track, a windmill at **Mirra Mitta bore** (37km from the roadhouse) draws piping-hot water out of the ground beside long-abandoned buildings; the water smells of tar and drains into cooler pools, providing somewhere to camp. By now you're crossing the polished gibber lands of the **Sturt Stony Desert**, and it's worth going for a walk to feel the cool wind and watch the dunes dancing in the heat haze away to the west. The low edge of **Coonchera Dune** to the right of the track (190km from the roadhouse) marks the start of a run along the mud pans between the sand hills; look for desert plants and dingoes. In two more hours you should be pulling up outside the Birdsville pub.

7

GETTING AROUND AND ACCOMMODATION   THE BIRDSVILLE TRACK

By car If there's been no rain, the 520km Birdsville Track is no obstacle to careful drivers during the winter: the biggest problem is getting caught in dried wheel ruts which can steer you off the road. Sections can be closed after rain. Check conditions online before travelling (ⓦ dpti.sa.gov.au).

Mungerannie Hotel Birdsville Track ☎ 08 8675 8317, ⓦ mungeranniehotel.com.au. The *Mungerannie Hotel* provides the only services on the Birdsville Track, with fuel, meals, cold beers and accommodation (simple en-suite rooms and a rustic campsite), plus a swimming pool. Camping per person __$15__, doubles __$80__

The Oodnadatta Track

The road from **Marree** to **Oodnadatta** is by far the most interesting of the three famous Outback tracks, mainly because abandoned sidings and fettlers' cottages from the *Old Ghan* provide frequent excuses to get out of the car and explore. Disintegrating sleepers lie by the roadside along parts of the route, otherwise embankments and rickety bridges are all that remain of the line.

Marree to William Creek

About 30km into the journey from Marree, you cross the 5614km-long **Dog Fence** (or Great Dingo Fence), designed to keep dingoes away from southern flocks, which stretches from the Nullarbor Plain northeast into Queensland. Shortly after, a collection of scrap-metal sculptures at the **Mutonia Sculpture Park** at Alberrie Creek rail siding becomes visible on the side of the track. Standing in stark contrast to its harsh desert surrounds, it is an interesting, if not bizarre, photo opportunity. Another 50km along, near **Curdimurka ruins**, the road runs within sight of **Lake Eyre South**, giving a flavour of its bigger sister if you can't get out there. Twenty-five kilometres later, a short track south ends below three conical hills – two of which, the Bubbler and the perfectly symmetrical Blanche Cup, have hot, bubbling **mound springs** at the top, created when water escaping from the artesian basin deposits heaps of mud and minerals. One of these bores is not far up the road at **Coward Springs** (see p.728).

William Creek

WILLIAM CREEK has a resident population of just three – and has a source of fuel, camping and relaxation in the hotel (see below), which serves as a hangout for stockmen from **Anna Creek Station**, the world's largest cattle property, covering an area the size of Belgium. A solar-powered phone outside faces the battered remains of a Black Arrow **missile** dragged off the Woomera Range. Off-road drivers can take a 70km track from here to Lake Eyre's western shore; in the other direction is a more passable road to Coober Pedy, though there's almost nothing to see on the way.

Oodnadatta

Unless you stay long enough to meet some locals, you'll probably feel that **OODNADATTA** survived the *Ghan*'s closure with little to show for it. Oodnadatta was founded as a railhead in 1890, where mail and baggage for further north had to make do with camel trains from here until the line to Alice Springs was completed in 1928. Now that has gone, the town has become a base for the Aranda community and 4WD expeditions heading into the Simpson Desert. If your visit coincides with the annual weekend of horseracing in May, helicopters will be circling the track, trying to dry it out, and the town will be deserted, so stop at the track, buy a pass and join in.

The *Pink Roadhouse* (see below) acts as a store, bank and café, and sells detailed sketch maps of the area. From Oodnadatta you can head north towards Dalhousie Springs and the Simpson Desert (4WD only), or west to the Stuart Highway at Coober Pedy or Marla.

GETTING AROUND   THE OODNADATTA TRACK

By car As with the roads to Birdsville and Innamincka, with care any sound vehicle can drive the route in dry winter weather. After rain, however, sections of road can become decidedly hazardous when fast-flowing creek crossings and slippery mud can cause road closures. As always, check road conditions before departing with the nearest police station or visit the Department of Planning, Transport and Infrastructure website (ⓦdpti .sa.gov.au/OutbackRoads) and be sure to abide by any closures or restrictions in place; failure to do so not only puts you (and those who may have to come to your aid) in danger, but it ruins the condition of the track for future use and can result in seriously hefty fines (upwards of $4000 per vehicle).

ACCOMMODATION AND EATING

Coward Springs Campsite Coward Springs ☏ 08 8675 8336, ⓦcowardsprings.com.au. At Coward Springs a corroded pipe spilling into ponds has created an artificial environment of grasses and palms, behind which sits a campsite with toilet blocks and showers but unpowered pitches, and a refreshing outdoor spa ($2 for nonguests) created from the spring. Camel tours are on offer too (June & July). Camping per person $12.50

Pink Roadhouse Oodnadatta ☏ 1800 802 074, ⓦpinkroadhouse.com.au. The focal point of Oodnadatta, the *Pink Roadhouse* has a campsite and basic, a/c wooden cabins, a restaurant serving the "Oodnaburger" (which features pineapple and beetroot among other accompaniments), a post office and a supermarket. You can also buy fuel. Un/powered sites $15/$20, cabins $110

William Creek Hotel William Creek ☏ 08 8670 7880, ⓦwilliamcreekhotel.com. Comfortable rooms and hearty meals are found at this famous hotel, whose bar, walls and ceiling are heavily decorated with cards and photographs of 4WD disasters. Accommodation ranges from basic campsites and cabins and fairly smart self-contained huts known as Camel Houses. You can get fuel here for the journey ahead. Un/powered sites $24/30, cabins $150, Camel Houses $250

The Simpson Desert

Apart from the track out to the Stuart Highway, the area north of Oodnadatta is strictly for 4WDs, with **Dalhousie Hot Springs** in the Witjira National Park a worthwhile destination, or the **Simpson Desert** for the ultimate off-road challenge. The route directly north, towards Finke and the Northern Territory, is relatively good as far as **Hamilton Homestead** (110km), though Fogarty's Claypan, around halfway, might present a sticky problem. From Hamilton the route is via **Eringa ruins** (160km) and **Bloods Creek bore** on the edge of **Witjira National Park**.

THE SIMPSON DESERT CROSSING

Crossing the approximately 550km of steep north–south dunes through the Simpson Desert between Dalhousie in South Australia and Birdsville in Queensland is the ultimate challenge for any off-roader. In late September, 4WD groups are joined by bikes attempting to complete the punishing **Simpson Desert Cycling Classic** (Ⓦ desertchallenge.org). In winter, a steady stream of vehicles moves from west to east (the easier direction since the dunes' eastern slopes are steeper and harder to climb), but there's no help along the way, so don't underestimate the difficulties; extensive 4WD experience is required. Convoys need to include at least one skilled mechanic and, apart from the usual spares, a long-handled shovel and a strong tow-rope. You'll also need more than adequate food and water (six litres a day per person), and of course fuel – around a hundred litres of diesel, or two hundred litres of petrol, if you take the shortest route.

The enjoyment is mostly in the driving, though there's more than sand to look at: trees and shrubs grow in stabilized areas and at dusk you'll find dune crests patrolled by reptiles, birds, small mammals and insects. Photographers can take advantage of clear skies at night to make timed exposures of the stars circling the heavens. At the uncapped spout of Purni Bore, 70km from Dalhousie, birdlife and reeds fringe a 27°C pool; camping facilities here include a shower and toilet. A wooden post battling to stay above shifting sand at Poeppel Corner (269km) marks the junction of Queensland, South Australia and the Northern Territory. After the corner the dunes become higher but further apart, separated by claypans covered in mulga and grassland. Big Red, the last dune, is also the tallest; once over this it's a clear 41km run to Birdsville.

The **Simpson Desert Regional Reserve**, linking the Witjira National Park to the Simpson Desert Conservation Park, is closed in summer (Dec–March). As with other areas, a Desert Parks Pass is required (☎ 1800 816 078, Ⓦ environment.sa.gov.au/parks).

7

From Bloods Creek you can detour 30km northeast to **Mount Dare Hotel** (see below). In winter the homestead is busy with groups of 4WDs arriving from or departing for the desert crossing; it's at least 550km to the next fuel stop at Birdsville in Queensland.

Dalhousie Hot Springs

From Mt Dare it's a rough and bleak drive southeast to **Dalhousie Hot Springs**, which forms a collection of over one hundred **mound springs** like Arabian oases. The largest spring, next to the **campsite**, is cool enough to swim in and hot enough to unkink your back. What survives of the vegetation simmers with birdlife, and as nothing flows into the springs, the presence of **fish** – some, like the Dalhousie hardyhead, unique to the system – has prompted a variety of improbable explanations. One theory is that fish eggs were swept up in dust storms and later fell with rain at Dalhousie, but it's more likely that fish were brought in during an ancient deluge or that the population survives from when the area was an inland sea.

While the main springs area is flat and trampled by years of abuse from campers and cars – stay on the marked paths here to avoid causing further erosion – trudging out to other groups over the salt and samphire-bush flats armed with a packed lunch and camera gives you a good overview of the region from the top of well-formed, overgrown mounds. More views can be had from the stony hills to the west, and from **Dalhousie Homestead**, 16km south of the springs along the Pedirka road. The homestead was abandoned after the *Ghan* line was laid down, and today the stone walls, undermined by rabbit burrows, are gradually falling apart in the extreme climate.

ACCOMMODATION

THE SIMPSON DESERT

Mount Dare Hotel 30km southwest of Bloods Creek ☎ 08 8670 7835, Ⓦ mtdare.com.au. You can park your caravan at one of the powered sites or stay overnight in one of the spartan cabins. Fuel and meals are available, and there's a small store for essentials. Powered sites $25, cabins $85

Melbourne and around

HOT-AIR BALLOONS OVER MELBOURNE

Melbourne and around

Melbourne is Australia's second-largest city, with a population of 4.25 million. Rivalry between Sydney and Melbourne is on an almost childish level – in every sphere from football to fashion and business – and in purely monetary terms, Sydney leads the race. That said, Melburnians never tire of pointing out that they inhabit the world's most "liveable city", which is famous for its thriving café culture, trendy laneways and dynamic inner suburbs. It is Melbourne's subtle charms, rather than in-your-face sights, that make it worth a visit – and will make you want to stay much longer than planned.

In many ways, Melbourne is the most European of all Australian cities: magnificent landscaped gardens and parks provide greenery near the centre, while the skyscrapers of the **Central Business District (CBD)** and flash public spaces like **Federation Square** contrast with Victorian-era facades and tree-lined boulevards. Large-scale immigration since World War II has shaken up the city's formerly self-absorbed, parochial mind-set for good. In the postwar era, whole villages moved here from Greece, furnishing the well-worn statistic that Melbourne is the third-largest Greek city after Athens and Thessaloniki. Further influxes of immigrants from Vietnam, Lebanon, Sudan, Turkey and Italy have transformed the city into a **foodie heaven**, and tucking into a different cuisine each night is one of its great treats.

Bordering the south side of the CBD, the muddy and, in former decades, much-maligned Yarra River lies at the centre of the massive developments that have transformed the face of the city, with new high-rises still popping up like mushrooms. Close to the river, the venerable **Melbourne Cricket Ground (MCG)** has been drawing sports fans from all over since it hosted the 1956 Olympic Games, while the redevelopment of the trendy waterfront **Southbank** and **Docklands** precincts continues today. Continue south of the river for the rambling **Royal Botanic Gardens**, which form the centrepiece of the **Domain Parklands** and carpet the southern end of the CBD with lush greenery. Melbourne's eclectic **suburbs** offer up a melange of different vibes, from arty Fitzroy to multicultural Richmond – the combination of which gives the city its distinctive "Melbourne" flavour.

The city's strong claim to being the nation's **cultural capital** is well founded: laced with a healthy dash of counterculture, its artistic life flourishes, culminating in the highbrow **Melbourne International Arts Festival** for two weeks in October and its slightly offbeat (and shoestring) cousin the Fringe Festival (see p.780). Throughout the year, there are jam-packed seasons of classical music, comedy and theatre, a wacky array of exhibitions in small galleries, enough art-house movies to last a lifetime, and the Writers' Festival in August showcasing Australian literary talent. Sport, especially Australian Rules football, is almost a religion here, while the Melbourne Cup in November is a public holiday, celebrated with gusto.

Highlights

❶ Ian Potter Centre: NGV Australia Terrific collection of Australian art on Fed Square, with galleries devoted to the indigenous communities. **See p.736**

❷ Chinatown The low-rise, narrow streets of Melbourne's Chinatown have changed little since the nineteenth century. **See p.741**

❸ State Library of Victoria Exhibitions and paintings in this beautiful domed building give essential background on the founding of Melbourne. **See p.741**

❹ Aussie Rules match at the MCG Join the cheering crowds for an action-packed footy game at the MCG. **See p.743**

❺ Heide Museum of Modern Art Enjoy great paintings in a sylvan setting at John and Sunday Reed's modernist home. **See p.757**

❻ Eating out Melbourne's love of food borders on obsession, and eating out in the city is a must. **See p.767**

❼ Penguin Parade, Phillip Island See thousands of Little penguins emerge from the sea and waddle up to their burrows. **See p.791**

❽ Yarra Valley Verdant scenery and some truly great wineries. **See p.794**

❾ Healesville Sanctuary Beautiful bushland zoo and wildlife sanctuary for injured and orphaned animals. **See p.796**

HIGHLIGHTS ARE MARKED ON THE MAPS ON P.734 & PP.738–739

Melbourne is an excellent base for day-trips out into the surrounding countryside. To the south, the **Mornington Peninsula** on the east side of **Port Phillip Bay** has farmland and wineries on gently rolling hills, and is home to some of the city's most popular beaches and surfing spots, while the placid waters of the bay are good for swimming. Western Port Bay, beyond the peninsula, encloses two fascinating islands – **French Island**, much of whose wildlife is protected by a national park, and **Phillip Island**, whose "Penguin Parade", when masses of Little penguins waddle ashore each night, is among Australia's biggest tourist attractions. Closest to the city are the quaint villages of the eucalypt-covered **Dandenong Ranges**, while the scenic **Yarra Valley**, in the northeast, is Victoria's answer to South Australia's Barossa Valley, and one of many wine-producing areas around Melbourne. On the western side of Port Phillip Bay, Victoria's second city, **Geelong**, and most of the **Bellarine Peninsula** are not quite as captivating as their Mornington counterparts, but they do give access to the west coast and the world-famous Great Ocean Road. Queenscliff, near the

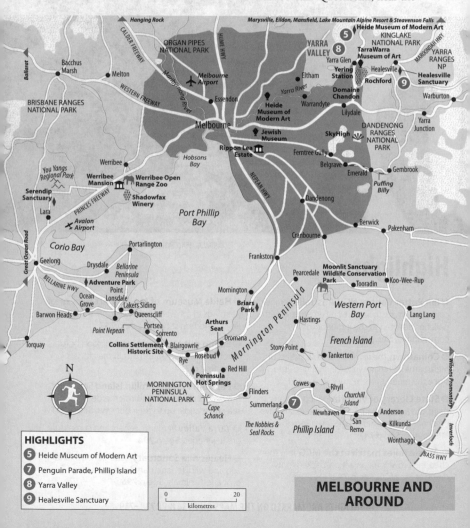

HIGHLIGHTS

5 Heide Museum of Modern Art

7 Penguin Parade, Phillip Island

8 Yarra Valley

9 Healesville Sanctuary

MELBOURNE AND AROUND

narrow entrance to Port Phillip Bay, with its beautiful, grand hotels, is a stylish (and expensive) weekend getaway.

Melbourne boasts a reasonably cool **climate**, although January and February are prone to barbaric hot spells when temperatures can climb into the forties. The threat of bushfires (see box, p.860) around this time can close off certain areas to the public.

Brief History

Melbourne and the region surrounding it have been inhabited for thousands of years, though the city itself has existed for only a fraction of that time. In 1803 **British** Lieutenant David Collins landed with a group of free settlers and a few hundred convicts at what is now Sorrento, but the location was abandoned less than a year later due to a lack of **fresh water**. Instead, the colonists sailed across the Bass Strait for an island known as Van Diemen's Land (now **Tasmania**).

It wasn't long before Tasmanians began crossing back over to the mainland in search of fresh pastures for their livestock, and in 1834 a small group chose to remain and pave the way for the establishment of **Melbourne**. Though the native Kulin Nation Aborigines bitterly resisted the burgeoning settlement evolved into the hub of a thriving pastoral community.

Charles La Trobe arrived from England in 1839 to administer the district, and under his guidance modern Melbourne rapidly began to take shape. With development focused on the north bank of the **Yarra River**, the city's population grew quickly and by 1840 had reached 10,000. Eleven years later, the Port Phillip District (as the area around Melbourne was known) officially demanded **separation** from the state of New South Wales. The new district of Victoria was formed – and just nine days afterwards, gold was discovered within its borders.

After the gold rush

Fortune-seekers flocked to Melbourne and the settlement boomed to become a **prosperous** and elegant city, whose inhabitants modelled their houses on middle-class England. Melbourne was now the **fastest-growing** and richest port in the British Empire; rail lines and cable trams were introduced to its streets and grandiose public developments such as the Royal Exhibition Building were constructed. Following **Federation** in 1901, Melbourne became Australia's political **capital**, a title it retained until Canberra became fully operational in 1927.

The 1930s were marked by rapid **industrial** development on the city's fringes and the growth of settlement in the suburbs; this continued postwar when Melbourne's population was boosted by a flood of **immigrant** workers, who transformed the city from a stereotypically British backwater into an international melting pot. In 1956, the highly successful **Olympic Games** further increased Melbourne's international standing. Multinational companies made the city their Australian base, and it remained the country's capital of business and finance until the focus shifted to **Sydney** in the early 1980s.

Melbourne today

The turn of the twenty-first century saw the creation of Federation Square and other urban public spaces. New cultural institutions – including the Melbourne Museum – began to appear in waves, and the city was named a UNESCO City of Literature in 2003. While Melbourne ultimately lost business to Sydney and politics to Canberra, its reputation as Australia's **cultural capital** continues to grow today.

Federation Square and around

Rising up from St Kilda Road in a gentle incline, the Plaza at **Federation Square** narrows into a horseshoe-shape where it's hemmed in by buildings including the **Ian**

Potter Centre: NGV Australia, one of the country's most interesting art museums, and the **Australian Centre for the Moving Image**. There are also numerous cafés and restaurants, usually buzzing with activity. Of the sights around Federation Square, Flinders Street Station, St Paul's Cathedral and the National Trust-listed painting *Chloe* (see opposite) are worthwhile diversions.

Federation Square

Occupying an entire block between Flinders Street and the Yarra River, **Federation Square** (or "Fed Square", as it's generally known), is considered the heart of Melbourne's CBD. Created in 2002 to provide the city with a single, central unifying focus, it was initially met with some resistance by Melburnians who baulked at the bold, contemporary architecture. Now, however, its bars and cafés are a popular after-work meeting spot, while the Plaza at its core is where crowds gather to check out live music, short art films and major sports events on a huge video screen.

Australian Centre for the Moving Image

Federation Square • Daily 10am–5pm • Admission fee for some films and exhibitions • ⓦ acmi.net.au

On the north side of Fed Square, the **Australian Centre for the Moving Image**, or ACMI, is devoted to exploring the moving image in all its forms, from film and television to video games and new media. Worth checking out is the screen gallery, featuring changing exhibitions of screen-based art. The ACMI also presents a wide range of programmes from cinema, film festivals and educative events to hip-hop concerts. An absorbing free permanent exhibition on the ground floor explores the evolution of the moving image, with a section devoted to Australian "voices" that highlights the impact it had on the Australian national identity.

Ian Potter Centre: NGV Australia

Federation Square • Daily 10am–5pm; free tour of the main collection daily at 11am, noon, 1pm & 2pm • Admission fee for some special exhibitions • ⓦ ngv.vic.gov.au

Walk from Flinders Street through the **Atrium** – a unique passageway of glass, steel and zinc – or from the Plaza through the narrow **Crossbar** to reach the **Ian Potter Centre: NGV Australia**, named in honour of Sir Ian Potter (1902–94), a local financier, philanthropist and patron of the arts. Occupying three floors, the centre showcases one of the best collections of Australian art in the country. The gallery is split between traditional and contemporary indigenous art, historic and modern Australian collections, and special temporary exhibitions. The stylish *Crossbar* **café** on the third floor has views of the Yarra and serves good snacks and drinks.

The building itself is as much a work of art as its exhibits, and is constructed from two overlapping wings forming a slightly crooked X and offering constantly shifting views, with glimpses of the Yarra and the parklands through the glass walls in the southern part of the building. The best way to get a handle on the work, as well as the building, is to participate in a **free guided tour** of the main collection. Additional tours focus on specific aspects of the collection.

Flinders Street Station

Cnr of Flinders and Swanston sts

The huge **Flinders Street Station**, the city's main suburban railway station, lies sandwiched between the southern edge of the CBD and the Yarra River, and is the gateway to the city for the million-plus commuters who pass through it daily. The current building dates back to the early 1900s and "under the clocks" – referencing its entrance with a row of clocks detailing train departures – is still a traditional Melbourne meeting place.

St Paul's Cathedral

Cnr of Flinders and Swanston sts • Mon–Fri 8am–6pm, Sat 9am–4pm, Sun 7.30am–7.30pm • Free • ☏ 03 9653 4333, ⓦ stpaulscathedral.org.au

Opposite Fed Square on the block between Swanston Street, Flinders Street and Flinders Lane is the splendid **St Paul's Cathedral**, built in the 1880s to a Gothic Revival design by English architect William Butterfield (who never actually visited Australia). Duck around the corner to Hosier Lane (between Flinders Street and Flinders Lane) for one of Melbourne's finest examples of famous **laneway street art** (see box, p.740).

Chloe

Cnr of Flinders and Swanston sts • Daily 10am–late • Free • ☏ 03 9650 3884, ⓦ youngandjacksons.com.au

The *Young & Jackson Hotel*, across from St Paul's Cathedral on Swanston Street, is now protected by the National Trust, not for any intrinsic beauty but as a showcase for a work of art that has become a Melbourne icon: **Chloe**, a full-length nude that now reclines upstairs in the comfortable *Chloe's Bar and Bistro*. Exhibited by the French painter Jules Lefebvre at the Paris Salon of 1875, it was sent to an international exhibition in Melbourne in 1881, where it caused quite a stir, and has been here ever since.

CBD

8

Seen from across the river, Melbourne's **Central Business District (CBD)** presents a spectacular modern skyline; what you notice from close up, however, are the florid nineteenth-century facades, grandiose survivors of the great days of the gold rush and after. The former Royal Mint on William Street near Flagstaff Gardens is one of the finest examples, but the main concentrations are to the south on **Collins Street** and along **Spring Street** to the east. At the centre of the CBD, trams jolt through the busy **Bourke Street Mall**. A stone's throw from these central thoroughfares, narrow lanes, squares and arcades with vibrant street art, hole-in-the-wall cafés, small restaurants, shops and boutiques add a cosy and intimate feel to the city.

Collins Street

North of Fed Square, **Collins Street** is the smart Melbourne address, becoming increasingly exclusive as you climb the hill from Spencer Street. At the western end of Collins Street the **Rialto Towers**, an Italianate-Gothic complex built in the 1890s now housing the luxury *Intercontinental Rialto Hotel*, sits adjacent to the massive **Rialto Towers**. Built in the 1980s, it was Melbourne's tallest structure until the Eureka Tower opened in 2006 (see p.745). Nearby, at no. 333, the former **Commercial Bank of Australia** has a particularly sumptuous interior, with a domed banking chamber and awesome barrel-vaulted vestibule that you can see for yourself during business hours.

Further up, shops such as the ever-crowded Tiffany & Co. at no. 267 become the focus of attention. Beyond this, on the corner of Collins and Swanston streets, the Neoclassical Melbourne **Town Hall** stands across the road from City Square. Continue northeast, past expensive boutiques, and Collins Place and the towering **Hotel Sofitel** next door dominate the upper part of Collins Street. Opposite stands one of the last bastions of Australian male chauvinism: the staid, men-only **Melbourne Club**. A block north, Little Collins Street runs parallel to its larger counterpart and is equally worth a stroll – particularly between Swanston and Elizabeth streets where quirky boutiques abound.

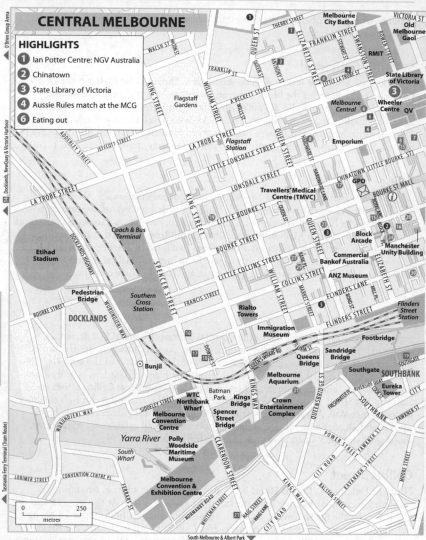

CENTRAL MELBOURNE

HIGHLIGHTS

1 Ian Potter Centre: NGV Australia
2 Chinatown
3 State Library of Victoria
4 Aussie Rules match at the MCG
6 Eating out

ACCOMMODATION					
Amora Hotel Riverwalk	14	Pensione Hotel	17	● EATING	
Art Series – The Blackman	22	Richmond Hill Hotel	20	A Little Bird Told Me…	4
Batman's Hill	16	St. Jerome's – The Hotel	6	Baby	33
Brady Hotel Central Melbourne	4	Urban Central	21	Bar Lourinha	16
Citadines Apart'Hotel	9	Victoria Hotel	11	Brother Baba Budan	17
City Centre Budget Hotel	8			Camy Shanghai Dumplings	15
Discovery Melbourne	3	● SHOPPING		Chin Chin	25
Exford Hotel	7	Basement Discs	2	Crossways Food for Life	20
Greenhouse Backpacker	13	Booktalk Café	7	Cumulus Inc.	22
Home at the Mansion	2	Federation Square		Dinner by Heston	31
Jasper Hotel	1	Book Market	4	Don Don	6
Langham	19	Haunted Bookshop	3	Flower Drum	13
Hotel Lindrum	12	Off the Hip	5	Fonda Mexican	21
Magnolia Court Boutique Hotel	10	Queen Victoria Market	1	Grossi Florentino	11
Mantra on Jolimont	15	Victorian Arts Centre		Ha Long Bay	3
Melbourne Central YHA	18	Sunday Market	6	Hardware Societe	8
Ovolo Laneways	5			Hofbrauhaus	12
				Hopetoun Tea Rooms	24

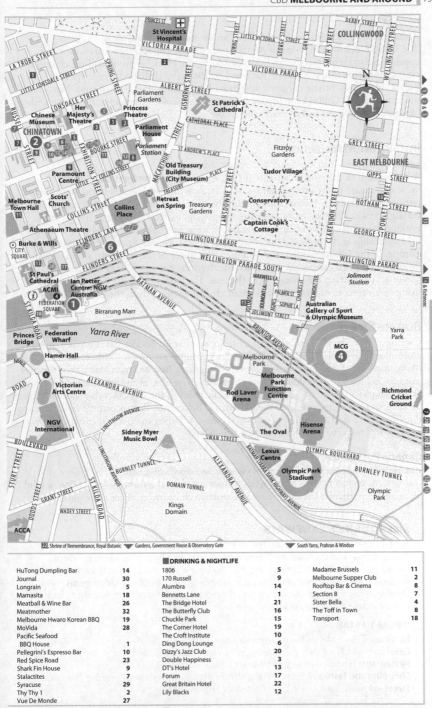

Shrine of Remembrance, Royal Botanic ▼ Gardens, Government House & Observatory Gate ▼ South Yarra, Prahran & Windsor

HuTong Dumpling Bar	**14**	
Journal	**30**	
Longrain	**5**	
Mamasita	**18**	
Meatball & Wine Bar	**26**	
Meatmother	**32**	
Melbourne Hwaro Korean BBQ	**19**	
MoVida	**28**	
Pacific Seafood		
BBQ House	**1**	
Pellegrini's Espresso Bar	**10**	
Red Spice Road	**23**	
Shark Fin House	**9**	
Stalactites	**7**	
Syracuse	**29**	
Thy Thy 1	**2**	
Vue De Monde	**27**	

■ DRINKING & NIGHTLIFE

1806	**5**	
170 Russell	**9**	
Alumbra	**14**	
Bennetts Lane	**1**	
The Bridge Hotel	**21**	
The Butterfly Club	**16**	
Chuckle Park	**15**	
The Corner Hotel	**19**	
The Croft Institute	**10**	
Ding Dong Lounge	**6**	
Dizzy's Jazz Club	**20**	
Double Happiness	**3**	
DT's Hotel	**13**	
Forum	**17**	
Great Britain Hotel	**22**	
Lily Blacks	**12**	

Madame Brussels	**11**
Melbourne Supper Club	**2**
Rooftop Bar & Cinema	**8**
Section 8	**7**
Sister Bella	**4**
The Toff in Town	**8**
Transport	**18**

Block Arcade

282–284 Collins St • Mon–Thurs 8am–6pm, Fri 8am–8pm, Sat & Sun 9am–5pm • Free • ⓦ theblock.com.au

The 1890s **Block Arcade** is one of Melbourne's grandest shopping centres, its name appropriately taken from the tradition of "doing the block" – promenading around the city's fashionable shopping lanes. Restored in 1988, the L-shaped arcade sports a mosaic-tiled floor, ornate columns and mouldings, and a glass-domed roof. Next door, the brand-new **St Collins Lane** luxury precinct at no. 260 is a modern alternative with top-notch restaurants and upmarket retail brands.

Immigration Museum

400 Flinders St, at William St • Daily 10am–5pm • $14 • ⓦ museumvictoria.com.au

A block south of the western stretch of Collins Street, the **Immigration Museum** is dedicated to one of the central themes of Australian history. Housed in the beautifully restored Old Customs House, the museum builds a vivid picture of immigration history through personal stories, music, moving images, light effects and interactive screens, evoking the experiences of being a migrant on a square-rigger in the 1840s, a passenger on a steamship at the beginning of the twentieth century and a postwar refugee from Europe. In the **Tribute Garden**, the outdoor centrepiece of the museum, a film of water flows over polished granite on which are engraved the names of 7000 migrants to Victoria, symbolizing the passage over the seas. The names of all the Koorie people living in Victoria prior to white settlement are listed separately at the garden's entrance.

Bourke Street

Carving a line down the centre of the city from west to east, **Bourke Street** offers a slightly more affordable experience than its Collins Street counterpart to the south. One of Melbourne's oldest and most well-known thoroughfares, **Bourke Street Mall** (ⓦ bourkestreet .com.au) is a tram-lined pedestrian street extending west from Swanston Street to Elizabeth Street that packs the crowds on weekends, public holidays and any other day with an excuse for shopping – bringing reason to the old saying "Busier than Bourke Street". In addition to the shops, you'll find a selection of cafés and bars – including the eternally buzzy *Pellegrini's Espresso Bar* (see p.767), Melbourne's first Italian bar.

General Post Office

350 Bourke St • Daily 10am–6pm, Fri till 8pm, Sun till 5pm • ☏ 03 9290 0200, ⓦ melbournesgpo.com

The western end of Bourke Street Mall is dominated by the **General Post Office**, a solid Neoclassical porticoed building with a distinctive clock tower. After a fire gutted most

---

MELBOURNE'S LANEWAYS

Nothing screams "Melbourne" quite like trams, four-seasons-in-one-day weather and the MCG. That is, nothing except a vibrant city **laneway**. Often missed by visitors, the multitude of character-filled backstreets crisscrossing the CBD are one of the city's greatest assets and the lifeblood of Melbourne's unique culture and identity. Some of the best **hidden gems** Melbourne has on offer are tucked away in the most unassuming of alleys, so don't be afraid to venture around corners to see what you uncover.

WHERE TO START

Bars Russell Place, Meyers Place, Liverpool Street, Tattersalls Lane
Cafés Somerset Place, Degraves Street, Centre Place, Little Lonsdale Street
Restaurants Hardware Lane/Street, Market Lane, Flinders Lane
Shopping and fashion Presgrave Place, Manchester Lane, Little Collins Street and Block Arcade
Street art Hosier Lane, Union Lane, Croft Alley, Higson Place

of its interior in 2003, it was restored and is now a light and airy shopping complex with high-end designer clothes and upmarket eateries.

Royal Arcade

355 Bourke St Mall • Mon–Thurs 9am–6pm, Fri 10am–8pm, Sat 9am–5pm, Sun 10am–5pm • ⦿ royalarcade.com.au

Running off Bourke Street Mall, the lovely **Royal Arcade** is Melbourne's oldest (1869), paved with black and white marble and lit by huge fanlight windows. A clock on which two 2m giants, Gog and Magog, strike the hours adds a welcome hint of the grotesque.

Chinatown

North of Bourke Street, and running parallel to it, is Little Bourke Street, with the majestic **Law Courts** by William Street at the western end, and **Chinatown** to the east between Exhibition and Swanston streets. Australia's oldest continuous Chinese settlement, Melbourne's Chinatown began with a few boarding houses in the 1850s (when the gold rushes attracted Chinese people in droves, many from the Pearl River Delta near Hong Kong) and grew as the gold began to run out and Chinese fortune-seekers headed back to the city. Today the area still has a low-rise, narrow-laned, nineteenth-century character, and it's packed with restaurants, stores and some of Melbourne's best-hidden laneway bars and restaurants.

Chinese Museum

22 Cohen Place • Daily 10am–4pm • $10 • ⦿ chinesemuseum.com.au

The **Chinese Museum**, in an old warehouse on Cohen Place, is concerned particularly with the Chinese role in the foundation and development of Melbourne, and is worth a visit for the 92m-long Dai Loong dragon alone, paraded each Chinese New Year and during the Moomba Festival (see p.779). The museum offers an interesting **Remembering Chinatown** self-guided audio tour of Chinatown using portable MP3 players and a guidebook.

QV

Lonsdale St • Mon–Thurs 10am–7pm, Fri 10am–9pm, Sat 10am–6pm, Sun 10am–5pm • ⦿ qv.com.au

North of Chinatown rises the bulky **QV**, named after the Queen Victoria Women's Hospital, which occupied the site from 1896 until the late 1980s. It now houses a shopping complex with a gym, supermarket, restaurants and bars. The building itself is an irregularly formed structure crisscrossed by open-air lanes and passageways dedicated to high-end fashion, with floor-to-ceiling glass walls.

State Library of Victoria

Library 328 Swanston St • Mon–Thurs 10am–9pm, Fri–Sun 10am–6pm; introductory tours Mon–Fri 10am–4pm • Free • ⦿ slv.vic.gov.au • **Wheeler Centre** 176 Little Lonsdale St • Mon–Fri 9am–5pm • Free • ☎ 03 9094 7809, ⦿ wheelercentre.com

To the western edge of QV is the **State Library of Victoria**. The building, dating from 1856, is a splendid example of Victorian architecture, and houses the state's largest public research and reference library. The interior has been painstakingly refurbished and is well worth a visit, in particular the **Cowen Gallery**, with its permanent display of paintings illustrating the changing look of Melbourne and Victoria; the **La Trobe Reading Room** with its imposing domed roof; and the **Dome Galleries**, which vividly tell the history of Victoria. The library houses a tresure-trove of paintings and rare and antiquarian books and newspapers, along with **Ned Kelly's armour** and death mask, and the famous rage-filled **Jerilderie letter**, which inspired Peter Carey's Booker Prize-winning novel *True History of the Kelly Gang*. There's also the MV Anderson **Chess Collection**: with almost 12,000 chess-related items it is reputedly one of the largest public collections in the world. Around the corner, the **Wheeler Centre** runs a lively programme of literary talks, readings and debates. The library has free public wi-fi.

Melbourne Central

Cnr La Trobe & Swanston sts • Mon–Wed, Sat & Sun 10am–7pm, Thurs & Fri 10am–9pm • ⓦ melbournecentral.com.au

Opposite the State Library is the refurbished **Melbourne Central** shopping complex, which mirrors the QV concept of alleys and passageways, and is lined with cafés and sushi bars. Housed under an iconic glass cone ceiling is the nineteenth-century Coop's Shot Tower, around which the centre is built. Encircling the Heritage-listed tower are three hundred fashion stores, boutiques and restaurants spread over five floors. There is an entertainment precinct on the third floor with a bowling alley and a **cinema complex**, and the subterranean basement contains Melbourne Central **train station** – one of four City Loop subway stops on Melbourne's train network.

Old Melbourne Gaol

377 Russell St • Daily 9.30am–5pm • $25 • **Night tours** from 8pm • $38; advance tour bookings required • ☎ 03 8663 7228, ⓦ oldmelbournegaol.com.au

The **Old Melbourne Gaol**, a block east of Swanston Street, is one of the most fascinating sights in the CBD. It's certainly the most popular, largely because Australian folk hero and bushranger **Ned Kelly** (see box, p.872) was hanged here in 1880 – the site of his execution and the beam from which he was hanged are on display, as is assorted armour worn by the Kelly gang. The various night tours use the spooky atmosphere of the prison to full effect.

The bluestone prison was built in stages from 1841 to 1864 – the gold rushes of the 1850s caused such a surge in lawlessness that it kept having to be expanded. A mix of condemned men, remand and short-sentence prisoners, women and "lunatics" (often, in fact, drunks) were housed here. Much has been demolished since the jail was closed in 1923, but the entrance and boundary walls survive.

The gruesome collection of **death masks** on show in the tiny cells bears witness to the nineteenth-century obsession with phrenology. Accompanying the masks are compelling case histories of the murderers and their victims. Most fascinating are the women: Martha Needle, who poisoned her husband and daughters (among others) with arsenic, and young Martha Knorr, the notorious "baby farmer", who advertised herself as a "kind motherly person, willing to adopt a child". After receiving a few dollars per child, she killed and buried them in her backyard. The jail serves up other macabre memorabilia, including a scaffold, various nooses and a triangle where malcontents were strapped to receive lashes of the cat-o'-nine-tails. Perhaps the ultimate rite of passage for visitors is the "Art of Hanging", an interpretive display that's part educational tool and part medieval snuff movie.

Queen Victoria Market

Cnr Elizabeth & Victoria sts • **Markets** Main: Tues & Thurs 6am–2pm, Fri 6am–5pm, Sat 6am–3pm, Sun 9am–4pm; Summer Night Market: Nov–March Wed 5–10pm; Winter Night Market: June–Aug Wed 5–10pm • **Hunt & Gather Food Tour**: Tues, Thurs, Fri & Sun 10am • $49 including food sampling, booking essential • ☎ 03 9320 5822, ⓦ qvm.com.au

Opened in the 1870s, **Queen Victoria Market** remains one of the best-loved of Melbourne's institutions. Its collection of huge, open-sided sheds and high-roofed decorative halls is fronted along Victoria Street by restored shops, with their original wrought-iron canopies. The market is a boisterous, down-to-earth affair where you can buy practically anything from new and secondhand clothes to fresh fish. Stallholders and shoppers seem just as diverse as the goods on offer: Vietnamese, Italian and Greek greengrocers pile their colourful produce high and vie for your attention, while the huge variety of deliciously smelly cheeses effortlessly draws customers to the old-fashioned deli hall.

Saturday morning marks a weekly social ritual as Melbourne's foodies turn out for their groceries, while Sunday is for clothing and shoe shopping. The guided **Hunt & Gather Food Tour** takes in all the culinary delights of the market, while the action-packed Night Markets have music stages, bars and over 200 stalls providing on-site cuisine from around the world, as well as clothing, jewellery and other crafty goods.

Parliament House

Spring St, East Melbourne • Mon–Fri 9am–5pm • **Parliament tours** Mon–Fri 9.30am, 10.30am, 11.30am, 1pm (express tour), 1.30pm, 2.30pm, 3.30pm & 4pm (express tour), on days when parliament is not sitting • Free • ☎ 03 9651 8568, ⦿ parliament.vic.gov.au • **Old Treasury Building** Mon–Fri & Sun 10am–4pm • Free • ☎ 03 9651 2233, ⦿ oldtreasurybuilding.org.au

Erected in stages between 1856 and 1930, the **Parliament House** and buildings have a theatrical presence, with a facade of giant Doric columns rising from a high flight of steps, and landscaped gardens on either side. Just south, the **Old Treasury Building** and adjacent State Government Office, facing the beautiful Treasury Gardens, are equally imposing. Completed in 1862 to a design by John James Clark, who was just 19 at the time, the Treasury was built to store the city's gold.

Fitzroy Gardens

Cnr Landsdown St & Wellington Parade, East Melbourne • **Captain Cook's Cottage** Daily 9am–5pm • $6.20 • **Conservatory** Daily 9am–5pm • Free • ⦿ fitzroygardens.com

East of Parliament House, the broad acres of **Fitzroy Gardens** run a close second to Carlton Gardens as a getaway from the CBD. Originally laid out in the shape of the Union Jack flag, the park's paths still just about conform to the original pattern, though the formal style has been fetchingly abandoned in between. The gardens are best appreciated on weekdays, as at the weekend you'll spend most of your time dodging the video cameras of wedding parties. The much-touted main attraction is really only for kitsch nostalgists: **Captain Cook's Cottage** was the family home of Captain James Cook, the English navigator who explored the southern hemisphere in three great voyages and first "discovered" the east coast of Australia. Otherwise, there are attractive flower displays at the **Conservatory**.

MCG and around

The **Melbourne Sports and Entertainment Precinct**, located 3km east of the city, contains a series of sport stadiums and venues including **Melbourne Park**, **Olympic Park** and the beloved **Melbourne Cricket Ground (MCG)**. It is considered Australia's premier sports precinct, and regularly hosts some of the biggest domestic and international sporting events, including the AFL Grand Final (Australian Rules football), Australian Open (tennis) and Boxing Day Test (cricket). The venues have also previously hosted the 1956 Summer Olympics and 2006 Commonwealth Games.

Melbourne Cricket Ground

Brunton Ave, in Yarra Park • **MCG tours** Daily between 10am–3pm; 1hr 15min; no tours on event days or public holidays • $23, or $31.50 combined with a museum ticket • ⦿ mcg.org.au • **National Sport Museum** Daily 10am–5pm, last admission 4pm • $23 • ⦿ nsm.org.au

East of the CBD lies **Yarra Park**, containing the hallowed **Melbourne Cricket Ground (MCG)**. Hosting state and international cricket matches and some of the top Aussie Rules football games, the "G", as it is affectionately referred to, is one of sports-mad Melburnians' best-loved icons. Home to the Melbourne Cricket Club since 1853, the complex became the centrepiece of the 1956 Olympic Games after it had been completely reconstructed – only the historic members' stand survived. The present-day MCG has a capacity of 100,000, boosted by the development of the Northern Stand, which was created for the 2006 Commonwealth Games, and houses the **National Sport Museum**, which contains various sports exhibitions.

Melbourne Park

Batman Ave • ⓦ mopt.com.au

From the MCG, three pedestrian bridges over Brunton Avenue lead to **Melbourne Park**, home to a further cluster of sporting venues, including the **Rod Laver Arena** and **Hisense Arena**, which host the Australian Open tennis championship in January. The latter can seat up to 10,500 people and has a retractable roof and moveable seating that allow for fully enclosed or open-air events such as cycling, tennis, basketball and concerts. On the other side of Swan Street lies the **Olympic Park** with the world-class AAMI soccer and rugby stadium.

Birrarung Marr

Batman Ave • Federation Bells chime 8–9am, 12.30–1.30pm & 5–6pm • ⓦ federationbells.com.au

Birrarung Marr forms a green link between the sports precinct of Melbourne Park and Federation Square, giving striking views of the city skyline, the sports arenas, river and parklands. Created from land previously occupied by railway lines, a swimming pool and a road, it now consists of grassy slopes, intersected by a long **footbridge** that crosses the entire park from the southeast to the northwest. The footbridge starts at a small, artificially created wetland area in the southeast by the river called the **Billabong** and leads over Red Gum Gully to the park's centrepiece, the **Federation Bells**, a collection of 39 bells ranging in size from a small handbell to a huge bell weighing a tonne, created to commemorate the Centenary of Federation in 2001. The bells are computer-controlled and normally ring three times a day.

Southbank and around

A kilometre from the CBD on the southern banks of the Yarra, the aptly named **Southbank** is an important cultural, entertainment and business hub. Once an unexciting industrial area, significant development in recent decades has seen the skyline and the population skyrocket. Bound by the Yarra River and St Kilda Road to the north and east and South Melbourne and South Wharf to the south and west, Southbank is the city's main arts precinct, with the **Victorian Arts Centre**, **Australian Centre for Contemporary Art** (ACCA) and the **National Gallery of Victoria International**. It is here that you will also find Melbourne's tallest building, **Eureka Tower**, and the vast **Crown Entertainment Complex**.

THE YARRA RIVER

Despite its nondescript appearance, the muddy **Yarra River** was – and still is – an important part of the Melbourne scene. Tidal movements of up to 2m meant frequent flooding, a problem only partly solved by artificially straightening the river and building up its banks. This also had the incidental benefit of reserving tracts of low-lying land as **recreational space**, now pleasingly crisscrossed by paths and cycle tracks. The best way to see the Yarra is on a cruise (see p.761), and you can **rent bikes** to explore the riverbanks (see p.760); on fine weekends, especially, the Yarra comes to life, with people messing about in boats, cycling and strolling.

Eureka Tower

7 Riverside Quay • Skydeck daily 10am–10pm, last admission 9.30pm • $20; The Edge $32 (including Skydeck admission) • Ⓦ eurekaskydeck.com.au

The riverside's most innovative development is the 92-storey **Eureka Tower**, located on the Southgate site and named after a landmark rebellion in Victoria's gold-rush era (the top levels are clad in gold). Finished in 2006 and towering 300m about the ground, it is the tallest building in Melbourne. Visitors can enjoy amazing views of the city and beyond from the 88th-floor **Skydeck**, which features the stomach-churning "skywalk" **The Edge**, a 3m glass cube that juts out over the city below.

Victorian Arts Centre

100 St Kilda Rd • **Theatres & Exhibition Tour** Mon–Sat 11am; 60min • $20 • **Backstage Tour** Sun 11am; 1hr 30min • $20; book tours online, by phone or from Theatres Building foyer box office • **Arts and crafts market** Sun 10am–4pm • **Famous Spiegeltent** Feb–April Ⓦ spiegeltent.net • ☎ 1300 182 183, Ⓦ artscentremelbourne.com.au

The **Victorian Arts Centre** comprises Hamer Hall, the Theatres Building and the Sidney Myer Music Bowl, an open-air venue across St Kilda Road in Kings Domain (see p.747). At the top of the Theatres Building is a 162m **spire** whose curved lower sections are meant to evoke the flowing folds of a ballerina's skirt. The **Theatres & Exhibition Tour** of the Gallery and State Theatre provides an insight into the history of the buildings and gives an overview of the architecture and design, while the **Backstage Tour** ventures behind the curtains. The centre also houses a Performing Arts Collection research facility covering everything from theatre to rock'n'roll, with exhibits including Dame Edna Everage's spectacles and Kylie's gold hotpants. Viewings are by appointment only, though snapshots of the collection are often displayed in the foyer and gallery spaces, as are splendid temporary exhibitions, normally focusing on the performance schedule. On Sunday the stalls of a good **arts and crafts market** line the pavement outside the arts centre, and between February and April each year the **Famous Spiegeltent** comes to town, hosting a packed schedule of music, comedy and cabaret.

National Gallery of Victoria (NGV) International

180 St Kilda Rd • **Gallery** Daily 10am–5pm • Free • Ⓦ ngv.vic.gov.au • **Persimmon restaurant** Daily 11am–4pm • ☎ 03 8620 2434 • **Gallery kitchen** and tearoom Daily 10am–5pm • ☎ 03 8620 2431

The bluestone building that is the **National Gallery of Victoria (NGV)**, Australia's oldest public art museum, houses a collection of international works under the name NGV International (its sister gallery, the Ian Potter Centre: NGV Australia is located at Federation Square). At the entrance is the **Waterwall** – a water curtain flowing down a glass wall 20m wide and 6m high – and the **Great Hall** on the ground floor, featuring a beautiful stained-glass ceiling, gives access to the landscaped **Sculpture Garden**. The ground floor contains three large rooms for temporary exhibitions. Level 1 has rooms displaying Asian art, and European paintings and sculpture from the fourteenth to the seventeenth centuries. Level 2 has paintings, sculpture and decorative arts from the seventeenth to the mid-twentieth centuries: Flemish and Dutch masters, including the Rembrandt Cabinet, are among the highlights here, while the contemporary era is represented using installations and photos on Level 3. There's also the swish mod-Oz **Persimmon restaurant** on ground level, the **Gallery Kitchen** on the same floor for drinks and snacks, and a **tearoom** on Level 1. NGV has a regular programme of international travelling exhibits, lectures, discussion groups, films and other activities – check out the gallery's What's On flyer or its website for details.

8

Australian Centre for Contemporary Art

111 Sturt St • Tues–Fri 10am–5pm, Sat & Sun 11–5pm • Free • ⓦ accaonline.org.au

South of NGV International, the distinctive, rusty steel facade of the **Australian Centre for Contemporary Art (ACCA)** is a sculpture in itself. ACCA has consistently challenging exhibitions of modern international and Australian art and places a strong emphasis on commissioning, rather than collecting, work.

Southgate

3 Southgate Ave • Daily 10am–late • ⓦ southgatemelbourne.com.au

One of the first developments in the riverside transformation, **Southgate**, immediately west of **Princes Bridge**, is an upmarket shopping complex with lots of smart cafés, restaurants, bars and a huge food court with very popular outdoor tables. Look out for *Ophelia*, the iconic mosaic sculpture commissioned for the opening of the site in 1992 – her sister sculpture *Angel* lives up the river at Birrarung Marr (see p.744).

Crown Entertainment Complex

8 Whiteman St • Daily 24hr • ⓦ crownmelbourne.com.au

Providing the lower Yarra's unavoidable focal point, the **Crown Entertainment Complex** is Australia's largest gambling and entertainment venue, stretching across 600m of riverfront west of Southgate between Queens Bridge and Spencer Street Bridge. Within the complex, you'll find a casino, three luxury hotels (*Crown Metropole, Crown Promenade* and *Crown Towers*), designer shopping boutiques and a variety of restaurants catering for a range of tastes and budgets.

Polly Woodside

21 South Wharf Promenade • Sat & Sun 10am–4pm, daily during school hols • $16 • ⓦ pollywoodside.com.au

The **Polly Woodside** is a small, barque-rigged sailing ship built in Belfast in 1885 for the South American coal trade. After circumnavigating the world 17 times, it was sold to the National Trust for one cent on retirement in 1968 and moored at South Wharf. There's a small dedicated **maritime museum** in a converted shed, where a video based on a real sailor's diary focuses on the hardships and occasional pleasures of life on board, and costumed guides help bring the experience to life.

Melbourne Convention and Exhibition Centre

1 Convention Centre Place • ☎ 03 9235 8000, ⓦ mcec.com.au

The **Melbourne Convention and Exhibition Centre** is a whimsical example of the city's dynamic new architectural style: facing the river is an immense 450m-long glass wall, while the street entrance has an awning resembling a ski jump propped up by wafer-thin pylons. The complex hosts a range of large-scale public and trade exhibitions, conventions and events, and is worth checking out for its "6 Star Green Star" environmental rating design.

Sea Life Melbourne Aquarium

Cnr of Flinders & King sts • Daily 9.30am–6pm, last admission 5pm • $40.50; Shark Dive Xtreme $299, bookings essential • ☎ 1800 026 576, ⓦ melbourneaquarium.com.au

Opposite the Crown Entertainment Complex is the **Melbourne Aquarium**, which harbours thousands of creatures from the Southern Ocean. Part of it is taken up by the Oceanarium tank, which holds over two million litres of water and contains 3200 animals from 150 species. There is also a great stingray-filled exhibit, crocodile lair and a glass room surrounded by shark-filled water. The curved, four-storey building also houses penguins and a hands-on learning centre, where visitors can get a fish-eye view of life underwater, with access to lecture halls and an amphitheatre, as well as cafés, a shop and a restaurant. You can also come nose-to-nose with a shark in the "**Shark Dive Xtreme**" experience, if you are game.

Docklands

On what was once the city's old dock area, **Docklands** is a large-scale commercial, residential and leisure development that's slowly rising to the west of Southern Cross Station. The constantly evolving face of the area is set to undergo further development in the coming years, but for now the restaurant promenade, the Melbourne Star observation wheel, the residential and entertainment precincts of **NewQuay** on Victoria Harbour, and the ever-expanding **Waterfront City** are very much open to the public and gaining in popularity among Melburnians.

O'Brien Group Arena

105 Pearl River Rd, Docklands • Daily 6am–late • $27 including skate hire, $11 Tues without skates • 15min lessons for beginners, free • ☎ 03 1300 756 699, ⓦ obriengrouparena.com.au

With two Olympic-sized skating rinks, the **O'Brien Group Arena** is Australia's largest ice sports and entertainment venue. The rinks can get quite crowded during school holidays, but if you can make the most of the later opening hours, you could have the place almost to yourself. During **ice hockey season**, you can catch either the Melbourne Mustangs or Melbourne Ice in regular matches.

Etihad Stadium

740 Bourke Street • Mon–Fri 8.30am–5pm, or 4hr prior to event starting time • ⓦ etihadstadium.com.au

At the heart of Docklands lies another of Melbourne's giant sporting venues, **Etihad Stadium** (formerly the Telstra Dome), a 54,000-seat venue for AFL, cricket, domestic and international soccer and rugby matches, as well as concerts by big-name artists. A wide pedestrian footbridge crosses the railway tracks at Southern Cross Station, connecting Etihad Stadium and the Docklands with Spencer Street and the older part of the city.

The Domain Parklands

Wedged between St Kilda Road and the Yarra River, the leafy Domain Parklands encompass Kings Domain, the Shrine of Remembrance and the Royal Botanic Gardens, furnishing the southern end of the CBD with verdant greenery.

Kings Domain

Across St Kilda Road from the National Gallery of Victoria, the grassy open parkland of **Kings Domain** encompasses the **Sidney Myer Music Bowl**, which serves as an outdoor music arena for the Victorian Arts Centre. Its amphitheatre shape projects the sound from the stage, so if you don't have tickets to Music Bowl events you can usually hear (but not see) the stage performances clearly from the perimeter – unsurprisingly, the area is a popular evening picnic spot.

8

Shrine of Remembrance

Birdwood Ave • Daily 10am–5pm • Free • Check website for details of regular exhibitions, talks and events • Tours daily 11am & 2pm • Free • ☎ 03 9661 8100, ⓦ shrine.org.au

The Shrine of Remembrance, in formal grounds in the southwestern corner of the Kings Domain, was built in 1934 to commemorate those who fought in various conflicts. It's a rather Orwellian monument, apparently half-Roman temple, half-Aztec pyramid. The shrine is designed so that at 11am on Remembrance Day (Nov 11) a ray of sunlight strikes the memorial stone inside – an effect that's simulated every half an hour. Regular exhibitions, talks and events are also worth checking out.

Royal Botanic Gardens

Birdwood Ave • Daily 7.30am–sunset • Free • ☎ 03 9252 2429, ⓦ rbg.vic.gov.au • Take any St Kilda Road tram (except route #1) and disembark at stop no. 20 (Domain Interchange/St Kilda Rd).

The **Royal Botanic Gardens** contain over eight thousand different plant species and over fifty thousand individual plants, as well as native wildlife such as cockatoos and kookaburras, in an extensive landscaped setting. Melbourne's much-maligned climate is perfect for horticulture: cool enough for temperate trees and flowers to flourish, warm enough for palms and other subtropical species, and wet enough for anything else.

Highlights include the **herb garden**, comprising part of the medicinal collection established in 1880; the **fern gully**, a lovely walk through shady ferns, with cooling mists of water on a hot summer's day; the large ornamental **lake** full of ducks, black swans and eels; and various **hothouses** where exotic cacti and fascinating plants such as the carnivorous pitcher plant thrive. Families should head to the dedicated **children's garden** (Wed–Sun 10am–sunset, daily during school holidays), which features snaking paths, bamboo thickets, water channels to jump in and a lily pond. The painstakingly restored **Observatory Gate**, a group of nineteenth-century Italianate buildings next door to the visitor centre, can be visited on one of the tours that leave from the centre (see below).

The *Jardin Tan* café (daily 8am–4pm) next to the visitor centre at Observatory Gate, and *The Terrace* (daily: May–Sept 9.45am–4pm; Oct–April 9am–5pm) by the lake both serve meals, snacks and cakes.

INFORMATION & TOURS

Tourist information The visitor centre is at the Observatory Precinct on Birdwood Ave (Mon–Fri 9am–5pm, Sat & Sun 9.30am–5pm), and has displays, maps and brochures.

Plays On summer evenings, plays are often performed in the gardens; check ⓦ rbg.vic.gov.au to see what's on. Swap popcorn for picnic baskets from mid-Dec to mid-March, when art-house, cult and classic films are projected onto a big outdoor screen at the Moonlight Cinema (enter at D Gate on Birdwood Ave; films start around 8.30pm; $19; ⓦ moonlight.com.au). Don't forget to take an extra layer of clothing, a rug and insect repellent.

Tours A range of seasonal and year-round tours can be booked through the visitor centre and leave from the Observatory Gate. The Discovery Walk gives a fine introduction to the history and horticultural diversity of the gardens (Tues–Sun 11am & 2pm; free). The Aboriginal Heritage Walk explores the traditional uses of plants for foods, medicine, tools and ceremonies (Sun–Fri 11am; $31, bookings essential on ☎ 03 9252 2429). Starry Southern Skies offers people a chance to gaze up at the stars and planets of the southern hemisphere through large telescopes (Mon 8–9.30pm in Sept, 9–10.30pm Oct–April; $24).

Melbourne's suburbs

It's in Melbourne's inner **suburbs** that you'll really get a feel for what life in this city is all about. Many have quite distinct characters, whether as ethnic enclaves or self-styled artists' communities. Browsing through markets and shops, cruising across Hobsons Bay, sampling the world's foods and, of course, sipping espresso, are the primary attractions. Café society finds its home to the north among the alternative galleries and secondhand shops of **Fitzroy**, while the Italian cafés on Lygon Street in nearby **Carlton** fuelled the Beat Generation with espresso, though these days boutiques far outnumber bookshops. Grungy **Richmond**, to the east, has both Vietnamese and Greek enclaves, is home to a number of good Middle Eastern restaurants, and has a diverse music scene in its many pubs. South of the river is the place for fashion and shopping, whether at wealthy **South Yarra**, alternative **Windsor**, or self-consciously hip **Prahran**. To the south, **St Kilda** has the advantage of a beachside location to go with its trendy but raucous

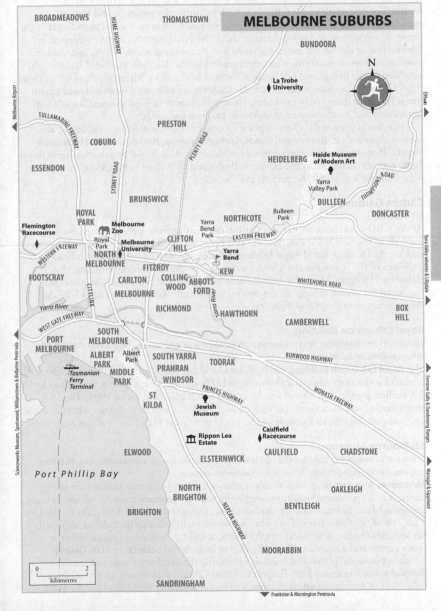

nightlife. To add some family-friendly stops to your itinerary, make for the well-designed **zoo** in Carlton, or **Scienceworks**, a hugely enjoyable interactive museum in Spotswood. Further out, the excellent **Heide Museum of Modern Art** is in Bulleen and, if you continue along in the same direction, Eltham hosts the artists' colony of **Montsalvat**.

Carlton

Tram #1, #3 or #8 from Swanston St; any tram bound for Melbourne University will deliver you within one block of Lygon St

Carlton lies just north of the CBD but, with its university presence and long-established Italian restaurant scene, it could be a million miles away. **Lygon Street** is the centre of the action, and it was here, in the 1950s, that espresso bars first opened in Melbourne; at the time these exotic spots had an unconventional allure, and the local intelligentsia soon made this street their second home. Victorian terraced houses provided cheap living, and this became the first of the city's "alternative" suburbs. These days, Carlton is no longer bohemian; its residents are older and wealthier, and Lygon Street has gone definitively upmarket, though the smart fashion shops still jostle with bookshops and an abundance of Italian restaurants and cafés.

Lygon Street itself is the obvious place to explore, but the elegant architecture also spreads eastwards to **Drummond Street**, **Carlton Gardens**, **Rathdowne and Nicholson streets**. Running along the western side of the university, Royal Parade gives onto **Royal Park**, with its memorial to the explorers Burke and Wills (see box, p.451), from where it's a short walk through the park to the zoo.

Carlton Gardens

1–111 Carlton St

At the CBD's northeast corner, the **Carlton Gardens** provide a green escape from the hubbub of the CBD. The Gardens are also home to the fantastic **Melbourne Museum** and World Heritage-listed **Royal Exhibition Building** – one of the oldest exhibition pavilions of the industrial era. On the south side of the Exhibition Building, the elaborate Hochgurtel fountain stands some 10m high and represents the power and success of the young colony. At the centre, four youths dance below symbols of the arts, science, commerce and industry.

Royal Exhibition Building

9 Nicholson St • Tours Mon–Fri 2pm; 1hr • $10; tours start and can be booked at the Melbourne Museum next door • ☎ 03 9270 5000, ⓦ museumvictoria.com.au/reb

The **Royal Exhibition Building** was built by David Mitchell (father of Dame Nellie Melba) for the International Exhibition of 1880, during which time it was visited by 1.5 million people. It is also where Australia's first parliament sat in 1901. The magnificent Neoclassical edifice, with its soaring dome and huge entrance portal, is the only substantially intact example in the world of a Great Hall from a major exhibition.

Melbourne Museum

11 Nicholson St • **Museum** Daily 10am–5pm • $14 • ☎ 03 8341 7777, ⓦ museumvictoria.com.au/melbournemuseum • **IMAX films** Daily, approximately every hour 9.45am–late • $20–32 • ⓦ imaxmelbourne.com.au

Melbourne Museum is an ultramodern, state-of-the-art place that makes a dramatic contrast to its nineteenth-century neighbour, with its geometric forms, vibrant colours, immense blade-like roof and a greenhouse accommodating a lush fern gully flanked by a canopy of tall forest trees. The museum, whose eight galleries include one especially for kids, also houses a 400-seat amphitheatre, a hall for major touring exhibitions, a study centre and a museum shop. Highlights include the **Science and Life Gallery**, which explores the plants and animals inhabiting the southern lands and seas; **Bunjilaka**, the Museum's First Peoples Cultural Centre, showcasing an extraordinary collection of Aboriginal artefacts from Victoria and further afield; and the **Australia**

Gallery, focusing on the history of Melbourne and Victoria, which features the (stuffed) legendary racehorse Phar Lap. Also of interest are the **Evolution Gallery**, which looks at the earth's history and holds an assortment of dinosaur casts, and the **Forest Gallery**, a living, breathing indoor rainforest containing over 8000 plants from more than 120 species, including 25m-tall gums, as well as birds, insects, snakes, lizards and fish. The **IMAX Melbourne**, attached to the museum, boasts one of the world's biggest movie screens. Up to eight different IMAX films, ranging from natural wonders to artificial marvels and spacewalks, are projected each day, some in 3D.

Melbourne Zoo

Elliott Avenue, Parkville • Daily 9am–5pm • $32.50, under-16s outside school holidays and weekends $16.30, otherwise free; Roar 'n' Snore $199, under-13s $150; call ☎ 1300 966 784 to book • ☎ 03 9285 9300 • ⓦ zoo.org.au/melbournezoo • Tram #55 from William St, or train to Royal Park station on Upfield line from Flinders St Station

When it opened in 1862, **Melbourne Zoo** was the first in Australia. Popular attractions include an **Orang-utan Sanctuary**, featuring a treetop boardwalk, as well as the **Gorilla Rainforest** and **Asian Rainforest**, part of the award-winning **Trail of the Elephants**, where you can meet the five resident elephants, learn about the life of a "mahout" or elephant keeper, and eat *nasi goreng* at the Asian food stalls. The Australian area contains a central lake with waterbirds, open enclosures for koalas and other animals and a bushland setting where you can walk among emus, kangaroos and wallabies. Strolling along the boardwalks of the **Great Flight Aviary** you'll come across rainforest, wetland and a scrub area with a huge gum tree where many birds nest. The dark **Platypus House** is also worth a look, since the mammals are notoriously difficult to see in the wild, and the **Butterfly House** is highly enjoyable. In summer, the zoo stays open until 9.30pm on selected nights (usually weekends) for its "Zoo Twilights" music programme, which hosts live bands playing on the central lawn. The zoo also runs the popular **Roar 'n' Snore** sleepover, where you get to sleep in safari tents in the Historic Elephant Enclosure and take an after-dark zoo tour. Meals and snacks are provided, as are tents, but bring your own bedding.

8

Fitzroy

Trams #11, #86, #96

In the 1970s, **Fitzroy** took over from Carlton as the home of the city's artistic community, and every year at the end of September, the area is awash with pop-up art installations, exhibitions and street performers as part of the colourful **Fringe Festival** – the alternative scene's answer to the highbrow Melbourne International Arts Festival (see p.780). The district's focus is **Brunswick Street** (tram #11 from Collins St), especially between **Gertrude Street**, home to trendy galleries, art spaces and boutiques, and **Johnston Street**, with its lively Spanish bars. In the shadow of Housing Commission tower blocks, funky secondhand shops rub shoulders with ethnic supermarkets and cafés packed with grungy students, hipsters and musicians.

Artists' Garden and Fitzroy Nursery

390 Brunswick St • Mon–Fri 9am–5.30pm, Sat & Sun 9.30am–5.30pm • Free • ⓦ fitzroynursery.com.au

Fitzroy's fringe art leanings are reflected in wacky street installations such as mosaic chairs, and sculptures like Mr Poetry. The eye-catching wrought-iron gate at the entrance to the **Fitzroy Nursery**, with its fairy-tale motif, sets the theme for the **Artists' Garden** above the nursery, which exhibits sculptures and other decorative items for garden use.

Rose Street Artists' Market

60 Rose St • Sat & Sun 11am–5pm • ⓦ rosestmarket.com.au

Fitzroy hosts the unique but pricey **Rose Street Artists' Market** where a rotation of over 600 fashion designers, painters, photographers, ceramicists, sculptors and other artists

FITZROY, CARLTON & COLLINGWOOD

● **EATING**

Abla's	9
Babka Bakery Café	6
Bimbo Deluxe	7
The Beaufort	5
Bluebonnet Barbecue	1
Brunetti	17
Charcoal Lane	10
D.O.C. Pizza & Mozzarella Bar	20
Easy Tiger	12
Fitz Curry Cafe	19
Huxtaburger	11
Jimmy Grants	18
Jimmy Watson's	15
Panama Dining Room	7
Po' Boy Quarter	16
Proud Mary	14
Rice Queen	2
Shakahari	12
Trotters	8
The Vegie Bar	3

■ **DRINKING & NIGHTLIFE**

Bar Open	1
The Curtin	12
The Everleigh	11
Gertrude Street Enoteca	4
Laird Hotel	13
The Lincoln	6
Naked For Satan	2
The Peel	7
The Rainbow	4
Sircuit	9
The Standard	5
The Tote	8

● **SHOPPING**

Abbotsford Convent Market	6
Brunswick Street Bookstore	5
Collingwood Farmers Market	7
Grub Street Bookshop	2
Hares & Hyenas	4
Northside Records	8
Polyester Records	1
Rose Street Artists' Market	3

■ **ACCOMMODATION**

169 Drummond Street	3
Downtowner on Lygon	6
Lygon Lodge	1
Melbourne Metro YHA	4
The Nunnery	2
Laird Hotel	5

N

FITZROY

CARLTON

COLLINGWOOD

Fitzroy Pool

Rose Street

Johnston Street

Smith Street

Brunswick Street

Lygon Street

Hanover Street

Bell Street

Melbourne Museum

St Vincent's Hospital

Royal Exhibition Building

Carlton Gardens

IMAX Theatre

Ian Potter Museum of Art

University of Melbourne

Old Melbourne Gaol

RMIT

Collingwood Station

Ofuroya (Japanese Bath House)

Northcote Social Club

▲ #86 to Bundoora RMIT (Tram Route)
▲ #11 to West Preston (Tram Route)
▲ #96 to East Brunswick (Tram Route)
▲ #1 & to East Coburg & #8 to Moreland (Tram Routes)
▲ #11 to South Melbourne Beach via CBD & #8 to Toorak via CBD (Tram Routes)
#11 to Victoria Harbour Docklands via CBD & #86 to Waterfront City Docklands via CBD (Tram Routes) ▶
#96 to St Kilda Beach via CBD (Tram Route) ▶

▲ 6 & 7

0 250 metres

sell their wares each weekend in one of seventy stalls. Running off Brunswick Street, Rose Street market is perfect for a wander after a lazy Brunswick Street brunch and the ideal place to pick up a unique souvenir.

Fitzroy Pool

160 Alexandra Parade • Mon–Fri 6am–8pm, Sat & Sun 8am–6pm, year-round • $6

Fitzroy Pool in the north of the suburb, is a popular summer meeting place where everyone from hipsters and families to Italian and Greek retirees come to strut their stuff and beat the summer heat. As well as the heated outdoor 50m lap pool, there is a toddlers' pool, gymnasium, fitness classes, spa and sauna.

Collingwood

Tram #86 from Bourke St

Smith Street, forming the boundary between Fitzroy and **Collingwood** to the east, has charity shops, ethnic butchers and cheap supermarkets among New Age bookshops, quirky cafés and revamped pubs. North of Johnston Street you'll see a clutch of sportswear factory-seconds outlets. Collingwood and the adjacent suburb of Abbotsford have a large **LGBT population**, with gay bars and clubs clustered on Peel, Gipps and Glasshouse streets.

Richmond

Tram #48 or #75

Bordered by the Yarra River, **Richmond** is the bustling heart of inner Melbourne's Vietnamese community. Its epicentre, Victoria Street, is lined with greengrocers, fishmongers and *pho* restaurants, while running parallel further south, Bridge Road is a bargain-shopper's paradise, dotted with clothing factory-seconds stores. Further south again, the clutch of bars and restaurants nestled around the corner of Swan and Church streets is a popular pit stop for football-goers en route to and from games at the nearby MCG.

South Yarra, Prahran and Windsor

South of the river, the suburbs of **South Yarra**, **Prahran** and **Windsor** are home to the city's biggest **shopping** area, both grungy and upmarket. The main drag, **Chapel Street**, spans the three suburbs, and provides an extensive range of retail, eating and drinking options – from expensive fashion designers and exclusive restaurants to secondhand charity stores and late-night snack haunts.

South Yarra

Trams #5, #6, #8 and #72 depart from Swanston St to Chapel St; alternatively, the Frankston, Pakenham, Cranbourne, Dandenong and Sandringham line trains all stop at South Yarra station

The **South Yarra** stretch of **Chapel Street** has long been considered a "Golden Mile" of trendy shopping, awash with boutiques and speciality stores, bistro bars full of beautiful people and cooler-than-thou nightclubs. These days, much of its exclusivity has been usurped by the arrival of generic clothing chains and slightly sleazy bars. While there is still a smattering of designer boutiques to be found, most of the cool kids have migrated south down the Chapel Street beat towards Prahran and Windsor.

Prahran

Trams #5, #6, Sandringham line train to Prahran station

Beyond Commercial Road in **Prahran** proper, Chapel Street focuses on street-smart fashion, becoming progressively more downmarket as it heads south. Landmarks

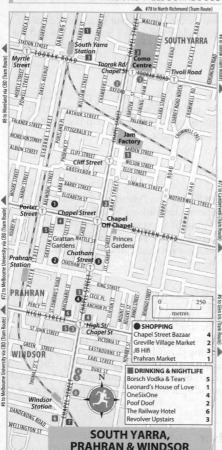

include **Prahran Market** (Tues, Thurs, Fri & Sat 7am–5pm, Sun 10am–3pm), an excellent, though expensive, food emporium (fish, meat, fruit, vegetables and delicatessen) plus cafés and a few clothes shops. On the western side of Chapel Street, **Chapel Street Bazaar** has an amazing array of secondhand clothes, Art Deco jewellery, furniture and bric-a-brac. Just opposite, tucked away in Little Chapel Street, **Chapel off Chapel** (ⓦchapeloffchapel.com.au) provides a venue for an eclectic mix of theatre performances, music and art exhibitions.

Greville Street

In the heart of Prahran, running west off Chapel Street, **Greville Street** was once the undisputed corridor of cutting-edge cool, with retro and designer boutiques, music outlets, bookshops and groovy bars and restaurants. While the hype has dissipated somewhat, the strip retains a unique vibrancy and is experiencing a quiet revival with new designers moving in. Look out for the return of the Sunday **Greville Village Market**, on the corner of Gratton Street in Gratton Gardens, with arts, crafts and secondhand clothes and jewellery.

Windsor

Trams #5, #64, Sandringham train to Windsor station

As Chapel Street crosses High Street the suburb changes to **Windsor** and becomes more interestingly eclectic. Secondhand stores and discount household appliance shops sit cheek by jowl with a growing number of worthwhile cafés and bars frequented by south-side locals. Busy Dandenong Road marks the boundary of Windsor and **East St Kilda**. Just across Dandenong Road on Chapel Street lies the **Astor Theatre**, a beautifully decorated cinema in an Art Nouveau building.

South Melbourne

Tram #1, #12, #96

Stretching southwest of the Yarra River is **South Melbourne**, whose focus is the excellent **South Melbourne Market**. South Melbourne's long and interesting history has seen this former gold-rush slum transform many times over before emerging as the gentrified inner-suburb it is today. Despite this, a number of 1960s-era housing commission towers still remain amid the restored Victorian terraces and semi-detached townhouses, as well as a handful of gold-rush-era prefabricated dwellings. These portable iron homes were constructed in England, shipped to Melbourne during the gold rush, and have been preserved by the National Trust as some of the few **prefabricated iron buildings** remaining in the world (399 Coventry St; entry and tour $6; first Sun of the month 1–4pm).

One block from the market, **Clarendon Street** is South Melbourne's main shopping precinct, and a fine example of a nineteenth-century streetscape.

South Melbourne Market

322–326 Coventry St, enclosed by York, Cecil and Coventry sts • Wed, Sat & Sun 8am–4pm, Fri 8am–5pm • Night Market Jan–March, Thurs 5.30–10pm • Cooking school information and booking on ☎ 03 9209 6295, ⓦ southmelbournemarket.com.au • Tram #96 from Bourke St

Opened in 1867, the **South Melbourne Market** is one of the city's oldest and most popular markets, with stalls selling everything from fruit and vegetables to clothes, homewares and continental delicacies. Outside on Cecil Street at market stall 91 is the famous South Melbourne "dimmy" (*dim sim*) stall – be prepared to queue. The market also runs a Cooking School with an ever-changing list of classes that focus on various cooking skills and cuisines, and a summer night market with street-food trucks, bars and live music.

Albert Park and Port Melbourne

Trams #1, #3a, #96

The exclusive suburb of **Albert Park** has the feel of a small village, with many lovely old terraced houses and **Dundas Place**, a shopping centre of mouthwatering delis and bakeries. At the end of Victoria Street, there's a beach with a narrow strip of sand that continues west to the up-and-coming suburb of **Port Melbourne** whose Station Pier (tram #109) is home to the *Spirit of Tasmania* ferry terminal and a number of good restaurants. In the shadow of St Kilda Road, Albert Park itself has a golf course and excellent aquatic centre, with its five pools (see p.782), BBQs, restaurant and a boating lake, and is usually teeming with joggers, cyclists and locals picnicking or playing a game of footy. Every year in March, thousands of people descend upon the park for the **Australian Grand Prix** (see p.47).

St Kilda

Trams #3, #3a, #12, #16, #96

If it's the bay you're heading for, then **St Kilda** is the obvious destination. The former seaside resort has an air of shabby gentility, which enhances its current paradoxical reputation as a sophisticated yet seedy suburb with raging nightlife. Running from St Kilda Road down to the Esplanade, **Fitzroy Street** is often touted as Melbourne's red-light district – usually pretty tame, though late at night not a comfortable place for women alone – and epitomizes this split personality, since it's lined with dozens of cafés and bars. On weekend nights, these and others throughout St Kilda are filled to overflowing with a style-conscious but fun crowd.

Acland Street

Acland Street, with its wonderful continental cake shops and bakeries, has a distinctly more cosmopolitan vibe than rowdy Fitzroy Street: it also features an attractive wooden and brick theatre, **Theatreworks** (see p.788), and the **Linden Centre of Contemporary Arts**, at no. 26 (Tues–Sun 11am–4pm, Wed until 8pm; ⓦlindenarts.org), which is set in a gracious colonial mansion and features painting, sculpture and photography shows. You can sit under the palm trees of **O'Donnell Gardens**, or nearby **St Kilda Botanical Gardens**, and eat your Acland Street goodies or vie for a seat at one of the dozens of bars and restaurants on the main drag.

8

St Kilda beach

The **beachfront** is a popular weekend promenade year-round, with separate cycling and walking paths stretching down to Elwood and Brighton, and a long pier. Near the base of the pier is the botched redevelopment of a historic site, the **St Kilda Sea Baths** (ⓦ stkildaseabaths.com.au), which dates back to 1931, as well as a mix of restaurants and bars, and a fitness centre with a kitsch Moorish twist. On Sunday, the **Esplanade Market** (10am–5pm) lines the waterfront on Upper Esplanade.

Luna Park

18 Lower Esplanade • School hols Mon–Wed & Sun 11am–8pm, Thurs–Sat 11am–11pm; May to mid-Sept Sat & Sun 11am–6pm; mid-Sept to April Fri 7–11pm, Sat 11am–11pm, Sun 11am–8pm • Free entry; $10.95 for individual rides or $49.95 unlimited rides day-ticket • ⓦ lunapark.com.au

St Kilda's most famous icon, **Luna Park**, is located on the Esplanade, and entered through the huge, laughing clown's face of "Mr Moon". Despite a couple of new attractions, there's nothing very high-tech about this 1912 amusement park: the Scenic Railway, the world's oldest operating roller-coaster, runs along bumpy wooden trestles and the Ghost Train wouldn't spook a toddler – but then that's half the fun.

Rippon Lea Estate

192 Hotham St • **Mansion** Sept–April daily 10am–5pm; May–Aug daily 10am–4pm • $15, garden only $10 • **Summer Sessions** Jan–March Sun 10am–4pm • $15 • ⓦ ripponleaestate.com.au

Rippon Lea Estate shows how Melbourne's wealthy elite lived a century ago. The 33-room mansion, which is protected by the National Trust, has magnificent gardens, complete with ornamental lake and fernery, and a way-over-the-top interior. The grounds are popular for picnics at weekends, and during summer when they host "Summer Sessions", afternoons of live music, bocce (types of bowls) and wine tasting.

Jewish Museum of Australia

26 Alma Rd, East St Kilda • Tues–Thurs 10am–4pm, Fri 10am–3pm, Sun 10am–5pm; closed Jewish holy days • $10 • ⑩ jewishmuseum .com.au • Tram #3 or #67 from Swanston St in the city to stop 32 on St Kilda Rd

The **Jewish Museum of Australia** houses permanent exhibitions focusing on Australian and world Jewish history, plus displays on Jewish beliefs and rituals, with an emphasis on festivals and customs. Interactive displays and over twenty thousand historical objects ensure an active calendar of temporary exhibitions too.

Western suburbs

Just a short drive over the Westgate Bridge from the CBD, the **suburbs** to the **west** of the city are home to some of Melbourne's most multicultural communities and are rapidly gaining in popularity for both Melburnians and tourists alike. African, Asian and Middle Eastern food is a major draw-card for the up-and-coming suburb of **Footscray**, while the far more gentrified bay-side suburb of **Williamstown** showcases the area's maritime and industrial heritage.

Scienceworks

2 Booker St, Spotswood • Daily 10am–4.30pm; Planetarium hourly shows 11am–3pm, 45min; Lightning Room shows noon–3pm • $14 entry, plus $6 each for Planetarium and Lightning Room • ☎ 03 9392 4800, ⑩ museumvictoria.com.au/scienceworks • Metro train to Spotswood station (Werribee or Williamstown line), or take the Williamstown ferry (see below) from Southbank

Inside a Space Age building, set in appropriately desolate wasteland, the displays and exhibitions at **Scienceworks** are ingenious, fun and highly interactive. In addition, the **Lightning Room** holds electrifying half-hour shows explaining the science behind fireworks and features high-voltage equipment capable of simulating real lightning bolts. The **Planetarium** displays state-of-the-art digital technology, taking visitors on a virtual journey through the galaxy.

Williamstown

Metro train (Williamstown line) or Williamstown ferry (☎ 03 9682 9555, ⑩ williamstownferries.com.au) to Williamstown station, or head out by car on the West Gate Freeway across the huge West Gate Bridge

Set on a promontory at the mouth of the Yarra, **Williamstown** is a strange mix of rich and poor; of industry, yachting marinas and working port. The street along the waterfront, named Nelson Place, is nowadays lined with restaurants and cafés. **Williamstown Craft Market** is held in the reserve between Nelson Place and the waterfront (third Sun of each month, 10am–4pm; ⑩ williamstowncraftmarket.com.au). The most enjoyable way to get to Williamstown is by ferry from Southgate.

Heide Museum of Modern Art

7 Templestowe Rd, Bulleen • **Museum** Tues–Sun 10am–5pm • $18, under-12s free • **Café Vue** Tues–Fri 10am–5pm, Sat & Sun 9am–5pm • ☎ 03 9850 1500, ⑩ heide.com.au • 14km from the city centre; Metro train to Heidelberg station (Hurstbridge line) then bus #903 (Mordialloc-bound) to Bridge St/Manningham Road stop (frequent services)

The **Heide Museum of Modern Art** was the home of Melbourne art patrons **John Reed** (1901–81) and **Sunday Reed** (1905–81), who in the mid-1930s purchased what was then a derelict dairy farm on the banks of the meandering Yarra River. During the following decades the Reeds fostered and nurtured the talents of young artists and played a central role in the emergence of Australian art movements such as the Angry Penguins, the Antipodeans and the Annandale Realists; the painters Sidney Nolan, John Perceval, Albert Tucker and Arthur Boyd were all members of the artistic circle at

Heide at one time or another. **Heide I** is the farmhouse where the Reeds lived from 1934 until 1967, while their airy modernist 1960s home **Heide II** shows work from the collection. The most prominent addition is the **Heide III** (Albert & Barbara Tucker Gallery), which features over two hundred artworks from Albert's personal collection. **Café Vue** draws on produce from the cottage garden; it also does a great hamper (pre-order) for consumption in the sculpture garden.

Montsalvat

7 Hillcrest Ave, Eltham • Daily 9am–5pm • $14, galleries included in ticket • Metro train to Eltham station (Hurstbridge line), then catch bus #582 (towards Noyra Rd) to Rockliffe St/Mt Pleasant Rd • ☎ 03 9439 7712, ⓦ montsalvat.com.au

Eltham, a bushy suburb about 24km from the city, is known for **arts and crafts**. Its reputation was established in 1935 when the charismatic painter and architect Justus Jorgensen moved to what was then a separate town and founded **Montsalvat**, a European-style artists' colony. Built with the help of his students and followers, the colony's eclectic design was inspired by medieval European buildings, with wonderful quirky results; Jorgensen died before it was completed and it has deliberately been left unfinished. He did, however, live long enough to see his community thrive, and to oversee the completion of the mud-brick Great Hall, whose influence is evident in other mud-brick buildings around Eltham. Today, Montsalvat contains two galleries and is still home to a colony of painters and craftspeople.

ARRIVAL AND DEPARTURE

MELBOURNE

BY PLANE

MELBOURNE AIRPORT (TULLAMARINE)

Tullamarine is Melbourne's main airport (☎ 03 9297 1600, ⓦ melbourneairport.com.au) and lies 25km northwest of the city. Terminal 1 handles domestic flights (Qantas only), Terminal 2 handles international ones, Terminal 3 is for domestic flights and is used by airlines including Virgin Australia and Regional Express (Rex), and Terminal 4 is for Tiger Airways and Jetstar domestic flights, as well as Regional Express arrivals.

Domestic destinations Adelaide (24–26 daily; 1hr); Alice Springs (daily; 2hr 55min); Brisbane (28 daily; 2hr 10min); Cairns (6–12 daily; 3hr 25min); Canberra (18 daily; 1hr 5min); Coffs Harbour (4 weekly; 1hr 50min); Darwin (3 daily; 3hr 55min); Gold Coast (15–16 daily; 2hr 5min); Hamilton Island (3 weekly; 3hr 10min); Hobart (14–15 daily; 1hr 15min); Launceston (9 daily; 1hr 5min); Newcastle (4 daily; 1hr 30min); Perth (16 daily; 4hr 10min); Sunshine Coast (2 daily; 2hr 15min); Sydney (78 daily; 1hr 25min); Townsville (daily; 3hr).

Skybus The Skybus (☎ 1300 759 287, ⓦ skybus .com.au) takes you to Southern Cross Station on Spencer St on the west side of the city (every 10min 6am–11.30pm, every 15–30min outside these times; 20min depending on traffic; $19 one-way, $38 return, valid for a year). If you book in advance, Skybus have a complimentary minibus service that picks up passengers from the coach terminal at Southern Cross Station and drops off at most of the hotels in the city centre and adjacent suburbs (Mon–Fri 6am–10.30pm, Sat & Sun 6am–7pm; free).

Taxi A taxi from Melbourne Airport costs between $45–60 to the city centre, $65 to St Kilda.

AVALON AIRPORT

Jetstar Airways, a budget subsidiary of Qantas, operates a limited number of domestic flights from Avalon Airport, situated just off the Princes Freeway, 55km southwest of Melbourne (☎ 03 5227 9100, ⓦ avalonairport.com.au).

Destinations Adelaide (2 weekly; 1hr 20min); Gold Coast (daily; 2hr 5min) Hobart (4 weekly; 1hr 15min); Sydney (5 daily; 1hr 25min).

Sita Coaches Coaches meet all arriving Jetstar flights and drop off passengers at Southern Cross Station (50min; one-way $22, return $42), as well as various suburbs and towns in the area if booked 48 hours in advance (☎ 03 9689 7999, ⓦ www.sitacoaches.com.au/avalon).

Taxi Taxis from Avalon Airport to the city are expensive: around $95–100 to the centre, $120 to St Kilda.

BY TRAIN

Southern Cross Station This is the main (and only central) Melbourne train station; it has a staffed information desk with all V/Line (within Victoria) train and bus timetables for up-to-date information.

Destinations Adelaide (2 weekly; 10hr); Alice Springs (weekly; 36hr via Adelaide); Ballarat (22 daily; 1hr 30min); Bendigo (20 daily; 2hr); Geelong (50 daily; 1hr); Perth (2 weekly; 45hr via Adelaide); Sydney via Albury (2 daily; 11hr 30min); Warrnambool (3 daily; 3hr 15min).

BY BUS

Greyhound Australia (Mon–Fri 8am–6pm, Sat 8am–4pm; ☏ 1300 473 946, ⓦ greyhound.com.au), V/Line (daily 6am–midnight; ☏ 1800 800 007, ⓦ vline.com.au) and Firefly buses (daily 6am–9.30pm; ☏ 1300 730 740, ⓦ fireflyexpress.com.au) all have terminals at Southern Cross Station. Some hotels pick up from Southern Cross Station.

Destinations Adelaide (3 daily; 10hr); Brisbane via Sydney (3 daily; 29hr); Sydney (5 daily; 13hr); Sydney via Canberra (2 daily; 14hr).

BY FERRY

Some hotels pick up from the Tasmanian ferry terminal located about 4km southwest of the city centre at Station Pier in Port Melbourne. The terminal is served by the #109 tram to Collins St in the CBD.

Ferries to Tasmania The ferry from Melbourne to Devonport in Tasmania, run by the *Spirit of Tasmania I* and *II* (Mon–Sat 8am–8.30pm, Sun 9am–8pm; ☏ 1800 634 906, ⓦ spiritoftasmania.com.au), takes around 11hrs. There's a nightly departure from Station Pier, Port Melbourne, at 7.30pm, plus additional departures at 9am and 9pm most Saturdays throughout the year, and selected days during mid-Dec to mid-Jan and school holidays. The cheapest one-way fares (unreserved seating) range from around $65 off-peak to $190 peak. For overnight sailings, shared four-bed male or female cabins are available from an additional $33, as are twin and family cabins for an additional $132–180. The fare for standard cars is normally $87; for motorbikes the cost is $60.

GETTING AROUND

Melbourne has an efficient system of trains, buses and trams, run by Public Transport Victoria (PTV). Call or log on to the PTV website for a range of public transport information including timetables and disability services (☏ 1800 800 007, ⓦ ptv.vic.gov.au). Unless you're going on a day-trip to the outer suburbs, you can get anywhere you need to, including St Kilda and Williamstown, on a Zone 1 ticket. Buses generally run 6am–11.30pm Mon–Sat, 7am–10pm Sun, and the Night Bus services offer departures from the CBD every 30min between 1.30am and 5.30am on weekends. Train and tram services operate from 5am to midnight, with night services running all night on Fri & Sat on all metropolitan train lines (depart Flinders St Station), and the #19, #67, #75, #86, #96 & #109 tram routes.

MYKI TICKETS (METRO, BUSES AND TRAMS)

Melbourne's ticket to travel on the city's trains, trams and buses comes in the form of myki, a reusable smartcard that stores value, and the only valid ticket on Melbourne's public transport network.

Visitor Value Pack You can buy a myki Visitor Value Pack ($14) from all major Metro train stations, airports, visitor information centres (including the Melbourne Visitor Centre at Federation Square; see p.761) and many hotels and hostels around Melbourne. The myki Visitor Value Pack includes a full-fare myki pre-loaded with $8 of "myki money" (enough for a full day of travel in Zone 1 of the Metro network) and offers discounts at 15 selected attractions around Melbourne.

Topping up To add value to your myki card, you can top up at myki machines located at Metro train stations, as well as the PTV Hub at Southern Cross Station near the corner of Spencer and Collins sts (Mon–Fri 7am–7pm, Sat & Sun 9am–6pm), all 7-Eleven stores and a range of other shops with the myki logo.

Touch on and off When travelling with myki, you need to "touch on" with the myki reader at train station entry points, or every time you board a bus or tram. When exiting a train station or bus you need to "touch off" to ensure the lowest fare, otherwise a 2hr Zone 1 & 2 fare ($3.90) will be deducted from your myki (there's no need to "touch off" on trams as they are all in Zone 1). You cannot top up or purchase myki passes from the drivers of trains or trams, but it is possible to do so on buses.

Types of fares Fares are calculated by the zone(s) you travel in and the time frame of your journey (either 2hr or full day); when you "touch on" and "touch off", the cheapest fare is automatically deducted from your myki. An entire journey in Zone 1 costs $3.90 for 2hr and $7.80 for a day-pass. An entire journey in Zone 2 is $2.70 for 2hr and $5.40 for a day-pass. Journeys in both Zones 1 & 2 cost $3.90 for 2hr, and $7.80 for a day-pass. All full fares are capped at $6 on weekends and public holidays.

BY TRAM

Melbourne's trams give the city a distinctive character and provide a pleasant, environmentally friendly way of getting around: the City Circle is particularly convenient, and free (see box, p.760).

Routes Trams run down the centre of the road; passengers can board trams from stops at the side of the road, or from central islands where present. Stops are signposted, and they often have a map with route numbers and times – the route number is displayed at the front of the tram.

Safety Although motorists are prohibited from passing trams that are stationary at stops, always look left as you disembark to make sure there are no vehicles approaching.

BY TRAIN

The Metro train network runs hourly throughout the night on weekends, and is the fastest way to reach distant suburbs. An underground loop system feeding into 16 suburban lines (City Loop) connects the city centre's five

8

MELBOURNE'S VINTAGE TRAMS

Melbourne's tram system dates back to 1885, and some of the trams are vintage wooden vehicles dating back as far as the 1920s. The vintage **City Circle tram** is a **free service** that runs in a loop along Flinders, Spring, Nicholson, La Trobe and Spencer sts. The **Colonial Tramcar Restaurant** is a converted 1927 tram offering a traditional silver- and white-linen restaurant service as you trundle around Melbourne.

City Circle tram Daily (except Christmas Day & Good Friday) every 12min, Mon–Fri 9.15am–9.15pm, Sat 9am–9.30pm, Sun 9am–6.30pm. Timetables and maps available on ⓦ ptv.vic.gov.au.

Colonial Tramcar Restaurant Starts at Normanby Rd near the Crown Casino, South Melbourne. The restaurant (no-smoking) offers a three-course early dinner (daily 5.45–7.15pm; $82) and a five-course dinner (8.35–11.30pm: Sun–Thurs $125, Fri & Sat $140), plus a four-course luncheon (daily 1–3pm; $85). All drinks are included. You'll usually need to reserve at least two to three weeks ahead, or up to three or four months in advance for Fri and Sat evenings (ⓣ 03 9695 4000, ⓦ tramrestaurant.com.au).

train stations: Southern Cross, which also serves as the station for interstate and country trains; Flagstaff, on the corner of La Trobe & William sts; Melbourne Central, on the corner of Swanston & La Trobe sts; Parliament, on Spring St; and Flinders St, the main suburban station.

Maps You can pick up train route maps at any City Loop station as well as many suburban stops.

Accessibility Trains and train stations are fully accessible for people using wheelchairs or with limited mobility, and there are lifts at all City Loop stations.

Safety New trains have a Passenger Emergency Intercom system that can be used to contact train staff (emergency use only), and all stations have a red emergency button. If the train is deserted, you'll feel safest if you sit in the front carriage nearest the driver.

Bikes on trains Bikes can be taken on Metro and V/Line trains free of charge, outside peak periods (Mon–Fri 7–9.30am & 4–6.30pm), if there's space available. If you're travelling with a reserved ticket on a V/Line service, you can check your bike on the train at least 30min prior to travelling.

BY BUS

Regular buses often run on the same routes as trams, as well as filling gaps where no train or tram lines run.

Night Bus Probably the most useful buses are the special after-midnight Night Bus services (every 30min Sat & Sun 12.30–5.30am), which depart from the CBD along 21 routes from the inner to the outer suburbs. CBD-bound buses depart suburban areas hourly throughout the night. See ⓦ ptv.vic.gov.au for timetables and routes.

BY CAR

Driving in Melbourne requires some care, mainly because of the trams. You can overtake a tram only on the left and must stop and wait behind it while passengers get on and off, as they step directly into the road (though there's no need to stop if there's a central pedestrian island). A peculiar rule has developed to accommodate trams at major intersections in the city centre: when turning right, you pull over to the left-hand lane (leaving the tram tracks clear for trams) and wait for the lights to change to amber before turning – a so-called "hook turn". Signs overhead indicate when this rule applies.

Rental Many car rental and campervan companies offer one-way rental. Rent-A-Bomb (ⓣ 13 15 53, ⓦ rentabomb .com.au) is a used-car company offering cheap rates, and Vroom Vroom Vroom (Mon–Fri 9am–5pm; ⓣ 1300 722 920, ⓦ vroomvroomvroom.com.au) compare deals on car and campervan hire.

BY BIKE

Cyclists should also watch out for tram lines – tyres can easily get wedged in them. This apart, Melbourne is perfect for cycling. There are 24 urban routes in and around the city, including the popular 35km Main Yarra Trail that follows the river out to the suburbs.

Maps and information The visitor centre at Federation Square (see opposite) has cycling maps which are also downloadable from the VicRoads website (ⓦ vicroads.vic.gov.au). The staff at Bicycle Network (Level 4, 246 Bourke St; Mon–Fri 9am–5pm; ⓣ 03 8376 8888, ⓦ bicyclenetwork.com.au) can assist with practical information; their website has a list of organized bike rides in Victoria and interstate.

Rental Rentabike at Federation Square (ⓣ 0417 339 203, ⓦ rentabike.net.au) offer bike rental for $15 (1hr), $35 (1 day) or $100 (weekly hire), as well as bike tours (see opposite).

INFORMATION

Volunteers in red uniforms – so-called City Ambassadors – roam the CBD between Elizabeth, Russell, La Trobe and Flinders sts (Mon–Sat 10am–4pm, Sun noon–3pm), and can assist with all kinds of tourist enquiries. *Melway*, available from all newsagents, is the city's best printed street directory.

Melbourne Visitor Centre In the northwest corner of Federation Square, the city's main visitor centre (daily 9am–6pm; ☎03 9658 9658, ⓦthatsmelbourne.com.au), directly opposite Flinders St, has brochures and maps galore about Melbourne and the rest of the state. The pocket-sized *Melbourne Walks* series is probably the most useful: each one describes a themed, self-guided walk (1hr 30min–2hr 30min) around the city and has a good reference map.

iVenture See Melbourne Card The iVenture discount sightseeing card is available at the Melbourne Visitor Centre (see above) and online at ⓦseemelbournepass.iventurecard .com. It provides free or discounted admission to more than 30 attractions ($95/145/179 for 3/5/7 attractions on the Flexi Pass, $199/219 for 3/7 day Unlimited Attraction Pass).

Greeter Service A free Greeter Service matches up visitors with local volunteers for 2–4 hours (starting from 9.30am), giving them an unparalleled insider's view of the city – book at least 24hr in advance up to four months ahead (☎03 9658 9658 Mon–Fri 7.30am–6pm or ☎03 9658 9942 Sat & Sun 9am–6pm).

Visit Victoria The Visit Victoria website provides a wealth of information on attractions, accommodation and events (ⓦvisitvictoria.com).

Visitor Information Booth Bourke Street Mall; Daily 9am–5pm.

Parks Victoria For information on national parks and conservation areas in Victoria (☎13 19 63, ⓦparkweb .vic.gov.au).

National Trust A good resource selling several historical walking-tour guides (Tasma Terrace, 4 Parliament Place, East Melbourne; Mon–Fri 9am–5pm; ☎03 9656 9800, ⓦnationaltrust.org.au).

TOURS

Freddy's Bike Tours (☎0431 610 431, ⓦfreddysbike tours.com.au) A good way of getting a handle on Melbourne is to join an All-in-One City Tour (4.5hr; $49 everything included, bookings essential). Tours depart from the Freddy's Bike Tours shop in Batman Park (next to the Melbourne Aquarium) at 11am daily between Oct and May and on weekends by request June to Sept.

Melbourne By Foot Comprehensive tours of the city led by knowledgeable local guides (☎1300 311 081, ⓦmelbournebyfoot.com). The Daily Cultural Walk (3hr; $40) covers many facets of Melbourne's unique culture, including street art, cafés, music and sport, with insights into local history. Alternatively, the Beer Lover's Tour on Thursdays and Saturdays (3hr; $85 including beer tastings and a burger) explores the city's long fascination with beer and pub culture, with a focus on beers from Victorian microbreweries.

8

RIVER AND BAY CRUISES

Most cruises ply the **Yarra River** and the upper reaches of Port Phillip Bay (called Hobsons Bay) between St Kilda and Williamstown at the mouth of the Yarra. A cruise on the western suburbs' **Maribyrnong River** reveals a side of Melbourne tourists don't usually get to see, and contrary to local (eastern suburbs) prejudices, it is not all factory yards and oil-storage containers either. The main departure points in the city for cruises along the Yarra River are **Federation Wharf**, at the southern end of Federation Square, **Southgate** and, further west, **Williamstown**. All cruises run weather permitting; in the cooler months (May–Sept) the last scheduled departures of the day may be cancelled.

Blackbird Maribyrnong Cruises (☎03 9689 6431, ⓦblackbirdcruises.com.au). Depart from Wingfield St and land at Footscray. The Maribyrnong River Cruise passes Flemington Racecourse, Footscray Park and various other parklands to Essendon and shows the tranquil and pretty side of the supposedly drab Western suburbs (2hr; departs Tues, Thurs, Sat & Sun 1pm; $20), while the Port of Melbourne Cruise takes in the industrial aspects of the lower Maribyrnong and Yarra rivers plus the Docklands development (1hr; departs Tues, Thurs, Sat & Sun at 4pm; $10). Take the train to Footscray station (Watergarden/Werribee line) or take bus #216/#219 from the city to Sunshine, and get off at bus stop 17.

City River Cruises (☎03 9650 2214, ⓦcityrivercruises. com.au). Offers five departures daily (10am–3.30pm; additional departures in summer; $23). Buy tickets at the Princes Bridge booth at the southern end of Flinders Street Station or via the website.

Melbourne River Cruises (☎03 8610 2600, ⓦmelbcruises.com.au). Run their city cruise five to six times daily, departing from Berth 5, Southgate and Federation Wharf. Tickets are available at the blue kiosks at Southgate or online. The River Garden Cruise (1hr 15min; $23) heads upriver past South Yarra and Richmond to Herring Island. The Port and Docklands Cruise (1hr 15min; $23) runs downriver past Crown Casino and Melbourne Exhibition Centre to the Westgate Bridge. Combined up- and downriver cruises cost $29. In addition, cruises to Williamstown and back (approx 1hr; $29) leave hourly (daily; 11.30am–3.30pm, less frequently in the cooler months).

Williamstown Ferries (☎03 9682 9555, ⓦwilliamstown ferries.com.au). Run between Williamstown and Southgate in the west of the city. Departures leave from Southgate's berth hourly between 10.30am and 4.30pm, or from Williamstown from 11.30am to 4.30pm ($18 one-way, or $28 return).

8

TOURS FROM MELBOURNE

There is a plethora of tour companies running trips from Melbourne. With options for the backpacker budget right up to luxury experiences, it's easy to organize day-trips to Phillip Island, the Yarra Valley, the Mornington Peninsula, the Grampians and the Great Ocean Road, as well as overnight (or longer) tours further afield.

Autopia Tours ☎ 03 9393 1333, ⓦ autopiatours .com.au. Long-established outfit running popular day-trips by minibus along the Great Ocean Rd ($135), to Phillip Island ($120) and the Grampians ($135), plus a combined tour to the Great Ocean Rd and the Grampians (3 days; $425), including dorm accommodation and most meals.

Bunyip Tours ☎ 1300 286 947, ⓦ bunyiptours.com. Nature-focused tours with lots of bushwalking, mainly to Wilson's Promontory (1–3 days; $125–439). The tours can be combined with the Phillip Island Penguin Parade on the way back to Melbourne. A three-day tour of the Great Ocean Rd and the Grampians costs $380, and a one-day sunset tour is $130, including lunch. Small groups.

Echidna Walkabout ☎ 03 9646 8249, ⓦ echidnawalkabout.com.au. Long-running upmarket ecotour operator, with very small groups and enthusiastic, extremely knowledgeable guides, focusing on native wildlife. The Koalas and Kangaroos In the Wild day-tour ($210) goes to Serendip Sanctuary and the You Yangs, southwest of Melbourne, while the four-day Wildlife Journey heads out to more remote parts of East Gippsland, and includes bushwalks; accommodation is in good-quality B&Bs ($1650).

Go West ☎ 03 9485 5290, ⓦ gowest.com.au. This small-group tour company is primarily aimed at the backpacker market, and offers day-trips to the Great Ocean Rd, Grampians, and Yarra Valley ($130), and to Phillip Island ($135); tours are very good value, entertaining and informative.

Groovy Grape ☎ 1800 661 177, ⓦ groovygrape.com.au. One-way tour specialist offering regular trips between Melbourne and Adelaide via the Great Ocean Rd and the Grampians (3 days; $435 including all meals and shared accommodation).

Melbourne's Best Tours ☎ 1300 130 550, ⓦ melbournetours.com.au. More conventional half-day and full-day tours to various destinations including Mt Buller ($125), and Ballarat and Sovereign Hill ($170). Max 24 people.

One Stop Adventures ☎ 03 9693 3704, ⓦ onestopadventures.com.au. One-way trips from Melbourne to Adelaide (2–6 days, $259–$879), Alice Springs (10 days, $1210), Brisbane (8 days, $1089), Cairns (26–41 days, $2189–$3639) and Darwin (17 days, $2069). The Sydney via Canberra tour (2 days $315) explores the high country, and includes overnight accommodation at an authentic Aussie farmstay.

Penguin Island Tours ☎ 03 9629 5888, ⓦ penguinislandtour.com.au. As the name suggests, it focuses primarily on day-trips to see penguins (from $119) and does it well, with good 24-seat minibuses equipped with DVD players.

ACCOMMODATION

The most obvious areas with a concentration of **accommodation** are the CBD, and the adjoining suburbs of North Melbourne, Carlton, Fitzroy, East Melbourne and Richmond. Some of the cheap accommodation areas on the fringes of the city centre are fairly dead at night, though they're within easy reach of all the action. South of the CBD, South Melbourne, Albert Park, South Yarra, St Kilda and Windsor (see map, p.734) are handy for both the city centre and the beach, and with lots of good eating options. St Kilda is very lively, if a bit rough around the edges, with a few hostels and a number of **motels** and **apartments**.

The most exclusive **hotels** are in the CBD, particularly around Collins St and the leisure precincts of Southgate and the Crown Casino, while there's a collection of revamped hotels around Southern Cross Station. For **last-minute discounts**, check out ⓦ wotif.com. Melbourne has plenty of **backpacker accommodation**, ranging from fairly basic, scruffy places to smart, custom-built **hostels** with all the mod cons. During winter, most hostel beds cost around $25, rising to around $35 in summer. Most hostels have separate dorms for females on request. Standard facilities include a kitchen, TV room, laundry, luggage storage and internet access. For those with their own transport, **campsite cabins** are an inexpensive option but they are located far from the city centre.

CENTRAL MELBOURNE

HOTELS AND MOTELS

Art Series – The Blackman 452 St Kilda Rd ☎ 03 9039 1444, ⓦ artserieshotels.com.au/Blackman; map pp.738–739. The hotel showcases the work of artist Charles Blackman, as well as providing boutique facilities in boldly designed suites and rooms, a French-inspired deli/café and an Italian restaurant. Studio $\overline{$220}$

Batman's Hill 623 Collins St ☎ 03 9614 6344, ⓦ batmanshill.com.au; map pp.738–739. An elegant exterior belies modern interior. The wide range of facilities includes bars, a restaurant and 24hr room service. $\overline{$149}$

ACCOMMODATION DURING SPORTING EVENTS

If you plan on staying during the big **sporting events**, be aware that virtually all accommodation tends to be booked out months in advance. This applies particularly during the Australian Open Tennis in Jan and the Formula 1 Grand Prix (mid-March); other events and times to avoid or prebook far in advance are the Melbourne Cup (first Tues in Nov & the preceding weekend) and the AFL Grand Final (last Sat in Sept).

Brady Hotel Central Melbourne 30 Little La Trobe St ☎03 9650 9888, ⓦbradyhotels.com.au; map pp.738–739. Offers 146 modern apartments and guest rooms located on the vibrant northern edge of the CBD. Facilities include a gym, business centre, café/bar and room service. **$140**

Citadines Apart'Hotel 131–135 Bourke St ☎03 6272 7272, ⓦcitadines.com.au; map pp.738–739. Good-value serviced apartments in a central location with fantastic views of the city. Suitable for long or short stays, with spacious bathrooms and clean, well-appointed kitchens. Facilities include a restaurant, fitness centre, swimming pool and sauna as well as a laundry service. **$160**

Jasper Hotel 489 Elizabeth St ☎03 8327 2777 or ☎1800 468 359, ⓦjasperhotel.com.au; map pp.738–739. A complete design makeover has raised this YWCA-owned hostel, across the road from Queen Victoria Market, to boutique hotel status. The 65 rooms are stylishly furnished with queen-size beds, flat-screen TVs and sleek bathrooms. Next door, *Jasper Kitchen* is open for breakfast and well-priced lunches. **$125**

Langham 1 Southgate Ave, Southbank ☎03 8696 8888, ⓦmelbourne.langhamhotels.com.au; map pp.738–739. A modern hotel minutes from Fed Square, with dazzling CBD views but old-fashioned service, with the benefits of a health club, spa and sauna. **$280**

Hotel Lindrum 26 Flinders St ☎03 9668 1111, ⓦhotellindrum.com.au; map pp.738–739. Named after Australia's most famous billiard player, Walter Lindrum, this luxurious five-storey boutique hotel has a distinct charm and comes with a private billiards room as well as a

lounge with open fireplace. The 59 rooms have recently been remodelled and feature commissioned Melbourne artwork and complimentary in-house movies. **$205**

★**Ovolo Laneways** 19 Little Bourke St ☎03 8692 0777, ⓦovolohotels.com; map pp.738–739. Located in the heart of Melbourne's theatre and restaurant district, this funky new hotel has a range of studios and suites with stylish urban decor. Throw in a host of unusual freebies including free minibar (restocked daily), loot bag of snacks, self-service laundry, Apple TV, happy hour at the bar, and iPads available on request, and you've got the *Ovolo*. The only downside is a lack of windows in some rooms. **$230**

Pensione Hotel 16 Spencer St ☎03 9621 3333 or ☎1800 816 168, ⓦpensione.com.au; map pp.738–739. This boutique hotel is popular with cost-conscious business types and travellers. Pleasant and well-maintained, it offers a variety of modern en-suite rooms, finished in soft tones – plus there's a bar, restaurant and rooftop sundeck. Some triple rooms have three single beds and are ideal for budget travellers. Check online for deals. **$124**

Victoria Hotel 215 Little Collins St ☎03 9669 0000, ⓦvictoriahotel.com.au; map pp.738–739. Huge refurbished hotel dating back to 1880 in central location, with its own café, bar, pool and sauna, and a wide range of rooms. Undercover parking available ($20/day). **$120**

BUDGET HOTELS AND HOSTELS

City Centre Budget Hotel 22 Little Collins St ☎03 9654 5401, ⓦcitycentrebudgethotel.com.au; map pp.738–739. Good option for those on a budget who want their own

8

FLAT-SHARING

If you're staying a while and are interested in **flat-sharing**, check the Saturday edition of *The Age* newspaper, as well as the notice boards of hostels, the *Galleon Café* (9 Carlisle St, St Kilda), Readings books and music stores (see p.781), as well as these websites:

EasyRoommate ⓦau.easyroommate.com
Flatmates ⓦflatmates.com.au/melbourne
Flatmate Finders ⓦflatmatefinders.com.au
Flate Share ⓦflatshare.com.au/melbourne
Gumtree ⓦgumtree.com.au
House Share Melbourne ⓦhousesharemelbourne.com.au
Locanto ⓦmelbourne.locanto.com.au
Realestate ⓦrealestate.com.au/share
Share Houses ⓦsharehouses.com.au/melbourne
Share Accommodation ⓦshare-accommodation.net

rooms (shared bathrooms), but the facilities of a hostel. The timber-floored rooms, all on the first and second floors (no lift), are nicely designed, and there's a great rooftop garden. Free tour-booking service are also available. $94

Discovery Melbourne 167 Franklin St ☎ 03 9329 7525, ⓦ discoverymelbourne.com; map pp.738–739. Large, clean hostel close to the Queen Victoria Market. Rooftop BBQ area, kitchen, laundry, cinema, bar and café all under one roof. Dorms $25, doubles $180

Exford Hotel 199 Russell St ☎ 03 9663 2697, ⓦ exfordhotel.com.au; map pp.738–739. Secure, good-value hostel in an extremely central position in Chinatown above a refurbished pub. The four- to ten-bed dorms are a little scruffy, though twins and doubles are better-looking, and there's a tiny sundeck with a BBQ. Shared facilities only. Dorms $31, doubles $90

Greenhouse Backpacker Level 6, 228 Flinders Lane ☎ 03 9639 6400, ⓦ greenhousebackpacker.com.au; map pp.738–739. Clean, very friendly place in a superb sixth-floor location in the heart of the CBD with spacious dorms (four–eight beds), singles and doubles. Good amenities and a pleasant rooftop garden with BBQ. Staff can help with finding work, and there's a travel desk. Rates include breakfast, and free wi-fi. Dorms $37, doubles $98

Melbourne Central YHA 562 Flinders St ☎ 03 9621 2523, ⓦ yha.com.au; map pp.738–739. Big, clean hostel occupying a five-storey building near Southern Cross and Flinders St stations. Facilities include a ground-floor bar and café and a roof terrace. Dorms $39, doubles $113

Urban Central 334 City Rd, Southbank ☎ 03 9693 3700, ⓦ urbancentral.com.au; map pp.738–739. Huge hostel on the city's edge, with modern-looking four-bed dorms, doubles/twins and family rooms, some en-suite. Secure and clean with well-appointed kitchen and cheap meal deals. There's a good travel information desk and affordable bar downstairs. Rates include free tea and coffee, daily breakfast and rice/pasta for meals. Dorms $35, doubles $115

NORTHERN SUBURBS

Downtowner on Lygon 66 Lygon St, Carlton ☎ 03 9663 5555, ⓦ downtowner.com.au; map p.752. Chain hotel with small but stylish en-suite rooms, some with spas, all with TV, tea- and coffee-making facilities. There's also a restaurant, bar and covered parking (included in rates). Ideally situated on Lygon St. $235

Lygon Lodge 220 Lygon St, Carlton ☎ 03 9663 6633, ⓦ lygonlodge.com.au; map p.752. Good motel in central Carlton with 60 attractive rooms, most with small kitchenette and balcony. Free off-street car parking. $135

Melbourne Metro YHA 78 Howard St, off Victoria St, North Melbourne ☎ 03 9329 8599, ⓦ yha.com.au; map p.752. Close to the bus terminal, this huge, modern hostel

– really more like a smart hotel – has family and double/twin rooms, with or without en suite, plus dorms (four–eight beds), and a host of other amenities: kitchen, rooftop garden with BBQ, internet lounge, car parking, plus an in-house travel agent. Dorms $37, doubles $112

★ **The Nunnery** 116 Nicholson St, Fitzroy ☎ 1800 032 635, ⓦ nunnery.com.au; map p.752. Attractive hostel in a former convent and an 1860s two-storey house, with Brunswick St cafés and Melbourne Museum close by. The building retains original stained-glass windows and a grand staircase, and has a range of budget dorms and doubles (shared bathroom) and a cosy TV lounge, courtyard, internet facilities and a kitchen. The newer guesthouse offers slightly more sedate boutique-style accommodation separate from the main building. Weekly rates available. Dorms $32, doubles $120.

EASTERN SUBURBS

Amora Hotel Riverwalk 649 Bridge Rd, Richmond ☎ 03 9246 1200, ⓦ amorahotels.com.au; map pp.738–739. Close to the city, but a world away when you are looking at the peaceful rustic setting of the Yarra River from the river-view rooms. Has good-value packages that include full-buffet breakfasts. Good online rates. $259

Home at the Mansion 80 Victoria Pd, East Melbourne ☎ 03 9663 4212, ⓦ homeatthemansion.com; map pp.738–739. Popular sixteen-room hostel situated in a character-filled heritage building. Offers a range of private and shared rooms, all with large stained-glass windows, flat-screen TV and security lockers. There's also an outdoor café/bar with nightly specials and events. Dorms $27 doubles $90

Magnolia Court Boutique Hotel 101 Powlett St, East Melbourne ☎ 03 9419 4222, ⓦ magnolia-court .com.au; map pp.738–739. Elegant Victorian-era hotel in a quiet street, within walking distance of the CBD. Some rooms come with a kitchenette, sitting room or balcony, and are set across two older, lovingly restored buildings and a newer motel section. Breakfast included. $135

Mantra on Jolimont 133 Jolimont Rd, East Melbourne ☎ 03 9940 2100, ⓦ mantra.com.au; map pp.738–739. Perfect location for sport and entertainment venues, and within walking distance of the CBD. Over 130 modern and bright rooms, most set up for self-catering with kitchen, laundry and lounge/dining areas. On-site pool, gym, restaurant and bar. Studios $100, apartments $110

Richmond Hill Hotel 353 Church St, Richmond, between Bridge Rd and Swan St ☎ 03 9428 6501 or ☎ 1800 801 618, ⓦ richmondhillhotel.com; map pp.738–739. Set in a stately Victorian mansion in a pretty garden, with spacious dining and sitting rooms. Some rooms come with a balcony; economy rooms have shared bathrooms. Doubles $110

SOUTHERN SUBURBS

22 Travellers Accommodation 22 Chapel St, Windsor ☎03 9533 6855, ⓦcsbackpackers.com.au; map p.754. This friendly hostel at the Windsor end of Chapel St, close to St Kilda, offers refurbished, clean dorms and en-suite doubles with free buffet breakfast, tea and coffee. Tight security, internet service and 24hr access. To get there, take the Sandringham-line train from Flinders St Station to Windsor station; the hostel is across the road. Dorms $40, doubles $100

Abode St Kilda 63 Fitzroy St, St Kilda ☎03 8598 0521, ⓦeasystay.com.au; map p.756. Good, secure studio apartments well situated for all the action of St Kilda and within a 5min walk of the beach. The recently refurbished studios are immaculate and come with a kitchenette with dishwasher. When booking, request a studio to the back of the block to avoid the inevitable Fitzroy Street noise. $122

★**Base** 17 Carlisle St, St Kilda ☎03 8598 6200, ⓦstayatbase.com; map p.756. This funky hostel, rated one of the best in Australia, is slick and well managed. There are plenty of communal areas including a bar, kitchen and common room, and all rooms are en-suite. For a few dollars more per night, there's even a girls-only Sanctuary floor (with six- to eight-bed dorms), which provides free champagne in the evening and rents out hair straighteners – this is boutique backpacking. Dorms $28, doubles $130

Claremont Guest House 189 Toorak Rd, South Yarra ☎03 9826 8000, ⓦhotelclaremont.com; map p.754. Restored 1886 Victorian guesthouse in the heart of South Yarra. Over 70 bright, airy dorms and private rooms with recently renovated shared bathrooms. Spotless facilities with super-friendly and helpful staff, laundry facilities, free wi-fi and breakfast included. More "flashpacker" than backpacker. Dorms $58, doubles $106

The Como Melbourne 630 Chapel St, South Yarra ☎03 9825 2222, ⓦcomomelbourne.com.au; map p.754. Stylish hotel that often plays host to visiting celebs and businesspeople. All 111 rooms are spacious, many with full kitchens and the usual facilities, plus the gigantic bathtubs come with a complimentary companion – the hotel's signature rubber duck. *The Como's SOBar* is good for a drink. $215

Cosmopolitan Hotel 2–8 Carlisle St, St Kilda ☎03 9534 0781, ⓦcosmopolitanhotel.com.au; map p.756. Located in the heart of St Kilda, just moments from Acland St, St Kilda Beach and CBD-bound trams, this 86-room hotel offers a range of spacious studios, suites and standard rooms, some with a balcony. Free wi-fi and on-site parking, as well as friendly staff. $137

Habitat HQ Hostel 333 St Kilda Rd ☎03 9537 3777, ⓦhabitathq.com.au; map p.756. Popular and clean, carbon-neutral hostel, offering private rooms with en suite, and four- to ten-bed dorms. Weekly events, free wi-fi and parking, plus a well-equipped kitchen, courtyard and in-house bar. Dorms $44, doubles $139

Hiigh Apartments 153B High St, Prahran ☎03 9533 6558, ⓦhiighapartments.com.au; map p.754. Just 50m from the cafés, bars and shops of Chapel St, these contemporary apartments are functional, albeit on the small side. Apartments contain equipped kitchen, lounge/dining area, balcony and a/c. Weekly rates available. $225

L'Emporia 31 Grattan St, Prahran ☎03 9973 4657, ⓦlemporia.com.au; map p.754. Spacious, modern and well-equipped apartments, all with kitchen, laundry facilities, cable TV and balconies – as well as city vistas from the higher floors. Just three minutes' walk to Chapel St, Prahran market and public transport. $175

★**The Prince** 2 Acland St, St Kilda ☎03 9536 1111, ⓦtheprince.com.au; map p.756. This boutique hotel housed within *The Prince* complex is one of St Kilda's trendiest places to lay your head. Minimalist bedrooms include huge TVs with cable and Bose sound systems, while bathrooms are stocked with deluxe MALIN+GOETZ skin products. Other facilities include a day-spa and relaxation centre, the elegant *Circa* restaurant, *The Prince Public Bar* (see p.774) and a club/band room. $172

Punthill South Yarra Grand 7 Yarra St, South Yarra ☎03 9916 8888, ⓦpunthill.com; map p.754. Stylish aparthotel-style accommodation in the heart of upmarket South Yarra. With Chapel Street's shopping just a block away, and more restaurants than you'll know what to do with, the location is perfect for exploring the southern suburbs and the nearby CBD. Most rooms boast impressive city or bay views from tastefully furnished balconies. $160

Ritz Backpackers 169B Fitzroy St, St Kilda ☎03 9525 3501, ⓦritzbackpackers.com; map p.756. If you like beer and love to party, then this is the place for you. Located in the heart of Fitzroy St (adjacent to a popular pub), with simple rooms. Tiny communal kitchen, but good facilities including a TV lounge, laundry, pool table, electronic security and free towels. Lots of activities and tours as well as free pancake breakfasts each morning. Dorms $31, doubles $90

CAMPING AND CARAVAN PARK

There are no campsites anywhere close to the centre; the nearest is the *Melbourne Big 4 Holiday Park*.

Melbourne Big4 Holiday Park 265 Elizabeth St, Coburg East ☎1800 802 678 or ☎03 9353 8222, ⓦmelbournebig4.com.au. Bus #526 to the city (daytime only, no service Sun). Shady park 10km north of the city, with cabins and camping, plus a communal kitchen and swimming pool. Un/powered sites $48/56, cabins $125

EATING

Melbourne is Australia's premier city for eating out. Sydney may be more style-conscious and Adelaide cheaper, but Melbourne has the best food and the widest choice of cuisines – many of which are showcased at the Food and Wine Festival each March (see p.779). In the CBD, Greek **cafés** line Lonsdale St between Swanston and Russell sts, while Little Bourke St is the home of Chinatown. Lygon St, in inner-suburb Carlton, is just one of many places across the city with a concentration of Italian **restaurants**. Nearby, Brunswick St in Fitzroy and Smith St in neighbouring Collingwood both have a huge variety of international cuisines as well as trendy bars and cafés. Indeed, Fitzroy and St Kilda, another gastronomically mixed bag, are the centres of bar and café society; St Kilda also has great restaurants, bakeries and delis, as does Jewish Balaclava (aka East St Kilda). In Richmond, Vietnamese places dominate Victoria St, but you'll also find cheap Middle Eastern and Burmese food.

Some licensed restaurants allow you to bring your own (**BYO**) drink, though check first. Most places only allow you to bring in wine, which usually incurs a corkage fee ($5–10 per bottle). If you're going to be around for a while, *The Age Cheap Eats*, and its more upmarket companion, *The Age Good Food Guide*, are books worth the investment. For those on a **budget** looking for the best food and drink specials, try the witty ⓦ thehappiesthour.com.

CITY CENTRE

You can still find the odd old-fashioned coffee lounge in the city – the type of place where you can get a milky cappuccino and grilled cheese on toast – but stylish cafés with smarter decor and more diverse menus now set the scene. Hardware Lane, Degraves St and Centre Place are fantastic examples of Melbourne's love for laneways and good coffee. The cheapest places to eat are food halls like those in the major department stores and Southgate by the river, while the QV complex on Lonsdale St also has several good options.

CAFÉS

A Little Bird Told Me … 29 Little La Trobe St ⓦ alittlebirdtoldmecoffee.tumblr.com; map pp.738–739. Chic Scandinavian-inspired decor and coffee to die for, thanks to talented baristas and a pedigree house coffee blend (Seven Seeds, for those playing at home). Large communal tables with quirky terrariums. A perfect spot to people-watch and snack on delicious carrot cake ($5). Mon–Fri 7am–5pm, Sat 9am–4pm.

★**Brother Baba Budan** 359 Little Bourke St ☎03 9606 0449; map pp.738–739. Other than cakes and pastries, they don't serve food at *Brother Baba Budan* – it's all about the coffee ($4), which is excellent. Primarily a takeaway joint, there are a few seats around a central communal table (in addition to the dozens hanging from the ceiling). Mon–Sat 7am–5pm, Sun 8am–5pm.

Hardware Societe 120 Hardware St ☎03 9078 5992; map pp.738–739. It may be tiny, but the French-and-Spanish-inspired menu pulls in the crowds. After a breakfast of baked eggs and chorizo ($18), the rows of baked goods that line the counter are hard to pass up. Attached is the Mini Marche, selling imported European treats. Mon–Fri 7.30am–3pm, Sat & Sun 8.30am–2pm.

Hopetoun Tea Rooms Shop 2, Block Arcade, 282 Collins St ☎03 9650 2777, ⓦ hopetountearooms.com; map pp.738–739.au. Traditional tea, scones and delicious cakes have been served in these elegant surroundings for

over a hundred years. Daily High Tea ($50) is extremely popular, so book ahead or miss out. Meals $20. Mon–Sat 8am–5pm, Sun 9am–5pm.

Pellegrini's Espresso Bar 66 Bourke St ☎03 9662 1885; map pp.738–739. Melbourne's first espresso bar is still an institution, with a classic 1950s interior and platefuls of cheap Italian fare (spag bol, risotto, meatballs) presented at the counter at lightning speed for around $18. Also good for coffee and home-made cakes. Mon–Sat 8am–11.30pm, Sun 11am–8pm.

RESTAURANTS

Bar Lourinha 37 Little Collins St ☎03 9663 7890, ⓦ barlourinha.com.au; map pp.738–739. It might look like a wine bar, but it's the tapas people come for. Dishes, such as house-made chorizo with Nicola potatoes, can be seen being made in the open kitchen ($8–28). Mon–Thurs noon–11pm, Fri–Sat noon–1am.

Chin Chin 125 Flinders Lane ☎03 8663 2000, ⓦ chinchinrestaurant.com.au; map pp.738–739. Big flavours and Southeast Asian share plates are the modus operandi at this hawker-style dining hall. If you can't decide what to eat, just say, "Feed Me" and, for $69, you'll be served a selection. Grab a drink at *GoGo Bar* downstairs before or after dinner and check out the Chin Chin Wall of Art in the laneway next to the restaurant. No bookings. Mains $26. Daily 11am–late.

Crossways Food for Life 123 Swanston St ☎03 9650 2939 ⓦ crosswaysfoodforlife.com.au; map pp.738–739. Indian-style vegetarian food prepared by Hare Krishna devotees, some practising vows of silence. At $7.95 for an all-you-can-eat set lunch/dinner, this is a cheap, healthy belly-filler in town. Mon–Sat 11.30am–8.00pm.

Cumulus Inc. 45 Flinders Lane ☎03 9650 1445, ⓦ cumulusinc.com.au; map pp.738–739. Hugely popular café-restaurant in a bright, airy dining hall at the top end of Flinders Lane. The contemporary menu includes an impressive six varieties of oyster and the restaurant's delectable signature, whole slow-roast lamb shoulder to

8

share ($75). Reservations only available for groups of more than six. Mon–Fri 7am–11pm, Sat & Sun 8am–11pm.

Dinner by Heston Level 3, 8 Whiteman St, Southbank ☏03 9292 5777, ⊕dinnerbyheston.com.au; map pp.738–739. Owned by celebrity chef Heston Blumenthal, the modern (and slightly eccentric) dishes here are inspired by their roots in medieval cuisine, such as the signature dish "Meat Fruit" (chicken liver parfait with mandarin; $38). Daily 5.30–11.00pm & Fri–Sat noon–2.30pm.

Don Don 198 Little Lonsdale St ☏03 9670 7113; map pp.738–739. Easily one of the cheapest, heartiest and best feeds for under $10 in Melbourne. *Don Don's* small menu is limited to a selection of "Don" varieties (short for "*donburi*", a Japanese rice dish; $7.50), but they do them extremely well. Daily 11am–9pm.

Grossi Florentino 80 Bourke St ☏03 9662 1811, ⊕grossiflorentino.com; map pp.738–739. A Melbourne institution. Downstairs, the grill restaurant (mains $40) and the adjacent cellar bar (counter meals $18) serve home-style pasta dishes, drinks and good coffee, while upstairs is a very pricey and elegant Italian restaurant (three-course set menu $140). Mon–Sat 7.30am–late.

Hofbrauhaus 18 Market Lane ☏03 9663 3361, ⊕hofbrauhaus.com.au; map pp.738–739. Head here for large servings of Bavarian fare, including whopping schnitzels. Help it all go down with some German beer on tap, because the other patrons will be. Also provides knee-slapping entertainment. Mains $25–45. Daily noon–late.

Journal 253 Flinders Lane ☏03 9650 4399, ⊕journalcafe.com.au; map pp.738–739. Sympathetically integrated into an education college – which uses the kitchen as a classroom – chic *Journal* has a limited menu of excellent Italian dishes. Breakfast around $10, mains $16. Mon–Wed 7am–9pm, Thurs–Fri 7am–11pm, Sat–Sun 7am–5pm.

★**Mamasita** 1/11 Collins St ☏03 9650 3821, ⊕mamasita.com.au; map pp.738–739. A meal at popular, bustling *Mamasita* is an experience in itself. The majority gluten-free Mexican menu consists of shared family-style meals (think sticky short ribs with jalapeño *crema*; $30) and smaller items such as tacos and quesadillas ($6). The extensive tequila and mescal lists could make it an outing your head won't soon forget. Mon–Sat noon–late, Sun 12.30pm–10pm.

★**Meatball & Wine Bar** 135 Flinders Lane ☏03 9654 7545, ⊕meatballandwinebar.com.au; map pp.738–739. Life is simple at *Meatball*: first, you select your balls (beef, pork, chicken, fish or veggie), then a sauce (red, white or green) and finally, something for under your balls (creamy polenta or Italian beans, for example). After, you may have room for ice cream sandwiched between two macaroons ($12). Meatballs $18. Mon–Fri 8am–1am, Sat & Sun 11am–1am.

Melbourne Hwaro Korean BBQ 562 Little Bourke St ☏03 9642 5659, ⊕hwaro.com.au; map pp.738–739.

Authentic Korean BBQ, as evidenced by the service bells on the tables and the hoards of Korean expats who frequent this place daily. The *kimchi* pancake ($15) is the best this side of Seoul. BBQ dishes from $15. Daily 5–11pm.

MoVida 1 Hosier Lane ☏03 9663 3038, ⊕movida.com; map pp.738–739.au. Tables are scarce at this busy tapas bar-restaurant, but grab a seat at the bar or on the couch and soak up the Spanish flavours. Spanish beers and wine complete the vibe. Tapas $4–12, set-menu banquet $80. Daily noon–late.

Red Spice Road 27 McKillop St ☏03 9603 1601, ⊕redspiceroad.com; map pp.738–739. Tasty, modern Southeast Asian cuisine dished up in generous servings. The dark wood floors and low red lighting, cast from what is possibly the biggest lantern in Melbourne, gives an intimate feel to the large communal tables. The daily banquets ($69–99) are the best way to sample a bit of everything. Daily noon–3pm, and 5pm–late.

Stalactites 177 Lonsdale St ☏03 9663 3316, ⊕stalactites.com.au; map pp.738–739. Operating for over thirty years, this recently spruced-up Greek restaurant serves giros ($27), *saganaki* (traditional deep-fried cheese, $12.50), souvlaki ($13.50) and moussaka ($26) all dished up in huge portions in a congenial dining area. Most Melburnians have eaten here at least once. Daily 24hr.

Syracuse 23 Bank Place ☏03 9670 1777, ⊕syracuserestaurant.com.au; map pp.738–739. Situated in a small laneway, *Syracuse's* bright interior is timeless, with its arched ceiling, large wall mirrors, bentwood chairs and wood racks stacked with wine bottles. Come for mouthwatering tapas (from 3pm), then follow it with fantastic cheese plates, accompanied by one of the many wines on offer, and finish up with crème caramel and coffee. Mains from $28. Mon–Fri 7am–late, Sat 6pm–late.

Vue De Monde Level 55, 525 Collins St ☏03 9691 3888, ⊕www.vuedemonde.com.au; map pp.738–739. Regarded as one of the country's best restaurants, where chef Shannon Bennett blends fine French cuisine with contemporary imagination. It's not cheap (four-course set menu $230, degustation $275), but you'd struggle to find better anywhere. An excellent-value lunchbox ($18) can be purchased next door at *Café Vue*. Lunch Thurs–Sat from noon, dinner daily 6–9pm.

CHINATOWN

Yum cha (also known as *dim sum*, a series of small delicacies served from trolleys) is available at lunchtime almost everywhere in Chinatown; on Sun it's a crowded ritual.

Camy Shanghai Dumplings 23 Tattersalls Lane ☏03 9663 8555; map pp.738–739. If you don't mind a queue for a cheap meal at a Melbourne institution, head here for large portions of authentic Chinese dumplings and noodles, and complimentary Chinese tea. No-frills service, bright lighting and plastic cups are the norm. BYO alcohol, or buy a Tsingtao in-house ($6). Mains under $10. Daily 11.30am–10pm.

Flower Drum 17 Market Lane, between Bourke & Little Bourke sts ☎03 9662 3655, ⓦflowerdrum .melbourne; map pp.738–739. The finest Chinese restaurant in Melbourne, if not Australia. Its sophisticated Cantonese cuisine (Peking duck, Hainanese pork, *yi-meen* noodles) and discreet service have garnered it a clutch of top awards. Naturally, this all comes at a price: expect to pay at least $120 for the four-course chef's menu. Mon–Sat noon–3pm & 6–11pm, Sun 6–10.30pm.

HuTong Dumpling Bar 14 Market Lane ☎03 9650 8128, ⓦhutong.com.au; map pp.738–739. Very popular three-storey dumpling bar – a little fancier than some of its counterparts, but the extra dollar or two is worth it. The *xiao long bao* (spiced pork dumpling) is a crowd favourite ($11.80/eight pieces), but the list of other regional specialities is equally appetizing. Daily 11.30am–3pm & 5.30–10.30pm.

Longrain 40–44 Little Bourke St ☎03 9671 3151, ⓦlongrain.com; map pp.738–739. In a lively converted warehouse at the top of Little Bourke St, *Longrain* is an explosion of flavours and noise. The modern Thai food packs punches of chilli, lime and coriander, and the slick service ensures you are in and out in time for the next sitting. The egg-net pork ($32) and green papaya salad ($15) will bring you back again. Daily 6pm–late, and Fri noon–3pm.

Shark Fin House 131 Little Bourke St ☎03 9663 1555, ⓦsharkfin.com.au; map pp.738–739. Award-winning *yum cha* specialists located in a converted three-storey warehouse that is the quintessential Chinese eating experience: preposterously loud, closely packed tables adrenaline-charged staff. Mains $28, banquet $38.80. Daily 11.30am–3pm & 5.30–11pm.

CARLTON

Lygon St, between Grattan and Elgin streets, is the hub of Carlton, mainly consisting of wall-to-wall Italian pizza and pasta restaurants spilling out onto the footpath, and on most evenings all but the most resolute-looking passers-by are accosted by their touts. Cheap Asian noodle bars on and around Lygon St cater to the large number of Asian students at Melbourne Uni and RMIT.

Abla's 109 Elgin St ☎03 9347 0006, ⓦablas.com.au; map p.752. A homely restaurant serving some of the best Lebanese food in town. The ten-course banquet for $60 is magnificent. Mains $28. Mon–Sat 6–10pm, also Thurs & Fri noon–3pm.

★ **The Beaufort** 421 Rathdowne St ☎03 9347 8171, ⓦthebeaufort.com.au; map p.752. Cocktails, good times and smoked ribs are the name of the game here, but vegetarians are looked after just fine too. Small BBQ menu done well. Share the "Feed Me Meats" options with a mate

for $35–55, coupled with a whisky from the extensive selection. Mon–Thurs 4pm–late, Fri–Sun 1pm–late.

Brunetti 380 Lygon St ☎03 9347 2801, ⓦbrunetti. com.au; map p.752. Back at its original home on Lygon St, what began as a cake shop 30 years ago is now a café, licensed restaurant, *paninoteca*, *gelateria* and *pasticceria* with an array of display cases filled with a mouthwatering selection of chocolates, pastries and cakes, plus coffee. Mini desserts from $2.50, mains $18. Daily 6am–late.

D.O.C. Pizza & Mozzarella Bar 295 Drummond St ☎03 9347 2998, ⓦdocgroup.net; map p.752. A far cry from the Lygon St trattorias, *D.O.C.* is modern, delicious and cool. Arguably some of the best pizzas in Melbourne are made here – perfectly crunchy thin crusts with uncomplicated toppings like prosciutto with buffalo mozzarella and tomato ($24.90). Pizza from $18. Mon–Wed 6pm–late, Thurs–Sun noon–late.

Jimmy Watson's 333 Lygon St ☎03 9347 3985, ⓦjimmywatsons.com.au; map p.752. Formerly a wine salon, this Lygon St icon has survived the vagaries of Melbourne's food and drinking trends. The strengths are its very good bar meals (mod-Oz cuisine) in convivial, atmospheric surroundings, and a superb wine list. Mains $25. Mon–Sat 11am–11pm, Sun 1–7pm.

Shakahari 201–203 Faraday St ☎03 9347 3848, ⓦshakahari.com.au; map p.752. Excellent and imaginative Asian-influenced vegetarian food such as satays, curries and *laksas* for around $22. Menu changes according to season. Mon–Fri noon–3pm & 6–9.30pm, Sat noon–3pm & 6–10.30pm Sun 6–10.30pm.

Trotters 400 Lygon St ☎03 9347 5657, ⓦtrotters .com.au; map p.752. Against the understated recycled timber backdrop, the trattoria-inspired menu here is unassumingly satisfying – think pan-fried gnocchi with pumpkin and burnt sage butter ($22). Mon–Fri 7.30am–late, Sat 8am–late, Sun 9am–9pm.

FITZROY

Fitzroy's focal point, grungy Brunswick St, is packed with great cafés and pubs, while running at right angles across it is Johnston St, known for its Spanish influence and late-night bars. Dissecting Brunswick St to the south, Gertrude St is fast becoming a chic hub for Melbourne's artistic community and has a couple of cool pubs and cafés.

Babka Bakery Café 358 Brunswick St ☎03 9416 0091; map p.752. A deservedly popular place: the home-made bread and cakes are divine, and Eastern European-inspired dishes from the changing blackboard menu are equally enticing. Try Russian *blintzes* for breakfast ($10) or lamb and dried apricot pie for lunch (sandwiches $13.50). Tues–Sun 7am–7pm.

Bimbo Deluxe 376 Brunswick St ☎03 9419 8600, ⓦbimbodeluxe.com.au; map p.752. An endless procession of super-cheap and delicious pizzas – which are

8

only $4 for lunch Mon–Fri & dinner Mon–Sat & all day Sun) plus a few other favourites keep the diners coming back again and again. The large, dimly lit bar out back keeps the drinkers and pool sharks happy. Excellent rooftop bar too. Daily 11.30am–late.

★ **Bluebonnet Barbecue** 32 St Georges Rd South ☎03 9972 1815, ⓦbluebonnetbbq.com.au; map p.752. This smokey Texan BBQ destination is all about the meat. Oak-smoked chicken, home-made sausages, slow-cooked pulled pork and a range of delicious veggie sides. The $42 set menu allows you to sample a bit of everything. Come hungry. Mon–Thurs 6am–10pm, Fri–Sun noon–3pm & 5–11pm.

Charcoal Lane 136 Gertrude St ☎03 9418 3400, ⓦcharcoallane.com.au; map p.752. From the efficient service, clean lines of the interior and contemporary Australian cuisine, you would never guess that *Charcoal Lane* is actually a social enterprise providing meaningful work for disengaged youth. Chef Andy Bedford's dishes (such as parma-ham-wrapped wallaby; $31) ooze with native flavours. Tues–Sat noon–3pm & 6–10pm.

Fitz Curry Cafe 44 Johnston St ☎03 9495 6119, ⓦfitzcurrycafe.com.au; map p.752. Small, no-frills curry house that dishes up delicious, organic food at low prices. Takeaway available. The malai kofta ($12.95) is sublime. Mains $14. Daily 5–10pm.

Jimmy Grants 113 Saint David St ☎03 8419 8800, ⓦjimmygrants.com.au; map p.752. Named after the Aussie rhyming slang for "immigrants", *Jimmy Grants* pays tribute to the Greek heritage of its owner, celebrity Masterchef judge George Calombaris. With a strong focus on no-fuss "souvas" (souvlaki; $12), the simple menu delivers. Sun–Thurs 10am–10pm, Fri & Sat 10am–11pm.

Panama Dining Room Level 3, 231 Smith St ☎03 9417 7663, ⓦthepanama.com.au; map p.752. Climb the nondescript stairwell from Smith St to the atmospheric loft that is the *Panama Dining Room*. A popular spot for Melburnians to catch up over after-work drinks and graze on the European food from the kitchen while looking out over city views. Mains $35. Daily 6pm–late.

★ **Rice Queen** 389 Brunswick St ☎03 9419 6624, ⓦricequeen.com.au; map p.752. Dripping with kitsch Asian decor and happy punters, *Rice Queen* serves up a dizzying mix of mod-oriental share dishes such as baby *banh mi* ($7) and Korean DIY tacos ($23). Out the back there's a private karaoke room for post-dinner/sake singalongs. Bookings recommended. Daily noon–late.

The Vegie Bar 380 Brunswick St ☎03 9417 6935, ⓦvegiebar.com.au; map p.752. Cheap, popular and hip place with simple, fresh vegetarian and vegan food. Licensed and BYO (wine only). Mains $15. Daily 11am–10pm.

COLLINGWOOD AND RICHMOND

Swan St, running from Church St towards Wattle Park, is home to Greek restaurants, while Victoria St, separating Richmond from Abbotsford, is lined with Vietnamese supermarkets, clothes shops and dozens of cheap, authentic restaurants. Adjacent Collingwood's Smith St also has a burgeoning café scene.

★ **Baby** 631 Church St, Richmond ☎03 9421 4599, ⓦbabypizza.com.au; map pp.738–739. This is one popular baby! The seasonal menu of over 20 artisan pizzas (the "Funghi" – a mix of buffalo taleggio, *fior di latte*, mushrooms and thyme – is a standout; $23.50) is topped with share platters as well as Italian-inspired breakfast options (try the pecorino, pea and mint poached eggs; $19.50). Mon–Fri 7am–11pm, Sat & Sun 8am–11pm.

Easy Tiger 96 Smith St, Collingwood ☎03 9417 2373, ⓦeasytiger.co; map p.752. A funky Thai restaurant with pleasingly minimal decor: there's just one long canteen table and a scattering of tables for two. Mains (seasonal) can include roast duck and watermelon salad or coconut braised Wagyu beef (both $34). Tues–Sun 6pm–late & Fri noon–2.30pm.

Fonda Mexican 428 Swan St, Richmond ☎03 9429 0085, ⓦfondamexican.com.au; map pp.738–739. Much like the bright decor, the Mexican street-food-inspired dishes at Fonda are colourful and leave a lasting impression. Order and pay at the bar canteen-style, and your margarita ($17) and quesadilla ($16) will be delivered to your table in a flash. Great food with no fuss. *Fonda* can also be found in the CBD and Windsor. Daily 11.30am–late.

Ha Long Bay 82 Victoria St, Richmond ☎03 9429 3268; map pp.738–739. If you're searching for a good Vietnamese restaurant on Victoria St, then this is it. Ignore the lurid lime walls and concentrate on choosing something from the long, long list of dishes. Cheap corkage, and most menu items less than $10. Daily 10am–11pm.

Huxtaburger 106 Smith St, Collingwood ☎03 9417 6328, ⓦhuxtaburger.com.au; map p.752. *Huxtaburger* is a takeaway that sells quality burgers, chips and beer – with a twist. The buns are brioche and the patties are made from grass-fed Wagyu beef. Serving sizes are a little smaller than normal pub fare. Burgers from $13. Daily 11.30am–10pm, Fri & Sat till 11pm.

Meatmother 167 Swan St, Richmond ☎03 9041 5359, ⓦmeatmother.com.au; map pp.738–739. As the name suggests, *Meatmother* is a celebration of all things carnivorous – even the cocktail list features bacon. The whole affair is kept pretty simple: just select your meats ($22–34) and sides ($8), or put your trust in "Mother's Mood" for maximum meat exposure ($45). Wed–Sun 5pm–late, Fri–Sun also noon–3pm.

Pacific Seafood BBQ House 240 Victoria St, Richmond ☎03 9427 8225, ⓦpacificbbqhouse.com.au; map pp.738–739. Despite the name, duck is a particular favourite here, though if that's not your taste, go to the tanks and pick which fish to devour. Great ambience (mains around $20). Licensed & BYO. Daily 11am–10.30pm.

Proud Mary 172 Oxford St, Collingwood ☎ 03 9417 5930, ⊚ proudmarycoffee.com.au; map pp.738–739. Daytime café that does sensational breakfasts ($18) and – some say – the best coffee in Melbourne, made with single-origin beans lovingly roasted in-house and concocted in a gleaming machine that offers a variety of espresso styles. Mon–Fri 7am–4pm, Sat & Sun 8am–4pm.

Po' Boy Quarter 295 Smith St, Collingwood ☎ 03 9419 2130, ⊚ poboyqarter.com; map pp.738–739.. Formerly operating as a creole food truck (Gumbo Kitchen), *Po' Boy Quarter*'s permanent home on Smith St serves New Orleans-style po' boys (stuffed baguettes; $12), gumbo ($13) and a range of cajun sides. Sun–Wed 11.30am–11pm, Thurs–Sat 11.30am–1am.

Thy Thy 1 Level 1, 142 Victoria St, Richmond ☎ 03 9429 1104; map pp.738–739. One of the most popular Vietnamese restaurants in Melbourne. The food, which includes crispy spring rolls, noodles and chicken dishes, is basic but great. Mains $13. Daily 10am–10pm.

SOUTH YARRA, PRAHRAN AND WINDSOR

Caffè e Cucina 581 Chapel St, South Yarra ☎ 03 9827 4139, ⊚ caffeecucina.com.au; map p.754. This became the benchmark for Melbourne's restaurant-café style when it opened in 1988, and has spawned a score of imitators with its wood panelling, cute little table lamps and a creative menu written up on a central blackboard. Today, it's still one of Melbourne's coolest eating spots, attracting a smart clientele and dishing up fantastic pasta. Mains $37. Daily noon–11pm.

★**Hawker Hall** 98 Chapel St, Windsor ☎ 03 8560 0090, ⊚ hawkerhall.com.au; map p.754. Taking its inspiration from the vibrant hawker centres of Singapore and Malaysia, *Hawker Hall* is an energetic beer hall & restaurant, dishing up share plates, to be washed down with any of the eighteen varieties of beer on tap. The pork and chive wontons are tops ($13.50). Mains $16. Daily 11am–late.

★**Lucky Coq** 179 Chapel St, Windsor ☎ 03 9525 1288, ⊚ luckycoq.com.au; map p.754. Renovated old pub with a grungy, bohemian feel. Serves excellent gourmet pizzas at selected times for just $4 (Mon–Fri 11.30am–4pm, Mon–Thurs also 7–11pm, Fri & Sat 7–9pm, Sun noon–11pm) and around $9 at other times. Its late opening hours make it the prime destination for partygoers. Mon–Fri 11.30am–3am, Sat & Sun noon–3am.

Misschu 276 Toorak Rd, South Yarra ☎ 03 9041 5848, ⊚ misschu.com.au; map p.754. *Misschu* has a compact menu specializing in rice-paper rolls, dumplings and vermicelli salads – all served up with quirky, tongue-in-cheek tuckshop flair. Among the favourites are Peking duck pancakes and BBQ pork *char sui* buns, which pair nicely with a slushy of frozen young coconut juice, lychees and fresh mint. Order with a form at the window. Mains $13. Mon–Fri 11am–11pm, Sat & Sun noon–11pm.

Parlour Diner 64 Chapel St, Windsor ☎ 03 9533 2006; map p.752. A modern twist on the all-American diner, dishing up burgers ($16), buttermilk fried chicken ($27), flat-top dogs ($12), curly fries ($7) and jalapeño poppers ($12). Sun–Thurs noon–10pm, Fri & Sat noon–11pm.

Yellow Bird 122 Chapel St, Windsor ☎ 03 9533 8983, ⊚ yellowbird.com.au; map p.752. A Chapel St institution that rarely seems to close, *Yellow Bird* is always catering to a bevvy of faithful locals. Inside, it's a mishmash of retro furniture, fake flowers and wacky trinkets. Out front, heaters and tables allow for people-watching and alfresco dining. A Mexican-infused menu, covering all-day breakfast to dinner and everything in between; the drinks list is equally thorough. Mains $16. Daily 8am–late.

SOUTH MELBOURNE, ALBERT PARK AND PORT MELBOURNE

The night-time scene in these suburbs is rather low-key, but there are cafés and delicatessens aplenty dishing up a mouthwatering selection of food during the day.

Andrew's Hamburgers 144 Bridport St, Albert Park ☎ 03 9690 2126, ⊚ facebook.com/andrewshamburgers. Much-loved and extremely low-key hamburger shop that serves them big and fatty with all the trimmings (around $12). Mon–Sat 11am–9pm.

Balderdash 295 Bay St, Port Melbourne ☎ 03 9077 3813, ⊚ balderdashcafe.com. Housed in this nineteenth-century pub is one serious coffee house. Breakfast and lunch are served more as an accompaniment to the coffee than the other way around, but you will enjoy the food nonetheless. Keep an eye out for lunch specials like paella or spiced lamb. Then have another coffee. Breakfast/lunch $18. Mon–Fri 7am–4pm, Sat & Sun 8am–4pm.

Chez Dre 285–287 (rear) Coventry St, South Melbourne ☎ 03 9690 2688, ⊚ chezdre.com.au. Hidden down an unassuming-looking alley off South Melbourne Market is a treasure-trove of French-inspired sweets: tarts, madeleines, gateaux and macarons that have been made in-house in the open kitchen. Hot food is also on the menu, with all-day breakfast dishes and a range of baguettes. Breakfast $16.50, *petit gateaux* $8.50. Mon–Fri 7am–4pm, Sat & Sun 8am–4pm.

Kamel 19 Victoria Ave, Albert Park ☎ 03 9696 1386, ⊚ kamelrestaurant.com. Cosy, Middle Eastern restaurant with a delectable menu. Delicious meze, seafood or grill dishes, and there's a good vegetarian selection. Daily 5–9pm, Fri–Sun also noon–3pm.

Peko Peko 190 Wells St, South Melbourne ☎ 03 9686 1109. Westernized Taiwanese food with a Japanese edge, in a casual yet lively setting. Start with something from the "small eat" menu, like the five spice tofu ($9), before digging into the signature "pop chicken" (crispy fried chicken cubes; $14). Warning: this dish is seriously addictive. Mon–Sat 11.30am–4pm & 5–9pm.

8

ST KILDA

This suburb's café scene and nightlife revolve around Acland St and Fitzroy St. While the former is good for browsing in shops and for pigging out on cakes, the latter has the edge on nightlife. Carlisle St is the spot for late breakfast and coffees.

Bala's Café 1C Shakespeare Grove ☎03 9534 6116, ⊛balas.com; map p.756. Excellent, cheap Thai and Indian takeaway food, including lassis and lots of stir-fried dishes with ultra-fresh ingredients. There are a few tables if you want to eat in, though it gets very busy at lunch and dinner. Mains $12. Daily noon–9.30pm.

The Banff 145 Fitzroy St ☎03 9525 3899, ⊛banffstkilda .com.au; map p.756. Excellent, cheap pizza and pasta in a cosy ski-lodge atmosphere. Outdoor dining spaces and weekday specials of $6 pizza (all day Mon & Tues and noon–5.30pm Wed–Fri) cooked in an open wood fire make this a year-round winner. Daily 8am–10pm.

Captain Baxter 10–18 Jacka Blvd, St Kilda Sea Baths ☎03 8534 8999, ⊛captainbaxter.com.au; map p.756. Dishing up fresh Asian-themed flavours, meals here are designed to share, such as grilled beef short ribs ($39) and yellow salmon curry ($36.50). The nautical decor fits perfectly with the beachfront locale, and there's a large outdoor deck for lounging and admiring the bay. Mon–Thurs 5pm–late, Fri–Sun noon–late.

Galleon Cafe 9 Carlisle St ☎03 9534 8934; map p.756. Breakfast, served until 4pm, is the big attraction in this retro daytime café, which is especially popular at weekends. The poached egg on sweet potato, basil and feta hash ($15) is amazing. Mains $15. Daily 7am–5pm.

★i Carusi II 231 Barkly St ☎03 9593 6033, ⊛icarusiii .com.au; map p.756. This little St Kilda favourite produces some of the finest artisan pizza in Melbourne. The focus is on deliciously crispy bases, perfect sauce and a few quality toppings – try the *quattro formaggi* (mozzarella, gorgonzola, fontina and parmigiano), or *fungi porcini* (tomato, mozzarella, mushroom and prosciutto; $24.50). Mon–Fri 6pm–late, Sat & Sun noon–late.

Le Bon Continental Cake Shop 93 Acland St ☎03 9534 2515; map p.756. Fifty-year-old store that never fails to tempt the hundreds of passers-by with its array of delicious Mediterranean-influenced cakes and pastries. Don't miss the vanilla slice ($6.50). Daily 8am–11pm.

Lentil as Anything 41 Blessington St ⊛lentilasanything .com; map p.756. Operating on an honesty system where diners choose how much to pay for their meals, this tiny kitchen turns out high-quality organic, vegetarian tucker in generous portions. All proceeds go to community projects that assist local migrants and refugees and create job opportunities for the long-term unemployed. Daily noon–9pm.

Newmarket Hotel 34 Inkerman St ☎03 9810 0087, ⊛newmarketstkilda.com.au; map p.756. Southern Californian street food with a fancy twist and big, bold flavours – think soft-shell crab tacos ($18), cured meats ($18) and rare-breed roasts ($36) from a smoking wood-fired oven. Mon–Thurs four-course special $49. Daily noon–late.

Radio Mexico 11–13 Carlisle St ☎03 9534 9990, ⊛radiomexico.com.au; map p.756. In the Mexican wave that's gripping Melbourne, *Radio Mexico* is a standout. The menu is based around fresh, affordable and fun small/share plates inspired by taco-truck fare. Pumping out meals from a kitchen that looks like a caravan, the service is fast-paced, but there can be a queue for a table, so get there early. The ceviche ($20) is worth the wait. Tacos $7.50, share dishes $20. Mon–Thurs 5pm–late, Fri–Sun noon–late.

Topolino's 87 Fitzroy St ☎03 9534 1925, ⊛topolinos .com.au; map p.756. A dimly lit and noisy St Kilda institution, that churns out cheap pizzas, generous portions of pasta and good cocktails until very late. Pizza $14, mains $26. Mon–Thurs 4pm–late, Fri–Sun noon–late.

Uncle 188 Carlisle St ☎03 9041 2668, ⊛unclestkilda .com.au; map p.756. The name is a throwback to the Vietnamese term of respect, which is also how the chefs treat their Vietnamese menu, which features excellent *pho* ($12) and traditional flavours (such as lemongrass & coconut scotch fillet; $34). Try the "Uncle knows best" chef's selection for $49. Mon–Tues 5pm–late, Wed–Sun noon–late.

DRINKING

Melbourne's fondness for a drink or three is reflected in its abundance of excellent **bars and pubs** – from places so obscure and cutting edge you'll only know they exist by word of mouth, to large establishments catering to broader and louder tastes. In general, bars stay **open** to around 1am during the week and 3am at weekends, while some clubs are open until 5am or 7am at the weekend. Some of the more upmarket places have **dress codes**. A number of places to drink are also listed under "Live music", (see p.775). For online guides to the city's drinking spots try ⊛melbournebars.com.au or ⊛barfinder.com.au, and for special offers and happy hours, visit ⊛thehappiesthour.com.

CENTRAL MELBOURNE

1806 169 Exhibition St ☎03 9663 7722, ⊛1806 .com.au; map pp.738–739. 1806 was named to pay tribute to the year the word "cocktail" was officially defined, but you may be forgiven for thinking it was related to the number of items on its ginormous cocktail menu. These

award-winning drinks are served with a history lesson on the menu of. Mon–Thurs 5pm–1am, Fri 5pm–1am, Sat 5pm–1am, Sun 6pm–1am.

Chuckle Park 322 Little Collins St ☎03 9650 4494 ⊛chucklepark.com.au; map pp.738–739. A cosy outdoor venue, where the bar is housed in a tiny retro caravan and drinks are served in cans and fancy plastic cups. The quirky decor has a backdrop of graffiti and hanging terrarium lanterns, and, of course, astroturf. Daily noon–1am.

The Croft Institute 21 Croft Alley ☎03 9671 4399 ⓦthecroftinstitute.com.au; map pp.738–739.Tucked behind a collection of smelly bins in a zigzagging Chinatown laneway, *The Croft Institute* has an intriguing laboratory theme that has punters drinking cocktails from syringes (sans needle). Three floors, with DJs playing funk, roots reggae and dancehall. Mon–Thurs 5pm–1am, Fri 5pm–3am Sat 8pm–3am.

Double Happiness 21 Liverpool St ☎03 9650 4488, ⓦdouble-happiness.com.au; map pp.738–739. A funky laneway bar with an opium den/communist propaganda theme. Sip on cocktails with names like "Great Leap Forward" and snack on steamed dumplings. Mon–Thurs 5pm–1am, Fri 5pm–3am, Sat 8pm–3am.

Lily Blacks 12 Meyers Place ☎03 9654 4887, ⓦlilyblacks .com.au; map pp.738–739. A cocktail lover's dream with a 1920s speakeasy approach to drinking and decor, *Lily Blacks'* bartenders are known for producing some of the most creative and zestful cocktails around. It's a popular after-work and late-night haunt. Mon–Thurs 5pm 3am, Fri 4pm–3am, Sat & Sun 6pm–3am.

Madame Brussels Level 3, 59 Bourke St ☎03 9662 2775, ⓦmadamebrussels.com; map pp.738–739. Feels like something out of a David Lynch film, with fake grass and florid wicker chairs – and that's inside. Outside, the fantastic tennis-club-themed terrace overlooks the city spires. Cocktails come in jugs. Daily noon–1am.

Melbourne Supper Club Level 1, 161 Spring St ☎03 9654 6300, ⓦfacebook.com/melbournesupperclub; map pp.738–739. Couch-filled lounge bar that manages to be both elegant and relaxed. Cocktails range from affordable to expensive, and there's an extensive wine list; a range of tasty snacks such as veal meatballs will keep the hunger at bay. Sun–Thurs 5pm–4am, Fri & Sat 5pm–6am.

★**Rooftop Bar & Cinema** Level 7, 252 Swanston St ☎03 9654 5304, ⓦrooftopcinema.com.au; map pp.738–739. The seven-storey climb (or lift) up Curtain House is certainly worth it for the views and atmosphere of the *Rooftop Bar*. Astroturf, deck chairs and sun umbrellas make it the perfect summer hangout, and gas heaters keep it surprisingly toasty in winter. From Dec to March, the Rooftop Cinema takes over from 8–11pm most nights. Tues–Sun noon–1am.

★**Section 8** 27–29 Tattersalls Lane ☎0432 291 588, ⓦsection8.com.au; map pp.738–739. *Section 8* is the quintessential Melbourne laneway bar. A shipping container with a window cut into it makes up the bar, and the chairs and tables are comprised entirely of wooden pallets and barrels. With mulled wine and gas heaters in the winter and pitchers of home-brewed Pirates' Punch in summer, it really is one of Melbourne's best city beer gardens. Mon–Wed 10am–11pm, Thurs & Fri

10am–1am, Sat noon–1am & Sun noon–11pm.

Sister Bella 22 Drewery Place (enter via Sniders Lane) ⓦsisterbella.com; map pp.738–739. Hard to find, but that's half the appeal. After locating the unassuming door of the tiny front room, head up the stairs to discover the hidey-hole bar that is *Sister Bella*. Pull up a wooden crate or grandma's floral armchair and enjoy snacking on a toastie. Mon–Sat 4pm–1am, Sun 4–11pm.

Transport Federation Square ☎03 9923 2090 ⓦtransporthotel.com.au; map pp.738–739. Enormous pub complex with a staggering range of beers and local wines. Noisy but fun with DJs and live music most nights, it attracts a mixed crowd. Daily 11am–late.

CARLTON AND FITZROY

Bar Open 317 Brunswick St, Fitzroy ☎03 9415 9601, ⓦbaropen.com.au; map p.752. Classic, shabby-chic Brunswick St bar with a reputation for its chilled-out vibe and dedication to live music (Wed–Sun), and there are often exhibitions showcasing the work of local artists. With the small outdoor beer garden and indoor couches, it feels more like someone's house than a bar. Daily 3pm–3am.

The Everleigh Level 1, 150 Gertrude St, Fitzroy ☎03 9416 2229, ⓦtheeverleigh.com; map p.752. A real bartenders' bar where 1920s American-style killer cocktails such as "The Professor" (a potent blend of gin, pomegranate, lime and absinthe) are whipped up under the vintage chandeliers. One of Melbourne's finest bars, it can be tricky to find, but worth the effort. Daily 5.30pm–1am.

Gertrude Street Enoteca 229 Gertrude St, Fitzroy ☎03 9415 8262, ⓦfacebook.com/gertrudeenoteca; map p.752. An attractive wine bar, where the walls are lined with bottles and books. There's a limited menu, but an enormous wine list. Daily 11am–11pm.

The Lincoln 91 Cardigan St, Carlton ☎03 9347 4666, ⓦhotellincoln.com.au; map p.752. Friendly, revamped corner pub where you can order inexpensive dishes from a blackboard menu in the dining room and wines by the glass from an excellent wine list. Sun–Thurs noon–11pm, Fri & Sat noon–midnight.

Naked for Satan 285 Brunswick St, Fitzroy ☎03 9416 2238, ⓦnakedforsatan.com.au; map p.752. Not a satan-worshipping nudist bar, but a good-time Fitzroy watering hole with a rooftop bar (*Naked in the Sky*). Downstairs, the decor is a mishmash: part distillery, part 1950s pin-up art gallery, part library reading room, but the atmosphere is invariably busy and upbeat. Absolut vodka is infused in-house with flavours like salted caramel or opium and rose, and $2 *pintxo* (snacks on toothpicks) are available around the clock. Sun–Thurs noon–midnight, Fri & Sat noon–1am.

The Standard 293 Fitzroy St, Fitzroy ☎03 9419 4793, ⓦthestandardhotel.com.au; map p.752. Old-school Fitzroy pub (dates back to the 1860s) that is always busy due to the laidback, unpretentious atmosphere and large,

8

leafy beer garden. Hearty pub grub is served at lunch and dinner with snacks available in between. The front bar is decorated with a collection of knick-knacks labelled "retro-funk" by the bartenders, and there is a surprising warren of rooms and nooks to explore. Mon & Tues 3–11pm, Wed–Sat noon–11pm, Sun noon–10pm.

RICHMOND

The Bridge Hotel 642 Bridge Rd, Richmond ☎ 03 9429 5734, ⊛ thebridgehotel.com.au; map pp.738–739. With humble roots as a traditional corner pub, the revamped *Bridge Hotel* retains an old-world charm while adding a dash of new-world flair. Fitted out with its very own street-art-filled laneway, each nook and cranny of this two-storey pub is decorated with a unique theme – from an American diner to photography studio and garden setting. Sun–Thurs noon–late, Fri–Sat noon–3am.

Great Britain Hotel 447 Church St, Richmond ☎ 03 9810 0082, ⊛ thegreatbritainhotel.com.au; map pp.738–739. An excellent pub, hugely popular with the student brigade, with an array of funky couches and chairs, pool tables and a beer garden for long, hot nights. Ask for their famous home-brewed beer on tap called PISS, or sample from the "Boozy Milkshakes" selection (think salted caramel with bourbon; $12). Mon–Thurs 4pm–1am, Fri noon–3am, Sat 4pm–3am, Sun 4pm–1am.

SOUTH YARRA AND WINDSOR

Borsch, Vodka & Tears 173 Chapel St, Windsor ☎ 03 9530 2694, ⊛ borschvodkaandtears.com; map p.754. Harking back to the owners' Polish heritage, *Borsch* specializes in Eastern Bloc vodkas and absinthe. Styled to resemble a Krakow cellar bar, the cosy interior is perfect for sampling the enormous variety of flavoured and infused, in shot, cocktail or hot-tea form. Get there early to nab a table. Mon–Fri 8am–late, Sat & Sun 9am–late.

Leonard's House of Love 3 Wilson St, South Yarra ☎ 0428 066 778, ⊛ leonardshouseoflove.com.au; map p.754. Imagine the interior of a 1970s ski chalet – pine surfaces, roaring fireplace, taxidermied hunting trophies and the like – and you'll get an idea of what *Leonard's House of Love* is about. Choose from one of the many nooks, or head out to the spacious beer garden and enjoy the scent of BBQ wafting from the kitchen. Daily noon–late.

ST KILDA

Elephant and Wheelbarrow 169 Fitzroy St ☎ 03 9534 7888; map p.756. Corny English-themed pub, enormously popular with backpackers looking for love and good times. Has cover bands at the weekend. Daily noon–late.

The Esplanade Hotel 11 Upper Esplanade, St Kilda ☎ 03 9534 0211, ⊛ espy.com.au; map p.756. A St Kilda institution, famous for its beachside views and grungy drinking scene. Bands play every night and there are inexpensive meals from *The Espy Kitchen* at the rear, plus pool tables and pinball machines. Mon–Wed & Sun noon–1am, Thurs & Fri noon–3am, Sat 8am–3am.

Freddie Wimpoles 125 Fitzroy St ☎ 03 9525 4041, ⊛ freddiewimpoles.com; map p.756. Housed in the Heritage-listed *George Hotel* building, this hunter-lodge-style bar with its dark woods, antler chandeliers and beer-can display wall is strangely not out of place. Beer is the hero, with 12 rotating taps and many more bottled varieties. Sun–Wed noon–1am, Thurs–Sat noon–3am.

★ **Iddy Biddy Bar** 35–39 Blessington St ☎ 03 9525 3320 ⊛ iddybiddy.com.au; map p.756. This friendly little local on a corner just off the Acland St beat draws in the crowds with regular live music, old-school arcade games, inviting couches and outdoor streetside seating. Beer and cider on tap flow alongside cheap daily meal and drink specials. Sun–Thurs 8am–11pm, Fri & Sat 8am–1am.

The Local Taphouse 184 Carlisle St ☎ 03 9537 2633, ⊛ thelocal.com.au; map p.756. You may not recognize many of the names on the regularly changing craft beer taps, let alone the bottled varieties, but the "beeristas" behind the bar are happy to guide you through your selection. With comedy and live music (Mon, Fri & Sat), trivia (Sun), beer education classes and festivals, as well as a lovely rooftop deck, there's little wonder why St Kilda locals are so loyal to this local. Daily noon–1am.

Misery Guts 19 Grey St ☎ 03 8590 6431, ⊛ miserygutsbar.com; map p.756. The combination of exclusively Australian beers on tap, a perfectly executed classic cocktail list, the best cheese toasties this side of the Yarra, and quirky old-school collectables leave very little to be miserable about. Wed–Mon 2pm–late.

Prince Public Bar 29 Fitzroy St ☎ 03 9536 1176, ⊛ princebandroom.com.au; map p.756. Defiantly local and no-frills, the downstairs public bar of the *Prince Bandroom* (see p.776) has an air of resistance in the face of St Kilda's gentrification. Frequented in equal parts by colourful local identities, visitors and desperadoes, it's a true St Kilda experience. Daily noon–late.

The Vineyard 71A Acland St ☎ 0410 612 926, ⊛ thevineyard.com.au; map p.756. In true St Kilda style, this Acland St staple has long been a place where yuppies and hipsters rub shoulders with "bogans" and "bikies", collectively watching the world go by from prime positions in the outdoor courtyard. Live music and DJs nightly. Go for a drink, stay for the atmosphere. Daily 10.30am–late.

NIGHTLIFE

Melburnians are spoiled for choice when it comes to their nocturnal activities. A big part of the city's status as Australia's "culture capital" can be attributed to the vibrant nightlife and live music scene on offer throughout the city.

ENTERTAINMENT LISTINGS AND BOOKING AGENCIES

Melbourne has a rich arts and music scene with live performances, fashion shows and art exhibits taking place across the city every night of the week; to find out **what's on**, grab *The Age* on Friday, when the newspaper publishes the small entertainment supplement, *EG*. *Broadsheet* (ⓦbroadsheet.com.au) is also a great source for what's on and what's new. Also check out free magazines *Beat* (ⓦbeat.com.au) and *The Music* (ⓦthemusic.com.au). *Melbourne Community Voice* is the go-to for all the happenings in the LGBT community (ⓦgaynewsnetwork.com.au; see box, p.777).

TICKETS

Tickets for most venues can be booked through Ticketmaster (ⓣ13 61 00, ⓦticketmaster.com.au), Ticketek (ⓣ13 28 49, ⓦticketek.com.au) or Moshtix (ⓣ1300 438 849, ⓦmoshtix.com.au); credit card bookings only. You can buy tickets half-price on the day of performance from Half Tix at Melbourne Town Hall (Mon 10am–2pm, Tues–Thurs 11am–6pm, Fri 11am–6.30pm, Sat 10am–4pm; ⓦhalftixmelbourne.com).

LIVE MUSIC

Melbourne has a thriving music scene, and just about every pub puts on some sort of show – often free – during the week. Grungy Richmond has a big concentration of music pubs, as does Fitzroy, while St Kilda is also a worthy area to head to for a range of live music. Most big clubs have a cover charge of around $10. Some backpacker hostels give vouchers for reduced or free admission to a rapidly changing array of venues. Free listings magazines such as *Beat* (ⓦbeat.com.au; see box above) are a good source of information about the local music scene.

CBD, CARLTON, FITZROY AND COLLINGWOOD

170 Russell 170 Russell St, CBD ⓦ170russell.com; map pp.738–739. Formerly *Billboards* nightclub, this spacious underground venue has been in the entertainment biz for nearly half a century. You can view acts in relative comfort from the bar, or head into the overheated mosh-pit below. A mainstay venue for high-profile local and international bands. Times and prices vary according to shows.

Bar Open 317 Brunswick St, Fitzroy ⓦbaropen.com.au; map p.752. You might encounter comedy, or visual performances here. With couches you won't want to get up from dotted over the two floors, it's a perfect place to see what Fitzroy music is all about. Daily 3pm–3am.

Bennetts Lane 25 Bennetts Lane, CBD ⓦbennettslane.com; map pp.738–739. One of Melbourne's most interesting jazz venues, now expanded to include a larger back room to complement the, 1950s-style cellar. Tickets from $18. Daily 8pm–late.

The Curtin 29 Lygon St, Carlton ⓦjohncurtinhotel.com; map p.752. Has a packed schedule of local emerging bands right up to international acts, covering genres from punk to rock and everything in between. There are free live gigs in the front bar on Saturday afternoons. Tickets from $10–25. Mon–Thurs noon–late, Fri–Sat noon–3am, Sun noon–11pm.

Ding Dong Lounge Level 1, 18 Market Lane, CBD ⓦdingdonglounge.com.au; map pp.738–739. A small and busy place that plays host to an impressive array of local and international bands. The focus is on punk and metal, as well as DJs spinning vintage and new wave rock. You won't find any Top 40 pop here. Wed–Sat 9pm–late.

Forum 154 Flinders St, CBD ⓦforummelbourne.com.au; map pp.738–739. One of the most recognized landmarks in Melbourne, the iconic Forum theatre has an extensive history in film, cabaret, comedy and live music. First opened in 1929, it is one of Melbourne's most unique and best live music venues, playing host to international and local bands, singers and comedians. Times and prices according to shows.

Northcote Social Club 301 High St, Northcote ⓦnorthcotesocialclub.com; map p.752. A much-loved local venue for alternative, indie and folk bands, located in the northeastern suburb of Northcote. The intimate band room is a hotbed for up-and-comers, with many now-famous acts starting out on this stage. Mon 4pm–late, Tues–Sun noon–late.

The Rainbow 27 St David St, Fitzroy ⓦtherainbow.com.au; map p.752. Comfy, intimate pub with a mellow atmosphere and interesting crowd, not to mention a good selection of live blues, jazz, funk and roots from local bands three or four nights a week, including Sat. Mon–Thurs 3pm–late, Fri–Sun noon–late.

The Toff in Town 252 Swanston St, CBD ⓦthetoffintown.com; map pp.738–739. Intimate performance space and club/bar on the second floor of Curtin House. Live music most nights, from pop to folk. Sun–Thurs 5pm–3am, Fri–Sat 5pm–5am.

The Tote 71 Johnston St, Collingwood ⓦthetotehotel.com; map p.752. A Melbourne institution for those who like their music loud and raw. Every night of the week, you'll hear bands plying their trade in the dark and dingy band room. With a nice beer garden (including BBQ), colourful characters and good happy hours (6–8pm weekdays), it's

8

easy to see why many consider this Melbourne's best place to hear music. Entry from $5. Daily 4pm–late.

RICHMOND AND ST KILDA

★ **The Corner Hotel** 57 Swan St, Richmond ☎03 9427 7300, ⓦcornerhotel.com; map pp.738–739. A packed schedule of big and small, local and international artists. Also has a great beer garden on the roof. Tues & Wed 4pm–late, Thurs–Sun noon–late.

Dizzy's Jazz Club 368 Bridge Rd, Richmond ☎04 7472 3076, ⓦdizzys.com.au; map pp.738–739. *Dizzy's* blasts out contemporary jazz courtesy of local, national and international acts. The main bar hosts bands nightly (Tues–Thurs 8pm, Fri & Sat 9pm), and fairly regular jazz jam sessions. Bar snacks and food available from the restaurant downstairs. Cover charge $14–20 generally applies. Tues–Thurs 5.30–11pm, Fri & Sat 5.30pm–12.30am.

★ **The Esplanade Hotel** 11 Upper Esplanade, St Kilda ⓦespy.com.au; map p.756. "The Espy" is the soul of St Kilda and of Melbourne's eclectic band scene (playing here is almost a rite of passage), hosting an interesting nightly line-up of bands in the front bar (free) and *Gershwin Room* (small admission charge). Mon–Wed noon–1am, Thurs & Fri noon–3am, Sat 8am–3am, Sun noon–1am.

The Prince Bandroom At The Prince, 29 Fitzroy St, St Kilda ☎03 9536 1168, ⓦprincebandroom.com.au; map p.756. Part of the refurbished *Prince* complex, this is another St Kilda icon that has undergone a face-lift to fit in with the smart cafés and restaurants at this end of Fitzroy St. Upstairs late-night venue with good bands – often free. Paid gigs usually $25–75. Opening hours vary according to line-up – see website for details.

CLUBS

Melbourne's club culture is as lively as its bar scene. The hot spots are Chapel St in South Yarra and the CBD, but clubs take root anywhere they can, from big commercial nights in the suburbs to obscure experimental sessions in inner-city laneways. International DJs visit frequently, and local talent keeps the scene thriving. The bigger the night, the bigger the cover charge, though it rarely tops $15 unless there's an international guest.

Alumbra Shed 9, Central Pier, 161 Harbour Esplanade, Docklands ☎03 8623 9666, ⓦalumbra.com.au; map pp.738–739. Pumping house music until the wee hours in a spectacular location, *Alumbra* is one of the city's most respected clubs. Fri–Sat 10pm–late, Sun 6pm–late.

The Butterfly Club 5 Carson Place, CBD ☎03 9663 8107, ⓦthebutterflyclub.com; map pp.738–739. New city location, same great dash of artsy cocktail bar mixed with a cabaret salon. *The Butterfly Club* is one of the more camp environments. Nightly cabaret. Tues–Sun 5pm–late.

Onesixone 161 High St, Prahran ☎03 9533 8433, ⓦonesixone.com.au; map p.754. For over a decade, *Onesixone* has been a popular spot for late-night antics. Its reasonably small size enables exclusivity, as does its occasional celebrity drop-ins. Thurs–Sat 9pm–late.

Revolver Upstairs 229 Chapel St, Prahran ☎03 9521 5985, ⓦrevolverupstairs.com.au; map p.754. There's live music in the band room most evenings, while most nights in the lounge room DJs spin electronic beats, reggae and dub sounds. Tues–Wed 5pm–4am, Thurs 5pm–6am, Fri 5pm–noon Sat, Sat 5pm–9am Mon.

LGBT VENUES AND CLUB NIGHTS

Melbourne's LGBT venues are concentrated around the areas of South Yarra and Prahran in the south, and Collingwood and Fitzroy in the north. While there are still several staunch LGBT-only bars (see box opposite), the trend is increasingly moving to mixed venues that are LGBT-friendly.

DT's Hotel 164 Church St, Richmond ☎03 9428 5724, ⓦfacebook.com/dtspub; map pp.738–739. Friendly pub that attracts a mixed-LGBT crowd and hosts drag shows every Sat as well as other themed events from BBQs to pool competitions. Daily happy hour drinks specials and music. Tues–Sat 4pm–late, Sun 2–11pm.

GH Hotel 1 Brighton Rd, St Kilda ☎03 9534 4189, ⓦghhotel.com.au; map p.756. Fabulous refurbished St Kilda LGBT institution hosting weekly events including games night (Tues), drag bingo (Wed) and a host of drag-related shows most nights. Daily 4pm–late.

Laird Hotel 149 Gipps St, Collingwood ☎03 9417 2832, ⓦlairdhotel.com; map p.752. Well-equipped men-only venue with two bars, DJs, a beer garden and games room; popular with the leather crowd. Cheap drinks until 10pm. Mon–Sat 5pm–late, Sun 4pm–late.

The Peel 113 Wellington St, at Peel St, Collingwood ☎03 9419 4762, ⓦthepeel.com.au; map p.752. *The Peel* packs the dance floor as far as the eye can see. Multiple bars and mirrors, drag queen DJs and unisex bathrooms. Check website for entry policy. Thurs–Sat 9pm–9am.

Poof Doof 386 Chapel St, South Yarra ☎03 9827 7379, ⓦpoofdoof.com; map p.754. This weekly club night held at *Chasers* nightclub draws in big LGBTIQ crowds with its huge dance floor, mesmerizing laser lights, and, of course, serious beats. Be prepared to party hard. Entry $20. Sat 10.30pm–late.

Sircuit 103 Smith St, Fitzroy ☎03 9416 3960, ⓦsircuit.com.au; map p.752. Predominantly a male crowd, it's men-only on Sat (and Mon–Tues in summer), mixed Wed, Thurs, Fri & Sun. Hosts a fun range of weekly and special events from pool comps (Wed) to underwear (and no underwear) parties. No cover charge for regular nights. Wed–Sun 7.30pm–late.

LGBT MELBOURNE

Melbourne's LGBT scene may not be as in-your-face as Sydney's, but it's almost as big, and is also less ghettoized. Fitzroy, Collingwood and Carlton, north of the river, and St Kilda, South Yarra and Prahran, to the south, boast a strong **gay** presence; Fitzroy, Northcote and Clifton Hill are the city's recognized stomping grounds for **lesbians**.

There is a selection of LGBT-friendly accommodation in these areas (see below) and a host of LGBT-specific club nights around town (see opposite).

LISTINGS

MCV (*Melbourne Community Voice*; ⓦgaynewsnetwork.com.au), a free paper published weekly, is available at LGBT venues.

FESTIVALS

The scene's annual highlight is the fabulous **Midsumma Festival** (mid-Jan to early Feb; ⓦmidsumma.org.au). Held annually since 1988, Midsumma provides an umbrella for a wide range of sporting, artistic and theatrical events, and includes Pride March. There's also the much-celebrated **Melbourne Queer Film Festival** in March (ⓦmqff.com.au), which is the largest LGBT film festival in the southern hemisphere and has been running since 1991.

ORGANIZATIONS, SUPPORT GROUPS, BOOKSHOPS AND RADIO STATIONS

MCV Publishes a free monthly magazine covering news, politics, LGBTIQ issues, health, entertainment and more. Pick it up from Melbourne Town Hall, various cafés and shops around the CBD and suburbs, or online at ⓦgaynewsnetwork.com.au.
Same Same Australian LGBTIQ society and culture website (ⓦsamesame.com.au). Covers local and international news and events, and hosts popular city-based forums.
Switchboard Victoria ☎1800 184 527, ⓦswitchboard.org.au (daily 3pm–midnight). Counselling, referral and information for the LGBTIQ community.
Hares and Hyenas 63 Johnston St, Fitzroy ☎03 9495 6589, ⓦhares-hyenas.com.au. LGBTI bookshop. Mon–Wed 9.30am–6.30pm, Thurs–Fri 9am–7pm, Sat 10am–7pm, Sun 11.30–6.30pm.
Joy 94.9 ⓦjoy.org.au. LGBTI radio station, with 24hr music ranging from classical to R&B and world music, plus news and updates about the arts and club scene.

ACCOMMODATION

For further accommodation possibilities other than those listed below, check out Gay Share (ⓦgayshare.com.au), which arranges house shares for LGBT visitors.

169 Drummond Street 169 Drummond St, Carlton ☎03 9663 3081, ⓦ169drummond.com.au; map p.752. Discreet B&B in a two-storey refurbished Victorian terrace house. Four rooms with en suite. **$135**
Art Series – The Cullen 164 Commercial Rd, Prahran ☎03 9098 1555, ⓦartserieshotels.com.au/ Cullen; map p.754. Boutique hotel featuring the works of Australian artist Adam Cullen. Close to the bars, clubs and cafés of Chapel St and Commercial Rd. **$186**
Laird Hotel 149 Gipps St, Abbotsford ☎03 9417 2832, ⓦlairdhotel.com; map p.752. One of Melbourne's oldest gay pubs, the *Laird* has large, comfortable rooms upstairs, some en-suite, for men only. Rates include Continental breakfast. The service is especially helpful with tips on where to eat and drink. Doubles **$120**, en suites **$140**.

CAFÉS AND MEETING PLACES

i25 espresso/bar 25 Blessington St, St Kilda ☎03 9996 1560, ⓦimbiss25.com.au; map p.756. Serves all-day breakfast, and home-made snacks near busy Acland St. Tuck into a delicious veggie roll ($7.50), or sip on a beautifully crafted latte ($3.50) with the slice of the day ($4). Daily 6.30am–3.30pm.
The Railway Hotel 29 Chapel St, Windsor ☎03 9510 4050, ⓦtherailway.com.au; map p.754. Sitting atop an iconic 24-hour bottle shop, *The Railway*'s sun-drenched deck is popular for its weekly Sunday Session parties, kicking off around 4pm, with a predominantly LGBT crowd. Drink specials between 5pm and 9pm. Snacks and share platters are the way to go – for $25, the whole roasted chicken with stuffing and gravy makes for an easy Sunday roast dinner with friends. Daily noon–late.

8

COMEDY

Melbourne is the comedy capital of Australia, home of the madcap Doug Anthony All Stars, Wogs Out of Work and comedians from TV shows such as *Kath and Kim* and *Have You Been Paying Attention*. The highlight of the comedy year is the **Melbourne International Comedy Festival** in April (see opposite).

Comedy Club@Athenaeum Theatre 188 Collins St, CBD ☎ 03 9650 1977, ⓦ thecomedyclub.com.au. Considered the home of Australia's comedy, this slick, cabaret-style space features largely mainstream comedians, and offers a decent dinner-and-show deal for $49. Shows $29 – book ahead. Fri & Sat 7–11pm.

The Comics Lounge 26 Errol St, North Melbourne ☎ 03 9348 9488, ⓦ thecomicslounge.com.au. Comedy shows six days a week; all formats from stand-up to cabaret. Hosts prominent local comedians plus a stand-up night for comedy newcomers on Tues. Mon–Sat 6.30pm–late.

THEATRE

Melbourne's standing as the centre of Australian **theatre** has been recognized since 1871, when visiting English novelist Anthony Trollope remarked on the city's excellent venues and variety of performances. Nowadays, you can see a host of quality productions most nights of the week, from big musicals to experimental drama.

Her Majesty's Theatre 219 Exhibition St, CBD ☎ 03 8643 3300, ⓦ hmt.com.au. Lavish musicals, from *Billy Elliot* to *Chicago*, in a fabulously ornate old theatre.

La Mama 205 Faraday St, Carlton ☎ 03 9347 6948, ⓦ lamama.com.au. A Carlton institution for over forty years, La Mama hosts low-budget, innovative works by local playwrights.

Malthouse 113 Sturt St, South Melbourne ☎ 03 9685 5111, ⓦ malthousetheatre.com.au. A renovated malthouse containing three venues – the Beckett Theatre, the larger Merlyn Theatre and the studio Tower Room – hosting guest performances, opera, dance, concerts and readings. The resident company – the Malthouse Theatre – produces contemporary Australian plays.

Playhouse Theatre Victorian Arts Centre, 100 St Kilda Rd ☎ 03 9281 8000, ⓦ artscentremelbourne.com.au.

One of the Victorian Arts Centre's Theatre Buildings, offering a wide-ranging choice of programmes, from musical comedy to Shakespeare, as well as plays by the renowned Melbourne Theatre Company.

Princess Theatre 163 Spring St, CBD ☎ 03 9299 9800, ⓦ marrinergroup.com.au. Established at the height of the gold rush, this small, exquisitely restored theatre is one of the city's best-loved venues, and stages musicals such as *Guys and Dolls* and other mainstream theatrical productions.

Regent Theatre 191 Collins St, near City Square, CBD ☎ 03 9299 9990, ⓦ marrinergroup.com.au. This lovingly restored old theatre puts on productions of big-name musicals such as *Wicked* and *Showboat*.

Theatre Works 14 Acland St, St Kilda ☎ 03 9534 4879, ⓦ theatreworks.org.au. Cutting-edge Australian plays in a reasonably large space, formerly a church hall.

CLASSICAL MUSIC, OPERA AND DANCE

The **Melbourne Symphony Orchestra** has a season from Feb to Dec based at Hamer Hall and the Melbourne Town Hall, while the **State Orchestra of Victoria** performs less regularly at Hamer Hall, often playing works by Australian composers. Ticket prices are around $30–80 for classical music performances, and $70–150 for opera.

Chunky Move 111 Sturt St ☎ 03 9645 5188, ⓦ chunkymove.com. Dance company that puts on contemporary dance productions at the adjacent CUB Malthouse, as well as dance classes at the studio.

Hamer Hall Victorian Arts Centre, 100 St Kilda Rd ☎ 03 9281 8000, ⓦ artscentremelbourne.com.au. Big-name concerts and performances by the Melbourne Symphony Orchestra.

Recital Centre Corner Southbank Boulevard & Sturt St, CBD ☎ 03 9699 3333, ⓦ melbournerecital.com.au. Part of the arts precinct, this imaginative new building contains two performance spaces and is a wonderful venue for chamber music.

State Theatre Victorian Arts Centre, 100 St Kilda Rd ☎ 03 9281 8000, ⓦ artscentremelbourne.com.au. Venue for the Victorian Opera and the Australian Ballet Company.

FILM

The Crown Casino, Melbourne Central and the Jam Factory in South Yarra have a number of **cinemas** showing blockbuster movies (cheap tickets available on Tues). The city's vibrant independent cinemas screen less obviously commercial English and foreign-language films; these cinemas tend to offer discounts on Mon. Two annual film festivals take place in the city – Melbourne International Film Festival and Melbourne Underground Film Festival (see opposite & p.780).

ACMI Federation Square ☎03 8663 2200, ⓦacmi .net.au. Film buff's cinema; often shows Australian movies.

Astor Theatre Corner of Chapel St & Dandenong Rd, St Kilda ☎03 9510 1414, ⓦastortheatre.com.au. Classic and cult movie double-bills in a beautiful Art Deco cinema.

Cinema Nova Lygon Court Plaza, 380 Lygon St, Carlton ☎03 9347 5331, ⓦcinemanova.com.au. A rabbit warren of small but comfortable cinemas specializing in art-house and European films. Also hosts Script Alive, where actors read unproduced screenplays. Cheap day Mon.

IMAX Rathdowne St, Carlton ☎03 9663 5454, ⓦimaxmelbourne.com.au. Adjacent to the Melbourne Museum, with a gigantic screen and film reels so big they require a forklift to move them. Shows both 2D and 3D films, mostly documentaries on inaccessible places or anything involving a Tyrannosaurus Rex, but also the

occasional mainstream film specially made in large format.

Moonlight Cinema In the Botanic Gardens on Dallas Brooke Drive ☎1300 551 908, ⓦmoonlight.com.au. Enter at D Gate on Birdwood Ave; films start around 8.30pm ($19). In summer, watching a film under the stars here can be a real treat.

Palace Cinema Como Corner of Toorak Rd & Chapel St, South Yarra ☎03 9827 7533, ⓦpalacecinemas.com.au. A plush, four-cinema complex with a swanky bar area. Screens international art-house releases and hosts Italian and Greek film festivals.

Rooftop Cinema 252 Swanston St, CBD ☎03 9654 5394, ⓦrooftopcinema.com.au. Part of the enticing Curtin House complex, which also contains the bar *Cookie* and the *Toff in Town* (see p.775). Art-house movies, classics and recent releases.

FESTIVALS AND EVENTS

As Australia's "culture capital", Melbourne plays host to a number of lively festivals throughout the year celebrating food, music, film, fashion, culture and the arts. The City of Melbourne council website That's Melbourne (ⓦthatsmelbourne.com. au) has an extensive festivals guide.

JANUARY–FEBRUARY

Australian Open ⓦausopen.com. The last two weeks of Jan see tennis royalty battle it out in the sweltering heat at this world-class grand-slam tournament.

Midsumma ⓦmidsumma.org.au. LGBT festival with arts and cultural events (see box, p.777).

St Kilda Festival ⓦstkildafestival.com.au. Runs for one week in early Feb featuring music, comedy and street performances as well as a huge street festival joining Fitzroy and Acland streets on the final Sun.

White Night ⓦwhitenightmelbourne.com.au. The CBD magically reinvents itself through lights, art and music from dusk till dawn for one night in February every year.

MARCH–APRIL

Brunswick Music Festival ⓦbrunswickmusicfestival. com.au. Takes places in the third week of March, concentrating on folk and world music.

Food and Wine Festival ⓦmelbournefoodandwine. com.au. For 18 days in March, over 250 food- and wine-themed events fill every corner of Melbourne and Victoria with diverse culinary and wine experiences as part of this internationally acclaimed festival.

Virgin Australia Melbourne Fashion Festival ⓦvamff.com.au. An annual two-week-long celebration of fashion and design with world-class runway shows, featuring Australia's established and emerging designers. Takes place in March at various venues around the city.

Melbourne International Comedy Festival ⓦcomedyfestival.com.au. Held in April. Based at the Town Hall in Swanston St, with performances at over fifty

venues around town. For one-off and festival-long performances and other venues, check out the website.

Melbourne Queer Film Festival ⓦmqff.com.au. Presents over a hundred LGBT features, shorts and documentaries (see box, p.777).

Moomba Festival ⓦthatsmelbourne.com.au. Held every March for sixty years, this festival has a rather commercial approach, featuring events such as firework displays and dragon-boat races on the banks of the Yarra River in Alexandra Gardens and Docklands.

MAY–JUNE

Melbourne International Jazz Festival ⓦmelbournejazz.com. The two-week world-class festival brings venues and city streets alive with the spirit of jazz.

Next Wave Festival ⓦnextwave.org.au. Held biennially over two weeks in the second half of May (even-numbered years), and celebrates Victoria's young artists, writers and musicians.

JULY–AUGUST

Melbourne International Film Festival ⓦmiff .com.au. Based at a number of cinemas around the city, the Melbourne International Film Festival, held annually in July–Aug, has been going for over fifty years.

Melbourne Writers' Festival ⓦmwf.com.au. Melbourne is one of only five UNESCO International Cities of Literature, and the two-week Melbourne Writers' Festival celebrates writers, readers and thinkers by hosting a range of free events around the city in late Aug.

8

8

SEPTEMBER–OCTOBER

AFL Grand Final ⓦafl.com.au. The Australian Football League Grand Final is held at the MCG (see p.743) on the last weekend of September each year. While getting tickets to the game is exceptionally difficult, the "footy fever" that engulfs the city is impossible to miss. If you don't have an invitation to one of the thousands of backyard BBQs taking place on the day, head to Fed Square (or any pub) to watch on the big screen.

Melbourne International Arts Festival ⓦfestival .melbourne. Presents a selection of visual and performing arts, featuring Australian and international performers as well as a host of free events at Federation Square and other places around the city during Oct.

Melbourne Fringe Festival ⓦmelbournefringe.com. au. More innovative than the Melbourne International Arts Festival, the Fringe is an independent, multi-art-form festival celebrating diversity and artistic expression.

Melbourne Underground Film Festival ⓦmuff .com.au. Much younger than the International Film Festival, MUFF, taking place in Sept, showcases avant-garde, cutting-edge films.

NOVEMBER–DECEMBER

Carols By Candlelight ⓦcarols.visionaustralia.org. Held on Christmas Eve at the Sidney Myer Music Bowl in Kings Domain (see p.747), Carols By Candlelight has been a Christmas institution since 1938. Popular Australian entertainers perform carols between 8pm and 11pm while the crowds join in. Proceeds go to Vision Australia. Tickets from $70.

Melbourne Christmas Festival Throughout December, the City Square, Federation Square and the Town Hall come to life with Christmas spirit. The kids (and big kids) can meet Santa and admire the giant Christmas tree. At night, the buildings light up with festive projections. All free.

Melbourne Cup Carnival ⓦflemington.com.au. Early Nov sees racing, celebrities and fashion converge on Flemington Racecourse. Culminates with the Melbourne Cup – the "race that stops the nation".

Melbourne Music Week ⓦthatsmelbourne.com.au/ mmw. Across nine days in mid-Nov, over one hundred events (many free) celebrate the bands, artists, venues and punters that make Melbourne a music-loving city.

SHOPPING

Melbourne's big two **department stores**, David Jones and Myer, are located off the Bourke Street Mall, though the city really excels with its independent, funky boutiques. Many places are open seven days a week, especially shops in suburban areas such as Carlton, Fitzroy, South Yarra and St Kilda.

CLOTHES

STREETS AND LANEWAYS

Bridge Rd, Richmond Between Punt Rd and Church St. This is Melbourne's inner-city bargain district: lots of factory outlets, clothes and shoe shops selling seconds, samples and end-of-season stock.

Brunswick St, Fitzroy This edgy street is interspersed with cafés, bars and "cutting-edge" hairstylists, and you'll find lots of small, trendy clothes boutiques and accessories shops. These are great for unusual hats, costume jewellery and "lifestyle" bric-a-brac – think unusually shaped wall clocks or whatever is the latest craze in interior decor. It's also the place to pick up vintage clothes.

Chapel St: South Yarra, Prahran and Windsor Lots of upmarket fashion outlets at the northern (South Yarra) end, getting progressively less expensive, younger and grungier towards Prahran and Windsor in the south.

City Arcades & Lanes In the laneways of the two city blocks bordered by Flinders, Swanston, Bourke & Elizabeth sts. Lots of boutiques and small shops, selling designer brands, unusual fashion and shoes.

Gertrude St Not as high-density as Brunswick St, but with some great independent boutiques and vintage stores.

Hardware St & Little Bourke St Lots of shops selling travel clothing and equipment; head here to kit yourself out for your skiing, hiking or rafting adventures.

Lygon St, Carlton Mainly lined with cafés and restaurants, but there are also a few good shoe shops and fashion retail outlets, most of them at the northern end between Grattan and Elgin sts.

Smith St, Collingwood/Fitzroy Has a number of secondhand clothing stores as well as footwear wholesalers and factory discount outlets, especially the section north of Johnston St.

SHOPPING MALLS

Emporium 287 Lonsdale St ⓦemporiummelbourne .com.au. A mix of local and international designers, with an extensive food court. Sat–Wed 10am–7pm, Thurs–Fri 10am–9pm.

Melbourne's GPO 350 Bourke St at Elizabeth St, CBD ⓦmelbournesgpo.com. This grand, magnificently restored Victorian building is home to high-fashion outlets. Mon–Thurs & Sat 10am–6pm, Fri 10am–8pm, Sun 11am–5pm.

QV Corner of Swanston & Lonsdale sts, CBD ⓦqv.com.au. The latest city development with boutiques clustered in the lanes running from Russell St towards Swanston St, selling high-fashion designer labels. Mon–Thurs 10am–7pm, Fri 10am–9pm, Sat 10am–6pm, Sun 10am–5pm.

BOOKS

The Avenue Bookstore 127 Dundas Place, Albert Park ⓣ03 9690 2227, ⓦavenuebookstore.com.au; map p.756. The stock in this shop is almost overwhelming

– both in subject range and sheer quantity – and the staff really know their stuff. Daily 9am–7pm.

Booktalk Café 91 Swan St, Richmond ☎03 9428 1977, ⓦbooktalk.net.au; map pp.738–739. Great deals on new and secondhand books with a fantastic café nestled within. Daily 8am–5.30pm.

Brunswick Street Bookstore 305 Brunswick St, Fitzroy ☎03 9416 1030, ⓦbrunswickstreetbookstore.com; map p.752. Good independent bookseller, renowned for its huge range of art and design titles, with occasional launches and readings. Daily 10am–9pm.

Grub Street Bookshop 379 Brunswick St, Fitzroy ☎03 9417 3117, ⓦfacebook.com/GrubStreetBookshop; map p.752. Secondhand and antiquarian books specializing in Australian and other fine art. Daily 11am–6pm.

Haunted Bookshop 15 McKillop St, CBD ☎03 9670 2585, ⓦhaunted.com.au; map pp.738–739. With dim lighting and red velour interiors, this is Australia's leading occult, paranormal and mystical bookshop. Mon–Sat noon–5.30pm.

Readings 112 Acland St, St Kilda ☎03 9525 3852, ⓦreadings.com.au; map p.756. This independent bookshop is one of Melbourne's best. Daily 10am–9pm.

MUSIC

Basement Discs 24 Block Place, off Little Collins St, CBD ☎03 9654 1110, ⓦbasementdiscs.com.au; map pp.738–739. Discreet underground space with an exhilarating range of jazz and blues showcased amid inviting sofas and listening stations. Mon–Fri 10am–6pm, Sat 10am–5pm, Sun 11am–5pm.

JB HiFi 282 Chapel St, Prahran ☎03 9514 7500, ⓦjbhifi.com.au; map p.754. Large music retailer selling CDs, vinyl and equipment. Mon–Fri 9am–9pm, Sat 9am–5pm, Sun 10am–5pm.

Northside Records 236 Gertrude St, Fitzroy ☎03 9417 7557, ⓦnorthsiderecords.com.au; map p.752. Choice inner-city music store specializing in cool funk, the latest hip-hop, jazz, electronica and Latin music on CD and vinyl. Mon–Wed 11am–6pm, Thurs & Fri 11am–7pm, Sat 11am–6pm, Sun 1–5pm.

Off the Hip Basement 381 Flinders Lane, CBD (enter via Tavistock Place) ☎03 9621 2044, ⓦfacebook.com/offthehiprecords; map pp.738–739. Specializing in Australian garage, powerpop and rock'n'roll. Hosts in-store performances. Tues 11am–3pm, Wed & Thurs 10am–5pm, Fri & Sat 11am–5pm.

Polyester Records 387 Brunswick St, Fitzroy ☎03 9419 5137, ⓦpolyesterrecords.com; map p.752. An independent record store that supports local and international independent music. They stock one of the largest ranges of new vinyl LPs in Melbourne as well as CDs, tickets, DVDs and books. Mon–Sat 10am–8pm, Sun 11am–6pm.

MARKETS

Abbotsford Convent 1 St Heliers St, Abbotsford ⓦabbotsfordconvent.com.au; map p.752. The Slow Food Farmers' Market (8am–1pm, fourth Sat of the month; $2) has a good number of stalls selling mostly organic produce in a fantastic setting on the banks of the Yarra River. The Collingwood Children's Farm is next door and is a great intermission. The Sunday Market (10am–4pm, fourth Sun of the month; $2) has an outdoor fashion market and indoor arts and crafts stalls.

Collingwood Farmers' Market Collingwood Children's Farm, 18 St Heliers St, Abbotsford ⓦfarm.org.au; map p.752. An idyllic leafy location on the Yarra and great produce including fruit, veg, honey and olive oils. Take a break at the café or snack on burgers or pancakes. Admission $2. Second Sat of the month, 8am–1pm.

Esplanade Market Upper Esplanade, St Kilda ⓦstkildaesplanademarket.com.au; map p.756. A Melbourne institution and particularly nice in warm weather: retreat to the beach afterwards or to one of the cafés on Fitzroy or Acland streets. Features works from artists, fresh produce, secondhand clothing and century-old bric-a-brac. Sun 10am–4pm.

Federation Square Book Market The Atrium, Fed Square ⓦfedsquare.com; map pp.738–739. Choose from over 5000 new and secondhand books in The Atrium at Federation Square. Sat 11am–5pm.

Prahran Market Commercial Rd, Prahran ⓦprahranmarket.com.au.; map p.754. Excellent, upmarket food emporium selling pricey fish, meat, fruit and vegetables. Tues & Thurs–Sat 7am–5pm, Sun 10am–3pm.

Queen Victoria Market Cnr Victoria & Elizabeth sts ⓦqvm.com.au; map pp.738–739. Probably the best-loved of Melbourne's fresh produce markets (see p.742).

Queen Vic Night Market Queen Victoria Market ⓦqvm.com.au/night-market; map pp.738–739. An exciting market with stalls selling unusual food, spices, deli items and gifts. Nov–March & June–Aug Wed 5–10pm.

Rose St Artists' Market 60 Rose St, Fitzroy ⓦrosestmarket.com.au; map p.752. Permanent weekend market with lots of creative types peddling art, fashion, jewellery and vintage pieces. *Young Bloods Diner* is the market eatery. Sat & Sun 11am–5pm.

St Kilda Twilight Market O'Donnell Gardens, cnr Acland St and Upper Esplanade, St Kilda ⓦstkildatwilightmarket.com; map p.756. Expect artworks, crafts, hand-designed fashion and jewellery, produce and foods of the world at this small but popular evening market in a beautiful location beneath the palm trees beside Luna Park. Trams #96, #16, #3 & #79 from the CBD. Thurs 5–10pm.

South Melbourne Market 322–326 Coventry St, enclosed by York, Cecil and Coventry sts, South Melbourne ⓦsouthmelbournemarket.com.au; map

8

p.756. Melbourne's second-oldest market sells a huge range of fresh fruit and vegetables, seafood, meat, deli goods, clothes, furniture and household items. Cecil St has some fantastic outlets serving crêpes and tapas – don't leave without trying "dimmies", delicious *dim sum* to take away. Wed, Sat & Sun 8am–4pm, Fri 8am–5pm.

DIRECTORY

Banks and exchange All major banks can be found on Collins St. Standard banking hours are generally Mon–Fri 9.30am–4pm (Fri till 5pm), although some branches of Westpac/Bank of Melbourne, including the one at the corner of Collins & Swanton streets, are open on Sat (10am–2pm). Branches of Travelex are at 261 Bourke St (Mon–Fri 9am–5pm, Sat 10am–4pm), 233 Collins St (same hours, except Sat 10am–2pm) and 136 Exhibition St (same hours, closed Sat).

Consulates UK, Level 17, 90 Collins St ☎03 9652 1600; USA, 553 St Kilda Rd ☎03 9526 5900.

Diving Dive Victoria (ⓦdivevictoria.com.au) has a list of members in Greater Melbourne who rent equipment, organize trips and offer dive courses.

Employment Try the Backpackers Resource Centre at *Discovery Melbourne* (see p.764), Backpacker Job Board (ⓦbackpackerjobboard.com.au), *Nomads St Kilda Hostel* "Work and Play" assistance (24 Grey St, St Kilda; ⓦjobs .nomadsworld.com). Most hostels in town have a jobs notice board.

Hospitals and medical centres Alfred Hospital, Commercial Rd, Prahran ☎03 9076 2000; Royal Children's Hospital, Flemington Rd, Parkville ☎03 9345 5522; Royal Melbourne Hospital, Grattan St, Parkville ☎03 9342 7000; St Vincent's Hospital, Victoria Parade, Fitzroy ☎03 9288 2211. Melbourne Sexual Health Centre, 580 Swanston St, Carlton ☎03 9341 6200, offers a free service. For vaccinations, anti-malaria tablets and first-aid kits, contact the Travel Doctor, 3rd Floor, 393 Little Bourke St ☎03 9935 8100, ⓦtraveldoctor.com.au.

Internet There are plenty of internet cafés throughout Melbourne, with most charging around $5/hr. Many hostels also have internet access and lots of cafés offer free wi-fi, as does the State Library (see p.741). For late-night venues in the CBD, try Dot Com Internet Café (349 Elizabeth St), N2C Internet Café (Shop 100, 200 Bourke St) or Sublink (6 Campbell Arcade, under Flinders St Station). In St Kilda, Laundry Room in Acland Court (Level 1, 158 Acland St) offers wi-fi and computer access along with laundry facilities.

Laundries Almost all hostels and hotels have their own. Commercial self-serve coin laundries include My Beautiful Laundrette, 153 Brunswick St, Fitzroy (daily 6.30am–9.30pm) and Blessington Street Laundrette, 22 Blessington St, St Kilda (daily 7.30am–9pm). Machines cost $3–8 per wash and driers $1 for 6–10min.

Victorian Arts Centre Sunday Market St Kilda Rd, CBD ⓦartscentremelbourne.com.au; map pp.738–739. Good crafts market on the footpath alongside the Victorian Arts Centre, extending to the underpass towards Southgate. Over 150 stalls selling handmade quality artwork, woodcarvings, ceramics, textiles and jewellery. Sun 10am–4pm.

Left luggage and luggage forwarding Most hotels store luggage without charge on the day of check in/out. Southern Cross Station has self-service lockers ($10–16/ day). Travellers Aid at Flinders St Station can store luggage between 8am–8pm from $5.50 per day.

Library The Redmond Barry Reading Room at the State Library of Victoria, 328 Swanston St (Mon–Thurs 10am–9pm, Fri–Sun 10am–6pm; see p.741), has current Australian and overseas magazines; the Newspaper Reading Room has Australian and overseas papers.

Pharmacies Mulqueeny Midnight Pharmacy, cnr of Williams & High sts, Prahran (24hr); Elizabeth Pharmacy, 125 Elizabeth St, City (Mon–Fri 7.30am–6.30pm, Sat 9.30am–5.30pm).

Police Melbourne East Police Station at 226 Flinders Lane, City (☎03 9637 1100); emergency ☎000.

Post office The GPO retail shop is located at 250 Elizabeth St (Mon–Fri 8.30am–5.30pm, Sat 9am–5pm, including the poste restante counter). Other post offices are generally open Mon–Fri 9am–5pm. For mail forwarding, contact a local post office (see p.740 for CBD location).

Skiing Auski Ski Hiring & Information Centre, 9–11 Hardware Lane ☎03 9670 1412, can advise on skiing conditions at Baw Baw, Buffalo, Mount Hotham, Mount Buller, Falls Creek and at Thredbo in New South Wales (Mon–Thurs 9.30am–5.30pm, Fri 9.30am–6pm, Sat 10am–4pm & Sun 11am–4pm).

Swimming pools City Baths, 420 Swanston St (Mon–Thurs 6am–10pm, Fri 6am–8pm, Sat & Sun 8am–6pm; $6.20 swim, $13 including sauna & spa, $21 gym, pool, sauna & spa; ☎03 9658 9011), has a 30m heated indoor pool for swimming, plus a pool for water aerobics. The outdoor 50m Fitzroy Pool, 160 Alexandra Parade, is very attractive and provides one of the cheapest swims in town at $6 (see p.753). In the state-of-the-art Melbourne Sports & Aquatic Centre, Aughtie Drive, off Albert Park Rd in Albert Park, there are several pools and water slides, as well as a spa (Mon–Fri 5.30am–10pm, Sat & Sun 7am–8pm; admission $8.20 or $10.90 including spa, sauna & steam room; ☎03 9926 1555, ⓦmsac.com.au). Take tram #96 from Bourke St in the city.

Taxis There are taxi ranks on Swanston St outside Flinders St Station and outside Spencer St station, and plenty to flag down. Call Silver Top Taxis (☎13 10 08) or Yellow Cabs (☎13 22 27).

Telephones There's a plethora of discount phonecards around, which can be used in any payphone for dirt-cheap international calls (as low as 2¢/min to the UK). They are sold in lots of shops, as well as internet cafés and some hostels. Read the small print before buying – watch out for flagfall billing in units of 3min or more and short expiry dates.

Travel agents For flight bookings: Flight Centre, 112 Flinders Lane (☎1300 830 434), plus many branches throughout the city; STA Travel, Shop 5, 240 Flinders St (☎03 9654 7266) and 144 Acland St, St Kilda (☎03 9525 3188), plus other branches throughout the city; Student Flights (☎1800 046 462, ⓦstudentflights.com.au), Shop 4, 250 Flinders St (☎1300 086 968). For travel agents: Backpackers World, Shop 1, 250 Flinders St

(Mon–Fri 10am–6pm, Sat & Sun 10am–5pm; ☎03 9654 8477, ⓦbackpackersworld.com); Peterpans Adventure Travel, 415 Elizabeth St (Mon–Fri 10am–6pm, Sat & Sun 10am–5pm; ☎1800 669 424, ⓦpeterpans .com.au.

Travellers Aid centre Level 3, 225 Bourke St (Mon–Fri 9am–5pm; ☎03 9654 2600, ⓦtravellersaid.org.au), plus Flinders St and Southern Cross stations.

Travellers with disabilities The Travellers Aid Society (ⓦtravellersaid.org.au) provides information for the disabled; Southern Cross (under Bourke St Bridge) and Flinders St (between platform 9 & 10, within the ticket area) stations offer assistance and internet facilities. They also rent mobility equipment and provide information and maps for getting around Melbourne.

Mornington Peninsula

The **Mornington Peninsula** curves right around Port Phillip Bay, culminating in Point Nepean, well to the southwest of Melbourne. The shoreline facing the bay is beach-bum territory, though the well-heeled denizens of **Sorrento** and **Portsea**, at the tip of the peninsula, might well resent that tag. On the largely straight, ocean-facing coast, **Mornington Peninsula National Park** encompasses some fine seascapes, with several walking trails marked out. The western side of the peninsula facing the shallow waters of **Western Port Bay** (and the French and Phillip islands) has a much quieter, rural feel. Heading north from the pleasant township of **Flinders**, the coastline of rocky cliffs flattens out to sandy beaches, while north of **Stony Point** are mudflats and salt marshes lined by white mangroves: not particularly visually appealing but an internationally recognized and protected habitat for migratory waterbirds. Away from the coast, the townships of **Arthurs Seat** and **Red Hill** make for an enjoyable day-trip or weekend getaway, with an abundance of wineries, walks and markets to explore.

8

ARRIVAL AND INFORMATION

You can get to the peninsula by **public transport** from Melbourne to Frankston. From there you can access the main beach resorts and towns along the Nepean Highway on the northern side, as well as Flinders and Hastings to the south. For a sightseeing trip taking in wineries, beaches and Arthurs Seat you'll need your own vehicle.

By train Catch a Metro train from Flinders St to Frankston (1hr), where you can change onto a train to Stony Point (35min) for connections to the Phillip and French islands.

By bus Take a train to Frankston station, from where the #788 Metro bus to Portsea stops at Mornington, Dromana and Sorrento; the #782 serves Flinders and the #783 Hastings. For more information call ☎1800 800 007 or go to ⓦptv.vic.gov.au.

By ferry The Peninsula Searoad (☎03 5258 3244, ⓦsearoad.com.au) car and passenger ferry service crosses Port Phillip Bay from Queenscliff on the Bellarine Peninsula to Sorrento on the Mornington Peninsula all year round (see p.784). For French Island and Phillip Island, Inter Island Ferries (☎03 9585 5730, ⓦinterislandferries.com.au) run services from Stony Point on the eastern side of the Mornington Peninsula.

By car From Melbourne, the fastest route (around 1hr) is along the Monash Freeway (M1) and Eastlink tollway (M3): take exit 28 onto the Mornington Peninsula Freeway (M11) and follow the signs to Arthurs Seat/ Dromana. For a more scenic coastal drive you can try the St Kilda Road/Nepean Highway (State Route 3) – it will take an extra 30min, depending on traffic.

Visitor information There are visitor information centres in Frankston (Pier Promenade; daily 9am–5pm; ☎1300 322 842), Dromana (359B Point Nepean Rd; daily 9am–5pm; ☎03 5987 3078), Mornington (320 Main St; Mon–Fri 9am–5pm, Sat–Sun 10am–4pm; ☎03 5975 1644) and Sorrento (corner George St & Ocean Beach Rd; daily 10am–4pm in summer, till 3pm in winter; ☎03 5984 1478).

The western coast

The peninsula starts at suburban Frankston, 40km from central Melbourne. From here on down, the western coast, flanked by the Nepean Highway, sports beach after beach, all crowded and traffic-snarled in summer.

Mornington

Fifteen kilometres beyond Frankston, the fishing port town of **MORNINGTON** preserves some fine old buildings along Mornington Esplanade. The namesake of the Peninsula, Mornington has a number of pleasant beaches as well as a charming Main Street lined by almost a kilometre of speciality shops, restaurants and cafés, and a produce and craft market held every Wednesday (9am–3pm).

Briars Park

450 Nepean Hwy, Mt Martha • **Park** 9am–5pm • Free • **1840s homestead** 10am–4pm; phone for tour times • Entry with tour guide $7 (no admittance without guide) • ☎ 03 5974 3686, ⓦ mornpen.vic.gov.au/activities/the-briars

Near Mount Martha, **Briars Park** holds an **1840s homestead**, complete with a collection of furniture and memorabilia given to the owner, William Balcombe, by Napoleon Bonaparte, who reportedly stayed with the family when they lived on the island of St Helena. There is also an enclosed wildlife reserve with woodlands and extensive **wetlands** visited by more than fifty species of waterbird, which can be observed at close distance from two hides. A number of signposted walking trails through these areas (ranging from 600m to 7km) start just west of the visitor centre.

Arthurs Seat State Park

Arthurs Seat Rd, 5.5km from Mornington Peninsula Visitor Information Centre • **Heronswood** 105 Latrobe Parade, Dromana • Daily 9am–5pm, café from 10am • $10 • for café bookings, call ☎ 03 5984 7318; ⓦ diggers.com.au • **Enchanted Maze Garden** 55 Purves Rd, Arthurs Seat • Daily 10am–6pm • $29; Tree Surfing $59 • ☎ 03 5981 8449, ⓦ enchantedmaze.com.au • **Arthurs Restaurant and Bar** 790 Arthurs Seat Rd, Arthurs Seat • ☎ 03 5981 4444, ⓦ arthurshotel.com.au

Inland from Dromana, where seaside development begins in earnest, the granite outcrop of **Arthurs Seat State Park** rises 305m, providing breathtaking views of Port Phillip Bay. You can drive up to the summit along a winding road dotted with great lookouts, with a good stop-off at **Heronswood**, a Gothic Revival homestead and garden with an excellent **café**. It provides wonderful **picnics** to enjoy under the conifers in the garden. Near the top is the **Enchanted Maze Garden**, which combines four landscaped mazes with theme gardens, a sculpture park and a "tree surfing" experience, as well as lots of family-oriented activities and a good restaurant. Alternatively, have a drink or a bite to eat at the revamped *Arthurs Restaurant and Bar*, opposite Arthurs Seat, which offers stunning 180-degree bay views.

Sorrento and Portsea

Beyond Arthurs Seat, the peninsula arcs and narrows: the sands around Sorrento and Portsea – two towns so close they are practically one – offer a choice between the rugged surf of the ocean ("back" beaches) or the calmer waters of the bay ("front" beaches). With some of the most expensive real estate outside the Melbourne CBD, **SORRENTO** is the traditional haunt of the city's rich during the "season" from Boxing Day to Easter. Well-to-do outsiders also make it their playground in January and on summer weekends (when accommodation is notoriously pricey and scarce), flocking here to swim, surf and dive at the bay and ocean beaches. Exploring beautiful rock formations and low-tide pools, and swimming with bottlenose dolphins and seals (see p.786) are some of Sorrento's less glitzy attractions on offer.

PORTSEA, just beyond Sorrento, is a haven for divers, with excellent dives of up to 40m off Port Phillip Heads; trips operate from the pier throughout the summer and there are a couple of good dive shops. Portsea Front Beach, on the bay by the pier, is wall-to-wall beautiful people, as is Shelley Beach, which also attracts playful dolphins.

WINERIES OF THE MORNINGTON PENINSULA

The inland area around **Arthurs Seat** and **Red Hill** is probably the most scenic: a bucolic landscape of rolling hills, orchards and paddocks. This is also where the bulk of the peninsula's two hundred or so **vineyards** are located. They produce superb, if pricey, Chardonnay, Pinot Grigio/Gris and Pinot Noir wines. As in the Yarra Valley, good restaurants, especially winery restaurants, have proliferated on the peninsula in recent years, some of them in truly spectacular settings.

Mornington Peninsula Wineries (ⓦ morningtonpeninsulawineries.com.au) provides detailed information on the region's wineries, as do the visitor information centres and attractions in the region. Pick up the Mornington Peninsula *Wine Food Farmgate Trail Map*, also available at information centres.

WINERIES

Foxeys Hangout 795 White Hill Rd, Red Hill ⓣ 03 5989 2022, ⓦ foxeys-hangout.com.au. Small, bustling cellar door with vineyard panorama views. Tapas-style share plates ($12) of modern Australian cuisine, served by friendly and knowledgeable staff. Fri, Sat & Sun 11am–5pm.

Max's at Red Hill 53 Shoreham Rd, Red Hill ⓣ 03 5931 0177, ⓦ maxsrestaurant.com.au. Attached to the Red Hill Estate winery, *Max's* offers a seasonal menu (two courses from $70 per person) with superb views over the hills and Western Port Bay. Daily noon–5pm, dinner also Fri & Sat 6.30pm–late.

Montalto Vineyard and Olive Grove 33 Shoreham Rd, Red Hill South ⓣ 03 5989 8412, ⓦ montalto. com.au. Scenic and upmarket, with an area of wetland home to over ninety species of bird and other wildlife; it has a lovely kitchen garden (two courses from $60 per person) and a sculpture-dotted walk through the property. Cellar door daily 11am–5pm; Piazza Café daily 11am–4pm.

Stillwater at Crittenden 25 Harrison's Rd, Dromana ⓣ 03 5981 9555, ⓦ stillwateratcrittenden.

com.au. High-quality, innovative cuisine showcasing the best seasonal and regional produce (mains from $34) in a stunning lakeside vineyard setting. Lunch daily 11am–4pm (except Mon and Tues between May–Oct), dinner Fri & Sat.

★ **Ten Minutes By Tractor** 1333 Mornington Flinders Rd, Main Ridge ⓣ 03 5989 6455, ⓦ tenminutesbytractor.com.au. Award-winning food and wine served in an immaculate setting. The degustation menu (from $144 per person) is worth splashing out on. Cellar door daily 11am–5pm; restaurant Wed–Sun noon–3pm and also Thurs–Sat from 6.30pm, Dec 27–Jan 26 daily noon–3pm and also Tues–Sat from 6.30pm.

T'Gallant 1385 Mornington Flinders Rd, Main Ridge ⓣ 03 5931 1300, ⓦ tgallant.com.au. A pioneer in the winery field, proclaiming itself "Tuscany on the Mornington Peninsula"; the winery's rustic *La Baracca Trattoria* serves pizzas ($16–32) and other simple dishes alongside a glass of Pinot Noir or Pinot Gris. Cellar door daily 9am–5pm; La Baracca Trattoria Mon–Fri noon–3pm, Sat & Sun noon–4pm.

BREWERY

Red Hill Brewery 88 Shoreham Rd, Red Hill South ⓣ 03 5989 2959, ⓦ redhillbrewery.com.au. If you're in the mood for a beer instead of wine, this brewery has an excellent range straight from the vat and does hearty food to accompany it (mains from $25). Fri–Sun 11am–6pm.

On the other shore, Portsea Ocean Beach has excellent surfing, and a hang-gliding pad on a rock formation known as London Bridge.

Collins Settlement Historic Site

On Point Nepean Hwy at Sullivan Bay, 2km before Sorrento ⓦ parkweb.vic.gov.au

In 1803, Captain David Collins attempted the first permanent European settlement at what is now the **Collins Settlement Historic Site**; the settlers struggled here for eight months before giving up and moving on to Tasmania. One of the convicts in the expedition was the infamous William Buckley who, having escaped, was adopted by the local Aborigines and lived with them for 32 years; his survival against all odds has been immortalized in the phrase "Buckley's chance". You can walk along the cliffs and around the pioneer cemetery; there's a signposted turn-off from the main road.

MORNINGTON PENINSULA MARKETS

As well as the beaches, the peninsula's **community markets** attract many city dwellers wishing to sample local fresh produce and the works and wares of talented craftspeople.

Boneo Community Market ⓦboneomarket.com. Third Sat of every month (8am–noon), at the Boneo Recreation Reserve, cnr Boneo and Limestone roads, Boneo.

Dromana Drive-in Market ⓦdromanadrivein .com.au/market.htm. Held on Sundays in summer at the Dromana drive-in cinema (Dec–Jan 8am–1pm) on the Bittern–Dromana Rd, just off the Mornington Peninsula Freeway.

Emu Plains Market ⓦemuplainsmarket.com.au. Coolart Rd, Balnarring, on the third Sat of every month

(Oct–April 9am–2pm).

Mornington Main Street Market ⓦfacebook .com/mainstreetmarketmornington. Every Wed on Main St, Mornington (9am–3pm).

Mornington Racecourse Market ⓦcraftmarkets. com.au. Racecourse Rd, Mornington (year-round, second Sun of the month 9am–2pm).

Red Hill Community Market ⓦcraftmarkets .com.au. First Sat of the month (Sept–May 8am–1pm) at Red Hill Recreation Reserve, Arthurs Seat Rd, 10km east of Dromana. One of the biggest and best.

ARRIVAL AND DEPARTURE

By ferry A reliable car and passenger ferry service operated by Peninsula Searoad (☎03 5258 3244, ⓦsearoad.com.au) runs across the mouth of the bay from Sorrento on the Mornington Peninsula to Queenscliff on the Bellarine Peninsula all year round (hourly 7am–6pm; late Dec–late Jan & Fri–Sun in Feb till 7pm; 45min). There is an additional 6am passenger

SORRENTO AND PORTSEA

service, which must be booked in advance. Return fares for pedestrians are $22, while cars cost $114 (including driver) plus $22 for each additional adult passenger. Motorbikes plus a rider are $65. No advance bookings are necessary (except for the 6am passenger service), but cars should be at the terminal 30–45min prior to departure.

TOURS AND ACTIVITIES

Diving and kayaking *Bayplay* (3755 Point Nepean Rd, Portsea; ☎03 5984 0888, ⓦbayplay.com.au) doubles as a PADI dive resort and offers dive courses (all levels) from its shop in Portsea. As well as a wide range of dives for novices and experienced divers, it also runs a guided sea-kayaking dolphin sanctuary trip along the coast (daily 3hr; $99); on most days, dolphins and seals come to frolic around the boats. It also provides a free booking service for all kinds of other activities including horseriding and surfing lessons.

Swimming with dolphins and seals This is one of Port Phillip Bay's prime attractions. Operators include the environmentally conscious Polperro Dolphin Swims (☎03 5988 8437 or ☎0428 174 160, ⓦpolperro.com.au), which takes the smallest groups, and Moonraker (☎03 5984 4211, ⓦmoonrakercharters.com.au). Both run, weather permitting, 3–4hr trips from Sorrento Pier twice daily during the season (Oct–April/May) for roughly the same prices: around $135 for swimmers, including wetsuit and snorkelling equipment, and $65 for sightseers.

ACCOMMODATION

Carmel of Sorrento 142 Ocean Beach Rd, Sorrento ☎03 5984 3512, ⓦcarmelofsorrento.com.au. Charming, sandstone B&B smack in the middle of town. Self-contained units also available. Min 2 nights at weekends in summer. $220

Hotel Sorrento 5 Hotham Rd, Sorrento ☎03 5984 8000, ⓦhotelsorrento.com.au. A charming, 1871 limestone hotel located in a secluded spot on a hill above the jetty. Try to stay in the "Heritage Suites" with sea views. Suites $280

Portsea Hotel 3746 Point Nepean Road, Portsea ☎03 5984 2213, ⓦportseahotel.com.au. An iconic Tudor building overlooking the historic Portsea Pier. Basic but comfortable rooms (some with shared bathroom)

close to the action of the rollicking nightlife at the pub lawn downstairs. Twins with shared bathroom $160, en suites $180

Portsea Village Resort 3765 Point Nepean Rd, Portsea ☎03 5984 8484, ⓦportseavillageresort .com.au. Boutique resort-style accommodation opposite the beach. One- to three-bedroom apartments with kitchen, and access to indoor and outdoor pools, tennis court and on-site restaurant. $325

Sorrento Beach Motel 780 Melbourne Rd, Sorrento ☎03 5984 1356, ⓦsorrentobeachmotel .com.au. Mid-level, well-managed yet quirky motel where the outside of each room looks like an old beach hut. $150

FROM TOP STREET ART, MELBOURNE (P.737); YARRA VALLEY VINEYARDS (P.794) >

EATING AND DRINKING

As is to be expected in this posh part of the peninsula, most **restaurants** tend to be on the pricey side, but some come with great views across the water. In winter, a lot of places have restricted opening times or are only open at weekends.

Cakes and Ale 102 Ocean Beach Rd, Sorrento ☎ 03 5984 4995, ⍟ cakes-and-ale.com.au. With more to it than simply cakes and ale, this busy restaurant with a hipster vibe serves up innovative and tasty dishes – think cured meats, cheese and an extensive wine list. Try the mouthwatering blue-cheese souffle ($15.50). Mon–Fri noon–late, Sat–Sun 11am–late.

Continental Hotel 21 Ocean Beach Rd, Sorrento ☎ 03 5984 2201, ⍟ continentalhotel.com.au. Good-looking old-timer with a spacious dining area, a few tables out front and a Mediterranean-influenced menu (mains from $26) featuring a range of Mornington Peninsula wines. Live music and a nightclub on Sat (9pm–3am). Restaurant Mon, Thurs–Fri 9am–10pm, Sat 8am–10pm, Sun 8am–4pm.

Hotel Sorrento 5 Hotham Rd, Sorrento ☎ 03 5984 8000, ⍟ hotelsorrento.com.au. Hotel-bar and a restaurant with a mod-Oz menu featuring seafood dishes and grills that are a cut above your average pub fare (mains from $26), and excellent views across the bay. Daily 7.30am–8.30pm.

Loquat 3183 Point Nepean Rd, Sorrento ☎ 03 5984 4444, ⍟ loquat.com.au. Charming converted cottage dishing up consistently good meals with a fine ambience and attentive service – a real winner on the peninsula. The $39 Friday special "Flatty and French" (flathead and chips) is a crowd-pleaser. Thurs–Sun 6pm–late.

Portsea Hotel 3746 Point Nepean Rd, Portsea ☎ 03 5984 2213, ⍟ portseahotel.com.au Ever-popular among seasonal holiday-makers, the main draw-card of the affectionately known "Portsea Pub" is the spacious beer garden, located atop a grassy, sun-drenched hill and with direct beach access. Gets very crowded during summer. Mains from around $27. Daily noon–late.

Point Nepean National Park

The tip of the Mornington Peninsula, with its fortifications, tunnels and former army base, is now classified as **Point Nepean National Park**, part of a patchwork of parks sprinkled over the southern end of the peninsula, collectively known as **Mornington Peninsula National Park**.

The Point Nepean Shuttle runs to the fortifications at Point Nepean, with four optional drop-offs for walks: the first, the **Walter Pisterman Heritage Walk** (1km), passes through coastal vegetation to the Port Phillip Bay shoreline; the second, the **Range Area Walk** (1.8km), leads to the top of Cheviot Hill, where you can look across to Queenscliff. The track then continues to **Cheviot Beach** where on December 17, 1967, **Harold Holt**, Australia's then prime minister, went for a swim in the rough surf of Bass Strait and disappeared, presumed drowned; his body was never found. The third walk, the **Fort Pearce and Eagle's Nest Heritage Trail** (2km), crosses through defence fortifications. A fourth walk, the **Bay Beach Walk** (2.8km), takes you around **Fort Nepean**, right at the tip of the peninsula. Built at the same time as Fort Queenscliff opposite to protect wealthy post-gold-rush Melbourne from the imagined threat of Russian invasion, the fort comprises two subterranean levels, whose tunnels lead down to the Engine House at water level.

ARRIVAL AND INFORMATION

POINT NEPEAN NATIONAL PARK

By bus The hop-on-hop-off shuttle service between the Visitor Centre and Fort Nepean departs from the Quarantine Station every 30min (10.30am–3.30pm; $10).

By car You can drive to Gunners car park (free), 2.5km into the park, and walk the rest of the way to Point Nepean. Vehicle access is available 8am–5pm.

By bike The park is accessible at all time by bike; you can rent a bicycle at the Point Nepean Information Centre within the park ($30.10 per day).

Visitor centre The information centre (daily 10am–5pm; ☎ 03 5984 6014) and Gunners car park are located at the Quarantine Station precinct within the park.

South and east coast

The Mornington Peninsula National Park spreads along the ocean coast and has a number of sights and activities to keep you occupied. The enjoyable two-day **Coastal Walk** (27km) runs from London Bridge along the coast to **Cape Schanck**, the site of an 1859 lighthouse (tours daily 10am–4pm; $16.50, book ahead; ☏ 1300 885 259). Here, walkways lead down to the sea along a narrow neck of land, providing magnificent coastal views. The nearby **Bushrangers Bay Walk** (5km; 2hr) heads from the cape to Main Creek, beginning along the clifftop and leading down to a wild beach facing Elephant Rock.

Moonlit Sanctuary Wildlife Conservation Park

550 Tyabb-Tooradin Rd • **Park** Daily 10am–5pm • $20 • **Night tour** from 7pm April–Sept & 8.30pm Oct–March; 1hr 30min • $42; booking essential • **Koala Encounters** from 11am, 1.15pm, 3pm; 30min • $15; booking essential • ☏ 03 5978 7935, ⓦ moonlitsanctuary.com.au

Set in bushland 15km southeast of Frankston, near the northern end of Western Port Bay, **Moonlit Sanctuary Wildlife Conservation Park** is home to lots of kangaroos, wallabies, emus and waterbirds. However, the park's emphasis is on conserving and breeding rare nocturnal Australian animals, so it's well worth coming late in the day to take part in their guided night tour. It offers the chance to see creatures such as spot-tailed quolls, southern bettongs, pademelons, squirrel gliders and tawny frogmouths.

Peninsula Hot Springs

140 Springs Lane, Rye • Daily 7.30am–10pm • Tues–Thurs $35, Fri–Mon $45; spa treatments also available • ☏ 03 5950 8777, ⓦ peninsulahotsprings.com

Tucked away in bushland, a world away from the summer chaos of Sorrento and Portsea, is one of the peninsula's most fiercely kept secrets – the **Peninsula Hot Springs**. Filled with natural thermal mineral waters channelled from deep underground, there are over twenty "bathing experiences" available to visitors, including a Turkish steam bath, a cave pool and a hilltop pool with striking 360-degree views. The Spa Dreaming Centre within the springs complex also offers pampering **spa treatments** including salt wraps, ancient healing stone therapies and Aboriginal-inspired Kodo full-body massages. Not to be missed.

8

TOURS AND ACTIVITIES

SOUTH AND EAST COAST

Horseriding Take horse rides along Gunnamatta Beach or through bushland with Gunnamatta Trail Rides, 150 Sandy Rd, Fingal. Beach rides $140 (2hr); ☏ 03 8609 6083, ⓦ gunnamatta.com.au.

Surfing Surfing lessons ($60 for 1hr 30min, equipment provided) are offered by the East Coast Surf School (226 Balnarring Rd, Merricks North; ☏ 0417 526 465, ⓦ eastcoastsurfschool.net.au) at various spots near Point Leo.

ACCOMMODATION

Views Cape Schanck 41 Trent Jones Dr, Cape Schanck ☏ 03 5988 6555, ⓦ viewscapeschanck.com.au. Secluded, modern accommodation with idyllic views of the ocean and sand dunes, as well as exceptional service. Cosy in the winter and breezy in the summer, a perfect romantic retreat. Luxurious on-site organic day-spa $280

French Island

FRENCH ISLAND, on the eastern side of the Mornington Peninsula, is well off the beaten track. A former prison farm, about two-thirds of the island is a national park, with the remaining third used as farmland. The island is renowned for its rich **wildlife**, especially its birds of prey and flourishing koala colony. Make sure you bring mosquito repellent. It can be difficult and expensive to bring a car onto the island (see below), but it's a great place to cycle, an activity that is encouraged, with all walking tracks open to bikes.

ARRIVAL AND INFORMATION

FRENCH ISLAND

By ferry Inter Island Ferries (☏ 03 9585 5730, ⓦ interislandferries.com.au) connect the Mornington Peninsula with French Island (15min) and Phillip Island (30min), departing from Stony Point, on the eastern side of the Mornington Peninsula, and travelling to Tankerton Jetty on French Island (seven daily Mon–Fri

7.10am–7.25pm, six on Sat 7.40am–6.20pm, and six on Sun 8.10am–6.20pm; $26 return, bikes $8). To get to Stony Point from Melbourne, take the Frankston train from Flinders St Station and either the Stony Point train extension, or bus #782 to Stony Point.

By car The only way to get a vehicle onto the island is via the French Island Barge (☎ 0428 880 729) from Corinella on the eastern coast of Western Port Bay (15min; $200 per car return). The two-car capacity barge operates daily, but only at high tide. Advanced bookings are essential. Alternatively, Stony Point Caravan Park (☎ 03 5983 9242) and Cowes Caravan Park (☎ 03 5952 2211) on Phillip Island can provide secure parking for $5 per 24 hours, depending on availability.

French Island National Park office ☎ 03 5980 1294. **Parks Victoria** ☎ 13 19 63, ⊕ parkweb.vic.gov.au.

TOURS

French Island Bus Tour ☎ 03 5980 1241, ⊕ frenchislandtours.com.au. Take the Inter Island Ferry from Stony Point (or Cowes on Phillip Island) to Tankerton jetty; tours meet the ferry and drop off at the jetty at the end (departs Tues, Thurs & Sun, and also Sat during school holidays; full-day $70, half-day $46, inclusive of ferry ticket). For a brief visit to French Island, it's best to book one of the afternoon tours covering the island's natural attractions and the historic prison.

ACCOMMODATION

Fairhaven Campsite Coast Road, French Island ☎ 13 19 63, ⊕ parkweb.vic.gov.au. A small, basic campsite operated by Parks Victoria, a 5km walk to the west of the island, which has a pit toilet and tank water, but no showers. Open fires not allowed. **Free**

French Island Glamping 59 Barge Access Rd, French Island, ☎ 0498 843 850, ⊕ frenchislandglamping .com.au. This "glamping" (glamorous camping) experience brings together the great outdoors and modern creature comforts, like huge bell tents equipped with bluetooth speakers, electric blankets and queen-sized beds. **$230**

McLeod Eco Farm McLeod Rd, French Island ☎ 03 5980 1224, ⊕ mcleodecofarm.com. Operating as a medium security prison for much of the 1900s, this property was transformed into a charming eco-farm in the 1990s. Accommodation is available in the former prison cells, now converted into twins with bunk beds, or in the slightly more expensive former officers' quarters with queen-sized beds; all have shared facilities. The farm is surrounded by the national park and has 8km of beach frontage; the very reasonable rates include a two-course organic meal and transfer from the ferry jetty 29km away. **$98** per person.

Tortoise Head Guest House Tankerton Road, French Island ☎ 03 5980 1234, ⊕ tortoisehead.net. Near the jetty, this small B&B offers accommodation in private or dormitory-style cabins with en suites and sea views. Unpowered campsites are also available. Moderately priced lunches and dinners are also available. Camping **$15**, dorms **$39**, doubles **$180**.

Phillip Island

The hugely popular holiday destination of **PHILLIP ISLAND** is famous above all for the nightly roosting of hundreds of Little penguins at Summerland Beach – the so-called **Penguin Parade** – but the island also boasts some dramatic coastline, plenty of surfing, fine swimming beaches, and a couple of well-organized wildlife parks.

Cowes, on the sheltered bay side, is the main town and a lively and attractive place to stay in summer. Other, smaller, communities worth a visit are **San Remo**, on the mainland; **Newhaven**, the first island community across the bridge; and **Rhyll**, on the northeast corner of the island.

San Remo

Just before the bridge linking the mainland to Phillip Island, the small township of **SAN REMO** has several accommodation and eating options, as well as a picturesque fishing fleet by its wharf and a cooperative selling fresh fish and crayfish. Pelican feeding takes place daily at midday at the jetty (free), where you may also be able to spot the resident family of giant stingrays.

Newhaven

NEWHAVEN has a large visitor centre, where you can book accommodation, pick up a free map and buy tickets for the Penguin Parade (see opposite), Churchill Island (see below), the Koala Conservation Centre (see p.792), or a combined parks pass for all three ($57), as well as ferry cruises.

Churchill Island

Heritage Farm daily 10am–5pm • $12.50 • ⓦ penguins.org.au

Tiny **CHURCHILL ISLAND**, accessible by a narrow bridge 1km north of Newhaven, is mostly occupied by a working **farm** and historic homestead in English-style gardens, surrounded by ancient moonah trees that are home to abundant birdlife. The farm puts on a range of daily activities including milking, sheepshearing and blacksmithing demonstrations, while a leisurely walk leads around the small island (2hr) from the Churchill Island Visitor Centre, with views of the unspoilt coastline; the visitor centre has a café.

Rhyll

Unlike most other places on the island, the fishing village of **RHYLL** has managed to retain a sleepy charm. There are a couple of cafés on the foreshore with splendid views of the tranquil, shallow waters of Western Port Bay and the South Gippsland coast; occupying the best position is the *Foreshore Bar and Restaurant* (see p.794).

The Conservation Hill Lookout, just off the Cowes–Rhyll Road further north, provides a good view of the **Rhyll Inlet**, a significant roosting and feeding ground for migratory wading birds that come from as far as Siberia. A **boardwalk** starting at the car park takes visitors into the middle of the inlet, a landscape of mangroves, salt marshes and mudflats.

8

Cowes

Phillip Island's main town, **COWES**, situated at the centre of the north coast, is busy, touristy and even bordering on tacky, though the sandy bays are sheltered enough for good swimming and there are several decent places to eat and stay around **The Esplanade**, a lively strip facing the jetty.

Phillip Island Nature Park

The **Phillip Island Nature Park** is located on the **Summerland Peninsula**, the narrow tip of land at the island's western extremity. The reason for the reserve is the **Little penguin**, the smallest of the penguins, found only in southern Australian waters and whose largest colony breeds at Summerland Beach (around two thousand penguins in the parade area, and twenty thousand on the island altogether).

Penguin Parade

Parade Nightly after dusk • General viewing $25.10, guided ranger tour $78, VIP tour $78 • **Penguin Parade Visitor Centre** 10am–an hour after sunset • Admission included in parade ticket • ☎ 03 5951 2800, ⓦ penguins.org.au

The **Penguin Parade** is inevitably horribly commercial, with four thousand visitors a night at the busiest time of the year (around Christmas, January and Easter). Spectators sit in concrete-stepped stadiums looking down onto a floodlit beach, with taped narrations in Japanese, Mandarin and English. But ecological disaster would ensue if the penguins weren't managed properly, and visitors would still flock here, harming the birds and eroding the sand dunes. As it is, all the money made goes back into research and looking after the penguins, and into facilities such as the excellent **Penguin Parade Visitor Centre**. The "Penguin Experience" here is a simulated underwater scene of the hazards of a penguin's life, and there are also interactive displays, videos and even nesting boxes where you can watch the chicks. To escape the majority of the crowds, you can choose the "**VIP Tour**" (with an exclusive, elevated viewing tower) or the "**Guided Ranger Tour**" (reserved front-row seats on the sand) options – both with a ranger on hand to answer questions.

The parade itself manages to transcend the setting, as the penguins come pouring onto the beach, waddling comically once they leave the water soon after dark; fifty minutes later the floodlights are switched off and it's all over, at which time (or before) you can move on to the extensive illuminated boardwalks over their burrows, enabling you to watch their antics after the parade finishes – they're active most of the night. The quietest time to observe them is during the cold and windy winter (you'll need water- or windproof clothing at any time of year).

The Nobbies and Seal Rocks

Daily 10am–1hr before sunset • Free

At the tip of the Summerland Peninsula is **Point Grant**, where **The Nobbies**, two huge rock stacks, are linked to the island at low tide by a wave-cut platform of basalt, affording views across to Cape Schanck on the Mornington Peninsula. The **Nobbies Centre** features informative displays about the surrounding ecotourism sites, as well as a café and gift shop. From the car park, a network of boardwalks lead across spongy greenery – vibrant in summer with purple and yellow flowers – along the rounded clifftops to a lookout over a blowhole. This is a wild spot, with views along the rugged southern coastline towards Cape Woolamai, a granite headland at the eastern end of the island. From September to April you may see muttonbirds (shearwaters) here – they arrive in September to breed and head for the same burrows each year, after an incredible flight from the Bering Strait in the Arctic Circle.

Two kilometres off Point Grant are **Seal Rocks**, two rocky islets with the largest-known colony of Australian fur seals, estimated to number around five thousand. It's possible to see seals all year round through the telescopes along the boardwalks ($2), though their numbers peak during the breeding season (late Oct to Dec). You can get a better view of the seals from the Nobbies Centre via cameras in the colony; there's also a café and children's play area. Cruises to Seal Rocks are available from Cowes (see opposite).

Koala Conservation Centre

1810 Phillip Island Tourist Rd, between Newhaven and Cowes • Daily 10am–5pm, extended hours in summer; 4pm feeding • $12.50 • ☎ 03 5951 2800, ⓦ penguins.org.au

The **Koala Conservation Centre** aims to keep the koala habitat as natural as possible while still giving people a close view. A treetop walk through a part of the bushland park allows visitors to observe the marsupials at close range. The rangers provide fresh gum leaves every afternoon – a very popular photo opportunity. You can learn about koalas in the excellent interpretive centre.

Phillip Island Wildlife Park

2115 Phillip Island Rd, 1km south of Cowes • Daily from 10am; call for closing times • $18 • ☎ 03 5952 2038, ⓦ piwildlifepark.com.au

Phillip Island Wildlife Park provides a shady sanctuary for Australian animals: beautiful dingoes, Tasmanian devils, fat and dozy wombats, as well as an aviary and a koala reserve. There are also freely ranging emus, Cape Barren geese, wallabies, eastern grey kangaroos and pademelons.

Phillip Island Grand Prix Circuit

Back Beach Rd, Ventnor • Circuit Daily 9am–5.30pm • Free • **Circuit tours** Daily 2pm; 1hr • $22 • **Go-karts** Daily 10am–5pm, subject to circuit availability • 10min session $35, 20min session $60, 30min session $80 ☎ 03 5952 9400, ⓦ phillipislandcircuit.com.au

Phillip Island is home to the **Phillip Island Grand Prix Circuit**, where the **Australian**

Motorcycle Grand Prix is held over three days in October (tickets from $35; ⓦmotogp .com.au). A History of Motorsport display at the circuit visitor centre features snapshots and memorabilia of the crazy exploits and heroics of Australia's early racers. Guided tours provide access to otherwise restricted areas, including the circuit control tower, pit lane, and winner's podium. Visitors can experience all the twists and turns of the famed circuit on a smaller-scale replica go-karting track.

ARRIVAL AND DEPARTURE   PHILLIP ISLAND

By bus and train V/Line buses to Cowes (via Koo-wee-rup) depart from Melbourne's Southern Cross Station approximately every 2hrs, 6am–9pm on weekdays and every 3hrs, 9am–6pm on weekends (2.5hrs; $14). You can also get a train from Southern Cross or Flinders St stations to Dandenong and then a bus to Cowes. However, there's no public transport on the island itself, so it can be tricky getting around and to the Penguin Parade, over 10km from Cowes.

By ferry Inter Island Ferries (ⓣ 03 9585 5730, ⓦ interislandferries.com.au) connect the Mornington Peninsula with French Island and Phillip Island (30min; $26 return, bikes $8), departing from Stony Point, on the eastern side of the Mornington Peninsula (Mon–Fri seven daily between 7.30am–7.45pm, Sat six between 8.30am

and 6.45pm, Sun six between 9am and 6.45pm), and from Cowes (Mon–Thurs three daily between 8.35am and 5.50pm, Fri four between 8.35am and 8.15pm, Sat three between 8.30am and 5.30pm, Sun three between 9am and 5.30pm).

By car If you're driving, head southeast from Melbourne on the Monash Freeway (M1) or Eastern Freeway (M3) to Dandenong, then follow the South Gippsland Highway (M420) to Lang Lang and from there the Bass Highway to Anderson, where the road heads directly west to San Remo and the bridge across to the island, a drive of approximately 1hr 30min in total. The scenic lookout about 4km before San Remo is worth stopping at for fantastic views of Western Port Bay and the surrounding countryside.

INFORMATION

Visitor centres There are visitor centres at Newhaven (895 Phillip Island Rd; daily 9am–5pm) and Cowes (91–97 Thompson Ave; daily 9am–5pm). Both centres can be

contacted on ⓣ 1300 366 422, ⓦ visitbasscoast.com.au. There is also a handy free iPhone app "Phillip Island Nature Parks Australia" with detailed island info.

TOURS

Joining a tour solves the problem of no public transport on the island. A few operators specializing in small groups (up to twenty people; see box, p.762) run day-tours of the island from Melbourne that include the Penguin Parade at dusk

and take in a winery, the Nobbies rock formations (see opposite) and a wildlife park (from around $100 including dinner and all entrance fees).

Wildlife Coast Cruises (ⓣ 1300 763 739, ⓦ wildlifecoastcruises.com.au) Offer various cruises from the Cowes Jetty, the best being the trip to Seal Rocks (2hr;

$78) to see the Australian fur seals close up, as well as the relaxing Twilight Bay cruise (90min; $48) which features regular dolphin sightings, and an onboard bar.

ACCOMMODATION

Out of season you shouldn't have any trouble finding somewhere to stay, but during the peak seasons – Christmas to Easter and the Moto GP in early Oct – accommodation nearly doubles in price and some places require weekly bookings. The Phillip Island tourist information centres in Newhaven and Cowes handle accommodation bookings for the island.

Amaroo Park 97 Church St, Cowes ⓣ 03 5952 2548, ⓦ amaroopark.com. Accommodation comprises studio and two-bedroom cabins, double or twin rooms with shared bathroom in a 1920s homestead, as well as powered sites; facilities include a heated swimming pool, Japanese restaurant and bike rental. En-suite studios $110, homestead doubles $120, family villas $150, powered sites $40

★**Clifftop** 1 Marlin St, Smiths Beach ⓣ 03 5952 1033, ⓦ clifftop.com.au. A stunning secluded location with views across the water on the south of the island are what

make this the best accommodation option. The eight suites are exquisitely decorated and offer everything for a perfect romantic getaway. $235

Glen Isla House 230 Church St, Cowes ⓣ 03 5952 1882, ⓦ glenisla.com. A lovely historic property with access to a sandy beach and tranquil gardens. Lots of home comforts and sumptuous classic decor. No under-12s. $275

The Island Accommodation 10–12 Phillip Island Tourist Rd, Newhaven ⓣ 03 5956 6123, ⓦ theislandaccommodation.com.au. This impeccably clean and well-appointed hostel has won awards for its ecofriendly design. Helpful staff have a wealth of local information to share. Dorms $35, doubles $135

Kaloha Holiday Resort Cnr Chapel & Steele sts, Cowes ☎ 03 5952 2179, ⓦ kaloha.com.au. Modern rooms, some with kitchenettes, as well as self-contained villas. Enjoy a cocktail from the veranda of the cosy on-site restaurant and bar while looking out over the lagoon-style swimming pool. Located in shady grounds just off a quiet beach. $170

Silverwater Resort 17 Potters Hill Rd, San Remo ☎ 03 5671 9300, ⓦ silverwaterresort.com.au. Luxury resort

rooms and apartments with sweeping views of Westernport Bay. Facilities include heated swimming pools, tennis court, gym and kids' play area. Doubles $250, apartments $275

The Waves 1 The Esplanade, Cowes ☎ 03 5952 1351, ⓦ thewaves.com.au. Self-contained modern studio apartments with spa bath and balcony, many overlooking beautiful Cowes beach opposite. Short walk to shops and restaurants on Thompson Ave and good proximity to all major island attractions. $270

EATING AND DRINKING

Foreshore Bar and Restaurant 11 Beach Rd, Rhyll ☎ 03 5956 9520, ⓦ theforeshore.com.au. Nautical decor and a soothing atmosphere combine nicely with great bay views at *Foreshore Bar and Restaurant*. Serves up treats such as dukkah-spiced lamb rump ($36.50) and has an extensive selection of wines. Mon–Fri 11am–3pm and 5–9pm (closed Tues Easter–Dec), Sat & Sun 11am–9pm.

Harry's on the Esplanade Level 1, 17 The Esplanade, Cowes ☎ 03 5952 6226, ⓦ harrysrestaurant.com.au. Excellent seafood and meat dishes with a European slant – from seven oysters four ways ($25) to pan-fried kangaroo fillet ($34) – in a nice setting on the Esplanade. March–Aug Tues–Sun 11.30am–9pm; Sept–Feb Tues–Fri 11.30am–9pm, Sat & Sun 10am–9pm.

Isola di Capri 2 Thompson Ave, Cowes ☎ 03 5952 2435, ⓦ isoladicapri.com.au. Friendly, moderately priced

Italian restaurant and *gelateria* at the corner of the Esplanade. The handmade gnocchi ($20) is a standout. Mon–Fri 4.30–9.30pm, Sat, Sun & public hols 11.30am–2pm & 4.30–9.30pm; *gelateria* daily noon–6pm.

Rusty Water Brewery 1821 Phillip Island Rd, Cowes ☎ 03 5952 1666, ⓦ rustywaterbrewery.com.au. Popular restaurant and brewery with extensive drinks menu and reputation for a mean beef rib-eye ($39). Live music on Fri. Wed–Sun noon–8.30pm.

Westernport Hotel 161 Marine Parade, San Remo ☎ 03 5678 5205, ⓦ thewesternport.com.au. Classic pub grub – "Parma" (Australian for *parmigiana* – chicken schnitzel with ham and cheese, $24.50), fish 'n' chips and steaks – in a sleek bistro setting. Good-sized portions, family-friendly. Live music on weekends. Mon–Sat 11.30am–1am, Sun 11.30am–11.30pm.

Yarra Valley and the Dandenongs

Northeast of Melbourne, the **Yarra Valley** stretches out towards the foothills of the Great Dividing Range, with **Yarra Glen** and **Healesville** the targets for excursions into the wine country and the superb forest scenery beyond. To the east, and still within the suburban limits, the cool **Dandenong Ranges** have been a popular retreat for city folk for over a century, with quaint villages, fine old houses, beautiful flowering gardens and shady forests of eucalypts and tree ferns. To get to all these destinations and to have a good look round, you really need your own vehicle.

Yarra Valley

Just half an hour's drive from Melbourne, the **Yarra Valley** is home to around eighty of Victoria's best small **wineries**. Wine country starts in outer suburbia north of the Maroondah Highway just before Lilydale (turn-offs are signposted). North of Lilydale, you can check out wineries (again, all signposted) along or near three routes – the Warburton Highway to the east, the Maroondah Highway to Healesville, and the Melba Highway, heading north past Yarra Glen.

Warburton

Heading along the Warburton Highway via Yarra Junction you come to **WARBURTON**, a pretty, old-fashioned town on the Upper Yarra River, whose cool

WINERIES OF THE YARRA VALLEY

The handy booklet *Wine Regions of Victoria* is available at visitor centres (free), or you can download the free smartphone app by the same name with descriptions, maps and journey planner function. If you intend to take a few swigs (and can't find a teetotal driver) it's best to join a **winery tour**. Wild Wombat Winery Tours (☏ 1300 945 396, ⓦ wildwombatwinerytours.com.au) picks up at 9.30am from central Melbourne (daily), visiting five wineries in the Yarra Valley ($120 including transport, tastings, and a good restaurant lunch with wine in the afternoon).

WINERIES

Yering Station 38 Melba Hwy, just south of Yarra Glen • ☏ 03 9730 0100, ⓦ yering.com. Yering Station is located on the site of the first vineyard planted in the area in 1838 and has a glass-walled restaurant offering views across the valley, plus a wine bar and a shop selling regional produce. The grounds also host the lively Yarra Valley Farmers' Market, selling fruit, vegetables and other valley produce such as smoked trout, honey and jams. On the same property is the *Chateau Yering Historic House Hotel* (see p.796). Mon–Fri 10am–5pm, Sat & Sun 10am–6pm; market third Sun of every month 9am–2pm.

Domaine Chandon 727 Maroondah Hwy, near the town of Coldstream • ☏ 03 9738 9200, ⓦ chandon.com.au. Möet & Chandon's Australian winery, Domaine Chandon, was established in 1986, joining successful Chandon estates in Argentina, Brazil and California. It produces fine *méthode champenoise* sparkling wine, which you can sample in a modern, bright tasting room with spectacular views of the Yarra Valley ($12 with cheese). Free tours of the winery take visitors through the winemaking process and Domaine Chandon's impressive history. It is also possible to self-guide around the tour route. Daily 10.30am–4.30pm.

Rochford 878 Maroondah Hwy at Hill Rd • ☏ 03 5957 3333, ⓦ rochfordwines.com.au. Rochford winery is known for its sparkling Pinot Chardonnay and specializes in locally produced food; it also hosts regular concerts in its gardens. The cellar door is open for wine tasting ($5) and purchases, and there's also *Isabella's Restaurant*, offering a fine-dining experience with expertly matched Rochford wines. Tasting packages can be booked in advance (with cheese or canapes; $15), and you can see the winery via a segway tour ($145). If you're feeling particularly extravagant, take to the skies with an early-morning hot-air balloon experience over the valley ($395, including breakfast). Vineyard and restaurant daily 9am–5pm; segway tour Mon–Fri on demand, Sat, Sun & public hols 10.30am & 2.30pm; hot-air balloon experience early morning on demand.

8

climate and hill-station atmosphere attract droves of urban dwellers seeking respite from the city. The town is also the final stop on the **Warburton Rail Trail** (ⓦ railtrails.org.au), a 40km cycling track that follows the former Warburton Railway from Lilydale.

Healesville and around

HEALESVILLE is a small, pleasant town nestled in the foothills of the Great Dividing Range. The town's main attraction is the renowned **Healesville Sanctuary**, a bushland zoo that is one of the state's primary locations for viewing and learning about native Australian wildlife. The nearby **TarraWarra Museum of Art** hosts an impressive collection of modern Australian visual art, and provides an enjoyable stop en route to the Sanctuary. Sadly, much of the area north of Healesville, including the village of **Marysville** and the picturesque **Steavenson Falls**, was completely devastated by the Black Saturday bushfires (see box, p.860). Areas affected include Maroondah Reservoir Park, Cathedral Range State Park, Kinglake National Park and Yarra Ranges National Park. These areas have been reopened to the public, and many Marysville businesses have slowly got up and running, but the rebuilding process will take some time. As you head east from Healesville on the Maroondah Highway, the scenery becomes progressively more attractive towards the **Lake Mountain Alpine Resort**.

TarraWarra Museum of Art

311–315 Healesville–Yarra Glen Rd, Healesville • Tues–Sun 11am–5pm • $7.50 • ☎ 03 5957 3100, ⓦ twma.com.au

The **TarraWarra Museum of Art** is located in a striking modern building, designed by the renowned Allan Powell and ranked among the top five architecturally significant landmarks in Melbourne. Showcasing Australian art from the mid-twentieth century onwards, the wide collection – most of which has been donated from the private collection of one couple, Eva and Marc Besen – has enough to keep you occupied for hours.

Healesville Sanctuary

Badger Creek Rd, Healesville • Daily 9am–5pm; Spirits of the Sky presentation noon & 2.30pm, weather permitting • $31.60 • ⓦ zoo. org.au/healesville • Take a train from Melbourne to Lilydale, then bus #685 to Healesville and a connecting bus #686 from there towards Badger Creek

The **Healesville Sanctuary** is home to more than two hundred species of Australian animals and a refuge for injured and orphaned ones, some of which are subsequently returned to the wild. It's a fascinating place in a beautiful setting, with a stream running through park-like grounds that are dense with gum trees and cool ferns, as well as 3km of walking tracks. The informative "Meet the Keeper" presentations are worth joining, especially the one featuring the birds of prey ("Spirits of the Sky").

Lake Mountain Alpine Resort

1071 Lake Mountain Rd, Marysville • Entry $56 per car • For seasonal opening times and ski rental information, see ⓦ lakemountainresort.com.au

Less than an hour from Healesville is Melbourne's closest alpine resort, **Lake Mountain Alpine Resort** (1400m), a very popular place for cross-country skiing, tobogganing, snow play, snow shoeing and snow mobile rides during the white season. Each year, "Christmas in July" is celebrated for two weeks during the school holidays with a range of family-friendly activities. During the warmer months, Lake Mountain is fantastic for mountain-bike riding, bushwalking and road cycling. Given the bushfire-prone nature of the area during the summer months, it is important to check for any fire warnings or fire bans with the Country Fire Authority (ⓦ cfa.vic.gov.au) or the Victorian Bushfire Information Line (VBIL; ☎ 1800 240 667) before departing on any cycling or walking trip.

ARRIVAL AND GETTING AROUND   THE YARRA VALLEY

By train For Healesville, take a Metro train from Melbourne to Lilydale and then bus #685.

By bus There's a daily bus #684 from Lilydale (1.20pm) to Eildon via Healesville and Marysville.

By car From Melbourne, follow the Eastern Freeway (M3) and Maroondah Highway (State Route 34) through Ringwood and Lilydale towards Yering in the Yarra Valley.

INFORMATION AND TOURS

Yarra Valley Visitor Centre The Old Courthouse, Harker St, Healesville 3777, just off the Maroondah Hwy (daily 9am–5pm) ☎ 03 5962 2600, ⓦ visityarravalley.com.au.

Marysville Visitor Centre 11 Murchison St, Marysville (daily 9am–5pm) ☎ 03 5963 4567, ⓦ marysvilletourism. com.

Parks Victoria information line ☎ 13 19 63, ⓦ parkweb.vic.gov.au.

ACCOMMODATION

Chateau Yering Historic House Hotel 42 Melba Hwy, Yering ☎ 03 9237 3333, ⓦ chateauyering.com.au. For real comfort and luxury, you can wine and dine at the hotel's more casual *Sweetwater Café* or the very posh *Eleonore's Restaurant*, then sink into a four-poster bed in one of the period-style rooms. **$415**

Yarra Valley Grand Hotel 19 Bell St, Yarra Glen ☎ 03 9730 1230, ⓦ yarravalleygrand.com.au. The splendidly restored nineteenth-century hotel has very welcoming en-suite rooms, including a three-level tower suite, as well as a restaurant with moderately priced lunches and dinners (open daily). **$205**

EATING AND DRINKING

De Bortoli 58 Pinnacle Lane, off the Melba Hwy at Dixon's Creek north of Yarra Glen ☎03 5965 2271, ⓦdebortoli.com.au. Occupies an unbeatable location, with views over gently rolling hills. This was one of the first places in the valley to offer gourmet food, such as pan-fried kingfish with saffron ($37), at its Italian-influenced restaurant along with its wine. Lunch from noon Thurs–Mon, dinner Sat from 6pm; bookings advised.

Healesville Hotel 256 Maroondah Hwy, Healesville ☎03 5962 4002, ⓦyarravalleyharvest.com.au. One of the many great eating options in the town itself, with its beer garden, bar menu and fancier restaurant, which serves dishes like roasted pork belly ($36), and sources meat from its own butcher. Daily noon–9pm.

★**Innocent Bystander** 336 Maroondah Hwy, Healesville ☎03 5962 6111, ⓦinnocentbystander. com.au. This buzzy café dishes up tasty pizza ($25), artisan cheese-tasting plates ($28) and baked goods, as well as wine and beer from adjacent *Giant Steps winery* (☎03 5962 6111, ⓦgiantstepswine.com.au). Sun–Thurs 9am–9pm, Fri & Sat 9am–10pm.

Yarra Valley Dairy 70 McMeikans Rd, Yering ☎03 9739 0023, ⓦyvd.com.au. Sells gourmet cheeses (free tastings) and serves superb cheese-based lunches – prices vary according to daily specials. Daily 10.30am–5pm.

Dandenong Ranges National Park

Like the Blue Mountains of New South Wales, the **Dandenong** hills are enveloped in a blue haze rising from the forests of gum trees. Rain ensures that the area stays cool and lush, while fine old houses and gardens add to the scenery. Easy bushwalks in the **Dandenong Ranges National Park** start from Upper Ferntree Gully, and are accessible by train or by car via the Burwood Highway. The most picturesque route is along the winding **Mount Dandenong Tourist Road**, which is lined with mountain ash trees and quaint little villages, many with small cafés, galleries or craft shops that make for a pleasant pit stop.

8

SkyHigh

26 Observatory Rd, Mt Dandenong • Mon–Fri 9am–10pm, Sat & Sun 8am–10pm • Free; cars $6; maze $6 • ☎ 03 9751 0443, ⓦskyhighmtdandenong.com.au • Take the Mount Dandenong Tourist Rd then turn left at Ridge Rd, or take bus #694/#698 from Ferntree Gully or Belgrave stations

Atop the Dandedong ranges, there are amazing views of Melbourne and beyond from the newly developed **SkyHigh** observatory, one of the park's most popular destinations. Arguably Victoria's best lookout point, SkyHigh also has a café and bistro, a maze, and immaculately kept gardens from which to take in the scene. Views of the starry night sky are equally breathtaking.

Puffing Billy

Departs from Puffing Billy station in Belgrave (1 Old Monbulk Rd), or from Gembrook or Lakeside • Puffing Billy to Lakeside $54 return; to Gembrook $71 return • ☎ 03 9757 0700, ⓦpuffingbilly.com.au

A pleasant way to enjoy the forests and fern gullies is to take a ride on the **Puffing Billy** steam train, which runs for 13km from the Puffing Billy station in Belgrave to Lakeside on Lake Emerald, stopping at Menzies Creek and Emerald: one train a day continues a further 9km from Lake Emerald to Gembrook. The Puffing Billy station is a short, signposted walk from **Belgrave** station (suburban trains).

Emerald Lake Park

Emerald Lake Rd, Emerald • Daily: mid-March to April & Oct to mid-Dec 9am–6pm; May–Sept 9am–4.30pm; mid-Dec to mid-March 8am–8pm; café daily 9am–4.30pm • ☎ 1300 131 683, ⓦemeraldlakepark.com.au • Bus #695 runs daily from the Belgrave train station to Emerald

Just outside Emerald, man-made **Emerald Lake Park**, adjacent to the station, has over 15km of bushwalks, paddleboats for rent, a water slide and a free swimming pool, as well as picnic and barbecue facilities, tearooms and a café.

ARRIVAL AND DEPARTURE

By train and bus From Mon to Sat, it's possible, although not exactly easy, to see the Dandenongs by public transport; catch a train from Melbourne to Upper Ferntree Gully station, then take bus #698, which runs via Mount Dandenong Tourist Rd to Olinda township and the SkyHigh observatory in the Dandenong Ranges.

DANDENONG RANGES NATIONAL PARK

Alternatively, take a train to Belgrave station, starting point of the Puffing Billy steam train (see p.797), and then bus #694 (Mon–Sat). Bus #688 runs from Olinda via the northern part of Mount Dandenong Tourist Rd to Croydon railway station, where you can catch a train back to Melbourne.

Geelong and Bellarine Peninsula

Southwest of Melbourne, the **Bellarine Peninsula**, together with the Mornington Peninsula to the east, separates Port Phillip Bay from the Bass Strait. The Bellarine does not receive the hoards of tourists that the Mornington Peninsula experiences over the summer months, and because of this, it is a quiet, peaceful place to escape. Once you've passed through **Werribee**, the **You Yangs** and the **Serendip Sanctuary**, the city of **Geelong** – the state's largest city after the capital – is the gateway to the peninsula and the Great Ocean Road, and a worthy stop-off point for an afternoon or a few days en route. The historic seaside village of **Queenscliff**, with its elegant Victorian-era hotels, stately churches and quaint fishermen's cottages, sits at the end of the peninsula and is the docking point for the Peninsula Searoad passenger and car ferry, linking Queenscliff and the Bellarine with Sorrento on the Mornington Peninsula.

Werribee

Werribee Park Shuttle departs from the Victorian Arts Centre, St Kilda Rd, at 9.30am • $35 return; advance booking required on ☎ 03 9748 5094, ⓦ werribeeparkshuttle.com.au • Metro train to Werribee station (Werribee line) then bus #439 to Werribee Mansion or the zoo

Head west from Melbourne towards Geelong – for the Bellarine Peninsula and Great Ocean Road – and it's just a short detour off the Princes Freeway to **WERRIBEE** for the Werribee Mansion and the Open Range Zoo. **Werribee Park Shuttle**, a private bus service, provides transport to Werribee Park.

Werribee Mansion

K Rd • **Mansion** May–Oct Mon–Fri 10am–4pm, Sat & Sun 10am–5pm; Nov–April daily 10am–5pm • $9.60 • Guides tours daily 11.30am • $19.20 (includes entry) • ☎ 03 8734 5100, ⓦ parkweb.vic.gov.au • **Victoria State Rose Garden** Daily 9.30am–5pm • Free • ⓦ vicstaterosegarden.com.au

Built in 1874–77 by Scottish squatters Thomas and Andrew Chirnside, who struck it rich on the back of selling sheep, the sixty-room mansion is the largest private residence in Victoria. Guides in period costume show you around the ornate homestead and the Victorian-era gardens; alternatively, free audioguides are available at the entrance. The grand sandstone building is surrounded by 25 acres of formal gardens, including the **Victoria State Rose Garden**, which is at its best between November and April when the five thousand rose bushes are in bloom.

Werribee Open Range Zoo

K Rd • **Zoo** Daily 9am–5pm • $32.50; safari tour (40min) included in ticket • **Off Road Safari** Daily at 11.45am; 1hr 30min • $55 • ⓦ zoo. org.au

Just down the road from Werribee Mansion are the extensive grounds of **Werribee Open Range Zoo**, home to giraffes, cheetahs, lions, rhinoceroses, hippopotamuses and monkeys, as well as kangaroos and emus. It's designed to resemble as closely as possible the natural habitats of the animals. There's a **safari tour** conducted by trained guides and an "**Off Road Safari**" through the park's African savannah.

Shadowfax Winery

K Rd • Daily 11am–5pm; restaurant Mon–Fri noon–3pm, Sat & Sun noon–4pm; cellar door daily 11am–5pm • Free • ☎ 03 9731 4420,
Ⓦ shadowfax.com.au

The **Shadowfax Winery** is an impressive box-like structure that offers cellar door
sales, glimpses of the winemaking process, and tastings in the underground barrel
hall, which is rich with the wonderful aromas of maturing wines. Along with
gourmet food from the deli, there's live music every Saturday and Sunday over
lunch at the restaurant.

You Yangs Regional Park

The small but rugged granite peaks that rise sharply out of the flat volcanic plains
between Melbourne and Geelong form the **You Yangs Regional Park**. Scramble to the
top of the highest, **Flinders Peak** (348m; approx 45min return), and you're rewarded
with fine views of Geelong and Port Phillip Bay. The You Yangs, as well as the nearby
Brisbane Ranges, are excellent places for spotting kangaroos, wallabies, koalas and
possums at dusk.

Serendip Sanctuary

20km north of Geelong at 100 Windermere Rd, Lara • Daily 10am–4pm • Free • Ⓦ parkweb.vic.gov.au • Nearest train station is Lara (V/
Line) from where it's a 30min walk

The **Serendip Sanctuary** is a square kilometre of bush, marsh and wetlands renowned
for its captive breeding programme of brolgas, magpie geese and Australian bustards.
These can be viewed on four self-guided walks ranging from 800m to 1.4km, along
walkways dotted with bird hides and observation areas. You can also observe
kangaroos, wallabies and emus in their natural habitat. Maps available from the
information centre.

Geelong

Approaching **GEELONG** via its industrial outskirts, you can be forgiven for wanting to
zip past the bland melange of fast-food outlets, petrol stations and suburban housing to
the beckoning seaside attractions of the Bellarine Peninsula and the Great Ocean Road
beyond. However, Geelong has made a big effort to shed its rust-bucket image, mainly
by revamping the waterfront. The city centre is a pleasant enough place to do some
exploring, combined with a lunch stop.

National Wool Museum

Geelong Wool Exchange, 26 Moorabool St • Mon–Fri 9.30am–5pm, Sat–Sun 10am–5pm • $9 • ☎ 03 5272 4701, Ⓦ geelongaustralia
.com.au/nwm

The **National Wool Museum**, housed in the Geelong Wool Exchange, a National
Trust-listed building, is worth a visit. It concentrates on the social history of
the wool industry, with reconstructions of typical shearers' quarters and a
millworker's 1920s cottage; wool is still auctioned off thirty days a year on the
exchange's top floor.

Geelong Art Gallery

55 Little Malop St • Daily 10am–5pm • Donation appreciated • ☎ 03 5229 3645 Ⓦ geelonggallery.org.au

Many of the town's best Victorian buildings are on **Little Malop Street**, including
the elegant **Geelong Art Gallery**, which has an extensive collection of paintings
by nineteenth-century Australian artists such as Tom Roberts and Frederick
McCubbin, plus twentieth-century Australian paintings, sculpture and
decorative arts.

8

Corio Bay

From Little Malop Street and Malop Street, Moorabool Street leads down to **Corio Bay** and the waterfront, with its renovated promenades, rotunda, fountains and a lovely nineteenth-century carousel. There's a lovely swimming enclosure at Eastern Beach with diving platforms and fun water play equipment.

Baywalk Bollards

Over a hundred sculptured **bollards** are installed around the Geelong waterfront along Eastern Beach. The bollards chronicle iconic city characters from the past and present, including dapper young ladies in neck-to-knee bathing costumes, 1930s lifesavers, a Geelong AFL footballer, jaunty sailors, fishermen and a town band.

Botanic Gardens

Daily 7.30am–5pm; *Tea House* daily 11am–3pm • Free

Nestled among the lawns and trees of Eastern Park, around ten minutes' walk from the city centre, are Geelong's **Botanic Gardens**. The entrance is through the latest addition to the gardens, the 21st Century Garden, which specializes in resilient native and exotic dry-climate plants. Beyond this are the historic gardens: begun in the late 1850s, they boast lawns, rare trees, a fernery and conservatory, fountains and sculptures, as well as the small *Tea House café*.

Narana Creations

410 Torquay Rd (Surfcoast Hwy), Grovedale • Mon–Fri 9am–5pm, Sat 10am–4pm • Free • ☏ 03 5241 5700, ⓦ narana.com.au

On the way to Torquay (see p.811), **Narana Creations**, a not-for-profit Aboriginal arts, crafts and cultural centre, is worth a brief stop. Paintings and various cultural artefacts including traditional boomerangs and *yidaki* (didgeridoos) are sold here, and visitors can sometimes listen to Dreamtime stories or didgeridoo playing.

ARRIVAL AND DEPARTURE   GEELONG

By train The easiest way to get to Geelong from Melbourne is by train (hourly from Southern Cross Station); the train station is situated northwest of the centre.

By bus To get to the Bellarine Peninsula from Geelong, take a McHarry's Buslines bus (☏ 03 5223 2111, ⓦ mcharrys.com.au) from the train station for Ocean Grove and Barwon Heads, Point Lonsdale via Queenscliff, St Leonards via Portarlington, and Grovedale via Torquay.

INFORMATION

Tourist information In addition to the visitor centre (daily 9am–5pm; ☏ 03 5283 1735, ⓦ visitgeelongbellarine. com.au) at the Wool Museum (see p.799), there's a helpful tourist information stall (Mon–Sat 9am–5pm) in the Market Square Shopping Centre, at the corner of Moorabool and Malop streets, and a booth on the waterfront (daily 10am–4pm) in front of the carousel. There's also a visitor centre at the Little River rest stop on the Princes Hwy, on the way to Geelong from Melbourne (daily 9am–5pm; ☏ 03 5283 1735).

ACCOMMODATION

Irish Murphy's 30 Aberdeen St ☏ 03 5221 4335, ⓦ irishmurphysgeelong.com.au. A small hostel above a lively Irish pub with newly renovated rooms and facilities. It has a kitchen, common room and free wi-fi for guests as well as a 20 percent discount on meals at the pub and restaurant downstairs. Just a 5min walk from the train station and a 10min walk from Geelong CBD. Dorms $35, doubles $80

Vue Apartments 6 Bellerine St ☏ 03 5202 1061, ⓦ vueapartments.com.au. Comfortable serviced apartments close to the waterfront, most rooms with park or bay views. On-site day spa, and in close proximity to public transport, shopping centre and restaurants. $225

EATING AND DRINKING

Fishermen's Pier At the bay end of Yarra St ☎ 03 5222 4100, ⓦ fishermenspier.com.au. Serves tasty, if pricey, seafood prepared in a range of styles, from African to Tuscan. Daily noon–2.30pm & 6–9pm.

Little Creatures Brewery 221 Swanston St ☎ 03 5202 4009, ⓦ littlecreatures.com.au. Set in a historic wool mill, the trendy crowd here creates a lively atmosphere. Sip on the signature pale ale ($10.50 pint) as you chow down on wood-fired pizza and share platters (don't miss the pulled pork sliders; $13). Mon–Tues 10am–5pm, Wed–Fri 10am–10pm, Sat–Sun 8am–10pm.

The Telegraph Hotel 2 Pakington St ☎ 03 5222 2471, ⓦ thetelegraphhotel.com.au. This 1800s landmark watering hole serves up hearty modern-Oz cuisine (meaning a bit of everything), from veggie Thai curry ($22) to chicken scallopini ($26). Be sure to leave room for the honeycomb berry sundae for dessert ($12). Daily 11am–11pm.

Wharf Shed Café 15 Eastern Beach Rd ☎ 03 5221 6645, ⓦ wharfshedcafe.com.au. A popular café/ restaurant in a converted boat shed in Geelong's waterfront precinct, which feeds cakes, pizzas and fish 'n' chips to the masses coming here on sunny weekends. Mon–Fri 11am–late, Sat & Sun 9am–late.

Queenscliff and around

From Geelong, the Bellarine Highway runs 31km southeast to **QUEENSCLIFF** through flat and not particularly scenic grazing country. Queenscliff is essentially a quiet fishing village on Swan Bay – with several quaint cottages on Fishermens Flat – which became a favourite holiday resort for Melbourne's wealthy elite in the nineteenth century. It then fell out of favour, but has recently begun to enjoy something of a revival as a popular place for a weekend away or a Sunday drive.

Fort Museum

King St • Tours Sat & Sun 1pm & 3pm; 1hr 30min • $12 • ☎ 03 5258 1488, ⓦ fortqueenscliff.com.au

Queenscliff's position near the narrow entrance to Port Phillip Bay made it strategically important: a **fort** here faces the one at Point Nepean. Planned during the Crimean War, but not completed until 1885, it was built in response to the perceived threat of a Russian invasion, and was used again during World War I and II. Its museum can only be visited on ninety-minute guided tours.

Queenscliffe Maritime Museum

Wharf Street • Daily 10.30am–4.30pm • $8 • ☎ 03 5258 3440, ⓦ maritimequeenscliffe.org.au

Among Queenscliff's attractions is the **Queenscliffe Maritime Museum**, which concentrates on the many shipwrecks caused by The Rip, a fierce current about 1km wide between Point Lonsdale and Point Nepean. Outside, a tiny fisherman's cottage is set up as it would have been in 1870, and there's a shed where an Italian fisherman painted, in naive style, all the ships he'd seen pass through from 1895 to 1947 (imaginatively including the *Titanic*).

Marine and Freshwater Discovery Centre

2A Bellarine Hwy • Mon–Fri 11am–3pm, 10am–4pm during school holidays • $8, children $5 • ☎ 03 5258 3344, ⓦ mdca.org.au

The **Marine and Freshwater Discovery Centre** provides educational services in a small aquarium stocked with local marine life. Also open to the public, it organizes a range of activities mainly during the summer holidays, such as marine biology cruises, rock pool rambles and snorkelling tours.

Bellarine Peninsula Railway

Peninsula Railway Sun (plus Tues & Thurs in school hols) 11am, 1.30pm & 3pm • Lakers Siding $10 one-way, $15 return; Drysdale $20 one-way, $30 return • ☎ 03 5258 2069, ⓦ bellarinerailway.com.au • **Blues Train** Sat 6.30–11.30pm • $99.70 return and meal (over-18s only) • ⓦ thebluestrain.com.au

Every Sunday, the **Bellarine Peninsula Railway** operates steam trips from the old Queenscliff Railway Station to Lakers Siding and Drysdale, 20km northwest. The railway also hosts the Blues Train on Saturday nights, a round trip with performances by Melbourne's leading blues and jazz musicians.

Point Lonsdale

From Queenscliff, it's about 5km to peaceful **Point Lonsdale**, whose most noticeable feature is its magnificent 1902 lighthouse, 120m high and visible for 30km out to sea. Below the lighthouse, on the edge of the bluff, is "Buckley's Cave" where William Buckley is thought to have lived at some stage during his thirty-year sojourn with the Aborigines.

Adventure Park

1251 Bellarine Hwy, Wallington • Daily: Jan 10am–6.30pm; Feb–April & Nov–Dec 10am–5pm, closed May–Oct • $42, children 90–120cm tall $32, under-90cm free • ☎ 03 5250 7200, ⓦ adventurepark.com.au • To get there by bus, phone McHarry's on ☎ 03 5223 2111 (approx 10min from Geelong or Queenscliff)

Ten kilometres or so west down the highway from Queenscliff, the **Adventure Park** boasts Victoria's only water park, and is a big hit with kids and adults alike. Spread over fifty acres of picturesque parkland, it has over twenty rides and provides everything from giant water slides and a raging river to minigolf, go-karts and paddleboats.

Portarlington

PORTARLINGTON, sitting on Port Phillip Bay about 14km north of Queenscliff, is famous for its sweet blue mussels and the annual Portarlington Mussel Festival (Newcombe St; second Sat in Jan). There's also a beautifully preserved steam-powered flour mill, spread over four storeys of solid stone, owned by the National Trust (mid-Sept to May Sat & Sun noon–4pm; $5).

ARRIVAL AND DEPARTURE
QUEENSCLIFF

By ferry A reliable car and passenger ferry service operated by Peninsula Searoad (☎03 5258 3244, ⓦ searoad.com.au) runs across the mouth of the bay from Queenscliff to Sorrento on the Mornington Peninsula all year round (hourly 7am–6pm, Boxing Day to end of daylight saving until 7pm; 45min). One-way fares for pedestrians are $11, while cars cost $62 (including driver) plus $11 for each adult passenger. Motorbikes plus a rider are $35. No advance bookings are necessary but cars should be at the terminal 30–45min prior to departure.

INFORMATION AND EVENTS

Queenscliff Visitor Centre 55 Hesse St (daily 9am–5pm; ☎031 5258 4843, ⓦ queenscliff.com.au).
Queenscliff Music Festival Held annually on the last weekend of Nov, featuring an eclectic mix of Australian contemporary music (folk, blues, world music, fusion), and draws ever-growing crowds (ⓦ qmf.net.au).

ACTIVITIES

Diving Dive among wrecks and marine life with the Queenscliff Dive Centre ($240 for one-day Scuba Experience; ☎03 5258 1188, ⓦ divequeenscliff.com.au).
Dolphin cruises Visit a seal colony or a gannet rookery and get the chance to swim with dolphins in Port Phillip Bay with Sea All Dolphin Swims (4hr; $145; twice daily Oct–May; ☎03 5258 3889, ⓦ dolphinswims.com.au).

Bike rental You can rent a bike from Big4 Beacon Resort (from $10; see below) and follow the Bellarine Rail Trail (map available from the information centres in Queenscliff and Geelong), a fabulous track running 33km from Queenscliff to Geelong through farming and coastal countryside, sharing some of the journey with the Bellarine Railway.

ACCOMMODATION

Big4 Beacon Resort 78 Bellarine Hwy ☎03 5258 1133, ⓦ beaconresort.com.au. Recently renovated holiday park with a heated pool. Powered sites $44, cabins $125, villas $175, apartments $252
Point Lonsdale Guest House 31 Point Lonsdale Rd, Point Lonsdale ☎03 5258 1142, ⓦ pointlonsdaleguest house.com.au. Originally constructed in 1884 to house the workers building the Point Lonsdale Lighthouse, this renovated guesthouse retains much old-world charm. The ship-cabin decor gives a distinct maritime theme in both

the older and newer parts of the building, which is kept spotlessly clean. $125

Queenscliff Dive Centre Lodge 37 Leamonth St, Queenscliff ☎03 5258 4188, ⓦdivequeenscliff.com. au. A good budget option, with facilities including a heated diver training pool, spa and BBQ area, as well as a sociable lounge with open fireplace. Breakfast included. Perfect for those undertaking courses with the dive school, but open to non-diving visitors as well. Dorms $35, doubles $120

Salt Loft 33 Hesse St, Queenscliff ☎0439 353 624, ⓦsalt-loft.com.au. Self-catering apartments with stunning water views from private balcony. All rooms with coffee machine and luxury bath products. Complimentary use of tandem bike to tour around. $260

Vue Grand 46 Hesse St, Queenscliff ☎03 5258 1544, ⓦvuegrand.com.au. Grand hotel with Spanish-style exterior and a fabulously ornate Victorian interior, plus an award-winning, but expensive, restaurant. $198

EATING AND DRINKING

Some of the town's best **places to eat** can be found along Hesse St. In addition to the options below are the gorgeous – but pricey – restaurants at the *Vue Grand* (lunch & dinner daily; see above).

Athelstane House 4 Hobson St, Queenscliff ☎03 5258 1024, ⓦathelstane.com.au. Modern Australian fare in a laidback atmosphere. Enjoy a sunny breakfast (from $10) on the deck or courtyard, and dinner (from $30) in the cosy dining room from the small, yet well-done menu. Mon–Fri 8–10am & 6–9pm, Sat–Sun 8–11am & 6–9pm.

Couta Boat Café 59 Hesse St, Queenscliff ☎03 5258 4600, ⓦqueenscliffinn.com.au. As it's based in the *Queenscliff Inn* – a gorgeously latticed 1902 Edwardian guesthouse – dining at the *Couta Boat* is as much of a historical experience as a culinary one. The menu features fresh local seafood and home-cooked favourites, made from locally sourced produce. Mains $28. Thurs–Mon noon–3pm.

Little Red Fox Eatery 600 Banks Rd ☎03 5245 7282, ⓦlittleredfoxeatery.com.au. A little further out of town, tucked away in the *Banks Road Vineyard*, with a seasonal menu sourced from local produce. The $70 five-course chefs table ($95 with matched wines) provides a good sample of the top menu items. Breakfast Sat–Sun, lunch Wed–Sun, dinner Fri–Sat.

Vue Street Bar 46 Hesse St ☎03 5258 1544, ⓦvuegrand.com.au. A trendy streetside bar on the terrace of the historic *Vue Grand* (see below). A rotating variety of speciality and microbrewery beers on tap (plus a range of over 70 bottled craft beers) are complemented by tasty bar snacks such as fish and chips ($19) and pizza ($18). Wed–Sat noon–8pm, Sun noon–3pm.

8

Victoria

TWELVE APOSTLES, GREAT OCEAN ROAD

9

Victoria

Australia's second-smallest state, Victoria is also the most densely populated and industrialized. Although you're never too far from civilization, there are many opportunities to sample the state's wilder days when it was a centre for gold prospectors and bushrangers. All routes radiate from Melbourne, and no destination is much more than seven hours' drive away. Sadly, many visitors see little of Victoria apart from its cultured capital and the Great Ocean Road, a winding 285km drive through spectacular coastal scenery. Others may venture to rugged Wilsons Promontory National Park (the "Prom"), three hours away on the coast of the mainly dairy Gippsland region, or to the Goldfields, where the nineteenth-century gold rush left its mark in the grandiose architecture of old mining towns such as Ballarat and Bendigo.

There is, however, much more to the state. Marking the end of the Great Dividing Range, the jagged sandstone ranges of the **Grampians**, with their Aboriginal rock art and dazzling springtime flora, rise from the monotonous **Wimmera** wheatfields and Western District wool country. To the north of the Grampians is the wide, flat Mallee region – scrub, sand dunes and dry lakes reaching to the **Murray River** and Mildura, an irrigated oasis supporting orchards and vineyards. In complete contrast, the **Victorian Alps** in the state's northeast have several winter **ski slopes**, high country that is also perfect for summer bushwalking and horseriding. In the foothills and plains below, where bushranger **Ned Kelly** once roamed, are some of Victoria's finest wineries (wine buffs should pick up a copy of *Wine Regions of Victoria*, available from the visitor centre in Melbourne and other towns). Beach culture is alive and well on the **coastline**, with some of Australia's best **surfing**.

Brief history

Seminomadic **Koories** have lived in this region for at least forty thousand years, establishing semipermanent settlements such as those of circular stone houses and fish traps at Lake Condah in western Victoria. Colonists, however, did not get off to an auspicious start: there was an unsuccessful attempt at settlement in the **Port Phillip Bay** area in 1803, but Van Diemen's Land (Tasmania) across Bass Strait was deemed more suitable. It was from Launceston that Port Phillip Bay was eventually settled, in 1834; other Tasmanians soon followed and **Melbourne** was established.

This occupation was in defiance of a British government edict forbidding settlement in the territory, then part of New South Wales, but **squatting** had already begun the previous year when Edward Henty arrived with his stock to establish the first white settlement at **Portland** on the southwest coast. A pattern developed of land-hungry

VICTORIAN ALPS

Highlights

❶ Great Ocean Road Wait until the sun sets and watch Little (fairy) penguins come out to play at the Twelve Apostles; Lorne and Port Fairy are the nicest bases en route. **See p.810**

❷ Goldfields Discover the mining memorabilia and grand architecture which grace the old gold towns of Ballarat and Bendigo. **See p.827**

❸ Wilsons Promontory National Park There's great bushwalking and fantastic coastal scenery at Victoria's favourite national park. **See p.860**

❹ Kelly Country Follow in the steps of Ned Kelly, Australia's most famous bush outlaw, in the historic towns of the northeast, the most appealing of which is beautiful Beechworth. **See p.874**

❺ Milawa Gourmet Region Excellent local produce washed down with great wines from Brown Brothers winery – against a backdrop of stunning scenery. **See p.875**

❻ Victorian Alps Perfect for skiing in winter, the Victorian Alps are ideal territory for summer bushwalking. **See p.876**

HIGHLIGHTS ARE MARKED ON THE MAP ON PP.808–809

9

settlers – generally already men of means – responding to Britain's demand for wool, and during the 1840s and 1850s what was to become Victoria evolved into a prosperous pastoral community with squatters extending huge grazing runs.

From the beginning, the Koories fought against the invasion of their land: 1836 saw the start of the **Black War**, as it has been called, a bloody guerrilla struggle against the settlers. By 1850, however, the Aboriginal people had been devastated – by disease as

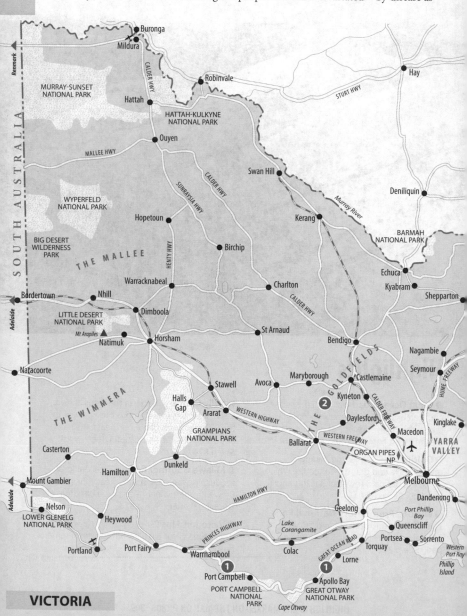

well as war – and felt defeated, too, by the apparently endless flood of invaders; their population is believed to have declined from around 15,500 to just 2300.

By 1851 the white population was large and confident enough to demand separation from New South Wales, achieved, by a stroke of luck, just nine days before **gold** was discovered in the new colony. The rich goldfields of Ballarat, Bendigo and Castlemaine brought an influx of hopeful migrants from around the world. More gold came from

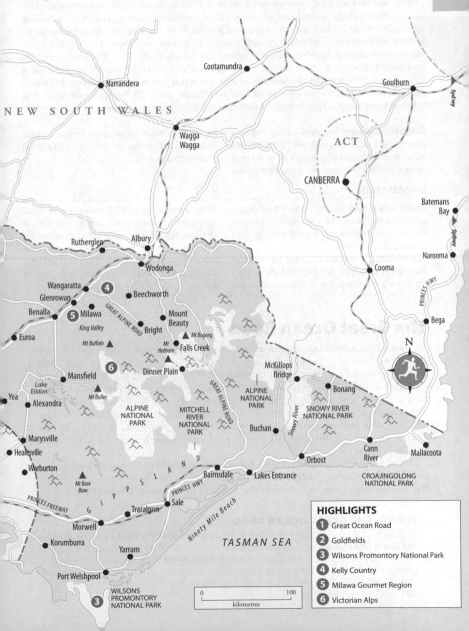

HIGHLIGHTS

1. Great Ocean Road
2. Goldfields
3. Wilsons Promontory National Park
4. Kelly Country
5. Milawa Gourmet Region
6. Victorian Alps

9

Victoria over the next thirty years than was extracted during the celebrated California gold rush, transforming Victoria from a pastoral backwater into Australia's financial capital. Following federation in 1901, Melbourne was the national political capital – a title it retained until Canberra became fully operational in 1927.

GETTING AROUND VICTORIA

Using your **own vehicle** is definitely most convenient, as some rural train and bus services are infrequent and quite a few places can only be reached by public transport with difficulty, if at all. Most public transport, by rail and road, is with **V/Line** and subsidiary country bus lines; Melbourne, Geelong and Warrnambool (for the Great Ocean Road), Bendigo (for the Goldfields and Murray region) and Ballarat (for western Victoria) are the main interchanges (☎ 1800 800 007, ⓦ vline .com.au). Virtually all trains depart from Melbourne's Southern Cross Station (see p.758). The NSW-operated TrainLink runs trains to Albury and other towns in the northeast, and Melbourne, and bus services to Echuca and Mildura from southern NSW train stations (ⓦ nswtrainlink.info). Greyhound Australia buses operate through Victoria from Sydney and Canberra, stopping in northeast Victorian towns (Wangaratta, Benalla and Seymour; ☎ 1300 473 946, ⓦ greyound.com.au). From Melbourne Airport (see p.758) there are frequent buses to Ballarat, Bendigo, Gippsland and Geelong.

Timetables and fares Timetables and fares frequently change – call Public Transport Victoria (PTV; ☎ 1800 800 007) or check the website (ⓦ ptv.vic.gov.au) for the latest information. The PTV website has an excellent journey planner which details all departure times and places, connections, and whether the service is by train or bus (V/line or other operator).

INFORMATION

Tourist information Tourism Victoria (ⓦ visitvictoria. com) has plentiful information on all areas of the state. Visit Parks Victoria (ⓦ parks.vic.gov.au) for details of the state's national parks and reserves.

Climate Winter is generally mild, and the occasional heatwaves in summer are mercifully usually limited to a few days in a row, though they can create bushfires that last for weeks (see box, p.860). The only problem is that of unpredictability. Spring and autumn days can be immoderately hot or cool, and rainy "English" weather can descend in any season. Weeks of heavy summer rain in early 2011 caused flooding in the state's north and west: forty towns were evacuated and eighty roads closed as rivers rose rapidly and broke their banks across the region.

The Great Ocean Road

The **Great Ocean Road** (ⓦ visitgreatoceanroad.org.au), Victoria's famous southwestern coastal route, starts at Torquay, just over 20km south of Geelong, and extends 285km west to Warrnambool. It was built between 1919 and 1932 as a scenic road to equal California's Pacific Coast Highway – and it certainly lives up to its reputation. The road was to be both a memorial to the soldiers who died in World War I and an employment scheme for those who returned. More than three thousand ex-servicemen laboured with picks and shovels, carving the road along Australia's most rugged and densely forested coastline; the task was speeded up with the help of the jobless during the Great Depression.

The road hugs the coastline between **Torquay** and **Apollo Bay** and passes through the popular holiday towns of **Anglesea** and **Lorne**, set below the Otway Ranges. From Apollo Bay it heads inland, through the towering forests of **Great Otway National Park**, before

---

HIKING THE GREAT OCEAN ROAD

Walking and hiking enthusiasts can tread two magnificent **walking tracks** along the coast: **the Great Ocean Walk** (ⓦ greatoceanwalk.com.au), a 104km track from Apollo Bay to the Twelve Apostles, and the long-established **Great South West Walk** (ⓦ greatsouthwestwalk. com), a superb 250km circuit starting from just outside Portland that heads southeast along the coast and back along the Glenelg River. A good source of information is Parks Victoria (☎ 13 19 63, ⓦ parks.vic.gov.au).

rejoining the coast at Princetown to wind along the shore for the entire length of **Port Campbell National Park**. This stretch from Moonlight Head to Port Fairy, sometimes referred to as the "Shipwreck Coast", is the most spectacular – there are two hundred known shipwrecks here, victims of imprecise mid-nineteenth century navigation tools, the rough Southern Ocean and dramatic rock formations such as the **Twelve Apostles**.

From **Warrnambool**, the small regional centre where the Great Ocean Road ends, the Princes Highway continues along the coast, through quaint seaside **Port Fairy** and industrial **Portland**, before turning inland for the final stretch to the South Australia border.

GETTING AROUND

THE GREAT OCEAN ROAD

By train There's a service from Melbourne to Warrnambool via Geelong (2–3 daily, 3hr 20min), with connecting V/Line buses to Port Fairy and Portland, and on to Mount Gambier in South Australia.

By bus A daily bus service operates from Geelong to Apollo Bay, calling at Torquay, Anglesea, Aireys Inlet and Lorne; the journey takes around 2hr 30min. On Mondays, Wednesdays and Fridays the service continues to Warrnambool (after a bus change in Apollo Bay) and makes a short photo-opportunity stop at the Twelve Apostles. Buses also travel in the reverse direction, from

Warrnambool to Geelong. Greyhound buses travel the Great Ocean Road on their three-day Melbourne–Adelaide trip.

By car If you don't have your own vehicle, it's worth considering one way car rental, available from the big-name companies in Melbourne. There are plenty of parking spots from which to admire the view, but with narrow roads, steep cliffs and hairpin bends, drivers need to keep their eyes glued to the road. In summer the road is filled with cyclists, although the route is only suitable for the experienced and adventurous.

TOURS

One-way **tours** between Melbourne and Adelaide, via the Great Ocean Rd, are a good way to take in the scenery. A few operators do one- or two-day **round trips** from Melbourne to the Great Ocean Rd, some with a Grampians option and/or transfer to Adelaide.

Adventure Tours ☎ 1300 654 604 or ☎ 03 8102 7800, ⓦ adventuretours.com.au. Two-day tours (from $295) from Melbourne to Adelaide, taking in the Great Ocean Road and the Grampians, and four-day tours (from $780) adding in Kangaroo Island; shared hostel accommodation

and some meals included.

Groovy Grape ☎ 1800 661 177, ⓦ groovygrape.com. au. Small and friendly Groovy Grape covers the Great Ocean Rd–Grampians route in a three-day tour ($425), including accommodation, all meals and national park entry fees.

Torquay

Gateway to the Great Ocean Road, **TORQUAY** is the centre of **surf culture** on Victoria's "surf coast" and two local beaches, **Jan Juc** and **Bells Beach**, are solidly entrenched in Australian surfing mythology. Many come for the excellent surfing, but the town also has some good restaurants and cafés, surf- and beach-wear shops, great walks, golf, day-spas and a generally lively atmosphere, particularly in summer. The big event here is the Rip Curl Pro (call Surfing Victoria on ☎ 03 5261 2907 or see ⓦ ripcurl.com.au), held at Bells Beach at Easter, which draws national and international contestants and thousands of spectators.

Point Impossible, just north of Torquay, is the start of the 44km **Surf Coast Walk** (ⓦ surfcoastwalk.com.au) to Fairhaven via Bells Beach, Anglesea and Aireys Inlet. The walk is rated moderate and the track is generally good.

Surf City Plaza

As you come into Torquay on the Surfcoast Highway – the main road to Torquay from Geelong – you'll see the **Surf City Plaza** shopping centre on your right, one of the best places in town to rent and buy surf gear. Left off the Great Ocean Road towards the beach, there's another cluster of shops, supermarkets and cafés around Gilbert Street. The **Surf World Museum** (daily 9am–5pm; $12; ☎ 03 5261 4606, ⓦ surfworld.com.au)

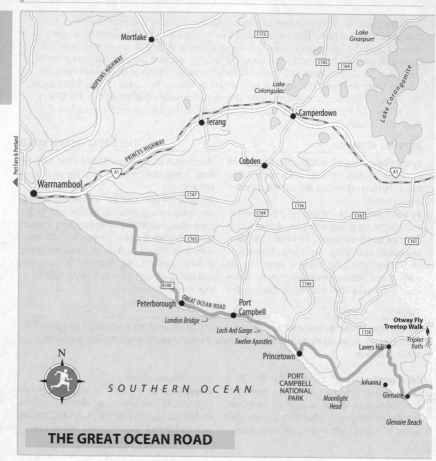

THE GREAT OCEAN ROAD

at the rear of the plaza features the Australian Surfing Hall of Fame, interactive videos that explain how waves are created, and displays about surfing history.

The beaches

A grassy public reserve shaded by huge Norfolk pines (with electric barbecues and picnic tables) runs along rocky **Fisherman's Beach** – worth a look for its magnificent sundial, made up of tiny mosaic tiles and shells representing Aboriginal Dreamtime stories – and **Front Beach**. The **Surf Beach** (or "back beach"), south of Cosy Corner (a headland separating Front and Surf beaches), is backed by rugged cliffs and takes a full belting from the Southern Ocean; it's patrolled in summer. **Jan Juc**, just south of Surf Beach across Torquay Golf Club, is also patrolled in season and has better swimming and surfing.

Tiger Moth World Adventure Park

Torquay Airport, 325 Blackgate Rd • Fri–Mon 10am–5pm • $12.50 • ☏ 03 5261 5100, �ⓦ tigermothworld.com.au

Tiger Moth World Adventure Park, a family amusement park 3km east of Torquay, has lots of mostly water-based attractions, but also offers skydives ($399) and **scenic flights** aboard vintage Tiger Moths, biplanes and modern aircraft. The modern

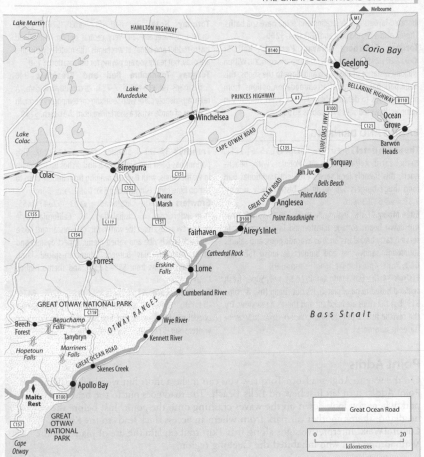

planes fly as far west as the Twelve Apostles, following the rugged coastline (1hr 30min return; $390pp; min 2 passengers).

ARRIVAL AND INFORMATION

By bus A daily bus from Geelong to Apollo Bay calls in at Torquay and other points in between. A weekday-only service (Mon, Wed, Fri) runs to Warrnambool with a bus change in Apollo Bay. Local buses run between Geelong and Torquay – McHarry's Buslines (☎03 5223 2111, ⓦmcharrys.com.au) has details.

Tourist information Torquay Visitor Information Centre

TORQUAY

in the Surfworld Museum, Surf City Plaza, Beach Rd (daily 9am–5pm; ☎03 5261 4219).

Watersports Anglesea-based Go Ride a Wave (☎1300 132 441, ⓦgoridewave.com.au) and Westcoast Adventure (☎03 5261 2241, ⓦwestcoastadventure.org) offer surfing classes and sea-kayaking in Torquay.

ACCOMMODATION

Grossmans Country Cottages 375 Grossmans Rd ☎03 5261 2656 or ☎0410 313 533, ⓦgrossmans .com.au. Excellent-value, fully equipped cottages on rolling hills, 5min out of town, with a real country-farm feel. Each cottage can sleep five people, and some have

sea views. There is also a tennis court and a spa centre. No internet. **$220**

Surf City Motel 35 The Esplanade ☎03 5261 3492, ⓦsurfcitymotel.com.au. Super location across from the beach, but prices are on the high side. The rooms have

9

assorted layouts and decoration and some have spa baths. There's also a heated pool and BBQ area. **$200**

Torquay Foreshore Caravan Park 35 Bell St ☎ 03 5261 2496, ⊛ torquaycaravanpark.com.au. Within walking distance of the beach and close to the shops, this huge park has an array of accommodation options, from powered sites to deluxe cabins. Popular with students in summer. Powered sites **$79**, cabins **$350**

Torquay Hotel 36 Bell St ☎ 03 5261 2001, ⊛ torquayhotel.com.au. Very central option, with good bistro fodder and bands at weekends. The motel-style rooms are okay, but really you are paying for the location. **$150**

Torquay Toongahra Bed and Breakfast 240 Grossmans Rd ☎ 0402 657 731, ⊛ torquaybnb.com. A relaxing, friendly place with soothing contemporary decor, in six acres of gardens just a short drive from the beach. **$150**

EATING AND DRINKING

The Beach Hotel 3 Stuart Ave, Jan Juc ☎ 03 5261 5111, ⊛ thebeachhoteljanjuc.com.au. Popular with beach-goers, this friendly local serves excellent traditional pub food (huge burgers $20.90) in its bistro. Daily noon–2.30pm & 6–8.30pm.

Café Moby 41 The Esplanade ☎ 03 5261 2339. Former run-down beach cottage transformed into a great café serving tasty breakfasts, such as avocado eggs, and salads, sourdough sandwiches and burgers at lunch ($8–15). Daily 7am–4pm (longer hours in summer).

Fisho's 34 The Esplanade ☎ 0407 534 124. Super-fresh seafood boxed to go or plated. It's not cheap (fish & chips $19) but the chips are hand cut and there's a sea view. Try the ceviche fish tacos ($20). Daily noon–3pm & 5–8pm (later in summer).

Frenchy's 17 The Esplanade ☎ 03 5261 2202. This parlour has been here since 1962, and dishes up ice cream in waffle cones, with flavours ranging from bubble gum to lemon lime twist (single scoop $5). Daily 9am–5pm.

Growlers 23 The Esplanade ☎ 03 5264 8455, ⊛ growlers.com.au. Inhabiting a Californian-style bungalow across from the water, this café-restaurant has a laidback beach vibe and varied menu. Expect oysters and other seafood, plus burgers, Moroccan-spiced lamb backstraps (mains from $18–37.50), and theme nights. Daily 8.30am–late.

Sandbah Café 21 Gilbert St ☎ 03 5261 6414, ⊛ sandbahcafe.com.au. This large and airy place serves good breakfasts, cakes and lunches, including warming winter soup ($12–20). Daily 7am–5pm.

Point Addis

On the way to Anglesea from Torquay, you can make a short but worthwhile detour to **Point Addis**; turn left just beyond Bells Beach. The road goes out to the headland car park where you look down on the waves crashing onto the point. Just before the headland, there's another car park from where an access track leads to the **Koorie Cultural Walk**. Interpretive signs along this 1km trail explain the use of plants by the Wathaurong clan who inhabited the Geelong region.

Anglesea

ANGLESEA is a pleasant place for a holiday, with the Anglesea River running through to the sea, and picnic grounds along its banks; its main claim to fame is a large population of **kangaroos**, which graze the golf course. Despite tourist development, the beach has retained its sand dunes and untouched aspect. Children can swim safely here, as the surf is fairly gentle, although the waves are high and powerful enough for body-surfing.

ARRIVAL AND ACTIVITIES
ANGLESEA

By bus A daily bus service from Geelong to Apollo Bay calls in at Anglesea and other points in between. A weekday-only service (Mon, Wed, Fri) runs to Warrnambool with a bus change in Apollo Bay.

Watersports Go Ride a Wave (☎ 1300 132 441, ⊛ gorideawave.com.au) are a long-established outdoor

activities company based in Anglesea with an outlet in Torquay, offering surfing lessons ($80/2hr or packages; gear included) as well as sea-kayaking instruction and trips exploring the coastline. Westcoast Adventure (☎ 03 5261 2241, ⊛ westcoastadventure.org) run surfing classes in Torquay and Anglesea ($60/2hr or packages, gear included).

ACCOMMODATION AND EATING

Anglesea Backpackers Hostel 40 Noble St ☎ 03 5263 2664, ⊛ angleseabackpackers.com. A small hostel located

between the river and the golf course, with two six-bed dorms and an en-suite double. Dorms **$35**, doubles **$115**

Anglesea Rivergums 10 Bingley Pde ☎03 5263 3066, ⓦanglesearivergums.com.au. On the river, this friendly clapperboard self-catering accommodation is a great place to unwind. There are two self-contained apartments (one with private access to the *Anglesea Hotel*). No internet. **$170**
Captain Moonlite 100 Great Ocean Rd ☎03 5263 2454, ⓦcaptainmoonlite.com.au.com. In the Surf Life Saving Club and with great beach and surf views, this all-day café dishes up delicious coastal European fare to good vibes. Mains (under $30) might include snapper with

cauliflower and currants. Jan–March daily 8am–9pm; April–July & Sept–Dec Fri 11am–9pm, Sat & Sun 8am–9pm.
Laneway 73 73 Great Ocean Rd ☎03 5263 3113. Inner-city Melbourne hangs out at the beach in this daytime café (home-made paninis and focaccias, coffee and cakes) and evening bistro, which promotes sustainable fishing, with dishes such as pan-seared snapper on Vietnamese salad ($36). There are pizzas, curries and steaks too. Café daily 7am–5pm; bistro Mon, Tues & Fri–Sun 6pm–late.

Aireys Inlet

From Anglesea the road goes inland for a few kilometres through scrubby bush. Beyond, the pretty red-capped **Split Point Lighthouse** (tours on the hour 10am–4pm in summer holidays, otherwise 11am–2pm; 45min; $14; ☎1800 174 045, ⓦsplitpointlighthouse .com.au) overlooks the small town of **AIREYS INLET**. With spectacular cliffs and beautiful sandy beaches, this is a popular spot for swimming and surfing.

ARRIVAL AND ACTIVITIES	**AIREYS INLET**
By bus A daily bus service from Geelong to Apollo Bay calls in at Aireys Inlet and other points in between. A weekday-only service (Mon, Wed, Fri) runs to Warrnambool with a bus change in Apollo Bay.	**Horseriding** Blazing Saddles (☎03 5289 7322, ⓦblazingsaddlestrailrides.com) operate rides through Great Otway National Park (from $50), plus beach rides and pony rides for kids.

ACCOMMODATION AND EATING

Aireys Inlet Holiday Park Great Ocean Rd ☎03 5289 6230, ⓦaicp.com.au. En-suite cabins, from top end to budget, nestled between the bush and the beach. Facilities include a heated pool and spa. **$210**
A La Grecque Cnr Great Ocean and Beach rds ☎03 5289 6922, ⓦalagrecque.com.au. Simple, seasonal ocean- and farm-fresh Greek food courtesy of the Talimanidis family, long-term Great Ocean Road foodies. Breakfast pastries, meze and mains (to $40), such as chargrilled lamb rump with heirloom carrots and sesame yoghurt. Daily

10am–2.30pm & 6pm–late.
Split Point Cottages 40 Hopkins St ☎03 5220 0500, ⓦsplitpointcottages.com.au. Four rammed-earth cottages with modern facilities, within walking distance to the beach. There's also an on-site tennis court and outdoor spa. Minimum stay two nights. **$220**
Willows Tea House 7 Federal St ☎03 5289 6830. Next to the lighthouse, this café and gift shop in the former lightkeeper's stables is famous for its home-made cakes and scones with cream and jam ($4). Daily 9am–4pm.

Lorne and around

Picturesquely set at the foot of the heavily forested **Otway Ranges**, on the banks of the Erskine River, **LORNE** has long been the premier Great Ocean Road holiday town. Only two hours' drive from the city, it's hugely popular with Melbourne weekenders who relish its surf scene and café society overlying an essentially middle-class 1930s resort. To complete the picture, lush **Great Otway National Park**, with its walking tracks, plunging falls and fern gullies, almost surrounds the town.

About a thousand people live in Lorne, but from Christmas until the end of January twenty thousand more pour in; if you arrive unannounced, you'll have no hope of finding even a camping spot. The three-day **Falls Festival** (ⓦfallsfestival .com), held over New Year, is celebrated with a big rock concert that attracts droves of teenagers, followed a few days later by the **Mountain to Surf Run** and one day later by the highlight of the peak season, the **Pier to Pub Swim** (ⓦlornesurfclub.com.au). It is said to be the largest blue-water swimming event in the world and attracts as many as four thousand competitors who race the 1200m from Lorne Pier to the main beach.

9

The town's beachfront is enlivened by the restored *Grand Pacific Hotel* with its 1870s facade, on a headland at the western end, and the modern terraced *Cumberland Lorne Resort*. Between the street and the beach is a foreshore with trampolines and a pool. The **surf beach** itself is one of Victoria's safest, protected from the Southern Ocean by two headlands, but in summer it gets very crowded.

Qdos

35 Allenvale Rd • Jan daily 8.30am–6pm, Feb–Dec Thurs–Mon 9am–5pm • ☎ 03 5289 1989, ⊚ qdosarts.com

The cultural highlight of Lorne is **Qdos**, set above the town, which stages prestigious temporary art shows and displays sculptures outdoors among the eucalypts. It's worth visiting for the setting alone, and the café (see opposite).

Erskine Falls

Surrounding Lorne are the lush forests of the **Otway Ranges**, which form part of Great Otway National Park (see p.819). Pockets of temperate rainforest, towering blue-gum forests, cliffs and waterfalls (there are ten around Lorne) characterize the Lorne section of the park, south of the Erskine River. The **Erskine Falls**, one of the most popular attractions, drop 30m into a fern-fringed pool – from the car park here the falls are a few minutes' walk through majestic trees and tall umbrella ferns; another 150m takes you down to the quiet, rocky Erskine River. Experienced hikers can walk through the bush from Lorne to the falls (7.5km one-way; a strenuous 3–4hr walk), starting from the *Erskine River Caravan Park* next to the bridge over the Erskine River, and following the river; after 1km you'll pass the Sanctuary, a natural rock amphitheatre, then Splitter Falls and Straw Falls, before reaching Erskine Falls.

Teddy's Lookout

Teddy's Lookout, in Queens Park, is a 3km walk from Lorne (up Otway St, turn left at the roundabout into George St); just follow the signposts. You end up high above the sea, with a view of the St George River below and the Great Ocean Road curving around the cliffs.

ARRIVAL AND INFORMATION LORNE

By bus A daily bus service from Geelong to Apollo Bay calls in at Lorne and other points in between. A weekday-only service (Mon, Wed, Fri) runs to Warrnambool with a bus change in Apollo Bay.

Tourist information The very helpful visitor centre at 15 Mountjoy Pde (daily 9am–5pm; ☎ 1300 891 152 or ☎ 03 5289 1152, ⊚ visitgreatoceanroad.org.au) has a good stock of leaflets, some on hiking routes.

Services Lorne Surf Shop rents out surf- and boogie-boards and wetsuits from 132 Mountjoy Pde (daily 9.30am–5pm; ☎ 03 5289 1600, ⊚ lornesurf.com.au).

ACCOMMODATION

Cumberland Lorne 150 Mountjoy Pde ☎ 03 5289 4444, ⊚ cumberland.com.au. Luxurious, fully equipped beachfront apartments, many with private balconies overlooking the water. Facilities include a gym, tennis and squash courts, indoor swimming pool, and surfboard and mountain-bike rental. $350

Cumberland River Holiday Park 2680 Great Ocean Rd, Cumberland River ☎ 03 5289 1790, ⊚ cumberlandriver.com.au. West of Lorne, this sylvan campsite has a great location on the river and near the beach, with BBQ facilities and excellent walks. No internet. Unpowered sites $70, safari tents $120, cabins $200

Grand Pacific Hotel & Apartments 268 Mountjoy Pde, opposite the pier at Point Grey ☎ 03 5289 1609, ⊚ grandpacific.com.au. This restored and refurbished Victorian building lives up to its name: it has great views over Loutit Bay from the bistro and the bar. The rooms have old-world charm but all the mod cons – some have spa baths – and it's worth shelling out a bit more for a room with sea views. There are also bright and airy modern, self-contained apartments. Doubles $180, apartments $230

Great Ocean Road Cottages 10 Erskine Ave ☎ 03 5289 1070, ⊚ greatoceanroadcottages.com. Well-designed, comfortable self-catering cottages, sleeping two to six people, in a lovely forest setting beside the Erskine River, just minutes from the main strip. No internet. $225

Lorne Backpackers 10 Erskine Ave ☎ 03 5289 1070, ⊚ greatoceanroadcottages.com. This excellent, attractive hostel shares the grounds with *Great Ocean Road Cottages*. The hostel section comprises two large timber buildings with dorms, double and queen rooms and balconies, and there's free use of laundry and boogie-boards. No internet. Dorms $35, doubles $90

★**Lorne Bush House Cottages & Eco Retreats** 1860 Deans Marsh Rd ☎03 5289 2477, ⓦlornebushcottages.com. This is in the hills behind Lorne, three minutes' drive from town, and offers a choice of two- to four-bedroom self-contained spa cottages

with open fires or safari-style tents for glamping, all with decks and most with views over eucalypt forest to the sea. There's also a ropes course, and wildlife abounds. Cottages $320, permanent tents $280

★**Ocean Lodge Motel & Apartments** 6 Armytage St ☎03 5289 1330, ⓦoceanlodgelorne.com.au. A few minutes' walk from the pier, this modern lodge sits in beautiful gardens and has spectacular views across the bay; there's a guest lounge with pool table and a tennis court. No internet. Motel unit $195, apartment $245

EATING AND DRINKING

There are great places to eat and drink everywhere in town – but they charge Melbourne prices and then some. Most licensed establishments allow you to bring your own wine but charge a hefty corkage fee.

Arab Espresso Bar 94 Mountjoy Pde ☎03 5289 1435. This beatnik hangout has been going strong since 1956. It sports minimalist decor and is still good for daytime snacks, and more substantial evening meals (most mains under $25). Mon–Fri 9am–9pm, Sat 8am–11pm, Sun 7.30am–10pm.

Ipsos 48 Mountjoy Pde ☎03 5289 1883. Contemporary Greek food at its simple best, from the next generation of the Talimanidis family, the long-term Great Ocean Road foodies behind *A La Grecque* in Aireys Inlet (see p.815). Share dishes include *kefalograviera*, crisp-fried hard cheese drizzled with ouzo and apricot reduction; mains from $28. Licensed. Daily except Tues noon–3pm & 6–9.30pm (may close over July).

Lorne Fish & Chips 42 Mountjoy Pde ☎03 5289 1843. Good for an inexpensive feast of that beachside favourite, fish and chips ($12). Eat in or takeaway. Daily 11am–7pm.

Lorne Hotel 176 Mountjoy Pde ☎03 5289 1409, ⓦlornehotel.com.au. Tasty bistro meals ($27–42), including a seafood platter for two, plus a sensational beer

garden overlooking the ocean. Live music Fri and Sat. Daily noon–late.

Lorne Pier Seafood Restaurant Pier Head ☎03 5289 1119. It's pricier than the average fish-and-chip shop, but this well-known seafood restaurant (mains around $30) is worth it for the setting alone. Licensed and BYO. Daily 10am–late.

★**Pizza Pizza** 2 Mountjoy Pde ☎03 5289 1007. This happening hole-in-the-wall beside the river turns out scrumptious classic and gourmet pizzas ($16.50). Eat "in" at clustered footpath tables or takeaway. Licensed and BYO. Cash only. Daily 6pm–late (usually); phone to check as hours change.

Qdos 35 Allenvale Rd ☎03 5289 1989, ⓦqdosarts .com. Tucked away in the eucalypt-clad hills above Lorne, this art-gallery-cum-café serves breakfast, light lunches (most mains under $20) and tasty home-made cakes in a relaxed atmosphere. Bookings advisable. Jan daily 8.30am–6pm; Feb–Dec Thurs–Mon 9am–5pm; closed part May and Aug (call for details).

Wye River

Between Lorne and Apollo Bay, wooded hills fall steeply into the ocean. If you can, stop for lunch and take advantage of the stunning ocean views at *Wye Beach Hotel* in the hamlet of **WYE RIVER**. On Christmas Day 2015, a bushfire destroyed 116 homes and holiday houses at Wye River and neighbouring Separation Creek. No lives were lost and the hotel and store (see below) survived and continue to operate, however many from the community don't plan to rebuild. Just beyond Wye River at **Kennett River**, you can detour up Grey River Road to spot koalas among the eucalypts; the road left of *Kafe Koala* winds up behind the town. Note that there's no public transport.

ACCOMMODATION AND EATING   WYE RIVER

Wye Beach Hotel ☎03 5289 0240, ⓦwyebeachhotel .com.au. Great ocean views, a bistro offering seafood, pub favourites and other dishes, and good coffee, plus comfortable motel-style accommodation. $160

★**The Wye General** ☎03 5289 0247, ⓦthewye general.com.au This beach-facing bakery, café and

general store is a terrific pit stop for brunch, scrumptious burgers on house-made brioche, and pizza (summer holidays only); you can pick up deli goods in the shop. Shop Mon–Fri 8am–4pm, Sat & Sun 8am–5.30pm; café daily 8am–4pm; extended hours in summer.

9

Beauchamp Falls

A possible detour off the Great Ocean Road – from Skenes Creek between Kennett River and Apollo Bay – is the scenic 30min drive north to **Beauchamp Falls**: the spectacular falls are a further 30min down a secluded walking track.

Apollo Bay

Fishing – commercial and recreational – is the main activity in **APOLLO BAY**. The town also marks the start of the **Great Ocean Walk** (ⓦgreatoceanwalk.com.au), a 104km track through forests and some of the state's most stunning coastal scenery. Note that sections of the track become impassable at high tide and in rough weather so make sure that you register with the visitor centre.

The town has an enjoyably alternative feel – lots of artists and musicians live here and both local pubs often have music at weekends. The weekly **Community Market** (Sat 9am–1pm) on the foreshore is well worth a browse and showcases locally produced arts and crafts as well as fresh produce.

ARRIVAL AND INFORMATION

By bus A daily bus service runs from Geelong to Apollo Bay. A weekday-only service (Mon, Wed, Fri) continues to Warrnambool via Port Campbell.

Tourist information The Great Ocean Road Visitor Information Centre, on the foreshore at the eastern end of town (daily 9am–5pm; ☎03 5237 6529, ⓦvisitgreatoceanroad.org.au), has helpful staff who can book accommodation. Enquire here for information about sightseeing tours (4WD or normal vehicle).

TOURS

Apollo Bay Aviation ☎03 5237 7600, ⓦapollobayaviation.com.au. Based at the Apollo Bay airfield south of town, this company operates scenic flights to a variety of destinations, including nearby Cape Otway and the Twelve Apostles (plane $280, helicopter $450, for 45min; ask about group rates), and further afield to King Island, Tasmania.

Apollo Bay Fishing and Adventure Tours ☎03 5237 7888, ⓦapollobayfishing.com.au. Fishing trips (from $60), seal watching (from $40) and scenic boat cruises.

Otway Eco Tours ☎0419 670 985, ⓦplatypustours .net.au. Operates out of the Otway town of Forrest, 37km northwest of Apollo Bay, and runs canoe trips in the densely forested hinterland to see platypus and glow-worms (two–six people; up to 3.5hr; $85) as well as walking and mountain-bike tours.

Otway Expeditions ☎0419 007 586, ⓦotwayexpeditions.tripod.com. Mountain-bike tours that go from the "rainforest to the beach" ($65, min 6 people).

ACCOMMODATION

A Room with a View 280 Sunnyside Rd, Wongarra ☎03 5237 0218, ⓦroomwithaview.com.au. Cosy, aptly named B&B accommodation, 14km east of town, with magnificent views of green rolling hills and the ocean, and gourmet breakfasts to set you up for the day. $260

★**Apollo Bay Eco YHA** 5 Pascoe St ☎03 5237 7899, ⓦyha.com.au. Easily the state's best budget-accommodation option. A million-dollar property with incredible facilities including a great sea-facing sun deck, and state-of-the-art kitchen and lounge rooms. Those not acquainted with such extravagance may want to stay here indefinitely. Dorms $30, doubles $99

Apollo Bay Holiday Park 27 Cawood St ☎03 5237 7111, ⓦapollobayholidaypark.com.au. Camping and van sites plus a wide range of cabins that sleep two to six people. The park is close to the beach and shops. Unpowered sites $25, cabins $90

Sandpiper Motel 3 Murray St ☎03 5237 6732, ⓦsandpiper.net.au. Only 50m from the beach, these stylish apartments (some with ocean views) offer luxury in the middle of everything. $220

Skenes Creek Lodge Motel 61 Great Ocean Rd, Skenes Creek ☎03 5237 6918, ⓦskenescreekmotel.com. Good mid-range motel in a garden setting above the main road, a 5min drive from Apollo Bay, with restaurant and ocean views. $100

Surfside Backpacker Cnr Great Ocean Rd & Gambier St ☎03 5237 7263, ⓦsurfsidebackpacker.com. A friendly place with small dorms and cheap doubles on a hill overlooking the beach at the southern end of town. Facilities include disabled access, pool table, outdoor BBQs and a large vinyl collection. Dorms $28, doubles $75

EATING AND DRINKING

In town, the places to eat are strung along the Great Ocean Road. To buy freshly caught seafood, go to the Fishermen's Co-op at the harbour (☎ 03 5237 6591; Mon–Fri 9.30am–3.30pm, Sat & Sun 10am–4.30pm).

Apollo Bay Hotel 95 Great Ocean Rd ☎ 03 5237 6250, ⓦ apollobayhotel.com.au. Great pub that offers delicious bistro meals (around $19), alfresco dining and pizzas till late, with an excellent beer garden facing the water. Daily 11am–11pm; food 11.30am–8pm.
Bay Leaf Café 131 Great Ocean Rd ☎ 03 5237 6740. Good breakfast pit stop where you can fuel for a very reasonable price (mains $10–30). Daily 7.45am–3pm, plus dinner 6pm–late in summer.
Chris's Beacon Point 2km up Skenes Creek Rd (#280), Skenes Creek ☎ 03 5237 6411, ⓦ chriss.com.au. This

renowned hilltop restaurant above Skenes Creek plates up Mediterranean dishes with a Greek accent amid ocean views. Seafood, such as local calamari, is the focus, but mains (to $36) might include the likes of bacon-wrapped veal with fennel-spiked jam. Mon–Fri 6pm–late, Sat & Sun noon–2pm & 6pm–late.
Thaihouse 18 Pascoe St ☎ 03 5237 6766. Good Thai–Vietnamese cuisine at average prices (mains $11–16) with outdoor tables for eating alfresco on balmy nights. Daily 5pm–late.

Great Otway National Park and around

Soon after Apollo Bay, the Great Ocean Road enters the 53,000-acre **Great Otway National Park**, stretching south along the coast from Anglesea and inland to Lavers Hill and beyond, taking in the lush Otway Ranges, one of the wettest places in Victoria. From **Maits Rest** car park, 15km west of Apollo Bay, you can stroll through a lovely fern gully, which gives a feel of the dense rainforest that once covered the entire range.

Cape Otway Lighthouse

Daily 9am–5pm • $19.50 • Tours daily from 9am; 45min; no extra fee • ☎ 03 5237 9240, ⓦ lightstation.com

Beyond the Maits Rest car park a turn-off leads to **Cape Otway Lighthouse**, 12km away on a sealed road, where there's a small café and pleasant accommodation in refurbished lighthouse-keepers' residences (see p.820). You can visit the lighthouse or join a guided tour, and might even see a migrating whale between June and September. Three kilometres north of Cape Otway, the side road to Blanket Bay is a good place to spot koalas.

Lavers Hill

Back on the main road, continue west to **Castle Cove**, where steps lead down to an unpatrolled beach. The road now turns inland again and stepped hills rise sharply from the road as it passes turn-offs to **Johanna**, one of Victoria's best-known surf beaches, before reaching **LAVERS HILL**, a tiny town with a good café and the highest point in the Otway Ranges.

Otway Fly Treetop Walk

360 Phillips Track, Weeaproinah • Daily 9am–5pm (last entry to walk is 4pm) • $25 • ☎ 03 5235 9200, ⓦ otwayfly.com

It's well worth detouring to the **Otway Fly Treetop Walk**, about fifteen minutes' drive east of Lavers Hill – just follow the road signs. A 600m steel-trussed walkway allows you to walk through temperate rainforest at canopy level, 25m above the ground. Abseiling and a zipline tour are also available and the Otway Fly Visitor Centre on top of the hill, 300m from the beginning of the walkway, has a good gourmet organic café and a souvenir shop.

ACCOMMODATION AND EATING   GREAT OTWAY NATIONAL PARK

CAPE OTWAY

Bimbi Park 90 Manna Gum Drive (halfway along the road to Cape Otway Lighthouse) ☎ 03 5237 9246, ⓦ bimbipark.com.au. The only caravan park actually

within the national park. The facilities and some of the cabins are quite basic but the setting is gorgeous – on a small farm with paddocks surrounded by bushland – and the caravan park offers excellent horseriding excursions,

9

including a ride to Station Beach (1hr 30min; $75), a 3km-long stretch of sand with freshwater springs and waterfalls. Cabins $115

Cape Otway Lightstation ☎03 5237 9240, ⓦlightstation.com. Pleasant accommodation in three refurbished lighthouse-keepers' residences that sleep two to sixteen people, simply but tastefully decorated and fully equipped. $275

★**Great Ocean Ecolodge** ☎03 5237 9297, ⓦgreatoceanecolodge.com. This restful solar-powered lodge sits in 165 acres of grassland and eucalypt forest abutting Great Otway National Park and is accessible on foot from the Great Ocean Walk. Five en-suite rooms share a guest lounge, dining room and library. Accommodation (two nights min) includes a guided dusk walk to see kangaroos, koalas, tiger quolls and other native animals, plus afternoon tea and a Continental breakfast; you can add dinners and picnic lunches (included in some packages). All profits support wildlife and environment conservation. $380

LAVERS HILL

Blackwood Gully Tea Rooms 1–15 Great Ocean Road ☎03 5237 3290. A good café serving breakfast, light snacks ($8–15) and Devonshire teas. There's also a gift shop on the premises. Daily 8am–6.30pm.

Fauna Australia Wildlife Retreat 5040 Colac–Lavers Hill Rd ☎03 5237 3234, ⓦfaunaaustralia.com.au. Located just outside Lavers Hill are these cosy cottages and units at a privately run Australian wildlife sanctuary – they also offer guided tours and serve refreshments. No internet. $150

The Shipwreck Coast

The 180km stretch of coast between lonely, windswept Moonlight Head and Port Fairy is known as the **Shipwreck Coast** (ⓦshipwreckcoast.com); it takes in the Twelve Apostles – the Great Ocean Road icon – and other well-known coastal formations such as Loch Ard Gorge and London Bridge. Most of the coast is protected under the auspices of Great Otway National Park and **Port Campbell National Park**. More than six hundred ships have come to grief in the coast's treacherous waters – two hundred or so of which have been found – and the **Historic Shipwreck Trail** links the sites of 53 wrecks between Moonlight Head and the South Australia border with informative plaques and signed walking paths. A brochure about the trail is available at all the visitor centres in the region.

The Twelve Apostles

The most awe-inspiring formations on the coast are the **Twelve Apostles** – gigantic limestone pillars, some rising 65m out of the water, which retreat in rows as stark reminders of the sea's power (the cliff faces erode about 2cm a year). The Twelve Apostles Visitor Centre (daily 10am–4.30pm) at the car park on the northern side of the road has a takeaway food kiosk, toilet facilities and welcome shelter from the winds blowing off the Southern Ocean. It features wall-length panels of sailcloth with scripted poems about the Shipwreck Coast's awesome, dangerous beauty. Covered walkways and a tunnel under the road lead to the lookout points and a short walk along the clifftop. Sunset here (summer around 9pm, winter 5.45pm) is a popular time for photographers and, unfortunately, crowds. Wait ten minutes or so after dusk, however, when the tourists have jumped back on their buses and left, and you'll be treated to another fantastic spectacle: hordes of Little penguins waddling onto the shore. Early morning, before the bus tours arrive, is another good time for photographs.

ARRIVAL, TOURS AND ACCOMMODATION
THE TWELVE APOSTLES

By bus A weekday-only bus (Mon, Wed, Fri) from Apollo Bay to Warrnambool stops for a photo opportunity at the Twelve Apostles.

12 Apostles Helicopters Great Ocean Rd ☎03 5598 8283, ⓦ12apostleshelicopters.com.au. For a bird's-eye view of the coast, take a helicopter ride from behind the Twelve Apostles Visitor Centre ($145/15min).

The 13th Apostle Backpacker Hostel 5 Post Office Rd, Princetown ☎03 5598 8062, ⓦthe13thapostle.com.au. This contemporary, purpose-built hostel provides pleasant and clean budget accommodation (singles, doubles, family and share rooms) in this tiny hamlet about 6km southeast of the Twelve Apostles. There is a general store and pub across the road. Dorms $25, doubles $60

Loch Ard Gorge

At underrated **Loch Ard Gorge**, a small network of clifftop walks and a staircase lead down to a beach to give you the chance to view the fantastic rock formations all around. It was here that the *Loch Ard*, an iron-hulled square rigger, hit a reef and foundered while transporting immigrants from England to Melbourne in the spring of 1878. Only two of the 53 people on board survived: Eva Carmichael and Tom Pearce, both in their late teens. They were swept into a long gorge and Tom dragged Eva into a cave in its western wall before going for help. A walkway leads down to the beach, covered with delicate pink kelp, and you can scramble over craggy rocks to the mouth of the cave where Eva sheltered, now a nesting site for small birds. The Loch Ard cemetery, where the ship's passengers and crew are buried, is on the clifftop overlooking the gorge. As you drive further, you pass more scenic points, with resonant names such as Blowhole and Thundercave, before reaching Port Campbell.

Port Campbell

PORT CAMPBELL is a quintessential coastal village on the edge of Port Campbell National Park and, at just 12km away, the main base for those visiting the Twelve Apostles. Ask at the visitor centre about the **Port Campbell Discovery Walk** (90min), which will take you along a clifftop to a viewpoint above Two Mile Bay. Port Campbell **beach** is a small sandy curve and the only safe swimming beach between Apollo Bay and Warrnambool; it is patrolled in season. The town climbs the hill behind the beach and is a pleasant place to while away an evening.

ARRIVAL, INFORMATION AND TOURS   PORT CAMPBELL

By bus A weekday-only bus (Mon, Wed, Fri) runs from Apollo Bay to Warrnambool via Port Campbell.
Tourist information The 12 Apostles Visitor Information Centre at 26 Morris St (daily 9am–5pm; ☎ 03 5598 6089 or ☎ 1300 137 255, ⓦ visit12apostles.com.au) has displays and information about the area and its national parks, and

can also book accommodation. Free wi-fi is also available.
Port Campbell Boat Charters 32 Lord St ☎ 03 5598 6366, ⓦ portcampbellboatcharters.com.au. Dives on shipwreck sites and fishing trips; they also rent out snorkelling or diving gear to those who want to go it alone (diving from $50, fishing trips from $70).

ACCOMMODATION

Loch Ard Motor Inn 18 Lord St ☎ 03 5598 6328, ⓦ lochardmotorinn.com.au. In a prime position opposite the beach; most of the simple yet comfortable rooms here have private patios facing the water. **$190**
Port Campbell Flashpackers & Guesthouse 54 Lord St ☎ 0407 696 559, ⓦ portcampbellguesthouse.com. A spacious modern place with bunk, double and family rooms and simple self-catering facilities; a good budget option. Dorms **$45**, doubles **$95**

Port Campbell Hostel 18 Tregea St ☎ 03 5598 6305, ⓦ portcampbellhostel.com.au. A pleasant, well-run hostel with a good kitchen, spacious common room and TV lounge, bright dorms, double/twins and family rooms. Dorms **$35**, doubles **$100**
Sea Foam Villas 14 Lord St ☎ 03 5598 6413, ⓦ seafoamvillas.com. Light-filled, well-equipped contemporary foreshore apartments with private balconies and sea views. Some have spas. **$185**

EATING AND DRINKING

Craypot Bistro Port Campbell Hotel, 40 Lord St ☎ 03 5598 6320. For regular Aussie food or a late-night drink (they close when the last person leaves), head to the good-quality bistro at this popular pub (mains up to $25). Daily noon–2pm & 6–8.30pm.
Port Campbell Take-Away 16 Lord St. The simply titled takeaway facing the foreshore is a favourite with surfers needing their fish-and-chip fix ($10–12 average). Cross the road to eat your food and watch waves wash ashore. Daily

8am–5.30pm.
Waves 29 Lord St ☎ 03 5598 6111, ⓦ wavesport campbell.com.au. Considered the best place in town, serving reliably good breakfasts, plus mod-Oz lunches and dinners such as local crayfish (in season) and Asian half chicken. Mains from $20; booking advised. You can also stay upstairs in colourful luxury suites with small private balconies. Daily 8am–8pm or 9.30pm, depending on the season.

9

London Bridge and the Grotto

Tourists could once walk across the double-arched rock formation known as **London Bridge**, a short distance west of Port Campbell. In mid-January 1990, however, the outer span collapsed and fell into the sea, minutes after two very lucky people had crossed it – they were eventually rescued from the far limestone stack by helicopter. As luck would have it, the couple were conducting an extramarital affair, and fled from the waiting media as soon as the helicopter arrived. Another good place to stop, just before Peterborough, is the **Grotto**, where a path leads from the clifftop to a rock pool beneath an archway.

Warrnambool

Attractively set on the sea at the end of the Great Ocean Road, **WARRNAMBOOL** is also the centre of rich **dairy country**. Spectacular coastline and fantastic beaches, cycling and walking trails, plus a good range of accommodation and cafés, make it a popular holiday destination.

Allansford Cheese World

Great Ocean Rd, Allansford • Mon–Fri 8.30am–5pm, Sat 9am–3pm, Sun 10am–3pm • ☎ 03 5565 3130, ⓦ cheeseworld.com.au

As well as selling cheese and gourmet products, this factory has free tastings and presentations throughout the day, a café serving teas and light lunches, and a fun, interactive local history museum featuring early 1900s farm implements and household items.

The Whale Nursery

Follow the signs off the Great Ocean Road • For more information see ⓦ visitwarrnambool.com.au

Lady Bay, where Warrnambool shelters, was first used by seal hunters and whalers in the early nineteenth century and was permanently settled from the early 1840s. **Southern right whales**, hunted almost to extinction, have begun to return in recent years. Every year between late May/June and September/early October whales come to the waters off Logans Beach to calve. Often they swim very close to the shore and can be viewed from specially constructed platforms at Logans Beach.

Flagstaff Hill Maritime Village

89 Merri St • Daily 9am–5pm • $16 • *Shipwrecked* nightly after dusk; $26; 70min; bookings essential • ☎ 1800 556 111, ⓦ flagstaffhill.com

The perils of shipping in the Shipwreck Coast's treacherous waters are the theme at State Heritage-listed **Flagstaff Hill Maritime Village**. The extensive grounds feature the Warrnambool Garrison, erected in 1887 when the fear of a Russian invasion was widespread, alongside historic lighthouses and a nineteenth-century coastal village arranged around the fort. Flagstaff Hill's *pièce de résistance*, however, is the sound-and-laser show, *Shipwrecked*, which recounts the story of the 1878 Loch Ard disaster (see p.821).

Warrnambool Art Gallery

26 Liebig St • Mon–Fri 10am–5pm, Sat & Sun noon–5pm • Free • ☎ 03 5559 4949, ⓦ thewag.com.au

This fine provincial gallery holds more than two thousand artworks, including European salon paintings of the 1800s, collections of Western District colonial paintings, contemporary Australian prints and indigenous artefacts. The gallery also showcases major exhibitions of Australian works and themed collections curated from around the world.

ARRIVAL AND INFORMATION

By train Trains run from Melbourne to Warrnambool via Geelong (2–3 daily; 3hr 20min), with connecting V/Line buses to Port Fairy and Portland, and on to Mount Gambier in South Australia.

By bus There is a once-a-weekday bus to Geelong via Apollo Bay and an infrequent service from Warrnambool to Hamilton via Port Fairy.

Destinations Apollo Bay (Mon, Wed & Fri; 3hr 30min); Ballarat (5 weekly; 3hr); Geelong (Mon, Wed & Fri; 6hr 35min); Hamilton (Sun–Fri 1–3 daily; 2hr 25min); Mount Gambier (1–2 daily; 2hr 35min); Port Fairy (4–5 daily; 40min); Portland (1–4 daily; 1hr 35min).

Tourist information The well-organized Warrnambool Visitor Centre (daily 9am–9pm; ☎ 03 5559 4620 or ☎ 1800 637 725, ⓦ visitwarrnambool.com.au) is part of the Flagstaff Hill complex at 89 Merri St.

ACCOMMODATION

Girt By Sea 52 Banyan St ☎0408 583 855, ⓦ girtbyseawarrnambool.com.au. This tastefully furnished B&B is in a restored nineteenth-century sandstone house, and is divided into two self-contained apartments that sleep two to five people. No internet. **$220**

Hotel Warrnambool Cnr Koroit & Kepler sts ☎03 5562 2377, ⓦ hotelwarrnambool.com.au. Inviting B&B pub accommodation in a historic town centre building; offering both en-suite and shared-facilities rooms in assorted rich colours. Continental breakfast included. **$110**

Lady Bay Resort 2 Pertobe Rd ☎03 5562 1662, ⓦ ladybayresort.com.au. Modern, self-contained apartments (with one or two bedrooms) located on the foreshore, with ocean views and a seasonally open outdoor pool. **$210**

Warrnambool Beach Backpackers 17 Stanley St ☎03 5562 4874, ⓦ beachbackperscom.au. The best backpacker hostel in town, less than a 5min walk from the beach, with large and smaller dorms and doubles. There's a common room, bar, bike and surfboard hire, and free boogie-boards. Dorms **$26**, doubles **$80**

EATING AND DRINKING

CAFÉS AND RESTAURANTS

Fishtales Café 63–65 Liebig St ☎03 5561 2957, ⓦ fishtalescafe.com.au. A relaxed, funky place with a huge menu, including pasta, burgers, seafood, steaks and Monday-night Sri Lankan curries (mains up to $25). Daily 6am–late.

Mack's Snacks 77 Liebig St ☎03 5562 2432. Open since 1948 and still serving up good-value burgers ($10), wraps, cakes and biscuits which you can enjoy in diner-like booths. Mon–Fri 9am–8.30pm, Sat 9am–3pm.

Nonna Casalinga 69 Liebig St ☎03 5562 2051. Settle in for simple and delicious cliché-free Italian dishes sourced from the chef's garden and surrounding countryside. Mains, such as porterhouse sandwiched between rosti and piled buttermilk onion rings, go up to $35. Tues–Sat 6pm–late.

Pippies by the Bay 91 Merri St ☎03 5561 2188, ⓦ pippiesbythebay.com.au. Beside the visitor centre at Flagstaff Hill and awash with ocean views, this award-winning restaurant serves mod-Oz cuisine with Italian influences (slow-cooked duck leg with caramelized bacon and onion and red wine jus, $32). Breakfast and lunch dishes are cheaper. Mon–Fri 10am–late, Sat 9am–late, Sun 9am–4pm.

Proudfoots Boathouse 2 Simpson St ☎03 5561 5055, ⓦ proudfootsboathouse.com.au. Out of town, this refurbished nineteenth-century timber boathouse on the Hopkins River houses a popular water-level restaurant and cool upstairs bar with great views. Modern Australian mains, including local lobster in season, from $25. Wed–Sat 10am–3pm & 6pm–late, Sun 10am–3pm.

BARS AND CLUBS

The Gallery Club 214 Timor St ☎03 5562 0741, ⓦ galleryclub.com.au. A stylish venue for cocktails and late-night entertainment, with four bars, two DJ areas and two outdoor areas. Cash only. Wed, Fri & Sun 10.30pm–3am.

The Loft 58 Liebig St ☎03 5561 0995, ⓦ theloftbar .com.au. The town's best music venue, with local and even international bands, trivia nights, dance classes and other events. Wed & Thurs 6pm–1am, Fri & Sat 4pm–1am, Sun 2–11pm.

Whalers Hotel 53 Liebig St ☎03 5562 8391, ⓦ thewhalershotel.com.au. A popular pub incorporating the funky *Highline Bar & Lounge*. There are above-average bistro meals (Tues–Sun) plus bands and DJs on Fri and Sat nights. Daily noon–late.

Port Fairy

Once an early port and whaling centre, **PORT FAIRY** is now a quaint and hugely appealing crayfishing, abalone and tourist town with a busy jetty, a harbour full of yachts and over fifty National Trust-listed buildings; it's an essential destination for history and architecture fans. Heavy breakers roll into the surrounding beaches, and on **Griffiths Island**, poised between the ocean and Port Fairy Bay, there's a **muttonbird** rookery with a specially constructed lookout where, between September and April, you can watch the birds roost at dusk.

For a historic small town, Port Fairy is quite a happening place, hosting numerous events (see below). With its village-like atmosphere and excellent **accommodation**, as well as good pubs, tearooms and restaurants, the town is a great place to break your journey between Melbourne and Adelaide.

The Port Fairy **Historical Society** at 30 Gipps St (mid July & Aug Sat 2–4pm; Sept to mid-July Wed & Sat 2–5pm, Sun 10.30am–12.30pm; $4; ☎03 5568 2263, ⓦhistoricalsociety.port-fairy.com), in the old courthouse by the river, displays costumes, photographs, shipwreck relics and other items relating to the town's pioneer history. Other attractions include the excellent links-style **golf course** (ⓦportfairygolf .com.au; $25 for nine holes, $40 for eighteen) which has awe-inspiring sea views.

ARRIVAL AND INFORMATION   PORT FAIRY

By bus Buses run from Warrnambool to Port Fairy – up to five services on weekdays, far fewer on weekends. There is also an infrequent service to Hamilton (see p.843) that originates in Warrnambool.

Tourist information The visitor centre on Bank St (daily 9am–5pm; ☎03 5568 2682, ⓦvisitportfairy-moyneshire .com.au) has details of all cottages, B&Bs and caravan parks. They also produce excellent leaflets detailing the Port Fairy Historic Town Walk and the Shipwreck and Maritime Heritage Walk, which take you around town to admire the many fine buildings and the sites of seventeen shipwrecks, sometimes visible.

Festivals In summer (Dec/Jan) the four-week-long Moyneyana Festival focuses on outdoor activities and music, with events such as a raft race on the Moyne River and its highlight, the Moyneyana New Year's Eve Parade. At Easter the annual Queenscliff to Port Fairy yacht race ends here, with a huge party. Music is big too: the Port Fairy Spring Music Festival (ⓦportfairyspringfest.com.au) in mid-October concentrates on classical music, with some opera and jazz thrown in for good measure, and the huge Port Fairy Folk Festival (ⓦportfairyfolkfestival.com) over the Labour Day long weekend in March takes over the entire town, with Australian and overseas acts playing world, roots and acoustic music; tickets are sold from September and go quickly.

ACCOMMODATION

Daisies by the Sea 222 Griffiths St ☎03 5568 2355, ⓦport-fairy.com/daisiesbythesea. A delightful B&B with two suites that look on to East Beach; the excellent breakfast is brought to your room. $160

Douglas Riverside 85 Gipps St ☎0450 832 792, ⓦdouglasriversideportfairy.com.au. There are a number of B&Bs in town, but the best are in quaint colonial cottages on the Moyne River, such as this family-run gem with rooms and apartments on the water. Double $180, apartments $350

Port Fairy YHA 8 Cox St ☎03 5568 2468, ⓦportfairyhostel.com.au. A well-run and super-friendly hostel in a lovely old house (built in 1843) in the town centre. Reception 9–10.30am & 5–9pm. Dorms $26, doubles $75

★**Seacombe House** 22 Sackville St ☎03 5568 1082, ⓦseacombehouse.com.au. One of many National Trust-listed buildings, with cheaper traditional guesthouse rooms including excellent-value singles, gorgeous but pricey modern motel units and nineteenth-century cottages with spas. The in-house restaurant is remarkable. $110

EATING AND DRINKING

Caledonian Inn 41 Bank St ☎03 5568 1044, ⓦcaledonianinnportfairy.com.au. Known as "The Stump", this is Victoria's oldest continually licensed pub (since 1844). It serves classic pub food such as steaks ($27) and pasta dishes ($18.50). Daily 11am–2pm & 5.30–8.30pm.

Coffin Sally 33 Sackville St ☎03 5568 2618, ⓦwww .coffinsally.com.au. Rock up to this surfer-meets-hipster place for a cocktail (fireside in winter) and great pizza (up to $18), served to chilled music. Daily 4pm–late (June–August takeaway only Mon & Tues).

Merrijig Kitchen 1 Campbell St ☎03 5568 2324, ⓦmerrijiginn.com. For something special, head to the acclaimed kitchen restaurant at the Merrijig Inn, a wonderful old tavern building. The changing menu is inspired by the best local artisan produce, with starters from $16 and mains from $34. Thurs–Mon 6pm–late.

Rebecca's Café 70–72 Sackville St ☎03 5568 2533. A bright and buzzy café serving breakfasts, light lunches, scrumptious cakes and great coffee (mains around $15). Daily 7am–5pm.

Fen 22 Sackville St ☎03 5568 3229, ⓦfenrestaurant .com.au. Expect inventive dishes with a multisensory impact and native Australian flavours from this dining experience within historic Seacombe House. Mains, such as local flathead fillets with butter-toasted macadamias, finger lime, blood orange and saltbush, cost around $40; five- and eight-course tasting menus $100 and $135. Tues–Sat 6.30–9.30pm.

Portland and around

PORTLAND likes to describe itself as the "Birthplace of Victoria". Indeed, there are many historic buildings, but unlike Port Fairy they don't add up to a coherent, captivating townscape. It's the last stop on the Victoria coast going west on the Princes Highway, but **Nelson**, a friendly fishing village further west, or **Port Fairy** make for more atmospheric overnight stops between Melbourne and Adelaide. The rugged coastal scenery to the southwest around Cape Nelson and Cape Bridgewater, however, is not to be missed.

Maritime Discovery Centre

Lee Breakwater Rd · Daily 9am–5pm · $7.40 · ☎ 03 5523 2671

The small **Maritime Discovery Centre** extends to the back of the visitor centre on the foreshore down from Bentinck Street. Its centrepiece is a life-sized model of a great white shark, caught 13km west of Cape Bridgewater in 1982. There is also a sperm whale skeleton and a motley assemblage of boat-building tools, memorabilia, photos and marine wildlife information.

Southwest along the coast

To the southwest of town, the scenery around craggy **Cape Nelson** and stormy **Cape Bridgewater** (Victoria's highest coastal cliffs) is stunning, including caves, blowholes, fascinating limestone pipes erroneously called a "petrified forest", and the beach at **Bridgewater Bay**, a wide, sandy arc from cape to cape. The best way to explore is along the walking tracks that start from the car park signposted left off the road to Cape Bridgewater. Bring good walking shoes – the volcanic rocks can be very sharp – and food and drink.

Seal Point

Contact the *Bridgewater Bay Café* in Bridgewater Bay (☎ 03 5526 7155, ⊛ bridgewaterbay.com.au) for information

Seal Point at Cape Bridgewater is home to about a thousand **fur seals**. Seals by Sea Tours (45min; $40; ☎ 03 5526 7247, ⊛ sealsbyseatours.com.au) operate cruises during which you can interact with these social creatures. They also offer caged snorkelling with the seals.

ARRIVAL AND INFORMATION   PORTLAND

By plane The airport is 13km out of town and best reached by taxi (about $30). There are daily flights to/from Melbourne's Essendon Airport (1hr 20min) with Sharp Airlines (⊛ sharpairlines.com.au).

By bus Warrnambool to Portland services operate daily, continuing to Mount Gambier in South Australia.

Destinations Mount Gambier (1–2 daily; 1hr 35min); Port Fairy (1–3 daily; 1hr); Warrnambool (1–2 daily; 1hr 35min).

Tourist information The excellent, anchor-shaped visitor centre (daily 9am–5pm; ☎ 1800 035 567, ⊛ visitportland .com.au) has pamphlets and maps galore, and staff can advise on local attractions, driving routes and the 250km Great South West Walk, which begins and ends here. The visitor centre also has a brochure for the Historical Buildings Walk, which starts at the former Customs House in Cliff St (near the southern end of Bentinck St) and takes in some of Portland's two hundred nineteenth-century buildings.

ACCOMMODATION

★**Annesley House** 60 Julia S ☎ 0429 852 235, ⊛ annesleyhouse.com.au. Built in 1878 as a doctor's surgery and residence, two-storey *Annesley House* blends old-world charm with modern amenities in its six elegant

serviced apartments. $175

Clifftop Accommodation 13 Clifton Court ☎ 03 5523 1126, ⊛ portlandaccommodation.com.au. Within walking distance of the main drag, these three spacious

---

THE PORTLAND CABLE TRAM

A restored and modified **vintage cable tram** (daily: summer 10am–4pm; winter 10am–3pm; $17.50; ⊛ portlandcabletrams.com.au) transports sightseers along the foreshore on a return trip of 7.4km, from the depot at Henty Park to the interesting Powerhouse Motor and Car Museum (daily; 10am–4pm, $5), Fawthrop Lagoon (home to pelicans), and through the Botanic Gardens.

en-suite rooms have cooking facilities and balconies overlooking Portland Bay; telescopes and binoculars are provided for whale watching. Adults only. $185

Gordon Hotel 63 Bentinck St ☎ 03 5523 1121. At the more affordable end of the market, this huge pub has simple rooms with shared facilities and the price includes a light breakfast; ask for a room with sea views. No internet. $75

EATING AND DRINKING

Clock by the Bay 1 Cliff St ☎ 03 5521 1254. This classy restaurant in the elegant old post office building delivers delicious French-influenced dishes, from a breakfast rosti to mains such as local deep-sea fish with citrus crumb, spicy sausage and white-bean ragout ($37). Cheaper lunch menu. Wed & Sun 9am–5pm, Thurs–Sat 9am–1am.

Gordon Hotel 63 Bentinck St ☎ 03 5523 1121. Good pub food for lunch and dinner at moderate prices (mains up to $20), with bands providing a musical accompaniment on weekends. Daily noon–8.30pm.

Lido Larder 5 Julia St ☎ 03 5521 1741. A great place for an espresso and a delicious light meal, such as a savoury tartlet ($8) or the daily special, such as chicken Kiev ($15), and scrumptious house-baked cupcakes – or stock up for a picnic. Mon–Fri 7.30am–5pm, Sat 8am–noon.

Lower Glenelg National Park

From Portland, the Princes Highway makes its uneventful way, via Heywood, to Mount Gambier in South Australia. After 120km it crosses the **Glenelg River** (which rises in the Grampians) at Dartmoor, a popular point to begin a four-day canoeing trip downstream to the river mouth at Nelson; ask about canoe rental at the Nelson Visitor Information Centre (see below). For most of the journey, the clear blue river flows through unspoilt **Lower Glenelg National Park** (ⓦparks.vic.gov.au) in a 60km gorge cut through limestone.

The **Princess Margaret Rose Cave** (daily 45min guided tours at 10am, 11am, noon, then hourly from 1.30pm to 4.30pm, fewer tours during winter; $20; ☎08 8738 4171, ⓦprincessmargaretrosecave.com), a huge chamber of actively growing stalactites and stalagmites, is the main cave in an extensive system and the only one open to the public. It lies beside the river where it loops round by the South Australia border. It can be reached by canoe, car (unsealed roads from both sides of the border lead to the caves) or on a cruise from Nelson (see below).

Nelson

NELSON, at the end of the coastal road and virtually on the Victoria/South Australia border, is well worth an overnight stay. A peaceful, friendly hamlet, it feels caught in a time warp, and there's little to do but wander along the coast, read on the beach, and **fish** or **canoe** on the Glenelg.

INFORMATION AND ACTIVITIES

Tourist information The Nelson Visitor Information Centre (daily 10am–12.30pm & 1.30–5pm; ☎08 8738 4051, ⓦnelsonvictoria.com.au), signposted just off Leake St, also covers Lower Glenelg National Park and the Discovery Bay Coastal Park, which protects the shoreline almost all the way from Portland to the border. Here you can get information on walks and activities in and around the town and in both parks. (Camping permits must be pre-purchased at ⓦparkstay.vic.gov.au.)

Services Nelson Kiosk (daily 7am–5pm; ☎08 8738 4061), on Kellet St, serves as the local service general store and post office.

Activities Nelson Boat and Canoe Hire, Kellet St (mid-Sept to mid-July daily 9am–5pm,; ☎08 8738 4048, ⓦnelsonboatandcanoehire.com.au), rent out canoes and kayaks (from $25/2hr). They also sell bait and fishing licences. Nelson River Cruises on Old Bridge Road (☎08 8738 4191, ⓦglenelgrivercruises.com.au) run cruises to Princess Margaret Rose Cave (daily in peak season, other times Sat & Sun and on some weekdays; departs 1pm; 3.5hr; $32.50, cave entry not included). Bookings are essential.

ACCOMMODATION AND EATING

Kywong Caravan Park North Nelson Rd ☎08 8738 4174, ⓦkywongcp.com. Set in bushland 1km north of town, with cheap en-suite and share-facility cabins as well as electric BBQs and a camp kitchen. $90

Nelson Cottage B&B 22 Kellett St ☎ 08 8738 4161, ⓦ nelsoncottage.com.au. This is the best option if you're staying overnight, with six comfortable rooms with shared facilities in an 1880s police station. Rates include a Continental breakfast. $90

Nelson Hotel Kellett St ☎ 08 8738 4011, ⓦ nelsonhotel .com.au. A true country pub with two dining rooms, serving up excellent fresh seafood and huge steaks (mains up to $25). They open daily for lunch in summer. Mon–Wed 6–8pm, Thurs–Sun noon–2pm & 6–8pm.

Pinehaven Motel Main Rd ☎ 08 8738 4041. A basic motel owned by the petrol station next door. The en-suite units are small but clean; overnight truck traffic can disrupt sleep. No internet. $80

Central Victoria: the Goldfields

Central Victoria is classic Victoria: a rich pastoral district, chilly in winter and hot in summer. Two grand provincial cities, **Ballarat** and **Bendigo**, whose fine buildings were funded by gold, draw large numbers of visitors, while, by contrast, the area's other charming centres, such as **Castlemaine** and **Maldon**, once prosperous gold towns in their own right, now seem too small for their extravagant architecture but attract history buffs, art aficionados and "foodies".

GETTING AROUND | CENTRAL VICTORIA: THE GOLDFIELDS

There's very good **transport** from Melbourne and Melbourne Airport with regular V/Line trains and buses to Bendigo, Ballarat and the other major Goldfields centres; a few local buses fill some gaps.

By train There are very frequent trains to Bendigo (via Castlemaine) and Ballarat, plus less frequent services to Ararat.

By car Your own transport is a big advantage as driving is the best way to link the two gold cities of Bendigo and Ballarat with towns and villages such as Maldon and Castlemaine.

Towards the Goldfields: the Calder Freeway and Calder Highway

You can take the Western Freeway or the train directly from Melbourne to Ballarat, but the route via the **Calder Freeway and Calder Highway** towards Bendigo, 150km

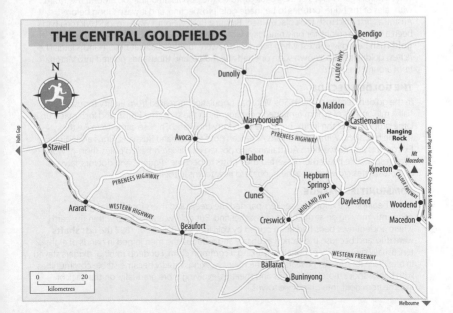

THE CENTRAL GOLDFIELDS

9

northwest of Melbourne, offers many attractions just off the main road. The railway to Bendigo, which continues to Swan Hill, follows the same route, calling at the major towns. Much of the southern area, such as the settlements of Gisborne and Woodend, is part of the Macedon Ranges region (information is available from ☎ 1800 244 711, ⓦ visitmacedonranges.com).

Organ Pipes National Park

April–Sept daily 8.30am–4.30pm; Oct–March Mon–Fri 8.30am–4.30pm, Sat & Sun 8.30am–6pm • ☎ 13 19 63, ⓦ parks.vic.gov.au

At Diggers Rest, 22km from Melbourne and just off the freeway, a short detour to the east will take you to tiny **Organ Pipes National Park**, designated a national park for its outstanding geological interest. The rock formations here form a series of basalt columns, created by lava cooling in an ancient river bed, that rise up to 20m above Jacksons Creek. The park can be explored along walking tracks and has picnic areas with tables.

Hanging Rock Recreation Reserve

South Rock Rd, 6km northeast of Woodend • Daily 9am–5pm; $10 per car, $4 per adult pedestrian • ☎ 1800 244 711

About 50km beyond the Organ Pipes, **Woodend** is a friendly, bustling place on weekends, with antique shops and cafés along the main street; it's also the jumping-off point for **Hanging Rock Recreation Reserve**. Rising 105m above the plain, the rock became famous because of the eerie 1975 film *Picnic at Hanging Rock*, based on the book by Joan Lindsay, about a group of schoolgirls who mysteriously go missing here on Valentine's Day 1900 after a picnic – a story many people falsely believed to be true. More about that story, as well as geological information about the rock, can be gleaned from the displays in the Hanging Rock Discovery Centre at its base; adjacent to it is a licensed café and a gift shop. You can walk around the base of the rock or climb to the summit with its massive boulders and crags in around an hour.

THE GOLD RUSHES

The California gold rushes of the 1840s captured the popular imagination around the world with tales of the huge fortunes to be made gold prospecting, and it wasn't long before Australia's first gold rush took place – near Bathurst in New South Wales in 1851. Victoria had been a separate colony for only nine days when gold was found at Clunes on July 10, 1851; the **gold rush** began in earnest when rich deposits were found in Ballarat nine months later. The richest goldfields ever known soon opened at Bendigo, and thousands poured into Victoria from around the world.

THE GOLDEN DECADE

In the golden decade of the 1850s, Victoria's population increased from eighty thousand to half a million, half of whom remained permanently in the state. The British and Irish made up a large proportion of the influx, but more than forty thousand Chinese came to make their fortune too, along with experienced American gold-seekers and Russians, Finns and Filipinos. Ex-convicts and native-born Australians also poured in, leaving other colonies short of workers; even respectable policemen deserted their posts to become "diggers", and doctors, lawyers and prostitutes crowded into the haphazard new towns in their wake.

COMMUNITIES EMERGE

In the beginning, the fortune-seekers panned the creeks and rivers for **alluvial gold**, constantly moving on at the news of another find. But gold was also deep within the earth, where ancient river beds had been buried by volcanoes. In Ballarat in 1852 the first **shafts** were dug, and because the work was unsafe and arduous, the men joined in bands of eight or ten, usually grouped by nationality, working a common claim. For deep mining, diggers stayed in one place for months or years, and the major workings rapidly became stable communities with banks, shops, hotels, churches and theatres, evolving more gradually, on the back of income from gold, into grandiose towns.

Bendigo

Rich alluvial gold was first discovered in **BENDIGO** in 1851, and, after the initial fields were exhausted, shafts were sunk into a gold-bearing quartz reef. Bendigo became the greatest goldfield of the time, and had the world's deepest mine. Mining continued here until 1954, long after the rest of central Victoria's goldfields were exhausted, so it's a city that has developed over a prosperous century: the nationwide department store Myer began here, as did Australia's first building society in 1858. Bigger and more magnificent than Ballarat (this is one of Victoria's largest regional cities with a population of just over 100,000, including a large number of university and other students), Bendigo has a thriving arts, culture, and food and wine scene. Its most visited sights are legacies of the mining days – the **Bendigo Joss House**, **Dai Gum San Chinese Precinct** and the **Central Deborah Gold Mine** – as well as the acclaimed **Bendigo Art Gallery**.

At the heart of Bendigo is vast, leafy **Rosalind Park**, and three important religious buildings constructed with money from gold-mining – All Saints Church (now View Hill Fellowship), St Paul's Cathedral and **Sacred Heart Cathedral**. The lively **View Street Arts Precinct**, climbing the hill beside Rosalind Park, features Bendigo Art Gallery, The Capital theatre and elaborate gold-rush buildings now housing antique and vintage stores, stylish wine bars, and restaurants. Further up View Street is the **Queen Elizabeth Oval**, with its historic redbrick grandstand, where you can watch Aussie Rules football on winter weekends and cricket in summer.

Bendigo is the end point of the **Goldfields Track** (ⓦgoldfieldstrack.com.au), a 210km walking and mountain-biking trail celebrating the movement of miners between diggings during the gold rush. Starting in Buninyong, outside Ballarat, and visiting Daylesford and Castlemaine, it takes about two weeks start to finish.

Sacred Heart Cathedral

Cnr Wattle & High sts • Crypt daily 9am–5pm

Local Catholics imported stonemasons from Italy and England, and their splendid craftsmanship is especially evident in the design and details of **Sacred Heart Cathedral**, begun in 1897 in English Gothic style. The interior has beautiful woodcarvings of the Twelve Apostles, and the crypt is the burial place of local bishops.

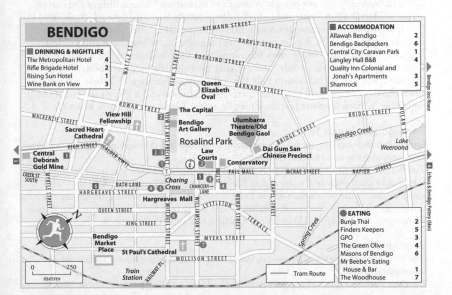

BENDIGO

DRINKING & NIGHTLIFE

The Metropolitan Hotel	4
Rifle Brigade Hotel	2
Rising Sun Hotel	1
Wine Bank on View	3

ACCOMMODATION

Allawah Bendigo	2
Bendigo Backpackers	6
Central City Caravan Park	1
Langley Hall B&B	4
Quality Inn Colonial and Jonah's Apartments	3
Shamrock	5

EATING

Bunja Thai	2
Finders Keepers	5
GPO	3
The Green Olive	4
Masons of Bendigo	6
Mr Beebe's Eating House & Bar	1
The Woodhouse	7

NIEMANN STREET
BARKLY STREET
ROSALIND STREET
WATTLE ST
VIEW STREET
Queen Elizabeth Oval
BARNARD STREET
ROWAN STREET
MACKENZIE STREET
View Hill Fellowship
The Capital
Sacred Heart Cathedral
Bendigo Art Gallery
Ulumbarra Theatre/Old Bendigo Gaol
BRIDGE STREET
NOLAN ST
Bendigo Creek
Lake Weeroona
HIGH STREET (CALDER HWY)
Rosalind Park
Central Deborah Gold Mine
Law Courts
Dai Gum San Chinese Precinct
Conservatory
PALL MALL
MCRAE STREET
NAPIER STREET
CREEK ST SOUTH
MYRTLE STREET
BATH LANE
Charing Cross
CHANCERY LANE
HARGREAVES STREET
Hargreaves Mall
WILLIAMSON STREET
LYTTLETON TERRACE
MUNDY STREET
CHAPEL STREET
Spring Creek
QUEEN STREET
KING STREET
MITCHELL STREET
MYERS STREET
Bendigo Market Place
St Paul's Cathedral
MOLLISON STREET
Train Station
RAILWAY PL
Tram Route
Bendigo Joss House
Echuca & Bendigo Pottery (6km)

0 250 metres

N

9

Pall Mall

Many of Bendigo's finest gold-rush buildings, none of which would look out of place in a capital city, stand along the grand avenue of **Pall Mall**. These include the law courts (1896) and the old Post Office building (1887) that now houses the visitor centre and the Post Office Gallery, featuring social history displays; the colossal four-storey **Hotel Shamrock** (1897) opposite is an extravagant example of Victorian gold-boom architecture.

The Capital – Bendigo's Performing Arts Centre

50 View St • Box office Mon–Fri 9.15am–5.15pm; Sat 10am–1pm; performance times vary • ☎ 03 5434 6100, ⓦ thecapital.com.au

Bendigo's Performing Arts Centre is a massive Neoclassical pile, which plays host to diverse shows – from classical music, opera and ballet to comedy, musicals and concerts. There are around 150 performances each year, and The Capital hosts a writer's festival (ⓦ bendigowritersfestival.com.au) each August.

Bendigo Art Gallery

42 View St • Daily 10am–5pm • Donation • ☎ 03 5434 6088, ⓦ bendigoartgallery.com.au

Housed in another beautifully restored nineteenth-century building with a modern addition, this is one of Australia's finest regional galleries, featuring an extensive collection of Australian painting from Bendigo's gold-rush days to the present; the gallery has a strong focus on acquiring contemporary works. There is also nineteenth-century British and European art acquired with all that gold, and the gallery hosts impressive travelling exhibitions, some international.

Dai Gum San Chinese Precinct

Bridge Street, one of Bendigo's oldest, was once **Chinatown**, home to the Chinese who came in their thousands in the 1850s and who knew Bendigo as *dai gum san* ("big gold mountain"); when the gold ran out, many turned to market gardening. As late as the 1960s old shops sporting faded Chinese signs were still in evidence, but now Chinese customs and ways of life are best seen in the beautiful **Dai Gum San Chinese Precinct** that links the Golden Dragon Museum with the Yi Yuan Gardens and Kuan Yin Temple. Spanning historic Bendigo Creek, this development features colourful Chinese symbolism and is undoubtedly the best place in Australia to experience Chinese history and culture.

The **Golden Dragon Museum** (1–11 Bridge St; daily 9.30am–5pm; $11; ☎ 03 5441 5044, ⓦ goldendragonmuseum.org) holds an impressive collection of costumes, textiles, furniture and Chinese processional regalia, including the world's oldest Imperial dragon Sun Loong, over 90m long and the highlight of the annual Easter Chinese Spring Festival parade, and another magnificent dragon, Loong. An extensive world-class exhibition tells the full story of Bendigo's Chinese community since the days of the gold rush; there are also tearooms and a gift shop. The tranquil adjoining **Yi Yuan Gardens** feature a temple to the Goddess of Mercy, **Kuan Yin**.

Bendigo Joss House Temple

Finn St , North Bendigo • Daily 11am–3pm or by prior arrangement • $6 • ☎ 03 5442 1685, ⓦ bendigojosshouse.com • Bus #7, which runs approximately hourly Mon–Fri, and the Vintage Talking Tram

The National Trust-listed **Bendigo Joss House** in North Bendigo was built by the Chinese in the 1860s and is the oldest Chinese temple still in use in Australia. The route to the shrine passes man-made Lake Weeroona, whose picnic grounds are the setting for the lovely *Boardwalk Restaurant & Café* (Mon–Fri 7.30am–4pm, Sat & Sun 8am–4pm; ☎ 03 5443 9855) in an old Chinese teahouse that overlooks the lake.

Bendigo Pottery

About 6km north of town, on the Midland Highway • Daily 9am–5pm • Museum $8; 30min wheel throwing $15 • ☎ 03 5448 4404, ⓦ bendigopottery.com.au

Bendigo Pottery, north of town, is Australia's oldest working **pottery centre**, dating back to 1858. In addition to the pottery shop, café, an antiques and collectables centre with more than forty stalls, and artisan outlets, the pottery includes an excellent interpretive museum. You can also watch demonstrations of hand throwing by potters and even make your own pot on a wheel.

Central Deborah Gold Mine

76 Violet St • Daily 9.30am–4.30pm • Above-ground admission $6.50 • Mine Experience Tour 4 daily, 10.30am–3pm; $30 • Underground Adventure tours (including a meal) daily 11am & 2pm; $85 • Nine Levels of Darkness tour (includes lunch) Mon–Fri 10.30am; $199 (min 2 required) • ☎ 03 5443 8322 (general enquiries), ☎ 03 5443 8255 (bookings), ⓦ central-deborah.com

The **Central Deborah Gold Mine** was the last Central Goldfields mine to close. You can explore the area above ground, including an interpretive museum, but it's worth taking the 75-minute underground **Mine Experience Tour** if you've never been down a mine; everybody is issued with a reassuring hard hat, complete with torch and generator. You descend to a depth of 60m in a lift, which takes 85 seconds – it would take thirty minutes to reach the bottom of some of the deepest shafts. The further down you go the hotter it gets, and at 60m it's warm and airless, dripping with water and muddy underfoot. If you want to scramble around the mine a bit longer, climb ladders, and perhaps operate a drill, you can join the **Underground Adventure** (2hr 30min) which descends to 85m, or the 3.5–4hr Nine Levels of Darkness that takes you to 228m and is Australia's deepest underground mine tour.

ARRIVAL AND DEPARTURE   BENDIGO

By train The train station is about 1km south of the historic town centre. Trains from Melbourne (via Castlemaine) run from early morning to late at night. There are also trains to Echuca and Swan Hill.

Destinations Echuca (1–3 daily; 1hr 20min); Melbourne night (hourly; 1hr 30min–2hr); Swan Hill (1–2 daily; 2hr 15min).

By bus Bendigo Airport Service runs buses to and from Melbourne Airport (5–7 daily; 2hr 15min); booking essential on ☎ 03 5444 3939 or ⓦ bendigoairportservice .com.au. Arriving and departing from Bendigo train station, buses run to Geelong (2 daily; 4hr 30min) via Ballarat (2hr 15min), with one service stopping at Castlemaine (50min) and Daylesford (1hr 20min); as well as to Horsham (daily; 3hr 20min) and Mildura (4 weekly; 5hr 45min). There is a limited service to Maldon (Wed; 1hr).

INFORMATION AND TOURS

Tourist information The visitor centre in the old post office building on Pall Mall (daily 9am–5pm; ☎ 1800 813 153, ⓦ bendigotourism.com) has a free accommodation-booking service, a range of walking and cycling maps, and offers free wi-fi.

Vintage Talking Tram Tour ☎ 03 5442 2821, ⓦ bendigotramways.com. A good way to get an overall impression of this large city is to take the Vintage Talking Tram Tour (daily 10am–4pm; departures on the hour from Central Deborah Gold Mine). The tram takes in several of the main attractions and the ticket includes a guided tour of the Bendigo Tram Depot, Australia's oldest working tram depot and workshop (1hr; $22.50, $17.50 without the depot tour).

ACCOMMODATION

Allawah Bendigo 45 View St ☎ 03 5441 7003, ⓦ allawahbendigo.com. This organization has a variety of stylish self-contained apartments, suites and maisonettes (self-contained rooms with kitchenettes and independent entries) around Bendigo. Some are purpose-built and others are in mid-to-late nineteenth-century buildings. Maisonettes $125, doubles $170, apartments $180

Bendigo Backpackers 33 Creek St South ☎ 03 5443 7680, ⓦ bendigobackpackers.com.au. Ultra-casual hostel in a town-centre weatherboard house, with spacious dorms, doubles, twins and family rooms. There's a big kitchen, an open fire in the lounge and a courtyard. Dorms $30, doubles $68

Central City Caravan Park 362 High St, Golden Square ☎ 03 5443 6937, ⓦ centralcitycaravanpark.com.au. Caravan and camping park with modern amenities and a pool. It's located 2.5km southwest of the CBD but there's a bus stop to town just outside. Wi-fi for an additional charge. Un/powered site $35/42, cabin $105

Langley Hall B&B 484 Napier St ☎ 0418 545 832, ⓦ langleyhall.com.au. A 1903 Edwardian mansion turned into a boutique B&B, featuring six gracious heritage rooms, charming common areas, and a leafy garden. No children. $165

Quality Inn Colonial and Jonah's Apartments 483–485 High St ☎ 03 5447 0122, ⓦ bendigocolonial.com.au.

9

A comfortable motel with contemporary rooms and three-bed apartments that belie the old-fashioned colonial-inspired exterior. There's also an indoor pool and spa, and a restaurant. Two-night minimum for apartments. Doubles $151, apartments $300

Shamrock Cnr Pall Mall & Williamson St ☎ 03 5443 0333, ⊚ hotelshamrock.com.au. Centrally located, this fabulous grand Victorian hotel has a range of accommodation, from standard, motel-like rooms to heritage spa suites with views over Pall Mall. $170

EATING

Bendigo is renowned for its restaurants, cafés, wine bars and general food and wine culture, and has several defined dining precincts, including View Street, Pall Mall, Bath Lane and Chancery Lane. The Bendigo Community Farmers' Market (2nd Sat of each month; ⊚ bcfm.org.au) provides another opportunity to sample the fine regional produce.

Bunja Thai 32 Pall Mall ☎ 03 5441 8566, ⊚ bunja .com.au. Set in a grand 1880s bank building, this Thai restaurant is a local favourite, with its delicious Thai tapas ($10), curries (from $20), banquet menus (starting at $35pp) and $12 lunch specials. Mon–Fri noon–2.30pm & 5.30pm–late, Sat 5.30pm–late.

Finders Keepers 20 Mitchell St ☎ 03 5443 5126, ⊚ finderskeepersbendigo.com.au. Bendigo's most beautiful café (with big picture windows and stained glass) is also one of its most popular, with scrumptious all-day breakfasts (from $7.50), home-made cakes, and a lovely upstairs balcony. Mon–Thurs 7am–5pm, Fri 7am–8pm, Sat & Sun 8am–4pm.

GPO 60–64 Pall Mall ☎ 03 5443 4343, ⊚ gpobendigo .com.au. A sleek contemporary space in a historic nineteenth-century building serving delicious tapas, pizza and other Mediterranean dishes to a chatty crowd of locals. Mains around $25. Daily 11.30am–late.

The Green Olive 11 Bath Lane ☎ 03 5442 2676. Excellent coffee (roasted on site), decadent cakes and light lunches, such as spicy quesadillas ($16), keep this casual café packed with locals. Mon–Fri 7am–4pm, Sat & Sun 8am–3pm.

★ **Masons of Bendigo** 25 Queen St ☎ 03 5443 3877, ⊚ masonsofbendigo.com.au. This fabulous restaurant focuses on fine central Victorian produce, maximizing the dining experience by offering share-style dishes, with a roaming menu for two people. Savoury bites are priced from $11 while larger plates (from $32) include superb lamb, duck, seafood and vegetarian dishes. There's a great wine list and a good beer selection. Tues–Sat noon–2pm & 6pm–late.

Mr Beebe's Eating House & Bar 17 View St ☎ 03 5441 5557, ⊚ mrbeebes.com.au. Way too laidback for its ornate heritage building (designed by the eponymous architect Mr Beebe), this casual place pulls people in with delicious terrines, parfaits, and sharing plates (from $14–40), such as chargrilled pork chop with quinoa and Kaiser salad with *pedro* jus and glazed fig. Multi-course tasting menus ($52–70) solve the dilemma of choosing. Daily 11am–late.

The Woodhouse 101 Williamson St ☎ 03 5443 8671, ⊚ thewoodhouse.com.au. A steakhouse specializing in red-gum chargrilled steaks (try the tender dry-aged Wagyu, $56) and excellent wood-fired pizzas (from $20). Mon–Fri noon–2pm & 5.30pm–late, Sat 5.30pm–late.

DRINKING AND NIGHTLIFE

The Metropolitan Hotel Cnr Bull & Hargreaves sts ☎ 03 5443 4916, ⊚ metrobendigo.com.au. Bendigo has a student-influenced nightlife during university terms and the *Metropolitan* is one of several pubs offering live music and DJs (Friday and Saturday nights). It also hosts trivia nights and karaoke. There's a sports bar, a courtyard, lots of beers on tap and wines by the glass. The in-house restaurant specializes in hand-pressed, oven-baked schnitzels from $16. Daily 11am–late.

Rifle Brigade Hotel 137 View St ☎ 03 5443 4092, ⊚ riflebrigadehotel.com.au. Recently restored to its gold-era glory, this inviting pub, with open fires in winter

and a courtyard, is also a great place to eat. The very jazzed up pub grub includes pomegranate-glazed chicken, braised beef spare ribs (both $24.50), paella ($28.50) and steaks. Daily 11am–late.

Rising Sun Hotel 84 Barnard St ☎ 03 5441 3833, ⊚ risingsunhotel.com.au. A stylish contemporary pub with a chic bar and bistro serving beers, cocktails and good bar snacks. Daily 11am–late.

Wine Bank on View 45 View St ☎ 03 5444 4655, ⊚ winebankonview.com. For after-work drinks, locals love this classy bar in an atmospheric old bank, which has a superb wine selection. The food is good too. Mon–Fri 8am–late, Sat 8.30am–1pm, Sun 8.30am–4pm.

Castlemaine

CASTLEMAINE, 39km southwest of Bendigo, is at the centre of the area once known as the Mount Alexander Goldfields. Between 1851 and 1861 this was the world's richest alluvial goldfield – 105,000kg of gold were found here (modest quantities are still found at Wattle Gully mine at nearby Chewton, Australia's oldest working gold mine). Castlemaine became the headquarters of the Government Camp for the area in 1852, and its impressive buildings were built over the next decade. Partly because of the **Castlemaine State Festival** (ⓦcastlemainefestival.com.au), Victoria's premier regional arts festival, which takes place over ten days in March or April in odd-numbered years, Castlemaine has a cultured and arty feel with around four hundred practising artists and artisans in the area, and numerous galleries and theatres around town.

Historic Castlemaine Market Building

Mostyn St • Daily 9am–5pm

The town's finest building is the 1862 **Castlemaine Market**, a wonderfully extravagant piece of Neoclassical architecture. Used as a market for more than a hundred years, it now houses the Visitor Information Centre and is used for exhibitions and functions.

Theatre Royal

30 Hargraves St • ☎ 03 5472 1196, ⓦ theatreroyalcstlemaine.com.au

The Heritage-listed 1858 (albeit with a 1930s facade) **Theatre Royal**, one of the oldest theatres in Australia, is magnificent; when the famous Lola Montez performed here, miners threw nuggets of gold at her in appreciation. The theatre presents art-house and mainstream films, live music and comedy, and has a street-level café (daily noon–8pm).

Buda

42 Hunter St • Wed–Sat noon–5pm, Sun 10am–5pm • $12 • ☎ 03 5472 1032, ⓦ budacastlemaine.org

Another stunning architectural attraction, a short distance from the centre, is **Buda**, a gracious home and garden built in 1861 by a retired Baptist missionary and extended by its subsequent owner Ernest Leviny, a Hungarian silversmith, in the 1890s. The house and gardens give an insight into the good life enjoyed in the gold-rush days, and on display are many works by Leviny and his daughters, including carved-wood hangings, silverware and embroidery, as is the family's art collection.

Castlemaine Art Gallery and Historical Museum

14 Lyttleton St • Mon, Wed–Fri 10am–5pm, Sat & Sun noon–5pm • $4 • ☎ 03 5472 2292, ⓦ castlemainegallery.com

The **Castlemaine Art Gallery and Museum** is also worth a visit. It specializes in Australian photographs and paintings, featuring many works by the Heidelberg School, notably Frederick McCubbin and Tom Roberts.

ARRIVAL AND DEPARTURE   CASTLEMAINE

By train There are frequent trains from Melbourne that continue to Bendigo (see p.829). Another option is the Victorian Goldfields Railway (Wed & Sun; more often during summer; single trip $30, return $45; ☎ 03 5470 6658, ⓦvgr.com.au), a tourist steam train, or diesel locomotive on days of severe fire warnings, which runs between Castlemaine and Maldon. The station is a block west of the main street.

By bus Castlemaine Bus Lines operate to Maldon and Bendigo (timetables and info available at ☎ 03 5472 1455, ⓦcastlemainebuslines.com.au). There are also buses to Ballarat (Mon–Fri daily; 1hr 30min). The buses depart from the train station.

INFORMATION

Tourist information The very helpful Castlemaine Visitor Information Centre in the Market Building on Mostyn St (daily 9am–5pm; ☎ 03 5471 1795 or ☎ 1800 171 888, ⓦmaldoncastlemaine.com.au) can arrange accommodation.

Markets If you're here on a Saturday, trek the 2km out along the Pyrenees Highway to Wesley Hill Community Market, a giant flea market selling local produce and crafts (7.30am–1pm). There are two markets on the first Sunday of each month: the Castlemaine Farmers Market takes place at Victory Park and features fine local produce and entertainment (9am–1pm; ⓦ castlemainefarmersmarket .org); and the Artists Market, in Western Reserve, showcases local art and design.

9

Festival Throughout the year, various gardens in the Castlemaine district open their doors to visitors, especially during the Festival of Gardens (ⓦfestivalofgardens.org), which takes place in even-numbered years during the November Melbourne Cup week.

ACCOMMODATION

Apple Annie's 31 Templeton St ☎03 5472 5311, ⓦappleannies.com.au. Two lovely period apartments full of colour, tucked behind *Apole Annie's Bakery Café*, a handy source of delicious food. Both apartments have open fires and the larger one has a tempting claw-footed bath. **$150**

Big 4 Castlemaine Gardens Holiday Park 1 Doran Ave ☎03 5472 1125, ⓦbig4.com.au. A leafy park just out of the town centre, but next to the open-air swimming pool and Botanic Gardens. Un/powered sites **$36/$38**, cabins **$125**

★ **Campbell St Lodge** 33 Campbell St ☎03 5472 3477, ⓦcampbellstlodge.com.au. Simple, old-fashioned rooms in a historic National Trust-listed town-centre house, and self-contained apartments in an adjoining building. Doubles **$115**, apartments **$175**

Claremont Coach House 7 Burnett Rd ☎0401 010 589, ⓦclaremontcoachhouse.com. A self-contained bare-brick coach house built in 1857 and a bedsit garden cottage (with limited cooking facilities) share their leafy setting with grand Claremont House (private), 3km north of the CBD near the Botanic Gardens. Both offer an inexpensive taste of history. **$100**

The Empyre Boutique Hotel 68 Mostyn St ☎03 5472 5166, ⓦempyre.com.au. Six super-stylish luxury suites with open fires, some opening on to the iron lace-trimmed balcony, in a charming 1860s town-centre building that reflects the area's rich history. Breakfast included **$285**

EATING AND DRINKING

Origini 213 Barker St ☎03 5472 1766, ⓦorigini.com.au. A slice of rustic Italy in a tiny town shop. Locals chat over coffees and unfussy food, including filled flatbreads and arguably the best minestrone outside Rome ($14); Friday is traditional pizza night ($20). Eat inside, on the footpath or in the garden. Mon–Thurs 8.30am–4.30pm, Fri 8am–late.

Railway Hotel 65 Gingell St ☎03 5472 1250, ⓦrailwayhotelcastlemaine.com.au. Traditional country-style pub, with locals propping up the bar and happy patrons in the bistro tucking into hearty grub, the highlight of which is the enormous succulent steaks (from $28). Mon–Fri 6pm–late, Sat & Sun noon–2.30pm.

re-Public 26 Templeton St ☎03 5472 1582, ⓦre-public.com.au. This award-winning indoor-outdoor café is the place for delicious breakfasts (from $10), gourmet open sandwiches and wraps ($15), and bigger dishes like battered rockling fillets ($26). Daily 8am–4pm.

Saff's 64 Mostyn St ☎03 5470 6722. Considered the best café in town, with special evening events including recitals and poetry readings. Food includes soup ($9.50) and burgers (from $16). Daily 7.30am–4.30pm.

Maldon

Some 17km northwest of Castlemaine is quaint **MALDON**, a tiny, peaceful town surrounded by low hills that boasts Victoria's most intact historic streetscape. Its combination of charming shops and B&Bs have made it an understandably popular weekend getaway from Melbourne.

Gold was found here in 1853 and the rich, deep alluvial reefs were mined until 1926. The main shopping street largely preserves its original appearance, with single-storey shopfronts shaded by awnings and decorated with iron lacework. Apart from enjoying the town's gift and craft shops, cafés and architecture, you can take an underground tour at the stunning candlelit **Carman's Tunnel goldmine** off Parkin's Reef Road, 3km south of town (Sat & Sun; tours depart at 1.30pm, 2.30pm & 3.30pm; 30–40min; $7.50; ☎03 5475 2656).

ARRIVAL AND INFORMATION   MALDON

By train The Victorian Goldfields Railway (Wed & Sun; more often during the summer; single trip $30, return $45; ☎03 5470 6658, ⓦvgr.com.au), a tourist steam train or diesel locomotive on days of severe fire warnings, runs between Castlemaine and Maldon. The station is about 1km northeast of the main street on the Bendigo road.

By bus Castlemaine Bus Lines runs services to Castlemaine (2–3 daily; 20min); the buses leave from the town centre, outside the *Kangaroo Hotel* (timetables and info available at ☎03 5472 1455, ⓦcastlemainebuslines.com.au).

OPPOSITE MURRAY RIVER NEAR MILDURA (P.851) >

9

MALDON FOLK FESTIVAL

During the long weekend before the Melbourne Cup (see p.48), things get busy as people head to town for the four-day **Maldon Folk Festival** (ⓦmaldonfolkfestival.com; full weekend $95, Sat, Sun or Mon only $60). Since its inception in 1974 the event has steadily grown, and apart from folk, it features blues, bluegrass and world music as well as theatre and dance. The festival takes place in more than twenty venues around the town, with free entertainment in the streets.

Tourist information Maldon Visitor Information Centre is in the Shire Gardens, 93 High St (daily 9am–5pm; ☎03 5475 2569, ⓦmaldoncastlemaine.com.au). Their website is useful for information on B&Bs and self-contained accommodation around Maldon.

ACCOMMODATION AND EATING

Berryman's Café and Tea Rooms 30 Main St ☎03 5475 2904. Home-style food, including all-day breakfasts, lunches (mains $7–16) and afternoon teas. The cakes and scones are home-made and gluten-free options are available. BYO. Mon 9am–late, Tues–Sun 9am–5pm.

Café Maldon 52 Main St ☎03 5475 2022. A bustling café, serving burgers, sandwiches, pies and salads, with vegetarian and gluten-free options (mains $5–12). Daily 8am–5pm.

The Grand 26 High St ☎0409 553 047, ⓦthegrandmaldon.com.au. Charming self-contained apartments in a historic building (one in the old stables). Breakfast provisions include locally baked bread. $160

Kangaroo Hotel 89 High St ☎03 5475 2214. Opposite the visitor centre, this is a good place for a drink and a bite to eat, with a cosy beer garden, live music some nights and reasonably priced pub favourites such as steaks and parmigianas (most dishes under $20). Daily noon–late.

Miss Pritchard's Pantry 31 High St ☎03 5475 2282. Locals and visitors alike fill this corner café, enjoying the good coffee and classic vinyl tunes; on weekends there's seating in a courtyard. The menu features the likes of breakfast rice pudding, savoury tarts ($12), luscious salads ($16) and more substantial dishes such as cauliflower and chickpea dumplings with spiced yoghurt ($15). Occasional themed dinners. Wed–Fri 9am–4pm, Sat & Sun 9am–5pm.

Daylesford and around

The attractive, hilly country around **DAYLESFORD** and neighbouring Hepburn Springs, just ninety minutes from Melbourne, is a popular weekend retreat known as the "spa capital of Australia". There are around seventy **mineral springs** within a 50km radius, more than thirty spas, and wellness retreats and healing centres aplenty; services range from natural therapies to tarot readings (enquire at the visitor centre or see ⓦspacountrycom.au). Daylesford grew from the Jim Crow gold diggings of 1851, but the large Swiss-Italian population quickly realized the value of the water from the mineral springs, which has been bottled since 1850.

Daylesford's well-preserved Victorian and Edwardian streets rise up Wombat Hill, where you'll find the Botanical Gardens, between Hill Street and Central Springs Road, whose lookout tower has panoramic views. Nearby, on the corner of Daly and Hill streets, is **The Convent** (daily 10am–4pm; $5; ☎03 5348 3211, ⓦconventgallery.com.au), a rambling former convent with three levels of galleries selling high-quality arts, crafts and antiques, and a café and a bar. There's a great Sunday market (8am–3pm) at Daylesford train station.

Lake Daylesford

A short distance south of the town centre on Vincent Street, **Lake Daylesford** is the location of Central Springs Reserve, which has several walking tracks and old-fashioned water pumps from which you can drink the mineral springs.

Lavandula Swiss Italian Farm

Shepherds Flat, 5km north of Hepburn Springs • Sept–May Fri–Tues 10.30am–5.30pm, June–Aug Sat & Sun 10.30am–5.30pm • $4 • ☎03 5476 4393, ⓦlavandula.com.au

With your own transport you can visit the **Lavandula Swiss Italian Farm**, and walk among historic stone farmhouses and through extensive gardens, lavender fields, and

ALTERNATIVE DAYLESFORD

Daylesford – once labelled "the world's funkiest town" by the British Airways inflight magazine – has a New Age, alternative atmosphere, with a large gay community. The town has several gay-friendly guesthouses, and on the second weekend in March it is the venue for **ChillOut** (☎03 5348 4516, ⓦchilloutfestival.com.au), Australia's largest rural gay and lesbian festival, featuring a street parade, music and cabaret, dance parties and a carnival at Victoria Park.

grape and olive groves. There's also a shop selling lavender and other products and *La Trattoria*, the farm's renowned Italian café, which serves teas and Mediterranean cuisine during Lavandula's hours.

Tuki trout farm

Smeaton, 23km west of Daylesford via Creswick • Daily 11am–6pm • $10, rod rental $6 • ☎03 5345 6233, ⓦtuki.com.au

At **Tuki trout farm** you can catch your own lunch from one of the six ponds and have it filleted and cooked for you while you wait – the activity is suitable for everyone from beginners to avid anglers. There is also a restaurant and shop selling trout and other local produce.

ARRIVAL AND INFORMATION

By bus Buses operate to Hepburn Springs (Mon–Fri 4 daily; 15min) and Ballarat (Sun–Fri 6 weekly; 55min); they leave from/arrive a block back from the main street.
Tourist information Daylesford Visitor Information Centre, servicing the whole area, is at 98 Vincent St in

DAYLESFORD AND AROUND

Daylesford (daily 9am–5pm; ☎03 5321 6123, ⓦvisitdaylesford.com); it has loads of brochures on local activities and accommodation, including B&Bs. Internet access is also available.

ACCOMMODATION

Book well in advance if you want **to stay** in Daylesford on a weekend. Bookings for apartments and houses are handled by Daylesford Accommodation Escapes (☎03 5348 1448, ⓦdabs.com.au) and Daylesford Getaways (☎03 5348 4422, ⓦdayget.com.au).

Daylesford Royal Hotel 27 Vincent St, Daylesford ☎03 5348 2205, ⓦdaylesfordroyalhotel.com. Stylishly refurbished Victorian pub with pleasant, centrally heated rooms and a one-bed suite, some with spa bath and access to the first-floor balcony. Breakfast included. **$180**
Daylesford Victoria Caravan Park 3021 Ballan Rd, Daylesford ☎03 5348 3821, ⓦdaylesfordvictoria caravanpark.com.au. With a nice parkland setting close to the lake, 1.7km from town, this park has unpowered and

powered sites plus fully self-contained cabins. Un/powered sites **$32/$34**, cabins **$145**
Tuki Retreat Smeaton (23km west of Daylesford via Creswick) ☎03 5345 6233, ⓦtuki.com.au. Spacious lodge-style self-contained stone cottages, all with open fireplaces and lake and valley views; some also have spa baths. In addition there is a three-bedroom restored weatherboard miner's cottage. Rates include breakfast. **$200**

EATING AND DRINKING

★**Belvedere Social** 82b Vincent St, Daylesford ☎03 5348 2088, ⓦbelveteresocial.com.au. Fabulous seasonal regional produce flavours the food and cocktail menus at this slightly industrial Art Deco bistro bar. Take your pick of hot and cold bites (up to $16), and larger "grown", "caught" and "raised" dishes, such as rare-breed pork cutlet with spiced apple ($35). A five-course "Feed Me" option is $75. Wed 3pm–late, Thurs–Sun 11am–late.
Koukla Café and Pizzeria 82 Vincent St, Daylesford ☎03 5348 2363, ⓦcafekoukla.com.au. A rustic-chic corner café, warmed by open fires in winter, dishing up

generous breakfasts, including a mushroom medley, and wood-fired pizzas from noon (from $20) with a juicy steak ($32) added for the dinner menu. There's a good craft beer and cider list. Daily 7am–late.
Lake House King St, nr the lake ☎03 5348 3329, ⓦlakehouse.com.au. Multi-award-winning restaurant that is regarded as one of the state's best. The cuisine is refined mod-Oz with a strong emphasis on using the freshest seasonal local produce. Lunch and dinner from $80 (two–four courses), tasting menu from $145. Daily noon–2.30pm & 6–9pm.

9

Mercato@Daylesford 32 Raglan St ☏ 03 5348 4488, ⓦ mercatorestaurant.com.au. Fine regional cuisine using local ingredients but inspired by flavours from around the world. Mains, such as kangaroo fillet with native pepperberry, bush tomato chutney and heirloom beetroots, start at around $35, or there's a degustation sampling menu for $130. Mon, Tues & Thurs 6pm–late, Fri–Sun noon–3pm & 6pm–late.

Pastry King Café 60 Vincent St ☏ 03 5348 1356. For the last 75 years or so this place has been baking delicious pies (average $6), muffins and other indulgences, perfect for picnic lunches by the lake. Daily 6am–5pm.

Sweet Decadence at Locantro 87 Vincent St ☏ 03 5348 3202. Handmade chocolates, light breakfasts and lunches, such as nachos and sandwiches (most under $15), coffee and cake served up in an old building full of character. Daily 9.30am–5pm.

Hepburn Springs

Buses from Daylesford operate weekdays only (4 daily; 15min)

Synonymous with spas and pampering, the charming hamlet of **HEPBURN SPRINGS**, set amid lush green hills 3km north of Daylesford, is a popular weekend retreat for stressed-out urbanites. From the bus stop, walk through shady Soldiers Memorial Park to Heritage-listed **Hepburn Mineral Springs Reserve**, a leafy park where you can taste three kinds of mineral water from old pumps. You can also take advantage of the pool, spa, steam room and massage facilities at the sleek **Hepburn Bathhouse & Spa** complex (Mon–Thurs 9am–6.30pm, Fri 9am–8pm, Sat 8am–8pm, Sun 8am–6.30pm; bathhouse entry from $32, contact the spa for treatment prices; ☏ 03 9999 9386, ⓦ hepburnbathhouse.com), which features an 1890s bathhouse. Bookings for the spa (unnecessary for the bathhouse) must be made well in advance, especially for weekends. There is also a café in the reserve.

ACCOMMODATION — HEPBURN SPRINGS

Continental House 9 Lone Pine Ave ☏ 0467 277 525, ⓦ continentalhouse.net.au. This renovated 1920s guesthouse and retreat has twelve en-suite rooms and a wood-panelled guest lounge with a chandelier, fireplace and cosy nooks. Yoga, massages and reiki are available on request. The rambling house sits in a wild garden, where kangaroos graze, on a hill above Mineral Springs Reserve. Whole-house bookings welcome. **$120**

The Dudley 101 Main Rd ☏ 03 5348 3033, ⓦ thedudley.com.au. This boutique hotel, in a garden setting, offers a choice of accommodation: four spacious en-suite B&B rooms in the elegant Federation-era main house and two self-contained suites in Dudley Cottage. All include breakfast – a gourmet event. **$500**

Hepburn Springs Chalet 78 Main Rd ☏ 03 5348 2344, ⓦ hepburnspringschalet.com.au. Unapologetically retro traditional guesthouse with a splash of kitsch; the rooms, all en suite, have everything you need but no frills. There's a casual guest lounge with open fire, plus a reading room, restaurant and in-house day-spa. **$160**

Peppers Mineral Springs Retreat Cnr Main Rd & Tenth St ☏ 03 5348 2202, ⓦ peppersprings.com.au. A gracious, grand retreat in a famous 1930s Art Deco hotel with classic, luxurious en-suite rooms; there's a mineral spa on site too. Tasty meals are available in the bar, and at the more elegant and expensive in-house restaurant, which showcases beef from the hotel's own farm. Rates include breakfast in the conservatory. **$335**

EATING AND DRINKING

Blue Bean Love Café 115 Main Rd ☏ 03 5348 2297. The hippest place in town, this likeable laidback spot offers all-day breakfasts and contemporary comfort food, with curry and burger nights ($16) and lashings of live music. Mon & Fri–Sun 8am–9pm, Tues–Thurs 8am–3pm.

The Old Hepburn Hotel 236 Main Rd ☏ 03 5348 2207, ⓦ oldhepburnhotel.com.au. Almost 2km further along Main Rd from the *Blue Bean Love Café*, this is a good choice for a drink in the beer garden or for tasty pub grub, such as chicken schnitzel or salt and pepper squid (most mains under $25), from the seasonal menu. Bands play on weekends. Mon–Thurs 6–8.30pm, Fri–Sun noon–2pm & 6–8.30pm.

Ballarat

BALLARAT is a grand provincial city that makes a memorable first impression, especially if approached from the west, via the Western Freeway, along the **Avenue of Honour**. Lined on both sides with more than 22km of trees and dedicated to the Ballarat soldiers who enlisted in World War I, this is Australia's longest such avenue. It ends at the massive **Arch of Victory**, through which you enter Sturt Street and the city. More than a quarter of all **gold** found in Victoria came from Ballarat's fabulously rich reef mines before they were exhausted in 1918. Nowadays, in addition to the more obvious tourist attractions and fine **architecture**, the town is interesting in its own right, with a large student population that gives the city a somewhat vibrant character and reasonably active nightlife.

Sturt and Victoria streets terminate on either side of the Bridge Mall, the central shopping area at the base of quaint **Bakery Hill** with its old shopfronts. Southeast of the city centre, Eureka Street runs towards the site of the **Eureka Stockade** (see box, p.841), with several museums and antique shops along the way. Main Road is crossed by Bradshaw Street, where you'll find **Sovereign Hill**, the re-created gold-rush town. Northwest of the centre, approached via Sturt Street, are the **Ballarat Botanical Gardens** and Lake Wendouree.

Lydiard Street

The most complete **nineteenth-century streetscape** is along Lydiard Street, which runs from the centre up past the train station, with historic multistorey edifices, terraced shopfronts with awnings, and wide verandas with decorative iron-lacework, mostly dating from the mid- to late nineteenth century. As you walk south from the Art Gallery along Lydiard Street you'll see more nineteenth-century architecture, including the former **Mining Exchange** (1888), which has been renovated to its original splendour and operates as the Mining Exchange Gold Shop; and the architecture of Her Majesty's Theatre (1875), in Lydiard Street beyond Sturt Street, proclaims its gold-rush-era heyday. Note the imposing Classical Revival **town hall** on Sturt Street, which dominates the city centre.

Art Gallery of Ballarat

40 Lydiard St North • Daily 10am–5pm • Free • Guided tours daily 2pm; free • ☎ 03 5320 5858, ⓦ artgalleryofballarat.com.au

Another superb building, the **Art Gallery of Ballarat** is Australia's oldest provincial art gallery, established in 1884. Its extensive collection is strong on colonial and

9

Heidelberg School paintings, displayed alongside the watercolours of S.T. Gill, a self-taught artist who painted scenes of gold-rush days in Ballarat. There is also a range of artistic responses to the Eureka Stockade event (see box opposite), including a series of pencil portraits by Sidney Nolan. In another part of the gallery is a reconstruction of the drawing room of the famous Lindsay family (whose best-known members are the artist Norman and the writer Jack), from nearby Creswick, with several of their paintings. Among the works in the upstairs galleries are two Fred Williams landscapes.

Ballarat Botanical Gardens

Conservatory daily 9am–5pm • Free • ☎ 03 5320 5500 • Bus #16 from Sturt St, near the Myer department store

The **Ballarat Botanical Gardens**, laid out in 1858, cover about half a square kilometre beside Lake Wendouree, just northwest of the city centre. Begonias grow so well in Ballarat that a Begonia Festival runs over the Labour Day long weekend in March. The Conservatory, an impressive glasshouse whose design was inspired by origami, is used to showcase the flowers and other floral displays throughout the year. Other highlights are the **Avenue of Big Trees**, with a California redwood among its monsters, and classical statuary donated by rich gold-miners, scattered about the gardens. Pride of place goes to *Benzoni's Flight from Pompeii*, housed in the Statuary Pavilion. Along Prime Minister Avenue there are busts of Australian prime ministers, reflecting the city's strong political past.

Museum of Australian Democracy at Eureka (MADE)

Daily 10am–5pm • $12 • ☎ 1800 287 113; ⓦ made.org • Bus #9 from the station and city centre

On the site of the Eureka Stockade (see box opposite), the state-of-the-art **Museum of Australian Democracy at Eureka** commemorates and honours the influential uprising; the original, frayed **Eureka Flag** is displayed in a purpose-built space, with subdued lighting to protect the precious relic. The museum also encompasses democracy worldwide, looking at civics, culture, history and citizenship through books, music and Martin Luther King's "I have a dream" speech, with many interactive and high-tech exhibits.

Ballarat Wildlife Park

250 Fussell St • Daily 9am–5.30pm • Animal shows Sat & Sun: generally 1.30–4pm • $31 • ☎ 03 5333 5933, ⓦ wildlifepark.com.au • Bus #9 from the station and city centre

The **Ballarat Wildlife Park** is home to more than eighty free-ranging kangaroos, plus wombats, koalas and assorted reptiles. The chance to get close to the cuddlier animals and have your photo taken (for an additional fee) is a highlight, and there are morning guided tours. Feeding times and the special animal presentations are definitely worth attending.

Sovereign Hill

Bradshaw Street • Daily 10am–5pm • $52.50, includes admission to the Gold Museum and Red Hill Mine • "Blood on the Southern Cross" nightly; 1hr 30min; $59, joint ticket for show and Sovereign Hill $111.50, for dinner and show $99; bookings essential • ☎ 03 5337 1199, ⓦ sovereignhill.com.au • Bus #9 from the station and city centre

The impressive recreated gold-mining township of **Sovereign Hill** is 1.5km southeast of the city centre. Planned around an actual mineshaft from the 1880s (guided

---

BALLARAT'S MINING HOTELS

There are still over forty old **hotels** in Ballarat – survivors of the hundreds that once watered the thirsty miners. Some of the finest date from the mid-1850s and are on Lydiard Street: *Craigs Royal Hotel*, opposite Her Majesty's Theatre, and the *George Hotel* at no. 27 are an integral part of Ballarat's architectural heritage. Sadly, during the 1970s, the council forced many old pubs to pull down verandas deemed unsafe, so very few survive in their original form. One that does is attached to the *Golden City Hotel* at 427 Sturt St, which took the council to the Supreme Court to save its magnificent wide veranda with original cast-iron decoration.

underground tours are available), the seventy-odd buildings and shops are modelled on those that lined Ballarat's main street in the 1850s, with a cast of characters in strikingly authentic period dress. There are diggings where you can learn how to pan for gold (and perhaps find a small memento), and a mining museum filled with steam-operated machinery. You can also have your picture taken in period get-up (for an extra fee), ride around the village on the horse-drawn coach, take in a show at the pretty theatre, watch a gold bar being smelted, and explore the tents and temple of the Chinese village. There's a spectacular outdoor evening **sound-and-light show**, "Blood on the Southern Cross", which makes use of the whole panorama of Sovereign Hill to tell the story of the Eureka Stockade.

Gold Museum

Daily 9.30am–5.30pm, in summer until 6pm • $12.50, but included in Sovereign Hill entry • Ⓦ goldmuseum.com.au

Opposite Sovereign Hill, the **Gold Museum** offers a good overview of the recreated settlement. It has an outstanding display of real gold, and a large collection of coins arranged in displays exploring the history and uses of gold. A small Eureka display details life on the goldfields and explains the appalling conditions that provoked the Eureka Stockade (see box below). Central to the display is a large painting of the rebellion by George Browning, a mid-nineteenth-century artist: it's interesting to spot the indigenous faces portrayed in the stockade, commonly labelled as a white armed uprising.

THE EUREKA STOCKADE

The **Eureka Stockade** is one of the most celebrated and controversial events in Australia's history and generally regarded as the only major act of white armed rebellion against a government the country has seen – however, some historians argue that Aboriginal people were involved in it as well. It was provoked by conditions in the goldfields, where diggers had to pay exorbitantly for their right to prospect for gold (as much as thirty shillings a month), without receiving in return any right to vote or any chance of a permanent right to the land they worked. The administration at Ballarat was particularly repressive, and in November 1854 local diggers formed the **Ballarat Reform League**, demanding full civic rights and the abolition of the licence fee, proclaiming that "the people are the only legitimate source of power". At the end of the month a group of two hundred diggers gathered inside a **stockade** of logs, hastily flung together, and determined to resist further arrests for non-possession of a licence. They were attacked at dawn on December 3 by police and troops; 22 died inside, and five members of the government forces also lost their lives.

MINER'S RIGHT

The movement was not a failure, however: the diggers had aroused widespread sympathy, and in 1855 licences were abolished, to be replaced by an annual **Miner's Right**, which carried the right to vote and to enclose land. The leader of the rebellion, Irishman Peter Lalor, eventually became a member of parliament.

EUREKA FLAG

With its white cross and five white stars on a blue background, representing the constellation of the Southern Cross, the **Eureka Flag** has become a symbol of empowerment – and indeed of many Australian protest movements: shearers raised it in strikes during the 1890s; wharfies used it before World War II in their bid to stop pig iron being sent to Japan; and today the flag is flown by a growing number of Australians who support the country's transformation to a republic. On a deeper level, all sorts of claims are made for the Eureka Rebellion's pivotal role in forming the Australian nation and psyche. The diggers are held up as a classic example of the Australian (male) ethos of mateship, as well as independence and anti-authoritarianism, while the gold rush in general is credited with overthrowing the hierarchical colonial order, as servants rushed to make their fortunes, leaving their masters and mistresses to fend for themselves. The flag is on display at the Museum of Australian Democracy at Eureka (see opposite).

9

Ballarat Bird World

408 Eddy Ave, Mount Helen • Sat & Sun 10am–5pm • $10 • ☎ 03 5341 3843, ⓦ ballaratbirdworld.com.au

The privately run **Ballarat Bird World** at Mount Helen, 7km south of Ballarat, is worth a detour. It has ten acres of landscaped bushland gardens, complete with a small rainforest and a waterfall, and more than two hundred birds including parrots and cockatoos from Australia, Asia, Africa and South America, some of which were bred here.

ARRIVAL AND INFORMATION

BALLARAT

By train There are very frequent trains from Melbourne to Ballarat (20 daily; 1hr 10min–1hr 30min), with some continuing to Ararat (see opposite). The station is fairly central, just off Lydiard Street.

By bus Buses run to Bendigo (some via Castlemaine and Daylesford), Hamilton via Dunkeld, Horsham and Warrnambool, arriving at and leaving from the train station. Greyhound Australia buses from Melbourne to Adelaide travel the Western Freeway and Western Highway via Ballarat, Ararat, Stawell and Horsham. Public transport buses in Ballarat and surrounds are operated by CDC Ballarat/Davis Bus Lines (see ⓦ cdcvictoria.com.au for map and timetables).

Destinations Bendigo (10 weekly; 2hr); Castlemaine (5 weekly; 2hr 5min); Daylesford (6 weekly; 45min); Geelong (2–3 daily; 1hr 30min); Hamilton (6 weekly; 2hr 20min); Horsham (1–3 daily; 2hr 40min); Mildura (6 weekly; 7hr 30min); Mount Gambier (5 weekly; 3hr 35min); Warrnambool (5 weekly; 3hr 5min).

Tourist information Ballarat Visitor Information Centre, located in the city centre at 43 Lydiard St North (daily 9am–5pm; ☎ 1800 446 633, ⓦ visitballarat.com.au), offers information and town maps, and can book accommodation; there is also free wi-fi.

ACCOMMODATION

Ansonia on Lydiard 32 Lydiard St South ☎ 03 5332 4698, ⓦ theansonialydiard.com.au. A lovely boutique hotel set in a heritage building in the historic precinct, offering elegant rooms, beautiful public spaces and a restaurant. $170

Big 4 Ballarat Goldfields Holiday Park 108 Clayton St ☎ 1800 632 237, ⓦ ballaratgoldfields.com.au. Well located, beside Sovereign Hill, this holiday park has good facilities for campers, including a kitchen, and cabins are also available. Powered sites $38, cabins $89

Comfort Inn Sovereign Hill Magpie St ☎ 03 5337 1159, ⓦ sovereignhill.com.au. There's a good choice of accommodation here, overlooking the recreated gold town, from budget shared bunk rooms to plush colonial-themed doubles. Dorms $33, doubles $190

Craigs Royal Hotel 10 Lydiard St South ☎ 03 5331 1377, ⓦ craigsroyal.com. The accommodation (forty or so boutique rooms and suites, some with spas) at this grand Victorian-era hotel is the city's most sumptuous – if you can't afford to stay, at least visit for a drink. $265

The Eastern 81 Humffray St ☎ 0427 440 661, ⓦ ballaratbackpackers.com. Eclectically decorated with vintage and repro furniture, this popular place has retro charm. There's a range of comfortable dorms, singles and doubles, all with shared bathroom, and facilities include a kitchen and a bar with boutique beer on tap and a pool table. Live music nights mean it can be noisy. Cash only. Dorms $35, doubles $80

The George Hotel 27 Lydiard St North ☎ 03 5333 4866, ⓦ georgehotelballarat.com.au. Lovely rooms and a stylish but casual restaurant, set in an early twentieth-century hotel with a three-level cast-iron veranda unique to Victoria. $180

Oscars 18 Doveton St ☎ 03 5331 1451, ⓦ oscarshotel.com.au. This trendily renovated Art Deco pub has thirteen contemporary rooms, some with spas, a couple of smart bars, an excellent café and a sunny courtyard. $150

EATING

Catfish Thai 42–44 Main Rd, Bakery Hill ☎ 03 5331 5248, ⓦ acatfishthai.com.au. One of Ballarat's best, this award-winning restaurant plates up delicious contemporary sharing Thai dishes from a changing menu including street food appetizers ($15) and spicy salads ($32); with whole-table banquets from $55/person. They also run cooking classes ($165). Tues–Sat 6pm–late.

Eclectic Tastes 2 Burnbank St ☎ 03 5339 9252. Eclectic doesn't describe just the food in this shop-turned-retro café, which is illuminated by lightshades made of disposable drink cups. The menu ranges from an above-standard BLT ($14) to pork and water-chestnut dumplings ($22), and there's great coffee. Mon–Fri 9am–4pm.

Europa Café 411 Sturt St ☎ 03 5338 7672, ⓦ europacafe.com.au. A buzzy spot serving good coffee, all day breakfast, cakes, snacks and light meals such as salads and risottos (from $15). Daily 7am–6pm.

Irish Murphy's 36 Sturt St ☎ 03 5331 4091, ⓦ murphysballarat.com.au. Popular with backpackers for its big food at small prices, decent beer and frequent live music (with minimal Irish kitsch). Mains from $18. Daily 11.30am–2pm & 6–9pm.

Kambei 501 Main Rd ☎ 03 5331 1468, ⓦ kambei.com. au. Flawless tempura (assorted costs $20) is the main act at this classic Japanese restaurant, popular with families and groups. Tues–Thurs 5–10pm, Fri & Sat noon–2.30pm &

5pm–10pm, Sun noon–2.30pm & 5pm–9pm.

L'Espresso 417 Sturt St ☎ 03 5333 1789. An arty café that attracts local uni students, intellectuals and musicians, with good coffee, tasty breakfasts (most less than $15), light meals and interesting wines by the glass. Daily 7.30am–6pm.

DRINKING, NIGHTLIFE AND ENTERTAINMENT

Thanks to a burgeoning student population – over twenty thousand are enrolled at the University of Ballarat, with a high percentage of them studying music, performing arts and fashion – the city has a buzzy live **music** and **club** scene. For up-to-date information about what's on, check the local paper and the events/what's-on section of ⓦ visitballarat.com.au. Most action takes place Wednesday to Sunday after 9pm. The elaborate Victorian-era Her Majesty's Theatre, at 17 Lydiard St South (☎ 03 5333 5888, ⓦ hermaj.com), stages all types of touring productions, while the grand Regent on the same street at no. 49 is an eight-screen **cinema** (☎ 03 5330 5555, ⓦ regententertainment.com.au).

BARS AND CLUBS

Freight Bar & Restaurant 49 Mair St ☎ 03 5333 5431 ⓦ freightbar.com.au. With three bars, a restaurant and open-air deck over two levels, this is a great place for a drink and/or something to eat. There are boutique beers, cocktails and a menu ranging from sliders ($18) to chargrilled eye fillet ($36). Tues–Sun 11am–late.

Karova Lounge Cnr Field & Camp sts ⓦ karovalounge .com. Ballarat's best live-music venue, where popular bands and solo acts from Melbourne and around the country play up to four nights a week – mostly hip-hop and rap-electronica. Wed–Sat 9pm–late.

Western Victoria

Several roads run west from the Goldfields to the South Australia border through the seemingly endless wheatfields of the **Wimmera region**. To the west of the farming centre of **Ararat** is the major attraction of the area, **Grampians National Park**, the southwestern tail end of the Great Dividing Range. Stawell and Horsham – the latter regarded as the capital of the Wimmera – make good bases, but **Halls Gap**, in a valley and surrounded by national park, is even better. North of Horsham is the wide, flat **Mallee** with its eponymous twisted mallee (a type of eucalyptus) scrub, sand dunes and salt lakes. This region, Victoria's small "Outback" with several state and national parks, extends from **Wyperfeld National Park** in the south, right up to Mildura's irrigated oasis on the Murray River. South of the Grampians is sheep country; following the Hamilton Highway from Geelong you'll end up at **Hamilton**, the major town and wool capital of the Western District, also accessible via **Dunkeld** on the southern edge of the Grampians.

GETTING AROUND   WESTERN VICTORIA

By train Trains run from Melbourne to Ararat via Ballarat. There are also morning trains from Melbourne to Bendigo, with a connecting bus to Horsham and on to Adelaide.

By bus Buses run from Ballarat (see p.838) to Ararat, Stawell (with a connection to Halls Gap), Hamilton via Dunkeld, Horsham and Warrnambool (see p.822).

Ararat and around

ARARAT, some 90km west from Ballarat, is an old goldfields town, with an abundance of grand Victorian architecture and a main street laid out to show off the best profiles of the nearby mountains: **Mount Ararat** in the west and the **Pyrenees Range** with **Mount Cole** in the east. The town was founded in 1857, when a group of seven hundred hopeful Chinese from Guangdong province in southern China, making the three-week trudge from the South Australian port of Robe to the central Victorian goldfields, stumbled across a fabulously rich, shallow alluvial goldfield, the **Canton Lead**.

9

Gum San Chinese Heritage Centre

31 Lambert St • Daily 11am–4pm • $10 • ☎ 03 5352 1078, ⓦ gumsan.com.au

The excellent **Gum San Chinese Heritage Centre** pays homage to the fact that Ararat is the only Australian town founded by the Chinese. It was designed by a Melbourne architect of Chinese origin and is a recreation of a two-storey southern Chinese temple set in a traditional Chinese garden. The exhibits, some interactive, recount the tale of the founding of the city and familiarize Western visitors with aspects of Chinese culture.

Langi Morgala Museum

48 Queen St • Tues–Thurs 10am–3pm, Sat 1–4pm • $5 • ☎ 03 5352 3117

The **Langi Morgala Museum** occupies an 1870s brick building banded with bluestone. Along with the usual pioneering displays, there's an important collection of Aboriginal artefacts.

J Ward Museum

Girdlestone St • Tours daily 10am, 11am, 1pm & 2pm • $15 • ☎ 03 5352 3357, ⓦ jward.org.au

A guided tour of the **J Ward Museum**, north of the railway tracks, gives a chilling insight into one of the darker aspects of the area's social history. The 1859 building started out as a prison, but from the mid-1880s it operated as a high-security ward of the Ararat Lunatic Asylum; criminally insane men were incarcerated here, in harsh conditions. The asylum was only closed in 1991.

Wineries

These days Ararat is the commercial centre for a sheep-farming and wine-producing area, the Grampians Wine Region; you can visit the cellar doors of local **wineries** such as Montara (Fri–Sun 11am–4pm; ☎ 03 5352 3868, ⓦ montara.com.au), 3km south along Chalamabar Road, and Mount Langi Ghiran (daily 10am–5pm; ☎ 03 5354 3207, ⓦ langi.com.au), on Vine Road north of Buangor, renowned for its superb whites and reds; to get here, turn north from the Western Highway towards Warrak.

ARRIVAL AND INFORMATION

ARARAT

By train Trains run from Melbourne to Ararat via Ballarat (Mon–Fri 3 daily, Sat & Sun 2 daily; 2hr 20min).
By bus There are buses from Ballarat (2–4 daily; 1hr 15min) and Stawell (Tues & Fri daily; 30min).
Tourist information The Visitor Information Centre, located within the train station on High St (daily 9am–5pm; ☎ 03 5355 0281, ⓦ ararat.vic.gov.au), provides information on the Grampians, can book local accommodation and has internet access.

ACCOMMODATION AND EATING

Ararat Southern Cross Motor Inn 96 High St ☎ 03 5352 1341, ⓦ ascmi.com.au. A good-value motel, opposite the train station, with fully renovated, spacious rooms with kitchenettes and cable TV. $140
Links Retreat 139 Golf Links Rd ☎ 0419 438 948, ⓦ linksretreat.com.au. Those seeking luxury and serenity should head to *Links Retreat*, a cosy bluestone-and-timber house with three guest rooms and full amenities, situated in bushland beside Chalambar Golf Course. $165
Shire Hall 240 Barkly St ☎ 03 5352 1280, ⓦ shirehallhotel.com.au. Cheap pub-style accommodation – but with doonas (quilts) – in a building erected in 1860, with shared facilities and a guest lounge. $60
Sicilians 102 Barkly St ☎ 03 5352 2627, ⓦ sicilians .com.au. Family-run restaurant serving good Italian/ Lebanese fare, including pizzas ($16–20), pasta and salads. Mon–Sat 11am–2.30pm & 6pm–late.
Vines Café & Bar 74 Barkly St ☎ 03 5352 1744. Good breakfasts, light meals (from around $15) and lots of local wines by the glass. Thurs–Tues 9am–5pm.

Stawell

STAWELL (pronounced "stall"), just over 30km northwest of Ararat, is an old mining settlement. Gold is still extracted here, but the town is most famous for the **Stawell Gift**, a grass-track sprint race offering big prize money ($40,000 to the winner) that has been held here every Easter, bar four years, since 1878. The **Stawell Gift Hall of Fame** at 6 Main St (daily 9am–5pm; $5; ☎03 5358 1326, ⓦstawellgift.com) charts the history of the race itself. Stawell is also the closest major town to the Grampians, and the departure point for the bus to Halls Gap.

ARRIVAL, INFORMATION AND EATING STAWELL

By bus There are buses to Halls Gap (1–2 daily; 35min) and to Ararat (1–2 daily; 30min), where you can make train connections to Ballarat (18 weekly; 1hr 30min) and Horsham (daily; 55min).

Tourist information The helpful Stawell & Grampians Visitor Information Centre is located in the Hall of Fame (daily 9am–5pm; ☎1800 330 080, ⓦgrampianstravel .com.au) and has a detailed brochure, *The Cultural Heritage*

Trail, listing all the town's notable buildings and landmarks from the mid- to late 1800s.

Town Hall Hotel 62 Main St ☎03 5358 1059. Built in 1874, this is a good place to stop for lunch, dinner or just a beer. The bistro serves traditional, moderately priced pub lunches and dinners such as steaks, burgers and chicken dishes (mostly under $20). Daily noon–2pm & 6pm–late.

The Grampians

Rising from the flat, volcanic plains of western Victoria's wheat and grazing districts, the sandstone ranges of the **GRAMPIANS**, with their weird rocky outcrops and stark ridges, seem doubly spectacular. In addition to their scenic splendour, in **Grampians National Park (Gariwerd)** you'll find a dazzling array of **flora**, with a spring and early summer bonanza of wild flowers; a wealth of **Aboriginal rock art**; an impressive **Aboriginal Cultural Centre**; waterfalls and lakes; and more than fifty **bushwalks** along nearly 200km of tracks. There are also several hundred kilometres of road, from sealed highway to unsealed and 4WD tracks, on which you can take **scenic drives** and **4WD tours**.

The **best times to come** are in autumn, spring and early summer when the waterfalls are in full flow and the wild flowers are blooming (although there's always something in flower year-round). Between June and August it can be cold and wet, while summers can be very hot, with the potential for bushfires in extreme weather conditions. If you're undertaking extended walks in summer, carry a portable radio to get the latest information on the fire risk: on **total fire ban days** no exposed flames – not even that from a portable gas stove – are allowed. Tracks and campsites may be off limits due to events such as fire, storms or maintenance, and the park can be closed on a day of extreme weather conditions, so always check at Brambuk the National Park and Cultural Centre in Halls Gap (see below).

Halls Gap

The small town of **Halls Gap**, 25km west of Stawell and on the eastern fringes of the Grampians, is ringed by national park. Its setting is gorgeous, in the long flat strip of the Fyans Valley surrounded by the soaring bush and rock of the Wonderland, Mount Difficult and Mount William ranges; there is an abundance of colourful birdlife here and you are guaranteed to see kangaroos all over town. Packed with accommodation and other facilities catering to park visitors, this is the obvious place to base yourself, especially if you don't have your own transport. The town's focus is the **Stony Creek Stores** dining and shopping complex on the main street; nearby there's a supermarket/ bottle shop and an ATM.

Brambuk the National Park and Cultural Centre

Just over 2km south of Halls Gap along Grampians Road • Daily 9am–5pm • Free • ☎03 5361 4000, ⓦbrambuk.com.au

The best place to start your visit is at **Brambuk the National Park and Cultural Centre**. It consists of two separate buildings: the first one mainly dispenses information on the national park and sells guidebooks and maps; don't miss the displays that trace the development of the Grampians over four hundred million years. There is also an outdoor Gariwerd Seasons display and the *Bushfoods Café*, where you can sample bushtucker in the form of kangaroo pie or a platter of roo, crocodile, emu, duck and traditional damper bread.

9

Aboriginal Cultural Centre

Behind the National Park and Cultural Centre Daily 9am–5pm • Free • ☎ 03 5361 4000, ⓦ brambuk.com.au • Gariwerd Dreaming Theatre shows run hourly from 10am–4pm; $5 • Most tours and walks are on demand only and must be booked in advance

With its undulating red-ochre tin roof, the **Aboriginal Cultural Centre** blends in wonderfully with the backdrop of bush and rocky ridge; its design incorporates many symbolic features important to the five Koorie communities who own and manage the centre. Exhibitions feature a poignant photographic history of the area's original inhabitants, while the Gariwerd Dreaming Theatre shows 35-minute presentations on the region's Aboriginal creation story and its geology, flora and fauna. There are also activities such as boomerang throwing (generally 3pm; $6) and didgeridoo workshops (generally 1pm; $6), as well as guided group tours – a 45-minute Bush Discovery Walk including bushtucker tasting in the café (generally 2pm; $9) plus three- and five-hour rock art/cultural tours (generally Mon–Fri at 9.30am; from $80; min two people).

Wonderland Range

The most popular section for visitors is the **Wonderland Range**, immediately to the west of Halls Gap. From the village you can head directly to **Venus Baths** (1.2km return). **The Pinnacle**, one of the most popular lookouts in the Grampians, is usually accessed from the Wonderland car park (just off Mount Victory Rd; the turn-off is signposted). The 4.2km return walk can be strenuous in some areas; wear sturdy shoes and always carry water. **Silverband Falls** is another Wonderland walk – a short and easy stroll that takes you through a shady forest to a delightful waterfall that flows all year round.

The Balconies

The other major features in the Grampians are the Balconies, Boroka Lookout, Mackenzie Falls and Zumsteins, all accessible via Mount Victory Road northwest of Halls Gap. The walk to the **Balconies** (1.6km return), formerly known as the **Jaws of Death**, begins from the Reed Lookout car park (the turn-off is signposted) and goes for about ten minutes through lichen-covered tea trees until you have reached the lookout over the Victoria Valley and towards the Balconies. The much-photographed rock formation consists of one ledge above another, forming the image of a reptile's elongated, open jaw.

Mount William

If you're reasonably fit, consider tackling the ninety-minute return walk to the top of **Mount William** (1168m; 3.5km return), the highest point in the park. This starts from the Mount William Road car park, for which you turn off 16km south of Halls Gap.

ROCK ART IN THE GRAMPIANS

It's estimated that the indigenous **Koorie people** lived in the area known to them as **Gariwerd** up to twenty thousand years ago. The area offered such rich food sources that the Koories didn't have to spend all their time hunting and food-gathering, and could therefore devote themselves to religious and cultural activities. Evidence of this survives in **rock paintings**, which are executed in a linear style, usually in a single colour (either red or white), but sometimes done by handprints or stencils. You can visit some of the rock shelters where Aboriginal people camped and painted on the sandstone walls, although many more are off limits for cultural reasons. One of the best is **Gulgurn Manja**, in the northern Grampians, 5km south of the Western Highway. Starting at the Hollow Mountain car park, it is reached by a signposted fifteen-minute walk. The name of this important site means "it is hands of young people", as many of the handprints here were done by children. In the southern Grampians is **Billimina**, a fifteen-minute walk above the *Buandik* campsite; it's an impressive rock overhang with clearly discernible, quite animated, red stick figures.

Extended walks

More challenging walks include one to Major Mitchell Plateau (3 days/2 nights, 40km), starting from the Sheep Hills car park on Grampians Tourist Road (3km south of Mt William Rd) but involving a difficult 500m climb to the plateau, and the Mount Difficult walk (2 days/1 night, 21km), which starts from Rose Gap and traverses a large, undulating, rocky plateau. The 144km, twelve-night Grampians Peaks Trail, running the length of the park, is under construction; find out which sections are open on the park website (ⓦparkweb.vic.gov.au). These walks are remote and registration through a trip intention at Brambuk the National Park and Cultural Centre Visitor Centre (see p.845) is required.

ARRIVAL AND INFORMATION

By bus There is a local service between Halls Gap and Stawell (1–2 daily; 35min) leaving from/arriving at the Halls Gap Visitor Centre.

Tourist information The friendly staff at the Halls Gap Visitor Centre (117 Grampians Rd; daily 9am–5pm; ☎ 1800 065 599, ⓦgrampianstravel.com.au) can advise on tours and activities. Brambuk the National Park and Cultural Centre (see p.845) provides walking guides and more detailed topographic maps; the easy-to-use Parks Victoria guides *Southern Walks*, *Northern Walks* and *Wonderland*

THE GRAMPIANS

Walks ($3.30 each) are good all-rounders and handy for short walks.

Walks Although most walking tracks are clearly defined and well signposted, it's a good idea to carry a compass if you're planning an overnight trek. Before beginning an extended walk, register at Brambuk the National Park and Cultural Centre (see p.845). Some walks start from Halls Gap village, while others branch off Victory and Grampian roads, making them difficult to get to without a car. You can drive on park roads to major points and then get out and walk.

TOURS AND ACTIVITIES

Absolute Outdoors Grampians Grampians Rd ☎ 03 5356 4556, ⓦabsoluteoutdoors.com.au. Absolute Outdoors offer climbing/abseiling tours (from $75), canoeing and kayaking trips (from $60), guided nature and night-time spotlight walks, plus mountain-bike tours; they also rent mountain bikes ($40/day).

GMAC (Grampians Mountain Adventure Company) 618 Brimpaen-Laharum Rd, Brimpaen ☎0427 747 047, ⓦgrampiansadventure.com.au. Trained and accredited by the Australian Climbing Instructors' Association, GMAC also operates at Mt Arapiles (west of Horsham) and can

cater for advanced levels. Half-day beginners' climbing instruction for $95.

Grampians Horse Riding Adventure Brimpaen ☎03 5383 9255, ⓦgrampianshorseriding.com.au. Located at Brimpaen in the Wartook Valley on the northwestern side of the Grampians, this outfit offers trail rides through the bush twice a day (10am & 2pm; 2hr 30min; $100).

Hangin' Out in the Grampians ☎03 5356 4535 or ☎0407 684 831, ⓦhanginout.com.au. Climbing tours with Hangin' Out start at $75 (4hr) and rise to $130 for full-day tours that include abseiling.

ACCOMMODATION

Although Halls Gap has lots of **accommodation** of every kind, during school holidays you'll need to book in advance. Note that many places will insist on long stays, and prices rise at weekends. Online bookings and prepayment (ⓦparkstay .vic.gov.au) are required for all but two of the **campsites** in the national park. The fee is $26.60 (for up to six people) per site per day. Very limited **bush camping** is allowed in the park; staff at Brambuk can advise (see p.845).

HOSTELS

Asses Ears Wilderness Lodge 130 Schmidts Rd, Brimpaen ☎03 5383 9215, ⓦassesearslodge .com.au. Great backpacker accommodation in eight six-berth timber en-suite cabins; double and four-bed cabins also available, and all are in a quiet location in the Wartook Valley on the northwestern side of the Grampians, 40min from Halls Gap. There's a licensed bar, inexpensive restaurant, swimming pool and pool table. The owners can drop you off for hikes and organize loads of activities. Rates include breakfast and linen. Dorms $23, cabins $72

Brambuk Backpackers Grampians Rd, Halls Gap ☎03 5356 4250, ⓦbrambuk.com.au/backpackers.htm. This hostel, within Grampians National Park, boasts a great lounge area with open fireplace. All rooms are en suites and rates include a light breakfast. Dorms $30, doubles $75

★**Grampians Eco YHA** Grampians Rd, Halls Gap ☎03 5356 4544, ⓦyha.com.au. Hostel built according to environmentally friendly principles, recycling waste water and using solar electricity and wood-burning stoves. It has excellent facilities, including cosy lounge rooms, large kitchens, internet access and spotless same-sex dorms. Office open 8–10am & 5–10pm. Dorms $42, doubles $115

9

Tim's Place 44 Grampians Rd, Halls Gap ☎03 5356 4288, ⓦtimsplace.com.au. Friendly small hostel with a lovely, homely feel. There are dorms, doubles and triple rooms in the main house, and decent studio apartments out the back. Extras include free use of sports equipment and mountain bikes. Dorms $30, doubles $80, apartments $110

HOTELS, APARTMENTS AND COTTAGES

Dulc Thryptomene Crt, Halls Gap ☎03 5356 4711, ⓦdulc.com.au. Nestled in bushland about 3km from town, these contemporary, split-level, open-plan one- and two-bedroom "cabins" have polished concrete floors, stainless steel kitchens, leather couches, big beds and luxurious toiletries. $300

★**Grampians Pioneer Cottages** 58 Pioneer Lane, off Birdswing Rd ☎03 5356 4402, ⓦgrampians pioneercottages.com.au. Five kilometres southeast of town, these five self-contained pioneer-style two- and three-bedroom cottages look either at the Grampians or east, over the plains. The red-gum, log, red-brick, mud-brick and stone cottages are individually designed; all have open fireplaces. There is also a communal outdoor kitchen. Bed linen is extra. $197

Mountain Grand 124 Grampians Rd, Halls Gap ☎03 5356 4232, ⓦmountaingrand.com.au. An elegant, refurbished 1930s-style guesthouse with ten comfortable en-suite rooms, some with spa. There are also lounge areas and a good restaurant. $166

CARAVAN PARKS

Halls Gap Caravan Park Cnr School & Grampians rds, Halls Gap ☎03 5356 4251, ⓦhallsgapcaravanpark .com.au. Opposite the shopping centre and so a bit noisy, but it's well equipped. There is a range of cabins and lots of camping space and many walks start here. Budget units $120, cabins $160

Halls Gap Lakeside Tourist Park 27 Tymna Drive, Halls Gap ☎03 5356 4281, ⓦhallsgaplakeside.com. Located four kilometres south of town on the banks of Lake Bellfield, this site features a heated outdoor pool. There are a range of options from tent pitches to spanking new, open-plan cabins for couples, with mountain views. Un/powered sites $33/39, cabins $105

EATING, DRINKING AND ENTERTAINMENT

Halls Gap's main **eating** options are located in the Stony Creek Stores shopping and dining complex on Grampians Rd, but around the area are some good country-style pubs worthy of a beer and a meal. For entertainment, there's **live jazz** at *Balconies Restaurant* (see below) every Saturday evening. An alternative **film festival** (ⓦhgff.com.au) comes to town in early November, and there's a jazz festival in early to mid-February (ⓦgrampiansjazzfestival.com.au).

Balconies Restaurant Mountain Grand Hotel, 124 Grampians Rd, Halls Gap ☎03 5356 4232. This hotel restaurant partners elegant surroundings with reasonably priced good-quality meals and wine. The menu might include dishes such as warm pepper-crusted kangaroo salad and alpine lake smoked trout; mains up to $30. Mon–Sat 6pm–late.

Halls Gap Hotel 2262 Grampians Rd (2km out of Halls Gap) ☎03 5356 4566, ⓦhallsgaphotel.com.au. Serves decent bistro meals (try the pie of the day off the specials board, $22.90), but people also come for the views from the veranda looking towards the mountains. Mon & Tues 6–8pm, Wed–Sun noon–2pm & 6–8pm.

Kookaburra Bar & Bistro 125 Grampians Rd, Halls Gap ☎03 5356 4222, ⓦkookaburrahotel.com.au. Dependable European and bistro-style dishes including baked duckling ($35), kangaroo fillet ($32) and home-made ice cream. Lighter pasta and salad dishes are also available. Bookings recommended. Tues–Fri 6pm–late, Sat & Sun noon–3pm & 6pm–late.

Livefast Lifestyle Café Stony Creek ☎03 5356 4400, ⓦlivefast.com.au. Light, bright café serving all-day breakfast (from $12), toasties ($7), grazing plates ($18), salads, gourmet beans and the best coffee in town. Gluten-free and vegetarian options are available and there's free wi-fi. Mon–Fri 7am–3pm, Sat & Sun 7am–4pm.

The Quarry Restaurant Stony Creek ☎03 5356 4858, ⓦquarryrestaurant.com.au. Popular spot in a pleasant garden setting and a fully licensed bar. A dish such as chargrilled chicken breast with chips and salad costs around $30. Bookings recommended. Daily 6pm–late; June–Aug closed Tues.

Hamilton

Three highways converge at **HAMILTON**, a civilized little city where you can see the Grampians from the main street. Its former claim to fame was as the "Wool Capital of the World" and the region still produces a substantial amount of Australia's wool. There are only a few things to distract you here.

The most worthwhile of the town's museums and galleries is **Hamilton Art Gallery** at 107 Brown St (Mon–Fri 10am–5pm, Sat 10am–noon & 2–5pm, Sun 2–5pm; entry by donation; ☎03 5573 0460, ⓦhamiltongallery.org), one of the state's finest provincial art galleries. Its collection of eighteenth-century watercolours of English pastoral scenes by Paul Sandby is the largest outside Britain.

The **Hamilton Botanic Gardens** at the corner of Thompson and French streets are also worth visiting (always open; ☎1800 807 056). First planted in 1870, and classified by the National Trust of Victoria, these delightful gardens feature sweeping lawns, lakes, fountains and a bird enclosure.

ARRIVAL AND INFORMATION
HAMILTON

By bus There are services from Ballarat (2 daily; 2hr 10min) via Dunkeld; and from Warrnambool (Sun–Fri 1–2 daily; 1hr 35min–2hr 15min).
Tourist information The friendly Hamilton Visitor

Information Centre on Lonsdale St (daily 9am–5pm; ☎1800 807 056, ⓦvisitsoutherngrampians.com.au) can book accommodation.

ACCOMMODATION AND EATING

Comfort Inn Grange Burn 142 Ballarat Rd ☎03 5572 5755, ⓦthegrangeburn.com.au. A comfortable property with 31 spacious, redbrick-lined rooms, a pool, picnic area and on-site restaurant. __$138__
Commercial Hotel 145 Thompson St ☎03 5572 4119. This simple yet central hotel with shared bathrooms is a good bet for budget travellers. It has good food and there are live music nights. __$40__
Darriwill Farm Café Restaurant 169 Gray St ☎03 5571 2088, ⓦdarriwillfarm.com.au. A town favourite serving breakfast as well as lunch and dinner; it's also a gourmet deli and kitchenware and gift shop. Mains, including vegetarian dishes, showcase local produce and start around $30. Café: Mon–Thurs 10am–5pm, Fri 10am–8.30pm, Sat 9.30am–3pm & 6pm–late; shop: Mon–Thurs 10am–5.30pm, Fri 10am–6pm, Sat 9.30am–3pm.
Lake Hamilton Motor Village & Caravan Park 8

Ballarat Rd ☎03 5572 3855, ⓦlakehamilton.com.au. In a pleasant riverside location, this place has 25 one- and two-bedroom self-contained cabins, a solar-heated pool and BBQs. Powered sites __$33__, cabins __$145__
Royal Mail Hotel 98 Parker St, Dunkeld ☎03 5577 2241, ⓦroyalmail.com.au. Foodies shouldn't miss the acclaimed and elegant *Royal Mail Hotel* restaurant at Dunkeld, 30km from Hamilton. There are two- ($75), three- ($95) and five-course ($125) chef's tasting menus, which draw on the hotel's own farm and vegetable gardens and change daily, but the pick is the signature eight-course menu ($165) paired with wines off a long list. Book well in advance. The *Parker Street Project*, in the former public bar, is a less expensive option, with delicious comfort food mains such as beef and kidney pie and steaks (up to $39). Restaurant: Wed–Sun 6.30pm–late; Project: daily noon–2.30pm & 6–9pm.

The Wimmera

The Wimmera, flat, dry and hot in summer, relies heavily on irrigation water from the Grampians for its vast wheat and barley fields; before irrigation and the invention of the stump jump plough, the area was little more than mallee scrub.

Horsham

The small city of **HORSHAM**, capital of the Wimmera, makes a good stopping point en route to Adelaide or the Murray region, with a number of motels along the main road. It has an idyllic picnic spot, complete with barbecues by the Wimmera River, but there's little else to detain you, though Grampians National Park (see p.845) is within striking distance, to the south. **Mount Arapiles**, 40km west, is one of Australia's most important **rock-climbing** centres, attracting climbers from around the world. There is also a great walk around the mountain and a tree-shaded camping area.

ARRIVAL, TOURS AND ACCOMMODATION
HORSHAM

By bus Buses run from Ararat (via Stawell), Bendigo (which continue to Adelaide) and Mildura (Henty Highway Coaches). *Destinations* Ararat (3–4 daily; 1hr 35min); Ballarat (1–2 daily; 2hr 40min); Bendigo (daily; 3hr 20min); Mildura (3 weekly; 5hr); Stawell (3–4 daily; 1hr 10min).

Rock-climbing The Climbing Company in Natimuk (☎03 5387 1329, ⓦclimbco.com.au), 15min from Horsham, offers beginner-to-advanced climbing and abseiling at Mt Arapiles. Half day $60 (min 4 people), full day $90 (min 3 people).

9

White Hart Hotel 55 Firebrace St ☎ 03 5382 1231. A central, cheap place, and the best of the town's pub accommodation with a good bistro, offering fourteen standard rooms with shared bathrooms. **$60**

The Mallee

The Mallee, Victoria's most sparsely populated region, begins north of Warracknabeal, from where the **Henty Highway** heads up to join the Sunraysia Highway and forges its way to Mildura. This area is flat and semi-arid, and very hot in summer, and there is little reason to visit unless you're a nature lover or travelling on to the Murray region (see below). Along the way are small dusty towns such as **Hopetoun** ("Gateway to the Mallee"). Fifty kilometres west of Hopetoun is **Wyperfeld National Park**, which at 365,000 hectares is one of Victoria's largest. The park's most famous resident is the endangered mallee fowl, an industrious ground dweller that builds a mound nest.

Beyond Hopetoun, the Henty Highway merges into the Sunraysia Highway. Heading north on the Sunraysia, you pass Ouyen, which doesn't warrant much time. Heading west on the Mallee Highway, the access track to the picturesque and fascinating **pink salt lakes** of **Murray-Sunset (Yanga-Nyawi) National Park** leads north from Linga.

Continuing north on the Calder Highway from Ouyen, you pass **Hattah-Kulkyne National Park**, just east of the highway; the park consists of dry mallee scrub, native woodland, and a lakes system lined with gums, all of which are surprisingly rich in birdlife. Lake Hattah is reached by turning off the highway at Hattah, 34km north of Ouyen, onto Hattah–Robinvale Road. From Hattah it's less than 70km to Mildura and the Murray River.

GETTING AROUND AND INFORMATION   THE MALLEE

By bus The only public transport service in the region is a Henty Highway Coach passenger and freight service between Horsham and Mildura (3 weekly in each direction; 5hr 30min) that stops at Hopetoun and other towns (☎ 0400 882 476, ⓦ hentyhighwaycoach.com.au).

Tourist information Visitor information is available in Hopetoun at 75 Lascelles St (Mon–Fri 9am–5pm) or the *Bon Bon Café* (see below). See also the websites ⓦ wimmeramalleetourism.com.au and ⓦ hopetounvictoria .com.au.

ACCOMMODATION AND EATING

Bon Bon Café 74 Austin St, Hopetoun ☎ 03 5083 3082. A surprising find in this small remote town, the welcoming *Bon Bon Café* serves good traditional café food, such as sandwiches, soup and salads (most dishes under $12). Daily 9am–5pm.

Wonga Campground Wyperfeld National Park

☎ 03 5395 7221. Bush camping is not allowed in Wyperfeld National Park, but a sealed road leads from Hopetoun via Yampeet to this shady campsite with picnic area, water (treat before drinking) and toilets; sites are for up to six people. Prepayment required (ⓦ pakstay.vic .gov.au). Unpowered sites **$26.60**

The Murray region

From its source close to Mount Kosciuszko high in the Australian Alps, the **Murray River** flows for about 2700km and forms the border between Victoria and New South Wales until it crosses into South Australia (someone got a ruler out for the rest of the border to the coast), and although the actual watercourse is in New South Wales, the Victoria bank is far more interesting and more populous. After the entire length was navigated in 1836, the river became the route along which cattle were driven from New South Wales to the newly established town of Adelaide, and later in the century there was a thriving paddle-steamer trade on the lower reaches of the river, from Wentworth on the New South Wales side (see p.296) and Mildura through to Echuca.

In 1864, **Echuca** was linked by railway to Melbourne, stimulating the river trade in the upper reaches, and subsequently becoming a major inland port. At the height of the paddle-steamer era, **Mildura** was still a run-down, rabbit-infested cattle station, but in 1887 the Chaffey brothers, brought over from Canada, instituted irrigation projects that now support dairy and vegetable farms, vineyards and citrus orchards throughout northwest Victoria. Between Mildura and Echuca, **Swan Hill** marks the transition to sheep, cattle and wheat country; the **Pioneer Settlement** here explores the extraordinarily hard lives of the early settlers. Upstream of Echuca the Murray flows through more settled regions, but also the Barmah wetlands, an ecosystem of international significance (see p.857).

Nowadays, **paddle steamers** cruise for leisure, and are the best way to enjoy the river and admire the magnificent **river red gums** lining its banks, as well as the huge array of birds and other wildlife that the Murray sustains. Renting a **houseboat** is also a relaxing (if expensive) way to travel.

Mildura

MILDURA has a mirage-like aura, its vineyards and orange orchards standing out from a hot, dry landscape. To the southwest is the evocatively named **Sunset Country**, with nothing but gnarled mallee scrub, red sand and pink salt lakes (reached via Linga on the Mallee Highway). Mildura makes a good winter getaway, but summer can be very hot. Many people use the town as a jumping-off point for Mungo National Park (see p.297). North of the train station, through the river parklands, the 90-year-old **Mildura Weir** system, designed to provide stable pools for irrigation and to enable year-round navigation, is a pleasant place to while away an hour or so.

Mildura Arts Centre

199 Cureton Ave • Daily 10am–5pm • Free • ☎ 03 5018 8330, ⓦ milduraartscentre.com.au

The **Mildura Arts Centre** consists of the historic home **Rio Vista**, the Mildura Regional Art Gallery, a theatre and a sculpture park. Rio Vista was built in 1889 for William Chaffey, who lived here with his first and second wives (both called Hattie Schell, the second the niece of the first) until he died in 1926. It's a lovely house, though rather ill-suited to the climate, and inside are various displays about the Chaffeys and Mildura's development. The art gallery's most important piece is *Woman Combing Her Hair at the Bath*, a pastel by Edgar Degas; it also has some excellent Australian sculpture.

ARRIVAL AND INFORMATION   MILDURA

Mildura is 555km from Melbourne, about as far as you can go in this small state; on the border of New South Wales, and a little more than 100km from South Australia, it's ideally located for onward transport to either.

By plane Mildura's airport is 11km out of town and best reached by taxi. Virgin Australia, Regional Express and Qantas Link fly from and to Melbourne daily (1hr 10min).

By bus V/Line buses run from Bendigo via Swan Hill, and Henty Highway Coach buses from Horsham (see p.849); TrainLink (NSW-operated) buses travel from Cootamundra train station over the border (ⓦ nswtrainlink.info). Locally, Buslink (☎ 03 5023 0274, ⓦ buslink.com.au) runs frequent services across the river to Wentworth via Buronga, around central Mildura and suburban areas further to the east and west, and south as far as Red Cliffs.

Destinations Ballarat (4 weekly; 7hr 35min); Bendigo (4 weekly; 5hr 45min); Horsham (3 weekly; 5hr); Swan Hill (6 weekly; 2hr 45min).

By car You can rent a car from, among others, Avis at Mildura Airport (☎ 03 5021 4442).

Tourist information The Mildura Visitor Information and Booking Centre is in the state-of-the-art Alfred Deakin Centre at Deakin Ave and 12th St (Mon–Fri 9am–5.30pm, Sat & Sun 9am–5pm; ☎ 03 5018 8380 or ☎ 1800 039 043, ⓦ visitmildura.com.au), which also houses a decent café and a library, with internet access. The visitor centre will book accommodation and supply free town maps: they also have particularly good information on the Murray-Sunset (Yanga-Nyawi) and Hattah-Kulkyne national parks.

Seasonal work Mildura has a good reputation as a place to find fruit-picking work; the grape harvest takes place from January to May but citrus fruit and vegetables are picked at other times of year. For details, contact MADEC Mildura, 126 Deakin Ave (☎ 03 5021 3472, ⓦ madec.edu .au), or call the Harvest Trail Service (see p.53).

9

Swimming A back-to-nature alternative to the swimming pool on Deakin Ave is available at the sandy swimming beach at Chaffey Bend. There are lifeguards in summer, but take local advice and beware of dangerous currents.

TOURS

Harry Nanya Tours ☎ 03 5027 2076, ⓦ harrynanya tours.com.au. Away from the river, the most outstanding natural attraction is Mungo National Park (see p.297), 110km across the border in New South Wales. Koorie tour operators belonging to the Paakantyi people lend their perspective on the park with Harry Nanya Tours, based just over the border in Wentworth (April–Oct all-day tour $180, $90 from Mungo).

Mildura Paddlesteamers Mildura Wharf ☎ 03 5023 2200, ⓦ paddlesteamers.com.au. The best short river cruise is on the PS *Melbourne* (daily 10.50am & 1.50pm; 2hr; $30), Mildura's only genuinely steam-driven paddle steamer. Built in 1912, it still has its original boiler and engine. The same company runs PV *Rothbury*, built in 1881 and in its day the fastest steamboat on the river; it's now been converted to diesel and takes people on cruises to local attractions, such as the 10.30am Thursday cruise to Trentham Estate Winery (5hr; $70 including lunch and wine tasting); there are also lunch and dinner cruises.

ACCOMMODATION

Mildura has an ever-increasing number of **hostels** to cater to the hordes of backpackers who come here looking for work. If you are staying longer, ask the hostel for their weekly rates. There are also numerous **houseboats** based in Mildura or across the river in Buronga or Wentworth. Mildura Houseboats (91–125 Etiwanda Ave, ☎ 03 5024 7790, ⓦ mildurahouseboats.com.au) offer large six- to twelve-berth self-contained houseboats with all mod cons; expect to pay from $1400 for three nights in peak season. Contact the Visitor Information Centre, or see ⓦ visitmildura.com.au/accommodation, for details of other operators.

Apex RiverBeach Holiday Park 435 Cureton Ave ☎ 03 5023 6879, ⓦ apexriverbeach.com.au. Nestled among river red gums along the riverbank, but still close to the main shops, these fully self-contained one- and two-bedroom cabins offer good value in a picturesque setting. $120

Mildura City Backpackers 50 Lemon Ave ☎ 03 5022 7922, ⓦ milduracitybackpackers.com.au. Sociable and homely heritage weatherboard house close to the town centre, with dorms and doubles and a good mix of workers and travellers passing through. Couch-sitting on the patio is a nightly event. $22

Mildura International Backpackers 5 Cedar Ave ☎ 0408 210 132, ⓦ mildurabackpackers.com.au. Work-orientated hostel with recreation area, two kitchens and an outdoor BBQ area, cable TV and laundry. The operators have work contacts, do all the paperwork required and organize transport. Rooms are twin-, three- and four-bedded. Cash only. Dorms $30, doubles $60

Mildura Stopover Guesthouse 9 Lemon Ave ☎ 03 5021 1980, ⓦ stopover.com.au. Despite the name, this place mostly houses long-term workers who want a clean place to stay with good facilities, including a sunny courtyard with BBQ. Doesn't have the party atmosphere of the other hostels, however. Cash only. Dorms $30, doubles $80

Quality Hotel Mildura Grand 7th St, opposite the train station ☎ 03 5023 0511, ⓦ qualityhotelmildura grand.com.au. Restored 1890s hotel, complete with ballroom, renowned gourmet restaurant (see below), gym, spa, sauna and outdoor pool. There are more than ninety rooms, ranging from contemporary standard doubles to a luxurious poolside suite with marble bathroom and spa. Breakfast is included. $155

EATING AND DRINKING

The Mildura region has a reputation for **fine cuisine**, mainly due to the presence of celebrity chef and author Stefano de Pieri and his superb *Stefano's* restaurant (see below). There are many cafés and restaurants on Langtree Ave, just south of the mall and known as "Feastreet". If you have your own transport, you can make an enjoyable outing to buy fruit and vegetables from surrounding farms.

CAFÉS AND RESTAURANTS

Hudak's Bakery Café Cnr 8th St & Langtree Mall ☎ 03 5023 1843, ⓦ hudaksbakery.com.au. Good Continental breads, pies, focaccia and cakes (most less than $10), with great seating on the outdoor balcony. Branches also at 15th St & Centro Mildura. Daily 7am–5.30pm.

Rendezvous Restaurant 34 Langtree Ave ☎ 03 5023 1571, ⓦ rendezvousmildura.com.au. Take your pick of three dining environments: casual downstairs, alfresco in the courtyard under the vines, or a laidback upstairs fine dining room (usually only open for dinner). The menu ranges from lunch focaccias ($15) to gorgonzola tart and chargrilled steaks ($30–40). Daily 7.30am–2.30pm & 5.30pm–late.

★**Stefano's** Quality Hotel Mildura Grand, 7th St,

opposite the train station ☎03 5022 0881, ⓦstefano .com.au. Tucked away in the hotel cellar, *Stefano's* is the crowning glory of *The Grand*'s four eating places. Founded by renowned chef Stefano de Pieri, it offers a degustation menu of northern Italian food that changes daily, but might includee risotto, cabbage pudding or wild rabbit terrine; dinner is either two ($45), three ($65) or five courses ($95). Bookings essential. Tues–Sat 7pm–late.

27 Deakin 27 Deakin Ave ☎03 5021 3627, ⓦstefano .com.au. Operated by Stefano de Pieri's family (see opposite), and just one of his shrines to food, this café and food store serves delicious breakfasts, lunches, coffee, cakes and bread, and sells gourmet grocery items and *Stefano's* famous preserves. Mon–Sat 7am–3pm, Sun 8am–noon.

Wirraway Bistro Mildura RSL, cnr Madden Ave & 10th St ☎03 5023 1187, ⓦwirrawaybistro.com. Returned and Services Club bistro open to the public and offering better than average dishes such as chicken Kiev and mixed grill plus more contemporary options, including a tasty Asian beef salad. Lunch and dinner mains are from $19.90. Daily noon–2pm & 6–8.30pm.

BARS AND PUBS

Mildura Brewery 20 Langtree Ave ☎03 5022 2988, ⓦmildurabrewery.com.au. Incredibly good beer straight from the giant vats visible from the tables, along with well-priced pub grub. Daily 10.30am–midnight.

O'Malley's Irish Tavern 46 Deakin Ave ☎03 5021 4236. A barn-like venue that fills up on weekends and has regular live music. The menu includes the likes of beef and Guinness pie and lamb shanks. Daily 11am–late.

Sandbar 45 Langtree Ave ☎03 5021 2181, ⓦthesandbar.com.au. Where the locals like to go for a drink and good pub grub, with an excellent courtyard, an outdoor stage and live music on weekends. Sun–Fri noon–late, Sat 11am–late.

Swan Hill

As you approach **SWAN HILL**, the landscape changes – this is cattle and sheep country, with wheatfields further north. The Murray here is shallow and tricky to navigate, so there's not much river traffic. Swan Hill is a service centre for the pastoral industry and has a typically solid, conservative atmosphere. Surprisingly, it's quite a multicultural place, having approximately ten percent of Victoria's Aboriginal population, and a large Italian community. The **Pioneer Settlement** is undoubtedly Swan Hill's main attraction. Next to the train station, hard to miss, is the fake 13m Murray Cod (built for a film and one of Australia's many "Big Things"), which doesn't really serve a purpose, but amuses tourists.

Swan Hill Regional Art Gallery

Horseshoe Bend • Tues–Fri 10am–5pm, Sat & Sun 11am–5pm • Entry by donation • ☎ 03 5036 2430, ⓦ gallery.swanhill.vic.gov.au

The purpose-built, riverside **Swan Hill Regional Art Gallery** specializes in Australian naïve art, modern Australian prints and drawings, and works of art that relate to the Swan Hill region – there are around four hundred pieces in the collection. The gallery also hosts good touring exhibitions.

Pioneer Settlement

Horseshoe Bend, about 1km south of the train station • Daily 9.30am–4.30pm • $29; combination ticket for settlement, sound-and-light show and PS *Pyap* cruise, $70 • Sound-and-light show (nightly from dusk; $22.50) • *Pyap* cruises 2.30pm (1hr; $22.50) • ☎ 03 5036 2410 or ☎ 1800 981 911, ⓦ pioneersettlement.com.au

Swan Hill's **Pioneer Settlement**, a reconstruction of a pioneering community, was the first of its kind in Australia and is still one of the best. There are more than fifty original and replica heritage buildings and many of the **shops** are functional – the baker, the printer, the haberdashery and the porcelain-doll shop – with assistants dressed in vaguely period costume. Generally, though, it's low-key and peaceful: you can wander through the barber's shop and the stock and station agents undisturbed, and pose for your own "wanted" poster at the print shop. You can also ride around the settlement in a 1924 Dodge or horse-drawn carriage for free. The 45-minute **sound-and-light show** in the evening is strikingly effective.

The settlement sits on the banks of the Marraboor River, a branch of the Murray, and a wooden bridge spans the river to Pental Island, which has assorted native flora

9

and fauna. A nineteenth-century **paddle steamer**, the PS *Pyap*, cruises from the settlement upriver past Murray Downs Homestead.

ARRIVAL AND INFORMATION

SWAN HILL

By train Trains travel to Swan Hill from Melbourne (6 weekly; 4hr 25min) via Bendigo.

By bus There are buses to Bendigo, and Mildura via Robinvale.

Destinations Albury (daily; 6hr); Bendigo (1–3 daily; 3hr 15min); Echuca (daily; 2hr); Mildura (daily; 3hr 20min).

Tourist information The Swan Hill Region Information Centre, across the road from the train station, on the corner of McCrae and Curlewis streets (daily 9am–5pm; ☎ 03 5032 3033 or ☎ 1800 625 373, ⓦ swanhillonline.com), has a free map of the town; it also sells tickets for attractions. Parks Victoria at 324 Campbell St (Mon–Fri 8.30am–5pm; ☎ 03 5036 4829) can provide you with information on camping in nearby Nyah-Vinefera Park.

ACCOMMODATION

Big 4 Riverside Caravan Park 1 Monash Drive ☎ 03 5032 1494, ⓦ big4riversideswanhill.com.au. A good, centrally located caravan park on the Murray River, with a range of cabins, some facing the water, that sleep two to eight people. **$140**

Ibis Styles Swan Hill 405 Campbell St ☎ 03 5032 2726, ⓦ swanhillresort.com.au. The most luxurious motel in town, with over sixty suites and rooms, some with spa baths, an indoor and outdoor pool and spa, gym and other sports facilities. **$142**

Jacaranda Motel & Holiday Units 179 Curlewis St ☎ 03 5032 9077, ⓦ jacarandaholidayunits.com.au. Good-value motel close to the centre, with spacious one- and two-bedroom self-contained units. There's also a pool and BBQ area. **$100**

EATING AND DRINKING

Java Spice 17 Beveridge St ☎ 03 5033 0511, ⓦ javaspice.com.au. Excellent spicy Thai food in a great outdoor setting. Soups from $11.50, mains from $21.50. Tues–Thurs 5–9.30pm, Fri–Sun 11.30am–2.30pm & 5–9.30pm.

Quo Vadis 255 Campbell St ☎ 03 5032 4408, ⓦ quovadisrestaurant.com.au. The best Italian restaurant in Swan Hill, an authentic pizzeria that serves mammoth pasta portions (from $22). Daily 5.30pm–late.

RSL Club 138 Curlewis St ☎ 03 5032 2359. This local club is a nice place for a cheap bistro-style meal, such as a roast of the day or chicken schnitzel (most less than $25), and a beer with the locals. Daily noon–2pm & 6–8.30pm.

Spoons Riverside 125 Monash Dve ☎ 03 5032 2601, ⓦ spoonsriverside.com.au. Relaxing river views, best from the deck, are matched with modern dishes using great local produce, such as twelve-hour-cooked saltbush lamb with preserved lemon, fig and almond ($33). Leave room for the signature fruit pudding dessert. Simpler and cheaper breakfast and lunch offerings are also on offer. Dinner bookings recommended. Sun–Wed 8am–11pm, Thurs–Sat 8am–11pm.

Echuca

ECHUCA, a lively and progressive place, is the most easily accessible river town from Melbourne – it's only three hours or so by bus or car, making it a popular weekend getaway. Echuca became the largest inland port in Australia after the railway line connected it with Melbourne in 1864. When the **missions** began to close in the 1930s, many Aboriginal families migrated to the Echuca area; they were forced to live on the fringes in badly constructed, flood-prone housing. Women commonly worked in the canneries and hospitals, and the men packed fruit, sheared sheep and did other labouring jobs.

The **Port of Echuca**, a popular tourist attraction where stores, pubs and businesses have been preserved, gives a good insight into the paddle-steamer era. Most people head to the port precinct, with its massive wharves and collection of old buildings, and several cruises ply along the river from here. The **town** itself is not too touristy and has retained much of its charm. There are two principal streets: High Street, the former main street, leads to Murray Esplanade and the wharf, and is the centre of tourist activity, with lots of cafés and boutiquey shops, while Hare Street, the present-day main street, is lined with more commercial buildings.

Port of Echuca

74 Murray Esplanade • Daily 9am–5pm • Discovery Centre $14; Discovery Centre and Cruise $35; Discovery Centre, museums entry and cruise $55 (boats depart daily at 10.15am, 11.30am, 1.15pm and 2.30pm), Port After Dark Tour (Wed, Fri & Sat nights) $19.50 • ☎ 03 5481 0500, ⊛ portofechuca.org.au

To enter the port and the old wharf area, you'll need to pay the Discovery Centre entrance fee. You can combine this with a cruise on the *Pevensey* or the *Alexander Arbuthnot* (see p.856); alternatively, the Port After Dark Tour reveals some of the precinct's darker secrets.

The magnificent red-gum **wharf**, constructed in 1865, was nearly half a kilometre long in its prime and is still fairly extensive. Three landing platforms at different levels allowed unloading, even during times of flooding, and there are wonderful views from the top, high over a bend in the river. At the lowest level, several **old paddle steamers** are moored, including the PS *Pevensey*, a 1911 cargo boat (see p.856), and the PS *Adelaide*, built in 1866 and the oldest wooden-hulled paddle steamer still operating anywhere in the world. In the Cargo Shed Museum there's a scale model of the working port, paddle-steamer models, interactive exhibits and an audiovisual presentation.

Back out on Murray Esplanade, which runs through the port area, is the **Star Hotel**, which was first licensed in 1867 and is a typical pioneer pub, a tiny one-storey building with a tin roof and veranda. As the river trade declined, the *Star* was de-licensed (in 1897), along with many of the other 79 hotels in town. Drinking on the premises became illegal, so the loyal clientele dug a tunnel to the street through which they could escape at the first hint of a police raid — you can examine this, along with the cellar. The two-storey weatherboard building set back on an angled block in Little Hopwood Street is Victoria's only Heritage-listed brothel – no longer in business.

Bridge Hotel

At the north end of the wharf complex, opposite Hopwood Gardens, is the **Bridge Hotel**, opened in 1859 but de-licensed in 1916. It was built by the founder of Echuca, Henry Hopwood, an ex-convict who also started a punt service across the Murray. The story goes that if the pub wasn't doing well he'd close the ferry down for a few hours, leaving prospective passengers with little else to do but drink.

Great Aussie Beer Shed

377 Mary Ann Rd • Sept to mid-July Sat & Sun 9.30am–5pm • $14 • ☎ 03 5480 6904, ⊛ greataussiebeershed.com.au

A unique attraction is the **Great Aussie Beer Shed**, which features more than sixteen thousand types of beer cans from around Australia and the world, as well as brewery- and beer-related items. The complex also houses heritage domestic and farm equipment; entry includes a fifteen-minute guided tour.

ARRIVAL AND INFORMATION ECHUCA

By train Trains operate from Melbourne via Bendigo (1–2 daily; 3hr 25min).

By bus V/Line buses run daily from Bendigo; there are also daily TrainLink (NSW-operated) buses from Albury and Wagga Wagga train stations over the border (⊛ nswtrainlink.info).

Destinations Albury (daily; 4hr 10min); Bendigo (1–2 daily; 1hr 20min); Melbourne (1–3 daily; 2hr 45min); Mildura (daily; 5hr 15min); Rutherglen (daily; 3hr 45min); Shepparton (daily; 1hr 25min); Swan Hill (daily; 2hr).

Tourist information The Visitor Information Centre, 2

Heygarth St (daily 9am–5pm; ☎ 03 5480 7555 or ☎ 1800 804 446, ⊛ echucamoama.com), sells tickets for the port complex and cruises, books accommodation and is an agent for V/Line and TrainLink bus tickets. Ask here about the many houseboats available to rent in the area.

Festivals Echuca and neighbouring Moama, across the river in New South Wales, have a couple of worthwhile festivals. In February, look out for the Riverboats Music Festival (⊛ riverboatsmusic.com.au) featuring paddle steamers, live music from top Australian artists and regional food and wine. There is also the July Winter Blues Festival (⊛ winterblues.com.au).

9

CRUISES

Echuca Paddlesteamers ☎03 5481 2832, ⓦechucapaddlesteamers.net.au. One-hour cruises are available on PS *Alexander Arbuthnot* and PS *Pevensey*. Cruises ($24.50) usually depart daily at 10.15am, 11.30am, 1.30pm and 2.45pm, but check in advance. There are additional weekend departures; phone or check the website for details.

Murray River Paddlesteamers ☎03 5482 5244, ⓦmurrayriverpaddlesteamers.com.au. One- to two-hour cruises are available on PS *Pride of the Murray*, PS *Canberra* and PS *Emmylou*, the latter a wood-fired paddle steamer that also offers overnight trips. Cruises are generally two to four times daily but departure times vary

– phone to check. From $25.

MV Mary Ann ☎03 5480 7000, ⓦmaryann.com.au. Lunch and dinner cruises, featuring mod-Oz cuisine (12.30pm, $45; 6.30pm, from $79).

Kingfisher Cruises ☎03 5855 2855, ⓦkingfishercruises.com.au. A two-hour eco-cruise (Mon, Wed, Thurs, Sat & Sun, generally departing at 10am or 10.30am, with additional departures during busy times; $37.50) through the Barmah wetlands some 30km upstream of Echuca. Part of the World Heritage-listed Barmah National Park, this region contains the world's largest single stand of river red gums, one of the major draws of the Murray River region.

ACCOMMODATION

Echuca Backpackers 410–424 High St ☎03 5480 7866, ⓦbackpackersechuca.com.au. Centrally located, with a/c dorms as well as en-suite twins/doubles at an affordable price. There's a small kitchen and courtyard, and the owner has employment contacts and can provide transport to places of work. Dorms $28, doubles $60

Echuca Gardens 103 Mitchell St ☎03 5480 6522, ⓦechucagardens.com. Accommodation in charming gypsy wagons, a guesthouse and a historic self-contained cottage in a very scenic location on the edge of Banyule State Forest. Min two-night stay. $80

Echuca Holiday Park Crofton St, Victoria Park ☎03 5482 2157, ⓦechucacaravanpark.com.au. A well-equipped riverfront caravan park with a swimming pool,

tennis courts and two kitchens. Un/powered sites $51/54, cabins $141.

Shamrock Hotel 579 High St ☎03 5482 1036, ⓦshamrockhotel.com.au. Grand old pub in the historic port district offering basic but cheap dorm-style rooms with shared facilities. There are also traditional pub-style double rooms. It can get loud on weekends when it turns into a drinking hole. Dorms $45, doubles $90

★**Steam Packet Inn** Cnr Leslie St & Murray Esplanade ☎03 5482 3411, ⓦsteampacketinn.com.au. A National Trust-classified nineteenth-century B&B with super-friendly service, offering traditionally decorated rooms in the heart of the old port. Cooked breakfast included. $155

EATING AND DRINKING

★**American Hotel** 239-249 Hare St ☎03 5480 0969, ⓦamericanhotelechuca.com.au. Renovated and extended, Echuca's oldest pub feeds folks three delicious meals a day, indoors and out. The menu has a distinct American accent, from tacos (three for $15.90) and gumbo to Kansas-style ribs ($30), plus burgers, steaks and a $15 Sunday roast. There's a rooftop bar, a deli, lots of local and imported beers and live music at weekends. Daily 7.30am–late; food: 8–11 am, 11.30am–2.30pm & 5.30–8.30pm.

Beechworth Bakery 513 High St ⓦbeechworthbakery. com.au. A branch of the original, very successful bakery from Beechworth. Sells a variety of breads baked in a wood-fired oven, pies (from $4.50), focaccias ($8.50), pastries and other treats. The sun deck is a good spot for breakfast or lunch. Daily 6am–6pm.

Fish in a Flash 602 High St ☎03 5480 0824. This inviting fish-and-chip shop has an excellent selection of fresh seafood, including some of the best battered tiger prawns this side of Melbourne (fish and chips from $9.90). Daily 8.30am–8pm.

★**Shebani's** 535 High St ☎03 5480 7075, ⓦshebani.com.au. Tuck into modern and traditional Mediterranean dishes amid colourful tiles and filigree lamps, or alfresco in the garden courtyard. The seasonal menu might include specials such as Moroccan goat-and-date tagine ($19.50). Daily 8am–4pm.

Wistaria 51 Murray Esplanade ☎03 5482 4210. Lovely Victorian house where you can get breakfast and light lunches (around $15–20 for both), Devonshire teas, coffee and cakes. Licensed. Daily 8am–5pm.

NIGHTLIFE AND ENTERTAINMENT

Echuca's workers', sports and other **clubs** serve cheap meals and drinks, presumably as an incentive to get you to their gambling machines – non-members can sign in as visitors. There are more clubs across the river in Moama (NSW). The Paramount Cinema & Performing Arts Centre at 392 High St has an auditorium and four cinemas with state-of-the-art facilities (☎03 5482 3399, ⓦechucaparamount.com).

Harvest Hotel 183 Hare St ☎03 5482 1266. If you're looking for somewhere with quiet corners, try this two-storey pub, which also offers reasonably priced bistro meals such as braised pork belly. Daily 11am–late.

Rojo OPT Bar 273 Hare St ☎03 5480 0150. A popular bar with DJs playing Top 40, commercial dance and rhythm and blues tunes, with changing drinks specials. Fri & Sat 9pm–4am.

Shamrock Hotel 579 High St ☎03 5482 1036, ⓦshamrockhotel.com.au. Atmospheric pub with the town's best beer garden, plus bands and DJs at weekends. Daily 11am–late.

Star Hotel 45 Murray Esplanade ☎03 5480 1181, ⓦstarhotelechuca.com.au. With two bars and a café, this historic pub is a good place to head for a drink and a wood-fired pizza. Daily 11am–late.

Kyabram Fauna Park

75 Lake Rd, Kyabram • Daily 9.30am–5.30pm • $20 • ☎03 5852 2883, ⓦkyabramfaunapark.com.au

Thirty kilometres southeast of Echuca, the small farming town of Kyabram's main attraction is **Kyabram Fauna Park**, a community-owned wildlife park divided into grassland for free-ranging kangaroos, wallabies, emus and other animals, and a huge wetland area. You can wander around the grassland area and through several aviaries; a two-storey observation tower affords views of the more than 140 species of native birdlife. Diamond pythons, tiger snakes, crocodiles and other not-so-sociable creatures can be viewed from a safe distance at the Reptile House.

Barmah and around

Some 30km upstream on the Murray, **BARMAH** is most easily reached by crossing into New South Wales at Echuca and heading north on the Cobb Highway, then turning east. This small river town is associated with red-gum milling, and with sleeper-cutting in the early railway days.

Barmah National Park

Between Barmah and Strathmerton; access to the twelve major entrance gates is available from Moira Lakes Road, Barmah–Picola Road and the Murray Valley Highway • ⓦparks.vic.gov.au

Ten kilometres out of town, the lovely Ramsar Convention-listed Barmah National Park contains the world's largest stands of **river red gum**, some of them 45m tall and five hundred years old. The forest runs along the Murray for more than 100km and stands in an extensive flood plain – **canoeing** among the trees at flood time (July–Nov) is a magical experience. During the wet season more than two hundred species of waterbird come here, and there's plenty of other wildlife; you might even see brumbies (wild horses). When it's dry you can tread several well-established walking tracks: the place was of special significance to the local Yorta Yorta Aboriginal people and you can still see fish traps, middens, and scars on trees where the bark was removed to make canoes. Yorta Yorta heritage and culture is explained through interpretive signage in the park's **Dharnya** area.

INFORMATION AND TOURS

Tourist information Contact the Nathalia Barmah Visitor Information Centre in Nathalia (73 Blake St; ☎03 5866 2289, ⓦnathaliabarmah.com.au).

Echuca Boat & Canoe Hire ☎03 5480 6208, ⓦechucaboatcanoehire.com. Arrange transport and rent canoes and kayaks from Echuca Boat & Canoe Hire (canoes from $20/hr, kayaks from $16/hr).

BARMAH AND AROUND

Kingfisher Cruises ☎03 5855 2855, ⓦkingfishercruises .com.au. A cruise in the MV *Kingfisher* – a flat-bottomed boat that glides over Barmah Lake and through stands of red gum – leaves from the visitors' area at the lake. Bookings are essential and departure times vary; contact the operator for details. From $37.50.

ACCOMMODATION

Bush camping is permitted in the park; contact Parks Victoria (☎13 19 63, ⓦparks.vic.gov.au) for details.

Barmah Caravan Park 7 Murray St ☎03 5869 3225. A

great site on the banks of the river among red gums, with a small, sandy beach for swimming, and a few cabins. Un/powered sites $20/25, cabins $95

9

Gippsland

GIPPSLAND stretches southeast of Melbourne from Western Port Bay to the New South Wales border, between the Great Dividing Range and Bass Strait. Green and well watered, it's been the centre of Victoria's dairy industry since the 1880s, although the Latrobe Valley (particularly around Morwell) is home to industrial areas, coal mines and power stations. South Gippsland has Victoria's most popular national park, **Wilsons Promontory**, or "The Prom", a hook-shaped landmass jutting out into the strait, with superb scenery and fascinating bushwalks. The region to the east, around the **Gippsland Lakes** and **Ninety Mile Beach**, is beautifully untouched, and just beyond Orbost–Marlo is the unspoilt coastline of **Croajingolong National Park** – with its rocky capes, high sand dunes and endless sandy beaches – which stretches to the New South Wales border. **Mount Baw Baw**, an alpine resort near

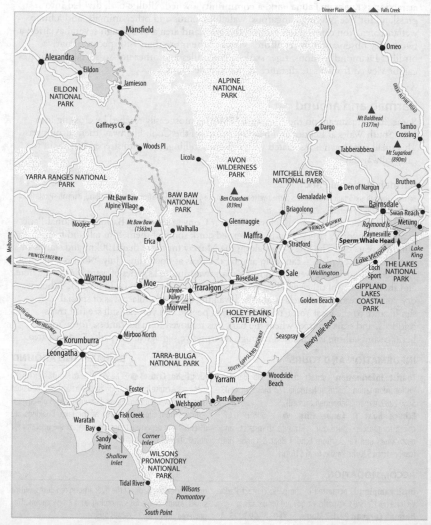

Mount Buffalo off the freeway from Moe (80km west of Sale), offering skiing and snowboarding in winter and bushwalking in summer, presents a very different face of Gippsland, as does the isolated gold town of **Walhalla**.

GETTING AROUND   GIPPSLAND

By train There are frequent trains from Melbourne to Bairnsdale.

By bus There are bus connections (up to 4 daily) from Traralgon Station to Sale (1hr) and Bairnsdale (1hr 45min), as well as daily (2–6) local services from Bairnsdale to Lakes Entrance, Orbost, Marlo and points between these towns. See individual towns for details. There is also a twice-weekly service from Bairnsdale to

Canberra via Lakes Entrance and Orbost (6hr 30min). Premier Motor Service (☎13 34 10, ⓦpremierms .com.au), a NSW-based bus company, runs a daily bus from Melbourne to Sydney along the coast, calling in at Sale, Bairnsdale, Lakes Entrance, Orbost and other stops. The bus leaves Melbourne at 5.45pm and gets to Lakes Entrance late at night.

By car Having your own car is essential for experiencing

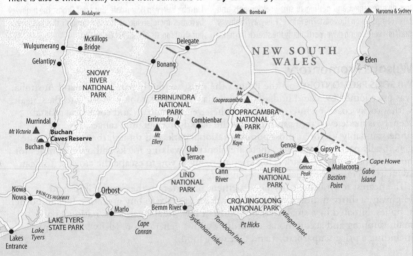

GIPPSLAND

9

BLACK SATURDAY BUSHFIRES

February 7, 2009 will be forever etched on most Victorians' minds as the start of Australia's worst ever **bushfires**. "**Black Saturday**", as it is known, killed more than 170 people and thousands of animals, destroyed more than a million acres of bushland, wiped out townships and left 7500 homeless. Residents in Victoria's southeast were told the day before to prepare for extreme conditions: forecast temperatures exceeding 47°C and winds of up to 120km/hr combined with tinder-dry land due to long-term drought and the previous week's heatwave. In the Gippsland region a fire started deliberately in Churchill quickly spread to surrounding areas. Fires also destroyed thousands of acres of bushland in Wilsons Promontory.

Always check with Parks Victoria (☎13 19 63, ⓦparks.vic.gov.au) before setting out during the summer months and familiarize yourself with bushfire safety tips (see box, p.42).

---

this diverse region and getting to small settlements and bush campsites on the coast. The Princes Freeway/Highway itself is a very boring drive, particularly the stretch from the Latrobe Valley to Bairnsdale, but after Orbost the highway becomes more scenic as it goes through the tall, dense eucalypt forests of Far East Gippsland.

Wilsons Promontory

WILSONS PROMONTORY, or "the Prom", the most southerly part of mainland Australia, was once joined by a land bridge to Tasmania. Its barbed hook juts out into Bass Strait, with a rocky coastline interspersed with sheltered sandy bays and coves; the coastal scenery is made even more stunning by the backdrop of granite ranges. It's understandably Victoria's most popular **national park**, and though the main campsite gets totally packed in summer, there are plenty of walking tracks and opportunities for bush camping, and the park is big enough to allow you to escape the crowds. You can swim at several of the beaches and even **surf**.

The nearest town is the dairying settlement of **Foster** on the South Gippsland Highway, a thirty-minute drive away and the best place to buy groceries, fuel and other supplies. Situated by a small river on Norman Bay, **Tidal River** is the national park's main camping and accommodation centre, with a general store (daily 9am–4pm) including a pricey supermarket and takeaway food.

Walks

Many short walks begin from Tidal River, including a track accessible to wheelchairs. During summer holidays and on weekends from November to the end of April, the tracks become extremely busy so show up early, and book well in advance if you intend to camp.

One of the best walks is the **Squeaky Beach Track** (1hr 30min return), which crosses Tidal River, heads uphill and through a tea-tree canopy, finally ending on a beach of pure, white quartz sand that really does squeak underfoot. The **Lilly Pilly Gully Nature Walk** (2hr return) is also very rewarding, as it affords an excellent overview of the diverse vegetation of "the Prom", from low-growing shrubs to heathland to open eucalypt forest, as well as scenic views. The walk starts at the Lilly Pilly Gully car park near Tidal River.

The longer tracks in the southern section of the park are well defined and mostly not too difficult; the campsites here have pit toilets and there is fresh water, although it is creek water so needs to be treated. The most popular walk is the one- to two-day (35.5km) **Sealers Cove–Refuge Cove–Waterloo Bay** circuit beginning and ending at Telegraph Saddle car park. Another spectacular two- or three-day loop, starting at Telegraph Saddle and ending at Tidal River, takes you to **Wilson's Promontory Lighthouse**, on a peninsula thrust south into the strait. (You can stay overnight in the restored nineteenth-century lightkeepers' cottages or camp; see opposite)

Although the longer (overnight) hikes in the remote north of the park are suitable only for experienced, properly equipped bushwalkers (as there are no facilities and limited fresh water), there are some well-signposted short walks (up to 3km).

ARRIVAL AND INFORMATION	WILSONS PROMONTORY

By bus The only public transport to Wilsons Promontory is a Friday afternoon (generally summer-only) bus from Foster to Tidal River – check with the national park visitor centre (see below). If you don't want to rent a car, you can take a V/Line train-and-bus combination from Melbourne's Southern Cross Station to Foster (3–4 daily; 2hr 40min); the *Prom Coast Backpackers YHA* (see below) can also arrange transport to the national park for $15–20 per person.

By car The easiest way to get here from Melbourne is to follow the South Gippsland Highway to Meeniyan, where

you turn right onto Route C444 which takes you to the park entrance. Once you enter the park, it's 30km to Tidal River on a sealed road.

Tourist information The national park visitor centre (daily 8.30am–4pm; ☎03 5680 9555 or ☎1800 350 552, ⓦ parks.vic.gov.au) at Tidal River is an obvious first stop. It has plenty of information, though not all of it is on display: the small booklet *Discovering the Prom* ($16.50) is invaluable if you're attempting any of the overnight walks.

TOURS

Bunyip Tours ☎03 9650 9680, ⓦ bunyiptours.com. This Melbourne-based ecotour operator and a long-established Prom specialist offers a two-day Wildlife Extravaganza (Tues & Sat, plus Thurs in summer; $349) to Wilsons Promontory and Phillip Island (see p.790); they also offer a one-day tour

to Wilsons Prom only (Wed & Sun, plus Fri in summer; $125).
Wildlife Coast Cruises ☎1300 763, 739, ⓦ wildlifecoastcruises.com.au. Full-day cruise around the Prom on a luxurious catamaran cruiser, departing from Port Welshpool, north of Wilsons Promontory ($245).

ACCOMMODATION

Detailed information on all sorts of **accommodation** close to Wilsons Promontory is available on ☎1800 458 382 and ⓦ promaccom.com.au. Accommodation in the park is arranged through the information centre (see above). Accommodation for Christmas until the end of January, Easter and long weekends is allocated via a ballot system for which you register online through the Parks Victoria website (ⓦ parks.vic.gov.au), although even outside these times many places are booked up to a year in advance. Staying in the very basic **huts** (use of the campsite's facilities; bed linen not supplied) works out at around $25 per person for groups of four to six people. The **camping area** has 484 unpowered pitches ($56; max eight people per site). Facilities include hot showers, a laundry, communal kitchen and summer outdoor cinema. Very comfortable **self-contained holiday cabins** sleep up to six people (from $235.10 for two), and the **Wilderness Retreats** ($319.30 for two), a cross between cabin and tent, have timber decks, lockable doors, queen beds and en suites. Self-contained Lightkeepers' Cottages ($141.31/person; 2 nights max) have fully equipped kitchens, lounges and two- to four-bed bunk rooms; bed linen can be hired to lighten your pack weight.

Prom Coast Backpackers YHA 40 Station Rd, Foster ☎03 5682 2171, ⓦ yha.com.au. This centrally located hostel is a good budget option. There are dorms, family rooms and doubles/twins and the operators can arrange transport to Wilsons Prom for a reasonable fee. Dorms $30,

doubles $70
Wilsons Promontory Motel 26 Station Rd, Foster ☎03 5682 2055, ⓦ wilsonspromontorymotel.com.au. A three-star motel in a good location, with twenty redbrick-walled rooms and a communal BBQ area. $110

Mount Baw Baw

The ski village at **MOUNT BAW BAW**, near the edge of Baw Baw National Park, is considerably south of Victoria's other resorts and one of the closest ski areas to Melbourne. It's a quiet little place, commanding magnificent views south over much of Gippsland and consisting mainly of private lodges. As at Mount Buffalo (see p.878), the ski runs are mainly for beginners and intermediates. There are seven ski tows here and, in addition to downhill skiing and snowboarding, you can ski cross-country on 10km of groomed trails.

Mount Baw Baw is also open in the summer and is ideal for bushwalking; there's also a full calendar of events, including trail running, mountain biking, car rallies and road cycling.

9

By bus The Mt Baw Baw Transport Service (☎ 03 5134 6876 or ⓦ mountainexperience.com/snow for bookings) provides an on-demand winter-only bus service from Moe train station (about an hour south) to the resort (from $60 return).

By car Mount Baw Baw is approximately two-and-a-half-hours from Melbourne. The best option is to take South Face Road – drive along the Princes Freeway to Moe, follow the signs to Walhalla and head through Erica, then follow signs for Mt Baw Baw, turning off at South Face Road. It's unsealed but allows all-weather access and amazing views along a wider, less winding road than the other routes.

Note that chains are required by law to be carried during the declared snow season and fitted when necessary.

Information For more detail on the area and accommodation options, which range from shared lodges to self-contained apartments and cabins, see ⓦ mountbawbaw.com.au. Resort entry (no charge outside the ski season) is $35/day weekdays and $52/day weekends; this can be purchased online at ⓦ mtbawbaw .alpineeasyaccess.com.au. A one-day lift pass costs $50 on weekdays, $80 at weekends. Up the mountain there is a restaurant (June–Sept daily 10am–late; Oct–May Fri 6.30pm–late, Sat & Sun 10am–late), plus a spa and sauna.

Walhalla

Tucked into a deep, narrow valley in the foothills of the Great Dividing Range, 48km northeast of Moe, **WALHALLA** is a relic of Victoria's gold-rush era; it was the last mainland community connected to the electricity grid – as late as 1998. From a peak population in the thousands in the 1880s, Walhalla is now home to fewer than twenty people – guardians of a tiny town that is packed with interest. While here, you can tour a mine and explore original weatherboard buildings, shops and mine sites strung along Stringer's Creek. In addition, there is a hillside cemetery and a hilltop cricket pitch – the locals levelled the hilltop and hitting a six means an energetic chase for fielders – plus a couple of cafés and a sweet shop.

Walhalla is the start of the Australian Alps Walking Track, which runs 655km through the alpine regions of Victoria, New South Wales and the Australian Capital Territory and takes about ten weeks start-to-finish. There are also shorter walks in the area and a network of 4WD tracks in the enfolding ranges.

A sealed road snakes up the valley into town but it's more fun rolling in on a steam train (bushfire risk permitting) on the Walhalla Goldfields Railway (Wed, Sat & Sun; ⓦ walhallarail.com.au), which travels 4km of restored track.

Tourist Information The Corner Store & Museum, Main Rd (☎ 03 5165 6250, ⓦ visitwalhalla.com.au), provides information, brochures and maps; their website lists a number of accommodation options.

Long Tunnel Extended Gold Mine Tours ☎ 03 5165 6259. Take a 45-minute tour deep underground to the original workings of one of Victoria's most successful mines. Mon–Fri 1.30pm, Sat & Sun noon, 1.30pm & 3pm; $20.

The Star Hotel Main Rd ☎ 03 5165 6262, ⓦ starhotel. com.au. A loving recreation of the original gold-era establishment that burned down in 1951, this two-storey hotel at the top of town has twelve spacious rooms, some opening onto the garden. There's a guest lounge and bar with an open fire and an in-house restaurant open Saturdays (and midweek subject to occupancy). **$250**

The Walhalla Lodge Hotel Main Rd ☎ 03 5165 6226. Affectionately called the "Wally Pub", this classic country hotel is the place for a cold beer, generous pub grub such as a mixed grill ($30), and a chat with locals and fellow travellers. Wed–Sun 11.30am–late; food Wed & Thurs noon–2pm & 6–7.30pm, Fri noon–2pm & 6–8pm, Sat & Sun noon–2.30pm & 6–8pm.

The Gippsland Lakes region

The **Gippsland Lakes**, Australia's largest system of inland waterways, are fed by the waters of, among others, the Mitchell, Nicholson and Tambo rivers, and are separated from the sea by Ninety Mile Beach. East of Yarram, the beach stretches long and straight towards **Lakes Entrance**, the commercialized focal point of the area and one of

Victoria's most popular holiday spots, with the foothills of the high country within easy reach to the north.

Sale and around

The large town of **SALE**, an old river port at the junction of the South Gippsland and Princes highways, is a good point from which to explore the coastal park and Ninety Mile Beach, a popular area for surf fishing. The town itself doesn't have a great deal for visitors, although there are museums and galleries, and a few good cafés and pubs.

From the village of Seaspray, 35km south, a coastal road hugs the shore for 20km to Golden Beach, from where a scenic drive heads through Gippsland Lakes Coastal Park to the small settlement of Loch Sport; here you're faced with the enviable dilemma of lakes on one side and ocean beaches with good surfing on the other. An unsealed road continues to Sperm Whale Head in The Lakes National Park, a good location for boating, water-skiing and fishing.

ARRIVAL AND INFORMATION   SALE AND AROUND

By bus V/Line buses run from Traralgon to Sale (up to 5 daily; 35min).

Tourist information The visitor centre (8 Foster St, Sale; daily 9am–5pm; ☎ 1800 677 520, ⓦ tourismwellington.

com.au) issues fishing licences and provides information about the Bataluk Cultural Trail (see box below). Information on The Lakes National Park is available from ⓦ parks.vic.gov.au, or the Sale office on ☎ 03 5143 8200.

ACCOMMODATION AND EATING

Cambrai Hostel 117 Johnston St, Maffra ☎ 03 5147 1600, ⓦ maffra.net.au/hostel. If you'd like to make friends with locals, stay off the beaten track at *Cambrai Hostel* in Maffra, a small dairy town, 20km off the Princes Highway in the foothills of the Great Dividing Range. Located in a lovely, refurbished house in the town centre, the hostel has dorms (six to eight beds) and doubles, a communal kitchen, comfy lounge and licensed bar. The owners offer prebooked pick-ups from the bus stop and have work contracts. They can also arrange walks and gold-panning in the high country. Weekly rates available. Dorms $34, doubles $80.

Captains Lodge International Cnr Warruk Way & Fiske St, Sale ☎ 03 5144 3766, ⓦ captainslodgeint. com. This friendly motel, a short way out of town, is a good option in Sale. There's a pool and gardens, plus bar and an Austrian/international restaurant. $105

Mister Raymond 268 Raymond St, Sale ☎ 03 5144 4007, ⓦ misterraymond.com.au. Hip restaurant serving good all-day breakfasts (from $8), lunches (try the Mexican beef salad $18), plus tapas-style Friday night dinners (with live music). The monthly themed five-course dinners are fun. Tues–Thurs & Sat 8am–3.30pm, Fri 8am–11pm.

Bairnsdale and around

The next major town along the highway east of Sale, **BAIRNSDALE** serves as another departure point for the lakes to the south – and for Mitchell River National Park, about 42km to the northwest via the Bairnsdale–Dargo Road; here you can view the magnificent river gorge from the cliff edge or explore it on walking tracks to the den of a mythical beast. Bairnsdale is the region's largest town but there's not much to do here; it is, however, a good place to stock up on groceries and other supplies.

An exhibition at the **Krowathunkooloong Keeping Place** (37–53 Dalmahoy St; usually Mon–Fri 9am–5pm but check; $6; ☎ 03 5150 0737), part of the Bataluk Cultural Trail (see box below), explains the history of the Gunaikurnai people. The **East Gippsland Art**

BATALUK CULTURAL TRAIL

Encompassing eleven sites, scattered between Yarram near Wilsons Promontory and Cape Conran in the east, the **Bataluk Cultural Trail** (ⓦ batalukculturaltrail.com.au) links places of cultural and spiritual significance to the Gunaikurnai people, the first inhabitants of the Gippsland coast who have lived here for more than thirty thousand years. The sites include shell middens and scarred trees; a cave, the Den of Nargun in Mitchell River National Park, 25km northwest of Bairnsdale; and the fascinating Krowathunkooloong Keeping Place in Bairnsdale.

9

Gallery (2 Nicholson St; Tues–Fri 10am–4pm, Sat 10am–2pm; free; ☎03 5153 1988, ⓦeastgippslandartgallery.org.au) is also worth a visit.

ARRIVAL AND INFORMATION

By bus V/Line buses run from Traralgon to Bairnsdale (up to 5 daily; 1hr 30min). From Bairnsdale, buses go to Lakes Entrance, Orbost and Marlo (2–4 daily). The V/Line Sapphire Coast Link bus and train service travels between Melbourne and Narooma on the NSW south coast four days a week.

BAIRNSDALE AND AROUND

Destinations Lakes Entrance (30min); Marlo (1hr 55min); Orbost (1hr 30min); Narooma/NSW (Sapphire Coast Link; 4 weekly, 5hr 35min).
Tourist information 240 Main St (daily 9am–5pm; ☎03 5152 3444, ⓦdiscovereastgippsland.com.au).

ACCOMMODATION

Big 4 Bairnsdale Holiday Park 139 Princes Hwy ☎1800 062 885, ⓦbairnsdaleholidaypark.com. Budget accommodation just west of town, set in landscaped gardens and with its own fauna park. Un/powered sites $40/50, cabins $115

Grand Terminus Hotel 98 McLeod St ☎03 5152 4040, ⓦgrandterminus.com.au. Affordable and comfortable accommodation in an 1880s corner pub with an iron-lace-trimmed veranda. The twelve en-suite single, double and family rooms are smallish but neatly decked out. $85

Paynesville

Eighteen kilometres south of Bairnsdale, **PAYNESVILLE** (ⓦvisitpaynesville.com.au) is a popular lakeside holiday town with canals and inlets, famous for its boating and other watersports. There are a few good cafés and restaurants here, and a pleasant walk along the waterfront.

A three-minute ferry ride away across the McMillan Straits is **Raymond Island**, which, with its prolific birdlife, kangaroos and large koala population – one of the biggest in Victoria – is an idyllic place to stay. The Raymond Island Ferry runs roughly every half-hour throughout the day (cars $10 return, foot passengers free; ☎0418 517 959).

ACCOMMODATION

PAYNESVILLE

Paynesville-based **Gippsland Lakes Escapes** (☎03 5156 0432, ⓦgippslandlakesescapes.com.au) offer a wide range of accommodation in Paynesville, Raymond Island and surrounds, suitable for all budgets and ranging from B&Bs and self-contained cottages to resorts.

Lake Gallery B&B 2A Backwater Court ☎0409 560 448, ⓦlakegallerybedandbreakfast.com. A gorgeous – if pricey – option is the luxurious *Lake Gallery B&B*, which

has two designer-decorated guest suites at the water's edge, a spa and its own jetty, plus an art gallery. Rates include breakfast. $200

Bruthen and around

To see a very different side of the Lakes region it's worth detouring to the attractive village of **BRUTHEN**, 22km inland from Bairnsdale on the Great Alpine Road. There are some antique shops, an 1860s general store and walking tracks here, but the main draw is **Bullant Brewery** (see below).

From Bruthen, you can take a forty-minute scenic drive along back roads to the Buchan Caves (see p.867), or continue to alpine ski resorts such as Dinner Plain, Falls Creek and Mount Beauty, via the Great Alpine Road. En route, the charming Gippsland "High Country" farming town of **Omeo**, 75km from Bruthen, offers horseriding and whitewater rafting (ⓦomeoregion.com.au).

EATING AND DRINKING

BRUTHEN

Bullant Brewery 46 Main St ☎03 5157 5307, ⓦbullantbrewery.com. Around eight varieties of craft beer are brewed here and you can sample some on a tasting tray. The food is good too, including pizzas (from

$10), burgers ($21), sharing plates ($38) and lamb, beef, chicken and seafood dishes (from $18). Wed, Thurs & Sun 11am–5pm, Fri & Sat 11am–10pm.

9

Lakes Entrance

LAKES ENTRANCE is named after the entrance to the Gippsland Lakes, an area cut through a sandy barrier between the lakes and the sea and formed about six thousand years ago. When first seen by white men in the 1840s, the outlet was a seasonal, intermittent gap, unsuitable for reliable trade. In 1889 the present stable entrance was opened 6km east of the old one: this artificial opening is dredged regularly to keep the entrance deep enough for boats to pass through.

Lakes Entrance is a big, slightly tawdry, tourist town, with loads of motels at either end as you enter from the highway; the foreshore with its marinas and gardens is, however, very pleasant. There are all sorts of attractions aimed at keeping families happy, including minigolf, walking trails and the **Griffiths Shell Museum** on the Esplanade (daily summer 9am–5pm, winter 10am–4pm; $8; ☎03 5155 1538), which fronts onto an arm of Lake King.

The town is also a big **fishing port** with around 25 active fishing boats: the Fishermen's Cooperative Wharf has a viewing platform where you can watch the catch being unloaded, and the town is renowned for its seafood.

Beaches, swimming, surfing and fishing are obviously the other big attractions here. Lakes Entrance Surf Beach, a substantial stretch of white sand patrolled in season by surf lifesavers and part of **Ninety Mile Beach**, is reached via a footbridge across the lake to Hummocks Reserve. A stand on the beach side of the footbridge rents canoes, paddleboats, aquabikes and catamarans.

ARRIVAL AND INFORMATION

By bus Buses run from Bairnsdale and Orbost to Lakes Entrance. The V/Line Sapphire Coast Link bus/train service between Melbourne and Narooma on the NSW south coast stops in Lakes Entrance.
Destinations Bairnsdale (2–4 daily; 45min); Orbost (2–4 daily; 45min); Narooma/NSW (Sapphire Coast Link; 4 weekly, 5hr 35min).

LAKES ENTRANCE

Tourist information The Lakes Entrance Visitor Centre (2 Marine Pde; daily 9am–5pm; ☎03 5155 1966, ⓦdiscovereastgippsland.com.au), on the Esplanade, provides local advice and tickets for lake cruises. They also book accommodation, a useful service in summer when the place gets very busy.

TOURS

Mako Fishing Charters ☎0412 699 394, ⓦmakofishingcharters.com. Lake ($60/3hr) and ocean ($150/5hr 30min) fishing on the *Panama II*, with all fishing gear and bait supplied.
Sea-Safari ☎0458 511 438, ⓦlakes-explorer.com.au. An eco-cruise on *Lakes Explorer* is very worthwhile. Run by "Skipper Pete", an environmentalist with a national parks background, these educational trips provide a glimpse into the region's wildlife, geology and history. Choose from the Ocean Entrance cruise ($15/1hr) or the Rigby Island Sea

Safari ($30/3hr) that takes you to a wildlife sanctuary and beyond. Cruises generally depart at 10am and sometimes in the afternoons – call to check.
Wyanga Park Winery lunch cruise ☎03 5155 1508, ⓦwyangapark.com.au. Of the many lake cruises on offer, one of the most popular is the Peel's Lake Cruises trip up North Arm to the *Wyanga Park Winery* – the most famous local winery – on the fringe of the Colquhoun Forest (45min; Wed & Sat with additional cruises in summer, $55, departs at 11am and includes a main meal and glass of wine at the winery café).

ACCOMMODATION

Big 4 Waters Edge Holiday Park 623 Esplanade ☎03 5155 1914, ⓦwatersedgepark.com. Holiday park with great amenities, including two pools, games room, playground and modern holiday cabins. **$135**
★**The Goat and Goose B&B** 16 Gay St ☎03 5155 3079, ⓦgoatandgoose.com. In a timber pole-framed house on a hill at the eastern end of town, this traditional B&B has great ocean views, and three of the four suites have spas. Breakfast included. **$198**
Kalimna Woods Kalimna Jetty Rd ☎03 5155 1957,

ⓦkilimnawoods.com.au. Four fully self-contained timber cottages in a bush setting, some with spas and log fires. **$150**
Waverley House Cottages 205 Palmers Rd ☎03 5155 1257, ⓦwaverleyhousecottages.com.au. Stylish self-contained one- and two-bedroom cottages with spas, a 5min drive from town and beside a golf course. There's also a pool, hot tub, covered BBQ area and communal lounge area with an open fire. Rates include a Continental breakfast basket (and chocolates) on first night only. Min three-night stay in peak season. **$260**

EATING AND DRINKING

Ferrymans Seafood Café Middle Boat Harbour ☎ 03 5155 3000, ⒲ferrymans.com.au. One of Lakes Entrance's best seafood restaurants in a great location on the water, with a seasonally changing menu and mains from $18.50. Daily 10am–late.

Henry's Winery Café Wyanga Park Winery, 246 Baades Rd (some 3km from town) ☎ 03 5155 1508, ⒲wyangapark.com.au. Excellent cuisine sourced from local producers, with dishes such as Lakes Entrance whiting fillets ($22) and spicy lamb ribs ($22). You can get here via a cruise (see opposite). Daily noon–2.30pm.

Footbridge Fish & Chips 19 Myer St ☎ 03 5155 2253. A standard fish-and-chip shop exterior belies the generous helpings of crisp battered fish and chips (around $10) parcelled up here. Gluten-free options available. Daily 8am–6.30pm.

Tres Amigos Mexican 521 Esplanade ☎ 03 5155 2977. A backpacker and surfer favourite, dishing out reasonably priced Mexican food (mains $15 to $30). Daily 6.30pm–late.

Metung

If the commercialism of Lakes Entrance turns you off, head for the more refined charms of **METUNG**, a pretty, affluent boating and holidaying village to the west. There are boats for rent, some pleasant waterfront walks, gift shops, delicious food, and even daily pelican feeding – this is a place to relax and unwind.

ARRIVAL AND INFORMATION · METUNG

By car Take the highway towards Bairnsdale then turn south on the side road at Swan Reach.

Tourist information The visitor centre at 50 Metung Rd (daily 9am–5pm; ☎ 03 5156 2969, ⒲metungtourism. com.au) can arrange boat rental and operates the Metung Accommodation service. Options include B&Bs, motels, apartments and houses – for after-hours accommodation enquiries call ☎ 0405 265 033.

ACCOMMODATION AND EATING

Bancroft Bites 57 Metung Rd ☎ 03 5156 2854, ⒲bancroftbites.com.au. A delightful licensed café serving good food and coffee. Lunches include a seafood hotpot ($21), steak sandwich ($19) and share platters ($38). Daily except Wed 8am–3pm.

★**McMillans of Metung Resort** 155 Metung Rd ☎ 03 5156 2283, ⒲mcmillansofmetung.com.au. Very comfortable, fully equipped villas and cottages of different sizes in a garden setting, with a solar-heated pool, tennis court and private jetty. $230

Metung Hotel Kurnai Ave ☎ 03 5156 2206, ⒲metunghotel.com.au. A cheaper option with six neat rooms with shared bathrooms. The pub also serves good-value lunches and dinners and has a fantastic outdoor table area on the water. $85

★**The Moorings at Metung** 44 Metung Rd ☎ 03 5156 2750, ⒲themoorings.com.au. Thirty or so luxury apartments with sun decks, plus cheaper motel-style units, most overlooking Bancroft Bay. There are also indoor and outdoor pools, a spa, tennis court and BBQ facilities, and the hotel has its own marina for those arriving by boat. Doubles $190, apartments $225

Nautica Shop 8/50 Metung Rd ☎ 03 5156 2345. Located beside the village green, this restaurant and bar is a great spot for coffee and home-made cakes, and more substantial meals featuring fresh local produce, the star of which is the seafood. Daily 8am–11pm.

Buchan

Beyond Lakes Entrance the small town of Nowa Nowa is where you turn north off the Princes Highway for the settlement of **BUCHAN**, in the foothills of the Victorian Alps. The area offers fishing, horseriding and other adventure activities, but is most famous for its beautiful caves.

Buchan Caves Reserve

Caves Rd · Guided tours daily, generally from 10am or 11am but times vary with the season · Single cave tour (Royal or Fairy) $21.50, both caves $32.20, Federal Cave $35.90 (bookings essential for Federal Cave) · ☎ 03 5162 1900, ⒲parks.vic.gov.au

The **Buchan Caves Reserve** boasts more than six hundred **caves**, the most famous of which – Royal Cave and Fairy Cave – can be seen on **guided tours**. Both show caves, which drip with beautiful limestone formations, are lit and have walkways. You can also book a more historical tour, wearing headlamp and helmet, of the less visited and

9

less decorated Federal Cave. In the extensive park surrounding the caves there's a national parks visitor centre, an icy, spring-fed swimming pool, a playground and walking tracks, plus lots of wildlife, predominantly kangaroos.

ACCOMMODATION

Accommodation is either in town or at Buchan Caves, where there is a variety of well-priced accommodation, from campsites to cabins to wilderness retreats (permanent, elevated tents; $187). Caves accommodation must be prebooked with Parks Victoria at ⓦ parkstay.vic.gov.au. You can find out about the options at the main Parks Victoria website (ⓦ parkweb.vic.gov.au).

Buchan Accommodation 16 Gelantipy Rd ⓣ 03 5155 9494, ⓦ buchanaccommodation.com. A collection of spacious one- and two-bedroom cabins with full amenities in garden and farm settings. $140

The Snowy River Loop

From Buchan you can continue north on the **Snowy River Loop**, although this is hilly and very remote country and the roads are generally narrow and winding – most are unsealed and they can be treacherous in adverse weather. A 4WD is highly recommended, and always check road conditions at the Omeo Visitor Information Centre (ⓣ 03 5159 1455) in advance.

From Buchan the road follows the Murrindal River and slowly winds up to the plateau of the Australian Alps and Snowy River National Park. Turning right at Wulgumerang, about 55km north of Buchan, enables you to make a scenic arc through part of **Snowy River National Park**, following the road towards Bonang; **Little River Falls** are well worth a stop on this stretch.

Further on, you descend into the valley of the Snowy River, which you cross at **McKillops Bridge**. The river's sandy banks here are a popular swimming spot, and are also the place to embark on a **rafting** trip through deep gorges, caves, raging rapids and tranquil pools. The road through Snowy River National Park continues until it meets the Bonang–Orbost road.

The winding road down from the plateau to the coast, still mostly unsealed, leads past **Errinundra National Park**, which protects magnificent wetland eucalypt forests as well as Victoria's largest surviving stand of **rainforest**. At **Errinundra Saddle**, in the heart of the park, there's a delightful picnic area and a self-guided boardwalk through the forest (about 40min) – look out for lyrebirds, masterful mimics with harp-shaped tails. Take special care while driving, as logging trucks use all the roads in the area.

ARRIVAL AND INFORMATION

SNOWY RIVER LOOP

By car The sealed road leading from Buchan into the Snowy River Loop ends at Wulgumerang, just before the turn-off to McKillops Bridge. You can continue straight up to Jindabyne in the Snowy Mountains of New South Wales – a spectacular drive – but about two-thirds of the road is unsealed and it can be rough; check conditions at the Omeo Visitor Information Centre (ⓣ 03 5159 1455) before setting out.

Tourist information See the Parks Victoria website (ⓦ parks.vic.gov.au) or contact the Orbost office (ⓣ 03 5161 1222) for information.

Outdoor activities Based at Gelantipy, Snowy River Expeditions (ⓣ 03 5155 0220, ⓦ karoondapark.com) offers good-value rafting (from $150), abseiling (beginner $40, day-session $145), rock climbing ($145), horseriding ($40/hr) and wild caving adventures ($40).

ACCOMMODATION

Karoonda Park Gelantipy ⓣ 03 5155 0220, ⓦ karoondapark.com. Run by Snowy River Expeditions, this small country hostel is situated on a beef and sheep farm and offers a variety of accommodation, from dorms to motel-style rooms and family cabins. No internet. Dorms $35, doubles $870, cabins $125

Marlo and around

The seaside village of **MARLO**, 73km east of Lakes Entrance, has a pub with decent food, a motel and caravan park, and a grocery store; this is also where the Snowy River enters the sea via a shallow lagoon complex. Further east, **Cape Conran Coastal Park** (ⓦparks.vic.gov.au) is definitely worth a visit, offering wild surf beaches, heathland and woodland, abundant wildlife and some great walks. There is no public transport to the park, so driving is the only option.

ACCOMMODATION AND EATING   MARLO AND AROUND

Cape Conran Cabins Banksia Bluff Camping Area, beyond East Cape, 18km east of Marlo ⓣ03 5154 8438, ⓦconran.net.au. Located just a short walk from the beach, these seven rustic cabins in Cape Conran Coastal Park sleep up to eight and have their own kitchen, shower and toilet. There are also powered campsites and tent-style wilderness retreats (unavailable in winter). Christmas holiday campsites are allocated by ballot. The managers can arrange surfing lessons and other activities. The cabins are self-catering

and there are few local places to eat, so stock up on supplies in the nearby town of Orbost (or Marlo) on the way through. Powered sites $38.90, cabins $230.90 (up to eight people), wilderness retreats $186.50

Marlo Hotel 19 Argyle Pde, Marlo ⓣ03 5154 8201, ⓦmarlohotel.com.au. Built in 1886, this delightful pub has a large balcony overlooking the estuary, plus good bistro-style meals, including local seafood. The Marlo also has a number of ocean-hued rooms, some with views. Daily noon–2pm & 6–8pm. $140

Mallacoota and around

Approached via Genoa, 47km east from Cann River along the Princes Highway, **MALLACOOTA** is an unspoilt village in a gorgeous location on the lake system of **Mallacoota Inlet** and surrounded by Croajingolong National Park. During the summer and Easter holidays this tranquil place becomes a bustling holiday resort. You can bushwalk and ride bikes, go fishing, and explore the beautiful waterways on your own or by renting a boat or canoe from local operators. Further afield you can tour **Point Hicks Lighthouse** (Fri–Mon generally 1pm; $7; ⓣ03 5158 4268, ⓦpointhicks.com.au), which also offers accommodation.

About 10km from Genoa, a turn-off to the left leads to **Gipsy Point**, an idyllic spot near the confluence of the Genoa and Wallagaraugh rivers on the upper reaches of Mallacoota Inlet.

INFORMATION AND ACTIVITIES   MALLACOOTA AND AROUND

Tourist information The very helpful volunteer-operated Mallacoota "Info Shed" is situated on the main wharf (generally daily 10am–4pm; ⓣ03 5158 0800, ⓦvisitmallacoota.com.au). The Parks Victoria office, on the corner of Allan and Buckland drives (daily 9.30am–3.30pm; ⓣ13 19 63, ⓦparks.vic.gov.au), has details of secluded camping spots and local bushwalks, and issues fishing licences. Parks Victoria also provide information on nearby Croajingolong National Park, a UNESCO Biosphere Reserve with beaches, heathland and eucalypt forests, which

begins southeast of the town at Sydenham Inlet and continues 100km along the coast to the state border.

Cruises Loch-Ard Cruises (ⓣ0418 615 282) offer two-hour cruises of the inlet for $28 and three hours for $38.

Outdoor activities Mallacoota Equipment Hire (ⓣ0488 329 611, ⓦmallacootahire.com) rents out bikes, kayaks and fishing equipment. Boat rental is also available from Mallacoota Hire Boats (ⓣ0438 447 558, ⓦmallacootahireboats.com), 200m to the left of the information shed.

ACCOMMODATION

Adobe Mudbrick Holiday Flats 17 Karbeethong Hill Ave ⓣ03 5158 0329, ⓦadobeholidayflats.com.au. Spacious, self-contained mud-brick apartments on a former chicken farm. Popular with couples. No internet. $145

Gipsy Point Lakeside Boutique Resort 261 Gipsy Point Rd, Gipsy Point ⓣ03 5158 8200, ⓦgipsy.com.au. A boutique resort set in a native garden by the Wallagaraugh River, with a pool, private jetty and attractive one- and three-bedroom apartments, some with spa, all

with water views or river frontage. $255

★**Karbeethong Lodge** 16 Schnapper Point Drive ⓣ03 5158 0411, ⓦkarbeethonglodge.com.au. A renovated, 1920s weatherboard guesthouse with ten singles and doubles, most en-suite, some opening onto the veranda. Has a lovely country feel. Continental breakfast included. $150

Mallacoota Foreshore Holiday Park Allan Drive ⓣ03 5158 0300. Great location, just metres from the water. Easily the best place in town to pitch a tent (there are no

9

cabins). Its office also offers good advice about where the fish are biting. Un/powered sites **$43/51**

Mallacoota Hotel Motel 51 Maurice Ave ☎03 5158 0455, ⓦmallacootahotel.com.au. Very central option on the main shopping strip, with motel rooms and fully self-contained family suites. There's also a bistro (see below) and a swimming pool. Fee for wi-fi. **$130**

Point Hicks Lighthouse ☎03 5156 0432, ⓦgippslandlakesescapes.com.au. Accommodation in the self-contained lighthouse-keeper's cottages (sleeping up to four people) in Croajingolong National Park, accessed via Cann River. Bookings must be made with Gippsland Lakes Escapes. Two-night minimum. No internet. **$375**

EATING AND DRINKING

Choices for food are very limited, although the standard is high. Note that some establishments close in winter.

Café 54 Maurice Avenue ☎03 5158 0646. A simple daytime café and takeaway with great burgers and other meals (up to $15), plus coffee and cakes. Daily 8am–5pm.

Croajingolong Café Allan Drive ☎03 5158 0098. Fronting the lake, and with outdoor seating for warm-weather grazing, *Croajingolong* serves tasty brunches, generous light meals, such as Moroccan beef salad (mains around $15), and good coffee. Daily 8.30am–4pm.

Mallacoota Hotel 51 Maurice Ave ☎03 5158 0455, ⓦmallacootahotel.com.au. Pub-bistro offering well-priced meals and cold beer, and there's live music in January. Mains start around $18, going up to $33 for a porterhouse steak. Daily noon–2pm & 6–8.30pm.

The northeast

The **Hume Freeway**, the direct route between Melbourne and Sydney, cuts straight through Victoria's northeast, known as the "High Country", passing towns such as Benalla, Glenrowan and Wangaratta, a sizeable place known for its jazz festival. **Rutherglen**, up against the state border, is a long-established wine-producing region. Head east for picturesque **Beechworth**, which is rich in history, with beautiful streetscapes, haunting attractions and a famous bakery. The northeast is also home to the Victorian Alps – ideal for **skiing** in winter and **bushwalking** and **mountain biking** at other times of the year.

GETTING AROUND   THE NORTHEAST

By train V/Line trains run three times daily from Melbourne to Wodonga and Albury (NSW) via Seymour, Benalla and Wangaratta.

By bus From Wangaratta there are buses to Glenrowan, Rutherglen, Beechworth, Bright and Mount Beauty.

On a tour There are plenty of walking and cycling trails for going it alone in the Victorian Alps, or you can organize a trip through outdoor tour operators such as Auswalk (☎03 9597 9767, ⓦauswalk.com.au) and Riding High Cycling Tours (☎03 5725 1343, ⓦridinghigh.com.au).

The Hume Freeway and Kelly Country

Part of this northeast region is known as **Kelly Country**, after legendary bushranger Ned Kelly (see box, p.872). **Benalla** and **Glenrowan** (where he was finally seized after a bloody shoot-out) still bear traces of the helmeted outlaw's activities, with Glenrowan wholeheartedly cashing in on his fame.

FRUIT-PICKING IN THE GOULBURN VALLEY

The rich plains of the **Goulburn Valley**, running through Seymour, Nagambie and Shepparton, are a popular area for backpackers looking for **seasonal work**. The small city of **Shepparton** is the operations centre for canned-fruit companies, with peaches, pears, apples and plums exported worldwide. Ask at the **Greater Shepparton Visitor Centre** at 90 Welsford St (daily 9am–5pm; ☎1800 808 839, ⓦdiscovershepparton.com.au) about fruit-picking work.

Seymour and around

SEYMOUR is the first major stop off the Hume Freeway out of Melbourne. An important train interchange, it's an uninspiring place, but nearby **Tahbilk Winery** (254 O'Neils Rd; Mon–Fri 9am–5pm, Sat & Sun 10am–4pm; ☎03 5794 2555, ⓦtahbilk .com.au), 6km southwest, is worth exploring. Victoria's oldest continually operating winery and vineyard, it opened in 1860, and its Shiraz and Marsanne vines have yielded more than 140 harvests. The well-preserved whitewashed buildings house the cellar door and an excellent café; there are also extensive grounds, with 4km of walking trails through regenerated wetlands.

Benalla

BENALLA, 92km northeast of Seymour, is a civilized town on the lake of the same name, formed by the Broken River, which runs through town and occasionally floods it. There's a major festival here every November, featuring live entertainment and a street parade, and it is a good base for visiting nearby Glenrowan.

The **Costume and Pioneer Museum** in the visitor centre (daily 9am–5pm; $5) displays a musty collection of women's dresses from the 1920s and bridal gowns from the late eighteenth century until the early twentieth century, along with a range of **Ned Kelly relics**, including the bloodstained green silk cummerbund he was awarded as a child for saving a friend from drowning, and which he was proudly wearing when captured.

The **Benalla Art Gallery** (Bridge St; daily except Tues 10am–5pm; free; ☎03 5760 2619, ⓦbenallaartgallery.com), in a lovely setting across the lake, has a fine collection of early twentieth-century and contemporary Australian art, including an Albert Tucker Kelly-gang painting, *Joe Byrne Exhibited at Benalla*. There's also a good café here (see below).

ARRIVAL AND INFORMATION   BENALLA

By train Trains run regularly from Melbourne to Benalla (3 daily; 2hr 20min).

Tourist information The helpful Benalla Visitor Information Centre, 14 Mair St (daily 9am–5pm; ☎03

5762 1749, ⓦenjoybenalla.com.au), has lots of pamphlets and information on the region, and can book accommodation. Their website features a useful *Ned Kelly Touring Route* brochure and map.

ACCOMMODATION AND EATING

Belmont Bed and Breakfast 80 Arundel St ☎03 5762 6575, ⓦbelmontbnb.com.au. You'll find a number of motels along Bridge St, though *Belmont Bed and Breakfast*, a charming 1900s house with elegantly furnished rooms, is more interesting by far. Continental breakfast included. **$160**

Benalla Gallery Café ☎03 5762 3777, ⓦbenallagallerycafe.com. This café in a serene location at the Benalla Art Gallery by the lake is one of the best places in town for something to eat during the day. Mains,

such as a warm chicken salad, range from $10–19. Daily except Tues 10am–4pm.

Georgina's Restaurant 100 Bridge St ☎03 5762 1334, ⓦgeorginas.net.au. Further up the price scale, *Georgina's* is the best option in town for excellent contemporary Australian cuisine. Mains, such as paprika-marinated free range chicken on corn fritters, start from $28. Tues, Wed & Sat 5.30pm–late, Thurs & Fri noon–2pm & 5.30pm–late.

Glenrowan

GLENROWAN, 29km beyond Benalla, was the site of the Kelly gang's last stand, which took place in Siege Street near the train station. A 6m-high effigy of Ned Kelly, in full iron-armour, greets you as you enter town, and there are many Kelly-related sites and attractions. The best of these is **Kate's Cottage Gift Shop & Souvenirs** (35 Gladstone St; daily 9am–5.30pm; $6; ☎03 5766 2448), featuring a museum – newspaper clippings, photographs, letters and other memorabilia – and a run-down replica of the Kelly home at the back. With its bare earth floor, bark roof and newspaper-lined walls, the homestead speaks volumes about the hard lives of the Kellys and many other families. An evocative audiotape narrates Ned's story from childhood and is interspersed with

9

folk songs inspired by his life. The original homestead, 9km west along Kelly Gap Road, is now nothing more than rubble and a brick chimney.

Glenrowan is also renowned for its fortified **wines** and full-bodied reds, particularly Shiraz. The area's most famous winery, Baileys of Glenrowan, established in 1870, offers tastings, and has a museum of winemaking and an excellent café (Taminick Gap Rd; daily 10am–5pm; ☏03 5766 1600, ⊚baileysofglenrowan.com.au).

Wangaratta

At the junction of the Ovens and King rivers, 16km from Glenrowan, **WANGARATTA** is a good base for visits to the Milawa and the King Valley gourmet regions (see box, p.875).

THE NED KELLY STORY

Even before **Ned Kelly** became widely known, folklore and ballads were popularizing free-ranging bushrangers as potent symbols of freedom and resistance to authority. Born in 1855, Ned Kelly was the son of an alcoholic rustler and a mother who sold illicit liquor. By the time he was 11 he was already in constant trouble with the police, who considered the whole family troublemakers. Constables in the area were instructed to "endeavour, whenever the Kellys commit any paltry crime, to bring them to justice... the object [is] to take their prestige away from them".

DAN KELLY

Ned became the accomplice of established bushranger **Harry Power**, and by his mid-teens had a string of warrants to his name. Ned's brother, Dan, was also wanted by the police, and on one fateful occasion, hearing that he had turned up at his mother's, a policeman set out, drunk and without a warrant, to arrest him. A scuffle ensued and the unsteady constable fell to the floor, hitting his head and allowing Dan to escape. The following day warrants were issued for the arrest of Ned (who was in New South Wales at the time) and Dan for attempted murder, and their mother was subsequently sentenced to three years' imprisonment.

ON THE RUN

From this point on, the **Kelly gang**'s crime spree accelerated and, following the death of three constables in a shoot-out at Stringybark Creek, the biggest manhunt in Australia's history began, with a £1000 reward offered for the gang's apprehension. On December 9, 1878, they robbed the bank at Euroa, taking £2000, before moving on to Jerilderie in New South Wales, where another bank was robbed and Kelly penned the famous **Jerilderie Letter**, describing the "big, ugly, fat-necked, wombat-headed, big-bellied, magpie-legged, narrow-hipped, splay-footed sons of Irish bailiffs or English landlords which is better known as Officers of Justice or Victoria Police" who had forced him onto the wrong side of the law.

After a year on the run, the gang formulated a grand plan: they executed Aaron Sherritt, a police informer, in Sebastopol, thus luring a train-bound posse of armed troopers from nearby Beechworth. The gang intended to derail this train at Glenrowan, with as much bloodshed as possible, before moving on to rob the bank at Benalla and barter hostages for the release of Kelly's mother. In the event, having already sabotaged the tracks, the gang commandeered the Glenrowan Inn and, in a moment of drunken candour, Kelly detailed his ambush to a schoolteacher who escaped, managing to save the special train. As the troopers approached the inn, the gang donned the home-made iron armour that has since become their motif. In the ensuing gunfight Kelly's comrades were either killed or committed suicide as the inn was torched, while Ned himself was wounded 28 times but taken alive, tried by the same judge who had incarcerated his mother, and sentenced to hang.

EXECUTION

Public sympathies lay strongly with Ned Kelly, and a crowd of five thousand gathered outside Melbourne Gaol on November 11, 1880, for his execution, believing that the 25-year-old bushranger would "die game". True to form, his last words are said to have been "Such is life". His extraordinary life and rebel spirit are best captured in Peter Carey's bravura *True History of the Kelly Gang* (see p.996).

It's most famous for the four-day **Wangaratta Jazz Festival** (ⓦwangarattajazz.com). Beginning on the Friday prior to the Melbourne Cup (run on the first Tuesday in November), this is one of Australia's premier jazz and blues events, attracting national stars and international legends. The town's other musical claim to fame is that **Nick Cave** spent much of his childhood here; he sang in the boy's choir in Wangaratta cathedral.

ARRIVAL AND INFORMATION   WANGARATTA

By train There are regular trains from Melbourne to Wangaratta (3 daily; 2hr 40min).

By bus Buses connect Wangaratta with Beechworth, Mount Beauty via Bright, and Rutherglen.

Destinations Beechworth (1–6 daily; 40min); Bright (1–3 daily; 1hr 30min); Mount Beauty (3 weekly; 2hr 30min);

Rutherglen (9 weekly; 30min).

Tourist information The staff at the Wangaratta Visitor Information Centre, 100 Murphy St (daily 9am–5pm; ☏1800 801 065, ⓦvisitwangaratta.com.au), can book tickets for the festival as well as local tours and accommodation.

ACCOMMODATION AND EATING

Café Derailleur 38 Norton St ☏03 5722 9589, ⓦcafederailleur.com.au This retro espresso bar in a tiny 1940s ex-railway café opposite the train station has the buzz of a Melbourne laneway café. Coffee is king but there's also great food, with all-day breakfasts, house-baked bread and cakes, and dishes (all under $22) such as pulled pork burgers with slaw, char sui dressing and lime mayonnaise. Mon–Wed 7am–3.30pm, Thurs & Fri 7am–4.30pm, Sat 7am–3pm, Sun 8am–3pm.

Parkview Motor Inn 56 Ryley St ☏03 5721 5655, ⓦparkviewmotorinn.com.au. Modern motel, with cable TV and free DVDs to borrow. There are standard and deluxe rooms, plus one- and two-bedroom apartments. $125

Pinsent Hotel 20 Reid St ☏03 5721 2183 ⓦpinsenthotel.com.au. A renovated nineteenth-century country pub with eleven surprisingly spacious en-suite

air-conditioned rooms and a bistro. Rates include a light breakfast. $90

Wangaratta RSL Victoria Pde ☏03 5721 2501. Great-value food and drinks are served at this typical Aussie club that offers steaks and chicken schnitzels, plus Malaysian dishes (most mains under $25). Mon–Fri noon–2pm & 6–8pm, Sat 10am–2pm & 6–8.30pm, Sun 10.30am–2pm & 6–8pm.

Watermarc 58 Faithful St ☏03 5722 4000, ⓦwatermarc.com.au. Part of the lively Ovens River precinct, this café-restaurant-bar boasts relaxing river views and a deck for alfresco dining. The modern Australian menu of wood-fired pizza and small and large ($26–35) plates showcases local produce and wines, all served by a young crew. Tues–Fri 10am–10pm, Sat 8am–10pm, Sun 8am–4pm.

Rutherglen

Northeast of Wangaratta, 32km west of Wodonga on the Murray River Highway, **RUTHERGLEN** is the heart of Victoria's oldest wine-producing region, renowned for its Durif (a red varietal) and excellent dessert wines, Muscat and Tokay. Most of the more than twenty **wineries** in the area (ⓦwinemakers.com.au) are fourth- or fifth-generation establishments with cellars full of character. The weather partly accounts for the quality of Rutherglen's sweet wines: the long, mild autumns allow the grapes to stay on the vines longer, producing higher sugar levels in the fruit. All the wineries are open for tastings (mostly free) and cellar-door sales (generally Mon–Sat 10am–5pm, Sun hours differ from place to place).

On the Queen's Birthday weekend in June the town hosts the **Winery Walkabout** – one of Australia's biggest wine-tasting festivals, when the new season's releases are presented to the public. Another festive event, the **Tastes of Rutherglen**, is held over Victoria's Labour Day weekend in mid-March, and sees some of the best local restaurants guest-starring at the wineries.

Rutherglen Wine Experience and Visitor Information Centre

57 Main St • Daily 9am–5pm • Free • ☏ 1800 622 871, ⓦ rutherglenvic.com

Local history museum, shop, café and visitor centre in one, **Rutherglen Wine Experience and Visitor Information Centre** has informative displays about the gold rush and the district's agricultural history, including winemaking. The shop sells local wines and arts and crafts, and there are stacks of brochures and information on touring the wineries.

9

They also rent bikes ($25/half day, $35/day, including helmet) and have downloadable cycle-route maps on their website.

ACCOMMODATION   RUTHERGLEN

Around three hours from Melbourne, Rutherglen is a popular weekend getaway, so **accommodation** can be hard to find at that time; you'll have no problem during the week.

Poachers Paradise Hotel Motel 97 Murray St ☎02 6032 7373, ⓦpoachersparadise.com.au. Behind the 1860s *Poachers Paradise Hotel* there are ten motel units with air conditioning and the usual mod cons; two have spas. The bar and bistro up front serves breakfast as well as hearty pub grub, with mains under $30. Daily noon–2pm, 6–8.30pm. **$129**

The Victoria Hotel 90 Main St ☎02 6032 8610, ⓦvictoriahotelrutherglen.com.au. You can't miss this 150-year-old town-centre hotel, which is full of character. It has standard doubles with shared bathroom, plus more expensive en suites and a two-bedroom suite. **$120**

The Walkabout Motel 15 Murray Valley Highway ☎02 6032 9572, ⓦwalkaboutmotel.com.au. A comfortable motel with standard and spa suites, the latter with brick walls and timber ceilings, plus self-contained cottages with veranda. Suites **$145**, cottages **$270**

EATING AND DRINKING

Parker Pies 88 Main St ☎02 6032 9605, ⓦparkerpies. com.au. An award-winning bakery and licensed café serving a myriad of excellent pies for a moderate cost, including venison and emu varieties, and even one featuring local Shiraz. Daily 8am–5pm.

Tuileries Restaurant Drummond St ☎02 6032 9033 ⓦtuileriesrutherglen.com.au. The place for an excellent range of local wines and highly recommended mod-Oz cuisine (mains from $31.50). There is also a casual daytime café (mains $13.50) and a wine bar. Café: daily noon–2pm; restaurant: daily 6.30pm–late; wine bar daily 6pm–late.

Beechworth

Some 35km east of Wangaratta, off the Great Alpine Road, in the foothills of the Victorian Alps, is **BEECHWORTH**, once the centre of the rich **Ovens gold-mining region**. The entire town of honey-coloured granite buildings is acknowledged by Heritage Victoria and the National Trust as being of historic significance, and the town and surrounding area is designated as **Beechworth Historic Park** (ⓦparks.vic.gov.au). The immaculately preserved architecture and compelling history, combined with great restaurants, boutiques and an engaging small-town atmosphere, make Beechworth a great spot for a couple of days.

Courthouse

Ford St • Daily 9.30am–4.30pm • Included in Golden Ticket (see opposite)

As is true of so many other towns in the northeast, Beechworth is rich in **Ned Kelly** history. Among the **government buildings** on Ford Street, part of the Beechworth Historic and Cultural Precinct, is the 1858 **courthouse** where his trial began (it was transferred to Melbourne); it has changed little since 1864, and was in use till 1989. As well as such horrors as manacles and a cat-o'-nine-tails, there's a display on the racy but hard life of Ellen Kelly, Ned's mother. Next door to the courthouse is a still-functioning Telegraph Station, and opposite, underneath the town hall, is the grim cell where Kelly's mentor, "Gentleman Bushranger" Harry Power, was imprisoned.

Burke Museum

Loch St • Daily 10am–5pm • Included in Golden Ticket (see opposite)

Don't miss the **Burke Museum**, dedicated to explorer Robert O'Hara Burke, one-time superintendent of police in Beechworth, who perished with William John Wills on their historic journey from Melbourne to the Gulf of Carpentaria (see box, p.451). The museum also has fascinating background on Beechworth's Chinese population (once making up more than a quarter of its residents) and there's a street of reconstructed nineteenth-century shops, as well as an Aboriginal collection and compelling Kelly memorabilia.

HIGH COUNTRY GOURMET REGIONS

The High Country area of Victoria, including the small town of Milawa, 15km southeast of Wangaratta on Snow Road, is renowned for the excellent quality of its locally produced food and wine, so much so that it has been dubbed the **Milawa Gourmet Region** (ⓦmilawagourmet.com).

Another major wine and gourmet area is the nearby **King Valley**, around 30km south of Milawa and centred around the small town of Whitfield. There are many cellar doors here, as well as fine Italian-inspired produce and dining – see ⓦkingvalleytourism.org.au and ⓦwinesofthekingvalley.com.au for more information.

Brown Brothers Winery 239 Milawa–Bobinawarrah Rd ⓣ03 5720 5500, ⓦbrownbrothers .com.au. If it's a tipple of something special you're after, try a tour of Brown Brothers Winery, situated just outside Milawa and clearly signposted; you'll also find a casual café and a great restaurant, *Patricia's Table* (daily noon–3pm; bookings essential on ⓣ03 5720 5540), which specializes in complementing Brown Brothers' wines with seasonal local foods such as spiced rolled goat; two courses $68, three courses $95. Daily 9am–5pm.

King River Café Snow Rd ⓣ03 5727 3461, ⓦkingrivercafe.com.au. A popular spot, specializing in local wines and good food, such as pizzas ($11) and wok-tossed duck and noodles ($30); the cakes and coffee are excellent, too. Mon 10am–3pm, Wed–Sun 10am–late.

Milawa Cheese Factory 17 Milawa–Bobinawarrah Rd ⓣ03 5727 3589, ⓦmilawacheese.com.au. In Milawa itself you can taste and purchase award-winning cheeses at this factory and enjoy breakfast or lunch at the excellent adjoining restaurant and bakery. Daily 9am–5pm.

Milawa Mustards 1597 Glenrowan–Myrtleford Road ⓣ03 5727 3202, ⓦmilawamustards .com.au. Taste and buy eighteen home-made seed mustard varieties, plus other condiments. Daily 10am–5pm.

The Olive Shop Snow Rd ⓣ03 5727 3887, ⓦtheoliveshop.com.au. Locally grown olives and extra virgin olive oil, plus tapenades and condiments. Daily 10am–5pm.

Gorge Scenic Drive

The 5km, one-way **Gorge Scenic Drive** (it is also a lovely walk or bike ride) begins at Sydney Road and ends at Bridge Street, on the town's western edge. It includes the famous Spring and Reid creeks, which supported eight thousand diggers in 1852, an old storehouse for blasting powder known as the **powder magazine**, and natural features such as Flat Rock, Telegraph Rock and Woolshed Falls. Come prepared for a dip in the natural **rock pools** accessed from the bridge. You can combine the gorge drive or walk with a visit to the cemetery, where the tall Chinese **burning towers** stand out among the colonial monuments.

ARRIVAL AND INFORMATION

BEECHWORTH

By bus V/Line operates a daily bus service from Wangaratta to Beechworth (1–3 daily; 40min); some services continue to Bright (1hr).

Tourist information The visitor centre is located in the fine old Town Hall at 103 Ford St (daily 9am–5pm; ⓣ1300 366 321, ⓦexplorebeechworth.com.au) and can book tours and accommodation, as well as provide you with pamphlets on places of interest, including the Gorge Scenic Drive. To visit all the sights, purchase a Golden Ticket ($25, valid for four consecutive days), which also includes two excellent walking tours, one on Ned Kelly and another about the gold rush.

ACCOMMODATION

1860 Luxury Accommodation 4 Surrey Lane ⓣ0408 273 783, ⓦ1860luxuryaccommodation.com. Old meets new in a relocated 1860s timber slab hut augmented with rescued and repurposed materials, including a blacksmith bellows coffee table. There's a king bed, leather lounges, high-spec kitchen and two-person bath. Min two nights on weekends. **$315**

Armour Motor Inn 1 Camp St ⓣ03 5728 1466, ⓦarmourmotorinn.com.au. Central motel, with 21 comfortable double, twin and family rooms, all with cable TV and some opening onto the garden. There's also a pool and sauna. Continental breakfast included. **$130**

★**Freeman on Ford** 97 Ford St ⓣ03 5728 2371, ⓦfreemanonford.com.au. Five-star rooms beautifully decorated in traditional Victorian and 1930s styles in the heart of town. A cooked breakfast and afternoon tea are

9

included, and there are guest lounges, a swimming pool and spa. A charming heritage option for those who can afford it. $295

The Old Priory 8 Priory Lane ☎03 5728 1024, ⓦoldpriory.com.au. Reasonably priced singles ($70) are the real drawing card of this historic B&B, which also offers budget group accommodation. If you want peace and quiet, it's best to come at the weekend, when the school groups have gone. $100

Tanswell's Commercial Hotel 50 Ford St ☎03 5728 1480. Beautiful old building on the town's main strip that offers traditional pub accommodation with reasonable double rooms (shared facilities) and an en-suite apartment. $135

EATING AND DRINKING

Beechworth Bakery 27 Camp St ⓦbeechworthbakery.com.au. This balconied bakery is an Australian icon, though the pies (around $5), bread, cakes and pastries are on the stodgy side. Daily 6am–7pm.

Beechworth Pantry 77 Ford St ☎03 5728 2456 ⓦbeechworthpantry.com.au. Occupying a double-fronted shop, this deli-coffee shop serves delicious sandwiches ($10), platters for two ($32–40), coffee, cakes, milkshakes and "spiders" (ice cream in flavoured lemonade). Its shelves are stocked with assorted delicious relishes and other regional foodstuffs. Daily 9am–5.30pm.

Bridge Road Brewers Ford St ☎03 5728 2703 ⓦbridgeroadbrewers.com.au. Occupying an old coach house behind *Tanswell's Commercial Hotel*, this is one of Australia's best craft breweries, with a range of fantastic ales and pizzas ($9.50–22), including gluten-free. Mon–Wed 11am–4pm, Thurs 11am–5pm, Fri–Sun 11am–10pm; food: Mon–Thurs noon–3pm, Fri–Sun noon–3 & 6pm–8.30pm.

The Ox and Hound Bistro 52 Ford St ☎03 5728 2123, ⓦoxandhound.com.au. A gold-era shop with a beautiful pressed metal ceiling and wicker chairs is the setting for classic Italian and French dishes featuring locally foraged foods. Mains (from $30) such as pan-fried trout with red cabbage might be followed by delicious house-made ice cream. Reservations recommended. Mon & Tues 6pm–late, Fri–Sun noon–2.30pm & 6pm–late.

Provenance 86 Ford St ☎03 5728 1786, ⓦtheprovenance.com.au. The stately *Provenance* in the gold-era Bank of Australasia building creates remarkable original à la carte (two courses $63, three courses $80) and degustation ($100) menus with a contemporary Japanese flavour. Bookings advisable. Wed–Sun 6.30pm–late.

The Victorian Alps

The **VICTORIAN ALPS**, the southern section of the Great Dividing Range, bear little resemblance to their European counterparts; they're too gentle, too rounded, and above all too low to offer really great **skiing**, although they remain a popular winter sports destination. In July and August there is usually plenty of snow and the resorts are packed out. Most people come for the downhill skiing, though **cross-country skiing** is also popular, particularly at Falls Creek, Dinner Plain, Mount Buffalo and **Lake Mountain** (ⓦlakemountainresort.com.au), 21km from Marysville (south of the main Alpine region). **Snowboarding** was first encouraged at Mount Hotham and is now firmly established everywhere. **Falls Creek**, **Mount Hotham** and **Mount Buller** are the largest and most commercial skiing areas, particularly the last, which is within easy reach of Melbourne; smaller resorts such as **Mount Baw Baw** in Gippsland (see p.861) are more suited to beginners.

The towns of **Mansfield**, **Bright** and **Mount Beauty** are good bases for exploring the Alps, and are great places to unwind. In summer there are activities such as hiking, horseriding and cycling; fewer facilities are open, but there are often great bargains to be had on rooms. If you're **driving**, you'll need snow chains in winter (they're compulsory in many parts), and you should heed local advice before venturing off the main roads.

Mansfield

MANSFIELD is located at the junction of the Maroondah and Midland highways, just a few kilometres north of Lake Eildon, 140km east of Seymour and 63km south of Benalla. As the main approach to Mount Buller, it's a lively place with good pubs, restaurants and a cinema. The annual highlight is the **Mansfield High Country Festival** (ⓦhighcountryfestival.com.au), which begins in late October and runs to Melbourne

BUSHWALKING IN ALPINE NATIONAL PARK

In summer, when the wild flowers are in bloom, the Alps are ideal **bushwalking** territory, as most of the high mountains (and the ski resorts) are contained within the vast **Alpine National Park**. The most famous of the walks is the 650km **Australian Alps Walking Track** (ⓦ australianalps.environment.gov.au) that begins at Walhalla, near Baw Baw National Park in Gippsland, and follows the ridges to Mount Kosciuszko in the Snowy Mountains of New South Wales, before continuing to Namadgi National Park in the Australian Capital Territory. If you are doing any serious bushwalking, you'll need to be properly equipped. Water can be hard to find, and the weather can change suddenly and unexpectedly: even in summer it can get freezing cold up here, especially at night. After prolonged dry spells, **bushfires** can also pose a very real threat, as was the case in 2009, when bushland and resorts were burnt.

Cup Day (first Tuesday in November). Activities include horseracing, parades, music and arts events.

ARRIVAL AND INFORMATION   MANSFIELD

By bus V/Line has a year-round bus service from Melbourne to Mansfield (1–2 daily; 3hr). There are also buses to Mount Buller in snow season.

Tourist information The helpful Mansfield Visitor Information Centre, 175 High St (daily 9am–5pm; ☏ 03 5775 7000 or ☏ 1800 039 049 for accommodation bookings, ⓦ mansfieldmtbuller.com.au), has oodles of information on all sights and activities in the Mansfield and Mount Buller region, including skiing and walks. Outside the snow season, you have a choice of horseriding, hiking, climbing, abseiling, hang-gliding, rafting, canoeing or 4WD tours.

Outdoor activities One of many local outfits, Stirling Experience (☏ 03 5777 6441, ⓦ stirlingexperience .com.au) offers winter and summer (such as walking and cycling) adventures around Mount Buller and neighbouring Mount Stirling.

ACCOMMODATION AND EATING

Alzburg Resort 39 Malcolm St ☏ 1300 885 448, ⓦ alzburg.com.au. A resort hotel with all mod cons, a restaurant and bar, and a variety of accommodation styles – from motel units to luxury penthouse apartments. **$190**

The Delatite Hotel Cnr High & Highett sts ☏ 03 5775 2004, ⓦ hoteldelatite.com.au. A true country pub with a bistro and clean rooms, some with shared facilities, which is popular with workers. Rates include Continental breakfast. **$90**

The Magnolia 190 Mount Buller Rd ☏ 03 5779 1000, ⓦ magnoliamansfield.com.au. Stylish B&B accommodation (three rooms, one three-bedroom apartment) in a charming early 1900s house. The restaurant serves Italian-style cuisine and is open for dinner Thurs–Sat from 6pm. Breakfast is included. **$120**

Mansfield Traveller's Lodge 116 High St ☏ 03 5775 1800, ⓦ mansfieldtravellerslodge.com.au. Friendly motel with neat rooms and a good backpackers' in a separate building next door. Dorms **$40**, doubles **$160**

The Produce Store 68 High St ☏ 03 5779 1404, ⓦ theproducestore.com.au. This excellent rustic store and café features baked goods, coffee, local wines and regional produce from its changing blackboard menu, with mains including lamb shank soup ($13–27). Mon–Thurs, Sat & Sun 9am–5pm, Fri 9am–late.

Mount Buller Resort

To reach **MOUNT BULLER RESORT**, 48km from Mansfield, you gradually ascend on the smooth, sealed Summit Road. With 7000 beds, 22 ski lifts and 80km of runs, the village has the greatest capacity of any Australian ski resort. The most popular summer activity here (ⓦ mtbuller.com.au/summer) is mountain biking, while neighbouring Mount Stirling offers hiking, horseriding and 4WD trails.

ARRIVAL AND INFORMATION   MOUNT BULLER

By bus During the ski season, Mansfield–Mount Buller Bus Lines, 137 High St, Mansfield (☏ 03 5775 2606, ⓦ mmbl .com.au), operate a transport service from Mansfield to Mount Buller up to ten times a day. They also run Ski Express from Melbourne to Mt Buller via Melbourne Airport (3 weekly; 3.5hr).

Tourist information For general information on Mount Buller and Mount Stirling, contact the Mansfield Visitor Information Centre (see above); Mansfield–Mt Buller High Country Reservations (☏ 1800 039 049,

9

Ⓦmansfieldmtbuller.com.au) and *Mount Buller Resort* (Ⓣ1800 285 537, Ⓦmtbuller.com.au) detail a wide range of accommodation for all budgets.

ACCOMMODATION AND EATING

Akla Ski Club 36 The Avenue Ⓣ0401 711 959, Ⓦakla.com.au. This comfortable self-catering timber lodge close to the village centre has five good-value en-suite four-bed rooms, a fully equipped kitchen and a communal lounge/dining area. **$270**

Arlberg Hotel 189 Summit Rd Ⓣ1800 032 380, Ⓦarlberg.com.au. Huge "ski-in/ski-out" property with a variety of rooms and five- to eight-bed self-contained apartments. Also has bars and restaurants to suit most budgets. **$285**

Buller Central Hotel The Avenue Ⓣ0499 004 946, Ⓦbullercentral.com.au. Unbeatable location in the centre of the village, with four-share rooms and one- and two bedroom apartments, plus large lounges. There's also a winter-only in-house Italian restaurant. Weekend rates (€950 peak season) include breakfast and two-course dinner. **$350**

Duck Inn 18 Goal Post Rd Ⓣ03 5777 6326, Ⓦduckinnmtbuller.com. Cosy boutique hotel with rooms that sleep from two to six people. Also has an excellent restaurant on the premises with mains around $38. Breakfast included, but wi-fi is an additional charge. **$420**

Bright and around

BRIGHT is at the centre of the picturesque Ovens Valley, between Mount Buffalo and Mount Beauty, about 75km southeast of Wangaratta on the Great Alpine Road. It began life as a gold-mining town in the 1850s and today has a faintly elegant air, with tall European trees lining the main street and filling the parks. A clear stream flows through Centenary Park, opposite the visitor centre, and in autumn the glorious colours of the changing leaves create a very un-Australian scene.

As the ski fields of Mount Hotham, Falls Creek and Mount Buffalo are less than an hour's drive away, Bright is a popular **ski base** in winter. In summer **outdoor activities** are on offer – such as paragliding, hang-gliding, caving, bushwalking, horseriding and cycling. For gentler-paced activity, try the two circular **walks** (5km) that lead out of town along the river.

Mount Buffalo National Park

Six kilometres northwest of Bright, you can turn off the Great Alpine Road into **Mount Buffalo National Park**, which encompasses a huge plateau around Mount Buffalo, and

---

SKIING IN THE VICTORIAN ALPS

The official start of the **ski season** is the Queen's Birthday long weekend in June, though there is often not enough snow cover until August, and it lasts through to early October. During the snow season, a daily entry fee of $37–43.50 per car applies, depending on the resort. As a rough guide to **costs**, lift tickets range from $50–115/day, while group **lessons** cost around $60–70. Full equipment rental is about $85/day. For **weather** and snow conditions go to Ⓦski.com.au. For accommodation, phone the central reservation hotlines of each mountain resort.

In addition to the resorts detailed here, there is also skiing at Mount Baw Baw in Gippsland (see p.861).

PACKAGES AND TOURS

Day-trip or weekend **packages** are the best way to go, and are far cheaper than trying to do it yourself. The best-value trips are organized by *Alzburg Resort* at Mansfield (Ⓣ1300 885 448, Ⓦalzburg.com.au). The day-tours leave Melbourne early in the morning and arrive at Mount Buller about two-and-a-half hours later, giving the opportunity for a full day's skiing (from $90, including entrance fees; a one-day lift/lesson ticket is $121 extra). There's also a "return another day" bus service, costing $190 and including entrance fees but not accommodation.

It's also worth checking out the area around Hardware Lane in Melbourne, where such companies as Auski at no. 9 (Ⓣ03 9670 1412, Ⓦauski.com.au) and Mountain Designs at 373 Little Bourke St (Ⓣ03 9670 3354, Ⓦmountaindesigns.com) can advise on skiing conditions at the resorts, and sell or rent equipment.

has a number of beautiful walking tracks and spectacular abseiling pitches, plus tobogganing and good cross-country skiing on 24km of marked trails. There is no public transport to the park so a car is essential. Accommodation can be found in Bright, or you can camp here at Lake Catani in the summer months (Nov–April; booking essential through Parks Victoria on ☎13 19 63 or ⓦparkstay.vic.gov.au).

Boynton's Feathertop Winery

6619 Great Alpine Rd, Porepunkah • Daily 10am–5pm • ☎03 5756 2356, ⓦboynton.com.au

For a change of pace, visit **Boynton's Feathertop Winery**, 10km northwest of Bright at Porepunkah, on the northeast slopes of the Ovens Valley. Enjoy the spectacular views of Mount Buffalo while sampling a house wine – they specialize in cool-climate wines. You can enjoy fine Mediterranean-inspired cuisine at the *Alfresco Dining Restaurant* (Thurs–Mon noon–3pm), which moves out onto the winery's terrace in the warmer months, and food platters are available from the deli (daily 10am–5pm).

Wandiligong

From Bright you follow a walking/cycling path (or drive) for 6km to **WANDILIGONG**, a beautiful National Trust-registered village, where you'll find the **Wandiligong Maze and Café** (11 White Star Rd; Wed–Sun 10am–4.30pm; closed Aug; $12; ⓦwandimaze .com.au). The hedge maze itself is a lot of fun, but the licensed café is a wonderful find, serving salads, freshly squeezed juices and home-made treats, in a tranquil garden setting.

ARRIVAL AND INFORMATION   BRIGHT

By bus V/Line operates a daily bus service to Bright from Wangaratta (1–3 daily; 1hr 30min) via Beechworth (1–3 daily; 1hr).

Tourist information The Alpine Visitor Information Centre at 119 Gavan St (daily 9am–5pm; ☎03 5755 0584 or ☎1800 111 885, ⓦvisitbright.com.au) has information on what's happening around town and can also book accommodation.

ACTIVITIES

Abseiling Adventure Guides Australia (☎03 5728 1804 or ☎0419 280 614, ⓦadventureguidesaustralia .com.au), run abseiling on Mt Buffalo, from learn-the-ropes beginner sessions (from $90) to a multi-pitch day on the 300m North Wall.

Bike rental Cyclepath, 74 Gavan St (☎03 5750 1442, ⓦcyclepath.com.au), rents mountain bikes from $35/hour or $50/day.

Paragliding Alpine Paragliding, 6 Ireland St (☎0407 573 879, ⓦalpineparagliding.com), organizes tandem flights for novices (from $130/10min), and introductory and full courses leading to a licence.

Skiing Adina Ski Hire, 15 Ireland St (☎03 5755 1177, ⓦadina.com.au), and Bright Ski Centre, 22 Ireland St (☎03 5755 1093, ⓦbrightskicentre.com.au), rent skiing and snowboarding equipment, offer package deals including off-mountain accommodation and transport to Mount Hotham, and have up-to-date snow and road reports.

ACCOMMODATION

Alpine Hotel 7 Anderson St ☎1300 581 117, ⓦalpinehotelbright.com.au. This charming redbrick place is the focal point of town, with motel units behind the main building, excellent breakfasts and good-value bistro meals. No internet. **$95**

Bright Riverside Holiday Park 4–10 Toorak Rd ☎03 5755 1118, ⓦbrhp.com.au. Great riverside location in the heart of town, offering good-value cabins (four to six people) and holiday units sleeping up to five. **$185**

★**The Buckland Luxury Retreat** McCormacks Lane, Buckland Valley ☎0419 133 318, ⓦthebuckland .com.au. Situated 12km out of town, this eco-oasis has four studio houses and a one-bed chalet all with first-class amenities in a very relaxing rural setting. Not cheap, but popular with the weekend getaway crowd. Generally two nights minimum; rates include full breakfast. No children. **$335**

Coach House Inn 100 Gavan St ☎1800 813 992, ⓦcoachhousebright.com.au. Mid-priced motel near the visitor centre with eighteen spacious one- and two-bedroom units with some character. Great communal BBQ gazebo area, plus a pool and restaurant. **$127**

Elm Lodge 6 Wood St ☎0430 075 678, ⓦelmlodge .com.au. Good value and centrally located, this place offers self-contained studios and one- and two-bedroom cottages in a beautiful garden. There's a free laundry, a BBQ area and facilities for washing and storing mountain bikes. **$150**

9

EATING AND DRINKING

Alpine Hotel 7 Anderson St ☎03 5755 1366, ⓦpubsbright.com. Good-value bistro meals (pizzas are a speciality, from $12.50) with a sunny beer garden; bands play on Sat nights. Daily noon–2pm & 5.30–8.30pm.

Bright Brewery 121 Great Alpine Rd (near visitor centre) ☎03 5755 1301, ⓦbrightbrewery.com. Popular brewery attracting crowds with its multi-award-winning beers, good salads, platters, meat mains and pizzas ($20–25) and a relaxed outdoor setting. Tasting tours available ($18) and there's live music on Sun afternoons. Daily noon–3pm & 5.30–8.30pm.

Coral Lee 8 Barnard St ☎03 5755 5113. This cute retro place sells the best coffee in town, plus oversized cakes and biscuits, and vegetarian meals. Most dishes $10–30. Mon–Sat 8.30am–5pm, Sun 8.30am–4pm.

Ginger Baker Wine Bar & Café 127 Great Alpine Rd ☎03 5755 2300, ⓦgingerbaker.com.au. Beside the Ovens River and with a large outdoor dining area, this funky café does great breakfasts ($8–17) and sharing plates (up to $15) for lunch and dinner. Mon–Wed, Fri & Sat 8am–3pm, Thurs & Sun 8am–3pm & 6–9pm.

Riverdeck Café 119 Gavan St ☎03 5755 2199. Hearty breakfasts and great deli salads and sandwiches with a lovely outdoor area facing the river. Most dishes $9–16. Daily 8.30am–5pm.

★**Simone's** 98 Gavan St ☎03 5755 2266, ⓦsimonesbright.com.au. One of rural Victoria's top Italian restaurants. Given the quality of the cooking the prices are reasonable, with starters around $25 and mains, including a honey caramelized local trout dish, up to $45. Or you can opt for a degustation menu ($110; bookings recommended). They also run a cooking school. Licensed and BYO. Tues–Sat 6.30pm–late.

Tani Eat & Drink 100 Gavan St ☎03 5728 6502, ⓦtanieatdrink.com.au. Informal, original café-bar delivering modern Japanese-influenced sharing dishes, such as miso-painted boned quail with fermented cabbage. Starters $6–10. Select two ($50) or three ($72) courses or go with their selection and tuck into a six-course set menu ($88). Wed–Sun 6pm–late.

Thirteen Steps 14 Barnard St ☎03 5750 1313, ⓦthirteensteps.com.au. An atmospheric underground bistro and wine bar offering dishes to share, such as crumbed buffalo mozzarella with ruby grapefruit, priced from $16–39. Thurs–Mon 6–11pm.

Mount Hotham

Beyond Harrietville, a pretty village of wide, tree-lined streets 25km southeast of Bright, a steep ascent takes you to **Mount Hotham** in Alpine National Park, the state's highest ski area and self-proclaimed "powder snow capital of Australia". All this actually means is that the snow here can be marginally less sticky than elsewhere. Victorian **snowboarding** started here, and **Mount Hotham Alpine Resort** offers lots of special facilities, equipment rental and lessons; the resort has 320 hectares of ski terrain and thirteen lifts.

Dinner Plain, a resort village 10km from the summit of Mount Hotham and about 1500m above sea level, has more of a cosy, alpine-village feel – complete with architect-designed timber houses that are meant to resemble cattlemen's mountain huts – than the somewhat unsightly Hotham resort. With 35km of groomed cross-country trails around the village and a 10km trail leading to Mount Hotham, Dinner Plain is really the domain of cross-country skiers.

ARRIVAL AND INFORMATION
MOUNT HOTHAM

By helicopter Helicopter shuttle-flights in winter link Mount Hotham with Falls Creek ($170 return; ☎1300 731 450, ⓦforestair.com.au), only seven minutes away by air, where you can ski or snowboard on the same lift pass.

Tourist information The following websites offer general information about the area: ⓦdinnerplain.com and ⓦmthotham.com.au. A few centres handle bookings for the mainly lodge-style accommodation: Hotham Holidays (☎1800 468 426, ⓦhothamholidays.com.au); Mount Hotham Accommodation (☎1800 657 547, ⓦmthothamaccommodation.com.au); and Dinner Plain (☎1800 670 019, ⓦdinnerplain.com).

GETTING AROUND

By bus During the ski season, buses ferry skiers around Mount Hotham Alpine Resort and to the start of cross-country trails and skiing areas (6.45am until late; free). A regular shuttle-bus ($20 return) also ferries downhill skiers from Dinner Plain to Mount Hotham.

Mount Beauty and Falls Creek

Some 30km east of Bright, in the Upper Kiewa Valley, the town of **MOUNT BEAUTY** lies at the base of the state's highest peak, Mount Bogong (1986m). **FALLS CREEK RESORT**, 32km further along, on the edge of the Bogong High Plains, has more of a village feel than its sister resort at Mount Hotham. It also has probably Victoria's **best skiing** and the largest snow-making system in Victoria to supplement any shortage of the real stuff. There are fifteen lifts, a wide variety of downhill pistes and good cross-country trails. **Snowboarding** is really big here, too, and in addition there are rides on snowmobiles and snowbikes, and a tube park for snowtubing, tobogganing and snowshoeing.

ARRIVAL AND INFORMATION   MOUNT BEAUTY AND FALLS CREEK

By helicopter Helicopter shuttle-flights in winter link Mount Hotham with Falls Creek ($170 return; ☎ 1300 731 450, ⓦ forestair.com.au), only seven minutes away by air, where you can ski or snowboard on the same lift pass.

Tourist information General information on the area is available from the Mount Beauty Visitor Information Centre

(daily 9am–5pm; ☎ 03 5755 0596, ⓦ visitmountbeauty. com.au) at 31 Bogong High Plains Rd, and the Falls Creek Visitor Information Centre (daily 10am–3pm, longer during the ski season; ☎ 03 5758 1200, ⓦ fallscreek .com.au).

ACCOMMODATION AND EATING

Falls Creek has a good range of lodges, apartments and resorts – for bookings and information, contact **Falls Creek Central Reservations** (☎ 1800 232 557, ⓦ fallscreek.com.au). The budget-conscious would do best to stay in Mount Beauty and travel to Falls Creek to ski: enquire about packages at the Mount Beauty Visitor Information Centre (see above). Falls Creek offers a host of dining options, with many of the pubs, **restaurants** and cafés staying open in summer.

Dreamers Spa Village 218 Kiewa Valley Hwy, Mt Beauty ☎ 03 5754 1222, ⓦ dreamersmtbeauty .com.au. Accommodation on this five-acre mountain-view property ranges from stone-and-timber studio spa rooms (not available during peak season) to luxurious split-level rammed earth three-bedroom eco-apartments featuring recycled timbers, some with private courtyards. They're not cheap but they're definitely special. Fee for wi-fi. $310

The Man Hotel 20 Slalom St, Falls Creek ☎ 03 5758 3362, ⓦ themanfallscreek.com.au. A cosy pub serving tasty gourmet pizzas (from $19) and other bistro-style

meals (under $25). There's also a lounge bar and live entertainment. Daily 4pm–late.

Mountain Creek Motel 6 Mountain Creek Rd, Tawonga (north of Mount Beauty) ☎ 03 5754 4247, ⓦ mountaincreekmotel.com. Standard motel units and bunk rooms, plus a guest kitchen, laundry, swimming pool and sauna/spa. Dorms $42, doubles $135

Skafferi Café & Produce Store 84 Bogong High Plains Rd, Mount Beauty ☎ 03 5754 4544, ⓦ skafferi.com.au. Great coffee and cakes and delicious Swedish food – herrings and meatballs, of course – served against a mountain backdrop. Mon & Thurs–Sun 8am–4pm.

Tasmania

CRADLE MOUNTAIN–LAKE ST CLAIR NATIONAL PARK

Tasmania

It used to be a "mainlander's" joke that Tasmania was twenty years behind the rest of Australia. And in some ways this island state remains old-fashioned, a trait that is charming and frustrating by turns. Yet increasingly Australians are beginning to wonder whether the joke might have been on them after all. The isolation that once stymied growth in Tasmania is now seen as an asset. More and more Aussies find themselves lured across the Bass Strait by the relaxed pace of life and outstanding wine and cuisine, as much as the state's famously pristine environment. An increasing number of luxury hotels have appeared, too – chintz and doilies in heritage stays are out, cool contemporary beach houses are in – and Australia's most cutting-edge gallery, MONA in Hobart, definitively refutes accusations that Tasmania is backwards. The Tasmanian landscape – vast swathes of rainforest that date back to the last ice age, jagged glaciated mountains and white-powder beaches – still brings many visitors to the island. Even if you're not particularly outdoorsy, the experience of visiting such a pure environment brings a tingle of exhilaration.

Tasmania has come a long way since it was known as Van Diemen's Land and was Britain's dumping ground for the worst of the worst convicts. Its name became so tainted with penal brutality that the state decided to rebrand when transportation ended in 1853. Until the past couple of decades, the island retained a reputation as somewhere brooding, almost gothic, and it was also renowned for its ties to the old country. Roughly the size of Ireland, Tasmania has rolling hills, hawthorn hedges and stone villages that recall England's West Country, largely in the midlands between its two largest cities, the capital Hobart and Launceston in the north.

Yet if anything defines (and divides) Tasmania it is the environment. This is the closest point in Australia to the Antarctic Circle; the next land west is Argentina, and air monitoring stations record the air in the state's northwest as the purest in the world. With forty percent of the island protected in parks and reserves, Tasmania is one of the cleanest places on earth. Much of the southwest is pure wilderness; a place of wild rivers, temperate rainforests, buttongrass plains and glacially carved mountains and tarns. Protected as a vast **World Heritage Area**, it offers some of the best wilderness walking and rafting in the world.

BAY OF FIRES

Highlights

❶ Hobart Whether at Salamanca Market or modern art sensation MONA, the state capital is quietly gaining a reputation for its alternative culture. **See p.889**

❷ Tasman Peninsula The infamous penal settlement at Port Arthur is haunting, but don't overlook the jaw-dropping coast, seen on bushwalks or an eco-cruise. **See p.913**

❸ Freycinet National Park Tasmania's great escape, whether the easy walk to Wineglass Bay or a four-day expedition deep into the bush. **See p.922**

❹ Bay of Fires A string of perfect beaches – azure sea and powder-white sands – with bush camps that are free to stay at for up to four weeks. **See p.926**

❺ Tamar Valley Tasmania's astonishingly pure environment is a natural provider of high-quality dining and drinking – and the vineyards of the Tamar Valley is one of the best regions to experience this. **See p.935**

❻ Cradle Mountain–Lake St Clair National Park Famed for the six-day Overland Track bushwalk, the park's rugged, glaciated landscape is also littered with rewarding day-hikes. **See p.953**

❼ Franklin River Raft one of the world's most thrilling whitewater roller-coasters and see first-hand why Australians fought to protect Tasmania's last wild river. **See p.963**

HIGHLIGHTS ARE MARKED ON THE MAP ON P.886

Cradle Mountain in the centre and Strahan on the west coast are the gateways from which most people experience the wild, and they form two stops on a much-travelled loop that includes capital Hobart, with its must-see Museum of Old and New Art and burgeoning food and arts scenes; convict history on the Tasman Peninsula; the string of beautiful beaches along the sunnier, drier east coast, the state's holiday playground; and Launceston, the state's second city and gateway to the vineyards of the Tamar Valley. Tick off the lot and you'll have a taste of the state. Yet those less-visited corners are equally appealing: places like the far south down to Cockle Creek, a blend of wilderness, scenery and food culture; the sparsely populated northeast corner, home to the mesmerizing Bay

HIGHLIGHTS

1. Hobart
2. Tasman Peninsula
3. Freycinet National Park
4. Bay of Fires
5. Tamar Valley
6. Cradle Mountain–Lake St Clair National Park
7. Franklin River

TASMANIA

of Fires beaches and **Mount William National Park**, a haven for Forester kangaroos; or small resorts in the northwest like pretty **Stanley** or the isolated shack villages at Arthur River. All are places to slow down; to discover astonishing scenery and wildlife, perhaps settle into a free bush camp for the night and revel in the purity of this environment.

Brief history

The Dutch navigator **Abel Tasman** sighted the island in 1642. Landing a party on its east coast, he named it **Van Diemen's Land** in honour of the governor of the Dutch East Indies. Early maps showed it connected to the mainland, and several eighteenth-century French and British navigators, including Bruny d'Entrecasteaux, William Bligh and James Cook did not prove otherwise. It was Matthew Flinders' discovery of the **Bass Strait** in 1798 that confirmed Tasmania as an island (and reduced the journey to Sydney by a week). In 1803, after a French expedition had been observed in the island's southern waters, it was decided to establish a second **colony** in Australia, and Lieutenant David Bowen settled with a group of convicts on the banks of the Derwent River at Risdon Cove. In the same year, Lieutenant-Colonel John Collins set out from England with another group to settle the Port Phillip district of what would become Victoria; after a few months they gave up and crossed the Bass Strait to join Bowen's group.

Hobart Town was founded in 1804 and the first **penal settlement** opened at Macquarie Harbour (Strahan) in 1821, followed by Maria Island and Port Arthur; they were mainly for convicts who had committed secondary offences after transportation. Lurid tales of the harsh conditions and violent regime enshrined Van Diemen's Land in British folklore as a prison-island hell. In truth, many convicts enjoyed higher standards of living than they had in British and Irish slums, and some free settlers made fortunes.

The environmental debate

Tasmania's recent history has been shaped not by the postwar industrialization and immigration that transformed the mainland, but by battles over **natural resources**. Forests, fast-flowing rivers and mountainous terrain meant that forestry and hydroelectricity schemes began early here. The flooding of **Lake Pedder** in 1972 for the HEC (Hydro Electricity Commission) led to the formation of the **Wilderness Society**, a conservation organization that went on to lead the largest civilian protest in Australian history in 1982 – the **Franklin Blockade** (see box, p.965), which saved one of Tasmania's last wild rivers and led to World Heritage status for a fifth of the state. Bitter controversy over the balance between conservation and exploitation of natural resources has long polarized the state's population between "greenies" and loggers.

Yet after more than thirty years of conflict, sometimes fought tree by tree, the future is still uncertain. After a moratorium on logging in 2010, the World Heritage area was extended by 170,000 hectares in June 2013 to include high-value old-growth forest in the **Styx Valley** (see p.907), the nearby Weld and Upper Florentine valleys, and the Great Western Tiers around Lake St Clair (see p.953). Simultaneously, a moratorium on logging remains in forests of the **Blue Tier** (see p.928). Yet although state forestry arm Forestry Tasmania seems to accept the need for reform, forced by a collapse in native timber markets, the battle continues. In early 2013, as timber prices slumped and prices for iron ore and bauxite soared through Asian demand, the federal government approved open-cut mining in the Tarkine region in the northwest (see box, p.951), also home to the largest Gondwanan rainforest in Australia. An appeal to the Federal Court by the Save the Tarkine movement (⊚ tarkine.org) was lost in mid-2015. In late 2014, the Tasmanian Government repealed the Tasmanian Forests Intergovernmental Agreement (widely seen as a forestry "peace deal" which protected old-growth forest) and removed 400,000 hectares of forest from reserve status. At the time of writing, other challenges were being faced, as summer bushfires raged through parts of Tasmania's west and north, razing more than 100,000 hectares, including about two per cent of the World Heritage areas.

10

NATIONAL PARKS AND BUSHWALKING

All **national parks** in Tasmania charge daily **entry fees**, which you can pay for online (W passes.parks.tas.gov.au) before arrival. A 24-hour pass costs $12 per pedestrian or cyclist, or $24 per vehicle (including up to eight passengers); and an eight-week Holiday Pass costs $30 per person or $60 per vehicle. This doesn't include camping fees, though many sites are free.

Tasmania's wilderness has always attracted thousands of **bushwalkers**, and many tracks are boardwalks to avoid erosion to the fragile park environments. The Tasmania Parks and Wildlife Service's website (W parks.tas.gov.au) offers walking guidelines, which are also available in the leaflet *Before You Walk* from the PWS desk at the Service Tasmania shops in Hobart (134 Macquarie St; ☏ 1300 135 513) and 26 other locations around the state. Detailed **Tasmaps** (from $6.95) of walking tracks are available in most visitor centres, outdoors shops and Service Tasmania outlets.

Never underestimate the Tasmanian wilderness. It can be dangerous – even lethal – if you're ill-prepared; the weather changes rapidly, and even on a warm day, hail, sleet or snow can suddenly descend in the highlands where hypothermia is a possibility even in summer. Never go alone, always inform others of your plans, and sign in and out of walks in the books provided at the start of a track. As a minimum, you'll need wet-weather gear, thermal clothing, walking boots, a sturdy tent, warm sleeping bag, fuel cooking stove, maps and a compass. Gear can be rented from shops in Hobart and Launceston.

WHEN TO GO

The weather Notwithstanding a record 41°C, it rarely gets above 30°C during the day in Tasmania, even in high summer, and the weather is notoriously changeable, particularly in the uplands, where it can sleet and snow at any time of year; the most stable month is Feb. Winter (June–Aug) can drop to freezing at night even in the more temperate east coast; daytime temperatures average 12°C. Wilderness walks are best left to the most experienced and well equipped at this time of year.

INFORMATION

Tourist information Excellent tourist offices (W discovertasmania.com.au) in gateways Hobart, Launceston and Devonport provide information on, and bookings for, transport, tours and accommodation statewide. *Tasmanian Travelways* (W travelways.com.au) is a handy, free listings magazine stocked by tourist offices and packed with information on everything from accommodation to attractions and bus timetables.

GETTING THERE

BY PLANE

Fierce competition between airlines means competitive prices for flights to Tasmania. A typical advance fare from Melbourne to Launceston one-way is $70–100, though websites can offer deals as low as $50. Virgin Australia (☏ 13 67 89, W virginaustralia.com/au) has direct services from Sydney, Melbourne and Brisbane to both Hobart and Launceston. Qantas (☏ 13 13 00, W qantas.com.au) has direct flights from Melbourne and Sydney to Hobart and from Melbourne to Launceston and Devonport. Qantas's budget arm, Jetstar (☏ 13 15 38, W jetstar.com.au), flies from Melbourne to Hobart and Launceston, from Brisbane to Launcest, and from Sydney to Hobart. Tiger Air (☏ 1300 174 266 or ☏ 07 3295 2104, W tigerair.com.au) flies from Melbourne to Hobart. Rex Airlines (☏ 13 17 13, W rex.com.au) flies from Melbourne to Burnie/Wynyard.
Brisbane to: Hobart (daily; 2hr 50min); Launceston (daily; 3hr 30min).

Melbourne to: Burnie (4 daily; 1hr 10min); Devonport (3 daily; 1hr 5min); Hobart (16 daily; 1hr); Launceston (10 daily; 1hr).
Sydney to: Hobart (5 daily; 1hr 50min); Launceston (daily; 1hr 35min).

BY FERRY

Entry by ferry is only worth considering if you have your own car or bike. It's a ten-hour trip across the Bass Strait on Spirit of Tasmania ferries (☏ 1800 634 906, W spiritoftasmania.com.au) from Port Melbourne to Devonport, and fares are rarely cheaper than flights. Evening sailings depart daily year-round; daytime services only operate a few times a week from September to April.
Fares Prices per person vary by season but are around $130. Cars under 2m in length cost $87 (one-way) while bikes/motorbikes cost $5/$60. For overnight sailings, you will also need to book either a cabin (shared or private) or a recliner chair (in a private lounge) in order to sleep. The costs soon add up.

TOUR AND EXPEDITION OPERATORS

Tasmania deserves at least a fortnight but if time and money are tight, tour operators will whisk you around the major sights. In addition, activity providers offer expeditions that are a holiday in their own right. All of those below include park entry fees and accommodation.

Green Island Tours ☎03 6376 3080, ⓦcycling-tasmania.com. Supported and self-guided cycle tours around the state, from five to thirteen days.

Jump Tours ☎03 6288 7030, ⓦjumptours .com.au. Young, lively backpacker tours that are among the cheapest available (though don't include meals), departing from Hobart and Launceston. Hostel accommodation with an opportunity to upgrade from dorms.

Pepper Bush Adventures ☎03 6352 2263, ⓦpepperbush.com.au. High-end bespoke tours with unique experiences and good tucker from one of the best wildlife guides in the state, Craig "Bushy" Williams. Based in Launceston.

Rafting Tasmania ☎0422 642 190, ⓦraftingtasmania.com.au. One of the most experienced providers of tours along the magic Franklin River – one of the world's greatest raft adventures over eight or ten days – but they also run day-trips on the King River, near Queenstown.

Tarkine Trails ☎0405 255 537, ⓦtarkinetrails .com.au. Speciality operator for the northwest Tarkine region; four- and six-day coastal and forest walks.

Tasmanian Expeditions ☎1300 666 856, ⓦtasmanianexpeditions.com.au. This Launceston-based company is the leading adventure provider in the state. Trips cover all wilderness walks (including some serious expeditions) and the company acts as a retailer for upmarket cabin-based walks, plus cycle and multi-activity trips.

Under Down Under Tours ☎1800 444 442, ⓦunderdownunder.com.au. Small-group hostel-based backpacker tours offering two- to eight-day trips taking in the major sights, with short walks in national parks, plus breakfasts. Also operates day-trips to major sights from Hobart and Launceston.

GETTING AROUND

Given the vagaries of the bus system and difficulty of reaching wilderness destinations, most travellers rent a car. Otherwise, several backpacker tours will whisk you (fairly rapidly) around the state's highlights, and guided adventure tour operators generally include transport from the cities.

BY BUS

Between them, main operators TassieLink (☎1300 300 520, ⓦtassielink.com.au) and Redline (☎1300 360 000, ⓦtasredline.com.au) cover major destinations. Services between the cities and larger towns are regular. Elsewhere they can be erratic, especially at weekends on the east and west coasts, and change again during school holidays. TassieLink's services to either end of the Overland Track benefits bushwalkers. In addition, private operators like Cradle Mountain Coaches in Devonport (☎03 6427 7626 or ☎0448 800 599, ⓦcradlemountaincoaches.com.au) run bushwalker transfers to central state walks, including the Cradle Mountain–Lake St Clair area and Walls of Jerusalem National Park.

BY CAR

A car is by far the most rewarding way to see the state.

Be aware that when you rent standard insurance only covers bitumen roads – few operators insure for dirt roads, which are safe enough if you drive slowly. Car hire companies will charge for mileage and distances are deceptive in Tassie – winding country roads mean trips take longer than their kilometre distances suggest. Drive cautiously at dusk and night, when wildlife is common on roads, and never argue with log trucks in forestry areas.

BY BIKE

Unlike other states, the shorter distances of Tasmania make cycling a viable option, although holiday traffic in summer demands careful thought about routes. Operators in Hobart and Launceston rent touring bikes, while Green Island Tours (☎03 6376 3080, ⓦcycling-tasmania.com) runs tours (see box below).

Hobart

Australia's most southerly city, state capital **HOBART** is small but beautifully sited. On one side is the broad Derwent River, with Mount Wellington rising behind the city, often dusted with snow in winter and a hint of the southwest wilderness beyond. Both conspire to give the city – despite its growing sophistication – a remote, frontier feel. For decades Hobart was derided as the backwater of Australia and the tourist experience was low-key; visitors came to eat and drink at the pubs near the old docks, or to browse the craft shops at the historic stone warehouses of Salamanca Place. But the opening of the MONA gallery in 2010 was a game-changer. Hobart has always had an alternative, creative streak, and today it hums with optimism and energy. Every weekend, interstate visitors fly in to see the gallery,

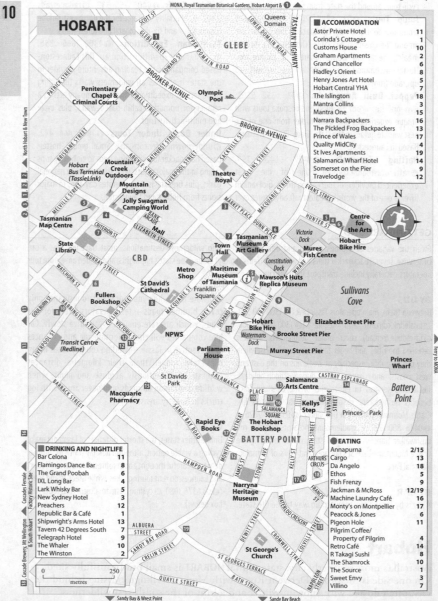

10

HOBART

■ ACCOMMODATION
Astor Private Hotel	11
Corinda's Cottages	1
Customs House	10
Graham Apartments	2
Grand Chancellor	6
Hadley's Orient	8
Henry Jones Art Hotel	7
Hobart Central YHA	7
The Islington	18
Mantra Collins	3
Mantra One	15
Narrara Backpackers	16
The Pickled Frog Backpackers	13
Prince of Wales	17
Quality MidCity	4
St Ives Apartments	19
Salamanca Wharf Hotel	14
Somerset on the Pier	9
Travelodge	12

■ DRINKING AND NIGHTLIFE
Bar Celona	11
Flamingos Dance Bar	8
The Grand Poobah	6
IXL Long Bar	4
Lark Whisky Bar	5
New Sydney Hotel	3
Preachers	12
Republic Bar & Café	1
Shipwright's Arms Hotel	13
Tavern 42 Degrees South	7
Telegraph Hotel	9
The Whaler	10
The Winston	2

● EATING
Annapurna	2/15
Cargo	13
Da Angelo	18
Ethos	5
Fish Frenzy	9
Jackman & McRoss	12/19
Machine Laundry Café	16
Monty's on Montpellier	17
Peacock & Jones	6
Pigeon Hole	11
Pilgrim Coffee/ Property of Pilgrim	4
Retro Café	14
R Takagi Sushi	8
The Shamrock	10
The Source	1
Sweet Envy	3
Villino	7

THE TASMANIAN TIGER

Few animals in Australia arouse such fascination as the **Tasmanian tiger (thylacine)**. The irony is that it's extinct. Probably. The peculiar, dog-like marsupial, which had a rigid tail, stripes, and a backwards-opening pouch, was hunted out of existence by sheep farmers fearful for their stock and encouraged by a bounty put on the creature's head from 1888 to 1909. The last animal is supposed to have died in Hobart Zoo in 1936. Yet thylacine sightings are still reported; ask around in remote areas of the northwest and southwest and someone will tell you they've seen one. And although Sydney's Australian Museum shelved plans to resurrect the species using DNA from pickled specimens in 2005, a research team at Pennsylvania University successfully sequenced the genetic data in 2008.

10

sample the profusion of smart restaurants, cafés and shops and enjoy the city's relaxed lifestyle.

This newly acquired gloss is laid over a fine architectural heritage, accounting for much of Hobart's appeal. Australia's second oldest city after Sydney, Hobart has escaped the worst excesses of developers, and its early buildings are better preserved than those in any other antipodean city. There's a wealth of Georgian architecture – more than ninety buildings are classified by the National Trust, most on Macquarie and Davey streets – while the urban village **Battery Point** has changed little in appearance since it was established in the mid nineteenth-century.

A couple of outstanding museums aside – not least MONA – Hobart has little that demands your attention, but much to enjoy. With its blossoming arts and food cultures, and its backdrops of water and historic buildings, the city has matured into a quirky, quietly self-assured capital. It's not nearly as contemporary as Sydney, Melbourne or even Perth, of course, nor would Hobartians want it to be. As they will be keen to tell you, its small size and relaxed pace make it one of Australia's most liveable capitals, and for visitors that makes it a great place in which to simply hang out. There are some great walks in its backyard, too.

The waterfront

Hobart is a city focused on its harbour. The core of the Central Business District (CBD)lies above **Sullivans Cove** and **Franklin Wharf**, the first commercial centre of Hobart, where merchants erected warehouses as the colony grew. Hobart developed into one of the world's great whaling centres in the 1830s, and to cater for the growing volume of shipping, a new wharf – **Princes Wharf** on the south side – was built, featuring a row of handsome sandstone warehouses on Salamanca Place. As the new wharf became the focus of port activity, the original wharf developed into an industrial centre of flour mills and factories.

Today the old docks are thriving: a fishing fleet still occupies **Victoria Dock**, and yachts share **Constitution Dock** with fish punts that sell fresh and cooked seafood alongside the Mures Fish Centre complex of restaurants and cafés. Elizabeth Street Pier meanwhile has acquired a slew of bars, restaurants and luxury hotel-apartments. Nearby Brooke Street Pier and Watermans Dock serve as the embarkation point for harbour **cruises** in all manner of craft, from replica brigantines to sleek modern catamarans.

Henry Jones Jam Factory

25 Hunter St • Free

Located within original stone warehouses, the former **Henry Jones Jam Factory** houses the **Centre for the Arts**, the University of Tasmania's art school, which is reached via a courtyard entrance. Here, the **Plimsoll Gallery** (daily noon–5pm; free; ☎03 6226 4300, ⓦutas.edu.au/plimsoll) occasionally hosts shows by contemporary Tasmanian artists. The bulk of the old factory has been redeveloped into a complex with the luxury *Henry Jones Art Hotel* (see p.897), a restaurant, bar and galleries. On the waterfront nearby,

10

sculptures and a plaque commemorate the links between Hobart and Antarctica, from the first expedition in 1839 when Captain James Clark Ross sailed from Hobart in the *Erebus* and *Terror* to locate the South Pole.

Tasmanian Museum and Art Gallery

Dunn Place • Tues–Sun 10am–4pm • Free • ☎ 03 6165 7000, ⓦ tmag.tas.gov.au

The interesting **Tasmanian Museum and Art Gallery** (aka **TMAG**) has an excellent collection that deserves half a day at least. The best place to start a visit is in the refurbished colonial bond store rather than the main building, going to the top floor to follow the story of colonial settlement told from the Aboriginal perspective in the exhibition **Our land: Parrawa, parrawa! Go away!** The exhibition continues, as Van Diemen's Land becomes Tasmania, with displays of Victorian furnishings, china and art from the homes of well-to-do merchants.

The main museum building ticks off many Tasmanian themes. One room is dedicated to the permanent exhibition "Ningina Tunapri" which celebrates **Tasmanian Aboriginal** culture and has replica shelters and reed boats, plus artefacts such as exquisite shell necklaces to provide a comprehensive account of the Aboriginal people, from their traditional lives to recent land-rights campaigns. Another room focuses on the extinct **Tasmanian tiger (thylacine)**, with famous footage of the island's last tigers, which died in Hobart Zoo in 1936 (see box, p.891). Upstairs on Level 2 is an excellent **gallery** of colonial art, featuring superb landscape paintings of Tasmania by the nineteenth-century artists **John Glover** and **W.C. Piguenit**, plus several iconic portraits of the well-known "last" Aborigines, painted by artists such as **Benjamin Duterrau** and **Thomas Bock** in the 1830s and 1840s. The same floor houses an "Islands to Ice" exhibit exploring Antarctic ecology and exploration – Tasmania has long been the launchpad for polar expeditions and maintains a scheduled air service to the continent during summer.

Maritime Museum of Tasmania

Cnr Argyle & Davey sts • Daily 9am–5pm • $9 • ☎ 03 6234 1427 • ⓦ maritimetas.org

The modest **Maritime Museum of Tasmania**, opposite TMAG, houses memorabilia, photographs and exhibits to introduce the history of Hobart as a maritime city. It's dominated by models of boats – the most impressive is a third-scale model of an open whaling boat – but includes a decent spread of shipping artefacts.

Mawson's Huts Replica Museum

Cnr Argyle and Morrison sts • Daily: Oct–April 9am–6pm; May–Sept 10am–5pm • $12 • ☎ 03 6231 1518 or ☎ 1800 551 422, ⓦ mawsons-huts-replica.org.au

These faithful replicas of the buildings that were used to shelter Antarctic explorer Douglas Mawson and his expedition team on the first Australasian expedition to the frozen continent in 1912–14 are designed to raise funds for the conservation of the originals. Opened in 2014, they recreate the living conditions of the explorers and have interesting displays about their work, the husky dogs that accompanied them, and the frozen continent they explored. The huts are gaining a reputation as one of Hobart's top attractions.

Salamanca Place

The focus of the waterfront for most visitors is **Salamanca Place**. Here, former merchants' warehouses and shipping offices are occupied by arts-and-crafts galleries, speciality shops, restaurants, cafés and pubs. The most rewarding spot to browse is the **Salamanca Arts Centre** at 77 Salamanca Place, a former jam-canning factory that houses a diverse range of galleries and outlets plus arts organizations such as the Peacock Theatre. Notwithstanding weekend nights, Salamanca Place is at its liveliest during the Saturday **Salamanca Market** (8am–3pm). Like Tassie itself, it's a friendly, alternative affair, with stalls full of Tassie crafts – woodwork from local timbers (often recycled), textiles and art – alongside bric-a-brac and secondhand books and clothes.

Off Salamanca Place is modern **Salamanca Square**, with a large fountain feature; the square is home to the long-standing (and excellent) Hobart Bookshop (see p.901).

Battery Point to Sandy Bay

Kellys Steps lead up from Salamanca Place to **Battery Point**, a suburb with an enduring village atmosphere. It takes its name from the battery of guns once sited on present-day **Princes Park**, protecting the harbour below, but is more famous for its cute colonial cottages. With the building of the wharf in the 1830s, a working-class community grew up behind Salamanca Place, and Battery Point was home to the waterfront workmen, then, later, merchants who built fine houses. Nowadays, pubs with names such as the *Shipwright's Arms* are the only reminder of the original population. Gentrification has transformed Battery Point into a prosperous urban village, with streets of immaculately restored historic cottages and the charming flower-filled green of **Arthurs Circus**. The former corner-store shops now host smart cafés and restaurants. There's a particular concentration of early buildings on De Witt and Cromwell streets.

St George's Church, on Cromwell, is the joint work of John Lee Archer (responsible for the nave, completed in 1838) and James Blackburn (the tower, added in 1847), the early colony's best-known architects. **Hampden Road** has more fine nineteenth-century mansions, including **Narryna** at no. 103 (Tues–Sat 10am–4.30pm, Sun noon–4.30pm; $10; ⊕narryna.com.au). The former home of a Scottish sea captain, the house-museum is furnished with period Georgian antiques.

The next suburb south is well-heeled **Sandy Bay**, home to the Royal Tasmanian Yacht Club, the Wrest Point Casino in an incongruous 1970s tower with a revolving restaurant, and a passable beach – a pleasant spot from which to watch weekend regattas.

The CBD

The city centre is small-scale, largely flat and eminently walkable. As well as shops, there's abundant historic architecture – an appealing mishmash of Georgian, Victorian and Art Deco between some Sixties eyesores. Macquarie and Davey streets have the most historic buildings, although there are a few minor sights along the streets north of Macquarie Street, particularly Murray and Campbell streets.

Franklin Square

Leafy **Franklin Square** spreads around its imposing statue of Sir John Franklin, the governor of Van Diemen's Land between 1837 and 1843, who achieved posthumous fame as an Arctic explorer after his ill-fated 1845 expedition to discover the Northwest Passage. The square marks the start of the sandstone Neoclassical buildings of the state government and law courts along Macquarie Street. The Murray Street intersection by St David's Cathedral is often cited as Australia's finest Georgian streetscape.

St Davids Park

St Davids Park was originally the graveyard of St David's Cathedral, but was converted to a park in the early twentieth century. It's a quiet spot, containing some important monuments, notably a huge memorial to the first governor, David Collins. Other early colonial gravestones have been removed and set into two sandstone walls at the bottom of the park.

State Library

91 Murray St • Mon–Fri 9.30am–5pm, Sat 9.30am–2pm • Free • ☎ 03 6233 7484, ⊕ linc.tas.gov.au

The **State Library** holds the **Allport Library and Museum of Fine Arts,** worth a visit if you have an interest in decorative arts. It displays a wealthy family's collection of eighteenth- and nineteenth-century furnishings, ceramics, silver and glass, paintings, prints and rare books relating to Australia and the Pacific.

Theatre Royal

29 Campbell St • Tours 11am Mon, Wed & Fri; $15 • ☏ 03 6233 299 or ☏ 1800 650 277, ⊛ theatreroyal.com.au

The **Theatre Royal** is Australia's oldest surviving theatre, built in 1837. It has an intimate interior decorated in Regency style, best seen while attending a performance. Otherwise, tours relate the history of the theatre, as well as thespian yarns.

Penitentiary Chapel and Criminal Courts

Cnr Brisbane & Campbell sts • Tours Mon–Fri 10am, 11.30am, 1pm & 2.30pm; Sat & Sun 12pm & 1pm • $15 • ☏ 03 6231 0911, ⊛ nationaltrust.org.au/places/the-tench

The **Penitentiary Chapel and Criminal Courts** – otherwise known as "The Tench" – is an interesting insight into another aspect of Hobart's convict history. Begun by Irish colonial architect John Lee Archer in the 1830s, the penitentiary chapel was built to dispense moral fibre as much as discipline and justice to the fledgling settlement's convict population. The complex also has two courtrooms, underground tunnels and tiny solitary cells where the early town's convicts were incarcerated and, in some cases, led out to the gallows. Entry is by tour only (90min), run by National Trust volunteers who describe the history as you wander through; there's also a lamplight ghost tour (Mon & Fri, 1hr; bookings (essential) online; $20).

Royal Tasmanian Botanical Gardens

Queens Domain • Daily: Oct–March 8am–6.30pm; April & Sept 8am–5.30pm; May–Aug 8am–5pm • Free • ☏ 03 6166 0451, ⊛ rtbg.tas.gov.au

Wedged between two busy highways north of the city centre, **Queens Domain** is a sparse, bush-covered hill traversed by walking and jogging tracks. At the base of the hill, on the Derwent, the trees suddenly become lush in the **Royal Tasmanian Botanical Gardens**. Pick up a leaflet outlining the gardens and its waymarked walks at any entrance or from the **visitor centre** at the west side of the park. It's about a thirty-minute walk from the city centre to the gardens via Davey or Liverpool streets.

MONA

655 Main Rd, Berridale, 12km from the CBD • Daily except Tues: Oct–April 10am–6pm; May–Sept 10am–5pm • $25 • ☏ 03 6277 9900, ⊛ mona.net.au • Buses #510, #520, #521 and #X20; MONA's MR-1 catamaran and the MONA Roma bus depart from an office on Brooke St quay several times a day; $20 return; ☏ 03 6223 6064

For many visitors – foreign and interstate alike – the astonishing **MONA** gallery provides the inspiration to visit Hobart in the first place, and the city's standing as a creative hub has rocketed since it opened in 2011. The subterranean "Museum of Old and New Art" is the personal vision of millionaire gambler **David Walsh**, who grew up in the nearby suburb of Glenorchy, and who once declared that he wanted MONA to "shock and offend". Changing exhibits seem selected to provoke as much as inspire: one of the more infamous is Belgian Wim Delvoye's digestive machine that "eats" rotting beef and defecates (regularly, at 2pm). Julius Popp's *Bit.Fall* became a favourite of Hobartians, reproducing words from current internet news searches as droplets to form a waterfall of words. Fulfilling the "Old" part of the title is Walsh's superb personal collection of **antiquities**. But in aiming to shock traditional Tasmanians' prudish sensibilities, Walsh has failed utterly – most people love MONA.

The vines of Morrilla Estate, surrounding the museum, still produce cool-climate wines, which you can taste and buy in the bar, along with organic ales from the on-site Moo Brew boutique brewery. You can also dine at the superb restaurant, *The Source* (see p.899) and stay at the luxury MONA Pavilions (see p.898).

Inland to Mount Wellington

There's a clutch of sites beneath "The Mountain", enough to make a day-trip southwest of the centre. Bus is the easiest way to get there, but you can also walk the two kilometres alongside the **Hobart Rivulet**, which goes to the brewery via the Female Factory site. The path starts at the car park beside Bodyworks on Molle Street (opposite Collins Street).

Cascades Female Factory Historic Site

16 Degraves St • Daily 9.30am–4pm • $5 • **Tours** Daily 10am–3pm (except 11am), 45min; $15 • *Her Story* Daily 11am, 45min; $20 • ☎ 03 6233 6656, ⓦ femalefactory.org.au • Buses #446, #447 and #449

10

Unlike the folklore associated with male convict history, the female experience is often overlooked. World Heritage listed in 2010, the **Cascades Female Factory Historic Site** attempts to rectify that. Sandstone walls are all that remain of a prison built in 1827 to house recidivist convict women, who were set to work washing and sewing. Information boards and a free leaflet interpret the ruins, but to bring the site to life join a tour: either a heritage tour with a guide or *Her Story*, an excellent two-hand theatre production that roams throughout the site to narrate its operation.

Cascade Brewery

140 Cascade Rd • Visitor centre daily 10am–4pm • Free • Brewery tours: several daily, times vary, 1hr 30min; $30, booking essential (long trousers and covered flat shoes required) • Heritage tours: Several daily, 1hr 30min; $20 • ☎ 03 6224 1117, ⓦ cascadebreweryco.com.au • Buses #446, #447 and #449

The seven-storey **Cascade Brewery** is the oldest in Australia. It's now owned by the Foster's Group but still uses traditional methods, taking advantage of the pure spring water that "cascades" down Mount Wellington. **Tours** to explain the brewery process are pretty active – there are 220 stairs – but you're rewarded at the end with a glass or three of draught beer in the original brewer's residence. Heritage tours relate the brewery's history on a tour of its three-acre gardens. The visitor centre contains a small **museum** of brewing paraphernalia, a souvenir shop and a bar with a beer garden.

Mount Wellington

Road access via Huon Rd and Pinnacle Rd to the summit • Buses #448 or #449 run to Fern Tree

In most images of Hobart, **Mount Wellington** (1270m) – or Kunanyi (its Aboriginal name, now used frequently) – looms in the background, sometimes snow-covered. In reality, it is often shrouded in heavy cloud or mist. It is a popular excursion, visited by sightseers who ascend on a 19km road as much as local walkers who see it as wilderness-lite (but still, maps are recommended for hikes). A **shuttle bus** runs tours to the top (daily 10.15am Sat) & 1.30pm; $30), as well as except providing one-way transport for walkers ($30; ☎0408 341 804). **Local buses** go as far as Ferndale suburb, from where you can pick up a walking route to the summit via Fernglade Track and Pinnacle Track before a tough push up on the Zig Zag Track. Allow three hours each way; more if you divert onto numerous side tracks such as the Organ Pipes Track beneath the mountain's awesome cliffs. There are picnic grounds at the beginning of the track at Fern Tree and about halfway up at **The Springs**, and drinkable water cascades from rocks as you climb. Whether reached by four wheels or two legs, the bare rocky summit offers an astonishing panorama: over the city and harbour, then out over vast tracts of bush and grass plains to Bruny Island in the south and Maria Island to the north. One of the most popular trips is to go up by bus then zoom down again by **mountain bike** on the Mount Wellington Descent (daily: Jan & Feb 10am, 1pm & 4pm; March–Dec 10am & 1pm; $75; ☎03 6274 1880, ⓦmtwellingtondescent.com.au).

ARRIVAL AND DEPARTURE HOBART

By plane Hobart's airport (☎03 6216 1600, ⓦhobartairport.com.au) is 17km east of the city near Cambridge and there are numerous flights from the mainland. Redline's Airporter Shuttle Bus ($18 one-way,

$32 return; bookings ☎1300 385 511) meets all flights and drops off at accommodation in central Hobart and the inner-city suburbs. A taxi into the city centre costs around $50.
By bus Redline Coaches go to Launceston via the Midlands

10

Highway, with connections to Devonport via Deloraine and on to Burnie, Wynyard and Stanley. Departures are from the Transit Centre, 230 Liverpool St (☎1300 360 000). TassieLink covers surrounding areas, services south, to the east and west coast. Most TassieLink buses depart from the Hobart Bus Terminal, 64 Brisbane St (☎1300 300 520). Some services leave from the Hydro building, 4 Elizabeth St (check the timetable and route maps online).

Destinations Bicheno (3–4 weekly; 4hr); Cygnet (3 on Thurs, daily rest of week; 55min); Deloraine (2–3 daily; 4hr); Devonport (1–3 daily; 5hr 30min); Dover (Mon–Fri 2 daily; 1hr 40min); Geeveston (Mon–Fri 6 daily, Sat & Sun 3 daily; 1hr 15min); Kettering (Mon–Fri 4 daily; 40min); Lake St Clair (4 weekly; 3hr); Launceston (3–4 daily; 2hr 30min); Port Arthur (Mon–Sat daily; 2hr 15min); Queenstown via Lake St Clair, with connections to Strahan (Sun–Fri daily; 5hr 45min); Richmond (Mon–Fri 9 daily, Sat daily; 45min); St Helens (Mon–Sat daily; 3hr 45min); Swansea (Mon–Sat 1–2 daily; 2hr 30min); Triabunna, for Maria Island (Mon–Sat 1–2 daily; 1hr 40min).

GETTING AROUND

By bus Metro buses (☎13 22 01, ⊛metrotas.com.au) ease getting to suburban destinations. The Metro Shop, 22 Elizabeth St, sells electronic Greencards (offering a twenty percent saving) and provides timetables, as do several newsagents; the area outside the GPO – Elizabeth St, Franklin Square and Macquarie St – is the bus interchange. Single tickets cost from $3.20; a daily fare cap of $9 (or $4.50 if boarding after 9am or on weekends) applies for Greencard users. The free Salamanca Shuttle (Sat 9am–2pm; ⊛hobartcity.com.au) loops around nine stops in the CBD to reach Salamanca Market every 10min.

By taxi Central ranks are outside the *Grand Chancellor* hotel and on Salamanca Place.

Bike rental Hobart Bike Hire, 35 Hunter St (Daily 9am–5pm; ☎0447 556 189, ⊛hobartbikehire.com.au) is the most central bike-hire option (find them in the alley between the *Henry Jones Art Hotel* and the Centre for The Arts). Rates are $35/24hr; daily and half-day rates available.

Taxis Combined Services ☎13 10 08; Yellow Cabs ☎13 19 24.

INFORMATION

Tourist information The Tasmanian Travel and Information Centre, at the corner of Davey and Elizabeth streets (daily 9am–5pm; ☎03 6238 4222, ⊛hobarttravelcentre.com.au), has information on current city tours and the rest of the state. **Bushwalking information** The Parks and Wildlife Service has an unmanned desk with information sheets at the Service Tasmania shop, 134 Macquarie St (Mon–Fri 9am–5pm; ☎1300 135 513). It stocks the full range of bushwalking maps, as does the Tasmanian Map Centre, 100 Elizabeth St (☎03 6231 9043).

TOURS AND CRUISES

For a small city there are a lot of tours going. For specialist-interest walking tours – food walks, art walks, ghost walks, historical walks – consult the tourist office (see above). Under Down Under and Jump (see box, p.889) run backpackers' day-trips by bus to regional sights such as the Tasman Peninsula, the Huon Valley and Mount Field National Park.

Bruny Island/Tasman Island Cruises Elizabeth St Pier ☎03 6293 1465, ⊛brunycruises.com.au, ⊛tasman cruises.com.au. Full-day tours (daily 7.45am; $195) to either Bruny Island or the Tasman Peninsula on an acclaimed eco-cruise along the coasts. Includes lunch and all transfers. The Tasman Island Cruise offers an extension to include Port Arthur ($225) or the Tasmanian Devil UnZoo ($215).

Hobart Yachts King's Pier ☎0438 399 477, ⊛hobartyachts.com.au. Sailing trips (3hr; $140) on the Derwent River with Tasmanian couple Mark and Marsha Stranger (and their crew) aboard the 62ft luxury cutter *Halsal IV*. Other tours include overnighters or five nights or more along the east coast or to Port Davey.

Lady Nelson Constitution Dock ☎03 6234 3348, ⊛ladynelson.org.au. Great-value short cruises (Sat & Sun 11am & 1pm, plus 3pm in summer; 1hr 30min; $30) aboard a replica of the ship that brought European settlement to Tasmania.

Peppermint Bay Cruise Brooke St Pier ☎1800 751 229, ⊛peppermintbaycom.au. High-end cruise ($98) down the D'Entrecasteaux Channel by catamaran for lunch in the top-notch *Peppermint Bay Restaurant*, Woodbridge.

Windeward Bound Elizabeth St Pier ☎0418 120 243, ⊛windewardbound.com. Afternoon sailing trips (3hr; $90 including light lunch) on Tasmania's largest tall ship, a 33m brigantine owned by a youth development charity.

ACCOMMODATION

Accommodation in Hobart is not especially cheap, especially during peak season when bookings are essential, with city centre and dockside **hotels** commanding premium prices. **Motels** are generally cheaper but situated in Sandy Bay, about 3km south of the centre. Backpackers' hostels can be fairly shabby – don't be afraid to ask to see a room but be aware that your options are limited in January.

10

WATERFRONT AND BATTERY POINT

HOTELS

Customs House Hotel Cnr Murray & Morrison sts, opposite Watermans Dock ☎03 6234 6645, ⓦcustomshousehotel.com. Compact, modestly stylish pub rooms in a former harbour warehouse, all en suite and the best with old stone walls. Good value for the location, though the front rooms with harbour views can be noisy at weekends. $110

Grand Chancellor 1 Davey St ☎03 6235 4535 or ☎1800 753 379, ⓦgrandchancellorhotels.com. Prime location for a large four-star resort favoured by older package tourists – an ugly exterior belies plush contemporary rooms. Facilities include restaurants, bars and a pool, plus parking. $280

★**Henry Jones Art Hotel** 25 Hunter St ☎03 6210 7700, ⓦthehenryjones.com. Hobart's first boutique hotel on the waterfront is still its best. Housed in a former colonial warehouse, this arty five-star exudes style in its use of timber furnishings and sandstone walls, while rooms feature huge beds and wet-room bathrooms. $320

Prince of Wales 55 Hampden Rd, Battery Point ☎03 6223 6355, ⓦprinceofwaleshotel.net.au. Overlook the 1960s architecture – an eyesore hereabouts – and the pub's twelve older motel-style rooms represent decent value for the location. Walk-up rates can be two-thirds of the price, which includes a light breakfast. $160

APARTMENTS

St Ives Apartments 67 St Georges Terrace, Battery Point ☎03 6221 5555, ⓦstivesapartments.com.au. A great location near Battery Point and Salamanca makes this block an appealing prospect. The mid-range rooms and apartments are clean and give a nod to modern style; excellent deals available online. $260

★**Salamanca Wharf Hotel** 13–17 Castray Esplanade ☎03 6224 7007, ⓦsalamancawharfhotel.com. Crisp contemporary studios and one-bed apartments finished in Tasmanian timbers. Close (but not too close) to the action on Salamanca Place, but without harbour views (hence the great price). All accommodation is serviced daily and comes with a kitchen and laundry. $215

Somerset on the Pier Elizabeth St Pier ☎03 6220 6600 or ☎1800 766 377, ⓦsomerset.com. An apartment hotel whose unrivalled pier location guarantees wonderful water views across Constitution Dock. Most of the split-level, bright, studio and one-bedroom apartments have balconies, all have kitchen and laundry, and there's a gym and sauna. $240

THE CBD

HOTELS

★**Astor Private Hotel** 157 Macquarie St ☎03 6234 6611, ⓦastorprivatehotel.com.au. You'll find bygone charm and an effusive welcome from irrepressible owner Tildy in this rambling, immaculately maintained 1920s hotel. Superb value for the central location, although the cheapest rooms share bathrooms. Rates include breakfast. $110

Mantra Collins 58 Collins St ☎03 6226 1111 or ☎131 517, ⓦhotelcollins.com.au. Housed within a renovated tower block, this has a location and cool metropolitan style to woo executives and style-conscious tourists. Floor-to-ceiling windows offer superb views of the harbour or Mount Wellington. Choose from hotel rooms or apartments, and book online for best rates. $209

Hadley's Orient 34 Murray St ☎03 6237 2999, ⓦhadleyshotel.com.au. One of the oldest hotels in Hobart, National Trust-listed and with a superb central location. A major renovation has restored some the old place's glory, with rooms now boasting Victorian-style furniture, brocade curtains and richly patterned fabrics. For an extra $20, it's worth upgrading to a Superior room for more space. $299

Quality MidCity Cnr Elizabeth & Bathurst sts ☎03 6234 6333 or ☎1800 030 966, ⓦhobartmidcity.com.au. There's bland though at least inoffensive decor in this anonymous mid-range chain hotel – think light-wood laminate furniture and swirly bed covers. Overlook that and the hotel is comfy enough and good value for the central location. $125

Travelodge 167 Macquarie St ☎03 6220 7100, ⓦtravelodge.com.au. Terrific central location and a bright modern decor make this a good choice. Budget rooms are very affordable, but it's worth spending a bit extra for more space if you're going to stay more than a couple of nights. Larger rooms have kitchenettes. $99

SELF-CATERING

Corinda's Cottages 17 Glebe St ☎03 6234 1590, ⓦcorindascottages.com.au. The loveliest heritage address in Hobart: three cottages around the cobbled yard and gardens of a manor with old beams, bric-a-brac and rustic charm by the cartful despite being a 20min walk from the centre. The owners also offer two glam ultramodern apartments next door as *2on2* (☎03 6234 1590, ⓦ2on2.com.au; $275). $265

Graham Apartments 15 Pirie St, New Town ☎03 6278 1333, ⓦgrahamapartments.com.au. Among the best-value self-contained apartments in Hobart, these are simple but comfortable motel-style apartments, 2.5km north of the centre but a 15min walk from the nightlife of North Hobart. $124

Mantra One Sandy Bay Road 1 Sandy Bay Rd ☎03 6221 6000, ⓦmantraonesandybayroad.com.au. A superb location equidistant from Salamanca Place and the city centre, opposite St David's Park, makes up for accommodation that is bland in style, though comfy and equipped with kitchenettes and laundry facilities. Some have scenic views. Cheaper last-minute deals available. $249

10

HOSTELS

Hobart Central YHA 9 Argyle St ☎03 6231 2660, ⓦyha.com.au. Spotless and small budget hotel and backpackers' a block's walk from the waterfront and CBD. As well as the four- to twelve-bed dorms, there are double rooms with en-suite bathrooms, which attract an older clientele, and one family room that sleeps four. A small kitchen and laundry are available. Service not always helpful, but new management (at time of writing) has that in their sights. Dorms $31, doubles $114

Narrara Backpackers 88 Goulburn St ☎03 6234 8801, ⓦnarrarabackpackers.com. Favoured by older travellers, this is an intimate home from home, with small but bright rooms, in good condition, and with a hugely helpful owner, Mo. Accommodation in dorms (including female-only), rooms, and a studio for four. Off-street parking available. Dorms $23, doubles $69, studio $119

The Pickled Frog Backpackers 281 Liverpool St ☎03 6234 7977, ⓦthepickledfrog.com. The party backpackers' in a former pub: think colourful graffitied walls and a young international crowd. Plus points include several lounge areas, a reception/bar area serving cheap beer and snacks, and free shuttles to some attractions. Negatives are that the larger dorms are fairly cramped. Dorms $24, doubles $70

THE SUBURBS

★**The Islington** 321 Davey St ☎03 6220 2123, ⓦislingtonhotel.com. This luxury boutique hotel, once a grand manor house, is sophisticated yet utterly relaxed, with rooms full of art and antiques creating a homely feel. Gorgeous accommodation, super-comfy beds, flawless staff, a superb in-house restaurant and serene gardens with views to Mount Wellington – outstanding in every respect. It's no wonder it's won a slew of accommodation awards. $475

★**MONA Pavilions** 3655 Main Rd, Berriedale ☎03 6277 9900, ⓦmona.net.au. It's possible to stay at MONA (see p.894) itself in one of the stylish and high-tech one- and two-bedroom pavilions. Named for Australian architects or artists, they come with a private wine cellar and touch-screen controls for everything from the lighting to the blinds. Each has a large balcony overlooking the Derwent estuary, and they are decorated with antiquities and artworks from the MONA collection. Expensive, but the price includes breakfast at *The Source* (see opposite), and entry to MONA. $650

EATING

Hobart's eating scene has never been more exciting, with critics celebrating its **concept restaurants** which, showcase seasonal, local ingredients. All very impressive, yet fish and chips eaten from fishermen's punts in Constitution Dock can provide as enjoyable a meal and old favourites retain the easy charm of Tassie dining. Salamanca Place offers the widest choice in the centre – a couple of superb options aside, the CBD is better for **cafés** – while the short bar-and-restaurant strip in North Hobart (aka "NoHo") is the choice of many Hobart locals.

WATERFRONT, BATTERY POINT AND SANDY BAY

Annapurna 93 Salamanca Place ☎03 6224 0400, ⓦannapurnaindiancuisine.com. Casual restaurant serving Indian food that's a good option for a cheap(ish), filling meal: tandoori prawns or traditional *rogan josh* and rice for around $19. A second outlet is at 305 Elizabeth St, North Hobart. Mon–Fri noon–3pm & 5–10pm, Sat & Sun 5–10pm.

Cargo 51 Salamanca Place ☎03 6223 7788, ⓦcargobarsalamanca.com.au. Hugely popular, partly due to its thin-crust pizzas in standard and exotic flavours – octopus salsa or salt-and-pepper-prawn pizza, anyone? – priced from $22, but also due to its outside bar and lounge-bar vibe inside. Sun–Fri 10.30am–late, Sat 7am–late.

Da Angelo 47 Hampden Rd ☎03 6223 7011, ⓦdaangelo.com. The cosy informal atmosphere and the outstanding, home-made pizzas and pasta make this neighbourhood Italian a mainstay of Hobart dining. The gnocchi are legendary. Mains average $22. Reservations recommended. Sun–Thurs 5–10pm, Fri noon–3pm & 5–11pm, Sat 5–11pm.

Fish Frenzy Elizabeth St Pier ☎03 6234 7788, ⓦfishfrenzy.com.au. Tasty fresh fish and chips – served in paper cones – from $18 (and more expensive fresh fish dishes) plus tables overlooking the yachts in Constitution Dock make for informal dining that's hard to beat. The locals will tell you that these are the best fish and chips in town, and they don't disappoint. Daily 11am–9pm.

Jackman & McRoss 57–59 Hampden St, Battery Point ☎03 6223 3186. A classy café, where New World sass meets traditional European café style, serving gourmet pastries and savouries for $8–14: fresh baguettes, frittatas and melt-in-the-mouth pies – the slow-cooked beef is legendary. A second café is in the CBD at 4 Victoria St. Mon–Fri 7am–6pm, Sat & Sun 7am–5pm; Victoria St Mon–Fri 7am–4.30pm.

Machine Laundry Café 12 Salamanca Square ☎03 6224 9922. An antidote to the slicker places in Salamanca, this buzzy, retro-styled café is deservedly popular. Café food such as ricotta hotcakes or roti wraps with scrambled eggs priced around $16; there are even a few washing machines. Daily 7.30am–5pm.

Monty's on Montpellier 37 Montpellier Retreat, Battery Point ☎03 6223 2511, ⓦmontys.com.au. Fine dining without the fuss; seasonal mod-Oz cuisine plus romantic dining in a cottage. It's a mite pricey at first glance – dishes like trevalla with local mussels average $32 – but worth every cent. Booking recommended. Tues–Sat 6pm–late.

★**Peacock & Jones** Hunter St ☎1800 375 692, ⓦpeacockandjones.com.au. A smart and buzzing addition to the Hobart dining scene, the open kitchen here produces small plates and main meals with an emphasis on local produce and seafood, including tasty oysters. Tapas dishes range from $11–19, with steaks and other heartier dishes at $35–42. Indoor seating is complemented by about five tables in the atrium of the Henry Jones factory, around a fireplace. Mon–Sat noon–10pm.

Retro Café 31 Salamanca Place ☎03 6223 3073. Bagels and poached eggs or pan-fried mushrooms and sourdough for breakfast, chicken bruschetta and burgers for lunch (average $17) and a grandstand view of the goings-on in Salamanca. A Hobart institution and, yes, there's a retro vibe to the interior. Mon–Fri 7.30am–6pm, Sat & Sun 8am–6pm.

CBD

Ethos Eat Drink 100 Elizabeth St ☎03 6231 1165, ⓦethoseatdrink.com. Edible flowers, a menu of ingredients (as well as dishes), vintage decor – welcome to the latest zeitgeist-stretching eatery, and this one in a colonial mews. The daily-changing menu might include beef carpaccio with radish wafers or grilled squid with a lemon dressing, all priced by size – around $9 to $30 from the à la carte menu; the six-course tasting menu is $72 (or $125 with matched wines). Reservations recommended. Tues–Sat 6pm–late.

★**Pigeon Hole** 93 Goulbourn St ☎03 6236 9306, ⓦpigeonholecafe.com.au. A fantastic little neighbourhood café whose vintage vibe is hip without ever flaunting it. Famous for sourdough breads, its terrific blackboard menu might include dishes like pork and fennel meatballs, hearty vegetable soup and beef short ribs, all for less than $20. Mon–Sat 8am–4.30pm.

Pilgrim Coffee/Property of Pilgrim 48 Argyle St ☎03 6236 1999. Two interconnected venues of hip warehouse style. One is a buzzy café with good coffee, the other offers breakfasts and gutsy, delicious dishes like Mexican black beans, hoisin duck (mains around $18) and sourdough fruit bread ($7). Mon–Fri 6.30am–4.30pm,

Sat & Sun 8am–2pm.

R Takagi Sushi 155 Liverpool St. Just a couple of tables, yet this place prepares some of the freshest sushi in town at some of the lowest prices: *nori maki* rolls cost around $5, or there's *tsuya* broth with vegetables and noodles. Mon–Fri 10.30am–5.30pm, Sat 10.30am–4pm, Sun 11.30am–3pm.

The Shamrock 195 Liverpool St ☎03 6234 3892. A shabby pub in looks, "The Shammie" packs 'em in, office worker and backpacker alike, for one of the cheapest feeds in Hobart: $10 pub favourites like schnitzels and roasts, plus daily specials like beef curry or flathead for $12. Daily 11am–late.

Villino Espresso 30 Criterion St ☎03 6231 0890, ⓦvillino.com.au. The finest coffee in Hobart, say many of this tiny place, which roasts its own beans; nibbles such as croissant and muffins are practically an afterthought. It's often busy, so for coffee on the go, visit its adjacent hole-in-the-wall outlet Ecru. A large latte or flat white will cost you $4. Mon–Fri 8am–4.30pm, Sat 9am–3pm.

NORTH HOBART AND THE SUBURBS

★**The Source** MONA, 651–5 Main Rd, Berriedale ☎03 6277 9904, ⓦmona.net.au/mona/restaurant. Sophisticated dining at MONA gallery (see p.894) and some of the finest cuisine in the state from chef Vince Trim. Super-fresh ingredients go into dishes that are works of art in themselves. Mains are around $35 for lunch, and dinner degustation menus start from $75 for three courses. Dishes might include a slow-cooked beef cheek, chargrilled octopus and pan-seared scallops. To finish, try the caramel and chocolate parfait, or baked figs with blue cheese and walnuts. Service is faultless. Mon, Wed, Thurs & Sun 7.30–10am & noon–3pm, Fri & Sat 7.30–10am, noon–3pm & 6–10pm.

Sweet Envy 341 Elizabeth St ☎03 6234 8805, ⓦsweetenvy.com. This little patisserie, run by a pastry chef who used to work with Gordon Ramsay, and his cake designer partner, is piled high with treats: macaroons, cupcakes, flaky almond croissants, fruit tarts and lavender cream cakes. There are also gourmet pies and coffee, plus astonishing ice creams. Cupcakes, slices and other sweet treats $3–6. Tues–Sat 8.30am–5pm.

DRINKING, NIGHTLIFE AND ENTERTAINMENT

In the heart of the city, Hobart's small **nightlife** scene centres on the water: Salamanca Place and Franklin's Wharf are boisterous good fun at weekends. To tap into the locals' scene try North Hobart – most pub **gig venues** appeal for a drink, too. Free gigs are staged in the open-air courtyard behind the Salamanca Arts Centre on Friday evenings (5.30–7.30pm) during "Rektango" sessions– a local institution.

WHAT'S ON AND TICKETS

Thursday's *Mercury* newspaper contains a gig guide. *The Dwarf* online gig guide (ⓦthedwarf.com.au) is a useful reference too.

Centretainment 53 Elizabeth St Mall ☎03 6234 5998, ⓦcentretainment.com.au. A one-stop shop for

all advance theatre and concert tickets.

PUBS AND BARS

Bar Celona 23 Salamanca Square ☎03 6224 7557, ⓦbarcelonahobart.com. This renovated sandstone warehouse is turned into a slick café by day and a bar on two

10

10

FESTIVALS AND EVENTS

Hobart's premier event is the finish of the **Sydney–Hobart yacht race** (see p.48). The two hundred or so yachts, which leave Sydney on December 26, start to arrive in Hobart on December 28, making for a lively New Year's Eve waterfront party. The race coincides with the state's largest festival, **The Taste of Tasmania** (Ⓦ thetasteoftasmania.com.au), an erstwhile food jamboree to promote Tasmanian produce that has morphed into a week-long party with music and theatre. The **Australian Wooden Boat Festival** (Ⓦ australianwoodenboatfestival.com.au) runs over three days in early February in odd-numbered years, and fills the docks with beautiful historic craft. In late October, the **Royal Hobart Show** agricultural festival provides four fun days of country fare.

MONA has recently added a couple of events to the Hobart calendar. **MONA FOMA** (Ⓦ mofo.net.au), aka **MOFO**, brings artists on the avant-garde side of rock, such as Nick Cave, DJs and performance artists to the city for three days in mid-January. And in June, MONA's winter solstice arts festival, **DARK MOFO**, sees the iconoclastic gallery run riot around the city for a week, with cutting-edge art installations at several sites.

levels by night. More civilized than many options in the Salamanca area, with DJs on the mezzanine level at weekends. Cocktails $16, wines from $8 a glass, and a range of beers (including plenty of Tassie brews) on offer. Mon–Thurs noon–midnight, Fri noon–1am, Sat 9am–1am, Sun 9am–midnight.

IXL Long Bar 25 Hunter St ☎03 6210 7700, Ⓦ thehenryjones.com. Cocktails ($19), craft beers and a decent choice of Tassie whiskies (from $12–38), the bar of the *Henry Jones Art Hotel* – all rough stone walls and exposed beams – is the most sophisticated spot for pre- or post-dining drinks. Wines by the glass $8–12. Sun–Thurs 5–10.30pm, Fri & Sat 3–10.30pm.

Lark Whisky Bar 14 Davey St ☎03 6231 9088, Ⓦ larkdistillery.com.au. The outlet for one of Tasmania's leading whisky producers, the bar also serves other Tassie malts plus a huge range of whiskies from around the world and an all-Tasmanian wine list. Lark whisky from $16. There's often live folk music on Fri evenings. Daily 10am–7pm, Fri until late.

New Sydney Hotel 87 Bathurst St ☎03 6234 4516, Ⓦ newsydneyhotel.com.au. Hobart's Irish pub, featuring live Celtic, blues and folk on most nights and a proud boast of no jukebox, pokies nor TV. There's also a fine selection of beers on tap, including Tassie craft beers and Guinness, and good gastropub-style meals such as steaks or lamb shoulder at around $26 a main. Mon–Thurs 3pm–late, Fri & Sat noon–late, Sun noon–9pm.

Preachers 5 Knopwood St ☎03 6223 3621. Drinking in a colonial garden cottage full of homely knick-knacks, summer evenings here can feel like a mellow house party. Good range of Tassie craft beers on draught. Mon–Thurs noon–10.30pm, Fri & Sat noon–midnight, Sun noon–8.30pm.

Shipwright's Arms Cnr Colville & Trumpeter sts, Battery Point ☎03 6223 1846, Ⓦ shipwrightsarms.com.au. Traditional old pub with a bar built by a shipwright, with seafaring memorabilia. A great choice for

atmosphere at weekends, when locals pile in for a natter and reasonably priced pub grub. Daily 11am–11pm.

Tavern 42 Degree South Elizabeth St Pier ☎03 6224 7742, Ⓦ tav42.com.au. A fine spot for summer evenings, this lounge bar has a great waterfront location, with tables laid either side of the pier, and an upmarket vibe that makes it popular with a style-conscious set. Also has a reliable good-value mod-Oz brasserie, with mains averaging $30. Mon–Thurs 7.30am–1am, Fri 7.30am–2am, Sat 8.30am–2am, Sun 8.30am–1am.

Telegraph Hotel 19 Morrison St ☎03 6234 6254. Cheap beer nights keep "The Tellie" absurdly popular with students and teenagers. It's usually rammed at weekends, when people pour in from the suburbs for the night, but also fills up midweek for special beer and food deals – steaks sometimes as cheap as $5. Mon–Thurs & Sun 5pm–midnight, Fri & Sat till 2am.

The Whaler 39 Salamanca Place ☎03 6200 1854, Ⓦ thewhaler.com.au. While not the rollicking pub it was in whaling days (perhaps a good thing), this traditional Tassie pub remains a mainstay of the Salamanca strip. The jury's still out with the locals as to whether the former *Knopwood's Retreat* will remain the popular boozer it used to be, but it's always been at its best when everyone spills onto the street on summer weekends. Sun–Thurs 11am–midnight, Fri & Sat 11am–1am.

The Winston 381 Elizabeth St, North Hobart ☎03 6231 2299, Ⓦ thewinston bar.com.au. Almost student-common-room in style, this is a relaxed pub to drop into the North Hobart scene – think shabby sofas and friendly drinkers supping a good range of craft beers. A small stage hosts occasional gigs in the singer-songwriter and folk vein. Mon–Thurs & Sun 4pm–midnight, Fri & Sat 4pm–2am.

LIVE MUSIC AND CLUBS

Flamingos Dance Bar 201 Liverpool St Ⓦ flamingosbar.com. Welcome to Tasmania's only dedicated gay club. It hosts the occasional drag or costume special, otherwise expect two floors of fun, with party anthems played for a young gay and straight crowd. Cover charge from $15. Fri & Sat from 10pm–5am.

The Grand Poobah 142 Liverpool St ☎03 6231 3363, ⓦfacebook.com/thegrandpoobahbar. Comedy, gigs, club nights, burlesque shows – the programming here is eclectic (and erratic – listings are on Facebook) though usually has an alternative slant. Can be fun despite a rather anonymous, youth-club-like venue. Cover charge $20. Wed 8pm–1am, Fri & Sat 9pm–4.30am.

★ **Republic Bar & Café** 299 Elizabeth St, North Hobart ☎03 6234 6954, ⓦrepublicbar.com. Hobart's best pub-gig venue attracts a friendly crowd for its reliable roster of local and Aussie touring acts. Expect garage rock, alt-folk, roots and blues acts on most nights of the week – check the website for what's on – usually for a cover charge of around $25. Mon & Tues 3pm–midnight, Wed, Thurs & Sun noon–midnight, Fri & Sat noon–3am.

MAJOR VENUES

Federation Concert Hall 1 Davey St ☎1800 001 190, ⓦtso.com.au. The modern(ish) 1100-seat venue by the docks that's home to the Tasmanian Symphony Orchestra. Concerts generally feature the major-name composers of the classical canon – Mozart, Chopin, Verdi, Bach, Britten – but also occasionally include modern avant-garde names like Berio. If you're a fan of orchestral pops you'll sometimes find that on the programme too.

Theatre Royal 29 Campbell St ☎03 6233 2299 or ☎1800 650 277, ⓦtheatreroyal.com.au. "A dream of a theatre" said Noël Coward when he played this lovely Regency-style place, founded in 1835. Today it hosts a broad spectrum of entertainment, from comedy nights to music, dance and serious drama.

Wrest Point 410 Sandy Bay Rd, Sandy Bay ☎1800 132 054, ⓦwrestpoint.com.au. Two gig venues – the Entertainment Centre and smaller Showroom – that host mainstream shows: music, including international touring rock acts and tribute shows, plus comedy.

THEATRE

Peacock Theatre Salamanca Arts Centre, 77 Salamanca Place ☎03 6234 8414, ⓦsalarts.org.au. One of the more interesting rep theatres in Tasmania, with the wall of an original colonial quarry as a backdrop to the intimate venue. It specializes in contemporary works produced by several performance companies.

The Playhouse Theatre 106 Bathurst St ☎03 6234 1536, ⓦplayhouse.org.au. The Hobart Repertory Theatre Society, an amateur not-for-profit group established in 1926, puts on at least five plays a year, anything from Shakespeare to *The Elephant Man*. Advance tickets through Centretainment (see p.899).

FILM

State Cinema 375 Elizabeth St, North Hobart ☎03 6234 6318, ⓦstatecinema.com.au. Hobartians fought hard to protect their repertory cinema from demolition, and now enjoy a diet of art-house and foreign films by international and Australian auteurs, with matinees to while away a wet day. There's also a decent bar. Adult tickets are $19; head there on Tuesday for $15 tickets.

Village Cinema Centre 181 Collins St ☎1300 555 400, ⓦvillagecinemas.com.au. Seven-screen multiplex for mainstream releases, with digital sound and stadium-style seating. Tickets $18.50.

DIRECTORY

Bookshops Ellison Hawker, 90 Liverpool St, has an excellent travel section. Fullers Bookshop, 131 Collins St, and The Hobart Bookshop, 22 Salamanca Square, are Hobart's two best literary bookshops. For secondhand books, try Rapid Eye Books, 36–38 Sandy Bay Rd, Battery Point.

Campervan rental National operators, like Britz, Hertz, Maui and Wicked, maintain bases at the airport. Local, budget operators include Tassie Motor Shacks Campervans (☎03 6248 4418, ⓦtassiemotorshacks.com) at Seven Mile Beach.

Camping and outdoor equipment Camping shops are on Elizabeth St near Bathurst St: Jolly Swagman Camping World, 107 Elizabeth St; Mountain Designs, 111 Elizabeth St; plus Mountain Creek Outdoors, 75–77 Bathurst St (☎03 6234 4395), which also offers gear rental.

Car rental Autorent-Hertz, at the airport and cnr Harrington & Bathurst sts (☎03 6391 8677 or ☎1300 030 222, ⓦautorent.com.au), also has campervans; Avis, Market Place (☎03 6214 1711) and at the airport (☎03 6248 5424), offers similar rates; Lo-Cost Auto Rent at 92 Harrington St (☎03 6231 0550, ⓦlocostautorent.com) has some older cars as well as newer models.

Environment Information about conservation programmes (including volunteering) from the Wilderness Society's campaign office at 130 Davey St (☎03 6224 1550, ⓦwilderness.org.au/tas). The international organization Conservation Volunteers (☎03 6231 1779, ⓦconservationvolunteers.com.au) has an office at 63 Melville St.

Hospital Royal Hobart Hospital, 48 Liverpool St ☎03 6166 8308.

Laundry Laundry Machine Café, 12 Salamanca Square (daily 7.30am–5pm).

Luggage Locker, 212 Liverpool St (daily 8am–5pm; ☎0407 368 618) from $7–15 per day or $25 per week (handy if you're bushwalking).

Pharmacy Macquarie Pharmacy, 180 Macquarie St (daily 8am–10pm; ☎ 03 6223 2347); North Hobart Pharmacy, 360–362 Elizabeth St (daily 8am–10pm; ☎ 03 6234 1136).

Post office GPO, cnr Elizabeth & Macquarie sts (Mon–Fri 8.30am–5.30pm, Sat 9am–12.30pm).

Around Hobart

10

Water, wilderness and wildlife – in many ways the landscapes around Hobart are Tasmania in miniature. Once the region that put the apple into the state's Apple Isle nickname, the bucolic D'Entrecasteaux Channel south of the capital has diversified in produce recently – nowadays this area has more than its fair share of artisan producers making fine cheeses and wines. Even **Bruny Island** across the D'Entrecasteaux Channel has acquired a foodie focus, but it's still better known as Hobart's favourite getaway because of its beautiful beaches, bushwalks and a superb eco-cruise – small wonder it's shifting rapidly upmarket. North of Hobart are two day-trips that sum up the diversity so close to the capital. Northwest, beyond the heritage town of New Norfolk, the forest and subalpine landscapes of the **Mount Field National Park** hint at the great southwest wilderness beyond, while **Richmond** northeast is all about the cosy character of a pretty historic village.

The Channel Highway

It's a lovely drive south of Hobart along the **Channel Highway** (B68). Unless you're here to eat there's little in the way of sights but much to enjoy as you hug the shore of the D'Entrecasteaux Channel, rolling through farmland and weatherboard villages before looping back alongside the Huon River to Huonville. Small wonder the place is full of city escapees seeking the good life. En route, Kettering is the gateway to beautiful Bruny Island.

Cygnet

Though the largest settlement in the area, **CYGNET** is really just an oversized village. It once earned its keep as the hub of a fruit-growing region – it remains a good spot to look for harvesting **work** from November to May and the occasional farmer still rolls in on a tractor. Yet the town has now mellowed into a quietly arty place, with a touch of the hippy about it. There are a number of galleries and two marvellous cafés to settle in. The atmosphere comes to the fore during the **Cygnet Folk Festival** (ⓦcygnetfolkfestival.org; tickets on sale via website from Sept) in mid-January when four thousand festival-goers descend for folk, world and roots gigs – expect relaxed, crafty and family-friendly rather than rocking.

ARRIVAL AND DEPARTURE   THE CHANNEL HIGHWAY

By bus Kettering (Mon–Fri 7 daily, Sat 2 daily; 50min) and Cygnet (Mon–Fri daily; 1hr 10min) are served by Metro Tas buses from Hobart. TassieLink also goes to Cygnet (Mon–Fri 2 daily, Sat & Sun 3 daily; 1hr).

ACCOMMODATION AND EATING

CYGNET

Cygnet Holiday Park 3 Mary Street ☎ 0418 532 160. This is a basic small site in the north end of the village with a simple amenities block; it's cheap and powered sites are available. The location directly opposite the *Cygnet Art Hotel* pub appeals too. Un/powered sites $15/30

★**Lotus Eaters Café** 10 Mary St ☎ 03 6295 1996. "Local" and "organic" are watchwords in this adorable café of mismatched furnishings, inside and out. You're here for the daily menus created from whatever is super-fresh: amazing soups with real depth ($14), local smoked trout, dill and mascarpone tart ($25), and salads. Great desserts too. Thurs–Mon 9am–4pm.

★**Red Velvet Lounge** 24 Mary St ☎ 03 6265 0466. Barn-like but cosy, this arty café is a real community hangout, with squishy sofas and a relaxed vibe. Outstanding breakfasts, fresh wholesome soups and a short daily menu of mains: delicious pastas or melt-in-the-mouth slow-roast lamb, pork or beef ($26). Gourmet pizzas at weekends. Wed, Thurs & Sun 9am–4pm, Fri & Sat 9am–4pm & 5–8.30pm.

Bruny Island

With its hauntingly beautiful beaches and superb coastline, **Bruny Island** feels far more distant than an hour from Hobart. Practically two islands joined by a narrow isthmus (where you can sometimes see Little penguins from a viewing platform), it's roughly 70km from end to end and has a population of only four hundred. The cost of taking a car across on the ferry from Kettering deters casual visitors, so the island has long been a backwater, a retreat to enjoy walks, a spot of fishing and abundant wildlife that includes Little penguins, short-tailed shearwaters and a unique island population of albino Bennett's wallabies. It also has an important place in the history of the Tasmanian Aborigines as the land of the Nuenonne people, which included Truganini (see box, p.924) and the first "Black station" for the forced resettlement of Aboriginal people in secluded **Barnes Bay**.

Yet in recent years, Bruny's isolation has raised its profile. On the southern part of the island – by far the most interesting compared to the pastoral north – there's now a growing food scene and high-end self-catering cottages have started to replace weekenders' shacks. That the island retains its sense of remoteness – its haunting landscapes, relaxed pace, even its sketchy mobile phone coverage – accounts for much of the appeal. Many people try to rush the island on a day-trip, but it rewards an overnight stay.

AROUND HOBART

10

Neck Game Reserve

On the isthmus that connects the two islands, the **Neck Game Reserve** acts as a sanctuary for Little penguins and muttonbirds, which inhabit rookeries in sand dunes. The birds return to their burrows at dusk during the nesting season (Sept–Feb for penguins, Sept–April for muttonbirds); a wooden boardwalk leads to a viewing platform and you'll find information on the birds' habits and on best practice for spotting them at its start. A stairway also ascends to a lookout with a small monument to **Truganini**, the Aboriginal woman who became the final survivor of the seventy-strong Nuenonne people whose traditional lands were Bruny Island (see box, p.924).

Adventure Bay

The main settlement on South Bruny, **ADVENTURE BAY** is the principal tourist centre but remains little more than a general store (that has fuel), with shacks and houses spread behind an astonishingly beautiful powder beach. The sheltered bay served as a safe refuge for early European explorers after the journey across the Southern Ocean. The private **Bligh Museum of Pacific Discovery** (876 Adventure Bay; ☎03 6263 1117; daily 10am–4pm but closes on occasion; $4) charts links with explorers such as James Cook, who called here on his last voyage, and the ill-fated Captain Bligh, who sailed on to mutiny. At the far end of the bay you reach the first of three sections of the **South Bruny National Park**, the Fluted Cape State Reserve. A steep climb to the top of the cape (2hr 30min return) provides superb ocean views. Visit at dusk and you may spot the endemic population of white wallabies.

The northwest coast

The west coast of Bruny, along the D'Entrecasteaux Channel, is less scenic but has **ALONNAH**, the main settlement on Bruny, with a general store and post office (petrol sold), plus the island's only pub and bottle shop, *Hotel Bruny*. Five kilometres south at **LUNAWANNA**, the general store sells basic groceries.

Cape Bruny Lighthouse and Cloudy Bay

Nowhere on Bruny Island feels more remote than its south tip, reached by a bumpy dirt road where the road forks south of Lunawanna. Here, the Labillardière State Reserve area occupies the western "hook" of the island; you can drive to the **Cape Bruny Lighthouse**, built in 1836, for stupendous views of ragged cliffs and empty ocean or strike out on a seven-hour walking trail which circuits the peninsula. Take the left turn instead from Lunawanna and you'll wind up at **Cloudy Bay**, the final chunk of the national park, with a great sweep of lonely surf beach. You can bush camp at the far end of the beach.

ARRIVAL AND DEPARTURE
BRUNY ISLAND

By ferry The ferry from Kettering sails at least eleven times daily (6.30am–7pm, 20min; $33 return per car, motorbikes and bicycles $6, foot passengers free). Metro buses from Hobart go to Kettering Ferry Terminal (Mon–Fri 7 daily, Sat 2 daily); alternatively, organized day-trips from Hobart are available.

INFORMATION

Tourist information The Bruny D'Entrecasteaux Visitor Centre at the Kettering ferry terminal (daily 9am–5pm; ☎03 6267 4494) supplies the usual flyers plus good free maps of the island. They'll book accommodation, mostly in self-catering cottages. Also check local agency sites for self-catering options: ⓦ brunyisland.com, ⓦ brunyisland.org.au or ⓦ brunyisland.net.au.

Groceries Stock up on vegetables in Kingston, near Hobart, or Cygnet, as island prices are high and choice limited, although gourmet picnic provisions are available at the Bruny Island Cheese Company (1km north of the isthmus).

GETTING AROUND AND TOURS

By car As there is no public transport on the island, you'll need your own car to get around. In terms of island driving times, allow 40min to get from the quay to Adventure Bay. Petrol is available at Adventure Bay, Alonnah and Lunawanna.

By bike If cycling, be aware that many of the island's roads are dusty, bumpy unsealed stretches for kilometres at a time.

TOURS

Bruny Island Cruises ☎ 03 6293 1465, ⌨ brunycruises. com.au. Former Bruny fisherman Rob Pennicott's Bruny Island Cruises operates award-winning wildlife cruises from Adventure Bay in speedboats beside the spectacular

cliffs; you'll see seals, possibly dolphins, maybe a southern right whale in late November or early December, plus abundant birdlife (mid-April to mid-Dec daily 11am, mid-Dec to mid-April daily 11am & 2pm; $135 or $150 pick-up from Kettering at 8.45am). Also available as a full-day trip from Hobart ($225, lunch included).

Inala Nature Tours ☎ 03 6293 1217, ⌨ inalanaturetours.com.au. Biologist and conservationist Dr Tonia Cochran, based at *Inala* (see below), provides bespoke nature tours, catering to niche interests if requested. Prices vary by requirement, but average around $140 per person per day.

10

ACCOMMODATION

HOSTELS AND SELF-CATERING

43 Degrees Waterfront, Adventure Bay ☎ 03 6293 1018, ⌨ 43degrees.com.au. Upmarket eco-accommodation in open-plan tunnel-like lodges, well located moments from the beach or by the cruise jetty of Adventure Bay. Accommodation is in studios and two-bedroom apartments, all with well-equipped kitchens, most with bay views from the deck. At the time of writing, some apartments were undergoing an upgrade to luxury spa suites. $190

Explorers Cottages Lighthouse Rd, 1km south of Lunawanna ☎ 03 6293 1271, ⌨ brunyisland.com. Comfy family holiday cottages on a bay, with wood combustion fires and a location that's well-placed for trips to the south or nipping to Adventure Bay, as well as meals in *Hotel Bruny*. Facilities include a communal laundry. $205

Inala 320 Cloudy Bay Rd ☎ 03 6293 1217, ⌨ inalaanaturetours.com.au. The place to come for wildlife: these two comfortable, spacious, self-contained

cottages are set on the private 1500-acre nature reserve of their conservationist owner. Lots of wallabies. $250

CAMPSITES AND CARAVAN PARKS

Parks and Wildlife Service bush camps are located throughout the island: at Neck Beach on the south side of the isthmus (pit toilet, untreated water); at either end of Cloudy Bay (pit toilet only); and above Jetty Beach (pit toilets, untreated water) near the island lighthouse. National park fees apply (in addition to camping fees) at all but Neck Beach. $10

Captain Cook Holiday Park Adventure Bay ☎ 03 6293 1128, ⌨ captaincookpark.com. The only budget option in Adventure Bay, this caravan park has a grandstand view of the beach opposite. Alongside basic caravans and two-bedroom cabins, there are also newer one-bedroom villas, and the site has a children's play area. You might also be lucky enough to see the park's resident white wallabies. Un/powered sites $25/30, cabins $150

EATING

Hotel Bruny Main Rd, Alonnah ☎ 03 6293 1148. Bruny's smartened-up pub stresses that it sources ingredients as fresh and local as possible. Expect Cloudy Bay oysters – done seven ways – along with pub-grub faves like crumbed calamari, chicken parmigiana, steak or fish and chips averaging $26 a plate. Daily 11am–10pm.

The Penguin Café 710 Main Rd, Adventure Bay ☎ 03 6293 1352. A simple menu – breakfasts, sandwiches, burgers and quiches – perks up hugely when fish arrives straight off the boat into this rustic café. Good coffee. Tues–Sun 9am–7pm.

Mount Field National Park and around

If the Hartz range feels too remote from the city, head for the high wilderness around Mount Field National Park, a high alpine area with glacial tarns (and an intermittent winter ski field) that is part of the Tasmanian Wilderness World Heritage Area. Not that you have to ascend: many visitors come solely for the magnificent stands of **swamp gum** (the tallest hardwood trees in the world) and **waterfalls** at the lower levels. Other impressive trees are further west in the Styx Valley (see p.907), a highly contested area of old-growth forest near Maydena. If you plan to stay overnight or hike here, the best option for supplies en route from Hobart is **New Norfolk**, 37km east of the park.

New Norfolk

Tasmania's third-oldest town, **NEW NORFOLK** was founded by Norfolk Islanders after the penal colony there was abandoned in 1807. Set on the banks of the Derwent, it's a pretty spot with lots of heritage buildings including oust houses used in local brewing. It's also home to one of Australia's oldest pubs, the *Bush Inn* (1825), Tasmania's oldest Anglican church, St Matthews (1823), and a number of good antique stores.

ARRIVAL AND INFORMATION   NEW NORFOLK

By bus TassieLink buses serve New Norfolk (Tues, Thurs, Fri & Sun daily; 45min) from Hobart on the West Coast route.
Tourist information The New Norfolk Visitor Information Centre is on Circle St (daily 10am–5pm; ☎ 03 6261 3700) and supplies the usual flyers and maps.

ACCOMMODATION AND EATING

★ **Woodbridge on Derwent** 6 Bridge St ☎ 03 6261 5566, ⊚ slh.com/hotels/woodbridgeonthederwent. Rated as one of Australia's top ten luxury hotels (by *Business Review Australia* magazine), this historic Georgian manor is a labour of love for owners Laurelle and John Grimley. It has eight fairly opulent rooms, all with river views, and a magnificent terraced garden that runs down to the riverbank. Some rooms have log fireplaces. The restaurant is open for breakfast and dinner. **$495**

Mount Field National Park

Russell Falls is Mount Field National Park's most famous sight; it cascades in two impressive waterfalls within easy reach of the ranger centre, along an easy twenty-minute circuit. Longer walks continue on to **Horseshoe Falls** (1hr) and **Lady Barron Falls** (3hr return). The best short walk around the visitor centre is the **Tall Trees Track** (1hr 30min), where huge swamp gums dominate; the largest date back to the early nineteenth century.

Lake Dobson

If you want to get away from the tour-group mobs, you'll find short walks along the Lake Dobson Road, which leads high up to **Lake Dobson**, 16km into the park in the area of the alpine moorlands and glacial lakes. From the lake car park, you can go on plenty of longer walks, including treks along the tarn shelf that take several days, with huts to stay in along the way. The walk to **Twilight Tarn**, with its historic hut, is one of the most rewarding (4hr return), or you can continue on for the full tarn-shelf circuit (6hr return). A shorter option is the **Pandani Grove Nature Walk** (with an accompanying leaflet available from the ranger station), a forty-minute circuit of the lake, including a section of tall **pandanus** – the striking heath plant, which, with its crown of long fronds, looks like a semitropical palm. You'll need your own transport to reach these higher walks.

ARRIVAL AND INFORMATION   MOUNT FIELD NATIONAL PARK

Since there is no public transport to the national park, a tour is the only option if you're without your own wheels.

Tours Under Down Under (☎ 03 6272 9884 or ☎ 1800 444 442, ⊚ underdownunder.com.au) takes in the lower park and Russell Falls on a whirlwind day-trip that includes a stop at the Bonorong Wildlife Sanctuary (see opposite), three times a week ($110).
Ranger station For park information and advice or to register for overnight hikes, drop in to the Mount Field Ranger Station at the entrance to the park (summer daily 9am–4pm, winter Mon–Fri 10am–3pm, Sat & Sun 9am–3.30pm; ☎ 03 6288 1149), which also has a café, shop and interpretive centre, with free pamphlets on walks in the park. There's also information here about walks in the Southwest National Park, several of which can be started from Scotts Peak Rd, which runs off the Gordon River Rd to the west of Mount Field.

ACCOMMODATION

Land of the Giant campsite Mount Field National Park ☎ 03 6288 1526. Run by Mount Field National Park rangers, this is a pretty, spacious campsite in the lower levels of the park, with pitches beside the forest or a river. Facilities are good too, including hot showers and free electric barbecues. Un/powered sites **$16/20**

Mount Field National Park cabins ☏ 03 6491 2271. Gathered in a bush clearing, the five hikers' cabins above Lake Dobson are as basic as they come – no power, light nor cooking facilities – but they sleep six and, assuming you're fully equipped, make an excellent base from which to explore the park's alpine regions. $45

Maydena and the Styx Valley

Long a forestry backwater, **Maydena**, twelve kilometres west of Mount Field National Park, has been at the sharp end of the conservation debate. The reason is the small town's proximity to the **Styx Valley**, aka the **"Valley of the Giants"**. Here, towering swamp gums (*Eucalyptus regnans*) – some over 95m tall and 5m wide at the base – have been growing for as long as four hundred years. This area of old-growth forest has suffered damage from logging activities but in 2013 conservationists celebrated when it was included as part of the expansion of the World Heritage Area of the Southwest National Park. You can pick up a map to the walking trails at the Wilderness Society's Hobart office or download it online (🌐wilderness.org.au/self-drive-guides). Access is by your own transport only, via unsealed Florentine Road, 2.5km beyond Maydena.

ACTIVITIES	MAYDENA AND THE STYX VALLEY

Rail trips At Maydena, the community-run Railtrack Riders ($30 round trip); ☏ 1300 720 507 or ☏ 0427 206864, 🌐 railtrackriders.com.au) operates a guided railway trip into the rainforest on a pedal-powered cart. The trip, to Florentine, takes about an hour to travel less than five kilometres.

Richmond and around

Surrounded by rolling countryside and wineries, **RICHMOND**, about 25km north of Hobart, is one of the oldest and best-preserved towns in Australia. It has the distinction of having Australia's oldest Roman Catholic church, **St John**, dating in part from 1837, and its oldest bridge, the arched-stone **Richmond Bridge**, constructed in 1823 using convict labour. Legend says the bridge is haunted by the ghost of George Grover, a work gang leader during its construction, who used his whip once too often and was beaten to death by the convicts, then thrown into the river.

Most of Richmond's houses date from the 1830s and 1840s, giving it an English village appearance, and many are now used as galleries, craft shops, cafés and cottage accommodation. Inevitably, Richmond is fairly touristy; despite this, it's a pleasant stop, a gentle Sunday stroll sort of place for browsing chic antique shops and dawdling over lunch.

A free leaflet detailing the old buildings is available from the visitor centre at Old Hobart Town (see p.908); a particular highlight is the National Trust-listed Oak Lodge at 8 Bridge St (daily 11.30am–3.30pm; donation), a handsome Georgian residence built in 1831.

Richmond Gaol

37 Bathurst St • Daily 9am–5pm • $9 • ☏ 03 6260 2127, 🌐 richmondgaol.com.au

Richmond's most important colonial sight is the sandstone **Richmond Gaol**, Australia's oldest intact example of an early prison. The prison's function was mostly to house prisoners in transit or those awaiting trial, and to accommodate convict road gangs working in the district; the east wing was designed to hold female convicts, who could not be accommodated at Port Arthur. One of its most infamous inmates was Ikey Solomon, reputedly the inspiration for the character of Fagin in Charles Dickens' Oliver Twist. Signs and audiovisuals explain the features of the jail, which now seems sombre but incongruously handsome.

Bonorong Wildlife Sanctuary

593 Briggs Rd, Brighton • Daily 9am–5pm • $26 • Free tours 11.30am & 2pm • ☏ 03 6268 1184, 🌐 bonorong.com.au

Efforts to pull the endangered Tasmanian devil back from the brink of extinction are what make this one of the state's most celebrated wildlife sanctuaries. Yet because

10

Bonorong specializes in the rehabilitation of orphaned and injured wildlife (hence the emphasis that this is not a zoo), it houses the full quota of unique Tassie wildlife: mobs of Forester kangaroos, pademelons and wallabies, plus quolls, possums, wombats and echidnas. It's located 18km west of Richmond, in Brighton, just west of Hobart's city limits, and makes a fulfilling day-trip from the capital if you have your own transport.

ARRIVAL AND INFORMATION

RICHMOND AND AROUND

By bus TassieLink runs services from Hobart to Richmond from Brisbane St terminus via Macquarie St (Mon–Fri 8 daily, Sat 2 daily; 1hr). For Bonorong Wildlife Sanctuary, Metro buses from Hobart get you to Brighton, but leave you 2km from the park itself.

On a tour The Hobart Shuttle Bus Company (☎ 0408 341 804, ⦻ hobartshuttlebus.com) runs tours from the visitor centre in Hobart (Sun–Fri 9am & 12.20pm, Sat 12.20pm;

$30), and operates a longer tour that includes Bonorong Wildlife Sanctuary.

Tourist information Leaflets on local sights, self-catering cottages and the like are available from the Old Hobart Town model village at 21 Bridge St (daily 9am–5pm; ☎ 03 6260 2502, ⦻ oldhobarttown.com). The tourism website ⦻ richmondvillage.com.au is useful for planning.

EATING

Ashmore on Bridge Street 34 Bridge St ☎ 03 6260 2238. There are modern international dishes like berry pancakes or daily frittata ($18) in this bright cheerful place.

Add in good coffee, wood floors and a chintz-free heritage building and you have a Richmond café par excellence. Daily 8.30am–4.30pm.

The far south

The Huonville Highway (A6) is the fast route to a great escape south of Hobart. Initially, it rolls through the pretty bucolic landscapes around Huonville. Yet the further you go, the more the landscape takes over. Forestry remains important around **Geeveston** and while some magnificent old-growth rainforests in surrounding valleys were included in the expansion of the World Heritage Area in 2013, the conservation battles in the area are unlikely to end soon. The **Tahune Forest AirWalk** is the leading tourism sight, though if you prefer your scenery without railings the alpine **Hartz Mountains National Park** may appeal. Arguably more inspiring still is **Cockle Creek**, the most southerly point accessible by road in Australia and the gateway into the Southwest National Park.

Huonville and around

HUONVILLE is the focus of the region but is missable except to stock up on supplies, pop into the regional visitor information centre just north of town and pick up park passes and walk information from the **Parks and Wildlife Service visitor centre** on Main Street, in the centre of town.

The Apple Shed

2064 Main Rd, Grove, 6km north of Huonville • Daily 10am–6pm, Fri till 9pm • $3 • ☎ 03 6266 4345

Housed in an old apple shed, on the Huon Highway (A6) at **Grove**, this museum focuses on the much-diminished apple industry hereabouts, with hundreds of varieties and weird apple paraphernalia on display to illustrate a huge export industry that peaked in the 1950s. A cellar door has cider tastings and a café serves light meals.

Franklin

Beyond Huonville is **FRANKLIN**, a bucolic place dating from 1839, with several fine old homes. The estuarial river along which timber was once exported brings a hint of the sea to the town, as does Franklin's chief attraction, the **Wooden Boat** Centre (daily except Sat 9.30am–4.30pm; $12; ☎03 6266 3586, place in woodenboatcentre.com), where you can see students work on hulls as part of courses in traditional boat-building and restoration. Boat tours on the Huon River are also available with Yukon Tours (daily 10.30am & 3pm; $50; ☎0498 578 535; ⓦyukon-tours.com.au). The ninety-minute cruises are aboard the restored Danish sailing ketch Yukon.

ARRIVAL AND INFORMATION

By bus TassieLink stops at Huonville, Grove and Franklin on its Hobart–Geeveston service (Mon–Fri 10 daily, Sat & Sun 6 daily).

Tourist information The Huon Valley Visitor Centre, 2km north of Huonville on Huon Hwy (daily: Oct–March 9am–5pm; April–Sept 10am–4pm; ☎03 6264 0326,

HUONVILLE AND AROUND

ⓦ huonvalley.tas.gov.au), is the best source of information on the entire area. The Parks and Wildlife Service visitor centre at 22 Main St, Huonville (Mon–Fri 9am–4.30pm; ☎03 6621 7026), sells maps, park passes and current information on walking conditions.

ACCOMMODATION AND EATING

HUONVILLE

Home Hill 38 Nairn St, Ranelagh ☎03 6264 1200, ⓦ homehillwines.com.au. The most sophisticated dining in the Huon Valley comes in this sleek vineyard restaurant, where seasonal menus showcase local produce, such as Bruny Island oysters and Huon rainbow trout and salmon. Main courses average $35. Views are as outstanding as the wines. Daily noon–3pm.

Huon Bush Retreats 300 Browns Road, 5km west of Ranelagh ☎03 6264 2233, ⓦhuonbushretreats.com. Retreat indeed – it's hard to believe you're only 40 minutes from Hobart in this private nature reserve with eco-cabins, luxury tepees and a few campsites deep within a rainforest crammed with wildlife. The eco-cabins have fully equipped kitchens, colourful interiors, a large lounge area with wood heater for cold nights, and the novelty of an outdoor bathtub. There are good walks in the area, too. Unpowered sites $30, tepees $135, cabins $205

FRANKLIN

Petty Sessions Gourmet Café 3445 Huon Hwy ☎03 6266 3488, ⓦpettysessions.com.au. A renowned abalone chowder, and scallop and fish pies are fixtures in Franklin's former courtroom, but this laidback café-restaurant also prepares seasonal dishes like grilled Huon River salmon, and honey-glazed pork belly; mains average $24. Daily: summer 10am–4pm & 6–8.30pm; winter 10am–4pm & 5.30–7.30pm

Riverview Cottage 3444 Huon Hwy ☎0416 140149, ⓦriverviewcottage.wordpress.com. There's modern romance in the four rooms of this heritage cottage, a marriage of French-inspired country decor and architectural charm. Note that two rooms share a bathroom; en suites are $10 extra. Breakfast includes fresh jams and eggs from the neighbour's hens. $125

Geeveston and around

Two huge upright logs serve as an entrance to sleepy and solid **GEEVESTON**, a forestry town in the heart of the Southern Forest. Logging in the nearby Weld and Florentine valleys has long been a source of bitter clashes between conservationists and the timber industry – in 2013 the greenies celebrated when some of the forests were awarded World Heritage listing. The **Forest and Heritage Centre** offers a fairly one-sided history of logging, with much talk about sustainable forests, and displays of local woodcrafts. The forest centre serves as a gateway to Forestry Tasmania's Tahune AirWalk attraction 26km away – buy tickets here in high summer to avoid queues at the site itself.

Tahune AirWalk

Arve Rd, 26km from Geeveston • daily: Oct–March 9am–5pm; April–Sept 10am–4pm • $28 • Eagle Hang Glider $16 • ☎03 6295 7170 or ☎1300 720 507, ⓦ adventureforests.com.au

From Geeveston, Arve Road buries away into the much-contested forests. En route are several short boardwalk trails through the magnificent swamp gum and eucalypt forests; most are only ten to twenty minutes long and are detailed on a free leaflet from the Forest and Heritage Centre in Geeveston (see p.910). Most visitors skip them in their hurry to reach the **Tahune AirWalk**, a $4.5-million project opened in

2001. Supported by twelve towers, its 597m walkway explores the tree canopy of the old-growth forest 25–48m high above the ground and above the confluence of the rivers, with magnificent views across to the Hartz Mountains. For more thrills (and an extra $16), the **Eagle** Hang Glider will whizz you across the forest along a cable while strapped beneath a hang-glider wing. Back at ground level, the visitor centre has interpretive forestry displays and several trails loop through the forest.

10

Hartz Mountains National Park

Twenty-four kilometres along Arve Road from Geeveston, a turn-off heads southwest to the **Hartz Mountains National Park**, a remote subalpine region of glacial lakes, rainforests and moorlands. A stony, unsealed track winds for 12km, with several stopping-off points; 2km from the end of the track is a very short walk to Waratah Lookout, which has great views over the Huon Valley and the Southern Forest. There are a couple of other short walks (under one hour) and longer walks for the more adventurous, including one to the sometimes-snowcapped Hartz Peak (1255m), but this is steep and difficult and recommended for very experienced walkers only. There's the potential for fog and snow at any time – come prepared and pick up a map of day-walks from the Forest and Heritage Centre in Geeveston or the PWS office in Huonville.

The **Picton River** skirts the Hartz Mountains from its source deep in the Southwest National Park; with its modest Grade 2–3 rapids, intermittent gentle sections and magnificent wilderness scenery, it's an easy, short (and affordable) **rafting** alternative to the Franklin River (see box, p.963).

ARRIVAL, INFORMATION AND ACTIVITIES   GEEVESTON AND AROUND

By bus TassieLink services go from Hobart to Geeveston via Huonville and Franklin (Mon–Fri 7 daily, Sat & Sun 3 daily). Note that there is no public transport to the Tahune AirWalk nor the Hartz Mountain National Park.

Tourist information The Forest and Heritage Centre, 15 Church St, Geeveston (daily 9am–5pm; ☏ 03 6297 1836, Ⓦforestandheritagecentre.com.au), has information on walks from Arve Rd, west of Geeveston, and hikes in the Hartz Mountain National Park.

Rafting Aardvark Adventures (☏ 03 6273 7722, Ⓦ aardvarkadventures.com.au) organizes rafting trips on the Picton River near the Tahune AirWalk for $155 per person.

ACCOMMODATION AND EATING

The Kermandie Port Huon ☏ 03 6297 1052, Ⓦkermandie.com.au. Vintage furnishings add character to the lovely en-suite rooms of this older hotel that was handsomely refurbished by a downshifter from Sydney in late 2012. Queens are worth the $10 extra, as most feature views of the marina opposite. **$140**

Sass Kermandie Hotel, Port Huon ☏ 03 6297 1052, Ⓦkermandie.com.au. The makeover of this hotel has brought metropolitan sassiness to the sleepy south Huon. There are tapas plates of local ingredients in the lounge bar or dishes like Tassie steak, wallaby filet or handmade gnocchi ($28) in the restaurant. Daily noon–2.30pm, 5.30–8pm.

Tahune Lodge Arve Rd, 26km west of Geeveston ☏ 1300 720 527, Ⓦadventureforests.com. The forest lodge of the Tahune AirWalk is a good option for backpackers and families on a budget. Sited within the forest, its modern hostel-style accommodation offers four-bed dorms, doubles and family rooms, and the room price includes entry to the AirWalk. Dorms **$50**, doubles **$115**

Dover and around

The scenery becomes increasingly wild as the road swings south of Geeveston to roll in after 21km at **DOVER**, an attractive fishing village set behind a large bay, **Port Esperance**. It's an appealingly backwoods sort of spot to kick back, with fishing boats moored off a jetty in the bay and wooded hills that peel back to the triangular outline of **Adamsons Peak** (1226m), snowcapped in winter. It's also by far the most comfortable gateway to Cockle Creek (see p.912). Note that **SOUTHPORT**, 20km

OPPOSITE HOBART (P.889) >

10

ALL ABOARD THE BUSH LINE

Once the **Ida Bay Railway** was just a hauler of timber for export. Today, the claim to fame of this tiny 1940s bush-train is that it is Australia's southernmost railway. Journeys embark south of Southport at Ida Bay and pootle through the bush to reach a lonely bit of coast. In theory it's a two-hour return journey, but this makes an ideal day-trip if you bring a picnic then catch a later train home (Dec–April daily 10am, noon & 2pm, plus 4pm in Jan; May–Dec Thurs, Fri, Sat & Sun 10am &12.30pm; $32; ☎ 03 6298 3110 or ☎ 0428 383 262, ⊛ idabayrailway.com.au).

further on, is the last stop for fuel and supplies on the road south, but the IGA supermarket in Dover has a better selection if you need to stock up.

Hastings Caves State Reserve

Around 6km west of Southport via Hastings Caves Rd • Springs 10.30am–4pm • $5, or included with cave tour • Cave tours 11.30am, 12.30pm, 2.15pm & 3.15pm; 45min • $24 • ☎ 03 6298 3209, ⊛ parks.tas.gov.au

Scenery aside, one reason to make the trek 21km south of Dover is the **Hastings Caves State Reserve**. Near the visitor centre, a thermal spring is fed into a shallow pool of around 28°C. It's no great shakes, but the setting is lush and there are several walks in the grounds. Around 5km further on in the foothills of Adamsons Peak are **Hastings Caves**, a series of richly decorated dolomite chambers formed around forty million years ago. Newdegate Cave, the best, is open daily for tours to show off its weird formations and weirder wildlife, including many species found nowhere else.

ARRIVAL AND DEPARTURE   DOVER AND AROUND

By bus TassieLink services go from Hobart via Huonville, Franklin and Geeveston to Dover (Mon–Fri 2 daily; 1hr 40min).

ACCOMMODATION AND EATING

Driftwood Holiday Cottages 51 Bay View Rd, Dover ☎ 03 6298 1441 or ☎ 1800 353 983, ⊛ driftwoodcottages.com.au. These well-appointed, self-contained studios and cottages offer spectacular views across Esperance Bay from their balconies. Each comes with nice extras, such as underfloor heating, a large breakfast hamper or wood burner. The new two-bedroom cottages have barbecues, and one has a double spa bath. Studios $170, cottages $325

Dover Beachside Tourist Park Kent Beach Rd, Dover ☎ 03 6298 1301, ⊛ dovertouristpark.com.au. Just around the corner from Driftwood and across the road from the bay, this small holiday park offers three- and four-star cabins and camping; it's the best budget option in town.

Un/powered sites $25/35, cabins $100

Far South Wilderness Camp Narrows Rd, Strathblane ☎ 03 6298 1922, ⊛ farsouthwilderness.com.au. True escapism on an inlet of the Esperance River. The main wilderness lodge can be taken over by school groups, but it also has cabins and a superb, modern forest lodge surrounded by bush that sleeps up to ten – think of it as a private backpackers'. $75

Post Office 6985 6985 Huon Hwy ☎ 03 6298 1905. Lemon seafood risotto, local fish, wallaby steaks, honey and ginger quail, and freshly made pizzas are typical of the simple, modern cuisine of this café-restaurant. The atmosphere is relaxed and inviting, the prices good at around $18 a pizza. Good just for a drink too. Thurs–Sat 4–8pm.

Cockle Creek

If bush camping for a few days is an essential part of the Tasmanian experience, the end of the road in Australia seems a logical place to do it. Cockle Creek Road, the country's most southerly road, threads past sheltered bays and coastal forests to **COCKLE CREEK** on lovely **Recherche Bay** (pronounced "research" by locals). The bay is named after the ship in which a French expedition under **Bruny D'Entrecasteaux**, sent to look for the missing La Perouse expedition (see p.109), dropped anchor for four weeks in 1792 and again in 1793. As well as important botanical research carried out by naturalist Labilladière, a garden was established and cordial meetings with the Aboriginal people were recorded.

Notwithstanding the haunting bay itself, which has lots of free camping spots along the shore, there's little here except a few shacks and caravans inhabited semipermanently by fishing-obsessed retirees, and an emergency phone. Yet it's a great spot to drop off the radar or as a gateway for day-trips (or longer) to the magnificent coastline of the **Southwest National Park** (see p.965). A wooden bridge across Cockle Creek leads to the park where an interpretive board provides an introduction to the area's fascinating history from Aboriginal, French, whalers' and settlers' perspectives. It's a five-minute walk to a bronze sculpture of a baby southern right whale.

10

ARRIVAL AND ACCOMMODATION   COCKLE CREEK

By bus Tasmanian Wilderness Experiences (☏ 01300 882 293, ⏉ twe.travel) runs bushwalker services from Hobart to Cockle Creek on request (reservations essential).

Accommodation The only accommodation is camping, with free spots scalloped along the shore. Campers can stay for up to one month. The downside is the lack of facilities: pit toilets and water only.

The Tasman Peninsula

The Tasman Peninsula is one of the most visited parts of the state. Everyone comes on a day-trip for the penal settlement of Port Arthur – the most popular attraction in Tasmania before the opening of Hobart's MONA gallery – yet this peninsula is worth a visit in its own right: there are superb **bushwalks** around its spectacular south and eastern coastline, incredible nature cruises and a good wildlife park. That your Port Arthur ticket is valid for two days is just one more reason to stay overnight. The fastest route from Hobart to the **Tasman Peninsula** is northeast along the Tasman Highway then across the **Sorell Causeway** to the small town of **Sorell**, your last chance for shopping and banking.

Eaglehawk Neck and around

The introduction to the Tasman Peninsula is **Eaglehawk Neck**, a spectacular sweep of white sand and bush whose narrow strip yokes the peninsula to "mainland" Tasmania. It's as historical as it is hauntingly beautiful: during the convict era, the neck was guarded by a chain of fierce dogs to prevent Port Arthur escapees fleeing the prison island. Of the original military station here, only the low, long timber **Officers' Quarters** (daily 9am–4pm; free) dating from 1832 survives. It has been turned into a mini-museum that documents the site's convict past with novel perspectives from the bored officers and their wives who were stationed here.

Some of the finest coastal features on the peninsula are around this area. Just to the north of the superb arc of sand is the **Tessellated Pavement**, its natural "cobbles" visible at low tide, and to the south, off the highway, is a **blowhole** that works in big swells, the huge **Tasman Arch** and the **Devils Kitchen**, a sheer rock cleft into which the sea

---

A WALK INTO THE SOUTHWEST NATIONAL PARK

For many visitors, **Cockle Creek** provides an accessible taste of Tasmania's south coast; an utterly remote region otherwise experienced only by hikers who tackle the **South Coast Track** (see p.966), an isolated nine-day haul that's for very experienced and well-prepared bushwalkers only. From the statue of the southern right whale, an easy walk to Fishers Point takes you around a headland (4km return; up to 2hr). But since you've come this far, it's better to make a day-trip of it and walk to South Cape Bay (4hr return; moderate difficulty). After a boardwalked though occasionally muddy hike through rainforest, you emerge at a sweep of wild surf beach where civilization feels long distant and the next land south is Antarctica. Magic.

surges. Much of this latter area falls within the **Tasman National Park** and marks the start (or end of) the **Tasman Trail**, a 16km clifftop walk that runs between the Devils Kitchen and **Fortescue Bay** (see below).

Tasmanian Devil Unzoo

Taranna • Daily: Oct–May 9am–6pm; June–Sept 9am–5pm • $33 multiple entry • ☎ 03 6250 3230, �🖜 tasmaniandevilunzoo.com.au

Southwest of Eaglehawk Neck at **Taranna**, the **Tasmanian Devil** Unzoo is a privately owned conservation park engaged in a breeding programme to help save the Tasmanian devil from extinction (see box, p.919). These iconic animals are fed around five times a day or you can go eye-to-eye with one in a bubble-like dome sunk at ground level. The site also has a decent spread of 'roos, wallabies and quolls, all fed daily. Your ticket permits multiple entries to the centre for the duration of your stay on the peninsula, allowing you to explore the area and then return for various feedings or falcon free-flight displays (times advertised at entrance). You can also take a ninety-minute 4WD tour ($79) with researchers to see how devils are being tracked in the surrounding countryside.

Fortescue Bay and the Tasman National Park

Perhaps the most beautiful bay on the peninsula is **Fortescue Bay**, a gorgeous cove of white sand and bush, accessed via a pitted 12km dirt road off the Arthur Highway south of Taranna. As well as being a beautiful (and popular) campsite within the Tasman National Park, it is the start of some of the finest walks in the state. Few are more spectacular than that to the cliffs of **Cape Huay** (4hr return from campsite), with its views over a dolerite stack known as the Candlestick. A separate extended walk from the bay goes all the way to **Cape Pillar**, where the 300m sea cliffs are said to be the highest in Australia. It's a two- or three-day return trip, requiring you to camp out overnight in the national park (fuel stoves only).

Port Arthur Historic Site

Port Arthur • Daily 8.30am–7pm • Passes including access to the site and various tours $37–85 • ☎ 1800 659 101, ⍉ portarthur.org.au

In 1830, **PORT ARTHUR** was selected to host a **prison settlement** on the "natural penitentiary" of the Tasman Peninsula, its "gate" at Eaglehawk Neck guarded by dogs. It was intended for convicts who committed serious crimes in New South Wales or Van Diemen's Land after transportation. The regime was never a subtle one: Van Diemen's Land **Lieutenant-Governor George Arthur** believed that a convict's "whole fate should be … the very last degree of misery consistent with humanity". However, his aim was to create "a machine to grind rogues honest". This was rehabilitation rather than

---

TASMAN PENINSULA ECO-CRUISES AND DIVING

An **eco-cruise** along the spectacular coastline of the Tasman Peninsula is highly recommended. Tours in high-speed boats hug the 200m cliffs and nose into sea caves – expect to see sea eagles, albatross, seals on Tasman Island, possibly dolphins, and if you're lucky, whales from September to December and April to May.

Eaglehawk Dive Centre 178 Pirates Bay Drive ☎ 03 6250 3566, ⍉ eaglehawkdive.com.au. Provides dive-boat charters (equipment included) into the spectacular dive sites of the Tasman coast: caves, shipwrecks, kelp forests and nearby seal colonies, with an underwater visibility of 15–30m.

Tasman Island Cruises ☎ 03 6250 2200, ⍉ tasmancruises.com.au. An award-winning outfit that sails out from Port Arthur to jet down to Tasman Island, then zip up the coast to Pirates Bay (Eaglehawk Neck), with a return by minibus (daily 10am; mid-Dec to mid-April also 2pm; 3hr; $125).

PORT ARTHUR HISTORIC SITE TOURS AND PASSES

All entry passes to the **Port Arthur Historic Site** include an overview tour and a cruise around the bay. Other tour options visit the **Isle of the Dead**, Port Arthur's cemetery from 1833 to 1877, to hear the tales of some of the 1100 convicts, asylum inmates, paupers and free men buried there; and the **Point Puer Boys' Prison**, which held transportees as young as nine.

TICKETS

The basic **ticket** ($37) provides access to the site, a 40-minute guided tour and a 25-minute harbour cruise; options include an audio tour ($6) and tours to Point Puer (2hr; $50 including entry) and the Isle of the Dead (1hr; $50 including entry).

GHOST TOURS

Small wonder that the site has been known for ghosts even when it was a penal settlement; over ten thousand sightings have been reported, most in the Parsonage and Separate Prison. **Ghost tours** by night ($25; 1hr 30min; reservation essential) tour the buildings by lamplight and titillate with ghoulish tales of convict-era horrors. An After Dark Pass ($69) adds a two-course dinner to the tour. The **Paranormal Investigation Experience** (last Sat of the month 7–10pm, or 9pm–midnight in summer; minimum age 18; $85) is a small group tour exploring the most haunted buildings of the site with scientific gizmos.

10

punitive punishment; work with the system and your years would slip past, fight it and you would be crushed.

The first 150 convicts established a timber industry, then Port Arthur became a self-supporting centre of industry, with shipbuilding, brickmaking, shoemaking, even agriculture. In a separate prison for boys at **Point Puer**, inmates were taught trades. Meanwhile, prison officers and their families enjoyed gardens, a drama club, a library and regular cricket. After transportation ended, psychological punishment replaced physical. The **Separate Prison**, based on Pentonville Prison in London, opened in 1852, where prisoners were held in tiny cells in isolation and silence, always referred to by numbers and hooded whenever they left their cells. The idea represented progressive penal ideas that let convicts contemplate their misdeeds, but by the time Port Arthur closed in 1877 it had its own **mental asylum** full of ex-convicts, as well as a geriatric home for ex-convict paupers.

Visiting the site

Popularized by Marcus Clarke's romantic tragedy *For the Term of His Natural Life* (1870), Port Arthur received visitors as soon as the prison closed in 1877, when former inmates provided guided tours. Today, the **Port Arthur Historic Site**, a hundred-acre area that takes in more than sixty buildings of the penal settlement and colonial period afterwards (buggies are available for those with mobility difficulties), is among the leading attractions in the state, with all the tour groups that implies; come as early as possible to escape the crowds, especially in summer. Yet a visit to the site remains essential to understand the convict history of Van Diemen's Land. Excellent introductory tours (included in all passes; 45min) stress that for many convicts, Port Arthur represented a fresh start; an escape from the slums of the industrial revolution or rural famine, with accommodation, regular meals and the first opportunity to learn a trade.

With a tour ticked off, you are free to explore the beautifully restored buildings at leisure, each with information boards on its past. Highlights include the English **church**, completed just three years after the site was opened (religion was central to Governor Arthur's idea of reform); the chilling **Separate Prison**, superbly restored to tell personal histories of those incarcerated and which doubles as a museum of the entire site; and the **Governor's House**, a miniature manor furnished in Georgian and late Victorian styles. Perhaps the greatest surprise is the World Heritage Site's appearance. With its sandstone British architecture, picket fences around pretty civilian cottages

10

and trim green lawns above a beautiful bay, it looks more like a serene, old-world university campus than a prison.

What's not widely discussed at Port Arthur is that it was also the site of a modern tragedy: Australia's worst mass murder. In April 1996, a lone gunman killed 35 people at the Port Arthur site and wounded 37 more. He was later sentenced to life imprisonment, never to be released. Those events led to the Australian government passing some of the strictest gun control laws in the world. A discreet memorial to those who died in the massacre is in the ruins of the former café, not far from the visitor centre, hidden behind trees and shrubbery, but easily found if you are looking for it. Visitors are asked not to ask guides about these events, as many still find it too devastating to talk about. There is a brochure available at the visitor centre.

Coal Mines Historic Site

Coal Mines Rd, via Premaydena • Free • ⊕ portarthur.org.au

Despite the ghoulish focus on penal servitude at Port Arthur, time in the coal mines of Lime Bay in the peninsula's northeast was equally brutal due to the punishing, dangerous nature of the work. The coal mined here (on average three tonnes a day) wasn't even of particularly good quality. Granted World Heritage status in 2010, the site remains low-key compared to Port Arthur; you are free to wander the ruins of the prisons and discover the solitary cells where offending troublesome convicts were held. An excellent guide leaflet from the Port Arthur Historic Site (available as a download) provides background and directions, as there is no public transport to the site.

ARRIVAL AND DEPARTURE THE TASMAN PENINSULA

By bus TassieLink's Hobart–Port Arthur service calls at all settlements en route to Port Arthur. Be aware that the only afternoon return is on Saturday, however (Mon–Sat 2 daily; 1hr 25min).

Tours Numerous privately operated tours of the Tasman Peninsula ease the logistics of a day-trip from Hobart for backpackers: Jump and Under Down Under (see box, p.889) run tours for $120 and $110 respectively. Tasman Island Cruises ($225) also operates a tour from Hobart, taking in the Port Arthur Historic Site and including a spot of eco-cruising (see box, p.914).

ACCOMMODATION

EAGLEHAWK NECK

Lufra Hotel and Apartments 380 Pirates Bay Drive ☏03 6250 3262, ⊕lufrahotel.com. There are three options here: basic budget rooms and better standards in the hotel; and self-contained studios and two-bedroom units that are well-equipped, modern(ish) and feature awesome views over the bay. Doubles $90, studios $160, apartments $230

FORTESCUE BAY

★ **Fortescue Bay camping** ☏03 6250 2433. Welcome to one of the loveliest national park campsites in Tasmania,

---

ONTO THE CENTRAL PLATEAU

A left-turn off the Midlands Highway around 45km north of Hobart leads onto the Lake Highway and up to Tasmania's forgotten highlands. Also accessible going south from Longford (see p.938) and Deloraine (see p.940), **the Central Plateau** (1440m max) is a sparsely populated flat landscape of moors, mists and glacial lakes. Given its reputation for frost, sleet and snowstorms in winter, it's probably no surprise that the area is almost empty. The only real town is **Bothwell**, en route up to the plateau, whose claims to fame include Australia's oldest golf course and a whisky distillery. Created by Scottish settlers in 1822, the Ratho Farm golf course welcomes visitors (green fees $40, club hire $20; ☏03 6259 5553 or ☏0497 644 916, ⊕rathofarm.com), while the Nante Estate distillery (daily 10am–4pm; ☏1800 746 453, ⊕nant.com) produces single malt (guided tours $15). The area is also celebrated for its thousands of lakes and its trout. On a fine weekend the resident population of a few hundred swells into thousands as fishermen head up to shacks around the best fishing lakes: **Great Lake**, **Lake Sorrell** and **Arthurs Lakes**.

spread among the gums behind the beach of Fortescue Bay and home to wildlife by the ton. Facilities include water, barbecues, firepits (firewood for sale), toilets and showers. National park entry fees apply; the sense of escapism is free. Camping $13

PORT ARTHUR

Port Arthur Holiday Park Garden Point Rd ☎03 6250 2340, ⓦportarthurhp.com.au. The best budget option on the peninsula provides lovely spacious camping pitches with a private fire/barbecue area, basic bunk rooms, plus simple en-suite cabins spread throughout its green site, all a 2km shore walk from the Port Arthur Historic Site. Reservation recommended in summer. Camping $31, dorms $30, cabins $135

Sea Change Safety Cove 425 Safety Cove Rd, 4km

EATING

Pavement 380 Pirates Bay Drive ☎03 6250 3262. The restaurant of the *Lufra Hotel* prepares a passable pub menu of standards such as chicken schnitzel, lamb shank or fish and chips (mains average $24). However, the million-dollar view over the beach of Eaglehawk Neck is worth the price alone. Live music on Sat. Daily 6–9pm.

Gabriel's on the Bay 6955 Arthur Hwy, Port Arthur

south of Port Arthur ☎03 6250 2719, ⓦsafetycove .com. There are few better escapes in peak season than this waterfront B&B. Alongside home-from-home en-suite rooms, expect ocean views, jaw-dropping sunrises and a quiet beach on the doorstep, plus charm in abundance from its friendly owners. Also has a two-bedroom self-contained flat. Doubles $200, flat $250

★**Stewarts Bay Lodge** 6955 Arthur Hwy ☎03 6250 2888, ⓦstewartsbaylodge.com.au. This resort has cabins in rustic and luxury varieties spread throughout the bush above a lovely bay, with a shoreline walking track to the Port Arthur Historic Site. Accommodation is in excellent one- to three-bed cabins (with a wide range of prices), and facilities include a good restaurant. A fine base from which to explore the peninsula. No wi-fi. $194

☎03 6250 2771. The restaurant of *Stewarts Bay Lodge* is the fine-dining address of the peninsula. Local produce is on the menu: Tassie oysters, scallops with pancetta, garlic and chilli, or smoked quail alongside steak or a seafood platter (mains average $33). As appealing is the beautiful bayside position. Mon & Thurs–Sun 8–10am, noon–2pm & 5.30–8.30pm; Tues & Wed 8am–10am & noon–2pm.

10

The Midland Highway

Anyone heading north via the **Midland Highway** rather than the east coast is generally in a hurry. The fast three-hour route between Hobart and Launceston more or less follows the coaching road between the colony's first towns. Those origins and the early colonial villages en route have led the tourist board to christen this The Heritage Highway. Former garrison and sheep towns, they are places to break up a journey rather than destinations in their own right. On the southern half of the route, keep a look out for the black silhouette sculptures that randomly appear in the landscape; there are sixteen of them.

Oatlands

Australia's greatest concentration of colonial **Georgian buildings** is the appeal of **OATLANDS**, the first stop north of Hobart. The 140 convict-constructed buildings are squeezed into just two square kilometres; the tourist office in town produces a free leaflet marking the highlights. Some are occupied by antique and crafts shops and galleries, painting a sheen of discreet prosperity onto this small, sleepy town.

Historic charm aside, the town's main sight, and also housing the tourist office, is the restored **Callington Mill** complex at 1 Mill Lane (daily 9am–5pm; $15; tours hourly 10am–3pm; ☎03 6254 1212, ⓦcallingtonmill.com.au). Built in 1821, the mill was abandoned in 1892 until its sails turned again in 2010, when it was scrubbed up and restored to working order, turning out flour, oats, bran and semolina. It's the only traditional European wind-powered mill in the southern hemisphere. The mechanics and outbuildings provide an interesting insight into colonial history, and on tours you'll hear about the (mis)fortune of its original owner.

10

By bus Redline's daily bus services between Hobart and Launceston stops in Oatlands (Mon–Fri 3 daily, Sat & Sun 2 daily; 1hr 10min).

Tourist information and tours With prior booking, the tourist office at 1 Mill Lane (daily 9am–5pm; ☎ 03 6254 1212) provides themed walking tours, including the Executioner's Trail of the military precinct and jail, which includes a visit to one of Australia's oldest courthouses (1829), and an Oatlands town tour (min 4 people; $15/person).

EATING

e.sense Patisserie Café 104 High St ☎ 03 6254 1263. Using flour ground at Callington Mill and organic ingredients, the artisan baker-owners of this pretty modern-rustic café produce gluten-free pies, pancakes, scones and more from their wood-fired oven. There's a huge range of teas, and organic coffee. May–Sept Wed–Sun 9am–5pm; Oct–April daily 9am–5pm.

Ross

Beyond Oatlands you drive north through sheep-grazing countryside, before turning to **ROSS**, 2km east of the highway. Settled by Scots, this is arguably Tasmania's – perhaps even Australia's – best-preserved colonial village; barely a modern shop sign intrudes on the air of bygone bucolic bliss, and honey-hued stone buildings line the lanes behind British elm trees. The time-honoured entry to Ross from the south is via **Ross Bridge**, designed by John Lee Archer in 1836 and famous for the tangled carvings – Celtic symbols, colonial characters, animals and flora – on its sandstone arches. So impressed was the colony governor, George Arthur, that he granted their convict stonemasons a free pardon.

Ross Female Factory

Cnr Bond & Portugal sts • Mon–Fri 9am–5pm, Sat & Sun 9.30am–5pm • Free

Over the crest of the hill above the Tasmanian Wool Centre are the remains of the **Female Factory**, one of the two female colonial prisons in Tasmania – the other is in Hobart (see p.895). Information displays in the overseer's cottage narrate the female convict experience; women were held at the prison before being assigned as servants. Only foundations remain of the former convict buildings. A path from here leads to the **colonial cemetery**.

The Tasmanian Wool Centre

48 Church St • Mon–Fri 9.30am–5pm, Sat & Sun 10am–5pm • Museum by donation • ☎ 03 6381 5466, ⓦ taswoolcentre.com.au

Casts of the original carvings on the Ross Bridge, now rather worn, can be seen at the **Tasmanian Wool Centre**, uphill from the village crossroads. It also acts as the town's visitor information centre and has displays on local history and the settlers' wool industry.

By bus Redline's daily bus services between Hobart and Launceston stop at Ross (Mon–Fri 3 daily, Sat & Sun 2 daily; 1hr 25min).

Tourist information In the Tasmanian Wool Centre, Church St (Mon–Fri 9.30am–5pm, Sat & Sun 10am–5pm; ☎ 03 6381 5466, ⓦ visitross.com.au).

ACCOMMODATION AND EATING

Colonial Cottages of Ross ☎ 03 6381 5354 or ☎ 0417 522 354, ⓦ rossaccommodation.com.au. Manages three heritage cottages sleeping from two to eight; expect rough sandstone or wood-panelled walls, traditional furnishings of iron and tester beds, and a free glass of port on arrival. If you prefer traditional B&B accommodation, there is also a house with two guest rooms plus a two-bedroom retreat (with separate entrance) available. All are furnished in colonial style (one with a four-poster bed). Doubles $140, cottages $180

Ross Caravan Park and Motel 2 High St ☎ 03 6381 5224, ⓦ rossmotel.com.au. As well as pitches, this small site spread along the Macquarie River by the bridge has simple "cabins" – actually self-contained rooms in stone cottages, which sleep up to four people – great for families or backpackers. With no linen provided and bathrooms at the caravan park, it's a bit like a private hostel. Check-in is at a motel 50m away that offers clean and good if rather bland four-star accommodation. Un/powered sites $26/34, cabins $70, doubles $135

Ross Hotel 35 Church St ☎ 03 6381 5445,

ⓦ rosshotel.com.au. The village's old pub (1835) is one of the few eating options in town, serving the usual chicken schnitzel or steaks (about $25). On a nice day, the pub's side garden is a lovely spot to sit. Upstairs are simple but acceptable heritage-style pub rooms with shared facilities. Daily noon–10pm; food noon–2pm & 6–8pm. **$75**

The east coast

If anywhere in Tasmania conforms to the Aussie stereotype of white beaches and azure seas beneath a cloudless sky, it is the **east coast**. Sheltered from the prevailing westerly winds and washed by warm currents (well, warm by local standards), this is the state's holiday playground; cheerful and unpretentious, not to mention sunnier and drier than elsewhere thanks to prevailing weather patterns. Small wonder it's popular – prices go up and accommodation is scarce from Christmas to mid-February during school summer holidays.

The Gold Coast this is not, however. The coastline itself remains relatively undeveloped, and the few settlements are small-fry fishing and holiday towns like **Swansea** and **Bicheno**. It speaks volumes that **St Helens**, gateway to the spectacular white beaches of the Bay of Fires, is the largest settlement with a population of just over two thousand. If even that seems too many, there are four national parks for escape, including **Maria Island** (the *whole* island), an entire peninsula at **Freycinet National Park** and staggeringly beautiful empty beaches in **Mount William National Park** at the northeast tip of the state. Come to kayak, surf, swim or just enjoy the salt-tanged atmosphere. And if that sounds good, the string of bush camps here lets you stay at the fringes of one beautiful beach after another, often without paying a cent.

10

GETTING AROUND   THE EAST COAST

By bus From Hobart, TassieLink tracks up the east coast via Triabunna, Swansea and the Coles Bay turn-off to Bicheno. Local bus companies fill in the gaps.
By bike Inevitably, most people tour by car; however, the winding coastal route makes for pleasant cycling, especially out of season. Just be warned of fast traffic on some sections of fairly narrow road and a brutal haul uphill between Hobart and Triabunna.

Maria Island National Park

Uninhabited save for its park ranger, **Maria Island** (pronounced "Ma-rye-a") is 15km off the east coast and accessed by ferry from Triabunna. The beaches are excellent, and the walks and mountain-bike rides are easy, with broad tracks and few hills to climb. Maria Island also appeals for its wildlife, especially the prolific **birdlife**, with over 130 species; it's the only

---

DEVILS IN DANGER

Made world-famous by the angry cartoon character "Taz", the **Tasmanian devil**, *Sarcophilus harrisii*, is actually a stocky nocturnal black-haired animal about the size of a squat bulldog. That makes it the world's largest **carnivorous marsupial**, with an appetite for carrion, reptiles and insects to match. The name was coined by European settlers who found the marsupial's call, ranging from a low groan to a banshee screech, positively demonic.

Yet devils need all the friends they can get right now. Devil Facial Tumour Disease (DFDT), a contagious cancer that is transmitted by saliva and causes fatal bulbous lesions, has spread across the state at around 15km a year since it was detected in northeast Tasmania in 1996. In the ensuing decade, there was a 95 percent decline in devil sightings. While geneticists race to map the twelve strains of the disease, the state's **Save the Tasmanian Devil Programme** (ⓦ tassiedevil.com.au) is pinning hopes on breeding colonies such as Trowunna Wildlife Park (see p.940) and Devils@Cradle (see p.954), as well as large disease-free enclosures in Tasmania and on the mainland. These programmes are the last line of defence for a top predator whose demise threatens to destabilize the entire Tasmanian ecosystem. The species went onto the "Endangered" list in 2010; not quite on the brink of extinction, perhaps, but close to the edge.

10

national park containing all eleven of the state's endemic bird species, including the rare forty-spotted pardalote and Cape Barren geese. A decision to transfer a small population of threatened Tasmanian devils to the island in 2013 (see box, p.919) only confirmed Maria's status as a Noah's Ark for native species. You can just about sample the island on a hurried day-trip, but if you fancy playing the castaway, treat yourself to at least an overnight stay.

Darlington

The ferry lands at **DARLINGTON**, actually just a jetty and a few buildings left over from Maria's time as a colonial **penal settlement**. Like a trial run for Port Arthur, it held convicts in a probation station from 1825 until 1850. The old commissariat store now serves as a visitor centre while the penitentiary itself is now an atmospheric **bunkhouse** (see below); the site won World Heritage accreditation from UNESCO in 2010.

Idling on the beaches aside, most visitors come to tackle the many short **walks** around Darlington. The **Fossil Cliffs** are a twenty-minute stroll from the ferry quay, or you can walk to the Painted Cliffs (2hr return), with its section of strangely sculpted sandstone. Hike up **Bishop and Clerk** (4hr return) for astounding ocean views from the dolerite pinnacle. The visitor centre at Darlington (see below) has a range of pamphlets with ideas for longer bushwalks.

The southern end

With a couple of days to spare – or one day on a bike – you can go past a superb beach at the island's narrow isthmus to the rarely visited **southern end** of the island, practically a second island of unspoilt forests and secluded beaches. As there's little water here, be sure to bring supplies with you.

ARRIVAL AND DEPARTURE   MARIA ISLAND

By bus TassieLink buses depart for Triabunna (from where ferries to the island depart) from Hobart: Mon–Fri 2 daily, Sat (school holidays only) 1 daily, Sun 1 daily; 1hr 25min–1hr 40min.

By ferry Maria Island Ferry (Dec–April daily 9am & 3.30pm; June–Aug daily 10.30am & 3pm; Sept–Nov Fri–Mon 10.30am & 3.30pm; 40min; return $35, bikes $10; ☎0419 746668, ✆mariaislandferry.com.au) departs from the quay at Triabunna, reached on the TassieLink east-coast service. Reservations are advised, especially in summer. Alongside the ferry fare, standard national park fees apply – if you have a car pass, bring the receipt.

INFORMATION

Tourist information A visitor centre by the quay on the Esplanade in Triabunna (daily Oct–April 9am–5pm; May–Sept 10am–4pm; ☎03 6257 1420) has information on the island. An unmanned centre at Darlington has information on island fauna and hikes; in theory opening times are between the first ferry to arrive and last to leave.

Bike hire The ferry company (on the waterfront at Triabunna, see above) hires mountain bikes and helmets for $25/day, and the ranger's office in Darlington also has a few mountain bikes for rent.

ACTIVITIES

Boat cruise East Coast Cruises (✆eastcoastcruises .com.au) circumnavigates the island on a full-day cruise around Maria's western cliffs, visiting sea caves and giving time to snorkel or kayak, before spending the afternoon at Darlington to see the convict ruins and wildlife (Nov–April daily 10am; 7hr; $220, lunch included).

Hiking The island hosts one of Tasmania's signature hikes, the Maria Island Walk (Oct–April; $2400; ☎03 6234 2999, ✆mariaislandwalk.com.au). This excellent four-day guided walk skirts the coastline to stop in luxury wilderness camps and a late nineteenth-century house in Darlington, with gourmet meals each night. Price includes transfers from Hobart; maximum of eight people.

ACCOMMODATION AND EATING

MARIA ISLAND
Bush camping away from Darlington is best at French's Farm or prettier Encampment Cove in the south of Maria, four hours' walk from Darlington. Non-treated rainwater is available at both, though both are fuel stove only. Note that you'll need to be self-sufficient if staying overnight on the island because no food is available.

★ **Penitentiary Bunkhouse** ☎03 6256 4772. The

convicts could never have imagined that reservations were essential to bed down in their old penitentiary. There's no denying the atmosphere of its basic stone-walled six-bed dorms, each with wood stoves, table and chairs, but note that there's no cooking equipment nor bedding. Dorms $15

Darlington Campsite ☎ 03 6257 1420. The island's best campsite, spread at the shoulder of the penitentiary not far from Darlington Bay, provides the full range of facilities: a public phone, toilets, showers ($1), fireplaces, cold-water taps and tank water for drinking. Free gas barbecues are provided in the dunes. Sites $13

TRIABUNNA

Triabunna is a nondescript, oversized village; it's only worth staying here if bus or ferry timetables demand so.

Gallery Artspaces Highway 7, Vicary St ☎ 03 6257 3311. Moroccan lamb, sourdough with falafel and feta wraps (average $12–16) are typical of the wholesome light lunches served in this gallery café, all freshly made. That the coffee's the best in town also makes it handy when waiting for the ferry. They'll also do lunch packs to take to the island with you. Daily 8.30am–4pm.

Tandara Hotel Motel Tasman Highway ☎ 03 6257 3333. These modernized motel units are bland in decor – the usual blond wood laminate and wetroom-style bathroom – but they are the most comfortable option in Triabunna and offer great value for money. $88

Triabunna Cabin and Caravan Park Vicary St ☎ 03 6257 3575, ⓦ mariagateway.com. One of the few "mainland" options for budget travellers is this small and fairly cramped caravan park. There are twenty caravan sites and a small lawn for camping, otherwise accommodation is in cabins or two en-suite studios (in the same cottage). Camping $30, studios $105, cabins $120

Swansea

On a sunny day, the 50km drive from Triabunna to **SWANSEA** is spectacularly beautiful, with brilliant white beaches, the intense aquamarine of Great Oyster Bay and views to the Freycinet Peninsula, where the contours of the Hazards Mountains shimmer in the distance. One of Tasmania's oldest settlements, Swansea was founded in the 1830s and retains some colonial architecture, and is today a low-key resort. There are a smattering of cafés and restaurants, and a beautiful 2km shore path from the centre that provides gorgeous views to the Freycinet Peninsula, especially at sunset.

For more detail on the settlement's past, the **Swansea Bark Mill Museum** (96 Tasman Hwy; daily 10am–4pm; $10) at the north end of the town has exhibits on the area's French connections and, as a centrepiece, the eponymous contraption that produced leather-tanner from black wattle bark.

ARRIVAL AND INFORMATION SWANSEA

By bus Swansea is on TassieLink's east-coast service that departs from Hobart: Mon, Wed, Fri, Sat & Sun daily; 2hr 15min.

Tourist information Cnr Franklin & Noyes sts (daily Oct–April 9am–5pm; May–Sept 10am–4pm; ☎ 03 6256 5072, ⓦ eastcoasttasmania.com).

ACCOMMODATION

Camping Options are limited for campers in Swansea. If you have your own transport there's good, free bush camping behind the beach at Mayfield Bay Coastal Reserve 10km south.

Meredith House & Mews 15 Noyes St ☎ 03 6257 8119, ⓦ meredith-house.com.au. Gay-friendly B&B in an antiques-filled chintz-free convict-built Georgian manor on a hill just off the main street; some rooms have views over the bay. In addition to the six rooms, the former mews has been renovated into four self-contained studios. Doubles $180, studios $225

Piermont Tasman Hwy, 3km south ☎ 03 6257 8131, ⓦ piermont.com.au. Chic escapism in fifteen luxury self-contained stone cottages, with walls of stone or rammed earth and a touch of the Mediterranean about their beautifully finished laidback decor; the best open directly onto a private beach. Also has six stylish spa suites. Cottages $355, suites $415

Swansea Backpackers Lodge Tasman Hwy, 600m north of centre ☎ 03 6257 8650, ⓦ swanseabackpackers.com.au. Arguably Tasmania's slickest hostel, this modern flashpackers' by the Bark Mill is more expensive than your average hostel but worth the extra dollars. It's spacious and spotless, with a smart stainless-steel kitchen and some excellent doubles. Dorms $39, doubles $85

Swansea Holiday Park 2 Bridge St ☎ 03 6257 8148, ⓦ swansea-holiday.com.au. The few pitches on this rather cramped caravan park are the best of a bad lot for campers; it also offers simple cabins that can sleep up to six. On the plus side, the location, just over the road from Jubilee Beach appeals. Powered sites $35, cabins $130

10

10

EATING

★**Kate's Just Desserts & Cafe** 12 Addison St, 1km south off Tasman Hwy ☎03 6257 8428, ⓦkatesberryfarm.com/cafe. A rustic and utterly adorable little café with wonderful views across Kate's boysenberry, blackberry, raspberry and strawberry farm to the bay beyond. Obviously, berries feature in home-made milkshakes and chocolate, but there are also ciabattas, crêpes and waffles, daily potpies and lunches like salmon chowder or Moroccan lamb. Just one warning: it's very popular. Daily 9.30am–4.30pm.

Piermont Tasman Hwy, 3km south ☎03 6257 8131. This award-winning restaurant has all the style and awesome ocean views of its chic boutique resort, with fine French cuisine to boot; five-course degustation menus ($100 including wine) feature dishes such as braised beef cheek or duck confit. Booking essential. Sept–July daily 6pm–late.

Saltshaker 11 Franklin St ☎03 6257 8488. There's one excellent reason to visit this cool city-style bistro – the vast view over Great Oyster Bay to the Freycinet Peninsula. But the nosh is tasty too; mostly modern light cooking such as calamari on rocket salad ($20) or crab pasta with spinach, red pepper and white wine dill sauce ($25). Daily 8am–6pm.

The Freycinet Peninsula

The fame of Wineglass Bay, the most celebrated beach in Tasmania, ensures a steady stream of visitors to **Freycinet National Park** (pronounced "fray-zin-ay") even in winter. It is one of the east coast's poster destinations, something that grants its gateway village, Coles Bay, a popularity out of all proportion to its size. Fortunately, the beach and national park beyond live up to the hype – there are beautiful beaches, thick bush, granite mountains that glow orange at sunset and some excellent walking, including what is arguably Tasmania's best introduction to multiday bushwalking (certainly its sunniest).

Friendly Beaches

If an epic wild beach is your kind of thing, spectacular **Friendly Beaches** is your kind of place. Though part of the national park, this long sweep of white sand, azure sea and bush remains quiet even in high summer, largely due to a location north of Coles Bay, but also because the sheer scale thins crowds. To get there, turn left at a sign on the Coles Bay road, around 8km after the turn-off from the Tasman Highway.

Coles Bay

Despite its visitor numbers and though shifting rapidly upmarket, **COLES BAY**, on the north edge of the Freycinet National Park, remains pleasingly low-key; its laidback scattering of beach houses and shacks on an inlet is more village than resort. Yet even here the scenery is spectacular due to **The Hazards**, three peaks – Amos, Dove and Mayson – that rise from the sea and are especially impressive at dawn and sunset when their pinky granite glows. There are **general stores** at each end of the village, one a post office with fuel, a pub, the *Illuka Holiday Centre* and a couple of cafés.

Freycinet National Park

The park begins just beyond Coles Bay at the **national park office**, which sells maps and booklets on day-walks. Here, too, is Richardsons Beach, the first of many idyllic little beaches further around the bay; Honeymoon Bay is gorgeous. Walking tracks into the park proper start at the **Walking Track Car Park**, a further 4km from the office. **Water** is scarce, so carry all you'll need or ask the rangers about safe streams. Shorter walks are well-marked: most walkers head off on the easy ascent to the lookout over exquisite **Wineglass Bay**, with its perfect curve of white beach. To make a half-day of it, continue down to the beach itself (2.6km return to the lookout, 1–2hr; 5km return to the beach, 2hr 30min–3hr 30min), then return by cutting across the isthmus and following the shore back. For longer hikes, the 27km **peninsula circuit** is excellent. You could blast it in 10hr, but it's best done over two days with a night at a **campsite** on **Cooks Beach** – a good dry run (literally) for longer Tassie hikes.

ARRIVAL AND INFORMATION

By bus TassieLink's east-coast service drops off at the turn-off to Coles Bay on the Tasman Highway, to connect with the Calow's Coaches service to Coles Bay and the National Park car park (Mon, Wed, Fri & Sun daily, bookings required; ☎03 6376 2161 or ☎0400 570 036, ⓦcalowscoaches.com).

Tourist information Both general stores stock a confetti

THE FREYCINET PENINSULA

of flyers for accommodation and activities. For more general information, check out ⓦfreycinetcolesbay.com. The excellent national park office (daily May–Oct 9am–4pm; Nov–April 8am–5pm; ☎03 6256 7000, ⓦparks.tas.gov.au) on the car park behind Richardson's Beach sells maps and will advise on walks and track conditions.

ACTIVITIES

Cruises Wineglass Bay Cruises, on the jetty of Coles Bay (☎03 6257 0355, ⓦwineglassbaycruises.com), runs a daily wildlife-spotting trip to Wineglass Bay, where you tuck into fresh local oysters and cheeses with a glass of bubbly (10am–2pm; $130).

Kayaking Freycinet Adventures, 2 Freycinet Drive (☎03 6257 0500, ⓦfreycinetadventures.com.au), runs some of Tasmania's finest kayak experiences for beginners: two

different three-hour sea-kayaking tours ($95; 2hr on the water) plus two- and four-day kayak expeditions around the peninsula (Dec–April; $295 & $1290 respectively).

Quad biking All4adventure, on the Esplanade as you enter Coles Bay (☎03 6257 0018, ⓦall4adventure.com.au), offers quad-bike tours of the northern national park – note that bike drivers must have a driving licence (daily 1pm, Nov–March 4.30pm as well; from $149 driver, $99 passenger).

ACCOMMODATION AND EATING

COLES BAY

Holiday agency Freycinet Rentals (5 East Esplanade; ☎03 6257 0320, ⓦfreycinetrentals.com) has a selection of holiday house rentals.

Big4 Illuka on Freycinet Holiday Park Esplanade ☎03 6257 0115 or ☎1800 786 512, ⓦbig4.com.au. This holiday park, opposite the beach and close to the stores and pub in central Coles Bay, has the full spread of budget accommodation, from camping in a dedicated upper area, to two-bedroom self-contained cabins and units that sleep up to six. Un/powered sites $30/40, cabins $135

Coles Bay Esplanade YHA Reserve Rd ☎03 6257 0115, ⓦyha.com.au. About 1km from the National Park, this hostel has the usual dorms and double/twin rooms, as well as family rooms. The hostel is in the centre of the township and is popular with families. It has an on-site restaurant and is very close to the beach. Dorms $27, doubles $70

Edge of the Bay 3.5km west of Coles Bay ☎03 6257 0102, ⓦedgeofthebay.com.au. Not as flash as its $2000-a-night neighbour *Saffire*, but a smart resort with similar gorgeous views of the Hazards from its self-catering cottages; either rustic or minimalist suites with water views. Its restaurant, *The Edge*, serves fine-dining dinners (6–10pm), such as Cape Grim steak ($38) or scallop paella ($32), all with beautiful bay views. $310

★**Tombolo** 6 Garnett St ☎03 6257 0124. The cutest café in Coles Bay, with art on the walls and a modern menu

of thin wood-fired pizzas (around $22, also takeaway) and fish and chips, plus posher nosh like local oysters. It's worth a visit just to linger over great coffee and the view of the Hazards. Daily 8.30am–4pm, Tues–Sun 6–8.30pm.

FREYCINET NATIONAL PARK

Freycinet Lodge ☎03 6256 7222, ⓦfreycinetlodge .com.au. With a gorgeous setting on the bay, this is the only resort in the national park. Cabins are nestled in the surrounding bushland, but none are far from the main lodge. All have one or two bedrooms with king-size beds, and some have balconies. They offer a very comfortable base from which to tackle the walking tracks on the doorstep. $219

Friendly Beaches campsite Far from the action in Coles Bay, this bush camp is rarely busy even in peak season. It's also basic, with just pit toilets, no water and fuel stove only. Focus instead on the fact that you're staying behind one of the most beautiful beaches in the state for the price of a national parks pass. Free

Richardsons Beach/Honeymoon Bay campsites ☎03 6256 7004, ⓦparks.tas.gov.au. Pitches right behind the beach yet only 10min from Coles Bay. The bad news is that these national park sites are so popular that pitches are allocated by ballot from mid-December to mid-February and over Easter. If you hope to camp during this period, apply via the website by the end of July. Un/powered sites $13/16

Bicheno

Halfway up the east coast, **BICHENO** (pronounced "bish-eno") lives a double life as a modest resort and a fishing town for crayfishing and abalone. The recreational fishing is excellent, too, as is the diving and surfing on Redbill Beach just north of the centre when swell conditions play ball. But even if you're not in the water the coastal scenery

10

THE ABORIGINAL PEOPLES OF TASMANIA

The demise of the **Aboriginal peoples of Tasmania** is one of the most tragic episodes of recent history. Ironically, were it not for American and British sealers and whalers, who had operated on Van Diemen's Land since 1793 and lived with Aboriginal women on the Furneaux Islands in the Bass Straits, the Tasmanian Aborigines could have disappeared entirely. The last full-blood Aboriginal Tasmanian was a woman called **Truganini**, who died at Oyster Cove, south of Hobart, in 1876. But a strong Aboriginal movement has grown up in Tasmania, giving hope to a restoration of indigenous cultural identity on the island.

Raised ocean levels after the last Ice Age separated the Aboriginal people of Tasmania from the mainland and caused isolation that was both genetic and **cultural**: for example, they couldn't make fire but kept alight smouldering fire sticks, and their weapons were simple clubs and spears not boomerangs. In terms of their **appearance**, the men wore their hair in long ringlets smeared with grease and red ochre, and women's heads were closely shaved. To keep warm, they used a paste of animal fat, ochre and charcoal.

FIRST WHITE SETTLEMENT

Upon **white settlement** in the early 1800s, there were reckoned to be about five thousand Aboriginal people in Tasmania, divided into **bands** who shared a language and culture, socialized, intermarried and – crucially – fought against other bands. They also traded and moved peacefully across neighbouring territory to share resources. Once the nomadic tribes realized that the white settlers were not going to "share" resources in this traditional exchange, confrontation was inevitable. Tit-for-tat skirmishes in the 1820s led state governor George Arthur to declare martial law in 1828, expelling all Aboriginal people from settled districts and giving settlers licence to shoot on sight. To end the bloodshed, the government planned to confine the remaining Aborigines on **Bruny Island**, and in 1830, a militia of three thousand settlers swept the island in a dragnet known as the **Black Line**.

DECLINE OF ABORIGINAL PEOPLE

The ploy failed, but betrayal between rival bands did the job instead and in 1834, the last 135 Aborigines were moved to a makeshift settlement on Flinders Island in the Bass Strait. Within four years most had died through disease or the harsh conditions. The 47 survivors were transferred to their final settlement at Oyster Cove, near Hobart, in 1837. The skeleton of that group's last survivor, Truganini, originally from Bruny Island, was displayed in the Tasmanian Museum until 1976, when her remains were finally cremated and scattered in the D'Entrecasteaux Channel.

PALAWA

The mixed-race descendants of the Aboriginal Tasmanians, known as the Palawa, were given a voice by the establishment of the **Tasmanian Aboriginal Centre (TAC)** in the 1970s. A push for land rights handed it control of historic areas of Flinders Island in 1999 and, in 2005, Cape Barren Island to its south. Pride in Aboriginal roots grew, too: in a 1981 census, 2700 Tasmanians ticked the Aboriginal box; by 2006 that number was 16,900. Ironically, this has riled the TAC, whose sympathies lie with the Bass Strait communities who can trace their lineage back to the late 1700s.

of granite foreshore and white beaches is beautiful. A 3.5km **Bicheno Foreshore Footway** takes in the lot as it runs along the coast from Redbill Point (reached via Gordon St) via beaches and The Gulch, as the narrow channel through **Governor Island Marine Nature Reserve** is known, then down a granite foreshore to a blowhole that spurts when a large swell surges in.

Walks aside, there are two attractions locally. In the centre **Bicheno Motorcycle Museum**, at 35 Burgess St (daily 9am–4pm; $9), is stuffed full of a private collectors' immaculate motorbikes. Otherwise, wildlife – including Tassie devils in a breeding and conservation centre – hops and scampers around **East Coast Natureworld** (daily 9am–5pm; $25; ⊚natureworld.com.au), 7km north of Bicheno on the Tasman Highway.

ARRIVAL AND INFORMATION

By bus TassieLink's east-coast service calls in at Bicheno on its way up from Hobart (Mon, Wed, Fri & Sun daily; 3hr). There is also a service to St Helens with Calows Coaches (Mon–Fri & Sun daily; ☎ 03 6376 2161, ⓦ calowscoaches .com), as well as buses to Coles Bay (Mon–Fri 5 daily).

Tourist information Bicheno's well-stocked, friendly visitor centre is in Foster St, beside the supermarket (daily Oct–April 9am–5pm; May–Sept 10am–4pm; ☎ 03 6375 1500, ⓦ eastcoasttasmania.com).

ACTIVITIES

Diving The marine reserve offers large caves and vertical rock faces with swim-throughs and drop-offs. Bicheno Dive Centre, opposite the Sea Life Centre at 2 Scuba Court (☎ 03 6375 1138, ⓦ bichenodive.com.au), runs trips and rents gear.

Marine-life cruises Bicheno Glass Bottom Boats, at the north end of The Gulch (☎ 03 6375 1294), run forty-minute

glass-bottom-boat tours of the marine reserve (Oct–April 2 daily; $25).

Wildlife spotting Wildlife can be seen on an evening tour to a penguin rookery with Bicheno Penguin Tours (☎ 03 6375 1333, ⓦ bichenopenguintours.com.au). Reserve at East Coast Surf, opposite the visitor centre (nightly; $30).

ACCOMMODATION

Bicheno Backpackers 11 Morrison St ☎ 03 6375 1651, ⓦ bichenobackpackers.com.au. Great small backpackers' where accommodation is split between four- and eight-bed dorms in a rustic cabin-like block and decent single, double and twin rooms opposite at the main site, plus a separate, more central flashpackers' with more modern (and more expensive) en suites for couples and a vibe like a private hostel, in two houses. Dorms $28, doubles $70

Bicheno by the Bay The Esplanade ☎ 03 6375 1171, ⓦ bichenobythebay.com.au. A family-friendly resort that appeals for its bushland setting as much as the location moments from the town centre and The Gulch. Notwithstanding a few hotel-style rooms, its mainstay is the A-frame cottages that sleep up to nine. There's also a heated swimming pool and a tennis court. Doubles $120, cabins $160

★**Bicheno Hideaway** 179 Harveys Farm Rd, signposted 3km south ☎ 03 6375 1312,

ⓦ bichenohideaway.com. Book in here for a few days' R&R. A nicely ramshackle bolthole in six acres of bushland, it has five cylindrical chalets in a boutique-rustic style above a private foreshore. They're certainly different, wonderfully laidback, and offer good value. $155

East Coast Holiday Park 4 Champ St ☎ 03 6375 1999, ⓦ bichenoholidaypark.com.au. Though rather suburban compared to the glorious scenery all around, this is a tidy, well-maintained holiday park that could not be more central; it's just off the arc of the main road. Un/powered sites $30/$35, doubles $105, cabins $138, cottages $165.

Wintersun Gardens Motel 35 Gordon St ☎ 03 6375 1225, ⓦ wintersunbicheno.com.au. Double and family rooms here are simple and the annual refurbishment keeps things fresh – the wetroom-style bathrooms are excellent. Families will appreciate the space of the apartments. Facilities include a small pool and barbecue. Nothing flash but good value. $100

EATING

Pasini's 2/70 Burgess St ☎ 03 6375 1076. In the centre of town, this is a café and wine bar as well as an Italian deli. No surprises, then, that it serves wood-fired pizzas and home-made pasta such as chilli fettucine

with local calamari (around $24), although it does rustle up a mean toasted sandwich and a warming seafood chowder. Mon–Sat 9am–9pm, Sun 9am–3pm.

St Marys

Some 30km north of Bicheno, just past Chain of Lagoons, a side road slips off the Tasman Highway and slaloms uphill over Elephant Pass to **ST MARYS**. A picturesque little Fingal Valley town surrounded by state forest, it's another world after the salt-tousled coast. It's rural, rather old-fashioned, definitely untouristy and also rather quirky, thanks to a small alternative community that frequents the crafts stores, the *Purple Possum Wholefoods Café* (see p.926), and the rocking live gigs at central *St Marys Hotel*. Aside from a break from the coast, St Marys offers a short walking track to the 832m peak of **South Sister**, accessed 6km up unsealed and winding German Town Road. You can camp for free on the raceground in Story Street.

10

By bus Calows Coaches (☎03 6376 2161 or ☎ 0400 570 036, ⟁calowscoaches.com) run to Bicheno, St Helens and Launceston (1–3 daily).

ACCOMMODATION AND EATING

Mount Elephant Pancake Barn Elephant Pass ☎03 6372 2263. They serve 38 varieties of pancake (about $20) in this Tassie institution, with its rustic cabin vibe—both savoury types like chicken satay and smoked salmon, and sweet such as banana, walnut and maple. Cash only. Daily summer 8am–6pm; winter 9am–4pm; closed first two weeks of August.

Purple Possum Wholefoods Café 5 Story St ☎03 6372 2655. Wholesome, healthy and home-made vegetarian food in a health-food-shop café. Many of the ingredients that go into its toasties, veggie pies, soups ($7.50), cakes and highly rated veggie burger ($18) are grown in the owner's garden. Nov–April Mon–Fri 9am–5pm, Sat 9am–3pm; May–Oct Mon–Fri 10am–4pm, Sat 11am–4pm.

★**Seaview Farm** 8km uphill on German Town Rd ☎03 6372 2341 or ☎0417 382 876, ⟁seaviewfarm.net. The peace and views at this biological farm are reason enough to divert off the coast. Choose from smart-rustic en-suite rooms or a lovely folksy cottage (sleeps seven) with a kitchen and woodburner. The owners sell their superb beef and you can pick herbs (and sometimes vegetables) from the garden. No children under 12 allowed. Doubles $130, cottage $300

St Helens and the Bay of Fires

The last stop before the Tasman Highway turns inland, **ST HELENS** is the largest town on the east coast. Don't get too excited – even with its shops, supermarkets and banks it's a low-key sort of place and is certainly no looker. Many visitors come solely to try their luck at the self-described "big game fishing capital of Tasmania". For most, however, the **Bay of Fires** and its string of beautiful beaches is the draw. The one tourist attraction in town, such as it is, is the **St Helens History Room** (daily 9am–5pm; $5; ☎03 6376 1744, ⟁visitsthelenstasmania.com.au) in the visitor centre at 61 Cecilia St, which documents local settler and especially Chinese mining history in the Blue Tier hills inland.

Bay of Fires Coastal Reserve

Perhaps the best reasons to visit St Helens are the sugary white beaches which arc before an aquamarine sea in the **Bay of Fires Coastal Reserve**. Explorer Tobias Furneaux coined the name in 1773 when he passed a coastline illuminated by the cooking fires of Aboriginal tribes. The reserve stretches north up the coast for over 30km, all the way to Eddystone Point, but most people are content to dawdle on those that scallop the coast north of **Binalong Bay**, 17km east of St Helens and still a sleepy village despite its magic setting. Beyond the beach at the village, beaches are accessed off the road to The Gardens, each with a basic bush camp behind. The Gardens, 13km north, is gentrifying fast, with holiday shacks being replaced by glass-walled holiday houses. Note that there's no transport to Binalong Bay but it's an easy cycle from St Helens.

Mount William National Park

The northern end of the Bay of Fires falls within the lower half of **Mount William National Park**; to get there take the rough road running inland north for 54km from St Helens to the pink-granite tower of the Eddystone Lighthouse. The northern end of the park is reached via Gladstone (east of Launceston) on an unsealed track to **Great Musselroe Bay**, where there's a free basic **campsite**. There are no real tracks within the park itself, but plenty of astonishingly beautiful beach and headland walking, and lots of Forester kangaroos.

By bus Calows Coaches (☎03 6376 2161, ⟁calowscoaches .com) goes to St Helens via St Marys from both Launceston (daily) and Bicheno (daily except Sat). There is no direct service from Hobart – take the TassieLink service to Bicheno and catch the connecting bus.

Tourist information St Helens' visitor centre is at 61 Cecilia St, north of the central crossroads, opposite the post office (daily 9am–5pm; ☎03 6376 1744); it is chock-full of maps and advice on walks in the neighbouring area, including the Blue Tier (see p.928).

ACTIVITIES

Bike hire East Lines (28 Cecilia St; ⓣ 03 6376 1720).

Tours Join skipper David Duggan and his daughter Alisha at Bay of Fires Eco Tours (ⓣ 0499 209 756, ⓦ bayoffiresecotours.com.au; daily 9.30am & 2pm; $85) for tours of Binalong Bay Gulch. David is a former abalone diver who knows these waters well, and their new operation takes small groups (max 18 passengers) to see wildlife including albatrosses, seals, dolphins and more. Some tours circle the amazing Sloop Rock, a feature of the Bay of Fires. Great for families.

Cooking classes Roz MacAllan at Kiss A Fish Cookery School (ⓣ 0418 433 667, ⓦ kissafishcookeryschool.com.au; Nov–April Sat; $210 half day, $350 full day) runs excellent and very personal hands-on cooking classes, using local produce and seafood, from the purpose-built commercial kitchen (complete with wood-fired oven) on the veranda of her beautiful home overlooking the bay at Binalong.

Fishing Skipper Rocky Carosi (ⓣ 0419 383 362, ⓦ rockycarosifishing.com) runs ocean game-fishing charters for up to eight people, though you'll need to join a group or be well-heeled if going alone (from $260pp or $1100 charter).

Walking One of Tassie's signature walking experiences, the Bay of Fires Lodge Walk (ⓣ 03 6392 2211, ⓦ bayoffires.com.au; Oct–May; $2300–2475 depending on season) is a luxury four-day guided beach trek, split between two days' walking and accommodation in a stylish ecolodge with an eco-spa and astounding sea views.

ACCOMMODATION

Opt for facilities and food options at St Helens or beach-bum escapism at Binalong Bay – the choice is yours. Bush camps are sited behind all beaches of the Bay of Fires. You'll need to rough it since facilities extend only to a pit toilet, but you have the state's blessing to stay for four weeks without paying a cent.

BINALONG BAY

Bed in the Treetops 124 Binalong Bay Rd ⓣ 03 6376 1318 or ⓣ 0408 518 418, ⓦ bedinthetreetops.com.au. Two luxury adults-only suites in two styles – mellow rustic and metropolitan chic – in a bushland retreat that's sited 1km from the Bay of Fires beaches. And yes, you gaze out across treetops. **$330**

ST HELENS

Big4 St Helens Holiday Park 2 Penelope St ⓣ 03 6376 1290 or ⓣ 1300 559 745, ⓦ big4.com.au. This tidy park is well-organized and excellent for families, and is a good choice if you prefer camping with comforts; in addition to sites, there are also studio units, holiday cabins and villas. It's located 2km south of the centre. Un/powered sites **$40/42**, studios **$130**, cabins **$150**, villas **$195**

Kellraine Units 72 Tully St ⓣ 03 6376 1169. The motel building is stuck in the 1970s, the location 1km from the centre on the Launceston road is not ideal, but there's no faulting the price of these simple, clean, self-contained units. A good option if a cabin is beyond the budget. **$85**

Tidal Waters Resort 1 Quail St ⓣ 03 6376 1999, ⓦ tidalwaters.com.au. There's nothing to quicken the pulse about this four-star resort on the bay, but it is St Helens' only full-facility hotel accommodation, with a large restaurant that spills out onto a sprawling deck overlooking the wetlands, and a small pool. Rooms are large; ask for one with a balcony overlooking the water for the best value for money. **$195**

EATING

Captain's Catch 1 Marina Parade, St Helens ⓣ 03 6376 1170. Once a fancier restaurant, this fishmongers and fish-n-chippy still has sit-down dining as well as takeaways, if you prefer to sit outside on the wharf wall. The outlook over the marina through the glass walls is part of the charm. Daily 11am–8.30pm.

Moresco Restaurant 64 Main Rd, Binalong Bay ⓣ 03 6376 8131. The signature dish of Tasmanian seafood broth sets the mood for this mod-Oz menu. Bingalong's newest kid on the block also offers such delights as gnocchi with roasted mushrooms, spinach, truffle oil and aged parmesan ($28) or slow-roast Cape Grim beef ($36) that's as good as the spectacular view of the beach. It also serves takeaway fish and chips – ideal if the sands are irresistible. Tues–Sun 9am–8pm.

St Helens to Scottsdale

From St Helens, the **Tasman Highway** cuts inland across the northeast highlands towards Launceston, 170km away. This is mostly dairy and forestry country, although there's the odd patch of rainforest and relics of a late 1800s tin-mining boom based around the **Blue Tier**, a mountain plateau north of the main road which was once a rich tin-mining area. Many of the towns here virtually disappeared after the mines finally closed in the 1950s, and many of the one-street settlements that remain are struggling.

10

So, this is a touring route with little reason to stop overnight – to make a trip out of it, however, you can follow a Trail of the Tin Dragon (ⓦtrailofthetindragon.com) that stops at historic sights of the immigrant Chinese miners who worked the Blue Tier.

The Blue Tier

The first slice of mining heritage, **Goshen**, straggled along the Tasman Highway, is little more than a few timber houses. So, turn off a kilometre further on and swing up to **Goulds Country**, to see the remaining buildings – all wooden – of what was once a town. The road continues past the site of another abandoned mining town, Lottah, and climbs up Poimena Road to the site of Poimena. In recent years, **the Blue Tier** has become the focus of an environmental campaign to preserve one of the few remaining old-growth forests left in the northeast: an ancient ecosystem of pure creeks that tumble through mossy forest. The easiest of several signposted walks taking between two and six hours is the boardwalked **Goblin Forest Walk** (wheelchair accessible; 20min), where interpretive boards reveal the former mining settlement there. There's also a thirty-minute walk to the 810m-high Blue Tier summit, Mount Poimena, for views right across the northeast to the coast.

INFORMATION AND ACTIVITIES   THE BLUE TIER

Walking information Get details on Blue Tier walks at the St Helens visitor centre (see p.926) or via conservation site ⓦ bluetier.org.

Mountain biking In recent years the area has been celebrated for its superb mountain biking, and on weekends you're likely to encounter many lycra-clad cyclists on the roads, in the cafés and in parks. The Blue Tier Descent trail winds over granite outcrops and slabs, through myrtle forests and tree ferns. It begins at Mount Poimena and ends at *Weldborough Hotel*. Launceston-based Mountain Bike Tasmania provides trips (see p.932) or you can hire bikes at The Corner Store in Derby (ⓦ mtbhire.com.au).

Pyengana and the Columba Falls State Reserve

Around 26km from St Helens on the Tasman Highway a left turn-off threads through a broad dairy valley to **PYENGANA**, home of the award-winning **Pyengana Cheese Factory** (daily: June–Aug 10am–4pm; Sept–May 9am–5pm; free), where you can watch the stuff being made, tuck in at the café (see opposite) or put together a picnic for the falls. Just further on is *The Pub in the Paddock* (see opposite), a real country local celebrated for its resident beer-drinking pigs; ask at the bar for a "pig beer" (don't worry, it's mostly water).

The road continues 10km further into the cool, temperate rainforest of the **St Columba Falls State Reserve**. An easy short stroll passes through tree ferns, sassafras and myrtle to the base of **St Columba Falls**, which at 90m are among the highest in Tasmania.

Weldborough

The Weldborough Pass (595m) is probably the most beautiful part of the drive west, not least because of a short walk through the **Weldborough Pass Scenic Reserve**, predominantly myrtle forest with tree ferns and blackwoods. Once the hub of the Chinese mining community – the cemetery has Chinese graves and a tower, in which paper prayer offerings were burned – **WELDBOROUGH** now consists solely of a few houses and the *Weldborough Hotel*, an historic and charming old pub with a nice line in craft brews; arguably the most appealing break en route west (see opposite).

Derby

It's hard to believe that **DERBY**, a one-street town with a touch of the frontier about it, was the booming centre of the profitable Briseis Tin Mine between 1876 and 1952. The well-presented **Tin Dragon Interpretation Centre** inside The Corner Store on Main Street (daily: Nov–April 9am–5pm; May–Oct 9am–3pm; $9 ☎03 6354 1062), is one of the few modern developments in a town that's been quietly closing down since the boom turned to bust. The centre provides a great history of tin-mining, but its most compelling exhibit is a documentary on a flood disaster in 1929 that all but destroyed Derby. The town is also home to one of Tasmania's newest mountain-bike trails, an 80km network that includes the 25km Blue Tier Descent and a couple of "black diamond" trails for experienced riders.

ACCOMMODATION AND EATING — **ST HELENS TO SCOTTSDALE**

Holy Cow Café St Columba Falls Rd, Pyengana ☏ 03 6373 6157. Ploughman's lunch, cheese platters or just cheese on toast stars in the barn-like café of the cheese factory, with views over dairy country. There are also home-made burgers and daily potpies (both $15) plus yummy ice cream. Daily: June–Aug 10am–4pm; Sept–May 9am–5pm.

The Pub in the Paddock St Columba Falls Hotel, St Columba Falls Rd, Pyengana ☏ 03 6373 6121. This rustic boozer from the 1880s, a snug cocoon of wood walls and open fires, rustles up no-nonsense pub grub like daily roasts ($20) and pork ribs (daily: bar noon–11pm; food noon–2pm & 6–8pm). $75. The hotel also has six simple rooms with valley views in an annexe.

★**Weldborough Hotel** Weldborough ☏ 03 6354 2223, ☏ weldborough.com.au. A must-visit for any beer buff, this splendid mining-era pub specializes in beers and ciders from Tasmania's microbreweries and prepares daily home-made tucker like beef and ale pie and curries (around $18). Add in pub rooms that blend historic character and modern(ish) style, bunks in two miners' cabins and camping, and you have a fine overnight break. (May–Sept Tues–Sun noon–3pm & 6–8pm; Oct–April daily noon–3pm & 6–8pm). Camping per person $10, dorms $35, doubles $90

Launceston and around

As the second-largest city after Hobart, with around 100,000 inhabitants, **LAUNCESTON** is the natural rival to the capital. Like Hobart, it is sited on a waterway, the Tamar River, and has plenty of historic architecture along with a matching colonial history; it has even acquired similar art and food cultures, and locals argue that their city stands up to comparison with Hobart. In truth though, Tasmania's "northern capital" remains an oversized provincial town. Not that that is such a terrible thing. A small scale means that nothing in the town – from the excellent gallery-museum and increasingly sophisticated restaurant and café scene to the rugged beauty of **Cataract Gorge** – is more than twenty minutes' walk away. And the surrounding vineyards of the **Tamar Valley** or the ice-shattered summit of **Ben Lomond National Park** are well within an hour's drive.

Queen Victoria Museum and Art Gallery

Cataract Gorge aside, the **Queen Victoria Museum and Art Gallery** (aka "**QVMAG**") is Launceston's star attraction. Exhibits are split between two sites: a multimillion-dollar redevelopment of railway yards at Inveresk, on the north bank of the river, has created space for a museum of sciences and history; art and decorative arts are displayed in the gallery, in a renovated, original Victorian pile on Wellington Street on the western fringe of the CBD.

QVMAG: Museum

2 Invermay Rd, Inveresk • Daily 10am–4pm • Free; charges for some touring exhibitions; planetarium $6 • ☏ 03 6323 3777, ☏ qvmag.tas .gov.au

The museum's interior – two-thirds of which is home to the University of Tasmania's **Academy of Arts** – has an incredible sense of space, which suits the scale of exhibits dedicated to science – dinosaurs, trains and planes soaring in the rafters – and history. A fascinating permanent exhibit includes remains of the extinct Tasmanian tiger (thylacine), including a rug made of thylacine skins. There's also an appealing array of objects from the colonial past, including convict items and personal items of bushrangers and explorers from Tassie's rollicking early history. More science is served

10

LAUNCESTON

■ ACCOMMODATION	
Arthouse	1
Balmoral on York	5
Clarion City Park	2
Hatherley Birrell Collection	4
Launceston Backpackers	6
Mantra Charles	7
Peppers Seaport Hotel	3
Red Feather Inn	8

■ DRINKING & NIGHTLIFE	
Alchemy	2
The Irish	4
New York Hotel	3
Royal Oak Hotel	1

● EATING	
Black Cow	4
Blue Café Bar	1
Brisbane Street Bistro	5
Fresh on Charles	11
Inside Café	6
Jailhouse Grill	9
Me Wah	2
Milkbar Café	8
Mud Bar & Restaurant	3
Pierre's Coffee House and Restaurant	7
Stillwater	10

by a **planetarium** and the child-friendly **Phenomena Factory** with hands-on science experiments. Even the former **railway workshops** have been transformed with a hugely atmospheric walkway through the old Blacksmith Shop in a large shed behind the main hall.

QVMAG: Gallery

2 Wellington St • Daily 10am–4pm • Free • ☎ 03 6323 3777, ⊛ qvmag.tas.gov.au

Despite being the third-oldest city in Australia, first settled in 1804, Launceston has hung on to little of its colonial Georgian architecture. What the city has in abundance is fine **Victorian architecture** from its boom as the hub of regional mineral exploration in the late 1800s. One of its showpieces is the original building of the museum and gallery; it was first opened in 1891 to mark half a century of Queen Victoria's reign.

Renovation has opened up exhibition spaces and returned some of the scale to the historic pile as the host of the city's permanent **gallery**. The gallery is well worth visiting for its landscapes by leading colonial painters of the nineteenth century – late Romantic works from John Glover, early dabbles with Impressionism by W.C. Piguenit – plus an iconic work by Robert Dowling, *Aborigines of Tasmania*, an already romanticized work (1859) considering that most of its subjects had by this times died following the tragic colonial policies of removing tribes. The museum also has a good collection of Tasmanian decorative arts plus displays of Chinese ceramics and the Guan Di temple, a fabulously intricate altar of the 1880s that Chinese immigrant miners installed in the *Weldborough Hotel* during the region's tin boom.

City Park

Tamar St • Daily 8am–5pm

City Park is one of Launceston's loveliest spaces. Established in the 1820s, it follows the models of a Victorian English park, with wrought-iron gates, a conservatory full of flowers and ferns, and a fountain erected to mark Queen Victoria's Diamond Jubilee in 1897. Locals refer to it as "Monkey Park" because of the Japanese macaques that romp around a small enclosure by the gates (daily 8am–4pm).

10

Design Tasmania Centre

Cnr Tamar & Brisbane sts • Mon–Fri 9.30am–5.30pm, Sat & Sun 10am–4pm • ☎ 03 6331 5506, ⊛ designtasmania.com.au

Established in 1976 to support and encourage Tasmanian designers, the **Design Tasmania Centre** is an essential stop for anyone with an interest in interior design. Both temporary exhibitions by individual designers and a permanent collection of modern pieces showcase the superb work of state designers, woodworkers and furniture-makers, most of whom draw inspiration from the surrounding environment. As good a reason to visit is the centre's retail outlet, which is stuffed full of beautiful crafts: expect woodwork, ceramics, homewares and jewellery in styles that range from cutting-edge to rustic chic. Not cheap, of course, but the quality is exceptional.

The old wharf area

The wharves on the North Esk River have disappeared, but **Custom House**'s Neoclassical pile remains on the Esplanade to testify to the port's prosperity during the boom of the late 1800s. Otherwise rather neglected, the **old wharf area** (which encompasses the area around the Esplanade and William Street) receives visitors for tours of **J. Boag & Son Brewery**, founded in 1881. Dressed in a fluoro jacket and safety glasses, you begin in the **Boag's Centre For Beer Lovers** at 39 William St (daily 11am, 1pm & 3pm; $33; bookings on ☎ 03 6332 6300 or ⊛ boags.com.au), then spend an hour in the brewery before returning to the gift shop for a small tasting of beers with snacks.

Cataract Gorge and beyond

Access to the central gorge by car is via York St then follow signs; alternatively, it is about a 20min walk from the city centre

Few cities have so magnificent a natural feature as **Cataract Gorge** so close to their centre. So wild is its beauty that walkers came to promenade along its banks as early as the 1880s, and continue to do so today. Only the tarmac paths, the occasional power line and the number of people strolling reveal that you're not deep in the bush. The gorge is especially atmospheric when illuminated at dusk.

Cataract Walk and Zig Zag track

Assuming you're walking in – and this is the most rewarding entry – access to the gorge is from two tracks on either side of Kings Bridge, which spans the mouth of the South Esk River. The easiest is the **Cataract Walk** (30min one-way), which begins by a small tollhouse and offers spectacular views of the gorge as it winds to the prim Victorian gardens at **Cliff Grounds**, where peacocks and a wrought-iron rotunda are a startling contrast to the gorge's wild beauty. **Zig Zag track** (25min one-way) from the south side of the gorge is steeper and wilder, its rocky path burrowing through the bush along the top of the gorge. It ends at the **First Basin**, a natural canyon pool opposite Cliff Grounds rather ruined by an ugly **swimming pool**, which was built to discourage people from swimming in the basin itself.

10

Launceston Basin Chair Lift

Embarkation from Cliff Grounds and First Basin • Daily: spring & autumn 9am–5pm; summer 9am–6pm; winter 9am–4.30pm • $12 one-way, $15 return

The **Launceston Basin Chair Lift** connects the First Basin to Cliff Grounds with a six-minute 308m ride, said to be the longest single-span chairlift in the world. It's a fun thing to do if heights don't bother you, and gives a good view of the whole basin area. You can also cross to the other side of the basin on foot via the **Basin Walk** directly underneath the chairlift, although this route is impassable when the river is in flood, or on the **Alexandra Suspension Bridge** just upstream of the basin.

Towards Trevallyn Dam

To make a day of the gorge, you can take a track from the Alexandra Suspension Bridge and continue to walk upriver to the narrower **Second Basin** and the disused **Duck Reach Power Station** (1hr 30min return; 9am–3pm; free), where there are a few displays about its past as Australia's first hydroelectric power station, built in 1885. You could continue a bit further to the large **Trevallyn State Recreation Area** (daily 8am–dusk) on the South Esk River, or the **Trevallyn Dam**, 6km west of the city centre, a popular place for **cable hang-gliding** (Dec–April daily 10am–5pm: May–Nov Mon–Fri by booking, Sat & Sun 10am–4pm; $20; ☎0419 311 198, ⓦcablehanggliding.com.au).

ARRIVAL AND DEPARTURE
LAUNCESTON

By plane Launceston Airport is 20km south of the city, near the town of Evandale. Direct flights from Melbourne, Sydney and Brisbane land here. The Airporter Shuttle Bus (☎01300 385 522) meets flights and drops off at accommodation for $15. A taxi costs about $45–50, and there are the usual car-rental agencies at the airport.

By bus Long-distance buses arrive at the Cornwall Square Transit Centre, cnr Cimitiere and St John sts, where both Redline and TassieLink have ticket offices and left-luggage facilities.

Destinations Burnie (1–2 daily; 2hr 30min); Cradle Mountain (Mon & Wed daily; 4hr); Deloraine (3 daily; 45min); Devonport (daily; 1hr 30min); Hobart (daily; 2hr 30min); Mole Creek (daily Mon–Fri; 1hr 30min); Strahan (daily Mon & Wed; 7hr).

GETTING AROUND AND INFORMATION

By the Tiger Bus Central Launceston is easily walkable. However, the municipal Tiger Bus is handy and free: from the car park at Inveresk QFMAG Museum a commuter service (Mon–Fri 7.30–9.45am & 4.15–6.30pm) loops into the CBD every 15min, with another touring the CBD every 30mins or so in the interim (Mon–Fri 10am–3.30pm).

By Metro city bus The standard city bus service is useful for scattered attractions or outlying accommodation. All buses arrive and depart from the bus stops at the Metro bus interchange (☎13 22 01, ⓦmetrotas.com.au), on St John St near the Brisbane Street Mall. Single tickets cost from $3.20; electronic Greencards are the best way to go for convenience and cheaper fares. Greencards can be bought from the MetroTas depot office at 168 Wellington St (Mon–Fri 8.30am–5pm).

By car If driving, note that most streets are one-way, and that Cameron St is interrupted by Civic Square, and Brisbane St by the Mall.

By bike ArtBikes (ⓦartbikes.com.au) are free for one day and available from the Design Tasmania Centre (cnr Brisbane St & Tamar St; Mon–Fri 9.30am–5.30pm; Sat & Sun 10am–4pm; ☎03 6331 5506).

Tourist information The helpful Launceston Visitor Information Centre, 68–72 Cameron St (Mon–Fri 9am–5pm, Sat & Sun 9am–1pm; ☎1800 651 827, ⓦdestinationlaunceston.com.au), can arrange good accommodation, tours and tickets in the area and state-wide.

TOURS AND CRUISES

Launceston Historic Walks ☎03 6331 2213. Local historian Robyn Jones runs ninety-minute guided walks through the inner city (Mon 4pm, Tues–Sat 10am; $15), sprinkled with tales of the characters who built and left their mark on Launceston.

Mountain Bike Tasmania ☎0447 712638, ⓦmountainbiketasmania.com.au. This organization runs guided mountain-bike trips in the Launceston city area and out to Ben Lomond National Park and the Blue Tier. The three-hour Trevallyn Reserve tour costs $120, while the six-hour Ben Lomond Descent is $225.

Pepperbush Adventures ☎03 6352 2263, ⓦpepperbush.com.au. Craig "Bushie" Williams runs some of the finest wildlife and activity tours in Tasmania. Day-trip options include wildlife tours with bushtucker – the Quoll Patrol is outstanding – guided walking on Ben

Lomond and Tamar Valley wine tastings. Prices are from $195 per person, and although they are expensive, these are utterly unique experiences.

Tamar River Cruises Home Point Parade ☎03 6334 9900, ⓦtamarrivercruises.com.au. Cheap cruises into the mouth of Cataract Gorge in a traditional-style steamer, plus longer trips sail up the Tamar (50min–4hr; longer cruises Sept–May only; $29–125). All depart from the quay at the confluence of the Tamar and North Esk rivers.

Tasmanian Expeditions ☎03 6339 3999 or ☎1300 666 856, ⓦtasmaniaexpeditions.com. This Launceston-based outfit organizes myriad activities in the area, from walks to epic wilderness hikes. For example, a day-tour rock climbing on the Dolerite crags in Cataract Gorge costs $250.

ACCOMMODATION

★**Arthouse** 20 Lindsay St ☎03 6333 0222 or ☎1800 041 135, ⓦarthousehostel.com.au. Impressive backpackers' on the north bank whose renovated Federation-era house offers spacious proportions, lots of natural light and historic character. Dorms are four- to eight-bed, some facing onto a front balcony; rooms are singles ($55), twins and doubles. Also has two kitchens and bike hire for guests. Dorms **$24**, doubles **$69**

Balmoral on York 19 York St ☎03 6331 8000, ⓦbalmoralonyork.com.au. One of the better budget hotels, this place located in an older block is bland but perfectly comfy, offering clean, modern(ish) rooms of the pale wood laminate variety. Great CBD views from the best rooms. **$135**

Clarion City Park Grand 22 Tamar St ☎03 6331 7633, ⓦchoicehotels.com.au. Don't be put off by the chain; favoured by executives and older travellers, this small central hotel offers spotless accommodation in just 31 rooms with classic-modern decor and heritage touches, and has welcoming staff. Some rooms have balconies and bathtubs. Also welcome is the free central parking. **$185**

Hatherley Birrell Collection 43 High St ☎0458 947727, ⓦhatherley.com.au. An "art and design experience" say the owners of this luxury accommodation in an 1830s mansion house, where rooms are individually styled, with bold colours and striking artwork. Attention to detail extends to great bathrooms, in-room breakfasts and superb in-room entertainment. The two "garden pavilions" are modern additions with equally lavish touches, such as bathtubs carved from volcanic stone. **$280**

Launceston Backpackers 103 Canning St ☎03 6334 2327, ⓦlauncestonbackpackers.com.au. Another decent hostel, a mite institutional, but spacious, clean and friendly. Dorms come in four- and six-bed varieties, while triples, twins and en-suite rooms are in an annexe. Good notice board for travel and work, plus in-house tour agency for trips. Dorms **$25**, doubles **$58**

★**Mantra Charles** 287 Charles St ☎03 6337 4100 or ☎1300 987 604, ⓦmantra.com.au. A 10min walk from the centre and moments from the foodie strip on Charles St, this converted Art Deco hospital marries designer decor with slick service under the banner of the Mantra chain. The result is contemporary luxury in spacious rooms or suites with a kitchenette. Book online for bargains; breakfast $30 extra. **$189**

★**Peppers Seaport** 28 Seaport Blvd ☎03 6345 3333 or ☎1300 987 600, ⓦpeppers.com.au. This is a smart contemporary hotel, built (tastefully) in the shape of a ship to fit its old dockland surroundings. Stays in the modern, neutral rooms or spacious suites with kitchenettes have a coastal holiday feel, if you book a river view. "City view" rooms treat you to a car park and four-lane highway. **$239**

Red Feather Inn 42 Main St, Hadspen, 10km southwest of Launceston ☎03 6393 6506, ⓦredfeatherinn.com.au. French country decor lends a relaxed air to this boutique B&B in a Georgian house; bathrooms are gorgeous. The village is a 15min drive from the CBD and Evandale – a luxurious base from which to explore the area. You'll be welcomed with a platter of local goodies and a bottle of Tasmanian wine on arrival. **$250**

EATING

Old Launceston Seaport, off Charles St, around *Peppers Seaport Hotel* (see above) or food court *Morty's*, corner of Brisbane & Wellington streets, provide a good spread of **eating and drinking options** in one location – the former offers marina-style waterfront dining, the latter cheap, international fast food.

Black Cow Cnr George & Paterson sts ☎03 6331 9333, ⓦblackcowbistro.com.au. Brasserie style belies the quality of cuisine at this venue run by the owners of *Stillwater* (see p.934). The reason to come is steak, most of it reared on the lush pasture at Cape Grim, northwest Tasmania, all aged at least 35 days. Not especially cheap at prices from $40 a go, but truly outstanding quality. Great wine list, too. It's very popular, so bookings are almost essential. Daily 5.30–10pm.

Blue Café Bar Inveresk Railyards, off Invermay Rd ☎03 6334 3133, ⓦbluecafebar.com.au. A lively art-college hangout, this café-restaurant benefits from the industrial chic of its former powerhouse. It prepares a classic mod-Oz menu: gourmet pizzas and fine mains like red curried duck and papaya salad ($26) or Flinders Island lamb rump, plus popular weekend breakfasts. Sun–Thurs 8am–4pm, Fri & Sat 8am–8.30pm.

Brisbane Street Bistro 24 Brisbane St ☎03 6333

10

10

0888, ⓦ brisbanestreetbistro.com. The latest venture by Terry Fidler, one of Tasmania's leading chefs, this award-winning small restaurant offers Tassie twists on classic European dishes like confit duck, pepper-crusted venison loin, and slow-cooked local lamb ($42), plus fine local wines. Factor in the relaxed atmosphere and this is a great choice for slow dining. To go all-out, order the six-course tasting menu ($95). Tues–Sat 6–11pm.

Fresh on Charles 178 Charles St ⓣ 03 6331 4299, ⓦ freshoncharles.com.au. Modern and creative vegetarian food like green tea noodles with tofu or lentil burgers with satay sauce average $19 in this multi-room café beloved by an alternative arty crowd. The decor shifts from mismatched mid-century modern furniture in the front rooms to hip sixties and seventies retro in a backroom bar area that hosts comedy and music. Mon–Thurs & Sat 8.30am–3pm, Fri 8.30am–3pm & 6–9pm.

Inside Cafe 10–14 Patterson St ⓣ 03 6331 7348, ⓦ insidecafe.com.au. Light and bright, and one half of a homewares shop, this is a pleasant setting with stone walls, wooden floors and a mix of bentwood chairs and couches. Dishes include braised lamb, warm smoked chicken salad with pistachio dukkah, and pulled-pork bagels; if you're just after a simple tea-and-toast breakfast, that's possible too. Average prices $12, but just a tad pretentious (is it wrong to expect the sardines to be fresh rather than presented in the tin?). Mon–Fri 7.30am–4pm, Sat 8am–3.30pm.

Jailhouse Grill 32 Wellington St ⓣ 03 6331 0466, ⓦ jailhousegrill.com.au. A popular choice among locals for an unpretentious meal out. It's famous for doing one thing well: charcoal-grilled dishes such as barbecued steak, pork ribs, wallaby, scallop kebabs and duck. Mains average $30. Mon–Wed 5.30–9.30pm, Thurs–Sun noon–3pm & 5.30–9.30pm.

★**Me Wah** 39–41 Invermay Rd, Invermay ⓣ 03 6331 1308, ⓦ mewah.com.au. Regularly voted one of the ten best Cantonese restaurants in Australia, this is a superb dining experience. For forty years, this elegant restaurant has been known for its courteous old-fashioned service and dishes to die for, and is decent value too at $26–32 for most mains. As well as stalwart dishes like Peking Duck, tempt

yourself with sea scallops steamed with ginger and spring onions, a tasty duck *sang choy bao*, or king prawns with Szechuan chilli sauce. There is also a second *Me Wah* in Hobart, but the Launceston one is the original. Tues–Sun 11.30am–2.30pm & 5–10pm.

Milkbar Café 139 St John St ⓣ 0457 762 378. This sweet little junkshop-chic café is attached to a crafts workshop. Expect delicious coffee – roasted on the premises – and organic teas, bagels, croissants, wraps and Turkish rolls (all under $10), along with daily specials chalked on a blackboard. Mon–Fri 8am–4.30pm.

★**Mud Bar & Restaurant** 28 Seaport Boulevard ⓣ 03 6334 5066, ⓦ mudbarandrestaurant.com. Part of the *Peppers Seaport* complex, this stylish restaurant overlooking the river – with a terrace for more balmy nights – offers up modern Oz-Asian fusion cuisine. Much more than just another hotel restaurant, *Mud* is another arm of the *Stillwater* stable (see below) and lives up to expectations. The mixed oyster plate ($40 dozen) is a work of art; mains average $38 and include slow-cooked spiced lamb with pumpkin and long beans. Daily 11am–10pm.

Pierre's Coffee House and Restaurant 88 George St ⓣ 03 6331 6835, ⓦ pierres.net.au. Established in the 1950s by a French immigrant, *Pierre's* is now a classy metropolitan-style brasserie with leather banquette seating. The menu has also moved upmarket – dishes include crispy pork belly ($33) – but there's still room for a beefburger ($25) on the lunch menu. Classy spot for a drink, too. Tues–Sat 8.30am–10pm.

★**Stillwater** 2 Bridge Rd ⓣ 03 6331 4153, ⓦ stillwater .com.au. Consistently one of Tassie's finest dining venues, this riverside café/restaurant and bar in a colonial mill oozes class. During the day, it's a deliciously lazy spot for breakfasts, lunch or coffee. Mains are around $27 at lunch; at night things shift up a gear to offer a seasonal five-course set chef's menu ($120) or à la carte offerings such as roasted duck breast, whole roasted quail or abalone congee (average main $42). May–Sept Sun–Tues 8.30am–3pm & Wed–Sat 8.30am–late; Oct–April Sun & Mon 8.30am–3pm & Tues–Sat 8.30am–late.

DRINKING AND NIGHTLIFE

Alchemy 90 George St ⓣ 03 6331 2526, ⓦ alchemylaunceston.com.au. Glass-fronted almost clubby bar with live music at weekends that styles itself as one of the city's more sophisticated drinking options. It also puts more of an emphasis on food, with a reliable steak ($27), parmas and pastas, plus cheap lunch deals for around $14. Tues–Sat 11am–late.

The Irish 211 Brisbane St ⓣ 03 6331 4440, ⓦ theirish1835.com.au. Guinness and several beers on tap? Tick. Live music every night? Tick. Faux Irish knick-knacks? Tick. All present and correct in Launceston's Irish

pub, which can be raucous good fun at weekends. It also rustles up the usual fish and chips, stews and pies (around $25). Daily noon–late; food daily noon–2pm & 5.30–8.30pm (till 9pm on Fri).

New York Hotel 122 York St ⓦ hotelnewyork.net.au. While nothing to shake the global super-clubs, this venue popular with late-teens and twenty-somethings is worth checking out for the occasional touring indie rock band that is slotted in between its mainstay of club nights. Wed 6pm–2am, Fri & Sat 5pm–5.30am.

Royal Oak Hotel 14 Brisbane St ⓣ 03 6331 5346.

Genial old boozer that seems more rural than city, with its long wooden bar and relaxed atmosphere. It also has live music of the blues, jazz, folk or singer-songwriter variety most nights and serves budget meals (mains around $19) in a separate, basic dining area. Daily noon–1am; food noon–3pm & 5–9pm.

DIRECTORY

Banks and foreign exchange Branches of major banks are at the bottom of Charles St.

Bookshop Fullers Bookshop, 93 St John St; Read-A-Lot, 45 George St (secondhand and exchange).

Camping equipment Allgoods has a store at 71–79 York St and another, called Tent City, at 60 Elizabeth St; gear rental available. Paddy Pallin, 110 George St, and Mountain Designs, 120 Charles St, focus on the top end of the market. All sell guidebooks and maps.

Car and campervan rental Europcar, airport and 80 Tamar St (☎ 03 6331 8200 or ☎ 13 13 90); Autorent Hertz, airport and 58 Paterson St (☎ 1300 030 222); Bargain Car Rentals, 276 Airport Rd (☎ 1300 729 230); Lo-Cost Auto Rent, 80 Tamar St (☎ 03 6334 3437).

Hospital Launceston General, 274–280 Charles St ☎ 03 6777 6777.

Internet The Digital Hub is on the ground floor of the State Library, Civic Square (Mon–Thurs 9.30am–6pm, Fri 9.30am–7pm Sat 9.30am–2pm). Cyber King, George St (Mon–Fri 8.30am–7.30pm, Sat & Sun 9.30am–6.30pm).

Post office 111 St John St ☎ 13 13 18.

Taxis Taxi ranks are on George St between Brisbane and Paterson sts, on St John St outside Princes Sq, and outside the Transit Centre. Taxis Combined ☎ 13 10 08.

The Tamar Valley

Beyond Launceston, the Tamar River broadens and meanders through the **Tamar Valley**. It's a region renowned for its wines – the vineyards here produce some of Tassie's finest (see box, p.936) – and for its bucolic scenery: orchards, farms and forested hills peel back either side of the reed-fringed river until it empties into the Bass Strait after 65km. Indeed, the countryside and wines are arguably the highlights; notwithstanding an excellent mine centre at Beaconsfield, the sights here are modest and there's little to warrant an overnight visit. For a day or so of touring from Launceston, however, this is lovely stuff.

West of the Tamar

The West Tamar Highway (A7) tracks above the river all the way to the Bass Strait where you'll hit splendid **Green's Beach**. It's worth stopping en route at **Brady's Lookout State Reserve** for magnificent views of the valley or detour to Rosevears to potter alongside the river – a good cycle route.

Beaconsfield

The largest town in the area is **BEACONSFIELD**, the centre of a gold rush in the late 1800s; the gold mine here only closed as recently as 2012. The **Beaconsfield Mine & Heritage Museum** (daily 9.30am–4.30pm; $15; ⓦbeaconsfieldheritage.com.au) is far more fascinating than its name suggests. Occupying the original late 1880s mine buildings, with their massive machinery, it is very well-presented and child-friendly – anyone for gold-panning? – taking in Tasmanian colonial history as much as mining in interactive displays. Most fascinating is the exhibit detailing the 2006 mine collapse which trapped two men for two weeks, before they were ultimately rescued.

Beauty Point

The traditional sights hereabouts are at **BEAUTY POINT** village, with a pretty river setting, less than ten minutes' drive from Beaconsfield. Here old warehouses on Inspection Head Wharf have been converted into **Seahorse World** (daily: Dec–April 9.30am–4pm; May–Nov 10am–3pm; regular 1hr tours; $22; ⓦseahorseworld.com.au) and the **Platypus House** (daily: June–Aug 10am–3.30pm; Sept–May 9.30am–3.30pm; regular 1hr tour; $25; ⓦplatypushouse.com.au). Both are a little tired, but are most people's only chance to see the creatures, not to mention small sharks and cuttlefish, and, along with the platypuses, echidnas. Both are good bets, too, if you have children to entertain.

10

By bus Manions Coaches (☎03 6383 1221, ⓦmanionscoaches.com.au) runs services up the west shore from Launceston (Mon–Fri 8 daily, Sat 3 daily) to Beaconsfield (40min) and Beauty Point (45min).

Tourist information The Tamar Visitor Centre (daily 8.30am–5pm; ☎03 6394 4454, ⓦdestinationlaunceston .com.au) is on the A7 in the centre of Exeter around 16km from Launceston.

ACCOMMODATION AND EATING

★**Rosevears Waterfront Tavern** 215 Rosevears Drive, Rosevears ☎03 6394 4074, ⓦrosevearstavern .com.au. One of Tassie's oldest pubs (1831) in one of its prettiest locations on the banks of the Tamar – this is the stuff summer-evening meals were made for. Expect seasonal mod-Oz cuisine such as crispy-skinned pork belly with garlic and almond couscous and a lime and pomegranate jus, but you'll also find beer-battered fish and chips, steak and pizza offerings (mains around $26). There's a small art gallery attached to the back of the pub, and they were building smart new accommodation

units on the hill behind at the time of research. Mon, Tues & Sun noon–2.30pm; Wed–Sat noon–2.30pm & 6–10pm.

Tamar Cove 4221 Main Rd, Beauty Point ☎03 6383 4375, ⓦtamarcove.com. On the main road as you enter the village, this has pleasant, modern, motel-style rooms with a small pool, plus an excellent small restaurant. The seafood chowder and seafood platter are the signature dishes. Restaurant daily 8am–10pm, closed Mon in winter. **$129**

George Town

On the eastern shore of the Tamar estuary, **GEORGE TOWN** should be a more compelling place. Instead, one of the oldest towns in Australia – it was founded before Launceston in 1804 – is missable except for the replica historic craft at the Bass & Flinders Centre (8 Elizabeth St; daily 10am–4pm; $10; ☎03 6382 3792, ⓦbassandflinders.org.au). Sited just above York Cove, where the first settlers landed, it has a Huon pine replica of HMAS *Norfolk* in which George Bass and Matthew Flinders embarked on a circumnavigation of Tasmania in 1798, plus a replica of the whale boat in which Captain James Kelly explored the state's west coast. Restoration of smaller craft is usually under way in a boat shed 200m away.

WINES IN THE TAMAR VALLEY

Fine soil, sun-soaked slopes and a warm(ish) climate have elevated the Tamar Valley into Tasmania's premier wine country. Growing areas cluster around Rosevears on the west bank and the **Pipers River area** east of George Town but are spread throughout the district. Armed with a *Tamar Valley Wine Route* brochure from the visitor centre in Launceston (ⓦtamarvalleywineroute.com.au), you could explore the countryside, dropping into whichever of the 32 **vineyards** takes your fancy, to sample crisp and fresh cool-climate wines – Pinot Noir and sparkling wines are specialities. Most are open daily 10am–5pm, though some close in July and August.

Goaty Hill 530 Auburn Rd, Kayena ☎01300 819 997, ⓦkgoatyhill.com. You can enjoy a gourmet cheese platter from the deck overlooking the vineyard as you taste the wonderful whites produced here, which include Riesling, Chardonnay, Sauvignon Blanc and a sparkling wine; there's also a Pinot Noir. Daily 11am–5pm.

Holm Oak 11 West Bay Rd, Rowella ☎03 6394 7577, ⓦholmoakvineyards.com.au. A family-owned winery, a little bit off the beaten track, but with wonderful views of the vineyards and orchards. Holm Oak produces cool-climate wines including Pinot Noir and Moscato (as well as their own cider). Children will enjoy tossing apples to Pinot the Pig in the garden

below the cellar door. Daily: June–Aug 11am–4pm; Sept–May 11am–5pm.

Velo Wines 755 West Tamar Highway, Legana ☎03 6330 3677, ⓦvelowines.com.au. Right at the entrance to the Tamar Valley, as you leave Launceston, Velo is named for its owner's other passion, cycling. Former Olympic road cyclist Micheal Wilson bought the 50-year-old vineyard in 2001 and set about becoming a qualified viticulturist. It now produces Cabernet Sauvignon and Pinot Noir, along with some other varietals including Riesling and Pinot Gris. The expansive modern restaurant overlooks the vineyard. Wed–Sun 11am–4pm.

10

Low Head

Five kilometres to the north, **LOW HEAD** is an adjunct of George Town and similarly salty. Here, the convict-built **Low Head Pilot Station** is the oldest working pilot station in Australia having been in operation since 1805. One of the former pilot cottages now houses a museum of maritime memorabilia (daily 10am–4pm; $5; ☎03 6382 1143, ⓦmuseum.lowhead.com). There's also a **Little penguin colony** at Low Head; tours are offered each evening at sunset (1hr; $22; bookings ☎0418 361 860, ⓦpenguintours .lowhead.com).

ARRIVAL, INFORMATION AND TOURS   GEORGE TOWN

By bus Lees Coaches (☎0400 937 440, ⓦleescoaches .com) covers the east shore from Launceston (Mon–Fri 4–5 daily, Sat 2 daily) to George Town (50min) and Low Head (1hr; booking required).

Tourist information The tourist office for George Town and Low Head (☎03 6382 1700, ⓦprovincialtamar.com. au; daily: June–Sept 9am–3pm; Oct–May 9am–4pm) is in a pavilion as you enter George Town from the south. You can hire bikes here ($25/day) to pedal along a shoreside path to Low Head, called the Kanamaluka Trail.

Seal and Sea Adventure Tours ☎03 6382 3452 or ☎0419 357 028, ⓦsealandsea.com. This George Town tour company runs diving and fishing charters, and cruises to a nearby fur seal colony on Tenth Island.

ACCOMMODATION AND EATING

Low Head Tourist Park 136 Low Head Rd ☎03 6382 1573, ⓦlowheadtouristpark.com.au. While there's precious little space for camping, this ticks all boxes for other forms of budget accommodation, with caravans, a mini-hostel in a self-contained unit, cabins and cottages, all with the river just over the road. Un/powered sites $17/37, dorms $28, cabins $95

Pier Hotel 5 Elizabeth St ☎03 6382 1300, ⓦpierhotel .com.au. The best motel-style rooms here look over the cove where settlement in northern Tasmania began. Locals know it best for the bistro; rather bare but serving good tucker like grilled fish with a rocket, pear and parmesan salad ($27). Restaurant daily noon–2pm & 6–9pm. $159

South of Launceston

Some of the earliest settlement in Australia's colonial history has left its mark throughout the hinterland around Launceston. With hawthorn hedgerows along the roadsides, English churches in historic villages like **Evandale**, and fine Georgian farming mansions around **Longford**, it might be easy to imagine you're somewhere in the old country (except for the gum trees and pink rosellas pecking in the grass). All make enjoyable day-trips with your own transport – there's no public transport to the sights, only the towns – and there's also fine bushwalking (plus occasional skiing) southeast at **Ben Lomond National Park**.

Evandale

"Where history comes alive" is the catchphrase of **EVANDALE**, 20km southeast of Launceston. On Sundays, visitors pour in for a popular country market, which offers pony rides, fresh produce, crafts, books and more (see p.938); the rest of the time the National Trust-classified village is a nicely sleepy sort of place, with a sprinkling of antiques and craft shops and colonial architecture that all but recreates village England. The **Evandale** Tourist Information **Centre** sells a *Heritage Walk* leaflet ($3), otherwise simply head to the heart of the village at the T-junction of Russell Street. Here, some of the old buildings bear descriptive plaques, and the **Clarendon Arms Hotel** (1847) has murals inside that depict early Tassie history. The bronze penny-farthing outside refers to Evandale's annual three-day Village Fair held on the last weekend in February, a historical rustic jamboree famous for its **National Penny Farthing Championships**; you'll pay $12 entry to watch but may feel it's worth it for the sight of lycra-clad riders on old bikes.

10

Clarendon Estate

234 Clarendon Station Rd, 8km south of Evandale • Clarendon House Sept–June Tues, Thurs & Sat 10am–4pm • $10 • Grounds daily 10am–4pm, $5

The National Trust-owned **Clarendon House** on the banks of the South Esk River speaks volumes about the prosperity of early colonial settlers. One of Australia's most impressive colonial mansions, the grand Neoclassical-style manor was built in 1838 by a wool-producer and furnished in Georgian style. Ghost tours are run on Thursdays at 8pm ($25). The gardens cover seven hectares and give access to the South Esk River, ideal for fishing and picnics. A feature of the gardens is an impressive avenue of elm trees.

ARRIVAL AND INFORMATION   EVANDALE

By bus TassieLink's services to Cressy (#740) and Longford (#741) from Launceston stop at Evandale (3 daily; 30min).
Tourist information 18 High St (daily 9.30am–4.30pm;

☎ 03 6391 8128; ⍈ evandaletasmania.com).
Market Held in Falls Park on Logan Rd, en route to Ben Lomond National Park (Sun 8am–1.30pm).

Longford

LONGFORD, 20km southwest of Launceston, is still very much a country town, but with a rich history evident in its fine buildings and pioneer cemeteries. The town was founded in 1807 to access the fine pasture hereabouts. Agricultural success led two farmers – the Archer brothers – to build superb colonial farming estates south of town: one rustic, the other rather aristocratic, and both World Heritage listed.

Brickendon Estate

236 Wellington St, 2km southeast of the centre via Woolmers Lane (C521) • Tues–Sun: Oct to mid-May 9.30am–5pm; mid-May to Sept 9.30am–4pm • $12.50 • ☎ 03 6392 1383, ⍈ brickendon.com.au

Set up from land granted to William Archer in 1824, **Brickendon Estate** is still run as a working sheep property by sixth-generation Archers. Earlier members of the family saw fit to keep the original buildings in which convicts worked out their sentences, thereby preserving the pretty farm village. To walk around the farm village, with its huge Dutch-style wooden barns, brick outbuildings such as the servants' quarters and blacksmith's, and the Victorian chapel, is like exploring a film set for a historic rural blockbuster. Friendly sheep, poultry, horses, goats and Aggie the pig will keep young children entertained. It's also possible to stay here, in both convict-built and newer farm cottages (see website for details). William Archer's brother Thomas had earlier established Woolmers Estate (see below) nearby.

Woolmers Estate

658 Woolmers Lane, 5.5km from Longford • 10am–4pm • $20; grounds only $14 • Tours 11.15am, 12.30pm, 2pm, plus 10am & 3.30pm Oct–April • ☎ 03 6391 2230, ⍈ woolmers.com.au

English settler Thomas Archer established his estate **Woolmers** in 1819 and it remained in the hands of his descendants until 1994. The original Georgian bungalow with its warren of dark rooms still stands, as does the impressive Italianate villa built by Thomas as he prospered in 1843. A guided **tour** of the house is fascinating as much for the family story as the interiors; the dining room is still set up as it was for a royal visit in 1868. Don't miss the splendid woolshed in the grounds, said to be Australia's oldest (1819). Seven cottages are available for overnight stays (see website for details). Archer's brother William had an equally impressive estate, Brickendon (see above), not far away.

ARRIVAL AND EATING   LONGFORD

By bus TassieLink's service to Cressy from Launceston stops at Longford (Mon–Fri 9 daily, Sat 3 daily; 55min) but there's no transport to the manors themselves.
Hubert & Dan 59 Wellington St ☎ 0458 822 308. The lunch menu at chef Danielle Lefrancois' smart café

includes halloumi veggie burgers, slow-cooked lamb sliders with grilled aubergine, aioli and spicy relish, and corn fritter "bombs" (all around $20), and the dinner menu changes each week. Mon–Fri 9am–4.30pm, Thurs 6–8pm.

JJ's Bakery & Old Mill Café 52 Wellington St ☎03 6391 2364. A handy place to stop if you need information as well as a pick-me-up coffee (good coffee, at that) and a bite to eat. It's a big place, with low ceilings and lots of atmosphere, turning out pies and pasties, cakes, sandwiches, salads and pizzas ($18). Service is quick and friendly, and there's a garden courtyard out the back. Daily 7am–5pm.

Ben Lomond National Park

The plateau of the **Ben Lomond Range**, over 1300m high and 84 square kilometres in area, lies entirely within **Ben Lomond National Park**, 50km southeast of Launceston. For most of the year, the area below **Legges Tor** (1572m), the second-highest point in Tasmania, offers rugged **bushwalking** across a subalpine plateau with magnificent vegetation. It's rarely visited by tourists, yet has the major plus of a road right onto the plateau; the hairpin route up, known as Jacobs Ladder, is as much of an attraction as the summit itself. Destinations for a walk include Legges Tor or the fabulously named Little Hell, with views of the dolerite cliff known as Stacks Bluff (both 1hr 30min return). From mid-June to August, the mountain hosts a modest ski scene, with six ski lifts and equipment rental at an alpine village beneath Legges Tor.

INFORMATION AND ACTIVITIES	**BEN LOMOND NATIONAL PARK**
Park ranger There is no visitor centre, so contact the ranger (☎03 6230 5312). **Mountain biking** A thrilling way to experience the mountain in summer is on the Ben Lomond Descent, a high-adrenaline downhill cycle from the plateau organized by Mountain Bike Tasmania (see p.932) in Launceston	(6–7hr; $225; includes equipment, packed lunch and transfers from Launceston). **Skiing** A snow report is posted in season on ⊕ski.com.au/reports/australia/tas/benlomond. Ski hire is available on the summit from Ben Lomond Snow Sports (☎03 6390 6185, ⊕skibenlomond.com.au).

ACCOMMODATION

Camping Bush camping is permitted anywhere in the national park, but a free camping area with six pitches and a toilet is signposted 1km inside the park boundary, 7km from the summit.

Deloraine and Walls of Jerusalem National Park

There's beautiful scenery west of Launceston. Tiny towns sit in rich farmland and beside green river vales, all rolling up to the wall-like **Great Western Tiers**, where Tasmania's Central Plateau drops abruptly to the surrounding plains. The area's main destination is **Deloraine**, which leads a double life as a farming and arts centre, and the nearby village of **Mole Creek**, gateway to the caves of Tassie's only underground national park. Both serve as a base for day-walks but the best walking hereabouts is in the Walls of Jerusalem National Park, which is fast gaining a reputation as an alternative to Cradle Mountain.

BUSHWALKS NEAR DELORAINE

Close to prime **bushwalking** areas in the Western Tiers, Deloraine doubles as a base for walkers. You can pick up information from the Deloraine visitor centre; they have a map of the Meander Forest Reserve that includes surrounding day-walks. Popular tracks include the stroll to **Alum Cliffs**, an impressive gorge in the Mersey River of Aboriginal significance (40min return) that's signposted on the road between Chudleigh and Mole Creek; a difficult walk to **Quamby Bluff**, renowned for its myrtle rainforest (6.5km; 6hr; beginning at Brodies Rd, off the Lake Highway); and the track to gorgeous **Liffey Falls** (8km; 3hr; beginning at the picnic ground 5km west of the tiny community of Liffey). Another excellent day-walk visits **Meander Falls** in the Meander Forest Reserve, about 25km south of Deloraine.

10

Deloraine and around

Draped over hills beside the **Meander River**, **DELORAINE** is a pleasant spot on the route west. The area was settled by Europeans in the 1830s, but Deloraine was a late starter, developing from 1846, and today it's National Trust classified, its backstreets stuffed with historic houses. But don't let that put you off – architecture is only a backdrop to this town's quietly bohemian vibe. Numerous arts and crafts galleries line the streets – for a taster there's Deloraine Creative Studios (61 Emu Bay Rd; 9.30am–5pm), the outlet for several local artists and craftworkers, and the largest of the many shops in town. For crafts overload, there's the **Tasmanian Craft Fair** in early November (see opposite), when around twenty thousand visitors browse and buy from the largest crafts gathering in Australia.

Yarns and folk museum

At the visitor centre, 98 Emu Bay Rd • Daily 9.30am–4pm • $8 • ☎ 03 6362 5280, ⓦ yarnsartworkinsilk.com

Given Deloraine's artsy bent, it's appropriate that its finest attraction is the "Yarns" exhibition in the visitor information centre, which showcases four fabulously detailed silk wall-hangings of seasonal local scenes. They're the work of over three hundred local artisans and each panel represents just under a year's work. Your ticket also gets you into a small museum of settler history but it's small beer by comparison.

Chudleigh

It's a lovely drive west beneath the western end of the Great Western Tiers to **CHUDLEIGH**, 24km from Deloraine. A little further on you can taste Tassie honey (and honey ice cream) at the **Honey Farm** at Chudleigh (daily except Sat 9am–5pm; free), where there are over fifty varieties to taste and buy.

Mole Creek Karst National Park

Cave tours (45min) daily every hour • Marakoopa Cave 10am–4pm • King Solomons Cave June–Oct 10.30am–4.30pm; May–Nov 11.30am–3.30pm • $19 • ☎ 03 6363 5133, ⓦ parks.tas.gov.au

Mole Creek, about 25km from Deloraine (via the village of Chudleigh), is a pleasingly rural backwater set in lovely scenery. The most celebrated sight, though, is subterranean; **Mole Creek Karst National Park** is a network of over two hundred caves around the town. Two spectacular ones are open to the public 14km west of Mole Creek: **Marakoopa Cave**, with huge caverns, streams, pools and glow-worms; and 6km further west the smaller but more richly decorative **King Solomons Cave**, with stalactites and stalagmites. It's touristy, with railings and concrete pathways, but provides a taster of what lies beneath the ground in the area. The caverns are a constant 9°C, so dress warmly. For more adventure, you can go caving with Wild Cave Tours (see opposite).

Trowunna Wildlife Park

1892 Mole Creek Rd, Mole Creek • Daily 9am–5pm • $22 • ☎ 03 6362 6162, ⓦ trowunna.com.au

Staff at the small **Trowunna Wildlife Park** at Mole Creek, about twelve minutes' drive from Deloraine, are passionate about breeding backup populations of Tasmanian devils (see box, p.919). Guided tours are run at 11am, 1pm and 3pm, finishing with a devil feeding session, and there are also wallabies, wombats (line up for a cuddle), pademelons, potoroos, quolls, snakes and plenty of birdlife.

ARRIVAL AND DEPARTURE

By bus TassieLink and Redline stop in Deloraine: Redline on a twice daily service; and TassieLink on its Launceston–West Coast service Mon & Wed (pick-ups only). The depot for both is the Deloraine visitor centre. Redline runs a daily service (Mon–Fri) from Launceston via Deloraine to Mole Creek. **Destinations:** Cradle Mountain (2 weekly; 2hr 35min); Devonport (2–3 daily; 40min); Hobart (2–4 daily; 4hr); Launceston (2–4 daily; 45min).

INFORMATION AND TOURS

Tourist information Deloraine's excellent Great Western Tiers Visitor Centre, at 98 Emu Bay Rd (daily 9am–5pm; ☎ 03 6362 5280, ⊚ greatwesterntiers.net.au), covers the entire Western Tiers region with accommodation bookings, maps and details on walks and arts outlets.

Events The annual Tasmanian Craft Fair (⊚ tascraftfair .com.au), the largest of its type in Australia, attracts around twenty thousand people over four days in early November. Book accommodation well In advance if you'll be visiting at the time.

Wild Cave Tours ☎ 03 6367 8142, ⊚ wildcavetours .com. Excellent half-day ($130) and full-day ($260) caving tours of Mole Creek caves that are inaccessible to other members of the public – a good introduction to caving.

10

ACCOMMODATION

Bluestone Grainstore 14 Parsonage St ☎ 03 6362 4722, ⊚ bluestonegrainstore.com.au. The smartest option in town, this B&B provides luxury rooms in an old stone granary that introduce a dash of city cool to sleepy Deloraine: expect crisp white walls and linen, pale wood furniture and leather headboards. **$165**

Bonney's Inn 17 West Parade ☎ 03 6362 2974, ⊚ bonneys-inn.com. Pleasant B&B in heritage-styled rooms in the oldest house in town, a Georgian residence beside the *Deloraine Hotel* that's full of character. If you're a light sleeper, ask for a room at the back, as trains rumble by in the night (just across the street). **$168**

Deloraine Apex Caravan Park West Parade ☎ 03 6362 2345. The camping site spreads along the Meander River just off the main street of Deloraine. While the flat ground appeals, amenities are clean but dated, and expect the sound of the goods trains rumbling past at night. Un/ powered sites **$25/30**

★ **Forest Walks Lodge** 669 Jackeys Marsh Rd, 10km south of Deloraine ☎ 03 6369 5150, ⊚ forestwalkslodge.com. An excellent base for walkers, this small ecolodge offers utter peace and far more style than you'd expect from its location buried deep in a valley among pristine bush. Its lovely owners provide guided walks and great meals. The finest escape in the area. **$140**

Mole Creek Caravan Park 2 Union Bridge Rd, Mole Creek ☎ 03 6363 1150, ⊚ molecreek.net.au. A pretty site with about fifty camping and caravan spots, beside a stream about four kilometres west of the village. Un/ powered sites **$20/25**

Mole Creek Guest House 100 Pioneer Drive, Mole Creek ☎ 03 6363 1399, ⊚ molecreekguesthouse.com.au. Charming guest rooms with country-cottage decor – think old iron bed frames, traditional bedspreads and vintage wardrobes – but all mod-cons (including en-suite bathrooms) make up the accommodation in this congenial guesthouse. There's also a three-bedroom cottage, ideal for families, and a café serving wood-fired pizzas and more. **$155**

EATING

Cruzin' in the 50s Diner 2 Railway St, Deloraine ☎ 03 6362 2978. A favourite with locals, this colourful outpost of Americana brings *Happy Days* to Deloraine. So, there's booth seating, vintage Americana decor, rock 'n' roll on the jukebox and a menu of burgers (from $16), fries, nachos and even malted milkshakes. Mon–Thurs 10am–4.30pm, Fri & Sat 10am–9pm, Sun 10am–5pm.

Deloraine Deli 36 Emu Bay Rd, Deloraine ☎ 03 6362 2127. This deli-café is the mainstay of Deloraine café society. Expect fresh quiches and gluten-free bagels at lunch, plus the likes of Tasmanian ocean trout with leek soubise or pork belly with roasted cauliflower at dinner (dinner mains average $24). Mon–Thurs 8.30am–5pm, Fri & Sat 8.30am–10pm, Sun 10am–4pm.

Pepperberry Café 100 Pioneer Drive, Mole Creek ☎ 03 6363 1399. A lovely relaxing spot for coffee, a lazy lunch or early dinner, attached to *Mole Creek Guest House*. Wood-fired pizzas ($21) are the mainstay, but they also offers pies, soups and pasta dishes. Local craft beers are available on tap. Sun–Thurs 10.30am–3pm, Fri & Sat 10.30am–7pm.

Walls of Jerusalem National Park

Part of the World Heritage Area, the **Walls of Jerusalem National Park** is one of Tassie's finest wilderness areas. It jigsaws into the Cradle Mountain area and shares many of its characteristics – a series of craggy dolerite peaks that enclose a central basin and miles of glaciated lakes, pencil pines and open moorland. What sets the Walls of Jerusalem apart from Cradle Mountain is the lack of visitors. Snow is possible even in January, so be well prepared. The most settled months are February and April.

As the Walls of Jerusalem is the only national park in Tasmania that you can't drive into, the walk in begins outside the park boundaries. The standard approach is from Mole Creek (see opposite), then south, following the Mersey River via the unsealed road east of Lake Rowallan to a car park. You ascend through forest into the park,

10

which has no ranger outpost (although rangers do patrol). However, tracks are well kept, with boardwalks laid in places, there's plenty of clean water to drink from the streams, and there are a couple of camping platforms with composting toilets – the old wooden trappers' huts are really for emergencies only.

For years the Walls was something of a walkers' secret. Now visitor numbers have so increased that there has been talk of summer quotas to preserve the delicate habitat. At the time of writing, this hadn't yet happened, but visit the PWS website (ⓦparks.tas .gov.au) for the most up-to-date information.

The central basin

On a very long day-trip, you can sample the park on a hike into the central basin – through **Herods Gate**, with views of Barn Bluff and Cradle Mountain to the northwest – and back. It's a 14km return hike, which takes around eight hours at a steady clip. To experience the park's magic you can stay overnight on wooden platforms at *Wild Dog Creek Campsite*. From here there are numerous routes to various peaks and lakes – **Mount David** offers especially stunning views – and an experienced walker could easily spend a happy week rootling around.

INFORMATION AND ACCOMMODATION	**WALLS OF JERUSALEM NATIONAL PARK**
Map You'll need the *Walls of Jerusalem National Park Map* ($12); pick up a copy before you go from outdoors shops in Launceston or buy one online at ⓦtasmap.tas.gov.au. **Tasmanian Expeditions** ☎ 1300 666 856 or ☎ 03 6339 3999, ⓦtasmanianexpeditions.com. Runs several multiday guided walks in the park, including one of day-walks from a base at Wild Dog Creek and a six-day	combined trip walk with Cradle Mountain. **Wild Dog Creek Campsite** Walls of Jerusalem National Park. The only established campsite in the national park is the *Wild Dog Creek Campsite*, with pitches on wooden platforms to protect the delicate habitat. Facilities include pit toilets and unfiltered water. <u>Free</u> (with NP pass)

The northwest coast

There's a real sense of heading into the wilderness as you travel along the northwest coast. After the cities of **Devonport** and **Burnie**, the towns grow smaller and more spaced out as you skip beside the Bass Strait to **Stanley**, a historic village in a spectacular setting. It serves as the best base for a visit to the area; a hub for day-trips to Wynyard, Boat Harbour Beach or the ragged coast of the Rocky Cape National Park.

Keep going beyond Stanley and civilization (and any form of public transport) starts to peter out, the roads get narrower, and finally you roll into dairy village **Marrawah**. Pushing on to **Arthur River**, you'll find just a few holiday shacks and houses around the river. Here, there's a sense of life at the edge; of settlements buffeted by what is officially the cleanest air in the world and a raw coastline pounded by waves that have rolled all the way from South America.

Devonport

DEVONPORT is the third-largest city in Tasmania, yet the port of the **Bass Strait ferry** is hardly the most inspiring welcome to the island. The small CBD is not a destination in itself and the rest of the town feels suburban. Unless you're heading here for the ferry, there's little reason to visit, although it's a useful transit hub for Cradle Mountain and the west coast.

Bass Strait Maritime Centre

8 Gloucester Ave • Daily 9am–5pm • $10 • ☎ 03 6424 7100, ⓦ bassstraitmaritimecentre.com.au

Split between a modern display hall and the old harbourmaster's cottage, the salty exhibits at this museum of Bass Strait shipping tell stories of shipwrecks, early colonial history and Devonport pioneer life. There are also a few rooms of maritime heritage and an interactive computer game ($2) to try to "dock" a steamer in historic Devonport. The centre runs sailing trips on a restored fishing ketch on Wednesdays and Sundays (2hr; $40), a good way to experience the force of nature that is Bass Strait.

Mersey Bluff

With a good beach, fine food, a great playground for children and views over the Bass Strait, there are worse places to lose half a day than Mersey Bluff, north of the CBD. Its knobble of rock was of significance to local Aborigines, who etched around 270 engravings onto the headland, possibly ten thousand years ago, and left middens. **Tiagarra Aboriginal Culture & Art Centre** (ⓦtiagarra.weebly.com), closed in 2014 but at the time of writing there was strong support for moves to reopen it. The building marks the start of a short trail to the carvings.

10

ARRIVAL AND DEPARTURE   DEVONPORT

By plane Devonport Airport is 10km east of the city and served by flights from Melbourne (2–4 daily; 1hr). A shuttle bus into Devonport (ⓣ0437 067 108; $14) coordinates with arrivals and also serves the surrounding area. A taxi into town will cost about $30 – it's a good idea to prebook (Taxis Combined ⓣ03 6424 1431 or ⓣ13 10 08).

By bus TassieLink services run to/from Hobart and the west coast via Sheffield and Cradle Mountain. Redline travels the west coast to Smithton. Both run services to Launceston.

Destinations Burnie (1–2 daily; 50min); Cradle Mountain via Sheffield (Dec–March daily, otherwise 2 weekly; 2hr

15min); Deloraine (2–3 daily; 1hr 30min); Hobart (1–2 daily; 4hr 30min); Launceston (2–5 daily; 1hr 30min); Queenstown (2 weekly; 5hr 20min).

By ferry *Spirit of Tasmania* ferries (see p.888) from Melbourne dock at a terminal in East Devonport, across the Mersey River from the city centre; Redline and TassieLink express buses for Launceston and Hobart connect with arrivals. The cute and historic little *Spirit of Devonport* passenger ferry runs a cross-river service to the port quay, bottom of Murray St near the terminal, on demand (just push the button on the pontoon and wait for the ferry to arrive (Mon–Fri 7am–5.30pm, Sat 9am–5pm; $2.50).

INFORMATION

Tourist information The Devonport Visitor Centre, on the CBD waterfront at 92 Formby Rd (Mon–Fri 7.30am–3.30pm, Sat & Sun 7.30–11.30am; ⓣ03 6424 4466, ⓦtasmaniasnorthwest.com.au), is an excellent resource for information and bookings statewide. It also

has internet access.

Outdoor supplies For bushwalking supplies and maps, there are outdoors shops at the junction of Rooke & Steele sts, or there's a huge Allgoods near the Bass Highway, at 6 Formby Rd.

ACCOMMODATION AND EATING

★ **Drift** 41 Bluff Road ⓣ03 6424 4695, ⓦdriftdevonport .com. With a location right on the beachfront, this Mersey Bluff restaurant/café is relaxed and casual, even welcoming barefoot clients. Whether it's burgers (from $10) or pizza in the café or more upmarket fare in the adjoining restaurant, everything is made with the freshest, northwest Tassie ingredients. This might mean dishes like wild mushroom risotto, pan-roasted duck breast, or a fish and prawn curry (around $30). Mon & Tues 10am–4pm, Wed–Fri 10am– late, Sat 8.30am–late, Sun 9am–late.

Laneway 2/38 Steele St ⓣ03 6424 4333, ⓦlane-way .com.au. This great licensed café-bistro feels more Melbourne than Devonport. With bare brick and eclectic decor, it's hip without showing off, serving up lunches such as lemon-pepper calamari or chicken Caesar salad ($20) – or a burger if you want something more hearty – plus excellent breakfasts with delicious juice and coffee. All in all, a great find. Mon–Fri 7am–5pm, Sat & Sun 7am–4pm.

Molly Malones 34 Best St ⓣ03 6424 1898, ⓦmollymalones.com.au. Beef and Guinness pie ($20), Irish stew, Tex-Mex and steak are typical of the rib-sticking pub-grub served in large portions in this Irish pub (daily: pub 11am–late; food daily 11.30am–3pm & 6–9pm). Above is a hostel; basic and fairly shabby in places but mostly clean and as central as it gets. Dorms $20, doubles $40

Quality Hotel Gateway 16 Fenton St ⓣ03 6424 4922, ⓦgatewayinn.com.au. The business travellers' choice, well-located in the heart of the CBD and the largest hotel in town. Compact refurbished studios in chain-hotel style as well as smarter "executive" and "spa" rooms with harbour views. $180

Tasman Backpackers 114 Tasman St ⓣ03 6423 2335, ⓦtasmanbackpackers.com.au. Spacious hostel in a former nurses' residence with mostly well-furnished twins and triples, a couple of en-suite doubles and five- to nine-bed dorms (including separate male and female dorms). A

20min walk from the river, but free pick-ups on request. They also have free bicycles for guests' use. Popular

Nov–May with harvest workers, so book early if travelling at this time of year. Dorms $24, doubles $66

Around Devonport

Standard practice is to use Devonport as a stepping-stone to Cradle Mountain or the west coast. Yet it warrants a pause if you have your own transport to explore the surrounding area, mainly for the chance to see some Aussie wildlife.

Latrobe

LATROBE, just 8km south of Devonport, put itself on the map as the self-proclaimed "Platypus Capital of the World", to which end an impressively tacky **Big Platypus** is plonked outside the **Australian Axeman's Hall of Fame** (daily 9am–4pm; free) on Bells Parade. This celebration of the Tasmanian spectator sport of wood-chopping is best visited on Sundays, when Latrobe – a sleepy place of antique and bric-a-brac shops – holds its weekly crafts market in the Axeman's arena.

Your best chance of spotting a real platypus is on a tour through the **Warrawee State Reserve**, 4km south of Latrobe. Landcare Platypus Tours run tours either at dawn or dusk, with all proceeds going to habitat maintenance (2hr; $10; ☎03 6246 1774 or book at the visitor centre in the Axeman's Hall of Fame).

Narawntapu National Park

One of the best places in Tasmania to see **wombats**, **Narawntapu National Park** is home to an abundance of marsupials; at dusk, **Forester kangaroos** and **Bennett's wallabies** emerge to graze the grassland behind Bakers Beach (good for swimming). You'll need your own transport to get out here; it's a meandering, 40km drive from Devonport via the B71 then C740 to the main entrance and information centre (summer daily, winter Mon–Fri; ☎03 6248 6277).

ACCOMMODATION
NARAWNTAPU NATIONAL PARK

Camping ☎03 6248 6277. Popular camping areas are sited at Springlawn and Bakers Point in the national park – check in at the visitor centre or self-register out of hours (summer daily 9am–5pm; winter Mon–Fri 9am–5pm).

Facilities include toilets and picnic tables, plus powered sites, electric barbecues and showers at Springlawn (tokens from visitor centre). Un/powered sites $13/$16

Sheffield

With its cute, old-fashioned looks and murals on every spare public wall, **SHEFFIELD**, 30km south of Devonport, picks up traffic en route to Cradle Mountain (see p.953). The scenery's gorgeous – a backdrop of farmland rolls to Mount Roland (1231m), a highly impressive mountain fin that glows when spotlit during sunset. Sheffield is a sleepy sort of place, now almost entirely devoted to tourism, with plenty of bric-a-brac outlets and cafés. In the mid-1980s, the town's rural economy was ailing, so the community hatched a plan to revive itself through **murals**. Since then, more than sixty works have been painted, most showing the history and folklore of the town, and new works are chosen in an international competition held annually in late March/early April. All entries are displayed in Mural Park for the following year.

ARRIVAL AND INFORMATION
SHEFFIELD

By bus TassieLink stops on its scheduled Launceston–Queenstown service via Cradle Mountain (Mon & Wed only; 2hr from Launceston).

Tourist information The Kentish Visitor Information Centre is at Pioneer Crescent precinct in the town centre

(Oct–April Mon–Fri 9am–5pm, Sat & Sun 10am–4pm; May–Sept Mon–Fri 9am–4pm, Sat & Sun 11am–3pm; ☎03 6491 1179, ⓦ sheffieldcradleinfo.com.au). The centre is a great source of regional information, hands out Sheffield mural maps and provides wi-fi access.

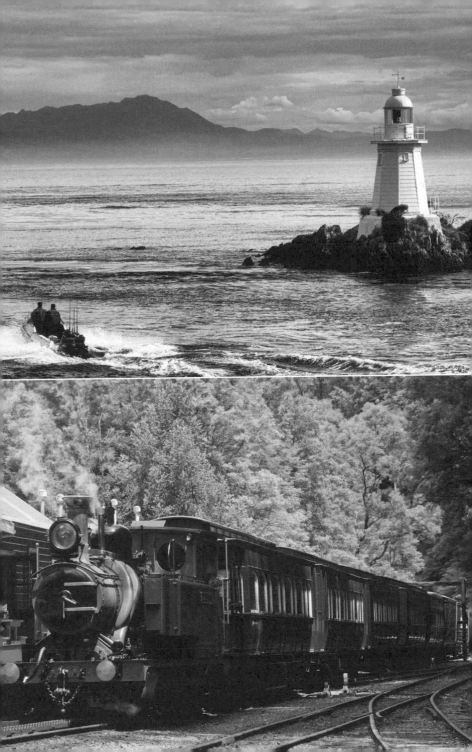

10

★**Glencoe** Barrington, 8km northwest of Sheffield ☎03 6492 3267, ⓦglencoeruralretreat.com.au. This country B&B, run by a French couple and set on an old dairy farm, offers utter relaxation in elegant modern country rooms with charm and style by the tonne. As well as breakfast, the owners prepare a three-course dinner for guests ($65, on request): expect French home cooking such as duck confit or slow-cooked lamb shank, and crème brulee. A great launchpad for Cradle Mountain. $175

T's Chinese Restaurant 83 Main St ☎03 6491 2244. "Mindblowing" said leading Aussie chef Anthony Lui of T's exquisite dumplings. Bloody delicious, say locals of this modest Chinese restaurant/takeaway run by the Zhao family. Either way, the accolades are probably down to the lamb, pork and beef sourced from the owners' farm. Truly "from paddock to plate". Daily 5–9pm.

Inland along the B17

The coast road provides the obvious option for touring. Yet with time to spare and your own transport you can circuit inland between Ulverstone and Penguin on the B17. As well as picturesque hop-growing countryside, the route passes a couple of child-friendly sights. Tours of the **Gunns Plains Caves** (hourly tours daily 10am–3.30pm; 50min; $15; ☎03 6429 1388, ⓦgunnsplainscaves.com.au) show off remarkable limestone formations which glow red when spotlit from behind. Beyond, there's native wildlife – including devils – in the **Wings Wildlife Park** (daily 10am–4pm; $22; ⓦwingswildlife.com.au). You can also visit just to picnic or wander among camels and bison ($6).

Penguin

Cheerful and unpretentious, **PENGUIN** is a bright and breezy little holiday town, with safe swimming beaches and a laidback vibe. It also has penguins – lots of them, grinning from bins on the main street and culminating in the 2m-high **Big Penguin** in the foreshore park. Ironically, real ones no longer come to town – they have set up new colonies near Ulverstone and Burnie. If you are driving from Devonport, the highway tracks west towards **Ulverstone**, an unremarkable holiday centre that is popular with families due to its beaches. A far more appealing drive is to pick up Penguin Road at Ulverstone, which hugs the scenic coastline for 12km all the way to Penguin.

By bus The Redline Bass Highway service between Devonport (45min) and Burnie (15min) stops in town once a day and twice on Fridays.

Tourist information The visitor centre, at 78 Main Rd (daily: May–Sept 9.30am–3.30pm; Oct–April 9am–4pm; ☎03 6437 1421) can provide more details about things to do in the area, including twilight penguin trips.

Jo & Co Café 74 Main Rd ☎03 6437 2101. A mainstay of the local café scene whose colourful and cluttered retro interior matches the laidback atmosphere of the town. The café menu is all unpretentious wholesome stuff – Devonshire teas, home-made soups, pancakes, burgers and lasagne – and good value at around $13 a main. Mon & Thurs–Sun 8am–3pm.

The Madsen 64 Main Rd ☎03 6437 2588, ⓦthemadsen.com. The most stylish stay in Penguin is very much in the boutique B&B vein; think restrained, elegant decor in charcoal grey, cream and chocolate, and beach views from some rooms. The spacious penthouse is ideal for a splurge, at $35 extra. $165

Penguin Holiday Apartments 99–101 Main Rd ☎03 6437 1900, ⓦpenguinholidayapartments.com. Though the breeze-block walls and simple kitchenettes of these doubles and family rooms are far from fancy, the motel-style accommodation here is central, cheap and, crucially, just behind the beach. Small wonder it's popular. $95

Burnie

Tasmania's fourth-largest city, **BURNIE**, 15km west of Penguin, was until recently a major industrial centre known for paper manufacture. The wane of the industry forced a rethink and Burnie now brands itself a "City of Makers" in an effort to highlight its creative credentials. It's had some success, too – while Burnie is unlikely ever to become a resort town, its showpiece Makers' Workshop is certainly worth a visit if you are en route west.

Little Penguin Observation Centre

Parsonage Point, West Beach • Tours daily Sept–March, one hour after dusk • Free • ☎ 0437 436 8033, ⓦ discoverburnie.net

A boardwalk links the city to the beachside **Little Penguin Observation Centre**, where Burnie locals have created a safe habitat for the Little penguins who waddle ashore here at around dusk – the hundreds of handmade "igloos" that they use as burrows. During penguin season (Sept–March), when the penguins are coming ashore to feed their chicks each night, the Friends of Burnie Penguins run free interpretive tours; just turn up around dusk. You might see some penguins at other times of year, but it's less likely, and certainly in much lower numbers.

Makers' Workshop

2 Bass Hwy • Daily 9am–5pm • Free • **Tours** every 45min from 9.15am • $15 • ☎ 03 6430 5831, ⓦ discoverburnie.net

The distinctive contemporary lines of the **Makers' Workshop** building beside the beach (and highway) are a landmark at the west end of town. The building is part museum, part arts centre, and was planned principally as a home for the community-based, nonprofit **Creative Paper Mill**. Its life-size handmade paper sculptures are on display in the central atrium, along with an exhibit on the paper industry, and you can have a go at papermaking on one of the workshop tours. A changing roster of artists – ceramicists, painters, jewellers and milliners – set up temporary workshops in one wing of the building to showcase their work, all of which is for sale. The work of around fifty other Tasmanian artists is sold in an excellent gift shop, and a cheese shop offers tastings of local prize-winning blues, creamy camemberts and sharp, crumbly cheddars.

Hellyers Road Distillery and around

153 Old Surrey Rd, 3km east of Burnie, off the Bass Highway • Daily 10am–4.30pm • **Tours** 10.30am–3pm, 40min • $17.50 • ☎ 03 6433 0439, ⓦ hellyersroaddistillery.com.au

The last two decades have seen a rise in Tasmanian whisky as producers take advantage of the exceptionally clean water and high-quality ingredients. Australia's largest producer of Aussie single malts, **Hellyers Road Distillery**, runs tours of its award-winning distillery plus sales (and tastings) in a visitor shop. While you're in the area, visit **Fernglade**, a peaceful, forested stretch of the Emu River known for its **platypus reserve**; the elusive marsupials are most active at dawn and after dusk. It's signposted a kilometre beyond off Old Surrey Road.

ARRIVAL AND INFORMATION   BURNIE

By plane Burnie Airport (ⓦ burnieairport.com.au) – actually in Wynyard, 20km northwest – has direct flights to/from Melbourne run by Regional Express (REX) airline. The usual car-rental agencies maintain bureaux at the airport, otherwise the Burnie Airbus (☎ 03 6431 2992) connects the airport with centre.

By bus Redline buses stop at Burnie (outside the Metro Cinemas on Wilmot St) en route west from Launceston and Devonport. Metro buses connect to Wynyard and Penguin from stops on Cattley St. TassieLink operates a

twice-weekly service between Burnie and Queenstown on Tuesdays and Fridays.

Destinations Hobart (1–2 daily; 5hr 45min); Launceston (1–2 daily; 2hr 20min); Penguin (Mon–Fri 8 daily, Sat 3 daily; 30min); Stanley (daily; 1hr).

Tourist information The Makers' Workshop, at 2 Bass Highway (daily 9am–5pm; ☎ 03 6430 5831, ⓦ discoverburnie.net), doubles as the tourist office, and can book you accommodation if you decide to stay overnight in town.

EATING

★**Another Mother** 14 Cattley St ☎ 03 6431 8000. Quirky and colourful, with a welcoming atmosphere and yummy, mostly vegetarian, fresh food, this is a great place,

set up by two local mums. The menu includes the likes of risotto with crunchy snow peas and pumpkin, veggie lasagne and home-made burgers, all around $14. Great

10

cakes and coffee, and they also do an all-day breakfast. Tues–Sat 9am–3pm.

Bayviews Burnie Surf Club, 2 North Terrace ☎03 6431 7999, ⓦbayviewsrestaurant.com.au. Burnie's fine-dining seafront address takes style cues from Sydney, both in the airy minimalist dining room and the mod-Oz menu of dishes such as herb-roasted local salmon with cauliflower puree, avocado mousse and fried capers for $36 or – in keeping with the setting – a seafood platter ($39). Mon–Wed 5pm–late, Thurs–Sat noon–3pm & 5pm–late.

Fish Frenzy Burnie Surf Club, 2 North Terrace ☎03 6432 1111, ⓦfishfrenzyburnie.com.au. Fish and chips, served in a paper cone, to be eaten on the beachfront. Add in scallops, calamari, oysters, and prices from $16 and it's no wonder this is a popular spot. Catch of the day is also available, and you can also eat in. Daily: 8am–9pm.

From Wynyard to Stanley

WYNYARD, another 19km along the old Bass Highway from Burnie, snuggles into lush pasture between the **Inglis River** and the sea. It's a sedate spot, with fishermen on the wharf by the river and little to thrill in the town itself aside from what is said to be Australia's largest collection of restored vintage Fords, including a rare 1903 Model A, the world's joint-equal oldest car: the **Wonders of Wynyard** exhibition is in the **Wynyard Visitor Information Centre** (see opposite; daily: Aug–April 9am–5pm; May–July 10am–4pm ; $8; ☎03 6443 8330, ⓦwondersofwynyard.com). In the vicinity are a couple of sights of geological interest.

Fossil Bluff

Three kilometres northwest of the centre is **Fossil Bluff**, a 275-million-year-old headland whose sedimentary rock contains fossilized seashells; one of the world's oldest fossil marsupials was discovered here. Its three major layers – Permian Tillite at the base, sandstone and finally a cap of basalt – can be examined at low tide from a beach.

Table Cape

One of the area's defining landmarks, **Table Cape** is the solidified plug of a prehistoric volcano which juts from the sea in the form of 170m-high cliffs. While impressive from a distance, it's at its best from a **lookout** on its summit, reached on a turning off the main road 4km west of the centre. Here you get magnificent views of the coast and around October a chequerboard of colours when **tulip fields** planted here bloom.

Boat Harbour Beach and Sisters Beach

Some 11km west of Wynyard, a turn-off from the Bass Highway winds down to **Boat Harbour Beach**. The original settlement of ramshackle holiday shacks has been marred by a large modern holiday-cabin complex, *Azzure,* but the sand remains pure white, the sea a beautiful pale turquoise. Attractive **Sisters Beach**, a few kilometres west of Boat Harbour, is far less developed; just a few houses in the bush spread behind a wilder beach.

Rocky Cape (Tangdimmaa) National Park

Stretching a mere 12km along the coast, from Sisters Beach to Rocky Cape, are the scrubby hills and sinewy coastline of **Rocky Cape National Park**, Tasmania's smallest national park. It was created in 1967 to preserve some remarkable **Aboriginal caves**: North Cave and South Cave at Rocky Cape itself were found to contain huge shell middens, bones and stone tools dating back eight thousand years, when the sea was several fathoms below its current level. Several walks in the park will take you to the caves, although they're of less appeal than the beautiful coastline: all rocky pools, safe swimming beaches and picnic areas, backed by heathland ablaze with flowers, including unique orchids in late spring. Road access is off the Bass Highway, around 20km west of Wynyard.

ARRIVAL AND INFORMATION

By plane Bizarrely for its size, Wynyard has Burnie Airport 10min from its centre (see p.947).

FROM WYNYARD TO STANLEY

By bus While Metro and Redline buses connect Wynyard with Burnie (and Stanley), the town does not really warrant the hassle of a visit by public transport as the surrounding destinations are only accessible with your own transport. **Tourist information** Wynyard Visitor Centre, beside a large car park behind the intersection of Jackson & Dodgin sts (daily Aug–April 9am–5pm; May–July 10am–4pm; ☎ 03 6443 8330, ⓦ visitwaratahwynyard.com.au).

Stanley

When first settled in 1826, **STANLEY** was described by Lieutenant-Governor Arthur as being "beyond the ramparts of the unknown". Nearly two centuries on, it somehow retains a suggestion of being at the edge of the world. Amazing, really, considering the thousands of holiday-makers who visit each year, delighting in the historic looks, cosy atmosphere and good beaches on either side of the pretty fishing village. The town remains utterly in awe of **The Nut**; the eighteenth-century colonial explorer Matthew Flinders called Stanley's landmark a "cliffy round lump in form resembling a Christmas cake", not a bad description of the solidified core of a prehistoric volcano rising sheer from the ocean to nearly 150m. **Circular Head**, as it's officially called (also the name for the surrounding municipality) provided shelter for the fledgling town, founded as the original headquarters of the **Van Diemen's Land Company** and the first settlement in northwest Tasmania. It has spread out from the original wharf area but remains a postcard-pretty core chock-full of small historic houses.

The Nut

Chairlift Sept–June daily 9.30am–5pm, weather permitting • $10 one-way, $16 return

The time-honoured tradition of any visit to Stanley is to ascend The Nut. The choice is either a stiff twenty-minute climb or a slow and gentle ride on the **chairlift**, reached via the ramp opposite the post office. At the summit a 2km trail tracks the edge of **The Nut State Reserve**, affording the best views over the town and port, and southeast as far as Table Cape.

Highfield Historic Site

Green Hills Rd • June–Aug Mon–Fri 9.30am–4.30pm; Sept–May daily 9.30am–4.30pm • $12 • ☎ 03 6458 1100, ⓦ historic-highfield.com.au

If The Nut demarcates Stanley on one side, Highfield bookends it on the other. Green Hills Road runs behind the beach then uphill to the original headquarters of the Van Diemen's Land Company, 2km north of the town, now open as the **Highfield Historic**

VDL AND WOOLNORTH TOURS

The **Van Diemen's Land Company (VDL)** was the brainchild of a group of well-connected individuals. Through a Royal Charter in 1825, they acquired 250,000 acres of the then-unexplored tip of Tasmania to produce fine wool on sheep farms. The *Tranmere* duly arrived at Circular Head with the personnel, livestock, supplies and equipment to create the township of Stanley.

The first flocks were grazed at Woolnorth on Cape Grim, a plateau of tussocky grass that was ideal – and also prime hunting land for the local Aborigines. When hunting parties began to take sheep, whites killed Aborigines in retaliation, and a vindictive cycle of killings began that culminated in 1827, with thirty unarmed Aborigines being killed by shepherds and their bodies thrown over the cliff (now euphemistically called "Suicide Bay").

In the 1840s the company changed its emphasis from wool to the sale and lease of its land, a fifth of which it still owns. In February 2016, the Australian government controversially approved the sale of VDL (then controlled by New Zealand company Tasman Farms and still Tasmania's largest dairy company) to Chinese company Moon Lake Investments. Today, VDL owns 25 dairy farms and 17,000 hectares of land in Tasmania, including Woolnorth Station on remote **Cape Grim**, where the Baseline Air Pollution Station records the air, carried thousands of kilometres across the Great Southern Ocean, as the cleanest in the world. Tours at **Woolnorth** take in the colonial homestead, Cape Grim and its 62-turbine wind farm. They depart from the wind farm gate at Bluff Point at 9.30am and 11.30am daily (2hr $66; ☎ 03 6452 1493, ⓦ woolnorthtours.com.au).

10

Site. Even though rooms are sparsely furnished with contemporary furniture, it's impressive as a time capsule of Regency design – you have to admire the chutzpah of VDL's aim to establish European high civilization in this utterly remote corner of the world. Interpretive boards provide a fascinating (and honest) history of the VDL Company and early development of the northwest, also providing detail from the perspective of local Aborigines.

The port area

Below Church Street and Alexander Terrace, the foreshore spreads along Wharf Road towards the fishing port. This was the original port for the VDL Company – the slate-roofed, blue-stoned **Van Diemen's Land Company Store** (now a boutique hotel; see below) was built in 1844 as the warehouse, while the contemporary bond store (now a restaurant), built with stone traditionally used as ships' ballast, sits beside the wharf. Further along at Fisherman's Dock, **Stanley Seaquarium** (June–Aug Sat & Sun 10.30am–3.30pm; Sept–May daily 10am–4pm; $12) has sharks, rays and a rock pool full of sea stars, sea cucumbers and hermit crabs – one to entertain the kids.

ARRIVAL AND INFORMATION   STANLEY

By bus Redline stops in Stanley on its west-coast route from Burnie via Wynyard (Mon–Fri daily; 1hr 15min). The bus depot is at the visitor centre.

Tourist information The excellent Stanley Visitor Centre is on the road into Stanley, at 45 Main Rd (daily 10am–5pm; ☎03 6458 1330 or ☎1300 138 229, ⓦstanley.com.au), and

serves as the visitor centre for the entire northwest region. **Stanley Seal Cruises** ☎0419 550 134, ⓦstanleysealcruises.com.au. Based in the harbour, Stanley Seal Cruises sails to an offshore colony of Australian fur seals, weather permitting (daily: Sept–April 10am & 3pm; May to mid-July 1pm; $55).

ACCOMMODATION

★@ **VDL Stanley** 16 Wharf Rd ☎03 6458 2032, ⓦatvdlstanley.com.au. The former VDL store (see above) has been beautifully renovated to create three glamorous suites, a tasteful union of hip interior design and historic architecture, with custom-designed Tasmanian furniture and art in the shared lounge. There's no reception; your key will be left for you to pick up. Also manages @ The Base, a nearby cottage with modern hotel-style rooms ($135). **$250**

The Ark 18 Wharf Rd ☎0421 695 224, ⓦthearkstanley .com.au. This B&B by the wharf is a superb blend of historic features – pressed metal ceilings and hardwood floors – and luxurious modern looks, calming muted colours and French furnishings. There are five relaxing, comfortable suites with bay views. **$178**

Beachside Retreat West Inlet 253 Stanley Highway, 2.5km south of the town centre ☎03 6458 1350, ⓦbeachsideretreat.com. Style and solitude in a

mini-complex of architect-designed luxury eco-cabins and beach houses, each secluded in a bush foreshore with glass walls looking out to a private beach. Book the Sea Eagle beach house for a hot tub in the sand dunes. **$218**

Stanley Cabin and Tourist Park Wharf Rd ☎03 6458 1266 or ☎1800 444 818, ⓦstanleycabinpark.com.au. Spread behind the beach a block from the high street, this is the only camping and budget option in town, so is perennially popular. As well as cosy twins in a tiny hostel, it offers motel-style rooms, and budget and spa cabins. Un/powered sites **$25/$30**, dorms **$26**, doubles **$90**, cabins **$110**

Stanley Hotel 19–21 Church St ☎1800 222 397, ⓦstanleytasmania.com.au. More than just a pub, with smart hotel-standard en suites ($140) that are worth the extra over the budget rooms, which share amenities; be warned, the latter are above the bar. **$70**

EATING

Hursey Seafood 2 Alexander Terrace ☎03 6458 1103, ⓦhurseyseafoods.com.au. You can't miss the big lobster on the roof of the Hursey building; head inside for takeaways (downstairs) or a sit-down feast overlooking the bay (upstairs). Apart from lobster, the signature fish is Stripey Trumpeter ($35), fresh from the tank. Half a small crayfish (freshwater lobster) will set you back $50, but there's plenty else to choose from (mains around $24). You can also buy fresh seafood to cook yourself. Daily:

restaurant 11.45am–2.15pm & 5.45–7.45pm; takeaway 11am–7pm.

★**Moby Dicks Breakfast Bar** 5 Church St ☎03 6458 1414. The most popular place in Stanley for breakfast, they pack them in here for the usual bacon-and-eggs offerings, as well as lighter fare (cereal and toast, waffles, pancakes). If you can't get enough seafood, there's also a "fisherman's breakfast" ($18) that includes smoked salmon with your poached eggs and spinach. Basic bacon, eggs, tomato and toast, $12. There's a deck outside overlooking the water. Daily 7.30am–noon.

Stanley Hotel Cnr Church & Victoria sts ☎03 6458 1161. This award-winning local pub serves fresh seafood and above-average bistro food – daily pies and seafood dishes for around $25 – in a lively lounge bar with terrace dining. Make a reservation or expect to wait in summer. There's also a bar menu in the public bar, which has an open fire, couches and a big screen TV screening sport. Daily 11.30am–3pm & 6–9pm.

Stanley's on the Bay 15 Wharf Rd ☎03 6458 1404. Slow-braised lamb shanks with mash, rich seafood chowder and fresh trevella (around $25) are typical of the quality cuisine here. Splash out $100 for the seafood platter for two. The decor is a nautical theme, complementing the stone walls and wooden ceilings of the historic Customs Bond Store it is housed in. Sept–June Mon–Sat 6–9pm.

Touchwood Cafe 31 Church St ☎03 6458 1342. Informal bistro for morning coffee and good-value lunches, using ingredients from the owner's farm. Home-baked cakes and muffins, and enormous "the Nut" scones with jam and cream, plus more substantial dishes like vegetarian lasagne or seafood chowder. Mains around $20. Tues–Sat 10am–4pm.

10

From Stanley into the Tarkine

Covering nearly a million acres in the northwest, the **Tarkine** is one of Tasmania's last frontiers. A blank space on the map stretching from south of Smithton down to Corinna and from the wild west coast to the Murchison Highway (A10), it is a mix of buttongrass plain, rigged coastline, primeval temperate rainforest and all-too-modern plantation forest; a dichotomy which neatly sums up what has become one of the most hotly contested battlefronts in Tasmania's long-running eco-wars (see box below). Arthur River (see p.952) and Corinna (see p.957) also edge the Tarkine and provide access to its wild interior. The best way to discover the magic of the forests, though, is to join a walking tour (see p.952). Be sure to fuel up at Marrawah before heading south; this is your last chance until Zeehan.

Tarkine Forest drives

South of **Smithton** – a nondescript forestry town ten kilometres west of Stanley – ten **forestry reserves**, ranging from rainforests to blackwood swamps and giant eucalypt

---

THE BATTLE FOR THE TARKINE

The **Tarkine** refers to the raw coast south of Arthur River and the plains of the Arthur Pieman Reserve (see p.952) as much as the fabled forests that spread east to the A10. The name was coined by conservationists after the local Tarkiner Aboriginal people in an effort to highlight Tasmania's largest unprotected wilderness; "greenies" had been pushing for a Tarkine National Park since the 1960s. Of its 593,000 acres of forest, seventy percent constitutes Australia's largest tract of temperate rainforest, second only in global significance to tracts in British Columbia: a "forgotten wilderness" of giant myrtle forests, wild rivers and bare granite mountains.

So environmentalists were horrified when a road was proposed through its heart from Arthur River to Corinna and on to Zeehan. Dubbed "**the Road to Nowhere**", the Western Explorer was constructed hastily and finished in 1996. During the run up to the Australian federal election in 2004, 180,000 acres of the Tarkine received protection from forestry, and awareness of the area grew as a moratorium on logging of ancient native forest was declared in 2011. The conservationists' push for a national park seemed unstoppable.

As it turns out, logging was the least of their worries. In February 2013, as Australia rode an Asian minerals boom, the government gave a green light to **open-cut mining** in the Tarkine – the area had been fabled for rich iron, tin and bauxite deposits since the early 1900s. The **Save the Tarkine** coalition brought about a legal challenge, which cited apocalyptic predictions for the Tasmanian devil in this, one of its last redoubts. But by August 2013, work on two of at least six mines had begun and in June 2015 Save the Tarkine's appeal to the Full Court against the Riley Creek mine approval was dismissed. Mass protests on a scale not seen since the Gordon River dam campaign have been proposed. For updates about campaigns and ways to help, visit the website of pressure group Save the Tarkine (⊛tarkine.org).

forests, are accessible on a circular driving route on unsealed roads via Kanunnah Bridge and Taytea Bridge on the C218 (90km return). All roads were originally created as access for logging – this is not raw wild Tarkine – yet allow a taste of the ancient biodiversity of these forests. Make stops at the **Julius River Forest Reserve** and the **Milkshakes Hills Forest Reserve**.

INFORMATION AND TOURS

FROM STANLEY INTO THE TARKINE

Tourist information Stanley Visitor Centre (see p.950) is your best pre-visit source of information, while Ⓦ discoverthetarkine.com.au is a good holiday planner. Forestry Tasmania has an office in Smithton on West Esplanade (Mon–Fri 9am–4pm; ☎ 03 6433 2665, Ⓦ forestrytas.com.au), which stocks leaflets with route information (also available as a download from the website). **Walking tours** Several companies now offer walking

tours of the area, including specialist conservation operator Tarkine Trails (Ⓦ tarkinetrails.com.au), which organizes four- and six-day expeditions (camp and vehicle based) through the forest or up the coast from Corinna; and Tasmanian Expeditions (☎ 1300 666 856 or ☎ 03 6331 9000, Ⓦ tasmanianexpeditions.com), which offers a five-day Tarkine and West Coast Explorer tour (including a Pieman River cruise), among others.

Arthur River and the Arthur Pieman Conservation Area

Just over 20km south of Marrawah, a scattering of holiday shacks at **ARTHUR RIVER** marks the start of one of the Tasmanian coast's great wilderness areas, where trees washed down the Frankland and Arthur rivers lie crashed against the windswept shoreline. From Gardiners Point – "**The Edge of the World**" – on the south side of the river mouth, the next land west is South America. Forget about swimming, however. Even walking along the beach can be an obstacle course. Upriver is the fringe of the fabled Tarkine Forest, complete with a spectacular array of birdlife and steep banks dense with native trees, although access is only by river cruise.

Road to Nowhere

Arthur River also marks the start of the fabulously wild **Arthur Pieman Conservation Area**, part of the Tarkine that is accessible via the controversial **Western Explorer** or "Road to Nowhere". Mostly dirt-track, the route grinds 114km south across buttongrass plains to Corinna (3–4hr) and while usually manageable in a 2WD car (insurance permitting), this is a remote, bumpy, dusty track with no settlements, no fuel until Zeehan 157km away and little help if you get into trouble. On such a poor road, speeds above 50km/h are ill-advised.

Sundown Point

One of the most rewarding stops south on the Western Explorer is this splendid beach 9km south of Arthur River, where you can see Aboriginal concentric circles chiselled onto a rock slab by the beach entry. You can drive there or allow a day for a return coastal walk from Arthur River.

INFORMATION

ARTHUR RIVER

Information and permits A PWS office as you enter Arthur River (daily 9am–5pm; ☎ 03 6457 1225) can advise on road conditions and issue permits for camping.
Supplies Note that supplies are minimal; a small store

opposite the Parks office (daily: summer 7.30am–8pm; winter 7.30am–4pm) has basic supplies but it's better to stock up in Smithton.

TOURS AND ACTIVITIES

AR Reflections River Cruises ☎ 03 6457 1288, Ⓦ arthurriver.com.au. Trips in a modern cruiser with a flybridge for 360-degree views (Sept–May daily 10.15am; 5hr; $95). Departing from the quay beside the bridge, the boat travels towards the river mouth and then loops for

15km upstream. There's also time off the boat at Warra Landing for a lunch of sandwiches, cake and Tassie cheeses, followed by a guided walk in the rainforest.
Arthur River Canoe & Boat Hire ☎ 03 6457 1312. Just before the bridge, this hire shop has Canadian canoes and

kayaks from $14/hr. They also run two- and four-day kayaking trips from $80.

MV George Robinson ☎03 6457 1158, ⓦarthurrivercruises.com. This traditional steamer departs from a quay beside the bridge and sails at stately pace 14km upriver to the confluence of the Arthur and Frankland rivers at Turks Landing, for a short bushwalk and barbecue lunch (Sept–May daily 10am; 5hr; $95).

ACCOMMODATION

Arthur River Beach House 24 Gardiner St ☎0438 454311. Epic sunsets and escapism are the options at one of the most luxurious offerings in the village, a spacious self-contained holiday house that sleeps up to six and is located opposite the river mouth (anglers love it, apparently). **$160**

Arthur River Cabin Park 1239 Arthur River Rd ☎03 6457 1212, ⓦarthurrivercabinpark.com. Not as natural as the PWS pitches in the village centre, this neat holiday park a kilometre north of the centre provides camping with comforts, plus good-value self-contained cabins. Un/powered sites **$27/30**, cabins **$90**

Arthur River campsites ☎03 6457 1225. PWS manage three serviced campsites: the most central is *Peppermint Campground* near the office, followed by the *Manuka Campground* just north. *Prickly Wattle* campsite is about two kilometres south of the community. All have pitches among the trees or in hollows behind the dunes; facilities include water, pit toilets and cold showers. Unpowered sites **$13**

Arthur River Holiday Units 4 Gardiner St ☎03 6457 1288, ⓦarthurriver.com. Owned by the AR Reflections cruise operator (package deals available; see opposite), these clean holiday cabins are well located in the heart of the village, though bedroom decor is so dated – all pink flowery bedspreads and some pine walls – that it's almost retro. **$130**

Cradle Mountain–Lake St Clair National Park

A jagged fin rising to an upturned crescent ridge, **Cradle Mountain**'s outline is so perfect it could have been designer-drawn. **Cradle Mountain–Lake St Clair National Park** is the best known of Tasmania's wilderness regions, and the park's 1612 square kilometres have loads to offer, including Australia's best bushwalk, the **Overland Track**. One of the most glaciated areas in Australia, this wild region of rivers, buttongrass plains and alpine moorland covers some of Tasmania's highest land and is punctuated by its highest point, **Mount Ossa** (1617m), one of many jagged dolerite peaks in the park. **Lake St Clair**, which bookends the park's southern end as Cradle Mountain does the northern, is the deepest freshwater lake in Australia at more than 200m.

Cradle Mountain is easily accessible from Devonport, Deloraine or Launceston, and the park's southern Lake St Clair end from Derwent Bridge on the Lyell Highway between Queenstown and Hobart. Most visitors spend a day around Cradle Mountain only – a breathtaking sight despite its popularity; the south is less obviously scenic even though good walks are within reach. The Overland Track (see box, p.954) threads between the two, attracting walkers from all over the world to lose themselves in pure wilderness and stunning scenery over six or more mud- and often leech-filled days of exhilarating exhaustion.

Cradle Mountain

Dove Lake and Cradle Mountain behind it is the must-see of any visit, but there are a couple of sights en route to make a day of it, all strung along the 13km access road, Cradle Mountain Road. The visitor centre and car park are two kilometres from the park boundary, where you'll find the ranger centre. The nine-kilometre boardwalk from the ranger centre to Dove Lake is not as scenic as other trails, so unless you're keen, save your energy for the summit and take the free shuttle bus.

Wilderness Gallery

Cradle Mountain Hotel, 3718 Cradle Mountain Rd, 2km south of Cradle Mountain turn-off • Daily 10am–6pm • $7 (free for guests at the hotel)

The first diversion en route into the park is the **Wilderness Gallery** of *Cradle Mountain Hotel*. It hangs stunning large-scale landscape photography of Tasmania by well-known and emerging local and international photographers, including the late, great

10

THE OVERLAND TRACK

Some moan that it's in danger of being loved to death, but most hikers agree that the **Overland Track** remains Australia's greatest extended bushwalk: 65km, unbroken by roads and passing through fields of wild flowers, and forests of deciduous beech, Tasmanian myrtle, pandanus and King Billy pine, with side walks leading to views of waterfalls and lakes, and starting points for climbs of the various mountain peaks. Most of the track is well-maintained boardwalk but you may still end up ankle-deep in mud. Along the route are six basic coal-stove- or gas-heated huts (not for cooking – bring your own stove), with composting toilets outside. But there's no guarantee there'll be space, so you need a good tent – they're usually warmer than huts, too – and a warm sleeping bag even in summer.

The direct walk generally takes six days – five, if you catch a boat from Narcissus Hut across Lake St Clair, or up to ten if you want to go on some of the side walks – and demands that walkers carry enough food and fuel for the duration, plus extra supplies in case you have an accident or bad weather sets in. All water en route is potable.

OVERLAND TRACK PRACTICALITIES

Around eight thousand people walk the track each year, most between November and April. While the track is at its most crowded from Christmas to the end of January, it is at its best during February and March when the weather has stabilized. Such is the route's popularity that a quota system has been introduced to regulate numbers to sixty departures a day between October and May. Walkers must book their place to walk (W overlandtrack.com.au) and pay $200 per person in addition to the park entry fee; your money goes to the park's conservation. During this period, the walk is north to south (Cradle Mountain to Lake St Clair) only, a good idea at any rate since it's more downhill than up.

During other months you can register in the national park offices at Cradle Mountain or Lake St Clair, where you receive an obligatory briefing and have your gear checked over; the walk cost in this period is just the cost of the national park entry fee ($30). At either end you can purchase Tasmap's *Cradle Mountain–Lake St Clair* map ($14.95) – an essential purchase despite the boardwalks – and pick up one of several guidebooks that are useful for novice walkers.

TOURS

With moderate fitness and experience, appropriate gear and a fair reserve of stamina, most walkers can tackle the track. However, guided tours will share the loads of tents and food, provide a richer appreciation of the wilderness and get someone else to do the cooking. Both of these depart from Launceston.

Tasmanian Expeditions 1300 666 856 or 03 6339 3999, tasmanianexpeditions.com.au. Runs the standard six-day trip, with variations, including trips that divert into Pine Valley and winter treks that require the use of snowshoes (6 days; $2095, full board and transfers from Launceston).

Cradle Mountain Huts 03 6392 2211, cradlehuts.com.au. Provides wilderness without the wild thanks to accommodation in private lodges – you'll have hot showers and a delicious meal before a proper bed each night (Oct–May; 6 days $3190–3570, full board departing and returning Launceston). They also offer a four-day option from Waldheim to Arm River (limited departures) for $2350–2600 (but be warned: you'll wish you had done it all). Highly recommended.

Tasmanian, **Peter Dombrovskis**, whose images instilled in the Australian consciousness the idea of Tasmania's wilderness as somewhere pure, almost mythic.

Devils@Cradle

3950 Cradle Mountain Rd, 3km south of Cradle Mountain turn-off • Daily 10am–4pm; feeding 5.30pm & 8.30pm • $18 • 03 6492 1491, W devilsatcradle.com

An excellent conservation and breeding centre, **Devils@Cradle** provides information and encounters with the beleaguered Tasmanian devil (see box, p.919). As they're nocturnal, the devils are at their best during the evening feeding times – ask, too, about night-time tours with rangers ($27.50).

Cradle Mountain Interpretation Centre

Cradle Mountain Rd, 4km south of Cradle Mountain turn-off • Daily 9.30am–4pm

Just within the park's boundary, an interpretive centre has displays on the park area's history, flora and fauna. It also marks the start of three boardwalked tracks: one to Dove Lake (9km; 2.5–3hr); one to the **Pencil Pine Falls** (20–30min); and an "Enchanted Walk" that follows a creek through rainforest to *Cradle Mountain Lodge* (20–30min).

Waldheim Chalet

5km into the park • Open 24hr • Free

"Forest Home" in German, **Waldheim Chalet** is a reconstruction of the King Billy pine chalet built by Austrian-Australian **Gustav Weindorfer** in 1912. It is now a museum devoted to the man who did more than anyone to promote this wilderness area and its value as a national park; appropriately, he is buried just outside. Ancient King Billy pines line the short forest walk from the hut (15min).

Dove Lake and the summit

Dove Lake, spectacularly sited beneath the jagged curve of Cradle Mountain itself, is an impressive site regardless of the tour groups that swamp the area in high summer. Most day-trippers are content to amble along the Dove Lake circuit (2–3hr), an easy gravelled walk around the shore of the lake. For something tougher and quieter – take the trail to Marion's Lookout (2–3hr), which ascends a slope on the west shore for a close-up view of Cradle Mountain, or, for a real challenge, embark on the steep day-walk to the summit itself (6hr return; seek advice from the ranger station at the Cradle Mountain Interpretation Centre first).

ARRIVAL AND DEPARTURE   CRADLE MOUNTAIN–LAKE ST CLAIR NATIONAL PARK

By bus The Launceston–Strahan TassieLink service via Deloraine, Devonport and Sheffield stops at the Cradle Mountain Transit Centre just outside the park, from where shuttle buses drive into the park. To ease logistics for Overland Track walkers it offers packages providing discounts on round-trip fares. Buses to Lake St Clair run between Hobart and Strahan. Buses run to Cradle Mountain twice a week April–Nov, and four times a week in the peak season for the Overland Track (Dec–March). From

Launceston to Cradle Mountain, the trip takes three hours. **By minibus** Several operators provide private-hire bushwalker transport: minibus taxis, basically. Charges are cheaper the more people are aboard. From Launceston, try Outdoor Tasmania (☏ 03 6391 8249, ✆ outdoortasmania .com.au) or Cradle Mountain Coaches (☏ 0448 800599, ✆ cradlemountaincoaches.com.au). If you're coming from Hobart, try Tasmanian Wilderness Experiences (☏ 1300 882 293 or ☏ 03 6261 4971, ✆ twe.travel).

GETTING AROUND AND INFORMATION

Getting around Cars and wilderness are not a good mix. So, in an effort to reduce traffic in the park, most parking is at the Cradle Mountain Transit Centre, also the stop for public buses, 2.5km from the park boundary but linked by frequent shuttle buses to Dove Lake (Oct to mid-May daily 8am–8pm; every 10–15min in summer). The bus ticket is included in the standard national park entry fee, which can be paid at the visitor centre. Although there's a second car park at the lake, be aware

that it fills early in summer.

Tourist information The Cradle Mountain Visitor Centre at the transit centre (daily 8.30am–4.30pm, until 5pm in Jan, reduced hours winter; ☏ 03 6492 1110, ✆ parks.tas.gov.au) provides information on day-walks in the surrounding area and acts as a registration point for the Overland Track (see box opposite). It also has a shop with hiking supplies plus walk guidebooks. There is also a national park visitor centre at Lake St Clair.

ACTIVITIES

Canyoning Cradle Mountain Canyons (4057 Cradle Mountain Rd; ☏ 1300 032 384, ✆ cradlemountaincanyons .com.au) takes advantage of gorges in the Dover River for canyoning trips. Excursions for beginners (half-day $105), as well as advanced adventurers (full-day $210).

Horseriding Cradle Mountain Horseriding (☏ 1300 656 069, ✆ cradlemountainhorseriding.com.au) provides two-hour rides ($120) on tracks just outside the national park area but enjoying similar views to those in the park; prices include collection from your accommodation.

Scenic flights Cradle Mountain Helicopters, based at the Cradle Mountain Transit Centre (⊕03 6492 1132, ⊚cradlemountainhelicopters.com.au), runs scenic helicopter flights over the park (weather permitting; 10min; $270 for three people).

ACCOMMODATION

Hotel accommodation is sited between the Cradle Mountain Visitor Centre and the Rangers' Interpretation Centre off Cradle Mountain Rd, the main road into the park. None of it is cheap, nor is it widely available in high summer, when reservations are essential. Camping is available outside the park boundary – pitching within it is forbidden unless at designated areas beside the Overland Track. There are fewer accommodation options at Lake St Clair.

★**Cradle Mountain Highlanders Cottages** 3876 Cradle Mountain Rd, 3.5km from Cradle Mountain turn-off ⊕03 6492 1116, ⊚cradlehighlander.com.au. The antithesis of bland hotel-style accommodation, these self-contained bush cabins offer varying degrees of comfort, from the cosy *Bushmans Hut* shack to two-bedroom spa chalets. Most have wood-burning stoves, but all are individually decorated in lovely rustic style and come at good prices. They will supply breakfast baskets if you order ahead. **$180**

Cradle Mountain Hotel 3718 Cradle Mountain Rd, 2km from Cradle Mountain turn-off ⊕03 6492 1404, ⊚cradlemountainhotel.com.au. Impressive public areas (including a billiards room, two libraries and a gift shop) and reasonable rates for standard rooms make this a good choice. All Deluxe and King rooms (with spa baths) have bush views; standard rooms overlook the car park. **$139**

★**Cradle Mountain Lodge** Cradle Mountain Rd, 100m outside park entrance ⊕1300 806 192 or ⊕03 6492 2103, ⊚cradlemountainlodge.com.au. Timber cabins offer luxury on the fringe of the national park, from contemporary-styled "Pencil Pine Cabins" to spacious "King Billy Suites", all with log or gas fires (though no cooking facilities). Facilities in the lodge include country-style lounges and a spa with outdoor hot tub. **$439**

Discovery Holiday Parks Cradle Mountain Rd, 2.5km from Cradle Mountain turn-off ⊕03 6492 1395, ⊚discoveryholidayparks.com.au. The only camping and backpackers' option and luckily it's a good one for outdoorsy types. There are four-bed dorms and family rooms in a YHA-affiliated hostel, well-maintained cabins and cottages that sleep up to six, and camping pitches buried deep in bush clearings. Un/powered sites **$42/$55**, dorms **$33**, cabins **$129**, cottages **$149**

Waldheim Cabins 5km into the park ⊕03 6491 2158, ⊚parks.tas.gov.au. This magical getaway leaves no doubt why Gustav Weindorfer (see p.955) chose to live here surrounded by nature. The only accommodation within the park, these self-catering hikers' huts for four to eight people offer basic facilities but are clean and ideal for retreating into nature. Pick up keys from the visitor centre (8.30am–4.30pm); they are left in a box outside the Cradle Mountain Interpretation Centre (see p.955) after hours. **$95**

EATING AND DRINKING

Cradle Mountain Lodge 100m from park entrance ⊕03 6492 2147, ⊚cradlemountainlodge.com.au. The lodge has two options for dining. The classy *Highland Restaurant* (reservations required) serves fine dining deep in the bush – seasonal gourmet menus (two courses $64) showcase state ingredients in dishes like salmon with smoked scallops, or wallaby steaks. The popular *Tavern Bar & Bistro*, meanwhile, rustles up more solid stuff: rib-eye beef on the bone, pork and veal ragu or spaghetti, averaging $27. Tavern Bar daily: 11.30am–late; food noon–4pm & 5–9pm; Highland Restaurant daily 6–9pm.

The west

It's the lure of wilderness that attracts a certain type of traveller to Tasmania: the thrill of walks in a pure environment and boat expeditions through primeval rainforest. For those who'd like a taste of this adventure, the west's holiday hub of **Strahan** is the place to head. Once a lonely fishing village at the edge of the world, Strahan was transformed into one of Tasmania's leading wilderness resorts almost overnight by a campaign to preserve the **Franklin River** (see p.965).

The fast road to Strahan is the **A10** which spears southwest of Burnie through tiny mining towns in various stages of atrophy to **Queenstown**, the rough 'n' ready heartland of west-coast mining. The road was built in the 1960s to improve access to the northwest forests and **logging** remains a major industry hereabouts. Along the route the extent of plantation forest may come as a shock, especially if you've become used to the lushness and biodiversity of the protected wilderness elsewhere. On the stretch from Strahan to Hobart, the A10 passes through the pristine wilderness of the UNESCO-listed **Franklin-Gordon Wild Rivers National Park** and the bottom edge of Cradle Mountain–Lake St Clair National Park; a section of road that's worth lingering over.

Waratah and around

Windswept **WARATAH**, 8km off the A10, was Tasmania's first mining town and peaked in the early twentieth century after thirty years of outrageously profitable tin-mining at nearby **Mount Bischoff**. The mine closed in 1947 and today Waratah is little more than a scattered collection of weatherboard cottages; worth a visit, if you're passing, to see the **mining museum** in the former courthouse in the centre (Sun–Tues 10am–3pm; free) and an old ore stamper (Mon–Fri 7.30am–4.30pm, Sat & Sun 8am–5pm; free) in a shed opposite. The town's most impressive feature is Waratah Falls, a waterfall that cascades into a gorge (best viewed from Kings Park), right in the middle of town.

Around 10km beyond Waratah is a gravel access road that takes you to a car park to meet the walking track to **Philosopher Falls** (1.5hr return). One of the iconic destinations of the Tarkine, long unmarked, it is now accessible on an excellent footpath that tracks a former mine waterway through beautiful myrtle forest to reach a viewing platform of the falls tumbling through ancient forest. The last fuel stop before Corinna is the former mining town of **Savage River**, 45km along the B23 from Waratah, before you head through the **Pieman River State Reserve.**

Corinna

It's hard to believe the few shacks at the old gold-mining settlement of **CORINNA** on the **Pieman River**, cocooned by dense rainforest, were once home to 2500 people in a brawling, boozy mine town. What remains is not just the only surviving example of an isolated mining village in Tasmania, it is one of the state's most appealing eco-resorts, superbly restored without sacrificing the deep tranquillity of the place. Several boardwalked **trails** (from fifteen minutes to five hours) loop through the surrounding thick forest, and you could also spend a happy day or two **kayaking** up the river and its tributaries, a superb way to experience the solitude and peace of the area. All in all, the antithesis to packaged wilderness resorts, and highly recommended.

ARRIVAL AND CRUISES
CORINNA

By car The "Fatman" – Tasmania's only surviving cable barge – crosses the Pieman River from Corinna (daily: summer 9am–7pm; winter 9am–5pm; car $25, bike $12.50), to enable you to continue on the C249 to Zeehan, and then on the B27 to Strahan.

Cruise Cruise downriver to the coast on the renovated Huon-pine MV *Arcadia II*, with an hour to wander along the wild west coast (4hr; $90 including lunch; ☎03 6446 1170).

ACCOMMODATION AND EATING

★**Corinna Wilderness Experience** ☎03 6446 1170, ⓦcorinna.com.au. Settle into one of the traditionally styled one- and two-bedroom cottages behind the Tarkine Hotel, or take over the five guesthouse style rooms in the Old Pub, and revel in a level of comfort the miners could barely have dreamed of. Each cottage has a veranda and a gas fire to keep out the chill; expect a digital detox, as there's no wi-fi or mobile phone signal here. There is a small camping area near the river, with purpose-built raised decks. Unpowered sites $40, cottages $220

The Tarkine Hotel Corinna Rd, Corinna. This rustic pub in the bush looks like it's been here forever, but was rebuilt in 2008. With a welcoming bar and the rustic *Tannin* restaurant, this is the only place around to dine without cooking for yourself. Fresh Tassie produce goes into the Pieman Pies, such as steak and pepper or chicken and lemon myrtle ($25), or plump for the tempura-battered prawns or Strahan salmon. Alternatively, just sit with a beer on the veranda and drink in the silence. Daily: bar noon–11pm; restaurant 11.30am–3pm & 6–9pm.

South toward Zeehan

If you skip the Waratah/Corinna side track off the A10, you slalom on through forest, past the turn-off to Cradle Mountain and through tiny **TULLAH**, 40km south of Waratah, which has fuel; and then the modest zinc-mining town of **ROSEBERY**, still eking out an existence through its mine. If you feel like stretching your legs, stop to take the hike to the 113m **Montezuma Falls** (3hr return), 8km south of the town.

10

Zeehan

ZEEHAN is living proof of the boom-and-bust of Tassie west-coast mining towns. The town became prosperous from silver-lead mines that opened in the 1880s and at its height "Silver City" had a population of ten thousand. It's hard to believe now; the mines began to fail by 1908, and despite a brief revival in the 1970s, when tin mines opened, Zeehan began a slow decline. But while boom-period buildings in the high street, notably the Gaiety Theatre, stand as memories of former glories, mining continues. In 2014, a mothballed nickel mine reopened and the town began to buzz again, but tourist dollars are still more than welcome. From here you can go direct to Strahan (47km) on the sealed B27 or switch back to the A10 to reach Strahan via Queenstown, 32km away.

West Coast Heritage Centre

114 Main St • Daily 10am–4.30pm • $15 • ☎ 03 6471 6225, ⓦ westcoastheritage.com.au

Fortunately for the town, its museum is a belter. Ticking many boxes, the **West Coast Heritage Centre** is a reinvention of the old pioneer museum, incorporating four heritage buildings into its complex: the old School of Mines and Metallurgy, Post Office, Police Station and the Gaiety Theatre. It has thirty themed exhibition spaces with displays on mining and regional history, plenty of historic photos – far more interesting than you'd expect – and a simulation of a mine. The Gaiety Theatre screens original Edwardian and period-styled movies; take a seat in what was Australia's largest theatre and where Lola Montez once trod the boards. Screened back to back, they include early telecasts of Aussie sports and *The Story of the Kelly Gang* (1906), the first feature film ever made anywhere. Outside are static displays of the steam engine that operated on mining railways.

Queenstown

No town in the state exemplifies Tasmanian mining quite like **QUEENSTOWN**. It was born through a gold mine on Mount Lyell in 1883 and lives by it still – the current mine, which can be visited on excellent tours (see opposite), was taken over in 1995 by **Copper Mines of Tasmania**, now part of Indian mining corporation Vedanta. Queenstown's infamous "**lunar landscape**" of red-brown rock was caused by a toxic combination of tree-felling, fire and acid rain that robbed the mountains of most vegetation by the 1930s. Regrowth has appeared on lower slopes since the smelters closed in 1969, but it's estimated that the damage will last some four hundred years. **Spion Kopf lookout**, reached off Hunter Street, behind the library on the through-road, offers good views of the open-cut mine slopes. The original 1883 mine is the Iron Blow 2km away, an impressively deep void seen from a cantilevered walkway. It's signposted off the Lyell Highway (towards Derwent Bridge).

Queenstown has an unpolished edge – compared to Strahan, it feels defiantly scruffy and things can get rowdy at weekends. That said, it attracts more than its share of tourism due to the historic West Coast Wilderness Railway from Strahan, which terminates here (see box opposite). A warning if you're heading east: there is no fuel between Queenstown and Derwent River 88km away.

THE WEST COAST WILDERNESS RAILWAY

In 2002 a $30-million investment saw trains once again rattle along the old **ABT Railway** between Queenstown and Strahan. The original railway was completed in 1896 to transport copper ore from Queenstown to Regatta Point in Strahan, but closed in 1963 when road transport became more economical. Reconstruction took three years (only six months less than it took the original workers to hack through the rainforest by hand), two of the line's four surviving steam locomotives were restored, and replica carriages were built using native woods. Known as the **West Coast Wilderness Railway** (☎03 6471 0100, ⓦwcwr.com.au), the line is a popular tourist trip that gives a great insight into the pioneering days of this area.

The railway runs three different trips. The full-day Queenstown Explorer (from $159) departs from Strahan, swinging through the King River Gorge and climbing up to Dubbil Barril on a 1:16 rack-and-pinion track system before stopping at Queenstown station (opposite the *Empire Hotel*) for an hour before the return journey. Try to secure a riverside seat; when facing forward, sit on the right-hand side from Strahan, or left from Queenstown. Two shorter loop trips also run from both Queenstown and Strahan (from $99).

10

Eric Thomas Galley Museum

Cnr Stricht & Driffield sts • May–Sept Mon–Fri 9.30am–5pm, Sat & Sun 12.30–5pm; Oct–April Mon–Fri 9.30am–4.30pm, Sat & Sun 12.30–4.30pm • $6 • ☎03 6471 1483

The best introduction to the region's mining heritage is found at the enjoyably old-fashioned **Eric Thomas Galley Museum**, which is set in a late 1800s miners' pub. Most rooms are given over to photographic displays of early pioneer life, depicting hard lives battled out in the bush when Queenstown was a months' travel from help, and proving that the patchy scrub on today's hills is a huge improvement on the early 1900s. Upstairs are idiosyncratic themed rooms stuffed with memorabilia – medical equipment, military uniforms, film projectors and the like.

ARRIVAL AND DEPARTURE   QUEENSTOWN

By bus TassieLink services run from Hobart (Tues, Thurs & Sun daily; 5hr 35min) and from Launceston via Deloraine and Cradle Mountain (Mon & Wed daily; 5hr 30min). Its daily service runs to Strahan (Sun–Fri daily; 45min) and to Burnie (Tues & Fri daily; 2hr 50min).

INFORMATION AND TOURS

Tourist information The Eric Thomas Galley Museum (see above) doubles as a visitor centre.

Mine tour A trip with Queenstown Heritage Tours (☎0407 049 612) into the depths of Mount Lyell is the must-do of Queenstown. Led by an enthusiastic guide, Anthony Coulson, you descend around 500m underground into a working mine wearing helmet and overalls to walk and be driven through 10km of tunnels. Bookings essential (daily 9am & 1.30pm; 3hr; $110). Anthony also runs a tour to the century-old Lake Margaret Hydro Power village (2hr 30min; $60).

ACCOMMODATION AND EATING

Unless you're stuck or fancy a night boozing in Queenstowns' rollicking pubs, Strahan has more appealing accommodation options for all budgets.

Café Serenade 40–42 Orr St ☎0458 712 199. The best café in Queenstown is surprisingly chic, with the likes of toasted focaccias with Tasmanian salmon, capers and spinach ($13), and home-baked scones on the menu. Daily curries and belly-buster breakfasts ($17) keep things grounded. Daily 9am–5pm.

Mt Lyell Anchorage 17 Cutten St ☎03 6471 1900, ⓦmtlyellanchorage.com. Three self-contained miners' cottages and four guest rooms in the main house (three with en suites, one with a private bathroom) provide a comfortable B&B choice just a few minutes walk from the centre of town. Rooms are large, with plantation shutters and heritage fittings. The owner prides herself on attention to detail, down to bathrobes, heated towel rails and electric blankets on the beds. **$160**

Penghana 32 The Esplanade ☎03 6471 2560, ⓦ penghana.com.au. The former Mt Lyell Mine manager's residence, a National Trust-listed Victorian pile from 1898 set in gardens and with views over the town, is now a gorgeous B&B. The six spotless guest rooms (five doubles and a twin) have high ceilings and traditional decor, and there's even a billiard room in addition to a guest lounge. Home-cooked dinners are available for guests on request. **$150**

Strahan and around

STRAHAN is not just the only town and port on Tassie's wild west coast; it is also one of the premier tourist destinations in Tasmania. "The best little town in the world", said the *Chicago Tribune* newspaper in 2011 of what is just an over-sized village. The reason is twofold: its setting on **Macquarie Harbour**, a body of water over six times the size of Sydney's harbour; and the surrounding southwestern wilderness.

Such is its fame that, in summer at least, Strahan has ceased to be "real" in the normal sense. For all the hype about a typical west-coast village, fishing is a sideshow to tourism. Strahan is on a different level from other towns in west Tasmania, with more agencies offering sightseeing trips and activities than in the rest of the area combined. What saves it from tackiness is that it remains an attractive place – the tourism infrastructure on the harbour is far from the eyesore it could have been – and the surrounding wilderness is as compelling as ever.

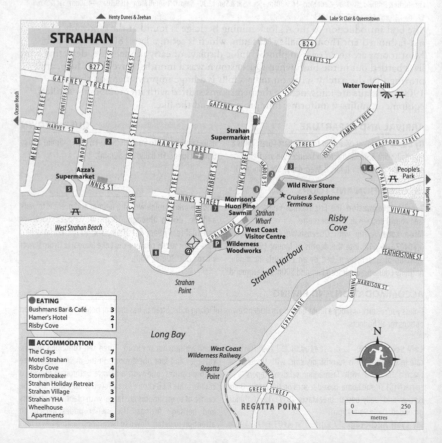

STRAHAN

▲ Henty Dunes & Zeehan   ▲ Lake St Clair & Queenstown

● EATING	
Bushmans Bar & Café	3
Hamer's Hotel	2
Risby Cove	1

■ ACCOMMODATION	
The Crays	7
Motel Strahan	1
Risby Cove	4
Stormbreaker	6
Strahan Holiday Retreat	5
Strahan Village	3
Strahan YHA	2
Wheelhouse Apartments	8

Brief history

Long before it became a wilderness gateway, the harbour held a penal settlement on **Sarah Island** – it can be visited on a Gordon River cruise (see p.962). During its operation from 1822 to 1833, this was the sink of the empire; home to the worst of the worst and infamous for its brutal treatment of prisoners – convicts nicknamed the narrow entrance to Macquarie Harbour **Hells Gates**. Abundant **Huon pine** facilitated logging and shipbuilding by convicts, and continued to attract loggers after 1830. Later, Strahan developed as an export port for nearby mines and was Tasmania's third-largest port by the late 1800s until larger ship sizes – not to mention wild weather – led to its demise. By 1970 the population had dwindled to three hundred, most involved in fishing for abalone, crayfish and shark.

In 1982, the **Franklin Blockade** campaign to preserve the **Gordon River** thrust Strahan into the international spotlight (see box, p.965). For Tasmanian and mainland Australians alike, the river represented an ideal of primeval, almost mythic, purity. One of Australia's last wild rivers, it threads through some of the planet's most ancient rainforest. On its banks are stands of Huon pines thought to be the second-oldest living things on earth: some trees have been estimated at more than ten thousand years old. **Cruises** on the Gordon River had run before the blockade, but the declaration of the **World Heritage Area** lured busloads of tourists to see the river for themselves.

Around the West Coast Visitor Centre

Exhibition at West Coast Visitor Centre • Esplanade • Daily: Oct–March 10am–5.30pm; April–Sept 10am–5pm • $2 • ☏ 1800 352 200, ⓦ westernwilderness.com.au

For a decent primer on the town, stop in the **West Coast Visitor Centre** on The Esplanade, built of tin and wood to reflect the area's boatbuilding and timber industries, for an **exhibition** addressing local themes such as Aboriginal heritage, convicts, logging, wilderness and eco-wars. Adjacent to the visitor centre in a corrugated-iron shed, **Morrison's Huon Pine Sawmill** (daily 8am–5pm; free) lets you watch local timbers being processed; they're then turned and sold as crafts in **Wilderness Woodworks** (daily 8am–5pm; free) on the other side of the visitor centre.

Outside the visitor centre is an **amphitheatre** where *The Ship that Never Was* is staged, an entertaining two-hander said to be Australia's longest-running production (late Sept–May daily 5.30pm; $20; ☏ 03 6471 7700). Written by local playwright/historian Richard Davey, it retells the bizarre true story of an 1834 convict escape from Sarah Island achieved by stealing the last ship ever built by the penal shipyard. Expect slapstick, much audience participation and a lot of fun.

Around the harbour

The heart of Strahan is the renovated 1930s frontage of The Esplanade. It has a touch of movie-set perfection about it (think *The Truman Show*), but wander off the main street and reality sets in. From there the **Strahan Historic Foreshore Walkway** tracks the shore of the harbour for 1.7km to **Regatta Point**, the terminal for the **West Coast Wilderness Railway** (see p.959); self-guided walk maps are available from the visitor centre. En route, an old sawmill at Risby Cove houses a crafts and art gallery (daily 8am–5pm; free) with work by state artists. It is opposite the **People's Park**, the starting point for a rainforest walk to **Hogarth Falls** (40min; 2km return). Walk the other way from the wharf to West Strahan Beach, in front of the holiday park, which is safe for a swim.

Ocean Beach and Henty Dunes

Six kilometres east of town, **Ocean Beach** is, at 30km, the longest beach in Tasmania but inspires less for its length than for what it represents. The next landmass west from here is Patagonia and waves offshore have been known to reach 26m high – swimming is most definitely not advised. The wind here can be biting too, so be sure to wrap up warm. Another reason to visit is for marvellous sunsets and to watch – from November

10

to February – the migratory **muttonbirds** roost at dusk; in peak season rangers talk visitors through the birds' astounding migration cycles to the Bering Sea. The beach stretches south all the way to **Macquarie Heads** (aka Hells Gates); you can drive there on an 11km teeth-jarring gravel road signposted off the Ocean Beach road.

The northern end of the beach is backed by **Henty Dunes**, which rise up to 30m high; not quite the Sahara but impressive nonetheless. Two fun ways to experience them are by quad-bike tours or by renting sandboards from 4Wheeler Quad Bikes on the Esplanade in Strahan (☎ 0419 508 175)

ARRIVAL AND INFORMATION

By bus TassieLink services run from Hobart via Lake St Clair, and from Launceston via Deloraine, Devonport, Sheffield and Cradle Mountain.
Destinations Hobart (Tues–Thurs, Fri & Sun daily; 5hr 35min); Launceston (Mon & Wed daily; 5hr 30min); Queenstown (Mon–Fri 1–2 daily, Sun daily; 45min).
Tourist information The West Coast Visitor Centre, on

STRAHAN AND AROUND

The Esplanade (daily: Oct–March 10am–6pm; April–Sept 10am–5pm; ☎ 1800 352 200 or ☎ 03 6472 6800, ⓦ westernwilderness.com.au), handles accommodation bookings and enquiries.
Bike rental You can rent mountain bikes from *Strahan Holiday Retreat*, at 10 Innes St (see opposite).

TOURS AND ACTIVITIES

The Bonnet Island Experience ☎ 03 6471 4300, ⓦ gordonrivercruises.com.au. This daily twilight cruise (2hr 30min; $105) sails at dusk to the wild island at Hells Gates to visit its lighthouse and watch penguins roost.
Gordon River Cruises ☎ 03 6471 4300, ⓦ gordonrivercruises.com.au. Past the turbulent Hells Gates, where the harbour and the Southern Ocean meet, this cruise takes you across Macquarie Harbour and up the calm waters of the Gordon River. There's time to get off and explore a rainforest boardwalk that leads to a 2000-year-old Huon pine. On the return journey, there's a stop for a guided tour of the former penal colony at Sarah Island. Several other shorter cruises are available, but this one (5hr 30min; from $105) is well worth doing.
West Coast Yacht Charters The Esplanade ☎ 03 6471 7422, ⓦ westcoastyachtcharters.com.au. The alternative to mass-tourism trips, with cruises aboard a 20m ketch.

Options are 2.5hr lunch or dinner cruises ($70 without food, otherwise $90), or excellent overnight adventures ($320–$350) 35km up the Gordon River – further than any other cruise – to Sir John Falls or including Sarah Island. All can include kayaking and fishing if you want. Cruises run Oct–April only.
World Heritage Cruises ☎ 03 6471 7174 or ☎ 1800 611 796, ⓦ worldheritagecruises.com.au. Five generations of the Grining family have been taking passengers onto the Gordon River since 1896. Today, the family firm sails across Macquarie Harbour and upriver to a landing stage for a 30min stop. Penal history marks the return, with stops at Sarah Island and a whiz through Macquarie Heads (Hells Gates). Includes buffet lunch or dinner (daily: late Jan to mid-July & mid-Aug to late Dec 9am; late Dec to late Jan 9am & 3.15pm; from $115; 5–6hr).

ACCOMMODATION

The Crays 11 Innes St & 59 The Esplanade ☎ 03 6471 7422, ⓦ thecraysaccommodation.com. Of the two sites for these holiday cabins that sleep up to eight, the best is The Esplanade opposite Risby Cove; quiet yet close to the action. Accommodation is simple and homely, with nice touches like fresh flowers, and teabags and milk to start you off. $180
Motel Strahan 3 Andrew St ☎ 03 6471 7555, ⓦ motelstrahan.com.au. What looks an unremarkable motel provides tasteful modern rooms at some of the best rates in town. The caveat is that it's 15min walk from the centre, but on the plus side that makes it quiet in high season – a good option for a short stay. $155
★ **Risby Cove** The Esplanade ☎ 03 6471 7572, ⓦ risby. com.au. Tucked away from the main town centre, a short distance from the summer tourist buzz, this former

sawmill, fully renovated using corrugated iron and salvaged Huon pine, now houses bright, modern(ish) one- and two-bedroom suites with balconies that make a virtue of their simplicity. "The Shack" suite overlooks a car park but is larger. $220
Stormbreaker The Esplanade ☎ 03 6471 7422, ⓦ westcoastyachtcharters.com.au. Although with little privacy, so not for everyone, West Coast Yacht Charters' 18m yacht nevertheless offers a most unusual stay in Strahan. On board, there is a twin in the bow, a double cabin aft, and eight single bunks in a shared crew quarters amidships. A bit like a floating hostel; prices are per person. Oct–April. $60
Strahan Holiday Retreat Cnr Andrew & Innes sts ☎ 03 6471 7442, ⓦ strahanholidaypark.com.au. One of two budget accommodation options in central Strahan

RAFTING ON THE FRANKLIN RIVER

To really experience the **Franklin-Gordon Wild Rivers National Park**'s utterly pristine scenery and awesome sense of remoteness, you need to **raft the Franklin River**. One of the great rivers of Australia, saved from destruction by protests in the early 1980s (see box, p.965) and the only major wild river in Tasmania, it races through canyons in grade 3 to 4 **rapids** – even grade 6 in places – and through thick inaccessible rainforest. No wonder this is known by rafters as one of the greatest paddle adventures in the world.

Rafting trips generally run between December and early April on five- to ten-day trips, depending on where you start. From **Collingwood River**, off the Lyell Highway, it takes about three days to raft the **Upper Franklin**, riding rapids through subalpine scenery. The **Middle Franklin** is a mixture of pools, deep ravines and wild rapids as the river makes a 50km detour around Frenchmans Cap. Limestone cliffs overhang the **Lower Franklin**, which involves a tranquil paddle through dense myrtle beech forests with flowering leatherwoods overhead, and **Kutikina Caves** and **Deena-reena** –Aboriginal sights that are only accessible to rafters.

Due to the dangers of the trip, visitors should go with a specialist **tour operator**. You don't have to be experienced to sign up – just fit, with lots of stamina and courage. It's not cheap, but this is an experience of a lifetime.

Franklin River Rafting ☏0422 642 190, ⓦfranklinriverrafting.com. Eight- ($2860) and ten-day ($3190) rafting expeditions, departing from Hobart and including all meals. The ten-day trip includes an optional day-walk to Frenchmans Cap (see p.964). October to April only.

Water by Nature ☏0408 242941 or ☏1800 111 142, ⓦfranklinrivertasmania.com. Water by Nature offers a five-day trip ($2090) on the Lower Franklin, a seven-day trip on the Upper Franklin ($2440), or ten days rafting the full navigable length of the river ($2980). The ten-day trip also includes the Frenchmans Cap (see p.964).

10

– the other is the YHA (see opposite) – there are sixty cottages and cabins, and a caravan ground (but no tent sites for camping) in a bushy area close to an estuarine beach and just a 15min walk from the wharf. Un/powered sites $15/30, cabins $99, cottages $115

Strahan Village The Esplanade ☏03 6471 4200, ⓦstrahanvillage.com.au. New ownership in 2014 has resulted in some needed renovations, smartening up the accommodation options here. These include "Hilltop" hotel rooms with superb harbour views, on the hill above the township (it's a five-minute walk down, perhaps a bit longer going back up). On the Esplanade, there are "Village" rooms upstairs in Hamer's Hotel, cottages (motel-style despite the cottage-look exteriors and white picket fences), and smarter (and more expensive) "Waterfront" rooms beside the harbour. $97

Strahan YHA 43 Harvey St ☏03 6471 7255, ⓦyha.com .au. A bush setting adds to the rustic vibe of this hostel, which even has a platypus in the creek on the property. There are four- and eight-bed dorms, twin rooms and three-bed family rooms. Facilities include a large kitchen, lounge and laundry. Only open Oct–April. Dorms $30, doubles $85

Wheelhouse Apartments 4 Frazer St ☏03 6471 7777, ⓦwheelhouseapartments.com.au. Architect-designed two-storey apartments on a hilltop, built with local timbers and whose portholes add a maritime air. While attention to detail is lacking and facilities are tired in places, what lets it off the hook is the finest harbour view in Strahan through floor-to-ceiling windows. No wi-fi. $320

EATING

Bushmans Bar & Café 1 Harold St ☏03 6471 7612. A new owner/chef has revamped the menu here and it's not quite what you'd expect from the name of the restaurant. Fine dining is the watchword, with dishes such as Sassafras rack of lamb with hazelnut purée and parmesan crumbs, or twice-cooked baby chicken with sticky black rice and chilli jam. Main dishes average $36. Tues & Wed 5.30pm–late, Thurs–Sat 5.30pm–late.

Hamer's Hotel The Esplanade ☏03 6471 4335. The pub, the hub of Strahan's social life, has an attached fairly bland, modern bistro, *Hamer's Grill* that prepares steaks and pork or lamb cutlets, and lighter bites such as asparagus and pea risotto or seafood fettucine for around $30 – not cheap but portions are large and quality respectable. There's also a slightly smaller and cheaper menu in the bar. Food daily noon–3pm & 5–8.30pm.

Risby Cove The Esplanade ☏03 6471 7572. Located in a restored sawmill, this is one of the best restaurants in town and perfect for a dinner date. Beef with roast garlic and truffle mash or blue eye (trevalla) on wasabi soufflé are typical of a seasonal mod-Oz menu; mains around $34. Daily 6–9pm.

10

Along the Lyell Highway (A10)

Between Queenstown and Derwent Bridge, the **Lyell Highway** (A10) slices through the heart of the **Franklin-Gordon Wild Rivers National Park**, in places tracking beside the Franklin River itself. It's a fabulous drive, a slideshow of wilderness scenery slipping past the windscreen. Several stops along the Lyell Highway are signposted en route to break up the journey with a short stroll, while **Lake St Clair**, the south end of the celebrated Cradle Mountain–Lake St Clair National Park, is a destination in its own right. But allow plenty of time, too, simply to pull over and take in the gorgeous views and appreciate the purity of this landscape.

Stops along the Lyell Highway

Beyond Lake Burbury, east of Queenstown, a car park at Nelson River bridge marks the start of an easy return walk through temperate rainforest to **Nelson Falls** (20min return), which tumbles 33m into a forest glade. Placards along the track pinpoint flora en route.

A little further on you catch a first glimpse of the white-quartzite dome of Frenchmans Cap, like a dusting of snow. For a more spectacular viewpoint that takes in the Franklin River Valley, **Donaghy's Hill Wilderness Lookout Walk** begins further along the highway on the right. Walk from the parking area along the old road to the top of the hill, where a sign marks the beginning of the forty-minute return track. The **track to Frenchmans Cap** itself is signposted from a car park a little further on; a tough three- or four-day return hike – but just a fifteen-minute jaunt to a suspension bridge over the Franklin River.

Continuing on the Lyell, you have another opportunity to see the Franklin on a ten-minute **Nature Trail**, at a point where the river is tranquil, as it flows around large boulders; there's a longer 25-minute circuit, too. You'll also find a picnic area with an **interpretive board** about the river.

Lake St Clair

The scenery at Lake St Clair, the south end of the Cradle Mountain–Lake St Clair National Park (see p.953), is less dramatic than at Cradle Mountain and correspondingly less busy. Most people treat it as a pause en route to Strahan or Hobart on the Lyell Highway, but there are good walks and cruises on the lake to justify a longer stop.

The gateway to the park is **Cynthia Bay**, at the south end of Lake St Clair 5km off the Lyell Highway. Here you'll find interpretive displays in a visitor centre with a shop. Several short **walks** around Lake St Clair are detailed on a board, from one-hour nature and Aboriginal heritage walks around the visitor centre to the **Labyrinth** at the north end of the lake, a magical area of tarns pooled in bush-draped rocks beneath miniature bluffs. It's well-named though – bring a map and ideally a compass.

The easy option to see the scenery is a **cruise** on Australia's deepest lake. Boats can drop you off at Narcissus Hut to walk back to the centre (5–6hr) or enter the Labyrinth; alternatively, get off at Echo Point to return on a three-hour bushwalk.

ARRIVAL, INFORMATION AND CRUISES   **LAKE ST CLAIR**

By bus TassieLink's service between Hobart (Tues, Thurs, Fri & Sun; 3hr) and Strahan (Tues, Thurs & Sun; 2hr 45min) stops at Lake St Clair.

Tourist information The national park visitor centre is beside the car park at Lake St Clair (daily 8am–5pm; ☎ 03 6289 1172).

Cruise Tickets for cruises on the lake are sold at the general store and *Lake St Clair Lodge* (☎ 03 6289 1137). In summer, it departs Cynthia Bay at 9am, 12.30pm & 3pm (times based on demand in winter); arriving at Echo Point 20min later – from there it's another 25min to Narcissus Hut (1hr 30min return; to Echo Point $35, to Narcissus Hut $40).

ACCOMMODATION AND EATING

Lake St Clair Lodge ☎ 03 6289 1137, ⊕ lakestclairlodge .com.au. Bush camping, hikers' huts, studios and cottages – they get a mixed clientele here by the lake. Campers get forest pitches near the water, hikers are in rustic hostel huts for two to four people; smart studio cabins and self-contained Lakeside Suites are a treat after the Overland Track, and cottages sleep up to six. Check-in is at the café beside the visitor centre, serving sandwiches, pies and modern dishes (daily: May–Sept 8am–4.30pm; Oct–April 8am–late). Sites **$25**, huts per person **$45**, doubles **$120**

Derwent Bridge

At the Lake St Clair turn-off, **Derwent Bridge** spreads along the highway. The reason to stop is **The Wall** (daily: May–Aug 9am–4pm; Sept–April 9am–5pm, closed August 6–19; $12; ☎ 03 6289 1134, ⊕ thewalltasmania.com) at the southern end of the village. It's a phenomenal work-in-progress by artist Greg Duncan: a frieze of a hundred 3m Huon-pine panels carved with detailed scenes of local history and nature, inside what looks like a giant tin shed. Started in 2005, the work will eventually be 100m in length; Greg was about three-quarters of the way through at the time of research. Note that no photography of any kind is allowed. There's a smart restaurant here if you're inclined to linger.

10

ACCOMMODATION AND EATING DERWENT BRIDGE

Derwent Bridge Wilderness Hotel Lyell Highway ☎ 03 6289 1144, ⊕ derwentbridgewildernesshotel .com.au. A barn-like building with fires in winter, artwork by The Wall's Greg Duncan and pub meals like fish and chips, steaks, pastas and curries costing around $25 (pub 8am–9.30pm; food noon–2pm & 6–8pm). Accommodation – backpacker singles and doubles plus rather pricey doubles, not all en-suite – is plain but comfy. Backpackers' **$35**, doubles **$140**

Southwest National Park

Even in a state as wild as Tasmania, the **Southwest National Park** is spoken of with something approaching reverence. A blank space on the map of arrow-sharp mountain ranges and broad grassy plains, nowhere else in the state so epitomizes the grandeur and spirit of the wilderness nor such edge-of-the-world isolation. For experienced bushwalkers, that escapism and rough terrain is a draw. If you're

AUSTRALIA'S ORIGINAL ECO-WAR

The future of the Tasmanian wilderness could have been very different had it not been for a bitter battle waged by environmentalists in the 1980s. In 1972 the flooding of **Lake Pedder** led to the formation of the **Wilderness Society**, which began a relentless campaign against the next target on the Hydro Electricity Commission's (HEC) agenda – a huge dam on the Lower Gordon River. The scheme had state government backing despite the catastrophic effect on Tasmania's last wild river, the Franklin. In a blocking manoeuvre, the whole southwest area was proposed for the World Heritage List. It was officially accredited on the same day that the Wilderness Society's **Franklin Blockade** began – December 14, 1982. The Tasmanian government had chosen to ignore the UNESCO accreditation.

For two months, protestors from all over Australia took to inflatable dinghies, paddling upriver from Strahan to stand in front of bulldozers in nonviolent protest. The **blockade** became a cause célèbre in Sydney and Melbourne and attracted international attention – British botanist David Bellamy was among the twelve hundred or so arrested for trespassing. During the course of the campaign, a new federal government was voted in, and in March 1983, following a trailblazing High Court ruling, it overruled the state's backing for the HEC plans. Although the blockade itself had failed to stop preparatory work on the dam, it had changed the opinion of many Australians forever and enshrined the value of Tasmanian wilderness at state and national levels.

10

thinking of joining them, being able to use a compass and read a map is as vital as a cheerful attitude to unpredictable weather even in summer – the southwest has more than two hundred days of rain a year. The surprise, then, is that you can get a taste of the Southwest National Park by driving in on the road beyond Maydena (see p.907) – the ranger for this end of the Southwest National Park is at Mount Field (see p.906), so drop in to ask about conditions. Admittedly, the scenery is not as spectacular as that on hikes deeper into the park. But the route includes vast panoramas and child-friendly walks like the **Creepy Crawly Nature Trail** 2km after the Scotts Peak turn: a taste of the forest elsewhere.

Gordon Dam

Daily: Nov–April 10am–5pm; May–Oct 11am–3pm • Free • ☎ 03 6280 1134

The definitive full stop at the end of the road west of Maydena is the Gordon Dam power station – the road was only built to enable its construction. Here, a Hydro Tasmania-run visitor centre details the mechanics of the hydroelectricity project. You're here really to walk along the curved dam wall itself – at 140m high, it's several metres higher than the Sydney Harbour Bridge. If you're after an even bigger adrenaline kick you can abseil down it on the world's highest commercial abseil, provided on demand by Aardvark Adventures (see below).

South Coast Track

If the Overland Track (see p.954) is Tasmania's premier inland bushwalk, the **South Coast Track** is its best coastal trek. At 85km, it's one of the longest tracks in the Southwest National Park, and at around seven days along one of the wildest coasts in Australia, one of the most challenging. The rewards are magnificent **beaches**, spectacular coastal scenery and Aboriginal middens, as much as a sense of escapism at the edge of the world – the next landmass south is Antarctica. Around a thousand people do the walk each year, 75 percent of them between December and March, most from Melaleuca east to Cockle Creek, so that the prevailing weather is at your back – the area is still exposed to cold southerly winds and frequent rain. In addition, sleet or snow is not unknown in summer on the exposed Ironbound Range (900m). Much of the route is now boardwalked, but you will need to be prepared for mud. Similarly, there are no huts en route, so tents and fuel stoves are essential, plus enough supplies for at least ten days in case you are stuck due to the weather.

ARRIVAL AND DEPARTURE — SOUTHWEST NATIONAL PARK

By plane There is no public transport into the park. Walkers for the South Coast Track must fly to Melaleuca from Hobart's airport with Par Avion ($290; ☎ 03 6248 5390, ⊛ paravion.com.au), then head for Cockle Creek, where you will need to phone for transport to pick you up. Dover Taxico (☎ 0429 982 006) provides transfers to Geeveston to connect with TassieLink buses ($200 for up to seven walkers, or $400 to Hobart).

INFORMATION

Park information The nearest visitor/ranger centre is at Mount Field National Park (see p.906). A useful website for information about walking the track is ⊛ southcoasttrack .com.au)

Maps and guides If you're walking the South Coast Track you will need the 1:100,000 *South Coast Walks* map and ideally the walking guide *South Coast Track* by bushwalk guru John Chapman.

SCENIC FLIGHTS AND ACTIVITIES

Abseiling Aardvark Adventures (☎ 03 6273 7722, ⊛ aardvarkadventures.com.au) runs abseiling trips down the Gordon Dam on demand (4–5hr; $210). The team can either meet you at the site or provide transfers from Hobart. **Kayaking** Roaring 40s Ocean Kayaking (☎ 1800 653 712, ⊛ roaring40skayaking.com.au) offers a number of amazing kayaking expeditions in the area. You're flown into Melaleuca then spend three to seven days exploring the area (Nov–April; seven-day trip $3250, three-day $2250).

Scenic flights Par Avion (☎ 03 6248 5390, ⓦ paravion .com.au) provides scenic flights over the area, with a stop in the wilderness and boat trip at Melaleuca Inlet ($350/4hr).

Trekking Tasmanian Expeditions (☎ 1300 666 856 or ☎ 03 6339 3999, ⓦ tas-ex.com) runs guided walks of the South Coast Track (Nov–May; nine days; $2295, incl transfers from Hobart, food and shared tent). You need to be fit, as each party member (max of ten) needs to haul their share of supplies – around 18–20kg – over 15km a day, though there is a rest day mid-route.

ACCOMMODATION

Ted's Beach Southwest National Park. Of several spots to bush camp in the area, all maintained by PWS, *Ted's Beach* spread along the shore of Lake Pedder, before you reach the Gordon Dam, is the most appealing. Though basic, it nevertheless provides free electric barbecues, non-treated water and toilets. **$13**

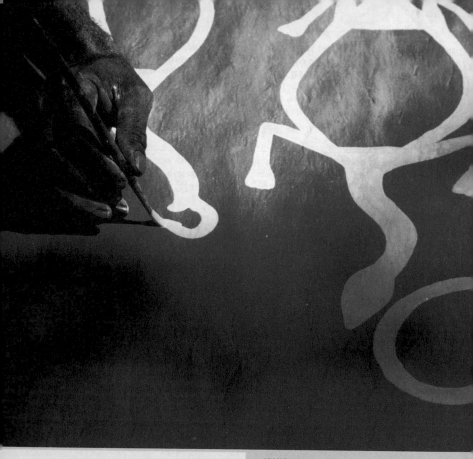

ABORIGINAL BARK PAINTING

Contexts

History

The first European settlers saw Australia as *terra nullius* – empty land – on the principle that Aborigines didn't "use" the country in an agricultural sense, a belief that remained uncontested in law until 1992. However, decades of archeological work, the reports of early settlers, and oral tradition, have established that humans have occupied Australia for a minimum of forty thousand years – proof that Australia's Aboriginal peoples shaped, controlled and used their environment as surely as any farmer. But two centuries of European rule shattered traditional Aboriginal life, and evidence of those earlier times mostly consists of cryptic art sites and legends.

While the treatment of Aboriginal people was shameful, as indeed are the conditions that many of them endure today, Australia has established a rock-solid parliamentary democracy and has successfully accommodated hundreds of thousands of people from all over the world. Migration has transformed the country, from the arrival of southern Europeans in the 1950s and 1960s to the more recent waves of people from Vietnam, Lebanon and India. Australia also resettles significant numbers of UN-registered refugees, and huge numbers of students come from China, Southeast Asia and India. Since 1945, more than 7 million people have settled in Australia; while there have been some tensions, the ability of all these people to live together is perhaps the country's best achievement.

From Gondwana to the Dreamtime

After the break-up of the supercontinent known as **Gondwana** into India, Africa, South America, Australasia and Antarctica, Australia moved away from the South Pole, reaching its current geographical location about fifteen million years ago. There was never a land link with the rest of Asia, and thus the country developed its unique fauna – **megafauna** (see box, p.985) flourished, along with widespread rainforests, until about fifty thousand years ago. Subsequent ice ages dried out the climate; by six thousand years ago the seas had stabilized at their present levels and Australia's environment was much as it is today, an arid centre with a relatively fertile eastern seaboard. **Humans** had been in Australia long before then, of course, most likely taking advantage of low sea levels to cross the Timor Trough into northern Australia, or island-hopping from Indonesia via New Guinea. The earliest human remains found in Australia (in New South Wales) are dated to around 40,000 BC, with scientists estimating that humans could have settled here 70,000 years ago.

The oldest known remains from central Australia are only 22,000 years old, so it's also plausible that initial colonization occurred around the coast, followed by later

70,000–40,000 BC	22,000 BC	1521–24	1606
The first humans settle in Australia	The interior of the country is colonized	Possible Portuguese expedition to Australia	The Dutch East India Company first travels the western coast of Cape York Peninsula

exploration of the interior – though it's just as likely that corrosive rainforests, which covered the centre until about twenty thousand years ago, obliterated all trace of earlier human habitation. When the European settlers arrived, the **thylacine** (Tasmanian tiger) had disappeared from the Australian mainland but still lived in Tasmania, while the **dingo**, an introduced canine, was prevalent on the mainland but unknown in Tasmania. This indicates that there was a further influx of people and **dogs** more recently than twelve thousand years ago, after rising sea levels separated Tasmania. The earliest inhabitants used crude **stone implements**, gradually replaced by more refined, lighter tools, **boomerangs**, and used core stones to flake "blanks", which were then fashioned into spearheads, knives and scrapers. **Trade networks** for rock, **ochre** (a red clay used for ceremonial purposes) and other products – shells and even wood for canoes – eventually stretched from New Guinea to the heart of the continent, following river systems away from the coast. **Rock art**, preserved in an ancient engraved tradition, and other more recent painted styles, seem to indicate that cultural links also travelled along these trade routes.

It's probable that the disappearance of the megafauna was accelerated by Aboriginal hunting, but the most dramatic change wrought by the original Australians was the controlled use of **fire** to clear forest. Burning promoted new growth and encouraged game, indirectly expanding grassland and favouring certain plants that evolved fire-reliant seeds and growth patterns. But while the Aborigines modified the environment for their own ends, their belief that land, wildlife and people were an interdependent whole maintained a balance between the population and natural resources. Tribes were organized and related according to complex kinship systems, reflected in the three hundred different **languages** known to exist at that time. Legends about the mythical **Dreamtime**, when creative forces shaped the landscape, provided verbal maps of tribal territory and linked natural features to the actions of these Dreamtime ancestors, who often had both human and animal forms.

The first Europeans

Prior to the sixteenth century, the only regular visitors to Australia were the **Malays**, who established seasonal camps while fishing the northern coasts for trepang, a sea slug, to sell to the Chinese. In Europe, the globe had been carved up between Spain and Portugal in 1494 under the auspices of Pope Alexander VI at the **Treaty of Tordesillas**, and all maritime nations subsequently kept their nautical charts secret, to protect their discoveries. It's possible, therefore, that the inquisitive **Portuguese** knew of **Terra Australis**, the Great Southern Land, soon after founding their colony in East Timor in 1516.

But while the precise date of "discovery" is contentious, it is clear that various nations were making forays into the area: the **Dutch** in 1606 and 1623, who were appalled by the harsh climate and inhabitants of Outback Queensland, and the **Spanish** in 1606, who were looking for both plunder and pagans to convert to Catholicism. The latter, guided by **Luis Vaes de Torres**, blithely navigated the strait between New Guinea and Cape York as if they knew it was there. As Torres hailed from Portugal it is indeed likely that he knew where he was; there's evidence that the Portuguese had **mapped** a large portion of Australia's northern coastline as early as 1536.

1642	1768–71	1770	1787
Dutch explorer Abel Tasman explores western Tasmania	English Lieutenant James Cook's expedition in HM *Endeavour*	Cook declares Australia *terra nullius*	The First Fleet of eleven ships departs from England on a mission to colonize Australia

Later in the seventeenth century, the Dutch navigators **Dirk Hartog**, **Van Diemen** and **Abel Tasman** added to maps of the east and north coasts, but eventually discarded "New Holland" as a barren, worthless country. William Dampier, a buccaneer who wrote popular accounts of his visit to Western Australia, first stirred British interest in 1697. However, it wasn't until the British captured the Spanish port of Manila, in the Philippines, in 1762, that detailed maps of Australia's coast fell into their hands; it took them six more years to assemble an expedition to the continent. Sailing in 1768 on the *Endeavour*, **Captain James Cook** headed to Tahiti, then proceeded to map New Zealand's coastline before sailing west in 1770 to search for the Great Southern Land.

The British sighted the continent in April 1770 and sailed north from Cape Everard to **Botany Bay**, where Cook commented on the Aborigines' initial indifference to seeing the *Endeavour*. When a party of forty sailors attempted to land, however, two Aborigines attacked them with spears; the British drove them off with musket fire. Continuing on up the Queensland coast, the British passed Moreton Bay and Fraser Island before entering the treacherous passages of the Great Barrier Reef where, on June 11, the *Endeavour* ran aground off Cape Tribulation. Cook managed to beach the ship safely at the mouth of the Endeavour River (present-day Cooktown), where the expedition set up camp while the ship was repaired.

Contact between Aborigines and whites during the following six weeks was tinged with a mistrust that never quite erupted into serious confrontation, and Cook took the opportunity to make notes in which he tempered romanticism for the "noble savage" with the sharp observation that European and Aboriginal values were mutually incomprehensible. The expedition was intrigued by some of Australia's wildlife, but otherwise unimpressed with the country, and was glad to sail onwards on August 5. With imposing skill, Cook successfully managed to navigate the rest of the reef, finally claiming possession of the country – which he named **New South Wales** – for King George III on August 21, at Possession Island in the Torres Strait.

Convicts

The expedition's reports didn't arouse much enthusiasm in London, however, and the disdainful attitude towards the Great Southern Land matched the opinion voiced by the Dutch more than a century before. However, after the loss of its American colonies following the **American War of Independence** in 1783, Britain was deprived of a handy location to offload convicted criminals. **Sir Joseph Banks**, botanist on the *Endeavour*, advocated Botany Bay as an ideal location for a **penal colony** that could soon become self-sufficient. The government agreed, and in May 1787 the **First Fleet**, packed with around 730 convicts (570 men and 160 women), set sail for Australia on eleven ships, under the command of **Captain Arthur Phillip**. Reaching Botany Bay in January 1788, Phillip deemed it unsuitable for his purposes and instead founded the settlement at **Sydney Cove**, on Port Jackson's fine natural harbour.

The early years at Sydney were not promising. The colonists suffered erratic weather and starvation, Aboriginal hostility, soil that was too hard to plough, and timber so tough it dented their axes. In 1790, supplies ran so low that a third of the population had to be transferred to a new colony on **Norfolk Island**, 1500km northeast. Even so, in the same year Britain dispatched a second fleet with a thousand more convicts – about a quarter of

1788	1798	1803	1808
Convicts clear ground at Sydney Cove	George Bass and Matthew Flinders circumnavigate Tasmania	Matthew Flinders circumnavigates Australia	The Rum Rebellion: the only successful coup in Australia's history

whom died en route. To ease the situation, Phillip granted packages of farmland to marines and former convicts before he returned to Britain in 1792. The first **free settlers** arrived the following year, and Britain's preoccupation with the French Revolutionary Wars meant a reduction in the number of convicts being transported to the colony, thus allowing a period of consolidation.

Meanwhile, **John Macarthur** manipulated the temporary governor into allowing his **New South Wales Corps**, which had replaced the marines as the governor's strong arm, to exercise considerable power in the colony. This was temporarily curtailed in 1800 by **Philip King**, who also slowed an illicit rum trade, encouraged new settlements and speeded production by allowing convicts to work for wages. Macarthur was forced out of the corps into the wool industry, importing Australia's first **sheep** from South Africa. He continued to stir up trouble though, which culminated in the **Rum Rebellion** of 1808, when merchant and pastoral factions, supported by the military, ousted **Governor William Bligh**. Britain finally took notice of the colony's anarchic state and appointed the firm-handed **Colonel Lachlan Macquarie**, backed by the 73rd Regiment, as Bligh's replacement in 1810. Macquarie settled the various disputes and brought eleven years of disciplined progress to the colony.

Labelled the "Father of Australia", for his vision of a country that could rise above its convict origins, Macquarie implemented enlightened policies towards former convicts or **emancipists**, enrolling them in public offices. He also attempted to educate, rather than exterminate, Aboriginal people and was the driving force behind New South Wales becoming a productive, self-sufficient colony. But he offended the landowner **squatters**, who were concerned that emancipists were being granted too many favours, and also those who regarded the colony solely as a place of punishment. In fact, conditions had improved so much that by 1819 New South Wales had become the major destination for voluntary emigrants from Britain.

In 1821, Macquarie was replaced as governor, and his successor, Sir Thomas Brisbane, was instructed to segregate, not integrate, convicts. To this end, when New South Wales officially graduated from being a penal settlement to a new British colony in 1823, convicts were used to colonize newly explored regions – Western Australia, Tasmania and Queensland – as far away from Sydney's free settlers as possible.

Explorers

Matthew Flinders had already circumnavigated the mainland in 1803 (and suggested the name "**Australia**", from the Latin *Australis*, meaning "southern") in his leaky vessel, the *Investigator*, and with the colony firmly established, expeditions began pushing inland from Sydney. In 1823, John Oxley, the Surveyor General, having previously explored newly discovered pastoral land west of the Blue Mountains, chose the **Brisbane River** in Queensland as the site of a new penal colony, thus opening up the fertile Darling Downs to future settlement. Meanwhile, townships were being founded elsewhere around the coast, eventually leading to the creation of **separate colonies** to add to that of Van Diemen's Land (Tasmania), settled in 1803 to ward off French exploration. Albany and Fremantle on the west coast were established in 1826 and 1829 respectively, followed by the Yarra River (Melbourne, Victoria) in 1835, and Adelaide (South Australia) in 1836.

1813	**1829**	**1851**	**1854**
Matthew Flinders calls New South Wales "Australia"	Australia claimed as a British territory and Perth is founded	Victorian gold rush begins	The Eureka Stockade, a rebellion of miners in Ballarat

But it was the possibilities of the **interior** – which some maintained concealed a vast inland sea – that captured the imagination of the government and squatters. Setting out from Adelaide in 1844, **Charles Sturt** was the first to attempt to cross the centre. Forced to camp for six months at a desert waterhole, where the heat melted the lead in his pencils and unthreaded screws from equipment, he managed to reach the aptly named Sturt's Stony Desert before scurvy forced him back to Adelaide. At the same time, **Ludwig Leichhardt**, a Prussian doctor, had more luck in his crossing between the Darling Downs and Port Essington, near Darwin, which he accomplished in fourteen months. Unlike Sturt, Leichhardt found plenty of potential farmland and returned a hero. He vanished in 1848, however, while again attempting to cross the continent. In the same year, the ill-fated **Kennedy** expedition managed the trek from Tully to Cape York in northern Queensland, but most of the party died, Kennedy included, as a result of poor planning, starvation and attack by Aborigines. Similarly, **Burke and Wills'** successful 1860–61 south-to-north traverse between Melbourne and the Gulf of Carpentaria in Queensland was marred by the death of the expedition leaders upon their return south, owing to bad organization and a series of unfortunate errors (see box, p.451). Finally, Australia's centre was located by **John McDouall Stuart** in 1860, who subsequently managed a safe return journey to Adelaide. Hopes of finding an inland sea were quashed, and the harsh reality of a dry, largely infertile interior began to dawn on developers.

Aboriginal response

British advances had been repulsed from the very first year of the colony's foundation; Governor Phillip reporting that "the natives now attack any straggler they meet unarmed". Forced off their traditional hunting grounds, which were taken by the settlers for agriculture or grazing, the Aborigines began stealing crops and spearing stock. Response from the British was brutal; the relatively liberal **Lieutenant-Governor George Arthur** ordered a sweep of Tasmania in 1830, to round up all Aboriginal people and herd them into **reserves**, a symbolic attempt to clear "the uncivilized" from the paths of progress. More direct action, such as the **Myall Creek Massacre** in 1838 (see box, p.276), when 28 Aborigines were roped together and butchered by graziers, created public outcry, but similar "**dispersals**" became commonplace wherever indigenous people resisted white intrusion. More insidious methods – such as poisoning waterholes or lacing gifts of flour with arsenic – were also employed by pastoralists angered over stock losses.

The Aboriginal people were not a single, unified society, and the British exploited existing divisions by creating the notorious **Native Mounted Police**, an Aboriginal force that aided and abetted the extermination of rival groups. By the 1890s, citing a perversion of Darwinian theory which held that Aboriginal people were less evolved than whites and so doomed to extinction, most states had followed Tasmania's example of "**protectionism**", relocating Aborigines into reserves that were frequently a long way from their traditional lands.

White Australia, Federation and war

Throughout the country, goldfields became centres of **nationalism**, peaking in Queensland in the 1880s, where the flames were fanned by the importation of

1860	1868	1869	1882
The Burke and Wills expedition, using camels to explore the interior	Convict transportation to Western Australia ends	Children of Australian Aboriginal and Torres Strait Islander descent are taken from their families by the state	Australia beats England in the first Ashes series

GOLD

The discovery of **gold** in Australia in 1851 had a dramatic bearing on Australia's future. The first major strikes in New South Wales and Victoria brought an immediate flood of hopeful miners from Sydney and Melbourne and, once the news spread overseas, from the USA and Britain. Gold opened up Australia's interior; as returns petered out in one area, prospectors moved on into uncharted regions to find more.

A new "level society", based on a "mateship" ethic, evolved on the goldfields. Yet the **diggers** were all too aware of their poor social and political rights. At the end of 1854, frustrations over mining licences erupted at **Eureka** (see p.838), where miners built a stockade and ended up being charged by mounted police. The Victorian goldfields also saw **racial tensions** directed against a new minority, the **Chinese**, who first arrived during the 1850s. Disheartened by diminishing returns and infuriated by the Chinese ability to find gold in abandoned claims, diggers stormed a Chinese camp at **Lambing Flat** in 1861. Troops were sent in to stop the riots, but the ringleaders were later acquitted by an all-white jury.

The gold rush came to an end in the 1870s, and many of the towns made rich in the boom are now charming and sedate holiday destinations, capitalizing on a colourful and at times harsh history. Their buildings, some based on Neoclassical temples, others with ornate balconies and multiple storeys, are a significant part of the country's **architectural heritage**. One of the most enjoyable to visit is **Ballarat**, specifically for its step-back-in-time outdoor museum (see p.840) where you can pan for gold and watch it being smelted. The rush may be long gone, but there are still dazzlingly rich pickings to be had: in 2013 a massive nugget was unearthed near Ballarat, weighing 5.5kg and worth more than half a million dollars.

Solomon Islanders to work on sugar plantations. Ostensibly to prevent slavery, but politically driven by recession and growing white unemployment, the government passed the 1901 Immigration Act – also known as the **White Australia Policy** – which greatly restricted non-European immigration.

Central government was first mooted in 1842, but new states were not keen to return to the control of New South Wales, lose interstate customs duties, or share the new-found mineral wealth. But by the end of the century they began to see advantages to **federation**, not least as a way to control indentured labour and present a united front against French, German and Russian expansion in the Pacific. A decade of wrangling by the states saw the formation of a High Court and a two-tier parliamentary system consisting of a House of Representatives and Senate, presided over by a prime minister. Each state would have its own premier, and Britain would be represented by a governor-general. Approved by Queen Victoria shortly before her death, the **Commonwealth of Australia** came into being on January 1, 1901.

It's notable that the Immigration Act was the first piece of legislation to be passed by the new parliament, and reflected the nationalist drive behind federation. Though the intent was to create an Australia largely of European – and preferably British – descent, the policy also sowed the seeds for Australian independence from the "Mother Country". The first pull away came as early as 1912, when the **Commonwealth Bank** opened, evidence that Australia was endeavouring to become less financially reliant on Britain. Centred entirely on white interests, the White Australia Policy ensured that Aboriginal people were not given the right to vote in state elections until 1962 and were not included in the

1894	1901	1913	1915	1932
South Australia becomes the third place in the world to give women the vote	Commonwealth of Australia founded on January 1	Foundation stone for the city of Canberra laid	Australian soldiers land at Gallipoli in Turkey	The Sydney Harbour Bridge opens

national census until 1967. The policy itself was repealed in 1973. The new government did, however, give white **women** the vote (and the option to stand for Parliament) in 1902, following South Australia's lead eight years earlier. And in 1907, the Australian Labor Party, which had grown out of the economic recession and union battles with the government during the 1890s, established the concept of a **minimum wage**.

Defence had also been a positive force behind federation. But even though the war between Japan and Russia in 1904 had highlighted the need to build its own defence force, Australia was largely unprepared for the outbreak of hostilities in Europe a decade later, owning little more than a navy made up of secondhand British ships. There was a patriotic rush to enlist in the army, and an opportunistic occupation of German New Guinea by Australian forces. However, the issue of compulsory conscription, raised by **Prime Minister Billy Hughes**, was twice defeated in referendums.

From the Australian perspective, the most important stage of the war occurred when Turkey gave its support to Germany in 1915. **Winston Churchill** formulated a plan to defend British shipping in the Dardanelles by occupying the **Gallipoli Peninsula**, and diverted Australian infantry bound for Europe. Between April and December 1915, wave after wave of Australian, New Zealand and British troops were mown down below Turkish gun emplacements, as they attempted to take control of the peninsula. By the end of the year, it became clear that Gallipoli was not going to fall, and the survivors were evacuated to fight on the Western Front. The long-term effect of the senseless slaughter was the first serious questioning of Anglo-Australian relations: should Australia have sacrificed so much (8141 soldiers died) to defend a (geographically) distant country's interests? Conversely, Gallipoli is still treated as a symbol of national identity and pride.

1918–39

After World War I, the Nationalist Party joined forces with the **Country Party** to assume government under the paternalistic and fiercely anti-socialist guidance of **Earle Page** and **Stanley Bruce**. The Country Party was formed as a result of the widening divisions between the growing urban population and farmers, who felt isolated and politically unrepresented. Under the coalition, pastoral industries were subsidized by overseas borrowing, allowing them to compete internationally, and technology began to close the gap between the city and the Outback. Radio and aviation developments saw the birth of **Qantas** and the **Royal Flying Doctor Service** in Queensland's remote west. Development also occurred in the cities: work started on the Sydney Harbour Bridge, and the new Commonwealth capital, **Canberra**, was completed.

On the social front, the USA stopped mass immigration in 1921, deflecting a flood of people from depressed **Southern Europe** to Australia, which the government countered by encouraging British immigrants with assisted passages. As the **Great Depression** set in during the early 1930s, Australia faced the collapse of its economic and political systems, with all the parties divided. Pressed for a loan, the Bank of England forced a restructuring of the Australian economy. Adding to national embarrassment, politics and sports became blurred during the 1932 "**body-line**" cricket series: the loan was made virtually conditional on the Australian cricket authorities

1940	1942	1945	1956
Scientists, under Australian Howard Florey, develop penicillin	Fall of Singapore: 16,000 Australians made prisoners of war. Bombing of Darwin by the Japanese	Australia is a founding member of the United Nations	Satirist Barry Humphries launches the career of Edna Everage

dropping their allegations that British bowlers were deliberately trying to injure Australian batsmen during the tour.

Meanwhile, worries about communism were succeeded by concern about the rise of fascism, as Mussolini and Hitler took power in Europe and Japanese forces invaded Manchuria – the **Tanaka memorial** in 1927 actually cited Australia as a target for future conquest by Japan. Australia assisted the immigration of refugees from central Europe, and – after a prolonged union battle – halted iron exports to Japan. When Prime Minister Joseph Lyons died in office, **Robert Menzies** was elected to the post, in time to side with Britain as hostilities were declared against Hitler in September 1939.

World War II and after

Just as in World War I, Australia cemented its national identity by getting involved on a global scale in World War II, but this time without Britain's involvement. Menzies' United Australia Party barely lasted long enough to form diplomatic ties with the USA – in case Germany overran Europe – before internal divisions saw the government crumble, replaced by **John Curtin** and his Labor Party in 1941.

Curtin, concerned about Australia's vulnerability after the Japanese attack on Pearl Harbor, made the radical decision of shifting the country's commitment in the war from defending Britain and Europe to fighting off an invasion of Australia from Asia. After the **fall of Singapore** in 1942 and the capture of sixteen thousand Australian troops, Curtin succeeded in ordering the immediate recall of Australians fighting in the Middle East. In February, the Japanese unexpectedly bombed Darwin, launched submarine raids against Sydney and Newcastle, and invaded New Guinea. Feeling abandoned and betrayed by Britain, Curtin appealed to the USA, who quickly adopted Australia as a base for coordinating Pacific operations under **General Douglas MacArthur**. Meanwhile, Australian troops in New Guinea halted Japanese advances along the **Kokoda trail** at Milne Bay, while the Australian and US navies slowed down the Japanese fleet in the **Battle of the Coral Sea** – which, thanks to modern cannon, was notable as the first naval engagement in which the two sides never even saw each other.

Australia came out of World War II realizing that, geographically, the country was closer to Asia than Europe, and that it could not count on Britain to help in a crisis. From this point on, Australia began to look to the USA and the Pacific, in addition to Britain, for direction. Another consequence of the war was that immigration was speeded up, fuelled by Australia's recent vulnerability. The government reintroduced assisted passages from Britain – the "ten-pound-poms" – and also accepted substantial numbers of European refugees.

With international right-wing extremism laid low by the war, the old fear of **communism** returned. When North Korea invaded South Korea in 1950, Australia, led by a revitalized Menzies and his new Liberal Party, was the first country after the USA to commit troops to counter communist forces. Menzies also sent soldiers and pilots to Malaya (as peninsular Malaysia was known at the time), where communist rebels had been fighting the British colonial administration almost since the end of World War II. At home, he opened up central Australia to British **atomic bomb tests** in the 1950s, because – echoing the beliefs of the first European colonists – "nobody lived there". A number of Aborigines were moved to reserves, but others

1962	1967	1971	1973	1975
Troops sent to Vietnam War	PM Harold Holt vanishes at Cheviot Beach	Neville Bonner becomes the first Aboriginal MP	The White Australia Policy ends; Sydney Opera House opens	The Great Barrier Reef Marine Park is established

– along with the British troops involved in the tests – suffered the effects of fallout, and the Aborigines' traditional lands were rendered uninhabitable. Wrangles with the British government over compensation, and the clearing of the test sites at **Maralinga** and **Emu Junction**, were finally settled in 1993.

Menzies was still in control when the USA became involved in **Vietnam**, and with conflict in Malaya all but over, Australia volunteered "advisers" to Vietnamese republican forces in 1962. Once fighting became entrenched, the government introduced conscription and – bowing to the wishes of the American president **Lyndon B. Johnson** – sent a battalion of soldiers into the fray in 1965, events that immediately split the country. Menzies quit politics the following year, succeeded by his protégé **Harold Holt**, who, rallying under the catchphrase "All the way with LBJ", willingly increased Australia's participation in the Vietnamese conflict. But as the war dragged on, world opinion shifted to seeing the matter as a civil struggle, rather than as a fight between democratic and communist ideologies, and in 1970 the government began scaling down its involvement. Roughly 60,000 Australian troops served in Vietnam in total; 521 were killed. Back at home, Aboriginal people were finally granted **civil rights** in 1967, and Holt mysteriously disappeared while swimming off the coast of Victoria, leaving the Liberals in turmoil and paving the way for a Labor win under **Gough Whitlam**, well regarded by the left, in 1972.

Whitlam's three years in office had far-reaching effects: he ended national service and participation in Vietnam, granted independence to **Papua New Guinea**, recognized the People's Republic of China, and instituted free health care and higher education systems. The end came in 1975, when a loans scandal involving the government led the conservative majority in the Senate to block supply bills, effectively stopping government expenditure. In an unprecedented move, the **governor-general John Kerr** (the largely ceremonial representative of the Crown overseeing Australian affairs) dismissed the government – a move that shocked many into questioning the validity of Britain's hold on Australia – and called an election, which Labor lost. In contrast, the following eight years were uneventful, culminating in the return of Labor in 1983 under the charismatic **Bob Hawke**, a former trade union leader. Labor's subsequent thirteen years and four terms in office were brought to a close under the leadership of Hawke's successor and former treasurer, **Paul Keating**. Although he was unpopular with some for his perceived arrogance, the Liberal party lost to Keating in the 1993 election. Keating was always a strong advocate of Australia being part of Asia, but news of a secret military agreement with Indonesia created a public backlash, in part resulting in a landslide victory for the **Liberal-National coalition**, led by **John Howard**, in 1996.

Into the twenty-first century

Howard's performance in the early years of office showed that his critics had underestimated his tenacity and political skills, honed by 22 years in federal politics. By 1998, Howard's political position was so secure that the coalition managed to be re-elected on what some considered a suicidal platform of **tax reform** through the implementation of a **GST**, or Goods and Services Tax. When Howard's prospects of winning the next election were slipping away in mid-2001, he successfully turned the country's attention to the ongoing issue of **refugees**, playing on fears of

1978	1985	1992	1996
First Sydney Gay and Lesbian Mardi Gras	Freehold of Uluru and Kata Tjuta granted to the Mutitjulu people	The Mabo Decision ends the concept of *terra nullius*	The Wik Decision holds that indigenous land rights survive the granting of pastoral leases

unfettered immigration. The election was a comfortable win for his coalition, and the opposition Labor Party was further diminished.

Defying public opinion, Howard vociferously supported the **war** in Iraq, and subsequently joined the "coalition of the willing" in the military attack on the country. In contrast to the government's rhetorical support, Australia's physical contribution to the war was actually quite small – two thousand troops, plus some warships and aircraft.

In federal elections in October 2004, the Liberals scored a resounding victory and Howard was elected prime minister for the fourth time. By December 2004, he had become Australia's **second-longest serving prime minister**, surpassed only by Menzies' eighteen years in office. Underpinned by an ongoing resources boom, the Australian economy appeared in very good shape; China's and India's ravenous demands for Australian minerals and metal ore boosted the price of its commodity exports. However, Australia had been running a **trade deficit** for almost five years and improvements were hampered by increased consumer spending on imports and by the worst drought on record. In April 2007, the Howard government announced there was a water crisis, and proposed the establishment of a **national water management scheme**.

The return of the Labor Party

After years of constant leadership struggles, the Australian Labor Party entered into the election year energized and revitalized under the leadership of Queenslander **Kevin Rudd**. A former diplomat, bureaucrat and business consultant, Rudd had a reputation for being a consummate negotiator and a shrewd politician. Next to Howard, Rudd appeared youthful, handled every challenge thrown at him by the Liberal Party with aplomb, and won with a massive swing to Labor.

ABORIGINAL RIGHTS

During the 1980s there were some advances under Labor in the area of **Aboriginal rights**. An ineffectual inquiry into Aboriginal deaths in custody was overshadowed in June 1992 when the High Court handed down the landmark **Mabo Decision**, legally overturning the concept of *terra nullius*. Eddie Mabo's claim that he could inherit land – previously designated by the government as "Crown Land" – on Murray Island (Mer) in the Torres Strait, was granted, and the Merriam were acknowledged as traditional landowners. Sadly, the remarkable and charismatic campaigner Eddie Mabo died before the ruling was given, having waited for years for the outcome. However, his legacy was the passing of the Native Title Act of 1993. Next came the **Wik Decision** in December 1996, which stated that native title and pastoral leases could coexist over the same area.

While Mabo and Wik had an effect – such as the handing back of the **Silver Plains** property on Queensland's Cape York to its traditional owners in 2000 – not all similar land claims are likely to succeed. A **Native Title Tribunal** was established to consider each case, but given former resettlement policies, claimants have an uphill struggle to prove constant association with the land. Nonetheless, a growing acknowledgement that Aboriginal people were in fact the land's original inhabitants, and the perception that they will eventually be re-enfranchised, has seen mining companies, farmers and, notably – and ironically, given its past record – the Queensland government, ignoring political and legal wrangles and making private land-use agreements with, or handovers to, local communities.

1999	2000	2003	2008
Australia votes no to becoming a Republic	27th Summer Olympic Games held in Sydney	Australian military deployed in the Iraq War	Prime Minister Kevin Rudd formally apologizes to the Aboriginal people for "past mistreatment"

Rudd ratified the Kyoto Protocol on climate change and then formally **apologized to the Australian Aborigines** in February 2008, a campaign promise fulfilled in a poignant ceremony. He withdrew Australian combat troops from Iraq, with a stinging rebuke of the former government's actions in sending troops "without a full and proper assessment".

But Rudd's popularity began to falter: he was widely thought to have made a range of promises, on everything from the environment to health care, which he wasn't capable of realizing. His behaviour, working impossible hours and expecting those around him to follow suit, caused several resignations and raised more doubts about his leadership. In June 2010, after behind-the-scenes manoeuvring, deputy prime minister Julia Gillard announced that she wished to **contest the leadership**: Rudd resigned and Gillard took over in a caretaker role.

The first female prime minister of Australia

Julia Gillard refused to move into the prime minister's residence in Canberra until she had been officially elected: the election was held in August 2010, but the result was too close to call – Labor and the Liberals won 72 seats each. After two weeks of power-brokering, two independent MPs decided to back Labor, and Gillard officially became Australia's **first female prime minister**.

Straight-talking Gillard won approval for her empathetic reaction to the appalling **floods** that hit Queensland in late 2010 and early 2011. A skilful parliamentarian and persuasive public speaker, she brought in an emissions trading scheme and mining tax, and strengthened paid parental leave.

With low unemployment figures, low interest rates, low inflation and a triple A credit rating, Australia under Gillard appeared to be thriving. But while the country bucked the global economic downturn which began in 2008, largely due to the strong trading relationship with China (and due to mining in particular), Gillard never calmed the squabbles within her party. Rudd continued to oppose Gillard from the sidelines, while the Murdoch press launched personal attacks on the prime minister, mocking her appearance, exaggerating her foibles and even deriding her partner. And many of the Labor Party faithful were sorely disappointed when she failed to support single-sex marriage and reduced financial support for single parents.

With tensions continuing, in June 2013 Gillard took the gamble of calling a leadership ballot. She lost, Rudd was reinstated as leader and Gillard **left party politics** after a relatively short term of office. Her achievement in becoming the country's first female prime minister will, as she put it herself in a gracious resignation speech, make things easier for the next female leader.

The power-wrangling within the Labor Party proved very damaging. In September 2013, the Liberal Party's **Tony Abbott** defeated Rudd in the general election, despite the lack of deeply felt support for his anti-immigration policies and his untenable status as a climate-change sceptic. Deeply unpopular, his approval rating dropped consistently and on September 14, 2015, Malcolm Turnbull, once chairman of the Australian Republican Movement, pushed for a leadership vote, defeating Abbott 54 votes to 44. In the national election of July 2016, Turnbull narrowly defeated the Labor Party once again to form a Liberal-led coalition government.

2009	2010	2013	2016
Massive bushfires sweep Victoria, with 173 fatalities	Julia Gillard becomes the first female prime minister of Australia	Kevin Rudd regains his role as PM, to be swiftly replaced by Tony Abbott	Malcolm Turnbull re-elected prime minister of Australia

Australia's indigenous peoples

While white Australians historically grouped the country's indigenous peoples under the term Aborigines, in recent years there has been wider recognition that there are many separate cultures that are as diverse but interrelated as those of Europe. Today, these cultures include, for example, urbanized Koorie communities in Sydney and Melbourne, seminomadic groups such as the Pintupi living in the western deserts, and the Yolngu people of eastern Arnhem Land, an area never colonized by settlers. If there is any thread linking these groups, it is the island continent they inhabit and, particularly in the north, the appalling state of health, education and opportunities they experience.

Colonization

From 1788, the estimated 750,000 indigenous people of Australia were gradually dispossessed of their lands and livelihoods by the British colonists who failed to recognize them as legitimate inhabitants. Australia was annexed to the British Empire on the basis that it was **terra nullius**, or uninhabited wasteland. (This legal fiction persisted until the High Court judged in the landmark Mabo and Wik rulings; see box, p.978.) Upon deciding that the country was unoccupied, successive waves of new settlers hastened to make it so. Violent conflicts between indigenous and recently arrived Australians resulted in the decimation of Aboriginal groups. The most widely known of these conflicts was the **unofficial war** waged against Tasmania's Aboriginal peoples, which resulted in the near-destruction of indigenous Tasmanians (see box, p.924). Historians estimate that twenty thousand Aborigines may have died in these mostly unrecorded battles.

Australia's geographical isolation meant that the introduction of European **diseases** was also a powerful agent in decimating the indigenous populations. Whole communities were wiped out by smallpox and malaria epidemics, and the diaries from the First Fleet record the rapid destruction from smallpox of the Aboriginal camps in the Sydney hinterland within a few years of the establishment of the colony. Those who didn't die fled the area, unwittingly infecting neighbouring groups as they went.

The interruption of traditional **food and water supplies** became progressively worse through the nineteenth and twentieth centuries as the pastoral industry expanded across rural Australia, and vast areas were stripped of vegetation to provide grazing land. Grazing animals drained established water sources, and dug up the flora on the soil surface with their hooves, contributing to erosion and salinity, and so creating dust bowls.

Australia's Aboriginal peoples have also been subjected to various forms of **incarceration**, ranging from prisons to apartheid-style reserves. Much of this systematic imprisonment was instigated between 1890 and 1950 as an official policy of **protection**, in response to the devastating impact of colonization. Missionaries and other well-meaning people believed that Aborigines were a dying race, and that it was a Christian duty to provide for them in their passing. Parliamentary records of the time reveal a harsher mentality. Aborigines were often viewed as a weak and degenerate people who exposed white settlers to physical and moral turpitude. For the wellbeing of Aborigines and settlers alike, state governments enacted legislation to appoint official **Protectors of Aborigines**, established reserves in rural areas, and moved Aboriginal people to them. In some parts of Australia these reserves were established on traditional lands, allowing people to continue to live relatively undisturbed. Elsewhere, notably Queensland, people were forcibly removed from their home areas and relocated in reserves throughout the state. Families were broken up and their ties with the land and spirits shattered. The so-called protectors had autonomy over those in their ward. For example, Aboriginal people required permits to marry or to move from one reserve to another, or were forced into indentured (or simply slave) labour to be paid in flour or tobacco. This treatment persisted in some areas until the late 1960s.

Aboriginal people are still absurdly overrepresented in Australia's prison population. In 1987, the situation led to a **Royal Commission into Aboriginal Deaths in Custody**, which reported to the Federal Parliament. It called for wide-ranging changes in police and judicial practice, and substantial changes to social programmes aimed at improving the lot of Aboriginal peoples in the areas of justice, health, education, economics and empowerment. But despite considerable government lip service paid to the recommendations of the Royal Commission, it has not resulted in any substantial change to incarceration rates.

From the 1920s, Aboriginal children fathered by European Australians but born to black mothers were removed and put into state institutions or with white foster parents as part of a policy of **assimilation**. The practice of "taking the children away" began in Victoria in 1886 and continued until 1969, and still haunts the lives of many Aboriginal Australians, now known as the **Stolen Generation**, who have lost contact with their natal families and their culture. Their plight was poignantly depicted in the 2002 film *Rabbit-Proof Fence* (see p.992). But despite the policy being the subject of a major government enquiry in 1997, and the subsequent media attention following the release of the report, it was only with the election of the Rudd government that there was finally an official **apology**.

Revitalization and setbacks

The **revitalization** of Aboriginal people and their culture effectively began in 1967, when a constitutional referendum overwhelmingly endorsed the rights of indigenous Australians as voting citizens, and gave the federal government the power to legislate for Aboriginal people. Prior to this referendum, Aboriginal people had the status of wards of each of the states. The referendum ushered in a new era of **self-determination** for Aboriginal people, evidenced by the establishment of the first Ministry for Aboriginal Affairs in the Whitlam Labor government of 1972–75.

After more than a hundred years of agitation, **land rights** were accorded to Aboriginal groups in the Northern Territory in 1976 under federal legislation. All the mainland states and territories now have provisions for Aboriginal land rights. Throughout the 1970s and 1980s, successive federal governments set up various representative bodies, including the notorious **Aboriginal and Torres Strait Islanders Commission** (**ATSIC**: 1990–2004). This statutory authority gave elected Aboriginal representatives effective control over many of the federal funding programmes directed at Aboriginal organizations and communities. Substantial funds were directed towards training for employment and improved health education. The reality was far different: corruption, nepotism and flawed or ill-considered projects conspired to bring about ATSIC's abolition in 2004 and a return to greater federal government control.

Along with ownership of land and some control over funding came opportunities for economic self-sufficiency and expansion previously unavailable to Aboriginal groups. In many parts of the country, this allowed Aborigines to buy the cattle stations on which they had worked without wages for many years. In central Australia, Aboriginal enterprises include TV and radio stations, transport companies, small airlines, publishing companies, tourist businesses and joint-venture mining operations.

Cooperative agreements with the Australian Nature Conservation Agency led to Aboriginal ownership and joint management of two of Australia's most important conservation reserves, **Uluru–Kata Tjuta** and **Kakadu** national parks in the Northern Territory. These arrangements recognize that Aboriginal owners retain an enormous understanding about the ecology of their traditional lands that are vital in the development of land-management plans.

In 2007, the Howard government brought in a significant change in policy. A report entitled *Little Children are Sacred* was released, pertaining to the issue of child abuse in Northern Territory indigenous communities. Howard's seven-point plan to combat the problem, labelled "**the intervention**", included a ban on alcohol in some communities as well as "voluntary" medical checks for sexual abuse for indigenous children younger than sixteen. While some saw these actions as a gross overreaction, as well as a ploy for re-election, many others supported it, including Aboriginal leaders.

Citizenship and its problems

Despite some successes, Australia's indigenous peoples are struggling against considerable disadvantages. With improved rights in the 1960s came a new-found unemployability (for example, few station owners were willing to pay black workers the same wage as white people), along with the legal right to purchase **alcohol**, a disastrous combination. Institutionalized welfarism compounded feelings of futility, as well as shame towards Aboriginal origins, and substance abuse has been heavily implicated in the destructive spiral sometimes observed in Outback towns (and some inner-city areas). The negative repercussions have been evident in sickness and death, violence and despair, exclusion from education and meaningful employment, as well as families and communities in disarray.

Poor health, alcohol and substance abuse continue to reduce substantially the life expectancy of Aborigines. About seventy percent of indigenous Australians die before they turn 65 (compared with just over twenty percent for other Australians), Aboriginal infant mortality is two to three times higher than for white babies, and the death rate from diabetes is six times higher. As with most areas of social service, health services for Aboriginal peoples have been the province of white professionals until recently; an essential focus of recent strategies has been to empower Aboriginal people by giving resources to them directly.

On the **positive** side, many communities are confronting the problems that alcohol is causing. Some choose to be "dry", not allowing alcohol to be brought into the community, and pressure is put on those who break the laws of the society.

The future

The process of **reconciliation** with its "rights"-based approach, as initiated by the Labor government under Keating, was always troubling to Prime Minister John Howard. Upon his re-election in 1998, "**practical reconciliation**" was the new catchphrase and essentially meant the delivery of welfare services through mainstream programmes.

The new "whole of government" approach meant the responsibility for the delivery of indigenous programmes was to be shared by several government departments. "**Mutual obligation**" and "**shared responsibility**" have been the new buzzwords, a rhetoric that echoed the ideas of Noel Pearson, the Aboriginal lawyer and community leader from the Cape York Peninsula, whose aim is to replace social welfare with social enterprise. On Cape York, he embarked on a community-based social-renewal project that includes having payments of benefits invested in enterprise activity rather than as an individual welfare cheque, with each individual and family making a commitment to contributing as well as receiving.

ABORIGINAL MUSIC

Aboriginal music is an increasingly powerful and invigorating seam in the fabric of world music. Its instruments and rhythms have a strong influence on contemporary Australian music, and there's probably no better example of the musical crossing of cultural boundaries than in the story of Australia's most recognizable instrument, the **didgeridoo**. Known also as a *yidaki*, or simply a "didge", this hollowed-out tree branch, when blown into, produces a resonant hum that can be punctuated by imitations of animal and bird noises. Its sound is uniquely evocative of the Australian landscape.

The big surprise for many visitors to Australia is the sheer **diversity** of Aboriginal music. From the big rock sound of the Warumpi Band, and the heartfelt guitar ballads of Archie Roach, to the cruisey island reggae of Saltwater and the echoes of an ancient culture in the work of Nabarlek (who sing mostly in their own language), there is no way of pigeonholing the music. One hot indigenous talent is Yilila, a band whose music – an energetic mix of pulsing didge, screaming guitar solos and funky bass – is based on the story of *Dhumbala* or Red Flag, which chronicles their ancestors' centuries-old relationship with Indonesian traders. At the other end of the spectrum is Geoffrey Gurrumul Yunupingu, a former member of Yothu Yindi and member of Saltwater whose uplifting debut album, *Gurrumul* (2008), won rave reviews and a handful of awards. Geoffrey was born blind and sings angelically in his native Yolngu tongue with just acoustic guitar and bass behind him.

FESTIVALS

Barunga Sports & Cultural Festival
ⓦbarungafestival.com.au. Biggest of the Aboriginal music festivals, this showcases up to forty bands, along with team sports, traditional dance, spear-throwing and didge-playing competitions. It's held at Barunga Community, 80km south of Katherine in the NT, over the Queen's Birthday holiday weekend in June (campsites with facilities are available).

Gattjirrk Milingimbi Cultural Festival
ⓦfacebook.com/GattjirrkFestival. The Milingimbi community's GattJirrk Cultural Festival in the Top End is purely a music event and, being harder to get to than Barunga, gets fewer white visitors. Dates for this one are hard to nail down, although it's always held sometime mid-year, on Milingimbi Island in the Crocodile archipelago. There are flights from Darwin, otherwise you need permission from the Northern Land Council (Darwin Head Office ☎08 8920 5100, ⓦnlc.org.au) to drive across Arnhem Land to Ramingining to catch a barge. Traditional music and dance are featured, along with gospel bands and lots of Arnhem Land rock.

Laura Dance Festival
ⓦlauradancefestival .com. The Laura Dance Festival, held every odd-numbered year in far north Queensland, attracts high-profile performers like the Warumpi Band and Christine Anu, plus all the local Murri bands. Held in June, there are usually quite a few backpackers and hippies about, as well as the local Murri community. It's about three hours' drive (on sealed roads) north from Cairns to Laura, a small town 60km west of Cooktown.

Yabun Survival Day
If you're in Sydney over summer, there's no better place to be on the Australia Day holiday (Jan 26) than at Yabun Survival Day festival at Victoria Park. This festival began as a highly political event, deliberately juxtaposed with the Australia Day festivities that mark the arrival of the First Fleet of "white invaders". It continues as a celebration of the survival of indigenous people and cultures in the face of white oppression, and draws many of the biggest names in indigenous music.

Aboriginal communities had to enter into **Shared Responsibility Agreements (SRA)** with government departments, committing to "behavioural change" or similar actions in exchange for funding for specified community infrastructure needs. The first SRA released in December 2004 was with Mulan, a remote community in Western Australia. The government agreed to install a petrol bowser, and in return the community agreed to make sure their children showered daily and looked after other health issues. In most cases, these SRAs were reported to be successful. At first glance, it seemed a common-sense approach – no more wasting of money by a corrupt organization rife with nepotism, no more "one size fits all" solutions. However, funds were distributed on a seemingly ad-hoc basis and with few mechanisms in place to check if and how its "mutual obligation" is fulfilled.

Many Aboriginal leaders do not favour government policies that specifically target their communities. In early 2009, a group of human rights lawyers lodged a complaint about "the intervention" with the United Nations Committee for the Elimination of Racial Discrimination: intervention was branded by the committee as inherently racist. Despite this outcome, Julia Gillard did not investigate or halt the policy. One of the most controversial aspects of the intervention was the suspension of the Racial Discrimination Act in the areas where it takes place. This was deemed by its supporters to be a necessary though problematic and arguably paternalistic decision.

Flora and fauna

Despite forty thousand years of human pressure and manipulation, accelerated in the last two centuries by the effects of introduced species, Australia's ecology and wildlife remain among the most distinctive on earth. They are also some of the most endangered: in the last two hundred years, more native mammals have become extinct here than on any other continent, and land clearing – particularly in Queensland – kills an estimated 7.5 million birds a year, bringing several species to the edge of extinction.

Australians love to tell stories about the **dangers** the bush holds for the inexperienced traveller. In reality, fearsome "drop bears" lurking in gums, fallen tree trunks that turn out to be giant snakes, bloodthirsty wild pigs, and other rampaging terrors are mostly confined to hotel bars, the product of suburban paranoia laced with a surprising naivety about the great outdoors. Apart from a couple of avoidable exceptions (see p.41), there's little to fear from Australia's wildlife.

Marsupials and monotremes

In the years after the demise of the dinosaurs, Australia split away from the rest of the world and the animals here evolved along different lines to anywhere else. As placental mammals gained the ascendancy in South America, Africa, Europe and Asia, it was the marsupials and monotremes that took over in Australia, alongside the megafauna (see box below). These orders are not exclusive to Australia (they're also found in New Guinea and South America), but it's here that they reached their greatest diversity and numbers.

   Marsupials are mammals that give birth to a partially formed embryo, which itself then develops in a **pouch** on the mother; this allows a higher breeding rate in good years. Easiest to find because they actively seek out people, **ringtail** and **brushtail possums** are common in suburbs and campsites, and often hard to avoid if they think there's a chance of getting some food. With a little persistence, you should encounter one of the several species of related **glider possum** on the edges of forests at dusk. **Kangaroos** and **wallabies** are the Australian answer to deer and antelope, and range from tiny, solitary rainforest species to the gregarious 2m-tall red kangaroo of the central plains – watching these creatures bouncing effortlessly across the landscape is an extraordinary sight. The arboreal, eucalyptus-chewing **koalas** and tubby,

---

ANCIENT AUSTRALIAN WILDLIFE

Australia has a **fossil record** that makes up in range what it lacks in quantity. Imprints of invertebrates from South Australia's **Ediacaran fauna**, dated to over 600 million years ago, are the oldest evidence of animal life in the world. On a larger scale, footprints and remains of several **dinosaur** species have been uncovered, and **opalized marine fossils** are unique to the country. Perhaps most intriguing is evidence of the **megafauna** – giant wildlife that included the 20m-long constricting snake montypythonoides, flightless birds bigger than an ostrich, a rhino-sized wombat, carnivorous kangaroos, and thylacoleo, a marsupial lion – which flourished until about thirty thousand years ago, overlapping with Aboriginal occupation. Climatic changes were probably responsible for their demise, but humans wiped out the **thylacine**, a dog-like marsupial with an oversized head, which vanished from the mainland after the introduction of dingoes, but survived in Tasmania until 1936 – the year it received government protection.

NATIONAL PARKS

Nearly ten percent of Australia's great outdoors is protected within national parks, many of them – such as **Kakadu** (NT), a vast area of natural beauty and Aboriginal rock art dating back tens of thousands of years – significant enough to be listed as World Heritage Sites. Another is the **Tasmanian wilderness**, at a fifth of the state's total area one of the largest conservation reserves in Australia; its 80km **Overland Track** from Cradle Mountain to Lake St Clair is one of the world's great walks – a challenging five or six days but worth it for the spectacular scenery every step of the way. Other equally spectacular parks include **Karajini** (WA), astonishing for its wild flowers, gorges and red dust, and the **Flinders Ranges** (SA), 300km north of Adelaide, renowned for the great kilometre-high natural bowl of **Wilpena Pound** and as the start of the **Heysen Trail**, a punishing 1200km walk. There are less visited, but equally rewarding, national parks too, such as **Mutawintji**, 130km northeast of Broken Hill in New South Wales, with secluded gorges, quiet waterholes and ancient galleries of Aboriginal rock art to be discovered in the caves and overhangs.

ground-dwelling **wombats** are smaller, less active and more sensitive to disturbance; this has made them more elusive, and has placed them on the endangered list as their habitat is cleared. Carnivorous marsupials are mostly shrew-sized today (though a lion equivalent probably survived into Aboriginal times, and fossils of meat-eating kangaroos have been found); two of the largest are spotted native cats or **quolls**, and Tasmania's indigenous **Tasmanian devil**, a terrier-sized scavenger. These creatures are currently suffering severe health problems (see p.919).

Platypuses and echidnas are the only **monotremes**, egg-laying mammals that suckle their young through specialized pores. Once considered a stage in the evolution of placental mammals, they're now recognized as a specialized branch of the family. Neither is particularly rare, but being nocturnal, shy and, in the case of the platypus, aquatic, makes them difficult to find. Ant-eating **echidnas** resemble a long-nosed, thick-spined hedgehog or small porcupine, and are found countrywide. **Platypuses** are confined to the eastern ranges and look like a blend of duck and otter, having a grey, rubbery bill, webbed feet, short fur, and a poison spur on males, a combination that seemed too implausible to nineteenth-century biologists, who initially denounced stuffed specimens as a hoax, assembled from pieces of other animals.

Introduced fauna

Of the **introduced mammals**, **dingoes** are descended from dogs, introduced to Australia by Aboriginal people in the last twelve thousand years – although there is some merit to the claim that they were introduced from Asia around 3500 to 4000 years ago. To keep them away from flocks, graziers built "vermin fences", which were connected by the Australian government to form a 5400km-long, continuous fence, allegedly the world's longest. The **Dingo Fence** stretches from South Australia into northwest Queensland and down to New South Wales. **Camels** have also become acclimatized to Australia since their introduction in the 1840s; they are doing so well in the central deserts that they are considered a pest. Australia is the only place where dromedaries still occur in the wild, and they are regularly exported to the Middle East. The blight that **hoofed mammals** – horses, cows, sheep and goats – have perpetrated on Australia's fragile fauna is horrendous. The damage caused by **rabbits** is equally pervasive, especially in the semi-desert areas where their cyclic population explosions can strip every shred of plant life from fragile dune systems.

Feral **cats**, which hunt for sport as well as necessity, are currently one of the greatest threats to indigenous fauna, primarily small marsupials and birds. An introduced amphibian, however, has turned out to be the most insidious and rapacious invader of all: the highly toxic **cane toad** (see opposite).

Reptiles, birds, bats and marine life

Australian **reptiles** come in all shapes and sizes. In the tropical parts of the country, the pale lizards you see wriggling across the ceiling on Velcro-like pads are **geckos**, and you'll find fatter, sluggish **skinks** – such as the stumpy blue-tongued lizard – everywhere. Other widespread species are **frill-necked lizards**, known for fanning out their necks and running on their hind legs when frightened, and the ubiquitous **goanna** family, which includes the monstrous perentie, third-largest lizard in the world. In central Australia, look out for the extraordinary **thorny devil** or moloch, an animal that seems part rock, part rosebush.

Crocodiles are confined to the tropics and come in two types. The shy, inoffensive **freshwater crocodile** grows to around 3m in length and feeds on fish and frogs. The larger, bulkier, and misleadingly named saltwater or **estuarine crocodile** can grow to 7m, ranges far inland (often in freshwater), and is the only Australian animal that constitutes an active threat to humans. Highly evolved predators, they should be given a very wide berth (see box, p.510). Despite their bad press, **snakes** are generally timid and pose far less of a problem, even though Australia has everything from constricting pythons through to three-quarters of the world's most venomous species.

With a climate that extends from temperate zones well into the tropics, Australia's **birdlife** is prolific and varied. Small **penguins** and **albatrosses** live along the south coast, while **riflebirds**, related to New Guinea's birds of paradise, and the **cassowary**, a colourful version of the ostrich, live in the tropical rainforests. The drabber **emu** prefers drier plains further west. Among the birds of prey, the countrywide **wedge-tail eagle** and the coastal **white-bellied sea eagle** are most impressive in their size. Both share their environment with the stately grey **brolga**, an Australian crane, and the even larger **jabiru stork**, with its chisel beak and pied plumage. **Parrots**, arguably the country's most spectacular birds, come in over forty varieties, and no matter if they're flocks of green budgerigars, outrageously coloured rainbow lorikeets, or white sulphur-crested cockatoos, they'll deafen you with their noisy song. Equally raucous are **kookaburras**, giant kingfishers found near permanent water. The quieter **tawny frogmouth**, an incredibly camouflaged cousin of the nightjar, has one of the most disgruntled expressions ever seen on a bird.

Huge colonies of **bats**, of orange, ghost and horseshoe varieties, congregate in caves and fill entire trees all over Australia. The **fruit bat**, or flying fox, is especially common in the tropics, where evenings can be spent watching colonies of the 1m-winged monsters heading out from their daytime roosts on feeding expeditions.

In addition to what you'll see on the Barrier Reef (covered in the Coastal Queensland chapter), **whales**, **turtles**, **dolphins**, **seals** and **dugongs** (sea cows) are part of the country's marine life, with humpback and southern right whales making a welcome return to the coasts in recent decades after being hunted close to extinction.

CANE TOADS

The most insidious of all Australia's invasive species has been the **cane toad**, imported from Latin America in the 1930s in a failed attempt to control cane beetle in the sugar-cane fields of north Queensland. Unfortunately, the toads turned out to be huge pests themselves. With no natural predators to halt their progress, they have waddled down the east coast to the north coast of New South Wales and across the top of the continent to the flood plains of the Top End, including Kakadu National Park. They are a disaster for native fauna – being highly toxic, the amphibians can kill anything that eats them. More positively, crows and magpies have developed the skill of flipping the toads onto their backs to devour the nonpoisonous intestines, great evidence of evolution in action. If the skill extends to other types of meat-eating bird, predation may at last keep the pesky cane toad at bay.

Flora

Australia's most distinctive and widespread **trees** are those that developed a **dependence on fire**. Some, like the seemingly limitless varieties of **eucalypt** or gum tree, need extreme heat to burst open button-shaped pods and release their seeds, and encourage fires by annually shedding bark and leaves, depositing a thick layer of tinder on the forest floor. Other shrubs with similar habits are **banksia**, **grevillia** and **bottlebrush**, with its distinctive bushy flowers and spiky seedpods, while those prehistoric survivors, palm-like **cycads** and **grass trees**, similarly depend on regular conflagrations to promote new growth. For thousands of years, Aborigines used controlled burn-offs to make the land more suitable for hunting, thereby possibly enhancing these fire-reliant traits.

Despite the country having extensive arid regions, there is no native equivalent to the cactus, although the dry, spiky **spinifex** or porcupine grass, the succulent **samphire** with its curiously jointed stem, and the aptly named **saltbush** come closest in their ability to survive extreme temperatures. After rain, smaller desert plants rush to bloom and seed, covering the ground in a spectacular blanket of colour, a phenomenon for which Australia's Outback regions are well known.

On a larger scale, the Outback is dotted with stands of hardy **mulgas** and **wattles**, which superficially resemble scrawny eucalypts but have different leaf structures, as well as scattered groups of bloated, spindly branched **bottle trees**, whose sweet, pulpy and moisture-laden cores can be used as emergency stock feed in drought conditions. The similar but far larger **boab**, found in the Kimberley and the northern part of the Northern Territory, is thought to be an invader from East Africa. **Mallee scrub** is unique to the southeastern Outback, where clearing of these tangled, bush-sized eucalypts for grazing has endangered both scrub and those animals that rely on it – the mound-building **mallee fowl** being the best known.

Mangrove swamps, found along the tropical and subtropical coasts, are tidal zones of thick grey mud and mangrove trees, whose interlocked aerial roots make an effective barrier to exploration. They've suffered extensive clearing for development, and it wasn't until recently that their importance to the estuarine life cycle won them limited government protection. Aboriginal people have always found them a rich source of animal and plant products.

Rainforest once covered much of the continent, but today only a small portion of its former abundance survives. Nevertheless, you'll find pockets everywhere, from Tasmania's richly verdant wilderness to the monsoonal examples of northern Queensland and the Top End in the Northern Territory. Trees grow to gigantic heights, as they compete with each other for light, supporting themselves in the poor soil with aerial or buttressed roots. The extraordinary **banyan** and **Moreton Bay fig** trees are fine examples of the two types. They support a huge number of plant species, with tangled **vines** in the lower reaches, and **orchids**, **elkhorns** and other epiphytes using larger plants as roosts. **Palms** and **tree ferns**, with their giant, delicately curled fronds, are found in more open forest, where there's regular water.

Some forest types illustrate the extent of Australia's prehistoric flora. **Antarctic beech** or *Nothafagus*, found south of Brisbane as well as in South America, along with native pines and **kauri** from Queensland, which also occur in New Zealand, are all evidence of the prehistoric supercontinent, Gondwana. Other "living fossils" include primitive marine **stromatolites** – algae corals – still found around Shark Bay, Western Australia, and in fossilized form in the central deserts.

As long as you don't eat them or fall onto the pricklier versions, most Australian plants are harmless – though in rainforests you'd want to avoid entanglement with spiky **lawyer cane** or wait-awhile vine (though it doesn't look like it, this is a climbing palm). Also watch out for the large, pale-green, heart-shaped leaves of the **stinging tree**, a scraggly "regrowth" plant found on the margins of cleared tropical rainforest. Even a casual brush delivers an agonizing and prolonged sting; if you're planning on bushwalking in the tropics, learn to recognize and avoid this plant.

Australian film

Australia has had a connection to film since federation. It is generally agreed (with deference to a 1900 Salvation Army promo, *Stations of the Cross*) that *The Story of the Kelly Gang*, made by Charles Tait in 1906, was the world's first feature-length film. Later, with the many cinematic testaments to the heroic disaster of Gallipoli, Australian silent cinema reached a creative peak. Raymond Longford was Australia's Spielberg of silents at this time, and his 1919 production of *The Sentimental Bloke* and its sequel, *Ginger Mick*, a year later, were popular and notably naturalist dramas about a woman's taming of her larrikin husband's proclivities. The themes of distrust of sophistication and the mythic spell of "the bush" began to make its mark on Australian productions – one still evident in Baz Luhrmann's *Australia* in 2008.

HUMOUR, BLACK COMEDY AND SATIRE

The Adventures of Priscilla, Queen of the Desert (Stephan Elliott, 1994). A queer romp across the Outback, prying into some musty corners of Australian social life along the way.

Babakiueria (Julian Pringler, 1988). A culture-reversing short-film spoof with Aborigines invading Australia and continuing with an anthropological-style study of white Australia. Well worth the search.

The Castle (Rob Sitch, 1997). A family's struggle to defend their home in the face of a trinity of suburban horrors: toxic-waste dumps, overhead power lines and airport developers.

Death in Brunswick (John Ruane, 1990). A black comedy about the misfortunes of a hapless dishwasher who becomes embroiled in a gangland killing.

Malcolm (Nadia Tass, 1985). A charming, offbeat comedy about a slow-witted tram driver in Melbourne.

Muriel's Wedding (P.J. Hogan, 1994). Kleptomaniac frump Muriel wastes away in an Abba-and-confetti dreamworld until ex-schoolchum Rhonda masterminds Muriel's escape from her awful family and ghastly seaside suburb of "Porpoise Spit". Great performances.

ADOLESCENT AND MISFIT ROMANCE

Better Than Sex (Jonathan Teplitzky, 2000). In this romantic comedy, Josh has only three days left until he returns to London, so a one-night, after-party fling with Cin shouldn't hold any complications.

Flirting (John Duigan, 1989). This sequel to *The Year My*

Voice Broke follows a young boy's adventures in boarding school. Superior coming-of-age film.

Lonely Hearts (Paul Cox, 1981). Following the death of his mother, 50-year-old Peter buys a new toupee and joins a dating agency. A sensitive portrayal of the ensuing, at

---

OZ ON THE BOX

Australian TV has finally shrugged off the twee image bestowed by umpteen episodes of *Neighbours* and *Home and Away*. First came the sexy, sassy *Secret Life of Us* (2001–05) set in Melbourne's St Kilda, then critically acclaimed *Love My Way* (2004–07), dealing with the emotional entanglements of 30-something Sydneyites. *Underbelly* (2007) was a gritty crime series covering real-life gangland killings on the dark side of Melbourne, seemingly a million miles from the wobbly furnishings and emotional blandness of *Neighbours*. And the 2011 TV adaption of *The Slap* (see p.997) was a pitch-perfect dive into the seamier side of the Melbourne suburbs, albeit with the main focus on sex rather than crime.

One of the most interesting developments in Australian TV though, is the seven-part series **First Australians** (2008). Drawing inspiration from individual stories, from Bennelong, taken to England in 1792, to land-rights campaigner Eddie Mabo, it covers the tragic history of relations between Australia's colonizers and its first people with thoughtfulness and subtlety.

times awkward, relationship. Other Paul Cox features include *Man of Flowers*, *My First Wife* and *Cactus*.

Looking for Alibrandi (Kate Woods, 2000). Light yet surprisingly layered story of a teenage Sydney girl dealing with suicide, high school, new love and immigrant cultural identity.

Love and Other Catastrophes (Emma-Kate Croghan, 1996). A youthful campus comedy with film-buff in-jokes and an energetic cast, set in and filmed at Melbourne Uni.

Mullet (David Caesar, 2001). A slow-motion plot set in a New South Wales south-coast fishing town where nothing happens until a mysterious prodigal son (Ben Mendelsohn) returns to mixed receptions from his family, former friends and fiancée.

Somersault (Cate Shortland, 2004). Having been caught kissing her mother's no-hoper boyfriend, 16-year-old Heidi (Abbie Cornish) runs away from home winding up in wintery Jindabyne in the snowfields of southern New South Wales. She tries to cobble together a new life there, but her strong sensuality, coupled with emotional fragility, gets her into new trouble. Fine acting and a great debut film.

Strictly Ballroom (Baz Luhrmann, 1991). Mismatched dancers who, together, dare to defy the prescribed routines of a ballroom dancing competition – all its frozen smiles and gaudy gown glory. A feel-good hit and the first feature from the successful director of *Moulin Rouge* (2001).

URBAN DYSFUNCTIONALS

Animal Kingdom (David Michôd, 2010). This much-praised and grim family drama about Melbourne's crime scene aims high, but is undermined by a blank central performance and a derivative script.

The Boys (Rowan Woods, 1998). This tense and powerful drama follows an ex-prisoner who terrorizes his dysfunctional family and coerces his unemployed brothers into a violent crime.

Careful, He Might Hear You (Carl Shultz, 1982). An absorbing tug-of-love drama set in 1930s Sydney with brilliant images by cinematographer John Seale.

Chopper (Andrew Dominik, 2000). Eric Bana brilliantly plays notorious criminal Mark "Chopper" Read, who ruthlessly dominates prison inmates and underworld associates alike. Based on Read's autobiography.

The Devil's Playground (Fred Schepisi, 1975). Burgeoning sexuality creates tension between pupils and their tutors in a Catholic seminary. A fine debut film.

Head On (Ana Kokkinos, 1998). Unemployed Ari (Alex Dimitriades) escapes living with his strict Greek parents by spending a hectic 24 hours nightclubbing, drug taking and graphically exploring his homosexuality.

Lantana (Ray Lawrence, 2001). Set in Sydney, this is a sometimes bleak but thought-provoking tale of trust and secrecy in marriage. Coincidences and consequences bind lives of strangers together in ways that are as twisting, tangled and tough as the Australian plant that provides the film's title. The strong cast includes Geoffrey Rush and Anthony LaPaglia.

The Last Days of Chez Nous (Gillian Armstrong, 1991). A middle-aged woman slowly loses her grip on her marriage and family.

Romper Stomper (Geoffrey Wright, 1991). A bleak account of the violent disintegration of a gang of Melbourne skin-heads, notable as Russell Crowe's big-screen debut.

Sweetie (Jane Campion, 1988). Part black comedy, part bleakly disturbing portrait of a bizarre suburban family.

OCKERDOM

The Adventures of Barry McKenzie (Bruce Beresford, 1972). Ultra-ocker comes to England to teach "pommie sheilas about real men". Ironically, Barry Humphries' satire got beer-spurting ovations from the very people he despised but set Beresford's career back a couple of years.

Australia (Baz Luhrmann, 2008). Hoity-toity English-woman Lady Sarah Ashley (Nicole Kidman) comes to Australia to find her pastoralist husband dead. Cue the independent cowboy (Hugh Jackman) and beautifully shot cattle drive. World War II, separation and melodrama follows. Whether you fall for director Baz Luhrmann's epic

or not, everyone fell under the spell of the Aboriginal character Nullah (newcomer Brandon Walters).

Crocodile Dundee (Peter Faiman, 1985). The acceptable side of genial ockerdom saw Paul Hogan sell Australian bush mystique to the mainstream and put Kakadu National Park firmly on the tourist agenda. Enjoyable once, but don't bother with the sequels.

Wake in Fright aka Outback (Ted Kotcheff, 1970). A horrifying gem in its uncut 114min version; a real *Deliverance* down under. A coast-bound teacher blows his fare in Outback Hicksville and his life slowly degenerates into a brutal, beer-sodden nightmare.

GRITTY AND DEFIANT WOMEN

The Babadook (Jennifer Kent, 2014). A widowed mother confronts the monster that preoccupies her son.

Celia (Ann Turner, 1988). A wonderful allegory that mixes a 1950s rabbit-eradication programme with a communist witch-hunt. Stubborn Celia is determined to keep her bunny.

Dance Me to My Song (Rolf de Heer, 1998). A unique and moving film written by and starring cerebral-palsy-sufferer Heather Rose as she is abused by her carer and falls in love.

The Getting of Wisdom (Bruce Beresford, 1977). Spirited Laura rejects the polite sensibilities and snobbery of an Edwardian boarding school.

Holy Smoke (Jane Campion, 1999). An unlikely but enjoyable desert encounter between Kate Winslet, at her bravura best as a member of an Indian cult, and grizzled Harvey Keitel, the "cult-exiter" sent by her family to bring her back to her senses.

My Brilliant Career (Gillian Armstrong, 1978). An early feminist questions and defies the expectations of 1890s Victoria.

Puberty Blues (Bruce Beresford, 1981). Two teenage beach girls refuse to accept their pushchair-and-shopping-trolley destiny.

Shame (Steve Jodrell, 1988). A woman lawyer on an Outback motorcycle trip breaks down in a small town and becomes embroiled in the town's secrets.

We of the Never Never (Igor Auzins, 1981). A good-looking version of Jeannie Gunn's autobiographical classic of early twentieth-century station life in the Top End.

MEN IN RUGGED CIRCUMSTANCES

Comrades (Bill Douglas, 1986). The second half of masterful, magical *Comrades* sees the Tolpuddle Martyrs exiled to Australia, a land of surreal, sometimes brutal, encounters and epic beauty.

The Dish (Rob Sitch, 2000). Light-hearted take on how Australia saved NASA during the broadcasting of the 1969 Apollo 11 moon landing from New South Wales' Parkes Space Observatory, and an aside on how the country's technological skills are often overlooked. Starring Sam Neill.

Gallipoli (Peter Weir, 1980). A deservedly classic buddy movie in which a young Mel Gibson strikingly evokes the Anzacs' cheery idealism and the tragedy of their slaughter.

The Man from Snowy River (George Miller, 1981). Men, horses and the land from A.B. ("Banjo") Paterson's seminal and dearly loved poem caught the overseas' imagination. A modern kangaroo western.

Plains of Heaven (Ian Pringle, 1982). A spookily atmospheric story of two weathermen in a remote meteorological station slowly losing their minds.

Sunday Too Far Away (Ken Hannam, 1973). A simple tale of macho shearers' rivalries in Outback South Australia, with a charismatic performance by a youthful, bottom-baring Jack Thompson.

THE OUTBACK

Cunnamulla (Dennis O'Rourke, 2000). Controversial and powerful documentary of malaise in Cunnamulla, an isolated Outback town, 800km west of Brisbane, featuring inhabitants' own stories of teen sex and hopelessness, frontier redneckery, racial tension, social dysfunction, and desperate longings for escape to distant cities.

Evil Angels (A Cry in the Dark) (Fred Schepisi, 1987). A dramatic retelling of the Azaria Chamberlain story; Ayers Rock (Uluru) and dingoes will never seem quite the same again. But it's Meryl Streep's atrocious Aussie accent and the line "the dingo's got my baby" that have become classics.

Picnic at Hanging Rock (Peter Weir, 1975). A richly layered tale about the disappearance of a party of schoolgirls and its traumatic aftermath.

The Proposition (John Hillcoat, 2005). Ray Winstone, Guy Pearce and Emily Watson in a Western-inspired tale of bloodshed and revenge, written by Nick Cave.

Razorback (Russell Mulcahy, 1984). Dark comedy exploiting urban paranoia of the Outback and featuring a remote township, a gigantic, psychotic wild pig, and some bloodthirsty nutters who run the local abattoir.

Red Dog (Kriv Stenders, 2011). True (and beautifully shot) story of the eponymous hound, immortalized by a statue in his home town. The dog, searching for his master, brings a mining town together.

Satellite Boy (Catriona McKenzie, 2012). Twelve-year-old Aboriginal Pete lives with his grandfather, Old Jagamarra, in an abandoned outdoor cinema. He walks to the city through epic Kimberley landscapes to try to save his home from developers, rediscovering lost bush skills en route.

Walkabout (Nicolas Roeg, 1971). Following their deranged father's suicide during a bush picnic, two children wander through the desert until an Aboriginal boy, David Gulpilil, guides them back to civilization.

Wolf Creek (Greg McLean, 2005). Three backpackers are stuck in the desert at nightfall, hundreds of kilometres from anywhere, when their car won't start. It appears help is at hand in the person of truck-driving Mick Taylor, but his aims are to never let them leave alive. Terrifying, and tasteless, considering the inspiration was the real backpacker murders of the 1990s.

ABORIGINAL AUSTRALIA

Bran Nue Day (Rachel Perkins, 2009). An eccentric 1950s-set musical about a young Aborigine escaping his Catholic school to return home – the weakest element is the music, the strongest the endearing cast.

The Chant of Jimmie Blacksmith (Fred Schepisi, 1977). Set in the 1800s, a mixed-race boy is forced onto the wrong side of the law. Based on the novel by Thomas

Keneally and powerfully directed.

Charlie's Country (Rolf de Heer, 2014): A man from a remote community in Arnhemland exposes the painful clash between white law and Indigenous people.

Dead Heart (Brian Brown, 1996). A long-overdue and regrettably overlooked thriller, set in an Aboriginal community near Alice Springs. Bravely gets its teeth into some juicy political and social issues.

The Fringe Dwellers (Bruce Beresford, 1985). An aspiring daughter persuades her family to move from the bush into a suburban white neighbourhood, with expected results.

Jedda, the Uncivilized (Charles Chauvel, 1955). An orphaned Aboriginal girl brought up by a "civilized" white family cannot resist her "tribal" urges when she is semi-voluntarily abducted by a black outlaw.

Manganinnie (John Honey, 1980). Set during the time of the "black drives" of 1830s Tasmania, a young Aboriginal girl gets separated from her family and meets a white girl in similar straits.

Rabbit-Proof Fence (Phillip Noyce, 2002). A moving film, with beautiful cinematography, set in 1930s Western Australia and based on a true "Stolen Generation" story. Three girls, daughters of absent white fathers and black mothers, are taken from their families according to the policy of the all-powerful Chief Protector of Aborigines to a settlement at Moore River, but manage to escape. The girls – Outback-cast unknowns giving emotive, natural performances – make their way over 2000km home following the fence, pursued by a tracker (David Gulpilil).

Samson and Deliliah (Warwick Thornton, 2009). An alternative, uncompromising romance about a petrol-sniffing Aboriginal kid in a tattered desert community.

Sapphires (Wayne Blair, 2012). A Sixties-set pic about four young Aboriginal girls who travel with their band *The Sapphires*, to sing for US troops in Vietnam.

Ten Canoes (Rolf de Heer, 2005). A goose-egg-hunting expedition in the Arafura Wetlands in Arnhem Land in tribal times: Dayindi (played by Jamie Gulpilil, son of David Gulpilil) fancies one of the wives of his older brothers – a threat to tribal law. To teach him a lesson, the older brother tells him a parable from the mythical past. The story weaves back and forth between the two timelines, with the Dreamtime events in colour, the goose-egg hunting in black and white. This beautifully photographed and humorously narrated film has a timeless appeal that transcends cultures, the result of close cooperation between de Heer, David Gulpilil and the Arnhem Land community of Ramingining.

The Tracker (Rolf de Heer, 2002). Set in 1922, this is something of a fable in an experimental form: "The Fanatic", a police officer who will stop at nothing, including cold-blooded massacre, leads "The Tracker" (David Gulpilil), "The Follower" (a young, green policeman) and "The Veteran", all in search of "The Accused", an indigenous man wanted for a white woman's murder. Violent massacre scenes are replaced by landscape paintings with a painful soundtrack, while songs (performed by Aboriginal musician Archie Roach) and narration convey the themes, creating a disturbing impression.

Yolngu Boy (Stephen Johnson, 2001). In Yolgnu country in Arnhem Land, Lorrpu, Milika and Bortj have always been an inseparable trio. But when adolescence hits, 15-year-old Bortj's petrol-sniffing rampages land him in jail; as Lorrpu and Milika become tribally initiated, Bortj finds himself outside his own culture and unable to become a man, and friendships and loyalties are tested. When the three embark on a (beautifully shot) 500km overland trek to Darwin, living off the land, distress gives way to joy ... until they hit the city.

PORTENTS OF DOOM

Cane Toads: an Unnatural History (Mark Lewis, 1988). An eccentric, original and amusing documentary about the violent feelings Queensland's venomous amphibians arouse and the real threat they may pose to Australia's ecology.

The Last Wave (Peter Weir, 1977). An eerie chiller about a lawyer defending an Aborigine accused of murder – and the powerful, elemental forces his people control.

Mad Max 2 (George Miller, 1981). The best of the trilogy, set in a near future, where loner Max protects an oil-producing community from fuel-starved crazies. Great machinery and stunts.

Tomorrow, When the War Began (Stuart Beattie, 2010). An action picture about teenagers banding together when their fictional town, Wirrawee, is invaded. Features some amazing Blue Mountains' locations.

Books

Australian writing came into its own in the 1890s, when a strong nationalistic movement produced writers such as Henry Lawson and the balladeer A.B. "Banjo" Paterson, who romanticized the bush and glorified the mateship ethos, while outstanding women writers, such as Miles Franklin and Barbara Baynton, gave a feminine slant to the bush tale and set the trend for strong female authorship. In the twentieth and twenty-first centuries, Australian novelists came to be recognized in the international arena: Patrick White was awarded a Nobel Prize in 1973, Peter Carey won the Booker Prize in 1988 and again in 2001, and Kate Grenville scored the 2001 Orange Prize for Fiction. The other great figure in contemporary Australian writing is Les Murray, whose poems are deep-rooted in rural Australia, but make joyous metaphysical leaps and bounds.

TRAVEL AND TRAVEL GUIDES

Peter Carey *30 Days in Sydney: a wildly distorted account*. Part of Bloomsbury Publishers' "The Writer and the City" project, where "some of the finest writers of our time reveal the secrets of a city they know best". Now based in New York, celebrated Australian writer Carey returns to his old stomping ground with the perspective only an expat can have, coupled with the ability of a great writer to vividly portray it.

Bruce Chatwin *The Songlines*. A semi-fictional account of an exploration into Aboriginal nomadism and mythology that turns out to be one of the more readable expositions of this complex subject, though often pretentious.

Sean Condon *Sean and David's Long Drive*. Australia's humorous answer to Kerouac's *On the Road*: Melbourne-based Condon and his friend David are fully fledged city dwellers when they set off on a tour around their own country, to come face to face with the dangers of crocs, tour guides and fellow travellers.

Robyn Davidson *Tracks*. A compelling account of a young woman's journey across the desert, accompanied only by four camels and a dog. Davidson manages to break out of the heroic-traveller mould to write with compassion and honesty of the people she meets and the doubts, dangers and loneliness she faces on her way. A classic of its kind.

Tony Horwitz *One for the Road*. Married to an Australian, Pulitzer Prize-winning American author Horwitz comes to live in Sydney, but pines for adventure and sets off to hitchhike through the Outback. Along the way he encounters colourful characters from Aborigines to jackeroos, and hard-drinking men in a multitude of bush pubs. A comical, perceptive account.

Howard Jacobson *In the Land of Oz*. Jacobson focuses his lucidly sarcastic observations on a round-Australia trip in the late 1980s that gets rather close to some home truths for most Australians' tastes.

Mark McCrum *No Worries*. Knowing nothing of the country except the usual clichés, McCrum arrives in 1990s Australia and makes his way around by plane, train, thumb and Greyhound, meeting a surprising cast of characters along the way. As he travels, the stereotypes give way to an insightful picture of modern Australia.

Ruth Park *Ruth Park's Sydney*. Prolific novelist Park's 1973 guide to the city has been fully revised and expanded. A perfect walking companion, full of personal insights, anecdotes and literary quotations.

Nicholas Shakespeare *In Tasmania*. During the seven years writing and researching a biography of Bruce Chatwin, British writer Shakespeare spent time in Australia following in his footsteps. Researching his family history, Shakespeare found living Tasmanian relatives. A brilliantly Chatwinesque book, where historical tales are woven with the writer's own experiences.

Alice Thomson *The Singing Line*. The great-great-granddaughter of Alice Todd, the woman after whom Alice Springs was named, retraces her ancestor's journey to central Australia. Nice change from the usual male-centric view of the early pioneers.

Mark Whittaker and Amy Willesee *The Road to Mount Buggery: a Journey through the Curiously Named Places of Australia*. Australia certainly has some unfortunate, banal and obscure place names, which Mark and Amy seek out on their journey, from Lake Disappointment to Cape Catastrophe. This entertaining, well-informed travelogue gives the fascinating stories behind the names.

AUTOBIOGRAPHY AND BIOGRAPHY

Julia Blackburn *Daisy Bates in the Desert.* For almost thirty years from 1913, Daisy Bates was Kabbarli, "the white-skinned grandmother", to the Aboriginal people with whom she lived in the desert. Blackburn's beautifully written biography interweaves fiction with fact to conjure up the life of one of Australia's most eccentric and misunderstood women.

Jill Ker Conway *The Road from Coorain.* Conway's childhood, on a drought-stricken Outback station during the 1940s, is movingly told, as is her battle to establish herself as a young historian in sexist, provincial 1950s Australia.

★**Robert Drewe** *The Shark Net.* Accomplished novelist and journalist, Drewe has written a transfixing memoir of his boyhood and youth in Perth, which segues into a literary true-crime story. Against a vividly drawn 1950s middle-class backdrop, Drewe shows how one man's random killing spree struck fear into the 'burbs of sunny, friendly and seemingly innocent Perth.

★**Albert Facey** *A Fortunate Life.* A hugely popular autobiography of a battler, tracing his progress from a bush orphanage to Gallipoli, through the Depression, another war and beyond.

Barry Hill *Broken Song: T.G.H. Strehlow and Aboriginal Possession.* As a child growing up on the Hermannsburg Mission in central Australia, Strehlow learnt the Aranda (Arrente) language. In 1932, the anthropologist began collecting Aranda songs, myths and tjurunga (sacred objects) for his book *Songs of Central Australia.* Resented by other anthropologists for his unique insight and access, Strehlow's was a fascinating career that ended in disgrace.

Eddie Mabo and Noel Loos *Edward Koiko Mabo: His Life and Struggle for Land Rights.* Mabo spent much of his life fighting for the autonomy of Torres Strait Islanders and in the process overthrew the concept of *terra nullius*, making his name a household word in Australia. Long interviews with the late black hero form the basis of this book and affectionately reveal the man behind the name.

David Malouf *12 Edmondstone Street.* An evocative autobiography-in-snatches of one of Australia's finest literary novelists, describing, in loving detail, the eponymous house in Brisbane where Malouf was born, life in the Tuscan village where he lives for part of each year, and his first visit to India.

Leah Purcell *Black Chicks Talking.* In an effort to overcome Aboriginal stereotypes, indigenous actor and writer Purcell gives insight into the lives of contemporary black women with this collection of lively, lengthy interviews, conducted with nine young females (all under 35).

Hazel Rowley *Christina Stead: a Biography.* Stead (1902–83) has been acclaimed as Australia's greatest novelist. After spending years in Paris, London and New York with her American husband, she returned to Australia in her old age.

SOCIETY AND CULTURE

Richard Baker *Land is Life: From Bush to Town – the Story of the Yanyuwa People.* The Yanyuwa people inhabited the Gulf of Carpentaria before the Europeans arrived, but most now live in the town of Borroloola. Historian Baker, assigned a "skin" in the Yanyuwa kinship system, gathered the people's oral history and produced this fascinating story told from the Yanyuwa point of view and time.

★**Geoffrey Blainey** *Triumph of the Nomads.* A fascinating account portraying Aboriginal people as masters and not victims of their environment by this controversial conservative historian.

Peter and Gibson Dunbar-Hall *Deadly Sounds Deadly Places.* Comprehensive guide to contemporary Aboriginal music in Australia, from Archie Roach to Yothu Yindi.

Monica Furlong *Flight of the Kingfisher: a Journey among Kukatja Aborigines.* Furlong lived among the Aboriginal people of the Great Sandy Desert; this is her account of Kukatja perceptions and spiritual beliefs.

Roslynn Haynes *Seeking the Centre: the Australian Desert in Literature, Art and Film.* The geographical and metaphorical impact of the desert on Australian culture is explored in this illustrated book, as is the connection Aboriginal people have with the desert.

David Headon *North of the Ten Commandments.* An anthology of Northern Territory writings from all perspectives and sources – an excellent literary souvenir for anyone who falls for the charms of Australia's "one percent" territory.

Donald Horne *The Lucky Country.* This seminal analysis of Australian society, written in 1976, has yet to be matched and is still often quoted.

HISTORY AND POLITICS

Robyn Annear *Nothing But Gold: the Diggers of 1852.* With an eye for interestingly obscure details and managing to convey a sense of irony without becoming cynical, this is a wonderfully readable account of the gold rushes of the nineteenth century, a period that perhaps did more than any other to shape the country's national character.

Len Beadell *Outback Highways.* Extracts from Len Beadell's half-dozen books, cheerfully recounting his life in the central Australian deserts as a surveyor, and his involvement in the construction of Woomera and the atomic bomb test sites.

★**John Birmingham** *Leviathan: the unauthorized biography of Sydney.* Birmingham's tome casts a contemporary eye over the dark side of Sydney's history, from nauseating accounts of Rocks' slum life and the 1900 plague outbreak, through the 1970s traumas of Vietnamese boat people (now Sydney residents) to scandals of police corruption.

John Marsden *The Rabbits*. This illustrated (by Shaun Tan) story about the British arriving in Australia is a great way to introduce both children and adults to the most important event in the continent's history.

Manning Clark *A Short History of Australia*. A condensed version of this leading historian's multi-volume tome, focusing on dreary successions of political administrations, and cynically concluding with the "Age of Ruins".

Inga Clendinnen *Dancing With Strangers*. Empathetic, almost poetically written account imagining the interaction of the British and the Aborigines (whom Clendinnen calls "Australians") in the five years after the arrival of the First Fleet.

Ann Curthoys *Freedom Ride: A Freedom Rider Remembers*. History professor Curthoys was one of the busload of young, idealistic, white university students who accompanied Aboriginal activist Charles Perkins (only 29 himself) on his revolutionary trip through northern New South Wales in 1965 to look at Aboriginal living conditions and root out and protest against racial discrimination.

David Day *Claiming a Continent: a New History of Australia*. Award-winning, general and easily readable history, concluding in 2000. The possession, dispossession and ownership of the land – and thus issues of race – are central to Day's narrative.

Colin Dyer *The French Explorers and the Aboriginal Australians*. From Bruny d'Entrecasteaux's (1793) to Nicolas Baudin's (1802) expeditions, the French explorers and onboard scientists kept detailed journals that provide a wealth of information on Aboriginal Australians, particularly those of Tasmania who d'Entrecasteaux noted "seem to offer the most perfect image of pristine society".

Bruce Elder *Blood on the Wattle: Massacres and Maltreatment of Aboriginal Australians Since 1788*. A heart-rending account of the horrors inflicted on the continent's indigenous peoples, covering infamous nineteenth-century massacres as well as more recent mid-twentieth-century scandals of the "Stolen Generation" children.

Tim Flannery (ed) *Watkin Trench 1788*. One of the most vivid accounts of early Sydney written by a 20-something captain of the marines, Watkin Trench, who arrived with the First Fleet. Trench's humanity and youthful curiosity shine through as he brings alive the characters who peopled the early settlement.

Robert Hughes *The Fatal Shore*. A minutely detailed epic of the origins of transportation and the brutal beginnings of white Australia.

Dianne Johnson *Lighting the Way: Reconciliation Stories*. Twenty-four very personal stories, written in a simple, engaging style, show Aboriginal and non-Aboriginal Australians working with each other, from community artworks to political activism. Positive and inspiring.

Mark McKenna *Looking for Blackfellas Point: an Australian History of Place*. This prize-winning book uncovers the uneasy history of Aborigines and European settlers on the far south coast of New South Wales and widens its scope to the enduring meaning of land to both Aboriginal and white Australians.

Alan Moorehead *Cooper's Creek*. A historian's dramatic retelling of the ill-fated Burke and Wills expedition that set out in 1860 to make the first south-to-north crossing of the continent. A classic story of exploration.

★**Sarah Murgatroyd** *The Dig Tree: the Story of Burke and Wills*. Murgatroyd's recent retelling of the Burke and Wills story is gripping and immaculately researched – she journeyed along the route, and utilized the latest scientific and historical evidence, and the text is complemented by maps, photos and paintings.

Rosemary Neill *White Out: How Politics is Killing Black Australia*. Outspoken book which asserts that the rhetoric of self-determination and empowerment excuses the wider society from doing anything to reduce the disparity between black and white Australian populations.

Cassandra Pybus *Community of Thieves*. Attempting to reconcile past and future, fourth-generation Tasmanian Pybus provides a deeply felt account of the near-annihilation of the island's Aboriginal people.

Henry Reynolds *The Other Side of the Frontier* and *The Law of the Land*. A revisionist historian demonstrates that Aboriginal resistance to colonial invasion was both considerable and organized. *The Whispering in Our Hearts* is a history of those settler Australians who, troubled by the treatment of Aboriginal people, spoke out and took political action. *Why Weren't We Told?* is his most personal, an autobiographical journey showing how he, like many generations of Australians, imbibed a distorted, idealized Australian history; it includes a moving story about his friendship with Eddie Mabo.

Portia Robinson *The Women of Botany Bay*. The result of painstaking research into the records of every female transported from Britain and Ireland between 1787 and 1828, Robinson tells with conviction and passion who these women really were.

Eric Rolls *Sojourners and Citizens* and *Flowers and the Wide Sea*. The first and second volumes of farmer-turned-historian Rolls' fascinatingly detailed history of the Chinese in Australia.

Anne Summers *Damned Whores and God's Police*. Stereotypical images of women in Australian society are explored in this ground-breaking reappraisal of Australian history from a feminist point of view.

ECOLOGY AND ENVIRONMENT

Col Bailey *Shadow of the Thylacine*. The author goes in search of the Tasmanian tiger, in an attempt to prove that the spectacularly striped and shy animal has survived its presumed extinction. A social history, as well as an ecological quest.

★**Tim Flannery** *The Future Eaters*. Paleontologist and environmental commentator Flannery poses that, as the first human beings migrated down to Australasia, the Aborigines, Maoris and other Polynesian peoples changed the region's flora and fauna in startling ways, and began consuming the resources needed for their own future.

Tim Flannery *Chasing Kangaroos: A Continent, a Scientist, and a Search for the World's Most Extraordinary Creature*. In another great piece of scientific journalism, Flannery painstakingly traces the history of Australia's hopping herbivore.

Josephine Flood *The Riches of Ancient Australia*. An indispensable and lavish guide to Australia's most famous landforms and sites. The same author's *Archaeology of the Dreamtime* provides background on the development of Aboriginal society.

Drew Hutton and Libby Connors *A History of the Australian Environmental Movement*. Written by a husband-and-wife team, Queensland academics and prominent in Green politics, this well-balanced book charts the progress of conservation attempts from 1860 to modern protests.

Peter Latz *Bushfires and Bushtucker: Aboriginal Plant Use in Central Australia*. Handbook with photos, published by an Aboriginal-owned press.

Ann Moyal *Platypus: the Extraordinary Story of How a Curious Creature Baffled the World*. When British and French naturalists were first introduced to the platypus, they were flummoxed: was it bird, reptile or mammal? And did it really lay eggs? Moyal, a science historian, provides a captivating look at the platypus – and Australian nature – through European eyes.

Tim Murray (ed) *Archeology of Australia*. The last thirty-odd years have seen many ground-breaking discoveries in Australian archeology, with three sites in particular of great significance: Kakadu in the Northern Territory, Lake Mungo in New South Wales, and South West Tasmania. A range of specialists contribute essays on the subject.

Mary White *The Greening of Gondwana*. Classic work on the evolution of Australia's flora and geography.

James Woodford *The Wollemi Pine: the Incredible Discovery of a Living Fossil from the Age of the Dinosaurs*. The award-winning environment writer at the *Sydney Morning Herald* tells the story of the 1994 discovery in Wollemi wilderness near Sydney. *The Secret Life of Wombats* begins as a fascinating account of the "wombat boy", a schoolboy so curious to find out about how wombats lived that he crawled into their burrows. In *The Dog Fence: a Journey through the Heart of the Continent* Woodford travels the 5400km length of the fence built to keep livestock safe from dingoes.

CONTEMPORARY FICTION

Thea Astley *The Multiple Effects of Rainshadow*. On an Aboriginal island reserve in 1930, a white woman dies in childbirth, and her husband goes on a shotgun-and-dynamite rampage. The novel traces the effects over the years on eight characters who witnessed the violent events, ultimately exploring the brutality and racism in Australian life.

Murray Bail *Eucalyptus*. Beautifully written novel with a fairytale-like plot. New South Wales farmer, Holland, has planted nearly every type of eucalyptus tree on his land. When his extraordinarily beautiful daughter Ellen is old enough to marry, he sets up a challenge for her legion of potential suitors, to name each tree.

John Birmingham *He Died with a Felafel in His Hand*. A collection of squalid and very funny tales emerging from the once-dissolute author's experience of flat-sharing hell in Brisbane.

Anson Cameron *Tin Toys*. The Aboriginal "Stolen Generation" issue explored through the tale of Hunter Carolyn, an unintentional artist who can change skin colour at will.

★**Peter Carey** *The True History of the Kelly Gang*. Carey's masterpiece: the brilliantly imagined tale of outlaw Ned Kelly revels in the antihero's mythic undertakings and salty language.

Steven Carroll *The Time We Have Taken*. The last book of a trilogy about a family living in suburban Melbourne from the 1950s through to the 1970s is a celebration of the minutiae of suburban life and won the 2008 Miles Franklin Literary Award.

Robert Drewe *The Savage Crows*. A writer whose own life is falling apart in a cockroach-ridden Sydney of the 1970s sets out to discover the grim truth behind Tasmania's "final solution".

Richard Flanagan *Death of a River Guide*. Narrator, environmentalist Aljaz Cosini, goes over his life and that of his family and forebears as he lies drowning in the Franklin River. Thoughtful writings about Tasmanian landscape, place, migration and the significance of history are the hallmark of Flanagan's novels. His nineteenth-century-set *Gould's Book of Fish: a Novel in Twelve Fish* delves into Tasmania's past as the brutal penal settlement of Van Diemen's Land. Flanagan's 2014 Booker-winning *The Narrow Road to Deep North* centres around the building of the Thai Burma railroad during World War II.

Tom Gilling *Miles McGinty*. Nineteenth-century Sydney comes alive in this riotous, entertaining love story of Miles, who becomes a levitator's assistant and begins to float on air, and Isabel, who wants to fly.

Peter Goldsworthy *Three Dog Night*. It takes three dogs to keep a person warm on a desert night, an allusion to the love triangle that emerges when psychiatrist Martin Blackman returns to Adelaide after a decade in London with his new, much-loved wife, and visits his oldest friend, the difficult Felix, a once-brilliant surgeon dying of terminal cancer. Felix is an initiated man who has lived with Aborigines in the central Australian desert; when Lucy accompanies him there, Martin must confront his insecurities.

Kate Grenville *The Idea of Perfection*, set in the tiny, fictional New South Wales town of Karakarook, and about two unlikely characters who fall in love, won the 2001 Orange Prize for Fiction. *The Secret River* was shortlisted for the Man Booker Prize in 2006 and won the Commonwealth Writers Prize. This historical novel explores the uneasy terrain of early white contact with Aborigines, telling the story of freed convict William Thornhill taking up land in the Hawkesbury with his family.

Chloe Hooper *A Child's Book of True Crime*. With a claustrophobic Tasmanian setting, this perverse, chilling novel is narrated by a young primary-school teacher having an affair with the married father of her smartest pupil. His writer-wife's true-crime book, about a love triangle that disintegrates into murder, leads the anxious teacher into imagining a child's-classic-Australian-literature-style version, with characters such as Kitty Koala and Wally Wombat.

Douglas Kennedy *The Dead Heart*. A best-selling comic thriller made into a film; an itinerant American journalist gets abducted by man-eating hillbillies in Outback Australia.

Michelle de Kretser *The Lost Dog*. This contemporary Australian love story and intriguing mystery is a layered work with sparkling writing and wonderful observations. It won the 2008 New South Wales Premier's Literary Awards' book of the year and the prize for best fiction.

Julia Leigh *The Hunter*. Intriguing, internationally acclaimed first novel about the rediscovery and subsequent hunt of the Tasmanian tiger; a faceless biotech company after thylacine DNA plays the bad guy.

David Malouf *The Conversations at Curlow Creek*. One of Australia's most important contemporary writers charts the developing relationship between two Irishmen the night before a hanging; one is the officer appointed to supervise the execution and the other the outlaw facing his death. *Remembering Babylon* is the moving story of a British cabin boy in the 1840s who, cast ashore, lives for sixteen years among the Aboriginal people of far north Queensland, and finally re-enters the British colonial world.

Andrew McGahan *The White Earth*. A haunting novel set in 1992 in Queensland's Darling Downs wheatfields as the Mabo land-rights case fills the news. After the death of his father, 8-year-old William and his unstable mother are invited to live on his ageing uncle's Kuran station. In order to prove himself worthy of his uncle's inheritance of the property, William is drawn into his uncle's dark world and association with the racist White League. Questions of Aboriginal dispossession and white belonging reverberate. The polemical tone of *Underground* (2006), a dystopian novel with a somewhat far-fetched plotline, set in a not too distant future in totalitarian Australia, invoked the ire of neo-conservative reviewers.

Alex Miller *Journey to the Stone Country*. A betrayed wife leaves her middle-class Melbourne existence and returns to tropical North Queensland, setting out on a journey with a childhood Aboriginal acquaintance into the stone country that is his tribe's remote heartland. However, dark secrets from the lives of their grandparents threaten what future they may have together. *Lovesong* the author's latest (and highly recommended) novel.

Elliot Perlman *Seven Types of Ambiguity*. The chain of events, secrets and lies stretching back a decade that lead to Simon Heywood kidnapping his ex-girlfriend's son are related by seven different narrators. Probing middle-class anxiety in a consumeristic, market-driven society, Perlman's conscience-driven writing can be moralistic at times, but at its best is clever and insightful, providing an intense social portrait of contemporary Melbourne.

Peter Temple *Truth*. A dark crime novel, set against the background of Victorian forest fires: the protagonist is flawed and troubled cop Stephen Villani.

Janette Turner Hospital *Oyster*. Disquieting novel set in the literally off-the-map, opal-mining, one-pub Queensland town of Inner Maroo, whose inhabitants are either rough-as-guts mining people, or religious fundamentalists. Her latest, *Orpheus Lost*, is also wonderful.

Christos Tsiolkas *The Slap*. A big brassy bestseller, memorable not so much for its examination of the morality of slapping a child – the novel's central event – but for a riveting exploration of sex, boredom and bitchiness in the Melbourne suburbs.

★**Tim Winton** *Cloudstreet*. A wonderful, faintly magical saga about the mixed fortunes of two families who end up sharing a house in postwar Perth. *Breath* is based in a small coastal community where two young boys learn to surf from an ageing thrill-seeker and learn plenty of life lessons along the way. Winton captures the spirit both of the time (early 1970s) and of surfing and the lure of the ocean – not an easy task.

Danielle Wood *The Alphabet of Light and Dark*. Set evocatively on Bruny Island, in melancholy Tasmanian-Gothic vein. Like the main character Essie, Wood's great-great-grandfather was superintendent of the Cape Bruny Lighthouse. Essie returns from Western Australia to the lighthouse after her grandfather's death to write her family history and becomes immersed in her ancestors' tragedies.

AUSTRALIAN CLASSICS

Barbara Baynton *Bush Studies*. A collection of nineteenth-century bush stories written from the female perspective.

Rolf Boldrewood *Robbery Under Arms*. The story of Captain Starlight, a notorious bushranger and rustler around the Queensland borders.

Marcus Clarke *For the Term of His Natural Life*. Written in 1870 in somewhat overblown prose, this romantic tragedy is based on actual events in Tasmania's once-notorious prison settlement.

Bryce Courtenay *Jessica*. Though this is not Courtenay's best-known work (that would be *The Power of One*), this heartbreaking story based on a true tale of murder and passion grips from the very beginning.

Miles Franklin *My Brilliant Career*. Written by one of Australia's foremost writers, this semi-autobiographical novel is about a spirited young girl in early twentieth-century Victoria who refuses to conform.

May Gibbs *Snugglepot and Cuddlepie*. A timeless children's favourite: the illustrated adventures of two little creatures who live inside gumnuts.

Xavier Herbert *Capricornia*. An indignant and allegorical saga of the brutal and haphazard settlement of the land of Capricornia (tropical Northern Territory thinly disguised).

George Johnston *My Brother Jack*. The first in a disturbing trilogy set in Melbourne suburbia between the wars, which develops into a semi-fictional attempt to dissipate the guilt Johnston felt at being disillusioned with, and finally leaving, his native land.

Thomas Keneally *The Chant of Jimmie Blacksmith*. A prize-winning novel that delves deep into the psyche of an Aboriginal outlaw, tracing his inexorable descent into murder and crime. Sickening, brutal and compelling.

Henry Lawson Ballads, poems and stories from Australia's best-loved chronicler come in a wide array of collections. A few to seek out are: *Henry Lawson Bush Ballads*, *Henry Lawson Favourites* and *While the Billy Boils – Poetry*.

Norman Lindsay *The Magic Pudding*. A whimsical tale of some very strange men and their grumpy, flavour-changing and endless pudding; a children's classic with

very adult humour.

Ruth Park *The Harp in the South*. First published in 1948, this first book in a trilogy is a well-loved tale of inner-Sydney slum life in 1940s Surry Hills.

A.B. ("Banjo") Paterson Australia's most famous bush balladeer, author of *Waltzing Matilda* and *The Man from Snowy River*, who helped romanticize the bush's mystique. Some of the many titles published include *Banjo Paterson's Favourites* and *Man from Snowy River and Other Verses*.

Katharine Susannah Pritchard *Coonardoo*. This wonderful book celebrates Outback life but also reveals the abuse of Aboriginal women, in particular, by white station owners. Pritchard was a founder of the Australian Communist Party.

Henry Handel Richardson *The Getting of Wisdom*. A gangly country girl's experience of a snobby boarding school in early twentieth-century Melbourne. Like Miles Franklin (see opposite), Richardson was female and wrote under a pseudonym.

★**Nevil Shute** *A Town Like Alice*. A wartime romance that tells of a woman's bravery, endurance and enterprise, both in the Malayan jungle and in the Australian Outback where she strives to create the town of the title.

Christina Stead *For Love Alone*. Set largely around Sydney Harbour, where the author grew up, this novel, set in the 1930s, follows the obsessive Teresa Hawkins, a poor but artistic girl from a large, unconventional family, who scrounges and saves in order to head for London and love.

Randolph Stow *The Merry-go-round in the Sea*. An endearing tale of a young boy growing up in rural Western Australia during World War II.

Kylie Tennant *Ride on Stranger*. First published in 1943, this is a humorous portrait of Sydney between the world wars, seen through the eyes of newcomer Shannon Hicks.

Patrick White *Voss*. This masterful and densely symbolic novel imagines the early settlement of Australia by whites, partly from an Aboriginal perspective.

ABORIGINAL WRITING

Faith Bandler *Welour, My Brother*. A novel by a well-known black activist describing a boy's early life in Queensland, and the tensions of a racially mixed community.

John Muk Muk Burke *Bridge of Triangles*. Powerful, landscape-driven images in this tale of a mixed-race child growing up unable to associate with either side of his heritage, but refusing to accept the downward spiral into despair and alcoholism adopted by those around him.

Evelyn Crawford *Over My Tracks*. Told to Chris Walsh,

this oral autobiography is the story of a formidable woman, from her 1930s childhood among the red sandhills of Yantabulla, through her Outback struggles as a mother of fourteen children, to her tireless work, late in life, with Aboriginal students, combating prejudice with education.

Nene Gare *The Fringe Dwellers*. A story of an Aboriginal family on the edge of town and society.

Ruby Langford *Don't Take Your Love to Town*. An autobiography demonstrating a black woman's courage and humour in the face of tragedy and poverty lived out in northern New South Wales and the inner city of Sydney.

Sally Morgan *My Place*. A widely acclaimed and best-selling account of a Western Australian woman's discovery of her black roots.

David Mowaljarlai and Jutta Malnic *Yorro Yorro*. Starry-eyed photographer Malnic's musings while recording sacred Wandjina sites in the west Kimberley and, more interestingly, Mowaljarlai's account of his upbringing and Ngarinyin tribal lore.

★**Mudrooroo** *Wildcat Falling*. The first novel to be published (in 1965) by an Aboriginal writer, under the name Colin Johnson, this is the story of a black teenage delinquent coming of age in the 1950s. *Doctor Wooreddy's Prescription for Enduring the Ending of the World* details the attempted annihilation of the Tasmanian Aborigines. Three of Mudrooroo's novels – *The Kwinkan* (1995), *The Undying* (1998) and *Underground* (1999) – are part of his magic-realist *Master of Ghost Dreaming* series.

Oodgeroo Noonuccal *My People*. A collection of verse by an established campaigning poet (previously known as Kath Walker).

Paddy Roe *Gularabulu*. Stories from the west Kimberley,

both traditional myths and tales of a much more recent origin.

Kim Scott *Benang*. Infuriated at reading the words of A.O. Neville, Protector of Aborigines in Western Australia in the 1930s, who planned to "breed out" Aborigines from Australia, author Scott wrote this powerful tale of Nyoongar history using Neville's own themes to overturn his elitist arguments.

Archie Weller *The Day of the Dog*. Weller's violent first novel, with its searing pace and forceful writing, came out in an angry burst after being released, at 23, from incarceration in Broome jail. The protagonist, in a similar situation, is pressured back into a criminal world by his Aboriginal peers and by police harassment. Weller's second novel, *Land of the Golden Clouds*, is an epic science-fiction fantasy, set 3000 years in the future, which portrays an Australia devastated by a nuclear holocaust and populated by warring tribes.

Alexis Wright *Carpentaria*. Childhood memories and stories that her Waanyi grandmother told her flowed into Wright's novel about the Gulf country – in title, subject and scope, reminiscent of Xavier Herbert's classic *Capricornia*, but from an Aboriginal point of view. Shortlisted for the Miles Franklin award in 2007.

SPECIALIST AND WILDLIFE GUIDES

Jack Absalom *Safe Outback Travel*. The bible for Outback driving and camping, full of sensible precautions and handy tips for preparation and repair.

John Chapman and Monica Chapman *Bushwalking in Australia*. The fourth edition of this bushwalking bible has detailed notes for 25 of the best bushwalks Australia-wide, accompanied by colour topographic maps and photographs. The authors also publish several other excellent walking guides, including the indispensable *South West Tasmania*.

David Clark *Big Things*. From the Big Banana to the Big Lobster, Clark provides a comprehensive guide to Australia's kitsch icons.

Catherine de Courcey and John Johnson *River Tracks: Exploring Australian Rivers*. A practical and up-to-date motoring guide to six river journeys, with lots of insider insight and history.

The Great Barrier Reef A lucid and lavishly illustrated *Reader's Digest* rundown on the Reef. Available both in coffee-table format and in a more portable, edited edition.

James Halliday *Australian Wine Companion*. Released every year, the venerable Halliday provides not only an authoritative guide to the best wines but to the hundreds of wineries themselves, making it a great companion when visiting any of Australia's wine regions.

David Hampshire *Living and Working in Australia: A Survival Handbook*. Given that so many people come to

Australia and don't want to leave, this is a handy book with information from everything from that pesky tax file number to negotiating permits and visa applications.

Tim Low *Bush Tucker: Australia's Wild Food Harvest* and *Wild Food Plants of Australia*. Guides to the bountiful supply of bushtucker that was once the mainstay of the Aboriginal diet; the latter is pocket-sized and contains clear photographs of over 180 plants, describing their uses.

Greg Pritchard *Climbing Australia: the Essential Guide*. Comprehensive guide for rock-climbers, covering everything from the major climbing sites to the best websites.

Peter and Pat Slater *Field Guide to Australian Birds*. Pocket-sized, and the easiest to use of the many available guides to Australian birds.

Nick Stock *The Penguin Good Australian Wine Guide*. Released every year in Australia, this is a handy book for a wine buff to buy on the ground, with the best wines and prices detailed.

Tyrone T. Thomas Regional bushwalking guides by local publisher Michelle Anderson Publishing. A series of ten local guides, from *50 Walks in North Queensland* to *120 Walks in Tasmania*, which make excellent trail companions.

Mark Warren *Atlas of Australian Surfing*. A comprehensive guide to riding the best of Australia's waves by this surfing "hall of fame" recipient. Includes plenty of tips, but omits a few "secret spots".

Australian English

The colourful variant of Australian English, or Strine, has its origins in the archaic cockney and Irish of the colony's early convicts as well as the adoption of words from the many Aboriginal languages. For such a vast country, the accent barely varies to the untutored ear; from Tasmania ("Tassie") to the northwest you'll find little variation in the national drawl, with a curious, interrogative ending to sentences fairly common – although Queenslanders are noted for their slow delivery. One of the most consistent tendencies of *strine* is to abbreviate words and then stick an "-o" or, more commonly, an "-ie" on the end: as in "bring your cozzie to the barbie this arvo". This informality extends to the frequent use of "bloody", "bugger" and "bastard", all used affectionately. There's also an endearing tendency to genderize inanimate objects as, for example, "she's buggered, mate" ("your inanimate object is beyond repair").

The country has its own excellent *Macquarie Dictionary*, the latest edition of which is the ultimate authority on the current state of Australian English. Also worth consulting are *The Dinkum Dictionary: The Origins of Australian Words* by Susan Butler, and *Word Map* by Kel Richards, a dictionary of Australian regionalisms.

Akubra Wide-brimmed felt hat; a brand name.

Anzac Australia and New Zealand Army Corps; every town has a memorial to Anzac casualties from both world wars.

Arvo Afternoon.

Back o'Bourke Outback.

Banana bender Resident of Queensland.

Barbie Barbecue.

Battler Someone who struggles to make a living, as in "little Aussie battler".

Beaut! or **You beauty!** Exclamation of delight.

Beg yours? Excuse me, say again?

Beyond the Black Stump Outback; back of beyond.

Billabong Waterhole in dry river bed.

Billy Cooking pot.

Bitumen Sealed road as opposed to dirt road.

Blowies Blow flies.

Bludger Someone who does not pull their weight, or a scrounger – as in "dole bludger".

Blue Fight; also a red-haired person.

Blundstones Leather, elastic-sided workmen's boots, now also a fashion item in some circles. Often shortened to "blundies".

Bonzer Good; a good thing.

Bottle shop Off-licence or liquor store.

Brumby Feral horse.

Buckley's No chance; as in "Hasn't got a Buckley's".

Budgie smugglers Men's tight-fitting Speedos.

Bugs Moreton Bay bug – type of crayfish indigenous to southern Queensland.

Bunyip Monster of Aboriginal legend; bogeyman.

Burl Give it a go; as in "give it a burl".

Bush Unsettled country area.

Bushranger Runaway convict; nineteenth-century outlaw.

Bushwhacker Someone lacking in social graces, a hick.

BYO Bring your own. Restaurant which allows you to bring your own alcohol.

Chook Chicken.

Chunder Vomit.

Cocky Small farmer; cow cocky, dairy farmer.

To come the raw prawn To try to deceive or make a fool of someone.

Coo-eee! Aboriginal long-distance greeting, now widely adopted as a kind of "yoo hoo!"

Corroboree Aboriginal ceremony.

Cozzies Bathers, swimmers, togs; swimming costume.

Crim Criminal.

Crook Ill or broken.

Crow eater Resident of South Australia.

Cut lunch Sandwiches.

Dag Nerd.

Daggy Unfashionable. Original meaning: faeces stuck on a sheep's rear end.

Daks or **strides** Trousers/pants.

Dam A man-made body of water or reservoir; not just the dam itself.

Damper Soda bread cooked in a pot on embers.

Dekko To look at; as in "take a dekko at this".

Derro Derelict or destitute person.

Didgeridoo Droning Aboriginal musical instrument made from a termite-hollowed branch.

Digger Old-timer, especially an old soldier.

Dill Idiot.

Dilly bag Aboriginal carry-all made of bark, or woven or rigged twine.

Dinkum True, genuine, honest.

Disposal store Store that sells used army and navy equipment, plus camping gear.

Dob in To tell on someone; as in "she dobbed him in".

Donga Sleeping quarters used often in the mining industry.

Drizabone Voluminous waxed cotton raincoat, originally designed for horseriding; a brand name.

Drongo Fool.

Drover Cowboy or station hand.

Dunny Outside pit toilet.

Esky Portable, insulated box to keep food or beer cold.

Fair dinkum or **dinky di** Honestly, truly.

Fossick To search for gold or gems in abandoned diggings.

Furphy A rumour or false story.

Galah Noisy or garrulous person; after the bird.

Galvo Corrugated iron.

Garbo Garbage or refuse collector.

G'day Hello, hi. Short for "good day".

Gibber Rock or boulder.

Give away To give up or resign; as in "I used to be a garbo but I gave it away".

Grog Alcoholic drink, usually beer.

Gub, gubbah Aboriginal terms for a white person.

Gutless wonder Coward.

Hoon A yob, delinquent. Also someone who drives recklessly.

Humpy Temporary shelter used by Aborigines and early pioneers.

Jackeroo Male station-hand.

Jilleroo Female station-hand.

Joey Baby kangaroo still in the pouch (also, less familiarly, a baby koala).

Koorie Collective name for Aboriginal people from southeastern Australia.

Larrikin Mischievous youth.

Lay by Practice of putting a deposit on goods until they can be fully paid for.

Like a shag on a rock Out on a limb.

Lollies Sweets or candy.

Manchester Linen goods.

Mate A sworn friend – one you'd do anything for – as essential as beer to the Australian stereotype.

Milk bar Corner shop, and often a small café.

Moleskins Strong cotton trousers worn by bushmen.

Never Never Outback, wilderness.

New Australian Recent immigrants; often a euphemism for Australians of non-British descent.

No worries That's OK; it doesn't matter; don't mention it.

Ocker Uncultivated Australian male.

Op shop Short for "Opportunity Shop"; a charity shop/thrift store.

Outback Remote, unsettled regions of Australia.

Paddock Field.

Panel van Van with no rear windows and front seating only.

Pashing Kissing or snogging, often in the back of a panel van.

Perve To leer or act as a voyeur (short for pervert); as in "What are you perving at?"

Piss Beer.

Pokies One-armed bandits; gambling machines.

Pommie or **Pom** Person of English descent – not necessarily abusive.

Rapt Very pleased, delighted.

Ratbag An eccentric person; also a term of mild abuse.

Ratshit or **shithouse** How you feel after a night on the piss.

Rego Vehicle registration document.

Ridji didge The real thing or genuine article.

Ripper! Old-fashioned exclamation of enthusiasm.

Rollies Roll-up cigarettes.

Root Vulgar term for sexual congress.

Rooted To be very tired or to be beyond repair; as in "she's rooted, mate" – "your [car] is irreparable".

Ropable Furious to the point of requiring restraint.

Roustabout An unskilled labourer in a shearing shed.

Sandgroper Resident of Western Australia.

She'll be right or **she'll be apples** Everything will work out fine.

Shoot through To pass through or leave hurriedly.

Shout To pay for someone, or to buy a round of drinks; as in "it's your shout, mate".

Sickie To take a day off work due to (sometimes alleged) illness; as in "to pull a sickie".

Singlet Sleeveless cotton vest. The archetypal Australian singlet, in navy, is produced by Bonds.

Skivvy Polo neck.

Slab 24-can carton of beer.

Smoko Tea break.

Snag Sausage.

Speedo Famous Australian brand of swimming costume; speedos (or sluggos) refers to men's swimming briefs.

Spunk Attractive or sexy person of either gender (but generally a young man); as in "what a spunk!" Can also be used as an adjective: spunky.

Squatter Historical term for early settlers who took up public land as their own.

Station Very large pastoral property or ranch.

Sticky beak Nosy person, or to be nosy; as in "let's have a sticky beak".

Stockman Cowboy or station hand.

Stubby Small bottle of beer.

Swag Large bedroll, or one's belongings.

Tall poppy Someone who excels or is eminent. "Cutting down tall poppies" is to bring overachievers back to earth – a national pastime.

Thongs Flip-flops or sandals.

Throw a wobbly Lose your temper.

Tinnie Can of beer, or a small aluminium boat.

Ute Short for "utility" vehicle; pick-up truck.

Wacko! Exclamation of enthusiasm.

Walkabout Temporary migration undertaken by Aborigines; also has the wider meaning of a journey.

Gone walkabout To go missing.

Warm fuzzies Feeling of contentment.

Waxhead Surfer.

Weatherboard Wooden house.

Whinger Someone who complains – allegedly common among Poms.

Wog Derogatory description for those of Mediterranean descent.

Wowser Killjoy.

Yabber To talk or chat.

Yabbie Freshwater crayfish.

Yakka Work, as in "hard yakka".

Yobbo Uncouth person.

Small print and index

A ROUGH GUIDE TO ROUGH GUIDES

Published in 1982, the first Rough Guide – to Greece – was a student scheme that became a publishing phenomenon. Mark Ellingham, a recent graduate in English from Bristol University, had been travelling in Greece the previous summer and couldn't find the right guidebook. With a small group of friends he wrote his own guide, combining a contemporary, journalistic style with a thoroughly practical approach to travellers' needs.

The immediate success of the book spawned a series that rapidly covered dozens of destinations. And, in addition to impecunious backpackers, Rough Guides soon acquired a much broader readership that relished the guides' wit and inquisitiveness as much as their enthusiastic, critical approach and value-for-money ethos. These days, Rough Guides include recommendations from budget to luxury and cover more than 120 destinations around the globe, from Amsterdam to Zanzibar, all regularly updated by our team of roaming writers.

Browse all our latest guides, read inspirational features and book your trip at **roughguides.com**.

Rough Guide credits

Editors: Helen Abramson, Emma Gibbs, Melissa Graham, Georgia Stephens
Layout: Ankur Guha
Cartography: Animesh Pathak
Picture editor: Aude Vauconsant
Proofreader: Susanne Hillen
Managing editor: Andy Turner

Assistant editor: Payal Sharotri
Production: Jimmy Lao
Cover photo research: Sarah Stewart-Richardson
Editorial assistant: Aimee White
Senior DTP coordinator: Dan May
Programme manager: Gareth Lowe
Publishing director: Georgina Dee

Publishing information

This twelfth edition published March 2017 by
Rough Guides Ltd,
80 Strand, London WC2R 0RL
11, Community Centre, Panchsheel Park,
New Delhi 110017, India
Distributed by Penguin Random House
Penguin Books Ltd, 80 Strand, London WC2R 0RL
Penguin Group (USA), 345 Hudson Street, NY 10014, USA
Penguin Group (Australia), 250 Camberwell Road,
Camberwell, Victoria 3124, Australia
Penguin Group (NZ), 67 Apollo Drive, Mairangi Bay,
Auckland 1310, New Zealand
Penguin Group (South Africa), Block D, Rosebank Office
Park, 181 Jan Smuts Avenue, Parktown North, Gauteng,
South Africa 2193
Rough Guides is represented in Canada by DK Canada, 320
Front Street West, Suite 1400, Toronto, Ontario M5V 3B6
Printed in Singapore
© Rough Guides 2017
Maps © Rough Guides

MIX
Paper from responsible sources
FSC™ C018179
www.fsc.org

Help us update

We've gone to a lot of effort to ensure that the twelfth
edition of **The Rough Guide to Australia** is accurate
and up-to-date. However, things change – places get
"discovered", opening hours are notoriously fickle,
restaurants and rooms raise prices or lower standards. If
you feel we've got it wrong or left something out, we'd like
to know, and if you can remember the address, the price,
the hours, the phone number, so much the better.

Please send your comments with the subject line
"Rough Guide Australia Update" to mail
@uk.roughguides.com. We'll credit all contributions and
send a copy of the next edition (or any other Rough Guide
if you prefer) for the very best emails.

Readers' updates

Thanks to all the readers who have taken the time to write in with comments and suggestions (and apologies if we've
inadvertently omitted or misspelt anyone's name):

Genie Bettencourt; Andrea Cantello; Paul Fero; Sabrina Gilard; John Halley; Chris Jubb; Martin Lewis; and Peter Lofting.

ABOUT THE AUTHORS

Melanie Ball's travel writing career fell off the back of an overland expedition truck between London and Johannesburg, and her articles and images have been published across Australia in newspapers and magazines in the thirty-odd years since. Melanie has lived in – and loved exploring – Victoria since she was a toddler.

Mark Chipperfield Raised on a farm in south Devon, Mark began travelling at 17 when he worked on a German freighter from Auckland to Rotterdam. Since then, he has worked as a news reporter, foreign correspondent and travel writer, with a special interest in Australia and the Pacific. He lives in Sydney.

Shafik Meghji An award-winning travel writer and journalist based in South London, Shafik Meghji has co-authored over thirty Rough Guides to destinations in Europe, Latin America, North Africa, Asia and Australasia. He writes regularly for print and digital publications, including the Guardian and the Huffington Post. Visit ⟁shafikmeghji.com and ⟁unmappedroutes.com. Twitter: @ShafikMeghji.

Lee Mylne is an award-winning travel journalist who has called Australia home for the past thirty years. Born in New Zealand, she's traipsed around the world in search of good stories for most of her adult life, and is the author of a dozen books and countless travel articles.

Helen Ochyra fell for Australia on her very first visit, when – and where – she also had her first travel article published. Helen has travelled around Australia extensively and especially loves Western Australia, where she has travelled from top to bottom in search of the perfect Outback pub, best beach break and most memorable glass of Margaret River red.

Amy Palfreyman After years of roaming the planet, Amy has finally re-planted her roots in her beloved hometown of Melbourne… for now. High school teacher by day and travel writer by night, she has lurked, notepad in hand, in the corners of just about every bar, club and restaurant the city has to offer. She is still tired, full and hung-over.

Phillip Tang grew up in Sydney on a typically Australian diet of pho and fish'n'chips. A degree in Chinese and Latin-American cultures launched him into travel and writing books about Asia, Australia and the Americas. For more information visit ⟁philliptang.co.uk.

Greg Ward has written Rough Guides to Southwest USA, Brittany and Normandy, Hawaii and Las Vegas; is the joint author of others including France, USA, Provence, Spain, Barcelona, Belize and Japan; has edited many more; and has written books on travel and music for several other publishers. For more information visit ⟁gregward.info.

Acknowledgements

Mark Chipperfield: Thanks go to Brooke Liebelt, tourism manager for Yorke Peninsula, who introduced me to that lovely part of South Australia and to the media and PR team at Destination NSW, especially Elissa Tyrrell and Belinda Winstanley, who helped me to re-explore several far flung parts of New South Wales. And a big thank you to Donna Ciaccia, from VisitCanberra, who provided invaluable support and advice for my trip to the capital. Lastly, I'd like to say "Whatawee?" ("How Are You?") to Tania Anderson, from Norfolk Island Tourism, who provided meticulous feedback on the section devoted to that Pacific island.

Shafik Meghji: Many thanks to: Emma Gibbs, Georgia Stephens and Helen Abramson at Rough Guides; YHA; Great Southern Railway; Jovanka Ristich; Rebecca Astier of Accor; Victor Cooper of Ayal Aboriginal Tours; Kakadu Cultural Tours; The Kangaroo Sanctuary in Alice Springs; Jean, Nizar and Nina Meghji; and Sioned Jones.

Lee Mylne: Grateful thanks to the many people and organisations who assisted with travel, advice and research. In Tasmania, special thanks to: Sherene Somerville at Tourism Tasmania; Ruth Dowty at East Coast Regional Tourism Organisation; Leanne Tyrrell; Destination Launceston; Rebecca Fitzgibbon at MONA; and Danny McKenzie at Port Arthur Historic Site. Also to Tracey Leitch for her assistance in the Tarkine, Corinna and Stanley; and to Roz MacAllen and John Potter for hospitality and advice in the Bay of Fires. For other introductions and help, thanks to Klick Communications, Sally Morgan and Silke Kerwick. In Outback Queensland, I'm hugely grateful to: Tourism & Events Queensland; Outback Queensland Tourism Association; Russell Boswell and Savannah Guides; Townsville Enterprise; and Southern Queensland Country Tourism. Thanks in particular to Mary-Clare Power and Jane Hodges for helping facilitate travel and give invaluable advice.

Helen Ochyra: Many thanks to Elen Thomas at Tourism WA for her continued support and the invaluable information she provided, as well as to the endlessly helpful Western Australian residents, business owners and tour operators who provided on-the-ground assistance of every variety. Thanks also, as ever, to Douglas for his boundless support – and for always carrying the bags!

Amy Palfreyman: Many thanks, as always, to my beautiful family and friends for making sure I never had to eat, drink or dance alone through the many hours of research that went into this guide. Thanks also to my students for not taking advantage of my forgetfulness in class during the heavy writing weeks. To the team at Rough Guides, the opportunity to showcase my wonderful city has been very much appreciated; thank you for trusting me with this gem.

Phillip Tang: Immense thanks to the wonderful Sydney experts Vek Lewis, Lisa N'Paisan, Venus Vamp and Waimei Garcia-Lee. Big thanks to Jack Kennerley and Seth Glossop for exploring the beaches, the night and the misty Blue Mountains with me. Much appreciation to Helen Abramson for keen editing eyes, hard work and patience.

Greg Ward: Thanks to the many wonderful people who made my time in Queensland so hugely enjoyable, including Megan Bell; Stacey Brant; Judy; Denis and Miles at the Broken River Resort; Brooke Hargraves; Joanne Hennessy; Darren and Jackie Keenan; Zak Kelly; Daniel Meek; Sarah Mullet; and Gigi and Andrea at the Pink Flamingo. Back home, thanks especially to friends and neighbours Alison and Cefn for so much advice and expertise, and to my dear wife Sam for everything and more. And finally, thanks to my editor Melissa Graham for being such a pleasure to work with, and to Helen Abramson and all at Rough Guides for keeping the whole thing running so smoothly.

Photo credits

301 Photoshot: Chameleons Eye / Rafael Ben-Ari
339 Getty Images: Photolibrary / Australian Scenics (b);
The Image Bank / Andrew Watson (t)
379 Robert Harding Picture Library: Konrad Wothe
(b); Matthew Williams-Ellis (tr). **SuperStock:** Prisma /
CCOphotostockBS (tl)
409 Getty Images: Peter Adams (t). **Robert Harding
Picture Library:** Karl Johaentges (b)
434–435 Robert Harding Picture Library: LOOK / Don
Fuchs
437 SuperStock: Universal Images Group
459 Dreamstime: David Hilcher (b) **Getty Images:** (t).
482–483 Getty Images: Michael Dunning
485 Getty Images: George Clerk
509 Alamy Stock Photo: Ingo Oeland (t); Andrew Watson
(b)
533 Fotolia (t). **Getty Images:** James Braund
(bl). **SuperStock:** David Wall (br)
554–555 Fotolia
557 Getty Images: Jeff Rotman
583 Getty Images: Orien Harvey (tr). **L Jake:** (tl, b)
617 Getty Images: Frances Andrijich (t); John Clutterbuck
(b)
650–651 SuperStock: Radius

653 Getty Images: Manfred Gottschalk
677 Getty Images: Bob Stefko
713 Fotolia (br). **Getty Images:** Bob Stefko (bl); Danita
Delimont (t)
730–731 Getty Images: Andrew Peacock
733 Fotolia
765 Dorling Kindersley: Karen Trist (tl). **Robert Harding
Picture Library:** Iain Masterton (b); Richard Nebesky (tr)
787 Fotolia (b). **L Jake** (t)
804–805 Fotolia
807 Getty Images: Richard I'Anson
835 Alamy Stock Photo: Alberto Campanile
865 Alamy Stock Photo: Andrew Bain (tl). **Robert
Harding Picture Library:** Don Fuchs (b). **SuperStock:** agf
photo (tr)
882–883 SuperStock: Radius
885 Getty Images: John White Photos
911 Getty Images: Jochen Schlenker
945 Getty Images: Glenn Van Der Knijff (b); Steve Daggar
Photography (t)
968 Getty Images: Penny Tweedie

Cover *Perry Sandhills, near Wentworth, New South Wales*
4Corners: Hans-Peter Merten

Index

Maps are marked in grey

Q

R

S

Map symbols

The symbols below are used on maps throughout the book

——— - -	State/province boundary	@	Internet café/access	☉	Statue/memorial	⫽	Mountain pass
— — —	Chapter division boundary	ⓘ	Information office	🐘	Zoo/wildlife park	🌲	Tree
▬▬▬	Motorway	◆	National park/reserve	🌴	Lighthouse	🌿	Viewpoint
———	Pedestrianized road	E	Embassy	🎋	Waterfall	卅	Picnic area
———	Road	⛽	Fuel station	🍇	Vineyard/winery	🏯	Chinese temple
⊓⊓⊓⊓⊓⊓	Steps	Å	Campsite	Cliff	Cliff	🏛	Stately home/palace
⋈⋈⋈⋈⋈	Unsealed road	⊤	Gardens	⌇⌇	Rocks	🏛	Monument
- - - - -	Footpath	P	Parking	Gorge	Gorge	♦	Museum
————	Wall	⊞	Hospital	Reef	Reef	▢	Market
———	Tram route	⊠	Post office	🕐	Crater	▥	Building
▬═▬═	Railway	⊠	Gate	⛺	Conservation hut	▧	Church (town maps)
●—- -—●	Cable car	♦	Place of interest	🕳	Cave	◯	Stadium
— — —	Ferry route	∴	Ruin	⚒	Mine	▢	Park
✈	Airport	🏌	Golf course	🏔	Butte	▢	Beach
✈	Domestic airport	❆	Ferris Wheel	⌣	Bridge	⊞	Cemetery
★	Bus stop	⛱	Swimming pool	▲	Mountain peak	▨	Marsh
◎	City rail	✡	Synagogue	〰	Mountain range	▨	Aboriginal land
⛴	Boat						

Listings key

■	Accommodation		
●	Eating		
■	Drinking & nightlife		
●	Shopping		

Long bus journey?
Phone run out of juice?

 TEST YOUR KNOWLEDGE WITH OUR ROUGH GUIDES TRAVEL QUIZ

1 Denim, the pencil, the stethoscope and the hot-air balloon were all invented in which country?

a. Italy
b. France
c. Germany
d. Switzerland

2 What is the currency of Vietnam?

a. Dong
b. Yuan
c. Baht
d. Kip

3 In which city would you find the Majorelle Garden?

a. Marseille
b. Marrakesh
c. Tunis
d. Malaga

4 What is the busiest airport in the world?

a. London Heathrow
b. Tokyo International
c. Chicago O'Hare
d. Hartsfield-Jackson
   Atlanta International

5 Which of these countries does not have the equator running through it?

a. Brazil
b. Tanzania
c. Indonesia
d. Colombia

6 Which country has the most UNESCO World Heritage Sites?

a. Mexico
b. France
c. Italy
d. India

7 What is the principal religion of Japan?

a. Confucianism
b. Buddhism
c. Jainism
d. Shinto

8 Every July in Sonkajärvi, central Finland, contestants gather for the World Championships of which sport?

a. Zorbing
b. Wife-carrying
c. Chess-boxing
d. Extreme ironing

9 What colour are post boxes in Germany?

a. Red
b. Green
c. Blue
d. Yellow

10 For three days each April during Songkran festival in Thailand, people take to the streets to throw what at each other?

a. Water
b. Oranges
c. Tomatoes
d. Underwear

 For more quizzes, competitions and inspirational features go to **roughguides.com**

1-b / 2-a / 3-b / 4-d / 5-b / 6-c / 7-d / 8-b / 9-d / 10-a